Rick Steves'®

BEST OF EUROPE 2006

EUROPE
0
350 mi
0
350 km
Trondheim
Ålesund
NORWAY
Lillehammer
SOGNEFJORD
Bergen
Oslo
Stavanger
Kristiansand
Inverness
HIGHLANDS
SCOTLAND
NORTHERN IRELAND
Oban
Glasgow
Edinburgh
North Sea
Århus
DENMARK
Legoland
Ærø
Lübeck
Hamburg
Derry
Belfast
LAKE DISTRICT
IRELAND
Aran Islands
Galway
Dublin
Blackpool
York
DINGLE PENINSULA
Cashel
Kinsale
Conwy
ENGLAND
NETHER-LANDS
WALES
Cardiff
COTSWOLDS
Cambridge
Bath
Amsterdam
Haarlem
London
Arnhem
GERMANY
CORNWALL
Bruges
Brussels
Rhine R.
Köln
BELGIUM
Frankfurt
Würzburg
Atlantic Ocean
Mont St. Michel
Honfleur
Bayeux
Rouen
Reims
Mosel
St. Goar
Nürnberg
Rothenburg
NORMANDY
Paris
LUX.
Baden-Baden
BRITTANY
Dinan
Chartres
Versailles
Strasbourg
Danube
Belle-Ile
LOIRE
Seine R.
ALSACE
BLACK FOREST
BAV
Colmar
Füssen
Loire R.
Amboise
Chinon
BURGUNDY
Reutte
SWITZ.
Bern
Innsbruck
Beaune
FRANCE
Gimmelwald
Geneva
DORDOGNE
Dordogne R.
Beynac
Chamonix
Rhône River
Aosta
LAKE DISTRICT
Bay of Biscay
Bordeaux
Lyon
Milan
Po
PIEDMONT
Santiago de Compostela
Albi
PROVENCE
Genoa
CINQUE TERRE
GALICIA
St. Jean-de-Luz
Bilbao
LANGUEDOC
Avignon
San Sebastián
Arles
Nice
Pisa
BASQUE
Ligurian Sea
Carcassonne
MONACO
Cassis
Porto
Douro R.
ANDORRA
Collioure
CATALUNYA
CORSICA (France)
Cadaques
Barcelona
Nazaré
Coimbra
Segovia
Salamanca
Madrid
PORTUGAL
Lisbon
Toledo
CASTILE LA MANCHA
Menorca
SPAIN
Évora
Consuegra
Majorca
SARDINIA (Italy)
Salema
Guadalquivir R.
Ibiza
ALGARVE
Sevilla
Mediterranean
ANDALUCÍA
Granada
Tarifa
COSTA DEL SOL
GIBRALTAR
Tangier
MOROCCO
ALGERIA
TUNISIA

SWEDEN
FINLAND
Savonlinna
Gulf of Bothnia
Turku
Helsinki
St. Petersburg
Volga River
RUSSIA
Uppsala
Tallinn
ESTONIA
Stockholm
Moscow
LATVIA
Riga
Göteborg
Visby
Kalmar
Öland
Växjö
Baltic Sea
LITHUANIA
Don River
Copenhagen
Vilnius
RUSSIA
Minsk
Gdańsk
BELARUS
Poznań
Toruń
Berlin
Warsaw
Kiev
POLAND
Elbe R.
Dnieper River
Oder River
Dresden
UKRAINE
Vistula R.
Auschwitz
Kraków
Prague
TATRA MTNS
CZECH REPUBLIC
Levoča
MOLDOVA
Český Krumlov
SLOVAKIA
Kishinév
Melk
Bratislava
Eger
Munich
Vienna
Segesta
Salzburg
Budapest
Hallstatt
AUSTRIA
HUNGARY
Sigisoara
Pécs
ROMANIA
SLOVENIA
DOLOMITES
Bled
Bran
Ljubljana
CROATIA
Bucharest
Venice
Zagreb
Black Sea
Plitvice
Belgrade
BOSNIA & HERZ.
Danube R.
Ravenna
SAN MARINO
Sarajevo
SERBIA & MONTENEGRO
BULGARIA
Split
Florence
Ancona
Sofia
Siena
Plovdiv
TUSCANY
Istanbul
Assisi
Rila
Dubrovnik
UMBRIA
Adriatic Sea
Skopje
Civita
MACEDONIA
Rome
Tiranë
VATICAN CITY
Thessaloniki
ITALY
ALBANIA
Bari
TURKEY
Naples
Meteora
Brindisi
Sorrento
GREECE
Aegean Sea
AMALFI COAST
Paestum
Corfu
Delphi
Ephesus
Tyrrhenian Sea
Sámos
Athens
Bodrum
Ionian Sea
Mykonos
Nafplion
Hydra
Naxos
Cefalù
Paros
Rhodes
PELOPONNESE
Palermo
SICILY
Taormina
Santorini
Finikoundas
Agrigento
Sea
Valletta
MALTA
GORGE OF SAMARIA
CRETE

NETHERLANDS
GERMANY
BELGIUM
LUXEMBOURG
FRANCE
SWITZERLAND
LIECHTENSTEIN
ITALY
HARZ MOUNTAINS
LORRAINE
LES VOSGES
ALSACE
BLACK FOREST
JURA MTNS.
APPENZELL
BERNER OBERLAND
TICINO
TIROL
BAVARIA
Hannover
Braunschweig
Magdeburg
Celle
Bergen-Belsen
Wolfsburg
Hameln
Goslar
Halberstadt
Aschersleben
Göttingen
Bad Bentheim
Hengelo
Rheine
Osnabrück
Bielefeld
Münster
Paderborn
Arnhem
Nijmegen
Emmerich
Essen
Dortmund
Duisburg
Venlo
Düsseldorf
Kassel
Korbach
Naumburg
Erfurt
Weimar
Eisenach
Bebra
Marburg
Maastricht
Aachen
Köln
Bonn
Liege
Remagen
Rhine
Wetzlar
Fulda
Suhl
Coburg
Burg Eltz
Koblenz
Boppard
St. Goar
Cochem
Beilstein
Zell
Bacharach
Bingen
Wiesbaden
Frankfurt
Mainz
Rudesheim
Main
Würzburg
Bamberg
Bayreuth
Weiden
Steinach
Trier
Mosel
Luxembourg City
Worms
Mannheim
Heidelberg
Nürnberg
Rothenburg
Thionville
Metz
Kaiserslautern
Saarbrücken
Castle Road
Dinkelsbühl
Romantic Road
Karlsruhe
Baden-Baden
Stuttgart
Nordlingen
Schwäbisch Gmünd
Ingolstadt
Donauworth
Toul
Nancy
Strasbourg
Kehl
Reutlingen
Tübingen
Ulm
Augsburg
Dachau
Munich
St Dié
Ribeauvillé
Kaysersberg
Hausach Open Air Museum
Colmar
Triberg
Furtwangen
Danube
Herrsching
Andechs Monastery
Landsberg
Eguisheim
Freiburg
Bad Krozingen
Meersburg
Ravensburg
Ronchamp
Staufen
Mulhouse
Rhinefalls
Konstanz
Lake Constance
Stein
Lindau
Kempten
Oberammergau
Füssen
Neuschwanstein
Belfort
Basel
Reutte
Zugspitze
Zürich
Appenzell
Bregenz
Ebenalp
Feldkirch
Ehrenberg
Fallerschein
Lech
Innsbruck
Stubai Gletscher
Besançon
Luzern
Zug
Buchs
Vaduz
Bludenz
Brenner Pass
Vipiteno
Neuchâtel
Murten
Bern
Lac de Neuchâtel
Avenches
Ballenberg Museum
Fluelen
Chur
Scuol
Reifenstein Castle
Frasne
Fribourg
Gruyères
Spiez
Inter-laken
Susten Pass
Glacier Express
Merano
Lausanne
Grindelwald
Jungfrau
Gimmelwald
Samedan
St. Moritz
Bolzano
Pontresina
Glurns
Montreux
Chillon
Lac Léman
Schilthorn
Geneva
Locarno
Sondrio
Martigny
Saas-Fee
Lugano
Lago Como
Trento
Matterhorn
Zermatt
Lago Maggiore
Varenna
Bernina Express
Annecy
Chamonix
Mont Blanc
Lago Lugano
Bellagio
Isar
A1
A2
A3
A4
A5
A6
A7
A8
A9
A12
A22
A27
A28
A30
A31
A35
A36
A40
A44
A45
A48
A57
A61
A67
A70
A73
A81
A95
E25
E40

GERMANY, AUSTRIA & SWITZERLAND
Freeway/Motorway
Major Roads
Major Rail Line
Airport
St. Goar Recommended Location*
Bebra Just passing through**
Ruin, Museum, Other Point of Interest
Castle/Monument/Palace
* Black locations are places of interest to tourists, sized by importance.
** Gray locations are not places of interest to tourists and are sized by population.
0 km 50 100 km
0 miles 50 miles
POLAND
CZECH REPUBLIC
AUSTRIA
SLOVAKIA
HUNGARY
CROATIA
SLOVENIA
SAXONY
BOHEMIA
MORAVIA
WACHAU
SALZKAMMERGUT
DOLOMITES
FRIULI
JULIAN ALPS
ALPE DI SIUSI
Berlin
Tegel
Potsdam
Sanssouci Palace
Brandenburg
Frankfurt an der Oder
Rzepin
Wittenberg
Cottbus
Zielona Góra
Zary
Lauchhammer
Leipzig
Halle
Moritzburg
Meissen
Dresden
Bad Schandau
Zittau
Boleslawiec
Zgorzelec
Gorlitz
Chemnitz
Seiffen
Glauchau
Decin
Ústí nad Labem
Litoměřice
Terezín
Plauen
Ruzyně
Karlovy Vary
Prague
Kutná Hora
Cheb
Marktredwitz
Marianské Lazne
Karlstejn Castle
Plzen
Štramberk
Olomouc
Kromeriz
Zlín
Tabor
Telc
Brno
Český Kubice
Furth
Veseli nad Luznici
Slavonice
Český Budejovice
Český Velenice
Gmund
Breclav
Kuty
Regensburg
Ober-traubling
Český Krumlov
Passau
Summerau
Durnstein
Krems
Vienna
Grinzing
Bratislava
Danube
Linz
Mauthausen
Melk
Schönbrunn Palace
St. Valentin
Attnang Puchheim
Puchberg
Eisenstadt
Schneeberg
Salzach
Herrenchiemsee
Chiemsee
Salzburg
Bad Ischl
Sopron
Esterhazy Palace
Rosenheim
Berchtesgaden
Hallstatt
Selzthal
Kufstein
Hallein
Stainach Irdning
Leoben
Bruck an der Mur
Szombathely
Worgl
Zell am See
Hinterhornalm
Hall
Kitzbuhel
Piber
Graz
Badgastein
Grossglockner Pass
Spielfeld
Spittal
Klagenfurt
Maribor
Nagykanizsa
Dobbiaco
Lienz
Jesenice
Cortina
Castelrotto
Tarvisio
Vršič Pass
Bled/Lesce
Koprivnica
Brnik
Lake Bled
Lake Bohinj
Ljubljana
Calalzo
Belluno
Udine
Zagreb
Pordenone
Palmanova
Postojna Caves
Škocjan Caves
VENETO

GREAT BRITAIN
CORNWALL
Tintagel
Exeter
Salisbury
Winchester
Southampton
Gatwick
Canterbury
Dover
Rye
SOUTH DOWNS
Portsmouth
Brighton
Hastings
Beachy Head
Lyme Bay
Weymouth
Bournemouth
Newport
ISLE OF WIGHT
St. Ives
Truro
Plymouth
Penzance
Land's End
Falmouth
St. Michael's Mount
ISLES OF SCILLY
English Channel
to Wexford, Ireland
to Cobh, Ireland
Guernsey (UK)
Cherbourg
Jersey (UK)
Dieppe
Etrétat
Le Havre
American Cemetery
D-DAY BEACHES
Arro-manches
Honfleur
Bayeux
Deauville
Rouen
St. Lô
Caen
Lisieux
Vernon
NORMANDY
Evreux
Mont St. Michel
Avranches
Roscoff
Morlaix
OUESSANT
Brest
St. Brieuc
St. Malo
Dol
Dinan
Pontorson
Fougères
Alençon
Chartres
BRITTANY
Quimper
Rennes
Laval
Le Mans
Lorient
Ile de Groix
Vannes
Redon
Quiberon
Carnac
Belle-Ile
La Flèche
LOIRE
Blois
Angers
Amboise
Langeais
Tours
Loire
Chenonceau
Nantes
Villandry
Chinon
Cholet
Ile de Noirmoutier
Loches
Ile d'Yeu
La Roche-sur-Yon
Les Sables-d'Olonne
Poitiers
Chauvigny
Niort
Ile de Re
LA CHARENTE
La Rochelle
Ile d'Oleron
Rochefort
Mortemart
Oradour-sur-Glane
Atlantic Ocean
Saintes
Limoges
Cognac
Angoulême
Gironde
Dordogne
St. Emilion
Périgueux
Brive-la-Gaillarde
DORDOGNE
Les Eyzies
Sarlat
Bordeaux
Font du Gaume
Beynac
Bergerac
Le Buisson
Arcachon
Rocamadour
DUNE DU PILAT
Peche Merle
Garonne
Cahors
AQUITAINE
Agen
Bay of Biscay
Montauban
COSTA VERDE
Llanes
Santander
St. Jean-de-Luz
Dax
Bilbao
San Sebastián
Biarritz
Toulouse
Guggenheim
Guernica
Hondarribia
Bayonne
BASQUE
Pau
St. Jean Pied du Port
Tarbes
Lourdes
LANG
Vitoria
Miranda de Ebro
Pamplona
CIRQUE DE GAVARNIE
Foix
Haro
RIOJA
Burgos
Santo Domingo Calzada
Logrono
PYRENEES
ANDORRA
Andorra la Vella
ORDESA NATIONAL PARK
Huesca
Palencia
SPAIN

FRANCE
0 km
50 km
100 km
0 miles
50 miles
Ostende
Bruges
Antwerp
Channel Tunnel
Dunkerque
Ghent
Brussels
Calais
Boulogne
St. Omer
Waterloo
FLANDERS
Lille
BELGIUM
Aachen
Liege
Namur
Arras
Cambrai
Aulnoye
Abbeville
WALLONIE
Cochem
Zell
Mosel
St. Goar
Bacharach
Rudesheim
Frankfurt
Wetzlar
Rhine
Amiens
St. Quentin
ARDENNES
Charleville Mézières
LUXEMBOURG
Trier
GERMANY
Laon
Beauvais
Luxembourg City
Kaiserslautern
Mannheim
Heidelberg
Senlis
Soissons
Longwy
Thionville
Chantilly
Reims
Verdun Battlefield
Giverny
Charles de Gaulle
Seine
Epernay
Metz
Saarbrücken
Paris
CHAMPAGNE
Châlons
Karlsruhe
Stuttgart
Disneyland Paris
LORRAINE
Baden-Baden
Versailles
Orly
Nancy
Seine
Vaux-le-Vicomte
St. Dizier
Toul
Strasbourg
Fontainebleau
Troyes
VOSGES
ALSACE
Ribeauvillé
BLACK FOREST
Freudenstadt
Chaumont
Kayserberg
Rhein
Orléans
Chablis
Colmar
Triberg
Laroche
Eguisheim
Freiburg
Auxerre
BURGUNDY
Culmont
Cheverny
Loire
Avallon
Ronchamp
Mulhouse
Meersburg
Chambord
Vézelay
LES VOSGES
Staufen
Guedelon
Semur-en-Auxois
Belfort
Zurich
Sancerre
JURA MTNS.
Vierzon
Besançon
SWITZERLAND
Bourges
Autun
Châteauneuf-en-Auxois
Dijon
Dol
Neuchâtel
Luzern
Bern
Lake Luzern
Châteauroux
Nevers
Le Creusot
Beaune
Lac de Neuchâtel
Avenches
Châlon-sur-Saône
Frasne
Fribourg
Interlaken
Moulins
Brançion
Gruyères
Cluny
Tournus
Vallorbe
Lausanne
BERNER OBERLAND
Gimmelwald
Montluçon
Montreux
Vichy
Mâcon
Bourg-en-Bresse
Guéret
Geneva
Locarno
FRANCE
BEAUJOLAIS
Roanne
Martigny
Lugano
Rhône
Chamonix
Clermont-Ferrand
Annecy
Mont Blanc
Lago Maggiore
Stresa
Lyon
SAVOIE
Mont Blanc Tunnel
Lago di Orta
AUVERGNE
Aosta
St. Etienne
Vienne
Chambéry
Bourg S.M.
Malpensa
Milan
Loire
Modane
PIEDMONT
Grenoble
Po
Le Puy-en-Velay
Torino
ITALY
Gouffre Padirac
Rhône
Valence
Briançon
Lot
Clelles
Pinerolo
LE LANGHE
Rodez
Mende
Montélimar
Gap
Barolo
St. Cirq Lapopie
PROVENCE
Cuneo
Genoa
GORGE DE L'ARDECHE
GORGES DU TARN
Vaison la Romaine
Savona
Cordes
Tarn
Millau
Orange
Châteauneuf-du-Pape
Digne
Finale
Pont du Gard
Albi
Uzès
Avignon
Isle sur la Sorgue
Nîmes
Les Baux
St. Rémy
Roussillon
Vence
Menton
Castres
St. Paul
Montpellier
Arles
LUBERON
GRAND CANYON DU VERDUN
Grasse
MONACO
Ligurian Sea
Caunes-Minervois
Minerve
CAMARGUE
Aix-en-Provence
Nice
Villefranche
Antibes
Carcassonne
Béziers
Cannes
to Bastia, Corsica
Marseille
CÔTE D'AZUR
Narbonne
Cassis
St. Tropez
Queribus & Peyrepertuse
Toulon
Mediterranean Sea
Perpignan
Collioure
to Porto Torres, Sardinia
L'Ile Rousse
Port Bou
to Ajaccio, Corsica
CORSICA (France)
Figueres
Cadaques

North Atlantic Ocean
Sea of the Hebrides
Irish Sea
St. George's Channel
Celtic Sea
IRELAND
NORTHERN IRELAND
Dublin
Belfast
Galway
Cork
Waterford
Wexford
Kilkenny
Limerick
Derry
Dingle
Tralee
Killarney
Kenmare
Bantry
Kinsale
Cobh
Midleton
Ardmore
Dungarvan
Clonmel
Cashel
Tipperary
Athlone
Mullingar
Sligo
Westport
Clifden
Leenane
Ballina
Donegal
Drogheda
Dundalk
Newry
Wicklow
Arklow
Enniscorthy
Rosslare
Kilkenny
Carlow
Tullamore
Portlaoise
Portarlington
Longford
Cavan
Enniskillen
Omagh
Belleek
Larne
Bangor
Portrush
Coleraine
Ennis
Shannon
Doolin
Kilronan
Salthill
Kinvarra
Macroom
Glengarriff
Skibbereen
Tintagel
Clovelly
St. Ives
Penzance
Plymouth
Truro
Falmouth
Fishguard
Milford Haven
Tenby
to Roscoff & Cherbourg, France
ISLES OF SCILLY

GREAT BRITAIN & IRELAND
0 km
50 km
100 km
0 miles
50 miles
Moray Firth
Inverness
Culloden Battlefield
Kyle
HIGHLANDS
Caledonian Canal
Loch Ness
Aviemore
Aberdeen
Fort William
Ben Nevis
Glencoe
Linnhe
Pitlochry
Crianlarich
Oban
Loch Awe
Perth
Dundee
Inveraray
St. Andrews
Stirling
Loch Lomond
Loch Fyne
M90
M9
Firth of Forth
Glasgow
M8
Edinburgh
Isle of Arran
Ardrossan
Troon
Carstairs
Holy Island
to Bergen, Norway
Berwick
Ayr
SCOTLAND
Bamburgh Castle
Jedburgh
LOWLANDS
BORDERS
Alnwick
Cairnryan
Dumfries
M74
Stranraer
Hadrian's Wall
Newcastle upon Tyne
Carlisle
M6
Beamish Open Air Museum
Penrith
Keswick
Durham
Buttermere
Ullswater
Dove Cottage
Ambleside
A1
Middlesbrough
Isle of Man
LAKE DISTRICT
Windermere
Staithes
Whitby
Douglas
Oxenholme
NORTH YORK MOORS
Pickering
Scarborough
Lancaster
Blackpool
PENNINES
York
Bridlington
North Sea
Preston
Southport
Leeds
M6
M62
Kingston
Holyhead
Liverpool
Manchester
M1
Anglesey
Conwy
Caernarfon
Betws-y-Coed
Mold
Chester
Snowdon
Ruthin
Crewe
MIDLANDS
Lincoln
Blaenau Ffestiniog
Llangollen
M1
SNOWDONIA NATIONAL PARK
Harlech
Nottingham
Shrewsbury
Telford
ENGLAND
King's Lynn
Ironbridge Gorge
Leicester
Aberystwyth
Norwich
Llandrindod Wells
Birmingham
Coventry
Peterborough
CAMBRIAN MTNS
Worcester
Warwick
Ely
EAST ANGLIA
Stratford
Northampton
to Esbjerg, Denmark
M5
Chipping Campden
Cambridge
WALES
COTSWOLDS
M1
Cheltenham
Moreton
Ipswich
Gloucester
Stow
Luton
Swansea
Tintern Abbey
Blenheim Palace
M40
Harwich
M4
Chepstow Castle
Oxford
Stansted
Hertford
Caerphilly
M11
Newport
Cirencester
Colchester
to Hoek van Holland, Netherlands
St. Fagans Folk Museum
Cardiff
Bristol Channel
Bristol
M4
Didcot
Windsor
London
Bath
Reading
Avebury
Greenwich
Southend-on-Sea
Heathrow
Wells
DEVON
Glastonbury
Stonehenge
M3
M2
Ramsgate
M23
M5
Salisbury
M20
Canterbury
to Ostende, Belgium
Winchester
Gatwick
Dover
Southampton
Folkestone
Exeter
Dorchester
SOUTH DOWNS
Channel Tunnel
Dunkerque
Portsmouth
Calais
Rye
Lyme Bay
DARTMOOR
Bournemouth
Weymouth
Hastings
Brighton
Newport
Torquay
Eastbourne
ISLE OF WIGHT
Beachy Head
Boulogne
English Channel
A26
A16
FRANCE
to Guernsey
to Cherbourg, France
to Ouistreham & Le Havre, France

SWITZERLAND
LIECH.
Vaduz
Brenner Pass
Vipiteno
Reifenstein Castle
Merano
Castelrotto
Bolzano
ALPE DI SIUSI
Glurns
Adige
TRENTINO ALTO ADIGE
Trento
Riva
Neuchâtel
Lac de Neuchâtel
Murten
Avenches
Bern
Luzern
Lake Luzern
Fribourg
Brienz
Interlaken
Spiez
Gruyères
BERNER OBERLAND
Lausanne
Mt. Schilthorn
Gimmelwald
Mt. Jungfrau
Lac Léman
Montreux
Château Chillon
Glacier Express
St. Moritz
Pontresina
TICINO
Bernina Express
Locarno
Saas Fee
Domodossola
Lugano
Lago di Como
Menaggio
Varenna
Bellagio
Lago Lugano
Matterhorn
Zermatt
Chamonix
Aiguille du Midi
Breuil-Cervinia
Lago Maggiore
Stresa
Chiasso
Como
Lecco
Lago d'Iseo
Lago di Garda
Mont Blanc
Courmayeur
Lago di Orta
Bergamo
Orio al Serio
Pré Didier
Aosta
AOSTA
Monza
Malpensa
Milan
Linate
Brescia
Sirmione
Verona
Vicenza
Desenzano
LOMBARDY
Mantua
Cremona
Po
Modane
Turin
Piacenza
Briançon
PIEDMONT
Asti
Parma
Modena
EMILIA ROMAGNA
Reggio Emilia
Alba
Barolo
Bologna
Monte Viso
Genoa
Santa Margherita
Sestri Levante
Levanto
Monterosso
Vernazza
Cuneo
Camogli
San Fruttuoso
Portofino
CINQUE TERRE
APUAN ALPS
ITALY
LIGURIA
Colle di Tonda Pass
Finale
La Spezia
Carrara
FRANCE
Portovenere
Pistoia
Amerigo Vespucci
Fiesole
Lucca
Viareggio
Florence
Pisa
Arno
CHIANTI
Vence
St. Paul
Nice
MONACO
Ventimiglia
Villefranche
Antibes
Cannes
Ligurian Sea
Galileo
Livorno
San Gimignano
Volterra
TUSCANY
Siena
St. Tropez
COTE D'AZUR
CAPRAIA
Montalcino
VIA AURELIA
ELBA
Bastia
L'Ile Rousse
to Marseille, France
CORSICA (France)
Ajaccio
Mediterranean Sea
Bonifacio
MADDALENA
S. Teresa
EMERALD COAST
ASINARA
SARDINIA (Italy)
Porto Torres
Sassari
Grotto of Neptune

ITALY
0 km
50 kilometers
0 miles
50 miles
AUSTRIA
Klagenfurt
San Candido
Cortina
Tarvisio
JULIAN ALPS
Bled
Lake Bohinj
Lake Bled
Brnik Airport
Ljubljana
DOLOMITES
Calalzo
FRIULI
Udine
SLOVENIA
Zagreb
Palmanova
Postojna Caves
Aquileia
Grado
Skocjan Caves
Lipica
CROATIA
Asolo
Trieste
Treviso
Piran
VENETO
Marco Polo
Rijeka
Padua
Venice
Pazin
Chioggia
ISTRIA
KRK
Po
Pula
CRES
RAB
BOSNIA & HERZ.
CROATIA
Ferrara
Ravenna
Adriatic Sea
Zadar
DUGI OTOK
Rimini
SAN MARINO
Pesaro
Sibenik
Split
Rubicon
San Leo
Trogir
Urbino
Falconara
Ancona
LE MARCHE
BRAC
Sansepolcro
HVAR
Arezzo
Gubbio
Macerata
Cortona
Monte-pulciano
L. Trasimeno
Assisi
to Dubrovnik, Croatia
Perugia
Spello
Pienza
Deruta
Ascoli Piceno
Bevagna
Montelfalco
Chiusi
UMBRIA
Orvieto
Todi
Spoleto
Mt. Gran Sasso
Pitigliano
Bagnoregio & Civita
Lago di Bolsena
Terni
Pescara
to Patras, Greece
Viterbo
L'Aquila
ABRUZZO
Orte
Rieti
Chieti
Tarquinia
Tiber
LAZIO
Termoli
Cerveteri
Tivoli
GARGANO PENINSULA
VATICAN CITY
Hadrian's Villa
ABRUZZO NAT'L PARK
Rome
MOLISE
Manfredonia
Fiumicino
Ciampino
Ostia Antica
Isernia
Campobasso
Foggia
Tyrrhenian Sea
Montecassino
Latina
Anzio
PUGLIA
Formia
Caserta
CAMPANIA
BASILICATA
Naples
Mt. Vesuvius
Pompeii
Herculaneum
Potenza
PONZA
ISCHIA
Positano
Sorrento
Amalfi
CAPRI
AMALFI COAST
Paestum
to Sicily
A2
A23
A27
A4
E45
S423
A14
A1
S2
A24
S1
A12
A25
A16

SPAIN & PORTUGAL
0 km
50 km
100 km
0 mi
50 mi
100 mi
Atlantic Ocean
Ferrol
Coruña
San Martin
Ribadeo
Canero
La Espina
Avilés
Oviedo
Gijón
COSTA VERDE
Santander
Santillana del Mar
Altamira Caves
Comillas
Santiago de Compostela
Cabo Finisterre
GALICIA
Lugo
ASTURIAS
Cangas
PICOS DE EUROPA
Potes
Fuente Dé
Piedrafita
CANTABRIA
Pontevedra
Vigo
Guillarei
Orense
Ponferrada
León
Cillervelo
Aguilar
Valencia
Viana do Castelo
S. Maria
Burgos
Becilla
Braga
Bragança
Benevente
Palencia
Lerma
DOURO
Porto
Amarante
Vila Real
Mirandela
Zamora
SPA
Valladolid
Aranda
Vila Nova
Pinhaõ
Douro
Peso da Regua
Pocinho
Medina del Campo
PORTUGAL
CASTILE-LEON
Aveiro
Viseu
Salamanca
Peñaranda
Mondego
Guarda
Segovia
La Granja
Vilar
Valley of the Fallen
Figueira da Foz
Coimbra
Conimbriga
Ciudad Rodrigo
Piedranita
Ávila
El Escorial
Barajas
Madrid
Batalha
Leiria
Plasencia
Nazaré
Tomar
Fatima
Valado
Castelo Branco
Tajo
Talavera de la Reina
Aranjuez
Alcobaça
Caldas da Rainha
Entroncamento
Valencia de Alcantara
Toledo
Óbidos
Cabo da Roca
Santarém
Tajo
Tejo
Portalegre
Cáceres
Trujillo
La Nava
Almoncid
CASTILE-LA
Sintra
Consuegra
Lisbon
Zorita
Estoril
Cascais
Elvas
Badajoz
Mérida
Puerto Lapice
Cromlech dos Almendres
Tomelloso
Setúbal
Cabo Espichel
Évora
Don Benito
Escoural
Anta do Zambujeiro
La Albuera
Ciudad Real
Manzanares
Casa Branca
EXTREMADURA
AVE High Speed Rail
Valdepeñas
ALENTEJO
Puertollano
Sines
Llerena
Alcarecejos
Cercal
Beja
Galaroza
Odemira
Funcheira
Córdoba
Linares
Vila do Bispo
Úbeda
ALGARVE
Italica
Sagres
Vila Real
Ayamonte
Carmona
Jaén
Tunes
Lagos
Salema
Loule
Faro
Cacela Velha
Huelva
Sevilla
Écija
ANDALUCÍA
Albufeira
Tavira
Guadalquivir
Utrera
Alhambra
WHITE HILL TOWNS
Bobadilla
Sanlucar
Jerez
Zahara
Antequera
Granada
Arcos
Grazalema
SIERRA NEVADA
COSTA DE LA LUZ
Rota
Cádiz
Benaojan
Ronda
Málaga
Frigiliana
Medina-Sidonia
Pileta Caves
Nerja
Nerja Caves
Motril
Marbella
Torremolinos
Salobreña
Fuengirola
Vejer
San Pedro
COSTA DEL SOL
Cabo Trafalgar
Algeciras
La Línea
Tarifa
GIBRALTAR (UK)
Strait of Gibraltar
Tangier
CEUTA (Spain)
MOROCCO
Tetouan
A3
A1
A6
A2
E1
A49
A4
A66
A92
E5

to Plymouth, England
Bay of Biscay
Bordeaux
Libourne
St. Emilion
Périgueux
DORDOGNE
Dordogne
Sarlat
Le Buisson
Beynac
Brive-la-Gaillarde
Aurillac
Lot
DUNE DU PILAT
Garonne
Cahors
Rodez
AQUITAINE
Agen
Montauban
Tarn
Dax
FRANCE
Albi
Toulouse
Castres
St. Jean-de-Luz
Biarritz
Bayonne
Hendaye
Irun
Lekeitio
Bilbao
San Sebastián
Guggenheim Museum
Guernica
BASQUE
St. Jean Pied du Port
Pau
Tarbes
Lourdes
LANGUEDOC
Minerve
Carcassonne
Narbonne
Miranda de Ebro
Vitoria
Pamplona
Canfranc
CIRQUE DE GAVARNIE
Foix
Haro
RIOJA
Logroño
PYRENÉES
Jaca
ORDESA NAT'L PARK
Torla
Ainsa
Andorra la Vella
ANDORRA
La Tour
Perpignan
Santo Domingo Calzada
Castejón
Collioure
Cerbère
Portbou
Puigcerda
Figueres
Dalí Museum
Cadaques
IN
ARAGON
Ebro
Huesca
Barbastro
Soria
Duero
Zaragoza
Lérida
CATALUNYA
Girona
Tossa
COSTA BRAVA
Almazan
Siguenza
Calatayud
Montserrat
Ebro
Mataró
Vilafranca
Barcelona
AVE High Speed Rail
Daroca
Sitges
El Prat de Llobregat
Molina
Alcañiz
Tarragona
Guadalajara
Monreal
Montalbán
Tortosa
COSTA DORADA
Delta Del Ebro
Sacedon
Morella
Teruel
Vinarós
Cuenca
Torrebaja
Alcazar
Castelló de la Plana
Ferries to Menorca
MANCHA
Motilla
Requena
Sagunto
ISLANDS
MALLORCA
Valencia
BALEARIC
Palma
Sotuélamos
Albacete
Alzira
IBIZA
Gandia
CABRERA
Alcaraz
Dénia
Ibiza
Alcoy
Jávea
Elche
Elda
FORMENTERA
Jumilla
Benidorm
Alicante
Caravaca
Elche
Murcia
COSTA BLANCA
Cúllar Baza
Lorca
La Manga
Cartagena
MTNS.
Mojacar
Almería
Mediterranean Sea
Algiers
ALGERIA
A8
A68
A1
A15
A68
N11
A2
A7
A7
A31
A7
A63
A62
N20
A71
A61
A64
A9
A7

LOW COUNTRIES
0 km
50 km
100 km
0 miles
50 miles
North Sea
Wadden Islands
Waddenzee
Afsluitdijk
Den Helder
Hindeloopen
Leeuwarden
Groningen
Emden
NETHERLANDS
Ijsselmeer
Open-Air Museum
Enkhuizen
Alkmaar
Hoorn
Edam
Zaanse Schans
Lelystad
Flevoland
Haarlem
Amsterdam
Keukenhof
Aalsmeer
Schiphol
Bad Bentheim
Hengelo
Scheveningen
The Hague
Leiden
Utrecht
Kröller-Muller Museum
Open-Air Museum
Delft
to Harwich, England
Hoek van Holland
Rotterdam
Arnhem
Waal
Maas
Nijmegen
Emmerich
Rhine
Delta Expo
Middelburg
Eindhoven
Essen
Duisburg
to Dover, England
Zeebrugge
Bruges
Ostende
Antwerp
Venlo
Düsseldorf
FLANDERS
Flanders Fields Museum
Ieper
Ghent
Brussels
Hasselt
Maastricht
GERMANY
Köln
Leuven
Waterloo
Aachen
Tournai
Lille
BELGIUM
Liege
Remagen
Meuse
Namur
Mons
Arras
Cambrai
Dinant
WALLONIE
La Roche
Cochem
Aulnoye
Zel
FRANCE
Bastogne
Vianden
ARDENNES
LUXEMBOURG
Mosel
St. Quentin
Trier
Charleville Mézières
Laon
Luxembourg City
Longwy
Soissons
Thionville
Senlis
Reims
Verdun Battlefield
Saarbrücken
Charles de Gaulle
A7
A28
A31
A30
A1
A2
A12
A15
A16
A27
A3
A57
A58
A67
A73
E40
E313
E17
E42
A26
E25
A61
A4

DENMARK
0 km
50 km
100 km
0 mi
50 mi
Oslo
Drammen
Drøbak
Kongsberg
Moss
Tønsberg
Sandefjord
Skien
Halden
NORWAY
Lake Vanern
Arendal
Kristiansand
Göta Canal
Skagen
Göteborg
Hirtshals
SWEDEN
Hjørring
Frederikshavn
E6
LÆSØ
Hanstholm
Ålborg
Thisted
Limfjorden
E45
DENMARK
Halmstad
Viborg
Grenå
JUTLAND
Ebeltoft
Kronborg
Helsing-borg
Ringkøbing
Herning
Silkeborg
Århus
Helsingør
SAMSØ
Frederiksborg
Skanderborg
Hillerød
Lund
Billund
Jelling
Louisiana
Copenhagen
Malmo
Legoland
Vejle
Roskilde
Dragør
Esbjerg
Open-Air Museum
E20
E29
E55
Trelleborg
to Harwich, England
Ribe
Odense
ZEALAND
FUNEN
Svendborg
LANGE-LAND
MØN
SYLT
ÆRØ
Møns Klint (cliffs)
Westerland
Ærøskøbing
Flensburg
FALSTER
Niebull
Rødby
Gedser
A7
Puttgarten
Schleswig
Stralsund
Husum
Kiel
GERMANY
Rostock

Rick Steves'®

BEST OF EUROPE 2006

CONTENTS

INTRODUCTION

Big Ben, the Eiffel Tower, and the Roman Colosseum. Yodeling in the Alps, Celtic harps in a pub, and a canal ride under the stars. Michelangelo's *David* and Mad King Ludwig's castles. Sunny Riviera beaches, medieval German towns, and Spanish streets that teem with people at night. Pasta and bratwurst, souvlaki and scones, Parisian crêpes and Tuscan grapes....

Europe is the world's most culture-rich continent. To wrestle it down to a manageable size, this book breaks Europe into its top destinations. It then gives you all the information and opinions necessary to wring the maximum value out of your limited time and money in each of them. If you plan to stay for two months or less in Europe, this book is all you need.

Experiencing Europe's culture, people, and natural wonders economically and hassle-free has been my goal for almost 30 years of traveling, tour guiding, and travel writing. With this book, I pass on to you the lessons I've learned, updated for 2006.

Rick Steves' Best of Europe is the crème de la crème of places featured in my Country Guides. It's balanced to include a comfortable mix of exciting cities and cozy towns: from Paris, London, and Rome to traffic-free Italian Riviera ports, alpine villages, and mom-and-pop châteaux. It covers the predictable biggies and mixes in a healthy dose of Back Door intimacy. Along with Leonardo in the Louvre, you'll enjoy Caterina in her cantina. I've been selective. For example, rather than listing countless medieval towns, I recommend only the best.

The best is, of course, only my opinion. But after nearly three decades of travel research, I've developed a sixth sense for what travelers enjoy.

European Almanac

Population: 365 million (the U.S. has 295 million).
Area: 915,000 square miles (roughly half of the continental U.S.).
Languages: Three main groups: Romance (Italian, Spanish, French), Slavic (Eastern Europe and Russia), and Germanic (German, Dutch, Scandinavian...and English). Most popular second languages are English and French.
Climate: Moderate, warmed by prevailing westerly sea winds. Average of about 65°F in summer, 40°F in winter.
Vegetation: In the north, a mix of conifers (pine and fir) and deciduous trees (oak, elm, and maple). Along the Mediterranean, there are olives, figs, and grapes.
Major Rivers: Danube, Rhine, Rhône, Po, and Seine.
Life Expectancy: About 77 years, among the highest in the world.
Religion: Largely Protestant in the North, Catholic in the South. Many Europeans claim no church affiliation.
Government: The European Union is a federation of independent nations. Formed as an economic trade bloc, it is increasingly a political body with elected representatives.
Gross Domestic Product: $12 trillion (U.S. GDP is $11 trillion).

This Information Is Accurate and Up-to-Date

This book is updated every year. Most publishers of guidebooks that cover a country from top to bottom can afford an update only every two or three years, and even then, the research is often by e-mail or letter. Since this book is selective, my researchers and I can personally update it each summer. The telephone numbers and hours of sights listed in this book are accurate as of mid-2005—but once you pin Europe down, it wiggles. For any updates, see www.ricksteves.com/update. Also at my Web site, check the Graffiti Wall (select "Rick Steves' Guidebooks," then your destination) for a huge, valuable list of reports and experiences—good and bad—from fellow travelers.

Use this year's edition. People who try to save a few bucks by traveling with an old book are not smart. They learn the seriousness of their mistake...in Europe. Your trip costs about $10 per waking hour. Your time is valuable. This guidebook saves lots of time.

About This Book

This book is organized by destinations. Each destination is covered as a mini-vacation on its own, filled with exciting sights and homey, affordable places to stay. In each chapter, you'll find the following:

Planning Your Time contains a suggested schedule, with thoughts on how to best use your limited time.

Orientation includes tourist information, city transportation, and an easy-to-read map designed to make the text clear and your arrival smooth.

Sights are rated: ▲▲▲—Don't miss; ▲▲—Try hard to see; ▲—Worthwhile if you can make it; No rating—Worth knowing about.

Sleeping and Eating includes descriptions, addresses, and phone numbers of my favorite budget hotels and restaurants.

Transportation Connections covers how to reach nearby destinations by train or bus.

The **appendix** is a traveler's tool kit, with telephone tips, a climate chart, and a list of U.S. embassies and national tourist offices.

Browse through this book, choose your favorite destinations, and link them up. Then have a great trip! You'll travel like a temporary local, getting the most out of every mile, minute, and dollar.

PLANNING

Trip Costs

Five components make up your trip cost: airfare, surface transportation, room and board, sightseeing/entertainment, and shopping/miscellany.

Airfare: Don't try to sort through the mess yourself. Get and use a good travel agent. A basic round-trip U.S.A.-to-Europe flight should cost $700–1,000 (even cheaper in winter), depending on where you fly from and when. Always consider saving time and money in Europe by flying "open jaw" (flying into one city and out of another, such as flying into London and out of Athens).

Surface Transportation: Your best mode depends upon the time you have and the scope of your trip. For many it's a Eurailpass (for prices, see sidebar on page 17). Train passes are normally available only outside of Europe. You may save money by simply buying tickets as you go (for more information, see "Transportation," below).

Drivers can figure $250 per person per week (based on 2 people splitting the cost of the car, tolls, gas, and insurance). Car rental is cheapest to arrange from the United States. Leasing, for trips over three weeks, is even cheaper.

Room and Board: You can easily manage in Europe in 2006 on an overall average of $100 a day per person for room and board (more for cities, less for towns). A $100-a-day budget allows $10 for lunch, $5 for snacks, $20 for dinner, and $65 for lodging (based on 2 people splitting the cost of a $130 double room that includes breakfast). That's doable. Students and tightwads will do it on $50 ($25 per bed, $25 for meals and snacks).

Sightseeing and Entertainment: In big cities, figure $5–10 per major sight, $3 for minor ones, and $25 for splurge experiences (e.g., tours, concerts, gelato binges). An overall average of $15 a day works for most. Don't skimp here. After all, this category directly powers most of the experiences all the other expenses are designed to make possible.

Shopping and Miscellany: Figure $1 per postcard and $2 per coffee, beer, and ice-cream cone. Shopping can vary in cost from nearly nothing to a small fortune. Good budget travelers find that this category has little to do with assembling a trip full of lifelong and wonderful memories.

When to Go

May, June, September, and October are the best travel months. Peak season (July and August) offers the sunniest weather and the most exciting slate of activities—but the worst crowds. During this busy time, it's best to reserve rooms well in advance, particularly for the big cities (see "Making Reservations," on page 25).

Off-season, October through April, expect generally shorter hours at attractions, more lunchtime breaks, fewer activities, and fewer guided tours in English. If you're traveling off-season, be careful to confirm opening times.

As a general rule of thumb any time of year, the climate north of the Alps is mild (like Seattle), while south of the Alps it's like Arizona. For specifics, check the Climate Chart in the appendix. If you wilt in the heat, avoid the Mediterranean in summer. If you want blue skies in the Alps, Britain, and Scandinavia, travel in the height of summer. Plan your itinerary to beat the heat (for a spring trip, start in the south and work north) but also to moderate culture shock (start in mild Britain and work south and east) and minimize crowds. Touristy places in the core of Europe (Germany, the Alps, France, Italy, and Greece) suffer most from crowds.

Sightseeing Priorities

Only have a week to "see" Europe? You can't, of course, but if you're organized and energetic you can see the two art-filled cultural capitals of London and Paris plus Europe's most magnificent landscape—the Swiss Alps.

Whether you have a week or longer, here are my recommended priorities. These itineraries are fast-paced, but doable by car or train and each allows about two nights in each spot. I've taken geographical proximity into account. Most work best if you fly "open jaw."

If you have...

Europe's Best Destinations

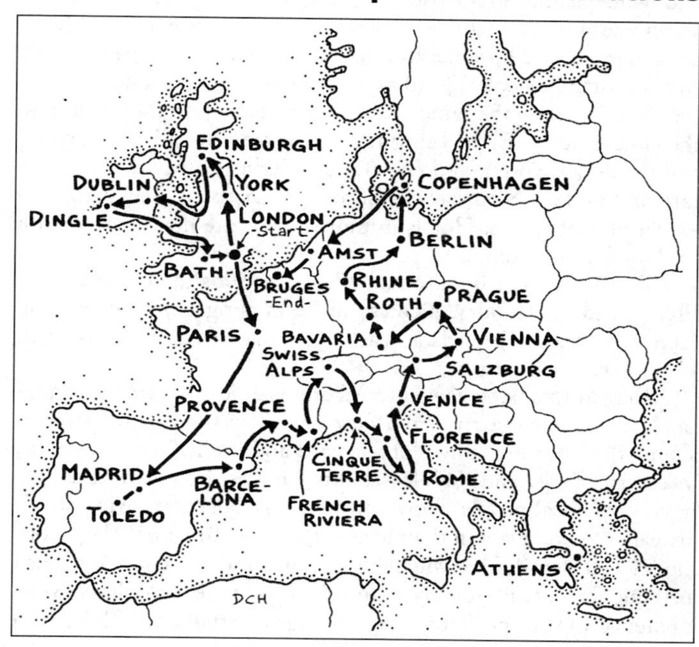

5 days: Paris, Swiss Alps
7 days, add: London
10 days, add: Rome
14 days, add: Rhine, Amsterdam, Haarlem
17 days, add: Venice, Florence
21 days, add: Cinque Terre, Rothenburg, Bavaria
28 days, add: Siena, Bath (a day each), Salzburg, Hallstatt, French Riviera
35 days, add: Provence, Barcelona, Madrid, Toledo
42 days, add: Vienna, Prague, Berlin
49 days, add: Copenhagen, York, Edinburgh
56 days, add: Dublin, Dingle, Bruges
60 days, add: Athens (splice it in from Rome or fly home from Athens).

Travel Smart

Your trip to Europe is like a complex play—easier to follow and really appreciate on a second viewing. While no one does the same trip twice to gain that advantage, reading this book's chapters on your intended destinations before your trip accomplishes much the same thing.

As you read this book, note the days of markets and festivals and when sights are closed. When setting up your itinerary, anticipate problem days. Mondays are bad in Florence, Tuesdays are bad in Paris. Museums and sights, especially large ones, usually stop admitting people 30–60 minutes before closing time.

Sundays have the same pros and cons as they do for travelers in the United States. Sightseeing attractions are generally open, shops and banks are closed, and city traffic is light. Rowdy evenings are rare on Sundays. Saturdays in Europe are virtually weekdays with earlier closing hours. Hotels in tourist areas are most crowded on Fridays and Saturdays.

Be sure to mix intense and relaxed periods in your itinerary. Plan ahead for laundry, picnics, and e-mailing home. Every trip (and every traveler) needs at least a few slack days. Pace yourself. Assume you will return.

Reread this book as you travel and visit local tourist information offices. Upon arrival in a new town, lay the groundwork for a smooth departure. Buy a phone card and use it for reservations, reconfirmations, and double-checking hours. Enjoy the friendliness of the local people. Slow down and ask questions. Most locals are eager to point you in their idea of the right direction. Wear your money belt, familiarize yourself with the local currency, and learn a simple formula to quickly estimate rough prices in dollars. Keep a notepad in your pocket for organizing your thoughts. Those who expect to travel smart, do.

RESOURCES

Tourist Offices

In the United States: Each country has a national tourist office in the U.S.A. (see the appendix for Web sites, phone numbers, and addresses). Before your trip, you can ask for the free general information packet and for specific information (such as city maps and schedules of upcoming festivals).

In Europe: The local tourist information office is your best first stop in any new city. Try to arrive, or at least telephone, before it closes. In this book, I'll refer to a tourist information office as a TI. Throughout Europe, you'll find TIs are usually well organized and English speaking.

As national budgets tighten, many TIs have been privatized. This means they become sales agents for big tours and hotels, and their "information" becomes unavoidably colored. While the TI has listings of all the rooms and is eager to book you one, use their room-finding service only as a last resort. Across Europe, room-finding services are charging commissions from hotels, taking fees from travelers, blacklisting establishments that buck their materialistic rules, and are unable to give hard opinions on the relative value of one place over another. The accommodations stakes are too high to go potluck through the TI. By using the listings in this book, you can avoid that kind of "help."

Rick Steves' Guidebooks, Public Television Shows, and Radio Shows

Rick Steves' Europe Through the Back Door gives you budget-travel skills, such as minimizing jet lag, packing light, planning your itinerary, traveling by car or train, finding rooms, changing money, avoiding rip-offs, buying a mobile phone, hurdling the language barrier, staying healthy, taking great photographs, using a bidet, and much more. The book also includes chapters on 38 of my favorite "Back Doors."

Country Guides: These annually-updated books offer you the latest on the top sights and destinations, with tips on how to make your trip efficient and fun. Here are the titles:

Rick Steves' Best of Europe
Rick Steves' Best of Eastern Europe
Rick Steves' England (new in 2006)
Rick Steves' France
Rick Steves' Germany & Austria
Rick Steves' Great Britain
Rick Steves' Ireland
Rick Steves' Italy
Rick Steves' Portugal
Rick Steves' Scandinavia
Rick Steves' Spain
Rick Steves' Switzerland

City and Regional Guides: Updated every year, these books focus on Europe's most compelling destinations. Along with specifics on sights, restaurants, hotels, and nightlife, you'll get self-guided, illustrated tours of the outstanding museums and most characteristic neighborhoods.

Rick Steves' Amsterdam, Bruges & Brussels
Rick Steves' Florence & Tuscany
Rick Steves' London
Rick Steves' Paris
Rick Steves' Prague & the Czech Republic
Rick Steves' Provence & the French Riviera
Rick Steves' Rome
Rick Steves' Venice

Rick Steves' Phrase Books: This series of practical and budget-oriented books covers French, German, Italian, Portuguese, Spanish, and French/Italian/German. You'll be able to ask the gelato man for a free taste, chat with your cabbie, and make hotel reservations over the phone.

And More Books: *Rick Steves' Europe 101: History and Art for the Traveler* (with Gene Openshaw) gives you the story of Europe's people, history, and art. Written for smart people who were sleeping in their history and art classes before they knew they were going to Europe, *101* helps Europe's sights come alive.

Rick Steves' Easy Access Europe, written for travelers with limited mobility, covers London, Paris, Bruges, Amsterdam, and the Rhine River.

Rick Steves' Postcards from Europe, my autobiographical book, packs 25 years of travel anecdotes and insights into the ultimate 2,000-mile European adventure.

My latest book, *Rick Steves' European Christmas,* covers the joys, traditions, and history of the holiday season in seven countries throughout Europe.

Public Television Shows: My series, *Rick Steves' Europe,* keeps churning out shows. Many of the 95 episodes feature destinations covered in this book.

Radio Shows: My new weekly radio show, which combines call-in questions (à la *Car Talk*) and interviews with travel experts, airs on public radio stations. For a schedule of upcoming topics, an archive of past programs, and details on how to call in, see www.ricksteves.com/radio.

More Guidebooks

You may want some supplemental information, especially if you'll be traveling beyond my recommended destinations. When you consider the improvements they'll make in your $3,000 vacation, $25 or $35 for extra maps and books is money well spent. Especially for several people traveling by car, the weight and expense are negligible.

The Lonely Planet guides to various European countries are thorough, well-researched (though not updated annually), and packed with good maps and hotel recommendations for low- to moderate-budget travelers. The hip, insightful Rough Guide series (by British researchers, not updated annually) and the highly opinionated Let's Go series (annually updated by Harvard students) are great for students and vagabonds. If you're a backpacker with a train pass and interested in the youth and night scene, get Let's Go. The popular, skinny green Michelin guides (covering most southern countries and French regions) are excellent, especially if you're driving. They're known for their city and sightseeing maps, dry but concise and helpful information on all major sights, and good cultural and historical background. English editions are sold locally at tourist shops and gas stations.

Maps

The black-and-white maps in this book, drawn by Dave Hoerlein, are concise and simple. Dave, who is well-traveled in Europe, has designed the maps to help you locate recommended places and get to the tourist offices, where you can pick up a more in-depth map (usually free) of the city or region. Better maps are sold at newsstands and bookstores—take a look before you buy to be sure the map has the level of detail you want. For drivers, I'd recommend a 1:200,000- or 1:300,000-scale map for each country. Train travelers can usually manage fine with the freebies they get with their train pass and at the local tourist offices.

PRACTICALITIES

Red Tape: Americans and Canadians need a passport but no visa and no shots to travel throughout Europe. Crossing borders is easy. Sometimes you won't even realize it's happened. When you do change countries, however, you change phone cards, postage stamps, gas prices, ways to flush a toilet, words for "hello," figurehead monarchs, and breakfast breads. Plan ahead for these changes (use up stamps and phone cards, brush up on the new language).

Time: In Europe—and in this book—you'll be using the 24-hour clock. After 12:00 noon, keep going—13:00, 14:00, and so on. For anything over 12, subtract 12 and add p.m. (14:00 is 2 p.m.). European time is generally six/nine hours ahead of the east/west coast of the U.S.A., though Great Britain and Ireland are five/eight hours ahead.

Metric: Outside of Britain, get used to metric. A liter is about a quart, four to a gallon. A kilometer is six-tenths of a mile. I figure kilometers to miles by cutting them in half and adding back 10 percent of the original (120 km: 60 + 12 = 72 miles, 300 km: 150 + 30 = 180 miles). For more on metric conversions, see the appendix.

Watt's Up? If you're bringing electrical gear, you'll need an adapter plug (2 round prongs for the Continent, 3 square ones for Britain and Ireland; sold cheap at travel stores in the United States). Travel appliances and electronic equipment often have convenient, built-in converters; look for a voltage switch marked 120V (U.S.) and 240V (Europe). If yours doesn't have a built-in converter, you'll have to buy an external one.

News: Americans keep in touch with the *International Herald Tribune* (published almost daily via satellite throughout Europe). Every Tuesday, the European editions of *Time* and *Newsweek* hit the stands with articles of particular interest to European travelers. Sports addicts can get their fix from *USA Today*. News in English will only be sold where there's enough demand: in big cities and tourist centers. Good Web sites include www.europeantimes.com and http://news.bbc.co.uk. If you're concerned about how some event might affect your safety as an American traveling abroad, call the U.S. consulate or embassy in the nearest big city for advice (see appendix for list).

Discounts: While discounts for sights and transportation are not listed in this book, seniors (60 and over), students (with International Student Identity Cards), and youths (under 18) may snare discounts—but only by asking. Some discounts (particularly for sights) are granted only to European residents.

MONEY

Exchange Rates

I've priced things in local currencies throughout this book.

Most countries in this book have adopted the euro currency: Austria, Belgium, France, Germany, Greece, Ireland, Italy, Spain, and the Netherlands:

1 euro (€) = $1.20, and €0.80 = about $1. To roughly convert prices in euros to dollars, add 20 percent: €20 is about $24, €50 is about $60, and so on. One euro is broken down into 100 cents. You'll find coins ranging from 1 cent to 2 euros, and bills from 5 euros to 500 euros.

Britain, Denmark, Switzerland, and the Czech Republic have kept their traditional currencies:

1 British pound (£) = about $1.80, and £0.55 = about $1. To roughly convert British pounds to dollars, you can double them: £5 is about $10 (actually $9).

1 Danish kroner (kr) = about 16 cents, and 6 kr = about $1. To translate Danish prices into dollars, divide by 6 (e.g., 100 kr = about $16).

1 Swiss franc (SF) = about 80 cents, and 1.25 SF = about $1. To estimate the dollar equivalent of prices in Swiss francs, subtract about one-fourth (e.g., 60 SF = about $45).

1 Czech koruna (Kč) = about 4 cents, and 25 Kč = about $1. To very roughly convert Czech crowns into dollars, drop the last digit and divide by three: 750 Kč = $25 (actually $30).

Banking

Bring plastic (ATM, credit, or debit cards) along with several hundred dollars in hard cash as an emergency backup. Traveler's checks are a waste of time and money.

To withdraw cash from a bank machine, you'll need a PIN code (numbers only, no letters on European keypads) and your bankcard. Before you go, verify with your bank that your card will work and alert them that you'll be making withdrawals in Europe; otherwise, the bank may not approve transactions if it perceives unusual spending patterns. Bring two cards in case one gets demagnetized or eaten by a machine. If you plan on getting cash advances with your regular credit card, be sure to ask the card company about fees before you leave.

Visa and MasterCard are more commonly accepted than American Express. Just like at home, credit or debit cards work easily at larger hotels, restaurants, and shops, but smaller businesses prefer payment in local currency.

Twelve European countries have adopted the euro currency, but some haven't, including Denmark, Britain, Switzerland, and the Czech Republic. If you're about to cross a border with spare coins you won't be able to use anywhere else, spend them on candy, souvenirs, gas, or a telephone call home.

Regular banks have the best rates for changing money and traveler's checks. For a large exchange, it pays to compare rates and fees. Post offices and train stations usually change money if you can't get to a bank.

You should use a money belt (a pouch with a strap that you buckle like a belt and wear under your clothes). Thieves target tourists. A money belt provides peace of mind, allowing you to carry lots of cash safely.

Don't be petty about withdrawing money. You don't need to waste time every few days tracking down a cash machine. Change a week's worth of money, get big bills, stuff them in your money belt, and travel!

Damage Control for Lost or Stolen Cards

If you lose your credit, debit, or ATM card, you can stop people from using your card by reporting the loss immediately to the respective global customer-assistance centers. Call these 24-hour U.S. numbers collect: Visa (tel. 410/581-9994), MasterCard (tel. 636/722-7111), and American Express (tel. 336/393-1111).

At a minimum, have the following information ready: the name of the financial institution that issued you the card, along with the type of card (classic, platinum, or whatever). Ideally, plan ahead and pack photocopies of your cards—front and back—to expedite their replacement. Providing the following information will allow for a quicker cancellation of your missing card: full card number, whether you are the primary or secondary cardholder, the cardholder's name exactly as printed on the card, billing address, home phone number, circumstances of the loss or theft, and identification verification (your birthdate, your mother's maiden name, or your Social Security number—memorize this, don't carry a copy). If you are the secondary cardholder, you'll also need to provide the primary cardholder's identification-verification details. You can generally receive a temporary card within two or three business days in Europe.

If you promptly report your card lost or stolen, you typically won't be responsible for any unauthorized transactions on your account, although many banks charge a liability fee of $50.

Tips on Tipping

Tipping in Europe isn't as automatic and generous as it is in the United States, but for special service, tips are appreciated, if not expected. As in the U.S., the proper amount depends on your resources, tipping philosophy, and the circumstance, but some general guidelines apply.

Restaurants: Tipping is an issue only at restaurants that have waiters and waitresses. If you order your food at a counter, don't tip.

At restaurants with wait staff, the service charge (10–15 percent) is usually listed on the menu and included in your bill. When the service is included, there's no need to tip beyond that, but if you like to tip and you're pleased with the service, you can round up the bill (but not more than 5 percent).

If the service is not included, tip up to 10 percent by rounding up or leaving the change from your bill. Leave the tip on the table or hand it to your server. It's best to tip in cash even if you pay with your credit card. Otherwise the tip may never reach your server.

Taxis: To tip the cabbie, round up. For a typical ride, round up to the next euro on the fare (to pay a €13 fare, give €14); for a long ride, to the nearest 10 (for a €75 fare, give €80). If the cabbie hauls your bags and zips you to the airport to help you catch your flight, you might want to toss in a little more. But if you feel like you're being driven in circles or otherwise ripped off, skip the tip.

Special services: It's thoughtful to tip a couple of euros to someone who shows you a special sight and who is paid in no other way (such as the man who shows you an Etruscan tomb in his backyard). Tour guides at public sights often hold out their hands for tips after they give their spiel. If I've already paid for the tour, I don't tip extra, though some tourists do give a euro or two, particularly for a job well done. I don't tip at hotels, but if you do, give the porter a euro for carrying bags and leave a couple of euros in your room at the end of your stay for the maid if the room was kept clean. In general, if someone in the service industry does a super job for you, a tip of a couple of euros is appropriate...but not required.

When in doubt, ask. If you're not sure whether (or how much) to tip for a service, ask your hotelier or the TI; they'll fill you in on how it's done on their turf.

VAT Refunds and Customs Regulations

VAT Refunds: Wrapped into the purchase price of your souvenirs is a Value-Added Tax (VAT) ranging from seven to 22 percent. If you make a purchase that meets your host country's minimum purchase requirement (an average of $100; see appendix) at a store that participates in the VAT refund scheme, you're entitled to get most of that tax back. Personally, I've never felt that VAT refunds are worth the hassle, but if you do, here's the scoop.

If you're lucky, the merchant will subtract the tax when you make your purchase (this is more likely if the store ships the goods to your home). Otherwise, you'll need to:

Begin your trip at www.ricksteves.com

At ricksteves.com you'll find a wealth of **free information** on destinations covered in this book, including fresh European travel and tour news every month and helpful "Graffiti Wall" tips from thousands of fellow travelers.

When you're there, the **online Travel Store** is a great place to save money on travel bags and accessories specially designed by Rick Steves to help you travel smarter and lighter. These include Rick's popular carry-on bags (wheeled and rucksack versions), money belts, day bags, totes, toiletries kits, packing cubes, clotheslines, locks, clocks, sleep sacks, adapters, and a wide selection of guidebooks, planning maps, and *Rick Steves' Europe* DVDs.

Traveling through Europe by rail is a breeze, but choosing the right railpass for your trip—amidst hundreds of options—can drive you nutty. At ricksteves.com you'll find **Rick Steves' Annual Guide to European Railpasses**—your best way to convert chaos into pure travel energy. Buy your railpass from Rick, and you'll get a bunch of free extras to boot.

Travel agents will tell you about mainstream tours of Europe, but they won't tell you about **Rick Steves' tours.** Rick Steves' Europe Through the Back Door travel company offers more than two dozen itineraries and 250+ departures reaching the best destinations in this book...and beyond. You'll enjoy the services of a great guide, a fun bunch of travel partners (with group sizes in the mid-20s), and plenty of room to spread out in a big, comfy bus. You'll find tours to fit every vacation size, from week-long city getaways (Paris, London, Venice, Florence, Rome), to 12–18 day country tours, to three-week "Best of Europe" adventures. For details, visit www.ricksteves.com or call 425/771-8303, ext. 217.

Get the paperwork. Have the merchant completely fill out the necessary refund document, typically called a "cheque." You'll have to present your passport at the store.

Have your cheque(s) stamped at the border by the customs agent who deals with VAT refunds. If you're in a European Union country, then you get the stamp at your last stop in the European Union. Otherwise, get your cheque stamped when you leave the country.

It's best to keep your purchases in your carry-on for viewing, but if they're too large or considered too dangerous (such as knives) to carry on, then track down the proper customs agent to inspect them before you check your bag. You're not supposed to use your purchased goods before you leave. If you show up at customs wearing your new kilt, officials might look the other way—or deny you a refund.

To collect your refund, you'll need to return your stamped documents to the retailer or its representative. Many merchants work with a service that has offices at major airports, ports, and border crossings, such as Global Refund (www.globalrefund.com) or Premier Tax Free (www.premiertaxfree.com). These services, which extract a four percent fee, usually can refund your money immediately in your currency of choice or credit your card (within two billing cycles). If you have to deal directly with the retailer, mail the store your stamped documents and then wait. It could take months.

Customs Regulations: You can take home $800 in souvenirs per person duty-free. The next $1,000 is taxed at a flat 3 percent. After that, you pay the individual item's duty rate. You can also bring in duty-free a liter of alcohol (slightly more than a standard-sized bottle of wine), a carton of cigarettes, and up to 100 cigars. As for food, anything in cans or sealed jars is acceptable. Skip dried meat, cheese, and fresh fruits and veggies. To check customs rules and duty rates, visit www.customs.gov.

TRANSPORTATION

By Car or Train?

Each has pros and cons. Cars are an expensive headache in big cities but give you more control for delving deep into the countryside. Groups of three or more go cheaper by car. If you're packing heavy (with kids), go by car. Trains are best for city-to-city travel and give you the convenience of doing long stretches overnight. By train, I arrive relaxed and well rested—not so by car. A EurailDrive pass allows you to mix train and car travel. When thoughtfully used, this pass economically gives you the best of both transportation worlds.

Traveling by Train

A major mistake Americans make is relating public transportation in Europe to the pathetic public transportation they're used to at home. By rail you'll have Europe by the tail. While many simply buy tickets as they go ("point to point"), the various train passes give you the simplicity of ticket-free, unlimited travel, and depending on how much traveling you do, often offer a tremendous savings over regular point-to-point tickets. The Eurailpass gives you several options (explained in the sidebar on page 17).

For a summary of railpass deals and point-to-point ticket options (available in the U.S. and in Europe), check our free Railpass Guide at www.ricksteves.com. If you decide to get a railpass, this guide will help you know you're getting the right one for your trip. To study train schedules in advance on the Web, look up http://bahn.hafas.de/bin/query.exe/en (Germany's excellent all-Europe timetable).

Eurailpass and Eurail Selectpass

The granddaddy of European railpasses, Eurail, gives you unlimited rail travel on the national trains of 17 European countries. That's 100,000 miles of track through all of western Europe, including Ireland, Greece, and Hungary (but excluding Great Britain and most of Eastern Europe). The pass includes many bonuses, such as free boat rides on the Rhine, Mosel, and lakes of Switzerland; several international ferries (Sweden-Finland and Italy-Greece, plus a 50 percent discount on the Ireland-France route); and a 60 percent discount on the Romantic Road bus tour through Germany.

The Eurail Selectpass covers any three, four, or five Eurail countries connected by rail or ferry (e.g., a three-country Selectpass could cover France, Italy, and Greece). Selectpasses are fine for a focused trip, but to see the Best of Europe, you'd do best with a Eurailpass. Either pass gives a 15 percent Saverpass discount to two or more companions traveling together.

Eurail Analysis

For an at-a-glance break-even point, remember that a one-month Eurailpass pays for itself if your route is Amsterdam-Rome-Madrid-Paris on first class or Copenhagen-Rome-Madrid-Copenhagen on second class. A one-month Eurail Youthpass saves you money if you're traveling from Amsterdam to Rome to Madrid and back to Amsterdam. Passes pay for themselves quicker in the north, where the cost per mile is higher. Check the "Europe by Rail: Dollars and Time" map on page 16 to see if your planned travels merit purchasing a train pass. If it's about even, go with the pass for the convenience of not having to wait in line to buy tickets and for the fun and freedom to travel "free."

Using one Eurailpass versus a series of country passes: While nearly every country has its own mini-version of the Eurailpass, trips covering several countries are usually cheapest with the budget whirlwind traveler's old standby, the Eurailpass, or its budget cousin, the Eurail Selectpass. This is because the more rail days included in a pass, the cheaper your per-day cost is. A group of country passes with a few rail days apiece will have a high per-day cost, while a Eurailpass with a longer life span offers a better deal overall. However, if you're traveling in a single country, an individual country railpass (such as Francerail or Germanrail) is often a better value than any of the Eurail passes.

EurailDrive Pass: The EurailDrive Pass is for those who want to combine train travel with the freedom of having a car a day here and a day there. Great areas for a day of joyriding include the Dutch

Europe by Rail: Dollars and Time

This map can help you determine if a railpass is right for you. Add up the ticket prices for your route. If your total is about the same or more than the cost of a pass, buy the pass (unless you like waiting in lines at train stations).

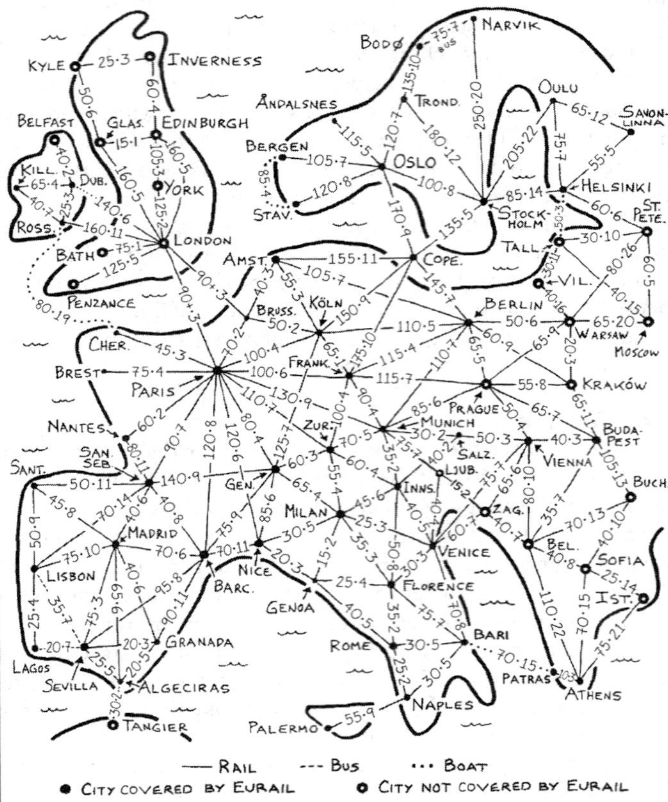

The first number between cities = approximate cost in $US for a 1-way, 2nd class ticket. The second number = number of hours the trip takes.

Important: These fares and times are based on the Eurail Tariff Guide. Actual prices may vary due to currency fluctuations and local promotions. Local competition can cut the actual price of some boat crossings (from Italy to Greece, for example) by 50% or more. For approximate 1st class rail prices, multiply the prices shown by 1.5.
Travel times and fares are for express trains where applicable.

Railpasses

Prices listed are for 2006. *Rick Steves' Guide to Eurail Passes* has the latest and can be found at www.ricksteves.com/rail. Prices subject to change.

EURAILPASSES

These passes cover all 18 Eurail countries: Austria, Belgium, Denmark, Finland, France, Germany, Greece, Hungary, Ireland, Italy, Luxembourg, Netherlands, Norway, Portugal, Romania, Spain, Sweden, and Switzerland.

	1st Class Individual	1st Class Saver	2nd Class Youth
10 days in 2 months flexi	$715	$608	$465
15 days in 2 months flexi	940	800	612
15 consecutive days	605	513	394
21 consecutive days	785	668	510
1 month consec. days	975	828	634
2 months consec. days	1378	1173	897
3 months consec. days	1703	1450	1108

FIRST CLASS EURAILDRIVE PASSES

4 first class rail days and 2 car days in a 2 month period in all 18 Eurail countries.

Car Categories	2 Adults	1 Adult	Extra Car Day	Extra Rail Day
Economy	$427	$475	$49	$45
Compact	443	506	65	45
Intermediate	450	521	75	45

Prices are per person. Third and fourth persons sharing car get a 4-day out of 2-month railpass for approximately $380 per person (kids 4-11 $190). You can add rail days (max 6) and car days (no limit).

FIRST CLASS SELECTPASS DRIVE

Any 3 days of rail travel + 2 days of Hertz or Avis car rental in 2 months within 3 connecting Eurail countries.

Car Categories	2 Adults	1 Adult	Extra Car Day	Extra Rail Day
Economy	$318	$365	$49	$40
Compact	332	395	65	40
Intermediate	335	410	75	40

Prices are per person. You can add rail days (max 7) and car days (no limit). A fourth or fifth country each adds about $35 to these prices. Third and fourth adults sharing the car pay $270 per person (kids 4-11 $135).

To order Rail and Drive passes, call your travel agent or Rail Europe at 800-438-7245.

SELECTPASSES

This pass covers travel in three, four, or five adjacent countries. For details, check out www.ricksteves.com/rail. Prices subject to change.

1st Class Individual	3 Countries	4 Countries	5 Countries
5 days in 2 months	$383	$428	$473
6 days in 2 months	423	468	513
8 days in 2 months	503	548	593
10 days in 2 months	580	625	670
15 days in 2 months			850

1st Class Saver	3 Countries	4 Countries	5 Countries
5 days in 2 months	$325	$363	$400
6 days in 2 months	360	398	435
8 days in 2 months	428	465	503
10 days in 2 months	493	530	568
15 days in 2 months			723

2nd Class Youth	3 Countries	4 Countries	5 Countries
5 days in 2 months	$249	$278	$307
6 days in 2 months	275	304	333
8 days in 2 months	325	354	383
10 days in 2 months	375	404	433
15 days in 2 months			553

Saverpass prices are per person for 2 or more people traveling together at all times. Youthpasses: Under age 26 only. Kids 4-11 pay half adult or saver fare; under 4: free.

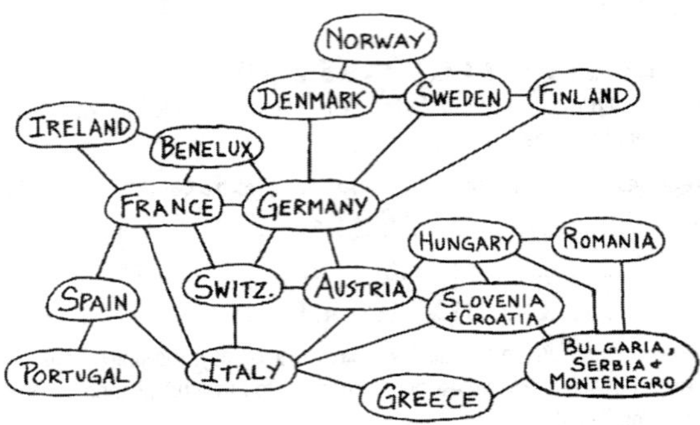

Selectpass diagram key:

*A **Selectpass** can be designed to connect a "chain" of any three, four, or five countries in this diagram linked by direct lines. (Examples that qualify: Norway-Sweden-Germany; Spain-France-Italy.) Each bubble counts as one country.*

countryside; Germany's Rhine or Bavaria; France's Provence; Italy's Tuscany and Umbria; or the Alps (for "car hiking"). When comparing prices, remember that each day of car rental comes with about $30 of extra expenses (CDW insurance, gas, parking), which you can divide among the people in your party.

Car Rental

It's cheaper to arrange European car rentals in the United States, so check rates with your travel agent or directly with the companies. Rent by the week with unlimited mileage. If you'll be renting for three weeks or more, ask your agent about leasing, which is a scheme to avoid insurance costs and taxes. Allow about $750 per person (based on two people sharing the car) to rent a small economy car for three weeks with unlimited mileage, including gas, parking, and insurance. I normally rent the smallest, least expensive model. Explore your drop-off options and costs. Drop-off in another country can be very expensive. You'll probably need to get separate car rentals for Britain, Ireland, and the Continent.

For peace of mind, I spring for the Collision Damage Waiver insurance (CDW, about $15 per day), but it has a high deductible hovering around $1,000–1,500. When you pick up your car, many car-rental companies will try to sell you "super CDW" at an additional cost of $7–15 per day to lower the deductible to zero.

Some credit cards offer CDW-type coverage for no charge to their customers. Quiz your credit-card company on the worst-case scenario. You have to choose between the coverage offered by your car-rental company and your credit-card company. This means that if you go with the credit-card coverage, you'll have to decline the CDW offered by the car-rental company. In this situation, some car-rental companies put a hold on your credit card for the amount of the full deductible (which can equal the value of the car). This is bad news if your credit limit is low--particularly if you plan on using that card for other purchases during your trip.

Another alternative is buying CDW insurance from Travel Guard for $9 a day (U.S. tel. 800-826-4919, www.travelguard.com). It's valid throughout Europe, but some car-rental companies refuse to honor it, especially in Italy and the Republic of Ireland. Oddly, residents of some states (including Washington) are not allowed to buy this coverage.

In sum, buying CDW—and the supplemental insurance to buy down the deductible, if you choose—is the easiest but priciest option. Using the coverage that comes with your credit card is cheaper, but can involve more hassle. If you're taking a short trip but not in Italy or Ireland, the cheapest solution is to buy Travel Guard's very affordable CDW. For longer trips, leasing is the best way to go.

Note that if you'll be driving in Italy, theft insurance (separate from CDW insurance) is mandatory. The insurance usually costs about $10–15 a day, payable when you pick up the car.

If you plan to drive your rental car into the Czech Republic, keep these tips in mind: State your travel plans up front to the rental company. Some won't allow any of their rental cars to enter Eastern European countries due to the high theft rate. Some won't allow certain types of cars: BMWs, Mercedes, and convertibles. Ask about extra fees—some companies automatically tack on theft and collision coverage for a Czech excursion. To avoid hassles at the Czech border, ask the rental agent to mark your contract with the company's permission to cross.

Driving

For much of Europe, all you need is your valid U.S. driver's license and a car. Confirm with your rental company if an international license is required in the countries you plan to visit. Those traveling in Austria, Germany, Greece, Italy, Portugal, Spain, and Eastern Europe should probably get an international driver's license (at your local AAA office—$10 plus the cost of two passport-type photos).

While gas is expensive, if you keep an eye on the big picture, paying $4 per gallon is more a psychological trauma than a financial one. I use the freeways whenever possible. They are free in the Netherlands and Germany. You'll pay a one-time road fee of about $25 as you enter Switzerland, about $7 for Austria, and about $3 for the Czech Republic. The Italian autostradas and French autoroutes are punctuated by tollbooths (charging about $1 for every 10 minutes). The alternative to these super-freeways often is being marooned in rural traffic. The autostrada/autoroute usually saves enough time, gas, and nausea to justify its expense. Mix scenic country-road rambling with high-speed autobahning, but don't forget that in Europe, the shortest distance between two points is the autobahn.

Parking: Parking is a costly headache in big cities. You'll pay about $20 a day to park safely. Ask at your hotel for advice. I keep a pile of coins in my ashtray for parking meters, public phones, launderettes, and wishing wells.

Cheap Flights

Connecting your itinerary by air is cheaper than you might think. Thanks to Europe's new budget airlines, you can get between many European cities for significantly less than $100 one-way. Some amazing promotional deals can even bring fares down into the single digits. The best deals are from major hub cities (especially London).

New budget airlines are continually being launched, but a handful of them are more established, including easyJet (www.easyjet.com), Ryanair (www.ryanair.com), and Virgin Express (www.virgin-express.com). Some good Web sites you can use to search routes on multiple cheap airlines include www.skyscanner.net, www.mobissimo.com, and www.sidestep.com.

Europe by Air works with 25 different European airlines, offering flights between 150 European cities in 30 countries. Using their "Flight Pass" system, each coupon for a nonstop flight costs $99 plus taxes and airport fees—which can be around $50 (U.S. tel. 888-321-4737, www.europebyair.com).

Be warned that these no-frills airlines can come with trade-offs: minimal customer service, non-refundable tickets, and stringent restrictions on the amount of baggage you're allowed to check without paying extra. Often you can only book these flights online. Also note that you'll sometimes fly out of less convenient, secondary airports. For example, Ryanair's England hub is Stansted Airport, the farthest of London's airports from the city center. Ryanair's service to Copenhagen, Denmark, lands you in a different (though nearby) country: Malmö, Sweden.

COMMUNICATING

Telephones

Smart travelers learn the phone system and use it daily to reserve or reconfirm rooms, find tourist information, or phone home. Many European phone booths take insertable phone cards rather than coins.

Phone Cards: There are two kinds of phone cards: insertable phone cards that you stick into the phone (which can only be used in phone booths), and international phone cards that can be used from virtually any phone (you dial a toll-free number and enter your PIN code). Both kinds of cards work only in the country where you bought them (for example, a Swiss phone card works when you're making calls in Switzerland, but is worthless in France).

You can buy **insertable phone cards** from post offices, newsstands, or tobacco shops. Slide the card into the phone, make your call, and the value is deducted from your card. These are a good deal for calling within Europe, but it's cheaper to make your overseas calls with an international phone card.

International phone cards, which come with a Personal Identification Number (PIN), allow you to call home at the rate of about a dime a minute. To use an international phone card, dial the toll-free access number listed on the card; then, at the prompt, enter your PIN code (also listed on card) and dial the number you want to call, whether it's local, long-distance, or international. These are sold at newsstands, exchange bureaus, souvenir shops, and mini-marts. There are many different brands. Ask for a cheap international telephone card. Stress "international" because some types permit only local calls. Buy a lower denomination in case the card is a dud.

If you use **coins** to make your calls, have a bunch handy. Or look for a **metered phone** ("talk now, pay later") in the bigger post offices. Avoid using hotel-room phones for anything other than local calls and international phone card calls.

Making Calls within a European Country: You'll save money by dialing direct. You just need to learn to break the codes. About half of all European countries use area codes; the other half uses a direct-dial system without area codes.

In countries that use area codes (such as Austria, Britain, Germany, Ireland, and the Netherlands), you dial the local number when calling within a city, and you add the area code if calling long distance within the country. For example, Berlin's area code is 030, and the number of one of my recommended Berlin hotels is 3150-3944. To call it from Frankfurt, dial 030/3150-3944.

To make calls within a country that uses a direct-dial system (Belgium, the Czech Republic, Denmark, France, Greece, Italy, Spain, and Switzerland), you dial the same number whether you're calling across the country or across the street.

Making International Calls: You always start with the international access code (011 if you're calling from America or Canada, or 00 from Europe), then dial the country code of the country you're calling (see chart in appendix).

What you dial next depends on the phone system of the country you're calling. If the country uses area codes, drop the initial zero of the area code, then dial the rest of the number. To call the Berlin hotel from Copenhagen, dial 00, 49 (Germany's country code), 30/3150-3944 (omitting the initial zero in the area code).

Countries that use direct-dial systems (no area codes) vary

in how they're accessed internationally by phone. For instance, if you're making an international call to Denmark, Italy, Spain, or the Czech Republic, simply dial the international access code, country code, and phone number. But if you're calling Belgium, France, or Switzerland, drop the initial zero of the phone number. Example: To call a Paris hotel (tel. 01 47 05 49 15) from London, dial 00, 33 (France's country code), then 1 47 05 49 15 (phone number without the initial zero).

To call my office from Europe, I dial 00 (Europe's international access code), 1 (U.S.A.'s country code), 425 (Edmonds' area code), and 771-8303.

Remember, European time is generally six/nine hours ahead of the east/west coast of the U.S.A., though Great Britain, Ireland, and Portugal are five/eight hours ahead.

U.S. Calling Cards: Calling home from Europe is easy but expensive with AT&T, MCI, or Sprint calling cards. Since direct-dial rates have dropped, U.S. calling cards are no longer a good value. It's also outrageously expensive to use your calling card to make calls between European countries. It's much cheaper to make your calls using an international phone card purchased in Europe.

Mobile Phones: American mobile phones work in Europe if they're GSM-enabled, tri-band (or quad-band), and on a calling plan that includes international calls. Some travelers prefer to buy mobile phones in Europe. For about $100, you can get a phone with $20 worth of calls that will work in the country where you purchased it. (You can buy more time at newsstands or mobile phone shops.) For about $125, you can get a phone that will work in most countries once you pick up the necessary chip per country (about $30 each). If you're interested, stop by any European shop that sells mobile phones (you'll see prominent store-window displays). Depending on your trip and budget, ask for a phone that works only in that country or one that can be used throughout Europe. If you're on a budget, skip mobile phones and use international phone cards instead.

E-mail and Mail

More and more hotels have e-mail addresses and Web sites (included in this book). I've listed some Internet cafés, but your hotelier or TI can steer you to the nearest Internet access point.

To arrange for mail delivery, reserve a few hotels along your route in advance and give their addresses to friends. Allow 10 days for a letter to arrive. Federal Express makes two-day deliveries—for a price. E-mailing and phoning are so easy that I've dispensed with mail stops all together.

SLEEPING

In the interest of smart use of your time, I favor hotels and restaurants handy to your sightseeing activities. Rather than list hotels scattered throughout a city, I describe my favorite two or three neighborhoods and recommend the best accommodations values in each.

Now that hotels are so expensive and tourist information offices' room-finding services are so greedy, it's more important than ever for budget travelers to have a good listing of rooms and call directly to make reservations. This book gives you a wide range of budget accommodations to choose from: hostels, bed-and-breakfasts, guest houses, pensions, small hotels, and splurges. I like places that are quiet, clean, small, central, traditional, friendly, and not listed in other guidebooks. Most places I list are a good value, having at least five of these seven virtues.

Rooms with private bathrooms are often bigger and renovated, while the cheaper rooms without bathrooms often will be on the top floor or not yet refurbished. Any room without a bathroom has access to a bathroom in the corridor (free unless otherwise noted). Rooms with tubs often cost more than rooms with showers. All rooms have a sink. Unless I note a difference, the cost of a room includes a continental breakfast. When breakfast is not included, the price is usually posted in your hotel room.

Before accepting a room, confirm your understanding of the complete price. The only tip my recommended hotels would like is a friendly, easygoing guest. I appreciate feedback on your hotel experiences.

Hotels

Most hotels listed in this book cluster around $70–100 per double, but can run as low as $15 for a bunk and as high as $200+ for a double with maximum plumbing and more. The cost is higher in big cities and heavily-touristed areas and lower off the beaten track. Three or four people can save money by requesting one big room. Traveling alone can get expensive: A single room is often only 20 percent cheaper than a double. If you'll accept a room with twin beds and you ask for a double, you may be turned away. Ask for "a room for two people" if you'll take a twin or a double.

Rooms are generally safe, but don't leave valuables lying around. More (or different) pillows and blankets are usually in the closet or available on request. Remember, in Europe towels and linen aren't always replaced every day. Drip-dry and conserve.

A very simple continental breakfast is almost always included. (Breakfasts in Europe, like towels and people, get smaller as you go south.) If you like juice and protein for breakfast, supply it yourself. I enjoy a box of juice in my hotel room and often supplement the

Sleep Code

I've divided the rooms into three categories, based on the price for a standard double room with bath:

$$$ **Higher Priced**
$$ **Moderately Priced**
$ **Lower Priced**

To give maximum information in a minimum of space, I use this code to describe accommodations listed in this book. Prices listed are per room, not per person. When there is a range of prices in one category, the price will fluctuate with the season, size of room, or length of stay.

S = Single room (or price for one person in a double).

D = Double or twin. Double beds are usually big enough for non-romantic couples.

T = Triple (often a double bed with a single bed moved in).

Q = Quad (an extra child's bed is usually less).

b = Private bathroom with toilet and shower or tub.

s = Private shower or tub only (the toilet is down the hall).

NSE = Does not speak English. Used only when it's unlikely you'll encounter English-speaking staff.

cash only = Does not accept credit cards; you'll need to pay with the local currency.

According to this code, a couple staying at a "Db-€90" hotel in Spain would pay a total of 90 euros (about $108) for a double room with a private bathroom. The hotel accepts credit cards or cash in payment; you can assume a hotel takes credit cards unless you see "cash only" in the listing.

skimpy breakfast with a piece of fruit and cheese.

Pay your bill the evening before you leave to avoid the time-wasting crowd at the reception desk in the morning.

Making Reservations

It's possible to travel at any time of year without reservations (especially if you arrive early in the day), but given the erratic accommodations values and the quality of the gems I've found for this book, I'd highly recommend calling for rooms at least a day or two in advance as you travel (your fluent receptionist will likely help you call your next hotel if you pay for the call). Even if a hotel clerk says the hotel is fully booked, you can try calling between 9:00 and 10:00 on the day you plan to arrive. That's when the hotel clerk knows who'll be checking out and just which rooms will be available. I've taken great pains to list telephone numbers with long-distance instructions (see "Telephones," above and in the appendix). Use the telephone and the convenient phone cards. Most hotels listed are accustomed to English-only speakers. A hotel receptionist will trust you and hold a room until 16:00 (4:00 p.m.) without a deposit, though some will ask for a credit-card number. Honor (or cancel by phone) your reservations. Long distance is cheap and easy from public phone booths. Don't let these people down—I promised you'd call and cancel if for some reason you won't show up. Don't needlessly confirm rooms through the tourist office; they'll take a commission.

If you know exactly which dates you need and really want a particular place, reserve a room well in advance before you leave home. To reserve from home, e-mail, call, or fax the hotel. Phone and fax costs are reasonable, e-mail is a steal, and simple English is usually fine. To fax, use the form in the appendix (or find it online at www.ricksteves.com/reservation). A two-night stay in August would be "2 nights, 16/8/06 to 18/8/06" (Europeans write the date in this order—day/month/year—and hotel jargon counts your stay from your day of arrival through your day of departure).

If you e-mail or fax a reservation request and receive a response with rates stating that rooms are available, this is not a confirmation. You must confirm that the rates are fine and that indeed you want the room. You'll often receive a response requesting one night's deposit. A credit-card number and expiration date will usually work. If you use your credit card for the deposit, you can pay with your card or cash when you arrive; if you don't show up, you'll be billed for one night. Ask about the cancellation policy when you reserve; sometimes you may have to cancel as much as two weeks ahead to avoid paying a stiff penalty. Reconfirm your reservations several days in advance for safety.

Bed-and-Breakfasts

You can stay in private homes throughout Europe and enjoy double the cultural intimacy for about half the cost of hotels. You'll find them mainly in smaller towns and in the countryside (so they are most handy for those with a car). In Germany, look for *Zimmer* signs. For Italian *affitta camere* and French *chambre d'hôte* (CH), ask at local tourist offices. Doubles cost about $50, and you'll often share a bathroom with the family. While your European hosts will rarely speak English (except in Switzerland, the Netherlands, Belgium, and Scandinavia), they will almost always be enthusiastic, delightful hosts.

Hostels

For $15–20 a night, you can stay at one of Europe's 2,000 hostels. While official hostels admit nonmembers for an extra fee, it's best to join the club and buy a youth hostel card before you go (call Hostelling International at 202/783-6161 or order online at www.hiayh.org). To increase your options, consider the many independent hostels that don't require a membership card (www.hostels.com). Except in Bavaria (where you must be under 27 to stay in an official hostel), travelers of any age are welcome as long as they don't mind dorm-style accommodations and making lots of traveling friends. Cheap meals are sometimes available, and kitchen facilities are usually provided for do-it-yourselfers. Expect crowds in the summer, snoring, and lots of youth groups giggling and making rude noises while you try to sleep. Family rooms and doubles are often available on request, but it's basically boys' dorms and girls' dorms. Many hostels are locked up from about 10:00 until 17:00, and a 23:00 curfew is often enforced. Hostelling is ideal for those traveling single: prices are per bed, not per room, and you'll have an instant circle of friends. More and more hostels are getting their business acts together, taking credit-card reservations over the phone and leaving sign-in forms on the door for each available room. If you're serious about traveling cheaply, get a card, carry your own sheets, and cook in the members' kitchens.

Camping

For $5–10 per person per night, you can camp your way through Europe. "Camping" is an international word, and you'll see signs everywhere. All you need is a tent and a sleeping bag. Good campground guides are published, and camping information is also readily available at local tourist information offices. Europeans love to holiday camp. It's a social rather than a nature experience and a great way for traveling Americans to make local friends. Camping is ideal for families traveling by car on a tight budget.

EATING

Europeans are masters at the art of fine living. That means eating long and eating well. Two-hour lunches, three-hour dinners, and endless hours sitting in outdoor cafés are the norm. Americans eat on their way to an evening event and complain if the check is slow in coming. For Europeans, the meal is an end in itself, and only rude waiters rush you.

Even those of us who liked dorm food will find that the local cafés, cuisine, and wines become a highlight of our European adventure. This is sightseeing for your palate, and even if the rest of you is sleeping in cheap hotels, your taste buds will want an occasional first-class splurge. You can eat well without going broke. But be careful: You're just as likely to blow a small fortune on a mediocre meal as you are to dine wonderfully for $15.

Send Me a Postcard, Drop Me a Line

If you enjoy a successful trip with the help of this book and would like to share your discoveries, please fill out the survey at www.ricksteves.com/feedback. I personally read and value all feedback.

Restaurants

When restaurant hunting, choose a place filled with locals, not the place with the big neon signs boasting "We Speak English and Accept Credit Cards." Look for menus posted outside; if you don't see one, move along.

For a no-stress meal in France and Italy, look for set-price *menus* (called the tourist menu, *menu del giorno, prix-fixe,* or simply *le menu*) that give you several choices of courses. At some restaurants, the *menu* is cheaper at lunch than dinner. Combination plates (*le plat* in France, *plato combinado* in Spain) provide house specialties at reasonable prices. For tips on tipping, see page 11.

Galloping gourmets bring a menu translator. The *Marling Menu Master,* available in French, Italian, and German editions, is excellent.

When you're in the mood for something halfway between a restaurant and a picnic meal, look for take-out food stands, bakeries (with sandwiches and small pizzas to go), delis with stools or a table, a department store cafeteria, or simple little eateries for fast and easy sit-down restaurant food.

Picnics

So that I can afford the occasional splurge in a nice restaurant, I like to picnic. In addition to the savings, picnicking is a great way to sample local specialties. And, in the process of assembling your meal, you get to plunge into local markets like a European.

Gather supplies early. Many shops close for a lunch break. While it's fun to visit the small specialty shops, a *supermarché* gives you more efficiency with less color for less cost.

Picnics (especially French ones) can be an adventure in high cuisine. Be daring: Try the smelly cheeses, midget pickles, ugly pâtés, and minuscule yogurts. Local shopkeepers sell small quantities of produce and even slice and stuff a sandwich for you.

A typical picnic for two might be fresh bread (half loaves on request), two tomatoes, three carrots, 100 grams of cheese (about a quarter-pound, called an *etto* in Italy), 100 grams of meat, two apples, a liter box of orange juice, and yogurt. Total cost for two: about $10.

When driving, I organize a backseat pantry in a cardboard box: plastic cups, paper towels, a water bottle (the standard disposable European half-liter plastic mineral water bottle works fine), a damp cloth in a resealable baggie, a Swiss army knife, and a petite tablecloth. To take care of juice once and for all, stow a rack of liter boxes of orange juice in the trunk. (Look for "100%" on the label or you'll get a sickly sweet orange drink.)

TRAVELING AS A TEMPORARY LOCAL

We travel all the way to Europe to enjoy differences—to become temporary locals. You'll experience frustrations. Certain truths that we find "God-given" or "self-evident," like cold beer, ice in drinks, bottomless cups of coffee, hot showers, body odor smelling bad, and bigger being better, are suddenly not so true. One of the benefits of travel is the eye-opening realization that there are logical, civil, and even better alternatives. A willingness to go local ensures that you'll enjoy a full dose of local hospitality.

If there is a negative aspect to the European image of Americans, we can appear loud, aggressive, impolite, rich, and a bit naive. While Europeans look bemusedly at some of our Yankee excesses—and worriedly at others—they nearly always afford us individual travelers all the warmth we deserve.

While updating this book, I heard over and over again that my readers are considerate and fun to have as guests. Thank you for traveling as temporary locals who are sensitive to the culture. It's fun to follow you in my travels.

Judging from all the positive comments I receive from travelers who have used this book, it's safe to assume you'll enjoy a great, affordable vacation—with the finesse of an experienced, independent traveler. Thanks, and happy travels!

BACK DOOR TRAVEL PHILOSOPHY

From *Rick Steves' Europe Through the Back Door*

Travel is intensified living—maximum thrills per minute and one of the last great sources of legal adventure. Travel is freedom. It's recess, and we need it.

Experiencing the real Europe requires catching it by surprise, going casual..."Through the Back Door."

Affording travel is a matter of priorities. (Make do with the old car.) You can travel—simply, safely, and comfortably—anywhere in Europe for $100 a day plus transportation costs. In many ways, spending more money only builds a thicker wall between you and what you came to see. Europe is a cultural carnival and, time after time, you'll find that its best acts are free and the best seats are the cheap ones.

A tight budget forces you to travel close to the ground, meeting and communicating with the people, not relying on service with a purchased smile. Never sacrifice sleep, nutrition, safety, or cleanliness in the name of budget. Simply enjoy the local-style alternatives to expensive hotels and restaurants.

Extroverts have more fun. If your trip is low on magic moments, kick yourself and make things happen. If you don't enjoy a place, maybe you don't know enough about it. Seek the truth. Recognize tourist traps. Give a culture the benefit of your open mind. See things as different but not better or worse. Any culture has much to share.

Of course, travel, like the world, is a series of hills and valleys. Be fanatically positive and militantly optimistic. If something's not to your liking, change your liking. Travel is addicting. It can make you a happier American as well as a citizen of the world. Our Earth is home to six billion equally important people. It's humbling to travel and find that people don't envy Americans. They like us, but with all due respect, they wouldn't trade passports.

Globe-trotting destroys ethnocentricity. It helps you understand and appreciate different cultures. Regrettably, there are forces in our society that want you dumbed down for their convenience. Don't let it happen. Thoughtful travel engages you with the world—more important than ever these days. Travel changes people. It broadens perspectives and teaches new ways to measure quality of life. Many travelers toss aside their hometown blinders. Their prized souvenirs are the strands of different cultures they decide to knit into their own character. The world is a cultural yarn shop, and Back Door travelers are weaving the ultimate tapestry. Come on, join in!

VIENNA

(Wien)

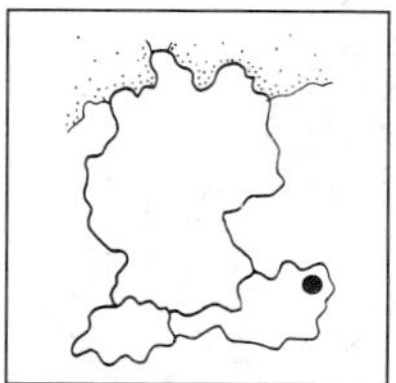

Vienna is a head without a body. For 640 years the capital of the once-grand Hapsburg Empire, she started and lost World War I, and with it her far-flung holdings. Today, you'll find an elegant capital of 1.6 million people (one-fifth of Austria's population) ruling a small, relatively insignificant country. Culturally, historically, and from a sightseeing point of view, this city is the sum of its illustrious past. The city of Freud, Brahms, Maria Theresa's many children, a gaggle of Strausses, and a dynasty of Holy Roman Emperors ranks right up there with Paris, London, and Rome.

Vienna has always been the easternmost city of the West. In Roman times, it was Vindobona, on the Danube facing the Germanic barbarians. In the Middle Ages, Vienna was Europe's bastion against the Ottoman Turks—a Christian breakwater against the riding tide of Islam (hordes of up to 200,000 Turks were repelled in 1529 and 1683). During this period, as the Turks dreamed of conquering what they called "the big apple" for their sultan, Vienna lived with a constant fear of invasion (and the Hapsburg court ruled from safer Prague). You'll notice none of Vienna's great palaces were built until after 1683, when the Turkish threat was finally over. While Vienna's old walls held out the Turks, World War II bombs destroyed nearly a quarter of the city's buildings. In modern times, neutral Austria and Vienna took a big bite out of the USSR's Warsaw Pact buffer zone. And today, Vienna is a springboard for newly popular destinations in Eastern Europe.

The truly Viennese person is not Austrian, but a second-generation Hapsburg cocktail, with grandparents from the distant corners of the old empire—Hungary, the Czech Republic, Slovakia,

Vienna Overview

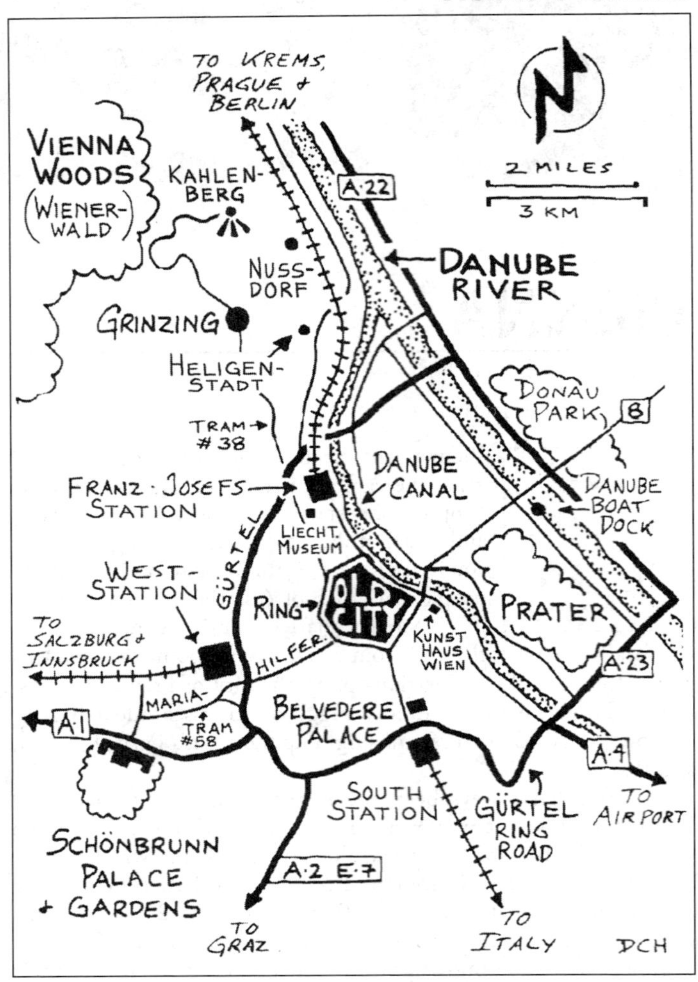

Poland, Slovenia, Croatia, Bosnia, Serbia, Romania, and Italy. Vienna is the melting-pot capital of a now-collapsed empire that, in its heyday, consisted of 60 million people—only 8 million of whom were Austrian.

In 1900, Vienna's 2.2 million inhabitants made it the world's fifth-largest city (after New York, London, Paris, and Berlin). But these days—with dogs being the preferred "child" and the average Viennese mother having only 1.3 children—the population is down to around 1.6 million.

The Hapsburgs, who ruled the enormous Austrian Empire from 1273 to 1918, shaped Vienna. Some ad agency has convinced Vienna to make Elisabeth, wife of Emperor Franz Josef—with her narcissism and struggles with royal life—the darling of the local tourist scene. You'll see "Sissy" all over town. But stay focused on the Hapsburgs who mattered: Maria Theresa (r. 1740–1780, see page 47) and Franz Josef (r. 1848–1916, see page 54) are the most important.

After the defeat of Napoleon and the Congress of Vienna in 1815 (which shaped 19th-century Europe), Vienna enjoyed its violin-filled belle époque, which shaped our romantic image of the city—fine wine, chocolates, cafés, and waltzes.

Planning Your Time

For a big city, Vienna is pleasant and laid-back. Packed with sights, it's worth two days and two nights on the speediest trip. To be grand-tour efficient, you could sleep in and sleep out on the train (Berlin, Kraków, Venice, Rome, the Swiss Alps, Paris, and the Rhine are each handy night trains away). I'd spend two days this way:

Day 1: 9:00–Circle the Ring by tram, following my "Do-It-Yourself Tram Orientation Tour" (page 38); 10:00–Drop by TI for any planning and ticket needs, then see the sights in Vienna's old center (using my self-guided commentary)—Monument Against War and Fascism, Kaisergruft crypt, Kärntner Strasse, St. Stephan's Cathedral, and Graben; 12:00–Finger sandwiches for lunch at Buffet Trzesniewski; 13:00–Tour the Hofburg and treasury; 16:00–Hit one more museum or shop, or browse and people-watch; 19:30–Choose classical music (concert or opera), House of Music museum, or *Heurige* wine garden.

Day 2: 9:00–Schönbrunn Palace (drivers: This is conveniently on the way out of town toward Salzburg; horse-lovers: You'll need to rearrange—or rush the palace—to see the Lipizzaner stallions' morning practice); 12:00–Back in central Vienna for lunch at Naschmarkt or Rosenberger Markt; 13:00–Tour the Opera; 14:00–Kunsthistorisches Museum; 16:00–Your choice of the many sights left to see in Vienna; Evening–See Day 1 evening options.

ORIENTATION

(area code: 01)

Vienna—Wien in German (pronounced "veen")—sits between the Vienna Woods (Wienerwald) and the Danube (Donau). To the southeast is industrial sprawl. The Alps, which arc across Europe from Marseille, end at Vienna's wooded hills, providing a popular playground for walking and sipping new wine. This greenery's momentum carries on into the city. More than half of Vienna is parkland, filled with ponds, gardens, trees, and statue-maker memories of Austria's glory days.

Think of the city map as a target. The bull's-eye is the cathedral, the first circle is the Ringstrasse, and the second is the Gürtel outerbelt. The old town—snuggling around towering St. Stephan's Cathedral south of the Danube—is bound tightly by the Ringstrasse. The Ring, marking what was the city wall, circles the first district (or *Bezirk*). The Gürtel, a broader ring road, contains the rest of downtown (*Bezirkes* 2–9).

Addresses start with the *Bezirk,* followed by street and building number. Any address higher than the ninth *Bezirk* is beyond the Gürtel, far from the center. The middle two digits of Vienna's postal codes show the *Bezirk*. The address "7, Lindengasse 4" is in the seventh district, #4 on Linden Street. Its postal code would be 1070. Nearly all your sightseeing will be done in the core first district or along the Ringstrasse. As a tourist, concern yourself only with this compact old center. When you do, sprawling Vienna suddenly becomes manageable.

Tourist Information

Vienna's one real tourist office is a block behind the Opera House at Albertinaplatz (daily 9:00–19:00, tel. 01/24555, press 2 for English info, www.info.wien.at). Confirm your sightseeing plans and pick up the free and essential city map with a list of museums and hours (also available at most hotels), the monthly program of concerts (called *Wien-Programm*—includes daily calendar and information on the contemporary cultural scene, including live music, jazz, walks, expositions, and evening museum options), the biannual city guide *(Vienna Journal)*, and the youth guide *(Vienna Hype)*. The TI also books rooms for a €2.90 fee. While hotel and ticket-booking agencies at the train stations and airport can answer questions and give out maps and brochures, I'd rely on the TI if possible.

Consider the TI's handy €3.60 ***Vienna from A to Z*** booklet. Every important building sports a numbered flag banner that keys into this guidebook. *A to Z* numbers are keyed into the TI's city map. When lost, find one of the "famous-building flags" and match its number to your map. If you're at a famous building, check the map to see what other key numbers are nearby, then check the *A to Z* book description to see if you want to go in. This system is especially helpful for those just wandering aimlessly among Vienna's historic charms.

The much-promoted €17 **Vienna Card** might save the busy sightseer a few euros. It gives you a 72-hour transit pass (worth €12.50) and discounts of 10–50 percent at the city's museums. (Note: seniors and students will do better with their own discounts.)

Arrival in Vienna

By Train at the West Station (Westbahnhof): Train travelers arriving from Munich, Salzburg, and Melk land at the Westbahnhof. The *Reisebüro am Bahnhof* books hotels (for a €4 fee), has maps, answers questions, and has a train info desk (daily 7:30–21:00). The Westbahnhof also has a grocery store (daily 5:30–23:00), ATMs, Internet access, change offices, and storage facilities. Airport buses and taxis wait in front of the station.

To get to the city center (and most likely, your hotel), take the U-3 metro (buy your ticket or transit pass—described below—from a *Tabak* shop in the station or from a machine). Blue U-3 signs lead down to the metro tracks (direction Simmering for Mariahilfer Strasse hotels or the center). If your hotel is along Mariahilfer Strasse, your stop is on this line (see page 80). If you're sleeping in the center or just sightseeing, ride five stops to Stephansplatz, escalate in the exit direction Stephansplatz, and you'll hit the cathedral. The TI is a five-minute stroll down the busy Kärntner Strasse pedestrian street.

By Train at the South Station (Südbahnhof): Those arriving from Italy and Prague land here. The Südbahnhof has all the services, left luggage, and a TI (daily 9:00–19:00). To reach Vienna's center, follow the S (Schnellbahn) signs to the right and down the stairs, and take any train in the direction Floridsdorf; transfer in two stops (at Landsstrasse/Wien Mitte) to the U-3 line, direction Ottakring, which goes directly to Stephansplatz and Mariahilfer Strasse hotels. Tram D also goes to the Ring, and bus #13A goes to Mariahilfer Strasse.

By Train at Franz Josefs Station: If you're coming from Krems (in the Danube Valley), you'll arrive at Vienna's Franz Josefs station. From here, take tram D into town. Better yet, get off your train at Spittelau (the stop before Franz Josefs) and use its handy U-Bahn station.

By Plane: Vienna's airport is 12 miles from the center (tel. 01/7007-22233, www.viennaairport.com). It's connected to the very central Wien-Mitte station by S-Bahn (S-7 yellow, €3, 2/hr, 24 min). A speedier new City Airport Train (CAT) connects the airport to Wien-Mitte (green signs, €9, 2/hr, 16 min, www.cityairporttrain.com). Express airport buses (parked immediately in front of the arrival hall, €6, 3/hr, 30 min, buy tickets from drivers) go conveniently to Schwedenplatz, Westbahnhof, and Südbahnhof, from where it's easy to continue by subway. Taxis into town cost about €35 (including €10 airport surcharge). Hotels arrange for fixed-rate car service to the airport (€30, 30-min ride).

Helpful Hints

Banking: ATMs are everywhere. Banks are open weekdays roughly from 8:00 to 15:00 (until 17:30 on Thu). After hours, you can change money at train stations, the airport, post offices, or the American Express office (Mon–Fri 9:00–17:30, Sat 9:00–12:00, closed Sun, Kärntner Strasse 21-23, tel. 01/5154-0456).

Internet Access: The TI has a list of Internet cafés. BigNet is the dominant outfit (www.bignet.at), with lots of stations at Kärntner Strasse 61 (daily 10:00–24:00) and Höher Markt 8–9 (daily 10:00–24:00). Surfland Internet Café is near the Opera (daily 10:00–23:00, Krugerstrasse 10, tel. 01/512-7701).

Post Offices: Choose from the main post office (Postgasse in center, open 24 hrs daily, handy metered phones), Westbahnhof (daily 6:00–23:00), Südbahnhof (daily 7:00–22:00), or near the Opera (Mon–Fri 7:00–19:00, closed Sat–Sun, Krugerstrasse 13).

English Bookstores: Consider the **British Bookshop** (Mon–Fri 9:30–18:30, Sat 9:30–17:00, closed Sun, at corner of Weihburggasse and Seilerstätte, tel. 01/512-1945; same hours at branch at Mariahilfer Strasse 4, tel. 01/522-6730) or **Shakespeare & Co.** (Mon–Sat 9:00–19:00, closed Sun, north of Höher Markt square, Sterngasse 2, tel. 01/535-5053).

Travel Agency: Intropa is convenient at Neuer Markt 8, with good service for flights and train tickets (Mon–Fri 9:00–18:00, Sat 10:00–13:00, closed Sun, tel. 01/513-4000). Train tickets come with a €2 service charge when purchased from an agency rather than at the station—a great convenience.

Getting Around Vienna

By Bus, Tram, and Metro: Take full advantage of Vienna's simple, cheap, and super-efficient transit system, which includes trams, buses, subway (U-Bahn), and faster suburban trains (S-Bahn, or *Schnellbahn*). I use the tram mostly to zip around the Ring (tram #1 or #2) and take the U-Bahn to outlying sights or hotels. Numbered lines (such as #38) are trams, and numbers followed by an *A* (such as #38A) are buses. The smooth, modern trams are Porsche-designed, with "backpack technology" locating the engines and mechanical hardware on the roofs for a lower ride and easier entry. Lines that begin with *U* (e.g., U-3) are U-Bahn lines (these metro routes are designated by the end-of-the-line stops). Blue lines are the speedier S-Bahns. Take a moment to study the eye-friendly city-center map on metro station walls to internalize how the transit system can help you. The free tourist map has essentially all the lines marked, making the too-big €1.50 transit map unnecessary (information tel. 01/790-9105).

Trams, buses, and the metro all use the same tickets. Buy your tickets from *Tabak* shops, station machines, *Vorverkauf* offices in the station, or on board (just on trams, single tickets only, more expensive). You have lots of choices:

- Single tickets (€1.50, €2 if bought on tram, good for 1 journey with necessary transfers)
- 24-hour transit pass (€5)
- 72-hour transit pass (€12)
- 7-day transit pass (€12.50, pass always starts on Mon)
- "8-day card" *(Acht Tage Karte)*—eight full days of free transportation for €24 (can be shared—for example, 4 people for 2 days each). With a per-person cost of €3/day (compared to €5/day for a 24-hour pass), this can be a real saver for groups.

Kids under 15 travel free on Sundays and holidays.

Stamp a time on your ticket as you enter the metro system, tram, or bus (stamp it only the first time for a multiple-use pass). Cheaters pay a stiff €44 fine if caught—and then they make you buy a ticket. Rookies miss stops because they fail to open the door. Push buttons, pull latches—do whatever it takes. Study the excellent wall-mounted street map before you exit the metro. Choosing the right exit—signposted from the moment you step off the train—saves lots of walking.

By Taxi: Vienna's comfortable, civilized, and easy-to-flag-down taxis start at €2.50. You'll pay about €7 to go from the Opera to the Westbahnhof. Pay only what's on the meter—any surcharges (other then the €2 fee added to fares when you telephone them) are just crude cabbie rip-offs.

By Car with Driver: Consider the luxury of having your own car and driver. Johann (John) Lichtl is a kind, honest, English-speaking cabbie who can take up to four passengers in his car (€25/1 hr, €20/hr for 2 or more hours, mobile 0676-670-6750). Consider using Johann to day-trip to the Wachau Valley (€100, up to 8 hrs), or to drive you to Salzburg with Wachau sightseeing en route (€180, up to 12 hours; other trips by negotiation).

By Bike: Vienna is a great city for biking—*if* you own a bike. Bike rental is a hassle (get list at TI). There are no bike-rental options in the center; the nearest is out at Prater Park (see page 69). The bikes you'll see parked in public racks all over town are part of a loaner system that is only workable for locals with mobile phones. The bike path along the Ring is wonderfully entertaining.

By Buggy: Rich romantics get around by traditional horse and buggy. The horse buggies, called *Fiakers,* clip-clop tourists on tours lasting 20 minutes (€40—old town), 40 minutes (€65—old town and the Ring), or one hour (€95—all of the above, but more thorough). You can share the ride and cost with up to five people. Because it's a kind of guided tour, before settling on a carriage, talk to a few drivers and pick one who's fun and speaks English.

TOURS

Walks—The TI's *Walks in Vienna* brochure describes Vienna's many guided walks. The basic 90-minute "Vienna First Glance" introductory walk is given daily throughout the summer (€11, 14:00 from near the Opera, in English and German, tel. 01/894-5363, www.wienguide.at).

Bus Tours—Yellow Cab Sightseeing offers a one-hour, €12, quickie double-decker bus tour with recorded commentary, departing at the top of each hour (10:00–17:00) from in front of the Opera (corner of Operngasse). Vienna Sightseeing offers hop-on, hop-off tours covering 13 predictable sightseeing stops (departures from Opera at top of each hour 10:00–17:00, recorded commentary). Given Vienna's excellent public transportation and this outfit's meager one-bus-per-hour frequency, I'd take this not to hop on and off, but only to get the narrated orientation drive through town (€20 for 24-hr ticket, or €12 if you stay on for the full 60-minute circular ride—skipping the hop-on, hop-off privileges). Their 3.5-hour Vienna city sights tour includes a visit to Schönbrunn Palace and a bus tour around town (€34; April–Oct 3/day—9:45, 10:30, and 14:00; Nov–March 2/day—9:45 and 14:00; call 01/7124-6830 to book this or get info on other tours). These leave from the Südbahnhof or, 30 minutes earlier, from the Opera.

Local Guides—The tourist board Web site (www.info.wien.at) has a long list of local guides with specialties and contact information. Lisa Zeiler is a good English-speaking guide (2-hr walks for €120—if she's booked, she can set you up with another guide, tel. 01/402-3688, lisa.zeiler@gmx.at). Ursula Klaus, an art scholar specializing in turn-of-the-century Vienna, enjoys tailoring tours to specific interests (especially music, art, architecture). She does half-day tours for €120 (tel. 01/522-8556, mobile 0676-421-4884, ursula.klaus@aon.at).

Do-It-Yourself Ringstrasse Tram Orientation Tour

In the 1860s, Emperor Franz Josef had the city's ingrown medieval wall torn down and replaced with a grand boulevard 190 feet wide. The road, arcing nearly three miles around the city's core, predates all the buildings that line it—so what you'll see is very "neo": neoclassical, neo-Gothic, and neo-Renaissance. One of Europe's great streets, it's lined with many of the city's top sights. Trams #1 and #2 and a great bike path circle the whole route—and so should you.

This self-guided tram tour, rated ▲▲, gives you a fun orientation and a ridiculously quick glimpse of the major sights as you glide by (€1.50, 30-min circular tour). Tram #1 goes clockwise; tram #2, counterclockwise. Most sights are on the outside, so use tram #2

Vienna

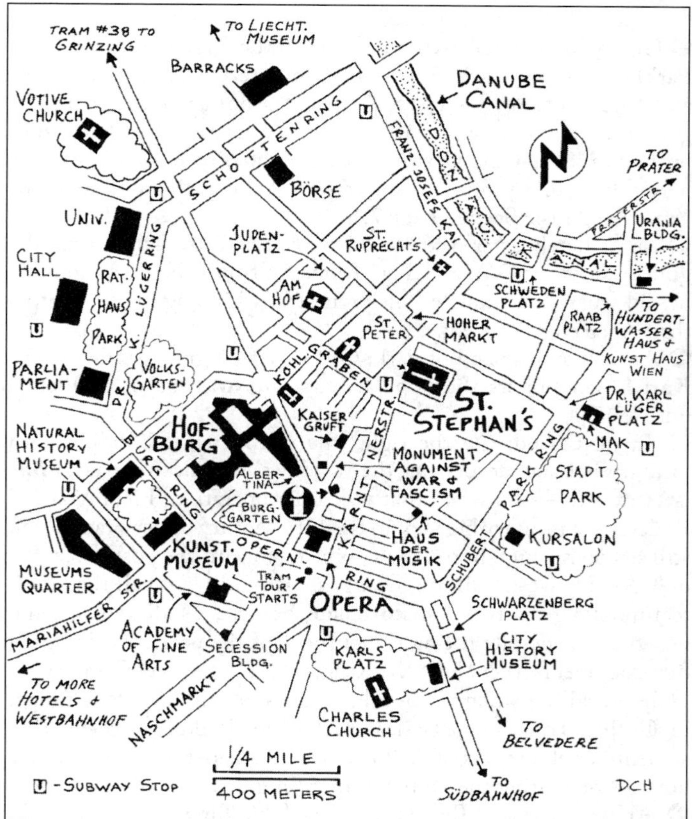

(sit on the right, ideally in the front seat of the front car; or—for maximum view and minimum air—sit in the bubble-front seat of the second car). Start immediately across the street from the Opera House. You can jump on and off as you go (trams come every 5 min). Read ahead and pay attention—these sights can fly by. Let's go:

➔ Immediately on the left: The city's main pedestrian drag, Kärntner Strasse, leads to the zigzag roof of **St. Stephan's Cathedral.** This tram tour makes a 360-degree circle around the cathedral, staying about this same distance from it.

➔ At first bend (before first stop): Look right, toward the tall fountain and the guy on a horse. Schwarzenberg Platz shows off its **equestrian statue** of Prince Charles Schwarzenberg, who fought Napoleon. Behind that is the Russian monument (behind the fountain), which was built in 1945 as a forced thanks to the Soviets for liberating Austria from the Nazis. Formerly a sore point, now it's just ignored. Beyond that (out of sight, on tram D route) is Belvedere Palace (see page 66).

➲ Going down Schubertring, you reach the huge **Stadtpark** (City Park) on the right, which honors many great Viennese musicians and composers with statues. At the beginning of the park, the gold-and-cream concert hall behind the trees is the **Kursalon,** opened in 1867 by the Strauss brothers, who directed many waltzes here. The touristy Strauss concerts are held in this building (see "Summer Music Scene," page 71).

➲ Immediately after next stop, look right: In the same park, the gilded statue of "Waltz King" **Johann Strauss** holds a violin as he did when he conducted his orchestra, whipping his fans into a three-quarter-time frenzy.

➲ At next stop at end of park: On the left, a green statue of **Dr. Karl Lüger** honors the popular man who was mayor of Vienna until 1910.

➲ At next bend: On the right, the quaint white building with military helmets decorating the windows was the **Austrian ministry of war**—back when that was a big operation. Field Marshal Radetzky, a military big shot in the 19th century under Franz Josef, still sits on his high horse. He's pointing toward the post office, the only Art Nouveau building facing the Ring. Locals call the architecture along the Ring "**historicism**" because it's all neo-this and neo-that—generally fitting the purpose of the particular building (for example, farther along the Ring, we'll see the neo-Gothic City Hall—recalling when medieval burghers ran the city government in Gothic days; a neoclassical parliament building—celebrating ancient Greek notions of democracy; and a neo-Renaissance opera house—venerating the high culture filling it).

➲ At next corner: The white-domed building over your right shoulder as you turn is the Urania, Franz Josef's 1910 **observatory.** Lean forward and look behind it for a peek at the huge red cars of the giant 100-year-old Ferris wheel in Vienna's Prater Park (fun for families, described on page 69).

➲ Now you're rolling along the **Danube Canal.** This "Baby Danube" is one of the many small arms of the river that once made up the Danube at this location. The rest have been gathered together in a mightier modern-day Danube, farther away. This neighborhood was thoroughly bombed in World War II. The buildings across the canal are typical of postwar architecture (1960s). They were built on the cheap, and are now being replaced by sleek, futuristic buildings. This was the site of the original Roman town, Vindobona. In three long blocks, on the left (opposite the BP station, be ready—it passes fast), you'll see the ivy-covered walls and round Romanesque arches of St. Ruprecht's, the oldest church in Vienna (built in the 11th century on a bit of Roman ruins). Remember, medieval Vienna was defined by that long-gone wall that you're tracing on this tour. Across the river is an OPEC headquarters, where oil ministers often meet to set prices. Relax for a few stops until the corner.

➲ Leaving canal, turning left up Schottenring, at first corner: A block down on the right, you can see a huge red-brick **castle**—actually a high-profile barracks built here at the command of a nervous Emperor Franz Josef (who found himself on the throne as an 18-year-old in 1848, the same year people's revolts against autocracy were sweeping across Europe).

➲ At next stop: On the left, the orange-and-white, neo-Renaissance temple of money—the **Börse**—is Vienna's stock exchange.

➲ Next stop, at corner: The huge, frilly, neo-Gothic church on the right is a "**votive church,**" built as a thanks to God when an 1853 assassination attempt on Emperor Franz Josef failed. Ahead on the right (in front of tram stop) is the **Vienna University** building (established in 1365, it has no real campus as the buildings are scattered around town). It faces (on the left, behind a gilded angel across the Ring) a chunk of the old **city wall.**

➲ At next stop, on right: The neo-Gothic City Hall, flying the flag of Europe, towers over **Rathaus Platz,** a festive site in summer, with a huge screen showing outdoor movies, operas, and concerts and a thriving food circus (see page 69—if you're hungry and it's thriving, hop off now). In the winter, the building becomes a huge Advent calendar, with 24 windows opening—one each day—as Christmas approaches. Immediately across the street (on left) is the **Burgtheater,** Austria's national theater.

➲ At next stop, on right: The neo-Greek temple of democracy houses the **Austrian Parliament.** The lady with the golden helmet is Athena, goddess of wisdom. The big construction mess is for the restoration of the building's grand ramp. Across the street (on left) is the imperial park called the **Volksgarten.**

➲ After the next stop on the right is the **Natural History Museum,** the first of Vienna's huge twin museums. It faces the **Kunsthistorisches Museum,** containing the city's greatest collection of paintings. The **MuseumsQuartier** behind them completes the ensemble with a collection of mostly modern-art museums. A hefty statue of Empress Maria Theresa squats between the museums, facing the grand gate to the **Hofburg,** the emperor's palace (on left, across the Ring). Of the five arches, only the center one was used by the emperor. (Your tour is essentially finished. If you want to jump out here, you're at many of Vienna's top sights.)

➲ Fifty yards after the next stop, on the left through a gate in the black-iron fence, is a statue of Mozart. It's one of many charms in the **Burggarten,** which until 1918 was the private garden of the emperor. Vienna had more than its share of intellectual and creative geniuses. A hundred yards farther (on left, just out of the park), the

German philosopher Goethe sits in a big, thought-provoking chair playing trivia with Schiller (across the street on your right). Behind the statue of Schiller is the Academy of Fine Arts.

➲ Hey, there's the **Opera** again. Jump off the tram and see the rest of the city.

SIGHTS

Vienna's Old Center

These sights, in the heart of Vienna, are listed in the order of a convenient self-guided walking tour through town.

▲▲▲Opera (Staatsoper)—The Opera, facing the Ring and near the TI, is a central point for any visitor. While the critical reception of the building 130 years ago led the architect to commit suicide, and though it's been rebuilt since the WWII bombings, it's still a dazzling place (€4.50, by guided 35-min tour only, daily in English; July–Aug at 11:00, 13:00, 14:00, 15:00, and often at 10:00 and 16:00; Sept–June fewer tours, afternoon only). Tours are often canceled for rehearsals and shows, so check the posted schedule or call 01/514-442-613.

The Vienna State Opera—with musicians provided by the Vienna Philharmonic Orchestra in the pit—is one of the world's top opera houses. There are 300 performances a year, but in July and August the singers rest their voices. Since there are different operas nearly nightly, you'll see big trucks out back and constant action backstage—all the sets need to be switched each day. Even though the expensive seats normally sell out long in advance, the opera is perpetually in the red and subsidized by the state.

Tickets for Seats: For ticket information, call 01/513-1513 (phone answered daily 10:00–21:00, www.wiener-staatsoper.at). If seats aren't sold out, last-minute tickets (for pricey seats—up to €100) are sold for €30 from 9:00 to 14:00 only the day before the show.

Standing Room: Unless Placido Domingo is in town, it's easy to get one of 567 *Stehplätze* (standing-room spots, €2 at the top or €3.50 downstairs). While the front doors open 60 minutes early, a side door (on the Operngasse side, the door under the portico nearest the fountain) is open 80 minutes before curtain time, giving those in the know an early grab at standing-room tickets. Just walk in straight, then head right until you see the ticket booth marked *Stehplätze* (tel. 01/5144-42419). If fewer than 567 people are in line, there's no need to line up early. You can even buy standing-room tickets after the show has started—in case you want only a little taste of opera. Dress is casual (but do your best) at the standing-room bar. Locals save their spot along the rail by tying a scarf to it.

Rick's Crude Tip: For me, three hours is a lot of opera. But just to see and hear the Opera House in action for half an hour is a treat. You can buy a standing-room spot and just drop in for part of the show. Ushers don't mind letting tourists with standing-room tickets in for a short look. Ending time is posted in the lobby—you could stop by for just the finale. If you go at the start or finish, you'll see Vienna dressed up. With all the time you save, consider stopping by...

Sacher Café—The home of every chocoholic's fantasy, the *Sachertorte*, faces the rear of the Opera. While locals complain that the cakes have gone downhill (and many tourists are surprised how dry they are), a coffee and slice of cake here can be €8 well invested. For maximum elegance, sit inside (daily 8:00–23:30, Philharmoniker Strasse 4, tel. 01/51456).

The U-Bahn station in front of the Opera is actually a huge underground shopping mall with fast food, newsstands, lots of pickpockets, and even an Opera Toilet Vienna experience (€0.50, *mit Musik*).

▲Monument Against War and Fascism—A powerful four-part statue stands behind the Opera House on Albertinaplatz. The split white monument, *The Gates of Violence,* remembers victims of all wars and violence, including the 1938–1945 Nazi rule of Austria. A montage of wartime images—clubs and WWI gas masks, a dying woman birthing a future soldier, chained slave laborers—sits on a pedestal of granite cut from the infamous quarry at Mauthausen, a nearby concentration camp. The hunched-over figure on the ground behind is a Jew forced to wash anti-Nazi graffiti off a street with a toothbrush. The statue with its head buried in the stone (Orpheus entering the underworld) reminds Austrians of the consequences of not keeping their government on track. Behind that, the 1945 declaration of Austria's second republic—with human rights built into it—is cut into the stone. This monument stands on the spot where several hundred people were buried alive while hiding in the cellar of a building demolished in a WWII bombing attack (see photo to right of park).

Austria was pulled into World War II by Germany, which annexed the country in 1938, saying Austrians were wannabe Germans anyway. But Austrians are not Germans—never were, never will be. They're quick to tell you that while Austria was founded in the 10th century, Germany wasn't born until 1870. For seven years during World War II (1938–1945), there was no Austria. In 1955, after 10 years of joint occupation by the victorious Allies, Austria regained total independence on the condition that it would be forever neutral (and never join NATO or the Warsaw Pact). To this day, Austria is outside of NATO (and Germany).

Vienna at a Glance

▲▲▲Opera Dazzling, world-famous opera house. **Hours:** Visit by guided 35-min tour only, daily in English; July–Aug at 11:00, 13:00, 14:00, 15:00, and often at 10:00 and 16:00; Sept–June fewer tours, afternoon only, call ahead to confirm tour times.

▲▲▲Hofburg Treasury The Hapsburgs' collection of jewels, crowns, and other valuables—the best on the Continent. **Hours:** Wed–Mon 10:00–18:00, closed Tue.

▲▲▲Kunsthistorisches Museum World-class exhibit of the Hapsburgs' art collection, including Raphael, Titian, Caravaggio, Bosch, and Brueghel. **Hours:** Tue–Sun 10:00–18:00, Thu until 21:00, closed Mon.

▲▲▲Schönbrunn Palace Spectacular summer residence of the Hapsburgs, similar in grandeur to Versailles. **Hours:** Daily April–Oct 8:30–17:00, July–Aug until 18:00, Nov–March 8:30–16:30, reservations recommended.

▲▲Albertina Museum Newly opened Hapsburg residence with ho-hum apartments and world-class permanent and temporary exhibits. **Hours:** Daily 10:00–18:00, Wed until 21:00.

▲▲St. Stephan's Cathedral Beautiful, enormous Gothic cathedral in the center of Vienna. **Hours:** Church doors open Mon–Sat 6:00–22:00, Sun 7:00–22:00, officially only open for tourists Mon–Sat 8:30–11:30 & 13:00–16:30, Sun 13:00–16:30.

▲▲Stephansplatz, Graben, and Kohlmarkt Atmospheric pedestrian squares and streets around the cathedral. **Hours:** Always open.

▲▲Hofburg Imperial Apartments Lavish main residence of the Hapsburgs. **Hours:** Daily 9:00–17:00.

▲▲Hofburg New Palace Museums Uncrowded collection of armor, musical instruments, and ancient Greek statues, in the elegant halls of a Hapsburg palace. **Hours:** Wed–Mon 10:00–18:00, closed Tue.

▲▲Kaisergruft Crypt for the Hapsburg royalty. **Hours:** Daily 9:30–16:00.

▲▲Belvedere Palace Elegant palace of Prince Eugene of Savoy, with a collection of 19th- and 20th-century Austrian art (including

Klimt). **Hours:** Tue–Sun 10:00–18:00, closed Mon.

▲▲**Haus der Musik** Modern musuem with interactive exhibits on Vienna's favorite pastime. **Hours:** Daily 10:00–22:00.

▲**Monument Against War and Fascism** Powerful four-part statue remembering victims of the Nazis. **Hours:** Always open.

▲**Kärntner Strasse** Vienna's lively main pedestrian drag, connecting the Opera with the cathedral. **Hours:** Always open.

▲**Lipizzaner Museum** Displays dedicated to the regal Lipizzaner Stallions; horse-lovers should check out their practice sessions. **Hours:** Museum open daily 9:00–18:00, stallions practice across the street roughly Feb–June and Sept–Oct, Tue–Sat 10:00–12:00 when the horses are in town, call to confirm.

▲**Augustinian Church** Hapsburg marriage church, now hosting an 11:00 Sunday Mass with wonderful music. **Hours:** Open daily.

▲**Imperial Furniture Collection** Eclectic collection of Hapsburg furniture. **Hours:** Tue–Sun 10:00–18:00, closed Mon.

▲**Naschmarkt** Sprawling, lively, people-filled outdoor market. **Hours:** Mon–Fri 7:00–18:00, Sat 6:00–18:00, closed Sun, closes earlier in winter.

▲**Natural History Museum** Big building facing Kunsthistorisches Museum, featuring the ancient Venus of Willendorf. **Hours:** Wed–Mon 9:00–18:30, Wed until 21:00, closed Tue.

▲**Academy of Fine Arts** Small but exciting collection with works by Bosch, Botticelli, Rubens, Guardi, and Van Dyck. **Hours:** Tue–Sun 10:00–18:00, closed Mon.

▲**Liechtenstein Museum** Recently re-opened Baroque art collection. **Hours:** Wed–Mon 9:00–20:00, closed Tue.

▲**KunstHausWien** Modern art museum dedicated to zany local artist/environmentalist Hundertwasser. **Hours:** Daily 10:00–19:00.

▲**Dorotheum** Vienna's highbrow auction house. **Hours:** Mon–Fri 10:00–18:00, Sat 9:00–17:00, closed Sun.

Across the square from the TI, you'll see what looks like a big terrace overlooking the street. This was actually part of Vienna's original defensive rampart. Above it is the sleek, controversial titanium canopy (called by locals the "diving board") that welcomes visitors to the newly restored...

▲▲Albertina Museum—This building was the residence of Maria Teresa's favorite daughter, Maria Christina, who was the only one allowed to marry for love rather than political strategy. Her many sisters were jealous. (Marie Antoinette had to marry the French king...and wound up beheaded.) Maria Christina's husband, Albert of Saxony, was a great collector of original drawings. He amassed an enormous assortment of works by Dürer, Rembrandt, Rubens, and others. Today, the Albertina presents wonderful exhibitions of these fine works, as well as allowing visitors to tour its elegant state rooms and enjoy temporary exhibits of other artists (€9, audioguide also available for both permanent and temporary exhibits, daily 10:00–18:00, Wed until 21:00, overlooking Albertinaplatz across from TI and Opera House, tel. 01/534-830, www.albertina.at).

The Albertina consists of three components. First, stroll through the Hapsburg state rooms (French classicism—lots of white marble). Top-quality facsimiles of the collection's greatest pieces hang in these rooms. Then browse the modern gallery, featuring special exhibitions of world-famous artwork—for specific dates and works to be displayed, visit www.albertina.at. Finally, the Albertina also displays selections from its own spectacular collection of works by Michelangelo, Rubens, Rembrandt, and Raphael, plus a huge sampling of precise drawings by Albrecht Dürer. Of Dürer's 400 original drawings that survived, Albert collected 300 of them. Most were sold or stolen over the ages, and today the collection is down to about 100. As the Albertina's collection is made up of fragile sketches and exquisite drawings—very sensitive to light—they are kept mostly in darkness and shown only rarely in rotation. The collection is vast, so you'll always see exciting originals, thoughtfully described in English.

▲▲Kaisergruft (Remains of the Hapsburgs)—The crypt for the Hapsburg royalty, a block down the street from the Monument Against War and Fascism, is covered in detail, along with other Hapsburg sights, on page 60.

▲Kärntner Strasse—This grand, mall-like street (traffic-free since 1974) is the people-watching delight of this in-love-with-life city. While it's mostly a crass commercial pedestrian mall with its famed elegant shops now long gone, locals know it's the same road crusaders marched down as they headed off for the Holy Land in the 12th century. Its name indicates that it points south, in the direction of the Austrian state of Kärnten.

Starting from the Opera, you'll find lots of action—shops,

Empress Maria Theresa (1717–1780) and Son Josef II (1741–1790)

Maria Theresa was the only woman to officially rule the Hapsburg Empire in that family's 700-year reign. She was a strong and effective empress (r. 1740–1780). People are quick to remember Maria Theresa as the mother of 16 children (10 survived). Imagine that the most powerful woman in Europe either was pregnant or had a newborn for most of her reign. Maria Theresa ruled after the Austrian defeat of the Turks, when Europe recognized Austria as a great power. (Her rival, the Prussian emperor, said, "When at last the Hapsburgs get a great man, it's a woman.")

The last of the Baroque imperial rulers, and the first of the modern rulers of the Age of Enlightenment, Maria Theresa marked the end of the feudal system and the beginning of the era of the grand state. She was a great social reformer. During her reign, she avoided wars and expanded her empire by skillfully marrying her children into the right families. For instance, after daughter Marie Antoinette's marriage into the French Bourbon family (to Louis XVI), a country that had been an enemy became an ally. (Unfortunately for Marie, her timing was off. Arriving in time for the Revolution, she lost her head.)

Maria Theresa was a great reformer and in tune with her age. She taxed the Church and the nobility, provided six years of obligatory education to all children, and granted free health care to all in her realm. Maria Theresa also welcomed the boy genius Mozart into her court.

The empress' legacy lived on in her son, Josef II, who ruled as emperor himself for a decade (1780–1790). He was an even more avid reformer, building on his mother's accomplishments. An enlightened monarch, Josef mothballed the too-extravagant Schönbrunn, secularized the monasteries, established religious tolerance within his realm, freed the serfs, made possible the founding of Austria's first general hospital, and promoted relatively enlightened treatment of the mentally ill. Josef was a model of practicality (for example, reusable coffins à la Amadeus, and no more than six candles at funerals)—and very unpopular with other royals. But his policies succeeded in preempting the revolutionary anger of the age, enabling Austria to avoid the turmoil that shook so much of the rest of Europe.

street music, the city casino (at #41), the venerable Lobmeyr Crystal shop (#26), American Express (#21), the Loos American bar (dark, plush, small, great €8 cocktails, Kärntnerdurchgang 10, tel. 01/512-3283), and then, finally, the cathedral. Where Kärntner Strasse hits the Graben (at #3), the Equitable Building (filled with lawyers, bankers, and insurance men) is a fine example of historicism from the turn of the century. Step in, climb the stairs, and imagine how slick the courtyard must have felt in 1900.

▲▲St. Stephan's Cathedral (Stephansdom)—This massive church is the Gothic needle around which Vienna spins. It has survived Vienna's many wars and symbolizes the city's freedom (church doors open Mon–Sat 6:00–22:00, Sun 7:00–22:00; officially only open for tourists Mon–Sat 8:30–11:30 & 13:00–16:30, Sun 13:00–16:30, otherwise closed for services; during services, you can enter back of church and get to north tower elevator, but unless you're attending Mass, you cannot enter main nave; entertaining €4 English tours daily April–Oct at 15:45, information board inside entry has tour schedules).

This is the third church to stand on this spot. The church survived the bombs of World War II, but, in the last days of the war, fires from the street fighting between Russian and Nazi troops leapt to the rooftop. The original timbered Gothic rooftop burned, and the cathedral's huge bell crashed to the ground. With a financial outpouring of civic pride, the roof of this symbol of Austria was rebuilt in its original splendor by 1952. The ceramic tiles are purely decorative (locals who contributed to the postwar reconstruction each "own" one for their donation).

The **grounds** around the church were a cemetery until Josef II emptied it as an "anti-plague" measure. (Inside, a few of the most important tombstones decorate the church walls.) You can still see the footprint of the old cemetery church in the pavement, today ignored by the human statues. Remains of the earlier Virgil Chapel (dating from the 13th century) are immediately under this (on display in the subway).

Study the church's **west end** (main entrance). You can see the original Romanesque facade (c. 1240) with classical Roman statues imbedded in it. Above are two stubby towers nicknamed "pagan towers" because they are built with Roman stones (with inscriptions just flipped around to expose the smooth sides). Two 30-foot-tall columns flank the main entry. If you stand back and look at the tops, you'll see that they symbolize creation (one's a penis, the other's a vagina).

Go inside. See the dramatic photos of **WWII damage** (with bricks neatly stacked and ready) in glass cases 20 yards opposite the south entrance (on the wall near 3a).

The nave is ringed with **chapels.** The church once had over a hundred. This was typical of Catholic churches, as each guild and leading family had their own chapel. The Tupperware-colored glass windows date from 1950. Before WWII, the entire church was lit with windows like the ones behind the altar. Those, along with the city's top art treasures, were hidden safely from the Nazis and bombs in salt mines. The altar painting of the stoning of St. Stephan is early Baroque, painted on copper.

St. Stephan's is proud to be Austria's national church. A **plaque** explains how each region contributed to the rebuilding after World War II: windows from Tirol, furniture from Vorarlberg, the floor from Lower Austria, and so on.

The Gothic sandstone **pulpit** in the middle of the nave (on left) is a realistic masterpiece carved from three separate blocks (find the seams). A spiral stairway winds up to the lectern, surrounded and supported by the four Latin Church fathers: Saints Ambrose, Jerome, Gregory, and Augustine. The railing leading up swarms with symbolism: lizards (animals of light) and battle toads (animals of darkness). The "Dog of the Lord" stands at the top, making sure none of those toads pollutes the sermon. Below the toads, wheels with three parts (the Trinity) roll up, while wheels with four parts (the four seasons, symbolizing mortal life) roll down. This work, by Anton Pilgram, has all the elements of the Flamboyant Gothic style in miniature. Gothic art was done for the glory of God. Artists were anonymous. But this was around 1500, and the Renaissance was going strong in Italy. While Gothic persisted in the North, the Renaissance spirit had already arrived. In the more humanist Renaissance, man was allowed to shine—and artists became famous. So Pilgram included a rare self-portrait bust in his work (the guy with sculptor's tools, in the classic "artist observing the world from his window" pose under the stairs).

You can ascend both **towers,** the north (via crowded elevator inside on the left) and the south (outside right transept, by spiral staircase). The north shows you a mediocre view and a big bell: the 21-ton Pummerin, cast from the cannon captured from the Turks in 1683, and supposedly the second biggest bell in the world that rings by swinging (locals know it as the bell that rings in the Austrian New Year; €4, daily 8:30–17:30, July–Aug until 18:00, Nov–March until 17:00). The 450-foot-high south tower, called St. Stephan's Tower, offers a far better view—343 tightly wound steps up the spiral staircase (€3, daily 9:00–17:30, this hike burns about 1 *Sachertorte* of calories). From the top, use your *Vienna from A to Z* to locate the famous sights.

The forlorn **Cathedral Museum** (Dom Museum, outside left transept past horses) gives a close-up look at piles of religious paintings, statues, and a treasury (€5, Tue–Sat 10:00–17:00, closed Sun–Mon, Stephansplatz 6, tel. 01/515-523-560).

▲▲Stephansplatz, Graben, and Kohlmarkt—The atmosphere of the church square, Stephansplatz, is colorful and lively. At nearby Graben Street (which was once a *Graben,* or ditch—originally the moat for the Roman military camp), top-notch street entertainers dance around an extravagant **plague monument** (at Bräuner Strasse). In medieval times, people did not understand the causes of plagues and figured they were a punishment from God. It was common for survivors to bribe or thank God with a monument like this one (c. 1690). Find Emperor Leopold, who ruled during the plague and made this statue in gratitude. (Hint: The typical inbreeding of royal families left him with a gaping underbite.) Below Leopold, Faith (with the help of a disgusting little cupid) tosses old naked women—symbolizing the plague—into the abyss.

Just before the plague monument is Dorotheergasse, leading to the Dorotheum auction house (see page 68). Just beyond the monument, you'll pass a fine set of **public WCs.** Around 1900, a local chemical maker needed a publicity stunt. He purchased two wine cellars under the Graben and hired Adolf Loos to design classy WCs in the Modernist style (complete with chandeliers and finely crafted mahogany) to prove that his chemicals really got things clean. The restrooms are clean to this day—so clean that they're used for poetry readings. Locals and tourists happily pay €0.50 for a quick visit. The Graben dead-ends at the aristocratic supermarket Julius Meinl am Graben (see page 87).

Turning left on **Kohlmarkt,** you enter Vienna's most elegant shopping street (except for "American Catalog Shopping" at #5, second floor), with the emperor's palace at the end. Strolling Kohlmarkt, daydream about the edible window displays at **Demel** (#14). Demel is the ultimate Viennese chocolate shop. During the summer, when the tables are moved outside, a room is filled with Art Nouveau boxes of Empress Sissy's choco-dreams come true: *Kandierte Veilchen* (candied violet petals), *Katzenzungen* (cats' tongues), and so on. The cakes here are moist (compared to the dry *Sachertortes*). The delectable window displays change about weekly, reflecting current happenings in Vienna. Inside, an impressive can-can of cakes is displayed to tempt visitors into springing for the €10 cake and coffee deal (point to the cake you want). You can sit inside, with a view of the cake-making, or outside, with the street action. Shops like this boast "K. u. K."—good enough for the *König und Kaiser* (king and emperor—same guy).

Just beyond Demel and across the street, at #1152, you can pop into a charming little Baroque **carriage courtyard,** with the surviving original carriage garages.

Kohlmarkt ends at **Michaelerplatz,** with a scant bit of Roman Vienna exposed at its center. On the left are the fancy Loden Plankl shop, with traditional formal wear, and the stables of the Spanish

Adolf Loos
(1870–1933)

Adolf Loos—Vienna's answer to Frank Lloyd Wright—famously condemned needless ornamentation, declaring, "Decoration is a crime." You can see three good examples of his work (all c. 1900 and described in this chapter) as you stroll the old center. Just off Kärntner Strasse is the Loos American Bar (Kärntnerdurchgang 10). On the Graben, you can descend into the finest public toilets in town. And facing Michaelerplatz, in front of the Hofburg entrance, is the Loos House (a.k.a. the "house without eyebrows").

Riding School. Study the grand entry facade to the Hofburg Palace—it's neo-Baroque from around 1900. The four heroic giants illustrate Hercules wrestling with his great challenges (much like the Hapsburgs, I'm sure). Opposite the facade, notice the modern Loos House (now a bank), which was built at about the same time. It was nicknamed the "house without eyebrows" for the simplicity of its windows. An anti–Art Nouveau statement (inspired by Frank Lloyd Wright and considered Vienna's first "modern" building), this was actually shocking at the time. To quell some of the outrage, the architect added flower boxes.

Enter the Hofburg Palace by walking through the gate, under the dome, and into the first square (In der Burg).

Vienna's Hofburg Palace

The complex, confusing, and imposing Imperial Palace, with 640 years of architecture, demands your attention. This first Hapsburg residence grew with the family empire from the 13th century until 1913, when the last "new wing" opened. The winter residence of the Hapsburg rulers until 1918, it's still the home of the Spanish Riding School, the Vienna Boys' Choir, the Austrian president's office, 5,000 government workers, and several important museums.

Rather than lose yourself in its myriad halls and courtyards, focus on three sections: the Imperial Apartments, Treasury, and Neue Burg (New Palace).

Hofburg Orientation from In der Burg Square: The statue is of Emperor Franz II, grandson of Maria Theresa, grandfather of Franz Josef, and father-in-law of Napoleon. Behind him is a tower with three kinds of clocks (the yellow disk shows the stage of the moon tonight). On the right, a door leads to the Imperial Apartments. Franz faces the oldest part of the palace. The colorful gate, which used to have a drawbridge, leads to the 13th-century Swiss Court (named for the Swiss mercenary guards once stationed

Vienna's Hofburg Palace

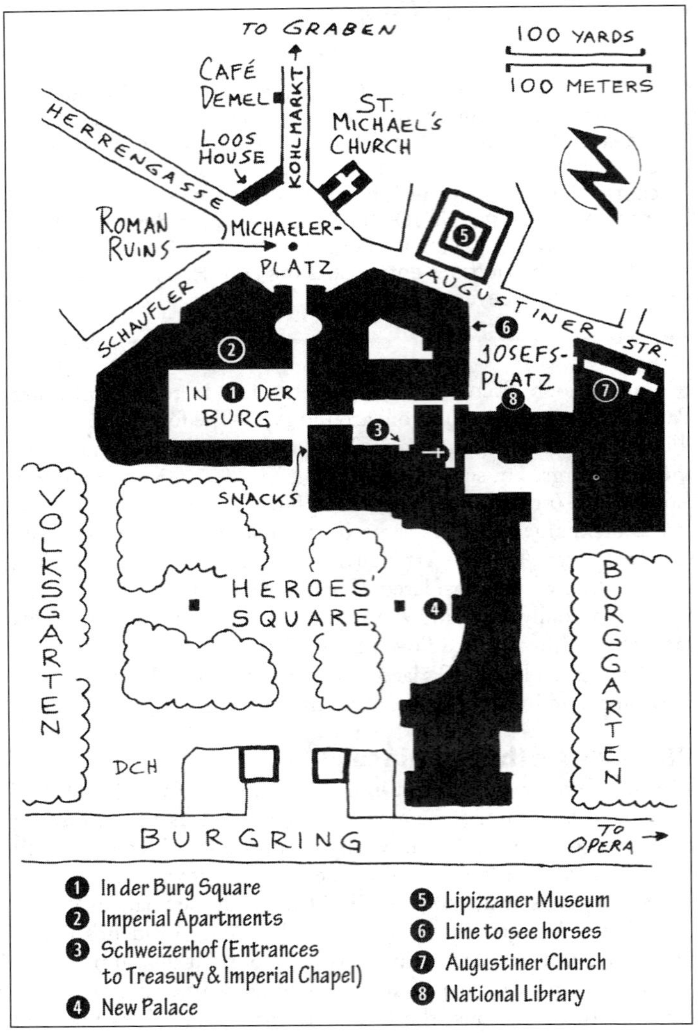

here), the Schatzkammer (treasury), and the Hofburgkapelle (palace chapel, where the Boys' Choir sings the Mass). For the Heroes' Square and the New Palace, continue opposite the way you entered In der Burg, passing through the left-most tunnel (with a tiny but handy sandwich bar—Hofburg Stüberl, Mon–Sat 7:00–17:00, Sun 10:00–15:00, your best bet if you need a bite or drink before touring the Imperial Apartments).

Sissy

Empress Elisabeth—Franz Josef's mysterious, narcissistic, and beautiful wife—is in vogue. Sissy was mostly silent. Her main goals in life seem to have been preserving her reputation as a beautiful empress, maintaining her Barbie Doll figure, and tending to her fairytale, ankle-length hair. In spite of severe dieting and fanatic exercise, age took its toll. After turning 30, she allowed no more portraits to be painted and was generally seen in public with a delicate fan covering her face (and bad teeth). Complex and influential, she was adored by Franz Josef, whom she respected. Her personal mission and political cause was promoting Hungary's bid for nationalism. Her personal tragedy was the death of her son Rudolf, the crown prince, by suicide. Disliking Vienna and the confines of the court, she traveled more and more frequently. Over the years, the restless Sissy and her hardworking husband became estranged. In 1898, while visiting Geneva, Switzerland, she was murdered by an Italian anarchist. Sissy has been compared to Princess Diana because of her beauty, bittersweet life, and tragic death. Her story is wonderfully told in the new Sissy Museum, now part of the Hofburg Imperial Apartments tour.

▲▲▲Imperial Apartments (Kaiserappartements)—These lavish, Versailles-type, "wish-I-were-God" royal rooms are the downtown version of the grander Schönbrunn Palace. If you're rushed and have time for only one palace, do this (€7.50, daily 9:00–17:00, last entry 16:30, from courtyard through St. Michael's Gate, just off Michaelerplatz, tel. 01/533-7570). Palace visits are a one-way romp through 20 rooms. You'll find some helpful English information within, and, with that and the following description, you won't need the €7.50 *Imperial Apartments and Sissy* museum guidebook. The included audioguide brings the exhibit to life. Tickets include the royal silver and porcelain collection *(Silberkammer)* near the turnstile. If touring the silver and porcelain, do it first to save walking.

Self-Guided Tour: Get your ticket, tour the silver and porcelain collection, climb the stairs, go through the turnstile, study the family tree tracing the Hapsburgs from 1273 to their messy WWI demise, and use the big model of the palace complex to understand the complex lay of the imperial land. Then head into the...

Sissy Museum: The first six rooms tell the life story of Empress Elisabeth's fancy world—her luxury homes and fairytale existence. While Sissy's life story is the perfect stuff of legends, the exhibit tries to keep things from getting too giddy, and doesn't add to the sugary, kitschy image that's been created. The exhibit starts with

Emperor Franz Josef

Franz Josef I—who ruled for 68 years (1848–1916)—was the embodiment of the Hapsburg Empire as it finished its six-century-long ride. Born in 1830, Franz Josef had a stern upbringing that instilled in him a powerful sense of duty and—like so many men of power—a love of things military. His uncle, Ferdinand I, was a dimwit, and, as the revolutions of 1848 were rattling royal families throughout Europe, the Hapsburgs replaced him, putting 18-year old Franz Josef on the throne. FJ put down the revolt with bloody harshness and spent the first part of his long reign understandably paranoid as social discontent simmered. FJ was very conservative. But worse, he figured wrongly that he was a talented military tactician, leading Austria into disastrous battles against Italy (which was fighting for its unification and independence) in the 1860s. His army endured severe, avoidable casualties. It was clear: FJ was a disaster as a general. Wearing his uniform to the end, he never saw what a dinosaur his monarchy was becoming, and never thought it strange that the majority of his subjects didn't even speak German. He had no interest in democracy and pointedly never set foot in Austria's parliament building. But, like his contemporary Queen Victoria, he was the embodiment of his empire—old-fashioned but sacrosanct. His passion for low-grade paperwork earned him the nickname "Joe bureaucrat." Mired in these petty details, he missed the big picture. He helped start a Great War that ultimately ended the age of monarchs. The year 1918 marked the end of Europe's big royal families: Hohenzollerns (Prussia), Romanovs (Russia), and Hapsburgs (Austria).

her assignation and traces the development of her legend, analyzing how her fabulous but tragic life could create a 19th-century Princes Diana from a rocky start (when she was disdained for abandoning Vienna and her husband, the venerable Emperor Franz Josef). You'll read bits of her poetic writing, catch snatches of movies made about her, see exact copies of her now-lost jewelry, and learn about her escapes, dieting mania, and chocolate bills. Admire Sissy's hard-earned thin waist (20 inches at age 16, 21 inches at age 50... after giving birth to 4 children). The black statue in the dark room represents the empress after the suicide of her son—aloof, thin, in black, with her back to the world.

After the Sissy rooms, a one-way route takes you through a series of royal rooms.

Waiting Room for the Audience Room: A map and mannequins from the many corners of the Hapsburg realm illustrate the multi-ethnicity of the vast empire. Every citizen had the right to meet privately with the emperor. Three huge paintings entertained guests while they waited. They were propaganda, showing crowds of commoners enthusiastic about their Hapsburg royalty. On the right: An 1809 scene of the emperor returning to Vienna, celebrating news that Napoleon had begun his retreat. Left: The return of the emperor from the 1814 Peace of Paris, the treaty that ended the Napoleonic wars. (The 1815 Congress of Vienna that followed was the greatest assembly of diplomats in European history. Its goal: to establish peace through a "balance of power" among nations. While rulers ignored nationalism in favor of continued dynastic rule, this worked for about 100 years, until a colossal war—World War I—wiped out the Hapsburgs and the rest of Europe's royal families.) Center: Less important, the emperor makes his first public appearance to adoring crowds after recovering from a life-threatening illness (1826). The chandelier—considered the best in the palace—is Baroque, made of Bohemian crystal.

Audience Room: Suddenly, you were face-to-face with the emp. The portrait on the easel shows Franz Josef in 1915, when he was over 80 years old. Famously energetic, he lived a spartan life dedicated to duty. He'd stand at the high table here to meet with commoners, who came to show gratitude or make a request. (Standing kept things moving.) On the table, you can read a partial list of 56 appointments he had on January 3, 1910 (family name and topic of meeting).

Conference Room: The emperor presided here over the equivalent of cabinet meetings. After 1867, he ruled the Austro-Hungarian Empire, so Hungarians sat at these meetings. The paintings on the wall show the military defeat of a popular Hungarian uprising...subtle.

Emperor Franz Josef's Study: The desk was originally between the windows. Franz Josef could look up from his work and see his lovely, long-haired, tiny-waisted Empress Elisabeth's reflection in the mirror. Notice the trompe l'oeil paintings above each door, giving the believable illusion of marble relief. Notice also all the family photos—the perfect gift for the dad/uncle/hubby who has it all.

The walls between the rooms are wide enough to hide servants' corridors (the door to his valet's room is in the back left corner). The emperor lived with a personal staff of 14: "three valets, four lackeys, two doormen, two manservants, and three chambermaids."

Emperor's Bedroom: This features his famous no-frills iron bed and portable washstand (necessary until 1880, when the palace got running water). While he had a typical emperor's share of mistresses, his dresser was always well-stocked with photos of Sissy. Franz Josef lived here after his estrangement from Sissy. An etching shows the empress—a fine rider and avid hunter—riding sidesaddle while jumping a hedge. The big, ornate stove in the corner was fed from behind. Through the 19th century, this was a standard form of heating.

Small Salon: This is dedicated to the memory of the assassinated Emperor Maximilian of Mexico (bearded portrait, Franz Josef's brother, killed in 1867). This was also a smoking room—necessary in the early 19th century, when smoking was newly fashionable (but only for men—never in the presence of women). Left of the door is a small button the emp had to buzz before entering the quarters of his estranged wife. You can go right in.

Empress' Bedroom and Drawing Room: This was Sissy's, refurbished neo-rococo in 1854. She lived here—the bed was rolled in and out daily—until her death in 1898.

Sissy's Dressing/Exercise Room: Servants worked two hours a day on Sissy's famous hair here. She'd exercise on the wooden structure. While she had a tough time with people, she did fine with animals. Her favorite dogs hang adorably on the wall.

Sissy's Bathroom: Detour into the behind-the-scenes palace. In the narrow passageway, you'll walk by Sissy's hand-painted-porcelain, dolphin-head WC (on the right). In the main bathroom, you'll see her huge copper tub (with the original wall coverings behind it). Sissy was the first Hapsburg to have running water in her bathroom (notice the hot and cold faucets). You're walking on the first linoleum ever used in Vienna—from around 1880. Next, enter the servants' quarters, with tropical scenes painted by Bergl in 1766. As you leave these rooms and re-enter the imperial world, look back to the room on the left.

Empress' Great Salon: The room is painted with Mediterranean escapes, the 19th-century equivalent of travel posters. The statue is of Elisa, Napoleon's oldest sister (by the neoclassical master, Canova). Turn the corner and pass through the anterooms of Alexander's apartments.

Red Salon: The Gobelin wall hangings were a 1776 gift from Marie Antoinette and Louis XVI in Paris to their Viennese counterparts.

Dining Room: It's dinnertime, and Franz Josef has called his extended family together. The settings are modest...just silver. Gold was saved for formal state dinners. Next to each name card was a menu with the chef responsible for each dish. (Talk about pressure.) While the Hofburg had tableware for 4,000, feeding 3,000 was a typical day. The cellar was stocked with 60,000 bottles of wine. The kitchen was huge—50 birds could be roasted on the hand-driven spits at once.

Through the shop, you're back on the street. Two quick lefts take you back to the palace square (In der Burg), where you can pass through the black, red, and gold gate and to the treasury.

▲▲▲Treasury (Weltliche und Geistliche Schatzkammer)—This "Secular and Religious Treasure Room" contains the best jewels on the Continent. Slip through the vault doors and reflect on the glitter of 21 rooms filled with scepters, swords, crowns, orbs, weighty robes, double-headed eagles, gowns, gem-studded bangles, and an eight-foot-tall, 500-year-old unicorn horn (or maybe the tusk of a narwhal)—which was considered incredibly powerful in the old days, giving its owner the grace of God. These were owned by the Holy Roman Emperor—a divine monarch. The well-produced, included audioguide provides a wealth of information (€8, Wed–Mon 10:00–18:00, closed Tue, follow Schatzkammer signs to the Schweizerhof, tel. 01/52524).

Room 2: The personal crown of Rudolf II has survived since 1602—it was considered too well-crafted to cannibalize for other crowns. This crown is a big deal because it's the adopted crown of the Austrian Empire, established in 1806 after Napoleon dissolved the Holy Roman Empire (an alliance of Germanic kingdoms so named because it tried to be the grand continuation of the Roman Empire). Pressured by Napoleon, the Austrian Francis II—who had been Holy Roman Emperor—became Francis I, Emperor of Austria. Francis I/II (the stern guy on the wall, near where you entered) ruled from 1792 to 1835. Look at the crown. Its design symbolically merges the typical medieval king's crown and a bishop's miter.

Rooms 3 and 4: These contain some of the coronation vestments and regalia needed for the new Austrian emperor.

Room 5: Ponder the Throne Cradle. Napoleon's son was born in 1811 and made king of Rome. The little eagle at the foot is symbolically not yet able to fly, but glory-bound. Glory is symbolized by the star, with dad's big *N* raised high.

Room 11: The collection's highlight is the 10th-century crown of the Holy Roman Emperor. The imperial crown swirls with symbolism "proving" that the emperor was both holy and Roman. The jeweled arch over the top is reminiscent of the parade helmet of ancient Roman emperors whose successors the HRE claimed to be. The cross on top says the HRE ruled as Christ's representative on earth. King Solomon's portrait (on the crown, right of cross) is Old Testament proof that kings can be wise and good. King David (next panel) is similar proof that they can be just. The crown's eight sides represent the celestial city of Jerusalem's eight gates. The jewels on the front panel symbolize the Twelve Apostles.

The nearby 11th-century Imperial Cross preceded the emperor in ceremonies. Encrusted with jewels, it carried a substantial chunk of *the* cross and *the* holy lance (supposedly used to pierce the side of Jesus while on the cross; both items displayed in the same glass case). This must be the actual holy lance, as Holy Roman Emperors actually carried this into battle in the 10th century. Look behind the cross to see how it was actually a box that could be clipped open and shut. You can see bits of the "true cross" anywhere, but this is a prime piece—with the actual nail hole.

The other case has jewels from the reign of Karl der Grosse (Charlemagne), the greatest ruler of medieval Europe. Notice Charlemagne modeling the crown (which was made a hundred years after he died) in the tall painting adjacent.

Room 12: The painting shows the coronation of Maria Theresa's son Josef II in 1764. He's wearing the same crown and royal garb you've just seen.

Room 16: Most tourists walk right by perhaps the most exquisite workmanship in the entire treasury, the royal vestments (15th century). Look closely—they are painted with gold and silver threads.

▲Heroes' Square (Heldenplatz) and the New Palace (Neue Burg)—This last grand addition to the palace, from just before World War I, was built for Franz Ferdinand but never used. (It was tradition for rulers not to move into their predecessor's quarters.) Its grand facade arches around Heroes' Square. Notice statues of the two great Austrian heroes on horseback: Prince Eugene of Savoy (who beat the Turks that had earlier threatened Vienna) and Archduke Charles (first to beat Napoleon in a battle, breaking Nappy's image of invincibility and heralding the end of the Napoleonic age). The frilly spires of Vienna's neo-Gothic City Hall break the horizon, and a line of horse-drawn carriages await their customers.

▲▲New Palace Museums: Armor, Music, and Ancient Greek Statues—The Neue Burg—technically part of the Kunsthistorisches Museum across the way—houses three fine museums (same ticket): an armory (with a killer collection of medieval weapons), historical musical instruments, and classical statuary from ancient Ephesus. The included audioguide brings the exhibits to life and lets you actually hear the fascinating old instruments in the collection being played. An added bonus is the chance to wander all alone among those royal Hapsburg halls, stairways, and painted ceilings (€7.50, Wed–Mon 10:00–18:00, closed Tue, almost no tourists, tel. 01/5252-4484).

More Hapsburg Sights near the Hofburg

Central Vienna has plenty more sights associated with the Hapsburgs. With the exception of the last one (on Mariahilfer Strasse), these are all near the Hofburg. Remember that the biggest Hapsburg sight of all, Schönbrunn Palace, makes a great half-day trip (4 miles from the center—see page 70).

Palace Garden (Burggarten)—This greenbelt, once the back yard of the Hofburg and now a people's park, welcomes people to loiter on the grass and is lively with office workers enjoying a break on nice days. The statue of Mozart facing the Ringstrasse is popular. The iron-and-glass pavilion now houses the recommended Palmenhaus Restaurant (see page 88) and a small but fluttery butterfly exhibit (€5, daily 10:00–17:00). The butterfly zone is delightfully muggy on a brisk off-season day, but trippy any time of year. If you tour it, notice the butterflies hanging out on the trays with rotting slices of banana. They lick the fermented banana juice as it beads, and then just hang out there in a stupor...or fly in anything but a straight line.

▲Lipizzaner Museum—A must for horse-lovers, this tidy museum in the Renaissance Stallburg Palace shows (and tells in English) the 400-year history of the famous riding school. Lipizzaner fans have a warm spot in their hearts for General Patton, who, at the end of World War II—knowing that the Soviets were about to take control of Vienna—ordered a raid on the stable to save the horses and ensure the survival of their fine old bloodlines. Videos show the horses in action on TVs throughout the museum. The "dancing" originated as battle moves: *pirouette* (quick turns) and *courbette* (on hind legs to make a living shield for the knight). The 45-minute movie in the basement theater also has great horse footage (showings alternate between German and English). These are very special horses—you'll notice they actually have "surnames," as all can be traced to the original six 16th-century stallions (€5, daily 9:00–18:00, Reitschulgasse 2 between Josefsplatz and Michaelerplatz, tel. 01/533-8658). Any time of day, you can see the horses prance on video in the museum's window.

Seeing the Lipizzaner Stallions: Seats for performances by Vienna's prestigious Spanish Riding School book up months in advance, but standing room is often available the same day (tickets-€35–105, standing room-€24–28, March–June and Sept–Oct Sun at 11:00, sometimes also Fri at 18:00, tel. 01/533-9031, www.srs.at). Luckily for the masses, training sessions with music in a chandeliered Baroque hall are open to the public (€11.50 at the door, roughly Feb–June and Sept–Oct, Tue–Sat 10:00–12:00 when the horses are in town). Tourists line up early at Josefsplatz, gate 2. Save money and avoid the wait by buying the €14.50 combo-ticket that covers both the museum and the training session (and lets you avoid that ticket line). Or, better yet, simply show up late. If you want to hang out with Japanese tour groups, get there early and wait for the doors to open at 10:00. But almost no one stays for the full two hours—except for the horses. As people leave, new tickets are printed continuously, so you can just waltz in with no wait at all. If you arrive at 10:45, you'll see the best action as one group of horses finishes and two more perform before they call it a day.

▲Augustinian Church (Augustinerkirche)—This is the Gothic and neo-Gothic church where the Hapsburgs latched, then buried, their hearts (weddings took place here and the royal hearts are in the vault). Don't miss the exquisite, tomb-like Canova memorial (neoclassical, 1805) to Maria Theresa's favorite daughter, Maria Christina, with its incredibly sad white-marble procession. The church's 11:00 Sunday Mass is a hit with music-lovers—both a Mass and a concert, often with an orchestra accompanying the choir. To pay, contribute to the offering plate and buy a CD afterwards. (Programs are available at the table by the entry all week.)

The church faces Josefsplatz, with its statue of the great reform emperor Josef II. The National Library (€3, next to the Augustinian Church) is worth a look.

▲▲Kaisergruft, the Remains of the Hapsburgs—Visiting the imperial remains is not as easy as you might imagine. These original organ donors left their bodies—about 150 in all—in the unassuming Kaisergruft (Capuchin Crypt), their hearts in the Augustinian Church (church open daily, but to see the goods you'll have to talk to a priest; Augustinerstrasse 3), and their entrails in the crypt below St. Stephan's Cathedral. Don't tripe.

Upon entering the Kaisergruft (€4, daily 9:30–16:00, last entry 15:40, behind Opera on Neuer Markt), buy the €0.50 map with a Hapsburg family tree and a chart locating each coffin.

The double coffin of Maria Theresa (1717–1780) and her husband is worth a close look for its artwork. Maria Theresa outlived her husband by 15 years—which she spent in mourning. Old and fat, she installed a special lift enabling her to get down into the crypt to be with her dead husband (even though he had been far from faithful). The couple recline—Etruscan style—atop their fancy lead coffin. At each corner are the crowns of the Hapsburgs—the Holy Roman Empire, Hungary, Bohemia, and Jerusalem. Notice the contrast between the rococo splendor of Maria Theresa's tomb and the simple box holding her more modest son, Josef II (at his parents' feet; for more on Joe II, see page 47).

Franz Josef (1830–1916) is nearby, in an appropriately austere military tomb. Flanking Franz Josef are the tombs of his son, the archduke Rudolf, and Empress Elizabeth. Rudolf and his teenage love committed suicide together in 1898 and—since the Church figured he forced her and was therefore a murderer—it took considerable legal hair-splitting to win Rudolf this spot (after examining his brain, it was determined that he was physically retarded and therefore incapable of knowingly killing himself and his girl). *Kaiserin* Elisabeth (1837–1898), a.k.a. Sissy, always gets the "Most Flowers" award.

In front of those three is the most recent Hapsburg tomb. Empress Zita was buried in 1989. Her burial procession was probably the last such Old Regime event in European history. The monarchy died hard in Austria.

While it's fun to chase down all these body parts, remember that the *real* legacy of the Hapsburgs is the magnificence of this city. Step outside. Look up. Watch the clouds glide by the ornate gables of Vienna.

▲Imperial Furniture Collection (Kaiserliches Hofmobiliendepot)—Bizarre, sensuous, eccentric, or precious, this is your peek at the Hapsburgs' furniture—from grandma's wheelchair to the emperor's spittoon—all thoughtfully described in English. The Hapsburgs had many palaces, but only the Hofburg was permanently furnished. The rest were furnished on the fly—set up and taken down by a gang of royal roadies called the "Depot of Court Movables" (Hofmobiliendepot). When the monarchy was dissolved in 1918, the state of Austria took possession of the Hofmobiliendepot's inventory—165,000 items. Now this royal storehouse is open to the public in a fine, new, sprawling museum. Don't go here for the *Jugendstil* furnishings. The older Baroque, rococo, and Biedermeier pieces are the most impressive and tied most intimately to the royals. Combine a visit to this museum with a stroll down the lively shopping boulevard, Mariahilfer Strasse (€7, Tue–Sun 10:00–18:00, closed Mon, Mariahilfer Strasse 88, tel. 01/5243-3570).

Near Karlsplatz

These sights cluster around Karlsplatz, just southeast of Ringstrasse (U-1, U-2, or U-4: Karlsplatz).

Karlsplatz—This fine and picnic-friendly square, with its Henry Moore sculpture in the pond, is ringed with sights. The Art Nouveau station pavilions—from the 19th-century municipal train system—are textbook *Jugendstil* by Otto Wagner (steel frame and decorative marble slabs with painted gold ornaments). One of Europe's first subway systems, it was built with a military purpose in mind: to move troops quickly in time of civil unrest—specifically, out to Schönbrunn Palace.

Charles Church (Karlskirche)—Charles Borromeo, a 16th-century bishop from Milan, was an inspiration during plague times. This "votive church" was dedicated to him in 1713, when an epidemic spared Vienna. The church offers the best Baroque in Vienna, with a unique combination of columns (showing scenes from the life of Charles Borromeo, à la Trajan's Column in Rome), a classic pediment, and an elliptical dome (€6 includes a skippable 1-room museum, audioguide, and visit to renovation site; Mon–Sat 9:00–12:30 & 13:00–18:00, Sun 13:00–18:00). The entry fee may seem steep, but remember that it funds the restoration.

Visitors ride the industrial lift to a platform at the base of the dome. Consider that the church was built and decorated with essentially the same scaffolding system. From there, you'll climb stairs to the steamy lantern at the extreme top of the church. At that dizzying height, you're in the clouds with cupids and angels. Many details that appear smooth and beautiful from ground level—such as gold leaf, rudimentary paintings, and fake marble—look rough and sloppy up close. It's surreal to observe the 3-D figures from an unintended angle. Faith, Hope, Charity, and Borromeo triumph and inspire while Protestants and their stinkin' books are trashed. Borromeo lobbies heaven for plague relief. At the very top, you'll see the tiny dove representing the Holy Ghost, surrounded by a cheering squad of nipple-lipped cupids.

Historical Museum of the City of Vienna (Wien Museum Karlsplatz)—This under-appreciated museum walks you through the history of Vienna with fine historic artifacts. You'll work chronologically from the ground floor (Roman artifacts, original statues from St. Stephan's Cathedral—c. 1350, with various Hapsburgs showing off the slinky hip-hugging fashion of the day) to the first floor (old city maps, booty from the Turkish siege, 1850 city model showing the town just before the wall was replaced by the Ring), to the second floor (city model from 1898 with new Ringstrasse, sentimental Biedermeier paintings and objets d'art, early-20th-century paintings including some by Gustav Klimt). The museum is worth the €4 admission (free Sun and Fri morning, open Tue–Sun 9:00–18:00, closed Mon, www.wienmuseum.at).

The Secession—This building, nicknamed the "golden cabbage" today (and "a temple for bullfrogs" when it was first built around the turn of the century), was created by the Vienna Secession movement, a group of non-conformist artists led by Gustav Klimt, Otto Wagner, and friends. The Secession, whose slogan was "To each age its art, and to art its liberty," first exhibited their "liberty-style" art here in 1897.

The young trees carved into the walls and its bushy "cabbage" rooftop are symbolic of renewal cycle. That spirit of turning away from traditions survives today, and the Secession still gives cutting-edge art a platform. While the staff hopes you take a look at the temporary exhibits (and the ticket includes this whether you like it or not), most tourists head for the basement, home to a small exhibit about the history of the building and the museum's highlight: Klimt's classic *Beethoven Frieze* (a.k.a. the "searching souls"). One of the masterpieces of Viennese Art Nouveau, this 105-foot-long fresco was a centerpiece of a 1902 homage to Beethoven exhibition. Sit down and read the free flier, which explains Klimt's still-powerful work. The theme, inspired by Beethoven's *Ninth Symphony*, features floating female figures "yearning for happiness." They drift and weave and search—like most of us do—through internal and external temptations and forces, falling victim to base and ungodly temptations, and losing their faith. Then, finally, they become fulfilled by poetry, music, and art as they reach the "Ideal Kingdom" where "True Happiness,

Art Nouveau Sights

Vienna gave birth to its own curvaceous brand of Art Nouveau around the early 1900s: Jugendstil ("youth style"). The TI has a brochure laying out Vienna's 20th-century architecture. The best of Vienna's scattered Jugendstil sights: the Belvedere Palace collection, the clock on Höher Markt (which does a musical act at noon), and the gilded, cabbage-domed Secession building at the Ring end of the Naschmarkt (see page 62).

Pure Bliss and Absolute Love" are found in a climactic embrace (€6, Tue–Sun 10:00–18:00, Thu until 20:00, closed Mon).

▲Naschmarkt—In 1898, the city decided to cover up its Vienna River. The long, wide square created was filled with a lively produce market that still bustles daily. From near the Opera, the Naschmarkt (roughly "Munchies Market") stretches along Wienzeile Street. The "belly of Vienna" comes with two parallel lanes—one lined with fun and reasonable eateries, and the other lined with the town's top-end produce and gourmet goodies. This is where top chefs like to get their ingredients. At the gourmet vinegar stall, you sample the vinegar like perfume—with a drop on your wrist. Farther from the center, the Naschmarkt becomes likeably seedy and surrounded by sausage stands, Turkish *döner kebab* stalls, cafés, and theaters. Each Saturday, it's infested by a huge flea market where, in olden days, locals would come to hire a monkey to pick little critters out of their hair (Mon–Fri 7:00–18:00, Sat 6:00–18:00, closed Sun, closes earlier in winter, U-4: Kettenbruckengasse). For a picnic park, pick up your grub here and walk over to Karlsplatz (described above).

More Sights in Vienna

▲▲▲Kunsthistorisches Museum—This exciting museum, across the Ring from the Hofburg Palace, showcases the grandeur and opulence of the Hapsburgs' collected artwork in a grand building (built as a museum in 1888). There are European masterpieces galore, all well-hung on one glorious floor, plus a fine display of Egyptian, classical, and applied arts.

Starting with the Italian wing of the museum, you get an immediate sense of the richness of this collection—you've walked right into the High Renaissance. Here, you'll see Raphael's graceful *Madonna of the Meadow* and Correggio's voluptuous *Jupiter and Io.* Meander through the Venetian Renaissance rooms to spend time with Titian, and land (with a thud) in the heart of Realism. (Caravaggio's still-shocking *David with the Head of Goliath* shows the artist was distinctly "a head" of his time.)

The Baroque rooms offer pudgy winged babies galore—quite

a contrast to the simple, direct, and down-to-earth Northern paintings by Dutch and Flemish artists only steps away. Enjoy Hieronymus Bosch's bizarrely crowded work and linger at the paintings by Peter Brueghel, the undisputed master of the slice-of-life village scene. Giuseppe Arcimboldo's *Summer* and *Winter* (with faces made of produce and fish, respectively) are always crowd-pleasers. Try the helpful, included audioguide for the full picture. Sadly, one of the jewels in the museum's crown is now missing. Cellini's *Salt Cellar,* a divine golden salt bowl valued at €50 million, was stolen in 2003 by expert thieves—to the anguish of the Vienna art world (€10, Tue–Sun 10:00–18:00, Thu until 21:00, closed Mon, tel. 01/525-240, www.khm.at; for my more detailed description of the top artwork, download www.ricksteves.com/kunst).

▲Natural History Museum—In the twin building facing the art museum, you'll find moon rocks, dinosaur stuff, and the fist-sized Venus of Willendorf—at 30,000 years old, the world's oldest sex symbol, found in the Danube Valley. This museum is a hit with children (€6.50, Wed–Mon 9:00–18:30, Wed until 21:00, closed Tue, tel. 01/521-770).

MuseumsQuartier—The vast grounds of the former imperial stables now corral several impressive, cutting-edge museums. Walk into the complex from the Hofburg side, where the main entrance (with visitors center) leads to a big courtyard with cafés, fountains, and revolving "installation lounge furniture," all surrounded by the quarter's various museums.

The **Leopold Museum** features modern Austrian art, including the largest collection of works by Egon Schiele (1890–1918) and a few drawings by Kokoschka and Klimt (€9, Wed–Mon 10:00–19:00, Thu until 21:00, closed Tue, behind Kunsthistorisches Museum, U-2 or U-3: Volkstheater/Museumsplatz, Museumsplatz 1–5, tel. 01/525-700, www.leopoldmuseum.org). Note that for these three artists, you'll do better in the Belvedere Palace (see below).

The **Museum of Modern Art** (Museum Moderner Kunst Stiftung Ludwig, a.k.a. "Mumok") is Austria's leading modern-art gallery. It's the striking lava-paneled building—three stories tall and four stories deep, offering seven floors of far-out art encased in very young stone. This huge, state-of-the-art museum displays revolving exhibits showing off art of the last generation—including Klee, Picasso, and Pop (€8, Tue–Sun 10:00–18:00, Thu until 21:00, closed Mon, tel. 01/525-001-440, www.mumok.at).

Rounding out the sprawling MuseumsQuartier are an architecture museum, Transeuropa, Electronic Avenue, children's museum, and the Kunsthalle Wien—an exhibition center for contemporary art (€7). Various combo-tickets are available for those interested in more than just the Leopold and Modern Art museums (visit www.mqw.at).

▲Academy of Fine Arts (Akademie der Bildenden Künste)—This small but exciting collection includes works by Bosch, Botticelli, and Rubens (quick, sketchy cartoons used to create his giant canvases); a Venice series by Guardi; and a self-portrait by a 15-year-old Van Dyck. It's all magnificently lit and well-described by the €2 audioguide, and comes with comfy chairs (€5, Tue–Sun 10:00–18:00, closed Mon, 3 blocks from Opera at Schillerplatz 3, tel. 01/5881-6225, www.akademiegalerie.at). The fact that this is a working art academy gives it a certain realness. As you wander the halls of the academy, ponder how history might have been different if Hitler—who applied to study architecture here but was rejected—had been accepted as a student. Before leaving, peek into the ground floor's central hall—textbook historicism, the Ringstrasse style of the late 1800s.

▲Liechtenstein Museum—The noble Liechtenstein family (who own only a tiny country, but whose friendship with the Hapsburgs goes back generations) amassed an incredible private art collection. Their palace was long a treasure for Vienna art lovers. Then, in 1938—knowing Hitler was intent on plundering artwork to create an immense "Führer Museum"—the family fled to their tiny homeland with their best art. Only in March of 2004 was the collection re-established in Vienna, and opened again to the adoring public. The Liechtensteins' "world of Baroque pleasures" includes the family's rare French rococo carriage (which was used for the family's grand entry into Paris—after being carted to the edge of town and assembled there; nearly all such carriages were destroyed in the French Revolution), a plush Baroque library, an inviting English Garden, and an impressive collection of paintings including a complete cycle of early Rembrandts (€10, €4 audioguide, Wed–Mon 9:00–20:00, closed Tue, tram D to Bauernfeldplatz, Fürstengasse 1, tel. 01/319-5767-252, www.liechtensteinmuseum.at).

▲KunstHausWien: Hundertwasser Museum—This "make yourself at home" museum is a hit with lovers of modern art. It mixes the work and philosophy of local painter/environmentalist Hundertwasser. Stand in front of the colorful checkerboard building and consider Hundertwasser's style. He was against "window racism." Neighboring houses allow only one kind of window. But 100H2O's windows are each different—and he encouraged residents to personalize them. He recognized "tree tenants" as well as human tenants. His buildings are spritzed with a forest and topped with dirt and grassy little parks—close to nature, good for the soul. Floors and sidewalks are irregular—to "stimulate the brain" (although current residents complain it just causes wobbly furniture and sprained ankles). Thus 100H2O waged a one-man fight—during the 1950s and 1960s, when concrete and glass ruled—to save the human soul from the city. (Hundertwasser claimed that "straight lines are godless.") Inside the museum, start with his interesting biography (which ends in 2000). His fun-loving paintings are half *Jugendstil* ("youth style") and half just kids' stuff. Notice the photographs from his 1950s days as part of Vienna's bohemian scene. Throughout the museum, notice the fun philosophical quotes from an artist who believed, "If man is creative, he comes nearer to his creator" (€8 for Hundertwasser Museum, €14 combo-ticket includes special exhibitions, half-price on Mon, open daily 10:00–19:00, extremely fragrant and colorful garden café, U-3: Landstrasse, Weissgerberstrasse 13, tel. 01/712-0491).

The KunstHausWien provides by far the best look at Hundertwasser. For an actual lived-in apartment complex by the green master, walk five minutes to the one-with-nature **Hundertwasserhaus** (free, at Löwengasse and Kegelgasse). This complex of 50 apartments, subsidized by the government to provide affordable housing, was built in the 1980s as a breath of architectural fresh air in a city of boring, blocky apartment complexes. While not open to visitors, it's worth visiting for its fun-loving and colorful patchwork exterior and the Hundertwasser festival of shops across the street. Don't miss the view from Kegelgasse to see the "tree tenants" and the internal winter garden residents enjoy.

Hundertwasser detractors—of which there are many—remind visitors that 100H2O was a painter, not an architect. They describe the Hundertwasserhaus as a "1950s house built in the 1980s," and colorfully painted with no real concern about the environment, communal living, or even practical comfort. Nearly all the original inhabitants got fed up with the novelty and moved out.

▲▲Belvedere Palace—This is the elegant palace of Prince Eugene of Savoy—the still-much-appreciated conqueror of the Turks. Eugene, a Frenchman considered too short and too ugly to be in the service of Louis XIV, offered his services to the Hapsburgs. While he was short and ugly indeed, he became the greatest military genius of his age. When you conquer cities, as Eugene did, you get really rich. He had no heirs, so the state got his property and Josef II established the Belvedere as Austria's first great public art gallery. Today, his palace boasts sweeping views and houses the Austrian gallery of 19th- and 20th-century art (€7.50, €2.50 audioguide, Tue–Sun 10:00–18:00, closed Mon, entrance at Prinz-Eugen-Strasse 27, tel. 01/7955-7134, www.belvedere.at). To get here from the center, catch tram D at the Opera (direction Südbahnhof, it stops at the palace gate).

Belvedere means "beautiful view." Sit at the top palace and look over the Baroque gardens, the mysterious sphinxes (which symbolized solving riddles and the finely educated mind of your host, Eugene), the lower palace, and the city. The spire of St. Stephan's Cathedral is 400 feet tall, and no other tall buildings are allowed within the first district. The hills—covered with vineyards—are where locals love to go to sample the new wine. (You can see Kahlenberg, from where you can walk down to several recommended *Heurigen* beyond the spire—see page 75.) These are the first of the Alps, which stretch from here all the way to Marseilles, France. The square you're overlooking was filled with people on May 15, 1955, as local leaders stood on the balcony of the Upper Palace (behind you) and proclaimed Austrian independence.

The Upper Palace was Eugene's party house. Today, like the Louvre in Paris (but much easier to enjoy), this palace contains a fine collection of paintings. The collection is arranged chronologically: on the first floor, you'll find historicism, Romanticism, Impressionism, Realism, tired tourism, expressionism, Art Nouveau, and early modernism. Each room tries to pair Austrian works from that period with much better-known European works. It's fun to see the work of artists like van Gogh, Munch, and Monet hung with their lesser-known Austrian contemporaries. As Austria became a leader in art around 1900, the collection gets stronger, with fine works by Gustav Klimt, Oskar Kokoschka, and Egon Schiele. The Klimt room shows how even in his early work, the face was vivid and the rest dissolved into decor. During his "golden period," this background became his trademark gold leaf studded with stones. The corner room shows a small exhibit on Prince Eugene, Archduke Franz Ferdinand, and the signing of the state treaty in 1955. Don't miss the poignant Schiele family portrait from 1918. His wife had died while he was still working on it. (He and his child were also soon taken by the influenza epidemic that swept through Europe after World War I.)

The upper floor shows off early-19th-century Biedermeier paintings (hyper-sensitive, super-sweet, uniquely Viennese Romanticism—the poor are happy, things are lit impossibly well, and folk life is idealized). Your ticket also includes the Austrian Baroque and Gothic art in the Lower Palace. Prince Eugene lived in that palace, but he's long gone and I wouldn't bother to visit.

▲▲Haus der Musik—Vienna's House of Music has a small first-floor exhibit on the Vienna Philharmonic, and upstairs you'll enjoy fine audiovisual exhibits on each of the famous hometown boys (Haydn, Mozart, Beethoven, Strauss, and Mahler). But the museum is unique for its effective use of interactive touch-screen computers and headphones to actually explore the physics of sound. You can twist, dissect, and bend sounds to make your own musical language, merging your voice with a duck's quack or a city's traffic roar. Wander through the "sonosphere" and marvel at the amazing acoustics—I could actually hear what I thought only a piano tuner could hear. Pick up a virtual baton to conduct the Vienna Philharmonic Orchestra (each time you screw up, the musicians put their instruments down and ridicule you). A computer will help you compose your own waltz by throwing dice. Really experiencing the place takes time. It's open late and makes a good evening activity (€10, daily 10:00–22:00, 2 blocks from Opera at Seilerstatte 30, tel. 01/51648, www.hdm.at).

▲Vienna's Auction House, the Dorotheum—For an aristocrat's flea market, drop by Austria's answer to Sotheby's, the Dorotheum. Its five floors of antique furniture and fancy knickknacks have been put up either for immediate sale or auction, often by people who inherited old things they don't have room for (Mon–Fri 10:00–18:00, Sat 9:00–17:00, closed Sun, classy little café on second floor, between Graben and Hofburg at Dorotheergasse 17, tel. 01/515-600). Fliers show schedules for actual auctions, which you are welcome to attend.

Judenplatz Memorial and Museum—The square called Judenplatz marks the location of Vienna's 15th-century Jewish community, one of Europe's largest at the time. The square, once filled with a long-gone synagogue, is now dominated by a blocky memorial to the 65,000 Austrian Jews killed by the Nazis. The memorial—a library turned inside out—symbolizes Jews as "people of the book" and causes one to ponder the huge loss of culture, knowledge, and humanity that took place between 1938 and 1945.

The Judenplatz Museum, while sparse, has displays on medieval Jewish life and a well-done video re-creating community scenes from five centuries ago. Wander the scant remains of the medieval synagogue below street level—discovered during the construction of the Holocaust memorial. This was the scene of a medieval massacre. Since Christians weren't allowed to lend money, Jews were Europe's moneylenders. As so often happened in Europe, when Christian locals fell too deeply into debt, they found a convenient excuse to wipe out the local ghetto—and their debts at the same time. In 1421, 200 of Vienna's Jews were burned at the stake. Others who refused a forced conversion committed mass suicide in the synagogue (€3, €7 combo-ticket includes a synagogue and Jewish Museum of the City of Vienna—see below, Sun–Thu 10:00–18:00, Fri 10:00–14:00, closed Sat, Judenplatz 8, tel. 01/535-0431).

Honorable Mentions—There's much, much more. The city map lists everything. If you're into Esperanto, undertakers, tobacco, clowns, firefighting, Freud, or the homes of dead composers, you'll find them all in Vienna. Several good museums that try very hard but are submerged in the greatness of Vienna include: **Jewish Museum of the City of Vienna** (€5, or €7 combo-ticket includes synagogue and Judenplatz Museum—listed above, Sun–Fri 10:00–18:00, Thu until 20:00, closed Sat, Dorotheergasse 11, tel. 01/535-0431, www.jmw.at), **Folkloric Museum of Austria** (Tue–Sun 10:00–17:00, closed Mon, Laudongasse 15, tel. 01/406-8905), and **Museum**

of Military History, one of Europe's best if you like swords and shields (Heeresgeschichtliches Museum, Sat–Thu 9:00–17:00, closed Fri, Arsenal district, Objekt 18, tel. 01/795-610). The vast **Austrian Museum of Applied Arts** (Österreichisches Museum für Angewandte Kunst, or "MAK") is Vienna's answer to London's Victoria and Albert collection. The museum shows off the fancies of local aristocratic society, including a fine *Jugendstil* collection (€8, free Sat, open Tue–Sun 10:00–18:00, Tue until 24:00, closed Mon, Stubenring 5, tel. 01/711-360, www.mak.at).

Top People-Watching and Strolling Sights

▲City Park (Stadtpark)—Vienna's City Park is a waltzing world of gardens, memorials to local musicians, ponds, peacocks, music in bandstands, and locals escaping the city. Notice the *Jugendstil* entrance at the Stadtpark U-Bahn station. The Kursalon, where Strauss was the violin-toting master of waltzing ceremonies, hosts daily touristy concerts in three-quarter time.

▲Prater—Since the 1780s, when the reformist Emperor Josef II gave his hunting grounds to the people of Vienna as a public park, this place has been Vienna's playground. While tired and a bit run-down these days, Vienna's sprawling amusement park still tempts visitors with its huge 220-foot-tall, famous, and lazy Ferris wheel *(Riesenrad)*, roller coaster, bumper cars, Lilliputian railroad, and endless eateries. Especially if you're traveling with kids, this is a fun, goofy place to share the evening with thousands of Viennese (daily 9:00–24:00 in summer, but quiet after 22:00, U-1: Praterstern). For a local-style family dinner, eat at Schweizerhaus (good food, great beer) or Wieselburger Bierinsel.

Sunbathing—Like most Europeans, the Austrians worship the sun. Their lavish swimming centers are as much for tanning as swimming. To find the scene, follow the locals to their "Danube Sea" and a 20-mile, skinny, man-made beach along Danube Island. It's traffic-free concrete and grass, packed with in-line skaters and bikers, with rocky river access and a fun park (easy U-Bahn access on U-1 to Donauinsel).

A Walk in the Vienna Woods (Wienerwald)—For a quick side-trip into the woods and out of the city, catch the U-4 to Heiligenstadt, then bus #38A to Kahlenberg, where you'll enjoy great views and a café overlooking the city. From there, it's a peaceful 45-minute downhill hike to the *Heurigen* of Nussdorf or Grinzing to enjoy some new wine (see "Vienna's Wine Gardens," page 75).

City Hall (Rathaus) Food Circus and Open-Air Cinema—A thriving people scene erupts each evening through the summer in front of the City Hall (Rathaus) on the Ring. You'll find lots of colorful food circus–type eateries and free movies or excellent concerts (see "Eating" and "Summer Music Scene," below).

Naschmarkt—Vienna's busy produce market is a great place for people-watching (see page 63).

Near Vienna: Schönbrunn Palace

Among Europe's palaces, only Schloss Schönbrunn (Schönbrunn Palace) rivals Versailles. Worth ▲▲▲ and located four miles from the center, it was the Hapsburgs' summer residence. It's big (1,441 rooms), but don't worry—only 40 rooms are shown to the public. (Today the families of 260 civil servants rent simple apartments in the rest of the palace.)

While the exterior is Baroque, the interior was finished under Maria Theresa in let-them-eat-cake rococo. The chandeliers are either of hand-carved wood with gold-leaf gilding or of Bohemian crystal. Thick walls hid the servants as they ran around stoking the ceramic stoves from the back, and so on. Most of the public rooms are decorated in neo-Baroque, as they were under Franz Josef (r. 1848–1916). When WWII bombs rained on the city and the palace grounds, the palace itself took only one direct hit. Thankfully, that bomb, which crashed through three floors—including the sumptuous central ballroom—was a dud.

Reservations and Hours: Schönbrunn suffers from crowds. To avoid the long delays in July and August (mornings are worst), make a reservation by telephone (tel. 01/8111-3239, answered daily 8:00–17:00). You'll get an appointment time and a ticket number. Check in at least 30 minutes early. Upon arrival, go to the group desk, give your number, pick up your ticket, and jump in ahead of the masses. If you show up in peak season without calling first, you deserve the frustration. Wait in line, buy your ticket, and wait until the listed time to enter (which could be tomorrow). Kill time in the gardens or coach museum (palace open daily April–Oct 8:30–17:00, July–Aug until 18:00, Nov–March 8:30–16:30). Crowds are worst from 9:30 to 11:30, especially on weekends and in July and August; it's least crowded from 12:00 to 14:00 and after 16:00.

Cost and Tours: The admission price is based on the tour you select. Choose between two audioguide tours: the Imperial Tour (22 rooms, €8, 35 min, Grand Palace rooms plus apartments of Franz Josef and Elisabeth—mostly 19th-century and therefore least interesting) or the Grand Tour (40 rooms, €10.50, 50 min, adds apartments of Maria Theresa—18th-century rococo). The Schönbrunn Pass Classic includes the Grand Tour, Gloriette viewing terrace, maze, privy garden, and the court bakery—complete with *Apfelstrudel* demo and tasting (€15, available April–Oct only; more info: www.schoenbrunn.at). I'd go for the Grand Tour.

Getting to the Palace: Take tram #58 from Westbahnhof directly to the palace, or ride U-4 to Schönbrunn and walk 400 yards. The main entrance is in the left side of the palace as you face it.

Palace Gardens—After strolling through all the Hapsburgs tucked neatly into their crypts, a stroll through the emperor's garden with countless commoners is a celebration of the natural evolution of civilization from autocracy into real democracy. As a civilization, we're doing well.

The sculpted **gardens** (with a palm house, €3.50, daily May–Sept 9:30–18:00, Oct–April 9:30–17:00) lead past Europe's oldest **zoo** (*Tiergarten,* built by Maria Theresa's husband for the entertainment and education of the court in 1752; €12, May–Sept daily 9:00–18:30, less off-season, tel. 01/877-9294) up to the **Gloriette,** a purely decorative monument celebrating an obscure Austrian military victory and offering a fine city view (viewing terrace-€2.30, included in €15 Schönbrunn Pass Classic, daily April–Sept 9:00–18:00, July–Aug until 19:00, Oct until 17:00, closed Nov–March). The park itself is free (daily sunrise to dusk, entrance on either side of the palace). A touristy choo-choo train makes the rounds all day, connecting Schönbrunn's many attractions.

Coach Museum Wagenburg—The Schönbrunn coach museum is a 19th-century traffic jam of 50 impressive royal carriages and sleighs. Highlights include silly sedan chairs, the death-black hearse carriage (used for Franz Josef in 1916, and most recently for Empress Zita in 1989), and an extravagantly gilded imperial carriage pulled by eight Cinderella horses. This was rarely used other than for the coronation of Holy Roman Emperors, when it was disassembled and taken to Frankfurt for the big event (€4.50; April–Oct daily 9:00–18:00; Nov–March Tue–Sun 10:00–16:00, closed Mon; last entry 30 min before closing, 200 yards from palace, walk through right arch as you face palace, tel. 01/877-3244).

ACTIVITIES

Summer Music Scene

As far back as the 12th century, Vienna was a mecca for musicians—both sacred and secular (troubadours). The Hapsburg emperors of the 17th and 18th centuries were not only generous supporters of music, but fine musicians and composers themselves. (Maria Theresa played a mean double bass.) Composers like Haydn, Mozart, Beethoven, Schubert, Brahms, and Mahler gravitated to this music-friendly environment. They taught each other, jammed together, and spent a lot of time in Hapsburg palaces. Beethoven was a famous figure, walking—lost in musical thought—through Vienna's woods. In the city's 19th-century belle époque, "Waltz King" Johann Strauss and his brothers kept Vienna's 300 ballrooms spinning.

This musical tradition continues into modern times, leaving some prestigious Viennese institutions for today's tourists to enjoy: the Opera, the Boys' Choir, and the great Baroque halls and churches, all busy with classical and waltz concerts.

Vienna is Europe's music capital. It's music *con brio* from October through June, reaching a symphonic climax during the Vienna Festival each May and June. Sadly, in July and August, the Boys' Choir, the Opera, and many more music companies are—like you—on vacation. But Vienna hums year-round with live classical music. In the summer, you have these basic choices:

2006: The Year of Mozart—Mozart, born in 1756, would be 250 years old in 2006 if he had taken better care of himself. Vienna and Salzburg will celebrate the occasion with a busy schedule of Mozart concerts (details at TI or at www.mozart2006.net).

Touristy Mozart and Strauss Concerts—If the music comes to you, it's touristy—designed for flash-in-the-pan Mozart fans. Powdered-wig orchestra performances are given almost nightly in grand traditional settings (€25–50). Pesky wigged-and-powdered Mozarts peddle tickets in the streets. They rave about the quality of the musicians, but you'll get second-rate chamber orchestras, clad in historic costumes, performing the greatest hits of Mozart and Strauss. These are casual, easygoing concerts with lots of tour groups. While there's not a local person in the audience, the tourists generally enjoy the evening. To sort through all your options, check with the ticket office in the TI (same price as on the street but with all venues to choose from). Savvy locals suggest getting the cheapest tickets, as no one seems to care if cheapskates move up to fill unsold pricier seats. Critics explain that the musicians are actually very good (often Hungarians, Poles, and Russians working a season here to fund an entire year of music studies back home), but that they haven't performed much together so aren't "tight." The Mozarthaus is a small room richly decorated in Venetian Renaissance style with intimate chamber-music concerts (€30, almost nightly at 19:30, near St. Stephan's Cathedral at Singerstrasse 7, tel. 01-911-9077).

Strauss Concerts in the Kursalon—For years, Strauss concerts have been held in the Kursalon, where the "Waltz King" himself directed wildly popular concerts 100 years ago (€32–49, 4 concerts nightly April–Oct, 1 concert nightly other months, tel. 01/512-5790). Shows are a touristy mix of ballet, waltzes, and a 15-piece orchestra in wigs and old outfits. For the cheap option, enjoy a summer-afternoon coffee concert (free if you buy a drink, weekends and maybe also weekdays July–Aug 15:00–17:00).

Serious Concerts—These events, including the Opera, are listed in the monthly *Wien-Programm* (available at TI). Tickets run from €36 to €75 (plus a stiff 22 percent booking fee when booked in advance or through a box office like the one at the TI). While it's easy to book tickets online long in advance, spontaneity is also workable, as there are invariably people with tickets they don't need selling them at face value or less outside the door before concert time. If you call a concert hall directly, they can advise you on the availability of (cheaper) tickets at the door. Vienna takes care of its starving artists (and tourists) by offering cheap standing-room tickets to top-notch music and opera (1 hr before show time).

Vienna's **Summer of Music Festival** (a.k.a. "KlangBogen") assures that even from June through September, you'll find lots of great concerts, choirs, and symphonies (special *KlangBogen* brochure at TI; get tickets at Wien Ticket pavilion off Kärntner Strasse next to Opera House, or go directly to location of particular event; Summer of Music tel. 01/42717, www.klangbogen.at).

Musicals—The Wien Ticket pavilion sells tickets to contemporary American and British musicals done in German language (€10–95 with €2.50 standing room), and offers these tickets at half price from 14:00 until 17:00 the day of the show. Or you can reserve (full-price) tickets for the musicals by calling up to one day ahead (call combined office of the 3 big theaters at tel. 01/58885).

Vienna Boys' Choir—The boys sing (heard but not seen, from a high balcony) at Mass in the Imperial Chapel (Hofburgkapelle) of the Hofburg (entrance at Schweizerhof, from Josefsplatz go through tunnel) 9:15–10:30 on Sundays, except in July and August. While seats must be reserved two months in advance (€5–29, reserve by fax, e-mail, or mail: fax from the U.S. 011-431-533-992-775, hmk@aon.at, or write Hofmusikkapelle, Hofburg-Schweizerhof, 1010 Wien; tel. for information only—cannot book tickets—01/533-9927), standing room inside is free and open to the first 60 who line up. Rather than line up early, you can simply swing by and stand in the narthex just outside, where you can hear the boys and see the Mass on a TV monitor. Boys' Choir concerts (on stage at the Musikverein) are also given Fridays at 16:00 in May, June, September, and October (€35–48, standing room goes on sale at 15:30 for €15, Karlsplatz 6, U-1, U-2, or U-4: Karlsplatz, tel. 01/5880-4141). They're nice kids, but, for my taste, not worth all the commotion. Remember, many churches have great music during Sunday Mass. Just 200 yards from the Boys' Choir chapel, Augustinian Church has a glorious 11:00 service each Sunday (see page 59).

Summer Music and Film Festival at the City Hall (Rathaus)—The park in front of the City Hall thrives nightly in July and August, as a huge screen is set up with top-end speakers to show films of great concerts. While it's not live, the quality is excellent and it's free—and single locals know this is the best pick-up place in town. Classical, opera, or jazz, there's a different concert every night. Go early to enjoy dinner in the park, as there are countless (mostly ethnic) stalls serving fun and cheap meals to the youthful gang (daily from 11:00 until late in July and Aug). Film schedules are at the TI.

Classical Music to Go—To bring home Beethoven, Strauss, or the Wiener Philharmonic on a top-quality CD, shop at Gramola on the Graben, Emi on Kärntner Strasse, or Virgin Megastore on Mariahilfer Strasse.

EXPERIENCES

Vienna's Cafés

In Vienna, the living room is down the street at the neighborhood coffeehouse. This tradition is just another example of Viennese expertise in good living. Each of Vienna's many long-established (and sometimes even legendary) coffeehouses has its individual character (and characters). These classic cafés are a bit tired, with a shabby patina and famously grumpy waiters who treat you like an uninvited guest invading their living room. Still, it's a welcoming place. They offer newspapers, pastries, sofas, quick and light workers' lunches, elegance, smoky ambience, and "take all the time you want" charm for the price of a cup of coffee. Order it *melange* (like a cappuccino), *brauner* (strong coffee with a little milk), or *schwarzer* (black). Americans who ask for a latte are mistaken for Italians and given a cup of hot milk. Rather than buy the *Herald Tribune* ahead of time, spend the money on a cup of coffee and read it for free, Vienna-style in a café.

My favorites are: **Café Hawelka,** with a dark, "brooding Trotsky" atmosphere, paintings by struggling artists who couldn't pay for coffee, a saloon-wood flavor, chalkboard menu, smoked velvet couches, an international selection of newspapers, and a phone that rings for regulars (Wed–Mon 8:00–2:00, Sun from 16:00, closed Tue, just off Graben, Dorotheergasse 6); **Café Central,** with *Jugendstil* decor and great *Apfelstrudel* (high prices and stiff staff, Mon–Sat 8:00–22:00, Sun 10:00–18:00, Herrengasse 14, tel. 01/533-376-326); the **Café Sperl,** dating from 1880 with furnishings identical to the day it opened, from the coat tree to the chairs (Mon–Sat 7:00–23:00, Sun 11:00–20:00 except closed Sun July–Aug, just off Naschmarkt near Mariahilfer Strasse, Gumpendorfer 11, tel. 01/586-4158); and the basic, untouristy **Café Ritter** (daily 7:30–23:30, Mariahilfer Strasse 73, U-3: Neubaugasse, near several recommended hotels, tel. 01/587-8237).

If **Starbucks** seems big in Vienna, it's because the Seattle-based coffee firm has decided to test the Euro-waters here. Apparently, they figured that Vienna—with its love of fine coffee—would be a tough market to crack...and if they could succeed here, they could take Europe. Locals report that Starbucks is popular with teenagers and tourists, but the coffee is overpriced, and "flavored" coffee is nonsense to Viennese connoisseurs. Even so, the "coffee to go" trend has been picked up by many bakeries and other joints.

Vienna's Wine Gardens *(Heurigen)*

The uniquely Viennese institution of *Heurige* is two things: a wine, and a place to drink it. When the Hapsburgs let Vienna's vintners sell their own new wine *(Heurige)* tax-free, several hundred families opened *Heurigen* (wine-garden restaurants clustered around the edge of town)—and a tradition was born. Today they do their best to maintain the old-village atmosphere, serving the homemade new wine (the last vintage, until November 11, when a new vintage year begins) with light meals and strolling musicians. Most *Heurigen* are decorated with enormous antique presses from their vineyards. Wine gardens might be closed on any given day; always call ahead to confirm, if you have your heart set on a particular place. (For a near-*Heurige* experience right downtown, drop by Gigerl Stadtheuriger—see "Eating," page 85.)

At any *Heurige,* fill your plate at a self-serve cold-cut buffet (€6–9 for dinner). Food is sold by the "*10 dag*" unit. (A *dag* is a decigram, so *10 dag* is 100 grams...about a quarter pound.) Dishes to look out for: *Stelze* (grilled knuckle of pork), *Fleischlaberln* (fried ground-meat patties), *Schinkenfleckerln* (pasta with cheese and ham), *Schmalz* (a spread made with pig fat), *Blunzen* (black pudding... sausage made from blood), *Presskopf* (jellied brains and innards), *Liptauer* (spicy cheese spread), *Kornspitz* (whole-meal bread roll), and *Kummelbraten* (crispy roast pork with caraway). Waitresses will then take your wine order (€2.20 per quarter liter, about 8 oz). Many locals claim it takes several years of practice to distinguish between *Heurige* and vinegar.

There are more than 1,700 acres of vineyards within Vienna's city limits, and countless *Heurige* taverns. For a *Heurige* evening, rather than go to a particular place, take a tram to the wine-garden district of your choice and wander around, choosing the place with the best ambience.

Getting to the *Heurigen:* You have three options: a 15-minute taxi ride, trams and buses, or a goofy tourist train.

Trams make a trip to the Vienna Woods quick and affordable. The fastest way is to ride U-4 to its last stop, Heiligenstadt, where trams and buses in front of the station fan out to the various neighborhoods. Ride tram D to its end point for Nussdorf. Ride bus #38A for Grinzing and on to the Kahlenberg viewpoint—#38A's end station. (Note that tram #38—different from bus #38A—starts at the Ring and finishes at Grinzing). To get to Neustift am Walde, ride U-6 to Nussdorfer Strasse and catch bus #35A. Connect Grinzing and Nussdorf with bus #38A and tram D (transfer at Grinzingerstrasse).

The **Heuriger Express** train is tacky but handy and relaxing, chugging you on a hop-on, hop-off circle from Nussdorf through Grinzing and around the Vienna Woods with a light narration

(€7.30, buy ticket from driver, 60 min, daily April–Oct 12:00–19:00, departs from end station of tram D in Nussdorf at the top of every hr, tel. 01/479-2808).

Here are a couple good *Heurige* neighborhoods:

Grinzing: Of the many *Heurige* suburbs, Grinzing is the most famous, lively...and touristy. Many people precede their visit to Grinzing by riding tram #38A from Schottentor (on the Ring) to its end (up to Kahlenberg for a grand Vienna view), and then ride 20 minutes back into the *Heurige* action. From the Grinzing tram stop, follow Himmelgasse uphill toward the onion-top dome. You'll pass plenty of wine gardens—and tour buses—on your way up. Just past the dome, you'll find the heart of the *Heurige.*

Heiligenstadt (Pfarrplatz): Between Grinzing and Nussdorf, this area features several decent spots, including the famous and touristy Mayer am Pfarrplatz (a.k.a **Beethovenhaus,** Mon–Sat 16:00–23:00, Sun 11:00–23:00, bus #38A stop: Fernsprechamt/ Heiligenstadt, walk 5 min uphill on Dübling Nestelbachgasse to Pfarrplatz 2, tel. 01/370-3361). This place has a charming inner courtyard with an accordion player and a sprawling backyard with a big children's play zone. Beethoven lived—and composed his *Sixth Symphony*—here in 1817. He hoped the local spa would cure his worsening deafness. **Weingut and Heuriger Werner Welser,** a block uphill from Beethoven's place, is lots of fun, with music nightly from 19:00 (open daily 15:30–24:00, Probusgasse 12, tel. 01/318-9797).

Nussdorf: A less-touristy district—characteristic and popular with locals—Nussdorf has plenty of *Heurige* ambience. Right at the end station of tram D, you'll find three long and skinny places side by side: **Schübel-Auer Heuriger** (Tue–Sat 16:00–24:00, closed Sun–Mon, Kahlenbergerstrasse 22, tel. 01/370-2222) is my favorite. Also consider **Heuriger Kierlinger** (daily 15:30–24:00, Kahlenbergerstrasse 20, tel. 01/370-2264) and **Steinschaden** (daily 15:00–24:00, Kahlenbergerstrasse 18, tel. 01/370-1375). Walk through any of these and you pop out on Kahlenbergerstrasse, where a walk 20 yards uphill takes you to some more eating and drinking fun: **Bamkraxler** ("Tree Jumper"), the only beer garden amid all these vineyards. It's a fun-loving, youthful place with fine keg beer and a regular menu—traditional, ribs, veggie, kids' menu—rather than the *Heurige* cafeteria line (€6–10 meals, kids' playground, Tue–Sat 16:00–24:00, Sun 11:00–24:00, closed Mon, Kahlenbergerstrasse 17, tel. 01/318-8800).

Sirbu Weinbau Heuriger is actually in the vineyards, high above Vienna with great city and countryside views, a top-notch buffet, a glass veranda, and a traditional interior for cool weather. This place is a bit more touristy, since it's more upmarket and famous as "the ultimate setting" (from 15:00, closed Sun, big children's play zone, Kahlenbergerstrasse 210, tel. 01/320-5928). It's high above regular transit service, but fun to incorporate into a little walking. Ideally, ride bus #38A to the end at Kahlenberg, and ask directions to the Heuriger (a 20-min walk downhill).

NIGHTLIFE

If old music and new wine aren't your thing, Vienna has plenty of alternatives. For an up-to-date rundown on fun after dark, get the TI's free *Vienna Hype* booklet.

Bermuda Triangle (Bermuda Dreieck)—The area known as the "Bermuda Triangle"—north of St. Stephan's Cathedral, between Rotenturmstrasse and Judengasse—is the hot local nightspot. You'll find lots of music clubs and classy pubs, or *Beisl* (such as Krah Krah, Salzamt, Bermuda Bräu, and First Floor—for cocktails with live fish). The serious-looking guards have nothing to do with the bar scene—they're guarding the synagogue nearby.

Gürtel—The Gürtel is Vienna's outer ring road. The arches of a lumbering viaduct (which carries a train track) are now filled with trendy bars, dance clubs, antique shops, and restaurants. To experience—or simply see—the latest scene in town, head out here. The people-watching—the trendiest kids on the block—makes the trip fun even if you're looking for exercise rather than a drink. Ride U-6 to Nussdorfer Strasse or Thaliastrasse and hike along the viaduct.

English Cinema—Two great theaters offer three or four screens of English movies nightly (€6–9): **English Cinema Haydn,** by my recommended hotels on Mariahilfer Strasse (Mariahilfer Strasse 57, tel. 01/587-2262, www.haydnkino.at); and **Artis International Cinema,** right in the town center a few minutes from the cathedral (Schultergasse 5, tel. 01/535-6570).

SLEEPING

My recommendations stretch mainly from the center (figure at least €100 for a decent double), along the likeable Mariahilfer Strasse (around €80), to the Westbahnhof (around €60). While few places in Vienna are air-conditioned (they are troubled by the fact that, per person, Las Vegas expends more energy keeping people cool than arctic Norway does to keep people warm), you can generally get fans on request. Even places with elevators often have a few stairs to climb, too.

These hotels loose big and you pay more if you find a room through Internet booking sites. Book direct by phone, fax, or e-mail and save. Most places will hold a room without a deposit if you promise to arrive before 17:00.

Sleep Code

(€1 = about $1.20, country code: 43, area code: 01)

S = Single, D = Double/Twin, T = Triple, Q = Quad, b = bathroom, s = shower only. English is spoken at each place. Unless otherwise noted, credit cards are accepted and breakfast is included.

To help you sort easily through these listings, I've divided the rooms into three categories, based on the price for a standard double room with bath:

$$$ Higher Priced—Most rooms €115 or more.
$$ Moderately Priced—Most rooms between €75–115.
$ Lower Priced—Most rooms €75 or less.

Within the Ring, in the Old City Center

You'll pay extra to sleep in the atmospheric old center, but if you can afford it, staying here gives you the best classy Vienna experience.

$$$ Pension Pertschy circles an old courtyard and is bigger and more hotelesque than the others listed here. Its 50 rooms are huge, but well-worn and a bit musty. Those on the courtyard are quietest (Sb-€77, small Db-€117, large Db-€170, cheaper off-season, extra bed-€30, non-smoking rooms, elevator, U-1 or U-3: Stephansplatz, Habsburgergasse 5, tel. 01/534-490, fax 01/534-4949, www.pertschy.com, pertschy@pertschy.com).

$$$ Pension Neuer Markt is a four-star place that feels family-run, with 37 quiet, comfy, old-feeling rooms in a perfectly central locale (Ss-€85, Sb-€105, smaller Ds-€96, Db-€125, prices can vary with season and room size, extra bed-€20, elevator, Seilergasse 9, tel. 01/512-2316, fax 01/513-9105, www.hotelpension.at/neuermarkt, neuermarkt@hotelpension.at).

$$$ Pension Aviano is another peaceful four-star place, with 17 comfortable rooms on the fourth floor above lots of old center action (Sb-€85, Db-€125–145 depending on size, 15 percent cheaper Nov–March, extra bed-€30, elevator, non-smoking rooms, between Neuer Markt and Kärntner Strasse at Marco d'Avianogasse 1, tel. 01/512-8330, fax 01/5128-3306, www.pertschy.com, aviano@pertschy.com).

$$$ Hotel Schweizerhof is a classy 55-room place with big rooms, three-star comforts, and a more formal ambience. It's centrally located midway between St. Stephan's Cathedral and the Danube canal (Sb-€84–88, Db-€109–131, Tb-€131–146, low prices are for July–Aug and slow times, elevator, can be noisy on weekends, Bauernmarkt 22, U-1 or U-3: Stephansplatz, tel. 01/533-1931, fax 01/533-0214, www.schweizerhof.at, office@schweizerhof.at).

Hotels and Restaurants in Central Vienna

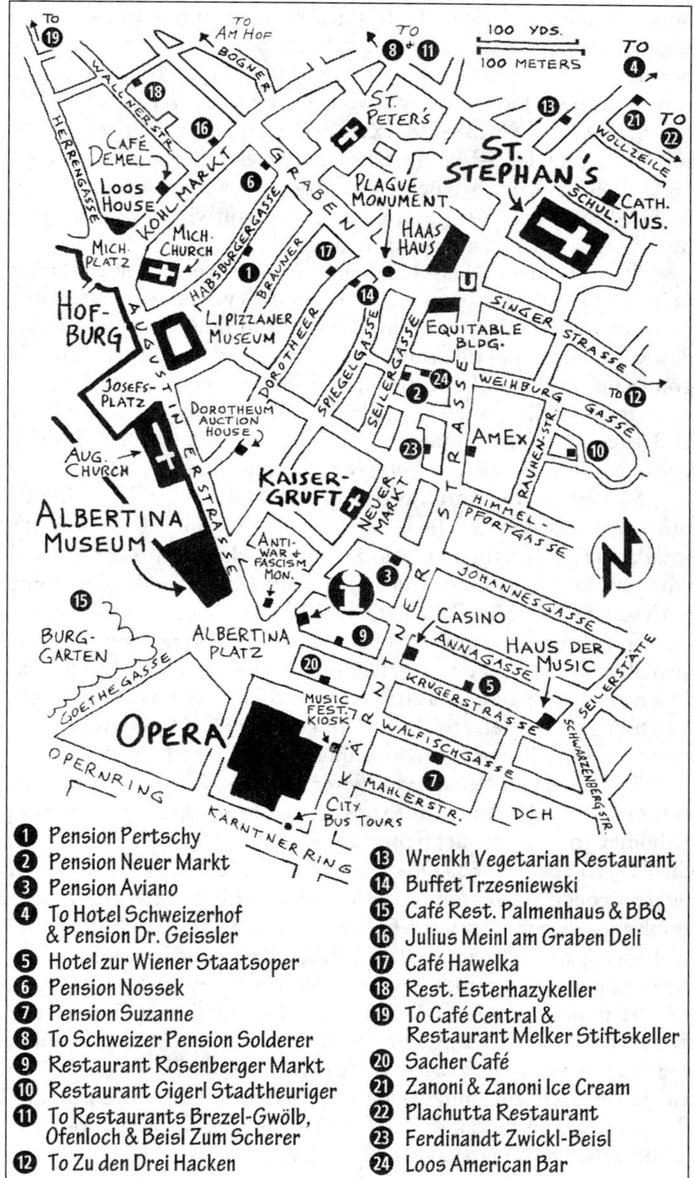

$$$ Hotel zur Wiener Staatsoper, the Schweizerhof's sister hotel, is quiet and rich. Its 22 tight rooms come with high ceilings, chandeliers, and fancy carpets on parquet floors—ideal for people whose hotel tastes are a cut above mine. The singles are tiny, with beds too short for anyone over six feet tall (Sb-€76–88, Db-€111–126, Tb-€133–148, extra bed-€22, cheaper prices are for July–Aug and Dec–March, fans on request, elevator, U-1, U-2, or U-4: Karlsplatz, a block from Opera at Krugerstrasse 11, tel. 01/513-1274, fax 01/513-127-415, www.zurwienerstaatsoper.at, office@zurwienerstaatsoper.at, manager Claudia).

$$ At **Pension Nossek,** an elevator takes you above any street noise into Frau Bernad's and Frau Gundolf's world, where the children seem to be placed among the lace and flowers by an interior designer. Right on the wonderful Graben, this is a particularly good value (30 rooms, S-€46–54, Ss-€58, Sb-€69–73, Db-€110, €25 extra for sprawling suites, extra bed-€35, cash only, elevator, U-1 or U-3: Stephansplatz, Graben 17, tel. 01/5337-0410, fax 01/535-3646, www.pension-nossek.at, reservation@pension-nossek.at).

$$ Pension Suzanne, as Baroque and doily as you'll find in this price range, is wonderfully located a few yards from the Opera. It's small, but run with the class of a bigger hotel; the 26 rooms are packed with properly Viennese antique furnishings. Streetside rooms come with some noise (Sb-€76, Db-€94–115 depending on size, 4 percent discount with cash, extra bed-€30, spacious apartment for up to 6 also available, discounts in winter, fans on request, elevator, a block from Opera, U-1, U-2, or U-4: Karlsplatz and follow signs for Opera exit, Walfischgasse 4, tel. 01/513-2507, fax 01/513-2500, www.pension-suzanne.at, info@pension-suzanne.at, manager Michael).

$$ Schweizer Pension Solderer, family-owned for three generations, is run by Anita. She runs an extremely tight ship, offering 11 homey rooms, parquet floors, and lots of tourist info (S-€38–42, Sb-€55–65, D-€58–65, Db-€78–87, Tb-€102–109, Qb-€126–131, prices depend on season and room size, cash only, entirely non-smoking, elevator, laundry-€11/load, U-2 or U-4: Schottenring, Heinrichsgasse 2, tel. 01/533-8156, fax 01/535-6469, www.schweizerpension.com, schweizer.pension@chello.at).

$$ Pension Dr. Geissler has 23 comfortable rooms on the eighth floor of a modern building about 10 blocks northeast of St. Stephan's, near the canal (S-€48, Ss-€68, Sb-€76, D-€60, Ds-€77, Db-€95, 20 percent less in winter, elevator, U-1 or U-4: Schwedenplatz, Postgasse 14, tel. 01/533-2803, fax 01/533-2635, www.hotelpension.at/dr-geissler, dr.geissler@hotelpension.at).

Hotels and Pensions along Mariahilfer Strasse

Lively Mariahilfer Strasse connects the Westbahnhof (West Station) and the city center. The U-3 line, starting at the Westbahnhof, goes down Mariahilfer Strasse to the cathedral. This very Viennese street is a tourist-friendly and vibrant area filled with local shops and cafés. Most hotels are within a few steps of a U-Bahn stop, just one or two stops from the Westbahnhof (direction from the station: Simmering).

$$$ NH Hotels, a Spanish chain, runs two stern, passionless business hotels a few blocks apart on Mariahilfer Strasse. Both rent ideal-for-families suites, each with a living room, two TVs, bathroom, desk, and kitchenette (rack rate: Db suite-€155, going rate usually closer to €100, plus €13 per person for optional breakfast, apartments for 2–3 adults, kids under 12 free, non-smoking rooms, elevator). The 78-room **NH Atterseehaus** is at Mariahilfer Strasse 78 (U-3: Zieglergasse, tel. 01/5245-6000, fax 01/524-560-015, nhatterseehaus@nh-hotels.com), and the **NH Wien** has 106 rooms at Mariahilfer Strasse 32 (U-3: Neubaugasse, tel. 01/521-720, fax 01/521-7215, nhwien@nh-hotels.com). The Web site for both is www.nh-hotels.com.

$$ Pension Corvinus is bright, modern, and warmly run by a Hungarian family: Miklos, Judit, and Zoltan. Its eight comfortable rooms are spacious, with small, compact bathrooms (Sb-€58, Db-€91, Tb-€105, extra bed-€26, non-smoking rooms, portable air-con-€10, elevator, free Internet access, parking garage-€11/day, on the third floor at Mariahilfer Strasse 57–59, tel. 01/587-7239, fax 01/587-723-920, www.corvinus.at, hotel@corvinus.at).

$$ Pension Mariahilf is a four-star place offering a clean, aristocratic air in an affordable and cozy pension package. Its 12 rooms are spacious but outmoded, with an Art Deco flair (Sb-€59–66, Db-€95–102, Tb-€124, lower prices are for longer stays, elevator, U-3: Neubaugasse, Mariahilfer Strasse 49, tel. 01/586-1781, fax 01/586-178-122, penma@inode.at).

$$ Haydn Hotel, in the same building as the Pension Corvinus (listed above), is a big, fancy, dark place with 40 spacious rooms that have seen better days (Sb-€58–70, Db-€90–100, suites and family apartments, extra bed-€30, air-con, elevator, free Internet access, Mariahilfer Strasse 57–59, tel. 01/587-44140, fax 01/586-1950, www.haydn-hotel.at, info@haydn-hotel.at, Nouri).

$$ Hotel Admiral is huge, quiet, and practical, with 80 large, comfortable rooms (Sb-€66, Db-€91, extra bed-€23, cheaper in winter, breakfast-€5 per person, free Internet access, free parking, U-2 or U-3: Volkstheater, a block off Mariahilfer Strasse at Karl Schweighofer Gasse 7, tel. 01/521-410, fax 01/521-4116, www.admiral.co.at, hotel@admiral.co.at).

$ Pension Hargita rents 24 generally small, bright, and tidy rooms (mostly twins) with Hungarian decor. This spick-and-span, well-run, well-located place is an excellent value (S-€35, Ss-€40, Sb-€52, D-€48, Ds-€55, Db-€63, Ts-€70, Tb-€76, Qb-€87,

Hotels and Restaurants Outside the Ring

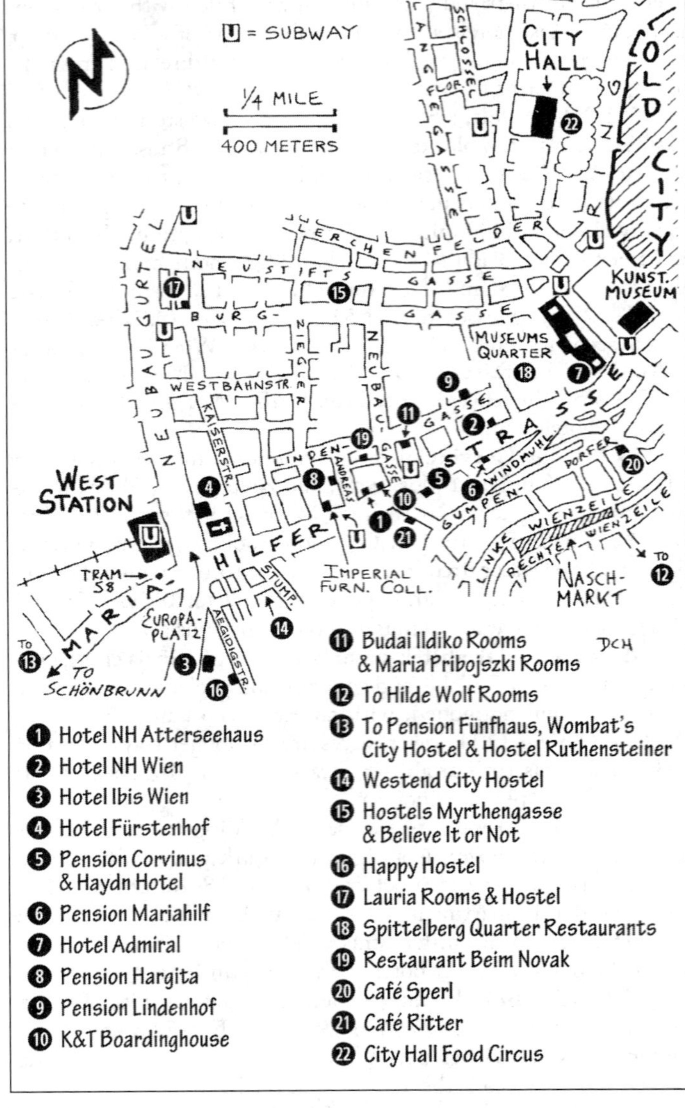

breakfast-€3, U-3: Zieglergasse, corner of Mariahilfer Strasse and Andreasgasse, Andreasgasse 1, tel. 01/526-1928, fax 01/526-0492, www.hargita.at, pension@hargita.at, classy Amalia). As the place has street noise, request a room in the back.

$ Pension Lindenhof rents 19 worn but clean rooms and is filled with plants (S-€29, Sb-€36, D-€49, Db-€65, cash only, elevator, U-3: Neubaugasse, Lindengasse 4, tel. 01/523-0498, fax 01/523-7362, pensionlindenhof@yahoo.com, Gebrael family, Zara and Keram SE).

$ K&T Boardinghouse rents four big, comfortable rooms facing the bustling Mariahilfer Strasse above a sex shop (Db-€65, Tb-€85, Qb-€105, 2-night minimum, no breakfast, air-con-€10, cash only, non-smoking, free Internet access, 3 flights up, no elevator, Mariahilfer Strasse 72, tel. 01/523-2989, fax 01/522-0345, www.kaled.at, kaled@chello.at, Tina SE).

$ *Private Rooms:* Two women rent rooms out of their dark and homey apartments in the same building at Lindengasse 39 (classic old elevator). Each has high ceilings and Old World furnishings, with two cavernous rooms sleeping two to four and a skinny twin room, all sharing one bathroom. These places are great if you're on a tight budget and wish you had a grandmother to visit in Vienna: **Budai Ildiko** lives on the mezzanine level and speaks English (S-€32, D-€45, T-€64, Q-€82, no breakfast but free coffee, cash only, laundry, apt. #5, tel. 01/523-1058, tel. & fax 01/526-2595, budai@hotmail.com). **Maria Pribojszki** lives on the first floor (D-€50, T-€66, Q-€88, breakfast-€4, cash only, apt. #7, tel. 01/523-9006, http://members.aon.at/bnb, bnb@aon.at).

$ Hilde Wolf, with the help of her grandson, Patrick, shares her homey apartment with travelers. Her four huge but stuffy rooms are like old libraries (S-€33, D-€48, T-€70, Q-€90, breakfast-€4, cash only, U-2: Karlsplatz, 3 blocks below Naschmarkt at Schleifmühlgasse 7, tel. 01/586-5103, fax 01/689-3505, www.schoolpool.at/bb). There's no sign or name at the street—she's on the first floor.

Near the Westbahnhof (West Station)

$$ Hotel Ibis Wien, a modern high-rise hotel with American charm, is ideal for anyone tired of quaint old Europe. Its 340 cookie-cutter rooms are bright, comfortable, and modern, with all the conveniences (Sb-€64, Db-€79, Tb-€94, €5 more per room May–June and Aug–Oct, breakfast-€9, non-smoking rooms, air-con, elevator, parking garage-€10/day, exit Westbahnhof to the right and walk 400 yards, Mariahilfer Gürtel 22-24, tel. 01/59998, fax 01/597-9090, h0796@accor.com).

$$ Hotel Fürstenhof, right across from the station, rents 58 spacious but borderline-musty rooms. This venerable hotel has an

Old World maroon-velvet feel (S-€44, Sb-€67–92, D-€62, small Db-€95, Db-€108, Tb-€114, Qb-€120, elevator, Internet access, Europaplatz 4, tel. 01/523-3267, fax 01/523-326-726, www.hotel-fuerstenhof.com, reception@hotel-fuerstenhof.com).

$ Pension Fünfhaus is big, clean, stark, and quiet—almost institutional. Although the neighborhood is rundown and comes with a few ladies loitering late at night, this 47-room place is a good value (S-€32, Sb-€40, D-€44, Db-€52, T-€66, Tb-€78, 4-person apartments-€90, cash only, closed mid-Nov–Feb, Sperrgasse 12, tel. 01/892-3545 or 01/892-0286, fax 01/892-0460, www.pension5haus.at, Frau Susi Tersch). Half the rooms are in the fine main building and half are in the annex, which has good rooms but is near the train tracks and a bit scary on the street at night. From the station, ride tram #52 or #58 two stops down Mariahilfer Strasse to the Kranzgasse stop, then backtrack two blocks to Sperrgasse.

Cheap Dorms and Hostels near Mariahilfer Strasse

$ Believe It or Not is a tiny, basic place with about the cheapest bunk beds in town in two coed rooms for up to 10 travelers. Hardworking and friendly Heny requires a minimum two-night stay and warns that this place is appropriate only for the young at heart (bed-€13.50, €10 Nov–Easter, cash only, locked up 10:00–12:30, no curfew, kitchen facilities, Myrthengasse 10, ring apt. #14, tel. 01/526-4658, www.believe-it-or-not-vienna.at, believe_it_or_not _vienna@hotmail.com).

$ Jugendherberge Myrthengasse is a well-run youth hostel (260 beds, €16–18 each in 3- to 6-bed rooms, includes sheets and breakfast, non-members pay €3.50 extra, always open, no curfew, lockers and lots of facilities, Myrthengasse 7, tel. 01/523-6316, fax 01/523-5849, hostel@chello.at).

$ Westend City Hostel, just a block from the Westbahnhof and Mariahilfer Strasse, is well-run and well-located, with 180 beds in 4- to 12-bed dorms (€17/bed including sheets, breakfast, and a locker, cash only, laundry, Internet access, Fügergasse 3, tel. 01/597-6729, fax 01/597-672-927, www.westendhostel.at, westendcityhostel@aon.at).

$ Happy Hostel rents five ramshackle yet homey apartments for two to five people beautifully located on a quiet street a couple blocks from the Westbahnhof and Mariahilfer Strasse (€25/person, Db-€50, no breakfast, Aegidigasse 19, tel. 01/208-2618, www.happyhostel.at, info@happyhostel.at).

$ Lauria Rooms and Hostel is a creative little place run by friendly Gosha, with two 10-bed dorms (boys and girls mixed, with lockers) and several other rooms sleeping two to six each (€13 dorm beds, around €20/person in other rooms, Kaiserstrasse 77, tram #5 or a 10-minute walk from Westbahnhof, tel. 01/522-2555, www.panda-vienna.at).

$ Other hostels with €16 beds and €40 doubles near Mariahilfer Strasse are **Wombat's City Hostel** (Grangasse 6, tel. 01/897-2336, www.wombats-hostels.com, wombats@chello.at) and **Hostel Ruthensteiner** (Robert-Hamerling-Gasse 24, tel. 01/893-4202, www.hostelruthensteiner.com, info@hostelruthensteiner.com).

EATING

The Viennese appreciate the fine points of life, and right up there with waltzing is eating. The city has many atmospheric restaurants. As you ponder the Eastern European specialties on menus, remember that Vienna's diverse empire may be gone, but its flavor lingers.

While cuisines are routinely named for countries, Vienna claims to be the only *city* with a cuisine of its own: Vienna soups come with fillings (semolina dumpling, liver dumpling, or pancake slices). *Gulasch* is a beef ragout of Hungarian origin (spiced with onion and paprika). Of course, Viennese schnitzel (Wiener schnitzel) is a breaded and fried veal cutlet. Another meat specialty is boiled beef *(Tafelspitz)*. While you're sure to have *Apfelstrudel,* try the sweet cheese strudel, too (*Topfenstrudel*—wafer-thin strudel pastry filled with sweet cheese and raisins).

On nearly every corner, you can find a colorful *Beisl.* These uniquely Viennese taverns are a characteristic cross between an English pub and a French brasserie—filled with poetry teachers and their students, couples loving without touching, housewives on their way home from cello lessons, and waiters who enjoy serving hearty food and good drink at an affordable price. Ask at your hotel for a good *Beisl.*

Wherever you're eating, some vocabulary helps. Try the *grüner Veltliner* (dry white wine), *Traubenmost* (a heavenly grape juice—alcohol-free but on the verge of wine), *Most* (the same thing but lightly alcoholic), and *Sturm* (stronger than *Most,* autumn only). The local red wine (called *Portugieser*) is pretty good. Since the Austrian wine is often sweet, remember the word *trocken* (dry). You can order your wine by the *Viertel* (quarter liter, 8 oz) or *Achtel* (eighth liter, 4 oz). Beer comes in a *Krügel* (half liter, 17 oz) or *Seidel* (0.3 liter, 10 oz). The *dag* you see in some prices stands for "decigram" (10 grams). Therefore, *10 dag* is 100 grams, or about a quarter pound.

Near St. Stephan's Cathedral

All of these places are within a five-minute walk of the cathedral.

Gigerl Stadtheuriger offers a near-*Heurige* experience (à la

Grinzing, see "Vienna's Wine Gardens," page 75)—often with accordion or live music—without leaving the city center. Just point to what looks good. Food is sold by the weight; 100 grams *(10 dag)* is about a quarter pound (cheese and cold meats cost about €3 per 100 grams, salads are about €2 per 100 grams; price sheet is posted on the wall to right of buffet line). They also have menu entrées, along with spinach strudel, quiche, *Apfelstrudel,* and, of course, casks of new and local wines. Meals run €7–11 (daily 15:00–24:00, indoor/outdoor seating, behind cathedral, a block off Kärntner Strasse, a few cobbles off Rauhensteingasse on Blumenstock, tel. 01/513-4431).

Am Hof square (U-3: Herrengasse) is surrounded by a maze of atmospheric medieval lanes; the following places are all within a block of the square. **Restaurant Ofenloch** serves good, old-fashioned Viennese cuisine with friendly service, both indoors and out. This 300-year-old eatery, with great traditional ambience, is central but not overrun with tourists (€12–18 main dishes, Tue–Sat 11:30–24:00, Mon 18:00–24:00, closed Sun, Kurrentgasse 8, tel. 01/533-8844). **Brezel-Gwölb,** a wonderfully atmospheric wine cellar with outdoor dining on a quiet square, serves delicious light meals, fine *Krautsuppe,* and old-fashioned local dishes. It's ideal for a romantic late-night glass of wine (daily 11:30–1:00, leave Am Hof on Drahtgasse, then take first left to Ledererhof 9, tel. 01/533-8811). Around the corner, **Beisl "Zum Scherer"** is just as untouristy and serves traditional plates for €10. Sitting outside, you'll face a stern Holocaust memorial. Inside comes with a soothing woody atmosphere and intriguing decor (Mon–Sat 11:00–24:00, closed Sun, Judenplatz 7, tel. 01/533-5164). Just below Am Hof, the ancient and popular **Esterhazykeller** has traditional fare deep underground or outside on a delightful square (Mon–Fri 11:00–23:00, Sat–Sun 16:00–23:00, self-service buffet in lowest cellar or from menu, Haarhof 1, tel. 01/533-2614).

These wine cellars are fun and touristy but typical, in the old center, with reasonable prices and plenty of smoke: **Melker Stiftskeller,** less touristy, is a *Stadtheurige* in a deep and rustic cellar with hearty, inexpensive meals and new wine (Tue–Sat 17:00–24:00, closed Sun–Mon and most of July, between Am Hof and Schottentor U-Bahn stop at Schottengasse 3, tel. 01/533-5530). **Zu den Drei Hacken** is famous for its local specialties (€10 plates, Mon–Sat 11:00–23:00, closed Sun, indoor/outdoor seating, Singerstrasse 28, tel. 01/512-5895).

Ferdinandt Zwickl-Beisl is an inviting little place with a user-friendly menu featuring the classic traditional *Beisl* plates, plus salads and vegetarian dishes. Choose between Old World, woody indoor seating and pleasant streetside seating (€7–10 plates, a block off the Kärntner Strasse mob scene at Neuer Markt 2, tel. 01/513-8991).

Wrenkh Vegetarian Restaurant and Bar is popular for its high vegetarian cuisine. Chef Wrenkh offers daily €8–10 lunch *menus* and €8–13 dinner plates in a bright, mod bar or in a dark, smoke-free, fancier restaurant (daily 11:30–24:00, Bauernmarkt 10, tel. 01/533-1526).

Buffet Trzesniewski is an institution—justly famous for its elegant and cheap finger sandwiches and small beers (€0.80 each). Three different sandwiches and a *kleines Bier (Pfiff)* make a fun, light lunch. Point to whichever delights look tasty (or grab the English translation sheet and take time to study your options). Pay for your sandwiches and a drink. Take your drink tokens to the lady on the right. Sit on the bench and scoot over to a tiny table when a spot opens up (Mon–Fri 8:30–19:30, Sat 9:00–17:00, closed Sun, 50 yards off Graben, nearly across from brooding Café Hawelka, Dorotheergasse 2, tel. 01/512-3291). This is a good opportunity (in the fall) to try the fancy grape juices—*Most* or *Traubenmost* (see above).

Julius Meinl am Graben, a posh supermarket right on the Graben, has been famous since 1862 as a top-end delicatessen with all the gourmet fancies. Along with the picnic fixings on the shelves, there's a café with light meals and great outdoor seating, a stuffy and pricey restaurant upstairs, and a take-away counter (shop open Mon–Fri 8:30–19:30, Sat 8:30–18:00, closed Sun; restaurant open Mon–Sat until 24:00, closed Sun; Am Graben 19, tel. 01/532-3334).

Akakiko Sushi: If you're just schnitzeled out, this small chain of Japanese restaurants with an easy sushi menu may suit you. The bento box meals are tasty. Three locations have no charm but are fast, reasonable, and convenient (€7–10 meals, all open daily 10:00–24:00): Singerstrasse 4 (a block off Kärntner Strasse near the cathedral), Heidenschuss 3 (near other recommended eateries just off Am Hof), and Mariahilfer Strasse 42–48 (fifth floor of Kaufhaus Gerngross, near many recommended hotels).

Plachutta Restaurant, with a stylish green-and-crème, elegant-but-comfy interior and breezy covered terrace, is famous for the best beef in town. You'll find an enticing menu with all the classic Viennese beef dishes, fine deserts, attentive service, and an enthusiastic local clientele. They've developed the art of beef to the point of producing popular cookbooks (€15–20 meals, daily 11:30–23:00, U-3: Stubentor, 10-min walk from St. Stephan's Cathedral, Wollzeile 38, tel. 01/512-1577).

***Ice Cream!*: Zanoni & Zanoni** is a very Italian *gelateria* run by an Italian family. They are mobbed by happy Viennese for their huge €2 cones to go, and for their fun outdoor seating (daily 7:00–24:00, 2 blocks up Rotenturmstrasse from cathedral at Lugeck 7, tel. 01/512-7979).

Near the Opera

Café Restaurant Palmenhaus, overlooking the Palace Garden (Burggarten—see page 58), tucked away in a green and peaceful corner two blocks behind the Opera in the Hofburg's back yard, is a world apart. If you want to eat modern Austrian cuisine with palm trees rather than tourists, this is it. And at the edge of a huge park, it's great for families (€8 2-course lunches available Mon–Fri, €15 dinners, open daily 10:00–2:00, serious vegetarian dishes, fish, extensive wine list, indoors in greenhouse or outdoors, tel. 01/533-1033). While nobody goes to the Palmenhaus for good prices, the **Palmenhaus BBQ,** a cool parkside outdoor pub just below that uses the same kitchen, is a wonderful value with more casual service (summer Wed–Sat from 20:00, closed Sun–Tue, open in good weather only, informal with €8 BBQ and meals posted on chalkboard).

Rosenberger Markt Restaurant is my favorite for a fast, light, and central lunch. Just a block toward the cathedral from the Opera, this place—while not cheap—is brilliant. Friendly and efficient, with special theme rooms for dining, it offers a fresh, smoke-free, and healthy cornucopia of food and drink (daily 10:30–23:00, lots of fruits, veggies, fresh-squeezed juices, addictive banana milk, ride the glass elevator downstairs, Maysedergasse 2, tel. 01/512-3458). You can stack a small salad or veggie plate into a tower of gobble for €2.80.

City Hall (Rathaus) Food Circus: During the summer, scores of outdoor food stands and hundreds of picnic tables are set up in the park in front of the City Hall. Local mobs enjoy mostly ethnic meals on disposable plates for decent-but-not-cheap prices. The fun thing here is the energy of the crowd, and a feeling that you're truly eating as the locals do...not schnitzel and quaint traditions, but trendy "world food" with people out having pure and simple fun in a fine Vienna park setting (July–Aug daily from 11:00 until late, in front of City Hall on the Ringstrasse).

Spittelberg Quarter

A charming cobbled grid of traffic-free lanes and Biedermeier apartments has become a favorite place for Viennese wanting a little dining charm between the MuseumsQuartier and Mariahilfer Strasse (handy to many recommended hotels; take Stiftgasse from Mariahilfer Strasse, or wander over here after you close down the Kunsthistorisches or Leopold Museum). Tables tumble down sidewalks and into breezy courtyards filled with appreciative locals enjoying dinner or a relaxing drink. Stroll Spittelberggasse, Schrankgasse, and Gutenberggasse and pick your favorite place. Don't miss the vine-strewn wine garden at Schrankgasse 1. **Amerlingbeisl,** with a casual atmosphere both on the cobbled street and in its vine-covered courtyard, is a great value (€7 plates, salads, veggie dishes, traditional specialties, long hours daily, Stiftgasse 8, tel. 01/526-1660). The neighboring **Plutzer Bräu** is also good (ribs, burgers, traditional dishes, Tirolean beer from the keg, daily 11:00–2:00, Schrankgasse 4, tel. 01/526-1215). For traditional Viennese cuisine with tablecloths, consider the classier **Witwe Bolte** (daily 11:30–15:00 & 17:30–23:30, Gutenberggasse 13, tel. 01/523-1450).

Near Mariahilfer Strasse

Mariahilfer Strasse is filled with reasonable cafés serving all types of cuisine. **Restaurant Beim Novak** serves tasty and well-presented Viennese cuisine away from the modern rush. While this small and intimate place, thoughtfully run by Maximilian, has no outdoor seating, the charming back room offers a relaxing atmosphere (€7 lunch specials, €10–15 plates, Mon–Fri 11:30–15:00 & 18:00–22:00, open Sat for dinner Sept–March, closed Sun and in Aug, a block down Andreasgasse from Mariahilfer Strasse at Richtergasse 12, tel. 01/523-3244).

Naschmarkt (described on page 63) is Vienna's best Old World market, with plenty of fresh produce, cheap local-style eateries, cafés, *döner kebab* and sausage stands, and the best-value sushi in town (Mon–Fri 7:00–18:00, Sat 6:00–18:00, closed Sun, closes earlier in winter, U-4: Kettenbrückengasse). Survey the lane of eateries at the end of the market nearest the Opera. The circa-1900 pub is inviting. Picnickers can buy their goodies at the market and eat on nearby Karlsplatz (plenty of chairs facing Charles Church).

TRANSPORTATION CONNECTIONS

Vienna has two main train stations: the Westbahnhof (West Station), serving Munich, Salzburg, Melk, and Budapest; and the Südbahnhof (South Station), serving Italy, Budapest, Prague, Poland, Slovenia, and Croatia. A third station, Franz Josefs, serves Krems and the Danube Valley (but Melk is served by the Westbahnhof). Metro line U-3 connects the Westbahnhof with the center, tram D takes you from the Südbahnhof and the Franz Josefs station to downtown, and tram #18 connects West and South stations. Train info: tel. 051-717 (to get an operator, dial 2, then 1).

From Vienna by Train to: Melk (hrly, 75 min, sometimes change in St. Pölten), **Krems** (hrly, 1 hr), **Salzburg** (hrly, 3 hrs), **Innsbruck** (every 2 hrs, 5.5 hrs), **Budapest** (6/day, 3 hrs), **Prague** (6/day, 4.5 hrs), **Český Krumlov** (5/day, 6–7 hrs, up to 3 changes), **Munich** (hrly, 5.25 hrs, change in Salzburg, a few direct trains), **Berlin** (2/day, 10 hrs, longer on night train), **Zürich** (3/day, 9 hrs),

Ljubljana (7/day, 6–7 hrs, convenient early-morning direct train, others change in Villach or Maribor), **Zagreb** (8/day, 6.5–10.5 hrs, 3 direct, others with up to 3 changes including Villach and Ljubljana), **Kraków** (4/day, 6.5–9 hrs, 2 direct including a night train departing at about 22:00, arriving around 6:00), **Warsaw** (4/day, 7.5–10 hrs, 2 direct including a night train), **Rome** (1/day, 13.5 hrs), **Venice** (3/day, 7.5 hrs, longer on night train), **Frankfurt** (4/day, 7.5 hrs), **Amsterdam** (1/day, 14.5 hrs).

To Eastern Europe: Vienna is the springboard for a trip to Prague, four hours away (€42 one-way, €84 round-trip, €53 round-trip with Eurail). Americans and Canadians do not need visas to enter the Czech Republic. Purchase tickets at most travel agencies. Eurail passholders bound for Prague must pay to ride the rails in the Czech Republic.

SALZBURG

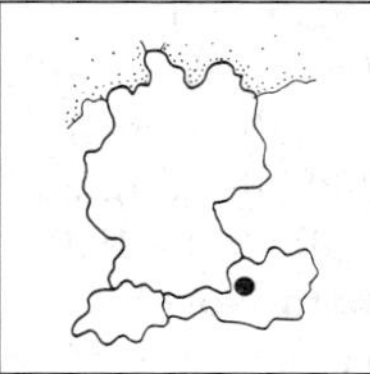

Salzburg is forever smiling to the tunes of Mozart and *The Sound of Music*. Thanks to its charmingly preserved old town, splendid gardens, Baroque churches, and Europe's largest intact medieval fortress, Salzburg feels made for tourism. It's a museum city with class. Vagabonds wish they had nicer clothes.

But even without Mozart and the von Trapps, Salzburg is steeped in history. In about A.D. 700, Bavaria gave Salzburg to Bishop Rupert for his promise to Christianize the area. Salzburg remained an independent state until Napoleon came (around 1800). Thanks in part to its formidable fortress, Salzburg managed to avoid the ravages of war for 1,200 years...until World War II. Much of the city was destroyed by WWII bombs (mostly around the train station), but the historic old town survived.

Eight million tourists crawl its cobbles each year. That's a lot of Mozart balls—and all that popularity has led to a glut of businesses hoping to catch the tourist dollar. Still, Salzburg is both a must and a joy.

Planning Your Time

While Vienna measures much higher on the Richter scale of sightseeing thrills, Salzburg is simply a touristy, stroller's delight. You'll probably need two nights here—nights are important for swilling beer in atmospheric local gardens and attending concerts in Baroque halls and chapels. Seriously consider one of Salzburg's many evening musical events (about €30–40). While the sights are mediocre, the town is an enjoyable Baroque museum of cobbled streets and elegant buildings. And to get away from it all, bike down the river or hike across the Mönchsberg.

The town of Hallstatt provides the best glimpse at the nearby Salzkammergut Lake District (see next chapter). A day trip from Salzburg to Hallstatt is doable, but involves about five hours of travel time and makes for a very long day (skip it in winter, when Hallstatt is pretty dead).

ORIENTATION

(area code: 0662)
Salzburg, a city of 150,000 (Austria's fourth largest), is divided into old and new. The old town, sitting between the Salzach River and the 1,600-foot-high hill called Mönchsberg, holds nearly all the charm and most of the tourists.

Tourist Information

Salzburg has three helpful TIs (main tel. 0662/8898-70, www.salzburg.info): at the **train station** (daily April–Sept 9:00–18:30, July–Aug until 19:30, Oct–March until 17:45, tel. 0662/8898-7340), on **Mozartplatz** in the old center (daily 9:00–18:00, July–Aug until 19:00, sometimes closed Sun in winter, tel. 0662/8898-7330), and at the **Salzburg Süd park-and-ride** (July–Aug daily 9:00–19:00, otherwise Mon–Sat 10:00–18:00, closed Sun, closed Nov–Easter, tel. 0662/8898-7360). At any TI, you can pick up a free city-center map (the €0.70 map has a broader coverage and more information on sights, but probably isn't necessary), the *Salzburg Card* brochure (listing sights with current hours and prices), and a bimonthly schedule of events. Book a concert upon arrival. The TIs also book rooms for a fee.

Salzburg Card: The TI sells the Salzburg Card, which covers all your public transportation (including elevator and funicular) and admission to all the city sights (including Hellbrunn Palace). The card is pricey (€22/24 hrs, €29/48 hrs, €34/72 hrs, €3 less Oct–May), but if you'd like to pop into all the sights without concern for the cost, this can save money and enhance your experience. Get this, feel the financial pain once, and the city's all yours.

Arrival in Salzburg

By Train: The little Salzburg station is user-friendly. The TI is at track 2A. Downstairs at street level, you'll find a place to store your luggage, buy tickets, and get train information. Bike rental is nearby (see "Getting Around Salzburg," below). The bus station is across the street (where buses #1, #5, #6, #25, and #51 go to the old center; get off at the first stop after you cross the river for most sights and city center hotels, or just before the bridge for Linzergasse hotels). Figure €7 for a taxi to the center. To walk downtown (15 min), leave the station ticket hall to the left and walk straight down Rainerstrasse, which leads under the tracks past Mirabellplatz, turning into Dreitaltigkeitsgasse. From here, you can turn left onto Linzergasse for many of the recommended hotels, or cross the Staatsbrücke bridge for the old town (and more hotels). For a more dramatic approach, leave the station the same way but follow the tracks to the river, turn left, and walk the riverside path toward the fortress.

By Car: Follow Zentrum signs to the center and park short-term on the street or longer under Mirabellplatz. Ask at your hotel for suggestions.

Helpful Hints

Festival: Salzburg celebrates the 250th birthday of her favorite son with Mozart 2006, a series of special events and concerts (Jan 27–Dec 5, 2006; details at www.mozart2006.net).

Internet Access: BigNet, a block off Mozartplatz at Judengasse 5, has 33 terminals (about €6/hr with regular promotions, daily 9:00–22:00, tel. 0662/841-470). Their ground-floor terminals are often full, but upstairs you'll find plenty of access.

Laundry: The launderette near my recommended Linzergasse hotels at the corner of Paris-Lodron Strasse and Wolf-Dietrich Strasse is handy (€10 self-service, €15 same-day full-service, Mon–Fri 7:30–18:00, Sat 8:00–12:00, closed Sun, tel. 0662/876-381).

American Express: AmEx has travel-agency services, but doesn't sell train tickets (Mon–Fri 9:00–17:30, closed Sat–Sun, Mozartplatz 5, tel. 0662/8080).

Getting Around Salzburg

By Bus: Single-ride tickets for central Salzburg *(Einzelkarte-Kernzone)* are sold on the bus for €1.80. At machines and *Tabak/Trafik* shops, you can buy cheaper single-ride tickets or a €3.40 day pass (*Tageskarte,* good for 24 hrs). To signal the driver you want to get off, press the buzzer on the pole. Bus info: tel. 0662/4480-6262.

By Bike: Salzburg is fun for cyclists. Top Bike rents bikes from two outlets—at the river side of the train station (leave left and walk 50 yards); and on the river next to Staatsbrücke bridge (€3.70/hr, €13/24 hrs, tel. 06272/4656, mobile 0676-476-7259, www.topbike.at, Sabine). Velo-Active rents bikes on Residenz Platz under the *Glockenspiel* in the old town (€4/hr, €12/24 hrs; mountain bikes-€6/hr, €18/24 hrs; daily 9:00–18:00 but hours unreliable—often you'll have to call or let the Panorama Tours man nearby help you, shorter hours off-season and in bad weather, passport number for security deposit, tel. 0662/435-595, mobile 0676-435-5950). Both companies offer 20 percent off with a valid train ticket or Eurailpass—ask for it.

Salzburg

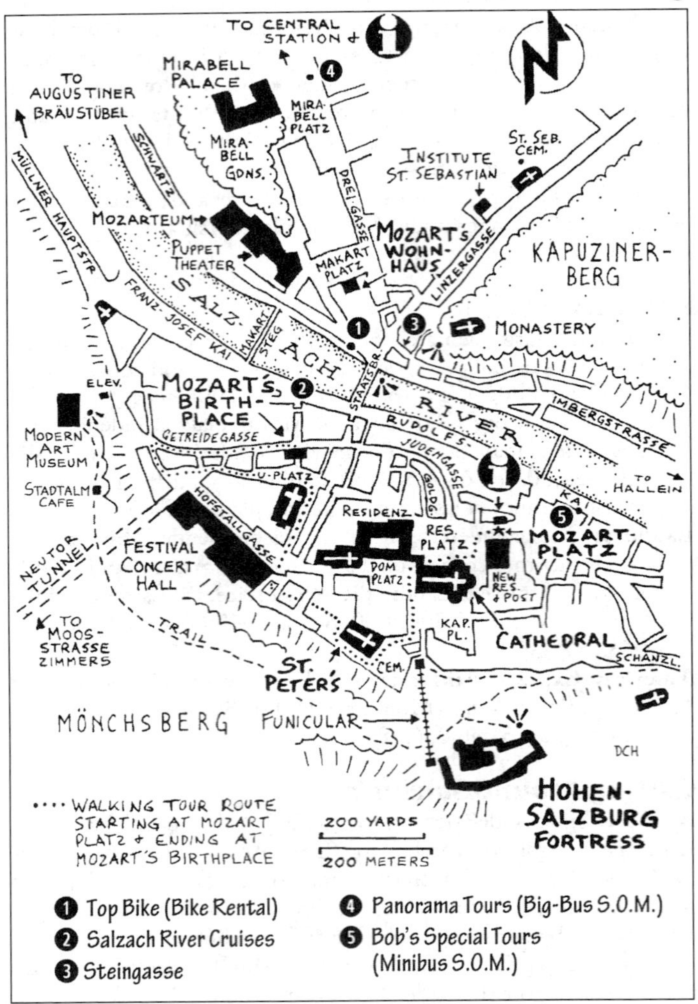

By Funicular and Elevator: The old town is connected to the top of the Mönchsberg mountain (and great views) via funicular and elevator (Web site for both: www.stadtbus.at). The **funicular** (FestungsBahn) whisks you up to the imposing Hohensalzburg fortress (for prices of various ticket options, see page 105). The **elevator** (MönchsbergAufzug) on the east side of the old town propels you to the recommended Gasthaus Stadtalm (see page 116 of "Sleeping," and page 121 of "Eating"), the Museum of Modern Art (see page 107), and wooded paths (€1.60 one-way, €2.60

round-trip, summer daily 9:00–21:00, off-season until 18:00).

By Taxi: Meters start around €3 (from train station to your hotel, allow about €8). As always, small groups can taxi for about the same price as riding the bus.

By Boat: Salzburg's Salzach River Cruises runs a basic 40-min round-trip cruise with recorded commentary (€11, April–Sept 8/day). For a longer cruise, ride to Hellbrunn and return by bus (€13, April–Sept 2/day). Boats leave from the old-town side of the river just downstream of the Staatsbrücke bridge (tel. 0662/8257-6912).

By Buggy: The horse buggies *(Fiaker)* that congregate at the Residenz Platz charge €35 for a 25-minute trot around the old town (www.fiaker-salzburg.at).

TOURS

For details on the popular *Sound of Music* bus tours around Salzburg and into the surrounding countryside, see page 107.

Walking Tours—The tourist office offers two-language, one-hour guided walks of the old town. They are informative, but you'll be listening to a half hour of German (€8, daily at 12:15, start at TI on Mozartplatz, tel. 0662/8898-7330—just show up and pay the guide). To save that money (and avoid all that German), you can easily do it on your own using my self-guided commentary (see "Sights," below).

Local Guides—Christiana Schneeweiss ("Snow White"), a hard-working young guide with a passion for fitting local history into the big picture, gives spirited half-day private tours for €75 (tel. 0664/340-1757, christiana.schneeweiss@aon.at). Barbel Schalber, one of Salzburg's senior guides, offers a two-hour walk packed with information and spicy opinions for €75 (tel. 0662/632-225, baxguide@utanet.at). Salzburg has many other good guides (to book, call tel. 0662/840-406).

SIGHTS

In the Old Town

I've linked the best sights in the old town into this handy self-guided orientation walk, rated ▲▲▲. Begin in the heart of town, just up from the river, near the TI on...

Mozartplatz—All the happy tourists around you probably wouldn't be here if not for the man honored by the statue here—Mozart (erected in 1842). Mozart spent much of his first 25 years (1756–1777) in Salzburg, the greatest Baroque city north of the Alps. But the city's much older. The Mozart statue actually sits on bits of Roman Salzburg. And the pink church of St. Michael overlooking the square is from A.D. 800. The first Salzburgers settled

Salzburg at a Glance

▲▲**Salzburg Cathedral** Glorious, harmonious, Baroque main church of Salzburg. **Hours:** May–Oct Mon–Sat 9:00–18:30, Sun 13:00–18:30, Nov–April Mon–Sat 10:00–17:00, Sun 13:00–17:00.

▲▲**Getreidegasse** Picturesque old shopping lane with characteristic wrought-iron signs. **Hours:** Always open.

▲▲**Mozart's Wohnhaus** Restored house where the composer lived, with the best Mozart exhibit in town. **Hours:** Daily 9:00–18:00, July–Aug until 19:00.

▲▲***Sound of Music* Tour** Cheesy but fun tour through the *S.O.M.* sights of Salzburg and the surrounding Salzkammergut Lake District, by minibus or big bus. **Hours:** Various options daily at 9:00, 9:30, and 14:00.

▲**Mozart's Birthplace** House where Mozart was born in 1756, featuring his instruments and other exhibits. **Hours:** Daily July–Aug 9:00–19:00, Sept–June 9:00–18:00.

▲**Mirabell Gardens and Palace** Beautiful palace complex with fine views, Salzburg's best concert venue, and *Sound of Music* memories. **Hours:** Gardens—always open; concerts—free in the park May–Aug Sun at 10:30 and Wed at 20:30, in the palace nearly nightly at 19:30, 20:00, or 20:30.

▲**Steingasse** Historic cobbled lane with trendy pubs. **Hours:** Always open.

right around here. Surrounding you are Café Glockenspiel, the American Express office, and the tourist information office (with a concert box office). Just around the downhill corner is a pedestrian bridge leading over the Salzach River to the quiet, most medieval street in town, Steingasse (see page 104).

Walk toward the cathedral and into the big square with the huge fountain.

Residenz Platz—Important buildings ringed this square when it was the ancient Roman forum...and they still do. Salzburg's energetic Prince-Archbishop Wolf Dietrich (who ruled from 1587–1612) was raised in Rome, counted the Medicis as his buddies, and had grandiose Italian ambitions for Salzburg. After a convenient fire destroyed the cathedral, he set about building "the Rome of the North." This square, with his new cathedral and palace, was the centerpiece of his Baroque dream city. A series of interconnecting

▲**St. Sebastian Cemetery** Baroque cemetery with graves of Mozart's wife and father, and other Salzburg VIPs. **Hours:** Daily April–Oct 9:00–18:30, Nov–March 9:00–16:00.

▲**Hohensalzburg Fortress** Imposing castle capping the Mönchsberg mountain overlooking town, with tourable grounds, impressive interior, commanding views, and good evening concerts. **Hours:** Grounds and interior open daily—mid-March–mid-June: grounds 9:00–18:00, interior 9:30–17:30; mid-June–mid-Sept: grounds 9:00–19:00, interior 9:30–18:00; mid-Sept–mid-March: grounds 9:00–17:00, interior 9:30–17:00; grounds are open until 21:30 on concert nights. Concerts occur nearly nightly at 19:30, 20:00, or 20:30.

▲**Hellbrunn Castle** Palace on the outskirts of town featuring gardens with trick fountains. **Hours:** Daily 9:00–17:30, July–Aug until 18:00 with palace tour or until 22:00 with fountain-only tour, April and Oct until 16:30, closed Nov–March.

St. Peter's Cemetery Atmospheric old cemetery with mini-gardens overlooked by cliff face with monks' caves. **Hours:** Cemetery—daily April–Sept 6:30–19:00, Oct–March 6:30–18:00; caves—May–Sept Tue–Sun 10:30–17:00, closed Mon, less off-season.

St. Peter's Church Romanesque church with rococo decor. **Hours:** Long hours daily.

squares—like you'll see nowhere else—lead from here through the old town.

For centuries, Salzburg's leaders were both important church officials *and* princes of the Holy Roman Empire, hence the title "prince-archbishop"—mixing sacred and secular authority. Wolf Dietrich misplayed his power and spent his last five years imprisoned in the Salzburg castle.

The fountain is as Italian as can be, with a Triton matching Bernini's famous Triton Fountain in Rome. Lying on a busy trade route to the south, Salzburg was well aware of the exciting things going on in Italy. Things Italian were respected (as in colonial America, when a bumpkin would "stick a feather in his cap and call it macaroni"). Local artists even Italianized their names in order to raise their rates.

Residenz—Dietrich's skippable palace is connected to the cathedral by a skyway. A series of ornately decorated rooms and an art gallery are open to visitors with time to kill (€7.30 includes both palace and gallery with audioguide for staterooms, daily 10:00–17:00, gallery closed Mon except July–Aug, tel. 0662/8042-2690).

Opposite the old Residenz is the new Residenz, which has long been a government administration building. Today it houses the central post office and the Heimatwerk, a fine shop showing off all the best local handicrafts (Mon–Fri 9:00–18:00, Sat 9:00–13:00, closed Sun). In 2006, Salzburg's grand history and art museum opens in this building.

Atop the new Residenz rings the famous...

Glockenspiel—This bell tower has a carillon of 35 17th-century bells (cast in Antwerp) that chimes throughout the day and plays tunes (appropriate to the month) at 7:00, 11:00, and 18:00. There was a time when Salzburg could afford to take tourists to the top of the tower to actually see the big barrel with adjustable tabs turn (like a giant music-box mechanism)...pulling the right bells in the right rhythm. Notice the ornamental top: an upside-down heart in flames surrounding the solar system (symbolizing that God loves all of creation).

Look back, past Mozart's statue, to the 4,220-foot-high Gaisberg—the forested hill with the television tower. A road leads to the top for a commanding view. Its summit is a favorite destination for local nature-lovers and kids learning to ski.

Walk under the prince-archbishop's skyway and step into Cathedral Square (Domplatz).

▲▲Salzburg Cathedral—This was one of the first Baroque buildings north of the Alps. It was finished in 1628, during the Thirty Years' War. (Pitting Roman Catholics against Protestants, this war devastated much of Europe and brought most grand construction projects to a halt.) Experts differ on what motivated the builders: to emphasize Salzburg's commitment to the Roman Catholic cause and the power of the Church here, or to show that there could be a peaceful alternative to the religious wars that were racking Europe at the time. Salzburg's archbishop was technically the top papal official north of the Alps, but the city managed to stay out of the war. With its rich salt production, it had enough money to rise above the warring parties and didn't need papal money.

The dates on the iron gates refer to milestones in the church's history: In 774, the previous church (long since destroyed) was founded by St. Virgil, to be replaced in 1628 by the church you see today. In 1959, the reconstruction was completed after a WWII bomb blew through the dome.

Step inside (donation requested, May–Oct Mon–Sat 9:00–18:30, Sun 13:00–18:30, Nov–April Mon–Sat 10:00–17:00, Sun

13:00–17:00). Enter the cathedral as if part of a festival procession—drawn toward the resurrected Christ by the brightly lit area under the dome, and cheered on by ceiling paintings of the Passion. Sit under the dome and imagine all four organs playing, each balcony filled with 14 musicians...glorious surround-sound. Mozart, who was the organist here for two years, would advise you that the acoustics are best in pews immediately under the dome. Study the symbolism of the decor all around you—intellectual, complex, and cohesive. Think of the altar in Baroque terms, as the center of a stage, with sunrays as spotlights in this dramatic and sacred theater.

Built in just 14 years (1614–1628), the church boasts harmonious architecture. When the pope visited in 1998, 5,000 people filled the cathedral (330 feet long and 230 feet tall). The baptismal font (dark bronze, left of the entry) is from the previous cathedral (c. 1320). Mozart was baptized here ("Amadeus" means "beloved by God"). Concert and Mass schedules are posted at the entrance; the Sunday Mass at 10:00 is famous for its music.

The **Cathedral Museum** (Dom Museum) has a rich collection of church art (entry at portico, €5, mid-May–Oct Mon–Sat 10:00–17:00, Sun 11:00–18:00, closed Nov–mid-May, tel. 0662/844-189).

Under the skyway, a stairway leads down to the *Domgrabungen*—an excavation site under the church with a few 2nd-century Christian Roman mosaics, and the foundation stones of the 8th-century church that stood here first (€2, daily 9:00–17:00, probably July–Aug only, tel. 0662/845-295).

From Cathedral Square to St. Peter's Cemetery: Cathedral Square is surrounded by "ecclesiastical palaces." The **statue of Mary** (1771) is looking away from the church, but if you stand in the rear of the square immediately under the middle arch, you'll see that she's positioned to be crowned by the two angels on the church facade.

From the cathedral, walk toward the fortress into the next square (passing the free underground public WCs and the giant chessboard), and head for the pond. This was a **horse bath**, the 18th-century equivalent of a car wash. Notice the puzzle above it—the artist wove the date of the structure into a phrase. It says, "Leopold the Prince Built Me," using the letters LLDVICMXVXI, which total 1732 (add it up...it works)—the year it was built. A small road (back by the chessboard) leads uphill to the fortress (and fortress lift). The stage is set up for the many visiting choirs who are unable to line up a gig. They are welcome to sing here anytime at all. With your back to the cathedral, leave the square through a gate on the right that reads *St. Peter*. It leads to a waterfall and St. Peter's Cemetery.

The **waterfall** is part of a canal system that has brought water into Salzburg from Berchtesgaden, 16 miles away, since the 13th century. Climb uphill a few steps to feel the medieval water power.

The stream, divided from here into smaller canals, was channeled through town to power factories (there were more than 100 watermill–powered firms as late as the 19th century), provide fire protection, and flush out the streets (Sat morning was flood-the-streets day). There's a good view of the funicular climbing up to the castle from here. Drop into the fragrant and traditional **bakery** at the waterfall. It's hard to beat their rocklike *Roggenbrot* (various fresh rolls for less than €1, Thu–Tue 7:00–17:30, Sat until 12:00, closed Wed).

Now step into...

St. Peter's Cemetery—This collection of lovingly tended mini-gardens abuts the Mönchberg's rock wall (free, silence is requested, daily April–Sept 6:30–19:00, Oct–March 6:30–18:00). Walk in about 50 yards to the intersection of lanes at the base of the cliff (marked by a stone ball). You're surrounded by three churches, each founded in the 6th century atop a pagan Celtic holy site. Look back toward the entry. The early-Gothic-style church was built in 1491—during the late Gothic period. (The old-school Gothic, rather then Baroque, implied allegiance to the Holy Roman Empire.) St. Peter's Church is closest to the stone ball. Notice the fine Romanesque stonework on the chapel nearest you, and the fancy rich guys' Renaissance-style tombs decorating its walls.

Wealthy as those guys were, they ran out of caring relatives. The graves surrounding you are tended by relatives. In Austria, grave sites are rented, not owned. Rent bills are sent out every 10 years. If no one cares enough to make the payment, you're gone. Notice that iron crosses were much cheaper than stone tombstones. While the cemetery where the von Trapp family hid out in *The Sound of Music* was actually in Hollywood, it was inspired by this one.

Look up the cliff. Legendary medieval hermit monks are said to have lived in the hillside—but "catacombs" they're not. For €1, you can climb lots of steps to see a few old caves, a chapel, and some fine views (May–Sept Tue–Sun 10:30–17:00, closed Mon, less off-season).

Continue downhill through the cemetery and out the opposite end. Just outside, hook right and drop into...

St. Peter's Church—Just inside, enjoy a carved Romanesque welcome: an arcade of palm trees leads to a fine tympanum showing Jesus on a rainbow flanked by Peter and Paul over a stylized tree of life and under a Latin inscription reading, "I am the door to life, and only through me can you find eternal life." Enter the nave and notice how the once purely Romanesque vaulting has since been iced with a sugary rococo finish. Up the right side aisle is the tomb of St. Rupert, with a painting showing Salzburg in 1750 (one bridge, salt ships sailing the river, and angels hoisting barrels of salt to heaven as St. Rupert prays for his city). On pillars farther up the aisle are faded bits of 13th-century Romanesque frescos.

Leaving the church, notice the Stiftskeller St. Peter restaurant (on the left—described under "Eating," page 119, and "Music Scene," page 111). Charlemagne ate here in A.D. 803—allowing locals to claim it's the oldest restaurant in Europe. Opposite where you entered the square, you'll see St. Rupert waving you into the next square (early-20th-century Bauhaus style, dorms for student monks), with a modern crucifix (1926) on the far wall. To the right of the crucifix (at #8), press the red button on the bronze door, enter, and see an unforgettable expressionist-carved crucifix (also from the 1920s, free, daily until 11:30).

The next square is...

Toscanini Hof—This square faces the 1925 Festival Hall. The hall's three theaters seat 5,000. This is where the nervous Captain von Trapp waited before walking onstage to sing "Edelweiss" just before he escaped with Maria and his family to Switzerland. On the left is the city's 1,500-space, inside-the-mountain parking lot; ahead, behind the Felsenkeller sign, is a tunnel (generally closed) leading to the actual concert hall; and to the right is the backstage of a smaller hall where carpenters are often building stage sets (door open on hot days).

Walk downhill through Max Reinhardt Platz, to the right of the church and past the public WC into...

Universitätsplatz—This square hosts a busy open-air produce market—Salzburg's liveliest (mornings Mon–Sat, best on Sat). Locals are happy to pay more here for the reliably fresh and top-quality produce (half of Austria's produce is now grown organically). The market really bustles on Saturday mornings, when the farmers are in town. Public marketplaces have fountains for washing fruit and vegetables. The fountain here (notice the little ones for smaller dogs and bigger dogs)—a part of the medieval water system—plummets down a hole and to the river. The sundial (over the water hole) is accurate (except for the daylight savings hour) and two-dimensional, showing both the time (obvious) and the date (less obvious). The fanciest facade overlooking the square is the backside of Mozart's Birthplace (described below).

Continue past the fountain to the end of the square, passing several characteristic and nicely arcaded medieval tunnel passages (on right) that connect the square to Getreidegasse. Cross the big road for a look at the giant horse troughs, adjacent the prince's stables. Paintings show the various breeds and temperaments of horses in his stable. Like Vienna, Salzburg had a passion for the equestrian arts. Take two right turns and you're at the start of...

▲▲Getreidegasse—This street was old Salzburg's busy, colorful main drag. (*Schmuck* means "jewelry.") Famous for its old wrought-iron signs (best viewed from this end), the street still looks much as it did in Mozart's day—though the elegant shops are mostly gone, replaced by chain outlets. On the right at #39, Sporer serves up homemade spirits (€1.30 per shot). *Nuss* is nut, *Marille* is apricot (typical of this region), and *Edle Brande* are the stronger schnapps. Austrian wines are sold by the *Achtel* (eighth of a liter). Notice the old doorbells—one per floor. At #40, Eisgrotte serves good ice cream. Across from Eisgrotte, a tunnel leads to Bosna Grill, the local choice for the very best sausage in town (see page 452). Farther along you'll pass McDonald's (with low-key medieval golden arches) and the Nordsee Restaurant (which was an even more controversial addition to this street than McDonald's). The knot of excited tourists and salesmen hawking goofy gimmicks mark the home of Salzburg's most famous resident...

▲Mozart's Birthplace (Geburtshaus)—Mozart was born here in 1756. It was in this building—the most popular Mozart sight in town—that he composed most of his boy-genius works. It's almost a pilgrimage. The place is filled with scores of scores, portraits, his first violin (picked up at age 5), the clavichord (a predecessor of the piano, with simple teeter-totter keys that played very softly) upon which he composed *The Magic Flute* and the *Requiem*, and a relaxing video concert hall. Exhibits explain the life of Wolfgang on the road and tell about Salzburg in Mozart's day (including a furnished middle-class apartment). It's all well-described in English (€6, or €9 for combo-ticket that includes Mozart's *Wohnhaus*, daily July–Aug 9:00–19:00, Sept–June 9:00–18:00, last entry 30 min before closing, Getreidegasse 9, tel. 0662/844-313). Note that Mozart's *Wohnhaus*, across the river, provides a more informative visit than this more-visited sight (see page 104).

When you're finished enjoying Getreidegasse and Mozart's Birthplace, you can continue this walk across the river (see below). To get there from Mozart's house, head for the river, jog left (past the fast-fish restaurant and free public toilets), and climb to the top of the Makartsteg pedestrian bridge.

Across the River

Salzach River—Survey Salzburg's river from the Makartsteg pedestrian bridge. It's called "salt river" not because it's salty, but because of the precious cargo it once carried—the salt mines of Hallein are just nine miles upstream. Salt could be transported from here all the way to the Danube, and on to Russia. The riverbanks and roads were built when the river was regulated in the 1850s. Before that, the Salzach was much wider and slower-moving. Houses opposite the old town fronted the river with docks and "garages" for boats. The grand buildings just past the bridge were built on reclaimed land in the late 19th century in the historicist style of Vienna's Ringstrasse.

Scan the cityscape. Notice all the churches. Salzburg, nicknamed the "Rome of the North," has 38 Catholic churches (plus 2 Protestant churches and a synagogue). Find the five streams gushing into the river. These date from the 13th century, when a river was split into five canals running through the town to power its mills. Hotel Stein (upstream, just left of next bridge) has a popular new roof-terrace café. Downstream, notice the Museum of Modern Art atop Mönchsberg, with a view café and a faux castle (actually a water reservoir). The Romanesque bell tower with the copper dome in the distance is the Augustine church, marking the best beer hall in town (the Augustiner Bräustübl—see page 122).

Cross the bridge, pass the Café Bazar (a fine place for a drink—see page 123), walk a block inland, and take a left past the heroic statues into...

▲Mirabell Gardens and Palace (Schloss)—The bubbly gardens laid out in 1730 for the prince-archbishop have been open to the public since 1850 (thanks to Emperor Franz Josef, who was rattled by the popular revolutions of 1848). The gardens are free and open until dusk. The palace is only open as a concert venue (see below). The statues and the arbor (far left) were featured in *The Sound of Music*. Walk through the gardens to the palace. Look back, enjoy the garden/cathedral/castle view, and imagine how the prince-archbishop must have reveled in a vista that reminded him of all his secular and religious power. Then go to the right side of the palace and find the horse.

The rearing Pegasus statue (rare and very well-balanced) is the site of a famous *Sound of Music* scene where the kids all danced before lining up on the stairs (with Maria just beyond). The steps lead to a small mound in the park (made of WWII rubble, and today a rendezvous point for Salzburg's gay community). With your back to the palace, climb the stairs and find two tough dwarfs (early volleyball players with spiked mittens) welcoming you to Salzburg's Dwarf Park. Cross the elevated walk (noticing the city's fortified walls) to meet statues of a dozen actual dwarfs who served the prince-archbishop—modeled after real people with real fashions in about 1600. This was Mannerist art, from the hyper-realistic age that followed the Renaissance.

There's plenty of **music,** both in the park and in the palace. A brass band plays free park concerts (May–Aug Sun at 10:30 and Wed at 20:30). To properly enjoy the lavish Mirabell Palace—once the prince-archbishop's summer palace, and now the seat of the mayor—get a ticket to a *Schlosskonzert* (my favorite venue for a classical concert—see page 112).

You could end the walk here, but if you want to visit one more Mozart sight, go a long block southeast to Makartplatz, where you'll find...

▲▲Mozart's Wohnhaus—This reconstruction of Mozart's second home (his family moved here when he was 17) is the most informative Mozart sight in town. The English-language audioguide (included with admission, 90 min) provides a fascinating insight into Mozart's life and music, with the usual scores, old pianos, and an interesting 30-minute-long film (#17 on your audioguide for soundtrack) that runs continuously (€6, or €9 for combo-ticket that includes Mozart's Birthplace in the old town, daily 9:00–18:00, July–Aug until 19:00, last tickets sold 60 min before closing, allow 1 hr minimum for visit, Makartplatz 8, tel. 0662/8742-2740).

You're a few blocks from the sights near Linzergasse (see below). Or head back over the river to enjoy some of the sights up on Salzburg's little mountain, Mönchsberg (see "Above the Old Town," below).

Across the River, near Linzergasse

▲Steingasse—This street, a block in from the river, was the only street in the Middle Ages going south to Hallein. Today it's wonderfully tranquil and free of Salzburg's touristy crush (if coming from Mozartplatz, cross the river via the Mozartsteg pedestrian bridge, cross the busy Imbergstrasse, jog left and go a block farther inland to a quiet cobbled lane, and turn left).

Stroll down this peaceful chunk of old Salzburg—once the only road on this side of the river. Just after the Maison de Plaisir at #24 (for centuries, a town brothel—open from 24:00), you'll find a magnificent view of the fortress across the river. Notice the red dome marking the oldest nunnery in the German-speaking world (established in 712) under the fortress and to the left. The real Maria from *The Sound of Music* taught in this nunnery's school. In 1927, she and Herr von Trapp were married in the church you see here (not the church filmed in the movie). He was 47. She was 22. Hmmmm.

At #19, find the carvings on the old door—notices from beggars to the begging community (more numerous after the economic dislocation caused by the wars over religion following the Reformation) indicating whether the residents would give or not. Notice the old-fashioned doorbells.

At #9, a plaque shows where Joseph Mohr, who wrote the words to "Silent Night," was born—poor and illegitimate—in 1792. Stairs lead from near here up to the monastery.

Across the street, on the corner you just passed, the wall is gouged out. This was left even after the building was restored so locals could remember the American GI who tried to get a tank down this road during a visit to #24.

By night, Steingasse is home to several trendy pubs (see "Steingasse Pub Crawl," page 123).

▲St. Sebastian Cemetery—Wander through this quiet place—so Baroque and so Italian (free, daily April–Oct 9:00–18:30, Nov–March 9:00–16:00, entry usually at Linzergasse 43). Mozart is buried in Vienna, his mom's in Paris, and his sister is in Salzburg's old town (St. Peter's)—but Wolfgang's father Leopold and his wife Constantia are buried here (from the Linzergasse entrance, take 17 paces and look left). When Prince-Archbishop Wolf Dietrich had the cemetery moved from around the cathedral and put here, across the river, people didn't like it. To help popularize it, he had his own mausoleum built as its centerpiece. Continue straight past the Mozart tomb to this circular building (English description at door).

Above the Old Town

These sights are atop the Mönchsberg, Salzburg's little mountain, hovering above the old town.

▲Hohensalzburg Fortress—Built on a rock 400 feet above the Salzach River, this fortress was never really used. That's the idea. It was a good investment—so foreboding, nobody attacked the town for a thousand years. One of Europe's mightiest, it dominates Salzburg's skyline and offers incredible views.

You can hike up or ride the funicular (€8.50 round-trip, includes admission to fortress grounds and exhibit; €5.60 one-way with fortress grounds and exhibit). Save money by not paying for the exhibit (which isn't worth seeing anyway): ask for *"ohne Almpassage"* and you get just the round-trip ride and the fortress grounds for €6.80. Or go in the evening—the funicular serves the "castle concert," running 300 nights a year until 21:30. Even if you're not seeing the concert, you can ride up and down and see the fortress courtyard for €3.20.

The fortress visit has three parts: a relatively dull courtyard with some fine views (€3.60 if you hike up, or included in various funicular fares), the Kuenburg Bastion (an overlook point accessed from the courtyard), and the palatial interior (worth the €3.60 extra admission). The fortress is open daily year-round (mid-March–mid-June: grounds 9:00–18:00, interior 9:30–17:30; mid-June–mid-Sept: grounds 9:00–19:00, interior 9:30–18:00; mid-Sept–mid-March: grounds 9:00–17:00, interior 9:30–17:00; last entry 30 min before closing, tel. 0662/8424-3011). On nights when there's a concert, the castle grounds are open until 21:30.

Courtyard: The courtyard is easy to tour on your own. Climb from the funicular to the inner courtyard. Immediately inside, circle left (counterclockwise, passing the audioguide booth with the only pricing scheme in Europe that charges you more to listen longer). The cannon were positioned to defend the city against the Turks. Skip the one-room marionette exhibit—you'll see more for free in its lobby than by paying €3 to go inside. The courtyard was the main square of a community of a thousand—which could be self-sufficient when necessary. The well dipped into a rain-fed cistern. The square was ringed by craftsmen, blacksmiths, bakers, and so on. The church is dedicated to St. George, the protector of horses (logical for an army church) and decorated by fine red marble reliefs (c. 1502). Behind the church is the top of the old lift that helped supply the church. (From here, steps lead back into the city, or to the "Mönchsberg Walk," described below.) Continue behind the church and turn left into the Kuenburg Bastion (once a garden) for fine city and castle views.

Kuenburg Bastion: Notice how the castle has three parts: the original castle inside the courtyard, the vast whitewashed walls (built when the castle was a residence), and the lower, beefed-up fortifications (built to defend against Turkish invasion). Survey Salzburg from here and think about fortifying an important city using nature. Mönchsberg naturally cradles the old town, with just a small gate between the mountain and the river needed to bottle up the place. The new town across the river needed a bit of a wall arcing from the river to its hill. Back then, only one bridge crossed the Salzach into town—with a fortified gate.

Back inside the castle courtyard, continue your circle. The Round Tower (1497) helps you visualize the inner original castle.

Fortress Palace Interior: You'll pay €3.60 to tour the interior. Tourists are allowed inside the palace only with an escort. You'll go one room at a time, listening to a 45-minute audioguide. The decorations are from around 1500—fantastic animals and plants inspired by tales of New World discoveries. While the interior furnishings are mostly gone—taken by Napoleon—the rooms survived as well as they did because no one wanted to live there after 1500, so the building was never modernized. Your tour includes a room dedicated to the art of "intensive questioning" ("softening up" prisoners, in current American military jargon)—filled with tools of that gruesome trade. You'll get a sneak preview of the room used for the nightly fortress concerts. The last rooms show music, daily life in the castle, and an exhibit dedicated to the Salzburg regiment in the World Wars. The highlight is the commanding city view from the top of a tower.

▲Mönchsberg Walk—For a great 30-minute hike, exit the fortress by taking the steep lane down from the castle courtyard. At the first intersection, right leads into the old town, and left leads across the Mönchsberg. The lane leads 20 minutes through the woods high above the city (stick to the high lanes, or you'll end up back in town), taking you to the Gasthaus Stadtalm Café (light meals, cheap beds—see page 116 of "Sleeping," and page 121 of "Eating"). From the Stadtalm, pass under the medieval wall and walk left along the wall to a tableau showing how it once looked. Take the switchback to the right and follow the lane downhill to the Museum of Modern Art (described below), where the elevator zips you back into town. If you stay on the lane past the elevator, you eventually pass the Augustine church that marks the rollicking Augustiner Bräustübl (see page 122).

In 1669, a huge Mönchsberg landslide killed more than 200 townspeople. Since then the cliffs have been carefully checked each spring and fall. Even today, you might see crews on the cliff, monitoring its stability.

Museum of Modern Art on Mönchsberg—The modern-art museum on top of Mönchsberg, built in 2004, houses Salzburg's Rupertinum Gallery, plus special exhibitions. While the collection is not worth climbing a mountain for, the restaurant has some of the best views in town (at top of Mönchsberg elevator, www.museumdermoderne.at).

More Salzburg Sights and Activities

▲▲Riverside or Meadow Bike Ride—The Salzach River has smooth, flat, and scenic bike paths along each side (thanks to medieval tow paths—cargo boats would float downstream and be dragged back up by horse). On a sunny day, I can think of no more shout-worthy escape from the city. The nearly four-mile path upstream to Hellbrunn Palace is easy, with a worthy destination (leave Salzburg on castle side). Perhaps the most pristine meadow farm-country route is the four-mile Hellbrunner Allee from Akademiestrasse. Even a quickie ride across town is a great Salzburg experience. In the evening, the riverbanks are a floodlit-spires world.

▲▲*Sound of Music* Tour—I took this tour skeptically (as part of my research chores) and liked it. It includes a quick but good general city tour, hits the *S.O.M.* spots (including the stately home, flirtatious gazebo, and grand wedding church), and shows you a lovely stretch of the Salzkammergut Lake District. This is worthwhile for *S.O.M.* fans and those who won't otherwise be going into the Salzkammergut. Warning: Many think rolling through the Austrian countryside with 30 Americans singing "Doe, a Deer" is pretty schmaltzy. Local Austrians don't understand all the commotion. Of the many companies doing the tour, consider Bob's Special Tours (usually uses a more intimate mini-bus) and the Panorama tours (more typical, professional big bus). Each one provides essentially the same tour (in English with a live and lively guide, 4 hrs, free hotel pick-up) for the same price. The *S.O.M.* tour for each company costs €35, but you'll get a €5 discount from either if you book direct and mention Rick Steves. Getting a spot is simple—just call and make a reservation. Note: Your hotel will be eager to call to reserve for you—to get their commission—but if

Sound of Music Debunked

Rather than visit the real-life sights from the life of Maria von Trapp and family, most tourists want to see the places where Hollywood chose to film this fanciful story. Local guides are happy not to burst any *S.O.M.* pilgrim's bubble, but keep these points in mind:

- "Edelweiss" is not a cherished Austrian folk tune or national anthem. Like all the "Austrian" music in the *S.O.M.*, it was composed for Broadway by Rodgers and Hammerstein. It was, however, the last composition that the famed team wrote together, as Hammerstein died in 1960—nine months after the musical opened.
- The *S.O.M.* implies that Maria was devoutly religious throughout her life, but Maria's foster parents raised her as a socialist and atheist. Maria discovered her religious calling while studying to be a teacher. After completing school, she joined the convent as a novitiate.
- Maria's position was not as governess to all the children, as portrayed in the musical, but specifically as governess and teacher for the Captain's second-oldest daughter, Maria, who was bedridden with rheumatic fever.
- The Captain didn't run a tight domestic ship. In fact, his seven children were as unruly as most. But he did use a whistle to call them—each kid was trained to respond to a certain pitch.
- Though the von Trapp family did have seven children, the show changed all their names and even their genders. Rupert, the eldest child, responded to the often-asked tourist question, "Which one are you?" with a simple, "I'm Leisl!"
- The family never escaped by hiking to Switzerland (which is a 5-hour drive away). Rather, they pretended to go on one of

you let them do it, you will not get the discount I've negotiated.

Minibus Option: Ninety percent of **Bob's Special Tours** use an eight-seat mini-bus and therefore have better access for old-town sights, promote a more casual feel, and spend less time waiting and picking up (buses leave from Bob's office along the river just east of Mozartplatz at Rudolfskai 38, daily at 9:00 and 14:00 year-round, tel. 0662/849-511, mobile 0664-541-7492, www.bobstours.com). Nearly all of Bob's tours stop for the luge ride when the weather is dry (mountain bobsled-€4 extra, confirm beforehand). Some travelers looking for Bob's tours at Mozartplatz have been hijacked by other companies...have Bob's pick you up at your hotel or meet the bus at their office.

Big-Bus Option: Salzburg Panorama Tours depart from their kiosk at Mirabellplatz daily at 9:30 and 14:00 year-round (book by calling 0662/874-029 or online at www.panoramatours.com).

their frequent mountain hikes. With only the possessions in their backpacks, they "hiked" all the way to the train station (it was at the edge of their estate) and took a train to Italy. The movie scene showing them climbing into Switzerland was actually filmed near Berchtesgaden, Germany...home to Hitler's Eagle's Nest, and certainly not a smart place to flee.

- The actual von Trapp family house exists...but it's not the one in the film. The mansion in the movie is actually two different buildings, one used for the front, the other for the back. The interiors were all filmed on Hollywood sets.
- For the film, Boris Levin designed a reproduction of the Nonnberg Abbey courtyard so faithful to the original (down to its cobblestones and stained-glass windows) that many still believe the cloister scenes were really shot at the abbey. And no matter what you hear in Salzburg, the graveyard scene (in which the von Trapps hide from the Nazis) was also filmed on the Fox lot.
- In 1956, a German film producer offered Maria $10,000 for the rights to her book. She asked for royalties, too, and a share of the profits. The agent explained that German law forbids film companies from paying royalties to foreigners (Maria had by then become a U.S. citizen). She agreed to the contract and unknowingly signed away all film rights to her story. Only a few weeks later, he offered to pay immediately if she would accept $9,000 in cash. Because it was more money than the family had seen in all of their years of singing, she accepted the deal. Later, she discovered the agent had swindled them—no such law existed.

Many travelers appreciate their more business-like feel, roomier buses, and slightly higher vantage point.

Other Tours: Both Bob's and Panorama Tours also offer an extensive array of other day trips from Salzburg (Berchtesgaden Eagle's Nest, salt mines, and Salzkammergut lakes and mountains are the most popular, with the same discount—€5 off with this book), all explained in their brochures, which litter hotel lobbies all over town.

▲Hellbrunn Castle—The attractions here are a garden full of clever trick fountains and the sadistic joy the tour guide gets from soaking tourists. (Hint: When you see a wet place, cover your camera.) After buying your ticket, you wait for the English tour, laugh and scramble through the entertaining 40-minute trick water toy tour, and are then free to tour the forgettable palace with an included audioguide (€7.50, daily 9:00–17:30, July–Aug until 18:00

Greater Salzburg

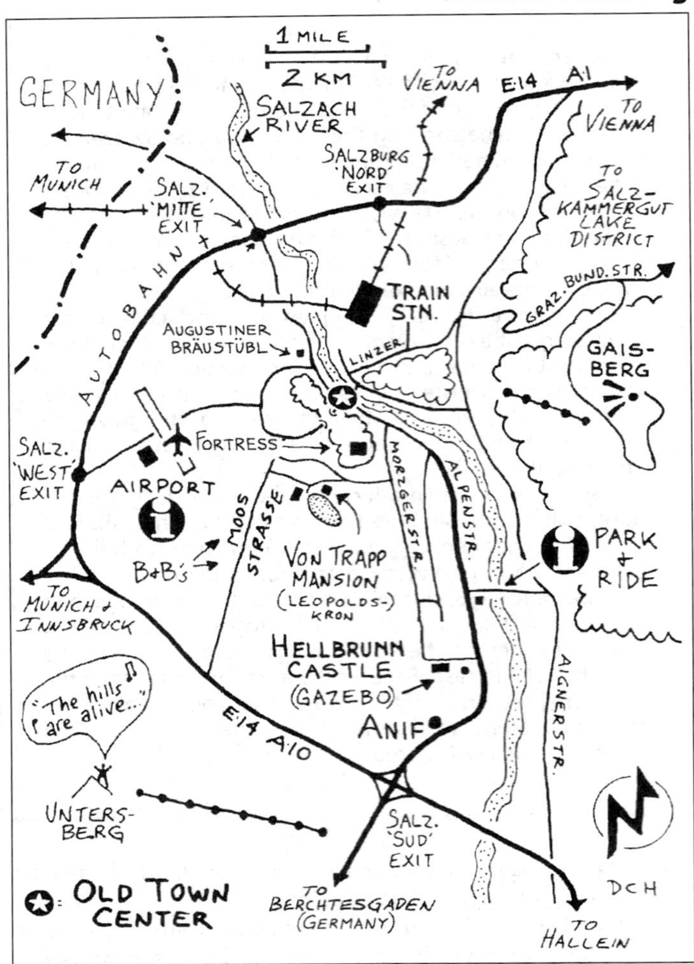

with palace tour or until 22:00 with €7 fountain-only tour, April and Oct until 16:30, closed Nov–March, tel. 0662/820-372, www.hellbrunn.at). Hellbrunn is nearly four miles south of Salzburg (bus #25 from station or from Staatsbrücke bridge in the center, 2/hr, 20 min). It's most fun on a sunny day or with kids, but, for many, it's a lot of trouble for a few water tricks. The Hellbrunn Baroque garden, one of the oldest in Europe, now features *S.O.M.*'s "I Am 16, Going on 17" gazebo.

ENTERTAINMENT

Music Scene

▲▲Salzburg Festival (Salzburger Festspiele)—Each summer, from late July to the end of August, Salzburg hosts its famous Salzburg Festival, founded in 1920 to employ Vienna's musicians in the summer. This fun and festive time is crowded, but there are plenty of beds (except for a few August weekends). There are three big halls: the Opera and Orchestra venues in the Festival House, and the Landes Theater where German plays are performed. Tickets for the big festival events are generally expensive (€50–100) and sold out well in advance (bookable from Jan). Most tourists think they're "going to the Salzburg Festival" by seeing smaller non-festival events that go on during the festival weeks. For these lesser events, same-day tickets are normally available (the ticket office on Mozartplatz, in the TI, prints a daily list of concerts and charges a 30 percent fee to book them). For specifics on this year's festival schedule and tickets, visit www.salzburgfestival.at, or contact the Austrian National Tourist Office in the United States (P.O. Box 1142, New York, NY 10108-1142, tel. 212/944-6880, fax 212/730-4568, www.austria-tourism.com, travel@austria.info). While I've never planned in advance, I've enjoyed great concerts with every visit.

▲▲Musical Events Year-Round—Salzburg is busy throughout the year, with 2,000 classical performances in its palaces and churches annually. Pick up the events calendar at the TI (free, bimonthly). Whenever you visit, you'll have a number of concerts (generally small chamber groups) to choose from.

Concerts at the Fortress (Festungskonzerte): There are nearly nightly concerts—Mozart's greatest hits for beginners—up at the fortress in the "prince's chamber," featuring small chamber groups (open seating after the first 5 more expensive rows, €30–36, at 19:30, 20:00, or 20:30, doors open 30 min early, tel. 0662/825-858 to reserve, pick tickets up at the door). The medieval-feeling chamber has windows overlooking the city, and the concert gives you a chance to enjoy the grand city view and a stroll through the castle courtyard. (The €8.50 round-trip funicular is discounted to €3.20 within an hour of the show.)

Concerts at the Mirabell Palace (Schlosskonzerte): The nearly nightly chamber music concerts at the Mirabell Palace are performed in a lavish Baroque setting. They come with more sophisticated programs and better musicians than the fortress concerts. Baroque music flying around a Baroque hall is a happy bird in the right cage (open seating after the first 5 more expensive rows, €30–36, at 19:30, 20:00, or 20:30, doors open 30 min early, tel. 0662/848-5860).

"Five O'Clock Concerts" (5-Uhr-Konzerte): These concerts—next to St. Peter's in the old town—are cheaper, since they feature young artists (€12, July–Sept at 17:00 daily except Wed, 45 min, tel. 0662/8445-7619, www.5-uhr-konzerte.com). While the series is formally named after the brother of Joseph Haydn, it offers music from various masters.

Marionette Theater: Salzburg's much-loved marionette theater offers operas with spellbinding marionettes and recorded music. Music-lovers are mesmerized by the little people on stage (€18–35, nearly nightly June–Sept except Sun, also some in May, tel. 0662/872-406, www.marionetten.at).

Mozart Dinner Concert: For those who'd like some classical music but would rather not sit through a concert, Stiftskeller St. Peter offers a traditional candlelit meal with Mozart's greatest hits performed by a string quartet and singers in historic costumes gavotting among the tables. In this elegant Baroque setting, tourists who clap between movements are treated to three courses of food (from Mozart-era recipes) mixed with three 20-minute courses of crowd-pleasing music (€45, almost nightly at 20:00, call to reserve at 0662/828-6950). For more details, see page 119.

***Sound of Music* Dinner Show:** The show at the Sternbräu Inn (see page 121) is Broadway in a dirndl with tired food. But it's a good show, and *S.O.M.* fans leave with hands red from clapping. A piano player and a hardworking quartet of singers perform an entertaining mix of *Sound of Music* hits and traditional folk songs (€43 includes a schnitzel and crisp apple strudel dinner at 19:30). You can also come by at 20:30, pay €31, skip the full dinner, and get the show with a few of my favorite things: apple strudel and coffee (nightly mid-May–mid-Oct, Griesgasse 23, tel. 0662/826-617, www.soundofmusicshow.com).

SLEEPING

Finding a room in Salzburg, even during its music festival (mid-July–Aug), is usually easy. Rates rise significantly (20–30 percent) during the music festival and sometimes also around Easter and Christmas; these higher prices do not appear in the ranges I've listed. You'll often be charged 10 percent extra for a one-night stay.

Linzergasse and Rupertgasse

These listings are in a pleasant neighborhood (with easy parking) a 15-minute walk from the train station (for directions, see "Arrival in Salzburg," above) and a 10-minute walk to the old town. If you're coming from the old town, simply cross the main bridge (Staatsbrücke) to the mostly traffic-free Linzergasse. If driving, exit

Sleep Code

(€1 = about $1.20, country code: 43, area code: 0662)
S = Single, **D** = Double/Twin, **T** = Triple, **Q** = Quad, **b** = bathroom, **s** = shower only, **SE** = Speaks English. Unless otherwise noted, credit cards are accepted and breakfast is included. All of these places speak English.

To help you sort easily through these listings, I've divided the rooms into three categories, based on the price for a standard double room with bath:

$$$ Higher Priced—Most rooms €90 or more.
$$ Moderately Priced—Most rooms between €60–90.
$ Lower Priced—Most rooms €60 or less.

the highway at Salzburg-Nord, follow Vogelweiderstrasse straight to its end, and turn right.

$$$ Altstadthotel Wolf Dietrich, around the corner from Linzergasse on pedestrian-only Wolf-Dietrich Strasse, is well located (with half its rooms overlooking St. Sebastian Cemetery) and a reasonable big-hotel option, if that's what you want (27 rooms, Sb-€69–89, Db-€120–160, rates depend on room size, family deals, €40 more during festival time, elevator, pool, sauna, garage-€12/day, Wolf-Dietrich Strasse 7, tel. 0662/871-275, fax 0662/882-320, www.salzburg-hotel.at, office@salzburg-hotel.at). Their annex across the street has 14 equally comfortable rooms (but no elevator, and therefore slightly cheaper prices).

$$$ Hotel Trumer Stube, three blocks from the river just off Linzergasse, has 20 clean, cozy rooms and a friendly, can-do owner (Sb-€60, Db-€100, Tb-€125, Qb-€140, top-floor rooms have lower ceilings and are €7 less expensive, non-smoking, elevator, Internet access, Bergstrasse 6, tel. 0662/874-776, fax 0662/874-326, www.trumer-stube.at, info@trumer-stube.at, pleasant Silvia SE).

$$$ Hotel Amadeus is a 500-year-old building with 25 comfortable rooms, half of them on the very peaceful back side overlooking the Mozart family tomb (most of the year: Sb-€60, Db-€92, Tb-€125; late July–Aug and Dec: Sb-€78, Db-€150, Tb-€175; free Internet access, Linzergasse 43, tel. 0662/871-401, fax 0662/876-1637, www.hotelamadeus.at, salzburg@hotelamadeus.at, Margo SE).

$$ Hotel Goldene Krone, about five blocks from the river, is big, quiet, and creaky-traditional but modern, with comforts rare in this price range (25 rooms, Sb-€60, Db-€88, Tb-€128, elevator, relaxing backyard garden, Linzergasse 48, tel. 0662/872-300, fax

Salzburg Center Hotels

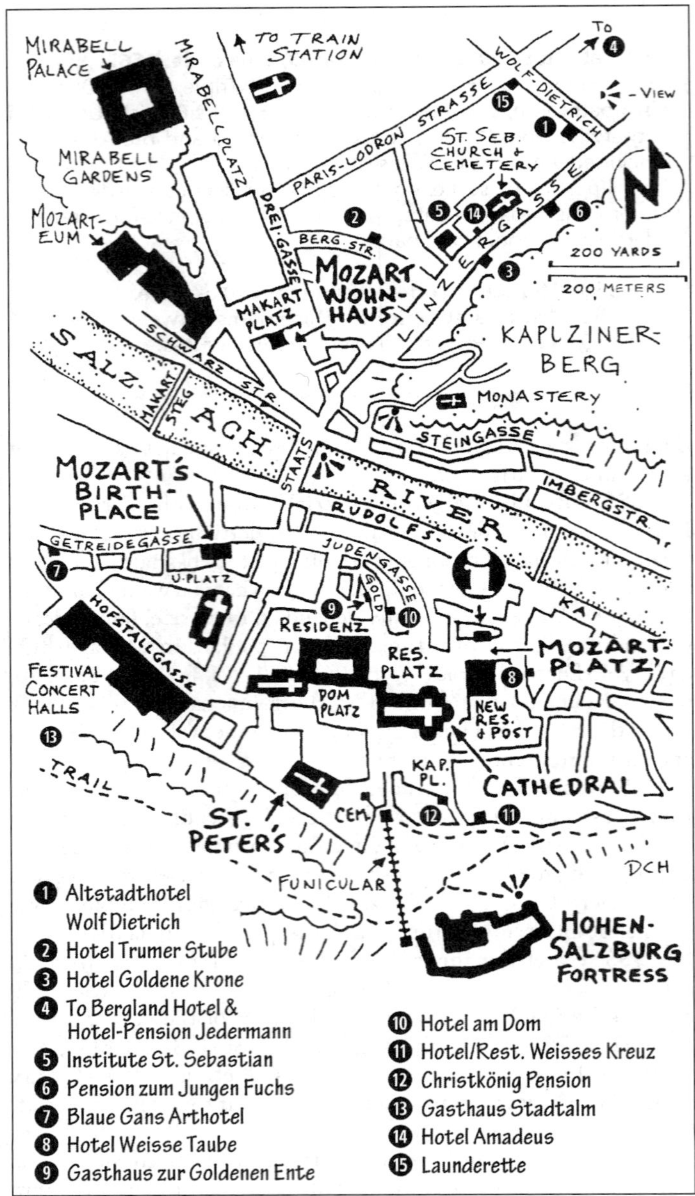

0662/8723-0066, office@hotel-goldenekrone.com, Claudia and Günther SE). Günther offers a free orientation talk on Salzburg by request. He also guides a just-for-fun, low-key, four-hour biking tour of untouristy Salzburg (€10, May–Sept in good weather only, Tue, Thu, and Sat at 14:00, must reserve ahead, minimum 4 people).

$$ ***Pensions on Rupertgasse:*** These two hotels are about five blocks farther from the river up Paris-Lodron Strasse to Rupertgasse, a breeze for drivers but with more street noise than the places on Linzergasse. They're both modern and well-run—good values if you don't mind being a bit away from the old town. **Bergland Hotel** is charming and classy, with comfortable neo-rustic rooms (Sb-€58, Db-€88, Tb-€105, Qb-€125, elevator, Internet access, English library, bike rental, Rupertgasse 15, tel. 0662/872-318, fax 0662/872-3188, www.berglandhotel.at, kuhn @berglandhotel.at, Kuhn family). The similar, boutique-like **Hotel-Pension Jedermann,** a few doors down, is also tastefully done and comfortable, with artsy decor and a backyard garden (Sb-€55, Db-€85, Tb-€105, Qb-€135, much more during music festival, Internet access, Rupertgasse 25, tel. 0662/873-241, fax 0662/873-2419, www.hotel-jedermann.com, office@hotel-jedermann.com).

$ Institute St. Sebastian is in a somewhat sterile but very clean historic building next to St. Sebastian Cemetery. From October through June, the institute houses female students from various Salzburg colleges, and also rents 40 beds for travelers. From July through September, the students are gone and they rent all 100 beds (including 20 doubles) to travelers. The building has spacious public areas, a roof garden, a piano guests are welcome to play, and some of the best rooms and dorm beds in town for the money. The immaculate doubles come with modern baths and head-to-toe twin beds (S-€29, Sb-€37, D-€50, Db-€57, Tb-€74, Qb-€88, elevator, includes breakfast, self-service laundry-€3/load, reception open daily July–Sept 7:30–12:00 & 13:00–22:00, Oct–June 8:00–12:00 & 16:00–21:00, Linzergasse 41, enter through arch at #37, tel. 0662/871-386, fax 0662/8713-8685, www.st-sebastian-salzburg.at, office@st-sebastian-salzburg.at). Students like the €18 bunks in 4- to 10-bed dorms (€2 less if you have sheets, no lockout time, free lockers, free showers). You'll find self-service kitchens on each floor (fridge space is free; request a key).

$ Pension zum Jungen Fuchs terrifies claustrophobes and titillates troglodytes. It's plain and sometimes smelly, but sleepable and wonderfully located in a funky, dumpy old building (16 rooms, S-€27, D-€40, T-€50, no breakfast, cash only, Linzergasse 54, tel. 0662/875-496).

In or above the Old Town

$$$ Blaue Gans Arthotel is ultra-modern, giving you a break from charming old Salzburg with artsy public spaces and 40 sleek but nothing-special rooms beautifully located at the far end of Getreidegasse (Sb-€100, standard Db-€140, bigger superior Db-€170, fancier suites, elevator, Getreidegasse 41, tel. 0662/842-4910, fax 0662/842-4919, www.blauegans.at, office@blauegans.at).

$$$ Gasthaus zur Goldenen Ente is in a 600-year-old building with medieval stone arches and narrow stairs. Located above a good restaurant, it's as central as you can be on a pedestrian street in old Salzburg. The 17 rooms are modern yet worn, and the service is uneven (most of the year: Sb-€68, Db-€90; late July–Aug and Dec: Sb-€78, Db-€135; extra person-€29, elevator, parking-€6/day, Goldgasse 10, tel. 0662/845-622, fax 0662/845-6229, www.ente.at, hotel@ente.at).

$$$ Hotel Weisse Taube is a big, quiet, old-feeling, 30-room place with more comfort than character, well-located about a block off Mozartplatz (Sb-€59, Db with shower-€93, bigger Db with bath-€106, elevator, Internet access, tel. 0662/842-404, fax 0662/841-783, Kaigasse 9, www.weissetaube.at, hotel@weissetaube.at).

$$$ Hotel am Dom, while pretty forgettable, is perfectly located—on Goldgasse a few steps from the cathedral. The 14 rooms are old and basic, but well-maintained (Sb-€76–79, Db-€79–117, extra bed-€33, prices slightly lower Nov–mid-June, non-smoking rooms, Goldgasse 17, tel. 0662/842-765, fax 0662/8427-6555, www.amdom.at, bach@salzburg.co.at).

$$ Hotel Restaurant Weisses Kreuz is a Tolkienesque little family-run place on a cobbled back street under the fortress. It's away from the crowds and offers a fine Balkan restaurant, four rooms, and a peaceful roof garden (small Db-€66, big Db-€90, Tb-€120, 10 percent more June–Aug, garage, Bierjodlgasse 6, tel. 0662/845-641, fax 0662/845-6419, weisses.kreuz@eunet.at).

$$ Christkönig Pension makes you feel like a guest of the bishop, with 25 rooms in a 14th-century church building just under the castle and behind the cathedral. You can even stay in the bishop's suite...if no one from the Vatican is visiting. This place offers a charming, quiet, and unique way to sleep well and cheaply in the old center (S-€34, Sb-€38, D-€62, Db-€75, €6 extra for 1-night stays, cash only, Kapitelplatz 2a, tel. 0662/842627, www.christkoenig-kolleg.at, christkoenig-pension@salzburg.co.at, Frau Anna Huemer).

$ Gasthaus Stadtalm is a local version of a mountaineer's hut and a great budget alternative. Snuggled in a forest on the remains of a 15th-century castle wall atop the little mountain overlooking Salzburg, it has magnificent town and mountain views. While the accommodations are designed-for-backpackers rustic, the price and view are the best in town—it's a fine experience (26 beds, €13.50/person in 2-, 4-, and 6-bed dorms, includes breakfast and shower, cash only, no lockers, bike rental-€6, open mid-April–Oct, 2 min from top of €2.60 round-trip Mönchsberg elevator, Mönchsberg 19-C, tel. & fax 0662/841-729, www.stadtalm.com, Peter and Roland SE).

Near the Train Station

$$ Pension Adlerhof, a plain and decent old place, is two blocks in front of the train station (left off Kaiserschutzenstrasse), but a 15-minute walk from the sightseeing action. It has a quirky staff, a boring location, and 35 stodgy-but-spacious rooms (Sb-€55, D-€52, Db-€78, Tb-€90, Qb-€112–120, 10 percent cheaper off-season and during slow times, cash only, elevator, Elisabethstrasse 25, tel. 0662/875-236, fax 0662/873-663, www.pension-adlerhof.com, adlerhof@pension-adlerhof.at).

$ International Youth Hotel, a.k.a. the "Yo-Ho," is the most lively, handy, and American of Salzburg's hostels (€16 in 6- to 8-bed dorms, €19 in dorms with bathrooms, Q-€17/person, Qb-€20/person, sheets included, cheap breakfast, 6 blocks from station toward Linzergasse and 6 blocks from river at Paracelsusstrasse 9, tel. 0662/879-649, fax 0662/878-810, www.yoho.at, office@yoho.at). This easygoing place speaks English first; has cheap meals, 160 beds, lockers, Internet access, laundry, tour discounts, and no curfew; plays *The Sound of Music* free daily at 10:30; runs a lively bar; and welcomes anyone of any age. The noisy atmosphere and lack of a curfew can make it hard to sleep.

Zimmer (Private Rooms)

These are generally roomy and comfortable and come with a good breakfast, easy parking, and tourist information. Off-season, competition softens prices. These are a bus ride from town, but, with a €3.40 transit day pass *(Tageskarte)* and the frequent service, this shouldn't keep you away. In fact, most will happily pick you up at the train station if you simply telephone them and ask. Most will also do laundry for a small fee for those staying at least two nights. I've listed prices for two nights or more. If staying only one night, expect a 10 percent surcharge.

Beyond the Train Station

Both of these places have easy free parking, are a 30-minute walk or easy bus ride into the center, and are happy to pick up when you arrive. They're a 10-minute walk from station: head for the river, cross the pedestrian Pioneer Bridge, turn right, and walk along the river a few minutes into a quiet suburban-feeling residential neighborhood.

$ Trude Poppenberger's three pleasant rooms share a long, mountain-view balcony (S-€25, D-€38, T-€57, Wachtelgasse 9, tel. & fax 0662/430-094, www.trudeshome.com, mail@trudeshome .com). From Pioneer Bridge, turn right, walk along the river 300 yards, cross the canal, go left on Linke Glanzeile for three minutes, and then turn right on Wachtelgasse to #9.

$ Brigitte Lenglachner rents six basic rooms with no public spaces (S-€24, D-€37, Db-€44, T-€50, Tb-€64, Qb-€88, bigger apartment, Scheibenweg 8, she pushes tours and charges a booking fee—save money and book your tours direct, tel. & fax 0662/438-044, bedandbreakfast4u@yahoo.de). From the Pioneer Bridge, walk along the river to the third street (Scheibenweg), turn left, and it's halfway down on the right.

On Moosstrasse

The busy street called Moosstrasse, southwest of Mönchsberg, is lined with *Zimmer.* (While it does come with lots of cows, *moos* means "moss.") Handy bus #16 connects Moosstrasse to the center frequently (Mon–Fri 4/hr until 17:00, then 2/hr; Sat 4/hr until 12:00, then 2/hr)—but service drops to a frustrating once per hour on Sundays. To get to these from the train station, take bus #1, #5, #6, or #25 to Makartplatz, where you'll change to #16. If you're coming from the old town, catch bus #16 from Hanuschplatz, just downstream of the Staatsbrücke bridge near the *Tabak* kiosk. Buy a €1.80 *Einzelkarte-Kernzone* ticket (for 1 trip) or a €3.40 *Tageskarte* (day pass, good for 24 hrs) from the streetside machine and punch it when you board the bus. The bus stop you use for each *Zimmer* is listed below. If you're driving from the center, go through the tunnel, continue straight on Neutorstrasse, and take the fourth left onto Moosstrasse. Drivers exit autobahn at *Süd* and then head in the direction of *Grodig.*

$ Frau Ballwein offers cozy, charming, and fresh rooms in two buildings, all with intoxicating view balconies (S-€23, D-€40, Db-€48–50, Tb-€65–70, family deals, cash only, farm-fresh breakfasts, non-smoking, small pool, Moosstrasse 69-A, bus stop: Gsengerweg, tel. & fax 0662/824-029, www.privatvermieter.com /haus-ballwein, haus.ballwein@gmx.net).

$ Helga Bankhammer rents four nondescript rooms in a farmhouse, with a real dairy farm out back (D-€44, Db-€48, no surcharge for 1-night stays, family deals, non-smoking, laundry about €5/load, Moosstrasse 77, bus stop: Marienbad, tel. & fax 0662/830-067, www.privatzimmer.at/helga.bankhammer, bankhammer@aon.at).

$ Haus Reichl, with three good rooms at the end of a long lane, feels the most remote (Db-€48, Tb-€66, Qb with balcony and view-€80, non-smoking, between Ballwein and Bankhammer B&Bs, 200 yards down Reiterweg to #52, bus stop: Gsengerweg, tel. & fax 0662/826-248, www.privatzimmer.at/haus-reichl, haus .reichl@telering.at). Elizabeth offers free loaner bikes for guests (20 min to the center).

$ Pension Bloberger Hof, while more a hotel than a *Zimmer*, is comfortable and friendly, with a rural location and 20 farmer-plush, good-value rooms. It's the farthest out, but reached by the same bus #16 from the center (Sb-€41–51, Db-€60, big new Db with balcony-€85, extra bed-€15, family apartment, non-smoking, restaurant for guests, free loaner bikes, free station pick-up if staying 3 nights, Hammerauerstrasse 4, bus stop: Hammerauerstrasse, tel. 0662/830-227, fax 0662/827-061, www.blobergerhof.at, office @blobergerhof.at).

EATING

Salzburg boasts many inexpensive, fun, and atmospheric places to eat. I'm a sucker for big cellars with their smoky, Old World atmosphere, heavy medieval arches, time-darkened paintings, antlers, hearty meals, and plump patrons. Most of these eateries are centrally located in the old town, famous with visitors, but also enjoyed by the locals.

Gasthaus zum Wilden Mann is the place if the weather's bad and you're in the mood for *Hofbräu* atmosphere and a hearty, cheap meal at a shared table in one small, smoky, well-antlered room (€6–8 daily specials, Mon–Sat 11:00–21:00, closed Sun, 2 min from Mozart's birthplace, enter from Getreidegasse 22 or Griesgasse 20, tel. 0662/841-787). For a quick lunch, get the *Bauernschmaus*, a mountain of dumplings, kraut, and peasant's meats (€8.50). Manager Robert runs the place with a Schwarzenegger-like energy.

Stiftskeller St. Peter has been in business for more than 1,000 years—it was mentioned in the biography of Charlemagne. It's classy and central as can be, serving uninspired traditional Austrian cuisine (€15–25 meals, daily 11:00–24:00, indoor/outdoor seating, next to St. Peter's Church at foot of Mönchsberg, restaurant tel. 0662/841-268). They host the Mozart Dinner Concert described in "Music Scene," on page 112 (€45, nearly nightly at 20:00, call 0662/828-6950 to reserve). Over the centuries, they've learned to charge for each piece of bread and not serve free tap water.

St. Paul's Stub'n Beer Garden is a secret—tucked away under the castle with an ignore-the-tourists-attitude (German-only menu). The food is better than a beer hall, and the young, local clientele fills its troll-like interior and breezy tree-shaded garden (€10 daily specials, €10–15 plates, Mon–Sat 17:00–22:00, closed Sun, Herrengasse 16, tel. 0662/843-220).

Triangel Restaurant, just across from the festival concert

Salzburg Center Restaurants

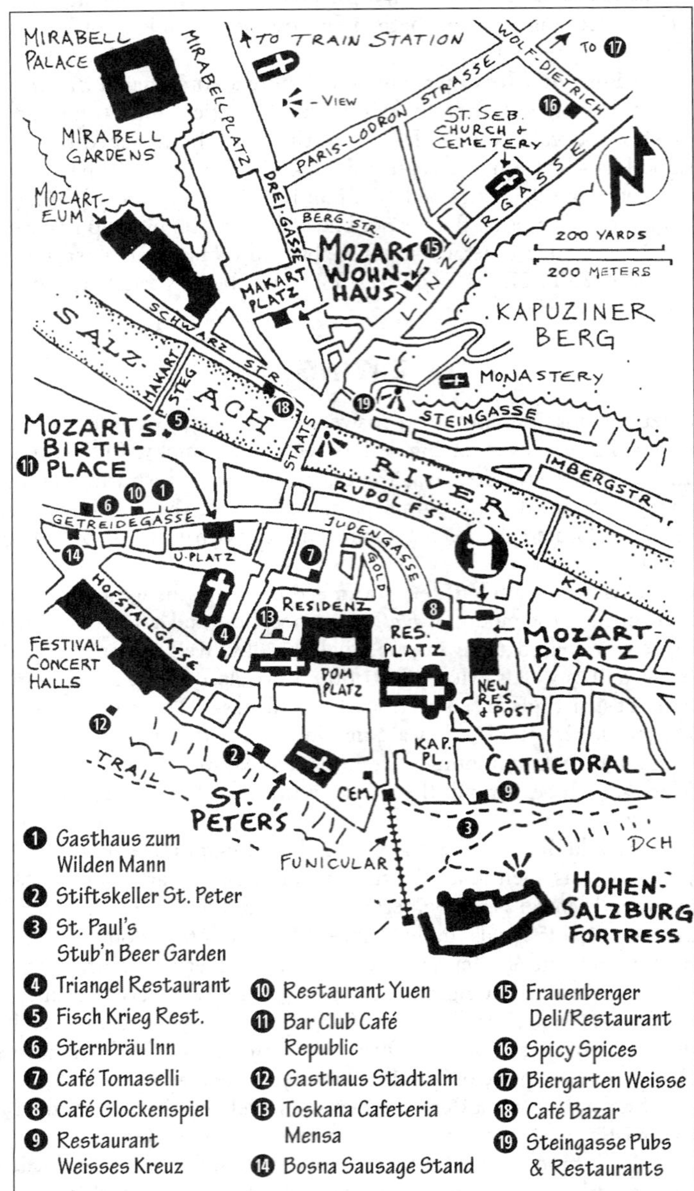

hall, caters to local students and artists. They serve simple regional cuisine, including a daily €5 lunch (2 choices: meat or vegetarian, available Tue–Fri 12:00–13:30; open Tue–Sat 11:00–24:00, closed Sun–Mon, good indoor and outdoor seating, Wiener Philharmonikergasse 7, tel. 0662/842-229).

Fisch Krieg Restaurant, on the river where the fishermen used to sell their catch, serves fast, fresh, and inexpensive fish with great riverside seating (€2 fishwiches to go, €7 meals, salad bar, Mon–Fri 8:30–18:30, Sat 8:30–13:00, closed Sun, Hanuschplatz 4, tel. 0662/843-732).

Sternbräu Inn is a sprawling complex of popular eateries (traditional, Italian, self-serve, and vegetarian) in a cheery garden setting—explore both courtyards before choosing a seat (most restaurants open daily 9:00–24:00). One fancy, air-conditioned room hosts the *Sound of Music* dinner show (see page 112).

Café Tomaselli (Alter Markt 9) and **Café Glockenspiel** (Mozartplatz 2) are the top places to see and be seen. While overpriced, these are good for lingering and people-watching. Each serves light meals and lots of drinks, keeps long hours daily, and has fine seating on the square, a view terrace upstairs, and indoor tables. Tomaselli (with its Kiosk annex across the way) offers better people-watching and a classier interior.

Restaurant Weisses Kreuz, nestled quietly behind the cathedral and under the fortress, serves good Balkan cuisine in a pleasant dining room or under an ivy-roofed front porch (€11 3-course *menu*, daily 11:30–14:45 & 17:00–22:45, closed Tue Oct–mid-June, Bierjodlgasse 6, tel. 0662/845-641).

Restaurant Yuen affords a break from the wurst, with good Chinese food and friendly service (€6 buffet until 15:00, €7 buffet 18:00–21:00, open daily, indoors or on quiet courtyard at Getreidegasse 24, tel. 0662/843-770).

Bar Club Café Republic, a hip hangout for local young people near the end of Getreidegasse, serves good food with indoor and outdoor seating. It's ideal if you want something mod, untouristy, and un-wursty (trendy breakfasts 8:00–18:00, Asian and international menu, €5–9 plates, lots of hard drinks, daily until late, music with a DJ Fri and Sat from 23:00, Anton Neumayr Platz 2, tel. 0662/841-613).

Gasthaus Stadtalm, the local mountaineer's hut, sits high above the old town on the edge of the cliff with cheap prices, good food, and great views. If hiking across Mönchsberg, make this your goal (traditional food, salads, cliffside garden seating or cozy-mountain-hut indoor seating, an indoor view table booked for a decade of New Year's celebrations, 2 min from top of €2.60 round-trip Mönchsberg elevator, Mönchsberg 19-C, tel. & fax 0662/841-729, Peter and Roland SE).

Eating Cheaply in the Old Town

Toskana Cafeteria Mensa is the students' lunch place, fast and cheap—with indoor seating and a great courtyard for sitting outside with students and teachers instead of tourists. They serve a daily soup and main course special for €3.50 (Mon–Fri 9:00–15:30, hot meals served 11:00–13:30 only, closed Sat–Sun, behind the Residenz, in the courtyard opposite Sigmund-Haffnergasse 16).

Sausage stands serve the local fast food. The best places (like those on Universitätsplatz) use the same boiling water all day, which gives the weenies more flavor. Key words: *Weisswurst*—boiled white sausage, *Bosna*—with onions and curry, *Käsekrainer*—with melted cheese inside, *Debreziner*—spicy Hungarian, *Frankfurter*—our weenie, *frische*—fresh ("eat before the noon bells"), and *Senf*—mustard (ask for sweet—*süss* or sharp—*scharf*). Only a tourist puts the sausage in a bun like a hot dog. Munch alternately between the meat and the bread (that's why you have 2 hands), and you'll look like a local. Generally, the darker the weenie, the spicier it is. Perhaps the best spicy sausage is at the 55-year-old **Bosna Stand,** run by the chatty Frau Ebner (€2.40, to go only, Mon–Fri 11:00–19:00, May–Dec also Sat 11:00–17:00, July–Dec also Sun 16:00–20:00, hiding down the tunnel marked #33 across from Getreidegasse 40).

Picnickers will appreciate the bustling morning **produce market** (daily except Sun) on Universitätsplatz, behind Mozart's house (see page 101).

Away from the Center

Augustiner Bräustübl, a monk-run brewery, is rustic and crude. It's closed for lunch, but on busy nights, it's like a Munich beer hall with no music but the volume turned up. When it's cool, you'll enjoy a historic setting with beer-sloshed and smoke-stained halls. On balmy evenings, it's a Monet painting with beer breath under chestnut trees in the garden. Local students mix with tourists eating hearty slabs of schnitzel with their fingers or cold meals from the self-serve picnic counter, while children frolic on the playground kegs. For your beer: Pick up a half-liter or full-liter mug (*schank* means self-serve price, *bedienung* is the price with waiter service), pay the lady, wash your mug, give Mr. Keg your receipt and empty mug, and you will be made happy. Waiters don't bring food—instead, go up the stairs, survey the hallway of deli counters, and assemble your own meal (or, as long as you buy a drink, you can bring in a picnic). For dessert—after a visit to the strudel kiosk—enjoy the incomparable floodlit view of old Salzburg from the nearby Müllnersteg pedestrian bridge and a riverside stroll home (open daily 15:00–23:00; about a 15-min walk along the river—with the river on your right—from the Staatsbrücke bridge, head up Müllner Hauptstrasse northwest along the river and ask for "Müllnerbräu," its local nickname; Augustinergasse 4, tel. 0662/431-246). Don't be fooled by second-rate gardens serving the same beer nearby. Augustiner Bräustübl is a huge, 1,000-seat place within the Augustiner brewery.

On or near Linzergasse

These cheaper places are near the recommended hotels on Linzergasse.

Frauenberger is a friendly, picnic-ready, and inexpensive deli, with indoor or outdoor seating. They'll make a sandwich to your specs (Mon 8:00–14:00, Tue–Fri 8:00–18:00, Sat 8:00–12:30, closed Sun, wurst grill open longer hours and on Sun, across from Linzergasse 16).

Spicy Spices is a trippy vegetarian-Indian restaurant where Suresh Syad serves tasty curry and rice take-out, samosas, organic salads, vegan soups, and fresh juices (€5 lunch specials, Mon–Sat 10:00–22:00, Sun 12:00–21:00, Wolf-Dietrich Strasse 1, tel. 0662/870-712).

Biergarten Weisse, close to the hotels on Rupertgasse and away from the tourists, is a long-time hit with locals (Mon–Sat 10:30–2:00, Sun 16:00–24:00, on Rupertgasse east of Bayerhamerstrasse, tel. 0662/872-246).

Café Bazar, overlooking the river between Mirabell Gardens and the Staatsbrücke bridge, is a great place for a classy drink with an old-town and castle view (Mon–Sat 7:30–24:00, closed Sun, Schwarzstrasse 3, tel. 0662/874-278).

Steingasse Pub Crawl

For a fun post-concert activity, crawl through medieval Steingasse's trendy pubs, open until the wee hours. This is a young and very hip scene: dark bars filled with well-dressed twentysomethings lazily smoking cigarettes and talking philosophy, with avant-garde Euro-pop throbbing on the soundtrack. Most of the pubs are in cellar-like caves...extremely atmospheric. (For more on Steingasse, see page 104.)

At the Linzergasse end of Steingasse are a couple of places that serve food and are lively earlier in the evening. **Pepe Gonzales,** with Mexican decor, serves tapas *con* cocktails (nightly 18:30–3:00, Steingasse 3, tel. 0662/873-662). Next door, **Shrimps** is the least claustrophobic of these places, with international cuisine (spicy shrimp sandwiches and salads, nightly 17:00–1:00, Steingasse 5).

A block farther down Steingasse, the scene doesn't get rolling until later. **Soulen Sprung** wins the "Best Atmosphere" award (nightly 21:00–4:00, Steingasse 13, tel. 0662/881-377). If the door's closed, ring the bell and enter its hellish interior—lots of stone and red decor, with mountains of melted wax beneath age-old candlesticks. Next door, the tiny **Fridrich,** with lots of mirrors and a silver ceiling fan, specializes in wine (nightly from 17:00, Steingasse 15, tel. 0662/876-218).

After you close down these four places, consider the next street down—the riverside Giselakai, also lined with trendy pubs.

TRANSPORTATION CONNECTIONS

By train, Salzburg is the first stop over the German–Austrian border. This means that if Salzburg is your only stop in Austria, and you're using a Eurail Selectpass that does not include Austria, you don't have to pay extra or add Austria to your pass to get here.

From Salzburg by Train to: Innsbruck (direct every 2 hrs, 2 hrs), **Vienna** (2/hr, 3.5 hrs), **Hallstatt** (every 2 hrs, 50 min to Attnang Puchheim, 20-min wait, then 90 min to Hallstatt), **Reutte** (every 2 hrs, 4 hrs, transfer to a bus in Innsbruck), **Munich** (2/hr, 1.5–2 hrs). Train info: tel. 051-717 (to get an operator, dial 2, then 1).

HALLSTATT

and the SALZKAMMERGUT

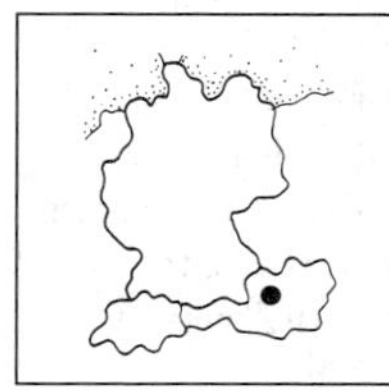

Commune with nature in Austria's Lake District. "The hills are alive," and you're surrounded by the loveliness that has turned on everyone from Emperor Franz Josef to Julie Andrews. This is *Sound of Music* country. Idyllic and majestic, but not rugged, it's a gentle land of lakes, forested mountains, and storybook villages, rich in hiking opportunities and inexpensive lodging. Settle down in the postcard-pretty, lake-cuddling town of Hallstatt.

Planning Your Time

While there are plenty of lakes and charming villages, Hallstatt is really the only one that matters. One night and a few hours to browse are all you'll need to fall in love. To relax or take a hike in the surroundings, give it two nights and a day. It's a relaxing break between Salzburg and Vienna.

ORIENTATION

(area code: 06134)

Lovable Hallstatt is a tiny town bullied onto a ledge between a selfish mountain and a swan-ruled lake, with a waterfall ripping furiously through its middle. It can be toured on foot in about 15 minutes. The town is one of Europe's oldest, going back centuries before Christ. The symbol of Hallstatt, which you'll see all over town, is two adjacent spirals—a design based on jewelry found in Bronze Age Celtic graves high in the nearby mountains.

The charms of Hallstatt are the village and its lakeside setting. Go there to relax, nibble, wander, and paddle. While tourist

Hallstatt

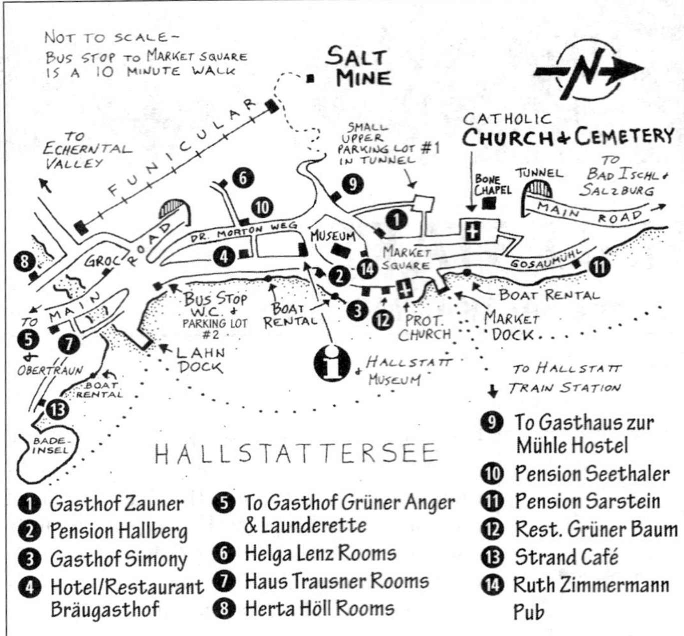

crowds can trample much of Hallstatt's charm in August, the place is almost dead in the off-season. The lake is famous for its good fishing and pure water.

Tourist Information

The friendly and helpful TI, on the main drag, can explain hikes and excursions, arrange private tours of Hallstatt (€65), and find you a room (April–Oct Mon–Fri 9:00–12:00 & 14:00–17:00; in July–Aug also Sat 10:00–16:00, closed Sun; Nov–March Mon–Fri 9:00–13:00, closed Sat–Sun; a block from Marktplatz toward lakefront parking, above post office, Seestrasse 169, tel. 06134/8208, www.inneres-salzkammergut.at, hallstatt@inneres-salzkammergut.at).

The TI offers a €5 walking tour of the town in English at 10:00 on Wednesdays and Saturdays in July and August (confirm schedule at TI).

Arrival in Hallstatt

By Train: Hallstatt's train station is a wide spot on the tracks across the lake. *Stefanie* (a boat) meets you at the station and glides scenically across the lake into town (€1.90, meets each train until about 18:30—don't arrive after that). The last departing boat-train connection leaves Hallstatt around 18:00, and the first boat goes in the morning at 6:50 (9:20 on Sun). Walk left from the boat dock for the TI and most hotels. Since there's no train station in town, the TI can help you find schedule information, or check www.oebb.at.

By Car: The main road skirts Hallstatt via a long tunnel above the town. Parking is tight mid-June through mid-October. Hallstatt has several numbered parking areas outside the town center. Parking lot #1 is in the tunnel above the town (swing through to check for a spot, free with guest card). Otherwise, several numbered lots are just after the tunnel. If you have a hotel reservation, the guard will let you drive into town to drop your bags (ask if your hotel has any in-town parking). It's a lovely 10- to 20-minute lakeside walk to the center of town from the lots. Without a guest card, you'll pay €4.20 per day for parking. Off-season parking in town is easy and free.

Helpful Hints

Internet Access: Try Hallstatt Umbrella Bar (€4/hr, summers only, weather permitting—since it's literally under a big umbrella, halfway between Lahn boat dock and Museum Square at Seestrasse 145).

Laundry: A small full-service launderette is at the campground up from the *Bade-Insel,* just off the main road (about €8/load, mid-April–mid-Oct daily 7:00–12:00 & 15:00–22:00, closed off-season, tel. 06134/83224). In the center, Hotel Grüner Baum does laundry for non-guests (€11/load, facing Market Square).

Bike Rental: Hotel Grüner Baum rents bikes (€6/half-day, €11/day).

Parks and Swimming: Green and peaceful lakeside parks line the south end of Lake Hallstatt. If you walk 10 minutes south of town to Hallstatt-Lahn, you'll find a grassy public park, playground, and swimming area *(Badestrand)* with a fun man-made play island *(Bade-Insel).*

Views: For a great view over Hallstatt, hike above Helga Lenz's *Zimmer* as far as you like (see page 133), or climb any path leading up the hill. The 40-minute steep hike down from the salt-mine tour gives the best views (see page 131).

Hallstatt Historic Town Walk

This short walk starts at the dock.

Boat Landing—There was a Hallstatt before there was a Rome. In fact, because of the importance of salt mining here, an entire epoch—the Hallstatt era, from 800 to 400 B.C.—is named for this important spot. Through the centuries, salt was traded and people came and went by boat. You'll still see the traditional *Fuhr* boats, designed to carry heavy loads in shallow water.

Towering above the town is the Catholic church. Its faded St. Christopher—patron saint of travelers with his cane and baby Jesus on his shoulder—watched over those sailing in and out. Until 1875, the only way into town was by boat. Then came the train and the road. The good ship *Stefanie* shuttles travelers back and forth from here to the Hallstatt train station immediately across the lake. The Bootverleih sign advertises boat rentals (see "Lake Trip," below).

Notice the one-lane road out of town (with the waiting time, width, and height posted). Until 1966, when a bigger tunnel was built above Hallstatt, all the traffic crept single file right through the town.

Look down the shore at the huge homes. Several families lived in each of these houses back when Hallstatt's population was about double its present 1,000; today, many of them rent rooms to visitors.

Parking is tight here in the tourist season. Locals and hotels have cards getting them into the prime town-center lot. From October through May, the barricade is lifted and anyone can park here. Hallstatt is snowbound for about three months each winter, but the lake hasn't frozen over since 1981.

See any swans? They've patrolled the lake like they own it since the 1860s, when Emperor Franz Josef and Empress Sissy—the Princess Di of her day—made this region their annual holiday retreat. Sissy loved swans, so locals made sure she'd see them here. During this period, the Romantics discovered Hallstatt, many top painters worked here, and the town got its first hotel.

Tiny Hallstatt has two big churches—Protestant (with a grassy lakeside playground) and Catholic up above (described below, with its fascinating bone chapel). After the Reformation, most of Hallstatt was Protestant. Then, under Hapsburg rule, it was mostly Catholic. Today, 60 percent of the town is Catholic.

Walk over the town's stream, past the Protestant church, one block to the...

Market Square—In 1750, a fire leveled this part of town. The buildings you see now are all late-18th-century and built of stone rather than flammable wood. Take a close look at the two-dimensional, up-against-the-wall pear tree (it likes the sun-warmed wall). The statue features the Holy Trinity. Continue a block past Gasthof Simony to the pair of phone booths and step into the...

Museum Square—Because 20th-century Hallstatt was of no industrial importance, it was untouched by World War II. But once upon a time, its salt was worth defending. High above, peeking out of the trees, is Rudolf's Tower (Rudolfsturm). Originally a 13th-century watchtower protecting the salt mines, and later the mansion of a salt-mine boss, it's now a restaurant with a great view. A zigzag trail connects the town with Rudolfsturm and the salt mines just beyond. The big, white houses by the waterfall were water-powered mills that once ground Hallstatt's grain. If you hike up a few blocks, you'll see the river raging through town. Around you are the town's TI, post office, a museum, city hall, and the Dachstein Sport shop (with a prehistoric basement, described below). The statue on the square is of the mine manager who excavated prehistoric graves around 1850. Much of the *Schmuck* (jewelry) sold locally is inspired by the jewelry found in the area's Bronze Age tombs.

For thousands of years, people have been leaching salt out of this mountain. A brine spring sprung here, attracting Bronze Age people around 1500 B.C. Later, they dug tunnels to mine the rock, which was 70 percent salt, dissolved it into a brine, and distilled out salt—precious for preserving meat (and making french fries so tasty). For a look at early salt-mining implements, visit the museum.

SIGHTS AND ACTIVITIES

▲▲Hallstatt's Catholic Church and Bone Chapel—The Catholic church overlooks the town from above. From near the boat dock, hike up the covered wooden stairway and follow signs to Kath. Kirche. The lovely church has 500-year-old altars and frescoes dedicated to St. Barbara (patron of miners) and St. Catherine (patron of foresters—lots of wood was needed to fortify the many miles of tunnels and boil the brine to distill out the salt). The last priest modernized parts of the church, but since Hallstatt is a UNESCO World Heritage Site, now they're changing it all back to its original state.

Behind the church, in the well-tended graveyard, is the 12th-century Chapel of St. Michael (even older than the church). Its bone chapel—or charnel house *(Beinhaus)*—contains more than 600 painted skulls. Each skull has been lovingly named, dated, and decorated (skulls with dark, thick garlands are oldest—18th century; those with flowers more recent—19th century). Space was so limited in this cemetery that bones had only 12 peaceful, buried years here before making way for the freshly dead. Many of the dug-up bones and skulls ended up in this chapel. They stopped this practice in the 1960s, about the same time the Catholic Church began permitting cremation (€1, daily mid-May–Sept 10:00–16:00, Easter–mid-May 11:00–16:00, Oct 10:00–17:00, weather permitting, closed Nov–Easter).

▲World Heritage Hallstatt Museum—This newly redone museum tells the story of Hallstatt—with a special focus on the Hallstatt period (800–400 B.C.), when this little village was the crucial salt-mining hub of a culture that spread from France to the

Salzkammergut

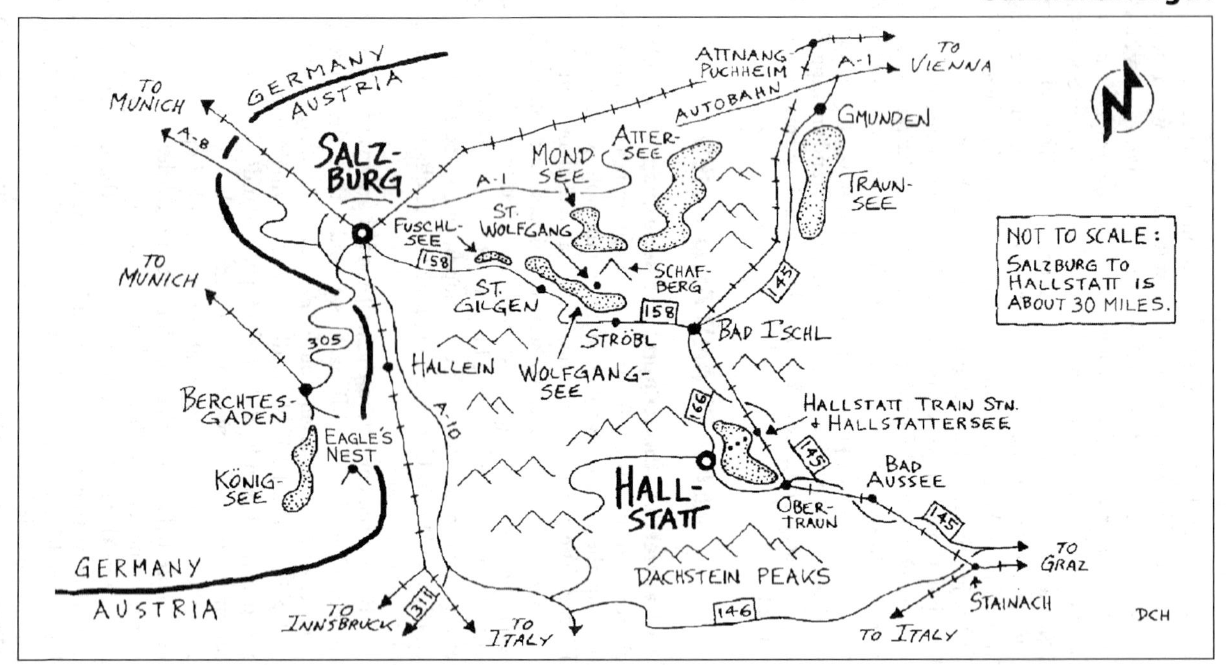

Balkans. Back then, Celtic tribes dug for precious salt, and Hallstatt was, as its name means, the "place of salt."

First you'll watch a video that takes you back in time 7,000 years. Then you'll walk through exhibits tracing the town's evolution to the present day. This fun museum—though pricey—is well organized into meaningful, bite-sized chunks. There are displays on everything from the region's flora and fauna to local artists and the surge in Hallstatt tourism during the Romantic age—and lots and lots of salt-mining artifacts. Everything's in German, but the €2 English guide explains most of it (€7, daily May–Sept 10:00–18:00, Oct–April 11:00–15:00, closed Mon, Seestrasse 56, adjacent to TI, tel. 06134/828-015). The Dachstein Sport shop across from the TI dug into a prehistoric site, and now its basement is another small museum (free).

▲Lake Trip—For a quick boat trip, you can ride *Stefanie* across the lake and back for €3.80. It stops at the tiny Hallstatt train station for 30 minutes, giving you time to walk to a hanging bridge and enjoy the peaceful, deep part of the lake. Longer lake tours are also available (€7/50 min, €8.50/90 min, www.hallstatt.net/schiffahrt, sporadic schedules—especially off-season—so check chalkboards by boat docks for today's times). Those into relaxation can rent a sleepy electric motorboat to enjoy town views from the water (two rental places: Riedler, next to ferry dock or across from Bräugasthof, tel. 06134/8320; or Hemetsberger, near Gasthof Simony or past bridge before Bad Insel, tel. 06134/8228; both daily in-season and in good weather until 19:00; boats have 2 speeds: slow and stop; €11/hr, spend an extra €3/hr for faster 500-watt boats).

▲▲Salt Mine Tour—If you have yet to pay a visit to a salt mine, Hallstatt's—which claims to be the oldest in the world—is a good one. You'll ride a steep funicular high above the town (funicular-€8.50 round-trip, €5.10 one-way, daily May–mid-Sept 9:00–18:00, Oct until 16:30, closed Nov–April), take a 10-minute hike, check your bag and put on old miners' clothes, hike 650 feet higher in your funny outfit to meet your guide, load onto the train, and ride into the mountain through a tunnel actually made by prehistoric miners. Inside, you'll watch a great video (English headsets), slide down two banisters, and follow your guide. While the tour is mostly in German, the guide is required to speak English if you ask—so ask (salt mine tour-€15.50, €21 combo-ticket includes entrance and round-trip funicular, can buy mine tickets at cable-car station, daily May–mid-Sept 9:30–16:30, Oct 9:30–15:00, closed Nov–April, the 16:00 funicular departure catches the last tour at 16:30, no children under age 4, rarely a long wait but arrive after 15:00 and you'll find no lines and a smaller group, tel. 06132/200-2400). The well-publicized ancient Celtic graveyard excavation sites nearby are really dead (precious little to see). If you skip the funicular, the scenic

40-minute hike back into town is (with strong knees) a joy.

At the base of the funicular, notice train tracks leading to the Erbstollen tunnel entrance. This lowest of the salt tunnels goes many miles into the mountain, where a shaft connects it to the tunnels you just explored. Today, the salty brine from these tunnels flows 25 miles through the world's oldest pipeline to the huge modern salt works (next to the highway) at Ebensee. You'll pass a stack of the original 120-year-old wooden pipes between the lift and the mine.

SLEEPING

Hallstatt's TI can almost always find you a room (either in town or at B&Bs and small hotels outside of town—which are more likely to have rooms available and come with easy parking). Mid-July and August can be tight. Early August is worst. Hallstatt is not the place to splurge—some of the best rooms are in *Zimmer,* just as nice and modern as the bigger hotels, at half the cost. A bed in a private home costs about €20 with breakfast. It's hard to get a one-night advance reservation. But if you drop in and they have a spot, one-nighters are welcome. Prices include breakfast, lots of stairs, and a silent night. "*Zimmer mit Aussicht?*" means "Room with view?"—worth asking for. The cheaper places don't take credit cards (like many businesses in town).

$$$ Gasthof Zauner is run by a friendly mountaineer, Herr Zauner, whose family has owned it since 1914. The 12 pricey, pine-flavored rooms on the main square are decorated with sturdy alpine-inspired furniture. Lederhosen-clad Herr Zauner recounts tales of local mountaineering lore, including his own impressive ascents (Sb-€46–53, Db-€84–98, prices depend on season and view, closed mid-Nov–mid-Dec, Marktplatz 51, tel. 06134/8246, fax 06134/82468, www.zauner.hallstatt.net, zauner@hallstatt.at).

$$$ Pension Hallberg-Tauchergasthof (Diver's Inn), across from the TI, has six big rooms and a funky mini-museum of WWII artifacts found in the lake (Sb-€40–75, Db-€60–110, rooms for up to 5 also available, price depends on size, cash preferred, tel. 06134/8709, fax 06134/20621, www.pension-hallberg.at.tf, hallberg@aon.at, Gerda the "Salt Witch" and Eckbert Winkelmann).

$$ Gasthof Simony, my 500-year-old favorite, is on the square, with a lake view, balconies, creaky wood floors, slippery rag rugs, antique furniture, a lakefront garden for swimming, and a huge breakfast. Reserve in advance. For safety, reconfirm your room and price a day or two before you arrive and call again if arriving late (S-€38, D-€45–50, Ds-€55–60, Db-€75–80, third person-€30 extra, cash preferred, Markt 105, tel. & fax 06134/8231, Susanna Scheutz SE).

Sleep Code

(€1 = about $1.20, country code: 43, area code: 06134)
S = Single, **D** = Double/Twin, **T** = Triple, **Q** = Quad, **b** = bathroom, **s** = shower only, **SE** = Speaks English, **NSE** = No English. Unless otherwise noted, credit cards are accepted, English is spoken, and breakfast is included.

To help you sort easily through these listings, I've divided the rooms into three categories, based on the price for a standard double room with bath:

$$$ **Higher Priced**—Most rooms €80 or more.
$$ **Moderately Priced**—Most rooms between €50–80.
$ **Lower Priced**—Most rooms €50 or less.

$$ Bräugasthof Hallstatt is another creaky, friendly old place—a former brewery—with eight clean, cozy, mostly lakeview rooms run by Susanna's sister and her family (Sb-€42, Db-€76, Tb-€110, Db/Tb cheaper for 3-night stays, just past TI on the main drag at Seestrasse 120, tel. 06134/8221, fax 06134/82214, www.brauhaus-lobisser.com, info@brauhaus-lobisser.com, Lobisser family).

$$ Gasthof Pension Grüner Anger is a practical and modern, away from the medieval town center—the only hotel in town that doesn't squeak and creak. It's big and quiet, with 11 rooms, a few blocks from the base of the salt-mine lift, and a 15-minute walk from Market Square (Sb-€35, Db-€63, €3 more per room July–Aug, €3 more for 1-night stays July–Aug, third person-€15, nonsmoking, Internet access, free parking, Lahn 10, tel. 06134/8397, fax 06134/83974, www.hallstatt.net/gruener.anger, anger@aon.at, Sulzbacher family).

$ Helga Lenz is a steep five-minute climb above the Pension Seethaler (look for the green *Zimmer* sign). This large, sprawling, woodsy house has a nifty garden perch, wins the "Best View" award, and is ideal for those who sleep well in tree houses and don't mind the ascent from town (S-€18—only available April–June and Oct, D-€32, Db-€38, T-€45, Tb-€54, 1-night stays-€2 per person extra, family room, cash only, closed Nov–March, Hallberg 17, tel. & fax 06134/8508, www.demregio.at/lenz, haus-lenz@aon.at).

$ Two ***Zimmer*** are a few minutes' stroll south of the center, just past the bus stop/parking lot and over the bridge: **Haus Trausner** has four clean, bright, new-feeling rooms (Ds-€35, Db-€38, less for more than 1 night, cash only, Lahnstrasse 27, tel. 06134/8710, trausner1@utanet.at, Maria Trausner SE), while **Herta Höll** rents out three rooms in a riverside house crawling with kids (Db-€40, apartment-€60, cash only, Malerweg 45, tel. 06134/8531, fax 06134/825-533, frank.hoell@aon.at).

$ Gasthaus zur Mühle Jugendherberge, below the waterfall, with the cheapest good beds in town, is popular for its great pizzas and cheap grub (46 beds, bed in 3- to 14-bed coed dorms-€11, D-€24, sheets-€3 extra, family quads, breakfast-€3, big lockers with a €20 deposit, closed Nov, reception closed Tue Sept–mid-May—so arrange in advance if arriving on Tue, below tunnel car park, Kirchenweg 36, tel. & fax 06134/8318, toeroe.f@magnet.at, run by Ferdinand Törö).

$ Pension Seethaler is a dark, homey old lodge with 45 beds and a breakfast room mossy with antlers, perched above the lake. The confusing floor plan is like an M. C. Escher house with fire hazards, and the staff won't win any awards for congeniality—*Zimmer* are friendlier and cheaper—but this place is a reasonable last resort (€18/person in S, D, T, or Q, €26/person in Db, Tb, or Qb, cash only, coin-op showers downstairs-€1/8 min, closed Nov, Dr. Morton Weg 22, find the stairs to the left of Seestrasse 116, at top of stairs turn left, tel. 06134/8421, pension-seethaler@aon.at).

$ Ancient-feeling **Pension Sarstein** has 25 beds in basic, dusty rooms with flower-bedecked, lakeview balconies, in a charming building run by friendly Isabelle Fischer. You can swim from her lakeside garden (S-€18, D-€36, Ds-€44, Db-€50, Ds and Db have balconies, 1-night stays-€2 per person extra, cash only, leave the boat dock to the right and walk 200 yards to Gosaumühlstrasse 83, tel. 06134/8217, NSE).

EATING

You can enjoy good food inexpensively, with delightful lakeside settings. While everyone cooks the typical Austrian fare, your best bet here is trout. *Reinanke* trout is from Lake Hallstatt. Restaurants in Hallstatt tend to have unreliable hours and close early on slow nights, so don't wait too long to get dinner.

Feed the swans while your trout is being cooked at **Restaurant Bräugasthof** (fun menu and tasty food, May–Oct daily 10:00–21:00, closed Nov–April, tel. 06134/20012, see "Sleeping," page 132). **Hotel Grüner Baum** is another lakefront option (May–Oct Tue–Sun 11:30–22:00, closed Mon and Nov–April, at bottom of Market Square, tel. 06134/8263).

While it lacks a lakeside setting, **Gasthof Zauner's** classy restaurant is well respected for its grilled meat and fish; the interior of its dining room is covered in real ivy that grows in through the windows (daily 11:30–14:30 & 17:30–22:00, closed Nov–mid Dec, reservations smart, see "Sleeping," page 132).

For the best pizza in town with a fun-loving local crowd, chow down cheap and hearty at **Gasthaus zur Mühle** (daily 11:00–14:00

& 17:00–21:00, closed Tue and no lunch mid-Oct–mid-May, see "Sleeping," page 134).

Locals like the smoky **Strand Café,** a 10-minute lakeside hike away, near the town beach, or *Bade-Insel* (April–Oct Tue–Sun 10:00–21:00, closed Mon and Nov–March, great garden setting on the lake, Seelande 102, tel. 06134/8234).

For your late-night drink, savor Market Square from the trendy little pub called **Ruth Zimmermann** (daily June–Oct 9:00–2:00, Nov–May 12:00–2:00, tel. 06134/8306).

TRANSPORTATION CONNECTIONS

From Hallstatt by Train to: Salzburg (hrly, 90 min to Attnang Puchheim, short wait, 50 min to Salzburg), **Vienna** (hrly, 90 min to Attnang Puchheim, short wait, 2.5 hrs to Vienna). Day-trippers to Hallstatt can check bags at the Attnang Puchheim station. (Note: Connections there and back can be very fast—about 5 min; have coins ready for the lockers at track 1.) Train info: tel. 051-717 (to get an operator, dial 2, then 1).

BRUGES

(Brugge)

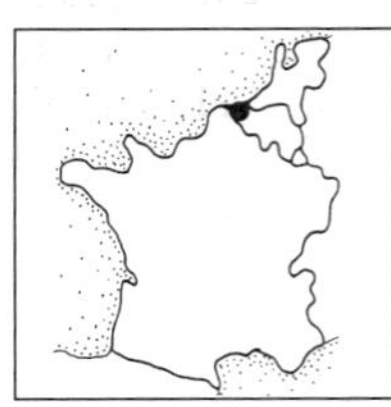

With Renoir canals, pointy, gilded architecture, vivid time-tunnel art, and stay-awhile cafés, Bruges is a heavyweight sightseeing destination, as well as a joy. Where else can you ride a bike along a canal, munch mussels and wash them down with the world's best beer, savor heavenly chocolate, and see Flemish Primitives and a Michelangelo, all within 300 yards of a bell tower that jingles every 15 minutes? And there's no language barrier.

The town is Brugge (BROO-ghah) in Flemish, and Bruges (broozh) in French and English. Its name comes from the Viking word for wharf. Right from the start, Bruges was a trading center. In the 11th century, the city grew wealthy on the cloth trade.

By the 14th century, Bruges' population was 35,000, as large as London's. As the middleman in sea trade between northern and southern Europe, it was one of the biggest cities in the world and an economic powerhouse. In addition, Bruges had become the most important cloth market in Northern Europe.

In the 15th century, while England and France were slogging it out in a 100-year war, Bruges was the favored residence of the powerful Dukes of Burgundy—and at peace. Commerce and the arts boomed. The artists Jan van Eyck and Hans Memling had studios here.

But by the 16th century, the harbor had silted up and the economy had collapsed. The Burgundian court left, Belgium became a minor Hapsburg possession, and Bruges' Golden Age abruptly ended. For generations, Bruges was known as a mysterious and dead city. In the 19th century, a new port, Zeebrugge, brought renewed vitality to the area. And in the 20th century, tourists discovered the town.

Today, Bruges prospers because of tourism: It's a uniquely well-preserved Gothic city and a handy gateway to Europe. It's no secret, but even with the crowds, it's the kind of city where you don't mind being a tourist.

Bruges' ultimate sight is the town itself, and the best way to enjoy it is to get lost on the back streets, away from the lace shops and ice-cream stands.

Planning Your Time

Bruges needs at least two nights and a full, well-organized day. Even non-shoppers enjoy browsing here, and the Belgian love of life makes a hectic itinerary seem a little senseless. With one day (other than a Monday, when all the museums are closed), the speedy visitor could do the Bruges blitz described below:

9:30	Climb the bell tower on the Market Square.
10:00	Tour the sights on the Burg Square.
11:00	Tour the Groeninge Museum.
12:00	Tour the Gruuthuse Museum.
13:00	Eat lunch and buy chocolates.
14:00	Take a short canal cruise (discount dock).
14:30	Visit the Church of Our Lady and see Michelangelo's Madonna and Child.
15:00	Tour the Memling Museum.
16:00	Catch the Straffe Hendrik Brewery tour (note that their last tour runs at 15:00 in winter).
17:00	Calm down in the Begijnhof courtyard.
18:00	Ride a bike around the quiet back streets of town or take a horse-and-buggy tour.
20:00	Lose the tourists and find dinner.

(If this schedule seems insane, skip the bell tower and the brewery—or stay another day.)

ORIENTATION

(area code: 050)

The tourist's Bruges (you'll be sharing it) is one square kilometer, contained within a canal, or moat. Nearly everything of interest and importance is within a convenient cobbled swath between the train station and Market Square (a 15-min walk). Many of my quiet, charming recommended accommodations lie just beyond Market Square.

Tourist Information

The main office is on Burg Square (April–Sept Mon–Fri 9:30–18:30, Sat–Sun 10:00–12:30 & 14:00–18:30; Oct–March Mon–Fri 9:30–17:00, Sat–Sun 9:30–13:00 & 14:00–17:00; lockers,

Bruges

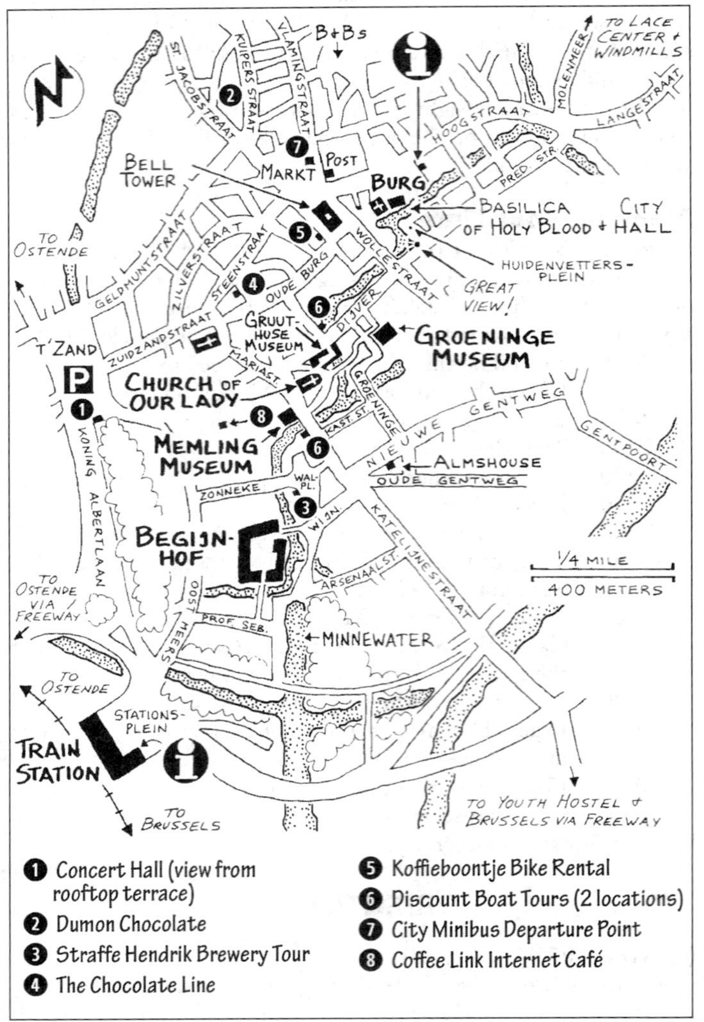

money-exchange desk, €0.30 WC in courtyard, tel. 050/448-686, www.brugge.be). The other TI is at the train station (generally Tue–Sat 10:00–13:00 & 14:00–17:00, closed Sun–Mon).

The TIs sell a great €1 Bruges visitors guide with a map and listings of all of the sights and services. You can also pick up a monthly English-language program called *events@brugge.* The TIs have information on train schedules and on the many tours available (see "Tours" below). Bikers will want the *5X on the Bike*

Around Bruges map/guide (€1.50) that shows five routes through the countryside. Many hotels give out free maps with more detail than the map the TIs sell.

Arrival in Bruges

By Train: Coming in by train, you'll see the square bell tower that marks the main square. Upon arrival, stop by the station TI to pick up the €1 Bruges visitors guide (map in centerfold). The station lacks ATMs, but has lockers (€2–3.50, daily 6:00–24:00).

The best way to get to the town center is by bus. All buses go directly to the Market Square. Simply hop on any bus, pay €1, and in four minutes, you're there. The €1 tickets are good for an hour. A day pass costs €3. Buses #4 and #8 go farther, to the northeast part of town (to the windmills and recommended places on Carmersstraat).

Note that nearly all city buses go directly from the train station to Market Square and fan out from there. They then return to Market Square (bus #2 stops at post office on square; other buses stop at library on nearby Kuiperstraat) and go directly back to the train station.

The **taxi** fare from the train station to most hotels is around €6 (tel. 050/334-444).

It's a 20-minute **walk** from the station to the center—no fun with your luggage. If you want to walk to Market Square, cross the busy street and canal in front of the station, head up Oostmeers, and turn right on Zwidzandstraat.

You can rent a **bike** at the station for the duration of your stay, but other bike rental shops are closer to the center (see "Helpful Hints," below).

By Car: Park at the train station for just €2.50 per day and take the bus into town. There are pricier (€9/day) underground parking garages at 't Zand and around town, and these garages are well-marked. Paid parking on the street in Bruges is limited to four hours. Driving in town is very complicated because of the one-way system.

Helpful Hints

ATMs: Although there are no cash machines at the train station, there are plenty in town: at the post office (Markt 5), Fortis Bank (Simon Stevins Plein 3), Fortis Bank (Hoogstraat 23), KBC (Steenstraat 38), and Fortis Bank (Vlamingstraat 78).

Internet Access: The relaxing **Coffee Link,** with mellow music and pleasant art, is centrally located, across from the Church of Our Lady (€2.20/30 min, daily 10:00–20:00 in summer, off-season until 19:00, 16 terminals, Mariastraat 38, tel. 050/349-973).

Post Office: It's on Market Square near the bell tower (Mon–Fri 9:00–18:00, Sat 9:30–12:30, closed Sun, tel. 050/331-411).

Store Hours: Shops are open 9:00–18:00, and a little later on Friday. Grocery stores are usually closed on Sunday. The main shopping street, Steenstraat, stretches from Market Square to the square called 't Zand. The Hema department store is at Steenstraat 73 (Mon–Sat 9:00–18:00, closed Sun).

Market Days: Wednesday morning (Market Square) and Saturday morning ('t Zand) are market days. On Saturday and Sunday, a flea market hops along Dijver in front of the Groeninge Museum.

Laundry: Bruges' most convenient place to do laundry is **Mister Wash** (daily 8:30–22:00, just off Market Square in an arcade at Sint Jakobsstraat 51, tel. 050/335-902). A less central launderette is at Gentpoortstraat 28 (daily 7:00–22:00).

Bike Rental: Koffieboontje, just under the bell tower, is extremely well organized and very handy. They take a credit-card imprint for a deposit, and you're on your way with a nearly new bike (€3/1 hr, €6/4 hrs, or €9/24-hr day, €6/day with an ISIC student card, free city maps and child seats, daily 9:00–22:00, the €15 "bike plus any 3 museums" deal could save enough to pay for lunch, Hallestraat 4, tel. 050/338-027, www.hotel-koffieboontje.be).

Other rental places are: **Fietsen Popelier** (€6/4 hrs, €9/24 hrs, new bikes, free map, no deposit, 50 yards from Church of Our Lady at Mariastraat 26, tel. 050/343-262), the less central **De Ketting** (cheap at €5/day, daily 9:00–19:30, Gentpoortstraat 23, tel. 050/344-196), and the **train station** (ticket window #3, daily 8:00–19:30, €9/day, €6.50/half day after 14:00, €20 deposit).

Best Town Views: The bell tower overlooking the Market Square rewards those who climb it with the ultimate town view. The best view without a climb is from the rooftop terrace of Bruges' concert hall (Concertgebouw). This seven-story building, built in 2002, is the city's only modern high-rise (daily 11:00–23:00, free elevator, on edge of old town on 't Zand).

TOURS

Of Bruges

Bruges by Boat—The most relaxing and scenic (though not informative) way to see this city of canals is by boat, with the captain narrating. Boats leave from all over town, run by different companies offering basically the same 30-minute tour (€5.50, 4/hr, daily 10:00–17:00). Two of the companies give an €0.80 discount with this book: Boten Stael (just over the canal from Memling Museum at Katelijnestraat 4, tel. 050/332-771) and Gruuthuse (Nieuwstraat 11, opposite the Groeninge Museum).

City Minibus Tour—City Tour Bruges gives a rolling overview of the town in an 18-seat, two-skylight minibus with dial-a-language headsets and video support (€11.50, 50 min). The tour leaves hourly from Market Square (10:00–20:00 in summer, until 18:00 in spring, until 17:00 in fall, less in winter, tel. 050/355-024, www.citytour.be). The narration, while clear, is slow-moving and a bit boring. But the tour is a lazy way to cruise past virtually every sight in Bruges.

Walking Tour—Local guides walk small groups through the core of town (€5, daily July–Aug, Sat–Sun only in June and Sept, no tours off-season, depart from TI at 14:30, 2 hrs). Though earnest, the tours are heavy on history and given in two languages, so they may be less than peppy. Still, to propel you beyond the pretty gables and canal swans of Bruges, they're good medicine. A private two-hour guided tour costs €45 (reserve at least 1 week in advance through TI, tel. 050/448-686); or contact Christian and Danielle Scharle (€50/2-hr walk, €100/3-hr driving tour, mobile 0476-493-203, tmb@skynet.be).

Horse-and-Buggy Tour—The buggies around town are ready to take you for a clip-clop tour (€28/30 min, price is per carriage, not per person).

From Bruges

Quasimodo Countryside Tours—This company offers those with extra time two excellent and entertaining all-day bus tours through the rarely visited Flemish countryside.

The "In Flanders Fields" tour concentrates on World War I battlefields, trenches, memorials, and poppy-splattered fields (April–Oct Tue–Sun 9:15–16:30, otherwise Sun, Tue, and Thu).

The other tour, "Triple Treat," focuses on Flanders' medieval past and rich culture, with tastes of chocolate, waffles, and beer (Mon, Wed, and Fri 9:15–16:30). Be ready for lots of walking.

Tours cost €48, or €38 if you're under 26 (includes a picnic lunch, 30-seat, non-smoking bus, reserve by calling tel. 050/370-470 or toll-free tel. 0800/97525, www.quasimodo.be). Buses leave from the Park Hotel on 't Zand.

Daytours In Flanders Fields Minibus Tours—Frank, the guide, loves leading small groups on this fascinating day trip. This tour is like Quasimodo's (listed above), but more expensive. The differences: seven travelers on a minibus rather than a big busload; hotel pickups (because the small bus is allowed in the town center); an included restaurant lunch, rather than a picnic; and a little more serious lecturing and a stricter focus on World War I. For instance, you actually visit the In Flanders Fields Museum in Ieper, called

Ypres in French. Tours cost €59 (book direct and mention this guidebook for a discount, Wed–Sun 9:00–17:00, no tours Mon and Tue, call 050/346-060 or toll-free 0800/99133 to book, www.visitbruges.com). They also offer an evening "Last Post" ceremony at the Menin Gate in Ypres (€35, daily 18:30–21:00).

Bruges by Bike—QuasiMundo Biketours Brugge leads daily bike tours in and around the city (€18, departs at 10:00, 5 miles, 2.5 hrs). Their other tour, "Border by Bike," goes through the nearby countryside to Damme (€18, departs at 13:00, 15 miles, 4 hrs, tel. 050/330-775, www.quasimundo.com). Book direct and mention this guidebook to get a discount. Both tours include bike rental, a light raincoat (if necessary), water, and a drink in a local café. Meet in front of the TI on Burg Square.

Bus and Boat Tour—The Sightseeing Line offers a bus trip to Damme and a boat ride back (€16.50, April–Sept daily at 14:00, 2 hrs, leaves from the post office at Market Square, tel. 050/355-024).

SIGHTS

These sights are listed in walking order from Market Square to Burg Square to the cluster of museums around the Church of our Lady to the Begijnhof (10-min walk from beginning to end).

▲Market Square (Markt)—Ringed by a bank, the post office, lots of restaurant terraces, great old gabled buildings, and the bell tower, this is the modern heart of the city (most city buses run from here to the train station). Under the bell tower are two great Belgian french-fry stands, a quadrilingual Braille description of the old town, and a metal model of the tower. In Bruges' heyday as a trading center, a canal came right up to this square.

Geldmuntstraat, just off the square, is a delightful street with many fun and practical shops and eateries.

▲▲Bell Tower (Belfort)—Most of this bell tower has presided over Market Square since 1300, serenading passersby with carillon music. The octagonal lantern was added in 1486, making it 290 feet high—that's 366 steps (daily 9:30–17:00, ticket window closes 45 min early, €0.30 WC in courtyard). The view is worth the climb and the €5.

▲▲Burg Square—This opulent square is Bruges' civic center, historically the birthplace of Bruges and the site of the 9th-century castle of the first Count of Flanders. Today, it's the scene of outdoor concerts and home to the TI (with a €0.30 WC). It's surrounded by six centuries of architecture.

▲Basilica of the Holy Blood—Originally the Chapel of Saint Basil, this church is famous for its relic of the blood of Christ, which, according to tradition, was brought to Bruges in 1150 after the Second Crusade. The lower chapel is dark and solid—a fine example

Museum Tips

Admission prices are steep, but they include great audioguides—so plan on spending some time and getting into it. For information on all the museums, call 050/448-711 or visit www.brugge.be/musea.

Combo-Tickets: The TIs and participating museums sell a museum combo-ticket (any 5 museums for €15). Since the Groeninge and Memling museums cost €8 each, art-lovers will save money with this pass. Another combo-ticket offers three museums and a bicycle for €15.

Black Monday: In Bruges, nearly all sights are open Tuesday–Sunday year-round 9:30–17:00 and are closed on Monday. If you're in Bruges on a Monday, consider a boat, bus, or walking tour.

of Romanesque style. The upper chapel (separate entrance, climb the stairs) is decorated Gothic (museum is next to upper chapel, museum entry-€1.50, April–Sept Thu–Tue 9:30–11:45 & 14:00–17:45, Oct–March Thu–Tue 10:00–11:45 & 14:00–15:45, Wed 10:00–11:45 only, Burg Square, tel. 050/336-792, www.holyblood.org).

▲City Hall's Gothic Room—Your ticket gives you access to a room full of old town maps and paintings and a grand, beautifully restored "Gothic Hall" from 1400. Its painted and carved wooden ceiling features hanging arches (€2.50, includes audioguide and admission to Renaissance Hall, daily 9:30–17:00, Burg 12).

Renaissance Hall (Brugse Vrije)—This elaborately-decorated room includes a grand Renaissance chimney carved from oak by Bruges' Renaissance man, Lancelot Blondeel in 1531. If you're into heraldry, the symbolism (explained in the free English flier) makes this room worth a five-minute stop. If you're not, you'll wonder where the rest of the museum is (€2.50, includes audioguide and admission to City Hall's Gothic Room, Tue–Sun 9:30–12:30 & 13:30–16:30, closed Mon, entrance in corner of square at Burg 11a).

▲▲▲Groeninge Museum—This museum houses a world-class collection of mostly Flemish art, from Memling to Magritte. While the museum has plenty of worthwhile modern art, the highlights are its vivid and pristine Flemish Primitives. ("Primitive" here means before the Renaissance.) Flemish art is shaped by its love of detail, its merchant patrons' egos, and the power of the Church. Lose yourself in the halls of Groeninge: Gaze across 15th-century canals, into the eyes of reassuring Marys, and through town squares littered with leotards, lace, and lopped-off heads (€8, includes audioguide, Tue–Sun 9:30–17:00, closed Mon, Dijver 12, tel. 050/448-751).

Bruges at a Glance

▲▲▲Groeninge Museum World-class collection of mainly Flemish art. **Hours:** Tue–Sun 9:30–17:00, closed Mon.

▲▲Bell Tower Overlooking Market Square, with 366 steps to a worthwhile view and a carillon close-up. **Hours:** Daily 9:30–17:00.

▲▲Burg Square Historic square with TI, sights, and impressive architecture. **Hours:** Always open.

▲▲Memling Museum/St. John's Hospital Art by the greatest of the Flemish Primitives. **Hours:** Tue–Sun 9:30–17:00, closed Mon.

▲▲Church of Our Lady Tombs and church art, including Michelangelo's *Madonna and Child*. **Hours:** Tue–Fri 9:30–12:20 & 13:30–16:50, Sat until 15:50, Sun 13:30–16:50 only, closed Mon.

▲▲Begijnhof Benedictine nuns' peaceful courtyard and Beguine's House museum. **Hours:** Courtyard always open, museum open daily 10:00–12:00 & 13:45–17:00, shorter hours off-season.

▲▲Straffe Hendrik Brewery Tour Fun and handy tour includes beer. **Hours:** Daily on the hour 11:00–16:00, Oct–March 11:00 and 15:00 only.

▲Gruuthuse Museum—The 15th-century mansion of a wealthy Bruges merchant displays period furniture, tapestries, coins, and musical instruments. Nowhere in the city do you get such an intimate look at the materialistic revolution of Bruges' glory days. With the help of the excellent and included audioguide, just browse through rooms of secular objects that are both functional and beautiful (€6, includes audioguide and entry to apse in Church of Our Lady, Tue–Sun 9:30–17:00, closed Mon, Dijver 17).

▲▲Church of Our Lady—The church stands as a memorial to the power and wealth of Bruges in its heyday. A delicate *Madonna and Child* by Michelangelo is near the apse (to the right if you're facing the altar). It's said to be the only Michelangelo statue to leave Italy in his lifetime (thanks to the wealth generated by Bruges' cloth trade). If you like tombs and church art, pay to wander through the apse (Michelangelo viewing is free, art-filled apse-€2.50, covered by €6 Gruuthuse admission, Tue–Fri 9:30–12:20 & 13:30–16:50, Sat until 15:50, Sun 13:30–16:50 only, closed Mon, Mariastraat).

▲▲Memling Museum/St. John's Hospital (Sint Janshospitaal)—The former monastery/hospital complex has two

▲▲Biking Explore the countryside and pedal to nearby Damme. **Hours:** Koffieboontje bike-rental shop open daily 9:00–22:00 (see page 140).

▲Market Square Main square that is the modern heart of the city, with carillon bell tower. **Hours:** Always open.

▲Basilica of the Holy Blood Romanesque and Gothic church housing a relic of the blood of Christ. **Hours:** April–Sept Thu–Tue 9:30–11:45 & 14:00–17:45, Oct–March Thu–Tue 10:00–11:45 & 14:00–15:45, Wed 10:00–11:45 only.

▲City Hall's Gothic Room Beautifully restored hall from 1400. **Hours:** Daily 9:30–17:00.

▲Gruuthuse Museum 15th-century mansion with furniture, tapestries, even a guillotine. **Hours:** Tue–Sun 9:30–17:00, closed Mon.

▲Chocolate Sample Bruges' specialty: Try Dumon, The Chocolate Line, Sweertvaegher, and on and on. **Hours:** Shops generally open 10:00–18:00.

entrances—one is to a welcoming visitors center (free), the other to the Memling Museum. The Memling Museum, in the monastery's former church, was once a medieval hospital and now contains six much-loved paintings by the greatest of the Flemish Primitives, Hans Memling. His *Mystical Wedding of St. Catherine* triptych is a highlight, as is the miniature gilded oak shrine to St. Ursula (€8 includes fine audioguide, Tue–Sun 9:30–17:00, closed Mon, across the street from the Church of Our Lady, Mariastraat 38).

▲▲Begijnhof—*Begijnhofs* (pronounced gutturally: buh-HHHINE-hof) were built to house women of the lay order called beguines, who spent their lives in piety and service (without having to take the same vows a nun would). For military or other reasons, there were more women than men in the medieval Low Countries. The order of beguines offered women (often single or widowed) a dignified place to live and work. When the order died out, many *begihnhofs* were taken over by towns for subsidized housing, but some became homes for nuns.

Bruges' Begijnhof—now inhabited by Benedictine nuns—almost makes you want to don a habit and fold your hands as you walk under its wispy trees and whisper past its frugal little homes. For a good slice of Begijnhof life, walk through the simple museum, the Beguine's House (€2, daily 10:00–12:00 & 13:45–17:00, fewer hours off-season, courtyard always open, English explanations, Beguine's House is left of entry gate).

Minnewater—Just south of the Begijnhof is Minnewater, an idyllic world of flower boxes, canals, and swans.

Almshouses—Walking from the Begijnhof back to the town center, you might detour along Nieuwe Gentweg to visit one of about 20 almshouses in the city. At #8, go through the door marked "Godshuis de Meulenaere 1613" (free) into the peaceful courtyard. This was a medieval form of housing for the poor. The rich would pay for someone's tiny room here in return for lots of prayers.

Avoid the Diamond Museum (at the start of Nieuwe Gentweg); it's less interesting than an encyclopedia (€6, daily 10:30–17:30, Katelijnestraat 43, tel. 050/342-056, www.diamondhouse.net).

Bruges Experiences: Beer, Chocolate, Lace, and Biking

▲▲Straffe Hendrik Brewery Tour—Belgians are Europe's beer connoisseurs. This fun, handy tour is a great way to pay your respects. The happy gang at this working family brewery gives entertaining and informative 45-minute, three-language tours (often by friendly Inge, €4 tour includes a beer, lots of very steep steps, great rooftop panorama, daily on the hour 11:00–16:00, 11:00 and 15:00 are your best times to avoid groups, Oct–March 11:00 and 15:00 only, 1 block past church and canal, take a right down skinny Stoofstraat to #26 on Walplein, tel. 050/332-697, www.halvemaan.be).

At Straffe Hendrik (Strong Henry), they remind their drinkers: "The components of the beer are vitally necessary and contribute to a well-balanced life pattern. Nerves, muscles, visual sentience, and a healthy skin are stimulated by these in a positive manner. For longevity and lifelong equilibrium, drink Straffe Hendrik in moderation!"

Their bistro, where you'll be given your beer (included with the tour), serves quick, hearty lunch plates. You can eat indoors with the smell of hops, or outdoors with the smell of hops. This is a great place to wait for your tour or to linger afterward.

▲Chocolate—Bruggians are connoisseurs of fine chocolate. You'll be tempted by chocolate-filled display windows all over town. While Godiva is the best big-factory/high-price/high-quality brand, there are plenty of smaller, family-run places in Bruges that offer exquisite handmade chocolates.

Perhaps Bruges' smoothest and creamiest chocolates are at **Dumon** (€1.75/100 grams). Madam Dumon and her children (Stefaan and Christophe) make their top-notch chocolate daily and sell it fresh just off Market Square (Thu–Tue 10:00–18:00, closed Wed, old chocolate molds on display in basement, Eiermarkt 6, tel. 050/346-282). Their *ganache,* a dark, creamy combo, wows chocoholics. The Dumons don't provide English labels because they believe it's best to describe their chocolates in person.

Locals and tourists alike flock to **The Chocolate Line** (€3.20/100 grams) for their *"gastronomique"* varieties—unique concoctions such as Havana cigar (marinated in rum, cognac, and Cuban tobacco leaves—so therefore technically illegal in the United States), lemon grass, ginger (shaped like a Buddha), saffron curry (a white elephant), and a spicy chili. My fave: the sheets of chocolate with crunchy roasted cocoa beans. The kitchen—busy whipping up 80 varieties—is on display in the back. Enjoy the window display, renewed monthly (Mon–Sat 9:30–18:00, Sun from 10:30, between Church of Our Lady and Market Square at Simon Stevinplein 19, tel. 050/341-090).

The smaller **Sweertvaegher,** near Burg Square, features top-quality chocolate (€2.65/100 grams) that's darker rather than sweeter, made with fresh ingredients and no preservatives (Tue–Sun 9:30–18:15, closed Mon, Philipstockstraat 29, tel. 050/338-367).

For a different experience, try chocolate fondue as a dessert at **'t Fonduehuisje** (€17–18.50-cheese or bourguignon fondue, €6.50-chocolate fondue, Fri–Wed 18:00–22:00, closed Thu, Wijngaardstraat 20, tel. 050/335-557).

Chocolate Museum—This museum explains why, in the ancient Mexican world of the Mayas and the Aztecs, chocolate was considered the drink of the gods (it's no surprise to me), and cocoa beans were used as a means of payment. With lots of information about the production of truffles, chocolates, hollow figures, and bars of chocolate, the museum ends in the "demonstration room," where you get to have a taste (€5, daily 10:00–17:00; the beautifully renovated building is a little hard to find—head to where Wijnzakstraat meets Sint Jansstraat at Sint Jansplein, behind Burg Square; tel. 050/612-237, www.choco-story.be).

Lace and Windmills by the Moat—A 10-minute walk from the center to the northeast end of town brings you to four windmills strung along a pleasant grassy setting on the "big moat" canal. The St. Janshuismolen windmill is open to visitors (€2, May–Sept daily 9:30–12:30 & 13:30–17:00, closed Oct–April, at the end of Carmersstraat, between Kruispoort and Dampoort, on Bruges side of the moat).

To actually see lace being made, drop by the nearby **Lace Centre (Kant Centrum),** where ladies toss bobbins madly while their eyes go bad (€2.50 includes afternoon demo and small lace museum, as well as adjacent Jeruzalem Church, Mon–Fri 10:00–12:00 & 14:00–18:00, until 17:00 on Sat, closed Sun, Peperstraat

3, tel. 050/330-072). The **Folklore Museum,** in the same neighborhood, is cute but forgettable (€3, daily 9:30–17:00, closed Mon, Balstraat 43, tel. 050/448-764-044). To find either place, ask for the Jeruzalem Church.

Two lace shops with good reputations are **'t Apostelientje** (Mon–Fri 9:30–18:00, Sat 9:30–17:00, Sun 10:00–13:00, tel. 050/337-860, Balstraat 11, near Lace Centre) and the **Little Lace Shop,** which has been run by the Muylle family for four generations and can offer lacemaking demonstrations (daily 10:00–18:00, Wijngaardstraat 32, near Begijnhof, tel. 050/336-406).

▲▲Biking—The Flemish word for bike is *fiets* (pron. feets). While the sights are close enough for easy walking, the town is a treat to bike through. And a bike quickly gets you into the dreamy back lanes without a hint of tourism. Take a peaceful evening ride through the back streets and around the outer canal. Consider keeping a bike for the duration of your stay. It's the way the locals get around in Bruges.

Rental shops have maps and ideas (see "Bike Rental" on page 140 for more info). The TI sells a handy *5X on the Bike Around Bruges* map/guide (€1.50) describing five different bike routes (10–18 miles) through the idyllic countryside nearby.

SLEEPING

Most places are located between the train station and the old center, with the most distant (and best) being a few blocks beyond Market Square to the north and east. B&Bs offer the best value (listed after "Hotels"). All include breakfast, are on quiet streets, and (with a few exceptions) keep the same prices throughout the year. Bruges is most crowded Friday and Saturday evenings Easter through October—with July and August weekends being worst.

Bruges is a great place to sleep, with Gothic spires out your window, no traffic noise, and the cheerily out-of-tune carillon heralding each new day at 8:00 sharp. (Thankfully, the bell tower is silent from 22:00–8:00.)

Hotels

$$$ Hotel Heritage offers 24 rooms in a completely modernized old building. It's tastefully decorated and has all the amenities. It's a great splurge (standard Db-€140, superior Db-€184, deluxe Db-€227, singles take a double for nearly the same cost, extra bed-€40, suites available, breakfast-€15, air-con, non-smoking, elevator, free Internet access, sauna, tanning bed, fitness room, bike rental for €6.50/half-day, Niklaas Desparsstraat 11, a block north of Market Square, tel. 050/444-444, fax 050/444-440, www.hotel-heritage.com, info@hotel-heritage.com, run by cheery

Sleep Code

(€1 = about $1.20, country code: 32)
S = Single, **D** = Double/Twin, **T** = Triple, **Q** = Quad, **b** = bathroom, **s** = shower only. Everyone speaks English. Unless otherwise noted, credit cards are accepted.

To help you easily sort through these listings, I've divided the rooms into three categories, based on the price for a standard double room with bath:

$$$ Higher Priced—Most rooms €110 or more.
$$ Moderately Priced—Most rooms between €75–110.
$ Lower Priced—Most rooms less than €75.

and hardworking Johan and Isabelle).

$$$ Hotel Egmond is quietly located in the middle of the melancholy Minnewater. Its eight 18th-century rooms have all the comforts (Sb-€92, small twin/b-€112, Db-€120–130, Tb-€150, cash only, for longer stays, ask about their apartments a few blocks away—€210–550, Minnewater 15, tel. 050/341-445, fax 050/342-940, www.egmond.be, info@egmond.be).

$$$ Crowne Plaza Hotel Brugge is the most modern, comfortable, and central hotel option. It's just like a fancy American hotel, with 96 air-conditioned rooms (Db-€254–276, prices drop as low as €200 on weekdays and off-season, breakfast-€21, elevator, pool, Burg 10, tel. 050/446-844, fax 050/446-868, www.crowneplaza.com).

$$ Hotel Adornes is small and classy—a great value. It has 20 comfy rooms with full, modern bathrooms in a 17th-century canalside house, and offers free parking (reserve ahead of time), free loaner bikes, and a cellar lounge with games and videos (Db-€95–120 depending upon size, singles take a double for nearly the same cost, Tb-€135, Qb-€145, elevator, near Van Nevel B&B—mentioned below—and Carmersstraat at St. Annarei 26, tel. 050/341-336, fax 050/342-085, www.adornes.be, hotel.adornes@proximedia.be, Nathalie runs the family business, Britt provides a warm welcome).

$$ Hotel Patritius, family-run and centrally located, is a grand, circa-1830, neoclassical mansion with 16 stately rooms, a plush lounge and breakfast room, and a courtyard garden (small Db-€85, Db-€90–110, Tb-€130, free parking, Riddersstraat 11, tel. 050/338-454, fax 050/339-634, www.hotelpatritius.be, hotel.patritius@proximedia.be, Garrett and Elvi Spaey).

$$ Hotel Botaniek has three stars, a box of chocolates in each of its nine rooms, and a quiet location a block from Astrid Park

Bruges Hotels

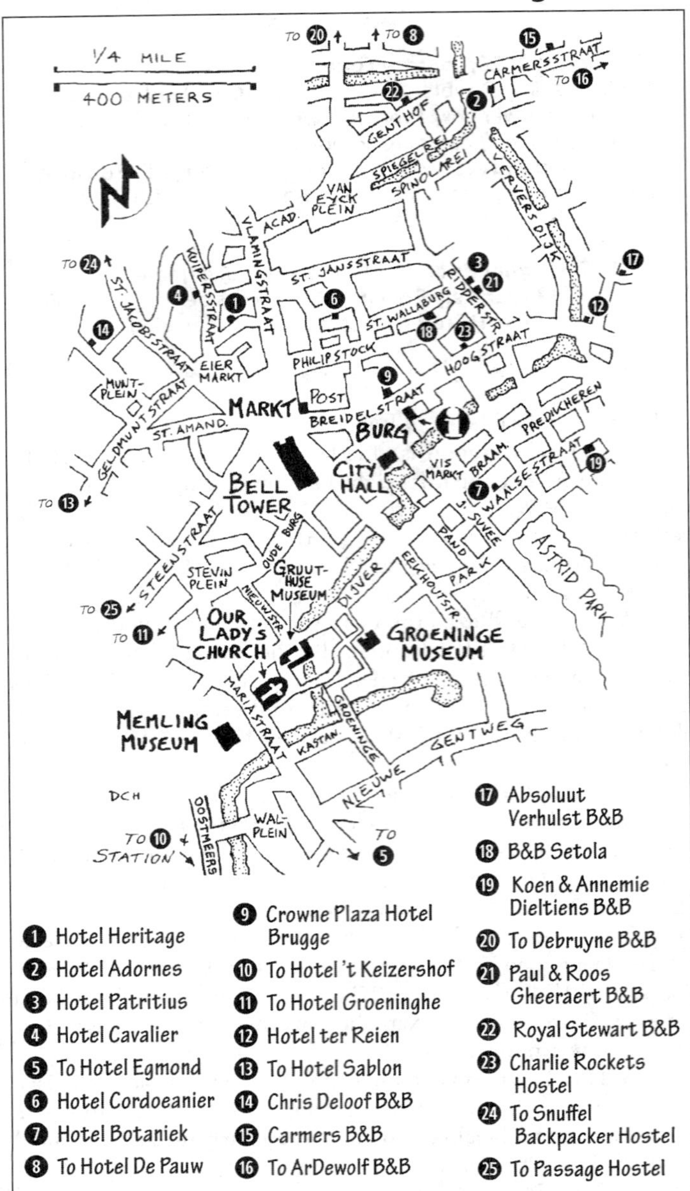

(Db-€93–97, Tb-€106, Qb-€115, more for 1-night stays, free boat ride for 3-night stays, 8 percent discount for 4-night stays, elevator, Waalsestraat 23, tel. 050/341-424, fax 050/345-939, www.botaniek .be, hotel.botaniek@pi.be).

$$ Hotel Groeninghe has eight charming, Old World rooms in a good location close to 't Zand. It's run by friendly Laurence (Sb-€70, Db-€85, Tb-€110, no elevator, Korte Vulderstraat 29, tel. 050/343-255, fax 050/340-769, www.hotelgroeninghe.be, hotelgroeninghe@pandora.be)

If you're in a jam, you might try these larger, well-located hotels of lesser value: **$$ Hotel ter Reien** (26 rooms, Sb-€75, Db-€80–120, Langestraat 1, tel. 050/349-100, hotel.ter.reien@online .be) and **$$$ Hotel Sablon** (the "oldest hotel in town," with 36 rooms, Sb-€89, Db-€110–120, Tb-€126, Noordzandstraat 21, tel. 050/333-902, info@sablon.be).

$ Hotel Cavalier, which has more stairs than character, rents eight decent rooms and serves a hearty buffet breakfast in a royal setting (Sb-€50–52, Db-€59–64, Tb-€73–78, Qb-€80–85, 2 lofty "backpackers' doubles" on 4th floor-€42 or €47, Kuipersstraat 25, tel. 050/330-207, fax 050/347-199, hotel.cavalier@skynet.be, run by friendly Viviane de Clerck).

$ Hotel Cordoeanier, a family-run place, rents 22 bright, simple, modern rooms on a quiet street two blocks off Market Square (Sb-€59–69, Db-€65–80, Tb-€75–85, Qb-€88–90, Quint/b-€101, higher prices are for bigger rooms, small groups should ask about "holiday house" across the street, Internet access, Cordoeanierstraat 16–18, tel. 050/339-051, fax 050/346-111, www.cordoeanier.be, info@cordoeanier.be, Kris, Veerle, Guy, and family).

$ Hotel de Pauw is tall, skinny, and family-run, with straightforward rooms, on a quiet street across from a church (Sb-€60, Db-€65–68, renovated Db-€75, free and easy street parking or pay garage, Sint Gilliskerkhof 8, tel. 050/337-118, fax 050/345-140, www.hoteldepauw.be, info@hoteldepauw.be, Philippe and Hilde).

Near the Train Station: **$ Hotel 't Keizershof** is a dollhouse of a hotel that lives by its motto, "Spend a night, not a fortune." It's simple and tidy, with seven small, cheery, old-time rooms split between two floors, with a shower and toilet on each (S-€25, D-€40, T-€62, Q-€72, cash only, free and easy parking, laundry service-€7.50, Oostmeers 126, a block in front of station, tel. 050/338-728, http://users.belgacom.net/hotel.keizershof, hotel. keizershof@belgacom.net, Stefaan and Hilde).

Bed-and-Breakfasts

These places, run by people who enjoy their work, offer a better value than hotels. Each is central, with lots of stairs and two or three doubles you'd pay €100 for in a hotel. Parking is generally easy on the street (pay 9:00–19:00, free overnight).

$$ Absoluut Verhulst is a great, modern-feeling B&B in a 400-year-old house, run by friendly Frieda and Benno (Sb-€50, Db-€75, huge and lofty suite-€95 for 2, €115 for 3, and €140 for 4, 1-night stays pay €10 extra per room, cash only, 5-min walk east of Market Square at Verbrand Nieuwland 1, tel. & fax 050/334-515, www.b-bverhulst.com, b-b.verhulst@pandora.be).

$ B&B Setola, run by Lut and Bruno Setola, offers three modern rooms and a spacious breakfast/living room in their house (Sb-€55, Db-€60, Tb-€80, 1-night stay is €10 extra per room, cash only, non-smoking, 6-min walk from Market Square, Sint Walburgastraat 12, tel. 050/334-977, fax 050/332-551, www.bedandbreakfast-bruges.com, setola@bedandbreakfast-bruges.com).

$ Koen and Annemie Dieltiens are a friendly couple who enjoy getting to know their guests while sharing a wealth of information on Bruges. You'll eat a hearty breakfast around a big table in their bright, comfortable house (Sb-€55, Db-€60, Tb-€80, 1-night stays pay €10 extra per room, cash only, non-smoking, tea and coffee facilities in room, Waalse Straat 40, 3 blocks southeast of Burg Square, tel. 050/334-294, fax 050/335-230, www.bedandbreakfastbruges.be, dieltiens@bedandbreakfastbruges.be). The Dieltiens also rent a cozy studio and apartment for 2–6 people in a nearby 17th-century house (2 people pay €375 per week for studio, €455 per week for apartment, prices higher for shorter stays and more people, 20 percent cheaper off-season).

$ Debruyne B&B, run by Marie-Rose and her architect husband, Ronny, offers artsy, original decor (check out the elephant-sized doors—Ronny's design) and genuine warmth. If Gothic is getting old, this is refreshingly modern (Sb-€55, Db-€60, Tb-€80, 1-night stay is €10 extra per room, cash only, non-smoking, free Internet, 7-min walk north of Market Square, Lange Raamstraat 18, tel. 050/347-606, fax 050/340-285, www.bedandbreakfastbruges.com, marie.debruyne@advalvas.be).

$ Paul and Roos Gheeraert live on the first floor, while their guests take the second. This neoclassical mansion with big, bright, comfy rooms is another fine value (Sb-€55, Db-€60, Tb-€80, cash only, strictly non-smoking; rooms have coffeemakers, TVs, and fridges; Riddersstraat 9, 4-min walk east of Market Square, tel. 050/335-627, fax 050/345-201, http://users.skynet.be/brugge-gheeraert, gheeraert.brugge@skynet.be). They also rent three modern, fully equipped apartments and a large loft nearby (Db-€60–80 for 2, third person-€10, 3-night minimum).

$ Chris Deloof's big, homey rooms are a good bet in the old center. Check out the fun, lofty A-frame room upstairs (Sb-€50, Ds/Db-€55, Tb-€70, pleasant breakfast room and a royal lounge, cash only, non-smoking, Geerwiynstraat 14, tel. 050/340-544, fax

050/343-721, www.sin.be/chrisdeloof, chris.deloof@pi.be). Chris also rents a nearby apartment (Qb-€70–80) and a holiday house for a family or group of up to five (€100–150).

$ The **Carmers B&B,** owned by the Van Nevel family, rents three attractive top-floor rooms with built-in beds in a 16th-century house (D-€50–53, Db-€60, third person-€17, cash only, non-smoking, 10-min walk from Market Square, or bus #4 or #8 from train station or Market Square to Carmersbridge, Carmersstraat 13, tel. 050/346-860, fax 050/347-616, www.brugesbb.com, robert.vannevel@advalvas.be). Robert, who works at the Memling Museum, enthusiastically shares the culture and history of Bruges with his guests.

$ ArDewolf's B&B is a family-friendly place warmly run by Nicole and Arnold in a stately, quiet neighborhood at the edge of the old town, near the windmills and moat (S-€35, D-€40, T-€60, Q-€70, Quint-€80, cash only, Oostproosse 9, tel. 050/338-366, www.ardewolf.be, ardewolf@pi.be). From the train station, take bus #4 to Sasplein. Walk to the path behind the first windmill and turn left on Oostproosse.

$ Royal Stewart B&B, run by Scottish Maggie and her husband, Gilbert, has three thoughtfully decorated rooms in a 17th-century house that was inhabited by nuns until 1953 (S-€35, D/Db-€57, cash only, pleasant breakfast rooms, non-smoking, Genthof 25-27, 5-min walk from Market Square, tel. & fax 050/337-918, r.stewart@pandora.be).

Hostels

Bruges has several good hostels offering beds for around €10–12 in two- to eight-bed rooms (singles go for about €15). Breakfast is about €3 extra. The American-style **Charlie Rockets** bar and hostel is the liveliest and most central (75 beds, €14.50 per bed, 2–6 per room, cash only, Hoogstraat 19, tel. 050/330-660, fax 050/343-630, www.charlierockets.com). The **Snuffel Backpacker Hostel** (€13–17, Ezelstraat 47, tel. 050/333-133, www.snuffel.be) and the funky **Passage** (€12, 4–7 per room, Dweerstraat 26, tel. 050/340-232; its hotel next door rents €25 singles, €40 doubles, www.passagebruges.com) are both small, loose, and central.

EATING

Bruges' specialties include mussels cooked a variety of ways (one order can feed two), fish dishes, grilled meats, and french fries. Don't eat before 19:30 unless you like eating alone. Tax and service are always included.

You'll find plenty of affordable, touristy restaurants on floodlit squares and along dreamy canals. Bruges feeds 3.5 million tourists

Bruges Restaurants

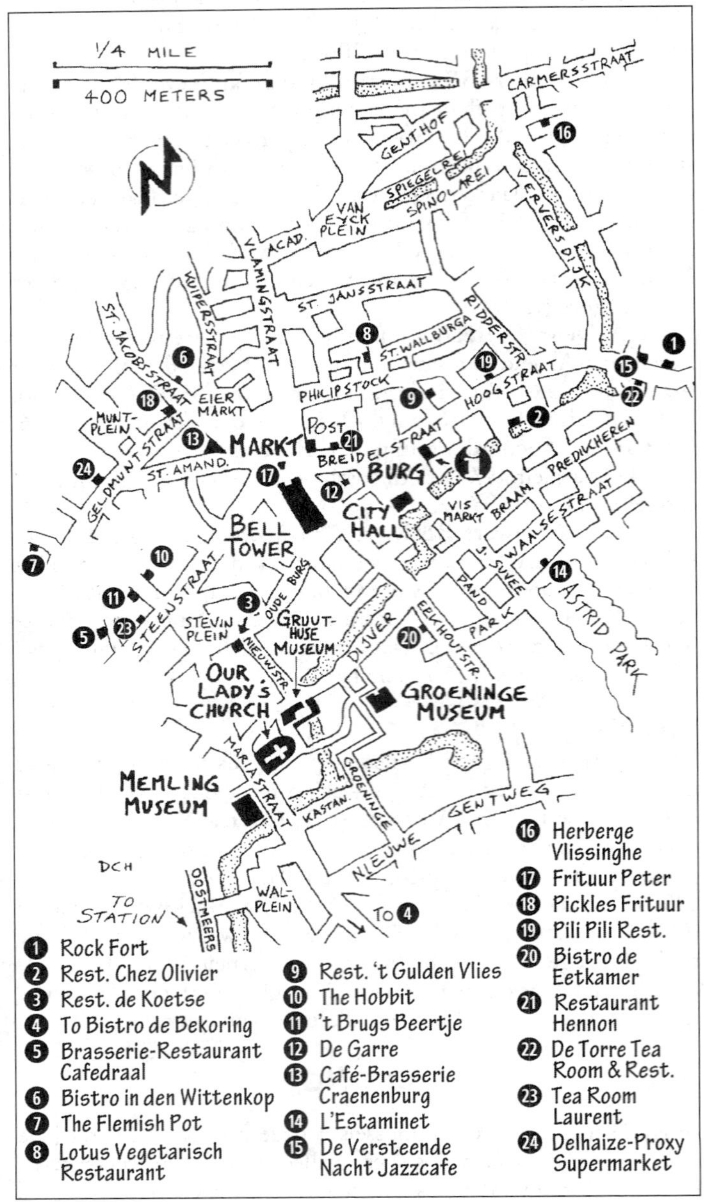

a year, and most are seduced by a high-profile location. These can be fine experiences for the magical setting and views, but the quality of food and service is low. I wouldn't blame you for eating at one of these places, but I won't recommend any. I prefer the candle-cool bistros that flicker on back streets.

Rock Fort is a chic, eight-table spot with a modern, fresh coziness and a high-powered respect for good food. Two young chefs, Peter and Hermes, give their French cuisine a creative twist. After just a few months in business, they became the talk of the town (€10 Tue–Fri lunch special with coffee, €15–20 beautifully presented dinner plates, Tue–Sat 12:00–14:30 & 18:00–23:00, closed Sun–Mon, great pastas and salads, reservations smart for dinner, Langestraat 15, tel. 050/334-113). They plan to open a tapas restaurant next door.

Restaurant Chez Olivier, with 10 classy, white-tableclothed tables, is considered the best fancy French cuisine splurge in town. While delicate Anne serves, her French husband, Olivier, is busy cooking up whatever he found freshest that day. While you can order à la carte, it's wise to go with the recommended daily *menu* (€34 for 3-course lunch, €45 for 3-course dinner, €55 for 4-course dinner, wine adds €15–20, Mon–Wed and Fri–Sat 12:00–13:30 & 19:00–21:30, closed Sun and Thu, reserve for dinner, Meestraat 9, tel. 050/333-659).

De Torre, a tea room and restaurant, has a fresh interior and a canalside terrace (€6–12 lunches, €20–33 dinners, Thu–Mon 10:00–22:00, closed Tue–Wed, Langestraat 8, tel. 050/342-946).

Pili Pili is a pasta place where Reinout and Tom prepare and serve dishes at very reasonable prices (€8.50 lunch plate with drink, €12.50 dinner, Thu–Tue 12:00–14:30 & 18:00–22:30, closed Sun afternoon and Wed, Hoogstraat 17, tel 050/491-149).

Restaurant de Koetse is a good bet for central, affordable, quality, local-style food. The feeling is traditional, yet fun and kid-friendly. The cuisine is Belgian and French, with a stress on grilled meat, seafood, and mussels (€27 3-course meals, €20 plates include vegetables and a salad, Fri–Wed 12:00–15:00 & 18:00–22:00, closed Thu, smoke-free section, wheelchair-accessible, Oude Burg 31, tel. 050/337-680).

Bistro de Eetkamer (the Living Room) has eight intimate tables and offers stay-awhile elegance, uppity service, and fine French/Italian cuisine—but only to those with a reservation (€42 fine 4-course *menu,* Thu–Mon 12:00–14:00 & 18:30–22:00, closed Tue–Wed, just south of Market Square, Eekhout 6, tel. 050/337-886).

Bistro de Bekoring, cute, candlelit, and Gothic, is tucked within two almshouses that were joined together. Rotund and friendly Chef Roland and his wife, Gerda, love serving traditional Flemish food from a small menu (€12 weekday lunch, €32 dinners,

Wed–Sat from 12:00 and from 18:30, closed Sun for dinner and all day Tue, out past Begijnhof at Arsenaalstraat 53, tel. 050/344-157).

Brasserie-Restaurant Cafedraal is boisterous and fun-loving, serving a local crowd good-quality, modern European cuisine, with an accent on French and fish. The high-ceilinged room is rustic but elegantly candlelit (€12 2-course lunches, €24 dinner plates, Mon–Sat 12:00–15:00 & 18:00–23:00, closed Sun, outdoor seating, Zilverstraat 38, tel. 050/340-845).

Bistro in den Wittenkop, very Flemish, is a cluttered, laid-back, old-time place specializing in the beer-soaked equivalent of beef bourguignon (€16–20 main courses, Tue–Sat 12:00–14:00 & 18:00–24:00, closed Sun–Mon, terrace in back, Sint Jakobsstraat 14, tel. 050/332-059).

The Flemish Pot (a.k.a. The Little Pancake House) is a cute restaurant serving delicious, inexpensive pancake meals (savory and sweet) and homemade *wafels* for lunch. Then, at 18:00, enthusiastic chefs Mario and Rik stow their waffle irons and pull out a traditional menu of vintage Flemish plates (€9–16.50 dinner menu, daily 10:00–22:00, just off Geldmuntstraat at Helmstraat 3, tel. 050/340-086).

Lotus Vegetarisch Restaurant serves good vegetarian lunch plates (€9 *plat du jour* offered daily), salads, and homemade chocolate cake in a smoke-free, pastel-elegant setting without a trace of tie-dye (Mon–Sat 11:45–14:00, closed Sun, just off Burg at Wapenmakersstraat 5, tel. 050/331-078).

Restaurant 't Gulden Vlies—romantic and candlelit, quiet and less "ye olde" than the other restaurants—serves when the others are closed. The menu is Belgian and French, with an imaginative flair (€14–18.50 plates, €16 3-course *menu*, €25 monthly menu, Wed–Sun 19:00–03:00, closed Mon–Tue, July open only Fri–Sun, Mallebergplaats 17, tel. 050/334-709).

The Hobbit is a popular grill house across the street from the recommended bar 't Brugs Beertje (see below). It features an entertaining menu, including all-you-can-eat spareribs with salad for €13—nothing fancy, just good, basic food in a fun, traditional setting (daily 18:00–24:00, Kemelstraat 8-10, tel. 050/335-520).

Bars Offering Light Meals, Beer, and Ambience

Stop into one of the city's atmospheric bars for a light meal or a drink with great Bruges ambience.

Any pub or restaurant carries the basic beers, but for a selection of more than 300 types, including brews to suit any season, drink at **'t Brugs Beertje.** For a light meal, consider their traditional cheese plate (Thu–Tue 16:00–24:00, closed Wed, Kemelstraat 5, tel. 050/339-616).

At **De Garre,** you can gain an appreciation of the Belgian beer culture. Rather than a noisy pub scene, it has a dressy, sit-down-and-focus-on-your-friend-and-the-fine-beer vibe (huge selection, daily 12:00–24:00, off Breidelstraat between Burg and Markt, on tiny Garre alley, tel. 050/341-029).

Café-Brasserie Craenenburg is one of the very few decent cafés on Markt Square, good for a coffee or beer in a historic setting (daily 8:00–23:00, Markt 16, tel. 050/333-402).

L'Estaminet is a youthful, jazz-filled eatery. Away from the tourists, it's popular with local students, who come for hearty €7 spaghetti (Tue–Sun 11:30–24:00, closed Mon, facing peaceful Astrid Park at Park 5, tel. 050/330-916).

De Versteende Nacht Jazzcafe is another youthful hang-out, serving tapas and cocktails on Langestraat 11 (€6–11 meals, Mon–Sat 19:00–24:00, closed Sun, live jazz on Wed from 21:00, tel. 050/343-293).

Herberge Vlissinghe, the oldest pub in town (1515), has hot snacks and a great atmosphere (Wed–Sun open from 11:00 on, closed Mon–Tue, Blekersstraat 2, tel. 050/343-737).

Fries, Fast Food, and Picnics

Local french fries *(frites)* are a treat. Proud and traditional *frituurs* serve tubs of fries and various local-style shish kebabs. Belgians dip their *frites* in mayonnaise, but ketchup is there for the Yankees (along with spicier sauces). For a quick, cheap, and scenic meal, hit a *frituur* and sit on the steps or benches overlooking Market Square, about 50 yards past the post office. The best fries in town are from **Frituur Peter**—twin take-away carts on the Market Square at the base of the bell tower (daily 10:00–24:00).

Pickles Frituur, a block off Market Square, is handy for sit-down fries. Its forte is greasy, fast, deep-fried Flemish corn dogs. The "menu 2" comes with three traditional gut bombs (Mon–Sat 11:30–24:00, closed Sun, at the corner of Geldmuntstraat and Sint Jakobstraat, tel. 050/337-957).

Delhaize-Proxy Supermarket is ideal for picnics (push-button produce pricer lets you buy as little as one mushroom, Mon–Sat 9:00–19:00, closed Sun, 3 blocks off the Market Square on Geldmuntstraat). For midnight munchies, you'll find Indian-run corner grocery stores.

Belgian Waffles

While Americans think of "Belgian" waffles for breakfast, the Belgians (who don't eat waffles or pancakes for breakfast) think of *wafels* as Liège-style (dense, sweet, eaten plain, and heated) and Brussels-style (lighter, often with powdered sugar or whipped cream and fruit, served in teahouses only in the afternoons from

14:00–18:00). You'll see waffles sold at restaurants and take-away stands.

For the best €1.50 Liège-style *wafels,* stop by **Restaurant Hennon**—their waffles and other dishes are made with fresh ingredients (€2.50–6 plates, closed Mon, between Market Square and Burg at Breidelstraat 16). You can also try **Tea Room Laurent** for waffles and pancakes (€4–8 plates, Steenstraat 79) and the **Flemish Pot** (listed above).

TRANSPORTATION CONNECTIONS

Trains

From Bruges by Train to: Brussels (2/hr, usually at :34 and :57, 1 hr, €10), **Ghent** (2/hr, 40 min), **Ostende** (3/hr, 15 min), **Köln** (6/day, 3.5 hrs), **Paris** (hrly via Brussels, 2.5 hrs, must pay supplement of €11 second class, €21 first class—even with a railpass), **Amsterdam** (hrly, 3.5 hrs, transfer in Antwerp or Brussels), **Amsterdam's Schiphol Airport** (hrly, 3.5 hrs, transfer in Antwerp or Brussels, €35). Train info: tel. 050/302-424.

By Eurostar to/from London: Bruges is an ideal "Welcome to Europe" stop after London. The Eurostar train connects Brussels and London within 2.5 hours (9/day). Take the Eurostar from London to Brussels, then transfer to Bruges (2/hr, 1 hr, entire trip is covered by same Eurostar ticket).

In 2005, full-fare one-way tickets cost $255 for second class and $375 for first class (full-fare tickets are exchangeable and fully refundable, even after your departure date). The cheaper second-class "Leisure" rates start at $90 one-way for midday, midweek travel (no refund or exchange). Railpass-holders get discounts ($75 one-way for second-class, $135 one-way for first-class). Seat availability is limited for each fare type. To find out the latest prices or to book a ticket, call U.S. tel. 800/EUROSTAR or visit www.ricksteves.com/eurostar or www.eurostar.com.

To order your Eurostar ticket in Belgium by phone, call 0900-10177 (expensive toll line costs €0.50/min from pay phone and €1.50/min from hotel); you can either pay with a credit card or simply reserve a seat and pay at the station at least an hour before the train leaves. You can buy a ticket in Belgium at major train stations (you'll get your ticket on the spot) or travel agencies (though most can't deliver until the next day). You can also purchase your ticket at any major train station in Europe.

PRAGUE

(Praha)

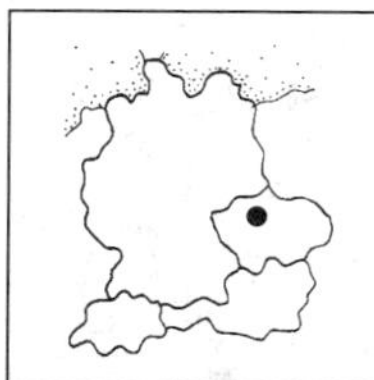

It's amazing what a decade and a half of freedom can do. Prague has always been historic. Now it's fun, too. No place in Europe has become so popular so quickly. And for good reason: Prague—the only Central European capital to escape the bombs of the last century's wars—is one of Europe's best-preserved cities. It's filled with sumptuous Art Nouveau facades, offers tons of cheap Mozart and Vivaldi, and brews the best beer in Europe. But even beyond its architecture and traditional culture, it's an explosion of pent-up entrepreneurial energy jumping for joy after 40 years of communist rule. Its low prices can cause you to jump for joy, too. Travel in Prague is like travel in Western Europe—15 years ago and for half the price.

Planning Your Time

Prague demands a minimum of two full days (with 3 nights, or 2 nights and a night train). From Munich, Berlin, and Vienna, it's about a six-hour train ride (you can also take a longer night train from Munich). From Budapest, Warsaw, or Kraków, it's a handy night train.

With two days in Prague, I'd spend a morning seeing the castle and a morning in the Jewish Quarter. Use your afternoons for loitering around the Old Town, Charles Bridge, and the Little Quarter, and split your nights between beer halls and live music. Keep in mind that Jewish sights close on Saturday.

Prague

M = METRO STN.
1/4 MILE
400 METERS
HRADČANY
PRAGUE CASTLE
MALÁ STRANA
STARÉ MĚSTO
NOVÉ MĚSTO
JOSEFOV
VLTAVA RIVER
PETŘÍN PARK
FUNICULAR
KAMPA ISLAND
CHARLES BRIDGE
KARLŮV MOST
OLD TOWN SQUARE
JEWISH CEM.
MUNICIPAL HOUSE
(OBECNÍ DŮM)
POWDER TOWER
MUCHA MUS.
MAIN POST
WENCESLAS SQUARE
VÁCLAVSKÉ NÁMĚSTÍ
MAIN TRAIN STN.
(HLAVNÍ NÁDRAŽÍ)
NATIONAL MUSEUM
MUZEUM
R.F.E.
PRAGUE MUNICIPAL MUSEUM
FLORENC
BUS STATION
NAT'L. THEATRE
TO DANCING HOUSE + VYŠEHRAD
TESCO
NÁRODNÍ TŘÍDA
MŮSTEK
STAROMĚSTSKÁ
MALOSTRANSKÁ
MALOSTRANSKÉ NÁM.
STARÉ ZÁMECKÉ SCHODY (STEPS)
ZÁMECKÉ SCHODY (STEPS)
HRAD. NÁM.
LORETA
STRAHOV MONASTERY
NAM REPUBLIKY
STARO. NÁM.
JANA PAL.
KAPROVA
KARLOVA
CELETNÁ
HYBERNSKÁ
NA PŘÍKOPĚ
NA POŘÍČÍ
PAŘÍŽSKÁ
ŽELEZNÁ
MELANTRICHOVA
MARTINSKÁ
BETLÉMSKÁ
NÁRODNÍ
SMETANOVO
MOST LEGIÍ
ÚJEZD
KARMELITSKÁ
MOSTECKÁ
LETENSKÁ
LETNA PARK
VALDŠTEJNSKÁ
NERUDOVA
ÚVOZ
VLAŠSKÁ
TRŽIŠTĚ
ST. NICH.
CHOTKOVA
MARIÁNSKÉ HRADBY
JELENÍ
MÁNESŮV MOST
ČECHŮV MOST
ŠTEFÁNIKŮV MOST
NA FRANTIŠKU
REVOLUČNÍ
WILSONOVA
OPLETALOVA
JERUZ.
RŮŽOVÁ
PANSKÁ
JINDŘIŠSKÁ
KŘIŽ.
DCH

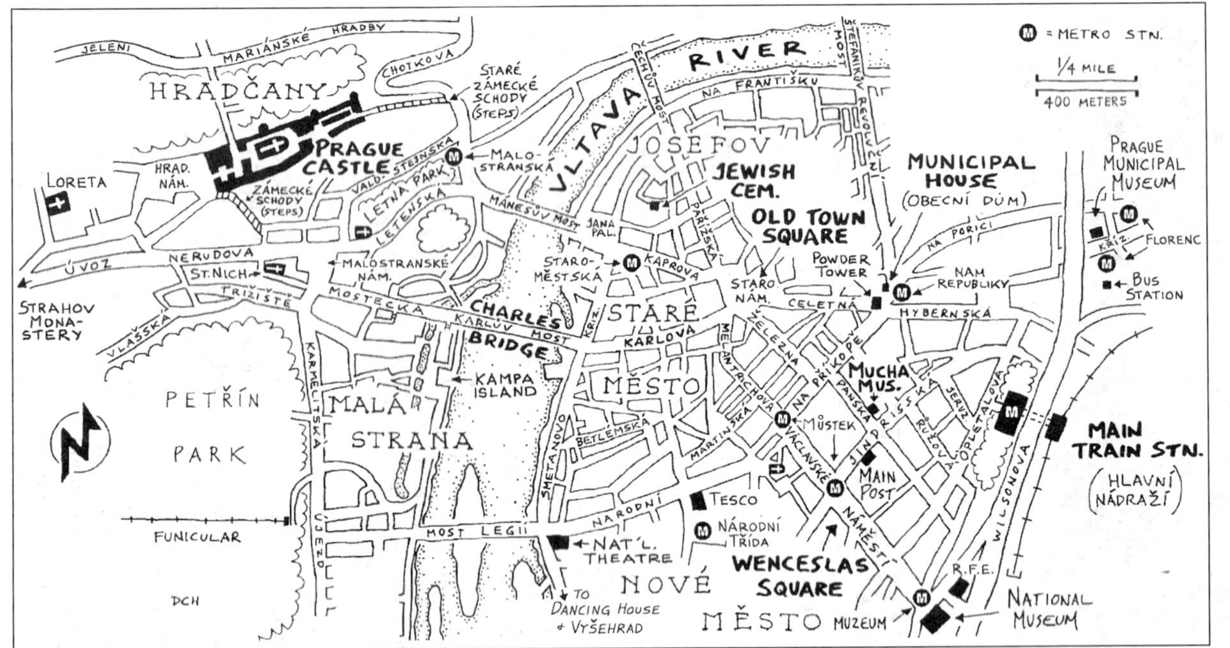

Prague Landmarks

English	Czech	Pronounced
Main Train Station	**Hlavní Nádraží**	hlav-nee nah-drah-zhee
Old Town	**Staré Město**	stah-reh myehs-toh
Old Town Square	**Staroměstské Náměstí**	star-roh-myehst-skeh nah-myehs-tee
New Town	**Nové Město**	noh-vay myehs-toh
Little Quarter	**Malá Strana**	mah-lah strah-nah
Jewish Quarter	**Josefov**	yoo-zehf-fohf
Castle Quarter	**Hradčany**	hrad-chah-nee
Charles Bridge	**Karlův Most**	kar-loov most
Wenceslas Square	**Václavske Náměstí**	vaht-slahf-skeh nah-myehs-tee
The River	**Vltava**	vul-tah-vah

ORIENTATION

Prague unnerves many travelers—it's behind the former Iron Curtain, and you've heard stories of rip-offs and sky-high hotel prices (both are a real problem, but avoidable if you're smart). Despite your fears, Prague is charming, safe, and ready to show you a good time. The language barrier is tiny. It seems every well-educated young person speaks English.

Locals call their town "Praha." It's big, with 1.2 million people, but focus on its relatively compact old center during a quick visit. As you wander, take advantage of brown street signs directing you to tourist landmarks.

The Vltava River divides the west side (castle and Little Quarter) from the east side (train station, Old Town, New Town, and most of the recommended hotels). Prague addresses come with references to a general zone. Praha 1 is in the old center on either side of the river. Praha 2 is in the new city, southeast of Wenceslas Square. Praha 3 and higher indicate a location farther from the center.

Tourist Information

TIs are at four key locations: **main train station** (roughly Easter–Oct Mon–Fri 9:00–19:00, Sat–Sun 9:00–16:00, but often closed; Nov–Easter Mon–Fri 9:00–18:00, Sat 9:00–15:00, closed Sun), **Old Town Square** (Easter–Oct Mon–Fri 9:00–19:00, Sat–Sun 9:00–18:00; Nov–Easter Mon–Fri 9:00–18:00, Sat–Sun

Rip-Offs in Prague

Prague's new freedom comes with new scams. There's no particular risk of violent crime—but green, rich tourists do get taken by con artists. Simply be on guard, particularly at these times: when traveling on trains (thieves thrive on overnight trains), changing money (tellers with bad arithmetic and inexplicable pauses while counting back your change), dealing with taxis (see "Getting Around Prague," page 167), paying in restaurants (see "Eating," page 207), and in seedy neighborhoods (see below).

Anytime you pay for something, make a careful note of how much it costs, how much you're handing over, and how much you expect back. Count your change. Someone selling you a phone card marked 190 Kč might first tell you it's 790 Kč, hoping to pocket the difference. Call the bluff, and they'll pretend it never happened.

Plainclothes policemen "looking for counterfeit money" are con artists. Don't show them any cash or your wallet. If you're threatened with an inexplicable fine by a "policeman," conductor, or other official, you can walk away, scare him away by saying you'll need a receipt (which real officials are legally required to provide), or ask a passerby if the fine is legit. On the other hand, do not ignore the plainclothes inspectors on the Metro and trams who have shown you their badge.

Pickpockets can be little children, or adults dressed as professionals or even as tourists. They target Western visitors. Many thieves drape jackets over their arms to disguise busy fingers. Thieves work the crowded and touristy places in teams. They use mobile phones to coordinate their bumps and grinds. Be careful if anyone creates a commotion at the door of a Metro or tram car (especially around the Národní and Vodičkova tram stops, or on the made-for-tourists trams #22 and #23)—it's a smokescreen for theft. Car theft is also a big problem in Prague (many Western European car-rental companies don't allow their rentals to cross the Czech border). Never leave anything valuable in your car—not even in broad daylight on a busy street. The sex clubs on Skořepka Steet, just south of Havelská Market, routinely rip off naive tourists and can be dangerous. They're filled mostly with Russian girls and German and Asian guys. Lately, this district has become the rage for British "stag" parties (happy to take cheap off-season flights to get to cheap beer and cheap girls). Be warned: Even on the street, aggressive girls can be all over gawkers.

This all sounds intimidating. But Prague is safe. It has its share of petty thieves and con artists, but very little violent crime. Don't be scared—just be alert.

9:00–17:00, tel. 224-482-018), below **Wenceslas Square** at Na Příkopě 20 (Easter–Oct Mon–Fri 9:00–19:00, Sat–Sun 9:00–17:00; Nov–Easter Mon–Fri 9:00–18:00, Sat 9:00–15:00, closed Sun, tel. 224-226-087), and the castle side of **Charles Bridge** (Easter–Oct daily 10:00–18:00, closed Nov–Easter). For general tourist information in English, dial 12444 (Mon–Fri 8:00–19:00).

The TIs offer maps, phone cards, information on guided walks and bus tours, and bookings for concerts, hotel rooms, and rooms in private homes. There are several monthly events guides—all of them packed with ads—including *Prague Guide* (29 Kč), *Prague This Month* (free), and *Heart of Europe* (free, summer only).

The English-language weekly *Prague Post* newspaper is handy for entertainment listings and current events (sold cheap at newsstands). The Prague Information Service's useful Web site is www.pis.cz.

Arrival in Prague

Upon arrival, be sure to buy a city map, with trams and Metro lines marked and tiny sketches of the sights for ease in navigating (30–70 Kč, many different brands, sold at kiosks, exchange windows, and tobacco stands). It's a mistake to try doing Prague without a good map—you'll refer to it constantly.

By Train: Most travelers coming from and going to major international destinations—as well as trains to and from Český Krumlov and some other Czech towns—use the main station, Hlavní Nádraží. Other trains use the secondary station, Nádraží Holešovice. (For information on getting to Prague, see "Transportation Connections," page 214.)

Upon arrival, get money. The stations have ATMs (best rates) and exchange bureaus (rates are generally bad, but can vary—compare by asking at 2 windows what you'll get for $100, but keep in mind that many of the windows are run by the same company). Then buy your map and confirm your departure plans. Consider arranging a room or tour through the AVE travel agency (branches in both stations—see "Sleeping," page 200). Anyone arriving on an international train will be met at the tracks by room hustlers, trying to snare tourists for cheap rooms.

Main Station (Hlavní Nádraží): This station's low-ceilinged hall contains a fascinating mix of travelers, kiosks, gamblers, loitering teenagers, and older riffraff. The creepy station ambience is the work of communist architects, who expanded a classy building to make it just big, painting it the compulsory dreary gray with reddish trim. An ATM is near the subway entrance. The station's left-luggage counter is reportedly safer than the lockers. The Wasteels office can help you figure out train connections, and sells cheap phone cards and tickets for anywhere in Europe (no commission;

Mon–Fri 9:00–17:00, Sat 9:00–16:00, closed Sun, tel. 224-641-954, www.wasteels.cz). The information office for Czech Railways (downstairs on the left) is less helpful, and the ticket windows downstairs don't give schedule information.

If you're killing time here (or you'd like a wistful glimpse of a more genteel age), go upstairs into the Art Nouveau hall. The station was originally named for Emperor Franz Josef. Later, it was named for President Woodrow Wilson, because his promotion of self-determination led to the creation of the free state of Czechoslovakia in 1918. Under the communists (who weren't big fans of Wilson), it was renamed simply the "Main Station." Here, under an elegant dome, you can sip coffee, enjoy music from the 1920s, watch boy prostitutes looking for work, and see new arrivals spilling into the city.

From the main station, it's a 10-minute **walk** to Wenceslas Square (turn left out of the station and follow Washingtonova to the huge National Museum, and you're there). You could instead catch **tram** #9 or, at night, tram #55 or #58; to find the stop, walk into the park in front of the station (nicknamed "Sherwood Forest," filled with thieves and homeless people at night), take a right, and walk two minutes. Or take the **Metro** (inside station, look for the red M with 2 directions: Háje or Ládví; catch a train to the Muzeum stop, then transfer to the green line—direction Dejvická—and get off at either Můstek or Staroměstská; these stops straddle the Old Town).

The train station **cabbies** are a gang of no-neck mafia thugs who will wait all day to charge an arriving tourist five times the regular rate. To get an honest cabbie, I'd walk a few blocks (or ride the Metro one stop) and hail one off the street. A taxi should get you to your hotel for no more than 200 Kč (see "Getting Around Prague," page 167); to avoid the train station taxi stand, call AAA Taxi (tel. 233-113-311).

Holešovice Station (Nádraží Holešovice): This station, slightly farther from the center, is suburban mellow. The main hall has all the services of the main station in a compact area. The friendly, little-frequented Internet café allows you to place cheap international calls through the Internet (7 Kč/min to the U.S., daily 8:00–19:30).

Outside the first glass doors, the ATM is on the left, the Czech Railways information office is on the right (daily 9:00–17:00), and the Metro is straight ahead (follow *Vstup,* which means "entrance"; take it 3 stops to the main station, 4 stops to the city-center Muzeum stop). Taxis and trams are outside to the right (allow 200 Kč for a cab to the center).

By Plane: Prague's new, tidy, low-key **Ruzyně Airport**—a delightful contrast to the old, hulking main train station—is 12

Prague's Four Towns

Until about 1800, the city was actually four distinct towns with four town squares separated by fortified walls.

Castle Quarter (Hradčany): Built regally on the hill, this was the home of the cathedral, monastery, castle, royal palace, and high nobility. Even today, you feel like clip-clopping through it in a fancy carriage. It has the high art and grand buildings, yet feels a bit sterile.

Little Quarter (Malá Strana): This Baroque town of fine homes and gardens was built by the aristocracy and merchant elite at the foot of the castle. The quarter burned in the 1500s and was rebuilt with the mansions of the generally domesticated European nobility, who moved in to be near the king. The tradition remains, as the successors of this power-brokering class—today's Parliament—now call this home.

Old Town (Staré Město): Charles Bridge connects the Little Quarter with the Old Town. A boom town in the 14th century, this has long been the busy commercial quarter—filled with merchants, guilds, and natural supporters of Jan Hus (folks who wanted a Czech stamp on their religion). Trace the walls of this town in the modern road plan (the Powder Tower is a remnant of a wall system that completed a fortified ring, half provided by the river). The marshy area closest to the bend—least inhabitable, and therefore allotted to the Jewish community—became the ghetto.

New Town (Nové Město): Nové Město rings the Old Town, cutting a swath from riverbank to riverbank, and is fortified with Prague's outer wall. In the 14th century, the king initiated the creation of this town, tripling the size of what would become Prague. Wenceslas Square was once the horse market of this busy, working-class district. When you cross the moat (Na Příkopě) that separates the Old and New Towns, you leave the tourists behind and enter the real, everyday town.

miles (about 30 min) west of the city center. The airport has ATM machines (avoid the change desks); desks promoting their transportation service (such as city transit and shuttle buses); kiosks selling city maps and phone cards; and a tourist service that has little printed material available. Airport info: tel. 220-113-314, operator tel. 220-111-111.

Getting to and from the airport is easy. You have several options:

- Dirt-cheap: Take bus #119 to the Dejvická Metro station, or #100 to the Zličín Metro station (20 min), then take the Metro into the center (12 Kč, info desk in airport arrival hall).
- Cheap: Take the Čedaz minibus shuttle to Náměstí Republiky,

across from Kotva department store (2/hr, pay 90 Kč directly to driver, info desk in arrival hall).

- Moderate: Take a Čedaz minibus directly to your hotel, with a couple of stops likely en route (360 Kč for a group of up to 4, tel. 220-114-296).
- Expensive: Catch a taxi. Cabbies wait at the curb directly in front of the arrival hall. Carefully confirm the complete price before getting in. It's a fixed rate of 600–700 Kč with no meter.

Helpful Hints

Internet Access: Internet cafés—which beg for business all along Karlova street, on the city side of the Charles Bridge—are commonplace. Consider Bohemia Bagel (see page 210).

Laundry: A full-service laundry near most of the recommended hotels is at Karolíny Světlé 10 (200 Kč/8-pound load, wash and dry in 2 hrs, Mon–Fri 7:30–19:00, closed Sat–Sun, 200 yards from Charles Bridge on Old Town side). Or surf the Internet while your undies tumble-dry at Korunní 14 (160 Kč/load wash and dry, Internet-2 Kč/min, daily 8:00–20:00, Praha 2, near Náměstí Míru Metro stop).

American Express: It's right on Wenceslas Square (foreign exchange daily 9:00–19:00; travel service Mon–Fri 9:00–18:00, Sat 9:00–12:00, closed Sun; Václavské Náměstí 56, Praha 1, tel. 222-211-136). AmEx also has offices on Celetná Street in the Old Town and on the Old Town Square.

Medical Help: A 24-hour pharmacy is at Palackého 5 (Praha 1, a block from Wenceslas Square, tel. 224-946-982). First aid and emergency medical service in the Czech Republic are free for everyone. For standard assistance, there are two state hospitals in the center: the General Hospital (open daily 24 hours, moderate wait time, U Nemocnice 2, Praha 2, use entry G, right above Karlovo Náměstí, tel. 224-962-564); and the Na Františku Hospital (go to the main entrance, Na Františku 1, on the embankment next to Hotel Intercontinental; for English assistance call Mr. Hacker between 8:00 and 14:00, tel. 222-801-278 or tel. 222-801-371, serious problems only). The reception staff may not speak English, but the doctors do.

For better-than-standard assistance in English (including dental service), consider the top-quality Hospital Na Homolce (less than 1,000 Kč for an appointment, from 8:00–16:00 call 252-922-146, after-hours emergency call 257-211-111, Roentgenova 2, Praha 5, bus #167 from Anděl Metro station).

The Canadian Medical Care Center is a small, private clinic with English-speaking Czech staff at Veleslavínská 1 in Praha 6 (tel. 235-360-133, after-hours emergency call 724-300-301, halfway between the city and the airport, 3,000 Kč for an appointment, 4,500 Kč for a home visit).

Local Help: Magic Praha is a tiny travel service run by hardworking Lída Šteflová. A charming Jill-of-all-trades who takes her clients' needs seriously, she's particularly helpful with accommodations and transfers throughout the Czech Republic, private tours, and side trips to historic towns. Lída, the best polka teacher in town, also arranges music evenings with the Prague Castle Orchestra—a fun-loving, mustachioed trio that plays a lively Czech mélange of Smetana, swing, old folk tunes, and 1920s cabaret songs (Národní 17, Praha 1, 5th floor, tel. & fax 224-230-914, tel. 224-232-755, mobile 604-207-225, www.magicpraha.cz, magicpraha@magicpraha.cz).

Athos Travel books rooms (see "Sleeping," page 200), rents cars, and has guides for hire (1–5 people-700 Kč/hr—see "Tours," page 169).

Best Views: Enjoy the "Golden City of a Hundred Spires" during the early evening, when the light is warm and the colors are rich. Good viewpoints include the terrace at the Strahov Monastery (above the castle), the top of St. Vitus Cathedral (at the castle), the top of either tower on Charles Bridge, the Old Town Square clock tower (elevator), the Restaurant u Prince terrace (see page 210), and the steps of the National Museum overlooking Wenceslas Square.

Getting Around Prague

You can walk nearly everywhere. But the Metro is slick, the trams fun, and the taxis quick and easy, once you're initiated. For details, pick up the handy transit guide at the TI.

Public Transportation: Affordable and excellent public transit is perhaps the best legacy of the communist era (locals ride all month for 275 Kč). The trams and Metro work on the same cheap tickets. Buy from machines (select ticket price, then insert coins), at kiosks, or at hotels. For convenience, buy all the tickets you think you'll need: 15-minute ticket with no transfer—8 Kč, 60-minute ticket with unlimited transfers—12 Kč, 24-hour ticket—70 Kč, three-day pass—200 Kč. Estimate conservatively. Remember, Prague is a great walking town, so unless you're commuting from a hotel far outside the center, you will likely find that individual tickets work best. The cheapo 8-Kč tickets are not good on night trams or night buses. The Metro closes at midnight, and the nighttime tram routes (identified with white numbers on blue backgrounds at tram stops) run all night in 30-minute intervals. Metro and tram tips: Navigate by signs listing end stations, and when you come to your stop, push the yellow button if the doors don't automatically open.

Prague Metro

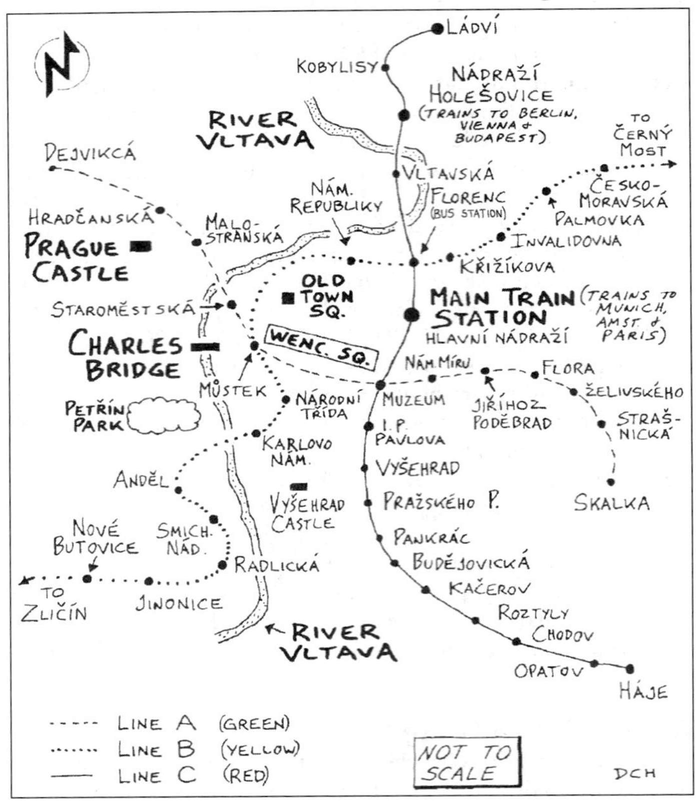

City maps show the tram, bus, and Metro lines. The three-line Metro system is handy and simple. Although it seems that all Metro doors lead to the neighborhood of Výstup, that's simply the Czech word for "exit." Trams are also easy to use; track your route with your city map. They run every five to 10 minutes in the daytime (a schedule is posted at each stop). Be sure to validate your ticket on the tram, bus, or Metro by sticking it in the machine (which stamps a time on it). There's a complete route planner at www.dp-praha.cz. Inspectors routinely ambush ticketless riders (including tourists) and fine them 400 Kč on the spot.

Taxis: Prague's taxis—notorious for hyperactive meters—are being tamed. Still, many cabbies are crooks who consider taking one sucker for a ride a good day's work. While most hotel receptionists and guidebooks advise avoiding taxis, I find Prague is a great taxi town and use them routinely. With the local rate, they're cheap (read the rates on the door: drop charge—30 Kč;

per-kilometer charge—22 Kč; and wait-time per-min charge—5 Kč). The key is to be sure the cabbie turns on the meter at the #1 tariff (look for the word *sazba,* meaning tariff, on the meter). Avoid cabs waiting at tourist attractions and train stations. Cabs labeled "AAA Taxi" and "City Taxi" are generally honest. I find that hailing a passing taxi generally gets me a fair price.

If a cabbie surprises you at the end with an astronomical fare, simply pay 200 Kč, which should cover you for a long ride anywhere in the center. Then go into your hotel. On the miniscule chance he follows you, the receptionist will take your side.

You're most likely to get a fair meter rate—which starts only when you take off—if you have a cab called from a hotel or restaurant (try AAA Taxi, tel. 233-113-311, or City Taxi, tel. 257-257-257; they're the most likely to have an English-speaking staff).

TOURS

Walking Tours—Prague Walks offers walking tours of the Old Town, the castle, the Jewish Quarter, and more (250–300 Kč, 90 min-3 hrs, tel. 261-214-603, mobile 723-262-980, www.praguewalks.com, pwalks@comp.cz). Consider their clever Good Morning Walk, which starts at 8:00 (April–Aug only), before the crowds hit. Several other companies offer good guided walks. For the latest, pick up the walking tour fliers at the TI.

Private Guides—Hiring your own personal guide can be an exceptional value in Prague, especially if you're traveling in a group. Guides meet you where you like and tailor the tour to your interests.

Šárka Pelantová, a wonderful young philosophy grad from a nearby town, runs "Personal Prague Guide" service. She expertly gets beyond the dates and famous buildings to provide insight into her culture, and is eager to build a walk around your interests (€13/hr, mobile 777-225-205, www.prague-guide.info, saraguide@volny.cz).

Katka Svobodová—a hardworking guide who knows her stuff and speaks excellent English—enjoys showing individuals and small groups around (400 Kč or €13 per hour, minimum 3 hrs, tel. 224-818-267, mobile 603-181-300, www.praguewalker.com, katerina@praguewalker.com).

Athos Travel's licensed guides can lead you on a general sightseeing tour or fit the walk to your interests: music, Art Nouveau, Jewish life, architecture, Franz Kafka, and more (1–5 people-700 Kč/hr, more than 5 people-800 Kč/hr, arrange tour at least 24 hrs in advance, tel. 241-440-571, info@athos.cz).

To get beyond Prague, call **Thomas Zahn,** who runs Pathways Guided Travel. Thomas, an American who married into the Czech Republic, specializes in helping Americans of Czech descent find

Prague at a Glance

▲▲▲**Old Town Square** Colorful, magical main square of Old World Prague, with fanciful, medieval clock tower (listed below). **Hours:** Always open.

▲▲▲**Charles Bridge** Atmospheric, statue-lined bridge connecting the Old Town to the castle. **Hours:** Always open.

▲▲▲**St. Vitus Cathedral** The Czech Republic's most important church, featuring a climbable tower and a striking stained-glass window by Art Nouveau artist Alfons Mucha. **Hours:** April–Oct daily except Sunday morning, 9:00–17:00, Nov–March until 16:00.

▲▲▲**Jewish Quarter** The best Jewish sight in Europe, featuring various synagogues and an evocative cemetery. **Hours:** Sun–Fri 9:00–18:00, closed Sat.

▲▲**Prague Castle** Traditional seat of Czech rulers, with St. Vitus Cathedral (see above), Old Royal Palace, Basilica of St. George, shop-lined Golden Lane, and fun toy museum (see below). **Hours:** April–Oct daily 9:00–17:00, Nov–March daily 9:00–16:00. Castle grounds: Daily 5:00–24:00.

▲▲**Mucha Museum** Likeable collection of Art Nouveau works by Czech artist Alfons Mucha. **Hours:** Daily 10:00–18:00.

▲▲**Wenceslas Square** Lively boulevard at the heart of modern Prague. **Hours:** Always open.

▲**Old Town Hall Astronomical Clock** Intricate landmark clock attracting throngs of gawking tourists. **Hours:** Always viewable; clock strikes daily on the hour 8:00–21:00, until 20:00 in winter.

▲**Strahov Monastery and Library** Baroque center of learning with ornate reading rooms and old-fashioned science exhibits. **Hours:** Daily 9:00–12:00 & 13:00–17:00.

▲**Havelská Market** Bustling open-air market, perfect for gathering a picnic. **Hours:** Daily 9:00–18:00.

▲**Toy and Barbie Museum** Teddy bears through the centuries, plus a whole floor of Barbies. **Hours:** Daily 9:30–17:30.

▲**Museum of Communism** The rise and fall of the regime, from start to Velvet finish. **Hours:** Daily 9:00–21:00.

their roots. He also organizes and leads creative, affordable (mostly 1-day and 2-day) excursions from Prague. Hiking, biking, horseback riding, or canoeing, you'll explore the unknown charms of the region with a small group and a committed guide. Explore Thomas' Web site for ways to connect with the rural Czech countryside and experience more than Prague on your visit (tel. 257-940-113, mobile 603-758-983, www.pathfinders.cz).

The **TI** also has plenty of private guides (for 3 hours: 1 person-1,200 Kč, 2 people-1,400 Kč, 3 people-1,600 Kč, 4 people-2,000 Kč, desk at Old Town Square TI, arrange and pay in person at least 2 hrs in advance, tel. 224-482-562, guides@pis.cz). For a listing of private guides, see www.guide-prague.cz.

Tram Joyride—Trams #22 and #23 (following the same route) both make a fine joyride through town. Consider it a scenic lead-up to touring the castle. Catch it at the Náměstí Míru Metro station; roll through a bit of the New Town, the Old Town, and across the river, and hop out just above the castle (at Hotel Savoy, stop: Pohořelec); then hike down the hill into the castle area.

Bus Tours—Cheap big-bus orientation tours provide an efficient once-over-lightly look at Prague and a convenient way to see the castle. But in a city as walkable as Prague, bus tours should be used only in case of rain, laziness, or both. Several companies have kiosks on Na Příkopě. Premiant City Tours offers 20 different tours, including several overview tours of the city (250 Kč/1 hr, 380 Kč/2 hrs, 750 Kč/3.5 hrs), the Jewish Quarter (700 Kč, 2 hrs), Prague by night, Bohemian glass, Terezín Concentration Camp memorial, Karlštejn Castle, Český Krumlov (1,750 Kč, 10 hrs), and a river cruise. The tours feature live guides and depart from near the bottom of Wenceslas Square at Na Příkopě 23. Get tickets at an AVE travel agency, hotel, on the bus, or at Na Příkopě 23 (tel. 224-946-922, mobile 606-600-123, www.premiant.cz). Tour salespeople are notorious for telling you anything to sell a ticket. Some tours, especially those heading into the countryside, can be in as many as four different languages. Hiring a private guide can be a much better value.

SIGHTS

The King's Walk (Královská Cesta)

The King's Walk—the ancient way of coronation processions—is touristy, but a Prague highlight. Follow this self-guided walk—pedestrian-friendly and full of playful diversions—to connect nearly all of the essential Prague sites (except the Jewish Quarter).

The king would be crowned in St. Vitus Cathedral in the Prague Castle, walk through the Little Quarter to the Church of St. Nicholas, cross Charles Bridge, and finish at the Old Town

The King's Walk

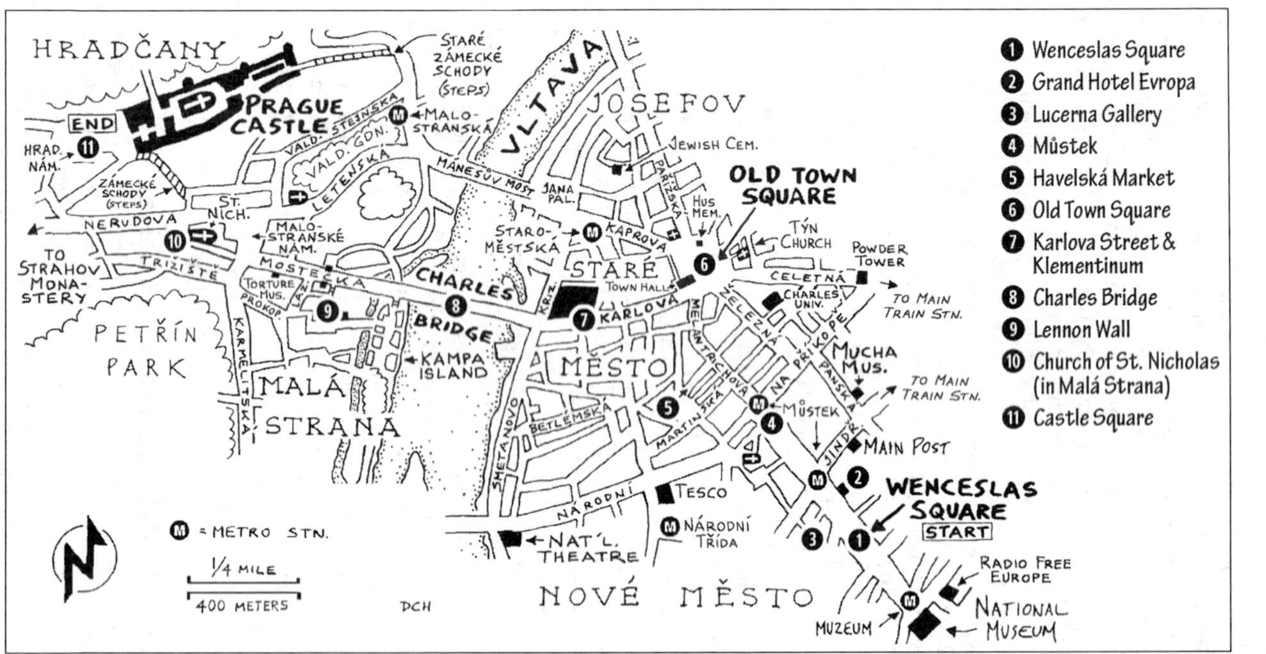

Square. If he hurried, he'd be done in 20 minutes. Like the main drag in Venice between St. Mark's and the Rialto Bridge, this walk mesmerizes tourists. Use it as a spine, but venture off it.

While you could cover this route in the same direction as the king, he's long gone, and it's a new morning in Prague—so we'll go in the opposite direction. Here are Prague's essential sights in walking order, starting at Wenceslas Square (where modern independence was proclaimed), proceeding through the Old Town and across the bridge, and finishing at the castle.

▲▲Wenceslas Square (Václavské Náměstí)—More a broad boulevard than a square (until recently, trams rattled up and down its parklike median strip), this city landmark is named for King Wenceslas, who is featured in the equestrian statue that stands at the top of the boulevard. The area originated as a horse market when the New Town was founded by the order of Charles IV.

The square functions as a stage for modern Czech history: The creation of the Czechoslovak state was celebrated here in 1918; in 1968, the Soviets put down huge popular demonstrations here; and in 1989, more than 300,000 converged here to claim their freedom. Starting at the top (Metro: Muzeum), stroll down the square:

The **National Museum** (Národní Muzeum) stands grandly at the top. While the museum is dull, it enjoys a powerful view, and the interior is richly decorated in the Czech Revival neo-Renaissance style that heralded the 19th-century rebirth of the Czech nation (80 Kč, May–Sept daily 10:00–18:00, Oct–April daily 9:00–17:00, halls of Czech fossils and animals). A major renovation of the entire building is in the works.

Stand behind the statue, facing the museum (uphill). The light-colored patches in the columns show where Russian bullets hit during the crackdown in 1968. Lowly masons—defying their communist bosses, who wanted the damage to be forgotten—showed their Czech spirit by intentionally mismatching their patches.

The nearby Metro stop (Muzeum) is the crossing point of two Metro lines. From here, you could roll a ball straight down the boulevard, through the heart of Prague to Charles Bridge.

Look at the ugly **communist-era building** to the left of the National Museum. This place housed the rubber-stamp Parliament back when they voted with Moscow. A Social Realist statue showing workers triumphing still stands at its base. It's now home to Radio Free Europe. After communism fell, RFE lost its funding and could no longer afford its Munich headquarters. As gratitude for its broadcasts—which kept the people of Eastern Europe in touch with real news—the current Czech government now rents the building to RFE for one crown a year. (As RFE energetically beams its American message deep into Islam from here, it has been threatened recently by Al-Qaeda, and a move is underway to

Central Prague

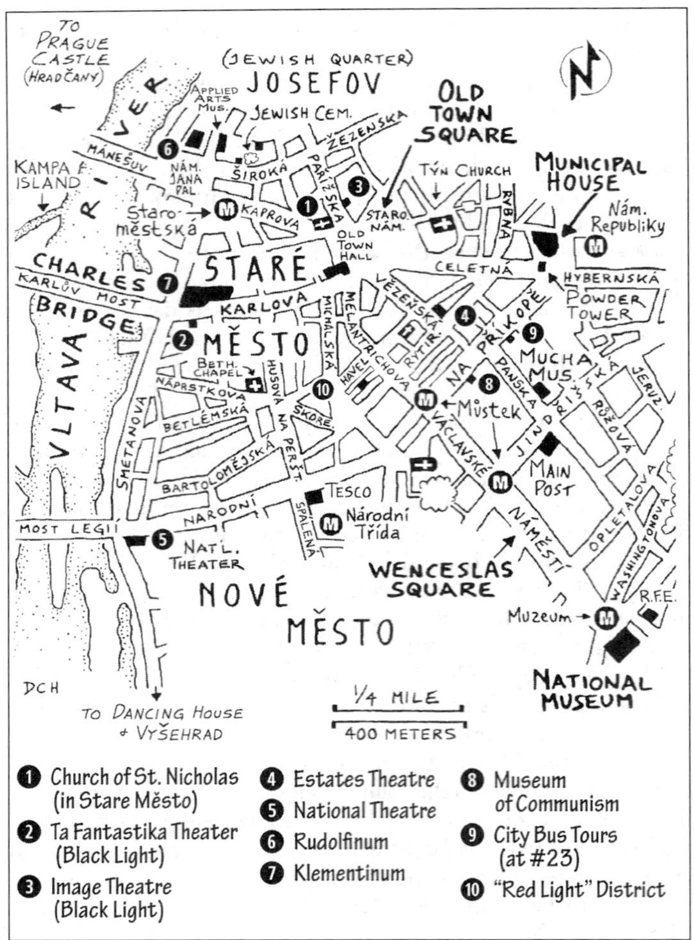

relocate it to an easier-to-defend locale.)

St. Wenceslas (Václav), commemorated by the statue, is the "good king" of Christmas carol fame. He was the wise and benevolent 10th-century duke of Bohemia. A rare example of a well-educated and literate ruler, he was credited by his people for Christianizing his nation and lifting up the culture. Wenceslas astutely allied the Czechs with Saxony, rather than Bavaria, giving the Czechs a vote when the Holy Roman Emperor was selected (and therefore more political clout). After being murdered in 929, Wenceslas became a symbol of Czech nationalism and statehood—and remains an icon of Czech unity whenever the nation has to rally. Supposedly, when the Czechs face their darkest hour, Wenceslas will come riding out of Blaník Mountain (east of Prague) with an army of knights to rescue the nation. In 1620, when Austria stripped Czechs of their independence, many people went to Blaník Mountain to see whether it was opening. They did the same at other critical points in their history (in 1938, 1948, and 1968)—but Wenceslas never emerged. Although now safely part of NATO and the EU, some Czechs are reluctant to be optimistic: If Wenceslas hasn't come out yet, the worst times must still lie ahead....

Study the statue. Wenceslas—always sporting the Czech flag—is surrounded by the four other Czech patron saints. Notice the focus on books. A small nation without great military power, the Czech Republic chose national heroes who enriched the culture by thinking, rather than fighting. This statue is a popular meeting point. Locals say, "I'll see you under the horse's tail."

Thirty yards below the big horse is a small garden with a low-key **memorial** "to the victims of communism"—such as Jan Palach. In 1969, a group of patriots decided that an act of self-immolation would stoke the fires of independence. Jan Palach, a philosophy student who loved life but wanted it with freedom, set himself on fire for the cause of Czech independence and died a few yards from this memorial (on the steps of the National Museum). Czechs are keen on anniversaries. Huge demonstrations swept the city on the 20th anniversary of Palach's death. These led, 10 months later, to the overthrow of the Czech communist government.

This grand square is a gallery of modern **architectural styles**. As you wander downhill, notice the fun mix, all post-1850: Romantic neo-Gothic, neo-Renaissance, and neo-Baroque from the 19th century; Art Nouveau from 1900; ugly functionalism from the mid-20th century (the "form follows function" and "ornamentation is a crime" answer to Art Nouveau); Stalin Gothic from the 1950s "communist epoch" (a good example is the Jalta building—halfway downhill on the right); and glass-and-steel buildings of the 1970s.

Walk a couple blocks downhill through the real people of Prague (not tourists) to **Grand Hotel Evropa,** with its hard-to-miss, dazzling, Art Nouveau exterior and plush café interior.

In November of 1989, this huge square was filled with more than 300,000 ecstatic Czechs believing freedom was at hand. Assembled on the balcony of the building opposite Grand Hotel Evropa (look for *KNIHY BOOKS* sign) was a priest, a rock star (famous for his unconventional style, which constantly unnerved the regime), Alexander Dubček (hero of the 1968 revolt), and Václav Havel (the charismatic playwright, newly released from prison, and every freedom-loving Czech's Mandela). Through a sound system provided by the rock star, Havel's voice boomed over the gathered masses, announcing the resignation of the politburo and saying the Republic of Czechoslovakia's freedom was imminent. Picture that cold November evening, with thousands of Czechs jingling their keychains in solidarity, chanting at the government, "It's time to go now!" (To quell this revolt, government tanks could have given it the Tiananmen Square treatment—which spilled lots of patriotic blood in China just 6 months earlier. Locals believe Gorbachev must have made a phone call recommending that blood not be shed over this.)

Havel, who became the nation's first post-communist president, ended his second (and, constitutionally, last) five-year term early in 2003. While he's still admired by Czechs, his popularity took a hit when he got married for the second time—to an actress 17 years his junior.

Immediately opposite Grand Hotel Evropa is the **Lucerna Gallery** (use entry marked *Divadlo Rokoko* and walk straight in). This is a grand mall from the 1930s with shops, theaters, a ballroom in the basement, and the fine Lucerna café upstairs. You'll see a sculpture—called *Wenceslas Riding an Upside-Down Horse*—hanging like a swing from a glass dome. Created in 1992 (3 years after freedom), it captured the topsy-turvy first days of free enterprise, and the scandal-ridden transition to privatization in a land with a weak legal system. Interestingly, the building (which also includes luxury apartments and offices) was built—and, until recently, owned—by the Havel family. Inside, you'll find a Ticketpro box office (with all available tickets, daily 9:30–18:00), a lavish 1930s Prague cinema (which shows artsy films in Czech with English subtitles or vice versa, 110 Kč), and the popular Lucerna Music Bar in the basement (nightly disco themes from the '70s, '80s, and '90s, 100 Kč, Tue–Sat from 21:00—see page 199).

If you're in the mood for a mellow hippie teahouse, consider a break at Dobrá Čajovna ("Good Teahouse") near the bottom of the square (#14; see page 213). Or, if you'd like an old-time wine bar, pop into the plain **Šenk Vrbovec** (nearby at #10); it comes with a whiff of the communist days, embracing the faintest bits of genteel culture in that age when refinement was sacrificed for the good of the working class. They serve traditional drinks, Czech keg wine, Moravian wines (listed on blackboard outside), *becherovka* (the 13-herb liqueur), and—only in autumn—*burčák* (young wine—grape juice halfway to wine).

The bottom of Wenceslas Square is called **Můstek**, which means "Bridge"; a bridge used to cross a moat here, allowing entrance into the Old Town (you can still see the original Old Town entrance down in the Metro station). Continuing straight, crossing that imaginary old bridge and moat, you enter the charm of Prague's Old Town. (Or, if you turn right at the bridge, you can stroll along the former moat on Na Příkopě, now a spacious pedestrian mall lined with stylish shops; for more on Na Příkopě and the nearby Municipal House, see pages 194 and 195.)

Heading straight from Můstek toward the Old Town Square, you'll find the...

▲Havelská Market—Central Prague's best open-air flower and produce market scene is a couple of blocks toward the Old Town Square from the bottom of Wenceslas Square (daily 9:00–18:00). Laid out in the 13th century for the German trading community, it still keeps hungry locals and vagabonds fed cheaply. Since many of those who produce their goods personally have a stall here, you'll be often dealing with the actual farmer or craftsperson. This is ideal for a healthy snack; merchants are happy to sell single pieces of fruit or vegetables, and you'll find a washing fountain and plenty of inviting benches midway down the street.

▲▲▲Old Town Square (Staroměstské Náměstí)—The focal point for most visits, this has been a market square since the 11th century. It became the nucleus of a town (Staré Město) in the 13th century, when its Town Hall was built. Today, the old-time market stalls have been replaced by cafés, touristy horse buggies, and souvenir hawkers.

The **Jan Hus Memorial,** erected in 1915 (500 years after the Czech reformer's martyrdom by fire), marks the center of the square and symbolizes the long struggle for Czech freedom (see "Hus and Luther" sidebar on page 178). Walk around the memorial. Jan Hus stands tall between two groups of people: victorious Hussite patriots, and Protestants defeated by the Hapsburgs. One of the patriots holds a cup—in the medieval Church, only priests could drink the wine at Communion. Since the Hussites fought for the right to take both the wine and the bread, the cup is their symbol. Behind Hus, a mother with her children represents the ultimate rebirth of the Czech nation. Hus was excommunicated and burned in Germany a century before the age of Martin Luther.

Do a quick **spin tour** in the center of the square to get a look at architectural styles: Gothic, Renaissance, Baroque, rococo, and Art Nouveau.

Spin clockwise, starting with the green domes of the Baroque Church of St. Nicholas. Originally Catholic, now Hussite, it's a popular venue for concerts. (There's another green-domed Church of St. Nicholas—also popular for concerts—by the same architect across the Charles Bridge in the Little Quarter.) The Jewish Quarter (Josefov) is a few blocks behind the church, down the uniquely tree-lined Paris street (Pařížská). Paris street, an eclectic cancan of mostly Art Nouveau facades, leads to a bluff that once sported a 100-foot-tall stone Stalin. Demolished in 1962 after Khrushchev exposed Stalin's crimes, it was recently replaced by a giant ticking metronome.

Hus and Luther

The word *catholic* means "universal." The Roman Catholic Church—in many ways the administrative ghost of the Roman Empire—is the only organization to survive from ancient times. For more than a thousand years, it enforced its notion that the Vatican was the sole interpreter of God's word on earth, and the only legitimate way to be a Christian was as a Roman Catholic. Jan Hus (c. 1369–1415) lived and preached 100 years before Martin Luther. Both were college professors, as well as priests. Both drew huge public crowds as they preached in their university chapels. Both promoted a local religious autonomy. And both helped establish their national languages. (Hus gave the Czechs their unique accents to enable the letters to fit the sounds.) Both got in big trouble. While Hus was burned, Luther survived. Living after Gutenberg, Luther was able to spread his message more cheaply and effectively, thanks to the new printing press. Since Luther was high-profile and German, killing him would have caused major political complications. While Hus may have loosened Rome's grip on Christianity, Luther orchestrated the Reformation that finally broke it. Today, both are revered as national heroes, as well as religious reformers.

Spin to the right past the Hus Memorial and the fine yellow Art Nouveau building. The large rococo palace on the right is part of the National Gallery—the temporary exhibits here tend to be the best in town. Notice the Gothic Týn Church (described below), with its fanciful spires flanking a solid gold effigy of the Virgin Mary. Lining the uphill side of the square is an interesting row of pastel houses with Gothic, Renaissance, and Baroque facades. The pointed, 250-foot-tall spire marks the 14th-century Old Town Hall, famous for its astronomical clock (described below).

In front of the Town Hall, **27 white inlaid crosses** mark the spot where 27 Protestant nobles, merchants, and intellectuals were beheaded in 1621 after rebelling against the Catholic Hapsburgs. The execution ended Czech independence for 300 years—and, for locals, it's still one of the grimmest chapters in their history. Until recently, Czechs walked around this sacred spot, avoiding stepping on it, and many would even stop to pay their respects. But today, the sacred soil is home to a hot-dog stand, and few notice the crosses in the pavement. Locals lament this transition: As the commercialized Old Town loses the power to evoke history, people trample over their own past here.

Týn Church—The towering Týn (teen) Church facing the Old Town Square was rebuilt fancier than the original—but enjoy it.

For 200 years after Hus' death, this was Prague's leading Hussite church. The lane leading to the church from the Old Town Square has a public WC and the most convenient box office in town (see Týnska Galerie listing under "Entertainment," page 197).

▲Old Town Hall Astronomical Clock—Ignore the ridiculous human sales racks, and join the gang for the striking of the hour (daily 8:00–21:00, until 20:00 in winter) on the 15th-century Town Hall clock. As you wait, see if you can figure out how the clock works.

With revolving disks, celestial symbols, and sweeping hands, this clock keeps several versions of time. Two outer rings show the hour: Bohemian time (Gothic numbers, counts from sunset—find the zero, next to 23...supposedly the time of tonight's sunset) and modern time (24 Roman numerals, XII at the top being noon, XII at the bottom being midnight). Five hundred years ago, everything revolved around the earth (the fixed middle background).

To indicate the times of sunrise and sunset, arcing lines and moving spheres combine with the big hand (a sweeping golden sun) and the little hand (the moon showing various stages). Look for the orbits of the sun and moon as they rise through day (the blue zone) and night (the black zone).

If this seems complex to us, it must have been a marvel 500 years ago. Heavily damaged during World War II, a lot of what you see today is a reconstruction.

The circle below (added in the 19th century) shows the zodiac, scenes from the seasons of a rural peasant's life, and a ring of saints' names—one for each day of the year, with a marker showing today's special saint.

Four statues flanking the clock represent 15th-century Prague's four biggest worries: invasion (a Turkish conqueror, his hedonism symbolized by a mandolin), death (a skeleton), greed (a miserly moneylender, who used to have "Jewish" features until after World War II), and vanity (enjoying the mirror). Another interpretation: Earthly pleasures brought on by vanity, greed, and hedonism are fleeting, because we are all mortal.

At the top of the hour (don't blink—the show is pretty quick): First, Death tips his hourglass and pulls the cord, ringing the bell; then the windows open, and the 12 apostles parade by, acknowledging the gang of onlookers; then the rooster crows; and then the hour is rung. The hour is often off because of daylight saving time (completely senseless to 15th-century clock-makers). At the top of the next hour, stand under the tower—protected by a line of banner-wielding, powdered-wigged concert salespeople—and watch the tourists.

Old Town Hall Tower, Hall, and Chapel—The main TI, left of the astronomical clock, contains a guides' desk and these two options: zipping up the only tower in town that has an elevator (40 Kč, fine views), or taking a 45-minute tour of the Gothic chapel and Town Hall, which includes a close-up of the 12 apostles and clock mechanism (50 Kč, 2/hr). A gallery inside the Town Hall features some of Prague's best temporary exhibits (especially photography— check in the office for schedule).

Next to the Old Town Hall, notice the elaborate Renaissance window on the house with the pink facade—the railings and the golden inscription *(Praga Caput Regni)* form Prague's most beautiful window.

Karlova Street—This street winds through medieval Prague from the Old Town Square to the Charles Bridge (it zigzags...just follow the crowds). This is a commercial gauntlet, and it's here that the touristy feeding-frenzy of Prague is most ugly. Street signs keep you on track, and *Karlův most* signs point to the bridge. Obviously, you'll find great people-watching on this drag, but few good values.

The exception is the colorful pub **U Tygra**, where you can rest your feet over a cheap Pilsner beer and watch locals (venture off 20 steps to the left, along Husova street). Bohumil Hrabal, the best modern Czech writer (best known for *Closely Watched Trains*), heard many of his famous stories from the regulars *(štamgast)* right here.

▲▲▲Charles Bridge (Karlův Most)—This much-loved bridge, commissioned by Charles IV in 1357, offers one of the most pleasant and entertaining 500-yard strolls in Europe. Until 1850, it was Prague's only bridge crossing the river. The bridge tower—once a tollbooth—is considered one of the finest Gothic gates anywhere. Climb it for a fine view...but nothing else (40 Kč, daily 10:00–19:00, as late as 22:00 in summer).

Be on the Charles Bridge when the sun is low for the best light, people-watching, and photo opportunities. Before the tacky commercialism and the camera-toting mobs get you down, remember the vacant gloom of this place before 1989. Think of the crowds of Charles Bridge as a celebration of freedom. (Better yet, arrive before 9:00 in the morning to have the place to yourself.)

The bridge is famous for its statues, but half of those you see today are replicas—the originals are in city museums and out of the polluted air. Two of the statues are worth a comment. First, the crucifix (facing the castle, near the start on the right) is the spot where convicts would pause to pray on their way to execution on the Old Town Square. Farther on (midstream, on right), the statue of John of Nepomuk—a Baroque saint of the Czech people—draws a crowd (look for the guy with the 5 golden stars around his head and the shiny dog). Back in the 14th century, John of Nepomuk was the priest to whom the queen confessed all her sins. The king wanted to know her secrets, but Father John dutifully refused to tell. He was tortured, eventually killed, and tossed off the bridge. When he hit the water, five stars appeared. The shiny plaque at the base of the statue depicts the heave-ho. Devout Catholics—from Mexico and Moravia alike—touch it for a wish to come true. You only get one chance in life for this wish, so think carefully before you touch. Notice the date on the inscription: This oldest statue on the bridge was unveiled in 1683, on the supposed 300th anniversary of the martyr's death.

From the end of the bridge (TI in tower on castle side), the street leads two blocks to the Little Quarter Square at the base of the huge Church of St. Nicholas. But before you head up there, consider a detour to...

Kampa Island and Lennon Wall—One hundred yards before the castle end of the Charles Bridge, stairs on the left lead down to the main square of Kampa Island (mostly created from the rubble of the Little Quarter, which was destroyed in an 1540 fire). The island features relaxing pubs, a breezy park, a new art gallery, and river access.

From the main square, Hroznová lane (on the right) leads to a bridge. To the left of the bridge, notice the high-water marks from the flood of August 2002. The water mill is one of many that once lined the canal here.

Fifty yards beyond the bridge is the **Lennon Wall** (Lennonova zeď)—the only chance in Prague to legally try your graffiti art. While the ideas of Lenin hung like a water-soaked trench coat upon the Czech people, the ideas of John Lennon gave many locals hope and a vision. When Lennon was killed in 1980, a memorial wall filled with graffiti spontaneously appeared. Night after night, the police would paint over the "All You Need Is Love" and "Imagine" graffiti. And day after day, it would reappear. Until independence came in 1989, travelers, freedom-lovers, and local hippies gathered here. Silly as it might seem, it's remembered as a place that gave hope to locals craving freedom. Even today, while the tension and danger associated with this wall is gone, the message stays fresh.

▲▲Little Quarter (Malá Strana)—This is the most characteristic, fun-to-wander old section of town. It's one of four medieval towns (along with Hradčany, Staré Město, and Nové Město) that united in the late 1700s to make modern Prague (see "Prague's Four Towns," page 165). It centers on the Little Quarter Square (Malostranské Náměstí), with the huge Church of St. Nicholas standing in the middle. For a short, vivid detour near the church, see the...

Torture Museum—This gimmicky moneymaker is similar to other European torture museums, but is nevertheless interesting, showing models of 60 gruesome medieval tortures, with well-written English descriptions (120 Kč, daily 10:00–22:00, just below Church of St. Nicholas at Mostecká 21, tel. 224-215-581).

Church of St. Nicholas (Kostel Sv. Mikuláše)—When the Jesuits came, they found the perfect piece of real estate for their church and its associated school—the Little Quarter Square. The Church of St. Nicholas (built 1703–1760 in the middle of the square) is the best example of High Baroque in town. It's giddy with curves and illusions. The altar features a lavish, gold-plated Nicholas flanked by the two top Jesuits: St. Ignatius Loyola and St. Francis Xavier.

Climb up the gallery through the staircase in the right transept to look at a collection of large canvases by Karel Škréta, the greatest Czech Baroque painter. Notice that at first glance, the canvases are utterly dark. But as sunbeams shine through the window, various parts of the painting brighten up. The painting is not two-dimensional; like a looking-glass, it's a play of light and darkness. This painting technique reflects a central Baroque belief: The world is full of darkness, and the only hope that makes it come alive comes from God.

For a good look at the city and the church's 250-foot dome, climb the tower for 30 Kč; the entrance is outside the right transept (church entry-50 Kč, daily 9:00–17:00, opens 30 min earlier for prayer; tower open April–Oct daily 10:00–18:00, closed off-season). The church is a concert venue in evenings; 400-Kč tickets are generally on sale at the door.

From here, hike 10 minutes uphill to the castle (and 5 min more to the Strahov Monastery).

Prague's Castle Area

Prague's castle—by some measures, the biggest on earth—is worth a half day of sightseeing. There are various ways to reach the castle and surrounding sights.

Getting to Prague Castle: Take **tram** #22 or #23, both of which go from the National Theater (Národní Divadlo) or Malostranská to the castle. You have two options: Get off at the stop Královský Letohrádek for the castle (see below); or stay on farther to Pohořelec to visit the Strahov Monastery (go uphill and through the gate toward the twin spires), and then hike down to the castle—this route is described under "Strahov Monastery and Library," below.

If you get off the tram at Královský Letohrádek, you'll see the **Royal Summer Palace** (Belvedér) across the street. This love gift—a Czech Taj Mahal—from Emperor Ferdinand I, who really did love his Queen Anne—is the finest Renaissance building in town. Notice that the reliefs, in good Renaissance style, are based on classical, rather than Christian, stories. The one depicted here is Virgil's *Aeneas.* The fountain in front of the palace features the most elaborate bronzework in the country. (If you stick your head under the bottom of the fountain, you'll find out why it's called the

Prague's Castle Area

"Singing Fountain.") From here, walk through the Royal Gardens (with fine views of the cathedral) to the gate, which leads you over the moat and into the castle grounds. Once the private grounds and residence (you'll see the building) of the communist presidents, these Royal Gardens were opened to the public with the coming of freedom under Václav Havel.

Hikers can follow the main cobbled road from Charles Bridge through the Little Quarter (the nearest subway stop is Malostranská). From the big church, hike uphill along Nerudova Street (described below). After about 10 minutes, a steep lane on the right leads to the castle. (If you continue straight, Nerudova becomes Úvoz and climbs to the Strahov Monastery and Library.)

▲Strahov Monastery and Library (Strahovský Klášter Premonstrátů a Strahovská Knihovna)—Twin Baroque domes high above the castle mark the Strahov Monastery (a 15-min hike uphill from Little Quarter, or 5-min walk from castle). If coming by tram, take tram #22 or #23 (from the National Theater or

Malostranská Metro station) to the Pohořelec stop, visit the monastery (go uphill 200 yards and through the gate into the monastery grounds), and then hike down to the castle.

The monastery had a booming economy of its own in its heyday (with vineyards and the biggest beer hall in town—still open). Its main church (dedicated to the Ascension of St. Mary) is an originally Romanesque structure decorated by the monks in textbook Baroque (usually closed, but look through the window inside the front door to see its interior).

The adjacent **library** offers a peek at how enlightened thinkers in the 18th century influenced learning (60 Kč, daily 9:00–12:00 & 13:00–17:00). Cases in the library gift shop show off illuminated manuscripts, some in old Czech. Two rooms are filled with 17th-century books under elaborately painted ceilings. Because the Czechs were a rural people with almost no high culture at this time, there were few books in the Czech language. The theme of the first and bigger hall is philosophy, with the history of man's pursuit of knowledge painted on its ceiling. The other hall focuses on theology. Notice the gilded locked case containing the *libri prohibiti* (prohibited books) at the end of the room. Only the abbot had the key, and you had to have his blessing to read these books—by Nicolas Copernicus and Jan Hus, even including the French encyclopedia. As the Age of Enlightenment began to take hold in Europe at the end of 18th century, monasteries still controlled the books. The hallway connecting these two library rooms was filled with cases illustrating the new practical approach to natural sciences. Find the baby dodo bird (which became extinct in the 17th century).

Just downhill from the monastery and through the gate, the views from the **monastery garden** are among the best in Prague. From the Panorama restaurant or the public perch below the tables, you can see the St. Vitus Cathedral (the centerpiece of the castle complex), the green dome of the Church of St. Nicholas (marking the center of the Little Quarter, or Malá Strana), the two dark towers fortifying the Charles Bridge, and the fanciful black spires of the Týn Church (marking the Old Town Square). On the horizon, the modern **Žižkov TV and radio tower** is meant to attract extraterrestrials to Prague.

Loreta Church (a.k.a. Loreta Shrine)—This church (between the castle and the Strahov Monastery) has been a hit with pilgrims for centuries, thanks to its dazzling bell tower, peaceful yet plush cloister, sparkling treasury, and much venerated "holy house" (90 Kč, Tue–Sun 9:00–12:15 & 13:00–16:30, closed Mon).

The central **Santa Casa** (holy house) was considered by some pilgrims to be part of Mary's home in Nazareth. Because many pilgrims returning from the Holy Land docked at the Italian port of Loreto, it's called the Loreta Shrine. The Santa Casa is the "little Bethlehem" of Prague. It has long been the departure point for Czech pilgrims setting out on the long, arduous journey to Europe's most important pilgrimage site, Santiago de Compostela, in northwest Spain.

The small Baroque church behind the Santa Casa is one of the most beautiful in Prague. The frescoes on the ceilings of the ambits illustrate a prayer to St. Mary. The Santa Casa itself, with only a few 15th-century frescoes and an old statue of Mary, might seem like a bit of a letdown, but consider that you're entering the holiest spot in the country for generations of believers. Upstairs, the highlight is a room full of jeweled worship aids in the treasury (well-described in English). Behind vault doors, you'll squint at a monstrance (Communion wafer holder) from 1699 with over 6,000 diamonds. Enjoy the short carillon concert at the top of the hour; from the lawn in front of the main entrance, you can see the racks of bells being clanged.

On the opposite side of the square is the **Černín palace,** the largest Baroque palace in town. It once belonged to one of the most cosmopolitan Czech families, and so, in 1918, it was turned into the Ministry of Foreign Affairs.

Walking down the street from the Loreta Square, you'll reach...

Castle Square (Hradčanské Náměstí)—The big square facing the castle feels like the castle's entry, but it's actually the central square of the Castle Quarter. Enjoy the awesome city view and the two entertaining string quartets that play regularly at the gate. (If the Prague Castle Orchestra is playing, say hello to friendly, mustachioed Josef and consider getting the group's terrific CD.) A tranquil café called Espresso Kajetánka (see page 211) hides a few steps down, immediately to the right as you face the castle. From here, stairs lead into the Little Quarter.

Castle Square was a kind of medieval Pennsylvania Avenue—the king, the most powerful noblemen, and the archbishop lived here. Look uphill from the gate. The Renaissance **Schwarzenberg Palace** (on the left, with the big rectangles scratched on the wall, now under renovation) was where the Rožmberks "humbly" stayed when they were in town from their Český Krumlov estates. The Schwarzenberg family (marvel at their coat of arms, made of human bones, in the ossuary in Kutná Hora) inherited the Krumlov estates and aristocratic prominence in Bohemia, and stayed in the palace until 20th century.

The archbishop still lives in the yellow rococo **palace** across the square (with the 3 white goose necks in the red field—the coat of arms of Prague archbishops).

Through the portal on the left-hand side of the palace, a lane leads to the **Sternberg Palace** (Šternberský Palác), filled with the National Gallery's skippable collection of European paintings—mostly minor works by Albrecht Dürer, Peter Paul Rubens, Rembrandt, and El Greco (100 Kč, Tue–Sun 10:00–18:00, closed Mon).

The Baroque sculpture in the middle of the square is a **plague column**, erected as a token of gratitude to the saints who saved the population from the epidemic, and an integral part of the main square of any Hapsburg town.

Survey the castle from this square—the tip of a 1,500-foot-long series of courtyards, churches, and palaces.

▲▲Prague Castle (Pražský Hrad)—For more than a thousand years, Czech leaders have ruled from the Prague Castle. It's huge and confusing—with plenty of sights not worth seeing. Keep things simple, rather than worry about rumors that you should spend all day here with long lists of museums to see. Five stops matter and are all explained here: St. Vitus Cathedral, Old Royal Palace, Basilica of St. George, the Golden Lane, and the toy museum.

Huge throngs of tourists turn the castle grounds into a sea of people during peak times; late afternoon is least crowded. The guard changes on the hour (5:00–23:00), with the most ceremony at noon. Walk under the fighting giants, under an arch, and into the second courtyard. The modern green awning with the golden winged cat (just past the ticket office) marks the offices of the Czech president.

Hours: Castle sights open April–Oct daily 9:00–17:00, Nov–March daily 9:00–16:00, last entry 15 min before closing; grounds open daily 5:00–24:00. Tel. 224-373-368 or 224-372-434.

Tickets: You can choose from three ticket routes. Route A costs 350 Kč and includes everything: the cathedral sights (apse, crypt, and tower—just looking around the front part of the cathedral is free), Old Royal Palace, Basilica of St. George, Powder Tower, Golden Lane (during peak sightseeing hours—it's free in the morning and evening), and an exhibition on the castle's building history. Route B (220 Kč) includes the cathedral sights and Old Royal Palace. Route C (50 Kč) gets you into the Golden Lane only, and Route D (50 Kč) into the Basilica of St. George only. For the thorough visit described below, opt for Route A. If you want to save time and money, buy Route D—tour the Basilica of St. George, wander the grounds, and explore the front half of the cathedral and peek into the tomb of Prince Wenceslas (this part of cathedral is free).

Tours: Hour-long tours in English depart from the main ticket office about three times a day, but cover only the cathedral and Old Royal Palace (80 Kč; reserve a week in advance if you want a private guide-400 Kč for up to 5 people, then 80 Kč per additional person, tel. 224-373-368). If you rent the worthwhile **audioguide** (200 Kč/2 hrs, 250 Kč/3 hrs), you won't be able to exit the castle area from the bottom, since you need to backtrack uphill to return the audioguide where you got it.

▲▲▲St. Vitus Cathedral (Katedrála Sv. Vita)—This Roman Catholic cathedral symbolizes the Czech spirit—it contains the tombs and relics of the most important local saints and kings, including the first three Hapsburg kings.

To **avoid crowds**, be at the entrance at 9:00, when the doors open. For 10 minutes, you'll have the sacred space for yourself (after about 9:15, tour guides shouting over each other turn the church into a hawkers' square). Otherwise, come here in the afternoon, when the church is still relatively full, but most tour groups are gone.

Before entering, check out the **facade**. What's up with the guys in suits carved into the facade below the big round window? They're the architects and builders who finished the church. Started in 1344, construction was stalled by wars and plagues. But, fueled by the 19th-century rise of Czech nationalism, Prague's top church was finished in 1929 for the 1,000th anniversary of the death of St. Wenceslas. While it looks all Gothic, it's actually two distinct halves: modern neo-Gothic and the original 14th-century Gothic. For 400 years, a temporary wall sealed off the unfinished cathedral.

Go inside (pickpocket alert) and find the third **stained-glass window** on the left. This masterful 1931 Art Nouveau window is by Czech artist Alfons Mucha (if you like this, you'll love the Mucha Museum in the New Town—see page 195). Notice Mucha's stirring nationalism: Methodius and Cyril are top and center (leaders in Slavic-style Christianity). Cyril is baptizing the mythic, lanky, long-haired Czech man. In the center is a kneeling boy and a prophesizing elder—that's young St. Wenceslas and his grandmother, St. Ludmila. In addition to being specific figures, these characters are also symbolic: The old woman, with closed eyes, stands for the past and the memory, while the young boy, with a penetrating stare, represents the hope and future of a nation. Notice how master designer Mucha draws your attention to these two figures through the use of colors—the dark blue on the outside gradually turns into green, then yellow, and finally the gold of the woman and the crimson of the boy in the center. In Mucha's color language, blue stands for the past, gold for the mythic, and red for the future. Along with all the meaning, Mucha's art is simply a joy to look at.

Show your ticket and circulate around the **apse.** You'll pass a carved wood relief of Prague in 1620 depicting the victorious Hapsburg armies entering the castle after the Battle of White Mountain, while the Protestant king Frederic escapes over the

Charles Bridge (before it had any statues). The second part of this Counter-Reformation wood relief, on the other side from the altar, captures the "barbaric" Protestant nobles destroying the Catholic icons in the cathedral after the Prague defeat.

A fancy, roped-off chapel (right transept) houses the **tomb of Prince Wenceslas,** surrounded by precious 14th-century murals showing scenes from his life, and a locked door leading to the crown jewels. The Czech kings used to be coronated right here in front of the coffin, draped in red.

You can climb 287 steps up the **spire** for one of the best views of the whole city (included in Route A or B ticket, or pay 20 Kč at the cathedral ticket window, April–Oct daily except Sun morning, 9:00–17:00, last entry 16:15, closes at 16:00 in winter).

Back Outside the Cathedral: Leaving the cathedral, turn left (past the public WC). The **obelisk** was erected in 1928—a single piece of granite celebrating the 10th anniversary of the establishment of Czechoslovakia. It was originally much taller, but broke in transit—an inauspicious start for a nation destined to last only 70 years. Up in the fat, green tower of the cathedral is the biggest Czech bell, nicknamed "Zikmund." In June 2002, it cracked—and two months later, the worst flood in recorded history hit the city. As members of a nation sandwiched between great powers, Czechs are deeply superstitious. Often unable to influence the course of their own history, they helplessly look at events as we might look at the weather and other natural phenomena—trying to figure out what fate has in store for them next.

Find the 14th-century **mosaic** of the *Last Judgment* outside on the right transept. It was built Italian-style by King Charles IV, who was modern, cosmopolitan, and ahead of his time. Jesus oversees the action, as some go to heaven and some go to hell. The Czech king and queen kneel directly below Jesus and the six patron saints. On coronation day, they would walk under this arch, which would remind them (and their subjects) that even those holding great power are not above God's judgment. The royal crown and national jewels are kept in a chamber (see the grilled windows) above this entryway, which was the cathedral's main entry for centuries, while the church was incomplete.

Across the square and 20 yards to the right, a door leads to the...

Old Royal Palace (Starý Královský Palác)—This was the seat of the Bohemian princes starting in the 12th century. While extensively rebuilt, the **large hall** is late Gothic, designed as a multipurpose hall for the old nobility. It's big enough for jousts—even the staircase was designed to let a mounted soldier gallop in. It was filled with market stalls, giving nobles a chance to shop without actually going into town. In the 1400s, the nobility met here to elect their king. This tradition survived until modern times, as the parliament crowded into this room until the late 1990s to elect the Czechoslovak (and later Czech) president. The last two elections happened in another, much more lavish hall in the castle. Look up at the flower-shaped, vaulted ceiling—far more elaborate than the simple cross ceiling in the cathedral.

On the right, enter the two small Renaissance rooms known as the "**Czech Office**." From these rooms, two governors used to oversee the Czech lands in the times when the Hapsburgs moved the capital to Vienna. In 1618, angry Czech Protestant nobles poured into these rooms and threw the two Catholic governors out of the window. This was the second of Prague's many defenestrations, and it sparked the Thirty Years' War. Look at the pictures illustrating the defenestration (a uniquely Czech solution to political discord, whereby offending politicians are literally tossed out of a window). The two governors landed—you could say, thankfully—in a pile of horse manure (there were royal stables under the window back then)...so, despite the height, they suffered only a broken arm. The Czech Estates Uprising lasted for two years and ended in the crushing defeat of the Czech army in the Battle of White Mountain, which marked the end of Czech freedom. Twenty-seven leaders of the uprising were executed, most of the old Czech nobility was dispossessed, and Protestants had to leave the country or convert to Catholicism.

Look down on the chapel from the end, and go out on the balcony for a fine Prague view. Is that Paris' Eiffel Tower in the distance? No, it's Petřín Tower, built for an exhibition in 1891 (200 feet tall, a quarter of the height of its Parisian big brother, built 2 years earlier). The spiral stairs on the left lead up to several rooms with painted coats of arms and no English explanations. The downstairs of the palace sometimes houses special exhibitions.

Across from the palace exit is the...

Basilica of St. George and Convent (Bazilika Sv. Jiří)—Step into the beautifully lit Basilica of St. George to see Prague's best-preserved Romanesque church. St. Wenceslas' mother, St. Ludmila, was reburied here in 973. The first Bohemian convent was established here near the palace.

Today, the **convent** next door houses the National Gallery's Collection of Old Masters (the best Czech paintings from Mannerism and Baroque periods, 100 Kč, Tue–Sun 10:00–18:00, closed Mon).

Continue walking downhill through the castle grounds. Turn left on the first street, which leads into the...

Golden Lane (Zlatá Ulička)—During the day, this street of old buildings, which originally housed goldsmiths, is jammed with tourists and lined with overpriced gift shops. Franz Kafka lived briefly at #22. There's a deli/bistro at the top and a convenient public WC at the bottom. In the morning and at night, the tiny street is empty and romantic.

▲Toy and Barbie Museum (Muzeum Hraček)—At the bottom of the castle complex, just after leaving the Golden Lane, a long wooden staircase leads to two entertaining floors of old toys and dolls thoughtfully described in English. You'll see a century of teddy bears, 19th-century model train sets, and an incredible Barbie collection (the entire top floor). Find the buxom 1959 first edition, and you'll understand why these capitalistic sirens of material discontent weren't allowed here until 1989 (50 Kč, not included in any castle tickets, daily 9:30–17:30).

After Your Castle Visit: Tourists squirt slowly through a fortified door at the bottom end of the castle. From there, you can follow the steep lane directly back to the riverbank (and the Malostranská Metro station). Or you can take a hard right and stroll through the long, delightful park to the top of the castle, where you'll find two more options: a staircase leading down into the Little Quarter, or a cobbled street taking you to the historic Nerudova Street—described below. (Halfway through that long park is a viewpoint overlooking the terraced gardens; you can zigzag down through the gardens into the Little Quarter—120 Kč, April–Oct daily 10:00–18:00.)

Nerudova Street—The steep, cobbled street leading to the castle is named for Jan Neruda, a gifted 19th-century journalist (and somewhat less talented fiction writer). It's lined with old buildings still sporting the characteristic doorway signs that served as street addresses. In 1777, in order to collect taxes more effectively, Hapsburg Empress Maria Theresa decreed that numbers be used instead of these quaint house names. The surviving signs are carefully restored and protected by law. Signs (e.g., the lion, 3 violinists, house of the golden suns) represent the family name, the occupation, or the various passions of the people who once inhabited the houses. This neighborhood is filled with old noble palaces, now generally used as foreign embassies.

Prague's Jewish Quarter (Josefov)

Prague's Jewish Quarter neighborhood and its well-presented, profoundly moving museum tell the story of the Jews of this region. For me, this is the most interesting Jewish sight in Europe (and worth ▲▲▲).

As the Nazis decimated Jewish communities in the region, Prague's Jews were allowed to collect and archive their treasures in this "museum." While the archivists ultimately died in concentration camps, their work survives. Seven sights scattered over a three-block area make up the tourists' Jewish Quarter. Six of the

Prague's Jewish Quarter

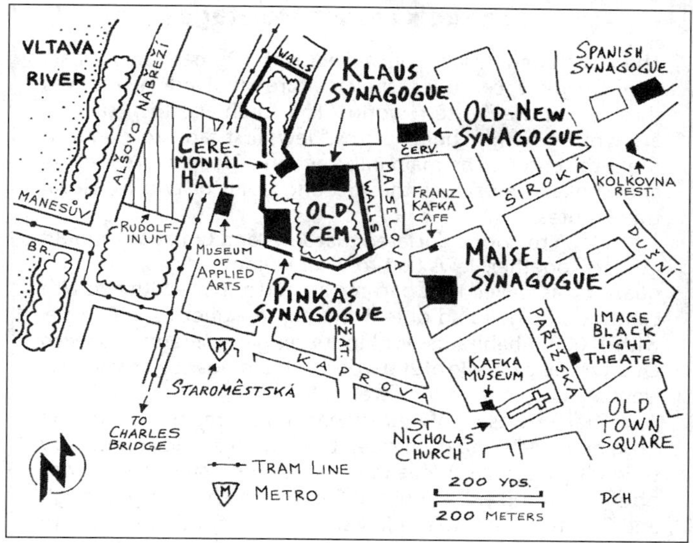

sights, called "the Museum," are treated as one admission. Your ticket comes with a map locating the sights and listing admission appointments—the times you'll be let in if it's very crowded. (Without crowds, ignore the times.) You'll notice plenty of security (stepped up since 9/11).

To visit all seven sights, you'll pay 500 Kč (300 Kč for the Museum and 200 Kč for the Old-New Synagogue; all sights open Sun–Fri 9:00–18:00, closed Sat—the Jewish Sabbath). There are occasional guided walks in English (40 Kč, 2.5 hrs, start at Maisel Synagogue, tel. 222-317-191). Most stops are described in English. The ticket lines at the cemetery and Pinkas Synagogue are longest. You'll likely save time if you buy your ticket at the Maisel Synagogue (the best place to start your visit, anyway).

Maisel Synagogue (Maiselova Synagóga)—This synagogue was built as a private place of worship for the Maisel family during the 16th-century golden age of Prague's Jews. Maisel was the financier of the Hapsburg king—and had lots of money. The synagogue's interior is decorated neo-Gothic. In World War II, it served as a warehouse for the accumulated treasures of decimated Jewish communities that Hitler planned to use for his "Museum of the Extinct Jewish Race." The one-room exhibit (the upstairs "women's gallery" is closed for renovation) shows a thousand years of Jewish history in Bohemia and Moravia. Well-explained in English, the topics covered include the origin of the Star of David, Jewish mysticism, discrimination, and the creation of Prague's ghetto. Notice the

Prague's Jewish Heritage

The Jewish people were dispersed by the Romans 2,000 years ago. Over the centuries, their culture survived in enclaves throughout the Western world: "The Torah was their sanctuary, which no army could destroy." Jews first came to Prague in the 10th century. The main intersection of Josefov (Maiselova and Široká streets) was the meeting point of two medieval trade routes.

When the pope declared that Jews and Christians should not live together, Jews had to wear yellow badges, and their quarter was walled in. It became a ghetto. In the 16th and 17th centuries, Prague had one of the biggest ghettos in Europe, with 11,000 inhabitants. Within its six gates, Prague's Jewish Quarter was a gaggle of 200 wooden buildings. It was said that "Jews nested, rather than dwelled."

The "outcasts" of Christianity relied mainly on profits from moneylending (forbidden to Christians) and community solidarity to survive. While their money protected them, it was often also a curse. Throughout Europe, when times got tough and Christian debts to the Jewish community mounted, entire Jewish communities were evicted or killed.

In the 1780s, Emperor Joseph II eased much of the discrimination against Jews. In 1848, the walls were torn down, and the neighborhood—named Josefov in honor of the emperor, who was less anti-Semitic than the norm—was incorporated as a district of Prague.

In 1897, ramshackle Josefov was razed and replaced with a new, modern town—the original 31 streets and 220 buildings became 10 streets and 83 buildings. This is what you'll see today: an attractive neighborhood of fine, mostly Art Nouveau buildings, with a few surviving historic Jewish buildings. By the 1930s, some 50,000 Jews lived in Prague. They were a hugely successful group, thanks largely to their ability to appreciate talent—a rare quality in the small Central European countries whose citizens, as the great Austrian novelist Robert Musil put it, "were equal in their unwillingness to let one another get ahead."

Of the 120,000 Jews living in the area in 1939, only 10,000 survived the Holocaust to see liberation in 1945. Today, only a couple of thousand Jews remain in Prague...but the legacy of their ancestors lives on.

eastern wall, with the holy ark containing the scroll of the Torah. The central case shows the silver ornamental Torah crowns that capped the scroll.

Spanish Synagogue (Španělská Synagóga)—This 19th-century, ornate, Moorish-style synagogue continues the history of the Maisel Synagogue, covering the 18th, 19th, and tumultuous 20th centuries. The upstairs is particularly intriguing (with c. 1900 photos of Josefov). The Spanish Synagogue is now used for classical concerts, often featuring the music of Jewish composers, such as Felix Mendelssohn and Gustav Mahler (ticket desk just outside at the door). The building also contains the Jewish public library, the only one of its kind in Prague.

Pinkas Synagogue (Pinkasova Synagóga)—A site of Jewish worship for 400 years, today this is a poignant memorial to the victims of the Nazis. The walls are covered with the handwritten names of 77,297 Czech Jews who were sent from here to the gas chambers of Auschwitz and other camps. (You'll hear the somber reading of the names as you ponder this sad sight.) Hometowns are in gold, family names are in red, followed in black by the individual's first name, birthday, and last date known to be alive. Notice that families generally perished together. Extermination camps are listed on the east wall. Climb six steps into the women's gallery. The names in poor condition near the ceiling are from 1953. When the communists moved in, they closed the synagogue and erased everything. With freedom, in 1989, the Pinkas Synagogue was reopened and all the names rewritten. The Synagogue closed briefly in 2003, as flood damage meant the names needed to be rewritten once again.

Upstairs is the **Terezín Children's Art Exhibit,** displaying art drawn by Jewish children who were imprisoned at Terezín Concentration Camp, and later perished. Terezín is a powerful day trip from Prague, easily accessible by tour bus (see page 171) or local bus (1-hr trip, departs Prague's Florenc station).

Old Jewish Cemetery (Starý Židovský Hřbitov)—As you wander among 12,000 evocative tombstones, remember that from 1439 until 1787, this was the only burial ground allowed for the Jews of Prague. Because of limited space, the Jewish belief that the body should not be moved once buried, and the sheer number of graves, tombs were piled atop each other. With its many layers, the cemetery became a small plateau. And as things settled over time, the tombstones got crooked. The Jewish word for cemetery means "House of Life." Like Christians, Jews believe that death is the gateway into the next world. Pebbles on the tombstones are "flowers of the desert," reminiscent of the old days when a rock was placed upon the sand gravesite to keep the body covered. You'll likely see pebbles atop scraps of paper containing prayers.

Ceremonial Hall (Obřadní Síň)—Leaving the cemetery, you'll find a neo-Romanesque mortuary house built in 1911 for the purification of the dead (on left). It's filled with a worthwhile exhibition, described in English, on Jewish burial traditions. A series of crude but instructive paintings show how the "burial brotherhood" took care of the ill and buried the dead. As all are equal before God, the rich and poor alike were buried in embroidered linen shrouds similar to the one you'll see on display.

Klaus Synagogue (Klauzová Synagóga)—This 17th-century synagogue (also at the exit of the cemetery) is the final wing of the Museum, devoted to Jewish religious practices. On the ground floor, exhibits explain the festive Jewish calendar. The central case displays a Torah (the first 5 books of the Bible) and solid silver pointers—necessary, since the Torah is not to be touched. Upstairs is an exhibit on the rituals of Jewish life (circumcision, bar and bat mitzvah, weddings, kosher eating, and so on).

Old-New Synagogue (Staronová Synagóga)—For more than 700 years, this has been the most important synagogue and central building in Josefov. Standing like a bomb-hardened bunker, it feels like it has survived plenty of hard times. Stairs take you down to the street level of the 13th century and into the Gothic interior. Built in 1270, it's the oldest synagogue in Central Europe.

The lobby (where you show your ticket) has two fortified old lockers—where the most heavily taxed community in medieval Prague stored its money in anticipation of the taxman's arrival. As 13th-century Jews were not allowed to build, this was constructed by Christians. The builders were good at four-ribbed vaulting, but since that resulted in a cross, it wouldn't work for a synagogue. Instead, they made the ceiling using clumsy five-ribbed vaulting.

The interior is pure 1300s. The Shrine of the Ark in front is the focus of worship. The holiest place in the synagogue, it holds the sacred scrolls of the Torah. The old rabbi's chair to the right remains empty out of respect. The red banner is a copy of the one the Jewish community carried through town during medieval parades. Notice the yellow pointed hat, which the pope in 1215 ordered all Jewish men to wear. Twelve is a popular number (e.g., 12 windows) because it symbolizes the 12 tribes of Israel. The horizontal, slit-like windows are an 18th-century addition allowing women to view the men-only services (separate 200-Kč admission includes worthwhile 10-minute tour—ask about it, Sun–Thu 9:30–18:00, Fri 9:30–17:00, closed Sat).

More Sights in the Old Town and the New Town

▲Na Příkopě—Na Příkopě (meaning "The Moat") follows the line of the Old Town wall, leading from Wenceslas Square right to a former gate in that wall, the Powder Tower (Prašná Brána, not worth touring). City tour buses leave from along this street, which offers plenty of shopping temptations (see "Shopping," page 199). The neo-Renaissance Òivnostenská Banka building on the corner of Nekázanka houses a modern bank in a classy, 19th-century ambience (enter and peek into the main hall upstairs).

▲Museum of Communism—The museum traces the story of communism in Prague: the origins, dream, reality, and nightmare; the cult of personality; and finally, the Velvet Revolution. Along the way, it gives a fascinating review of the Czech Republic's 40-year stint with Soviet economics. You'll find propaganda posters, busts of communist All-Stars (Marx, Lenin, Stalin), a photograph of the massive stone Stalin that overlooked Prague until 1962, and re-created slices of communist life—from a bland store counter to a typical classroom (with a poem on the chalkboard extolling the virtues of the tractor). Don't miss the 20-minute video showing how the Czech people chafed under the big red yoke from the 1950s through 1989—it plays continuously (180 Kč, daily 9:00-21:00, Na Příkopě 10, above a McDonald's and next to a casino—Lenin would turn over in his grave, tel. 224-212-966, www.museumofcommunism.com).

▲Municipal House (Obecní Dům)—The Municipal House is the "pearl of Czech Art Nouveau" (built 1905–1911, next to Powder Tower). It features Prague's largest concert hall, a great Art Nouveau café, and two other restaurants. Pop in and wander around the lobby of the concert hall. Walk through to the ticket office on the ground floor. Most days, there are guided tours through the Municipal House that show you all the halls worth seeing. Then choose your place for a meal or drink (see "Eating," page 207).

Standing in front of the Municipal House, you can survey four different styles of architecture. First, enjoy the pure Art Nouveau of the Municipal House itself. Featuring a goddess-like Praha presiding over a land of peace and high culture, the *Homage to Prague* mosaic on the building's striking facade stoked cultural pride and nationalist sentiment. Across the street, the classical fixer-upper from 1815 was the customs house (soon to be renovated). The stark national bank building (Česká Národní Banka) is textbook functionalism ("ornament is a crime") from the 1930s. And the big, black Powder Tower was the Gothic gate of the town wall, built to house the city's gunpowder. Crossing under it, you join the beaten path as Celetná Street leads to the Old Town Square.

▲▲Mucha Museum (Muchovo Muzeum)—This is one of Europe's most enjoyable little museums. I find the art of Alfons Mucha (MOO-kah, 1860–1939) insistently likeable. See the crucifixion scene he painted as an eight-year-old boy. Read how this popular Czech artist's posters, filled with Czech symbols and expressing his people's ideals and aspirations, were patriotic banners that aroused the national spirit. And check out the photographs of his models. With the help of this abundant supply of slinky models, Mucha was a founding father of the Art Nouveau movement. Prague isn't much on museums, but, if you're into Art Nouveau, this one is great. Run by Mucha's grandson, it's two blocks off Wenceslas Square and wonderfully displayed on one comfortable floor. Give it a once-over-lightly, just looking at the probing and haunting eyes of Mucha's models (120 Kč, daily 10:00–18:00, Panská 7, tel. 224-233-355, www.mucha.cz). While the exhibit is well-described in English, the 30-Kč English brochure on the art is a good supplement. The included 30-minute video is definitely worthwhile (English and Czech showings alternate, ask upon entry).

Bethlehem Chapel (Betlémská Kaple)—Emperor Charles IV founded the first university in Central Europe, and this was the university's chapel. Around the year 1400, priest and professor Jan Hus preached from the pulpit here (see "Hus and Luther" sidebar, page 178). While meant primarily for students and faculty, Hus' Masses were open to the public. Hus proposed that the congregation should be more involved in worship (e.g., actually drink the wine at Communion) and have better access to the word of God through services and scriptures written in the people's language, instead of Latin. Standing-room-only crowds of more than 3,000 were the norm when Hus preached. The stimulating, controversial ideas debated at the university spread throughout the city and, after Hus' death at the stake, sparked off the bloodiest civil war in Czech history. Each subsequent age has interpreted Hus to its liking: For the Protestants, Hus was the founder of the first Protestant church (though he was actually an ardent Catholic); for the revolutionaries, this critic of the power of the Church was a proponent of social equality; for the nationalists, the Czech preacher was the defender of the language; and for the communists, Hus was the first communist ideologue.

Today's chapel is a 1950s reconstruction of the original. Try the unbelievably bad acoustics inside—it demonstrates the sloppy work sponsored by the communists (tiny upstairs exhibit and big chapel with English info sheets available, 35 Kč, April–Oct daily 10:00–18:30; Nov–March Tue–Sun 10:00–17:30, closed Mon and during university functions; on Bethlehem Square—Betlémská Náměstí, tel. 224-248-595).

Klub Architektů, across from the entry, has an intriguing atmosphere and good food (see "Eating," page 207).

The Dancing House (Tančící Dům)—Prague has some delightful modern architecture. If ever a building could get your toes tapping, it would be this one, nicknamed "Fred and Ginger" by American architecture buffs. This metallic samba is the work of Frank Gehry (who designed the equally striking Guggenheim Museum in Bilbao, Spain, and Seattle's Experience Music Project). Eight-legged Ginger's wispy dress and Fred's metal mesh head are easy to spot (2 bridges down from Charles Bridge where Jiráskův bridge hits Nové Město, tram #17).

A pleasant, 10-minute, riverside walk from the Dancing House (towards the Charles Bridge) is the grand **National Theater** (Národní Divadlo). Opened in 1883, this theater was the first truly Czech venue in Prague, and from the very start was nicknamed the "Cradle of Czech Culture." The productions are heavily subsidized—the state pours more money into this single theater than into all of Czech film production. It is the best place in town for opera or ballet.

Across the street from the theater is the formerly venerable haunt of Prague's intelligentsia, **Grand Café Slavia,** a Vienna-style coffeehouse fine for a meal or drink with a view of the river.

ENTERTAINMENT

Prague booms with live (and inexpensive) theater, classical, jazz, and pop entertainment. Everything's listed in several monthly cultural events programs (free at TI) and in the *Prague Post* newspaper.

You'll be tempted to gather fliers as you wander through the town. Don't. To really understand all your options (the street Mozarts are pushing only their concert), drop by the **Týnská Galerie** box office at Týn Church on the Old Town Square. The event schedule posted on their wall clearly shows what's playing today and tomorrow, including tourist concerts, Black Light Theater, and marionette shows, with photos of each venue and a map locating everything (daily 10:00–19:00, tel. 224-826-969).

Ticketpro at Rytířská 31 (between the Havelská Market and the Estates Theater) sells tickets for the serious concert venues and most music clubs (daily 8:00–12:00 & 12:30–16:30; also has a booth in the Tourist Center at Rytířská 12, daily 9:00–20:00).

Black Light Theater—A kind of mime/modern dance variety show, Black Light Theater has no language barrier and is, for many, more entertaining than a classical concert. Unique to Prague (though somewhat comparable to the Canadian Cirque du Soleil), Black Light Theater originated in the 1960s as a playful and mystifying theater of the absurd. The two main venues are **Ta Fantastika** (*Aspects of Alice* at 21:30, more poetic, more puppets, traditional, a little artistic nudity, 620 Kč, reserved seating, near Charles Bridge at Karlova 8, tel. 222-221-366, www.tafantastika.cz) and **Image**

Theatre (more mime and absurd—"It's precisely the fact that we are all so different that unites us," shows at 18:00 and 20:00, 450 Kč, open seating—arrive early to grab a good spot, just off Old Town Square at Pařížská 4, tel. 222-314-448, www.imagetheatre.cz). Shows last about 90 minutes. Avoid the first four rows, which get you close enough to ruin the illusion. The other black light theaters advertising around town aren't as good.

Tourist Concerts—Each day, six or eight classical concerts designed for tourists fill delightful Old Town halls and churches with music of the crowd-pleasing sort: Vivaldi, Best of Mozart, Most Famous Arias, and works by local boy Antonín Dvořák. Concerts typically cost 400–1,000 Kč, start anywhere from 13:00 to 21:00, and last one hour. Common venues are two sites at the Little Quarter Square (at the Baroque Church of St. Nicholas and in the Prague Academy of Music in Liechtenstein Palace); in the Klementinum's Chapel of Mirrors; at the Old Town Square (in a different Church of St. Nicholas); and in the stunning Smetana Hall in the Municipal House (Obecní Dům). The artists vary from excellent to amateur.

To ensure quality, head for the Monday 17:00 concert at **St. Martin in the Wall** (Martinská street in the Old Town), where Prague's best professional musicians gather every week to tune in and chat with each other (400 Kč).

Serious Concerts—True music-lovers should consider the best symphonic venue, the **Rudolfinum** (the Prague Philharmonic, on Palachovo Náměstí, on the Old Town side of Mánes bridge). Concerts in the large Dvořák Hall or the small Suk Hall usually start at 19:30 (also afternoons on weekends). The ticket office is on the right side, under the stairs (250–1,000 Kč, open until few minutes before the show starts).

The **National Theatre** (Národní Divadlo, on the New Town side of Legií bridge)—with a must-see neo-Renaissance interior—is best for opera and ballet (shows from 19:00, 300–1,000 Kč, tel. 224-912-673, www.nationaltheatre.cz). The **Estates Theatre** (Stavovské Divadlo) is where Mozart premiered and personally directed many of his most beloved works. *Don Giovanni*, *The Marriage of Figaro*, and *The Magic Flute* are on the program a couple of times each month (shows from 20:00, 800–1,400 Kč, on square called Ovocný Trh, tel. 224-214-339, www.estatestheatre.cz). The ticket office for both of these theatres is in the little square (Ovocný Trh) behind the Estates Theatre.

The **State Opera** (Státní Opera) focuses on Verdi (tickets in the theatre, shows at 19:00 or 20:00, 400–1,200 Kč, on 5. Května—the busy street between the main train station and Wenceslas Square, tel. 224-227-693).

World-class musicians are in town during the **Prague Spring** (from May 12 to the beginning of June, www.festival.cz) and **Prague Autumn** (mid-Sept–mid-Oct, www.pragueautumn.cz) music festivals.

For any of these concerts, locals dress up, but many tourists wear casual clothes—as long as you don't show up in sneakers and ripped jeans, you'll be fine.

Music Clubs—Young locals keep Prague's many music clubs in business. Most clubs are neighborhood institutions with decades of tradition, generally holding only 100–200 people. Live rock and Bob Dylan–style folk are what younger generations go for. A number of good jazz clubs attract a diverse audience, from 18 to 80. In the last decade, ethnic music has also become hugely popular: Gypsy bands, Moravian poets, African drummers, Cuban boleros, and Moroccan divas often sell out even the largest venues. You can buy tickets at the club, or, for most places, at the Ticketpro offices (see above).

The **Lucerna Music Bar** is popular for disco nights (music nightly from 21:00, around 100 Kč cover, at the bottom of Wenceslas Square, in the basement of Lucerna Gallery, Vodičkova 36, tel. 224-217-108). Friday and Saturdays are the "1980s Party," featuring the silly pop songs of the last years under communism. The scene is a big, noisy dance hall with a giant video screen. While young and trendy, it offers cheap prices, and even older tourists mix in easily. **Malostranská Beseda,** on the Little Town Square, was known in the communist era for playing host to underground rock bands, semi-legal bards, and daring jazzmen—a stark contrast to the regime-pampered pop-stars. Today, Beseda is the only club in the center with daily live performances, and the crowd tends to be a bit older than in the other clubs (shows from 20:30, about 150-Kč cover, Malostranské Náměstí 21, tel. 257-532-092).

Cruises—Prague isn't great for a boat tour. Still, the hour-long Vltava River cruises, which leave from near the castle end of Charles Bridge about hourly (100 Kč), are scenic and relaxing, though not informative. Consider renting a small rowboat or paddle boat on the island by the National Theater, so you can float between the swans at your own pace (about 60 Kč/hr, bring photo ID for deposit).

SHOPPING

Prague's entire Old Town seems designed to bring out the shopper in visitors. Shop your way from the Old Town Square up Celetná to the Powder Tower, then along Na Příkopě to the bottom of Wenceslas Square (Václavské Náměstí).

Celetná is lined with big stores selling all the traditional Czech goodies. Celetná Crystal, about midway down the street, sells the largest selection of affordable crystal. You can get the glass safely shipped home directly from the shop (for larger purchases, you can get a refund of the VAT tax; for information on VAT Refunds, see page 12).

Na Příkopě has a couple of good modern malls. The best is Slovansky Dům (Na Příkopě 22), where you wander deep past a 10-theater multiplex into a world of classy restaurants and designer shops surrounding a peaceful, parklike inner courtyard. Another modern mall is Černá Růže (Na Příkopě 12). Next door is Mosers, where you can climb upstairs to peruse its museum-like crystal showroom.

SLEEPING

Peak time is during the months of May, June, September, and October, and during Christmas and Easter holidays. July and August are not too bad. Expect crowds on weekends. I've listed peak-time prices. If you're traveling in July or August, you'll find slightly lower rates. Prices tend to go up even more on holidays. English is spoken everywhere. Reserve by phone or e-mail. Generally, you'll give your credit-card number to guarantee a room reservation.

Room-Booking Services

Prague is awash with fancy rooms on the push list; private, small-time operators with rooms to rent in their apartments; and roving agents eager to book you a bed and earn a commission. You can save about 30 percent by showing up in Prague without a reservation and finding accommodations upon arrival. If you're driving,

Sleep Code

(25 Kč = about $1, €1 = $1.20, country code: 420)
S = Single, **D** = Double/Twin, **T** = Triple, **Q** = Quad, **b** = bathroom, **s** = shower only. Unless otherwise noted, credit cards are accepted and breakfast is included. Some hotels quote prices in euros.

To help you sort easily through these listings, I've divided the rooms into three categories based on the price for a standard double room with bath:

$$$Higher Priced—Most rooms 4,000 Kč (€133) or more.
$$Moderately Priced—Most rooms between 3,000–4,000 Kč (€100–133).
$Lower Priced—Most rooms 3,000 Kč (€100) or less.

Prague Hotels

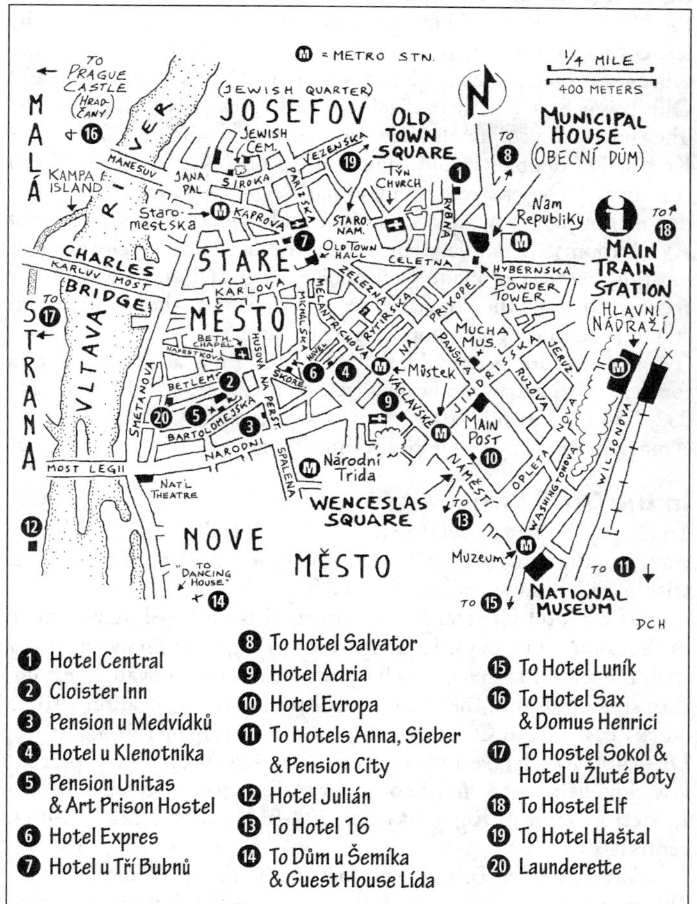

you'll see booking agencies as you enter town. Generally, if you book here, your hosts can come and lead you to their place.

Athos Travel, run by Filip Antoš, will find the right room for you from among 140 properties (ranging from hostels to 5-star hotels), 90 percent of which are in the historical center. Or use their handy Web site, which allows you to search for a room based on various criteria (best to arrange in advance during peak season, can also help with last-minute booking off-season, tel. 241-440-571, fax 241-441-697, www.athos.cz, info@athos.cz).

AVE, at the main train station (Hlavní Nádraží), is a less personable but helpful booking service (daily 6:00–23:00, tel. 251-551-011, fax 251-555-156, www.avetravel.cz, ave@avetravel.cz). With the tracks at your back, walk down to the orange ceiling and past the "Meeting Point" (don't go downstairs)—their office is in the left corner by the exit to the rip-off taxis. AVE has several other offices—at Holešovice station, the airport, Wenceslas Square, and Old Town Square. Their display board shows discounted hotels. They have a slew of hotels and small pensions available ($80/2,000-Kč pension doubles in old center, $40/1,000-Kč doubles a Metro ride away). You can reserve by e-mail (using your credit card as a deposit) or just show up at the office and request a room. Many of AVE's rooms are not very convenient to the center; be clear on the location before you make your choice. They sell taxi vouchers for those who want the convenience of a ride from the station's taxi stand, though they cost double the fair rate.

For a more personal touch, contact Lída at **Magic Praha** for help with accommodations (tel. & fax 224-230-914, tel. 224-232-755, mobile 604-207-225, www.magicpraha.cz, magicpraha @magicpraha.cz, see "Helpful Hints," page 166).

In the Old Town

You'll pay higher prices to stay in the Old Town, but for many travelers, the convenience is worth the expense. These places are all within a 10-minute walk of the Old Town Square.

$$$ Hotel Central is a sentimental favorite—I stayed there in the communist days. Like the rest of Prague, it's now changing with the times: Its 69 rooms have recently been renovated, leaving it fresh and bright. The place is well-run, and the location—three blocks east of the Old Town Square—is excellent (Sb-3,800 Kč, Db-4,400 Kč, deluxe Db-4,600 Kč, Tb-4,900 Kč, 30–40 percent less Nov–Feb, 5 percent discount for cash, elevator, Rybná 8, Praha 1, Metro: Náměstí Republiky, tel. 224-812-041, fax 222-328-404, central@orfea.cz).

$$$ Cloister Inn is well-located, with 75 modern rooms. The exterior is more concrete than charm—the building used to be shared by a convent and a secret-police prison—but inside, it's newly redone and plenty comfortable (Sb-4,000 Kč, Db-4,200 Kč, Tb-5,000 Kč, elevator, free Internet access and coffee, Konviktská 14, Praha 1, tel. 224-211-020, fax 224-210-800, www.cloister-inn .com, cloister@cloister-inn.com).

$$ Pension u Medvídků has 31 comfortably renovated rooms in a big, rustic, medieval shell with dark wood furniture. Upstairs, you'll find lots of beams to smack into (Sb-2,300 Kč, Db-3,500 Kč, Tb-4,500 Kč, extra bed-500 Kč, "historical" rooms 10 percent more, apartment 20 percent more, prices flex with season, Internet access-70 Kč/hr, Na Perštýně 7, Praha 1, tel. 224-211-916, fax 224-220-930, www.umedvidku.cz, info@umedvidku.cz). The pension runs a popular beer-hall restaurant that has live music most Fridays and Saturdays until 23:00.

$$ Hotel u Klenotníka, with 11 modern, comfortable rooms in a plain building, is three blocks off the Old Town Square (Sb-2,500 Kč, Db-3,800 Kč, Tb-4,500 Kč, Rytířská 3, Praha 1, tel. 224-211-699, fax 224-221-025, www.uklenotnika.cz, info@uklenotnika.cz).

$$ Hotel u Tří Bubnů ("Three Drums") is new, filling one of the oldest buildings in town, 50 yards toward the river from the Old Town Square. Its 18 rooms are spacious, with high ceilings and wooden beams (Db-3,900 Kč, extra bed-1,000 Kč, U Radnice 8, tel. 224-214-855, fax 224-236-100, www.utribubnu.cz, utribubnu@volny.cz).

$$ Hotel Haštal, on a quiet, hidden square in the Old Town, is also new. Its 20 rooms combine the elegance of the Old World (this was a popular hotel in the 1920s) with the amenities of the 21st century (Sb-3,000 Kč, Db-3,600 Kč, Tb-4,200 Kč, Haštalská 16, tel. 222-314-335, info@hastal.com, www.hastal.com).

$ Pension Unitas rents 35 small, tidy, youth hostel–type rooms with plain, minimalist furnishings and no sinks (S-1,100 Kč, D-1,400 Kč, T-1,750 Kč, Q-2,000 Kč, T and Q are cramped with bunks in D-sized rooms, easy reservations without a deposit, non-smoking, quiet hours 22:00–7:00, Bartolomějská 9, Praha 1, tel. 224-221-802, fax 224-217-555, www.unitas.cz, unitas@unitas.cz). They run a fine little youth hostel in the former prison downstairs (see "Youth Hostels," page 206).

$ Hotel Expres rents 29 simple rooms and brings a continental breakfast to your room (S-1,000 Kč, Sb-2,600 Kč, D-1,400 Kč, Db-2,800 Kč, Tb-3,400 Kč, 5 percent discount for cash, elevator, Skořepka 5, Praha 1, tel. 224-211-801, fax 224-223-309, www.pragueexpreshotel.cz, info@pragueexpreshotel.cz). While a good value, this place is in a red light zone and comes with late-night music from nearby clubs on weekends.

$ Hotel Salvator rents 30 comfortable rooms on a quiet street above a fun South American restaurant (D-1,850 Kč, Db-2,850 Kč, Qb-3,850 Kč, extra bed-500 Kč, elevator, Truhlářská 10, 3 min from Republic Square, Metro: Náměstí Republiky, tel. 222-312-234, fax 222-316-355, www.salvator.cz).

On Wenceslas Square

$$$ Hotel Adria, with a prime Wenceslas Square location, cool Art Nouveau facade, and 88 completely modern and business-class rooms, is your big-time, four-star, central splurge (Db-€220 but often discounted, air-con, elevator, minibars...the works, Václavské Náměstí 26, tel. 221-081-111, fax 221-081-300, www.adria.cz, accom@adria.cz).

$$$ Hotel Evropa is in a class by itself. This landmark place, famous for its wonderful 1903 Art Nouveau facade, is the centerpiece of Wenceslas Square. But someone pulled the plug on the hotel about 50 years ago, and it's a mess. It offers haunting beauty in all the public spaces, 92 dreary and ramshackle rooms, and a weary staff. They're waiting for a billion-crown investor to come along and rescue the place, but for now, they offer some of the cheapest rooms on Wenceslas Square (S-1,600 Kč, Sb-3,000 Kč, D-2,600 Kč, Db-4,000 Kč, T-3,100 Kč, Tb-5,000 Kč, some rooms have been very slightly refurbished, some remain in unrefurbished old style, they cost the same either way, every room is different, elevator, Václavské Náměstí 25, Praha 1, tel. 224-228-117, fax 224-224-544, www.evropahotel.cz, info@evropahotel.cz).

East of the Center, in Vinohrady

$$$ Hotel Sieber, with 20 rooms, is in an upscale residential neighborhood (near the former royal vineyards, or Vinohrady). It's a classy, four-star, business-class hotel that does a good job of being homey and welcoming (Sb-4,480 Kč, Db-4,800 Kč, extra bed-1,000 Kč, 20 percent discount Fri-Sun, elevator, air-con, 3-min walk to Metro: Jiřího z Poděbrad, or tram #11, Slezská 55, Praha 3, tel. 224-250-025, fax 224-250-027, www.sieber.cz, reservations@sieber.cz).

$$ Hotel Anna, with 24 bright, pastel, and classically charming rooms, is a bit closer in—10 minutes by foot east of Wenceslas Square (Sb-2,300 Kč, Db-3,100 Kč, Tb-3,900 Kč, 20 percent cheaper off-season, non-smoking rooms, elevator, Budečská 17, Praha 2, Metro: Náměstí Míru, tel. 222-513-111, fax 222-515-158, www.hotelanna.cz). The hotel runs a cheaper but similarly pleasant annex, the **Dependence,** two blocks away (Sb-1,860 Kč, Db-2,560 Kč, cheaper off-season, no elevator but all rooms on first floor, reception and breakfast at main hotel).

$ Hotel Luník, with 35 rooms, is a dignified but friendly, no-nonsense place out of the medieval, faux-rustic world in a normal, pleasant business district. It's two Metro stops from the main station (Metro: I.P. Pavlova) or a 10-minute walk from Wenceslas Square (Sb-2,050 Kč, Db-2,900 Kč, Tb-3,350 Kč, 20 percent cheaper Nov–March, elevator, some street noise, Londýnská 50, Praha 2, tel. 224-253-974, fax 224-253-986, www.hotel-lunik.cz, recepce@hotel-lunik.cz).

$ Hotel Pension City is tucked away in a typical Prague apartment house in a quiet, circa-1900s area near some of Vinohrady's best pubs and restaurants. Red carpets lead to enormous bathrooms and large rooms with nostalgic furnishings from the 1970s. Signs posted on the walls will tell you exactly where to step, where not to step, what is permitted, and what isn't (Sb-1,670 Kč, Db-2,320 Kč, Tb-2,610 Kč, 25 percent cheaper off-season, Belgická 10, Prague 2, Metro: Náměstí Míru, tel. 222-521-606, www.hotelcity.cz).

Away from the Center

Moving just outside the Old Town saves you money—and gets you away from the tourists and into some more workaday residential neighborhoods. These listings (great values compared to Old Town hotels) are all within a five- to 15-minute tram or Metro ride from the center.

$$ Hotel Julián, an oasis of professional, predictable decency in a quiet, untouristy neighborhood, is a five-minute taxi or tram ride from the action on the castle side of the river. Its 32 spacious, fresh, well-furnished rooms and big, homey public spaces hide behind a noble neoclassical facade. The staff is friendly and helpful (Sb-3,500 Kč, Db-3,800 Kč, Db suite-4,500 Kč, extra bed-900 Kč, family room, 13 percent less July–Aug, elevator, free tea and coffee in room, Internet access, parking lot, Elišky Peškové 11, Praha 5, tel. 257-311-150, reception tel. 257-311-145, fax 257-311-149, www.julian.cz, casjul@vol.cz). Free lockers and a shower are available for those needing to check out early, but stay until late (e.g., for an overnight train). Mike's Chauffeur Service, based here, is reliable and affordable (see page 214).

$$ Hotel 16, a stately little place with an intriguing Art Nouveau facade, high ceilings, and a clean, sleek interior, rents 14 fine rooms (Sb-2,500 Kč, Db-3,400 Kč, Db suite-3,900 Kč, Tb-4,600 Kč, 10 percent cheaper off-season, back/quiet rooms face the garden, front/noisier rooms face the street, air-con, elevator, 10-min walk south of Wenceslas Square, Metro: I.P. Pavlova, Kateřinská 16, Praha 2, tel. 224-920-636, fax 224-920-626, www.hotel16.cz, hotel16@hotel16.cz).

$ Dům u Šemíka, a friendly hotel named for a heroic mythical horse, is in a residential neighborhood just below Vyšehrad Castle, a 10-minute tram ride from the center (25 rooms, Sb-1,700 Kč, Db-2,100–2,650 Kč, apartment-2,800–4,850 Kč depending on size, extra bed-700 Kč; from the center, take tram #18 to Albertov, then walk 2 blocks uphill; or take tram #7 to Výtoň, go under rail bridge, and walk 3 blocks uphill to Vratislavova 36; Praha 2, tel. 224-920-736, fax 224-911-602, www.usemika.cz).

$ Guest House Lída, with 12 homey and spacious rooms, fills a big house in a quiet residential area a 30-minute walk or 15-minute tram ride from the center. Jan and Jiří Prouza, who run the place, are a wealth of information and know how to make people feel at home (small Db-1,440 Kč, Db-1,760 Kč, Tb-2,110 Kč, 10 percent cheaper Nov–March, cash only, family rooms, top-floor family suite with kitchenette, garage parking-200 Kč/day, Metro: Pražského Povstání; exit Metro and turn left on Lomnicka between the Metro station and big blue glass ČSOB building, follow Lomnicka for 500 yards, then turn left on Lopatecka, go uphill, and ring bell at Lopatecka #26, no sign outside; Praha 4, tel. & fax 261-214-766, lida@login.cz). The Prouza brothers also rent four apartments across the river, equally far away (Db-1,500 Kč, Tb-1,920 Kč, Qb-2,100 Kč).

Across the River, near the Castle

$$$ Hotel Sax, on a quiet corner a block below the Little Quarter action, will delight the artsy yuppie with its 22 rooms, fruity atrium, and modern, stylish decor (Sb-3,700 Kč, Db-4,400 Kč, Db suite-5,100 Kč, extra bed-1,000 Kč, cheaper off-season, elevator, near Church of St. Nicholas, 1 block below Nerudova at Jánský Vršek 3, Praha 1, reserve long in advance, tel. 257-531-268, fax 257-534-101, www.sax.cz, hotel@sax.cz).

$$$ Residence Domus Henrici, just above Castle Square, is a quiet retreat that charges—and gets—top prices for its eight smartly appointed rooms, some of which include good views (Ds-5,100 Kč, Db-5,600–6,200 Kč depending on size, extra bed-900 Kč, less off-season, pleasant terrace, Loretánská 11, Praha 1, tel. 220-511-369, fax 220-511-502, www.domus-henrici.cz, henrici@hidden-places.com). This is a five-minute walk above the castle gate in a quiet, elegant area.

$$$ Hotel u Žluté Boty ("By the Yellow Boot") is the most charming small hotel in Prague, hiding on a small lane in the Little Quarter. Each of its seven rooms has a completely different feel: Some preserve the 16th-century wooden ceilings, some feel like mountain lodges, and others are a bit marred by an insensitive 1970s adaptation. The manager's husband is a distinguished artist whose paintings (for sale) embellish the dining room and halls. The only drawback of this hotel are its thin walls—you'll know exactly what your neighbors are arguing about (Sb-3,700 Kč, Db-4,200 Kč, Tb-4,900 Kč, 25 percent less off-season, Jánský Vršek 11, tel. 257-532-269, fax 257-534-134, www.zlutabota.cz, hotel@zlutabota.cz).

Youth Hostels

$ Hostel Sokol, plain and institutional, with 100 beds, is peacefully located just off the parklike Kampa Island in the Tryš House buildings (the seat of the Czech Sokol Organization). Big, WWI hospital–style rooms are lined with single beds and lockers (8–14 per room, 350 Kč per bed, D-900 Kč, cash only, no breakfast, easy to reserve by phone or e-mail without deposit, open 24/7, members' kitchen, Nosticova 2, Praha 1, tel. 257-007-397, fax 257-007-340, www.sokol-cos.cz, hostel@sokol-cos.cz). From the main train station, ride tram #9 to Újezd. From the Holešovice station, take tram #12 to Újezd.

$ Art Prison Hostel fills a former prison in the basement of Pension Unitas (see page 203). With tiny, high windows and no plumbing, the rooms are stark—but not as stark as when Václav Havel did time here (64 beds, S-1,000 Kč, D-1,100 Kč, dorm beds in 4- to 5-bed cells for 370 Kč, includes sheets and breakfast, easy reservations without deposit if arriving by 17:00, no curfew, non-smoking, shared, modern facilities, lockers, Bartolomějská 9, tel. 224-221-802, www.unitas.cz, unitas@unitas.cz).

$ Hostel Elf, a fun-loving, ramshackle place covered with noisy, self-inflicted graffiti, has cheap, basic beds, a helpful staff, and lots of creative services—kitchen, free luggage room, laundry, no lockout, free tea, cheap beer, a terrace, and lockers (dorm beds-260–340 Kč, D-820 Kč, includes sheets and breakfast, on a train line a 10-min walk from main train station and Florenc bus station, Husitská 11, Praha 3, tel. 222-540-963, www.hostelelf.com, info@hostelelf.com).

EATING

A big part of Prague's charm is enjoyed wandering aimlessly through the winding old quarters, marveling at the architecture, watching the people, and sniffing out fun restaurants. You can eat well here for very little money. What you'd pay for a basic meal in Vienna or Munich will get you an elegant feast in Prague. Choose between traditional, dark Czech beer-hall ambience; elegant *Jugendstil,* early-20th-century atmosphere; ethnic; or hip and modern.

Watch out for scams. Many restaurants put more care into ripping off green tourists (and even locals) than in their cooking. Tourists are routinely served cheaper meals than what they ordered, given a menu with a "personalized" price list, charged extra for things they didn't get, or shortchanged. Avoid any menu without clear and explicit prices. Carefully examine your itemized bill and understand each line (a 10 percent service charge is sometimes added—in that case, there's no need to tip extra). Be careful of waiters padding the tab: Tax is always included in the price, so it shouldn't be tacked on later. Part with very large bills only if necessary, and deliberately count your change. Never let your credit card out of your sight, and check the numbers carefully. Make it a habit to get cash from an ATM to pay for your meals. Remember, there are two parallel worlds in Prague: the tourist town and the real city. Generally, if you walk two minutes away from the tourist flow, you'll find better value, ambience, and service.

In the Old Town

Art Nouveau Restaurants

The sumptuous Art Nouveau concert hall—**Municipal House** (Obecní Dům)—has three special restaurants: a café, a French

Prague Restaurants

restaurant, and a beer cellar (Náměstí Republiky 5). The dressy café, **Kavarna Obecní Dům,** is drenched in chandeliered, Art Nouveau elegance (light, pricey meals and drinks with great atmosphere and bad service, 250-Kč hot meal special daily, open daily 7:30–23:00, live piano or jazz trio 16:00–20:00, tel. 222-002-763). **Francouzska Restaurace,** the fine and formal French restaurant, is in the next wing (700- to 1,000-Kč meals, daily 12:00–16:00 & 18:00–23:00, tel. 222-002-777). **Plzeňská Restaurace,** downstairs, brags it's the most beautiful Art Nouveau pub in Europe (cheap meals, great atmosphere, daily 11:30–23:00, tel. 222-002-780).

Restaurant Mucha is touristy, with decent Czech food in a formal Art Nouveau dining room (300-Kč meals, daily 12:00–24:00, Melantrichova 5, tel. 224-225-045).

Cheap, Uniquely Czech Places near Old Town Square

Prices go way down when you get away from the tourist areas. At least once, eat in a restaurant with no English menu.

Pivnice u Zeleného Stromu ("At the Green Tree") is a new beer garden/cellar in an old building serving great beer and inexpensive traditional cuisine from a fun, imaginative menu. The courtyard is quiet, and the cellar is bright and fresh (good veggies, daily 11:00–23:00, next to Bethlehem Chapel at Betlémská Náměstí 6, tel. 222-220-228).

Klub Architektů is a modern student hangout with a medieval cellar serving cheap vegetarian meals, hearty salads, and a few "gourmet entrées" next to Bethlehem Chapel (Betlémská Náměstí 169, tel. 224-401-214).

U Medvídků, which started out as a brewery in 1466, has been a huge and popular beer hall since the 19th century. The food, beer, and service are fine, and the ambience is bright, noisy, and not too smoky (daily 11:30–23:00, a block toward Wenceslas Square from Bethlehem Square at Na Perštýně 7, tel. 224-211-916).

Plzeňská Restaurace u Dvou Koček ("By the Two Cats") is a typical Czech pub with cheap, no-nonsense, hearty Czech food and beer, and—once upon a time—a local crowd. Sandwiched between the two red light district streets, the restaurant's name is a bit ambiguous (200 Kč for 3 courses and beer, serving original Pilsner Urquell with accordion music nightly until 23:00, under an arcade, facing tiny square between Perlová and Skořepka Streets).

Restaurace Mlejnice is a fun little pub strewn with farm implements and happy eaters, tucked away just out of the tourist crush two blocks from the Old Town Square (order carefully and understand your itemized bill, daily 11:00–24:00, between Melantrichova and Òelezná at Kožná 14, reservations smart in evening, tel. 224-228-635).

Country Life Vegetarian Restaurant is a bright, easy, nonsmoking cafeteria with a well-displayed buffet of salads and veggie hot dishes. It's midway between the Old Town Square and the bottom of Wenceslas Square. They are serious about their vegetarianism, serving only plant-based, unprocessed, and unrefined food (Mon–Thu 8:30–19:00, Fri 8:30–18:00, Sun 11:00–18:00, closed Sat, through courtyard at Melantrichova 15/Michalská 18, tel. 224-213-366).

Česká Kuchyně ("Czech Kitchen") is a blue-collar cafeteria serving steamy, old-Czech cuisine to a local clientele. There's no English inside, so—if you want apple charlotte, but not tripe soup—be sure to review the small English menu in the window outside before entering. Note the numbers of the dishes you'd like that correspond to the Czech menu you'll see inside. Pick up your tally sheet as you enter, grab a tray, point liberally to whatever you'd like, and keep the paper to pay as you exit. It's extremely cheap... unless you lose your paper (daily 9:00–20:00, across from Havelská Market at Havelská 23, tel. 224-235-574).

Bohemia Bagel is hardly authentic Czech—exasperated locals insist that bagels have nothing to do with Bohemia. Owned by an American, this trendy place caters mostly to youthful tourists, with good sandwiches (100–125 Kč), a little garden out back, and Internet access (1.50 Kč/min). It's close to the Old Town Square (daily 7:00–24:00, locations at Újezd 16, tel. 257-310-529, and Masná 2, tel. 224-812-560, www.bohemiabagel.cz).

Havelská Market, surrounded by colorful little eateries, offers piles of picnic fixings (see page 177).

Ethnic Restaurants for Local Yuppies near the Old Town Square

With the recent economic boom, young professional Czechs have money to eat out, and trendy little ethnic eateries are popping up everywhere. Within the space of a couple of blocks, you can eat your way around the world. Two blocks north of Old Town Square (up Dlouhá Street), wander along Rámová Street to Haštalská Square. You'll pass the **Ariana** (Afghan), **Orange Moon** (Thai/Indian), **Chez Marcel** (French), and **Dahab** (fancy or cheap Moroccan buffet, daily 12:00–24:00, Dlouhá 33, tel. 224-827-375).

Dining with an Old Town Square View

Restaurant u Prince Terrace, in the five-star U Prince Hotel, facing the astronomical clock, is designed for foreign tourists. A sleek elevator takes you to its rooftop, where every possible inch is used to serve good food (fish, Czech, and international) to its guests. The view is arguably the best in town—especially at sunset, when a reservation is smart. The menu is a fun and impressively affordable mix, with photos to make ordering easy (daily until 24:00, Staroměstské Náměstí 29, tel. 224-213-807).

Above the Castle

To locate the following restaurants, see the map on page 183.

Malý Buddha ("Little Buddha") serves delightful food—especially vegetarian—and takes its theme seriously. You'll step into a mellow, low-lit escape of bamboo and peace to be served by people with perfect complexions and almost no pulse. Ethnic eateries like this are trendy with young Czechs (Tue–Sun 13:00–22:30, closed Mon, non-smoking, from the castle hike up the hill nearly to the monastery, Úvoz 46, tel. 220-513-894).

U Hrocha ("By the Hippo"), a very local little pub packed with beer-drinkers and smoke, serves simple, traditional meals—basically meat dishes with bread. Just below the castle near Little Quarter Square, it's actually the haunt of many members of Parliament—located just around the corner (daily 12:00–23:00, chalkboard lists daily meals in English, Thunovská 10).

Espresso Kajetánka, just off Castle Square, is a pricey café worth considering for the view and convenience (daily 10:00–20:00, on Ke Hradu, tel. 257-533-735).

In the Jewish Quarter

To locate these restaurants, see the map on page 208.

Kolkovna is a big, new, woody-yet-modern place catering to locals and serving a fun mix of Czech and international cuisine (ribs, salads, cheese plates, good beer, daily 11:00–24:00, across from Spanish Synagogue at V Kolkovně 8, tel. 224-819-701).

Franz Kafka Café is pleasant for a snack or drink (daily 10:00–21:00, a block from the cemetery, Široká 12).

Fine Dining near the River in the New Town

Restaurant Žofín is a Prague institution, taking you back to the era of waltzing elegance. Nicknamed for Franz Josef's mother, Sofia, it shares a circa-1880 palace with a famous ballroom on a small island south of Charles Bridge (mostly traditional, 3-course *menus* range from simple/310 Kč to gourmet/990 Kč, huge and reasonable wine list, plain garden tables or sumptuous reserve-in-advance indoor tables, Slovanský Island, reach island by bridge south of National Theater, tel. 224-934-548).

La Perle de Prague fills the seventh and eighth floors of Frank Gehry's wild and modern Dancing House building with Prague's high society and top-end visitors enjoying a fine river view and gourmet French cuisine. It's white-tablecloth dressy and offers terrace seating in good weather. While few tables are actually by the window, be sure to enjoy a pre-dinner drink or sip your last glass of wine upstairs, next to Fred Astaire's wire-mesh head, on the roof terrace (500-Kč business lunch, 900-Kč dinner *menu*, daily 12:00–14:00 & 19:00–22:30, reservations required to even get in the elevator, 15-min walk south of Charles Bridge, Tancící Dům, Rašínovo Nábřeží 80, tel. 221-984-160, www.laperle.cz).

Grand Café Slavia, across from the National Theater (facing the Legií Bridge on Národní Street), is a fixture in Prague, famous as a hangout for its literary elite. Today, it's a bit tired, with an Art Deco interior, lousy piano entertainment, and celebrity photos on the wall. But its cheap and fun menu, filled with interesting traditional dishes (meals, sweets, coffees, liqueurs—including absinthe for 55 Kč), make it a fun stop (daily 8:00–23:00, sit nearest the river). Notice the *Drinker of Absinthe* painting on the wall (and on the menu)—with the iconic Czech writer struggling with reality.

In the Little Quarter

Restaurace Rybářský Klub, on Kampa Island, is run by the Society of Czech Fishermen and serves the widest and tastiest selection of freshwater fish in Prague, at reasonable prices. Dine on fish cream soup, pike, trout, carp, or catfish under the imaginative artwork of local Malá Strana painter Kuba (3-course meal for around 300 Kč, daily 12:00–23:00, U Sovových Mlýnů 1, tel. 257-534-200).

Restaurace David, with two little 18th-century rooms hiding on a small cobblestone street opposite the American embassy, is the best place in town for an elegant meal. The exquisite cuisine—a mix of Czech and European styles, ranging from game to roasted duck and liver—is served in the most artistic of arrangements, and the waiters move around with the grace of the 19th century (most meals 600–1,000 Kč, reservations highly recommended, Tržiště 21, tel. 257-533-109).

In Vinohrady and Žižkov

Café Medúza ("Jellyfish"), an authentic, between-the-world-wars café with plush sofas and pictures of 1930s movie stars, draws a crowd of dreamy young Czechs enjoying coffee, cigarettes, cheap lunch specials, and dark Svijany beer (Mon–Fri 11:00–1:00, Sat–Sun 12:00–1:00, Belgická 17, Metro: Náměstí Míru, from Metro stop walk a bit down and look for Belgická on your left, tel. 222-515-107).

At **Hlučná Samota** ("Too Loud a Solitude"), the wooden floor and brick walls are dedicated to the great Czech writer Bohumil Hrabal. Though he never visited here, Hrabal would surely be delighted by some of the most beautiful waitresses in Prague, as well as the rich mix of Czech and Italian cuisine (including honey ducks, spinach salmon, and Prague's own Staropramen beer to wash it all down). An outdoor lunch—under the shade of linden trees on the quiet, circa-1900 Zagreb street—can easily stretch out into an all-afternoon affair (daily 11:00–23:00, Záhřebská 14, tel. 222-522-839, www.hlucnasamota.cz).

Restaurace U Sadu, on Škroupa square below the Žižkov TV Tower, is popular with young Czechs in the summer. An outdoor lunch on this quiet square under a futuristic monument must be one of the most atmospheric eating options in Prague. The restaurant up in the TV tower itself is expensive, but gives you Neil Armstrong's perspective on Prague.

Hospůdka nad Viktorkou, named for this neighborhood's soccer team, is around the corner on Bořivojova street. This quintessentially blue-collar Žižkov pub features occasional live performances by local bands, a warm glass terrace in the winter, and a little courtyard with a shady canopy of chestnut trees in the summer. Sipping a beer while chatting with locals in this purest of Prague institutions—you'll feel like you've really found the true Prague.

Drinks

Beer

For many, *pivo* (beer) is the top Czech tourist attraction. After all, the Czechs invented lager in nearby Plzeň (Pilsen in German) This is the famous Pilsner Urquell, a great lager on tap everywhere. Two classic places to enjoy a Pilsner Urquell are **U Zlateho Tygra** ("The Golden Tiger"), just south of Karlova on Husova (daily 15:00–23:00—often jam-packed) and **Hostinec u Pinkasů,** in the dead-end alley just off the bottom of Wenceslas Square.

Be sure to venture beyond Pilsner Urquell. There are plenty of other good Czech beers. Budvar is the local Budweiser, but it's not related to the American brew.

Czechs are among the world's biggest beer drinkers—adults drink about 80 gallons a year. The big degree symbol on bottles and menus marks the beer's heaviness, not its alcohol content (12 degrees is darker, 10 degrees lighter). The smaller figure shows alcohol content. Order beer from the tap (*tocene* means "draft," *sudove pivo* means "keg beer"). A *pivo* is large (0.5 liter, or 17 oz); a *malé pivo* is small (0.3 liter, or 10 oz). Men customarily order the large size.

In many restaurants, a beer hits your table like a glass of water in the United States. *Pivo* for lunch has me sightseeing for the rest of the day on Czech knees. *Na Zdraví* is "cheers" in Czech. Later they say *Nádraží* (which means "train station").

Tea

Many Czech people are bohemian philosophers at heart and prefer the mellow, smoke-free environs of a teahouse to the smoky, traditional beer hall. Young Czechs are much more interested in traveling to exotic destinations like Southeast Asia, Africa, or Peru than to Western Europe, so Oriental teahouses set their minds into vacation mode.

While there are teahouses all over town, a fine example in a handy locale is Prague's original one, established in 1991: **Dobrá Čajovna** ("Good Teahouse," Mon–Sat 10:00–21:30, Sun 14:00–21:30, near the base of Wenceslas Square, opposite McDonald's at Václavské Náměstí 14, www.cajovna.com). This teahouse, just a few steps off the bustle of the main square, takes you into a very peaceful world that elevates tea to an almost religious ritual. At the desk, you'll be given an English menu and a bell. Grab a seat and study the menu, which lovingly describes each tea. The menu lists a world of tea (very fresh, prices by the small pot), "accompaniments" (such as Exotic Miscellany), and light meals "for hungry tea-drinkers." When you're ready to order, ring your bell to beckon a tea monk—likely a member of the "Lovers of Tea Society."

TRANSPORTATION CONNECTIONS

Getting to Prague: Centrally located Prague is a logical gateway between Western and Eastern Europe. If you're coming from the West and using a Eurailpass, you must purchase tickets to cover the portion of the journey from the Czech border into Prague (buy at station before you board train for Prague). Or supplement your pass with a Prague Excursion pass, giving you passage from any Czech border station into Prague and back to any border station within seven days (first class-€50, second class-€40, youth second class-€30). EurAide, a travel agency with offices in Berlin (see page 553) and Munich, also sells these passes for a bit less from their American office (U.S. tel. 941/480-1555, fax 941/480-1522, www.euraide.de/ricksteves). From the East, Prague has convenient night-train connections with Budapest, Kraków, and Warsaw (see below).

For Czech train and bus schedules, see www.vlak-bus.cz. Train info tel. 221-111-122 (little English).

From Prague by Train to: Český Krumlov (8/day, 1/day direct, 4 hrs, verify departing station), **Berlin** (5/day, 5 hrs), **Munich** (3/day with changes, 6 hrs; 1 direct night train), **Frankfurt** (4 direct/day, 6 hrs), **Vienna** (3/day, 5 hrs), **Budapest** (5 direct/day, 7 hrs), **Kraków** (1 direct night train/day, 8.5 hrs; otherwise transfer in Katowice, Wrocław, or Ostrava-Svinov, 8–11 hrs), **Warsaw** (2/day direct, including 1 night train, 9–12 hrs; or 1/day, 9 hrs, with transfer in Ostrava-Svinov).

By Bus to: Český Krumlov (7/day, 3.5 hrs, from Florenc station; an easy, direct 3-hr bus leaves at about 9:00).

By Car with a Driver: Mike's Chauffeur Service is a reliable, family-run little company with fair and fixed rates around town and beyond. Friendly Mike's motto is, "We go the extra mile for you" (round-trip fares with waiting time included: Český Krumlov-3,500 Kč, Terezín-1,700 Kč, Karlštejn-1,500 Kč, up to 4 people, minibus also available, tel. 241-768-231, mobile 602-224-893, www.mike-chauffeur.cz, mike.chauffeur@cmail.cz). On the way to Krumlov, Mike will stop at no extra charge at Hluboká Castle or České Budějovice, where the original Bud beer is made. Mike offers a "Panoramic Transfer to Vienna" for 7,000 Kč (depart Prague at 8:00, arrive Český Krumlov at 10:00, stay up to 6 hrs,

1-hr scenic Czech riverside-and-village drive, then 2-hr Autobahn to your Vienna hotel, maximum 4 people). Mike also offers a similar "Panoramic Transfer to Budapest" for 10,000 Kč (2 hrs to Český Krumlov, then 1 hr scenic drive to Linz, followed by 5-6 hrs on the expressway to Budapest).

COPENHAGEN

(København)

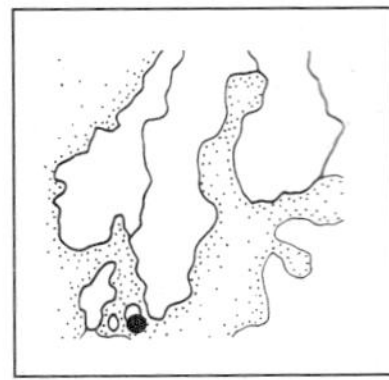

Copenhagen, Denmark's capital, is the gateway to Scandinavia. And now, with the bridge connecting Sweden and Denmark (creating the region's largest metropolitan area), Copenhagen is energized and ready to dethrone Stockholm as Scandinavia's powerhouse city. A busy day cruising the canals, wandering through the palace, and taking an old-town walk will give you your historical bearings. Then, after another day strolling the Strøget (Europe's first and greatest pedestrian shopping mall), biking the canals, and sampling the Danish good life, you'll feel right at home. Copenhagen is Scandinavia's cheapest and most fun-loving capital. So live it up.

Planning Your Time

A first visit deserves a minimum of two days.

Day 1: Catch a 10:30 city walking tour (departs from TI May–Sept daily except Sun; see "Tours," below). After lunch at Riz-Raz, visit the Use It information center and catch the relaxing canal-boat tour out to *The Little Mermaid* and back. Enjoy the rest of the afternoon tracing Denmark's cultural roots in the National Museum (touring the Victorian Apartment if possible) and visiting the Ny Carlsberg Glyptotek art gallery (some wings closed until mid-2006) or the National Art Museum (Impressionists and Danish artists). Spend the evening strolling Strøget (follow my self-guided walk, described on page 226).

Day 2: At 10:00, go neoclassical at Thorvaldsen's Museum. At 11:00, take the 50-minute guided tour of Denmark's royal Christiansborg Palace. After a *smørrebrød* lunch in a park, spend the afternoon seeing the Rosenborg Castle/crown jewels and the Museum of Danish Resistance. Spend the evening at Tivoli Gardens.

ORIENTATION

Nearly all of your sightseeing is in Copenhagen's compact old town. By doing things by bike or on foot, you'll stumble into some charming bits of Copenhagen that many miss. I rent a bike for my entire visit (for the cost of about a single cab ride per day) and park it safely in my hotel courtyard. I get anywhere in the town center literally faster than by taxi. The city is an absolute delight by bike.

For most visitors, the core of the town is the axis formed by the train station, Tivoli Gardens, Rådhuspladsen (City Hall Square), and the Strøget pedestrian street. Bubbling with street life and colorful pedestrian zones, this main drag is fun. But be sure to get off the Strøget.

You need to remember one character in Copenhagen's history: Christian IV. Ruling from 1588 to 1648, he was Denmark's Renaissance king and a royal party animal. The personal energy of this "Builder King" sparked a golden age when Copenhagen prospered and many of the city's grandest buildings were erected. Locals love to tell stories of everyone's favorite king, whose drinking was legendary.

Tourist Information

Copenhagen This Week is a free, handy, and misnamed monthly guide to the city, worth reading for its good maps, museum hours with telephone numbers, sightseeing tour ideas, shopping suggestions, and calendar of events, including free English tours and concerts (online at www.ctw.dk). This is *the* essential listing of everything in town, and it's always the most up-to-date information in print. While the "TIs" are really just an advertising agency (see below), you should be ready to roll with a map and *Copenhagen This Week*—both free and available at TIs and most hotels. The Danish Tourist Board's Web site also has a wealth of information on activities and events in Copenhagen (www.visitdenmark.com).

Wonderful Copenhagen, as the tourist office is called, is a for-profit company. This colors the advice and information it provides. Mindful of this, drop by to get a city map and *Copenhagen This Week,* browse the racks of brochures, and get your questions answered (July–Aug Mon–Sat 9:00–20:00, Sun 9:00–18:00, May–June Mon–Sat 9:00–18:00, closed Sun, Sept–April Mon–Fri 9:00–16:00, Sat 9:00–14:00, closed Sun, across from train station on Vesterbrogade 4A, tel. 70 22 24 42, www.visitcopenhagen.dk). They also book rooms for a 75-kr fee. The TI (unlike the excellent "Use It" service described below) only posts information from

Copenhagen Overview

outfits that pay for the shelf space. You'll find this week's entertainment program for Tivoli on posts outside Tivoli's main entrance (around the corner from the TI).

Use It is a better information service (10-min walk from train station). Government-sponsored, it caters to Copenhagen's young but welcomes budget travelers of any age. It's a friendly, driven-to-help, energetic, no-nonsense source of budget-travel information, offering a free room-finding service, free Internet access, and free short-term luggage lockers. Their free annual *Playtime* publication has Back Door–style articles on Copenhagen and the Danish culture, special budget tips, and self-guided tours. Read it! They book private rooms (350-kr doubles, no booking fee). From the station, head down Strøget, and then turn right on Rådhustræde for three blocks to #13 (mid-June–mid-Sept daily 9:00–19:00, otherwise

Mon–Wed 11:00–16:00, Thu 11:00–18:00, Fri 11:00–14:00, closed Sat–Sun, tel. 33 73 06 20, www.useit.dk).

The **Copenhagen Card,** which includes free entry to many of the city's sights, can save you some money if you're sightseeing like crazy (199 kr for 24 hours, the 72-hour version for 399 kr also covers outlying sights and public transportation).

Arrival in Copenhagen

By Train: The main train station is called Hovedbanegården (HOETH-bahn-gorn). It's a temple of travel and a hive of travel-related activity, offering lockers (35 kr/day), a checkroom (*garderobe,* 40 kr/day per backpack, Mon–Sat 5:30–24:00, Sun 6:00–24:00), a post office (Mon–Fri 8:00–21:00, Sat 9:00–16:00, Sun 10:00–16:00), a grocery store (daily 8:00–24:00), 24-hour thievery, and the best bike-rental shop in town (see "Getting Around Copenhagen," page 220). The station has ATMs and long-hours FOREX exchange desks (daily 8:00–21:00, FOREX is the least expensive place in town to change money). Showers for 10 kr are available in the public rest rooms at the back of the station.

While you're in the station, reserve your overnight train seat or *couchette* out at the Rejse-bureau (Mon–Fri 10:00–17:00, closed Sat–Sun, tel. 33 54 55 10). Some international rides and IC (fast) trains require reservations (usually 23–51 kr). If you have a railpass, you must make your reservations at the *Billetsalg* office (Mon–Fri 9:00–18:00, Sat–Sun 10:00–17:00). The *Kviksalg* office sells tickets within Denmark (plus the regional train to Malmö, Sweden). This "quick sale" office will also help you with reservations for international trips if the *Billetsalg* office is closed, and you're departing by train within one hour or early the next day (daily 5:45–23:30).

To get to the recommended Christianshavn B&Bs from the train station, catch bus #2A or #48 (15 kr, 4/hr, in front of station on near side of Bernstorffsgade, with back to the station heading to right, get off at stop just after *Knippelsbro*—Knippels Bridge). Note the time the bus departs, and then stop by the TI (across the street) and pick up a free Copenhagen city map that shows bus routes.

By Plane: Kastrup, Copenhagen's international airport, is a traveler's dream, with a TI, baggage check, bank, post office, shopping mall, grocery store, and bakery. You can use dollars or euros at the airport—but you'll get change back in kroner (airport info tel. 32 47 47 47, SAS info tel. 70 10 20 00). Need to kill a night at the airport? The Transfer Hotel, under the transit hall, rents compact fetal rest cabins. Called *hvilekabiner,* they are especially handy for early flights, but you must have a ticket, and if you stay there, you're stuck in the transit area (Sb-415 kr, Db-620 kr for 8 hrs, prices vary for 2- to 16-hr periods, reception open daily 5:30–23:30, easy telephone reservations, sauna and showers available at a cost for non-guests, tel. 32 31 24 55, fax 32 31 31 09, transferhotel@cph.dk).

Getting Downtown from the Airport: Taxis are fast, civil, accept credit cards, and, at about 200 kr to the town center, are a reasonable deal for foursomes. The slick and easy Air Rail train links the airport with the train station, as well as the Nørreport stations (25 kr, 3/hr, 12 min). City bus #250S gets you downtown to the Rådhuspladsen (at the train station) in 30 minutes for 25 kr (6/hr, across the street and to the right as you exit airport).

If you're going from the airport to Christianshavn, just hop on bus #2A, which takes you right through the middle of Christianshavn (30 min). Or you could take the Air Rail shuttle to Nørreport, then change to the Metro for Christianshavn (same 25-kr ticket works for entire trip). In a few years, the Metro will connect the airport and Christianshavn directly in 10 minutes.

Helpful Hints

Emergencies: Dial 112 and specify fire, police, or ambulance. Emergency calls from public phones are free.

U.S. Embassy: It's at Dag Hammerskjölds Alle 24 (tel. 35 55 31 44).

Pharmacy: Steno Apotek is across from the train station (open 24 hrs daily, Vesterbrogade 6c, tel. 33 14 82 66).

Telephones: Use the telephone liberally. Everyone speaks English, and *Copenhagen This Week* and this book list phone numbers for everything you'll be doing. All telephone numbers in Denmark are eight digits, and there are no area codes. Calls anywhere in Denmark are cheap; calls to Norway and Sweden cost 6 kr per minute from a booth (half that from a private home). Get a phone card (sold at newsstands, starting at 30 kr). To make inexpensive international calls, buy a phone card (with a scratch-off personal identification number). The Go Bananas card is particularly reliable (sold at kiosks for 100 kr—giving you more than 100 minutes of talk time to the United States, same card good in Germany, Denmark, Sweden, and Norway).

Jazz Festival: The Copenhagen Jazz Festival—10 days starting the first Friday in July—puts the town in a rollicking slide-trombone mood. The Danes are Europe's jazz enthusiasts, and this music festival fills the town with happiness. The TI prints up an extensive listing of each year's festival events, or get the latest at www.jazzfestival.dk. There's also an autumn jazz festival the first week of November.

Getting Around Copenhagen

By Bus, S-tog, and Metro: It's easy to navigate Copenhagen with its fine buses, Metro, and S-tog, a suburban train system with stops in the city (Eurail valid on S-tog). A 17-kr two-zone ticket (pay as you board buses, buy from station ticket offices or vending machines for the Metro) gets you an hour's travel within the center. Consider the blue two-zone *klippekort* (105 kr for 10 1-hr rides and the 24-hour pass (100 kr, validate day pass in yellow machine on bus or at station, both sold at stations and the TI). Assume you'll be within the middle two zones. Buses go every five to eight minutes during daytime hours. Bus drivers are patient, have change, and speak English. City maps list bus and subway routes. Locals are friendly and helpful. The HUR Kundecenter (big black building) on Rådhuspladsen (City Hall Square) is very helpful and has a fine, free map showing all the bus routes (tel. 36 13 14 15).

Copenhagen's super-futuristic Metro line connects Christianshavn and Nørreport (2 stops on S-tog from main train station). Eventually the Metro will run from Copenhagen to the airport and on to Ørestad, the industrial and business center created after the Øresund Bridge was built between Denmark and Sweden (for the latest, see www.m.dk).

By Bus Tour: Open Top Tour buses do a hop-on, hop-off 60-minute circle connecting the city's top sights (for details, see "Tours," page 222).

By Taxi: Taxis are plentiful, easy to call or flag down, and pricey (24-kr drop charge, and then 10 kr per kilometer, credit cards accepted). For a short ride, four people spend about the same by taxi as by bus (for example, 50 kr from train station to recommended Christianshavn B&Bs). Calling 35 35 35 35 will get you a taxi within minutes...with the meter already way up there.

Free Bikes: From May through November, 2,000 clunky but practical little bikes are scattered around the old-town center (basically the terrain covered in the Copenhagen map in this chapter). Simply locate one of the 150 racks, unlock a bike by popping a 20-kr coin into the handlebar, and pedal away. When you're done, plug your bike back into any other rack and your deposit coin will pop back out (if you can't find a rack, just abandon your bike and a homeless person will take it back and pocket your coin). These simple bikes come with theft-proof parts (unusable on regular bikes) and—they claim—computer tracer chips embedded in them so that bike patrols can retrieve strays. These are funded by advertisements painted on the wheels and by a progressive electorate.

Copenhagen's radical city bike program is a clever idea. But in practice, it doesn't work great for sightseers. It's hard to find bikes in working order, and when you get to the sight and park your bike, it'll be gone by the time you're ready to pedal on. (There's a 20-kr deposit coin as an incentive for any kid to pick up city bikes not plugged back into their special racks.) Use the free bikes for a one-way pedal here and there. But if you really want to bike efficiently, pay to rent one.

Good Bikes: For a comfortable bike that's yours for the duration and in great working order, rent one at the main train station's Cykelcenter (75 kr/24 hrs, cheaper for longer if paid in advance, Mon–Fri 8:00–17:30, Sat 9:00–13:00, July–Aug open Sun 9:00–13:00, otherwise closed Sun, no helmets, tel. 33 33 86 13). Cykelcenter also has a shop at the Østerport S-tog station (same prices, Mon–Fri 8:00–18:00, Sat 9:00–13:00, closed Sun, tel. 33 33 85 13). Cyclists see more, save time and money, and really feel like locals.

TOURS

▲▲▲Walking Tours—Once upon a time, American **Richard Karpen** visited Copenhagen and fell in love with the city (and one of its women). Now, dressed as Hans Christian Andersen, he leads daily 90-minute tours that wander in and out of buildings, courtyards, backstreets, and unusual parts of the old town. Along the way, he gives insightful and humorous background on the history and culture of Denmark, Copenhagen, and the Danes.

Richard offers three entertaining walks: "Castles and Kings," "Royal Copenhagen," and "Romantic Copenhagen." Each walk is a little more than a mile with breaks, and covers different parts of the historic center (75 kr apiece, kids under 12 free, departs from TI May–Sept Mon–Sat at 10:30). His tours, while all different, complement each other and are of equal introduction value.

Richard also does excellent tours of Rosenborg Castle (50 kr, doesn't include castle entry, Mon and Thu at 13:30, 90 min, led by dapper Renaissance "Sir Richard," meet outside castle ticket office). No reservations are needed for Richard's tours—just show up.

For details, pick up Richard's schedule in *Copenhagen This Week,* at the TI, or see www.copenhagenwalks.com.

Go with the Danes: These Danish guides give a fine basic two-hour introductory walk to Copenhagen (100 kr, Sat–Sun at 10:00, confirm schedule in *Copenhagen This Week,* tours start outside TI across from train station, simply show up, www.copenhagen-walkingtours.dk). This outfit also runs tours of Rosenborg Castle (60 min, Sun and Tue at 13:30 in July and Aug).

Copenhagen History Tours: Christian Donatzky, a charming young Dane with a master's degree in history, offers three walking tours. On Saturday at 10:00, the "Reformed Copenhagen" tour covers Copenhagen from 1400–1600—the era before, during, and after the Protestant Reformation. On Sunday at 10:00, the "Commercial Copenhagen" tour focuses on 1600–1800, when Copenhagen became an international business center. On Monday at 18:00 is the "Hans Christian Andersen's Copenhagen" tour (1800–2000), set in a time when Denmark turned democratic. The tours are thoughtfully designed, and those with a serious interest in

Copenhagen

Okm .5 1
Omi 1/4 1/2
Pedestrian Streets + Squares
S-Train
Metro
Canal Tour
Vesterport Stn.
To Brewery
Central Station
Rådhus-pladsen
Tivoli
To Airport
Tietgens Gade
Ny Carlsberg Glyptotek
H. C. Andersens Blvd.
Vesterbrogade
Voldgade
City Hall
Danish Design Center
Nat'l. Mus.
Radhusstræde
Use It
Strøget
Vestergade
Nørre Voldgade
Ørsteds Park
Nørre-port
Israels Plads
Nørregade
St Peters Church
Skt. Pederssstr.
Gråbrødre Torv
Fiolstræde
Købmagergade
Round Tower
Trin. Church
Erotica Museum
Post
Gothersgade
Rosenborg Castle
Kongens Have
St. Nikolai Church
Magasin
Thorvaldsens Museum
Christiansborg Palace
Slotsholmen
Royal Library
Christiansbrygge
Børsen
Harbor
Torve
Knippelsbro
Holmens Canal
Havnegade
Holbergsgade
Royal Theatre
Kongens Nytorv
Store Kongensgade
Fred. Church
To Østerport Stn.
Bredgade
Sankt Annæ Plads
Nyhavn
To Amalienborg, Mermaid, + Ferry to Norway
Hydrofoil to Malmö
Christianshavn
DCH

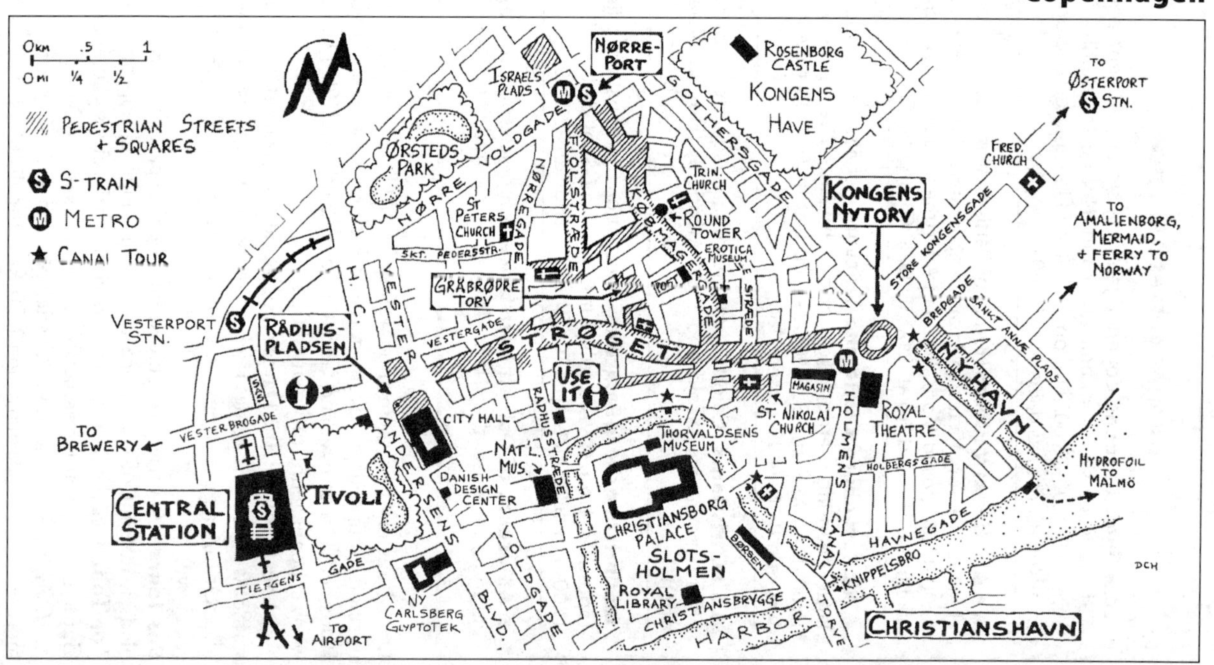

Copenhagen at a Glance

▲▲▲Tivoli Gardens Copenhagen's classic amusement park, with rides, music, food, and other fun. **Hours:** Mid-April–mid-Sept daily 11:00–23:00, later on Fri, Sat, and in summer, also open mid-Nov–Christmas daily 11:00–22:00.

▲▲▲National Museum History of Danish civilization with tourable 19th-century Victorian Apartment. **Hours:** Museum Tue–Sun 10:00–17:00, closed Mon; Victorian Apartment tours Sat and Sun (likely also Thu and Fri) at 12:00, 13:00, 14:00, and 15:00.

▲▲▲Rosenborg Castle and Treasury Renaissance castle of larger-than-life "warrior king" Christian IV. **Hours:** Daily June–Aug 10:00–17:00, May and Sept 10:00–16:00, Oct 11:00–15:00, Nov–April Tue–Sun 11:00–14:00, closed Mon.

▲▲▲Christiania Colorful counterculture squatters' colony where marijuana is sold and smoked openly. **Hours:** Always open.

▲▲Christiansborg Palace Royal reception rooms with dazzling tapestries. **Hours:** Visit only with tour, May–Sept daily at 11:00, 13:00, and 15:00; Oct–April Tue, Thu, Sat, and Sun at 15:00.

▲▲Museum of Danish Resistance Chronicle of Denmark's struggle against the Nazis. **Hours:** May–mid-Sept Tue–Sat

Danish history find them time well spent (70 kr, 60–90 min each in small groups, depart from statue of Bishop Absalon on Højbro Plads between Strøget and Christiansborg Palace, tel. 28 49 44 35, www.copenhagenhistorytours.dk).

Local Guides: The Danish tour guide organization has a huge staff of well-trained guides ready to show you around (www.guides.dk). Or hire a guide from Go with the Danes (1,000 kr/2-hr tour, see above).

Bus Tours—A variety of guided bus tours depart from Rådhuspladsen in front of the Palace Hotel. The hop-on, hop-off **Open Top Tour** does the basic 60-minute circle of the city sights—Tivoli Gardens, the royal Christiansborg Palace, National Museum, *The Little Mermaid,* Rosenborg Castle, Nyhavn sailors' quarter, and more—with a taped narration (120 kr, 2/hr, 140 kr for access to all 3 tour lines, ticket good for 48 hrs, April–Oct daily 9:30–17:00; you can get off, see a sight, and catch a later bus; bus departs City Hall below the *Lur Blowers* statue—to the left of City Hall—or at many other stops throughout city, pay driver, tel. 32 54 06 06,

10:00–16:00, Sun 10:00–17:00, off-season Tue–Sat 10:00–15:00, Sun 10:00–16:00, closed Mon.

▲**City Hall (Rådhus)** Copenhagen's landmark, packed with Danish history and topped with a tower. **Hours:** Mon–Fri 8:00–17:00, open Sat only for tours, closed Sun.

▲**Thorvaldsen's Museum** Works of the Danish neoclassical sculptor. **Hours:** Tue–Sun 10:00–17:00, closed Mon.

▲**Ny Carlsberg Glyptotek** Scandinavia's top art gallery, featuring Egyptians, Greeks, Etruscans, French, and Danes. **Hours:** Tue–Sun 10:00–16:00, closed Mon.

▲**National Art Museum** Good Danish and Impressionist collections. **Hours:** Tue–Sun 10:00–17:00, Wed until 20:00, closed Mon.

▲**Amalienborg Palace Museum** Quick and intimate look at Denmark's royal family. **Hours:** May–Oct daily 10:00–16:00, Nov–April Tue–Sun 11:00–16:00.

▲**Our Savior's Church** Spiral-spired church with bright Baroque interior. **Hours:** April–Aug Mon–Sat 11:00–16:30, Sun 12:00–16:30, closes off-season at 15:30.

run by Copenhagen Excursions—www.sightseeing.dk). The same company also runs jaunts into the countryside, with themes such as Vikings, castles, and Hamlet.

▲▲**Harbor Cruise and Canal Tours**—Two companies offer essentially the same live, three-language, 50-minute tours through the city canals. Both boats leave at least twice an hour from near Christiansborg Palace, cruise around the palace and Christianshavn area, and then proceed into the wide-open harbor. It's a relaxing way to see *The Little Mermaid* and munch a lazy picnic during the slow-moving narration.

The low-overhead **Netto-Bådene** tour boats leave from Holmen's Bridge in front of the palace and from Nyhavn (25 kr, late-April–Sept daily 10:00–17:00, later in summer, sign at dock shows next departure, 2–5/hr, dress warmly—boats are open-top until Sept, tel. 32 54 41 02, www.havnerundfart.dk). Don't mix up the boats—this cheaper line advertises less. Its Nyhavn dock is midway down the canal (on the city side), while the expensive boat is at the head of the canal.

The pricey option, **DFDS Canal Tours,** does the same tour for 50 kr (departs from Gammel Strand, 200 yards away, and from Nyhavn, April–mid-Oct daily 10:00–17:00). They also offer unguided "water bus" hop-on, hop-off tours for 45 kr (mid-May–early Sept 10:15–16:45, tel. 33 93 42 60).

Go with Netto. There's no reason to pay double.

Bike Tours—City Safari offers three-hour guided bike tours of Copenhagen, a general city intro including Christiania (200 kr includes bike, in English and Danish as needed, tours available upon pre-booking either by mail or phone, show up 10 min in advance at Danish Center for Architecture, Gammel Dok Storehouse, Strandgade 27B, tel. 33 23 94 90, www.citysafari.dk, or ask at Use It; energetic Steen is a one-man show and speaks fine English).

Self-Guided Walk: Strøget and Copenhagen's Heart and Soul

Start from **Rådhuspladsen (City Hall Square),** the bustling heart of Copenhagen, dominated by the tower of the City Hall. This was Copenhagen's fortified west end. For 700 years, Copenhagen was contained within its walls. In the mid-1800s, 140,000 people were packed inside. The overcrowding led to hygiene problems. (A cholera outbreak killed 5,000.) It was clear: The walls needed to come down...and they did.

In 1843, magazine publisher Georg Carstensen convinced the king to let him build a pleasure garden outside the walls of crowded Copenhagen. The king quickly agreed, knowing that happy people care less about fighting for democracy. **Tivoli Gardens** became Europe's first great public amusement park. When the train lines came, the station was placed just beyond Tivoli. Those formidable walls faded away, surviving only in echoes—a circular series of roads and remnants of moats, now people-friendly city lakes.

The **City Hall,** or Rådhus, is worth a visit (Mon–Fri 8:00–17:00, open Sat only for tours, closed Sun; described on page 233). Old **Hans Christian Andersen** sits to the right of City Hall, almost begging to be in another photo (as he used to in real life). Climb onto his well-worn knee. (While up there, you might take off your shirt for a racy photo, as many Danes enjoy doing.)

On a pedestal left of City Hall, note the *Lur Blowers* sculpture honoring the earliest warrior Danes. The *lur* is a horn that was used 3,500 years ago. The ancient originals (which still play) are displayed in the National Museum. (City tour buses leave from below these Vikings.)

The golden **weather girls** high up on the tower (marked *Philips* in blue) opposite the Strøget's entrance tell the weather: on a bike (fair) or with an umbrella. These two have been called the only women in Copenhagen you can trust. But for years, they've been

Self-Guided Walk: Strøget and Copenhagen's Heart and Soul

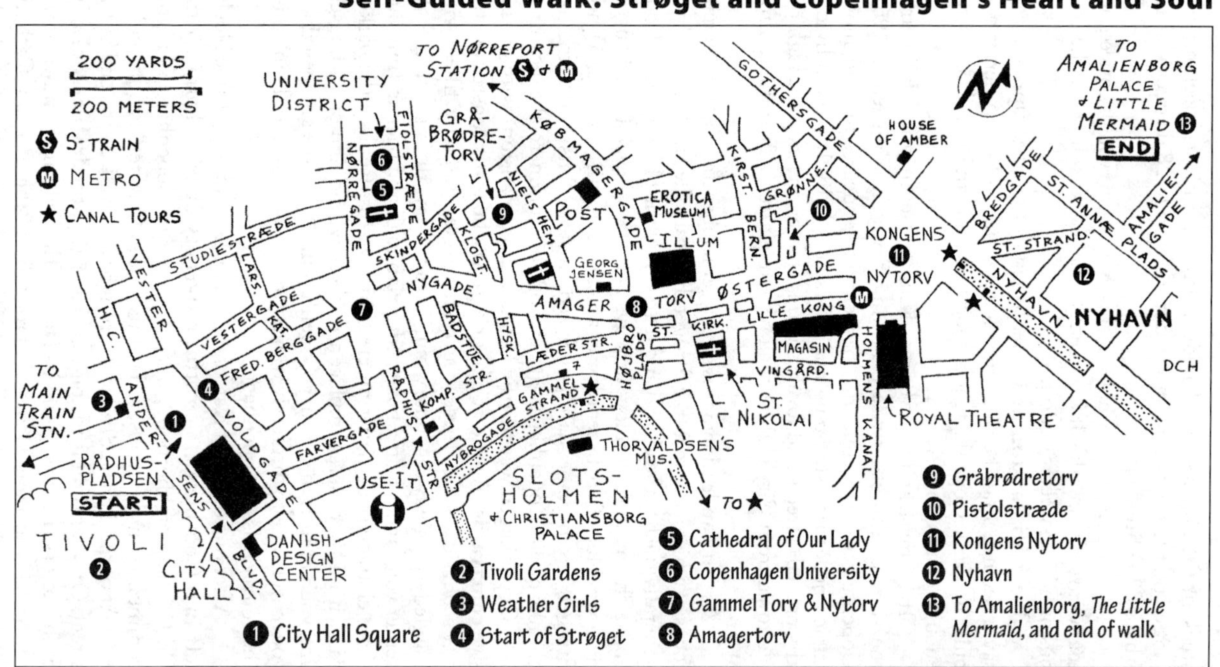

stuck in the almost-sunny mode...with the bike just peeking out. Notice that the red temperature dots only go to 28 degrees Celsius (that's 82 Fahrenheit).

Here in the traffic hub of this huge city, you'll notice...not many cars. Denmark's 180 percent tax on car purchases makes the bus or bike a sweeter option.

The **SAS building** is Copenhagen's only skyscraper. Locals say it seems so tall because the clouds hang so low. When it was built in 1960, Copenhageners took one look and decided—that's enough of a skyline.

The American trio of Burger King, 7-Eleven, and KFC marks the start of the otherwise charming **Strøget.** Finished in 1962, Copenhagen's experimental, tremendously successful, and most-copied pedestrian shopping mall is a string of lively (and individually named) streets and lovely squares that bunny-hop through the old town from City Hall to the Nyhavn quarter, a 20-minute stroll away.

As you wander down this street, remember that the commercial focus of a historic street like Strøget drives up the land value, which generally trashes the charm and tears down the old buildings. Look above the modern window displays and street-level advertising to discover bits of 19th-century character that still survive. While Strøget has become hamburgerized, historic bits and attractive chunks of old Copenhagen are just off this commercial cancan.

Copenhagen was fortified around large mansions with expansive **courtyards.** As the population grew, the walls constricted the city's physical size. These courtyards were gradually filled with higgledy-piggledy secondary buildings. Today, throughout the old center you can step off a busy pedestrian mall and back in time into these characteristic half-timbered time-warps. Replace the parked car with a tired horse, replace the bikes with a line of outhouses, and you are in 19th-century Copenhagen. If you see an open door, you're welcome to discreetly wander in and look around. Don't miss the courtyards of Copenhagen.

After one block (at Kattesundet), make a side-trip three blocks left into Copenhagen's colorful **university district.** Formerly the old brothel neighborhood, later the heart of Copenhagen's hippie community in the 1960s, today this "Latin Quarter" is Soho chic.

At Sankt Peders Stræde, turn right and walk to the end of the street. On your right is the big neoclassical **Cathedral of Our Lady.** Stand across the street from its facade. The Reformation Memorial celebrates the date Denmark broke from the Roman Catholic Church and became Lutheran (1536). Walk around and study the reliefs of great Danish reformers protesting from their pulpits. The relief facing the church shows King Christian III, who, after being influenced by Luther in his German travels (and realizing the advantages of being the head of his own state church), oversaw the town council meeting that decided on this break. Because of 1536, there's no Mary in the Cathedral of Our Lady.

The cathedral's **facade** is a Greek temple. (To the right in the distance, notice more neoclassicism—the law courts.) You can see why golden-age Copenhagen (early 1800s) fancied itself a Nordic Athens. Old Testament figures (King David and Moses) flank the cathedral's entryway. Above, John the Baptist stands where you'd expect to see Greek gods. He invites you in...to the New Testament.

Enter the cathedral—a world of neoclassical serenity (free, open daily 7:30–17:00). This pagan temple now houses Christianity. The nave is lined by the 12 apostles (all clad in Roman togas)—masterpieces by the great Danish sculptor Bertel Thorvaldsen. They lead to a statue of the risen Christ—standing where the statue of Caesar would have been. Rather than wearing an imperial toga, Jesus wears his burial shroud and says, "Come to me." The marvelous acoustics are demonstrated in free organ concerts each Saturday at noon. This is where Copenhagen gathers for extraordinary events. After September 11, 2001, the queen, her government, and the entire diplomatic core held a memorial service here.

Head back outside. If you face the facade and look to the left, you'll see **Copenhagen University**—home of 30,000 students. The king began the university in the 17th century to stop the Danish brain drain to Paris. Today tuition is free (but room, board, and beer are not). Locals say it's easy to get in...but (given the wonderful lifestyle) very hard to get out.

Step up the middle steps of the university's big building and enter a colorful lobby, starring Athena and Apollo. The frescoes celebrate high thinking, with themes such as the triumph of wisdom over barbarism. Notice how harmoniously the architecture, sculpture, and painting work together. Outside, busts honor great minds from the faculty, including (at the end) Niels Bohr—a professor who won the 1922 Nobel Prize for theoretical physics. He evaded the clutches of the Nazi science labs by fleeing to America in 1943, where he helped develop the atomic bomb.

Rejoin Strøget (down where you saw the law courts) at **Gammel Torv** and **Nytorv** (Old Square and New Square). This was the old town center. In Gammel Torv, the Fountain of Charity (Caritas) is named for the figure of Charity on top. It has provided drinking water to locals since the early 1600s. Featuring a pregnant woman squirting water from her breasts next to a boy urinating, this was just too much for people of the Victorian age. They corked both figures and raised the statue to what they hoped would be out of view. The Asian-looking kiosk was one of the city's first community telephone centers from the days before phones were privately owned. Look at the reliefs ringing its top: an airplane with bird wings (c. 1900) and two women talking on the newfangled phone. (It was thought business would popularize the telephone, but actually it was women... Now, 100 years later, look at the mobile phones.)

While Gammel Torv was a place of happiness and merriment, Nytorv was a place of severity and judgment. Walk to the small raised area in front of the old, ancient Greek–style former City Hall. Do a 360. The entire square is neoclassical. Read the old Danish on the City Hall facade: "With Law Shall Man Land Build." Look down at the pavement and read the plaque: "Here stood the town's Kag (whipping post) until 1780."

Next, walk down **Amagertorv,** prime real estate for talented street entertainers and pickpockets (past the Gad Bookstore—excellent selection of English-language guidebooks and cookbooks), to the stately brick Holy Ghost church. The fine spire is typical of old Danish churches. Under the stepped gable was a medieval hospital run by monks. A block behind the church (walk down Valkendorfsgade and through a passage under a rust-colored building) is the leafy and caffeine-stained **Gråbrødretorv** (Grey Friars' Square)—a popular place for an outdoor meal or drink in the summer—surrounded by fine old buildings. At the end of the square, the street Niels Hemmingsens Gade returns (past the Copenhagen Jazz House, a good place for live music nightly—see page 247) to Strøget. Continue down the pedestrian street, with its fine inlaid Italian granite stonework, to the next square with the stork fountain (actually a heron). The Victorian WCs here (steps down from fountain, 2 kr) are a delight.

Amagertorv—the next stretch of Strøget—is a highlight for shoppers. A line of Royal Copenhagen stores here sell porcelain (with demos), glassware, jewelry, and silverware. Illums Bolighus is known for modern design (Mon–Sat 10:00–18:00, Sun 12:00–17:00). From here, you can see the imposing Parliament building, Christiansborg Palace, and an equestrian statue of Bishop Absalon, the city's founder (canal boat tours depart nearby). A block toward the canal, running parallel to Strøget, starts Strædet, which is a second Strøget featuring cafés, antique shops, and no fast food. North of Amagertorv, a broad pedestrian mall, Købmagergade, leads past the Museum of Erotica to Christian IV's Round Tower and the Latin Quarter (university district). Café Norden overlooks the fountain—a smoky but good place for a coffee with a view. The second floor offers the best vantage point.

The final stretch of Strøget leads to **Pistolstræde** (leading off Strøget to the left from Østergade at #24), a cute lane of shops in restored 18th-century buildings. Wander back into the half-timbered section. The Kransekagehuset bakery (see "Eating," page 255) has a rack of tourist fliers including the very handy-for-shoppers

Local Life, which highlights small specialty shops in the area.

Continuing along Strøget, you'll pass McDonald's (good view from top floor) and major department stores (Illum and Magasin—see "Shopping," page 246) to Kongens Nytorv.

Kongens Nytorv, the biggest square in town, is home to the Royal Theatre, French embassy, and venerable Hotel D'Angleterre. The statue in the middle of the square celebrates Christian V who, in the 1670s, enlarged Copenhagen by adding this "King's New Square" (Kongens Nytorv). The entire center is a happy skating rink for three months each winter.

On the right (just before the Metro station, at #19), Hviids Vinstue, the town's oldest wine cellar (from 1723), is a colorful if smoky spot for an open-face sandwich and a beer (3 sandwiches and a beer for 50 kr at lunchtime). Wander around inside, if only to see the old photos.

Just off Kongens Nytorv (30 yards from Hviids Vinstue) is the entrance to the futuristic Metro. Ride the escalators down and up to see the latest in Metro design (automated cars, no driver...sit in front to watch the tracks coming at you).

Head back up to ground level. Across the square is the trendy harbor of Nyhavn.

Nyhavn is a recently gentrified sailors' quarter. (Hong Kong is the last of the nasty bars from the rough old days.) With its trendy cafés, jazz clubs, and tattoo shops (pop into Tattoo Ole at #17—fun photos, very traditional), Nyhavn is a wonderful place to hang out. The canal is filled with glamorous old sailboats of all sizes. Any historic sloop is welcome to moor here in Copenhagen's ever-changing boat museum. Hans Christian Andersen lived and wrote his first stories here (in the red double-gabled building on the right at #20). Wander the quay, enjoying the frat-party parade of tattoos (hotter weather reveals more tattoos). Celtic and Nordic mythological designs are in (as is bodybuilding, by the looks of things). The place thrives—with the cheap-beer drinkers dockside and the richer and older ones looking on from comfier cafés.

A note about all this public beer-drinking: There's no more beer consumption here than in the United States; it's just out in public. Many young Danes can't afford to drink in a bar. So they "picnic drink" their beers in squares and along canals, spending a quarter of the bar price for a bottle from a nearby kiosk (just past the bridge on the right).

Just past the first bridge, a line of people wait for the best ice cream around—packed into fresh-baked waffles (look through the window to see the waffle iron in action).

Continuing north along the harborside (from end of Nyhavn canal, turn left), you'll stroll a delightful waterfront promenade to the modern fountain of Amaliehaven Park (immediately across the harbor from the new opera house).

The orderly **Amalienborg Palace and Square** is a block inland, behind the fountain. Queen Margrethe II and her family live in the mansion to your immediate left as you enter the square from the harborside. Her son and heir to the throne, Crown Prince Frederik, recently moved into the mansion directly opposite his mother's. While the guards change with royal fanfare at noon only when the queen is in residence, they shower every morning. The small Amalienborg Palace Museum offers an intimate look at royal living (see page 242). If in need of a very traditional cheap lunch, head inland two blocks just past the Marble Church, to Svend Larsen's Smørrebrød (fine little 8-kr open-face sandwiches to go, St. Kongensgade 83, Mon–Fri 8:00–14:00, closed Sat–Sun).

From the square, Amaliegade leads north to Kastellet (Citadel) Park and Denmark's fascinating WWII-era Museum of Danish Resistance (see "Near *The Little Mermaid*," page 242). A short stroll past the Gefion fountain (illustrating the myth of the goddess who was given one night to carve a chunk out of Sweden to make into Denmark's main island, Zealand—which you're on) and an Anglican church built of flint brings you to the overrated, overfondled, and overphotographed symbol of Copenhagen, ***Den Lille Havfrue—The Little Mermaid.***

You can get back downtown on foot, by taxi, or on bus #1A, #15, or #19 from Store Kongensgade on the other side of Kastellet Park, or bus #29 from behind the Museum of Danish Resistance on Langelinie Street.

SIGHTS

Near the Train Station

▲▲▲Tivoli Gardens—The world's grand old amusement park—since 1843—is 20 acres, 110,000 lanterns, and countless ice cream cones of fun. You pay one admission price and find yourself lost in a Hans Christian Andersen wonderland of rides, restaurants, games, marching bands, roulette wheels, and funny mirrors. Tivoli doesn't try to be Disney. It's wonderfully and happily Danish.

Cost, Hours, Location: The park is open every day—but only from about April 10 to September 20 (daily 11:00–23:00, later on Fri, Sat, and in summer, 65 kr gets you in, tel. 33 15 10 01, www.tivoli.dk). Rides range in price from 15 to 70 kr (195 kr for all-day pass). All children's amusements are in full swing by 12:00; the rest of the amusements open by 16:30. Tivoli is across from the train station. If you're catching an overnight train, this is *the* place to spend your last Copenhagen hours. Tivoli also opens for a Christmas Market (mid-Nov–Christmas daily 11:00–22:00—with ice skating on Tivoli Lake).

Entertainment in Tivoli: Upon arrival (through main entrance, on right in shop), pick up a map and events schedule. Take a moment to sit down and plan your entertainment for the evening. Events are spread between 15:00 and 23:00; the 19:30 concert in the concert hall can be free or may cost up to 500 kr, depending on the performer (box office tel. 33 15 10 12). If the Tivoli Symphony is playing, it's worth paying for. The ticket box office is outside, just to the left of the main entrance (daily 11:00–20:00, if you buy a concert ticket you get into Tivoli for free). You'll also find the daily events schedule on the posts outside the main entrance.

Free concerts, pantomime theater, ballet, acrobats, puppets, and other shows pop up all over the park, and a well-organized visitor can enjoy an exciting evening of entertainment without spending a single krone beyond the entry fee. The children's theater, Valmuen, plays excellent traditional fairy tales daily at 12:00, 13:00, and 14:00. Friday evenings feature a (usually free) rock or pop show at 22:00. On Saturday from late April through late September, fireworks light up the sky at 23:45. The park is particularly romantic at dusk, when the lights go on.

Eating at Tivoli: Inside the park, expect to pay amusement-park prices for amusement park–quality food. **Søcafeen,** by the lake, allows picnics if you buy a drink. The *pølse* (sausage) stands are cheap. **Færgekroen** is a good lakeside place for typical Danish food, beer, and an impromptu sing-along with a bunch of drunk Danes. The Croatian restaurant, **Hercegovina,** overlooks a leafy section of the amusement park and serves a 129-kr lunch buffet (mostly cold, 12:00–16:00) and a 169-kr dinner buffet (salads, veggies, and lots and lots of meat, daily 17:00–22:00, music nightly after 19:00). For a cake and coffee, consider the **Viften** café. **Georg,** to the left of the concert hall, has tasty 45-kr sandwiches and 150-kr dinners (which include a glass of wine).

▲Rådhus (City Hall)—This city landmark, between the train station/Tivoli/TI and Strøget pedestrian mall, offers private tours and trips up its 345-foot-tall tower. It's draped, inside and out, in Danish symbolism. The city's founder, Bishop Absalon, stands over the door. The polar bears climbing on the rooftop symbolize the giant Danish protectorate of Greenland.

Step inside. The lobby has racks of tourist information (city maps and *Copenhagen This Week*). The building was inspired by the City Hall in Siena, Italy (with the necessary addition of a glass roof). Huge functions fill this grand hall (the iron grill in the center of the floor is an elevator for bringing up 1,200 chairs) while the busts of four illustrious local boys—the fairy-tale-writer Hans Christian Andersen, the sculptor Bertel Thorvaldsen, the physicist Niels Bohr, and the building's architect Martin Nyrop—look on. Underneath the floor are national archives dating back to 1275, popular with Danes researching their family roots. The City Hall is free and open to the public (Mon–Fri 8:00–17:00, open on Sat only for tours—see below, closed Sun). You can wander throughout the building and into the peaceful garden out back. Guided English-language **tours** get you into more private, official rooms (30 kr, 45 min, year-round Mon–Fri at 15:00, Sat at 10:00 and 11:00).

Tourists romp (in groups with an escort) up the **tower**'s 300 steps for the best aerial view of Copenhagen (20 kr, June–Sept: Mon–Fri 10:00, 12:00, and 14:00, Sat 12:00; Oct–May: Mon–Sat 12:00, tel. 33 66 25 82).

▲▲Christiansborg Palace—A complex of government buildings stands on the ruins of Copenhagen's original 12th-century fortress: the Parliament, Supreme Court, prime minister's office, royal reception rooms, royal library, several museums, and the royal stables.

While the current palace dates only from 1928 and the royal family moved out 200 years ago, the building is the sixth to stand here in 800 years and is rich with tradition. The information-packed 50-minute English-language tours of the royal reception rooms are excellent. As you slip-slide on protect-the-floor slippers through 22 rooms, you'll gain a good feel for Danish history, royalty, and politics. (For instance, the family portrait of King Christian IX shows why he's called the "father-in-law of Europe"—with children eventually becoming or marrying royalty in Denmark, Russia, Greece, Britain, France, Germany, and Norway.) The highlight is the dazzling set of modern tapestries—Danish-designed but Gobelin-made in Paris. This gift, given to the queen on her 60th birthday in 2000, celebrates 1,000 years of Danish history with wild wall-hangings from the Viking age to our chaotic times (admission by tour only, 40 kr, May–Sept daily at 11:00, 13:00, and 15:00; Oct–April Tue, Thu, Sat, and Sun at 15:00; from equestrian statue in front, go through wooden door, past entrance to Christiansborg Castle ruins, into courtyard, and up stairs on right; tel. 33 92 64 92).

Christiansborg Castle Ruins—An exhibit in the scant remains of the first fortress built by Bishop Absalon, the 12th-century founder of Copenhagen, lies under the palace. There's precious little to see, but it's old and well described (20 kr, May–Sept daily 9:30–15:30; Oct–April Tue, Thu, Sat, and Sun 9:30–15:30, closed Mon, Wed, and Fri; good 1-kr guide). Early birds note that this sight opens 30 minutes before other nearby sights.

▲Thorvaldsen's Museum—This museum, which has some of the best swoon-worthy art you'll see anywhere, tells the story and shows the monumental work of the great Danish neoclassical sculptor Bertel Thorvaldsen (1770–1844). Considered Canova's equal among neoclassical sculptors, Thorvaldsen spent 40 years in Rome. He was lured home to Copenhagen with the promise to showcase his work in a fine museum—which opened in the revolutionary year of 1848 as Denmark's first public art gallery. The ground floor showcases his statues (pull open the little black "information" cases for descriptions). Upstairs, get into the mind of the artist by perusing his personal possessions and the private collection of paintings from which he drew inspiration (30 kr, free Wed, open Tue–Sun 10:00–17:00, closed Mon, well-described, located in neoclassical building with colorful walls next to Christiansborg Palace, tel. 33 32 15 32).

Royal Library—Copenhagen's "Black Diamond" library is a striking building made of shiny black granite, leaning over the harbor at the edge of the palace complex. Wander through the old and new sections, read a magazine, and enjoy a classy—and pricey—lunch (restaurant, café, library hours: Mon–Sat 10:00–19:00, closed Sun, tel. 33 47 43 63).

▲▲▲National Museum—Focus on the excellent and curiously enjoyable Danish collection, which traces this civilization from its ancient beginnings. Exhibits are laid out chronologically and described in English. Pick up the museum map. The audioguide (25 kr) describes the highlights but adds little to the printed descriptions you'll find inside. Start with "Denmark's Old Tide" at room #1 (right of entrance, through glass tunnel), and follow the numbers through the "prehistory" section circling the ground floor—oak coffins with still-clothed and -armed skeletons from 1300 B.C., ancient and still-playable *lur* horns, the 2,000-year-old Gundestrup Cauldron of art-textbook fame, lots of Viking stuff, and a bitchin' collection of well-translated rune stones. Then go upstairs, find room 101, and carry on to find fascinating material on the Reformation, an exhibit on everyday town life in the 16th and 17th centuries, and, in room 126, a unique "cylinder perspective" of the noble family (from 1656) and two peep shows. The next floor takes you into modern times, with historic toys and a slice-of-Danish-life 1600–2000 gallery where you'll see everything from rifles and old bras to early jukeboxes (50 kr, free Wed, Tue–Sun 10:00–17:00, closed Mon, mandatory bag check—10-kr coin deposit, cafeteria, enter at Ny Vestergade 10, tel. 33 13 44 11).

▲National Museum's Victorian Apartment—The museum inherited an incredible Victorian apartment just around the corner, a tour of which is included with your admission. The wealthy Christensen family managed to keep its plush living quarters a 19th-century time capsule until the granddaughters passed away in 1963. Since then, it's been part of the National Museum with all but two of its rooms looking like they did around 1890. Visit it if the tour schedule works for you (45-min tours leave from museum ticket desk Sat and Sun at 12:00, 13:00, 14:00, and 15:00; tours also likely at those times on Thu and Fri).

▲Ny Carlsberg Glyptotek—Scandinavia's top art gallery is an impressive example of what beer money can do. Because of ongoing renovation until mid-2006, some collections (Danish painting, French and Danish sculpture) will not be on view—but the admission price will be reduced to soften the blow. The museum has intoxicating Egyptian, Greek, and Etruscan collections; a fine sample of early 19th-century Danish golden-age painting (may not be viewable); and a heady, if small, exhibit of 19th-century French paintings (in the new "French Wing," including Géricault, Delacroix, Manet, Impressionists, and Gauguin before and after Tahiti). Linger with marble gods under the palm leaves and glass dome of the very soothing winter garden. Designers, figuring Danes would be more interested in a lush garden than in classical art, used this wonderful space as leafy bait to cleverly introduce locals to a few Greek and Roman statues. (It works for tourists, too.) One of the original Rodin *Thinker*s (wondering how to scale the Tivoli fence?) is in the museum's backyard (20 kr, free Wed and Sun, Tue–Sun 10:00–16:00, closed Mon, 2-kr English brochure/guide, classy cafeteria under palms, behind Tivoli at Dantes Plads 7, tel. 33 41 81 41, www.glyptoteket.dk).

Danish Design Center—This center, its building a masterpiece in itself, shows off the best in Danish design as well as top examples from around the world, including architecture, fashion, and graphic arts. A visit to this low-key display case for sleek Scandinavian design offers an interesting glimpse into the culture. The basement showcases the Industrial Design prizewinners from 1965 through 1999. Here's a sample English description: "He taught the materials to do things not even they realized they were able to do" (40 kr, Mon–Fri 10:00–17:00, Wed until 21:00, Sat–Sun 11:00–16:00, across from Tivoli at H. C. Andersen Boulevard 27, tel. 33 69 33 69, www.ddc.dk). The boutique next to the ticket counter features three themes: travel light (chic travel accessories and gadgets), modern Danish classics, and books and posters. The café on the main level, under the atrium, serves light lunches (60–100 kr).

Hovedbanegården—Copenhagen's great train station is a fascinating mesh of Scandinavian culture and transportation efficiency. Even if you're not a train traveler, check it out (see "Arrival in Copenhagen," page 219). Notice how the classical music effectively keeps the junkies away from the back door.

Rosenborg Castle and Nearby

▲▲▲Rosenborg Castle and Treasury—This finely furnished Dutch Renaissance–style castle was built by Christian IV in the early 1600s as a summer castle. Open to the public since 1838, it houses the Danish crown jewels and 500 years of royal knickknacks, including some great Christian IV memorabilia, such as the shrapnel (removed from his eye and forehead after a naval battle) that he had made into earrings for his girlfriend. Because nothing is explained in English, a tour—or the following self-guided tour—is essential.

Cost, Hours, Location: 60 kr, daily June–Aug 10:00–17:00, May and Sept 10:00–16:00, Oct 11:00–15:00, Nov–April Tue–Sun 11:00–14:00, closed Mon. S-tog: Nørreport, tel. 33 15 32 86.

Tours: Richard Karpen leads fascinating 90-minute tours in princely garb (May–Sept Mon and Thu at 13:30, 50 kr plus your palace entrance, see "Tours," on page 222). **Go with the Danes** offers similar tours (60 min, Sun and Tue at 13:30 in July and Aug). If these don't work for you, follow this self-guided tour through the castle and treasury that I've woven together from the highlights of Richard's walk.

Self-Guided Tour: You'll tour the first floor room by room, then climb to the third floor for the big throne room. After a quick sweep of the middle floor, finish in the basement for the jewels. Begin the tour on the ground floor, in the Audience Room.

Ground floor: Here in the **Audience Room,** all eyes were on Christian IV. Today, your eyes should be on him, too. Take a close look at his bust by the fireplace. Check this guy out—earring and fashionable braid, a hard drinker, hard lover, energetic statesman, and warrior king. Christian IV was dynamism in the flesh, wearing a toga: a true Renaissance guy. During his reign, the size of Copenhagen doubled. Rosenborg was his favorite residence, and where he chose to die. You're surrounded by Dutch paintings (the Dutch had a huge influence on 17th-century Denmark). Note the smaller statue of the 19-year-old king, showing him jousting jauntily on his coronation day. The astronomical clock—with musical works and moving figures—did everything you can imagine.

The **study** (nearest where you entered) was small (and easy to heat). Kings did a lot of corresponding. We know a lot about Christian because 3,000 of his handwritten letters survive. The painting shows eight-year-old Christian—after his father died, but still too young to rule. A portrait of his mother hangs above the boy, and opposite is a portrait of Christian in his prime.

In the **bedroom,** paintings show the king as an old man...and as a dead man. In the case are the clothes he wore when wounded in battle. Riddled with shrapnel, he lost an eye. No problem for the warrior king with a knack for heroic publicity stunts: He had the shrapnel bits taken out of his eye and forehead made into earrings. (They hang in the case above the blood-stained cloth.) Christian lived to be 70 and fathered 26 children (with two wives and one mistress).

The next room displays **wax casts** of royal figures. This was the way famous and important people were portrayed back then. The **chair** is a forerunner of the whoopee cushion. When you sat on it, metal cuffs pinned your arms down, allowing the prankster to pour water down the back of the chair (see hole)—making you "wet your pants." When you stood up, the chair made embarrassing tooting sounds.

The next room has a particularly impressive inlaid **marble floor.** Imagine the king meeting emissaries here in the center, with the emblems of Norway (right), Denmark (center), and Sweden (left) behind him.

The end room was a **dining room.** Study the box made of amber (petrified tree resin, 30–50 million years old). The tiny figures show a healthy interest in sex. (You might want to shield children from the more graphic art in the case next to the door you just passed.) By the window (opposite where you entered), a hole in the wall let the music performed by the band in the basement waft in. (Who wants the actual musicians in the dining room?) The audio hole was also used to call servants.

The **long hall** leading to the staircase exhibits an intriguing painting of Frederick III being installed as the absolute monarch. Study it closely for slice-of-life details. Next, a sprawling family tree makes it perfectly clear that Christian IV comes from good stock. Note the tree is labeled in German—the second language of the realm.

The queen had a hand-pulled elevator, but you'll need to hike up two flights of stairs to the top-floor throne room.

Throne room (top floor): The **Long Hall**—considered one of the best-preserved Baroque rooms in Europe—was great for banquets. The decor trumpets the great accomplishments of Denmark's great kings. The four corners of the ceiling feature the four continents known at the time. (America was still considered pretty untamed—notice the decapitated head with the arrow sticking out of it.) In the center, of course, is the proud seal of the Danish Royal Family. The tapestries are from the late 1600s, designed for this room. Effective propaganda, they show the Danes defeating their Swedish rivals on land and at sea. The king's throne was made of "unicorn horn" (actually narwhal tusk from Greenland)—believed to bring protection from evil and poison. It was about the most precious material in its day. The queen's throne is of hammered silver—the 150-pound lions are 300 years old.

The small room to the left holds a delightful **royal porcelain** display with Chinese, French, German, and Danish examples of the "white gold." For five centuries, Europeans couldn't figure out how the Chinese made this stuff. The difficulty in just getting it back to Europe in one piece made it precious. The Danish pieces, called "Flora Danica" (on the left as you enter) are from a huge royal set showing off the herbs and vegetables of the realm.

On your way back down, the **middle floor** is worth a look:

Circling counterclockwise, you'll see more fine clocks, fancy furniture, and royal portraits. In the first room, notice the double portrait of the king and his sister. The queen enjoyed her royal lathe (with candleholders for lighting and pedals to spin it hidden away below). The small mirror room (on the side) was where the king played Hugh Hefner—using mirrors on the floor to see what was under those hoop skirts. In hidden cupboards, he had a fold-out bed and a handy escape staircase.

Back outside, find the stairs leading down to the...

Royal Danish Treasury (castle basement): The palace was a royal residence for a century and has been the royal vault right up until today. As you enter, peek into the royal **wine cellar,** with thousand-liter barrels, to right of ticket checker. Then continue into the treasury.

The diamond- and pearl-studded **saddles** were Christian IV's—the first for his coronation, the second for his son's wedding. When his kingdom was nearly bankrupt, Christian had these constructed lavishly—complete with solid-gold spurs—to impress visiting dignitaries and bolster Denmark's credit rating.

Next case: **tankards.** Danes were always big drinkers, and to drink in the top style, a king had narwhal steins (#4030 and #4031). Note the fancy Greenland Inuit (Eskimo) on the lid. The case is filled with exquisitely carved ivory.

Next case: What's with the mooning snuffbox (#4063)? Also, check out the amorous whistle (#4064).

Case in corner: The 18th century was the age of **brooches.** Many of these are made of freshwater pearls. Find the fancy combination toothpick and ear spoon (#1140). A queen was caught having an affair after 22 years of royal marriage. Her king gave her a special present: a golden ring—showing the hand of his promiscuous queen shaking hands with a penis (#4146).

Step downstairs, away from all this silliness. Passing through the serious vault door, you come face to face with a big, jeweled **sword.** The tall, two-handed, 16th-century coronation sword was drawn by the new king, who cut crosses in the air in four directions, symbolically promising to defend the realm from all attacks. The cases surrounding the sword contain everyday items used by the king (all solid gold, of course). What looks like a trophy case of gold records is actually a collection of dinner plates with amber centers (#5032).

Go down the steps. In the center case is Christian IV's **coronation crown** (from 1596, 7 pounds of gold and precious stones, #1524), which some consider to be the finest Renaissance crown in Europe. Its 12 gables radiate symbolism. Find the symbols of justice (sword and scales), fortitude (a woman on a lion with a sword), and charity (a woman nursing—meaning the king will love God and his people as a mother loves her child). The pelican, which famously pecks its own flesh to feed its children, symbolizes God sacrificing his son, just as the king would make great sacrifices for his people. Climb the footstool to look inside—it's as exquisite as the outside. The shields of various Danish provinces remind the king that he's surrounded by his realms.

Circling the cases along the wall (right to left), notice: the fine enameled lady's goblet with traits of a good woman spelled out in Latin (#5128); above that, an exquisite prayer book (with handwritten favorite prayers, #5134); the big solid-gold baptismal basin (#5262) hanging above tiny boxes that contained the royal children's umbilical chords (handy for protection later in life, #5272); and royal writing sets with wax, seals, pens, and ink (#5320).

Go down a few more steps into the lowest level of the treasury and last room. The two **crowns** in the center cases are more modern (from 1670), lighter, and more practical—just gold and diamonds without all the symbolism. The king's is only four pounds, and the queen's is a mere two.

The cases along the walls show off the **crown jewels.** These were made in 1840 of diamonds, emeralds, rubies, and pearls from earlier royal jewelry. The saber (#5540) shows emblems of the 19 provinces of the realm. The sumptuous pendant features a 19-carat diamond cut (like its neighbors) in the 58-facet "brilliant" style for maximum reflection. Imagine these on the dance floor. The painting shows the coronation of Christian VIII at Frederiksborg Chapel in 1840. The crown jewels are still worn by the queen on special occasions several times a year.

▲Rosenborg Gardens—The Rosenborg Castle is surrounded by the royal pleasure gardens and, on sunny days, a minefield of sunbathing Danish beauties and picnickers. While "ethnic Danes" grab the shade, the rest of the Danes worship the sun. When the royal family is in residence, there's a daily changing-of-the-guard mini-parade from the Royal Guard's barracks adjoining Rosenborg Castle (at 11:30) to Amalienborg Castle (at 12:00). The Queen's Rose Garden (across the moat from the palace) is a royal place for a picnic (cheap open-face sandwiches to go at Sos's Smørrebrød, nearby at the corner of Borgergade and Dronningens Tværgade, Mon–Fri 8:00–14:00, closed Sat–Sun). The fine statue of Hans Christian (H. C., pronounced *hoe see*) Andersen in the park, actually erected in his lifetime (and approved by him), is meant to symbolize how his stories had a message even for adults.

▲National Art Museum (Statens Museum for Kunst)—The museum fills an impressive building with Danish and European paintings from the 14th century through today. Of most interest is the Danish golden age of paintings and those from the late 19th and early 20th centuries. Its Impressionist collection is impressive (with works by Manet, Monet, Renoir, Cézanne, Gauguin, and van Gogh). It's complemented with works by Danish artists, who, inspired by the Impressionists, introduced that breezy movement to Scandinavia. Make a point to meet the "Skagen" artists. They gathered in the fishing village of Skagen on the northern tip of Denmark, surrounded by the sea and strong light, and painted heroic folk fishermen themes in the late 1800s (50 kr, extra for special exhibitions, Tue–Sun 10:00–17:00, Wed until 20:00, closed Mon, Sølvgade 48, tel. 33 74 84 94).

Near Strøget

Museum of Erotica—This museum's focus is the love life of *Homo sapiens.* Better than the Amsterdam equivalent, it offers a chance to visit a porn shop and call it a museum. It took some digging, but they've put together a history of sex from Pompeii to the present day. Visitors get a peep into the world of 19th-century Copenhagen prostitutes and a chance to read up on the sex lives of Mussolini, Queen Elizabeth, Charlie Chaplin, and Casanova. After reviewing a lifetime of Playboy centerfolds and an entire room filled with Marilyn Monroe, visitors sit down for the arguably artistic experience of watching the "electric *tabernakel,*" a dozen silently slamming screens of porn (worth the 79-kr entry fee only if fascinated by sex, they'll try to charge you 99 kr with optional graphic booklet, daily May–Sept 10:00–23:00, Oct–April 11:00–20:00, a block north of Strøget at Købmagergade 24, tel. 33 12 03 11). Copenhagen's dreary little red light district along Istedgade behind the train station has withered away to almost nothing. If you came to Copenhagen to sightsee sex...it's in the museum.

Round Tower—Built in 1642 by Christian IV, the tower connects a church, library, and observatory (the oldest functioning observatory in Europe) with a ramp that spirals up to a fine view of Copenhagen (20 kr, June–Aug Mon–Sat 10:00–20:00, Sun 12:00–20:00, Sept–May Mon–Sat 10:00–17:00, Sun 12:00–17:00, nothing to see inside but the ramp and the view, just off Strøget on Købmagergade).

Near *The Little Mermaid*

▲▲Museum of Danish Resistance (Frihedsmuseet)—The compelling story of Denmark's heroic Nazi-resistance struggle (1940–1945) is well explained in English, from Himmler's eyepatch to fascinating tricks of creative sabotage (40 kr, free on Wed, open May–mid-Sept Tue–Sat 10:00–16:00, Sun 10:00–17:00, off-season Tue–Sat 10:00–15:00, Sun 10:00–16:00, closed Mon; guided tours at 14:00 Tue, Thu, and Sun in the summer; on Churchillparken between Amalienborg Palace and *The Little Mermaid,* bus #26 from Langelinie or bus #1, #6, #19, or #29 from farther away, tel. 33 13 77 14).

▲Amalienborg Palace Museum—While Queen Margrethe II and her family live quite privately in one of the four mansions that make up the palace complex, another mansion has been open to the public since 1994. It displays the private studies of four kings of the House of Glucksborg, who ruled 1863–1972. Your visit is short—six or eight rooms on one floor. But it affords an intimate and unique peek into Denmark's royal family (45 kr, May–Oct daily 10:00–16:00, Nov–April Tue–Sun 11:00–16:00, enter on side of palace square farthest from the harbor, tel. 33 12 08 08).

Amalienborg Palace Changing of the Guard—This noontime event is boring in the summer when the queen is not in residence—the guards just change places. For more information about the palace and Amalienborg Square, see page 232.

Christianshavn

▲Our Savior's Church (Vor Frelsers Kirke)—The church's bright Baroque interior (1696), with its pipe organ supported by the royal elephants, is worth a look (free, helpful English flier, April–Aug Mon–Sat 11:00–16:30, Sun 12:00–16:30, off-season closes 1 hr earlier, bus #2A, #8, #19, or Metro: Christianshavn, Sankt Annægade 29, tel. 32 57 27 98). You can climb the unique spiral spire for great views of the city and of the Christiania commune below (20 kr, 400 steps, 311 feet high, closed in bad weather and Nov–March).

▲▲▲Christiania—In 1971, the original 700 Christianians established squatters' rights in an abandoned military barracks just a 10-minute walk from the Danish parliament building. A generation later, this "free city" still stands—an ultra-human mishmash of idealists, hippies, potheads, nonmaterialists, and happy children (250 kids, 250 dogs, and 600 adults). There are even a handful of Willie Nelson–type seniors among the 180 remaining here from the original takeover. And an amazing thing has happened: The place has become the third-most-visited sight among tourists in Copenhagen. Move over, *Little Mermaid.*

Pusher Street is Christiania's main drag. Get beyond this touristy side of Christiania, and you'll find a fascinating, ramshackle world of moats and earthen ramparts, alternative housing, cozy tea houses, carpenter shops, hippie villas, children's playgrounds, peaceful lanes, and people who believe that "to be normal is to be in a straightjacket." Be careful to distinguish between real Christianians and Christiania's motley guests—druggies (mostly from other countries) who hang out here in the summer for the freedom. Part of the original charter guaranteed that the community would stay open to the public.

The Community: Christiania is broken into 14 administrative

Christiania

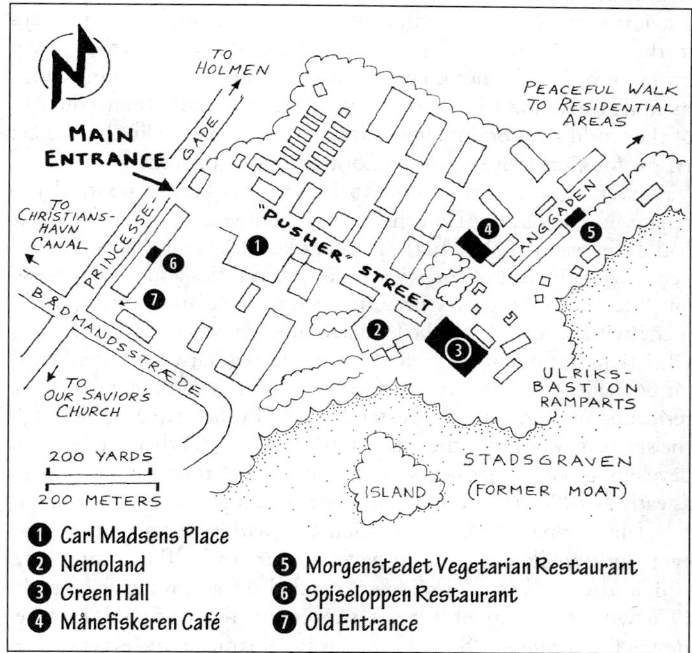

neighborhoods on a former military base. The land is still owned by Denmark's Ministry of Defense. Locals build their homes but don't own the land. There's no buying or selling of property. When someone moves out, the community decides who will be invited in to replace that person. A third of the adult population works on the outside, a third works on the inside, and a third doesn't work much at all. There are nine rules: no cars, no hard drugs, no guns, no explosives, and so on. The Christiania flag is red and yellow because when the original hippies took over, they found a lot of red and yellow paint on site. The three yellow dots in the flag are from the three "i"s in Christiania.

The community pays the city about $1 million a year for utilities and has about $1 million a year more to run its local affairs. A few "luxury hippies" have oil heat, but most use wood or gas. The ground here was poisoned by its days as a military base, so nothing is grown in Christiania. The community has one mailing address (for 25 kr/month, you can receive mail here). A phone chain provides a system of communal security (they have had bad experiences calling the police). Each September 26, the day those first squatters took over the barracks here in 1971, Christiania has a big birthday bash.

Tourists are entirely welcome here, because they've become a major part of the economy. Visitors react in very different ways to the place. Some see dogs, dirt, and dazed people. Others see a haven of peace, freedom, and no taboos. Locals will remind judgmental Americans (whose country incarcerates more than a quarter of the world's prison inmates) that a society must make the choice: Allow for alternative lifestyles...or build more prisons.

Even since its inception, Christiania has been a political hot potato. No one in the Danish establishment wanted it. And no one had the nerve to mash it. In the last decade, Christiania has connected better with the rest of society—paying its utilities and taxes, and so on. But since taking over in 2001, Denmark's conservative government (with pressure from the United States) has vowed to "normalize" Christiania, and in recent years police have regularly conducted raids on pot sellers. In January 2004, to minimize governmental hassles, residents tore down the hash stands along Pusher Street. (Although the shops may be gone, the merchants remain.) And there's talk about developing posh apartments to replace existing residences—perhaps as early as 2006, according to one government plan.

Many predict that Christianians will withstand the government's challenge, as they have in years past. The community, which also calls itself Freetown, fended off a similar attempt in 1976 with the help of fervent supporters from around Europe. *Bevar Christiania*—"Save Christiania"—banners fly everywhere, and locals are confident that their free way of life will survive. As history has shown, the challenge may just make that hippie haven a bit stronger.

Orientation Tour: Passing under the gate, take Pusher Street directly into the community. The first square—a kind of market square (souvenirs and marijuana-related stuff)—is named Carl Madsens Place, honoring the lawyer who took the squatters' case to the Danish supreme court in 1976 and won. Beyond that is Nemoland (a food circus, on the right). A huge warehouse called the Green Hall (Den Gronne Hal) is a recycling center (where people get most of their building material) that does double duty at night as a concert hall and as a place where children work on crafts. On the left, a lane leads to the Månefiskeren café, and beyond that, to the Morgenstedet vegetarian restaurant. Going straight on Pusher Street takes you to the ramparts that overlook the lake. A walk or bike ride through Christiania is a great way to see how this community lives. (When you leave, look up—the sign above the gate says, "You are entering the EU.")

Smoking Marijuana: Beefy marijuana plants stand on proud pedestals at the market square. The open-air food circus (or the canal-view perch above it, on the earthen ramparts) creates just the right ambience for losing track of time.

While hard drugs are out and government crackdowns continue, marijuana is still sold and smoked happily (cheap, in joints or loose, bars have bongs). Local dealers are friendly, talkative, and helpful to Americans. They claim you're safe within Christiania. You can buy and smoke marijuana legally anytime of year, but don't take it out of the neighborhood or you'll risk arrest. Because of the possibility of losing its favored trade status with America, Denmark is required by Uncle Sam to make an occasional bust of someone leaving the "free city" with pot.

About hard drugs: For the first few years, junkies were tolerated. But that led to violence and polluted the mellow ambience residents envisioned. In 1979, the junkies were expelled—an epic confrontation in the community's folk history now—and since then, the symbol of a fist breaking a syringe is as prevalent as the leafy marijuana icon. Hard drugs are emphatically forbidden in Christiania.

Eating in Christiania: The people of Christiania appreciate good food and count on tourism as a big part of their economy. Consequently, there are plenty of decent eateries. Most of the restaurants are closed on Monday (the community's weekly holiday). **Pusher Street** has a few grungy but tasty falafel stands. **Nemoland** is a fun food circus with Thai food, fast hippie food, and great tented outdoor seating. Its stay-a-while atmosphere comes with backgammon, foosball, bakery goods, and fine views from the ramparts. **Morgenstedet** is a good, cheap vegetarian café (60-kr meals, Tue–Sun 12:00–21:00, closed Mon, left after Pusher Street). **Månefiskeren** (Moonfisher Bar) looks like a Brueghel painting—from 2006—with billiards, chess, light meals, and drinks. **Spiseloppen** is *the* classy, good-enough-for-Republicans restaurant in the community (closed Mon, described in "Eating," page 254).

Hours and Tours: Christiania is open all the time (main entrance is down Prinsessegade behind Vor Frelsers' spiral church spire in Christianshavn). You're welcome to snap photos, but ask residents before you photograph them. Guided tours leave from the front entrance of Christiania at 15:00 (just show up, 30 kr, 90 min, daily late June–Aug, Sat–Sun rest of year, in English and Danish, tel. 32 57 96 70). For a private tour, contact Nina Pontoppidan. Nina and her husband have been part of the community since its early days, and she charges 180 kr for a 90-minute tour (tel. 32 57 69 51, pontoppidan@mail.mira.dk).

Greater Copenhagen

Carlsberg Brewery—Denmark's beloved source of legal intoxicants, Carlsberg welcomes you to its Visitors Center for a self-guided tour and a half-liter of beer (free, Tue–Sun 10:00–16:00, closed Mon, bus #18, enter at Gamle Carlsbergvej 11 around corner from brewery entrance, tel. 33 27 13 14).

Open-Air Folk Museum (Frilandsmuseet)—This park is filled with traditional Danish architecture and folk culture (50 kr, free Wed, open April–Sept Tue–Sun 10:00–17:00, closed Mon and off-season, outside of town in the suburb of Lyngby, S-tog: Sorgenfri and 10-min walk to Kongevejen 100, tel. 33 13 44 11).

Bakken—Danes gather at Copenhagen's other great amusement park, Bakken (free, April–Aug daily 12:00–24:00, S-tog: Klampenborg then walk 10 min through the woods, tel. 39 63 73 00, www.bakken.dk—in Danish only).

Dragør—Consider a trip a few minutes out of Copenhagen to the fishing village of Dragør (bus #250S or #5A from station 5 stops at Sundbyvesterplads, change to #350A).

SHOPPING

Shops are generally open Monday through Friday from 10:00 to 19:00 and Saturday from 9:00 to 16:00. While the big department stores dominate the scene, many locals favor the characteristic, small artisan shops and boutiques that are listed in the *Local Life* flier. You can't get this flier at the TI, but keep your eyes peeled for it (for example, at the bus info center on Rådhuspladsen and at the bakery on Pistol Street).

For a street's worth of shops selling **"Scantiques,"** wander down Ravnsborggade from Nørrebrogade.

Copenhagen's colorful **flea markets** are small but feisty and surprisingly cheap (Sat May–Nov 8:00–14:00 at Israels Plads, Fri and Sat May–Sept 8:00–17:00 along Gammel Strand and on Kongens Nytorv). For other street markets, ask at the TI.

The city's top **department stores** (Illum at Østergade 52, tel. 33 14 40 02; and Magasin at Kongens Nytorv 13, tel. 33 11 44 33) offer a good, if expensive, look at today's Denmark. Both are on Strøget and have fine cafeterias on their top floors. The department stores and the Politiken Bookstore on Rådhuspladsen have a good selection of maps and English travel guides.

Shoppers who like jewelry look for amber, known as "gold of the North." Globs of this petrified sap wash up on the shores of all the Baltic countries. **House of Amber** has a shop and a tiny two-room museum with about 50 examples of prehistoric insects trapped in the amber (remember *Jurassic Park*?) under magnifying glasses (25 kr, daily 10:00–18:00, 50 yards off Nyhavn at Kongens Nytorv 2).

If you buy anything substantial (more than 300 kr, about $50) from a shop displaying the **Danish Tax-Free Shopping** emblem, you can get a refund of the Value Added Tax, roughly 25 percent of the purchase price (VAT is MOMS in Danish). If you have your purchase mailed, the tax can be deducted from your bill. For details, call 32 52 55 66, and see the information on VAT refunds on page 12.

NIGHTLIFE

For the latest on the city's hopping jazz scene, inquire at the TI, study your *Copenhagen This Week* booklet, or pick up the "alternative" *Playtime* magazine at Use It. To locate the following places, see the map on pgae 76. The **Copenhagen Jazz House** is a good bet for live jazz (around 90 kr, Tue–Thu and Sun at 20:30, Fri–Sat at 21:30, closed Mon, Niels Hemmingsensgade 10, tel. 33 15 26 00 for the schedule in Danish, www.jazzhouse.dk). For blues, try the **Mojo Blues Bar** (50 kr Fri–Sat, otherwise no cover, nightly 20:00–5:00, music starts at 22:00, Løngangsstræde 21c, tel. 33 11 64 53). Christiania always seems to have something musical going on after dark. **Tivoli** has evening entertainment daily from mid-April through mid-September until 23:00 (see page 232).

If you'd rather dance, join Denmark's salsa wave at **Sabor Latino Salsa Club.** Located one block south of Rådhuspladsen, it offers free salsa lessons in English. Salsa dancing is surprisingly easy to learn in this friendly environment, and you'll get a chance to know the fun-loving Danes (free on Thu, 50 kr Fri–Sat, Thu–Sun 21:00–3:00, free lesson 22:00–23:00, closed Mon–Wed, no reservation required, wear comfortable shoes, Vestervoldgade 85, tel. 26 16 46 96).

SLEEPING

I've listed a few big business-class hotels, the best budget hotels in the center, cheap rooms in private homes in great neighborhoods an easy bus ride from the station, and a few backpacker dorm options.

Big Copenhagen hotels have an exasperating pricing policy. Their high rack rates are actually charged only about 20 or 30 days a year (unless you book in advance and don't know better). Hotels are swamped at certain times and need to keep their gouging options open. Therefore, you need to check their Web site for deals or be bold enough to simply show up and let the TI (for a 75-kr fee) find you a room on their push list. The TI swears that, except for maybe 10 days a year, they can land you a deeply discounted room in a three- or four-star business-class hotel in the center. That means a 1,400-kr American-style comfort double for about 800 kr, including a big buffet breakfast.

Sleep Code

(6 kr = about $1, country code: 45)
S = Single, **D** = Double/Twin, **T** = Triple, **Q** = Quad, **b** = bathroom, **s** = shower. Breakfast is generally included at hotels but not at private rooms or hostels. Unless otherwise noted, credit cards are accepted. Everybody speaks English.

To help you sort easily through these listings, I've divided the rooms into three categories, based on the price for a standard double room with bath during high season:

$$$ **Higher Priced**—Most rooms 1,000 kr or more.
$$ **Moderately Priced**—Most rooms between 450–1,000 kr.
$ **Lower Priced**—Most rooms 450 kr or less.

Hotels in Central Copenhagen

Prices include breakfast unless noted otherwise. All are big, modern places with elevators and non-smoking rooms upon request, and all accept credit cards. Beware, many hotels have rip-off phone rates even for local calls. The Mayfair, Webers, Sophie Amalie, and Ibis hotels are big and soulless. The rest are smaller, cheaper, and more characteristic.

$$$ Ibsens Hotel is an elegant 118-room hotel in a charming neighborhood away from the main train station commotion and a short walk from the old center (Sb-935–1035 kr, Db-1,150–1350 kr, discounted rooms available May–June and Aug–Sept—ask about these and other discounts when booking or check their Web site for the latest offers, Vendersgade 23, S-tog: Nørreport, tel. 33 13 19 13, fax 33 13 19 16, www.ibsenshotel.dk, hotel@ibsenshotel.dk).

$$$ Hotel Mayfair is a comfortable but sterile place on a quiet street three blocks behind the station (Sb-1,295 kr, Db-1,395 kr rack rate but Db often go for 800 or 900 kr, a half a block away from busy Vesterbrogade at Helgolandsgade 3, tel. 33 31 48 01, fax 33 23 96 86, www.choicehotels.dk, info.mayfair@comfort.choicehotels.dk).

$$$ Webers Scandic Hotel faces busy Vesterbrogade (some noisy rooms), but has a peaceful garden courtyard and a modern, inviting interior (high-season rack rates: small Sb-1,145 kr, Sb-1,395 kr, Db-1,545 kr, but ask about summer/weekend rates June–Aug and Fri–Sun all year—you can save 20–30 percent depending on availability, sauna, exercise room, particularly expensive phone rates, Vesterbrogade 11B, tel. 33 31 14 32, fax 33 31 14 41, www.scandic-hotels.com, webers@scandic-hotels.com).

$$$ Sophie Amalie Hotel is a classy and modern Danish-style hotel a block from the big cruise-ship harbor and a block from trendy

Copenhagen Hotels

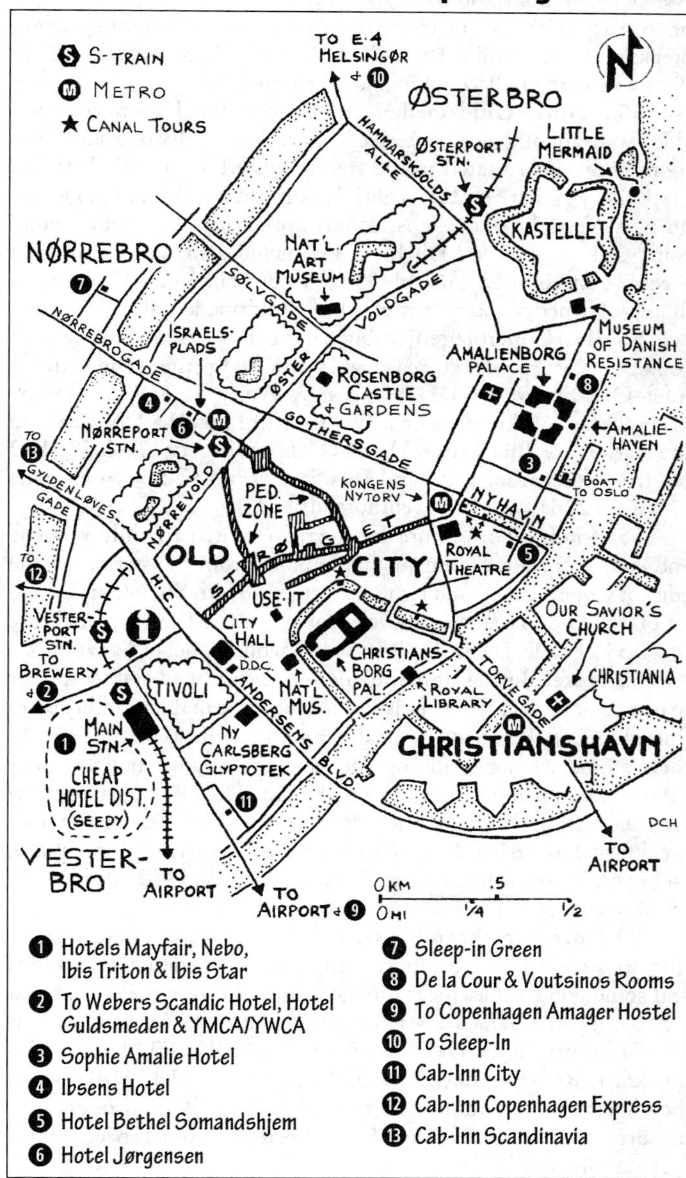

1. Hotels Mayfair, Nebo, Ibis Triton & Ibis Star
2. To Webers Scandic Hotel, Hotel Guldsmeden & YMCA/YWCA
3. Sophie Amalie Hotel
4. Ibsens Hotel
5. Hotel Bethel Somandshjem
6. Hotel Jørgensen
7. Sleep-in Green
8. De la Cour & Voutsinos Rooms
9. To Copenhagen Amager Hostel
10. To Sleep-In
11. Cab-Inn City
12. Cab-Inn Copenhagen Express
13. Cab-Inn Scandinavia

Nyhavn (134 rooms, Sb-875/1,075/1,275 kr, Db-1,075/1,175/1,275 kr, prices vary with size of room from pretty tight to very spacious, breakfast-115 kr, Sankt Annæ Plads 21, tel. 33 13 34 00, fax 33 11 77 07, www.remmen.dk, booking.hsa@remmen.dk).

$$$ Hotel Guldsmeden, a boutique hotel with comfortable, well-appointed rooms, feels more like a B&B than a 64-room hotel. It's situated in the trendy Vesterbro district, between Frederiksborg park and the central train station. Although located on busy Vesterbrogade, most rooms are clustered around a quiet courtyard (Sb-995 kr, Db-1,295 kr, includes breakfast, Internet access, Vesterbrogade 66, tel. 33 22 15 00, fax 33 22 15 55, www.hotelguldsmeden.dk, reception@hotelguldsmeden.dk).

$$ Ibis Copenhagen, a big chain, has several hotels with cookie-cutter rooms at reasonable prices in the center (mid-June–Oct: Sb-599 kr, Db-799 kr, Nov–April: Sb-599 kr, Db-659 kr, breakfast-60 kr, elevator). Two identical hotels a block behind the station are **Ibis Triton Hotel** (Helgolandsgade 7, tel. 33 31 32 66, triton@accorhotel.dk) and **Ibis Star Hotel** (Colbjornsensgade 13, tel. 33 22 11 00, star@accorhotel.dk).

$$ Hotel Nebo, a secure-feeling refuge with a friendly welcome and comfy, spacious rooms, is half a block from the station on the edge of Copenhagen's red light district (S-460 kr, Sb-760 kr, D-690 kr, older Db-860 kr, cheaper Oct–April, extra bed-150 kr, Istedgade 6, tel. 33 21 12 17, fax 33 23 47 74, www.nebo.dk, nebo@email.dk).

$$ Hotel Bethel Somandshjem is a calm and stately former seamen's hotel facing the boisterous Nyhavn canal and offering 30 fine rooms at the most reasonable rack rates in town. A third of their rooms are non-smoking and newly renovated, but the older rooms are a bit more spacious (Sb-595 kr, Db-745 kr, harborview Db-795 kr, big Db on corner-895 kr, extra bed-150 kr, includes breakfast, bus #650S from station or Metro to Kongens Nytorv, facing bridge over the canal at Nyhavn 22, tel. 33 13 03 70, fax 33 15 85 70 www.hotel-bethel.dk).

$$ Hotel Jørgensen is a friendly little 30-room hotel beautifully located just off Nørreport with some cheap, depressing rooms and some good-value, nicer rooms. While the lounge is classy and welcoming, the halls are a narrow, tangled maze (basic S-475 kr, Sb-575 kr, very basic D-575 kr, more elegant Db-700 kr, includes breakfast, Romersgade 11, tel. 33 13 81 86, fax 33 15 51 05, www.hoteljoergensen.dk, hoteljoergensen@mail.dk). They also rent 135-kr dorm beds to those under 35 (6–14 beds in rooms, sheets-30 kr, includes breakfast).

A Danish Motel-6

$$ Cab-Inn is a radical innovation: identical, mostly collapsible, tiny but comfy, cruise ship–type staterooms, all bright, molded, and shiny with TV, coffeepot, shower, and toilet. Each room has a single bed that expands into a twin with one or two fold-down bunks on the walls. The staff will hardly give you the time of day, but it's tough to argue with this efficiency (Sb-510 kr, Db-630 kr, Tb-750 kr, Qb-870 kr, breakfast-50 kr, easy parking-60 kr, www.cabinn.dk). There are two virtually identical Cab-Inns in the same neighborhood (a 15-min walk northwest of the station): **Cab-Inn Copenhagen Express** (86 rooms, Danasvej 32–34, tel. 33 21 04 00, fax 33 21 74 09, express@cabinn.com) and **Cab-Inn Scandinavia** (201 rooms, "Commodore" rooms have a real double bed for 100 kr extra, Vodroffsvej 55, tel. 35 36 11 11, fax 35 36 11 14, scandinavia@cabinn.com). A third location recently opened just south of Tivoli: **Cab-Inn City** (350 rooms, Mitchellsgade 14, tel. 33 46 16 16, fax 33 46 17 17, city@cabinn.com).

Rooms in Private Homes

Lots of travelers seem shy about rooms in private homes. Don't be. I almost always sleep in a private home. And, at 450 kr or so per double, they're a great value. The experience is as private or as social as you want it to be, offering great "at home in Denmark" opportunities in good neighborhoods (in Christianshavn and near Amalienborg Palace) for a third of the price of hotels. You'll get a key and come and go as you like. Always call ahead—they book in advance. All speak English and afford a fine peek into Danish domestic life. Rooms generally have no sink. While they usually don't include breakfast, you'll have access to the kitchen. If their rooms are booked up, they can often find you a place with a neighbor. You can trust the quality of their referrals. If you still can't snare a place, remember that the TI or Use It would love to send you to one from their stable of locals renting out rooms. For more listings, visit www.bbdk.dk.

Private Rooms in Christianshavn

This area is a never-a-dull-moment hodgepodge of the chic, artistic, hippie, and hobo, with historic fixed-up warehouses in the shadow of government ministries. Colorful with shops, cafés, and canals, Christianshavn is an easy 10-minute walk to the center and has good bus connections to the airport and downtown. The bus stop is just outside the 7-Eleven on Torvegade. Take bus #2A or #48 to City Hall or the main train station and #2A to the airport. The Metro connects Christianshavn and Nørreport (2 stops on S-tog from main train station).

$ Annette and Rudy Hollender enjoy sharing their 300-year-old home with my readers. Even with a long and skinny staircase, sinkless rooms, and two rooms sharing one toilet/shower, it's a comfortable and cheery place to call home (S-350 kr, D-450 kr,

Christianshavn

T-625 kr, cash only, closed Nov–April, half a block off Torvegade at Wildersgade 19, Metro: Christianshavntorv, tel. 32 95 96 22, hollender@city.dk).

$ Chicken's Private Pension rents basic rooms in a funky old house, with steep stairs and rustic furniture. It's right on Christianshavn's main drag (S-350 kr, D-450 kr, T-625 kr, Q-800 kr, extra bed-125 kr, kitchen available for breakfast on your own, cash only, Torvegade 36, Metro: Christianshavntorv, tel. 32 95 32 73, mobile 20 41 32 73, www.chickens.dk, morten@chickens.dk, Morton Frederiksen).

South of Christianshavn: **$$ Gitte Kongstad** rents two apartments, each taking up an entire spacious floor in her 100-year-old house. You'll have a kitchen, little garden, Internet connection, and your own bike as you settle comfortably far from the big-city intensity (Sb-400 kr, Db-475 kr, extra bed-150 kr, cash only, family-friendly, bus #2A from airport, bus #12 or #13 from station, and just 75 yards from Metro stop: Lergravsparken, Badensgade 2, tel. & fax 32 97 71 97, mobile 21 65 75 22, g.kongstad@post.tele.dk). You'll feel at home here, and the bike ride into town (or to the beach) is a snap.

Lower-Priced Private Rooms a Block from Amalienborg Palace

Amaliegade is a stately cobbled street in a quiet neighborhood (a 10-min walk north of Nyhavn and Strøget). You can look out your window and see the palace guard changing. Catch bus #1A or #15 from the station to Fredericiagade.

$ The following people are artistic and professional folks who each rent out two rooms in their utilitarian, modern, and very Danish flats: **Puk and Holger De la Cour** (S-375 kr, D-425 kr with do-it-yourself breakfast, extra bed-150 kr, cash only, kitchen/lounge available, Amaliegade 34, 4th floor, tel. 33 12 04 68, mobile 23 72 96 45, holgerdelacour@private.dk) and **Line** (pronounced LEE-nuh) **Voutsinos** (2 double rooms, 1 with queen bed, 1 with 2 large single beds, D-425 kr, includes breakfast, extra bed-150 kr, cash only, family deals, May–Sept only, Amaliegade 34, 3rd floor, tel. & fax 33 14 71 42, line.voutsinos@privat.dk).

Hostels

Copenhagen energetically accommodates the young vagabond on a shoestring. The Use It office (see page 218) is your best source of information. Each of these places charges about 100 kr per person for a bed and breakfast. Some don't allow sleeping bags, and if you don't have your own hostel bedsheet, you'll usually have to rent one for about 30 kr. IYHF hostels normally sell non-cardholders a guest pass for 25 kr.

$ The modern **Copenhagen Amager Hostel** (IYHF) is huge (528 beds), with 300-kr doubles, 390-kr triples, 460-kr quads, and five-bed dorms at 95 kr per bed (membership required, sheets-35 kr, no curfew, excellent facilities, breakfast-45 kr, dinner-65 kr, Internet access, self-serve laundry). It's on the edge of town, but the Metro gets you within a 10-minute walk (Metro: Balla Center). By bus, it's 30 minutes from the center (#250S with change to #100S, direction: Svanmøllen S, Vejlands Allé 200, tel. 32 52 29 08, fax 32 52 27 08, www.danhostel.dk).

$ The following two big, grungy, central crash pads are open in July and August only: **Danish YMCA/YWCA** (dorm bed-90 kr, 4- to 10-bed rooms, breakfast-25 kr, sheets-15 kr, Valdemarsgade 15, 10-min walk from train station or bus #6, tel. 33 31 15 74) and **Sleep-In** (dorm bed-110 kr, sheets-30 kr, 4- or 6-bed cubicles in a huge 286-bed room, no curfew, breakfast-20 kr, lockers, always has room and free condoms, Blegdamsvej 132, bus #1, #6, or #14 to Triangle stop and look for sign, tel. 35 26 50 59, www.sleep-in.dk, copenhagen@sleep-in.dk).

$ Sleep-in Green, the "ecological hostel," is very young, cool, and open mid-April through October (100-kr bunks, organic breakfast-30 kr, in a quiet spot a 15-min walk from center or catch bus 5A from station to Ravnsborggade, off Nørrebrogade at Ravnsborggade 18, tel. 35 37 77 77, www.sleep-in-green.dk).

EATING

Cheap Meals

For a quick lunch, try a *smørrebrød,* a *pølse,* or a picnic. Finish it off with a pastry.

Smørrebrød

Denmark's 300-year-old tradition of open-face sandwiches survives. Find a *smørrebrød* take-out shop and choose two or three that look good (about 10 kr each). You'll get them wrapped and ready for a park bench. Add a cold drink, and you have a fine, quick, and very Danish lunch. Tradition calls for three sandwich courses: herring first, then meat, and then cheese. Downtown, you'll find these handy local alternatives to Yankee fast-food chains:

Near Kongens Nytorv: Try Tria Cafe (Mon–Fri 8:00–14:00, closed Sat–Sun, Gothersgade 12).

Near the Round Tower: Café Halvvejen is good for sit-down *smørrebrød* (lunch only, on Krystalgade).

Near Gammeltorv/Nytorv: Sorgenfri offers a local experience in a dark, woody spot just off Strøget (Mon–Sat 11:00–21:00, Sun 12:00–21:00, Brolæggerstræde 8, tel. 33 11 58 80). Or consider Domhusets Smørrebrød (Mon–Fri 7:00–14:30, closed Sat–Sun, Kattesundet 18, tel. 33 15 98 98).

Near Amalienborg Palace: Head inland two blocks just past the Marble Church to Svend Larsen's Smørrebrød (8-kr sandwiches to go, Mon–Fri 8:00–14:00, closed Sat–Sun, St. Kongensgade 83).

Near Rosenborg Palace: Sos's Smørrebrød delights local office workers (Mon–Fri 8:00–14:00, closed Sat–Sun, at corner of Borgergade and Dronningens Tværgade). The nearby Rosenborg Gardens are perfect for your picnic.

The Pølse

The famous Danish hot dog, sold in *pølsevogn* (sausage wagons) throughout the city, is another typically Danish institution that has resisted the onslaught of our global, Styrofoam-packaged, fast-food culture. Study the photo menu for variations. These are fast, cheap, tasty, and—like their American cousins—almost worthless nutritionally. Even so, what the locals call the "dead man's finger" is the dog Danish kids love to bite.

There's more to getting a *pølse* than simply ordering a hot dog. Employ these handy phrases: *rød* (red, the basic weenie), *medister* (spicy, better quality), *knæk* (short, stubby, tastier than *rød*), *ristet* (fried), *brød* (a bun, usually smaller than the sausage), *svøb* ("swaddled" in bacon), *Fransk* (French style, buried in a long skinny hole in the bun with sauce), and *flottenheimer* (a fat one with onions and sauce). *Sennep* is mustard and *ristet løg* are crispy, fried onions. Wash everything down with a *sodavand* (soda pop).

By hanging around a *pølsevogn,* you can study this institution. Denmark's "cold feet cafés" are a form of social care: People who have difficulty finding jobs are licensed to run these wiener-mobiles. As they gain seniority, they are promoted to work at more central locations. Danes like to gather here for munchies and *pølsesnak*—the local slang for empty chatter (literally, "sausage talk").

Picnics

Throughout Copenhagen, small delis *(viktualiehandler)* sell fresh bread, tasty pastries, juice, milk, cheese, and yogurt (drinkable, in tall liter boxes). Two of the largest supermarket chains are **Irma** (in arcade on Vesterbrogade next to Tivoli) and **Super Brugsen. Netto** is a cut-rate outfit with the cheapest prices. The little grocery store in the main train station is expensive but handy (daily 8:00–24:00).

Pastry

Find your way to the famous Danish pastries by looking for the golden pretzel sign hanging over the door or windows—it's the Dane's age-old symbol for a bakery. Danish pastries, called *wienerbrød* (Vienna bread) in Denmark, are named for the Viennese bakers who brought the art of pastry-making to Denmark, where the Danes say they perfected it. Try these bakeries: **Nansens** (on corner of Nansensgade and Ahlefeldtsgade, near Ibsens Hotel), **Kransekagehuset** (on Pilestræde—Pistol Street, just off Strøget, near Kongens Nytorv; for their cheaper takeout, go around the corner to Ny Ostergade 9), and **Lagekagehuset** (on Torvegade in Christianshavn). For a genteel bit of high-class 1870s Copenhagen, pay a lot for a coffee and a fresh danish at **Conditori La Glace,** just off Strøget at Skoubogade 3.

Dining with the Danes

For a unique experience and a great opportunity to meet locals in their homes, consider dining with a Danish family. You get a homey two-course meal with lots of conversation. Some effort is made to match your age and interests (but not occupations). Book in advance, by phone or online. **Dine with the Danes** costs 350 kr per person (reserve at least a day in advance, tel. 26 85 39 61, www.dinewiththedanes.dk). **Meet the Danes** charges 395 kr per person (tel. 33 46 46 46, www.meetthedanes.dk).

Restaurants

In the Center

Det Lille Apotek ("The Little Pharmacy") is a reasonable, candlelit place. It's been popular with locals for 200 years, and now it's also quite touristy (sandwich lunches, traditional dinners for 120–170 kr nightly from 17:30; just off Strøget, between Frue Church and Round Tower at St. Kannikestræde 15; tel. 33 12 56 06). Their specialty is "Stone Beef," a big slab of tender, raw steak plopped down in front of you on a scalding-hot lava stone. Flip it over a few times and it's cooked within minutes.

Riz-Raz Vegetarian Buffet has two locations in Copenhagen: around the corner from the canal boat rides at Kompagnistræde 20 (tel. 33 15 05 75) and across from Det Lille Apotek at Store Kannikestræde 19 (tel. 33 32 33 45). At both places, you'll find a healthy all-you-can-eat Mediterranean/vegetarian buffet lunch for 59 kr (daily 11:30–16:00) and an even bigger dinner buffet for 69 kr (16:00–24:00). The dinner has to be the best deal in town. And they're happy to serve free water with your meal.

Café Norden, smoky and very Danish with fine pastries, overlooks Amagertorv by the swan fountain. They have good light meals and salads and great people-watching from window seats on the second floor (order at the bar upstairs).

Kobenhavner Cafeen, cosy yet classy, dishes up traditional food at a reasonable price. Their lunch specials are served until 17:00, when the more expensive dinner menu kicks in (daily until 22:00, 2 blocks off Nytorn at Badstuestraede 10, tel. 33 32 80 81).

Bryggeriet Apollo, just outside the main entrance to Tivoli, offers pub atmosphere Danish-style. Beer is brewed on the premises while the kitchen cranks out generous portions of meat-and-potatoes dishes for reasonable prices (140–200-kr dinners, Mon–Sat 11:30–22:00, Sun 15:00–24:00, Vesterbrogade 3, tel. 33 12 33 13). Order a one-liter mug of beer and they take a surprising security deposit.

Hercegovina, a Croatian restaurant with folksy seating overlooking a leafy section of Tivoli, serves a 129-kr lunch buffet (mostly cold, 12:00–16:00) and a 169-kr dinner buffet (salads, veggies, and lots and lots of meat, including a lamb on a spit, daily 17:00–22:00, music nightly after 19:00). While this is technically in Tivoli, diners can get in from the outside by going through the restaurant's office (facing the train station, next to the TI). You can eat here without a Tivoli ticket, but you will not be allowed into the park.

Copenhagen Restaurants

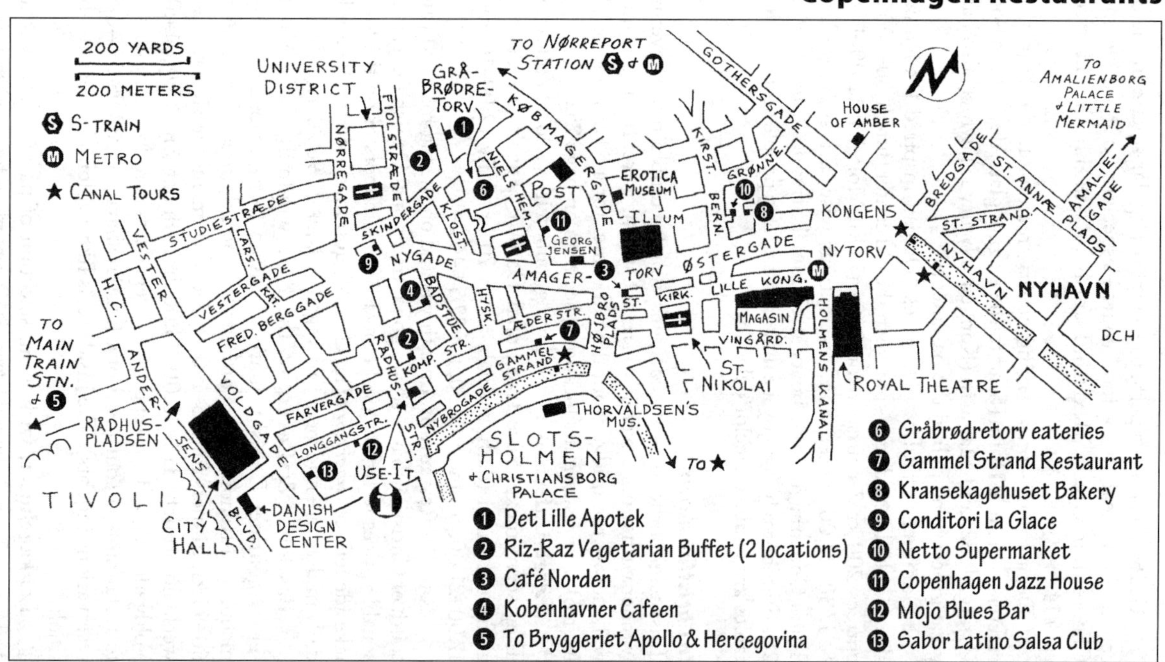

Gråbrødretorv is perhaps the most popular square in the old center for a meal. It's a food court—especially in good weather. Choose from Greek, Mexican, Danish, or a meal in the old streetcar #14.

Department stores serving cheery, reasonable meals in their cafeterias include **Illum** (head to the elegant glass-domed top floor, Østergade 52) and **Magasin** (Kongens Nytorv 13), which also has a great grocery and deli in the basement.

Gammel Strand, which serves "Danish-inspired French cuisine," is ideal for a dressy splurge in the old center (lunch-80–200 kr, entrees-200 kr, 3-course menu-300–450 kr, Mon–Sat 12:00–15:00 & 17:30–22:00, closed Sun, reservations wise, across from Canal Tours Copenhagen tour boats at Gammel Strand 42, tel. 33 91 21 21). Outdoor tables enjoy a canal and strolling people scene. Indoor tables are white-tablecloth elegant.

In Christianshavn

This neighborhood is so cool, it's worth combining an evening wander with dinner even if you're not staying here. It's a 10-minute walk across the bridge from the old center (or a 3-min ride on the Metro). For restaurants locations, see map on page 252.

Færge Cafeen is a fun-loving pub with a local following. They serve inexpensive traditional Danish specialties indoors or along the canal (daily specials about 70 kr, daily 12:00–16:00 & 17:00–21:00, Strandgade 50, tel. 32 54 46 24).

Ravelin Restaurant, on a tiny island on the big road 100 yards south of Christianshavn, serves good, traditional Danish food at reasonable prices to happy local crowds. Dine indoors or on the lovely lakeside terrace (*smørrebrød* lunches-40–100 kr, dinners-100–200 kr, daily mid-April–mid-Sept, Torvegade 79, tel. 32 96 20 45).

Bastionen & Løven, at the little windmill (Lille Mølle), serves gourmet Danish: nouveau cuisine from a small but fresh menu, on a Renoir terrace or in its Rembrandt interior (lunches for 60–95 kr, dinners for 145–190 kr, 3-course menu for 310 kr, 135-kr weekend brunch, daily 10:00–24:00, brunch Sat–Sun 10:00–14:00, Voldgade 50, walk to end of Torvegade and follow ramparts up to restaurant, at south end of Christianshavn, tel. 32 95 09 40 for reservations indoors). The inside feels like a colonial mansion—but smoky.

Lagkagehuset, with a big selection of pastries, sandwiches, and excellent fresh-baked bread, is a great place for breakfast (takeout coffee and pastries for 15 kr, Torvegade 45). **Spicy Kitchen** serves cheap and good Indian food (Torvegade 56).

Spiseloppen ("The Flea Eats") is a wonderfully classy place in Christiania. It serves great 140-kr vegetarian meals and 160–220-kr meaty ones by candlelight. It's gourmet anarchy—a good fit for

Christiania, the free city/squatter town (restaurant open Tue–Sun 17:00–22:00, closed Mon, live music Fri and Sat, reservations often necessary on weekends; 3 blocks behind spiral spire of Vor Frelser's church, on top floor of old brick warehouse, turn right just inside Christiania's gate, enter the wildly empty warehouse, and climb the graffiti-riddled stairs; tel. 32 57 95 58). Beware, the people at the next table are likely to light up a joint while waiting for their ribs. Other, less-expensive Christiania eateries are listed above (see page 245).

Near Nørreport

These places—near the recommended Ibsens and Jørgensens hotels—are all close enough to survey before making a choice.

Kost Bar serves good-sized portions of pub fare indoors or outdoors (60-kr salads, 50–75 kr for lunch, 75–120 kr for dinner, daily 11:00–24:00, later on weekends, Vendersgade 16, tel. 33 33 00 35).

Café Klimt, which draws a young, hip, but sometimes heavy-smoking crowd, offers omelettes, sandwiches, and modern world cuisine (50–100 kr, daily 10:00–24:00, later Fri–Sat, Frederikborggade 29, tel. 33 11 76 70).

Café Marius, with a jazzy elegance, dressy indoor tables, and casual sidewalk seating, is popular for its homemade pasta, hearty burgers, and big salads. Marius is from Chicago, so don't expect traditional Danish here (85–135-kr plates, brunch served daily with American-style pancakes, daily 12:00–23:00, Nørre Farimagsgade 55, tel. 33 11 83 83).

TRANSPORTATION CONNECTIONS

From Copenhagen by Train to: Hillerød/Frederiksborg (6/hr, 40 min), **Roskilde** (1–3/hr, 30 min), **Odense** (2/hr, 1.75 hrs), **Helsingør** (3/hr, 50 min), **Malmö** (3/hr, 35 min), **Ærøskøbing** (5/day, 2.5 hrs to Svendborg with a transfer in Odense, then 75-min ferry crossing to Ærøskøbing), **Stockholm** (11/day, 5 hrs on X2000 high-speed train, night service via Malmö 23:10–6:10; take regional train to Malmö first, but if you get off at Malmö Syd, you'll miss your connection—wait for Malmö C, for Central), **Växjö** (5/day, 3 hrs), **Kalmar** (5/day, 4 hrs), **Oslo** (2/day departing 8:20 and 13:36, 8–9 hrs, you must change in Göteborg, Sweden; no night train), **Berlin** (4/day, 9 hrs, via Hamburg), **Amsterdam** (2/day, 11 hrs), and **Frankfurt/Rhine** (4/day, 8 hrs). Convenient overnight trains from Copenhagen run to Stockholm, Amsterdam, and Frankfurt, some with one connection. National train info tel. 70 13 14 15. International train info tel. 70 13 14 16. Cheaper bus trips are listed at Use It (see page 218).

PARIS

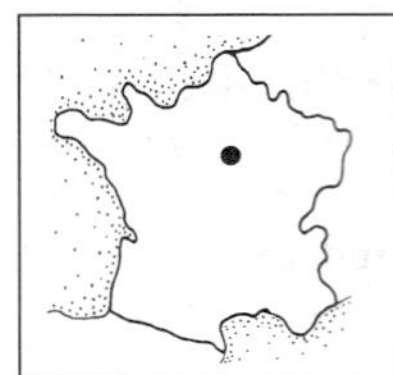

The City of Light has been a beacon of culture for centuries. As a world capital of art, fashion, food, literature, and ideas, it stands as a symbol of all the fine things that human civilization can offer.

Paris offers sweeping boulevards, chatty crêpe stands, chic boutiques, and world-class art galleries. Sip decaf with deconstructionists in a sidewalk café, then step into an Impressionist painting in a tree-lined park. Climb Notre-Dame and rub shoulders with the gargoyles. Cruise the Seine, zip up the Eiffel Tower, and saunter down the avenue des Champs-Elysées. Master the Louvre and Orsay museums. Save some after-dark energy for one of the world's most romantic cities.

Some see the essentials and flee, overwhelmed. But with the proper approach and a good orientation, you'll fall head over heels for Europe's capital.

Planning Your Time: Paris in One, Two, or Three Days

Day 1

Morning: Follow my self-guided "Historic Core of Paris Walk" (see page 277), featuring Ile de la Cité, Notre-Dame, the Latin Quarter, and Sainte-Chapelle.

Afternoon: Visit the Pompidou Center (at least from the outside), then walk to the Marais neighborhood, visit place des Vosges, and consider touring any of three museums nearby: Carnavalet Museum (city history), Jewish Art and History Museum, or Picasso Museum.

Evening: Cruise the Seine River or take the "Paris Illumination" nighttime bus tour.

Day 2

Morning: Visit Arc de Triomphe, then saunter down the Champs-Elysées.

Afternoon: Have lunch in the Tuileries (several lunch cafés in the park), then tour the Louvre.

Evening: Enjoy the Trocadéro scene and a twilight ride up the Eiffel Tower.

Day 3

Morning: Tour the Orsay Museum.

Afternoon: Either tour the nearby Rodin Museum and Napoleon's Tomb or visit Versailles (take RER-C train direct from Orsay).

Evening: Visit Montmartre and the Sacré-Cœur basilica.

ORIENTATION

Paris (city center pop. 2,150,000) is split in half by the Seine River, divided into 20 *arrondissements* (proud and independent governmental jurisdictions), circled by a ring-road freeway (the *périphérique*), and speckled with Métro stations. You'll find Paris easier to navigate if you know which side of the river you're on, which *arrondissement* you're in, and which subway (Métro) stop you're closest to. If you're north of the river (the top half of any city map), you're on the Right Bank *(rive droite)*. If you're south of it, you're on the Left Bank *(rive gauche)*. The bull's-eye of your Paris map is Notre-Dame, which sits on an island in the middle of the Seine. Most of your sightseeing will take place within five blocks of the river.

Arrondissements are numbered, starting at the Louvre and moving in a clockwise spiral out to the ring road. The last two digits in a Parisian zip code are the *arrondissement* number. The abbreviation for the Métro stop is "Mo." In Parisian jargon, Napoleon's tomb is on *la rive gauche* (the Left Bank) in the *7ème* (7th *arrondissement*), zip code 75007, Mo: Invalides. Paris Métro stops are used as a standard aid in giving directions, even for those not using the Métro. As you're tracking down addresses, these words and pronunciations will help: *place* (plahs; square), *rue* (roo; road), *avenue* (ah-vuh-noo), *boulevard* (boo-luh-var), *pont* (pohn; bridge), and Métro (may-troh).

Tourist Information

Avoid the Paris TIs because of their long lines, short information, and charge for maps. This chapter, the *Pariscope* magazine

Paris Overview

Paris train stations & destinations

1. Gare St. Lazare: To Normandy (also Vernon/Giverny)
2. Gare Nord: To London, Brussels, Amsterdam & N. France (also Chantilly & Auvers-sur-Oise)
3. Gare L'Est: To E. France, S. Germany, Switzerland & Austria
4. Gare du Lyon: To Italy & SE France (also Fontainebleau & Melun/Vaux-le-Vicomte)
5. Gare d'Austerlitz: To SW France, Loire Valley & Spain
6. Gare Montparnasse: To SW France, Loire Valley, Normandy & Brittany (also Chartres)

(described below), and one of the freebie maps available at any hotel (or in the front of this book) are all you need. Paris' TIs share a single phone number: 08 92 68 30 00 (from the United States, dial 011 33 8 92 68 30 00).

If you must visit a TI, there are several locations: **Grands Magasins** (Mon–Sat 9:00–18:30, closed Sun, near Opéra Garnier at 11 rue Scribe), **Gare de Lyon** (Mon–Sat 8:00–20:00, closed Sun), **Montmartre** (daily 10:00–19:00, place du Tertre), at the **Eiffel Tower** (May–Sept daily 11:00–18:42, closed Oct–April), and at the **Louvre** (Wed–Mon 10:00–19:00, closed Tue). Both **airports** have handy information offices (called ADP) with long hours and short lines (see "Transportation Connections," page 356).

For a complete schedule of museum hours and English-language museum tours, pick up the free *Musées, Monuments Historiques, et Expositions* booklet from any museum.

Web Sites: Paris' TIs have an official Web site (www.parisinfo.com) offering practical information on hotels, special events, museums, children's activities, fashion, nightlife, and more. Two other Web sites that are entertaining and at times useful are www.bonjourparis.com (which claims to offer a virtual trip to Paris, featuring interactive French lessons, tips on wine and food, and news on the latest Parisian trends) and the similar www.paris-anglo.com (with informative stories on visiting Paris, plus a directory of over 2,500 English-speaking businesses).

Pariscope: The *Pariscope* weekly magazine (or one of its clones, €0.40 at any newsstand) lists museum hours, art exhibits, concerts, festivals, plays, movies, and nightclubs. Smart tour guides and sightseers rely on this for the latest listings.

Maps: While Paris is littered with free maps, they don't show all the streets. You may want the huge Michelin #10 map of Paris. For an extended stay, I prefer the pocket-size, street-indexed *Paris Pratique* or Michelin's *Paris par Arrondissement* (both about €6, sold at newsstands and bookstores in Paris). Before you buy a map, look at it to make sure it has the level of detail you want.

Bookstores: There are many English-language bookstores in Paris where you can pick up guidebooks (for nearly double their American prices). Most carry this book. My favorite is the friendly Red Wheelbarrow Bookstore in the Marais neighborhood, run by charming Penelope and Abigail (main store at 22 rue St. Paul, Mon–Sat 10:00–19:00, Sun 14:00–19:00; children's bookstore nearby at 13 rue Charles V, Wed–Sun 10:00–19:00, closed Mon–Tue; Mo: St. Paul for both, tel. 01 42 77 42 17). Others include Shakespeare and Company (daily 12:00–24:00, some used travel books, 37 rue de la Bûcherie, across the river from Notre-Dame, Mo: St. Michel, tel. 01 43 26 96 50), W.H. Smith (Mon–Sat 10:00–19:00, 248 rue de

Daily Reminder

Monday: These sights are closed today—Orsay, Rodin, Marmottan, Montmartre Museum, Carnavalet, Catacombs, and Versailles; the Louvre and Eiffel Tower are more crowded because of this. Napoleon's Tomb is closed the first Monday of each month (except July–Sept). Some small stores don't open until 14:00. Street markets such as rue Cler and rue Mouffetard are dead today. Some banks are closed. It's discount night at most cinemas.

Tuesday: Many museums are closed today, including the Louvre, Picasso, Cluny, and Pompidou Center. The Eiffel Tower, Orsay, and Versailles are particularly busy today.

Wednesday: All sights are open (Louvre until 21:45). The weekly *Pariscope* magazine comes out today. Most schools are closed, so many kids' sights are busy. Some cinemas offer discounts.

Thursday: All sights are open except the Sewer Tour. The Orsay is open until 21:45. Department stores are open late.

Friday: All sights are open except the Sewer Tour (Louvre until 21:45). Afternoon trains and roads leaving Paris are crowded; TGV train reservation fees are higher.

Saturday: All sights are open (except the Jewish Art and History Museum). The fountains run at Versailles (July–Sept); otherwise, avoid weekend crowds at area châteaux and Impressionist sights. Department stores are jammed. The Jewish Quarter is quiet.

Sunday: Some museums are free the first Sunday of the month—and therefore more crowded (e.g., Louvre, Rodin, Pompidou, Cluny, and Picasso). Several museums offer reduced prices every Sunday (Orsay plus Cluny and Rodin—other than first Sun, when they're free). Napoleon's Tomb is open until 19:00 in summer, and the fountains run at Versailles (early April–early Oct). Most of Paris' stores are closed on Sunday, but shoppers will find relief in the Marais neighborhood's lively Jewish Quarter and in Bercy Village, where many stores are open. Look for organ concerts at St. Sulpice and possibly other churches. The American Church often hosts a free evening concert at 18:00 (Sept–May only). Many recommended restaurants in the rue Cler neighborhood are closed for dinner.

Rivoli, Mo: Concorde, tel. 01 44 77 88 99), and Brentanos (closed Sun, 37 avenue de l'Opéra, Mo: Opéra, tel. 01 42 61 52 50).

American Church: The American Church is a nerve center for the American émigré community. It distributes a free, handy, and insightful monthly English-language newspaper called the *Paris Voice*, which has useful reviews of concerts, plays, and current events; find it at about 200 locations in Paris (www.parisvoice.com). Also available is an advertisement paper called *France–U.S.A. Contacts* (www.fusac.fr), full of useful information for those seeking work or long-term housing. The church faces the river between the Eiffel Tower and Orsay Museum (reception open Mon–Sat 9:30–22:30, Sun 9:00–19:30, 65 quai d'Orsay, Mo: Invalides, tel. 01 40 62 05 00).

Arrival in Paris

By Train: Paris has six train stations, all connected by Métro, bus, and taxi (see page 357). All have ATMs, banks or change offices, information desks, telephones, cafés, newsstands, and clever pickpockets. Most have lockers *(consigne automatique),* listed per station; see page 357. Hop the Métro to your hotel (see "Getting Around Paris," below).

By Plane: For detailed information on getting from Paris' airports to downtown Paris (and vice versa), see "Transportation Connections" on page 356.

Helpful Hints

Heightened Security *(Plan Vigipirate)*: You may notice an abundance of police at monuments, on streets, and on the Métro, as well as security checks to enter many public buildings. This is part of Paris' anti-terror plan. The police are helpful, the security lines move quickly, and there are fewer pickpocket problems on the Métro.

Theft Alert: Métro and RER lines that serve high-profile tourist sights are popular with thieves. Wear a money belt, put your wallet in your front pocket, loop your day bag over your shoulders (consider wearing it in front), and keep a tight grip on your purse or shopping bag. Muggings are rare but do occur. If you're out late, avoid the dark riverfront embankments and any place where the lighting is dim and pedestrian activity is minimal.

Paris Museum Pass: This worthwhile pass, covering most sights in Paris, is available at major Métro stations, TIs, and museums. For information, see page 266.

Museum Strategy: When possible, visit key museums first thing (when your energy is best) and save other activities for the afternoon. Arriving 20 minutes before major museums open is

The Paris Museum Pass

In Paris, there are two classes of sightseers—those with a Paris Museum Pass, and those who stand in line. Serious sightseers save time and money by getting this pass.

Most of the sights listed in this chapter are covered by the pass (see list below), except for the Eiffel Tower, Montparnasse Tower, Marmottan Museum, Opéra Garnier, Notre-Dame treasury, Jacquemart-André Museum, Jewish Art and History Museum, Grande Arche de La Défense, Jeu de Paume and Grand Palais exhibition halls, Catacombs, *Paris Story* film, Montmartre Museum, Dalí Museum, and the ladies of Pigalle.

The pass pays for itself with four major admissions and gets you into most sights with no lining up to buy tickets (2 consecutive days-€30, 4 consecutive days-€45, 6 consecutive days-€60, no youth or senior discount). It's sold at museums, main Métro stations (including Ecole Militaire and Bastille), and TIs (even at airports). Try to avoid buying the pass at a major museum (such as the Louvre), where supply can be spotty and lines long.

The pass isn't activated until the first time you use it (you write the starting date on the pass). Think and read ahead to make the most of your pass, since some museums are free (e.g., Carnavalet and Victor Hugo's House), many sights are discounted on Sundays, and your pass must be used on consecutive days. The free directory that comes with your pass lists the current hours of sights, phone numbers, and the price kids pay (where applicable—see below).

The pass isn't worth buying for children and teens, as most museums are free for those under 18 (teenagers may need to show proof of age). Of the museums that charge for children, some allow kids in free if their parent has a Museum Pass, while others charge admission, depending on age (the cutoff age varies from 5 to 18). If a sight is free for kids, they can skip the line with their passholder parents.

Included sights you're likely to visit (and admission prices without the pass): Louvre (€8.50), Orsay Museum (€7), Sainte-

line-time well spent. Remember, most museums require you to check daypacks and coats, and important museums have metal detectors that will slow your entry. If you're still ahead of the pack when you get inside, consider hustling to the most popular works first. The Louvre, Orsay, and Pompidou are open on selected nights (see "Paris at a Glance," page 274), making for peaceful visits with fewer crowds.

Useful Telephone Numbers: American Hospital—01 46 41 25 25; English-speaking pharmacy—01 45 62 02 41 (Pharmacie les Champs, 24 hrs, 84 avenue des Champs-Elysées, Mo: Georges

Chapelle (€6.10), Arc de Triomphe (€7), Les Invalides/Napoleon's Tomb (€7), Conciergerie (€6.10), Panthéon (€7), Sewer Tour (€4), Cluny Museum (€5.50), Pompidou Center (€7), Notre-Dame towers (€6.10), Archaeological Crypt (€3.50), Picasso Museum (€5.50), Rodin Museum (€5), L'Orangerie Museum (when it re-opens, about €6), Maritime Museum (€7). Outside Paris, the pass covers the Palace of Versailles (€7.50, plus its Trianon châteaux-€5).

Tally up what you want to see—and remember, an advantage of the pass is that you skip to the front of some lines, which saves hours of waiting, especially in summer. (Nevertheless, everyone must pass through the slow-moving, metal-detector lines at some sights, and a few places, such as Notre-Dame's tower, can't accommodate a bypass lane.) With the pass, you'll pop freely into sights that you're walking by (even for a few minutes) that otherwise might not be worth the expense (e.g., Archaeological Crypt, Conciergerie, and the Panthéon).

Museum Tips: The Louvre and many other museums are closed on Tuesday. The Orsay, Rodin, Marmottan, Carnavalet, Catacombs, Victor Hugo's House, and Versailles are closed Monday. Some museums offer reduced prices on Sunday. Most sights stop admitting people 30–60 minutes before closing time, and many begin shutting down rooms 45 minutes before.

For the fewest crowds, visit very early, at lunch, or very late. Most museums have slightly shorter hours October through March. French holidays can really mess up your sightseeing plans on Jan 1, May 1, July 14, Nov 1, Nov 11, and Dec 25.

The best Impressionist art museums are the Orsay (page 291), Marmottan (page 296), and L'Orangerie (due to reopen in 2007).

Many museums also host optional temporary exhibitions, which are not covered by the Paris Museum Pass (generally €3–5 extra). You can find good information on many of Paris' sights on the French TI's official Web site: www.parisinfo.com/museum_monuments.

V); Police—17; U.S. Embassy—01 43 12 22 22; Paris and France directory assistance—12.

Street Safety: Parisian drivers are notorious for ignoring pedestrians. Look both ways (many streets are one-way) and be careful of seemingly quiet bus/taxi lanes. Don't assume you have the right of way, even in a crosswalk. When crossing a street, keep your pace constant and don't stop suddenly. By law, drivers must miss pedestrians by one meter—a little more than a yard (1.5 meters in the countryside). Drivers carefully calculate your speed and won't hit you, provided you don't alter your route or pace.

Watch out for a lesser hazard: *merde.* Parisian dogs decorate the city's sidewalks with 16 tons of droppings per day. People get injured by slipping in it.

Toilets: Carry small change for pay toilets, or walk into any sidewalk café like you own the place and find the toilet in the back. The restrooms in museums are free and the best you'll find, and if you have a Museum Pass, you can drop into almost any museum for the toilets. Modern, sanitary, street-booth toilets provide both relief and a memory (coins required, don't leave small children inside unattended). Keep toilet paper or tissues with you, as some toilets are poorly supplied.

Parking: Drivers pay to park curbside (except Sunday year-round, or any day in Aug). There are good parking garages under Ecole Militaire, St. Sulpice Church, Les Invalides, the Bastille, and the Panthéon for about €20–25 per day. Some hotels offer parking for less—ask.

Getting Around Paris

By Métro: In Paris, you're never more than a 10-minute walk from a Métro station. Europe's best subway allows you to hop from sight to sight quickly and cheaply (runs daily 5:30–24:30). Learn to use it.

Pickpockets and Panhandlers: Thieves spend their days in the Métro. Be on guard. For example, if your pocket is picked as you pass through a turnstile, you end up stuck on the wrong side while the thief strolls away. Stand away from Métro doors to avoid being a target for a theft-and-run just before the doors close. Any jostling or commotion, especially when boarding or leaving trains, is likely the sign of a thief or a team of thieves in action. Make any fare inspector show proof of identity (ask locals for help if you're not certain).

Paris has a huge homeless population and higher than 11 percent unemployment; expect a warm Métro welcome from panhandlers, musicians, and those selling magazines produced by the homeless community.

Tickets and Passes: One ticket (€1.40) takes you virtually anywhere in the system. Tickets are also good on the RER suburban trains (see below) and on city buses, although one ticket cannot be used to transfer between subway and bus or between different bus routes. Save 30 percent by buying a ***carnet*** (car-nay) of 10 tickets for €10.50 (a single ticket is €1.40, kids 4–10 pay €5 for a *carnet*). Buy tickets at any Métro station from a human or a machine (some machines also accept credit cards).

If you're staying in Paris for a week or more, consider the **Carte Orange** (kart oh-rahnzh) for about €15, which gives you free run of the bus and Métro system for one week, starting Monday and ending Sunday; ask for the Carte Orange *hebdomadaire* and supply a passport-size photo. The month-long version costs about

€50; request a Carte Orange *mensuel* (good from the first day of the month to the last). These passes cover only central Paris. You can pay more for passes covering regional destinations (like Versailles), but for most visitors, this is a bad value (buy individual tickets for longer-distance destinations). All passes can be purchased at any Métro station, most of which have photo booths where you can get the photo required for the pass. Despite what some Métro agents say, Carte Orange passes are definitely not limited to residents; if you're refused, simply go to another station to buy your pass.

The overpriced **Paris Visite** passes were designed for tourists and offer minor reductions at minor sights (1 day-€9, 2 days-€14, 3 days-€19, 5 days-€28), but you'll get a better value with a cheaper *carnet* of 10 tickets or a Carte Orange.

How the Métro Works: To get to your destination, determine the closest "Mo" stop and which line or lines will get you there. The lines have numbers, but they're best known by their end-of-the-line stops. (For example, the La Défense/Château de Vincennes line, also known as line 1, runs between La Défense in the west and Vincennes in the east.) Once in the Métro station, you'll see blue-and-white signs directing you to the train going in your direction (e.g., "*direction:* La Défense"). Insert your ticket in the automatic turnstile, pass through, reclaim your ticket, and *keep it until you exit the system*. Fare inspectors regularly check for cheaters and accept absolutely no excuses.

Transfers are free and can be made wherever lines cross. When you transfer, look for the *correspondance* (connections) signs when you exit your first train, then follow the proper direction sign.

While the Métro whisks you quickly from one point to another, be prepared to walk significant distances within stations to reach your platform (most noticeable when you transfer). Escalators are usually available for vertical movement, but they're not always in working order. To limit excessive walking, avoid transferring at these sprawling stations: Montparnasse-Bienvenüe, Chatelet-Les Halles, Charles de Gaulle-Etoile, Gare du Nord, and Bastille.

Before taking the *sortie* (exit) to leave the Métro, check the helpful *plan du quartier* (map of the neighborhood) to get your bearings, locate your destination, and decide which *sortie* you want. At stops with several *sorties,* you can save lots of walking by choosing the best exit.

After you exit the system, toss or tear your used ticket so you don't confuse it with your unused ticket—they look virtually identical.

By RER: The RER (Réseau Express Régionale; air-ay-air) is the suburban arm of the Métro, serving destinations further out of the center (Versailles and the airports). These routes are indicated by thick lines on your subway map and identified by letters A, B, C, etc.

Paris

TO LA DEFENSE
ARC DE TRIOMPHE
AVE KLEBER
CHAMPS ELYSEES
JACQUEMART ANDRÉ MUSEUM
BLVD.
HAUSSMANN
9
TO MONTMARTRE & SACRE COEUR
8
MADELEINE
OPERA GARNIER
PLACE CONCORDE
PLACE VENDOME
PALAIS ROYAL
2
GRAND PALAIS
PETIT PALAIS
BATEAUX MOUCHES
TROCADERO
TUILERIES GARDEN
1
RUE DE RIVOLI
SEINE R.
EIFFEL TOWER
SEWER TOUR
R. SAINT DOMINIQUE
BLVD.
ORSAY
LOUVRE
FORUM LES HALLES
PLACE CHATELET
POMPIDOU
JEWISH MUSEUM
PICASSO MUSEUM
MARAIS
CARNAVALET MUSEUM
3
PERE LACHAISE CEM.
PLACE REPUBLIQUE
BLVD ST MARTIN
BLVD MAGENTA
SEBASTOPOL BLVD
GARE DE L'EST
10
CANAL ST. MARTIN
7
RUE CLER
INVALIDES
RODIN MUSEUM
PARC DU CHAMP DE MARS
ECOLE MILITAIRE
TO VERSAILLES
BLVD. SAINT GERMAIN
STE. CHAPELLE
ILE CITE
HOTEL DE VILLE
R. ST. ANTOINE
4
PLACE DES VOSGES
OPERA
PLACE BASTILLE
NOTRE-DAME
LATIN QUARTER
CLUNY MUS.
SORBONNE
PANTHEON
ILE ST LOUIS
5
RUE MOUFFETARD
ST. SULPICE
6
LUX. GDN.
BLVD. RASPAIL
BLVD. ST. MICHEL
1/2 MILE
.5 KM
BOLD NUMBERS INDICATE ARRONDISSEMENTS (DISTRICTS)
DCH

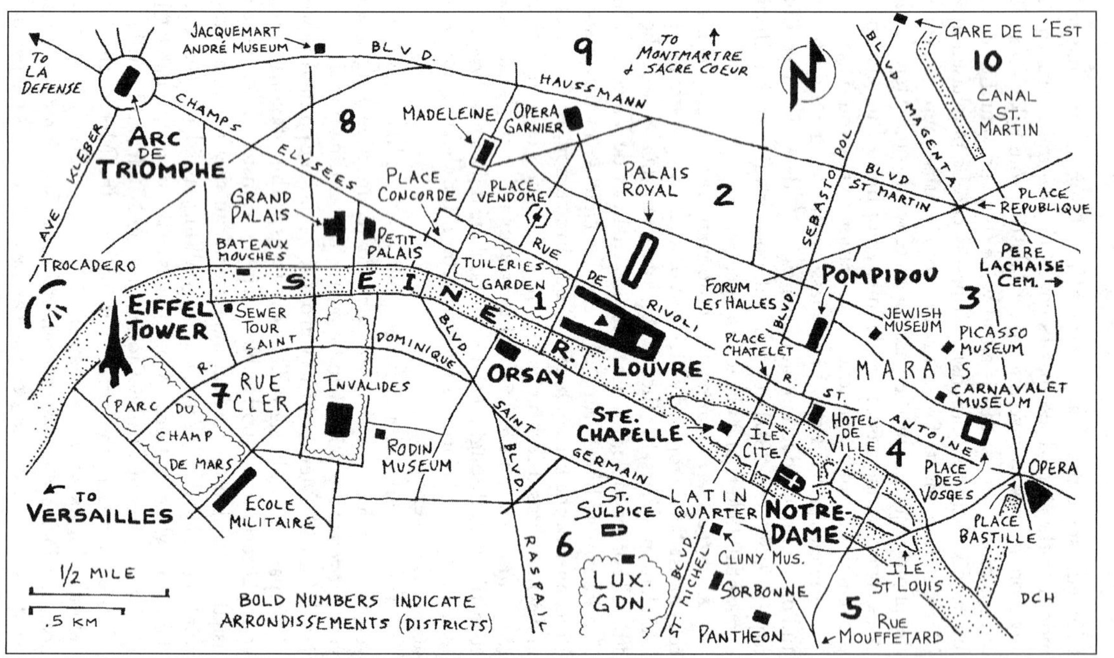

Key Words for the Métro and RER

- *direction* (dee-rek-see-ohn): direction
- *ligne* (leen-yuh): line
- *correspondance* (kor-res-pohn-dahns): transfer
- *sortie* (sor-tee): exit
- *carnet* (kar-nay): cheap set of 10 tickets
- *Pardon, madame/monsieur* (par-dohn, mah-dahm/mes-yur): Excuse me, lady/bud.
- *Je descend* (juh day-sahn): I'm getting off.
- *Donnez-moi mon porte-monnaie!* (duh-nay-mwah mohn port-moh-nay): Give me back my wallet!

Etiquette

- When waiting at the platform, get out of the way of those exiting their train. Board only once everyone is off.
- Avoid using the hinged seats near the doors when the car is jammed; they take up valuable standing space.
- In a crowded train, try not to block the exit. If you're blocking the door when the train stops, step out of the car and to the side, let others off, then get back on.
- Talk softly in the cars. Listen to how quietly Parisians can communicate and follow their lead.
- On escalators, stand on the right, pass on the left.

Some suburban routes are operated by France's railroad (SNCF), and are called **Transilien**; they function the same way and use the same tickets as the RER. On Transilien trains (but not RER trains), railpasses are accepted (show your pass at a ticket window to get a free ticket to get through the turnstiles).

Within the city center, the RER works like the Métro but can be speedier (if it serves your destination directly) because it makes fewer stops. Métro tickets are good on the RER when traveling in the city center. (You can transfer between the Métro and RER systems with the same ticket.) But to travel outside the city (to Versailles or the airport, for example), you'll need to buy a separate, more expensive ticket at the station window before boarding. Unlike in the Métro, you need to insert your ticket in a turnstile to exit the RER lines. Also unlike the Métro, not every train stops at every station along the way; check the sign over the platform to see if your destination is listed as a stop (*toutes les gares* means it makes all stops along the way), or confirm with a local before you board.

By City Bus: The trickier bus system is worth figuring out. Métro tickets are good on buses and the Métro, though you can't use the same ticket to transfer between the two systems. One ticket gets you anywhere in central Paris, but if you transfer buses or leave the city center (shown as zone 1 on the diagram onboard the bus), you must validate a second ticket. While the Métro shuts down about 24:30, some buses continue much later.

Enter buses through the front door. Punch your Métro ticket in the machine behind the driver, or pay the higher cash fare. Get off buses using the rear door. Even if you're not certain you've figured it out, do some joyriding (outside of rush hour: Mon–Fri 8:00–9:30 & 17:30–19:30). Lines #24, #63, #87, and #69 are a few of Paris' most scenic routes, and make a great introduction to the city. Buses #69 and #87 are particularly handy. The #69 runs east–west between the Eiffel Tower and Père Lachaise Cemetery by way of rue Cler (recommended hotels), quai d'Orsay, the Louvre, and the Marais (more recommended hotels). Bus #87 also links the Marais and rue Cler areas, as well as the Luxembourg Garden neighborhood (with more recommended hotels). The #87 stays mostly on the Left Bank, connecting the Eiffel Tower, St. Sulpice, Luxembourg Garden, St. Germain-des-Prés, the Latin Quarter, and the Bastille.

Schedules are posted at bus stops. Handy bus-system maps *(plan des autobus)* are available in any Métro station (and in the €6 *Paris Pratique* map book—see "Tourist Information," above). Big system maps, posted at each bus and Métro stop, display the routes. Individual route diagrams show the exact routes of the lines serving that stop. Major stops are displayed on the side of each bus. The handiest bus routes are listed for each recommended hotel neighborhood (see "Sleeping," page 319).

By Taxi: Parisian taxis are reasonable—especially for couples and families. The meters are tamper-proof. Fares and supplements (described in English on the back windows) are straightforward. There's a €5.20 minimum. A 10-minute ride (e.g., Bastille to Eiffel Tower) costs about €10 (versus about €1 to get anywhere in town using a *carnet* ticket on the Métro). You can try waving down a taxi, but it's easier to ask for the nearest taxi stand (*"Où est une station de taxi?"*; oo ay oon stah-see-ohn duh taxi). Taxi stands are indicated by a circled T on many city maps, including Michelin's #10 Paris. A typical taxi takes three people (maybe 4, if you're polite and pay about €3 extra); groups of up to five can use a *grand taxi,* which must be booked in advance—ask your hotel to call. If a taxi is summoned by phone, the meter starts as soon as the call is received, adding €3–4 to the bill. Higher rates are charged at night from 19:00 to 7:00, all day Sunday, and to either airport. There's a €1 charge for each piece of baggage and for train station pick-ups. To tip, round up to the next euro (minimum €0.50). Taxis are tough to find on Friday and Saturday nights, especially after the Métro closes (around 24:30). If you need to catch a train or flight early in the morning, book a taxi the day before.

TOURS

Bus Tours—Paris Vision offers bus tours of Paris, day and night (advertised in hotel lobbies); their "Paris Illumination" night tour is much more interesting (see "Nightlife," page 317).

Far better daytime bus tours are the hop-on, hop-off double-decker buses that connect Paris' main sights while providing running commentary. You can hop off at any stop, tour a sight, then catch a later bus. These are ideal in good weather, when you can sit on top. (See also "Batobus" under "Boat Tours," below.)

Two companies provide hop-on, hop-off bus service: **L'Open Tours** and **Les Cars Rouges;** pick up their brochures showing routes and stops from any TI or on their buses. You can start either tour at nearly any of the major sights, such as the Eiffel Tower (both companies stop on avenue Joseph Bouvard).

L'Open Tours uses yellow buses and provides more extensive coverage on four different routes, rolling by most of the important sights in Paris. Their Paris Grand Tour offers the best introduction. Tickets are good for any route. Buy your tickets from the driver (1-day ticket-€25, 2-day ticket-€28, kids 4–11 pay €13 for 1 or 2 days, allow 2 hours per tour). Two or three buses depart hourly from about 10:00 to 18:00; expect to wait 10–20 minutes at each stop (stops can be tricky to find—look for yellow signs). You'll see these bright-yellow, topless, double-decker buses all over town (tel. 01 42 66 56 56, www.paris-opentour.com).

Les Cars Rouges' bright red buses offer largely the same service with fewer stops on a single Grand Tour Route, for a bit less money (2-day ticket: adult-€23, kids 4–12 pay €12; tel. 01 53 95 39 53, www.carsrouges.com).

Boat Tours—Several companies offer one-hour boat cruises on the Seine (by far best at night). The huge, mass-production **Bateaux-Mouches** or **Bateaux Parisien** boats are convenient to rue Cler hotels (depart every 20–30 min from the pont de l'Alma's right bank, or from just in front of the Eiffel Tower, respectively; €7, kids 4–12 pay €4, daily 10:00–22:30, useless recorded explanations in 6 languages and tour groups by the dozens, tel. 01 40 76 99 99). The smaller and more intimate **Vedettes du Pont-Neuf** depart only once an hour from the center of Pont-Neuf (2/hr after dark), but they come with a live guide giving explanations in French and English and are convenient to Marais and Luxembourg area hotels (€10, kids 4–12 pay €5, tel. 01 46 33 98 38).

From April through October, the **Batobus** hop-on, hop-off boats on the Seine connect eight popular stops every 15–25 minutes: Eiffel Tower, Champs-Elysées, Orsay/place de la Concorde, Louvre, Notre-Dame, St. Germain-des-Prés, Hôtel de Ville, and Jardin des Plantes. Pick up a schedule at any stop (or TI) and use the

Paris at a Glance

▲▲▲Louvre Europe's oldest and greatest museum, starring Mona Lisa and Venus di Milo. **Hours:** Wed–Mon 9:00–18:00, closed Tue. Most wings open Wed and Fri until 21:45.

▲▲▲Orsay Museum 19th-century art, including Europe's greatest Impressionist collection. **Hours:** June 20–Sept 20 Tue–Sun 9:00–18:00; Sept 21–June 19 Tue–Sat 10:00–18:00, Sun 9:00–18:00; Thu until 21:45 year-round, closed Mon.

▲▲▲Eiffel Tower Paris' soaring exclamation point. **Hours:** Daily March–Sept 9:00–24:00, Oct–Feb 9:30–23:00.

▲▲▲Arc de Triomphe Triumphal arch with viewpoint, marking start of Champs-Elysées. **Hours:** Outside always open; inside open daily April–Sept 10:00–23:00, Oct–March 10:00–22:30.

▲▲▲Sainte-Chapelle Gothic cathedral with peerless stained glass. **Hours:** Daily March–Oct 9:30–18:00, Nov–Feb 9:00–17:00.

▲▲▲Versailles The ultimate royal palace, with Hall of Mirrors, vast gardens, a grand canal, and smaller palaces. **Hours:** May–Sept Tue–Sun 9:00–18:30, Oct–April Tue–Sun 9:00–17:30, closed Mon. Gardens open early (7:00) and smaller palaces open late (12:00).

▲▲Notre-Dame Cathedral Paris' most beloved church, with towers and gargoyles. **Hours:** Church daily 8:00–18:45; tower daily April–Sept 9:30–19:30, Oct–March 10:00–17:30; treasury daily 9:30–17:30.

▲▲Sacré-Cœur White basilica atop Montmartre with spectacular views. **Hours:** Daily 7:00–23:00.

▲▲Napoleon's Tomb The emperor's imposing tomb, flanked by army museums. **Hours:** April–Sept daily 10:00–18:00, summer Sun until 19:00, Oct–March daily 10:00–17:00, closed first Mon of month except July–Sept.

▲▲Rodin Museum Works by the greatest sculptor since Michelangelo. **Hours:** April–Sept Tue–Sun 9:30–17:45; Oct–March Tue–Sun 9:30–16:45, closed Mon.

▲▲Marmottan Museum Untouristy art museum focusing on Monet. **Hours:** Tue–Sun 10:00–18:00, closed Mon.

▲▲**Pompidou Center** Modern art in colorful building with city views. **Hours:** Wed–Mon 11:00–21:00, closed Tue.

▲▲**Jacquemart-André Museum** Art-strewn mansion. **Hours:** Daily 10:00–18:00.

▲▲**Cluny Museum** Medieval art with unicorn tapestries. **Hours:** Wed–Mon 9:15–17:45, closed Tue.

▲▲**Carnavalet Museum** Paris' history wrapped up in a 16th-century mansion. **Hours:** Tue–Sun 10:00–18:00, closed Mon.

▲▲**Jewish Art and History Museum** Displays history of Judaism in Europe. **Hours:** Mon–Fri 11:00–18:00, Sun 10:00–18:00, closed Sat.

▲▲**Deportation Memorial** Monument to Holocaust victims, near Notre-Dame. **Hours:** Daily April–Sept 10:00–12:00 & 14:00–19:00, Oct–March 10:00–12:00 & 14:00–17:00.

▲▲**Champs-Elysées** Paris' grand boulevard. **Hours:** Always open.

▲▲**Picasso Museum** World's largest collection of Picasso's works. **Hours:** April–Sept Wed–Mon 9:30–18:00; Oct–March Wed–Mon 9:30–17:30, closed Tue.

▲**Opéra Garnier** 19th-century opera house open for tours. **Hours:** Daily 10:00–17:00 except during performances.

▲**La Défense and La Grande Arche** Paris' modern arch on outskirts of city. **Hours:** Elevator daily 10:00–19:00.

▲**Catacombs** Underground tunnels lined with bones. **Hours:** Tue–Sun 10:00–17:00, closed Mon.

▲**Paris Sewer Tour** The lowdown on Paris plumbing. **Hours:** May–Sept Sat–Wed 11:00–17:00, Oct–April Sat–Wed 11:00–16:00, closed Thu–Fri.

boats as a scenic alternative to the Métro (€11 for unlimited use for 1 day, €13 for 2 days, under 12 about 50 percent less, www.batobus.com). Boats run from 10:00 to 19:00 (and until 21:00 June–Sept).

Canauxrama runs a 2.5-hour cruise on a peaceful canal without the Seine in sight, starting from place de la Bastille and ending at Bassin de la Villette (near Mo: Stalingrad). The first segment of your trip is through a tunnel, as the canal runs under boulevard Richard Lenoir for about 20 blocks (€14, kids-€9, seniors and students-€11, departs at 9:45 and 14:30 across from Opéra Bastille, just below boulevard de la Bastille, opposite #50, where the canal meets place de la Bastille, tel. 01 42 39 15 00).

Walking Tours—The company **Paris Walks** offers a variety of excellent two-hour walks, led by British or American guides, nearly daily for €10 (Peter and Oriel Caine, tel. 01 48 09 21 40 for recorded schedule in English, fax 01 42 43 75 51, see www.paris-walks.com for their complete schedule and private tour options, paris@paris-walks.com). Tours focus on the Marais, Montmartre, Ile de la Cité and Ile St. Louis, and Hemingway's Paris. Ask about their family-friendly tours. Call a day or two ahead to learn their schedule and starting point. No reservations are required. These are thoughtfully prepared, relaxing, and humorous. Don't hesitate to stand close to the guide to hear.

Private Guides—For many, Paris merits hiring a Parisian as your personal guide. **Arnaud Servignat**, who runs Global Travel Partners, is an excellent licensed local guide (€215/half-day, €335/day; also does car tours of the countryside around Paris for €300/half-day, €505/day; tel. 06 68 80 29 05, fax 01 42 57 00 38, arnaud.servignat@noos.fr). Elizabeth Van Hest is another likeable and capable guide (€170/half-day, €250/day, tel. 01 43 41 47 31, e.van.hest@noos.fr). Paris Walks can also set you up with one of their guides; some are trained to work with families and children (see "Walking Tours," above).

Bike Tours—Fat Tire Bike Tours attract a younger crowd for fun and frolicking three- to four-hour guided rides through Paris. These are well done and surprisingly informative, whether by day (€24, March–Nov daily at 11:00, also at 15:00 June–July) or by night (€28, April–Oct daily at 19:00, cash only, in English, no bikes or reservations needed, meet at south pillar of Eiffel Tower, tel. 01 56 58 10 54, www.fattirebiketours.com). They also offer bike tours of Giverny (€65) and of Versailles (€50, mid-April–mid-Oct, depart at 9:30, mid-May–July Tue–Sun, otherwise Sun, Tue, and Thu, meet at office near Eiffel Tower, 24 rue Edgar Faure, Mo: Dupleix). Fat Tire's pricey new **Segway Tours** are making a splash with an older clientele (€70, April–Oct daily at 10:30 and 18:00, www.parissegwaytours.com).

Excursion Tours—Many companies offer minivan and big bus tours to regional sights, including all of the day trips described in this book. **Paris Walks** (mentioned above) is the best, with educational though infrequent tours of the Impressionist artist retreats of Giverny and Auvers-sur-Oise (€47–56, includes admissions, tel. 01 48 09 21 40 for recording in English, www.paris-walks.com).

Paris Vision and **Touringscope** both offer mass-produced, full-size bus and minivan tours to several popular regional destinations, including the Loire Valley, Champagne region, D-Day beaches, and Mont St. Michel. Minivan tours are more expensive but more personal, given in English, and offer convenient pick-up at your hotel (€130–200/person). Their full-size bus tours are multilingual and cost about half the price of a minivan tour—worth it for some simply for the ease of transportation to the sights (about €60, destinations include Versailles, Chartres, and Giverny). Paris Vision's full-size buses depart from 214 rue de Rivoli (Mo: Tuileries, tel. 01 42 60 30 01, fax 01 42 86 95 36, www.parisvision.com); Touringscope's leave from 11 boulevard Haussmann (Mo: Opéra or Chausée d'Antin, tel. 01 53 34 11 94, www.touringscope.com).

Historic Core of Paris Walk

(This information is distilled from the Historic Paris Walk chapter in *Rick Steves' Paris*, by Gene Openshaw, Steve Smith, and Rick Steves.)

Allow four hours for this self-guided tour, including sightseeing. Start where the city did—on the Ile de la Cité. Face Notre-Dame and follow the dotted line on the map on page 278. To get to Notre-Dame, ride the Métro to Cité, Hôtel de Ville, or St. Michel and walk to the big square facing the...

▲▲Notre-Dame Cathedral—This 700-year-old cathedral is packed with history and tourists. Study its sculpture and windows, take in a Mass, eavesdrop on guides, and walk all around the outside (free, daily 8:00–18:45; treasury-€2.50, not covered by Museum Pass, daily 9:30–17:30; ask about free English tours, normally Wed and Thu at 12:00 and Sat at 14:30; Mo: Cité, Hôtel de Ville, or St. Michel). Climb to the top for a great view of the city; you get 400 steps for only €6.10 (daily April–Sept 9:30–19:30, Oct–March 10:00–18:00, last entry 45 min before closing, covered by Museum Pass though you can't bypass line, arrive early to avoid long lines). There are clean toilets in front of the church near Charlemagne's statue.

The **cathedral facade** is worth a close look. The church is dedicated to "Our Lady" (Notre-Dame). Mary is center stage—cradling Jesus, surrounded by the halo of the rose window. Adam is on the left and Eve is on the right.

Historic Core of Paris

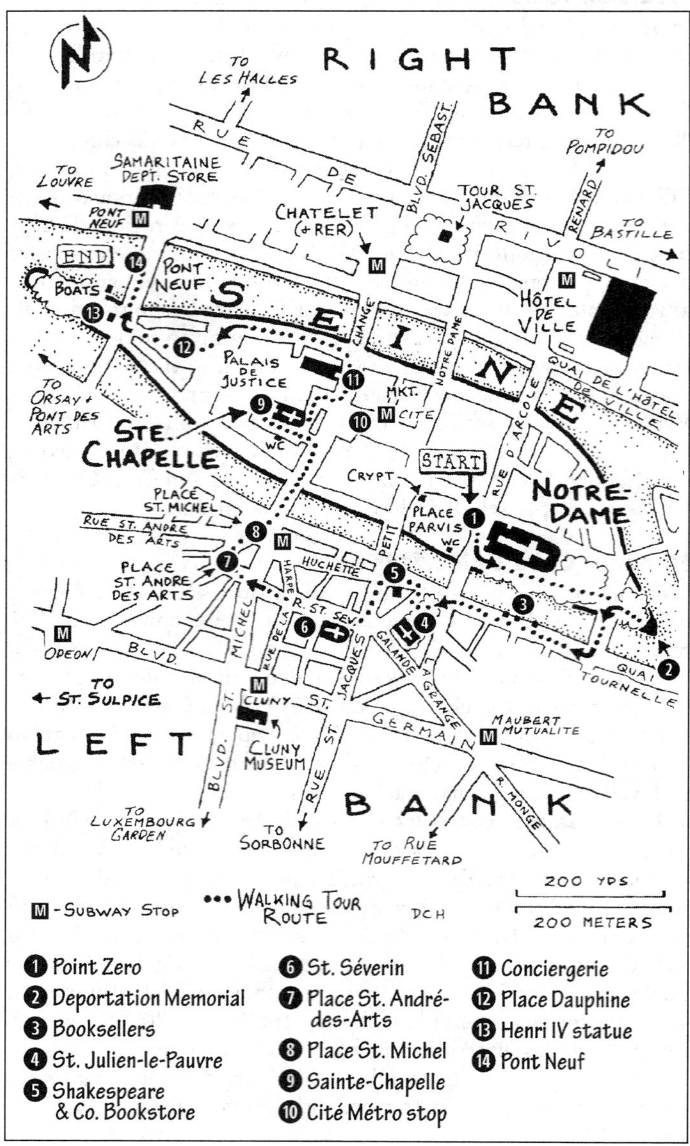

Below Mary and above the arches is a row of 28 statues known as the Kings of Judah. During the French Revolution, these biblical kings were mistaken for the hated French kings. The citizens stormed the church, crying, "Off with their heads!" All were decapitated, but have since been recapitated.

Speaking of decapitation, look at the carving above the doorway on the left. The man with his head in his hands is St. Denis. Back when there was a Roman temple on this spot, Christianity began making converts. The 4th-century bishop of Roman Paris, Denis, was beheaded. But these early Christians were hard to keep down. The man who would become St. Denis got up, tucked his head under his arm, and headed north until he found just the right place to meet his maker: Montmartre. (Although the name "Montmartre" comes from the Roman "Mount of Mars," later generations—thinking of their beheaded patron St. Denis—preferred a less pagan version, "Mount of Martyrs.") The Parisians were convinced of this miracle, Christianity gained ground, and a church soon replaced the pagan temple.

Medieval art was OK if it embellished the house of God and told Bible stories. For a fine example, move to the base of the central column (at the foot of Mary, about where the head of St. Denis could spit if he were really good). Working around from the left, find God telling a barely created Eve, "Have fun, but no apples." Next, the sexiest serpent I've ever seen makes apples à la mode. Finally, Adam and Eve, now ashamed of their nakedness, are expelled by an angel. This is a tiny example in a church covered with meaning.

Now move to the right and study the carving above the **central portal**. It's the end of the world, and Christ sits on the throne of Judgment (just under the arches, holding his hands up). Below him an angel and a demon weigh souls in the balance. The "good" stand to the left, looking up to heaven. The "bad" ones to the right are chained up and led off to a six-hour tour of the Louvre on a hot day. The "ugly" ones must be the crazy, sculpted demons to the right, at the base of the arch.

Wander through the interior. You'll be routed around the ambulatory, much as medieval pilgrims would have been. Don't miss the rose windows filling each of the transepts. Back outside, walk around the church through the park on the riverside for a close look at the flying buttresses.

The neo-Gothic, 300-foot **spire** is a product of the 1860 reconstruction. Around its base are apostles and evangelists (the green men) as well as Eugène-Emmanuel Viollet-le-Duc, the architect in charge of the work. Notice how the apostles look outward, blessing the city, while the architect (at top, seen from behind the church) looks up, admiring his spire.

The **archaeological crypt** is a worthwhile 15-minute stop with your Museum Pass (€3.50, Tue–Sun 10:00–18:00, closed Mon, enter 100 yards in front of cathedral). You'll see Roman ruins, trace the street plan of the medieval village, and see diagrams of how the earliest Paris grew and grew, all thoughtfully explained in English.

If you're hungry near Notre-Dame, the nearby Ile St. Louis has inexpensive *crêperies* and grocery stores open daily on its main drag. Plan a picnic for the quiet, bench-filled park immediately behind the church (public WC available).

Behind Notre-Dame, squeeze through the tourist buses, cross the street, and enter the iron gate into the park at the tip of the island. Look for the stairs and head down to reach the...

▲▲Deportation Memorial (Mémorial de la Déportation)—This memorial to the 200,000 French victims of the Nazi concentration camps draws you into their experience. As you descend the steps, the city around you disappears. Surrounded by walls, you have become a prisoner. Your only freedom is your view of the sky and the tantalizing glimpse of the river below.

Enter the single-file chamber ahead. Inside, the circular plaque in the floor reads, "They went to the end of the earth and did not return." A hallway stretches in front of you, lined with 200,000 lighted crystals, one for each French citizen that died. Flickering at the far end is the eternal flame of hope. The tomb of the unknown deportee lies at your feet. Above, the inscription reads, "Dedicated to the living memory of the 200,000 French deportees sleeping in the night and the fog, exterminated in the Nazi concentration camps."

Above the exit as you leave is the message you'll find at all Nazi sights: "Forgive, but never forget." (Free, daily April–Sept 10:00–12:00 & 14:00–19:00, Oct–March 10:00–12:00 & 14:00–17:00, east tip of the island Ile de la Cité, behind Notre-Dame and near Ile St. Louis, Mo: Cité.)

Ile St. Louis—Look across the river to the Ile St. Louis. If the Ile de la Cité is a tug laden with the history of Paris, it's towing this classy little residential dinghy laden only with boutiques, famous sorbet shops, and restaurants (see "Eating," page 341). This island wasn't developed until much later (18th century). What was a swampy mess is now harmonious Parisian architecture. The pedestrian bridge, pont St. Louis, connects the two islands, leading right to rue St. Louis-en-l'Ile. This spine of the island is lined with interesting shops. A short stroll takes you to the famous Berthillon ice-cream parlor (#31). Loop back to the pedestrian bridge along the parklike quays (walk north to the river and turn left). This walk is about as peaceful and romantic as Paris gets.

Before walking to the opposite end of the Ile de la Cité, loop through the Latin Quarter (as indicated on the map on page 297).

Ile St. Louis

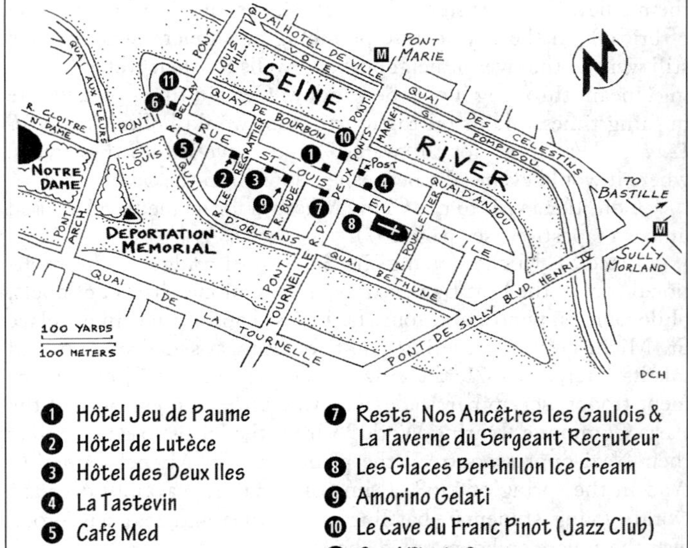

From the Deportation Memorial, cross the bridge onto the Left Bank and enjoy the riverside view of Notre-Dame, window-shopping among the green book stalls and browsing through used books, vintage posters, and souvenirs. At the little park and church (over the bridge from the front of Notre-Dame), venture inland a few blocks, basically arcing through the Latin Quarter and returning to the island two bridges down at place St. Michel.

▲Latin Quarter—This neighborhood's touristic fame relates to its intriguing artsy, bohemian character. This was perhaps Europe's leading university district in the Middle Ages—home, since the 13th century, to the prestigious Sorbonne University. Back then, Latin was the language of higher education. And, since students here came from all over Europe, Latin served as their linguistic common denominator. Locals referred to the quarter by its language: Latin.

The neighborhood's main boulevards (St. Michel and St. Germain) are lined with far-out bookshops, street singers, and jazz clubs. While still youthful and artsy, the area has become a tourist ghetto filled with cheap North African eateries. The cafés that were once the haunts of great poets and philosophers are now the hangout of tired tourists. For colorful wandering or café sitting, afternoons and evenings are best (Mo: St. Michel).

Walking along rue St. Séverin, you can still see the shadow of the medieval sewer system (the street slopes into a central channel of bricks). In the days before plumbing and toilets, when people still went to the river or neighborhood wells for their water, "flushing" meant throwing it out the window. Certain times of day were flushing times. Maids on the fourth floor would holler, *"Garde de l'eau!"* ("Watch out for the water!") and heave it into the streets, where it would eventually be washed down into the Seine.

Consider a visit to the Cluny Museum for its medieval art and unicorn tapestries (see page 297).

Place St. Michel (facing the St. Michel bridge) is the traditional core of the Left Bank's artsy, liberal, hippie district of poets, philosophers, winos, and tourists. In less commercial times, place St. Michel was a gathering point for the city's malcontents and misfits. Here, in 1871, the citizens took the streets from government troops, set up barricades *Les Miz*–style, and established the Paris Commune. During World War II, the locals rose up against their Nazi oppressors (read the plaques by St. Michel fountain). And in the spring of 1968, a time of social upheaval all over the world, young students—battling riot batons and tear gas—took over the square and demanded change.

From place St. Michel, look across the river and find the spire of Sainte-Chapelle church and its weathervane angel (below). Cross the river on pont St. Michel and continue along boulevard du Palais. On your left, you'll see the high-security doorway to the Sainte-Chapelle. You'll need to pass through a metal detector to get into the Sainte-Chapelle complex. Once past security, restrooms are ahead on the left. The line into the church may be long. (Museum Pass–holders can bypass this line; pick up an English info flier.) Enter the humble ground floor of...

▲▲▲Sainte-Chapelle—This triumph of Gothic church architecture is a cathedral of glass like no other. It was speedily built from 1242 to 1248 for Louis IX (the only French king who is now a saint) to house the supposed Crown of Thorns. Its architectural harmony is due to the fact that it was completed under the direction of one architect in only six years—unheard of in Gothic times. (Notre-Dame took more than 200 years to build.)

The design clearly shows an Old Regime approach to worship. The basement was for staff and other common folk. Royal Christians worshipped upstairs. The ground-floor paint job, a 19th-century restoration, is a reasonably accurate copy of the original.

Climb the spiral staircase to the **Chapelle Haute**. Fill the place with choral music, crank up the sunshine, face the top of the altar, and really believe that the Crown of Thorns is there, and this becomes one awesome space.

"Let there be light." In the Bible, it's clear: Light is divine.

Sainte-Chapelle

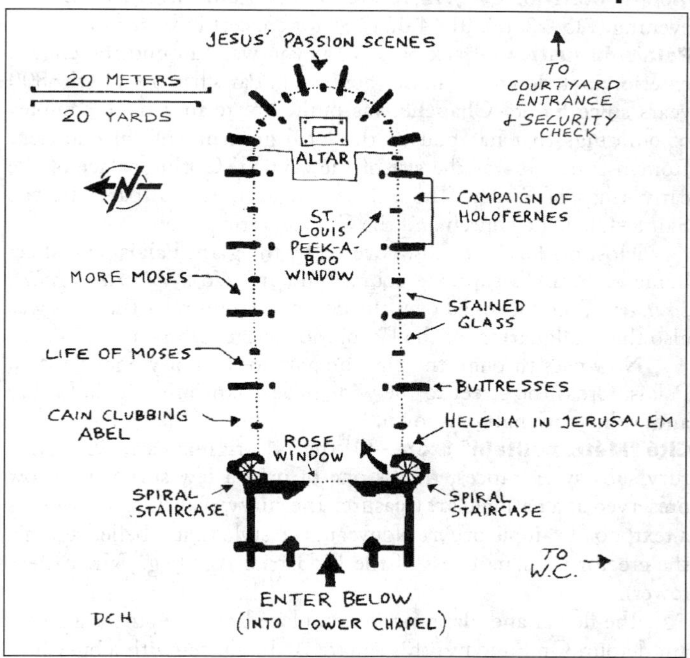

Light shining through stained glass was a symbol of God's grace shining down to earth. Gothic architects used their new technology to turn dark stone buildings into lanterns of light. The glory of Gothic shines brighter here than in any other church.

There are 15 separate panels of stained glass (6,500 square feet—two-thirds of it 13th-century original), with more than 1,100 different scenes, mostly from the Bible.

The altar was raised up high to better display the relic—the Crown of Thorns—around which this chapel was built. The supposed crown cost King Louis three times as much as this church. Today, it is kept in the Notre-Dame treasury and shown only on Fridays during Lent.

Louis IX's little private viewing window is in the wall to the right of the altar. Louis IX, both saintly and shy, liked to go to church without dealing with the rigors of public royal life. Here, he could worship while still dressed in his jammies.

Lay your camera on the ground and shoot the ceiling. Those ribs growing out of the slender columns are the essence of Gothic.

Books in the gift shop explain the stained glass in English. (€6.10 entry fee, €9 combo-ticket covers Conciergerie, both covered by Museum Pass, daily March–Oct 9:30–18:00, Nov–Feb

9:00–17:00, Mo: Cité).There are concerts almost every summer evening (€15–23, tel. 01 44 07 12 38 for concert information).

Palais de Justice—Back outside, as you walk around the church exterior, look down and notice how much Paris has risen in the 800 years since Sainte-Chapelle was built. You're in a huge complex of buildings that has housed the local government since ancient Roman times. It was the site of the original Gothic palace of the early kings of France. The only surviving medieval parts are the Sainte-Chapelle church and the Conciergerie prison.

Most of the site is now covered by the giant Palais de Justice, home of France's supreme court (built in 1776). "*Liberté, Egalité, Fraternité,*" emblazoned over the doors, is a reminder that this was also the headquarters of the Revolutionary government.

Now pass through the big iron gate to the noisy boulevard du Palais. Cross the street to the wide pedestrian-only rue de Lutèce and walk about halfway down.

Cité "Métropolitain" Stop—Of the 141 original early-20th-century subway entrances, this is one of only a few survivors—now preserved as a national art treasure. The curvy, plantlike ironwork is a textbook example of Art Nouveau, the style that rebelled against the erector-set squareness of the Industrial Age (e.g., Mr. Eiffel's tower).

The flower and plant market on place Louis Lépine is a pleasant detour. On Sundays, this square is all aflutter with a busy bird market. And across the way is the Prefecture de Police, where Inspector Clouseau of *Pink Panther* fame used to work, and where the local resistance fighters took the first building from the Nazis in August of 1944, leading to the Allied liberation of Paris a week later.

Pause here to admire the view. Sainte-Chapelle is a pearl in an ugly architectural oyster. We'll double back to the Palais de Justice, turn right and enter the...

Conciergerie—Though barren inside, this former prison echoes with history. It's a gloomy place. Kings used it to torture and execute failed assassins. The leaders of the Revolution put it to similar good use. A tower along the river, called "the babbler," was named for the painful sounds that leaked from it.

Marie-Antoinette was imprisoned here. During a busy eight-month period in the Revolution, she was one of 2,600 prisoners kept here on the way to the guillotine. You can see Marie-Antoinette's cell, which houses a collection of her mementos. In another room, a list of those made "a foot shorter at the top" by the "national razor" includes ex-King Louis XVI, Charlotte Corday (who murdered Jean-Paul Marat in his bathtub), and the chief revolutionary who got a taste of his own medicine, Maximilien de Robespierre (€6.10,

€9 combo-ticket covers Sainte-Chapelle, both covered by Museum Pass, daily April–Sept 9:30–18:30, Oct–March 10:00–17:00, good English descriptions).

Back outside, turn left on boulevard du Palais and head toward the river (north). On the corner is the city's oldest public clock. The mechanism of the present clock is from 1334, and even though the case is Baroque, it keeps on ticking.

Turn left onto quai de l'Horloge and walk west along the river, past the round medieval tower called "the babbler." The bridge up ahead is the pont Neuf, where we'll end this walk. At the first corner, veer left into a sleepy triangular square called place Dauphine. Marvel at how such quaintness could be lodged in the midst of such greatness as you walk through the park to the end of the island (the departure point for Seine river cruises offered by Vedettes du Pont-Neuf; see page 273). At the equestrian statue of Henry IV, turn right onto the bridge and take refuge in one of the nooks on the Eiffel Tower side.

Pont Neuf—This "new bridge" is now Paris' oldest. Built during Henry IV's reign (around 1600), its 12 arches span the widest part of the river. The fine view includes the park on the tip of the island (note Seine tour boats), the Orsay Museum, and the Louvre. These turrets were originally for vendors and street entertainers. In the days of Henry IV, who originated the promise of "a chicken in every pot," this would have been a lively scene.

As for now, you can tour the Seine by boat, shop at the Samaritaine (across the bridge), continue to the Louvre, or head to the beach *(plage)*.

Paris *Plage* and In-Line Skaters—Since 2001 Paris officials have removed cars from a key section of busy Right Bank express lanes to make room for an artificial beach (mid-July–mid-Aug). Tons of sand are poured over black asphalt, then sprinkled lightly with beach chairs and changing rooms, and *voilà!*—a summer scene that the Beach Boys would appreciate (though you can't swim in the river). The faux beach extends two miles along the Seine on voie Georges Pompidou (just north of the Ile de la Cité), from pont des Arts to pont de Sully, with three main sub-areas: one sandy, one grassy, and one with wood decking. You'll also find climbing walls, a swimming pool, trampolines, a library, beach volleyball, badminton, and Frisbee areas.

The same riverside highway also provides a long fun-filled traffic-free zone for joggers, bicyclists, and in-line skaters (mid-July–mid-Aug Sun–Fri 9:00–16:00). For even more high-rolling fun, thousands of rollerbladers take to the streets Fridays at 22:30 and summer Sunday afternoons as police close off various routes in different parts of downtown (ask at your hotel or a TI).

SIGHTS

Paris Museums near the Tuileries Garden

Paris' grandest park, the Tuileries Garden, was once the private property of kings and queens. Today it links the museums of the Louvre, L'Orangerie, Jeu de Paume, and the Orsay.

▲▲▲Louvre—This is Europe's oldest, biggest, greatest, and second-most-crowded museum (after the Vatican). Housed in a U-shaped, 16th-century palace (accentuated by a 20th-century glass pyramid), the Louvre is Paris' top museum and one of its key landmarks. It's home to *Mona Lisa*, *Venus de Milo,* and hall after hall of Greek and Roman masterpieces, medieval jewels, Michelangelo statues, and paintings by the greatest artists from the Renaissance to the Romantics (mid-1800s).

Touring the Louvre can be overwhelming, so be selective. Consider taking a tour (see "Tours," below), or follow my self-guided tour at the end of this listing. Focus on the **Denon Wing** (south, along the river): Greek sculptures, Italian paintings (by the likes of Raphael and da Vinci), and—of course—French paintings (neoclassical and Romantic). For extra credit, tackle the **Richelieu Wing** (north, away from the river), with works from ancient Mesopotamia (today's Iraq), as well as French, Dutch, and Northern art; or the **Sully Wing** (connecting the other two wings), with Egyptian artifacts and more French paintings.

Cost: €8.50, €6 after 18:00 on Wed and Fri, free on first Sun of month, covered by Museum Pass. Tickets good all day; reentry allowed. The new self-serve ticket machines are faster than the ticket windows (accepts euro notes, coins, and Visa cards, not MasterCard).

Hours: Wed–Mon 9:00–18:00, closed Tue. Most wings open Wed and Fri until 21:45. Upon arrival, head straight for the Denon Wing, which contains the biggies: *Mona Lisa, Venus de Milo,* and more. Galleries start closing 30 minutes early. Evening visits are peaceful and the pyramid glows after dark. Galleries start shutting down 30 minutes early. The last entry is 45 minutes before closing. Crowds are worst on Sun, Mon, Wed, and mornings. Wed and Fri evenings are cheaper and quieter.

Information: Tel. 01 40 20 53 17, recorded info tel. 01 40 20 51 51, www.louvre.fr. Pick up the free *Louvre Plan Information* in English at the information desk under the pyramid as you enter.

Crowd-Beating Tips: There is no grander entry than through the pyramid, but metal detectors (not ticket-buying lines) create a long line at times. There are several ways to avoid the line. Museum Pass–holders can use the group entrance in the pedestrian passageway between the pyramid and rue de Rivoli (under the arches, a few steps north of the pyramid, find the uniformed guard at the

Paris Museums near the Tuileries Garden

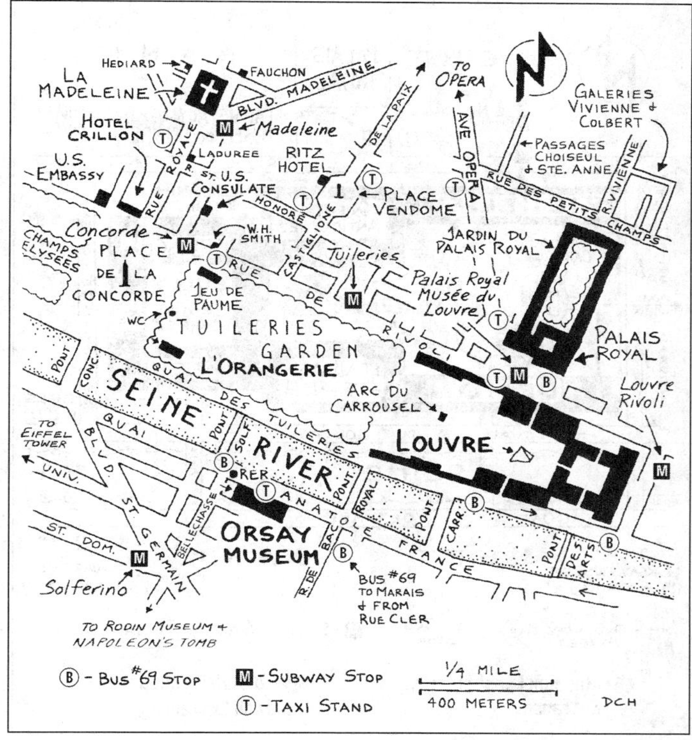

entrance, with the escalator down). Otherwise, you can enter the Louvre from its (usually less-crowded) underground entrance, accessed through the "Carrousel du Louvre" shopping mall. Enter the mall at 99 rue de Rivoli (the door with the red awning, daily 8:30–23:00) or directly from the Métro stop Palais Royal-Musée du Louvre (stepping off the train, exit to the left, following signs to Carrousel du Louvre-Musée du Louvre). The taxi stand is across rue de Rivoli next to the Métro station.

Tours: The 90-minute English-language tours leave three times daily except Sun (normally at 11:00, 14:00, and 15:45, €6 plus your entry ticket, tour tel. 01 40 20 52 63). Digital audioguides (available for €5 at entries to the three wings, at top of escalators) give you a directory of about 130 masterpieces, allowing you to dial a rather dull commentary on included works as you stumble upon them.

Underground Louvre: To explore the subterranean shopping mall, enter through the pyramid, walk toward the inverted pyramid, and uncover a post office, a handy TI and SNCF (train

The Louvre

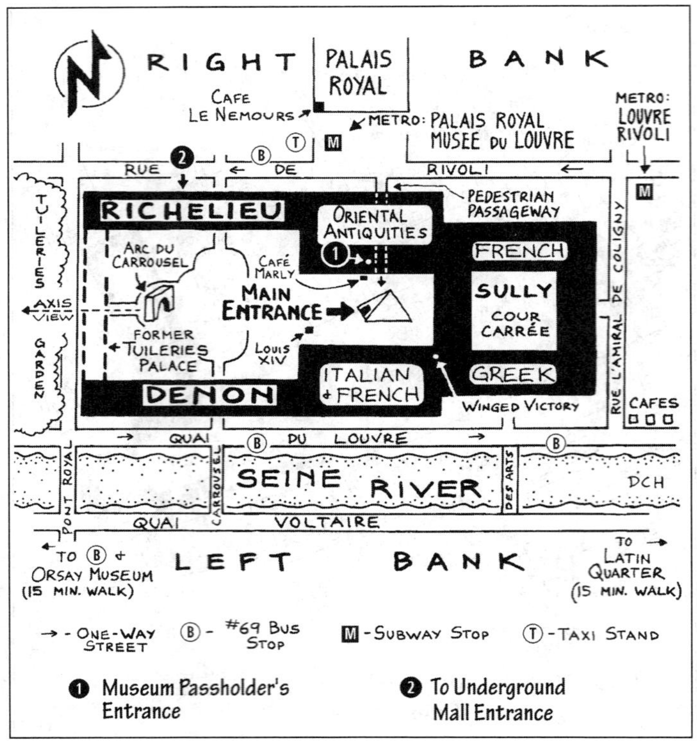

tickets) office, glittering boutiques and a dizzying assortment of good-value eateries (up the escalator), and the Palais Royal-Musée du Louvre Métro entrance. Stairs at the far end take you right into the Tuileries Garden, a perfect antidote to the stuffy, crowded rooms of the Louvre.

Self-Guided Tour: Start in the Denon wing and visit the highlights, in the following order (thanks to Gene Openshaw for his help with this).

Wander through the **ancient Greek and Roman works** to see the Parthenon frieze, Pompeii mosaics, Etruscan sarcophagi, and Roman portrait busts. You can't miss lovely *Venus de Milo (Aphrodite).* This goddess of love (c. 100 B.C., from the Greek island of Melos) created a sensation when she was discovered in 1820. Most "Greek" statues are actually later Roman copies, but Venus is a rare Greek original. She, like Golden Age Greeks, epitomizes stability, beauty, and balance. Later Greek art was Hellenistic, adding motion and drama. For a good example, see the exciting *Winged Victory of Samothrace* (*Victoire de Samothrace,* on the landing). This statue of a woman with wings, poised on the prow of a ship, once stood on a hilltop to commemorate a great naval victory. This is the *Venus de Milo* gone Hellenistic.

The **Italian collection** is on the other side of the Winged Victory. The key to Renaissance painting was realism, and for the Italians "realism" was spelled "3-D." Painters were inspired by the realism and balanced beauty of Greek sculpture. Painting a 3-D world on a 2-D surface is tough, and after a millennium of Dark Ages, artists were rusty. Living in a religious age, they painted mostly altarpieces full of saints, angels, Madonnas-and-bambinos, and crucifixes floating in an ethereal gold-leaf heaven. Gradually, though, they brought these otherworldly scenes down to earth. The Italian collection—including the *Mona Lisa*—is scattered throughout rooms *(salles)* 3 and 4, in the long Grand Gallery, and in adjoining rooms. These paintings are likely to be moving targets while the room they usually occupy (Salle des Etats) is renovated. *Mona Lisa* and other Italian Renaissance works described here will be close by. Just ask.

Two masters of the Italian High Renaissance (1500–1600) were Raphael (see his *La Belle Jardinière*, showing the Madonna, Child, and John the Baptist) and Leonardo da Vinci. The Louvre has the greatest collection of Leonardos in the world—five of them, including the exquisite *Virgin, Child, and St. Anne*, the neighboring *Madonna of the Rocks,* and the androgynous *John the Baptist.* His most famous, of course, is the *Mona Lisa.*

Leonardo was already an old man when François I invited him to France. Determined to pack light, he took only a few paintings. One was a portrait of Lisa del Giocondo, the wife of a wealthy Florentine merchant. When Leonardo arrived, François I immediately fell in love with the painting and made it the centerpiece of the small collection of Italian masterpieces that would, in three centuries, become the Louvre museum. He called it *La Gioconda.* We know it as a contraction of the Italian for "my lady Lisa"—*Mona Lisa.* Warning: François I was impressed, but *Mona* may disappoint you. She's smaller and darker than you'd expect, engulfed in a huge room, and hidden behind a glaring pane of glass.

Mona's overall mood is one of balance and serenity, but there's also an element of mystery. Her smile and long-distance beauty are subtle and elusive, tempting but always just out of reach, like strands of a street singer's melody drifting through the Métro tunnel. *Mona* doesn't knock your socks off, but she winks at the patient viewer.

Now for something **neoclassical**. Notice the fine work, such as *The Coronation of Napoleon* by Jacques-Louis David, near *Mona* in the Salle Daru. Neoclassicism, once the rage in France (1780–1850), usually features Greek subjects, patriotic sentiment, and a clean, simple style. After Napoleon quickly conquered most of Europe, he insisted on being made emperor (not merely king) of this "New Rome." He staged an elaborate coronation ceremony in Paris, and rather than let the pope crown him, he crowned himself. The setting is the Notre-Dame Cathedral, with Greek columns and Roman arches thrown in for effect. Napoleon's mom was also added, since she couldn't make it to the ceremony. A key on the frame describes who's who in the picture.

The **Romantic** collection, in an adjacent room (Salle Mollien), has works by Théodore Géricault *(The Raft of the Medusa)* and Eugène Delacroix *(Liberty Leading the People)*. Romanticism, with an emphasis on motion and emotion, is the complete flip side of neoclassicism, though they both flourished in the early 1800s. Delacroix's *Liberty*, commemorating the stirrings of democracy in France, is also a fitting tribute to the Louvre, the first museum opened to the common rabble of humanity. The good things in life don't belong only to a small wealthy part of society, but to all. The motto of France is *"Liberté, Egalité, Fraternité"*—liberty, equality, and brotherhood.

Exit the room at the far end (past the café) and go downstairs, where you'll bump into the bum of a large, twisting male nude who looks like he's just waking up after a thousand-year nap. The two *Slaves* (1513–1515) by Michelangelo are a fitting end to this museum—works that bridge the ancient and modern worlds. Michelangelo, like his fellow Renaissance artists, learned from the Greeks. The perfect anatomy, twisting poses, and idealized faces look like they could have been done 2,000 years earlier. Michelangelo said that his purpose was to carve away the marble to reveal the figures God put inside. The *Rebellious Slave*, fighting against his bondage, shows the agony of that process and the ecstasy of the result.

Jeu de Paume (Galerie Nationale du Jeu de Paume)—This museum hosts rotating exhibits of top contemporary artists (€6, not covered by Museum Pass, Tue 12:00–21:30, Wed–Fri 12:00–19:00, Sat–Sun 10:00–19:00, closed Mon, on place de la Concorde, just inside Tuileries Garden on rue de Rivoli side, Mo: Concorde).

▲Musée de l'Orangerie—This Impressionist museum, lovely as a water lily, is due to reopen sometime in 2007. (For the latest, ask at any Paris TI.) When it opens, you can step out of the tree-lined, sun-dappled Impressionist painting that is the Tuileries Garden, and into L'Orangerie (loh-rahn-zheh-ree), a little *bijou* of select works by Utrillo, Cézanne, Renoir, Matisse, and Picasso. On the ground floor, you'll find a line of eight rooms dedicated to these artists. Downstairs is the finale: Monet's water lilies. The museum's collection is small enough to enjoy in a short visit, but complete enough to see the bridge from Impressionism to the

Moderns. And it's all beautiful (located in Tuileries Garden near place de la Concorde, Mo: Concorde). If you need a Monet fix before L'Orangerie reopens, visit the Marmottan Museum (see page 296).

▲▲▲Orsay Museum—The Musée d'Orsay (mew-zay dor-say) houses French art of the 1800s (specifically, art from 1848 to 1914), picking up where the Louvre leaves off. For us, that means Impressionism. The Orsay houses the best general collection anywhere of Edouard Manet, Claude Monet, Pierre-Auguste Renoir, Edgar Degas, Vincent van Gogh, Paul Cézanne, and Paul Gauguin.

The museum shows art that is also both old and new, conservative and revolutionary. You'll start on the ground floor with the Conservatives and the early rebels who paved the way for the Impressionists, then head upstairs to see how a few visionary young artists bucked the system, revolutionized the art world, and paved the way for the 20th century.

For most visitors, the most important part of the museum is the Impressionist collection upstairs. Here, you can study many pictures you've probably seen in books, such as Manet's *Luncheon on the Grass*, Renoir's *Dance at the Moulin de la Galette*, Monet's *Gare St. Lazare*, James Abbott McNeill Whistler's *Portrait of the Artist's Mother*, van Gogh's *The Church at Auvers-sur-Oise*, and Cézanne's *The Card Players*. As you approach these beautiful, easy-to-enjoy paintings, remember that there is more to this art than meets the eye.

Impressionism 101: The camera threatened to make artists obsolete. A painter's original function was to record reality faithfully, like a journalist. Now a machine could capture a better likeness faster than you could say Etch-A-Sketch.

But true art is more than just painted reality. It gives us reality from the artist's point of view, putting a personal stamp on the work. It records not only a scene—a camera can do that—but the artist's impressions of that scene. Impressions are often fleeting, so the artist has to work quickly.

The Impressionist painters rejected camera-like detail for a quick style more suited to capturing the passing moment. Feeling stifled by the rigid rules and stuffy atmosphere of the Academy, the Impressionists took as their motto, "Out of the studio, into the open air." They grabbed their berets and scarves and took excursions to the country, where they set up their easels on riverbanks and hillsides, or sketched in cafés and dance halls. Gods, goddesses, nymphs, and fantasy scenes were out; common people and rural landscapes were in.

The quick style and simple subjects were ridiculed and called childish by the "experts." Rejected by the Salon, the Impressionists

Orsay Museum—Ground Floor

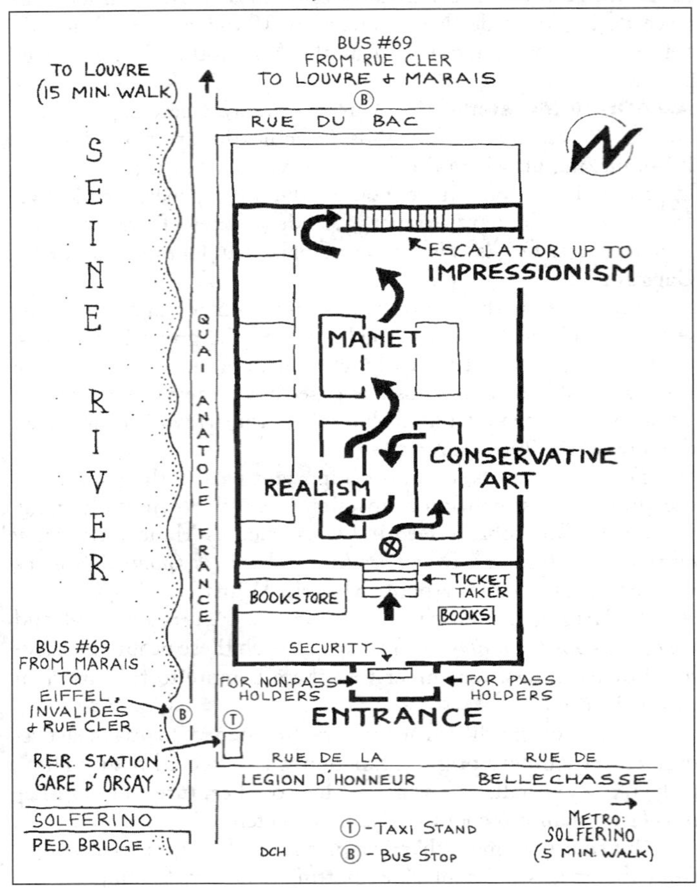

staged their own exhibition in 1874. They brashly took their name from an insult thrown at them by a critic, who laughed at one of Monet's impressions of a sunrise. During the next decade, they exhibited their own work independently. The public, opposed at first, was slowly drawn in by the simplicity, color, and vibrancy of Impressionist art.

Cost: €7; €5 after 16:15 and on Sun, free first Sun of month, covered by Museum Pass. Tickets are good all day. Museum Pass–holders can enter quickly on the right side of the building, ticket-buyers enter along the left (river) side.

Hours: June 20–Sept 20 Tue–Sun 9:00–18:00, Sept 21–June 19 Tue–Sat 10:00–18:00, Sun 9:00–18:00, Thu until 21:45 year-round, always closed Mon. Last entry is 45 min before closing. The

Impressionist galleries start closing at 17:15, frustrating unwary visitors. Note that the Orsay is crowded on Tuesday, when the Louvre is closed.

Location: The Orsay sits above the RER-C stop called Musée d'Orsay. The nearest Métro stop is Solférino, three blocks south of the Orsay. Bus #69 from the Marais neighborhoods stops at the museum on the river side (quai Anatole France); from the rue Cler area, it stops behind the museum on the rue du Bac. A taxi stand is in front of the museum on quai Anatole France.

Information: The booth inside the entrance gives free floor plans in English. Tel. 01 40 49 48 41, www.musee-orsay.fr.

Tours: Audioguides are €5. English-language guided tours usually run daily (except Sun) at 11:30 (90-min tours-€6). Tours in English focusing on the Impressionists are offered Tuesdays at 14:30 (€6, sometimes also on other days).

Cafés: The elegant second-floor restaurant has a pricey but *très* elegant restaurant, serving tea and coffee from 15:00–17:30. A simple fifth-floor café is sandwiched between the Impressionists; above it is an easy self-service place.

Southwest Paris: The Eiffel Tower Neighborhood

▲▲▲Eiffel Tower (La Tour Eiffel)—It's crowded and expensive, but this 1,000-foot-tall ornament is worth the trouble. In hot weather, it's six inches taller. It covers 2.5 acres and requires 50 tons of paint. Its 7,000 tons of metal are spread out so well at the base that it's no heavier per square inch than a linebacker on tiptoes. Visitors to Paris may find *Mona Lisa* to be less than expected, but the Eiffel Tower rarely disappoints, even in an era of skyscrapers.

Built a hundred years after the French Revolution (and in the midst of an Industrial one), the tower served no function but to impress. Bridge-builder Gustave Eiffel won the contest for the 1889 Centennial World's Fair by beating out such rival proposals as a giant guillotine. To a generation hooked on technology, the tower was the marvel of the age, a symbol of progress and man's ingenuity. To others it was a cloned-sheep monstrosity. The writer Guy de Maupassant routinely ate lunch in the tower just so he wouldn't have to look at it.

Delicate and graceful when seen from afar, the Eiffel is massive—even a bit scary—from close up. You don't appreciate the size until you walk toward it; like a mountain, it seems so close but takes forever to reach.

There are three observation platforms, at 200, 400, and 900 feet; the higher you go, the more you pay. Each requires a separate elevator (and line), so plan on at least 90 minutes if you want to go to the top and back. For most, the view from the second level is plenty.

Eiffel Tower to Les Invalides

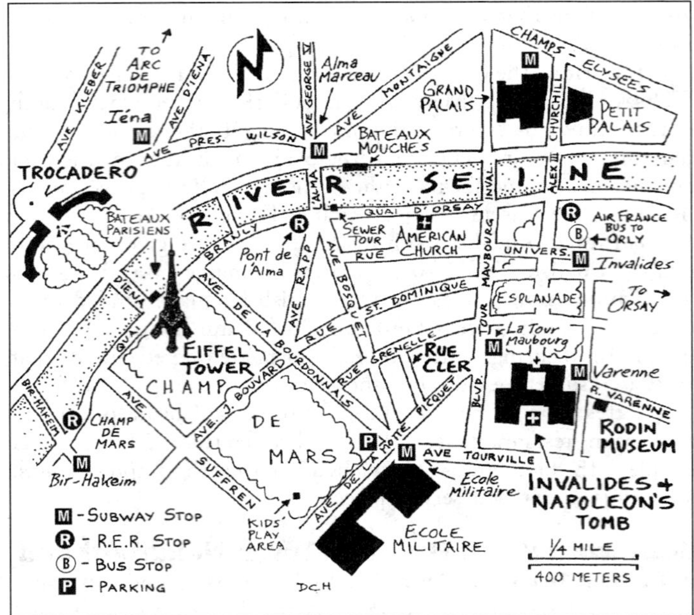

A TI/ticket booth is between the Pilier Nord (north pillar) and Pilier Est (east pillar). The stairs (yes, you can walk up partway) are next to the Jules Verne restaurant entrance (allow $300 per person for the restaurant, reserve 3 months in advance). A sign in the cheek-to-jowl elevator tells you to beware of pickpockets.

As you ascend through the metal beams, imagine being a worker, perched high above nothing, riveting this giant erector set together. On top, all of Paris lies before you, with a panorama guide. On a good day, you can see for 40 miles.

The **first level** has exhibits, a post office (daily 10:00–19:00, cancellation stamp will read Eiffel Tower), a snack bar, WCs, and souvenirs. Read the informative signs (in English) describing the major monuments, see the entertaining free movie on the history of the tower, and don't miss a century of fireworks—including the entire millennium blast—on video. Then consider a drink or a sandwich overlooking all of Paris at the snack café (outdoor tables in summer) or at the city's best view bar/restaurant, Altitude 95 (see page 345).

The **second level** has the best views (walk up stairway to get above netting), a cafeteria, and WCs.

While you'll save no money, consider taking the elevator up and the stairs down (from second level) for good exercise and views.

Cost and Hours: It costs €4 to go to the first level, €7.50 to the second, and €11 to go all the way (not covered by Museum Pass). On a budget? You can climb the stairs to the second level for only €3.50 (daily March–Sept 9:00–24:00, Oct–Feb 9:30–23:00, last entry 1 hour before closing, shorter lines at night, can catch Bateaux-Parisiens boat for Seine cruise at base of tower, Mo: Trocadéro, RER: Champ de Mars-Tour Eiffel, tel. 01 44 11 23 23, www.tour-eiffel.fr).

Crowd-Beating Tips: To avoid most crowds, go early (by 8:45) or late in the day (after 18:00, after 20:00 May–Aug, last entry 1 hr before closing); weekends are worst. Ideally you'd arrive with some light and stay as it gets dark.

Best Views: The best place to view the tower is from **Trocadéro Square** to the north; it's a 10-min walk across the river, a happening scene at night, and especially fun for kids. Consider arriving at the Trocadéro Métro stop for the view, then walking toward the tower. Another great viewpoint is the long, grassy field, **Parc du Champ de Mars**, to the south (great for dinner picnics). However impressive it may be by day, the tower is an awesome thing to see at twilight, when it becomes engorged with light, and virile Paris lies back and lets night be on top.

National Maritime Museum (Musée National de la Marine)—This extensive museum houses an amazing collection of ship models, submarines, torpedoes, cannonballs, *beaucoup de* bowsprits, and naval you-name-it—including a small boat made for Napoleon. You'll find some English information on the walls. The €3 audioguide is an essential investment for *Master and Commander* types; kids like the museum either way (adults-€7, kids-€4, covered by Museum Pass, Wed–Mon 10:00–18:00, closed Tue, on left side of Trocadéro Square with your back to Eiffel Tower, www.musee-marine.fr).

▲Paris Sewer Tour (Les Egouts de Paris)—This quick and easy visit takes you along a few hundred yards of underground water tunnel lined with interesting displays, well-described in English, that explain the evolution of the world's longest sewer system. (If you straightened out Paris' sewers, they would reach beyond Istanbul.) Don't miss the slideshow, the fine WCs just beyond the gift shop, and the occasional tour in English (€4, covered by Museum Pass, May–Sept Sat–Wed 11:00–17:00, Oct–April Sat–Wed 11:00–16:00, closed Thu–Fri, located where pont de l'Alma greets the Left Bank, Mo: Alma-Marceau, RER: Pont de l'Alma, tel. 01 53 68 27 81).

▲▲Napoleon's Tomb and Army Museum (Les Invalides)—The emperor lies majestically dead inside several coffins under a grand dome—a goose-bumping pilgrimage for historians. Napoleon is surrounded by the tombs of other French war heroes and a fine military museum in Hôtel des Invalides. Check out the interesting

World War II wing. Follow signs to the "crypt" to find Roman Empire-style reliefs that list the accomplishments of Napoleon's administration. The restored dome glitters with 26 pounds of gold (€7, covered by Museum Pass, April–Sept daily 10:00–18:00, summer Sun until 19:00, Oct–March daily 10:00–17:00, closed the first Mon of every month except July–Sept; Mo: La Tour Maubourg or Varenne, tel. 01 44 42 37 72, www.invalides.org).

▲▲**Rodin Museum (Musée Rodin)**—This user-friendly museum is filled with passionate works by the greatest sculptor since Michelangelo. You'll see *The Kiss, The Thinker, The Gates of Hell,* and many more.

Well-displayed in the mansion where the sculptor lived and worked, exhibits trace Rodin's artistic development, explain how his bronze statues were cast, and show some of the studies he created to work up to his masterpiece (the unfinished *Gates of Hell*). Learn about Rodin's tumultuous relationship with his apprentice and lover, Camille Claudel. Mull over what makes his sculptures some of the most evocative since the Renaissance. And stroll the gardens, packed with many of his greatest works (including *The Thinker*). The beautiful gardens are ideal for artistic reflection...or a picnic.

Cost, Hours, Location: €5, €3 on Sun, free first Sun of month, covered by Museum Pass. You'll pay €1 to get into the gardens only—which may be Paris' best deal, as many works are on display there. April–Sept Tue–Sun 9:30–17:45, closed Mon, gardens close 18:45, Oct–March Tue–Sun 9:30–16:45, closed Mon, gardens close 17:00. It's at 77 rue de Varenne, near Napoleon's Tomb (Mo: Varenne, tel. 01 44 18 61 10, www.musee-rodin.fr).

▲▲**Marmottan Museum (Musée Marmottan Monet)**—In this private, intimate, untouristy museum, you'll find the best collection anywhere of works by Impressionist headliner Claude Monet. Follow Monet's life through over a hundred works, from simple sketches to the *Impression: Sunrise* painting that gave his artistic movement its start—and a name. You'll also enjoy classic Monet canvases featuring the water lilies from his garden at Giverny.

Cost, Hours, Location: €7, not covered by Museum Pass, Tue–Sun 10:00–18:00, last entry is 17:30, closed Mon, 2 rue Louis Boilly, Mo: La Muette, follow brown museum signs 6 blocks down chaussée de la Muette through park to museum, tel. 01 44 96 50 33, www.marmottan.com.

Post-Museum Stroll: Wander down one of Paris' most pleasant (and upscale) shopping streets, the rue de Passy (2 blocks up chaussée de la Muette in opposite direction from La Muette Métro stop).

Southeast Paris: The Latin Quarter

This Left Bank neighborhood, just opposite Notre-Dame, is the Latin Quarter. (For more information and a walking tour, see

The Latin Quarter

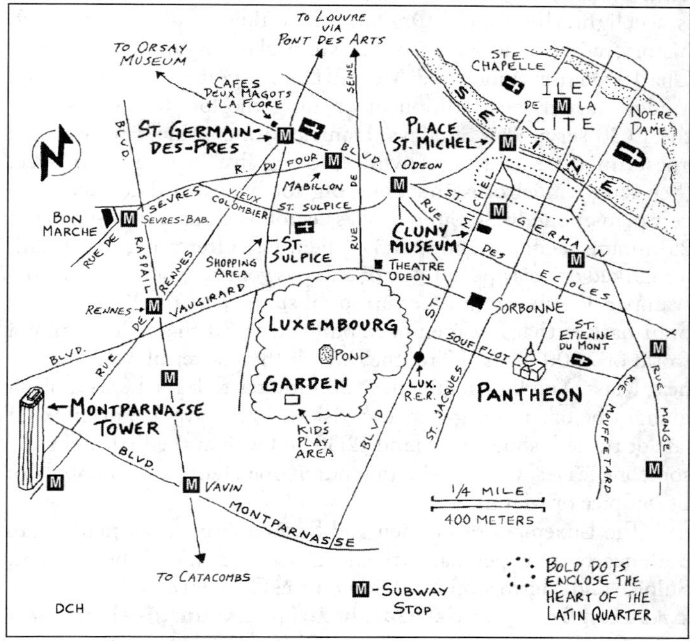

the "Latin Quarter," page 281, part of the Historic Core of Paris Walk.)

▲▲Cluny Museum (Musée National du Moyen Age)—This treasure-trove of Middle Age ("Moyen Age") art fills the old Roman baths, offering close-up looks at stained glass, Notre-Dame carvings, fine goldsmithing and jewelry, and rooms of tapestries. The star here is the exquisite "Lady and the Unicorn" tapestry: In five panels, a delicate-as-medieval-can-be noble lady introduces a delighted unicorn to the senses of taste, hearing, sight, smell, and touch.

Cost, Hours, Location: €5.50, €4 on Sun, free first Sun of month, covered by Museum Pass, Wed–Mon 9:15–17:45, closed Tue, near corner of boulevards St. Michel and St. Germain; Mo: Cluny-La Sorbonne, St. Michel, or Odéon; tel. 01 53 73 78 16, www.musee-moyenage.fr.

St. Germain-des-Prés—A church was first built on this site in A.D. 452. The church you see today was constructed in 1163 and is all that's left of a once sprawling and influential monastery. The colorful interior reminds us that medieval churches were originally painted in bright colors. The surrounding area hops at night with venerable cafés, fire-eaters, mimes, and scads of artists (free, daily 8:00–20:00, Mo: St. Germain-des-Prés).

▲St. Sulpice Organ Concert—For pipe-organ enthusiasts, this is a delight. The Grand Orgue at St. Sulpice Church has a rich history, with a succession of 12 world-class organists (including Charles-Marie Widor and Marcel Dupré) going back 300 years. Widor started the tradition of opening the loft to visitors after the 10:30 service on Sundays. Daniel Roth continues to welcome guests in three languages while playing five keyboards at once. (See www.danielrothsaintsulpice.org for his exact dates and concert plans.) The 10:30 Sunday Mass is followed by a high-powered 25-minute recital at about 11:35. Then, just after noon, the small, unmarked door is opened (left of entry as you face the rear). Visitors scamper like sixteenth notes up spiral stairs, past the 19th-century Stairmasters that five men once pumped to fill the bellows, into a world of 7,000 pipes. Here, they watch the master play during the next Mass. You'll generally have 30 minutes to kill (there's a plush lounge) before the organ plays; visitors can leave at any time. If late or rushed, show up around 12:30 and wait at the little door. As someone leaves, you can slip in (church open daily 7:30–19:30, Mo: St. Sulpice or Mabillon).

The Luxembourg Garden and St. Germain street market are both nearby and open daily (the St. Germain market is between St. Sulpice and Métro stop Mabillon on rue Clément).

▲▲Luxembourg Garden (Jardin du Luxembourg)—Paris' most beautiful, interesting, and enjoyable garden/park/recreational area is a great place to watch Parisians at rest and play (open daily until dusk, Mo: Odéon, RER: Luxembourg). It's ideal for families. These private gardens are property of the French Senate (housed in the château) and have special rules governing their use (e.g., where cards can be played, where dogs can be walked, where joggers can run, when and where music can be played). The brilliant flower beds are completely changed three times a year, and the boxed trees are brought out of the orangery in May. Challenge the card and chess players to a game (near the tennis courts), rent a toy sailboat, or find a free chair near the main pond and take a breather. Notice any pigeons? The story goes that a poor Ernest Hemingway used to hand-hunt (read: strangle) them here. Paris Walking Tours offers a good tour of the park (see "Tours," page 273).

The grand, neoclassical-domed Panthéon, now a mausoleum housing the tombs of several great Frenchmen, is a block away and only worth entering if you have a Museum Pass.

If you enjoy the Luxembourg Garden and want to see more, visit the nearby, colorful Jardin des Plantes (Mo: Jussieu or Gare d'Austerlitz, RER: Gare d'Austerlitz) and the more elegant Parc Monceau (Mo: Monceau).

Montparnasse Tower (La Tour Montparnasse)—The 59-story superscraper is cheaper and easier to get to the top of than the Eiffel

Tower, with the added bonus of offering one of Paris' best views—the Eiffel Tower is in sight and the Montparnasse Tower isn't. Buy the €3 photo guide to the city, then go to the rooftop and orient yourself. As you zip 56 floors in 38 seconds, watch the altitude meter above the door. Up top, enjoy the surreal scene with a man in a box and a helipad surrounded by the window-cleaner track. Then scan the city, noticing the lush courtyards hiding behind grand street fronts. Downstairs you'll find fascinating historic black-and-white photos and a plush little theater playing *Paris Like Never Seen* (free, 12 min, shows continuously). You'll float past unseen visual delights, spiraling down the Eiffel Tower as the French narration explains, "Paris is radiant and confident, like a lover who finally took her blouse off."

Cost, Hours, Location: €8.50, not covered by Museum Pass, daily April–Sept 9:30–23:30, Oct–March 9:30–22:30, disappointing after dark, entrance on rue de l'Arrivée, Mo: Montparnasse-Bienvenüe.

▲Catacombs—These underground tunnels contain the anonymous bones of six million permanent Parisians. In 1785, the Revolutionary Government of Paris decided to relieve congestion and improve sanitary conditions by emptying the city cemeteries (which traditionally surrounded churches) into an official ossuary. The perfect locale was the many miles of underground tunnels from limestone quarries, which were, at that time, just outside the city. For decades, priests led ceremonial processions of black-veiled, bone-laden carts into the quarries, where the bones were stacked into piles five feet high and as much as 80 feet deep behind neat walls of skull-studded tibiae. Each transfer was completed with the placement of a plaque indicating the church and district from which that stack of bones came and the date they arrived.

From the entry, a spiral staircase leads 60 feet down. Then you begin a one-mile subterranean walk. After several blocks of empty passageways, you ignore a sign announcing: "Halt, this is the empire of the dead." Along the way, plaques encourage visitors to reflect upon their destiny: "Happy is he who is forever faced with the hour of his death and prepares himself for the end every day." You emerge far from where you entered, with white-limestone-covered toes, telling anyone in the know you've been underground gawking at bones. Note to wannabe Hamlets: An attendant checks your bag at the exit for stolen souvenirs. A flashlight is handy. Being under 6'2" is helpful.

Cost, Hours, Location: €5, not covered by Museum Pass, Tue–Sun 10:00–17:00, ticket booth closes at 16:00, closed Mon, 1 place Denfert-Rochereau, tel. 01 43 22 47 63. Take the Métro to Denfert-Rochereau, then find the lion in the big traffic circle; if he looked left rather than right, he'd stare right at the green entrance to the Catacombs.

Northwest Paris: Champs-Elysées, Arc de Triomphe, and Beyond

▲▲Place de la Concorde and the Champs-Elysées—This famous boulevard is Paris' backbone, and has the greatest concentration of traffic. All of France seems to converge on the place de la Concorde, the city's largest square. It was here that the guillotine took the lives of thousands—including King Louis XVI and Marie-Antoinette. Back then it was called the place de la Revolution.

Catherine de Médicis wanted a place to drive her carriage, so she started draining the swamp that would become the avenue des Champs-Elysées. Napoleon put on the final touches, and it's been the place to be seen ever since. The Tour de France bicycle race ends here, as do all parades (French or foe) of any significance. While the boulevard has become a bit hamburgerized, a walk here is a must. Take the Métro to the Arc de Triomphe (Mo: Charles de Gaulle-Etoile) and saunter down the Champs-Elysées (Métro stops every few blocks: Franklin D. Roosevelt, George V, and Charles de Gaulle-Etoile).

▲▲▲Arc de Triomphe—Napoleon had the magnificent Arc de Triomphe commissioned to commemorate his victory at the battle of Austerlitz. There's no triumphal arch bigger (165 feet high, 130 feet wide). And, with 12 converging boulevards, there's no traffic circle more thrilling to experience—either from behind the wheel or on foot (take the underpass).

The foot of the arch is a stage on which the last two centuries of Parisian history have played out—from the funeral of Napoleon, to the goose-stepping arrival of the Nazis, to the triumphant return of Charles de Gaulle after the Allied liberation. Ponder the Tomb of the Unknown Soldier (from World War I, at base of arch), where the flame is rekindled daily at 18:30. Find François Rude's famous relief, "La Marseillaise" (on the right pillar), showing a shouting Lady Liberty rallying weary troops.

The 284 steps lead to a cute museum about the arch, sweeping skyline panoramas, and a mesmerizing view down onto the traffic that swirls around the arch.

Cost, Hours, Location: €7, covered by Museum Pass, daily April–Sept 10:00–23:00, Oct–March 10:00–22:30, Mo: Charles de Gaulle-Etoile, use underpass to reach arch. At the arch, the elevator—which is only for people with disabilities—goes to the museum but not to the top.

▲Opéra Garnier—This grand palace of the belle époque was built for Napoleon III and finished in 1875. From the grand avenue de l'Opéra, once lined with Paris' most fashionable haunts, the newly restored facade seems to say "all power to the wealthy." And Apollo, holding his lyre high above the buidling, seems to declare "this is a temple of the highest arts." While huge, the actual theater

Northwest Paris: Champs-Elysées, Arc de Triomphe, and Beyond

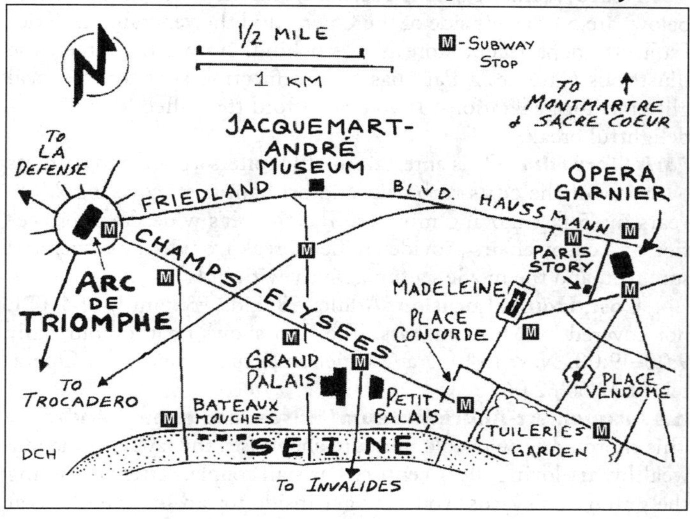

seats only 2,000. The real show was before and after, when the elite of Paris—out to see and be seen—strutted their elegant stuff in the extravagant lobbies. Think of the grand marble stairway as a theater itself. As you wander the halls and gawk at the decor, imagine the place filled with the beautiful people of the day. The massive foundations straddle an underground lake (creating the mysterious world of the *Phantom of the Opera*). Tourists can peek from two boxes into the actual red-velvet theater, where they see Marc Chagall's colorful ceiling (1964) playfully dancing around the eight-ton chandelier. Note the box seats next to the stage—the most expensive in the house, with an obstructed view of the stage... but just right if you're there only to be seen. The elitism of this place prompted President François Mitterand to have a people's opera house built in the 1980s (symbolically on place de la Bastille, where the French Revolution started in 1789). This left the Opéra Garnier home only to ballet and occasional concerts (usually no performances from mid-July to mid-Sept). While the library/museum is of interest to opera buffs, anyone will enjoy the second-floor grand foyer and Salon du Glacier, iced with decor typical of 1900.

Cost, Hours, Location: €6, not covered by Museum Pass, daily 10:00–17:00, July–Aug until 18:00, closed during performances, 8 rue Scribe, Mo: Opéra, tel. 01 40 01 22 53, www.opera-de-paris.fr.

Tours: There are English tours of the building on most afternoons (€10, includes entry, 90 min, call to confirm, tour ticket window at opposite end of entry from regular ticket booth).

Nearby: American Express, a TI, and the *Paris Story* film (see below) are on the left side of the Opéra, and the venerable Galeries Lafayette department store is just behind. Across the street, the illustrious Café de la Paix has been a meeting spot for the local glitterati for generations. If you can afford the coffee, this offers a delightful break.

***Paris Story* Film**—This entertaining film offers a good and painless overview of the city's turbulent and brilliant past, covering 2,000 years in 45 fast-moving minutes. The theater's widescreen projection and cushy chairs provide an ideal break from bad weather and sore feet, and the movie's a fun activity with kids.

Cost, Hours, Location: Adults-€8, kids-€5, family of 4-€21, not covered by Museum Pass. The film shows on the hour daily 9:00–19:00. Next to Opéra Garnier at 11 rue Scribe, Mo: Opéra, tel. 01 42 66 62 06.

▲▲Jacquemart-André Museum (Musée Jacquemart-André)—This thoroughly enjoyable museum showcases the lavish home of a wealthy, art-loving, 19th-century Parisian couple. After wandering the grand boulevards, you now get inside for an intimate look at the lifestyles of the Parisian rich and fabulous. Edouard André and his wife Nélie Jacquemart—who had no children—spent their lives and fortunes designing, building, and then decorating a sumptuous mansion. What makes this visit so rewarding is the fine audioguide tour (in English, free with admission). The place is strewn with paintings by Rembrandt, Botticelli, Uccello, Mantegna, Bellini, Boucher, and Fragonard—enough to make a painting gallery famous. Plan on spending an hour with the audioguide.

Cost, Hours, Location: €8.50, not covered by Museum Pass, daily 10:00–18:00, elegant café, boulevard Haussmann, Mo: Miromesnil or St Philippe de Roule, tel. 01 45 62 11 59, www.musee-jacquemart-andre.com/jandre.

Petit Palais (and its Musée des Beaux-Arts)—The free museum will likely be closed for renovation through 2006. When it reopens, you'll find a broad collection of paintings and sculpture from the 1600s to the 1900s. To some it feels like a museum of second-choice art, as the more famous museums in Paris have better collections from the same periods. Others find a few diamonds in the rough from Monet, Renoir, Boudin, and more; some interesting Art Nouveau pieces; and a smattering of works by Dutch, Italian, and Flemish Renaissance artists (across from Grand Palais, avenue Winston Churchill, just west of place de la Concorde, tel. 01 40 05 56 78).

Grand Palais—This grand exhibition hall, built for the 1900 World's Fair, is busy with generally worthwhile temporary exhibits. Get details on the current schedule from TIs or in *Pariscope* magazine (€9, not covered by Museum Pass, avenue Churchill, Mo: Rond Point or Champs-Elysées).

▲View from Hôtel Concorde-Lafayette—For a remarkable Parisian panorama, take the Métro to the pedestrian-unfriendly Porte Maillot stop, then follow *Palais de Congrés* signs to the glass-and-steel tower that houses this luxury hotel. Take an elevator in the rear of the lobby to floor 33, walk one flight up, and enter a sky-high world of semi-circular booths (rooftop bar open 17:30–02:00, €8 beers, €6 espressos, and jaw-dropping views, best before dark). If it's clear and the sun's about to set, spring for a drink—the ride was free (rooms start at €400, 3 place du General Koening, tel. 01 40 68 50 68, www.concorde-lafayette.com).

▲La Défense and La Grande Arche—On the outskirts of Paris, the centerpiece of Paris' ambitious skyscraper complex (La Défense) is the Grande Arche. Inaugurated in 1989 on the 200th anniversary of the French Revolution, it was dedicated to human rights and brotherhood. The place is big—38 floors holding offices for 30,000 people on more than 200 acres. Notre-Dame Cathedral could fit under its arch. The complex at La Défense is an interesting study in 1960s land-use planning. More than 100,000 workers commute here daily, directing lots of business and development away from downtown and allowing central Paris to retain its more elegant feel. This makes sense to most Parisians, regardless of whatever else they feel about this controversial complex. You will enjoy city views from the Grande Arche elevator.

Cost, Hours, Location: Grande Arche elevator-€7.50, kids-€6, family deals, not covered by Museum Pass, daily 10:00–19:00, RER or Mo: La Défense, follow signs to Grande Arche, tel. 01 49 07 27 57. The entry price includes art exhibits and a film on the Arche's construction.

Northeast Paris: The Marais Neighborhood and More

The Marais neighborhood extends along the Right Bank of the Seine from the Pompidou Center to the Bastille. It contains more pre-revolutionary lanes and buildings than anywhere else in town and is more atmospheric than touristy. It's medieval Paris. This is how much of the city looked until, in the mid-1800s, Napoleon III had Baron Haussmann blast out the narrow streets to construct broad boulevards (wide enough for the guns and ranks of the army, too wide for revolutionary barricades), thus creating modern Paris. Originally a swamp *(marais)* during the reign of Henry IV, this area became the hometown of the French aristocracy. In the 17th century, big shots built their private mansions *(hôtels)*, close to Henry IV's place des Vosges. When strolling the Marais, stick to the west–east axis formed by rue Sainte-Croix de la Bretonnerie,

Northeast Paris: The Marais Neighborhood and More

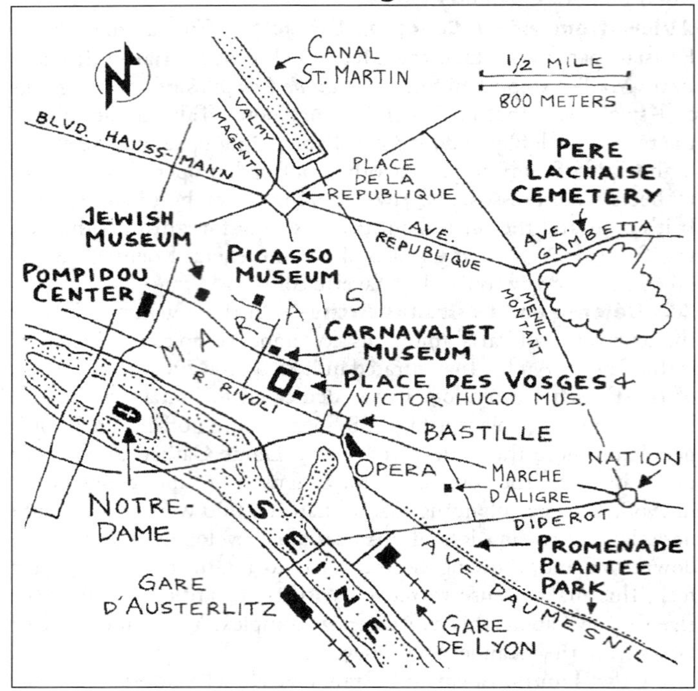

rue des Rosiers (heart of Paris' Jewish community), and rue St. Antoine. On Sunday afternoons, this trendy area pulses with shoppers and café crowds.

▲Place des Vosges—Study the architecture in this grand square: nine pavilions per side. Some of the brickwork is real, some is fake. Walk to the center, where Louis XIII sits on a horse surrounded by locals enjoying their community park. Children frolic in the sandbox, lovers warm benches, and pigeons guard their fountains while trees shade this retreat from the glare of the big city. Henry IV built this centerpiece of the Marais in 1605. As hoped, this turned the Marais into Paris' most exclusive neighborhood. As the nobility flocked to Versailles in a later age, this too was a magnet for the rich and powerful of France. With the Revolution, the aristocratic elegance of this quarter became working-class, filled with gritty shops, artisans, immigrants, and Jews. **Victor Hugo** lived at #6, and you can visit his house (free, Tue–Sun 10:00–18:00, closed Mon, 6 place des Vosges, tel. 01 42 72 10 16). Leave the place des Vosges through the doorway at southwest corner of the square (near the three-star Michelin restaurant, l'Ambrosie) and pass through the elegant **Hôtel de Sully** (great example of a Marais mansion) to rue St. Antoine.

▲▲Pompidou Center (Centre Pompidou)—One of Europe's greatest collections of far-out modern art is housed in the Musée National d'Art Moderne, on the fourth and fifth floors of this colorful, exoskeletal building. Once ahead of its time, this 20th-century (remember that century?) art has been waiting for the world to catch up with it. After so many Madonnas-and-Children, a piano smashed to bits and glued to the wall is refreshing.

The Pompidou Center and its square are lively, with lots of people, street theater, and activity inside and out—a perpetual street fair. Kids of any age enjoy the fun, colorful fountain called *Homage to Stravinsky*, next to the Pompidou Center. Don't miss the free exhibits on the ground floor of the Center. Ride the escalator for a great city view from the top (ticket or Museum Pass required), and consider the good mezzanine-level café.

Cost, Hours, Location: €7, free first Sun of month, covered by Museum Pass, Wed–Mon 11:00–21:00, closed Tue, Mo: Rambuteau, tel. 01 44 78 12 33, www.centrepompidou.fr.

Lunch: You'll find the cool Café La Mezzanine on Level 1 of the Pompidou and the snobby Chez Georges view restaurant on Level 6. Across from the entrance/exit, on rue Rambuteau, is the cheap, efficient Flunch self-service cafeteria. My favorite places line the Stravinsky fountain: Dame Tartine and Crêperie Beaubourg (to the right as you face the museum entrance).

▲▲Jewish Art and History Museum (Musée d'Art et Histoire du Judaïsme)—This fascinating museum is located in a beautifully restored Marais mansion and tells the story of Judaism throughout Europe, from the Roman destruction of Jerusalem to the theft of famous artworks during World War II.

The museum illustrates the cultural unity maintained by this continually dispersed population. You'll learn about the history of Jewish traditions from bar mitzvahs to menorahs, and see the exquisite traditional costumes and objects around which daily life revolved. Don't miss the explanation of "the Dreyfus affair," a major event in early 1900s French politics. You'll also see photographs of and paintings by famous Jewish artists, including Chagall, Modigliani, and Soutine. A small but moving section is devoted to the deportation of Jews from Paris.

Helpful, free audioguides and many English explanations make this an enjoyable history lesson (red numbers on small signs indicate the number you should press on your audioguide). Move along at your own speed.

Cost, Hours, Location: €7, includes audioguide, not covered by Museum Pass, Mon–Fri 11:00–18:00, Sun 10:00–18:00, closed Sat, 71 rue du Temple, Mo: Rambuteau or Hôtel de Ville a few blocks farther away, tel. 01 53 01 86 60, www.mahj.org.

▲▲Picasso Museum (Musée Picasso)—Tucked into a corner of the Marais and worth ▲▲▲ if you're a Picasso fan, this museum contains the world's largest collection of Picasso's paintings, sculptures, sketches, and ceramics, and includes his small collection of Impressionist art. The art is well-displayed in a fine old mansion with a peaceful garden café. The room-by-room English introductions help make sense of Picasso's work—from the Toulouse-Lautrec-like portraits at the beginning of his career to his gray-brown Cubist period to his return-to-childhood, Salvador Dalí-like finish. The well-done €3 English guidebook helps Picassophiles appreciate the context of his art and learn more about his interesting life. Most will be happy reading the posted English explanations while moving at a steady pace through the museum—the ground and first floors satisfied my curiosity.

Cost, Hours, Location: €5.50, free first Sun of month, covered by Museum Pass, April–Sept Wed–Mon 9:30–18:00, Oct–March Wed–Mon 9:30–17:30, closed Tue, 5 rue de Thorigny, Mo: St. Paul or Chemin Vert, tel. 01 42 71 25 21, www.musee-picasso.fr.

▲▲Carnavalet Museum (Musée Carnavalet)—The tumultuous history of Paris is well portrayed in this converted Marais mansion. Explanations are in French only, but many displays are fairly self-explanatory. You'll see paintings of Parisian scenes, French Revolution paraphernalia, old Parisian store signs, a small guillotine, a model of 16th-century Ile de la Cité (notice the bridge houses), and rooms full of 17th-century Parisian furniture.

Cost, Hours, Location: Free, Tue–Sun 10:00–18:00, closed Mon; avoid lunchtime (12:00–14:00), when many rooms close; 23 rue de Sévigné, Mo: St. Paul, tel. 01 44 59 58 58.

▲Promenade Plantée Park—This two-mile-long, narrow garden walk on a viaduct was once used for train tracks and is now a joy. Part of the park is elevated. At times, you'll walk along the street until you pick up the next segment. The shops below the viaduct's arches make for entertaining window-shopping.

Cost, Hours, Location: Free, opens Mon–Fri at 8:00, Sat–Sun at 9:00, closes at sunset. It runs from place de la Bastille (Mo: Bastille) along avenue Daumesnil to Saint-Mandé (Mo: Michel Bizot). From place de la Bastille (follow "Sortie Opéra" or "Sortie rue de Lyon" from Bastille Métro station), walk down rue de Lyon with the Opéra immediately on your left. Find the steps up the red brick wall a block after the Opéra.

▲Père Lachaise Cemetery (Cimetière du Père Lachaise)—Littered with the tombstones of many of the city's most illustrious dead, this is your best one-stop look at the fascinating, romantic world of "permanent Parisians." More like a small city, the cemetery is confusing, but maps will direct you to the graves of Frédéric

Chopin, Molière, Edith Piaf, Oscar Wilde, Gertrude Stein, Jim Morrison, Héloïse and Abélard, and more (helpful €2 maps sold at flower stores near either entry).

Cost, Hours, Location: Free, Mon–Sat from 8:00, Sun from 9:00, closes at dusk. It's down rue Père Lachaise from Mo: Gambetta, or across the street from the Père Lachaise Métro stop (also reachable via bus #69).

North Paris: Montmartre

▲▲Sacré-Cœur and Montmartre—The five-domed, Roman-Byzantine basilica of Sacré-Cœur took 44 years to build (1875–1919). It stands on a foundation of 83 pillars sunk 130 feet deep, necessary because the ground beneath was honeycombed with gypsum mines. The exterior is laced with gypsum, which whitens with age.

For an unobstructed panoramic view of Paris, climb 260 feet up the tight and claustrophobic spiral stairs to the top of the **dome** (church free, open daily 7:00–23:00; €5 to climb dome, daily June–Sept 9:00–19:00, Oct–May 10:00–18:00).

One block from the church, the **place du Tertre** was the haunt of Henri de Toulouse-Lautrec and the original bohemians. Today, it's mobbed with tourists and unoriginal bohemians, but it's still fun (go early in the morning to beat the crowds).

To get to Montmartre, take the Métro to the Anvers stop (one more Métro ticket buys your way up the funicular and avoids the stairs) or the closer but less scenic Abbesses stop. A taxi to the top of the hill saves time and avoids sweat. For restaurant recommendations, see "Eating," page 341.

Pigalle—Paris' red-light district, the infamous "Pig Alley," is at the foot of butte Montmartre. *Oo la la.* It's more shocking than dangerous. Walk from place Pigalle to place Blanche, teasing desperate barkers and fast-talking temptresses. In bars, a €150 bottle of cheap champagne comes with a friend. Stick to the bigger streets, hang on to your wallet, and exercise good judgment. Cancan can cost a fortune, as can con artists in topless bars. After dark, countless tour buses line the streets, reminding us that tour guides make big bucks by bringing their groups to touristy nightclubs like the famous Moulin Rouge (Mo: Pigalle or Abbesses).

Disappointments de Paris

Here are a few negatives to help you manage your limited time:

La Madeleine is a big, neoclassical church with a postcard facade and a postbox interior.

Paris' **Panthéon** (nothing like Rome's) is another neoclassical edifice filled with the mortal remains of great Frenchmen.

The **Bastille** is Paris' most famous non-sight. The square is there, but confused tourists look everywhere and can't find the famous prison of Revolution fame. The building's gone, and the square is good only as a jumping-off point for Promenade Plantée Park (see previous page).

Finally, much of the **Latin Quarter** is a frail shadow of its once-bohemian self. The blocks nearest the river (across from Notre-Dame) are more Tunisian, Greek, and Woolworth's than old-time Paris. The neighborhood merits a wander, but you're better off focusing on the area around boulevard St. Germain and rue de Buci, and on the streets around the Maubert-Mutualité Métro stop.

PALACE OF VERSAILLES

Every king's dream, Versailles was the residence of the French king and the cultural heartbeat of Europe for about 100 years—until the Revolution of 1789 ended the notion that God deputized some people to rule for Him on Earth. Louis XIV spent half a year's income of Europe's richest country turning his dad's hunting lodge into a palace fit for a divine monarch. Louis XV and Louis XVI spent much of the 18th century gilding Louis XIV's lily. In 1837, about 50 years after the royal family was evicted, King Louis Philippe opened the palace as a museum. Europe's next-best palaces are Versailles wannabes.

Cost: There are several different parts of the palace, each with a separate admission. The **State Apartments,** which are the most essential component, costs €7.50 (€5.50 after 15:30, covered by Museum Pass). Guided tours cost extra; see the "Touring Versailles from A to D" sidebar, page 312.

The **gardens** are normally €3 (not covered by Museum Pass), except on summer weekends, when the fountains blast and the price shoots up to €6 (see "Fountain Spectacles," page 311).

Entering the **Grand and Petit Trianon Palaces** costs €5 together (both covered by Museum Pass).

Two types of **all-day Versailles passes** are available for those without a Paris Museum Pass. Unless you plan to visit most of the sights within Versailles, neither of these passes is worth considering. Of the two, the better value is the **Versailles Pass**, which covers your train fare from Paris and gives you priority access to these entrances: State Apartments, the King's Private Apartments, both Trianon Palaces, the gardens, and Les Grand Eaux Musicales (see "Fountain Spectacles," below; note that these run only on summer weekends). The pass also includes an audioguide (€21, sold at Paris train stations, RER stations that serve Versailles, and FNAC department stores). The **Versailles Passport** covers the same sights and services, except for the train fare from Paris (€20, sold at Versailles TI, listed in "Information," below).

Versailles

WALKING TIMES

Train Station to Château = 10 min.
Château to Grand Trianon = 30 min.
Grand Trianon to Hamlet = 20 min.
Le Hamlet to Château = 30 min.

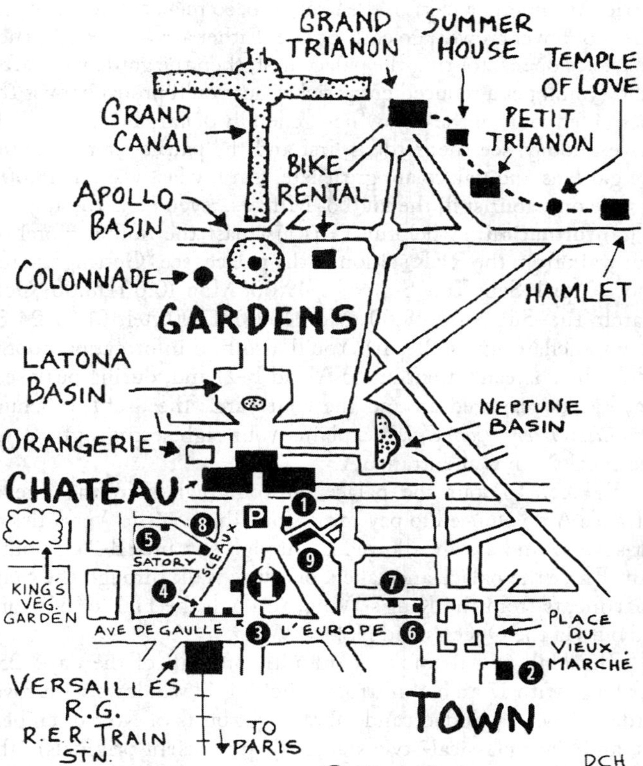

GRAND TRIANON
SUMMER HOUSE
TEMPLE OF LOVE
GRAND CANAL
PETIT TRIANON
BIKE RENTAL
APOLLO BASIN
COLONNADE
HAMLET
GARDENS
LATONA BASIN
NEPTUNE BASIN
ORANGERIE
CHATEAU
SATORY
SCEAUX
KING'S VEG. GARDEN
AVE DE GAULLE
L'EUROPE
PLACE DU VIEUX MARCHÉ
VERSAILLES R.G. R.E.R. TRAIN STN.
TO PARIS
TOWN
DCH

1. Hôtel de France
2. Hôtel le Cheval Rouge
3. Hôtel Ibis Versailles
4. Hôtel du Palais
5. Hôtel d'Angleterre
6. Rest. la Bœuf à la Mode
7. Rest. A la Côte Bretonne
8. Rest. le Limousin
9. Equestrian Performances

Hours: The **palace** is open May–Sept Tue–Sun 9:00–18:30, Oct–April Tue–Sun 9:00–17:30, closed Mon (last entry 30 min before closing). The **Grand and Petit Trianon Palaces** are open April–Oct Tue–Sun 12:00–18:00, Nov–March Tue–Sun 12:00–17:00, closed Mon. The **gardens** are open daily from 7:00 (8:00 in winter) to sunset (as late as 21:30 or as early as 17:30).

In summer, Versailles is especially crowded around 10:00 and 13:00, and all day Tuesday and Sunday. Remember, the crowds gave Marie-Antoinette a pain in the neck, too, so relax and let them eat cake. For fewer crowds, go early or late: Either arrive by 9:00 (when the palace opens, touring the palace first, then the gardens) or after 15:30 (you'll get a reduced entry ticket but you'll probably miss the last guided tours of the day, which generally depart at 15:00). If you arrive midday, see the gardens first and the palace later, at 15:00. The gardens and palace are great late. On my last visit, at 18:00 I was the only tourist in the Hall of Mirrors...even on a Tuesday.

Information: A helpful TI is just past the Sofitel Hôtel on your walk from the RER station to the palace (see "Getting There," below; April–Sept Tue–Sun 9:00–19:00, Mon 10:00–18:00, Oct–March Tue–Sun 9:00–18:00, Mon 10:00–17:00, tel. 01 39 24 88 88, www.chateauversailles.fr). You'll also find information booths inside the château (at entrances A and B-2) and, during peak season, kiosks scattered around the courtyard. The useful brochure *Versailles Orientation Guide* explains your sightseeing options. A free checkroom is at entrance A.

Palace: To tour the palace on your own, join the line at entrance A if you need to pay admission. Those with a Versailles or Paris Museum Pass are allowed in through entrance B-2 without a wait. Enter the palace and take a one-way walk through the State Apartments from the King's Wing, through the Hall of Mirrors, and out via the Queen's and Nobles' Wing.

The Hall of Mirrors was the ultimate hall of the day—250 feet long, with 17 arched mirrors matching 17 windows with royal garden views, 24 gilded candelabra, eight busts of Roman emperors, and eight classical-style statues (7 are ancient originals). The ceiling is decorated with stories of Louis' triumphs. Imagine this place filled with silk gowns and powdered wigs, lit by thousands of candles. The mirrors—a luxury at the time—were a reflection of an era when aristocrats felt good about their looks and their fortunes. In another age altogether, this was the room in which the Treaty of Versailles was signed, ending World War I.

Before going downstairs at the end, take a stroll clockwise around the long room filled with the great battles of France murals. If you don't have *Rick Steves' Paris* (buy in the United States), the guidebook called *The Châteaux, The Gardens, and Trianon* gives a room-by-room rundown.

Getting Around the Gardens: It's a 30-minute hike from the palace, down to the canal, past the two Trianon palaces to the Hamlet. The fast-looking, slow-moving tram for tired tourists leaves from behind the château (north side) and serves the Grand Canal and the Trianon palaces. You can hop on and off as you like (€5, 4/hr, 4 stops but not the Hamlet, commentary is nearly worthless). A horse carriage also departs from the north side of the palace. Or you can rent bikes near the Grand Canal (1 hr-€6).

Palace Gardens: The gardens offer a world of royal amusements. Outside the palace is *l'orangerie.* Louis, the only person who could grow oranges in Paris, had a mobile orange grove that could be wheeled in and out of his greenhouses according to the weather. A promenade leads from the palace to the Grand Canal, an artificial lake that, in Louis' day, was a mini-sea with nine ships, including a 32-cannon warship. France's royalty used to float up and down the canal in Venetian gondolas.

While Louis cleverly used palace life at Versailles to "domesticate" his nobility, turning otherwise meddlesome nobles into groveling socialites, all this pomp and ceremony hampered the royal family as well. For an escape from the public life at Versailles, they built more intimate palaces as retreats in their garden. Before the Revolution there was plenty of space to retreat—the grounds were enclosed by a 25-mile-long fence.

The beautifully restored **Grand Trianon Palace** is as sumptuous as the main palace, but much smaller. With its pastel-pink colonnade and more human scale, this is a place you'd like to call home. The nearby **Petit Trianon**, which has a fine neoclassical exterior and an interior that can be skipped, was Marie-Antoinette's favorite residence (see "Cost" and "Hours," above).

You can almost see princesses bobbing gaily in the branches as you walk through the enchanting forest, past the white marble temple of love (1778) to the queen's fake-peasant **Hamlet** (*le Hameau;* interior not tourable). Palace life really got to Marie-Antoinette. Sort of a back-to-basics queen, she retreated further and further from her blue-blooded reality. Her happiest days were spent at the Hamlet, under a bonnet, tending her perfumed sheep and her manicured gardens in a thatch-happy wonderland.

Fountain Spectacles: Classical music fills the king's backyard, and the garden's fountains are in full squirt, July–Sept on Sat and early April–early Oct on Sun (schedule for both days: 11:00–12:00 & 15:30–17:00 & 17:20–17:30). On these "spray days," the gardens cost €6 (not covered by Paris Museum Pass but covered by Versailles passes, ask for a map of fountains). Louis had his engineers literally reroute a river to fuel these fountains. Even by today's standards, they are impressive. Pick up the helpful brochure of the fountain show ("Les Grandes Eaux Musicales") at any information booth

Touring Versailles from A to D

Versailles' highlights are the State Apartments (including the magnificent Hall of Mirrors) and the gardens, dotted with the Trianon Palaces—both covered on our self-guided tour. Versailles aficionados should spend extra time and money to see the lavish King's Private Apartments, the Opera House, and more, which can be visited only with an audioguide or live guide.

Whether you have a Paris Museum Pass or one of the Versailles passes or you've paid admission (€7.50) to enter the palace, you have to pay extra to take a tour. If you pay the €7.50 admission, keep your ticket as proof you've paid for the palace entry, in case you decide to take a guided tour after you've wandered through Versailles by yourself.

Stand in the courtyard to orient yourself to Versailles' entrances:

Entrance A—State Apartments, Self-Guided Tour: If you don't have a Museum Pass and you want to tour the palace on your own (or with a €4 audioguide), join the line at entrance A. Enter the palace and take a one-way walk through the State Apartments from the King's Wing, through the Hall of Mirrors, and out via the Queen's and Nobles' Wing.

Entrance B-2: This entrance is for Museum Pass–holders who want to tour the palace on their own (following the €4 audioguide).

Entrance C—King's Private Apartments: If you lack a Museum Pass, enter here to tour Louis XIV's private bedroom, other rooms, and the Hall of Mirrors, with the help of a dry but informative audioguide (€4).

Entrance C-2: Same as C but for passholders.

Entrance D—Various Guided Tours: You can select a one-hour live tour from a variety of themes, such as the daily life of a king or the lives of such lesser-known nobles as the well-coiffed Madame de Pompadour (€4, join first English tour available). Or consider the 90-minute tour (€6) of the King's Private Apartments (Louis XV, Louis XVI, and Marie-Antoinette) and the chapel. This tour, which is the only way visitors can see the sumptuous Opera House, can be long depending on the quality of your guide.

For a live tour, make reservations immediately upon arrival, as tours can sell out by 13:00 (first tours generally begin at 10:00, last tours depart usually at 15:00 but as late as 16:00).

The Gardens: If you want to visit these first, go around the left side of the palace. The spacious gardens stretch for miles behind the palace, featuring landscaped plots, statues, bubbling fountains, a Grand Canal, and several smaller palaces, interesting both outside and in.

Entrance to Versailles

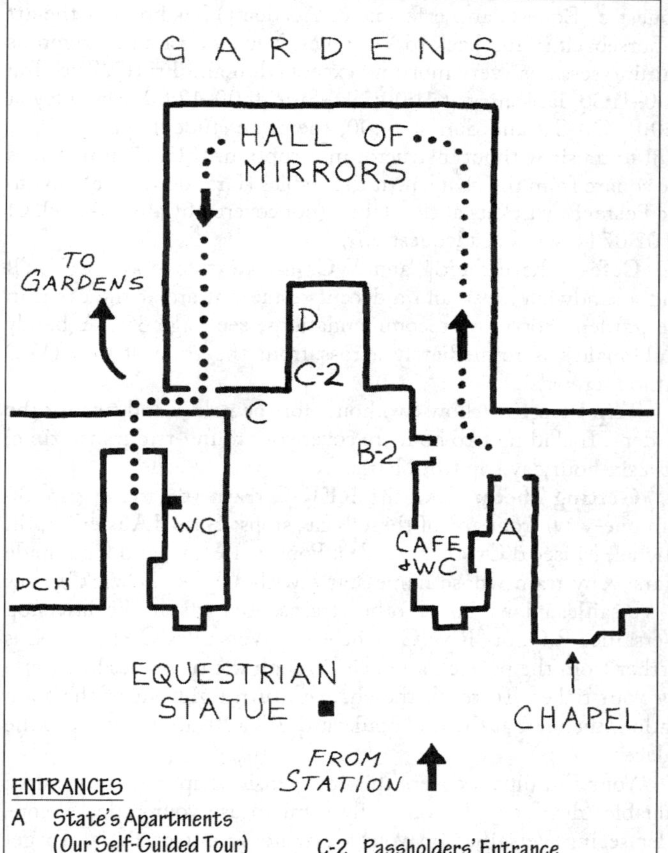

ENTRANCES

- A State's Apartments (Our Self-Guided Tour)
- B-2 Museum Passholders' Entrance
- C King's Private Apartments (with Audioguide)
- C-2 Passholders' Entrance for King's Private Apartments
- D Various Guided Tours
- • • • = Tour Route

for a guide to the fountains. Also ask about the impressive *Les Fêtes de Nuit* nighttime spectacle (July–mid-Sept some Sat).

Equestrian Performances: The Academie du Spectacle Equestre (Equestrian Performance Academy) has brought the art of horseback riding back to Versailles. You can watch its rigorous training sessions every morning except Mon and Fri (€7, Tue–Thu 9:00–11:30, last entry at 11:00; Sat–Sun 10:00–12:00, last entry at 11:00). On Sat and Sun at 14:00, the same students parade their stuff to music without instructor interruptions (€15, 75 min) across the square from the château, at the stables (Grande Ecurie) next to the Poste. Buy tickets at the stables (not covered by any pass, tel. 01 39 02 07 14, www.acadequestre.fr).

Cafés: The cafeteria and WCs are next to door A. You'll find a sandwich kiosk and a decent restaurant are at the canal in the garden. For more recommendations, see page 355. A handy McDonald's is immediately across from the train station (WC without crowds).

Trip Length: Allow two hours for the palace and two for the gardens. Including two hours to cover your round-trip transit time, it's a six-hour day trip from Paris.

Getting There: Take the **RER-C train** (€6 round-trip, 30 min one-way) from any of these RER stops: Gare d'Austerlitz, St. Michel, Musée d'Orsay, Invalides, Pont de l'Alma, and Champ de Mars. Any train whose name starts with a V (e.g., "Vick") goes to Versailles; don't board other trains. Get off at the last stop (Versailles R.G. or "Rive Gauche"—not Versailles C.H., which is farther from the palace), and exit through the turnstiles by inserting your ticket. To reach the château, turn right out of the train station, then left at the first boulevard. It's a 10-minute walk to the palace.

Your Eurailpass covers this inexpensive trip, but it uses up a valuable "flexi" day. If you really want to use your railpass, consider seeing Versailles on your way into or out of Paris. To get free passage, show your railpass at an SCNF ticket window—for example, at the Invalides or Musée d'Orsay RER stop—and get a *contremarque de passage*. Keep this ticket to exit the system.

When returning to Paris from Versailles, look through the windows past the turnstiles for the departure board. Any train leaving Versailles serves all downtown Paris RER stops on the C line (they're marked on the schedule as stopping at *"toutes les gares jusqu'à Austerlitz,"* meaning "all stations up to Austerlitz").

Taxis for the 30-minute ride between Versailles and Paris cost about €25–30.

To reach Versailles from Paris by **car,** get on the *périphérique* freeway that circles Paris and take the toll-free autoroute A-13 toward Rouen. Follow signs into Versailles, then look for *château* signs and park in the huge pay lot in front of the palace. The drive takes about 30 minutes one-way.

Town of Versailles: After the palace closes and the tourists go, the prosperous, wholesome town of Versailles feels a long way from Paris. The central market thrives on place du Marché on Sunday, Tuesday, and Friday until 13:00 (leaving the RER station, turn right and walk 10 min). Consider the wisdom of picking up or dropping your rental car in Versailles rather than in Paris. In Versailles, the Hertz and Avis offices are at Gare des Chantiers (Versailles C.H., served by Paris' Montparnasse station). Versailles makes a fine home base; see Versailles accommodations and recommended restaurants under "Sleeping" (page 319) and "Eating" (page 341).

SHOPPING

Even staunch anti-shoppers may be tempted to partake in chic Paris. Wandering among the elegant and outrageous boutiques provides a break from the heavy halls of the Louvre, and, if you approach it right, a little cultural enlightenment.

Here are some tips for avoiding *faux pas* and making the most of the experience.

French Etiquette: Before you enter a Parisian store, remember the following points.

- In small stores, always greet the clerk by saying "*Bonjour,*" plus the appropriate title (*Madame, Mademoiselle,* or *Monsieur*). When leaving, say, "*Au revoir, Madame/Mademoiselle/Monsieur.*"
- The customer is not always right. In fact, figure the clerk is doing you a favor by waiting on you.
- Except for in department stores, it's not normal for the customer to handle clothing. Ask first.
- Observe French shoppers. Then imitate.

Department Stores: Like cafés, department stores were invented here (surprisingly, not in America). Parisian department stores, monuments to a more relaxed and elegant era, begin with their spectacular perfume sections. Helpful information desks are usually nearby (pick up the handy store floor plan in English). Most stores have a good selection of souvenirs and toys at fair prices and reasonable restaurants; some have great view terraces. Choose from these four great Parisian department stores: Galeries Lafayette (behind old Opéra Garnier, Mo: Opéra), Printemps (next-door to Galeries Lafayette), Bon Marché (Mo: Sèvres-Babylone), and Samaritaine (near pont Neuf, Mo: Pont Neuf).

Boutiques: I enjoy window-shopping, pausing at cafés, and observing the rhythm of neighborhood life. While the shops are more intimate, sales clerks are more formal—mind your manners.

Here are four very different areas to explore:

A stroll from Sèvres-Babylone to St. Sulpice allows you to sample smart, classic clothing boutiques while enjoying one of Paris' prettier neighborhoods—for sustenance along the way, there's La Maison du Chocolat at 19 rue de Sèvres, selling handmade chocolates in exquisitely wrapped boxes.

The ritzy streets connecting place de la Madeleine and place Vendôme form a miracle mile of gourmet food shops, jewelry stores, four-star hotels, perfumeries, and exclusive clothing boutiques. Fauchon, on place de la Madeleine, is a bastion of over-the-top food products, hawking €7,000 bottles of Cognac (who buys this stuff?). Hédiard, at #21, across the square from Fauchon, is an older, more appealing, and accessible gourmet food shop. Next door, La Maison des Truffes sells black mushrooms for about €180 a pound, and white truffles from Italy for €2,500 a pound.

For more eclectic, avant-garde stores, peruse the artsy shops between the Pompidou Center and place des Vosges in the Marais (along rue Ste. Croix de la Bretonnerie and rue des Rosiers).

For a contemporary, more casual, and less frenetic shopping experience, and to see Paris' latest urban renewal project, take the Métro to Bercy Village, a once-thriving wine warehouse district that has been transformed into an outdoor shopping mall (Mo: Cour St. Emilion).

Flea Markets: Paris hosts several sprawling weekend flea markets (*marché aux puces,* mar-shay oh poos; literally translated, since *puce* is French for flea). These oversized garage sales date back to the Middle Ages, when middlemen would sell old, flea-infested clothes and discarded possessions of the wealthy at bargain prices to eager peasants. Today, some travelers find them claustrophobic, crowded, monster versions of those back home, though others find their French diamonds-in-the-rough and return happy.

The Puces St. Ouen (poos sahn-wahn) is the biggest and oldest of them all, with more than 2,000 vendors selling everything from flamingos to faucets (Sat 9:00–18:30, Sun–Mon 10:00–18:30, Mo: Porte de Clingancourt).

Street Markets: Several traffic-free street markets overflow with flowers, produce, fish vendors, and butchers, illustrating how most Parisians shopped before there were supermarkets and department stores. Good market streets include the rue Cler (Mo: Ecole Militaire), rue Montorgueil (Mo: Etienne Marcel), rue Mouffetard (Mo: Cardinal Lemoine or Censier-Daubenton), and rue Daguerre (Mo: Denfert-Rochereau). Browse these markets to collect a classy picnic (open daily except Sun afternoons and Mon, also closed for lunch 13:00–15:00).

Souvenir Shops: Avoid souvenir carts in front of famous monuments. Prices and selection are better in shops and department stores. The riverfront stalls near Notre-Dame sell a variety of used books, magazines, and tourist paraphernalia in the most romantic setting.

Whether you indulge in a new wardrobe, an artsy poster, or just one luscious pastry, you'll find that a shopping excursion provides a priceless slice of Parisian life.

NIGHTLIFE

Paris is brilliant after dark. Save energy from your day's sightseeing and get out at night. Whether it's a concert at Sainte-Chapelle, an elevator up the Arc de Triomphe, or a late-night café, experience the City of Light when it's lit up. If a **Seine River cruise** sounds appealing, check out "Tours," on page 273.

Pariscope magazine (see "Tourist Information," page 263), offers a complete weekly listing of music, cinema, theater, opera, and other special events. *Paris Voice* newspaper, in English, has a monthly review of Paris entertainment (available at any English-language bookstore, French-American establishments, or the American Church, www.parisvoice.com).

Music

Jazz Clubs: With a lively mix of American, French, and international musicians, Paris has been an internationally acclaimed jazz capital since World War II. You'll pay €10–25 to enter a jazz club (1 drink may be included; if not, expect to pay €5–10 per drink; beer is cheapest). See *Pariscope* magazine under "Musique" for listings, or better, the American Church's *Paris Voice* paper for a good monthly review, or drop by the clubs to check out the calendars posted on their front doors. Music starts after 21:00 in most clubs. Some offer dinner concerts from about 20:30 on. Here are several good bets:

Caveau de la Huchette, a characteristic old jazz club, fills an ancient Latin Quarter cellar with live jazz and frenzied dancing every night (about €10 admission on weekdays, €14 on weekends, €6 drinks, Tue–Sun 21:30–2:30 or later, closed Mon, 5 rue de la Huchette, Mo: St. Michel, recorded info tel. 01 43 26 65 05, www.caveaudelahuchette.fr).

For a hotbed of late-night activity and jazz, go to the two-block-long rue des Lombards, at boulevard Sébastopol, midway between the river and the Pompidou Center (Mo: Châtelet). **Au Duc des Lombards,** right at the corner, is one of the most popular and respected jazz clubs in Paris, with concerts generally at 21:00 (42 rue des Lombards, tel. 01 42 33 22 88). **Le Sunside** offers more traditional jazz—Dixieland and big band—and fewer crowds, with concerts generally at 21:00 (60 rue des Lombards, tel. 01 40 26 21 25).

At the more down-to-earth and mellow **Le Cave du Franc Pinot,** you can enjoy a glass of chardonnay at the main-floor wine bar, then drop downstairs for a cool jazz scene. They have good dinner-and-jazz values as well—allow about €50 per person (closed Sun–Mon, located on Ile St. Louis where pont Marie meets the island, 1 quai de Bourbon, Mo: Pont Marie, tel. 01 46 33 60 64).

Classical Concerts: For classical music on any night, consult *Pariscope* magazine; the "Musique" section under "Concerts Classiques" lists concerts (both free and with fee). Look for posters at tourist-oriented churches. From March through November, these churches regularly host concerts: St. Sulpice, St. Germain-des-Prés, Ste. Madeleine, St. Eustache, St. Julien-le-Pauvre, and Sainte-Chapelle. It's worth the €15–23 entry for the pleasure of hearing Mozart while surrounded by the stained glass of the tiny Sainte-Chapelle (it's unheated—bring a sweater). Look also for daytime concerts in parks, such as the Luxembourg Garden. Even the Galeries Lafayette department store offers concerts. Many concerts are free *(entrée libre),* such as the Sunday atelier concert sponsored by the American Church (Sun 18:00, not every week, Sept–May, 65 quai d'Orsay, Mo: Invalides, RER: Pont de l'Alma, tel. 01 40 62 05 00).

Opera: Paris is home to two well-respected opera venues. The Opéra Bastille is the massive modern opera house that dominates place de la Bastille. Come here for state-of-the-art special effects and modern interpretations of classic ballets and operas. In the spirit of this everyman's opera, unsold seats are available at a big discount to seniors and students 15 minutes before the show (Mo: Bastille, tel. 01 43 43 96 96). The Opéra Garnier, Paris' first opera house, hosts opera and ballet performances. Come here for less expensive tickets and grand belle époque decor (Mo: Opéra, tel. 01 44 73 13 99). For tickets, call 01 44 73 13 00, go to the opera ticket offices (open 11:00–18:00), or best, reserve on the Web at www.opera-de-paris.fr (French only, for both opera houses).

After-Dark Bus Tours

Several companies offer evening tours of Paris. I've described two here. These trips are sold through your hotel (brochures in lobby) or directly at the offices listed below. You save no money by buying direct.

Paris Illumination Tours, run by Paris Vision, connect all the great illuminated sights of Paris with a 100-minute bus tour in 12 languages. The double-decker buses have huge windows, but the most desirable front seats are reserved for customers who've bought tickets for the overrated Moulin Rouge. Left-side seats are marginally better. Visibility is fine in the rain.

You'll stampede on with a United Nations of tourists, get an audioguide, and listen to a tape-recorded spiel, which is interesting but occasionally hard to hear. Uninspired as it is, this provides an entertaining first-night overview of the city at its floodlit and scenic best. Bring your city map to stay oriented as you go. You're always on the bus except for one five-minute cigarette break at the Eiffel Tower viewpoint (adults-€26, kids under 11 ride free, departures 19:00–21:30 depending on time of year, usually April–Oct only, departs from Paris Vision office at 214 rue de Rivoli, across the street from Mo: Tuileries, tel. 01 42 60 30 01, fax 01 42 86 95 36, www.parisvision.com).

Touringscope offers the same kind of bus tour but with live guides (they try to keep the different languages to no more than three). This smaller, "we try harder" company offers better service and if their big buses don't fill up, they'll send you in a more personal minivan (buses depart from 11 boulevard Haussmann, Mo: Opéra or Chausée d'Antin-La Fayette, tel. 01 53 34 11 94, www.touringscope.com).

SLEEPING

I've focused most of my recommendations on three safe, handy, and colorful neighborhoods: the village-like rue Cler (near the Eiffel Tower), the artsy and trendy Marais (near place de la Bastille), and the lively and Latin yet classy Luxembourg (on the Left Bank). Before reserving, read the descriptions of the three neighborhoods closely. Each offers different pros and cons, and your neighborhood is as important as your hotel for the success of your trip.

Reserve ahead for Paris—the sooner the better. Conventions clog Paris in September (worst), October, May, and June (very tough). In August, when Paris is quiet, some hotels offer lower rates to fill their rooms (if you're planning to visit Paris in the summer, the extra expense of an air-conditioned room can be money well spent). For advice on booking rooms, see "Making Reservations" in this book's introduction.

Old, characteristic, budget Parisian hotels have always been cramped. Retrofitted with elevators, toilets, and private showers (as most are today), they are even more cramped. Even three-star hotel rooms are small and often not worth the extra expense in Paris. Some hotels include the hotel tax (*taxe du séjour*, about €1 per person per day), though most will add this to your bill.

Recommended hotels have an elevator unless otherwise noted. Quad rooms usually have two double beds. Because rooms with double beds and showers are cheaper than rooms with twin beds and baths, room prices vary within each hotel.

Continental breakfasts run about €6–9, buffet breakfasts (baked

Sleep Code

(€1 = about $1.20, country code: 33)
S = Single, **D** = Double/Twin, **T** = Triple, **Q** = Quad, **b** = bathroom, **s** = shower only, * = French hotel rating system (0-4 stars). Hotels with two or more stars are required to have an English-speaking staff. Nearly all hotels listed here will have someone who speaks English. You can assume a hotel takes credit cards unless you see "cash only" in the listing.

To help you sort easily through these listings, I've divided the rooms into three categories based on the price for a standard double room with bath:

$$$ **Higher Priced**—Most rooms €150 or more.
$$ **Moderately Priced**—Most rooms between €100–150.
$ **Lower Priced**—Most rooms €100 or less.

goods, cereal, yogurt, and fruit) cost about €8–14. Café or picnic breakfasts are cheaper, but hotels usually give unlimited coffee.

Get advice from your hotel for safe parking (consider long-term parking at either airport—Orly is closer—and a taxi in). Garages are plentiful (€20–25/day, with special rates through some hotels). Self-serve launderettes are common; ask your hotelier for the nearest one (*"Où est un laverie automatique?"*, ooh ay uh lah-vay-ree auto-mah-teek).

Rue Cler

Rue Cler is a safe, tidy, village-like pedestrian street. It's so French that when I step out of my hotel in the morning, I feel like I must have been a poodle in a previous life. How such coziness lodged itself between the high-powered government district and the wealthy Eiffel Tower and Invalides areas, I'll never know. This is a neighborhood of wide, tree-lined boulevards, stately apartment buildings, and lots of Americans. The American Church, American Library, American University, and many of my readers call this area home.

Become a local at a rue Cler café for breakfast or join the afternoon crowd for *une bière pression* (a draft beer). On rue Cler, you can eat and browse your way through a street full of pastry shops, delis, cheese shops, and colorful outdoor produce stalls. Afternoon *boules* (lawn bowling) on the Esplanade des Invalides is a relaxing spectator sport (look for the dirt area to the upper right as you face Les Invalides). The manicured gardens behind the golden dome of Les Invalides are free, peaceful, and filled with flowers (at southwest corner of grounds, close at about 19:00). Take an evening stroll above the river through the parkway between pont de l'Alma and pont des Invalides.

For an after-dinner cruise on the Seine, it's a 15-minute walk to the river and the Bateaux-Mouches (see page 273). For a post-dinner cruise on foot, saunter into Champ de Mars park to admire the glowing Eiffel Tower.

Cross the Champ de Mars park to mix it up with bargain-hunters at the twice-weekly open-air market, **Marché Boulevard de Grenelle,** under the Métro a few blocks southwest of Champ de Mars park (Wed and Sun until 12:30, between Mo: Dupleix and Mo: La Motte-Picquet-Grenelle). The Epicerie de la Tour **grocery** is open until midnight (197 rue de Grenelle). Rue St. Dominique is the area's boutique-browsing street. **Cyber World Café** is at 20 rue de l'Exposition (open daily 12:00–22:00, Sun until 20:00, tel. 01 53 59 96 54).

Your neighborhood **TI** is at the Eiffel Tower (May–Sept daily 11:00–18:42, closed Oct–April, all-Paris TI tel. 08 36 68 31 12). There's a **post office** at the end of rue Cler on avenue de la Motte-Picquet, and a handy **SNCF train office** at 78 rue St. Dominique (Mon–Fri 9:00–19:00, Sat 10:00–12:30 & 14:00–18:00, closed Sun).

The **American Church and Franco-American Center** is the community center for Americans living in Paris, and should be one of your first stops if you're planning to stay awhile (reception open Mon–Sat 9:00–22:00, Sun 9:00–19:30, 65 quai d'Orsay,tel. 01 40 62 05 00). Pick up a copy of *Paris Voice* for a monthly review of Paris entertainment, and *France–U.S.A. Contacts* for information on housing and employment through the community of 30,000 Americans living in Paris. The interdenominational services at 11:00 on Sunday, the coffee hour after church, and the free Sunday concerts (Sept–May 18:00, not every week) are a great way to make some friends and get a taste of émigré life in Paris.

Key **Métro** stops are Ecole Militaire, La Tour-Maubourg, and Invalides. The **RER-C** line runs from the Pont de l'Alma and Invalides stations, serving Versailles to the west; Auvers-sur-Oise to the north; and the Orsay Museum, Latin Quarter (St. Michel stop), and Austerlitz train station to the east.

Smart travelers take advantage of these helpful **bus routes** (see Rue Cler Hotels map, previous page, for stop locations): Line #69 runs along rue St. Dominique and serves Les Invalides, Orsay, Louvre, Marais, and Père Lachaise Cemetery. Line #63 runs along the river (the quai d'Orsay), serving the Latin Quarter along boulevard St. Germain to the east, and Trocadéro and the Marmottan Museum to the west. Line #92 runs along avenue Bosquet north to the Champs-Elysées and Arc de Triomphe (far better than the Métro) and south to the Montparnasse Tower. Line #87 runs on

Rue Cler Hotels

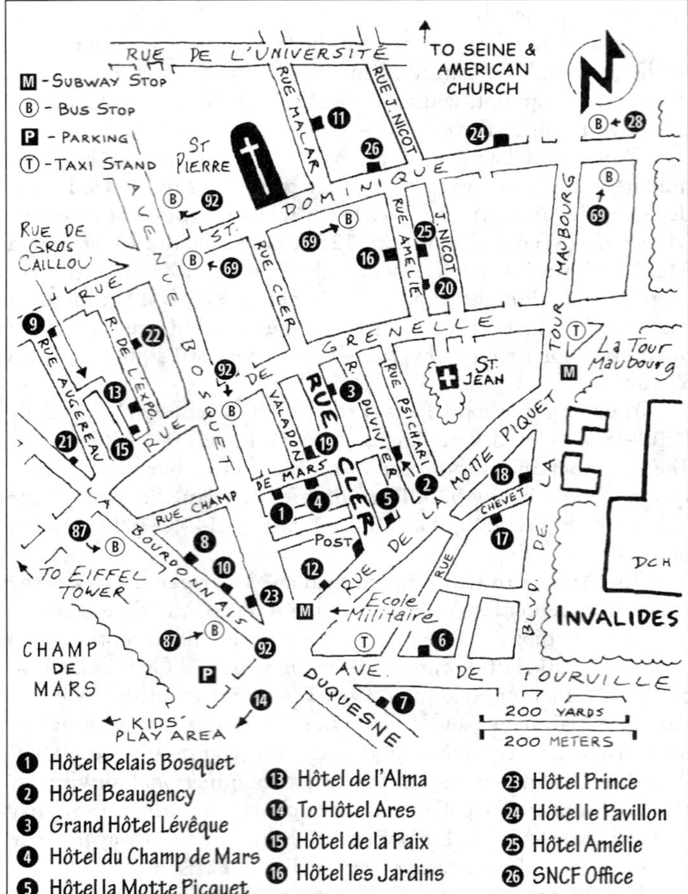

1 Hôtel Relais Bosquet
2 Hôtel Beaugency
3 Grand Hôtel Lévêque
4 Hôtel du Champ de Mars
5 Hôtel la Motte Picquet
6 Hôtels le Tourville & de Turenne
7 Hôtel Splendid
8 Hôtel de la Bourdonnais
9 Hôtel Londres Eiffel
10 Eber-Mars Hôtel
11 Hôtel de la Tulipe
12 Hôtel Royal Phare
13 Hôtel de l'Alma
14 To Hôtel Ares
15 Hôtel de la Paix
16 Hôtel les Jardins Eiffel
17 Hôtel Muguet
18 Hôtel de l'Empereur
19 Hôtel du Cadran
20 Best Western Eiffel Park
21 Hôtel Kensington
22 Hôtel de la Tour Eiffel
23 Hôtel Prince
24 Hôtel le Pavillon
25 Hôtel Amélie
26 SNCF Office

BUS ROUTES

28 Bus to Gare St. Lazare
69 Bus to Orsay, Louvre & Marais
92 Bus to Arc de Triomphe
87 Bus to Lux. Garden

avenue de la Bourdonnais and serves St. Sulpice, Luxembourg Garden, and the Sèvres-Babylone shopping area (also more convenient than Métro for these destinations). Line #28 runs on boulevard de la Tour-Maubourg and serves Gare St. Lazare.

Sleeping in the Rue Cler Neighborhood

(7th *arrondissement,* Mo: Ecole Militaire or La Tour-Maubourg) Rue Cler is the glue that holds this handsome neighborhood together. From here you can walk to the Eiffel Tower, Napoleon's Tomb, the Seine River, and the Orsay and Rodin museums. Hotels here are relatively spacious and a good value, considering the elegance of the neighborhood and the higher prices of the more cramped hotels in other central areas.

Many of my readers stay in this neighborhood. If you want to disappear into Paris, choose a hotel away from the rue Cler, or in the other neighborhoods I list. And if nightlife matters, sleep elsewhere. The first five hotels listed below are within Camembert-smelling distance of rue Cler; the others are within a 5- to 10-minute stroll.

The Heart of Rue Cler

$$$ Hôtel Relais Bosquet*** is modern, spacious, and a bit upscale, with snazzy, air-conditioned rooms, electric darkness blinds, and big beds. Gerard and his staff are politely formal and friendly (standard Db-€150, spacious Db-€170, Sb- €20 less, ask about occasional promotional rates, extra bed-€20, parking-€14, 19 rue du Champ de Mars, tel. 01 47 05 25 45, fax 01 45 55 08 24, www.relaisbosquet.com, hotel@relaisbosquet.com).

$$$ Hôtel la Motte Picquet*,** at the end of rue Cler, is an elaborately decorated, plush place with 18 adorable and spendy rooms. Most face a busy street but the twins are on the quieter side (Sb-€115–125, standard Db-€130, bigger Db with air-con-€165, 30 avenue de la Motte-Picquet, tel. 01 47 05 09 57, fax 01 47 05 74 36, www.paris-hotel-mottepicquet.com, book@hotelmottepicquetparis.com).

$$ Hôtel Beaugency*,** on a quieter street a short block off rue Cler, has 30 small, cookie-cutter rooms, a helpful staff, and a lobby you can stretch out in (Sb-€95, Db-€115, Tb-€130, air-con, 21 rue Duvivier, tel. 01 47 05 01 63, fax 01 45 51 04 96, www.hotel-beaugency.com, infos@hotel-beaugency.com).

Warning: The next two hotels listed here are busy with my readers (reserve long in advance).

$ Grand Hôtel Lévêque** is ideally located, with a helpful staff (Christophe and female Pascale SE), a singing maid, and a Starship *Enterprise* elevator. The simple but well-designed rooms have all the comforts, including air-conditioning and ceiling fans (S-€57, Db-€87–110, Tb-€125 for 2 adults and 1 child only, breakfast-€8, first breakfast free for readers of this book, 29 rue Cler, tel. 01 47 05 49 15, fax 01 45 50 49 36, www.hotel-leveque.com, info@hotel-leveque.com).

$ Hôtel du Champ de Mars**, with charming pastel rooms and helpful English-speaking owners Françoise and Stephane, is a homier rue Cler option. This plush little hotel has a Provence-style, small-town feel from top to bottom. Rooms are small, but comfortable and an excellent value. Single rooms can work as tiny doubles (Sb-€70, Db-€76–85, Tb-€98, 30 yards off rue Cler at 7 rue du Champ de Mars, tel. 01 45 51 52 30, fax 01 45 51 64 36, www.hotel-du-champ-de-mars.com, stg@club-internet.fr).

Near Rue Cler, Close to Ecole Militaire Métro

The following listings are a 5- to 10-minute walk from rue Cler, near Métro stop Ecole Militaire or RER stop Pont de l'Alma.

$$$ Hôtel le Tourville**** is the most classy and expensive of my rue Cler listings. This four-star place is surprisingly intimate, from its designer lobby and vaulted breakfast area to its pretty but small pastel rooms (small standard Db-€165, superior Db-€215, Db with private terrace-€240, junior suite for 3-4 people-€310–330, air-con, 16 avenue de Tourville, tel. 01 47 05 62 62, fax 01 47 05 43 90, www.hoteltourville.com, hotel@tourville.com).

$$$ Hôtel de la Bourdonnais*** is a *très* Parisian place, mixing Old World elegance with professional service, comfortable public spaces, and mostly spacious, traditionally decorated rooms (avoid the few *petite* rooms, Sb-€125, Db-€155, Tb-€175, Qb-€195, 5-person suite-€210, air-con, Internet access, 111 avenue de la Bourdonnais, tel. 01 47 05 45 42, fax 01 45 55 75 54, www.hotellabourdonnais.fr, hlb@hotellabourdonnais.fr).

$$ Hôtel Prince**, across avenue Bosquet from the Ecole Militaire Métro stop, has good-enough rooms, air-conditioning, and reasonable rates (Sb-€76, Db-€90–120, Tb-€130, 66 avenue Bosquet, tel. 01 47 05 40 90, fax 01 47 53 06 62, www.hotel-paris-prince.com).

$ Eber-Mars Hôtel**, on a busy street with oak-paneled public spaces, is a good midrange value with larger-than-average rooms and a beam-me-up-Jacques coffin-sized elevator (standard Db-€80, large Db-€95–115, Tb-€140, Qb-€160, pricey €10 breakfast, 117 avenue de la Bourdonnais, tel. 01 47 05 42 30, fax 01 47 05 45 91, www.hotelebermars.com, reservation@hotelebermars.com).

$ Hôtel Royal Phare** is a simple place facing the busy Ecole Militaire Métro stop with a "we try harder" staff. The 34 rooms are unimaginative with pink-pastel decor; those on the courtyard are quietest (Sb-€68, Db-€72–82, Tb-€105, 40 avenue de la Motte-Picquet, tel. 01 47 05 57 30, fax 01 45 51 64 41, www.hotel-royalphare-paris.com, royalphare-hotel@wanadoo.fr).

$ Hôtel de Turenne**, is a basic, well-located place with the cheapest air-conditioned rooms I found. While the rooms could use some work, the price is right. There are five truly single rooms and several connecting rooms good for families (Sb-€63, Db-€72–85, Tb-€100, extra bed-€10, 20 avenue de Tourville, tel. 01 47 05 99 92, fax 01 45 56 06 04, hotel.turenne.paris7@wanadoo.fr).

Near Rue Cler, Closer to Rue St. Dominique (and the Seine)

$$ Hôtel Londres Eiffel*** is my closest listing to the Eiffel Tower and Champ de Mars park. It offers immaculate, warmly decorated rooms, cozy public spaces, Internet access, and air-conditioning. The helpful staff takes good care of their guests. It's less convenient to the Métro (10-min walk); handy bus #69 and the RER stop Pont de l'Alma are better options (Sb-€99–105, Db-€110–145, deluxe Db-€175, Tb-€165–195, extra bed-€20, 1 rue Augerau, tel. 01 45 51 63 02, fax 01 47 05 28 96, www.londres-eiffel.com, info@londres-eiffel.com).

$$ Hôtel de la Tulipe*** is a unique place three blocks from rue Cler toward the river, with friendly Bernhard behind the desk. The smallish but artistically decorated rooms—each one different—come with little, stylish bathrooms and surround a seductive wood-beamed lounge and a peaceful, leafy courtyard (Db-€110–140, Tb-€180, 2-room suite-€250, no elevator, no air-con, 33 rue Malar, tel. 01 45 51 67 21, fax 01 47 53 96 37, www.paris-hotel-tulipe.com).

$ Hôtel de l'Alma** is a basic place but well-located on "restaurant row," with cheery rooms, small bathrooms, a *petite* courtyard, and reasonable rates (Sb-€85, Db-€95, includes breakfast, 32 rue de l'Exposition, tel. 01 47 05 45 70, fax 01 45 51 84 47, www.alma-paris-hotel.com, Carine SE).

Near Métro: La Tour-Maubourg

The next three listings are within two blocks of the intersection of avenue de la Motte-Picquet and boulevard de la Tour-Maubourg.

$$$ Hôtel les Jardins Eiffel***, on a quiet street, feels like a modern motel, but earns its three stars with professional service, its own parking garage, a spacious lobby, and 80 comfortable (if unimaginative), air-conditioned rooms—some with private balconies (ask for a room *avec petit balcon*). Even better: Readers of this book get free buffet breakfasts (Sb-€100–136, Db-€115–165, extra bed-€25–35 or free for a child, parking-€20/day, Internet access, 8 rue Amélie, tel. 01 47 05 46 21, fax 01 45 55 28 08, www.hoteljardinseiffel.com, paris@hoteljardinseiffel.com).

$$ Hôtel Muguet**, a peaceful, stylish, and immaculate refuge, gives you three-star comfort for a two-star price. This delightful place offers 48 tasteful, air-conditioned rooms, a greenhouse lounge, and a small garden courtyard. The hands-on owner, Catherine, gives her guests a restful and secure home in Paris (Sb-€90, Db-€100–108, Tb-€140, 11 rue Chevert, tel. 01 47 05 05 93, fax 01 45 50 25 37, www.hotelmuguet.com, muguet@wanadoo.fr).

$ Hôtel de l'Empereur** lacks intimacy but is roomy and a fair value. Its 38 pleasant rooms come with real wood furniture, and all the comforts except air-conditioning. Streetside rooms have views but some noise; fifth-floor rooms have small balconies and Napoleonic views (Sb-€70–80, Db-€80–100, Tb-€120, Qb-€140, 2 rue Chevert, tel. 01 45 55 88 02, fax 01 45 51 88 54, www.hotelempereur.com, contact@hotelempereur.com).

The Other Side of Champ de Mars Park

To stay in a peaceful neighborhood with many qualities of the rue Cler area (in the 7th *arrondissement*), cross Champ de Mars park and enter the 15th *arrondissement*. While it's a 10- to 15-minute walk to rue Cler, you get more space for your money and fewer fellow Americans.

$$ Hôtel Ares*** is handsome and situated on a quiet street a block toward the river from avenue de le Motte-Picquet. It has a classy lobby with elbow room, and pastel-soft rooms you can stretch out in (Sb-€115, Db-€135, Tb-€170, Qb-€200, between avenue de Suffren and boulevard de Grenelle—not to be confused with rue de Grenelle that crosses rue Cler, from the Métro follow rue d'Ouessant one block and turn right, 7 rue du Général de Larminat, Mo: La Motte-Picquet–Grenelle, tel. 01 47 34 74 04, fax 01 47 34 48 56, www.paris-hotel-ares.com, aresotel@easynet.fr).

Lesser Values in the Rue Cler Area

Given this fine area, these are acceptable last choices.

$$$ Hôtel du Cadran***, while perfectly located, has a nice lobby but little charm in its tight and narrow rooms (Db-€152–170, air-con, 10 rue du Champ de Mars, tel. 01 40 62 67 00, fax 01 40 62 67 13, www.hotelducadran.com).

$$$ Hôtel Splendid*** is Art Deco modern, professional, and worth your while if you land one of its three suites with great Eiffel Tower views. Sixth-floor rooms have small terraces and sideways tower views, all rooms seem pricey and need sprucing up. Ask about their occasional promotional rates (Db-€134–165, Db with balcony and view-€180, Db suite-€200–230, 29 avenue de Tourville, tel. 01 45 51 24 77, fax 01 44 18 94 60, www.hotels-exclusive.com/hotels/splendid, splendid@club-internet.fr).

$$$ Best Western Eiffel Park***, is a dead-quiet, concrete business hotel with all the comforts, a friendly staff, 36 pleasant if unexceptional rooms, and a nifty and spacious rooftop terrace (Db-€135–185, occasional promotional rates, 17 bis rue Amélie, tel.

01 45 55 10 01, fax 01 47 05 28, 68, www.eiffelpark.com, reservation@eiffelpark.com).

$$ Hôtel Amélie,** in a skinny building, is a midrange possibility with no lobby, no elevator, and shabby halls but decent rooms (Db-€95–105, 5 rue Amélie, tel. 01 45 51 74 75, fax 01 45 56 93 55, www.hotelamelie.com, hotelamelie@wanadoo.fr).

$ Hôtel Kensington** has miniscule rooms and little personality, but is a fair value (Sb-€55, Db-€70–86, 79 avenue de la Bourdonnais, tel. 01 47 05 74 00, fax 01 47 05 25 81, www.hotel-kensington.com, hk@hotel-kensington.com).

$ Hôtel de la Tour Eiffel** is a modest little place with fairly priced rooms, but cheap furnishings and foam mattresses (Sb-€70, Db-€85, Tb-€105, 17 rue de l'Exposition, tel. 01 47 05 14 75, fax 01 47 53 99 46, hte7@wanadoo.fr).

$ Hôtel de la Paix **, located away from the fray on a quiet street, is a reasonable value but is poorly managed and asks for full payment up front (Sb-€68, Db-€98–110, Tb-€120, good breakfast, 19 rue du Gros-Caillou, tel. 01 45 51 86 17, fax 01 45 55 93 28, hotel.de.la.paix@wanadoo.fr).

$ Hôtel le Pavillon** is quiet, with basic rooms, no elevator, and cramped halls in a charming location (Sb-€80, Db-€90; Tb, Qb, or Quint/b-€135; 54 rue St. Dominique, tel. 01 45 51 42 87, fax 01 45 51 32 79, PatrickPavillon@aol.com).

The Marais

Those interested in a more Soho/Greenwich Village locale should make the Marais their Parisian home. Only 15 years ago, it was a forgotten Parisian backwater, but now the Marais is one of Paris' most popular residential, tourist, and shopping areas. This is jumbled, medieval Paris at its finest, where classy stone mansions sit alongside trendy bars, antique shops, and fashion-conscious boutiques. The streets are a fascinating parade of artists, students, tourists, immigrants, and babies in strollers munching baguettes. The Marais is also known as a hub of the Parisian gay and lesbian scene. This area is *sans doute* livelier (and louder) than the rue Cler area.

In the Marais, you have these sights close at hand: Picasso Museum, Carnavalet Museum, Victor Hugo's House, Jewish Art and History Museum, and the Pompidou Center. You're also a manageable walk from Paris' two islands (Ile St. Louis and Ile de la Cité), home to Notre-Dame and the Sainte-Chapelle. The Opéra Bastille, Promenade Plantée park, place des Vosges (Paris' oldest square), Jewish Quarter (rue des Rosiers), and nightlife-packed rue de Lappe are also walkable. (Sight descriptions are listed in "Sights," page 286.)

The Marais has two good **open-air markets**: the sprawling

Marais Hotels

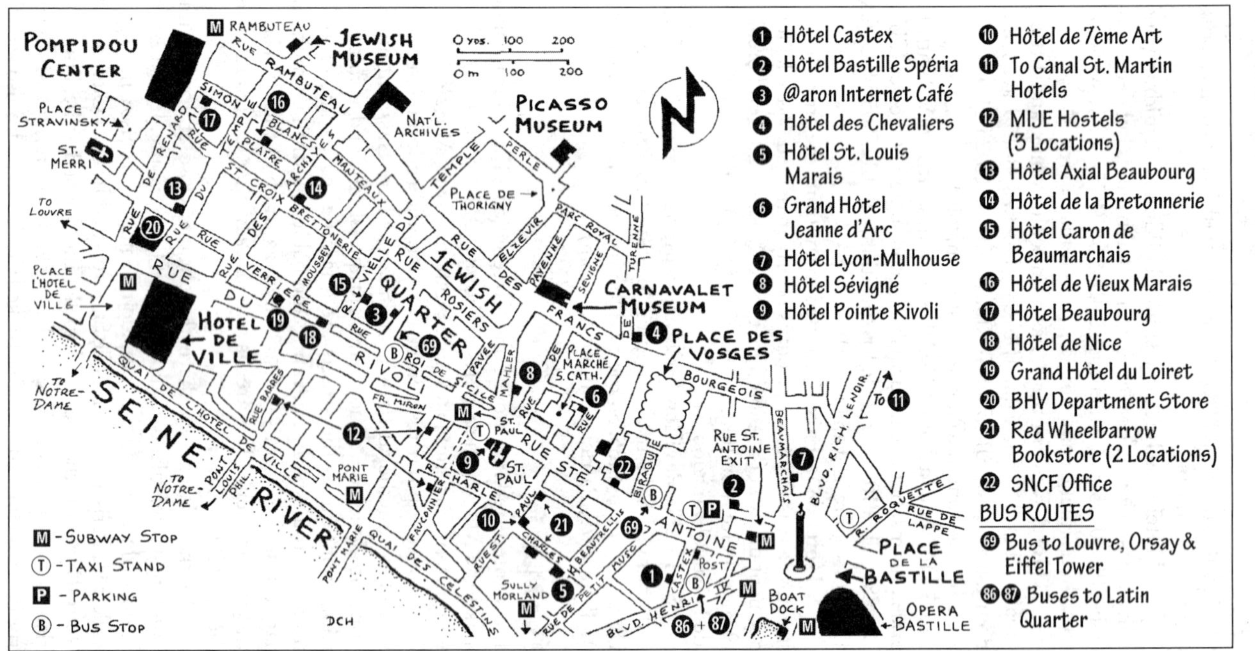

Marché de la Bastille on place de la Bastille (Thu and Sun until 12:30) and the more intimate, very local Marché de la place d'Aligre (daily 9:00–12:00, a few blocks behind Opéra on place d'Aligre). Two little **grocery shops** are open until 23:00 on rue St. Antoine (near intersection with rue Castex).

The nearest **TIs** are in the Louvre (Wed–Mon 10:00–19:00, closed Tue) and Gare de Lyon (Mon–Sat 8:00–20:00, all-Paris TI tel. 08 36 68 31 12). Most banks and other services are on the main drag, rue de Rivoli, which becomes rue St. Antoine. For your Parisian Sears, find the **BHV** next to the Hôtel de Ville. Marais **post offices** are on rue Castex and on the corner of rue Pavée and rue des Francs Bourgeois. A rare **Internet café**, @aron, is at 3 rue des Ecouffes (tel. 01 42 71 05 07). The Marais is home to the friendliest English-language bookstore in Paris, Red Wheelbarrow Bookstore, with two stores (main store at 22 rue St. Paul, daily 10:00–19:00, Sun open at 14:00; children's bookstore at 13 rue Charles V, open Wed–Sun 10:00–19:00, closed Mon–Tue). These kind folks sell most of my books.

Métro service to the Marais neighborhood is excellent, with direct service to the Louvre, Champs-Elysées, Arc de Triomphe, La Défense (all on line 1), rue Cler area (line 8 from Bastille stop) and four major train stations: Gare de Lyon, Gare du Nord, Gare de l'Est, and Gare d'Austerlitz. Key Métro stops in the Marais are, from east to west: Bastille, St. Paul, and Hôtel de Ville (Sully-Morland, Pont Marie, and Rambuteau stops are also handy). There are also several helpful **bus routes**: Line #69 on rue St. Antoine takes you to the Louvre, Orsay, and Rodin museums, plus Napoleon's Tomb, and ends at the Eiffel Tower. Line #86 runs down boulevard Henri IV, crossing Ile St. Louis and serving the Latin Quarter along boulevard St. Germain. Line #87 follows a similar route but extends to the Eiffel Tower and rue Cler neighborhood. Line #96 runs on rues Turenne and François Miron and serves the Louvre and boulevard St. Germain (near Luxembourg Garden), ending at the Gare Montparnasse. Line #65 gets you to the Gare d'Austerlitz, Gare de l'Est, and Gare du Nord train stations from place de la Bastille.

You'll find **taxi stands** on place de la Bastille, on the north side of rue St. Antoine (where it meets rue Castex), and on the south side of rue St. Antoine (in front of St. Paul church).

Sleeping in the Marais Neighborhood

(4th *arrondissement*)

The Marais runs from the Pompidou Center to the Bastille (a 15-min walk), with most hotels located a few blocks north of the main east-west drag, the rue de Rivoli/rue St. Antoine. It's about 15 minutes on foot from any hotel in this area to Notre-Dame, Ile St.

Louis, and the Latin Quarter. Strolling home (day or night) from Notre-Dame along the Ile St. Louis is marvelous.

$$ Hôtel des Chevaliers*,** a pretty little boutique hotel one block northwest of place des Vosges, offers small, pleasant rooms with modern comforts, including air-conditioning. Eight of its 24 rooms are off the street and quiet—worth requesting (Sb-€125–135, Db-€140–150, 30 rue de Turenne, Mo: St. Paul, tel. 01 42 72 73 47, fax 01 42 72 54 10, info@hoteldeschevaliers.com).

$$ Hôtel Castex*,** well-situated on a quiet street near the place de la Bastille, feels Spanish from the formal entry to the red-tiled floors and dark wood accents. A clever system of connecting rooms allows families total privacy between two rooms, each with its own bathroom. Rooms are narrow but tasteful and air-conditioned, and the elevator is big by Parisian standards. Your fourth night is free in August and from November through February—except around New Year's Eve (Sb-€95–115, Db-€120–140, Tb-€190–220, just off place de la Bastille and rue St. Antoine, 5 rue Castex, Mo: Bastille, tel. 01 42 72 31 52, fax 01 42 72 57 91, www.castexhotel.com, info@castexhotel.com).

$$ Hôtel Bastille Spéria*,** a short block off the place de la Bastille, offers business-type service. The 42 well-configured rooms are modern and comfortable with big beds and air-conditioning. Walls are thin and the elevator operates at glacial speed but it's English-language-friendly, from the *International Herald Tribune*s in the lobby to the history of the Bastille posted in the elevator (Sb-€100, Db-€125–140, child's bed-€20, excellent buffet breakfast-€12.50, 1 rue de la Bastille, Mo: Bastille, tel. 01 42 72 04 01, fax 01 42 72 56 38, www.hotel-bastille-speria.com, info@hotel-bastille-speria.com).

$$ Hôtel St. Louis Marais** is a tiny, welcoming place, lost on a quiet residential street between the river and rue St. Antoine. The lobby is inviting and the 20 rooms are cozy but not air-conditioned (small Sb-€59, standard Sb-€91, small Db-€107, standard Db-€125, Tb-€140, no elevator but only three floors, ask about newer street-level annex rooms, bargain-priced parking-€12, 1 rue Charles V, Mo: Sully Morland, tel. 01 48 87 87 04, fax 01 48 87 33 26, www.saintlouismarais.com, slmarais@noos.fr).

$ Hôtel de 7ème Art,** two blocks south of rue St. Antoine toward the river, is a relaxed, Hollywood-nostalgia place, run by hip, friendly, young people, with a full-service café-bar and Charlie Chaplin murals. Its 23 rooms lack imagination, but are comfortable and a fair value. The large rooms are American-spacious (small Db-€80, standard Db-€90–105, large Db-€115–140, extra bed-€20, 20 rue St. Paul, Mo: St. Paul, tel. 01 44 54 85 00, fax 01 42 77 69 10).

$ Grand Hôtel Jeanne d'Arc,** a well-tended hotel with

thoughtfully appointed rooms, is ideally located for (and very popular with) connoisseurs of the Marais. Rooms on the street can be noisy until the bars close. Sixth-floor rooms have a view, and corner rooms are wonderfully bright in the City of Light, though no rooms are air-conditioned. Reserve this place way ahead (Sb-€57–70, Db-€80, larger twin Db-€95, Tb-€113, good Qb-€130, 3 rue de Jarente, Mo: St. Paul, tel. 01 48 87 62 11, fax 01 48 87 37 31, www.hoteljeannedarc.com, information@hoteljeannedarc.com).

$ Hôtel Lyon-Mulhouse**, with half of its 40 pleasant rooms on a busy street off place de la Bastille, is a fair value. Its bigger, quieter rooms at the back are worth the extra euros (Sb-€65, Db-€70–75, twin Db-€85–90, Tb-€100, Qb-€120, no air-con, 8 boulevard Beaumarchais, Mo: Bastille, tel. 01 47 00 91 50, fax 01 47 00 06 31, hotelyonmulhouse@wanadoo.fr).

$ Hôtel Sévigné**, is a sharp little air-conditioned place with lavender halls, tidy, comfortable rooms at very fair prices, and an owner of few words (Sb-€64, Db-€74–86, Tb-€100, 2 rue Malher, Mo: St. Paul, tel. 01 42 72 76 17, fax 01 42 78 68 26, www.le-sevigne.com, contact@le-sevigne.com).

$ Hôtel Pointe Rivoli*, across from the St. Paul Métro stop, is a jumbled, treehouse of rooms in the thick of the Marais, with Paris' steepest stairs (no elevator) and modest rooms at reasonable rates (Sb-€70, Db-€80, Tb-€115, air-con planned so rates may increase, 125 rue St. Antoine, Mo: St. Paul, tel. 01 42 72 14 23, fax 01 42 72 51 11, pointerivoli@libertysurf.fr).

$ MIJE Youth Hostels: The Maison Internationale de la Jeunesse et des Etudiants (MIJE) runs three classy old residences, clustered a few blocks south of rue St. Antoine. Each is well-maintained with simple, clean, single-sex, one- to four-bed rooms for travelers of any age. None has an elevator or double beds, each has Internet access, and all rooms have showers. You can stay seven days maximum and prices given are per person and favor single travelers (2 people can find a double in a very simple hotel for similar rates). You can pay more to have your own room, or pay less and room with as many as three others (Sb-€43, Db-€33, Tb-€30, Qb-€28, cash only, includes breakfast but not towels, which you can get from a machine for €9; required membership card-€2.50 extra/person; rooms locked 12:00–15:00 and at 1:00). The hostels are: **MIJE Fourcy** (€11 dinners available to anyone with a membership card, 6 rue de Fourcy, just south of rue de Rivoli), **MIJE Fauconnier** (11 rue du Fauconnier), and the best, **MIJE Maubisson** (12 rue des Barres). They all share the same contact information (tel. 01 42 74 23 45, fax 01 40 27 81 64, www.mije.com) and Métro stop (St. Paul). Reservations are accepted, though you must arrive by noon or call the morning of arrival to confirm a later time.

Near the Pompidou Center

These hotels are farther west and closer to the Pompidou Center than to place de la Bastille. Métro stop Hôtel de Ville works well for all of these hotels, unless a closer stop is noted.

$$$ Hôtel Axial Beaubourg*,** a block from Hôtel de Ville toward the Pompidou Center, has a minimalist lobby and 28 pricey but plush rooms, many with wood beams. If you cancel with less than seven days' notice, you'll lose your one-night deposit (standard Db-€165, big Db-€200, air-con, 11 rue du Temple, tel. 01 42 72 72 22, fax 02 42 72 03 53, www.axialbeaubourg.com, infos@axialbeaubourg.com).

$$$ Hôtel Caron de Beaumarchais*** feels like a folk museum, with its 20 sweet little rooms and a lobby cluttered with bits from an elegant 18th-century Marais house. Short antique collectors love this place (small back-side Db-€145, larger Db on the front-€160, air-con, Internet access, 12 rue Vieille du Temple, tel. 01 42 72 34 12, fax 01 42 72 34 63, www.carondebeaumarchais.com, hotel@carondebeaumarchais.com).

$$$ Hôtel de la Bretonnerie*,** three blocks from the Hôtel de Ville, makes a fine Marais home. It has an on-the-ball staff, a big, welcoming lobby, elegant decor, and tastefully-appointed rooms with an antique, open-beam warmth (perfectly good standard "classic" Db-€110, bigger "charming" Db-€145, Db suite-€180, Tb-€170, Tb suite-€205, Qb suite-€245, between rue Vieille du Temple and rue des Archives at 22 rue Ste. Croix de la Bretonnerie, tel. 01 48 87 77 63, fax 01 42 77 26 78, www.bretonnerie.com, hotel@bretonnerie.com, Francoise SE).

$$ Hôtel de Vieux Marais** is tucked away on a quiet street two blocks east of the Pompidou Center and charges top euro in high season for its efficient rooms (Db-€115, €145 March-mid July, extra bed-€24, air-con, just off rue des Archives at 8 rue du Plâtre, Mo: Rambuteau or Hôtel de Ville, tel. 01 42 78 47 22, fax 01 42 78 34 32, www.vieuxmarais.com, hotel@vieuxmarais.com).

$$ Hôtel Beaubourg*** is a good three-star value on a quiet street in the shadow of the Pompidou Center. Its 28 rooms are wood-beam comfy and air-conditioned, and the inviting lounge is warm and pleasant (Db-€125–148, twins are considerably larger than doubles, includes breakfast, 11 rue Simon Le Franc, Mo: Rambuteau, tel. 01 42 74 34 24, fax 01 42 78 68 11, www.hotelbeaubourg.com, htlbeaubourg @hotellerie.net).

$$ Hôtel de Nice,** on the Marais' busy main drag, is a turquoise-and-rose, "Marie-Antoinette does tie-dye" place. Its narrow halls are littered with paintings and covered with carpets, and its 23 non-air-conditioned rooms are filled with thoughtful touches and include tight bathrooms. Twin rooms, which cost the same as doubles, are larger and on the street side—but have effective double-paned windows (Sb-€74, Db-€105, Tb-€128, Qb-€140, extra bed-€20, 42 bis rue de Rivoli, tel. 01 42 78 55 29, fax 01 42 78 36 07, www.hoteldenice.com, contact@hoteldenice.com).

$ Grand Hôtel du Loiret** is centrally-located, spartan, and basic, though the rooms are better than you might think (S-€48, Sb-€65, Db-€64–84, Tb-€95, 8 rue des Mauvais Garçons, tel. 01 48 87 77 00, fax 01 48 04 96 56, hotelduloiret@hotmail.com).

Near the Marais, on Ile St. Louis

The peaceful, residential character of this river-wrapped island, its brilliant location, and its homemade ice cream have drawn Americans for decades, allowing hotels to charge dearly for their rooms. There are no budget values here, but the island's coziness and proximity to the Marais, Notre-Dame, and the Latin Quarter compensate for higher rates. The hotels listed below are shown on the map on page 281. All are on the island's main drag, the rue St. Louis-en-l'Ile, where I list several restaurants (see page 351). Use Mo: Pont Marie or Sully-Morland.

$$$ Hôtel du Jeu de Paume****, located in a 17th-century tennis center, is the most expensive hotel I list in Paris. When you enter its magnificent lobby, you'll understand why. Greet Scoop, the hotel dog, then ride the glass elevator for a half-timbered-tree-house experience, and marvel at the cozy lounges. The 30 quite comfortable rooms are carefully designed and *très* tasteful, though small for the price (you're paying for the location and public spaces). Most face a small garden and all are pin-drop peaceful (Sb-€160, standard Db-€225, larger Db-€240–270, deluxe Db-€295, Db suite-€480, 54 rue St. Louis-en-l'Ile, tel. 01 43 26 14 18, fax 01 40 46 02 76, www.jeudepaumehotel.com).

The following two hotels are owned by the same person. For both, if you must cancel, do so a week in advance or pay fees:

$$$ Hôtel de Lutèce*** is the better, cozier value on the island, with a sit-a-while wood-paneled lobby, a fireplace, and warmly designed air-conditioned rooms. Twin rooms are larger and the same price as double rooms (Db-€162, Tb-€180, 65 rue St. Louis-en-l'Ile, tel. 01 43 26 23 52, fax 01 43 29 60 25, www.hotel-ile-saintlouis.com, lutece@hotel-ile-saintlouis.com).

$$$ Hôtel des Deux Iles*** is brighter and more colorful with marginally smaller rooms (Db-€162, 59 rue St. Louis-en-l'Ile, tel. 01 43 26 13 35, fax 01 43 29 60 25, 2isles@hotel-ile-saintlouis.com).

Luxembourg

This neighborhood revolves around Paris' loveliest park and adds quick access to the city's best shopping streets and grandest café-hopping. Sleeping in the Luxembourg area is a true Left Bank experience. The Luxembourg Garden, boulevard St. Germain,

Cluny Museum, and Latin Quarter are all within easy walking distance. Here you get the best of both worlds: youthful Left Bank energy and the classy trappings that surround the monumental Panthéon and St. Sulpice church.

Having the Luxembourg Garden at your back door allows strolls through meticulously-cared-for flowers, a great kids' play area, and a purifying escape from city traffic. Place St. Sulpice offers an elegant, pedestrian-friendly square and some of Paris' best boutiques. Sleeping in the Luxembourg area also puts several movie theaters at your fingertips (at Odéon Métro stop), as well as lively cafés on the boulevard St. Germain, rue de Buci, place de la Sorbonne and place de la Contrescarpe, all of which buzz with action until late.

Admire the Panthéon and Sorbonne University from the outside, observe Daniel Roth play the magnificent organ at St. Sulpice church (see page 298), and peek inside the beautiful St. Etienne-du-Mont church. The colorful **street market** at the south end of rue Mouffetard is a worthwhile 10–15 minute walk down from these hotels (Tue–Sat 8:00–12:00 & 15:30–19:00, Sun 8:00–12:00, closed Mon, 5 blocks south of place de la Contrescarpe, Mo: Place Monge). The nearest **TI** is at the Louvre. Handy **Internet service** is between the Luxembourg Garden and Panthéon at 17 rue Soufflot (XS Arena, always open). The **Village Voice** bookstore carries a full selection of English-language books (including mine) and is near St. Sulpice (6 rue Princesse, tel. 01 46 33 36 47).

Métro lines #10 and #4 serve this area. Key stops are Cluny-La Sorbonne, Mabillon, Odéon and St. Sulpice. RER line B provides direct service to Charles de Gaulle airport and Gare du Nord trains from the Luxembourg station. Buses #63, #86, and #87 run eastbound through this area on boulevard St. Germain and westbound along rue des Ecoles, stopping on place St. Sulpice. Lines #63 and #87 provide a direct connection to the rue Cler area; Line #63 serves the Orsay, Invalides, Rodin and Marmottan museums. Lines #86 and #87 run to the Marais.

Sleeping in the Luxembourg Neighborhood

While it takes only 15 minutes to walk from one end of this neighborhood to the other, I've located the hotels by the key monument they are close to (St. Sulpice Church, the Odeon Theater, and the Panthéon). No hotel is farther than a 5-minute walk from the Luxembourg Garden.

Hotels Near St. Sulpice Church
(6th *arrondissement*)

These hotels are all within a block of St. Sulpice, and two blocks from the famous boulevard St. Germain. This is nirvana for boutique-minded shoppers. Métro stops St. Sulpice and Mabillon are equally close. See the map on page 336.

$$$ Hôtel Relais St. Sulpice***, on the small street just behind St. Sulpice church, feels like a cozy bar with a melt-in-your-chair lounge and 26 beautifully designed, air-conditioned rooms, most of which surround a leafy glass atrium. The dazzling breakfast room sits below the atrium near the sauna (Db-€170–180–195–210 depending on size, most Db-€170–180, beefy buffet breakfast-€12, 3 rue Garancière, tel. 01 46 33 99 00, fax 01 46 33 00 10, www.relais-saint-sulpice.com, relaisstsulpice@wanadoo.fr).

$$$ Hôtel la Perle*** is a pricey pearl in the thick of the lively rue des Canettes a block off place St. Sulpice. At this snappy, modern hotel, glass doors slide onto the traffic-free street, and a fun lobby built around a central bar and atrium greets you. Rooms are plush, air-conditioned, and wood-beamed (standard Db-€173, bigger Db-€195, luxury Db-€235, 14 rue des Canettes, tel. 01 43 29 10 10, fax 01 43 34 51 04, www.hotellaperle.com, booking@hotellaperle.com).

$$ Hôtel Bonaparte** sits between boutiques, a few steps from place St. Sulpice, on the smart rue Bonaparte. While the 29 air-conditioned rooms don't live up to the handsome entry, they are homey, comfortable, and generally spacious with big bathrooms, molded ceilings, and clashing bedspreads (Sb-€92–138, Db-€120, big Db-€154, Tb-€158, 61 rue Bonaparte, tel. 01 43 26 97 37, fax 01 46 33 57 67).

$$ Hôtel le Récamier** feels like grandma's house, tucked in the corner of place St. Sulpice. Flowery wallpaper, dark halls, and spotless, just-what-you-need rooms (with no TV!)—some with views of the square—make this a good, if somewhat pricey Paris refuge. How such a low-key place escaped the trendy style of other hotels in this chic area, I'll never know (S-€97, Sb-€110, D-€104, Db-€124–144, Tb-€176, Qb-€218, includes breakfast, 3 bis place St. Sulpice, tel. 01 43 26 04 89, fax 01 46 33 27 73, e-mail address? You need a computer first).

Near the Odéon Theater

These hotels are between the Odéon Métro stop and Luxembourg Garden (5 blocks east of St. Sulpice) and may have rooms when others don't. In addition to the Odéon Métro, the RER line B Luxembourg stop is a short walk away.

$$ Hôtel Michelet Odéon** sits shyly in a corner of place de l'Odéon, a block from the Luxembourg Garden. Most of the spacious, simple rooms have views and all have creaky floors (Db-€95–115, Tb-€135, Qb-€150, 6 place de l'Odéon, tel. 01 53 10 05 60, fax 01 46 34 55 35, www.hotelmicheletodeon.com, hotel@micheletodeon.com).

$$ Grand Hôtel des Balcons** has an inviting lobby and spick-and-span rooms with interesting colors and generous space.

Hotels and Restaurants near St. Sulpice and the Odeon Theater

1. Hôtel Relais St. Sulpice
2. Hôtel la Perle
3. Hôtel Bonaparte
4. Hôtel le Récamier
5. Hôtel Michelet Odéon
6. Grand Hôtel des Balcons & Hôtel Delavigne
7. Au Bon Saint-Pourcain
8. Chez Diane
9. Brasserie Fernand
10. La Crêpe Rit du Clown
11. Chez Georges
12. Le Café de Flore & Les Deux Magots
13. Café Bonaparte
14. Café le Procope

Some rooms have narrow balconies (Db-€100–120, big Db-€150, big Tb-€180, a block below the Odéon theater, 3 Casimir-Delavigne, tel. 01 46 34 78 50, fax 01 46 34 06 27, www.balcons.com, resa@balcons.com).

$$ Hôtel Delavigne*** has a warm lobby and appealing rooms (Db-€115–130, Tb-€130–145, tel. 01 43 29 31 50, fax 01 43 29 78 56, 1 rue Casimir-Delavigne, www.hoteldelavigne.com, resa@hoteldelavigne.com).

Near the Panthéon

Use Métro: Cluny-La Sorbonne or RER-B: Luxembourg for the first five hotels listed. The first two wannabe-four-star hotels face the Panthéon's right transept and are owned by the same family (ask about their promotional rates, which may be available anytime, even during some summer weeks). The rates are high and the rooms aren't big, but the quality is tops.

$$$ Hôtel du Panthéon*** welcomes you with a wood-beamed, cozy lobby and 32 country-French-cute rooms with air-conditioning and every possible comfort. Fifth-floor rooms have sliver balconies, but sixth-floor rooms have the best views (Sb/Db-€175–215–240, Tb-€200–225–244, price varies by season, highest price is for peak weeks, check Web site for specials, 19 place du Panthéon, tel. 01 43 54 32 95, fax 01 43 26 64 65, www.hoteldupantheon.com, hoteldupantheon@wanadoo.fr).

$$$ Hôtel des Grands Hommes*** was built to look good—and it does. The lobby is to be admired but not enjoyed, and the 31 rooms reflect an interior designer's dream. Rooms are generally tight but adorable, with great attention to detail and little expense spared. Fifth- and sixth-floor rooms have balconies; sixth-floor balconies, with grand views, are big enough to use. For more luxury, splurge for a suite (Sb/Db-€175–215–240, Db suite-€250–390, price varies by season and week, check Web site for deals, air-con, 17 place du Panthéon, tel. 01 46 34 19 60, fax 01 43 26 67 32, www.hoteldesgrandshommes.com, reservation@hoteldesgrandshommes.com).

$$ Hôtel des Grandes Ecoles*** is idyllic. A short alley leads to three buildings protecting a flower-filled garden courtyard, preserving a sense of tranquility that is rare in a city this size. Its 51 rooms are reasonably spacious and comfortable, many with large beds. This romantic place is deservedly popular, so call well in advance, though reservations are not accepted more than four months ahead (Db-€110–120, a few bigger rooms-€135, extra bed-€20, parking-€30, 75 rue du Cardinal Lemoine, Mo: Cardinal Lemoine, tel. 01 43 26 79 23, fax 01 43 25 28 15, www.hotel-grandes-ecoles.com, hotel.grandes.ecoles@wanadoo.fr, mellow Marie speaks some English, Maman does not).

$$ Hôtel des 3 Collèges** is a welcoming, well-run place with charm (Db-€90, bigger Db-€114–134, Tb-€150, 16 rue Cujas, tel. 01 43 54 67 30, fax 01 46 34 02 99, www.3colleges.com, hotel@3colleges.com).

$ Hôtel Cluny Sorbonne** is smartly managed, a good deal, and conveniently located across from the famous university, just below the Panthéon. Rooms are clean and comfortable with wood furnishings (standard Db-€85, big Db-€100, really big Db-€140, 8 rue Victor Cousin, tel. 01 43 54 66 66, fax 01 43 29 68 07, www.hotel-cluny.fr, cluny@club-internet.fr).

$ Hôtel de Senlis** is a fair deal, hiding quietly below the Panthéon, with modest rooms, carpeted walls, and metal closets. Most rooms have beamed ceilings, and all rooms could use a decorator with taste (Sb-€69, Db-€74–88, Tb-€95, Qb-€110, 7 rue Malebranche, Mo: Cluny-La Sorbonne, tel. 01 43 29 93 10, fax 01 43 29 00 24, www.hoteldesenlis.fr, hoteldesenlis@wanadoo.fr).

$ Hôtel du Brésil,** one block from Luxembourg Garden, has little character and some smoky rooms but reasonable rates, making it an acceptable choice (Sb-€68, Db-€74–85, 10 rue le Goff, RER-B: Luxembourg, tel. 01 43 54 76 11, fax 01 46 33 45 78, www.hoteldubresil.fr, hoteldubresil@wanadoo.fr).

$ Hôtel des Médicis is as cheap, stripped-down, and basic as it gets, with a soiled linoleum charm, a happy owner, and a great location. Request Jim Morrison's old room, if you dare (S-€16, D-€31–35, 214 rue St. Jacques, Mo: Cluny La Sorbonne or RER-B Luxembourg, tel. 01 43 54 14 66, hotelmedicis@aol.com, Denis SE).

$ Hôtel Central*, wedged between two cafés, has a smoky, dingy reception, a steep, slippery stairway, so-so beds, and basic-but-cheery-if-somewhat-mildewed rooms. To an optimist, this hotel defines unpretentiousness; to a pessimist, it's a dive with a charming location. Either way, it's cheap. All rooms have showers, but toilets are down the hall (Ss-€32–37, Ds-€45–50, cash only, no elevator, 6 rue Descartes, Mo: Cardinal Lemoine, tel. 01 46 33 57 93, sweet Pilar NSE).

$ Y&H Hostel is easygoing and English-speaking, with Internet access, kitchen facilities, and basic but acceptable hostel conditions (beds in 4-bed rooms-€23, beds in double rooms-€26, includes breakfast, sheets-€2.50, cash only, rooms closed 11:00–16:00 but reception stays open, 2:00 curfew, reservations require deposit, 80 rue Mouffetard, Mo: Place Monge, tel. 01 47 07 47 07, fax 01 47 07 22 24, www.youngandhappy.fr, smile@youngandhappy.fr).

At the Bottom of Rue Mouffetard

These places are away from the Seine and other tourists, in an appealing work-a-day area. They require a longer walk or Métro

Hotels and Restaurants near the Pantheon

ride to sights but often have rooms when other places are booked up. The rue Mouffetard is the bohemian soul of this area, running south from its heart, place de la Contrescarpe, to rue de Bazeilles. Two thousand years ago it was the principal Roman road south to Italy. Today, this small, meandering street has a split personality. The lower half thrives in the daytime as a pedestrian shopping street. The upper half sleeps during the day but comes alive after dark, teeming with bars, restaurants, and nightlife. Use Métro stops Censier-Daubenton or Les Gobelins.

$ Port-Royal-Hôtel* has only one star, but don't let that fool you. This 46-room place is polished bottom to top and has been well-run by the same proud family for 67 years. You could eat off the floors of its spotless, comfy rooms. Ask for a room away from the street (S-€39–51, D-€51, big hall showers-€2.50, Db-€75, Tb-€89, cash only, requires cash deposit, climb stairs from rue Pascal to busy boulevard de Port-Royal, 8 boulevard de Port-Royal, Mo: Les Gobelins, tel. 01 43 31 70 06, fax 01 43 31 33 67, www.portroyalhotel.fr.st).

$ Hôtel de l'Espérance** is a solid two-star value. It's quiet, pink, fluffy, and comfortable, with thoughtfully appointed rooms, complete with canopy beds and a flamboyant owner (Sb-€70, Db-€78–86, 15 rue Pascal, Mo: Censier-Daubenton, tel. 01 47 07 10 99, fax 01 43 37 56 19, hotel.esperance@wanadoo.fr).

$ Hôtel de France** is set on a busy street, with adequately comfortable rooms, fair prices, and a charming owner, Madame Margo. The best and quietest rooms are *sur le cour* (on the courtyard), though streetside rooms are okay (Sb-€66, Db-€76–85, 108 rue Monge, Mo: Censier Daubenton, tel. 01 47 07 19 04, fax 01 43 36 62 34, hotel.de.fce@wanadoo.fr).

Versailles

For a laid-back alternative to Paris within easy reach of the big city by RER train (5/hr, 30 min), Versailles, with easy, safe parking and reasonably priced hotels, can be a good overnight stop. Get a map of Versailles at your hotel or at the TI.

Hôtel de France***, in an 18th-century townhouse, offers four-star value, with air-conditioned, appropriately royal rooms, a pleasant courtyard, comfy public spaces, a bar, and a restaurant (Db-€145, Tb-€180, Qb-€240, just off parking lot across from château, 5 rue Colbert, tel. 01 30 83 92 23, fax 01 30 83 92 24, www.hotelfrance-versailles.com, hotel-de-france-versailles@wanadoo.fr).

Hôtel le Cheval Rouge**, built in 1676 as Louis XIV's stables, now houses tourists. It's a block behind the place du Marché in a quaint corner of town on a large, quiet courtyard with free parking and sufficiently comfortable rooms (Sb-€66, Db-€70–85, Tb-€100, Qb-€106, 18 rue André Chénier, tel. 01 39 50 03 03, fax 01 39 50 61

27, www.chevalrouge.fr.st, chevalrouge@club-internet.fr).

Hôtel Ibis Versailles** offers modern comfort, but no air-conditioning (Db-€72–82 weekday, cheaper weekend rates can't be reserved ahead, across from RER station, 4 avenue du Général de Gaulle, tel. 01 39 53 03 30, fax 01 39 50 06 31).

Hôtel du Palais, facing the RER station, has clean, sharp rooms—the cheapest I list in this area. Ask for a quiet room off the street (Db-€56, extra person-€11, piles of stairs, 6 place Lyautey, tel. 01 39 50 39 29, fax 01 39 50 80 41, hotelpalais@ifrance.com).

Hôtel d'Angleterre,** away from the frenzy, is a tranquil old place with smiling, Polish-born Madame Kutyla in control. Rooms are comfortable and spacious. Park nearby in the château lot (Db-€68–90, price rises with size of room, extra bed-€15, just below palace to the right as you exit, 2 rue de Fontenay, tel. 01 39 51 43 50, fax 01 39 51 45 63, hotel.angleterre.versailles@wanadoo.fr).

EATING

Paris is France's wine and cuisine melting pot. While it lacks a style of its own (only French onion soup is truly Parisian), it draws from the best of France. Paris could hold a gourmet Olympics and import nothing.

Picnic or go to bakeries for quick take-out lunches, or stop at a café for a lunch salad or *plat du jour,* but linger longer over dinner. Cafés are happy to serve a *plat du jour* (garnished plate of the day, about €10–16) or a chef-like salad (about €9) day or night, while restaurants expect you to enjoy a full dinner. Restaurants open for dinner around 19:00, and small local favorites get crowded after 21:00. Most of the restaurants listed below accept credit cards.

To save piles of euros, review the budget eating tips in this book's introduction and consider dinner picnics (great take-out dishes available at charcuteries). My recommendations are centered around the same three great neighborhoods for which I list accommodations (above); you can come home exhausted after a busy day of sightseeing and have a good selection of restaurants right around the corner. And evening is a fine time to explore any of these delightful neighborhoods, even if you're sleeping elsewhere.

Restaurants

If you are traveling outside of Paris, save your splurges for the countryside, where you'll enjoy regional cooking for less money. Many Parisian department stores have huge supermarkets hiding in the basement and top-floor cafeterias that offer affordable, low-risk, low-stress, what-you-see-is-what-you-get meals. The three neighborhoods highlighted in this book for sleeping in Paris are also pleasant areas to window-shop for just the right restaurant,

Price Code

To help you choose among these listings, I've divided the restaurants into three categories, based on the price per person for a typical meal without wine.

$$$ Higher Priced—Most meals €30 or more.
$$ Moderately Priced—Most meals between €20–30.
$ Lower Priced—Most meals under €20.

as is the Ile St. Louis. Most restaurants we've listed in these areas have set-price *menus* between €15 and €30. In most cases, the few extra euros you pay are well-spent, and open up a variety of better choices. You decide.

Good Picnic Spots: For great people-watching, try the Pompidou Center (by the *Homage to Stravinsky* fountains), the elegant place des Vosges (closes at dusk), the gardens at the Rodin Museum, and Luxembourg Garden. The Palais Royal (across the street from the Louvre) is a good spot for a peaceful, royal picnic.

For a romantic picnic place, try the pedestrian bridge (pont des Arts) across from the Louvre, with its unmatched views and plentiful benches; the Champ de Mars park under the Eiffel Tower; and the western tip of Ile St. Louis, overlooking Ile de la Cité. Bring your own dinner feast, and then watch the riverboats and the Eiffel Tower light up the city for you.

In the Rue Cler Neighborhood

The rue Cler neighborhood caters to its residents. Its eateries, while not destination places, have an intimate charm. My favorites are small mom-and-pop places that love to serve traditional French food at good prices to a local clientele. You'll generally find great dinner *menus* for €20–30 and *plats du jour* for around €12–15. Eat early with tourists or late with locals.

Closer to Ecole Militaire, Between Rue de la Motte Picquet and Rue de Grenelle

$$$ Café de l'Esplanade, the latest buzz, is your opportunity to be surrounded by chic, yet older and sophisticated Parisians enjoying top-notch traditional cuisine as foreplay. There's not a tourist in sight. It's a sprawling place—half its tables, with well-stuffed chairs, fill a plush, living-room-like interior, and the other half are lined up outside under its elegant awning facing the street and car park. Dress competitively, as this is *the* place to be seen in the 7th *arrondissement* (€20 *plats du jour*, plan on €45 plus wine for dinner,

Rue Cler Restaurants

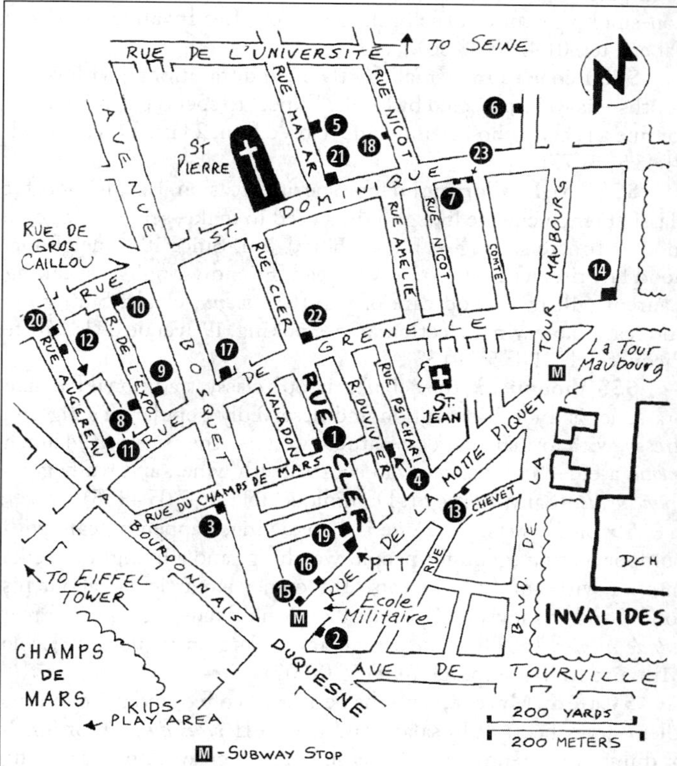

1. Café du Marché
2. Le Comptoir du Septième
3. Café le Bosquet
4. Léo le Lion
5. L'Affriolé & L'Ami Jean
6. Au Petit Tonneau
7. Brasserie Thoumieux
8. Le P'tit Troquet & La Casa di Sergio
9. Restaurant la Serre
10. La Fontaine de Mars
11. La Varangue
12. Chez Agnès
13. Le Florimond
14. Café de l'Esplanade
15. La Terrasse du 7eme
16. Fauchon Deli
17. Real McCoy
18. Pourjauran Bakery
19. Petite Brasserie PTT
20. Café Constant
21. Le Toulouse
22. Café la Roussillon
23. O'Brien's Pub

open daily, reserve ahead—especially if you want a curbside table, non-smoking room in the back, bordering Les Invalides at 52 rue Fabert, tel. 01 47 05 38 80).

$$$ Léo le Lion—small, softly lit, and traditional, with velvet booths—is well respected by locals. Expect to spend €45 per person for fine à la carte choices and wine (closed Sun, 23 rue Duvivier, tel. 01 45 51 41 77).

$$$ Save **Le Florimond** for a special occasion. Locals come for classic French cuisine like grandma used to make, served with care in an intimate setting—and so should you. Since it's a neighborhood favorite, it's best to reserve ahead. Friendly English-speaking Laurent will take good care of you (€32 *menu*, closed Sun, good and reasonable wine selection, non-smoking, 19 avenue de la Motte Picquet, tel. 01 45 55 40 38).

$$$ Thoumieux, the neighborhood's classy, traditional Parisian brasserie, is a local institution and deservedly popular. It's big and dressy, with formal but good-natured waiters. They serve a €14 lunch *menu*, a €31–33 dinner *menu* (3 courses with wine), and really good *crème brûlée* (daily, 79 rue St. Dominique, tel. 01 47 05 49 75).

$$ La Terrasse du 7ème is a sprawling, happening café with outdoor seating (good for people-watching) and a living room-like interior with comfy love-seats. The owner is particular about his food—and it shows (daily until 02:00, no fixed-price *menu*, great *salade niçoise*, they'll make a vegetarian plate on request, at Ecole Militaire Métro stop, tel. 01 45 55 00 02).

$ Café du Marché, with the best seats, coffee, and prices on rue Cler, serves hearty €10 salads and good €11 *plats du jour* for lunch or dinner to a trendy, smoky, mainly French crowd. This easygoing café is ideal if you want a light dinner (good dinner salads) or a more substantial but simple meal. Arrive before 19:30; it's packed at 21:00. A chalkboard lists the plates of the day—each a meal (Mon–Sat 11:00–23:00, closes at 17:00 on Sun, at the corner of rue Cler and rue du Champ de Mars, at 38 rue Cler, tel. 01 47 05 51 27).

$ Le Comptoir du Septième is owned by the Café du Marché folks and offers similar dishes and prices with better (but smoky) indoor seating (daily, 39 avenue de la Motte Picquet, at Ecole Militaire Métro stop, tel. 01 45 55 90 20).

$ Petite Brasserie PTT is popular with postal workers, offering traditional café fare at reasonable prices next to the PTT (post office) on rue Cler (closed Mon, opposite 53 rue Cler).

$ Café le Bosquet is a vintage Parisian brasserie with dressy waiters and a classic interior, or sidewalk tables on a busy street. Come here for a bowl of French onion soup, a salad, or a three-course *menu* (€18) and mix it up with waiters Didier and Antoine. Vegetarian dishes are possible—ask (closed Sun, many choices from a fun menu, the house red wine is plenty good, corner of rue du Champ de Mars and avenue Bosquet, at 46 avenue Bosquet, tel. 01 45 51 38 13).

Between Rue Grenelle and the River

$$$ Altitude 95 is in the Eiffel Tower, 95 meters (about 300 feet) above the ground (€21–31 lunches, €50 dinners, dinner seatings daily at 19:00 and 21:00, reserve well ahead for a view table; before you ascend to dine, drop by the booth between the north/*nord* and east/*est* pillars to buy your Eiffel Tower ticket and pick up a pass that enables you to skip the line; tel. 01 45 55 20 04, fax 01 47 05 94 40).

$$$ At **L'Affriolé**, you'll compete with young professionals for a table. This small and trendy place is well deserving of its rave reviews. Menu selections change daily, and the wine list is extensive, with some good bargains (€32 *menu*, closed Sun–Mon, 17 rue Malar, tel. 01 44 18 31 33).

$$$ Au Petit Tonneau is a souvenir of old Paris. Fun-loving owner-chef Madame Boyer prepares everything herself, wearing her tall chef's hat like a crown as she rules from her family-style kitchen. The small dining room is plain and doesn't look like it's changed in the 25 years she's been running the place. Her steaks and lamb are excellent (allow €28 for 2 courses, €35 3-course *menu*, open daily, can get smoky—come early, 20 rue Surcouf, tel. 01 47 05 09 01).

$$ Le P'tit Troquet is a petite place taking you back to Paris in the 1920s, gracefully and earnestly run by Dominique. The delicious three-course €29 *menu* comes with fun, traditional choices (closed Sun, 28 rue de l'Exposition, tel. 01 47 05 80 39).

$$ La Casa di Sergio is *the* place for gourmet Italian cuisine served family-style. Only Sergio could make me enthusiastic about Italian food in Paris. Sergio, a people-loving Sicilian, says he's waited his entire life to open a restaurant like this. Eating here involves a little trust...just sit down and let Sergio spoil you (€26–36 *menus*, open daily, 20 rue de l'Exposition, tel. 01 45 51 37 71).

$$ La Fontaine de Mars is a longtime favorite for locals, charmingly situated on a classic, tiny Parisian street and jumbled square. It's a happening scene, with tables jammed together for the serious business of good eating. Reserve in advance or risk eating upstairs without the fun street-level ambience (allow €40 per person with wine, open nightly, where rue de l'Exposition and rue St. Dominique meet, at 129 rue St. Dominique, tel. 01 47 05 46 44).

$$ Chez Agnès, the smallest restaurant listed in this book, is not for everyone. Small and flowery, it's a family-style place. Eccentric but sincere Agnès (with dog Gypsy at her side) does it all—in her minuscule kitchen, and serving, too—without a word of English. Don't come for a quick dinner; and don't come if you don't like dogs (€23 *menu*, closed Mon, 1 rue Augereau, tel. 01 45 51 06 04).

$$ L'Ami Jean is the place to go for excellent Basque specialties at fair prices—and everyone knows it. You must call ahead (try for an early reservation, when most Parisians won't dine), or join the crowd on the sidewalk and wait. The chef has made his reputation on the quality of his cuisine, not on the dark, simple decor (closed Sun–Mon, 27 rue Malar, tel. 01 47 05 86 89).

$ Café Constant is a tiny, two-level place that feels more like a small bistro, serving reasonably priced dishes in a lively setting. Though new, it has already established a loyal clientele (closed Sun, corner of rue Augereau and rue St. Dominique, next to recommended Hotel Londres Eiffel).

$ La Varangue is an entertaining one-man show featuring English-speaking Phillipe, who ran a French catering shop in Pennsylvania for three years, then returned to Paris to open his own place. He lives upstairs, and clearly has found his niche serving a Franco-American clientele who are all on a first-name basis. The food is cheap and basic (don't come here for a special dinner), the tables are few, and he opens early (at 17:30). Norman Rockwell would dig his tiny dining room (€10 *plats du jour* and a €15 *menu,* closed Sun, always a veggie option, 27 rue Augereau, tel. 01 47 05 51 22).

$ Le Toulouse is a cheap and easygoing food store-restaurant serving southwest French cuisine (featuring duck, *cassoulet*, and hearty salads) in a modern setting (closed Sun, 86 rue St Dominique, tel. 01 45 56 04 31).

$ Restaurant la Serre is reasonably priced and worth considering (*plats du jour* €11–15, closed Sun–Mon, good onion soup and duck specialties, 29 rue de l'Exposition, tel. 01 45 55 20 96, Margot).

Picnicking in Rue Cler

The rue Cler is a moveable feast that gives "fast food" a good name. The entire street is clogged with connoisseurs of good eating. Only the health-food store goes unnoticed. A festival of food, the street is lined with people whose lives seem to be devoted to their specialty: polished produce, rotisserie chicken, crêpes, or cheese.

For a magical picnic dinner at the Eiffel Tower, assemble it in no fewer than five shops on rue Cler and then go lounge on the best grass in Paris, with the dogs, Frisbees, a floodlit tower, and a cool breeze in the parc du Champ de Mars.

Asian delis (generically called *Traiteur Asie*) provide tasty, low-stress, low-price, takeout treats (€6 dinner plates, the one on rue Cler near rue du Champ de Mars has tables). There's a **Greek deli** with outdoor seats on rue Cler across from Grand Hôtel Lévêque. The elegant **Fauchon *charcuterie*** offers mouthwatering meals to go (open daily until 23:00, at Ecole Militaire Métro stop). **Real McCoy** is a little shop selling American food and sandwiches (closed Sun,

194 rue de Grenelle). There are small **late-night groceries** at 186 and 197 rue de Grenelle (open nightly until midnight).

Breakfast in Rue Cler

Café la Roussillon serves American breakfasts for €7.50 and a dynamite Sunday brunch for €15 (daily, at corner of rue de Grenelle and rue Cler, tel. 01 45 51 47 53). The **Pourjauran** bakery, offering great baguettes, hasn't changed in 70 years (20 rue Jean Nicot). The **bakery** at 112 rue St. Dominique is worth the detour, with classic decor and tables where you can enjoy your *café au lait* and croissant.

Nightlife in Rue Cler

This sleepy neighborhood is not the place for night owls, but there are a few notable exceptions. **Café du Marché** and its brother, **Le Comptoir du Septième** (both listed above), hop with a Franco-American crowd until about midnight, as does the flashier **Café la Roussillon** (nightly, at corner of rue de Grenelle and rue Cler). **O'Brien's Pub** is a relaxed Parisian rendition of an Irish pub (77 avenue St. Dominique).

In the Marais Neighborhood

The trendy Marais is filled with locals enjoying good food in colorful and atmospheric eateries. The scene is competitive and changes all the time. Here is an assortment of places—all handy to recommended hotels—that offer good food at reasonable prices, plus a memorable experience. For maximum ambience, go to the place des Vosges or place du Marché Ste. Catherine (several places listed below in each of these squares).

Dining on Romantic Place des Vosges

$$$ Ma Bourgogne is a good match for the classy place des Vosges, boasting a certain snob appeal. You'll sit under arcades in a whirlpool of Frenchness as bowtied and black-aproned waiters serve you traditional Burgundian specialties: steak, *coq au vin,* lots of French fries, escargot, and great red wine. Service at this institution comes with food but few smiles (€32 *menu*, open daily, dinner reservations smart, cash only, at northwest corner at #19, tel. 01 42 78 44 64).

$ Café Hugo, named for the square's most famous resident, sits across the square. It serves the same arcade ambience for less (standard café fare like onion soup, omelets, and salads for €6–10; €13 *plats du jour;* open daily).

$ Nectarine, next to Café Hugo, is a peaceful teahouse serving healthy salads, quiches, and inexpensive *plats du jour* both day and night. Its fun menu lets you mix and match omelets and crêpes (daily, 16 place des Vosges, tel. 01 42 77 23 78).

Near the Bastille

$$ Brasserie Bofinger, an institution for over a century, is famous for fish and traditional cuisine with Alsatian flair. You're surrounded by brisk, black-and-white-attired waiters in plush rooms reminiscent of the Roaring Twenties. The non-smoking room is best—under the grand 1919 *coupole*. You'll see boys shucking and stacking seafood platters out front before you enter. Their €33 three-course (with wine) *menu* is a good value (daily and nightly, reservations smart, 5 rue de la Bastille, don't be confused by the lesser "Petite" Bofinger across the street, tel. 01 42 72 87 82).

$$ Chez Janou, a Provençal bistro, tumbles out of its corner building and fills its broad sidewalk with happy eaters. At first glance, you know this is a find. But don't let the crowd intimidate you—inside and out, it's relaxed and charming. The style is French Mediterranean, with an emphasis on vegetables (€14 *plats du jour* that change with the season, open daily, two blocks beyond place des Vosges at 2 rue Roger Verlomme, tel. 01 42 72 28 41).

$$ L'Impasse, a relaxed bistro on a quiet alley, serves an enthusiastically French, €28 three-course *menu*. Françoise, a former dancer and artist, runs the place *con brio* (closed Sun, 4 impasse de Guéménée, tel. 01 42 72 08 45). The restaurant is next to a self-serve launderette (open nightly until 21:30—clean your clothes while you dine).

$$ Bistrot les Sans Culottes, a zinc-bar classic on lively rue de Lappe, serves traditional French cuisine with a proper respect for fine wine (€25 3-course *menu*, closed Mon, 27 rue de Lappe, tel. 01 48 05 42 92). Stay out past your bedtime. Eat here. Then join the rue de Lappe party.

$ Au Temps des Cerises, a *très* local wine bar, is fun for its colorful lunch of cheese or cold meats with good wine (Mon–Fri until 20:00, closed Sat–Sun, at rue du Petit-Musc and rue de la Cerisaie).

$ Vins des Pyrénées is a younger, livelier place with fun ambience, inexpensive meals, some smoke, and a reasonable wine list (daily, 25 rue Beautreillis, tel. 01 42 72 64 94).

In the Heart of the Marais

$$$ L'Excuse, one of the neighborhood's top restaurants, is a good splurge for a romantic, dressy evening in a hushed atmosphere with lounge-lizard music. The elegant nouveau cuisine focuses on what's fresh, with plates that are petite but creative, and presented with panache (€37 *menu*, cheaper at lunch, closed Sun–Mon, reserve ahead, request downstairs—ideally by the window, 14 rue Charles V, tel. 01 42 77 98 97).

$$ *On place du Marché Ste. Catherine:* This tiny square, just off rue St. Antoine, is an international food festival cloaked in

Marais Restaurants

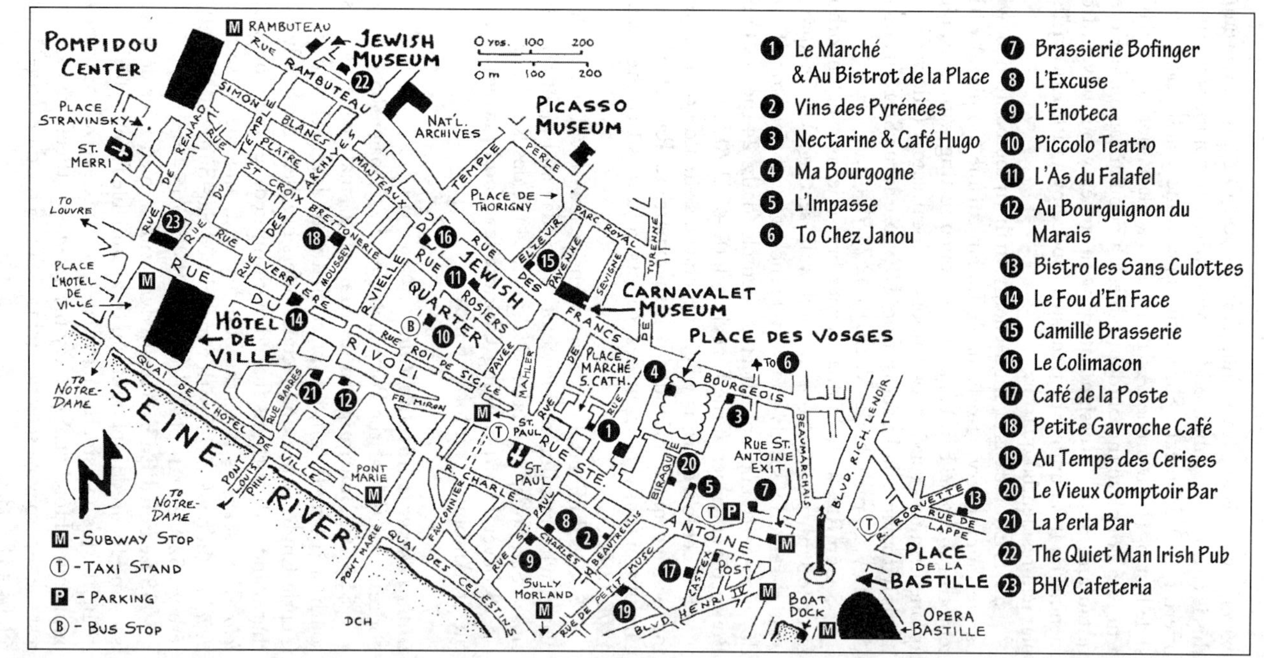

extremely Parisian, leafy-square ambience. On a balmy evening, this is clearly a neighborhood favorite, with five popular restaurants offering €20–30 meals. Survey the square and you'll find French-style bistros (Le Marché, Au Bistrot de la Place, both open daily), a fun Italian place (no outdoor tables), a popular Japanese/Korean restaurant, and a Russian eatery with an easy but adventurous menu. You'll eat under the trees surrounded by a futuristic-in-1800 planned residential quarter.

$$ L'Enoteca is a high-energy, half-timbered Italian wine bar–restaurant serving reasonable Italian cuisine (no pizza) with a tempting *antipasti* bar. It's a relaxed, open setting with busy, blue-aproned waiters serving two floors of local eaters (allow €30 for meals with wine, daily, across from L'Excuse at rue St. Paul and rue Charles V, 25 rue Charles V, tel. 01 42 78 91 44).

$ Camille, a traditional corner brasserie, is a neighborhood favorite with great indoor and sidewalk seating. White-aproned waiters serve €9 salads and very French *plats du jour* for €15 to a down-to-earth but sophisticated clientele (daily, 24 rue des Francs Bourgeois at corner of rue Elzévir, tel. 01 42 72 20 50).

$ Piccolo Teatro is where vegetarians should go for a good, inexpensive meal. Friendly British expatriate Rachel will take care of you (daily, near rue des Rosiers, 6 rue des Ecouffes, tel. 01 42 72 17 79).

$ L'As du Falafel serves inexpensive Jewish cuisine on plastic plates, with bustling ambience or to go (day and night until late, closed Sat, €6 "special falafel" is great, 34 rue des Rosiers).

$ Several hard-working **Chinese fast-food places** are along rue St. Antoine, great for a €6 meal.

Dining Closer to Hôtel de Ville

For restaurants near the Pompidou Center, see page 305.

$$$ Au Bourguignon du Marais, a small wine bar–bistro south of rue de Rivoli, is a place that wine-lovers shouldn't miss. Gentle English-speaking Jacques offers excellent Burgundy wines that blend well with his fine, though limited, selection of *plats du jour*. The escargots were the best I've had, and the dessert was... *délicieux* (allow €35–45 with wine, closed Sat–Sun, call by 19:00 to reserve, 52 rue Francois Miron, tel. 01 48 87 15 40).

$$ Le Fou d'En Face, with dynamite ambience inside and out, is a wine-focused restaurant run by an amiable fellow who loves his lot in life. It's on a small square barely off rue de Rivoli near the recommended Hôtel de Nice. Try the *pot-au-feu* (beef stew-€19), and test the superb wine selection (closed Sun, 3 rue du Bourg-Tibourg, tel. 01 48 87 03 75).

$$ Le Colimacon is a romantic little place twirled around its spiral stairs *(colimacon)*. They offer two-course (€18) or three-course

(€23) *menus* of traditional cuisine, including *magret de canard aux fruits de saison*—duck breast with a sauce of seasonal fruit (closed Tue, reservations required, 44 rue Vieille du Temple, tel. 01 48 87 12 01).

$ BHV Department Store's fifth-floor cafeteria provides an escape from the busy streets below, nice views, and no-brainer, point-and-shoot cafeteria cuisine (Mon–Sat 11:30–18:00, closed Sun, at intersection of rue du Temple and rue de la Verrerie, one block from Hôtel de Ville).

$ Petite Gavroche is a charmingly basic place offering dirt-cheap French cooking (€9 *plats du jour*, 15 rue Ste. Croix de la Bretonnerie, tel. 01 48 87 74 26).

Picnicking in the Marais

Picnic at peaceful place des Vosges (closes at dusk) or on the Ile St. Louis *quais* (see below). Stretch your euros at the basement supermarket of the **Monoprix** department store (closed Sun, near place des Vosges on rue St. Antoine). Two small grocery shops are open until 23:00 on rue St. Antoine (near intersection with rue Castex).

Breakfast in the Marais

For an incredibly cheap breakfast, try ***Hilaire boulangerie-pâtisserie,*** where the hotels buy their croissants (coffee machine-€0.70, cheap baby quiches, 1 block off place de la Bastille, corner of rue St. Antoine and rue de Lesdiguières).

Nightlife in the Marais

The best scene is the dizzying array of wacky eateries, bars, and dance halls on rue de Lappe. This street is what the Latin Quarter wants to be. Just east of the stately place de la Bastille, it's one of the wildest night spots in Paris. Sitting amid the chaos like a van Gogh painting is the popular, time-warp **Bistrot les Sans Culottes** (see above).

Trendy cafés and bars—popular with gay men—also cluster on rue Vieille du Temple, rue des Archives, and rue Ste. Croix de la Bretonnerie (close at about 02:00). Rue de Rosiers bustles with youthful energy. **Le Vieux Comptoir** is tiny, lively, and just hip enough (off place des Vosges at 8 rue de Birague). **Vins des Pyrénées** is young and fun (see above). **La Perla** is full of Parisian yuppies in search of the perfect margarita (26 rue François Miron). The **Quiet Man** is a traditional Irish pub with happy hour from 16:00 to 20:00 (5 rue des Haudriettes).

Ile St. Louis

The Ile St. Louis is a romantic and peaceful place to window-shop for plenty of promising dinner possibilities. Cruise the island's main street for a variety of options, from cozy *crêperies* to Italian places (intimate pizzeria and upscale) to typical brasseries (several with fine outdoor seating facing the bridge to Ile de la Cité). After dinner, sample Paris' best sorbet. Then stroll across to the Ile de la Cité to see an illuminated Notre-Dame. All listings below line the island's main drag, the rue St. Louis-en-l'Ile (see map on page 281). Consider skipping dessert to enjoy a stroll licking the best ice cream in Paris.

$$$ Le Tastevin is a little mother-and-son-run place serving top-notch traditional French cuisine with white-tablecloth, candlelit elegance under heavy wooden beams. The *menus* start with three courses at about €30 and offer plenty of classic choices that change with the season to ensure freshness (daily, good wine list, 46 rue St. Louis-en-l'Ile, tel. 01 43 54 17 31; owner Madame Puisieux speaks just enough English, while her son tends the kitchen).

$$ Nos Ancêtres les Gaulois and **La Taverne du Sergeant Recruteur**, next door to each other on rue St. Louis-en-l'Ile, are famous for their rowdy, medieval cellar atmosphere. They serve all-you-can-eat buffets with straw baskets of raw veggies (cut whatever you like with your dagger), massive plates of pâté, a meat course, and all the wine you can stomach for €36–38. The food is just food; burping is encouraged. If you want to eat a lot, drink a lot of wine, and holler at your friends while receiving smart-aleck buccaneer service, these food fests can be fun. Nos Ancêtres les Gaulois, or "Our Ancestors the Gauls," has bigger tables and seems made-to-order for local stag parties (daily from 19:00, at #39, tel. 01 46 33 66 07). If you'd rather be surrounded by drunk tourists than locals, pick La Taverne du Sergeant Recruteur. The "Sergeant Recruiter" used to get young Parisians drunk and stuffed here, then sign them into the army (daily from 19:00, #41, tel. 01 43 54 75 42).

$$ La Brasserie de l'Ile St. Louis is situated at the prow of the island's ship as it faces Ile de la Cité, offering purely Alsatian cuisine (try the *choucroute garni* for €17), served in Franco-Germanic ambience with no-nonsense brasserie service (closed Wed, no reservations, 55 quai de Bourbon, tel. 01 43 54 02 59).

$ Café Med, closest to Notre-Dame at #77, is best for inexpensive salads, crêpes, and light €12 *menus* in a tight but cheery setting (daily, limited wine list, tel. 01 43 29 73 17, charming Eva SE). There's a similar *crêperie* just across the street.

Riverside Picnic

On sunny lunchtimes and balmy evenings, the *quai* on the Left Bank side of Ile St. Louis is lined with locals who have more class than money, spreading out tablecloths and even lighting candles for elegant picnics. Otherwise, it's a great walk for people-watching.

Ice-Cream Dessert

Half the people strolling Ile St. Louis are licking an ice cream cone, because this is the home of *les glaces Berthillon.* The original **Berthillon** shop, at 31 rue St. Louis-en-l'Ile, is marked by the line of salivating customers (closed Mon–Tue). It's so popular that the wealthy people who can afford to live on this fancy island complain about the congestion it causes. For a less-famous but at-least-as-tasty treat, the homemade Italian gelato a block away at **Amorino Gelati** is giving Berthillon competition (no line, bigger portions, easier to see what you want, and they offer little tastes—Berthillon doesn't need to, 47 rue St. Louis-en-l'Ile, tel. 01 44 07 48 08). Having some of each is a fine option.

In the Luxembourg Neighborhood

Sleeping in the Luxembourg neighborhood puts you near many exciting dining and after-hours options. Because my hotels for this area cluster around the Panthéon and St. Sulpice Church, I've organized restaurants the same way. Restaurants near the Panthéon tend to be calm, those around St. Sulpice more boisterous; it's a short walk from one area to the other. Anyone sleeping in this area is close to the inexpensive eateries that line the always-bustling rue Mouffetard. You're also within a 15-minute walk of the *grands cafés* of St. Germain and Montparnasse.

Near the Panthéon

For locations, see page 339.

$$ Les Vignes du Panthéon, on a quiet street a block from the Panthéon, is a homey, formal, traditional place with a zinc bar, original flooring, white tablecloths, and soft ambience. It serves a mostly local clientele and will make you feel you're truly in Paris (allow €28 for à la carte, closed Sun, English menu posted outside, 4 rue des Fossés St. Jacques, tel. 01 43 54 80 81).

$$ Terra Neva, a few doors up from Les Vignes du Panthéon, has a privileged position on a broad sidewalk along a peaceful street with views to the Panthéon's facade. Join the loyal clientele for Italian specialties. Two can easily split the big *antipasti* (ask for mozzarella with it), and each get a pasta main course for about €22 per person (closed Sun, limited and pricey wine list, 18 rue des Fossés St Jacques, tel. 01 43 54 83 09). The *other* Italian place across the street (one letter difference in name) serves more basic, cheaper pizzas and pastas.

$$ Restaurant Perraudin is a welcoming, family-run, red-checkered-tablecloth place. Gentle M. Rameau serves classic *cuisine bourgeoise* with an emphasis on Burgundian dishes. The decor is classic turn-of-the-century, with big mirrors and old wood paneling (*bœuf bourguignon* is a specialty here, €28 *menus*, closed

Sat–Sun, between the Panthéon and Luxembourg Garden at 157 rue St Jacques, tel. 01 46 33 15 75).

$ Le Soufflot is my favorite outdoor café between the Panthéon and Luxembourg Garden, with a nifty library-like interior and outdoor tables on a wide sidewalk with point-blank views of the Panthéon. The cuisine is café-classic: salads, omelets, and *plats du jour* (daily, a block below the Panthéon on the right side of rue Soufflot as you walk toward Luxembourg Garden, tel. 01 43 26 57 56).

$ Le Volcan, a few blocks behind the Panthéon, has a wood floor, wood-counter-cozy front room, and a reasonable menu with dinners from €16 (10 rue Thouin, tel. 01 46 33 38 33).

On Rue Mouffetard

$ Café Delmas, at the top of rue Mouffetard on picturesque place de la Contrescarpe, is *the* place to see and be seen. Come here for a before- or after-dinner drink on the broad outdoor terrace, or for typical café cuisine (salads-€12, *plats*-€15, great chocolate ice cream, open daily).

$ Le Jardin d'Artemis is one of the better values right on rue Mouffetard, serving traditional French specialties with a Greek touch in a cozy setting (no outside tables, €17–26 *menus*, closed Tue, 34 rue Mouffetard, tel. 01 45 35 17 47).

$ Cave de la Bourgogne serves reasonably-priced café fare at the bottom of rue Mouffetard, with picture-perfect tables on an raised terrace and a warm interior (specials listed on chalkboards, open daily, 144 rue Mouffetard).

$ Le Jardin des Pates is popular with less-strict vegetarians, serving pastas and salads at fair prices (daily, near Jardin des Plantes, 4 rue Lacépède, tel. 01 43 31 50 71).

Near St. Sulpice Church

For locations, see page 336.

$$$ Au Bon Saint-Pourcain is to be saved for a special night. Soft lights and a few outside tables greet passers-by, while those who duck inside become part of the club. Reserve ahead for this tiny place, which serves traditional cuisine, hiding on a quiet lane between St. Sulpice Church and the Luxembourg Garden (à la carte only, allow €45 per person with wine, daily, 10 bis rue Servandoni, tel. 01 43 54 93 63).

$$ Chez Diane is an antique bistro on the same street a block closer to Luxembourg Garden serving French classics with a light-hearted spirit (menus from €26, closed Sun, 25 rue Servandoni, tel. 01 46 33 12 06).

Rue des Canettes and Rue Guisarde: For an entirely different experience, roam the streets between the St. Sulpice Church and boulevard St. Germain, abounding with restaurants, *crêperies*, wine bars, and jazz haunts. Find rue des Canettes and rue Guisarde, and window-shop the many Franco-Italian places. Every place does a brisk business, and it's hard to distinguish one from the other. **Brasserie Fernand** is lined with tiny tables packed with folks enjoying €10–15 plates of traditional French food (closed Sun, 13 rue Guisarde, tel. 01 43 54 61 47). For crêpes, try **La Crêpe Rit du Clown** (Mon–Sat 12:00–23:00, closed Sun, 6 rue des Canettes, tel. 01 46 34 01 02). And for a bohemian pub with a cigarette-rolling gang surrounded by black-and-white photos of the artsy and revolutionary French Sixties, have a drink at **Chez Georges** (cheap drinks from time-warp menu upstairs, cool little street-side table nook; downstairs for mostly gay jazz dance cellar, open 14:00–2:00, closed Sun–Mon and in Aug, 11 rue des Canettes).

In Montmartre

Montmartre is extremely touristy, with many mindless mobs following guides to cancan shows. But the ambience is undeniably fun, and an evening up here overlooking Paris is a quintessential experience in the City of Light. Along the touristy main drag (and just off it), several fun piano bars serve reasonable crêpes with great people-watching.

$$ Restaurant Chez Plumeau, just off the jam-packed place du Tertre, is a touristy yet cheery, moderately priced place with great seating on a tiny characteristic square (€28 *menu*, elaborate €15 salads, closed Wed, place du Calvaire, tel. 01 46 06 26 29).

$ L'Eté en Pente Douce hides under generous branches below the crowds on a classic neighborhood corner, with fine indoor and outdoor seating, €10 *plats du jour* and salads, veggie options, and good wines (daily, 23 rue Muller, many steps below Sacré-Cœur to the left as you leave, down the stairs below the WC, tel. 01 42 64 02 67).

In Versailles

In the pleasant town center, around place du Marché Notre-Dame, you'll find a variety of reasonably priced restaurants, cafés, and a few cobbled lanes (market days Sun, Tue, and Fri until 13:00). The square is a 15-minute walk from the château (veer left when you leave château). From the place du Marché, consider shortcutting to Versailles' gardens by walking 10 minutes west down rue de la Paroisse. The château will be to your left after entering, and the main gardens, Trianon Palaces, and Hamlet straight ahead. The quickest way to the château's front door is along avenue de St. Cloud and rue Colbert.

The following restaurants serve good food and are open daily for lunch or dinner. The first two are located on or near place du Marché Notre-Dame. **La Bœuf à la Mode** is a bistro with traditional cuisine right on the square (2-course *menu*-€20, 3-course *menu*-€25, 4 rue au Pain, tel. 01 39 50 31 99). **A la Côte Bretonne** is the place to go for crêpes in a friendly, cozy setting (a few steps off the square on traffic-free rue des Deux Portes at #12, tel. 01 39 51 18 24).

Rue Satory, a pedestrian-friendly street lined with restaurants, is on the south side of the château near Hôtel d'Angleterre (10-min walk, angle right out of the château). **Le Limousin** is a warm, traditional restaurant on the corner nearest the château, with mostly meat dishes (€35–40 with wine, daily, lamb is a specialty, 4 rue de Satory, tel. 01 39 50 21 50).

TRANSPORTATION CONNECTIONS

Trains

Paris is Europe's rail hub, with six major train stations, each serving different regions: Gare de l'Est (eastbound trains), Gare du Nord (northern France and Europe), Gare St. Lazare (northwestern France), Gare d'Austerlitz (southwestern France and Europe), Gare de Lyon (southeastern France and Italy), and Gare Montparnasse (northwestern France and TGV service to France's southwest). Any train station can give you schedule information, make reservations, and sell tickets for any destination. Buying tickets is handier from an SNCF neighborhood office—including those at the Louvre, Invalides, Orsay, Versailles, and airports—or at your neighborhood travel agency. It's worth the small fee. Look for SNCF signs in their window, which indicate they sell train tickets.

Schedules change by season, weekday, and weekend. Verify train schedules shown in this book (to study ahead on the Web, check http://bahn.hafas.de/bin/query.exe/en). The nationwide information line for train schedules and reservations is tel. 3635. Dial this four-digit number, then press "3" for reservations or ticket purchases when you get the message. Press 321 for Eurostar information or 322 for Thalys. This incredibly helpful, time-saving service costs €0.34 per minute from anywhere in France (ask for an English-speaking agent and hope for the best, allow 5 min per call). The time and energy you save easily justifies the telephone torture, particularly when making seat reservations (note that phoned reservations must be picked up at least 30 min prior to departure).

All six train stations have Métro, bus, and taxi service. All have banks or change offices, ATMs, information desks, telephones, cafés, newsstands, and clever pickpockets. Because of security concerns, not all have baggage check, though those with this service are identified below. Each station offers two types of rail service: long distance to other cities, called *Grandes Lignes* (major lines); and suburban service to outlying areas, called *banlieue* or RER. Both *banlieue* and RER trains serve outlying areas and the airports; the only difference is that *banlieue* lines are operated by SNCF (France's train system, called Transilien) and RER lines are operated by RATP (Paris' Métro and bus system). You may also see ticket windows identified as *Ile de France;* these are for Transilien (SNCF) trains serving destinations outside Paris in the Ile de France region (usually no longer than an hour from Paris).

Paris train stations can be intimidating, but if you slow down, take a deep breath, and ask for help, you'll find them manageable and efficient. Bring a pad of paper for clear communication at ticket/info windows. All stations have helpful *accueil* (information) booths; the bigger stations have roving helpers, usually in red vests. They're capable of answering rail questions more quickly than the information or ticket windows.

Station Overview

Here's an overview of Paris' major train stations. Métro and RER trains, as well as buses and taxis, are well-marked at every station. When arriving by Métro, follow signs for *Grandes Lignes*-SNCF to find the main tracks.

Gare du Nord

This vast station serves cities in northern France and international destinations north of Paris, including Copenhagen, Amsterdam, and the Eurostar to London, as well as two of the day trips described in this book (Chantilly and Auvers-sur-Oise).

Arrive early to allow time to navigate this station. From the Métro, follow *Grandes Lignes* signs (main lines) and keep going up until you reach the tracks at street level. *Grandes Lignes* depart from tracks 3–21, suburban *(banlieue)* lines from tracks 30–36, and RER trains depart from tracks 37–44 (tracks 41–44 are 1 floor below). Glass train information booths *(accueil)* are scattered throughout the station and information-providing staff circulate to help (all rail staff are required to know English).

The tourist information kiosk opposite track 16 is a hotel reservation service for Accor chain hotels (they also have free Paris maps). Information booths for the **Thalys** (high-speed trains to Brussels and Amsterdam) are opposite track 8. All non-Eurostar ticket sales are opposite tracks 3–8. Passengers departing on **Eurostar** (London via Chunnel) must buy tickets and check in on the second level, opposite track 6. (Note: Britain's time zone is one hour earlier; times listed on Eurostar tickets are local times—Parisian time for departing Paris and the British time you'll arrive in London.) Monet-esque views over the trains and peaceful, air-conditioned cafés hide on the upper level, past the Eurostar ticket windows (find the cool view WCs down the steps in the café). Baggage check, taxis, and rental cars are at the far end, opposite track 3 and down the steps.

Key destinations served by Gare du Nord *Grandes Lignes*: **Brussels** (12/day, 1.5 hrs, see "To Brussels and Amsterdam by Thalys Train," page 361), **Bruges** (18/day, 2 hrs, change in Brussels, one direct), **Amsterdam** (10/day, 4 hrs, see "To Brussels and Amsterdam by Thalys Train," page 361), **Copenhagen** (1/day, 16 hrs, two night trains), **Koblenz** (6/day, 5 hrs, change in Köln), and **London** (Eurostar via Chunnel, 17/day, 3 hrs, tel. 08 36 35 35 39).

By *banlieue*/RER lines: **Chantilly-Gouvieux** (hrly, fewer on weekends, 35 min), **Charles de Gaulle Airport** (2/hr, 30 min, runs 5:30–23:00, track 4), **Auvers-sur-Oise** (2/hr, 1 hr, transfer at Pontoise).

Gare Montparnasse

This big and modern station covers three floors, serves lower Normandy and Brittany, and offers TGV service to the Loire Valley and southwestern France, as well as suburban service to Chartres. At street level, you'll find a bank, and ticket windows for Ile de France trains in the center, just past the escalators. Baggage check may re-open in 2005. (If this happens, it will be on the mezzanine between levels 1 and 2.)

Most services are provided on the second (top) level, where the *Grandes Lignes* arrive and depart. Ticket windows and an information booth are to the far left (with your back to glass exterior). *Banlieue* trains depart from tracks 10–19. The main rail information office is opposite track 15. Taxis and car rentals are to the far left as you leave the tracks. Air France buses to Orly and Charles de Gaulle airports stop in front of the station, down the escalators and outside.

Key destinations served by Gare Montparnasse: Chartres (20/day, 1 hr, *banlieue* lines), **Pontorson/Mont St. Michel** (5/day, 4.5 hrs, via Rennes, then take bus from Pontorson; or take train to Pontorson via Caen, then bus from Pontorson), **Dinan** (7/day, 4 hrs, change in Rennes and Dol), **Bordeaux** (14/day, 3.5 hrs), **Sarlat** (5/day, 6 hrs, change in Bordeaux, Libourne, or Souillac), **Toulouse** (11/day, 5 hrs, most require change, usually in Bordeaux), **Albi** (7/day, 6–7.5 hrs, change in Toulouse, also night train), **Carcassonne** (8/day, 6.5 hrs, most require changes in Toulouse and Bordeaux, direct trains take 10 hrs), and **Tours** (14/day, 1 hr).

Gare de Lyon

This huge and bewildering station offers TGV and regular service to southeastern France, Italy, and other international destinations (for more trains to Italy, see "Gare de Bercy," next page). Frequent *banlieue* trains serve Melun (near Vaux-le-Vicomte) and Fontainebleau (some depart from the main *Grandes Lignes* level, more frequent departures are from one level down, follow RER-D signs, and ask at any *accueil* or ticket window where the next departure leaves from). Don't leave this station without relaxing in Le Train Bleu Restaurant, up the stairs opposite track G.

Grande Lignes trains arrive and depart from one level, but are divided into two areas (tracks A-N and 5-23). They are connected by the long platform along tracks A and 5, and by the hallway adjacent to track A and opposite track 9. This hallway has all the services, including ticket windows, ticket information, banks, shops, and access to car rental. *Banlieue* ticket windows are just inside the hall adjacent to track A *(billets Ile de France). Grandes Lignes* and *banlieue* lines share the same tracks. A tourist office (Mon–Sat 8:00–18:00, closed Sun) and a train information office are both opposite track L. From the RER or Métro, follow signs for *Grandes Lignes Arrivées* and take the escalator up to reach the platforms. Train information booths *(accueil)* are opposite tracks A and 11. Baggage check is down the stairs opposite track 13. Taxi stands are well-signed in front of the station and one floor below. For a quieter waiting area, follow *Consigne* (baggage check) signs down one floor from opposite track 13.

Air France buses to Montparnasse and Charles de Gaulle airport stop outside the main entrance to the station (opposite tracks A to L). Walk across the parking lot and the stop is opposite the European café (€11.50, 2/hr, normally at :15 and :45 after the hour).

Key destinations served by Gare de Lyon: Vaux-le-Vicomte (train to Melun, hrly, 30 min), **Fontainebleau** (nearly hrly, 45 min), **Beaune** (12/day, 2.5 hrs, most require change in Dijon), **Dijon** (15/day, 1.5 hrs), **Chamonix** (9/day, 9 hrs, change in Lyon and St. Gervais, 1 night train from Gare d'Austerlitz), **Annecy** (14/day, 4–7 hrs), **Lyon** (16/day, 2.5 hrs), **Avignon** (9/day in 2.5 hrs, 6/day in 4 hrs with change), **Arles** (14/day, 5 hrs, most with change in Marseille, Avignon, or Nîmes), **Nice** (14/day, 5.5–7 hrs, many with change in Marseille), **Venice** (3/day, 3/night, 11–15 hrs, most require changes), **Rome** (2/day, 5/night, 15–18 hrs, most require changes), and **Bern** (9/day, 5–11 hrs, most require changes, night train).

Gare de Bercy

This smaller station handles some night train service to Italy during renovation work at the Gare de Lyon (Mo: Bercy, one stop east of Gare de Lyon on line 14).

Gare de l'Est

This single-floor station (with underground Métro) serves eastern France and European points east of Paris. Train information booths are at tracks 1 and 26; the info booth at track 18 is for Transilien trains serving suburban areas; ticket windows are in the big hall opposite track 8; luggage storage *(Consigne)* is through the hall opposite track 12; Métro access is opposite track 18.

Key destinations served by Gare de l'Est: Colmar (12/day, 5.5 hrs, change in Strasbourg, Dijon, or Mulhouse), **Strasbourg** (14/day, 4.5 hrs, many require changes), **Reims** (12/day, 1.5 hrs), **Verdun** (5/day, 3 hrs, change in Metz or Chalon), **Munich** (5/day, 9 hrs, some require changes, night train), **Vienna** (7/day, 13–18 hrs, most require changes, night train), **Zürich** (10/day, 7 hrs, most require changes, night train), and **Prague** (2/day, 14 hrs, night train).

Gare St. Lazare

This relatively small station serves upper Normandy, including Rouen and Giverny. All trains arrive and depart one floor above street level. Follow signs to *Grandes Lignes* from the Métro to reach the tracks. Ticket windows are in the first hall at departure level. *Grandes Lignes* (main lines) depart from tracks 17–27; *banlieue* (suburban) trains depart from 1–16. The train information office *(accueil)* is opposite track 15. There's a post office (PTT) along track 27, and WCs are opposite track 19. There is no baggage check. You'll find many shops and services one floor below the departure level.

Key destinations served by Gare St. Lazare: Giverny (train to Vernon, 5/day, 45 min—then bus or taxi 10 min to Giverny), **Rouen** (15/day, 75 min), **Honfleur** (6/day, 3 hrs, via Lisieux, then bus), **Bayeux** (9/day, 2.5 hrs, some with change in Caen), and **Caen** (12/day, 2 hrs).

Gare d'Austerlitz

This small station provides non-TGV service to the Loire Valley, southwestern France, and Spain. All tracks are at street level. The information booth is opposite track 17, and all ticket sales are in the hall opposite track 10. Baggage check, WCs, and car rental are near track 27, along the side of the station, opposite track 21. To get to the Métro, you must walk outside and along either side of the station.

Key destinations served by Gare d'Austerlitz: Amboise (8/day in 2 hrs, 12/day in 1.5 hrs with change in St. Pierre-des-Corps), **Chamonix** (1 night train, day trains from Gare de Lyon) **Cahors** (7/day, 5–7 hrs, most with changes), **Barcelona** (1/day, 9 hrs, change in Montpellier, night trains), **Madrid** (2 night trains only, 13–16 hrs), and **Lisbon** (1/day, 24 hrs).

Buses

The main bus station is the Gare Routière du Paris-Gallieni (28 avenue du Général de Gaulle, in suburb of Bagnolet, Mo: Gallieni, tel. 01 49 72 51 51). Buses provide cheaper—if less comfortable and more time-consuming—transportation to major European cities. Eurolines' buses depart from here (tel. 08 36 69 52 52, www.eurolines.com). Eurolines has a couple of neighborhood offices: in the Latin Quarter (55 rue St. Jacques, tel. 01 43 54 11 99) and in Versailles (4 avenue des Sceaux, tel. 01 39 02 03 73).

To Brussels and Amsterdam by Thalys Train

The pricey Thalys train has the monopoly on the rail route (for a cheaper option, try the Eurolines bus; see above). Without a railpass, you'll pay about €80–100 second-class for the Paris–Amsterdam train (compared to €45 by bus) or about €60–80 second-class for the Paris–Brussels train (compared to €25 by bus). Even with a railpass, you need to pay for train reservations (second class-€14, first class-€30). Book at least a day ahead as seats are limited. Or hop on the bus, Gus.

To London by Eurostar Train

The fastest and most convenient way to get from the Eiffel Tower to Big Ben is by rail. Eurostar, a joint service of the Belgian, British, and French railways, is the speedy passenger train zips you (and up to 800 others in 18 sleek cars) from downtown Paris to downtown London (12–15/day, 2.5 hrs) faster and easier than flying. The actual tunnel crossing is a 20-minute, black, silent, 100-mile-per-hour non-event. Your ears won't even pop. Eurostar trains also run directly to London from Charles de Gaulle Airport (requires change in Lille) or Disneyland Paris (1/day direct, more often with transfer at Lille).

Eurostar Fares

Channel fares (essentially the same between London and Paris or Brussels) are reasonable but complicated. Prices vary depending on when you travel, whether you can live with restrictions, and whether you're eligible for any discounts (youth, seniors, and railpass-holders all qualify). Rates are lower for round trips and off-peak travel (midday, midweek, low-season, and low-interest). Fares are always changing. For specifics, visit www.ricksteves.com/eurostar.

As with airfares, the most expensive and flexible option is a **full-fare ticket** with no restrictions on refundability (even refundable after the departure date; for a one-way trip, figure around $345 in first class, $249 second class). A first-class ticket comes with a meal (a dinner departure nets you more grub than breakfast)—but it's not worth the extra expense.

Also like the airlines, **cheaper tickets** come with more restrictions—and are limited in number (so they sell out more quickly; for second-class, one-way tickets, figure $90–200). Non-full-fare tickets have severe restrictions on refundability (best-case scenario: you'll get 25 percent back, but with the cheapest options you'll get nothing). But several do allow you to change the specifics of your trip once before departure.

Those traveling with a railpass for Britain, France, or Belgium should look first at the **passholder** fare, an especially good value for one-way Eurostar trips (around $75).

Buying Eurostar Tickets

Refund and exchange restrictions are serious, so don't reserve until you're sure of your plans. If you're confident about the time and date of your crossing, order ahead from the United States. Only the most expensive ticket (full fare) is fully refundable, so if you want to have more flexibility, hold off—keeping in mind that the longer you wait, the more likely the cheapest tickets will sell out (you might end up having to pay for first class).

You can check and book fares by phone or online in the United States (order online at www.ricksteves.com/eurostar, prices listed in dollars; order by phone at U.S. tel. 800/EUROSTAR) or in France (French tel. 08 92 35 35 39, www.eurostar.com, prices listed in euros). These are different companies, often with slightly different prices and discount deals on similar tickets; if you order from the United States, check out both. (If you buy from a U.S. company, you'll pay for ticket delivery in the United States; if you book with the European company, you'll pick up your ticket at the train station.) In Europe, you can buy your Eurostar ticket at any major train station in any country, at neighborhood SNCF offices, or at any travel agency that handles train tickets (expect a booking fee).

Note that France's time zone is one hour later than Britain's. Times listed on tickets are local (Parisian time of departure and the British time of arrival in London).

Airports

Charles de Gaulle Airport

Paris' primary airport has two main terminals: T-1 and T-2, and two lesser terminals, T-3 and T-9. Air Canada, SAS, United, US Airways, KLM, Northwest, and Lufthansa all normally use T-1. Air France, British Airways, Continental, American, Alitalia, and KLM normally use T-2. Smaller airlines use T-3 and charter flights leave from T-9. Airlines sometimes switch terminals, so verify your terminal before flying. Terminals are connected every few minutes by a free *navette* (shuttle bus). The RER (Paris commuter train with links to the Metro) stops at T-2 and T-3 terminals, and the TGV (tay-zhay-vay, stands for *train à grande vitesse*) station is at T-2. There is no baggage storage at the airport. Beware of pickpockets on *navettes* between terminals and especially on RER trains. Do not take an unauthorized taxi from the men greeting you on arrival. Official taxi stands are well-signed.

Those flying to or from the United States will almost certainly use T-1 or T-2. Below is information for each terminal. For flight information, call 01 48 62 22 80. For the latest information on either of Paris' airports, check www.adp.fr.

Terminal 1 (T-1): This circular terminal has one main entry and covers three floors—arrival (*arrivées*, top floor), departure (*départs*, one floor down) and shops/boutiques (basement level). For information on getting to Paris, see "Transportation between Charles de Gaulle Airport and Paris," below.

Arrival level: You'll find a variety of services at these gates.

- Gate 36: Called *Meeting Point*, this gate has an ADP (a quasi-tourist office) that sells Museum Passes, offers free maps, and provides tourist/hotel information (daily 7:00–22:00). A nearby *Relay* store sells phone cards. To find the shuttle buses *(navettes)* for Terminal 2 and the RER trains to Paris, take the elevator down to level *(niveau)* 2, then walk outside (line #1 serves T-2 including the TGV station; line #2 goes directly to the RER station).
- Gate 34: Outside are Air France buses to Paris and Orly Airport.
- Gate 32: ATMs. Outside are Roissy Buses to Paris (buy tickets inside at gate 30 or from driver).
- Gate 20: Taxis outside.
- Gate 16: A bank with lousy rates for currency exchange.
- Gates 10–24: Car-rental offices.

Departure level (*niveau* 3): This is limited to flight check-in, though you will find ADP information desks here. Those departing from T-1 will find restaurants, a PTT (post office), a pharmacy, boutiques, and a handy grocery store one floor below the ticketing desks (*niveau* 2 on the elevator).

Terminal 2 (T-2): This long, horseshoe-shaped terminal is dominated by Air France and divided into several sub-terminals (or halls), each identified by a letter. You can walk from one hall to the other. Halls are connected to the RER, the TGV station, and T-1 every five minutes via free *navettes* (shuttle buses, line #5 runs to T-1).

Here's where you should find these key carriers: Air France, Continental, and American Airlines—Hall A; British Airways—Hall B; Delta—Hall C; more Air France, KLM, and Alitalia—Hall F.

The RER and TGV stations are below the Sheraton Hotel (access by *navettes* or on foot). Stops for *navettes*, Air France buses, and Roissy Buses are all well-marked and near each Hall (see "Transportation between Charles de Gaulle Airport and Paris," below). ADP information desks are located near gate 5 in each Hall. Car-rental offices, post offices, pharmacies, and ATMs *(point d'argent)* are also well-signed.

Transportation between Charles de Gaulle Airport and Paris: Three efficient public-transportation routes, taxis, and airport shuttle vans link the airport's terminals with central Paris. All are well-marked, and stops are centrally located at all terminals. If you're carrying lots of baggage—or are just plain tired—airport shuttle vans or taxis are well worth the extra cost.

To get to the rue Cler area, the Roissy bus and Métro combination is the most convenient public transport route. To reach the Marais, your best option is the Air France bus to Gare de Lyon, with a quick trip on Métro line #1. Both routes are described below. For the Luxembourg area, take RER-B to the Luxembourg stop. All your options into Paris are well-marked, but if you have trouble, ask any airport employee.

RER trains stop near T-1 and at T-2, cost €8, and run every 15 minutes, with stops in central Paris at Gare du Nord, Châtelet-Les Halles, St. Michel, and Luxembourg. When coming from Paris to the airport, T-1 is the first RER stop at Charles de Gaulle; T-2 is the second stop. Beware of pickpockets preying on jet-lagged tourists on these trains; wear your moneybelt. The other transportation options described below have far fewer theft problems.

Roissy Buses run every 15 minutes to Paris' Opéra Garnier (€8.50, 40–60 min). You'll arrive at a bus stop on rue Scribe at the American Express office, on the left side of the Opéra building. To get to the Métro entrance, turn left out of the bus, heading towards the front of the Opéra. For rue Cler hotels, take the #8 Métro line (direction: Balard) to La Tour Maubourg or Ecole Militaire. For hotels in the Marais neighborhood, take the same #8 line (direction: Créteil Préfecture) to the Bastille stop.

Air France bus routes serve central Paris about every 15–30 minutes (to Arc de Triomphe and Porte Maillot-€10, 40 min; to Montparnasse Tower/train station-€11.50, 60 min; or to the Gare de Lyon station-€11.50, 40 min). To reach Marais hotels from Gare de Lyon, take Métro line 1 (direction La Défense) to the Bastille, St. Paul, or Hôtel de Ville stops.

Taxis will run €40–50 with bags, more if traffic is bad. If taking a cab to the airport, ask your hotel to call for you (the night before if you must leave early) and specify that you want a real taxi *(un taxi normal)* and not a limo-service that costs €20 more. Remember, you pay a bit more on Sundays, before 7:00, and after 19:00.

Airport shuttles offer a less stressful trip between either of Paris' airports and downtown, ideal for single travelers or families of four or more (taxis are limited to three). Reserve from home and they'll meet you at the airport. Airport shuttles cost about €30–40 for one person, €40–45 for two, and €60–65 for three. Some offer deals if you do a round trip and most are more expensive at night (20:00–6:00). Plan on a 30-minute wait if you ask them to pick you up at the airport. Be clear on where and how you are to meet your driver. If you're planning to use an airport shuttle service to get from Paris to the airport, book your trip at least a day in advance (most hoteliers will make the call for you).

Choose between three options: **Golden Air**—among the most reliable of the many shuttles—ask for the Rick Steves discount (tel. 01 34 10 12 92, fax 01 34 10 93 89, www.paris-airport-shuttle-limousine.com, goldenair@goldenair.net), **Airport Connection** (tel. 01 44 18 36 02, fax 01 45 55 85 19, www.airport-connection.com), and **Paris Airports Service** (tel. 01 55 98 10 80, fax 01 55 98 10 89, www.parisairportservice.com).

Sleeping at or near Charles de Gaulle Airport: **Hôtel Ibis****, outside the RER Roissy Rail station at T-3 (the first RER stop coming from Paris), offers standard and predictable accommodations (Db-€80–90, near *navette* stop, free shuttle bus to all terminals, tel. 01 49 19 19 19, fax 01 49 19 19 21, www.ibishotel.com, h1404@accor-hotels.com). **Novotel***** is next door and the next step up (Db-€125–160, tel. 01 49 19 27 27, fax 01 49 19 27 99, www.novotel.com).

The small village of Roissy, which gave its name to the airport (Roissy Charles de Gaulle), has better-value chain hotels with shuttle service to the airport (6/hr, 10 min). There, you'll also find a real village to shop for your last Parisian dinner or an early-morning café breakfast. Choose from **Hotel Campanile** (Db-€65, tel. 01 34 29 80 40, fax 01 34 29 80 39, www.campanile.fr, roissy@campanile.fr) or **Hotel Kyriad** (Db-€85, tel. 01 34 29 00 00, fax 01 34 29 00 11, www.kyriad.fr, roissy@bleumarine.fr).

To avoid rush-hour traffic, drivers can consider sleeping north of Paris in the pleasant medieval town of **Senlis** (15 min north of airport) at **Hostellerie de la Porte Bellon** (Db-€60–75, central at 51 rue Bellon, near rue de la République, tel. 03 44 53 03 05, fax 03 44 53 29 94).

Orly Airport

This airport feels small. Orly has two terminals: Sud (south) and Ouest (west). International flights arrive at Sud. Arriving in Orly, you'll exit Sud's baggage claim (near gate H) and see signs directing you to city transportation, car rental, and so on. Turn left to enter the main terminal area, and you'll find exchange offices with bad rates, an ATM, the ADP (a quasi-tourist office that offers free city maps and basic sightseeing information, open until 23:00), and an SNCF rail desk (until 18:00, sells train tickets and even Eurailpasses, next to ADP). Downstairs are a sandwich bar, WCs, a bank (same bad rates), a newsstand (buy a phone card), and a post office with great rates for cash or American Express traveler's checks. Car-rental offices are located in the parking lot in front of the terminal. For flight info on any airline serving Orly, call 01 49 75 15 15. For information on either of Paris' airports, visit www.adp.fr.

Transportation between Orly Airport and Paris: Several efficient public transportation routes, taxis, and a couple of airport shuttle services link Orly with central Paris. The gate locations listed below apply to Orly Sud, but the same transportation services are available from both terminals.

The **Air France bus** (outside gate K) runs to Paris' Invalides Métro stop (€8, 4/hr, 30 min) and is handy for those staying in or near the rue Cler neighborhood (from Invalides bus stop, take the Métro two stops to Ecole Militaire to reach recommended hotels, see RER train info, next page).

Bus #285 (also called Jetbus, outside gate H, €5.30, 4/hr) is the quickest way to the Paris subway and the best way to the Marais and Luxembourg neighborhoods. Take Jetbus to the Villejuif Louis Aragon Métro stop and buy a *carnet* (book) of 10 Métro tickets. To reach the Marais neighborhood, take the Métro to the Sully Morland stop. For the Luxembourg area, take the same train to the Censier-Daubenton or Place Monge stops. If you're going to the airport, make sure before you board the Métro that your train is heading to Villejuif Louis Aragon (not Mairie d'Ivry), as the route splits at the end of the line.

The **Orlybus** (outside gate H, €6, 3/hr) takes you to the Denfert-Rochereau RER-B line and the Métro, offering subway access to central Paris, including the Latin Quarter and Notre-Dame Cathedral, as well as the Gare du Nord train station.

These routes provide access to Paris via **RER trains**: an ADP shuttle bus takes you to RER-C, with connections to Gare d'Austerlitz, St. Michel/Notre-Dame, Musée d'Orsay, Invalides, and Pont de l'Alma stations (outside gate G, 4/hr, €5.50). The **Orlyval trains** are overpriced (€9) and require a transfer at the Antony stop to reach RER-B (serving Luxembourg, Châtelet-Les Halles, St. Michel, and Gare du Nord stations in central Paris).

Taxis are to the far right as you leave the terminal, at gate M. Allow €25–35 with bags for a taxi into central Paris.

Airport shuttle minivans are ideal for single travelers or families of four or more (see "Charles de Gaulle Airport," above, for the companies to contact; from Orly, figure about €23/1 person, €30/2 people, less for larger groups and kids).

Sleeping near Orly Airport: Two chain hotels, owned by the same company, are your best option near Orly. **Hôtel Ibis**** is reasonable, basic, and close by (Db-€60, tel. 01 56 70 50 60, fax 01 56 70 50 70, www.ibishotel.com, h1413@accor-hotels.com). **Hôtel Mercure***** provides more comfort for a higher price (Db-€120–135, tel. 01 49 75 15 50, fax 01 49 75 15 51, h1246@accor-hotels.com). Both have free shuttles to the terminal.

PROVENCE

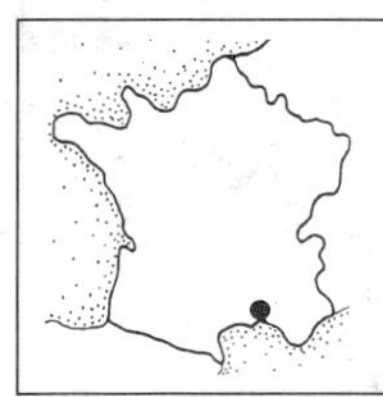

This magnificent region is shaped like a giant wedge of quiche. From its sunburned crust, fanning out along the Mediterranean coast from Nîmes to Nice, it stretches north along the Rhône Valley to Orange. The Romans were here in force and left many ruins—some of the best anywhere. Seven popes; great artists such as van Gogh, Cézanne, and Picasso; and author Peter Mayle all enjoyed their years in Provence. The region offers a splendid recipe of arid climate (except for occasional vicious winds, known as the mistral), captivating cities, exciting hill towns, dramatic scenery, and oceans of vineyards.

Explore the ghost town that is ancient Les Baux and see France's greatest Roman ruin, Pont du Gard. Spend your starry, starry nights where van Gogh did, in Arles. Uncover its Roman past, then find the linger-longer squares and café corners that inspired Vincent. Youthful but classy Avignon bustles in the shadow of its brooding pope's palace. It's a short hop from Arles or Avignon into the splendid scenery and villages that make Provence so popular today.

Planning Your Time

Make Arles or Avignon your sightseeing base, particularly if you have no car. Arles has a blue-collar quality and good-value hotels, while Avignon (three times larger than Arles) feels sophisticated and offers more nightlife and shopping. Italophiles prefer smaller Arles, while poodles pick urban Avignon.

You'll want a full day for sightseeing in Arles (best on Wed or Sat, when the morning market rages), a half day for Avignon, and a day or two for the villages and sights in the countryside.

Provence

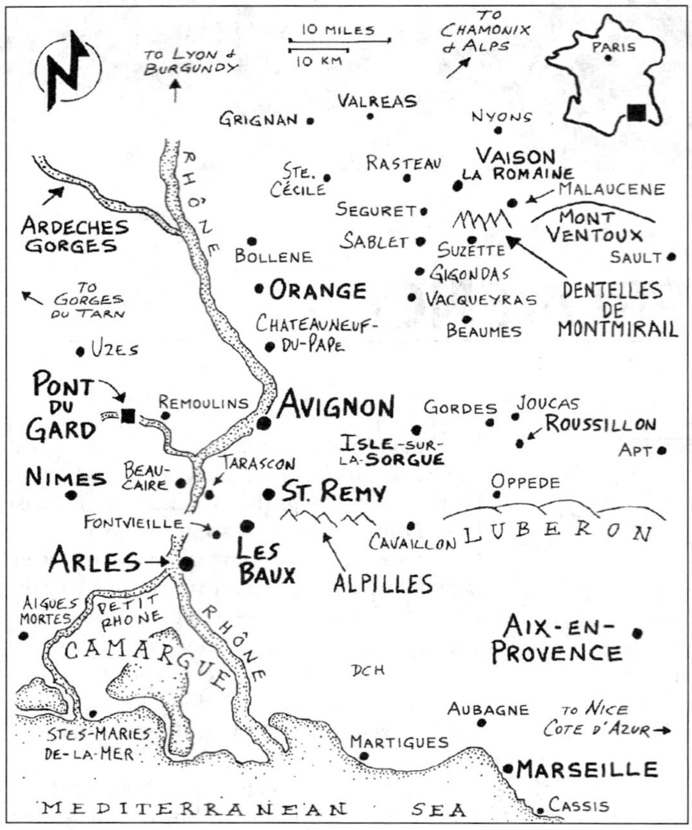

Getting Around Provence

By Car: The yellow Michelin map of this region is essential for drivers. Avignon (population 100,000) is a headache for drivers; Arles (population 35,000) is easier, though it still requires go-cart driving skills. Park only in well-watched spaces, and leave nothing in your car.

By Train or Bus: Travelers relying on public transportation will find their choices limited. Public transit is good between cities and decent to some towns, but marginal at best to the villages.

Frequent trains link Avignon and Arles (about 30 min between each). Buses connect smaller towns, but Les Baux can be reached only by taxi or tour.

St. Rémy offers the most accessible small-town experience. St. Rémy and the Pont du Gard are also connected by bus from Avignon.

Le Mistral

Provence lives with its vicious mistral winds, which blow 30 to 60 miles per hour, about 100 days out of the year. Locals say it blows in multiples of threes: three, six, or nine days in a row. *Le mistral* clears people off the streets and turns lively cities into virtual ghost towns. You'll likely spend a few hours taking refuge—or searching for cover.

When *le mistral* blows, it's everywhere, and you can't escape. Peter Mayle said it could blow the ears off a donkey. Locals say it ruins crops, shutters, and roofs (look for the stones holding tiles in place on many homes). They'll also tell you that this pernicious wind has driven many crazy (including young Vincent van Gogh). A weak version of the wind is called a *mistralet*.

Le mistral starts above the Alps and Massif Central Mountains and gathers steam as it heads south, gaining momentum as it screams over the Rhône Valley (which acts like a funnel between the Alps and Pyrénées) before exhausting itself as it hits the Mediterranean. While this wind rattles shutters throughout the Riviera and Provence, it's strongest over the Rhône Valley...so Avignon, Arles, and the Côtes du Rhône villages bear its brunt. While wiping the dust from your eyes, remember the good news: *Le mistral* brings clear skies.

Tours of Provence

It's possible to take half-day or full-day excursions to most of the sights described in this book from Arles or (better) Avignon. Local TIs have brochures on all of these excursions and can help you make a reservation. Here are two options:

Visit Provence—This tour company, based in Avignon, offers a great variety of half-day or full-day guided tours in eight-seat minivans (€50/half day, €100/day). For example, a half-day tour to both the Châteauneuf-du-Pape vineyards, with wine-tasting, and to Orange (includes Triumphal Arch, Roman Theater, and audioguide for Theater) costs €50. Other day trips include: Les Baux/Arles and St. Rémy/Les Baux/Pont du Gard. Not all tours include entry fees for sights, but reservations are required for all. Ask about their cheaper large-coach excursions (tel. 04 90 14 70 00, www.provence-reservation.com).

Lieutaud—This company operates cheap, unguided, big-bus excursions from Arles and Avignon to many hard-to-reach places at a fraction of the price you'd pay for a taxi. Different half-day and full-day trips are available every day, but no admission fees are included. Here are a few examples: Pont du Gard (€15/half-day, runs twice weekly, usually Tue and Thu); Vaison la Romaine and Orange (€19/half-day, 1 weekly, usually Mon); St. Rémy Wednesday morning market (€15/half-day); and Nîmes, Arles, and the Camargue (€28/day, usually Fri). They also offer weekly excursions to Les Baux or the Luberon, including Gordes and Roussillon (tel. 04 90 86 36 75, www.cars-lieutaud.fr).

Cuisine Scene in Provence

The almost extravagant use of garlic, olive oil, herbs, and tomatoes makes Provence's cuisine France's liveliest. To sample it, order anything *à la Provençale*. Among the area's spicy specialties are ratatouille (a thick mixture of vegetables in an herb-flavored tomato sauce), *brandade* (a salt cod, garlic, and cream mousse), aioli (a garlicky mayonnaise, often served atop fresh vegetables), tapenade (a paste of pureed olives, capers, anchovies, herbs, and sometimes tuna), *soupe au pistou* (vegetable soup with basil, garlic, and cheese), and *soupe à l'ail* (garlic soup). Look also for *riz Camarguaise* (rice from the Camargue) and *taureau* (bull meat). Banon (wrapped in chestnut leaves) and Picodon (nutty taste) are the native cheeses. The region's sheep's milk cheese, Brousse, is creamy and fresh. Provence also produces some of France's great wines at relatively reasonable prices. Look for Gigondas, Sablet, Côtes du Rhône, and Côte de Provence. If you like rosé, try the Tavel. This is the place to splurge for a bottle of Châteauneuf-du-Pape.

Remember, restaurants serve only during lunch (11:30–14:00) and dinner (19:00–21:00, later in bigger cities); cafés serve food throughout the day.

Arles

By helping Julius Caesar defeat Marseille, Arles (pronounced arl) earned the imperial nod and was made an important port city. With the first bridge over the Rhône River, Arles was a key stop on the Roman road from Italy to Spain, the Via Domitia. After reigning as the seat of an important archbishop and a trading center for centuries, the city became a sleepy place of little importance in the 1700s. Vincent van Gogh settled here a hundred years ago, but left only a chunk of his ear (now gone). American bombers destroyed much of Arles in World War II, as the townsfolk hid out in its underground Roman galleries. Today, Arles thrives again, with its evocative Roman ruins, an eclectic assortment of museums, made-for-ice-cream pedestrian zones, and squares that play hide-and-seek with visitors. It's an understandably popular home base from which to explore France's trendy Provence region.

ORIENTATION

Arles faces the Mediterranean and turns its back on Paris. While the town is built along the Rhône, it completely ignores the river (the part of Arles most damaged by Allied bombers in World War II, and therefore the least charming today).

Landmarks hide in Arles' medieval tangle of narrow, winding streets. Virtually everything is close—but first-time visitors can walk forever to get there. Hotels have good, free city maps, and Arles provides helpful street-corner signs that point you toward sights and hotels. Racing cars enjoy Arles' medieval lanes, turning sidewalks into tightropes and pedestrians into leaping targets.

Tourist Information

The main TI is on the ring road, esplanade Charles de Gaulle (April–Sept daily 9:00–18:45, Oct–March Mon–Sat 9:00–17:45, Sun 10:30–14:30, tel. 04 90 18 41 20). There's also a TI at the train station (open year-round, Mon–Sat 9:00–13:00, closed Sun). Both charge €1 to reserve hotel rooms. Pick up the good city map, note the bus schedules, and get English information on nearby destinations such as the Camargue wildlife area. Ask about bullfights and bus excursions to regional sights (see "Helpful Hints," below). Ask if buses to Les Baux have been reinstated.

Excursions from Arles: The TI can book bus excursions to many destinations that require a car to reach. These are the best half-day excursions I saw: Pont du Gard and Les Baux for €50, Luberon villages for €50, and Camargue for €36. An all-day trip to the lavender fields is offered in summer for €100 (go only in late June–July, when fields are blooming). See "Tours of Provence," page 369.

Arrival in Arles

By Train and Bus: The train and bus stations are next to each other on the river, a 10-minute walk from the town center (baggage storage not available). Get what you need at the train station TI before leaving. To reach the old town, turn left out of either station and walk 10 blocks, or take bus #3 from the shelter right across from the train station (2/hr, €0.80, buy ticket from driver). Taxis generally do not wait at either station, but you can summon one by asking the TI or calling 04 90 96 90 03 (rates are fixed, allow €8–10 to any hotel I list).

By Car: Follow signs to *Centre-Ville*, then follow signs toward Gare SNCF (train station). You'll come to a huge roundabout (place Lamartine) with a Monoprix department store to the right. Park along the city wall or in nearby lots; pay attention to *No Parking* signs on Wednesday and Saturday until 13:00 (violators will be towed to make way for Arles' huge outdoor produce markets). Some hotels have limited parking. Theft is a big problem; leave nothing in your car. From place Lamartine, walk into the city between the two stumpy towers.

Helpful Hints

Market Days: The big days are Wednesday and Saturday.

Supermarket: A big, handy **Monoprix** supermarket/department store is on place Lamartine (Mon–Sat 8:30–19:25, closed Sun).

Internet Access: Cyber City is central (daily 10:00–22:00, 41 rue du Quatre Septembre, tel. 04 90 96 87 76).

Laundry: One launderette is at 12 rue Portagnel; another is nearby at 6 rue de la Cavalerie, near place Voltaire (both daily 7:00–21:00, you can stay later to finish if you're already inside, English instructions).

Bike Rental: Try the **Peugeot** store (15 rue du Pont, tel. 04 90 96 03 77). Riding to Les Baux (20 miles round-trip, very steep climb) is possible from Arles—provided you're in great shape.

Car Rental: Avis is at the train station (tel. 04 90 96 82 42), **Europcar** and **Hertz** are downtown (2 bis avenue Victor Hugo, Europcar tel. 04 90 93 23 24, Hertz tel. 04 90 96 75 23), and **National** is just off place Lamartine toward the station (4 avenue Paulin Talabot, tel. 04 90 93 02 17).

Local Guide: Jacqueline Neujean, an excellent guide, knows Arles like the back of her hand (2 hrs/€90, tel. 04 90 98 47 51).

Cooking Courses: Friendly American **Madeleine** organizes a fun variety of wine appreciation and cooking courses from her B&B in the city center. See Maison d'Hôtes en Provence under "Sleeping," in Arles section (page 383).

Serious Coffee or Tea: Recharge at **Café de la Major** (closed Sun, near Forum Square at 7 bis rue Réattu, tel. 04 90 96 14 15).

Public Pools: Arles has three public pools (indoor and outdoor). Ask at the TI or your hotel.

Getting Around Arles

Everything's within walking distance. Only the Ancient History Museum requires a long walk (you can take the bus instead, €0.80, details in sight listing, below). The elevated riverside walk provides Rhône views and a direct (if odorous) route to the Ancient History Museum, with an easy return to the train station. Keep your head up for *Starry Night* memories, but eyes down for decorations by dogs with poorly trained owners.

Arles' **taxis** charge a set fee of about €8, but only the Ancient History Museum is worth a taxi ride (figure €30 each way to Les Baux, tel. 04 90 96 90 03).

SIGHTS AND ACTIVITIES

The worthwhile **monument pass** *(le pass monuments)* covers Arles' many sights and is valid for one week (adults-€13.50, under 18-€12, sold at each sight). Otherwise, it's €3–4 per sight and €5.50 for the Ancient History Museum. While any sight is worth a few minutes, many aren't worth the individual admission. Start at the Ancient History Museum for a helpful overview, then dive into the sights (ideally in the order described below). Remember, many begin closing rooms 30 minutes early.

▲▲▲Ancient History Museum (Musée de l'Arles Antique)—Begin your town visit here—it's Roman Arles 101. Models and original sculptures (with meager help from the English brochure) re-create the Roman city, making work-a-day life and culture easier to imagine.

You're greeted by an impressive row of pagan and early-Christian sarcophagi (2nd through 5th centuries). These would have lined the Via Aurelia outside the town wall. Pagan sarcophagi show simple slice-of-Roman-life scenes, while the Christian ones feature Bible stories. In the early days of the Church, Jesus was often portrayed beardless and as the good shepherd, with a lamb over his shoulder.

Next, you'll find models of every Roman structure in Arles you can visit today. These are the highlight for me, as they breathe a little life into buildings as they looked 2,000 years ago. Find the Forum model, and commit it to memory for when you visit the real thing later. Check out the pontoon bridge (over the widest, and therefore slowest, part of the river), find the arena (with its moveable stadium cover, which sheltered spectators from sun or rain), and locate Arles' chariot racecourse (where you are now). While virtually nothing is left of the racecourse (a.k.a. circus), the model shows that it must have rivaled Rome's Circus Maximus. Looking at the model, you can see that an emphasis on sports—with huge stadiums at the edge of town—is not unique to modern America. The model of the entire city puts it all together, illustrating how little Arles seems to have changed over two millennia—warehouses still on the opposite side of the river, and houses clustered around the city center.

All of the statues are original, except for the greatest—the *Venus of Arles*—which Louis XIV took a liking to and had moved to Versailles. It's now in the Louvre (and, as locals say, "When it's in Paris...bye-bye"). Jewelry, fine metal and glass artifacts, and well-crafted mosaic floors make it clear that Roman Arles was a city of art and culture.

Built at the site of the chariot racecourse (the arc of which is built into the parking lot), this air-conditioned, all-on-one-floor

Arles

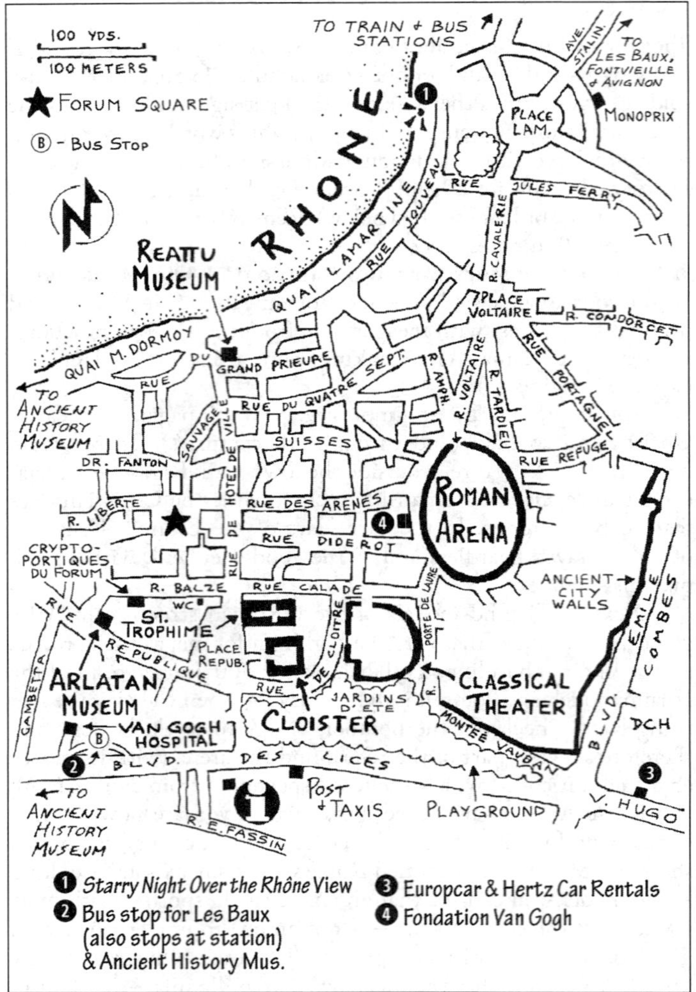

museum is a 25-minute walk from Arles along the river, or a bus ride with a short walk (€5.50, March–Oct daily 9:00–19:00, Nov–Feb daily 10:00–17:00, tel. 04 90 18 88 88, www.arles-antique.org—in French only).

Bus #1 gets you within a five-minute walk. Catch the bus in downtown Arles on boulevard des Lices (€0.80, pay driver, runs every 20 min, daily except Sun); to find the museum, exit left off the bus and then keep right, passing Hôtel Mercure. To return by bus, cross the bridge in front of museum and keep right, passing

Hôtel Mercure; the bus stop (look for glass shelter) will be on your left across from the next roundabout; you want direction: Trebon.

To reach the museum by foot from the city center, turn left at the river and take the riverside path to the big modern building just past the new bridge. The museum can call a taxi for your return (allow €8–10).

▲▲Forum Square (Place du Forum)—Named for the Roman forum that once stood here, this square was the political and religious center of Roman Arles. Still lively, this café-crammed square is popular for a *pastis*. The bistros on the square, while no place for a fine dinner, can put together a good enough salad or *plat du jour*—and when you sprinkle on the ambience, that's €10 well spent.

At the corner of Grand Hôtel Nord-Pinus, a plaque shows how the Romans built a foundation of galleries to make the main square level. The two columns are all that survive of a temple. Steps leading to the entrance are buried (the Roman street level was about 20 feet below you).

The statue on the square is of Frédéric Mistral. This popular poet, who wrote in the local dialect rather than French, was a champion of Provençal culture. After receiving the Nobel Prize in Literature in 1904, Mistral used his prize money to preserve and display the folk identity of Provence. He founded the regional folk museum (see Arlatan Museum, below) at a time when France was rapidly centralizing. (The famous local mistral—literally, "master"—wind has nothing to do with his name.)

The bright-yellow café is the famous subject of one of Vincent van Gogh's first works in Arles. While his painting showed the café in a brilliant yellow from the glow of gas lamps, the facade was bare limestone, just like the other cafés on this square. The café's current owners have painted it to match van Gogh's version...and cash in on the Vincent-crazed hordes who pay too much to eat or drink here.

Cryptoportiques du Forum—The only Baroque church in Arles (admire the wooden ceiling) provides a dramatic entry to this underground system of arches and vaults that supported the southern end of the Roman Forum (and hid French resistance fighters during World War II). The galleries of arches demonstrate the extent to which Roman engineers would go to follow standard city plans: If the land doesn't suit the blueprint, change the land. While remarkable, there's not much to it beyond the initial "Oh, wow!" (€3.50, May–Sept daily 9:00–12:00 & 14:00–18:00, April and Oct daily 9:00–11:30 & 14:00–17:30, Nov–March daily 10:00–11:30 & 14:00–16:30, leave Forum Square with Grand Hôtel Nord-Pinus on your right and turn right on rue Balze.)

▲▲St. Trophime Church, Cloisters, and Republic Square (Place de la République)—This church, named after a 3rd-century bishop of Arles and located on a fun square, sports the finest Romanesque main entrance (west portal) I've seen anywhere. Get a good view of it from...

Republic Square: This square used to be called "place Royale"...until the French Revolution. The obelisk was the centerpiece of Arles' Roman Circus. The lions at its base are the symbol of the city, whose slogan is "far from the anger of the lion." This is a popular gathering place for young Arlesians at night. Find a seat and watch the peasants—pilgrims, locals, and street musicians. There's nothing new about this scene.

Tympanum (on church facade): Like a Roman triumphal arch, the church trumpets the promise of Judgment Day. The tympanum (the semicircular area above the door) is filled with Christian symbolism. Christ sits in majesty, surrounded by symbols of the four evangelists: Matthew—the winged man, Mark—the winged lion, Luke—the ox, and John—the eagle. The 12 apostles are lined up below Jesus. It's Judgment Day...some are saved, and others aren't. Notice the condemned (on the right)—a chain gang doing a sad bunny-hop over the fires of hell. For them, the tune trumpeted by the three angels at the very top is not a happy one. Below the chain gang, St. Stephen is being stoned to death, with his soul leaving through his mouth and instantly being welcomed by angels. Ride the exquisite detail back to a simpler age. In an illiterate medieval world, long before the vivid images of our Technicolor time, this was a neon billboard over the town square. (A chart just inside the church on the right helps explain the carvings.)

Inside St. Trophime: The tall, 12th-century Romanesque nave is decorated by a set of tapestries showing scenes from the life of Mary (17th century, from French town of Aubusson). Immediately to the left of the entry, a chapel is built on an early-Christian sarcophagus from Roman Arles (from around A.D. 300). On its right side, the three Magi give gifts to baby Jesus, and a frieze below shows the flight to Egypt. Under the left transept, another Roman sarcophagus shows Jews hopping over the Red Sea as they leave Egypt. Amble around the Gothic apse and check out the relic chapel. This church is a stop on the ancient pilgrimage route to Santiago de Compostela in northwest Spain. For 800 years, pilgrims on their way to Santiago have paused here. Even today, modern-day pilgrimages are advertised near the church's entry (church entry is free, May–Sept daily 9:00–18:30, March–April and Oct daily 9:00–17:30, Nov–Feb daily 10:00–16:30).

The adjacent **cloisters** are the best in Provence (enter from square, through courtyard to right of church). Enjoy the sculpted capitals of the rounded 12th-century Romanesque columns and the pointed 14th-century Gothic columns. The second floor offers only a view of the cloisters from above (€3.50, same hours as church).

To get to the next sight, the Classical Theater, face the church, walk left, then take the first right on rue de la Calade.

Classical Theater (Théâtre Antique)—Precious little survives from this Roman theater, which served as a handy town quarry throughout the Middle Ages. Walk to a center aisle and pull up a stone seat. Built in the 1st century B.C., this theater seated 10,000. To appreciate its original size, look to the upper left side of the tower and find the protrusion that supported the highest of three seating levels. Today, 3,000 can attend events in this restored facility. Two lonely Corinthian columns look out from the stage over the audience. The orchestra section is defined by a semicircular pattern in the stone. Stepping up onto the left side of the stage and look down to the narrow channel that allowed the curtain to disappear below, like magic. Go backstage and browse through broken bits of Rome, and loop back to the entry behind the grass (€3, you can see much of the theater by peeking through the fence for free, May–Sept daily 9:00–11:30 & 14:00–18:30, April and Oct daily 9:00–11:30 & 14:00–17:30, Nov–March 10:00–11:30 & 14:00–16:30). A block uphill is the...

▲▲▲Roman Arena (Amphithéâtre)—Nearly 2,000 years ago, gladiators fought wild animals here to the delight of 20,000 screaming fans. Today, local daredevils fight wild bulls. In Roman times, games were free (sponsored by city bigwigs) and fans were seated by social class. The many exits allowed for rapid dispersal after the games—fights would break out among frenzied fans if they couldn't leave quickly. Through medieval times and until the early 1800s, the arches were bricked up, and the stadium became a fortified town—with 200 humble homes crammed within its circular defenses. Three of the medieval towers survive (the one above the ticket booth is open and rewards those who climb it with a good view). To see two still-sealed arches, complete with cute medieval window frames, turn right as you leave, walk to the Andaluz restaurant, and look back (€4, May–Sept daily 9:00–18:00, March–April and Oct daily 9:00–17:30, and Nov–Feb daily 10:00–16:30). Bullfight posters around the Arena advertise upcoming spectacles.

Turn left out of the arena and find...

▲▲Fondation Van Gogh—Refreshing to any art lover, and especially interesting to van Gogh fans, this small gallery features pieces by major contemporary artists and pays homage to Vincent through thought-provoking interpretations of his works. Many pieces are explained in English by the artists. The black-and-white photographs (both art and shots of places Vincent painted) complement the paintings (€7, not covered by monument pass, great collection of van Gogh prints and postcards for sale in free entry area, April–mid-Oct daily 10:30-20:00, mid-Oct–March Tue–Sun 11:00–17:00, closed Mon, facing Roman Arena at 24 bis

Van Gogh in Arles

"The whole future of art is to be found in the south of France."
—Vincent van Gogh, 1888

Vincent was 35 years old when he arrived in Arles in 1888, and it was here that he discovered the light that would forever change him. Coming from the gray skies and flatlands of the Netherlands and Paris, he was bowled over by everything Provençal—jagged peaks, gnarled olive trees, brilliant sunflowers, and the furious wind. Van Gogh worked in a flurry in Arles, producing more paintings than at any other period in his too-brief career—over 200 in just a few months. (The fact that locals pronounced his name "vahn-saw van gog" had nothing to do with his psychological struggles here.)

Sadly, none of van Gogh's paintings remain in Arles—but you can still visit the places that inspired him. Around downtown Arles, you'll find 17 steel-and-concrete van Gogh **"easels"** that mark places Vincent painted, including the *Café at Night* on Forum Square. Each comes with a photo of the actual painting and provides fans with a fun opportunity to compare the scene then and now. The TI has a €1 brochure that locates all the easels.

The **hospital** where Vincent was sent to treat his self-inflicted ear wound is today a cultural center (called *Espace Van Gogh* and *Mediathèque*). It surrounds a garden that the artist loved (and the only flower garden I've seen in Arles). Only the courtyard is open to the public; find the "easel" to see what Vincent painted here (free, near the Arlatan Museum on rue President Wilson). Vincent was sent from here to the mental institution in nearby St. Rémy (see page 410) before Dr. Paul Gachet invited him to Auvers-sur-Oise, near Paris.

From place Lamartine, walk to the river, then look toward the town to find where Vincent set his easel for this ***Starry Night over the Rhône*** painting, where stars boil above the skyline of Arles. Riverfront cafés that once stood here were destroyed by bridge-seeking bombs in World War II, as was the bridge whose remains you see on your right.

rond-point des Arènes, tel. 04 90 49 94 04, www.fondationvangogh-arles.org).

▲Arlatan Museum (Musée Arlaten/Museon Arlaten)—Built on the remains of the Roman Forum (see the courtyard), this museum houses the treasures of daily Provençal life. It was given to Arles by Nobel Prize winner Frédéric Mistral (see Forum Square, above). Mistral's vision was to give locals an appreciation of their cultural roots, presented in tableaux that unschooled villagers could understand—"a veritable poem for the ordinary people who cannot read." Even though there are no English descriptions, the museum offers a unique and intimate look at local folk culture from the 18th and 19th centuries.

A one-way route takes you through 30 rooms. The first few rooms display folk costumes chronologically until about 1900, when traditional dress was replaced by the modern nondescript norm. You'll then see fine freestanding wedding armoires (given to brides by parents, filled with essentials to begin a new home). Finely crafted wooden cages—called *panetières*—hung from walls and kept bread away from mice. *Santons* were popular figurines, giving nativity scenes a Provençal look. The second floor shows local history, and a large room covers lifestyles of residents of the marshy Camargue. A fascinating case shows antique Coursa Provençal bullfighting memorabilia, including a stuffed champion bull named Lion, who died of old age.

The last two rooms are the collection's pride and joy. In one, a rich mom is shown with her newborn. Her friends visit with gifts representing four physical and moral qualities hoped for in a new baby—good as bread, full as an egg, wise as salt, and straight as a match. The cradle is fully stocked with everything needed to raise an infant in 1888.

The next room shows "the great supper"—a traditional feast served on Christmas Eve before midnight Mass. It's 1860, and everything on the table is locally produced. Traditionally, 13 sweets—for Jesus and the 12 apostles—were served. Grandma and grandpa warm themselves in front of the fireplace; grandpa pours wine on a log for good luck in the coming year (€4, pick up excellent English brochure, April–Sept daily 9:30–12:30 & 14:00–18:00, Oct–March daily until 17:00, 29 rue de la République, tel. 04 90 96 08 23).

Réattu Museum (Musée Réattu)—Housed in a beautiful 15th-century mansion, this mildly interesting, mostly modern art collection includes 57 Picasso drawings (some two-sided, and all done in a flurry of creativity—I liked the bullfights best), a room of Henri Rousseau's Camargue watercolors, and an unfinished painting by the neoclassical artist Jacques Réattu, none with English explanations (€4, extra for special exhibits, May–Sept daily 9:00–12:00 & 14:00–18:30; March–April and Oct until 17:00; Nov–Feb daily 13:00–17:00; 10 rue du Grand Prieuré, tel. 04 90 96 37 68).

▲▲Wednesday and Saturday Markets—Twice a week in the morning, Arles' ring road erupts into an open-air market of fish, flowers, produce, and you-name-it. The Wednesday market runs along boulevard Emile Combes, between place Lamartine and Avenue Victor Hugo; the segment nearer place Lamartine is all about food, the upper half is about clothing, tablecloths, purses, etc.... The Saturday market is along boulevard des Lices near the

TI. Join in, buy flowers, try the olives, sample some wine, and swat a pickpocket; both markets are open until 12:00. On the first Wednesday of the month, it's a grand flea market.

Much of the market has a North African feel, thanks to the Algerians and Moroccans who live in Arles. They came to do the lowly city jobs that locals didn't want, and now mostly do the region's labor-intensive agricultural jobs (picking olives, harvesting fruit, and working in local greenhouses).

▲▲Bullfights (Courses Camarguaises)—Occupy the same seats fans have used for nearly 2,000 years, and take in Arles' most memorable experience—a bullfight *à la provençale* in the ancient arena. These are more sporting than bloody Spanish bullfights. The bulls of Arles (who, locals stress, "die of old age") are billed even more boldly than their human foes in the posters. A bull has a ribbon *(cocarde)* above its forehead, laced between its horns. The bullfighter, with a special hook, has 15 minutes to snare the ribbon. Local businessmen encourage a fighter by hollering out how much money they'll pay for the *cocarde*. If the bull pulls a good stunt, the band plays the famous "Toreador Song" from *Carmen*. The following day, newspapers have reports on the fight, including how many *Carmens* the bull earned.

Three classes of bullfights—determined by the experience of the fighters—are advertised in posters: The *course de protection* is for rookie bullfighters. The *trophée de l'Avenir* comes with better fighters. And the *trophée des As* features top professionals. During Easter and the fall rice harvest festival (Féria du Riz), the arena hosts actual Spanish bullfights (look for *corrida*) with outfits, swords, spikes, and the whole gory shebang (tickets €5–10, Easter–Oct on Sat, Sun, and holidays). Don't pass on a chance to see *Toro Piscine*, a silly spectacle for warm summer evenings where the bull ends up in a swimming pool (uh huh, get more details at TI). Nearby villages stage bullfights in small wooden bullrings nearly every weekend; the TI has the latest schedule.

SLEEPING

Hotels are a great value here; many are air-conditioned, though few have elevators.

$$$ Hôtel d'Arlatan***, built over the site of a Roman basilica, is classy in every sense of the word. It has sumptuous public spaces, a tranquil terrace, a designer pool, a turtle pond, and antique-filled rooms, most with high, wood-beamed ceilings and stone walls. In the lobby of this 15th-century building, a glass floor looks down into Roman ruins (standard Db-€88, bigger Db-€105–125, still bigger Db-€145, Db/Qb suites-€180–250, excellent buffet breakfast-€11, air-con, elevator, parking-€11, 26 rue Sauvage, 1 block

Sleep Code

(€1 = about $1.20, country code: 33)
S = Single, **D** = Double/Twin, **T** = Triple, **Q** = Quad,**b** = bathroom, **s** = shower only, **SE** = Speaks English, **NSE** = No English, * = French hotel rating system (0–4 stars). Unless otherwise noted, credit cards are accepted.

To help you sort easily through these listings, I've divided the rooms into three categories based on the price for a standard double room with bath:

$$$ **Higher Priced**—Most rooms €90 or more.
$$ **Moderately Priced**—Most rooms between €60–90.
$ **Lower Priced**—Most rooms €60 or less.

below Forum Square, tel. 04 90 93 56 66, fax 04 90 49 68 45, www.hotel-arlatan.fr, hotel-arlatan@wanadoo.fr, SE).

The next three hotels are worthy of three stars; each is an exceptional deal:

$$ Hôtel de l'Amphithéâtre**, a carefully decorated boutique hotel, is just steps from the Roman Arena. Public spaces are very sharp, with a museum quality, and the owners pay attention to every detail of your stay. The Belvedere room for €140 has the best view over Arles I've seen (Db-€52–72, superior Db-€82, Tb-€92, Qb-€120, air-con, elevator, parking-€5, 5 rue Diderot, one block from Arena, tel. 04 90 96 10 30, fax 04 90 93 98 69, www.hotelamphitheatre.fr, contact@hotelamphitheatre.fr, helpful Fabrice and Denis SE).

$$ Hôtel du Musée** is a quiet, delightful manor-home hideaway with 20 comfortable, air-conditioned rooms, a flowery two-tiered courtyard, and a snazzy art-gallery lounge. The rooms in the new section are worth the few extra euros and steps. Claude and English-speaking Laurence are gracious owners. The price ranges listed are for rooms in the old (lower rates) or new buildings (Sb-€43–50, Db-€55–65, Tb-€65–80, Qb-€80, buffet breakfast-€7, elevator, parking-€7, 11 rue du Grand Prieuré, follow signs to Réattu Museum, tel. 04 90 93 88 88, fax 04 90 49 98 15, www.hoteldumusee.com.fr, contact@hoteldumusee.com.fr).

$$ Hôtel Calendal**, located between the Roman Arena and Classical Theater, is Provençal chic and does everything right, with smartly appointed rooms—some with views overlooking the Arena—surrounding a large, palm-shaded courtyard. They even have my Provence video on DVD in the lobby. Enjoy the great buffet breakfast (€8), the salad-and-pasta-bar lunch buffet (€14), and the seductive ambience. Price ranges reflect room size (Db facing street-€45–70, Db facing garden-€72–85, Db with

Arles' Hotels and Restaurants

balcony-€90–100, air-con, Internet access, reserve ahead for parking-€10, 5 rue Porte de Laure, just above Arena, tel. 04 90 96 11 89, fax 04 90 96 05 84, www.lecalendal.com, contact@lecalendal.com, SE).

$$ Hôtel de la Muette,** with eager-to-please owners (NSE), is a good choice when the places listed above are full. Located in a quiet corner of Arles, the place is well-kept, with stone walls, wood beams, and air conditioning (Db-€55–60, Tb-€60–70, Qb-€80, no elevator, 15 rue de Suisses, tel. 04 90 96 15 39, fax 04 90 49 73 16, http//perso.wanadoo.fr/hotel-muette, hotel.muette@wanadoo.fr).

$$ Maison d'Hôtes en Provence, run by engaging American Madeleine and her soft-spoken French husband, Erique, combines an interesting B&B experience—four spacious and funky but comfortable rooms—with optional Provençal cooking workshops. Foodies should check out their Web site for its appealing and affordable range of gourmet classes (Db-€65, extra person-€15, good family room, across from launderette at 11 rue Portagnel, tel. & fax 04 90 49 69 20, www.cuisineprovencale.com, actvedel@wanadoo.fr).

$ Hôtel Régence,** one of the best deals in Arles, has a riverfront location, immaculate and comfortable rooms, good beds, safe parking, and easy access to the train station (Db-€35–48, Tb-€40–57, Qb-€60–67, choose riverview or quieter courtyard rooms, most with shower, air-con, no elevator but only two floors, excellent buffet breakfast-€5, Internet access, 5 rue Marius Jouveau, from place Lamartine, turn right immediately after passing between towers, tel. 04 90 96 39 85, fax 04 90 96 67 64, www.hotel-regence.com, contact@hotel-regence.com, the gentle Nouvions speak some English).

$ Hôtel Acacias**, just off place Lamartine inside the old city walls, is a modern, pastel paradise, with smallish, reasonably priced rooms with all the comforts, including cable TV and hairdryers (Db-€46–55, Tb-€61–79, Qb-€78–87, buffet breakfast-€6, air-con, elevator, 1 rue Marius Jouveau, tel. 04 90 96 37 88, fax 04 90 96 32 51, www.hotel-acacias.com, contact@hotel-acacias.com, Christophe and Sylvie SE).

$ Hôtel Voltaire* rents 12 small and spartan rooms with ceiling fans and nifty balconies overlooking a caffeine-stained square. It's perfect for starving artists, a block below the arena. Smiling owner Mr. Ferran (fur-ran) loves the States (his dream is to travel there), and hopes you'll add to his postcard collection. He also serves daily lunch and dinner; see "Eating," below (D-€28, Ds-€30, Db-€36, 1 place Voltaire, tel. 04 90 96 49 18, fax 04 90 96 45 49, levoltaire13@aol.com).

$ Hôtel le Rhône* greets you with neon yellow outside and hardworking owners inside—Benedicte and Hervé, refugees from northern France. Their 11 cute, spotless little rooms are decorated with cheery colors (D-€26, Ds-€31, Db-€38–40, some rooms have balconies over the square, 11 place Voltaire, tel. 04 90 96 43 70, fax 04 90 93 87 03, hotellerhone@wanadoo.fr).

EATING

You can dine well in Arles on a modest budget—in fact, it's hard to blow a lot on dinner here (all my listings have *menus* for €22 or less). The bad news is that restaurants here change regularly, so double-check my suggestions. All restaurants listed have outdoor seating, except La Bohème. Before dinner, go local on Forum Square and enjoy a *pastis*. This anise-based apéritif is served straight in a glass with ice, plus a carafe of water—dilute to taste.

On or near Forum Square

Great atmosphere and mediocre food at fair prices await on Forum Square. A half block below the Forum on rue du Dr. Fanton lies a lineup of these three tempting places:

Le 16, with warm ambience inside and out, is ideal for a fresh salad or one-course dinner. It offers a daily *plat du jour* and seasonal *menu* (closed Sat–Sun, just below Forum Square on 16 rue du Dr. Fanton, tel. 04 90 93 77 36).

La Paillotte, a few doors down, has rosy tablecloths under wood-beamed comfort inside, a nice terrace outside, and fine regional cuisine at affordable prices (€15–21 *menus*, closed Wed, 28 rue Dr. Fanton, tel. 04 90 96 33 15).

Au Bryn du Thym, almost next door, is reliable and specializes in traditional Provençal cuisine. Arrive early for an outdoor table (€19 *menu*, closed Tue, 22 rue Dr. Fanton, tel. 04 90 49 95 96).

La Bohème seems lost a block above Forum Square. Here you dine under a long, vaulted ceiling with good budget options (€14 vegetarian *menu*, €18 Provençal *menu*, closed Sun–Mon, 6 rue Balze, tel. 04 90 18 58 92).

La Cuisine de Comptoir (marked CDC) is the place urbanites go to lose that Provençal décor and pretend they're in Paris. It's a cool little bistro serving light *tartine* dinners (dishes served over toasted bread) at inexpensive prices (closed Sun, just off Forum Square's lower end at 10 rue de la Liberté, tel. 04 90 96 86 28).

Near the Roman Arena

For about the same price as on Forum Square, you can enjoy regional cuisine with a point-blank view of the arena. Of the two restaurants sitting side by side, I prefer **Le Pistou.** Arrive early to get an outdoor table with a view (*menus* from €18, closed Tue, at top of Arena, 30 rond-point des Arènes, tel. 04 90 18 20 92).

On the same block as the recommended Hôtel Calendal lies a mini-restaurant row, with several reasonable options. **Lou Caleu** is the best (though not cheapest), with very Provençal cuisine and *menus* at €18 and €26 (closed Mon, 27 rue Porte de Laure, tel. 04 90 49 71 77).

La Giraudière, a few blocks below the Arena on place Voltaire, is mauve and pretty and offers reliable regional cuisine under a heavy-beamed ceiling (€22–35 *menus*, closed Tue, air-con, tel. 04 90 93 27 52).

The recommended **Hôtel Calendal** hosts an all-you-can-eat salad-and-pasta bar (daily 12:00–16:00 for €14); the selection is as good as the quality. Retreat from the city and enjoy a healthy lunch in the hotel's palm-shaded garden.

The recommended **Hôtel Voltaire** serves a nothing-fancy three-course dinner (or lunch) for €11 and hearty salads for €8–10 (try *salade Fermiere*) daily on place Voltaire.

Dessert

For the best ice cream in Arles, find **Soleilei**, with all-natural ingredients and unusual flavors, such as *fadoli* (olive oil; daily, across from recommended La Vitamine restaurant at 9 rue du Dr. Fanton).

TRANSPORTATION CONNECTIONS

From Arles by Bus to: Nîmes (5/day, 1 hr), **St. Rémy** (6/day, 45 min), **Camargue/Stes-Maries-de-la-Mer** (5/day Mon–Sat, 4/day Sun, 1 hr). There are two bus stops in Arles: the Centre-Ville stop is at 16 boulevard Clemenceau (2 blocks below main TI, next to Café le Wilson); the other is at the train station. Bus info: tel. 04 90 49 38 01 (NSE). Ask about buses to **Les Baux** (it's possible they will be reinstated by the time you read this).

From Arles by Train to: Paris (17/day, two direct TGVs in 4 hrs, 15 with transfer in Avignon in 5 hrs), **Avignon Centre-Ville** (11/day, 20 min, afternoon gaps), **Avignon TGV** (2/hr, 20 min, take SNCF bus), **Nîmes** (9/day, 25 min), **Orange** (4/day direct, 35 min, more with transfer in Avignon), **Aix-en-Provence Centre-Ville** (10/day, 2 hrs, requires at least one transfer in Marseille), **Marseille** (20/day, 1 hr), **Carcassonne** (6/day, 3 hrs, 3 with transfer in Narbonne), **Beaune** (10/day, 4.5 hrs, 9 with transfer in Nîmes or Avignon and Lyon), **Nice** (11/day, 4 hrs, 10 with transfer in Marseille), **Barcelona** (2/day, 6 hrs, transfer in Montpellier), **Italy** (3/day, transfer in Marseille and Nice; from Arles, it's 4.5 hrs to Ventimiglia on the border, 8 hrs to Milan, 9.5 hrs to Cinque Terre, 11 hrs to Florence, and 13 hrs to Venice or Rome).

Avignon

Famous for its nursery rhyme, medieval bridge, and brooding Palace of the Popes, contemporary Avignon (ah-veen-yohn) bustles and prospers behind its mighty walls. During the 68 years (1309–1377) that Avignon starred as the Franco Vaticano, it grew from a quiet village into the thriving city it remains today. With its large student population and fashionable shops, today's Avignon is an intriguing blend of youthful spirit and urban sophistication. Street performers entertain the international crowds who fill Avignon's ubiquitous cafés and trendy boutiques. If you're here in July, be prepared for the rollicking theater festival (be sure to reserve your hotel months in advance). Clean, sharp, and popular with tourists, Avignon is more impressive for its outdoor ambience than for its museums and monuments. See the Palace of the Popes, then explore the city's thriving streets and beautiful vistas from the parc des Rochers des Doms.

ORIENTATION

The cours Jean Jaurés, which turns into rue de la République, runs straight from the train station to place de l'Horloge and the Palace of the Popes, splitting Avignon in two. The larger eastern half is where the action is. Climb to the parc des Rochers des Doms for a fine view, enjoy the people scene on place de l'Horloge, meander the backstreets (see "Discovering Avignon's Backstreets," page 393), and lose yourself in a quiet square. Avignon's shopping district fills the traffic-free streets where rue de la République meets place de l'Horloge.

Tourist Information

The main TI is between the train station and the old town, at 41 cours Jean Jaurés (April–Oct Mon–Sat 9:00–18:00, Sun 9:00–17:00; Nov–March Mon–Fri 9:00–18:00, Sat 9:00–17:00, Sun 10:00–12:00; longer hours during July festival, tel. 04 32 74 32 74, www.avignon-tourisme.com). Other branch offices may be open at either in the Palace of the Popes or at the St. Bénezet Bridge (rue Ferruce, but slow, with just one person working).

At any TI, get the good tear-off map and pick up the free and handy *Guide Pratique* (info on car and bike rental, hotels, and museums) as well as their Avignon "passion" map and guide, which includes several good (but tricky-to-follow) walking tours. It comes with the free **Avignon Passion Pass** (valid 15 days). Get the pass stamped when you pay full price at your first sight, and then receive reductions at the others; for example, €2 less at Palace of the Popes and €3 less at Petit Palais.

Avignon

Petit Palais Museum
River
St. Benezet Bridge
Blvd. St-Lazare
To Lyon via D-225 & A-7
Rochers des Doms (Park)
Pond
Rhone
R. Fer.
Blvd. du Rhone
Place du Palais
Palace of the Popes
Walls
R. Grottes
R. Balance
Pont Daladier
To Villeneuve
St. Etienne
Legat
Pey.
Croix
R. Carnot
To 6
Old City
Rempart Loulle
Rue
Place de l'Horloge
St. Pierre
Passage L'Orat.
St. Agricol
March.
Syn.
Roug.
Fourb.
Vieux
Pl. Pie
R. Thiers
Joseph
R. de la Republique
R. Bonneterie
Market
Rue
Calvet Museum
R. Roi Rene
3 Fau-cons
Fondation Angladon
R. Teint.
Des Lices
Vernet
Water-wheel
Fabre
Rue
Blvd. Raspail
St. Michel
Perd.
Cours Jaures
Old City Walls
To Nimes via A-9
Post
Cours JFK
DCH
Blvd. St. Roch
200 Yards
200 Meters
Bus Stn.
P - Parking
B - Bus Stop
Train Stn. "Centre-Ville"
To Arles
1 Best View of Bridge & Stairs to Ramparts
2 More Views & Orientation Table
3 TGV Shuttle Stop
4 TGV Shuttle Stop on Market Days
5 Launderette
6 To Shakespeare Bookshop

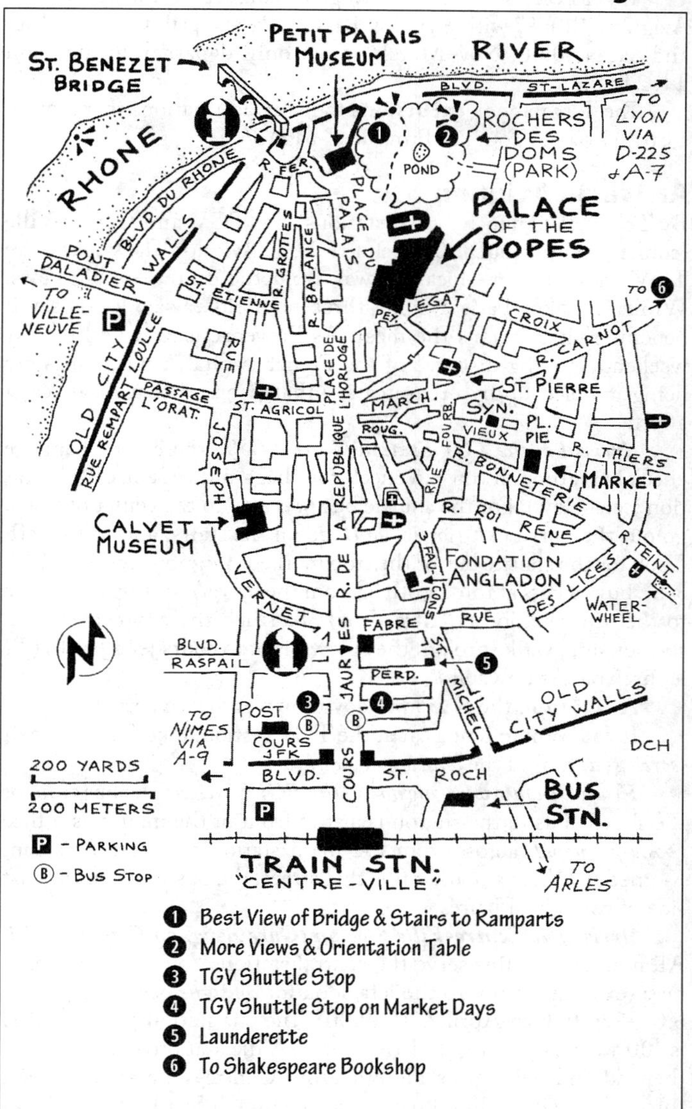

The TI offers informative English-language **walking tours** of Avignon (€10, €7 with Avignon Passion Pass; April–Oct Tue, Thu, and Sat at 10:00; Nov–March on Sat only, depart from the main TI, 2 hrs).

The TI can book **excursions** to many destinations that require a car. Also see "Tours of Provence," page 369.

Arrival in Avignon

By Train: Avignon has two stations, the TGV and Centre-Ville (connected by frequent €1.10 shuttle bus). Avignon's new space-age TGV train station—located away from the center—is big news. While it makes Paris a zippy three-hour ride away, locals say it benefits rich Parisians the most. As Provence is now within easy weekend striking distance of the French capital, rural homes are being gobbled up by urbanites at inflated prices that locals can't afford.

Arrival at the TGV Station (Gare TGV): There is no baggage check here, though you can check your bags at the Centre-Ville station (see below). For the shuttle bus *(navette)* to the center of town, go out the north exit *(sortie nord)*, down the stairs, and to the left. Look for the shuttle bus or the stop marked Avignon Centre (€1.10, 3/hr, buy tickets at info booth or from the driver). It drops you close to the other station (Centre-Ville). To reach the city center from the bus stop, walk through the city walls onto cours Jean Jaurés (TI is three blocks down at #41).

A taxi from the station to downtown Avignon costs €12.

If you want to rent a car at the TGV station, take the south exit *(sortie sud)* to find the *location de voitures.*

From Downtown Avignon to the TGV Station: The bus stop for the shuttle bus to the station is just in front of the main post office (*poste principal,* across from the main station on cours Président Kennedy). When a market fills that street, the bus waits on the east side of cours Jean Jaurés.

Arrival at Centre-Ville Station (Gare Avignon Centre-Ville): All non-TGV trains serve the central station. You can check bags here (exit the station to the left, look for *consignes* sign, May–Sept 6:00–22:00, Oct–April 7:00–19:00). The bus station *(gare routière)* is 100 yards to the right of the Centre-Ville station as you leave it (beyond and below Ibis Hôtel). From Centre-Ville station, walk through the city walls onto cours Jean Jaurés. The TI is three blocks down at #41.

By Car: Drivers entering Avignon should follow *Centre-Ville* and *Gare SNCF* (train station) signs. Park either near the walls for free (on boulevard Saint-Roch near Porte de la République), or, more securely, in a parking garage or a lot (€4/half-day, €7/day). The Palace of the Popes is just inside the walls where the "ruined"

St. Bénezet Bridge meets the city, and there's a TI in season. Leave nothing in your car. Hotels have advice for smart overnight parking.

Helpful Hints

Book Ahead for July: During the July theater festival, rooms are rare—reserve very early, or stay in Arles (page 380) or St. Rémy (page 411).

Internet Access: Consider **Webzone** (daily 14:00–24:00, 25 rue Carnot), or ask your hotelier for the nearest Internet café.

English Bookstore: Try **Shakespeare Bookshop** (Tue–Sat 9:30–12:30 & 14:00–18:30, closed Mon, 155 rue Carreterie, in Avignon's northeast corner, tel. 04 90 27 38 50).

Launderette: The launderette at 66 place des Corps-Saints (where rue Agricol Perdiguier ends) is near most hotels (daily 7:00–20:00).

Bike Rental: Consider **Provence Bike** at the bus station *(gare routière)* for bikes and scooters (52 boulevard St. Roch, tel. 04 90 27 92 61, www.provence-bike.com).

Car Rental: The TGV station has the most car-rental agencies (open long hours daily); the Centre-Ville station has fewer companies and shorter hours.

Tourist Trains: Two little trains, designed for tired tourists, leave regularly from the Palace of the Popes (mid-March–mid-Oct daily 10:00–19:00). One does a town tour (€7, 2/hr, 45 min, English commentary) and the other choo-choos you sweat-free to the top of the park, high above the river (€2, schedule depends on demand, no commentary).

Commanding City Views: Walk or drive across the Daladier Bridge (pont Daladier) for a great view of Avignon and the Rhône River. You can see other great views from the top of Parc des Rochers des Doms and from the end of the famous broken bridge, St. Bénezet (pont St. Bénezet).

SIGHTS

I've listed sights in the best order to visit, and have added a short walking tour of Avignon's backstreets to get you beyond the surface. Entries are listed at full price and also with the discount card (Avignon Passion Pass). Start your tour where the Romans did, on place de l'Horloge, and find a seat on a stone bench in front of City Hall (Hôtel de Ville).

Place de l'Horloge—The square, which was the town forum during Roman times and the market square through the Middle Ages, is Avignon's café square. (Restaurants here come with a fun ambience, but they also have high prices and low-quality meals.) Named for a medieval clock tower that the City Hall now hides, this square's present popularity arrived with the trains in 1854. Walk a few steps to the center and look down the main drag, rue de la République. When trains arrived in Avignon, proud city fathers wanted a direct, impressive way to link the new station to the heart of the city (just like in Paris)—so they plowed over homes to create the rue de la République, and widened place de l'Horloge.

Walk past the merry-go-round (public WCs behind), veer right, walk into Palace Square, and then walk uphill past the Palace of the Popes and enter...

Palace Square (Place du Palais)—This grand square surrounds the forbidding Palace of the Popes, the Petit Palais Museum, and the cathedral.

In the 1300s, the Vatican moved the entire headquarters of the Catholic Church to Avignon. The Church bought Avignon and gave it a complete face-lift. Along with clearing out vast spaces like this square, and building this three-acre palace, the Church erected more than three miles of protective wall, with 39 towers, "appropriate" housing for cardinals (read: mansions), and residences for the entire Vatican bureaucracy. The city was Europe's largest construction zone. Avignon's population grew from 6,000 to 25,000 in short order. (Today, 13,000 people live within the walls.) The limits of pre-pope Avignon are outlined on the TI map. Rue Joseph Vernet, rue Henri Fabre, rue des Lices, and rue Philonarde all follow the route of the city's earlier defensive wall.

The Petit Palais (Little Palace) seals the uphill end of the square and was built for a cardinal; today, it houses medieval paintings (museum described below). The church to the left of the Palace of the Popes is Avignon's cathedral. It predates the Church's purchase of Avignon by 200 years. Its small size reflects Avignon's modest, pre-pope population. The gilded Mary was added in 1859.

Notice the stumps in front of the Conservatoire National de Musique. Nicknamed "*bites,*" slang for the male anatomy, they effectively keep cars from double-parking in areas designed for people. Many of the metal ones slide up and down by remote control to let privileged cars come and go.

Petit Palace Museum (Musée du Petit Palais)—This palace displays the Church's collection of medieval Italian painting and sculpture. All 350 paintings deal with Christian themes. A visit here before going to the Palace of the Popes helps furnish and people that otherwise barren building (€6, €3 with Avignon Passion Pass, Oct–May Wed–Mon 9:30–13:00 & 14:00–17:30; June–Sept Wed–Mon 10:00–13:00 & 14:00–18:00, closed Tue year-round; at north end of the Palace Square, tel. 04 90 86 44 58).

▲▲Park (Parc des Rochers des Doms), Ramparts, and St. Bénezet Bridge (Pont St. Bénezet)—With a short loop, you can enjoy a park, hike to a commanding river view, walk a bit of the wall, and visit Avignon's beloved broken bridge.

Park: Hike (or catch the tourist train, see "Helpful Hints," above) from the Palace of the Popes to the rocky top where Avignon was first settled. While the park itself is a delight, with many lookout points, don't miss the climax—a grand view of the Rhône River Valley and the broken bridge. On the largest terrace in the north side of the park, an orientation table explains the view; all around the terrace, several tableaux provide a little history in English.

On a clear day, the tallest peak you see is Mont Ventoux ("windy mountain"). St. André Fortress (across the river) was built by the French in 1360, shortly after the Pope moved to Avignon, to counter the papal incursion into this part of Europe. The fortress was in the kingdom of France. Avignon's famous bridge was a key border crossing, with towers on either end—one French and one Vatican.

To find the highest view, where all the teenage lovers hang out, climb the rocky stairs behind the fountain on the north side of the park (watch your step). In the center of the park, you'll also find a small café and public WCs.

Ramparts: From the viewpoint closest to the bridge, find the stairs leading down onto the only bit of the rampart you can walk on. When the pope came in the 1360s, small Avignon had no town wall...so he built one (restored in the 19th century).

St. Bénezet Bridge: This bridge, whose construction and location were inspired by a shepherd's religious vision, is the "pont d'Avignon" of nursery-rhyme fame. The ditty (which you've probably been humming all day) dates back to the 15th century: *Sur le pont d'Avignon / on y danse, on y danse / sur le pont d'Avignon / on y danse tout en rond* ("On the bridge of Avignon, we dance there, we dance there, on the bridge of Avignon, we dance there all in a circle").

But the bridge is a big deal even outside of its kiddie-tune fame. This was the only bridge crossing the mighty Rhône in the Middle Ages, until it was knocked down by a flood. While only four arches survive today, the bridge was huge: Imagine a 22-arch, 3,000-foot-long bridge extending from Vatican territory to the lonely Tower of Philip the Fair, which marked the beginning of France. A Romanesque **chapel** on the bridge is dedicated to St. Bénezet. While there's not much to actually see on the bridge, the audioguide included in the €4 combo-ticket (available with the Palace of the Popes admission) tells a good story. It's also just fun to be in the breezy middle of the river, with a fine city view (April–Oct daily 9:00–19:00, July until 21:00, Aug–Sept until 20:00, Nov–March daily 9:30–17:45, last ticket sold 30 min before closing, tel. 04 90 27 51 16).

As you exit down the stairs, dip into the tiny and free museum, **Musée du Pont,** for some bridge history (daily 9:00–22:00, €0.50 WCs in same courtyard).

To get to the Palace of the Popes from here, exit the courtyard to the right and follow rue Ferruce straight ahead (don't take a right on rue Ferruce toward the river). After a block, look for the brown signs leading you left under the passageway, and up the stairs to the Palace Square.

▲Palace of the Popes (Palais des Papes)—In 1309, a French pope was elected (Pope Clement V). At the urging of the French king, His Holiness decided he'd had enough of unholy Italy. So, he loaded up his carts and moved to Avignon for a steady rule under a supportive king. The Catholic Church literally bought Avignon (then a two-bit town), and popes resided here until 1403. From 1378 on, there were twin popes, one in Rome and one in Avignon, causing a schism in the Catholic Church that wasn't fully resolved until 1417.

The papal palace is tourable. The included audioguide leads you through the one-way route and does a decent job of overcoming the lack of furnishings, teaching the basic history while allowing you to tour this largely empty palace at your own pace. As you wander, remember that this palace—the biggest surviving Gothic palace in Europe—was built to accommodate 500 people as the administrative center of the Vatican and home of the pope (you'll walk through his personal quarters, frescoed with happy hunting scenes). In the Napoleonic age, the palace was a barracks, housing 1,800 soldiers. You can see cuts in the wall where high ceilings gave way to floor beams.

The film auditorium shows a continuous 20-minute video in French that features images of the papal court, both in the Vatican and in Avignon. Nearby, a staircase leads to the tower for a view and windswept café.

A room at the end of the tour is dedicated to the region's wines, of which the pope was a fan. Sniff Le Nez du Vin (54 tiny bottles designed to develop your "nose"). Châteauneuf-du-Pape is a nearby village where the pope summered in the 1320s. Its famous wine is a direct descendant of his wine. You're welcome to taste some here (free, or split the €6 tasters' deal, which comes with a souvenir tasting cup).

You'll exit to the rear of the palace, where my backstreets walking tour begins (below). To return to the Palace Square, make two rights after exiting (€10, €8 with Avignon Passion Pass, combo-ticket available with St. Bénezet Bridge, April–Oct daily 9:00–19:00, July daily until 21:00, Aug–Sept daily until 20:00, Nov–March daily 9:30–17:45, last entry one hour before closing, tel. 04 90 27 50 74, www.palais-des-papes.com).

▲▲**Discovering Avignon's Backstreets**—Use the map in this book or the TI map to navigate this easy, level, 30-minute walk. This self-guided tour begins in the small square behind the Palace of the Popes, where visitors exit. (If you skipped the interior of the Palace of the Popes, walk down the Palace Square with the palace to your left, and take the first left down the narrow, cobbled rue Peyrolerie; notice how it was cut through the rock. You'll pop out into a small square behind the Palace of the Popes. Veer left and you're ready to go.)

Hôtel la Mirande: Located on the square, Avignon's finest hotel welcomes visitors. Find the atrium lounge and consider a coffee break amid the understated luxury (afternoon tea with a pastry, €15, is served 15:00–18:00). Inspect the royal lounge and dining room (recommended on page 400); cooking courses are offered in the basement below. Rooms start at €300.

Turn left out of the hotel and left again on rue Peyrolerie (Street of Coppersmiths), then take your first right on rue des Ciseaux d'Or. On the small square ahead, you'll find the...

Church of St. Pierre: The original chestnut doors were carved in 1551, when tales of New World discoveries raced across Europe (notice the Indian headdress). The fine Annunciation (lower left) shows Gabriel giving Mary the exciting news in impressive Renaissance 3-D.

Follow the alley to the left, which turned into a tunnel when it was covered with housing as the town's population grew. It leads into what was the cloister of St. Pierre (place des Châtaignes), named for chestnut trees, but now replaced by plane trees. Continue around the church.

With the church on your right, cross busy place Carnot to the Banque Chaix. The building opposite, with its beams showing, is a rare vestige from the Middle Ages. Notice how the building widens the higher it gets. A medieval loophole based taxes on ground-floor area—everything above was tax-free. Walking left down the pedestrian street, rue des Fourbisseurs (Street of Animal Furriers), notice how the top floors almost meet. Fire was a constant danger in the Middle Ages, as flames leapt easily from one home to the next. In fact, the lookout guard's primary responsibility was watching for fires, not the enemy. Virtually all of Avignon's medieval homes have been replaced by safer structures.

Turn left on traffic-free rue du Vieux Sextier (Street of the Balance, for weighing items); another left under the first arch leads to...

Avignon's Synagogue: Jews first came to Avignon with the diaspora of the 1st century. Avignon's Jews were nicknamed "the Pope's Jews" because of the protection that the Pope offered to Jews expelled from France. While this synagogue dates from the 1220s, in Revolutionary times it was completely rebuilt in a neoclassical, Greek-temple style by a non-Jewish architect. This is the only synagogue under a rotunda that you'll see anywhere. The ark holding the Torah is in the east, next to a list of Jews deported from here to Auschwitz in 1942, after Vichy France was gobbled up by the Nazis. To visit the synagogue, press the buzzer, and friendly Rabbi Moshe Aman will be your guide (Mon–Thu 10:00–12:00 & 15:00–17:00, Fri 10:00–12:00, closed Sat–Sun).

From here, retrace your steps to rue du Vieux Sextier. Cross it, then go through the arch and down the yellow alley. Turn left on rue de la Bonneterie ("street of hosiery"), which leads to the big, boxy...

Market (Les Halles): In 1970, the open-air market was replaced by this modern one, which may be ugly, but provides plenty of parking upstairs. Step inside for a sensual experience of organic breads, olives, and festival-of-mold cheeses. The rue des Temptations cuts down the center. The cafés and cheese shops are on the left—as far as possible from the stinky fish stall on the right (Tue–Sun until 13:00, closed Mon).

Continue on five minutes from Les Halles, on rue de la Bonneterie, which eventually becomes...

Rue des Teinturiers: This Street of the Dyers is Avignon's headquarters for all that's hip. You'll pass the Gray Penitents chapel. The facade shows the GPs, who dressed up in robes and pointy hoods to do their anonymous good deeds back in the 13th century (long before the KKK dressed this way).

You'll see the work of amateur sculptors, who have carved whimsical car barriers out of limestone. Earthy cafés, galleries, and a small stream (a branch of the Sorgue River) with waterwheels line this tie-dyed street. This was the cloth industry's dyeing and textile center in the 1800s. Those stylish Provençal fabrics and patterns you see for sale everywhere started here, after a pattern imported from China.

Waterwheel: At the waterwheel, imagine the Sorgue River, which hits the mighty Rhône here in Avignon, being broken into several canals in order to turn 23 such wheels. Around 1800, this powered the town's industries. The little cogwheel above the big one could be shoved into place, kicking another machine into gear behind the wall.

Across from the wheel at #41, **La Cave Breysse** would love to serve you a fragrant glass of regional wine (€2.50 per glass). Choose from the blackboard by the bar that lists all the bottles open today. You're welcome to take it out and sit by the canal (wine with salads and lunch plates, flexible hours, normally Tue–Sat 11:00–15:00, wine only Tue–Sat 18:00–22:30, closed Sun–Mon, Christine Savory and Tim Sweet SE).

To get back to the real world, double back on rue des Teinturiers, turning left on rue des Lices, which traces the first medieval wall—*lices* is the no-man's-land along a wall. You'll pass a four-story arcaded building that was a home for the poor in the 1600s, an army barracks in the 1800s, a fine arts school in the 1900s, and a deluxe condominium today (much of this neighborhood is going high-class residential). Eventually, you'll return to rue de la République, Avignon's main drag.

More Sights

Fondation Angladon-Dubrujeaud—This museum mixes a small but enjoyable collection of art from Post-Impressionists (including Paul Cézanne, Vincent van Gogh, Honoré Daumier, Edgar Degas, and Pablo Picasso) with re-created art studios and furnishings from many periods. It's a quiet place with a few superb paintings (€6, €4 with Avignon Passion Pass, Tue–Sun 13:00–18:00, closed Mon year-round and Tue in winter, 5 rue Laboureur, tel. 04 90 82 29 03, www.angladon.com).

Calvet Museum (Musée Calvet)—This museum impressively displays its wide-ranging collection, covering prehistory to 20th-century art with no English information. You'll find everything from Neolithic artifacts to medieval tapestries to porcelain plates to Impressionist paintings (€6, €3 with Avignon Passion Pass, Wed–Mon 10:00–13:00 & 14:00–18:00, closed Tue, on quieter west half of town at 65 rue Joseph Vernet; its antiquities collection is a few blocks away at 27 rue de la République—same hours and ticket; tel. 04 90 86 33 84).

Near Avignon in Villeneuve-lès-Avignon

▲Tower of Philip the Fair (Tour Philippe-le-Bel)—Built to protect access to St. Bénezet Bridge in 1307, this massive tower offers the best view over Avignon and the Rhône basin. It's best late in the day (€1.60, €0.90 with Avignon Passion Pass, April–Sept daily 10:00–12:30 & 14:00–18:30; Oct–Nov and March Tue–Sun 10:00–12:00 & 14:00–17:00, closed Mon and Dec–Feb; tel. 04 32 70 08 57). To reach the tower from Avignon, you can drive (5 min, cross Daladier Bridge, follow signs to Villeneuve-lès-Avignon); take a boat (Bateau-Bus departs from Mireio Embarcadère near Daladier Bridge); or take bus #11 (2/hr, catch bus across from Centre-Ville train station, in front of post office on cours Président Kennedy).

SLEEPING

(€1 = about $1.20, country code: 33)

Hotel values are distinctly better in Arles, though these are all solid values. Avignon is particularly popular during its July festival, when you must book ahead and can expect inflated prices. (Note that only a few hotels have elevators; specifically, the first three listed near place de l'Horloge.)

Near Centre-Ville Station

The next three listings are a 10-minute walk from the main train station; turn right off cours Jean Jaurés on rue Agricol Perdiguier.

$$ Hôtel Colbert** is a fine midrange bet. Parisian escapees Patrice and Annie, who both speak English, are your hosts. They care for this restored manor house, and it shows, from the peaceful patio to the warm room decor throughout (Sb-€43–53, Db-€60–70, Tb-€70–90, air-con, 7 rue Agricol Perdiguier, tel. 04 90 86 20 20, fax 04 90 85 97 00, www.lecolbert-hotel.com, colbert.hotel@wanadoo.fr).

At **$$ Hôtel le Splendid***, ever-smiling Madame Prel-Lemoine rents 17 cheery rooms with good beds, ceiling fans, and small bathrooms (Sb-€42–45, Db-€54–64, 17 rue Agricol Perdiguier, tel. 04 90 86 14 46, fax 04 90 85 38 55, www.avignon-splendid-hotel.com, contact@avignon-splendid-hotel.com).

$ Hôtel du Parc*, across the street at #18, is a little less sharp, but cheaper than Hôtel le Splendid, with entertaining Avignon native Madame Rous thrown in for free. Rooms have pretty stone walls; the best overlook the park. Madame bakes all her own bread and pastry for breakfast (S-€28, Ss-€35, D-€35, Ds-€44, Db-€48, Tb-€65, no TVs or phones, tel. 04 90 82 71 55, fax 04 90 85 64 86, hotel.du.parc.84@wanadoo.fr).

In the Center, near Place de l'Horloge

At **$$$ Hôtel d'Europe******, you can be a vagabond in the palace at Avignon's most prestigious address—if you get one of the 15 surprisingly reasonable "standard rooms." Enter into a fountain-filled courtyard, linger in the lounges, and enjoy every comfort. The hotel is located on handsome place Crillon, near the river (standard Db-€134, spacious Db standard-€164, first-class Db-€224, deluxe Db-€312, superior Db-€420, breakfast-€25, elevator, Internet access, garage-€16, 12 place Crillon, near Daladier Bridge, tel. 04 90 14 76 76, fax 04 90 14 76 71, www.heurope.com, reservations@heurope.com, SE).

$$$ Hôtel Mercure Cité des Papes*** is a modern hotel chain within spitting distance of the Palace of the Popes. It has 73 smartly designed, smallish rooms, musty halls, air-conditioning, elevators, and all the comforts (Db-€113–130, extra bed-€14, many rooms have views over place de l'Horloge, 1 rue Jean Vilar, tel. 04 90 80 93 00, fax 04 90 80 93 01, h1952@accor-hotels.com, SE).

$$$Hôtel Pont d'Avignon*** is nearby, just inside the walls, near St. Bénezet Bridge (87 rooms, same chain, same price, rue

Ferruce, tel. 04 90 80 93 93, fax 04 90 80 93 94, h0549@accor-hotels.com, SE).

$$ Hôtel de Blauvac** and friendly owner Veronica offer 16 mostly spacious, high-ceilinged rooms (many with an additional upstairs loft) and a sky-high atrium. It's a grand old manor home near the pedestrian zone (Sb-€60–70, Db-€65–75, Tb €80–90, Qb-€95, €10 less off-season, 11 rue de la Bancasse, 1 block off rue de la République, tel. 04 90 86 34 11, fax 04 90 86 27 41, www.hotel-blauvac.com, blauvac@aol.com).

$$ Hôtel Danieli** is a Hello-Dolly fluffball of a place that rents 29 colorful and comfortable rooms on the main drag. It has air-conditioning and lots of tour groups (Sb-€61–73, Db-€72–85, Tb-€83–100, Qb-€100–120, elevator, 17 rue de la République, tel. 04 90 86 46 82, fax 04 90 27 09 24, www.hotel-danieli-avignon.com, contact@hotel-danieli-avignon.com, kind owner Madame Shogol SE).

$$ Hôtel Médiéval** is burrowed deep a few blocks from the St. Pierre church in a massive stone mansion with a small flower-filled garden. The 34 unimaginative yet adequate rooms have firm beds (Db-€56–70, Tb-€79, kitchenettes available but require 3-day minimum stay, 15 rue Petite Saunerie, 5 blocks east of place de l'Horloge, behind Church of St. Pierre, tel. 04 90 86 11 06, fax 04 90 82 08 64, hotel.medieval@wanadoo.fr).

Chambre d'Hôte

$$$ Villa Agapè, just off busy place de l'Horloge, right in the center of town, is an oasis of calm and good taste. Run by helpful Madame de La Pommeraye, the villa has three handsomely decorated rooms, a peaceful courtyard, and a soaking pool to boot (Db-€100–140, extra person-€30, includes breakfast, 2-night minimum in high season; from place de l'Horloge, walk one block toward the TI and train sation and turn right on rue St. Agricol, it's on the left above the pharmacy, ring buzzer, 13 rue St. Agricol; tel. 04 90 85 21 92, fax 06 07 98 71 30, www.villa-agape.com, michele@villa-agape.com). For a week-long stay, ask about renting her entire house, where you get Madame's room, study, kitchen, and everything.

Sleeping Cheaply near Avignon

$ Auberge Bagatelle's hostel/campground offers dirt-cheap beds, a lively atmosphere, a busy pool, a café, a grocery store, a launderette, great views of Avignon, and campers for neighbors (dorm bed-€12, D-€25, across Daladier Bridge on the island l'Ile de la Barthelasse, bus #10 from main post office, tel. 04 90 86 30 39, fax 04 90 27 16 23, camping.bagatelle@wanadoo.fr).

Avignon's Hotels and Restaurants

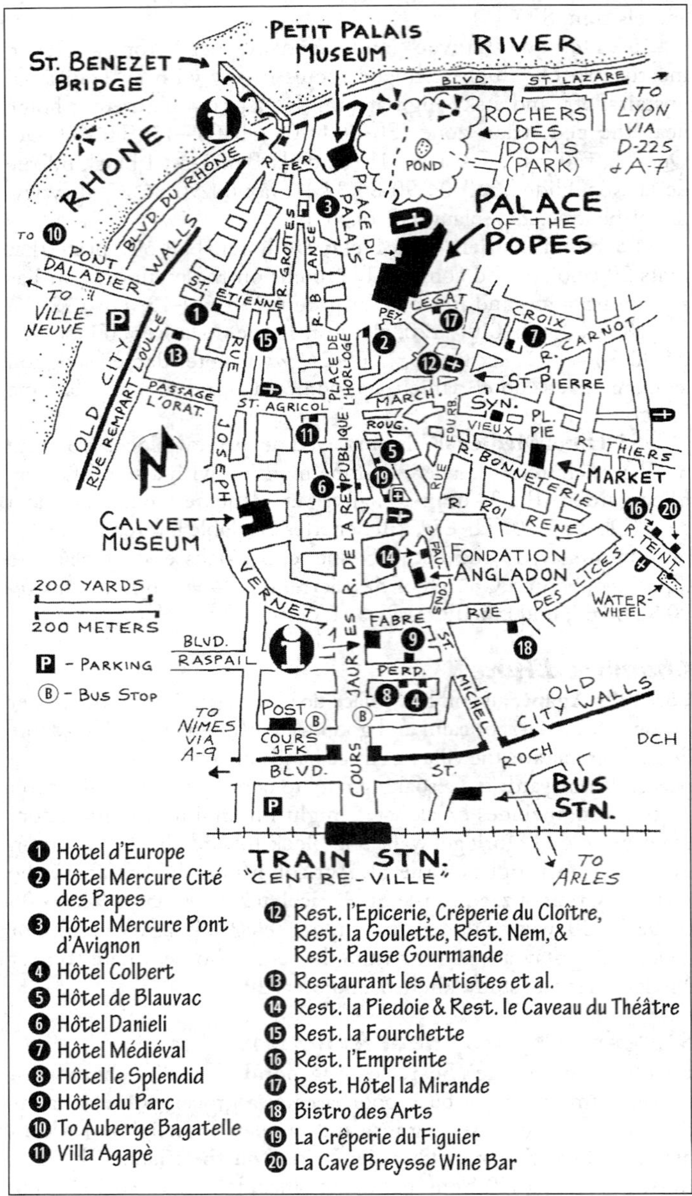

EATING

Skip the overpriced places on place de l'Horloge (Les Domaines and La Civette near the carousel are the least of evils here), and find a more intimate location for your dinner. Avignon has many delightful squares filled with tables ready to seat you.

Near the Church of St. Pierre

This church has enclosed squares on both sides, offering outdoor yet intimate ambience.

L'Epicerie is charmingly located and popular, with the highest-quality cuisine around St. Pierre church, including a good selection of à la carte items (€20 main dishes, closed Sun, cozy interior good in bad weather, 10 place St. Pierre, tel. 04 90 82 74 22).

Pass under the arch by L'Epicerie restaurant and enter enchanting place des Châtaignes, filled with the tables of four restaurants: **Crêperie du Cloître** (big salad and main-course crêpe for about €13, closed Sun–Mon); **Restaurant la Goulette** (Tunisian specialties, *tagine* or couscous-€17, closed Mon); **Restaurant Nem,** tucked in the corner of the square (Vietnamese, family-run, *menus* from €10, closed Tue–Wed); and **Pause Gourmande** (lunch only, *plats du jour*-€7, always a veggie choice, closed Sun).

Crillon Square (Place Crillon)

This large, open square just off the river provides more atmosphere than quality. Several cafés offer inexpensive bistro fare with *menus* from €14, *plats* from €12, and many tables to choose from. **Restaurant les Artistes** is one of several (daily, 21 place Crillon, tel. 04 90 82 23 54).

Elsewhere in Avignon

Bistro des Arts, with a colorful interior and pleasant service, is a good choice for Provençal dishes (daily, 24 rue des Lices, tel. 04 90 85 67 21).

La Crêperie du Figuier has good crêpes and salads that won't break the bank (dinner crêpe or salad for €11, closed Sun, 3 rue du Figuier, tel. 04 90 82 60 67).

At **La Piedoie,** a few blocks northeast of the TI, eager-to-please owner-chef Thierry Piedoie serves fine traditional and Provençal dishes in an intimate, elegant setting (€36 *menu*, closed Wed, interior seating only, 26 rue des Trois Faucons, tel. 04 90 86 51 53).

Le Caveau du Théâtre is the antithesis of its neighbor, La Piedoie, with wild posters decorating a carefree interior. Wine and good-value dishes are the specialties (€13 *plats*, €18 *menus*, fun ambience for free, closed Sun, 16 rue des Trois Faucons, tel. 04 90 82 60 91).

La Fourchette is cozy, indoor-only, traditional, and well-respected. It's a block from place de l'Horloge toward the river (*menus* from €29, closed Sat–Sun, 17 rue Racine, tel. 04 90 85 20 93).

L'Empreinte is good for North African cuisine in a trendy location (copious couscous for €11–16, takeout and veggie options available, daily, 33 rue des Teinturiers, tel. 04 32 76 31 84).

Hôtel la Mirande is the ultimate Avignon splurge. Reserve ahead here for understated elegance and Avignon's top cuisine (€28 lunch *menu*, €50 dinner *menu*, €85 tasting *menu*, closed Tue–Wed, behind Palace of the Popes, 4 place de la Mirande, tel. 04 90 86 93 93, fax 04 90 86 26 85, www.la-mirande.fr).

TRANSPORTATION CONNECTIONS

Trains

Remember, there are two train stations in Avignon: the new suburban TGV station and the Centre-Ville station in the city center (€1.10 shuttle buses connect to both stations, 3/hr, 10 min). Only the Centre-Ville station has baggage check. Car rental is available at both stations (better at TGV). Some cities are served both by slower local trains from the Centre-Ville station and by faster TGV trains from the TGV station; I've listed the most convenient stations for each trip.

From Avignon's Centre-Ville station to: Arles (12/day, 20 min), **Orange** (10/day, 15 min), **Nîmes** (14/day, 30 min), **Isle-sur-la-Sorgue** (6/day, 30 min), **Lyon** (10/day, 2 hrs), **Carcassonne** (8/day, 7 with transfer in Narbonne, 3 hrs), **Barcelona** (2/day, 6 hrs, transfer in Montpellier).

From Avignon's TGV station to: Arles (2/hr, by SNCF bus, 30 min), **Nice** (10/day, 4 hrs, a few direct, most require transfer in Marseille), **Marseille** (10/day, 70 min), **Aix-en-Provence TGV** (10/day, 75 min), **Lyon** (12/day, 1.5 hrs, also from Centre-Ville station—see above), **Paris'** Gare de Lyon (14/day, 3 with transfer in Lyon, 2.5 hrs), **Paris'** Charles de Gaulle airport (7/day, 3 hrs).

Buses

The bus station (*gare routière*, tel. 04 90 82 07 35) is just past and below the Ibis Hôtel to the right as you exit the train station (information desk open Mon–Fri 10:15–13:00 & 14:00–18:00, Sat 8:00–12:00, closed Sun). Nearly all buses leave from this station. The biggest exception is the SNCF bus service that runs from the Avignon TGV station to Arles (10/day, 30 min). The Avignon TI has schedules. Service is reduced or nonexistent on Sunday and holidays.

From Avignon by Bus to: Pont du Gard (5/day in summer, 3/day off-season, 40 min), **St. Rémy** (6/day, 45 min, handy way to visit its Wed market); **Isle-sur-la-Sorgue** (5/day, 45 min); **Vaison la Romaine** (2–3/day during school year, called *période scolaire*, 1/day otherwise and 1/day from TGV station, 90 min).

Pont du Gard

Throughout the ancient world, aqueducts were like flags of stone that heralded the greatness of Rome. A visit to this sight still works to proclaim the wonders of that age. This perfectly preserved Roman aqueduct was built as *the* critical link of a 30-mile canal that, by dropping one inch for every 350 feet, supplied nine million gallons of water per day (about 100 gallons per second) to Nîmes—one of ancient Europe's largest cities. Though most of the aqueduct is on or below the ground, at the Pont du Gard it spans a canyon on a massive bridge—one of the most remarkable surviving Roman ruins anywhere.

Getting to the Pont du Gard

By Bus: Buses run to Pont du Gard (Rive Gauche) from Avignon (5/day summer, 3/day off-season, 40 min.

Bus stops are at the traffic roundabout 300 yards from the Pont du Gard. The stop from Avignon and to Nîmes is on the opposite side of the roundabout from the Pont du Gard; the stop from Nîmes and to Avignon is on the same side as the Pont du Gard, just to the left as you enter the traffic circle. Make sure you're waiting for the bus on the correct side of the traffic circle.

By Car: Pont du Gard is an easy 25-minute drive due west of Avignon (follow signs to Nîmes) and 45 minutes northwest of Arles (via Tarascon). The Rive Gauche parking is off D-981, which leads from Remoulins to Uzès. (Parking is also available on the Rive Droite side, but it's farther away from the museum.)

ORIENTATION

There are two riversides to the Pont du Gard: the left and right banks (Rive Gauche and Rive Droite). Park on the Rive Gauche, where you'll find the museums, ticket booth, cafeteria, WC, and shops—all built into a modern plaza. You'll see the aqueduct in two parts: first, a fine new museum complex, then the actual river gorge spanned by the ancient bridge.

Cost: While it's free to see the aqueduct itself, the various optional activities each have a cost: parking (€5), museum (€6), informative 25-minute film (€3, see below), and a kids' space called Ludo (€4.50, scratch-and-sniff experience in English of various aspects of Roman life and the importance of water). The new extensive outdoor *garrigue* natural area, featuring historic crops and landscapes of the Mediterranean, is free (though €4 gets you a helpful English booklet). All are designed to give the sight more meaning—and they do—but for most visitors, only the museum is worth paying for. The €10 combo-ticket—which covers all sights and parking—is best for drivers. If you get the combo-ticket, check the movie schedule; the 25-minute film is silly, but offers good information in a flirtatious French style...and a cool, entertaining, and cushy break. During summer months, a free sound-and-light show plays at night against the Pont du Gard.

Hours: The museum is open daily (Easter–Nov 9:30–19:00, mid-June–Aug until 21:30, Dec–Easter until 18:00, closed most of Jan, tel. 08 20 09 33 30). The aqueduct itself is free and open until 22:00 (same hours as parking lot).

Canoe Rental: Consider seeing the Pont du Gard by canoe. Collias Canoes will pick you up at the Pont du Gard (or elsewhere, if prearranged) and shuttle you to the town of Collias. You'll float down the river to the nearby town of Remoulins, where they'll pick you up and take you back to the Pont du Gard (2-person canoe-€27, usually 2 hrs, though you can take as long as you like, tel. 04 66 22 85 54, SE).

SIGHTS

▲Museum—This state-of-the-art museum's multimedia approach (well-described in English) shows how water was an essential part of the Roman "art of living." You'll see examples of lead pipes, faucets, and siphons; walk through a rock quarry; learn how they moved those huge rocks into place; and learn how those massive arches were made. While actual artifacts from the aqueduct on display are few, the exhibit shows the immensity of the undertaking, as well as the payoff. Imagine the excitement as this extravagant supply of water finally tumbled into Nîmes. A relaxing highlight is the scenic video helicopter ride along the entire 30-mile course of the structure, from its start at Uzès all the way to the Castellum in Nîmes.

▲▲▲Viewing the Aqueduct—A parklike path leads to the aqueduct. Until a few years ago, this was an actual road—adjacent to the aqueduct—that has spanned the river since 1743. Before you cross the bridge, pass under it and hike 350 feet along the riverbank for a grand viewpoint from which to study the second-highest standing Roman structure (Rome's Colosseum is 2 yards taller).

This was the biggest bridge in the whole 30-mile-long aqueduct. It seems exceptional because it is: The arches are twice the width of standard aqueducts, and the main arch is the largest the Romans ever built—80 feet (so it wouldn't get its feet wet). The bridge is about 160 feet high, and was originally about 1,100 feet long. Today, 12 arches are missing, reducing the length to 790 feet.

While the distance from the source (in Uzès) to Nîmes was only 12 miles as the eagle flew, engineers chose the most economical route, winding and zigzagging 30 miles. The water made the trip in 24 hours with a drop of only 40 feet. Ninety percent of the aqueduct is on or under the ground, but a few river canyons like this required bridges. A stone lid hides a four-foot-wide, six-foot-tall chamber lined with waterproof mortar that carried a stream for over 400 years. For 150 years, this system provided Nîmes with good drinking water. Expert as the Romans were, they miscalculated the backup caused by a downstream corner, and had to add the thin extra layer you can see just under the lid to make the channel deeper.

The bridge and the river below provide great fun for holiday-goers. While parents suntan on inviting rocks, kids splash into the gorge from under the aqueduct. Some daredevils actually jump from the aqueduct itself—not knowing that crazy winds scrambled by the structure cause painful belly flops, and sometimes even accidental death. For the most refreshing view, float flat on your back under the structure (bring a swimsuit and sandals for the rocks).

The appearance of the entire gorge changed in 2002, when a huge flood flushed lots of greenery downstream. Those floodwaters put Roman provisions to the test. Notice the triangular-shaped buttresses at the lower level—designed to split and divert the force of any flood *around* the feet of the arches, rather than *into* them. The 2002 floodwaters reached the top of those buttresses. Anxious park rangers winced at the sounds of trees crashing onto the ancient stones...but the arches stood strong.

The stones that jut out—giving the aqueduct a rough, unfinished appearance—supported the original scaffolding. The protuberances were left, rather than cut off, in anticipation of future repair needs. The lips under the arches supported the wooden templates that allowed the stones of the round arches to rest on something until the all-important keystone was dropped into place. Each stone weighs four to six tons. The structure stands with no mortar—taking full advantage of the innovative Roman arch, made strong by gravity.

Hike over the bridge for a closer look. Across the river, a high trail (marked Panorama) leads upstream and offers commanding views. On the exhibit side of the structure, a trail marked Accès l'Aqueduc leads up to surviving stretches of the aqueduct. For a peaceful walk alongside the top of the aqueduct (where it's on land and no longer a bridge), follow the red-and-yellow markings. Remains of this part are scant because of medieval cannibalization—frugal builders couldn't resist the pre-cut stones as they constructed local churches. The ancient quarry (about a third of a mile downstream on the exhibit side) may open in 2006—ask.

Les Baux

Crowning the rugged Alpilles (ahl-pee) Mountains, this rock-capping castle town is a memorable place to visit. Even with the tourist crowds, the place evokes a strong community that lived a rugged life—thankful more for their top-notch fortifications than their dramatic views. While mobbed with tourists through most of the day, the town is a more peaceful scene for those arriving by 9:00 or after 17:00. Sunsets are dramatic, and nights in Les Baux-de-Provence are pin-drop peaceful. After dark, the castle is closed—but beautifully illuminated.

Les Baux is actually two visits in one: castle ruins on an almost lunar landscape, and, below, a medieval town packed with shops, cafés, and tourist knickknacks. See the castle, then savor or blitz the lower town on your way out. There's no free parking; get as close to the top as you can, and pay €4 (good for 3 days, take ticket and pay at machine next to telephone and bakery about 30 steps below town entry).

One cobbled street leads into town, where you're greeted first by the **TI** (April–Sept daily 9:00–19:00, Oct–March 9:00–12:00 & 13:00–18:00, in Hôtel de Ville, tel. 04 90 54 34 39). The main drag leads directly to the castle (15-min uphill walk).

Getting to Les Baux

By Bus: Longtime bus service with Arles was canceled in 2004 for "local political reasons." It might be reinstated—someday—ask. Consider taking a bus to St. Rémy (about €4 from Arles or Avignon), and then a taxi from there (figure €15 one-way). This allows you to combine two worthwhile stops while saving euros.

By Taxi: Figure €30 for a taxi one-way from Arles (tel. 06 80 27 60 92).

By Foot: Les Baux is a beautiful three-hour hike from St. Rémy; see "Hike to Les Baux" on page 411.

By Car: Les Baux is a 20-minute drive from Arles. From Arles, follow signs to Avignon, then Les Baux. Drivers can combine Les Baux with St. Rémy (15 min away).

SIGHTS

The Castle Ruins

Many of the ancient walls of Les Baux's striking castle still stand in testament to the proud past of this village. The climbing is fun, the views are sensational, and the mistral wind just might blow your socks off. Buy your ticket in the old olive-mill room, and study the museum exhibits (models of the town in the 13th and 16th centuries, interesting photos showing the town before tourism and today). Pick up the informative and included audioguide.

A 12th-century regional powerhouse, Les Baux was razed in 1632 by a paranoid Louis XIII, who was afraid of these trouble-making upstarts. The sun-bleached "dead city" ruins are carved into, out of, and on top of a rock 650 feet above the valley floor. As you wander out on the wind-blown field past kid-thrilling medieval siege weaponry, try to imagine 6,000 people living behind stone walls on this cliff. Notice the water-catchment system (a slanted field that caught rain water and drained it into a cistern—necessary during a siege). In the little chapel across from the museum, the slideshow ("Van Gogh, Gauguin, and Cézanne: Painting in the Land of the Olive Trees") provides a relaxing 10-minute interlude. Early July through late August, medieval events take place in the open area (visitors' crossbow shooting range might reopen in 2006, check at TI as you enter; castle entry-€7, Easter–Oct daily 9:00–19:00, July–Aug until 20:00, Nov–Easter daily 9:30–17:00).

Lower Town

You can shop and eat your way back to your car or the bus station through the new town. Or you can take your first left, go downhill, and check out these minor but fun sights as you descend from the castle:

Yves Brayer Museum (Musée Yves Brayer)—This is an appealing exhibit of paintings (van Gogh–like Expressionism, without the tumult) by Yves Brayer, who spent his final years in the 1970s here in Les Baux (€4, daily 10:00–12:30 & 14:00–18:30).

Downhill, around the corner, is...

St. Vincent Church—This 12th-century Romanesque church was built short and wide to fit the terrain. The center chapel on the right houses the town's traditional Provençal processional chariot. Each Christmas Eve a ram pulled this cart—holding a lamb, symbolizing Jesus, and surrounded by candles—to this church.

In front of the church is the old-town "laundry"—with a pig-snout faucet and 14th-century stone washing surface with drains designed for short women.

Around the corner, toward a great view, is the...

Chapel of Penitents—Notice the nativity scene painted by Yves Brayer, which shows the local legend that Jesus was born in Les Baux.

Staying left as you round the old laundry and heading downhill, you'll pass plenty of cafés with wonderful views. You'll see the

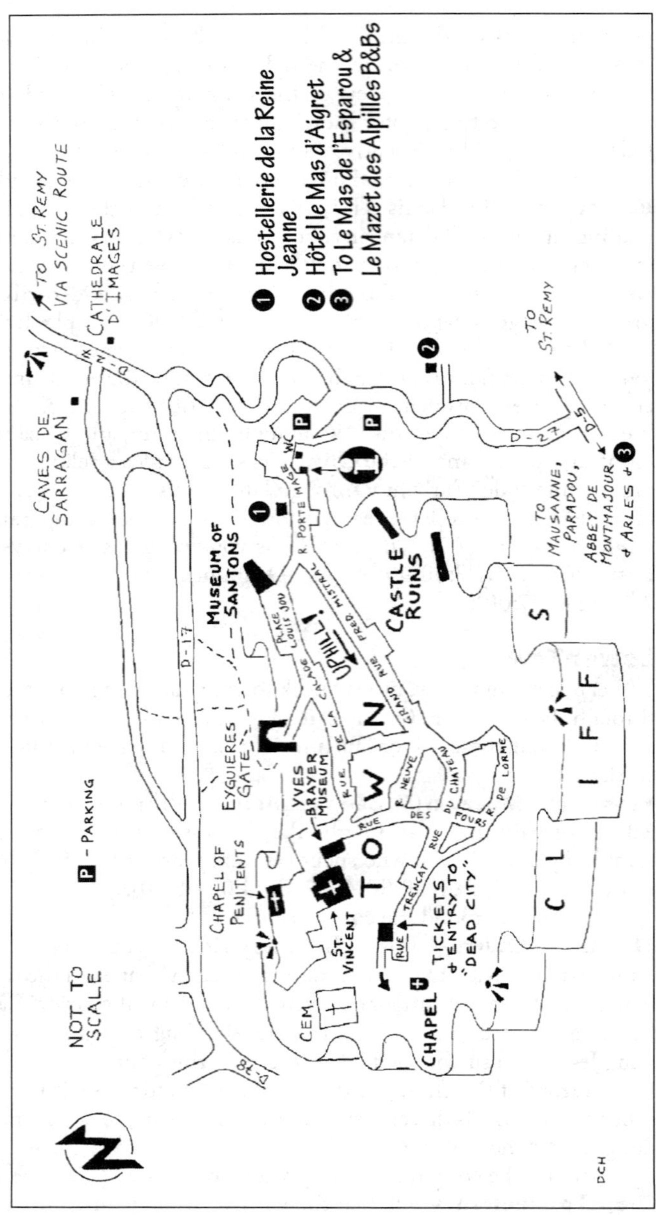
Les Baux
1 Hostellerie de la Reine Jeanne
2 Hôtel le Mas d'Aigret
3 To Le Mas de l'Esparou & Le Mazet des Alpilles B&Bs
TO ST. REMY VIA SCENIC ROUTE
CATHEDRALE D'IMAGES
CAVES DE SARRAGAN
MUSEUM OF SANTONS
R. PORTE MAGE
WC
TO ST. REMY
D-27
D-5
TO MAUSANNE, PARADOU, ABBEY DE MONTMAJOUR & ARLES & 3
CASTLE RUINS
PLACE LOUIS JOU
UPHILL!
RUE FRED. MISTRAL
GRAND RUE
RUE DE LA CALADE
D-17
EYGUIERES GATE
YVES BRAYER MUSEUM
R. NEUVE
RUE DU CHATEAU
R. DE LORME
RUE DES FOURS
TOWN
CLIFFS
P - PARKING
CHAPEL OF PENITENTS
ST. VINCENT
RUE TRENCAT
TICKETS & ENTRY TO "DEAD CITY"
CEM.
CHAPEL
NOT TO SCALE
D-78
DCH

town's fortified wall and one of its two gates. Farther below, you'll come to the...

Museum of Santons—The museum displays a collection of *santons*, popular folk figurines, which decorate local Christmas mangers (free entry). Notice how the nativity scene proves once again that Jesus was born in Les Baux. These painted clay dolls show off local dress and traditions. Find the old couple leaning into *le mistral* wind.

Near Les Baux

A half mile beyond Les Baux, D-27 leads to dramatic views of the hill town, with pullouts and walking trails at the pass, and two sights that fill cool, cavernous caves in former limestone quarries that date back to the Middle Ages. (The limestone is easy to cut, but gets hard and nicely polished when exposed to the weather.)

Caves de Sarragan—Occupied by the Sarragan Winery (which invites you in for a taste), the best views of Les Baux can be seen from its parking lot. While this place looks like it's designed for groups, the friendly, English-speaking staff welcomes individuals (free, April–Sept daily 10:00–12:00 & 14:00–19:00, Oct–March until 18:00, tel. 04 90 54 33 58).

Cathédrale d'Images—In a similar cave nearby, it offers a mesmerizing sound-and-slide show. Its 48 projectors flash countless images set to music on the quarry walls as visitors wander around, immersed in the year's theme (€7, daily 10:00–18:00). The D-27 continues to St. Rémy and makes a good loop if you return via D-5 from St. Rémy.

Speaking of quarries, in 1821, the rocks and soil of the area were discovered to contain an important mineral for the making of aluminum. It was named after the town—bauxite.

SLEEPING

In or near Les Baux

(€1 = about $1.20, country code: 33)

$$$ Le Mas d'Aigret*** crouches barely past Les Baux on the road to St. Rémy. Lie on your back and stare up at the castle walls rising beyond your swimming pool in this mini-oasis. Most of the average-sized, artfully designed rooms have private terraces and views over the valley, and the restaurant is troglodyte-chic (non-view Db-€100, larger Db with balcony-€135, Tb-€175, prices include breakfast, air-con, some daytime road noise with view rooms, €30 *menu* at restaurant, tel. 04 90 54 20 00, fax 04 90 54 44 00, www.masdaigret.com, contact@masdaigret.com, SE).

$$ Le Mas de l'Esparou *chambre d'hôte*, a few minutes below Les Baux, is welcoming and kid-friendly, with three spacious rooms, squishy mattresses, a swimming pool, table tennis, and distant views of Les Baux. Jacqueline loves her job, and her lack of English only makes her more animated. Monsieur Roux painted the artwork in your room and has a gallery in Les Baux (Db-€62, extra person-about €16, cash only, between Les Baux and Maussane les Alpilles on D-5, look for white sign with green lettering, tel. & fax 04 90 54 41 32, NSE).

$ Hostellerie de la Reine Jeanne**, an exceptional value, offers comfy rooms 150 feet to your right after the main entry to the live city, where you can watch the sun set and rise from Les Baux (standard Ds-€47, standard Db-€51, Db with view deck-€63, cavernous family suite-€92, air-con in some rooms, ask for *chambre avec terrasse*, good *menus* from €20, tel. 04 90 54 32 06, fax 04 90 54 32 33, www.la-reinejeanne.com, reine.jeanne@wanadoo.fr, affable Alain SE).

$ Le Mazet des Alpilles is a small home with three tidy air-conditioned rooms, just outside the unspoiled village of Paradou, five minutes below Les Baux. It may have space when others don't (Db-€53, ask for largest room, child's bed available, cash only, follow brown signs from D-17, in Paradou look for route de Brunelly, tel. 04 90 54 45 89, fax 04 90 54 44 66, lemazet@wanadoo.fr, charming Annick speaks just enough English).

St. Rémy

Sophisticated and sassy, St. Rémy-de-Provence gave birth to Nostradamus and cared for a distraught artist. A few minutes from the town center, you can visit the once thriving Roman city called Glanum, the mental ward where Vincent van Gogh was sent after lopping off his lobe, and an art center dedicated to his memory. Best of all, elbow your way through its raucous Wednesday market (until 12:30). A racecourse-like ring road hems in a pedestrian-friendly center that's well-stocked with fine foods and the latest Provençal fashions.

The **TI** on place Jean Jaurés is two blocks toward Les Baux from the ring road (Mon–Sat 9:30–12:30 & 14:00–19:00, Sun 10:00–12:00 & 15:00–17:00, tel. 04 90 92 05 22). Parking in St. Rémy is tricky and always comes with a fee; it's easiest at the TI lot. From the TI, it's a 15-minute walk to Glanum and Clinique St. Paul (van Gogh's mental hospital).

Getting to St. Rémy

By Bus: Buses run from Arles and Avignon to St. Rémy (6/day, 45 min). If arriving at St. Rémy by bus, get off on the ring road, just before the turnoff to Les Baux and the TI.

St. Rémy Area

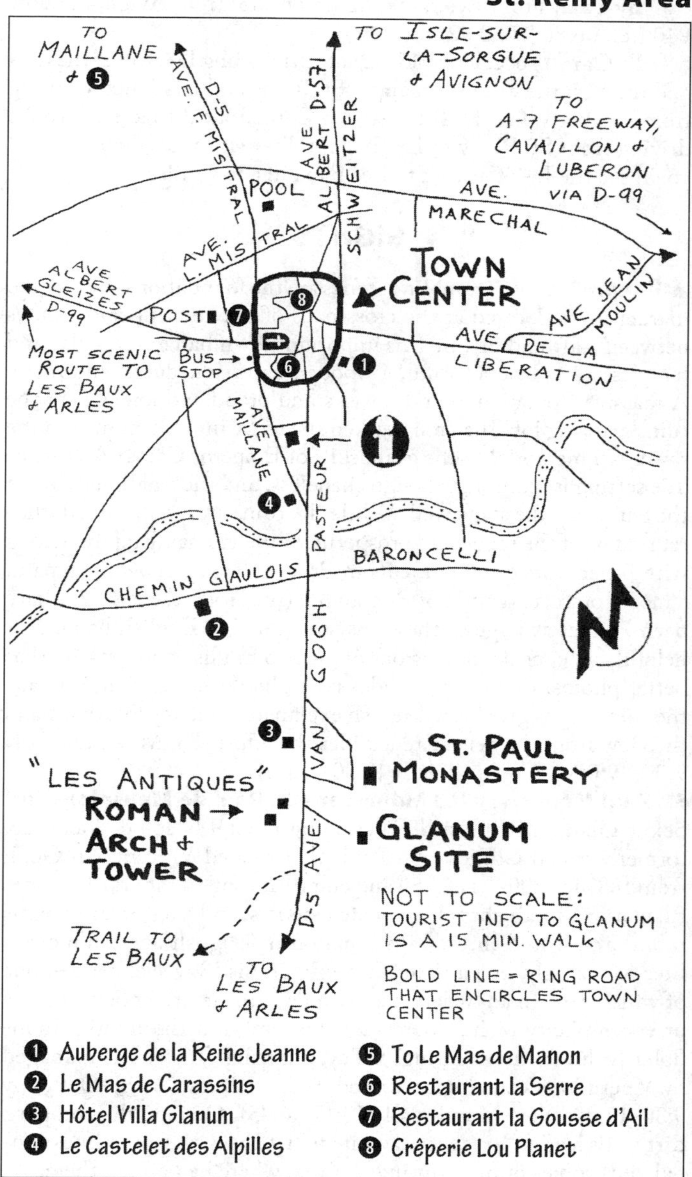

1 Auberge de la Reine Jeanne
2 Le Mas de Carassins
3 Hôtel Villa Glanum
4 Le Castelet des Alpilles
5 To Le Mas de Manon
6 Restaurant la Serre
7 Restaurant la Gousse d'Ail
8 Crêperie Lou Planet

By Taxi: From Les Baux, figure on €15; from Avignon, allow €40 (tel. 06 80 27 60 92).

By Car: A spectacular 15-minute drive along D-27, over the hills and through the woods, separates St. Rémy and Les Baux. Coming from Les Baux, find D-27 by passing Cathédrale d'Images. If you're driving from St. Rémy to Les Baux, follow signs for Tarascon, and you'll see the D-27 turnoff to Les Baux in a few miles.

SIGHTS

▲Glanum—These crumbling stones are the foundations of a Roman market town, located at the crossroads of two ancient trade routes between Italy and Spain. This important town had grand villas and temples, a basilica, a forum, a wooden dam, aqueducts, and more. A massive Roman arch and tower stand proud and lonely near the ruins' parking lot. The arch marked the entry into Glanum, and the tower is a memorial to the grandsons of Emperor Caesar Augustus. The setting is stunning, though shadeless, and the small museum at the entry sets the stage well. While the ruins are, well, ruined, they remind us of the range and prosperity of the Roman Empire. Along with other Roman monuments in Provence, they allow us to paint a more complete picture of Roman life (the city is estimated to have been 7 times as large as the ruins you see). The English handout is helpful, but consider buying one of the two English booklets (one has better photos, the other provides much better background). Inside the ruins, signs give basic English explanations at key locations, and the view from the belvedere justifies the effort (€6, May–Aug daily 9:00–19:00, Sept–April daily 10:30–17:00).

St. Paul Monastery (Le Monastère St. Paul de Mausole)—Just below Glanum is the still-functioning mental hospital (Valetudo, formerly called Clinique St. Paul) that treated Vincent van Gogh from 1889 to 1890. Pay €3.50 and enter Vincent's temporarily peaceful world: a small chapel, intimate cloisters, and a re-creation of his room. You'll find limited information in English about Vincent's life. Amazingly, he painted 150 works in his 53 weeks here—none of which remain anywhere nearby today. The contrast between the utter simplicity of his room (and his life) and the multimillion-dollar value of his paintings today is jarring. The site is managed by Valetudo, a center specializing in art therapy (April–Oct daily 9:30–19:00, Nov–March daily 10:15–16:45). Outside the complex, dirt trails lead to Vincent's favorite footpaths with (sometimes vandalized) copies of his paintings located where he painted them.

Food Lovers' Guide to St. Rémy—Wednesday is market day in St. Rémy, but you don't have to fast until then. Foodies will appreciate the three shops that gather on the ringroad in St. Rémy, near the turnoff to Les Baux.

Start at Olive-Huiles du Monde, where you can saddle up to a wine-bar-like setting and sample the best olive oil in this area; also check out the fine display of other products made from olive oil (daily 10:00–13:00 & 15:00–19:00, 16 boulevard Victor Hugo).

Le Petit Duc, across the road, offers a remarkable introduction to antique cookies. Let friendly owner Anne, who speaks English, take you on a tour (daily 10:00–13:00 & 15:00–19:00, 7 boulevard Victor Hugo).

Just one whiff of Joel Durand's chocolate will lure chocoholics inside. Ask for a sample, and learn the letter-coded system (daily 10:00–19:00, 3 boulevard Victor Hugo, next door to Le Petit Duc).

Centre d'Art Présence Vincent van Gogh—Here you'll find a permanent tribute to the painter (including some reproductions), as well as rotating exhibits reflecting the enormous influence of his work on contemporary artists (€3.50, Tue–Sun 10:30–12:30 & 14:30–18:30, closed Mon, inside the ring road on rue Estrine, tel. 04 90 92 34 72).

Hike to Les Baux—These directions will help you find your way on the lovely three-hour hike from St. Rémy to Les Baux (for more details, ask at TI). Start from the signposted slope opposite the Glanum entry. Follow the goat path up into the mountain, and arrive at the chimney. Go down the iron ladder, and you'll come to a lake. Walk around the lake on the left-hand side, turning left along the Mas de Gros cart track. A mile later, turn right on Sentier des Crêtes and follow the yellow markings to Les Baux. You'll end on the paved road in Val d'Enfer.

SLEEPING

(€1 = about $1.20, country code: 33)

$$$ Le Mas de Carassins***, a 15-minute walk from the center, is impeccably run by friendly Paris refugees Michel and Pierre. Luxury is affordable here. They pay attention to every aspect of the hotel, from the generously sized pool and gardens to the muted room decor to the optional €26 weekday-only dinner (standard Db-€98, bigger Db-€115, deluxe Db-€120, suite-€165, extra bed-€15, air-con, table tennis, look for signs 200 yards toward Les Baux from TI, 1 Chemin Gaulois, tel. 04 90 92 15 48, fax 04 90 92 63 47, www.hoteldescarassins.com, info@hoteldescarassins.com).

$$ Le Castelet des Alpilles*** is a slightly tired and Old World place, but the location is good (a few blocks toward Les Baux from the TI), the price is fair, and the rooms are plenty comfortable. Rooms are generally big and airy, and the balcony rooms have views of the Alpilles (Db-€65, Db with air-con and view balcony-€87, 6 place Mireille, tel. 04 90 92 07 31, fax 04 90 92 52 03, www.castelet-alpilles.com, hotel.castel.alpilles@wanadoo.fr).

$$ Hôtel Villa Glanum,** right across from the Glanum ruins, with some traffic noise, is a 15-minute walk from the town center. Rooms are small and unimaginative, yet adequate. The best rooms, which come with higher rates, are in bungalows around the pretty pool (Db-€62–82, Tb-€85–100, Qb-€105–120, cheaper off-season, 46 avenue van Gogh, tel. 04 90 92 03 59, fax 04 90 92 00 08, www.villaglanum.com, villa.glanum@wanadoo.fr).

$$ Auberge de la Reine Jeanne** is more central, if less personal. The 11 traditionally decorated, spotless, and spacious rooms (with big beds) take a backseat to the popular restaurant. Some rooms overlook a courtyard filled with tables and umbrellas (Db-€59–68, Tb/Qb-€76, €25 *menu* in fine restaurant, on right side of ring road a few blocks after you enter from Les Baux, 12 boulevard Mirabeau, tel. 04 90 92 15 33, fax 04 90 92 49 65, aubergereinejeanne@wanadoo.fr).

$$ Le Mas de Manon *chambre d'hôte* has rooms two miles from St. Rémy, off a bamboo-lined lane in a lush locale. Salty owners Marie-Odile (SE) and Claude (forget it) run this restored farmhouse, with modern rooms at fair prices. A stay here includes all the comforts and a pretty little garden (Db-€60, includes breakfast, cash only, leave St. Rémy toward Maillane on D-5 and look for signs after 2 miles, Chemin des Lones, tel. & fax 04 32 60 09 86, mobile 06 09 44 92 22, masdemanon@libertysurf.fr).

EATING

St. Rémy is packed with fine restaurants, each trying to outdo the others. Join the evening strollers and compare. To dine well in an interior courtyard packed with plants, try **La Serre,** where everything from bread to pâté is homemade (€22 *menu*, closed Mon, a block from where the road to Les Baux meets the ringroad in the old center, 8 rue de la Commune, tel. 04 90 92 37 21).

La Gousse d'Ail is no secret, but even so, it's a reliable and warm place for a mini-splurge (*menus* from €30, on the ring road just after the turnoff to Maillane at 6 boulevard Marceau, closed Thu, tel. 04 90 92 16 87).

Crêperie Lou Planet, on pleasant place Favier, is cheap and peaceful (daily until 20:00, behind Hôtel de Ville).

THE FRENCH RIVIERA

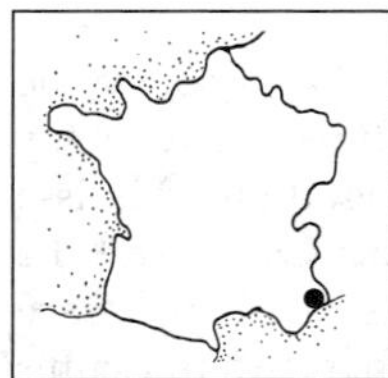

A hundred years ago, celebrities from London to Moscow flocked here to socialize, gamble, and escape the dreary weather at home. The belle époque is today's tourist craze, as this most sought-after, fun-in-the-sun destination now caters to budget travelers as well. Some of the Continent's most stunning scenery and intriguing museums lie along this strip of land—as do millions of heat-seeking tourists. Nice has world-class museums, a grand beachfront promenade, a seductive old town, and all the drawbacks of a major city (traffic, crime, pollution, etc.). But the day trips possible from Nice are easy and varied: Monte Carlo welcomes everyone, with cash registers open; Antibes has a romantic port and silky-sandy beaches; and the hill towns present a breezy and photogenic alternative to the beach scene. Evenings on the Riviera, a.k.a. the Côte d'Azur, were made for a promenade and outdoor dining.

Choosing a Home Base

My favorite home bases are Nice, Antibes, and Villefranche-sur-Mer.

Nice is the region's capital and France's fifth-largest city. With convenient train and bus connections to most regional sights, this is the most practical base for train travelers. Urban Nice also has a full palette of museums, a beach scene that rocks, the best selection of hotels in all price ranges, and good nightlife options. A car is a headache in Nice, though it's easily stored at one of the many parking garages.

Nearby **Antibes** is smaller, with a bustling center, the best sandy beaches I found, good walking trails, and the Picasso Museum. It has frequent train service to Nice and Monaco, and it's easy for drivers.

Villefranche-sur-Mer is the romantic's choice, with a serene setting and small-town warmth. It has finely-ground pebble beaches, good public transportation to Nice and Monaco, easy parking, and hotels in most price ranges.

Planning Your Time

Most should plan a full day for Nice and at least a half day each for Monaco and Antibes. Monaco has a unique energy at night (sights are closed, but crowds are few; consider dinner here), and Antibes is best during the day (good beaches, hiking, and Picasso Museum).

Helpful Hints

Museum Pass: The **Riviera Carte Musées** pass, a good value only for serious museumgoers, includes admission to many major Riviera museums, such as Nice's Chagall and Matisse museums, Antibes' Picasso Museum and Fort Carré, and the International Museum of Perfume in Grasse. This will save you money if you're planning to visit more than two museums in a day, or several museums over a few days (€10/1 day, €17/3 days, €27/7 days, buy at any participating sight).

Events: The Riviera is famous for staging major events. Unless you're actually taking part in the festivities, these events give you only room shortages and traffic jams. Here are the three biggies: Nice Carnival (Feb), the Grand Prix of Monaco (May), and the Cannes Film Festival (May).

Getting Around the Riviera

Nice is perfectly located for exploring the Riviera by public transport. Villefranche-sur-Mer and Antibes are within a 60-minute bus or train ride of each other.

Minivan Excursions: The TI and most hotels have information on minivan excursions from Nice (€50–60/half day, €80–110/day). **Med-Tour** is one of many (tel. 04 93 82 92 58 or 06 73 82 04 10, www.med-tour.com); **Tour Azur** is a bit pricier (tel. 04 93 44 88 77 or 06 71 90 76 70, www.tourazur.com); and **Revelation Tours** specializes in English tours (tel. 04 93 53 69 85 or 06 60 02 98 42, www.revelation-tours.com). All companies also offer private tours by the day or half day (check with them for their outrageous prices, about €90/hr).

Bus Station: At Nice's efficient bus station on boulevard Jean

The French Riviera

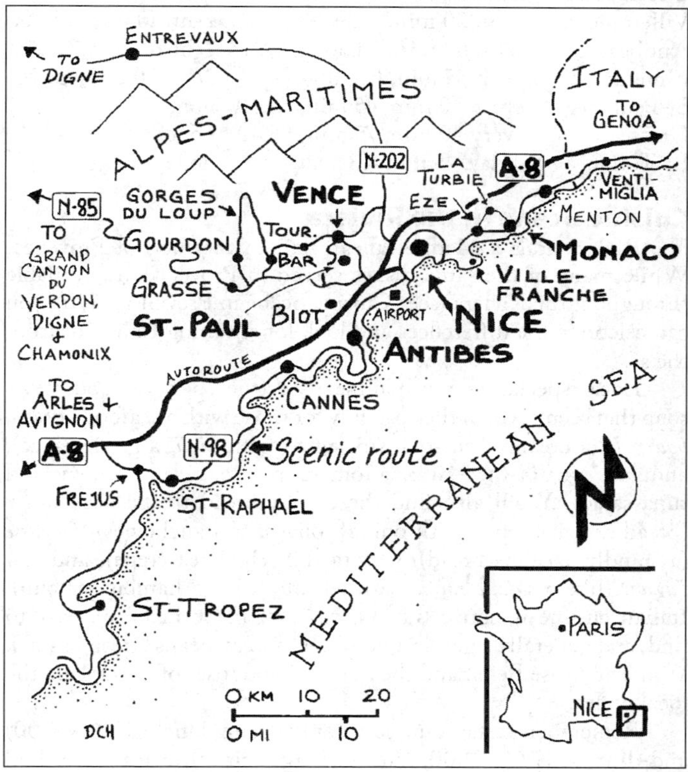

Jaurès, you'll find a baggage check (called *messagerie,* €2.50/bag, Mon–Sat 8:00–18:00, closed Sun), a snack bar with sandwiches and drinks, clean WCs (€0.50), and several bus companies. Get schedules and prices from the helpful English-speaking clerk at the information desk in the bus station (tel. 04 93 85 61 81). Buy tickets from the driver on the bus.

Schedules: Here's an overview of public transport options to key Riviera destinations with direct service from Nice. Two bus companies, RCA and Cars Broch, provide service on the same route between Nice, Villefranche-sur-Mer, and Monaco (RCA buses run more frequently). For any bus destination between Nice and Monaco (marked here with a *), you'll pay the same one-way or round-trip (free return only with same company, remember to keep your ticket). For other destinations, the one-way price is listed. Self-serve ticket machines in train stations make ticket purchases easy and fast.

Destination	Bus from Nice	Train from Nice
Villefranche	4/hr, 20 min, €1.80*	2/hr, 10 min, €1.60
Antibes	3/hr, 60 min, €4.30	2/hr, 25 min, €3.70
Monaco	4/hr, 45 min, €3.90*	2/hr, 20 min, €3.20
St-Paul	every 40 min, 45 min, €4.30	none
Grasse	every 40 min, 75 min, €6.40	none
La Turbie	4/day, 45 min, €3	none

Cuisine Scene in the Riviera

The Riviera adds a Mediterranean flair to the food of Provence. While many of the same dishes served in Provence are available throughout the Riviera (see "Cuisine Scene in Provence," 370), you can celebrate the differences and look for anything Italian or from the sea.

Local specialties are bouillabaisse (the spicy seafood stew-soup that seems worth the cost only for those with a seafood fetish), *bourride* (a creamy fish soup thickened with *aioli*, a garlic sauce), and *salade niçoise* (nee-swaz; a tomato, potato, olive, anchovy, and tuna salad). You'll also find these tasty bread treats: *pissaladière* (bread dough topped with onions, olives, and anchovies), *fougasse* (a spindly, lacelike bread), *socca* (a thin chickpea crêpe), and *pan bagnat* (like a *salade niçoise* stuffed into a huge hamburger bun). Italian cuisine is native (ravioli was first made in Nice), easy to find, and generally a good value (*pâtes fraîches* means "fresh pasta"). White and rosé Bellet and the rich reds and rosés of Bandol are the local wines.

Remember, restaurants serve only during lunch (11:30–14:00) and dinner (19:00–21:00, later in bigger cities); cafés serve food throughout the day.

Art Scene in the Riviera

The list of artists who have painted the Riviera reads like a Who's Who of 20th-century art. Pierre-Auguste Renoir, Henri Matisse, Marc Chagall, Georges Braque, Raoul Dufy, Fernand Léger, and Pablo Picasso all lived and worked here—and raved about the region's wonderful light. Their simple, semi-abstract, and—most importantly—colorful works reflect the Riviera. You'll experience the same landscapes they painted in this bright, sun-drenched region, punctuated with views of the "azure sea." Try to imagine the Riviera with a fraction of the people and development you see today.

But the artists were mostly drawn to the uncomplicated lifestyle of fishermen and farmers that has reigned here since time began. As the artists grew older, they retired in the sun, turned their backs on modern art's "isms," and painted with the wide-eyed wonder of children, using bright primary colors, basic outlines, and simple subjects.

Well-organized modern art museums (such as the Picasso Museum in Antibes, and the Chagall and Matisse museums in Nice, described in this chapter) litter the Riviera, allowing art-lovers to appreciate these artists' works while immersed in the same sun and culture that inspired them. Many of the museums were designed to blend the art with the surrounding views, gardens, and fountains, thus highlighting that modern art is not only stimulating, but sometimes simply beautiful.

Nice

Nice (sounds like niece), with its spectacular Alps-to-Mediterranean surroundings, eternally entertaining seafront promenade, and fine museums, is an enjoyable big-city highlight of the Riviera. In its traffic-free old city, Italian and French flavors mix to create a spicy Mediterranean dressing. Nice may be nice, but it's hot and jammed in July and August (reserve ahead). Get a room with air-conditioning *(une chambre avec climatisation)*. Everything you'll want to see in Nice is walkable or a short bus ride away.

ORIENTATION

Most sights and hotels recommended in this book are near avenue Jean Médecin, between the train station and the beach. It's a 20-minute walk from the train station to the beach (or a €10 taxi ride), and a 20-minute walk along the promenade from the fancy Hôtel Negresco to the heart of Old Nice.

You'll no doubt experience the inconvenience of construction in Nice. Three sleek tramway lines are being built (including one that will run along the promenade des Anglais). It's a huge project, and the first line won't open until 2006 at the earliest. Be ready for traffic reroutes and detours in many places.

Tourist Information

Nice's helpful TI has three locations: at the **airport** (mid-June–mid-Sept daily 8:00–21:00, mid-Sept–mid-June closed Sun); next to the **train station** (mid-June–mid-Sept Mon–Sat 8:00–20:00, Sun 9:00–19:00; mid-Sept–mid-June Mon–Sat 8:00–19:00, Sun 9:00–18:00); and facing the **beach** at 5 promenade des Anglais (mid-Sept–mid-June Mon–Sat 9:00–18:00, closed Sun; mid-June–mid-Sept Mon–Sat 8:00–20:00, Sun 9:00–19:00; tel. 08 92 70 74 07 costs €0.34/min, www.nicetourisme.com). Pick up the free Nice map (which lists all the sights, with hours and bus lines), the extensive *Practical Guide to Nice*, and information on regional day trips (such as city maps).

Art-lovers should consider buying a **museum pass** for sights in Nice or throughout the Riviera (sold at any participating sight). The Riviera Carte Musées pass covers many regional sights, including four museums in Nice (Chagall, Matisse, Fine Arts, and Modern and Contemporary Art; €10/1 day, €17/3 days, €27/7 days; for more information, see page 414). A Nice-only museum pass, Carte Passe-Musées 7 Jours, is also available (€6/7 days, does not include Chagall Museum).

Arrival in Nice

By Train: All trains stop at Nice's one main station (Nice-Ville, baggage check available, but closes at 17:45 and all day Sun and holidays). Avoid the suburban stations, and never leave your bags unattended. The TI is next door (to the left as you exit the station), car rental is to the right, and taxis are in front. To reach most of my recommended hotels, turn left out of the station, then right on avenue Jean Médecin. To get near the beach and the promenade des Anglais from the station, continue on foot for 20 minutes down avenue Jean Médecin, or take bus #15 or #17, which both run frequently to place Massena (bus #17 continues to the bus station, *gare routière*). Get off at place Massena and walk five minutes through Old Nice to the beach.

By Car: Driving into Nice from the west (such as from Provence), take the first Nice exit (for the airport—called *Côte d'Azur, Central*) and follow signs for *Nice Centre* and *Promenade des Anglais*. Try to avoid arriving at rush hour, when the promenade des Anglais grinds to a halt (Mon–Fri 17:00–19:30). Hoteliers know where to park (allow €10–18/day). The parking garage at the Nice Etoile shopping center on avenue Jean Médecin is handy to many of my hotel listings (ticket booth on 3rd floor, about €18/day, €10 from 20:00–8:00). All on-street parking is metered.

By Plane: For information on Nice's airport, see "Transportation Connections," page 441.

Helpful Hints

Theft Alert: Nice is notorious for pickpockets. Have nothing important on or around your waist, unless it's in a money belt tucked out of sight (thieves target fanny packs); don't leave anything visible in your car; be wary of scooters when standing at intersections; don't leave things unattended on the beach while swimming; and stick to main streets in Old Nice after dark.

U.S. Consulate: You'll find it at 7 avenue Gustave V (tel. 04 93 88 89 55, fax 04 93 87 07 38).

Canadian Consulate: It's at 10 rue Lamartine (tel. 04 93 92 93 22).

Medical Help: Riviera Medical Services has a list of English-speaking physicians. They can help you make an appointment or call an ambulance (tel. 04 93 26 12 70).

Museums: Most Nice museums are closed Tuesdays (except the Modern and Contemporary Art Museum) and free the first Sunday of the month. For information on Nice's museum passes, see "Tourist Information," above.

Supermarket: The big **Monoprix** on avenue Jean Médecin and rue Biscarra has a wide selection of food and cold drinks (closed Sun).

Internet Access: Consider **Web Nice** (daily 9:00–23:00, 25 bis promenade des Anglais, tel. 04 93 88 72 75), **Cyber Café Bio** (cheaper if you buy food or drink, daily 9:00–22:00, near the station at 16 rue Paganini, tel. 04 9 16 89 81), or **Maxi Web** (Mon–Sat 8:00–20:00, closed Sun, 6 bis avenue Durante, tel. 04 93 16 95 56). All three places have familiar American keyboards.

English Bookstore: The Cat's Whiskers has a great selection (closed Sun, 26 rue Lamartine, near recommended Hôtel du Petit Louvre, tel. 04 93 80 02 66).

English Radio: Tune into Riviera-Radio at FM 106.5.

American Express: AmEx faces the beach at 11 promenade des Anglais (where the promenade intersects with Rue du Congrès, tel. 04 93 16 53 53).

Laundry: The self-service **Point Laverie** is at the corner of Rue Alberti and Rue Pastorelli, next to Hôtel Vendôme (open daily).

Renting a Bike (and Other Wheels): Roller Station rents bikes (*vélos*, €5/hr, €10/half-day, €15/day), in-line skates (*rollers*, €5/day), and mini-scooters (*trotinettes,* €5/hr, €6/half day, €9/day). You'll need to leave an ID as deposit (daily 10:00–19:00, across from seaside promenade at 49 quai des Etats-Unis, another location at 10 rue Cassini near place Garibaldi, tel. 04 93 62 99 05).

Rocky Beaches: To make life tolerable on the rocks, swimmers should buy a pair of the cheap plastic beach shoes sold at many shops (flip-flops fall off in the water).

Views: For panoramic views, climb Castle Hill (see page 427).

Getting Around Nice

While walking gets you to most places, you'll want to ride the bus to the Chagall and Matisse museums. Bus fare is €1.40, and an all-day pass is €4.

Taxis are expensive but handy for the Chagall and Matisse museums and the Russian Church (figure €10–14 from promenade des Anglais). They normally only pick up at taxi stands *(tête de station)* or if you call (tel. 04 93 13 78 78).

The hokey tourist train is handy for getting to the castle (see "Tours," page 421).

Nice

CIMIEZ
MATISSE MUSEUM
ROMAN RUINS
1/4 MILE
400 METERS
P - PARKING
AVE. DE CIMIEZ
GARE DE SUD TRAIN STN.
TO ENTREVAUX
AVE. MALAUSSENA
CHAGALL MUSEUM
TO 1
RUSSIAN CATH.
FREEWAY
RAIMBALDI
MODERN ART MUSEUM
ELEVATED
AVE. THIERS
JEAN MEDECIN
NOTRE-DAME
DU BOUTAGE
CIMIEZ
PLACE GARIBALDI
RUE BARLA
TO 2
TRAIN STN.
DURANTE
BUS STN.
FAURE
CASSINI
GAMBETTA BLVD.
BLVD HUGO
PLACE MASSENA
AVE. JAURES
TO 3
CONGRES
RUE MASSENA
BLVD.
OLD NICE
CHATEAU
PORT
HOTEL NEGRESCO
COURS SALEYA
TO AIRPORT
4
AMEX
ELEVATOR
PROMENADE DES ANGLAIS
QUAI D. ETATS-UNIS
BEACHES
TOURIST TRAIN PICK-UP
BELLANDA TOWER
TO ANTIBES, CANNES & VENCE
TO VILLEFRANCHE, MONACO & ITALY
DCH
MEDITERRANEAN SEA
1 To High Corniche (sky-high route to Monaco)
2 To Middle Corniche (middle route, best for Monaco & Eze-le-Village)
3 To Low Corniche (low route to Villefranche-sur-Mer)
4 Start of Old Nice Walk

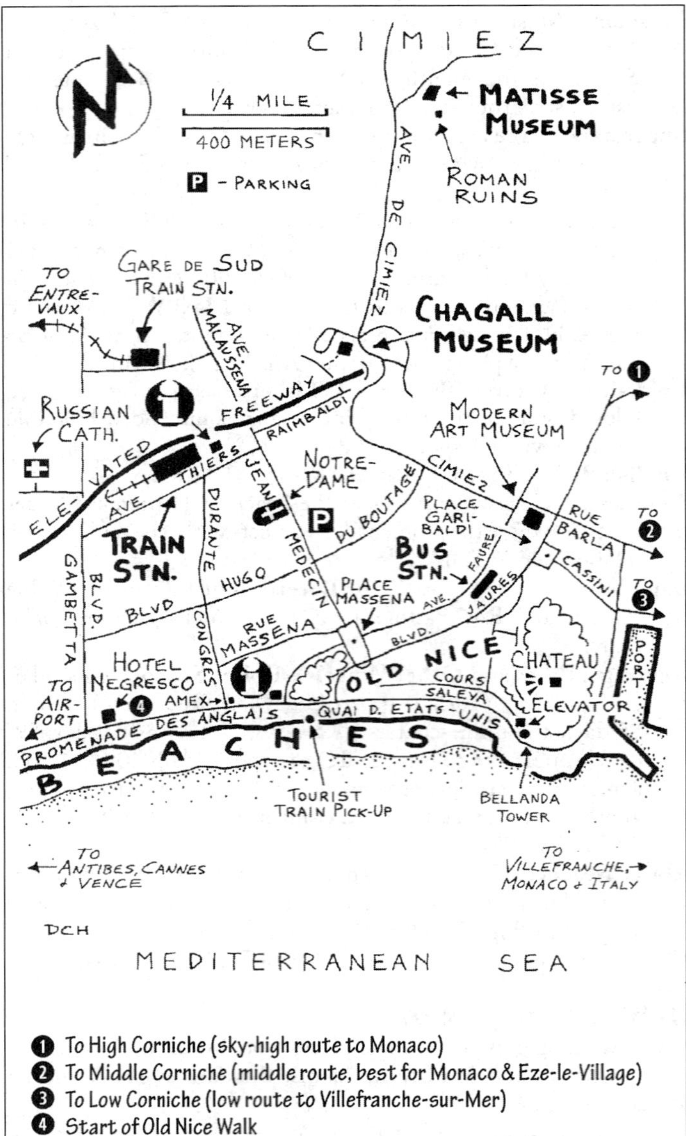

TOURS

Bus Tour—Le Grand Tour Bus provides an expensive hop-on, hop-off option on an open-deck bus with headphone commentary. The full route (about 90 min) includes the promenade des Anglais, old port, Cap de Nice, and the Chagall and Matisse museums on Cimiez Hill (€17/1-day pass, €19/2-day pass, cheaper for seniors and students, €10 for last tour of the day at about 18:45, hourly departures, buy tickets on bus, main stop is on promenade des Anglais, across from plage Beau Rivage, look for signs, tel. 04 92 29 17 00).
Tourist Train—For €6, you can spend 40 embarrassing minutes on the tourist train tooting along the promenade, through the old town, and up to the castle, with a taped English narration. This is a sweat-free way to get to the castle (every 30 min, meet train opposite Albert I park on promenade des Anglais, tel. 04 93 62 85 48).
Segway Tours—The latest technology to reach the Riviera is now available for three-hour English rolls through Nice. These stand-up scooter tours are relaxing, fun, and surprisingly informative (€45, March–Nov daily at 10:30, night tour at 18:30, cash only, reservations required, ages 12 and up, meet at 15 promenade des Anglais in front of Lido Plage, tel. 01 56 58 10 54, www.citysegwaytours.com).
Walking Tour—The TI on the promenade des Anglais organizes guided walking tours of Old Nice from May through October (€12, 1/week, usually Sat mornings, reservations necessary, tel. 08 92 70 74 07).
Local Guide—Pascale Rucker tailors excellent tours in and around Nice to your interests. You can book in advance or on short notice (€80/half-day, €140/day, tel. 04 93 87 77 89, mobile 06 16 24 29 52).

Nice in the Buff: A Walk Through Old Nice

This fun and informative self-guided walking tour gives a helpful introduction to Nice's bicultural heritage and most interesting neighborhoods. It's best done early in the morning (while the outdoor market still thrives). Allow about two hours at a leisurely pace, with a stop for coffee and a *socca* (chickpea crêpe).

Our tour begins on promenade des Anglais (near the landmark Hôtel Negresco) and ends in the heart of Old Nice (Vieux Nice).

Promenade des Anglais: Welcome to the Riviera. There's something for everyone along this four-mile-long seafront circus. Watch the Europeans at play, admire the azure Mediterranean, anchor yourself to a blue bench, and prop your feet up on the made-to-order guardrail. Later in the day, come back to join the evening parade of tans along the promenade.

For now, stroll like the belle époque English aristocrats for whom the promenade was built. The broad sidewalks of the promenade des Anglais (literally, "Walkway of the English") were

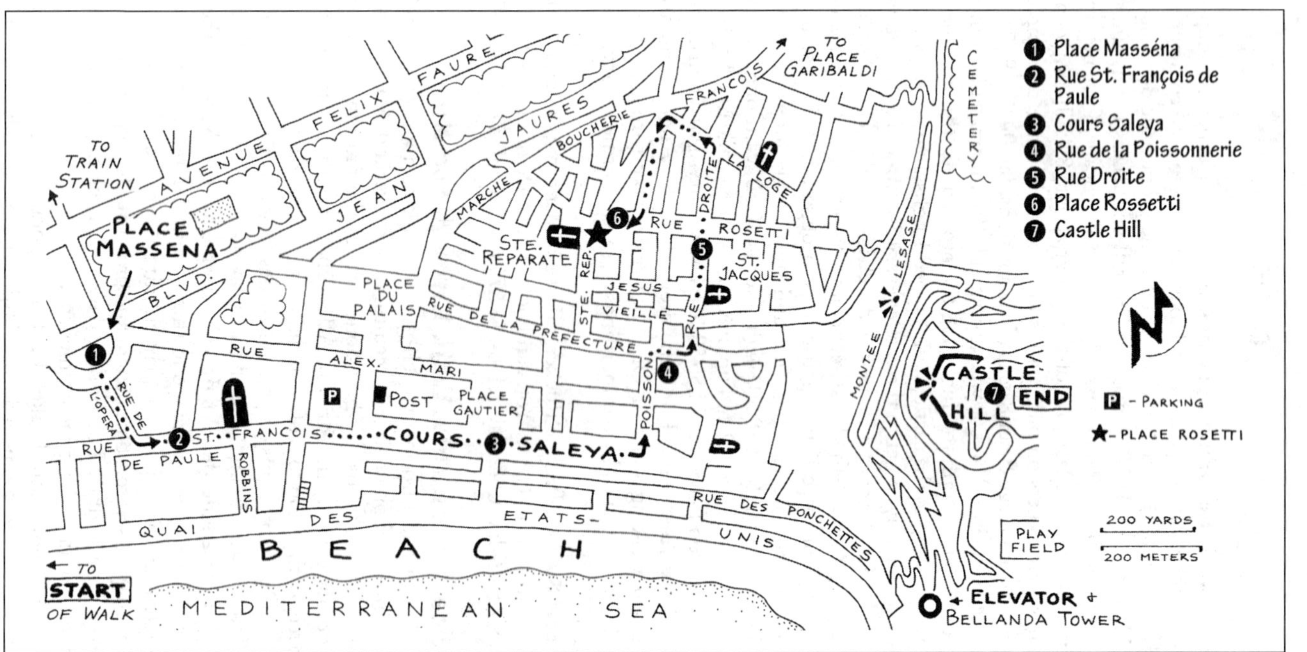
A Walk Through Old Nice
1 Place Masséna
2 Rue St. François de Paule
3 Cours Saleya
4 Rue de la Poissonnerie
5 Rue Droite
6 Place Rossetti
7 Castle Hill
P - PARKING
★ - PLACE ROSETTI
200 YARDS
200 METERS
TO START OF WALK
END
TO TRAIN STATION
TO PLACE GARIBALDI
PLACE MASSENA
CEMETERY
CASTLE HILL
ELEVATOR & BELLANDA TOWER
PLAY FIELD
MONTEE LESAGE
BEACH
MEDITERRANEAN SEA
QUAI DES ETATS-UNIS
RUE DES PONCHETTES
COURS SALEYA
PLACE GAUTIER
POST
PLACE DU PALAIS
RUE ALEX. MARI
RUE DE LA PREFECTURE
STE. REPARATE
RUE DE PAULE
ST. FRANCOIS
ROBBINS
RUE DE L'OPERA
BLVD. JEAN JAURES
AVENUE FELIX FAURE
MARCHE
BOUCHERIE
FRANCOIS
RUE DROITE
RUE ROSETTI
ST. JACQUES
LA LOGE
JESUS
VIEILLE
STE. REP.
POISSON

financed by wealthy English tourists who wanted a safe place to stroll and admire the view. The walk was paved in marble in 1822 for aristocrats who didn't want to dirty their shoes or smell the fishy gravel. This grand promenade leads to the old town and Castle Hill.

Start at the pink-domed...

Hôtel Negresco: Nice's finest hotel (also a historic monument) offers the city's most expensive beds and a free "museum" interior (always open—provided you're dressed decently, absolutely no beach attire). March straight through the lobby (as if you're staying there) into the exquisite Salon Royal. The chandelier hanging from the Eiffel-built dome is made of 16,000 pieces of crystal. It was built in France for the Russian czar's Moscow palace...but because of the Bolshevik Revolution in 1918, he couldn't take delivery. Read the explanation of the dome and saunter around counterclockwise: The bucolic scene, painted in 1913 for the hotel, sets the tone. Nip into the toilets for either a turn-of-the-century powder room or a Battle of Waterloo experience. The chairs nearby were typical of the age (cones of silence for an afternoon nap sitting up).

On your way out, pop into the Salon Louis XIV (right of entry lobby as you leave), where the embarrassingly short Sun King models his red platform boots (English descriptions explain the room).

Walk around the back to see the hotel's original entrance (grander than today's)—in the 19th century, classy people stayed out of the sun, and any posh hotel that cared about its clientele would design its entry on the shady north side.

Cross promenade des Anglais, turn left, and—before you begin your seaside promenade—grab a bench at the...

Bay of Angels (Baie des Anges): The body of Nice's patron saint, Réparate, was supposedly escorted into this bay by angels in the 4th century. Face the water. To your right is the airport, built on a landfill. On that tip of land way beyond the runway is Cap d'Antibes. Until 1860, Antibes and Nice were in different countries—Antibes was French, but Nice was a protectorate of the Italian kingdom of Savoy-Piedmont, a.k.a. the Kingdom of Sardinia. (During that period, the Var River—just west of Nice—was the geographic border between these two peoples.) In 1850, the people here spoke Italian and ate pasta. As Italy was uniting, the region was given a choice: Join the new country of Italy or join France (which was enjoying good times under the rule of Napoleon III). The vast majority voted in 1860 to go French...and *voilà!*

To the far left lies Villefranche-sur-Mer (marked by the tower at land's end—and home to lots of millionaires), then Monaco, then Italy. Behind you are the foothills of the Alps (les Alpes Maritimes), which gather threatening clouds that leave the Côte d'Azur alone to enjoy the sunshine more than 300 days each year. While half a million people live here, pollution is carefully treated—the water is routinely tested and very clean.

Now head to the left and begin...

Strolling the Promenade: The block next to Hôtel Negresco has a lush park and the Masséna Museum (city history, closed for renovation). Nearby sit two other belle époque establishments: the West End and Westminster hotels—English names to help those original guests feel at home. These hotels represent Nice's arrival as a tourist mecca a century ago, when the combination of leisure time and a stable economy allowed tourists to find the sun even in winter.

Even a hundred years ago, there was already sufficient tourism in Nice to justify building its first casino (a leisure activity imported from Venice). An elegant casino stood on pilings in the sea until the Germans destroyed it during World War II. While that's gone, you can see the striking 1920s Art Nouveau facade of the Palais de la Mediterranean, a grand casino and theater. Only the facade survives, and today it fronts a luxury condominium. The less charming Casino Ruhl is farther along (just before the park). Anyone can drop in for some one-armed-bandit fun, but for the tables at night, you'll need to dress up and bring your passport.

Albert I Park is named for the Belgian king who enjoyed wintering here. While the English came first, the Belgians and Russians were also huge fans of 19th-century Nice. The 1960 statue in the park commemorates Nice's being part of France for 100 years.

Walk into the park and continue down the center of the grassy strip between the two boulevards, all the way to place Masséna. The modern sculpture you pass—representing the curve of the French Riviera—is an answer to a prayer for local skateboarders. Walk to the fountains and face them. (To save water, they get high pressure only after 17:00.)

Place Masséna: You're standing on Nice's river, the Paillon (covered since the 1800s). Turn around. You can track the river's route under the green parkway you just walked; it meets the sea at the Casino Ruhl. For centuries, this river was Nice's natural defense. A fortified wall ran along its length to the sea. With the arrival of tourism in the 1800s, Nice expanded over and beyond the river. The rich red coloring of the buildings around you was the preference of Nice's Italian rulers.

Cross the square to the right, towards the Caisse d'Epargne bank and the curved buildings. Follow the steps that lead down past the three palm trees and to rue de l'Opéra (between the curved buildings). Walk down rue de l'Opéra, turning left on...

Rue St. François de Paule: You've entered Old Nice. Peer into the Alziari olive oil shop at #14 (opposite the city hall). Dating from 1868, the shop produces top-quality, stone-ground olive oil.

The proud owner, Gilles Piot, claims that stone wheels create less acidity (since metal grinding builds up heat). Locals fill their own containers from the huge vats (the cheapest one is peanut oil, not olive oil). Consider a gift for the olive-oil-lover on your list. A block down on the left (#7), Pâtisserie Auer's grand old storefront has changed little since the pastry shop opened in 1820. The writing on the window says, "Since 1820 from father to son." The royal medallions on the back wall remind shoppers that Queen Victoria fed her sweet tooth here. Across the street is Nice's grand opera house, from the same era. Imagine this opulent jewel buried deep in the old town of Nice back in the 19th century. With all the fancy big-city folks wintering here, the rough-edged town needed some high-class entertainment. The four statues on top represent theater, dance, music, and singing.

Continue on, sifting your way through tacky souvenirs to the cours Saleya (koor sah-lay-yuh).

Cours Saleya: Named for its broad exposure to the sun *(soleil)*, this commotion of color, sights, smells, and people has been Nice's main market square since the Middle Ages (produce market held daily until 13:00—except on Monday, when an antique market takes over the square). Amazingly, part of this square was a parking lot until 1980, when the mayor of Nice had an underground parking garage built.

The first section is devoted to freshly cut flowers that seem to grow effortlessly and everywhere in this ideal climate. Carnations, roses, and jasmine are local favorites in what has been the Riviera's biggest flower market since the 19th century. Fresh flowers are perhaps the best value in this otherwise pricey city.

The boisterous produce section trumpets the season with mushrooms, strawberries, white asparagus, zucchini flowers—whatever's fresh gets top billing.

Place Pierre Gautier (also called Plassa dou Gouvernou—bilingual street signs include the old Niçoise language, an Italian dialect) is where the actual farmers set up stalls to sell their produce and herbs directly. For a good overall view, climb the steps closest to the water (stepping over the trash sacks) above the Grand Bleu restaurant.

From your perch, look up to the hill that dominates to the east. The city of Nice was first settled there by Greeks circa 400 B.C. In the Middle Ages, a massive castle stood there, with turrets, high walls, and soldiers at the ready. With the river guarding one side and the sea the other, this mountain fortress seemed strong—until Louis XIV leveled it in 1706. Nice's medieval seawall ran along the lineup of two-story buildings where you're standing. Now look across place Pierre Gautier to the large "palace." This Ducal Palace was where the kings of Sardinia (the city's Italian rulers until about

1860) would reside when in Nice. Today, it's police headquarters.

Resume your stroll down the center of cours Saleya, stopping when you see La Cambuse restaurant on your left. In front, hovering over the black barrel fire with the paella-like pan on top, is the self-proclaimed Queen of the Market, Thérèse (tehr-ehz). When she's not looking for a husband, Thérèse is cooking *socca,* Nice's chickpea crêpe specialty. Spend €2 for a wad of *socca* (careful—it's hot, but good). If she doesn't have a pan out, that means it's on its way (watch for the frequent scooter deliveries). Wait in line...or else it'll all be gone when you return.

Continue down cours Saleya. The fine golden building at the end is where Henri Matisse lived for 17 years. Turn left at the Civette du Cours café, and head down...

Rue de la Poissonnerie: Look up at #4. Adam and Eve are squaring off, each holding a zucchini-like gourd. This scene (post-apple) represents the annual rapprochement in Nice to make up for the sins of a too-much-fun Carnival (Mardi Gras). Nice residents have partied hard during Carnival for more than 700 years. The iron grill above the door allows air to enter the building, but keeps out uninvited guests. You'll see lots of these open grills in Old Nice. They were part of an ingenious system of sucking in cool air from the sea, through the homes, and out through vents in the roof. Across the street, check out the small Baroque church dedicated to St. Rita, the patron saint of desperate causes. She holds a special place in locals' hearts, and this church is the most popular in Nice.

Turn right on the next street, then left on "Right" Street (rue Droite), into a world that feels like Naples.

Rue Droite: In the Middle Ages, this straight, skinny street provided the most direct route from wall to wall, or river to sea. Stop at Esipuno's bakery (at place du Jésus). Thirty years ago, this baker was voted the best in France, and his son now runs the place. Notice the firewood stacked by the oven. Farther along, at #28, Thérèse (whom you met earlier) cooks her *socca* in the wood-fired oven before she carts it to her barrel on cours Saleya. The balconies of the mansion in the next block mark the Palais Lascaris (1647), a rare souvenir from one of Nice's most prestigious families (free, Wed–Mon 10:00–18:00, closed Tue, worth touring for a peek at 1700s Baroque Italy high life, look up and make faces back at the guys under the balconies).

Turn left on the rue de la Loge, then left again on rue Mascoïnat, to reach...

Place Rossetti: The most Italian of Nice's piazzas, place Rossetti feels more like Rome than Nice. This square comes alive after dark. Fenocchio is popular for its many gelato flavors. Walk to the fountain and stare back at the church. This is the Cathedral of St. Réparate—an unassuming building for a major city's cathedral.

The cathedral was relocated here in the 1500s, when Castle Hill was temporarily converted to military-only. The name comes from Nice's patron saint, a teenage virgin named Réparate, whose martyred body floated to Nice in the 4th century, accompanied by angels (remember the Bay of Angels?). The interior is overwhelmingly Baroque. Remember that Baroque was a response to the Protestant Reformation. With the Catholic Church's "Counter-Reformation," the theatrical energy of churches was cranked up—with reenergized, high-powered saints and eye-popping decor.

Back outside the cathedral, the steps leading up rue Rossetti are the most direct path from here to Castle Hill (15 min straight up). If you're pooped, wander back down to quai des Etats-Unis near the beach and ride the elevator (next to Hôtel Suisse, where bayfront road curves right, open daily 10:00–18:00, until 20:00 in summer, one-way-€0.70, round-trip-€1).

Castle Hill (Colline du Château): This hill—in an otherwise flat city center—offers good views over Nice, the port (to the east), the foothills of the Alps, and the Mediterranean. The views are best at sunset or whenever the weather's really clear (park closes at 20:00 in summer, earlier off-season). Until the 1100s, the city of Nice was crammed onto this hilltop, as it was too risky to live in the flatlands below, where marauders were on the rampage. Today, you'll find a waterfall, a playground, two cafés (fair prices), and a cemetery—but no castle—on Castle Hill.

To walk back downtown, follow signs from just below the upper café to Vieille Ville (not Le Port), and turn right at the cemetery, then look for the walkway down on your left.

ACTIVITIES

▲▲Strolling the Promenade des Anglais—Sauntering along Nice's four-mile seafront promenade is a must. From the days when wealthy English tourists lined the seaside with grand hotels, to today as a favorite spot for Europeans to enjoy some fun in the sun—this stretch is *the* place to be in Nice.

▲Wheeling the Promenade—Get a bike and ride along the coast in both directions (about 30 min each way). Roller Station rents bikes, in-line skates, and mini-scooters (see "Helpful Hints," above). Both of the following paths start along the promenade des Anglais.

The path to the west stops just before the airport at perhaps the most scenic *boules* courts in France. Stop and watch the old-timers while away their afternoon tossing those shiny metal balls.

In the other direction, you'll round the hill—passing a scenic cape and the town's memorial to both World Wars—to the harbor of Nice, with a chance to survey some fancy yachts. Pedal around the harbor and follow the coast past the Corsica ferry terminal (you'll need to carry your bike up a flight of steps). From there, the path leads to a delightful, tree-lined residential district.

Relaxing at the Beaches—Nice is where the masses relax on the rocks. After settling into the smooth pebbles, you can play beach volleyball, table tennis, or *boules*; rent paddleboats, personal watercraft, or windsurfing equipment; explore ways to use your zoom lens as a telescope; or snooze on comfy beach beds with end tables. You can rent a spot on the beach (mattress and chaise lounge-€12, umbrella-€4, towel-€3). Many hotels have special deals with certain beaches for discounted rental (check with your hotel for details). Consider lunch in your bathing suit (€10 salads and pizzas in bars and restaurants all along the beach). For a peaceful cup of coffee on the beach, stop here first thing in the morning before the crowds hit. *Plage Publique* signs explain the 15 beach no-nos (translated in English).

SIGHTS

Museums

You can get a free pass for bus #15 when traveling between the Chagall and Matisse museums. Ask at either of these museums for this free ticket, which saves you a 20- to 30-minute walk (it's uphill from Chagall to Matisse).

▲▲▲Chagall Museum (Musée National Marc Chagall)—Even if you're suspicious of modern art, this museum—with the largest collection of Chagall's work in captivity anywhere—is a delight. After World War II, Chagall returned from the United States to settle in nearby Vence. Between 1954 and 1967, he painted a cycle of 17 large murals designed for, and donated to, this museum. These paintings, inspired by the biblical books of Genesis, Exodus, and the Song of Songs, make up the "nave," or core, of what Chagall called the "House of Brotherhood."

Each painting is a lighter-than-air collage of images that draw from Chagall's Russian-folk-village youth, his Jewish heritage, biblical themes, and his feeling that he existed somewhere between heaven and earth. He believed that the Bible was a synonym for nature, and that color and biblical themes were key ingredients for understanding God's love for his creation. Chagall's brilliant blues and reds celebrate nature, as do his spiritual and folk themes .

Notice the focus on couples. To Chagall, humans loving each other mirrored God's love of creation. Chagall enjoyed the love of two women in his long life—his first wife, Bella, then Valentina, who gave him a second wind as he was painting these late works. Chagall was one of the few "serious" 20th-century artists to portray unabashed love. Where the Bible uses the metaphor of earthly, physical, and sexual love to describe God's love for humans, Chagall uses unearthly colors and a mystical ambience to celebrate human love. Chagall's canvases are hard to interpret on a literal level, but they capture the rosy spirit of a man in love with life.

On your way out, be sure to visit the three Chagall stained-glass windows in the auditorium (depicting God's creation of the universe).

Cost and Hours: €5.50, covered by Riviera Carte Musées pass, Oct–June Wed–Mon 10:00–17:00, July–Sept Wed–Mon 10:00–18:00, closed Tue, tel. 04 93 53 87 31, www.musee-chagall.fr. For information on getting to the museum, see page 419.

▲▲Matisse Museum (Musée Matisse)—This museum, worth ▲▲▲ for his fans, contains the world's largest collection of Matisse paintings. It offers a painless introduction to the artist, whose style was shaped by Mediterranean light and by fellow Côte d'Azur artists Pablo Picasso and Pierre-Auguste Renoir.

Henri Matisse, the master of leaving things out, could suggest a woman's body with a single curvy line—leaving it to the viewer's mind to fill in the rest. Ignoring traditional 3-D perspective, he used simple dark outlines saturated with bright blocks of color to create recognizable but simplified scenes composed into a decorative pattern to express nature's serene beauty. You don't look "through" a Matisse canvas, like a window; you look "at" it, like wallpaper.

Matisse understood how colors and shapes affect us emotionally. He could create either shocking, clashing works (Fauvism) or geometrical, balanced, harmonious ones (later works). While other modern artists reveled in purely abstract design, Matisse (almost) always kept the subject matter at least vaguely recognizable. He used unreal colors and distorted lines not just to portray what an object looks like, but also to express the object's inner nature (even inanimate objects). Meditating on his paintings helps you connect with nature—or so Matisse hoped.

As you wander the museum, look for motifs, including fruit, flowers, wallpaper, and interiors of sunny rooms—often with a window opening onto a sunny landscape. Another favorite subject is the odalisque (harem concubine)—usually shown sprawled in seductive poses and with a simplified, masklike face.

Notice works from his different periods. Room 9 houses paintings from his formative years as a student. In Room 10, his work evolves through many stages, becoming simpler with time. Upstairs, in and around Room 17, you'll find sketches and models of his famous Chapel of the Rosary in nearby Vence and related religious work. On the same floor, there are rooms dedicated to his paper cutouts and his *Jazz* series. Throughout the building are souvenirs from his travels, which inspired much of his work.

The museum is in a 17th-century Genoese villa, set in an olive grove amid the ruins of the Roman city of Cemenelum. Part of the ancient Roman city of Nice, Cemenelum was a military camp that housed as many as 20,000 people.

Cost and Hours: €4, covered by Riviera Carte Musées pass, Wed–Mon 10:00–18:00, closed Tue, tel. 04 93 81 08 08, www.musee-matisse-nice.org.

Getting to the Matisse Museum: It's a confusing but manageable 45-minute walk from the top of avenue Jean Médecin (and the train station). And it's a 20- to 30-minute walk from the Chagall Museum.

Buses #15 and #17 serve the Matisse and Chagall Museums from the eastern side of avenue Jean Médecin (#15 runs more frequently-6/hr, #17-3/hr, €1.40). The bus stop for Matisse (called Arènes) is on avenue de Cimiez, two blocks up from Chagall. If connecting the museums by bus, ask for a free bus pass with your museum ticket.

To **walk** to the Matisse Museum, go to the train-station end of avenue Jean Médecin and turn right onto boulevard Raimbaldi along the overpasses, then turn left under the overpasses onto avenue Raymond Comboul. Once under the overpass, angle to the right up avenue de l'Olivetto to the alley (with the big wall on your right). A pedestrian path soon emerges, and it leads up and up to signs for both Chagall and Matisse.

Modern and Contemporary Art Museum (Musée d'Art Moderne et d'Art Contemporain)—This ultramodern museum features an enjoyable collection of art from the 1960s and 1970s, including works by Andy Warhol and Roy Lichtenstein, and offers frequent special exhibits.

Cost, Hours, Location: €4, covered by Riviera Carte Musées pass, Tue–Sun 10:00–18:00, closed Mon, on promenade des Arts near bus station, tel. 04 93 62 61 62, www.mamac-nice.org.

Molinard Perfume Museum—The Molinard family has been making perfume in Grasse (about an hour's drive from Nice) since 1849. Their Nice store has a small museum in the back illustrating the story of their industry. Back when people believed water spread the plague (Louis XIV supposedly bathed less than once a year), doctors advised people to rub fragrances into their skin and then powder their bodies. Back then, perfume was a necessity of everyday life.

Room 1 shows photos of the local flowers used in perfume production. Room 2 shows the earliest (18th-century) production method. Petals would be laid on a bed of animal fat. After baking in the sun, the fat would absorb the essence of the flowers. Petals would be replaced daily for two months until the fat was saturated. Models and old photos show the later distillation process (660 pounds of lavender would produce only a quarter-gallon of essence). Perfume is "distilled like cognac and then aged like wine." Room 3 shows the desk of a "nose." Of the 150 real "noses" (top perfume creators) in the world, more than 100 are French. You are welcome to enjoy the testing bottles before heading into the shop.

Cost, Hours, Location: Free, daily 10:00–19:00, sometimes closed Mon off-season, just between beach and place Masséna at 20 rue St. François de Paule, tel. 04 93 62 90 50, www.molinard.com.

Other Nice Museums—These museums are decent rainy-day options. The **Fine Arts Museum** (Musée des Beaux-Arts), with 6,000 works from the 17th to 20th centuries, will satisfy your need for a fine-arts fix (€4, covered by Riviera Carte Musées pass, Tue–Sun 10:00–18:00, closed Mon, 3 avenue des Baumettes, western end of Nice, tel. 04 92 15 28 28). The **Archaeological Museum** (Musée Archeologique) displays Roman ruins and various objects from the Romans' occupation of this region (€4, Wed–Mon 10:00–18:00, closed Tue, near Matisse Museum at 160 avenue des Arènes, tel. 04 93 81 59 57). Nice's city museum, **Museum Masséna** (Musée Masséna), may reopen in 2006.

More Sights

Russian Cathedral (Cathédrale Russe)—Nice's Russian Orthodox church—claimed to be the finest outside Russia—is worth a visit. Five hundred rich Russian families wintered in Nice in the late 19th century. Since they couldn't pray in a Catholic church, the community needed a worthy Orthodox house of worship. Czar Nicholas I's widow saw the need and provided the land (which required tearing down her house). Czar Nicholas II gave this church to the Russian community in 1912. (A few years later, Russian comrades—who didn't winter on the Riviera—assassinated him.) Here in the land of olives and anchovies, these proud onion domes seem odd. But, I imagine, so did those old Russians.

Step inside (pick up English info sheet). The one-room interior is filled with icons and candles, and the old Russian music adds to the ambience. The icon wall divides things between the spiritual world and the temporal world of the worshippers. Only the priest can walk between the two worlds, by using the "Royal Door." Take a close look at items lining the front (starting in the left corner). The angel with red boots and wings—the protector of the Romanov family—stands over a symbolic tomb of Christ. The tall, black, hammered-copper cross commemorates the massacre of Nicholas II and his family in 1918. Notice the Jesus icon near the Royal Door. According to a priest here, as the worshipper meditates, staring deep into the eyes of Jesus, he enters a lake where he finds his soul. Surrounded by incense, chanting, and your entire community...it could happen. Farther to the right, the icon of the Virgin and Child is decorated with semi-precious stones from the Ural Mountains. Artists worked a triangle into each iconic face—symbolic of the Trinity.

Cost, Hours, Location: €2.50, daily 9:00–12:00 & 14:30–18:00, closes 17:00 off-season, chanted services Sat at 17:30 or 18:00, Sun at 10:00, no tourist visits during services, no shorts, 10-min walk behind station at 17 boulevard du Tzarewitch, tel. 04 93 96 88 02.

SLEEPING

Don't look for charm in Nice. Go for modern and clean, with a central location and, in summer, air-conditioning. I've divided my sleeping recommendations into three areas: between the train station and Nice Etoile shopping center, near Old Nice and the beaches, and in a more stately area between the station and promenade des Anglais (by boulevard Victor Hugo).

Reserve early for summer visits. The rates listed here are for April through October. Prices generally drop €10–20 from November through March, and can increase dramatically during the Nice Carnival (Feb), Monaco's Grand Prix (May), and the Cannes film festival (May). June is convention month, and Nice is one of Europe's top convention cities—so book ahead.

Near the Train Station

Most hotels near the station are overrun, overpriced, and loud. Here are the pleasant exceptions (most are between Old Nice and the train station, near avenue Jean Médecin and boulevard Victor Hugo). For parking, ask your hotelier, or see "Arrival in Nice—By Car," page 418.

Sleep Code

(€1 = about $1.20, country code: 33)
S = Single, **D** = Double/Twin, **T** = Triple, **Q** = Quad,**b** = bathroom, **s** = shower only, * = French hotel rating (0–4 stars). Hotels speak English, have elevators, and accept credit cards unless otherwise noted.

To help you sort easily through these listings, I've divided the rooms into three categories based on the price for a standard double room with bath:

$$$ **Higher Priced**—Most rooms €95 or more.
$$ **Moderately Priced**—Most rooms between €65–95.
$ **Lower Priced**—Most rooms €65 or less.

Nice Hotels

1 Hôtel Excelsior
2 Hôtel Vendome & Launderette
3 Hôtel Clémenceau & Hôtel St. Georges
4 Hôtel du Petit Louvre
5 Hôtel Aria
6 Hôtel Masséna & Hôtel le Guitry
7 Hôtel Suisse
8 Hôtel Lafayette
9 Hôtel Mercure
10 Hôtel le Royal
11 Hôtel Lorrain
12 Hôtel Windsor
13 Hôtel les Cigales
14 Hôtel Splendid & Hôtel Gounod
15 Hôtel l'Oasis
16 To Hôtel Villa Eden
17 Cat's Whiskers Bookstore
Rue Massena Pedestrian Zone
1/4 Mile
.5 KM
Train Station
To Chagall & Matisse Museums
Nice Etoile
Bus Stn.
Place Garibaldi
Place Massena
Parc Albert I
Old Nice
Chateau
Elevator
Hotel Negresco
Promenade des Anglais
Quai des Etats-Unis
Beaches
Elevated Freeway
Cours Saleya
Amex
To 16

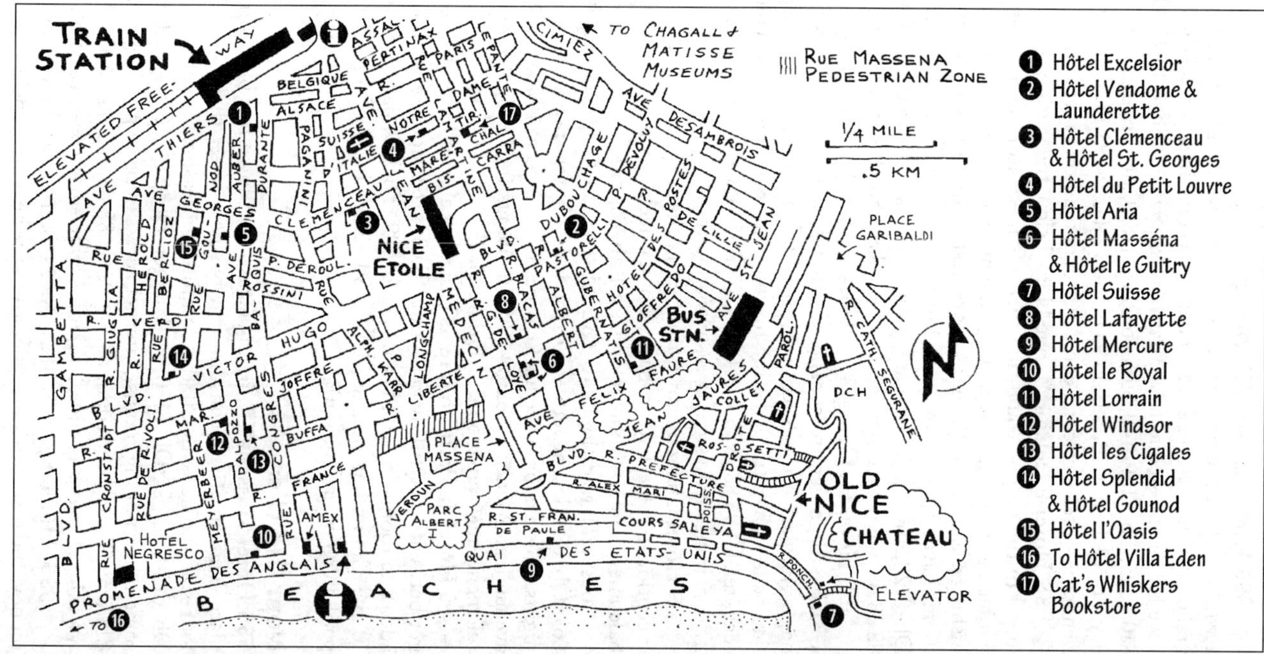

$$$ Hôtel Vendôme***, a mansion set off the street, gives you a whiff of the belle époque, with pink pastels, high ceilings, and grand staircases. Rooms are modern and come in all sizes. The best have balconies—request *"une chambre avec balcon"* (Sb-€88–95, Db-€105–125, Tb-€120–140, buffet breakfast-€10, air-con, parking-€10/day, 26 rue Pastorelli, tel. 04 93 62 00 77, fax 04 93 13 40 78, www.vendome-hotel-nice.com, contact@vendome-hotel-nice.com).

$$ Hôtel Excelsior***, one block below the station, is a diamond in the rough. You'll find turn-of-the-century decor, a small but lush garden courtyard, and pleasant rooms with real wood furnishings. Rooms on the garden are best in the summer; streetside rooms have balconies and get winter sun (standard Db-€90, *prestige* Db-€120, air-con, 19 avenue Durante, tel. 04 93 88 18 05, fax 04 93 88 38 69, www.excelsiornice.com, excelsior.hotel@wanadoo.fr).

$$ Hôtel St. Georges**, a block away, is big and bright, with a backyard garden, reasonably clean and comfortable rooms, and happy Jacques at the reception (Sb-€59, Db-€69, Tb with 3 separate beds-€87, extra bed-€16, air-con, 7 avenue Georges Clémenceau, tel. 04 93 88 79 21, fax 04 93 16 22 85, www.hotelsaintgeorges.fr, nicefrance.hotelstgeorges@wanadoo.fr).

$ Hôtel Clémenceau**, run by the charming La Serres, is an exceptional value with a basic, homey feel. Rooms—some with balconies, some without closets, all air-conditioned—are mostly spacious and traditional (S-€31, Sb-€43, D-€43, Db-€58, Tb-€69, Qb-€84, kitchenette-€8 extra and only for stays of at least 3 nights, no elevator, 3 avenue Georges Clémenceau, 1 block west of avenue Jean Médecin, tel. 04 93 88 61 19, fax 04 93 16 88 96, hotel-clemenceau@wanadoo.fr, Marianne).

$ Hôtel du Petit Louvre* is basic, but a good hostel-like budget bet, with playful owners (the Vilas), art-festooned walls, and adequate rooms (S-€38, Ds-€44, Db-€49, Tb-€57, pay on arrival, 10 rue Emma Tiranty, tel. 04 93 80 15 54, fax 04 93 62 45 08, petilouvr@wanadoo.com).

Near Old Nice

$$$ Hôtel Masséna****, in an elegant building a few blocks from place Masséna, is a consummate business hotel that offers 100 four-star rooms with all the comforts at reasonable rates (small Db-€120, larger Db-€150, still larger Db-€215, extra bed-€30, some non-smoking rooms, Internet access, reserve parking ahead-€18/day, 58 rue Giofreddo, tel. 04 92 47 88 88, fax 04 92 47 88 89, www.hotel-massena-nice.com, info@hotel-massena-nice.com).

$$$ Hôtel Suisse*** has Nice's best ocean views for the money, and is surprisingly quiet given the busy street below. Rooms are comfortable, with air-conditioning and modern conveniences.

Old Nice Hotels and Restaurants

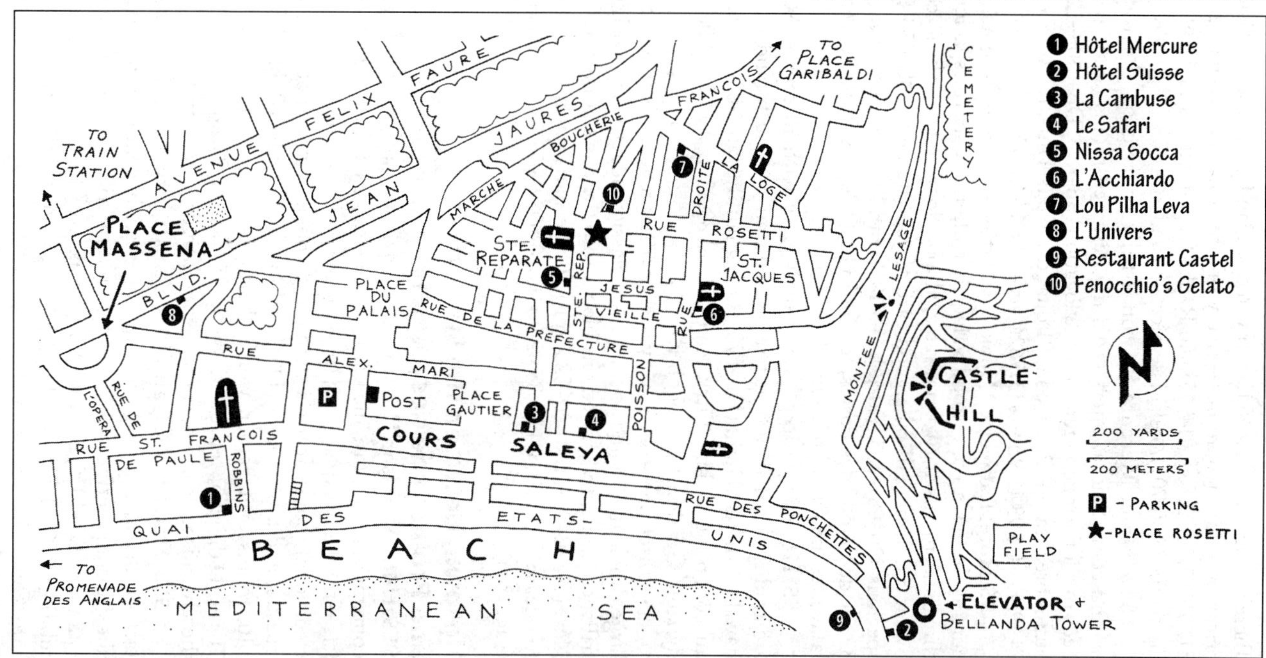

There's no reason to sleep here if you don't land a view, so I've listed prices only for view rooms—many of which have balconies (Db-€120–155, breakfast-€14, 15 quai Rauba Capeu, tel. 04 92 17 39 00, fax 04 93 85 30 70, hotelsuisse.nice@wanadoo.fr).

$$$ Hôtel Mercure***, wonderfully situated on the water behind cours Saleya, offers tastefully designed rooms (some with beds in a loft) at good rates for the location (Sb-€94, Db-€108–120, buffet breakfast-€12, air-con, 91 quai des Etats-Unis, tel. 04 93 85 74 19, fax 04 93 13 90 94, h0962@accor-hotels.com).

$$ Hôtel Lafayette*** looks big and average from the outside, but inside, it's a cozy, good value that offers 18 sharp, spacious, three-star rooms at two-star rates, all one floor up from the street. Sweet Sandrine will take good care of you (standard Db-€77–93, spacious Db-€87–105, extra bed-€18, central air-con, no elevator, 32 rue de l'Hôtel des Postes, tel. 04 93 85 17 84, fax 04 93 80 47 56, lafayette@nouvel-hotel.com).

$$ Hôtel le Guitry*** is a small place with 16 rooms. Half are traditional, half are just renovated and *très* plush, and a few have little natural light (Db-€70–90, big family room-€125, central air-con, 6 rue Sacha Guitry, tel. 04 93 80 83 83, fax 04 93 13 02 91, dynamo Geraldine S enough E).

$ Hôtel Lorrain** is very basic, with kitchenettes in all of its large, linoleum-floored rooms. It's a classic budget place, with no frills, conveniently located one block from the bus station and Old Nice (Db-€48, extra bed-€25, 6 rue Gubernatis, push top buzzer to release door, tel. 04 93 85 42 90, fax 04 93 85 55 54, hotellorrain @aol.com).

Uptown, Between the Station and Promenade des Anglais

$$$ Hôtel Windsor*** is a snazzy, well-run garden retreat with contemporary rooms, including some—designed by modern artists—that defy explanation (pass on the *artiste* rooms and ask for a traditional room). It has a swimming pool and gym (both free for guests), and a €10 sauna (Db-€105–155, extra bed-€20, breakfast-€10, rooms over garden worth the higher price, Internet access, 11 rue Dalpozzo, tel. 04 93 88 59 35, fax 04 93 88 94 57, www.hotelwindsornice.com, contact@hotelwindsornice.com).

$$$ Hôtel Les Cigales*** is a smart little pastel place with tasteful decor, 19 newly renovated rooms, air-conditioning, and a slick upstairs terrace, all well-managed by friendly Mr. Valentino (standard Db-€115, big Db-€160, breakfast-€10, 16 rue Dalpozzo, tel. 04 97 03 10 70, fax 04 97 03 10 71, www.hotel-lescigales.com, infos@hotel-lescigales.com).

$$$ Hôtel Splendid**** is a worthwhile splurge if you miss your Hilton. The rooftop pool, whirlpool tub, and panoramic breakfast room alone almost justify the cost...but throw in good rooms (some non-smoking), a free gym, Internet access, and air-conditioning, and you're as good as home (Db-€225, deluxe Db with terrace-€250, suites-€335, breakfast-€16, free breakfast with minimum 3-night stay, parking-€19/day, 50 boulevard Victor Hugo, tel. 04 93 16 41 00, fax 04 93 16 42 70, www.splendid-nice.com, info@splendid-nice.com).

$$$ Hôtel Gounod*** is behind Hôtel Splendid and shares the same owners, who allow its clients free access to Hôtel Splendid's pool, whirlpool tub, and other amenities. Don't let the lackluster lobby fool you. Its fine rooms are big, air-conditioned, and richly decorated, with high ceilings—though they can be musty (Db-€125–140, palatial 4-person suites-€215, breakfast-€10, parking-€12/day, 3 rue Gounod, tel. 04 93 16 42 00, fax 04 93 88 23 84, www.gounod-nice.com, info@gounod-nice.com).

$$$ Hôtel Aria*** is a soft-yellow, very sharp, big-city refuge with 30 comfortable rooms, half of which overlook a small park. This place is well run and a good value (Db-€95–110, junior suite-€150, extra bed-€20, buffet breakfast-€9, air-con, 15 avenue Auber, tel. 04 93 88 30 69, fax 04 93 88 11 35, www.aria-nice.com, reservation@aria-nice.com).

$$$ Hôtel le Royal*** stands shoulder-to-shoulder on the promenade des Anglais with the big boys (hôtels Negresco and Westminster). It feels like a retirement-home-turned-hotel (don't expect an enthusiastic reception), but offers solid comfort with air-conditioning at €100–200 less than its more famous neighbors. The mini-suites are well worth the extra euros (seaview rooms: Sb-€100, Db-€130, Db mini-suite €150; city-facing rooms: Sb-€80, Db-€100; 23 promenade des Anglais, tel. 04 93 16 43 00, fax 04 93 16 43 02, royal@vacancesbleues.com).

$$$ Hôtel l'Oasis*** is just that. This orange-pastel hotel sits away from the street, surrounding a large, flowery courtyard. Its 40 non-smoking rooms are also calming, with air-conditioning, earth tones, pleasing fabrics, sharp bathrooms, and reasonable rates. This hotel works with an English travel agency, so many guests are British, and the place is often booked long in advance (Sb-€75, Db-€90–120, Tb-€120, prices include breakfast, 23 rue Gounod, tel. 04 93 88 12 29, fax 04 93 16 14 40).

$$ Hôtel Villa Eden** is the one little belle époque time-warp place among the sprawling waterfront hotels lining the promenade des Anglais. This former mansion of a Russian aristocrat now rents 13 rooms with a faded and charming, family-run ambience. It's set back enough to lose the street noise and much of the sea view, but if you want to be close to the beach, this is a good budget option (Db-€63–69, extra bed-€15, 10-minute walk beyond Hôtel Negresco, bus #12 or #23 from station, 99

Promenade des Anglais, tel. 04 93 86 53 70, fax 04 93 97 67 97, hotelvillaeden@caramail.com).

EATING

My recommended restaurants are concentrated in the same neighborhoods as my favorite hotels. The promenade des Anglais is ideal for picnic dinners on warm, languid evenings, and the old town is perfect for restaurant-shopping. Gelato-lovers should save room for **Fenocchio** (on place Rossetti in Old Nice, 86 flavors from tomato to lavender, daily until 23:30). Ice cream cone in hand, you can join the evening parade along the Mediterranean (best view at night is from east end of quai des Etats-Unis, on tip below Castle Hill).

Old Nice, on or near Cours Saleya

Nice's dinner scene converges on cours Saleya (koor sah-lay-yuh)—entertaining enough in itself to make the generally mediocre food of its restaurants a good value. It's a fun, festive place to compare tans and mussels. Even if you're eating elsewhere, wander through here in the evening.

La Cambuse offers a refined setting and fine cuisine for those who want to eat on cours Saleya without sacrificing quality (allow €30–40 per person, open daily, at #5, tel. 04 93 80 82 40).

Le Safari has the best "eating energy" on the cours Saleya and serves all afternoon (open daily, at Castle Hill end at #1, tel. 04 93 80 18 44).

Nissa Socca offers good, cheap Italian cuisine and a lively atmosphere a few blocks from cours Saleya (Mon–Sat from 19:00, closed Sun, arrive early, a block off place Rossetti on rue Ste. Réparate, tel. 04 93 80 18 35).

L'Acchiardo, deeper in the old city, is a budget traveler's friend, with simple, hearty, traditional cuisine at bargain prices in a homey setting (€13 dinner *plats*, closed Sat–Sun, 38 rue Droite, tel. 04 93 85 51 16).

Lou Pilha Leva offers a fun, *très* cheap dinner option with *niçoise* specialties and outdoor-only benches. Order your food from one side and drinks from the other (open daily, located where rue de la Loge and Centrale meet in Old Nice).

L'Univers, a block off place Masséna, has earned a Michelin star while maintaining a warm ambience. This elegant place is as relaxed as a "top" restaurant can be, from its casual decor to the tasteful dinnerware. But when the artfully presented food arrives, you know this is high cuisine (*menus* from €40, closed Sun, 53 boulevard Jean Jaurès, tel. 04 93 62 32 22, plumailunivers@aol.com).

Restaurant Castel is your best beach option. Eating here, you almost expect Don Ho to grab a mike. You're right on the beach

Nice Restaurants

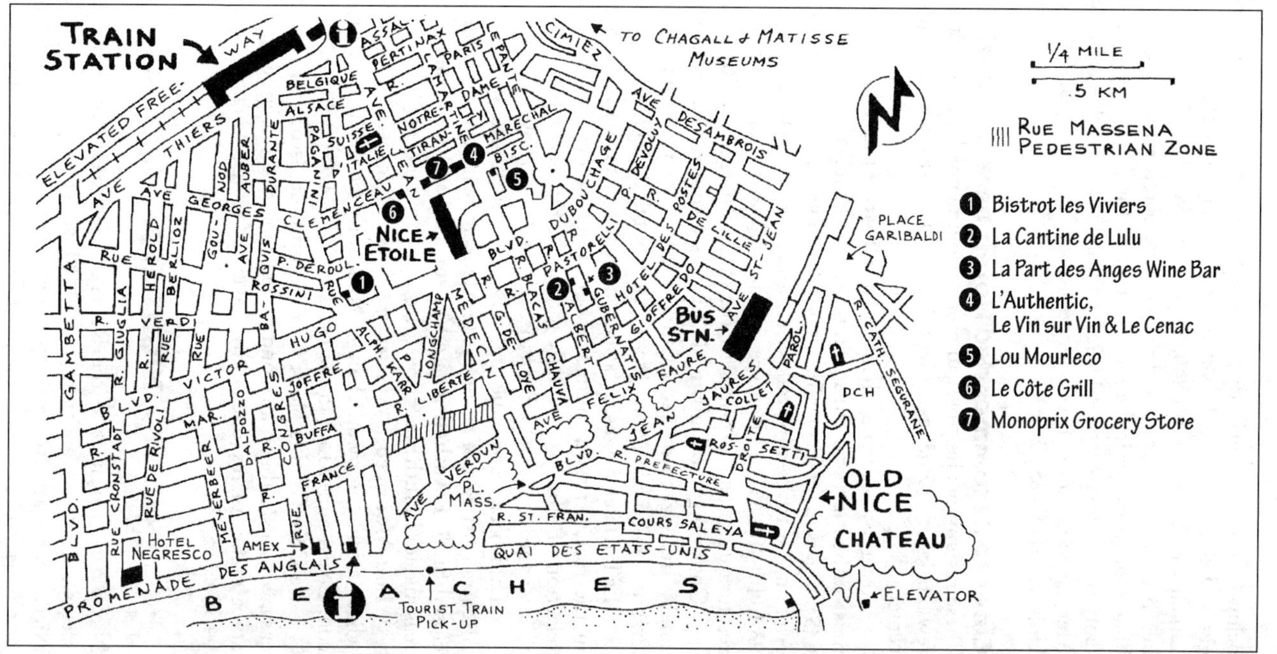

below Castle Hill, perfectly positioned to watch evening swimmers get in their last laps as the sky turns pink and city lights flicker on. Lunch views are unforgettable—you can even have lunch at your beach chair if you've rented one. Arrive before sunset and linger long enough to merit the few extra euros the place charges (open daily, salads and pastas-€13–15, main courses-€24, Panaché de la Mer is a good sampling of seafood and vegetables, 8 quai des Etats-Unis, tel. 04 93 85 22 66).

Close to Recommended Hotels near the Station

These restaurants lie closer to most recommended hotels, within a few blocks of avenue Jean Médecin, near the Nice Etoile shopping center.

Reserve ahead at enchanting little **Bistrot Les Viviers** for the most authentic *niçoise* cuisine in this book. Fish is their forte (allow €35 per person for dinner, lunch *menus* from €16, closed Sun, 22 rue Alphonse Karr, 5-min walk west of avenue Jean Médecin, tel. 04 93 16 00 48). Make sure to reserve for the *bistrot*, not their stuffier restaurant next door (prices are the same, ambience is different).

Charming **La Cantine de Lulu** is a fine value, wonderfully small, and Czech-owned, with homemade recipes from Nice to Prague (closed Sat–Mon, 26 rue Alberti, tel. 04 93 62 15 33).

La Part des Anges, an atmospheric wine shop with a few tables in the rear, serves a limited, mouthwatering menu with a large selection of wines (open daily for lunch, Fri–Sat only for dinner, reserve ahead, 17 rue Gubernatis, tel. 04 93 62 69 80).

Laid-back cafés line up along the broad sidewalk on rue Biscarra (just east of avenue Jean Médecin behind Nice Etoile, all closed Sun). **L'Authentic**, **Le Vin sur Vin**, and **Le Cenac** are all reasonable (L'Authentic is best, Le Cenac is cheapest).

Lou Mourleco is *niçoise traditionnel.* Because it serves only what's fresh, the menu changes constantly (*menus* from €20, air-con, closed Sun–Mon, 15 rue Biscarra, tel. 04 93 80 80 11).

Le Côte Grill, a block from Nice Etoile, is bright, cool, and easy, with a salad bar, air-conditioned rooms, and a large selection at reasonable prices (open daily, 1 avenue Georges Clémenceau, tel. 04 93 82 45 53).

NIGHTLIFE

Nice's bars play host to the Riviera's most happening late-night scene, full of jazz and rock 'n' roll. Most activity focuses on Old Nice, near place Rossetti. Plan on a cover charge or expensive drinks. If you're out very late, avoid walking alone. The plush and smoky bar at Hôtel Negresco is fancy-cigar old English.

TRANSPORTATION CONNECTIONS

For train and bus schedules from Nice to nearby towns, see "Getting Around the Riviera," page 414. Note that most long-distance train connections to other French cities require a change in Marseille.

From Nice by Train to: Marseille (19/day, 2.75 hrs), **Cassis** (7/day, 3 hrs, transfer in Toulon or Marseille), **Arles** (11/day, 3.5 hrs, 10 with change in Marseille), **Avignon** (10/day, 4 hrs, a few direct, most require transfer in Marseille), **Paris**' Gare de Lyon (14/day, 5.5–7 hrs, 6 with change in Marseille), **Aix-en-Provence** TGV station (10/day, 3.5 hrs, transfer in Marseille probable), **Chamonix** (4/day, 11 hrs, 2–3 transfers), **Beaune** (7/day, 7 hrs, transfer in Lyon), **Munich** (2/day, 12 hrs with 2 transfers, one night train with a transfer in Verona), **Interlaken** (1/day, 12 hrs), **Florence** (4/day, 7 hrs, transfers in Pisa and/or Genoa, night train), **Milan** (4/day, 5–6 hrs, 3 with transfers), **Venice** (3/day, 3/night, 11–15 hrs, 5 require transfers), **Barcelona** (3/day, 11 hrs, long transfer in Montpellier, or a direct night train).

Nice's Airport (Aéroport de Nice Côte d'Azur)

Nice's easy-to-navigate airport is on the Mediterranean, about 20 minutes west of the city center. Planes go about hourly to Paris (1-hr flight, about the same price as a train ticket). There are two terminals (1 and 2) used by domestic and international flights. Both terminals have TIs, banks, taxis, and buses to Nice (www.nice.aeroport.fr, tel. 08 20 42 33 33 or 04 89 88 98 28).

Taxis into the center are expensive, charging €30 to Nice hotels and €50 to Villefranche-sur-Mer. Taxis stop outside door *(Porte)* A-1 at Terminal 1 and outside Porte A-3 at Terminal 2.

Three **bus** lines run from both terminals into Nice. Bus #99 runs nonstop to the main train station (€3.50, 2/hr, 8:00–21:00, 30 min, drops you within a 10-min walk of many recommended hotels); the yellow "NICE" bus #98 goes to the bus station (*gare routière*, €3.50, 3/hr, 30 min) and will also take you to the train station upon request 6:00–8:00 and after 21:00 (ask driver for "*la gare SNCF*"). The slower, cheaper local bus #23 serves stops between the airport and train station (€1.40, 4/hr, 50 min, direction: St. Maurice).

Buy tickets in the **bus information office** (Terminal 1 only) or from the driver. To reach the bus information office and bus stops at Terminal 1, turn left after passing customs and exit the doors at the far end (buses #98 and #99 use platform 1, bus #23 uses platform 6). Buses serving Terminal 2 are well-signed to the right as you exit (bus #98 stops at platform 5, bus #99 uses platform 4, and bus #23 uses platform 6).

To get to **Villefranche-sur-Mer** from the airport, take the yellow "NICE" bus #98 to the bus station *(gare routière),* and transfer to the Villefranche-sur-Mer bus (bus #100, €1.70, 4/hr).

Buses also run hourly directly from the airport to **Antibes** (line #200, €8, 20 min) and to **Monaco** (line #110 express on the freeway, €14, 50 min).

Villefranche-sur-Mer

Villefranche offers travelers an easygoing slice of small-town Mediterranean life just 15 minutes from more high-powered Nice and Monaco. This town feels Italian—with soft orange buildings, steep, narrow streets spilling into the sea, and pasta with pesto. Luxury yachts glisten in the bay, a reminder to those lazing along the harborfront that Monaco is just down the coast. Sand-pebble beaches, a handful of interesting sights, and quick access to Cap Ferrat keep visitors just busy enough.

Originally a Roman port, Villefranche was overtaken by 5th-century barbarians. Villagers fled into the hills, where they stayed and farmed their olives. In 1295, the Duke of Provence—like much of Europe—was threatened by the Saracen Turks. He asked the hillside olive farmers to move down to the water and establish a front line against the invaders—denying them a base from which to attack Nice. In return for tax-free status, they stopped farming, took up fishing, and established *Ville-* (town) *franche* (without taxes). Since there were many such towns, this one was specifically "Tax-free town on the sea" *(sur Mer).* Around 1560, the Duke of Savoy built the town an immense citadel (which you can still tour). Today—because two-thirds of its 8,000 people call this their primary residence—Villefranche feels more like a real community than neighboring Riviera towns.

ORIENTATION

Tourist Information

The TI is in Jardin François Binon, below the main bus stop (July–Aug daily 9:00–19:00, Sept–June Mon–Sat 9:00–12:00 & 14:00–18:30, closed Sun, a 20-min walk or €10 taxi from train station, tel. 04 93 01 73 68, www.villefranche-sur-mer.com). Pick up the brochure detailing a self-guided walking tour of Villefranche and information on boat rides. If you plan to visit Cap Ferrat, ask for the simple brochure-map showing the walks around this peninsula (see "The Three Corniches: Villefranche to Monaco," page 448).

Villefranche-sur-Mer

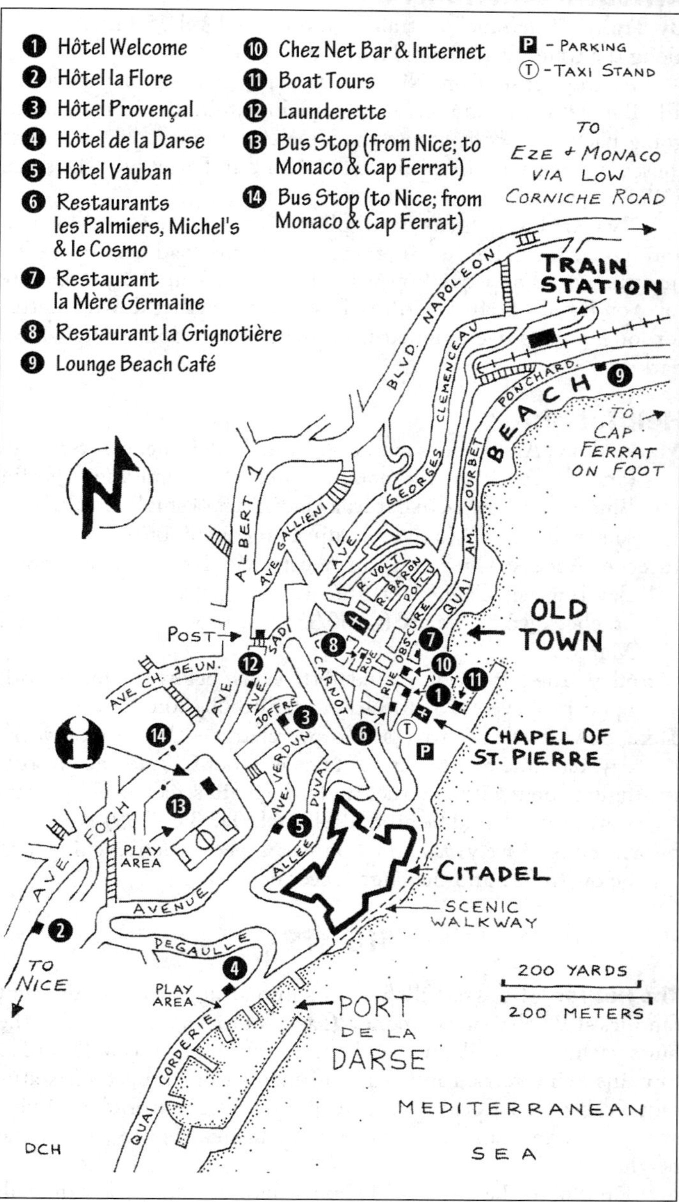

Arrival in Villefranche

By Train: Villefranche's train station is a level 15-minute walk along the water from the old town (taxi-€10).

By Bus: Buses from Nice and Monaco drop you just above the TI. The old town and most hotels are downhill. The stop for buses going back to Nice is across the street from where you were left (buses run every 10–15 min). Bus #111 to Cap Ferrat uses the same Villefranche stops.

By Car: From Nice's port, follow signs for Menton, Monaco, and Basse Corniche. In Villefranche, take the road next to the TI into the city. For a quick visit to the TI, park at the nearby pay lot. You'll find the free Parking Fossés a bit farther down—better for longer visits (well-signed from main road). Some hotels have parking.

Helpful Hints

Market Day: An antiques market enlivens Villefranche on Sundays (on place Amélie Pollonnais by Hôtel le Welcome and in Jardin Binon by the TI). On Saturday mornings, a small food market sets up by the TI (only in Jardin François Binon).

Internet Access: Chez Net, an "Australian International Sports Bar Internet Café," is a fun place to get a late-night drink or check your e-mail (€2.50/15 min, open daily, place du Marché).

Laundry: The self-service launderette is just below the main road, opposite 6 avenue Sadi Carnot (daily 8:00–20:00).

Taxi: Beware of taxi drivers who overcharge—the normal weekday, daytime rate to central Nice is about €30; to the airport, figure about €50; and the trip to the main street level from the waterfront should be around €10 (tel. 04 93 6 70 19).

Sports Fans: Lively *boules* action takes place each evening just below the TI and the huge soccer field.

SIGHTS

The Harbor—Browse Villefranche's miniscule harbor. Only eight families still fish to make money. Gaze out to sea and marvel at the huge yachts that call this bay home. (You might see well-coiffed captains being ferried in by dutiful mates to pick up their statuesque call girls.) Local guides keep a list of the world's 100 biggest yachts and talk about some of them like they're part of the neighborhood.

Parallel to the beach and about a block inland, you can walk the mysterious rue Obscura—a covered lane running 400 feet along the medieval rampart.

Chapel of St. Pierre (Chapelle Cocteau)—This chapel, decorated by artist, poet, and filmmaker Jean Cocteau, is the town's cultural highlight. A mean fisherwoman collects a €2 donation for the fishermen's charity, then sets you free to enjoy the chapel's small but delightful interior. In 1955, Jean Cocteau covered the barrel-vaulted chapel with heavy black lines and pastels. Each of the Cocteau scenes—the Gypsies of Stes-Maries-de-la-Mer who dance and sing to honor the Virgin; girls wearing traditional outfits; and three scenes from the life of St. Peter—are explained in English (€2, Tue–Sun 9:30–12:00 & 15:00–19:00, closed Mon, below Hôtel Welcome).

Citadel—The town's immense castle was built by the Duke of Savoy to defend against the French in the 1500s. When the region joined France in 1860, it became just a barracks. In the 20th century, with no military use, the city started using the citadel to house its police station, City Hall, and two art galleries.

Church—The town church features a fine crucifix—carved, they say, from a fig tree by a galley slave in the 1600s.

Boat Rides (Promenades en Mer)—These little cruises, with English handouts, are offered one or two days a week (June–Sept only, €11/1 hr, €16/2 hrs, across from Hôtel Welcome, tel. 04 93 76 65 65).

Beach Walk—A pleasant walk under the citadel, along a nearly beach-level rampart, connects the yacht harbor with the old town and beach. Stroll Villefranche's waterfront beyond the train station away from the town for postcard views back to Villefranche and a quieter beach (ideal picnic benches); consider extending your walk to Cap Ferrat (see page 448). Even if you're sleeping elsewhere, consider an ice-cream-licking village stroll here.

SLEEPING

(€1 = about $1.20, country code: 33)

There's a handful of hotels to choose from in Villefranche. The ones I list have at least half of their rooms with sea views—well worth paying extra for. The rooms at both of my first two listings, while different in cost, are about the same in comfort. Hôtel Welcome sits on the harbor in the center; Hôtel la Flore is a 10-minute walk from the old town, but has a pool and free parking.

$$$ Hôtel Welcome*** is right on the water in the old town—all 36 balconied rooms overlook the harbor. You'll pay top price for all the comforts in a very smart, professional hotel that seems to do everything right, and couldn't be better located ("comfort" Db-€164, bigger "superior" Db-€189, suites-€299–340, extra bed-€35, buffet breakfast-€12, air-con, parking garage-€16/day, 1 quai Amiral Courbet, tel. 04 93 76 27 62, fax 04 93 76 27 66, www.welcomehotel.com, resa@welcomehotel.com.).

$$$ Hôtel la Flore*** is for you if your idea of sightseeing is to enjoy the view from your bedroom deck, the dining room, or the pool (Db with no view-€90–125, Db with view and deck-€135, Db mini-suite-€195, extra bed-€34, Qb loft with huge terrace-€220, prices 10–15 percent cheaper Oct–March, air-con, elevator, pool, free parking, fine restaurant, just off main road high above harbor, 5 boulevard Princesse Grace de Monaco, 2 blocks from TI towards Nice, tel. 04 93 76 30 30, fax 04 93 76 99 99, www.hotel-la-flore.fr, hotel-la-flore@wanadoo.fr, SE).

$$$ Hôtel la Fiancée du Pirate is best for drivers, as it's above Villefranche on the Middle Corniche. Friendly Nadine (SE) offers 15 clean and comfortable rooms. Choose between larger rooms inside the building with air-conditioning (Db-€95–120), or view rooms on the garden patio (Db-€115–135, no air-con). There's a pool, garden, spacious *salon de thé*, breakfast terrace with partial views of Cap Ferrat and the sea, and even a small children's play area (8 boulevard de la Corne d'Or, Moyenne Corniche N7, tel. 04 93 76 67 40, fax 04 93 76 91 04, www.fianceedupirate.com, info@fianceedupirate.com).

$$ Hôtel le Provençal** is a big place crying out for an interior designer. The uninspired yet comfortable-enough rooms are a fair value, with some fine views and balconies (Db-€63–110, most around €80, Tb-€80–120, extra bed-€10, skip cheaper non-view rooms, air-con, right below the main road, a block from TI at 4 avenue Maréchal Joffre, tel. 04 93 76 53 53, fax 04 93 76 96 00, www.hotelprovencal.com, provencal@riviera.fr).

$ Hôtel la Darse**, a shy and unassuming little hotel sitting in the shadow of its highbrow brothers, offers a simple, low-key alternative right on the water at Villefranche's old port. The dull hallways disguise rooms that are quiet and reasonably comfortable; those facing the sea have million-dollar-view balconies (non-view Db-€52–62, view Db-€64–76, extra bed-€10, from TI walk or drive down avenue Général de Gaulle to the old Port de la Darse, tel. 04 93 01 72 54, fax 04 93 01 84 37, hoteldeladarse@wanadoo .fr, SE). Major renovations are planned—the hotel might be closed until spring, and prices could increase.

$ Hôtel Vauban*, two blocks down from the TI, is a curious place that makes me feel like I'm in a brothel, with 15 basic rooms and decor as Old World as the owner (non-view Db-€45, view Db-€70, cash only, 11 avenue Général de Gaulle, tel. 04 93 76 62 18, e-what?, NSE).

EATING

Comparison-shopping is half the fun of dining in Villefranche. Make an event out of a pre-dinner stroll through the old city. Check what looks good on the lively place Amélie Pollonnais above the Hôtel Welcome, saunter the string of candlelit places lining the waterfront, and consider the smaller, cheaper eateries embedded in the old city's walking streets.

Les Palmiers is a beachy place buzzing with cheery diners (hearty salads and pizza-€9, open daily, on place Amélie Pollonnais, tel. 04 93 01 71 63).

Michel's, on the other side of the fountain, is more romantic and stylish (allow €35–40 per person, closed Tue, tel. 04 93 76 73 24).

Le Cosmo Restaurant is next door, with great tables overlooking the harbor and the Cocteau chapel's facade (floodlit after some wine, Cocteau pops). It serves nicely presented gourmet dishes with less fun but better quality than Les Palmiers (fine salads and pastas-€10, great Bandol red wine, open daily, place Amélie Pollonnais, tel. 04 93 01 84 05).

La Mère Germaine, right on the harborfront, is the only place in town classy enough to lure a yachter ashore. It's dressy, with fine service and a harborside setting. The name comes from when the current owner's grandmother fed hungry GIs in World War II. Try the bouillabaisse, served with panache (€57 per person, or a mini-version for €39, €34 *menu*, open daily, reserve harborfront table, tel. 04 93 01 71 39).

Disappear into Villefranche's walking streets and find cute little **La Grignotière,** serving a €29 *gourmet menu* (open daily, 3 rue Poilu, tel. 04 93 76 79 83).

Lounge Beach Café, on the beach below the train station, is worth considering for the best view of Villefranche and decent food at reasonable prices. This place also works well for lunch or a drink with a view (salads, pastas, and à la carte, open daily, tel. 04 93 01 72 57).

Souris Gourmande ("Gourmet Mouse") is handy for a sandwich, to take away or eat there (daily 11:30–19:30, closed Fri in winter, behind Hôtel Welcome, €4 made-to-order sandwiches... be patient and get to know your chef, Albert). Sandwich in hand, there are plenty of great places to enjoy a harborside sit.

TRANSPORTATION CONNECTIONS

The last bus leaves Nice for Villefranche at about 19:45; the last bus from Villefranche to Nice leaves at about 21:00; and one train runs later (24:00).

From Villefranche by Train to: Monaco (2/hr, 10 min), **Nice** (2/hr, 10 min), **Antibes** (2/hr, 40 min).

By Bus to: Cap Ferrat (6/day, 10 min), **Monaco** (4/hr, 25 min), **Nice** (4/hr, 15 min).

The Three Corniches:
Villefranche to Monaco

Nice, Villefranche-sur-Mer, and Monaco are linked with three coastal routes: the Low, Middle, and High Corniches. The roads are nicknamed for the decorative frieze that runs along the top of a building (cornice). Each Corniche offers sensational views and a different perspective on this exotic slice of real estate.

Low Corniche: The *Basse Corniche* (often called *Corniche Inférieure*) strings ports, beaches, and villages together for a traffic-filled ground-floor view. It was built in the 1860s (along with the new train line) to bring people to the casino in Monte Carlo. When this Low Corniche was finished, many hill-town villagers came down and started the communities that line the sea today. Before 1860, the population of the coast between Villefranche-sur-Mer and Monte Carlo was zero.

Middle Corniche: The *Moyenne Corniche* is higher, quieter, and far more impressive. It runs through Eze and provides breath-taking views over the Mediterranean, with several scenic pullouts (the pullout above Villefranche-sur-Mer is particularly stunning).

High Corniche: Napoleon's crowning road-construction achievement, the *Grande Corniche,* caps the cliffs with staggering views from almost 1,600 feet above the sea. It is actually the Via Aurelia, used by Romans to conquer the West.

Villas: Driving from Villefranche-sur-Mer to Monaco, you'll come upon impressive villas. A particularly grand entry leads to the sprawling estate built by King Leopold II of Belgium in the 1920s. Those driving up to the Middle Corniche will look down on this yellow mansion that fills an entire hilltop with a lush garden. This estate was later owned by the Agnelli family (of Fiat fame and fortune), and then by the Safra family (American bankers).

The Best Route: For a ▲▲▲ route, **drivers** should take the Middle Corniche from Nice to Eze, follow signs to the High Corniche *(Grande Corniche/La Turbie)* from there, and after La Turbie, drop down into Monaco. **Buses** travel each route; the higher the Corniche, the less frequent the buses (roughly 5/day on Middle and High, 2/hr on Low; get details at Nice's bus station).

The following villages and sights are listed from west to east, as you'll reach them, from Villefranche-sur-Mer to Monaco.

▲Cap Ferrat—This peninsula decorates Villefranche-sur-Mer's sea views. An exclusive, largely residential community, it's a peaceful eddy off the busy Nice–Monaco route (Low Corniche). You could spend a day on this peninsula, wandering the port village of St. Jean-Cap-Ferrat, and walking on sections of the beautiful trails that follow the coast. The **TI** is between the port and Villa Ephrussi

Villefranche, Monaco, and the Corniches

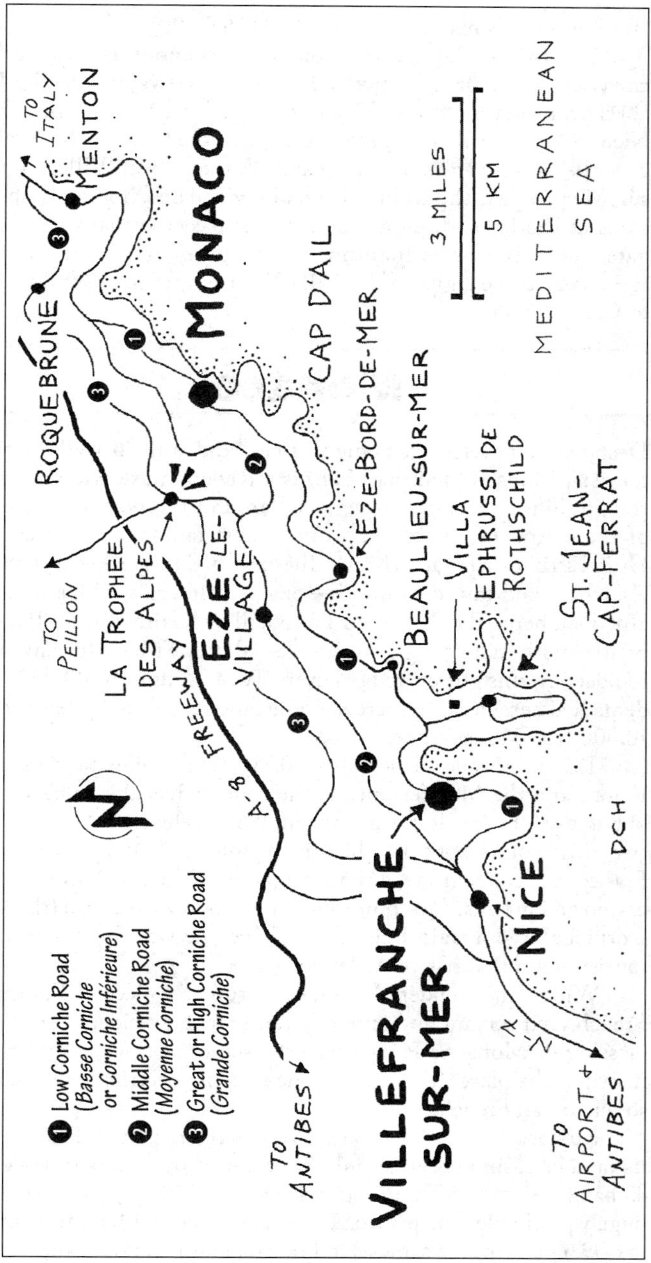

(at 59 avenue Denis Séméria, tel. 04 93 76 08 90).

Getting to Cap Ferrat from Villefranche: You can go by **car** (Low Corniche) or **taxi** (allow €15 one-way); ride the **bus** (#111 from main stop in Villefranche, 6/day, 10 min; bus from Nice to Monaco also drops you at edge of the Cap—4/hr, 5 min); or **walk** (50 min from Villefranche). Walkers from Villefranche-sur-Mer go past the train station along the beach and climb the steps at the far end. Continue straight past the mansions (with gates more expensive than my entire house) and make the first right. You'll see signs to the Villa Ephrussi de Rothschild, then to Cap Ferrat's port.

Monaco

Despite overdevelopment, high prices, and wall-to-wall daytime tourists, Monaco (mah-nah-koh) is a Riviera must. Monaco is on the go. Since 1929, cars have raced around the port and in front of the casino in one of the world's most famous auto races, the Grand Prix of Monaco (May). The new breakwater—constructed elsewhere and towed in by sea—enables big cruise ships to actually dock here. The district of Fontvieille, reclaimed from the sea, bristles with luxury high-rise condos. But don't look for anything too deep in this glittering tax haven. Two-thirds of its 30,000 residents live here because there is no income tax—leaving fewer than 10,000 true Monegasques.

This miniscule principality (0.75 square mile) borders only France and the Mediterranean. The country has always been tiny, but it used to be...less tiny. In an 1860 plebiscite, Monaco lost two-thirds of its territory when the region of Menton voted to join France. To compensate, France suggested Monaco build a fancy casino and promised to connect it to the world with a road (the Low Corniche) and a train line. This opened the way for a high-class tourist boom that has yet to let up.

While "independent," Monaco is run as a piece of France. A French civil servant appointed by the French president—with the blessing of Monaco's Prince Albert—serves as state minister and manages the place. Monaco's phone system, electricity, water, and so on, are all French.

Monaco is a business, and Prince Albert is its CEO. While its famous casino provides only 5 percent of the state's revenue, its 43 banks—which offer an attractive way to hide your money—are hugely profitable. The prince also makes money with a value-added tax (19.6 percent, the same as in France), plus real estate and corporate taxes.

The glamorous romance and marriage of Prince Albert's parents, the American actress Grace Kelly and Prince Rainier added to Monaco's fairy-tale mystique. Grace Kelly first came to Monaco to star in the 1955 Hitchcock film *To Catch a Thief*, in which she was filmed racing along the Corniches. Later, she married her prince and adopted the country. Tragically, Monaco's much-loved Princess Grace died in a car wreck on that same Corniche in 1982. Prince Rainier died in 2005.

It's a special place...there are more people in Prince Albert's philharmonic orchestra (about 100) than in his army (about 80 guards). His princedom is well-guarded, with police and cameras on every corner. (They say you could win a million dollars at the casino and walk through the wee hours to the train station without a worry.) Stamps are so few, they increase in value almost as soon as they're printed. And collectors snapped up the rare Monaco versions of euro coins (with the late Prince Rainier's portrait) so quickly that many locals have never even seen one.

ORIENTATION

The principality of Monaco consists of three distinct tourist areas: Monaco-Ville, Monte Carlo, and La Condamine. Monaco-Ville fills the rock high above everything else. This is the oldest section, home to Prince Albert's palace and all the sights except the casino. Monte Carlo is the area around the casino. And La Condamine is the port (which divides Monaco-Ville and Monte Carlo). You may also pass through a fourth, less-interesting area, Fontvieille.

Buses #1 and #2 link all areas (one ticket-€1.40, four tickets-€3.50, until 21:00, 10/hr, less on Sun). From the port (and train station), it's a 15-minute walk to the Prince's Palace or to the casino (40 min from palace to casino).

Telephone Tip: To call Monaco from France, dial 00, then 377 (Monaco's country code) and the eight-digit number. Within Monaco, simply dial the eight-digit number.

Tourist Information

The main TI is near the casino (2 boulevard des Moulins, Mon–Sat 9:00–19:00, Sun 10:00–12:00), but there's a handier branch in the train station (daily in summer 8:00–19:30, less off-season, tel. 00-377/92 16 61 16 or 00-377/92 16 61 66, www.monaco-tourisme.com). From June to September, you'll find information kiosks in the Monaco-Ville parking garage and on the port.

Arrival in Monaco

By Bus from Nice and Villefranche: There are three stops in Monaco, in order from Nice: in front of a tunnel at the base of

Monaco

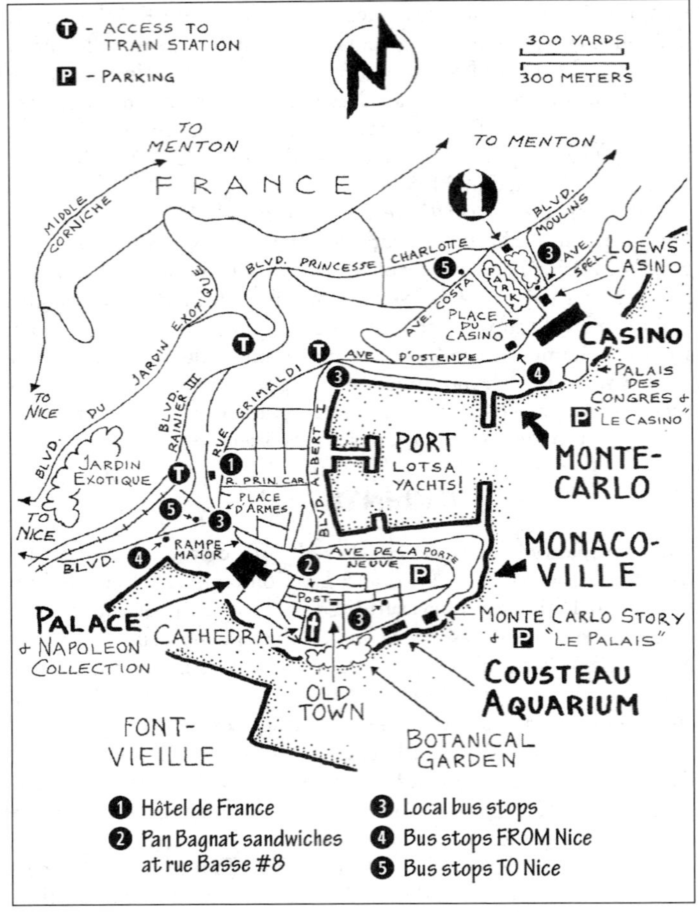

Monaco-Ville (place d'Armes), on the port, and below the casino (on avenue d'Ostende). The first stop is the best starting point. From there, you can walk up to Monaco-Ville and the palace (10 min straight up), or catch a local bus (lines #1 or #2). To reach the bus stop and steps up to Monaco-Ville, cross the street right in front of the tunnel and walk with the rock on your right for about 200 feet.

Keep your receipt for the return ride to Nice or Villefranche (RCA buses run twice as often as Cars Broch). The bus stop back to Nice is across the major road from your arrival point, at the light. The last bus leaves Monaco for Nice at about 20:00 (last train leaves about 23:30).

By Train from Nice: The train station is in central Monaco, about a 10-minute walk to the casino in Monte Carlo or the port, and 25 minutes to the palace in Monaco-Ville.

This is a long, underground station with many services. The TI, baggage check, and ticket windows are up the escalator at the Italy end of the station. There are three exits: two from the train platform level (one at each end) and one from above the platforms, up the escalator, past the TI. To walk to the casino, use this upper exit (go past TI, then up the elevator, then exit station and turn left on boulevard Princesse Charlotte and turn right on rue Iris; allow 10 min).

To reach Monaco-Ville and the palace from the station, take one of the two platform-level exits. The exit near the Italy end of the platform leads to the port and the bus stop for city buses #1 and #2, serving Monaco-Ville and the casino (follow *Sortie la Condamine* and go down two escalators, then go left, following Access Port signs). The port is a few blocks downhill from this exit, from which you can walk another 20 minutes to the palace (or casino, though this is the longer way there). The other platform-level exit is at the Nice end of the tracks (signed *Sortie Fontvieille*), which takes you along a long tunnel (TI annex at end) to the foot of Monaco-Ville; from here, it's a 15-minute walk to the palace.

To take the short-but-sweet coastal **walking path** into Monaco's Fontvieille district, get off the train one station before Monaco, in Cap d'Ail. Turn left out of the little station and walk 50 yards up the road, then turn left, going downstairs and under the tracks. Turn left onto the coastal trail, and hike the 20 minutes to Fontvieille. Once you reach Fontvieille, it's a 15-minute uphill hike to Monaco's sights.

By Car: Follow *Centre-Ville* signs into Monaco, then follow the red-letter signs to parking garages at *Le Casino* (for Monte Carlo) or *Le Palais* (for Monaco-Ville). The first hour of parking is free; the next costs €3.50.

Getting Around Monaco

In addition to the city bus system (described under "Orientation," above), here are your other transportation options.

Tourist Train: "Azur Express" tourist trains begin at the aquarium and pass by the port, casino, and palace (€6, 30 min, 2/hr, 10:30–18:00 in summer, 11:00–17:00 in winter depending on weather, taped English commentary, tel. 00-377/92 05 64 38).

Taxis: If you've lost track of time at the casino, you can call the 24-hour taxi service (tel. 00-377/93 15 01 01)...provided you still have enough money to pay for the cab home.

SIGHTS

Monaco-Ville

All of Monaco's sights (except for the casino) are in Monaco-Ville, packed within a few Disney-esque blocks. From anywhere in Monaco, you can get to the palace square, place du Palais (Monaco-Ville's sightseeing ground zero), by taking bus #1 or #2 to place de la Visitation (leave bus to the right and walk straight 5 min, passing a fountain). If you're walking up from the port, the well-marked lane leads directly to the *Palais*.

Palace Square (Place du Palais)—This square is the best place to get oriented to Monaco, as it offers views on both sides of the rock. Facing the palace, go to the right and look out over the city. This little, pastel Hong Kong look-alike was born on this rock in 1215 and has managed to remain an independent country for most of its nearly 800 years. Looking beyond the glitzy port, notice the faded green roof above and to the right: the casino that put Monaco on the map.

Now walk to the statue of the monk grasping a sword near the palace. Meet **François Grimaldi**, a renegade Italian dressed as a monk, who captured Monaco in 1297 and began the dynasty that still rules the principality. Prince Albert is his great-great-great-great...grandson, which makes Monaco's royal family Europe's longest-lasting dynasty.

Walk to the opposite side of the square and the Louis XIV **cannonballs**. Down below is Monaco's newest area, Fontvieille, where much of its post-WWII growth has been. Prince Rainier continued (some say, was obsessed with) Monaco's economic growth, creating landfills (topped with homes, such as Fontvieille), flashy ports, new beaches, and the new rail station. Thanks to Prince Rainier's efforts, tiny Monaco became a member of the United Nations.

You can buy Monaco stamps (popular collectibles, or mail from here) at the post office (PTT) a few blocks down rue Comte Félix Gastaldi.

Prince's Palace (Palais Princier)—A medieval castle sat where Monaco's palace is today. Its strategic setting has had a lot to do with Monaco's ability to resist attackers. Today, Prince Albert lives in the palace; princesses Stephanie and Caroline live just down the main street. The palace guards protect the prince 24/7, and still stage a Changing of the Guard ceremony with all the pageantry of an important nation (daily at 11:55, fun to watch, but jam-packed). Automated and uninspired tours (in English) take you through part of the prince's lavish palace in 30 minutes. The rooms are well-furnished and impressive, but interesting only if you haven't seen a château lately (€6, June–Sept daily 9:30–18:00, Oct daily 10:00–17:00, closed Nov–May, tel. 00-377/93 25 18 31).

Napoleon Collection—Napoleon occupied Monaco after the French Revolution. This is the prince's private collection of what Napoleon left behind: military medals, swords, guns, letters, and, most interesting, his hat. I found this collection more appealing than the palace (€4, June–Sept daily 9:30–18:00, Oct daily 10:00–17:00, Dec–May Tue–Sun 10:30–12:30 & 14:00–17:00, closed Mon, next to palace entry).

Cathedral of Monaco (Cathédrale de Monaco)—The somber cathedral, rebuilt in 1878 to show Monaco cared for more than just its new casino, is where centuries of Grimaldis are buried. Circle behind the altar (counterclockwise). The last tomb—Gratia Patricia, MCMLXXXII—is where Princess Grace was buried in 1982. Prince Rainier joined her here on April 15, 2005 (cathedral open daily 8:30–19:00, until 18:00 in winter).

As you leave the cathedral, step across the street and look down on the newly-reclaimed Fontvieille district and the fancy condos that contribute to the incredible population density of this miniscule country. The adjacent and immaculately maintained Jardin Botanique offer more fine views and a good place to picnic.

Cousteau Aquarium (Musée Océanographique)—Prince Albert I built this impressive, cliff-hanging aquarium in 1910 as a monument to his enthusiasm for things from the sea. One wing features Mediterranean fish; tropical species swim around the other (all well-described in English). Jacques Cousteau directed the aquarium for 17 years. The fancy Albert I Hall upstairs houses the museum (no English), featuring models of Albert and his beachcombers hard at work (aquarium and museum-€12, kids-€6, April–June and Sept daily 9:30–19:00, July–Aug 9:30–19:30, Oct–March 10:00–18:00, at opposite end of Monaco-Ville from palace, down the steps from Monaco-Ville bus stop, tel. 00-377/93 15 36 00, www.oceano.mc).

Monte Carlo Story—The informative 35-minute film gives a helpful account of Monaco's history and offers a comfortable soft-chair break from all that walking (€6.50, usually on the hour, Jan–June and Sept–Oct daily 14:00–17:00, July–Aug 14:00–18:00, closed Nov–Dec, you can join frequent extra showings for groups, English headphones; from aquarium, take escalator into parking garage, then take elevator down and follow signs).

Monte Carlo

▲Casino—Monte Carlo, which means "Charles' Hill" in Spanish, is named for the local prince who presided over Monaco's 19th-century makeover. Begin your visit to Europe's most famous casino in the park above the traffic circle. In the mid-1800s, olive groves stood here. Then, with the construction of this casino, spas, and easy road and train access, one of Europe's poorest countries was on the Grand Tour map—*the* place for the vacationing aristocracy to play. Today, Monaco has the world's highest per-capita income.

The casino is designed to make the wealthy feel comfortable while losing money. Charles Garnier designed this casino (with an opera house inside) in 1878, in part to thank the prince for his financial help in completing Paris' Opéra Garnier (which Garnier also designed). The central doors provide access to slot machines, private gaming rooms, and the opera house. The private gaming rooms occupy the left wing of the building.

Count the counts and Rolls-Royces in front of Hôtel de Paris (built at the same time), then strut inside past the slots to the sumptuous atrium. This is the lobby for the opera house (open only for performances). There's a model of the opera at the end of the room, and marble WCs on the right. Anyone over 21 (even in shorts, if before 20:00) can get as far as the one-armed bandits (push button on slot machines to claim your winnings), though you'll need decent attire to go any further. After 20:00, shorts are off-limits anywhere.

The scene, flooded with camera-toting tourists during the day, is great at night—and downright James Bond–like in the private rooms. The park behind the casino offers a peaceful café and a good view of the casino's rear facade and of Monaco-Ville.

If paying an entrance fee to lose money is not your idea of fun, access to all games in the new, plebeian, American-style Loews Casino, adjacent to the old casino, is free.

Cost and Hours: The first rooms, Salons Européens, open at 12:00 and cost €10 to enter. The glamorous private game rooms—where you can rub elbows with high rollers—open at 16:00, others not until 21:00, and cost an additional €10 (and you must show your passport). A tie and jacket (necessary in the evening) can be rented at the bag check for €30 plus a €40 deposit. Dress standards for women are far more relaxed (only tennis shoes are a definite no-no, tel. 00377/92 16 20 00, www.casino-monte-carlo.com).

Take the Money and Run: The return bus stop to Nice is at the top of the park above the casino on avenue de la Costa. To return to the train station from the casino, walk up the parkway in front of the casino, turn left on boulevard des Moulins, turn right on impasse de la Fontaine, climb the steps, and turn left on boulevard Princesse Charlotte (entrance to train station is next to Parking de la Gare; look for *Gare SNCF* sign).

SLEEPING AND EATING

(€1 = about $1.20, country code: 377)

For many, Monaco is best after dark.

The perfectly pleasant **$$ Hôtel de France**** is reasonable (Sb-€72, Db-€94, includes breakfast, 6 rue de la Turbie, near west exit from train station, tel. 00-377/93 30 24 64, fax 00-377/92 16 13 34, hotel-france@monte-carlo.mc).

Several cafés serve basic fare at reasonable prices (day and night) on the port, along the traffic-free rue Princesse Caroline. In Monaco-Ville, you'll find good *pan bagnat* and other sandwiches at 8 rue Basse, just off the palace square.

TRANSPORTATION CONNECTIONS

From Monaco by Train to: Nice (2/hr, 20 min), **Villefranche-sur-Mer** (2/hr, 10 min), **Antibes** (2/hr, 45 min).

By Bus to: Nice (4/hr, 40 min), **Villefranche-sur-Mer** (4/hr, 25 min).

The last bus leaves Monaco for Villefranche-sur-Mer and Nice at about 20:00; the last train leaves Monaco for Villefranche-sur-Mer and Nice at about 23:30.

Antibes

Antibes has a down-to-earth, easygoing ambience that's rare for this area. Its old town is postcard-perfect: a cluster of red-tiled roofs rising above the blue Mediterranean, watched over by twin medieval lookout towers and wrapped in a rampart. Visitors making the 30-minute trip from Nice browse Europe's biggest yacht harbor, snooze on a sandy beach, loiter through an enjoyable old town, stumble upon characteristic markets, and climb to a castle filled with Picassos.

Though it's much smaller than Nice, Antibes has a history that goes back just as far. Both towns were founded by Greek traders in the 5th century B.C. To the Greeks, Antibes was "Antipolis"—the town *(polis)* opposite *(anti)* Nice. For the next several centuries, Antibes remained in the shadow of its neighbor. By the turn of the 20th century, the town was a military base—so the rich and famous partied elsewhere. But when the army checked out after World War I, Antibes was "discovered" and enjoyed a particularly roaring '20s—with the help of party animals like Rudolph Valentino and the rowdy-yet-very-silent Charlie Chaplin. Fun-seekers even invented water skiing right here in the 1920s.

ORIENTATION

Antibes' old town lies between the port and boulevard Albert 1er and avenue Robert Soleau. Place Nationale is the old town's hub of activity. Lively rue Aubernon connects the port and the old town. Stroll along the sea between the Picasso Museum and place Albert

Antibes

To Fort Carre & Nice
Train Stn.
Port Vauban
Ave du 11 Nov.
Vieux Port
Ave. de la Liberation
Ave. de Verdun
Best Parking
Arch
Ave. Robert
Ave. Thiers
Ave Mistral
Blvd. d'Aiguillon
Andre
Place Nationale
Thuret
R. Aub.
Saleurs
Palm.
Clem.
Sade
Plage de la Gravette
Tourist Train Pick-Up
Rue de la Republique
Vauban
Soleau
Close
Cathedral
Cours Massena
Grasse
Rev.
Picasso Museum
Chateau Grimaldi
Place de Gaulle
Bus Stn.
Blvd. Wilson
Blvd. Albert 1er
Amiral de
Prom.
History & Archaeology Museum
Gen. Maizieres
Square Albert 1er
Rue Bourgeois
To 1
Blvd. Leclerc
200 Yards
200 Meters
B - Minibus Stop
P - Parking
To Plage Salvis, Cap d'Antibes & 5
1 To Hôtel le Mas Djoliba
2 Auberge Provençale
3 Modern Hôtel
4 Hôtel Relais du Postillon
5 To Hôtel Beau Site
6 Hôtel le Cameo
7 Restaurant le Vauban
8 Restaurant l'Ecureuil
9 Restaurant Chez Juliette
10 Restaurant les Vieux Murs
11 Le Café Jardin
12 Heidi's English Bookshop
13 Market Hall
14 Launderette

1er (where boulevard Albert 1er meets the water); the best beaches lie just beyond place Albert 1er, and the path is beautiful. Good play areas for children are on place des Martyrs de la Résistance (close to recommended Hôtel Relais du Postillon).

Tourist Information

There are two TIs. The most convenient is located in the old town, just inside the walls at 21 boulevard d'Aguillon (unpredictable hours, generally June–Aug daily 9:00–21:00, Sept–May Mon–Fri 10:00–12:00 & 14:00–17:00, closed Sat–Sun, tel. 04 93 34 65 65, www.antibes-ville.com). The big Maison de Tourisme is in the newer city, east of the old town where boulevard Albert 1er and rue de la République meet at 11 place Général de Gaulle (July–Aug daily 9:00–19:00, Sept–June Mon–Sat 9:00–12:30 & 13:30–18:00, closed Sun, tel. 04 92 90 53 00, www.antibes-juanlespins.com). At either TI, pick up the excellent city map and the interesting brochure with a walking tour of old Antibes (in English). The Nice TI has Antibes maps; plan ahead.

Arrival in Antibes

By Train: To get to the port (5-min walk), cross the street in front of the station and follow avenue de la Libération downhill. To reach the main TI in the modern city (15-min walk), exit right from the station on avenue Robert Soleau; follow *Maison du Tourisme* signs to place Général de Gaulle. Or hop on the free minibus (see "Getting Around Antibes," below; exit station to the right and cross the street to the park).

By Bus: The bus station is at the edge of the old town on place Guynemer, a block below the TI (info desk open Mon–Sat 8:30–12:00 & 14:30–17:30, closed Sun, public WCs around back).

By Car: Day-trippers should follow *Centre-Ville* and *Vieux Port* signs, and park near the old town walls—as close to the beach as you can (first 30 min free, then about €4/3 hrs, €8/day). Enter the old town through the last arch on the right. If you're sleeping here, hotels are signed; get advice from your hotelier on where to park.

Getting Around Antibes

A free **minibus** (*Minibus Gratuit* or *Navette Gratuite*) circles Antibes (Mon–Sat 7:30–19:30, not on Sun). There are four different circuits, two of which are useful for tourists. Line #1 goes from Fort Carré to the old port, the old town, the ramparts, and back again (every 15 min). Line #2 connects the train station to the main TI at place de Gaulle and to the port every 25 mins. Stops are tricky to find—look for bus stop signs around town (the TI has a small map).

A **tourist train** offers several circuits around old Antibes, the port, and the ramparts (€6.50, departs from place de la Poste, ask about schedule, tel. 06 03 35 61 35). It even has daily departures to Juan-les-Pins (see "Sights," page 462).

To call a **taxi**, dial 04 93 67 67 67.

Helpful Hints

Laundry: A full-service launderette is near the market hall on rue de la Pompe (Mon–Sat 9:00–12:00 & 14:30–19:00, closed Sun).

Bookstore: Heidi's English Bookshop has a great selection of new and used books (daily 10:00–19:00, 24 rue Aubernon).

Introductory Walking Tour of Antibes

This quick walk will help you get your bearings. Begin at the train station (or harborside parking lot), and stroll the **harbor** along avenue de Verdun. Locals claim that this is Europe's biggest yacht harbor, with 1,600 stalls. At the end of the yachts (quai des Pêcheurs), you'll see the pathetic remains of a once-hearty fishing fleet. The Mediterranean is getting fished out. Most of the seafood you'll eat here comes from fish farms or the Atlantic.

Cross through the old gate under the ramparts to enter the **old town**. Because Antibes was the last fort before the Italian border, the French king made sure the ramparts were strong and well-defended. Today, the town is the haunt of a large community of English, Irish, and Aussie boaters who help crew the giant yachts of the rich and famous. (That explains the Irish pubs and English bookstores.) Drop by the cute, shell-shaped **plage de la Gravette**, an adorable public beach tucked right in the middle of old Antibes.

Continue following the ramparts to the 16th-century, white-stone **Château Grimaldi**. The castle stands on prime real estate: This site has been home to the acropolis of the Greek city of Antipolis, a Roman fort, and a medieval bishop's palace. This château was the home of the Grimaldi family (who still rule Monaco), and today it houses the Picasso Museum (listed below). The neighboring **cathedral** is built over a Greek temple.

Notice the two **towers**. They symbolized society's two dominant land-owning classes: the Church and the nobility. (In 1789, the Revolution changed all that.) From the bluff below the castle, you can see **Cap d'Antibes** crowned by its lighthouse and studded with mansions.

The ramparts lead to the **History and Archaeology Museum** (see below). Just before that (at rue du Haut Castelet), hook inland and explore the charming, cobbled **pedestrian zone** around rue du Haut Castelet and rue du Bas Castelet. Poking around Antibes' peaceful back lanes, gradually work your way back to the entertaining covered **market hall** on cours Masséna.

SIGHTS

▲▲Picasso Museum (Musée Picasso)—In the early 20th century, Antibes' castle (Château Grimaldi) was home to an obscure little museum that nobody cared about. Then its director had a brainstorm: Offer the castle to Pablo Picasso as a studio. Picasso lived in the castle for four months in 1946, where he cranked out an amazing amount of art—and the resulting collection put Antibes on the tourist map.

Sitting serenely where the old town meets the sea, this museum offers a remarkable collection of Picasso's work: paintings, sketches, and ceramics. Picasso said that if you want to see work from his Antibes period, you'll have to see it in Antibes. You'll understand why Picasso liked working here. Several photos of the artist and a movie of him hard at work (when making art, he said he was "working" rather than "painting") make this already intimate museum even more so. In his famous *La Joie de Vivre* (the museum's highlight), there's a new love in Picasso's life, and he's feelin' groovy.

The museum also displays works by Nicolas de Stael (1914–1955), who spent his final lonely winter in Antibes near the château, where he committed suicide by jumping out a window. There's also a sculpture terrace overlooking the Bay of Antibes, featuring works by local artists (such as Germaine Richier), as well as by Picasso's friend Joan Miró *(Sea Goddess)*.

Cost and Hours: €5, covered by Riviera Carte Musées pass, June–Sept Tue–Sun 10:00–18:00, July–Aug Wed and Fri until 20:00; Oct–May Tue–Sun 10:00–12:00 & 14:00–18:00, always closed Mon (tel. 04 92 90 54 20).

History and Archaeology Museum (Musée d'Histoire et d'Archéologie)—Displaying Greek, Roman, and Etruscan odds and ends, this is the only place to get a sense of this city's ancient roots. I liked the 2,000-year-old lead anchors (€3, no English explanations, June–Sept Tue–Sun 10:00–18:00, July–Aug Wed and Fri until 20:00; Oct–May Tue–Sun 10:00–12:00 & 14:00–18:00, always closed Mon; on the water between Picasso Museum and place Albert 1er).

▲Market Hall (Marché Provençal)—The daily market bustles under a 19th-century canopy, with flowers, produce, Provençal products, and beach accessories (in old town behind Picasso Museum on cours Masséna). The market wears many appealing hats: produce daily except Monday until 13:00; handicrafts Thursday through Sunday in the afternoon; and romantic outdoor dining in the evenings.

Other Markets—Antibes' lively antique/flea market fills place Nationale and place Audiberti (next to the port) on Saturdays (7:00–18:00). Its clothing market winds through the streets around the post office (rue Lacan) on Thursdays (9:00–18:00).

Fort Carré—This impressively situated citadel, dating from 1487, was the last fort inside France. It protected Antibes from Nice, which until 1860 was part of Italy. You can tour this unusual four-pointed fort—at its height, it held 200 soldiers—but there's precious little to see inside. People visit for the stunning views (€3, covered by Riviera Carte Musées pass, includes tour, June–Sept daily 10:15–17:30, Oct–May daily 10:15–16:00).

Scenic footpaths link the fort to the port along the sea. It's a 30-minute portside walk from the old town to the fort (or taxi there and walk back). By foot or car, follow avenue du 11 Novembre around the port, stay on the main road (walkers can follow path by sports fields), then park on the beach just after the soccer field. A signed dirt path leads to Fort Carré. Keep following green-lettered signs to *Le Fort/Sens de la Visite*.

Beaches (Plages)—The best beaches stretch between Antibes' port and Cap d'Antibes, and the very best (plage de la Salis and plage du Ponteil) are just south of place Albert 1er. All are golden and sandy. Plage de la Salis is busy in summer, but it's manageable, with snack stands every so often and views of the old town. The closest beach to the old town is at the port (plage de la Gravette) and remains relatively calm in any season.

Juan-les-Pins—This village, across the Cap d'Antibes isthmus from Antibes, is where the action is in the evenings. It's a modern beach resort with good beaches, plenty of lively bars and restaurants, and a popular jazz festival in July. Buses, trains, and even a tourist train (see "Getting Around Antibes," above) make the 10-minute connection to and from Antibes constantly.

SLEEPING

(€1 = about $1.20, country code: 33)

The best Antibes hotels require a car or taxi—central pickings are slim in this city, where most hoteliers seem more interested in their restaurants.

Outside the City Center

$$$ Hôtel Pension le Mas Djoliba*** is a good splurge, but best for drivers (since it's a 15-min walk from the beach and old Antibes, and a 25-min walk from the train station). Reserve early for this tranquil, bird-chirping, flower-filled manor house where no two rooms are the same. After a busy day of sightseeing, dinner by the pool is a treat (they request that you dine here May–Sept). You'll be in good hands with sweet Stephanie serving and Sylvan cooking with market-fresh products (Db with breakfast and dinner-€80–96 per person, Db room only-€85–125, several good family rooms-€160–170, suite-€210, breakfast-€10, 29 avenue de Provence; from boulevard Albert 1er, look for blue signs and turn right up avenue Gaston Bourgeois; tel. 04 93 34 02 48, fax 04 93 34 05 81, www.hotel-djoliba.com, hotel.djoliba@wanadoo.fr).

$$ Hôtel Beau Site*** is my only listing on Cap d'Antibes, a 10-minute drive from the old town. It's a fine value if you want to get away, but not *too* far away. This place is a sanctuary, with friendly owners (Nathalie SE), a pool, a big patio, and easy parking. The 30 plush and well-cared-for rooms are priced fairly (standard Db-€67–77, bigger Db-€87–92, extra bed-€25, bikes available, 141 boulevard Kennedy, tel. 04 93 61 53 43, fax 04 93 67 78 16, www.hotelbeausite.net, hbeausit@club-internet.fr). From the hotel, it's a 10-minute walk down to the crowded plage de la Garoupe and a nearby hiking trail.

In the City Center

$$ Modern Hôtel** this spick-and-span, well-run place is in the pedestrian zone. The 17 standard-size rooms, each with air-conditioning and pleasing decor, are an excellent value (Sb-€55–60, Db-€64–76, €10 more in summer, 1 rue Fourmillière, tel. 04 92 90 59 05, fax 04 92 90 59 06).

$$ Hôtel Relais du Postillon**, on a thriving square, offers 15 small, tastefully designed rooms, all with names instead of numbers, accordion bathrooms in need of TLC, and owners who take more pride in their well-respected restaurant (Db-€46–84, price depends on size and whether you're facing courtyard or park, *menus* from €32, 8 rue Championnet, tel. 04 93 34 20 77, fax 04 93 34 61 24, postillon@atsat.com, SE).

$$ Auberge Provençale*, on charming place Nationale, has a popular restaurant and seven Old World rooms (those on the square get all the noise, day and night), with nonexistent management and a couldn't-care-less-if-you-stayed-here attitude (Db-€63–85, Tb-€72–94, Qb-€110, reception in restaurant, 61 place Nationale, tel. 04 93 34 13 24, fax 04 93 34 89 88). Their huge loft room, named "Céline," faces the back and comes with a royal canopy bed and a dramatic open-timbered ceiling for no extra charge.

$ Hôtel le Cameo** is a rambling, refreshingly non-aggressive old place above a bustling bar (where you'll find what reception there is). The public areas are dark, but the nine very simple, linoleum-lined rooms are almost huggable. All open onto the delightful place Nationale, which means you don't sleep until the restaurants close (Ds-€50, Db-€60, Ts-€59, Tb-€69, 5 place Nationale, tel. 04 93 34 24 17, fax 04 93 34 35 80, NSE).

EATING

The old town is crawling with possibilities. Lively place Nationale is filled with tables and tourists (great ambience), while locals seem to prefer the restaurants along the market hall. Take a walk and judge for yourself, considering these suggestions. Romantics and those on a budget should buy a picnic dinner and head for the beach.

Le Vauban is near the port, with an appealing interior and reasonably-priced salads and *plats* (*menus* from €20, open daily, 7 rue Thuret, tel. 04 93 34 33 05).

Le Café Jardin, serves simple food and has a quiet, hidden garden terrace behind the café (look for *Jardin* sign pointing through a door in the back, left of café; open Mon–Sat for lunch only, also open for dinner July–Aug, always closed Sun, 8 rue James Close, tel. 04 93 34 42 66).

L'Ecureuil (or "Casa Amando" in Spanish) is a fun, inexpensive place to try paella in the traffic-free zone. Señor and Madame Carramal are the friendly owners—he's Spanish, which explains why the paella is so *bueno* (closed Sun–Mon, 17 rue Fourmillière, tel. 04 93 34 07 97).

The recommended hotels **Auberge Provençale** (seafood specialties) and **Relais du Postillon** (cozier decor and an interior courtyard) both offer well-respected cuisine with *menus* for €30–35 (both open daily).

Chez Juliette, just off place Nationale, offers budget meals (*menus* from €14, closed for lunch and on Mon, rue Sade, tel. 04 93 34 67 37).

Les Vieux Murs is the place to splurge in Antibes for regional specialties. Its candlelit, red-tone, *très romantique* interior overlooks the sea (€40 *menu*, open daily June–mid-Sept, closed Tue off-season, along ramparts beyond Picasso Museum at 25 promenade Amiral de Grasse, tel. 04 93 34 06 73).

TRANSPORTATION CONNECTIONS

TGV and local trains serve Antibes' little station.

From Antibes by Train to: Cannes (2/hr, 15 min), **Nice** (2/hr, 25 min), **Villefranche-sur-Mer** (2/hr, 40 min), **Monaco** (2/hr, 60 min), **Marseille** (16/day, 2.25 hrs).

By Bus to: Cannes (3/hr, 25 min), **Nice Airport** (1/hr, 40 min), **Biot** (2/hr, 20 min).

BAVARIA AND TIROL

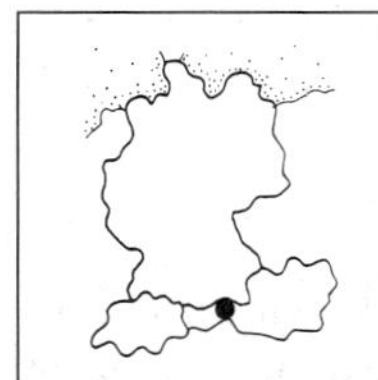

Two hours south of Munich, between Germany's Bavaria and Austria's Tirol, is a timeless land of fairytale castles, painted buildings shared by cows and farmers, and locals who still yodel when they're happy.

In Germany's Bavaria, stop by the Wieskirche, a textbook example of Bavarian rococo bursting with curly curlicues, and browse through Oberammergau, Germany's woodcarving capital and home of the famous Passion Play. Tour "Mad" King Ludwig's ornate Neuschwanstein Castle, Europe's most spectacular.

In Austria's Tirol, hike to the ruined Ehrenberg castle, scream down a ski slope on an oversized skateboard, and then catch your breath for an evening of yodeling and slap dancing.

In this chapter, I'll cover Bavaria first, then Tirol. Austria's Tirol is easier and cheaper than touristy Bavaria. My favorite home base for exploring Bavaria's castles is actually in Austria, in the town of Reutte. Füssen, in Germany, is a handier home base for train travelers.

Planning Your Time

While Germans and Austrians vacation here for a week or two at a time, the typical speedy American traveler will find two days' worth of sightseeing. With a car and more time, you could enjoy three or four days. If the weather's good and you're not going to Switzerland, be sure to ride a lift to an Alpine peak.

By Car: A good schedule for a one-day circular drive from Reutte is 7:30–Breakfast, 8:00–Depart hotel, 8:30–Arrive at Neuschwanstein to pick up tickets for two castles (which you reserved by telephone several days earlier, pick up at ticket center—see below; if traveling Oct–March, castles don't open until 10:00 so start an hour later), 9:00–Tour Hohenschwangau, 11:00–Tour Neuschwanstein, 13:00–Drive to the Wieskirche (20-min stop) and on to Linderhof, 14:30–Tour Linderhof, 16:30–Drive along scenic Plansee back into Austria, 17:30–Back at hotel, 19:00–Dinner at hotel and perhaps a folk evening. In peak season, you might arrive later at Linderhof to avoid the crowds. The next morning, you could stroll through Reutte, hike to the Ehrenberg ruins, and ride the luge on your way to Innsbruck, Munich, Switzerland, Venice, or wherever.

By Public Transportation: Train travelers can use Füssen as a base and bus or bike the three miles to Neuschwanstein. Reutte is connected by bus with Füssen (except Sun; taxi €28 one-way). If you're based in Reutte, you can bike to the Ehrenberg ruins (just outside Reutte) and to Neuschwanstein Castle/Tegelberg luge (90 min). A one-way taxi from Reutte to Neuschwanstein costs about €32. Or, if you stay at the recommended Gutshof zum Schluxen hotel, you can hike through the woods to Neuschwanstein (60 min).

Getting Around Bavaria and Tirol

By Car: This region is ideal by car. All the sights are within an easy 60-mile loop from Reutte or Füssen. Even if you're doing the rest of your trip by train, consider renting a car for the day here (as cheap as €50/day; see "Car Rental," page 470).

By Public Transportation: It can be frustrating. Local bus service in the region is spotty for sightseeing. If you're rushed and without wheels, Reutte, the Wieskirche, Linderhof, and the luge rides are probably not worth the trouble, but the Tegelberg luge near Neuschwanstein is within walking distance of the castle.

Füssen (with a 2-hr train ride to/from Munich every hour, some with a transfer in Buchloe) is three miles from Neuschwanstein Castle with easy bus and bike connections (see "Getting to the Castles from Füssen or Reutte," page 474). Reutte is a 30-minute bus ride from Füssen (Mon–Fri 6/day, Sat 2/day, none Sun, €3.20; taxis from Reutte to the castles are €32 one-way; to Füssen, €28).

Buses also run from Füssen to Oberammergau (4–5/day, less off-season, 1.5 hr, some with transfer in Echelsbacher Brücke; bus often marked Garmisch, confirm with driver that bus will stop in Oberammergau). From Munich, visiting Oberammergau directly by train is easier (hrly, 1.75 hrs, change in Murnau) than going to Füssen to catch the bus.

Füssen to Linderhof by public transportation will burn most of a valuable sightseeing day; you'll spend more time on the bus (or waiting for it) than you will at the castle. Skip Linderhof—or rent a car for the day. If you must go, take an early bus to Oberammergau,

Highlights of Bavaria and Tirol

which has direct bus connections to Linderhof (4/day in summer, less off-season, 30 min).

Confirm all bus schedules in Füssen by checking the big board at the bus stop across from the train station, buying a bus timetable (€0.30) at the TI or train station, or calling 08362/939-0505. For longer-distance bus trips (such as to Garmisch or Linderhof), you'll save money if you buy a *Tagesticket* (day pass).

By Bike: This is great biking country. Shops in or near train stations rent bikes for €8–15 per day. The ride from Reutte to Neuschwanstein and the Tegelberg luge (90 min) is great for those with the time and energy.

By Thumb: Hitchhiking, always risky, is a slow-but-possible way to connect the public-transportation gaps.

Füssen

Füssen has been a strategic stop since ancient times. Its main street sits on the Via Claudia Augusta, which crossed the Alps (over Brenner Pass) in Roman times. The town was the southern terminus of a medieval trade route now known among modern tourists as the "Romantic Road." Dramatically situated under a renovated castle on the lively Lech River, Füssen recently celebrated its 700th birthday.

Unfortunately, Füssen is overrun by tourists in the summer. Traffic can be exasperating. Apart from Füssen's cobbled and arcaded town center, there's little real sightseeing here. The striking-from-a-distance **castle** houses a boring picture gallery. The mediocre **City Museum** in the monastery below the castle exhibits lifestyles of 200 years ago and the story of the monastery, and offers displays on the development of the violin, for which Füssen is famous (€2.50, €3 includes castle gallery, April–Oct Tue–Sun 10:00–17:00, Nov–March Tue–Sun 13:00–16:00, closed Mon, English descriptions, tel. 08362/903-145).

Füssen's newest attraction, the **Model Railroad Museum** (Modelleisenbahn-Museum ZeitscHieneN), is small and overpriced but interesting, featuring model trains of all types—including, probably, the one you rode to town. The collection, gathered over a lifetime by brothers Ulf and Falk Haase, was donated by their mom to the town under the condition that this museum would be built (€4.50, Mon–Fri 10:00–18:00, Sat 10:00–14:00, closed Sun, Kemptener Strasse 7, tel. 08362/929-678).

Halfway between Füssen and the border (as you drive, or a woodsy walk from the town) is the **Lechfall,** a thunderous waterfall (with a handy WC).

ORIENTATION

(area code: 08362)

Füssen's train station is a few blocks from the TI, the town center (a cobbled shopping mall), and all my hotel listings (see "Sleeping," page 478). If necessary, the **TI** can help you find a room (June–mid-Sept Mon–Fri 8:30–18:30, Sat 10:00–13:00, Sun 10:00–12:00, less off-season, 3 blocks down Bahnhofstrasse from station, tel. 08362/93850, fax 08362/938-520, www.fuessen.de). After hours, the little self-service info pavilion (7:00–24:30) near the front of the TI features an automated room-finding service.

Arrival in Füssen: Exit left as you leave the train station (lockers available) and walk a few straight blocks to the center of town and the TI. To get to Neuschwanstein or Reutte, catch a bus from in front of the station.

Füssen

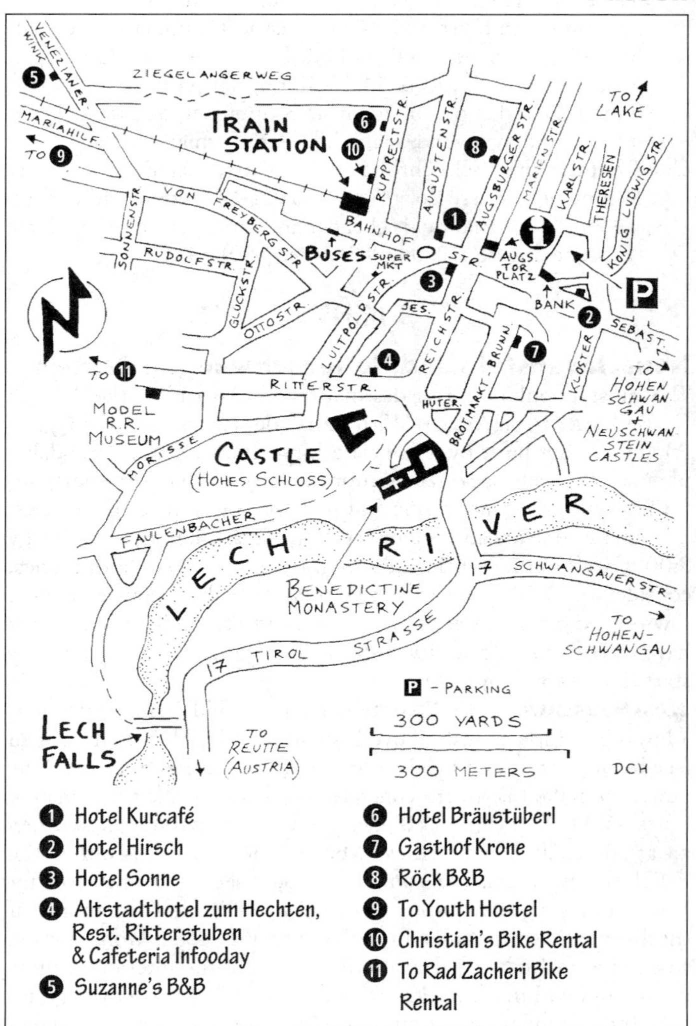

Helpful Hints

Internet Access: Try Videoland (€2/30 min, €3/hr, Mon–Sat 16:00–22:00, Sun 16:00–20:00, Luitpoldstrasse 11, tel. 08362/38300).

Bike Rental: Rent from friendly Christian at Preisschranke, next to the train station (€8/24 hrs, May–Sept Mon–Sat 9:00–19:00, Oct–April Mon–Fri 10:00–18:00, Sat 10:00–15:00, closed Sun, tel. 0178-374-0219 or 0176-2205-3080). Rad Zacherl has a bigger selection, but a less convenient location (€8/24 hrs, mountain bikes-€15/24 hrs, passport number for deposit, May–Sept Mon–Fri 9:00–18:00, Sat 9:00–13:00, Oct–April Mon–Fri 9:00–12:00 & 14:00–18:00, Sat 9:00–13:00, closed Sun, 1.25 miles out of town at Kemptener Strasse 119, tel. 08362/3292, www.rad-zacherl.de—in German only).

Car Rental: Peter Schlichtling (€50/24 hrs, includes insurance, Kemptener Strasse 26, tel. 08362/922-122, www.schlichtling.de—in German only) is cheaper and more central than Hertz (Füssenerstrasse 112, tel. 08362/986-580).

SIGHTS

Neuschwanstein and Hohenschwangau Castles

The most popular tourist destination in Bavaria is the "King's Castles" *(Königsschlösser)*. With fairytale turrets in a fairytale Alpine setting built by a fairytale king, they are understandably popular. The well-organized visitor can have a great four-hour visit. Others will just stand in line and perhaps not even see the castles. The key: Phone ahead for a reservation (details below) or arrive by 8:00 to wait in line for tickets (you'll have time to see both castles, consider fun options nearby—mountain lift, luge course, Füssen town—and get out by early afternoon). Off-season (Oct–June), you have a little more flexibility, but it's still a good idea to get an early start (try to arrive by 9:00).

▲▲▲**Neuschwanstein Castle**—Imagine "Mad" King Ludwig as a boy, climbing the hills above his dad's castle, Hohenschwangau (see below), dreaming up the ultimate fairytale castle. He had the power to make his dream concrete—and stucco. Neuschwanstein (noysh-VAHN-shteen) was designed by a painter first...then an architect. It looks medieval, but it's only about as old as the Eiffel Tower. It feels like something you'd see at a home show for 19th-century royalty. Built from 1869 to 1886, it's the epitome of the Romanticism popular in 19th-century Europe. Construction stopped with Ludwig's death (only a third of the interior was finished), and within six weeks, tourists were paying to go through it.

Today, guides herd groups of 60 through the castle, giving an interesting—if rushed—30-minute tour. You'll go up and down more than 300 steps, through lavish Wagnerian dream rooms, a royal state-of-the-19th-century-art kitchen, the king's gilded-lily bedroom, and his extravagant throne room. You'll visit 15 rooms with their original furnishings and fanciful wall paintings. After the tour, you'll see a room lined with fascinating drawings (described in English) of the castle plans, construction, and drawings from 1883 of Falkenstein—a whimsical, over-the-top, never-built castle that makes Neuschwanstein look stubby. Falkenstein occupied Ludwig's

Neuschwanstein and Hohenschwangau

fantasies the year he died. Following the tour, a 20-minute slide show (alternating German and English) plays continuously. If English is on, pop in. If not, it's not worth waiting for.

Mary's Bridge (Marienbrücke)—Before or after the Neuschwanstein tour, climb up to Mary's Bridge to marvel at Ludwig's castle, just as Ludwig did. This bridge was quite an engineering accomplishment 100 years ago. From the bridge, the frisky can hike even higher to the Beware—Danger of Death signs and an even more glorious castle view. (Access to the bridge is closed in bad winter weather, but many travelers walk around the barriers to get there—at their own risk, of course.) For the most interesting descent from Neuschwanstein (15 min longer and extremely slippery when wet), follow signs to the Pöllat Gorge.

▲▲Hohenschwangau Castle—Standing quietly below Neuschwanstein, the big yellow Hohenschwangau Castle was Ludwig's

"Mad" King Ludwig

Ludwig II (a.k.a. "Mad" King Ludwig), a tragic figure, ruled Bavaria for 23 years until his death in 1886 at the age of 41. Politically, his reality was to "rule" either as a pawn of Prussia or a pawn of Austria. Rather than deal with politics in Bavaria's capital, Munich, Ludwig frittered away most of his time at his family's hunting palace, Hohenschwangau. He spent much of his adult life constructing his fanciful Neuschwanstein Castle—like a kid builds a tree house—on a neighboring hill upon the scant ruins of a medieval castle. Although Ludwig spent 17 years building Neuschwanstein, he lived in it only 172 days. Ludwig was a true Romantic living in a Romantic age. His best friends were artists, poets, and composers such as Richard Wagner. His palaces are wallpapered with misty medieval themes—especially those from Wagnerian operas. Eventually he was declared mentally unfit to rule Bavaria and taken away from Neuschwanstein. Two days after this eviction, Ludwig was found dead in a lake. To this day, people debate whether the king was murdered or committed suicide.

boyhood home. Originally built in the 12th century, it was ruined by Napoleon. Ludwig's father, Maximilian, rebuilt it, and you'll see it as it looked in 1836. It's more lived-in and historic, and excellent 30-minute tours actually give a better glimpse of Ludwig's life than the more-visited and famous Neuschwanstein Castle tour.

Cost and Hours: Each castle costs €9, a *Königsticket* for both castles costs €17, and children under 18 are admitted free (castles open April–Sept daily from 9:00 with last tour departing at 18:00, Oct–March daily from 10:00 with last tour at 16:00).

Getting Tickets for the Castles: Every tour bus in Bavaria converges on Neuschwanstein, and tourists flush in each morning from Munich. A handy reservation system (see below) sorts out the chaos for smart travelers. Tickets come with admission times. (Miss this time and you don't get in.) To tour both castles, you must do Hohenschwangau first (logical, since this gives a better introduction to Ludwig's short life). You'll get two tour times: Hohenschwangau and then, two hours later, Neuschwanstein.

If you arrive late and without a reservation, you'll spend two hours in the ticket line and may find all tours for the day booked. A **ticket center** for both Neuschwanstein and Hohenschwangau is located at street level between the two castles (daily April–Sept 8:00–17:00, Oct–March 9:00–15:00, last tickets sold for Neuschwanstein 60 min before closing, for Hohenschwangau 30 min before closing; the TI might relocate here for 2006). First tours start around 9:00. Arrive by 8:00 and you'll likely be touring by 9:00. Warning: During the summer, tickets for English tours can run out by 16:00.

It's best to reserve ahead in peak season (July–Sept, especially Aug). You can make reservations a minimum of 24 hours in advance by contacting the ticket office by phone (tel. 08362/930-830), e-mail (info@ticket-center-hohenschwangau.de), or booking online (www.ticket-center-hohenschwangau.de). Tickets reserved in advance cost €1.60 extra (per person, per castle), and ticket holders must be at the ticket office well before the appointed entry time (30 min for Hohenschwangau, 60 min for Neuschwanstein, allowing time to make your way up to the castle). Remember that many of the businesses are owned by the old royal family, so they encourage you to space the two tours longer than necessary in hopes that you'll spend a little more money. Insist on the tightest schedule—with no lunch break—if you don't want too much down time.

Services: The helpful TI, bus stop, ATM, and telephones cluster around the main intersection (TI open daily April–June 9:00–17:00, July–Sept 9:00–18:00, Oct–March 9:00–16:00, tel. 08362/819-810, www.schwangau.de). The TI may have moved to the ticket center between the castles by 2006.

The "village" at the foot of Europe's Disney castle feeds off the droves of hungry, shop-happy tourists. The Bräustüberl cafeteria serves the cheapest grub (often with live folk music). The Alpsee is ideal for a picnic, but there are no grocery shops in the area. Your best bet is getting food to go from one of the many bratwurst stands (between the ticket center and TI) for a lazy lunch at the lakeside park or in one of the old-fashioned rowboats (rented by the hour in summer).

Getting to the Castles: From the ticket booth, Hohenschwangau is an easy 10-minute climb. Neuschwanstein is a steep 30-minute hike. To minimize hiking to Neuschwanstein, you can take a shuttle bus (from in front of Hotel Lisl, just above ticket office and to the left) or horse-drawn carriage (from in front of Hotel Müller, just above ticket office and to the right), but neither gets you to the castle doorstep. The frequent shuttle buses drop you off at Mary's Bridge, leaving you a steep 10-minute downhill walk from the castle—be sure to see the view from Mary's Bridge before hiking down to the castle (€1.80 up; €2.60 round-trip not worth it since you have to hike up to bus stop for return trip). Carriages (€5 up, €2.50 down) are slower than walking and they stop below Neuschwanstein, leaving you a five-minute uphill hike. Note: If it's less than an hour until your Neuschwanstein tour time, you'll need to hike, and even at a brisk pace, it still takes 30 minutes. For a lazy, varied, and economical plan, ride the bus to Mary's Bridge for the view, hike down to the castle, and then catch the carriage from there back down.

Getting to the Castles from Füssen or Reutte: If arriving by **car,** note that road signs in the region refer to the sight as *Königsschlösser,* not Neuschwanstein. There's plenty of parking (all lots-€4). Get there early, and you'll park where you like. Lot E—past the ticket center and next to the lake—is my favorite.

From **Füssen,** those without cars can catch the roughly hourly **bus** (€1.55 one-way, €3.10 round-trip, 10 min, note times carefully on the meager schedule, catch bus at train station), take a **taxi** (€8.50 one-way), or ride a rental **bike** (3 miles).

From **Reutte,** take the bus to Füssen (Mon–Fri 6/day, Sat 2/day, none Sun, €3.20, 30 min), then hop a city bus to the castle.

For a romantic twist, hike or mountain-bike from the trailhead at the recommended hotel **Gutshof zum Schluxen** in Pinswang (see page 490). When the dirt road forks at the top of the hill, go right (downhill), cross the Austria–Germany border (marked by a sign and deserted hut), and follow the narrow paved road to the castles. It's a 60- to 90-minute hike or a great circular bike trip (allow 30 min; cyclists can return to Schluxen from the castles on a different 30-min bike route via Füssen).

Near Neuschwanstein Castle

▲Tegelberg Gondola—Just north of Neuschwanstein is a fun play zone around the mighty Tegelberg gondola. Hang gliders circle like vultures. Their pilots jump from the top of the Tegelberg Gondola. For €15, you can ride the lift to the 5,500-foot summit and back down (May–Oct daily 9:00–17:00, Dec–April daily 9:00–16:30, closed Nov, frequency depends on demand, last lift goes up 10 min before closing time, in bad weather call first to confirm, tel. 08362/98360). On a clear day you get great views of the Alps and Bavaria and the vicarious thrill of watching hang gliders and parasailors leap into airborne ecstasy. Weather permitting, scores of adventurous Germans line up and leap from the launch ramp at the top of the lift. With one leaving every two or three minutes, it's great spectating. Thrill seekers with exceptional social skills may talk themselves into a tandem ride with a parasailor. From the top of Tegelberg, it's a steep 2.5-hour hike down to Ludwig's castle. Avoid the treacherous trail directly below the gondola. At the base of the gondola, you'll find a playground, a cheery eatery, and a very good luge ride (below).

▲Tegelberg Luge—Next to the lift is a luge course. A luge is like a bobsled on wheels (for more details, see page 487). This stainless-steel track is heated, so it's often dry and open when drizzly weather shuts down the concrete luges. It's not as scenic as Bichlbach and Biberwier (see "The Luge," page 487), but it's handy (€2.50/ride, 6-ride sharable card-€10, July–Sept daily 10:00–18:00, otherwise same hours as gondola, in winter sometimes opens later due to wet track, in bad weather call first to confirm, tel. 08362/98360). A funky cable system pulls riders (in their sleds) to the top without a ski lift.

More Sights in Bavaria

These are listed in driving order from Füssen.

▲▲Wies Church (Wieskirche)—Germany's greatest rococo-style church, this "church in the meadow" is newly restored and looking as brilliant as the day it floated down from heaven. Overripe with decoration but bright and bursting with beauty, this church is a divine droplet, a curly curlicue, the final flowering of the Baroque movement (donation requested, summer daily 8:00–19:00, winter daily 8:00–17:00, parking-€1, tel. 08862/932-930, www.wieskirche.de).

This pilgrimage church is built around the much-venerated statue of a scourged (or whipped) Christ, which supposedly wept in 1738. The carving—too graphic to be accepted by that generation's church—was the focus of worship in a peasant's barn. Miraculously, it wept—empathizing with all those who suffer. Pilgrims came from all around. A tiny and humble chapel was built to house the statue in 1739. (You can see it where the lane to the church leaves the parking lot.) Bigger and bigger crowds came. Two of Bavaria's top rococo architects, the Zimmermann brothers, were commissioned to build the Wieskirche that stands here today.

Follow the theological sweep from the altar to the ceiling: Jesus whipped, chained, and then killed (notice the pelican above the altar—recalling a pre-Christian story of a bird that opened its breast to feed its young with its own blood); the painting of a baby Jesus posed as if on the cross; the sacrificial lamb; and finally, high on the ceiling, the resurrected Christ before the Last Judgment. This is the most positive depiction of the Last Judgment around. Jesus, rather than sitting on the throne to judge, rides high on a rainbow—a symbol of forgiveness—giving any sinner the feeling that there is still time to repent, with plenty of mercy on hand. In the back, above the pipe organ, notice the empty throne—waiting for Judgment Day—and the closed door to paradise.

Above the entrances to both side aisles are murky glass cases with 18th-century handkerchiefs. People wept, came here, were healed, and no longer needed their hankies. Walk up either aisle flanking the high altar to see votives—requests and thanks to God (for happy, healthy babies, and so on). Notice how the kneelers are positioned so that worshippers can meditate on scenes of biblical miracles painted high on the ceiling and visible through the ornate tunnel frames. A priest here once told me that faith, architecture, light, and music all combine to create the harmony of the Wieskirche.

Two paintings flank the door at the rear of the church. One

shows the ceremonial parade in 1749 when the white-clad monks of Steingaden carried the carved statue of Christ from the tiny church to its new big one. The second painting, from 1757, is a votive from one of the Zimmermann brothers, the artists and architects who built this church. He is giving thanks for the successful construction of the new church.

The Wieskirche is 30 minutes north of Neuschwanstein. The northbound Romantic Road bus tour stops here for 15 minutes. You can take a bus from Füssen to the Wieskirche, but you'll spend more time waiting for the bus back than you will seeing the church. By car, head north from Füssen, turn right at Steingaden, and follow the signs. Take a commune-with-nature-and-smell-the-farm detour back through the meadow to the parking lot.

If you can't visit Wieskirche, visit one of the other churches that came out of the same heavenly spray can: Oberammergau's church, Munich's Asamkirche, Würzburg's Hofkirche Chapel (at the Residenz), the splendid Ettal Monastery (free and near Oberammergau), and, on a lesser scale, Füssen's cathedral.

If you're driving from Wieskirche to Oberammergau, you'll cross the Echelsbacher Bridge, which arches 230 feet over the Pöllat Gorge. Thoughtful drivers let their passengers walk across (for the views) and meet them at the other side. Any kayakers? Notice the painting of the traditional village woodcarver (who used to walk from town to town with his art on his back) on the first big house on the Oberammergau side, a shop called Almdorf Ammertal. It has a huge selection of overpriced carvings and commission-hungry tour guides.

▲Oberammergau—The Shirley Temple of Bavarian villages, exploited to the hilt by the tourist trade, Oberammergau wears way too much makeup. If you're passing through anyway, it's worth a wander among the half-timbered *Lüftlmalerei* houses frescoed (in a style popular throughout the town in the 18th century) with Bible scenes and famous fairytale characters. Browse through woodcarvers' shops—small art galleries filled with very expensive whittled works. The beautifully frescoed Pilat's House on Ludwig-Thomas-Strasse is a living workshop full of woodcarvers and painters in action (free; May–Oct, Dec, and Feb Mon–Sat 13:00–18:00; closed Nov, Jan, March–April and Sun). Or see folk art at the town's Heimatmuseum (Tue–Sun 14:00–18:00, closed Mon; **TI** open June–Oct Mon–Fri 8:30–18:00, Sat–Sun 13:00–17:00; Nov–May Mon–Fri 8:30–18:00, Sat 8:30–12:00, closed Sun, tel. 08822/92310, www.oberammergau.de).

Oberammergau Church: Visit the church, a poor cousin of the one at Wies. This church looks richer than it is. Put your hand on the "marble" columns. If they warm up, they're fakes—"stucco marble." Wander through the graveyard. Ponder the deaths that two wars dealt Germany. Behind the church are the photos of three Schneller brothers, all killed within two years in World War II.

Passion Play: Still making good on a deal the townspeople struck with God when they were spared devastation by the Black Plague several centuries ago, once each decade Oberammergau presents its Passion Play. For 100 summer days in a row, the town performs an all-day dramatic story of Christ's crucifixion (in 2000, 5,000 people attended per day). Until the next performance in 2010, you'll have to settle for reading the book, seeing Nicodemus tool around town in his VW, or browsing through the theater's exhibition hall (€2.50, German tours daily 10:00–17:00, tel. 08822/945-8833 or 08822/32278). English speakers get little respect here, with only two theater tours a day scheduled (often at 11:00 and 14:00). They may do others if you pay the €25 or gather 20 needy English speakers.

Sleeping in Oberammergau: **$$ Hotel Bayerischer Löwe** is central, with a good restaurant and 18 comfortable rooms (Db-€56, cash only, Dedlerstrasse 2, tel. 08822/1365, fax 08822/882, www.bayerischerloewe.com—in German only, gasthof.loewe@freenet.de, family Reinhofer). **$$ Gasthof zur Rose** is a big, central, family-run place with 21 rooms (Sb-€33, Db-€56, Tb-€71, Qb-€82, kids under 14 cheaper—ask, Dedlerstrasse 9, tel. 08822/4706, fax 08822/6753, gasthof-rose@t-online.de). **$ Frau Magold's** three bright and spacious rooms are twice as nice as the cheap hotel rooms, for much less money (Db-€37–43, cash only, immediately behind Gasthof Zur Rose at Kleppergasse 1, tel. & fax 08822/4340, NSE). The **$ youth hostel** on the river is a short walk from the center (€15 beds, includes breakfast and sheets, tel. 08822/4114, fax 08822/1695).

Getting to Oberammergau: From Füssen to Oberammergau, four to five buses run daily (fewer in winter, 1.5 hrs). Trains run from Munich to Oberammergau (hrly, 1.75 hrs, change in Murnau). Drivers entering the town from the north should cross the bridge, take the second right, and park in the free lot a block beyond the TI. Leaving town, head out past the church and turn toward Ettal on Road 23. You're 20 miles from Reutte via the scenic Plansee. If heading to Munich, Road 23 takes you to the autobahn, which gets you there in less than an hour.

▲▲Linderhof Castle—This homiest of "Mad" King Ludwig's castles is small and comfortably exquisite—good enough for a minor god. Set in the woods 15 minutes from Oberammergau and surrounded by fountains and sculpted, Italian-style gardens, it's the only palace I've toured that actually had me feeling envious. Don't miss the grotto, which is located outside and uphill from the palace; 15-minute tours are included with the palace ticket (€7, daily April–Sept 9:00–18:00, Oct–March 10:00–16:00, last tours

30 min before closing, parking-€2.50, fountains often erupt on the hour, English tours every 30 min or when 15 gather—sparse off-season, so you may have to wait, tel. 08822/92030). Plan for lots of walking and a two-hour stop to fully enjoy this royal park. Pay at the entrance and get an admission time. Visit outlying sights in the garden to pass any wait time. The outside of the palace is undergoing a long-term renovation, with lots of scaffolding. But the interior, freshly refurbished, is glorious. Without a car, getting to (and home from) Linderhof is a huge headache—skip it (but diehards can find details in "Getting Around Bavaria and Tirol," page 466).

▲▲Zugspitze—The tallest point in Germany is a border crossing. Lifts from Austria and Germany travel to the 10,000-foot summit of the Zugspitze. You can straddle the border between two great nations while enjoying an incredible view. Restaurants, shops, and telescopes await you at the summit.

On the German side, the 75-minute trip from Garmisch costs €43 round-trip; family discounts are available (buy a combo-ticket for cogwheel train to Eibsee and cable-car ride to summit, drivers can park for free at cable-car station at Eibsee, daily 8:15–14:15 to go up, last cable car down at 17:30, tel. 08821/7970). Allow plenty of time for afternoon descents: If bad weather hits in the late afternoon, cable cars can be delayed at the summit, causing tourists to miss their train from Eibsee back to Garmisch. Hikers enjoy the easy six-mile walk around the lovely Eibsee (German side, 5 min downhill from cable-car *Seilbahn*).

On the Austrian side, from the less-crowded Talstation Obermoos above the village of Erwald, the tram zips you to the top in 10 minutes (€32 round-trip, cash only, goes every 20 min, late May–Oct daily 8:40–16:40, tel. in Austria 05673/2309, www.zugspitze.com).

The German ascent from Garmisch is easier for those without a car, but buses do connect the Erwald train station and the Austrian lift nearly every hour.

SLEEPING

In Füssen

To locate these hotels, see map on page 469.

Though I prefer sleeping in Reutte (see page 488), convenient Füssen is just three miles from Ludwig's castles and offers a cobbled, riverside retreat. It's very touristy, but it has plenty of rooms. All recommended places are within a few blocks of the train station and the town center. Parking is easy at the station.

$$$ Hotel Kurcafé is deluxe, with 30 spacious rooms and all of the amenities. The standard rooms are comfortable, and the

Sleep Code

(€1 = about $1.20, country code: 49, area code: 08362)
S = Single, **D** = Double/Twin, **T** = Triple, **Q** = Quad, **b** = bathroom, **s** = shower only, **SE** = English spoken, **NSE** = No English spoken. Unless otherwise noted, credit cards are accepted, English is spoken, and breakfast is included.

To help you sort easily through these listings, I've divided the rooms into three categories, based on the price for a standard double room with bath:

- **$$$ Higher Priced**—Most rooms €85 or more.
- **$$ Moderately Priced**—Most rooms between €50–85.
- **$ Lower Priced**—Most rooms €50 or less.

Prices listed are for one-night stays. Most places give about a 5 to 10 percent off for two-night stays—always request this discount. Competition is fierce, and off-season prices are soft. High season is mid-June through September. Rooms are generally about 12 percent less in shoulder season and much cheaper in off-season.

newer, bigger rooms have elegant touches and fun decor—like canopy drapes and cherubic frescoes over the bed (Sb-€83, standard Db-€99, bigger Db-€114–139 depending on size, Tb-€125, Qb-€139, 4-person suite-€159, €10 more for weekends and holidays, cheaper off-season, non-smoking rooms, elevator, parking-€5/day, on tiny traffic circle a block in front of station at Bahnhofstrasse 4, tel. 08362/930-180, fax 08362/930-1850, www.kurcafe.com, info@kurcafe.com, Schöll family).

$$$ Hotel Hirsch is a big, romantic, old tour-class hotel with 53 rooms on the main street in the center of town. Their standard rooms are fine, and their theme rooms are a fun splurge (Sb-€56–82, standard Db-€87–133, theme Db-€118–162, prices depend on room size and demand, cheaper Nov–March and during slow times, only the expensive theme rooms are non-smoking, family rooms, elevator, free parking, Kaiser-Maximilian Platz 7, tel. 08362/93980, fax 08362/939-877, www.hotelhirsch.de, info@hotelhirsch.de).

$$$ Hotel Sonne, in the heart of town, rents 32 mod, institutional, yet comfy rooms (Sb-€85, Db-€105, Tb-€129, cheaper Oct–mid-June, non-smoking rooms, elevator, kitty-corner from TI at Reichenstrasse 37, tel. 08362/9080, fax 08362/908-100, www.hotel-sonne.de, info@hotel-sonne.de).

$$ Altstadthotel zum Hechten offers all the modern comforts in a friendly, traditional shell right under Füssen Castle in the old-town pedestrian zone (35 rooms, S-€30, Sb-€45, D-€60, Db-€75–80, Tb-€100, Qb-€112, free parking, cheaper off-season and for longer stays, non-smoking rooms, fun miniature bowling alley in basement, nearby church bells ring hourly at night; from TI, walk down pedestrian street, take second right to Ritterstrasse 6, tel. 08362/91600, fax 08362/916-099, www.hotel-hechten.com, hotel.hechten@t-online.de, Pfeiffer and Tramp families).

$$ Suzanne's B&B is run by a plain-spoken, no-nonsense American woman who strikes some travelers as brusque. Suzanne runs a tight ship, offering lots of local travel advice, backyard-fresh eggs, local cheese, a children's yard, laundry (€25/load), and bright, woody, spacious rooms (Db-€80, Tb-€115, Qb-€145, suite from €120 can hold up to 10—ask for details; attic special: €70 for 2, €100 for 3, €120 for 4; cash only, Internet access €5/hr, non-smoking, exit station right and backtrack 2 blocks along tracks, cross tracks at Venetianerwinkel to #3, tel. 08362/38485, fax 08362/921-396, www.suzannes.de, svorbrugg@t-online.de). Her kid-friendly loft has very low ceilings (you'll crouch), a private bathroom (you'll crouch), and up to six beds.

$$ Hotel Bräustüberl has 16 decent rooms at fair rates attached to a gruff, musty, old beer hall–type place. Don't expect much service (S-€25, Sb-€47, D-€50, Db-€64–78, cash only, Rupprechtstrasse 5, a block from station, tel. 08362/7843, fax 08362/923-951, brauereigasthof-fuessen@t-online.de).

$$ Gasthof Krone, a rare bit of pre-glitz Füssen in the pedestrian zone, has dumpy halls and stairs and big, time-warp rooms at good prices (S-€28, D/Ds-€52, extra bed-€29, €3 more per person for 1-night stays, reception in restaurant, from TI head down pedestrian street, take first left to Schrannengasse 17, tel. 08362/7824, fax 08362/37505, www.krone-fuessen.de—in German only, info@krone -fuessen.de).

$$ Wilhelm and Elisabeth Röck, a sweet old couple, rent out two rooms in their home a block from the TI (D-€51, Db-€52, cash only, non-smoking, Augsburgerstrasse 7, tel. 08362/6353, just enough English spoken).

$ Füssen Youth Hostel, a fine, German-run place, welcomes travelers under 27 (€17-dorm beds in 2- to 6-bed rooms, D-€40, €3 more for non-members, includes breakfast and sheets, non-smoking, laundry-€3.50/load, dinner-€5, office open 7:00–12:00 & 17:00–23:00, from station backtrack 10 min along tracks, Mariahilferstrasse 5, tel. 08362/7754, fax 08362/2770, jhfuessen @djh-bayern.de).

In Hohenschwangau, near Neuschwanstein Castle

Inexpensive farmhouse *Zimmer* (B&Bs) abound in the Bavarian countryside around Neuschwanstein, offering drivers a decent value.

Look for *Zimmer Frei* signs ("room free," or vacancy). The going rate is about €50–65 for a double, including breakfast.

$$ Beim "Landhannes" is a hundred-year-old working dairy farm run by Johann and Traudl Mayr. They rent six creaky, well-antlered rooms and keep flowers on the balconies, big bells in the halls, and cows in the yard (Sb-€30, Ds-€50, Db-€60, 20 percent discount for 3 or more nights, cash only, poorly signed in the village of Horn on the Füssen side of Schwangau, look for the farm 100 yards in front of Hotel Kleiner König, Am Lechrain 22, tel. 08362/8349, fax 08362/819-646, www.landhannes.de, mayr@landhannes.de).

$$ Sonnenhof is a big, woody, old house with four spacious, traditionally decorated rooms and a cheery garden. It's a 15-minute walk through the fields to the castles (S-€25, D-€45, Db-€55, cash only, at Pension Schwansee on the Füssen–Neuschwanstein road, follow the small lane 100 yards to Sonnenweg 11, tel. 08362/8420, Frau Görlich SE).

$$ Alpenhotel Meier is a small, family-run hotel with 15 rooms in a bucolic setting within walking distance of the castles, just beyond the lower parking lot (Sb-€46, Db-€77, plus €1.35 "tourist tax" per person, non-smoking rooms, all rooms have porches or balconies, family rooms, sauna, easy parking, just before tennis courts at Schwangauerstrasse 37, tel. 08362/81152, fax 08362/987-028, www.alpenhotel-allgaeu.de, alpenhotelmeier@web.de, Frau Meier SE).

$$ Romantic Pension Neuschwanstein, in the shadow of the castle, offers seven rooms in a historic home. Just a three-minute walk from the ticket booth, you enjoy proximity to the castle without all the hustle and bustle. This charming house is a little tired—but at 103 years old, you would be, too. Many of the rooms have balconies, and friendly Frau Strauss—who welcomes her guests as her mother did before her—is happy to share her garden with you (S-€29–35, Sb-€39, Db-€67, more for 1-night stays, cash only, free parking, Pfleger Rothut Weg 2, tel. & fax 08362/81102, info@albrecht-neuschwanstein.de).

EATING

In Füssen

Füssen's old town and main pedestrian drag are lined with a variety of eateries. Three good places cluster on Ritterstrasse, just under the castle, off the top of the main street:

Ritterstuben offers reasonable and delicious fish, salads, veggie plates, and a fun kids' menu (€6–12 meals, Tue–Sun 11:30–14:30 & 17:30–23:00, closed Mon, Ritterstrasse 4, tel. 08362/7759). Demure, English-speaking Gabi serves while her husband cooks.

Zum Hechten Restaurant serves hearty, traditional Bavarian fare and specializes in pike *(Hecht)* pulled from the Lech River

(€8–12 meals, Thu–Tue 11:00–14:00 & 17:00–20:30, closed Wed, Ritterstrasse 6).

Infooday is a clever and modern self-service eatery that sells its hot meals and salad bar by weight and offers English newspapers (filling salad-€3, meals-€5, Mon–Fri 10:30–18:30, Sat 10:30–14:30, closed Sun, Ritterstrasse 6).

Hotel Kurcafé's fine restaurant, right on Füssen's main traffic circle, has good and reasonable weekly specials, plus a tempting bakery (daily 11:30–14:30 & 17:30–22:00, choose between a traditional dining room and a pastel "winter garden," €11 Bavarian BBQ on Fri nights, live Bavarian zither music most Fri–Sat during dinner, tel. 08362/930-180).

TRANSPORTATION CONNECTIONS

From Füssen to: Neuschwanstein (hrly buses, 10 min, €1.50 one-way, €3 round-trip; taxis cost €8.50 one-way), **Reutte** (by bus, Mon–Fri 6/day, Sat 2/day, none Sun, 30 min, €3.20 one-way; taxis cost €28 one-way), **Munich** (hrly trains, 2 hrs, some change in Buchloe). Train info: tel. 11861 (€0.46/min).

The northbound **Romantic Road bus** departs Füssen for Hohenschwangau (and eventually Rothenburg) at 9:50 (having arrived in Füssen about 5 min earlier). The southbound Romantic Road bus departs Füssen for Munich at 19:15 (having arrived in Füssen about 10 min earlier). The bus stop is at Füssen's train station. Railpasses get you a 60 percent discount on the Romantic Road bus (and the ride does not use up a day of a Flexipass). For more information, see page 514 in the Rothenburg chapter.

Reutte

(€1 = about $1.20)

Reutte (ROY-teh, with a rolled *r*), a relaxed Austrian town of 5,700, is located 20 minutes across the border from Füssen. It's far from the international tourist crowd, but popular with Germans and Austrians for its climate. Doctors recommend its "grade 1" air. Reutte's one claim to fame with Americans: As Nazi Germany was falling in 1945, Hitler's top rocket scientist, Werner von Braun, joined the Americans (rather than the Russians) in Reutte. You could say the American space program began here.

Reutte isn't featured in any other American guidebook. While its generous sidewalks are filled with smart boutiques and lazy coffeehouses, its charms are subtle. It was never rich or important. Its castle is ruined, its buildings have painted-on "carvings," its churches are full, its men yodel for each other on birthdays, and lately, its energy is spent soaking its Austrian and German guests in *Gemütlichkeit.* Most guests stay for a week, so the town's attractions are more time-consuming than thrilling. If the weather's good, hike to the mysterious Ehrenberg ruins, ride the luge, or rent a bike. For a slap-dancing bang, enjoy a Tirolean folk evening. For accommodations, see Tirol's "Sleeping" section, page 488.

ORIENTATION

(area code: 05672)

Tourist Information: Reutte's TI is a block in front of the train station (Mon–Fri 8:00–12:00 & 14:00–17:00, Sat 8:30–12:00, closed Sun, tel. 05672/62336 or, from Germany, 00-43-5672/62336, www.reuttetourism.at). Go over your sightseeing plans, ask about a folk evening, pick up city and biking maps and the *Sommerprogramm* events schedule (German only), and ask about discounts with the hotel guest cards. Their "Information" booklet has a good self-guided town walk.

Laundry: Don't ask the TI about a launderette. Unless you can infiltrate the local campground, Hotel Maximilian, or Gutshof zum Schluxen (see page 490), the town has none.

SIGHTS AND ACTIVITIES

Ehrenberg Castle Ensemble

Just a mile outside of Reutte is the Ehrenberg Castle Ensemble *(Festungsensemble Ehrenberg),* the brooding ruins of four castles that once made up the largest fort in Tirol (built for defense against the Bavarians). Today, these castles are gradually being turned into a European Castle Museum, showing off 500 years of military architecture in one swoop (due to be completed in 2007, www.ehrenberg.at). The European Union is helping fund the project because it promotes the heritage of a multinational region—Tirol—rather than a country (the EU's vision is for a zone of regions rather than nations).

Three of the castles cluster together; the fourth (Fort Claudia) is across the valley, though all four used to be connected by walls. The first three—the easiest and most interesting to visit—are described below, from lowest to highest. New signs throughout the castle complex will help you find your way and explain some background on the region's history, geology, geography, culture, flora, and fauna.

Getting to the Castle Ensemble: The Klause, Ehrenberg, and Schlosskopf castles are on the road to Lermoos and Innsbruck. These are a pleasant walk or a short bike ride from Reutte; bikers can use the *Radwanderweg* along the Lech River (the TI has a good map).

Reutte

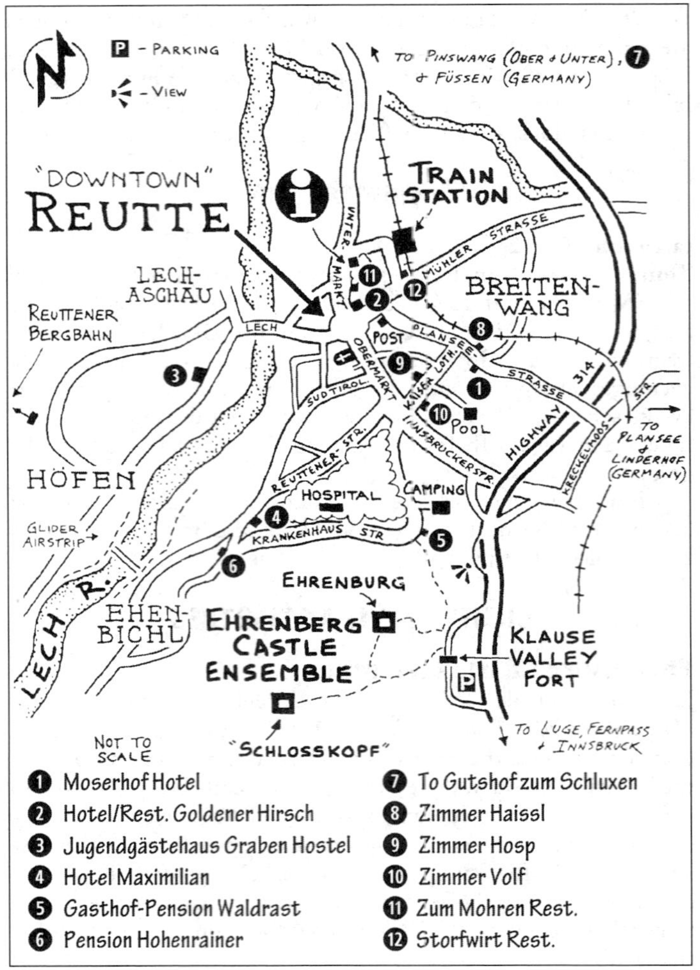

▲**Klause Valley Fort**—At the parking lot at the base of the ruin-topped hill, you'll find the recently modernized remains of a Gothic fortification. It was located on the medieval salt road (which used to be the ancient Roman road, Via Claudia Augusta). Beginning in the 14th century, this fort controlled traffic and levied tolls on all that passed through this strategic valley. Today it houses a 60-minute **sound-and-light show** *(son et lumière)* about the castles (€10). You'll sit inside the shell of the old castle while the 2,000-year history of this valley's fortresses is projected on the old stone walls and modern screens around you. By early 2006, this will also be the home to an extensive museum about the "castle ensemble." If you're hungry, drop by the nearby café/guest house, Gasthof Klause (closed Mon), which offers a German-language flier and a wall painting of the intact castle.

▲▲**Ehrenberg Ruins**—Ehrenberg, a 13th-century rock pile, provides a great contrast to King Ludwig's "modern" castles and a super opportunity to let your imagination off its leash. Hike up 20 minutes from the parking lot for a great view from your own private ruins. Facing the hill from the parking lot, find the gravelly road at the Klause sign. Follow the road to the saddle between the two hills. From the saddle, notice how the castle stands high on the horizon. This is Ehrenberg (which means "mountain of honor"), the first of the four ensemble castles, built in 1296. Thirteenth-century castles were designed to stand boastfully tall. With the advent of gunpowder, castles dug in. Notice the **ramparts** around you. They are from the 18th century. Approaching Ehrenberg castle, look for the small door to the left. It's the night entrance (tight and awkward, therefore safer against a surprise invasion). While hiking up the hill, you go through two doors. Castles allowed step-by-step retreat, giving defenders time to regroup and fight back against invading forces.

Before making the final and steepest ascent, follow the path around to the right to a big, grassy courtyard with commanding views and a fat, newly restored **turret.** This stored gunpowder and held a big cannon that enjoyed a clear view of the valley below. In medieval times, all the trees approaching the castle were cleared to keep an unobstructed view.

Look out over the valley. The pointy spire marks **Breitenwang,** which was a stop on the ancient Via Claudia Augusta. In A.D. 46, there was a Roman camp there. In 1489, after the Reutte bridge crossed the Lech River, Reutte (marked by the onion-domed church) was made a market town and eclipsed Breitenwang in importance. Any gliders circling? They launch from just over the river in Höfen (see "Flying and Gliding," page 486).

For centuries, this castle was the seat of government—ruling an area called the "judgment of Ehrenberg" (roughly the same as today's "district of Reutte"). When the emperor came by, he stayed here. In 1604, the ruler moved downtown into more comfortable quarters and the castle was no longer a palace.

Climb the steep hill to the top of the castle. Take the high ground. There was no water supply here, just kegs of wine, beer, and a cistern to collect rain.

Ehrenberg repelled 16,000 Swedish soldiers in the defense of Catholicism in 1632. Ehrenberg saw three or four other battles, but its end was not glorious. In the 1780s, a local businessman bought the castle in order to sell off its parts. Later, when vagabonds moved in, the roof was removed to make squatting miserable. With the roof gone, deterioration quickened, leaving this evocative shell and a whiff of history.

▲Schlosskopf—If you have energy left after conquering Ehrenberg, hike up to the mighty Schlosskopf (literally "castle head"). When the Bavarians captured Ehrenberg in 1703, the Tiroleans climbed up to the bluff above it to rain cannonballs down on their former fortress. In 1740, a mighty new castle—designed to defend against modern artillery—was built on this same sky-high strategic location. By 2001, the castle was completely overgrown with trees—you couldn't see it from Reutte. But today the trees are shaved away, and the castle has been excavated. The Castle Ensemble project is reconstructing the original equipment used to build this fortress (such as wooden cranes)—and is using those same means to restore parts of it. By 2007, Schlosskopf will be partially rebuilt, and the 18th-century construction equipment will retire and become part of the exhibit.

In Reutte

Folk Museum (Heimatsmuseum)—Reutte's Heimatmuseum, offering a quick look at the local folk culture and the story of the castles, is more cute than impressive. Ask to borrow the packet of information in English (€2, May–Oct Tue–Sun 10:00–17:00, closed Mon and Nov–April, in the bright green building on Untermarkt, around corner from Hotel Goldener Hirsch, tel. 05672/72304).

▲▲Tirolean Folk Evening—Ask the TI or your hotel if there's a Tirolean folk evening scheduled. Usually on Thursdays in the summer (July–mid-Sept), Reutte or a nearby town puts on an evening of yodeling, slap dancing, and Tirolean frolic worth the €8–10 and short drive. Off-season, you'll have to do your own yodeling. There are also weekly folk concerts in the park (July–Aug only, ask at TI). For listings of these and other local events, pick up a copy of the German-only *Sommerprogramm* schedule at the TI.

▲Flying and Gliding—For a major thrill on a sunny day, drop by the tiny airport in Höfen across the river, and fly. A small single-prop plane can buzz the Zugspitze and Ludwig's castles and give you a bird's-eye peek at Reutte's Ehrenberg ruins (2 people for 30 min-€110, 1 hr-€220, tel. 05672/62827, phone rarely answered and then not in English, so your best bet is to show up at the Höfen airport on good-weather afternoons). Or, for something more angelic, how about *Segelfliegen*? For €36, you get 30 minutes in a glider for two (you and the pilot). Just watching the towrope launch the graceful glider like a giant, slow-motion rubber-band gun is exhilarating (May–mid-Sept 12:00–19:00, in good but breezy weather only, find someone in the know at the "Thermic Ranch," tel. 05672/71550 or 05672/64010, or mobile 0676/711-0100).

Swimming—Plunge into Reutte's Olympic-size Alpenbad

swimming pool to cool off after your castle hikes (€6, June–mid-Sept daily 10:00–21:00, mid-Nov–May Tue–Sun 14:00–21:00, closed Mon and mid-Sept–mid-Nov; indoor/outdoor pools, big water slide, mini-golf, playground on-site, 5 min on foot from Reutte center, head out Obermarkt and turn left on Kaiser Lothar Strasse, tel. 05672/62666).

Reuttener Bergbahn—This mountain lift swoops you high above the tree line to a starting point for several hikes and an alpine flower park, with special paths leading you past countless local varieties (€9 one-way, €13 round-trip, flowers best in late July, lift usually mid-May–Oct daily 9:00–11:50 & 13:00–16:30, tel. 05672/62420, www.reuttener-seilbahnen.at—in German only).

Near Reutte

▲▲The Luge (Sommerrodelbahn)—Near Lermoos, on the road from Reutte to Innsbruck, you'll find two exciting luge courses, or *Sommerrodelbahn.* To try one of Europe's great €6 thrills, take the lift up, grab a sled-like go-cart, and luge down. The concrete course banks on the corners, and even a novice can go very, very fast. Most are cautious on their first run, speed demons on their second...and bruised and bloody on their third. A woman once showed me her journal illustrated with her husband's dried five-inch-long luge scab. He disobeyed the only essential rule of luging: Keep both hands on your stick. To avoid getting into a bumper-to-bumper traffic jam, let the person in front of you get way ahead before you start. No one emerges from the course without a windblown hairdo and a smile-creased face. Both places charge the same price (€6 per run, 5- and 10-trip discount cards) and shut down at the least hint of rain (call ahead to make sure they're open; you're more likely to get luge info in English if you call the TIs, listed below). If you're without a car, these are not worth the trouble (consider the luge near Neuschwanstein instead—see "Tegelberg Luge," page 474).

The Short and Steep Luge: Bichlbach, the first course (330-foot drop over a 2,600-foot course), is four miles beyond Reutte's castle ruins. Look for a chairlift on the right, and exit on the tiny road at the Almkopfbahn Rosthof sign (June–Sept daily 10:00–17:00, sometimes opens in spring and fall—especially weekends—depending on weather, call first, tel. 05674/5350, or contact the local TI at tel. 05674/5354).

The Longest Luge: The Biberwier *Sommerrodelbahn* is a better luge and, at 4,250 feet, the longest in Austria (15 min farther from Reutte than Bichlbach, just past Lermoos in Biberwier—the first exit after a long tunnel). The only drawbacks are its short season and hours (open late-May–June Sat–Sun 9:00–16:30 only, closed Mon–Fri, July–Sept daily 9:00–16:30, call first, tel. 05673/2323 or 05673/2111, TI tel. 05673/2922).

SLEEPING

Reutte is a mellow Füssen with fewer crowds and easygoing locals with a contagious love of life. Come here for a good dose of Austrian ambience and lower prices. Those with a car should make their home base here; those without should consider it. (To call Reutte from Germany, dial 00-43-5672, then the local number.) You'll drive across the border without stopping. Reutte is popular with Austrians and Germans, who come here year after year for one- or two-week vacations. The hotels are big, elegant, and full of comfy, carved furnishings and creative ways to spend lots of time in one spot. They take great pride in their restaurants, and the owners send their children away to hotel-management schools. All include a great breakfast, but few accept credit cards. Most places give about a 5 percent discount for stays of two nights or longer.

In Reutte

To locate these hotels, see map on page 484.

$$ Moserhof Hotel is a plush Tirolean splurge with 30 new-feeling rooms and polished service and facilities, including an elegant dining room (Sb-€54, Db-€84, extra bed-€35, these special prices only if you reserve ahead and ask for Rick Steves rates, almost all rooms have balconies, free parking, elevator, Internet access-€3/hr; from downtown Reutte, follow signs to village Breitenwang, it's just after church at Planseestrasse 44, tel. 05672/62020, fax 05672/620-2040, www.hotel-moserhof.at, info@hotel-moserhof.at, Hosp family).

$$ Hotel Goldener Hirsch, located in the center of Reutte just two blocks from the station, is a grand old hotel renovated with Tirolean *Jugendstil* flair. It boasts 56 rooms and one lonely set of antlers (Sb-€56, Db-€82, Tb-€115, Qb-€124–140, 2-night discounts, family rooms, elevator, quality food in their restaurant, known for local specialties and vegetarian *Gemüseplatte,* closed Mon, tel. 05672/62508, fax 05672/625-087, www.goldener-hirsch .at—in German only, info@goldener-hirsch.at, Monika, Helmut, and daughters Vanessa and Nina all SE).

$ The homey **Jugendgästehaus Graben** hostel has two to six beds per room and includes breakfast and sheets. Frau Reyman and her son Rudy keep the place traditional, clean, and friendly, and serve a great €6.50 dinner for guests only. This is a super value. If you've never hostelled and are curious (and have a car or don't mind a bus ride), try it. They accept non-members of any age (dorm bed-€19, Db-€45, cash only, non-smoking rooms, Internet access, laundry service, no curfew, less than 2 miles from Reutte, bus connection to Neuschwanstein via Reutte; from downtown Reutte, cross bridge and follow main road left along river, or take

Sleep Code

(€1 = about $1.20, country code: 43, area code: 05672)
S = Single, **D** = Double/Twin, **T** = Triple, **Q** = Quad, **b** = bathroom, **s** = shower only, **SE** = English spoken, **NSE** = No English spoken. Unless otherwise noted, credit cards are accepted, English is spoken, and breakfast is included.

To help you sort easily through these listings, I've divided the rooms into three categories, based on the price for a standard double room with bath:

$$$ Higher Priced—Most rooms €85 or more.
$$ Moderately Priced—Most rooms between €50–85.
$ Lower Priced—Most rooms €50 or less.

Prices listed are for one-night stays. Most places give about a 5 to 10 percent off for two-night stays—always request this discount. Competition is fierce, and off-season prices are soft. High season is mid-June through September. Rooms are generally about 12 percent less in shoulder season and much cheaper in off-season.

the bus—1 bus/hr until 19:30, ask for Graben stop, no buses Sun; Graben 1, tel. 05672/626-440, fax 05672/626-444, www.hoefen.at—in German only, jgh-hoefen@tirol.com).

In Ehenbichl

The next three listings are a couple miles upriver from Reutte in the village of Ehenbichl, under the Ehrenberg ruins. From central Reutte, go south on Obermarkt and turn right on Reuttenerstrasse, following signs to Ehenbichl.

$$ Hotel Maximilian is a great value. It includes free bicycles, table tennis, a children's playroom, and the friendly service of the Koch family. Daughter Gabi speaks flawless English. The Kochs host many special events, and their hotel has lots of wonderful extras such as a sauna, a masseuse, and a beauty salon (Sb-€35–42, Db-€70–80, family deals, fast Internet access, laundry service-€7/load even for non-guests, good restaurant, tel. 05672/62585, fax 05672/625-8554, www.maxihotel.com, maxhotel@netway.at). They rent cars to guests only (1 VW Golf, 1 VW van, book in advance).

$$ Gasthof-Pension Waldrast, separating a forest and a meadow, is run by the farming Huter family and their huge, friendly dog, Bari. The place feels hauntingly quiet and has no restaurant, but it does offer 10 nice rooms with sitting areas and castle-view balconies (Sb-€30, Db-€51–55, Tb-€66, Qb-€88, cash only, non-smoking, less than 1 mile from Reutte, just off main drag toward Innsbruck, past campground and under castle ruins on Ehrenbergstrasse, tel. & fax 05672/62443, www.waldrasttirol.com—in German only, info@waldrasttirol.com).

$ Pension Hohenrainer is a big, no-frills alternative to Hotel Maximilian—a quiet, good value with 12 modern rooms and some castle-view balconies (Sb-€23–28, Db-€41–50, cheaper for longer stays, free Internet access, follow signs up the road behind Hotel Maximilian into village of Ehenbichl, tel. 05672/62544 or 05672/63262, fax 05672/62052, www.hohenrainer.at, hohenrainer@aon.at).

In Pinswang

The village of Pinswang is closer to Füssen (and Ludwig's castles), but still in Austria.

$$ Gutshof zum Schluxen, run by helpful Hermann, gets the Remote Old Hotel in an Idyllic Setting award. This family-friendly working farm offers modern rustic elegance draped in goose down and pastels, and a chance to pet a rabbit and feed the deer. Its picturesque meadow setting will turn you into a dandelion picker, and its proximity to Neuschwanstein will turn you into a hiker. King Ludwig II himself is said to have slept here (Sb-€41, Db-€82, extra person-€22, 10 percent discount for 4 nights or more, Internet access, self-service laundry, free pickup from Reutte and Füssen, good restaurant, fun bar, mountain bike rental, between Reutte and Füssen in village of Pinswang, tel. 05677/8903, fax 05677/890-323, www.schluxen.com, welcome@schluxen.com).

Private Homes in Breitenwang

The Reutte TI has a list of 50 private homes that rent out generally good rooms *(Zimmer)* with facilities down the hall, pleasant communal living rooms, and breakfast. Most charge €15 per person per night and speak little or no English. Reservations are nearly impossible for one- or two-night stays, but short stops are welcome if you just drop in and fill available gaps. Most *Zimmer* charge around €1.50 extra for heat in winter (worth it). The TI can always find you a room when you arrive.

Right next door to Reutte is the older and quieter village of Breitenwang. It has all the best *Zimmer,* the recommended Moserhof Hotel (above), and a bakery (a 20-min walk from Reutte train station—at post office roundabout, follow Planseestrasse past onion dome to pointy straight dome; unmarked Kaiser Lothar Strasse is first right past this church).

The following *Zimmer* (all reasonably priced, rated **$**) are comfortable and quiet, have few stairs, and are within two blocks of the Breitenwang church steeple: **Helene Haissl** (the best of the bunch, D-€30, 2-night discounts, cash only, children's loft room available, beautiful troll-filled garden, free bikes, laundry service, across from big Alpenhotel Ernberg at Planseestrasse 63, tel. 05672/67913); **Walter and Emilie Hosp** (3 rooms in a modern house, D-€40, D-€36 for 2 nights or more, extra person-€15, cash only, Kaiser Lothar Strasse 29, tel. 05672/65377); and **Irene and Rudolf Volf** (3 rooms closer to Reutte's main drag, D-€40, D-€30 for 2 nights, cash only, Kaiser Lothar Strasse 2, tel. 05672/65066).

EATING

The hotels here take great pride in serving local cuisine at reasonable prices to their guests and the public. Rather than go to a cheap restaurant, try a hotel. Most offer €8–14 dinners from 18:00 to 21:00 and are closed one night a week. Reutte itself has plenty of inviting eateries—traditional, ethnic, fast food, grocery stores, and delis.

Restaurant Goldener Hirsch, located in the hotel of the same name, offers local specialties in a traditional setting. If you need a break from Tirolean food, try the tasty vegetable plate, *Gemüseplatte* (€8–12, closed Mon, Mühlerstasse 1, tel. 05672/62508).

Zum Mohren, known for its grill and game specialties, is located in the heart of Reutte. Check the menu for regionally inspired dishes featuring fresh asparagus, mushrooms, or whatever is in season (€8–14, Mon–Sat 11:00–24:00, closed Sun, Untermarkt 26, tel. 05672/623 45, www.mohren.at—in German only).

Storfwirt is the place for a quick lunch or light dinner. You can get the usual sausages here, as well as baked potatoes, salads, and pizza. Check for daily lunch or dinner specials (€3–7, Mon–Fri 8:00–24:00, Sat 17:00–24:00, closed Sun, Schrettergasse 15, tel. 05672/625-3920).

TRANSPORTATION CONNECTIONS

From Reutte by Train to: Innsbruck (7/day, 2.5 hrs, change in Garmisch and sometimes also in Mittenwald), **Munich** (hrly, 2.5–3 hrs, change in Garmisch, Pfronten-Steinach, or Kempten), **Garmisch** (every 2 hrs, 1 hr).

By Bus to: Füssen (Mon–Fri 6/day, Sat 2/day, none Sun, 30 min, €3.20, buses depart from in front of the train station, pay driver). Taxis cost €28 one-way.

By Car into Reutte from Germany: Skip the north *(Nord)* exit and take the south *(Süd)* exit into town. While Austria requires a toll sticker for driving on its highways (€8/10 days, buy at the border, gas stations, car-rental agencies, or *Tabak* shops), those just dipping into Tirol from Bavaria do not need one.

ROTHENBURG

and the ROMANTIC ROAD

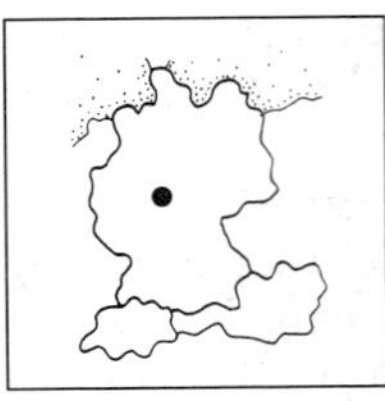

From Munich or Füssen to Frankfurt, the Romantic Road takes you through Bavaria's medieval heartland, a route strewn with picturesque villages, farmhouses, onion-domed churches, Baroque palaces, and walled cities.

Linger in Rothenburg (ROE-ten-burg), Germany's best-preserved walled town. Countless travelers have searched for the elusive "untouristy Rothenburg." There are many contenders (such as Michelstadt, Miltenberg, Bamberg, Bad Windsheim, and Dinkelsbühl), but none holds a candle to the king of medieval German cuteness. Even with crowds, overpriced souvenirs, Japanese-speaking night watchmen, and, yes, even *Schneeballen,* Rothenburg is best. Save time and mileage and be satisfied with the winner.

Planning Your Time

The best one-day drive through the heartland of Germany is the Romantic Road. The road is clearly marked for drivers, and well described in the free brochure available at any TI. Those without wheels can take the bus tour; see page 514 for details (railpass holders get a 60 percent discount, so the entire Frankfurt–Munich trip costs €38). Apart from Würzburg, with its Prince Bishop's Residenz, the only stop worth more than a few minutes is Rothenburg. Twenty-four hours is ideal for this town. With two nights and a day, you'll be able to see the essentials and actually relax a little.

Rothenburg

In the Middle Ages, when Frankfurt and Munich were just wide spots on the road, Rothenburg ob der Tauber was Germany's second-largest free imperial city, with a whopping population of 6,000. Today, it's her best-preserved medieval walled town, enjoying tremendous tourist popularity without losing its charm. Get medievaled in Rothenburg.

During Rothenburg's heyday, from 1150 to 1400, it was the crossing point of two major trade routes: Tashkent–Paris and Hamburg–Venice. Today, the great trade is tourism; two-thirds of the townspeople are employed to serve you. Too often, Rothenburg brings out the shopper in visitors before they've had a chance to see the historic town. True, this is a great place to do your German shopping, but appreciate the town's great history and sights first. While 2.5 million people visit each year, a mere 500,000 spend the night. Rothenburg is most enjoyable early and late, when the tour groups are gone. Rothenburg is very busy through the summer and in the Christmas Market month of December. Spring and fall are great, but it's pretty bleak from January through March—when most locals are hibernating or on vacation.

Rothenburg in a day is easy, with five essential experiences: the Medieval Crime and Punishment Museum, the Riemenschneider wood carving in St. Jakob's Church, the town walking tour, a walk along the wall, and the entertaining Night Watchman's Tour. With more time, there are several mediocre but entertaining museums, walking and biking in the nearby countryside, and lots of cafés and shops. Make a point to spend at least one night. The town is yours after dark, when the groups vacate and the town's floodlit cobbles wring some romance out of any travel partner.

ORIENTATION

(area code: 09861)

To orient yourself in Rothenburg, think of the town map as a human head. Its nose—the castle garden—sticks out to the left, and the neck is the skinny lower part, with the hostel and some of the best hotels in the Adam's apple. The town is a joy on foot. No sight or hotel is more than a 15-minute walk from the train station or each other.

Most of the buildings you'll see were built by 1400. The city was born around its long-gone castle—built in 1142, destroyed in 1356—which was located on the present-day site of the castle garden. You can see the shadow of the first town wall, which defines the oldest part of Rothenburg, in its contemporary street plan. A few

Rothenburg

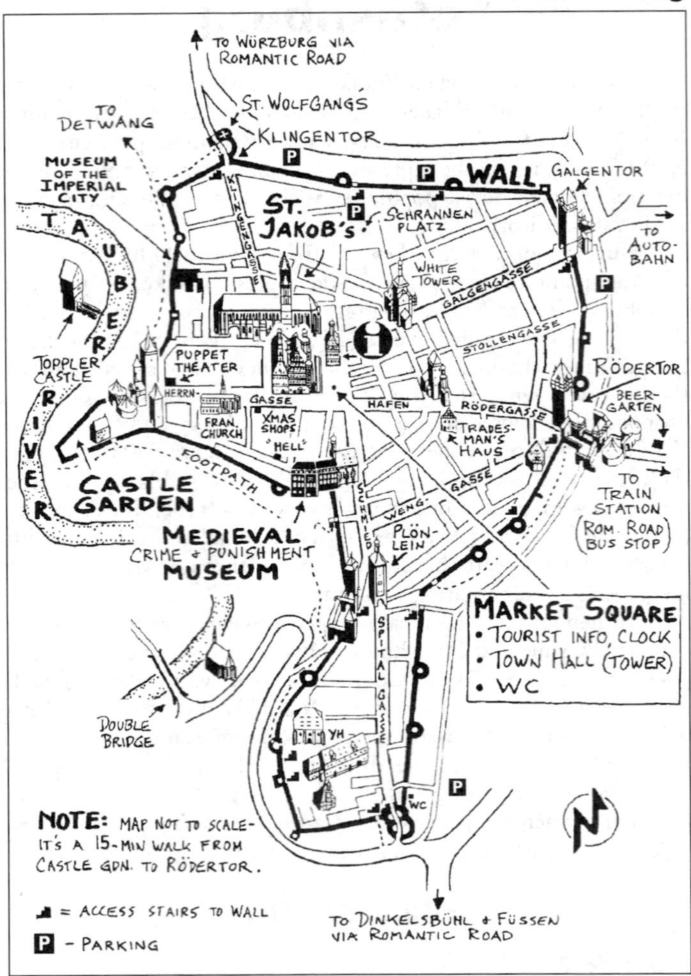

gates from this wall still survive. The richest and biggest houses were in this central part. The commoners built higgledy-piggledy (read: picturesque) houses farther from the center, near the present walls.

Tourist Information

The TI is on Market Square (April–Oct Mon–Fri 9:00–12:00 & 13:00–18:00, Sat–Sun 10:00–15:00, Nov–March shorter hours and closed Sun, tel. 09861/404800, www.rothenburg.de). If there's a long line, just raid the rack where they keep all the free pamphlets. The map and guide comes with a virtual walking guide to the town. The *Information* monthly guide lists all the events and entertainment. Ask about the daily English walking tour at 14:00 (€4, April–Oct; see "Tours," below). There's free Internet access in the TI lobby (just one terminal). Visitors who arrive late can check the handy map with all hotels—highlighting which ones still have rooms available, with a free direct phone connection to them—it's just outside the door. The best town map is available free with this book at the Friese shop, two doors west from the TI (toward St. Jakob's Church; see "Shopping," page 503).

Arrival in Rothenburg

By Train: It's a 10-minute walk from the station to Rothenburg's Market Square (following the brown Altstadt signs, exit left from station, turn right on Ansbacher Strasse, and head straight into the Middle Ages). Day-trippers can leave luggage in station lockers (€2, on platform) or at the Friese shop on Market Square. Arrange train and *couchette*/sleeper reservations at the travel agency in the station (no charge for quick questions, Mon–Fri 9:00–18:00, Sat 9:00–13:00, closed Sun, tel. 09861/7711). The nearest WCs are at the snack bar next door to the station. Taxis wait at the station (€5 to any hotel).

By Car: Driving in town can be a nightmare, with many narrow, one-way streets. Park outside the walls and walk five minutes to the center. Parking lots line the town walls and range from free (the P5 parking lot just outside Klingentor) to €4 per day. Only those with a hotel reservation can park within the walls after hours (but not during festivals; easiest entry often via Spittaltor).

Helpful Hints

Laundry: A handy launderette is near the station off Ansbacher Strasse (€5.50/load, includes soap, English instructions, opens at 8:00, last load in Mon–Fri at 18:00, Sat at 14:00, closed Sun, Johannitergasse 9, tel. 09861/2775).

Swimming: Rothenburg has a fine modern recreation center with an indoor/outdoor pool and sauna. It's just a few minutes' walk down the Dinkelsbühl Road (*Hallenbad*, adult-€3, child-€1.70, swimsuit and towel rental-€2 each, Mon 14:00–21:00, Tue–Thu 9:00–21:00, Fri–Sun 9:00–18:00, Nordlingerstrasse 20, tel. 09861/4565).

Bike Rental: You can rent bikes at Rad & Tat (€2.50/hr, €7.50/half-day, €10/full day, Mon–Fri 9:00–18:00, Sat 9:00–14:00, closed Sun, Bensenstrasse 17, outside of town near corner of Bensenstrasse and Erlbacherstrasse, passport number required, tel. 09861/87984, Daniel Lorenz SE).

Festivals: Rothenburgers dress up in medieval costumes, and beer gardens spill out into the street to celebrate Mayor Nusch's

Meistertrunk victory (June 2–5 in 2006, see story below under "Meistertrunk Show" on page 498) and 700 years of history in the Imperial City Festival (Sept 1–3 in 2006, with fireworks).

Christmas Market: Rothenburg is dead in November, January, and February, but December is its busiest month—the entire town cranks up the medieval cuteness with concerts and costumes, shops with schnapps, stalls filling squares, hot spiced wine, giddy nutcrackers, and mobs of earmuffed Germans. Christmas markets are big all over Germany, and Rothenburg's is considered one of the best. The festival takes place each year in the four weeks leading up to the last Sunday before Christmas (Dec 1–22 in 2006). Virtually all sights listed in this chapter are open longer hours during these four weeks. Try to avoid Saturdays and Sundays, when big-city day-trippers really clog the grog.

TOURS

▲▲Night Watchman's Tour—This tour is flat-out the most entertaining hour of medieval wonder anywhere in Europe. The Night Watchman (a.k.a. Hans Georg Baumgartner) jokes like a medieval Jerry Seinfeld as he lights his lamp and takes tourists on his one-hour rounds, telling slice-of-gritty-life tales of medieval Rothenburg (€4, April–Dec nightly at 20:00, in English, meet at Market Square, www.nightwatchman.de). This is the best evening activity in town. If you miss it, you can pick up a copy of the DVD at the Friese shop near the TI.

Old Town Historic Walk—The TI on Market Square offers 90-minute guided walking tours in English (€4, April–Oct daily at 14:00 from Market Square). Take this for the serious history of Rothenburg and to make sense of the town's architecture. Alternatively, you can hire your own **private guide**—a local historian who will really bring the ramparts alive. Gisela Vogl (€53/90 min, €70/2 hr, tel. 09861/4957, werner.vogl@t-online.de) and Anita Weinzierl (tel. 09868/7993, anitaweinzierl@aol.com) are both good. Martin Kamphans, a potter, also works as a guide (tel. 09861/7941, kamphans@t-online.de).

Horse-and-Buggy Rides—These give you a relaxing 30-minute clip-clop through the old town, starting from Market Square or Schrannenplatz (private buggy for €30, or wait for one to fill up for €5 per person).

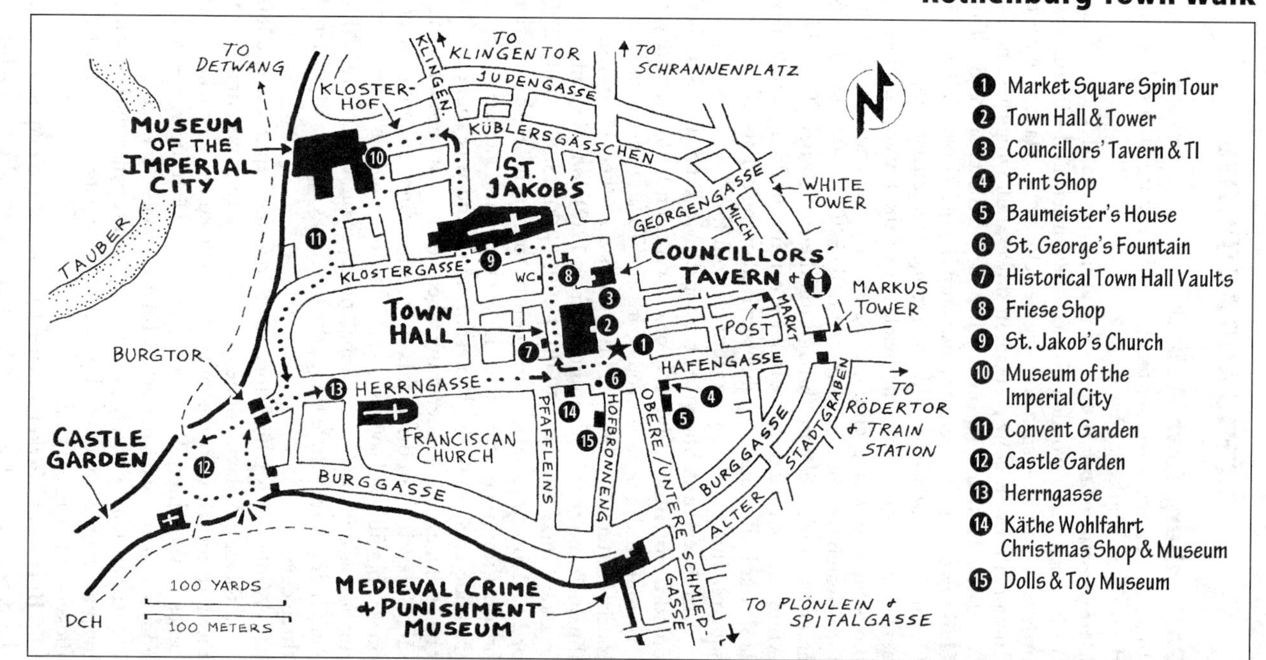
Rothenburg Town Walk
1 Market Square Spin Tour
2 Town Hall & Tower
3 Councillors' Tavern & TI
4 Print Shop
5 Baumeister's House
6 St. George's Fountain
7 Historical Town Hall Vaults
8 Friese Shop
9 St. Jakob's Church
10 Museum of the Imperial City
11 Convent Garden
12 Castle Garden
13 Herrngasse
14 Käthe Wohlfahrt Christmas Shop & Museum
15 Dolls & Toy Museum
TO DETWANG
TO KLINGENTOR
TO SCHRANNENPLATZ
KLOSTER-HOF
KLINGEN.
JUDENGASSE
KÜBLERSGÄSSCHEN
MUSEUM OF THE IMPERIAL CITY
ST. JAKOB'S
GEORGENGASSE
MILCH
WHITE TOWER
TAUBER
KLOSTERGASSE
WC
COUNCILLORS' TAVERN + i
MARKUS TOWER
TOWN HALL
POST
MARKT
HAFENGASSE
BURGTOR
HERRNGASSE
TO RÖDERTOR + TRAIN STATION
CASTLE GARDEN
FRANCISCAN CHURCH
PFAFFLEINS
HOFBRONNENG
OBERE / UNTERE SCHMIED-GASSE
BURGGASSE
STADTGRABEN
ALTER
BURGGASSE
100 YARDS
100 METERS
DCH
MEDIEVAL CRIME + PUNISHMENT MUSEUM
TO PLÖNLEIN + SPITALGASSE

SIGHTS AND ACTIVITIES

Rothenburg Town Walk

This one-hour walk weaves together Rothenburg's top sights. Start the walk on Market Square.

Market Square Spin Tour—Stand at the bottom of Market Square (10 feet below the wooden post on the corner) and—ignoring the little white arrow—spin 360 degrees clockwise, starting with the Town Hall tower. Now do it again slower, following these notes:

Town Hall and Tower: Rothenburg's tallest spire is the **Town Hall tower.** At 200 feet, it stands atop the old Town Hall, a white, Gothic, 13th-century building. Notice the tourists enjoying the best view in town from the black top of the tower (€1 and a rigorous but interesting climb, 214 steps, narrow and steep near the top—watch your head, April–Oct daily 9:30–12:30 & 13:30–17:00, enter on Market Square through middle arch of new Town Hall). After a fire burned down part of the original building, a **new Town Hall** was built alongside what survived of the old one (fronting the square). This is in Renaissance style from 1570.

Meistertrunk Show: At the top of Market Square stands the proud **Councillors' Tavern** (clock tower from 1466). In its day, the city council drank here. Today, it's the TI and the focus of most tourists' attention when the little doors on either side of the clock flip open and the wooden figures (from 1910) do their thing. Be on Market Square at 11:00, 12:00, 13:00, 14:00, 15:00, 20:00, 21:00, or 22:00 for the ritual gathering of the tourists to see the less-than-breathtaking reenactment of the Meistertrunk story. In 1631, the Catholic army took the Protestant town and was about to do its rape, pillage, and plunder thing when, as the story goes, the mayor said, "Hey, if I can drink this entire three-liter tankard of wine in one gulp, will you leave us alone?" The invading commander, sensing he was dealing with an unbalanced person, said, "Sure." Mayor Nusch drank the whole thing, the town was saved, and he slept for three days.

While this is a nice story, it was dreamed up in the late 1800s for a theatrical play designed to promote a romantic image of the town. In actuality, Rothenburg was occupied and ransacked several times in the Thirty Years' War, and it never recovered—which is why it's such a well-preserved time capsule today. Hint: For the best show, don't watch the clock; watch the open-mouthed tourists gasp as the old windows flip open. At the late shows, the square flickers with camera flashes.

Bottom of Market Square: On the bottom end of the square, the cream-colored building has a fine **print shop** (upstairs—see "Shopping," page 504). Adjoining that is the **Baumeister's Haus,** a touristy restaurant with a fine courtyard (see "Eating," page 510), featuring a famous Renaissance facade with statues of the seven virtues and the seven vices—the former supporting the latter. The statues are copies; the originals are in the Museum of the Imperial City (listed below). The green house below that is the former house of the 15th-century Mayor Toppler (it's now the recommended Greifen Gasthof); next to it is a famous Scottish restaurant (with arches). Keep circling to the big 17th-century **St. George's fountain.** The long metal gutters slid, routing the water into the villagers' buckets. Rothenburg's many fountains had practical functions beyond providing drinking water. The water was used for fighting fires, and some fountains were stocked with fish during times of siege. Two fine buildings behind the fountain show the old-time lofts with warehouse doors and pulleys on top for hoisting. All over town, lofts were filled with grain and corn. A year's supply was required by the city so they could survive any siege. The building behind the fountain is an art gallery (free, usually daily 11:00–17:00) showing off the work of Rothenburg's top artists. To the right is an old-time pharmacy mixing old and new in typical Rothenburg style.

The broad street running under the Town Hall tower is **Herrngasse.** The town originated with its castle (built in 1142 but now long gone; only the castle garden remains). Herrngasse connected the castle to Market Square. The last leg of this circular walking tour will take you from the castle garden up Herrngasse to where you now stand. For now, walk a few steps down Herrngasse to the arch under the Town Hall tower (between the new and old town halls). On the left wall are the town's measuring rods—a reminder that medieval Germany was made of 300 independent little countries, each with its own weights and measures. Merchants and shoppers knew that these were the local standards: the rod (4.3 yards), the *Schuh* (or shoe, roughly a foot), and the ell (from elbow to fingertip—4 inches longer than mine...try it). Notice the protruding cornerstone. These are all over town—originally to protect buildings from reckless horse carts (and vice versa). Under the arch, you'll find the...

▲Historical Town Hall Vaults—This museum gives a waxy but good look at Rothenburg during the Catholics-vs.-Protestants Thirty Years' War. With fine English descriptions, it offers a look at "the fateful year 1631," a replica of the famous Meistertrunk tankard, and a dungeon complete with three dank cells and some torture lore (€2, April–Oct daily 9:30–17:30, less off-season, tel. 09861/94280).

From the museum, walk toward St. Jakob's Church (just northwest of Market Square). You'll pass the public WC (on your left) and the recommended **Friese shop** (see "Shopping," page 504) tucked into the small square on your right.

Outside the church, you'll see a scene of Jesus praying at Gethsemane, a common feature of Gothic churches. Downhill, notice the nub of a sandstone statue—a rare original, looking pretty bad after 500 years of weather and, more recently, pollution. Original statues are now in the city museum. Better-preserved statues you see on the church are copies. If it's your wedding day, take the first entrance. Otherwise, use the second (downhill) door to enter...

▲▲St. Jakob's Church—Built in the 14th century, this church has been Lutheran since 1544. Take a close look at the 12 Apostles altar in front (from 1546, left permanently in its open festival-day position). Below Christ are statues of six saints. St. James (Jakob in German, pronounced YAH-kohp) is the one with the shell. He's the saint of pilgrims, and this church was a stop on the medieval pilgrimage route to Santiago (St. James in Spanish) de Compostela in Spain. Study the painted panels—ever see Peter with spectacles? Around the back of the altarpiece (upper left) is a great painting of Rothenburg's Market Square in the 15th century—looking like it does today. Before leaving the front of the church, notice the old medallions above the carved choir stalls featuring the coats of arms of Rothenburg's leading families and portraits of city and church leaders.

Stairs in the back of the church, behind the pipe organ, lead to the artistic highlight of Rothenburg and perhaps the most wonderful wood carving in all of Germany: the glorious 500-year-old, 35-foot-high *Altar of the Holy Blood.* Tilman Riemenschneider, the Michelangelo of German woodcarvers, carved this from 1499 to 1504 to hold a precious rock-crystal capsule, set in a cross that contains a scrap of tablecloth miraculously stained in the shape of a cross by a drop of communion wine. Below, in the scene of the Last Supper, Jesus gives Judas a piece of bread, marking him as the traitor, while John lays his head on Christ's lap. Everything is portrayed exactly as described in the Bible. On the left: Jesus enters Jerusalem. On the right: Jesus prays in the Garden of Gethsemane. Notice how Judas, with his big bag of cash, could be removed from the scene—illustrated by photos on the wall nearby—as was the tradition for the four days leading up to Easter (€1.50, April–Oct Mon–Sat 9:00–17:15, Sun 10:45–17:15, Nov–March daily 10:00–12:00 & 14:00–16:00, free helpful English info sheet).

For an interesting walk to the nearby Museum of the Imperial City (listed below), leave the church and, from its outside steps, walk around the corner to the right and under the chapel. Go two blocks down **Klingengasse** and stop at **Klosterhof Street.** (I've marked your spot with a small circular plaque in the middle of the road.) Looking down Klingengasse, you see the Klingentor (cliff tower). This tower was Rothenburg's water cistern. From 1595 until 1910, a copper cistern high in the tower provided clean spring water to the privileged. To the right of Klingentor is a good stretch of wall rampart to walk. To the left, the wall is low and simple, lacking a rampart because it guards only a cliff. Now find the shell decorating a building on the street corner next to you. That's the symbol of St. James (pilgrims commemorated their visit to Santiago de Compostela with a shell), indicating that this building is associated with the church. Walk under the shell, down Klosterhof (passing the colorful Altfränkische Weinstube; see "Eating," page 512) to the Museum of the Imperial City, housed in the former Dominican convent. Cloistered nuns used the lazy Susan embedded in the wall (to the right of museum door) to give food to the poor without being seen.

▲▲Museum of the Imperial City (Reichsstadt Museum)—You'll get a scholarly sweep through Rothenburg's history here. Highlights include *The Rothenburg Passion,* a 12-panel series of paintings from 1492 showing scenes leading up to Christ's crucifixion (in the *Konventsaal*); an exhibit of Jewish culture through the ages in Rothenburg *(Judaika);* a 14th-century convent kitchen *(Klosterküche);* romantic paintings of the town *(Gemäldegalerie);* and the fine Baumann collection of weapons and armor. Follow the Rundgang Tour signs (€3, €6 combo-ticket that includes Medieval Crime and Punishment Museum saves a whopping €0.20, daily April–Oct 10:00–17:00, Nov–March 13:00–16:00, English info sheet and descriptions, no photos, tel. 09861/939-043, www.reichsstadtmuseum.rothenburg.de).

Leaving the museum for the Castle Garden (listed below), go around to the right and into the **convent garden** (free, same hours as museum)—a peaceful place to work on your tan...or mix a poison potion. Angle left through the nun's garden (site of the now-gone Dominican church), eventually leaving via an arch at the far end. But enjoy the herb garden first. Monks and nuns, who were responsible for concocting herbal cures in the olden days, often tended herb gardens. Smell (but don't pick) the *Pfefferminze, Juniper* (gin), *Chamomilla* (disinfectant), and *Origanum.* Don't smell the plants in the poison corner (potency indicated by the number of crosses...like spiciness stars in a Chinese restaurant).

Exiting opposite where you entered, you see the back end of an original barn (behind a mansion fronting Herrngasse). Go downhill to the town wall (view through bars). This part of the wall takes advantage of the natural fortification provided by the cliff, and is therefore much smaller than the ramparts. Angle left along the wall to Herrngasse, then right under the tower *(Burgtor).* Notice the tiny "eye of the needle" door cut into the big door. If trying to get into town after curfew, you could bribe the guard to let you through this door (which was small enough to keep out any fully armed attackers).

Step through the gate and outside the wall. Look around and imagine being locked out in the year 1400. This was a wooden drawbridge (see the chain slits above). Notice the "pitch nose" mask—designed to pour boiling Nutella on anyone attacking. High above is the town coat of arms: a red castle *(roten Burg)*.

Castle Garden—The garden before you was once that red castle (destroyed in the 14th century). Today it's a picnic-friendly park with a viewpoint at the far end (considered the best place to kiss by romantic local teenagers). But the views of the lush Tauber River Valley below (a.k.a. Tauber Riviera) are just as good from either side of the tower on this near end of the park. To the right, a path leads down to the village of Detwang (you can see the church spire below)—a town even older than Rothenburg. To the left is a fine view of the fortified Rothenburg. Return to the tower, cross carefully under the pitch nose, and hike back up Herrngasse to your starting point.

Herrngasse—Many towns have a Herrngasse, where the richest patricians and merchants (the *Herren*) lived. Predictably, it's your best chance to see the town's finest old mansions. Strolling back to Market Square, you'll pass the old-time puppet theater (German only, on left), the Franciscan church (from 1285, oldest in town, on right), and the Eisenhut Hotel (Rothenburg's fanciest, worth a peek inside, on right). The shop next door at #11 retains the original old courtyard. The Käthe Wohlfahrt Christmas Villages shops (at Herrngasse 1 and across the street, see "Shopping," page 504) is your last, and perhaps greatest, temptation before reaching your starting—and ending—point: Market Square.

Museums within a Block of Market Square

▲▲Medieval Crime and Punishment Museum—This museum is the best of its kind, full of fascinating old legal bits and *Kriminal* pieces, instruments of punishment and torture—even a special cage complete with a metal gag for nags. As a bonus, you get exhibits on marriage traditions and witches. Follow the yellow arrows. Exhibits are tenderly described in English (€3.20, €6 combo-ticket includes €3 Museum of the Imperial City, daily April–Oct 9:30–18:00, Nov and Jan–March 14:00–16:00, Dec 13:00–16:00, last entry 45 min before closing, fun cards and posters, Burggasse 3-5, tel. 09861/5359, www.kriminalmuseum.rothenburg.de).

▲Dolls and Toy Museum—Two floors of historic *Kinder* cuteness is a hit with many. Pick up the free English binder for an extensive description of the exhibits (€4, family ticket-€10, daily March–Dec 9:30–18:00, Jan–Feb 11:00–17:00, just off Market Square, downhill from the fountain at Hofbronnengasse 13, tel. 09861/7330).

▲German Christmas Museum—Herr Wohlfahrt's passion is collecting and sharing historic Christmas decorations. This excellent museum, upstairs in the giant Käthe Wohlfahrt Christmas Villages shop, features a unique and thoughtfully described collection of Christmas-tree stands, mini-trees sent in boxes to WWI soldiers at the front, early Advent calendars, old-time Christmas cards, 450 clever ways to crack a nut, and a look at tree decorations through the ages—including the Nazi era and when you were a kid (€4, April–Dec daily 10:00–17:30, Jan–March only Sat–Sun 10:00–18:00, hours often change off-season, Herrngasse 1, 09861/409-365).

More Sights and Activities in Rothenburg

▲▲Walk the Wall—Just over a mile and a half around, providing great views and a good orientation, this walk can be done by those under six feet tall and without a camera in less than an hour. The hike requires no special sense of balance. This covered walk is a great option in the rain. Photographers go through lots of film, especially before breakfast or at sunset, when the lighting is best and the crowds are fewest. The best fortifications are in the Spitaltor (south end). Walk from there counterclockwise to the "forehead" (note on the Rothenburg map how the town outline looks like a head). Climb the Rödertor en route. The names you see along the way are people who donated money to rebuild the wall after World War II and those who've recently donated €1,000 per meter for the maintenance of Rothenburg's heritage.

▲Rödertor—The wall tower nearest the train station is the only one you can climb. It's worth the 135 steps for the view and a fascinating rundown on the bombing of Rothenburg in the last weeks of World War II, when the east part of the city was destroyed (€1, unreliable hours, usually open daily but closed for lunch April–Oct, closed Nov–March, photos of WWII damage with English translations). If you climb this, you can skip the Town Hall tower.

Sightseeing Lowlights—St. Wolfgang's Church is a fortified Gothic church built into the medieval wall at Klingentor. Its dungeon-like passages and shepherd's-dance exhibit are pretty lame (€1.50, April–Sept Wed–Mon 11:00–13:00 & 14:00–17:00, Oct until 16:00, closed Tue and Nov–March). The cute-looking Farming Museum (Bäuerliches Museum) next door is even worse. The 700-year-old Tradesman's House (Rothenburger Handwerkerhaus) shows the everyday life of a Rothenburger in the town's heyday (€2.20, April–Oct daily 9:00–18:00, Nov–Dec Mon–Fri 14:00–16:00, Sat–Sun 10:00–16:00, closed Jan–March, Alter Stadtgraben 26, near Markus Tower, tel. 09861/94280).

SHOPPING

Be warned...Rothenburg is one of Germany's best shopping towns. Do it here and be done with it. Lovely prints, carvings, wineglasses, Christmas-tree ornaments, and beer steins are popular.

The Käthe Wohlfahrt Christmas trinkets phenomenon is spreading across the half-timbered reaches of Europe. In Rothenburg, tourists flock to two **Käthe Wohlfahrt Christmas Villages** (on either side of Herrngasse, just off Market Square). This Christmas wonderland is filled with enough twinkling lights to require a special electric hookup, instant Christmas mood music (best appreciated on a hot day in July), and American and Japanese tourists hungrily filling little woven shopping baskets with €5–8 goodies to hang on their trees. Let the spinning flocked tree whisk you in, but pause at the wall of Steiffs, jerking uncontrollably and mesmerizing little kids. (OK, I admit it, my Christmas tree sports a few KW ornaments.) Note: Prices are padded with tour-guide incentives (Mon–Fri 9:00–18:00, Sat 9:00–16:00, Sun 10:00–18:00, tel. 09861/4090, www.wohlfahrt.de). The **Christmas Museum** upstairs (see page 502) is very good but dumps you back in the store, compelled now by the fascinating history to buy even more. Factor this likely extra expense into the museum's already steep €4 admission fee.

The **Friese shop** offers a charming contrast (just off Market Square, west of TI, on corner across from public WC). Cuckoo with friendliness, trinkets, and souvenirs, it gives shoppers with this book tremendous service: a 10 percent discount, 16 percent tax deducted if you have it mailed, and a free map (normally €1.50). Anneliese, who runs the place with her sons Frankie and Berni and grandson Rene (who played American football), charges only her cost for shipping and money exchange, and lets tired travelers leave their bags in her back room for free. For fewer crowds and better service, visit after 14:00 (Mon–Sat 8:00–17:00, Sun 9:30–17:00, tel. 09861/7166, fax 09861/936-619, friese-kabalo@gmx.de).

The Ernst Geissendörfer **print shop** sells fine prints, etchings, and paintings. Show this book for 10 percent off marked prices on all cash purchases (or minimum €50 credit-card purchases) and a free shot of German brandy to sip while you browse (Mon–Sat 10:00–18:00, Sun 10:00–17:00, late Dec–April, closed Sun, enter through bear shop on corner where Market Square hits Schmiedgasse, go up one floor, tel. 09861/2005).

For characteristic wineglasses, wine-making gear, and the real thing from the town's oldest wine-makers, drop by the **Weinladen am Plönlein** (daily 8:30–18:00, Plönlein 27—see "Wine Drinking in the Old Center," page 513, for info on wine-tasting).

Shoppers who mail their goodies home can get handy €2.50 boxes at the **post office** in the shopping center across from the train station (Mon–Fri 9:00–17:00, Sat 9:30–12:00, closed Sun).

Those who prefer to eat their souvenirs shop the *Bäckereien* (bakeries). Their succulent pastries, pies, and cakes are pleasantly distracting...but skip the bad-tasting Rothenburger *Schneebälle.*

SLEEPING

Rothenburg is crowded with visitors, but most are day-trippers. Except for the rare Saturday night and festivals (see "Festivals," page 495), finding a room is easy throughout the year.

Many hotels and guesthouses will pick up tired heavy-packers at the station. You may be greeted at the station by *Zimmer* skimmers who have rooms to rent. If you have reservations, resist them and honor your reservation. But if you haven't booked ahead, try talking yourself into one of these more desperate bed-and-breakfast rooms for a youth-hostel price. Be warned: These people are notorious for taking you to distant hotels and then charging you for the ride back if you decline a room.

If you're driving and unable to find your place, stop and give them a call. They will likely rescue you.

In the Old Town

$$$ Gasthof Greifen, once the home of Mayor Toppler, is a big, traditional, 600-year-old place with large rooms and all the comforts. It's run by a fine family staff and creaks with rustic splendor (small Sb-€38, Sb-€48, Db-€60–82, Tb-€97–102, Qb-€117–122, 10 percent off for 3-night stay, self- or full-service laundry, free and easy parking, half a block downhill from Market Square at Obere Schmiedgasse 5, tel. 09861/2281, fax 09861/86374, www.gasthof-greifen.rothenburg.de, info@gasthof-greifen.rothenburg.de, Brigitte and Klingler family). The family also runs a restaurant, serving basic meals in the garden or dining room.

$$$ Hotel Gerberhaus, a classy new hotel in an old building, is warmly run by Inge and Kurt, who mix modern comforts into 20 bright and airy rooms while maintaining a sense of half-

Sleep Code

(€1 = about $1.20, country code: 49, area code: 09861)
S = Single, **D** = Double/Twin, **T** = Triple, **Q** = Quad, **b** = bathroom, **s** = shower only, **SE** = Speaks English, **NSE** = No English. Unless otherwise noted, credit cards are accepted, English is spoken, and breakfast is included.

To help you sort easily through these listings, I've divided the rooms into three categories, based on the price for a standard double room with bath:

$$$ Higher Priced—Most rooms €65 or more.
$$ Moderately Priced—Most rooms between €40–65.
$ Lower Priced—Most rooms €40 or less.

Rothenburg Hotels

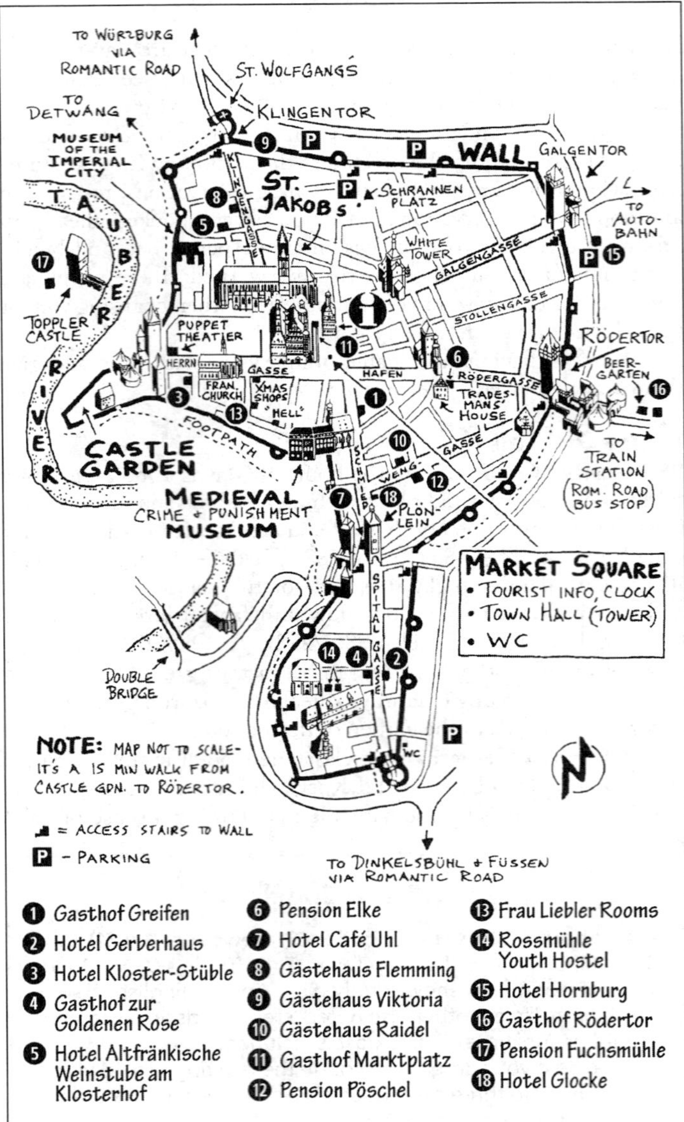

timbered elegance. Enjoy the pleasant garden in back (Sb-€48–56, Db-€56–79, Tb-€94–99, Qb-€104–114, prices depend on room size, 2-room apartment with kitchen-€89/2 people, €120/4 people, 5 percent off and a free *Schneeball* if you stay 2 nights and pay cash, most rooms non-smoking, some rooms with canopied 4-poster *Himmel* beds, free Internet access, laundry-€4/load, Spitalgasse 25, tel. 09861/94900, fax 09861/86555, www.gerberhaus.rothenburg.de, gerberhaus@t-online.de). The downstairs café and beer garden serve good soups, salads, and light lunches.

$$$ Hotel Kloster-Stüble, deep in the old town near the castle garden, is my classiest listing. Jutta greets her guests while husband Rudolf does the cooking, and Erika (SE) is the fun and energetic first mate who really runs the show. In 2004, the hotel expanded into the building next door, adding a breakfast room and eight gorgeous, modern rooms within the historic shell (Sb-€55–60, Db-€75–90, Tb-€110–115, family rooms-€110–155, ask about the luxurious apartment with kitchen and balcony or suites-€105 for 2 or up to €215 for 6, €3 extra on weekends, family deals, kids under 5 free, Heringsbronnengasse 5, tel. 09861/6774, fax 09861/6474, www.klosterstueble.de, hotel@klosterstueble.de).

$$$ Hotel Glocke, owned by the Thürauf family since 1898, is a clean, family-friendly place just blocks from Market Square. Their 24 comfortable rooms above their fine restaurant feature lots of traditional, woodsy accents, but are a bit pricey. Frau Thürauf runs a tight ship, making a great effort to make her guests feel welcome (Db-€80–105, depending on size, family rooms, in-house garage €4.50/day, Plönlein 1, tel. 09861/958-990, fax 09861/958-9922, www.glocke-rothenburg.de, glocke.rothenburg@t-online.de).

$$ Gasthof zur Goldenen Rose is a classic, family-run place—simple, traditional, comfortable, and a great value—where scurrying Karin serves breakfast and stately Henni (SE) keeps everything in good order. The hotel has one shower per floor, but the rooms are clean, and you're surrounded by cobbles, flowers, and red-tiled roofs (S-€21, D-€36, Ds-€46, Db-€49, some triples, spacious family apartment-€107/4 people, €128/5 people, kid-friendly, streetside rooms can be noisy, closed Jan–Feb, Spitalgasse 28, tel. 09861/4638, fax 09861/86417, www.thegoldenrose.de, info@thegoldenrose.de). The Favetta family also serves good, reasonably priced meals (restaurant closed Wed). Keep your key to get in after hours (side gate in alley).

$$ Hotel Altfränkische Weinstube am Klosterhof is the place for well-heeled bohemians. Mario and lovely Hanne rent six cozy rooms above their dark and smoky pub in a 600-year-old building. It's an upscale, *Monty Python* atmosphere, with TVs, modern showers, open-beam ceilings, and *Himmel* beds—canopied four-poster "heaven" beds (Sb-€45, Db-€55–65, Db suite-€75,

Tb-€70, prefer cash, kid-friendly, off Klingengasse at Klosterhof 7, tel. 09861/6404, fax 09861/6410, www.romanticroad.com/altfraenkische-weinstube). Their pub is a candlelit classic, serving hot food until 22:30 and closing at 1:00 in the morning. Drop by on Wednesday evening (19:30–24:00) for the English Conversation Club (see "Meet the Locals," page 513).

$$ Pension Elke, run by the spry Erich Endress and his son Klaus, rents 10 bright, airy, and comfy rooms above the family grocery store (S-€25, Sb-€35, D-€38–46, Db-€58–62, prices depend on size, extra bed-€15, cash only, reception in grocery store until 19:00, otherwise go around corner onto Alter Stadtgraben to first door on left and ring bell at top of stairs, near Markus Tower at Rodergasse 6, tel. 09861/2331, fax 09861/935-355, www.pension-elke-rothenburg.de—in German only, info@pension-elke-rothenburg.de).

$$ Hotel Café Uhl offers 10 fine rooms over a bakery (Sb-€30–35, Db-€50–65, prices depend on size, third person-€18, fourth person-€13, non-smoking rooms, parking-€4/day, reception in café, closed Jan, Plönlein 8, tel. 09861/4895, fax 09861/92820, www.hotel-uhl.de, info@hotel-uhl.de, Paul and Robert the baker SE).

$$ Gästehaus Flemming has seven tastefully modern, fresh, and comfortable rooms and a peaceful garden behind St. Jakob's Church (Sb-€45, Db-€55, Tb-€75, cash only, Klingengasse 21, tel. 09861/92380, fax 09861/976-384, www.gaestehaus-flemming.de, gaestehaus-flemming@t-online.de, Regina SE).

$$ Gästehaus Viktoria is a cheery little place right next to the town wall. Its three rooms overflow with furniture, ribbons, and silk flowers, and lovely gardens surround the house (Db-€45–50, Tb-€60, cash only, a block from Klingentor at Klingenschutt 4, tel. 09861/87682, Hanne SE).

$$ Gästehaus Raidel, a creaky 500-year-old house filled with beds and furniture all handmade by friendly Herr Raidel himself, rents 14 large rooms with cramped facilities down the hall. The ambience makes me want to sing the *Addams Family* theme song—but it works in a pinch (S-€19, Sb-€29, D-€39, Db-€49, Tb-€70, cash only, Wenggasse 3, tel. 09861/3115, fax 09861/935-255, best to reserve through Web site at www.romanticroad.com/raidel, gaestehaus-raidel@t-online.de, Herr Raidel SE).

$$ Gasthof Marktplatz, right on Market Square, rents nine tidy rooms with 1970s-era wallpaper and unenthusiastic staff (S-€21, D-€38, Ds-€43, Db-€48, T-€50, Ts-€57, Tb-€62, cash only, Grüner Markt 10, tel. & fax 09861/1662, www.gasthof-marktplatz.de, Herr Rosner SE). The maddening Town Hall bells ring throughout the night.

$$ Pension Pöschel is friendly, with six bearskin-cozy rooms in a concrete but pleasant building and an inviting garden out back (S-€20, D-€35, Db-€45, T-€45, Tb-€55, small kids free, cash only,

Wenggasse 22, tel. 09861/3430, pension.poeschel@t-online.de, Bettina SE).

$ Frau Liebler rents two large, modern, ground-floor rooms with kitchenettes and hardwood floors (Db-€40, cash only, breakfast in room, off Market Square behind Christmas shop, Pfaffleinsgasschen 10, tel. 09861/709-215, fax 09861/709-216).

$ ***Hostel:*** Here in Bavaria, hostelling is limited to those under 27, except for families traveling with children under 18. The fine **Rossmühle Youth Hostel** has 184 beds in two buildings. The droopy-eyed building (the old town horse mill, used when the town was under siege and the river-powered mill was inaccessible) houses groups and the office. The adjacent hostel is mostly for families and individuals (dorm beds-€19, bunk-bed Db- €43, includes breakfast and sheets, dinner-€5.40, self-serve laundry-€4, entrance on Rossmühlgasse, tel. 09861/94160, fax 09861/941-620, www.rothenburg.jugendherberge.de, jhrothenburg@djh-bayern.de). Reserve long in advance.

Outside the Wall

The first two places are a hundred yards outside the wall on the train-station side of town (less than a 10-min walk from the center) and are among the nicest rooms I recommend in town. The third is a rustic adventure below the town in what feels like a wilderness.

$$$ Hotel Hornburg, a grand 100-year-old mansion with groomed grounds and 10 spacious, tastefully decorated rooms, is a two-minute walk outside the wall and a super value (Sb-€52–67, Db-€69–98, Tb-€90–115, ground-floor rooms, non-smoking rooms, family-friendly, avoid if you're allergic to dogs, parking-€3/day; if walking, exit station and go straight on Ludwig-Siebert Strasse, turn left on Mann Strasse until you're 100 yards from town wall; if driving, exit station but go left on Vorm Würzburger Tor; Hornburgweg 28, tel. 09861/8480, fax 09861/5570, www.hotel-hornburg.de, hotelhornburg@t-online.de, friendly Gabriele and Martin SE).

$$$ Gasthof Rödertor offers 15 decent rooms in a quiet setting one block outside the Rödertor. This guesthouse has an inviting breakfast room with a farmhouse flair, a popular beer garden, and a restaurant dedicated to the potato (see "Beer Gardens and Discos," page 512). Guest rooms in an annex inside the wall are slightly cheaper (Db-€65–80, Tb-€70–105, Qb-€90–125, Ansbacher Strasse 7, tel. 09861/2022, fax 09861/86324, www.roedertor.com, hotel@roedertor.com, Frau Teutscher and her daughter Katie SE).

$$ Pension Fuchsmühle is a B&B in a renovated old mill on the river below the castle end of Rothenburg. The place is a work-in-progress, with kids and a linoleum-floor feel, but if you want a rustic, countryside experience, it's great. Alex and Heidi

Molitor rent six rooms and take good care of their guests (Sb-€37, Db-€55, Tb-€75, Qb-€85, extra bed-€15, €5 less after 3 nights, non-smoking, healthy farm-fresh breakfasts, piano, free tours of mill, free pickup at station, across the street from Toppler's little castle at Taubertalweg 103, tel. 09861/92633, www.fuchsmuehle.de, fuchsmuehle@t-online.de). It's a steep but pleasant 15-minute hike from the Fuchsmühle to Market Square. The Molitors provide flashlights for your return after dark.

EATING

Most restaurants serve meals only 11:30–13:30 and 18:00–20:00. Places listed are within a five-minute walk of Market Square. While all survive on tourism, many still feel like local hangouts. Your choices are typical Franconian or ethnic.

Traditional Franconian Restaurants

Restaurant Glocke, a *Weinstube* (wine bar) popular with locals, is run by Rothenburg's oldest wine-makers, the Thürauf family. Their seasonal menu is complemented by their family wine, served under an atmospheric, big-beamed ceiling. The menu is in German only because the friendly staff wants to explain your options in person. Don't miss their €4.20 deal to sample five Franconian wines (€10–15, Mon–Sat 10:30–23:00, Sun 10:30–14:00, vegetarian options, Plönlein 1, tel. 09861/958-990).

At **Zur Goldenen Rose,** Reno cooks up traditional German fare at good prices, as Henni stokes your appetite (Tue 11:30–14:00, Thu–Mon 11:30–14:00 & 17:30–20:30, closed Wed, Spitalgasse 28; leafy garden terrace out back open in sunny weather).

Extremely picturesque and touristy, **Baumeister Haus,** tucked deep behind a streetside pastry counter and antlered dining room, fills an inviting courtyard with people who don't understand a German menu (€8–15, daily 8:00–23:00, closes earlier off-season and when slow, a few doors below Market Square, Obere Schmiedgasse 3, tel. 09861/94700).

For cellar dining under medieval murals and pointy pikes, consider **Bürgerkeller,** where Herr Terian and his family pride themselves in quality local cuisine and offer a small but inviting menu and reasonable prices (€7–14, daily 11:30–14:00 & 18:00–21:00, near bottom of Herrngasse at #24, tel. 09861/2126).

Reichs-Küchenmeister is a typical big-hotel restaurant, but on a balmy evening, its pleasant tree-shaded terrace overlooking St. Jakob's Church is hard to beat (€8–16, daily 11:00–22:00, non-smoking room, nouveau German menu, some veggie choices, Kirchplatz 8, tel. 09861/9700).

Rothenburg Restaurants

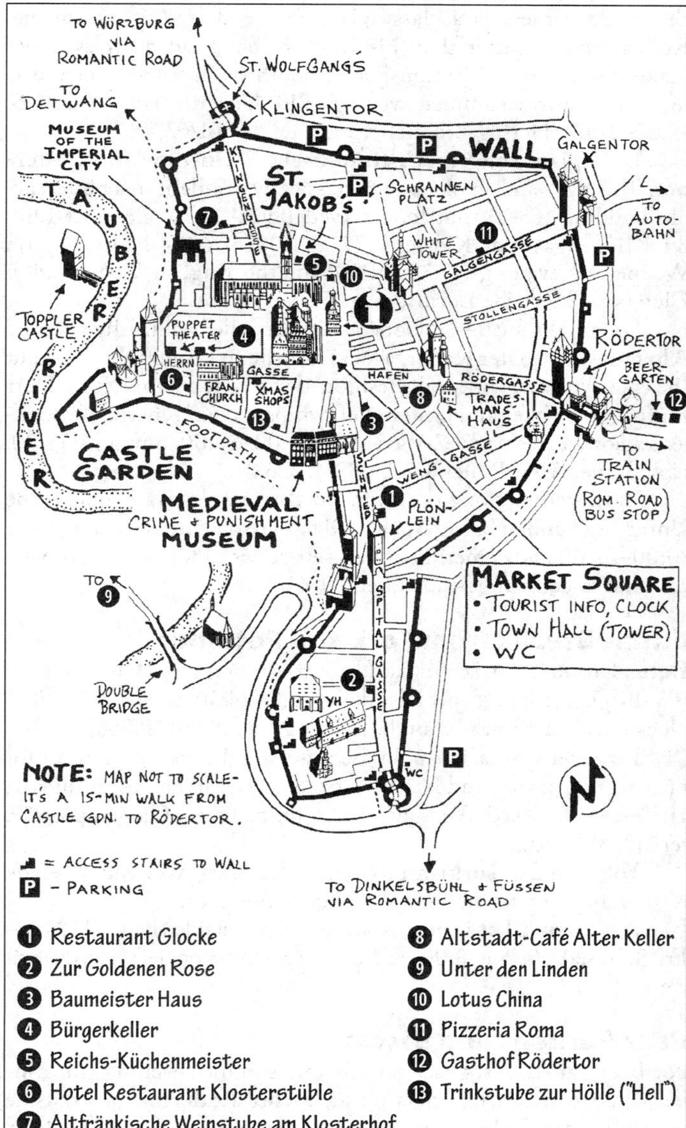

1. Restaurant Glocke
2. Zur Goldenen Rose
3. Baumeister Haus
4. Bürgerkeller
5. Reichs-Küchenmeister
6. Hotel Restaurant Klosterstüble
7. Altfränkische Weinstube am Klosterhof
8. Altstadt-Café Alter Keller
9. Unter den Linden
10. Lotus China
11. Pizzeria Roma
12. Gasthof Rödertor
13. Trinkstube zur Hölle ("Hell")

Hotel Restaurant Klosterstüble, deep in the old town near the castle garden, is a classy place for good traditional cuisine. Rudy's food is better than his English, but head waitress Erika makes sure communication goes smoothly. The shady terrace is nice on a warm summer evening (€10–15, daily 11:00–14:00 & 18:00–21:00, Heringsbronnengasse 5, tel. 09861/6774).

Bohemians enjoy the **Altfränkische Weinstube am Klosterhof.** This dark and smoky pub is classically candlelit in a 600-year-old building (€5–11, hot food served 18:00–22:30, closes at 1:00, off Klingengasse at Klosterhof 7, tel. 09861/6404). Drop by on Wednesday evening (19:30–24:00) for the English Conversation Club (see "Meet the Locals," page 513).

For a light meal—indoors or out—try the beautifully restored **Altstadt-Café Alter Keller,** a local favorite. It's central but without the crazy crowds, with walls festooned with old pots and jugs. Herr Hufnagel, a baker and pastry chef, whips up giant meringue cookies and other treats (€3–7, Wed–Mon 11:00–20:00, Sun until 18:00, closed Tue, Alter Keller 8, tel. 09861/2268).

In the valley along the river, worth the 20-minute hike, is the **Unter den Linden** beer garden (daily in season with decent weather 10:00–22:00 and sometimes later, self-service food and good beer, call first to confirm it's open, tel. 09861/5909).

Ethnic Breaks from Pork and Potatoes

Lotus China is a peaceful world apart, serving good Chinese food (€8–10 plates, lunch specials, daily 11:30–14:30 & 17:30–23:00, 2 blocks behind TI near church, Eckele 2, tel. 09861/86886).

Pizzeria Roma is smoky because it's the locals' favorite for €6.50 pizza, pastas, and Italian wine. Service can be slow (Thu–Tue 11:30–24:00, closed Wed, also has schnitzel fare, Galgengasse 19, tel. 09861/4540).

You'll find a **Turkish** place on Schrannengasse and a **Greek** restaurant just outside the wall opposite Spitaltor.

A **supermarket** is near Rödertor, just outside the wall (Mon–Fri 8:00–20:00, Sat 8:00–16:00, closed Sun, on left as you exit wall).

Beer Gardens and Discos

For beer-garden festivities on a balmy summer evening (for dinner or beer), Rothenburgers pick **Gasthof Rödertor,** just outside the wall through the Rödertor gate (May–Sept daily 17:00–24:00, look for wood gate). Their *Kartoffeln Stube* inside is dedicated to the potato (€6–10, daily 11:30–14:00 & 17:30–23:00, tel. 09861/2022).

Two popular **discos** are just down the street: Black Out (Ansbacher 15, in alley next to Sparkasse bank, open Wed and Fri–Sat 22:00–3:00, closed Sun–Tue and Thu) and Club 23 (around corner from bank on Adam Hörber Strasse, open Thu–Sat from 22:00, closed Sun–Mon, tel. 09861/933-045).

Wine Drinking in the Old Center

Trinkstube zur Hölle ("Hell") is dark and foreboding, but they offer thick wine-drinking atmosphere with lots of locals and a short menu until late (a block past Medieval Crime and Punishment Museum on Burggasse, with devil hanging out front, tel. 09861/4229). Mario's **Altfränkische Weinstube** (see "Traditional Franconian Restaurants," page 510) is similarly atmospheric. Wine-lovers enjoy **Restaurant Glocke**'s *Weinstube* (recommended above); for €4.20, you can sample five of their Franconian wines—choose dry or half-dry (Mon–Sat 10:30–23:00, Sun 10:30–14:00, Plönlein 1, tel. 09861/958-990). You're welcome to enjoy just the wine without eating.

Meet the Locals

For a rare chance to mix it up with locals who aren't selling anything, bring your favorite slang and tongue twisters to the **English Conversation Club** at Mario's Altfränkische Weinstube am Klosterhof (Wed 19:30–24:00, Anneliese from Friese shop and Hermann the German are regulars; see restaurant listed under "Traditional Franconian Restaurants," above). This group of intrepid linguists celebrated their 1,000th meeting in 2003.

TRANSPORTATION CONNECTIONS

From Rothenburg by Bus: The Romantic Road bus tour takes you in and out of Rothenburg each day (April–Oct), heading to Munich (via Füssen) or Frankfurt. See the schedule and tour description below.

By Train: A tiny train line connects Rothenburg to the outside world via **Steinach** (almost hrly, 15 min). If you plan to arrive in Rothenburg by train, note that the last train to Rothenburg departs nightly from Steinach at 20:30 (if you arrive in Steinach after 20:30, call one of the **taxi** services for a €22 ride to Rothenburg; ideally order the taxi at least an hour in advance: tel. 09861/2000, 09861/7227, or 09861/95100). For those leaving Rothenburg by train, the first train to Steinach departs at 6:00, the last at 20:00.

From Steinach by Train to: Rothenburg (almost hrly, 15 min, last train at 20:00), **Würzburg** (hrly, 1 hr), **Nürnberg** (2/hr, 1–1.5 hr, most change in Ansbach or Neustadt an der Aisch), **Munich** (hrly, 3 hrs, 2 changes), **Frankfurt** (hrly, 2.5 hrs, change in Würzburg). Train connections in Steinach are usually within a few minutes (to Rothenburg generally from track 5). Train info: tel. 11861 (€0.46/min).

Romantic Road

The Romantic Road (Romantische Strasse) winds you past the most beautiful towns and scenery of Germany's medieval heartland. Once Germany's medieval trade route, now it's the best way to connect the dots between Füssen, Munich, and Frankfurt (www.romantischestrasse.de).

Wander through quaint hills and rolling villages, and stop wherever the cows look friendly or a town fountain beckons. My favorite sections are from Füssen to Landsberg and Rothenburg to Weikersheim. (If you're driving with limited time, connect Rothenburg and Munich by autobahn.) Caution: The similarly promoted "Castle Road," which runs between Rothenburg and Mannheim, sounds intriguing but is nowhere near as interesting.

Throughout Bavaria, you'll see colorfully ornamented maypoles decorating town squares. Many are painted in Bavaria's colors, white and blue. The decorations that line each side of the pole symbolize the crafts or businesses of that community. Each May Day, they are festively replaced. Traditionally, rival communities try to steal each other's maypole. Locals will guard their new pole night and day as May Day approaches. Stolen poles are ransomed only with lots of beer for the clever thieves.

Getting Around the Romantic Road

By Bus: The Deutsche Touring company runs buses daily between Frankfurt and Munich (via Füssen) in each direction (April–Oct, tel. 069/790-350, www.deutsche-touring.com). Confirm departures and arrivals when you buy your ticket, because schedules aren't posted and special events can temporarily change bus-stop locations and schedules.

Buses usually leave from train stations (in towns large enough to have one) but are not well signed. The ride costs €95 and takes 13 hrs if you go all the way from Frankfurt to Munich (pay cash on the bus, luggage storage costs a few extra euros). You can get a 60 percent discount if you have a German railpass, Eurailpass, or Eurail Selectpass (if Germany is one of the selected countries). Students and seniors—without a railpass—get a 10 percent discount. Buses stop too briefly in Rothenburg (about 20 min) and Dinkelsbühl (about 20–40 min), and just long enough to use the WC at a few other attractions. The grim drivers usually hand out maps and brochures and play a tape-recorded narration of the journey highlights in English. Bus reservations are almost never necessary. But they are free and easy, and, technically, without one you can lose your seat to someone who has one (call 069/790-350 to reserve). You can start and stop where you like. There is no easier way to travel across Germany and get such

Romantic Road Bus Schedule

The following times are based on the 2005 schedule. Check www.euraide.de/ricksteves for any changes.

North to South

Depart Frankfurt	08:00
Depart Würzburg	10:00
Arrive Rothenburg Old Town (Schrannenplatz)	11:50
Depart Rothenburg Old Town	12:10
Arrive Dinkelsbühl	12:50
Depart Dinkelsbühl	13:30
Depart Augsburg	16:05
Depart Füssen	19:15
Arrive Munich	21:00

South to North

Depart Munich	08:00
Depart Füssen	09:50
Arrive Wieskirche	11:00
Depart Wieskirche	11:15
Depart Augsburg	14:00
Arrive Dinkelsbühl	16:05
Depart Dinkelsbühl	16:25
Arrive Rothenburg Old Town (Schrannenplatz)	17:05
Depart Rothenburg Old Town	17:30
Depart Würzburg	19:35
Arrive Frankfurt	21:00

a hearty dose of its countryside. But if you prefer urban sights and speedy trains, this can seem like a glorified Greyhound ride with a beverage service (free coffee, €1 for cold drinks).

By Car: Follow the brown Romantische Strasse signs and the free tourist brochure (available all over the place) that describes the journey.

SIGHTS

Along the Romantic Road

These sights are listed from north to south.

Frankfurt—The northern terminus of the Romantic Road is in this country's Manhattan (covered in *Rick Steves' Germany & Austria 2006*).

▲▲Würzburg—This historic city, though freshly rebuilt since World War II, is worth a stop for its impressive Prince Bishop's

The Romantic Road

Residenz, the bubbly Baroque chapel (Hofkirche) next door, and the palace's sculpted gardens. The helpful TI is on the Marktplatz (April–Dec Mon–Fri 10:00–18:00, Sat 10:00–14:00, May–Oct also Sun 10:00–14:00; Jan–March Mon–Fri 10:00–16:00, Sat 10:00–13:00, closed Sun, tel. 0931/372-398, www.wuerzburg.de).

The Residenz is a Franconian Versailles, with grand rooms, 3-D art, and a recently-restored tennis-court-sized fresco by Tiepolo (€5, April–Oct daily 9:00–18:00, Nov–March daily 10:00–16:00, last entry 30 min before closing, no photos, tel. 0931/355-1712). English tours are offered daily at 11:00 and 15:00 (May–Oct, confirm at TI or call ahead). The elaborate Hofkirche chapel is next door (as you exit the palace, go left) and the entrance to the picnic-worthy garden is just beyond. Easy parking is available. Don't confuse the Residenz (a 15-min walk southeast of the train station) with Marienberg fortress on the hilltop.

Weikersheim—This untouristy town has a palace with fine Baroque gardens (luxurious picnic spot), a folk museum, and a picturesque town square.

▲**Herrgottskapelle**—This peaceful church is graced with Tilman Riemenschneider's greatest carved altarpiece (Easter–Oct daily 9:15–17:30, less off-season, tel. 07933/508). Across the street is the Fingerhut (thimble, literally "finger hat") museum (€2, April–Oct daily 9:00–18:00, less off-season, tel. 07933/370). The southbound Romantic Road bus stops here for 15 minutes, long enough to see one or the other. The church and museum are a mile south of Creglingen (TI tel. 07933/631, www.creglingen.de—German only).

▲▲▲**Rothenburg**—See above for information on Germany's best medieval town.

▲**Dinkelsbühl**—Rothenburg's little sister is cute enough to merit a short stop. A moat, towers, gates, and a beautifully preserved medieval wall surround this town. Dinkelsbühl's history museum is meager and without a word of English. The Kinderzeche children's festival celebrates the success of the local children who pleaded with the Swedish army during the Thirty Years War, convincing them to spare the town. The festival turns Dinkelsbühl wonderfully on end for a week at the end of July. The helpful TI on the main street sells maps with a short walking tour and can help find rooms (Mon–Fri 9:00–18:00, Sat 10:00–13:00 & 14:00–16:00, Sun 10:00–13:00, shorter hours off-season, tel. 09851/90240, www.dinkelsbuehl.de).

Nördlingen—Known for its 15-mile-wide valley that was carved by a meteor 15 million years ago, Nördlingen separates the Schwabian and Franconian Alps. (The town also gained fame as the "grain basket" because of its rich soil.) Apollo astronauts did research and field training here; if you visit the museum dedicated to the study of the meteor (Rieskrater Museum), so can you (daily 10:00–12:00 & 13:30–16:30, closed Mon, Eugene Shoemaker Platz 1, tel. 09081/273-8220).

Augsburg—Founded more than 2,000 years ago by Emperor Augustus, Augsburg enjoyed its heyday in the 15th and 16th centuries. Today, it's Bavaria's third largest city, and the place where the idea for the "Romantic Road" originated.

Röttenbuch—This nondescript village has an impressive church in a lovely setting. The bus stops here only on request.

Landsberg am Lech—Like many towns in this area, Landsberg (on the river Lech) has its roots in salt trade. Every four years, the town returns to its medieval roots and hosts the Ruethen Pageant. The town, founded the same year as Munich (1158), was shaped by the architect Dominikus Zimmerman (of Wieskirche fame). Adolf Hitler wrote *Mein Kampf* while serving his prison sentence here after the Beerhall Putsch of 1923 (when Hitler and his followers unsuccessfully attempted to take over the government of Bavaria).

▲▲**Wieskirche**—This is Germany's most glorious Baroque-rococo church, beautifully restored and set in a sweet meadow. Heavenly! Northbound Romantic Road buses from Füssen stop here for 15 minutes. (See the Bavaria and Tirol chapter.)

Füssen—This town, a stop on the Romantic Road and three miles from the stunning Neuschwanstein Castle, is worth a stop on any sightseeing agenda. (See the Bavaria and Tirol chapter for description and accommodations.)

RHINE VALLEY

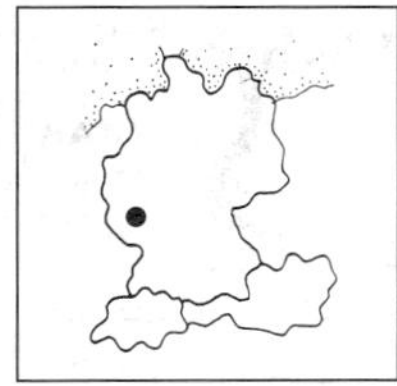

The Rhine Valley is storybook Germany, a fairytale world of legends and robber-baron castles. Cruise the most castle-studded stretch of the romantic Rhine as you listen for the song of the treacherous Loreley. For hands-on castle thrills, climb through the Rhineland's greatest castle, Rheinfels, above the town of St. Goar. Castle connoisseurs will enjoy the fine interior of Marksburg Castle. Spend your nights in a castle-crowned village, either Bacharach or St. Goar.

Planning Your Time

For a good look, cruise in, tour a castle or two, sleep in a genuine medieval town, and take the train out. If you have limited time, cruise less and explore Rheinfels Castle.

Ideally, spend two nights here, sleep in Bacharach, cruise the best hour of the river (from Bacharach to St. Goar), and tour the Rheinfels Castle. Those with more time can ride the riverside bike path. With two days and a car, go castle-hopping.

The Rhine

Ever since Roman times, when this was the empire's northern boundary, the Rhine has been one of the world's busiest shipping rivers. You'll see a steady flow of barges with 1,000- to 2,000-ton loads. Tourist-packed buses, hot train tracks, and highways line both banks.

Many of the castles were "robber-baron" castles, put there by petty rulers (there were 300 independent little countries in

Rhine Overview

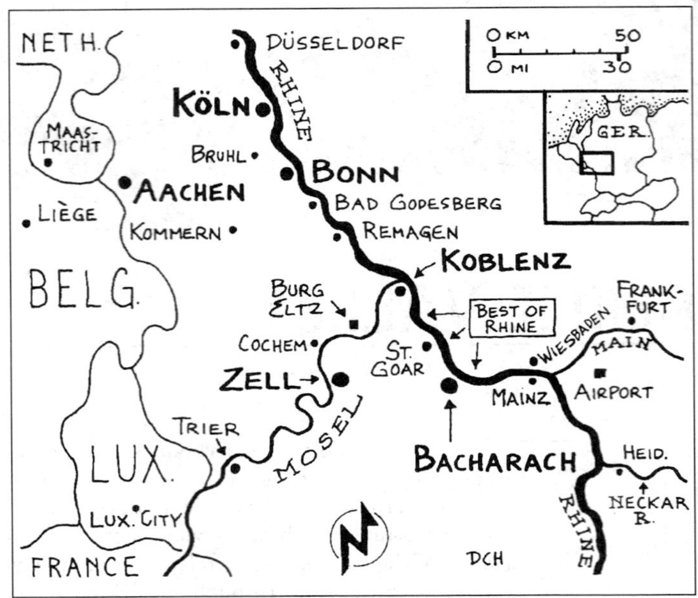

medieval Germany) to levy tolls on passing river traffic. A robber baron would put his castle on, or even in, the river. Then, often with the help of chains and a tower on the opposite bank, he'd stop each ship and get his toll. There were 10 customs stops in the 60-mile stretch between Mainz and Koblenz alone (no wonder merchants were early proponents of the creation of larger nation-states).

Some castles were built to control and protect settlements, and others were the residences of kings. As times changed, so did the lifestyles of the rich and feudal. Many castles were abandoned for more comfortable mansions in the towns.

Most Rhine castles date from the 11th, 12th, and 13th centuries. When the pope successfully asserted his power over the German emperor in 1076, local princes ran wild over the rule of their emperor. The castles saw military action in the 1300s and 1400s, as emperors began reasserting their control over Germany's many silly kingdoms.

The castles were also involved in the Reformation wars, in which Europe's Catholic and Protestant dynasties fought it out using a fragmented Germany as their battleground. The Thirty Years' War (1618–1648) devastated Germany. The outcome: Each ruler got the freedom to decide if his people would be Catholic or Protestant, and one-third of Germany was dead. Production of Gummi bears ceased entirely.

The French—who feared a strong Germany and felt the Rhine was the logical border between them and Germany—destroyed most of the castles prophylactically (Louis XIV in the 1680s, the revolutionary army in the 1790s, and Napoleon in 1806). They were often rebuilt in neo-Gothic style in the Romantic age—the late 1800s—and today are enjoyed as restaurants, hotels, hostels, and museums.

For information on Rhine castles, visit www.burgen-am-rhein.de. For more on the Rhine, visit www.loreleytal.com (heavy on hotels but has maps, photos, and a little history).

Getting Around the Rhine

While the Rhine flows north from Switzerland to Holland, the scenic stretch from Mainz to Koblenz hoards all the touristic charm. Studded with the crenellated cream of Germany's castles, it bustles with boats, trains, and highway traffic. Have fun exploring with a mix of big steamers, tiny ferries *(Fähre),* trains, and bikes.

By Boat: While many travelers do the whole trip by boat, the most scenic hour is from St. Goar to Bacharach. Sit on the top deck with your handy Rhine map-guide (or the kilometer-keyed tour in this chapter) and enjoy the parade of castles, towns, boats, and vineyards.

There are several boat companies, but most travelers sail on the bigger, more expensive, and romantic Köln-Düsseldorfer (K-D) line (free with a consecutive-day Eurailpass or with dated Eurail Flexipass, Eurail Selectpass, or German railpass—but it uses up a day of any Flexipass, otherwise about €8.40 for the first hour, then progressively cheaper per hour; the recommended Bacharach–St. Goar trip costs €8.40 one-way, €10.20 round-trip; half-price days: Tue for bicyclists, Mon and Fri for seniors over 60, tel. 06741/1634 in St. Goar, tel. 06743/1322 in Bacharach, www.k-d.com). Boats run daily in both directions April through October, with no boats off-season. Complete, up-to-date schedules are posted in any station, Rhineland hotel, TI, bank, current Thomas Cook Timetable, or at www.euraide.de/ricksteves. Purchase tickets at the dock up to five minutes before departure. (Confirm times at your hotel the night before.) The boat is rarely full. Romantics will plan to catch the old-time *Goethe,* which sails each direction once a day (see "Rhine Cruise Schedule," page 522; confirm time locally).

The smaller Bingen-Rüdesheimer line is slightly cheaper than K-D (railpasses not valid, buy tickets on boat, tel. 06721/14140, www.bingen-ruedesheimer.com), with three two-hour round-trip St. Goar–Bacharach trips daily in summer (about €7.50 one-way, €9.50 round-trip; departing St. Goar at 11:00, 14:10, and 16:10; departing Bacharach at 10:10, 12:00, and 15:00).

By Car: Drivers have these options: 1) Skip the boat; 2) Take a

Rhine Cruise Schedule

Boats run May through September and on a reduced schedule for parts of April and October; no boats run November through March. These times are based on the 2005 schedule. Check www.euraide.de/ricksteves (boats heading from north to south) for any changes.

Koblenz	*Boppard*	*St. Goar*	*Bacharach*
→			
—	9:00	10:15	11:25
*9:00	*11:00	*12:20	*13:35
11:00	13:00	14:15	15:25
14:00	16:00	17:15	18:25
←			
13:10	11:50	10:55	10:15
14:10	12:50	11:55	11:15
—	13:50	12:55	12:15
18:10	16:50	15:55	15:15
*20:10	*18:50	*17:55	*17:15

**Riding the "Nostalgic Route," you'll take the 1913 steamer* Goethe, *with working paddle wheel and viewable engine room (departing Koblenz at 9:00 and Bacharach at 17:15).*

round-trip cruise from St. Goar or Bacharach; 3) Draw pretzels and let the loser drive, prepare the picnic, and meet the boat; 4) Rent a bike, bring it on the boat for free, and bike back; or 5) Take the boat one-way and return by train. When exploring by car, don't hesitate to pop onto one of the many little ferries that shuttle across the bridgeless-around-here river (see below).

By Ferry: While there are no bridges between Koblenz and Mainz, you'll see car-and-passenger ferries (usually family-run for generations) about every three miles. Ferries near St. Goar and Bacharach cross the river every 10 minutes daily in the summer from about 6:00 to 20:00, connecting Bingen–Rüdesheim, Lorch–Niederheimbach, Engelsburg–Kaub, and St. Goar–St.Goarshausen (adult-€1, car and driver-€2.80, pay on the boat).

By Bike: You can bike on either side of the Rhine, but for a designated bike path, stay on the west side, where a 35-mile path runs between Koblenz and Bingen. The stretch between St. Goar and Bingen hugs the riverside and is road-free (note that it can be closed temporarily if canal work needs to be done, in which case cyclists can just use the road). I'd join the in-line skaters along the interesting six-mile stretch between St. Goar and Bacharach. In St. Goar, Hotel am Markt rents bikes to its guests (€5/day). In

Bacharach, you can rent bikes at Pension Malerwinkel if you're a guest (€6/day) or get a free loaner bike if you're staying at Pension Winzerhaus.

Consider taking a bike on the Rhine boats (free with ticket) and then biking back, or designing a circular trip using the fun and frequent shuttle ferries. A good target might be Kaub (where a tiny boat shuttles sightseers to the better-from-a-distance castle on the island).

By Train: Hourly milk-run trains down the Rhine hit every town: St. Goar–Bacharach, 12 min; Bacharach–Mainz, 60 min; Mainz–Frankfurt, 45 min. Some train schedules list St. Goar but not Bacharach as a stop, but any schedule listing St. Goar also stops at Bacharach. Tiny stations are not staffed—buy tickets at the platform machines (best bet) or on the train (this is a lesser choice because you risk being fined €40 for not having a ticket; be sure to seek out the conductor immediately upon boarding rather than waiting for him/her to come to you). Prices are cheap (for example, €2.60 between St. Goar and Bacharach).

SIGHTS

The Romantic Rhine

These sights are listed from north to south, Koblenz to Bingen.

▲▲▲Der Romantische Rhein Blitz Zug Fahrt—One of Europe's great train thrills is zipping along the Rhine in this fast train tour. Here's a quick and easy, from-the-train-window tour (also works for car, bike, or best by boat; you can cut in anywhere) that skips the syrupy myths filling normal Rhine guides.

Sit on the left (river) side of the train or boat going south from Koblenz. While nearly all the castles listed are viewed from this side, clear a path to the right window for the times I yell, "Cross over!"

You'll notice large black-and-white kilometer markers along the riverbank. I erected these years ago to make this tour easier to follow. They tell the distance from the Rhinefalls, where the Rhine leaves Switzerland and becomes navigable. Now the river-barge pilots have accepted these as navigational aids as well. We're tackling just 36 miles (58 kilometers) of the 820-mile-long (1,320 kilometer) Rhine. Your Blitz Rhine Tour starts at Koblenz and heads upstream to Bingen. If you're going the other direction, it still works. Just hold the book upside down.

Km 590—Koblenz: This Rhine blitz starts with Romantic Rhine thrills—at Koblenz. Koblenz is not a nice city (it was really hit hard in World War II), but its place as the historic *Deutsche Eck* (German corner)—the tip of land where the Mosel joins the Rhine—gives it a certain historic charm. Koblenz, from the Latin for "confluence," has Roman origins. Walk through the park,

Best of the Rhine

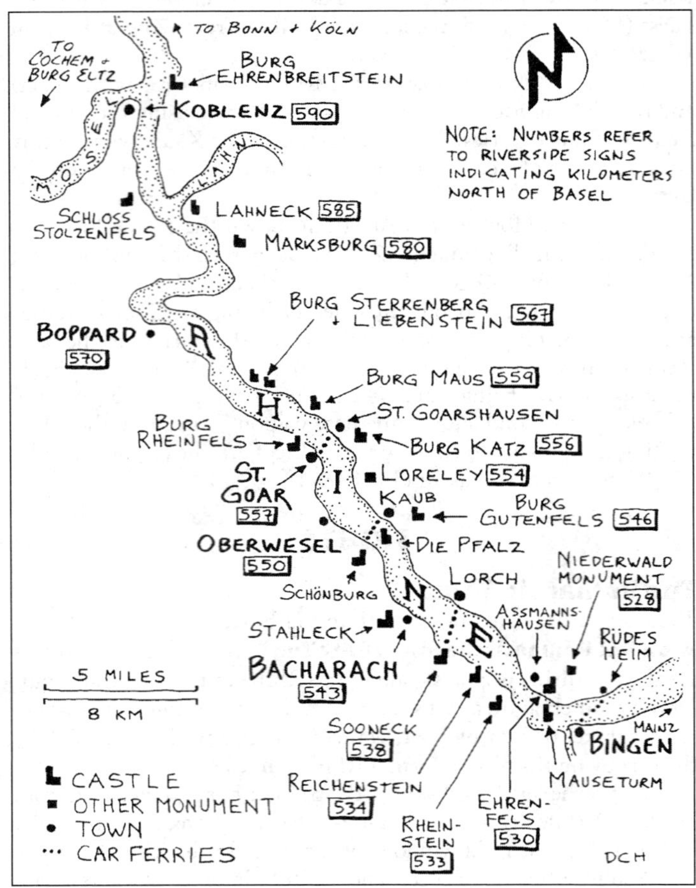

noticing the reconstructed memorial to the kaiser. Across the river, the yellow Ehrenbreitstein Castle now houses a hostel. It's a 30-minute hike from the station to the Koblenz boat dock.

Km 585—Burg Lahneck: Above the modern autobahn bridge over the Lahn River, this castle *(Burg)* was built in 1240 to defend local silver mines; the castle was ruined by the French in 1688 and rebuilt in the 1850s in neo-Gothic style. Burg Lahneck faces another Romantic rebuild, the yellow Schloss Stolzenfels (out of view above the train, a 10-min climb from tiny parking lot, open for touring, closed Mon).

Km 580—Marksburg: This castle (black and white with the 3 modern chimneys behind it, just after town of Spay) is the best-looking of all the Rhine castles and the only surviving medieval castle on the Rhine. Because of its commanding position, it was never attacked. It's now open as a museum with a medieval interior second only to the Mosel's Burg Eltz (see self-guided tour of Marksburg, page 530). The three modern smokestacks vent Europe's biggest car-battery recycling plant just up the valley.

Km 570—Boppard: Once a Roman town, Boppard has some impressive remains of 4th-century walls. Notice the Roman towers and the substantial chunk of Roman wall near the train station, just above the main square.

If you visit Boppard, head to the fascinating church below the main square. Find the carved Romanesque crazies at the doorway. Inside, to the right of the entrance, you'll see Christian symbols from Roman times. Also notice the painted arches and vaults. Originally most Romanesque churches were painted this way. Down by the river, look for the high-water *(Hochwasser)* marks on the arches from various flood years. (You'll find these flood marks throughout the Rhine and Mosel Valleys.)

Km 567—Burg Sterrenberg and Burg Liebenstein: These are the "Hostile Brothers" castles across from Bad Salzig. Take the wall between the castles (actually designed to improve the defenses of both castles), add two greedy and jealous brothers and a fair maiden, and create your own legend. Burg Liebenstein is now a fun, friendly, and affordable family-run hotel (9 rooms, Db-€98, suite-€120, giant king-and-the-family room-€195, easy parking, tel. 06773/308 or 06773/251, www.castle-liebenstein.com, hotel-burg-liebenstein@rhinecastles.com, Nickenig family).

Km 560: While you can see nothing from here, a 19th-century lead mine functioned on both sides of the river with a shaft actually tunneling completely under it.

Km 559—Burg Maus: The Maus (mouse) got its name because the next castle was owned by the Katzenelnbogen family. (*Katz* means "cat.") In the 1300s, it was considered a state-of-the-art fortification...until Napoleon had it blown up in 1806 with state-of-the-art explosives. It was rebuilt true to its original plans around 1900. Today, the castle hosts a falconry show (€6.50, daily at 11:00 and 14:30, 20-min walk up, tel. 06771/7669, www.burg-maus.de—in German only).

Km 557—St. Goar and Rheinfels Castle: Cross to the other side of the train. The pleasant town of St. Goar was named for a 6th-century hometown monk. It originated in Celtic times (really old) as a place where sailors would stop, catch their breath, send home a postcard, and give thanks after surviving the seductive and treacherous Loreley crossing. St. Goar is worth a stop to explore its mighty Rheinfels Castle. (For information, a guided castle tour, and accommodations, see page 541.)

Km 556—Burg Katz: Burg Katz (Katzenelnbogen) faces St. Goar from across the river. Together, Burg Katz (built in 1371) and Rheinfels Castle had a clear view up and down the river, effectively controlling traffic. There was absolutely no duty-free shopping on the medieval Rhine. Katz got Napoleoned in 1806 and rebuilt around 1900. Today, it's under a rich and mysterious Japanese ownership. It's technically a hotel—Germany wouldn't allow its foreign purchase for private use—but it's so expensive, nobody's ever stayed there. Below the castle, notice the derelict grape terraces—worked since the 8th century, but abandoned only in the last generation. The Rhine wine is particularly good because the slate absorbs the heat of the sun and stays warm all night, resulting in sweeter grapes. Wine from the flat fields above the Rhine gorge is cheaper and good only as table wine. The wine from the steep side of the Rhine gorge—harder to grow and harvest—is tastier and more expensive.

About Km 555: A statue of the Loreley, the beautiful but deadly nymph (see next listing for legend), combs her hair at the end of a long spit—built to give barges protection from vicious icebergs that occasionally rage down the river in the winter. The actual Loreley, a cliff, is just ahead.

Km 554—The Loreley: Steep a big slate rock in centuries of legend and it becomes a tourist attraction, the ultimate Rhinestone. The Loreley (flags on top, name painted near shoreline), rising 450 feet over the narrowest and deepest point of the Rhine, has long been important. It was a holy site in pre-Roman days. The fine echoes here—thought to be ghostly voices—fertilized the legendary soil.

Because of the reefs just upstream (at kilometer 552), many ships never made it to St. Goar. Sailors (after days on the river) blamed their misfortune on a *wunderbares Fräulein* whose long blonde hair almost covered her body. Heinrich Heine's *Song of Loreley* (the Cliffs Notes version is on local postcards) tells the story of a count who sent his men to kill or capture this siren after she distracted his horny son, causing him to drown. When the soldiers cornered the nymph in her cave, she called her father (Father Rhine) for help. Huge waves, the likes of which you'll never see today, rose from the river and carried Loreley to safety. And she has never been seen since.

But alas, when the moon shines brightly and the tour buses are parked, a soft, playful Rhine whine can still be heard from the Loreley. As you pass, listen carefully ("Sailors...sailors...over my bounding mane").

Km 552: Killer reefs, marked by red-and-green buoys, are called the "Seven Maidens." Okay, one more goofy legend: The prince of Schönburg Castle (*ober* Oberwesel) had seven spoiled daughters who always dumped men because of their shortcomings. Fed up, he invited seven of his knights up to the castle and demanded that his daughters each choose one to marry. But they complained that each man had too big a nose, was too fat, too stupid, and so on. The rude and teasing girls escaped into a riverboat. Just downstream, God turned them into the seven rocks that form this reef. While this story probably isn't entirely true, there's a lesson in it for medieval children: Don't be hard-hearted.

Km 550—Oberwesel: Cross to the other side of the train. Oberwesel was a Celtic town in 400 B.C., then a Roman military station. It now boasts some of the best Roman-wall and medieval-tower remains on the Rhine, and the commanding Schönburg Castle. Notice how many of the train tunnels have entrances designed like medieval turrets—they were actually built in the Romantic 19th century. OK, back to the river side.

Km 546—Burg Gutenfels and Pfalz Castle, the Classic Rhine View: Burg Gutenfels (see white-painted Hotel sign) and the shipshape Pfalz Castle (built in the river in the 1300s) worked very effectively to tax medieval river traffic. The town of Kaub grew rich as Pfalz raised its chains when boats came and lowered them only when the merchants had paid their duty. Those who didn't pay spent time touring its prison, on a raft at the bottom of its well. In 1504, a pope called for the destruction of Pfalz, but a six-week siege failed. Notice the overhanging outhouse (tiny white room—with faded medieval stains—between two wooden ones). Pfalz is tourable but bare and dull (€2 ferry from Kaub, €2.10 entry, April–Sept Tue–Sun 9:00–13:00 & 14:00–18:00, Oct–March until 17:00, last entry 60 min before closing, closed Mon and Dec, tel. 06774/570 or 0172/262-2800).

In Kaub, a green statue honors the German general Blücher. He was Napoleon's nemesis. In 1813, as Napoleon fought his way back to Paris after his disastrous Russian campaign, he stopped at Mainz—hoping to fend off the Germans and Russians pursuing him by controlling that strategic bridge. Blücher tricked Napoleon. By building the first major pontoon bridge of its kind here at the Pfalz Castle, he crossed the Rhine and outflanked the French. Two years later, Blücher and Wellington teamed up to defeat Napoleon once and for all at Waterloo.

Km 544—"The Raft Busters": Immediately before Bacharach, at the top of the island, buoys mark a gang of rocks notorious for busting up rafts. The Black Forest is upstream. It was poor, and wood was its best export. Black Foresters would ride log booms down the Rhine to the Ruhr (where their timber fortified coal-mine shafts) or to Holland (where logs were sold to shipbuilders). If they could navigate the sweeping bend just before Bacharach and then survive these "raft busters," they'd come home reckless

Rhine River Trade and Barge-Watching

The Rhine is great for barge-watching. There's a constant parade of action, and each boat is different. Since ancient times, this has been a highway for trade. Today, the world's biggest port (Rotterdam) waits at the mouth of the river.

Barge workers are almost a subculture. Many own their own ships. The captain (and family) live in the stern. Workers live in the bow. The family car often decorates the bow like a shiny hood ornament. In the Rhine town of Kaub, there was a boarding school for the children of the Rhine merchant marine—but today it's closed, since most captains are Dutch, Belgian, or Swiss. The flag of the boat's home country flies in the stern (German; Swiss; Dutch—horizontal red, white, and blue; or French—vertical red, white, and blue). Logically, imports go upstream (Japanese cars, coal, and oil) and exports go downstream (German cars, chemicals, and pharmaceuticals). A clever captain manages to ship goods in each direction.

Tugs can push a floating train of up to five barges at once. Upstream it gets steeper and they can push only one at a time. Before modern shipping, horses dragged boats upstream (the faint remains of towpaths survive at points along the river). From 1873 to 1900, they laid a chain from Bonn to Bingen, and boats with cogwheels and steam engines hoisted themselves upstream. Today, 265 million tons travel each year along the 530 miles from Basel on the Swiss border to Rotterdam on the Atlantic.

Riverside navigational aids are of vital interest to captains who don't wish to meet the Loreley. Boats pass on the right unless they clearly signal otherwise with a large blue sign. Since downstream ships can't stop or maneuver as freely, upstream boats are expected to do the tricky do-si-do work. Cameras monitor traffic all along and relay warnings of oncoming ships by posting large triangular signals before narrow and troublesome bends in the river. There may be two or three triangles per signpost, depending upon how many "sectors," or segments, of the river are covered. The lowest triangle indicates the nearest stretch of river. Each triangle tells whether there's a ship in that sector. When the bottom side of a triangle is lit, that sector is empty. When the left side is lit, an oncoming ship is in that sector.

The **Signal and Riverpilots Museum,** located at the signal triangles at the upstream edge of St. Goar, explains how barges are safer, cleaner, and more fuel-efficient than trains or trucks (Wed and Sat 14:00–17:00, outdoor exhibits always open).

and likely horny, the German folkloric equivalent of American cowboys after payday.

Km 543—Bacharach and Burg Stahleck: Cross to the other side of the train. Bacharach is a great stop (see details and accommodations below). Some of the Rhine's best wine is from this town, whose name means "altar to Bacchus." Local vintners brag that the medieval Pope Pius II ordered Bacharach wine by the cartload. Perched above the town, the 13th-century Burg Stahleck is now a hostel.

Km 540—Lorch: This pathetic stub of a castle is barely visible from the road. Notice the small car ferry (3/hr, 10 min), one of several along the bridgeless stretch between Mainz and Koblenz.

Km 538—Castle Sooneck: Cross back to the other side of the train. Built in the 11th century, this castle was twice destroyed by people sick and tired of robber barons.

Km 534—Burg Reichenstein, and **Km 533—Burg Rheinstein:** Stay on the other side of the train to see two of the first castles to be rebuilt in the Romantic era. Both are privately owned, tourable, and connected by a pleasant trail.

Km 530—Ehrenfels Castle: Opposite Bingerbrück and the Bingen station, you'll see the ghostly Ehrenfels Castle (clobbered by the Swedes in 1636 and by the French in 1689). Since it had no view of the river traffic to the north, the owner built the cute little *Mäuseturm* (mouse tower) on an island (the yellow tower you'll see near the train station today). Rebuilt in the 1800s in neo-Gothic style, it's now used as a Rhine navigation signal station.

Km 528—Niederwald Monument: Across from the Bingen station on a hilltop is the 120-foot-high Niederwald monument, a memorial built with 32 tons of bronze in 1877 to commemorate "the reestablishment of the German Empire." A lift takes tourists to this statue from the famous and extremely touristy wine town of Rüdesheim.

From here, the Romantic Rhine becomes the industrial Rhine, and our tour is over.

More Rhine Sights

▲▲Marksburg Castle—Thanks to its formidable defenses, invaders decided to give Marksburg a miss. This best-preserved castle on the Rhine can be toured only with a guide, and tours are generally in German only (4/hr in summer, 1/hr in winter). Still, it's an awesome castle, and my self-guided walking tour (below) fits the 50-minute German-language tour (€4.50, family card-€12.50, daily April–Oct 10:00–18:00, last tour departs at 17:00, Nov–March 11:00–17:00, last tour at 16:00, call ahead to see if a rare English tour is scheduled, tel. 02627/206, www.marksburg.de). Marksburg caps a hill above the Rhine town of Braubach (a short hike or shuttle train from the boat dock).

Self Guided Tour: Our tour starts inside the castle's first gate.

1. Inside the First Gate: While the dramatic castles lining the Rhine are generally Romantic rebuilds, Marksburg is the real McCoy—nearly all original construction. It's littered with bits of its medieval past, like the big stone ball that was swung on a rope to be used as a battering ram. Ahead, notice how the inner gate—originally tall enough for knights on horseback to gallop through—was made smaller, and therefore safer from enemies on horseback. Climb the Knights' Stairway carved out of slate rock and pass under the murder hole—handy for pouring boiling pitch on invaders. (Germans still say someone with bad luck "has pitch on his head.")

2. Coats of Arms: Colorful coats of arms line the wall just inside the gate. These are from the noble families who have owned the castle since 1283. In that year, financial troubles drove the first family to sell to the powerful and wealthy Katzenelnbogen family (who made the castle into what you see today). When Napoleon took this region in 1803, an Austrian family who sided with the French got the keys. When Prussia took the region in 1866, control passed to a friend of the Prussians who had a passion for medieval things—typical of this Romantic period. Then it was sold to the German Castles Association in 1900. Its offices are in the main palace at the top of the stairs.

3. Romanesque Palace: White outlines mark where the larger original windows were located, before they were replaced by easier-to-defend smaller ones. On the far right, a bit of the original plaster survives. Slate, which is soft and vulnerable to the elements, needs to be covered—in this case, by plaster. Because this is a protected historic building, restorers can use only the traditional plaster methods...but no one knows how to make plaster that works as well as the 800-year-old surviving bits.

4. Cannons: The oldest cannon here—from 1500—was back-loaded. This was advantageous, because many cartridges could be preloaded. But since the seal was leaky, it wasn't very powerful. The bigger, more modern cannons—from 1640—were one piece and therefore airtight, but had to be front-loaded. They could easily hit targets across the river from here. Stone balls were rough, so they let the explosive force leak out. The best cannonballs were stones covered in smooth lead—airtight and therefore more powerful and more accurate.

5. Gothic Garden: Walking along an outer wall, you'll see 160 plants from the Middle Ages—used for cooking, medicine, and witchcraft. The *Schierling* (hemlock, in the first corner) is the same poison that killed Socrates.

6. Inland Rampart: This most vulnerable part of the castle had a triangular construction to better deflect attacks. Notice the factory in the valley. In the 14th century, this was a lead, copper, and silver mine. Today's factory—Europe's largest car-battery recycling plant—uses the old mine shafts as vents (see the 3 modern smokestacks).

7. Wine Cellar: Since Roman times, wine has been the traditional Rhineland drink. Because castle water was impure, wine—less alcoholic than today's beer—was the way knights got their fluids. The pitchers on the wall were their daily allotment. The bellows were part of the barrel's filtering system. Stairs lead to the...

8. Gothic Hall: This hall is set up as a kitchen, with an oven designed to roast an ox whole. The arms holding the pots have notches to control the heat. To this day, when Germans want someone to hurry up, they say, "give it one tooth more." Medieval windows were made of thin alabaster or animal skins. A nearby wall is peeled away to show the wattle-and-daub construction (sticks, straw, clay, mud, then plaster) of a castle's inner walls. The iron plate to the left of the next door enabled servants to stoke the heater without being seen by the noble family.

9. Bedroom: This was the only heated room in the castle. The canopy kept in heat and kept out critters. In medieval times, it was impolite for a lady to argue with her lord in public. She would wait for him in bed to give him what Germans still call "a curtain lecture." The deep window seat caught maximum light for needlework and reading. Women would sit here and chat (or "spin a yarn") while working the spinning wheel.

10. Hall of the Knights: This was the dining hall. The long table is an unattached plank. After each course, servants could replace it with another preset plank. Even today, when a meal is over and Germans are ready for the action to begin, they say, "Let's lift up the table." The "action" back then was traveling minstrels who sang and told of news gleaned from their travels.

Notice the outhouse—made of wood—hanging over thin air. When not in use, its door was locked from the outside (the castle side) to prevent any invaders from entering this weak point in the castle's defenses.

11. Chapel: This chapel is still painted in Gothic style with the castle's namesake, St. Mark, and his lion. Even the chapel was designed with defense in mind. The small doorway kept out heavily armed attackers. The staircase spirals clockwise, favoring the sword-wielding defender (assuming he was right-handed).

12. Linen Room: Around 1800, the castle—with diminished military value—housed disabled soldiers. They'd earn a little extra money working raw flax into linen.

13. Two Thousand Years of Armor: Follow the evolution of armor since Celtic times. Because helmets covered the entire head, soldiers identified themselves as friendly by tipping their visor up with their right hand. This evolved into the military salute that is still used around the world today. Armor and the close-range weapons along the back were made obsolete by the invention of the rifle. Armor was replaced with breastplates—pointed (like the castle itself) to deflect enemy fire. This design was used as late as the start of World War I. A medieval lady's armor hangs over the door. While popular fiction has men locking their women up before heading off to battle, chastity belts were actually used by women as protection against rape when traveling.

14. The Keep: This served as an observation tower, a dungeon (with a 22-square-foot cell in the bottom), and a place of last refuge. When all was nearly lost, the defenders would bundle into the keep and burn the wooden bridge, hoping to outwait their enemies.

15. Horse Stable: The stable shows off bits of medieval crime and punishment. Cheaters were attached to stones or pillories. Shame masks punished gossipmongers. A mask with a heavy ball had its victim crawling around with his nose in the mud. The handcuffs with a neck hole were for the transport of prisoners. The pictures on the wall show various medieval capital punishments. Many times the accused was simply taken into a torture dungeon to see all these tools and, guilty or not, confessions spilled out of him. On that cheery note, your tour is over.

The Myth of the Loreley Visitors Center—This lightweight exhibit reflects on Loreley, traces her myth, and explores the landscape, culture, and people of the Rhine Valley. Displays in English describe the history well. Maybe by the time you visit, the echo megaphones in the little theater will tell the legend in English rather than only German (€1, April–Oct daily 10:00–18:00, often closed Nov–March, tel. 06771/9100, www.loreley-touristik.de). From the exhibit, a five-minute walk (marked as 30 minutes) takes you to the impressive viewpoint overlooking the Rhine Valley from atop the famous rock. From there, it's a steep 15-minute hike down to the riverbank.

Hiking to the Visitors Center and Top of the Loreley: For a good two-hour hike from St. Goar up to the Loreley, catch the ferry across to the village of St. Goarshausen (€1.50 round-trip, 6/hr until 20:00, then 2/hr May–Oct until 23:00, Nov–April until 21:00). Then follow green Burg Katz (Katz Castle) signs up Burgstrasse under the train tracks to find steps on right *(Loreley über Burg Katz)* leading to the Katz Castle (now a private hotel for Japanese elite) and beyond. Traverse the hillside, always bearing right toward the river. You'll pass through a residential area, hike down a 50-yard path through trees, then cross a wheat field until you reach the Loreley Visitors Center (shops and restaurants, see above) and rock-capping viewpoint. From here, it's a steep 15-minute hike down to the river, where a riverfront trail takes you back to St. Goarshausen and the St. Goar ferry.

Bacharach

Once prosperous from the wine and wood trade, Bacharach (BAHKH-ah-rahkh, with a guttural *kh* sound) is now just a pleasant half-timbered village of a thousand people working hard to keep its tourists happy.

Tourist Information: The TI is on the main street in the Posthof courtyard next to the church (April–Oct Mon–Fri 9:00–17:00, Sat 10:00–16:00, Sun 10:00–14:00, Nov–March Mon–Fri 9:00–12:00, closed Sat–Sun, Internet access-€6/hr, Oberstrasse 45, from train station turn right and walk 5 blocks down main street with castle high on your left, tel. 06743/919-303, www.bacharach.de or www.rhein-nahe-touristik.de, Herr Kuhn and his team SE). The TI stores bags for day-trippers and provides ferry schedules. For accommodations, see "Sleeping," page 537.

Shopping: The **Jost** beer-stein stores carry most everything a shopper could want. One shop is across from the church in the main square, the other—which offers more deals—is a block away at Rosenstrasse 16 (Mon–Fri 8:30–18:00, Sat 8:30–17:00, Sun 10:00–17:00, Rosenstrasse shop closed Sun, ships overseas, 10 percent discount with this book, tel. 06743/1224, www.phil-jost-germany.com). Herr and Frau Jost share sightseeing advice, send faxes, and reserve German hotels for travelers (reasonable charge for phone and fax fees). **Woodburn House,** which engraves woody signs and knickknacks, lets travelers store bags while they look for a room, and gives readers with this book a 10 percent discount (across from Altkölnischer Hof, Oberstrasse 60, tel. 06743/1655, Frances Geuss SE). The **post office** is on Oberstrasse between the train station and the TI (Mon–Fri 9:00–12:00 & 15:00–18:00, Sat 9:00–12:00, closed Sun).

Local Guides: Get acquainted with Bacharach by taking a walking tour. Charming Herr Rolf Jung, retired headmaster of the Bacharach school, is a superb English-speaking guide (€30, 90 min, call to reserve, tel. 06743/1519). If Herr Jung is not available, the TI has a list of other English-speaking guides, or take the self-guided walk, described below.

Introductory Bacharach Walk

Start at the Köln-Düsseldorfer ferry dock (next to a fine picnic park). View the town from the parking lot—a modern landfill.

Bacharach

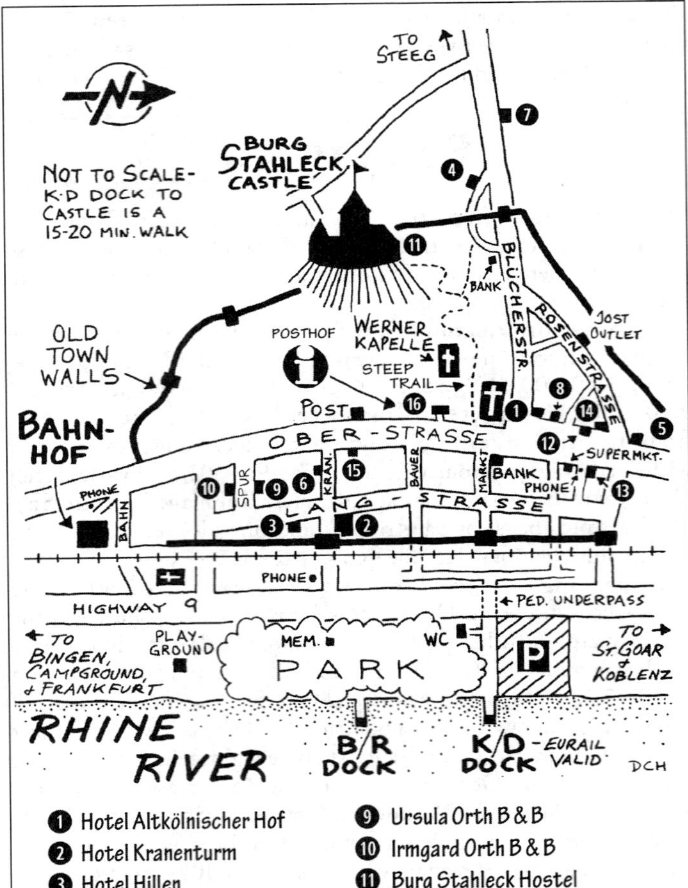

1. Hotel Altkölnischer Hof
2. Hotel Kranenturm
3. Hotel Hillen
4. Pension im Malerwinkel
5. Pension Binz
6. Pension Lettie
7. Pension Winzerhaus
8. Theilacker B & B
9. Ursula Orth B & B
10. Irmgard Orth B & B
11. Burg Stahleck Hostel
12. Altes Haus Restaurant
13. Kurpfälzische Münze Restaurant
14. Weingut Zum Grüner Baum
15. Weingut Karl Heidrich
16. Rhineland Museum

The Rhine used to lap against Bacharach's town wall, just over the present-day highway. Every few years the river floods, covering the highway with several feet of water. The **castle** on the hill is a youth hostel. Two of its original 16 towers are visible from here (up to 5 if you look really hard). The huge roadside wine keg declares this town was built on the wine trade.

Reefs up the river forced boats to unload upriver and reload here. Consequently, Bacharach became the biggest wine trader on the Rhine. A riverfront crane hoisted huge kegs of prestigious "Bacharach" wine (which in practice was from anywhere in the region). The tour buses next to the dock and the flags of the biggest spenders along the highway remind you that today's economy is basically founded on tourism.

At the big town map and public WC (€0.30, daily 9:00–18:00), take the underpass, ascend on the right, make a U-turn, then—if you are less than 2.3 meters tall—walk under the train tracks through the medieval gate (1 out of an original 15 14th-century gates) and to the two-tone Protestant **church,** which marks the town center.

From this intersection, Bacharach's main street (Oberstrasse) goes right to the half-timbered, red-and-white Altes Haus (from 1368, the oldest house in town) and left way down to the train station. To the left (or south) of the church, a golden horn hangs over the old **Posthof** (TI, free WC upstairs in courtyard open from 11:00). The post horn symbolizes the postal service throughout Europe. In olden days, when the postman blew this, traffic stopped and the mail sped through. This post station dates from 1724, when stagecoaches ran from Köln to Frankfurt.

Step into the courtyard—once a carriage house and inn that accommodated Bacharach's first VIP visitors. Notice the fascist eagle (from 1936, on the left as you enter) and the fine view of the church and a ruined chapel above. The Posthof is the home of the **Rhineland Museum,** which hopes to open in 2006 with a cultural landscape exhibit on the Rhine Valley. Manager Bitz's vision even includes wine-tasting (www.mittelrheintal.de).

Two hundred years ago, Bacharach's main drag was the only road along the Rhine. Napoleon widened it to fit his cannon wagons. The steps alongside the church lead to the castle. Return to the church, passing the **Italian Ice Cream** café, where friendly Mimo serves his special invention: Riesling wine–flavored gelato (quite tasty, €0.60 per scoop, opposite Posthof at Oberstrasse 48).

Inside the church (daily 9:30–18:00, English info on table near door), you'll find grotesque capitals, brightly painted in medieval style, and a mix of round Romanesque and pointed Gothic arches. Left of the altar, some medieval frescoes survive where an older Romanesque arch was cut by a pointed Gothic one.

Continue down Oberstrasse past the Altes Haus to the **old mint** *(Münze),* marked by a crude coin in its sign. Across from the mint, the wine garden of Fritz Bastian is the liveliest place in town after dark (see "Eating," page 540). Above you in the vineyards stands a ghostly black-and-gray tower—your destination.

Take the next left (Rosenstrasse) and wander 30 yards up to the **well.** Notice the sundial and the wall painting of 1632 Bacharach with its walls intact. Climb the tiny-stepped lane behind the well up into the vineyard and to the tower. The slate steps lead to a small path through the vineyard that deposits you at a viewpoint atop the stubby remains of the old town wall (if signs indicate that the path is closed, get as close to the tower base as possible).

A grand medieval town spreads before you. When Frankfurt had 15,000 residents, medieval Bacharach had 4,000. For 300 years (1300–1600), Bacharach was big, rich, and politically powerful.

From this perch you can see the chapel ruins and six surviving **city towers.** Visually trace the wall to the castle. The castle was actually the capital of Germany for a couple of years in the 1200s. When Holy Roman Emperor Frederick Barbarossa went away to fight the Crusades, he left his brother (who lived here) in charge of his vast realm. Bacharach was home of one of seven electors who voted for the Holy Roman Emperor in 1275. To protect their own power, these elector-princes did their best to choose the weakest guy on the ballot. The elector from Bacharach helped select a two-bit prince named Rudolf von Hapsburg (from a no-name castle in Switzerland). The underestimated Rudolf brutally silenced the robber barons along the Rhine and established the mightiest dynasty in European history. His family line, the Hapsburgs, ruled much of Central Europe until 1918.

Plagues, fires, and the Thirty Years' War (1618–1648) finally did Bacharach in. The town, with a population of about a thousand, has slumbered for several centuries. Today, the castle houses commoners—40,000 overnights annually by youth hostelers.

In the mid-19th century, painters such as J. M. W. Turner and writers such as Victor Hugo were charmed by the Rhineland's romantic mix of past glory, present poverty, and rich legend. They put this part of the Rhine on the old "grand tour" map as the "Romantic Rhine." Victor Hugo pondered the ruined 15th-century chapel that you see under the castle. In his 1842 travel book, *Rhein Reise (Rhine Travels),* he wrote, "No doors, no roof or windows, a magnificent skeleton puts its silhouette against the sky. Above it, the ivy-covered castle ruins provide a fitting crown. This is Bacharach, land of fairy tales, covered with legends and sagas." If you're enjoying the Romantic Rhine, thank Victor Hugo and company.

To get back into town, take the level path that leads along the wall up the valley past the next tower. Then cross the street into the parking lot. Pass Pension Malerwinkel on your right, being careful not to damage the old arch with your head. Follow the creek past a delightful little series of half-timbered homes and cheery gardens known as "Painters' Corner" *(Malerwinkel).* Resist looking into some pervert's peep show (on the right) and continue downhill back to the village center. Nice work.

SLEEPING

See map on page 534 for locations. Ignore guest houses and restaurants posting Recommended by Rick Steves signs. If they're not listed in the current edition of this book, I do not recommend them.

$$$ Hotel Altkölnischer Hof, a grand old building near the church, rents 20 rooms with modern furnishings (and some balconies) over an Old World restaurant. Public rooms are old-time elegant (Sb-€48–70, small or dark Db-€65, bright new Db-€72–82, new Db with balcony-€80–105, elevator, closed Nov–March, tel. 06743/1339, fax 06743/2793, www.hotel-bacharach-rhein.de, altkoelnischer-hof @t-online.de). Ask about their four spacious, newly-renovated apartments in a historic building nearby.

$$ Hotel Kranenturm offers castle ambience without the climb—a good combination of hotel comfort with *Zimmer* coziness, a central location, and a medieval atmosphere. Run by hardworking Kurt Engel and his intense but friendly wife, Fatima, this hotel is actually part of the medieval fortification. Its former *Kran* (crane) towers are now round rooms. When the riverbank was higher, cranes on this tower loaded barrels of wine onto Rhine boats. Hotel Kranenturm is 15 feet from the train tracks, but a combination of medieval sturdiness, triple-paned windows, and included earplugs makes the riverside rooms sleepable (Sb-€40–44, Db-€55–62, bigger Db-€58–65, castle or riverview Db-€70–80, Tb-€80–95, honeymoon special-€90–105, lower price is for off-season or stays of at least 3 nights in high season, family deals, cash preferred; for these special rates, book direct, not through TI; Rhine views come with ripping train noise, back rooms are quieter, kid-friendly, Internet access-€5/hour and laundry service-€12.50/load for guests only, Langstrasse 30, tel. 06743/1308, fax 06743/1021, hotel-kranenturm@t-online.de). Kurt, a good cook, serves €6–18 dinners; try his ice-cream special for dessert. Trade travel stories on the terrace with new friends over dinner, letting screaming trains punctuate your conversation. Drivers park along the highway at the Kranenturm tower. If arriving by train, walk down Oberstrasse, then turn right on Kranenstrasse.

$$ Hotel Hillen, a block south of the Hotel Kranenturm, has less charm and similar train noise, with spacious rooms, good food, and friendly owners. They installed new windows to minimize train noise, but to get a room on the quiet side ask for *ruhige Seite* (S-€28, Sb-€36, D-€42, Ds-€52, Db-€57, Tb-€75, 5 percent less after 3 nights, closed Nov–March, family rooms, Langstrasse 18, tel. 06743/1287, fax 06743/1037, hotel-hillen@web.de, kind Iris speaks some English).

$$ Pension im Malerwinkel sits like a grand gingerbread house just outside the wall at the top end of town in a little neighborhood so charming it's called "Painters' Corner" *(Malerwinkel)*. The Vollmer family's 20-room place is super-quiet and comes with a sunny garden on a brook and easy parking (Sb-€35, Db-€55–58 for 1 night, €50 for 2 nights, €48 for 3 nights, cash only, some rooms have balconies but most face parking lot, bike rental-€6/day, from town center go uphill and up the valley 5 min until you pass the old town gate and look left to Blücherstrasse 41, tel. 06743/1239, fax 06743/93407, www.im-malerwinkel.de—in German only, pension @im-malerwinkel.de).

$$ Pension Binz offers four large, bright rooms and a plain apartment in a serene location (Sb-€33, Db-€51, third person-€18, apartment with 2-night minimum-€61, fine breakfast, Koblenzer Strasse 1, tel. 06743/1604, pension.binz@freenet.de, cheery Karla speaks a little English).

$ At **Pension Lettie,** effervescent and eager-to-please Lettie offers four bright rooms. Lettie speaks good English (she worked for the U.S. Army before they withdrew) and does laundry—€10.50 per load (Sb-€34, Db-€45, Tb-€62, family room for 4-€80, for 5-€95, for 6-€105, studio apt-€50, discount for 2-night stays, 6 percent more if paying with credit card, strictly non-smoking, buffet breakfast with waffles and eggs, no train noise, a few doors inland from Hotel Kranenturm, Kranenstrasse 6, tel. 06743/2115, fax 06743/947564, pension.lettie@t-online.de).

$ Pension Winzerhaus, a 10-room place run by friendly Sybille and Stefan, is 200 yards up the valley from the town gate, so the location is less charming, and the train noise is replaced by street noise. But the parking is easy, and rooms are simple, clean, and modern (Sb-€30, Db-€45, Tb-€60, Qb-€65, cash only, free bikes for guests, non-smoking rooms, Blücherstrasse 60, tel. 06743/1294, fax 06743/937-779, winzerhaus@compuserve.de).

$ Herr und Frau Theilacker run a cozy, German-feeling *Zimmer* just off the main street with four comfortable rooms, vine-covered trellises, and a breakfast room filled with family photos. They're likely to have a room when others don't (S-€18, D-€36, cash only, in town center behind Altkölnischer Hof, take short lane between Altkölnischer Hof and Altes Haus straight ahead to Oberstrasse 57, no outside sign, tel. 06743/1248, NSE).

Sleep Code

(€1 = about $1.20, country code: 49, area code: 06743)
S = Single, **D** = Double/Twin, **T** = Triple, **Q** = Quad, **b** = bathroom, **s** = shower only, **SE** = Speaks English, **NSE** = No English. All hotels speak some English. Breakfast is included and credit cards are accepted unless otherwise noted.

To help you sort easily through these listings, I've divided the rooms into three categories, based on the price for a standard double room with bath:

$$$ **Higher Priced**—Most rooms €70 or more.
$$ **Moderately Priced**—Most rooms between €50–70.
$ **Lower Priced**—Most rooms €50 or less.

The Rhine is an easy place for cheap sleeps. *Zimmer* and *Gasthäuser* with €20 beds abound (and *Zimmer* normally discount their prices for longer stays). Rhine-area hostels offer €14 beds to travelers of any age. Each town's TI is eager to set you up, and finding a room should be easy any time of year (except for winefest weekends in Sept and Oct). Bacharach and St. Goar, the best towns for an overnight stop, are 10 miles apart, connected by milk-run trains, riverboats, and a riverside bike path. Bacharach is a much more interesting town, but St. Goar has the famous castle (see "St. Goar," page 541). Parking in Bacharach is simple along the highway next to the tracks (3-hr daytime limit is generally not enforced) or in the boat parking lot. Parking in St. Goar is tighter; ask at your hotel.

$ *Orth* Zimmer: Delightful sisters-in-law run two fine little B&Bs across the lane from each other (from station walk down Oberstrasse, turn right on Spurgasse, look for Orth sign). **Ursula Orth** rents five rooms and speaks a smidge of English (Sb-€22, D-€31, Db-€34, Tb-€45, cash only, rooms 4 and 5 on ground floor, Spurgasse 3, tel. 06743/1557). **Irmgard Orth** rents two fresh rooms. She speaks no English but is exuberantly cheery and serves homemade honey with breakfast (Sb-€20, Db-€34, cash only, Spurgasse 2, tel. 06743/1553; to get the listed rates, book direct instead of using the TI).

$ Jugendherberge Stahleck hostel is a 12th-century castle on the hilltop—500 steps above Bacharach—with a royal Rhine view. Open to travelers of any age, this is a gem with eight beds and a private modern shower and WC in most rooms. A steep 20-minute climb on the trail from the town church, the hostel is warmly run by Evelyn and Bernhard Falke (FALL-kay), who serve hearty €6 all-you-can-eat buffet dinners. The hostel pub serves cheap local wine until midnight (€17 dorm beds with breakfast and sheets, €3.10 extra for non-members or in a double, couples can share one of five €44 Db, no smoking in rooms, open all day but 22:00 curfew, laundry machine, beds normally available but call and leave your name, they'll hold a bed until 18:00, tel. 06743/1266, fax 06743/2684, jh-bacharach@djh-info.de). If driving, don't go in the driveway; park on the street and walk 200 yards.

EATING

You can easily find inexpensive (€10–15), atmospheric restaurants offering indoor and outdoor dining. The first three places are neighbors.

Altes Haus, the oldest building in town, serves reliably good food with Bacharach's most romantic atmosphere (€9–15, Thu–Tue 12:00–15:30 & 18:00–21:30, closed Wed and Dec–Easter, dead center by the church, tel. 06743/1209). Find the cozy little dining room with photos of the opera singer who sang about Bacharach, adding to its fame.

Kurpfälzische Münze is more expensive, but it's a popular standby for its sunny terrace and classy candlelit interior (€7–21, daily 10:00–22:00, in the old mint, a half-block down from Altes Haus, tel. 06743/1375).

Hotel Kranenturm is another good value, with hearty meals and good main-course salads (restaurant closed Nov–Feb, see hotel listing on page 537).

Wine-Tasting: Drop in on entertaining Fritz Bastian's **Weingut zum Grüner Baum** wine bar (also offers soup and cold cuts, good ambience indoors and out, just past Altes Haus, Mon–Wed and Fri from 13:00, Sat–Sun from 12:00, closed Thu and Feb–mid-March, tel. 06743/1208). As the president of the local vintner's club, Fritz is on a mission to give travelers an understanding of the subtle differences among the Rhine wines. Groups of 2–6 people pay €13.50 for a "carousel" of 15 glasses of 14 different white wines, one lonely red, and a basket of bread. Your mission: Team up with others who have this book to rendezvous here after dinner. Spin the lazy Susan, share a common cup, and discuss the taste. Fritz insists, "After each wine, you must talk to each other."

For a fun, family-run wine shop and *Stube* in the town center, visit **Weingut Karl Heidrich** (on Oberstrasse, directly in front of Hotel Kranenturm), where American Susanne and German Markus proudly share their family's wine.

St. Goar

St. Goar is a classic Rhine town—its hulk of a castle overlooking a half-timbered shopping street and leafy riverside park busy with sightseeing ships and contented strollers. From the boat dock, the main drag—a pedestrian mall without history—cuts through town before winding up to the castle. Rheinfels Castle, once the mightiest on the Rhine, is the single best Rhineland ruin to explore.

Tourist Information: The helpful St. Goar TI, which books rooms and offers a free baggage-check service, is on the pedestrian street, three blocks from the K-D boat dock and train station (Mon–Fri 8:00–12:30 & 14:00–17:00, Sat 10:00–12:00, Nov–April until 16:30, closed Sat–Sun; from train station, go downhill around church and turn left on Heer Strasse; tel. 06741/383).

St. Goar's waterfront park is hungry for a picnic. The small Edeka **supermarket** on the main street is great for picnic fixings (July–Sept Mon–Fri 8:00–18:00, Sat 8:00–16:00, Sun 10:00–14:00; Oct–June Sat 8:00–13:00, closed Sun).

The friendly and helpful Montag family runs the Hotel Montag (Michael) and three **shops** (steins—Misha, Steiffs—Maria, and cuckoo clocks—Marion), all at the base of the castle hill road. The stein shop under the hotel has Rhine guides, fine steins, and copies of this year's *Rick Steves' Germany & Austria* guidebook. All three shops offer 10 percent off any of their souvenirs (including Hummels) for travelers with this book (€5 minimum purchase). On-the-spot VAT refunds cover about half your shipping costs (if you're not shipping, they'll give you VAT form to claim refund at airport). The hotel offers expensive coin-op **Internet** access (€8/hr).

SIGHTS

St. Goar's Rheinfels Castle

Sitting like a dead pit bull above St. Goar, this mightiest of Rhine castles rumbles with ghosts from its hard-fought past. Burg Rheinfels *was* huge—once the biggest castle on the Rhine (built in 1245). It withstood a siege of 28,000 French troops in 1692. But in 1797, the French revolutionary army destroyed it. The castle was used for ages as a quarry, and today—while still mighty—it's only a small fraction of its original size. This hollow but interesting shell offers your single best hands-on ruined-castle experience on the river.

Cost and Hours: €4, family card-€10, mid-March–Sept daily 9:00–18:00, last entry at 17:00, Oct–mid-March only Sat–Sun 11:00–17:00—weather permitting.

Tours and Information: Call in advance or gather 10 English-speaking tourists and beg to get an English tour—perhaps from

St. Goar

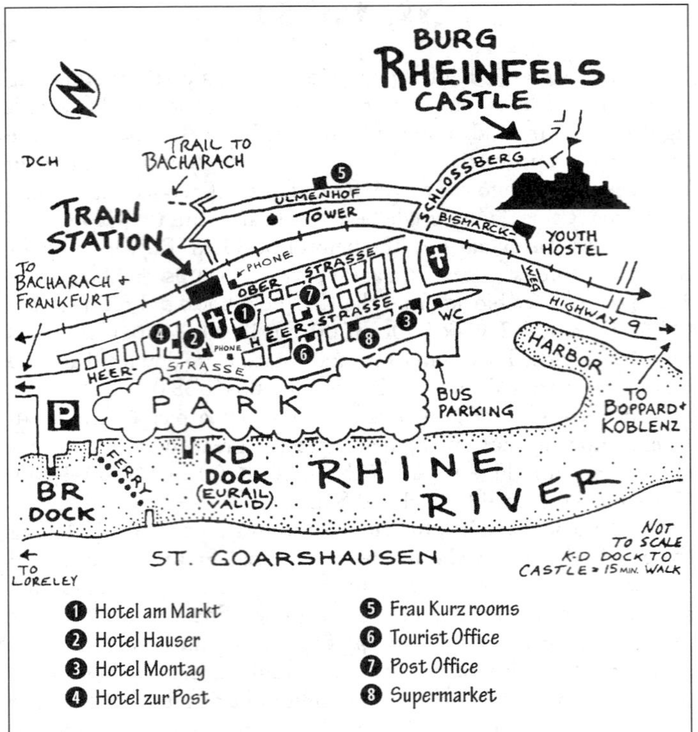

Günther, the "last knight of Rheinfels" (tel. 06741/7753). Otherwise, follow my self-guided tour below. The castle map is mediocre; the English booklet is better, with history and illustrations (€2). If it's damp, be careful of slippery stones. A handy WC (€0.30) is in the castle courtyard under the stairs to the restaurant entry.

Let There Be Light: If planning to explore the mine tunnels, bring a flashlight, buy a tiny one (€3 at entry), or do it by candlelight (museum sells candles with matches, €0.50).

Getting to the Castle: From St. Goar's boat dock or train station, take a steep 15-minute hike, a €5 taxi ride, an €8 minibus tour (tel. 06741/7011), or the kitschy "tschu-tschu" tourist train (€2 one-way, €3 round-trip, 7 min to the top, daily 10:00–17:00, 3/hr, runs from square between station and dock, also stops at Hotel Montag, complete with lusty music, tel. 06741/2030).

Self-Guided Tour: Rather than wander aimlessly, visit the castle by following this tour: From the ticket gate, walk straight. Pass *Grosser Keller* on the left (where we'll end this tour) and walk through an internal gate past the *zu den gedeckten Wehrgängen* sign

St. Goar's Rheinfels Castle

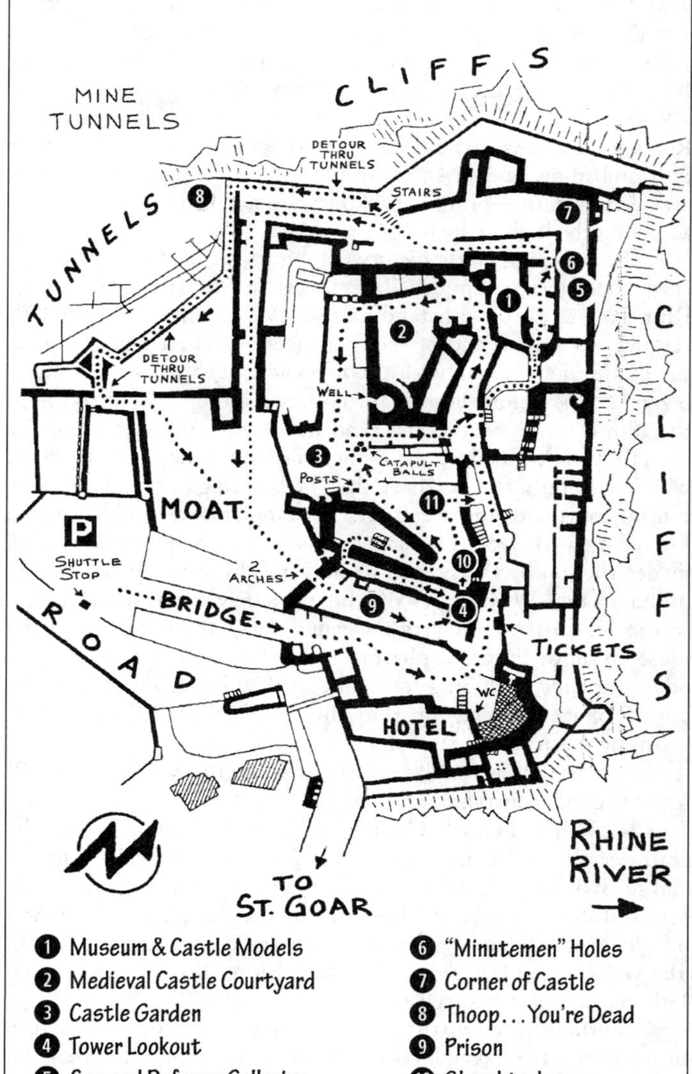

1. Museum & Castle Models
2. Medieval Castle Courtyard
3. Castle Garden
4. Tower Lookout
5. Covered Defense Galleries
6. "Minutemen" Holes
7. Corner of Castle
8. Thoop... You're Dead
9. Prison
10. Slaughterhouse
11. Big Cellar

on the right (where we'll pass later) uphill to the museum (daily 9:30–12:00 & 13:00–17:30) in the only finished room of the castle.

❶ **Museum and Castle Model:** The seven-foot-tall carved stone immediately inside the door (marked *Keltische Säule von Pfalzfeld*)—a tombstone from a nearby Celtic grave—is from 400 years before Christ. There were people here long before the Romans...and this castle. Find the old wooden library chair near the tombstone. If you smile sweetly, the man behind the desk may demonstrate—pull the back forward and it becomes stairs for accessing the highest shelves.

The sweeping castle history exhibit in the center of the room is well described in English. The massive fortification was the only Rhineland castle to withstand Louis XIV's assault during the 17th century. At the far end of the room is a model reconstruction of the castle (not the one with the toy soldiers) showing how much bigger it was before French revolutionary troops destroyed it in the 18th century. Study this. Find where you are (hint: Look for the tall tower). This was the living quarters of the original castle, which was only the smallest ring of buildings around the tiny central courtyard (13th century). The ramparts were added in the 14th century. By 1650, the fortress was largely complete. Ever since its destruction by the French in the late 18th century, it's had no military value. While no WWII bombs were wasted on this ruin, it served St. Goar as a quarry for generations. The basement of the museum shows the castle pharmacy and an exhibit of Rhine-region odds and ends, including tools and an 1830 loom. Don't miss the photos of ice-breaking on the Rhine—which, thanks to global warming, hasn't been necessary since 1963.

Exit the museum and walk 30 yards directly out, slightly uphill into the castle courtyard.

❷ **Medieval Castle Courtyard:** Five hundred years ago, the entire castle circled this courtyard. The place was self-sufficient and ready for a siege with a bakery, pharmacy, herb garden, brewery, well (top of yard), and livestock. During peacetime, 300–600 people lived here; during a siege, there would be as many as 4,000. The walls were plastered and painted white. Bits of the original 13th-century plaster survive.

Continue through the courtyard and out *Erste Schildmauer,* turn left into the next courtyard, and walk straight to the two old, wooden, upright posts. Find the pyramid of stone catapult balls on your left.

❸ **Castle Garden:** Catapult balls like these were too expensive not to recycle—they'd be retrieved after any battle. Across from the balls is a well—essential for any castle during the age of sieging. Look in. The old posts are for the ceremonial baptizing of new members of the local trading league. While this guild goes back centuries, it's now a social club that fills this court with a huge wine party the third weekend of each September.

If weary, skip to #5; otherwise, climb the cobbled path up to the castle's best viewpoint—up where the German flag waves.

❹ **Highest Castle Tower Lookout:** Enjoy a great view of the river, the castle, and the forest. Remember, the fortress once covered five times the land it does today. Notice how the other castles (across the river) don't poke above the top of the Rhine canyon. That would make them easy for invading armies to see.

Return to the catapult balls, walk down the road, go through the tunnel, veer left through the arch marked *zu den gedeckten Wehrgängen,* go down two flights of stairs, and turn left into the dark, covered passageway (Covered Defense Galleries). From here, we will begin a rectangular walk taking us completely around the perimeter of the castle.

❺ & ❻ **Covered Defense Galleries with "Minutemen" Holes:** Soldiers—the castle's "minutemen"—had a short commute: defensive positions on the outside, home in the holes below on the left. Even though these living quarters were padded with straw, life was unpleasant. A peasant was lucky to live beyond age 45.

Continue straight through the dark gallery and to the corner of the castle, where you'll see a white painted arrow at eye level. Stand with your back to the arrow on the wall.

❼ **Corner of Castle:** Look up. A three-story, half-timbered building originally rose beyond the highest stone fortification. The two stone tongues near the top just around the corner supported the toilet. (Insert your own joke here.) Turn around and face the wall. The crossbow slits below the white arrow were once steeper. The bigger hole on the riverside was for hot pitch.

Follow that white arrow along the outside to the next corner. Midway you'll pass stairs on the right leading down *zu den Minengängen* (sign on upper left). Adventurers with flashlights can detour here (see "Optional Detour—Into the Mine Tunnels," page 547). You may come out around the next corner. Otherwise, stay with me, walking level to the corner. At the corner, turn left.

❽ **Thoop...You're Dead:** Look ahead at the smartly placed crossbow slit. While you're lying there, notice the stonework. The little round holes were for scaffolds used as they built up. They indicate this stonework is original. Notice also the fine stonework on the chutes. More boiling pitch...now you're toast, too.

Continue along the castle wall around the corner. At the railing, look up the valley and uphill where the sprawling fort stretched. Below, just outside the wall, is land where attackers would gather. The mine tunnels are under there, waiting to blow up any attackers (read below).

Continue along the perimeter, jog left, go down five steps and into an open field, and walk toward the wooden bridge. You may detour here into the passageway (on right) marked *13 Hals Graben.* The "old" wooden bridge is actually modern. Angle left through two arches (before the bridge) and through the rough entry to the *Verliess* (prison) on the left.

❾ **Prison:** This is one of six dungeons. You walked through an entrance prisoners only dreamed of 400 years ago. They came and went through the little square hole in the ceiling. The holes in the walls supported timbers that thoughtfully gave as many as 15 residents something to sit on to keep them out of the filthy slop that gathered on the floor. Twice a day, they were given bread and water. Some prisoners actually survived longer than two years in here. While the town could torture and execute, the castle only had permission to imprison criminals in these dungeons. Consider this: According to town records, the two men who spent the most time down here—2.5 years each—died within three weeks of regaining their freedom. Perhaps after a diet of bread and water, feasting on meat and wine was simply too much.

Continue through the next arch, under the white arrow, then turn left and walk 30 yards to the *Schlachthaus.*

❿ **Slaughterhouse:** Any proper castle was prepared to survive a six-month siege. With 4,000 people, that's a lot of provisions. The cattle that lived within the walls were slaughtered in this room. The castle's mortar was congealed here (by packing all the organic waste from the kitchen into kegs and sealing it). Notice the drainage gutters. "Running water" came through from drains built into the walls (to keep the mortar dry and therefore strong...and less smelly).

Back outside, climb the modern stairs to the left. A skinny, dark passage (yes, that's the one) leads you into the...

⓫ **Big Cellar:** This *Grosser Keller* was a big pantry. When the castle was smaller, this was the original moat—you can see the rough lower parts of the wall. The original floor was 13 feet deeper. The drawbridge rested upon the stone nubs on the left. When the castle expanded, the moat became this cellar. Halfway up the walls on the entrance side of the room, square holes mark spots where timbers made a storage loft, perhaps filled with grain. In the back, an arch leads to the wine cellar (sometimes blocked off) where finer wine was kept. Part of a soldier's pay was wine...table wine. This wine was kept in a single 180,000-liter stone barrel (that's 47,550 gallons), which generally lasted about 18 months.

The count owned the surrounding farmland. Farmers got to keep 20 percent of their production. Later, in more liberal feudal times, the nobility let them keep 40 percent. Today, the German government leaves the workers with 60 percent...and provides a few more services.

You're free. Climb out, turn right, and leave. For coffee on a great view terrace, visit the Rheinfels Castle Hotel, opposite the entrance (WC at base of steps).

Optional Detour—Into the Mine Tunnels: Around 1600, to protect their castle, the Rheinfellers cleverly booby-trapped the land just outside their walls by building tunnels topped with thin slate roofs and packed with explosives. By detonating the explosives when under attack, they could kill hundreds of invaders. In 1626, a handful of underground Protestant Germans blew 300 Catholic Spaniards to—they figured—hell. You're welcome to wander through a set of never-blown-up tunnels. But be warned: It's 600 feet long, assuming you make no wrong turns; it's pitch-dark, muddy, and claustrophobic, with confusing dead-ends; and you'll never get higher than a deep crouch. It cannot be done without a light (flashlights available at entrance—see above). At stop #6 of the above tour, follow the stairs on the right leading down *zu den Minengängen* (sign on upper left).

The *Fuchsloch* sign welcomes you to the foxhole. Walk level (take no stairs) past the first steel railing (where you hope to emerge later) to the second steel railing. Climb down. The "highway" in this foxhole is three feet high. The ceiling may be painted with a white line indicating the correct path. Don't venture into the narrower side aisles. These were once filled with the gunpowder. After a small decline, take the second right. At the T-intersection, go right (uphill). After about 10 feet, go left. Take the next right and look for a light at the end of the tunnel. Head up a rocky incline under the narrowest part of the tunnel and you'll emerge at that first steel railing. The stairs on the right lead to freedom. Cross the field, walk under the bigger archway, and continue uphill toward the old wooden bridge. Angle left through two arches (before the bridge) and through the rough entry to the *Verliess* (prison) on the left. Rejoin the tour here at stop #8.

SLEEPING

(€ = about $1.20, country code: 49, area code: 06741)

$$$ Hotel Montag, with 28 rooms, is on the castle end of town just across the street from the world's largest free-hanging cuckoo clock. Manfred and Maria Montag and their son Mike speak New Yorkish. Even though the hotel gets a lot of bus tours, it's friendly, laid-back, and comfortable (Sb-€35–45, Db-€70–80, Tb-€90–100, coin-op Internet access-€8/hr, Heer Strasse 128, tel. 06741/1629, fax 06741/2086, hotelmontag@01019freenet.de). Check out their adjacent crafts shop (heavy on beer steins).

$$$ Rheinfels Castle Hotel is the town splurge. Actually part of the castle but an entirely new building, this luxurious

57-room place is good for those with money and a car (Db-€135–165 depending on river views and balconies, extra adult bed-€37, extra bed for kids aged 7–11—€25, kids under 7 free, elevator, free parking, indoor pool and sauna, dress-up restaurant, Schlossberg 47, tel. 06741/8020, fax 06741/802-802, www.schlosshotel-rheinfels.de—German only, info@burgrheinfels.de).

$$ Hotel am Markt, well-run by Herr and Frau Velich, is rustic, with all the modern comforts. It features a hint of antler with a pastel flair, 18 bright rooms, and a good restaurant where the son does the cooking. It's a good value and a stone's throw from the boat dock and train station (S-€35, Sb-€43, standard Db-€59, bigger riverview Db-€69, Tb-€82, Qb-€88, cheaper off-season, March–mid–April and Oct–mid-Nov pay 2 nights get third night free, closed mid-Nov–Feb, Am Markt 1, tel. 06741/1689, fax 06741/1721, www.hotelammarkt1.de—in German only, hotel.am.markt@gmx.de). Rental bikes are available to guests (€5/day).

$$ Hotel Hauser, facing the boat dock, is another good deal, warmly run by another Frau Velich. Its 12 rooms sit over a fine restaurant (S-€21.50, D-€45, Db-€50, great Db with Rhine-view balconies-€56, Db cheaper off-season, costs more with credit card, small bathrooms, restaurant, Heer Strasse 77, tel. 06741/333, fax 06741/1464, www.hotelhauser.de, hotelhauser@t-online.de).

$$ Hotel zur Post, with creaky parquet floors, less-than-warm management, and 12 forgettable, well-worn rooms, is a lesser value but a block off the riverfront (Sb-€37, Db-€62, a block from station at Bahnhofstrasse 3, tel. 06741/339, fax 06741/2708, www.hotelzurpost-online.de, zurposthotel@gmx.de, family Bergweiler).

$ Frau Kurz offers St. Goar's best *Zimmer* deal, with a breakfast terrace, garden, fine view, and homemade marmalade (S-€22, D-€38, Db-€44, showers-€2.60, more for 1-night stays, cash only, free and easy parking, confirm prices, honor your reservation or call to cancel, Ulmenhof 11, tel. & fax 06741/459, www.gaestehaus-kurz.de, some English spoken). It's a steep five-minute hike from the train station (exit left from station, take immediate left at the yellow phone booth, pass under tracks to paved path, go up stairs and follow zigzag path to Ulmenhof, *Zimmer* is just past tower).

$ St. Goar Hostel, the big beige building under the castle (on road to castle, veer right just after railroad bridge) has a 22:00 curfew (but you can borrow the key) and hearty €6 dinners (S-€17, dorm beds-€14, up to 10 beds per room, includes breakfast, cash only, open all day, check-in preferred 17:00–20:00 but must check in by 20:00, Bismarckweg 17, tel. 06741/388, fax 06741/2869, st-goar@diejugendherbergen.de).

EATING

Hotel am Markt serves tasty traditional meals (with plenty of game and fish, or try their specialties—roast wild boar and homemade cheesecake) at fair prices (€5–16) with good atmosphere and service. For your Rhine splurge, walk, taxi, or drive up to **Rheinfels Castle Hotel** for its incredible view terrace in an elegant setting (€15–20 dinners, daily 18:30–21:15, reserve a table by the window, see hotel listing above).

TRANSPORTATION CONNECTIONS

Milk-run trains stop at all Rhine towns each hour starting as early as 6:00. Koblenz, Boppard, St. Goar, Bacharach, Bingen, and Mainz are each about 15 minutes apart. From Koblenz to Mainz takes 75 minutes. To get a faster big train, go to Mainz (for points east and south) or Koblenz (for points north, west, and along Mosel). Train info: tel. 11861 (€0.46/min).

From Mainz by Train to: Bacharach/St. Goar (hrly, 1 hr), **Cochem** (hrly, 2.5 hrs, change in Koblenz), **Köln** (3/hr, 90 min, change in Koblenz), **Baden-Baden** (hrly, 1.5 hrs), **Munich** (hrly, 4 hrs), **Frankfurt** (3/hr, 45 min), **Frankfurt Airport** (4/hr, 25 min).

From Koblenz by train to: Köln (4/hr, 1 hr), **Berlin** (2/hr, 5.5 hrs, up to 2 changes), **Frankfurt** (3/hr, 1.5 hrs, 1 change), **Cochem** (2/hr, 50 min), **Trier** (2/hr, 2 hrs), **Brussels** (12/day, 4 hrs, change in Köln), **Amsterdam** (12/day, 4.5 hrs, up to 5 changes).

From Frankfurt by Train to: Bacharach (hrly, 1.5 hrs, change in Mainz; first train to Bacharach departs at 6:00, last train at 20:45), **Koblenz** (hrly, 90 min, changes in Mannheim or Wiesbaden), **Rothenburg** (hrly, 3 hrs, transfers in Würzburg and Steinach), **Würzburg** (hrly, 2 hrs), **Nürnberg** (hrly, 2 hrs), **Munich** (hrly, 4 hrs, 1 change), **Amsterdam** (8/day, 5 hrs, up to 3 changes), **Paris** (9/day, 6.5 hrs, up to 3 changes).

From Bacharach by Train to: Frankfurt Airport (hrly, 1.5 hrs, change in Mainz, first train to Frankfurt airport departs about 5:40, last train 21:30).

BERLIN

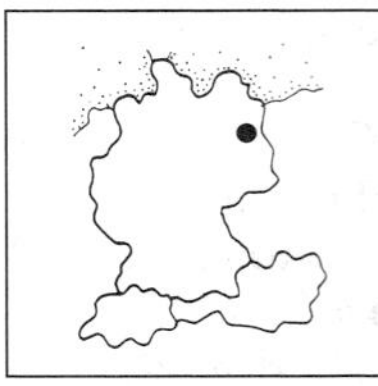

No tour of Germany is complete without a look at its historic and reunited capital, a construction zone called Berlin. Stand over ripped-up tracks and under a canopy of cranes and watch the rebirth of a European capital. Enjoy the thrill of walking over what was the Wall and through the Brandenburg Gate.

Berlin has had a tumultuous recent history. After the city was devastated in World War II, it was divided by the Allied powers: The American, British, and French sectors became West Berlin, and the Soviet sector, East Berlin. The division was set in stone when the East built the Berlin Wall in 1961. The Wall lasted 28 years. In 1990, less than a year after the Wall fell, the two Germanys officially became one. When the dust settled, Berliners from both sides of the once-divided city faced the monumental challenge of reunification.

The last decade has taken Berlin through a frenzy of rebuilding. And while there's still plenty of work to be done, a new Berlin is emerging. Berliners joke they don't need to go anywhere because the city's always changing. Spin a postcard rack to see what's new. A five-year-old guidebook on Berlin covers a different city.

Reunification has had its negative side, and locals are fond of saying "the Wall survives in the minds of some people." Some "Ossies" (impolite slang for Easterners) miss their security. Some "Wessies" miss their easy ride (military deferrals, subsidized rent, and tax breaks). For free spirits, walled-in West Berlin was a citadel of freedom within the East.

The city government has been eager to charge forward with little nostalgia for anything that was Eastern. Big corporations and the national government have moved in, and the dreary swath of

Berlin Sightseeing Modules

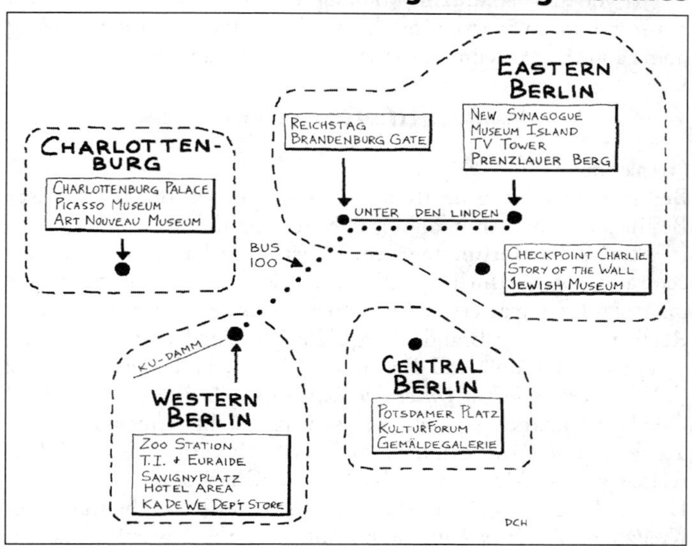

land that was the Wall and its notorious "death strip" has been transformed. City planners are boldly taking Berlin's reunification and the return of the national government as a good opportunity to make Berlin a great capital once again.

Planning Your Time

Because of Berlin's inconvenient location, try to enter and/or leave by either night train or plane. I'd give Berlin two days and spend them this way:

Day 1: Begin your day getting oriented to this huge city: Either take the 10:00 "Discover Berlin" guided walking tour offered by Original Berlin Walks (see page 559); or follow my "Do-It-Yourself Orientation Tour" by bus to the Reichstag (page 561), then continue by foot down Unter den Linden (page 567). Focus on sights along Unter den Linden today, including the Reichstag dome (most crowded 10:00–16:00), Pergamon Museum, and Egyptian Museum.

Day 2: Today concentrate on the sights in central Berlin, and in eastern Berlin south of Unter den Linden. Spend the morning lost in the paintings at the Gemäldegalerie. After lunch, hike via Potsdamer Platz to the *Topography of Terror* exhibit and along the surviving Zimmerstrasse stretch of Wall to the Museum of the Wall at Checkpoint Charlie. With extra time, consider visiting the Jewish Museum.

If you are maximizing your sightseeing, you could squeeze a hop-off, hop-on bus tour into Day 1. Remember that the Reichstag dome and the Museum of the Wall are open late.

ORIENTATION

(area code: 030)
Berlin is huge, with nearly four million people. But the tourist's Berlin can be broken into four digestible chunks:

1. Eastern Berlin: The former East Berlin has the highest concentration of worthwhile sights and colorful neighborhoods. The main sightseeing artery is the famous ***Unter den Linden*** boulevard: Reichstag building, Brandenburg Gate, Museum Island (Pergamon, Egyptian Museum, and Berlin Cathedral), and Alexanderplatz (TV Tower). ***South of Unter den Linden*** you'll find the delightful Gendarmenmarkt square, most Nazi sights (including the *Topography of Terror* exhibit), the Jewish Museum, the best Wall-related sights (Museum of the Wall at Checkpoint Charlie and East Side Gallery), and the colorful Turkish neighborhood of Kreuzberg. ***North of Unter den Linden*** are these worth-a-wander neighborhoods: around Oranienburger Strasse (New Synagogue), Hackescher Markt, and Prenzlauer Berg (several recommended hotels).

2. Central Berlin: The new city center—Potsdamer Platz, Kulturforum museums, and the giant Tiergarten park.

3. Western Berlin: The area around the Bahnhof Zoo train station and the grand Kurfürstendamm Boulevard, nicknamed "Ku'damm" (transportation hub, tours, information, shopping, and recommended hotels).

4. Charlottenburg Palace Area: The palace and nearby museums (Picasso, Art Nouveau), on the western edge of the city center.

Tourist Information

Berlin's TIs are run by a for-profit agency working for the city's big hotels, which colors the information they provide. The main TI is five minutes from Bahnhof Zoo, in the Europa Center (with Mercedes symbol on top, enter outside to left at Budapester Strasse 45, Mon–Sat 10:00–19:00, Sun 10:00–18:00, tel. 030/250-025, www.berlin-tourism.de). Smaller TIs are in the Brandenburg Gate (daily 10:00–18:00, longer in summer) and at the base of the TV Tower at Alexanderplatz (daily 10:00–18:00, longer in summer).

The TIs sell a good city map (€0.50), the *Berlin Programm* (a €1.60 comprehensive German-language monthly that lists upcoming events and museum hours, www.berlin-programm.de), the Museumspass (a.k.a. *Schaulust*, €12/3 days—see "Helpful Hints," below), and the German-English bimonthly *Berlin Calendar* magazine (€1.60, with timely features on Berlin and a partial calendar of events). The TIs also offer a €3 room-finding service (but only to hotels that give them kickbacks—many don't). Most hotels have free city maps.

EurAide's information office, located in the Bahnhof Zoo Reisezentrum (in front of train station, by taxi stand), provides an excellent service. They have answers to all your questions about Berlin or train travel around Europe. It's staffed by Americans (so communication is simple), and they have a knack for predicting your needs, then publishing free fliers to serve them (Mon–Fri 9:00–12:30 & 13:30–17:00, closed Sat–Sun and all Jan, great opportunity to get future *couchette* reservations nailed down ahead of time, Prague Excursion passes available—see "Transportation Connections" on page 599, www.euraide.com). EurAide also gives out a good, free city map and sells all public-transit tickets (including the €5.60 day pass) and the Welcome Card (see "Getting Around Berlin," page 555)—making a trip to the TI probably unnecessary. To get the most out of EurAide, have your questions ready before your visit.

Arrival in Berlin

By Train at Bahnhof Zoo: Berlin's central station is called Bahnhof Zoologischer Garten (because it's near Berlin's famous zoo), or "Zoo" for short (rhymes with "toe"). Coming from Western Europe, you'll probably land at Zoo. It's small, well organized, and handy (lockers and baggage check available in back of station).

Upon arrival by train, orient yourself like this: Inside the station, follow signs to Hardenbergplatz. Step into this busy square filled with city buses, taxis, the transit office, and derelicts. The Original Berlin Walks start from the curb immediately outside the station at the top of the taxi stand (see "Tours," page 559). Between you and the McDonald's across the street is the stop for bus #100 (departing to the right for my "Do-It-Yourself Orientation Tour," page 561). Turn right and tiptoe through the riffraff to the eight-lane highway, Hardenbergstrasse. Walk to the median strip and stand with your back to the tracks. Ahead you'll see the black, bombed-out hulk of the Kaiser Wilhelm Memorial Church and the Europa Center (Mercedes symbol spinning on roof), which houses the main TI. Just ahead on the left, amid the traffic, is the BVG transport information kiosk (where you can buy a €5.60 day pass covering the subway and buses, and pick up a free subway map). If you're facing the church, my recommended western Berlin hotels are behind you to your right (see page 590).

If you're staying at my western Berlin hotels, but you arrive at one of Berlin's other train stations (trains from most of Eastern Europe arrive at Ostbahnhof), no problem: Ride another train (fastest option) or the S-Bahn or U-Bahn (runs every few min) to Bahnhof Zoo and pretend you arrived here.

By Plane: See "Transportation Connections," page 600.

Helpful Hints

Monday Activities: Most museums are closed on Monday. Save Monday for Berlin Wall sights, the Reichstag dome, my "Do-It-Yourself Orientation Tour" and strolling Unter den Linden (see below), walking/bus tours, the Jewish Museum, churches, the zoo, or shopping along Kurfürstendamm (Ku'damm) Boulevard or at the Kaufhaus des Westens (KaDeWe) department store. (When Monday is a holiday—as it is several times a year—museums are open then and closed Tuesday.)

Museums: All **state museums,** including the Pergamon and Gemäldegalerie (plus others as noted in "Sights," page 563), are free for the last four hours on Thursdays (that is, if it closes at 18:00, it's free from 14:00 on; www.museen-berlin.de). There are two different types of discount passes for Berlin's state museums (different from the mostly private museums and sights covered by the WelcomeCard—see "Getting Around Berlin," below). The state museums are covered by a **one-day ticket** (*Tageskarte,* €10, not valid for special exhibitions, purchase at participating museums, not sold at TI). Entry to most of these museums costs €6–8, so the day ticket pays for itself if you visit at least two museums. Even better, consider the three-day ***"Schaulust" Museumspass,*** which covers most of the state museums (including the Pergamon and Gemäldegalerie) as well as several others (including the Jewish Museum). Only €2 more than the day ticket, it's valid for three times as long and is an excellent value if you'll be doing at least two days of museum-hopping (€12, not valid for special exhibitions, purchase at TI or participating museums). Note that if a museum is closed on one of the days of your Museumspass, you have access to that museum on the fourth day to make up for lost time.

Medical Help: If you need to see a doctor, dial "Call a Doc" at tel. 01804-2255-2362 (www.calladoc.com), a non-profit referral service designed for tourists. Payment is arranged between you and the doctor, and is likely far more affordable than similar care in the United States.

Travel Agency: Last Minute Flugbörse can help you find a flight in a hurry (next to TI in Europa Center, tel. 030/2655-1050, www.lastminuteflugboerse.de).

Addresses: Many Berlin streets are numbered with odd and even numbers on the same side of the street, often with no connection to the other side (for example, Ku'damm #212 can be across the street from #14). To save steps, check the white street signs on curb corners; many list the street numbers covered on that side of the block.

Internet Access: You'll find cheap, fast Internet access at easy-Internetcafé (daily 24 hrs, Ku'damm 224, 10-min walk from Bahnhof Zoo and near recommended western Berlin hotels, buy ticket at self-service machines, instructions in English).

Laundry: Schnell und Sauber Waschcenter is a handy launderette near my recommended western Berlin hotels (daily 6:00–23:00, €5–9 wash and dry, Leibnizstrasse 72, 4 blocks west of Savignyplatz, near intersection with Kantstrasse). Near my recommended hotels in Prenzlauer Berg, try Holly's Wasch-Theke (€5–9 wash and dry, includes detergent, daily 7:00–23:00, last load in at 21:30, attached café, Kollwitzstrasse 93, tel. 030/443-9210).

Festival: Be aware of the Love Parade, a huge techno-Woodstock that overwhelms the city with (mostly gay) love in mid-July—either you'll love it or hate it.

Getting Around Berlin

Berlin's sights spread far and wide. Right from the start, commit yourself to the fine public-transit system.

By Subway and Bus: The U-Bahn (*Untergrund-Bahn,* Berlin's subway), S-Bahn (*Schnell-Bahn,* or "fast train," mostly above ground and with fewer stops), *Strassenbahn* (streetcars), and all buses are consolidated into one "BVG" system that uses the same tickets. Here are your options:

- Basic ticket *(Einzel Fahrschein)* for two hours of travel in one direction on buses or subways—€2 (*Erwachsener* means "adult"—anyone 14 or older).
- A cheap short-ride ticket *(Kurzstrecke Erwachsener)* for a single short ride of six bus stops or three subway stations, with one transfer—€1.20.
- A day pass *(Tageskarte)* covering zones A and B, the city proper—€5.60 (good until 3:00 the morning after). To get out to Potsdam, you need a ticket covering zone C—€6. (For longer stays, a 7-day *Tageskarte* is also available—€22, or €28 including zone C; or buy 2 WelcomeCards, see below.)
- The Berlin/Potsdam **WelcomeCard** gives you three days of transportation in zones A, B, and C, and those same three days of minor discounts on lots of minor and a few major museums (including Checkpoint Charlie), sightseeing tours (including the recommended Original Berlin Walks), and music and theater events (€21, valid for an adult and up to 3 kids younger than 14). The WelcomeCard is a good deal for a three-day visit (since 3 1-day transit passes alone cost only €4.20 less than the WelcomeCard) and worth considering for a two-day visit.

Berlin at a Glance

▲▲▲Reichstag Germany's historic Parliament building, topped with a striking dome you can ascend. **Hours:** Daily 8:00–24:00, last entry 22:00.

▲▲▲Museum of the Wall at Checkpoint Charlie Moving museum near the former site of the famous border checkpoint between the American and Soviet sectors, with stories of brave escapes during the Cold War and the gleeful days when the wall fell. **Hours:** Daily 9:00–22:00.

▲▲▲Gemäldegalerie Germany's top collection of 13th- through 18th-century European paintings, featuring Dürer, Van Eyck, Rubens, Titian, Raphael, Caravaggio, and more. **Hours:** Tue–Sun 10:00–18:00, Thu until 22:00, closed Mon.

▲▲Brandenburg Gate One of Berlin's most famous landmarks, a multi-arched gateway, at the former border of East and West. **Hours:** Always open.

▲▲Unter den Linden Leafy boulevard through the heart of former East Berlin, lined with some of the city's top sights. **Hours:** Always open.

▲▲Pergamon Museum On Museum Island (just off Unter den Linden), featuring the fantastic second-century B.C. Greek Pergamon Altar. **Hours:** Tue–Sun 10:00–18:00, Thu until 22:00, closed Mon.

▲▲Berlin Wall Mostly gone, but parts of the wall are still visible, including the East Side Gallery and a chunk near the Topography of Terror (former SS and Gestapo headquarters). **Hours:** Always open.

▲▲Jewish Museum Berlin User-friendly museum celebrating Jewish culture, in a highly conceptual building. **Hours:** Daily 10:00–20:00, Mon until 22:00.

▲▲Gendarmenmarkt Inviting square bounded by twin churches, a chocolate shop, and a concert hall. **Hours:** Always open.

▲▲New Synagogue Largest prewar synagogue in Berlin, destroyed by Nazis, with a facade that has since been rebuilt. **Hours:** Sun–Thu 10:00–18:00, Fri 10:00–14:00, closed Sat, May–Aug

Sun–Mon until 20:00 and Fri until 17:00.

▲▲Egyptian Museum On Museum Island, the proud home of the exquisite 3,000-year-old bust of Queen Nefertiti. **Hours:** daily 10:00–18:00.

▲Kaiser Wilhelm Memorial Church Evocative destroyed church in the heart of the former West Berlin, with a modern annex. **Hours:** Church open Mon–Sat 10:00–16:00, closed Sun, annex open daily 9:00–19:00.

▲Kurfürstendamm West Berlin's main boulevard (nicknamed Ku'damm), packed with tourists and upscale shops. **Hours:** Always open.

▲Käthe Kollwitz Museum Features the black-and-white art of the local artist who conveyed the suffering of Berlin's stormiest century. **Hours:** Wed–Mon 11:00–18:00, closed Tue.

▲Kaufhaus des Westens (KaDeWe) The "department store of the West"—the biggest on the Continent—is where East Berliners flocked when the wall came down. **Hours:** Mon–Fri 10:00–20:00, Sat 9:30–20:00, closed Sun.

▲Potsdamer Platz The Times Square of old Berlin, long a postwar wasteland, now rebuilt with huge glass skyscrapers (can ascend 300-foot-tall Kollhoff tower), an underground train station, and—covered with a huge canopy—the Sony Center mall with eateries. **Hours:** Always open.

▲Musical Instruments Museum Impressive collection of historic instruments. **Hours:** Tue–Fri 9:00–17:00, Sat–Sun 10:00–17:00, closed Mon.

▲Charlottenburg Palace Skippable Baroque Hohenzollern palace on the edge of town. **Hours:** Tue–Sun 10:00–17:00, closed Mon.

▲Berggruen Collection Notable works by Picasso, Matisse, van Gogh, Cézanne, and Paul Klee. **Hours:** Tue–Fri 10:00–18:00, Sat–Sun 11:00–18:00, closed Mon.

▲Bröhan Museum Collection of Art Nouveau and Art Deco furnishings. **Hours:** Tue–Sun 10:00–18:00, closed Mon.

- The **CityTourCard** covers public transportation in zones A and B, plus some museum discounts (€14.50/48 hrs, €18.90/72 hrs, www.citytourcard.com). While it's cheaper than the WelcomeCard, it doesn't include zone C (which most visitors don't need unless they're going to Potsdam), and the discounts are not quite as good as the WelcomeCard's—for example, the CityTourCard doesn't include discounts to the Checkpoint Charlie Museum or Original Berlin Walks.

Buy your U- or S-Bahn tickets from machines at stations or at the BVG pavilion in front of Bahnhof Zoo (English instructions). To use the machine, first select the type of ticket you want, then load in the coins or paper. Punch your ticket in a red or yellow clock machine to validate it (or risk a €40 fine). The double-decker buses are a joy (can buy ticket on bus), and the subway is a snap. The S-Bahn (but not U-Bahn) is free with a validated Eurailpass (but it uses a flexi-day).

Sections of the U- or S-Bahn sometimes close temporarily for repairs. In this situation, a bus route replaces the train (*Ersatzverkehr,* or "replacement transportation").

By Taxi: Taxis are easy to flag down, and taxi stands are common. A typical ride within town costs €10–16, and a cross-town trip (for example, Zoo to Alexanderplatz) will run you around €25. A local law designed to help people get safely and affordably home from their subway station late at night is handy for tourists any time of day: A short ride of no more than two kilometers (1.25 miles) is a flat €3. (Ask for "*Kurzstrecke, drei euro, bitte.*") To get this cheap price, you must hail a cabbie on the street rather than go to a taxi stand (from a stand, it's a minimum €5 charge). Cabbies aren't crazy about the law, so insist on the price and be sure to keep the ride short.

By Bike: Be careful—in Berlin, motorists don't brake for bikers (and bikers don't brake for pedestrians). Fortunately, some roads and sidewalks have special red-painted bike lanes. Just don't ride on the regular sidewalk—it's *nicht erlaubt* (not allowed—that's "verboten" to you and me).

In western Berlin, you can rent good bikes at the **Bahnhof Zoo** left-luggage counter (in back of station, next to lockers; comes with lock, air pump, and mounted basket, €10/day, €23/3 days, €35/7 days, daily 6:15–21:00, passport required, €50 cash deposit); in the east, go to **Fahrradstation** at Hackesche Höfe (€15/day, Mon–Fri 8:00–20:00, Sat 10:00–16:00, closed Sun, Rosenthaler Strasse 40, tel. 030/2045-4500) or at the Friedrichstrasse S-Bahn station (same hours, but also open Sun 10:00–18:00).

TOURS

▲▲▲**City Walking Tours**—The Original Berlin Walks offers a variety of worthwhile tours led by enthusiastic guides who are native English speakers. The company, run by Englishman Nick Gay, offers a three-hour **Discover Berlin** introductory walk daily year-round at 10:00 and also at 14:30 from April through October for €12 (€9 if you're under 26 or with WelcomeCard). Just show up at the taxi rank in front of Bahnhof Zoo (or 20 min later in eastern Berlin's Hackescher Markt S-Bahn station, outside Häagen-Dazs). Their high-quality, high-energy guides also offer other tours: **Infamous Third Reich Sites** (€12, €9 with WelcomeCard, at 10:00 May–Sept Wed, Fri, and Sat–Sun; March–April and Oct Sat–Sun only; departs from Bahnhof Zoo meeting point only), **Jewish Life in Berlin** (€12, €9 with WelcomeCard, Mon at 10:00 May–Sept), **Potsdam** (€15, €11.20 with WelcomeCard, see page 587), and **Nightlife** (€9, see page 589). Many of the Third Reich and Jewish history sights are difficult to pin down without these excellent walks. Also consider their six-hour trip to the **Sachsenhausen Concentration Camp,** intended "to challenge preconceptions," according to Nick (€15, €11.20 with WelcomeCard, at 10:15 May–Sept Tue, Thu, and Sat–Sun; March–April and Oct Tue and Sat; departs from Bahnhof Zoo meeting point only, requires transit day ticket with zone C—or buy from guide, call office for specifics). Confirm tour schedules at EurAide or by phone with Nick or his wife and partner, Serena (private tours also available, tel. 030/301-9194, www.berlinwalks.com, info@berlinwalks.de).

For a more exhaustive (or, for some, exhausting) walking tour of Berlin, consider **Brewer's Berlin Tours,** run by Terry, a former British embassy worker in East Berlin, and his well-trained staff. These daily tours—especially the in-depth Total version—are legendary for their length, and best for those with a long attention span and a serious interest in Berlin (€10 for either tour, all-day Total Berlin starts at 10:30 and can last 5–8 hrs, 4-hr Classic Berlin starts at 12:30, both meet at New Synagogue, Oranienburger Strasse 28/30, U-Bahn: Oranienburger Tor, look for red sign, also does Potsdam tours twice weekly, mobile 0179-739-5389, www.brewersberlin.com).

▲**City Bus Tours**—For bus tours, you have two choices:

1. Full-blown bus tours. Contact Severin & Kühn (€22, 3 hrs, daily at 10:00 and 14:00, live guides in 2 languages, from Ku'damm 216, tel. 030/880-4190), or take BVG buses from Ku'damm 18 (€20, 2.5 hrs, leave every 30–60 min daily 10:00–17:00, tel. 030/885-9880).

2. Hop-on, hop-off circle tours. Several companies make a circuit of the city (City-Circle Sightseeing is good, offered by

Berlin

1/2 MILE
1 KM
TO PRENZLAUER BERG
T.V. TOWER
ALEXANDER-PLATZ
RATHAUS
NIKOLAI CHURCH
TO OST-BAHNHOF TRAIN STN.
MUSEUM ISLAND
DOM
NEW SYN.
ORANIEN-BURG
BRANDEN-BURG GATE
LEHRTER BAHNHOF
SPREE R.
REICHS-TAG
VICTORY COLUMN
STRASSE DES 17 JUNI
UNTER DEN LINDEN
PARISER PLATZ
FRIEDRICH STR.
LEIPZIG. STRASSE
EBERT
TIERGARTEN
GEMÄLDEGALERIE
BAUHAUS MUSEUM
GERMAN RESIST. MUSEUM
REMAINS OF WALL
MUSEUM OF THE WALL
KOCHSTR.
JEWISH MUSEUM BERLIN
ORANIEN STR.
KREUZBERG
POTSDAMER PLATZ
LIB.
NAT'L GALL
POTSDAM STR.
ERNST REUTER PLATZ
ZOO STN.
ZOO
SAVIGNY-PLATZ
HARD.
KU'DAMM
EUROPA CENTER
KUFURSTEN STR.
KLEIST.
KADEWE
LIETZEN- STR.
KOLLWITZ MUSEUM
MEMORIAL CHURCH
YORCKSTR.
LANDWEHR CANAL
• = S-BAHN STN.
.... = COURSE OF FORMER WALL
DCH

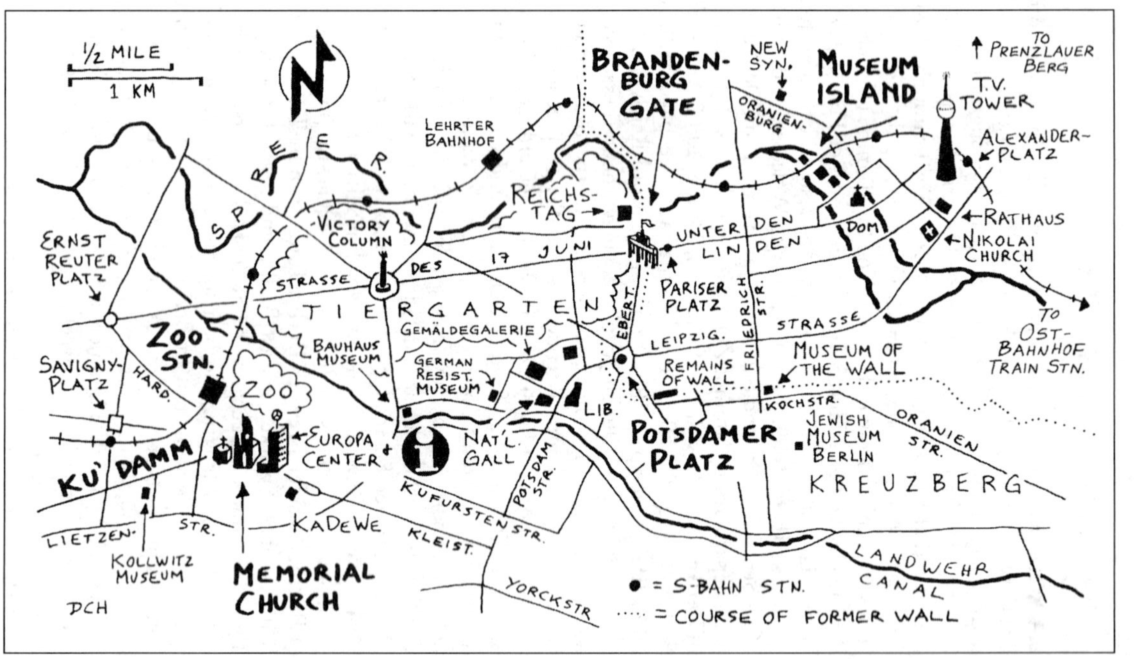

Severin & Kühn). The TI has all the brochures. The tours offer unlimited hop-on, hop-off privileges for their routes (about 14 stops) with a good recorded commentary (€18, daily 10:00–18:00, last bus leaves from Ku'damm at 16:00, 2–4/hr, 2-hr loop). Just hop on where you like and pay the driver. On a sunny day when some double-decker buses go topless, these are a photographer's delight, cruising slowly by just about every top sight in town.

Do-It-Yourself Orientation Tour: Bus #100 from Bahnhof Zoo to the Reichstag

This tour narrates the route of convenient bus #100, which connects my recommended hotel neighborhood in western Berlin with the sights in eastern Berlin. If you have the €18 and two hours for a hop-on, hop-off bus tour (described above), take that instead. But this short €2 bus ride is a fine city introduction. Bus #100 is a sightseer's dream, stopping at Bahnhof Zoo, Europa Center/Hotel Palace, Victory Column (Siegessäule), Reichstag, Brandenburg Gate, Unter den Linden, Pergamon Museum, and ending at Alexanderplatz. While you could ride it to the end, it's more fun to get out at the Reichstag and walk down Unter den Linden at your own pace (using my self-guided commentary on page 567). When combined with the self-guided stroll down Unter den Linden, this tour merits ▲▲▲. Before you take this bus into the East, consider checking out the sights in the West (see page 583).

The Tour Begins: Buses leave from Hardenbergplatz in front of the Bahnhof Zoo (and nearly next door to the Europa Center TI, in front of Hotel Palace; take it in the direction of Mollstrasse and Prenzlauer Allee). Buses come every 10 minutes, and single tickets are good for two hours—so take advantage of hop-on-and-off privileges. Climb aboard, stamp your ticket (giving it a time), and grab a seat on top. This is about a 10-minute ride. Note: The upcoming stop will light up on the reader board inside the bus.

➔ On your left and then straight ahead, before descending into the tunnel, you'll see the bombed-out hulk of the **Kaiser Wilhelm Memorial Church,** with its postwar sister church (described below) and the **Europa Center.** This is the west-end shopping district, a bustling people zone with big department stores nearby. When the Wall came down, East Berliners flocked to this area's department stores (especially KaDeWe, described below). Soon after, the biggest, swankiest new stores were built in the East. Now the West is trying to win those shoppers back by building even bigger and better shopping centers around Europaplatz. Across from the Zoo station, the under-construction Zoofenster tower will be taller than all the buildings you see here.

Emerging from the tunnel, on your immediate right you'll see the Berlin tourist information office.

➲ At the stop in front of Hotel Palace: On the left, the elephant gates mark the entrance to the **Berlin Zoo** and its aquarium (described on page 585).

➲ Driving down Kurfürstenstrasse, you'll pass several Asian restaurants—a reminder that, for most, the best food in Berlin is not German. Turning left, with the huge Tiergarten park in the distance ahead, you'll cross a canal and see the famous **Bauhaus Archive** (an off-white, blocky building) on the right. The Bauhaus movement ushered in a new age of modern architecture that emphasized function over beauty, giving rise to the blocky steel-and-glass skyscrapers in big cities around the world. On the left is Berlin's new embassy row. The big turquoise wall marks the communal home of all five Nordic embassies.

➲ The bus enters a 400-acre park called the **Tiergarten,** packed with cycling paths, joggers, and nude sunbathers. The **Victory Column** (Siegessäule, with the gilded angel, described on page 580) towers above this vast city park that was once a royal hunting grounds, now nicknamed the "green lungs of Berlin."

➲ On the left, a block after leaving the Victory Column: The 18th-century, late-rococo **Bellevue Palace** is the German White House. Formerly a Nazi VIP guest house, it's now the residence of the federal president (whose power is mostly ceremonial). If the flag's out, he's in.

➲ Driving along the Spree River: This park area was a residential district before World War II. Now, on the left-hand side, it's filled with the buildings of the **national government.** The huge brick "brown snake" complex was built to house government workers—but it didn't sell, so now its apartments are available to anyone. A Henry Moore sculpture entitled *Butterfly* floats in front of the slope-roofed House of World Cultures (Berliners have nicknamed this building "the pregnant oyster"). The modern tower (next on left) is a carillon with 68 bells (1987).

➲ While you could continue on bus #100, it's better on foot from here. Leap out at the **Platz der Republik.** Through the trees on the left you'll see Germany's new and sprawling chancellery. Started during the more imperial rule of Helmut Kohl, it's now considered overly grand. The big park is the Platz der Republik, where the Victory Column stood until Hitler moved it. The gardens were recently dug up to build underground train tracks to serve Berlin's new main train station (the Lehrter Bahnhof, across the field). Watch your step—excavators found a 250-pound undetonated American bomb.

➲ Just down the street stands the **Reichstag.** As you approach the old building with the new dome, look for the row of slate slabs imbedded in the ground (looks like a fancy slate bicycle rack). This is a memorial to the 96 politicians who were murdered and persecuted because their politics didn't agree with Chancellor Hitler's. Each slab is marked with a name and the party that politician belonged to—mostly KPD (Communists) and SPD (Socialists).

Throughout Berlin, you'll see posters advertising a play called *Ich bin's nicht, Adolf Hitler es gewesen (It wasn't me, Adolf Hitler did it).* The photo is of a model by Hitler's architect Albert Speer of what Berlin was to look like when the Nazis controlled the planet. Hitler planned to rename his capital city "Germania Metropolis." The enormous dome is the Great Hall of the People. Below it and to the right is the tiny Reichstag. Imagine this huge 950-foot-high dome dwarfing everything in Berlin (in the field to your left as you face the Reichstag).

Now visit the Reichstag (open late, no lines in evening), described below.

SIGHTS

Eastern Berlin

Along Unter den Linden

These sights line the famous Unter den Linden—the main boulevard that leads through the heart of former downtown East Berlin. I've arranged them in the order of a convenient self-guided orientation walk, picking up where my "Do-It-Yourself Orientation Tour" (above) leaves off. Allow a comfortable hour for this walk from the Reichstag to Alexanderplatz, including time for lingering (but not museum stops).

▲▲▲Reichstag Building—The Parliament building—the heart of German democracy—has a short but complicated and emotional history. When it was inaugurated in the 1890s, the last emperor, Kaiser Wilhelm, disdainfully called it the "house for chatting." It was from here that the German Republic was proclaimed in 1918. In 1933, this symbol of democracy nearly burned down. While the Nazis blamed a Communist plot, some believe that Hitler himself planned the fire, using it as a handy excuse to frame the Communists and grab power. As World War II drew to a close, Stalin ordered his troops to take the Reichstag from the Nazis by May 1 (the workers' holiday). More than 1,500 Nazis made their last stand here—extending World War II by two days. On April 30, 1945, it fell to the Allies. It was hardly used from 1933 to 1999. For the building's 101st birthday in 1995, the Bulgarian-American artist Christo wrapped it in silvery-gold cloth. It was then wrapped again in scaffolding, rebuilt by British architect Lord Norman Foster, and turned into the new parliamentary home of the Bundestag (Germany's lower house). To many Germans, the proud resurrection of the Reichstag—which no longer has a hint of Hitler—symbolizes the end of a terrible chapter in German history.

The **glass cupola** rises 155 feet above the ground, and a double staircase winds 755 feet to the top for a grand view. Inside the dome, a cone of 360 mirrors reflects natural light into the legislative chamber below. Lit from inside at night, this gives Berlin a memorable night-light. The environmentally friendly cone also helps with air circulation, drawing hot air out of the legislative chamber and pulling in cool air from below.

Hours: Free, daily 8:00–24:00, last entry 22:00, most crowded 10:00–16:00 (wait in line to go up—good street musicians, metal detectors, no big luggage allowed, some hour-long English tours when parliament is not sitting, tel. 030/2273-2152, www.bundestag.de).

Line-Beating Tip: Those with table reservations at the Dachgarten rooftop restaurant don't wait in the long lines. Go straight to the front and tell them you have a reservation. Reserve in advance by phone or e-mail (€15–26 entrées with a view, daily 9:30–16:30 & 18:30–24:00, tel. 030/2262-9933, kaeferreservierung.berlin@feinkost-kaefer.de).

Self-Guided Tour: As you approach the building, look above the door, surrounded by stone patches from WWII bomb damage, to see the motto and promise: *Dem Deutschen Volke* ("to the German people"). The open, airy lobby towers 100 feet high, with 65-foot-tall colors of the German flag. Glass doors show the **central legislative chamber.** The message: There will be no secrets in government. Look inside. The seats are "Reichstag blue," a lilac-blue color designed by the architect to brighten the otherwise gray interior. The German eagle (a.k.a. the "fat hen") spreads his wings behind the podium. Notice the doors marked "Yes," "No," and "Abstain"...the Bundestag's traditional "sheep jump" way of counting votes (for critical and close votes, all 669 members leave and vote by walking through the door of their choice).

Ride the elevator to the base of the glass **dome.** Take time to study the photos and read the circle of captions—an excellent exhibit telling the Reichstag story. Then study the surrounding architecture: a broken collage of old on new, like Germany's history. Notice the dome's giant and unobtrusive sunscreen that moves as necessary with the sun. Peer down through the skylight to look over the shoulders of the elected representatives at work. For Germans, the best view is down—keeping a close eye on their government.

Start at the ramp nearest the elevator and wind up to the top of the **double ramp.** Take a 360-degree survey of the city as you hike: First, the big park is the **Tiergarten,** the "green lungs" of Berlin. Beyond that is the **Teufelsberg,** or Devil's Hill (built of rubble from the bombed city in the late 1940s and famous during the Cold War as a powerful ear of the West—notice the telecommunications tower on top). Given the violent and tragic history of Berlin—a city blown apart by bombs and covered over by bulldozers—locals say, "You have to be suspicious when you see the nice, green park." Find the **Victory Column** (Seigessäule, moved by Hitler in the 1930s from in front of the Reichstag to its present position in the Tiergarten). Next, scenes of the new Berlin spiral into your view—**Potsdamer Platz,** marked by the conical glass tower that houses Sony's European headquarters. The yellow building to the right is the Berlin Philharmonic Concert Hall. Continue circling left, and find the green chariot atop the **Brandenburg Gate.** A monument to Gypsy victims of the Holocaust will be built between the Reichstag and Brandenburg Gate. (Gypsies, as disdained by the Nazis as were the Jews, lost the same percentage of their population to Hitler.) Another Holocaust memorial will be built just south of Brandenburg Gate. Next, you'll see **former East Berlin** and the city's next huge construction zone, with a forest of 300-foot-tall skyscrapers in the works. Notice the TV Tower (with the Pope's Revenge—explained on page 573), the Berlin Cathedral's massive dome, the red tower of the city hall, the golden dome of the New Synagogue, and the Reichstag's **Dachgarten Restaurant** ("Roof Garden"—see above). Follow the train tracks in the distance to the left toward a huge construction zone marking the future central Berlin train station, Lehrter Bahnhof. Just in front of it, alone in a field, is the Swiss Embassy. This used to be surrounded by buildings, but now it's the only one left. Complete your spin tour with the blocky **Chancellery,** nicknamed by locals "the washing machine." It may look like a pharaoh's tomb, but it's the office and home of Germany's most powerful person, the chancellor.

Let's continue our walk and cross what was the Berlin Wall. Leaving the Reichstag, turn left around the building. You'll see the Brandenburg Gate ahead on your right. Stay on the park side of the street for a better view of the gate. As you cross at the light, look down and notice the double row of cobblestones—this marks where the Wall used to be.

▲▲Brandenburg Gate (Brandenburger Tor)—The historic Brandenburg Gate (1791) is the last survivor of 14 gates in Berlin's old city wall (this one led to the city of Brandenburg). The gate was the symbol of Prussian Berlin...and later the symbol of a divided Berlin. It's crowned by a majestic four-horse chariot with the Goddess of Peace at the reins. Napoleon took this statue to the Louvre in Paris in 1806. When the Prussians got it back, she was renamed the Goddess of Victory.

The gate sat unused, part of a sad circle dance called the Wall, for more than 25 years. Now postcards all over town show the ecstatic day—November 9, 1989—when the world enjoyed the sight of happy Berliners jamming the gate like flowers on a parade

The Berlin Wall

The 100-mile "Anti-Fascist Protective Rampart," as it was called by the East German government, was erected almost overnight in 1961 to stop the outward flow of people (3 million leaked out between 1949 and 1961). The 13-foot-high Wall *(Mauer)* had a 16-foot tank ditch, a no-man's-land (or "death strip") that was 30 to 160 feet wide, and 300 sentry towers. During its 28 years, there were 1,693 cases when border guards fired, 3,221 arrests, and 5,043 documented successful escapes (565 of these were East German guards).

The carnival atmosphere of those first years after the Wall fell is gone, but hawkers still sell "authentic" pieces of the Wall, DDR (East German) flags, and military paraphernalia to gawking tourists. When it fell, the Wall was literally carried away by the euphoria. What managed to survive has been nearly devoured by a decade of persistent "Wall peckers."

Americans—the Cold War victors—have the biggest appetite for Wall-related sights, and a few bits and pieces remain for us to seek out. Pick up the free brochure *Berlin: The Wall,* available at EurAide or the TI, which traces the history of the Wall and helps you find the remaining chunks and other Wall-related sights in Berlin. You can also rent a *Hear We Go* audioguide about the Wall, at Checkpoint Charlie, which guides you from the checkpoint along Zimmerstrasse to Potsdamer Platz, and then brings you back via Leipziger Strasse and Mauerstrasse (€7, 80 min).

float. Pause a minute and think about struggles for freedom—past and present. (There's actually a "quiet room" built into the gate for this purpose, daily 11:00–18:00.) Around the gate, look at the information boards with pictures of how much this area changed throughout the 20th century. The latest chapter: The shiny white gate was completely restored in 2002. The TI within the gate is open daily 10:00–18:00.

Ponder the fact that you're standing in what was the so-called "death strip." Now cross through the gate, into...

▲Pariser Platz—This "Paris Square" was once filled with important government buildings—all bombed to smithereens in World War II. For decades, it was an unrecognizable, deserted no-man's-land. But now, sparkling new banks, embassies (the French Embassy rebuilt where it was before World War II), and a swanky hotel have filled in the void.

Face the gate and look to your left. The **U.S. Embassy** once stood here, and a new one will stand in the same spot (due to be completed in 2006). This new embassy has been controversial; for safety's sake, Uncle Sam wanted it away from other buildings, but the Germans preferred it in its original location. A compromise was reached, building the embassy by the gate—but rerouting several major roads to reduce the security risk. The new **Holocaust memorial,** consisting of more than 2,500 gravestone-like pillars, was completed in 2005 and stands behind the new embassy.

Just to the left, the **DZ Bank building** is by Frank Gehry, the unconventional American architect famous for Bilbao's golden Guggenheim, Prague's Dancing House, and Seattle's EMP. Gehry fans might be surprised at the DZ Bank building's low profile. Structures on Pariser Platz are expected to be bland so as not to draw attention away from the Brandenburg Gate. (The glassy facade of the Academy of Arts, next to Gehry's building, is controversial for that very reason.) For your fix of the good old Gehry, step into the lobby and check out its undulating interior.

Brandenburg Gate, the center of old Berlin, sits on a major boulevard, running east–west through Berlin. The western segment, called Strasse des 17. Juni, stretches for four miles from the Victory Column (past the flea market—see page 580) to the Olympic Stadium. But we'll follow this city axis in the opposite direction, east, up what is known as Unter den Linden—into the core of old imperial Berlin and past what was once the palace of the Hohenzollern family who ruled Prussia and then Germany. The palace—the reason for just about all you'll see—is a phantom sight, long gone (though some Berliners hope to rebuild it). Alexanderplatz, which marks the end of this walk, is near the base of the giant TV Tower hovering in the distance.

▲▲Unter den Linden—This is the heart of former East Berlin. In Berlin's good old days, Unter den Linden was one of Europe's grand boulevards. In the 15th century, this carriageway led from the palace to the hunting grounds (today's big Tiergarten). In the 17th century, Hohenzollern princes and princesses moved in and built their palaces here so they could be near the Prussian emperor.

Named centuries ago for its thousand linden trees, this was the most elegant street of Prussian Berlin before Hitler's time and the main drag of East Berlin after his reign. Hitler replaced the venerable trees—many 250 years old—with Nazi flags. Popular discontent actually drove him to replant linden trees. Today, Unter den Linden is no longer a depressing Cold War cul-de-sac, and its pre-Hitler strolling café ambience is returning.

As you walk toward the giant TV Tower, the big building you see jutting out into the street on your right is the **Hotel Adlon.** It hosted such notables as Charlie Chaplin, Albert Einstein, and Greta Garbo. (This was where Garbo said, "I want to be alone," during the filming of *Grand Hotel.*) Destroyed in World War II, the grand Adlon was rebuilt in 1996. See how far you can get inside.

Unter den Linden

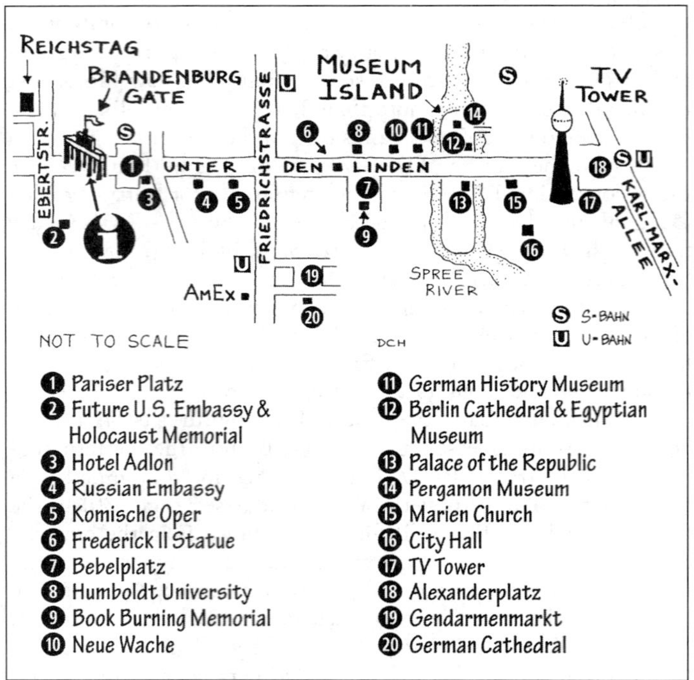

The Unter den Linden S-Bahn station ahead of you is one of Berlin's former **ghost subway stations.** During the Cold War, most underground train tunnels were simply blocked at the border. But a few Western lines looped through the East. To make a little hard Western cash, the Eastern government rented the use of these tracks to the West, but the stations (which happened to be in East Berlin) were strictly off-limits. For 28 years, the stations were unused, as Western trains slowly passed through, seeing only eerie DDR (East German) guards and lots of cobwebs. Literally within days of the fall of the Wall, these stations were reopened, and today they are a time warp (with dreary old green tiles and original signage). Go down into the station, walk along the track, and exit on the other side, following signs to Russische Botschaft...the Russian Embassy.

The **Russian Embassy** was the first big postwar building project in East Berlin. It's built in the powerful, simplified, neoclassical style Stalin liked. While not as important now as it was a few years ago, it's immense as ever. It flies the Russian white, red, and blue. Find the hammer-and-sickle motif decorating the window frames. Continuing past the Aeroflot Airline offices, look across the street to the right to see the back of the **Komische Oper** (Comic Opera;

program and view of ornate interior posted in window). While the exterior is ugly, the fine old theater interior—amazingly missed by WWII bombs—survives. The shop ahead on your right is an amusing mix of antiques, local guidebooks, knickknacks, and East Berlin nostalgia souvenirs.

The West lost no time in consuming the East; consequently, some are feeling a wave of nostalgia—or *Ost*-algia—for the old days of East Berlin. In recent local elections, nearly half of East Berlin's voters—and 6 percent of West Berliners—voted for the old Communist Party. One symbol of that era has been given a reprieve. As you continue to Friedrichstrasse, look at the DDR-style pedestrian lights, and you'll realize that someone had a sense of humor back then. The perky red and green men—*Ampelmännchen*—were under threat of replacement by the far less jaunty Western signs. Fortunately, the DDR signals will be kept after all.

At **Friedrichstrasse,** look right. Before the war, the Unter den Linden/Friedrichstrasse intersection was the heart of Berlin. In the 1920s, Berlin was famous for its anything-goes love of life. This was the cabaret drag, a springboard to stardom for young and vampy entertainers like Marlene Dietrich. (Born in 1901, Dietrich starred in the first German "talkie" and then headed straight to Hollywood.) Over the last few years, this boulevard—lined with super department stores (such as Galeries Lafayette, with its cool marble and glass waste-of-space interior, Mon–Sat 9:30–20:00, closed Sun; belly up to its amazing ground-floor viewpoint) and big-time hotels (such as the Hilton and Four Seasons)—has slowly begun to replace Ku'damm as the grand commerce and café boulevard of Berlin. (More recently, the West is retaliating with some new stores of its own.) Across from Galeries Lafayette is American Express (handy for any train-ticket needs, Mon–Fri 9:00–19:00, Sat 10:00–13:00, closed Sun, travel agency tel. 030/201-7400; for traveler's checks, call tel. 0800-185-3100).

If you continued down Friedrichstrasse, you'd wind up at the sights listed in "South of Unter den Linden," below—including the Museum of the Wall at Checkpoint Charlie (a 10-min walk from here). But for now, continue along Unter den Linden. You'll notice big, colorful **water pipes** around here, and throughout Berlin. As long as the city remains a big construction zone, it will be laced with these drainage pipes—key to any building project. Berlin's high water table means any new basement comes with lots of pumping out.

Continue down Unter den Linden a few more blocks, past the large equestrian statue of Frederick II ("the Great"), and turn right into the square called **Bebelplatz.** Stand on the glass window in the center. (Construction of an underground parking lot might prevent you from reaching the glass plate.)

Frederick the Great—who ruled from 1740 to 1786—established Prussia as a military power. This square was the center of the "new Rome" Frederick envisioned. Much of Frederick's palace actually survived World War II but was torn down by the communists since it symbolized the imperialist past. Now some Berliners want to rebuild the palace, from scratch, exactly as it once was. Other Berliners insist that what's done is done.

Bebelplatz is bounded by great buildings. The German State Opera was bombed in 1941, rebuilt to bolster morale and to celebrate its centennial in 1943, and bombed again in 1945. The former state library is where Lenin studied much of his exile away (climb to the second floor of the library to see a stained-glass window depicting his life's work with almost biblical reverence; there's a good café with light food, Tim's Canadian Deli, downstairs). The round Catholic St. Hedwig's Church—nicknamed the "upside-down teacup"—was built to placate the subjects of Catholic lands Frederick added to his empire. (Step inside to see the cheesy DDR government renovation.)

Humboldt University, across Unter den Linden, was one of Europe's greatest. Marx and Lenin (not the brothers or the sisters) studied here, as did Grimm (both brothers) and more than two dozen Nobel Prize winners. Einstein, who was Jewish, taught here until taking a spot at Princeton in 1932 (smart guy).

Look down through the glass you're standing on: The room of empty bookshelves is a memorial to the notorious Nazi **book burning.** It was on this square in 1933 that staff and students from the university threw 20,000 newly forbidden books (like Einstein's) into a huge bonfire on the orders of the Nazi propaganda minister Joseph Goebbels.

Continue down Unter den Linden. The next square on your right holds the Opernpalais' restaurants (see page 598 of "Eating"). On the university side, the Greek temple–like building is the **Neue Wache** (the emperor's "New Guardhouse," from 1816). When the Wall fell, this memorial to the victims of fascism was transformed into a new national memorial. Look inside, where a replica of the Käthe Kollwitz statue, *Mother with Her Dead Son,* is surrounded by thought-provoking silence. This marks the tombs of Germany's unknown soldier and the unknown concentration camp victim. The inscription in front reads, "To the victims of war and tyranny." Read the entire statement in English (on wall, right of entrance).

After the Neue Wache, the next building you'll see is the **German History Museum** (Deutsches Historisches Museum, €2, daily 10:00–18:00, tel. 030/203-040, www.dhm.de). I find its I. M. Pei–designed annex with a spiraling glass staircase more interesting than the collection (to find the annex, go down the street—Hinter dem Giesshaus—to the left of the museum).

Just before the bridge, wander left along the canal through a tiny but colorful arts-and-crafts market (weekends only, a larger flea market is just outside the Pergamon Museum; see page 580). Canal tour boats leave from here. Then go back out to the main road and cross the bridge to...

Museum Island (Museumsinsel)—This island, home of Germany's first museums, is gradually being renovated to consolidate the art collections of East and West Berlin (see below). For 300 years, the island's big square, the **Lustgarten,** has flip-flopped between being a military parade ground and a people-friendly park, depending upon the political tenor of the time. In 1999, it was made into a park again (read the history posted in corner opposite church). On a sunny day, it's packed with relaxing locals and is one of Berlin's most enjoyable public spaces.

The towering church is the century-old **Berlin Cathedral** (Berliner Dom, €4, €5 includes access to dome gallery, Mon–Sat 9:00–19:00, Sun 12:00–19:00, on summer Thu church—but not dome gallery—open until 22:00, www.berliner-dom.de; May–Sept organ concerts offered most Wed–Fri at 15:00, free with regular admission; for other concerts, visit ticket office on Lustgarten side, Mon–Fri 10:00–17:30, closed Sat–Sun, tel. 030/2026-9136). Inside, the great reformers (Luther, Calvin, and company) stand around the brilliantly restored dome like stern saints guarding their theology. Frederick I rests in an ornate tomb (right transept, near entrance to dome). The 270-step climb to the outdoor dome gallery is tough, but offers pleasant, breezy views of the city at the finish line (last entry 30 min before closing, dome closes in bad weather and at 17:00 in winter). The crypt downstairs is not worth a look.

Across Unter den Linden is the decrepit **Palace of the Republic** (with the copper-tinted windows). A symbol of the communist days, it was East Berlin's parliament building and futuristic entertainment complex. Although it officially has a date with the wrecking ball, many Easterners want it saved, and its future is still uncertain.

Berlin hopes to make Museum Island into one of the finest museum complexes in the world. They've got a good headstart with the excellent Pergamon Museum (see below). Berlin's Egyptian Museum, with the famous bust of Queen Nefertiti, moved into the nearby Altes Museum in August, 2005 (see page 572). You could visit any of the following museums—the Pergamon, Egyptian Museum, or Old National Gallery—before continuing our walk. Once you're finished, skip down to " Museum Island to Alexanderplatz," below, to resume the walk.

▲▲Pergamon Museum—Of all the island's museums, the Pergamon is the best, followed by the Egyptian Museum. Its highlight is the fantastic Pergamon Altar. From a second-century B.C.

Greek temple, the altar shows the Greeks under Zeus and Athena beating the giants in a dramatic pig pile of mythological mayhem. Check out the action spilling onto the stairs. The Babylonian Ishtar Gate (glazed blue tiles from the 6th century B.C.) and many ancient Greek and Mesopotamian treasures are also impressive (€8, covered by Museumspass, free Thu after 18:00, open Tue–Sun 10:00–18:00, Thu until 22:00, closed Mon, courtyard café, behind Museum Island's red-stone museum of antiquities, Am Kupfergraben, tel. 030/2090-5577 or 030/209-050). The excellent audioguide (free with admission, but €4 during free Thu extended hours) covers the museum's highlights. Don't mind the scaffolding. Renovation projects (due to last until 2008) may cause small sections of the museum to close temporarily in 2006, but the museum will remain open.

▲▲Egyptian Museum (Agyptische Museum)—The museum offers one of the great thrills in art appreciation—gazing into the still-young and beautiful face of 3,000-year-old Queen Nefertiti, the wife of King Akhenaton (€8, covered by Museumspass, free Thu after 14:00, open daily 10:00–18:00, free English audioguide, inside Altes Museum at Bodenstrasse 1–3, tel. 030/2090-5201).

This bust of Queen Nefertiti (c. 1340 B.C.) is perhaps the most famous piece of Egyptian art in Europe. Discovered in 1912, it shows the Marilyn Monroe of the early 20th century, with all the right beauty marks: long neck, symmetrical face, and just the right makeup (she's called "Berlin's most beautiful woman"). The bust never left its studio, but served as a master model for all other portraits of the queen. (That's probably why the left eye was never inlaid.) Buried for over 3,000 years, she was found by a German team who, by agreement with the Egyptian government, got to take home any workshop models they found. Although this bust is not representative of Egyptian art, it has become a symbol for Egyptian art by popular acclaim.

Old National Gallery (Alte Nationalgalerie)—This gallery shows 19th-century German Romantic art: man against nature, Greek ruins dwarfed in enchanted forests, medieval churches, and powerful mountains (€8, covered by Museumspass, free Thu after 18:00, open Tue–Sun 10:00–18:00, Thu until 20:00, closed Mon, tel. 030/2090-5801).

Museum Island to Alexanderplatz: Continue walking down Unter den Linden. Before crossing the bridge (and leaving Museum Island), look right. The pointy twin spires of the 13th-century Nikolai Church mark the center of medieval Berlin. This Nikolai-Viertel (district) was restored by the DDR and was trendy in the last years of socialism. Today, it's dull and, with limited time, not worth a visit.

As you cross the bridge, look left in the distance to see the gilded **New Synagogue,** rebuilt after WWII bombing (see page

578). Across the river to the left of the bridge is the construction site of a new shopping center with a huge aquarium in the center. The elevator will go right through the middle of an undersea world.

Walk toward **Marien Church** (from 1270, interesting but very faded old *Dance of Death* mural inside door) at the base of the TV Tower. The big, red-brick building past the trees on the right is the **City Hall,** built after the revolution of 1848 and arguably the first democratic building in the city. In the park are grandfatherly statues of Marx and Engels (nicknamed by locals "the old pensioners"). Surrounding them are stainless-steel monoliths depicting the struggles of the workers of the world.

The 1,200-foot-tall **TV Tower** (Fernsehturm) offers a fine view from halfway up (€7, daily March–Oct 9:00–1:00, Nov–Feb 10:00–24:00, tel. 030/242-3333). The tower offers a handy city orientation and an interesting view of the flat, red-roofed sprawl of Berlin—including a peek inside the city's many courtyards *(Höfe).* Consider a kitschy trip to the observation deck for the view and lunch in its revolving restaurant (reservations smart for dinner, same phone number). Built (with Swedish know-how) in 1969, the tower was meant to show the power of the atheistic state at a time when DDR leaders were having the crosses removed from church domes and spires. But when the sun shined on their tower, the greatest spire in East Berlin, a huge cross, reflected on the mirrored ball. Cynics called it "The Pope's Revenge." East Berliners dubbed the tower the "Big Asparagus." They joked that if it fell over, they'd have an elevator to the West.

Farther east, pass under the train tracks into **Alexanderplatz.** This area—especially the Kaufhof department store—was the commercial pride and joy of East Berlin. Today, it's still a landmark, with a major U- and S-Bahn station.

Our orientation stroll is finished. For a ride through workaday eastern Berlin, with its Lego-hell apartments (dreary even with their new face-lifts), hop back on bus #100 from here. It loops five minutes to the end of the line and then, after a couple minutes' break, heads on back. (This bus retraces your route, finishing at Bahnhof Zoo.) Or consider extending this foray into eastern Berlin, to...

Karl-Marx-Allee—The buildings along Karl-Marx-Allee in East Berlin (just beyond Alexanderplatz) were completely leveled by the Red Army in 1945. When Stalin decided this main drag should be a showcase street, he had it rebuilt with lavish Soviet aid and named it Stalin Allee. Today this street, done in the bold "Stalin Gothic" style so common in Moscow in the 1950s, has been restored (and named after Karl Marx)—providing a rare look at Berlin's communist days. Cruise down Karl-Marx-Allee by taxi, or ride the

U-Bahn to Strausberger Platz and walk to Schillingstrasse. There are some fine Social Realist reliefs on the buildings, and the lamp-posts incorporate the wings of a phoenix (rising from the ashes) in their design.

South of Unter den Linden

The following sights—heavy on Nazi and Wall history—are listed roughly north to south (as you reach them from Unter den Linden).

▲▲Gendarmenmarkt—This delightful and historic square is bounded by twin churches, a tasty chocolate shop, and the concert hall (designed by Schinkel, the man who put the neoclassical stamp on Berlin and Dresden) for the Berlin symphony. In summer, it hosts a few outdoor cafés, *Biergartens,* and sometimes concerts. The name of the square—part French and part German—reminds us that in the 17th century, a fifth of all Berliners were French émigrés, Protestant Huguenots fleeing Catholic France. Back then, tolerant Berlin was a magnet for the persecuted. The émigrés vitalized the city with new ideas and know-how.

The German Cathedral (described below) on the square has an exhibit worthwhile for history buffs. The French Cathedral (Franzosischer Dom) offers a humble museum on the Huguenots (€1.50, Tue–Sun 12:00–17:00, closed Mon) and a chance to climb 254 steps to the top for a grand city view (€1.50, daily 9:00–19:00).

Fassbender & Rausch, on the corner near the German Cathedral, is Europe's biggest chocolate store. After 150 years of chocolate-making, this family-owned business proudly displays its sweet delights—250 different kinds—on a 55-foot-long buffet. Truffles are sold for about €0.50 each. The shop's evangelical Herr Ostwald (a.k.a. Benny) would love you to try his best-seller: tiramisu (Mon–Fri 10:00–20:00, Sat 10:00–18:00, Sun 12:00–20:00, corner of Mohrenstrasse at Charlottenstrasse 60, tel. 030/2045-8440).

German Cathedral (Deutscher Dom)—This cathedral houses the thought-provoking *Milestones, Setbacks, Sidetracks* (Wege, Irrwege, Umwege) exhibit, which traces the history of the German parliamentary system. The exhibit is well done and more interesting than it sounds. There are no English descriptions, but you can follow a fine and free 90-minute audioguide (passport required for deposit) or buy the detailed €10 guidebook (free, June–Aug Tue–Sun 10:00–19:00, Tue until 22:00, closed Mon; Sept–May Tue–Sun 10:00–18:00, Tue until 22:00, closed Mon; on Gendarmenmarkt just off Friedrichstrasse, tel. 030/2273-0431).

▲▲▲Museum of the Wall at Checkpoint Charlie (Mauermuseum Haus am Checkpoint Charlie)—While the famous border checkpoint between the American and Soviet sectors is long gone, its memory is preserved by one of Europe's most

Eastern Berlin

interesting museums: the House at Checkpoint Charlie. During the Cold War, it stood defiantly—spitting distance from the border guards—showing off all the clever escapes over, under, and through the Wall.

Today, while the drama is over and hunks of the Wall stand like victory scalps at its door, the museum still tells a gripping history of the Wall, recounts the many ingenious escape attempts (early years—with a cruder wall—saw more escapes), and includes plenty of video and film coverage of those heady days when people-power tore down the Wall (€9.50, assemble 10 tourists and get in for €5.50 each, €3 audioguide, discount with WelcomeCard but not covered by Museumspass, cash only, daily 9:00–22:00, U-6 to Kochstrasse or—better from Zoo—U-2 to Stadtmitte, Friedrichstrasse 43–45,

Hitler and the Third Reich

While many come to Berlin to see Hitler sights, these are essentially invisible. The German Resistance Museum is in German only and difficult for the tourist to appreciate (see page 580). The *Topography of Terror* (SS and Gestapo headquarters) is a fascinating exhibit but—again—only in German, and all that remains of the building is its foundation (see below). (Both museums have helpful audioguides in English.) Hitler's bunker is completely gone (near Potsdamer Platz). Your best bet for "Hitler sites" is to take the Infamous Third Reich Sites walking tour offered by Berlin Walks (see "Tours," page 559). EurAide has a good flier listing and explaining sites related to the Third Reich.

tel. 030/253-7250, www.mauermuseum.de). If you're pressed for time, this is a good after-dinner sight. With extra time, consider the €7 "Hear We Go" audioguide about the Wall that takes you outside the museum (80 min).

Where Checkpoint Charlie once stood, notice the thought-provoking post with larger-than-life posters of a young American soldier facing east and a young Russian soldier facing west. Around you are reconstructions of the old checkpoint. It's not named for a person, but for Number Three—as in Alpha (at the East–West German border, a hundred miles west of here), Bravo (as you enter Berlin proper), and Charlie (the most famous because it was the only place where foreigners could pass). A few yards away (on Zimmerstrasse), a glass panel describes the former checkpoint. From there, a double row of cobbles in Zimmerstrasse traces the former path of the Wall (these innocuous cobbles run throughout the city). Follow it one very long block to Wilhelmstrasse, a surviving stretch of Wall, and the...

Topography of Terror (Topographie des Terrors)—The park behind the Zimmerstrasse/Wilhelmstrasse bit of Wall marks the site of the command center of Hitler's Gestapo and SS. Because of the horrible things planned here, the rubble of these buildings will always be left as rubble. The SS, Hitler's personal bodyguards, grew to become a state-within-a-state, with its talons in every corner of German society. Along an excavated foundation of the building, an exhibit tells the story of National Socialism and its victims in Berlin (free, info booth open daily May–Sept 10:00–20:00, Oct–April 10:00–18:00 or until dark, free English audioguide, requires passport as a deposit, available only until 18:45 in summer, tel. 030/2548-6703, www.topographie.de).

Across the street (facing the Wall) is the **German Finance**

Ministry (Bundesministerium der Finanzen). Formerly the headquarters of the Nazi Luftwaffe (Air Force), this is the only major Hitler-era government building that survived the war's bombs. The communists used it to house their—no joke—Ministry of Ministries. Walk up Wilhelmstrasse (to the north) to see an entry gate (on your left) that looks much like it did when Germany occupied nearly all of Europe. On the north side of the building (farther up Wilhelmstrasse, at corner with Leipziger Strasse) is a wonderful example of communist art. The mural (from the 1950s) is classic Social Realism, showing the entire society—industrial laborers, farmworkers, women, and children—all happily singing the same patriotic song. This was the communist ideal. For the reality, look at the ground in the courtyard in front of the mural to see an enlarged photograph from a 1953 uprising here against the communists—quite a contrast.

▲▲Jewish Museum Berlin (Jüdisches Museum Berlin)—This museum is one of Europe's best Jewish sights. The highly conceptual building is a sight in itself, and the museum inside—an overview of the rich culture and history of Europe's Jewish community—is excellent. The Holocaust is appropriately remembered, but it doesn't overwhelm this celebration of Jewish life.

Designed by American architect Daniel Libeskind (who is re-developing New York City's World Trade Center site), the zinc-walled building's zigzag shape is pierced by voids symbolic of the irreplaceable cultural loss caused by the Holocaust. Enter the museum through the 18th-century Baroque building next door, then go through an underground tunnel to reach the main exhibit. While underground, you can follow the Axis of Exile to a disorienting slanted garden with 49 pillars, or to the Axis of Holocaust, an eerily empty tower shut off from the outside world.

When you emerge from underground, climb the stairs to the engaging, thought-provoking, and accessible museum. There are many interactive exhibits (spell your name in Hebrew) and pieces of artwork (the *Fallen Leaves* sculpture in the building's largest void is especially powerful), and it's all very kid-friendly (peel the giant garlic and climb through a pomegranate tree). English explanations interpret both the exhibits and the design of the very symbolic building. The museum is in a nondescript residential neighborhood a 10-minute walk from the Checkpoint Charlie museum, but it's well worth the trip (€5, covered by Museumspass, discount with WelcomeCard, daily 10:00–20:00, Mon until 22:00, closed on Jewish holidays, tight security includes bag check and metal detectors; U-Bahn line 1, 6, or 15 to Hallesches Tor, take exit marked Jüdisches Museum, exit straight ahead, then turn right on Franz-Klühs-Strasse, museum is 5 min ahead on your left at Lindenstrasse 9; tel. 030/2599-3300, www.jmberlin.de).

The museum has a good café/restaurant (€9 daily specials, lunch 12:00–16:00, snacks at other times, tel. 030/2593-9760).

East Side Gallery—The biggest remaining stretch of the Wall is now "the world's longest outdoor art gallery." It stretches for nearly a mile and is covered with murals painted by artists from around the world. The murals are routinely whitewashed so new ones can be painted. This segment of the Wall makes a poignant walk. For a quick look, take the S-Bahn to Ostbahnhof station (follow signs to Stralauerplatz exit; once outside, TV Tower will be to your right; go left and at next corner look to your right—Wall is across the busy street). The gallery only survives until a land-ownership dispute can be solved, when it will likely be developed like the rest of the city. (Given the recent history, imagine the complexity of finding rightful owners of all this suddenly-very-valuable land.) If you walk the entire length, you'll find a small Wall souvenir shop at the end (they'll stamp your passport with the former East German stamp) and a bridge crossing the river to a subway station at Schlesisches Tor (in Kreuzberg).

Kreuzberg—This district—once abutting the dreary Wall and inhabited mostly by poor Turkish guest laborers and their families—is still run-down, with graffiti-riddled buildings and plenty of student and Turkish street life. It offers a gritty look at melting-pot Berlin in a city where original Berliners are as rare as old buildings. Berlin is the fourth-largest Turkish city in the world, and Kreuzberg is its "downtown." But to call it a "little Istanbul" insults the big one. You'll see *döner kebab* stands, shops decorated with spray paint, and mothers wearing scarves. For a dose of Kreuzberg without getting your fingers dirty, joyride on bus #129 (catch it near Jewish Museum). For a colorful stroll, take the U-Bahn to Kottbusser Tor and wander—ideally on Tuesday and Friday between 12:00 and 18:00, when the Turkish Market sprawls along the Maybachufer riverbank.

North of Unter den Linden

While there are few major sights to the north of Unter den Linden, this area has some of Berlin's trendiest, most interesting neighborhoods.

▲▲New Synagogue (Neue Synagogue)—A shiny gilded dome marks the New Synagogue, now a museum and cultural center on Oranienburger Strasse. Only the dome and facade have been restored, and a window overlooks a vacant field marking what used to be the synagogue. The largest and finest synagogue in Berlin before World War II, it was desecrated by Nazis on "Crystal Night" (Kristallnacht) in 1938, bombed in 1943, and partially rebuilt in 1990. Inside, past tight security, there's a small but moving exhibit on the Berlin Jewish community through the centuries with some good English descriptions (ground floor and first floor). On its facade, the *Vergesst es nie* message—added by East Berlin Jews in 1966—means "Never forget." East Berlin had only a few hundred Jews, but now that the city is united, the Jewish community numbers about 12,000 (€3, Sun–Thu 10:00–18:00, Fri 10:00–14:00, closed Sat, May–Aug Sun–Mon until 20:00 and Fri until 17:00, last entry 30 min before closing, U-Bahn: Oranienburger Tor, Oranienburger Strasse 28/30, tel. 030/8802-8300 and press 1, www.cjudaicum.de).

A block from the synagogue, walk 50 yards down Grosse Hamburger Strasse to a little park. This street was known for 200 years as the "street of tolerance" because the Jewish community donated land to Protestants so that they could build a church. Hitler turned it into the "street of death" *(Todes Strasse),* bulldozing 12,000 graves of the city's oldest Jewish cemetery and turning a Jewish nursing home into a deportation center. Note the two memorials—one erected by the former East Berlin government and one built later by the city's unified government. Somewhere nearby, a plainclothes police officer keeps watch over this park.

▲Oranienburger Strasse—Berlin is developing so fast, it's impossible to predict what will be "in" next year. The area around Oranienburger Strasse is definitely trendy (but is being challenged by hip Friedrichshain, farther east, and Prenzlauer Berg, described below).

While the area immediately around the synagogue is dull, 100 yards away things get colorful. The streets behind Grosse Hamburger Strasse flicker with atmospheric cafés, *Kneipen* (pubs), and art galleries.

At night, techno-prostitutes line Oranienburger Strasse. Prostitution is legal here, but there's a big debate about taxation. Since they don't get unemployment insurance, why should they pay taxes?

Hackescher Markt—This neighborhood, near Oranienburger Strasse, is worth exploring. A block in front of the Hackescher Markt S-Bahn station is **Hackesche Höfe,** with eight courtyards bunny-hopping through a wonderfully restored 1907 *Jugendstil* building. It's full of trendy restaurants, theaters, and cinema (playing movies in their original languages). This is a fine example of how to make huge city blocks livable—Berlin's apartments are organized around courtyard after courtyard off the main roads.

Prenzlauer Berg—Young, in-the-know locals agree that this is one of Berlin's most colorful up-and-coming neighborhoods (roughly between Helmholtzplatz and Kollwitz Platz and along Kastanienallee, U-Bahn: Senefelderplatz and Eberswalder Strasse). This part of the city was largely untouched during World War II, but its buildings slowly rotted away under the communists. Since the Wall fell, it's been overrun with laid-back hipsters, energetic young families, and clever entrepreneurs who are breathing life back into its classic old apartment blocks, deserted factories, and long-forgotten breweries. Though it's a few blocks farther out than the neighborhoods described above, it's a fun place to explore and have a meal (see page 599) or spend the night (see page 594).

Natural History Museum (Museum für Naturkunde)—This place is worth a visit just to see the largest dinosaur skeleton ever assembled. While you're there, meet "Bobby" the stuffed ape (€3.50, Tue–Fri 9:30–17:00, Sat–Sun 10:00–18:00, closed Mon, last entry 30 min before closing, U-Bahn line 6 to Zinnowitzer Strasse, Invalidenstrasse 43, tel. 030/2093-8591).

Central Berlin

Tiergarten Park and Victory Column (Siegessäule)—Berlin's "Central Park" stretches two miles from Bahnhof Zoo to Brandenburg Gate. Its centerpiece, the Victory Column, was built to commemorate the Prussian defeat of France in 1870. The pointy-helmeted Germans rubbed it in, decorating the tower with French cannons and paying for it all with francs received as war reparations. The three lower rings commemorate Bismarck's victories. I imagine the statues of Moltke and other German military greats—which lurk in the trees nearby—goose-stepping around the floodlit angel at night. Originally standing at the Reichstag, the immense tower was actually moved to this position by Hitler in 1938 to complement his anticipated victory parades. At the first level, notice how WWII bullets chipped the fine marble columns. Climbing its 285 steps earns you a breathtaking Berlin-wide view and a close-up look at the gilded angel made famous in the U2 video (€2.20, April–Sept Mon–Thu 9:30–18:30, Fri–Sun 9:30–19:00, Oct–March daily 9:30–17:30, closes in the rain, WCs for paying guests only, no elevator, bus #100, tel. 030/8639-8560). From the tower, the grand Strasse des 17. Juni (named for a workers' uprising against the DDR government in the 1950s) leads east to the Brandenburg Gate.

Flea Market—A colorful flea market with great antiques, more than 200 stalls, collector-savvy merchants, and fun German fast-food stands thrives weekends beyond the Victory Column on Strasse des 17. Juni (S-Bahn: Tiergarten).

German Resistance Memorial (Gedenkstätte Deutscher Widerstand)—This memorial and museum tells the story of the German resistance to Hitler. The Benderblock was a military headquarters where an ill-fated attempt to assassinate Hitler was plotted (the actual attempt occurred in Rastenburg, eastern Prussia). Stauffenberg and his co-conspirators were shot here in the courtyard. While posted explanations are in German only, the spirit that haunts the place is multilingual (free, Mon–Fri 9:00–18:00, Thu until 20:00, Sat–Sun 10:00–18:00, free and good English audioguide with passport, €3 printed English translation, no crowds, near Kulturforum just south of Tiergarten at Stauffenbergstrasse 13, enter in courtyard, door on left, main exhibit is on third floor, bus #129, tel. 030/2699-5000).

▲Potsdamer Platz—The Times Square of Berlin, and possibly the busiest square in Europe before World War II, Potsdamer Platz was cut in two by the Wall and left a deserted no-man's-land for 40 years. Today, this immense commercial/residential/entertainment center, sitting on a futuristic transportation hub, is home to the European corporate headquarters of several big-league companies. The new Potsdamer Platz was a vision begun in 1991, when it was announced that Berlin would resume its position as capital of Germany. Sony, Daimler-Chrysler, and other major corporations have turned it once again into a center of Berlin. While most of the complex just feels big (the arcade is like any huge, modern, American mall), the entrance to the complex and Sony Center Platz are worth a visit.

For an overview of the new construction, and a scenic route to Sony Center Platz, go to the east end of Potsdamer Strasse, facing the skyscrapers (the opposite end from Kulturforum, at main intersection of Potsdamer Strasse/Leipziger Strasse and Ebert Strasse/Stressemanstrasse, U-Bahn: Potsdamer Platz). Find the green hexagonal clock tower with the traffic lights on top. This is a replica of the first automatic **traffic light** in Europe, which once stood at the six-street intersection of Potsdamer Platz. On either side of Potsdamer Strasse, you'll see enormous cubical entrances to the brand-new underground Potsdamer Platz train station (due to open in 2006). Near these entrances, notice the **glass cylinders** sticking out of the ground. The mirrors on the tops of the tubes move with the sun to collect light and send it underground. Now go in one of the train station entrances and follow signs to Sony Center. (While you're down there, look for the other ends of the big glass tubes.)

You'll come up the escalator into **Sony Center** under a grand canopy. At night, multicolored floodlights play on the underside of this tent. Office workers and tourists eat here by the fountain, enjoying the parade of people. The modern Bavarian Lindenbrau beer hall—the Sony boss wanted a *Bräuhall*—serves good traditional food (€5–16, big salads, 3-foot-long taster boards of 8 different beers, daily 11:00–24:00, tel. 030/2575-1280). The adjacent Josty Bar is built around a surviving bit of a venerable hotel that was a meeting place for Berlin's rich and famous before the bombs (daily 9:00–24:00, tel. 030/2575-9702). You can browse the futuristic Sony Style Store, visit the Filmhaus (a museum with an exhibit on

Marlene Dietrich), and do some surfing at Web Free TV (on the street).

Across Potsdamer Strasse, you can ride what's billed as "the fastest elevator in Europe" to skyscraping rooftop **views.** You'll travel at nearly 30 feet per second to the top of the 300-foot-tall Kollhoff tower (€3.50, Tue–Sun 11:00–20:00, closed Mon, in red-brick building at Potsdamer Platz 1, tel. 030/2529-4372, www.panoramapunkt.de).

Kulturforum

Just west of Potsdamer Platz, with several top museums and Berlin's concert hall, is the city's cultural heart (admission to all sights covered by €10 state museums day ticket, or 3-day €12 Museumspass; phone number for all museums: tel. 030/266-2951). Of its sprawling museums, only the Gemäldegalerie is a must. To reach the Kulturforum, take the S- or U-Bahn to Potsdamer Platz, then walk along Potsdamer Platz and Potsdamer Strasse. From the Zoo station, you can also take bus #200 to Philharmonie. Across Potsdamer Strasse from the Kulturforum is the huge National Library (free English periodicals).

▲▲▲Gemäldegalerie—Germany's top collection of 13th- through 18th-century European paintings (more than 1,400 canvases) is beautifully displayed in a building that's a work of art in itself. Follow the excellent free audioguide. The North Wing starts with German paintings of the 13th to 16th centuries, including eight by Dürer. Then come the Dutch and Flemish—Jan Van Eyck, Brueghel, Rubens, Van Dyck, Hals, and Vermeer. The wing finishes with German, English, and French 18th-century art, such as Gainsborough and Watteau. An octagonal hall at the end features a fine stash of Rembrandts. The South Wing is saved for the Italians—Giotto, Botticelli, Titian, Raphael, and Caravaggio (€6, free Thu after 18:00, open Tue–Sun 10:00–18:00, Thu until 22:00, closed Mon, clever little loaner stools, great salad bar in cafeteria upstairs, Matthäikirchplatz 4).

New National Gallery (Neue Nationalgalerie)—This features 20th-century art, with ever-changing special exhibits (€6–8 depending on exhibit, free Thu after 18:00, open Tue–Fri 10:00–18:00, Thu until 22:00, Sat–Sun 11:00–18:00, closed Mon, café downstairs).

Museum of Arts and Crafts (Kunstgewerbemuseum)—Wander through a thousand years of applied arts—porcelain, fine *Jugendstil* (Art Nouveau) furniture, Art Deco, and reliquaries. There are no crowds and no English descriptions (€3, free Thu after 14:00, open Tue–Fri 10:00–18:00, Sat–Sun 11:00–18:00, closed Mon).

▲Musical Instruments Museum (Musikinstrumenten Museum)—This impressive hall is filled with 600 exhibits from the 16th century to modern times. Wander among old keyboard instruments and funny-looking tubas. There's no English, aside from a €0.10 info sheet, but it's fascinating if you're into pianos (€3, free Thu after 13:00, Tue–Fri 9:00–17:00, Sat–Sun 10:00–17:00, closed Mon, low-profile white building east of the big, yellow Philharmonic Concert Hall, tel. 030/254-810).

Poke into the lobby of Berlin's **Philharmonic Concert Hall** and see if there are tickets available during your stay (ticket office open Mon–Fri 15:00–18:00, Sat–Sun 11:00–14:00, must purchase tickets in person, box office tel. 030/2548-8132).

Western Berlin

Western travelers still think of Berlin's "West End" as the heart of the city. While it's no longer that, the West End still has the best infrastructure to support your visit and works well as a home base. Here are a few sights within an easy walk of your hotel and the Zoo station.

▲Kurfürstendamm—West Berlin's main drag, Kurfürstendamm boulevard (nicknamed "Ku'damm"), starts at Kaiser Wilhelm Memorial Church and does a commercial cancan for two miles. In the 1850s, when Berlin became a wealthy and important capital, her new rich chose Kurfürstendamm as their street. Bismarck made it Berlin's Champs-Elysées. In the 1920s, it became a chic and fashionable drag of cafés and boutiques. During the Third Reich, as home to an international community of diplomats and journalists, it enjoyed more freedom than the rest of Berlin. Throughout the Cold War, economic subsidies from the West made sure that capitalism thrived on Ku'damm. And today, while much of the old charm has been hamburgerized, Ku'damm is still a fine place to feel the pulse of the city and enjoy the elegant shops (around Fasanenstrasse), department stores, and people-watching.

▲Kaiser Wilhelm Memorial Church (Gedächtniskirche)—The church was originally a memorial to the first emperor of Germany, who died in 1888. Its bombed-out ruins have been left standing as a memorial to the destruction of Berlin in World War II. Under a fine mosaic ceiling, a small exhibit features interesting photos about the bombing and before-and-after models of the church (free, Mon–Sat 10:00–16:00, closed Sun, www.gedaechtniskirche.com).

After the war, some Berliners wanted to tear the church down and build it anew. Instead, it was decided to keep the ruin as a memorial, and stage a competition to design a modern add-on section. The winning selection—the short, modern building (1961) next to the church—offers a world of 11,000 little blue windows (free, daily 9:00–19:00). The blue glass was given to the church by the French as a reconciliation gift. For more information on both churches, pick up the English booklet (€2.60).

Western Berlin

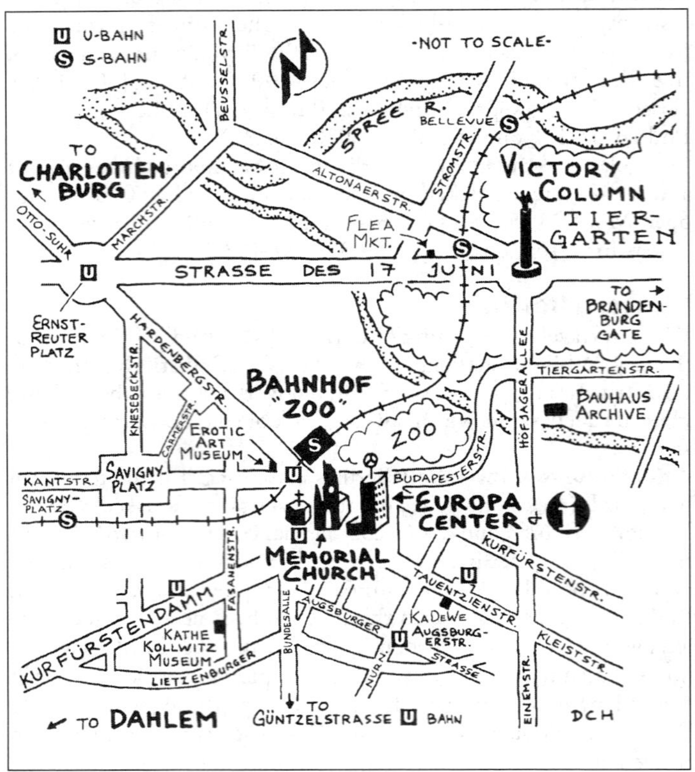

The lively square between the churches and the Europa Center (a shiny high-rise shopping center built as a showcase of Western capitalism during the Cold War) usually attracts street musicians.

▲Käthe Kollwitz Museum—This local artist (1867–1945), who experienced much of Berlin's stormiest century, conveys some powerful and mostly sad feelings about motherhood, war, and suffering through the black-and-white faces of her art (€5, €1 pamphlet has English explanations of a few major works, Wed–Mon 11:00–18:00, closed Tue, a block off Ku'damm at Fasanenstrasse 24, tel. 030/882-5210, www.kaethe-kollwitz.de).

▲Kaufhaus des Westens (KaDeWe)—The "department store of the West," with a staff of 2,100 to help you sort through its vast selection of 380,000 items, claims to be the biggest department store on the Continent. You can get everything from a haircut and train ticket (basement) to souvenirs (third floor). The theater and concert box office on the sixth floor charges an 18 percent booking fee, but they know all your options (cash only). The sixth floor is also a world of gourmet taste treats. The biggest selection of deli and exotic food in Germany offers plenty of classy opportunities to sit down and eat. Ride the glass elevator to the seventh floor's glass-domed Winter Garden self-service cafeteria—fun but pricey (Mon–Fri 10:00–20:00, Sat 9:30–20:00, closed Sun, U-Bahn: Wittenbergplatz, tel. 030/21210, www.kadewe.com). The Wittenbergplatz U-Bahn station (in front of KaDeWe) is a unique opportunity to see an old-time station. Enjoy its interior.

Berlin Zoo—More than 1,400 different kinds of animals call Berlin's famous zoo home—or so the zookeepers like to think. Germans enjoy seeing the pandas at play (straight in from the entrance). I enjoy seeing the Germans at play (€10 for zoo or world-class aquarium, €15 for both, children half price, daily 9:00–18:30, Nov–Feb until 17:00, aquarium closes at 18:00, feeding times—*Fütterungszeiten*—posted on map just inside entrance, enter near Europa Center in front of Hotel Palace or opposite Bahnhof Zoo on Hardenbergplatz, Budapester Strasse 34, tel. 030/254-010).

Erotic Art Museum—This offers three floors of graphic (mostly 18th-century) Oriental art, a tiny theater showing erotic silent movies from the early 1900s, and a special exhibit on the queen of German pornography, the late Beate Uhse. This amazing woman, a former test pilot for the Third Reich and groundbreaking purveyor of condoms and sex ed in the 1950s, was the female Hugh Hefner of Germany and CEO of a huge chain of porn shops. If you're traveling far and are sightseeing selectively, the sex museums in Amsterdam or Copenhagen are much better. This one, though well described in English, is little more than prints and posters (€5, daily 9:00–24:00, last entry 23:00, hard-to-beat gift shop, at corner of Kantstrasse and Joachimstalerstrasse, a block from Bahnhof Zoo, tel. 030/886-0666). If you just want to see sex, you'll see much more for half the price in a private video booth next door.

Charlottenburg Palace Area

The Charlottenburg district—with two fine museums across the street from a palace—makes a good side-trip from downtown. Ride U-2 to Sophie-Charlotte Platz and walk 10 minutes up the tree-lined boulevard Schlossstrasse (following signs to Schloss), or—much faster—catch bus #145 (direction Spandau) direct from Bahnhof Zoo.

For a Charlottenburg lunch, the **Luisen Bräu** is a comfortable brewpub restaurant with a copper and woody atmosphere, good local "microbeers" (*dunkles* means "dark," *helles,* "light"), and traditional German grub (€5–8 meals, daily 9:00–24:00, fun for groups, across from palace at Luisenplatz 1, tel. 030/341-9388).

Charlottenburg Palace Area

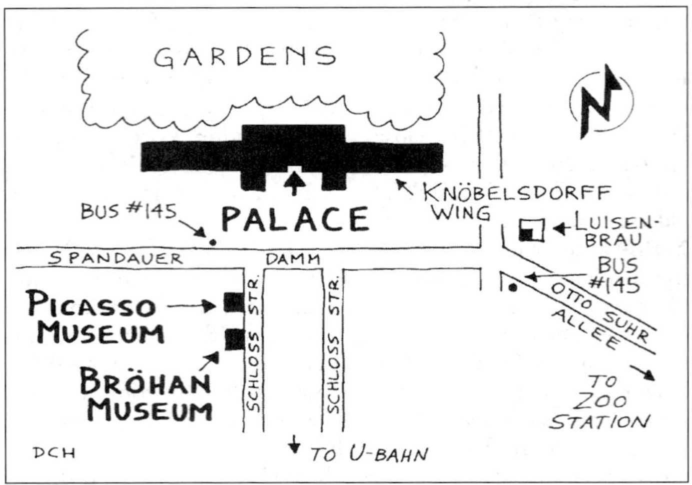

▲**Charlottenburg Palace (Schloss Charlottenburg)**—If you've seen the great palaces of Europe, this Baroque Hohenzollern palace comes in at about number 10 (behind Potsdam, too). It's even more disappointing since the main rooms can be toured only with a German guide (€8 includes 50-min tour, €2 to see just upper floors without tour, €7 to see palace grounds excluding tour areas, last tour 1 hour before closing, cash only, Tue–Sun 10:00–17:00, closed Mon, tel. 030/320-911).

The **Knöbelsdorff Wing** features a few royal apartments. Go upstairs and take a substantial hike through restored-since-the-war, gold-crusted white rooms (€5 depending on special exhibitions, free English audioguide, Tue–Fri 10:00–18:00, Sat–Sun 11:00–18:00, closed Mon, last entry 30 min before closing, when facing the palace walk toward the right wing, tel. 030/3209-1202).

▲**Berggruen Collection: Picasso and His Time**—This tidy little museum is a pleasant surprise. Climb three floors through a fun and substantial collection of Picassos. Along the way, you'll see plenty of notable works by Matisse, van Gogh, and Cézanne. Enjoy a great chance to meet Paul Klee (€6, covered by Museumspass, free Thu after 14:00, open Tue–Fri 10:00–18:00, Sat–Sun 11:00–18:00, closed Mon, Schlossstrasse 1, tel. 030/326-9580).

▲**Bröhan Museum**—Wander through a dozen beautifully furnished *Jugendstil* (Art Nouveau) and Art Deco living rooms, a curvy organic world of lamps, glass, silver, and posters. English descriptions are posted on the wall of each room on the main floor. While you're there, look for the fine collection of Impressionist paintings by Karl Hagemeister (€4–6 depending on special exhibits, covered by Museumspass excluding special exhibits, Tue–Sun 10:00–18:00, closed Mon, Schlossstrasse 1A, tel. 030/3269-0600, www.broehan-museum.de).

Near Berlin

▲Potsdam Palaces—Featuring a lush park strewn with the extravagant whimsies of Frederick the Great, the sleepy town of Potsdam has long been Berlin's holiday retreat. Frederick's super-rococo Sanssouci Palace is one of Germany's most dazzling. His equally extravagant New Palace, built to disprove rumors that Prussia was running out of money after the costly Seven Years' War, is on the other side of the park (it's a 30-min walk between palaces). The Potsdam **TI** is a fine source of information (April–Oct Mon–Fri 9:00–19:00, Sat–Sun 10:00–16:00, less off-season, 5-min walk from Potsdam S-Bahn station, walk straight out of station and take first right onto An der Orangerie, Friedrich-Ebert Strasse 5, tel. 0331/275-5850).

Your best bet for seeing Sanssouci Palace is to take the Potsdam TI's walking tour (see below). Otherwise, to make sense of all the ticket and tour options for the two palaces, stop by the palaces' information office (across the street from windmill near Sanssouci entrance, helpful English-speaking staff, tel. 0331/969-4202).

Sanssouci Palace: Even though *sans souci* means "without a care," it can be a challenge for an English speaker to have an enjoyable visit. The palaces of Vienna, Munich, and even Würzburg offer equal sightseeing thrills with far fewer headaches. While the grounds are impressive, the interior of Sanssouci Palace can be visited only by a one-hour tour in German (with a borrowed English text), and these tours get booked up quickly. The only English option is the Potsdam TI's tour (see below).

If you take a German tour of Sanssouci, you must be at the palace in person to get your ticket and the appointment time for your tour. In the summer, if you arrive by 9:00, you'll get right in. If you arrive after 10:00, plan on a wait. If you arrive after 12:00, you may not get in at all (€8, April–Oct Tue–Sun 9:00–17:00, closed Mon, Nov–March Tue–Sun 9:00–16:00, closed Mon).

New Palace (Neues Palais): Use the English texts to tour Frederick's New Palace (€5, plus €1 for optional live tour in German, April–Oct Sat–Thu 9:00–17:00, closed Fri, Nov–May Sat–Thu 9:00–16:00, closed Fri). If you also want to see the king's apartments, you must take a required 45-minute tour in German (€6, offered May–Oct daily at 11:00 and 14:00). Off-season (Nov–April), the king's apartments are closed, and you can visit the rest of the New Palace only on a German tour (€5); it can take up to an hour for enough people to gather.

Greater Berlin

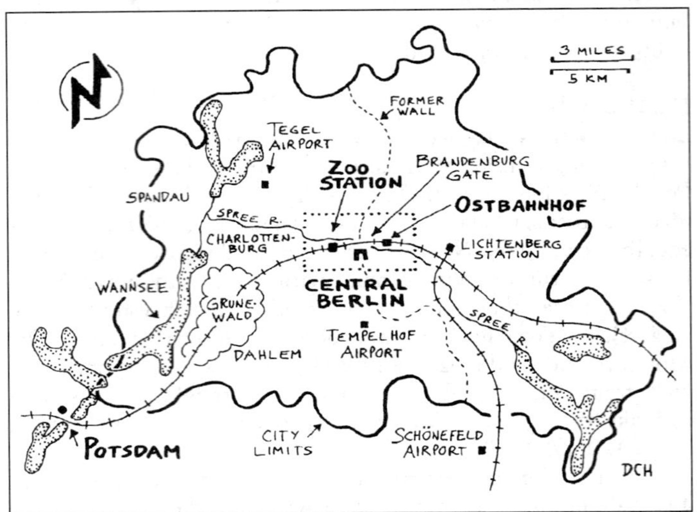

Walking Tours: The Potsdam TI's handy walking tour includes Sanssouci Palace, offering the only way to get into the palace with an English-speaking guide (€26 covers walking tour, palace, and park, 11:00 daily except Mon, 3.5 hrs, departs from Film Museum across from TI—walk straight out of Potsdam S-Bahn station and take first right onto An der Orangerie, reserve by phone, in summer reserve at least 2 days in advance, tel. 0331/275-5850).

A "Discover Potsdam" walking tour (which doesn't include Sanssouci Palace) is offered by Original Berlin Walks and led by a native English-speaking guide. The tour leaves from Berlin's Zoo station at 9:40 on Saturdays May through October (€15, or €11.20 if under age 26 or with WelcomeCard, meet at taxi stand at Zoo station, public transportation not included but can buy ticket from guide, no booking necessary, tel. 030/301-9194). The guide takes you to Cecilienhof Palace (site of postwar Potsdam conference attended by Churchill, Stalin, and Truman), through pleasant green landscapes to the historic heart of Potsdam for lunch, and to Sanssouci Park.

What to Avoid: Potsdam's much-promoted Wannsee boat rides are torturously dull.

Getting to Potsdam: Potsdam is easy to reach from Berlin (17 min on direct Regional Express/RE trains from Bahnhof Zoo every 30 min, or 30 min direct on S-Bahn line 7 from Bahnhof Zoo to Potsdam station; round-trip covered by €6 transit day pass with zones A, B, and C). If you're taking the Potsdam TI's tour, walk to the Film Museum from the Potsdam S-Bahn stop (see

"Walking Tours," above). If not taking the TI tour, catch bus #695 from the Potsdam station to the palaces (3/hr, 20 min). Use the same bus #695 to shuttle between the sights in the park. For a more scenic approach, take tram #96 or #X98 from the Potsdam station to Luisenplatz, then walk 15 minutes through the park and enjoy a classic view of Sanssouci Palace.

NIGHTLIFE

Berlin is a happening place for nightlife—whether it's nightclubs, pubs, jazz music, cabaret, hokey-but-fun German variety shows, theater, or concerts. Tourists stroll the Ku'damm after dark.

Berlin Programm lists a nonstop parade of concerts, plays, exhibits, and cultural events (€1.60, in German, www.berlin-programm.de); the *Ex-Berliner* (€2, www.ex-berliner.com) and the TI-produced *Berlin Calendàr* (€1.60) have less information, but are in English (all sold at kiosks and TIs). For the young and determined sophisticate, *Zitty* and *Tip* are the top guides to alternative culture (in German, sold at kiosks). Also pick up the free schedules *Flyer* and *030* in bars and clubs. The free *New Berlin* magazine—available at EurAide, Starbucks, and hostels—provides English-language inside scoop on nightlife, cheap eats, and hostels (www.newberlinmagazine.com).

Visit KaDeWe's ticket office for your music and theater options (sixth floor, 18 percent fee but access to all tickets, see page 584). Ask about "competitive improvisation" and variety shows.

Jazz—For jazz (blues and boogie, too) near my recommended Savignyplatz hotels in western Berlin, consider **A Trane Jazz Club** (daily, 21:00–2:00, Bleibtreustrasse 1, tel. 030/313-2550) and **Quasimodo Live** (Kantstrasse 12a, under Delphi Cinema, tel. 030/312-8086). For quality blues and New Orleans–style jazz, stop by **Ewige Lampe** (from 21:00, Niebuhrstrasse 11a).

Cabaret—Bar Jeder Vernunft offers modern-day cabaret a short walk from the recommended hotels in western Berlin. This variety show under a classic old tent perched atop a modern parking lot is a hit with German speakers, but can still be worthwhile for those who don't speak the language (as some of the music shows are in a sort of "Dinglish"). Even some Americans perform here periodically. Tickets are generally around €15, and shows change regularly (performances start at 20:30, closed Sun, seating can be a bit cramped, south of Ku'damm at Schaperstrasse 24, tel. 030/883-1582, www.bar-jeder-vernunft.de).

German Variety Show—To spend an evening enjoying Europe's largest revue theater, consider Revue Berlin at the Friedrichstadt Palast. The show basically depicts the history of Berlin, and is choreographed in a funny and musical way that's popular with the

Lawrence Welk–type German crowd. It's even entertaining for your entire English-speaking family (€13–51, Tue–Sat 20:00, also Sat–Sun at 16:00, U-Bahn: Oranienburger Tor, tel. 030/284-8830, www.friedrichstadtpalast.de).

Nightclubs and Pubs—Oranienburger Strasse's trendy scene (page 579) is being eclipsed by the action at Friedrichshain (farther east). To the north, you'll find the hip Prenzlauer Berg neighborhood, packed with everything from smoky pubs to small art bars and dance clubs (best scene is around Helmholtsplatz, U-Bahn: Eberswalder Strasse; see page 579).

Tour—Original Berlin Walks offers a Nightlife Berlin tour that goes beyond just a pub crawl, since the guides offer history along the way (€9, May–Sept on Tue, Thu, Sat, and Sun at 22:30, meet at Häagen-Dazs at Hackescher Markt S-Bahn station).

SLEEPING

When in Berlin, I sleep in the former West, on or near Savignyplatz. While Bahnhof Zoo and Ku'damm are no longer the center of Berlin, the trains, TI, and walking tours are all still handy to Zoo. And the streets around the tree-lined Savignyplatz (a 10-min walk behind the station) have a neighborhood charm. While towering new hotels are being built in the new center, simple, small, friendly, good-value places abound here. My listings are generally located a couple of flights up in big, run-down buildings. Inside, they're clean, quiet, and spacious enough so that their well-worn character is actually charming. Rooms in back are on quiet courtyards.

As an alternative, I've also listed some suggestions in eastern Berlin's youthful and increasingly popular Prenzlauer Berg neighborhood, as well as a couple other possibilities elsewhere.

Berlin is packed and hotel prices go up on holidays, including Green Week in mid-January, Easter weekend, the first weekend in May, Ascension weekend in May, the Love Parade (mid-July), Germany's national holiday (Oct 2–4), Christmas, and New Year's.

During slow times, the best values are actually business-class rooms on the push list booked through the TI. But as the world learns what a great place Berlin is to visit, a rising tide of tourists will cause these deals to fade away.

Western Berlin

Near Savignyplatz and Bahnhof Zoo

These hotels and pensions are a 5- to 15-minute walk from Bahnhof Zoo (or take S-Bahn to Savignyplatz). Hotels on Kantstrasse have street noise. Ask for a quieter room in back. The area has an artsy charm going back to the cabaret days in the 1920s, when it was the center of Berlin's gay scene. Of the accommodations listed in this

Sleep Code

(€1 = about $1.20, country code: 49, area code: 030)
S = Single, **D** = Double/Twin, **T** = Triple, **Q** = Quad, **b** = bathroom, **s** = shower only, **SE** = Speaks English, **NSE** = No English. Unless otherwise noted, credit cards are accepted, English is spoken, and breakfast is included.

To help you sort easily through these listings, I've divided the rooms into three categories, based on the price for a standard double room with bath:

$$$ Higher Priced—Most rooms €120 or more.
$$ Moderately Priced—Most rooms between €85–120.
$ Lower Priced—Most rooms €85 or less.

area, Pension Peters offers the best value for budget travelers.

$$$ Hotel Askanischerhof is the oldest *Zimmer* in Berlin, posh as can be with 16 sprawling, antique-furnished rooms. Photos on the walls brag of famous movie-star guests. Frau Glinicke offers Old World service and classic Berlin atmosphere (Sb-€95–110, Db-€117–145, extra bed-€25, free parking, non-smoking rooms, elevator, Ku'damm 53, tel. 030/881-8033, fax 030/881-7206, www.askanischer-hof.de, info@askanischer-hof.de).

$$$ Hecker's Hotel is an ultramodern, four-star business hotel with 69 rooms and all the sterile Euro-comforts (Sb-€125, Db-€150, breakfast-€15, weekends breakfast included, all rooms €200 during conferences, non-smoking rooms, elevator, parking-€9-12/day, between Savignyplatz and Ku'damm at Grolmanstrasse 35, tel. 030/88900, fax 030/889-0260, www.heckers-hotel.com, info@heckers -hotel.com).

$$$ Hotel Astoria is a friendly, three-star, business-class hotel with 32 comfortably furnished rooms and affordable summer and weekend rates (high season Db-€117–128; prices drop to Sb-€86–97, Db-€94–118 during low season of July–Aug, Nov–Feb, or any 2 weekend nights or if slow; breakfast-€10 extra, rooms with showers are cheaper than rooms with baths, non-smoking floors, elevator, free Internet access, parking-€13/day, around corner from Bahnhof Zoo at Fasanenstrasse 2, tel. 030/312-4067, fax 030/312-5027, www.hotelastoria.de, info@hotelastoria.de).

$$ Hotel Pension Savoy, under new ownership, rents 16 comfortable and colorfully decorated rooms with all the amenities. You'll love the cheery old pastel breakfast room. Most rooms overlook a quiet courtyard (Sb-€69–79, Db-€99–109, extra person-€34–46, elevator, Meinekestrasse 4, tel. 030/881-3700, fax 030/8847-1610, www.hotel-pension-savoy.de, info@hotel-pension-savoy.de).

Savignyplatz Neighborhood

$$ Hotel Atlanta has 30 newish rooms in an older building with big leather couches, half a block south of Ku'damm. It's next to Gucci, on an elegant shopping street (Ss-€40–70, Sb-€60–99, Db-€80–120, Tb-€100–140, Qb-€120–160, non-smoking rooms, Fasanenstrasse 74, tel. 030/881-8049, fax 030/881-9872, www.hotelatlanta.de, mail@hotelatlanta.de).

$$ Hotel Carmer 16, with 30 bright, airy rooms, feels like a big, professional hotel with all the comfy extras but a cold reception staff (Sb-€72, Db-€93–122, extra person-€20, some rooms have balconies, elevator and a few stairs, beauty parlor and mini-spa upstairs, Carmerstrasse 16, tel. 030/3110-0500, fax 030/3110-0510, carmer16@t-online.de).

$$ Hotel-Pension Funk, the former home of a 1920s silent-movie star, is delightfully quirky. Kind manager Herr Michael Pfundt offers 14 elegant old rooms with rich Art Nouveau furnishings (S-€34–57, Ss-€41–72, Sb-€52–82, D-€52–82, Ds-€72–93,

Db-€82–113, extra person-€23, cash preferred, Fasanenstrasse 69, a long block south of Ku'damm, tel. 030/882-7193, fax 030/883-3329, www.hotel-pensionfunk.de, berlin@hotel-pensionfunk.de).

$$ Hotel Bogota has 125 unique rooms and several large lounges in a sprawling old maze of a building that once housed the Nazi Chamber of Culture. (After the war, German theater stars were "de-Nazified" here before they could go back to work.) Photographer Helmut Newton lived here for two years, and Benny Goodman is rumored to have played here in the 1920s. Today pieces of the owner's modern-art collection lurk around every corner. Take a peek at the bizarre collage in the atrium, with mannequins suspended from the ceiling (S-€44, Ss-€55–57, Sb-€66–72, D-€66–69, Ds-€74–77, Db-€94–98, extra bed-€20, children under 12 free, non-smoking rooms, elevator, bus #109 from Bahnhof Zoo to Schlüterstrasse 45, tel. 030/881-5001, fax 030/883-5887, www.hotelbogota.de, hotel.bogota@t-online.de).

$$ Hotel Pension Alexandra has 10 pleasant rooms on a tree-lined street between Savignyplatz and Ku'damm. Expect the usual high ceilings and marble entryway found in these turn-of-the-century buildings, but with added touches—most rooms and the elegant breakfast room are decorated with original antique furniture (Ss-€50–72, Sb-€58–82, Ds-€63–82, Db-€65–99, extra bed-€25–35, Wielandstrasse 32, tel. 030/881-2107, fax 030/885-7780, www.alexandra-berlin.de, mail@alexandra-berlin.de).

$ Pension Peters, run by a German-Swedish couple, is sunny and central, with a cheery breakfast room. Decorated sleek Scandinavian, with every room renovated, it's a winner (S-€36, Ss-€47, Sb-€58, D-€51, Ds-€68, Db-€78–83, extra bed-€10, kids under 12 free, family room, cash preferred, Internet access, 10 yards off Savignyplatz at Kantstrasse 146, tel. 030/3150-3944, fax 030/312-3519, www.pension-peters-berlin.de, penspeters@aol.com, Annika and Christoph SE). The same family also runs a larger hotel just outside of Berlin (see Hotel Pankow on page 596) and rents apartments (ideal for small groups and longer stays).

$ Hotel Pension Columbus, run by the König family, fills a sprawling floor of a grand building with modest, well-worn, but clean rooms (S-€40–45, Ss-€55, Sb-€65, D-€65, Ds-€75, Db-€85, elevator, Meinekestrasse 5, tel. 030/881-5061, fax 030/881-3200, www.columbus-berlin.de, info@columbus-berlin.de).

$ Pension Alexis is a classic Old World four-room pension in a stately 19th-century apartment run by Frau and Herr Schwarzer. The shower and toilet facilities are old and cramped, but this, more than any other Berlin listing, has you feeling at home with a faraway aunt (S-€43, D-€65, T-€97, Q-€128, cash only, big rooms, handheld showers, Carmerstrasse 15, tel. 030/312-5144, enough English spoken).

$ Hotel Crystal Garni is professional and offers small, well-worn, comfortable rooms and a *vollkorn* breakfast room (S-€36, Sb-€41, D-€47, Ds-€57, Db-€66–77, elevator, a block past Savignyplatz at Kantstrasse 144, tel. 030/312-9047, fax 030/312-6465, run by John and Dorothy Schwarzrock and Herr Vasco Flascher).

South of Ku'damm

Several small hotels are nearby in a charming, café-studded neighborhood 300 yards south of Ku'damm (near intersection of Sächsische Strasse and Pariser Strasse, bus #109 from Bahnhof Zoo, direction: Airport Tegel). They are less convenient from the station than most of the Savignyplatz listings above. The last three places are all in the same building and run by the same family (the Visnaps).

$$ Hotel-Pension Bella, a clean, simple place with high ceilings, rents nine big, comfortable rooms but is a lesser value (Ss/Sb-€45–65, Ds-€70–85, Db-€80–90, extra person-€10, apartment also available, elevator, bus #249 from Zoo, Ludwigkirchstrasse 10a, tel. 030/881-6704, fax 030/8867-9074, www.pension-bella.de, info@pension-bella.de).

$$ Hotel Austriana, with 25 modern and bright rooms, is energetically run by the Visnap family (S-€33–43, Ss-€41–48, Sb-€49–67, Ds-€62–69, Db-€78–89, Ts-€78–96, Qs-€96–104, prices higher for holidays and conferences, half the rooms have balconies, elevator, Pariser Strasse 39, tel. 030/885-7000, fax 030/8857-0088, www.hotel-pension-austriana.de, austriana@t-online.de).

$ Insel Rügen Hotel has 31 rooms and ornate Eastern decor (S-€29–35, Ss-€34–40, D-€40–50, Ds-€55–65, Db-€65–85, elevator, Pariser Strasse 39, tel. 030/884-3940, fax 030/8843-9437, www.insel-ruegen-hotel.de, info@insel-ruegen-hotel.de).

$ Hotel-Pension-Curtis offers 10 hip, piney, basic rooms (S-€25–30, Ds-€50–60, Ts-€70–80, Qs-€72–90, cash only, elevator, Pariser Strasse 39, tel. 030/883-4931, fax 030/8843-9437, www.insel-ruegen-hotel.de, info@insel-ruegen-hotel.de).

Eastern Berlin

In Prenzlauer Berg

If you want to sleep in the former East Berlin, set your sights on the youthful, colorful, fun Prenzlauer Berg district. After decades of neglect, this corner of the East has quickly come back to life. Gentrification has brought Prenzlauer Berg great hotels, fine ethnic and German eateries (see page 599), and a happening nightlife scene. Prenzlauer Berg is about a mile and a half north of Alexanderplatz, roughly between Kollwitz Platz and Helmholtzplatz, and to the west, along Kastanienallee (known affectionately as "Casting Alley" for its share of beautiful people). The handiest U-Bahn stops are Senefelderplatz at the south end of the neighborhood and Eberswalder Strasse at the north end. For more on Prenzlauer Berg, see page 579.

$$$ Myer's Hotel is a boutique-hotel splurge offering simple, small, but elegant rooms and gorgeous public spaces, including a patio and garden. Details done right and impeccable service set this place apart. This peaceful hub—off a quiet courtyard and tree-lined street just a 10-minute walk from Kollwitz Platz or the nearest U-Bahn stop (Senefelderplatz)—makes it hard to believe you're in a capital city (Sb-€80–130, Db-€100–165, Metzer Strasse 26, tel. 030/440-140, fax 030/4401-4104, www.myershotel.de, info@myershotel.de).

$$ Hotel Jurine (yoo-REEN) is a pleasant business-style hotel whose friendly staff aims to please. Enjoy the breakfast buffet surrounded by modern art, or relax in the lush backyard (Sb-€75, Db-€90, Tb-€130, extra bed-€35, prices can double during conventions, breakfast-€13, parking garage-€12/day, 10-min walk to U-Bahn: Senefelderplatz, Schwedter Strasse 15, tel. 030/443-2990, fax 030/4432-9999, www.hotel-jurine.de, mail@hotel-jurine.de).

$$ Hotel Kastanienhof is a simple place offering fine but slightly overpriced rooms. The hotel is centrally located, making getting around Berlin a cinch, and it's near the hip Eberswalder Strasse bar scene (Sb-€73–93, Db-€98–108, Kastanienallee 65, tel. 030/443-050, fax 030/4430-5111, www.hotel-kastanienhof-berlin.de, info@hotel-kastanienhof-berlin.de).

$$ Apartments am Kollwitz Platz is typical of Prenzlauer Berg: an old, decrepit building that was gutted and remodeled, resulting in bright, clean, new-feeling spaces. It's in a quiet courtyard off a charming street speckled with cafés and shops; each room comes with a small kitchenette (Sb-€60, Db-€90, cash only, minimum 2-night stay, no breakfast, most rooms non-smoking, Wörther Strasse 20, tel. 030/4404-3641, fax 030/442-6433, www.hvp-pensionen.de, info@hvp-pensionen.de).

$ Transit Loft is technically a hostel, but feels more like an upscale budget hotel. Located in a refurbished factory, it offers clean, bright, modern, new-feeling, mostly-blue rooms with an industrial touch. The reception—staffed by friendly, hip Berliners—is open 24 hours, with a bar serving drinks all night long (dorm bed-€19, Sb-€59, Db-€69, Tb-€90, sheets and breakfast included, no age limit, cheap Internet access, fully wheelchair-accessible, Greifswalder Strasse 219; U-Bahn: Alexanderplatz, then tram #2, #3, or #4 to Hufelandplatz; tel. 030/4849-3773, fax 030/4405-1074, www.transit-loft.de, loft@hotel-transit.de).

$ Lette'm Sleep is a typical 50-bed youth hostel. It's not going to win any awards for cleanliness, but it's funky and relaxed, and fronts Helmholtzplatz—smack in the middle of Berlin's coolest neighborhood (dorm beds-€15–19, D with small kitchen area-€48,

Db apartment-€66, sheets-€3 extra, no breakfast but communal kitchen, lockers, free Internet access, bike rental, Lettestrasse 7, tel. 030/4473-3623, fax 030/4473-3625, www.backpackers.de, info@backpackers.de).

On Unter den Linden

$$$ Hotel Unter den Linden is ideal for those nostalgic for the days of Soviet rule—although nowadays, at least the management tries to be efficient and helpful. Formerly one of the best hotels in the DDR, this huge, blocky place, right on Unter den Linden in the heart of what was East Berlin, is reasonably comfortable and reasonably priced. Built in 1966, with prison-like corridors, it has 331 modern, plain, and comfy rooms (Sb-€67–87, Db-€109–123, non-smoking rooms, Unter den Linden 14, at intersection with Friedrichstrasse, tel. 030/238-110, fax 030/2381-1100, www.hotel-unter-den-linden.de, reservation@hotel-unter-den-linden.de).

Away from the Center

$ Hotel Pankow is a fresh, colorful 43-room place run by friendly Annika and Christoph (from the Pension Peters, above). It's a 30-minute commute north of downtown but a good value (S-€31, Sb-€46, D-€41, Db-€61, T-€51, Tb-€71, Q-€61, Qb-€81, family rooms, 2 children under 16 free in room with parents, elevator, Internet access, free parking in lot or €3/day in garage, tram in front of hotel takes you to the center in 30 min, Pasewalker Strasse 14-15, tel. 030/486-2600, fax 030/4862-6060, www.hotel-pankow-berlin.de, hotelpankow@aol.com).

Hostels

Berlin is known among budget travelers for its fun, hip hostels. Here are four good bets (all prices listed per person): **Studentenhotel Meininger 10** (€23/person, includes sheets and breakfast, cash only, no curfew, elevator, free parking, near City Hall on JFK Platz, Meiningerstrasse 10, U-Bahn: Rathaus Schoneberg, tel. 030/7871-7414, fax 030/7871-7412, www.meininger-hostels.de), **Mitte's Backpacker Hostel** (€15 dorm beds, S-€30–35, D-€23–28, T-€21, Q-€20, sheets-€2.50, no breakfast, could be cleaner, no curfew, Internet access, laundry, bike rental, English newspapers, U-Bahn: Zinnowitzerstrasse, Chauseestrasse 102, tel. 030/2839-0965, fax 030/2839-0935, www.backpacker.de, info@backpacker.de), **Circus** (dorm bed-€15–18, S-€28–32, D-€21–24, T-€18–20, Q-€16–18, 2-person apartment with kitchen-€65–75, 4-person apartment-€115–130, breakfast-€4, sheets-€2, cash only, no curfew, Internet access, 2 locations, U-Bahn: Rosa-Luxemburg Platz, Rosa-Luxemburg Strasse 39, or U-Bahn: Rosenthaler Platz, Weinbergsweg 1a, both tel. 030/2839-1433, fax 030/2839-1484, www.circus-berlin.de, info@circus-berlin.de), or **Clubhouse** (dorm bed-€14, bed in 5- to 7-bed room-€17, S-€32, D-€23, T-€20, breakfast-€3, sheets-€2, cash only, Internet access, on second floor, nightclub below, in hip Oranienburger Strasse area, S- or U-Bahn: Friedrichstrasse, Kalkscheunenstrasse 4-5, tel. 030/2809-7979, fax 030/2809-7977, www.clubhouse-berlin.de, info@clubhouse-berlin.de).

EATING

Don't be too determined to eat "Berlin-style." The city is known only for its mildly spicy sausage. Still, there is a world of restaurants in this ever-changing city to choose from. Your best approach may be to choose a neighborhood, rather than a particular restaurant.

For quick and easy meals, colorful pubs—called *Kneipen*—offer light meals and the fizzy local beer, *Berliner Weiss*. Ask for it *mit Schuss* for a shot of fruity syrup in your suds. If the kraut is getting wurst, try one of the many Turkish, Italian, or Balkan restaurants. Eat cheap at *Imbiss* snack stands, bakeries (sandwiches), and falafel/kebab places. Bahnhof Zoo has several bright and modern fruit-and-sandwich bars and a grocery (daily 6:00–24:00).

Western Berlin

Near Savignyplatz

Several good places are on or within 100 yards of Savignyplatz. Take a walk and survey these: **Dicke Wirtin** is a smoky old pub with traditional old-Berlin *Kneipe* atmosphere, famously cheap *Gulaschsuppe,* and salads (daily 12:00–4:00, just off Savignyplatz at Carmerstrasse 9, tel. 030/312-4952). **Die Zwölf Apostel** is trendy for leafy candlelit ambience and Italian food. A dressy local crowd packs the place for €10 pizzas and €15–30 meals. Late-night partygoers appreciate Apostel's great breakfast (daily, 24 hrs, cash only, outside seating in summer until 10:00, immediately across from Savignyplatz S-Bahn entrance, Bleibtreustrasse 49, tel. 030/312-1433). **Ristorante San Marino,** on the square, is another good Italian place, serving cheaper pasta and pizza (daily 11:00–1:00, Savignyplatz 12, tel. 030/313-6086). **Zillemarkt Restaurant,** which feels like an old-time Berlin beer garden, serves traditional Berlin specialties in the garden or in the rustic candlelit interior (€10 meals, daily 10:00–24:00, near the S-Bahn tracks at Bleibtreustrasse 48a, tel. 030/881-7040).

Weyers Café Restaurant, serving quality international and German cuisine, is a great value and worth a short walk. It's sharp, with white tablecloths, but not stuffy. On a sunny day, its patio is packed with locals (€10 dinner plates, daily 8:00–2:00, seating indoors or outside on the leafy square, Pariser Strasse 16, reservations smart after 20:00, tel. 030/881-9378).

Ullrich Supermarkt is the neighborhood grocery store (Mon–Sat 9:00–22:00, closed Sun, Kantstrasse 7, under the tracks near Bahnhof Zoo). There's plenty of fast food near Bahnhof Zoo and on Ku'damm.

Near Bahnhof Zoo

Self-Service Cafeterias: The top floor of the famous department store, **KaDeWe**, holds the Winter Garden Buffet view cafeteria, and its sixth-floor deli/food department is a picnicker's nirvana. Its arterials are clogged with more than 1,000 kinds of sausage and 1,500 types of cheese (Mon–Fri 10:00–20:00, Sat 9:30–20:00, closed Sun, U-Bahn: Wittenbergplatz). **Wertheim** department store, a half-block from the Kaiser Wilhelm Church, has cheap food counters in the basement and a city view from its fine self-service cafeteria, Le Buffet, located up six banks of escalators (Mon–Sat 9:30–20:00, closed Sun, U-Bahn: Ku'damm). **Marche,** a chain that's popped up in big cities all over Germany, is another inexpensive, self-service cafeteria within a half block of the Kaiser Wilhelm Church (Mon–Thu 8:00–22:00, Fri–Sat 8:00–24:00, Sun 10:00–22:00, plenty of salads, fruit, made-to-order omelettes, Ku'damm 14, tel. 030/882-7578).

At Bahnhof Zoo: **Terrassen am Zoo** is a good restaurant right in the station, offering peaceful decency amidst a whirlwind of travel activity (daily 6:00–22:00, upstairs, next to track 1, tel. 030/315-9140).

Eastern Berlin

Along Unter den Linden

The Opernpalais, preening with fancy prewar elegance, hosts a number of pricey restaurants. Its **Operncafé** has the best desserts and the longest dessert bar in Europe (daily 8:00–24:00, across from university and war memorial at Unter den Linden 5, tel. 030/202-683); sit down and enjoy perhaps the classiest coffee stop in Berlin. The beer and tea garden in front has a cheap food counter (from 10:00, depending on weather).

Near Pergamon Museum

Deponie3 is a trendy Berlin *Kneipe* usually filled with students from nearby Humboldt University. Garden seating in the back is nice if you don't mind the noise of the S-Bahn passing directly above you. The interior is a cozy, wooden wonderland of a bar, serving basic sandwiches, salads, and daily specials (€3–7 breakfasts, €5–11 lunches and dinners, sometimes with live music, open Mon–Fri from 9:00, Sat–Sun from 10:00, Georgenstrasse 5, 1 block from Pergamon under S-Bahn tracks, tel. 030/2016-5740). Georgenstrasse is home to other good restaurants, including a branch of Die Zwölf Apostel (daily until 24:00, described under "Near Savignyplatz," above).

Near Checkpoint Charlie

Lekkerbek, a busy little bakery and cafeteria, sells inexpensive and tasty salads, soups, pastas, and sandwiches (Mon–Fri 6:00–18:00, Sat 7:00–13:00, closed Sun, a block from Checkpoint Charlie museum at U-Bahn: Kochstrasse, Friedrichstrasse 211, tel. 030/251-7208). For a classier sit-down meal, try **Café Adler,** across the street from the museum (€4–9, Mon–Sat 10:00–24:00, Sun 10:00–19:00, Friedrichstrasse 20b, tel. 030/251-8965).

In Prenzlauer Berg

Prenzlauer Berg is packed with fine restaurants—German, ethnic, and everything in between. (For more on this district, see page 579.) If you want to just wander, plenty of good places cluster around Helmholtzplatz. Otherwise, here are a few suggestions.

The **KulturBrauerei** complex of buildings offers a smorgasbord of eateries and activities. This former home to the Schultheiss brewery hosts a pool hall, concert venues, nightclubs, and restaurants (open daily, Knaackstrasse 97, U-Bahn: Eberswalder Strasse, tel. 030/4431-5152, www.kulturbrauerei-berlin.de).

Prater Biergarten offers a mellower, outdoor ambience. This self-service place isn't the typical yodeling-and-lederhosen Bavarian beer garden—in addition to the wurst and beer are fine wine and snacks like olives, nuts, and pickles (Mon–Sat 18:00–24:00, Sun 10:00–24:00, just around the corner from KulturBrauerei at Kastanienallee 7, tel. 030/448-5688).

Knoppke's Imbiss has been a Berlin institution for over 70 years—it was family-owned even during DDR times. Locals say Knoppke's cooks up the best *Currywurst* (grilled hot dog with curry-infused ketchup) in town (Mon–Fri 4:30–20:00, closed Sat–Sun, Schönhauser Allee 44A). Don't be fooled by the Currystation at the foot of the stairs coming out of the station; Knoppke's is actually across the street, under the tracks.

TRANSPORTATION CONNECTIONS

Berlin has three train stations (with more on the way). Bahnhof Zoo was the West Berlin train station and still serves Western Europe: Frankfurt, Munich, Hamburg, Paris, and Amsterdam. The Ostbahnhof (former East Berlin's main station) still faces east, serving Prague, Warsaw, Vienna, and Dresden. The Lichtenberg Bahnhof (eastern Berlin's top U- and S-Bahn hub) also handles a few eastbound trains. Expect exceptions. All stations are conveniently connected by subway and even faster by train. Train info: tel. 11861 (€0.46/min).

From Berlin by Train to: Dresden (every 2 hrs, 2.25 hrs), **Frankfurt** (14/day, 5 hrs), **Munich** (14/day, 7 hrs, 10 hrs overnight), **Köln** (hrly, 6.5 hrs), **Amsterdam** (4/day, 7 hrs), **Budapest** (2/day, 13 hrs; 1 goes via Czech Republic and Slovakia, so Eurail is not valid), **Copenhagen** (4/day, 8 hrs, change in Hamburg), **London** (4/day, 15 hrs), **Paris** (6/day, 13 hrs, change in Köln, 1 direct night train), **Zürich** (12/day, 10 hrs, 1 direct night train), **Prague** (4/day, 5 hrs, no overnight trains), **Warsaw** (4/day, 8 hrs, 1 night train from Lichtenberg station; reservations required on all Warsaw-bound trains), **Kraków** (2/day, 10 hrs), **Vienna** (2/day, 12 hrs via Czech Republic; for second-class ticket, Eurailers pay an extra €23 if under age 26 or €31 if age 26 or above; otherwise, take the Berlin–Vienna via Passau train—nightly at 20:00).

Eurailpasses don't cover the Czech Republic. The **Prague Excursion pass** picks up where Eurail leaves off, getting you from any border into Prague and then back out to Eurail country again within seven days (first class-€50, second class-€40, youth second class-€30, buy from EurAide at Berlin's Bahnhof Zoo or Munich's Hauptbahnhof and get reservations—€3—at the same time).

There are **night trains** from Berlin to Amsterdam, Munich, Köln, Brussels, Paris, Vienna, Budapest, Kraków, Warsaw, Stuttgart, Basel, and Zürich, but there are no night trains from Berlin to anywhere in Italy or Spain. A *Liegeplatz,* or berth (€15–36), is a great deal; inquire at EurAide at Bahnhof Zoo for details. Beds cost the same whether you have a first- or second-class ticket or railpass. Trains are often full, so reserve your bed a few days in advance from any travel agency or major train station in Europe. Note: Since the Paris–Berlin night train goes through Belgium, railpass holders cannot use a Eurail Selectpass to cover this ride unless they've selected Belgium.

Berlin's Three Airports

Allow €20 for a taxi ride to or from any of Berlin's airports. **Tegel Airport** handles most flights from the United States and Western Europe (4 miles from center, catch the faster bus #X9 to Bahnhof Zoo, or bus #109 to Ku'damm and Bahnhof Zoo for €2; bus TXL goes to Alexanderplatz in East Berlin). Flights from the east and on Buzz Airlines usually arrive at **Schönefeld Airport** (12.5 miles from center, short walk to S-Bahn, catch S-9 to Zoo station). **Templehof Airport**'s future is uncertain (in Berlin, bus #119 to Ku'damm or U-Bahn 6 or 7). The central telephone number for all three airports is 01805-000-186. For British Air, call 01805-266-522, Delta at 01803-337-880, SAS at 01803-234-023, or Lufthansa at 01803-803-803.

LONDON

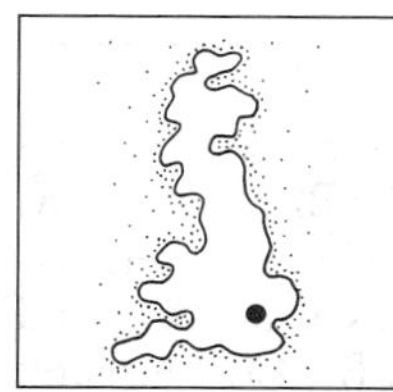

London is more than 600 square miles of urban jungle. With nine million struggling people—many of whom don't speak English—it's a world in itself and a barrage on all the senses. On my first visit I felt very, very small.

London is more than its museums and landmarks. It's a living, breathing, thriving organism...a coral reef of humanity. The city has changed dramatically in recent years, and many visitors are surprised to find how "un-English" it is. Whites are now a minority in major parts of the city that once symbolized white imperialism. Arabs have nearly bought out the area north of Hyde Park. Chinese take-outs outnumber fish-and-chips shops. Many hotels are run by people with foreign accents (who hire English chambermaids), while outlying suburbs are home to huge communities of Indians and Pakistanis. With the English Channel Tunnel complete and union with Europe inevitable, many locals see even more holes in their bastion of Britishness. London is learning—sometimes fitfully—to live as a microcosm of its formerly vast empire.

With just a few days here, you'll get no more than a quick splash in this teeming human tidal pool. But with a good orientation, you'll find London manageable and fun. You'll get a sampling of the city's top sights, history, and cultural entertainment, and a good look at its ever-changing human face.

Blow through the city on the open deck of a double-decker orientation tour bus and take a pinch-me-I'm-in-London walk through the West End. Ogle the crown jewels at the Tower of London, hear the chimes of Big Ben, and see the Houses of Parliament in action. Cruise the Thames River and take a spin on the London Eye Ferris Wheel. Hobnob with the tombstones in Westminster

London Neighborhoods

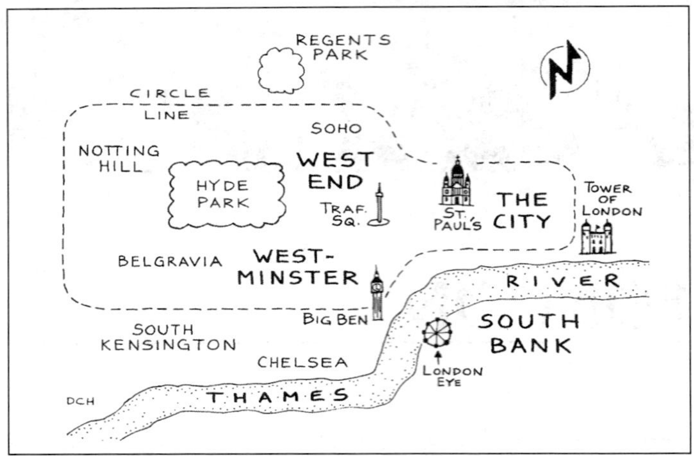

Abbey, enjoy Shakespeare in a replica of the Globe Theatre, and stand in awe over the original Magna Carta at the British Library. Visit with Leonardo, Botticelli, and Rembrandt in the National Gallery. Whisper across the dome of St. Paul's Cathedral and rummage through our civilization's attic at the British Museum. And sip your tea with pinky raised and clotted cream all over your scone. Spend one evening at a theater and the others catching your breath.

Planning Your Time

The sights of London alone could easily fill an entire trip. It's a great one-week getaway, worth four busy days at least.

Here's a suggested schedule:

Day 1: 9:00–Tower of London (Beefeater tour, crown jewels), 12:00–Munch a sandwich on the Thames while cruising from the Tower to Westminster Bridge, 13:00–Follow the self-guided Westminster Walk (see page 618) with a quick visit to the Churchill Museum and Cabinet War Rooms, 15:30–Trafalgar Square and National Gallery, 18:30–Dinner in Soho. Take in a play or 19:30 concert at St. Martin-in-the-Fields.

Day 2: 9:00–Take a hop-on, hop-off bus tour (consider hopping off near the end for the 11:30 Changing of the Guard at Buckingham Palace), 12:30–Covent Gardens for lunch and people-watching, 14:00–Tour the British Museum. Have a pub dinner before a play, concert, or evening walking tour.

Days 3 and 4: Choose among these remaining London highlights: Tour Westminster Abbey, British Library, Imperial War Museum, the two Tates (Tate Modern on the south bank for modern art, Tate Britain on the north bank for British art), St. Paul's Cathedral, or the Museum of London; take a spin on the London Eye Ferris Wheel or a cruise to Kew or Greenwich; do some serious shopping at one of London's elegant department stores or open-air markets; or take another historic walking tour.

After considering nearly all of London's tourist sights, I have pruned them down to just the most important (or fun) for a first visit of up to seven days. You won't be able to see all of these, so don't try. You'll keep coming back to London. After 25 visits myself, I still enjoy a healthy list of excuses to return.

ORIENTATION

(area code: 020)

To grasp London comfortably, see it as the old town in the city center without the modern, congested sprawl. The Thames River runs roughly west to east through the city, with most of the visitor's sights on the north bank. Mentally, maybe even physically, trim down your map to include only the area between the Tower of London (to the east), Hyde Park (west), Regent's Park (north), and the Thames (south). (This is roughly the area bordered by the Tube's Circle Line.) This three-mile stretch between the Tower and Hyde Park (about a 90-min walk)—looking like a milk bottle on its side (see page 607)—holds 80 percent of the sights mentioned in this book.

London is a collection of neighborhoods:

The City: Shakespeare's London was a walled town clustered around St. Paul's Cathedral. Today, it's the modern financial district.

Westminster: This neighborhood includes Big Ben, Parliament, Westminster Abbey, and Buckingham Palace, the grand government buildings from which Britain is ruled.

The West End: Lying between Westminster and the City (that is, at the "west end" of the original walled town), this is the center of London's cultural life. Trafalgar Square has major museums. Piccadilly Circus and Leicester Square host tourist traps, cinemas, and nighttime glitz. Soho and Covent Garden are thriving people-zones housing theaters, restaurants, pubs, and boutiques.

The South Bank: Until recently, the entire south bank of the Thames River was a run-down, generally ignored area, but now it's the hottest real estate in town, with upscale restaurants, major new sightseeing attractions, and pedestrian bridges allowing easy access from the rest of London.

Residential Neighborhoods to the West: Though they lack major tourist sights, Mayfair, South Kensington, Notting Hill, Chelsea, and Belgravia are home to London's wealthy and trendy, as well as many shopping streets and enticing restaurants.

Tourist Information

The **Britain and London Visitors Centre** is the best tourist information service in town (Mon–Fri 9:00–18:30, Sat–Sun 10:00–16:00, phone not answered after 17:00 Mon–Fri and not at all Sat–Sun, booking service, just off Piccadilly Circus at 1 Lower Regent Street, tel. 020/8846-9000, www.visitbritain.com, www.visitlondon.com). If you're traveling beyond London, take advantage of the Centre's well-equipped England desk. Bring your itinerary and a checklist of questions. Pick up these publications: *London Planner* (a great free monthly that lists all the sights, events, and hours), walking-tour schedule fliers, a theater guide, "Central London Bus Guide," and the Thames River Services brochure.

The Britain and London Visitors Centre sells long-distance bus tickets and passes, train tickets (convenient for reservations), and tickets to plays (20 percent booking fee). They also sell **Fast Track tickets** to some of London's attractions (at no extra cost), allowing you to skip the queue at the sights. These can be worthwhile for places that sometimes have long ticket lines, such as the Tower of London, London Eye Ferris Wheel, and Madame Tussaud's Wax Museum. While the Visitors Centre books rooms, you can avoid their £5 booking fee by calling hotels direct (see "Sleeping," page 655).

The **London Pass** provides free entrance to most of the city's sights, but since many museums are free, it's hard to justify the purchase. Still, fervent sightseers can check the list of covered sights and do the arithmetic (£23/1 day, £36/2 days, £44/3 days, £61/6 days, includes 128-page guidebook, tel. 0870-242-9988 for purchase instructions, www.londonpass.com).

Nearby you'll find the **Scottish Tourist Centre** (May–Sept Mon–Fri 9:30–18:30, Sat 10:00–17:00, off-season Mon–Fri 10:00–18:00, Sat 12:00–17:00, closed Sun, Cockspur Street, tel. 0845-225-5121, www.visitscotland.com) and the slick **French National Tourist Office** (Mon–Fri 10:00–18:00, Sat until 17:00, closed Sun, 178 Piccadilly Street, tel. 0906-824-4123).

Unfortunately, **London's Tourist Information Centres** (which present themselves as TIs at major train and bus stations and airports) are now simply businesses selling advertising space to companies with fliers to distribute.

Local bookstores sell London guides and maps; **Bensons Map Guide** is the best (£2.50, also sold at newsstands).

Arrival in London

By Train: London has eight train stations, all connected by the Tube (subway) and all with ATMs, exchange offices, and luggage storage. From any station, ride the Tube or taxi to your hotel.

By Bus: The bus ("coach") station is one block southwest of Victoria Station, which has a TI and Tube entrance.

By Plane: For detailed information on getting from London's airports to downtown London, see "Transportation Connections" (page 675).

Helpful Hints

Pedestrian Safety: Cars drive on the left side of the road, so before crossing a street, I always look right, look left, then look right again just to be sure.

Medical Problems: Local hospitals have 24-hour-a-day emergency care centers where any tourist who needs help can drop in, and after a wait, be seen by a doctor. The quality is good and the price is right (free). Your hotel has details. St. Thomas' Hospital, immediately across the river from Big Ben, has a fine reputation.

U.S. Embassy: It's at 24 Grosvenor Square (for passport concerns, open Mon–Fri 8:30–17:30, closed Sat–Sun, Tube: Bond Street, tel. 020/7499-9000).

Theft Alert: The Artful Dodger is alive and well in London. Be on guard, particularly on public transportation and in places crowded with tourists. Tourists, considered naive and rich, are targeted. More than 7,500 handbags are stolen annually at Covent Garden alone.

Changing Money: ATMs are the way to go. While regular banks charge several pounds to change traveler's checks, American Express offices offer a fair rate and will change any brand of traveler's checks for no fee. Handy AmEx offices are near Piccadilly (June–Sept Mon–Sat 9:00–18:00, Sun 10:00–17:00; Oct–May Mon–Sat 9:00–17:30, Sun 10:00–17:00; 30 Haymarket, tel. 020/7484-9610; refund office 24-hr tel. 0800/521-313). Marks & Spencer department stores give good rates with no fees.

Avoid changing money at exchange bureaus. Their latest scam: They advertise very good rates with a same-as-the-banks fee of 2 percent. But the fine print explains that the fee of 2 percent is for buying pounds. The fee for selling pounds is 9.5 percent. Ouch!

Sights: Free museums include the British Museum, British Library, National Gallery, National Portrait Gallery, Tate Britain (British art), Tate Modern (modern art), Imperial War Museum, Victoria and Albert Museum, Natural History Museum, Science Museum, and the Royal Air Force Museum London. Some, like the British Museum, request a £2–3 donation, but whether you contribute or not is up to you. Special exhibitions cost extra.

It's smart to telephone first to check hours and confirm plans, especially off-season, when hours shrink.

Internet Access: The astonishing easyInternetcafé chain offers up to 500 computers per store and is open long hours daily. Depending on the time of day, a £2 ticket buys anywhere from 80 minutes to six hours of computer time. The ticket is valid for four weeks and multiple visits at any of their five branches: Victoria Station (across from front of station, near taxis and buses, long lines), Trafalgar Square (456 Strand), Tottenham Court Road (#9–16), Oxford Street (#358, opposite Bond Street Tube station), and Kensington High Street (#160–166). They also sell 24-hour, seven-day, and 30-day passes (www.easyinternetcafe.com).

Travel Bookstores: Stanfords Travel Bookstore, in Covent Garden, is good and stocks current editions of my books (Mon–Fri 9:00–19:30, Sat 10:00–19:00, Sun 12:00–18:00, 12 Long Acre, tel. 020/7836-1321). There are two impressive Waterstone's bookstores: the biggest in Europe on Piccadilly (Mon–Sat 10:00–22:00, Sun 12:00–18:00, 203 Piccadilly, tel. 020/7851-2400) and one on the corner of Trafalgar Square (Mon–Sat 9:30–21:00, Sun 12:00–18:00, next to Costa Café, tel. 020/7839-4411).

Left Luggage: As security concerns heighten, train stations have replaced their lockers with left-luggage counters. Each bag must go through a scanner (just like at the airport), so lines can be long. Expect a wait to pick up your bags, too (each item-£5/24 hrs, daily 7:00–24:00). You can also check bags at the airports (£4/day). If leaving London and returning later, you may be able to leave a box or bag at your hotel for free—assuming you'll be staying there again.

Getting Around London

To travel smart in a city this size, you must get comfortable with public transportation. London's excellent taxis, buses, and subway system make a private car unnecessary. In fact, the new "congestion charge" of £5 levied on any private car entering the city center has been effective in cutting down traffic-jam delays and bolstering London's public transit. The revenue raised subsidizes the buses, which are now cheaper, more frequent, and even more user-friendly than before. Today, the vast majority of vehicles in the city center are buses, taxis, and service trucks. (Drivers, for all the details on the congestion charge, see www.cclondon.com.)

By Taxi: London is the best taxi town in Europe. Big, black, carefully regulated cabs are everywhere. I've never met a crabby cabbie in London. They love to talk, and they know every nook and cranny in town. I ride in one each day just to get my London questions answered. Rides start at £2. Connecting downtown sights is quick and easy and will cost you about £4 (for example, St. Paul's

London

ZOO
REGENT'S PARK
EUSTON STN.
KING'S CROSS STN.
ST. PANCRAS STN.
BRITISH LIB.
TO CAMBRIDGE
MUSEUM OF LONDON
LIVERPOOL ST. STN.
TO BATH
MARBLE ARCH + SPEAKER'S CORNER
PADDINGTON STN.
THEATRE DIST. + LEICESTER SQ.
BRITISH MUSEUM
HIGH
HOLBORN
ST. PAUL'S
TOWER OF LONDON
FLEET
CITY
COVENT GARDEN
TO HEATHROW AIRPORT
NOTTING HILL
OXFORD
SOHO
SHAFTESBURY
STRAND
EMBANKMENT
BAYS WATER
NOTT. HILL GATE
PICC. CIRCUS
ST. KATH. DOCK
HYDE PARK
KENS. GARDENS
PICCADILLY
PALL MALL
VICT.
WATER-LOO
GLOBE
TATE MODERN
CITY HALL
RIVER
ALBERT HALL
HOLLAND PARK
KNIGHTSBRIDGE
GREEN
ST JAMES'S
LONDON EYE
TRAFALGAR SQUARE + NATL. GALL.
TOWER BRIDGE
TO GREEN-WICH
KENS. HIGH ST.
SOUTH
BUCK. PALACE
VICTORIA
VICTORIA + ALBERT MUSEUM
HARRODS
WESTMINSTER
KENSINGTON
BUS STN.
VICT. STN.
TATE BRITAIN
BROMPTON ROAD
CHELSEA
PARLIAMENT, BIG BEN + WESTMINSTER ABBEY
1 MILE
1 KM
THAMES
TO LONDON BRIDGE (ARIZONA)
TO KEW GARDENS + HAMPTON COURT PALACE
TO GATWICK AIRPORT
DCH

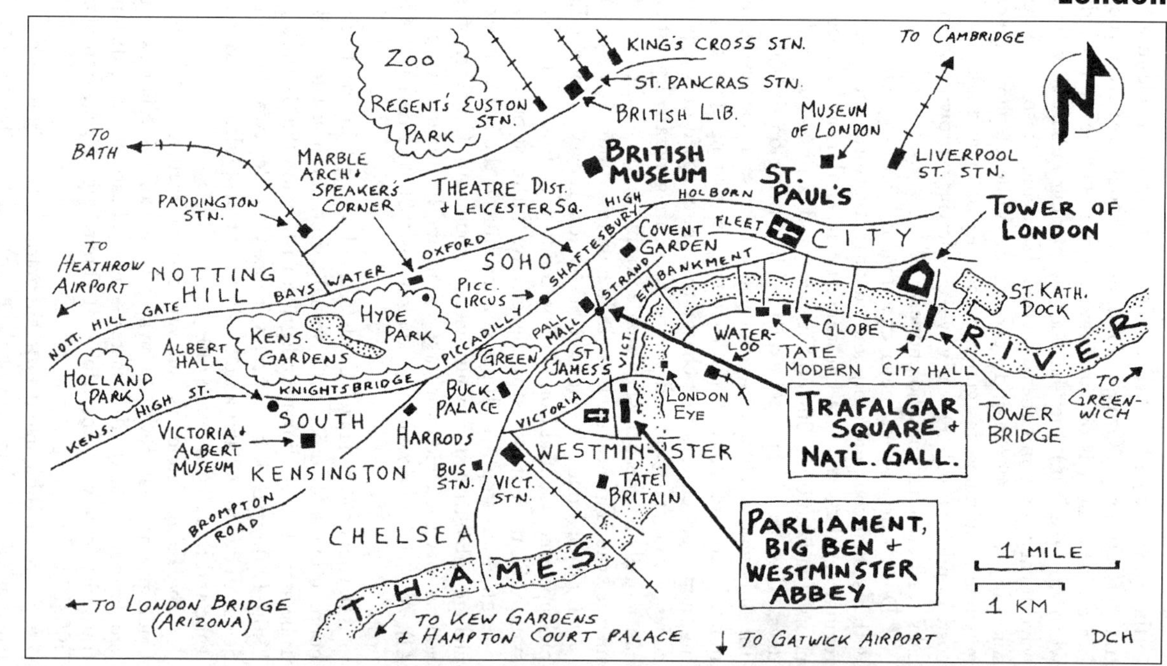

to the Tower of London). For a short ride, three people in a cab travel at Tube prices. Groups of four or five should taxi everywhere. If a cab's top light is on, just wave it down. (Drivers flash lights when they see you.) They have a tiny turning radius, so you can wave at cabs going in either direction. If waving doesn't work, ask someone where you can find a taxi stand. While telephoning a cab gets one in minutes, it's generally not necessary and adds to the cost. London is such a great wave-'em-down taxi town that most cabs don't even have a radio phone.

Don't worry about meter cheating. British cab meters come with a sealed computer chip and clock that ensures you'll get the regular tariff #1 most of the time, tariff #2 during "unsociable hours" (daily 18:00–6:00 and Sat–Sun), and tariff #3 only on holidays. All extra charges are explained in writing on the cab wall. The only way a cabbie can cheat you is to take a needlessly long route. There are alternative cab companies driving normal-looking, non-metered cars that charge fixed rates based on the postal codes of your start and end points. These are generally honest and can actually be cheaper when snarled traffic drives up the cost of a metered cab. Tip a cabbie by rounding up (maximum 10 percent).

By Bus: London's extensive bus system is easy to follow. Just pick up a free "Central London Bus Guide" map from a TI or Tube station. Signs at stops list routes clearly. On most buses (marked on sign at bus stop), you'll pay at a machine at the bus stop (exact change only), then show your ticket as you board. On other buses, you can pay the conductor (take a seat, and he'll come and collect £1). Any ride in downtown London costs £1. The best views are upstairs.

If you have a Travel Card (see below), get in the habit of hopping buses for quick little straight shots, even just to get to a Tube stop. During bump-and-grind rush hours (8:00–10:00 and 16:00–19:00), you'll go faster by Tube. Consider two special bus deals: all day for £2 and a ticket six-pack for £4 (also see "London Tube and Bus Passes," page 610).

By Tube: London's subway system (called the Tube or Underground, but never "subway") is one of this planet's great people-movers and the fastest—and cheapest—long-distance transport in town (runs Mon–Sat about 5:00–24:00, Sun about 7:00–23:00).

Survey a Tube map (free at any station). Each line has a name (such as Circle, Northern, or Bakerloo) and two directions (indicated by the end-of-the-line stop). Find the line that will take you to your destination, and figure out roughly what direction (north, south, east, west) you'll need to go to get there.

In the Tube station, feed your ticket into the turnstile, reclaim it, and hang onto the ticket—you'll need it to get through the

Handy Buses

Since the institution of London's "congestion charge" for cars, the bus system is faster, easier, and cheaper than ever. Tube-oriented travelers need to make a point to get over their tunnel vision, learn the bus system, and get around fast and easy.

Here are some of the most useful routes:

Route #9: Harrods to Hyde Park Corner to Piccadilly Circus to Trafalgar Square.

Routes #11 and #24: Victoria Station to Westminster Abbey to Trafalgar Square (#11 continues to St. Paul's).

Route #RV1: Tower of London to Tower Bridge to Tate Modern/Shakespeare's Globe to London Eye/Waterloo Station/County Hall Travel Inn accommodations to Trafalgar Square to Covent Garden (a scenic joyride).

Route #15: Paddington Station to Oxford Circus to Regent Street/TI to Piccadilly Circus to Trafalgar Square to Fleet Street to St. Paul's to Tower of London.

Route #188: Waterloo Station/London Eye to Trafalgar Square to Covent Garden to British Museum.

In addition, several buses (including #6, #12, #13, #15, #23, #139, and #159) make the corridor run from Trafalgar, Piccadilly Circus, and Oxford Circus to Marble Arch.

turnstile at the end of your journey. Find your train by following signs to your line and the (general) direction it's headed (such as Central Line: east).

Since some tracks are shared by several lines, you'll need to double-check before boarding a train: First, make sure your destination is one of the stops listed on the sign at the platform. Also, check the electronic signboards that announce which train is next, and make sure the destination (the end-of-the-line stop) is the one you want. Some trains, particularly on the Circle and District lines, split off for other directions, but each train has its final destination marked above its windshield. When in doubt, ask a local or a blue-vested staff person for help.

Trains run roughly every three to 10 minutes. If one train is absolutely packed and you notice another to the same destination is coming in three minutes, you can wait to avoid the sardine experience. The system can be fraught with construction delays and breakdowns, so pay attention to signs and announcements explaining necessary detours, etc. The Circle Line is notorious for problems. Bring something to do to make your waiting time productive.

You can't leave the system without feeding your ticket to the turnstile. Hang onto your ticket. (The turnstile will either eat your now-expired single-trip ticket, or spit your still-valid pass back out.)

Save walking time by choosing the best street exit—check the maps on the walls or ask any station personnel. "Subway" means "pedestrian underpass" in "English." For Tube and bus information 24 hours a day, call 020/7222-1234 (www.transportforlondon.gov.uk; for Tube only, visit www.thetube.com, has journey planner). And always...mind the gap.

Cost: Any ride in Zone 1 (on or within the Circle Line, including virtually all my recommended sights and hotels) costs £3. Tube tickets are also valid on city buses.

You can avoid ticket-window lines in Tube stations by buying tickets from coin-op or credit-card machines; practice on the punchboard to see how the system works (hit "Adult Single" and your destination). These tickets are valid only on the day of purchase.

Again, nearly every ride, if purchased individually, will be £3. Most travelers will save money by getting a Tube and bus pass. Beware: Overshooting your zone nets you a £10 fine.

London Tube and Bus Passes: Consider using the following passes, valid on both the Tube and buses (all passes are available for more zones, can be purchased as easily as a normal ticket at any station, and can get you a 30 percent discount on most Thames cruises).

If you figure you'll take three rides in a day, a day pass is a good deal. The **One-Day Travel Card,** covering Zones 1 and 2, gives you unlimited "off-peak" travel for a day, starting after 9:30 on weekdays and anytime on weekends (£4.70). The all-zone version of this card costs £6 (and includes Heathrow Airport). The unrestricted version, covering six zones (including Heathrow) at all times, costs £12. Families save with the Kid for a Quid deal (an adult with a Travelcard pays £1 extra per kid).

The new **Three-Day Travel Card** covers Zones 1 and 2 any time of day for £15.

The **7-Day Travel Card** costs £21.40 and covers Zones 1 and 2.

You'll likely see signs advertising the new **Oyster Card**, designed for commuters or tourists staying four days or more. The prepaid, rechargeable pass is good for Tube and/or bus trips, depending on what version you buy. There's a £10 minimum to get or add to a card, and you'll pay a £3 deposit to use the card (refundable at any Tube station ticket office). When using an Oyster Card, make sure you touch the card to the yellow scanner when you enter and exit the Tube. For specifics, visit www.oystercard.com.

Daily Reminder

Sunday: Some sights don't open until noon. The Tower of London is especially crowded today. Hyde Park Speakers' Corner rants from early afternoon until early evening. These are closed: Banqueting House, Sir John Soane's Museum, and legal sights (Houses of Parliament and Old Bailey; the City is dead). Evensong is at 15:00 at Westminster Abbey (plus free organ recital at 17:45) and 15:15 at St. Paul's (plus free organ recital at 17:00); both churches are open during the day for worship but closed to sightseers. Many stores and theaters are closed. Street markets flourish: Camden Lock, Spitalfields, Greenwich, and Petticoat Lane.

Monday: Virtually all sights are open except for Apsley House, the Theatre Museum, Sir John Soane's Museum, and a few others. The St. Martin-in-the-Fields church offers a free 13:00 concert. At Somerset House, the Courtauld Gallery is free until 14:00. Vinopolis is open until 21:00.

Tuesday: All sights are open; the British Library is open until 20:00. St. Martin-in-the-Fields has a free 13:00 concert.

Wednesday: All sights are open, plus evening hours at Westminster Abbey (until 19:45, but no evensong), the National Gallery (until 21:00), and Victoria and Albert Museum (until 22:00).

Thursday: All sights are open, British Museum until 20:30 (selected galleries), National Portrait Gallery until 21:00. St. Martin-in-the-Fields hosts a 19:30 evening concert (for a fee).

Friday: All sights are open, British Museum until 20:30 (selected galleries only), National Portrait Gallery until 21:00, Vinopolis is open until 21:00, Tate Modern and Saatchi Gallery until 22:00. Best street market: Spitalfields. St. Martin-in-the-Fields offers two concerts (13:00–free, 19:30–fee).

Saturday: Most sights are open except legal ones (Old Bailey; Houses of Parliament—open summer Sat for tours only; skip the City). Vinopolis is open until 21:00, Tate Modern and Saatchi Gallery until 22:00. Best street markets: Portobello, Camden Lock, Greenwich. Evensong is at 15:00 at Westminster Abbey, 17:00 at St. Paul's. St. Martin-in-the-Fields hosts a concert at 19:30 (fee).

Notes: Evensong occurs daily at St. Paul's (Mon–Sat at 17:00 and Sun at 15:15) and daily except Wednesday at Westminster Abbey (Mon–Tue and Thu–Fri at 17:00, Sat–Sun at 15:00). London by Night Sightseeing Tour buses leave from Victoria Station every evening at 19:30 and 21:30. The London Eye Ferris Wheel spins nightly until 21:00 in summer, until 20:00 in winter (closed Jan).

London at a Glance

▲▲▲British Museum The world's greatest collection of artifacts of Western civilization, including the Rosetta Stone and the Parthenon's Elgin Marbles. **Hours:** Daily 10:00–17:30, Thu–Fri until 20:30 but only a few galleries open after 17:30.

▲▲▲National Gallery Remarkable collection of European paintings (1250–1900), including Leonardo, Botticelli, Velázquez, Rembrandt, Turner, van Gogh, and the Impressionists. **Hours:** Daily 10:00–18:00, Wed until 21:00.

▲▲▲British Library Impressive collection of the most important literary treasures of the Western world, from the Magna Carta to Handel's *Messiah*. **Hours:** Mon–Fri 9:30–18:00, Tue until 20:00, Sat 9:30–17:00, Sun 11:00–17:00.

▲▲▲Westminster Abbey Britain's finest church and the site of royal coronations and burials since 1066. **Hours:** Mon–Fri 9:30–15:45, Wed also until 19:00, Sat 9:30–13:45, closed Sun to sightseers but open for services.

▲▲▲St. Paul's Cathedral The main cathedral of the Anglican Church, designed by Christopher Wren, with a climbable dome and daily evensong services. **Hours:** Mon–Sat 8:30–16:30, closed Sun except for worship.

▲▲▲Tower of London Historic castle, palace, and prison, today housing the crown jewels and a witty band of Beefeaters. **Hours:** March–Oct Mon–Sat 9:00–18:00, Sun 10:00–18:00; Nov–Feb Tue–Sat 9:00–17:00, Sun–Mon 10:00–17:00.

▲▲▲London Eye Ferris Wheel Enormous observation wheel, dominating—and offering commanding views over—London's skyline. **Hours:** April–mid-Sept daily 9:30–21:00, mid-Sept–March 9:30–20:00, closed Jan.

▲▲▲Tate Modern Works by Monet, Matisse, Dalí, Picasso, and Warhol displayed in a converted powerhouse. **Hours:** Daily 10:00–18:00, Fri–Sat until 22:00.

▲▲Tate Britain Collection of British painting from the 16th century through modern times, including works by William Blake, the Pre-Raphaelites, and J. M. W. Turner. **Hours:** Daily 10:00–17:50.

▲▲Houses of Parliament London's famous neo-Gothic landmark, topped by Big Ben and occupied by the Houses of Lords and Commons. **Hours:** House of Commons—Mon 14:30–22:30, Tue–Thu 11:30–19:30, Fri 9:30–15:00; House of Lords—Mon–Wed 14:30–22:30 or until they finish, Thu from 12:00 on, sometimes Fri from 10:00.

▲▲Imperial War Museum Examines the military history of the bloody 20th century. **Hours:** Daily 10:00–18:00.

▲▲Churchill Museum and Cabinet War Rooms Underground WWII headquarters of Churchill's war effort. **Hours:** Daily April–Sept 9:30–18:00, Oct–March 10:00–18:00.

▲▲National Portrait Gallery Who's Who of British history, featuring portraits of this nation's most important historical figures. **Hours:** Daily 10:00–18:00, Thu–Fri until 21:00.

▲▲Buckingham Palace Britain's royal residence with the famous Changing of the Guard. **Hours:** Palace—Aug–Sept only, daily 9:30–17:00; Guard—almost daily in summer at 11:30, every other day all year long.

▲▲Shakespeare's Globe Timbered, thatched-roofed reconstruction of the Bard's original wooden "O." **Hours:** Actor-led tours mid-May–Sept Mon–Sat 9:30–12:30, Sun 9:30–11:30; virtual tours daily 12:30–16:00; actor tours also Oct–mid-May daily 10:30–17:00. Plays are also held here.

▲▲Victoria and Albert Museum The best collection of decorative arts anywhere. **Hours:** Daily 10:00–17:45, Wed and last Fri of the month until 22:00 except mid-Dec–mid-Jan.

▲▲Somerset House Grand 18th-century civic palace housing three fine art museums: Courtauld Gallery (decent painting collection), Hermitage Rooms (rotating exhibits from famous St. Petersburg museum), and the Gilbert Collection (decorative arts). **Hours:** Daily 10:00–18:00.

▲▲Old Operating Theatre 19th-century hall where surgeons performed amputations for an audience of aspiring med students. **Hours:** Daily 10:30–17:00.

▲▲Vinopolis: City of Wine Offers a breezy history of wine with plenty of tasting opportunities. **Hours:** Daily 12:00–18:00, Fri–Sat and Mon until 21:00.

TOURS

▲▲▲Hop-on, Hop-off Double-Decker Bus Tours—Two competitive companies (Original and Big Bus) offer essentially the same tours with buses that have either live (English-only) guides or a tape-recorded, dial-a-language narration. This two-hour, once-over-lightly bus tour drives by all the famous sights, providing a stress-free way to get your bearings and at least see the biggies. You can sit back and enjoy the entire two-hour orientation tour (a good idea if you like the guide and the weather), or hop on and hop off at any of the nearly 30 stops and catch a later bus. Buses run about every 10–15 minutes in summer, every 20 minutes in winter. It's an inexpensive form of transport as well as an informative tour. Buses operate daily (from about 9:00 until early evening in summer, until late afternoon in winter) and stop at Victoria Street (1 block north of Victoria Station), Marble Arch, Piccadilly Circus, Trafalgar Square, and elsewhere.

Each company offers a core two-hour overview tour, two other routes, and a narrated Thames boat tour covered by the same ticket (buy ticket from driver, credit cards accepted at major stops such as Victoria Station, ticket good for 24 hrs, bring a sweater and a camera). Pick up a map from any flier rack or from one of the countless salespeople and study the complex system. Note: If you start at Victoria Station at 9:00, you'll finish near Buckingham Palace in time to see the Changing of the Guard (at 11:30); ask your driver for the best place to hop off. Sunday morning—when the traffic is light and many museums are closed—is a fine time for a tour. The last full loop leaves Victoria at 17:00. Both companies have entertaining as well as boring guides. The narration is important. If you don't like your guide, jump off and find another. If you like your guide, settle in for the entire loop.

Original London Sightseeing Bus Tour: Live-guided buses have a Union Jack flag and a yellow triangle on the front of the bus. If the front has many flags or a green or red triangle, it's a tape-recorded multilingual tour—avoid it, unless you have kids who'd enjoy the entertaining recorded kids' tour (£16, £2.50 discount with this book, limit 2 discounts per book, they'll rip off the corner of this page—raise bloody hell if they don't honor this discount, ticket good for 24 hours, tel. 020/8877-1722, www.theoriginaltour.com). Your ticket includes a 50-minute round-trip boat tour from Westminster Pier or Waterloo Pier (departs hourly, tape-recorded narration).

Big Bus Hop-on, Hop-off London Tours: These are also good. For £18, you get the same basic tour plus coupons for three different one-hour London walks and the scenic and usually entertainingly guided Thames boat ride (normally £5.40) between

Westminster Pier and the Tower of London. The pass and extras are valid for 24 hours. Buses with live guides are marked in front with a picture of an orange bus; buses with tape-recorded spiels display a picture of a blue bus and headphones. While the price is steeper, Big Bus guides seem more dynamic than the Original guides (daily 8:30–18:00, winter until 16:30, from Victoria Station, tel. 020/7233-9533, www.bigbus.co.uk).

At Night: The London by Night Sightseeing Tour runs basically the same circuit as the other companies, but after hours. While the narration is pretty lame (the driver does little more than call out the names of famous places as you roll by), the views at twilight are grand (£9, pay driver or buy tickets at Victoria Station or Paddington Station TI, April–Oct only, 2-hr tour with live guide, departs at 19:30 and 21:30 from Victoria Station, Taxi Road, at front of station near end of Wilton Road, tel. 020/8646-1747, www.london-by-night.net).

▲▲Walking Tours—Several times a day, top-notch local guides lead (often big) groups through specific slices of London's past. Schedule fliers litter the desks of TIs, hotels, and pubs. *Time Out* lists many, but not all, scheduled walks. Simply show up at the announced location, pay £5.50, and enjoy two chatty hours of Dickens, the Plague, Shakespeare, Legal London, the Beatles, Jack the Ripper, or whatever is on the agenda. Original London Walks, the dominant company, lists its extensive daily schedule in a beefy, plain, black-and-white *The Original London Walks* brochure (walks offered year-round—even Christmas, private tours for £90, tel. 020/7624-3978, for a recorded listing of today's walks call 020/7624-9255, www.walks.com). They also run **Explorer day trips,** a good option for those with limited time and transportation (different trip daily: Stonehenge/Salisbury, Oxford/Cotswolds, York, Bath, and so on).

Beatles: Fans of the still–Fabulous Four can take one of the Beatles walks (5/week, offered by Original London Walks, above), visit the Beatles Shop (daily, 231 Baker Street, next to Sherlock Holmes Museum, Tube: Baker Street, tel. 020/7935-4464), or go to Abbey Road and walk the famous crosswalk (at intersection with Grove End, Tube: St. John's Wood).

Private Guides—Standard rates for London's registered guides are £97 for four hours, £146 for eight hours (tel. 020/7403-2962, www.touristguides.org.uk). Robina Brown leads tours of small groups in her Toyota Previa (£200/3 hrs, £300–450/day, tel. 020/7228-2238, www.driverguidetours.com, robina@driverguidetours.com). Brit Lonsdale, an energetic mother of twins, is another registered London guide (£89/half-day, £142/day, tel. 020/7386-9907, brittl@ntlworld.com).

London Duck Tours—A bright-yellow amphibious vehicle takes a gang of 30 tourists past some famous sights on land (Big Ben, Buckingham Palace, Piccadilly Circus), then splashes into the Thames for a 30-minute cruise (£17, at least 2/hr, daily 10:00–18:00, 75 min, live commentary, these book up in advance, departs from Chicheley Street behind County Hall near London Eye Ferris Wheel, Tube: Waterloo or Westminster, tel. 020/7928-3132, www.londonducktours.co.uk).

▲▲Cruises—Boat tours with entertaining commentaries sail regularly from many points along the Thames. It's confusing, since there are several companies offering essentially the same thing. Your basic options are downstream (to the Tower and Greenwich), upstream (to Kew Gardens and Hampton Court), and round-trip scenic-tour cruises. Most people depart from the Westminster Pier (at the base of Westminster Bridge under Big Ben). You can catch most of the same boats (with less waiting) from Waterloo Pier at the London Eye Ferris Wheel across the river. For pleasure and efficiency, consider combining a one-way cruise (to Kew, Greenwich, or wherever) with a Tube ride back. While Tube and bus tickets don't work on the boats, a Travel Card can snare you a 33 percent discount on most cruises (just show the card when you pay for the cruise). Children and seniors also get discounts. You can purchase drinks and scant, pricey snacks on board. Buy boat tickets at the small ticket offices on the docks. Clever budget travelers pack a small picnic and munch while they cruise.

Here are some of the most popular cruise options:

To Tower of London: City Cruises boats sail 30 minutes to the Tower from Westminster Pier (£5.40 one-way, £6.50 round-trip, one-way included with Big Bus London tour; covered by £8.70 "River Red Rover" ticket that includes Greenwich—see next paragraph; 3/hr during June–Aug daily 9:40–20:40, 2/hr and shorter hours rest of year).

To Greenwich: Two companies head to Greenwich from Westminster Pier. Choose between **City Cruises** (£6.60 one-way, £8.20 round-trip; or get their £8.70 all-day, hop-on, hop-off "River Red Rover" ticket to have option of getting off at London Eye and Tower of London; June–Aug daily 10:00–17:00, less off-season, every 40 min, 70 min to Greenwich, usually narrated only downstream—to Greenwich, tel. 020/7740-0400, www.citycruises.com) and **Thames River Services** (£6.60 one-way, £8.20 round-trip, April–Oct daily 10:00–16:00, July–Aug until 17:00, has shorter hours and runs every 40 min rest of year, 2/hr, 50 min, usually narrated only to Greenwich, tel. 020/7930-4097, www.westminsterpier.co.uk).

To Kew Gardens: Westminster Passenger Services Association leaves for Kew Gardens from Westminster Pier (£9 one-way, £15

Thames Boat Piers

While Westminster Pier is the most popular, it's not the only dock in town. Consider all the options:

Westminster Pier, at the base of Big Ben, offers round-trip sightseeing cruises and lots of departures in both directions.

Waterloo Pier, at the base of London Eye Ferris Wheel, is a good, less-crowded alternative to Westminster, with many of the same cruise options.

Embankment Pier is near Covent Garden, Trafalgar Square, and Cleopatra's Needle (the obelisk on the Thames). You can take a round-trip cruise from here, or catch a boat to the Tower of London and Greenwich.

Tower Millennium Pier is at the Tower of London. Boats sail west to Westminster Pier or east to Greenwich.

Bankside Pier (near Tate Modern and Shakespeare's Globe) and **Millbank Pier** (near Tate Britain) are connected to each other by the "Tate to Tate" ferry service.

round-trip, 4/day, generally departing 10:30–14:00, 90 min, narrated for 30 min, tel. 020/7930-2062, www.wpsa.co.uk). Some boats continue on to **Hampton Court Palace** for an additional £3 (and 90 min). Because of the river current, you'll save 30 minutes cruising from Hampton Court back into town.

Round-Trip Cruises: Fifty-minute round-trip cruises of the Thames leave hourly from Westminster and Embankment Piers (£7, included with Original London Bus tour—listed above, tape-recorded narration, Catamaran Circular Cruises, tel. 020/7987-1185). The London Eye Ferris Wheel operates its own "River Cruise Experience," offering a similar 45-minute circular tour from Waterloo Pier (must be done in combination with Ferris Wheel, £21.50 includes both, reservations recommended, tel. 0870-443-9185, www.ba-londoneye.com).

From Tate to Tate: This boat service for art-lovers connects the Tate Modern and Tate Britain in 18 scenic minutes, stopping at the London Eye Ferris Wheel en route (£3.40 one-way/£5 for day ticket; with a Travel Card it's £2.30 one-way/£3.40 day ticket; buy ticket at gallery desk or on board, departing every 40 min from 10:00–17:00, tel. 020/7887-8008).

On Regent's Canal: Consider exploring London's canals by taking a cruise on historic Regent's Canal in north London. The good ship *Jenny Wren* offers 90-minute guided canal-boat cruises from Walker's Quay in Camden Town to Little Venice (£6.80, March–Oct daily 12:30 and 14:30, Sat–Sun also 10:30 and 16:30, Walker's Quay, 250 Camden High Street, Tube: Camden Town, tel. 020/7485-4433 or 020/7485-6210, www.walkersquay.com).

While in Camden Town, stop by the popular Camden Lock Market to browse through trendy arts and crafts (daily 10:00–18:00, busiest on weekends, a block from Walker's Quay).

Westminster Walk

Just about every visitor to London strolls the historic Whitehall boulevard from Big Ben to Trafalgar Square. Beneath London's modern traffic and big-city bustle lies 2,000 fascinating years of history. This three-quarter-mile, self-guided orientation walk (see map on page 619) gives you a whirlwind tour and connects the sights listed in this section.

Start halfway across **Westminster Bridge** (❶) for that "Wow, I'm really in London!" feeling. Get a close-up view of the **Houses of Parliament** and **Big Ben** (floodlit at night). Downstream you'll see the **London Eye Ferris Wheel.** Down the stairs to Westminster Pier are boats to the Tower of London and Greenwich.

En route to Parliament Square, you'll pass a **statue of Boadicea** (❷), the Celtic queen defeated by Roman invaders in A.D. 60.

To thrill your loved ones (or bug the envious), call home from a pay phone near Big Ben at about three minutes before the hour. You'll find a phone on Great George Street, across from **Parliament Square.** As Big Ben chimes, stick the receiver outside the booth and prove you're in London: Ding dong ding dong...dong ding ding dong.

Wave hello to Churchill in Parliament Square (❸). To his right is **Westminster Abbey** with its two stubby, elegant towers.

Walk north up Parliament Street, which turns into Whitehall (❹), toward Trafalgar Square. You'll see the thought-provoking **Cenotaph** (❺) in the middle of the street, reminding passersby of Britain's many war dead. To visit the Cabinet War Rooms (described below), take a left before the Cenotaph, on King Charles Street.

Continuing on Whitehall, stop at the barricaded and guarded **10 Downing Street** to see the British "White House" (❻), home of the prime minister. Break the bobby's boredom: ask him a question.

Nearing Trafalgar Square, look for the **Horse Guards** behind the gated fence (Changing of the Guard Mon–Sat 11:00, Sun at 10:00, dismounting ceremony daily at 16:00) and the 17th-century **Banqueting House** across the street (❼; described below).

The column topped by Lord Nelson marks **Trafalgar Square** (❽). The stately domed building on the far side of the square is the **National Gallery** (free) which has a classy café upstairs in the Sainsbury wing. To the right of the National Gallery is **St. Martin-in-the-Fields Church** and its Café in the Crypt.

To get to Piccadilly from Trafalgar Square, walk up Cockspur

Westminster Walk

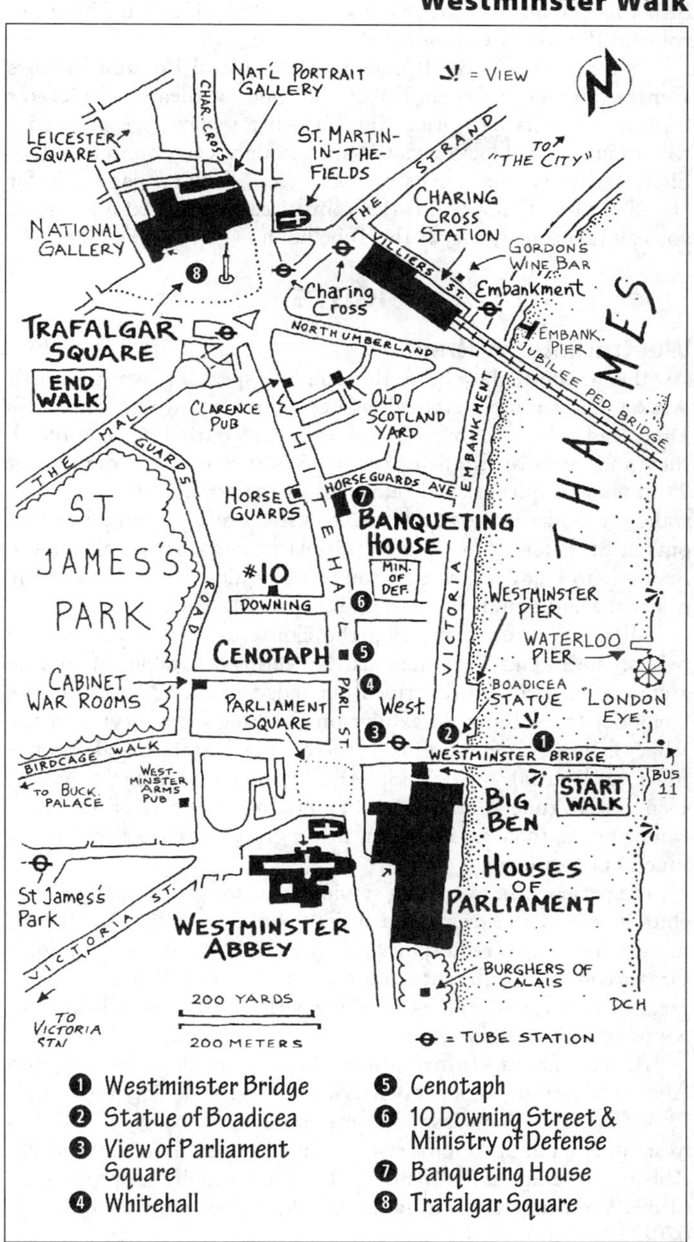

Street to Haymarket, then take a short left on Coventry Street to colorful **Piccadilly Circus.**

Near Piccadilly you'll find the **Britain and London Visitors Centre** (on Lower Regent Street) and piles of theaters. **Leicester Square** (with its half-price "tkts" booth for plays, see page 652) thrives just a few blocks away. Walk through seedy **Soho** (north of Shaftesbury Avenue) for its fun pubs (see "Eating," page 668, for "Food is Fun" Dinner Crawl). From Piccadilly or Oxford Circus, you can take a taxi, bus, or the Tube home.

SIGHTS

Westminster Abbey

As the greatest church in the English-speaking world (worth ▲▲▲), Westminster Abbey has been the place where England's kings and queens have been crowned and buried since 1066. A thousand years of English history—3,000 tombs, the remains of 29 kings and queens, and hundreds of memorials—lie within its walls and under its stone slabs. Like a stony refugee camp huddled outside St. Peter's Pearly Gates, this place has a story to tell and the best way to enjoy it is with a **tour** (audioguide-£3, live-£4; many prefer the audioguide because it's self-paced).

Three tiny **museums** ring the cloisters: the Chapter House (where the monks held their daily meetings, notable for its fine architecture and well-described but faded medieval art), the Pyx Chamber (containing an exhibit on the king's treasury), and the Abbey Museum (which tells of the abbey's history, royal coronations, and burials). Look into the impressively realistic eyes of Henry VII's funeral effigy (one of a fascinating series of wax-and-wood statues that, for three centuries, graced royal coffins during funeral processions).

Experience an **evensong** service—awesome in a nearly empty church (weekdays except Wed at 17:00, Sat–Sun at 15:00). The 40-minute **free organ recital** on Sunday at 17:45 is another highlight. Organ concerts (different from the Sunday recital) held here are great and inexpensive; look for signs with schedule details (or visit www.westminster-abbey.org).

Cost, Hours, Information: £7.50, includes cloisters and Abbey Museum; abbey open Mon–Fri 9:30–15:45, Wed until 19:00, Sat 9:30–13:45, last entry 60 min before closing, closed Sun to sightseers but open for services; cloisters open daily 8:00–18:00: Abbey Museum daily 10:30–16:00. Photography is prohibited. (Tube: Westminster or St. James's Park, call for tour schedule, tel. 020/7222-7110.)

The main entrance, on the Big Ben side, often has a sizable line; visit early or late to avoid tourist hordes. Midmornings are most crowded. On weekdays after 15:00 it's less crowded; come then and stay for the 17:00 evensong. Since the church is often closed to the public for special services, it's wise to call first.

For a free peek inside and a quiet sit in the nave, you can tell a guard at the west end (where the tourists exit) that you'd like to pay your respects to Britain's Unknown Soldier. If the guard is nice, he might let you slip in.

Between the Abbey and Trafalgar Square

▲▲Houses of Parliament (Palace of Westminster)—This neo-Gothic icon of London, the royal residence from 1042 to 1547, is now the meeting place of the legislative branch of government. Tourists are welcome to view debates in either the bickering House of Commons or the genteel House of Lords (in session when a flag flies atop the Victoria Tower). While the actual debates are generally extremely dull, it is a thrill to be inside and see the British government inaction (House of Commons: Mon 14:30–22:30, Tue–Thu 11:30–19:30, Fri 9:30–15:00, generally less action and no lines after 18:00, use St. Stephen's entrance, Tube: Westminster, tel. 020/7219-4272 for schedule, www.parliament.uk). The House of Lords has more pageantry, shorter lines, and less interesting debates (Mon–Wed 14:30–22:30 or until they finish, Thu from 12:00 on, sometimes Fri from 10:00 on, tel. 020/7219-3107 for schedule, and visit www.parliamentlive.tv for a preview). If there's only one line outside, it's for the House of Commons. Go to the gate and tell the guard you want the Lords (that's the second "line" with no people in it; it just takes a few minutes and both are worth seeing). You may pop right in—that is, after you've cleared the security gauntlet. Once you've seen the Lords (hide your HOL flier), you can often slip directly over to the House of Commons and join the gang waiting in the lobby. Inside the lobby, you'll find an announcement board with the day's lineup for both houses.

Just past security to the left, study the big dark **Westminster Hall,** which survived the 1834 fire. The hall was built in the 11th century and its famous self-supporting hammer-beam roof was added in 1397. The Houses of Parliament are located in what was once the Palace of Westminster, long the palace of England's medieval kings, until it was largely destroyed by fire in 1834. The palace was rebuilt in the Victorian Gothic style (a move away from neoclassicism back to England's Christian and medieval heritage, true to the romantic age). It was completed in 1860.

Houses of Parliament tours are offered in August and September (£7, 75 min, roughly Mon, Tue, Fri, and Sat 9:15–16:30; Wed and Thu 13:15–16:30; to avoid waits, book in advance through First Call, tel. 0870-906-3773, www.firstcalltickets.com, no booking fee). Meet your Blue Badge guide (at the Sovereign's

Entrance—far south end) for a behind-the-scenes peek at the royal chambers and both Houses.

The **Jewel Tower** is the only other part of the old Palace of Westminster to survive (besides Westminster Hall). It contains a fine little exhibit on Parliament (1st floor—history, 2nd floor—Parliament today) with a 25-minute video and lonely, picnic-friendly benches (£2, daily April–Sept 10:00–17:00, across street from St. Stephen's Gate, tel. 020/7222-2219).

Big Ben, the clock tower (315 feet high), is named for its 13-ton bell, Ben. The light above the clock is lit when the House of Commons is sitting. The face of the clock is huge—you can actually see the minute hand moving. For a good view of it, walk halfway over Westminster Bridge.

▲▲Churchill Museum and Cabinet War Rooms—This is a fascinating walk through the underground headquarters of the British government's fight against the Nazis in the darkest days of the Battle for Britain. The 27-room nerve center of the British war effort was used from 1939 to 1945. Churchill's room, the map room, and other rooms are just as they were in 1945. For all the blood, sweat, toil, and tears details, pick up an audioguide at the entry and punch in numbers as you go. Your ticket includes the new Churchill Museum, a multimedia celebration of the prime minister recently voted the greatest Briton ever (£10, April–Sept daily 9:30–18:00, Oct–March daily 10:00–18:00, last entry 45 min before closing, on King Charles Street, 200 yards off Whitehall, follow the signs, Tube: Westminster, tel. 020/7930-6961, www.iwm.org.uk).

For a nearby pub lunch, try the Westminster Arms (food served downstairs, on Storeys Gate, a couple of blocks south of War Rooms).

Horse Guards—The Horse Guards change daily at 11:00 (10:00 on Sun), and there's a colorful dismounting ceremony daily at 16:00. The rest of the day, they just stand there—terrible for camcorders (on Whitehall, between Trafalgar Square and #10 Downing Street, Tube: Westminster). While Buckingham Palace pageantry is canceled when it rains, the horse guards change regardless of the weather.

▲Banqueting House—England's first Renaissance building was designed by Inigo Jones around 1620. It's one of the few London landmarks spared by the 1698 fire and the only surviving part of the original Palace of Whitehall. Don't miss its Rubens ceiling, which, at Charles I's request, drove home the doctrine of the legitimacy of the divine right of kings. In 1649—divine right ignored—Charles I was beheaded on the balcony of this building by a Cromwellian Parliament. Admission includes a restful 20-minute audiovisual history, which shows the place in banqueting action; a 30-minute audio tour—interesting only to history buffs; and a look at the exquisite banqueting hall (£4, Mon–Sat 10:00–17:00, closed Sun, last entry at 16:30, subject to closure for government functions, aristocratic WC, immediately across Whitehall from the Horse Guards, Tube: Westminster, tel. 020/7930-4179). Just up the street is Trafalgar Square.

Trafalgar Square

▲▲Trafalgar Square—London's recently renovated central square, the climax of most marches and demonstrations, is a thrilling place to simply hang out. Lord Nelson stands atop his 185-foot-tall fluted granite column, gazing out to Trafalgar, where he lost his life but defeated the French fleet. Part of this 1842 memorial is made from his victims' melted-down cannons. He's surrounded by giant lions, hordes of people, and—until recently—even more pigeons. London's mayor, Ken Livingstone, nicknamed "Red Ken" for his passion for an activist government, decided that London's "flying rats" were a public nuisance and evicted the venerable seed salesmen (Tube: Charing Cross).

▲▲▲National Gallery—Displaying Britain's top collection of European paintings from 1250 to 1900—including works by Leonardo, Botticelli, Velázquez, Rembrandt, Turner, van Gogh, and the Impressionists—this is one of Europe's great galleries. While the collection is huge, following the route suggested on the map on page 624 will give you my best quick visit. The audioguide tours (suggested £4 donation) are the best I've used in Europe. Don't miss the Micro Gallery, a computer room even your dad would enjoy (closes 30 min earlier than museum); you can study any artist, style, or topic in the museum and even print out a tailor-made tour map.

Cost, Hours, Information: Free, daily 10:00–18:00, Wed until 21:00, free 1-hour overview tours daily at 11:30 and 14:30 plus Wed at 18:30. Photography is prohibited. It's on Trafalgar Square (Tube: Charing Cross or Leicester Square, tel. 020/7839-3321, www.nationalgallery.org.uk).

▲▲National Portrait Gallery—Put off by halls of 19th-century characters who meant nothing to me, I used to call this "as interesting as someone else's yearbook." But a selective walk through this 500-year-long who's who of British history is quick and free and puts faces on the story of England. A bonus is the chance to admire some great art by painters such as Holbein, Van Dyck, Hogarth, Reynolds, and Gainsborough. The collection is well described, not huge, and in historical sequence, from the 16th century on the 2nd floor to today's royal family on the ground floor.

Some highlights: Henry VIII and wives; several fascinating portraits of the "Virgin Queen" Elizabeth I, Sir Francis Drake, and Sir Walter Raleigh; the only real-life portrait of William

National Gallery Highlights

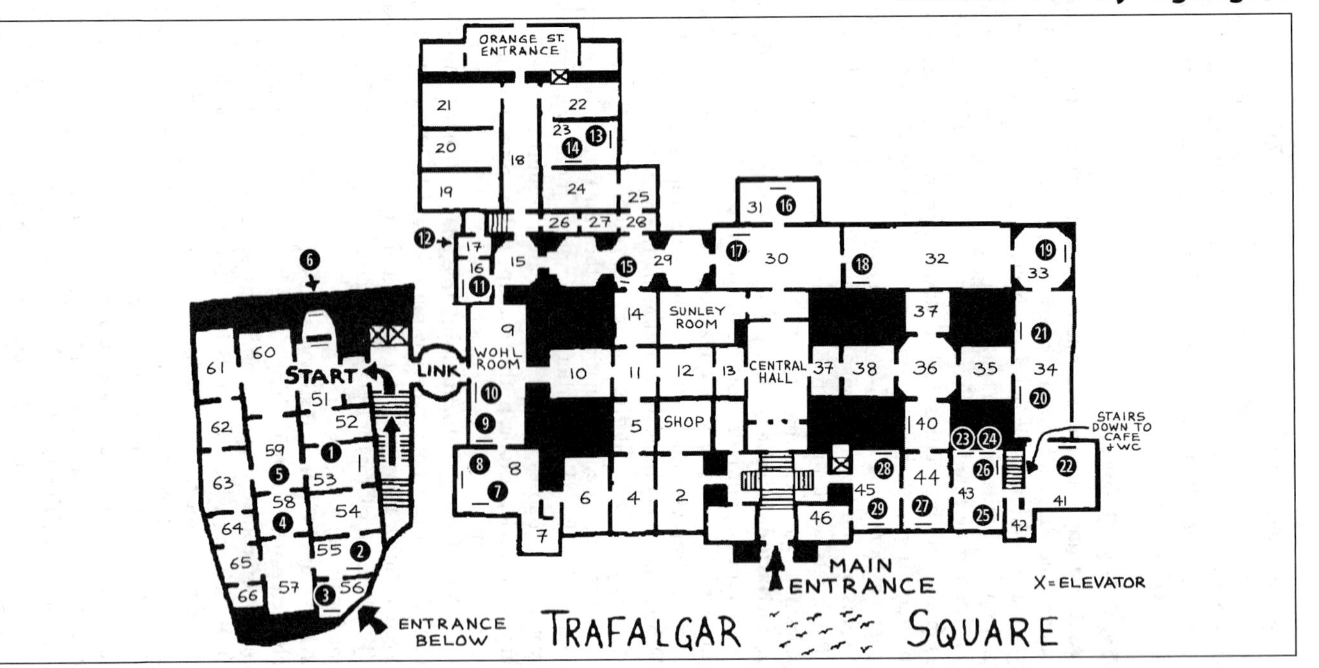

National Gallery Highlights Key

MEDIEVAL & EARLY RENAISSANCE

1. Wilton Diptych
2. UCCELLO *Battle of San Romano*
3. VAN EYCK *Arnolfini Marriage*

ITALIAN RENAISSANCE

4. BOTTICELLI *Venus and Mars*
5. CRIVELLI *Annunciation with St. Emidius*

HIGH RENAISSANCE

6. LEONARDO DA VINCI *Virgin and Child* (painting and cartoon)

NATIONAL GALLERY MAIN BUILDING - HIGH RENAISSANCE

7. MICHELANGELO *Entombment*
8. RAPHAEL *Pope Julius II*

VENETIAN RENAISSANCE

9. TITIAN *Bacchus and Ariadne*
10. TINTORETTO *Origin of the Milky Way*

NORTHERN PROTESTANT ART

11. VERMEER *Young Woman*
12. "A PEEPSHOW"
13. REMBRANDT *Belshazzar's Feast*
14. REMBRANDT *Self-Portrait*

BAROQUE & ROCOCO

15. RUBENS *The Judgment of Paris*
16. VAN DYCK *Charles I on Horseback*
17. VELAZQUEZ *The Rokeby Venus*
18. CARAVAGGIO *Supper at Emmaus*
19. BOUCHER *Pan and Syrinx*

BRITISH

20. CONSTABLE *The Hay Wain*
21. TURNER *The Fighting Téméraire*
22. DELAROCHE *The Execution of Lady Jane Grey*

IMPRESSIONISM & BEYOND

23. MONET *Gare St. Lazare*
24. MONET *The Water-Lily Pond*
25. MANET *The Waitress (Corner of a Café-Concert)*
26. RENOIR *Boating on the Seine*
27. SEURAT *Bathers at Asnières*
28. VAN GOGH *Sunflowers*
29. CEZANNE *Bathers*

NOTE: Paintings 6, 7, and 8 may be in Room 2.

Shakespeare; Oliver Cromwell and Charles I with his head on; self-portraits and other portraits by Gainsborough and Reynolds; the Romantics (Blake, Byron, Wordsworth, and company); Queen Victoria and her era; and the present royal family, including the late Princess Diana.

The excellent audioguide tours (£3 donation requested) describe each room (or era in British history) and more than 300 paintings. You'll learn more about British history than art and actually hear interviews with 20th-century subjects as you stare at their faces.

Cost, Hours, Information: Free, daily 10:00–18:00, Thu–Fri until 21:00. It's 100 yards off Trafalgar Square (around corner from National Gallery, opposite Church of St. Martin-in-the-Fields, tel. 020/7306-0055, www.npg.org.uk). The elegant Portrait Restaurant on the top floor comes with views and high prices; the cheaper Portrait Café is in the basement.

▲St. Martin-in-the-Fields—This church, built in the 1720s with a Gothic spire atop a Greek-type temple, is an oasis of peace on the wild and noisy Trafalgar Square (free, donations welcome, open daily, www.smitf.com). St. Martin cared for the poor. "In the fields" was where the first church stood on this spot (in the 13th century), between Westminster and the City. Stepping inside, you still feel a compassion for the needs of the people in this community. A free flier provides a brief yet worthwhile self-guided tour. The church is famous for its concerts. Consider a free lunchtime concert (Mon, Tue, and Fri at 13:00) or an evening concert (£8–18, Thu–Sat and some Tue and Wed at 19:30, box office tel. 020/7839-8362, church tel. 020/7766-1100). Downstairs, you'll find a ticket office for concerts, a gift shop, a brass-rubbing center, and a fine support-the-church cafeteria (see "Eating," page 666).

More Top Squares: Piccadilly, Soho, and Covent Garden

For a "Food is Fun" dinner crawl from Covent Garden to Soho, see "Eating," page 668.

▲▲Piccadilly Circus—London's most touristy square got its name from the fancy ruffled shirts—*picadils*—made in the neighborhood long ago. Today, the square is surrounded by fascinating streets swimming with youth on the rampage. For overstimulation, drop by the extremely trashy **Pepsi Trocadero Center's** "theme park of the future" for its Segaworld virtual-reality games, nine-screen cinema, and thundering IMAX theater (admission to Trocadero is free; individual attractions cost £2–8; before paying full price for IMAX, look for a discount ticket at brochure racks at the TI or hotels; located between Coventry and Shaftesbury, just off Piccadilly). Chinatown, to the east, has swollen since the British colony of Hong Kong gained its independence and was returned to China in 1997. Nearby

London's Top Squares

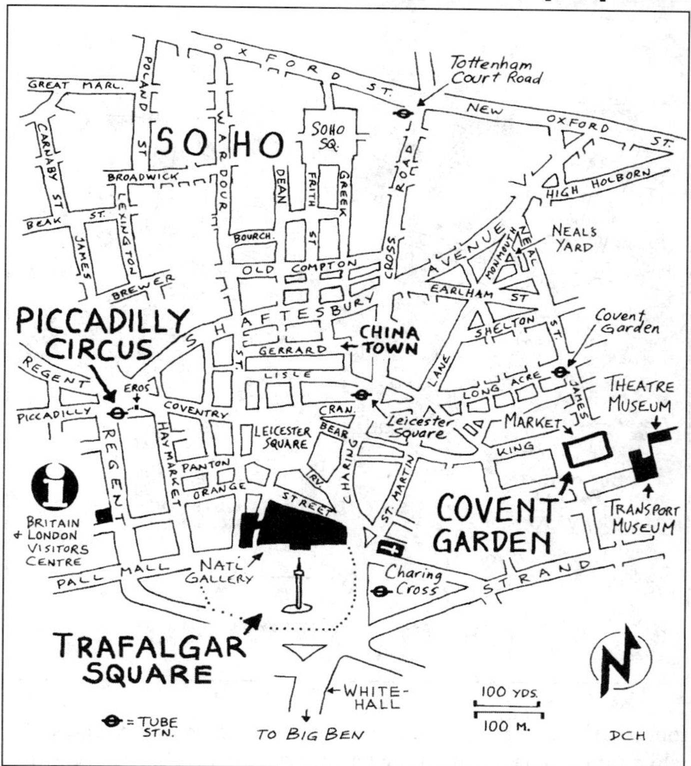

Shaftesbury Avenue and Leicester Square teem with fun-seekers, theaters, Chinese restaurants, and street singers.

Soho—North of Piccadilly, seedy Soho is becoming trendy and is well worth a gawk. But Soho is also London's red-light district, where "friendly models" wait in tiny rooms up dreary stairways and voluptuous con artists sell strip shows. While venturing up a stairway to check out a model is interesting, anyone who goes into any one of the shows will be ripped off. Every time. Even a £5 show in a "licensed bar" comes with a £100 cover or minimum (as it's printed on the drink menu) and a "security man." You may accidentally buy a £200 bottle of bubbly. And suddenly, the door has no handle.

Telephone sex is hard to avoid these days in London. Phone booths are littered with racy fliers of busty ladies "new in town." Some travelers gather six or eight phone booths' worth of fliers and take them home for kinky wallpaper.

▲▲Covent Garden—This boutique-ish shopping district is a people-watcher's delight, with cigarette eaters, Punch-and-Judy acts,

Central London

food that's good for you (but not your wallet), trendy crafts, sweet whiffs of marijuana, two-tone hair (neither natural), and faces that could set off a metal detector (Tube: Covent Garden). For better Covent Garden lunch deals, walk a block or two away from the eye of this touristic hurricane (check out the places north of the Tube station along Endell and Neal Streets).

Museums near Covent Garden

▲▲Somerset House—This grand 18th-century civic palace offers a marvelous public space, three fine-art collections, and a riverside terrace (between the Strand and the Thames). The palace once housed the national registry that records Britain's births, marriages, and deaths ("where they hatch 'em, match 'em, and dispatch 'em"). Step into the courtyard to enjoy the fountain. Go ahead...walk through it. The 55 jets get playful twice an hour. (In the winter, this becomes a popular ice-skating rink with a toasty café for viewing.)

Surrounding you are three small and sumptuous sights: the Courtauld Gallery (paintings), the Gilbert Collection (fine arts), and the Hermitage Rooms (the art of czarist Russia). All three are open the same hours (daily 10:00–18:00, last entry 17:15, £5 per sight, £8 for any 2 sights, £12 for all 3, easy bus #6, #9, #11, #13, #15, or #23 from Trafalgar Square, Tube: Temple or Covent Garden, tel. 020/7848-2526 or 020/7845-4600, www.somerset-house.org.uk). The Web site lists a busy schedule of tours, kids' events, and concerts. The riverside terrace is picnic-friendly (deli inside lobby).

The **Courtauld Gallery** is less impressive than the National Gallery, but its wonderful collection of paintings is still a joy. The gallery is part of the Courtauld Institute of Art, and the thoughtful description of each piece of art reminds visitors that the gallery is still used for teaching. You'll see medieval European paintings and works by Rubens, the Impressionists (Manet, Monet, Degas), Post-Impressionists (such as van Gogh and Cézanne), and more (£5, free Mon until 14:00, downstairs cafeteria, cloak room, lockers, and WC).

The **Hermitage Rooms** offer a taste of Romanov imperial splendor. As Russia struggles and tourists are staying away, someone had the bright idea of sending the best of its art to London to raise some hard cash. These five rooms host a different collection every six months, with a standard intro to the czar's winter palace in St. Petersburg (£5, tel. 020/7420-9410). To see what's on, visit www.somerset-house.org.uk/attractions/hermitage.

The **Gilbert Collection** displays 800 pieces of the finest in European decorative arts, from diamond-studded gold snuffboxes to intricate Italian mosaics. Maybe you've seen Raphael paintings and Botticelli frescoes...but this lush collection is refreshingly different (£5, includes free audioguide with a highlights tour and a helpful loaner magnifying glass).

▲London Transport Museum—This wonderful museum is a delight for kids. Whether you're cursing or marveling at the buses and Tube, the growth of Europe's biggest city has been made possible by its public transit system. Watch the growth of the Tube, then sit in the simulator to "drive" a train (£6, kids under 16 free, Sat–Thu 10:00–18:00, Fri 11:00–18:00, 30 yards southeast of Covent Garden's marketplace, tel. 020/7565-7299).

Theatre Museum—This earnest museum, worthwhile for theater buffs, traces the development of British theater from Shakespeare to today (free, Tue–Sun 10:00–18:00, closed Mon, free guided tours at 12:00 and 14:00, a block east of Covent Garden's marketplace down Russell Street, tel. 020/7943-4700, www.theatremuseum.org.uk).

North London

▲▲▲British Museum, Great Court, and Reading Room—Simply put, this is the greatest chronicle of civilization...anywhere. A visit here is like taking a long hike through Encyclopedia Britannica National Park. Entering on Great Russell Street, you'll step into the Great Court, the glass-domed hub of a two-acre cultural

British Museum

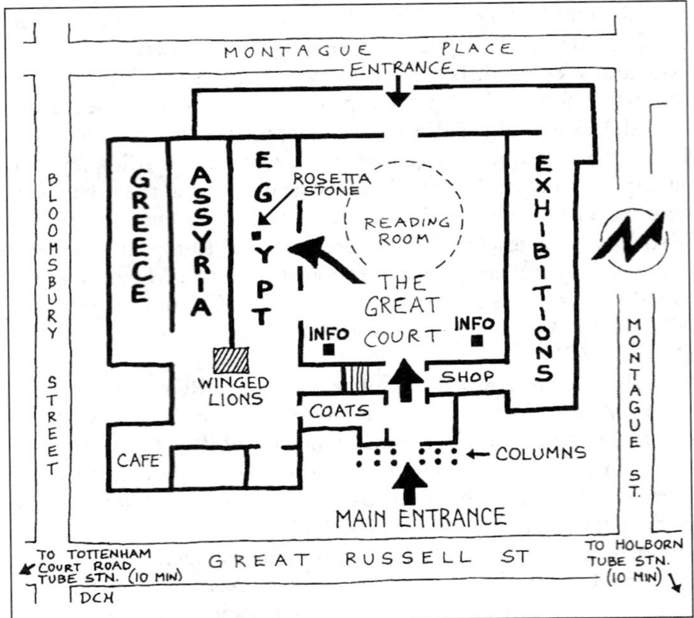

complex, containing restaurants, shops, and lecture halls plus the Round Reading Room.

The most popular sections of the museum fill the ground floor: Egyptian, Mesopotamian, and ancient Greek—with the famous Elgin Marbles from the Athenian Parthenon. Huge winged lions (which guarded Assyrian palaces 800 years before Christ) guard these great ancient galleries. For a brief tour, connect these ancient dots:

Start with the **Egyptian.** Wander from the Rosetta Stone past the many statues. At the end of the hall, climb the stairs to mummy land.

Back at the winged lions, explore the dark, violent, and mysterious **Assyrian** rooms. The Nimrud Gallery is lined with royal propaganda reliefs and wounded lions.

The most modern of the ancient art fills the **Greek** section. Find Room 11 behind the winged lions and start your walk through Greek art history with the simple and primitive Cycladic fertility figures. Later, painted vases show a culture really into partying. The finale is the Elgin Marbles. The much-wrangled-over bits of the Athenian Parthenon (from 450 B.C.) are even more impressive than they look. To best appreciate these ancient carvings, take the audioguide tour (available in this gallery).

Be sure to venture upstairs to see artifacts from **Roman Britain** (Room 50) that surpass anything you'll see at Hadrian's Wall or elsewhere in Britain. Nearby, the Dark Age Britain exhibits offer a worthwhile peek at that bleak era; look for the Sutton Hoo Burial Ship artifacts from a 7th-century royal burial on the east coast of England (Room 41). A rare Michelangelo cartoon is in Room 90. The **Great Court** is Europe's largest covered square—bigger than a football field. This people-friendly court—delightfully out of the London rain—was for 150 years one of London's great lost spaces... closed off and gathering dust. While the vast British Museum wraps around the court, its centerpiece is the stately **Reading Room**—famous as the place Karl Marx hung out while formulating his ideas on communism and writing *Das Kapital*. The Reading Room—one of the fine cast-iron buildings of the 19th century—is open to the public, but there's little to see that you can't see from the doorway.

Hours and Location: The British Museum is free (£3 donation requested, daily 10:00–17:30, plus Thu–Fri until 20:30—but from 17:30 only selected galleries and the Reading Room are open, least crowded weekday late afternoons, Great Russell Street, Tube: Tottenham Court Road, tel. 020/7323-8000, recorded info tel. 020/7388-2227, www.thebritishmuseum.ac.uk). The Reading Room is free and open daily 10:00–17:30 (Thu–Fri until 20:30). Computer terminals within the Reading Room offer COMPASS, a database of information about selected museum items (also available on their Web site, listed above). The Great Court has longer opening hours than the museum (daily 9:00–18:00, Thu–Sat until 23:00).

Tours: Guided **eyeOpener tours** (free, nearly hourly 11:00–15:30, 50 min) are each different, focusing on one particular subject within the museum. These leave throughout the day and can make the visit much more meaningful. There are also three types of **audioguide tours:** Top 50 Highlights (90 min, pick up at Great Court information desks), the Parthenon Sculptures (60 min, pick up at desk outside Parthenon Galleries), and the family tour, with themes such as "bodies, board games, and beasts" (length varies, pick up at Great Court information desks). To rent an audioguide (£3.50), you'll need to leave a photo ID (and sometimes a £10 deposit).

▲▲▲British Library—The British Empire built its greatest monuments out of paper. And it's in literature that England made her lasting contribution to civilization and the arts. Britain's national archives has more than 12 million books, 180 miles of shelving, and the deepest basement in London. But everything that matters for your visit is in one delightful room labeled "The Treasures." This room is filled with literary and historical documents that changed the course of history. You'll trace the evolution of European maps

British Library Highlights

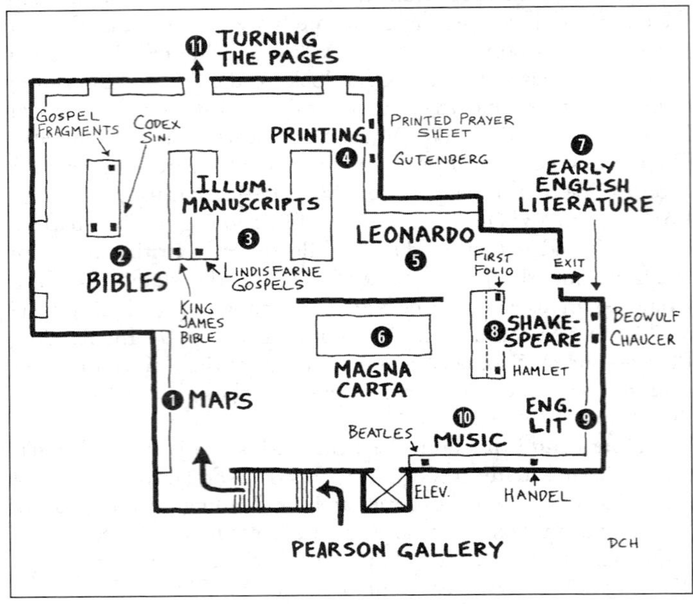

over 800 years. Follow the course of the Bible—from the earliest known gospels (written on scraps of papyrus) to the first complete Bible to the original King James version and the Gutenberg Bible. You'll see Leonardo's doodles, the Magna Carta, Shakespeare's First Folio, the original *Alice in Wonderland* in Lewis Carroll's handwriting, and manuscripts by Beethoven, Mozart, Lennon, and McCartney. Finish in the fascinating *Turning the Pages* exhibit, which lets you actually browse through virtual manuscripts of a few of these treasures on a computer (free, Mon–Fri 9:30–18:00, Tue until 20:00, Sat 9:30–17:00, Sun 11:00–17:00; 60-min tours for £6 usually offered Mon, Wed, and Fri–Sun at 15:00, Sat 10:30, and Sun 11:30; call 020/7412-7332 to confirm schedule and reserve; for £3.50 audioguide, leave photo ID and £20 deposit; room can be chilly—bring sweater; Tube: King's Cross, turn right out of station and walk a block to 96 Euston Road, library tel. 020/7412-7000, www.bl.uk). The ground-floor café is next to a vast and fun pull-out stamp collection, and the cafeteria upstairs serves good hot meals.

▲**Madame Tussaud's Waxworks**—This is expensive but dang good. The original Madame Tussaud did wax casts of heads lopped off during the French Revolution (such as Marie Antoinette's). She took her show on the road and ended up in London. And now it's much easier to be featured. The gallery is one big who's who photo-op—a huge hit with the kind of travelers who skip the British

Museum. Don't miss the gallery of has-been heads that no longer merit a body (such as Sammy Davis Jr. and Nikita Khruschev). After looking a hundred famous people in their glassy eyes and surviving a silly hall of horror, you'll board a Disney-type ride and cruise through a kid-pleasing "Spirit of London" time trip (£12–22 depending on time slot and season, children-£15, also flexes according to time, under 5 free, tickets include entrance to the London Planetarium, Mon-Fri 9:30–17:30, Sat–Sun 9:00–18:00, last entry 30 min before closing, Marylebone Road, Tube: Baker Street). The waxworks are popular. Avoid a wait by either booking ahead to get a ticket with an entry time (tel. 0870-400-3000, online at www.madame-tussauds.com for a £2 fee, or at no extra cost at the Britain and London Visitors Centre or the TIs at Victoria and Waterloo train stations) or arriving late in the day—90 minutes is plenty of time for the exhibit.

Sir John Soane's Museum—Architects and fans of eclectic knick-knacks love this quirky place (free, Tue–Sat 10:00–17:00, first Tue of the month also 18:00–21:00, closed Sun–Mon, £3 guided tours Sat at 14:30, 5 blocks east of British Museum, Tube: Holborn, 13 Lincoln's Inn Fields, tel. 020/7405-2107).

Buckingham Palace

▲Buckingham Palace—This lavish home has been Britain's royal residence since 1837. When the queen's at home, the royal standard flies (a red, yellow, and blue flag); otherwise the Union Jack flaps in the wind (£13 for state apartments and throne room, open Aug–Sept only, daily 9:30–17:00, only 8,000 visitors a day—to get an entry time, come early or for £1 extra you can book ahead by phone or online, Tube: Victoria, tel. 020/7321-2233, www.the-royal-collection.com/royaltickets, www.royal.gov.uk, buckinghampalace@royalcollection.org.uk).

Royal Mews—Actually the queen's working stables, the "mews" are open to visitors to wander, talk to the horse-keeper, and see the well-groomed horses. Marvel at the gilded coaches paraded during royal festivals, see fancy horse gear—all well described—and learn how skeptical the attendants were when the royals first parked a car in the stables (£6, April–Oct 11:00–16:00, closed Nov–March, Buckingham Palace Road, tel. 020/7321-2233).

▲▲Changing of the Guard at Buckingham Palace—The guards change with much fanfare at 11:30 almost daily in the summer and at a minimum, every other day all year long (no band when wet). Each month it's either daily or on odd or even days. Call 020/7321-2233 for the day's plan. Join the mob behind the palace (the front faces a huge and extremely private park). You'll need to be early or tall to see much of the actual Changing of the Guard, but for the pageantry in the street, you can pop by at 11:30. Stake out the high ground on the circular Victoria Monument for the best overall view. The marching troops and bands are colorful and even stirring, but the actual Changing of the Guard is a nonevent. It is interesting, however, to see nearly every tourist in London gathered in one place at the same time. Hop into a big black taxi and say, "Buck House, please." The show lasts about 30 minutes: Three troops parade by, the guard changes with much shouting, the band plays a happy little concert, and then they march out. On a balmy day, it's a fun happening.

For all the pomp with none of the crowds, see the colorful **Inspection of the Guard** ceremony at 11:00 in front of the **Wellington Barracks,** 500 yards east of the palace on Birdcage Walk. Afterward, stroll through nearby St. James's Park (Tube: Victoria, St. James's Park, or Green Park).

West London

▲Hyde Park and Speakers' Corner—London's "Central Park," originally Henry VIII's hunting grounds, has more than 600 acres of lush greenery, a huge man-made lake, the royal Kensington Palace (not worth touring), and the ornate neo-Gothic Albert Memorial across from the Royal Albert Hall. Early afternoons on Sunday (until early evening), Speakers' Corner offers soapbox oratory at its best (Tube: Marble Arch). "The grass roots of democracy" is actually a holdover from when the gallows stood here, and the criminal was allowed to say just about anything he wanted to before he swung. I dare you to raise your voice and gather a crowd—it's easy to do.

In 2004, the Princess Diana Memorial Fountain was opened in Hyde Park, in honor of the "People's Princess" who once lived in nearby Kensington Palace. The low-key circular stream is in the eastern part of the park, near the Serpentine Gallery. (Don't be confused by signs to the Diana Princess of Wales Children's Playground, also found within the park.)

▲Apsley House (Wellington Museum)—Having beaten Napoleon at Waterloo, the Duke of Wellington was once the most famous man in Europe. He was given London's ultimate address, #1 London. His newly refurbished mansion offers one of London's best palace experiences. An 11-foot-tall marble statue (by Canova) of Napoleon, clad only in a fig leaf, greets you. Downstairs is a small gallery of Wellington memorabilia (including a pair of Wellington boots). The lavish upstairs shows off the duke's fine collection of paintings, including works by Velázquez and Steen (£4.50, Tue–Sun 10:00–17:00, until 16:00 in winter, closed Mon, well described by included audioguide, 20 yards from Hyde Park Corner Tube station, tel. 020/7499-5676, www.english-heritage.org.uk). Hyde Park's pleasant and picnic-wonderful rose garden is nearby.

▲▲Victoria and Albert Museum—The world's top collection of

West London

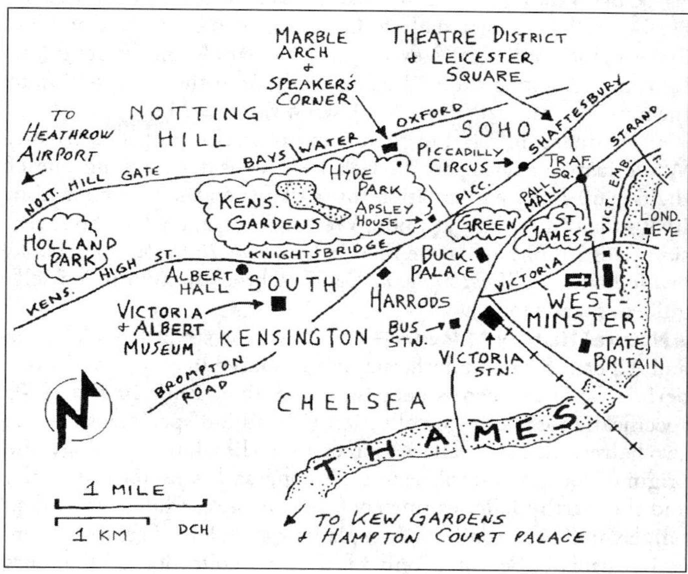

decorative arts (vases, stained glass, fine furniture, clothing, jewelry, carpets, and more) is a surprisingly interesting assortment of crafts from the West as well as Asian and Islamic cultures.

The V&A grew out of the Great Exhibition of 1851—that ultimate festival celebrating the greatness of Britain. After much support from Queen Victoria and Prince Albert, it was renamed after the royal couple.

Many visitors start with the **British Galleries** (upstairs)—a one-way tour stretching through 400 years of British lifestyles, almost a museum in itself.

In Room 46 are the plaster casts of **Trajan's Column,** a copy of Rome's 140-foot spiral relief telling the story of the conquest of Romania. (The V&A's casts are copies made for the benefit of 19th-century art students who couldn't afford a railpass.) Plaster casts of **Renaissance sculptures** (Room 46B) let you compare Michelangelo's monumental *David* with Donatello's girlish *David;* see also Ghiberti's bronze Baptistery doors that inspired the Florentine Renaissance.

In Room 48A are **Raphael's "cartoons,"** seven huge watercolor designs by the Renaissance master for tapestries meant for the Sistine Chapel. The cartoons were sent to Brussels, cut into strips (see the lines), and placed on the looms. Notice that the scenes, the Acts of Peter and Paul, are the reverse of the final product (lots of left-handed saints).

Cost, Hours, Location: Free, £3 donation requested, possible fee for special exhibits, daily 10:00–17:45, open every Wed and last Fri of month until 22:00 except mid-Dec–mid-Jan. (Tube: South Kensington, a long tunnel leads directly from the Tube station to the museum, tel. 020/7942-2000, www.vam.ac.uk).

The museum has 150 rooms and over 12 miles of corridors. While just wandering works well here, consider catching one of the free 60-minute orientation **tours** (daily, on the half-hour from 10:30–15:30, also daily at 13:00, Wed at 16:30, and a half-hour version at 18:30) or buying the fine £5 *Hundred Highlights* guidebook, or the handy £1 *What to See at the V&A* brochure (outlines 5 self-guided, speedy tours).

▲Natural History Museum—Just down the street from Victoria and Albert, this mammoth museum is housed in a giant and wonderful Victorian, neo-Romanesque building. Built in the 1870s specifically for the huge collection (50 million specimens), it has two halves: the Life Galleries (creepy-crawlies, human biology, the origin of species, "our place in evolution," and awesome dinosaurs) and the Earth Galleries (meteors, volcanoes, earthquakes, and so on). Exhibits are wonderfully explained, with lots of creative interactive displays. Pop in, if only for the wild collection of dinosaurs and the roaring *Tyrannosaurus rex.* Free 45-minute highlights tours occur daily about every hour from 11:00 to 16:00 (free, possible fee for special exhibits, Mon–Sat 10:00–18:00, Sun 11:00–18:00, last entrance 17:30, a long tunnel leads directly from South Kensington Tube station to museum, tel. 020/7942-5000, exhibit info and reservations tel. 020/7942-5011, www.nhm.ac.uk).

▲Science Museum—A sister to the Natural History Museum, next door, this sprawling wonderland for curious minds is kid-perfect. It offers hands-on fun, from moon walks to deep-sea exploration, with trendy technology exhibits, an IMAX theater (£7–10 tickets for grownups, kids less), cool rotating themed exhibits, and a kids' zone in the basement (free, daily 10:00–18:00, Exhibition Road, tel. 0870-870-4868).

East London: The City

▲▲The City of London—When Londoners say "The City," they mean the one-square-mile business, banking, and journalism center that 2,000 years ago was Roman Londinium. The outline of the Roman city walls can still be seen in the arc of roads from Blackfriars Bridge to Tower Bridge. Within the City are 23 churches designed by Christopher Wren, mostly just ornamentation around St. Paul's Cathedral. Today, while home to only 5,000 residents, the City thrives with over 500,000 office workers coming and going daily. It's a fascinating district to wander on weekdays, but since almost nobody actually lives there, it's dull in

East London: The City

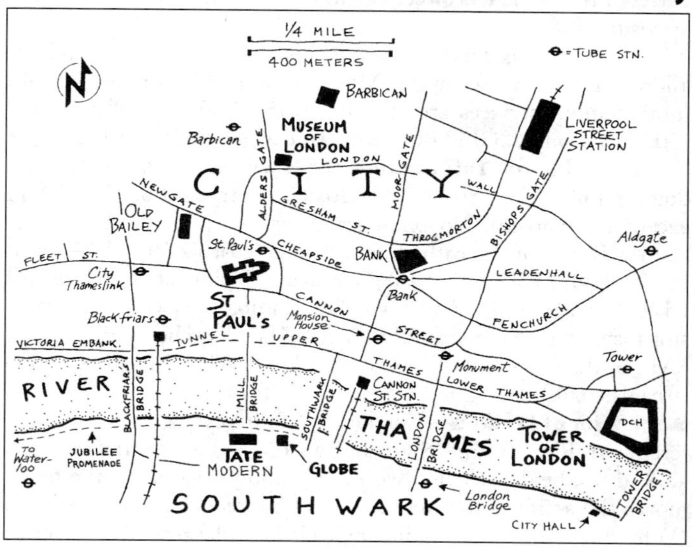

the evenings and on Saturday and Sunday.

▲Old Bailey—To view the British legal system in action—lawyers in little blond wigs speaking legalese with a British accent—spend a few minutes in the visitors' gallery at the Old Bailey (free, no kids under 14, Mon–Fri 10:30–13:00 & 14:00–16:30 most weeks, closed Sat–Sun, reduced hours in Aug; no bags, mobile phones, or cameras, but small purses OK; you can check your bag at the bagel shop across the street—or any other entrepreneurial place nearby—for £1; Tube: St. Paul's, 2 blocks northwest of St. Paul's on Old Bailey Street, follow signs to public entrance, tel. 020/7248-3277).

▲▲▲St. Paul's Cathedral—Wren's most famous church is the great St. Paul's, its elaborate interior capped by a 365-foot dome. The crypt (included with admission) is a world of historic bones and memorials, including Admiral Nelson's tomb and interesting cathedral models. The great West Door is opened only for great occasions, such as the wedding of Prince Charles and the late Princess Diana in 1981. Stand in the back of the church and imagine how Diana felt before making the hike to the altar with the world watching. Sit under the second-largest dome in the world and eavesdrop on guided tours.

Since World War II, St. Paul's has been Britain's symbol of resistance. Despite 57 nights of bombing, the Nazis failed to destroy the cathedral, thanks to the St. Paul's volunteer fire watch, who stayed on the dome. Climb the dome for a great city view and some fun in the Whispering Gallery—where the precisely designed barrel of the dome lets sweet nothings circle audibly around to the opposite side.

The **evensong** services are free, but nonpaying visitors are not allowed to linger afterward (Mon–Sat at 17:00, Sun at 15:15, 40 min). Sunday services are at 8:00, 10:15, 11:30 (sung Eucharist), 15:15 (evensong), and 18:00, with a **free organ recital** at 17:00.

Cost, Hours, Information: £7, includes church entry and dome climb, Mon–Sat 8:30–16:30, last entry 16:00, closed Sun except for worship. No photography is allowed. Ninety-minute "Super Tours" of the cathedral and crypt cost £2.50 (Mon–Sat at 11:00, 11:30, 13:30, and 14:00—confirm schedule at church or call tel. 020/7236-4128; £3.50 for 1-hour audioguide which covers 17 stops, available Mon–Sat 9:15–15:30). There's a cheery café in the crypt of the cathedral (Tube: St. Paul's, tel. 020/7236-4128, www.stpauls.co.uk).

▲Museum of London—London, a 2,000-year-old city, is so littered with Roman ruins that when a London builder finds Roman antiquities, he doesn't stop work. He simply documents the finds, moves the artifacts to a museum, and builds on. If you're asking, "Why did the Romans build their cities underground?" a trip to the creative and entertaining London Museum is a must. Stroll through London history from pre-Roman times through the 1920s. This regular stop for the local school kids gives the best overview of London history in town (free, Mon–Sat 10:00–18:00, Sun 12:00–18:00, Tube: Barbican or St. Paul's, tel. 0870-444-3852).

Geffrye Decorative Arts Museum—Walk through a dozen English front rooms dating from 1600 to 1990 (free, Tue–Sat 10:00–17:00, Sun 12:00–17:00, closed Mon, Tube: Liverpool Street, then bus #149 or #242 north to 136 Kingsland Road, tel. 020/7739-9893).

▲▲▲Tower of London—The Tower has served as a castle in wartime, a king's residence in peace time, and, most notoriously, as the prison and execution site of rebels. You can see the crown jewels, take a witty Beefeater tour, and ponder the executioner's block that dispensed with troublesome heirs to the throne and a couple of Henry VIII's wives. The crown jewels, dating from the Restoration, are the best on Earth—and come with hour-long lines for most of the day. To avoid the crowds, arrive when the Tower opens and go straight for the jewels, doing the Beefeater tour and White Tower later—or do the jewels after 16:30.

Cost, Hours, Information: £13.50, one-day combo-ticket with Hampton Court Palace-£18, March–Oct Mon–Sat 9:00–18:00, Sun 10:00–18:00; Nov–Feb Tue–Sat 9:00–17:00, Sun–Mon 10:00–17:00; last entry 60 min before closing. The long but fast-moving ticket line is worst on Sunday. No photography is allowed of the jewels or in chapels. (Tube: Tower Hill, tel. 0870-751-5177, recorded info tel. 0870-756-6060, booking tel. 0870-756-7070.) You can avoid the long lines by picking up your ticket at any London TI or the Tower Hill Tube station ticket office.

Ceremony of the Keys: Every night at precisely 21:30, with pageantry-filled ceremony, the Tower of London is locked up (as it has been for the last 700 years). To attend this free 30-minute event, you need to request an invitation at least two months before your visit. Write to Ceremony of the Keys, H.M. Tower of London, London EC3N 4AB. Include your name; the addresses, names, and ages of all people attending (up to 6 people, nontransferable, no kids under 8 allowed); requested date; alternative dates; and two international reply coupons (buy at U.S. post office—if your post office doesn't have the $1.75 coupons in stock, they can order them; the turn-around time is a few days).

More Sights Next to the Tower of London—The best remaining bit of London's **Roman Wall** is just north of the tower (at Tower Hill Tube station). The impressive Tower Bridge is freshly painted and restored; for more information on this neo-Gothic maritime gateway to London, you can visit the **Tower Bridge Experience** for its 1894–1994 history exhibit and a peek at its Victorian engine room (£5.50, family-£10 and up, daily 10:00–1830, last entry at 17:30, good view, poor value, enter at the northwest tower, tel. 020/7403-3761). The chic **St. Katharine Yacht Harbor,** just east of Tower Bridge, has mod shops and the classic old Dickens Inn, fun for a drink or pub lunch. Across the bridge is the South Bank, with the upscale Butlers Wharf area, new City Hall, museums, and promenade.

South London, on the South Bank

The South Bank is a thriving arts and cultural center tied together by a riverside path. This popular, pub-crawling walk—called the Jubilee Promenade—stretches from the Tower Bridge past Westminster Bridge, where it offers grand views of the Houses of Parliament. (The promenade hugs the river except just east of London Bridge, where it cuts inland for a couple of blocks.)

City Hall—Opened in 2002 just south of Tower Bridge, the glassy, egg-shaped building near the south end of Tower Bridge is London's City Hall, designed by Lord Norman Foster, the architect who worked on London's Millennium Bridge and Berlin's Reichstag. An interior spiral staircase allows visitors to watch the action below in the Assembly Chamber. Stop by the Visitors Centre on the lower ground floor, with a handy cafeteria. A top-floor observation deck known as "London's Living Room" is open for tours, usually on Monday morning (phone-in reservation required), and on occasional weekends 10:00–16:30 (Visitors Centre open Mon–Fri 8:00–20:00, enter from Queen's Walk, Tube: London Bridge

The South Bank

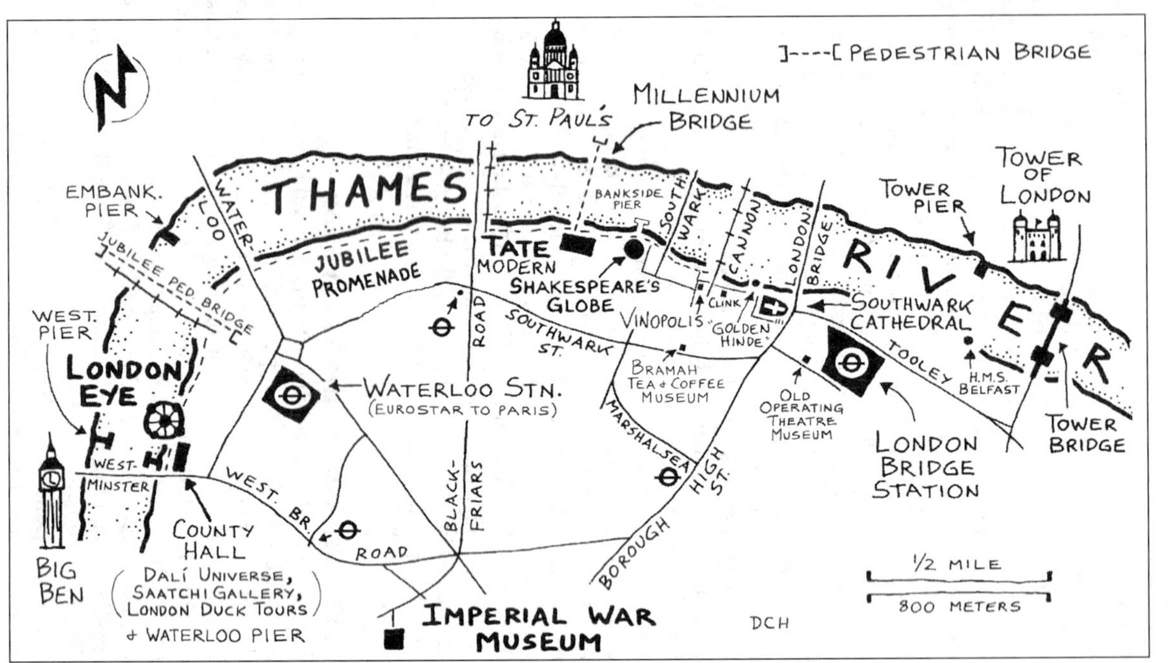

station plus 10-min walk, or Tower Hill station plus 15-min walk, call or check Web site to confirm tour times and opening hours, tel. 020/7983-4100, www.london.gov.uk).

▲▲▲London Eye Ferris Wheel—Built by British Airways, the wheel towers above London opposite Big Ben. This is the world's highest observational wheel, giving you a chance to fly British Airways without leaving London. Designed like a giant bicycle wheel, it's a pan-European undertaking: British steel and Dutch engineering, with Czech, German, French, and Italian mechanical parts. It's also very "green," running extremely efficiently and virtually silently. Twenty-five people ride in each of its 32 air-conditioned capsules for the 30-minute rotation (each capsule has a bench, but most people stand). From the top of this 450-foot-high wheel—the highest public viewpoint in the city—Big Ben looks small. You go around only once; save a shot on top for the glass capsule next to yours. Its original five-year lease has been extended to 25 years, and it looks like this will become a permanent fixture on the London skyline. Thames boats come and go from here using the Waterloo Pier at the foot of the wheel.

Cost, Hours, Location: £11.50, April–mid-Sept daily 9:30–21:00, mid-Sept–March 9:30–20:00, closed Jan for maintenance, Tube: Waterloo or Westminster, www.ba-londoneye.com (5 percent discount for booking online).

You can generally just buy your ticket and walk on (never more than a 30-min wait, worst on weekends and school holidays). If you want to book a ticket (with an assigned time) in advance, call or go online (automated booking tel. 0870-500-0600 or www.ba-londoneye.com). Upon arrival, you either pick up your prebooked ticket (if you've reserved ahead) or wait in the line inside to buy tickets. Then you join the ticket-holders' line at the wheel (starting 10 min before your assigned half-hour time slot).

Dalí Universe—Cleverly located next to the hugely popular London Eye Ferris Wheel, this exhibit features 500 works of mind-bending art by Salvador Dalí. While pricey, it's entertaining if you like Surrealism and want to learn about Dalí (£9, audioguide-£2.50, daily 10:00–18:30, generally summer evenings until 20:00, last entry 1 hour before closing, tel. 020/7620-2720).

▲Saatchi Gallery—The contemporary art gallery at the base of the London Eye features young British artists. Rather than halls of staid canvases, the collection displays many installations, each in their own room, giving the place a kind of funhouse, macabre atmosphere. Exhibits are changed routinely. Here are several I've seen: Damien Hirst's vision of mortality (live insects feeding on a rotting cow's head, then dying on a bug zapper); Ron Mueck's *Dead Dad,* an ultra-realistic (half-size) corpse in silicon and acrylic; and Tracey Emin's installation of her messy bedroom.

Visitors may be put off or simply grossed out. It's "just conceptual art," but the concepts are realized on a large scale, with big money and ultra-modern technical know-how, and displayed in a wood-paneled Edwardian-era setting. You may not like it, you may be offended, you may find it passé—but it's something to e-mail home about (£8.75, daily 10:00–20:00, Fri–Sat until 22:00, last entry 45 min before closing, located next to London Eye, Tube: Waterloo or Westminster).

▲▲Imperial War Museum—This impressive museum covers the wars of the last century, from heavy weaponry to love notes and Varga Girls, from Monty's Africa campaign tank to Schwartzkopf's Desert Storm uniform. You can trace the development of the machine gun, watch footage of the first tank battles, see one of over a thousand V2 rockets Hitler rained on Britain in 1944 (each with over a ton of explosives), hold your breath through the gruesome WWI trench experience, and buy WWII–era toys in the fun museum shop. The "Secret War" section gives a fascinating peek into the intrigues of espionage in World Wars I and II. The section on the Holocaust is one of the best on the subject anywhere. Rather than glorify war, the museum does its best to shine a light on the powerful human side of one of mankind's most persistent traits (free, daily 10:00–18:00, 90 min is enough time for most visitors, Tube: Lambeth North or bus #12 from Westminster, tel. 020/7416-5000).

The museum is housed in what was the Royal Bethlam Hospital. Also known as "the Bedlam asylum," the place was so wild it gave the world a new word for chaos: "bedlam." Back in Victorian times, locals—without trash-talk shows and cable TV—came here for their entertainment. The asylum was actually open to the paying public on weekends.

▲▲▲Tate Modern—Dedicated in the spring of 2000, the striking museum across the river from St. Paul's opened the new century with art from the old one. Its powerhouse collection of Monet, Matisse, Dalí, Picasso, Warhol, and much more is displayed in a converted powerhouse. Each year, the main hall features a different monumental installation by a prominent artist (free, fee for special exhibitions, daily 10:00–18:00, Fri–Sat until 22:00—a good time to visit, audioguide-£2, free 1-hr guided tours, call to confirm schedule, view café on top floor; cross the Millennium Bridge from St. Paul's, or Tube: Southwark plus a 10-min walk; or connect by ferry from Tate Britain for £3.40—see specifics on page 617; tel. 020/7887-8008, www.tate.org.uk).

▲Millennium Bridge—The pedestrian bridge links St. Paul's Cathedral and the Tate Modern across the Thames. This is London's first new bridge in a century. When it first opened, the $25 million bridge wiggled when people walked on it, so it promptly closed for a $7 million stabilization; now it's stable and back open (free).

Crossing the Thames on Foot

You can cross the Thames on any of the bridges that carry car traffic over the river, but London's two pedestrian bridges are more fun. The Millennium Bridge connects the sedate St. Paul's Cathedral with the great Tate Modern. The Golden Jubilee Bridge (consisting of 2 walkways that flank a railway trestle) links bustling Trafalgar Square on the North Bank with the London Eye Ferris Wheel and Waterloo Station on the South Bank. Replacing the old, run-down Hungerford Bridge, the Golden Jubilee Bridge—well-lit with a sleek, futuristic look—makes this busy route safer and more popular.

Nicknamed "a blade of light" for its sleek minimalist design—370 yards long, four yards wide, stainless steel with teak planks—it includes clever aerodynamic handrails to deflect wind over the heads of pedestrians.

▲▲Shakespeare's Globe—The original Globe Theater has been rebuilt, half-timbered and thatched, as it was in Shakespeare's time. (This is the first thatched roof in London since they were outlawed after the Great Fire of 1666.) The Globe originally accommodated 2,000 seated and another 1,000 standing. (Today, slightly smaller and leaving space for reasonable aisles, the theater holds 900 seated and 600 groundlings.) Its promoters brag that the theater melds "the three A's"—actors, audience, and architecture—with each contributing to the play. Open as a museum and a working theater, it hosts authentic old-time performances of Shakespeare's plays. The theater can be toured when there are no plays. The Globe's exhibition on Shakespeare is the world's largest, with interactive displays and film presentations, a sound lab, a script factory, and costumes.

Cost, Hours, Information: £8.50; mid-May–Sept Mon–Sat 9:30–12:30, Sun 9:30–11:30, includes 30-min actor-led tour offered on the half-hour; also open daily 12:30–16:00, but no tours available in the afternoons; Oct–mid-May daily 10:30–17:00, 30-min tour offered on the half-hour (on the South Bank directly across Thames over Southwark Bridge from St. Paul's; Tube: London Bridge plus a 10-min walk; tel. 020/7902-1500; www.shakespeares-globe.org). For details on seeing a play, see page 649. The Globe Café is open daily (10:00–18:00, tel. 020/7902-1433).

Bramah Tea and Coffee Museum—Aficionados of tea or coffee will find this small museum fascinating. It tells the story of each drink almost passionately. The owner, Mr. Bramah, comes from a big tea family and wants the world to know how the advent of commercial television, with breaks not long enough to brew a proper pot of tea, required a faster hot drink. In came the horrible

English instant coffee. Tea countered with finely chopped leaves in tea bags, and it's gone downhill ever since (£4, daily 10:00–18:00, 40 Southwark Street, Tube: London Bridge plus 3-min walk, tel. 020/7403-5650, www.bramahmuseum.co.uk). Its café, which serves more kinds of coffees and teas than cakes, is open to the public (same hours as museum). The #RV1 bus zips you to the museum easily and scenically from Covent Gardens.

▲▲Old Operating Theatre Museum and Herb Garret—Climb a tight and creaky wooden spiral staircase to a church attic where you'll find a garret used to dry medicinal herbs, a fascinating exhibit on Victorian surgery, cases of well-described 19th-century medical paraphernalia, and a special look at "anesthesia, the defeat of pain." Then you stumble upon Britain's oldest operating theater, where limbs were sawed off way back in 1821 (£4.75, daily 10:30–17:00, Tube: London Bridge, 9a St. Thomas Street, tel. 020/7955-4791, www.thegarret.org.uk).

▲▲Vinopolis: City of Wine—While it seems illogical to have a huge wine museum in London, Vinopolis makes a good case. Built over a Roman wine store and filling the massive vaults of an old wine warehouse, the museum offers an excellent audioguide with a light yet earnest history of wine. Sipping various reds and whites, ports, and champagnes—immersed in your headset as you stroll—you learn about the libation from its Georgian origins to Chile, including a Vespa ride through Chianti country in Tuscany. Allow some time, as the included audioguide takes 90 minutes—the sipping can slow things down wonderfully (£12.50 with 5 tastes, £15 with 10, don't worry...for £2.50 you can buy 5 more tastes inside, daily 12:00–18:00, Mon and Fri–Sat until 21:00, last entry 2 hrs before closing, Tube: London Bridge, between the Globe and Southwark Cathedral at 1 Bank End, tel. 0870-241-4040 or 020/7940-8301, www.vinopolis.co.uk).

More South Bank Sights, in Southwark

These sights, while mediocre, are worth knowing about. The area stretching from the Tate Modern to London Bridge, known as Southwark (SUTH-uck), was for centuries the place Londoners would go to escape the rules and decency of the city and let their hair down. Bear-baiting, brothels, rollicking pubs and theater—you name the dream, and it could be fulfilled just across the Thames. A run-down warehouse district through the 20th century, it's been gentrified with classy restaurants, office parks, pedestrian promenades, major sights (such as the Tate Modern and Shakespeare's Globe), and this colorful collection of lesser sights. The area is easy on foot and a scenic—though circuitous—way to connect the Tower of London with St. Paul's.

Southwark Cathedral—While made a cathedral only in 1905, it's been the neighborhood church since the 13th century and comes with some interesting history (free but £4 donation suggested, Mon–Fri 7:30–18:00, Sat–Sun & holidays 8:30–18:00, last entry 30 min before close, evensong services Tue, Thu, Fri at 17:30 and Sun at 15:00, photo permit-£2.50, audioguide-£2.50, tel. 020/7367-6700, www.dswark.org/cathedral).

The Clink Prison Museum—Proudly the "original clink," this was where law-abiding citizens threw Southwark troublemakers until 1780. Today, it's a low-tech torture museum filling grotty old rooms with papier-mâché gore. Unfortunately, there's little to seriously deal with the fascinating problem of law and order in Southwark, where 18th-century Londoners went for a good time (overpriced at £5, daily 10:00–18:00, July–Sept until 21:00, 1 Clink Street, tel. 020/7378-1558, www.clink.co.uk).

***Golden Hinde* Replica**—This is a full-size replica of the 16th-century warship in which Sir Francis Drake circumnavigated the globe from 1577 to 1580. Commanding this ship, Drake earned the reputation as history's most successful pirate. The original is long gone, but this boat has logged more than 100,000 miles, including its own voyage around the world. While the ship is fun to see, its interior is not worth touring (£3.50, daily 10:00–17:30, may be closed if rented out for birthday parties, school groups, or weddings, tel. 0870-011-8700, www.goldenhinde.co.uk).

HMS *Belfast*—"The last big-gun armored warship of World War II" clogs the Thames just upstream from the Tower Bridge. This huge vessel—now manned with wax sailors—thrills kids who always dreamed of sitting in a turret shooting off their imaginary guns. If you're into WWII warships, this is the ultimate...otherwise, it's just lots of exercise with a nice view of Tower Bridge (£7, daily March–Oct 10:00–18:00, Nov–Feb 10:00–17:00, tel. 020/7940-6300).

South London, on the North Bank

▲▲Tate Britain—One of Europe's great art houses, Tate Britain specializes in British painting from the 16th century through modern times. The museum has a good representation of William Blake's religious sketches, the Pre-Raphaelites' realistic art, and J. M. W. Turner's swirling works (free, £2 donation requested, daily 10:00–17:50, last entry at 17:00).

The museum offers a fine, free, and necessary **audioguide** plus free **tours** (normally Mon–Fri at 11:00—16th, 17th, and 18th centuries; at noon—19th century; at 14:00—Turner; at 15:00—20th century; Sat–Sun at noon and 15:00—highlights; call to confirm schedule, tel. 020/7887-8000, recorded info tel. 020/7887-8008, www.tate.org.uk). No photography is allowed. (Tube: Pimlico, then 7-min walk; or arrive directly at museum by taking bus #88 from Oxford Circus or #77A from National Gallery, or more fun, the £3.40 ferry from Tate Modern—see specifics on page 617.)

Greater London

▲Kew Gardens—For a fine riverside park and a palatial greenhouse jungle to swing through, take the Tube or the boat to every botanist's favorite escape, Kew Gardens. While to most visitors the Royal Botanic Gardens of Kew are simply a delightful opportunity to wander among 33,000 different types of plants, to the hard-working organization that runs the gardens, it's a way to promote understanding and preservation of the botanical diversity of our planet. The Kew Tube station drops you in an herbal little business community, a two-block walk from Victoria Gate (the main garden entrance). Pick up a map brochure and check at the gate for a monthly listing of best blooms.

Garden-lovers could spend days exploring Kew's 300 acres. For a quick visit, spend a fragrant hour wandering through three buildings: the Palm House, a humid Victorian world of iron, glass, and tropical plants built in 1844; a Waterlily House that would impress Monet; and the Princess of Wales Conservatory, a modern greenhouse with many different climate zones growing countless cacti, bug-munching carnivorous plants, and more (£8.50, £6 at 15:00 or later, Mon–Fri 9:30–18:30, Sat–Sun 9:30–19:30, until 16:30 or sunset off-season, galleries and conservatories close at 17:30, a £3.50 narrated floral 35-minute joyride on little train departs on the hour until 16:00 from Victoria Gate, Tube: Kew Gardens, boats run between Kew Gardens and Westminster Pier—see page 616, tel. 020/8332-5000, www.rbgkew.org.uk). For a sun-dappled lunch, walk 10 minutes from the Palm House to the Orangery (£6 hot meals, daily 10:00–17:30).

▲Hampton Court Palace—Fifteen miles up the Thames from downtown (£15 taxi ride from Kew Gardens) is the 500-year-old palace of Henry VIII. Actually, it was the palace of his minister, Cardinal Wolsey. When Wolsey, a clever man, realized Henry VIII was experiencing a little palace envy, he gave the mansion to his king. The Tudor palace was also home to Elizabeth I and Charles I. Sections were updated by Christopher Wren for William and Mary. The stately palace stands overlooking the Thames and includes some impressive Tudor rooms, including a Great Hall with magnificent hammer-beam ceiling. The industrial-strength Tudor kitchen was capable of keeping 600 schmoozing courtesans thoroughly—if not well—fed. The sculpted garden features a rare Tudor tennis court and a popular maze.

The palace, fully restored after a 1986 fire, tries hard to please, but it doesn't quite sparkle. From the information center in the main courtyard, visitors book times for tours with tired costumed guides

Greater London

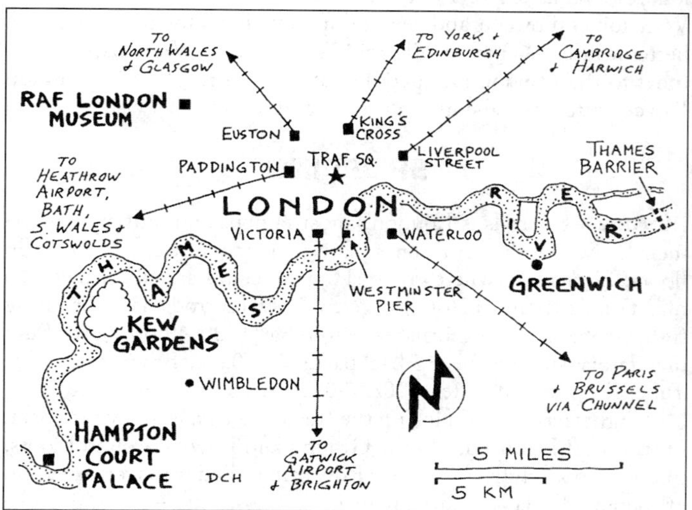

or pick up audioguides for self-guided tours of various wings of the palace (all free). The Tudor Kitchens, Henry VIII's Apartments, and the King's Apartments are most interesting. The Georgian Rooms are pretty dull. The maze in the nearby garden is a curiosity some find fun (maze free with palace ticket, otherwise £3.50). The palace costs £12 (1-day combo-ticket with Tower of London-£18, Mon 10:15–18:00, Tue–Sun 9:30–18:00, Nov–March until 16:30, tel. 020/8781-9500, recorded info tel. 0870-752-7777).

The train (2/hr, 30 min) from London's Waterloo station drops you just across the river from the palace. Consider arriving at or departing from the palace by boat (connections with London's Westminster Pier, see page 617); it's a relaxing, scenic three-hour cruise past two locks and a fun new/old riverside mix.

Royal Air Force Museum London—A hit with aviation enthusiasts, this huge aerodrome and airfield contain planes from World War II's Battle of Britain up through the Gulf War. You can climb inside some of the planes, try your luck in a cockpit, and fly with the Red Arrows in a flight simulator (free, daily 10:00–18:00, café, shop, parking, Tube: Colindale—top of Northern Line Edgware branch, Grahame Park Way, tel. 020/8205-2266, www.rafmuseum.org.uk).

Disappointments of London

On the South Bank, the London Dungeon, a much-visited but amateurish attraction, is just a highly advertised, overpriced haunted house—certainly not worth the £15.50 admission, much less your valuable London time. It comes with long and rude lines. Wait for Halloween and see one in your hometown to support a better cause. "Winston Churchill's Britain at War Experience" (next to the London Dungeon) wastes your time. The Kensington Palace State Apartments are lifeless and not worth a visit.

SHOPPING

Harrods—Harrods is London's most famous and touristy department store. With a million square feet of retail space on seven floors, it's a place where some shoppers could spend all day. (To me, it's a department store.) Big yet classy, Harrods has everything from elephants to toothbrushes (Mon–Sat 10:00–19:00, closed Sun, mandatory storage for big backpacks-£2.50, on Brompton Road, Tube: Knightsbridge, tel. 020/7730-1234, www.harrods.com).

Sightseers should pick up the free *Store Guide* at any info post. Here's what I enjoyed: On the Ground and Lower Ground Floors, find the Food Halls, with their Edwardian tiled walls, creative and exuberant displays, and staff in period costumes—not quite like your local supermarket back home.

Descend to the Lower Ground Floor and follow signs to the Egyptian Escalator, where you'll find a memorial to Dodi Fayed and Princess Diana. Photos and flowers honor the late princess and her lover (the son of Harrods' owner), who both died in a car crash in Paris in 1997. See the wineglass from their last dinner and the engagement ring that Dodi purchased the day before they died.

Ride the Egyptian Escalator—lined with pharaoh-headed sconces, papyrus-plant lamps, and hieroglyphic balconies (Harrods' owner is from Egypt)—to the fourth floor. From the escalator, make a U-turn left and head to the far corner of the store (toys) to find child-sized luxury cars that actually work. A junior Jaguar or Mercedes will set you back about $13,000. The child's Hummer ($30,000) is as big as my car.

Also on the Fourth Floor is the Georgian Restaurant. Enjoy a fancy tea under a skylight as a pianist tickles the keys of a Bösendorfer, the world's most expensive piano (tea-£19, includes finger sandwiches and pastries, served after 15:45).

Many of my readers report that Harrods is overpriced (its £1 toilets are the most expensive in Europe, but free toilets are available), snooty, and teeming with American and Japanese tourists. Still, it's the palace of department stores. The nearby Beauchamp Place is lined with classy and fascinating shops.

Harvey Nichols—Once Princess Diana's favorite, "Harvey Nick's" remains the department store *du jour* (Mon–Tue and Sat 10:00–19:00, Wed–Fri until 20:00, Sun 12:00–18:00, near Harrods, Tube: Knightsbridge, 109 Knightsbridge, www.harveynichols.com).

Want to pick up a little £20 scarf for the wife? You won't do it here, where they're more like £200. The store's fifth floor is a veritable food fest, with a gourmet grocery store, a fancy (smoky) restaurant, a Yo! Sushi bar, and a lively café. Consider a take-away tray of sushi to eat on a bench in the Hyde Park rose garden two blocks away.

Toys—The biggest toy store in Britain is **Hamleys,** with seven floors buzzing with 28,000 toys, managed by a staff of 200. At the "Bear Factory," kids can get a made-to-order teddy bear by picking out a "bear skin," and watch while it's stuffed and sewn (Mon–Sat 9:00–20:00, Thu until 21:00, Sun 12:00–18:00, 188 Regent Street, tel. 0870-333-2455, www.hamleys.com).

Street Markets—Antique buffs, people-watchers, and folks who brake for garage sales love to haggle at London's street markets. There's good early-morning market activity somewhere any day of the week. The best are **Portobello Road** (Mon–Wed and Fri–Sat 8:00–18:30, closes at 13:00 on Thu, closed Sun, Tube: Notting Hill Gate, near recommended B&Bs, tel. 020/7229-8354) and **Camden Lock Market** (daily 10:00–18:00 (Tube: Camden Town, tel. 020/7284-2084, www.camdenlock.net). The TI has a complete, up-to-date list. Warning: Markets attract two kinds of people—tourists and pickpockets.

Famous Auctions—London's famous auctioneers welcome serious bidders. You can preview estate catalogs or browse auction calendars online. For questions—or to set up a private appointment—contact **Sotheby's** (Mon–Fri 9:00–16:30, closed Sat–Sun, 34–35 New Bond Street, Tube: Oxford Circus, tel. 020/7293-5000, www.sothebys.com) or **Christie's** (Mon–Fri 9:00–16:30, Sun 14:00–17:00, closed Sat, 8 King Street, Tube: Green Park, tel. 020/7839-9060, www.christies.com).

ENTERTAINMENT

Theater (a.k.a Theatre)

London bubbles with top-notch entertainment seven days a week: plays, movies, concerts, exhibitions, walking tours, shopping, and children's activities.

For the best list of what's happening and a look at the latest London scene, pick up a current copy of *Time Out* (£2.50, www.timeout.com) or *What's On In London* (£1.60, www.whatsoninlondon.co.uk) at any newsstand. The TI's free, monthly *London Planner* covers sights, events, and plays at least as well. For plays, also visit www.officiallondontheatre.co.uk. For a chatty, *People Magazine*–type Web site on London's entertainment, check www.thisislondon.com.

Choose from classical, jazz, rock, and far-out music, Gilbert and Sullivan, tango lessons, comedy, Baha'i meetings, poetry read-

What's On in the West End

Here are some of the perennial favorites that you're likely to find among the West End's evening offerings. If spending the time and money for a London play, I like a full-fledged high-energy musical.

Generally you can book tickets for free at the box office or for a £2 fee by telephone or online.

Musicals

Chicago—A chorus-girl-gone-bad forms a nightclub act with another murderess to bring in the bucks (£15–42.50, Mon–Thu and Sat 20:00, Fri 20:30, matinees Fri 17:00 and Sat 15:00, Adelphi Theatre, Strand, Tube: Covent Garden or Charing Cross, booking tel. 020/7344-0055, www.chicagothemusical.com).

Mamma Mia!—This high-energy spandex-and-platform-boots musical weaves together 20 or 30 ABBA hits to tell the story of a bride in search of her real dad as her promiscuous mom plans her Greek Isle wedding. The production has the audience dancing by its happy ending (£25–49, Mon–Thu and Sat 19:30, Fri 20:30, matinees Fri 17:00 and Sat 15:00, Prince of Wales Theatre, Coventry Street, Tube: Piccadilly Circus, booking tel. 0870-850-0393).

Les Misérables—Claude-Michel Schönberg's musical adaptation of Victor Hugo's epic follows the life of Jean Valjean as he struggles with the social and political realities of 19th-century France. This inspiring mega-hit takes you back to the days of France's struggle for a just and modern society (£10–45, Mon–Sat 19:30, matinees Wed and Sat 14:30, Queen's Theatre, Shaftesbury Avenue, Tube: Piccadilly Circus, box office tel. 020/7494-5040, www.lesmis.com).

ings, spectator sports, theater, and the cinema. In Leicester Square, you'll find movies that have yet to be released in the States—if Hugh Grant is attending an opening-night premiere in London, it will likely be at one of the big movie houses here.

London's theater rivals Broadway's in quality and can beat it in price. Choose from Shakespeare, musicals, comedy, thrillers, sex farces, cutting-edge fringe, revivals starring movie celebs, and more. London does it all well. I prefer big, glitzy—even bombastic—musicals over serious chamber dramas, simply because London can deliver the lights, sound, dancers, and multimedia spectacle I rarely get back home.

Most theaters, marked on tourist maps, are found in the West End between Piccadilly and Covent Garden. Box offices, hotels, and TIs offer a handy free *Theatre Guide* (also at www.londontheatre.co.uk). Performances are nightly except Sunday, usually with one or two matinees a week (Shakespeare's Globe is the rare theater

Phantom of the Opera—A mysterious masked man falls in love with a singer in this haunting Andrew Lloyd Webber musical about life beneath the stage of the Paris Opera (£15–45, Mon–Sat 19:30, matinees Tue and Sat 14:30, Her Majesty's Theatre, Haymarket, Tube: Piccadilly Circus, booking tel. 0870-890-1106, www.thephantomoftheopera.com).

The Lion King—In this Disney extravaganza featuring music by Elton John, Simba the lion learns about the delicately balanced circle of life on the savanna (£17.50–40, Tue–Sat 19:30, matinees Wed and Sat 14:00 and Sun 15:00, Lyceum Theatre, Wellington Street, Tube: Charing Cross or Covent Garden, booking tel. 0870-243-9000 or 020/7344-4444, theater info tel. 020/7420-8112, www.thelionking.co.uk).

Thrillers

The Mousetrap—Agatha Christie's whodunit about a murder in a country house continues to stump audiences after 50 years (£11.50–30, Mon–Sat 20:00, matinees Tue 14:45 and Sat 17:00, St. Martin's Theatre, West Street, Tube: Leicester Square, box office tel. 0870-162-8787).

The Woman in Black—The chilling tale of a solicitor who is haunted by what he learns when he closes a reclusive woman's affairs (£12.50–32.50, Mon–Sat 20:00, matinees Tue 15:00 and Sat 16:00, Fortune Theatre, Russell Street, Tube: Covent Garden, box office tel. 020/7369-1737, www.thewomaninblack.com).

that does offer performances on Sunday, mid-May–Sept). Tickets range from about £8 to £40. Matinees are generally cheaper and rarely sell out.

To book a seat, simply call the theater box office directly, ask about seats and available dates, and buy a ticket with your credit card. You can call from the United States as easily as from England (check www.officiallondontheatre.co.uk, the American magazine *Variety*, or photocopy your hometown library's London newspaper theater section). Arrive about 30 minutes before the show starts to pick up your ticket and to avoid lines.

For a booking fee, you can reserve online (www.ticketmaster.co.uk or www.firstcalltickets.com) or call Keith Prowse Ticketing, formerly Global Tickets (U.S. tel. 800/223-6108). While booking through an agency is quick and easy, prices are inflated by a standard 25 percent fee. Ticket agencies (whether in the United States, at London's TIs, or scattered throughout the city) are scalpers with an address. If you're buying from an agency, look at the ticket carefully (your price should be no more than 30 percent over the printed face value; the 17.5 percent VAT is already included in the face value) and understand where you're sitting according to the floor plan (if your view is restricted, it will state this on the ticket; for floor plans of the various theaters, see www.theatremonkey.com). Agencies are worthwhile only if a show you've just got to see is sold out at the box office. They scarf up hot tickets, planning to make a killing after the show is sold out. U.S. booking agencies get their tickets from another agency, adding even more to your expense by involving yet another middleman. Many tickets sold on the street are forgeries. Although some theaters have booking agencies handle their advance sales, you'll stand a good chance of saving money and avoiding the middleman by simply calling the box office directly to book your tickets (international phone calls are cheap and credit cards make booking a snap).

Theater Lingo: stalls (ground floor), dress circle (first balcony), upper circle (second balcony), balcony (sky-high third balcony), slips (cheap seats on the fringes). Many cheap seats have a restricted view (behind a pillar).

Cheap Theater Tricks: Most theaters offer cheap returned tickets, standing-room, matinee, and senior or student standby deals. These "concessions" are indicated with a "conc" or "s" in the listings. Picking up a late return can get you a great seat at a cheap-seat price. If a show is "sold out," there's usually a way to get a seat. Call the theater box office and ask how.

Many theaters are so small that there's hardly a bad seat. After the lights go down, scooting up is less than a capital offense. Shakespeare did it.

Half-Price "tkts" Booth: This famous ticket booth at **Leicester Square** sells discounted tickets for top-price seats to shows on the push list the day of the show only (£2.50 service charge per ticket, Mon–Sat 10:00–19:00, Sun 12:00–15:30, matinee tickets from noon, lines often form early, list of shows available online, www.tkts.co.uk). Most tickets are half-price; other shows are discounted 25 percent.

Here are some sample prices: A top-notch seat to *Chicago* costs £40 bought directly from the theater, but only £22.50 at Leicester (LESS-ter) Square. The cheapest balcony seat (bought from the theater) is £15. Half-price tickets can be a good deal, unless you want the cheapest seats or the hottest shows. But check the board; occasionally they sell cheap tickets to good shows. For example, a first-class seat to the long-running *Les Misérables* (which rarely sells out) costs £45 when bought from the theater ticket office, but you'll save 25 percent and pay £36.50 at the tkts booth. Note that the real half-price booth (with its new "tkts" name) is a freestanding kiosk at the edge of the garden in Leicester Square. Several dishonest outfits nearby advertise "official half-price tickets." Avoid these. A second tkts booth has opened at the Canary Wharf Docklands Light Railway (DLR) Station; the freestanding kiosk is located near platforms #4 and #5 above the DLR concourse (Mon–Sat 11:30–18:00, closed Sun, Tube: Canary Wharf).

West End Theaters—The commercial (non-subsidized) theaters cluster around Soho (especially along Shaftesbury Avenue) and Covent Garden. With a centuries-old tradition of pleasing the masses, these present London theater at its glitziest. See the "What's On in the West End" sidebar.

Royal Shakespeare Company—If you'll ever enjoy Shakespeare, it'll be in Britain. The RSC performs at various theaters around London and in Stratford year-round. To get a schedule, contact the RSC (Royal Shakespeare Theatre, Stratford-upon-Avon, tel. 01789/403-444, www.rsc.org.uk).

Shakespeare's Globe—To see Shakespeare in a replica of the theater for which he wrote his plays, attend a play at the Globe. This thatch-roofed, open-air, round theater performs the plays much as Shakespeare intended (with no amplification). The play's the thing from mid-May through September (usually Tue–Sat 14:00 and 19:30, Sun at either 13:00 and 18:30 or 16:00 only, Mon at 19:30, tickets can be sold out months in advance). You'll pay £5 to stand and £13–29 to sit (usually on a backless bench; only a few rows and the pricier Gentlemen's Rooms have seats with backs). The £5 "groundling" tickets, while the only ones open to rain, are most fun. Scurry in early to stake out a spot on the stage's edge leaning rail, where the most interaction with the actors occurs. You're a crude peasant. You can lean your elbows on the stage, munch a picnic dinner, or walk around. I've never enjoyed Shakespeare as much as here, performed as it was meant to be in the "wooden O." Plays can be long. Many groundlings leave before the end. If you like, hang out an hour before the finish and beg or buy a ticket from someone leaving early (groundlings are allowed to come and go).

For information on plays or the £8.50 tours (see page 643), contact the theater at tel. 020/7902-1500 (or see www.shakespeares-globe.org). To reserve tickets for plays, call or drop by the box office (Mon–Sat 10:00–18:00, until 20:00 on day of show, at Shakespeare's Globe at New Globe Walk entrance, tel. 020/7401-9919). If you reserve online (www.wayahead.com/shakespeares-globe), be warned your ticket price will have an added booking fee.

The theater is on the South Bank directly across the Thames over the Millennium Bridge from St. Paul's Cathedral (Tube: Mansion House or London Bridge). The Globe is inconvenient for public transport, but the courtesy phone in the lobby gets a minicab in minutes. (These have set fees—e.g., £8 to South Kensington—but generally cost less than a metered cab and provide fine and honest service.) During theater season, there's a regular supply of black cabs outside the main foyer on New Globe Walk.

Fringe Theatre—London's rougher evening-entertainment scene is thriving, filling pages in *Time Out*. Choose from a wide range of fringe theater and comedy acts (generally £5).

Classical Music

For easy, cheap, or free concerts in historic churches, check the TIs' listings for **lunch concerts,** especially:

- Wren's St. Bride's Church, with free lunch concerts Mon–Fri at 13:15 (church tel. 020/7427-0133, www.stbrides.com).
- St. James at Piccadilly, with concerts on Mon, Wed, and Fri at 13:10 (suggested donation £3, info tel. 020/7381-0441, www.st-james-piccadilly.org).
- St. Martin-in-the-Fields, offering free concerts on Mon, Tue, and Fri at 13:00, church tel. 020/7766-1100, www.smitf.com).

St. Martin-in-the-Fields also hosts fine evening concerts by candlelight (£8–18, Thu–Sat at 19:30, sometimes also on other nights, box office tel. 020/7839-8362).

At St. Paul's Cathedral, **evensong** is held Monday through Saturday at 17:00 and on Sunday at 15:15. At Westminster Abbey, it's sung weekdays at 17:00 (but not on Wed) and Saturday and Sunday at 15:00. Free **organ recitals** are held on Sunday at Westminster Abbey (17:45, 30 min, tel. 020/7222-7110) and at St. Paul's (17:00, 30 min, tel. 020/7236-4128).

For a fun **classical event** (mid-July–early Sept), attend a "Prom Concert" (shortened from "Promenade Concert") during the annual festival at the Royal Albert Hall. Nightly concerts are offered at give-a-peasant-some-culture prices to "Promenaders"—those willing to stand throughout the performance (£4 standing-room spots sold at the door, £7 restricted-view seats, most £22 but depends on performance, Tube: South Kensington, tel. 020/7589-8212, www.royalalberthall.com).

Some of the world's best **opera** is belted out at the prestigious Royal Opera House, near Covent Garden (box office tel. 020/7304-4000, www.royalopera.org) and at the less-formal Sadler's Wells Theatre (Rosebery Avenue, Islington, Tube: Angel, info tel. 020/7863-8198, box office tel. 0870-737-7737, www.sadlerswells.com).

Evening Museum Visits

Many museums are open an evening or two during the week, offering fewer crowds. Here are the late nights for some of the major attractions:

- Vinopolis—Mon and Sat until 21:00 (see page 644).
- British Library—Tue until 20:00 (see page 631).
- National Gallery—Wed until 21:00 (see page 623).
- British Museum—Thu–Fri until 20:30, selected galleries and Reading Room only (see page 629).
- National Portrait Gallery—Thu–Fri until 21:00 (see page 623).
- Tate Modern—Fri–Sat until 22:00 (see page 642).
- Victoria and Albert Museum—Every Wed and last Fri of month until 22:00 (except mid-Dec–mid-Jan; see page 634).

Walks, Bus Tours, and Cruises

See "Tours" (on page 614) for information on walking tours (some are held in the evening), the London by Night bus tour, and Regent's Canal cruise.

During the summer, boats sail as late as 21:00 between Westminster Pier (near Big Ben) and the Tower of London. (For details, see page 616.)

A handful of outfits run Thames River evening cruises with four-course meals and dancing. London Showboat offers the best value (£53, April–Oct Wed–Sun, departs 19:00 from Westminster Pier, Thu–Sat evening cruises through the winter, 3.5 hrs, tel. 020/7740-0400, www.citycruises.com). For more on cruising, get the "Thames River Services" brochure from a London TI.

SLEEPING

London is expensive. For £70 ($135), you'll get a double with breakfast in a safe, cramped, and dreary place with minimal service and the bathroom down the hall. For £90 ($175), you'll get a basic, clean, reasonably cheery double in a usually cramped, cracked-plaster building with a private bath, or a soulless but comfortable room without breakfast in a huge Motel 6–type place. My London splurges, at £100–150 ($195–295), are spacious, thoughtfully appointed places you'd be happy to entertain or make love in. Hearty English or generous buffet breakfasts are included unless otherwise noted, and TVs are standard in rooms.

Reserve your London room with a phone call or e-mail as soon as you can commit to a date. To call a London hotel from the United States or Canada, dial 011-44-20 (London's area code without the initial zero), then the local eight-digit number. Some hotels will hold a room until 16:00 without a deposit, although most places will ask you for a credit-card number. The pricier ones have expensive cancellation policies (such as no refund if you cancel with less than 2 weeks' notice). Some fancy £120 rooms rent for a third off if you arrive late on a slow day and ask for a deal.

Sleep Code

(£1 = about $1.80, country code: 44, area code: 020)
S = Single, **D** = Double/Twin, **T** = Triple, **Q** = Quad,**b** = bathroom, **s** = shower only, **no CC** = Credit Cards not accepted. Unless otherwise noted, credit cards are accepted, and prices include a generous breakfast and all taxes.

To help you sort easily through these listings, I've divided the rooms into three categories based on the price for a double room with bath:

$$$ **Higher Priced**—Most rooms £100 or more.
$$ **Moderately Priced**—Most rooms between £70–100.
$ **Lower Priced**—Most rooms £70 or less.

Victoria Station Neighborhood, Belgravia

The streets behind Victoria Station teem with budget B&Bs. It's a safe, surprisingly tidy, and decent area without a hint of the trashy, touristy glitz of the streets in front of the station. Here in Belgravia, your neighbors include Andrew Lloyd Webber and Margaret Thatcher (her policeman stands outside 73 Chester Square). Decent eateries abound (see "Eating," page 671).

Cheaper rooms are relatively dumpy. Don't expect £90 cheeriness in a £60 room. Off-season, it's possible to save money by arriving late without a reservation and looking around. Competition softens prices, especially for multinight stays. On hot summer nights, request a quiet back room.

All the recommended hotels are within a five-minute walk of the Victoria Tube, bus, and train stations. Nearby is a garage (£15-per-day with a hotel voucher), a **launderette** (daily 8:00–20:30, self-service or full service, past Warwick Square at 3 Westmoreland Terrace, tel. 020/7821-8692), and a little dance club (**Club D'Jan,** music from 23:30, £8 includes drink, Thu–Sat, 63 Wilton Road).

$$$ Lime Tree Hotel, enthusiastically run by David and Marilyn Davies and their daughter Charlotte, comes with 30 spacious and thoughtfully decorated rooms and a fun-loving breakfast room (Sb-£65–80, Db-£100–125, Tb-£140–160, family room-£150–175, possible discount with cash, all rooms non-smoking, quiet garden, David deals in slow times and is creative at helping travelers in a bind, 135 Ebury Street, tel. 020/7730-8191, fax 020/7730-7865, www.limetreehotel.co.uk, info@limetreehotel.co.uk).

$$$ Quality Hotel Westminster is big, modern (but with tired carpets), well-located, and a good bet for no-nonsense comfort (Db-£130, check for various Web specials, drop-ins can ask for "saver

Victoria Station Neighborhood

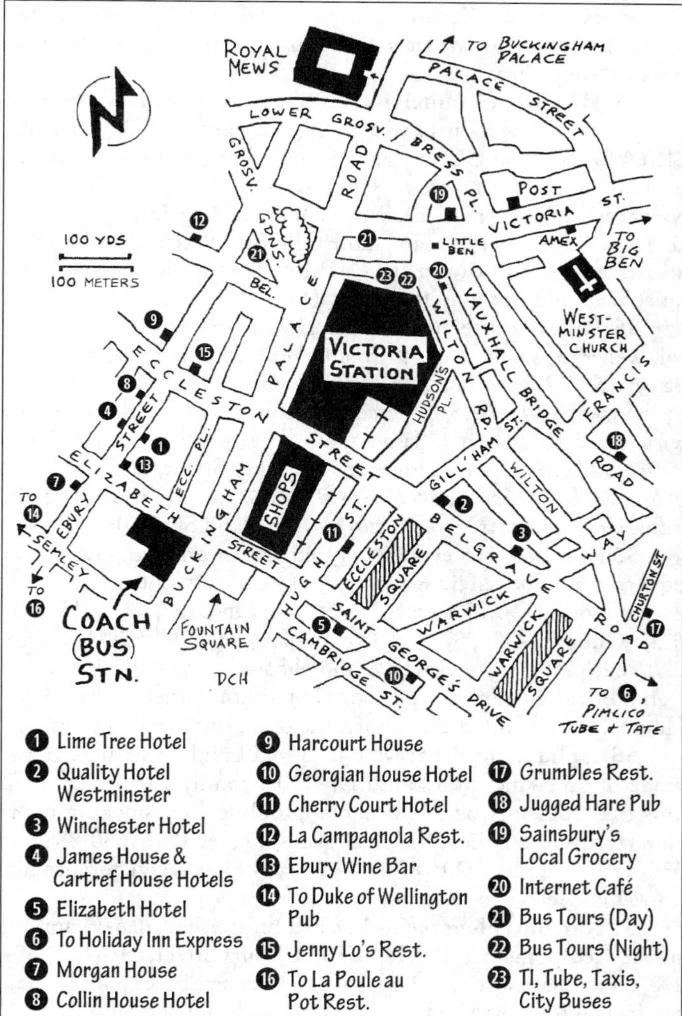

prices" on slow days, breakfast extra or bargained in, non-smoking floor, elevator, 82 Eccleston Square, tel. 020/7834-8042, fax 020/7630-8942, www.hotels-westminster.com, enquiries@hotels-westminster.com).

$$ Winchester Hotel is family-run and perhaps the best value, with 18 fine rooms and a caring management (Db-£85, Tb-£110, Qb-£140, no CC, no groups, no infants, 17 Belgrave Road, tel. 020/7828-2972, fax 020/7828-5191, www.winchester-hotel.net, winchesterhotel17@hotmail.com, commanded by Jimmy with his able first mates: Juanita, Ian, and Paul). The Winchester also rents apartments—with kitchenettes, sitting rooms, and beds on the quiet back side—around the corner (£125–230).

$$ James House and **Cartref House** are two nearly identical, well-run, smoke-free, 10-room places on either side of Ebury Street (S-£52, Sb-£62, D-£70, Db-£85, T-£90, Tb-£110, family bunk-bed Qb-£135, 5 percent discount with cash, all rooms with fans, no smoking, James House at 108 Ebury Street, tel. 020/7730-7338; Cartref House at 129 Ebury Street, tel. 020/7730-6176, fax for both: 020/7730-7338, www.jamesandcartref.co.uk, info@jamesandcartref.co.uk, run by Derek and Sharon).

$$ Elizabeth Hotel is a stately old place overlooking Eccleston Square, with fine public spaces and 40 well-worn but spacious and decent rooms (D-£75, small Db-£92, big Db-£102, Tb-£115, Qb-£125, Quint/b-£130, 37 Eccleston Square, tel. 020/7828-6812, fax 020/7828-6814, www.elizabethhotel.com, info@elizabethhotel.com). Be careful not to confuse this hotel with the nearby Elizabeth House. This one is big and comfy, the other small and dumpy.

$$ Holiday Inn Express fills an old building with 52 fresh, modern, and efficient rooms (Db-£105, family rooms, up to 2 kids free, some discounts for booking online, non-smoking floor, elevator, Tube: Pimlico, 106 Belgrave Road, tel. 020/7630-8888 or 0800-897-121, fax 020/7828-0441, www.hiexpressvictoria.co.uk, info@hiexpressvictoria.co.uk).

$$ Harcourt House rents 10 newly refurbished, neo-Victorian, smoke-free rooms (Sb-£60, Db-£80, 50 Ebury Street, tel. 020/7730-2722, www.harcourthousehotel.co.uk, harcourthouse@talk21.com, run by helpful David and Glesni Wood and cute dog Suki).

$$ Morgan House rents 11 good rooms and is entertainingly run, with lots of travel tips and friendly chat—especially about the local rich and famous—by Rachel Joplin (S-£46, D-£66, Db-£86, T-£86, family suites-£110–122 for 3–4 people, 120 Ebury Street, tel. 020/7730-2384, fax 020/7730-8442, www.morganhouse.co.uk, morganhouse@btclick.com).

$$ Collin House Hotel, clean, simple, and efficiently-run, offers 12 basic rooms with woody, modern furnishings (Sb-£55, D-£68, Db-£82, T-£95, non-smoking rooms, 104 Ebury St, tel. &

fax 020/7730-8031, www.collinhouse.co.uk, booking@collinhouse.co.uk, absentee owner).

$ Cherry Court Hotel, run by the friendly and industrious Patel family, rents 12 small, basic, air-conditioned rooms in a central location (Sb-£45, Db-£54, Tb-£75, Qb-£90, Quint/b-£105, paying with credit card costs 5 percent extra, fruit-basket breakfast in room, non-smoking, free Internet access, peaceful garden patio, 23 Hugh Street, tel. 020/7828-2840, fax 020/7828-0393, www.cherrycourthotel.co.uk, bookings@cherrycourthotel.co.uk).

$ Georgian House Hotel has 50 once-grand, now basic rooms and a cheaper top floor that works well for backpackers (S-£30, tiny D on 4th floor-£45, Db-£72, top floor Db-£60, Tb-£90, Qb-£100, Internet access, 35 St. George's Drive, tel. 020/7834-1438, fax 020/7976-6085, www.georgianhousehotel.co.uk, reception@georgianhousehotel.co.uk).

Big, Cheap, Modern Hotels

These places—popular with budget tour groups—are well-run and offer elevators and all the modern comforts in a no-frills, practical package. The doubles for £65–105 are a great value for London. Mid-week prices are generally higher than weekend rates.

$$ Jurys Inn rents 200 compact, comfy rooms near King's Cross station (Db/Tb-£104, 2 adults and 2 kids—under age 12—can share 1 room, breakfast extra, non-smoking floors, 60 Pentonville Road, Tube: Angel, tel. 020/7282-5500, fax 020/7282-5511, www.jurysdoyle.com).

$$ Premier Travel Inn London County Hall, literally down the hall from a $400-a-night Marriott Hotel, fills one end of London's massive former County Hall building. This place is wonderfully located near the base of the London Eye Ferris Wheel and across the Thames from Big Ben. Its 300 slick rooms come with all the necessary comforts (Db-£85 for 2 adults and up to 2 kids under age 15, couples can request a bigger family room—same price, breakfast extra, book in advance, no-show rooms are released at 16:00, elevator, some smoke-free and easy-access rooms, 500 yards from Westminster Tube stop and Waterloo Station, Belvedere Road, you can call central reservations at 0870-242-8000 or 0870-238-3300, you can fax 020/7902-1619 but you might not get a response, it's easiest to book online at www.travelinn.co.uk).

$$ Premier Travel Inn London Southwark, with 55 rooms, is near Shakespeare's Globe on the South Bank (Db for up to 2 adults and 2 kids-£76, Bankside, 34 Park Street, tel. 0870-990-6402, www.premiertravelinn.co.uk).

$$ Premier Lodge King's Cross, with 276 rooms, is just east of King's Cross station on York Way (Db-£83, non-smoking rooms available, breakfast extra, 24-hour reception, elevator, tel.

0870-990-6414, fax 0870-990-6415, central reservations 0870-242-8000, www.travelinn.co.uk).

Other **$$ Premier Travel Inns** charging £70–85 per room include **London Euston** (big, blue, Lego-type building packed with families on vacation on handy but noisy street, 141 Euston Road, Tube: Euston, tel. 0870-238-3301), **London Kensington** (11 Knaresboro Place, Tube: Earl's Court or Gloucester Road, tel. 0870-238-3304), **Tower Bridge** (Tower Bridge Road, inconveniently located a 10-min walk from Tube stop, Tube: London Bridge, tel. 0870-238-3303), and **London Putney Bridge** (farther out, 3 Putney Bridge Approach, Tube: Putney Bridge, tel. 0870-238-3302). For any of these, call 0870-242-8000, fax 0870-241-9000, or best, book online at www.travelinn.co.uk.

$$ Hotel Ibis London Euston, which feels a bit classier than a Premier Travel Inn, is located on a quiet street a block behind Euston Station (380 rooms, Db-£80, breakfast extra, no family rooms, non-smoking floor, 3 Cardington Street, tel. 020/7388-7777, fax 020/7388-0001, www.ibishotel.com, h0921@accor-hotels.com).

"South Kensington," She Said, Loosening His Cummerbund

To live on a quiet street so classy it doesn't allow hotel signs, surrounded by trendy shops and colorful restaurants, call "South Ken" your London home. Shoppers like being a short walk from Harrods and the designer shops of King's Road and Chelsea. When I splurge, I splurge here. Sumner Place is just off Old Brompton Road, 200 yards from the handy South Kensington Tube station (on Circle Line, 2 stops from Victoria Station, direct Heathrow connection). There's a taxi rank in the median strip at the end of Harrington Road. The handy Wash & Dry **launderette** is on the corner of Queensberry Place and Harrington Road (daily 8:00–21:00, bring 20p and £1 coins).

$$$ Aster House, run by friendly and accommodating Simon and Leona Tan, has won the "best B&B in London" award twice in the last five years. It has a sumptuous lobby, lounge, and breakfast room. Its rooms are comfy and quiet, with TV, phone, and air-conditioning. Enjoy breakfast or just lounging in the whisper-elegant Orangery, a Victorian greenhouse (Sb-£90, Db-£130, bigger Db-£160, deluxe 4-poster Db-£175, entirely non-smoking, 3 Sumner Place, tel. 020/7581-5888, fax 020/7584-4925, www.asterhouse.com, asterhouse@btinternet.com). Simon and Leona offer free loaner mobile phones to their guests.

$$$ Five Sumner Place Hotel has received several "Best Small Hotel in London" awards. The 13 rooms in this 150-year-old building are tastefully decorated, and the breakfast room is a conservatory/greenhouse (Sb-£100, Db-£153, third bed-£22; TV,

South Kensington Neighborhood

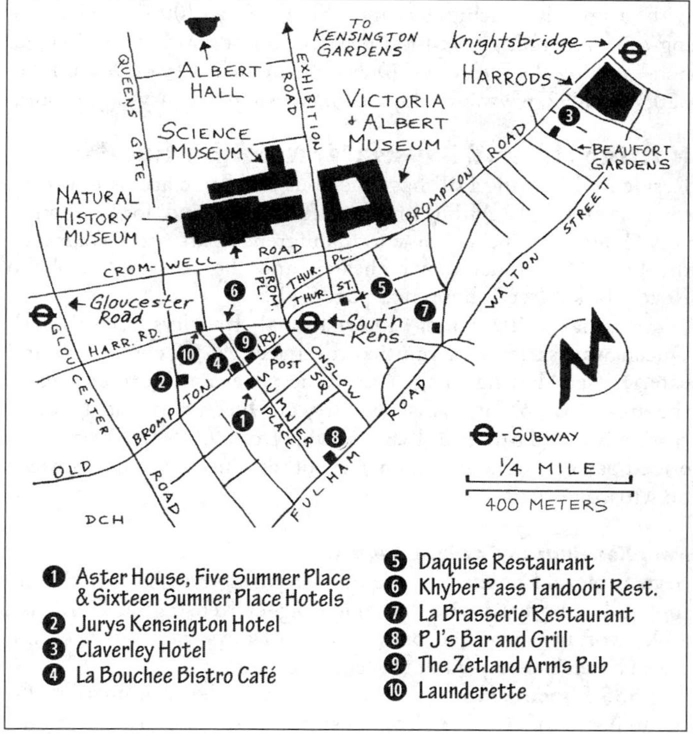

phone, and fridge in room by request; non-smoking rooms, elevator, 5 Sumner Place, tel. 020/7584-7586, fax 020/7823-9962, www.sumnerplace.com, reservations@sumnerplace.com, owners John and Barbara Palgan, helpful manager Tom Tyranowicz).

$$$ Sixteen Sumner Place, for well-heeled travelers, has over-the-top formality and class packed into its 42 rooms, plush lounges, and tranquil garden. It's in a labyrinthine building, with modern Italian decor throughout (Db-£170–220—but soft, breakfast in your room, elevator, 16 Sumner Place, tel. 020/7589-5232, fax 020/7584-8615, U.S. tel. 800/553-6674, www.numbersixteenhotel.co.uk, reservations@numbersixteenhotel.co.uk).

$$$ The Claverley, two blocks from Harrods, is on a quiet street similar to Sumner Place. The 30 fancy, dark-wood-and-marble rooms come with all the comforts (S-£70, Sb-£80–110, Db-£120–190 depending on size, sofa-bed Tb-£190–215, plush lounge, non-smoking rooms, elevator, 13–14 Beaufort Gardens, Tube: Knightsbridge, tel. 020/7589-8541, fax 020/7584-3410, U.S. tel. 800/747-0398, www.claverleyhotel.co.uk, reservations@claverleyhotel.co.uk).

$$$ Jurys Kensington Hotel is big, stately, and impersonal, with a greedy pricing scheme (Sb/Db/Tb-£100–240 depending on "availability," ask for a deal, breakfast extra, piano lounge, non-smoking floor, elevator, Queen's Gate, tel. 020/7589-6300, fax 020/7581-1492, www.jurysdoyle.com, kensington@jurysdoyle.com).

Notting Hill and Bayswater Neighborhoods

Residential Notting Hill has quick bus and Tube access to downtown, is on the A2 Airbus line from Heathrow, and, for London, is very "homely." It's also home to many trendy bars and restaurants, the historic Coronet movie theater, and the famous Portobello Road Market (see "Shopping," page 649).

Popular with young international travelers, Bayswater's Queensway street is a multicultural festival of commerce and eateries (see "Eating," page 672). One of several **launderettes** in the area is Brookford Wash & Dry, at Queensway and Bishop's Bridge Road (daily 7:00–19:30, service from 9:00–17:30, computerized pay point takes all coins). Another self-serve launderette is on Moscow Road.

Near Kensington Gardens Square

Several big old hotels line the quiet Kensington Gardens Square (not to be confused with the much bigger Kensington Gardens), a block off bustling Queensway, north of Bayswater Tube station. These hotels are very quiet for central London.

$$$ Phoenix Hotel, a Best Western modernization of a 125-room hotel, offers American business-class comforts; spacious, plush public spaces; and big, fresh, modern-feeling rooms (Sb-£99, Db-£130, Tb-£165, Qb-£185, flaky "negotiable" pricing list, discount for online bookings, elevator, 1–8 Kensington Gardens Square, tel. 020/7229-2494, fax 020/7727-1419, U.S. tel. 800/528-1234, www.phoenixhotel.co.uk, info@phoenixhotel.co.uk).

$$ Garden Court Hotel rents 34 comfortable, smoke-free rooms. It's newly refurbished and has a garden (S-£40, Sb-£62, D-£64, Db-£92, T-£84, Tb-£114, Q-£94, Qb-£135, elevator, 30 Kensington Gardens Square, tel. 020/7229-2553, fax 020/7727-2749, www.gardencourthotel.co.uk, info@gardencourthotel.co.uk).

$$ Kensington Gardens Hotel laces 16 decent rooms together in a tall, skinny place with lots of stairs and no lift (Ss-£45–50, Sb-£50–55, Db-£75, Tb-£95, book by phone or e-mail rather than through pricier Web site, 9 Kensington Gardens Square, tel. 020/7221-7790, fax 020/7792-8612, www.kensingtongardenshotel.co.uk, info@kensingtongardenshotel.co.uk, charming Rowshanak).

$$ Vancouver Studios offers 45 modern rooms with fully equipped kitchenettes (utensils, stove, microwave, and fridge)

Notting Hill and Bayswater Neighborhoods

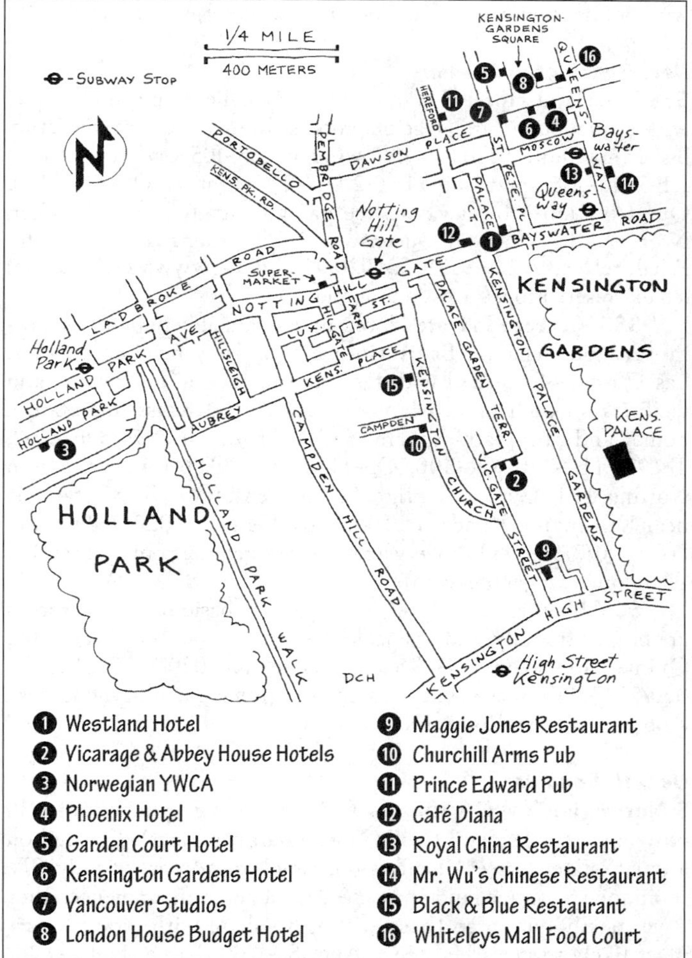

rather than breakfast (small Sb-£65, small Db-£85, big Db-£95, Tb-£120, extra bed-£18, 10 percent discount with week-long stay or more, call to confirm reservation a night or two before, lounge and garden, near Kensington Gardens Square at 30 Prince's Square, tel. 020/7243-1270, fax 020/7221-8678, www.vancouverstudios.co.uk, info@vancouverstudios.co.uk).

$ London House Budget Hotel is a threadbare, nose-ringed slumber mill renting 240 beds in 93 stark rooms (S-£43, Sb-£48, twin-£57, Db-£71, dorm bed-£16, prices flex downward with demand, includes continental breakfast, lots of school groups, 81

Kensington Gardens Square, tel. 020/7243-1810, fax 020/7243-1723, www.londonhousehotel.com, londonhousehotel@yahoo.co.uk).

Near Kensington Gardens

$$$ Westland Hotel is comfortable, convenient, and hotelesque, with a fine lounge and spacious rooms. Rooms are recently refurbished and quite plush (Sb-£80–90, Db-£95–105, cavernous deluxe Db-£110–125, sprawling Tb-£120–140, gargantuan Qb-£135–160, Quint/b-£150–170; elevator, free garage with 6 spaces; between Notting Hill Gate and Queensway Tube stations; 154 Bayswater Road, tel. 020/7229-9191, fax 020/7727-1054, www.westlandhotel.co.uk, reservations@westlandhotel.co.uk).

$$$ Vicarage Private Hotel, understandably popular, is family-run and elegantly British in a quiet, classy neighborhood. It has 17 rooms furnished with taste and quality, a TV lounge, and facilities on each floor. Mandy, Richard, and Krassi maintain a homey and caring atmosphere (S-£46, Sb-£70, D-£76, Db-£102, T-£93, Tb-£130, Q-£100, Qb-£140, no CC, 6-min walk from Notting Hill Gate and High Street Kensington Tube stations, near Kensington Palace at 10 Vicarage Gate, tel. 020/7229-4030, fax 020/7792-5989, www.londonvicaragehotel.com, reception@londonvicaragehotel.com).

$$ Abbey House Hotel, next door, is basic but its 16 rooms are bright, friendly, and sleepable (S-£45, D-£74, T-£90, Q-£100, Quint-£110, no CC, 11 Vicarage Gate, tel. 020/7727-2594, fax 020/7727-1873, www.abbeyhousekensington.com, abbeyhousedesk@btconnect.com, Rodrigo).

Near Holland Park

$ Norwegian YWCA (Norsk K.F.U.K.) is for women under 30 only (and men under 30 with Norwegian passports). Located on a quiet, stately street, it offers non-smoking rooms, a study, TV room, piano lounge, and an open-face Norwegian ambience. They have mostly quads, so those willing to share with strangers are most likely to get a bed (July–Aug: Ss-£32, shared double-£30/bed, shared triple-£25/bed, shared quad-£21/bed, includes breakfast and sack lunch; Sept–June: same prices also include dinner; 52 Holland Park, tel. 020/7727-9897, fax 020/7727-8718, www.kfuk.dial.pipex.com, kfuk.hjemmet@kfuk-kfum.no). With each visit, I wonder which is easier to get—a sex change or a Norwegian passport?

Other Neighborhoods

Near Covent Garden: **$$$ Fielding House Hotel,** located on a charming, quiet pedestrian street just two blocks east of Covent Garden, offers 24 no-nonsense rooms, bright orange hallways, and lots of stairs (Db-£100–115, Db with sitting room-£130, no breakfast, no smoking, no kids under 13, 4 Broad Court, Bow Street, tel. 020/7836-8305, fax 020/7497-0064, www.the-fielding-hotel.co.uk).

Near Baker Street: **$$$ The 22 York Street B&B** offers a less hotelesque alternative in the center, renting 18 stark, hardwood, comfortable rooms (Db-£100, Tb-£141, strictly smoke-free, social breakfast, inviting lounge; from Baker Street Tube station, walk 2 blocks down Baker Street and take a right, 22 York Street; tel. 020/7224-3990, fax 020/7224-1990, www.22yorkstreet.co.uk, michael@22yorkstreet.co.uk, energetically run by Liz and Michael).

Near Buckingham Palace: **$$ Vandon House Hotel,** run by the Central College in Iowa, is packed with students most of the year, but its 33 rooms are rented to travelers from late May through August at great prices. The rooms, while institutional, are comfy, and the location is excellent (S-£43, D-£68, Db-£84, Tb-£99, Qb-£118, only single beds, non-smoking, elevator, on a tiny road 2 blocks west of St. James Park Tube station, near east end of Petty France Street at 1 Vandon Street, tel. 020/7799-6780, fax 020/7799-1464, www.vandonhouse.com, info@vandonhouse.com).

Near Euston Station: The **$$ Methodist International Centre,** a modern, youthful, Christian residence, fills its lower floors with international students and its top floor with travelers. Rooms are modern and simple yet comfortable, with fine bathrooms, phones, and desks. The atmosphere is friendly, safe, clean, and controlled; it also has a spacious lounge and game room (Sb-£67, Db-£84, 2-course buffet dinner-£11, non-smoking rooms, elevator, on a quiet street a block west of Euston Station, 81–103 Euston Street—not Euston Road, Tube: Euston Station, tel. 020/7380-0001, fax 020/7387-5300, www.micentre.com, acc@micentre.com). In June, July, and August, when the students are gone, they also rent simple £38 singles.

Hostels

$ The **St. Christopher's Inn** hostel network offers £15–25 beds at six locations throughout London, including Southwark, Shepherd's Bush, Camden, and Greenwich. For details, see www.st-christophers.co.uk.

$ The **City of London Youth Hostel,** near St. Paul's, is clean, modern, friendly, and well-run. You'll pay £15 per bed in an 11-bed dorm, about £25 for a bed in their three- to eight-bed rooms, or £30 for a single room (£2 extra if you have no hostel card, 193 beds, cheap meals, open 24 hrs, Tube: St. Paul's, 36 Carter Lane, tel. 020/7236-4965, fax 020/7236-7681, www.yha.org.uk, city@yha.org.uk).

Near Gatwick and Heathrow Airports

Near Gatwick Airport: **$ London Gatwick Airport Premier Travel Inn** rents cheap rooms at the airport (Db-£55, tel. 0870-238-3305, www.premiertravelinn.co.uk). **$ Gatwick Travelodge** has budget rooms two miles from the airport (Db-£50, breakfast extra, Church Road, Lowfield Heath, Crawley, tel. 0870-191-1531, www.travelodge.co.uk).

$ Barn Cottage, a converted 16th-century barn, sits in the peaceful countryside, with a tennis court, small swimming pool, and a good pub within walking distance. It has two wood-beamed rooms, antique furniture, and a large garden that makes you forget Gatwick is 10 minutes away (S-£45, D-£60, no CC, can drive you to airport or train station for £8, Church Road, Leigh, Reigate, Surrey, tel. 01306/611-347, warmly run by Pat and Mike Comer).

$ Wayside Manor Farm is another rural alternative to a bland airport hotel. This four-bedroom countryside place is a 10-minute drive from Gatwick (Db-£65, Norwood Hill, near Charlwood, tel. 01293/862-692, www.wayside-manor.com, info@wayside-manor.com).

Near Heathrow Airport: It's so easy to get to Heathrow from central London, I see no reason to sleep there. But for budget beds near the airport, consider **$ Heathrow Ibis** (Db-£65, Db-£45 on Fri–Sun nights, breakfast extra, cheap shuttle bus to/from terminals except T-4, 112 Bath Road, tel. 020/8759-4888, fax 020/8564-7894, www.ibishotel.com, h0794@accor-hotels.com).

EATING

If you want to dine (as opposed to eat), check out the extensive listings in the weekly entertainment guides sold at London newsstands (or catch a train for Paris). The thought of a £40 meal in Britain generally ruins my appetite, so my London dining is limited mostly to easygoing, fun, but inexpensive alternatives. I've listed places by neighborhood—handy to your sightseeing or hotel.

Pub grub is the most atmospheric budget option. Many of London's 7,000 pubs serve fresh, tasty buffets under ancient timbers, with hearty lunches and dinners for £6–8.

Ethnic restaurants—especially Indian and Chinese—are popular, plentiful, and cheap. Most large museums (and many churches) have inexpensive, cheery cafeterias. Of course, picnicking is the fastest and cheapest way to go. Good grocery stores and sandwich shops, fine park benches, and polite pigeons abound in Britain's most expensive city.

Near Trafalgar Square

To locate the following restaurants, see the map on page 669.

St. Martin-in-the-Fields Café in the Crypt is just right for a tasty meal on a monk's budget, sitting on somebody's tomb in an ancient crypt (£6–8 cafeteria plates, cheaper sandwich bar, Mon–Wed 10:00–20:00, Thu–Sat 10:00–23:00, Sun 12:00–20:00, profits go to the church, no CC, underneath St. Martin-in-the-Fields church on Trafalgar Square, tel. 020/7839-4342).

The Chandos Pub's Opera Room floats amazingly apart from the tacky crush of tourism around Trafalgar Square. Look for it opposite the National Portrait Gallery (corner of William Street and St. Martin's Lane) and climb the stairs to the Opera Room. This is a fine Trafalgar rendezvous point—smoky, but wonderfully local. They serve traditional, plain-tasting £6–7 pub lunches and dinners (kitchen open Sun–Wed 11:00–19:00, Thu–Sat until 18:00, order and pay at the bar, tel. 020/7836-1401).

The International is a mod complement to The Chandos (just across the street), offering a bright and spacious retreat for local office workers oblivious to all the touristy hubbub nearby. The ground-floor bar has two-for-one bar meals daily (12:00–17:00). The classy restaurant upstairs serves modern European cuisine (daily, 2-course menu £10, 3 courses £13, 116 St. Martins Lane, tel. 020/7257-8626).

At **Gordon's Wine Bar,** a simple, steep staircase leads into a candlelit 15th-century wine cellar filled with dusty old bottles, faded British memorabilia, and local nine-to-fivers. At the buffet, choose a hot meal or a fine plate of cheeses and various cold cuts. (One £7 cold plate and a couple of glasses of wine provide a light, economical meal for two.) Then step up to the wine bar and consider the many varieties of wine and port available by the glass at excellent prices. The low, carbon-crusted vaulting deeper in the back seems to intensify the Hogarth-painting atmosphere. While it's crowded, you can normally corral two chairs and grab the corner of a table (arrive before 17:30 to get a seat, Mon–Sat 11:00–23:00, Sun 12:00–22:00, 2 blocks from Trafalgar Square, bottom of Villiars Street at #47, Tube: Embankment, tel. 020/7930-1408). On hot days, the crowd spills out into a leafy back patio.

The Clarence Pub, down Whitehall, a block south of Trafalgar Square toward Big Ben, is touristy but atmospheric with decent grub (£8 meals, daily 11:00–22:00, indoor/outdoor seating). Nearby are several cheaper cafeterias and pizza joints.

Sherlock Holmes Pub, a block from Trafalgar Square, sounds touristy but is the haunt of government workers and locals awaiting trains at Charing Cross Station. Fans of the fictional detective will appreciate the pub's location in the former Northumberland Hotel (featured in Holmes stories and one of author Sir Arthur Conan Doyle's haunts) and the fact that Old Scotland Yard was just across the street. Upstairs in the restaurant area is a replica of 221-B Baker Street (Mon–Sat 11:00–23:00, Sun 12:00–22:30, pub fare downstairs, restaurant meals served upstairs at lunch and dinnertime, 10 Northumberland Street, Tube: Charing Cross/ Embankment, tel. 020/7930-2644).

Crivelli's Garden Restaurant, serving a classy lunch in the National Gallery, is a good place to treat your palate to pricey, light Mediterranean cuisine (£15 lunches, daily 10:00–17:00, 1st floor of Sainsbury Wing). For something more Dickensian, try **Hamptons Wine Bar** (Mon–Fri 11:30–23:00, closed Sat–Sun, around the corner at 15 Whitcomb Street, tel. 020-7839-2823).

Near Piccadilly

Hungry and broke in the theater district? Head for Panton Street (off Haymarket, 2 blocks southeast of Piccadilly Circus) for cheap Thai, Chinese, and two famous London eateries. **Stockpot** is a mushy-peas kind of place, famous and rightly popular for its edible, cheap meals (daily 7:00–22:00, 38 Panton Street). The **West End Kitchen** (across the street at #5, same hours and menu) is a direct competitor that's just as good. Vegetarians prefer the **Woodland South Indian Vegetarian Restaurant,** across from the West End Kitchen. For a £5 Chinese meal, **Mr. Wu's** buffet is on Old Compton Street. And **Pizza Express** has many branches offering a gut-busting £5 buffet.

The palatial **Criterion Brasserie** serves a special £15 two-course "Anglo-French" menu (or £18 for 3 courses) under gilded tiles and chandeliers in a dreamy Byzantine church setting from 1880. It's right on Piccadilly Circus but a world away from the punk junk. The house wine is great and so is the food (specials available Mon–Sat 12:00–14:30 & 17:30–19:00, closed Sun lunch, tel. 020/7930-0488). After 19:00, the menu becomes really expensive. Anyone can drop in for coffee or a drink.

The "Food is Fun" Dinner Crawl: From Covent Garden to Soho

London has a trendy, generation-X scene that most Beefeater-seekers miss entirely. For a multicultural, movable feast, consider exploring these. Start around 18:00 to avoid lines, get in on early specials, and find waiters willing to let you split a meal. Prices, while reasonable by London standards, add up. Servings are large enough to share. All are open nightly.

The Dinner Crawl for Two: Arrive before 18:00 at **Belgo Centraal** and split the early-bird dinner special: a kilo of mussels, fries, and dark Belgian beer. At **Yo! Sushi,** have beer or sake and a few dishes. Slurp your last course at **Wagamama Noodle Bar.** Then, for dessert, people-watch at Leicester Square, where the serf's always up.

The "Food is Fun" Dinner Crawl

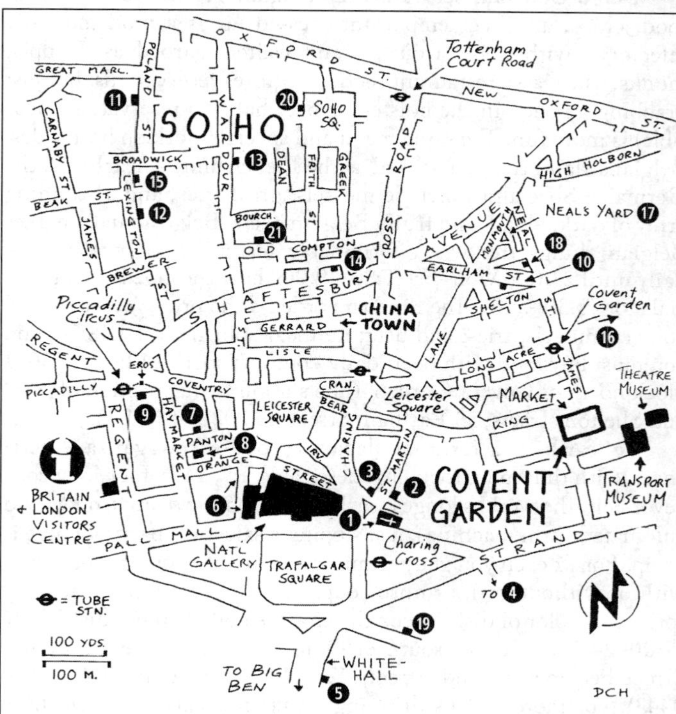

1. St. Martin-in-the-Fields Café in the Crypt
2. The Chandos Pub
3. The International Pub & Rest.
4. Gordon's Wine Bar
5. The Clarence Pub
6. Crivelli's Garden Rest. & Hamptons Wine Bar
7. Stockpot & West End Kitchen
8. Woodland South Indian Vegetarian Rest.
9. Criterion Brasserie
10. Belgo Centraal
11. Yo! Sushi
12. Wagamama Noodle Bar
13. Soho Spice Indian Rest.
14. Y Ming Chinese Rest.
15. Andrew Edmunds & Mildred's Vegetarian Rest.
16. To Zilly Fish Too Rest.
17. Neal's Yard Eateries
18. Food for Thought Café
19. Sherlock Holmes Pub
20. Pizza Express
21. Mr. Wu's Chinese Buffet

Belgo Centraal serves hearty Belgian specialties. It's a seafood, chips, and beer emporium dressed up as a mod monastic refectory—with noisy acoustics and waiters garbed as Trappist monks. The classy restaurant section requires reservations, but just grabbing a bench in the boisterous beer hall (no reservations possible) is more fun. The same menu and specials work on both sides. Belgians claim they eat as well as the French and as heartily as the Germans. Specialties include mussels, great fries, and a stunning array of dark, blond, and fruity Belgian beers. Belgo actually makes Belgian things trendy—a formidable feat (£10–14 meals; open daily until 23:00; Mon–Fri 17:30–19:00 "beat the clock" meal specials for £5.30–7.00—the time you order is the price you pay—and you get mussels, fries, and beer; no meal-splitting after 18:30, and you must buy food with beer; daily £6 lunch special 12:00–17:30; 1 block north of Covent Garden Tube station at intersection of Neal and Shelton streets, 50 Earlham Street, tel. 020/7813-2233).

Yo! Sushi is a futuristic Japanese-food-extravaganza experience. With thumping rock, Japanese cable TV, a 195-foot-long conveyor belt, the world's longest sushi bar, a robotic drink trolley, and automated sushi machines, just sipping a sake on a bar stool here is a trip. For £1 each you get unlimited tea, water (from spigot at bar, with or without gas), or miso soup. Grab dishes as they rattle by (priced by color of dish; check the chart: £1.50–3.50 per dish, daily 12:00–24:00, 2 blocks south of Oxford Street, where Lexington Street becomes Poland Street, 52 Poland Street, tel. 020/7287-0443). For more serious drinking on tatami mats, go downstairs into "Yo Below." (If you like Yo, there are several locations around town, including a handy branch a block from the London Eye on Belvedere Road, as well as outlets within Selfridges and Harvey Nichols department stores.)

Wagamama Noodle Bar is a noisy, pan-Asian, organic slurpathon. As you enter, check out the kitchen and listen to the roar of the basement, where benches rock with happy eaters. Everybody sucks. Stand against the wall to feel the energy of all this "positive eating" (£10 meals, daily 12:00–24:00, crowded after 20:00, nonsmoking, 10-A Lexington Street, tel. 020/7292-0990 but no reservations taken). If you like this place, there are now handy branches all over town, including near the British Museum (Streatham Street), High Street Kensington (#26), in Harvey Nichols (109 Knightsbridge), Covent Garden (Tavistock Street), Leicester Square (Irving Street), Piccadilly Circus (Norris Street), Fleet Street (#109), and between St. Paul's and the Tower of London (22 Old Broad Street).

Soho Spice Indian is where modern Britain meets Indian tradition—fine cuisine in a trendy, jewel-tone ambience. Unlike many Indian restaurants, when you order an entrée here (£10–15), it comes with side dishes (nan, dal, rice, vegetables). The £15 "tandoori selections" meal is the best "variety" dish and big enough for two (daily 12:00–22:30, non-smoking section, 5 blocks north of Piccadilly Circus at 124 Wardour Street, tel. 020/7434-0808).

Y Ming Chinese Restaurant, across Shaftesbury Avenue from the ornate gates, clatter, and dim sum of Chinatown, has clean European decor, serious but helpful service, and authentic Northern Chinese cooking (good £10 meal deal offered 12:00–18:00—last order at 18:00, Mon–Sat 12:00–23:30, closed Sun, 35 Greek Street, tel. 020/7734-2721).

Andrew Edmunds Restaurant is a tiny, candlelit place where you'll want to hide your camera and guidebook and act as local as possible. This great little place—with a jealous and loyal clientele—is the closest I've found to Parisian quality in a cozy restaurant in London. The modern European cooking with a creative seasonal menu is worth the splurge (3 courses for £25, daily 12:30–15:00 & 18:00–22:45, reservations are generally necessary—request ground floor rather than basement, 46 Lexington Street in Soho, tel. 020/7437-5708).

Mildred's Vegetarian Restaurant, across from Andrew Edmunds, has cheap prices, an enjoyable menu, and a plain-yet-pleasant interior filled with happy eaters (£6 meals, Mon–Sat 12:00–23:00, closed Sun, 45 Lexington Street, tel. 020/7494-1634).

The fun **Zilli Fish Too,** with a modern, bright setting near Covent Garden, serves up fresh seafood with a twist of Italy (2 courses-£15, 3 for £19, daily 12:00–15:00 & 17:30–23:30, 8 Wild Street, at corner of Great Queen Street, 2 blocks north of Covent Garden, tel. 020/7240-0011).

Neal's Yard is *the* place for cheap, hip, and healthy eateries near Covent Garden. The neighborhood is a tabouli of fun, hippie-type cafés. One of the best is **Food for Thought,** packed with local health nuts (good £5 vegetarian meals, Mon–Sat 12:00–20:30, Sun 12:00–17:00, non-smoking, 2 blocks north of Covent Garden Tube station, 31 Neal Street, tel. 020/7836-0239).

Near Recommended Victoria Station Hotels

Here are places a couple of blocks southwest of Victoria Station where I've enjoyed eating (see map on page 657).

La Campagnola, small and seriously Italian, is Belgravia's favorite budget Italian restaurant (£8–16 meals, Mon–Sat 12:00–15:00 & 18:00–23:30, closed Sun, 10 Lower Belgrave Street, tel. 020/7730-2057).

Ebury Wine Bar, filled with young professionals, provides a classy atmosphere, delicious £15–18 meals, and a £14 two-course special from 18:00–19:30 (Mon–Fri 11:00–23:00, Sat 12:00–23:00, Sun 18:00–22:00, 139 Ebury Street, at intersection with Elizabeth

Street, near bus station, tel. 020/7730-5447). Several cheap places are around the corner on Elizabeth Street (#23 for take-out or eat-in, super-absorbent fish-and-chips, and a Spanish *tapas* place across from that).

The Duke of Wellington pub is good, if somewhat smoky, and dominated by local drinkers. It's the neighborhood place for dinner (£6 meals, daily 11:00–15:00 & 18:00–21:00, 63 Eaton Terrace, at intersection with Chester Row, tel. 020/7730-1782).

Jenny Lo's Tea House is a simple, budget place serving up reliably tasty £5–8 eclectic Chinese-style meals to locals in the know (Mon–Fri 11:30–15:00 & 18:00–22:00, Sat 18:00–22:00, closed Sun, no CC, 14 Eccleston Street, tel. 020/7259-0399).

La Poule au Pot, ideal for a romantic splurge, offers a classy, candlelit ambience with well dressed patrons and expensive but fine country-style French cuisine (£15 lunch, £25 dinners, daily 12:30–14:30 & 18:45–23:00, Sun until 22:00, leafy patio dining, reservations smart, end of Ebury at intersection with Pimlico, 231 Ebury Street, tel. 020/7730-7763).

Grumbles brags it's been serving "good food and wine at non-scary prices since 1964." Offering a delicious mix of "modern eclectic French and traditional English," this hip and cozy little place is *the* spot to eat well in this otherwise workaday neighborhood (£12–22 meals, £12 lunch specials, reservations wise, self-serve launderette across the street open evenings, 2 nice sidewalk tables, daily 12:00–14:30 & 18:00–22:30, half a block north of Belgrave Road at 35 Churton Street, tel. 020/7834-0149).

The Jugged Hare Pub is in a lavish old bank building, its vaults replaced by kegs of beer and a fine kitchen. They have a fun, traditional menu with more fresh veggies than fries, and a plush and vivid pub scene good for a meal or just a drink (£7 meals, daily 12:00–21:00, 172 Vauxhall Bridge Road, tel. 020/7828-1543).

If you miss America, there's a mall-type **food court** at Victoria Place, upstairs in Victoria Station; **Café Rouge** seems to be the most popular here (£8–11 dinners, daily 9:30–22:30).

Groceries in and near Victoria Station: A large grocery, **Sainsbury's Local,** is on Victoria Street in front of the station, just past the buses (daily 6:00–24:00). In the station you'll find another, smaller Sainsbury's (at rear entrance, on Eccleston Street) and a couple other late-hours mini-markets.

Near Recommended Notting Hill and Bayswater Hotels

Queensway is lined with lively and inexpensive eateries. See the map on page 663.

Maggie Jones, exuberantly rustic and very English, serves my favorite £20 London dinner. You'll get fun-loving if brash service, and solid English cuisine, including huge plates of crunchy vegetables—by candlelight. Avoid the stuffy basement on hot summer nights, and request upstairs seating for the noisy but less cramped section. If you eat well once in London, eat here—and do it quick, before it burns down (daily 12:30–14:30 & 18:30–23:00, less expensive lunch menu, reservations recommended, friendly staff, 6 Old Court Place, just east of Kensington Church Street, near High Street Kensington Tube stop, tel. 020/7937-6462).

The **Churchill Arms** pub and **Thai Kitchens** is a local hangout, with good beer and old-English ambience in front and hearty £6 Thai plates in an enclosed patio in the back. You can eat the Thai food in this tropical hideaway or in the smoky but wonderfully atmospheric pub section. Arrive by 18:00 to avoid a line (Mon–Sat 12:00–21:30, Sun 12:00–16:00, 119 Kensington Church Street, tel. 020/7792-1246).

Prince Edward Pub serves good pub grub in a quintessential pub setting (£8 meals, Mon–Sat 12:00–14:30 & 18:00–21:00, Sun 12:00–18:00, indoor/outdoor seating, 2 blocks north of Bayswater Road at the corner of Dawson Place and Hereford Road, 73 Prince's Square, tel. 020/7727-2221).

Café Diana is a healthy little eatery serving sandwiches and Middle Eastern food. It's decorated with photos of Princess Diana, who used to drop by for pita sandwiches (daily 8:00–22:30, 5 Wellington Terrace, on Bayswater Road, opposite Kensington Palace Garden Gates—where Di once lived, tel. 020/7792-9606).

Black and Blue is a trendy bistro serving British/continental fusion cuisine to local hipsters. Follow the crowds to the gas torches and patio seating (£10–12 meals, Mon–Sat 12:00–23:00, Sun 12:00–22:30, 215 Kensington Church Street, tel. 020/7727-0004).

Royal China Restaurant is filled with London's Chinese, who consider this one of the city's best eateries. It's dressy in black, white, and chrome, with candles, brisk waiters, and fine food (£7–9 dishes, dim sum until 17:00, Mon–Thu 12:00–23:00, Fri–Sat 12:00–23:30, Sun 11:00–22:00, 13 Queensway, tel. 020/7221-2535).

Mr. Wu's Chinese Restaurant serves a 10-course buffet in a cramped little cafeteria. Just grab a plate and help yourself (£5, daily 12:00–23:00, check quality of buffet—right inside entrance—before committing, pickings can get slim, across from Bayswater Tube station, 54 Queensway, tel. 020/7243-1017).

Whiteleys Mall Food Court offers a fun selection of ethnic and fast-food eateries in a delightful mall (good salads at Café Rouge, second floor, corner of Porchester Gardens and Queensway).

Supermarket: **Europa** is a half-block from the Notting Hill Gate Tube stop (Mon–Sat 8:00–23:00, Sun 12:00–18:00, 112 Notting Hill Gate, near intersection with Pembridge Road).

Near Recommended South Kensington Hotels

Popular eateries line Old Brompton Road and Thurloe Street (Tube: South Kensington). See the map on page 661.

La Bouchee Bistro Café is a classy, hole-in-the-wall touch of France serving early-bird, three-course £13 meals before 19:00 and *plats du jour* for £8 all *jour* (daily 12:00–23:00, Sun until 22:00, 56 Old Brompton Road, tel. 020/7589-1929).

Daquise, an authentic-feeling 1930s Polish time-warp, is ideal if you're in the mood for kielbasa and kraut. It's likeably dreary—fast, cheap, family-run, and a much-appreciated part of the neighborhood (£10 meals, £8 lunch special includes wine, daily 11:30–23:00, non-smoking, 20 Thurloe Street, tel. 020/7589-6117).

Khyber Pass Tandoori Restaurant is a nondescript but handy place serving great Indian cuisine. Locals in the know travel to eat here (£12 dinners, daily 12:00–14:30 & 18:00–23:30, 21 Bute Street, tel. 020/7589-7311).

The Zetland Arms serves good pub meals upstairs in their nonsmoking restaurant (£6–10 meals, hearty £9 specials, table service, Mon–Fri 18:00–22:30, Sat–Sun 13:00–22:30, 2 Bute Street, tel. 020/7589-3813).

La Brasserie fills a big, plain room painted "nicotine yellow," with ceiling fans, a Parisian atmosphere, and good, traditional French cooking at reasonable prices (salads and veggie plates for £10, 2-course menus for £15 and £18, nightly until 23:00, 272 Brompton Road, tel. 020/7581-3089).

PJ's Bar and Grill is lively with the yuppie Chelsea crowd for a good reason. Traditional "New York brasserie"–style yet trendy, it has dressy tables surrounding a centerpiece bar. It serves pricey, cosmopolitan cuisine from a menu that changes with the seasons (£20 meals, nightly until 24:00, 52 Fulham Road, at intersection with Sydney Street, tel. 020/7581-0025).

Elsewhere in London

Between St. Paul's and the Tower: The **Counting House,** formerly an elegant old bank, offers great £7 meals, nice homemade meat pies, fish, and fresh vegetables (Mon–Fri 12:00–20:00, closed Sat–Sun, gets really busy with the buttoned-down 9-to-5 crowd after 12:15, near Mansion House in the City, 50 Cornhill, tel. 020/7283-7123).

Near St. Paul's: **Degustibus Sandwiches** is where a top-notch artisan bakery meets the public, offering fresh, you-design-it sandwiches, salads, and soups with simple seating or take-out picnic sacks (great parks nearby), just a block below St. Paul's (Mon–Fri 7:00–17:00, closed Sat–Sun, from church steps follow signs to youth hostel a block downhill, 53 Carter Lane, tel. 020/723-60056, Claire).

Near the British Library: Drummond Street (running just west of Euston Station) is famous in London for very cheap and good Indian and vegetarian food. Consider **Chutneys** and **Ravi Shankar** for a good *thali.*

TRANSPORTATION CONNECTIONS

Heathrow Airport

London's Heathrow Airport is the world's fourth busiest. Think about it: 63 million passengers a year on 425,000 flights from 170 destinations riding 90 airlines, like some kind of global maypole dance. While many complain about Heathrow, I think it's a great, user-friendly airport. Read signs, ask questions. For Heathrow's airport, flight, and transfers information, call the switchboard at tel. 0870-000-0123 (www.baa.co.uk). It has four terminals: T-1 (mostly domestic flights, with some European), T-2 (mainly European flights), T-3 (mostly flights from the United States), and T-4 (British Air transatlantic flights and BA flights to Paris, Amsterdam, and Athens). Taxis know which terminal you'll need.

Each terminal has an airport information desk, car-rental agencies, exchange bureaus, ATMs, a pharmacy, a **VAT refund desk** (tel. 020/8910-3682; you must present the VAT claim form from the retailer here to get your tax rebate on items purchased in Britain, see page 12 for details), and a **baggage-check desk** (£5.50/day, daily 6:00–23:00 at each terminal). Get online 24 hours a day at Heathrow's **Internet cafés** (T-4, mezzanine level) and at wireless "hotspots" in its departure lounges (T-1, T-3, and T-4). There are **post offices** in T-2 and T-4. Each terminal has cheap **eateries** (such as the cheery Food Village self-service cafeteria in T-3).

Heathrow's small **TI,** even though it's a for-profit business, is worth a visit to pick up free information: a simple map, the *London Planner,* and brochures (daily 8:30–18:00, 5-min walk from T-3 in Tube station, follow signs to Underground; bypass queue for transit info to reach window for London questions). If you're riding the Airbus into London, have your partner stay with the bags at the terminal while you head over to the TI.

If you're taking the Tube into London, buy a one-day Travel Card pass to cover the ride (see below).

Transportation to London from Heathrow Airport

By Tube (Subway): For £4, the Tube takes you the 14 miles to downtown London in 50 minutes on the Picadilly Line with stops (among others) at South Kensington, Leicester Square, and King's Cross Station (6/hr; depending on your destination, may require a change, www.thetube.com). Even better, buy a £5.40 one-day Travel Card that covers your trip into London and all your Tube travel for the day (starting at 9:30). Buy it at the ticket window at the Tube. You can hop on the Tube at Terminals 1, 2, or 3. From Terminal 4, which is undergoing some construction work until the fall of 2006, you reach the Tube by taking a 5-min shuttle bus ride to Hatton Cross Tube station.

By Airport Bus: The National Express Airbus, which may be discontinued, runs between the airport and London's King's Cross station, and serves the Notting Hill and Bayswater neighborhoods (£10, £15-round-trip, 2/hr, 60 min, runs 5:00–21:15, departs from each terminal, buy ticket from driver, tel. 08705-757-747, www.nxairport.com). The Tube works fine, but with baggage, I prefer the Airbus (assuming it serves my hotel neighborhood) because there are no connections underground and there's a lovely view from the top of the double-decker bus. Ask the driver to remind you when to get off. For people heading to the airport, exact pickup times are clearly posted at each bus stop.

By Airport Shuttle Bus: Hotelink offers door-to-door service (Heathrow-£15 per person, Gatwick-£22 per person, book the day before departure, buy online and save £1–2, tel. 01293/532-244, www.hotelink.co.uk, reservations@hotelink.co.uk).

By Taxi: Taxis from the airport to West and Central London cost about £45 and take about one hour. For four people traveling together, this can be a deal. Hotels can often line up a cab back to the airport for about £30. For the cheapest taxi to the airport, don't order one from your hotel. Simply flag down a few and ask them for their best "off-meter" rate.

By Heathrow Express Train: This slick train service zips you between Heathrow Airport and London's Paddington Station. At Paddington Station, you're in the thick of the Tube system, with easy access to any of my recommended neighborhoods—Notting Hill Gate is just two stops away. It's only 15 minutes to downtown from Terminals 1, 2, and 3, and 20 minutes from Terminal 4 (at the airport, you can use the Express as a free transfer between terminals). Buy your ticket to London before you board or pay a £2 surcharge to buy it on the train (£13, but ask about discount promos at Heathrow ticket desk, kids under 16 ride half-price, under 5 ride free, covered by BritRail pass, 4/hr, daily 5:10–23:30, tel. 0845-600-1515, www.heathrowexpress.co.uk). A Go Further ticket (£15) includes one Tube ride from Paddington to get you to your hotel (valid only on same day and in Zone 1, saves time). For one person on a budget, combining the Heathrow Express with either a Tube or taxi ride (between your hotel and Paddington) is nearly as fast and half the cost of taking a cab directly to (or from) the airport.

Buses from Heathrow to Bath

Direct buses run daily from Heathrow to Bath (11/day, 2.5 hrs,

£14, tel. 08705-757-747). BritRail passholders may prefer the 2.5-hour Heathrow-Bath bus/train connection via Reading (£10 for bus, rail portion free with pass, otherwise £33 total, payable at desk in terminal): first catch the twice-hourly RailAir Link shuttle bus to Reading (RED-ding), then hop on the hourly express train to Bath.

Most Heathrow buses depart from the common area serving Terminals 1, 2, and 3 (a 5-min walk from any of these terminals), although some depart from T-4 (bus tel. 08705-747-777).

Gatwick Airport

More and more flights, especially charters, land at Gatwick Airport, halfway between London and the southern coast (recorded airport info tel. 0870-000-2468).

Express trains—clearly the best way into **London** from here—shuttle conveniently between Gatwick and London's Victoria Station (£12, £23.50 round-trip, children under 5 free, 4/hr during day, 1–2/hr at night, 30 min, runs 24 hrs daily, can purchase tickets on train at no extra charge, tel. 0845-850-1530, www.gatwickexpress.co.uk). You can save a few pounds by taking South Central rail line's slower and less frequent shuttle between Victoria Station and Gatwick (£8, 3/hr, 1/hr midnight–4:00, 45 min, tel. 08457-484-950, www.southcentraltrains.co.uk).

To get to **Bath** from Gatwick, you can catch a bus to Heathrow and the bus to Bath from there. By train, the best Gatwick-Bath connection involves a transfer in Reading (2.5 hrs, irregular schedule; avoid transfer in London, where you'll have to change stations).

London's Other Airports

If you're flying into or out of **Stansted** (airport tel. 0870-0000-303), you can take the Airbus between the airport and downtown London's Victoria Coach Station (£10, 2/hr, 1.5 hrs, runs 4:00–24:00, picks up and stops throughout London, tel. 0845-850-0150, www.nxairport.com), or take the Stansted Express train (£14, connects to London's Liverpool Station, 40 min, 2–4/hr, 5:00–23:00, tel. 0845-850-0150, www.stanstedexpress.com). Stansted is expensive by cab; figure £80 one-way from central London.

For **Luton** (airport tel. 01582/405-100, www.london-luton.com), take the easyJet bus, which runs between the airport and Hendon Central Tube stop (£1, open to non-easyJet passengers, 40 min, runs 7:15–20:00, www.easybus.co.uk); Green Line's bus #757, which links the airport and London's Victoria Station at Buckingham Palace Road—stop 6 (£9, £8 for easyJet passengers, 2/hr, 1–1.25 hrs depending on time of day, runs 4:30–24:00, tel. 0870-608-7261, www.greenline.co.uk); or connect by rail to London's St. Pancras station (£11, runs 5:00-23:00, 25 min).

There's a slim chance you'd use **London City Airport** (tel. 020/7646-0088, www.londoncityairport.com). Blue shuttle buses connect the airport to the Liverpool Street Station (£6 one-way, 30 min), a hub for the Tube.

Connecting London's Airports

The **National Express Central Bus Station** offers direct Jetlink bus connections from **Heathrow** to **Gatwick Airport** (2/hr, 70 min or more, depending on traffic), departing just outside arrivals at all terminals (£16 one-way, £21 round-trip). To make a flight connection between Heathrow and Gatwick, allow three hours between flights.

More and more travelers are taking advantage of cheap flights out of London's smaller airports. A handy National Express bus runs between Heathrow, Gatwick, Stansted, and Luton airports—easier than having to cut through the center of London. Buses are frequent (less so between Stansted and Luton) and cheap: Heathrow-Luton is 1.5 hours direct and costs £16. Check schedules at www.nxairport.com.

Discounted Flights from London

Although bmi british midland has been around the longest, the others generally offer cheaper flights.

With **bmi british midland,** you can fly inexpensively to destinations in the U.K. and beyond (fares start around £30 one-way to Edinburgh, Paris, Brussels, or Amsterdam; or around £50 one-way to Dublin; prices can be higher, but there can also be much cheaper Internet specials—check online). For the latest, call British tel. 0870-607-0555 or U.S. tel. 800-788-0555 (check www.flybmi.com and their subsidiary, bmi baby, at www.bmibaby.com). Book in advance. Although you can book right up until the flight departs, the cheap seats will have sold out long before, leaving the most expensive seats for latecomers.

With no frills and cheap fares, **easyJet** flies from Luton, Stansted, and Gatwick. Prices are based on demand, so the least popular routes make for the cheapest fares, especially if you book early (tel. 0870-600-0000, www.easyjet.com).

Ryanair is a creative Irish airline that prides itself on offering the lowest fares. It flies from London (mostly Stansted airport) to often obscure airports in Dublin, Glasgow, Frankfurt, Stockholm, Oslo, Venice, Turin, and many others. Sample fares: London-Dublin—£78 round-trip (sometimes as low as £25), London-Frankfurt—£67 round-trip (Irish tel. 0818-303-030, British tel. 0871-246-0000, www.ryanair.com). Because they offer promotional deals any time of year, it's not essential that you book long in advance to get the best deals.

Virgin Express is a British-owned company with good rates (book by phone and pick up ticket at airport an hour before your flight, tel. 020/7744-0004, www.virgin-express.com). Virgin Express flies from London Heathrow and Brussels. From its hub in Brussels, you can connect cheaply to Barcelona, Madrid, Nice, Malaga, Copenhagen, Rome, or Milan (round-trip from Brussels to Rome for as little as £105). Their prices stay the same whether or not you book in advance.

Trains and Buses

London, Britain's major transportation hub, has a different train station for each region. Waterloo handles the Eurostar to Paris. King's Cross covers northeast England and Scotland (tel. 08457-225-225). Paddington covers west and southwest England (Bath) and South Wales (tel. 08457-000-125). For the others, call 08457-484-950 (or visit www.eurostar.com; £5 booking fee for telephone reservations). Note that for security reasons, stations offer a left-luggage service (£5/day) rather than lockers.

National Express' excellent bus service is considerably cheaper than trains. (To be put on indefinite hold, call 08705-808-080, or visit www.nationalexpress.com or the bus station a block southwest of Victoria Station.)

To Bath: Trains leave London's Paddington Station twice every hour between 7:00 and 19:00 (at :15 and :45 after each hour) for the 90-minute ride to Bath (costs £30 if you leave after 9:30 any day but Fri, when it's £40).

To get to Bath via Stonehenge, consider taking a guided bus tour from London to Stonehenge and Bath and abandoning the tour in Bath. Evan Evans' tour is fully guided for £53 (includes admissions). The tour leaves from the Victoria Coach station every morning at 8:45 (you can stow your bag under the bus), stops in Stonehenge (45 min), and then stops in Bath for lunch and a city tour before returning to London (offered year-round). You can book the tour at the Victoria Coach station, the Evan Evans' office (258 Vauxhall Bridge Road, near Victoria Coach station, tel. 020/7950-1777, U.S. tel. 866/382-6868, www.evanevans.co.uk, reservations@evanevanstours.co.uk), or the Green Line Travel Office (4a Fountain Square, across from Victoria Coach station, tel. 0870-608-7261, www.greenline.co.uk). Golden Tours also runs a fully guided Stonehenge-Bath tour for a similar price (departs from Fountain Square, located across from Victoria Coach Station, tel. 020/7233-6668, U.S. tel. 800/456-6303, www.goldentours.co.uk, reservations@goldentours.co.uk).

To Points North: Trains run hourly from London's King's Cross Station, stopping in **York** (2 hrs), **Durham** (3 hrs), and **Edinburgh** (4.5 hrs).

To Dublin, Ireland: The boat/bus journey takes between 9 and 10 hours and goes all day or all night (£29–57, 2/day, tel. 08705-143-219, www.eurolines.com). Consider a cheap 70-minute Ryanair flight instead (see above).

Crossing the Channel by Eurostar Train

The fastest and most convenient way to get from the Eiffel Tower to Big Ben is by rail. Eurostar, a joint service of the Belgian, British, and French railways, is the speedy passenger train zips you (and up to 800 others in 18 sleek cars) from downtown London to downtown Paris (12–15/day, 2.5 hrs) faster and easier than flying. The actual tunnel crossing is a 20-minute, black, silent, 100-mile-per-hour non-event. Your ears won't even pop. Eurostar trains also run directly from London to Disneyland Paris (1/day direct, more often with transfer at Lille).

Eurostar Fares

Channel fares (essentially the same between London and Paris or Brussels) are reasonable but complicated. Prices vary depending on when you travel, whether you can live with restrictions, and whether you're eligible for any discounts (youth, seniors, and railpass holders all qualify). Rates are lower for round trips and off-peak travel (midday, midweek, low-season, and low-interest). Fares are always changing. For specifics, visit www.ricksteves.com/eurostar.

As with airfares, the most expensive and flexible option is a **full-fare ticket** with no restrictions on refundability (even refundable after the departure date; for a one-way trip, figure around $375 in first class, $225 second class). A first-class ticket comes with a meal (a dinner departure nets you more grub than breakfast)—but it's not worth the extra expense.

Also like the airlines, **cheaper tickets** come with more restrictions—and are limited in number (so they sell out more quickly; for second-class, one-way tickets, figure $90–200). Non-full-fare tickets have severe restrictions on refundability (best-case scenario: you'll get 25 percent back, but with the cheapest options you'll get nothing). But several do allow

Eurostar Routes

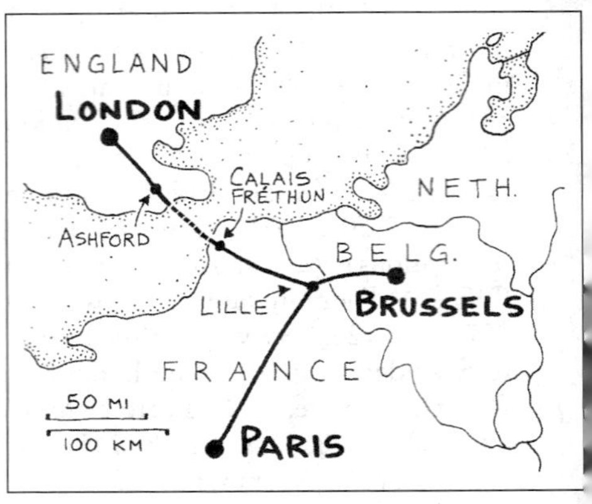

you to change the specifics of your trip once before departure.

Those traveling with a railpass for Britain, France, or Belgium should look first at the **passholder** fare, an especially good value for one-way Eurostar trips (around $75). In Britain, passholder tickets can be issued only at the Eurostar office in Waterloo Station or the American Express office in Victoria Station—not at any other stations. You can also order them by phone (see below), then pick them up at Waterloo Station.

Buying Eurostar Tickets

Refund and exchange restrictions are serious, so don't reserve until you're sure of your plans. If you're confident about the time and date of your crossing, order ahead from the United States. Only the most expensive ticket (full fare) is fully refundable, so if you want to have more flexibility, hold off—keeping in mind that the longer you wait, the more likely the cheapest tickets will sell out (you might end up having to pay for first class).

You can check and book fares by phone or online in the United States (order online at www.ricksteves.com/eurostar, prices listed in dollars; order by phone at U.S. tel. 800/EUROSTAR) or in Britain (British tel. 08705-186-186, www.eurostar.com, prices listed in euros). These are different companies, often with slightly different prices and discount deals on similar tickets; if you order from the United States, check out both. (If you buy from a U.S. company, you'll pay for ticket delivery in the United States.) In Europe, you can buy your Eurostar ticket at any major train station in any country or at any travel agency that handles train tickets (expect a booking fee).

Note that Britain's time zone is one hour earlier than France's. Times listed on tickets are local times (departure from London is British time, arrival in Paris in French time).

Crossing the Channel without Eurostar

By bus and boat or by train and boat: The old-fashioned way of crossing the Channel is cheaper than crossing by Eurostar. It's also twice as romantic, complicated, and time-consuming. You'll get better prices arranging your trip in London than you would in the United States. Taking the bus is cheapest, and round-trips are a bargain.

By **bus** to Paris, Brussels, or Amsterdam from Victoria Coach Station (via boat or Chunnel): £39 one-way, £50 round-trip for economy fares booked at least two days in advance; 8 hrs to Paris—5/day; 9 hrs to Brussels—5/day; 12 hrs to Amsterdam—4/day; day or overnight, on Eurolines (tel. 08705-143-219, www.eurolines.com).

The **Hoverspeed ferry** runs between Dover, England, and Calais, France (tel. 08705-240-241 or 0870-240-8070, www.hoverspeed.com). Hoverspeed sells London-Paris rail and ferry packages: £44 one-way; £56 round-trip with five-day return; and £67 round-trip over more than five days. You can buy this package deal in person at Waterloo and Charing Cross stations. If you book by phone (number listed above), you must book at least two weeks in advance, and the ticket will be mailed to you (no ticket pickup at station for bookings by phone).

By **P&O ferry** from Dover to Calais: £21 one-way or round-trip with five-day return; £41 round-trip over more than five days (tel. 0870-520-2020, www.poferries.com). Prices are for the ferry only; you need to book your own train tickets—see P&O's Web site for details.

By plane: Typical fares are £110 regular, less for student standby. Check with the budget airlines for cheap round-trip fares to Paris (see "Discounted Flights from London," page 678).

BATH

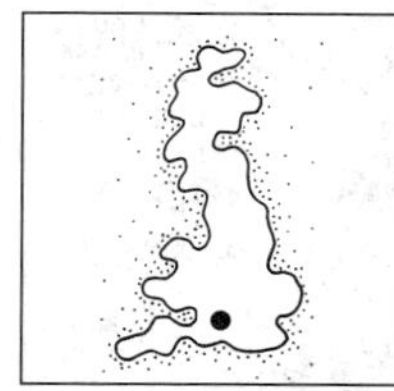

The best city to visit within easy striking distance of London is Bath—just a 90-minute train ride away. Two hundred years ago, this city of 85,000 was the trendsetting Hollywood of Britain. If ever a city enjoyed looking in the mirror, Bath's the one. It has more "government-listed" or protected historic buildings per capita than any other town in England. The entire city, built of the creamy warm-tone limestone called "Bath stone," beams in its cover-girl complexion. An architectural chorus line, it's a triumph of the Georgian style. Proud locals remind visitors that the town is routinely banned from the "Britain in Bloom" contest to give other towns a chance to win. Bath's narcissism is justified. Even with its mobs of tourists (2 million per year), Bath is a joy to visit.

Long before the Romans arrived in the 1st century, Bath was known for its hot springs. The importance of Bath has always been shaped by the healing allure of its 116-degree mineral hot springs. Romans called the popular spa town Aquae Sulis. The town's importance carried through Saxon times, when it had a huge church on the site of the present-day abbey and was considered the religious capital of Britain. Its influence peaked in 973 with King Edgar's sumptuous coronation in the abbey. Later Bath prospered as a wool town.

Bath then declined until the mid-1600s, when it was just a huddle of huts around the abbey, with hot, smelly mud and 3,000 residents, oblivious to the Roman ruins 18 feet below their dirt floors. Then, in 1687, Queen Mary, fighting infertility, bathed here. Within 10 months she gave birth to a son...and a new age of popularity for Bath.

The revitalized town boomed as a spa resort. Ninety percent

Bath

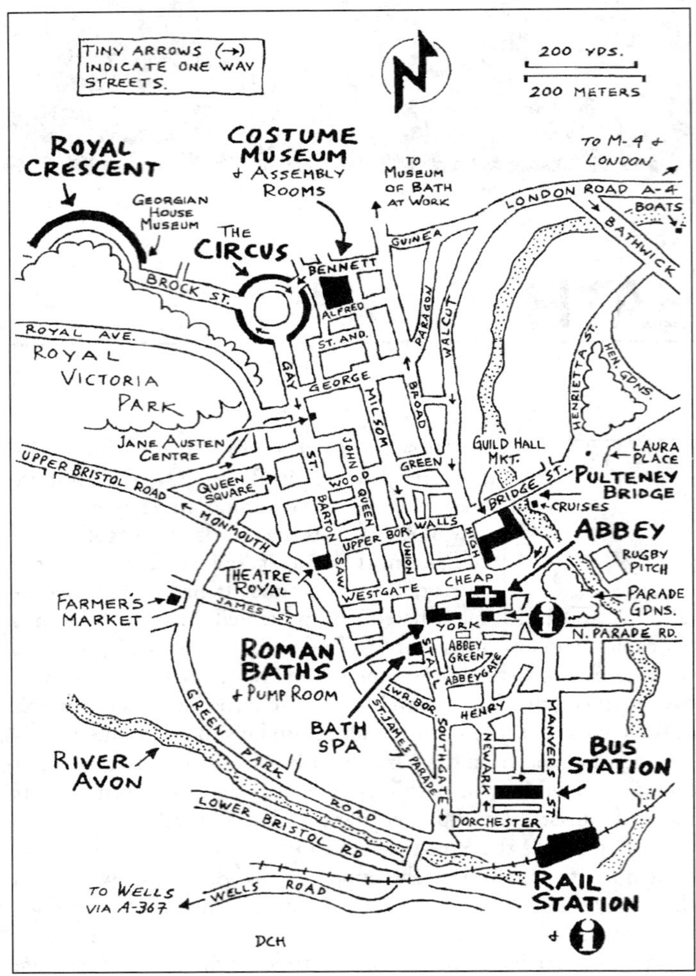

of the buildings you'll see today are from the 18th century. Local architect John Wood was inspired by the Italian architect Andrea Palladio to build a "new Rome." The town bloomed in the neoclassical style, and streets were lined not with scrawny sidewalks but with wide "parades," upon which the women in their stylishly wide dresses could spread their fashionable tails.

Beau Nash (1673–1762) was Bath's "master of ceremonies." He organized both the daily regimen of the aristocratic visitors and the city, lighting and improving street security, banning swords, and opening the Pump Room. Under his fashionable baton, Bath became a city of balls, gaming, and concerts—the place to see and be seen in England. This most civilized place became even more so with the great neoclassical building spree that followed.

The buzz in the early 21st century is that the venerable baths will be in the spotlight again. With the opening of a new spa (expected in 2006) tapping Bath's soothing hot springs, the town will once again attract visitors in need of a cure or a soak.

Planning Your Time

Bath deserves two nights even on a quick trip. There's plenty to do and it's a joy to do it.

Here's how I'd spend the day in Bath:

9:00–Tour the Roman Baths; 10:30–Catch the free city walking tour; 12:30–Picnic on the open deck of a Bath tour bus; 14:00–Free time in the shopping center of old Bath; 15:30–Tour the Costume Museum; 18:00–Pub grub dinner or classy meal; 20:00–Bizarre Bath comedy walk.

ORIENTATION

(area code: 01225)

Bath's town square, three blocks in front of the bus and train station, is a bouquet of tourist landmarks, including the abbey, Roman and medieval baths, and the royal Pump Room.

Tourist Information

The TI is in the abbey churchyard (Mon–Sat 9:30–17:00, Sun 10:00–16:00, tel. 0870-420-1278, www.visitbath.co.uk). Pick up the 50p Bath mini-guide (includes a map) and the free, info-packed *This Month in Bath.* Browse through scads of fliers, books, and maps. Skip their room-finding service (£5 fee and your host is nicked 10 percent) and book direct.

Arrival in Bath

The Bath **train station** has small-town charm, a national and international tickets desk, and a privately run tourism office masquerading as a TI. The **bus station** is immediately in front of the train station. To get to the TI from either station, walk two blocks up Manvers Street and turn left at the triangular "square," by following the small TI arrow on a signpost. My recommended B&Bs are all within a 10- to 15-minute walk or a £3.50 taxi ride from the station.

Helpful Hints

Festivals: The Bath Literature Festival is an open book from March 4–12, 2006 (www.bathlitfest.org.uk). The Bath International

Music Festival bursts into song from late May to early June (classical, folk, jazz, contemporary; for the line-up, see www.bathmusicfest.org.uk), overlapped by the eclectic Bath Fringe Festival (theater, walks, talks, bus trips; www.bathfringe.co.uk). The Jane Austen Festival unfolds genteelly mid- to late-September (www.janeaustenfestival.co.uk). Bath's festival box office sells tickets for most events, and can tell you exactly what's on tonight (2 Church Street, tel. 01225/463-362, www.bathfestivals.org.uk). Bath's local paper, the *Bath Chronicle,* publishes a "What's On" event listing on Fridays (www.thisisbath.com).

Car Rental: Hertz and Enterprise are each handy to central Bath. Europcar advertises it's in Bath but is outside of town. Avis is a mile from the Bristol train station; you'd need to rent a car to get there. Enterprise, which provides a pickup service for customers to and from their hotels (at Lower Bristol Road in Bath, tel. 01225/443-311) and Hertz (just outside Bath train station, tel. 01225/442-911) offer roughly these rates: £35/day, £70/weekend, and £140/week. Most offices close Saturday afternoon and all day Sunday, which complicates weekend pickups.

Internet Access: The top two Internet places are a block in front of the train station: Click Café (free 2-min e-mail check, daily 10:00–22:00, on Manvers Street, tel. 01225/481-008) and RetailerInternet.com (closed Sun, 128 Walcot Street, tel. 01225/445-999).

Laundry: The **Spruce Goose Launderette** is around the corner from the recommended Brock's Guest House on the pedestrian lane called Margaret's Buildings (daily 8:00–21:00, self-service or full-service on same day if dropped off at 8:00, tel. 01225/483-309). Anywhere in town, **Speedy Wash** can pick up your laundry for same-day service (£9.50/bag, Mon–Fri 7:30–17:30, most hotels work with them, tel. 01225/427-616). East of Pulteney Bridge, the humble **Lovely Wash** is on Daniel Street (daily 9:00–21:00, self-service only).

TOURS

Of Bath

▲▲▲Walking Tours—Free two-hour tours are offered by **The Mayor's Corps of Honorary Guides,** led by volunteers who want to share their love of Bath with its many visitors. Their chatty, historical, and gossip-filled walks are essential for your understanding of this town's amazing Georgian social scene. How else will you learn that the old "chair ho" call for your sedan chair evolved into today's "cheerio" farewell? Tours leave from in front of the

Pump Room (free, no tips, year-round daily at 10:30 plus Sun–Fri at 14:00; evening walks offered May–Sept at 19:00 on Tue, Fri, and Sat). Advice for theater-goers: Guides stop to talk outside the Theatre Royal. You can skip out a moment, pop into the box office, and snare a great deal on a play for tonight (see "Nightlife" on page 695 for details).

For **Ghost Walks** and **Bizarre Bath** tours, see "Nightlife," page 696.

For a **private tour,** call the local guides' bureau (£46/2 hrs, tel. 01225/337-111).

The **Great Bath Pub Crawl,** a relaxed stroll through the town, gives an insight into pubs: "the busy man's recreation, the idle man's business, the melancholy man's sanctuary, and the stranger's welcome" (£5, tours May–Sept nightly at 20:00, depart from outside the centrally-located Parade Park Hotel, 10 North Parade, tel. 01225/310-364, www.greatbathpubcrawl.com, info@greatbathpubcrawl.com).

Taxi Tours—Local taxis, driven by good talkers, go where big buses can't. A group of up to four can rent a cab for an hour (around £20) and enjoy a fine, informative, and—with the right cabbie—entertaining private joyride. It's probably cheaper to let the meter run than to pay for an hourly rate, but ask the cabbie for advice.

▲▲City Bus Tours—Four copy-cat companies fill Bath with exhaust as their nearly empty buses loop constantly through the city. Any of these is a fine and worthwhile tour (basically £6.50–9 for a 45-min figure-eight loop with hop-off, hop-on privileges, good for 24 hours). Jump on anytime, pay the driver, climb upstairs, and enjoy the rapid-fire spiel of your live guide (17 signposted pick-up points, generally 4/hr from 9:30–17:00, more frequent and with longer hours in summer). On a sunny day, this is a multitasking tourist's dream-come-true: You can munch a sandwich, work on a tan, snap great photos, and learn a lot all at the same time. Save money by doing the bus tour first—ticket stubs get you minor discounts at many sights. Pick from these four competing companies:

City Sightseeing (red-orange buses): Tickets on this bus line cost more (£9) but are good for 48 hours. They run a second "Skyline" route outside of town, handy for those wanting to visit the American Museum (see page 695). City Sightseeing bought out Guide Friday, the originators of the hop-on, hop-off buses; until GF's green-and-cream buses are phased out, tickets are valid on both types of buses.

Heritage (yellow buses): With fine live guides, Heritage buses run the basic 45-minute route cheaper than the rest at £7.

First Group/Bath Bus Panoramic ("Barbie" colored buses): Your 24-hour ticket from First is also good for the public bus

Bath at a Glance

▲▲▲**Roman and Medieval Baths** Ancient baths that gave the city its name, tourable with good audioguide. **Hours:** Daily April–Sept 9:00–18:00, July–Aug until 22:00, Oct–March 9:00–17:00.

▲▲▲**Costume Museum** 400 years of fashion under one roof, plus opulent Assembly Rooms. **Hours:** Daily June–Sept 11:00–18:00, Oct–May 11:00–17:00.

▲▲▲**Museum of Bath at Work** Gadget-ridden, circa-1900 engineer's shop, foundry, factory, and office, best enjoyed with a live tour. **Hours:** April–Oct daily 10:30–17:00, weekends only in winter.

▲▲**Royal Crescent and the Circus** Stately Georgian (neoclassical) buildings from Bath's late-18th-century glory days. **Hours:** Always viewable.

▲▲**Georgian House at No. 1 Royal Crescent** Best opportunity to explore the interior of one of Bath's high-rent Georgian beauties. **Hours:** Mid-Feb–Oct Tue–Sun 10:30–17:00, closes at 16:00 in Nov, closed Mon and Dec–mid-Feb.

▲**Pump Room** Swanky Georgian hall, ideal for a spot of tea or a taste of unforgettably "healthy" spa water. **Hours:** Daily 9:30–12:00 for coffee, 12:00–14:30 for lunch, 14:30–17:30 for high tea (open for dinner July–Aug only).

system; it's valid for a trip to the American Museum and even out to Wells—a nice bonus (£8.50, tel. 01225/313-222).

Classic City Tours (red with white stripe): These just-the-basics tour buses are technically "public service vehicles"—a loophole they use to be able to run the same routes as transit buses. Consequently, tour buses are required to take passengers across town for the normal £1 fare. Tourists have the right to hop on, ask for a "single fare," and pay £1 (hop-on, hop-off tour–£6.50, tel. 07721/559-686).

Of Stonehenge, Avebury, the Cotswolds, and More

Bath is a good launchpad for visiting Wells, Avebury, Stonehenge, and more.

Mad Max Minibus Tours—Operating daily from Bath, Maddy and Paul offer thoughtfully-organized, informative tours that run with a maximum group size of 16 people. Their **stone circles and villages** full-day tour (8:45–16:30) covers 110 miles and visits Stonehenge, the Avebury Stone Circle, and two cute villages—

▲**Abbey** 500-year-old Perpendicular Gothic church, graced with beautiful fan vaulting and stained glass. **Hours:** Mon–Sat 9:00–18:00, Sun usually 13:00–14:30 & 15:30–17:30, closes at 16:30 in winter.

▲**Pulteney Bridge and Palace Gardens** Shop-strewn bridge and relaxing riverside gardens. **Hours:** Bridge—always open; gardens—April–Sept daily 10:00–19:00, June–Aug until 20:00, shorter hours off-season.

▲**American Museum** An insightful look at colonial/early-American lifestyles, with 18 furnished rooms complete with guides eager to talk. **Hours:** April–Oct Tue–Sun 14:00–17:30, closed Mon and Nov–March.

Jane Austen Centre Exhibit on 19th-century Bath-based novelist, best for her fans. **Hours:** Mon–Sat 10:00–17:30, Sun 10:30–17:30.

Building of Bath Museum Architecture buff's guide to Bath. **Hours**: Tue–Sun 10:30–17:00, closed Mon.

Thermae Bath Spa Long-delayed, brand-new relaxation center, putting the bath back in Bath. **Hours:** May open in 2006.

Lacock and Castle Combe, which is the southernmost Cotswold village and is as sweet as they come (£22.50, cash only, Stonehenge admission not included).

Mad Max also offers the **Cotswold Discovery** full-day tour, a picturesque romp through the countryside, with stops in the Cotswolds' quainter villages, including Stow-on-the-Wold, Stanton, Stanway, Tetbury, and the Coln Valley. If you request this in advance, you can use the tour as transportation to get to Stow and bring your luggage along (£25, runs Sun, Tue, and Thu 8:45–17:15). Their short tour of **Stonehenge and Bradford-on-Avon** leaves daily at 14:00 and ends at 17:30 (£12.50, Stonehenge entry extra).

All tours depart from Bath at the Glass House shop on the corner of Orange Grove, a one-minute walk from the Abbey. Arrive a few minutes before your departure time. Only cash is accepted as payment.

It's better to book ahead for these popular tours via e-mail (www.madmaxtours.com, maddy@madmax.abel.co.uk) rather than by phone (Mon–Fri 8:00–18:00, tel. 01225/464-323). Please honor or cancel your seat reservation.

More Bus Tours—If Mad Max is booked up, don't fret. Plenty of companies in Bath offer tours of varying lengths, prices, and destinations. Note that the cost of admission to sites is usually not included with any tour. **Scarper Tours** runs a minibus tour to Stonehenge (£12.50, departs daily 9:30 & 13:30, tel. 07739/644-155, www.scarpertours.com). **Heritage City Guided Tour** offers a Stonehenge Express trip out to the rocks and back (£14, 2.25 hrs, departs Grand Parade daily at 10:00 and 14:00, mobile 07977-792-9486). **Celtic Horizons** runs day tours to a variety of destinations and charges a flat fee for up to eight people (Stonehenge-£60, Avebury area-£70, Cotswolds-£100–160, tel. 01373/461-784, www.celtichorizons.com, alan@celtichorizons.com).

SIGHTS

▲▲▲Roman and Medieval Baths—In ancient Roman times, high society enjoyed the mineral springs at Bath. From Londinium, Romans traveled so often to Aquae Sulis, as the city was called, to "take a bath" that finally it became known simply as Bath. Today, a fine museum surrounds the ancient bath. It's a one-way system leading you past well-documented displays, Roman artifacts, mosaics, a temple pediment, and the actual mouth of the spring, piled high with Roman pennies. Enjoy some quality time looking into the eyes of Minerva, goddess of the hot springs. The included self-guided tour audioguide makes the visit easy and plenty informative. For those with a big appetite for Roman history, in-depth 40-minute tours leave from the end of the museum at the edge of the actual bath (included with ticket, on the hour, a poolside clock is set for the next departure time). The water is so green because of the lead—don't drink it. You can revisit the museum after the tour (£9, £12 combo-ticket includes Costume Museum—a £3 savings, family combo-£32, combo-tickets good for 1 week, April–Sept daily 9:00–18:00, July–Aug until 22:00—last entry an hour before, Oct–March until 17:00, tel. 01225/477-784, www.romanbaths.co.uk). The museum and baths are a delight to visit in the evening—romantic, gas-lit, and all yours. After visiting the Roman Baths, drop by the attached Pump Room for a spot of tea, or to gag on the water.

▲Pump Room—For centuries, Bath was forgotten as a spa. Then, in 1687, the previously barren Queen Mary bathed here, became pregnant, and bore a male heir to the throne. A few years later Queen Anne found the water eased her gout. Word of its wonder waters spread, and Bath was back on the aristocratic map. High society soon turned the place into one big pleasure palace. The

Pump Room, an elegant Georgian hall just above the Roman baths, offers the visitor's best chance to raise a pinky in this Chippendale grandeur. Drop by to sip coffee or tea or enjoy a light meal (daily 9:30–12:00 for morning coffee, 12:00–14:30 for lunch—£14 2-course menu, 14:30–17:30 for traditional high tea—£10, £7 tea/coffee and pastry available anytime except during lunch, open for dinner July–Aug only; live music daily—string trio 10:00–12:00, piano 12:00–14:30, string trio 15:00–17:00; tel. 01225/444-477). Above the newspaper table and sedan chairs, a statue of Beau Nash himself sniffles down at you.

The Spa Water: This is your chance to sip a famous (but forgettable) "Bath bun" and split (and spit) a 50p drink of the awful curative water. The water is served from the King's Spring by appropriately attired Martin, who's ready to minuet (but refuses to gavotte). He explains that the water is 10,000 years old and marinated in wonderful minerals. It's pumped from nearly 100 yards deep, where there's no oxygen, making the water bacteria-free. Convenient public WCs are in the entry hallway that connects the Pump Room with the baths.

Thermae Bath Spa—After simmering unused for a quarter-century, Bath's natural thermal springs will once again offer R&R for the masses. The state-of-the-art leisure and curative spa, housed in a complex combining old buildings with controversial new, blocky architecture, is scheduled to open (after numerous delays) in 2006. The only natural thermal spa in the United Kingdom, it will include an open-air rooftop thermal pool and all the "pamper thyself" extras—aromatherapy steam rooms, mud wraps, and various healing-type treatments and classes. Swimwear is required (daily 9:00–22:00, £17/2 hrs, £23/4 hrs, £35/full day; treatments, massage, and solarium cost extra—ranging from £26–68; 100 yards from Roman and medieval baths on Beau Street, tel. 01225/331-234, www.thermaebathspa.com for the latest).

▲Abbey—The town of Bath wasn't much in the Middle Ages, but an important church has stood on this spot since Anglo-Saxon times. In 973, Edgar was crowned here. Dominating the town center, the present church—the last great medieval church of England—is 500 years old and a fine example of Late Perpendicular Gothic, with breezy fan vaulting and enough stained glass to earn it the nickname "Lantern of the West." The glass, red-iron gas-powered lamps, and heating grates on the floor are all remnants of the 19th century. The window behind the altar shows 52 scenes from the life of Christ. A window to the left of the altar shows that coronation of Edgar in 973 (worth the £2.50 donation, Mon–Sat 9:00–18:00, Sun usually 13:00–14:30 & 15:30–17:30, closes at 16:30 in winter, handy flyer narrates a self-guided 19-stop tour, www.bathabbey.org). Posted on the door is the schedule for concerts, services, and

evensong (Sun at 15:30 year-round, plus most Sat in Aug at 17:00). The facade (c. 1500, but mostly restored) is interesting for some of its carvings. Look for the angels going down the ladder. The statue of Peter (to the left of the door) lost his head to mean iconoclasts; it was re-carved out of his once super-sized beard. Take a moment to appreciate the abbey's architecture from the Abbey Green square.

A small but worthwhile exhibit, the abbey's **Heritage Vaults** tell the story of Christianity in Bath since Roman times (£2.50, Mon–Sat 10:00–16:00, last entry 15:30, closed Sun, entrance just outside church, south side).

▲Pulteney Bridge, Parade Gardens, and Cruises—Bath is inclined to compare its shop-lined Pulteney Bridge to Florence's Ponte Vecchio. That's pushing it. But to best enjoy a sunny day, pay £1.30 to enter the Parade Gardens below the bridge (April–Sept daily 10:00–19:00, June–Aug until 20:00, shorter hours off-season, includes deck chairs, ask about concerts held some Sun at 15:00 in summer, tel. 01225/394-041). Taking a siesta to relax peacefully at the riverside provides a wonderful break (and memory).

Across the bridge at Pulteney Weir, tour boat companies run **cruises** (£5, up to 7/day if the weather's good, 50 min to Bathampton and back, WCs on board). Just take whatever boat is running. Avon Cruisers actually stop in Bathampton (allowing you to hop off and walk back); Pulteney Cruisers come with a sundeck ideal for picnics.

Guildhall Market, located across from Pulteney Bridge, is a frumpy time warp in this affluent place, but it's fun for browsing and picnic shopping. Its cheap Market Café is recommended under "Eating," page 704.

The Victoria Art Gallery, also across from Pulteney Bridge, fills a fine room with paintings from the 18th and 19th centuries (free and includes audioguide, daily 10:00–17:00, WC, next to the Market).

▲▲Royal Crescent and the Circus—If Bath is an architectural cancan, these are the knickers. These first Georgian "condos" by John Wood (the Elder and the Younger) are well explained in the city walking tours. "Georgian" is British for "neoclassical," or dating from the 1770s. As you cruise the Crescent, pretend you're rich. Pretend you're poor. Notice the "ha ha fence," a drop-off in the front yard that acted as a barrier, invisible from the windows, for keeping out sheep and peasants. The refined and stylish Royal Crescent Hotel sits unmarked in the center of the crescent. You're welcome to (politely) drop in to explore its fine ground floor public spaces. A gracious and traditional cream tea is served in the garden out back (£11, daily 12:00–17:30).

Picture the round Circus as a colosseum turned inside out. Its Doric, Ionic, and Corinthian capital decorations pay homage to its

Greco-Roman origin and are a reminder that Bath (with its 7 hills) aspired to be "the Rome of England." The frieze above the first row of columns has hundreds of different panels, each representing the arts, sciences, and crafts. The first floor was high off the ground, to accommodate aristocrats on sedan chairs and women with Cher-like hairdos. The tiny round windows on the top floors were the servants' quarters. While the building fronts are uniform, the backs are higgledy-piggledy, infamous for their "hanging loos." Stand in the middle of the Crescent among the grand plane trees, on the capped old well. Imagine the days when there was no indoor plumbing and the servant girls gathered here to fetch water—this was gossip central. Standing on the well, your clap echoes three times around the circle (try it).

▲▲Georgian House at No. 1 Royal Crescent—This museum (corner of Brock Street and Royal Crescent) offers your best look into a period house. It's worth the £4 admission to get behind one of those classy exteriors. The volunteers in each room are determined to fill you in on all the fascinating details of Georgian life... like how high-class women shaved their eyebrows and pasted on carefully trimmed strips of furry mouse skin in their place. On the bedroom dresser sits a bowl of black beauty marks and a hair scratcher from those pre-shampoo days. Fido spent his days in the kitchen treadmill powering the rotisserie (mid-Feb–Oct Tue–Sun 10:30–17:00, closes at 16:00 in Nov, closed Mon, and Dec–mid-Feb, "no stiletto heels, please," tel. 01225/428-126, www.bath-preservation-trust.org.uk).

▲▲▲Costume Museum—One of Europe's great museums, it displays 400 years of fashion—one frilly decade at a time—and is housed within Bath's Assembly Rooms. Follow the excellent included audioguide tour and allow two hours (£6, £12 combo-ticket covers Roman Baths—saving you £3, family combo-£32, daily June–Sept 11:00–18:00, Oct–May 11:00–17:00, last entry 1 hour before closing, tel. 01225/477-789, www.museumofcostume.co.uk).

The **Assembly Rooms,** which you can see for free en route to the museum, are big, grand, empty rooms. Card games, concerts, tea, and dances were held here in the 18th century, before the advent of fancy hotels with grand public spaces made them obsolete. Note the extreme symmetry (pleasing to the aristocratic eye) and the high windows (which assured their privacy). After the Allies bombed the historical and well-preserved German city of Lübeck, the Germans picked up a Baedeker guide and chose a similarly lovely city to bomb: Bath. The Assembly Rooms—gutted in this war time tit-for-tat by WWII bombs—have since been restored to their original splendor. (Only the chandeliers are original.)

Below the Costume Museum (left as you leave, 20 yards away) is one of the few surviving sets of iron house hardware. "Link boys" carried torches through the dark streets, lighting the way for big shots in their sedan chairs as they traveled from one affair to the next. The link boys extinguished their torches in the black conical "snuffers." The lamp above was once gas-lit. The crank on the left was used to hoist bulky things to various windows (see the hooks). Few of these sets survived the dark days of the WWII Blitz, when most were collected, melted down, and turned into weapons to power the British war machine.

▲▲▲Museum of Bath at Work—This is the official title for Mr. Bowler's Business, a 1900s engineer's shop, brass foundry, and fizzy-drink factory with a Dickensian office. It's just a pile of meaningless old gadgets until a volunteer guide lovingly resurrects Mr. Bowler's creative genius. Also featured are various Bath creations through the years, including a 1914 car and the versatile plasticine (proto-Play-Doh, handy for clay-mation and more). Don't miss the fine "Story of Bath Stone" in the basement. While there are included audioguides, the live tours are the key (wonderful 45-minute tours go regularly). If rushed, join one already in session (£3.50, April–Oct daily 10:30–17:00, last entry at 16:00, weekends only in winter, 2 blocks up Russell Street from Assembly Rooms, steep uphill hike, tel. 01225/318-348).

Jane Austen Centre—This exhibition focuses on Jane Austen's five years in Bath (around 1800), and the influence Bath had on her writing. While the exhibit is thoughtfully done and a hit with "Janeites," there is little of historic substance here. You'll walk through a Georgian town house that she didn't live in and see mostly enlarged reproductions of things associated with her writing. The museum describes various places from two novels set in Bath (*Persuasion* and *Northanger Abbey*). After a live intro (15 min, 3/hr) explaining how this romantic but down-to-earth girl dealt with the silly, shallow, and arrogant aristocrat's world where "the doing of nothings all day prevents one from doing anything," you see a 15-minute video and wander through the rest of the exhibit (£4.65, Mon–Sat 10:00–17:30, Sun 10:30–17:30, 40 Gay Street between Queen's Square and the Circus, tel. 01225/443-000, www.janeausten.co.uk). Avid fans gather in mid- to late-September for the annual Bath Jane Austen Festival (readings and lectures, www.janeaustenfestival.co.uk).

If you're male and feeling left out, head one door downhill from the museum and look through the window. You'll see a fine delftware-decorated powder bowl designed for men to touch up their wigs.

The Building of Bath Museum—This museum offers an intriguing look behind the scenes at how the Georgian city was actually built. It's just a couple rooms of exhibits, but those interested in construction—inside and out—find it very much worth the £4 (Tue–Sun 10:30–17:00, closed Mon, above the Circus on a street called "The Paragon," tel. 01225/333-895).

▲**American Museum**—I know, you need this in Bath like you need a Big Mac. But this museum offers a compelling look at colonial and early-American lifestyles. Each of 18 completely furnished rooms (from the 1600s to the 1800s) is hosted by an eager guide waiting to fill you in on the candles, maps, bedpans, and various religious sects that make domestic Yankee history surprisingly interesting. One room is a quilter's nirvana (£6.50, April–Oct Tue–Sun 14:00–17:30, closed Mon and Nov–March, nice arboretum, at Claverton Manor, tel. 01225/460-503, www.americanmuseum.org). The museum is outside of town and a headache to reach if you don't have a car (10-min walk from bus #18).

ACTIVITIES

Walking—The Bath Skyline Walk is a six-mile wander around the hills surrounding Bath (leaflet at TI). Plenty of other scenic paths are described in the TI's literature. For additional options, get *Country Walks around Bath,* by Tim Mowls (£4.50 at TI).

Hiking the Canal to Bathampton—An idyllic towpath leads from the Bath train station along an old canal to the sleepy village of Bathampton. Immediately behind the station, cross the footbridge and see where the canal hits the river. Turn left, noticing the series of industrial-age locks, and walk along the towpath, giving thanks that you're not a horse pulling a barge. You'll be in Bathampton in less than an hour, where a classic pub awaits with a nice lunch or room-temp beer.

Boating—The Bath Boating Station, in an old Victorian boathouse, rents boats and punts (£5 per person/first hr, then £1.50/additional hr, April–Sept daily 10:00–18:00, Forester Road, 1 mile northeast of center, tel. 01225/466-407).

Swimming—The Bath Sports and Leisure Centre has a fine pool for laps as well as lots of water slides and entertaining gadgets for kids (£3, daily 8:00–22:00 but kids' hours are limited, call for open swim times, just across North Parade Bridge, tel. 01225/462-565).

Shopping—There's great browsing between the abbey and the Assembly Rooms (Costume Museum). Shops close at 17:30, some have longer hours on Thursday, and many are open on Sunday (11:00–17:00). Explore the antique shops lining Bartlett Street just below the Assembly Rooms.

NIGHTLIFE

Events are listed in *This Month in Bath* (free, available at TI) and "What's On," appearing Fridays in the local newspaper, the *Bath Chronicle* (www.thisisbath.com).

▲▲▲Bizarre Bath Street Theater—For an immensely entertaining walking-tour comedy act "with absolutely no history or culture," follow J. J. or Noel Britten on their creative and entertaining Bizarre Bath walk. This 90-minute "tour," which plays off local passersby as well as tour members, is a belly laugh a minute (£5, April–Sept nightly at 20:00, smaller groups Mon–Thu, heavy on magic, careful to insult all minorities and sensitivities, just racy enough but still good family fun, leave from Huntsman pub near the abbey, confirm at TI or call 01225/335-124, www.bizarrebath.co.uk).

▲Plays—The 18th-century Theatre Royal, newly restored and one of England's loveliest, offers a busy schedule of London West End-type plays, including many "pre-London" dress-rehearsal runs (£11–25, generally start at 19:30 or 20:00, tel. 01225/448-844, box office open Mon–Sat 10:00–8:00, www.theatreroyal.org.uk). Forty nosebleed spots on a bench (misnamed "standby seats") go on sale at noon on the day of each performance (£5, pay cash at box office or call and book with credit card, 2 tickets maximum). Or, you can snatch up any unsold seat in the house for £10 a half hour before "curtain up."

A handy cheap-sightseers' tip: During the free Bath walking tour, your guide stops here. Pop into the box office, ask what's playing tonight, and see if there are many seats left. If the play sounds good and if plenty of seats remain unsold, you're fairly safe to come back 30 minutes before curtain time to buy a ticket at that £10 price. Oh...and if you smell jasmine, it's the ghost of Lady Grey, a mistress of Beau Nash.

Evening Walks—Take your choice: comedy (Bizarre Bath, described above), history, or ghost. The free city walks (such a standard every day and described above) are now offered summer evenings (May–Sept 19:00 on Tue, Fri, and Sat, 2 hrs, leave from Pump Room). Ghost Walks are a popular way to pass the after-dark hours (£5, 20:00, 2 hrs, unreliably Mon–Sat April–Oct; in winter Fri only; leave from Garrick's Head pub near Theatre Royal, tel. 01225/463-618, www.ghostwalksofbath.co.uk). York and Edinburgh—which have houses thought to be actually haunted—are better for these walks.

Summer Nights at the Baths—In July and August, you can stretch your sightseeing day at the Roman Baths, open nightly until 22:00 (last admission 21:00), when they're far less crowded and more atmospheric, with their gas lamps flaming.

Pubs—Pubs aren't what they used to be in Bath. Most pubs in the center are very noisy, catering to a rowdy twenty-something crowd. But on the top end of town you can still find some classic, old places with inviting ambience and live music.

The Bell has a jazzy, pierced-and-tattooed, and bohemian feel, but with a mellow older crowd. They serve pizza in the garden out back (live music Mon and Wed evenings and Sun lunch, 103 Walcot Street, tel. 01225/460-426).

The Farmhouse fills its spacious and laid-back interior with live jazz, nightly from 21:00 (open mic on Tue, top of Landsdown Road, tel. 01225/316-162).

The **Star Pub** is less inviting and more cramped, but it's much appreciated by local beer lovers for its fine ale and "no machines or music to distract from the chat." It's called a "spit 'n' sawdust" place. And its long bench, nicknamed "death row," still comes with a complimentary pinch of snuff from tins on the ledge (top of Paragon Street, tel. 01225/425-072).

The **Old Green Tree Pub** is a rare, quiet traditional pub right in the town center (locally brewed real ales, non-smoking room, no children, Green Street, tel. 01225/448-259; also recommended under "Eating," page 702, for lunch).

SLEEPING

Bath is a busy tourist town. To get a good B&B, make a telephone reservation in advance. Competition is stiff, and it's worth asking any of these places for a weekday, three-nights-in-a-row, or off-season deal. Friday and Saturday nights are tightest, especially if you're staying only one night, since B&Bs favor those staying longer. If staying only Saturday night, you're very bad news to a B&B hostess. At B&Bs (and cheaper hotels), expect lots of stairs and no lifts.

B&Bs near the Royal Crescent

These listings are all a 15-minute uphill walk or an easy £3.50 taxi ride from the train station. Or take any hop-on, hop-off bus tour from the station, and get off at the stop nearest your B&B (for Brock's, Assembly Rooms, and Marlborough Lane listings hop off at Royal Avenue; confirm with driver), check in, then finish the tour later in the day. All of these B&Bs are non-smoking. Marlborough Lane places have easier parking, but are less centrally located.

$$$ The Town House, overlooking the Assembly Rooms, is genteel and homey, with three fresh, mod rooms that have a hardwood stylishness. In true B&B style, you'll enjoy breakfast at a big family table with the other guests (Db-£80, Fri and Sat Db-£90, 2-night minimum, 7 Bennett Street, tel. & fax 01225/422-505, www.thetownhousebath.co.uk, stay@thetownhousebath.co.uk, Alan and Brenda Willey).

$$$ Elgin Villa rents five comfy, well-maintained rooms (Ss-£35, Sb-£50, Ds-£50, Db-£80, Tb-£92, Qb-£112, more expensive for 1 night, discounted for 3 nights, continental breakfast served in room, 6 Marlborough Lane, tel. & fax 01225/424-557,

Sleep Code

(£1 = about $1.80, country code: 44, area code: 01225)
S = Single, **D** = Double/Twin, **T** = Triple, **Q** = Quad, **b** = bathroom, **s** = shower only, **no CC** = Credit Cards not accepted. Unless otherwise indicated, you can assume credit cards are accepted.

To help you sort easily through these listings, I've divided the rooms into three categories based on the price for a standard double room with bath:

$$$ Higher Priced—Most rooms £80 or more.
$$ Moderately Priced—Most rooms between £50–80.
$ Lower Priced—Most rooms £50 or less.

www.elginvilla.co.uk, stay@elginvilla.co.uk, Anna Rutherford).

$$ Brock's Guest House puts the bubbles in your Bath experience. Marion Dodd has redone her Georgian town house (built by John Wood in 1765) in a way that would make the great architect proud. It's located between the prestigious Royal Crescent and the courtly Circus (6 rooms, Db-£70–80, deluxe Db-£90, Tb-£95, reserve with credit card far in advance, little library on top floor, 32 Brock Street, tel. 01225/338-374, fax 01225/334-245, www.brocksguesthouse.co.uk, marion@brocksguesthouse.co.uk).

$$ Parkside Guest House has five thoughtfully appointed Edwardian rooms and a spacious back garden (Db-£68, 11 Marlborough Lane, tel. & fax 01225/429-444, www.parksidebandb.co.uk, post@parksidebandb.co.uk, Erica and Inge Lynall).

$ Woodville House, warmly run by Anne Toalster, is a grandmotherly little house with three tidy, charming rooms sharing two WCs and a TV lounge. Breakfast is served at a big, family-style table (D-£40, 2-night minimum, no CC, some parking, below the Royal Crescent at 4 Marlborough Lane, tel. 01225/319-335, matoalster@freenet.co.uk).

$ Prior House B&B, with four well-kept rooms, is run by hardworking Lynn Shearn (D-£50, Db-£55, 3 Marlborough Lane, tel. 01225/313-587, fax 01225/443-543, www.greatplaces.co.uk/priorhouse, priorhouse@greatplaces.co.uk).

B&Bs East of the River

These smoke-free listings are a 10-minute walk from the city center and generally a better value (but are less conveniently located).

$$$ The Ayrlington, next door to a lawn-bowling green, has attractive rooms with Asian decor and hints of a more genteel time. Though this well-maintained hotel fronts a busy street, it's

Bath Hotels

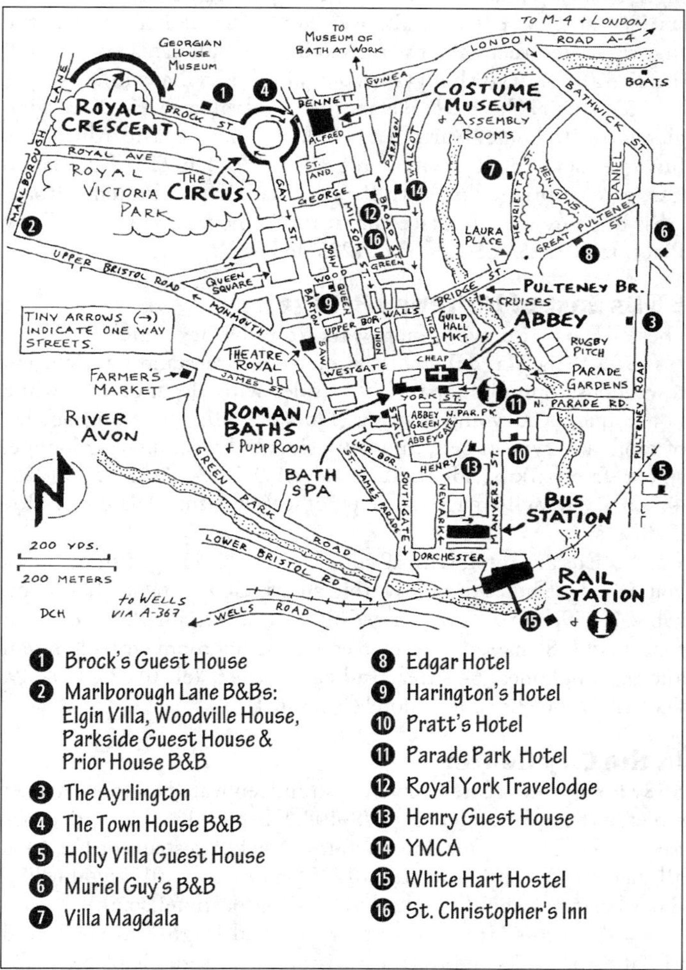

quiet and tranquil. Rooms in the back have pleasant views of sports greens and Bath beyond. For the best value, request a standard double with a view of Bath (huge price range due to varying sizes of rooms and policy of charging 30 percent more on Fri, Sat, and Sun, Db-£80–180—see Web site for specifics; fine garden, easy parking, 24-25 Pulteney Road, tel. 01225/425-495, fax 01225/469-029, www.ayrlington.com, mail@ayrlington.com).

$$ Holly Villa Guest House, with a cheery garden, six bright rooms, and a cozy TV lounge, is enthusiastically and thoughtfully run by Jill and Keith McGarrigle (Ds-£50, small Db-£55, big Db–£65, Tb-£75–85, no CC, easy parking; 8-min walk from station and city center—walk over North Parade Bridge, take the first right, and then take the second left; 14 Pulteney Gardens, tel. 01225/310-331, www.hollyvilla.com, jill@hollyvilla.com).

$$ Muriel Guy's B&B is another good value, mixing Georgian glamour with homey warmth and modern, artistic taste. Muriel is a fun and endearing live wire (5 rooms, S-£30, Db-£55, Tb-£65, no CC; go over bridge on North Parade Road, left on Pulteney Road, cross to church, Raby Place is first row of houses on hill; 14 Raby Place, tel. 01225/465-120, fax 01225/465-283).

B&Bs East of Pulteney Bridge

These B&Bs are a five-minute walk from the city center.

$$$ Villa Magdala rents 18 rooms in a freestanding Victorian town house opposite a park. It sparkles with elegance and, while hotelesque, is cozy and inviting (Db-£85–140, depending on size of room and type of bed; in quiet residential area, inviting lounge, smoke-free, parking, Henrietta Road, tel. 01225/466-329, fax 01225/483-207, www.villamagdala.co.uk, office@villamagdala.co.uk, Roy and Lois).

$$ Edgar Hotel, with 18 simple rooms and lots of stairs, gives you a budget-hotel option in this smart Georgian neighborhood (Sb-£40–50, Db-£60–85, Tb-£100, Qb-£110, smaller rooms on top, avoid #18 on ground level, pleasant sitting room with old organ and gramophones, 64 Great Pulteney Street, tel. 01225/420-619, fax 01225/466-916, edgar-hotel@pgen.net).

In the City Center

$$$ Harington's Hotel rents 13 fresh and renovated rooms on a quiet street in the town center (Sb-£78–108, Db-£98–138, high prices are for Fri–Sat; smoke-free, lots of stairs, attached restaurant-bar open all day, 10 Queen Street, tel. 01225/461-728, fax 01225/444-804, www.haringtonshotel.co.uk, post@haringtonshotel.co.uk).

$$$ Pratt's Hotel is as proper and old English as you'll find in Bath. Its creaks and frays are aristocratic. Its public places make you want to sip a brandy, and its 46 rooms are bright and spacious (Sb-£90, Db-£130, advance reservations get highest rate, drop-ins after 16:00 often snare Db for £75, dogs-£7.50 but children free, attached restaurant-bar, elevator, 4 blocks from station on South Parade, tel. 01225/460-441, fax 01225/448-807, www.forestdale.com, pratts@forestdale.com).

$$ Parade Park Hotel rents 35 modern, basic rooms in a very central location (S-£38, D-£55, small Db-£65, large Db–£85, Tb-£90, Qb-£120, smoke-free, lots of stairs, lively bar downstairs and noisy seagulls, 10 North Parade, tel. 01225/463-384, fax 01225/442-322, www.paradepark.co.uk, info@paradepark.co.uk).

$$ Royal York Travelodge—which offers 66 American-style, characterless yet comfortable rooms—worries B&Bs with its reasonable prices (Db-£60, £70 on Fri–Sun, Tb-same prices, up to 2 kids sleep free, breakfast extra, non-smoking rooms available, 1 York Building, George Street, tel. 01225/448-999, central reservation tel. 08700-850-950, www.travelodge.co.uk). This is especially economic for families of four (who enjoy the Db price).

$$ Henry Guest House is a plain, clean, vertical, eight-room place. It's two blocks in front of the train station on a quiet side street, run by a couple who genuinely cares about your travel experience (S-£30, D-£60, T-£75, family deals, no CC, lots of narrow stairs, 3 showers and 2 WCs for everybody, 6 Henry Street, tel. 01225/424-052, fax 01225/316-669, www.thehenry.com, enquiries@thehenry.com, helpful Sue and Derek).

Dorms

$ The **YMCA,** central on a leafy square, has 200 beds in industrial-strength rooms (S-£22, twin-£34, beds in big dorms-£11–13, £2 more per person on Fri and Sat, includes continental breakfast, cheap lunches, lockers, Internet access, dorms closed 10:00–16:00, down a tiny alley off Broad Street on Broad Street Place, tel. 01225/460-471, fax 01225/462-065, www.bathymca.co.uk, reservation@bathymca.co.uk).

$ White Hart Hostel is a simple place offering adults and families good, cheap beds in two- to six-bed dorms (£12.50/bed, Db-£50, family rooms, no breakfast, smoke-free, kitchen, 5-min walk behind train station at Widcombe—where Widcombe Hill hits Claverton Street, tel. 01225/313-985, www.whitehartbath.co.uk, run by Jo).

$ St. Christopher's Inn, in a prime, central location, is part of a chain of low-priced, high-energy hubs for backpackers looking for beds and brews (60 beds in 4- to 12-bed rooms-£15–19, deals sometimes available online; lively and affordable restaurant and bar downstairs, Internet access, laundry, lounge with video, 9 Green Street, tel. 01225/481-444, www.st-christophers.co.uk). Their beds are so cheap because they know you'll spend money on their beer.

EATING

Bath is bursting with quaint and stylish eateries. There's something for every appetite and budget—just stroll around the center of town. A picnic dinner of deli food or take-out fish-and-chips in the Royal Crescent Park is ideal for aristocratic hoboes. Reserve a table on Friday and Saturday evenings. Save money by eating before 19:00.

Between the Abbey and the Station

Three fine and popular places share North Parade Passage, a block south of the abbey:

Tilley's Bistro, popular with locals, serves healthy French, English, and vegetarian meals with candlelit ambience. Their fun menu lets you build your meal, choosing from an interesting array of £7 starters (Mon–Sat 12:00–14:30 & 18:30–23:00, closed Sun, reservations smart, non-smoking, North Parade Passage, tel. 01225/484-200).

Sally Lunn's House is a cutesy, quasi-historic place for traditional English meals, tea, pink pillows, and lots of lace (£15–20, nightly, smoke-free, 4 North Parade Passage, tel. 01225/461-634). Their forte is a variety of cream teas and buns (£7, until 18:00). Lunch customers get a free peek at the basement Kitchen Museum (otherwise 30p).

Crystal Palace Pub, with typical pub grub under rustic timbers or in the sunny courtyard, is a handy standby (meals-£7, meals Mon–Sat 11:00–20:00, Sun 12:00–16:00, smoke-free, children welcome on patio until 16:30 but not indoors, 11 Abbey Green, tel. 01225/482-666).

Between the Abbey and the Circus

George Street is lined with cheery eateries: Thai, Italian, wine bars, and so on.

Loch Fyne Restaurant, a Scottish fish place with a bright, airy, and youthful atmosphere, fills a former bank. The fish is fresh, prices are reasonable (£10–14), the energy is high, and it doesn't feel like a chain (24 Milsom Street, tel. 01225/750-120).

Martini Restaurant, a hopping, purely Italian place, has class and jovial waiters (entrées-£12, pizzas-£7, plenty of veggie options, daily fish specials, extensive wine list, daily 12:00–14:30 & 18:00–22:30, reservations smart, smoke-free section, 9 George Street, tel. 01225/460-818, Nunzio, Franco, and Luigi).

The Eastern Eye is unique, serving decent Indian cuisine in an exquisite Georgian room under a triple-domed ceiling. The architecture almost overwhelms the food—and that's not a bad thing (daily 12:00–14:30 & 18:00–23:00, 8 Quiet Street, tel. 01225/422-323).

Old Green Tree Pub, in the old town center, serves good lunches in a characteristic pub setting (real ales on tap, non-smoking room, lunch only 12:00–14:45, no children, Green Street, tel. 01225/448-259). As Bath is not a good pub-grub town, this is likely the best you'll do in the center.

Two big, noisy chain restaurants offer decent, inexpensive food to a loyal local following: **Browns** fills an old police station just across from the Abbey, serving English food throughout

Bath Restaurants

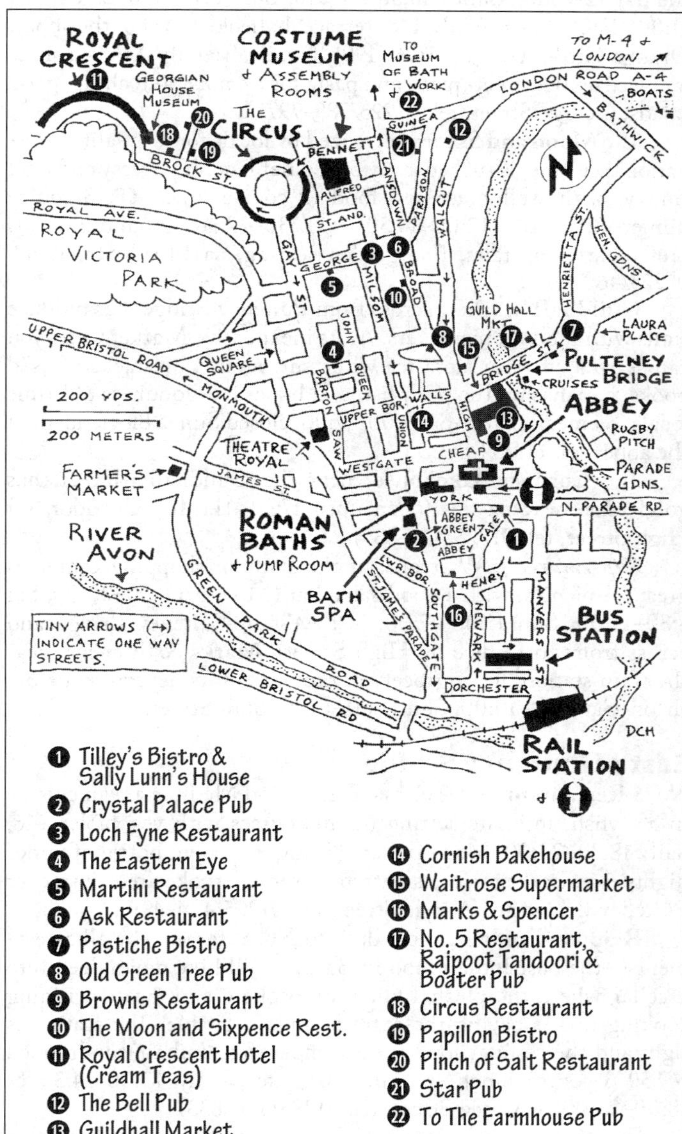

the day (2-courses until 18:30 for £10, Sun–Fri 12:00–23:00, Sat 11:00–23:00, kid-friendly, nice terrace, half-block east of the abbey, Orange Grove, tel. 01225/461-199). Family-friendly **Ask** is a similar place up the street (pizza and pasta for £7, noisy and cheap, good salads, George Street, tel. 01225/789-997).

The Moon and Sixpence, prized by locals for its quality international cuisine, is tucked away on a quiet lane. It's dressy and a bit smoky, with well presented food (2-course lunch-£8, 3-course dinner-£25, daily 12:00–14:30 & 17:30–22:30, ground floor is preferable to upstairs, fine garden seating, 6a Broad Street, tel. 01225/460-962).

Guildhall Market, across from Pulteney Bridge, has produce stalls with food for picnickers. At its inexpensive Market Café, you can slurp a curry or sip a tea while surrounded by stacks of used books, bananas on the push list, and honest-to-goodness old-time locals (£4 meals, Mon–Sat 9:00–17:00, closed Sun, a block north of the abbey, on High Street).

The **Cornish Bakehouse,** near the Guildhall Market, has good take-away pasties (open until 17:30, 11a The Corridor, off High Street, tel. 01225/426-635).

Supermarkets: **Waitrose,** at the Podium shopping center, is great for picnics, with a good salad bar (Mon–Fri 8:30–20:00, Sat 8:30–19:00, Sun 11:00–17:00, just west of Pulteney Bridge and across from post office on High Street). **Marks & Spencer,** near the train station, has a grocery at the back of its department store (Mon–Sat 9:00–10:00, Sun 11:00–17:00, Stall Street).

East of Pulteney Bridge

No. 5 Restaurant serves classic French and Mediterranean cuisine in a stylish, intimate setting (main courses with vegetables-£16, daily 18:30–22:00, Mon–Tue are "bring your own bottle of wine" nights—no corkage fee, smart to reserve, smoke-free, just over Pulteney Bridge at 5 Argyle Street, tel. 01225/444-499).

Rajpoot Tandoori, next door to No. 5, serves—by all assessments—the best Indian food in Bath. You'll hike down deep into a cellar where the plush Indian atmosphere and award-winning cooking makes paying the extra pounds palatable. The seating is tight and the ceilings low, but it's smoke-free and air-conditioned (£7.50 3-course lunch special, £10 plates, daily 12:00–14:30 & 18:00–23:00, 4 Argyle Street, tel. 01225/466-833).

The Boater Pub offers a £5 lunch in its pleasant beer garden overlooking the river. It's popular with rowdy twentysomethings for its good ales and riverside perch (lunch only, otherwise snacks, Mon–Sat 11:00–23:00, Sun 12:00–20:30, 9 Argyle Street, tel. 01225/464-211).

The feisty **Pastiche Bistro** offers inexpensive English food (2-course lunch-£5, 2-course dinner-£10, just east of Pulteney Bridge at 16 Argyle Street, tel. 01225/442-323).

Between the Circus and Royal Crescent

Circus Restaurant, a good value, gives modern English cuisine a Mediterranean twist. You'll get meat, fish, or veggies with an intimate, candlelit, Mozartean ambience. The three-course dinner special for £20 includes tasty vegetables and a selection of fine desserts (Wed–Sun 12:00–14:00 & 18:30–22:00, closed Tue lunch and all day Mon, reservations smart, 34 Brock Street, tel. 01225/318-918, Natasha serves while Adrian cooks).

Papillon Bistro is small, fun, and unpretentious, dishing up "modern-rustic cuisine from the south of France." It has cozy indoor and outdoor seating on a fine pedestrian lane (2-course meal-£8.50 from 12:00–18:30, 2-course dinners-£15–20, closed Sun–Mon, smart to reserve, 2 Margaret's Buildings, tel. 01225/310-064).

Pinch of Salt is a splurge, offering "world cuisine" in an uppity space—tight and trendy with mod decor—just off Brock Street (main courses-£14–17, closed Sun, 11 Margaret's Buildings, tel. 01225/421-251).

TRANSPORTATION CONNECTIONS

Bath's train station is called Bath Spa (train info: tel. 08457-484-950). The National Express bus office (Mon–Sat 8:00–17:30, closed Sun, bus info: tel. 08705-808-080) is one block in front of the train station.

From London to Bath: To get from London to Bath and see Stonehenge to boot, consider an all-day organized **bus tour** from London (and skip out of the return trip; see page 679 in the London chapter).

From Bath to London: You can catch a **train** to London's Paddington Station (2/hr, 90 min, £33–39 one-way after 9:30), or save money—but not time—by taking the National Express **bus** to Victoria Station (nearly hourly, a little over 3 hrs, one-way-£13, round trip-£21, www.nationalexpress.com).

From Heathrow to Bath: See page 676.

From Bath to London's airports: You can reach **Heathrow** by a train-and-bus combination (take train to Reading—runs hourly, catch airport shuttle bus from there—runs twice hourly, allow 2.5 hrs, £33, cheaper for BritRail passholders) or by National Express bus (11/day, 2.5 hrs, £14, tel. 08705-757-747). You can get to **Gatwick** by bus (nearly twice hourly, 4.5 hrs, £20) or by train (hrly, 3 hrs, transfer in Reading or Clapham Junction).

YORK

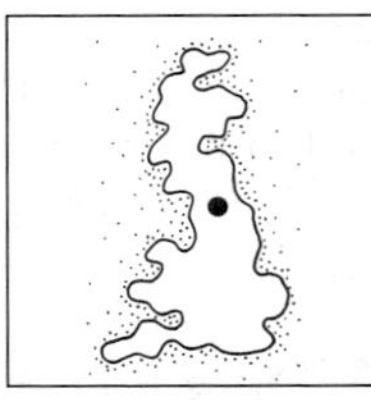

Historic York is loaded with world-class sights. Marvel at the York Minster, England's finest Gothic church. Ramble the Shambles, York's wonderfully preserved medieval quarter. Enjoy a walking tour led by an old Yorker. Hop a train at Europe's greatest railway museum, travel to the 1800s in the York Castle Museum, and head back a thousand years to Viking York at the Jorvik exhibit.

York has a rich history. In A.D. 71, it was Eboracum, a Roman provincial capital—the northernmost city in the Empire. Constantine was actually proclaimed emperor here in A.D. 306. In the 5th century, as Rome was toppling, a Roman emperor sent a letter telling England it was on its own, and York became Eoforwic, the capital of the Anglo-Saxon kingdom of Northumbria. A church was built here in 627, and the town became an early Christian center of learning. The Vikings later took the town, and from the 9th through the 11th centuries, it was a Danish trading center called Jorvik. The invading and conquering Normans destroyed then rebuilt the city, fortifying it with a castle and the walls you see today. Medieval York, with 9,000 inhabitants, grew rich on the wool trade and became England's second city. Henry VIII used the city's fine Minster as his Anglican Church's northern capital. The Archbishop of York is second only to the Archbishop of Canterbury in the Anglican Church. In the Industrial Age, York was the railway hub of North England. When it was built, York's train station was the world's largest. Today York's leading industry is tourism.

Planning Your Time

York rivals Edinburgh as the best sightseeing city in Britain after London. It deserves two nights and a day. For the best 36 hours, follow this plan: Catch the 18:45 city walking tour on the evening of your arrival (evening tours offered mid-June through Aug). The next morning, be at the Castle Museum at 9:30 when it opens—it's worth a good two hours. Then browse and sightsee through the day. Train buffs love the National Railway Museum, and scholars give the Yorkshire Museum high ratings. Tour the Minster at 16:00 before catching the 17:00 evensong service (16:00 on Sun). Finish your day with an early evening stroll along the wall and perhaps through the abbey gardens. This schedule assumes you're there in the summer (evening orientation walk) and that there's an evensong on. Confirm your plans with the TI.

ORIENTATION

(area code: 01904)

The sightseer's York is small. Virtually everything is within a few minutes' walk: sights, train station, TI, and B&Bs. The longest walk a visitor might take (from a B&B across the old town to the Castle Museum) is 15 minutes.

Bootham Bar, a gate in the medieval town wall, is the hub of your York visit. (In York, a "bar" is a gate and a "gate" is a street. Go ahead, blame the Vikings.) At Bootham Bar and on Exhibition Square facing it, you'll find the TI; the starting points for most walking tours and bus tours; handy access to the medieval town wall; and Bootham Street, which leads to the recommended B&Bs. When finding your way, navigate by sighting the tower of the Minster or the strategically placed green signposts pointing out all places of interest to tourists.

Tourist Information

The TI at Bootham Bar sells a £1 *York Map and Guide*. Ask for the free monthly *What's On* guide and the *York MiniGuide,* which includes a map and some discounts (April–Oct Mon–Sat 9:00–18:00, Sun 10:00–17:00, likely 10:00–16:00 off-season, WCs next door, tel. 01904/621-756). The TI books rooms for a £4 fee (and takes 10 percent from your host). The train-station TI is smaller but provides all the same information and services (same hours as main TI).

York Day Pass: The TI sells a pass that covers most York sights (but not Jorvik or the Castle Museum), major sights in the region, and the city hop-on, hop-off bus tour. If you take the bus tour and are a busy sightseer, it can save money (£17/1 day, £25/2 days, £32/3 days).

Arrival in York

The train station, which stores luggage for day-trippers (£4, Mon–Sat 8:00–20:30, Sun 9:00–20:30, platform 1), is a five-minute **walk** from town. From the station, turn left down Station Road and follow the crowd toward the Gothic towers of the Minster. After the bridge, a block before the Minster, signs to the TI send you left on St. Leonard's Place. Recommended B&Bs are a five-minute walk from there. (For a shortcut to B&B area from the train station, walk 1 block toward the Minster, cut through parks to riverside, cross railway bridge/pedestrian walkway, cross parking lot for B&Bs on St. Mary's Street, or duck through pedestrian walkway under tracks to B&Bs on Sycamore and Queen Anne's Road.)

Taxis zip new arrivals to their B&B for £3. (To summon one, call tel. 01904/623-332 or tel. 01904/638-833; they don't start the meter until you get in.)

Helpful Hints

Study Ahead: York has a great Web site: www.visityork.org.

Festivals: The Viking Festival features *lur* horn-blowing, warrior drills, and re-created battles (late Feb). The Late Music Festival is in March...if it starts on time. The Early Music Festival (medieval minstrels, Renaissance dance, and so on) zings its strings in mid-July (www.ncem.co.uk/yemf.shtml). And the York Festival of Food and Drink takes a bite out of the middle of September (www.yorkfestivaloffoodanddrink.com). Book a room well in advance during festival times and weekends any time of year.

Internet Access: Get online at the creaky, hip, and funky Evil Eye Café (daily 10:00–23:00, 10 terminals, 42 Stonegate) or Gateway Internet Exchange (Mon–Wed 10:00–20:00, Thu–Sat 10:00–23:00, Sun 12:00–16:00, 26 Swinegate, tel. 01904/646-446).

Laundry: Near the Bootham B&Bs, Regency Dry Cleaning is expensive (£4/kilogram—about 2 lbs, Mon–Fri 8:30–18:00, Sat 9:00–17:00, closed Sun, drop off by 9:30 for same-day service, 75 Bootham, at intersection with Queen Anne's Road, tel. 01904/613-311). The next-nearest place is Washeteria Launderette, a long 15-minute walk away (self-service or drop-off, 124 Haxby Road, tel. 01904/623-379).

Bike Rental: Trotters, just outside Monk Bar, rents bikes and has free cycling maps (£10/day, tandem-£30/day, helmets-£2, Mon–Sat 9:00–17:30, Sun 10:00–16:00, tel. 01904/622-868). Europcar at the train station also rents bikes (£10/day, platform 1, tel. 01904/656-181). The riverside path is pleasant.

Car Rental: In York, you'll find: Avis (Mon–Sat, closed Sat afternoon and Sun, 3 Layerthorpe, tel. 01904/610-460); Hertz (April–Sept daily, Sat–Sun until 13:00, at train station, tel. 01904/612-586); Sixt (Mon–Sat, closed Sun, inconveniently 3 miles out of town at Clifton Moor Industrial Estate, tel. 01904/479-715); Budget (daily, Sat and Sun only 9:00–11:00, a mile past recommended B&Bs at Clifton 82, tel. 01904/644-919); and Europcar (Mon–Fri 8:00–18:00, Sat–Sun until 13:00, train station platform 1, tel. 01904/656-181). Beware, car-rental agencies close Saturday afternoon and some close all day Sunday—when drop-offs are OK, but picking up is impossible.

TOURS

▲▲▲Walking Tours—Charming local volunteer guides give energetic, entertaining, and free two-hour walks through York (daily at 10:15 all year, plus 14:15 April–Oct, plus 18:45 mid-June–Aug, from Exhibition Square across from TI). These tours often go long because the guides love to teach and tell stories. You're welcome to cut out early—but say so or they'll worry, thinking they lost you.

There are many other commercial York walking tours. YorkWalk Tours, for example, has reliable guides and many themes from which to choose, such as Roman York, City Walls, or Snickelways—small alleys (£5, tel. 01904/622-303, www.yorkwalk.co.uk, TI has schedule). The ghost tours, all offered after nightfall, are more fun than informative. Haunted Walk relies a bit more on storytelling and history than on masks and surprises (£3, April–Nov nightly at 20:00, 90 min, just show up, depart from Exhibition Square, across street from TI, end in the Shambles, tel. 01904/621-003).

▲Hop-on, Hop-off Bus Tours—With one £8 ticket, you can jump on or off your choice of the two tours circling York. The tours generally follow the same route. The main difference is that the Guide Friday York Tour is longer and has live guides (green bus, 60-min loop, with a few extra stops, including York Racecourse and Rowntree Park), and the City Sightseeing tour has recorded narration (red bus, 45 min). Both tours cover secondary York sights that the city walking tours skip—the mundane perimeter of town (pay driver cash, can also buy from TI with credit card, departures every 10 min or more from 9:00 until around 17:00, less frequent off-season, Guide Friday tours don't run Nov–March, tel. 01904/655-585). While you can hop on and off all day, the tours are of no real value from a transportation-to-the-sights point of view because York is so compact. I'd catch either tour at the Bootham Bar TI and ride it for an orientation all the way around or get off at the Railway Museum, skipping the last five minutes.

Boat Cruise—The York Boat does a lazy 60-minute lap along the River Ouse (£6.50, Feb–Nov daily from 10:30 on, 4/day in summer, narrated cruise, leaves from Lendal Bridge and King's Staith landing) and also offers themed evening cruises—ghost, dinner, floodlit, and so on (boat rentals possible, tel. 01904/628-324).

SIGHTS

York Minster

The pride of York, and worth ▲▲▲, this largest Gothic church north of the Alps (540 feet long, 200 feet tall) brilliantly shows that the High Middle Ages were far from dark. The word "minster" means a place from which people go out to minister or spread the word of God. As it's the seat of a bishop, it's also a cathedral. While Henry VIII destroyed the great abbeys, this was not part of a monastery and therefore left standing. It seats 2,000 comfortably; on Christmas and Easter, over 4,000 worshipers pack the place. Today, over 250 employees and 300 volunteers work to preserve its heritage and welcome the half-million visitors each year.

Cost, Hours, Tours: The cathedral opens daily for worship at 7:00 and for sightseeing Mon–Sat from 9:00 and Sunday from 12:30, when they begin charging £4.50 admission. The closing time flexes with the season (roughly May–Oct at 18:30, earlier off-season—call for details, tel. 01904/557-216). The tower (£2.50) and undercroft (£3, or £6.50 combo-ticket includes undercroft and cathedral entry) have shorter hours, typically opening a half-hour later and closing a half-hour earlier than the Minster.

When you enter, go directly to the welcome desk, pick up the worthwhile "Welcome to the York Minster" flier, and ask when the next free guided 60-minute **tour** departs (2/hr, 9:30–14:00, they go even with just 1 or 2 people; you can join one in progress, or if none is scheduled, request a departure). The helpful Minster guides, wearing blue armbands, are happy to answer your questions.

Evensong and Church Bells: To experience the cathedral in musical and spiritual action, attend an evensong (Mon–Sat 17:00, Sun 16:00, 45 min). When the choir is off on school break (mid-July–Aug), visiting choirs usually fill in (confirm at church or TI). Arrive 10 minutes early and wait just outside the choir in the center of the church. You'll be ushered in and can sit in one of the big wooden stalls. If you're a fan of church bells, you'll experience ding-dong ecstasy on Sunday morning (around 10:00) and the Tuesday-evening practice (19:30–21:30). Stand in front of the church's west portal and imagine the gang pulling on a dozen ropes (halfway up the right tower—you can actually see the ropes through a little window).

Self-Guided Tour: Upon entering, head left, to the back (west end) of the church. Stand in front of the grand **west door** (used only on Sundays) on the "Deo Gratias 627–1927" plaque—a place of worship for 1,300 years, thanks to God. On the door, the list of bishops goes unbroken back to the 600s. The statue of Peter with the key and Bible is a reminder that the church is dedicated to St. Peter, and the key to Heaven is found through the word of God.

York

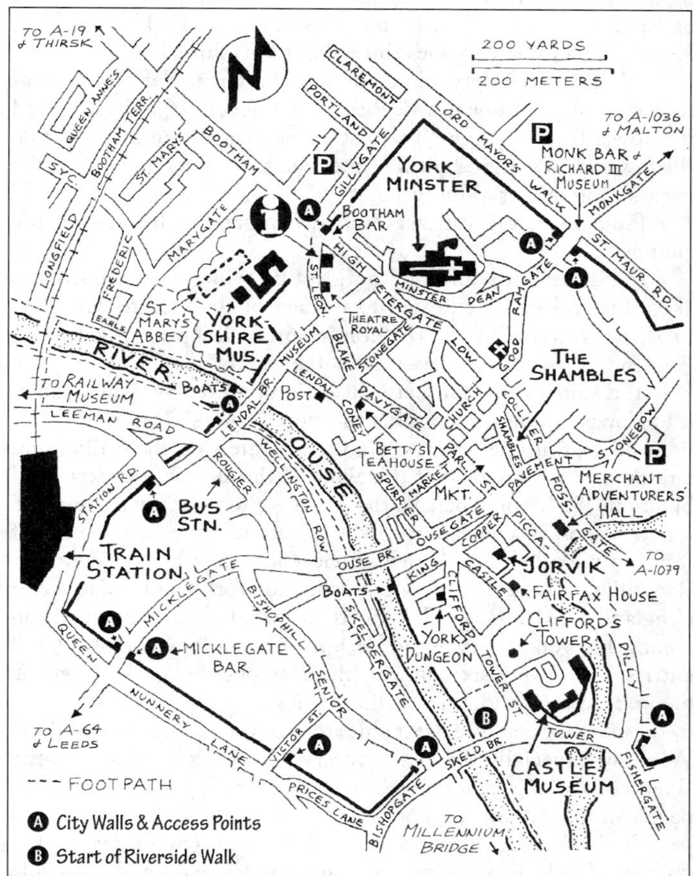

While the Minster sits on the remains of a Romanesque church (c. 1100), today's church was begun in 1220 and took 250 years to complete. King Edward I and II used it as a base, actually holding parliament here in the Chapter House (rather than in London) while fighting Scotland.

Looking down the church, your first impression might be the spaciousness and brightness of the **nave** (built 1280–1350). The nave—from the middle period of Gothic, called "Decorated Gothic"—is one of the widest Gothic naves in Europe. Rather than risk a stone roof, builders spanned the space with wood. Colorful shields on the arcades are the coats of arms of nobles who helped Edward I fight the Scots. The coats of arms in the clerestory (upper-level) glass represent the nobles who helped Edward II in the same fight. There's more medieval glass in this building than in the rest of England combined. This precious glass survived World War II—hidden in stately homes throughout Yorkshire.

Walk to the very center of the church, under the **central tower.** Look up. Look down. Read about how gifts and skill saved this tower from collapse. (The first tower collapsed in 1407.) While the tower is 60 yards tall, it was intended to be much taller. Use the neck-saving mirror to marvel at it.

From here, you can survey many impressive features of the church:

In the **north transept,** the grisaille windows—dubbed the "Five Sisters"—are dedicated to women of the empire who died in all wars. Made in 1250 (before colored glass was produced in England), these contain over 100,000 pieces of glass.

The **south transept** features the tourists' entry, where stairs lead down to the undercroft. The new "bosses" (carved medallions decorating the point where the ribs meet on the ceiling) are a reminder that the roof of this wing of the church was destroyed by fire in 1984. Some believe the fire was God's angry response to a new bishop, David Jenkins, who questioned the literal truth of Jesus' miracles. Others blame an electricity box hit by lightning. Regardless, the entire country came to York's aid. Blue Peter (England's "Mr. Rogers" back then) conducted a competition among his young viewers to design new bosses. Out of 30,000 entries, there were six winners (the blue ones—e.g., man on the moon, feed the children, save the whales).

Look back at the west end to marvel at the **Great West Window,** especially the stone tracery. While its nickname is the "Heart of York," it represents the sacred heart of Christ and reminds people of his love for the world.

Find the **dragon** on the right of the nave (two-thirds of the way up). While no one is sure of its purpose, it pivots and has a hole through its neck—so it was likely a mechanism designed to raise a lid on a baptismal font.

The **choir screen** is an ornate wall of carvings separating the nave from the choir. It's lined with all the English kings from William I (the Conqueror) to Henry VI (during whose reign it was carved, 1461). Numbers indicate the years each reigned. To say "it's slathered in gold leaf" sounds impressive, but the gold's very thin... a nugget the size of a sugar cube is pounded into a sheet the size of driveway.

Step into the **choir,** where Mass is held daily. All the carving was redone after an 1829 fire, but its tradition of glorious evensong services (sung by choristers from the Minster School) goes all the way back to the 8th century.

The astronomical clock in the **north transept** commemorates

York at a Glance

▲▲▲Minster York's pride and joy, and one of England's finest churches, with stunning stained-glass windows, textbook Decorated Gothic design, and moving evensong services. **Hours:** Open for worship daily from 7:00 and for sightseeing Mon–Sat from 9:00, Sun from 12:30; flexible closing time (roughly May–Oct at 18:30, earlier off-season); shorter hours for tower and undercroft; evensong services Mon–Sat 17:00, Sun 16:00, sometimes no services mid-July–Aug.

▲▲▲Castle Museum Excellent, far-ranging collection includes replica of 19th-century street and everyday objects from Victorian times to the present. **Hours:** Daily 9:30–17:00.

▲▲National Railway Museum Train buff's nirvana, tracing the history of all manner of rail-bound transport. **Hours:** Daily 10:00–18:00.

▲▲Yorkshire Museum Sophisticated archaeology museum with York's best Viking exhibit—plus Roman, Saxon, Norman, and Gothic artifacts. **Hours:** Daily 10:00–17:00.

▲The Shambles Atmospheric old butcher's quarter, with colorful, tipsy medieval buildings. **Hours**: Always open.

▲Jorvik Cheesy, crowded, but not-quite-Disney-quality exhibit/ride exploring Viking lifestyles and artifacts. **Hours:** Daily April–Sept 10:00–17:00, Oct–March until 16:00.

▲Fairfax House Glimpse into an 18th-century Georgian house, with enjoyably chatty docents. **Hours:** Mon–Thu and Sat 11:00–17:00, Sun 13:30–17:00, Fri by tour only at 11:00 and 14:00.

the 18,000 airmen who died in World War II flying from bases here in northern England. The Book of Remembrance contains all those names.

A corridor that functions as a small church museum leads to the Gothic, octagonal **chapter room**—the traditional meeting place of the governing body (or chapter) of the Minster. It's remarkable (almost frightening) for its breadth without an interior support. The fanciful carvings decorating the canopies above the stalls date from 1280 (80 percent are originals) and are some of the Minster's finest. Above the doorway, the Virgin holds baby Jesus while standing on the devilish serpent. Grates still send hot air

England's Anglican Church

The Anglican Church came into existence in 1534 when Henry VIII declared that he, and not Pope Clement VII, was the head of England's Catholics. The Pope had refused to allow Henry to divorce his wife to marry his mistress Anne Boleyn (which Henry did anyway, resulting in the birth of the future Elizabeth I). Still, Henry regarded himself as a faithful Catholic—just not a *Roman* Catholic—and made relatively few changes in how and what Anglicans worshipped.

Henry's son Edward VI instituted many of the changes that Reformation Protestants were bringing about in continental Europe (emphasis on preaching, people in the pews actually reading the Bible, clergy being allowed to marry, and a more "Protestant" liturgy in English from the revised Book of Common Prayer, 1549). The next monarch, Edward's sister Mary I, returned England to the Roman Catholic Church (1553), earning the nickname of "Bloody Mary" for her brutal suppression of Protestant elements. When Elizabeth I succeeded Mary (1558), she soon broke from Rome again. Today, many regard the Anglican Church as a compromise between the Catholic and Protestant traditions.

Is York's Minster the leading Anglican church in England? Yes and no (but mostly no). After a long feud, the archbishops of Canterbury and York agreed that York's bishop would have the title "Primate of England" and Canterbury's would be the "Primate of All England," directing Anglicans on the national level.

up robes of attendees on cold winter mornings. A model of the wooden construction illustrates the impressive 1285 engineering.

The **east end** is square, lacking a semi-circular apse, typical of England's Perpendicular Gothic style (15th century). The window, the size of a tennis court, is a carefully designed ensemble of biblical symbolism with God the Father presiding over ranks of saints and angels on the top; nine rows of 117 panels telling Bible stories in the middle; and a row of bishops and kings on the bottom. A chart (on the right, with a tiny, more helpful chart within—locate panels with color-coded numbers) highlights the core Old Testament scenes in this hard-to-read masterpiece. Enjoy the art close up on the chart, then step back and find the real thing. Because of its immense size, there's an extra layer of supportive stonework, making parts of it wide enough to walk along. In fact, for special occasions, the choir sings from the walkway halfway up the window. Monuments (almost no graves) were once strewn throughout the church, but in the Victorian age, they were gathered into the east end, where you see them today.

Tower and Undercroft: There are two extra sights to consider, both accessed from the south transept. You can scale the 275-step **tower** for the panoramic view (£2.50). The **undercroft** consists of the crypt, treasury, and foundations (£3 including audioguide, or £6.50 combo-ticket for Minster and crypt but not tower). The crypt is an actual bit of the Romanesque church, featuring 12th-century Romanesque art, excavated in modern times. The foundations give you a chance to climb down—archaeologically and physically—through the centuries to see the roots of the much smaller, but still huge, Norman church (Romanesque, 1100) that stood on this spot and, below that, the Roman excavations. As you wander, ponder the fact that Constantine was proclaimed Roman emperor here in A.D. 306. Peek also at the modern concrete save-the-church foundations.

Wall Walk from the Minster

After seeing the Minster, consider the following stroll up along a segment of York's wall.

Roman Column—The column that stands just across from the Minster was erected in 1971 to commemorate the 1,900th anniversary of the Roman founding of Eboracum (later called York). Across the street is a statue of the emperor Constantine. Constantine was in York when his father died. The troops declared him emperor, and six years later, he went to Rome and claimed his throne. In 312, Constantine legalized Christianity, and in 314, York got its first bishop. Today's Minster stands upon the remains of a Roman fort.

Study the Minster. You're looking at the glory of Gothic. The main tower was intended to hold a towering spire—too much. Even without all that extra weight, the church stands today only with the help of big, modern braces holding the foundation together.

Hike past the west portal of the Minster and down the street to...

Bootham Bar—This is one of four gates on York's medieval walls (free, open until dusk). The 12th-century walls are three miles long. Norman kings built the walls to assert control over North England. This was a center for Romans, Normans, and Henry VIII (16th century). In the 19th century, York was a center of industry (and hub of the railway system).

Now climb up on...

The Wall—Hike along the top of the wall behind the Minster to the first corner. Notice the pivots in the crenellations (square notches at the top of a medieval wall), which once held wooden hatches that provided cover for archers. At the corner, you can see the moat outside and a fine view of the Minster, with its truncated main tower and the pointy rooftop of its chapter house. The roofing—traditionally lead—melts during a fire and cascades to the ground.

Continue on to the next gate, **Monk Bar.** Keep an eye on the 12th-century guards, with their stones raised and primed to protect the town. Descend the wall at Monk Bar and step past the portcullis and outside the city's protective wall. Lean against the last bollard and gaze up at the tower, imagining 10 archers behind the arrow slits.

Walking back into town from here, you'll find a number of good eateries on Goodramgate (see "Eating," page 725). At the first corner, College Street leads right to the east end of the Minster along St. Williams College (1461) and the home of bishops and priests.

More Sights

▲The Shambles—This is the most colorful old street in the half-timbered, traffic-free core of town. Walk to the midway point, at the intersection with Little Shambles. Ye olde downtown York feels made for window-shopping, street musicians, and people-watching. This 100-yard-long street was once the "street of the butchers" (the name is derived from *shammell*—a butcher's cutting block). In the 16th century, it was busy with red meat. On the hooks under the eaves once hung rabbit, pheasant, beef, lamb, and pigs' heads. Fresh slabs were displayed on the fat sills. People lived above—as they did even in Roman times. The soil here wasn't great for building. Notice how things settled in the absence of a good soil engineer.

Little Shambles leads to the frumpy Newgate Market (popular for cheap produce and clothing), created in the 1960s with the demolition of a bunch of lanes as colorful as the Shambles. Return to the Shambles a little farther along, through a covered lane (or "snickelway"). Study the 16th-century oak carpentry—mortar and tenon joints with wooden plugs rather than nails.

For a cheap lunch, consider the cute, tiny **St. Crux Parish Hall.** This medieval church is now used by a medley of charities selling tea, homemade cakes, and light meals. They each book the church for a day, often a year in advance. Chat up the volunteers (Mon–Sat 10:00–16:00, closed Sun, at bottom end of the Shambles, at intersection with Pavement).

▲▲▲Castle Museum—Truly one of Europe's top museums, this is a Victorian home show, the closest thing to a time-tunnel experience England has to offer. Even a speedy museum-goer will want a couple hours here. It includes the 19th-century Kirkgate (a collection of old shops well stocked exactly as they were 150 years ago), a "From Cradle to Grave" clothing exhibit, and a fine costume collection. The one-way plan assures you'll see everything: a working water mill, prison cells with related exhibits, the domestic side of WWII, Victorian toys, and a century of swimsuit fashions. Bring 20p coins to jolt a mechanical Al Jolson into song. The museum's £3 guidebook isn't necessary, but makes a fine souvenir. The museum proudly offers no audioguides, as its living guides in each room are enthusiastic about talking—engage them (£6, daily 9:30–17:00, gift shop, parking, cafeteria midway through museum, tel. 01904/650-335, www.yorkcastlemuseum.org.uk; at the bottom of the hop-on, hop-off bus route; museum can call you a taxi—worthwhile if hurrying up to the railway museum).

Clifford's Tower, across from the Castle Museum, is all that's left of York's 13th-century castle, the site of a 1190 massacre of local Jews (read about this at base of hill). If you climb inside, there are fine city views from the top of the ramparts (not worth the £2.50, daily April–Sept 10:00–18:00, Oct–March until 16:00).

▲Jorvik—Take the "Pirates of the Caribbean," sail them north and back 1,000 years, and you get Jorvik—more a ride than a museum. Innovative 20 years ago, the commercial success of Jorvik (YOR-vik) inspired copycat ride/museums all over England. You'll ride a little Disney-type train car for 20 minutes through the re-created Viking street of Coppergate. It's the year 975, and you're in the village of Jorvik. Next, your little train takes you through the actual excavation site that inspired the reconstructed village. Everything is true to the dig—even the faces of the models are derived by computer from skulls dug up here. Finally you'll browse through a small gallery of Viking shoes, combs, locks, and other intimate glimpses of that redheaded culture. The exhibit on bone archaeology is fascinating (£7.20, daily April–Sept 10:00–17:00, Oct–March until 16:00, tel. 01904/643-211, www.vikingjorvik.com).

Midday lines can be an hour long in the peak of summer. Avoid the line by going very early or very late in the day, or by pre-booking (call tel. 01904/543-403, you're given a time slot, £1 booking fee). Some love this attraction, while others call it a gimmicky rip-off. If you're looking for a grown-up museum, the Viking exhibit at the Yorkshire Museum is far better. If you're thinking Disneyland with a splash of history, Jorvik's fun. To me, Jorvik is a commercial venture designed for kids, with nearly as much square footage devoted to its shop as to the museum.

▲▲National Railway Museum—If you like model railways, this is train-car heaven. The thunderous museum shows 200 illustrious years of British railroad history. Fanning out from a grand roundhouse is an array of historic cars and engines, including Queen Victoria's lavish royal car and the very first "stagecoaches on rails." A working steam engine is sliced open, showing cylinders, driving wheels, and smoke box in action. There's much more, including exhibits on dining cars, post cars, sleeping cars, train posters, and videos. At the Works section, you can see live train switchboards. And don't miss the English Channel Tunnel video (showing the first handshake at breakthrough). Purple-shirted "explainers" are everywhere, eager to talk trains. This biggest and best railroad museum anywhere is interesting even to people who think "Pullman" means "don't push" (free, £3 audioguide with 60 bits of railroad lore is worthwhile for train buffs, daily 10:00–18:00, snack bar sells Thomas the Tank Engine lunch sacks, tel. 01904/621-261).

A cute little "street train" shuttles you between the Minster and the Railway Museum (£1.50 each way, Easter–Oct, leaves Railway Museum every 30 min from 12:00 to 17:00 at the top and bottom of the hour; leaves the town— from Duncombe Place, 100 yards in front of the Minster—every 30 min, :15 and :45 min after the hour).

▲▲Yorkshire Museum—Located in a lush, picnic-perfect park next to the stately ruins of St. Mary's Abbey, Yorkshire Museum is the city's forgotten, serious "archaeology of York" museum. While the hordes line up at Jorvik, the best Viking artifacts are here—with no crowds and a better historical context. A stroll around this museum takes you through Roman (wonderfully described battle-bashed skull in first case), Saxon (great Anglo-Saxon helmet from A.D. 750), Viking, Norman, and Gothic York. There's an extensive section on abbey life before the dissolution. Its prize piece is the delicately etched 15th-century pendant called the Middleham Jewel—for which the museum raised $4 million to buy. The 20-minute video about the creation of the abbey plays continuously and is worth a look (£4, daily 10:00–17:00, tel. 01904/687-687). Before leaving, enjoy the evocative ruins of the abbey in the park (destroyed by Henry VIII in 16th century).

▲Fairfax House—This well-furnished building is perfectly Georgian inside, with docents happy to talk with you. It's compact and bursting with insights into aristocratic life in 18th-century England. Pianists may be allowed to actually pluck the harpsichord (£4.50, Mon–Thu and Sat 11:00–17:00, Sun 13:30–17:00, Fri by tour only at 11:00 and 14:00—the tours are worthwhile, on Castlegate, near Jorvik, tel. 01904/655-543).

Theatre Royal—A full variety of dramas, comedies, and works by Shakespeare is put on to entertain the locals in either the main theater or the little 100-seat theater-in-the-round (£8–17, almost nightly at 19:30, closed much of Aug, tickets easy to get, on St. Leonard's Place next to TI and a 5-min walk from recommended B&Bs, booking tel. 01904/623-568). Those under 25 get tickets for only £3.50.

Traditional Tea—York is famous for its elegant teahouses. Drop into one around 16:00 for tea and cakes. Ladies love **Betty's Teahouse,** where you pay £6 for a Yorkshire Cream Tea (tea and scones with clotted Yorkshire cream and strawberry jam) or £10 for a full traditional English afternoon tea (tea, delicate sandwiches, scones, and sweets). Your table is so full of doily niceties that the food is served on a little three-tray tower. While you'll pay a little extra here (and the food's nothing special), the ambience and people-watching are hard to beat (daily 9:00–21:00, piano music nightly 18:00–21:00, non-smoking, St. Helen's Square; fine view of street scene from a window seat on the main floor, downstairs near WC is a mirror signed by WWII bomber pilots—read the story). If there's a line, it moves quickly (except at dinner time). Wait for a seat by the windows on the ground level rather than sit in the much bigger basement.

A Riverside Walk—The New Walk is a mile-long, tree-lined, riverside lane created in the 1730s as a promenade for York's dandy class to stroll, see, and be seen. With the creation of York's Millennium Bridge, it's now possible to take this walk, cross over, and return to York passing through Rowntree Park (a great Edwardian park with lawn bowling for the public, plus family fun including a playground and adventure rides for kids). This hour-long walk is a great way to enjoy a dose of countryside from York. It's clearly described in the TI's "New Walk" flier (50p). You start from the riverside under Skeldergate Bridge (near the Castle Museum), walk away from town for a mile until you hit a modern bridge, cross the river, and walk home.

Honorable Mentions

York has a number of other sights and activities (described in TI material) that, while interesting, pale in comparison to the biggies.

Hall of the Merchant Adventurers—Claiming to be the finest medieval guildhall in Europe (from 1361), it's basically a vast half-timbered building with marvelous exposed beams and 15 minutes' worth of interesting displays about life and commerce back in the days when York was England's second city (£2, Mon–Sat 9:00–17:00, Sun 12:00–16:00, shorter hours off-season, below the Shambles off Piccadilly, tel. 01904/654-818).

Richard III Museum—This is interesting only for Richard III enthusiasts (£2, daily March–Aug 9:00–20:00, Sept–Oct 9:30–18:00, Nov–Feb until 16:00, Monk Bar, tel. 01904/634-191).

York Dungeon—It's gimmicky, but if you insist on papier-mâché gore, it's better than the London Dungeon (£8.95, daily 10:00–17:30, less off-season, 12 Clifford Street, tel. 01904/632-599).

Lawn Bowling Green—Visitors are welcome to watch the action—best in the evenings—at the green on Sycamore Place; you can buy a pint of beer (near recommended B&Bs, tell them which B&B you're staying at). Another green is in front of the Coach House Hotel Pub on Marygate.

SHOPPING

With its medieval lanes lined with classy as well as tacky little shops, York is a hit with shoppers. I find the **antique malls** interesting. Three places within a few blocks of each other are filled with stalls and cases owned by antique dealers from the countryside. The malls sell the dealers' bygones on commission. Serious shoppers do better heading for the countryside, but York's shops are a fun browse: The Antiques Centre York (daily 9:00–18:00, 41 Stonegate, tel. 01904/635-888), the antique mall at 2 Lendal (Mon–Sat 10:00–17:00, closed Sun, tel. 01904/641-582), and the Red House Antiques Centre (daily 9:30–17:30, as late as 19:00 in summer, a block from Minster at Duncombe Place, tel. 01904/637-000).

SLEEPING

I've listed peak-season, book-direct prices. Don't use the TI. Outside of July and August, some prices go soft. B&Bs will sometimes turn away one-night bookings, particularly for peak-season Saturdays. (York is worth 2 nights anyway.) Remember to book ahead during festival times (Feb, March, mid-June, mid-July, and mid-Sept—see "Helpful Hints," page 708) and weekends year-round.

B&Bs near Bootham

These recommendations are in the handiest B&B neighborhood, a quiet residential area just outside the old-town wall's Bootham gate, along the road called Bootham. All are within a five-minute walk of the Minster and TI and a 10-minute walk or taxi ride (£3) from the station. If driving, head for the cathedral and follow the medieval wall to the gate called Bootham Bar. The street called Bootham leads away from Bootham Bar.

Sleep Code

(£1 = about $1.80, country code: 44, area code: 01904)
S = Single, **D** = Double/Twin, **T** = Triple, **Q** = Quad, **b** = bathroom, **s** = shower only, **No CC** = Credit Cards not accepted. You can assume credit cards are accepted unless otherwise noted.

To help you sort easily through these listings, I've divided the rooms into three categories based on the price for a standard double room with bath (during high season):

$$$ Higher Priced—Most rooms £90 or more.
$$ Moderately Priced—Most rooms between £60–90.
$ Lower Priced—Most rooms £60 or less.

York Hotels and Restaurants

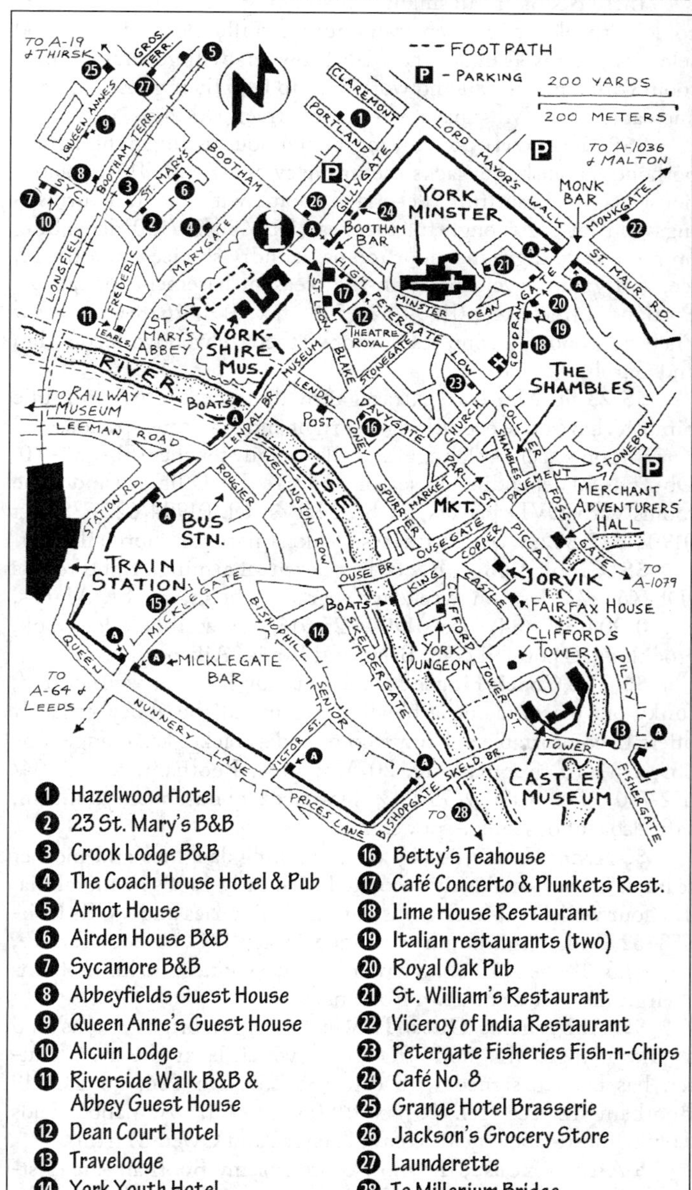

These B&Bs are all small, non-smoking, and family-run. They come with plenty of steep stairs but no traffic noise. For a good selection, call well in advance. B&B owners will generally hold a room with a phone call and work hard to help their guests sightsee and eat smartly. Most have permits for street parking.

$$$ The Hazelwood, my most hotelesque listing in this neighborhood, is plush, but lacks the intimacy of a B&B. This spacious house has 14 beautifully decorated rooms with modern furnishings and lots of thoughtful touches (Db-£80/90/100 depending on room size, 2 ground-floor rooms, laundry service-£5; a fridge, ice, and great travel library in the pleasant basement lounge; 24 Portland Street, tel. 01904/626-548, fax 01904/628-032, www.thehazelwoodyork.com, reservations@thehazelwoodyork.com, Ian and Caroline).

$$ 23 St. Mary's is extravagantly decorated. Chris and Julie Simpson have done everything just right and offer nine spacious and comfy rooms, a classy lounge, and all the doily touches (Sb-£34–40, Db-£64–80 depending on season and size, DVD library and some rooms with DVD players, 23 St. Mary's, tel. 01904/622-738, fax 01904/628-802, www.23stmarys.co.uk, stmarys23@hotmail.com).

$$ Crook Lodge B&B has seven charming, tight rooms (Db-£64–72, less on weekdays, parking, quiet, 26 St. Mary's, tel. 01904/655-614, fax 01904/625-915, www.crooklodge.co.uk, crooklodge@hotmail.com, Brian and Louise Aiken).

$$ The Coach House Hotel is a labyrinthine, well-located, funky old place, facing a bowling green and the abbey walls. It offers 12 comfortable old-time rooms and a crackerjack lounge (Sb-£35, Db-£70, free parking, 20 Marygate, Bootham, tel. 01904/652-780, fax 01904/679-943, www.coachhousehotel-york.com, info@coachhousehotel-york.com).

$$ Arnot House, run by a hardworking daughter-and-mother team, is homey and lushly decorated with early-1900s memorabilia. The four well-furnished rooms have little libraries and VCRs (Db-£58–62, 2-night minimum stay, video library, 17 Grosvenor Terrace, tel. & fax 01904/641-966, www.arnothouseyork.co.uk, kim.robbins@virgin.net, Kim and Ann Robbins).

$$ Abbeyfields Guest House has eight bright rooms and a quiet lounge. This doily-free place, which lacks the usual clutter, has been designed with care (Sb-£39, Db-£66, no CC, 19 Bootham Terrace, tel. & fax 01904/636-471, www.abbeyfields.co.uk, guest@abbeyfields.co.uk, Richard and Gwen Martin).

$ Airden House, the most central of my Bootham-area listings, is clean and simple, with eight spacious rooms and a cozy TV lounge (D-£48, Db-£56, no CC, 1 St. Mary's, tel. 01904/638-915, www.airdenhouse.co.uk, info@airdenhouse.co.uk, Graham and Lynda Scarisbrick).

$ The Sycamore is a fine value, with six homey rooms at the end of a dead-end street opposite a fun-to-watch bowling green (D-£46, Db-£50–60, family room-£60–70, ask about discounts, no CC, 19 Sycamore Place off Bootham Terrace, tel. 01904/624-712, www.thesycamore.co.uk, Elizabeth).

$ Queen Anne's Guest House has seven clean, cheery rooms (May–Sept: D-£42, Db-£44; Oct–April: D-£32, Db-£34; family room, lounge, 24 Queen Anne's Road, tel. 01904/629-389, fax 01904/619-529, www.queen-annes-guesthouse.co.uk, queen.annes@btopenworld.com, John and Linda).

$ Alcuin Lodge has five fine rooms and solid-wood furnishings (1 small top-floor D-£40, Db-£45–50, 15 Sycamore Place, tel. 01904/632-222, fax 01904/626-630, collinsonzoe@aol.com, Zoe Collinson and Lea Thomlinson).

B&Bs Along the Riverside

Hillery Summers runs two simple, well-worn workers' cottages fronting the River Ouse midway between the train station and the Minster. Each comes with small rooms, steep stairs, narrow hallways, a delightful front garden, and no traffic noise. Both face a pleasant pedestrian path; front rooms overlook the river, while back rooms watch a sprawling car park (see prices below, 2.5 percent extra to pay with credit card, Internet access, laundry, free parking, fax 01904/671-743, www.guesthouseyork.co.uk). **$$ Riverside Walk B&B** has 12 rooms (Db-£54–64, 8 Earlsborough Terrace, tel. 01904/620-769). **$$ Abbey Guest House,** with four rooms, is a bit cheaper since you have to walk next door to Riverside Walk for breakfast (D-£52, Db-£62, free parking, 14 Earlsborough Terrace, tel. 01904/627-782).

Hotels in the Center

$$$ Dean Court Hotel, facing the Minster, is a big, stately Best Western hotel with classy lounges and 40 comfortable rooms (small Db-£120, standard Db-£145, superior Db-£160, spacious deluxe Db-£175, some non-smoking rooms, tearoom, restaurant, elevator to most rooms, Duncombe Place, tel. 01904/625-082, fax 01904/620-305, www.deancourt-york.co.uk).

$ Travelodge offers 90 identical, affordable rooms near the Castle Museum (Db-£60, kids' bed free, some non-smoking rooms, 90 Piccadilly, central reservations tel. 0870-085-0950, www.travelodge.co.uk).

$ York Youth Hotel is a well-run hostel, with a kitchen, launderette, game room, and 120 beds (S-£25, bunk-bed D-£36, beds in 4- to 6-bed dorms-£15, beds in larger dorms-£12, less for multi-night stays, family rates, same-sex or coed possible, no breakfast, 10-min walk from station at 11 Bishophill Senior Road, tel.

01904/625-904, fax 01904/612-494, www.yorkyouthhotel.com).

$ York Backpackers Hostel offers cheap beds a few minutes' walk from the train station. The jovial staff welcomes backpackers and budget travelers of any age, with 24-hour access, no lockouts, and a guests-only bar in the basement, complete with support beams made of reclaimed ship timbers (£14 beds, 18- to 20-bed dorms, 88 Mickelgate, tel. 01904/627-720, www.yorkbackpackers.co.uk, mail@yorkbackpackers.co.uk).

EATING

York is bursting with inviting eateries. Picnic and light-meals-to-go options abound, and it's easy to find a churchyard, bench, or riverside perch upon which to munch cheaply. Perhaps the best picnic spot in town on a sunny day is under the evocative 12th-century ruins of St. Mary's Abbey in the Museum Gardens (near Bootham Bar).

There's a pub serving grub on every street. The only traditional chippie left in the center is **Petergate Fisheries** (good, cheap take-away fish-and-chips, daily 11:00–18:00, 95 Low Petergate).

Near the Minster

Café Concerto, a casual bistro with a fun menu, has an understandably loyal following (soup, sandwich, and salad meals-£8; fancier dinners-£15; daily 10:00–22:00, non-smoking, smart to reserve for dinner, facing the Minster, 21 High Petergate, tel. 01904/610-478).

Plunkets Restaurant is a bit oxymoronic—serving Tex-Mex cuisine among B&W glamour photos with dark, hardwood, candlelit English ambience—but the food is fine (daily 12:00–23:00, £6.50 early-bird special—main course and a beer or wine until 18:00, no reservations and often a line on weekends, 9 High Petergate, tel. 01904/637-722).

St. Williams Restaurant is just behind the great east window of the Minster in a wonderful half-timbered, 15th-century building (read the history on the menu). This is where the priests use their meal card. It serves quick and tasty lunches and elegant candlelit dinners (English and Mediterranean dishes, lunch 12:00–14:30, 3-course £15 specials 17:30–18:45, £15 plates, daily April–Sept, closed Sun–Mon Oct–March, College Street, tel. 01904/634-830). Outside seating with a Minster view is fine when balmy.

Betty's Teahouse, a favorite among local ladies, is popular for its traditional English afternoon tea (which works as a meal—£10 for tea, delicate sandwiches, scones, and sweets; for details, see page 718).

On and near Goodramgate, in the Old Town Center

Royal Oak Pub, a traditional, mellow old English pub, serves £6 meals throughout the day with hand-pulled ale. They happily swap out the peas and potatoes for more interesting vegetables—just ask (meals daily 11:00–20:00, three cozy rooms—one non-smoking, hearty meat dishes, homemade desserts, Goodramgate, a block inside Monk Bar, tel. 01904/653-856).

Lime House Restaurant is a small, modern, candlelit place serving international dishes and always a good vegetarian plate (lunch plates-£7, dinner plates-£12–15, 10 percent off orders before 19:15, Tue–Sat 12:00–14:00 & 18:00–21:30, closed Sun–Mon, 55 Goodramgate, tel. 01904/632-734).

Two popular Italian places along Goodramgate offer pizzas and pastas for £7: **Little Italy** is a little more intimate (#12, closed Mon, tel. 01904/623-539), while **Caesars** is bright and boisterous (#27, nightly, tel. 01904/670-914).

The Viceroy of India, just outside Monk Bar (and therefore outside the tourist zone), serves great Indian food at good prices to locals in the know. If you've yet to eat Indian on your trip, do it here (£8 plates, Mon–Fri 18:00–24:00, Sat–Sun 12:00–24:00, friendly staff, out Monk Bar to 26 Monkgate, tel. 01904/622-370, Mahmood welcomes you).

Near Bootham Bar and Your B&B

Café No. 8 is your best bistro choice on Gillygate, serving modern European comfort food, veggie options, and a shady little garden out back if the weather's good. Chef Ragnell lets what's fresh in the market shape his menu (£5–7 lunches, £10–14 dinners, daily except Sun and Mon eves, 8 Gillygate, tel. 01904/653-074).

The Coach House, while well-worn, serves good-quality food with fresh vegetables in a lounge that can be smoky (£8–11, nightly 18:30–21:00, attached to a classic old guesthouse, 20 Marygate, tel. 01904/652-780).

The **Grange Hotel Brasserie,** a couple of blocks from the B&Bs, is classier than a pub and serves a smattering of traditional European dishes. Eat downstairs rather than in the pricey main-floor restaurant (£9–13 main dishes, Mon–Sat 12:00–14:00 & 18:00–22:00, Sun 19:00–22:00, 1 Clifton, tel. 01904/644-744).

Jackson's grocery store is open daily 7:00–23:00 (near B&Bs, 50 yards outside Bootham Bar, on Bootham).

TRANSPORTATION CONNECTIONS

From York by Train to: Durham (hrly, 45 min), **Edinburgh** (2/hr, 2.5 hrs), **London** (2/hr, 2 hrs), **Bath** (hrly, 5 hrs, change in Bristol), **Cambridge** (nearly hrly, 2 hrs, change in Peterborough), **Birmingham** (2/hr, 2.5 hrs), **Keswick** (with transfers to Penrith then bus, 4.5 hrs). Train info: tel. 08457-484-950.

Connections with London's Airports: Heathrow (hrly, allow 2.5–3 hrs, from airport take Heathrow Express train to London's Paddington Station, tube to King's Cross, train to York—2/hr, 2 hrs), **Gatwick** (from Gatwick catch low-profile Thameslink train to King's Cross-Thameslink station in London; from there, walk 100 yards to King's Cross Station, train to York—2/hr, 2 hrs).

Buses: The **York Bus Information Centre** is at 20 Hudson Street, near the train station (Mon–Fri 8:30–17:00, closed Sat–Sun, tel. 01904/551-400, phone answered Mon–Sat 8:00–20:00, Sun 8:00–14:00).

EDINBURGH

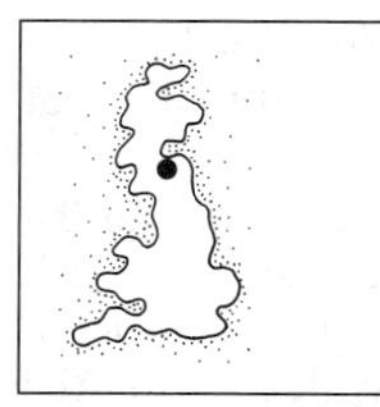

Edinburgh is the historical and cultural capital of Scotland. Once a medieval powerhouse sitting on a lava flow, it sprouted into Europe's first great grid-planned modern city. Today the colorful home of Robert Louis Stevenson, Sir Walter Scott, and Robert Burns is Scotland's showpiece and one of Europe's most entertaining cities. Historic, monumental, fun, and well-organized, it's a tourist's delight—especially in August, when the Edinburgh Festival takes over the town.

Promenade down the Royal Mile through Old Town. Historic buildings pack the Royal Mile between the grand castle (on the top) and the Palace of Holyroodhouse (on the bottom). Medieval skyscrapers stand shoulder to shoulder, hiding peaceful courtyards connected to High Street by narrow lanes or even tunnels. This colorful jumble is the tourist's Edinburgh.

Edinburgh (ED'n-burah) was once the most crowded city in Europe—famed for its skyscrapers and filth. The rich and poor virtually lived atop one another. In the Age of Enlightenment, a magnificent Georgian city (today's New Town) was laid out to the north, giving Edinburgh's upper class a respectable place to promenade. Georgian Edinburgh—like the city of Bath—shines with broad boulevards, straight streets, square squares, circular circuses, and elegant mansions decked out in colonnades, pediments, and sphinxes in the proud neoclassical style of 200 years ago.

While the Georgian city celebrated the union of Scotland and England (with streets and squares named after English kings and emblems), "devolution" is the latest trend. For the past several centuries, Scotland was ruled from London, and parliament had not met in Edinburgh since 1707. In a 1998 election, the Scots voted to gain more autonomy and bring their parliament home. In 2000, Edinburgh resumed its position as home to the Scottish Parliament (although London still calls the strategic shots). A strikingly modern new parliament building, which opened in 2004, is one more jewel in Edinburgh's crown.

Planning Your Time

While the major sights can be seen in a day, I'd give Edinburgh two days and three nights.

Day 1: Tour the castle. Then consider catching one of the city bus tours (from a block below the castle at The Hub/Tolbooth church) for a 60-minute loop, returning to the castle. Wander down the Royal Mile, having lunch, going to museums, shopping, and taking a walking tour (one leaves at 14:00 from Mercat Cross in August). Finish your sightseeing day with a tour of the Palace of Holyroodhouse, at the bottom of the Mile.

Day 2: Tour the Museum of Scotland. After lunch, stroll through the Princes Street Gardens and the National Gallery of Scotland. Then tour the good ship *Britannia.*

Evenings: Options include various "haunted Edinburgh" walks, literary pub crawls, live music in pubs (folk is rare—but still out there), or a touristy bagpipe-music evening. Or just settle down in a pub and sample the whisky and local beers while meeting the natives and attempting to understand their Scottish accents.

ORIENTATION

(area code: 0131)

The center of Edinburgh holds the Princes Street Gardens park and Waverley Bridge, where you'll find the TI, Princes Mall, train station, bus info office (starting point for most city bus tours), National Gallery, and a covered dance-and-music pavilion. Weather blows in and out—bring your sweater. Locals say the bad weather is one of the disadvantages of living so close to England.

Tourist Information

The crowded TI is as central as can be atop the Princes Mall and train station (May–June and Sept Mon–Sat 9:00–19:00, Sun 10:00–19:00; July–Aug daily 9:00–20:00; April–Oct Mon–Wed 9:00–17:00, Thu–Sat until 18:00, Sun 10:00–17:00, ATM outside entrance, tel. 0845-225-5121). The staff is knowledgeable and eager to help, but much of their information—including their assessment of museums and even which car-rental companies "exist"—is skewed by tourism payola.

Buy a map (the £1 version—if it's in stock—or the excellent £4 Collins Illustrated Edinburgh map, which comes with opinionated commentary and locates virtually every major shop and sight). If you're interested in late-night music, ask for the free monthly entertainment *Gig Guide*. The *Essential Guide to Edinburgh* (£1), while not truly essential, lists additional sights and services.

Book your room direct, using my listings, without the TI's help (as the TI takes 10 percent plus a £3 finder's fee, and B&Bs charge more for rooms booked through the TI). Browse the racks—tucked away in hallway at back of TI—for brochures on the various Scottish folk shows, walking tours, and regional bus tours.

Connect@edinburgh, a small Internet café, is beyond the brochure racks (see "Helpful Hints," below). The best monthly entertainment listing, *The List,* sells for £2.20 at newsstands.

Arrival in Edinburgh

Arriving by **train** at Waverley Station puts you in the city center and below the TI. High-security luggage storage is near platform 1 (£5/24 hrs, daily 7:00–23:00). Taxis queue almost trackside. The ramp they come and go on leads to Waverley Bridge. If there's a long taxi line, it's faster to hike the ramp and hail one on the street. From the station, "Way Out to Princes Street" signs lead up to the TI and the city bus stop (for bus directions from here to my recommended B&Bs, see page 754).

Both Scottish Citylink and National Express buses use the **bus station** (which has luggage lockers) two blocks north of the train station on St. Andrew Square in the New Town.

Edinburgh's slingshot-of-an-**airport** is 10 miles northwest of the center and well-connected by taxi (£15, 30 min to the center) and shuttle bus (LRT Airlink bus #100 to Waverley Bridge, £3.30, or £4.20 with all-day Airsaver city-bus pass, 6/hr, 30 min, roughly 5:00–24:00). Flight info: tel. 0870-040-0007; bmi british midland: tel. 0870-607-0555 (www.flybmi.com); British Airways: tel. 0870-850-9850 (www.ba.com).

Helpful Hints

Sunday Activities: Many minor sights close on Sunday, but the major sights are open. Sunday is a good day for a Royal Mile walking tour or a city bus tour (which go faster in light Sunday traffic). Arthur's Seat is lively with locals on weekends.

Internet Access: Get online at **easyInternetcafé** (daily 7:00–23:00, 450 terminals, a block from National Gallery at 58 Rose Street); **Connect@edinburgh** (in the TI, Mon–Sat 9:00–19:00, closed Sun, shorter hours off-season); **Elephant House Café** (4 stations, 24 George IV Bridge, off top of Royal Mile, see page 759); and **Hotel Ceilidh-Donia** (see page 757).

Car Rental: Except for Budget, these places have offices in the town center and at the airport: Avis (5 West Park Place, tel.

0131/337-6363, airport tel. 0131/344-3900), Europcar (24 East London Street, tel. 0131/557-3456, airport tel. 0131/333-2588), Hertz (10 Picardy Place, tel. 0131/556-8311, airport tel. 0131/333-1019), and Budget (airport only, tel. 0131/333-1926).

Local Guide: Ken Hanley wears his kilt as if pants don't exist and loves sharing his passion for Edinburgh and Scotland. A licensed Blue Badge guide, Ken comes equipped with a car and all the great stories (£60/half-day, £100/day, tel. 0131/666-1944, mobile 07710-342-044, www.small-world-tours.co.uk, k.hanley@blueyonder.co.uk).

Getting Around Edinburgh

Nearly all of Edinburgh's sights are within walking distance of each other.

City **buses** are handy (about 80p/ride, buy tickets on bus, LRT transit office at Old Town end of Waverley Bridge has schedules and route maps, tel. 0131/555-6363). Tell the driver where you're going, have change handy (buses require exact change—you lose any excess), take your ticket as you board, and ping the bell as you near your stop. Double-deckers come with fine views upstairs. Two companies handle the city routes: LRT (or Lothian) does most of it, and First does the rest. (To get from the city center to the recommended B&Bs on Dalkeith Road, you can catch LRT buses #14, #30, and #33, or First bus #86; for details, see page 754.) Day passes sold by each company are valid only on their buses (£2.50, or £2 after 9:30 weekdays and all day weekends, buy from driver). Buses run from about 6:00 to 23:00.

The 1,300 **taxis** cruising Edinburgh's streets are easy to flag down (a ride between downtown and B&B district costs about £5). As they can turn on a dime, hail them in either direction.

TOURS

In Edinburgh

Royal Mile Walking Tours—**Mercat Tours** offers 90-minute guided walks of the Mile—more entertaining than historic (£7.50, daily at 10:30, from Mercat Cross on the Royal Mile, tel. 0131/557-6464). The guides, who enjoy making a short story long, ignore the big sights and take you behind the scenes with piles of barely historic gossip, bully-pulpit Scottish pride, and fun but forgettable trivia. They also offer a variety of other tours.

In August only, the **Voluntary Guides Association** leads free two-hour tours of Edinburgh (generally departing daily around 10:00 and 14:00, check at TI or call for a schedule, tel. 0131/664-7180 or 0131/556-8854).

Edinburgh

MORAY PLACE
QUEEN ST. GARDENS
QUEEN
GEORGIAN HOUSE
HILL
CHARLOTTE SQ.
CASTLE
GEORGE
FREDERICK
ROSE
HANOVER
DAVID
ST ANDREW SQ.
NEW TOWN
1/4 MILE
400 METERS
TO ROYAL BOTANIC GARDEN
TO BRITANNIA & LEITH
BUS STN.
YORK PLACE
LEITH
CALTON HILL
PRINCES MALL & TRAIN STN.
NAT'L. MONUMENT
PRINCES STREET
SCOTT MON.
PRINCES ST. GARDENS
LOTHIAN
MOUND
WAVERLEY BRIDGE
NORTH BRIDGE
CALTON REGENT RD.
ROAD
PALACE OF HOLYROOD-HOUSE
MARKET
NEW
NAT'L. GALLERY
EDINBURGH CASTLE
THE ROYAL MILE
IV
QUEEN'S GALLERY
TO HAYMARKET STN.
MORRISON
BREAD
GRASS-MARKET
GEORGE
BRIDGE
ST. GILES
SCOTTISH PARLIAMENT
ST. MARYS
DYNAMIC EARTH
COW-GATE
HOLYROOD RD
FOUNTAINBRIDGE
OLD TOWN
SOUTH BRIDGE
PLEASANCE
QUEENS DRIVE
HIKE TO ARTHUR'S SEAT
SALISBURY CRAGS
MUSEUM OF SCOTLAND
TO DALKEITH ROAD
DCH
1 Edinburgh Festival tickets
2 Fringe Festival tickets

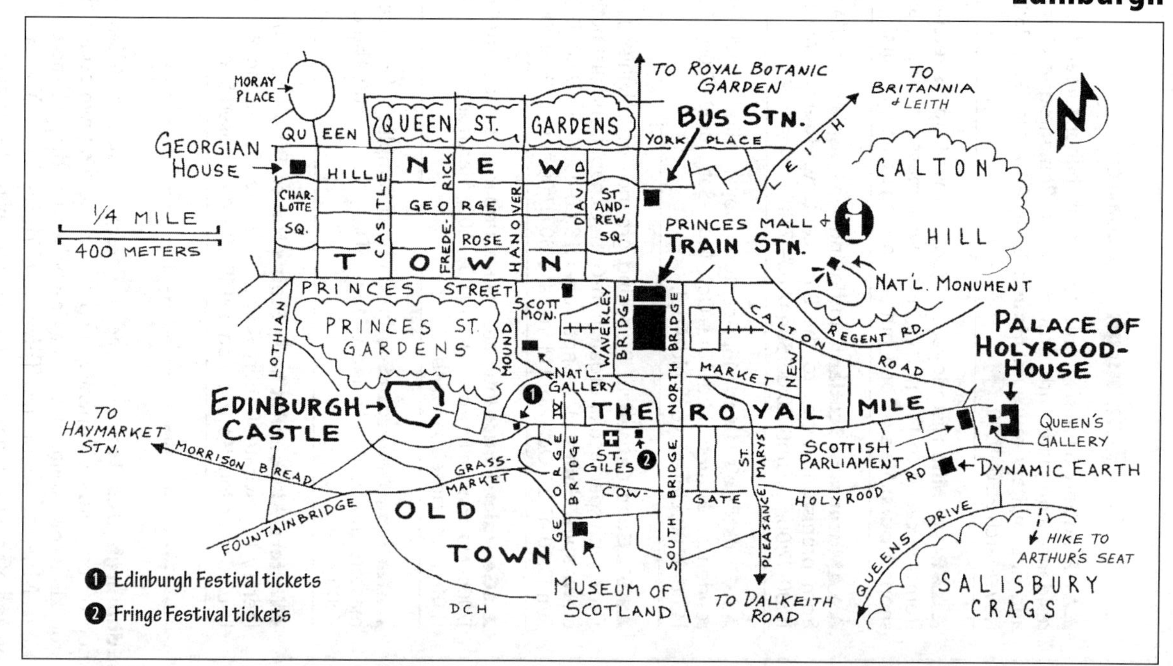

Edinburgh at a Glance

▲▲▲Edinburgh Castle Iconic 11th-century hilltop fort and royal residence complete with Crown Jewels, Romanesque chapel, and fine military museum. **Hours:** Daily April–Oct 9:30–18:00, Nov–March 9:30–17:00.

▲▲▲Royal Mile Historic road—good for walking—stretching from the castle to the palace, lined with museums, pubs, and shops. **Hours:** Always open, but best during business hours.

▲▲▲Museum of Scotland Intriguing, well-displayed artifacts from prehistoric times to the 20th century. **Hours:** Mon–Sat 10:00–17:00, Tue until 20:00, Sun 12:00–17:00.

▲▲Gladstone's Land 16th-century Royal Mile merchant's residence. **Hours:** Mid-April–Oct Mon–Sat 10:00–17:00, Sun 14:00–17:00, closed Nov–mid-April.

▲▲St. Giles Cathedral Preaching grounds of Calvinist John Knox, with spectacular organ, neo-Gothic chapel, and distinctive crown spire. **Hours:** May–Sept Mon–Fri 9:00–19:00, Sat 9:00–17:00, Sun 13:00–17:00; Oct–April Mon–Sat 9:00–17:00, Sun 13:00–17:00.

▲▲Georgian House Intimate peek at upper-crust life in the late 1700s. **Hours:** Daily April–Oct 10:00–17:00, March and Nov–Dec 11:00–15:00, closed Jan–Feb.

▲▲National Gallery of Scotland Choice sampling of European masters and Scotland's finest. **Hours:** Daily 10:00–17:00, Thu until 19:00.

▲Writers' Museum at Lady Stair's House Tribute to Scottish literary triumvirate: Robert Burns, Sir Walter Scott, and Robert Louis Stevenson. **Hours:** Mon–Sat 10:00–17:00, closed Sun.

Edinburgh Bus Tours—Three different 60-minute, hop-on, hop-off bus tours, all operated by LRT, circle the town center and stop along one route at the biggies: Waverley Bridge, the castle, Royal Mile, Georgian New Town, and Princes Street. You can hop on and off at any stop with one ticket all day (pick-ups about every 10–15 min). To compare your options, talk to the guides and drivers at the Waverley Bridge starting point. Why three different tours, all owned by the same big company? It has to do with local anti-monopoly laws.

The ride comes with informative narration. Two of the tours

▲**Museum of Childhood** Five stories of historic fun. **Hours:** Mon–Sat 10:00–17:00, closed Sun.

▲**John Knox House** Reputed 16th-century digs of the great reformer. **Hours:** Mon–Sat 10:00–17:00, closed Sun.

▲**People's Story** Proletarian life from the 18th to 20th centuries. **Hours:** Mon–Sat 10:00–17:00, closed Sun.

▲**Museum of Edinburgh** Historic mementos, from the original National Covenant scribed on animal skin to early golf balls. **Hours:** Mon–Sat 10:00–17:00, closed Sun.

▲**Scottish Parliament Building** Controversial new headquarters for the recently-returned Parliament. **Hours:** Mon and Fri 10:00–18:00, Tue–Thu 9:00–19:00, Sat–Sun 10:00–16:00, shorter hours off-season and when Parliament is in recess.

▲**Palace of Holyroodhouse** The queen's splendid home-away-from-home, with lavish rooms, 12th-century abbey, and gallery with rotating exhibits. **Hours:** Daily 9:30–18:00, Nov–April until 16:30.

▲**Georgian New Town** Elegant 1776 subdivision spiced with trendy shops, bars, and eateries. **Hours:** Always open.

▲**Sir Walter Scott Monument** Climbable tribute to the famed novelist. **Hours:** March–Oct Mon–Sat 9:00–18:00, Sun 10:00–18:00, Nov–Feb daily 10:00–15:00.

▲***Britannia*** The royal yacht with a history of distinguished passengers, a 15-minute trip out of town. **Hours:** Daily April–Sept 9:30–18:00, Oct–March 10:00–17:00.

have live guides: Mac Tours' City Tour (live Mon–Fri with "vintage buses") and Edinburgh Tour (always live). Avoid the City Sightseeing Tours, which have a recorded narration (better for non-English speakers). The tours have virtually the same route, cost, and frequency (£8.50, tickets give 10 percent discount off castle admission, valid 24 hours, buy on bus, tel. 0131/220-0770). Buses run daily year-round; in peak season, they leave Waverley Bridge daily between around 9:15 and 19:00 (mid-June–early Sept; hours shrink off-season). On sunny days they go topless (the buses), but they also suffer from traffic noise and exhaust fumes.

All three tours also offer £13 combo-tickets that include their *Britannia* Tour—a hop-on, hop-off route that stops at the Royal Botanic Garden, docks, and the *Britannia* royal yacht (£8.50, *Britannia* admission extra, departs Waverley Bridge every 15–30 min, live guide, tel. 0131/220-0770). If your main interest is seeing the *Britannia,* you'll save money taking a regular bus instead (see page 748).

From Edinburgh

Many companies run day trips to regional sights. Study the brochures at the TI's rack.

Heart of Scotland Tours offers various itineraries, but the best are the experience- and information-packed day trips of the Highlands and Loch Ness (£31, departures Wed and Sat–Sun, 8:00–20:00, leaves from 25 Waterloo Place near Waverley Station, fewer tours off-season, reserve at least a day ahead by phone or online, tel. 0131/558-8855, www.heartofscotlandtours.co.uk, run by Nick Roche). The tour gives those with limited time a chance to experience the wonders of Scotland's wild and legend-soaked Highlands in a long day (14- or 24-seat bus, talkative driver, good sound system). This Highlands joyride keeps a tight schedule, punctuated by several 30- to 90-minute stops. You'll see the vast and brutal Rannoch Moor; Glencoe, still evocative with memories of the clan massacre; views of Britain's highest mountain, Ben Nevis; Fort Augustus on Loch Ness (at the 90-min stop here, you can take the optional £6 boat ride or, if not into Nessie, enjoy free time in town); a scenic walk in the woods; and a 45-minute tea or pub break in the fine little village of Dunkeld. You'll learn a bit about Edinburgh to boot as you drive in and out.

SIGHTS

Edinburgh Castle

The fortified birthplace of the city 1,300 years ago, this imposing symbol of Edinburgh—worth ▲▲▲—sits proudly on a rock high above the city. While the castle has been both a fort and a royal residence since the 11th century, most of the buildings today are from its more recent use as a military garrison. This fascinating and multifaceted sight deserves several hours of your time.

Cost, Hours, Services: £9.50, daily April–Oct 9:30–18:00, Nov–March 9:30–17:00, last entrance 45 min before closing, tel. 0131/225-9846. The clean WC at the entry annually wins "British Loo of the Year" awards (marvel at the plaques near men's room; the one-way mirrors peeking into the women's sink area are now shuttered—thanks in part to readers of this book complaining). The Red Coat Cafeteria and Jacobite Room is a handy cafeteria in the castle (see "Eating," page 759).

Getting There: While regular city buses drop you far below (at the top of the Royal Mile, near the Camera Obscura), taxis take you right to the esplanade, in front of the gate. A new castle bus does a circuit through central Edinburgh, beginning at George Street (near train station) and leaving you at the castle's esplanade (£1, July–Aug only, daily 10:00–8:00, 4/hr in peak times, driver also sells £10 "Fast track ticket" for castle allowing you to bypass the line, though at 50p extra it's only worth considering in Aug, Edinburgh's busiest time).

Entry Gate: Start with the wonderfully droll 20-minute guided introduction tour (free with admission, 2–4/hr, departs from entry, see clock for next departure; few tours run off-season). The audioguide is excellent, with four hours of quick-dial digital descriptions of the sights, including the National War Museum of Scotland (£3, pay at ticket office, pick up at entry gate before meeting the live guide).

The castle has five essential stops: Crown Jewels, Royal Palace, Scottish National War Memorial, St. Margaret's Chapel (with a city view), and the excellent National War Museum of Scotland. The first four are at the highest and most secure point—on or near the castle square, where your introductory guided tour ends (and the sights described below begin). Consider the National War Museum of Scotland (50 yards below the cafeteria and big shop) a separate sight and worth a serious look.

1. Crown Jewels: There are two ways to see the jewels. You can go in directly from the courtyard, but there's often a line. To avoid the line, enter the building around to the left (next to WC), where you'll get to the jewels via the "Honors of Scotland" exhibition—a kid-friendly series of displays (which often moves at a very slow shuffle) telling the story of the crown jewels and how they survived the harrowing centuries.

Scotland's Crown Jewels—though not as impressive as England's—are older and at least as treasured by the locals. While Oliver Cromwell destroyed England's jewels, the Scots managed to hide theirs. Longtime symbols of Scottish nationalism, they were made in Edinburgh—in 1540 for a 1543 coronation—out of Scottish diamonds, gems, and gold...some say the personal gold of King Robert the Bruce melted down. They were last used to crown Charles II in 1651. When the Act of Union was forced upon the Scots in 1707—dissolving Scotland's parliament into England's to create the United Kingdom—part of the deal was that the Scots could keep their jewels locked up in Edinburgh. The jewels remained hidden for more than 100 years. In 1818, Sir Walter Scott and a royal commission rediscovered them intact. In 1999, for the first time in nearly three centuries, the crown of Scotland was brought from the castle for the opening of the Scottish Parliament (see photos on the wall where the "Honors of Scotland" exhibit meets the Crown Jewels room; a smiling Queen Elizabeth presides over the historic occasion).

The **Stone of Scone** sits plain and strong next to the jewels. This big gray chunk of rock is the coronation stone of Scotland's ancient kings (9th century). Swiped by the English, it sat under the coronation chair at Westminster Abbey from 1296 until 1996. Queen Elizabeth finally agreed to let the stone go home—on one condition: that it be returned to Westminster Abbey in London for all future coronations. With major fanfare, Scotland's treasured Stone of Scone returned to Edinburgh on Saint Andrew's Day, November 30, 1996. Talk to the guard for more details.

2. The Royal Palace: Scottish royalty lived here only when safety or protocol required (preferring the Palace of Holyroodhouse at the bottom of the Royal Mile). The Royal Palace, facing castle square under the flagpole, has two historic yet unimpressive rooms (through door marked "1566") and the Great Hall (separate entrance from opposite side of square; see below). Enter the **Mary Queen of Scots room,** where in 1566 the queen gave birth to James VI of Scotland, who later became King James I of England. The Presence Chamber leads into **Laich Hall** (Lower Hall), the dining room of the royal family.

The **Great Hall** was the castle's ceremonial meeting place in the 16th and 17th centuries. In later times, it was a barracks and a hospital. While most of what you see is Victorian, two medieval elements survive: the fine hammer-beam roof and the big iron-barred peephole (above fireplace on right). This allowed the king to spy on his subjects as they partied.

3. The Scottish National War Memorial: This commemorates the 149,000 Scottish soldiers lost in World War I, the 58,000 lost in World War II, and the 750 (and counting) lost in British battles since. Each bay is dedicated to a particular Scottish regiment. The main shrine, featuring a green Italian-marble memorial that contains the original WWI rolls of honor, sits—almost religiously—on an exposed chunk of the castle rock. Above you, the archangel Michael is busy slaying the dragon. The bronze frieze accurately shows the attire of various wings of Scotland's military. The stained glass starts with Cain and Abel on the left and finishes with a celebration of peace on the right. To appreciate how important this place is, consider that one out of every three adult Scottish men died in World War I.

4. St. Margaret's Chapel: The oldest building in Edinburgh is dedicated to Queen Margaret, who died here in 1093 and was sainted in 1250. Built in 1130 in the Romanesque style of the Norman invaders, it's wonderfully simple, with classic Norman

British, Scottish, and English

Of course, Scotland and England are comfortably tied together in a union no one seriously challenges. But history is clearly seen through two very different filters.

If you tour a British-oriented sight, such as the National War Museum of Scotland, you'll find things told in a "happy union" way. The official line: In 1707, it was clear to England and Scotland that it was in their mutual interest to dissolve the Scottish government and fold it into Britain, ruled from London. But talk to a cabbie or your B&B host, and you may get a different spin. In a clever move by England to deflate the military power of its little sister, Scottish Highlanders were sent to fight and die for Britain—in disproportionately higher numbers than their English counterparts. Poignant propaganda posters in the National War Museum of Scotland show a happy lad with the message: "Hey, look! Willie's off to Singapore with the Queen's own Highlanders."

The deep-seated rift shows itself in sports, too. While the English may refer to a British team in international competition as "English," the Scots are careful to call it "British." If a Scottish athlete does well, the English call him "British." If he screws up...he's a clumsy Scot.

zigzags decorating the round arch that separates the tiny nave from the sacristy. Used as a powder magazine for 400 years, very little survives. You'll see an 11th-century gospel book of St. Margaret's and small windows featuring St. Margaret, St. Columba (who brought Christianity to Scotland via Iona), and William Wallace (the brave-hearted defender of Scotland). The place is popular for weddings—and, since it seats only 20, it's particularly popular with brides' fathers.

Mons Meg—a huge and once-upon-a-time frightening 15th-century siege cannon that fired 330-pound stones nearly two miles—stands in front of the church.

Belly up to the banister (outside the chapel below the cannon) to enjoy the grand view. Below you are the guns—which fire the one o'clock salute—and a sweet little line of doggie tombstones, marking the soldiers' pet cemetery. Beyond stretches the Georgian New Town (read the informative plaque).

5. The National War Museum of Scotland: This thoughtfully covers four centuries of Scottish military history. Instead of the usual musty, dusty displays of endless armor, this museum has an interesting mix of short films, uniforms, weapons, medals, mementos, and eloquent excerpts from soldiers' letters. A pleasant surprise just when you thought your castle visit was about over, this rivals any military museum you'll see in Europe. There are three videos to look for (all run constantly): an excellent 13-minute sweeping introduction (upstairs from entrance), a five-minute bagpipe demo (TV screen), and a moving silent tribute to all who fought and died for Britain (near the end).

Leaving the castle, turn around and look back at the gate. There stand King Robert the Bruce (on the left, 1274–1329) and Sir William Wallace (Braveheart—on the right, 1270–1305). Wallace—now famous, thanks to Mel Gibson—fought long and hard against English domination before being executed in London. His body was cut to pieces and paraded through the far corners of jolly olde England. Bruce beat the English at Bannockburn in 1314. Bruce and Wallace still defend the spirit of Scotland. The Latin inscription above the gate between them reads, more or less, "What you do to us...we will do to you."

Along the Royal Mile

The Royal Mile—worth ▲▲▲—is one of Europe's most interesting historic walks. Consisting of a series of four different streets—Castlehill, Lawnmarket, High Street, and Canongate (each with its own set of street numbers), the Royal Mile is actually 200 yards longer than a mile. And every inch is packed with shops, cafés, and lanes leading to tiny squares.

Start at the top and amble down to the palace. These sights are listed in walking order. Bus #35 runs along the Mile, handy for going up after you've hit bottom. Entertaining 90-minute guided walks bring the legends and lore of the Royal Mile alive (described under "Tours," above).

As you walk, remember that originally there were two settlements here, divided by a wall: Edinburgh lined the ridge from the castle at the top. The lower end, Canongate, was outside the wall until 1856. By poking down the many side alleys, you'll find a few surviving rough edges of an Old Town well on its way to becoming a touristic mall. See it now. In a few years it'll be all tartans and shortbread, with tourists slaloming through the postcard racks on bagpipe skateboards.

Royal Mile Terminology: A "close" is a tiny alley between two buildings (originally with a door that closed it at night). A close usually leads to a "court," or courtyard. A "land" is a tenement block of apartments. A "pend" is an arched gateway. A "wynd" is a narrow, winding lane. And "gate" is from an old Scandinavian word for street.

Castle Esplanade—At the top of the Royal Mile, the big parking lot leading up to the castle was created as a military parade ground in 1816. It's often cluttered with bleachers for the Military Tattoo—a spectacular massing of the bands, filling the square

Royal Mile

PRINCES ST. GARDENS
WRITERS' MUSEUM
LADY STAIR'S HOUSE
TO TRAIN STATION
NOT TO SCALE - CASTLE TO PALACE OF HOLYROODHOUSE IS ABOUT 1 MILE
CANONGATE CHURCH
WHITE HORSE CLOSE
PALACE OF HOLYROOD-HOUSE
(BOTTOM OF ROYAL MILE)
CASTLE
(TOP OF ROYAL MILE)
GLADSTONE'S LAND
BANK ST.
ST GILES + MERCAT CROSS
COCKBURN ST.
NORTH BRIDGE
JOHN KNOX HOUSE
PEOPLE'S STORY
ABBEY
CAMERA OBSCURA
ESPLANADE
LAWNMKT.
HIGH
STREET
CANONGATE
MUS. OF EDINBURGH
HOLYROOD RD.
QUEEN'S GALLERY
GOOD RESTAURANTS + ANTIQUE SHOPS
VICTORIA
GEORGE IV BR.
TRON KIRK
MUSEUM OF CHILDHOOD
DYNAMIC EARTH
SCOTTISH PARLIAMENT
COWGATE
OLD PARLIAMENT HOUSE
SOUTH BRIDGE
GRASSMARKET
FOLK MUSIC PUBS
CHAMBERS
MUSEUM OF SCOTLAND
HOLYROOD PARK + ARTHUR'S SEAT
DCH
1 MacDonald Hotel
2 Jurys Inn
3 Ibis Hotel
4 Travelodge
5 Deacon Brodie's Pub
6 Lower Aisle Restaurant (in St. Giles)
7 Filling Station Restaurant
8 Dubh Prais Restaurant
9 Always Sunday Food Co. & Fringe Festival Ticket Office
10 The Tea Room
11 Clarinda's Tea Room
12 Elephant House Café & The Outsider Rest.
13 The World's End Pub
14 Whistlebinkies Pub
15 The Hub Festival Ticket Office
16 Greyfriars Bobby Statue
17 Trail to Arthur's Seat
18 Scotch Whisky Heritage Centre

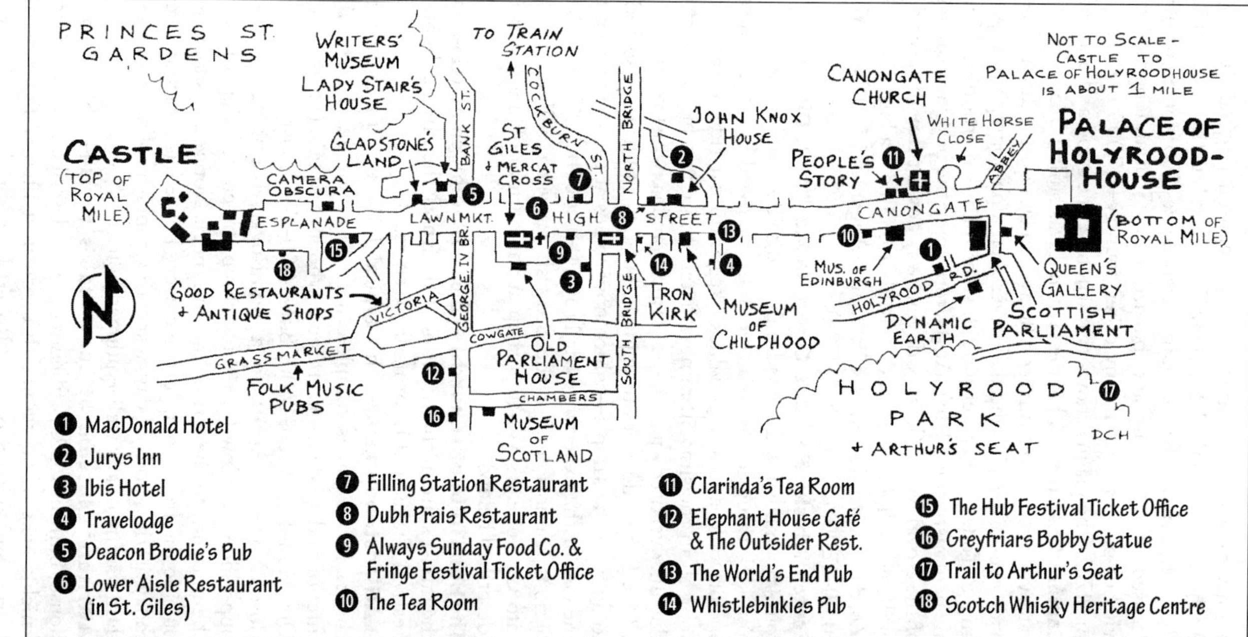

nightly for most of August (see "Edinburgh Festival," page 750). At the bottom, on the left (where the square hits the road), a plaque above the tiny witch's fountain memorializes 300 women who were accused of witchcraft and burned here. Scotland burned more witches per capita than any other country—17,000 between 1479 and 1722. The plaque shows two witches: one good and one bad.

Camera Obscura—A big deal when it was built in 1853, this observatory topped with a mirror reflected images onto a disc before the wide eyes of people who had never seen a photograph or captured image. Today you can climb 100 steps for an entertaining 15-minute demonstration (3/hr). At the top, enjoy the best view anywhere of the Royal Mile. Then work your way down through three floors of illusions, holograms, and early photos. This is a big hit with kids (£6, daily April–Oct 9:30–18:00, July–Aug until 19:30, Nov–March 10:00–17:00, tel. 0131/226-3709).

Scotch Whisky Heritage Centre (a.k.a. "Malt Disney")—This touristy ambush is designed only to distill £8 out of your pocket. You kick things off with a wee dram followed by a video history, a short talk, and a little whisky-keg train-car ride before finding yourself in the shop 50 minutes later. Those in a hurry are offered the unadvertised quickie—a sample and a whisky-keg ride for £3.50. People do seem to enjoy it, but that might have something to do with the sample—which now comes at the start rather than the end of the experience (daily 10:00–17:00, tel. 0131/220-0441). Serious connoisseurs of the Scottish firewater will want to pop into Cadenhead's Whisky Shop at the bottom of the Royal Mile (described below).

The Hub (Tolbooth Church)—The neo-Gothic church (1844) with the tallest spire in the city is now known as The Hub, Edinburgh's Festival Ticket and Information Centre.

▲▲Gladstone's Land—This typical 16th- to 17th-century merchant's house comes complete with an almost-lived-in furnished interior and guides in each room who love to talk (£5, mid-April–Oct Mon–Sat 10:00–17:00, Sun 14:00–17:00, last entry at 16:30, closed Nov–mid-April). For a good Royal Mile photo, lean out the upper-floor window (or simply climb the curved stairway outside the museum to the left of the entrance). Notice the snoozing pig outside the front door. Just like every house has a vacuum cleaner today, in the good old days a snorting rubbish collector was a standard feature of any well-equipped house.

▲Writers' Museum at Lady Stair's House—This aristocrat's house, built in 1622, is filled with well-described manuscripts and knickknacks of Scotland's three greatest literary figures: Robert Burns, Sir Walter Scott, and Robert Louis Stevenson. Edinburgh's high society would gather in homes like this in the 1780s to hear the great poet Burns read his work. Burns' work is meant to be read aloud rather than in silence. In the Burns room, you can hear his poetry—worth a few minutes for anyone, and essential for fans (free, Mon–Sat 10:00–17:00, closed Sun).

Wander around the courtyard here. Edinburgh was a wonder in the 17th and 18th centuries. Tourists came here to see its sky-scrapers, which towered 10 stories and higher. No city in Europe was so densely populated—or polluted—as "Auld Reekie."

Deacon Brodie's Pub—Read the "Doctor Jekyll and Mister Hyde" story of this pub's notorious namesake on the wall facing Bank Street. Then, to see his spooky split personality, check out both sides of the hanging signpost.

Heart of Midlothian—Near the street in front of the cathedral, a heart-shaped outline in the brickwork marks the spot of a gallows and a prison (now long gone). Traditionally, locals stand on the rim of the heart and spit into it. Hitting the middle brings good luck. Go ahead...do as the locals do.

▲▲St. Giles Cathedral—This is Scotland's most important church. Its ornate spire—the Scottish crown steeple from 1495—is a proud part of Edinburgh's skyline. As the church functions as a kind of Westminster Abbey of Scotland, the interior is fascinating (May–Sept Mon–Fri 9:00–19:00, Sat 9:00–17:00, Sun 13:00–17:00; Oct–April Mon–Sat 9:00–17:00, Sun 13:00–17:00; ask about concerts—some are free, usually Thu at 13:10; café and WC downstairs, see "Eating," page 760; tel. 0131/225-9442). Cathedral guides are strolling around waiting for you to engage them in conversation. You'll be glad you did.

Stepping inside, find John Knox's statue. Look into his eyes for 10 seconds from 10 inches away, and think of the Reformation struggles of the 16th century. Knox, the great reformer and founder of austere Scottish Presbyterianism, first preached here in 1559. His insistence that every person should be able to read the word of God gave Scotland an educational system 300 years ahead of the rest of Europe. Thanks partly to Knox, it was Scottish minds that led the way in math, science, medicine, and engineering. Voltaire called Scotland "the intellectual capital of Europe."

Knox preached Calvinism. Consider that the Dutch and the Scots both embraced this creed of hard work, thrift, and strict ethics. This helps explain why Scots are so different from the English (and why the Dutch and the Scots—both famous for their thriftiness and industriousness—are so much alike).

The oldest parts of the cathedral—the four massive central pillars—date from 1120. After the English burned the cathedral in 1385, it was rebuilt bigger and better than ever, and in 1495, its famous crown spire was completed. During the Reformation—when Knox preached here (1559–1572)—the place was simplified and whitewashed. Before this, with the emphasis on holy services provided by priests, there were lots of little niches. With the new focus on sermons rather than rituals, the grand pulpit took center stage. The organ (1992, Austrian-built, one of Europe's finest) comes with a glass panel in the back for peeking into the mechanism.

Knox had the church's fancy medieval glass replaced with clear glass. And 19th-century Victorians had Knox's glass replaced with the brilliantly colored glass you see today.

The modern window filling the west wall celebrates Scotland's favorite poet, Robert Burns. It was made in 1985 by an Icelandic artist (Leifur Breidfjord). The green of the lower level symbolizes the natural world—God's creation. The middle zone with the circle shows the brotherhood of man; Burns was a great internationalist. The top is a rosy red sunburst of creativity, reminding Scots of Burns' famous line, "My love is like a red, red rose"—part of a song near and dear to every Scottish heart. Why honor this "live fast and die young" Romantic here? This is Scotland's top church, and even this prodigal son has a place...a big place.

To the right of the Burns window is a fine pre-Raphaelite window. Like most in the church, it's a memorial to an important patron (in this case, John Marshall). From here stretches a great swath of war memorials.

The neo-Gothic **Chapel of the Knights of the Thistle** (in the far right corner, from 1911), with its intricate wood-carving, was built in two years entirely with Scottish materials and labor. It is the private chapel of the Knights of the Thistle, the only Scottish chivalric order, and it's used about once a year to inaugurate new members. Scotland recognizes its leading citizens by bestowing upon them a membership. The queen presides over the ritual from her fancy stall, marked by her British coat of arms—a heraldic zoo of symbolism. Are there bagpipes in heaven? Find the tooting angel above the door to the right.

John Knox is buried out back—with appropriate austerity—under the parking lot, at spot 23. The statue among the cars shows King Charles II riding to a toga party back in 1685. Near parking spot 15, enter the...

Old Parliament House—Step in to see the grand hall with its fine 1639 hammer-beam ceiling and stained glass. This hall housed the Scottish Parliament until the Act of Union in 1707 (explained in history exhibition under the big stained-glass depiction of the initiation of the first Scottish High Court in 1532). It now holds the law courts and is busy with wigged and robed lawyers hard at work in the old library (peek through the door) or pacing the hall deep in discussion. The friendly doorman is helpful (free, public welcome Mon–Fri 9:00–17:00, best action midmornings Tue–Fri, open-to-the-public trials 10:00–16:00—doorman has the day's docket, enter behind St. Giles Cathedral).

Mercat Cross—This chunky pedestal, on the downhill side of St. Giles, holds a slender column topped with a white unicorn. Royal proclamations have been read here since the 14th century. The tradition survives. In 1952, three days (traditionally the time it took for a horse to speed here from London) after the actual event, a town crier heralded the news that England had a new queen. Today Mercat Cross is the meeting point of various walking tours—both historic and ghostly.

A few doors downhill is the...

Police Information Center—This center provides a pleasant police presence (say that three times) and a little local law-and-order history to boot (free, May–Aug daily 10:00–21:30, less off-season). Pick up *For the Record*, the police brag mag ("Thirteen murders in the last year...and all of them solved!"). Ask the officer on duty about the grave-robber William Burke's skin and creative poetic justice, Edinburgh-style.

Cockburn Street—This street was cut through High Street's dense wall of medieval skyscrapers in the 1860s to give easy access to the Georgian New Town and the train station. Notice how the sliced buildings were thoughtfully capped with facades in a faux-16th-century Scottish baronial style. In the Middle Ages, only tiny lanes (like the Fleshmarket Lane just uphill from Cockburn Street) interrupted the long line of Royal Mile buildings.

Tron Kirk—This fine old building across from Cockburn Street, used as a sales base for a local walking-tour company, sits over an old excavation site. It houses a free Old Town history display (daily 10:00–17:30). (Perhaps even more important, just above Tron Kirk is a Starbucks with fine streetside tables and a spacious upstairs lounge.)

Continue downhill 100 yards to the...

▲Museum of Childhood—This five-story playground of historical toys and games is rich in nostalgia and history (free, Mon–Sat 10:00–17:00, closed Sun). Just downhill is a fragrant fudge shop offering delicious free samples.

▲John Knox House—Intriguing for Reformation buffs, this fine 16th-century house offers a well-explained look at the life of the great reformer (£3, Mon–Sat 10:00–17:00, closed Sun, 43 High Street, tel. 0131/556-9579). While some contend Knox never actually lived here, preservationists called it "his house" to save it from the wrecking ball in 1850.

The World's End—For centuries, a wall halfway down the Royal Mile marked the end of Edinburgh and the beginning of Canongate, a community associated with Holyrood Abbey. Today, where the Mile hits St. Mary's and Jeffrey Streets, High Street becomes Canongate. Just below John Knox House (at #43), notice the hanging sign showing the old gate. At the intersection, find the brass bricks that trace the gate (demolished in 1764). Look down St. Mary's Street to see a surviving bit of that old wall. Then, entering Canongate, you leave what was Edinburgh and head for...

Cadenhead's Whisky Shop—The shop is not a tourist sight. It's a firm, founded in 1842, that prides itself on bottling good malt whisky from kegs straight from the best distilleries, without all the compromises that come with profitable mass production (coloring with sugar to fit the expected look, watering down to lessen the alcohol tax, and so on). Those drinking from Cadenhead-bottled whiskies will enjoy the distilleries' product as the owners of the distilleries themselves do—pure, not as the sorry public does. If you want to learn about whisky—and perhaps pick up a bottle—they love to talk (Mon–Sat 10:30-17:30, closed Sun, 172 Canongate, tel. 0131/556-5864).

▲People's Story—This interesting exhibition traces the lot of the working class through the 18th, 19th, and 20th centuries (free, Mon–Sat 10:00–17:00, closed Sun, tel. 0131/529-4057). Curiously, while this museum is dedicated to the proletariat, immediately around the back (embedded in the wall of the museum) is the tomb of Adam Smith—the author of *Wealth of Nations* and the father of modern capitalism (1723–1790).

▲Museum of Edinburgh—Another old house full of old stuff, this one is worth a look for its early Edinburgh history and handy ground-floor WC. Don't miss the original copy of the National Covenant (written in 1638 on an animal skin), sketches of pre-Georgian Edinburgh (which show a lake, later filled in to become Princes Street Gardens when the New Town was built), and early golf balls. "Balls," said the queen, "If I had two, I'd be king." The king laughed. He had to. (Free, Mon–Sat 10:00–17:00, closed Sun.)

White Horse Close—Step into this 17th-century courtyard (bottom of Canongate, on the left, a block before the Palace of Holyroodhouse). It was from here that the Edinburgh stagecoach left for London. Eight days later, the horse-drawn carriage pulled into its destination: Scotland Yard.

Across the street is the new...

▲Scottish Parliament Building—Scotland's parliament originated in 1293, was dissolved by England in 1707, and returned in 2000. Their extravagant, and therefore controversial, new digs opened in 2004. The Catalan architect Enric Miralles mixed wild angles, lots of light, eyesore windows, and local stone into a startling complex that would, as he envisioned, "arise from the sloping base of Arthur's Seat and arrive into the city almost surging out of the rock." For a conversation starter, ask a local what he or she thinks about the place.

For a peek at the new building and a lesson in how the Scottish Parliament works, drop in and find the visitors' desk (free, April–Oct Mon and Fri 10:00–18:00, Tue–Thu 9:00–19:00—or 10:00–18:00 if Parliament is in recess, Sat–Sun 10:00–16:00; Nov–March Mon and Fri–Sun 10:00–16:00, Tue–Thu 9:00–19:00—or 10:00–18:00 if Parliament is in recess; last entry 45 min before closing). You can sign up to witness the Scottish Parliament's debates (usually Wed 14:30–17:30, Thu 9:30–12:30 & 14:30–17:30, tel. 0131/348-5411). For details and updates on visiting, see www.scottish.parliament.uk.

Queen's Gallery—The museum features rotating exhibits of drawings from the royal collection. For over five centuries, the royal family has amassed a wealth of art treasures. While the queen keeps most in her many private palaces, she shares an impressive load of it here, with exhibits changing about every six months. Though it's just two rooms, it can be exquisite, and generally comes with a well-done audioguide (£5, £11 combo-ticket includes Palace of Holyroodhouse, daily 9:30–18:00, Nov–April until 16:30, on the palace grounds, to the right of the palace entrance).

▲Palace of Holyroodhouse—Since the 14th century, this palace has marked the end of the Royal Mile. The queen spends a week here each summer. The abbey—part of a 12th-century Augustinian monastery—stood here first. It was named for a piece of the cross brought here as a relic by Queen (and later Saint) Margaret. As Scotland's royalty preferred living here to the blustery castle on the rock, the palace evolved over time.

Consider touring the interior (£8, £11 combo-ticket includes Queen's Gallery, palace guidebook-£4.50, daily 9:30–18:00, Nov–April until 16:30, last entry 45 min before closing, tel. 0131/556-7371; palace closed when the queen is at home—generally for a week around July 1—and whenever a prince drops in). The building, rich in history and decor, is filled with elegantly furnished rooms and a few darker, older rooms with glass cases of historic bits and Scottish pieces that locals find fascinating. Bring the palace to life with the included one-hour audioguide. You'll learn which of the kings featured in the 110 portraits lining the Great Gallery are real and which are fictional, what touches were added to the bedchambers to flatter King Charles II, and why the exiled Comte d'Artois took refuge in the palace. You'll also hear a goofy reenactment of the moment when conspirators—dispatched by Mary Queen of Scots' jealous second husband—stormed into the queen's chambers and stabbed her male secretary.

After exiting, you're free to stroll through the ruined abbey and the queen's gardens. Hikers: Note that the wonderful trail up Arthur's Seat starts just across the street from the gardens.

Dynamic Earth—This immense exhibit tells the story of our planet, filling several underground floors under a vast Gore-Tex tent. It's pitched, appropriately, at the base of the Salisbury Crags. The exhibit is designed for younger kids and does the same thing an American science exhibit would do—but with a charming Scottish accent. Standing in a time tunnel, you watch time rewind from Churchill to dinosaurs to the big bang. After several short films on stars, tectonic plates, and ice caps, you're free to wander past salty pools, a re-created rain forest, and various TV screens. End your visit with a 12-minute video finale (£9, family deals, daily 10:00–18:00, last ticket sold 70 min before closing, on Holyrood Road, between the palace and mountain, tel. 0131/550-7800). Dynamic Earth is a stop on the hop-on-hop-off bus route.

▲▲▲Museum of Scotland—This huge museum has amassed more historic artifacts than everything I've seen in Scotland combined. It's all wonderfully displayed with fine descriptions offering a best-anywhere hike through the history of Scotland. Start in the basement and work your way through the story: prehistoric, Roman, Viking, the "birth of Scotland," Edinburgh's witch-burning craze, clan massacres, all the way to life in the 20th century. Free audioguides offer a pleasant (if slow) description of various rooms and exhibits, and even provide mood music for your wanderings (free, Mon–Sat 10:00–17:00, Tue until 20:00, Sun 12:00–17:00; free 30-min intro tours generally at 10:30, 12:30, and 15:30; 2 long blocks south of Royal Mile from St. Giles Cathedral, Chambers Street, off George IV Bridge, tel. 0131/247-4422, www.nms.ac.uk).

The **Royal Museum,** next door, fills a fine iron-and-glass Industrial Age building (built to house the museum in 1851) with all the natural sciences as it "presents the world to Scotland." It's great for school kids, but of no special interest to foreign visitors (free, same hours as Museum of Scotland).

Greyfriars Bobby—The underwhelming yet famous statue of Greyfriars Bobby (Edinburgh's favorite dog—a terrier immortalized by Disney who stood by his master's grave for 14 years) is across the street from the Museum of Scotland. Every business nearby is named for the pooch that put the fidelity into Fido.

Bonnie Wee Sights in the New Town

Cross Waverley Bridge and walk through the Georgian New Town. According to the 1776 plan, it was three streets (Princes, George, and Queen) flanked by two squares (St. Andrew and Charlotte), woven together by alleys (Thistle and Rose). George Street—20 feet wider than the others (so a four-horse carriage could make a U-turn)—was the main drag. And, while Princes Street has gone down-market, George Street still maintains its old grace. The entire elegantly planned New Town—laid out when George was king—celebrated the hard-to-sell notion that Scotland was an integral part of the United Kingdom. The streets and squares

Scottish Words

aye	yes	**inch, innis**	island
ben	mountain	**inver**	river, mouth
bonnie	beautiful	**kyle**	strait
cairn	pile of stones	**loch**	lake
cellotape	Scotch tape	**neeps**	turnips
creag	rock, cliff	**tattie**	potato

haggis rich assortment of oats and sheep organs stuffed into a chunk of sheep intestine, liberally seasoned, boiled, and eaten mostly by tourists. Usually served with "neeps and tatties." Tastier than it sounds.

are named after the British royalty (Hanover was the royal family surname). Even Thistle and Rose streets are emblems of the two happily paired nations. Rose Street, mostly pedestrian-only, is famous for its rowdy pubs. Where it hits St. Andrew Square, Rose Street is flanked by the venerable Jenners department store and a Sainsbury's supermarket. Sprinkled with popular restaurants and bars, the stately New Town is turning trendy.

▲▲**Georgian House**—This refurbished Georgian house, set on Edinburgh's finest Georgian square, is a trip back to 1796. A volunteer guide in each of the five rooms shares stories and trivia—from the kitchen in the basement to the fully-stocked medicine cabinet in the bedroom. Start your visit with two interesting videos that cover architecture and Georgian lifestyles (40 min total, shown in basement, £5 entry, daily April–Oct 10:00–17:00, March and Nov–Dec 11:00–15:00, closed Jan–Feb, 7 Charlotte Square, tel. 0131/226-3318). A walk down George Street after your visit here can be fun for the imagination.

▲▲**National Gallery of Scotland**—The elegant neoclassical building has a delightfully small but impressive collection of European masterpieces, from Raphael, Titian, and Peter Paul Rubens to Thomas Gainsborough, Claude Monet, and Vincent van Gogh. And it offers the best look you'll get at Scottish paintings. The gallery's free, but investing £2 in the fine audioguide makes the museum's highlights yours as well (daily 10:00–17:00, Thu until 19:00, tel. 0131/624-6200). The Royal Scottish Academy, next door, hosts temporary art exhibits. After your National Gallery visit, if the sun's out, enjoy a wander through Princes Street Gardens.

Princes Street Gardens—The grassy park, a former lakebed, separates Edinburgh's New and Old Towns and offers a wonderful escape from the city. Once the private domain of the local wealthy, it was opened to the public in about 1870—not as a democratic gesture, but because it was thought that allowing the public into the park would increase sales for the Princes Street department stores. Join the local office workers for a picnic lunch break. There are also cheap concerts (£2, Mon and Tue at 19:30 in June–July, at Ross Bandstand), plus the oldest floral clock in the world.

The big lake, Nord Loch, was drained around 1800 as part of the Georgian expansion of Edinburgh. Before that, the lake was the town's sewer, water reservoir, and handy place for drowning witches. Much was written about the town's infamous stink (a.k.a. the "flowers of Edinburgh"), and the town's nickname, "Auld Reekie," referred to both the smoke of its industry and the stench of its squalor.

While the Loch is now long gone, memories of the countless women drowned as witches remain. With their thumbs tied to their ankles, they'd be lashed to dunking stools. Those who survived the ordeal were considered "aided by the devil" and burned as witches. If they died, they were innocent and given a good Christian burial. Until 1720, Edinburgh was Europe's witch-burning mecca—as little as a birthmark could condemn you.

▲Sir Walter Scott Monument—Built in 1840, this elaborate neo-Gothic monument honors the great author, one of Edinburgh's many illustrious sons. Scott, who died in 1832, is considered the father of the Romantic historical novel. The 200-foot monument shelters a marble statue of Scott and his dog Maida, surrounded by busts of 16 great Scottish poets and 64 characters from his books. Scott was a great dog lover. Of the 30 dogs he had in his lifetime, his favorite was the deerhound Maida. Climbing 287 steps earns you a fine city view (£2.50, March–Oct Mon–Sat 9:00–18:00, Sun 10:00–18:00, Nov–Feb daily 10:00–15:00, tel. 0131/529-4068).

Near Edinburgh

▲*Britannia*—This much-revered vessel, which carted around Britain's royal family for more than 40 years and 900 voyages before being retired in 1997, is permanently moored at the Ocean Terminal Shopping Mall in Edinburgh's Port of Leith. It's open to the public and worth the 15-minute bus or taxi ride from the center. Explore the museum, filled with engrossing royal-family-afloat history. Then, armed with your included audioguide, you're welcome aboard. You'll tour the bridge, dining room, and living quarters, and follow in the historic footsteps of such notables as Churchill, Gandhi, and Reagan. It's easy to see how the royals must have loved the privacy this floating retreat offered (£8, daily April–Sept 9:30–18:00, Oct–March 10:00–17:00, last entry 90 min before closing, tel. 0131/555-5566, www.royalyachtbritannia.co.uk). To get here from Edinburgh, catch LRT bus #22, #34, or #35 at Waverley Bridge (£2.50 round-trip). If you're doing a city bus tour, consider the combo-ticket that includes transportation to see the *Britannia* (see page 734).

Edinburgh Crystal—Blowing, molding, cutting, polishing, and engraving, you'll see it all on a Edinburgh Crystal Company glassworks tour (£3.50, daily 10:00–15:30). There's a shop full of "bargain" second-quality pieces and a cafeteria. Take LRT bus #37 or #37A from South Bridge, or drive 10 miles south of town on A701 to Penicuik (in town look for Tesco and follow the signs). You can schedule a more expensive "VIP tour" (£10) where you actually blow glass and cut crystal (tel. 01968/675-128).

Royal Botanic Garden—Britain's second-oldest botanical garden, established in 1670 for medicinal herbs, is now one of Europe's best (free, daily March and Sept–Oct 9:30–18:00, April–Aug 9:30–19:00, Nov–Feb 9:30–16:00, 90-min "rain forest to desert" tours April–Sept daily at 11:00 and 14:00 for £2.50, a mile north of center at Inverleith Row, city tour bus to *Britannia* also stops here—see page 734, tel. 0131/552-7171, www.rbge.org.uk).

ACTIVITIES

▲▲Arthur's Seat Hike—A 45-minute hike up the 822-foot volcanic mountain (surrounded by a fine park overlooking Edinburgh) starts from the Palace of Holyroodhouse and rewards you with a commanding view. You can run up like they did in *Chariots of Fire,* or just stroll. At the summit you'll enjoy commanding views of the town and surroundings. On May Day, be on the summit at dawn and wash your face in the morning dew (it's supposedly very good for your complexion).

From the parking lot below the Palace of Holyroodhouse, two trails go up. Take the wide path on the left (easier grade, through the abbey ruins and "Hunter's Bog"). After making the summit, you can return along the other path (to the right, with the steps), which skirts the base of the cliffs.

Those staying at my recommended B&Bs can enjoy a pre-breakfast or late-evening hike starting from the other side (in June, the sun comes up early, and it stays light until nearly midnight). From the Commonwealth Pool, take Holyrood Park Road, turn right (on Queen's Drive), and continue to a small parking lot. From here, it's a 20-minute hike.

Drivers can drive up most of the way from behind (follow the one-way street from palace, park by little lake and hike up).

Brush Skiing—If you'd rather be skiing, the Midlothian Ski Centre in Hillend has a hill on the edge of town with a chairlift, two slopes, a jump slope, and rentable skis, boots, and poles. While you're actually skiing over what seems like a million toothbrushes, it feels like snow skiing on a slushy day. Beware: Local doctors are used to treating an ailment called "Hillend Thumb"—thumbs dislocated when people fall here and get tangled in the brush (£7.50/first hr, then £3/hr, includes gear, Mon–Fri 9:30–21:00, Sat–Sun 9:30–19:00, closed last 2 weeks of June, LRT bus #4 from Princes Street—garden side, tel. 0131/445-4433). It closes if it snows.

▲Royal Commonwealth Games Swimming Pool—The immense pool is open to the public, with a well-equipped fitness center (£6, includes swim), sauna (£10), and a coffee shop overlooking the pool (pool admission only-£3.50, Mon–Fri 6:00–21:30, Sat 6:00–7:45 & 10:00–16:30, Sun 10:00–16:30, closed 9:00–10:00 every Wed, no towels or suit rentals, tel. 0131/667-7211).

More Hikes—You can hike along the river (called Water of Leith) through Edinburgh. Locals favor the stretch between Roseburn and Dean Village, but the 1.5-mile walk from Dean Village to the Royal Botanic Garden is also good. This and other hikes are described in the TI's *Walks in and around Edinburgh* (ask for the free 1-page flier, not their £2 guide to walks).

Shopping—The streets to browse are Princes Street (the elegant old Jenners department store is nearby on Rose Street, at St. Andrew Square), Victoria Street (antiques galore), Nicolson Street (south of the Royal Mile for a line of interesting second-hand stores), and the Royal Mile (touristy but competitively priced). Shops are usually open from 9:00 to 17:30 (later on Thu, some closed Sun).

Edinburgh Festival

One of Europe's great cultural events, Edinburgh's annual festival turns the city into a carnival of the arts. There are enough music, dance, drama, and multicultural events to make even the most jaded traveler drool with excitement. Every day is jammed with formal and spontaneous fun. A riot of festivals—official, fringe, book, film, and jazz and blues—rage simultaneously for about three weeks each August, with the Military Tattoo starting a week earlier (the best overall Web site is www.edinburghfestivals.co.uk). Many city sights run on extended hours, and those along the Royal Mile that normally close on Sunday open in the afternoon. It's a glorious time to be in Edinburgh.

The **official festival** (mid-Aug–early Sept) is the original, more formal, and most likely to get booked up. Major events sell out well in advance. The ticket office is at **The Hub,** located in the former Tolbooth Church, near the top of the Royal Mile (tickets-£4–55, booking from mid-April, office open Mon–Sat 10:00–17:00 or longer, in Aug until 20:00 plus Sun 10:00–17:00, tel. 0131/473-2000, fax 0131/473-2003). You can also book online at www.eif.co.uk.

The less-formal **Fringe Festival** features "on the edge" comedy and theater (most of Aug, ticket/info office just below St. Giles Cathedral on the Royal Mile, 180 High Street, tel. 0131/226-0026, bookings tel. 0131/226-0000, can book online from late June on, www.edfringe.com). Tickets are usually available at the door, but popular shows can sell out.

The **Military Tattoo** is a massing of the bands, drums, and bagpipes with groups from all over what was the British Empire. Displaying military finesse with a stirring lone-piper finale, this grand spectacle fills the castle esplanade nightly except Sunday, normally from a week before the festival starts until a week before it finishes (most of Aug, Mon–Fri at 21:00, Sat at 19:30 and 22:30, £9–30, booking starts in Dec, Fri–Sat shows sell out first, all seats generally sold out 2 months ahead, some scattered same-day tickets may be available; office open Mon–Fri 10:00–16:30, during Tattoo open until show time and Sat 10:00–22:30 and Sun 12:00–17:00; 33 Market Street, behind Waverley train station, tel. 0131/225-1188, www.edinburgh-tattoo.co.uk). If nothing else, it's a really big show.

If you do manage to hit Edinburgh during the festival, book a room far in advance and extend your stay by a day or two. Once you know your dates, reserve tickets to any show that you really want to see. Call and order your ticket with your credit-card number (see Hub contact info, above). Pick up your ticket at the office the day of the show. Several publications—including the festival's official schedule, the *Edinburgh Festivals Guide Daily, The List,* the *Fringe Program,* and the *Daily Diary*—list and evaluate festival events.

Other summer festivals: jazz and blues (tel. 0131/467-5200, www.jazzmusic.co.uk), film (tel. 0131/229-2550, www.edfilmfest .org.uk), and books (tel. 0131/228-5444, www.edbookfest.co.uk).

NIGHTLIFE

▲Ghost Walks—These walks are an entertaining and cheap night out (offered nightly, usually around 19:00 and 21:00, easy socializing for solo travelers). The theatrical and creatively staged **Witchery Tours,** the most established outfit, offers two different walks: "Ghosts and Gore" and "Murder and Mystery" (£7, 90 min, leave from top of Royal Mile near castle esplanade, reservations required, tel. 0131/225-6745, www.witcherytours.com). **Auld Reekie Tours** offers a scary array of walks daily and nightly (£7, 90 min, pick up brochure or visit www.auldreekietours.co.uk). Auld Reekie is into the paranormal, witch covens, and pagan temples, taking groups into the "vaults" under the old bridges "where it was so dark, so crowded, and so squalid that the people there knew each other not by how they looked, but by how they sounded, felt, and smelt. If you had a candle, you weren't poor enough to live in the vaults. Then the great fire came. They crowded in, thinking that a brick refuge like this wouldn't burn...and they all roasted. To this day, creepy things happen in the haunted vaults of Edinburgh." If you want more, there's plenty of it (complete with screaming Gothic "jumpers").

▲▲Literary Pub Tour—This two-hour walk is interesting even if you think Sir Walter Scott was an arctic explorer. You'll follow the witty dialogue of two actors as they debate whether the great literature of Scotland was high art or the creative recreation of fun-loving louts fueled by a love of whisky. You'll wander from the Grassmarket, over the Old Town to the New Town, with stops in three pubs as your guides share their takes on Scotland's literary greats. The tour meets at the Beehive Pub on Grassmarket (£8, book online and save £1, June–Sept nightly at 19:30, April–May and Oct Thu–Sun, Nov–March Fri only, call 0131/226-6665 to confirm, www.edinburghliterarypubtour.co.uk).

Scottish Folk Evenings—These £35–40 dinner shows, generally for tour groups intent on photographing old cultural clichés, are held in huge halls of expensive hotels. (Prices are bloated to include 20 percent commissions.) Your "traditional" meal is followed by a full slate of swirling kilts, blaring bagpipes, and Scottish folk dancing with an "old-time music hall" emcee. If you like Lawrence Welk, you're in for a treat. You can sometimes see the show without dinner for about two-thirds the price. The TI has fliers on all the latest venues.

Prestonfield House offers its Scottish folk evening with or without dinner Sunday to Friday. For £28, you get the show with two drinks and a wad of haggis (20:00–22:00); £40 buys you the same, plus a four-course meal and wine (be there at 19:00). It's in the stables of "the handsomest house in Edinburgh," which now houses the recommended Rhubarb Restaurant (Priestfield Road, a 10-min walk from Dalkeith Road B&Bs, tel. 0131/225-7800, www.prestonfield.com).

Theater—Even outside of festival time, Edinburgh is a fine place for lively and affordable theater. Pick up *The List* for a complete rundown of what's on (£2.20 at newsstands).

▲Live Music in Pubs—Edinburgh used to be a good place for traditional folk music, but in the last few years, pub owners—out of economic necessity—are catering to college-aged customers more interested in beer-drinking. Pubs that were regular venues for folk music have gone pop. Rather than list places likely to change their format in a few months, I'll simply recommend the monthly *Gig Guide* (free at TI, accommodations, and various pubs, www.gigguide.co.uk). This simple little sheet lists 8 or 10 places each night that have live music. Listings are divided by genre (pop, rock, world, and folk). Generally, several bars feature live folk music every night.

Pubs in the Old Town: The **Grassmarket** neighborhood (below the castle) is sloppy with live music and rowdy people spilling out of the pubs and into what was once upon a time a busy market square. It's fun to just wander through this area late at night and check out the scene at pubs such as Finnegan's Wake, Biddy Mulligan, and White Hart Inn. By the music and crowds you'll know where to go...and where not to. Have a beer and follow your ear. On the Royal Mile, **Whistlebinkies** is famous for live music (South Bridge, tel. 0131/557-5114, www.whistlebinkies.com).

Pubs near Dalkeith Road B&Bs: Three fine and classic pubs (without a lot of noisy machines and rowdy twentysomethings) cluster within 100 yards of each other around the intersection of Duncan Street and Causewayside, near the Dalkeith Road B&B neighborhood (see "Sleeping," below). **Leslie's Pub,** sitting between a working-class and an upper-class neighborhood, has two sides. Originally the gang would go in on the right to gather around the great hardwood bar, glittering with a century of *Cheers* ambience. Meanwhile, the more delicate folks would slip in on the left, with its discreet doors, plush snugs, and ornate ordering windows. Since 1896, this Victorian classic has been appreciated for both its "real ales" and a huge selection of whiskies—the menu is six pages of fine Scotch. (Leslie's is a block downhill from the others at 49 Ratcliffe Terrace.) The **Old Bell Pub,** with a nostalgic sports-bar vibe, serves only drinks after 19:00 (see "Eating," page 764). **Swany's Pub,** perhaps a little less welcoming then the others, is a quintessential smoky hangout for the working-class boys of the neighborhood—with some fun characters to get to know. **Bierex,** a much younger and noisier scene a few blocks away, is a favorite among young people for its cheap drinks (132 Causewayside, see "Eating," page 764).

SLEEPING

The advent of big, cheap hotels has made life tough for B&Bs. Still, book ahead, especially in August, when the annual festival fills Edinburgh. Conventions, school holidays, and weekends can make finding a room tough at almost any time of year. For the best prices, book directly rather than through the TI, which charges a higher room fee and levies a £3 booking fee. "Standard" rooms, with toilets and showers a tissue-toss away, save you £10 a night.

B&Bs Off Dalkeith Road

These B&Bs—south of town near the Royal Commonwealth Pool, just off Dalkeith Road—are all top-end, sporting three or four stars. While pricey, they come with uniformly friendly hosts and great cooked breakfasts, and are a good value for people with enough money. At these not-quite interchangeable places, character is provided by the personality quirks of the hosts.

All listings are non-smoking, on quiet streets, and within a two-minute walk of a bus stop (see "Getting There," below). While

Sleep Code

(£1 = about $1.80, country code: 44, area code: 0131)
S = Single, **D** = Double/Twin, **T** = Triple, **Q** = Quad, **b** = bathroom, **s** = shower only, **no CC** = Credit Cards not accepted. You can assume credit cards are accepted unless otherwise noted.

To help you sort easily through these listings, I've divided the rooms into three categories based on the price for a standard double room with bath (during high season):

$$$ Higher Priced—Most rooms £90 or more.
$$ Moderately Priced—Most rooms between £50–90.
$ Lower Priced—Most rooms £50 or less.

you won't find phones in the rooms, several offer Internet access. Most can provide triples or even quads for families.

Prices listed are for most of peak season; if there's a range, prices slide up with summer demand. Everyone charges about 10 percent more than these prices in August (when B&Bs are unlikely to accept bookings for 1-night stays). Conversely, in winter, when there's no demand, prices get really soft. These prices are for cash; expect a 3 to 5 percent fee for using your credit card.

Near the B&Bs, you'll find plenty of good eateries (see "Eating," page 762); several good, classic pubs (see "Nightlife," above); and easy, free parking. If you bring in "take out" food, your host would probably prefer you eat it in the breakfast room rather than muck up your room—ask.

The nearest laundry option is **Sun Dial launderette** (along the bus route to the city center at 13 South Clerk Street, opposite Queens Hall, self-service or drop-off, open daily, evening hours unpredictable—call to check, tel. 0131/667-0549).

Getting There: This comfortable, safe neighborhood is a 10-minute bus ride from the Royal Mile. From the train station, TI, or Sir Walter Scott Monument, cross Princes Street and wait at the bus stop next to the Disney shop opposite the TI (80p, use exact change—no change given if you pay more; catch LRT buses #14, #30, and #33, or First bus #86; tell driver your destination is "Dalkeith Road," ride 10 min to first or second stop—depending on B&B—after the pool, ping the bell, and hop out). These buses also stop at the corner of North Bridge and High Street on the Royal Mile. Buses run from 6:00 (9:00 on Sun) to 23:00. Taxi fare between the train station or Royal Mile and the B&Bs is about £5. Taxis are easy to hail on Dalkeith Road.

Listings: The quality of all these B&Bs is more than adequate. Prices are a bit steep, but the cheaper places are often just as good

Edinburgh, Our Neighborhood

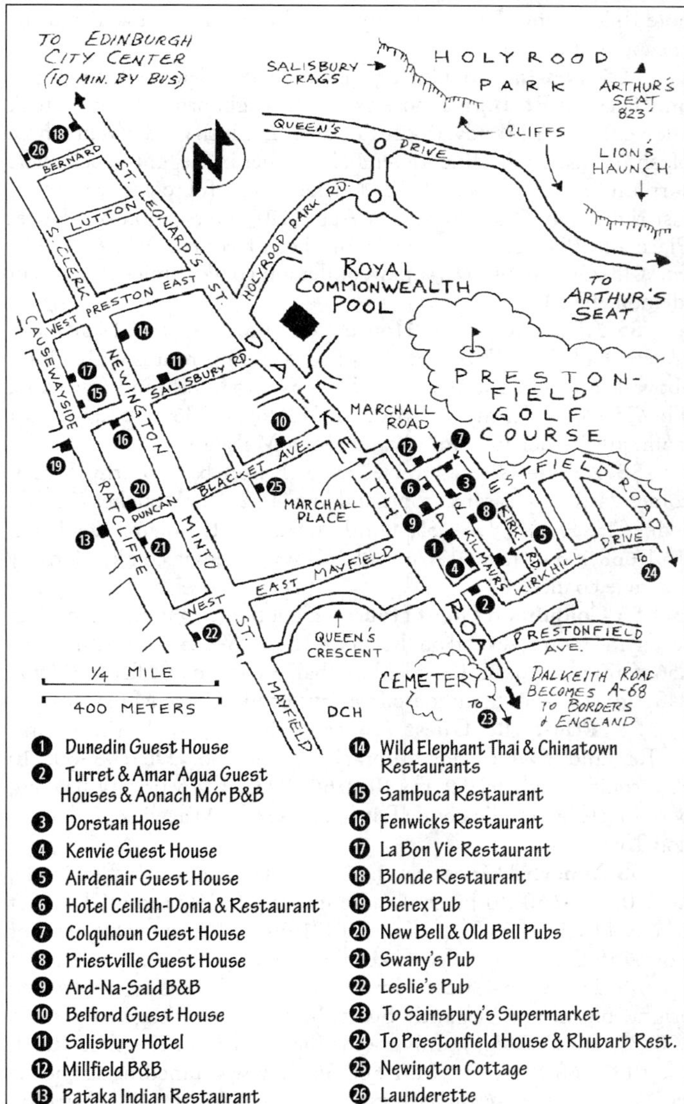

as the more expensive ones. Consider the lower-priced B&Bs, and note that among the moderately-priced (**$$**) places, I've listed the cheaper options first.

$$$ Newington Cottage is a deluxe place—Edinburgh's only five-star B&B. In a more exclusive neighborhood (signs aren't allowed) but still handy, this little palace in a lush garden rents three plush rooms. You'll dine under a chandelier in elegant neoclassical surroundings. Your host, Freda Mickel, is careful to get everything just right (Db-£80–100, Db in Aug-£110, intersection of Blacket Place and Blacket Avenue at 15 Blacket Place, tel. 0131/668-1935, fax 0131/667-4644, www.newcot.demon.co.uk, fmickel@newcot.demon.co.uk).

$$ Airdenair Guest House, offering views and homemade sweets made by Jill's parents, has five attractive rooms with a lofty above-it-all feeling (Sb-£25–35, Db-£52, Db in July and Aug–£60, Tb-£75–90, 29 Kilmaurs Road, tel. 0131/668-2336, www.airdenair.com, jill@airdenair.com, Jill and Doug McLennan).

$$ Kenvie Guest House, expertly run by Dorothy Vidler, comes with six pleasant rooms and lots of personal touches (1 small twin-£45, D-£47, Db-£55, family deals, 16 Kilmaurs Road, tel. 0131/668-1964, fax 0131/668-1926, www.kenvie.co.uk, dorothy@kenvie.co.uk).

$$ Colquhoun Guest House, in another elegant building, has seven fine rooms, several on the ground floor (S-£25–28, D-£44, Db-£56, family room, no CC, 5 Marchhall Road, tel. & fax 0131/667-8481, grace@colquhounhouse.freeserve.co.uk, Grace McAinsh).

$$ Priestville Guest House is homey, with six rooms, VCRs, and a free video library (D-£44–56, Db-£48–60, 10 Priestfield Road, tel. & fax 0131/667-2435, www.priestville.com, bookings@priestville.com, Trina and Colin Warwick and their dog Torrie).

$$ Aonach Mór has seven simple, pleasant rooms (S-£25–45, D-£50, Db-£60, 10 percent more in Aug, family rooms, Internet access, 14 Kilmaurs Terrace, tel. 0131/667-8694, www.aonachmor.com, info@aonachmor.com, keen Ross and Kathleen Birnie).

$$ Dunedin Guest House (dun-EE-din) is a fine value: bright, plush, and elegantly Scottish, with seven huge rooms (S-£30–35, Db-£60–70, family rooms for up to 5, 8 Priestfield Road, tel. 0131/668-1949, fax 0131/668-3636, www.dunedinguesthouse.co.uk, reservations@dunedinguesthouse.co.uk, Marsella Bowen).

$$ Turret Guest House is teddy-on-the-beddy cozy, with a vast bay-windowed family room (8 rooms, S-£25–37, D-£50–56, Db-£60–74, Internet access, 8 Kilmaurs Terrace, tel. 0131/667-6704, fax 0131/668-1368, www.turretguesthouse.co.uk, contact@turretguesthouse.co.uk, Jimmy and Fiona Mackie).

$$ Amar Agua Guest House is an inviting Victorian home

away from home—complete with a friendly Dalmatian. It's given a little extra sparkle by its energetic young proprietors, Dawn-Ann and Tony Costa (7 rooms, S-£25–35, Db-£60–70, free Internet access, 10 Kilmaurs Terrace, tel. 0131/667-6775, fax 0131/667-7687, www.amaragua.co.uk, rickstevesguest@amaragua.co.uk).

$$ Ard-Na-Said B&B is an elegant 1875 Victorian house with a comfy lounge and six classy rooms (Db-£60–70, 4-poster bed £10 more, family room, 5 Priestfield Road, tel. 0131/667-8754, www.ardnasaid.co.uk, jim@ardnasaid.co.uk, Jim and Olive Lyons).

$$ Dorstan House is more hotelesque and formal—with a few extra comforts—but still friendly and relaxed. Several of its 14 thoughtfully decorated rooms are on the ground floor (S-£20–40, Sb-£30–50, Ds-£40–70, Db-£50–80, family rooms, laundry service, 7 Priestfield Road, tel. 0131/667-6721, fax 0131/668-4644, www.dorstan-hotel.demon.co.uk, reservations@dorstan-hotel.demon.co.uk, Richard and Maki Stott).

$$ Hotel Ceilidh-Donia rents 14 cheery, tricked-out rooms with a pleasant back deck, a bar, and the only restaurant in the immediate area (Sb-£40, Db-£80, free Internet access for guests and diners, laundry service, 14 Marchhall Crescent, tel. 0131/667-2743, www.hotelceilidh-donia.co.uk, reservations@hotelceilidh-donia.co.uk; Max, Annette, and Alan).

$ Belford Guest House is a tidy, homey place offering seven good rooms and a warm welcome (D-£40, Db-£50, family deals, 5 percent off with cash, 13 Blacket Avenue, tel. 0131/667-2422, fax 0131/667-7508, www.belfordguesthouse.com, tom@belfordguesthouse.com, Tom Borthwick).

$ The Salisbury, more like a hotel than its neighbors, fills a classy old Georgian building with eight rooms, a large lounge, and a dumbwaiter in the breakfast room (Sb-£30–35, Db-£50, Db in July and Aug–£60, 45 Salisbury Road, tel. & fax 0131/667-1264, www.salisburyguesthouse.co.uk, brenda-wright@btconnect.com, Brenda Wright).

$ Millfield B&B, run graciously by Liz Broomfield, is thoughtfully furnished with antique class, a rare sit-and-chat ambience, and a comfy TV lounge. Since the showers are down the hall, you'll get spacious rooms and great prices (S-£22–25, D-£40–44, T-£50–60, no CC, reconfirm reservation by phone, 12 Marchhall Road, tel. & fax 0131/667-4428). Decipher the breakfast prayer by Robert Burns. Then try the "Taste of Scotland" breakfast option. See how many stone (14 pounds) you weigh in the elegant throne room.

Big, Modern Hotels

The last three of these listings are cheap as hotels go and offer more comfort than character. The first one's a splurge. In each case I'd skip the institutional breakfast and eat out.

$$$ MacDonald Hotel, my only fancy listing, is an opulent four-star splurge with 156 rooms up the street from the new parliament building. With its classy marble-and-wood decor, fitness center, and pool, it's hard to leave. On a gray winter day in Edinburgh, this could be worth it. Prices can vary wildly (Db-£110, includes breakfast, near bottom of Royal Mile, across from Dynamic Earth, Holyrood Road, tel. 0131/550-4500, fax 0131/550-4545, www.macdonaldhotels.co.uk).

$$$ Jurys Inn, a cookie-cutter place with 186 dependably comfortable rooms, is capably run and well-located a short walk from the station (Sb, Db, and Tb-all £95 Fri–Sat, £75 Sun–Thu, much cheaper off-season, breakfast-£9, 2 kids sleep free, non-smoking rooms, some views, pub/restaurant, on quiet street just off Royal Mile, 43 Jeffrey Street, tel. 0131/200-3300, fax 0131/200-0400, www.jurys.com).

$$ Ibis Hotel, mid-Royal Mile behind Tron Kirk, is well-run and perfectly located. It has 98 soulless but clean and comfy rooms drenched in prefab American charm (Db in June–Sept-£70, discounted in off-season, lousy continental breakfast-£5, non-smoking rooms, elevator, 6 Hunter Square, tel. 0131/240-7000, fax 0131/240-7007, www.ibishotels.com, h2039@accor.com).

$$ Travelodge has 193 no-nonsense rooms all decorated in dark blue and a great location. All rooms are the same, and suitable for two adults with two kids or three adults. While sleepable, it has a cheap feel with a quickly revolving staff (Sb, Db, and Tb-all £70, cheaper off-season, breakfast-£7, 33 St. Mary's Street, a block off Royal Mile, tel. 08700-850-950, www.travelodge.co.uk). Travelodge offers a swinging £25-per-room deal for a limited number of midweek bookings on their Web site.

Hostels

Edinburgh's cheap hostels are well-run and open to all, but they're scruffy and don't include breakfast. They do offer Internet access, laundry facilities, and £12–14 (unless otherwise noted) bunk beds in 8- to 16-bed single-sex dorms (about a £9–12 savings per person over B&Bs).

These three sister hostels are popular crash pads for young backpackers—youthful, hip, and beautifully located in the noisy center (www.scotlands-top-hostels.com): **High Street Hostel** (laundry-£2.50, kitchen, 8 Blackfriars Street, just off High Street/Royal Mile, tel. 0131/557-3984); **Royal Mile Backpackers** (105 High Street, tel. 0131/557-6120); and **Castle Rock Hostel** (just below the castle and above the pubs, 15 Johnston Terrace, tel. 0131/225-9666).

Brodies 2 Backpacker Hostel, spartan, clean, and beautifully located in the middle of the Royal Mile, rents 70 cheap beds in 4- to

8-bed dorms (£15–20 per bed, lockers, kitchen, free Internet access, laundry, 93 High Street, tel. 0131/556-2223, www.brodieshostels.co.uk). Older travelers feel more comfortable here than in the above hostels.

For more regulations and less color, try the two IYHF hostels: **Bruntsfield Hostel** (6–12 beds/room, near golf course, 7 Bruntsfield Crescent; buses #11, #15, #16, and #17 from Princes Street; tel. 0131/447-2994) and **Edinburgh Hostel** (4–10 beds/room, 5-min walk from Haymarket station, 18 Eglinton Crescent, tel. 0131/337-1120).

EATING

Along the Royal Mile

Historic pubs and doily cafés with reasonable, unremarkable meals abound. While the eateries along this most-crowded stretch of the city are invariably touristy, the scene is fun and competition makes a well-chosen place a good value. Here are some handy, affordable options for a good bite to eat (listed in downhill order; for locations, see map on page 739).

The Red Coat Café and Jacobite Room is a big, bright, efficient cafeteria in the heart of the castle (£6 quick, healthy meals). Punctuating the two parts of your castle visit (the castle itself and the impressive National War Museum of Scotland) with a break here is smart.

The Hub, a classy place in the old Tolbooth Church at the top of the Mile, serves gourmet sandwiches and fine desserts. While it's a bit pricey, the food is delightfully presented, the service is smart, and you're supporting the Edinburgh Festival (which owns the restaurant, and also has its booking office here). Sit in the bright-yellow Gothic interior or outside, with a wonderful Royal Mile perch (£6 sandwiches, inexpensive lunch menu is stowed at 17:30, £15 dinners from 18:00, open Mon–Fri 9:30–21:00, Sat–Sun 9:30–18:00, Castlehill, tel. 0131/473-2067).

The Elephant House, two blocks out of the touristy zone, is where locals browse newspapers in the stay-a-while back room, listen to soft rock, and sip coffee or munch a light meal. The friendly staff explain their enticing buffet line most of the day, then switch to table service after 18:00 (vegetarian-friendly, daily 8:00–23:00, 4 computers with cheap and fast Internet access, 2 blocks south of Royal Mile near Museum of Scotland at 21 George IV Bridge, tel. 0131/220-5355). It's easy to imagine J. K. Rowling annoying waiters with her baby pram while spending long afternoons gathering ideas for her Harry Potter saga in cafés like this.

The Outsider, also without a hint of Royal Mile tourism, is a sleek spot serving modern Mediterranean and Southeast Asian cuisine (good fish and stir-fry) in a minimalist maxi-chic setting. Cobble together a fun meal of £7-10 plates from their creative and trendy menu. As you'll be competing with local yuppies, reserve for dinner (daily 12:00–24:00, ground floor is non-smoking, 30 yards up from Elephant House at 15 George IV Bridge, tel. 0131/226-3131).

Deacon Brodie's Tavern is a sloppy pub serving soup, sandwiches, and snacks on the ground floor and basic £9 pub meals upstairs in the restaurant. While painfully touristy, it's dead center on the Mile with a fun history (daily 12:00–22:00, kids are welcome upstairs, tel. 0131/225-6531).

St. Giles Cathedral Lower Aisle, hiding under the landmark church, is *the* place for paupers to munch prayerfully. Stairs on the back side of the church lead into the basement, where you'll find simple, light lunches from 11:45 and coffee with cakes all day (Mon–Fri 9:00–16:30, Sun 10:00–13:30, closed Sat).

Always Sunday Food Company is a tiny place with a wonderful formula. It's a flexible fantasy of Scottish and Mediterranean hot dishes, fresh salads, smoked salmon, sharp cheese, homemade desserts, and so on. You're invited to mix and match at their user-friendly, create-a-lunch buffet line. They use healthy ingredients and are hip to any diet concerns. Sit inside or people-watch from Royal Mile tables outside (£5 lunches, daily 8:00–18:00, 30 yards below St. Giles Cathedral at 170 High Street, tel. 0131/622-0667).

The Filling Station, a big, noisy eatery decorated with old car parts, has an American-type menu and rocks at night. Behind its youthful bar stretches a family-friendly dining hall where you'll get pizza, pasta, and burgers for £7–10 (daily 12:00–23:30, 235 High Street, near North Bridge, tel. 0131/226-2488).

Dubh Prais Scottish Restaurant is a dressy eight-table place filling a cellar 10 steps and a world away from the High Street bustle. The owner-chef, James McWilliams, proudly serves Scottish "fayre" at its very best (including gourmet haggis). The daily specials are not printed, to guard against "zombie waiters." They like to get to know you a bit by explaining things (£8.50 2-course lunches Tue–Fri 12:00–14:00, £27 dinners Tue–Sat 18:30–22:30, closed Sun–Mon, reservations smart at night, opposite Radisson SAS Hotel at 123 High Street, tel. 0131/557-5732).

The World's End Pub, a colorful old place, dishes up hearty £5 meals from a creative menu in a fun, dark, and noisy space (daily 11:00–21:00, 4 High Street, tel. 0131/556-3628).

The Tea Room is a fragile hole-in-the-wall serving light lunches, scones, and fine tea in yellow elegance (daily 10:30–16:30, next to Museum of Edinburgh at 158 Canongate). Next door, **Bene's** fries up good, greasy fish-and-chips to go (munch in graveyard across street).

Clarinda's Tea Room, near the bottom of the Royal Mile, is charming and girlish—a fine and tasty place to relax after touring the Mile or the Palace of Holyroodhouse (quiche, salad, and soup lunches for £5, Mon–Sat 9:00–16:45, Sun 10:00–16:45, 69 Canongate, tel. 0131/557-1888). It's great for tea and cake anytime.

In the New Town

While most of your sightseeing will be along the Royal Mile, it's important that your Edinburgh experience stretches beyond this happy tourist gauntlet. Just a few minutes away, in the Georgian town, you'll find a bustling world of real office workers, students, and pensioners doing their thing. At mid-day that includes eating. Simply hiking over to one of these places will give you a good helping of Edinburgh today. All these places are within a few minutes' walk of the TI and main Waverley Bridge tour bus depot.

Café Royal is a movie producer's dream pub—the perfect *fin de siècle* setting for a coffee, beer, or light meal. (In fact, parts of *Chariots of Fire* were filmed here.) Drop in, if only to admire the 1880 tiles featuring famous inventors (daily 12:00–14:00 & 19:00–late, 2 blocks from Princes Mall on West Register Street, tel. 0131/556-4124). There are two eateries here: the pub (basic £6 meals) and the dressier restaurant, specializing in fish and game (2-course lunch with wine for £15, £20 plates, reserve for dinner as it's quite small and understandably popular).

The Dome Restaurant serves decent meals around a classy bar and under the elegant 19th-century skylight dome of what was a fancy bank. With soft jazz and dressy, white-tablecloth ambience, it feels a world apart (£12 plates until 17:00, £17 dinners until 22:00, daily 12:00–22:00, modern international cuisine, open for a drink anytime under the dome or in the adjacent Art Deco bar, 14 George Street, tel. 0131/624-8624, reserve for dinner). Notice the facade of this former bank building—the various ways to make money fill the pediment with all the nobility of classical gods.

The St. Andrew's Church Undercroft, in the basement of a fine old church, is the cheapest place in town for lunch (£2 sandwich and soup, Mon–Fri 12:00–14:00, on George Street, just off St. Andrew Square). Your tiny bill helps support the good work of the Church of Scotland.

Henderson's Salad Table and Wine Bar has fed a generation of New Town vegetarians hearty cuisine and salads (3-course lunch for £9, Mon–Sat 8:00–22:45, closed Sun, non-smoking, strictly vegetarian, pleasant live music nightly, always jazz on weekends, between Queen and George streets at 94 Hanover Street, tel. 0131/225-2131). Henderson's two different seating areas use the same self-serve cafeteria line. For the same healthy food with more elegant seating and table service, eat at the attached **Henderson's Bistro.**

Edinburgh's New Town

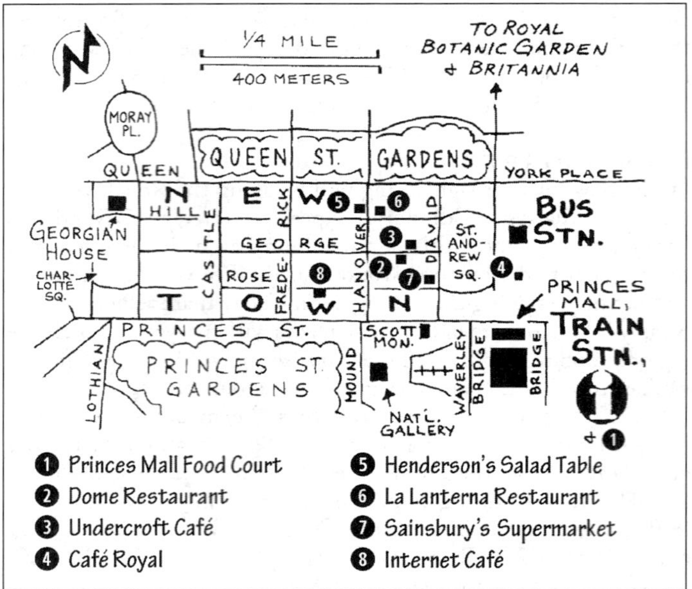

Ristorante La Lanterna is packed with local office workers who enjoy good southern Italian cuisine with friendly service (£5 pastas, £12 plates, pricier at dinner, no pizza, Mon–Sat 12:00–14:30 & 17:30–22:30, closed Sun, dinner reservations wise, 2 blocks off Princes Street, 83 Hanover Street, tel. 0131/226-3090, attentive Antonietta oversees the action).

Princes Mall Food Court, below the TI and above the station, is a circus of sticky fast-food joints littered with paper plates and shoppers (Mon–Sat 8:30–18:00, Thu until 19:00, Sun 11:00–17:00). If you'd prefer pubs, browse nearby Rose Street.

Supermarket: The glorious **Sainsbury's** supermarket, with a tasty assortment of take-away food and specialty coffees, is just one block from the Sir Walter Scott Monument and the lovely picnic-perfect Princes Street Gardens (Mon–Sat 7:00–22:00, Sun 10:00–20:00, on corner of Rose Street, on St. Andrew Square, across the street from Jenners, the classy department store).

Dalkeith Road Area, near Your B&B

All these places are within a 10-minute walk of my recommended B&Bs. Most are on or near the intersection of Newington and East Preston Streets. For locations, see map on page 755.

The nearest supermarkets aren't near. **Sainsbury's** is a 10-minute walk or a quick bus ride down Dalkeith Road away from town in the Cameron Toll shopping complex (Mon–Sat 7:30–22:00, Sun 8:00–19:00, tel. 0131/666-5200). There's also a **Tesco** between this neighborhood and the Royal Mile (Mon–Sat 7:00–24:00, Sun 9:00–22:00, 5 long blocks south of the Royal Mile, on Nicolson, just south of intersection with West Richmond Street).

Scottish/French Restaurants

These classy little eight-table places feature "Auld Alliance" cuisine—Scottish cooking with a French flair (seasoned with a joint historic disdain for England). They offer small menus with three or four items per course for two- or three-course meals (about £10 for a 2-course lunch, £20 for a 3-course dinner). For a cozy drink after dinner, visit the recommended pubs in the area (see "Nightlife," page 753).

Fenwicks is cozy and reliable, with tasty Scottish and continental food and no French fries. It's pricey, but this little linoleum, brown, and woody bistro is considered a good value by locals (main course-£13–16, 3-course £20 *menu*, daily 12:00–14:00 & 18:00–late, 15 Salisbury Place, tel. 0131/667-4265).

La Bon Vie Brassiere is candlelit chic with an enticing menu. This upmarket place serves modern Scottish/French cuisine (early special: a *plat du jour* with coffee-£5 until 19:00, later the 4-course gourmet *menu* is £20, you can B.Y.O. wine for £2 cork fee; daily 12:00–14:00 & 18:00–22:00, 49 Causewayside, tel. 0131/667-1110).

Blonde Restaurant, with a more eclectic and European menu, is less expensive, bigger, and more crowded than the others, with no set-price dinners. It's a bit out of the way, but a hit with locals (about £14 for 2 courses, good vegetarian options, Tue–Sun 12:00–14:30 & 18:00–22:00, closed Mon, 75 St. Leonard's Street, tel. 0131/668-2917).

Hotel Ceilidh-Donia serves well-prepared fish, meat, and vegetarian dishes in a flagstone-floored, high-ceilinged space with a small, friendly adjoining pub. The decor is likeably kitschy with attitude, and the garden seating is a delight (£10 plates with good vegetables, dinner from 18:30, closed Sun, free Internet access for customers, 14 Marchhall Crescent, tel. 0131/667-2743). This is the only place in the immediate neighborhood of the recommended B&Bs.

Scottish Grub and Pubs

The New Bell serves up filling modern Scottish fare, from steak and salmon to haggis, in a Victorian living room setting above the lovable Old Bell Pub. Along with wonderfully presented meals, you'll enjoy white tablecloths, oriental carpets on hardwood floors, and a relaxing spaciousness under open beams (2-course £11 special until 18:45, £13 plates 17:30–22:00, open daily always a veggie option, 233 Causewayside, tel. 0131/668-2868).

The Old Bell Pub, with an old-time sports-bar ambience—fishing, golf, horses—serves simpler £7 pub meals from the same fine kitchen on the ground floor. This is a classic snug pub, littered with evocative knickknacks. It comes with fine sidewalk seating and a mixed-age crowd (nightly, last meal order at 19:00, then drinks only, 233 Causewayside, tel. 0131/668-2868).

Bierex, a youthful pub, is the neighborhood favorite for modern dishes, camaraderie, and cheap booze. It's a spacious, bright, mahogany-and-leather place popular for its long and varied happy hours (£6 plates, daily 10:00–24:00, food served 10:00–21:00, Fri–Sat until 20:00, 132 Causewayside, tel. 0131/667-2335).

Rhubarb Restaurant is the hottest thing in Old World elegance. It's in "Edinburgh's most handsome house"—a riot of antiques, velvet, tassels, and fringes. The plush rhubarb color theme reminds visitors that this was the place where rhubarb was first grown in Britain. It's a 10-minute walk past the other recommended eateries behind Arthur's Seat, in a huge estate with big, shaggy Highland cows enjoying their salads *al fresco.* While most spend a wad here (plates around £20), smart budget travelers time their visit to take advantage of the great off-hours two-course meal for £14 (served 12:00–15:00, 18:00–19:00, and 22:00–23:00, reserve in advance and dress up if you can, in Prestonfield House, Priestfield Road, tel. 0131/225-1333, www.rhubarb-restaurant.com). For details on the Scottish folk evening offered here, see "Nightlife," page 752.

The noisy **Poolside Café** at the huge Commonwealth Pool on Dalkeith Road has sandwiches, soup, and salads for hungry swimmers and budget travelers alike (Mon–Fri 10:00–18:00, Sat–Sun 11:00–17:00, pass the entry without paying).

Ethnic Options

Pataka Indian Restaurant is a tight little 10-table "Indian bistro" with attentive service and great food. With big portions and small prices, it's understandably popular with locals (£7 dishes, daily 12:00–14:00 & 17:30–23:30, also offers take-away, 190 Causewayside, tel. 0131/668-1167).

Wild Elephant Thai Restaurant is a small, hardworking eatery that locals consider the best around for Thai (main dishes £6–10, £10 3-course meal until 20:00, open daily 17:00–23:00, also does take-away, 21 Newington Road, tel. 0131/662-8822).

Chinatown is an energetic little place that packs a lot of happy eating into its one small dining room (£6–9, Tue–Fri 12:00–14:00 & 17:30–23:00, Sat–Sun 17:30–23:30, closed Mon, reservations smart on weekend nights, take-away food 25 percent cheaper, 13 Newington Road, tel. 0131/662-0555).

Sambuca Italian Restaurant dishes up good pizza and pasta in a lively bistro where the only decor is the food and the only music is the sound of contented eaters (£7 pasta and pizza, £8–10 dishes, Mon–Sat 12:30–14:30 & 17:00–late, Sun 17:00–10:00, 103 Causewayside, tel. 0131/667-3307).

TRANSPORTATION CONNECTIONS

From Edinburgh by Train to: Glasgow (4/hr, 60 min, £7 one-way, £9 round-trip), **Inverness** (7/day, 4 hrs), **Oban** (3/day, 4.5 hrs, change in Glasgow), **York** (2/hr, 2.5 hrs), **London** (hrly, 5 hrs), **Durham** (hrly, 2 hrs, less frequent in winter), **Newcastle** (hrly, 1.5 hrs), **Keswick**/Lake District (south past Carlisle to Penrith, then catch bus to Keswick, 6/day, fewer Sun, 40 min), **Birmingham** (6/day, 4.5 hrs), **Crewe** (6/day, 3.5 hrs), **Bristol**/near Bath (hrly, 6-7 hrs). Train info: tel. 08457-484-950, www.gner.co.uk.

By Bus to: Oban (4/day, 4 hrs, not on Sun), **Fort William** (1/day, 4 hrs), **Inverness** (hrly, 4 hrs), **Blackpool** (Fri, Sat, Mon only, requires change in Glasgow, 5 hrs), **York** (1/day at 9:45, 5 hrs). For bus info, call Scottish Citylink (tel. 08705-505-050, www.citylink.co.uk) or National Express (tel. 08705-808-080). You can get info and tickets at the bus desk inside the Princes Mall TI.

ATHENS

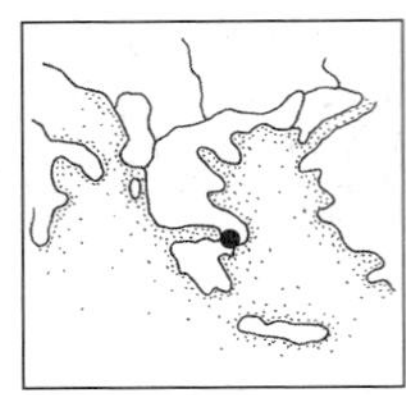

A century and a half ago, Athens was a humble city of about 8,000 people huddled at the base of the Acropolis. Today it's the teeming home of about four million Greeks.

One out of every three Greeks packs into this city—not because of its charm, but in hopes of good employment. The city is famous for its sprawl, noise, and pollution. The best advice to tourists has long been to see the big sights, then get out. But over the last decade or so, the city has made a concerted effort to curb pollution, clean up and pedestrianize the streets, spiff up the museums, and invest in one of Europe's better public transit systems. And with the 2004 Olympic Games powering even more urban upgrades, Athens feels like a different place to those who backpacked here in the days of Jackie and Ari O.

Even so, the conventional wisdom still holds true: Athens is a great city to see...but not to linger in. See the big sights (Acropolis, Ancient Agora, National Archaeological Museum), enjoy the shopping, eating, and strolling ambience of the Plaka (19th-century old town), and move on.

Planning Your Time

Athens' top sights, the Acropolis/Ancient Agora and the National Archaeological Museum, deserve a half day each. Two days total is plenty of time for the casual tourist to see the city's main attractions.

Day 1: In the morning, follow my "Welcome to Athens" self-guided walk (see page 773). Spend midday in the markets (shopping in the Plaka, browsing in the Central Market, and wandering through the flea market). Grab a souvlaki lunch near Monastiraki.

Athens Overview

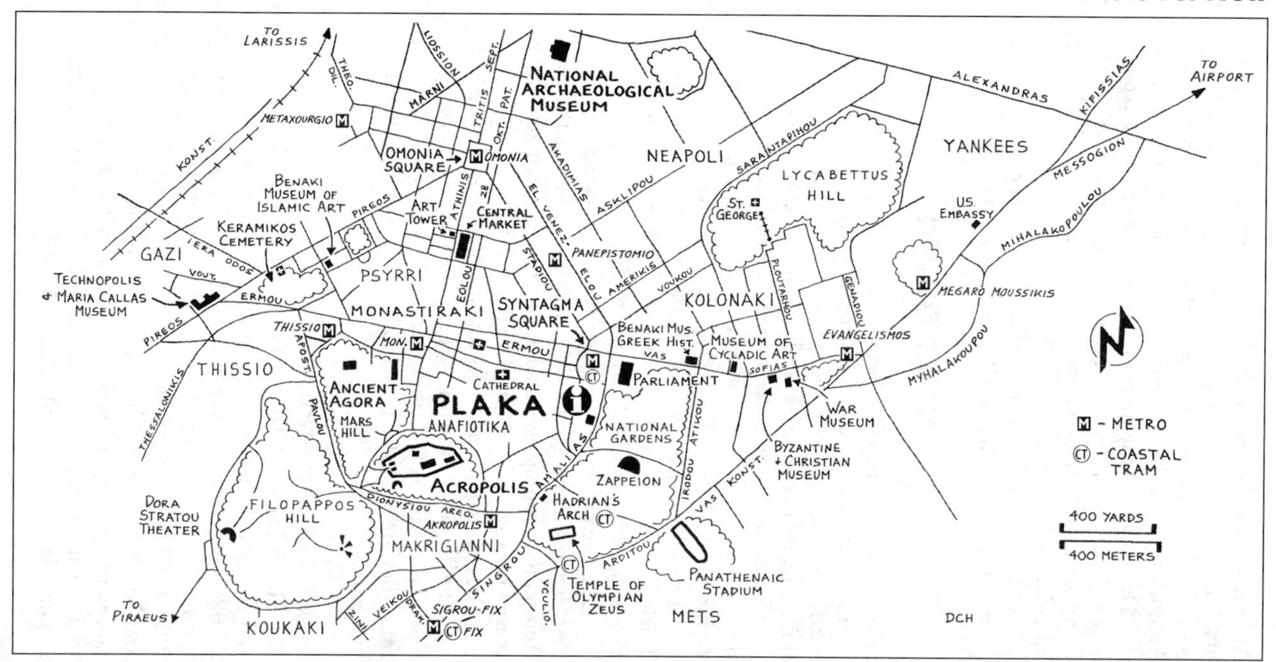

After lunch, do the ancient biggies—tour the Ancient Agora, then the Acropolis (confirming carefully how late the Acropolis is open). Be the last person off the Acropolis. Stroll down the Dionysiou Areopagitou into the Plaka for your evening meal and music.

Day 2: Spend the morning visiting museums or exploring the Plaka. After lunch, head to the National Archaeological Museum. Consider a bus tour to see the sunset at Cape Sounion's Temple of Poseidon (see "Tours," page 773).

Classical scholars and art-lovers will want more time to visit more of the archaeological sites, museums, and galleries.

ORIENTATION

Ninety-five percent of Athens is noisy, polluted modern sprawl, jammed with characterless concrete suburbs, poorly planned and hastily erected to house the city's rapidly expanding population. But forget all that, and pretend the old center is all there is.

For the sightseer, Athens is small. With the major exception of the National Archaeological Museum, everything of importance is within a few blocks of the Acropolis. This city-within-a-city takes in the districts of Monastiraki, Plaka, Syntagma, Kolonaki, Psyrri, Thisio, and Gazi to the north of the Acropolis, and Koukaki, Pangrati, Mets, and Makrigianni to the south.

The narrow, winding streets of the Plaka can be confusing at first, but you can't get too lost with a monument the size of the Acropolis looming overhead to keep you oriented. Street signs everywhere are in both Greek and English.

A good map is a necessity for enjoying Athens on foot. The fine map the TI gives out works great. One way or another, get a good map and use it. Note that due to the inexact science of translating from the Greek to the Roman alphabet, spellings of street names may vary.

Tourist Information

The Greek National Tourist Organization (EOT) covers Athens and the rest of the country (Mon–Fri 9:00–22:00, Sat–Sun 9:00–20:00, shorter hours in winter; from top of Syntagma Square facing the Parliament, head right a few blocks south to Amalias 26; tel. 210-331-0392, www.gnto.gr, info-desk@gnto.gr). Pick up their free and handy city map. They also have listings of museums, entertainment options, bus and train information, and ferry schedules to destinations throughout Greece. EOT also has an office at the airport (daily 8:00–22:00, tel. 210-353-0445).

Arrival in Athens

By Bus: Athens has two main intercity bus stations. Buses from the Peloponnese arrive at Terminal A (4 miles northwest of the center; bus #051 runs between the terminal and the junction of Zinonos and Menandrou, near Omonia Square, 4/hr, 5:00–24:00). A taxi from Terminal A to Syntagma should cost no more than €10 at any time. If you're arriving from Delphi, you'll be dropped at Terminal B (just over a mile north of Omonia Square, off Liossion; bus #024 goes from Liossion to Syntagma Square). The city plans to eventually combine these intercity bus stations at a new terminal in the Moschato area, near Piraeus.

By Train: Athens' new intercity train station is 13 miles north of the city center at Arharnon. Frequent suburban trains zip travelers from here into the city center and out to Piraeus.

By Plane: Metro Line 3 connects the airport with the city center. For information about Athens' Elefthérios Venizélos International Airport, see page 806.

Getting Around Athens

By Metro: The Metro is the best way to travel around central Athens. Trains run about every five minutes (5:00–24:00, www.ametro.gr). Buy the €0.70 tickets at machines or from ticket windows. Be sure to stamp your ticket in the machine before boarding. Those riding without a ticket (or with an unstamped ticket) are subject to stiff fines. The €3 public-transit day pass generally isn't worthwhile.

There are three lines:

Line 1 (green) runs from the port of Piraeus to the northern suburbs. Important stops include Monastiraki (city center), Plateia Viktorias (National Archaeological Museum), and Irini (Olympic Stadium—this stop may be closed in 2006). You can transfer to Line 2 at Omonia, and to Line 3 at Monastiraki.

Line 2 (red) runs from Sepolia in the northwest to Dafni in the southeast. By 2006, this line may have been extended at either end. Important stops include Larissis (train station), Syntagma (city center), and Akropoli (Acropolis and Makrigianni). Transfer to Line 1 at Omonia, and to Line 3 at Syntagma.

Line 3 (blue) runs from Monastiraki to the airport. Important stops are Syntagma and Evangelismos (Byzantine and War museums). Transfer to Line 1 at Monastiraki, and to Line 2 at Syntagma.

By Bus: Athens' buses are slow and overcrowded. Avoid them unless you're connecting the two intercity bus stations. Buy the €0.45 tickets in advance, either from a special ticket kiosk or from one of the many regular kiosks that dot the streets. Tickets must be validated in the orange machines as you board.

By Coastal Tram: The Athens Coastal Tram starts at Syntagma

Athens Public Transportation

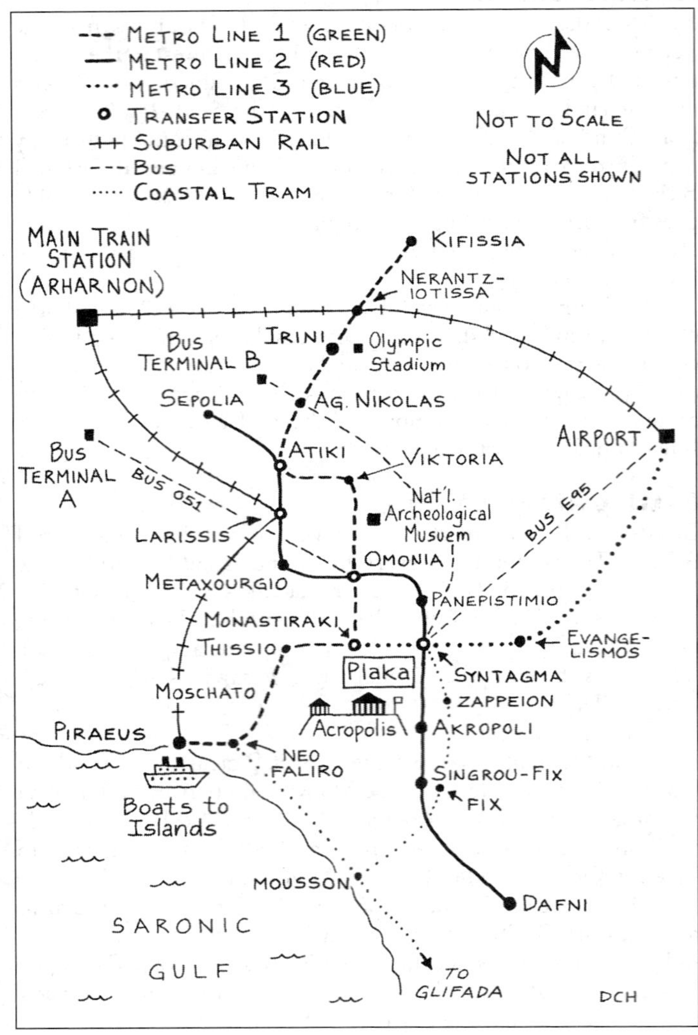

and runs 18 miles through the neighborhoods of Neos Kosmos and Nea Smyrni, emerging at the sea near Paleo Faliro. From there, it splits to either the Stadium and Olympic coastal complex in Neo Faliro, or past the marinas and beaches to Glyfada Square (€0.60; €0.40 transfers from other public transport within 90 min).

By Train: A suburban train network fans out from the new Athens Central Station at Arharnon. The line south to Piraeus stops at Larissis station, providing access to the Metro system.

Another line runs to the airport, stopping at the Olympic Stadium on the way.

By Taxi: Athens is a great taxi town. Its yellow taxis are cheap and helpful (€0.75 to start, then €0.25 per km, plus surcharges: €0.60 from ports and train and bus stations, €1 from the airport). While the day rate (tariff 1 on the meter) is €0.25 per kilometer, the rate doubles between midnight and 5:00 in the morning (tariff 2). Baggage costs €0.30 for each item over 10 kg (about 22 pounds). The minimum fare of €1.50 covers most journeys in central Athens.

Athens' cabbies double up—picking up more customers heading the same way—so there's no guarantee that you'll have the cab to yourself. Unfortunately, sharing the cab doesn't mean sharing the fare. The cabbie makes more and the passengers save nothing. Still, this makes it easier to find an available cab. You can simply hail any empty cab, or wave at a cab with a customer going your way and tell them where you're going. (If your destination works for the cabbie, he'll welcome you in.) Hotels routinely call cabs for guests (for a hefty €2 surcharge).

Helpful Hints

Theft Alert: Be wary of pickpockets at all times, particularly in crowds, at the Sunday Flea Market, on the Metro between the city and Piraeus, and at the port.

Bar Alert: Single male travelers are strongly advised to stay away from bars recommended by strangers encountered on the street. It sounds like an easy trap to avoid, but the steady flow of victims suggests otherwise. A dozen or so con men cruise the streets around the Plaka and Syntagma Square, looking for likely dupes. They are pros who speak multiple languages and specialize in putting travelers at ease. They pretend that they, too, are strangers in town who just happen to have stumbled upon a "great little bar." Your newfound friend will then take you to one of the area's sleazy bars and keep buying bottles of overpriced Champagne for the friendly girls that inevitably appear—and insist that you "share" the bill.

Telephones: All OTE phone booths work with cards (€3, €6, or €9; 3 min costs €0.30)—not coins. Cheap international phone cards work fine for both local and international calls. Both types of cards are sold at news kiosks.

Emergency: The "Tourist Police" is a special branch of the Greek police force responsible for handling problems such as disputes with hotels, restaurants, and other tourist services (available daily 24 hours; in the suburb of Koukaki, south of the Acropolis, at Veikou 43-45; tel. 210-920-0724). They also act as a contact point between tourists and other branches of the police force. The tourist police also staff a 24-hour information service (tel. 171) for emergency help. U.S. citizens can call tel. 210-721-2951 for emergency medical aid.

Embassies: The United States Embassy is at Leoforos Vasilissis Sofias 91 (tel. 210-721-2951, www.usembassy.gr), near the Megalo Musikis Metro station. The Canadian Embassy is nearby at Genadiou 4 (tel. 210-727-3400).

Bookshops: Eleftheroudakis is Greece's largest bookshop, with a floor for travel guides and maps and an entire floor for English books (Mon–Fri 9:00–20:00, Sat 9:00–17:00, closed Sun, Panepistimiou 17, Syntagma, tel. 210-331-4180). They run a smaller branch in the Plaka (Nikis 20, tel. 210-322-9388). The Compendium Bookstore stocks only English-language books (includes second-hand section, Mon–Fri 9:00–20:00, Sat 9:00–17:00, closed Sun, Nikis 28, Plaka, tel. 210-322-1248).

Car Rental: Syngrou Avenue is Athens' "rental car lane," with all the big companies (and piles of little ones) competing fiercely for your business. Syngrou is an easy walk from the Plaka and recommended hotels. Budget travelers can often negotiate great deals by visiting a few rental places and haggling.

Laundry: Plaka Laundrette charges €8 to wash, dry, and fold an 11-pound load (June–Sept Mon–Sat 8:00–20:00, Sun 8:00–15:00; Oct–May Mon–Sat 8:00–18:00, Sun 10:00–14:00; Angelou Geronta 10, tel. 210-321-3102).

Internet Access: EasyInternetcafé at Syntagma Square is handy and open all the time (bottom of square, right of McDonald's, enter through Everest). **Bits and Bytes** is also always open (Kapnikarea 19, Plaka). Across the street from the National Archaeological Museum, the **Museum Internet Café** has very fast access and the inviting atmosphere of a sprawling Starbucks (daily 9:00–24:00, on the left as you face the museum at Patision 46, tel. 210-883-3418). Hanging out here while sipping and surfing is a joy after a museum visit.

American Express: The main American Express office is at Ermou 2, just off Syntagma Square (Mon–Fri 8:30–16:00, Sat 8:30–13:30, closed Sun, tel. 210-324-4979). Its foreign-exchange office is 100 yards downhill at Ermou 7 (tel. 210-322-3380).

Post Offices: The most convenient post office for travelers is at Syntagma Square (Mon–Fri 7:30–20:00, Sat 7:30–14:00, closed Sun, bottom of the square, at corner with Mitropoleos). Smaller neighborhood offices include Monastiraki (Mon–Fri 7:30–14:00, closed Sat–Sun, Mitropoleos 58) and Makrigianni (Mon–Fri 7:30–14:00, closed Sat–Sun, Dionysiou Areopagitou 7). Overseas parcels over four pounds have to be inspected and mailed from the special Parcel Post Office (Mon–Fri 7:30–14:00, closed Sat–Sun, in the arcade between Amerikis and Voukourestiou, near Syntagma Square).

TOURS

Bus Tours—Four main companies run bus tours around Athens: Hop In Sightseeing (Zanni 29, in Piraeus, tel. 210-428-5500, www.hopin.com), CHAT (Xenofontos 9, tel. 210-322-3137, www.chatours.gr), GO Tours (Athanassiou 20, tel. 210-921-9555), and Key Tours (Kalirois 4, tel. 210-923-3166).

Hop In is popular for its fleet of deluxe, modern buses, and because it runs its tours only in English—so you don't have to listen to guides repeating themselves in a string of different languages. It offers a basic four-hour city tour, including a guided tour of the Acropolis, for €46 (€64 extended version includes National Archaeological Museum). Evening activities include a 90-mile round-trip drive down the coast to Cape Sounion to see the sunset at the Temple of Poseidon (€32, 4 hrs—not worth the time if you'll be seeing ancient sites elsewhere in Greece), and a night city tour that finishes with folk dancing at a taverna (€52). Hop In also offers one-day tours to Delphi and to Mycenae, Nafplio, and Epidavros (either tour €82 with lunch; €72 for tour only), and two-day tours to the monasteries of Meteora (€142).

It's convenient to book tours through your hotel; most act as a booking agent for at least one tour company. While they are in business to snare a commission, some offer substantial discounts on the listed prices as a service to their guests.

Walking Tours—For those who prefer to explore on foot, **City Walking Tours** offers a choice of five different walks (€29 per tour, all depart daily at 9:15, meet outside Syntagma Metro Station in Syntagma Square, walks last 3–4 hours, office open Mon–Fri 10:00–17:00, closed Sat–Sun, tel. 210-884-7269, mobile 694-585-9662).

For a **private local guide**, contact the Union of Official Guides (tel. 210-322-9705, about €140 per half-day).

Welcome to Athens Walk: Syntagma and Plaka

This self-guided walking tour is a great way to link the major attractions of the fascinating old Plaka district and surrounding areas. It starts at Syntagma Square, finishes at Monastiraki (near Ancient Agora, markets, and good restaurants), and involves about 45 minutes of actual walking. Allow closer to three hours if you intend to explore along the way.

Syntagma Square: In 1830, the Plaka was the nucleus of Athens. Syntagma Square (now the heart of the city) was on the outskirts of town. It was created in 1834 as part of a grand plan drawn up by the bevy of Bavarian architects called in by King Otto's father, Ludwig I, to create a worthy capital for newly independent Greece.

Plaka

TO KERAMIKOS CEMETERY
MONASTIRAKI SQUARE
TO OMONIA SQUARE & NATIONAL ARCHAEOLOGICAL MUSEUM
CHURCH OF KAPNIKAREA
HOTEL GRANDE BRETAGNE
TO BENAKI MUSEUM OF GREEK HISTORY
ERMOU
THISSIO
THISS.
AG. FIL.
ADRIANOU
TEMPLE OF HEPHAESTUS
MON.
IFESTOU
ATHINAS
EOLOU
EVANG.
PERIKLEOUS
LEKA
VOULIS
STADIOU
AMER.
EL. VENEZELOU
VOUKO.
NAT'L. BANK
VAS. SOFIAS
PANDROSSOU
KAP.
MITRO.
POST
CATHEDRAL
SYNTAGMA SQUARE
PARLIAMENT
STOA OF ATTALOS (MUSEUM)
VRISSAKI
AREOS
HADRIAN'S LIBRARY
DEX.
POLEOS
AGIOS ELEF.
ANCIENT AGORA
PIKLIS
TZAMI
POP. INSTR. MUSEUM
APOLONOS
FILELINON
XENO.
AMALIAS
TOMB OF THE UNKNOWN WARRIOR
PANATHENAIC WAY
DIOG.
ROMAN AGORA
TOWER OF THE WINDS
AG. FILO.
THOUK.
NIKIS
PALACE OF GIANTS
POLI.
LYSS.
FLESSA
NIKODIMOU
JEWISH MUSEUM
NATIONAL GARDEN
APOSTOLOU
CHURCH OF HOLY APOSTLES
DIOSKOURON
PANOS
KLEPSID.
ALM.
MINI.
IPER.
KEK.
ERE.
PRIT.
THEORIAS
EPI.
KYDATHINEON
ANAFIOTIKA
MARS HILL
M - METRO
CT - COASTAL TRAM
TRIPO.
ST. GEORGE
MUSEUM OF GREEK FOLK ART
PARTHENON
STRATONOS
THESPIDOS
DEDALOU
ZAPPEION
PAVLOU
ST. CATH.
BYRON STATUE
VAS.
GOURA
ACROPOLIS
MON. OF LYSICRATES
LISS.
200 YARDS
200 METERS
DIONYSIOU
HADRIAN'S ARCH
TO FILOPAPPOS HILL
ROB. GALI
AREOPAGITOU
THRAS.
VIRO.
FRIN.
OLGAS
DCH
AKROPOLI
MAK.

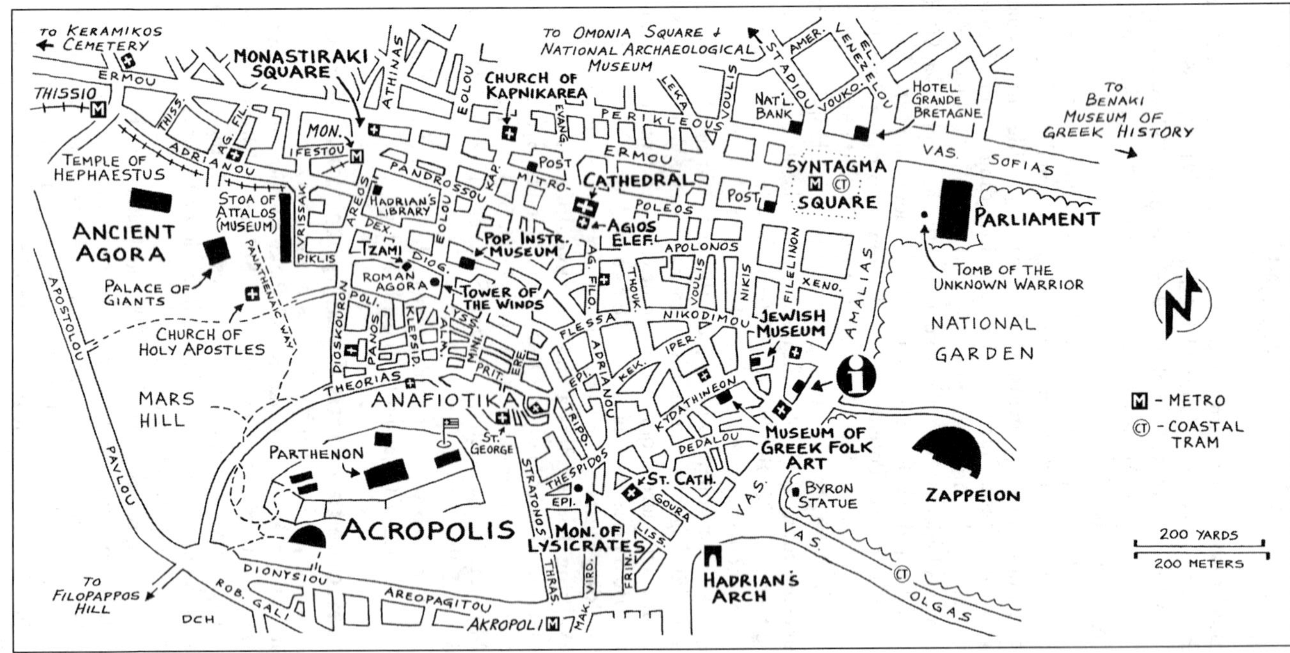

Imagine the original Syntagma Square: a big front yard for the new royal palace, with the country's leading families building mansions around the square. The Hotel Grand Bretagne, the adjacent Hotel King George II, the palatial Zappeion in the National Garden, and the stately architecture lining Queen Sophia Street behind the palace (now embassies and museums) are all surviving examples of these early mansions.

Originally known as Plateia Vasileos Othon, the square became known as Syntagma ("constitution") after a riotous crowd gathered here on September 3, 1843, demanding a constitution. King Otto, giving a speech from the balcony of the Royal Palace overlooking the square (now the Greek Parliament), gave his people—whose ancestors invented the concept—democracy.

Syntagma Square is also worth a footnote in Cold War history. In December 1944, Greek police fired on a communist demonstration here, killing several protesters and sparking battles all over the city between newly arrived British troops (in Athens to support the return of the right-wing monarchy) and members of the Greek resistance (mostly communists). When Britain could no longer afford to aid the Greek government against the communists, the United States took over. President Harry Truman explained this policy in a 1947 address to Congress, which became the basis for the Truman Doctrine—pledging American aid to countries fighting communism, and shaping U.S. foreign policy for the next 50 years.

Breathe deep and ponder the fact that until 1990, Athens was the most polluted city in Europe. It could turn your hanky black in hours. But over the last decade and half, a concerted effort has cleaned up the air. Traffic—while still pretty extreme—is limited: even- and odd-numbered license plates are prohibited in the center on alternate days. (Wealthy locals get around this restriction by owning two cars—one with even plates, the other with odd.) While car traffic is down, motorcycles are exempt...and their usage is up. Central-heating fuel is more expensive and much cleaner these days (as required by European Union regulations), more of the city center is pedestrianized, and the city's public transport is top notch.

Today the city's busiest subway station dumps people into the café-filled square. Plane trees (chosen for their resilience against pollution and the generous shade they provide) make Syntagma a breezy and restful spot. Around the square, you'll find Athens' most venerable hotel (Grande Bretagne), the American Express office, buses to the airport (parked in front of the City Bank), a TI (a block away), and the start of the new Athens Coastal Tram.

Hike across the busy street at the top of Syntagma Square for a close look at...

The Story of Athens

By the time of the Greek War of Independence (1821–1827), Athens had declined to little more than a rural backwater on the fringes of the Ottoman Empire. Its population had shrunk to about 2,000 people occupying a cluster of red-tiled Turkish houses on the northern side of the Acropolis (the area now known as the Plaka).

When it came to choosing a capital for the new nation, Athens wasn't even considered. The first choice was Nafplio in the Peloponnese, which the Turks had also favored as a seat of government. It would probably have stayed that way, if it weren't for the assassination of Greece's first president, Ioannis Kapodistrias, in 1831. His death resulted in the decision to install an outsider, 17-year-old Prince Otto of Bavaria, as the first king of Greece.

Otto was as wet behind the ears as any teenager, and was heavily influenced by his forceful father, King Ludwig I of Bavaria (grandfather of "Mad" King Ludwig of Neuschwanstein Castle fame; see page 472). Ludwig I—a great admirer of classical Athens—insisted that the city become the capital in 1834. It was also Ludwig who was responsible for the shape of the new Athens, ferrying in teams of Bavarian architects to create a plan of broad avenues and grand neoclassical buildings—much as they had done in Munich.

The character of Athens changed once more in 1923, when the defeat of the occupying Greek army in Turkey resulted in a forced population exchange between the two rivals. The population of Athens doubled overnight, and any thought of town planning went out the window as authorities scrambled to throw up cheap apartment blocks to house the newcomers.

The belated industrialization of Greece in the 1950s, coupled with the hard times of the Nazi occupation and civil war (when villagers could no longer afford to feed themselves, so had to flock to the city), sparked a wave of migration from rural areas. The trend continues to this day, and over a third of Greece's population now lives in the greater Athens area.

Parliament: Greece's imposing parliament building, where 300 representatives (elected every 4 years) tend to the business of state, overlooks Syntagma Square.

The origins of this "palace of democracy" couldn't have been less democratic. It was built as the royal palace by a Bavarian architect, who was under instructions to design a suitably grand home for the new royal couple, Otto and Amalia, recently arrived from Nafplio.

It was completed in 1842 at a time of rapidly escalating tensions between the new Bavarian elite and frustrated leaders of the War of Independence. If the palace was designed to impress, then the effect was quite the opposite. The conspicuous consumption angered impoverished locals.

The palace may have looked luxurious, but life here was no fun. The design was terribly impractical: impossible to heat in winter, and with only one bathroom among its 365 rooms. Imagine the lines. The palace, badly damaged by fire in 1909 and refurbished in the 1930s, has been the home of the Greek Parliament since 1935.

In front of the Parliament buildings is the...

Tomb of the Unknown Warrior: This monument is guarded by the much-photographed evzones, a special infantry unit of the Greek army. These colorful characters are clad in the traditional pleated kilt *(fustanella),* white britches, and pom-pom shoes made famous by the *klephts,* the mountain fighters who battled so ferociously in the War of Independence. The soldiers' skirts have 400 pleats...one for each year of Turkish/Ottoman occupation (and don't you forget it). The evzones change guard every hour on the hour, with a full changing-of-the-guard ceremony, complete with marching band, at 11:00 on Sundays.

From the bottom of Syntagma, stroll down...

Ermou Street: This pedestrian mall leads from Syntagma (next to McDonald's and American Express) down into the Plaka, and west to the Keramikos cemetery and the Gazi district. Just a few years ago, this street epitomized all that was terrible about Athens: lousy building codes, tacky neon signs, trucks double-parked, and terribly noisy traffic. When Ermou was first pedestrianized in 2000, merchants were upset. Now they love the ambience created as countless locals stroll through what has become a people-friendly shopping zone. This has traditionally been the street of women's shops (Akadimias is the "men's shopping street"). Many of the department stores on Ermou are housed in impressive neoclassical mansions, and talented street performers (many of them former music professionals from Eastern Europe) provide an entertaining soundtrack.

Ermou leads downhill to the...

Church of Kapnikarea: A classic Byzantine church (11th century, often closed), Kapnikarea is based on a Greek cross (like a plus sign inside a circle, symbolizing the perfection of God) rather than the Latin cross that's common in Western Europe. Telltale signs of a Byzantine church include round arches over the windows, bricks with the mortar surrounding the stones, and a domed cupola symbolizing heaven (always painted inside with the omnipotent "Pantocrator" God blessing us on Earth from its very top). The glass-and-gold-leaf mosaic around the door, while 20th century, is in the traditional style. Notice the focus on the eyes, which were considered a mirror of the soul and a symbol of its purity. The church is named for the tax on the cloth merchants that once lined this square.

At the church, turn left and proceed downhill on Kapnikareas Street two blocks to the busy intersection with Pandrossou Street. Ahead is the Roman Agora. On the right, Pandrossou Street Market leads to Monastiraki Square. (We'll backtrack to here later to finish this walk, going from this intersection through the shopping street.)

But for now, we'll circle clockwise on our Plaka tour. Turn left and walk (passing the recommended Hermion Restaurant, on the right) up the pedestrian street to the cathedral.

Cathedral (Mitropoli): This church was built with the arrival of King Otto in 1842. A statue of Damaskinos, archbishop of Greece from 1891–1949, faces the cathedral (generally open daily 8:00–13:00 & 16:30–20:00). As you enter any Greek Orthodox church, join the locals in the standard ritual: Drop a coin in the wooden box, pick up a candle, say a prayer, light the candle, and place in the candelabra. Make the sign of the cross and kiss the icon (in this case, of Jesus). Notice the lipstick smudges on the icon's protective glass. Also notice the candle recycle box behind the candelabra. Orthodox churches come with an altar screen dividing the lay community and the priests. The spiritual heavy lifting takes place behind the screen, where the priests turn the bread and wine into the body and blood of Jesus. Then they open the doors and serve it to their faithful flock—spooning the wine from a challis while holding a cloth under each chin so as not to drop any on the floor. Traditionally, women worshipped apart from men in the balconies upstairs. Women got the vote in Greece in 1954, and since about that time, they've been able to worship in the prime, ground-floor real estate with their men. The scaffolding has decorated this unremarkable church since the earthquake of 1989.

Leaving the cathedral, hook left to a smaller but much more historic...

Byzantine Church of Agios Elefthérios: The marble bits were scavenged from the Ancient Agora in the 12th century. The carved reliefs above the door are part of a calendar of ancient Athenian festivals, thought to have been carved in the 2nd century A.D. The church is sometimes referred to as "the old cathedral," because it was used by the archbishops of Athens after they were evicted from the Parthenon by the Turks. Step inside for pure 12th-century Orthodox architectural beauty.

Behind this little church, turn right, following Agia Filotheis, then (after a little jog right) continue along the pedestrians-only Adrianou, a touristy market street. Head uphill until you reach a small square with palm trees, the Byzantine Church of St. Catherine, and the small, ancient Greek excavation (look down at street level from 2,000 years ago). At the traffic street ahead, look left (Hadrian's Arch, described below), but go right to the...

Monument of Lysicrates: This elegant marble monument is the sole survivor of many such monuments that once lined this ancient "Street of the Tripods." It was so called because the monuments came with bronze tripods that displayed grand ornamental pottery vases and cauldrons (like those you'll see in the museums) as trophies. These ancient "Oscars" were awarded to winners of choral and theatrical competitions staged at the Theater of Dionysus on the southern side of the Acropolis. This lonely monument was erected in 334 B.C. by "Lysicrates of Kykyna, son of Lysitheides"—proud sponsor of the winning choral team that year. Excavations around the monument uncovered the foundations of other monuments, which are now reburied under a layer of red sand awaiting further study.

Passing the monument to the left, follow Epimenidou up the steps to the top. At the fork, head right up Stratonos, which leads around the base of the Acropolis. Pass the small St. George of the Rock Church, going straight, and continue gradually uphill. As you immerse yourself in a maze of tiny whitewashed houses, follow signs that point to the Acropolis. This is the community of...

Anafiotika: This charming "village" is Anafiotika. Literally "little Anafi," it was built by people from the tiny Cycladic island of Anafi who came to Athens looking for work after independence. In this delightful spot, nestled beneath the walls of the Acropolis, the city seems miles away. Weave through narrow paths lined with flowers and dotted with cats dozing peacefully in the sunshine. While ancestors of the original islanders still live here, Anafiotika is slowly becoming a place for wealthy locals to have an "island cottage" in the city. As you wander through the oleanders, notice the male fig trees—no fruit—that keep flies and mosquitoes away. Smell the chicken-manure fertilizer, peek into delicate little yards, enjoy the blue doors and maroon shutters...it's a transplanted Cycladic world.

Follow signs to the Acropolis (no matter how unlikely the direction might seem) until you emerge on a concrete ramp at the edge of the houses. This part of the walk circles the Acropolis. Turn right and head downhill back into the Plaka. At the traffic street, head left on the path leading to the Acropolis. After about 30 yards, just before the souvenir shack, turn right. Follow a series of stairs (a lane called Klepsidras) on their perfectly straight course until they dead-end at a black iron fence overlooking...

The Roman Agora and the Tower of the Winds: The Romans conquered Greece around 150 B.C. and stayed for centuries. This square was the commercial center of Roman Athens, with a colonnade providing shade for shoppers browsing the many stores that fronted it. Centuries later, the Ottoman Turks made this their grand bazaar. The mosque survives (although its minaret, like all minarets in town, was torn down by the Greeks when they won independence in the 19th century). The only building of any importance for sightseers is on the far right—the Tower of the Winds. Circle right for a closer look.

The octagonal Tower of the Winds, built in the 1st century B.C., was an ingenious combination of clock, weather vane, and guide to the planets. It's named after the beautiful relief carvings that depict the ancient Greek symbols for the eight winds. While even local guides don't know which is which, the reliefs are still beautiful. As you walk down the hill, you'll see reliefs depicting a boy with a harp, a boy with a basket of flowers (summer wind), a relief with a circle, and a guy blowing a conch shell—he's imitating Boreas, the howling winter winds from the north. The tower was capped with a weathervane in the form of a bronze Triton (half-man, half-fish) that spun to indicate which wind was blessing or cursing the city at the moment.

Bronze rods protruded from the walls and acted as sundials to indicate the time. And when the sun wasn't shining, time was told by the tower's sophisticated water clock, powered by water piped in from springs on the Acropolis. Under Turkish rule, dervishes used the tower as a place of whirling and prayer.

Since you can see the tower from the outside, and there's little else to see inside, going into the Roman Agora is not that important (€2, included in €12 Acropolis ticket, daily 8:00–20:00). But if you buy your €12 Acropolis ticket here (see Acropolis ticket sidebar, page 784), you can avoid lines at the Acropolis and pop into this sight essentially for free for a look at all the sides of the Tower of the Winds (a plaque explains this cool monument).

From the tower, head downhill on Eolou. After passing the excavation site of Hadrian's Library (on the left), you'll return to the intersection we stopped at earlier. Remembering that this crowded lane is worked by expert pickpockets, head left down Pandrosou to...

Monastiraki Square: Stand in the center of the square for this clockwise orientation spin-tour: To the right of the market street (where you entered) stands a former mosque (look for the Arabic script over the door). Known as the Tzami, it was a place of worship from the 15th to 19th centuries, was briefly used as a barracks and jail, and today houses the Museum of Traditional Greek Ceramics (may be closed, Areos 1 at Pandrosou, tel. 210-324-2066). Behind the mosque stand the Corinthian columns of Hadrian's Library (2nd century A.D.). The Acropolis towers behind the library; if you walk toward the library and then turn right, you'll reach the Greek agora.

The yellow train station was Athens' original British-built, 19th-century train station—neoclassical with a dash of Byzantium—and functions today as a Metro station. Just past the station, a road leads downhill into the flea market (antiques, jewelry, cheap clothing, artifacts from the Nazi occupation, and so on). If locals need a screw for an old lamp, they know they'll find it here. Opposite the Acropolis, Athinas Street leads straight to Omonia Square, past the bustling Central Market (5-min walk up the street). The small church in the square is the Church of the Virgin (12th-century Byzantine, mostly restored with a much more modern bell tower). The street behind the church is clogged with locals chowing down on the best souvlaki in town (see "Eating," page 803).

Your tour is over. You could conveniently explore the flea market, the central market, the nearby Keramikos cemetery, or dive into the Ancient Agora (described below). Alternatively, you could dive into a spicy souvlaki.

SIGHTS

The Agora: Athens' Ancient Market

While the Acropolis was the ceremonial showpiece, it was the agora that was the real heart of ancient Athens. Today, it's worth ▲▲▲. For some 800 years, from its foundation in the 6th century B.C. to its destruction by the Herulians in A.D. 267, it was the hub of all commercial, political, and social life, as well as home to the city's principal administrative and legislative buildings.

The agora was a lively place, where the pace seldom slackened—much like modern Athens. Crowds would gather here to listen to philosophers, such as the great Socrates, who spent much of his life here preaching the virtues of "nothing to excess," and urging listeners to "know thyself." The apostle Paul stopped here on his way to Corinth in A.D. 49.

The agora was never restored to its original role after the visit of the ransacking Herulians, and was slowly taken over by private housing. By the 18th century, it had become a flourishing Turkish residential district. The American School of Archaeology then arrived in the 1950s, forced everyone out of their houses and businesses, and demolished buildings that had stood for centuries—all so they could dig here.

Apart from the Temple of Hephaestus, little survives from the classical agora, but it remains a wonderful place to get a feel for the ancient city, nestled in the shadow of the Acropolis. Unlike the crowded Acropolis, the agora is a quiet, generally deserted place to wander and ponder the wonders of ancient Athens.

Cost, Hours, Location: Don't pay the €4 admission if you're going to the Acropolis, as it's included in the €12 Acropolis ticket—see page 784. The Ancient Agora is open April–Sept daily 8:00–19:00, Oct–March daily 8:30–15:00, main entrance from Adrianou, tel. 210-321-0185.

Self-Guided Tour: This tour will help you find meaning in the evocative rubble of the agora. Except for the temple and the museum in the rebuilt Stoa of Attalos, there are few "sights." As you wander, read about the various ruins from posted info panels scattered helpfully throughout the site (thanks to the 2004 Olympics).

Panathenaic Way: From the modern entrance, the Panathenaic Way runs straight through the agora (exiting on the far side) up toward the Acropolis. In ancient times, this was the ceremonial route followed by the grand parade at the Great Panathenaic Festival; today's tourists use the path to connect the sights of the agora. If you're seeing the Acropolis after the agora, you'll basically follow the Panathenaic Way with a sightseeing loop or two en route. From the top of the ramp, find the modern Stoa of Attalos on your left (with the Agora Museum) and the Temple of Hephaestus on your right. Use the chart at the ramp to orient yourself. Stop by the Stoa of Attalos to visit the museum, then proceed straight up the Middle Stoa road to the Temple, returning to the Panathenaic Way via the three giants of the Gymnasium. Finally, head past the wall and church up to the Acropolis exit.

Stoa of Attalos: The Stoa of Attalos was faithfully reconstructed in the 1950s by the American School of Archaeology to resemble the original stoa (covered walkway and hangout area), which was built by King Attalos II of Pergamum (159–138 B.C.). Imagine ancient Greeks (their hard labor done by slaves) lounging around in the shade provided by fine buildings like this. Notice the pillars designed to encourage leaning—with fluting starting only above six feet for the comfort of your favorite philosopher. The portico is supported by 45 columns—Doric on the ground floor and Ionic on the upper gallery. Upstairs are the workshops and offices of the American School of Archaeology, which continues its work.

Ten of the original 21 ground-floor rooms have been replaced by a small hall housing the **Agora Museum.** Taking this well-described chronological stroll through art from 3,200 B.C., you'll get a fun glimpse of life in ancient Athens (seeing a cute little baby's commode, a voting machine, and a barbeque).

Leaving the Stoa of Attalos, walk straight along the "Middle Stoa" lane, pass a fine Corinthian capital and a well, cross an aqueduct, and climb past the scant remains of what were the state administrative buildings to the...

Temple of Hephaestus: This is the only temple anywhere in the ancient Greek world with a completely intact roof. As it was used as a church for centuries, it was never cannibalized for its stone. It stands on a low hill at the western edge of the agora, where it was built in 449 B.C. When the great buildings of the Acropolis were begun, it was all hands on deck up there, and work on the Temple of Hephaestus was interrupted. Notice how the frieze was only finished on the side facing the agora (it's blank elsewhere). Like the Parthenon, it's a Doric temple, but with none of the refinements (elaborate carvings, fancy math to overcome the optical illusions) of that greater work. It was dedicated to Hephaestus, god of the forge, and was originally surrounded by metal foundries and workshops. These were demolished by the Romans, who surrounded the temple with formal gardens, which are preserved with the same kinds of plants today.

Athenians like to call this temple the "Theseion" because its frieze once featured carved reliefs depicting the feats of Theseus. In Mycenaean lore, Theseus was a superhero—slayer of the Minotaur and savior of Athens. The frieze also depicted the Labors of Hercules.

In A.D. 1300, the temple was converted into the Church of Agios Georgios. The last service held here was on December 13, 1834, in honor of King Otto's arrival in Athens.

There's an exit behind the Temple of Hephaestus for those wanting the smooth, paved walkway up to the Acropolis, rather than the rough climb through the agora.

In front of the temple, a lane passes three giants on pedestals (described below) before leading back to the Panathenaic Way.

The Palace of the Giants: This was once fronted by a line of fierce merman statues (three of which survive today). It's Roman, not Greek—but as one of the few things standing in the agora, it's a popular stop. The so-called "Palace of the Giants" was once a school, or "gymnasium" (which comes from the Greek word for "naked"—young men exercised naked during PE here). A plaque explains the complicated history of this building.

Back at the Panathenaic Way, turn right and walk toward the Acropolis. To the left, just past the Stoa of Attalos, stands the **Herulian Wall.** This rough wall—made from scrap stone—was thrown up hastily in A.D. 267 in an effort to keep the Herulians at bay.

On the right is the...

Church of the Holy Apostles: This charming little church was built in the 11th century to commemorate St Paul's teaching in the agora. It contains some fine Byzantine frescoes. Standing inside, look up at Pancrator God, try a chant (testing to find the rooms' resonant frequency), and notice the remains of the marble altar screen with holes once filled by icons.

Your tour is finished. Exit the agora uphill from the church (on the way to the Acropolis—described below) or back where you entered.

Acropolis Ticket

The €12 Acropolis ticket also gives you entry to five other major ancient sites: the Ancient Agora, the Roman Agora, the ancient Keramikos cemetery, the Temple of Olympian Zeus, and the Theater of Dionysus. The ticket is valid for four days. If you see only the Acropolis, you'll still pay €12. Buying the ticket at a sight other than the Acropolis can help you avoid long lines.

The Acropolis

In this age of superlatives, it's hard to overstate the historic and artistic importance of the Acropolis. It's surely the most important ancient sight in the Western world—and obviously worth ▲▲▲. Crowned by the mighty Parthenon, the Acropolis (literally, "high city") rises gleaming like a beacon above the gray concrete drudgery of modern Athens, a lasting testament to ancient Greece's glorious Golden Age in the 5th century B.C.

The Acropolis has been the heart of Athens since the beginning of recorded time. The first settlers arrived here in neolithic times, drawn by the permanent springs. It developed into a powerful Mycenaean city, associated with the mythical superhero Theseus. The Mycenaeans ruled from a palace that stood between where the Parthenon and the Erechtheion stand today (all that's left is an embankment of huge "Cyclopean" stones).

People lived on the Acropolis until 510 B.C. Then the Delphic Oracle booted them out, ruling that the Acropolis should be dedicated to the gods. Everything on the Acropolis was destroyed by the Persians before the Battle of Salamis (480 B.C.). Athens' improbable victory at Salamis, which followed an equally stunning land victory at Marathon 10 years earlier, saw Athens at the very peak of its power. Cash poured in from other city-states and islands keen to be allied to the winning side. The greatest of ancient architects, Pericles, spared no expense as he set about transforming the Acropolis into a complex of lavishly decorated temples worthy of the city's protector, Athena.

The four major monuments—the Parthenon, Erechtheion, Propylaia, and Temple of Athena Nike—survive in remarkably good condition given the battering they've taken over the centuries. The greatest challenge now is to save them from the modern menaces of acid rain and pollution.

Cost, Hours, Location: €12, free on Sun Nov–March and on national holidays. The site is open April–Oct daily 8:00–19:00 and Nov–March daily 8:00–16:30; tel. 210-321-0219, www.culture.gr. The main entrance is at the western side of the Acropolis; a new entrance for people with disabilities is located just to the north.

The Acropolis

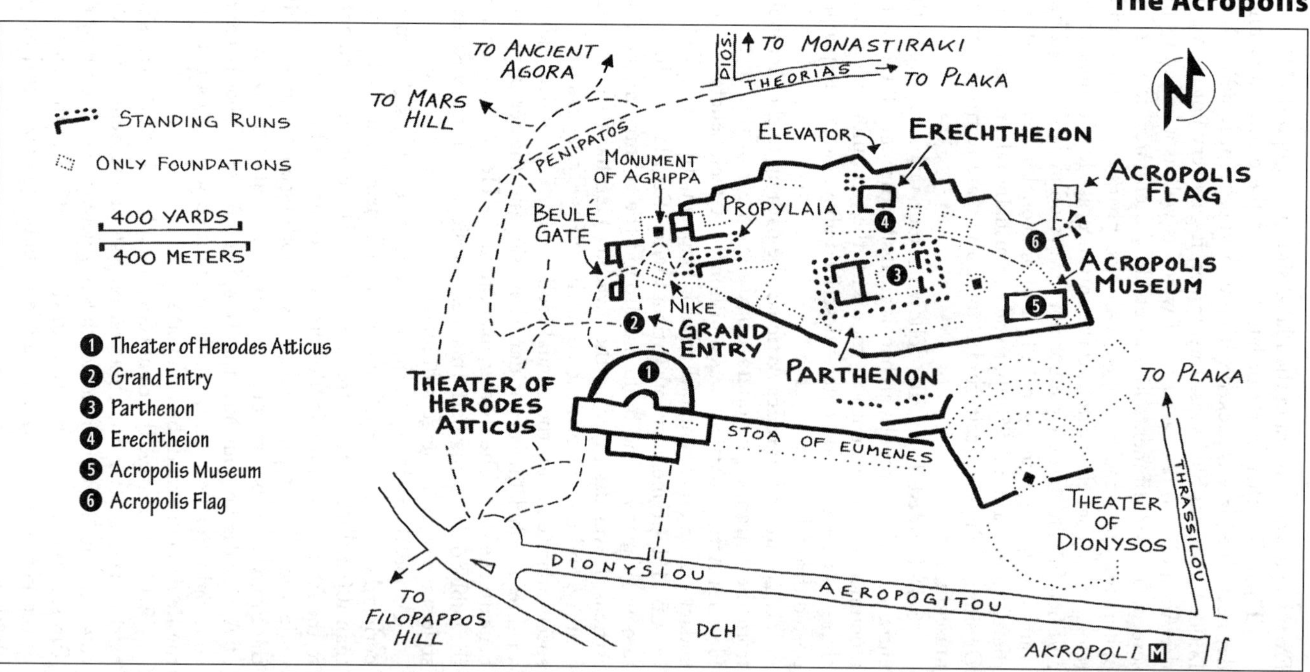

From the Roman Agora in the Plaka, signs point uphill.

Tips: Get there early or late to avoid the crowds and midday heat. The place is packed with tour groups from 10:30 to about 13:00. Wear sensible shoes. In summer, it gets very hot on top of the Acropolis, so take a bottle of water as well as a hat and sunscreen. The refreshments kiosk outside the entrance is your last opportunity to get a drink. No backpacks or bags are allowed inside (cloakroom just below gate). At the entrance, ask for the substantial and helpful site guide (free but not always offered). You can hire your own tour guide—generally a professional archaeologist—at the entrance (around €50, but you can usually talk them down). Or simply follow my self-guided tour. There are restrooms at the museum.

Self-Guided Tour: The following tour takes you from the entrance to the Acropolis archaeological site, through all the major monuments. Supplement this tour with the free information brochure (ask for it as you enter—described above) and info plaques posted throughout.

1. Theater of Herodes Atticus: The path up to the Acropolis from the entrance gate offers a bird's-eye view of the Theater of Herodes Atticus. Atticus was a billionaire Greek benefactor, legendary orator, and friend of Emperor Hadrian. This theater—built in A.D. 161 in memory of Atticus' wife, Regilla—is the most famous of many grand buildings around the country financed by Atticus. It was destroyed by the invading Herulians after about a century, and only reconstructed in the 1950s. Today it's used as a spectacular venue for the annual Hellenic Festival, which features an international line-up of dance, music, and theater performed beneath the stars. The theater, also called the Herodion, is open to the public only during performances (see sidebar). It has a Roman-style stage with the stage wall intact.

As locals climb up past the many olive trees, they sigh, remembering the trees as "the gift of Athena to Athens." Greece has more than 100 million of these trees. Stop at the base of the grand entry to the Acropolis, at the foot of the many columns of the Propylaia, under the tall, gray stone pedestal with nothing on it. Facing uphill, the Propylaia is before you, the empty pedestal of the Monument of Agrippa is on your left, the Temple of Athena Nike is *not* on your right (it's been temporarily dismantled for restoration), and the Beulé Gate stands behind you.

2. Grand Entry: The **Beulé Gate** (you'll walk through it as you exit) is named after French archaeologist Ernest Beulé, who discovered it in 1852 during demolition of a defensive wall built by the Turks. It was built by the Romans in A.D. 267 after the departure of the Herulians, using the rubble of buildings destroyed by the invaders.

The Hellenic Festival

The annual Hellenic Festival offers the opportunity to watch world-class performances of dance, music, and theater at the ancient Theater of Herodes Atticus, nestled spectacularly below the floodlit Acropolis. The festival keeps getting bigger and bigger, and now extends from May to September. For this year's festival program, see www.hellenicfestival.gr. The Web site also has information about performances at the famous Theater of Epidavros in the Peloponnese (3 hours west of Athens). Tickets go on sale three weeks before the performance. They can be bought over the phone by credit card or at the festival box office (Mon–Fri 8:30–16:00, Sat 9:00–14:30, closed Sun, tel. 210-928-2900, in the arcade at Panepistimiou 39, opposite the National Library). Tickets also are sold at the theater box office on the day of the performance.

While the **Monument of Agrippa** is long gone, its 25-foot-high stone pedestal remains. The grand pedestal gives a good indication of the scale of the bronze statue of the Roman general Agrippa, riding a chariot, that once stood here. It was erected in 27 B.C., after Agrippa's victory in a chariot race at the Panathenaic games.

Unfortunately, the exquisite **Temple of Athena Nike** is currently in pieces. This perfectly proportioned little temple, which normally stands on a small spur to the right of the Propylaia (as you face uphill), was dismantled in 2003 for restoration work. Gods willing, they'll put it back in 2007. This is the third time in its 2,400-year history that the temple has been taken apart. The Turks pulled it down at the end of the 17th century and used the stone elsewhere, but it was reassembled after independence. It was taken apart for renovations in 1935, and put back together in 1939. Unfortunately, that work did more harm than good—the steel rods used to hold things together expanded, damaging the stone. This time the restorers are determined to do the job properly, using titanium instead of steel. The temple's designer, Callicrates, one of the architects of the Parthenon, would doubtless be wondering what all the fuss is about. He had to make do with lead when he pieced together the original (427–424 B.C.). It was built to house a statue thanking Athena for victory ("Nike") over the Persians.

The entrance to the Acropolis couldn't be through just any old gate; it had to be the grandest gate ever built. That's the **Propylaia,** constructed in about 435 B.C. and laid out in alignment with the Parthenon. The Propylaia's large central hallway is flanked by two wings on either side, each with its own gate. The largest gate, in the center, opened onto Panathenaic Way, which was the ceremonial path from the Ancient Agora to the Erechtheion (used for the annual Great Panathenaic Festival, the main event on the city's religious calendar). The Propylaia remained intact until the Franks arrived in the 13th century and converted it into a palace. It later became the home of the Turkish ruler of Athens, and then a storehouse for gunpowder. The Propylaia was seriously damaged in 1645 when the gunpowder magazine was struck by lightning and exploded.

Stepping through the Propylaia, you're greeted by the...

3. Parthenon: The Parthenon is the showstopper—the finest temple in the ancient world, standing like a beacon on the highest point of the Acropolis (about 500 feet above sea level). It's impressive enough today, but just try to imagine how awesome the Parthenon must have looked when it was completed 2,500 year ago. This largest Doric temple in Greece, measuring 101 feet by 228 feet, with eight fluted Doric columns at each end and 17 along each side, was completed in just nine years (447–438 B.C.).

It's big, sure. But what makes the Parthenon truly exceptional is the extraordinary sophistication of the design. Architects Ictinus and Callicrates, working under the supervision of the master sculptor Pheidias, used a whole bag of optical tricks to bring the building to life. Any architect understands that a long, flat baseline on a building will give the illusion of sagging, and parallel columns will look like they are falling away from each other. To create a building that looked harmonious, the architects actually calculated bends in the construction, taking into consideration the optical illusions and giving the viewer the sense that all was straight and well. The Parthenon actually curves upwards in the middle, and its columns tilt ever so slightly inwards (one of the reasons why the Parthenon has withstood earthquakes so well). If you extended the columns up several miles, they'd eventually touch. Another trick was to use thicker columns at the corners, which made them appear all the same size. It's amazing to think that all this was planned and implemented in stone so long ago.

The Parthenon was built from the very finest materials and decorated with carved scenes of epic tales from Greek mythology created by master sculptors Agoracritos and Alcamenes. The carvings were painted in vivid colors. The best known of these sculptures are the controversial Elgin Marbles, which were removed from the temple's frieze by Englishman Lord Elgin in 1801 and now reside in London's British Museum, despite repeated requests for their return.

The Parthenon housed an enormous gold and ivory statue of Athena Polias ("Athena of the City") that was the work of the master Pheidias himself, completed in 432 B.C. Standing 40 feet high, the statue was considered a wonder of the ancient world. The original (which stood at the end closest to the Propylaia) was taken to Constantinople by the Byzantine emperor Theodosius in A.D. 426, and subsequently vanished. We know what it looked like from a Roman copy (the Athena Varvakeion, on display in Athens' National Archaeological Museum—see page 793).

The Parthenon survived intact until A.D. 267, when the Herulians hit town. Before moving on, they did some pretty serious looting and plundering. Fortunately, they satisfied themselves by demolishing only an interior colonnade.

In the 5th century A.D., the temple became a Byzantine Orthodox church, and its interior was decorated with colorful Christian frescoes. It remained a church for almost a thousand years, including a period as a Roman Catholic cathedral under Frankish rule.

In 1458, the Turks arrived and converted the Parthenon into a mosque, adding a minaret. The Turks had no respect for the sacred history of the place. They tore down stones just for the lead clamps that held them in place, in order to make bullets. (The exasperated Greeks offered them bullets if they'd stop destroying the temple.) The Turks also used it to store gunpowder, leading to the greatest catastrophe in the temple's long history. In 1687, a Venetian army laid siege to the Acropolis. The Venetians weren't worried about the architecture. As far as they were concerned, it was a lucky hit that triggered the massive explosion that ripped the center out of the Parthenon and wiped out the Turkish defenders.

Much work has been done in recent times to stabilize and restore the building. The present work began in 1984, meaning that they've been at it more than twice as long as it took to build in the first place.

Across the street stands the...

4. Erechtheion: The Erechtheion—with its much-loved and much-photographed Porch of the Caryatids, lined with stone ladies—was the most important religious building on the Acropolis. It was built in 406 B.C. on the spot where Athena and Poseidon fought for the naming rights to the city. Athena won by producing an olive tree, a symbol of prosperity. The temple gets its strange name from the mythical Athenian King Erechthonius, supposedly buried under the Caryatid porch.

The stones in front of the Caryatid porch, marking the oldest ruins on the Acropolis, are the remains of 6th-century B.C. Archaic buildings. They sit upon a "Cyclopean" foundation built during the Mycenaean period (1400 B.C.). As you approach the Erechtheion (left of Caryatids), you'll see the huge stones of the Mycenaean construction.

The Erechtheion is a complex structure, with three rooms built across a steep slope. The biggest (and least interesting) of these is the main temple, which is divided into two rooms *(cellae)*: one for

Athena and one for Poseidon, side by side to show that they were still friends. The northern porch—with its six slim, elegant, Ionic columns—is the face that the Erechtheion shows to the Plaka. Legend has it that the large crack at the center of the floor was caused by Poseidon's trident during his contest with Athena, but lightning is a more likely culprit.

Finally, we come to the Porch of the Caryatids, facing the Parthenon. It's a wonderfully inspired piece of architecture, with six beautiful maidens functioning as columns. These are faithful copies of the originals, five of which are on display here in the Acropolis Museum. The sixth was removed by the sticky-fingered Lord Elgin in 1805, shipped to London (on the same boat as Lord Byron), and currently lives at the British Museum. The Caryatids are so called because they were supposedly modeled on women from the town of Karyai (modern Karyes), near Sparta in the Peloponnese, who were famous for their upright posture and noble character.

The Erechtheion was part of Pericles' grand plan for the Acropolis. But construction was delayed by the outbreak of the Peloponnesian Wars with Sparta. Work began in 421 B.C., and it was finally completed in 395 B.C.

The elevator behind the Erechtheion was constructed for the Paralympics in 2004. It has been kept to lift people with disabilities from the Plaka up to the Acropolis.

5. Acropolis Museum: The small museum, housing a wonderful collection of Acropolis statuary, is an essential stop on any visit. Most of the finds actually predate the Golden Age and the Parthenon. Before the Battle of Salamis, the Persians destroyed the temples standing on the Acropolis. The rubble from these buildings provided a foundation for later building. This so-called "Persian rubble" provided later archaeologists a bonanza of Archaic-period (650–450 B.C.) discoveries that you'll see here.

The first rooms show off these oldest statues. Later, in Room IV, don't miss the beautiful *korai* (maidens) statues. Room VIII contains about 32 feet of the 525-foot-long Parthenon's frieze—the only section that remained following the 1687 explosion and the visit of stony-souvenir-loving Lord Elgin. It shows part of the Panathenaic procession, including the gods receiving all those offerings (panel 856). The highlight is the last room, featuring the five remaining original Caryatids. A plaster model stands in place of the sixth, which was removed by Lord Elgin. Modern pollution ground their features down to the rough faces you see today. Photographs from 1950 show these Caryatids with crisp facial features. In half a century of Industrial Age pollution, they experienced more destruction than in the previous 2,000 years. In 1998 they were brought inside, out of the acidic air, so thankfully they'll get no worse.

The latest on the continuing struggle by the Greeks to get their Parthenon reliefs back home: The British Museum has agreed to build a branch of their museum in Athens (near the Akropoli Metro station) and to offer the Parthenon reliefs on an extended loan there. But the new Greek government, elected in 2004, has put the project on hold.

Walking beyond the museum, to the far end of the Acropolis, climb to the base of the dramatic Greek flag.

6. Acropolis Flag: When the Nazis occupied Athens in April 1941, the evzone who guarded this flag was ordered by the Nazis to remove it. He calmly took it down, wrapped himself in it, and jumped to his death. A few weeks later, two heroic teenagers, Manolis Glezos and Apostolis Santas, scaled the wall, took down the Nazi flag, and raised the Greek flag. This was one of the first well-known acts of resistance against the Nazis, and the boys' bravery is honored by a plaque near the base of the flag. To this day, Greeks from just about anywhere in Athens see this flag and think of their hard-won independence.

From this viewpoint, look inland at Lycabettus Hill, crowned by the Church of St. George. The white bits on the Pentelican Mountains behind are quarries. The monuments of the Acropolis were built of marble quarried from these mountains—and the stone used to restore the monuments comes from these same, still-active quarries. While the new, white patches you see on the buildings as they are restored seem to be a different stone, they're exactly the same, and will age to fit the stately temples of the Acropolis.

Spinning clockwise (to the right), find: The parliament building (facing Syntagma Square), the National Garden behind it, the Panathenaic Stadium, the yellow Zappeion, the Temple of Olympian Zeus, and Hadrian's Arch. The Aegean Sea glimmers in the distance, beckoning you to the islands (but the only island visible is Aegina). The Parthenon blocks your view of the port of Piraeus (where boats to the islands embark). The Ancient Agora spreads below the Acropolis, and the sprawl of modern Athens paints the surrounding hills in a rash of white.

In 1830, Athens' population was about 5,000. By 1900, it was 600,000. In the 1920s, with the influx of Greeks from Turkey, the population surged to 1.5 million—and the city boomed. With the boom times in the 1950s and 1980s, the city grew to about four million. From this perch, you're looking at the homes of four out of every 10 Greeks. (If that makes you thirsty, there's a water fountain between you and the museum.)

The knobby, wind-swept hill in front of the Acropolis crawling with tourists is **Mars Hill,** made famous by the apostle Paul. This first great Christian missionary and author of about half of the New Testament preached to the Athenians here. While Athenians were famously open-minded, Paul encountered a skeptical audience and only netted a couple of converts. A new metal staircase is now in place, giving visitors an alternative to the famously slippery stone one.

National Archaeological Museum

The National Archaeological Museum is far and away the top ancient Greek art collection anywhere, well worth ▲▲▲. The museum takes you chronologically from 7,000 B.C. to A.D. 500 through beautifully displayed and described exhibits and in air-conditioned comfort.

Cost, Hours, Location: €10, April–Oct Tue–Sun 8:00–19:00, Mon 12:30–19:00; Nov–March Tue–Sun 8:00–15:00, Mon 10:30–17:00. It's at Oktovriou-Patission 44, 10-min walk from Plateia Viktorias Metro station, also many buses, tel. 210-821-7717, www.culture.gr. Photos are allowed, but no flash and no goofy poses in front of statues. The delightful basement cafeteria spills out onto a shady and restful courtyard. While there are no audioguides, live guides hang out in the lobby waiting to give you a €35, hour-long tour.

Orientation: The core rooms (3–6) cover prehistory and Aegean civilizations (7000–1050 B.C.). They include artifacts from the Aegean islands (the first city-states) and Troy, wall paintings from Thera, and the treasures of Royal Tombs from Mycenae. You'll see early clay fertility symbols—big women, which are basically huge thighs and breasts lumped together and worshipped (from about 5,000 B.C.). Then, 2,000 years later, thin is in as Cycladic fertility symbols evolved from Vaginolins to marble Twiggies (c. 3000 B.C.).

The central room shows off the funerary art looted from Mycenaean graves: the famous Mask of Agamemnon, finely decorated weapons, and jewelry, all buried with bodies.

Rooms 7–33 display Greek sculpture from the 8th century B.C. to the 4th century A.D., with many *Kouroi* (male nudes) and gravestone reliefs. This is the finest collection in existence, allowing you to watch art evolve from stiff, to balanced, to Hellenistic. Walk once around fast for the time-lapse effect: stiff Egyptian, balanced *David*-like, Golden Age, wet T-shirt, buckin' bronco Hellenistic. Then go around again for a closer look.

The collection also includes vases and painted pottery (upstairs, rooms 49–56), bronze statuary (ground floor, rooms 36–39), and Egyptian (rooms 40 and 41).

Highlights: Track down these top sights in the museum.

Mask of Agamemnon: The celebrated Mask of Agamemnon, a gold death mask unearthed at Mycenae by Heinrich Schliemann, is a popular favorite.

The Warrior Vase: Despite all the fuss about the Mask of Agamemnon, it was this beautiful 12th-century B.C. clay krater, or large vase (#1426), that Schliemann rated as his greatest find. It shows women (including a Ringo Starr–looking woman on the left) gathered to wave goodbye to a group of warriors heading off to war with their fancy armor and duffle bags hanging from their spears. While this provided the world with its first glimpse of a Mycenaean soldier, it's a timeless scene, repeated countless times in our generation.

Vaphio Cups: The exquisite Vaphio gold cups, with scenes of men taming wild bulls, are regarded as the finest examples of Mycenaean art. They were found in a tomb at Vaphio, near Sparta (2 small cups in a glass case at the back end of the central room).

Minoan Frescos: The museum's second biggest crowd-puller is its collection of magnificent frescos, uncovered at the ancient Minoan settlement of Akrotiri on the island of Santorini (Thira). These are upstairs in room 48.

Poseidon of Artemision: This stunning bronze statue, cast in 450 B.C., depicts the mighty god of the sea about to hurl his trident. It was discovered in the sea off Cape Artemision in 1928.

Horse and Jockey of Artemision: The Horse and Jockey of Artemision, cast in the 2nd century B.C., was discovered at the same time as the statue of Poseidon. The detail is astonishing, right down to the concerned look on the jockey's face.

Statue of Athena Varvakeion: In room 20, you'll see the most famous copy of the statue of Athena Polias by Pheidias, which once stood in the Parthenon (c. 450 B.C.). It portrays Athena, dressed in flowing golden robes, seated on a throne holding out a small figure of Nike (goddess of victory) in her right hand and a spear in her left.

Pottery: The museum's collection traces the development of pottery from the Bronze Age, through the Protogeometric and Geometric periods, to the emergence of the famous Attic black-figured pottery of the 6th century B.C., and red-figured pottery, which reached the peak of perfection during Pericles' rule in the middle of the 5th century B.C.

More Sights

National Gardens—The National Gardens, which extend south from the Parliament, are a wonderfully cool retreat from the traffic-clogged streets of central Athens. Covering an area of around 40 acres, they were planted in 1839 as the palace gardens, created for the pleasure of Queen Amalia. The gardens were opened to the public in 1923 (free, open daily from dawn to dusk).

Zappeion—Just south of the National Gardens stands the grand mansion known as the Zappeion, surrounded by formal gardens of its own. Finished in 1888, it was designed by the Danish architect

Theophilus Hansen, who was known (along with his brother Christian) for his neoclassical designs. The financing was provided by the Zappas brothers, Evangelos and Konstantinos, who were two of the prime movers in the campaign to revive the Olympic Games. It housed the International Olympic Committee during the first modern Olympics in 1896, hosted the fencing competition, and served as a media center during the 2004 Olympics. During the "diaspora" (a period during Ottoman rule), the Greek elite, intelligentsia, and aristocracy fled the country. They returned after independence (1827) and built grand mansions such as this. Today the Zappeion is a conference and exhibition center (gardens free and always open; building only open during exhibitions for a fee, Vas Amalias, Metro: Akropoli or Evangelismos, tel. 210-323-7830). To most Athenians, the Zappeion is best known as the site of the Aigli Village outdoor cinema (see "Nightlife," page 798).

Panathenaic (a.k.a. "Olympic") Stadium—This gleaming marble stadium has many names. Officially it's the Panathenaic Stadium, built in the 4th century B.C. to host the Panathenaic Games. Sometimes it's referred to as the Roman Stadium, because it was rebuilt by the great Roman benefactor Herodes Atticus in the 2nd century A.D., using the same prized Pentelic marble that was used in the Parthenon. It is this magnificent white marble that is responsible for the name that everyone agrees on: Kalimarmara (beautiful marble) Stadium. It was restored to its Roman condition in preparation for the first modern Olympics in 1896. It saw Olympic action again in 2004, when its unique horseshoe-shaped design provided a grand finish for the marathon. In ancient times, 50,000 filled the stadium without seats. Today, the same number of spectators can sit down (free, daily 8:30–14:00, located southeast of the Zappeion off Vas Konstantinou, Metro: Akropoli or Evangelismos, tel. 210-325-1744).

Temple of Olympian Zeus (Olympieion)—This largest temple in ancient Greece took almost 700 years to finish. It was begun late in the 6th century B.C. during the rule of the tyrant Peisistratos. But the task proved beyond him. The temple lay abandoned, half-built, for centuries until the Roman emperor Hadrian arrived to finish the job in A.D. 131. Although only 15 of the original 104 Corinthian columns remain standing, their sheer size (a towering 56 feet high) is enough to create a powerful impression of the temple's scale. The fallen column was toppled by a storm in 1852. The temple once housed a suitably oversized statue of Zeus, head of the Greek gods who lived on Mount Olympus, and an equally colossal statue of Hadrian (€2, covered by €12 Acropolis ticket, daily 8:30–15:00, Vas Olgas 1 at Vas Amalias, Metro: Akropoli, tel. 210-922-6330).

Arch of Hadrian—This grand archway lies just west of the Temple of Olympian Zeus, facing the Plaka and Acropolis. Its once-brilliant-white Pentelic marble is stained by the exhaust fumes from some of Athens' worst traffic. It was built by Hadrian in A.D. 132 to celebrate the completion of the Temple of Olympian Zeus, and marked the dividing line between the ancient city and Hadrian's new "Roman" city. An inscription on the west side informs the reader, "This is Athens, ancient city of Theseus," while the opposite frieze carries the message, "This is the city of Hadrian, and not of Theseus." This must have been a big deal for Hadrian, as the emperor himself came here to celebrate the inauguration (free, always viewable, Vas Amalias and Dionsiou Areopagitou, Metro: Akropoli).

Central Market—For a colorful and fragrant stroll through work-a-day Athens, sort through the dripping-fresh meat, fish, sticky figs, exotic nuts, spices, and a world of olives at this massive central food market. The market, with lots of immigrant color mixed in, is a barrage on all your senses (Mon–Sat 7:00–15:00, closed Sun, on Athinas between Sofokleous and Evripidou, Metro: Omonia or Monastiraki). Modern-art lovers should pop into the **Art Tower,** which rises above the market and offers eight stimulating floors of contemporary galleries (free, Wed–Fri 15:00–20:00, Sat 12:00–16:00, closed Sun–Tue, Armodiou 10, tel. 210-324-9626, www.artower.gr).

Keramikos Cemetery—Named for the ceramics workshops that used to surround it, this is a vast place to wander among marble tombstones from the 7th century B.C. onward. To see some of the original monuments, check whether the on-site Oberlender Museum has been reopened after its recent renovation (€2, covered by €12 Acropolis ticket, daily 8:00–19:00, Ermou 148, Metro: Thisio).

Museum of Cycladic Art—The Goulandris Museum of Cycladic Art shows off the largest collection of Cycladic art anywhere, collected by one of Greece's richest shipping families. This art of the Aegean city-states, predating the Golden Age by 2,000 years, gives an insight into the matriarchal cultures of the Greek island of Delos, where this great civilization originated. If you like fertility symbols, this museum will float your boat (€5, Mon and Wed–Fri 10:00–16:00, Sat 10:00–15:00, closed Sun, Tue, and many religious holidays, Neofytou Douka 4, Metro: Evangelismos, tel. 210-722-8321, www.cycladic.gr).

Museum of Greek Folk Art—Buried conveniently in the Plaka, this fine little museum offers a classy break from the folk kitsch on sale throughout that neighborhood. Four small floors display four centuries (17th–20th) of embroidery, traditional costumes, carvings, and shadow-theater puppets—all well-described in English. The ethnographic photo essay on the first floor (which has been listed as "temporary" for nearly a decade) is poetic. "In the coffee shop, there is room for everybody and everything: wise political words, incredible nautical tales, and memories." The well-described photos give you a fun trip around the country's most remote and traditional corners. Wonderful folk costumes from each region fill the top floor (€2, Tue–Sun 10:00–14:00, closed Mon, across from the church of Metamorphosis at Kydathineon 17, Metro: Akropoli or Syntagma, tel. 210-322-9031, www.culture.gr).

Benaki Museum of Greek History and Culture—This exquisite collection of 36 galleries on four floors takes you on a fascinating air-conditioned walk through the ages. The first exhibit kicks things off by saying, "Around 7000 B.C., the greatest revolution in human experience took place: the change from the hunting-and-gathering economies of the Paleolithic Age to the farming economy of the Neolithic Age...." You'll see fine painted vases, gold wreaths of myrtle leaves worn on heads 2,300 years ago, and evocative Byzantine icons and jewelry. Romantic art depicts Greece's stirring and successful 19th-century struggle for independence (€6, Mon, Wed, Fri, and Sat 9:00–17:00, Thu 9:00–24:00, Sun 9:00–15:00, closed Tue, no audioguide but well-described in English, classy rooftop café, Koumbari 1, across from back corner of the National Garden, tel. 210-367-1000, www.benaki.gr). The Benaki gift shop is considered a fine place to buy jewelry.

Benaki Museum of Islamic Art—This new museum, in the Psyrri district, showcases an 8,000-piece collection in two renovated neoclassical buildings. It's one of the few European museums dedicated to Islamic art. Highlights include beautifully painted ceramics, a 10th-century gold belt, a rare 14th-century astrolabe, and an entire marble room from a 17th-century Cairo mansion (€5, Tue and Thu–Sun 9:00–15:00, Wed 9:00–21:00, closed Mon, northeast of Keramikos cemetery at Agion Asomaton 22 at Dipylou, Metro: Thisio, tel. 210-325-1311, www.benaki.gr).

There is yet another Benaki that hosts temporary exhibits with a more modern-contemporary flavor (**Benaki Pireos Street Annex**, €3–5, Wed–Thu 9:00–17:00, Fri–Sun 10:00–22:00, closed Mon–Tue, Pireos 138, tel. 210-345-3111, www.benaki.gr).

Technopolis—Located in the gritty Gazi district, at the western end of the recently pedestrianized Ermou street, this new development was built on a 19th-century gasworks. It hosts an eclectic assortment of cultural events, including art exhibits, rock concerts, and experimental theater. The still-standing smokestacks are illuminated in red after dark, giving an eerie impression of its former industrial activity. The only permanent exhibit within Technopolis is a museum dedicated to diva **Maria Callas,** who had her heart broken when Ari left her for Jackie O (free, Mon–Fri 10:00–16:00, closed Sat–Sun, Pireos 100, Metro: Thisio, tel. 210-346-0981).

Jewish Museum—Before the Nazi occupation and the near-annihilation of Greece's Jews, many Jewish communities traced their roots back to medieval Spain's Sephardic diaspora and, before that, to classical Greece. The impressive collection highlights Jewish art and artifacts from the 5th century B.C., as well as documentation of the Holocaust (€3, Mon–Fri 9:00–14:30, Sun 10:00–14:00, closed Sat, Nikis 39 at Kydathineon, in the Plaka, Metro: Syntagma, tel. 210-322-5582, www.jewishmuseum.gr).

Museum of Greek Popular Instruments—This is one of the most entertaining museums in Athens. You can wander around listening to different instruments and styles of music through headphones at each exhibit, as well as examine over 1,200 instruments dating from the 18th century (free, Tue and Thu–Sun 10:00–14:00, Wed 12:00–18:00, closed Mon, Diogenous 1–3, in the Plaka, near Roman Forum, Metro: Monastiraki, tel. 210-325-0198, www.culture.gr, melmoke@otenet.gr).

Byzantine and Christian Museum—Traces the story of the Byzantine Empire, from Emperor Constantine's move from Rome to Byzantium (which he renamed Constantinople, now known as Istanbul) in A.D. 324 until the fall of Constantinople to the Ottoman Turks in 1453. It's mostly the story of early Christianity within the story of Byzantium, with exhibits shaped by the notion that "art is more than aesthetics...it's also a testament to a culture." The collection is arranged thematically with exhibits such as the Christianization of pagan temples, Christians in the face of death, and so on (€4, Tue–Sun 8:30–15:00, closed Mon, call ahead to check for periodic closures, Vasilissis Sofias 22, Metro: Evangalismos, tel. 210-721-1027).

National War Museum—This huge museum documents the history of Greek warfare, from Alexander the Great to today. Exhibits feature everything from ancient swords and armor to modern tanks and fighter jets (free, Tue–Sun 9:00–14:00, closed Mon, scant English descriptions but audioguide available, Rizari 2–4 at Vasilissis Sofias, Metro: Evangelismos, tel. 210-725-2974).

SHOPPING

Flea Market: The famous Monastiraki Flea Market stretches west of Monastiraki Square, along Ifestou and its side streets. It's a fun place for tourists and pickpockets to browse, but it's not ideal for buying gifts for the friends back home—unless they like flea-bitten junk. You'll see fake designer clothes, antiques, dusty books, and lots of stuff that might raise eyebrows at the airport (best on Sun, 8:00–15:00, Metro: Monastiraki or Thisio).

Souvenirs: There are countless souvenir shops in the Plaka area, mainly along Adrianou and Pandrossou, selling the full range of tourist paraphernalia: T-shirts, calendars, playing cards, plaster copies of famous statues, and so on. Competition is hot between shops, so there's room to bargain—especially if you're buying several items.

Jewelry: Serious buyers tell me that Athens is the best place in Greece to buy jewelry, particularly at the shops along Adrianou. The choices are much better than you'll find elsewhere, and—if you know how to haggle—so are the prices. The best advice is to take your time, and don't be afraid to walk away. The sales staff gets paid by commission, and they hate to lose a potential customer. Most of the stores have a similar selection, which they buy from factory wholesalers. More special artist-owned shops include **Byzantino,** which made the jewelry worn by Greek dancers in the closing ceremonies of the 2000 Sydney Olympics (Adrianou 120, tel. 210-324-6605, run by Kosta and American Laura). The Benaki Museum gift shop is also popular for jewelry.

Sandals: The place to buy real leather sandals is Stavros Melissinos, the famous "poet sandal-maker" of Athens (at Pandrosou 89, near Monastiraki Square). You'll find an assortment of styles priced from €20–28 per pair, as well as free copies of his poems (Mon–Sat 10:00–14:00 & 16:00–19:00, Sun 10:00–14:00, Pandrosou 89, tel. 210-321-9247). When the Beatles came to his shop in 1968, Melissinos was asked why he didn't ask for their autographs. He replied, "Why did they not ask for mine? I will be around long after the Beatles." He was right.

Carpets: The shops around the Plaka sell Turkish-style carpets, but generally don't stock Greek ones. For Greek carpets, look at the National Welfare Organization's Hellenic Folk Art Gallery, behind Plateia Mitropoleos. It has a good selection of shaggy flokati carpets, as well as knotted carpets, colorful kilims, and cushion covers embroidered with traditional folk designs. What's more, the profits go toward preservation of traditional handicrafts (Tue–Fri 9:00–20:00, Mon and Sat 9:00–15:00, closed Sun, Ipatias 6 at the corner of Apollonos, tel. 210-325-0524).

NIGHTLIFE

Strolling—The big news for people who enjoy an evening stroll is the Dionysiou Areopagitou, a wonderful and instantly popular new pedestrian boulevard arcing around the back side of the Acropolis. As the sun goes down, it's busy with locals (lovers, families, seniors, children at play) and visitors alike. You can actually walk entirely around the Acropolis, although much of the circuit is rougher than this fine paved stretch.

Outdoor Cinema—The Aigli Village Cinema is a cool, classic outdoor theater in the National Gardens (at the Zappeion), playing the latest blockbusters with a great sound system (€7, cash only, call 210-336-9369 for schedule and to see if it's played with original soundtrack). Cine Paris is another large, outdoor movie venue, and comes with the added bonus of an Acropolis view (€7, cash only, in the Plaka and on the roof of Kydathineon 22, tel. 210-324-8057).

Psyrri Night Life Zone—Psyrri, until recently famous only for being run-down, has emerged as the trendy nightclub, café, and restaurant zone. As the rustic old crafts shops survive, the mix of trendy and crusty gives the area a unique charm. The best action is around three squares: Agion Asomaton, Iroon, and Agion Anargyron.

Folk Dancing—The Dora Stratou Theater on Filopappos Hill is *the* place to go for real folk dancing. The company—the best in Greece—was originally formed to record and preserve the country's many traditional dances. Their repertoire includes such favorites as the graceful *kalamatianos* circle dance, the *syrtaki* (immortalized by Anthony Quinn in *Zorba the Greek*), and the dramatic solo *zimbetikos* (€15, late May–early Oct Tue–Sat at 21:30, Sun 20:15, no show Mon, 80 min, Dora Stratou Theater, Filopappos Hill, signposted from western end of Dionysiou Areopagitou, Metro: Akropoli, tel. 210-324-4395, after 19:30 call 210-921-4650, www.grdance.org).

SLEEPING

Although there are dozens of hotels around central Athens, prices are steep and good values are rare. Small, inexpensive hotels in the Plaka are few, listed in all the guidebooks, and filled with other tourists. Reserve ahead, especially in the summer months. If you're organized and planning in advance, it's worth checking out the hotel brochures at U.S. travel agencies.

You'll probably find cheaper deals (special rates offered to travel agencies or groups) for some of the hotels listed here. But don't be sucked in by some of the *very* cheap, too-good-to-be-true deals: Most of those are located in the sleazy suburbs around Omonia Square, or down in the coastal suburbs of Glyfada and Voula—far from the places you've come to see. You'll pay a premium to stay near the Acropolis...and it's worth it.

Consider using a Greek travel agency to find you a room. They know the city well, and these two places have a good reputation for their customer service: **Fantasy Travel** (south of Syntagma Square at Xenofontos 8, tel. 210-322-8410, fax 210-322-2624, www.fantasytravelofgreece.com) and **Dolphin Hellas Travel** (in Makrigianni at Syngrou 16, tel. 210-922-7772, fax 210-923-2101, www.greecetravel.com/dolphinhellas). Hotels give low rates to travel agencies to encourage them to send their clients. So the perception that you save money by booking directly with the hotel is a false one. By booking with a reliable Greek travel agency you can get the hotel and the services of the travel agency for ferry tickets,

Sleep Code

(€1 = about $1.20, country code: 30)
S = Single, **D** = Double/Twin, **T** = Triple, **Q** = Quad, **b** = bathroom, **s** = shower only, **NSE** = No English. Unless otherwise noted, credit cards are accepted, and most hotels require a credit-card number to guarantee your reservation.

To help you easily sort through these listings, I've divided the rooms into three categories, based on the price for a standard double room with bath:

$$$ **Higher Priced**—Most rooms €100 or more.
$$ **Moderately Priced**—Most rooms between €70–100.
$ **Lower Priced**—Most rooms €70 or less.

schedules, tours, and information. If you go to www.hotelsofgreece.com, every C-category hotel in the Athens section is within a half mile of the Acropolis or the Plaka and is less than €100 a night for a double.

One final word: Athens is a noisy city, and Athenians like to stay out late. I've tried to recommend places in quieter areas, but that's not always possible. Many hotels renovated for the Olympics, adding "soundproof" doors and windows that can be successful at blocking out noise. Still, light sleepers should be ready to use earplugs.

North of the Acropolis: Monastiraki, Plaka, and Syntagma

$$$ Hotel Grande Bretagne, a five-star place with 320 sprawling and elegantly furnished rooms, is considered the best hotel in Greece. It's *the* place to head if you have royal blood—or wish you did—and feel like being treated that way for a few days. Built in 1862 to accommodate visiting heads of state, it ranks among the grand hotels of the world. It became a hotel in 1874, and it still retains its 19th century elegance. No other hotel in Athens can boast such a rich history (Sb-€215, Db-€250–350, American-style breakfast-€28, air-con, overlooking Syntagma Square at Vassileos Georgiou 1, Metro: Syntagma, tel. 210-333-0000, fax 210-322-8034, www.grandebretagne.gr). If you'd rather just eat here, consider their rooftop restaurant (see "Eating," below).

$$$ Hotel Plaka and **Hotel Hermes** are decent business-class hotels well-located in the Plaka. They're both owned by the same company, and have rooms at the same price. The Hotel Plaka has a roof terrace, while the Hotel Hermes is closest to Syntagma on a quiet street (April–June and Oct: Sb-€115, Db-€145, Tb-€170; a bit higher July–Sept, 30 percent lower Nov–March; Hotel

Plaka Hotels

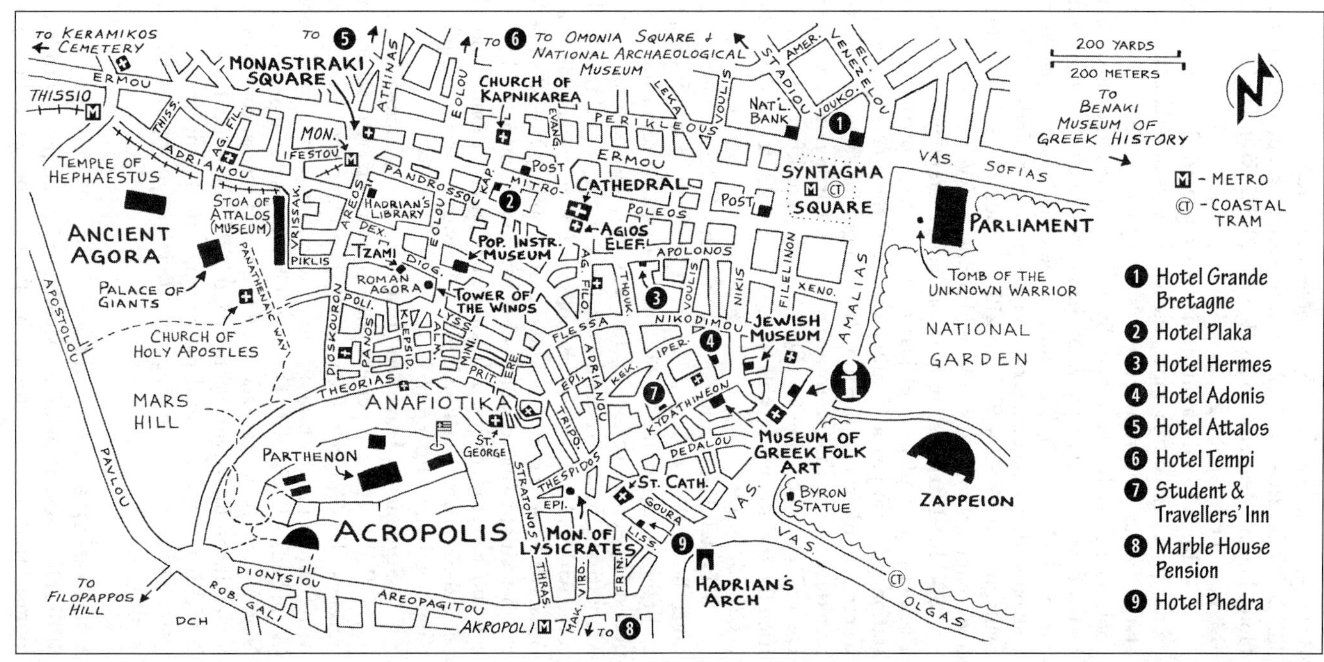

Plaka—on the corner of Mitropoleos and Kapnikarea, tel. 210-322-2096, fax 210-322-2412, www.plakahotel.gr, plaka@tourhotel; Hotel Hermes—at Apollonos 19, tel. 210-323-5514, fax 210-3222-412, www.hermeshotel.gr).

$$ Hotel Adonis, a small, modern hotel with 26 rooms, stands on the quiet, traffic-free upper reaches of Kodrou, right in the heart of the Plaka. Understandably, it's a popular place, and is often booked long in advance, especially in the summer. The rooms on the fourth floor have good views of the Acropolis, as does the rooftop bar (Sb-€50, Db-€77, Tb-€100, 40 percent cheaper Nov–March, cash only, air-con, includes roof-terrace breakfast, Kodrou 3, Metro: Syntagma, tel. 210-324-9737, fax 210-323-1602, owner Spiros doesn't like computers so there's no e-mail address or Web site).

$$ Hotel Attalos, an 80-room budget standby, is located on a sometimes-scruffy street just north of the Monastiraki Metro station. It's also just a 15-minute walk to the Acropolis, near the Central Market and the hip Psyrri nightlife scene. Enjoy your breakfast on the roof, with a view of the Parthenon (Sb-€54–64, Db-€67–80, Tb-€80–96, Qb-€96–115, breakfast-€8, air-con, friendly and knowledgeable staff, Athinas 29, tel. 210-391-2801, fax 210-324-3124).

$ Hotel Tempi, run by Yiannis and Katerina, offers traditional hospitality at prices that won't break the bank. It's popular and family-run, with 24 clean and comfortable rooms on a quiet pedestrians-only section of Eolou street, just 250 yards from Monastiraki Metro station. Ask for a room at the front—they come with balconies that overlook the flower markets on Plateia Agia Irini and have views of the Acropolis (Db-€58, Tb-€70, cheaper singles and doubles with bathroom down the hall, air-con, no elevator, communal kitchen/breakfast room, Eolou 29, tel. 210-321-3175, fax 210-325-4179, www.travelling.gr/tempihotel, tempihotel@travelling.gr).

$ Student & Travellers' Inn is the best backpacker place in the Plaka, and the perfect place to meet up with other young travelers. The 33 rooms come in all shapes and sizes, from dorms with communal bathrooms to private, air-conditioned rooms (dorm beds-€18, Sb-€50, Db-€60, Tb-€75, prices 20 percent lower Nov–March, breakfasts start at €3, Internet access, courtyard bar, Kydathineon 16, Metro: Syntagma, tel. 210-324-4808, fax 210-321-0065, www.studenttravellersinn.com, info@studenttravellersinn.com). An in-house travel agency specializes in trips to the Greek islands.

South of the Acropolis

$ Marble House Pension is a small, family-run place with 16 cozy rooms. Hidden away behind a brilliant red bougainvillea vine at the end of a cul-de-sac, it has to be the quietest hotel in Athens. It's well worth the walk (Sb-€40, Db-€46, Tb-€53, cheaper Oct–April or in doubles and triples with bathroom down the hall, breakfast-€5, ceiling fans, 10-min walk from Syngrou-Fix Metro at Zini 35a, tel. 210-923-4058 or 210-922-8294, fax 210-922-6461, www.marblehouse.gr, info@marblehouse.gr).

$ Hotel Phedra, overlooking a peaceful square of ancient ruins and a Byzantine Church, offers 21 of the best budget rooms in the Plaka (Sb-€50, D-€50, Db-€60, Tb-€72, less off-season, breakfast extra, air-con, 2 blocks from Hadrian's Arch at Lissikratous 6, tel. 210-323-8461, fax 210-322-7795).

EATING

Around Syntagma Square

Neon Café, a slick, modern, cafeteria-style eatery facing Syntagma Square, is designed for the traveler in a hurry. You'll find a daily selection of Greek favorites as well as salads and pastas (daily 7:00–1:00 in the morning, on the southwestern side of Syntagma Square at Mitropoleos 3, tel. 210-324-6873). While not cheap, it's efficient and air-conditioned. Head upstairs for a non-smoking section with a view.

Fast Food Eleni, west of Syntagma on unglamorous Perikleos, is one of central Athens' best-kept secrets. Most of the customers are workers from the surrounding shops and offices, who come here for the daily specials (such as roast pork with lemon and potatoes, €5.50) as well as for the fast food (Mon–Sat 11:00–17:00, closed Sun, 200 yards west of Syntagma Square at Perikleos 19).

Hotel Grande Bretagne's Roof Garden Restaurant is considered by many the finest chance in town to dine in Old World elegance—on a roof garden with grand Acropolis and city views (nightly from 19:00, reservations required, Greek and Mediterranean cuisine, €15 pastas, €30 main dishes, €60–75 *menus,* north side of Syntagma Square, tel. 210-333-0750, after 19:00 call 210-333-0766).

Around the Plaka

Diners—Greeks and tourist alike—flock to the Plaka. The food is generally mediocre, but the Plaka makes up for that in ambience. Unless stated otherwise, all the restaurants listed here are open daily for lunch and dinner. Credit cards are not always accepted, so bring cash.

Taverna O Thespis is a rare place that feels like the good old days in the Plaka. It's tucked away above the crowds up quiet Thespidos street, with tables cascading down a series of breezy terraces. Dine on traditional specialties like *bekri meze*—pork with

Plaka Restaurants

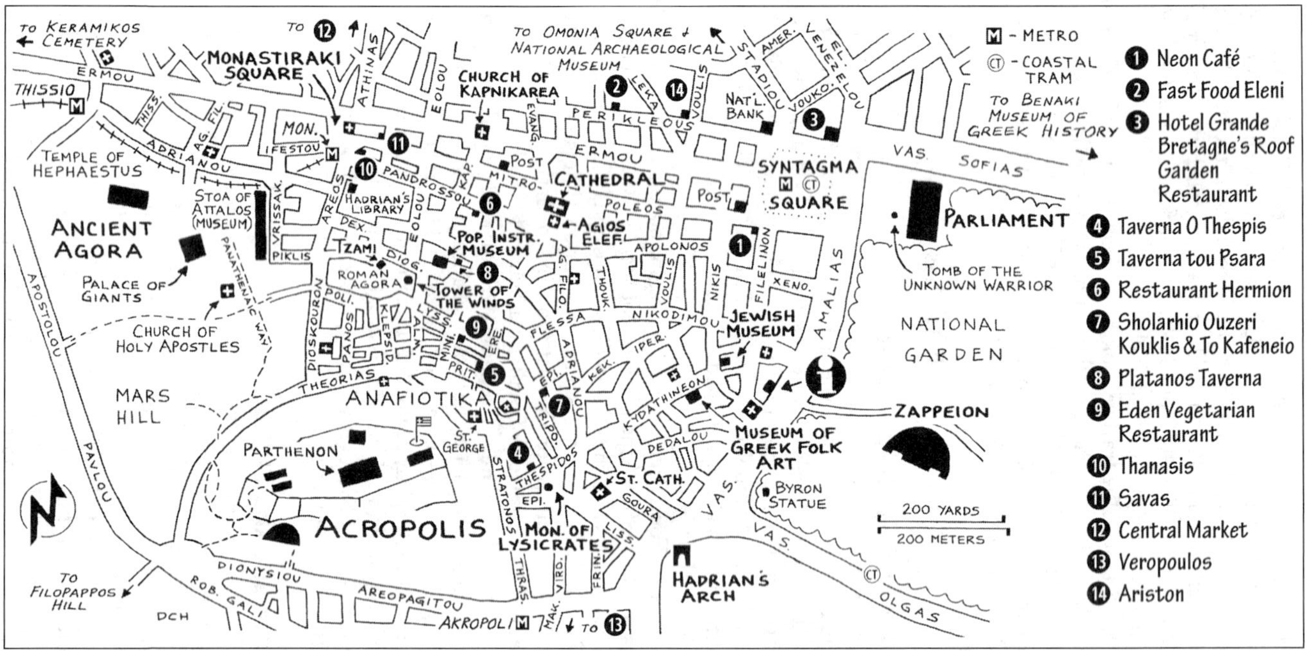

spicy sauce (€10 main dishes, daily 11:00–24:00, Thespidos 18, tel. 210-323-8242).

Taverna tou Psara is another good bet just above the hustle and bustle. The appetizers here are especially good: You can order a good selection of *mezedes* (appetizers) and forget about a main course. The outdoor terrace has views over the city and live folk music (€10–13 main dishes, daily 11:00–24:00, signposted off Tripodon at Eretheos 16, tel. 210-321-8734).

Restaurant Hermion is a dressy wicker place tucked away in a quiet arcade off busy Pandrosou, offering a choice of outdoor seating in a small, private square, or a cool air-conditioned interior. Under a canvas canopy surrounded by potted plants, you forget you're in a big city. The menu offers a large range of salads, and lots of fish (€10–15 main dishes, daily 11:00–24:00; with back to cathedral, leave the square downhill to the left, going 50 yards down Pandrosou to Zeus sign, then follow arcade passageway to Pandrosou 15; tel. 210-324-7148).

Sholarhio Ouzeri Kouklis is a fun, inexpensive place ideal for groups wanting to try a variety of traditional *mezedes* and drink good homemade booze on a breezy perch at the top of the Plaka. Since 1935, the Kouklis family has been making ouzo liquor (that's what an *ouzeri* is) and running their restaurant—which maintains a 1930s atmosphere to this day. The waiter comes around with a big platter of dishes, and you choose what you like (€3–4 per plate). Drinks are cheap, dessert is free, and the four-person €40 special is worth considering. As the plates are pretty big, this is most fun with a group of four or more (Mon–Sat 11:00–24:00, closed Sun, under the Acropolis at Tripodon 14 and Lisiou, tel. 210-324-7605).

To Kafeneio, just below Ouzeri Kouklis, is another good choice, with a traditional atmosphere—air-conditioned in the summer and fireplace-cozy in the winter. If you sit outside, the steep angle of the street may have you rethinking that second glass of ouzo (daily 11:00–24:00, Epiharmou 1 at Tripodon, tel. 210-324-6916). Don't confuse this restaurant in the Plaka with another, similarly named establishment in the Kolonaki district.

Platanos Taverna, on a peaceful courtyard next to the Museum of Greek Popular Instruments, is a good place for a quiet, unhurried meal. The interior decor has a 1940s feel, with interesting old pictures—but in good weather, I'd rather eat outside under the plane trees (Mon–Sat 12:00–17:00 & 19:00–24:00, closed Sun, Diogenous 4, tel. 210-322-0666).

Eden Vegetarian Restaurant, Athens' first vegetarian eatery (since 1982), enjoys mixing Greek and international dishes. The creative and inviting menu offers vegetarian versions of such Greek favorites as *mousakas* and *stifado* (€12 meals, Wed–Mon 12:00–24:00, closed Tue, Lyssiou 12, tel. 210-324-8858, www.edenveg.gr).

Fast Food and Picnics

On Monastiraki Square: The best place to head for fast food is the bottom end of Mitropoleos, where it meets Monastiraki Square. This is souvlaki heaven, with several frantic restaurants spilling into the street keeping hordes of hungry, mostly local eaters happy. For €6 you get a pile of *sis kebabs* on pita bread. Meat shaved from a gyro is cheaper. A gyro souvlaki sandwich to go can be as cheap as €1.50. Greek salads are hearty, and the wine, beer, and ouzo is cheap. **Thanasis** is famous for its special souvlaki, made from a traditional recipe that combines ground beef and lamb with Thanasis' secret blend of seasonings. Get it wrapped in pita bread to go (€1.50), or sit down to a plate of four (€6, daily 10:00–2:00 in the morning, Mitropoleos 69, tel. 210-324-4705). Across the street, another old favorite, **Savas,** has both a restaurant and a counter offering a choice of gyros to go: ground beef, pork, or chicken (all €1.50). The guys here can fill and wrap a gyro before you can blink. Ask for yours to be served *ap'ola* (with everything) and it'll come loaded with salad and garlicky *tzatziki* sauce (daily 10:00–3:00 in the morning, Mitropoleos 86, tel. 210-324-5048).

Markets: The lively Central Market is about 500 yards north of Plateia Monastirakiou on Athinas. You'll find the best and cheapest selection of whatever's in season at the fruit and vegetable stalls, which spread downhill to the left, flanked by shops selling feta from the barrel and a dozen different kinds of olives. The meat and fish markets are housed in the neoclassical building across the street, behind a row of shops specializing in dried fruit and nuts. Try the roasted almonds and the delicious white figs from the island of Evia. There are no big supermarkets close to the Plaka, but there are several small grocery stores that stay open long hours (7:00–22:00) and stock enough to throw together a decent picnic. To the south of the Acropolis, try **Veropoulos** (Mon–Fri 8:00–20:00, Sat 8:00–6:00, closed Sun, just uphill from Veikou at Parthenonos 6).

Ariston is one of the best places for *spanakopita* (spinach pie), *tiropita* (cheese pie), *kreatopita* (lamb pie), and *meletzanitopita* (eggplant pie). This is the cheapest and most filling meal in town, and much healthier than a souvlaki. It's been open since 1910 and also offers a wide assortment of pastries (2 blocks from Syntagma at Voulis 10).

TRANSPORTATION CONNECTIONS

Elefthérios Venizélos International Airport

Athens is served by Elefthérios Venizélos International Airport at Spata, 17 miles east of Athens (tel. 210-353-0000, www.aia.gr). **Olympic Airways** (www.olympic-airways.gr) flies to Iraklio on Crete (6/day), Paros (3/day), (Naxos (1/day), Sámos (3/day), and Santorini/Thira (4/day). Olympic's head office is at Leoforos Syngrou 96 (tel. 210-356-9111, toll-free tel. 801-114-4444), but you're better off using a travel agent. **Aegean Airlines** (www.aegeanair.com) has flights to Iraklio (6/day) and Santorini/Thira (4/day). Aegean has an office on Syntagma Square (Othonos 10, tel. 210-331-5502, toll-free tel. 801-112-0000).

There are several ways to get between the airport and downtown: **Metro** Line 3 zips you downtown in 45 minutes for €8. Express **bus** #E95 operates 24 hours daily between the airport and Syntagma Square (about 2/hr, 60–90 min depending on traffic). The downtown bus stop is outside the National Gardens on Amalias, on the eastern side of Syntagma Square. Bus #E96 operates between the airport and Plateia Karaiskaki in Piraeus (also runs 24 hrs daily, about every 40 min). A ticket for either bus costs €3, and is valid for 24 hours on all Athens transit. A **taxi** costs €20–25, depending on traffic. People on package trips are met at the airport by a cabbie who takes them to their hotel and helps get them settled in for about €75. Recently private English-speaking cabbies have been providing this same service to anyone for about €55.

By Boat from Piraeus

Piraeus, six miles southwest of central Athens, has been the port of Athens since ancient times. Today it's the main port for services to the Greek islands, making it the busiest passenger port in the Mediterranean.

Orientation: All ferry, hydrofoil, and catamaran services leave from Great Harbor (Megas Limin), which is the largest of three harbors surrounding the Piraeus Peninsula. Zea Marina (Limin Zeas) and the picturesque Mikrolimano (small harbor), on the eastern side of the peninsula, are for private yachts. The action at Great Harbor is centered on chaotic Plateia Karaiskaki, which juts out into the harbor right at the middle of the waterfront.

Getting to Piraeus: The **Metro** is by far the easiest way to get between Piraeus' Great Harbor and central Athens. There are trains to Monastiraki every 10 minutes between 6:00–24:00. Warning: The section between Piraeus and Monastiraki is notorious for pickpockets, so take extra care of your valuables and wear a money belt. There are suburban **trains** every 30 minutes to Athens' Central Station at Arharnon. In Piraeus, the Metro and train stations are 100 yards apart at the northeastern corner of the waterfront on Akti Kalimassioti. **Bus** #E96, connecting Piraeus to the airport, arrives and departs at the southwestern corner of Plateia Karaiskaki. There are no intercity buses to or from Piraeus.

Ferry Connections: For the latest information on ferry services, pick up a weekly schedule from the Greek National Tourist Organization offices in Athens or at the airport. Inquire

Piraeus

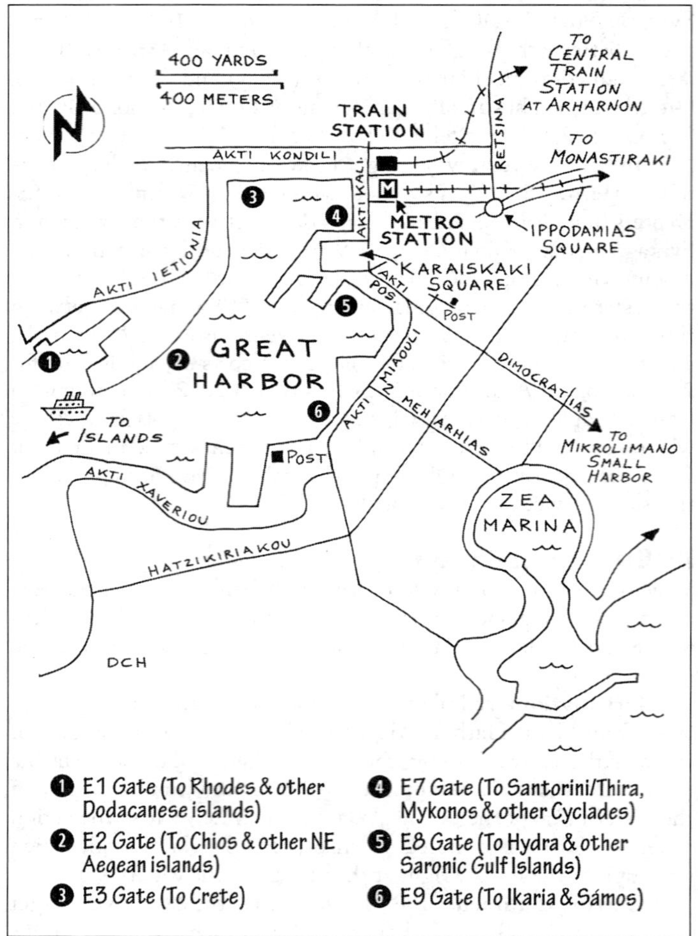

locally about ferry departure points in the immediate area.

To the Cyclades: Paros (6/day, 5 hrs), **Naxos** (6/day, 6 hrs), **Santorini/Thira** (4/day, 9 hrs). The best service is offered by Blue Star Ferries (www.bluestarferries.com). Its comfortable and modern boats are fitted with special stabilizers that provide a very smooth ride and enable them to keep sailing in winds of up to "force nine" on the local Beaufort scale.

To Crete: Iraklio (2/day, 10 hrs). The sleek Minoan Lines fleet (www.minoan.gr) is better than ANEK Lines (www.anek.gr)

To the Saronic Gulf Islands: Aegina (hrly, 1.25 hrs), **Poros** (4/day, 2.5 hrs), **Hydra** (2/day, 3.5 hrs), and **Spetses** (1/day, 4.5 hrs).

To the Northeast Agean Islands: Sámos (2/day, 13 hrs).

Hydrofoil and Catamaran Connections: Faster hydrofoils and catamarans also leave from Piraeus.

To the Cyclades: Paros (2/day, 3.5 hrs), **Naxos** (1/day, 4 hrs), and **Santorini/Thira** (1/day, 4.75 hrs). All these services are operated by Hellas Flying Dolphins (tel. 210-419-9000, www.dolphins.gr).

To the Saronic Gulf Islands: Aegina (hrly, 35 min), **Poros** (4/day, 1 hr), **Hydra** (6/day, 1.75 hrs), and **Spetses** (6/day, 2.5 hrs). Most of these services are operated by Hellas Flying Dolphins (see above).

To the Northeast Agean: Sámos (6/wk, 7 hrs). This service is operated by Nel Lines (www.nel.gr) using the futuristic-looking Aeolis Express, which is technically a high-speed ferry rather than a catamaran.

DUBLIN

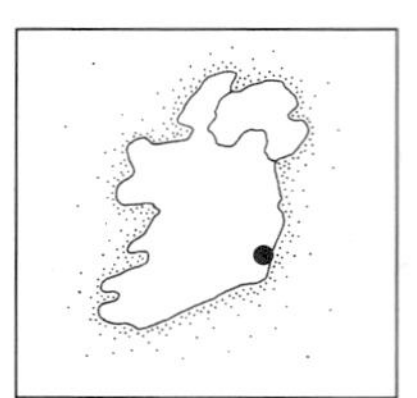

With reminders of its stirring history and rich culture on every corner, Ireland's capital and largest city is a sightseer's delight. Dublin's fair city will have you humming, "Cockles and mussels, alive, alive-O."

Founded as a Viking trading settlement in the 9th century, Dublin grew to be a center of wealth and commerce second only to London in the British Empire. Dublin, the seat of English rule in Ireland for 700 years, was the heart of a "civilized" Anglo-Irish area (eastern Ireland) known as "the Pale." Anything "beyond the Pale" was considered uncultured and almost barbaric...purely Irish.

The Golden Age of English Dublin was the 18th century. The British Empire was on a roll, and Dublin was right there with it. Largely rebuilt during this Georgian era, Dublin—even with its tattered edges—became an elegant and cultured capital.

Then nationalism and human rights got in the way. The ideas of the French Revolution inspired Irish intellectuals to buck British rule, and after the Rebellion of 1798, life in Dublin was never quite the same. But the 18th century left a lasting imprint on the city. Squares and boulevards in the Georgian style (that's British for "neoclassical") gave the city an air of grandness. The National Museum, National Gallery, and many government buildings are in the Georgian section of town. Few buildings (notably Christ Church Cathedral and St. Patrick's Cathedral) survive from before this Georgian period.

In the 19th century, with the closing of the Irish Parliament, the famine, and the beginnings of the struggle for independence, Dublin was treated—and felt—more like a colony than a partner. The tension culminated in the Easter Rising of 1916, independence ritain, and the tragic civil war. With many of its elegant left in ruins, Dublin emerged as the capital of the only for- olony in Europe.

While bullet-pocked buildings and dramatic statues keep nories of Ireland's recent struggle for independence alive, it's m time now, and the city is looking to a bright future. Locals enjoying the strong "Celtic Tiger" economy, while visitors enjoy a big-town cultural scene wrapped in a small-town smile.

Planning Your Time

On a three-week trip through Ireland, Dublin deserves three nights and two days. Consider this aggressive sightseeing plan:

Day 1: 10:30-Trinity College guided walk; 11:00-Book of Kells and Old Library; 12:00-Browse Grafton Street and have lunch there, or picnic on Merrion Square; 13:30-Visit Number Twenty-Nine Georgian House; 15:00-National Museum; 17:00-Return to hotel, rest, have dinner—eat well for less during early-bird specials; 19:30-Evening walk (musical or literary); 22:00-Irish music in Temple Bar area.

Day 2: 10:00-Dublin Castle tour; 11:00-Choose between self-guided O'Connell Street Stroll or guided historical walking tour; 13:00-Lunch; 14:00-Kilmainham Jail; 15:30-Visit Guinness Storehouse brewery and finish with view of city; Evening-Catch a play, concert, or Comhaltas traditional music in Dun Laoghaire.

ORIENTATION

(area code: 01)

Sprawling greater Dublin is home to over a million people—nearly a third of the country's population. But the center of touristic interest is a tight triangle between O'Connell Bridge, St. Stephen's Green, and Christ Church Cathedral. Within this triangle, you'll find Trinity College (home to the Book of Kells), Grafton Street (top pedestrian shopping zone), Temple Bar (trendy and touristy nightlife center), Dublin Castle, and the hub of most city tours and buses. The only major sights outside your easy-to-walk triangle are the Kilmainham Jail and the Guinness Storehouse (both west of the center).

The River Liffey cuts the town in two. Focus on the southern half, where nearly all your sightseeing will take place. Dublin's wide main drag, O'Connell Street, starts north of the river at the Parnell monument and runs south, down to the central O'Connell Bridge. After crossing the bridge, it continues south as the major city axis (as Westmoreland Street and then Grafton Street) to St. Stephen's Green.

The suburban port of Dun Laoghaire (DUN-leary; described on page 844) lies south of Dublin, 20 minutes away by DART commuter train. Travelers connecting by ferry to Holyhea Wales—or those just looking for a mellow town to sleep in outs of urban Dublin—can easily home-base here.

Tourist Information

Dublin's main tourist information office (TI) is a big shop with little to offer other than promotional fliers and long lines (Mon–Sat 9:00–17:30, Sun July–Sept only 10:30–15:00, located in a former church on Suffolk Street, 1 block off Grafton Street, tel. 01/605-7700, www.visitdublin.com). It has a car-rental agency, bus-info desk, café, and traditional knickknacks. But perhaps its greatest value is the chance to peruse the rack opposite the info counter and pick up brochures for destinations throughout Ireland. There's also a TI at the airport (daily 8:00–22:00) and one at the Dun Laoghaire ferry terminal (Mon–Sat 10:00–13:00 & 14:00–18:00, closed Sun).

While you can buy the TI's lousy map for €0.50, its free newspaper, *The Guide to Dublin,* has the same one on its staple page. The handy *Dublin's Top Visitor Attractions* booklet has a small map and the latest on all of the town's sights—many more than I list here (€3, sold at TI bookshop without any wait). For a schedule of happenings in town, check the minimal calendar of events inside *The Guide to Dublin* newspaper (free at TI).

The excellent *Collins Illustrated Dublin Map* (€6 at TIs and newsstands) is the ultimate city map, listing just about everything of interest, along with helpful opinions.

Dublin Pass: This new sightseeing pass can be a good deal if you like to visit lots of sights quickly (€29/1 day, €49/2 days, €59/3 days, cheaper for kids, sold at all 3 TIs but not at sights, www.dublinpass.com). The pass might save you a little time, because it allows you to bypass ticket-buyer lines—though the lines at included sights generally aren't very long. It covers museums, churches, literature-related sights, and expensive stops like the Guinness Storehouse and the Old Jameson Distillery, plus the Aircoach airport bus (but not Airlink). However, the pass doesn't include the famous Book of Kells or any bus tours or walking tours, and many of the sights it claims to "cover" (such as the National Gallery and the Chester Beatty Library) are actually free.

Arrival in Dublin

By Train: Dublin has two stations. Heuston Station, on the west end of town, serves west and southwest Ireland (30-min walk from O'Connell Bridge; take taxi or bus #90 instead, see below). Connolly Station—which serves the north, northwest, and Rosslare—is closer to the center (10-min walk from O'Connell Bridge). Each station has a baggage-check facility and ATMs.

The two train stations are connected by the red line of the

Greater Dublin

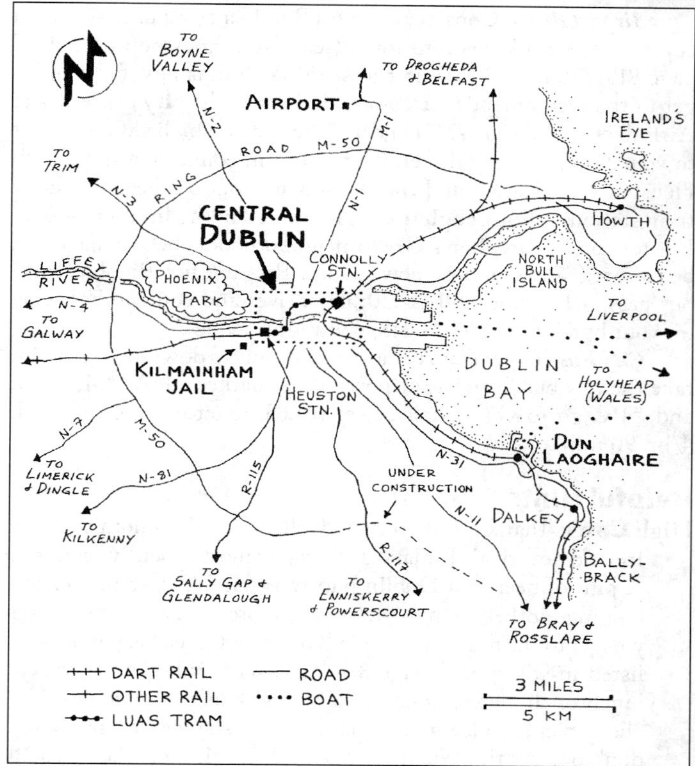

new Luas commuter train (see "Getting Around Dublin," page 815) and by bus. Bus #90 runs along the river, linking both train stations, the bus station, and the city center (€0.85, 6/hr). When you're leaving Dublin and you want to reach Heuston Station from the city center, catch bus #90 on the south side of the river; to get to Connolly Station and the Busaras bus station from the city center, catch #90 on the north side of the river.

By Bus: Bus Éireann, Ireland's national bus company, uses the Busaras Central Bus Station next to Connolly Station (10-min walk or short bus ride to the city center; see bus #90 info in "By Train," above).

By Ferry: Irish Ferries docks at the mouth of the River Liffey (near the town center), while the Stena Line docks at Dun Laoghaire (easy DART train connections into Dublin, 4/hr, 20 min).

By Plane: The airport has ATMs, change bureaus, car-rental agencies, baggage check, a café, and a supermarket at the parking lot. Taxis from the airport into Dublin cost about €25, taxis to Dun Laoghaire will run about €40.

Airport Buses: Consider buying a Rambler city-bus pass, which covers the Airlink bus into town (see "Getting Around Dublin," page 815)—but read this first to see if Airlink is best for you. To get to the recommended accommodations in the **city center,** take Airlink bus #748 (not #747) and ask the driver which stop is closest to your hotel (€5, pay driver, 2/hr, 40 min, connects airport with Heuston train station and the Busaras bus station, near Connolly train station). **Dun Laoghaire** is also served by Airlink (bus #746). But for the **St. Stephen's Green** neighborhood, the Aircoach is a better bet (€7, covered by new Dublin Pass but not Rambler city-bus pass, 4/hr, runs 5:30–22:30; pay driver and confirm best stop for your hotel, tel. 01/844-7118, www.aircoach.ie).

City Bus: To get from the airport cheaply to downtown Dublin, take the city bus from the airport; buses marked #16A, #41, #41B, and #41C go to O'Connell Street (€1.65, exact change required, 4/hr, 90 min).

Helpful Hints

High Costs: Thanks to its recent "Celtic Tiger" economic boom, Ireland now rivals Finland as Europe's most expensive country. A pint of beer in a Dublin pub can cost €4. Restaurants and lodging—other than hostels—are more expensive the closer you get to the touristy Temple Bar district (see cheaper options listed in "Sleeping," page 834). Look for pub grub "carvery" lunch or dinner options (usually less than €10), and consider cheap picnics once in a while. If you're staying at a big hotel, don't pay for the expensive optional €10–15 breakfast—you'll likely find a nearby local café that serves breakfast for half that. If you're doing a lot of sightseeing, the Dublin Pass can save money (see "Tourist Information," above).

Tourist Victim Support Service: This thoughtful service can be helpful if you run into any problems (Mon–Sat 10:00–18:00, Sun 12:00–18:00, tel. 01/478-5295).

U.S. Embassy: It's on 42 Elgin Road in the Ballsbridge neighborhood (Mon–Fri 8:30–17:00 for passport concerns, tel. 01/668-7122 or 01/668-8777, www.usembassy.ie).

Internet Access: There are Internet cafés on nearly every street. South of the River Liffey, try Central Cybercafé (Mon–Fri 9:00–22:00, Sat–Sun 10:00–21:00, 6 Grafton Street, tel. 01/677-8298). Global Internet Café is north of the Liffey (Mon–Fri 8:00–23:00, Sat 9:00–23:00, Sun 10:00–23:00, 8 Lower O'Connell Street, tel. 01/878-0295).

Laundry: Capricorn Launderette, a block southwest of Jurys Inn Christ Church on Patrick Street, is full-service only. Allow four hours and about €9 for a load (Mon–Fri 7:30–20:00, Sat

9:00–18:00, closed Sun, tel. 01/473-1779). The All-American Launderette offers self- and full-service options (Mon–Sat 8:30–19:00, Sun 10:00–18:00, 40 South Great George's Street, tel. 01/677-2779).

Festivals: St. Patrick's Day is a five-day extravaganza in Dublin (www.stpatricksday.ie). June 16 is Bloomsday, dedicated to the Irish author James Joyce and featuring the Messenger Bike Rally. On rugby weekends (about 4 per year), hotels raise their prices and are packed. Book ahead during festival times and for any weekend.

Getting Around Dublin

You'll do most of Dublin on foot. Big, green buses are cheap and cover the city thoroughly. Most lines start at the four quays (pron. "keys"), or piers, nearest O'Connell Bridge. If you're away from the center, nearly any bus takes you back downtown. Tell the driver where you're going, and he'll ask for €0.85, €1.25, €1.45, or €1.65, depending on the number of stops. Bring exact change or lose any excess.

Passes: The bus office at 59 Upper O'Connell Street has free "route network" maps and sells Rambler and Short-Hop city-bus passes. The three-day Rambler costs €10 and covers the Airlink airport bus (but not Aircoach buses or DART trains). The three-day Short Hop pass, which costs €15, includes DART trains (but not Airlink or Aircoach buses). Passes are also sold at each TI (bus info tel. 01/873-4222).

DART: Speedy commuter trains run along the coast, connecting Dublin with Dun Laoghaire's ferry terminal and recommended B&Bs. Think of the DART line as a giant "C" that serves coastal suburbs from Bray in the south to Howth in the north (€1.80, 4/hr, 20 min, runs 6:30–23:30, tel. 01/703-3504, www.irishrail.ie).

LUAS: The city's new light rail and subway system has two main lines (red and green) that serve inland suburbs. The more useful line for travelers is the red line, connecting the Connolly and Heuston train stations (€1.30, 6/hr, runs 5:30–00:30, tel. 1-800-676-464, www.luas.ie).

Taxi: Cabbies are honest, plentiful, friendly, and good sources of information (€2.75 minimum fare, €0.50 surcharge per bag, figure €7 or less for most downtown rides, €30 per hour for a guided joyride from most any cab).

TOURS

While the physical treasures of Dublin are mediocre by European standards, the city has a fine story to tell, and people with a natural knack for telling it. It's a good town for walking tours, and the competition is fierce. Pamphlets touting creative walks are posted all

Dublin

To Airport
Hugh Lane Gallery
Dublin Writers' Museum
Garden of Remembrance
Summerhill
To Croke Park & GAA Museum
Parnell Square
Amiens
St. Mary's Pro-Cathedral
Smithfield Village & Distillery
Dorset
Church
Market
Moore
O'Connell
Connolly Station
To Phoenix Park
Mary's Lane
Henry St.
Talbot St.
Capel St.
Post
Four Courts
Abbey St.
Abbey Theatre
Bus Station
River
Ha'penny Bridge
O'Connell Bridge
Customs House
Guinness Storehouse
Famine Memorial
George's Dock
Liffey
Heuston Station
Temple Bar
Townsend St.
Tara St. Stn.
Cornmarket
Dame
College
James's
Christ-Church Cathedral & Dublinia
To Kilmainham Jail
Beatty Library
Trinity College
Georges
St.
Nassau
Duke
Dublin Castle
Pearse Stn.
Grafton
Nat'l Gallery
St. Patrick's
Dart Rail to Dun Laoghaire
Oscar Wilde Mon.
* Not to scale - O'Connell Bridge to Christchurch St. Stephen's Green, or Parnell Square is a 15 min. walk
St. Stephen's Green
Nat'l Museum
Merrion Square
To Northumberland Road B&B's
Baggot St.
#29 Georgian House
DCH

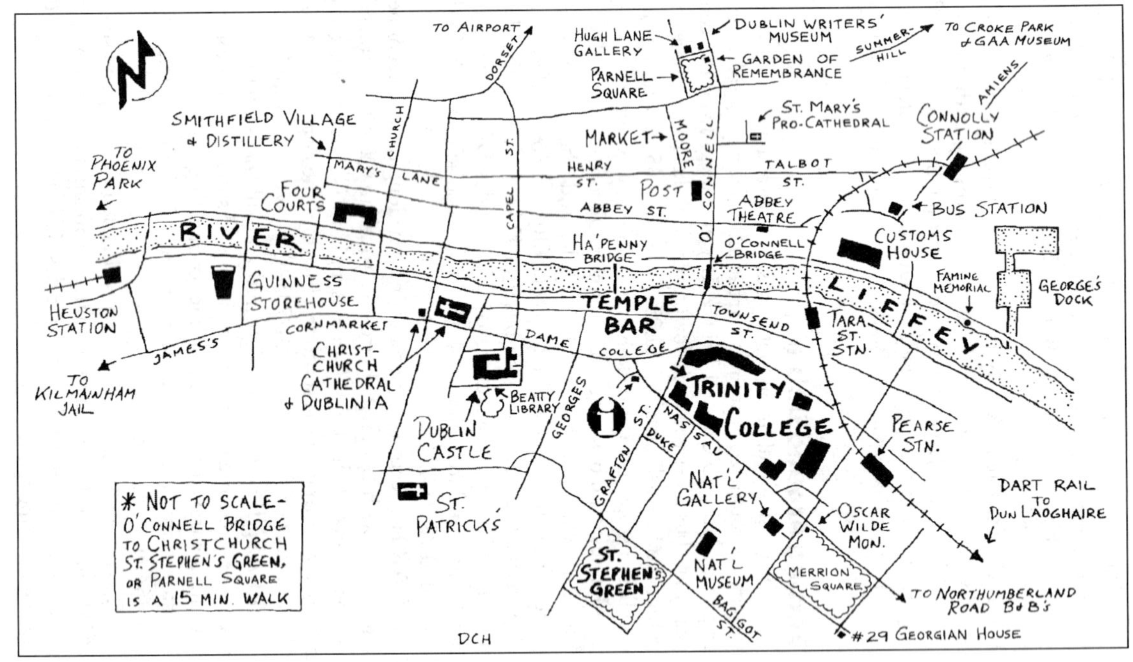

over town. There are medieval walks, literary walks, 1916 Easter Rising walks, Georgian Dublin walks, and more. The evening walks are great ways to meet other travelers.

▲▲Historical Walking Tour—This is your best introductory walk. A group of hardworking history graduates—many of whom claim to have done more than just kiss the Blarney Stone—enliven Dublin's basic historic strip (Trinity College, Old Parliament House, Dublin Castle, and Christ Church Cathedral). You'll get the story of their city, from its Viking origin to the present. Guides speak at length about the roots of Ireland's struggle with Britain. As you listen to your guide's story, you stand in front of buildings that aren't much to see, but are lots to talk about (April–Sept daily at 11:00 and 15:00; Oct–March only Fri, Sat, and Sun at 12:00). From May to September, the same group offers more focused tours (1916 Easter Rising "Terrible Beauty" walks, juicy slice-of-old-life Dublin "Sexual History of Ireland" walks, and gritty "Architecture and Society" walks; call for current schedule). All walks last two hours and cost €10 (depart from front gate of Trinity College, private tours available, tel. 01/878-0227, mobile 087-830-3523, www.historicalinsights.ie).

The 1916 Rebellion company offers, as you might guess, **1916 Rebellion Walks** (€10, 2 hrs, mid-April–Sept Mon–Sat at 11:30 and 14:30, Sun at 13:00, depart from International Bar at 23 Wicklow Street, mobile 086/858-3847, www.1916rising.com).

▲Dublin Literary Pub Crawl—Two actors take 30 or so tourists on a walk, stopping at four pubs. Half the time is spent enjoying their entertaining banter, which introduces the novice to the high *craic* (conversation) of Joyce, O'Casey, and Yeats. The two-hour tour is punctuated with 20-minute pub breaks (free time). While the beer lubricates the social fun, it dilutes the content of the evening (€11, April–Nov daily at 19:30, plus Sun at noon; Dec–March Thu–Sun only; you can normally just show up, but call ahead in July–Aug, when it can fill up; meet upstairs in Duke Pub, off Grafton on Duke Street, tel. 01/670-5602, www.dublinpubcrawl.com).

▲▲Traditional Irish-Music Pub Crawl—This is similar to the Literary Pub Crawl, but features music. You meet upstairs at 19:30 at Gogarty's Pub (Temple Bar area, corner of Fleet and Anglesea) and spend 40 minutes each in the upstairs rooms of three pubs listening to two musicians talk about, play, and sing traditional Irish music. While having only two musicians makes the music a bit thin (Irish music aficionados will tell you you're better off just finding a good session), the evening, though touristy, is not gimmicky. It's an education in traditional Irish music. The musicians demonstrate a few instruments and really enjoy introducing rookies to their art (€11, beer extra, April–Oct nightly, Nov and Feb–March Thu–Sat only, no tours Dec–Jan, allow 2.5 hrs, expect

Dublin at a Glance

▲▲▲National Museum Interesting collection of Irish treasures from the Stone Age to today. **Hours:** Tue–Sat 10:00–17:00, Sun 14:00–17:00, closed Mon.

▲▲▲Kilmainham Gaol Historic jail used by the British as a political prison, today a moving museum honoring the suffering of the Irish people. **Hours:** April–Sept daily 9:30–18:00, Oct–March 9:30–17:00.

▲▲▲Trinity Old Library Contains the exquisite illuminated manuscript, the Book of Kells, the most important piece of art from the Dark Ages. **Hours:** June–Sept Mon–Sat 9:30–17:00, Sun 9:30–16:30; Oct–May Mon–Sat 9:30–17:00, Sun 12:00–16:30.

▲▲Trinity College Ireland's most famous school, best visited with a 30-minute tour led by one of its students. **Hours:** Late May–Sept daily 10:30–15:30, weather permitting.

▲▲Dublin Castle The city's historic 700-year-old castle, featuring ornate English state apartments, tourable only with a guide. **Hours:** Two tours per hour, Mon–Fri 10:00–17:00, Sat–Sun 14:00–17:00.

▲▲Number Twenty-Nine Georgian House Restored 18th-century house providing an intimate glimpse of middle-class Georgian life. **Hours:** Tue–Sat 10:00–17:00, Sun 14:00–17:00, closed Mon.

▲▲Grafton Street The city's liveliest pedestrian shopping mall. **Hours:** Always open.

▲▲O'Connell Bridge Landmark bridge spanning the River Liffey at the center of Dublin. **Hours:** Always open.

up to 50 tourists, tel. 01/475-3313, www.discoverdublin.ie).

▲Hop-on, Hop-off Bus Tours—Two companies (Dublin City Tours and City Sightseeing/Guide Friday) offer hop-on, hop-off bus tours of Dublin, doing virtually identical 90-minute circuits, allowing you to get on or off at your choice of about 19 stops. Buses are mostly topless, with running live commentaries. Both companies go to the Guinness Storehouse, but City Sightseeing/Guide Friday buses stop at Kilmainham Jail (instead of Phoenix Park). Buy your ticket on board. Each company's map, free with your ticket,

▲▲O'Connell Street Dublin's grandest promenade and main drag, packed with history and ideal for a stroll. **Hours:** Always open.

▲Dublin Experience Decent but overpriced 45-minute slideshow offering a historic introduction to Dublin. **Hours:** June–Sept daily, showings on the hour 10:00–17:00, closed Oct–May.

▲Chester Beatty Library American expatriate's eclectic collection of mostly non-Western artifacts. **Hours:** Mon–Fri 10:00–17:00, Sat 11:00–17:00, Sun 13:00–17:00, Oct–April closed Mon.

▲National Gallery Fine collection of top Irish painters and European masters. **Hours:** Mon–Sat 9:30–17:30, Thu until 20:30, Sun 12:00–17:30.

▲Guinness Storehouse The home of Ireland's national beer, with a museum of beer-making, a gallery of clever ads, and the spectacular Gravity Bar with panoramic city views. **Hours:** Daily 9:30–17:00.

▲Gaelic Athletic Association Museum High-tech museum of traditional Gaelic sports like hurling and Irish football. **Hours:** Mon–Sat 9:30–17:00, Sun 12:00–17:00.

▲St. Stephen's Green Relaxing park surrounded by fine Georgian buildings. **Hours:** Always open.

▲Merrion Square Enjoyable and inviting park with a fun statue of Oscar Wilde. **Hours:** Always open.

▲Temple Bar Dublin's trendiest neighborhood, with shops, cafés, theaters, galleries, pubs, and restaurants—a great spot for live traditional music. **Hours:** Always open.

details various discounts you'll get at Dublin's sights (usually the Guinness Storehouse, Viking Splash tour, Old Jameson Distillery, Dublin Writers' Museum, Dublinia, Christ Church Cathedral, and others). Your ticket is valid for 24 hours from the time you buy it (daily, 4/hr 9:30–17:30, until 18:30 in summer). **Dublin City Tour** runs the green-and-cream buses with drivers that do the narration (€12.50, tel. 01/873-4222). **City Sightseeing** (red buses) and **Guide Friday** (yellow buses) cost more, but come with a guide and a driver, rather than a driver who guides (€14, tel. 01/872-9010).

▲Viking Splash Tours—If you'd like to ride in a WWII amphibious vehicle—driven by a Viking-costumed guide who's as liable to spout history as he is to growl—this is for you. The tour starts with a group roar from the Viking within us all. At first, the guide talks as if he were a Viking ("When we came here in 841..."), but soon the patriot emerges as he tags Irish history onto the sights you pass. Near the end of the 75-minute tour (punctuated by occasional group roars at passersby), you don a life jacket for a slow spin up and down a boring canal. Kids who expect a Viking splash may feel they've been trapped in a classroom, but historians will enjoy the talk more than the gimmick (€16, Feb–Nov daily 10:30–17:00, none Dec–Jan, depart about hourly from Bull Alley beside St. Patrick's Cathedral, ticket office at 64–65 Patrick Street, on gray days boat is covered, but still breezy—dress warmly, tel. 01/707-6000, www.vikingsplashtours.com).

SIGHTS

Trinity College

Founded in 1592 by Queen Elizabeth I to establish a Protestant way of thinking about God, Trinity has long been Ireland's most prestigious college. Originally the student body was limited to rich Protestant males. Women were admitted in 1903, and Catholics—though allowed entrance by the school much earlier—were given formal permission to study at Trinity in the 1970s. Today, half of Trinity's 12,500 students are women, and 70 percent are culturally Catholic (although only about 20 percent of Irish youth are churchgoing).

▲▲Trinity College Tour—Trinity students organize and lead 30-minute tours of their campus (look for ticket-seller on a stool just inside the gate). You'll get a rundown on the mostly Georgian architecture; a peek at student life, both in the early days and today; and enjoy the company of your guide, a witty Irish college kid (€10, includes €7.50 fee to see Book of Kells, where the tour leaves you; late May–Sept daily 10:30–15:30, departs roughly every 45 min, weather permitting).

▲▲▲Book of Kells in the Trinity Old Library—The only Trinity campus interior welcoming tourists (just follow the signs) is the Old Library, with its precious Book of Kells. The first-class *Turning Darkness into Light* exhibit puts the 680-page illuminated manuscript in its historical and cultural context, preparing you to see the original book and other precious manuscripts in the treasury. The exhibit is a one-way affair leading to the actual treasury, which shows only four books under glass in one display case. Make a point to spend at least half an hour in the exhibit (before reaching the actual Book of Kells). Especially interesting are the video clips showing the exacting care that went into the monk-uscripts and the ancient art of bookbinding.

Written on vellum (baby calfskin) in the 8th or early 9th century—probably by Irish monks in Iona, Scotland—this enthusiastically decorated copy of the four Gospels was taken to the Irish monastery at Kells in A.D. 806 after a series of Viking raids. Arguably the finest piece of art from what is generally called the Dark Ages, the Book of Kells shows that monastic life in this far fringe of Europe was far from dark. It has been bound into four separate volumes, and at any given time, two of the four gospels are on display. The crowd around the one glass case with the treasures can be off-putting, but hold your own and get up close. You'll see four richly decorated, 1,200-year-old pages—two text and two decorated cover pages. The library treasury also displays two other books—likely the Book of Armagh (A.D. 807) and the Book of Durrow (A.D. 680)—neither of which can be checked out.

Next, a stairway leads upstairs to the 200-foot-long main chamber of the Old Library (from 1732), stacked to its towering ceiling with 200,000 of the library's oldest books. Here, you'll find one of a dozen surviving original copies of the Proclamation of the Irish Republic. Patrick Pearse read these words outside the General Post Office on April 24, 1916, starting the Easter Rising that led to Irish independence. Read the entire thing...imagining that it's yours. Notice the inclusive opening phrase and the seven signatories (each of whom was executed). Another national icon is nearby: the oldest surviving Irish harp, from the 15th century.

Cost and Hours: €7.50; included in €10 Trinity College tour—see above; €10.50 combo-ticket covers *Dublin Experience* movie—see below; June–Sept Mon–Sat 9:30–17:00, Sun 9:30–16:30; Oct–May Mon–Sat 9:30–17:00, Sun 12:00–16:30 (tel. 01/608-2308). A long line often snakes out of the building. Minimize long waiting times by avoiding the midday crunch (roughly 11:30–14:30).

▲*Dublin Experience*—This 45-minute fancy slideshow giving a historic introduction to Dublin is one more tourist movie with the sound turned up. It's good—offering a fine, sweeping introduction to the story of Ireland—but pricey, riding on the coattails of the Book of Kells. Considering that the combo-ticket gets you this for half price, it's not a bad value (€4.50, included in €10.50 combo-ticket with Book of Kells/Old Library, June–Sept daily, showings on the hour 10:00–17:00, closed Oct–May, in modern arts building across from Trinity Old Library).

South of the River Liffey

▲▲Dublin Castle—Built on the site of the first Viking fortress, this castle was the seat of British rule in Ireland for 700 years. Located where the Poddle and Liffey Rivers came together, making a black pool (*dubh linn* in Irish), Dublin Castle was the official residence of the viceroy who implemented the will of the British royalty. In this stirring setting, in 1922, the Brits handed power over to Michael Collins and the Irish. Today, it's used for fancy state and charity functions. The 45-minute tours offer a room-by-room walk through the lavish state apartments of this most English of Irish palaces. The tour finishes with a look at the foundations of the Norman tower and the best remaining chunk of the 13th-century town wall (€5, 2/hr, Mon–Fri 10:00–17:00, Sat–Sun 14:00–17:00, tel. 01/677-7129).

▲Chester Beatty Library—Chester Beatty was a rich American mining engineer who retired to Ireland in 1950, later becoming its first honorary citizen. He left his priceless and eclectic collection to his adopted homeland as a public charitable trust.

More an exotic parade of non-Irish treasures than a library, these two floors of rare texts and collectibles sprouted from over 2,000 years of Eastern religions, Islam, and Christianity. You'll see books carved out of jade, ornate snuff bottles, rhino-horn cups, and even the oldest surviving copy of St. Paul's letter to the Romans (A.D. 180). Other highlights include a graceful Burmese book written on palm leaves—bound together to unfold like an accordion—and a densely ornamental sunburst motif from a 500-year-old Iranian Koran (free entry, Mon–Fri 10:00–17:00, Sat 11:00–17:00, Sun 13:00–17:00, Oct–April closed Mon, tel. 01/407-0750, www.cbl.ie). Enter the library via Dublin Castle's pedestrian arch, across Dame Street from the Olympia Theatre; walk straight ahead crossing the courtyard/parking lot, turn right behind the church and castle turret, walk straight for 75 yards, and enter on the left, just past the walled gardens. It's in the modern addition to the Dublin Castle clock tower building.

Dublin City Hall—The first neoclassical building in this very neoclassical city stands proudly overlooking Dame Street, in front of the gate to Dublin Castle. Built in 1779 as the Royal Exchange, it introduced the neoclassical style (then very popular on the Continent) to Ireland. Step inside (it's free) to feel the prosperity and confidence of Dublin in her 18th-century glory days. In 1852, it became the City Hall. Under the grand rotunda, a cycle of heroic paintings tells the city's history. Pay your respects to the 18-foot-tall statue of Daniel O'Connell (the great orator and liberator who won Catholic emancipation in 1829 from the much-depised Protestants over in London). The greeter sits like the Maytag repairman at the information desk, eager to give you more information. Downstairs is a simple *Story of the Capital* exhibition—storyboards and video clips of Dublin's history (€4, covered by Dublin Pass, Mon–Sat 10:00–17:00, Sun 14:00–17:00).

Dublinia—This tries valiantly, but fails, to be a "bridge to Dublin's medieval past." The amateurish look at the medieval town starts with a walk through dim rooms of tableaux, followed by several halls of

South Dublin

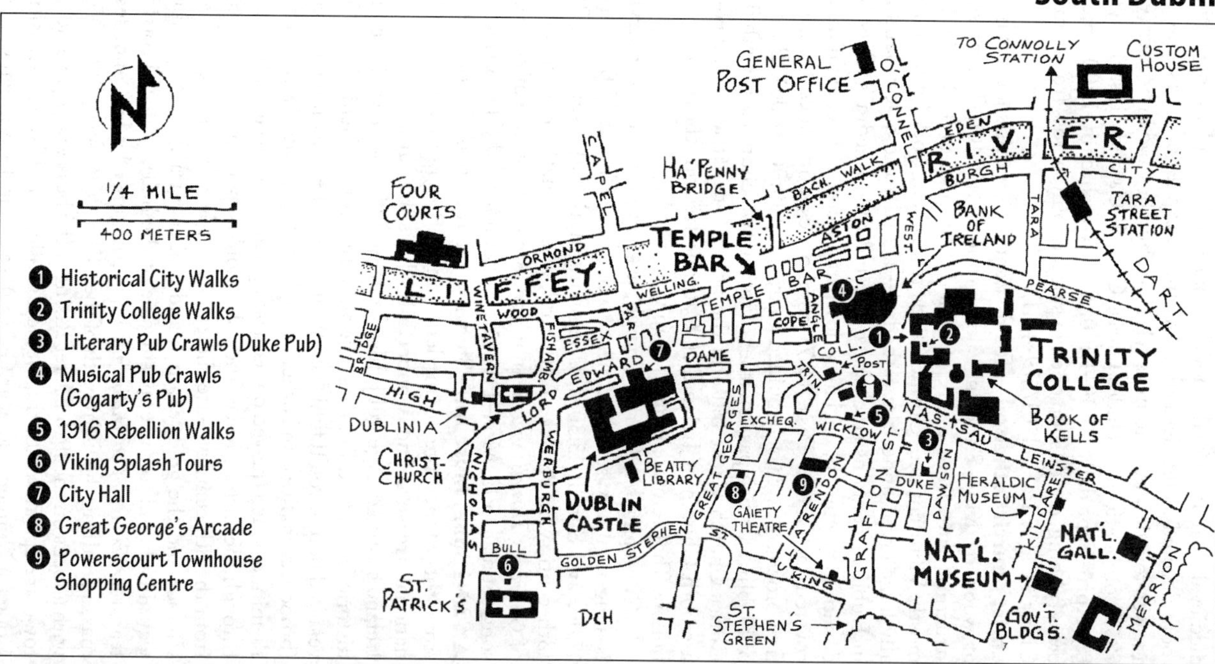

medieval exhibits, a scale model of old Dublin, and an interesting room devoted to medieval fairs. Then, after piles of stairs, you get a tower-top view of Dublin's skyline of churches and breweries (€6, €8.75 combo-ticket includes Christ Church Cathedral, saving you €3; April–Sept daily 10:00–17:00, Oct–March daily 11:00–16:00, brass rubbing, coffee shop open in summer only, across from Christ Church Cathedral, tel. 01/679-4611).

Christ Church Cathedral—The first church on this spot was built of wood by King Sitric in Viking times (c. 1040). The present structure dates from a mix of periods: Norman and Gothic, but mostly Victorian neo-Gothic (1870s restoration work). The unusually large crypt under the cathedral—actually the oldest building in Dublin—contains stocks, statues, and the cathedral's silver (€5 donation to church, includes downstairs crypt silver exhibition, covered by Dublin Pass, €8.75 combo-ticket includes Dublinia, free brochure with self-guided tour, daily 10:00–17:00). Because of Dublin's British past, neither of its top two churches is Catholic. Christ Church Cathedral and the nearby St. Patrick's Cathedral are both Church of Ireland. In Catholic Ireland, these sights feel hollow. They're more famous than visit-worthy.

Evensong: At Christ Church, a 45-minute evensong service is sung regularly several times a week (Tue–Thu at 18:00, Sat at 17:00, and Sun at 15:30; less regularly during the summer). The 13th-century St. Patrick's Cathedral, where Jonathan Swift (author of *Gulliver's Travels*) was dean in the 18th century, also offers evensong (Sun at 15:15, Mon–Fri at 17:30, but not Wed July–Aug).

▲▲▲National Museum—Showing off the treasures of Ireland from the Stone Age to modern times, this museum is itself a national treasure and wonderfully digestible under one dome. Ireland's Bronze Age gold fills the center. Up four steps, the prehistoric Ireland exhibit rings the gold. In a corner (behind a 2,000-year-old body), you'll find the treasury with the most famous pieces (brooches, chalices, and other examples of Celtic metalwork) and an 18-minute video (played on request), giving an overview of Irish art through the 13th century. The collection's superstars—both dating from the 8th century—are the exquisite silver and bronze Ardagh Chalice and the gold, enamel, and amber Tara Brooch. Jumping way ahead (and to the opposite side of the hall), a special corridor features *The Road to Independence,* with guns, letters, and death masks recalling the fitful birth of the "Terrible Beauty" (1900–1921, with a focus on the 1916 Easter Rising). The best Viking artifacts in town are upstairs with the medieval collection. If you'll be visiting Cong (in Connemara, near Galway), seek out the original Cross of Cong (free entry, Tue–Sat 10:00–17:00, Sun 14:00–17:00, closed Mon, good café, Kildare Street 2, between Trinity College and St. Stephen's Green). Greatest-hits tours are given several times a day

(€2, 40 min, tel. 01/677-7444 in morning for schedule).

▲National Gallery—Along with a hall featuring the work of top Irish painters, this has Ireland's best collection of European masters. It's impressive—although not nearly as extensive as those in London or Paris (free, Mon–Sat 9:30–17:30, Thu until 20:30, Sun 12:00–17:30, call for times of guided tours on weekends, Merrion Square West, tel. 01/661-5133, www.nationalgallery.ie).

▲▲Grafton Street—Once filled with noisy traffic, Grafton Street is today Dublin's liveliest pedestrian shopping mall. A five-minute stroll past street musicians takes you from Trinity College up to St. Stephen's Green (and makes you wonder why American merchants are so terrified of a car-free street). Walking by a buxom statue of "sweet" Molly Malone (known by locals as "the tart with the cart"), you'll soon pass two venerable department stores: the Irish Brown Thomas and the English Marks & Spencer. An alley leads to the Powerscourt Townhouse Shopping Centre, which tastefully fills a converted Georgian mansion. The huge, glass-covered St. Stephen's Green Shopping Centre and the peaceful and green Green itself mark the top of Grafton Street.

▲St. Stephen's Green—This city park, originally a medieval commons, was enclosed in 1664 and gradually surrounded with fine Georgian buildings. Today, it provides 22 acres of grassy refuge for Dubliners. On a sunny afternoon, it's a wonderful world apart from the big city.

▲▲Number Twenty-Nine Georgian House—The carefully restored house at Number 29 Lower Fitzwilliam Street gives an intimate glimpse of middle-class Georgian life—which seems pretty high-class. From the sidewalk, descend the stairs to the basement-level entrance (at the corner of Lower Fitzwilliam and Lower Mount Streets). Start with an interesting 12-minute video (you're welcome to bring in a cup of coffee from the café) before joining your guide, who takes you on a fascinating 35-minute walk through this 1790 Dublin home (€3.50, covered by Dublin Pass, tours leave regularly, Tue–Sat 10:00–17:00, Sun 14:00–17:00, closed Mon, tel. 01/702-6165).

▲Merrion Square—Laid out in 1762, this square is ringed by elegant Georgian houses decorated with fine doors—a Dublin trademark—with elegant knobs and knockers. The park, once the exclusive domain of the residents, is now a delightful public escape. More inviting than St. Stephen's Green, it's ideal for a picnic. If you want to know what "snogging" is, walk through the park on a sunny day, when it's full of smooching lovers. Oscar Wilde, lounging wittily on the corner nearest the town center and surrounded by his clever quotes, provides a fun photo op.

▲Temple Bar—This was a Georgian center of craftsmen and merchants. As it fell on hard times in the 19th century, the lower rents attracted students and artists, giving the neighborhood a bohemian flair. With recent government tax incentives and lots of development money, the Temple Bar district has become a thriving cultural (and beer-drinking) hotspot. Today, this much-promoted center of trendy shops, cafés, theaters, galleries, pubs with live music, and restaurants feels like the heart of the city. Dublin's "Left Bank"—which, like Paris', is on the south shore of the river—fills the cobbled streets between Dame Street and the River Liffey. ("Bar" means a walkway along the river.) The central **Meeting House Square** (just off Essex Street) hosts free street theater, as well as a lively organic-produce market and a book market (Sat 10:00–18:00). The square is surrounded by interesting cultural centers.

These days, the downsides to Temple Bar are noise and high prices. Crowded summer weekend nights can be a real zoo, with loud "hen" (bachelorette) parties in funky hats promenading the main drag, as drunken party dudes shout from pub doorways to get their attention. Be aware that a pint of beer here is fast approaching €5, at least €1 more than at less glitzy pubs just a couple blocks away (north of the Liffey river or south of Dame Street).

For a listing of events and galleries, visit the **Temple Bar Properties** office and ask for their free annual TASCQ Guide (18 Eustace Street, www.templebar.ie). Rather than follow particular pub or restaurant recommendations (mine are below, under "Eating"), venture down a few side lanes off the main drag to see what looks good.

The pedestrian-only **Ha' Penny Bridge,** named for the half-pence toll people used to pay to cross it, leads from Temple Bar over the River Liffey to the opposite bank and more sights.

North of the River Liffey

▲▲O'Connell Bridge—This bridge spans the River Liffey, which has historically divided the wealthy, cultivated south side from the poorer, cruder north side. While there's plenty of culture north of the river, even today, "the north" is considered rougher and less safe.

From the bridge, look upriver (west) as far upstream as you can. The big concrete building on the left in the distance houses the city planning commission. Maddening to locals, this eyesore is in charge of making sure new buildings in the city are built in good taste. It squats on the still buried precious artifacts of the first Viking settlement established in Dublin in the 9th century.

Across the river stands the Four Courts, today's Supreme Court building, shelled and burned in 1922 during the tragic civil war that followed Irish independence. Irreplaceable birth records were lost as the national archives office burned, making it challenging for those with Irish roots to trace their ancestry today. The closest bridge upstream—the elegant, iron Ha' Penny Bridge—leads

North Dublin

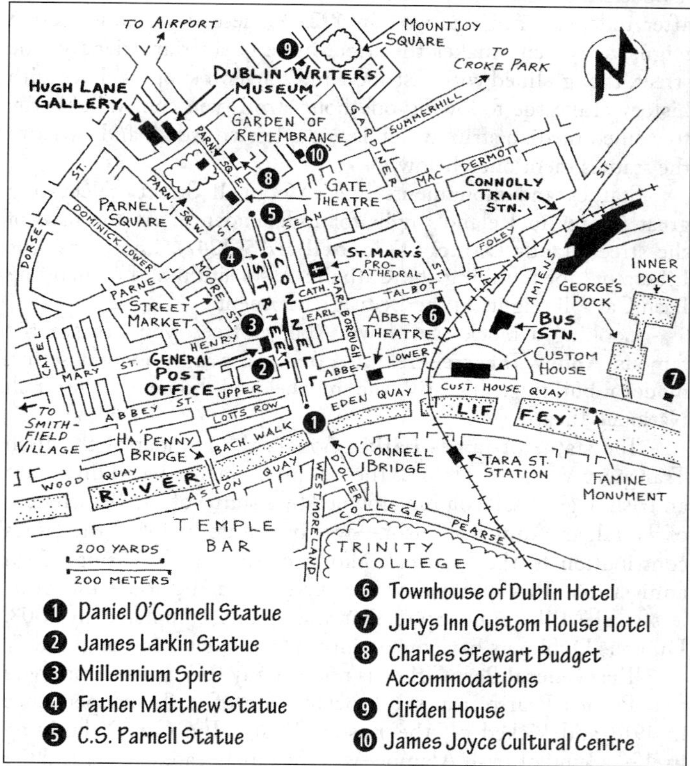

left into the Temple Bar nightlife district. Just beyond the old-fashioned, 19th-century bridge is Dublin's pedestrian Millennium Bridge, inaugurated in 2000. (Note that buses leave from O'Connell Bridge—specifically, Aston Quay—for the Guinness Storehouse and the Kilmainham Jail.)

Turn 180 degrees and look downstream to see the tall Liberty Hall union headquarters—for now, the tallest building in the Republic (16 stories tall, some say in honor of the 1916 Easter Uprising)—and lots of cranes. Booming Dublin is developing downstream. The Irish (forever clever tax fiddlers) have subsidized and revitalized this formerly dreary quarter with great success. A short walk downstream along the north bank leads to a powerful series of modern statues memorializing the Potato Famine of 1845–1849.

▲▲O'Connell Street Stroll—Dublin's grandest street leads from O'Connell Bridge through the heart of north Dublin. Since the 1740s, it has been a 45-yard-wide promenade. Ever since the first O'Connell Bridge connected it to the Trinity side of town in 1794, it's been Dublin's main drag. (But it was only named O'Connell after independence was won in 1922.) These days, construction reigns, as the city makes the street more pedestrian-friendly. The street, though lined with fast-food and souvenir shops, echoes with history. Take the following one-hour stroll (you can walk on the tree-lined median strip, which is wide, less crowded, and closer to the statues mentioned below):

Statues and monuments line O'Connell Street, celebrating great figures in Ireland's fight for independence. At the base of the street stands **Daniel O'Connell** (1775–1847), known as "the Liberator" for founding the Catholic Association and demanding Irish Catholic rights in the British Parliament.

Looking a block east down Abbey Street, you can see the famous **Abbey Theatre**—rebuilt after a fire into a nondescript, modern building. It's still the much-loved home of the Irish National Theatre.

The statue of **James Larkin** honors the founder of the Irish Transport Workers' Union. The one monument that didn't wave an Irish flag—a tall column crowned by a statue of the British hero of Trafalgar, Admiral Nelson—was blown up in 1966...the IRA's contribution to the local celebration of the Easter Rising's 50th anniversary. This spot is now occupied by the 300-foot-tall, stainless steel Millennium Spire that was finally completed in 2003. Dubious Dubliners have nicknamed it "the stiletto in the ghetto."

The **General Post Office** is not just any P.O. It was from here that Patrick Pearse read the Proclamation of Irish Independence in 1916 and kicked off the Easter Rising. The G.P.O. building itself—a kind of Irish Alamo—was the rebel headquarters and the scene of a five-day bloody siege that followed the proclamation. Its pillars remain pockmarked with bullet holes. Step inside and trace the battle by studying the well-described cycle of 10 paintings that circle the main hall (open for business and sightseers Mon–Sat 8:00–20:00, closed Sun).

The busy **Moore Street Market** is nearby (Mon–Sat 8:00–18:00, closed Sun). To get there, detour left two blocks after the Post Office down people-filled Henry Street, then wander to the right into the market. Many of its merchants have staffed the same stalls for 30 years. Start a conversation. It's a great work-a-day scene. You'll see lots of mums with strollers—a reminder that Ireland is Europe's youngest country, with about 40 percent of the population under the age of 25.

Back on O'Connell Street, cross back onto the median strip and continue your walk. The lampposts display the colorful three-castle city seal. The Latin motto below the seal states, "Happy the city where citizens obey." Flames rise from the castles, symbolizing the citizens' zeal to defend Dublin.

St. Mary's Pro-Cathedral, a block east of O'Connell down Cathedral Street, is Dublin's leading Catholic church. But, curiously, it's not a cathedral, even though the pope declared Christ Church one in the 12th century—and later, St. Patrick's. (Stubbornly, the Vatican has chosen to ignore the fact that Christ Church and St. Patrick's haven't been Catholic for centuries.) Completed in 1821, it's done in the style of a Greek temple.

Continuing up O'Connell Street, you'll find a statue of **Father Matthew,** a leader of the temperance movement of the 1830s who, some historians claim, was responsible for enough Irish peasants staying sober to enable Daniel O'Connell to organize them into a political force. (Perhaps understanding this dynamic, the U.S.S.R. was careful to keep the price of vodka affordable.) The fancy Gresham Hotel is a good place for an elegant tea or beer.

Charles Stewart Parnell stands boldly at the top of O'Connell Street. The names of the four ancient provinces of Ireland and all 32 Irish counties (North *and* South, since this was erected before Irish independence) ring the monument, honoring the member of Parliament who nearly won Home Rule for Ireland in the late 1800s. (A sex scandal cost Parnell the support of the Church, which let the air out of any chance for a free Ireland.)

Continue straight up Parnell Square East. At the **Gate Theatre** (on the left), Orson Welles and James Mason got their professional acting debuts.

The **Garden of Remembrance** (past Gate Theater, 1 block up on left, daily 8:30–18:00) honors the victims of the 1916 Rising. The park was dedicated in 1966 on the 50th anniversary of the uprising that ultimately led to Irish independence. The bottom of the cross-shaped pool is a mosaic of Celtic weapons, symbolic of how the early Irish would proclaim peace by throwing their weapons into a lake or river. The Irish flag flies above the park: green for Catholics, orange for Protestants, and white for the hope that they can live together in peace. Across the street...

The **Dublin Writers' Museum** fills a splendidly restored Georgian mansion. No other country so small has produced such a wealth of literature. As interesting to fans of Irish literature as it is boring to those who aren't, this three-room museum features the lives and works of Dublin's great writers (€6.50, covered by Dublin Pass, Mon–Sat 10:00–17:00, Sun 11:00–17:00, June–Aug Mon–Fri until 18:00, helpful audioguide available, 18 Parnell Square North, tel. 01/872-2077). With hometown wits such as Swift, Yeats, Joyce, and Shaw, there is a checklist of residences and memorials to see. Aficionados of James Joyce's work may want to hike 400 yards east to visit the **James Joyce Cultural Centre** (Mon–Sat 9:30–17:00, Sun 12:30–17:00, 35 North Great George's Street, tel. 01/878-8547). There's more Joyce memorabilia in Dun Laoghaire at the **James**

Joyce Museum (see page 845). Next door to the Dublin Writers' Museum is the...

Hugh Lane Municipal Art Gallery, in a grand neoclassical building, has a fine, bite-sized selection of Pre-Raphaelite, French Impressionist, and 19th- and 20th-century Irish paintings (free, Tue–Thu 9:30–18:00, Fri–Sat 9:30–17:00, Sun 11:00–17:00, closed Mon, tel. 01/874-1903). Sir Hugh went down on the *Lusitania* in 1915; due to an unclear will, his collection is shared by this gallery and the National Gallery in London.

Tucked in the back of the gallery is the **Francis Bacon Studio,** reconstructed here in its original (messy) state from its London location at the time of the artist's death in 1992. Born in Dublin and inspired by Picasso, Bacon reflected his belief that "chaos breeds energy" in his shocking paintings. This compact space contains touch-screen terminals, display cases of personal items, and a few unfinished works. The 10-minute film interview of Bacon may fascinate like-minded viewers...and disquiet others (€7, same hours as rest of gallery).

Your walk is over. Here on the north end of town, it's convenient to visit the Gaelic Athletic Association Museum at Croke Park (described on page 832, a 30-min walk or short taxi ride away). Otherwise, hop on your skateboard and return to the river.

Dublin's Smithfield Village

The neighborhood is worth a look for "Cobblestores" (a redeveloped Duck Lane lined with fancy crafts and gift shops), the Old Jameson Distillery whiskey tour, and a chimney observatory with big Dublin views. The sights are clustered close together, two blocks north of the river behind the Four Courts—the Supreme Court building.

The Old Jameson Distillery—Whiskey fans enjoy visiting the old distillery. You get a 10-minute video, 20-minute tour, and a free shot in the pub. Unfortunately, the "distillery" feels fake and put together for tourists. If you do take this tour, volunteer energetically when offered the chance to take the "whiskey taste test" at the end (€8.50, covered by Dublin Pass, daily 9:00–18:00, last tour at 17:30, Bow Street, tel. 01/807-2355).

The Chimney—Built in 1895 for the distillery, the chimney is now an observatory. Ride the elevator 175 feet up for a Dublin panorama not quite as exciting as the view from the Guinness Storehouse's Gravity Bar (overpriced at €6, covered by Dublin Pass, Mon–Sat 10:00–17:00, Sun 11:00–17:00, tel. 01/817-3838).

Outer Dublin

The jail and the Guinness Storehouse are the main sights outside of the old center. Combine them in one visit.

▲▲▲Kilmainham Gaol (Jail)—Opened in 1796 as the Dublin County Jail and a debtors' prison, and considered a model in its day, this jail was used frequently as a political prison by the British. Many of those who fought for Irish independence were held or executed here, including leaders of the rebellions of 1798, 1803, 1848, 1867, and 1916. National heroes Robert Emmett and Charles Stewart Parnell each did time here. The last prisoner to be held here was Eamon de Valera, who later became president of Ireland. He was released on July 16, 1924, the day Kilmainham was finally shut down. The buildings, virtually in ruins, were restored in the 1960s. Today, it's a shrine to the Nathan Hales of Ireland.

Start your visit with a guided tour (1 hr, 2/hr, includes 25 min in prison chapel for a rebellion-packed video, spend waiting time in museum). It's touching to tour the cells and places of execution while hearing tales of terrible colonialism and heroic patriotism alongside Irish schoolkids who know these names well. The museum is an excellent exhibit on Victorian prison life and Ireland's fight for independence. Don't miss the museum's dimly lit Last Words 1916 hall upstairs, which displays the stirring last letters patriots sent to loved ones hours before facing the firing squad (€5, covered by Dublin Pass, April–Sept daily 9:30–18:00, Oct–March daily 9:30–17:00, last entry 1 hr before closing; €5 taxi, or bus #51b, #78a, or #79 from Aston Quay or Guinness, tel. 01/453-5984). You could taxi to the jail, then catch the bus from there to Guinness (leaving the prison, take 3 rights, crossing no streets, to the bus stop, and hop bus #51b or #78a). Another option is taking the City Sightseeing/Guide Friday hop-on, hop-off bus, which stops at both the jail and the Guinness Storehouse.

▲Guinness Storehouse—A visit to the Guinness Storehouse is, for many, a pilgrimage. Arthur Guinness began brewing the famous stout here in 1759. By 1868, it was the biggest brewery in the world. Today, the sprawling brewery fills several city blocks. Around the world, Guinness brews more than 10 million pints a day. The home of Ireland's national beer welcomes visitors, for a price, with a sprawling new museum (but there are no tours of the actual working brewery). The museum fills the old fermentation plant, used from 1902 through 1988, vacated, and then opened in 2000 as a huge, shrine-like place. Step into the middle of the ground floor and look up. A tall, beer-glass-shaped glass atrium—14 million pints big—leads past four floors of exhibitions and cafés to the skylight. Then look down at Arthur's original 9,000-year lease enshrined under glass in the floor...quite a bargain. Atop the building, the Gravity Bar provides visitors with a commanding 360-degree view of Dublin—with vistas all the way to the sea—and a free beer. The actual exhibit makes brewing seem more grandiose than it is, and treats Arthur like the god of human happiness. Highlights are the cooperage (with old film clips showing the master wood-keg-makers plying their now extinct trade), a display of the brewery's clever ads, and the Gravity Bar, which really is spectacular (€13.50, covered by Dublin Pass, includes a €4 pint, daily 9:30–17:00, enter on Bellevue Street, bus #78a from Aston Quay near O'Connell Bridge, or bus #123 from Dame Street and O'Connell Street, tel. 01/408-4800). Both hop-on, hop-off bus tours stop here.

▲**Gaelic Athletic Association Museum**—The GAA was founded in 1884 as an expression of an Irish cultural awakening. It was created to foster the development of Gaelic sports, specifically Irish football and hurling, and to ban English sports, such as cricket and rugby—but it played an important part in the fight for independence. This museum, at the newly expanded 82,000-seat Croke Park Stadium, offers a high-tech, interactive introduction to Ireland's favorite games. Relive the greatest moments in hurling and Irish-football history. Then get involved. Pick up a stick and try hurling, kick a football, and test your speed and balance. A 15-minute film clarifies the connection between sports and Irish politics (€6, covered by Dublin Pass, Mon–Sat 9:30–17:00, Sun 12:00–17:00; on game Sundays, museum is open 12:00–17:00 to Cusack stand ticket-holders only, as other sections of stands are blocked from museum entry; museum located under the new stand at Croke Park, from O'Connell Street walk 20 min or catch bus #3, #11, #11a, #16, #16a, or #123; tel. 01/819-2323). The €9.50 museum-plus-stadium-tour option is worth it only for rabid fans who yearn to know which locker room is considered the unlucky one (1 hr, tour also covered by Dublin Pass).

Hurling and Irish Football at Croke Park—Actually seeing a match here, surrounded by incredibly spirited Irish fans, is a fun experience. Hurling is like airborne hockey with no injury timeouts, and Irish football looks like a rugged form of soccer. Matches are held on most Sunday afternoons from May to September. Tickets (€20–55) are available at the stadium, except during championships (tel. 01/836-3222, www.gaa.ie).

Greyhound Racing—For an interesting lowbrow look at local life, consider going to the dog races and doing a little gambling (€8, generally Wed, Thu, and Sat at 20:00, Shelbourne Park, tel. 01/668-3502). Greyhounds race on the other days at Harold's Cross Racetrack (€8, Mon, Tue, and Fri at 20:00, tel. 01/497-1081).

SHOPPING

Shops are open roughly Monday to Saturday from 9:00 to 18:00, and until 20:00 on Thursday. They have shorter hours on Sunday (if they're open at all). The best shopping area is Grafton, with its neighboring streets and arcades (such as the fun Great George's

Arcade between Great George's and Drury Streets), and nearby shopping centers (Powerscourt and St. Stephen's Green). Francis Street creaks with antiques.

For a street market, consider Mother Redcaps (Fri–Sun all day, bric-a-brac, antiques, crafts, Back Lane, Christ Church). For produce, noise, and color, visit Moore Street (Mon–Sat 8:00–18:00, near General Post Office). For raw fish, get a whiff of Michan Street (Tue–Sat 7:00–15:00, behind Four Courts building).

On Saturdays at Temple Bar's Meeting House Square, it's food in the morning (from 9:00) and books in the afternoon (until 18:00). Temple Bar is worth a browse any day for its art, jewelry, new-age paraphernalia, books, music, and gift shops.

ENTERTAINMENT

Ireland has produced some of the finest writers in both English and Irish, and Dublin houses some of Europe's finest theaters. While Handel's *Messiah* was first performed in Dublin (1742), these days Dublin is famous for its rock bands (U2, Thin Lizzy, Sinead O'Connor, and Live Aid founder Bob Geldof's band, the Boomtown Rats, all got started here).

Theater—**Abbey Theatre** is Ireland's national theater, founded by W. B. Yeats in 1904 to preserve Irish culture during British rule (26 Lower Abbey Street, tel. 01/878-7222, www.abbeytheatre.ie). **Gate Theatre** does foreign plays, as well as Irish classics (Cavendish Row, tel. 01/874-4045, www.gate-theatre.ie). The **Gaiety Theatre** offers a wide range of quality productions (King Street South, tel. 01/677-1717, www.gaietytheatre.com). **Point Theatre,** once a railway terminus, is now the country's top live-music venue (East Link Bridge, tel. 01/836-3633, www.thepoint.ie). At the **National Concert Hall,** the National Symphony Orchestra performs most Friday evenings (Earlsfort Terrace, off St. Stephen's Green, tickets €8–22, tel. 01/475-1666, www.nch.ie). Street theater takes the stage in Temple Bar on summer evenings.

Pub Action—Folk music fills the pubs, and street entertainers are everywhere. The Temple Bar area thrives with music—traditional, jazz, and pop. Although it's pricier than the rest of Dublin, it really is *the* comfortable and fun place for tourists and locals (who come here to watch the tourists). **Gogarty's Pub** (corner of Fleet and Anglesea, tel. 01/671-1822) has top-notch sessions upstairs nightly from 21:00. Use this as a kick-off for your Temple Bar evening.

A 10-minute hike up the river west of Temple Bar takes you to a twosome with a local and less touristy ambience. The **Brazen Head**, famous as Dublin's oldest pub, is a hit for an early dinner and late live music (nightly from 21:30, tel. 01/677-9549), with atmospheric rooms and a courtyard made to order for balmy evenings (on Bridge Street). **O'Shea's Merchant Pub**, just across the street, is encrusted in memories and filled with locals taking a break from the grind. They have live traditional music nightly (the front half is a restaurant, the magic is in the back half—enter on Bridge Street, tel. 01/679-3797).

To sample truly traditional Irish song and dance, consider heading to Comhaltas Ceoltoiri Éireann in nearby Dun Laoghaire (see "Dun Laoghaire," page 844).

SLEEPING

Dublin is popular, and rooms can be tight. Book ahead for weekends any time of year, particularly in summer and during major sporting events. Prices are often discounted on weeknights (Mon–Thu) and from November through February.

Big and practical places (both cheap and moderate) are most central at Christ Church, on the edge of Temple Bar. For classy, older Dublin accommodations, you'll stay a bit farther out (southeast of St. Stephen's Green). The most economical non-hostel lodging is north of the River Liffey (page 838).

For a small-town escape with the best budget values, take the convenient DART train (at least 3/hr, 20 min) to nearby Dun Laoghaire (see page 844).

Near Christ Church

These hotels face Christ Church Cathedral, a five-minute walk from the best evening scene at Temple Bar, and 10 minutes from the sightseeing center (Trinity College and Grafton Street). The cheap hostels in this neighborhood have some double rooms. Full Irish breakfasts, which cost €10–15 at the hotels, are half the price at the many small cafés nearby; consider Bagel Haven (beside Kinlay House, hidden on Cow's Lane).

$$ Harding Hotel is a hardwood, 21st-century, Viking-style place with 53 institutional-yet-hotelesque rooms. The rooms are simpler than Jurys (below), but they're also more intimate (Sb-€64, Db-€89–106, Tb-€114–131, breakfast-€10, Copper Alley, across street from Christ Church, tel. 01/679-6500, fax 01/679-6504, www.hardinghotel.ie, harding.hotel@kinlaygroup.ie).

$$ Jurys Christ Church Inn (like its sisters across town, in Galway, and in Belfast) is central and offers business-class comfort in all of its 182 identical rooms. This no-nonsense, modern, American-style hotel chain has a winning keep-it-simple-and-affordable formula. If ye olde is getting old (and you don't mind big tour groups), there's no better value in town. All rooms cost the same: €108 Sun–Thu (or €117 Fri–Sat) for one, two, or three adults or two adults and two kids (breakfast extra). Each

Sleep Code

(€1 = about $1.20, country code: 353, area code: 01)
S = Single, **D** = Double/Twin, **T** = Triple, **Q** = Quad, **b** = bathroom, **s** = shower only. Breakfast is included and credit cards are accepted unless otherwise noted. To locate hotels, see map on page 836.

To help you easily sort through these listings, I've divided the rooms into three categories, based on the price for a standard double room with bath:

- **$$$ Higher Priced**—Most rooms €130 or more.
- **$$ Moderately Priced**—Most rooms between €70–130.
- **$ Lower Priced**—Most rooms €70 or less.

room has a modern bathroom, direct-dial telephone, and TV. Two floors are strictly non-smoking. Request a room far from the noisy elevator (book long in advance for weekends, parking-€12/day, Christ Church Place, tel. 01/454-0000, fax 01/454-0012, U.S. tel. 800/423-6953, www.jurysdoyle.com, info@jurysdoyle.com). Another Jurys is near the Connolly train station (see page 838).

$ Kinlay House, around the corner from Harding Hotel, is the backpackers' equivalent—definitely the place to go for cheap beds in a central location and an all-ages-welcome atmosphere. This huge, red-brick, 19th-century Victorian building has 149 metal, prison-style beds in spartan, non-smoking rooms. There are singles, doubles, and four- to six-bed coed dorms (good for families), as well as a few giant dorms. It fills up most days. Call well in advance, especially for singles, doubles, and summer weekends (S-€44–52, D-€54–64, Db-€58–68, dorm beds-€18–26, includes continental breakfast, kitchen access, launderette-€7.50, Internet access-€4/hr, left luggage, travel desk, TV lounge, small lockers, lots of stairs, Christ Church, 2–12 Lord Edward Street, tel. 01/679-6644, fax 01/679-7437, www.kinlayhouse.ie, kinlay.dublin@kinlaygroup.ie).

$ Four Courts Hostel is a 256-bed hostel beautifully located immediately across the river from the Four Courts, a five-minute walk from Christ Church and Temple Bar. It's bare and institutional (as hostels are), but spacious and well-run, with a focus on security and efficiency (dorm beds-€15–17, S-€45, Sb-€50, bunk D-€60, bunk Db-€66, includes small breakfast, girls' floor and boys' floor, non-smoking, elevator, free Internet access, game room, laundry service, some parking, left luggage room, 15–17 Merchant's Quay, bus #748 from airport, #90 from train or bus station, tel. 01/672-5839, fax 01/672-5862, www.fourcourtshostel.com, info@fourcourtshostel.com).

Dublin Hotels

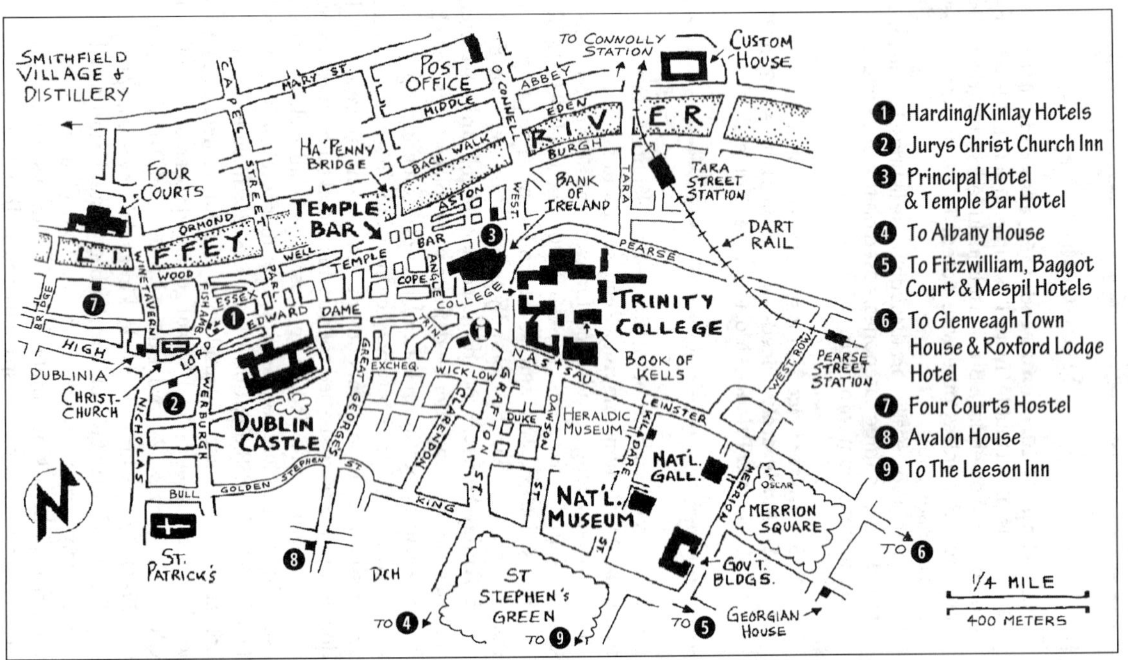

Between Trinity College and Temple Bar

$$$ Principal Hotel Fleet Street rents 70 decent rooms. For its size, it has an intimate feel with character (Sb-€106–127, Db-€130–169, often midweek deals, breakfast-€13.50, non-smoking rooms, request a quiet room off the street, 19-20 Fleet Street, tel. 01/670-8122, fax 01/670-8103, www.principalhotel.com). Rather than buying the spendy hotel breakfast, walk around the corner to Bewley's on Westmoreland Street.

$$$ Temple Bar Hotel is a 130-room, business-class place, very centrally located midway between Trinity College and the Temple Bar action (Sb-€150, Db-€195, Tb-€255, midweek discounts, non-smoking rooms, Fleet Street, Temple Bar, tel. 01/677-3333, fax 01/677-3088, www.templebarhotel.com, reservations@tbh.ie).

$$ Trinity College turns its 800 student-housing rooms on campus into no-frills, affordable accommodations in the city center each summer (mid-June–Sept, S-€55, Sb-€66, D-€110, Db-€128, all doubles are twins, includes continental breakfast, cooked breakfast-€3 extra, tel. 01/608-1177, fax 01/671-1267, www.tcd.ie/accom, reservations@tcd.ie).

Near St. Stephen's Green

$$$ Albany House's 43 rooms come with classic furniture, high ceilings, Georgian elegance, and some street noise. Book early and request one of the four huge "superior" rooms, which are the same price as standard rooms (Sb-€100–130, Db-€140–180, €120 in slow times, Tb-€170–210, includes breakfast, back rooms are quieter, non-smoking, just 1 block south of St. Stephen's Green at 84 Harcourt Street, tel. 01/475-1092, fax 01/475-1093, http://indigo.ie/~albany, albany@indigo.ie).

$$$ Baggot Court Guest House has 11 fine rooms, but no lounge (Sb-€90–100, Db-€120–165, Tb-€150–210, non-smoking, free parking, 92 Lower Baggot Street, tel. 01/661-2819, fax 01/661-0253, www.baggotcourt.com, baggot@indigo.ie).

$$ The Fitzwilliam has an inviting lounge and rents 13 decent rooms cheaper than the Baggot Court, a block farther away (Sb-€65–75, Db-€100–130, children under 16 sleep free, 41 Upper Fitzwilliam Street, tel. 01/662-5155, fax 01/676-7488, www.fitzwilliamguesthouse.ie, info@fitzwilliamguesthouse.ie).

$ Avalon House, near Grafton Street, rents 281 backpacker beds (dorm beds-€15–30, S-€30–34, Sb-€33–37, twin D-€56–64, twin Db-€60-70, includes continental breakfast, elevator, Ireland bus tickets, Internet access, launderette, a few minutes off Grafton Street at 55 Aungier Street, tel. 01/475-0001, fax 01/475-0303, www.avalon-house.ie).

Away from the Center, East of St. Stephen's Green

$$$ Roxford Lodge Hotel is a memorable splurge in a quiet residential neighborhood a 20-minute walk from Trinity College, with 20 tastefully decorated, whirlpool-tub-laden rooms. The €300 executive suite is honeymoon-worthy (Sb-€90, Db-€140, Tb-€165, Qb-€200, secure parking, 46 Northumberland Road, tel. 01/668-8572, fax 01/668-8158, www.roxfordlodge.ie, roxfordlodge@eircom.net).

$$$ Mespil Hotel is a huge, modern, business-class hotel renting 256 identical three-star rooms (most with a double and single bed, phone, TV, voicemail, and modem hookup) at a good price, with all the comforts. This is a cut above Jurys Inn, for a little more money (Sb, Db, or Tb-€150, breakfast-€15, elevator, non-smoking floors, apartments for week-long stays, 10-min walk southeast of St. Stephen's Green or bus #10, Mespil Road, tel. 01/488-4600, fax 01/667-1244, www.leehotels.com, mespil@leehotels.com).

$$$ The Leeson Inn, with 22 crisply uncluttered rooms, stands proudly Georgian in a great location a five-minute walk south of St. Stephen's Green (Sb-€75–109, Db-€109–149, Tb-€129–169, Qb-€179–189; small first-come, first-served parking lot; 24 Lower Leeson Street, tel. 01/662-2002, fax 01/662-1567, www.leesoninndowntown.com, info@leesoninndowntown.com).

$$ Glenveagh Town House rents 13 rooms—Victorian upstairs and modern downstairs—southeast of the city center, a 20-minute walk from Trinity College (Sb-€75, Db-€100–130, less in slow times, includes breakfast, parking, 31 Northumberland Road, tel. 01/668-4612, fax 01/668-4559, www.glenveagh.ie, glenveagh@eircom.net). Catch bus #5, #6, #7, #8, or #45 down Northumberland Road into downtown Dublin (every 10 min).

North of the River Liffey

To locate these hotels, see map on page 827.

$$ Townhouse of Dublin, with 80 small, stylish rooms (some with pleasant views into a central garden courtyard), hides behind a brick Georgian facade one block north of the Customs House (Sb-€70, Db-€115, Tb-€130; small first-come, first-served parking lot; 47–48 Lower Gardiner Street, tel. 01/878-8808, fax 01/878-8787, www.townhouseofdublin.com, info@townhouse.com)

$$ Jurys Inn Custom House, on Custom House Quay, offers the same value as the Jurys at Christ Church. Bigger (with 234 rooms) and not quite as well-located (in a boring neighborhood, a 10-min riverside hike from O'Connell Bridge), this Jurys is more likely to have rooms available (Db-€108 Sun–Thu, or €117 Fri–Sat, tel. 01/607-5000, fax 01/829-0400, U.S. tel. 800/423-6953, www.jurysdoyle.com, info@jurysdoyle.com).

$$ Clifden House is a good value, with 15 unpretentious, neatly kept rooms on a gritty Georgian street around the corner from once swanky Mountjoy Square (Sb-€38–60, Db-€70–110, Tb-€90–130, Qb-€90-140, non-smoking, some parking in back, 32 Gardiner Place, tel. 01/874-6364, fax 01/874-6122, www.clifdenhouse.com, bnb@indigo.ie).

$$ Charles Stewart Budget Accommodations is a big, basic place offering lots of forgettable rooms, many long and narrow, with head-to-toe twins, in a great location for a good price (S-€32, Sb-€50–64, D-€60–76, Db-€65–89, Tb-€100–121, Qb-€120–140, frequent midweek discounts, includes cooked breakfast, just beyond top end of O'Connell Street at 5–6 Parnell Square, tel. 01/878-0350, fax 01/878-1387, www.charlesstewart.ie, info@charlesstewart.ie).

EATING

As Dublin does its boom-time jig, fine and creative eateries are popping up all over town. While you can get decent pub grub for €12 on just about any corner, consider saving pub grub for the countryside. And there's no pressing reason to eat Irish in cosmopolitan Dublin. The city's good restaurants are packed from 20:00 on, especially on weekends. Eating early (17:00–19:00) saves time and money (as many better places offer an early-bird special).

Quick and Easy Around Grafton Street

Cornucopia is a small, earth-mama-with-class, proudly vegetarian, self-serve place two blocks off Grafton. It's friendly and youthful, with hearty €8 lunches and €10 dinner specials (Mon–Sat 8:30–20:00, Sun 12:00–19:00, 19 Wicklow Street, tel. 01/677-7583).

O'Neill's offers dependable €10 carvery lunches in a labyrinth of a pub with a central location, across from the main TI (daily 12:00–21:30, Suffolk Street, tel. 01/679-3656).

Graham O'Sullivan Restaurant and Coffee Shop is a cheap, cheery cafeteria serving soup and sandwiches with a salad bar and unpretentious ambience (Mon–Fri 8:00–18:30, Sat 9:00–17:00, Sun 9:00–16:30, 12 Duke Street). Two pubs on the same street—**The Duke** and **Davy Burns**—serve pub lunches. (The nearby Cathach Rare Books shop at 10 Duke Street displays a rare edition of *Ulysses,* among other treasures, in its window.)

Bewley's Café is an old-time local favorite offering light meals from €8 and full meals from €12. Sit on the ground floor among Harry Clarke windows and Art Deco lamps, or upstairs in the bright atrium decorated by local art students (self-service Mon–Sat 7:30–20:00, Sun 8:00–20:00, 78 Grafton Street, tel. 01/635-5470). For a taste of witty Irish lunch theater, check out **Bewley's Café Theatre** upstairs, where you can catch an hour performance with soup and a sandwich for only

Dublin Restaurants

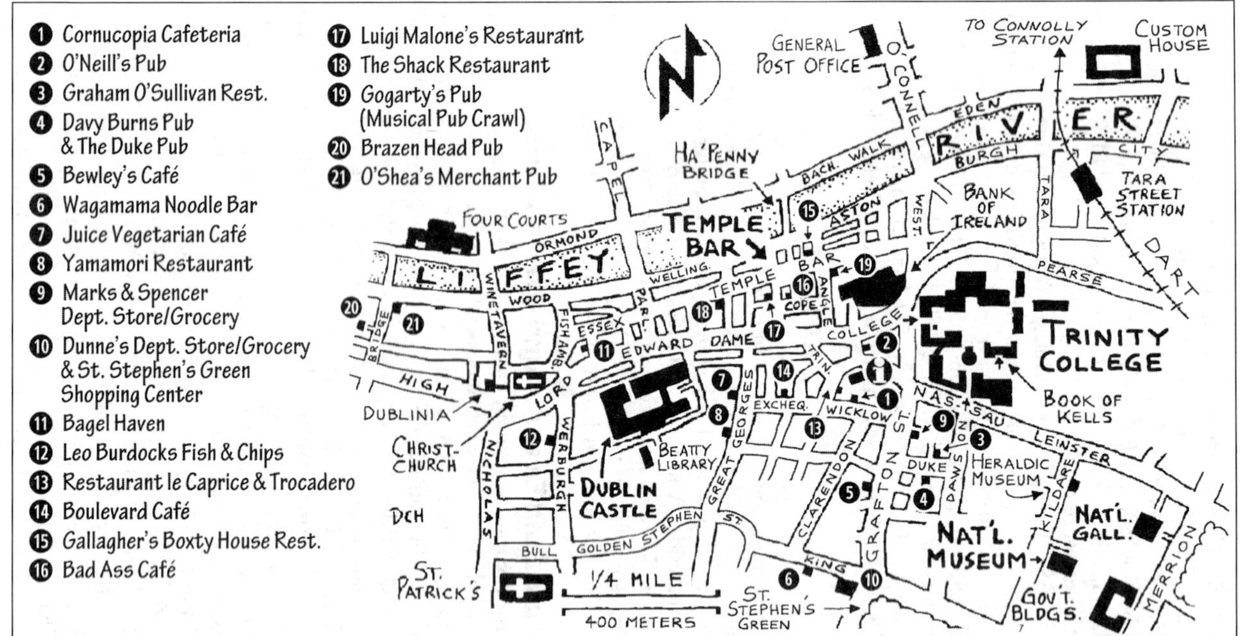

€12 (daily at 13:00 during a play's run, doors open 12:45, booking info tel. 086-878-4001, best to call ahead to see what's on).

Wagamama Noodle Bar, like its popular sisters in London, is a pan-Asian slurpathon with great and healthy noodle and rice dishes (€10–15) served by walkie-talkie-toting waiters at long communal tables (daily 12:00–23:00, no reservations, often a line, South King Street, underneath St. Stephen's Green Shopping Centre, tel. 01/478-2152).

South Great George's Street is lined with hardworking little eateries. **Juice** keeps vegetarians happy (daily 11:00–22:00, 73 South Great George's Street, tel. 01/475-7856).

Yamamori is a plain, bright, and modern Japanese place serving seas of sushi and noodles (€9 lunches daily 12:30–17:30, €13–18 dinners nightly 17:30–23:00, 71 South Great George's Street, tel. 01/475-5001).

Supermarkets: **Marks & Spencer** department store (on Grafton Street) has a fancy grocery store in the basement with fine takeaway sandwiches and salads (Mon–Fri 9:00–19:00, Thu until 21:00, Sat 9:00–19:00, Sun 12:00–18:30). Locals prefer **Dunne's** department store for its lower prices (same hours, grocery in basement, in St. Stephen's Green Shopping Centre).

Fast and Cheap near Christ Church

Many of Dublin's **late-night grocery stores** (such as the Spar off the top of Dame Street on Parliament Street) sell cheap salads, microwaved meat pies, and made-to-order sandwiches. A €7 picnic dinner back at the hotel might be a good option after a busy day of sightseeing.

Bagel Haven does fresh bagel sandwiches and healthy fruit salads. Get it to go and enjoy a picnic with a Georgian view in one of Dublin's grassy squares (€3.50–5 breakfasts, €5–8 lunches, Mon–Fri 7:30–16:00, Sat 10:00–17:00, Sun 10:00–16:00, hidden beside Kinlay House on Cow's Lane, tel. 01/675-9900).

Leo Burdocks Fish & Chips is popular with locals (takeout only, daily 12:00–24:00, 2 Werburgh Street, off Christ Church Square).

Classy Restaurants and Cafés

These three restaurants are located within a block of each other, just south of Temple Bar and Dame Street, near the main TI.

Le Caprice is a fine, relaxing Italian place, with a wall of celebrities-who-ate-here photos, a good wine selection, and a friendly staff (€20–26 meals, Tue–Sun 17:30–23:15, closed Mon, 12 St. Andrew Street, tel. 01/679-4050). Consider their €19 early-bird special if your plans will take you elsewhere by 20:00.

Trocadero, across the street, serves beefy European cuisine to locals interested in a slow, romantic meal. The dressy, red-velvet interior is draped with photos of local actors. Come early, or make a reservation. This place is a favorite with Dublin's theatergoers (€18–29 meals, Mon–Sat 17:00–24:00, closed Sun, 3 St. Andrew Street, tel. 01/677-5545). The three-course early-bird special at €20 is a fine value (17:00–19:00, leave by 20:00).

Boulevard Café is mod, local, trendy, and likeable, serving Mediterranean cuisine, heavy on the Italian. They serve salads, pasta, and sandwiches for around €8, three-course lunch specials for €13 (offered Mon–Sat 12:00–16:00), and dinner plates for €13–23 (café open Mon–Sat 12:00–24:00, closed Sun, 27 Exchequer Street, smart to reserve for dinner, tel. 01/679-2131).

At Temple Bar

Gallagher's Boxty House is touristy and traditional, a good, basic value with creaky floorboards and old Dublin ambience. Its specialty is boxties—the generally bland-tasting Irish potato pancake filled and rolled with various meats, veggies, and sauces. The "Gaelic Boxty" is liveliest (€14–20, also serves stews and corned beef, Mon–Fri 9:00–23:00, Sat–Sun 10:00–23:00, 20 Temple Bar, reservations wise, tel. 01/677-2762).

Bad Ass Café is a grunge diner (where Sinead O'Connor was once a waitress) serving cowboy/Mex/veggie/pizzas to old and new hippies. No need to dress up (€8 lunches and €12–18 dinners, kids' specials, daily 11:30–24:00, Crown Alley, just off Meeting House Square, tel. 01/671-2596).

Luigi Malone's, with its fun atmosphere and varied menu of pizza, ribs, pasta, sandwiches, and fajitas, is just the place to take your high-school date (€12–24, daily 12:00–23:00, corner of Cecila and Fownes Streets, tel. 01/679-2723).

The Shack, while a bit pricey and touristy, has a reputation for good quality and serves traditional Irish, chicken, seafood, and steak dishes (€16–26 entrées, daily 11:00–23:00, in the center of Temple Bar, 24 East Essex Street, tel. 01/679-0043).

TRANSPORTATION CONNECTIONS

Within Ireland

From Dublin by Bus to: Belfast (6/day, 3 hrs), **Trim** (10/day, 1 hr), **Ennis** (13/day, 4.5 hrs), **Galway** (13/day, 3.5 hrs), **Limerick** (13/day, 3.5 hrs), **Tralee** (7/day, 6 hrs), **Dingle** (4/day, 8 hrs, €23, transfer at Tralee). Bus info: tel. 01/836-6111.

By Train from Heuston Station to: Tralee (5/day, 4 hrs, talking timetable tel. 01/805-4266), **Ennis** (2/day, 4 hrs), **Galway** (5/day, 3 hrs, talking timetable tel. 01/805-4222).

By Train from Connolly Station to: Rosslare (5/day, 3 hrs), **Portrush** (7/day, 5 hrs, transfer in Belfast), **Belfast** (8/day, 2 hrs, tel. 01/836-3333).

Dublin Airport: The airport is well-connected to the city center seven miles away; see "Arrival in Dublin," page 812. Airport info: tel. 01/814-1111, www.dublin-airport.com.

Between Ireland and Britain

Spend a few minutes online researching your transportation options across the Irish Sea. Most airline and ferry companies routinely offer discounts (often as much as €10) for tickets purchased from their Web sites.

Dublin and London: The journey by boat plus train or bus takes 7–12 hours, all day or all night (bus: 4/day, €25–42, British tel. 08705-143-219, www.eurolines.co.uk; train: 4/day, €61–118, Dublin train info: tel. 01/836-6222, British train info: 01/703-1884).

If you're going directly to London, flying is your best bet. Check **Ryanair** first (90 min, Irish tel. 01/609-7878, www.ryanair.com). Other options include **British Airways** (toll-free tel. in Ireland 1-800-62647, in U.S. 800/247-9297, www.britishairways.com), **Aer Lingus** (tel. 01/886-8888, www.aerlingus.com), and **bmi british midland** (Irish tel. 01/407-3036, U.S. tel. 800/788-0555, www.flybmi.com). To get the lowest fares, ask about round-trip ticket prices and book months in advance (though Ryanair offers deals nearly all of the time).

Dublin and Liverpool: SeaCat has ferries for car and foot passengers (4 hrs, daily, €28-32 one-way for foot passengers, tel. 800-805-055, www.steam-packet.com). Car-only ferries are operated by both P&O Irish Sea Ferries (7.5 hrs, daily, tel. 01/407-3434, www.poirishsea.com) and Norse Merchant (8 hrs, Mon–Sat, closed Sun, tel. 01/819-2999, www.norsemerchant.com). Check in one to two hours before the sailing time—call to confirm details.

Dublin and Holyhead: Irish Ferries sails between Dublin and Holyhead in North Wales (dock is a mile east of O'Connell Bridge, 5/day: 2 slow, 3 fast; slow boats—3.25 hrs, €30 one-way walk-on fare; fast boats—1.75 hrs, €40; Dublin tel. 01/638-3333, Holyhead tel. 08705-329-129, www.irishferries.com).

Dun Laoghaire and Holyhead: Stena Line sails between Dun Laoghaire (near Dublin) and Holyhead in North Wales (3/day, 2 hrs on HSS *Catamaran,* €30–44 one-way walk-on fare, €4 extra if paying with credit card, reserve by phone—they book up long in advance on summer weekends, Dun Laoghaire tel. 01/204-7777, recorded info tel. 01/204-7799, can book online at www.stenaline.ie).

Dun Laoghaire

Dun Laoghaire (DUN-leary) is seven miles south of Dublin. This beach resort, with the ferry terminal for Wales and easy connections to downtown Dublin, is a great small-town base for the big city.

For the view, hike out to the lighthouse at the end of the interesting East Pier. The Dun Laoghaire harbor was strategic enough to merit a Martello tower, one in a line built to defend against an expected Napoleonic invasion (the tower now houses a museum, see below). By the mid-19th century, the huge breakwaters—reaching like two muscular arms into the Irish Sea—were completed, protecting a huge harbor. Ships sailed regularly from here to Wales (60 miles away), and the first train line in Ireland connected the terminal with Dublin. While still a busy transportation hub, today the nearly mile-long breakwaters are also popular with strollers, bikers, birders, and fishermen.

Getting to Dun Laoghaire

While buses run between Dublin and Dun Laoghaire, the **DART** commuter train is much faster (4/hr, 20 min, runs Mon–Sat about 6:30–23:30, Sun from 9:00, €1.80 one-way, €3.20 round-trips are good same day only, Eurail valid but uses a flexi-day; for a longer stay, consider the €15 Short Hop 3-day bus-and-rail ticket covering DART and Dublin buses). If you're coming from Dublin, catch a DART train marked "Bray" and get off at the Sandycove or Dun Laoghaire stop, depending on which B&B you choose; if you're leaving Dun Laoghaire, catch a train marked "Howth" to get to Dublin, and get off at the central Tara Street station.

The **taxi** fare from Dun Laoghaire to central Dublin is about €25; to the airport, about €40. Try ABC Taxi service (tel. 01/285-5444). With easy, free parking and DART access into Dublin, this area is ideal for those with **cars** (which cost €20/day to park in Dublin).

ORIENTATION

The Dun Laoghaire **TI** is in the ferry terminal (Mon–Sat 10:00–18:00 year-round, closed Sun). The Net House Café provides a fast **Internet** connection 24 hours a day (€2.50/30 min, 28 Upper George's Street). The Jeeves **laundry** is located in the village of Sandycove (Mon–Sat 8:30–18:00, closed Sun, full-service only, 34 Glasthule Road, next to Daniel's Restaurant and Wine Bar, tel. 01/230-1120).

SIGHTS

James Joyce Museum—The Martello tower at Sandycove is the setting for the opening of the novel *Ulysses.* Literary fans will find memorabilia at the James Joyce Museum in the tower (€6.25, covered by Dublin Pass, ask about discount with DART ticket, Feb–Oct Mon–Sat 10:00–17:00, Sun 14:00–18:00, closed Nov–Jan, tel. 01/280-9265).

ENTERTAINMENT

For an evening of pure Irish music, song, and dance, check out the **Comhaltas Ceoltoiri Éireann**, an association working to preserve this slice of Irish culture. It got started when Elvis and company threatened to steal the musical heart of the new generation. Judging by the pop status of traditional Irish music these days, Comhaltas accomplished its mission. Their "Seisiun" evening is a stage show mixing traditional music, song, and dance (€10, July–Aug Mon–Thu at 21:00, followed by informal music session at 22:30). On Fridays all year long, they have a *ceilidh* (KAY-lee), where everyone does set dances. This style, the forerunner of square dancing, evolved from the French Quadrille dances of 200 years ago, with two couples making up a "set" (€8 includes friendly pointers, 21:30–00:30). At 21:00 on Tuesdays and Wednesdays (free) and Saturdays (€3), there are informal sessions by the fireside. All musicians are welcome. Performances are held in Cuturlann na Éireann, near the Seapoint DART stop, or take bus #7 from Dun Laoghaire, at 32 Belgrave Square, Monkstown (tel. 01/280-0295, www.comhaltas.com). Their bar is free and often filled with music.

SLEEPING

(€1 = about $1.20, country code: 353, area code: 01)

Near the Sandycove DART Station

These listings are within several blocks of the Sandycove DART station and a seven-minute walk to the Dun Laoghaire DART station/ ferry landing.

$ Seaview B&B, a modern house run by Mrs. Kane, has three big, cheery rooms and a welcoming guests' lounge. While a few blocks farther out than the others, it's worth the walk for its bright and friendly feeling (Db-€75, cash only, strictly non-smoking, just above Rosmeen Gardens at 2 Granite Hall, tel. & fax 01/280-9105, seaviewbedandbreakfast@hotmail.com).

$ Windsor Lodge rents four fresh, inviting rooms on a quiet street a block off the harbor and a block from the DART station (Db-€60–80, Tb-€90, family deals, cash only, non-smoking, 3

Dun Laoghaire

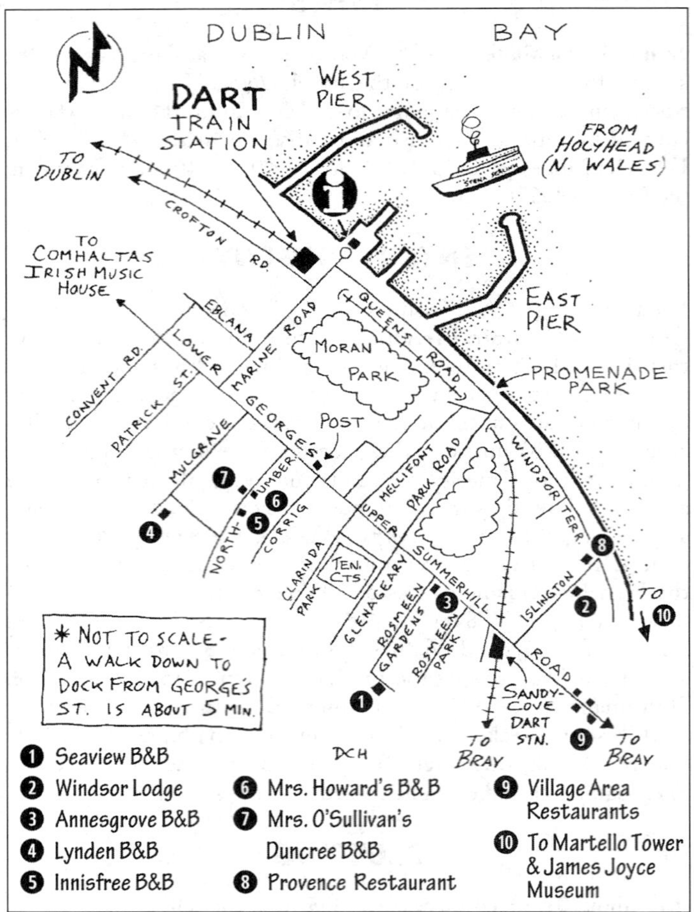

Islington Avenue, Sandycove, tel. & fax 01/284-6952, winlodge @eircom.net, Mary O'Farrell).

$ Annesgrove B&B has four tidy rooms decorated in beige and brown (S-€50, D-€60, Db-€70, Tb-€90, cash only, parking, close to park and beach, 28 Rosmeen Gardens, tel. 01/280-9801, Anne D'Alton).

Near the Dun Laoghaire DART Station

$ Lynden B&B, with a classy, 150-year-old interior hiding behind a somber front, rents four big rooms (S-€40, Sb-€45–50, D-€56, Db-€70, cash only, past Mulgrave Street to 2 Mulgrave Terrace, tel. 01/280-6404, fax 01/230-2258, lynden@iol.ie, Maria Gavin).

$ Innisfree B&B has a fine lounge and six big, slightly frayed rooms (D-€50, Db-€58, from George's Street, hike up the plain but quiet Northumberland Avenue to #31, tel. 01/280-5598, fax 01/280-3093, innismyth@eircom.net, Brendan and Mary Smyth).

On the same street, you'll find two places renting four big, well-worn rooms each: **$ Mrs. Howard's B&B** (S-€35, Sb-€40, D-€56, Db-€62, cash only, TV lounge, 36 Northumberland Avenue, tel. 01/280-3262, corahoward2003@yahoo.co.uk) and **$ Mrs. O'Sullivan's Duncree B&B** (D-€56, Db-€62, cash only, family room, non-smoking, 16 Northumberland Avenue, tel. 01/280-6118).

EATING

If staying in Dun Laoghaire, I'd definitely eat here and not in Dublin. Glasthule (called simply "the village" locally, just down the street from the Sandycove DART station) has a stunning array of fun, hardworking little restaurants.

Bistro Vino is the rage lately, with cozy, candlelit, Mediterranean ambience and great pasta and seafood (€14–23 meals, €20 early-bird special 17:00–19:00, daily 17:00–23:00, arrive early or have a reservation, 56 Glasthule Road, tel. 01/280-6097).

Reubens serves fish and pasta in a casual setting opposite the Eagle House pub (€11–18 meals, daily 10:00–22:00, 57 Glasthule Road, tel. 01/236-5971).

The big **Eagle House** pub dishes up hearty €9–16 pub meals (until 21:30) in a wonderful atmosphere. This is a super local joint for a late drink. The nearby **Daniel's Restaurant and Wine Bar** is less atmospheric but also good (€18–24 meals, Tue–Sun 18:00–23:00, closed Mon, 34 Glasthule Road, tel. 01/284-1027).

Provence, a classy little French restaurant with occasional live piano music, faces the water and serves fine cuisine (€28–35 main courses, €20 2-course early-bird special before 19:00, Tue–Sat 17:00–22:00, closed Sun–Mon, 1 Martello Terrace, directly down from Sandycove DART station, reservations smart, tel. 01/280-8788).

Walters Public House and Restaurant is a bright, modern place above a pub, offering good food to a dressy crowd (€16–24 meals, €15 early-bird special before 19:00, daily 17:30–22:30, 68 Upper George's Street, tel. 01/280-7442).

George's Street, Dun Laoghaire's main drag three blocks inland, has plenty of eateries and pubs, many with live music. A good bet for families is the kid-friendly **Bits and Pizza** (daily 12:00–24:00, off George's Street at 15 Patrick Street, tel. 01/284-2411).

DINGLE PENINSULA

Dingle Peninsula, the westernmost tip of Ireland, offers just the right mix of far-and-away beauty, ancient archaeological wonders, and isolated walks or bike rides—all within convenient reach of its main town. Dingle town is just large enough to have all the necessary tourist services and a steady nocturnal beat of Irish folk music.

Although crowded in summer, Dingle still feels like the fish and the farm really matter. Forty fishing boats sail from Dingle, tractor tracks dirty its main drag, and a faint whiff of peat fills its nighttime streets.

For more than 25 years, my Irish dreams have been set here on this sparse but lush peninsula, where locals are fond of saying, "The next parish is Boston." There's a feeling of closeness to the land on Dingle. When I asked a local if he was born here, he thought for a second and said, "No, it was about six miles down the road." When I told him where I was from, a faraway smile filled his eyes, and he looked out to sea and sighed, "Ah, the shores of Americay." I asked his friend if he'd lived here all his life. He said, "Not yet."

Dingle feels so traditionally Irish because it's a *Gaeltacht,* a region where the government subsidizes the survival of the Irish language and culture. While English is always there, the signs, menus, and songs come in Gaelic. Children carry hurling sticks to class, and even the local preschool brags "ALL Gaelic."

Of the peninsula's 10,000 residents, 1,500 live in Dingle town. Its few streets, lined with ramshackle but gaily painted shops and pubs, run up from a rain-stung harbor always busy with fishing boats and yachts. Traditionally, the buildings were drab gray or

Dingle Peninsula
DINGLE PENINSULA
TO GALWAY & THE BURREN
N 69
TRALEE
N 21
KERRY AIRPORT
KILLARNEY
TO CORK, ROSSLARE & DUBLIN
MUCKROSS HOUSE & FARMS
DCH
TO KENMARE
BLENNER-VILLE
MILL-TOWN
R-561
NAT'L PARK
KERRY PENINSULA
"RING OF KERRY"
N 70
N-86
CONOR PASS
N-86
MINARD CASTLE
INCH
LIS-POLE
DINGLE TOWN
GALLARUS ORATORY
DUNQUIN
BLASKET ISLANDS
ATLANTIC OCEAN
10 MILES
10 KM
TO BOSTON

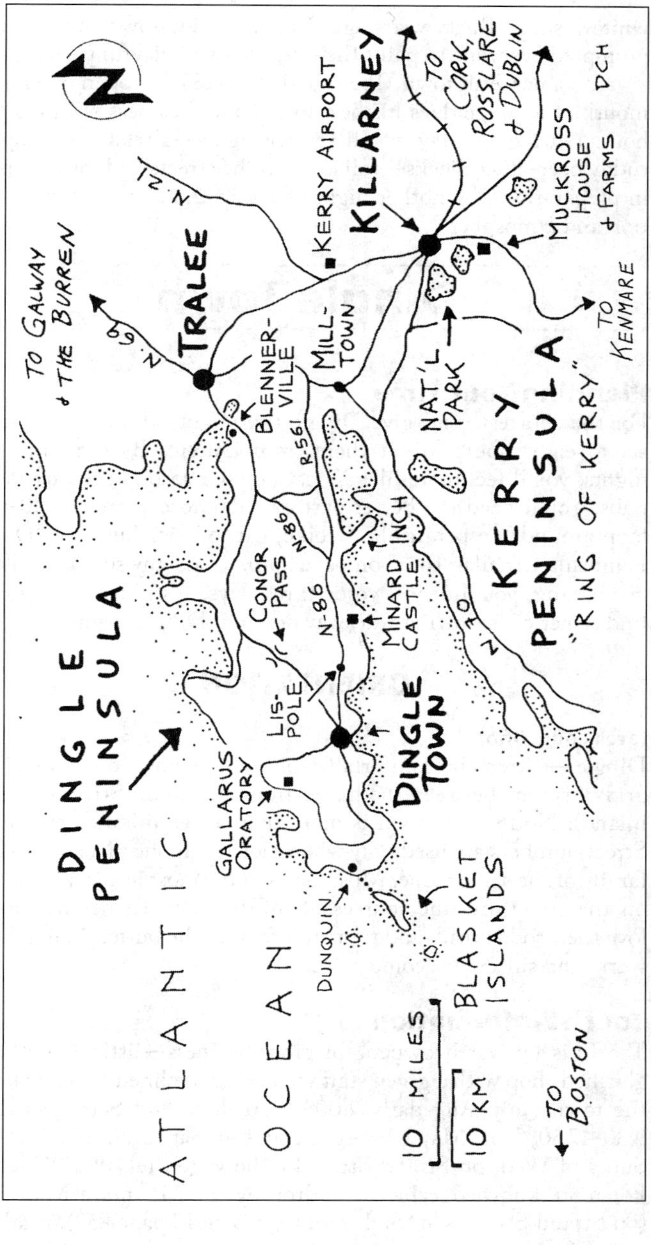

whitewashed. Thirty years ago, Ireland's "tidy town" competition prompted everyone to paint their buildings in playful pastels.

It's a peaceful town. The courthouse (1832) is open one hour a month. The judge does his best to wrap up business within a half hour. During the day, you'll see teenagers—already working on ruddy beer-glow cheeks—roll kegs up the streets and into the pubs in preparation for another night of music and *craic* (fun conversation and atmosphere).

Dingle Town

Planning Your Time

For the shortest visit, give Dingle two nights and a day. It takes six to eight hours to get there from Dublin. By spending two nights, you'll feel more like a local on your second evening in the pubs. You'll need the better part of a day to explore the 30-mile loop around the peninsula by bike, car, or tour bus (see "Dingle Peninsula Circular Tour" on page 864). To do any serious walking or relaxing, you'll need two or three days. It's not uncommon to find Americans slowing way, way down in Dingle town.

ORIENTATION

(area code: 066)

Dingle—extremely comfortable on foot—hangs on a medieval grid of streets between the harborfront and Main Street (3 blocks inland). Nothing in town is more than a five-minute walk away. Street numbers are used only when more than one place is run by a family of the same name. Most locals know most locals, and people on the street are fine sources of information. Remember, locals love their soda bread, and tourism provides the butter. You'll find a warm and sincere welcome.

Tourist Information

The TI is a privately owned, for-profit business—little more than a glorified shop with a green staff who are disinclined to really know the town (July–Aug daily 9:00–19:00, June and Sept–Oct daily 9:30–17:30; Nov–May Mon–Tue and Thu–Sat 10:00–17:00, closed Sun and Wed; on Strand Street by the water, tel. 066/915-1188). For more knowledgeable help, drop by the Mountain Man shop (on Strand Street, see "Sights and Activities," page 852) or talk to your B&B host.

Helpful Hints

Before You Go: The local Web site (www.dingle-peninsula.ie) lists festivals and events.

Crowds: Crowds trample Dingle's charm throughout July and August. The absolute craziest times are the Dingle Races (2nd weekend in Aug), Dingle Regatta (3rd weekend in Aug), and the Blessing of the Boats (end of Aug, beginning of Sept). The first Mondays in May, June, and August are bank holidays, giving Ireland's workers three-day weekends—and ample time to fill up Dingle. The town's metabolism (prices, schedules, activities) rises and falls with the tourist crowds, so October through April is sleepy.

Banking: Two banks in town, both on Main Street, offer the same rates (Mon 10:00–17:00, Tue–Fri 10:00–16:00, closed Sat–Sun) and have cash machines. The TI happily changes cash and traveler's checks at mediocre rates. Expect to use cash (rather than credit cards) to pay for most peninsula activities.

Internet Access: Dingle Internet Café is on Main Street (€2.60/30 min, April–Sept Mon–Fri 10:00–22:00, Sat 13:00–20:00, Sun 14:00–20:00, shorter hours Oct–March, tel. 066/915-2478, www.dingleinternetcafe.ie).

Post Office: It's on Main Street near Benners Hotel (Mon–Fri 9:00–17:30, Sat 9:00–13:00, closed Sun).

Laundry: Dingle Cleaners is full-service only—drop off before 10:00 and pick up dried and folded late that afternoon (€8–12 depending on load size, Mon–Sat 9:30–18:00, closed Sun, beside Moran's Market and gas station, tel. 066/915-0680, mobile 087-793-5621).

Bike Rental: Bike rental shops abound. The cheapest is at Kirrary B&B (€8/day, Greys Lane, see "Sleeping," page 857), or try Paddy's Bike Hire (€10/day or €1 more for 24 hrs, €12 for better bikes, daily 9:00–19:00, on Dykegate next to Grapevine Hostel, tel. 066/915-2311). Foxy John's (Main Street), Mountain Man (no helmets), and the Ballintaggert Hostel also rent bikes. If you're biking the peninsula, get a bike with skinny street tires, not slow and fat mountain-bike tires. Plan on leaving €10, plus a driver's license or passport, as a security deposit.

Dingle Activities: The Mountain Man, a hiking shop run by a local guide, Adrian Curran, is a clearinghouse for information on hiking, biking, horseback riding, climbing, peninsula tours, and trips to the Blasket Islands (the shop is the Dingle town contact for the Dunquin–Blasket Islands boats and shuttle-bus rides to the harbor via Moran's taxi service—see "Blasket Islands," page 871). Give them a call a few days ahead of time to see which guided, scenic, mountain day-hikes are scheduled (July–Sept daily 9:00–21:00, Oct–June 9:00–18:00, just off harbor at Strand

Street, tel. 066/915-2400, www.themountainmanshop.com).

Travel Agency: Maurice O'Connor at Galvin's Travel Agency can book plane tickets, as well as boat rides to France (Mon–Fri 9:30–18:00, Sat 9:30–17:00, closed Sun, John Street, tel. 066/915-1409).

Farmers Market: On most Saturdays (10:00–14:00), local farmers fill the St. James churchyard on Main Street with their fresh produce and homemade marmalade.

SIGHTS AND ACTIVITIES

▲▲The Harry Clark Windows of Diseart—Just behind Dingle's St. Mary Church stands St. Joseph's Convent and Diseart (dee-ZHART), containing a beautiful neo-Gothic chapel built in 1884. The sisters of this order, who came to Dingle in 1829 to educate local girls, worked heroically during the famine. During Mass in the chapel, the Mother Superior would sit in the covered stall in the rear, while the sisters—filling the carved stalls—chanted responsively.

The chapel was graced in 1922 with 12 windows—the work of Ireland's top stained-glass man, Harry Clark. Long appreciated only by the sisters, these special windows—showing six scenes from the life of Christ—are now open to the public. The convent has become a center for sharing Christian Celtic culture and spirituality (free, Mon–Fri 9:30–13:00 & 14:00–17:00, closed Sat–Sun, tel. 066/915-2476, www.diseart.ie).

Enjoy a meditative 15 minutes following the free audioguide that explains the chapel one window at a time. The scenes (clockwise from the back entrance) are: the visit of the Magi, the Baptism of Jesus, "Let the little children come to me," the Sermon on the Mount, the Agony in the Garden, and Jesus appearing to Mary Magdalene. Each face is lively and animated in the imaginative, devout, medieval, and fun-loving art of Harry Clark, whom locals talk about as if he's the kid next door.

▲Fungie—In 1983, a dolphin moved into Dingle Harbor and became a local celebrity. Fungie (FOON-gee, with a hard *g*) is now the darling of the town's tourist trade and one reason you'll find so many tour buses parked along the harbor. With a close look at Fungie as bait, tour boats are thriving. The hardy little boats motor seven to 40 passengers out to the mouth of the harbor, where they troll around looking for Fungie. You're virtually assured of seeing the dolphin, but you don't pay unless you do (€12, kids-€6, 1-hr trips depart 10:00–19:00 depending on demand, behind TI at Dolphin Trips office, tel. 066/915-2626). To actually swim with Fungie, rent wetsuits at Bresnan's B&B (Cooleen Street, tel. 066/915-1967) and catch the early-morning 8:00–10:00 trip (€35 includes a wetsuit—unless you've packed your own).

▲Oceanworld—The aquarium offers a little peninsula history, 300 different species of local fish in thoughtfully described tanks, and the easiest way to see Fungie the dolphin...on video. Walk through the tunnel while fish swim overhead. The only creatures not local—other than you—are the sharks. The aquarium's mission is to teach, and you're welcome to ask questions. The petting pool is fun. Splashing attracts the rays, which are unplugged (€9, families-€25, daily July–Aug 10:00–20:30, May–June and Sept 10:00–18:00, Oct–April 10:00–17:00, cafeteria, just past harbor on west edge of town, tel. 066/915-2111).

Dingle Area

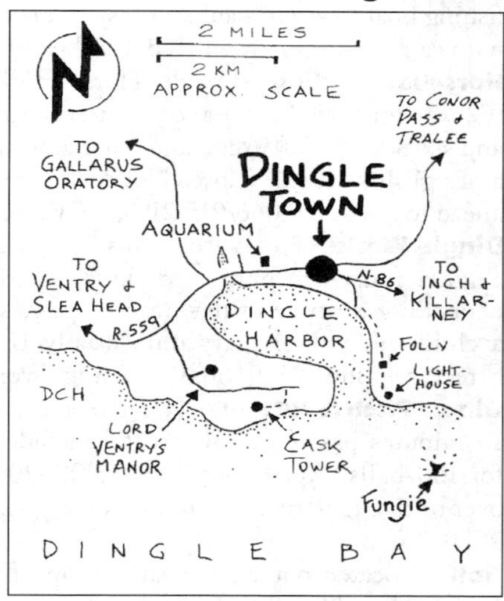

▲Short Harbor Walk from Dingle—For an easy stroll along the harbor out of town (and a chance to see Fungie, 90 min round-trip), head east from the roundabout past the Esso station. Just after Bambury's B&B, take a right, following signs to Skelligs Hotel, and go left at the Irish Coast Guard station on the bay. At the beach, climb the steps over the wall and follow the seashore path to the mouth of Dingle Harbor (marked by a tower—some 19th-century fat cat's folly). Ten minutes beyond that is a lighthouse. This is Fungie's neighborhood. If you see tourist boats out, you're likely to see the dolphin. The trail continues to a dramatic cliff.

The **harbor** was built on land reclaimed (with imported Dutch expertise) in 1992. The string of old stone shops facing the harbor was the loading station for the narrow-gauge railway that hauled the fish from Dingle to Tralee (1891–1953). Make a point to walk out to the end of the breakwater—newly paved, and illuminated at night. The Eask Tower on the distant hill is a marker that was built in 1847 during the famine as a make-work project. In pre-radar days, it helped ships locate Dingle's hidden harbor. The fancy mansion across the harbor is Lord Ventry's 17th-century manor house (see "Dingle Peninsula Circular Tour," page 864).

Sailing—The Dingle Marina Centre offers diving, sailing, traditional currach rowing, and a salty little restaurant. Sailors can join the club for a day to sail (€22, July–Aug, tel. 066/915-1984). Currachs—

stacked behind the building—are Ireland's traditional lightweight fishing boats, easy to haul and easy to make. Cover a wooden frame with canvas (originally cowhide) and paint with tar—presto.

Horseback Riding—Dingle Horse Riding takes out beginners (€26/hr for a trail ride) and experienced riders on four-hour (€95) and six-hour (€130) excursions. Bob along beaches or mountains on an English-style ride (closed Nov–Feb, 5-min drive from Dingle, call ahead to book, tel. 066/915-2199, www.dinglehorseriding.com).

Dingle World of Leisure—This is a health club for adults and a good rainy-day option for kids, offering bowling (€18–30/hr depending on time of day), arcade games, a swimming pool, and a children's indoor playground (daily 11:00–23:00, just off John Street, tel. 066/915-0660, www.dingleworldofleisure.com).

Dingle Pitch & Putt—For 18 scenic holes and a driving range, hike 10 minutes past Oceanworld (€5 includes gear, driving range €5 for 100 balls, April–Oct daily 10:00–20:00, closed Nov–March, over bridge take first left and follow signs, Milltown, tel. 066/915-2020).

Golf—Located out west, near the tip of the Dingle peninsula in Ballyferriter (9 miles from Dingle town), Ceann Sibeal/Dingle Links offers an enjoyable round of golf in a hard-to-beat setting (€50–70 green fees, open daily, tel. 066/915-6255, www.dinglelinks.com).

Shopping—Dingle is filled with shops showing off local craftsmanship. The **West Kerry Craft Guild**—a co-op selling the work of 15 local artists—is a delight even if you're just browsing. The prices here are very good, since you're buying directly from the artists (June–Aug daily 10:00–18:00, Sept–May daily 11:00–17:00, 18 Main Street, tel. 066/915-2976). The **Niamh Utsch Jewelry** shop next door is much respected for its unique work. **Lisbeth Mulcahy Weaver**, filled with traditional but stylish woven wear, is also the Dingle sales outlet of the well-known potter from out on Slea Head (Mon–Sat 9:00–18:00, Sun 10:00–18:00, Green Street, tel. 066/915-1688).

NIGHTLIFE

▲▲▲Music in Dingle Pubs—Even if you're not into pubs, take a nap and then give these a whirl. Dingle is renowned among traditional musicians as a place to get work ("€40 a day, tax-free, plus drink"). The town has piles of pubs. There's music every night, and rarely a cover charge. The scene is a decent mix of locals, Americans, and Germans. Music normally starts around 21:30, and the last call for drinks is "half eleven" (23:30), sometimes later on weekends. For a seat near the music, arrive early. If the place is chockablock, power in and find breathing room in the back. By

The Voyage of St. Brendan

It has long been part of Irish lore that St. Brendan the Navigator (A.D. 484–577) and 12 followers sailed from the southwest of Ireland to the "Land of Promise" (what is now North America) in a currach—a wood-frame boat covered with ox hide and tar. According to a 10th-century monk who poetically wrote of the journey, St. Brendan and his crew encountered a paradise of birds, were attacked by a whale, and suffered the smoke of a smelly island in the north before finally reaching their Land of Promise.

The legend and its precisely described locations still fascinate modern readers. A British scholar of navigation, Tim Severin, re-created the entire journey from 1976 to 1977. He and his crew set out from Brendan Creek in County Kerry in a currach. The prevailing winds blew them to the Hebrides, the Faeroe Islands, Iceland, and finally to Newfoundland. While this didn't successfully prove that St. Brendan sailed to North America, it did prove that he could have.

St. Brendan fans have been heartened by an intriguing archaeological find in Connecticut. Called the "Gungywamp," the site includes a double circle of stones and a beehive-like chamber built in the same manner as the stone *clochans* huts on the Dingle Peninsula. The Gungywamp beehive chamber has been carbon-dated to approximately A.D. 600. Outside the chamber, a stone slab is inscribed with a cross that resembles the unique style of the Irish cross.

According to his 10th-century biographer, "St. Brendan sailed from the Land of Promise home to Ireland. And from that time on, Brendan acted as if he did not belong to this world at all. His mind and his joy were in the delight of heaven."

midnight, the door is usually closed, and the chairs are stacked.

While two pubs, the **Small Bridge Bar** (An Droichead Beag) and **O'Flaherty's**, are the most famous for their good beer and folk music, make a point to wander the town and follow your ear. Smaller pubs may feel a bit foreboding to a tourist, but people—locals as well as travelers—are out for the *craic.* Irish culture is very accessible in the pubs; they're like highly interactive museums waiting to be explored. But if you sit at a table, you'll be left alone. Stand or sit at the bar, and you'll be engulfed in conversation with new friends. Have a glass in an empty, no-name pub and chat up the publican. Pubs are no longer smoky, but can be stuffy and hot, so leave your coat at home. The more offbeat pubs are more likely to erupt into leprechaun karaoke.

Pub Crawl—The best pub crawl is along Strand Street to O'Flaherty's (see map on page 862). **Murphy's** is lively, offering rock as well as ballads and traditional music. O'Flaherty's has a high ceiling and is dripping in old-time photos and town memorabilia—it's touristy, but lots of fun, with nightly music in the summer. **John Benny Moriarty's** has dependably good traditional music sessions, with John himself joining in on accordion when he's not pouring pints.

Then head up Green Street. **Dick Mack**, across from the church, is nicknamed "the last pew." This is a tiny leather shop by day, expanding into a pub at night, with several rooms, a fine snug (private booth, originally designed to allow women to drink discreetly), reliably good beer, and strangely fascinating ambience. Notice the Hollywood-type stars on the sidewalk, recalling famous visitors. Established in 1899, this place is now run by the grandson of the original Dick Mack. A painting in the window shows Dick Mack II with the local gang.

Green Street climbs to Main Street, where two more Dick Mack–type places are filled with locals deep in conversation (but without music): **Foxy John's** (a hardware shop by day) and **O Currain's** (across the street, a small clothing shop by day).

A bit higher up Main Street is **McCarthy's Pub**, a smoke-stained relic. It's less touristy and has some fine traditional music sessions and occasional plays on its little stage. Wander downhill to the **Small Bridge Bar** at the bottom. With live music nightly, it's popular for good reason. While the tourists gather around the music, poke around the back and do an end run around the wall, which leads to a window nook actually closest to the musicians. Occasionally, musicians sell CDs of their tunes, which can be a nice keepsake of your time in Ireland.

Off-season: From October through April, the bands play on, though at fewer pubs: Small Bridge Bar (live music nightly), John Benny Moriarty's (Mon, Wed, Thu), McCarthy's (Fri, Sat), and Murphy's (Sat).

Music shops: Danlann Gallery sells musical instruments and woodcrafts (Mon–Fri 10:00–18:00, later in summer, "flexible" on weekends, owner makes violins, Green Street). Siopa an Phiobaire, exclusively a music shop, sells traditional wind instruments (Mon–Fri 10:00–17:00, closed Sat–Sun, Craft Centre, on edge of town a few minutes' walk past Oceanworld, tel. 066/915-1778). Dingle Bodhrans sells homemade traditional goatskin drums and gives lessons (1-hour lesson-€40, Mon–Sat 10:30–18:00, closed Sun, Green Street, enter red iron gate of small alley opposite church, tel. 087-245-7689, Andrea).

Folk Concerts—Top local musicians offer a quality evening of live, acoustic, classic Irish music in the fine little St. James Church on Main Street (€10 advance purchase, €12 at the door; Mon, Wed, and Fri at 19:30, May–Sept only; mobile 087/982-9728, see sign on church gate or drop by Murphy's Ice Cream shop for details).

If you're not a night owl (music in pubs doesn't begin until 21:30) or prefer not to be packed into a pub with the distractions of conversation, then this is your best opportunity to hear Irish traditional music in a more controlled environment.

Dancing—Some pubs host "set dancing" with live music. Your two best possibilities are the Small Bridge Bar or John Benny Moriarty's pub (see above), but ask at the TI for more suggestions.

Theater—Dingle's great little theater is The Phoenix on Dykegate. Its film club (50–60 locals) meets here Tuesdays year-round at 20:30 for coffee and cookies, followed by a film at 21:00 (€6 for film, anyone is welcome). The leader runs it almost like a religion, with a sermon on the film before he rolls it. The regular film schedule for the week is posted on the door.

SLEEPING

$$$ Heaton's Guesthouse, big, peaceful, and American in its comforts, is on the water just west of town, at the end of Dingle Bay—a five-minute walk past Oceanworld on The Wood. The 16 thoughtfully appointed rooms come with all the amenities (Db-€86–128, suite Db-€130–180, creative breakfasts, parking, The Wood, tel. 066/915-2288, fax 066/915-2324, www.heatonsdingle.com, heatons@iol.ie, Cameron and Nuala Heaton).

$$$ Benners Hotel was the only place in town a hundred years ago. It stands bewildered by the modern world on Main Street, with sprawling public spaces and 52 abundant, overpriced rooms (Db-€200 July–Aug, €160 May–June, €150 Sept–May, discounts on Web site, tel. 066/915-1638, fax 066/915-1412, www.dinglebenners.com, info@dinglebenners.com).

$$ Greenmount House sits among chilly palm trees in the

Sleep Code

(€1 = about $1.20, country code: 353, area code: 066)

S = Single, **D** = Double/Twin, **T** = Triple, **Q** = Quad, **b** = bathroom, **s** = shower only. Breakfast is included and credit cards are accepted unless otherwise noted. To locate hotels, see map on page 858.

To help you easily sort through these listings, I've divided the rooms into three categories, based on the price for a standard double room with bath:

$$$ Higher Priced—Most rooms €100 or more.
$$ Moderately Priced—Most rooms between €60–100.
$ Lower Priced—Most rooms €60 or less.

Dingle Hotels and Services

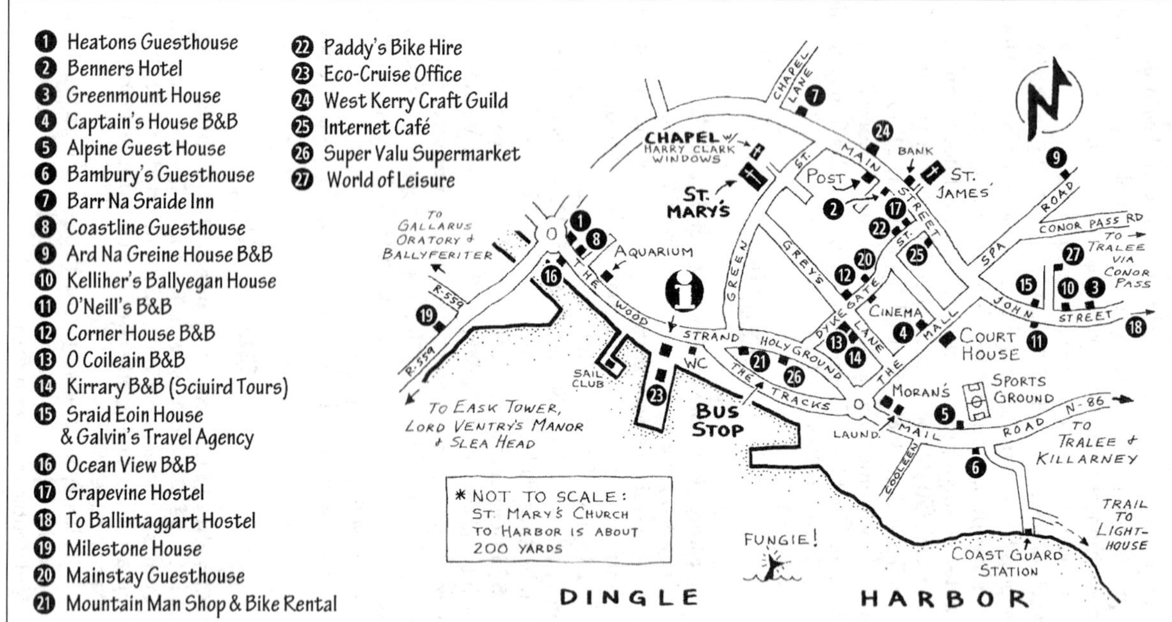

countryside at the top of town. A five-minute hike up from the town center, this guesthouse commands a fine view of the bay and mountains. John and Mary Curran run one of Ireland's best B&Bs, with five superb rooms (Db-€75–95—top price through the summer) and seven sprawling suites (Db-€100–150) in a modern building with lavish public areas and breakfast in a solarium (reserve in advance, no children under 8, most rooms at ground level, parking, top of John Street, tel. 066/915-1414, fax 066/915-1974, www.greenmount-house.com, info@greenmount-house.com).

$$ Captain's House B&B is a shipshape place in the town center, fit for an admiral, with eight classy rooms, peat-fire lounges, a stay-awhile garden, and a magnificent breakfast in the conservatory. Mary, whose mother ran a guest house before Dingle was discovered, loves her work and is very good at it (Sb-€50–60, Db-€80–100, great suite-€140–160, The Mall, tel. 066/915-1531, fax 066/915-1079, captigh@eircom.net, Jim and Mary Milhench).

$$ Alpine Guest House looks like a Monopoly hotel, but that means it's comfortable and efficient. Its 13 spacious, bright, and fresh rooms come with wonderful sheep-and-harbor views, a cozy lounge, a great breakfast, and friendly owners (Db-€70–95, Tb-€85–130, prices vary with room size and season, 10 percent discount with this book through 2005, no smoking, parking, Mail Road, tel. 066/915-1250, fax 066/915-1966, www.alpineguesthouse.com, alpinedingle@eircom.net, Paul). If you're driving into town from Tralee, you'll see this a block uphill from the Dingle roundabout and Esso station.

$$ Bambury's Guesthouse, big and modern, with views of grazing sheep and the harbor, rents 12 airy, comfy rooms (Db-€70–110, prices depend on size and season, family deals; coming in from nearby Tralee, it's on your left on Mail Road, 2 blocks before Esso station; tel. 066/915-1244, fax 066/915-1786, http://bamburysguesthouse.com, info@bamburysguesthouse.com).

$$ Milestone House is a 15-minute walk out of town (at mile 0.8 on the "Dingle Peninsula Circular Tour" in this chapter—see page 864). It has warmly decorated rooms, great views of Dingle harbor, and an ancient boundary stone in the front yard. Friendly Barbara Carroll is a font of sightseeing tips (Sb-€40–45, Db-€60–70, Tb-€90–105, Qb-€110–120, parking, tel. & fax 066/915-1831, www.iol.ie/~milstone, milestonedingle@eircom.net).

$$ Mainstay Guesthouse is smack-dab in the center of town, with 14 modest rooms, a cheery breakfast area, and an inviting back garden (Sb-€48–58, Db-€76–96, Tb-€114–144, non-smoking, tel. 066/915-1598, fax 066/915-2376, www.mainstaydingle.com, info@mainstaydingle.com, Gus and Ruth Cero).

$$ Barr Na Sraide Inn, central and hotelesque, has 22 comfortable rooms (Db-€70–100, family deals, self-service laundry, bar, parking, past McCarthy's pub, Upper Main Street, tel. 066/915-1331, fax 066/915-1446, www.barrnasraide.com, barrnasraide@eircom.net).

$$ Coastline Guesthouse, on the water next to Heaton's Guesthouse (listed above), is a modern, sterile place with seven bright, spacious rooms (Db-€70–90, Tb-€100–140, non-smoking, parking, The Wood, tel. 066/915-2494, fax 066/915-2493, www.coastlinedingle.com, coastlinedingle@eircom.net, Vivienne O'Shea).

$$ Ard Na Greine House B&B is a charming, windblown, modern house on the edge of town. Mrs. Mary Houlihan rents four well-equipped, comfortable rooms (with fridges) to non-smokers only (Sb-€52, Db-€70, Tb-€80, parking, 8-min walk up Spa Road, 3 doors beyond Hillgrove Hotel, tel. 066/915-1113).

$$ Kelliher's Ballyegan House is a big, plain building with six fresh, comfortable rooms on the edge of town, and great harbor views (Db-€70, Tb-€100, cash only, non-smoking, parking, Upper John Street, tel. 066/915-1702, Hannah and James Kelliher).

$$ O'Neill's B&B is a homey, friendly place with six decent rooms on a quiet street at the top of town (Db-€75, family deals, cash only, strictly non-smoking, parking, John Street, tel. 066/915-1639, Mary O'Neill).

$$ Corner House B&B is my longtime Dingle home. It's a simple, traditional place with five large, uncluttered rooms, run with a twinkle and a grandmotherly smile by Kathleen Farrell (S-€40, D-€75, T-€90, plenty of plumbing, but it's down the hall, cash only, reserve with a phone call and reconfirm a day or 2 ahead, central as can be on Dykegate Street, tel. 066/915-1516). Mrs. Farrell, one of the original three B&B hostesses in a town now filled with them, is a great storyteller.

$$ Collins B&Bs: The following two B&Bs, which take up a quiet corner in the town center, are run by the same Collins—Coileain in Gaelic—family that does archaeological tours of the peninsula (see "Sciuird Archaeology Tours," page 871). Both offer fine rooms (O Coileain's are a bit bigger), cheap bike rental (€8/day), identical prices (Db-€70–74), and a homey friendliness. **O Coileain B&B** is run by a young family—Rachel, Michael, and their two cute little girls (tel. 066/915-1937, archeo@eircom.net). **Kirrary B&B**, just over the fence, is grandma's place, with a homey charm (good place to rent bikes, tel. 066/915-1606, collinskirrary@eircom.net, Eileen Collins).

$$ Sraid Eoin House offers four modest but pleasant, top-floor rooms above Galvin's Travel Agency (Db-€65–70, Tb-€90–100, John Street, tel. 066/915-1409, fax 066/915-2156, sraideoinhouse@hotmail.com, friendly Kathleen and Maurice O'Connor).

$ Ocean View B&B rents three tidy rooms (2 with views) in a humble little waterfront row house overlooking the bay (S-€28, D-€46, welcome treat on arrival, 5-min walk from center, 100 yards past Oceanworld at 133 The Wood, tel. 066/915-1659, thewood@gofree.indigo.ie, Mrs. Brosnan).

Hostels: **$ Grapevine Hostel** is clean and friendly, quietly yet very centrally located, with a cozy fireplace lounge and a fine members' kitchen. Each four- to eight-bed dorm has its own bathroom. Dorms are coed, but there's a female-only room (26 beds, €15–17 per person, Db-€40, laundry-€5, open all day, Dykegate Lane, tel. 066/915-1434, www.grapevinedingle.com, hostel@grapevinedingle.com, run by Siobhan—sheh-vahn).

$ Ballintaggart Hostel, a backpackers' complex, is housed in a stylish old manor house used by Protestants during the famine as a soup kitchen (for those hungry enough to renounce Catholicism). It comes complete with laundry service (€6), a classy study, a family room with a fireplace, and a resident ghost (130 beds, €14 in 10-bed dorms, €18 beds in Qb, Db-€50, no breakfast, but there's a kitchen, a mile east of town on Tralee Road, tel. 066/915-1454, fax 066/915-2207, www.dingleaccommodation.com, info@dingleaccommodation.com). Ask the Tralee bus to drop you here before arriving in Dingle.

EATING

For a rustic little village, Dingle is swimming in good food.

Budget Tips: The Super Valu supermarket/department store, at the base of town, has everything and stays open late (Mon–Sat 8:00–21:00, Sun 8:00–19:00, daily until 22:00 in June–Aug). Smaller groceries are scattered throughout the town, such as Centra on Main Street (Mon–Sat 8:00–21:00, Sun 8:00–18:00). Consider a grand view picnic out on the end of the newer pier (as you face the harbor, it's the pleasure-boat pier on your right).

Fancy restaurants serve early-bird specials from 18:00 to 19:00. Many "cheap and cheery" places close at 18:00, and pubs do good €12 dinners all over town. Most pubs stop serving food around 21:00 (to make room for their beer drinkers).

James G. Ashe Pub and Restaurant, an old-fashioned joint, is popular with locals for traditional Irish food at great prices. Try their beef-and-Guinness stew (€10 lunches, €15–22 dinners, lunch 12:00–16:00, dinner 18:00–21:00, Main Street, tel. 066/915-0989).

The Old Smokehouse, serving happy locals in a rustic, woody setting, offers the best moderate-value meals in town, with fresh Dingle Bay fish and good vegetables (€16–24 dinner plates, daily 18:00–22:00, corner of Main Street and The Mall, tel. 066/915-1061).

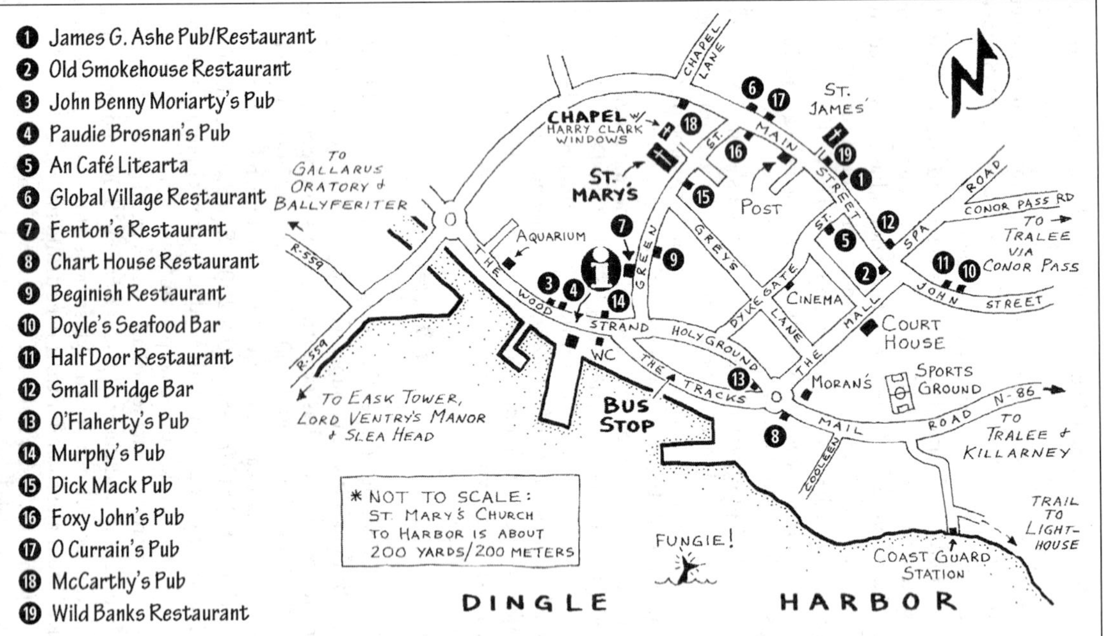

Dingle Restaurants
1 James G. Ashe Pub/Restaurant
2 Old Smokehouse Restaurant
3 John Benny Moriarty's Pub
4 Paudie Brosnan's Pub
5 An Café Litearta
6 Global Village Restaurant
7 Fenton's Restaurant
8 Chart House Restaurant
9 Beginish Restaurant
10 Doyle's Seafood Bar
11 Half Door Restaurant
12 Small Bridge Bar
13 O'Flaherty's Pub
14 Murphy's Pub
15 Dick Mack Pub
16 Foxy John's Pub
17 O Currain's Pub
18 McCarthy's Pub
19 Wild Banks Restaurant
To Gallarus Oratory & Ballyferiter
R-559
To Eask Tower, Lord Ventry's Manor & Slea Head
Chapel Lane
Chapel w/ Harry Clark Windows
St. Mary's
Aquarium
The Wood
Strand
WC
Bus Stop
Green
Grey's
St.
Main Street
Post
St. James'
Holy Ground
The Tracks
Dyke Gate Lane
Cinema
St.
The Mall
Moran's
Court House
Sports Ground
Spa Road
Conor Pass Rd
To Tralee via Conor Pass
John Street
N-86
Mail Road
To Tralee & Killarney
Coolleen
Coast Guard Station
Trail to Lighthouse
Fungie!
* Not to scale: St. Mary's Church to Harbor is about 200 yards/200 meters
Dingle Harbor

John Benny Moriarty's is a waterfront pub dishing up traditional Irish fare (food daily 12:30–21:30, music after 21:30, The Pier). **Paudie Brosnan's** pub, a few doors down, has fresh mussels.

An Café Litearta, a likeable eatery hidden behind an inviting bookstore, serves tasty soup and sandwiches to a good-natured crowd of Gaelic-speakers (Mon–Sat 10:00–18:00, closed Sun, tel. 066/915-2204, Dykegate Street).

At the **Global Village Restaurant,** Martin Bealin concocts his favorite dishes, gleaned from his travels around the world. It's an eclectic, healthy, meat-eater's place popular with locals for its interesting cuisine (€18–24 dinners, good salads and great Thai curry, daily 17:00–21:30, top of Main Street, tel. 066/915-2325 or 087/917-7700).

Fenton's is a good place for seafood meals with a memorable apple-and-berry-crumble dessert (€18–27 main courses, 3-course meals-€27, early-bird specials before 19:00, Tue–Sun 18:00–21:30, closed Mon, reservations smart, on Green Street down the hill below the church, tel. 066/915-2172 or 087/248-2487).

The **Stone House Restaurant**, on the Slea Head loop, offers good meals in a great atmosphere. It's a worthy choice for those looking for an out-of-the-way dinner and a 20-minute scenic drive. It's right across the road from the Dunbeg fort, at mile 7.7 on the "Dingle Peninsula Circular Tour"—see page 864 (open Wed–Mon 12:30–15:30 for €8–12 lunches and 18:30–22:00 for €17–23 dinners, closed Tue, dinner reservations essential, tel. 066/915-9970).

Dingle's Five Fancy Restaurants

Chart House Restaurant serves contemporary cuisine with a menu dictated by what's fresh and seasonal. Settle back into the sharp, clean, lantern-lit, harborside ambience (€28 dinners, June–Sept daily 18:30–22:00, Oct–May closed Tue, at roundabout at base of town, tel. 066/915-2255).

Beginish Restaurant, serving modern European fare with a fish forte in an elegant Georgian setting, is probably your best dressy splurge meal in town (€21–29 plates, Wed–Sun 18:00–21:30, closed Mon–Tue, you'll be glad you reserved ahead, Green Street, tel. 066/915-1588).

Wild Banks Restaurant is named for nearby fishing grounds, and Chef Laura Walker does a great job preparing the local catch. There's a nice wine selection, and the white-chocolate crème brûlée dessert gets raves (€25–29 dinners, €24 early-bird 3-course meals before 20:00, Tue–Sun 18:00-21:30, closed Mon, halfway down Main Street, tel. 066/915-2888).

Two of Dingle's long-established top-notch restaurants—**Doyle's Seafood Bar** (more famous, with excellent seafood and service, tel. 066/915-1174) and **The Half Door** (heartier portions, also open for lunch Mon–Sat 12:30–14:00, tel. 066/915-1600)—are neighbors on John Street. They're in the guidebooks for good reason, and therefore filled with tourists. Both have the same dinner hours (Mon–Sat 18:00–21:30, closed Sun), offer an early-bird special (3-course meal-€36, 18:00–19:00), and take reservations (wise).

TRANSPORTATION CONNECTIONS

The nearest train station is in Tralee, 30 miles away.

From Dingle by bus to: Galway (5/day, 6.5 hrs), **Dublin** (5/day, 8 hrs), **Rosslare** (2/day, 9 hrs), **Tralee** (6/day, 75 min, €9); fewer departures on Sundays. Most bus trips out of Dingle require at least one or two (easy) transfers. Dingle has no bus station and only one bus stop, on the waterfront behind the Super Valu supermarket (bus info tel. 01/830-2222, or call Tralee station at 066/712-3566).

Airports

Kerry Airport, a 45-minute drive from Dingle town (just off the main road from Killarney to Tralee), offers connecting flights via **Dublin** on Aer Arann, **London Stansted** on Ryanair (www.ryanair.com), and even **Frankfurt-Hahn** on Ryanair (tel. 066/976-4644, www.kerryairport.ie).

Shannon Airport, the major airport in Western Ireland, has direct flights to **Dublin** (2–3/day, 30 min) and **London** (6/day, 1 hr). Ryanair and Aer Lingus (www.aerlingus.ie) fly out of Shannon. Airport info: tel. 061/471-444. Shannon Airport TI: tel. 061/471-664 (daily 6:30–18:00, June–Sept until 19:00). Shannon Airport also has easy bus connections to **Limerick** (nearly hrly, 1 hr, can continue to Tralee—2 hrs, and Dingle—1.25 hrs more), **Ennis** (nearly hrly, 45 min), and **Galway** (every 2 hrs, 2 hrs). Bus info: tel. 061/313-333, www.buseireann.ie.

Dingle Peninsula Circular Tour

A sight worth ▲▲▲, the Dingle Peninsula loop trip is about 30 miles long (must go in clockwise direction). It's easy by car, or it's a demanding three hours by bike—if you don't stop.

While you can take the basic guided tour of the peninsula (see "Tours," page 871), the self-guided route below makes it unnecessary. A fancy map is also unnecessary, if you follow my instructions.

Self-Guided Tour by Bike or Car

I've keyed in mileage to help locate points of interest. If you're driving, as you leave Dingle, reset your odometer at Oceanworld. Even if you get off track or are biking, you can calculate distances between points from my mileage key. To get the most out of your circle trip, read through this entire section before departing. Then go step by step (staying on R559 and following The Slea Head Drive signs). Roads are very congested in August.

The Dingle Peninsula is 10 miles wide and runs 40 miles from Tralee to Slea Head. The top of its mountainous spine is Mount Brandon—at 3,130 feet, the second-tallest mountain in Ireland. While only tiny villages lie west of Dingle town, the peninsula is home to 500,000 sheep.

Leave Dingle town west along the waterfront (0.0 miles at Oceanworld). There's an eight-foot tide here. The seaweed was used to make formerly worthless land arable. (Seaweed is a natural source of potash—organic farming before it was trendy.) Across the water, the fancy Milltown House B&B (with flags) was Robert Mitchum's home for a year during the filming of *Ryan's Daughter*. Look for the narrow mouth of this blind harbor (where Fungie frolics) and the Ring of Kerry beyond that. Dingle Bay is so hidden, ships needed the tower (1847) on the hill to find its mouth.

0.4 miles: At the roundabout, turn left over the bridge. The hardware store building on the right was a corn-grinding mill in the 18th century.

0.8 miles: The Milestone B&B is named for the stone pillar (*gallaun* in Gaelic) in its front yard. This may have been a prehistoric grave or a boundary marker between two tribes. The stone goes down as far as it sticks up. The peninsula, literally an open-air museum, is dotted with more than 2,000 such monuments dating from the Neolithic Age (4000 B.C.) through early Christian times. Another stone pillar stands in the field across the street in the direction of the yellow manor house of Lord Ventry (in the distance).

Lord Ventry, whose family came to Dingle as post–Cromwell War landlords in 1666, built this mansion in about 1750. Today, it houses an all-Gaelic boarding school for 140 high-school girls.

As you drive past the Ventry estate, you'll pass palms, magnolias, and exotic flora introduced to Dingle by Lord Ventry. The Gulf Stream causes the mild climate (it never snows), which supports subtropical plants. Consequently, fuchsias—imported from Chile and spreading like weeds—line the roads all over the peninsula and redden the countryside from June to September. And over 100 inches of rain a year give this area its "40 shades of green."

Ten yards past the Tobair Michael B&B (on left) a tiny white wall with a blue marker marks the St. Michael's Well. A

Dingle Peninsula Circular Tour

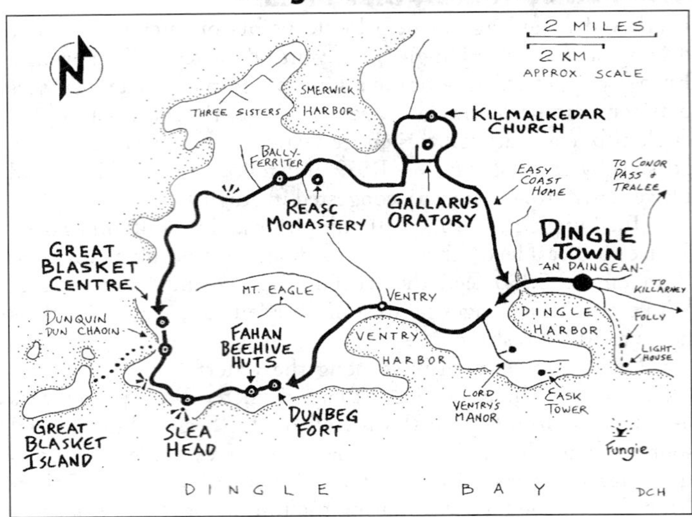

Christianized Celtic holy well, it's still the site of a Mass on St. Martin's day. St. Martin was the Christian antidote to pagan holy places. Generally, when you see something dedicated to him, it sits upon something that pre-Christian people worshipped.

3 miles: Stay off the "soft margin" as you enjoy views of Ventry Bay, its four-mile-long beach (to your right as you face the water), and distant Skellig Michael, which you'll see all along this part of the route. Skellig Michael—jutting up like France's Mont St. Michel—contains the rocky remains of an 6th-century monastic settlement. Next to it is a smaller island, Little Skellig—a breeding ground for gannets (seagull-like birds with 6-foot wingspans). In 1866, the first transatlantic cable was laid from nearby Valentia Island to Newfoundland. It was in use until 1965. Mount Eagle (1,660 feet), rising across the bay, marks the end of Ireland. In the village of Ventry, Gaelic is the first language. The large hall at the end of the village is used as a classroom, where big-city students come on field trips to be immersed in the Gaelic language.

4.7 miles: The rushes on either side of the road are the kind used to make the local thatched roofs. Thatching, which nearly died out because of the fire danger, is more popular now that anti-flame treatments are available. Black-and-white magpies fly.

5.3 miles: The Irish football star Paidi O Se (Paddy O'Shea) is a household name in Ireland. He now trains the Kerry team and runs the pub on the left. (Easy beach access from here.)

5.6 miles: The blue house hiding in the trees 100 yards off the road on the left (view through the white gate) was kept cozy by Tom Cruise and Nicole Kidman during the filming of *Far and Away.*

6.6 miles: *Taisteal go Mall* means "go slowly"; there's a red-colored, two-room schoolhouse on the right (20 students, 2 teachers). On the left is the small Celtic and Prehistoric Museum, a strange private collection of prehistoric artifacts with no real connection to Dingle (overpriced at €5, daily 10:00–17:00).

6.9 miles: The circular mound on the right is a late-Stone Age ring fort. In 500 B.C., it was a petty Celtic chieftain's headquarters, a stone-and-earth stockade filled with little stone houses. These survived untouched through the centuries because of superstitious beliefs that they were "fairy forts." While this is unexcavated, recent digging has shown that people have lived on this peninsula since 4000 B.C.

7.3 miles: Look ahead up Mount Eagle at the patchwork of stone-fenced fields.

7.7 miles: Dunbeg Fort, a series of defensive ramparts and ditches around a central *clochan,* though ready to fall into the sea, is open to tourists. There are no carvings to be seen, but the small *(beg)* fort *(dun)* is dramatic (€2, daily 9:30–20:00, descriptive handout). Forts like this are the most important relics left from Ireland's Iron Age (500 B.C. to A.D. 500). Since erosion will someday take this fort, it has been excavated.

Along the road, you'll see a new stone-roofed house built to blend in with the landscape and the region's ancient rock-slab architecture (A.D. 2000). It's the Stone House Restaurant, serving good lunches (daily 12:30–15:30, tel. 066/915-9970).

7.8 miles: Just 50 yards up the hill is a cottage abandoned by a family named Kavanaugh 150 years ago, during the famine. It still contains their original furniture. Gabriel Kavanaugh proudly displays his Kerry livestock in an adjacent pen, including some local red deer—once plentiful, but now rare (€3, tel. 066/915-6241).

8.2 miles: A group of beehive huts, or *clochans,* is a short walk uphill (€2, daily 9:30–19:00, WC). These mysterious stone igloos, which cluster together within a circular wall, are a better sight than the similar group of beehive huts a mile down the road. Look over the water for more Skellig views.

Farther on, you'll ford a stream. There has never been a bridge here; this bit of road—nicknamed the "upside-down bridge"—was designed as a ford.

9.2 miles: Pull off to the left at this second group of beehive huts. Look downhill at the scant remains of the scant home that was burned as the movie equivalent of Lord Ventry tried to evict the tenants in *Far and Away*. Even without Hollywood, this is a bleak and godforsaken land. Look above at the patches of land slowly made into farmland by the inhabitants of this westernmost piece of Europe. Rocks were cleared and piled into fences. Sand and seaweed were laid on the clay, and in time, it was good for grass. The created land, if at all tillable, was generally used for growing potatoes; otherwise, it was only good for grazing. Much has fallen out of use now. Look behind at the Ring of Kerry in the distance, and ahead at the Blasket Islands.

9.9 miles: At Slea Head, marked by a crucifix, a pullout, and great views of the Blasket Islands (described on page 871), you turn the corner on this tour. On stormy days, the waves are "racing in like white horses."

10.4 miles: Pull into the little parking lot (at Dunchaoin sign) to view the Blaskets and Dunmore Head (the westernmost point in Europe) and review the roadside map (which traces your route) posted in the parking lot. The scattered village of Dunquin has many ruined rock homes abandoned during the famine. Some are fixed up, as this is a popular place these days for summer homes. You can see more good examples of land reclamation, patch by patch, climbing up the hillside. Mount Eagle was the first bit of land Charles Lindberg saw after crossing the Atlantic on his way to Paris in 1927. Villagers here were as excited as he was—they had never seen anything so big in the air. Ahead, down a road on the left, a plaque celebrates the 30th anniversary of the filming of *Ryan's Daughter*.

11.9 miles: The Blasket Islanders had no church or cemetery on the island. This was their cemetery. The famous Blasket storyteller Peig Sayers (1873–1958) is buried in the center. At the next intersection, drive down the little lane that leads left (100 yards) to a small stone marker commemorating the 1588 shipwreck of the *Santa Maria de la Rosa* of the Spanish Armada. Below that is the often tempestuous Dunquin Harbor, from which the Blasket ferry departs. Island farmers—who, on a calm day, could row across in 20 minutes—would dock here and hike 12 miles into Dingle to sell their produce. When transporting sheep, farmers would lash the sheep's pointy little hoofs together and place them carefully upside down in the currach—so they wouldn't puncture the frail little craft's canvas skin.

12 miles: Back on the main road, follow signs to the Great Blasket Centre.

13.5 miles: Leave the Slea Head Road left for the Great Blasket Centre (described on page 872).

13.7 miles: Back at the turnoff, head left (sign to Louis Mulcahy Pottery).

14.5 miles: Passing land that was never reclaimed, think of the work it took to pick out the stones, pile them into fences, and bring up sand and seaweed to nourish the clay and make soil for growing potatoes. Look over the water to the island aptly named the "Sleeping Giant"—see his hand resting happily on his beer belly.

15.1 miles: The view is spectacular. Ahead, on the right, study the top fields, untouched since the planting of 1845, when the potatoes didn't grow, but rotted in the ground. The faint vertical ridges of the potato beds can still be seen—a reminder of the famine (easier to see a bit later). Before the famine, 40,000 people lived on this peninsula. After the famine, the population was so small that there was never again a need to farm so high up. Today, only 10,000 live on the peninsula. Coast downhill. The distant hills are crowned by lookout forts built back when Britain expected Napoleon to invade.

18.3 miles: Ballyferriter (Baile an Fheirtearaigh), established by a Norman family in the 12th century, is the largest town on this side of Dingle. The pubs serve grub, and the old schoolhouse is a museum (€2, Easter–Sept daily 10:00–16:30, closed off-season). The early-Christian cross next to the schoolhouse looks real. Tap it...it's fiberglass—a prop from *Ryan's Daughter*.

19.1 miles: At the T junction, signs direct you to Dingle ("An Daingean, 11 km") either way. Go left, via Gallarus (and still following Slea Head Way). Take a right over the bridge, still following signs to Gallarus.

19.5 miles: Just beyond the bridge, you'll pass the Tigh Bhric pub and market (great pub-grub lunches, tel. 066/915-6325). Just a few yards before the sign to Mainistir Riaise (Reasc monastic enclosure), detour right up the lane. After 0.2 miles (the unsigned turnout on your right), you'll find the scant remains of the walled Reasc Monastery (dating from the 6th–12th centuries). The inner wall divided the community into sections for prayer and business (cottage industries helped support the monastery). In 1975, only the stone pillar was visible, as the entire site was buried. The layer of black felt marks where the original rocks stop and the excavators' reconstruction begins. The stone pillar is Celtic (c. 500 B.C.). When the Christians arrived in the 5th century, they didn't throw out the Celtic society. Instead, they carved a Maltese-type cross over the Celtic scrollwork. The square building was an oratory (church—you'll see an intact oratory at the next stop). The round buildings would have been *clochans*—those stone, igloo-type dwellings. The monastery ran cottage industries with a double-duty kiln. Just outside the wall (opposite the oratory, past the duplex *clochan*, at the bottom end), find a stone hole with a passage facing the southwest wind. This was the kiln—fanned by the wind, it was used for cooking and drying grain. Locals would bring their grain to be dried and ground, and the monks would keep a tithe. With the arrival of the Normans in the 12th century, these small religious communities were replaced by relatively big-time state and church governments.

20 miles: Return to the main road, continue to the right.

21.1 miles: At the big hotel (Smerwick Harbor), turn left, following the sign to Gallarus Oratory.

21.8 miles: At the big building (with camping sign), go right and follow the sign for the oratory where you'll find a small tourist center—with a shop, WC, and video theater. For €3, you get a 17-minute video overview of Dingle Peninsula's historic sights.

The Gallarus Oratory, built about 1,300 years ago, is one of Ireland's best-preserved early-Christian churches. Shaped like an upturned boat, its finely fitted drystone walls are still waterproof. Notice the holes once used to secure covering at the door and the fine alternating stonework on the corners.

From the oratory, the little lane leads directly up and over the hill, home to Dingle. To complete this tour, however, you should return to the main road and continue (following sign to An Mhuirioch).

22.9 miles: Turn right at the fork and immediately take a right (at the blue shop sign) at the next fork. Pass a 19th-century church.

24.2 miles: The ruined Kilmalkedar church was the Norman center of worship for this end of the peninsula. It was built when England replaced the old monastic settlements in an attempt to centralize their rule. The 12th-century Irish Romanesque church is surrounded by a densely populated graveyard (which, over the centuries, has risen noticeably above the surrounding fields). In front of the church, you'll find the oldest medieval tombs, a stately early-Christian cross (substantially buried by the rising graveyard and therefore oddly proportioned), and a much older ogham stone. This stone, which had already stood here 900 years when the church was built, is notched with the mysterious, Morse-code-type ogham script used from the 3rd to 7th centuries. It marked a grave, indicating this was a pre-Christian holy spot. The hole was drilled through here centuries ago as a place where people would come to seal a deal—standing on the graves of their ancestors and in front of the house of God, they'd "swear to God" by touching fingers through this stone. You can still use this to renew your marriage vows (free, B.Y.O. spouse). The church fell into ruin during the Reformation. As Catholic worship went underground until the early 19th century, Kilmalkedar was never rebuilt.

24.6 miles: Continue uphill, overlooking the water. You'll pass another "fairy fort" (Ciher Dorgan) dating back to 1000 B.C. (free, go through the rusty "kissing gate").

25.5 miles: At the crest of the hill, enjoy a three-mile coast back into Dingle town (in the direction of the Eask Tower).

28.3 miles: *Tog Bog E* means "take it easy." At the T junction, turn left. Then turn right at the roundabout.

29 miles: You're back into Dingle town. Well done.

TOURS

▲▲Sciuird Archaeology Tours—Sciuird (SCREW-id; Irish for "excursion") tours are offered by a father-son team with Dingle history—and a knack for sharing it—in their blood. Tim Collins, who's a retired Dingle police officer, and his son Michael give serious, 2.5-hour minibus tours (€20, departing at 10:30 and 14:00, depending upon demand). Drop by the Kirrary B&B (at Dykegate and Grey's Lane) or call 066/915-1606 to put your name on the list. Call early. Tours fill quickly in summer. Off-season (Oct–April), you may have to call back to see if the necessary five people signed up to make a bus go. While skipping the folk legends and the famous sights (such as Slea Head), your guide will drive down tiny farm roads (the Gaelic word for road literally means "cow path"), over hedges, and up ridges to hidden Celtic forts, mysterious stone tombs, and forgotten castles with sweeping seaside views. The running commentary gives an intimate peek into the history of Dingle. Sit as close to the driver as possible to get all the information. They do two completely different tours: west (Gallarus Oratory) and east (Minard Castle and a wedge tomb). I enjoyed both. Dress for the weather. In a gale storm with horizontal winds, Tim kept saying, "You'll survive it."

More Minibus Tours—Moran's Tour, which does a quickie minibus tour around the peninsula, offers meager narration and a short stop at the Gallarus Oratory (€17 to Slea Head, normally May–Sept at 10:00 and 14:00 from Dingle TI, 2.5 hrs; Moran's is at Esso station at roundabout, tel. 066/915-1155 or mobile 087-275-3333). There are usually enough seats, though it's best to book a day ahead. But if no one shows up, consider a private Moran taxi trip around the peninsula (€70 for 4 people, cabbie narrates 2.5-hour ride).

Eco-Cruises—Dingle Marine Eco Tours offers a 2.5-hour, birds-and-rocks boat tour of the peninsula. The guided tour sails either east toward Minard Castle or west toward the Blasket Islands (€25, April–Sept, departs 16:00, weather permitting, office around corner from TI, tel. 066/915-0768).

Blasket Islands

This rugged group of six islands off the tip of Dingle Peninsula seems particularly close to the soul of Ireland. The population of Great Blasket Island, as many as 160 people, dwindled until the government moved the last handful of residents to the mainland in 1953. Life here was hard. Each family had a cow, a few sheep, and a plot of potatoes. They cut their peat from the high ridge and harvested fish from the sea. There was no priest, pub, or doctor. These people formed the most traditional Irish community of the 20th century—the symbol of antique Gaelic culture.

A special closeness to an island—combined with a knack for vivid storytelling—is inspirational. From this primitive but proud fishing/farming community came three writers of international repute, whose Gaelic work—basically tales of life on Great Blasket—has been translated into many languages. You'll find *Peig* (by Peig Sayers), *Twenty Years a-Growing* (Maurice O'Sullivan), and *The Islander* (Thomas O'Crohan) in shops everywhere.

In the summer, there's a café and hostel (open May–Sept, mobile 086-852-2321) on Great Blasket Island, but it's little more than a ghost town overrun with rabbits on a peaceful, grassy, three-mile-long poem.

Getting to the Blasket Islands

The 40-passenger Blasket ferry runs hourly, and in summer, every half hour, depending on weather and demand (€20 round-trip, April–mid-Oct 10:00–18:00, no boats mid-Oct–March). There may be a bus from Dingle town to Dunquin—leaving in the morning and picking up in the late afternoon—coordinated with the ferry schedule (also €17 taxi service by Moran, tel. 066/915-1155; Dunquin ferry tel. 066/915-6422). Dunquin has a fine hostel (tel. 066/915-6121).

In summer, a fast, 12-passenger boat called the *Peig Sayers* runs between Dingle town and the Blaskets. The ride (which may include a quick look at Fungie) traces the spectacular coastline all the way to Slea Head, in a boat designed to slice expertly through the ocean chop. Because of the tricky landing at Great Blasket's primitive and tiny boat ramp, any substantial swell can make actually going ashore impossible (€30 same-day round-trip, departs from the sailing pier in Dingle at 9:00, 11:00, 13:00, and 15:00, includes 40-min ride with free time to explore island; or €70 overnight trip, includes dinner, a bed in the island's hostel, and breakfast; for info, call Mary at 066/915-1344 or mobile 087-672-6100).

Great Blasket Centre

This ▲▲ state-of-the-art Blasket and Gaelic heritage center gives visitors the best look possible at the language, literature, and way of life of the Blasket Islanders. See the fine 20-minute video (shows on the half hour), hear the sounds, read the poems, browse through old photos, and then gaze out the big windows at those rugged islands, and imagine. Even if you never got past limericks, the poetry of these people—so pure and close to each other and nature—will have you dipping your pen into the cry of the birds (€3.50, Easter–Oct daily 10:00–18:00, July–Aug until 19:00, closed Nov–Easter, cafeteria, on the mainland facing the islands, well-signposted, tel. 066/915-6444). Visit this center before visiting the islands.

ROME

(Roma)

Rome is magnificent and brutal at the same time. Your ears will ring. If you're careless, you'll be run down or pickpocketed. You'll be frustrated by the kind of chaos that only an Italian can understand. You may even come to believe Mussolini was a necessary evil.

But Rome is required, and if your hotel provides a comfortable refuge; if you pace yourself; if you accept—and even partake in—the siesta plan; if you're well-organized for sightseeing; and if you protect yourself and your valuables with extra caution and discretion, you'll do fine.

Two thousand years ago, the word Rome meant civilization itself. Everything was either civilized (part of the Roman Empire, Latin- or Greek-speaking) or barbarian. Today, Rome is Italy's political capital, the capital of Catholicism, and the center of the ancient world, littered with evocative remains. As you peel through its fascinating and jumbled layers, you'll find Rome's buildings, cats, laundry, traffic, and 2.6 million people endlessly entertaining. And then, of course, there are its magnificent sights.

Tour St. Peter's, the greatest church on earth, and scale Michelangelo's 328-foot-tall dome, the world's largest. Learn something about eternity by touring the huge Vatican Museum. You'll find the story of creation—bright as the day it was painted—in the restored Sistine Chapel. Do the "Caesar Shuffle" through ancient Rome's Forum and Colosseum. Savor Europe's most sumptuous building, the Borghese Gallery, and take an early evening "Dolce Vita Stroll" down the Via del Corso with Rome's beautiful people. Enjoy an after-dark walk from Campo de' Fiori to the Spanish Steps, lacing together Rome's Baroque and bubbly nightspots.

Planning Your Time

For most travelers, Rome is best done quickly. It's a great city, but it's exhausting. Time is normally short, and Italy is more charming elsewhere. To "do" Rome in a day, consider it as a side-trip from Orvieto or Florence, and maybe before the night train to Venice. Crazy as that sounds, if all you have is a day, it's a great one.

Rome in a day: Vatican (two hours in the museum and Sistine Chapel and one hour in St. Peter's), taxi over the river to the Pantheon (picnic on its steps), then hike over Capitol Hill, through the Forum, and to the Colosseum. Have dinner on Campo de' Fiori and dessert on Piazza Navona.

Rome in two to three days: Day one, do the "Caesar Shuffle" from the Colosseum and Forum over Capitol Hill to the Pantheon. After a siesta, join the locals strolling from Piazza del Popolo to the Spanish Steps (see my self-guided "Dolce Vita Stroll," page 933). Have dinner near your hotel.

On the second day, see the Vatican City (St. Peter's, climb the dome, and tour the Vatican Museum). Spend the evening walking from Campo de' Fiori—an atmospheric place for dinner—to the Trevi Fountain and Spanish Steps (see "Night Walk Across Rome," page 935). With a third day, add the Borghese Gallery (reservations required) and the National Museum of Rome.

ORIENTATION

Sprawling Rome actually feels manageable once you get to know it. The old core, with most of the tourist sights, sits in a diamond formed by the train station (in the east), the Vatican (west), the Borghese Gardens (north), and the Colosseum (south). The Tiber River runs through the diamond from north to south. It takes about an hour to walk from the train station to the Vatican.

Consider Rome in these layers:

The ancient city had a million people. The best of the classical sights stand in a line from the Colosseum to the Pantheon (see map on page 892).

Medieval Rome was little more than a hobo camp of 50,000—thieves, mean dogs, and the pope, whose legitimacy required a Roman address. The medieval city, a colorful tangle of lanes, lies between the Pantheon and the river.

Window-shoppers' Rome twinkles with nightlife and ritzy shopping near Rome's main drag, Via del Corso—in the triangle formed by Piazza del Popolo, Piazza Venezia, and the Spanish Steps. (See Dolce Vita Stroll map, page 934.)

Vatican City, west of the Tiber, is a compact world of its own with two great, huge sights: St. Peter's Basilica and the Vatican Museum. (See Vatican City map, page 911.)

Trastevere, the seedy, colorful, wrong-side-of-the-river neighborhood/village, is Rome at its crustiest—and perhaps most "Roman." (See Trastevere map, page 918.)

Baroque Rome is an overleaf that embellishes great squares throughout the town with fountains and church facades.

Since no one is allowed to build taller than St. Peter's dome, the city has no modern skyline. Until last year, the Tiber River was ignored. After the last floods (1870), the banks were built up very high and Rome turned its back on its naughty river. It was not until 2003 that a boat service was launched, giving the river a bit more attention.

Tourist Information

While Rome has several main tourist information offices, the dozen or so TI kiosks scattered around the town at major tourist centers are handy and just as helpful. If all you need is a map, forget the TI and get one at your hotel or a newsstand kiosk.

You'll find helpful tourist offices—especially if they're not too busy—at the airport (daily 8:00–19:00, tel. 06-6595-6074) and at the train station (daily 8:00–21:00; near track 3, accessible from platforms or lobby, marked *Informazioni Turistiche/Tourist Info,* tel. 06-4890-6300, combined with travel agency).

Smaller TIs (daily 9:00–18:00) include kiosks near the Forum (on Piazza del Tempio della Pace), at Via del Corso (on Largo Goldoni), in Trastevere (on Piazza Sonnino), on Via Nazionale (at Palazzo delle Esposizioni), at Castel Sant' Angelo, and at Santa Maria Maggiore. For more information, call 06-3600-4399 (daily 9:00–19:00).

At any TI, ask for a city map, a listing of sights and hours (in the free *Museums of Rome* booklet), and *Passepartout,* the free seasonal entertainment guide for evening events and fun. Don't book rooms through a TI; you'll save money by booking direct.

The tourism promotion office, near Piazza della Repubblica's huge fountain, covers the city and the region. It's a five-minute walk out the front of the train station (Mon–Sat 9:00–19:00, closed Sun, Via Parigi 5, free Internet access, but only to sites regarding Rome tourism, www.romaturismo.com, tel. 06-360-64399). It's air-conditioned and less crowded than the TIs but more focused on promotion than information, and therefore less helpful. It does have seats and a study table.

Roma c'è is a cheap little weekly entertainment guide with a useful English section (at the back) on musical events (new edition every Thu, sold at newsstands for €1, www.romace.it, Web site in Italian).

Rome Overview

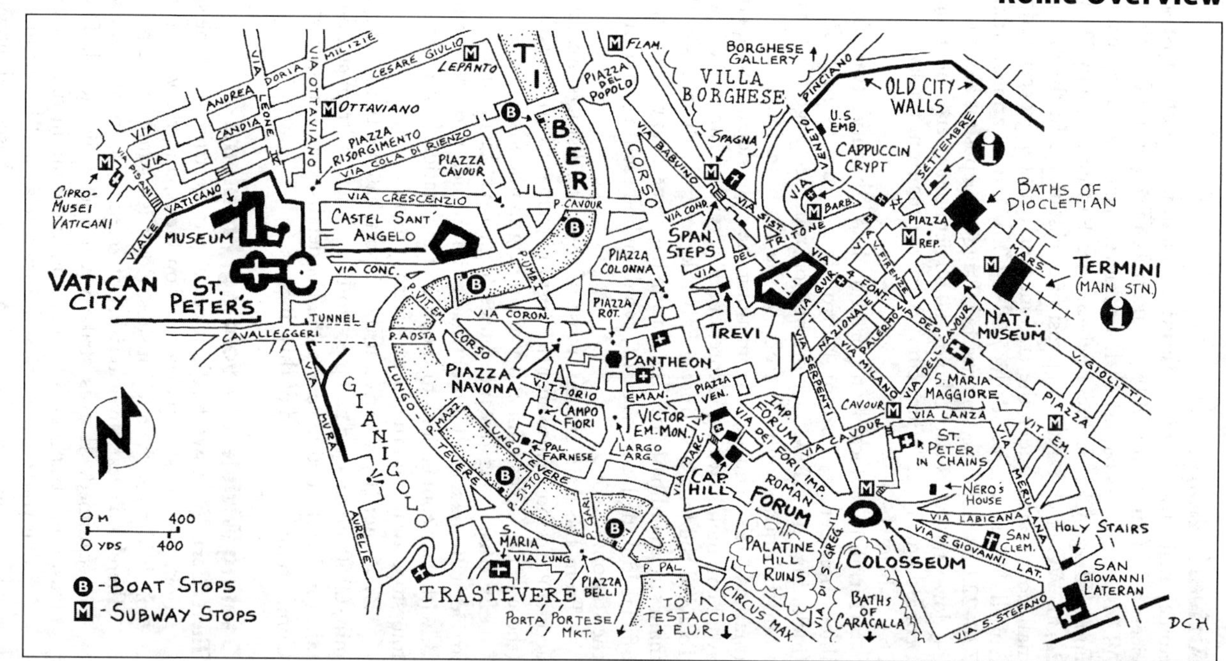

Arrival in Rome

Rome's main train station, **Termini,** is a minefield of tourist services: a TI (daily 8:00–21:00), train info office (daily 7:00–21:00), ATMs, late-hours banks, 24-hour thievery, and the handy, cheery Food Village Chef Express Self-Service Ristorante (daily 11:00–22:30, WC at entrance, near east end of station). In the modern mall downstairs, under the station, you'll find a grocery (oddly named "Drug Store," daily 7:00–24:00) and pharmacy (daily 7:30–22:00, public showers nearby). Luggage deposit is along track 24, downstairs (€3.80 for 5 hours, €0.60 per hour after). The train to Leonardo da Vinci/"Fiumicino" Airport runs from tracks 25 and 26 (see below).

Termini is a local transportation hub. The city's two Metro lines intersect at Termini Metro station (downstairs). Buses (including the ATAC city orientation tour, see page 890) leave from the square right in front of the main station hall. Taxis (marked "Taxi") queue in front along the right side of the square; avoid con men hawking "express taxi" services in unmarked cars. To avoid the long taxi line, simply hike out past the buses to the main street and hail one. The station has some sleazy sharks with official-looking business cards; avoid anybody selling anything at the station.

From the train station, most of my hotel listings are easily accessible by foot (those near the Termini train station) or by Metro (those in the Colosseum and Vatican neighborhoods).

By Bus: Long-distance buses (e.g., from Siena and Assisi) arrive at Rome's small **Tiburtina** station, which is on Metro line B, with easy connections to the main train station (a straight shot four stops away) and the entire Metro system.

By Plane: If you arrive at the airport, catch a train (2/hr, 30 min, €9.50, credit card accepted) to Rome's central train station or take (or share) a taxi to your hotel. For details, see "Transportation Connections" at the end of this chapter.

Dealing With (and Avoiding) Problems

Theft Alert: With sweet-talking con artists meeting you at the station, well-dressed pickpockets on buses, and thieving gangs of children at the ancient sites, Rome is a gauntlet of rip-offs. There's no great physical risk, but green or sloppy tourists will be scammed. Thieves strike when you're distracted. Don't trust kind strangers. Keep nothing important in your pockets. Assume you're being stalked. (Then relax and have fun.) Be most on guard while boarding and leaving buses and subways. Thieves crowd the door, then stop and turn while others crowd and push from behind. The sneakiest thieves are well-dressed businessmen (generally with something in their hands); lately

Greater Rome

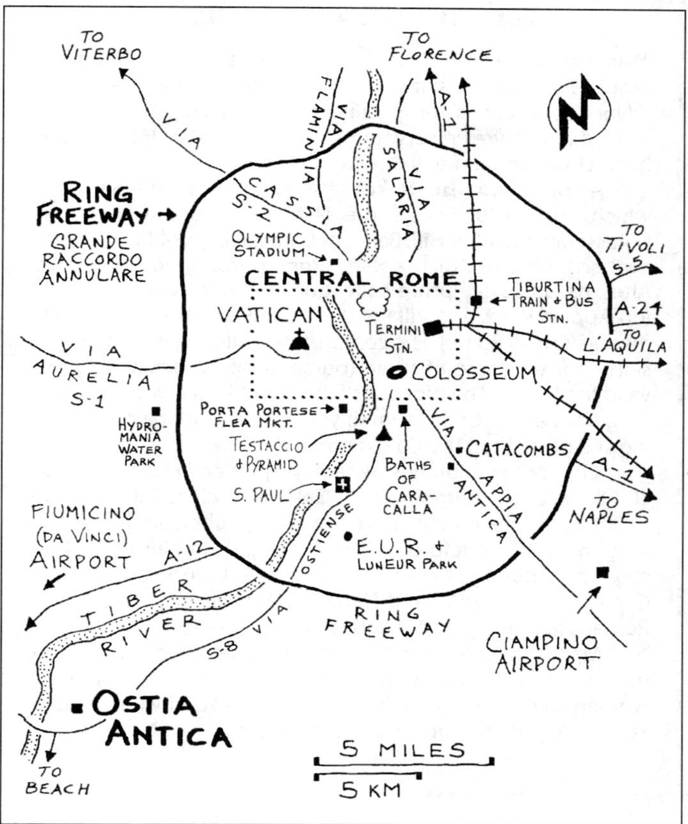

many are posing as tourists with fanny packs, cameras, and even Rick Steves guidebooks! Scams abound: Don't give your wallet to self-proclaimed "police" who stop you on the street, warn you about counterfeit (or drug) money, and ask to see your wallet. If a bank machine eats your ATM card, see if there's a thin plastic insert with a tongue hanging out that thieves use to extract it.

If you know what to look out for, the gangs of children picking the pockets and handbags of naive tourists are no threat but an interesting, albeit sad, spectacle. Gangs of city-stained children (sometimes as young as 8–10 years old), too young to be prosecuted but old enough to rip you off, troll the tourist crowds around the Colosseum, Forum, Piazza Repubblica, and train and Metro stations. Watch them target tourists who are overloaded with bags or distracted with a

Tips on Sightseeing in Rome

Museums: Plan ahead. The marvelous Borghese Gallery requires reservations; it's safest to make reservations well in advance of your trip (for specifics, see page 905). The only other sight that requires reservations—Nero's Golden House—has been closed indefinitely due to water damage.

A special **combo-ticket** (also called Archeologia Card), which costs €20, covers the National Museum of Rome, Colosseum, Palatine Hill, Baths of Caracalla, Crypt Balbi (medieval art), Museum of the Bath (Roman inscriptions), Palazzo Altemps (so-so sculpture collection), Tomb of Cecilia Metella (on Appian Way), and Villa of the Quintilli (barren Roman villa on outskirts of Rome). The combo-ticket allows you to see nine sights for the price of three (purchase at participating sites, valid for 7 days). The big plus of this ticket is that you avoid the long lines at the Colosseum (if you purchase it at a participating site other than the Colosseum).

Churches: Churches generally open early (around 7:00), close for lunch (roughly 12:00–15:00), and close late (around 19:00). Kamikaze tourists maximize their sightseeing hours by visiting churches before 9:00 and seeing the major sights that stay open during the siesta (St. Peter's, Colosseum, Forum, Capitol Hill Museum, and National Museum of Rome) while Romans are taking it cool and easy.

Many churches have "modest dress" requirements, which means no bare shoulders, miniskirts, or shorts—for men, women, or children. This dress code is only strictly enforced at St. Peter's and St. Paul's Outside the Walls.

video camera. The kids look like beggars and hold up newspapers or cardboard signs to confuse their victims. They scram like stray cats if you're onto them. A fast-fingered mother with a baby is often nearby. The terrace above the bus stop near the Colosseum Metro stop is a fine place to watch the action and maybe even pick up a few moves of your own.

Reporting Losses: To report lost or stolen passports and documents or to make an insurance claim, you must file a police report (at the train station with Polizia at track 1 or with Carabinieri at track 20; offices are also at Piazza Venezia). To replace a passport, file the police report, then go to your embassy (see below). To report lost or stolen credit cards, see page 11.

Embassies: The U.S. Embassy is on Via Vittorio Veneto 119/A (Mon–Fri 8:30–13:00 & 14:00–17:30, closed Sat–Sun, tel. 06-46741, www.usembassy.it) and the Canadian Embassy is at Via Zara 30 (tel. 06-445-981, www.canada.it).

Emergency Numbers: Police—tel. 113. Ambulance—tel. 118.

Hit and Run: Walk with extreme caution. Scooters don't need to stop at red lights, and even cars exercise what drivers call the "logical option" of not stopping if they see no oncoming traffic. As noisy gasoline-powered scooters are replaced by electric ones, they'll be quieter (hooray) but more dangerous for pedestrians. Follow locals like a shadow when you cross a street (or spend a good part of your visit stranded on curbs). When you do cross alone, don't be a deer in the headlights. Find a gap in the traffic and walk with confidence while making eye contact with the approaching driver—they will slow down as long as they can tell where you intend to go.

Staying/Getting Healthy: The siesta is a key to survival in summertime Rome. Lie down and contemplate the extraordinary power of gravity in the Eternal City. I drink lots of cold, refreshing water from Rome's many drinking fountains (the Forum has three). There's a pharmacy (marked by a green cross) in every neighborhood, including a handy one in the train station (daily 7:30–22:00, located downstairs, at west end), and a 24-hour pharmacy on Piazza dei Cinquecento 51 (next to train station on Via Cavour, tel. 06-488-0019). Embassies can recommend English-speaking doctors. Consider MEDline, a 24-hour home medical service (tel. 06-808-0995, doctors speak English). Anyone is entitled to free emergency treatment at public hospitals. The hospital closest to the train station is Policlinico Umberto 1 (entrance for emergency treatment on Via Lancisi, translators available, Metro: Policlinico). The American Hospital, a private hospital on the edge of town, is accustomed to helping Yankees (tel. 06-225-571).

Helpful Hints

Museum Prices: These can be upped when museums host special exhibits (no price break if you skip exhibit).

Train Tickets: Get train tickets and railpass-related reservations and supplements at travel agencies, rather than dealing with the congested train station. The cost is either the same or there's a minimal charge. Your hotel can direct you to the nearest travel agency. Quo Vadis, near the Vatican, is helpful (Via della Conciliazione, 22-24, tel. 06-6880-4941, fax 06-6880-3191, qv.viaggi@tiscalinet.it). Or purchase train tickets from the American Express office near the Spanish Steps (Mon–Fri 9:00–17:30, closed Sat–Sun, Piazza di Spagna 38, tel. 06-67641).

Bookstore: Try American Bookstore (Via Torino 136, Metro: Repubblica, tel. 06-474-6877), Almost Corner Bookshop in Trastevere (Via del Moro 45, tel. 06-583-6942), and the Anglo-American Bookshop (Via della Vite 102, tel. 06-679-5222).

Internet Access: Your hotelier can direct you to an Internet access point near your hotel. The city's biggest Internet café is easy Internetcafé, centrally located on Piazza Barberini (access from €0.50, open 24/7, 250 terminals, www.easyinternetcafe.com).

Laundry: Ask your hotelier for the nearest launderette (usually open daily 8:00–22:00, about €6 to wash and dry a 15-pound load). The Bolle Blu chain comes with Internet access (near train station at Via Milazzo 20, Via Palestro 59, and Via Principe Amedeo 116, tel. 06-446-5804).

Web sites on Rome: www.romaturismo.com (music, exhibitions, and events, in English), www.wantedinrome.com (job openings and real estate, but also festivals and exhibitions, in English), and www.vatican.va (the pope's Web site, in English).

Getting Around Rome

Sightsee on foot, by city bus, or by taxi. I've grouped your sightseeing into walkable neighborhoods.

Public transportation is efficient, cheap, and part of your Roman experience. It starts running around 5:30 and stops around 23:30, sometimes earlier. After midnight, there are a few very crowded night buses, and taxis become more expensive and hard to get. Don't try to hail one—go to a taxi stand.

Buses and subways use the same ticket. You can buy tickets at newsstands, tobacco shops (*tabacchi,* marked by a black-and-white "T" sign), or at major Metro stations or bus stops, but not on board. Since many Metro stations have no human ticket-sellers and the machines are either broken or require exact change (helps to put in smallest coin first), it's easier to buy a few tickets above ground at newsstands or *tabacchi* (€1, good for 75 min, valid for one Metro ride, including transfers, and unlimited buses) or an all-day bus/Metro pass (€4, for more info, visit www.atac.roma.it, or call 800-431-784). One-week transit passes cost €16. Stamp your ticket before using it (machines are near subway turnstiles and on buses—watch others and imitate).

Buses (especially the touristy #64) and the subway are havens for thieves and pickpockets. Assume any commotion is a thief-created distraction. If one bus is packed, there's likely a second one on its tail with far fewer crowds and thieves.

By Metro: The Roman subway system (Metropolitana) is simple, with two clean, cheap, fast lines that intersect at Termini train station. While much of Rome is not served by its skimpy subway, these stops are helpful:

Termini—train station, National Museum of Rome, recommended hotels

Repubblica—Baths of Diocletian/Octagonal Hall, TI, recommended hotels

Metropolitana: Rome's Subway

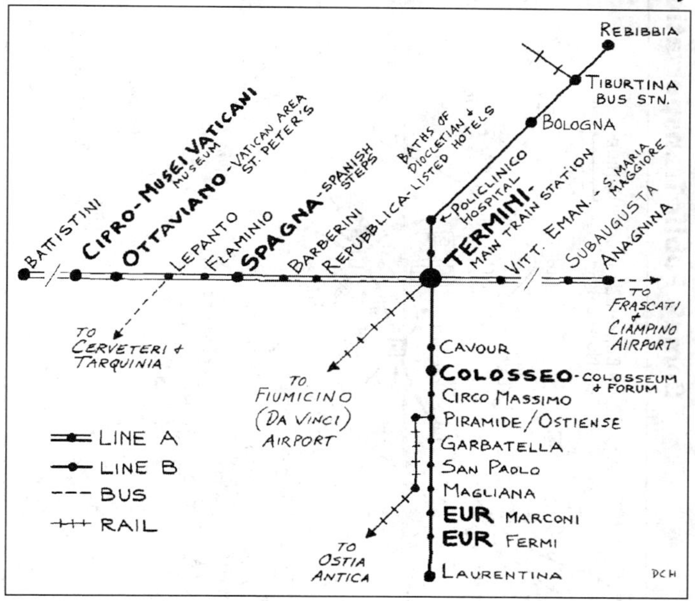

Barberini—Cappuccin Crypt, Trevi Fountain
Spagna—Spanish Steps, Villa Borghese, classy shopping area
Flaminio—Piazza del Popolo, start of recommended Dolce Vita Stroll down Via del Corso
Ottaviano—St. Peter's and Vatican City
Cipro-Musei Vaticani—Vatican Museum, recommended hotels
Colosseo—Colosseum, Roman Forum, recommended hotels
E.U.R.—Mussolini's futuristic suburb

Note that first and last compartments are generally less crowded.

By Bus: Bus routes are clearly listed at the stops. Try asking the TI for a bus map (bus info: tel. 06-4695-2027). There are two types of tickets: Most tickets have a bar code and must be stamped on the bus in the yellow box with the digital readout (be sure to retrieve your ticket); the other, smaller boxes with horizontal slots are used for the old-style skinny tickets, which are being phased out. Punch your ticket as you board (even if you've already stamped it for the Metro)—or you are cheating. Riding without a stamped ticket on the bus, while relatively safe, is stressful. Inspectors fine even innocent-looking tourists €52. If the validation machine won't work, you can write the date, time, and bus number on the ticket. Ideally, buy a bunch of tickets from a tobacco shop or newsstand

Rome's Public Transportation

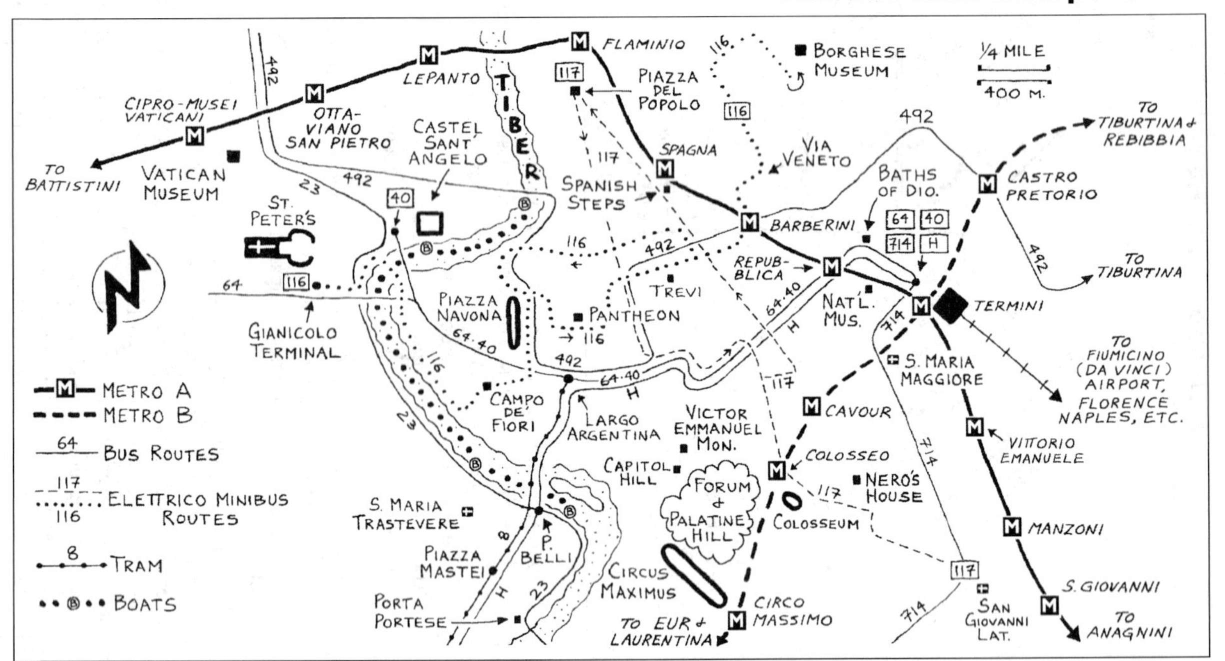

first thing so you can hop a bus without first having to search for a tobacco shop that's open.

Here are a few buses worth knowing about:

#64—Termini (train station), Piazza della Repubblica (sights), Via Nazionale (recommended hotels), Piazza Venezia (near Forum), Largo Argentina (near Pantheon), and St. Peter's Basilica. Ride it for a city overview and to watch pickpockets in action (can get horribly crowded).

#40—This express route is especially helpful—it's essentially the same route as #64, but with fewer stops, crowds, and pickpockets.

#8—This tram connects Largo Argentina with Trastevere (get off at Piazza Mastai, just after crossing the Tiber River).

#H—Express connecting Termini train station and Trastevere, with a few stops on Via Nazionale (for Trastevere, get off at Piazza Belli, just after crossing the river).

#492—Stazione Tiburtina (bus station), Piazza Barberini, Piazza Venezia, Piazza Cavour (Castel Sant' Angelo), and Piazza Risorgimento (near Vatican Museum).

#714—Termini (train station), Santa Maria Maggiore, San Giovanni in Laterano, and Terme di Caracalla (Baths of Caracalla).

#23—Links Vatican with Trastevere, stopping at Porta Portese (Sunday flea market), Trastevere (Piazza Belli), Castel Sant' Angelo, the Vatican Museum (nearest stop is Via Leone IV).

Rome has cute *elettrico* minibuses that wind through the narrow streets of old and interesting neighborhoods (daily, fewer on Sun). These are handy for sightseeing and fun for simply joyriding:

Elettrico #116—Through the medieval core of Rome from Ponte Vittorio Emanuele II (near Castel Sant' Angelo) to Campo de' Fiori to Piazza Barberini via the Pantheon and on to the Villa Borghese.

Elettrico #117—San Giovanni in Laterano, Colosseo, Via dei Serpenti, Trevi Fountain, Piazza di Spagna, and Piazza del Popolo.

By Taxi: I use taxis in Rome more often than in other cities. They're reasonable and useful for efficient sightseeing in this big, hot city. Taxis start at about €2.50 and charge about €1 per kilometer from there (surcharges of €1 on Sun, €2.75 for night hours of 22:00–7:00, €1 surcharge for luggage, €7.25 extra for airport, tip by rounding up to the nearest euro). Sample fares: Train station to Vatican-€9; train station to Colosseum-€6; Colosseum to Trastevere-€7. Three or four companions with more money than time should taxi almost everywhere. It's tough to wave down a taxi in Rome. Find the nearest taxi stand by asking a passerby or a clerk in a shop, *"Dov'è* (doh-vay) *una fermata dei tassi?"* (Some are listed on my maps.) Taxis listing their telephone number on the door have fair meters—use them. To save time and energy, have your hotel call a taxi; the meter starts when the call is received. To call a cab on your own, dial 06-3570, 06-4994, or 06-88177.

When you arrive at the train station or airport, beware of hustlers conning naive visitors into unmarked rip-off "express taxis." Only use official taxis, with a "taxi" sign and phone number marked on the door. By law, they must display a multilingual official price chart. If you have any problems with a taxi, making a show of writing down the taxi number (to file a complaint) can motivate a driver to quickly settle the matter.

By Boat: Battelli di Roma, a new boat service, slowly floats its way down the Tiber—re-energizing the city's neglected river (single ride-€1, day pass-€2.30, tour-€10, boats depart hourly, daily 8:00–19:30, maybe until 24:00 in summer, tel. 06-678-9361, www.battellidiroma.it).

You can access the docks from the following bridges: Ponte Duca d'Aosta, Ponte Risorgiamento, Ponte Cavour (Ara Pacis), Ponte Sant' Angelo (Vatican), Ponte Sisto (Trastevere), or Calata Anguillara (Isola Tiburtina).

The same company runs a variety of boat tours that leave from Ponte Sant' Angelo: guided river tours in English (€10, 4/day, but since the river is far below the level of the city, don't expect much of a view); a full-day excursion to Ostia Antica (€40, daily, includes lunch and guided tour, departs around 9:00 and returns in afternoon, confirm times); and a dinner cruise (steep price of €43, daily, book in advance).

TOURS

Context Rome—Americans Paul Bennett and Lani Bevacqua offer walking tours for travelers with longer-than-average attention spans. Their orientation walks lace together lesser-known sights from antiquity to the present. Tours vary in length from two to four hours and range in price from €25–60. Try to book in advance, since their groups are limited to six and fill up fast (tel. 06-482-0911, 888/467-1986 in the U.S., www.contextrome.com).

If you're interested in weeklong classes on Rome, look into the Institute for Roman Culture, an innovative, educational organization run by Tom Rankin and his colleague, archaeologist Darius Arya (see www.romanculture.org for prices, details, and booking).

Through Eternity—This company offers four walking tours, all led by native English speakers. The tours include St. Peter's and the Vatican Museum (€40, museum entry not included, 5 hrs, most days); the Colosseum and Roman Forum (€25, 2.5 hrs, daily); and Rome at Twilight (€25, nightly). Call or visit their Web site to get the schedule and to book in advance (max of 20 people, private tours

Daily Reminder

Sunday: These sights are closed: Vatican Museum (except for the last Sunday of the month, when it's free and crowded) and the Catacombs of San Sebastian. E.U.R.'s Museum of Roman Civilization closes early in the afternoon. The old center is delightfully quiet.

Monday: Many sights are closed: National Museum of Rome, Borghese Gallery, Capitol Hill Museum, Octagonal Hall (at Baths of Diocletian), Etruscan Museum, Castel Sant' Angelo, Trajan's Market, Montemartini Museum, Protestant Cemetery, E.U.R.'s Museum of Roman Civilization, and Ostia Antica.

All of the ancient sights (e.g., Colosseum and Forum) and the Vatican Museum, among others, are open. The Baths of Caracalla close early in the afternoon.

Tuesday: All sights are open in Rome except for Nero's Golden House. This isn't a good day to side-trip to Naples, because its Archaeological Museum is closed.

Wednesday: All sights are open except for the Catacombs of San Callisto.

Thursday: All sights are open except for Galleria Doria Pamphilj and the Cappuccin Crypt.

Friday/Saturday: All sights are open in Rome.

to Tivioli and Pompeii, tel. 06-700-9336, mobile 347-336-5298, 10 percent discount if booked online, www.througheternity.com, info@througheternity.com, Rob Allyn).

Rome Walks—These guides (many of them students) give tours in fluent English to small groups (2–8 people). Sample tours include Colosseum/Forum/Palatine Walk (€48, includes admission to Colosseum, 3 hrs), Scandal Tour (€30, 2 hrs to dig up the dirt on Roman emperors, royalty, and popes), Vatican City Walk (€52, includes admission to Vatican Museum, 4 hrs), and a Twilight Rome Evening Walk (€25, all the famous squares that offer lively people scenes, 2 hrs). They also do private tours to Hadrian's Villa and Villa d'Este. See their Web site for the latest (www.romewalks.com) and book in advance by e-mail (info@romewalks.com) or phone (mobile 347-795-5175, Annie). You'll need to give your hotel name and phone number. Your guide will call or e-mail you to let you know the meeting place.

Roman Odyssey Tours—Another ex-pat tour company, Roman Odyssey, offers various two- to three-hour, €20 walks. To get folks hooked, they often give free 40-minute tours of St. Peter's Square and Basilica (tel. 06-580-9902, mobile 328-912-3720, for a listing of tours see www.romanodyssey.com, Rahul).

Rome at a Glance

▲▲▲**Vatican Museum** Four miles of the art of Western Civilization, culminating in the Sistine Chapel. **Hours:** March–Oct Mon–Fri 8:45–16:45 and Sat 8:45–13:45, Nov–Feb Mon–Sat 8:45–13:45, closed on numerous religious holidays and Sun, except last Sun of the month.

▲▲▲**St. Peter's Basilica** Most impressive church on earth, with Michelangelo's *Pietà* and dome. **Hours:** Daily April–Sept 7:00–19:00, Oct–March 7:00–18:00. Dome: Daily April–Sept 8:00–17:45, Oct–March 8:00–16:45.

▲▲▲**Roman Forum** Ancient Rome's main square, with ruins and grand arches. **Hours:** Daily 9:00–19:00 or an hour before dark.

▲▲▲**Colosseum** Huge stadium where gladiators fought. **Hours:** Daily 9:00–19:00 or until an hour before dark.

▲▲▲**Pantheon** The defining domed temple. **Hours:** Mon–Sat 8:30–19:30, Sun 9:00–18:00, holidays 9:00–13:00.

▲▲▲**National Museum of Rome** Greatest collection of Roman sculpture anywhere. **Hours:** Tue–Sun 9:00–19:45, closed Mon.

▲▲▲**Borghese Gallery** Bernini sculptures and paintings by Caravaggio, Raphael, and Titian in a Baroque palazzo. Reservations mandatory. **Hours:** Tue–Sun 9:00–19:00, Sat maybe until 23:00 June–Sept, closed Mon.

▲▲**Catacombs** Layers of tunnels with tombs, mainly Christian, outside the city. **Hours:** Daily 8:30–12:00 & 14:30–17:30, until 17:00 in winter (San Callisto closed Wed and Feb, San Sebastian closed Sun and Nov).

▲▲**Capitol Hill Museum** Ancient statues, mosaics, and expansive view of Forum. **Hours:** Tue–Sun 9:00–20:00, closed Mon.

▲▲**Capitol Hill** Hilltop square designed by Michelangelo with museum, grand stairway, and Forum overlooks. **Hours:** Always open.

▲**Trajan's Column** Tall column with narrative relief, on Piazza Venezia. **Hours:** Always viewable.

▲**Nero's Golden House** Sparse remains of Emperor Nero's sprawling home. This sight has been closed indefinitely—up to two years—due to water damage.

▲**Mamertine Prison** Prison that held Saints Peter and Paul. **Hours:** Daily 9:00–12:30 & 14:00–17:00.

▲**Arch of Constantine** Honors Emperor Constantine, who legalized Christianity. **Hours:** Always open.

▲**Palatine Hill** Ruins of emperors' palaces, Circus Maximus view, and museum. **Hours:** Daily 9:00–19:00 or until an hour before dark.

▲**Castel Sant'Angelo** Hadrian's Tomb turned castle, prison, papal refuge, now museum. **Hours:** Tue–Sun 9:00–20:00, maybe June–Sept Sat 21:00–23:45, closed Mon.

▲**Baths of Diocletian** Once ancient Rome's immense public baths, now a Michelangelo church—Church of Santa Maria degli Angeli—and the Octagonal Hall, a room with minor ancient Roman sculpture. **Hours:** Church—Mon–Sat 7:00–18:30, Sun 8:00–19:30. Octagonal Hall—Tue–Sat 9:00–14:00, Sun 9:00–13:00, closed Mon.

▲**Museum of Roman Civilization** Lifeless museum, but has a 3-D model of ancient Rome and plaster copies of Rome's scattered ruins gathered in one place. **Hours:** Tue–Sat 9:00–18:15, Sun 9:00–13:30, closed Mon.

▲**Montemartini Museum** 400 Roman statues in a 1932 electric power plant. **Hours:** Tue–Sun 9:30–19:00, closed Mon.

▲**Galleria Doria Pamphilj** Fancy palace packed with art. **Hours:** Fri–Wed 10:00–17:00, closed Thu.

▲**Cappuccin Crypt** A crypt, newly opened after renovation, decorated with the bones of 4,000 monks. **Hours:** Fri–Wed 9:00–12:00 & 15:00–18:00, closed Thu.

▲**St. Peter-in-Chains** Church with Michelangelo's *Moses*. **Hours:** Daily 7:00–12:30 & 15:30–18:00.

▲**Santa Maria della Vittoria** Church with Bernini's swooning *St. Teresa in Ecstasy*. **Hours:** Daily 7:00–12:00 & 15:30–19:00.

▲**Trevi Fountain** Baroque hotspot—bring coins to ensure a return trip to Rome. **Hours:** Always open.

▲**Villa Borghese** Central Park of Rome, with lake, Borghese Gallery, and Etruscan Museum. **Hours:** Always open.

Private Guides—Consider a personal tour. Any of the tour companies I list can provide a guide. I work with Francesca Caruso, a licensed Italian guide who speaks excellent English and loves to teach and share her appreciation of her city (€100 for 2 hrs or more—she happily stretches the tour to half a day for eager students, individuals, and small groups; chris.fra@mclink.it).

Hop-on, Hop-off Bus Tour—The ATAC city bus tour, also called Trambus, offers a quick, cheap orientation tour of Rome on big, red double-decker buses with an open-air upper deck. In under two hours, you'll have 80 sights pointed out to you (by a live guide in English and maybe one other language). You can get out at any of the nine stops and catch a later bus (though stops are poorly marked and the included map is useless). The stops are: Via Veneto, Via Tritone, Ara Pacis, Piazza Cavour, St. Peter's Square, Corso Vittorio Emanuele (for Piazza Navona), Piazza Venezia, Colosseum, and Via Nazionale. While the guide's spiel is limited to simple identification of the sights, this tour provides an efficient and economical orientation to Rome (mobbed mid-day, not ideal in bad weather). Bus #110 departs every 30 minutes—at the top and bottom of the hour—from in front of the Termini train station (runs daily March–Sept 9:00–20:00, Oct–Feb 10:00–18:00, tel. 06-4695-2252). Buy the €13 ticket (or pay €20 for combo-ticket with Archeobus—see below) at the info kiosk marked "i" near platform D, or purchase it on the bus and pay about 10 percent more.

Archeobus—This hop-on, hop-off bus runs hourly from Termini out to the Appian Way. While this is a handy way to see the sights down this ancient Roman road, it's sometimes crowded and the service can be sporadic. The trip, in an air-conditioned minibus, includes a basic, uninspired two-hour tour (longer if there's traffic) in Italian and English (€8, €20 combo-ticket with the hop-on, hop-off bus tour—see above; tickets sold at platform D in front of train station or at green kiosk on Piazza Venezia, hourly departures from station and Piazza Venezia 9:45–16:45, tel. 06-4695-4695).

SIGHTS

From the Colosseum Area to Capitol Hill

Beware of gangs of young thieves, particularly between the Colosseum and the Forum; they're harmless if you know their tricks (see "Theft Alert," page 878).

▲St. Peter-in-Chains Church (San Pietro in Vincoli)—Built in the 5th century to house the chains that held St. Peter, this church is most famous for its Michelangelo statue. Check out the much-venerated chains under the high altar, then focus on Moses (free, daily 7:00–12:30 & 15:30–18:00, modest dress required). The church is a 10- to 15-minute walk north of the Colosseum (Metro stop: Colosseo, exit Metro stop to the left and climb the staircase that's roughly 50 yards away, then work your way slowly uphill; or get off at Metro: Cavour, exit Metro and go up steep flight of steps, take a right at the top and walk a block).

Pope Julius II commissioned Michelangelo to build a massive tomb, with 48 huge statues, crowned by a grand statue of this egomaniacal pope. The pope had planned to have his tomb placed in the center of St. Peter's Basilica. When Julius died, the work had barely been started, and no one had the money or necessary commitment to Julius to finish the project. Michelangelo finished one statue—Moses—and left a few unfinished statues: Leah and Rachel flanking Moses in this church, the *Prisoners* (now in Florence's Accademia), and the *Slaves* (now in Paris' Louvre).

This powerful statue of Moses—mature Michelangelo—is worth studying. The artist worked on it in fits and starts for 30 years. Moses has received the Ten Commandments. As he holds the stone tablets, his eyes show a man determined to stop his tribe from worshiping the golden calf and idols...a man determined to win salvation for the people of Israel. Why the horns? Centuries ago, the Hebrew word for "rays" was mistranslated as "horns."

▲Nero's Golden House (Domus Aurea)—The barren remains of Emperor Nero's "Golden House" were recently closed indefinitely due to water damage. The original entrance to the gold-leaf-encrusted house was all the way over at the Arch of Titus in the Forum. Nero's massive estate once sprawled across the valley (where the Colosseum now stands) and up the hill—the part you tour today. Larger even than Bill Gates' place, it was a pain to vacuum. A colossal, 100-foot-tall bronze statue of Nero towered over everything. The estate incorporated an artificial lake (where the Colosseum was later built) and a forest stocked with game. It was decorated with the best multicolored marble and the finest frescoes. No expense was too great for Nero—his mistress soaked daily in the milk of 500 wild asses kept for her bathing pleasure.

Nero (ruled A.D. 54–68) was Rome's most notorious emperor. He killed his own mother, kicked his pregnant wife to death, crucified St. Peter, and—most galling to his subjects—was a bad actor. When Rome burned in A.D. 64, Nero was accused of torching it to clear land for an even bigger house. The Romans rebelled and Nero stabbed himself in the neck, crying, "What an artist dies in me!"

While only hints of the splendid, colorful frescoes survive, the towering vaults and the sheer immensity of the place are impressive. As you wander through rooms that are now underground (but originally were not), look up at the holes in the ceiling. Ponder how much of old Rome still hides underground...and why the subway is limited to two lines.

When the sight reopens, visits are allowed only with an escort

Ancient Rome

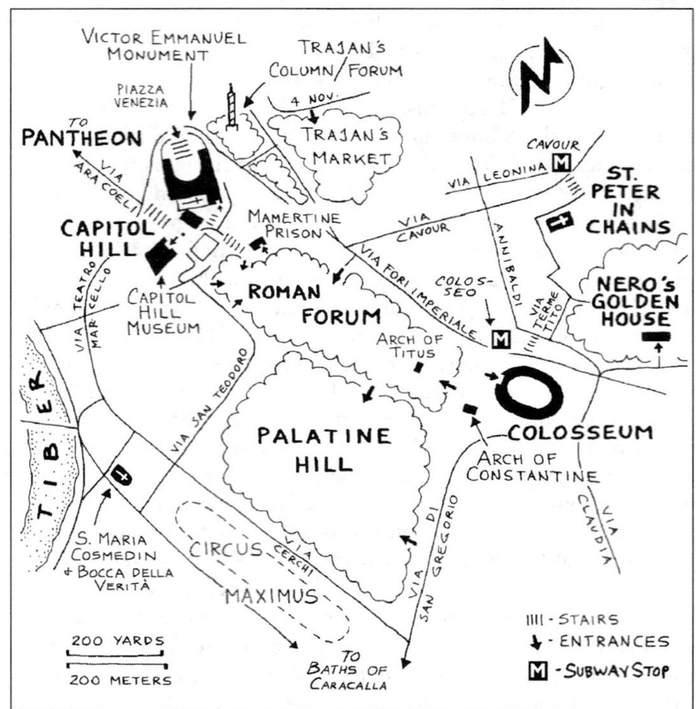

(30 people, about every 30 min) and a mandatory reservation (€5 admission plus €1.50 reservation fee, Wed–Mon 9:00–19:45, last entry at 18:40, closed Tue). Schedule your visit online at www.pierreci.it or by calling 06-3996-7700 during office hours (Mon–Sat 9:00–13:30 & 14:30–17:00). Guided tours in English are also offered twice daily for €8.50; request a tour when you book your reservation. Audioguides cost €2, but listen to the intro before entering or you'll be forever behind. If you show up without a reservation, you could luck out and be allowed in (chances are best on a late afternoon on a weekday). Nero's House is near the Metro Colosseo stop and 200 yards northeast of Colosseum; go through a park gate, up a hill, and it's on the left.

▲▲▲Colosseum—This 2,000-year-old building is *the* great example of Roman engineering. Using concrete, brick, and their trademark round arches, Romans constructed much larger buildings than the Greeks. But in deference to the higher Greek culture, they finished their no-nonsense megastructure by pasting all three orders of Greek columns (Doric, Ionic, and Corinthian) as exterior decorations. The Flavian Amphitheater's popular name,

"Colosseum," comes from the colossal statue of Nero that once stood in front of it.

Romans were into "big." By putting two theaters together, they created a circular amphitheater. They could fill and empty its 50,000 numbered seats as quickly and efficiently as we do our superstadiums. Teams of sailors hoisted canvas awnings over the stadium to give fans shade. This was where ancient Romans, whose taste for violence was the equal of modern America's, enjoyed their Dirty Harry and *Terminator.* Gladiators, criminals, and wild animals fought to the death in every conceivable scenario. The floor of the Colosseum is missing, exposing underground passages. Animals were kept in cages here and then lifted up in elevators; they'd pop out from behind blinds into the arena. The gladiator didn't know where, when, or by what he'd be attacked.

Cost, Hours, Location: €8 (includes Palatine Hill visit within 24 hours; also covered by €20 combo-ticket); there's often a €2 surcharge for special exhibits. A dry-but-fact-filled audioguide is available at the ticket office (€4 for 2 hours of use). Guided tours in English depart several times per day and last about one hour (€4). The Colosseum is open daily 9:00–19:00, or until an hour before sunset (tel. 06-3996-7700). Metro: Colosseo.

Outside the entrance of the Colosseum, vendors sell handy little *Rome: Past and Present* books with plastic overlays to un-ruin the ruins (marked €11, price soft). A WC is behind the Colosseum (facing ticket entrance, go right; WC is under stairway). Caution: For a fee, the incredibly crude modern-day gladiators snuff out their cigarettes and pose for photos. They take easy-to-swindle tourists for too much money. Watch out if you tangle with these guys (they're armed...and accustomed to getting as much as €100 from naive Asian tourists).

Avoid Long Lines: Instead of waiting in line (sometimes as long as an hour) at the Colosseum to purchase a ticket, you have several good alternatives:

1. Buy your ticket at either of the two rarely crowded Palatine Hill entrances near the Colosseum—there's one inside the Forum and another on Via di San Gregorio (facing Forum entry, with Colosseum at your back, go left on street). This €8 ticket includes entry to both the Colosseum and Palatine (valid for 24 hours). With ticket in hand, you can walk right by the long ticket line, through the turnstile, and into the Colosseum.

2. Consider buying a €20 combo-ticket at a less-crowded sight. The combo-ticket covers the Colosseum, Palatine Hill, National Museum of Rome, Museum of the Bath, Baths of Caracalla, and more. Buy it at any of the included sights.

3. You can book a tour on the spot from hustlers who rescue individuals from the line by selling tours that include tickets

Colosseum Area

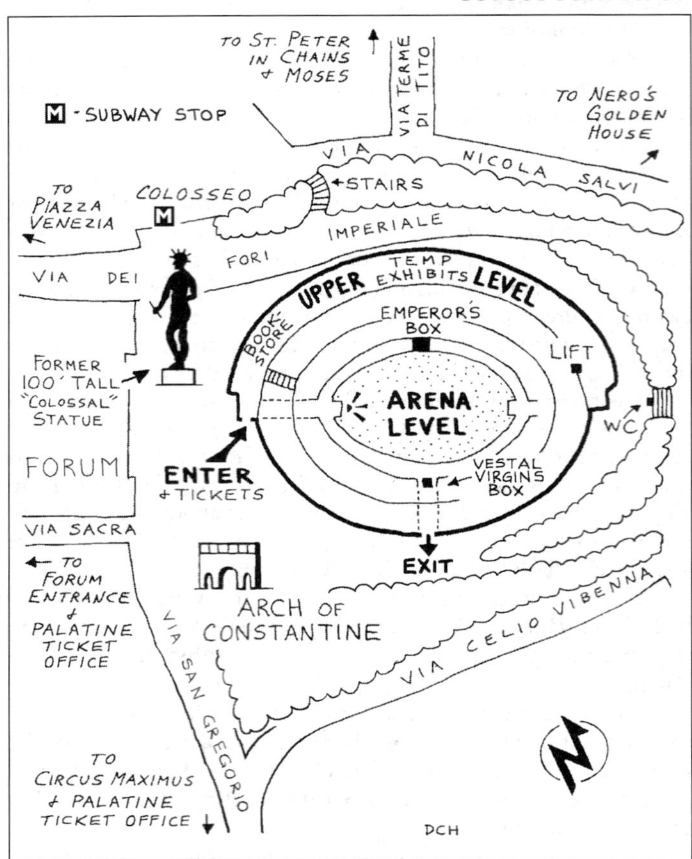

they already have. This will cost you a few euros (€15 for the tour including the €8 ticket), but can save time and comes with a brief guided tour. Beware—American students working for the guides will tell you that there's a long line, when sometimes there is none at all. (It can be hard for you to instantly judge the length of the line because it's tucked into the Colosseum arcade.)

▲Arch of Constantine—The arch, next to the Colosseum, marks one of the great turning points in history—the military coup that made Christianity mainstream. In A.D. 312, Emperor Constantine defeated his rival Maxentius in one crucial battle. The night before, he had seen a vision of a cross in the sky. Constantine became sole emperor and legalized Christianity. With this one battle, a once-obscure Jewish sect with a handful of followers was now the state religion of the entire Western world. In A.D. 300, you could be killed for being a Christian; later, you could be killed for not being one. Church enrollment boomed.

By the way, don't look too closely at the reliefs decorating this arch. By the 4th century, Rome was on its way down. Rather than struggle with original carvings, the makers of this arch plugged in bits and pieces scavenged from existing monuments. The arch is newly restored and looking great. But any meaning read into the stone will be very jumbled.

▲▲▲Roman Forum (Foro Romano)—This is ancient Rome's birthplace and civic center, and the common ground between Rome's famous seven hills (free, daily 9:00–19:00 or an hour before dark, Metro: Colosseo, tel. 06-3996-7700). A €4 audioguide helps decipher the rubble (rent at gift shop at entrance on Via dei Fori Imperiali). Guided tours in English are offered nearly hourly (€4); ask for information at the ticket booth at the Palatine Hill (near Arch of Titus). See "Roman Forum Walk," page 927.

▲Palatine Hill—The hill above the Forum contains scanty remains of the imperial palaces and the foundations of Rome, from Iron Age huts to the legendary house of Romulus (under corrugated tin roof in far corner). We get our word "palace" from this hill, where the emperors chose to live. The Palatine was once so filled with palaces that later emperors had to build out. (Looking up at it from the Forum, you see the substructure that supported these long-gone palaces.) The Palatine museum has sculptures and fresco fragments but is nothing special. From the pleasant garden, you'll get an overview of the Forum. On the far side, look down into an emperor's private stadium and then beyond at the dusty Circus Maximus, once a chariot course. Imagine the cheers, jeers, and furious betting. But considering how ruined the ruins are, the heat, the hill to climb, the €8 entry fee, and the relative difficulty in understanding what you're looking at, the Palatine Hill is a disappointment.

Cost, Hours, Location: €8, includes Colosseum visit within 24 hours, also covered by €20 combo-ticket, daily 9:00–19:00, or one hour before sunset, Metro: Colosseo. The main entrance and ticket office—which also sells Colosseum tickets, enabling smart sightseers to avoid that long line—is near the Arch of Titus and Colosseum. Another Palatine entrance is on Via di San Gregorio.

Audioguides cost €4. Guided tours in English are offered once daily (€3.50); ask for information at the ticket booth.

▲Mamertine Prison—This 2,500-year-old, cistern-like prison, which once held the bodies of Saints Peter and Paul, is worth a look (donation requested, daily 9:00–12:30 & 14:00–17:00, at the foot of Capitol Hill, near Forum's Arch of Septimius Severus). When you step into the room, you'll hit a modern floor. Ignore that and look up at the hole in the ceiling, from which prisoners were lowered. Then take the stairs down to the level of the actual prison floor.

Downstairs, you'll see the column to which Peter was chained. It's said that a miraculous fountain sprang up in this room so Peter could convert and baptize his jailers, who were subsequently martyred as well. The upside-down cross commemorates Peter's upside-down crucifixion.

Imagine humans, amid fat rats and rotting corpses, awaiting slow deaths. On the walls near the entry are lists of notable prisoners (Christian and non-Christian) and the ways they were executed: *strangolati*, *decapitato*, *morto di fame* (died of hunger)....

▲Trajan's Column, Market, and Forum—This offers the grandest column and best example of "continuous narration" from antiquity. Over 2,500 figures scroll around the 130-foot-high column, telling of Trajan's victorious Dacian campaign (circa A.D. 103, in present-day Romania), from the assembling of the army at the bottom to the victory sacrifice at the top. The ashes of Trajan and his wife were held in the mausoleum at the base while the sun once glinted off a polished bronze statue of Trajan at the top. Today, St. Peter is on top. Study the propaganda that winds up the column like a scroll, trumpeting Trajan's wonderful military exploits. You can see this close up for free (always open and viewable, just off Piazza Venezia, across the street from the Victor Emmanuel Monument). Viewing balconies once stood on either side, but it seems likely Trajan fans came away only with a feeling that the greatness of their emperor and empire was beyond comprehension (for a rolled-out version of the column's story, visit the Museum of Roman Civilization at E.U.R., page 926). This column marked **"Trajan's Forum,"** which was built to handle the shopping needs of a wealthy city of over a million. Commercial, political, religious, and social activities all mixed in the forum.

For a fee, you can go inside **Trajan's Market** (boring) and part of Trajan's Forum. The market was once filled with shops selling goods from all over the Roman Empire (€6.20, summer Tue–Sun 9:00–18:30, winter Tue–Sun 9:00–16:30, closed Mon, tel. 06-679-0048). Trajan's Column is just a few steps off Piazza Venezia, on Via dei Fori Imperiali, across the street from the Victor Emmanuel Monument. Trajan's Forum stretches southeast of the column toward the Colosseum. The entrance to Trajan's Market is uphill from the column on Via IV Novembre.

Time Elevator Roma—The cheesy and overpriced visit starts with a stand-up Italian-only 15-minute intro, followed by a 30-minute multi-screen show with seats jolting through the centuries. Equipped with headphones, you get nauseous in a comfortable, air-conditioned theater as the history of Rome unfolds before you—from the founding of the city, through its rise and fall, to its impressive Renaissance rebound and up to the present (€11, daily 11:00–19:30, shows every 30 min, no kids under 5, Via dei

S.S. Apostoli 20, just off Via del Corso, 3-min walk from Piazza Venezia, tel. 06-9774-6243, www.time-elevator.it).

Capitol Hill Area

There are several ways to get to the top of Capitol Hill (also called "Capitoline Hill"). If you're coming from the north (Piazza Venezia), take Michelangelo's impressive stairway to the right of the big, white Victor Emmanuel Monument. Coming from the south (the Forum), take either the steep staircase or the winding road, which converge near the top of the hill at a great Forum overlook, she-wolf statue, and refreshing water fountain. Block the spout with your fingers; water spurts up for drinking. Romans, who call this *il nasone* (the big nose), joke that a cheap Roman boy takes his date out for a drink at *il nasone*. Near the *nasone* is a back-door entrance to the Victor Emmanuel Monument (see Monument listing, page 899).

▲▲Capitol Hill (Campidoglio)—This hill, once the religious and political center of ancient Rome, is still the home of the city's government. The mayoral palace and the Capitol Hill Museum (listed below) border Michelangelo's Renaissance square. The square's centerpiece is a copy of the famous equestrian statue of Marcus Aurelius (the original is behind glass in the adjacent museum).

Michelangelo intended that people approach the square from his grand stairway off Piazza Venezia. From the top of the stairway, you see the new Renaissance face of Rome with its back to the Forum. Michelangelo gave the buildings the "giant order"—huge pilasters make the existing two-story buildings feel one-storied and more harmonious with the new square. Notice how the statues atop these buildings welcome you and then draw you in. The terraces just downhill (past either side of the mayor's palace) offer fine views of the Forum.

▲▲Capitol Hill Museum—This museum encompasses two buildings (Palazzo dei Conservatori and Palazzo Nuovo) connected by an underground passage that leads to the vacant Tabularium and a panoramic overlook of the Forum (€8 ticket covers both buildings, valid 3 hrs from entrance time, Tue–Sun 9:00–20:00, last entry 60 min before closing, closed Mon, audioguide-€4, tel. 06-3996-7800).

To identify the museum's two buildings, face the equestrian statue on Capitol Hill Square (with your back to the grand stairway leading up to the square). The Palazzo Nuovo (where you start this self-guided tour) is on your left; the Palazzo dei Conservatori (where you buy your ticket and finish) is on your right (closer to the river). Ahead is the Palazzo Senatorio (mayoral palace, not open to public); below it—and out of sight—are the Tabularium and underground passage connecting the two museum buildings.

Capitol Hill Museum Overview

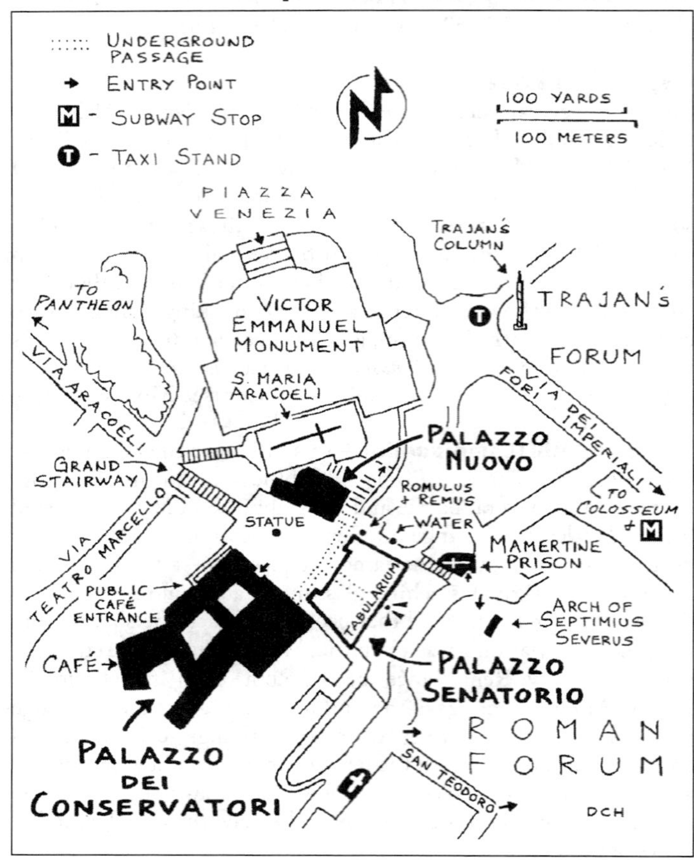

Buy your ticket (and rent the optional audioguide) at Palazzo dei Conservatori.

The **Palazzo dei Conservatori** is one of the world's oldest museums, at 500 years old. Outside the entrance, notice the marriage announcements and, possibly, wedding-party photo ops. Inside the courtyard, have a look at giant chunks of a statue of Emperor Constantine; when intact, this imposing statue held court in the Basilica of Constantine in the Forum. The museum is worthwhile, with lavish rooms and several great statues. Tops is the original (500 B.C.) Etruscan *Capitoline Wolf* (the little statues of Romulus and Remus were added in the Renaissance). Don't miss the *Boy Extracting a Thorn* or the enchanting *Commodus as Hercules.* The second-floor painting gallery—except for two Caravaggios—is forgettable. The café upstairs, with a splendid patio with city views, is lovely at sunset.

Connect the two museums with the underground passage that leads to the **Tabularium.** Built in the 1st century A.D., this once held the archives of ancient Rome. The word *Tabularium* comes from tablet, on which the Romans wrote their laws. You won't see any tablets, but you will see a superb head-on view of the Forum from the windows.

The **Palazzo Nuovo** houses mostly portrait busts of forgotten emperors. But it has three must-see statues: the *Dying Gaul,* the *Capitoline Venus* (both on the first floor up), and the original gilded bronze equestrian statue of Marcus Aurelius (behind glass in museum courtyard). This greatest surviving equestrian statue of antiquity was the original centerpiece of the square. While most such pagan statues were destroyed by Dark Age Christians, Marcus was mistaken for Constantine (the first Christian emperor) and therefore spared.

Glimpses of Ruins from Capitol Hill to Piazza Venezia—Leaving Capitol Hill, descend the stairs leading to Piazza Venezia. At the bottom of the stairs, look left several blocks down the street to see a condominium actually built around surviving ancient pillars and arches of Teatro Marcello—perhaps the oldest inhabited building in Europe.

Still at the bottom of the stairs, look up the long stairway to your right (which pilgrims climb on their knees) at the Santa Maria in Aracoeli church for a good example of the earliest style of Christian church. While pilgrims find it worth the climb, sightseers can skip it. As you walk toward Piazza Venezia, look down into the ditch on your right to see the ruins of an ancient apartment building from the 1st century A.D.; part of it was transformed into a tiny church (faded frescoes and bell tower). Rome was built in layers—almost everywhere there is an earlier version beneath your feet.

Piazza Venezia—This vast square is the focal point of modern Rome. The Via del Corso, which starts here, is the city's axis, surrounded by Rome's classiest shopping district. In the 1930s, Mussolini whipped up Italy's nationalistic fervor here from a balcony above the square (to your left with your back to Victor Emmanuel Monument). Fascist masses filled the square screaming, "Four more years!"—or something like that. In 1945, they shot and hung Mussolini from a meat hook in Milan.

Victor Emmanuel Monument—This oversized monument to Italy's first king—built to celebrate the 50th anniversary of the country's unification—was part of Italy's push to overcome the new country's strong regionalism and to create a national identity. Open to the public, it offers a grand view of the Eternal City (free, 242 punishing steps to the top).

Romans think of the 200-foot-high, 500-foot-wide monument not as an altar of the fatherland, but as "the wedding cake," "the typewriter," or "the dentures." It wouldn't be so bad if it weren't sitting on a priceless acre of ancient Rome and if they had chosen better marble (this is too in-your-face white and picks up the pollution horribly). Soldiers guard Italy's *Tomb of the Unknown Soldier* as the eternal flame flickers. At the tomb, stand with your back to the flame and see how Via del Corso bisects Rome.

Note: There is a clever little back door access from the top of Capitol Hill, leading directly to the top of the Victor Emmanuel Monument, saving you lots of uphill stair-climbing (go up wide steps in left corner of the square, near the drinking fountain and she-wolf statue, pass through iron gate at top of steps, and enter small unmarked door on the right).

Pantheon Area

To get to the Pantheon, walk (it's a 10- to 15-min walk from the Forum), take a taxi, or catch a bus. Bus #64 carries tourists and pickpockets daily and frequently between the train station and Vatican City, stopping at Largo Argentina, a few blocks south of the Pantheon. The *elettrico* minibus #116 runs between Campo de' Fiori and Piazza Barberini via the Pantheon (daily, fewer on Sun).

▲▲▲Pantheon—For the greatest look at the splendor of Rome, antiquity's best-preserved interior is a must (free, Mon–Sat 8:30–19:30, Sun 9:00–18:00, holidays 9:00–13:00, tel. 06-6830-0230). Because the Pantheon became a church dedicated to the martyrs just after the fall of Rome, the barbarians left it alone, and the locals didn't use it as a quarry. The portico is called "Rome's umbrella"—a fun local gathering in a rainstorm. Walk past its one-piece granite columns (biggest in Italy, shipped from Egypt) and through the original bronze doors. Sit inside under the glorious skylight and enjoy classical architecture at its best.

The dome, 142 feet high and wide, was Europe's biggest until the Renaissance. Michelangelo's dome at St. Peter's, while much higher, is about three feet smaller. The brilliance of this dome's construction astounded architects through the ages. During the Renaissance, Brunelleschi was given permission to cut into the dome (see the little square hole above and to the right of the entrance) to analyze the material. The concrete dome gets thinner and lighter with height—the highest part is volcanic pumice.

This wonderfully harmonious architecture greatly inspired Raphael and other artists of the Renaissance. Raphael, along with Italy's first two kings, chose to be buried here.

As you walk around the outside of the Pantheon, notice the "rise of Rome"—about 15 feet since it was built. The nearest WCs are at McDonald's and at bars on the square. Great gelato is nearby,

Pantheon Area

at **Giolitti's** (Via Uffici del Vicario 40, see page 939).

▲▲Churches near the Pantheon—The **Church of San Luigi dei Francesi** has a magnificent chapel painted by Caravaggio (free, but bring coins to buy light, Fri–Wed 7:30–12:30 & 15:30–19:00, Thu 7:30–12:30, sightseers should avoid Mass at 7:30 and 19:00).

The only Gothic church in Rome is **Santa Maria sopra Minerva,** with a little-known Michelangelo statue, *Christ Bearing the Cross* (free, daily 7:00–12:00 & 15:30–19:00, on a little square behind Pantheon, to the east). The **Church of St. Ignazio,** several blocks east of the Pantheon, is a riot of Baroque illusions with a false dome (free, daily 7:00–12:30 & 16:00–19:00). A few blocks away, back across Corso Vittorio Emmanuele, is the rich and Baroque **Gesu Church,** headquarters of the Jesuits in Rome (free, daily 7:00–12:30 & 16:00–19:15). Modest dress is recommended at all churches.

▲Galleria Doria Pamphilj—This gallery, filling a palace on Piazza del Collegio Romano, offers a rare chance to wander through a noble family's lavish rooms with the prince who calls this downtown mansion home. Well, almost. Through an audioguide, the prince lovingly narrates his family's story, including how the Doria Pamphilj (pahm-FEEL-yee) family's cozy relationship with the pope inspired the word "nepotism." Highlights include paintings by Caravaggio, Titian, and Raphael, and portraits of Pope Innocent X by Velázquez (on canvas) and Bernini (in marble). The fancy rooms of the palace are interesting, with a mini-Versailles-like hall of mirrors and paintings lining the walls to the ceiling in the style typical of 18th-century galleries (€8, includes worthwhile audioguide, Fri–Wed 10:00–17:00, closed Thu, from Piazza Venezia walk 2 blocks up Via del Corso and take a left, tel. 06-679-7323, www.doriapamphilj.it).

Piazza di Pietra (Piazza of Stone)—This square was actually a quarry set up to chew away at the abandoned Roman building. You can still see the holes hungry medieval scavengers chipped into the columns to steal the metal pins that held the slabs together (2 blocks toward Via del Corso from Pantheon).

▲Trevi Fountain—This bubbly Baroque fountain, worth ▲ by day and ▲▲ by night, is a minor sight to art scholars but a major nighttime gathering spot for teens on the make and tourists tossing coins. (For more information, see page 939.)

East Rome, near the Train Station

These sights are within a 10-minute walk of the train station. By Metro, use the Termini stop for the National Museum and the Piazza Repubblica stop for the rest.

▲▲▲National Museum of Rome in Palazzo Massimo—This museum houses the greatest collection of ancient Roman art anywhere, and includes busts of emperors and a Roman copy of the *Greek Discus Thrower*. The ground floor is a historic yearbook of marble statues from the 2nd century B.C. to the 2nd century A.D., with rare Greek originals.

The first floor is peopled by statues from the 1st through 4th centuries A.D. To see the second-floor collection of frescoes and mosaics that once decorated Roman villas, you must reserve an entry time for a free, 45-minute tour led by an Italian- and English-speaking guide; if interested, book the next available tour when you buy your ticket. Finally, descend into the basement to see fine gold jewelry, dice, an abacus, and vault doors leading into the best coin collection in Europe, with fancy magnifying glasses maneuvering you through cases of coins from ancient Rome to modern times.

Cost and Hours: €6, covered by €20 combo-ticket, Tue–Sun 9:00–19:45, closed Mon, last entry 45 min before closing. An audioguide costs €4 (buy ticket first, then get audioguide at bookshop). The museum is about 100 yards from the Termini train station (Metro: Termini). As you leave the station, it's the sandstone-brick

East Rome

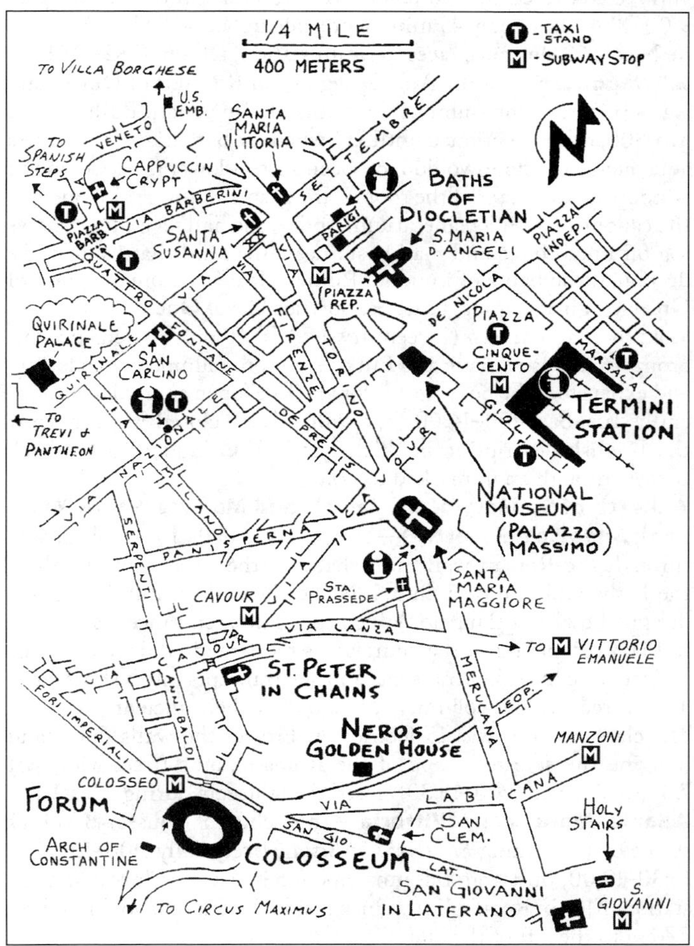

building on your left. Enter at the far end, at Largo di Villa Peretti (tel. 06-481-4144).

▲Baths of Diocletian—Around A.D. 300, Emperor Diocletian built the largest baths in Rome. This sprawling meeting place, with baths and schmoozing spaces to accommodate 3,000 bathers at a time, was a big deal in ancient Rome. While much of it is still closed, three sections are open: the Octagonal Hall, the Church of St. Mary of the Angels and Martyrs (both face Piazza della Repubblica—see below), and the skippable Museum of the Bath, which displays ancient Roman inscriptions on tons of tombs and tablets, but has nothing on the baths despite its name (museum entry-€5, covered by €20 combo-ticket, audioguide-€4, Tue–Sun 9:00–19:45, last entry 45 min before closing, closed Mon, Viale E. de Nicola 79, entrance faces Termini station, tel. 06-4782-6152).

▲Octagonal Hall—The Aula Ottagona, or Rotunda of Diocletian, was a private gymnasium in the Baths of Diocletian. Built around A.D. 300, these functioned until 537, when the barbarians cut Rome's aqueducts. The floor would have been 23 feet lower (look down the window in the center of the room). The graceful iron grid supported the canopy of a 1928 planetarium. Today, the hall's a gallery, showing off fine bronze and marble statues—the kind that would have decorated the baths of imperial Rome. Most are Roman copies of Greek originals...gods, athletes, portrait busts. One merits a close look: the *Boxer at Rest* (1st century B.C.). Textbook Hellenistic, this bronze statue is realistic and full of emotion. Slumped over, losing, and exhausted, the boxer gasps for air (free, open sporadically, generally Tue–Sat 9:00–14:00, Sun 9:00–13:00, closed Mon, borrow the English-description booklet, handy WC hidden in the back corner through an unmarked door).

▲Church of St. Mary of the Angels and Martyrs (Santa Maria degli Angeli e dei Martiri)—From Piazza della Repubblica, step through the Roman wall into what was the great central hall of the baths and is now a church (since the 16th century) that was designed by Michelangelo. When the church entrance was moved to Piazza Repubblica, the church was reoriented 90 degrees, turning the nave into long transepts and the transepts into a short nave. The 12 red granite columns still stand in their ancient positions. The classical floor was 15 feet lower. Project the walls down and imagine the soaring shape of the Roman vaults (free, Mon–Sat 7:00–18:30, Sun 8:00–19:30, closed to sightseers during Mass).

▲Santa Maria della Vittoria—This church houses Bernini's statue of a swooning *St. Teresa in Ecstasy* (free; daily 7:00–12:00 & 15:30–19:00; on Largo Susanna, about 5 blocks northwest of train station, Metro: Repubblica). Once inside the church, you'll find St. Teresa to the left of the altar.

Teresa has just been stabbed with God's arrow of fire. Now, the angel pulls it out and watches her reaction. Teresa swoons, her eyes roll up, her hand goes limp, she parts her lips...and moans. The smiling, cherubic angel understands just how she feels. Teresa, a 16th-century Spanish nun, later talked of the "sweetness" of "this intense pain," describing her oneness with God in ecstatic, even erotic, terms.

Bernini, the master of multimedia, pulls out all the stops to make this mystical vision real. Actual sunlight pours through the alabaster windows; bronze sunbeams shine on a marble angel holding a golden arrow. Teresa leans back on a cloud and her robe ripples from within, charged with her spiritual arousal. Bernini has created a little stage-setting of heaven. And watching from the "theater boxes" on either side are members of the family that commissioned the work.

Santa Susanna Church—The home of the American Catholic Church in Rome, Santa Susanna holds Mass in English daily at 18:00 and Sunday at 9:00 and 10:30. Their excellent Web site in English, www.santasusanna.org, contains tips for travelers and a long list of convents that rent out rooms. They arrange papal audiences (see page 910) and have an English library with my Venice, Florence, and Rome guidebooks (Via XX Settembre 15, near recommended Via Firenze hotels, Metro: Repubblica, tel. 06-4201-4554).

North Rome: Villa Borghese and nearby Via Veneto

▲Villa Borghese—Rome's scruffy "Central Park" is great for people-watching (plenty of modern-day Romeos and Juliets). You can take a rowboat out on the lake or visit the two museums listed below.

▲▲▲Borghese Gallery—This private museum, filling a cardinal's mansion in the park, offers one of Europe's most sumptuous art experiences. Because of the gallery's slick mandatory reservation system, you'll enjoy its collection of world-class Baroque sculpture—including Bernini's *David* and his excited statue of Apollo chasing Daphne, as well as paintings by Caravaggio, Raphael, Titian, and Rubens—with manageable crowds.

The essence of the collection is the connection of the Renaissance with the classical world. Notice the 2nd-century Roman reliefs with Michelangelo-designed panels above either end of the portico as you enter. The villa was built in the early 17th century by the great art collector Cardinal Borghese, who wanted to prove that the glories of ancient Rome were matched by the Renaissance.

In the main entry hall, opposite the door, notice the thrilling relief of the horse falling (1st century A.D., Greek). Pietro Bernini, father of the famous Bernini, completed the scene by adding the rider.

Each room seems to feature a Baroque masterpiece. The best of all is in Room 3: Bernini's *Apollo and Daphne.* It's the perfect Baroque subject—capturing a thrilling, action-filled moment. In the mythological story, Apollo races after Daphne. Just as he's about to reach her, she turns into a tree. As her toes turn to roots and branches spring from her fingers, Apollo is in for one rude surprise. Walk slowly around. It's more air than stone.

Cost and Hours: €8.50, includes €2 reservation fee, Tue–Sun 9:00–19:00, Sat sometimes until 23:00 June–Sept, closed Mon. No photos are allowed.

North Rome

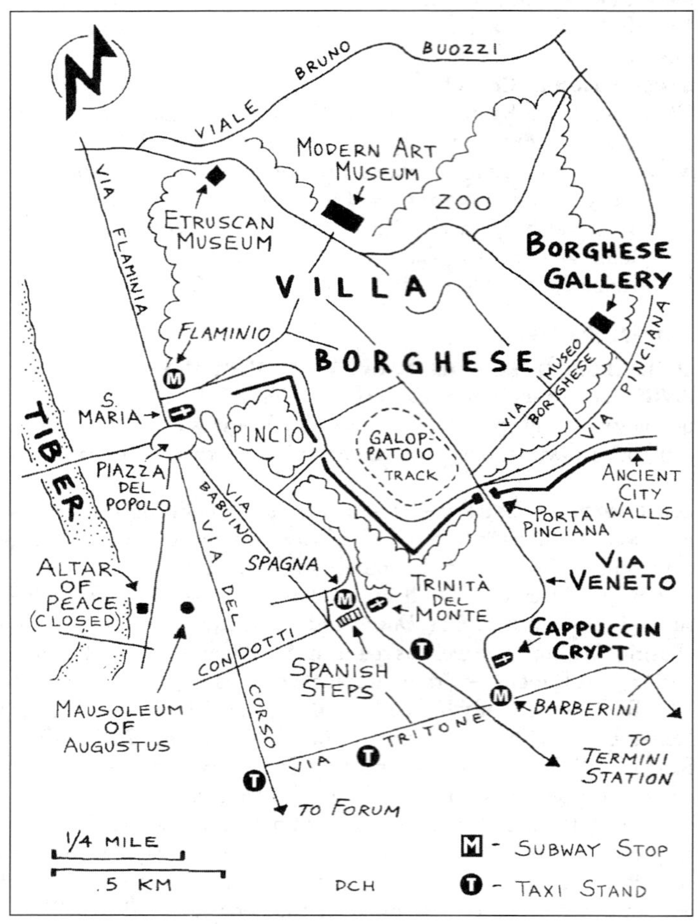

Reservations: Reservations are mandatory and easy to get in English by booking online (www.ticketeria.it) or calling 06-328-101 (if you get an Italian recording, press 2 for English; office hours: Mon–Fri 9:00–18:00, Sat 9:00–13:00, office closed Sat in Aug and Sun year-round). Every two hours, 360 people are allowed to enter the museum. Entry times are 9:00, 11:00, 13:00, 15:00, and 17:00 (plus 19:00 and 21:00 if open late on Sat June–Sept). Reserve a *minimum* of several days in advance for a weekday visit, at least a week ahead for weekends. When you reserve, request a day and time, and you'll get a claim number. While you'll be advised to come 30 minutes before your appointed time, you can arrive a few minutes beforehand. But don't cut it too close, as no-show tickets are sold to stand-bys.

If you don't have a reservation, try calling to see if there are any openings, or just show up and hope for a cancellation. Reservations are tightest at 11:00 and on weekends. No-shows are released a few minutes after the top of the hour. Generally, out of 360 reservations, a few will fail to show (but more than a few may be waiting to grab them).

Visits are strictly limited to two hours. Concentrate on the ground floor, but leave yourself 30 minutes for the paintings of the Pinacoteca upstairs (highlights are marked by the audioguide icons). The fine bookshop and cafeteria are best visited outside your two-hour entry window.

Tours: Guided English tours are offered at 9:10 and 11:10 for €5; reserve with entry reservation (or consider the excellent audioguide tour for €4).

Location: The museum is in the Villa Borghese park. A taxi can get you within 100 yards of the museum (tell the cabbie your destination: gah-leh-REE-ah bor-GAY-zay). Otherwise, take the Metro to Spagna and from there, it's a 15-minute walk through the park.

Etruscan Museum (Villa Giulia Museo Nazionale Etrusco)—The Etruscan civilization thrived in this part of Italy around 600 B.C., when Rome was an Etruscan town. The Etruscan civilization is fascinating, but the Villa Giulia Museum is extremely low-tech and in a state of disarray. I don't like it, and fans of the Etruscans will prefer the Vatican Museum's section. Still, the Villa Giulia does have the famous "husband and wife sarcophagus" (a dead couple seeming to enjoy an everlasting banquet from atop their tomb—6th century B.C. from Cerveteri); the *Apollo from Veii* statue (of textbook fame); and an impressive room filled with gold sheets of Etruscan printing and temple statuary from the Sanctuary of Pyrgi (€4, Tue–Sun 8:30–19:30, closed Mon, closes earlier off-season, Piazzale di Villa Giulia 9, tel. 06-322-6571).

▲Cappuccin Crypt—If you want to see artistically arranged bones, this is the place. Newly opened after renovation, this macabre crypt gives "interior decorating" a new meaning. It's below the church of Santa Maria della Immacolata Concezione on Via Veneto, just up from Piazza Barberini. The bones of more than 4,000 monks who died between 1528 and 1870 are in the basement, all lined up for the delight—or disgust—of the always-wide-eyed visitor. The soil in the crypt was brought from Jerusalem 400 years ago, and the monastic message on the wall explains that this is more than just a macabre exercise. Pick up a few of Rome's most interesting postcards (donation, Fri–Wed 9:00–12:00 & 15:00–18:00, closed Thu, Metro: Barberini, tel. 06-487-1185). A painting of St. Francis by Caravaggio is upstairs.

Just up the street you'll find the American Embassy, Federal Express, and fancy Via Veneto cafés filled with the poor and envious looking for the rich and famous.

Ara Pacis (Altar of Peace)—Now surrounded by a high fence, this may reopen in 2006 after restoration. In 9 B.C., after victories in Gaul and Spain, Emperor Augustus celebrated the beginning of the Pax Romana (the Roman empire at peace) by building this altar of peace. Peace is almost worshiped here. The north and south walls show a procession with realistic portraits of the imperial family in Greek Hellenistic style. It's a memorable combination of Roman grandeur and Greek elegance. Even during restoration, the altar can sometimes be seen through the windows (a long block west of Via del Corso on Via di Ara Pacis, on east bank of river near Ponte Cavour, nearest Metro: Spagna).

West Rome: Vatican City Area

▲▲▲St. Peter's Basilica—There is no doubt: This is the richest and most impressive church on earth. To call it vast is like calling God smart. Marks on the floor show where the next-largest churches would fit if they were put inside. The ornamental cherubs would dwarf a large man. Birds roost inside, and thousands of people wander about, heads craned heavenward, hardly noticing each other. Don't miss Michelangelo's *Pietà* (behind bulletproof glass) to the right of the entrance. Bernini's altar work and seven-story-tall bronze canopy *(baldacchino)* are brilliant.

For a quick walk through the basilica, follow these points (see map on page 909):

❶ The atrium is larger than most churches. Notice the historic doors (the Holy Door, on the right, won't be opened until the next Jubilee Year, in 2025—see point 13 on page 912).

❷ The purple, circular porphyry stone marks the site of Charlemagne's coronation in A.D. 800 (in the first St. Peter's church that stood on this site). From here, get a sense of the immensity of the church, which can accommodate 95,000 worshipers standing on its six acres.

❸ Michelangelo planned a Greek-cross floor plan rather than the Latin-cross standard in medieval churches. A Greek cross, symbolizing the perfection of God, and by association the goodness of man, was important to the humanist Michelangelo. But accommodating large crowds was important to the Church in the fancy Baroque age, which followed Michelangelo, so the original nave length was doubled. Stand halfway up the nave and imagine the stubbier design Michelangelo had in mind.

❹ View the magnificent dome from the statue of St. Andrew. See the vision of heaven above the windows: Jesus, Mary, a ring of saints, rings of angels, and, on the very top, God the Father.

St. Peter's Basilica

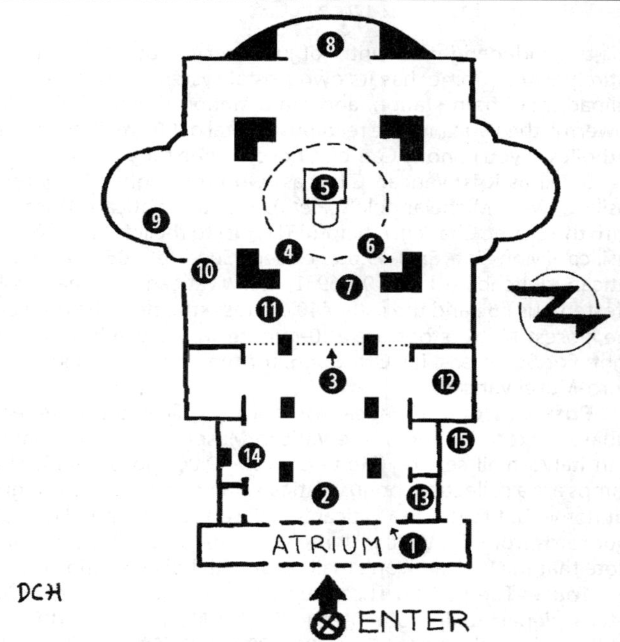

1. Holy Door
2. Charlemagne's Coronation Site, 800 A.D.
3. Extent of original "Greek Cross" Church Plan
4. St. Andrew Statue & View of Dome
5. Main Altar (Directly over Peter's Tomb)
6. Stairs Down to Crypt (Entrance May Move)
7. St. Peter Statue (With Kissable Toe)
8. BERNINI—Dove Window & "Throne of Peter"
9. St. Peter's Crucifixion Site
10. Museum Entrance
11. RAPHAEL—Transfiguration (Mosaic Copy)
12. Blessed Sacrament Chapel
13. MICHELANGELO—Pietà
14. Elevator to Roof and Dome-Climb (Possible Indoor Location)
15. Elevator to Roof and Dome-Climb (Possible Outdoor Location)

Vatican City

This tiny independent country of just over 100 acres, contained entirely within Rome, has its own postal system, armed guards, helipad, mini-train station, and radio station (KPOP). Politically powerful, the Vatican is the religious capital of 800 million Roman Catholics. If you're not a Catholic, become one for your visit.

Small as it is, Vatican City has two huge sights: St. Peter's Basilica (with Michelangelo's *Pietà*) and the Vatican Museum (with the Sistine Chapel). A helpful TI is just to the left of St. Peter's Basilica (Mon–Sat 8:30–19:00, closed Sun, tel. 06-6988-1662; Vatican switchboard tel. 06-6982, www.vatican.va). The thief-infested bus #64 and the safer #40 express stop near the basilica. The closest Metro stops are a 10-minute walk away from either sight: For St. Peter's, it's Ottaviano; for the Vatican Museum, it's Cipro-Musei Vaticani.

Post Office: The Vatican post, with offices on St. Peter's Square (next to TI) and in the Vatican Museum, is more reliable than Italy's mail service (Mon–Sat 8:30–19:00, closed Sun). The stamps are a collectible bonus. Vatican stamps are good throughout Rome, but to use the Vatican's mail service, you need to mail your cards from the Vatican; write your postcards ahead of time. (Note that the Vatican won't mail cards with Italian stamps.)

Tours: The Vatican TI conducts free 90-minute tours of St. Peter's (depart daily from TI at 14:15, also Mon, Wed, and Fri at 15:00, confirm schedule at TI, tel. 06-6988-1662). Tours are the only way to see the Vatican Gardens; book at least a day in advance by calling 06-6988-4676 (€9, Mon–Sat 10:00–12:00, tours start at Vatican Museum tour desk and finish on St. Peter's Square). To tour the necropolis of St. Peter's and the saint's tomb, call the Excavations Office at 06-6988-5318 a minimum of a week before your visit (€8, 2 hrs, office open Mon–Fri 9:00–17:00).

Seeing the Pope: Your best chances for a sighting are on Sunday and Wednesday. The pope usually gives a blessing at noon on Sunday from his apartment on St. Peter's Square (except summer, when he speaks at his summer residence at Castel Gandolfo 25 miles from Rome; train leaves Rome's Termini station). St. Peter's is easiest (just show up) and, for most, enough of a "visit." Those interested in a more formal appearance (but not more intimate), can get a ticket for the Wednesday blessing (at 10:30) when the pope, arriving in his bulletproof Popemobile, greets and blesses

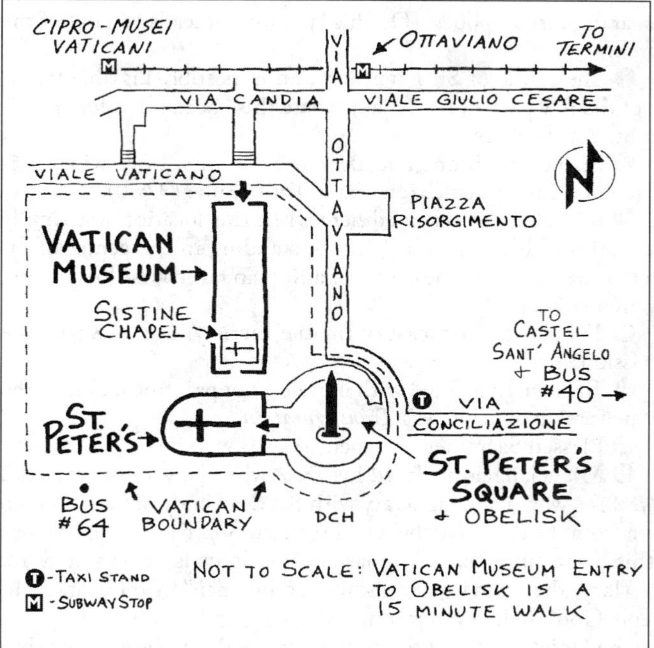

the crowds at St. Peter's from a balcony or canopied platform on the square (except in winter, when he speaks at 10:30 in the 7,000-seat Aula Paola VI Auditorium, next to St. Peter's Basilica). This requires a ticket—arrange it in advance through your hotel or the Santa Susanna Church (they get it and you pick it up the day before at their church between 17:00 and 18:45, Via XX Settembre 15, near recommended Via Firenze hotels, Metro: Repubblica, tel. 06-4201-4554, www.santasusanna.org). To find out the pope's schedule or to book a free spot for the Wednesday blessing (either for a seat on the square or in the auditorium), call 06-6988-4631. The weekly entertainment guide *Roma c'è* always has a "Seeing the Pope" section. If you only want to see the Vatican—but not the pope—minimize crowd problems by avoiding these times.

❺ The main altar sits directly over St. Peter's tomb and under Bernini's 70-foot-tall bronze canopy.

❻ The stairs lead down to the crypt to the foundation, chapels, and tombs of popes. (Do this last, since it leads you out of the church.)

❼ The statue of St. Peter, with an irresistibly kissable toe, is one of the few pieces of art that predate this church. It adorned the first St. Peter's church.

❽ St. Peter's throne and Bernini's starburst dove window is the site of a daily Mass (Mon–Sat at 17:00, Sun at 17:30).

❾ St. Peter was crucified here when this location was simply "the Vatican Hill." The obelisk now standing in the center of St. Peter's square marked the center of a Roman racecourse long before a church stood here.

❿ For most, the treasury (in the sacristy) is not worth the admission.

⓫ The church is filled with mosaics, not paintings. Notice the mosaic version of Raphael's *Transfiguration*.

⓬ Blessed Sacrament Chapel.

⓭ Michelangelo sculpted his *Pietà* when he was 24 years old. A *pietà* is a work showing Mary with the dead body of Christ taken down from the cross. Michelangelo's mastery of the body is obvious in this powerfully beautiful masterpiece. Jesus is believably dead, and Mary, the eternally youthful "handmaiden" of the Lord, still accepts God's will...even if it means giving up her son.

The Holy Door (just to the right of the *Pietà*) was bricked shut at the end of the Jubilee Year 2000 and won't be opened until 2025. Every 25 years, the Church celebrates an especially festive year derived from the Old Testament idea of the Jubilee Year (originally every 50 years), which encourages new beginnings and the forgiveness of sins and debts. In the Jubilee Year 2000, Pope John Paul II tirelessly—and with significant success—promoted debt relief for the world's poorest countries.

⓮ An elevator leads to the roof and the stairway up the dome (€5, allow an hour to go up and down; this entrance is sometimes closed, in which case you'll find another elevator just outside the basilica on the north side of St. Peter's). The dome, Michelangelo's last work, is (you guessed it) the biggest anywhere. Taller than a football field is long, it's well worth the sweaty climb for a great view of Rome, the Vatican grounds, and the inside of the basilica—particularly heavenly while there is singing. Look around—Rome has no modern skyline. No building is allowed to exceed the height of St. Peter's. The elevator takes you to the rooftop of the nave. From there, a few steps take you to a balcony at the base of the dome looking down into the church interior. After that, the one-way, 323-step climb (for some people claustrophobic) to the cupola

Is the Pope Catholic?

Rome's tour guides, who introduce tourists to the city's great art and Christian history, field a lot of interesting questions and comments from their groups. Here are a few of their favorites:

- Was John Paul II the son of John Paul I?
- Who's the guy on the cross?
- Oh, to be here in Rome...where our Lord Jesus walked.
- Is this where Christ fought the lions?
- This guy who made so many nice things, Rene Sance, who is he? (Say it fast, and you'll get the gist.)
- What's the Sistine Chapel worth in U.S. dollars?
- How did Michelangelo get Moses to pose for him?
- What's Michelangelo doing now?

begins. The rooftop level (below the dome) has a gift shop, WC, drinking fountain, and a commanding view.

Dress Code: The church strictly enforces its dress code: no shorts or bare shoulders (applies to men, women, and children); no miniskirts. You might be required to check any bags at a free cloakroom near the entry.

Hours of Church: Daily May–Sept 7:00–19:00, Oct–April 7:00–18:00. All are welcome to join in the hour-long Mass at the front altar (Mon–Sat at 8:30, 10:00, 11:00, 12:00, and 17:00; Sun and holidays 9:00, 10:30, 12:10, 13:00, 16:00, & 17:30). The church often closes on Wednesday mornings during papal audiences. This place is particularly moving at 7:00, while tourism is still sleeping. Volunteers who want you to understand and appreciate St. Peter's give free 90-minute tours (depart from TI daily at 14:15; also Mon, Wed, and Fri at 15:00; confirm schedule and meet tour at TI outside entrance to basilica, tel. 06-6988-1662); the tours are generally excellent but non-Christians can find them preachy. Seeing the *Pietà* is neat; understanding it is divine.

Cost and Hours of Dome: The view from the dome is worth the climb (€5 elevator plus 323-step climb, allow an hour to go up and down, daily April–Sept 8:00–17:45, Oct–March 8:00–16:45).

▲▲▲Vatican Museum—The four miles of displays in this immense museum—from ancient statues to Christian frescoes to modern paintings—are topped by the Raphael Rooms and Michelangelo's glorious Sistine Chapel. (If you have binoculars, bring them.)

Even without the Sistine, this is one of Europe's top three or four houses of art. It can be exhausting, so plan your visit carefully, focusing on a few themes. Allow two hours for a quick visit, three or four for time to enjoy it. The museum has a nearly impossible-not-to-follow, one-way system. Tip: The Sistine Chapel has an exit (optional) that leads directly to St. Peter's Basilica, saving you the 10-minute walk back to the Vatican Museum exit; if you want to squirt out at the Sistine, see the Pinacoteca painting gallery first (described below) and don't get an audioguide (which needs to be returned at the entry/exit).

Start, as civilization did, in Egypt and Mesopotamia. Next, the Pio Clementino collection features **Greek and Roman statues.** Decorating its courtyard are some of the best Greek and Roman statues in captivity, including the *Laocoön* group (1st century B.C., Hellenistic) and the *Apollo Belvedere* (a 2nd-century Roman copy of a Greek original). The centerpiece of the next hall is the *Belvedere Torso* (just a 2,000-year-old torso, but one that had a great impact on the art of Michelangelo). Finishing off the classical statuary are two fine 4th-century porphyry sarcophagi; these royal purple tombs were made (though not used) for the Roman emperor Constantine's mother and daughter. They were Christians—and therefore outlaws—until Constantine made Christianity legal (A.D. 312). The tombs, crafted in Egypt at a time when a declining Rome was unable to do such fine work, have details that are fun to study.

After long halls of tapestries, old maps, broken penises, and fig leaves, you'll come to what most people are looking for: The Raphael Rooms (or *stanza*) and Michelangelo's Sistine Chapel.

These outstanding works are frescoes. A fresco (meaning "fresh" in Italian) is technically not a painting. The color is mixed into wet plaster, and, when the plaster dries, the painting is actually part of the wall. This is a durable but difficult medium, requiring speed and accuracy, as the work is built slowly, one patch at a time.

After fancy rooms illustrating the "Immaculate Conception of Mary" (in the 19th century, the Vatican codified this hard-to-sell doctrine, making it a formal part of the Catholic faith) and the triumph of Constantine (with divine guidance, which led to his conversion to Christianity), you enter the first room completely done by **Raphael** and find the newly restored *School of Athens*. This is remarkable for its blatant pre-Christian classical orientation, especially since it originally wallpapered the apartments of Pope Julius II. Raphael honors the great pre-Christian thinkers—Aristotle, Plato, and company—who are portrayed as the leading artists of Raphael's day. The bearded figure of Plato is Leonardo da Vinci. Diogenes, history's first hippie, sprawls alone in bright blue on the stairs, while Michelangelo broods in the foreground—supposedly added late. Apparently, Raphael snuck a peek at the Sistine Chapel and decided that his arch-competitor was so good he had to put their personal differences aside and include him in this tribute to the artists of his generation. Today's St. Peter's was under construction as Raphael was working. In the *School of Athens*, he gives us a sneak preview of the unfinished church.

Next (unless you detour through the refreshingly modern Catholic art section) is the brilliantly restored **Sistine Chapel.** This is the pope's personal chapel and also the place, upon the death of the ruling pope, a new pope is elected. The College of Cardinals meets here and votes four times a day until a two-thirds-plus-one majority is reached and a new pope is elected.

The Sistine is famous for Michelangelo's pictorial culmination of the Renaissance, showing the story of creation, with a powerful God weaving in and out of each scene through that busy first week. This is an optimistic and positive expression of the High Renaissance and a stirring example of the artistic and theological maturity of the 33-year-old Michelangelo, who spent four years on this work.

Later, after the Reformation wars had begun and after the Catholic army of Spain had sacked the Vatican, the reeling Church began to fight back. As part of its Counter-Reformation, a much older Michelangelo was commissioned to paint the *Last Judgment* (behind the altar). Brilliantly restored, the message is as clear as the day Michelangelo finished it: Christ is returning, some will go to hell and some to heaven, and some will be saved by the power of the rosary.

In the recent and controversial restoration project, no paint was added. Centuries of dust, soot (from candles used for lighting and Mass), and glue (added to make the art shine) were removed, revealing the bright original colors of Michelangelo. Photos are allowed (without a flash) elsewhere in the museum, but as part of the deal with the company who did the restoration, no photos are allowed in the Sistine Chapel.

For a shortcut, a small door at the rear of the Sistine Chapel—likely labled "Exit for private tour groups only"—allows groups and individuals (without an audioguide) to escape directly to St. Peter's Basilica. If you exit here, you're done with the museum. The Pinacoteca is the only important part left. Consider doing it at the start. Otherwise it's a 10-minute, heel-to-toe slalom through tourists from the Sistine Chapel to the entry/exit.

After this long march, you'll find the **Pinacoteca** (the Vatican's small but fine collection of paintings, with Raphael's *Transfiguration*, Leonardo's unfinished *St. Jerome*, and Caravaggio's *Deposition*), a cafeteria (long lines, mediocre food), and the underrated early-Christian art section, before you exit via the souvenir shop.

Cost and Hours: €12, March–Oct Mon–Fri 8:45–16:45, Sat 8:45–13:45; Nov–Feb Mon–Sat 8:45–13:45, closed Sun except last Sun of the month (when it's free, crowded, and open 8:45–13:45). Last entry is about 90 minutes before the closing time. The Sistine Chapel sometimes shuts down 30 minutes early.

The museum is generally hot and crowded. The most crowded days are Saturday, the last Sunday of the month, Monday, rainy days, and any day before or after a holiday closure. Afternoons and Wednesday mornings are best.

The museum is closed on many holidays (mainly religious ones) including—for 2006—Jan 1 (New Year's) and 6 (Epiphany), Feb 11 (Vatican City established), March 19 (Saint Joseph), April 16 and 17 (Easter and Easter Monday), May 1 (Labor Day) and 25 (Ascension Thursday), June 15 (Corpus Christi Day) and 29 (Saints Peter and Paul), Aug 15 and either Aug 14 or 16 (Assumption of the Virgin), Nov 1 (All Saints' Day), and Dec 8 (Immaculate Conception) and 25–26 (Christmas). Other holidays may pop up—search for "closed dates" at www.vatican.va to confirm hours.

Modest dress (no short shorts or bare shoulders) is appropriate and often required. Museum tel. 06-6988-4947.

Tours: A tour in English is offered once daily at 11:00 (€16.50, 2 hrs, tel. 06-6988-4466 to reserve). You can rent a €5 audioguide (but if you do, you lose the option of taking the shortcut from the Sistine Chapel to St. Peter's, because the audioguide must be returned at the Vatican Museum entrance).

▲Castel Sant' Angelo—Built as a tomb for the emperor; used through the Middle Ages as a castle, prison, and place of last refuge for popes under attack; and today, a museum, this giant pile of ancient bricks is packed with history.

Ancient Rome allowed no tombs, not even the emperor's, within its walls. So Hadrian grabbed the most commanding position just outside the walls and across the river and built a towering tomb (circa A.D. 139) well within view of the city. His mausoleum was a huge cylinder (210 by 70 feet) topped by a cypress grove and crowned by a huge statue of Hadrian himself riding a chariot. For nearly a hundred years, Roman emperors (from Hadrian to Caracalla in A.D. 217) were buried here.

In the year 590, the Archangel Michael appeared above the mausoleum to Pope Gregory the Great. Sheathing his sword, the angel signaled the end of a plague. The fortress that was Hadrian's mausoleum eventually became a fortified palace, renamed for the "holy angel."

In 1277, the pope built the elevated corridor connecting Castel Sant' Angelo with the Vatican. Since Rome was repeatedly plundered by invaders, Castel Sant' Angelo was a handy place of last refuge for threatened popes.

After you walk around the entire base of the castle, take the small staircase down to the original Roman floor. In the atrium, study the model of the castle in Roman times and imagine the niche in the wall filled with a towering "welcome to my tomb" statue of Hadrian. From here, a ramp leads to the right, spiraling 410 feet. While some of the original brickwork and bits of mosaic survive, the marble veneer is long gone (notice the holes in the wall that held it in place). At the end of the ramp, stairs climb to the room where the ashes of the emperors were kept. These stairs continue to the top, where you'll find the papal apartments. Don't miss the Sala del Tesoro (treasury), where the wealth of the Vatican was locked up in a huge chest. Do miss the 58 rooms of the military museum. The views from the top are great—pick out landmarks as you stroll around—and a restful coffee with a view of St. Peter's is worth the price.

Cost, Hours, Tours: €5, Tue–Sun 9:00–20:00, maybe also June–Sept Sat 21:00–23:45, closed Mon. You can take an English-language tour with an audioguide (€4) or live guide (€4.50, Sun at 14:30, confirm tour times, tel. 06-3996-7600, Metro: Lepanto or bus #64, near Vatican City).

Ponte Sant' Angelo—The bridge leading to Castel Sant' Angelo was built by Hadrian for quick and regal access from downtown to his tomb. The three middle arches are actually Roman originals and a fine example of the empire's engineering expertise. The statues of angels are copies of original Berninis—textbook Baroque. In medieval times, this was the only bridge in the area connecting St. Peter's and the Vatican with downtown Rome. Nearly all pilgrims passed this bridge to and from the church. Its shoulder-high banisters recall a tragedy. On a Jubilee Year festival in 1450, the crowd got so huge that the mob pushed out the original banisters, causing nearly 200 to fall to their deaths off the bridge.

Southwest Rome: Trastevere

Trastevere is the colorful neighborhood across *(tras)* the Tiber *(tevere)* River. Trastevere (trahs-TAY-veh-ray) offers the best look at medieval-village Rome. The action unwinds to the chime of the church bells. Go there and wander. Wonder. Be a poet. This is Rome's Left Bank.

This proud neighborhood was long a working-class area. Now that it's becoming trendy, high rents are driving out the source of so much color. Still, it's a great people scene, especially at night. Stroll the back streets (for restaurant recommendations, see "Eating," page 952).

To get to Trastevere, taxi or ride the bus (from Vatican area—#23 or #492; or from Via Nazionale hotels—take the #40 express to Piazza Belli just over bridge, or catch #64, #70, #115, or #640 to Largo Argentina, then transfer to tram #8 and get off at Piazza Mastai, the stop just after the river).

Sta. Maria in Trastevere Church—One of Rome's oldest churches, this was made a basilica in the 4th century, when Christianity was legalized (free, Mon–Sat 7:30–13:00 & 15:00–19:00, Sun 7:30–19:00). It was the first church dedicated to the Virgin Mary. The portico (covered area just outside the door) is decorated with

Trastevere

T - Taxi Stand
Villa Farnesina
Sights
1 Santa Maria in Trastevere
2 Villa Farnesina
Hotel/Restaurants
3 Hotel Santa Maria
4 Casa San Giuseppe
5 Trattoria da Lucia
6 Osteria Ponte Sisto
7 Gelateria alla Scala
Tiber River
Isola Tiberina
Hosp.
Teatro di Marcello
Ponte Rotto Ruins
Pierleoni
Fab
Cestio
Ponte Palantino
Ripa
To Porta Portese
S. Cecelia
Genovesi
Salumi
V. Lung.
Anguillara
Piazza Belli
Ponte Garibaldi
Lungo. Cenci
Via Arenula
To Largo Argentina
Lungo Vallati
Via Capo di Ferro
V. Pettinari
To Campo de' Fiori
V. Giulia
Tebaldi
Ponte Sisto
Piazza Trilussa
+ Fountain
Lungo Raphael
Sanzio
V. Renelli
Via Lungaretta
San Crisogono
Viale Trastevere
Arco S. Calisto
Manar
Via Luciano
Piazza S. Maria
Santa Maria in Trastevere
Paglia
S. Egidio
Moro
Via D. Ren.
V. Politeama
Vic. Cinque
V. Pelliccia
Vic. Bologna
V. Bell.
V. Ponte Sisto
V. D. Scala
Vic. Scala
V. Leo.
Vic. Mattonato
Via Garibaldi
To Gianicolo Hill
Lungara
Corsini
To Botanical Gardens
Lungo. Farnesina
To Vatican
100 Yards
100 Meters
DCH

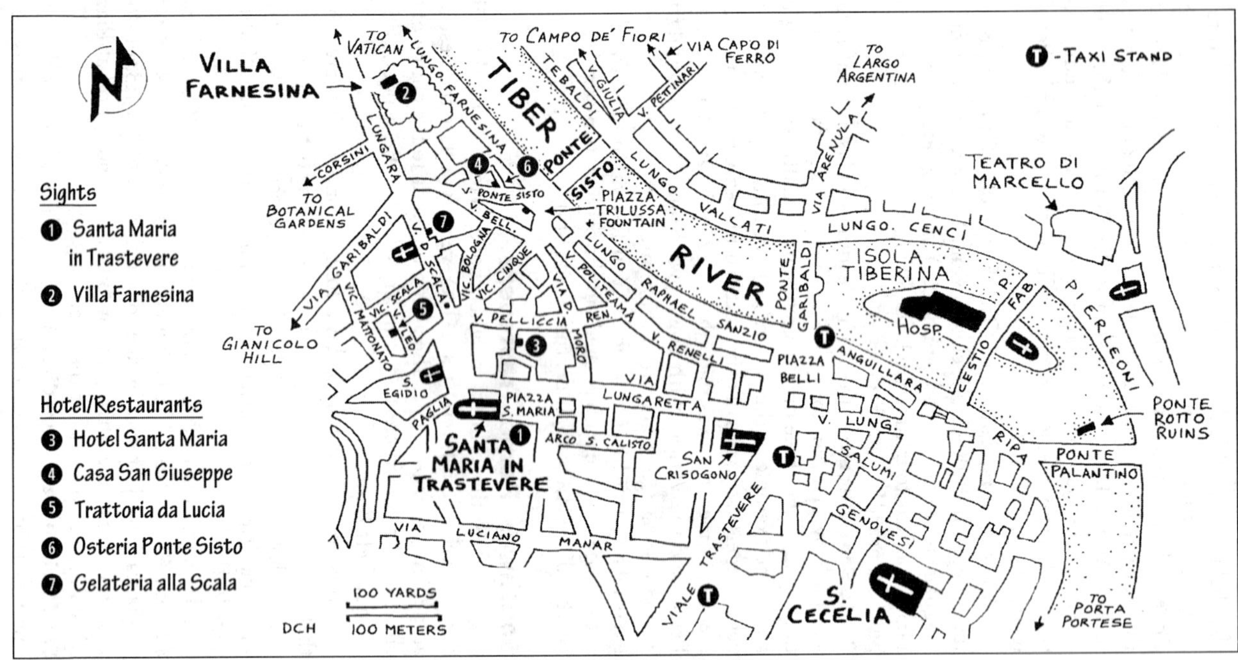

fascinating ancient fragments filled with early Christian symbolism. Most of what you see today dates from around the 12th century, but the granite columns come from an ancient Roman temple, and the ancient basilica floor plan (and ambience) survive. The 12th-century mosaics behind the altar are striking and notable for their portrayal of Mary—the first to show her at the throne with Jesus in Heaven. Look below the scenes from the life of Mary to see ahead-of-their-time mosaics (by Cavallini, from 1300), predating the Renaissance by 100 years.

The church is on Piazza di Santa Maria. While today's fountain is from the 17th century, there has been a fountain here since Roman times.

Villa Farnesina—This sumptuous 16th-century Renaissance villa, built for a wealthy Sienese banker, is decorated with paintings by Peruzzi and a lovesick Raphael (€5, Mon–Sat 9:00–13:00, closed Sun, Via della Lungara).

Linking Trastevere with the "Night Walk Across Rome"—You can walk from Trastevere to Campo de' Fiori to link up with the beginning of the "Night Walk Across Rome" (see page 935): From Trastevere's church square (Piazza di Santa Maria), take Via del Moro to the river and cross at Ponte Sisto, a pedestrian bridge with a good view of St. Peter's dome. Continue straight ahead for one block. Take the first left, which leads down Via di Capo di Ferro through the scary and narrow darkness to Piazza Farnese, with the imposing Palazzo Farnese. Michelangelo contributed to the facade of this palace, now the French Embassy. The fountains on the square feature huge, one-piece granite hot tubs from the ancient Roman Baths of Caracalla. One block from there (opposite the palace) is the atmospheric square of Campo de' Fiori.

South Rome

If you visit Ostia Antica (see page 926), you can maximize sightseeing efficiency by visiting any of the sights in south Rome on your return.

▲St. Paul's Outside the Walls (Basilica San Paolo Fuori le Mura)—This was the last major construction project of Imperial Rome (c. 380) and the largest church in Christendom until St. Peter's. After a tragic 19th-century fire, St. Paul's was rebuilt in the same general style and size as the original. Step inside and feel as close as you'll get in the 21st century to experiencing a monumental Roman basilica. Marvel at the ceiling and imagine building it with those massive wood beams in A.D. 380.

It feels sterile, but in a good way—like you're already in heaven. Along with St. Peter's Basilica, San Giovanni in Laterano, and Santa Maria Maggiore, this church is part of the Vatican rather than Italy. St. Paul is supposed to be buried under the altar (without his head, which San Giovanni in Laterano has).

Alabaster windows light the vast interior, 5th-century mosaics decorate the triumphal arch leading to the altar, and mosaic portraits of all 264 popes, from St. Peter to John Paul II, ring the place—with blank spots ready for future popes. Find John Paul II (to right of the high altar: Jo Paulus II, no date) and John Paul I (to his right, with a reign of one month and three days). The church was built upon the grave of the apostle Paul (who was decapitated two miles from this spot). Wander the ornate yet peaceful cloister—decorated with fragments from early Christian tombs and sarcophagi of people who wanted to be buried close to Paul (closed 13:00–15:00).

The courtyard leading up to the church is typical of early Christian churches; even the first St. Peter's had this kind of welcoming zone (free, daily 7:00–18:00, modest dress code enforced, Via Ostiense 186, Metro: San Paolo).

▲Montemartini Museum (Musei Capitolini Centrale Montemartini)—This museum houses a dreamy collection of 400 ancient statues, set evocatively in a classic 1932 electric power plant among generators and *Metropolis*-type cast-iron machinery. While the art is not as famous as the collections you'll see downtown, the effect is fun and memorable—and you'll encounter absolutely no tourists (€4.20, €9.90 combo-ticket includes Capitol Hill Museum, Tue–Sun 9:30–19:00, closed Mon, Via Ostiense 106, a short walk from Metro: Garbatella, tel. 06-3996-7800).

Baths of Caracalla (Terme di Caracalla)—Today it's just a shell—a huge shell—with all of its sculptures and most of its mosaics moved to museums. Inaugurated by Emperor Caracalla in A.D. 216, this massive complex could accommodate 1,600 visitors at a time. Today you'll see a two-story, roofless brick building surrounded by a garden, bordered by ruined walls. The two large rooms at either end of the building were used for exercise. In between the exercise rooms was a pool flanked by two small mosaic-floored dressing rooms. Niches in the walls once held statues. In its day, this was a remarkable place to hang out. For ancient Romans, the baths were a social experience.

The Baths of Caracalla functioned until Goths severed the aqueducts in the 6th century. In modern times, operas were performed here from 1938–1993. To keep the ruins from becoming more ruined, the performances were discontinued (€5, covered by €20 combo-ticket, Mon 9:00–14:00, Tue–Sun 9:00–one hour before sunset, audioguide-€4, good €8 guidebook can be read in shaded garden while sitting on a chunk of column, Metro: Circus Maximus, and a 5-min walk south along Via delle Terme di Caracalla, tel. 06-3996-7700). The baths' statues are displayed elsewhere: several are in Rome's Octagonal Hall and the immense

Toro Farnese (a marble sculpture of a bull surrounded by people) snorts in Naples' Archaeological Museum.

Testaccio—Four fascinating but lesser sights cluster at the Piramide Metro stop between the Colosseum and E.U.R., in the gritty Testaccio neighborhood. (This is a quick and easy stop as you return from E.U.R. or when changing trains en route to Ostia Antica.)

Working-class since ancient times, the Testaccio neighborhood has recently gone trendy-bohemian. Visitors wander through an awkward mix of yuppie and proletarian worlds, not noticing—but perhaps feeling—the "keep Testaccio for the Testaccians" graffiti. This has long been the neighborhood of slaughterhouses, and its restaurants are renowned for their ability to cook up the least palatable part of the animals...the fifth quarter. For a meal you won't forget, try **Trattoria "Da Oio" a Casa Mia** (closed Sun, Via Galvani 43, tel. 06-578-2680).

Pyramid of Gaius Cestius: The Marc Antony/Cleopatra scandal (around 30 B.C.) brought exotic Egyptian styles into vogue. A rich Roman magistrate, Gaius Cestius, had a pyramid built as his tomb. Made of brick covered in marble, it was completed in just 330 days (as stated in its Latin inscription) and fell far short of Egyptian pyramid standards. Later incorporated into the Aurelian Wall, it's now next to the Piramide Metro stop.

Porta Ostiense: This formidable gate (also next to Piramide Metro stop) is from the Aurelian Wall, begun in the 3rd century under Emperor Aurelius. The wall, which encircled the city, was 12 miles long and 26 feet high, with 14 main gates and 380 72-foot-tall towers. Most of what you'll see today is circa A.D. 400, but the barbarians reconstructed the gate later, in the 6th century.

If you climb up (enter nearest the pyramid) you can enjoy a free ramble along the ramparts and exhibits and models of Ostia Antica (Rome's ancient port; see page 926) and the Ostian Way. (For more on the wall, visit the Museum of the Walls at Porta San Sebastian; see "Ancient Appian Way," below.)

Protestant Cemetery: The *Cimitero Acattolico per gli Stranieri al Testaccio* (cemetery for the burial of non-Catholic foreigners) is a tomb-filled park, running along the wall just beyond the pyramid. From the Piramide Metro stop, walk between the pyramid and the Roman gate on Via Persichetti, then go left on Caio Cestio to the gate of the cemetery. Ring the bell (donation box, Tue–Sat 9:00–18:00, Sun 9:00–14:00, closed Mon and an hour early in winter).

Originally, none of the Protestant epitaphs were allowed to make any mention of heaven. Signs direct visitors to the graves of notable non-Catholics who died in Rome since 1738. Many of the buried were diplomats. And many, such as poets Shelley and Keats, were from the Romantic Age. They came on the Grand

Tour and—"captivated by the fatal charms of Rome," as Shelley wrote—never left. Head left toward the pyramid to find Keats' tomb, in the far corner. Keats died in his 20s, unrecognized. He wanted to be unnamed on a tomb which read "Young English Poet, 1821. Here lies one whose name was writ in water." To see Keats' tomb if the cemetery is closed, look through the tiny peephole on Via Caio Cestio, 10 yards off Via Marmarata.

Inside the cemetery (nearest the pyramid), look down on Matilde Talli's cat hospice (flier at the gate). Volunteers use donations to care for these "Guardians of the Departed" who "provide loyal companionship to these dead."

Notice the beige travertine post office from 1932 (across the big street from cemetery). This is textbook Mussolini Fascist architecture. The huge X design on the stairwells celeebrates the 10th anniversary of the dictator's reign.

Monte Testaccio: Just behind the Protestant Cemetery (as you leave, turn left and continue two blocks down Caio Cestio) is a 115-foot-tall ancient trash mountain. It's made of broken *testae*—earthenware jars used to haul mostly wine 2,000 years ago, when this was a gritty port warehouse district. For 500 years, rancid oil vessels were discarded here. Slowly, Rome's lowly eighth hill was built. Because the caves dug into the hill stay cool, trendy bars, clubs, and restaurants compete with gritty car-repair places for a spot. The neighborhood was once known for a huge slaughterhouse and a Gypsy camp that squatted inside an old military base. Now it's home to the Villagio Globale, a site for concerts and techno-raves. The night scene at Monte Testaccio after 21:00 is youthful and lively with restaurants and clubs, but the neighborhood can be rough (Metro: Piramide).

Ancient Appian Way (Via Appia Antica)

Since the 4th century B.C., this has been Rome's gateway to the East. The first section was perfectly straight. It was the largest, widest, fastest road ever, the wonder of its day, called the "Queen of Roads." Eventually, this most important of Roman roads stretched 430 miles to the port of Brindisi—where boats sailed for Greece and Egypt. Twenty-nine such roads fanned out from Rome. Just as Hitler built the autobahn system in anticipation of empire maintenance, the emperors realized the military and political value of a good road system. A central strip accommodated animal-powered vehicles, and elevated sidewalks served pedestrians. As it left Rome, the road was lined with tombs and funerary monuments. Imagine a funeral procession passing under the pines and cypress and past a long line of pyramids, private mini-temples, altars, and tombs.

Hollywood created the famous image of the Appian Way lined with the bodies of Spartacus and his gang of defeated and crucified slave rebels. This image is only partially accurate. Spartacus was killed in battle.

Tourist's Appian Way: The road starts less than two miles south of the Colosseum at the massive San Sebastian Gate. The Museum of the Walls, located at the gate, offers an interesting look at Roman defense and a chance to scramble along a stretch of the ramparts (€2.60, Tue–Sat 9:00–19:00, Sun 9:00–14:00, closed Mon, tel. 06-7047-5284). Half a mile down the road are the two most historic and popular catacombs, those of San Callisto and San Sebastian (described below). Beyond that, the road becomes pristine and traffic-free, popular for biking and hiking.

To reach the Appian Way, take the Archeobus from Piazza Venezia (see "Archeobus," page 890) or take the Metro to the Colli Albani stop, then catch bus #660 to Via Appia Antica—its last stop and the start of an interesting stretch of the ancient road (the segment between the 3rd and 11th milestones is best). At the bus stop, you'll find Caffè dell' Appia Antica (Via Appia Antica 175), which serves light lunches and rents bikes (lots of fun). From here you can walk 15 minutes (or bike) to the Catacombs of San Callisto.

▲▲Catacombs—The catacombs are burial places for (mostly) Christians who died in ancient Roman times. By law, no one was allowed to be buried within the walls of Rome. While pagan Romans were into cremation, Christians preferred to be buried. But land was expensive and most Christians were poor. A few wealthy, landowning Christians allowed their property to be used as burial places.

The 40 or so known catacombs circle Rome about three miles from its center. From the 1st through the 5th centuries, Christians dug an estimated 375 miles of tomb-lined tunnels, with networks of galleries as many as five layers deep. The tufa stone—soft and easy to cut, but which hardened when exposed to air—was perfect for the job. The Christians burrowed many layers deep for two reasons: to get more mileage out of the donated land and to be near martyrs and saints already buried there. Bodies were wrapped in linen (like Christ's). Since they figured the Second Coming was imminent, there was no interest in embalming the body.

When Emperor Constantine legalized Christianity in A.D. 313, Christians had a new, interesting problem. There would be no more persecuted martyrs to bind them together and inspire them. Thus the early martyrs and popes assumed more importance, and Christians began making pilgrimages to their burial places in the catacombs.

In the 800s, when barbarian invaders started ransacking the tombs, Christians moved the relics of saints and martyrs to the safety of churches in the city center. For a thousand years, the catacombs were forgotten. Around 1850, they were excavated and became part of the Romantic Age's Grand Tour of Europe.

When abandoned plates and utensils from ritual meals were

found, 18th- and 19th-century Romantics guessed that persecuted Christians hid out in these candlelit galleries. This legend grew—even though it was untrue. They are simply early Christian burial grounds. With a million people in Rome, the 10,000 early Christians didn't need to camp out in the catacombs. They hid in plain view, melting into obscurity within the city itself.

The underground tunnels, while empty of bones, are rich in early Christian symbolism, which functioned as a secret language. The dove represented the soul. You'll see it quenching its thirst (worshiping), with an olive branch (at rest), or happily perched (in paradise). Peacocks, known for their "incorruptible flesh," embodied immortality. The shepherd with a lamb on his shoulders was the "good shepherd," the first portrayal of Christ as a kindly leader of his flock. The fish was used because the first letters of these words—"Jesus Christ, Son of God, Savior"—spelled "fish" in Greek. And the anchor is a cross in disguise. A 2nd-century bishop had written on his tomb: "All who understand these things, pray for me." You'll see pictures of people praying with their hands raised up—the custom at the time.

Catacomb tours are essentially the same. Which one you take is not important. The **Catacombs of San Callisto** (a.k.a. Callixtus), the official cemetery for the Christians of Rome and burial place of 3rd-century popes, is the most historic. Sixteen bishops (early popes) were buried here. Buy your €5 ticket and wait for your language to be called. They move lots of people quickly. If one group seems ridiculously large (over 50 people), wait for the next tour in English (Thu–Tue 8:30–12:00 & 14:30–17:30, closed Wed and Feb, closes at 17:00 in winter, Via Appia Antica 110, tel. 06-5130-1580). Dig this: The catacombs have a Web site—www.catacombe.roma.it—that focuses mainly on San Callisto, featuring photos, site info, and a history.

The **Catacombs of San Sebastian** (Sebastiano) are 300 yards farther down the road (€5, Mon–Sat 8:30–12:00 & 14:30–17:30, closed Sun and Nov, closes at 17:00 in winter, Via Appia Antica 136, tel. 06-785-0350).

E.U.R.

In the late 1930s, Italy's dictator, Benito Mussolini, planned an international exhibition to show off the wonders of his fascist society. But these wonders brought us World War II, and Il Duce's celebration never happened. The unfinished mega-project was completed in the 1950s and now houses government offices and big, obscure museums.

If Hitler and Mussolini won the war, our world might look like E.U.R. (ay-oor). Hike down E.U.R.'s wide, pedestrian-mean boulevards. Patriotic murals, aren't-you-proud-to-be-an-extreme-

E.U.R.

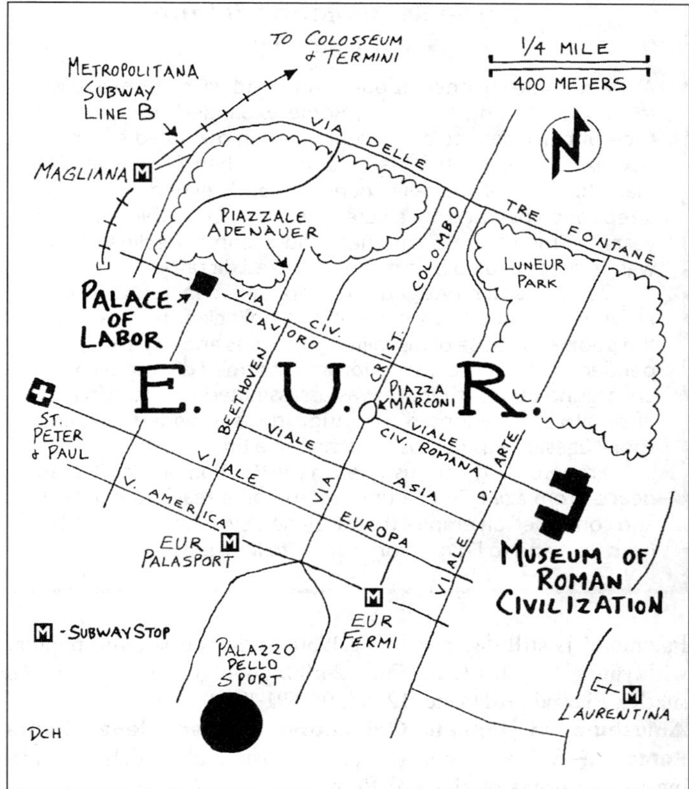

right-winger pillars, and stern squares decorate the soulless, planned grid and stark office blocks. Boulevards named for Astronomy, Electronics, Social Security, and Beethoven are more exhausting than inspirational. Today E.U.R. is worth a trip for its Museum of Roman Civilization (described below).

The Metro skirts E.U.R. with three stops (10 min from the Colosseum). Use E.U.R. Magliana for the "Square Colosseum" and E.U.R. Fermi for the Museum of Roman Civilization (both described below). Consider walking 30 minutes from the palace to the museum through the center of E.U.R.

From the Magliana subway stop, stairs lead uphill to the **Palace of the Civilization of Labor (Palazzo della Civiltà del Lavoro)**, the essence of fascist architecture. With its giant, no-questions-asked, patriotic statues and its black-and-white simplicity, this is E.U.R.'s tallest building and landmark. It's understandably nicknamed the "Square Colosseum." Around the corner, Café

Rome—Republic and Empire
(500 B.C.–A.D. 500)

Ancient Rome spanned about a thousand years, from 500 B.C. to A.D. 500. During that time, Rome expanded from a small tribe of barbarians to a vast empire, then dwindled slowly to city size again. For the first 500 years, when Rome's armies made her ruler of the Italian peninsula and beyond, Rome was a republic governed by elected senators. Over the next 500 years, a time of world conquest and eventual decline, Rome was an empire ruled by a military-backed dictator.

Julius Caesar bridged the gap between republic and empire. This ambitious general and politician, popular with the people because of his military victories and charisma, suspended the Roman constitution and assumed dictatorial powers around 50 B.C., then he was assassinated by a conspiracy of senators. His adopted son, Augustus, succeeded him, and soon "Caesar" was not just a name but a title.

Emperor Augustus ushered in the Pax Romana, or Roman peace (from A.D. 1–200), a time when Rome reached her peak and controlled an empire that stretched even beyond Eurail—from Scotland to Egypt, from Turkey to Morocco.

Palombini is still decorated in a 1930s style and is quite popular with young Romans (daily 7:00–24:00, good gelato, pastries, and snacks, Piazzale Adenauer 12, tel. 06-591-1700).

▲Museum of Roman Civilization (Museo della Civilta Romana)—With 59 rooms of plaster casts and models illustrating the greatness of classical Rome, this vast and heavy museum gives a strangely lifeless, close-up look at Rome. Each room has a theme, from military tricks to musical instruments. One long hall is filled with casts of the reliefs of Trajan's Column. The highlight is the 1:250-scale model of Constantine's Rome—circa A.D. 300 (€6.20, Tue–Sat 9:00–18:15, Sun 9:00–13:30, closed Mon, Piazza G. Agnelli; from Metro: E.U.R. Fermi, take Via America, turn right and walk past McDonald's, at T intersection, go left uphill about 3 blocks on Via dell' Arte, you'll see huge museum columns on right; tel. 06-592-6041).

Near Rome

▲▲Ostia Antica—For an exciting day trip less than an hour from downtown Rome, pop down to the ancient Roman port of Ostia Antica. It's similar to Pompeii, but a lot closer and, in some ways, more interesting. Because Ostia was a working port town, it shows a more complete and gritty look at Roman life than does wealthy Pompeii. Wandering around today, you'll see the remains of the docks, warehouses, apartment flats, mansions, shopping arcades, and baths that served a once thriving port of 60,000 people. Later, Ostia became a ghost town, and is now excavated. Start at the 2,000-year-old theater, buy a map, explore the town, and finish with its fine little museum.

Getting There: From downtown Rome, it's a 45-minute combination Metro/train ride to Ostia Antica. It'll cost you just one Metro ticket each way (€2 total round-trip). From Rome, take the Metro (line B) to the Piramide stop (consider popping out to see the ancient Roman pyramid tomb, listed above in South Rome sights). Exit and walk to the left, following signs for the "Ferrovia Roma–Lido" train (4/hr, keep your Metro ticket handy, overhead signs direct you to correct platform), which you'll ride to Ostia Antica (the stop before Lido Nord). At the train station at Ostia Antica, cross the road via the blue sky-bridge and walk straight down Via della Stazione di Ostia Antica, continuing straight until you reach the parking lot. The entrance is on the left.

Cost and Hours: €4, Tue–Sun 8:30–18:00 in summer; you can linger on the grounds until 19:00; 8:30–16:00 in winter, closed Mon; good audioguide—not always available. The well-done audioguide costs €5 (tel. 06-5635-8099).

SELF-GUIDED WALKS

Here are three walks that give you a moving picture of Rome, an ancient yet modern city. You'll walk through history ("Roman Forum Walk"), take a refreshing early evening stroll ("The Dolce Vita Stroll"), and enjoy the thriving night scene ("Night Walk Across Rome").

Roman Forum Walk

The Roman Forum (Foro Romano) was the political, religious, and commercial center of the city. Rome's most important temples and halls of justice were here. This was the place for religious processions, elections, political demonstrations, important speeches, and parades by conquering generals. As Rome's Empire expanded, these few acres of land became the center of the civilized world.

Cost, Hours, Location: Free, daily 9:00–19:00 or until an hour before dark, Metro: Colosseo, tel. 06-3996-7700. You can rent a €4 audioguide at the gift shop at the entrance on Via dei Fori Imperiali. Tours in English are offered almost hourly (€4); ask at the ticket booth at Palatine Hill (near Arch of Titus). Just like at the Colosseum, street vendors sell small *Rome: Past and Present* books with plastic overlays that restore the ruins (marked €11, offer less).

The Tour Begins: Walk through the entrance nearest the Colosseum, hiking up the ramp marked "Via Sacra." Stand next to the triumphal...

Roman Forum Walk

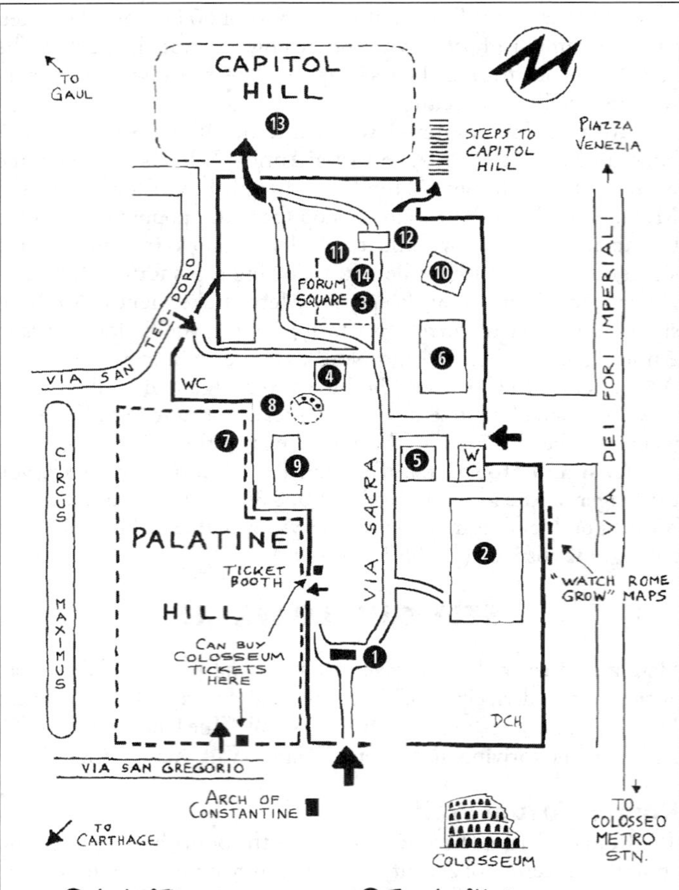

1. Arch of Titus
2. Basilica of Constantine
3. Forum's Main Square
4. Temple of Julius Caesar
5. Temple of Antoninus and Faustina
6. Basilica Aemilia
7. Caligula's Palace
8. Temple of Vesta
9. House of the Vestal Virgins
10. Curia (Senate House)
11. Rostrum
12. Arch of Septimius Severus
13. Temple of Saturn
14. Column of Phocas

❶ **Arch of Titus (Arco di Tito):** The arch commemorated the Roman victory over the province of Judea (Israel) in A.D. 70. The Romans had a reputation as benevolent conquerors who tolerated the local customs and rulers. All they required was allegiance to the empire, which could be shown by worshiping the emperor as a god. No problem for most conquered people, who already had half a dozen gods on their prayer lists anyway. But the Israelites' god was jealous and refused to let his people worship the emperor. Israel revolted. After a short but bitter war, the Romans defeated the rebels, took Jerusalem, sacked their temple, and brought home 50,000 Jewish slaves...who were forced to build this arch.

Start down the Via Sacra into the Forum. After just a few yards, turn right and follow a path uphill to the three huge arches of the...

❷ **Basilica of Constantine (a.k.a. Basilica Maxentius):** These gigantic arches represent only one third of the original Basilica of Constantine, a mammoth hall of justice. The arches were matched by a similar set along the Via Sacra side (only a few squat brick piers remain). Between them ran the central hall, which was spanned by a roof 130 feet high—about 55 feet higher than the side arches you see. (The stub of brick you see sticking up began an arch that once spanned the central hall.) The hall itself was as long as a football field, lavishly furnished with colorful inlaid marble, a gilded bronze ceiling, fountains, and statues, and filled with strolling Romans. At the far (west) end was an enormous marble statue of Emperor Constantine on a throne. (Pieces of this statue, including a hand the size of a man, are on display in Rome's Capitol Hill Museum.)

This basilica was begun by the emperor Maxentius, but after he was trounced in battle, the victor—Constantine—completed the massive building.

Now stroll deeper into the Forum, down the Via Sacra, through the trees. Many of the large basalt stones under your feet were walked on by Caesar Augustus 2,000 years ago. Pass by the only original bronze door still swinging on its ancient hinges (green, on right) and continue between ruined buildings until the Via Sacra opens up to a flat, grassy area.

❸ **The Forum's Main Square:** The original Forum, or main square, was this flat patch about the size of a football field, stretching to the foot of Capitol Hill. Surrounding it were temples, law courts, government buildings, and triumphal arches.

Rome was born right here. According to legend, twin brothers Romulus (Rome) and Remus were orphaned in infancy and raised by a she-wolf on top of Palatine Hill. Growing up, they found it hard to get dates. So they and their cohorts attacked the nearby Sabine tribe and kidnapped their women. After they made peace, this marshy valley became the meeting place and then the trading center for the scattered tribes on the surrounding hillsides.

At the near (east) end of the main square (the Colosseum is to the east) find the foundations of a temple now capped with a peaked wood-and-metal roof. This is...

❹ **The Temple of Julius Caesar (Tempio del Divo Giulio, or "Ara di Cesare"):** Julius Caesar's body was burned on this spot (under the metal roof) after his assassination.

Caesar (100–44 B.C.) changed Rome—and the Forum—dramatically. He cleared out many of the wooden market stalls and began to ring the square with even grander buildings. Caesar's house was located behind the temple, near that clump of trees. He walked right by here on the day he was assassinated ("Beware the Ides of March!" warned a street-corner Etruscan preacher).

Though popular with the masses, not everyone liked Caesar's urban design or his politics. When he assumed dictatorial powers, he was ambushed and stabbed to death by a conspiracy of senators, including his adopted son, Brutus *(Et tu, Brute?).*

The funeral was held here, facing the main square. The citizens gathered and speeches were made. Mark Antony stood up to say (in Shakespeare's words), "Friends, Romans, countrymen, lend me your ears. I come to bury Caesar, not to praise him." When Caesar's body was burned, the citizens who still loved him threw anything at hand on the fire, requiring the fire department to come put it out. Later, Emperor Augustus dedicated this temple in his name, making Caesar the first Roman to become a god.

Behind and to the left of the Temple of Julius Caesar are the 10 tall columns of the...

❺ **Temple of Antoninus and Faustina:** The respected Emperor Antoninus (A.D. 138–161) built this temple—originally called the Temple of Faustina—in honor of his late beloved wife. After the emperor's death, the temple became a monument to them both.

The 56-foot-tall Corinthian (leafy) columns must have been awe-inspiring to out-of-towners who grew up in thatched huts. Although the temple has been reconstructed as a church, you can still see the basic layout—a staircase led to a shaded porch (the columns), which admitted you to the main building (now a church) where the statue of the god sat.

Picture the Forum covered with dirt as high as the green door—as it was until excavated in the 1800s.

There's a ramp next to the Temple of A. and F. Walk halfway up it and look to the left to view the...

❻ **Basilica Aemilia:** A basilica was a Roman hall of justice. In a society that was as legal-minded as America is today, you needed a lot of lawyers—and a big place to put them. Citizens came here to work out matters such as inheritances and building permits, or to sue somebody.

Notice the layout. It was a long, rectangular building. The stubby columns all in a row form one long, central hall flanked by two side aisles. Medieval Christians required a larger meeting hall for their worship services than Roman temples provided, so they used the spacious Roman basilica (hall of justice) as the model for their churches. Cathedrals from France to Spain to England, from Romanesque to Gothic to Renaissance, all have the same basic floor plan as a Roman basilica.

Return again to the Temple of Julius Caesar. Notice the ruts in the stone street in front of the temple—carved by chariot wheels. To the right of the temple are the three tall Corinthian columns of the Temple of Castor and Pollux. Beyond that is Palatine Hill—the corner of which may be...

❼ Caligula's Palace (a.k.a. the Palace of Tiberius): Emperor Caligula (ruled A.D. 37–41) had a huge palace on Palatine Hill overlooking the Forum. It actually sprawled down the hill into the Forum (some supporting arches remain in the hillside), with an entrance by the Temple of Castor and Pollux.

Caligula tortured enemies, stole senators' wives, and parked his chariot in handicap spaces. But Rome's luxury-loving emperors only added to the glory of the Forum, with each one trying to make his mark on history.

To the left of the Temple of Castor and Pollux, find the remains of a small, white, circular temple...

❽ The Temple of Vesta: This was Rome's most sacred spot. Rome considered itself one big family, and this temple represented a circular hut, like the kind Rome's first families lived in. Inside, a fire burned, just as in a Roman home. And back in the days before lighters and matches, you never wanted your fire to go out. As long as the sacred flame burned, Rome would stand. The flame was tended by priestesses known as Vestal Virgins.

Around the back of the Temple of Vesta, you'll find two rectangular brick pools. These stood in the courtyard of...

❾ The House of the Vestal Virgins: The Vestal Virgins lived in a two-story building surrounding a central courtyard with these two pools at one end. Rows of statues to the left and right marked the long sides of the building. This place was the model—both architecturally and sexually—for medieval convents and monasteries.

The six Vestal Virgins, chosen from noble families before they reached the age of 10, served a 30-year term. Honored and revered by the Romans, the Vestals even had their own box opposite the emperor in the Colosseum.

As the name implies, a Vestal took a vow of chastity. If she served her term faithfully—abstaining for 30 years—she was given a huge dowry, honored with a statue (like the ones at left), and allowed to marry (life begins at 40?). But if the Romans found any Virgin who wasn't, she was strapped to a funeral car, paraded through the streets of the Forum, taken to a crypt, given a loaf of bread and a lamp...and buried alive. Many women suffered the latter fate.

Head to the Forum's west end (opposite the Colosseum). Stop at the big, reconstructed brick building (on right) with the triangular roof. If the door's open, look in.

❿ **The Curia:** The Senate House (Curia) was the most important political building in the Forum. Though this current building is a 1930s reconstruction, this was the site of Rome's official center of government since the birth of the republic. Three hundred senators, elected by the citizens of Rome, met here to debate and create the laws of the land. Their wooden seats once circled the building in three tiers; the Senate president's podium sat at the far end. The marble floor is from ancient times. Listen to the echoes in this vast room—the acoustics are great.

(Note: Although Julius Caesar was assassinated in "the Senate," it wasn't here—the Senate was temporarily meeting across town.)

Go back down the Senate steps to the metal guardrail and look right to a 10-foot-high wall at the base of Capitol Hill marked...

⓫ **Rostrum (Rostra):** Nowhere was Roman freedom more apparent than at this "Speaker's Corner." The Rostrum was a raised platform, 10 feet high and 80 feet long, decorated with statues, columns, and the prows of ships.

Rome's orators, great and small, came here trying to draw a crowd and sway public opinion. Mark Antony rose to offer Caesar the laurel-leaf crown of kingship, which Caesar publicly (and hypocritically) refused while privately becoming a dictator. Men such as Cicero railed against the corruption and decadence that came with the city's newfound wealth. In later years, daring citizens even spoke out against the emperors, reminding them that Rome was once free.

The big arch to the right of the Rostrum is...

⓬ **Arch of Septimius Severus:** In imperial times, the Rostrum's voices of democracy would have been dwarfed by images of empire such as the huge, six-story-high Arch of Septimius Severus (A.D. 203). The reliefs commemorate the African-born emperor's battles in Mesopotamia. Near ground level, see curly-haired Severus marching captured barbarians back to Rome for the victory parade. Despite Severus' efficient rule, Rome's empire was crumbling under the weight of its own corruption, disease, decaying infrastructure, and the constant attacks by foreign "barbarians."

Pass underneath the Arch of Septimius Severus and turn left.

Rome Falls

Again, Rome lasted 1,000 years—500 years of growth, 200 years of peak power, and 300 years of gradual decay. The fall had many causes, among them the barbarians who pecked away at Rome's borders. Christians blamed the fall on moral decay. Pagans blamed it on Christians. Socialists blamed it on a shallow economy based on spoils of war. (George W. Bush blamed it on Democrats.) Whatever the reasons, the far-flung empire could no longer keep its grip on conquered lands, and it pulled back. Barbarian tribes from Germany and Asia attacked the Italian peninsula and even looted Rome itself in A.D. 410, leveling many of the buildings in the Forum. In 476, when the last emperor checked out and switched off the lights, Europe plunged into centuries of ignorance, poverty, and weak government—the Dark Ages.

But Rome lived on in the Catholic Church. Christianity was the state religion of Rome's last generations. Emperors became popes (both called themselves Pontifex Maximus), senators became bishops, orators became priests, and basilicas became churches. The glory of Rome remains eternal.

On the slope of Capitol Hill are the eight remaining columns of the...

⓭ **Temple of Saturn:** These columns framed the entrance to the Forum's oldest temple (497 B.C.). Inside was a humble, very old wooden statue of the god Saturn. But the statue's pedestal held the gold bars, coins, and jewels of Rome's state treasury, the booty collected by conquering generals.

Standing here, at one of the Forum's first buildings, look east at the lone, tall...

⓮ **Column of Phocas:** This is the Forum's last great monument (A.D. 608), a gift from the powerful Byzantine Empire to a fallen empire—Rome. After Rome's 1,000-year reign, the city was looted by Vandals, the population of a million-plus shrank to 10,000, and the once-grand city center—the Forum—was abandoned, slowly covered up by centuries of silt and dirt. In the 1700s an English historian named Edward Gibbon stood here. Hearing Christian monks singing at these pagan ruins, he looked out at the few columns poking up from the ground, pondered the "Decline and Fall of the Roman Empire," and thought, "Hmm, that's a catchy title...."

The Dolce Vita Stroll

This is the city's chic stroll, from Piazza del Popolo (Metro: Flaminio) down a wonderfully traffic-free section of Via del Corso,

The Dolce Vita Stroll

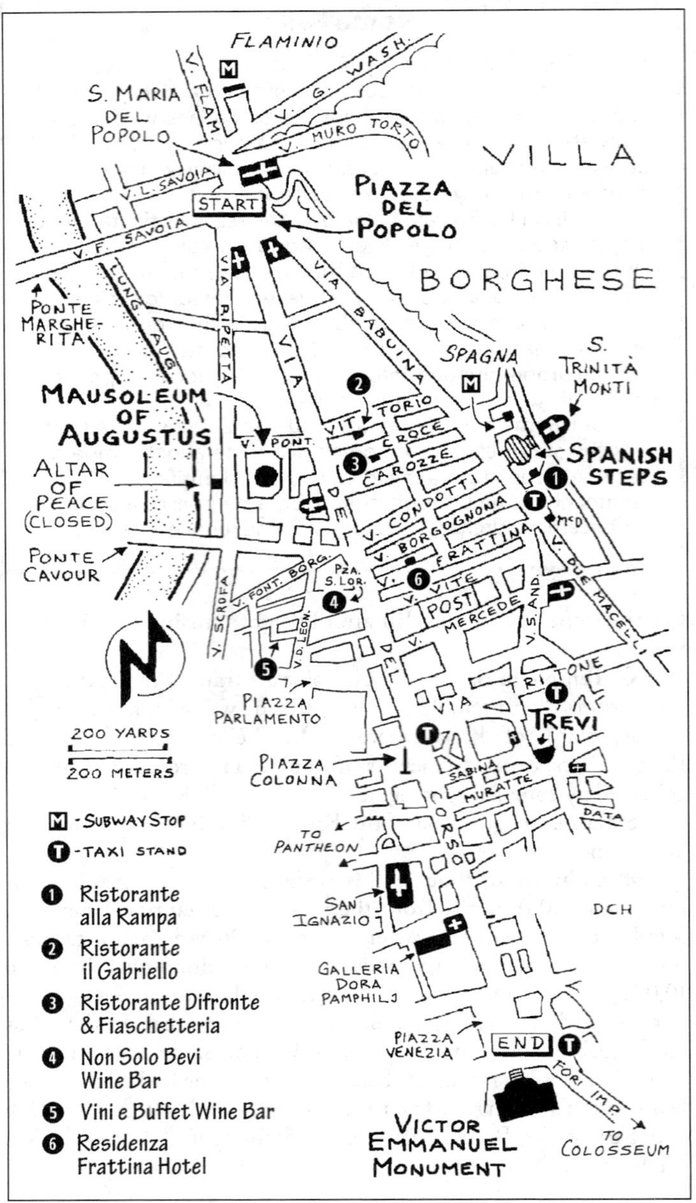

and up Via Condotti to the Spanish Steps each evening around 18:00 (Sat and Sun are best). Shoppers, people-watchers, and flirts on the prowl fill this neighborhood of Rome's most fashionable stores (open after siesta 16:30–19:30). Throughout Italy, early evening is time to stroll.

Start on **Piazza del Popolo**. The delightfully car-free square is marked by an obelisk that was brought to Rome by Augustus after he conquered Egypt. (It used to stand in the Circus Maximus.) In medieval times, this area was just inside Rome's main entry.

The Baroque church of **Santa Maria del Popolo,** on the square, contains Raphael's Chigi Chapel (KEE-jee, third chapel on left) and two Caravaggio paintings (the side paintings in chapel left of altar). The church is open daily (Mon–Sat 7:00–12:00 & 16:00–19:00, Sun 8:00–13:30 & 16:30–19:30, next to gate in the old wall, on far side of Piazza del Popolo, to the right as you face gate).

From Piazza del Popolo, shop your way down **Via del Corso.** If you need a rest or a viewpoint, join the locals sitting on the steps of various churches along the street.

At Via Pontefici, historians turn right and walk a block to see the massive, rotting, round-brick **Mausoleum of Augustus,** topped with overgrown cypress trees. Beyond it, next to the river, is Augustus' Ara Pacis, or Altar of Peace (might reopen in 2006 after renovation).

From the mausoleum, return to Via del Corso and the 21st century, continuing straight until **Via Condotti.** Shoppers, take a left on Via Condotti to join the parade to the **Spanish Steps.** The streets that parallel Via Condotti to the south (Borgognona and Frattini) are just as popular. You can catch a taxi home at the taxi stand a block south of the Spanish Steps (at Piazza Mignonelli, near American Express and McDonald's).

Historians: Ignore Via Condotti and forget the Spanish Steps. Continue a half-mile down Via del Corso—straight since Roman times—to the Victor Emmanuel Monument. Climb Michelangelo's stairway to his glorious (especially when floodlit) square atop Capitol Hill. From the balconies at either side of the mayor's palace, catch the lovely views of the Forum as the horizon reddens and cats prowl the unclaimed rubble of ancient Rome.

Night Walk Across Rome: Campo de' Fiori to the Spanish Steps

Rome can be grueling. But a fine way to enjoy this historian's rite of passage is an evening walk lacing together Rome's floodlit night spots and fine urban spaces with real-life theater vignettes.

Sitting so close to a Bernini fountain that traffic noises evaporate; jostling with local teenagers to see all the gelato flavors;

Night Walk Across Rome

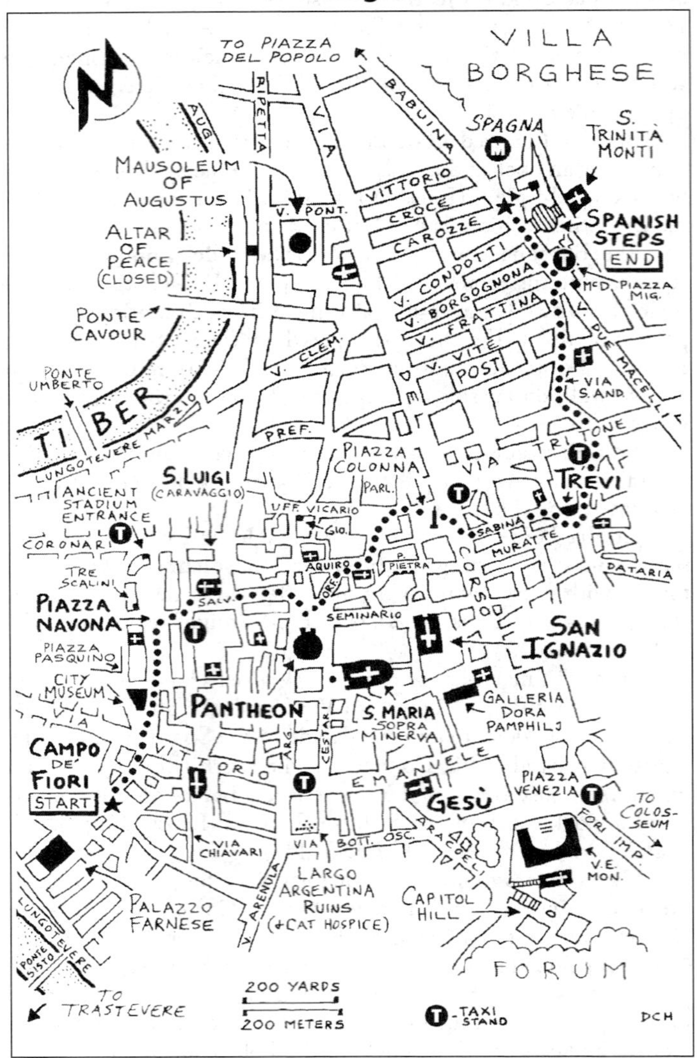

enjoying lovers straddling more than the bench; jaywalking past flak-proof-vested *polizia;* and marveling at the ramshackle elegance that softens this brutal city for those who were born here and can imagine living nowhere else—these are the flavors of Rome best tasted after dark.

Start at the **Campo de' Fiori** (Field of Flowers), my favorite outdoor dining room after dark (see "Eating," page 953). The statue of Giordano Bruno, an intellectual heretic who was burned on this spot in 1600, marks the center of this great and colorful square. Bruno overlooks a busy produce market in the morning and strollers after sundown. This neighborhood is still known for its free spirit and occasional demonstrations. When the statue of Bruno was erected in 1889, local riots overcame Vatican protests against honoring a heretic. Bruno faces his nemesis, the Vatican Chancellory (the big white building in the corner a bit to his right), while his pedestal reads: "And the flames rose up."

At the east end of the square (behind Bruno), the ramshackle apartments are built right into the old outer wall of ancient Rome's mammoth Theater of Pompey. This entertainment complex covered several city blocks, stretching from here to Largo Argentina. Julius Caesar was assassinated in the Theater of Pompey, where the Senate was renting space.

The square is lined with and surrounded by fun eateries. Bruno faces La Carbonara, the only real restaurant on the square. The Forno, next door to the left, is a popular place for hot and tasty take-out *pizza bianco* (plain pizza bread).

If Bruno did a hop, step, and jump forward, then turned right on Via dei Baullari and marched 200 yards, he'd cross the busy Corso Vittorio Emanuele and find **Piazza Navona.** Rome's most interesting night scene features street music, artists, fire-eaters, local Casanovas, ice cream, fountains by Bernini, and outdoor cafés (worthy of a splurge if you've got time to sit and enjoy the human river of Italy).

This oblong square retains the shape of the original racetrack that was built by the emperor Domitian. (If you want to see the ruins of the original entrance, exit the square at the north end, take an immediate left, and look down to the left 25 feet below the current street level.) Since ancient times, the square has been a center of Roman life. In the 1800s the city would flood the square to cool off the neighborhood.

The **Four Rivers fountain** in the center is the most famous fountain by the man who remade Rome in Baroque style, Gian Lorenzo Bernini. Four burly river gods (representing the four continents that existed in 1650) support an obelisk, while the water of the world gushes everywhere. The Nile has his head covered (since the headwaters were unknown then). The Ganges holds an oar. The Danube turns to admire the obelisk, which Bernini had moved here from a stadium on the Appian Way. And the Rio de la Plata from Uruguay tumbles backward in shock, wondering how he ever made the top four. Bernini enlivens the fountain with horses plunging through the rocks and exotic flora and fauna from these newly discovered lands. Homesick Texans may want to find the armadillo. (It's the big, weird armor-plated creature behind the Plata river statue.)

The Plata river god is gazing upward at the church of Saint Agnes, worked on by Bernini's former student turned rival, Francesco Borromini. Borromini's concave facade helps reveal the dome and epitomizes the curved symmetry of Baroque. Tour guides say that Bernini designed his river god to look horrified at Borromini's work. Or he may be shielding his eyes from St. Agnes' nakedness, as she was stripped before being martyred. But the fountain was completed two years before Borromini even started work on the church.

At the **Tre Scalini** café (near the fountain), sample some *tartufo* "death by chocolate" ice cream, world-famous among connoisseurs of ice cream and chocolate alike (€4 to go, €8 at a table, closed Wed). Seriously admire a painting by a struggling artist. Request "Country Roads" from an Italian guitar player, and don't be surprised when he knows it. Listen to the white noise of gushing water and exuberant humans.

Leave Piazza Navona directly across from Tre Scalini café, go east past rose peddlers and palm readers, jog left around the guarded building, and follow the brown sign to the Pantheon. The Pantheon is straight down Via del Salvatore (cheap pizza place on left just before the Pantheon, WC at McDonald's).

Sit for a while under the floodlit and moonlit **Pantheon's** portico. The 40-foot single-piece granite columns of the Pantheon's entrance show the scale the ancient Romans built on. The columns support a triangular, Greek-style roof with an inscription that says that "M. Agrippa" built it. In fact, it was built *("fecit")* by Emperor Hadrian (A.D. 120), who gave credit to the builder of an earlier structure. This impressive entranceway gives no clue that the greatest wonder of the building is inside—a domed room that inspired later domes, including Michelangelo's St. Peter's and Brunelleschi's Duomo (in Florence). Notice how the pavement slants down from McDonald's to the Pantheon, showing how high modern Rome has built on ancient rubble.

With your back to the Pantheon, veer to the right down Via Orfani. After passing Bar Pantheon, you'll see **Tazza d'Oro Casa del Caffè,** one of Rome's top coffee shops, dating back to the days when this area was licensed to roast coffee beans. Locals come here for its fine *granita di caffè con panna*. Look back at the fine view of the Pantheon from here. Then take Via Orfani to Piazza Capranica.

Piazza Capranica is home to the big, plain, Florentine Renaissance-style Palazzo Capranica. Big shots, like the Capranica family, built stubby towers on their palaces—not for any military use, but just to show off. Leave the piazza to the right of the palace, between the palace and the church. Via in Aquiro leads to a 6th-century B.C. **Egyptian obelisk** (taken as a trophy by Augustus after his victory in Egypt over Mark Antony and Cleopatra). Walk into the guarded square past the obelisk and face the huge parliament building.

A short detour to the left (past Albergo National) brings you to Rome's most famous gelateria. **Gelateria Caffè Pasticceria Giolitti** is cheap to go or elegant and splurge-worthy for a sit among classy locals (open daily until very late, Via Uffici del Vicario 40); get your gelato in a cone *(cono)* or cup *(coppetta)*.

Piazza Colonna features a huge 2nd-century column honoring Marcus Aurelius. The big, important-looking palace—headquarters of the deputies (or cabinet) of the prime minister. The **Via del Corso** is named for the Berber horse races—without riders—that took place here during Carnevale until the 1800s when a horse trampled a man to death in front of a horrified queen. Historically the street was filled with meat shops. When it became Rome's first gaslit street in the 1800s, "nastier" shops were banned and replaced by classier boutiques, jewelers, and antique dealers. Today, every evening most of Via del Corso is closed to traffic and it becomes a wonderful parade of Romans out for an evening stroll. Cross Via del Corso, Rome's noisy main drag, jog right (around the Y-shaped shopping gallery from 1928), and head down Via dei Sabini to the roar of the water, light, and people of the Trevi Fountain.

The **Trevi Fountain** shows how Rome took full advantage of the abundance of water brought into the city by its great aqueducts. This watery Baroque avalanche was completed in 1762 by Nicola Salvi, hired by a pope who was celebrating the reopening of the ancient aqueduct that powers it. Salvi used the palace behind the fountain as a theatrical backdrop for the figure of "Ocean," who represents water in every form. The statue surfs through his wet kingdom—with water gushing from 24 spouts and tumbling over 30 different kinds of plants—while Tritone blows his conch shell. (From here, the water goes underground, then bubbles up again at Bernini's Four Rivers Fountain in Piazza Navona.)

The magic of the square is enhanced by the fact that no streets directly approach it. You can hear the excitement as you approach and then, bam, you're there. The scene is always lively, with lucky Romeos clutching dates while unlucky ones clutch beers. Romantics toss a coin over their shoulder, thinking it will give them a wish and assure their return to Rome. That may sound silly, but every year I go through this touristic ritual...and it actually seems to work.

Take some time to people-watch (whisper a breathy *bello* or *bella*) before leaving. Face the fountain, then go past it on the right down Via delle Stamperia to Via del Triton. Cross the busy street and continue to the Spanish Steps (ask, *"Dov'è Piazza di Spagna?"—Spagna* rhymes with "lasagna"), a few blocks and thousands of dollars of shopping opportunities away.

The Piazza di Spagna, with the very popular **Spanish Steps,** is named for the Spanish Embassy to the Vatican, which has been here for 300 years. It's been the hangout of many Romantics over the years (Keats, Wagner, Openshaw, Goethe, and others). The British poet John Keats pondered his mortality, then died in the pink building on the right side of the steps. Fellow Romantic Lord Byron lived across the square at #66.

The Sinking Boat Fountain at the foot of the steps, which was done by Bernini or his father, Pietro, is powered by an aqueduct. All of Rome's fountains are aqueduct-powered; their spurts are determined by the water pressure provided by the various aqueducts. This one, for instance, is much weaker than Trevi's gush.

The piazza is a thriving night scene. Window-shop along Via Condotti, which stretches away from the steps. This is where Gucci and other big names cater to the trendsetting jet set. Facing the Spanish Steps, you can walk right about a block to tour one of the world's biggest and most lavish McDonald's (salad bar, WC). There's a taxi stand in the courtyard outside McDonald's; or, if you'd prefer, the Spagna Metro stop (usually open until 23:30) is just to the left of the Spanish Steps, ready to zip you home.

SLEEPING

The absolute cheapest beds (dorms or some cramped doubles) in Rome are €20 in small, backpacker-filled hostels. A nicer hotel (around €130 with a bathroom and air-con) provides an oasis and refuge, making it easier to enjoy this intense and grinding city. If you're going door to door, prices are soft—so bargain. Built into a hotel's official price list is a kickback for a room-finding service or agency; if you're coming direct, they pay no kickback and may lower the price for you. Many hotels have high-season (mid-March–June, Sept–Oct) and low-season prices. If traveling outside of peak times, ask about a discount. Room rates are lowest in sweltering August. Easter, September, and Christmas are most crowded and expensive. On Easter (April 16 in 2006) and other major religious holidays, the entire city can get booked up.

English works in all but the cheapest places. Traffic in Rome roars. My challenge: To find friendly places on quiet streets. With

Sleep Code

(€1 = about $1.20, country code: 39)
S = Single, **D** = Double/Twin, **T** = Triple, **Q** = Quad, **b** = bathroom, **s** = shower only, **SE** = Speaks English, **NSE** = No English. Breakfast is included in all but the cheapest places. You can assume a hotel takes credit cards unless you see "cash only" in the listing.

To help you sort easily through these listings, I've divided the rooms into three categories based on the price for a standard double room with bath:

$$$ **Higher Priced**—Most rooms €180 or more.
$$ **Moderately Priced**—Most rooms between €115–180.
$ **Lower Priced**—Most rooms €115 or less.

the recent arrival of double-paned windows and air-conditioning, night noise is not the problem it was. Even so, light sleepers should always ask for a *tranquillo* room. To get the best deal, reserve directly, without using a room-finding service. And many places offer a small discount if you pay in hard cash.

Most hotels are eager to connect you with a shuttle service to the airport. It's reasonable and easy for departure, but upon arrival, I think it's simplest to catch a cab or the train.

Almost no hotels have parking, but nearly all have a line on spots in a nearby garage (about €24/day).

Bed-and-breakfasts are booming in Rome, offering comfy doubles in the old center for €70–110. The Beehive is a good contact for booking B&Bs in Rome (www.cross-pollinate.com, page 945).

Rome has many **convents** that rent out rooms; the beds are twins and English is often in short supply, but the price is right. I list four nun-run places below: the divine Suore di Santa Elisabetta and the possibly-still-being-renovated Pensione per Pelligrini (both near Basilica Santa Maria Maggiore, see page 943), friendly Casa San Giuseppe (in Trastevere, page 950), and the most user-friendly, Casa per Ferie Santa Maria alle Fornaci dei Padri Trinitari (near the Vatican, page 952). For more, see the Santa Susanna Church's Web site (www.santasusanna.org, select "Coming To Rome").

On Via Firenze

I generally stay on Via Firenze because it's safe, handy, central, and relatively quiet. It's a 10-minute walk from the central train station and airport shuttle, and two blocks beyond Piazza della Repubblica and the TI. The Defense Ministry is nearby, and you've got heavily armed guards watching over you all night.

The neighborhood is well connected by public transportation (with the Repubblica Metro stop nearby). Virtually all the city buses that rumble down Via Nazionale (#64, #70, #115, #640, and the #40 express) take you to Piazza Venezia (Forum) and Largo Argentina (Pantheon). From Largo Argentina, electric trolley #8 goes to Trastevere (get off at first stop after crossing the river) and the #64 (jammed with people and thieves) and the #40 express both continue to St. Peter's.

A 24-hour **pharmacy** near the recommended hotels is Farmacia Piram (Via Nazionale 228, tel. 06-488-4437).

$$ Residenza Cellini is a gorgeous six-room place that feels like the guest wing of a neoclassical palace. It offers "ortho/anti-allergy beds" and four-star comforts and service (Db-€175, larger Db-€195, extra bed-€25, €30 discount off-season—Aug plus mid-Nov–mid-March, air-con, elevator, Via Modena 5, tel. 06-4782-5204, fax 06-4788-1806, www.residenzacellini.it, residenzacellini@tin.it, Barbara, Gaetano, and Donato SE).

$$ Hotel Oceania is a peaceful slice of air-conditioned heaven. This 15-room, manor house-type hotel is spacious and quiet, with spotless, tastefully decorated rooms, run by a pleasant father-and-son team. While Armando (the dad) serves world-famous coffee, Stefano (the son) works to give their hotel all the extra touches. He just added a plasma TV with surround sound to his lounge for guests to watch classic movies set in Rome...and Italy episodes from my TV series (Sb-€118, Db-€148, Tb-€178, Qb-€205, additional 25 percent off in Aug and winter, large roof terrace, family suite, Via Firenze 38, 3rd floor, tel. 06-482-4696, fax 06-488-5586, www.hoteloceania.it, info@hoteloceania.it, Anna and Stefano SE).

$$ Hotel Aberdeen, which perfectly combines high quality and friendliness, is warmly run by Annamaria, with support from cousins Sabrina and Cinzia and sister Laura. The 37 comfy, modern, air-conditioned, and smoke-free rooms are a terrific value. Enjoy the frescoed breakfast room (Sb-€97, Db-€140, Tb-€160, Qb-€175, 30 percent less in Aug and winter, check Web site for deals, Via Firenze 48, tel. 06-482-3920, fax 06-482-1092, www.travel.it/roma/aberdeen, hotel.aberdeen@travel.it, SE).

$$ Residence Adler offers breakfast on a garden patio, wide halls, and eight quiet, simple, and air-conditioned rooms in a good location. It's run the old-fashioned way by a charming family (Db-€125, Tb-€160, Qb-€190, Quint/b-€205, additional 5 percent off with cash, 15 percent off in Aug and winter, elevator, Via Modena 5, 2nd floor, tel. 06-484-466, fax 06-488-0940, www.hoteladler-roma.com, info@hoteladler-roma.com, gracious Sr. Brando Massini NSE but tries).

$$ Hotel Nardizzi Americana offers 18 simple, pleasant, air-conditioned rooms and a delightful rooftop terrace. While loosely run, it's a fine value (Sb-€105, Db-€125, Tb-€155, Qb-€170, 10 percent discounts for off-season and long stays, additional 10 percent off with cash, elevator, Via Firenze 38, 4th floor, tel. 06-488-0035, fax 06-488-0368, www.hotelnardizzi.it, info@hotelnardizzi.it, SE).

Between Via Nazionale and Basilica Santa Maria Maggiore

$$ Hotel Sonya is a small, family-run, but impersonal place with 23 well-equipped rooms, a central location, and decent prices (Sb-€93, Db-€130, Tb-€145, Qb-€165, Quint/b-€180, 5 percent discount for cash, 10 percent discount in low season, air-con, elevator, faces the opera at Via Viminale 58, Metro: Repubblica or Termini, tel. 06-481-9911, fax 06-488-5678, www.hotelsonya.it, info@hotelsonya.it, Francesca SE).

$$ Hotel Pensione Italia, in a busy, interesting, and handy locale, is placed safely on a quiet street next to the Ministry of the Interior. Thoughtfully run by Andrea, Nadine, and Gabriele, it has 31 comfortable, clean, bright, non-smoking rooms (Sb-€85, Db-€120, Tb-€155, Qb-€175, all rooms 30 percent off mid-July–Aug and Nov–Feb, most rooms have fans, air-con-€8/day, elevator, Via Venezia 18, just off Via Nazionale, Metro: Repubblica or Termini, tel. 06-482-8355, fax 06-474-5550, www.hotelitaliaroma.com, info@hotelitaliaroma.com, SE). They have eight decent annex rooms across the street.

$ Hotel Montreal, run with care, is a bright, solid, business-class place on a big street a block southeast of Santa Maria Maggiore (soft prices, these are the max: Db-€115 but €90 in July–Aug, Tb-€140 but €120 in July–Aug, air-con, elevator, good security, 1 block from Metro: Vittorio, 3 blocks west of train station, Via Carlo Alberto 4, Metro: Termini or Vittorio Emanuele, tel. 06-445-7797, fax 06-446-5522, www.hotelmontrealroma.com, info@hotelmontrealroma.com, SE).

$ Suore di Santa Elisabetta is a heavenly Polish-run convent with a peaceful garden and tidy rooms. Often booked long in advance, it's a super value (S-€36, Sb-€45, D-€58, Db-€76, Tb-€96, Qb-€116, 23:00 curfew, elevator, fine view roof terrace, a block southwest of Basilica Santa Maria Maggiore at Via dell' Omata 9, Metro: Termini or Vittorio Emanuele, tel. 06-488-8271, fax 06-488-4066, ist.it.s.elisabetta@libero.it, SE).

$ Pensione per Pelligrini, another convent, is scheduled to reopen in 2006 after renovation. It's several blocks south of Basilica Santa Maria Maggiore (new prices not yet set, just off Piazza Vittorio Emanuele II, Istituto Buon Salvatore, Via Leopardi 17, no

Hotels in East Rome

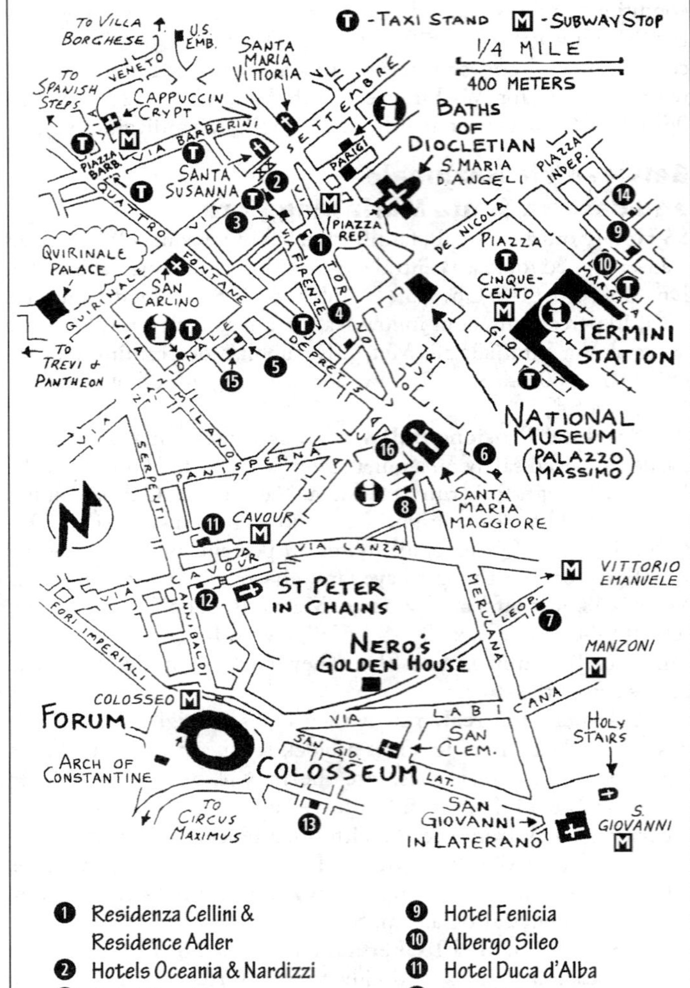

1. Residenza Cellini & Residence Adler
2. Hotels Oceania & Nardizzi
3. Hotel Aberdeen
4. Hotel Sonya
5. Hotel Pensione Italia
6. Hotel Montreal
7. Pensione per Pelligrini
8. Suore di Santa Elisabetta
9. Hotel Fenicia
10. Albergo Sileo
11. Hotel Duca d'Alba
12. Hotel Paba
13. Hotels Lancelot & Capo d'Africa
14. The Beehive Hostel
15. Gulliver's House Hostel
16. Casa Olmata Hostel

sign, Metro: Vittorio Emanuele, tel. 06-446-7147 or 06-446-7225, fax 06-446-1382, Sister Anna Maria SE).

$ Casa Olmata is a ramshackle, laid-back backpackers' place a block southwest of Basilica Santa Maria Maggiore, midway between the Termini train station and Colosseum (dorm beds-€20, S-€38, bunk bed D-€44, one queen-size D-€57, lots of stairs, laundry service, free Internet access, video rentals, games, rooftop terrace with views and nearly free dinner parties, dinners twice weekly, communal kitchen, Via dell' Olmata 36, 3rd floor, Metro: Vittorio Emanuele, tel. 06-483-019, fax 06-486819, www.casaolmata.com, info@casaolmata.com, Mirella and Marco).

$ Gulliver's House Rome is a fun little hostel in a safe and handy locale, run by helpful Simon and Sara. Its 24 beds in cramped quarters work fine for backpackers. They host English movie evenings nightly in their lounge—warm up with my TV shows on Rome (€20 per bunk bed in 8-bed dorm, one D-€70, cash only, closed 12:00–16:00, 1:00 curfew, small kitchen, Via Palermo 36, tel. 06-481-7680, www.gulliversshouse.com, stay@gulliversshouse.com). They also offer five fun, funky double rooms at **Gulliver's Place** farther north, in a large, secure building next to a university (D-€70, Db-€80, Tb-€100, air-con, elevator, Metro: Castro Pretorio, you'll find out the address upon booking, reserve through Gulliver's House—tel. 06-481-7680, www.gulliversplace.com, SE).

Sleeping Cheaply, Northeast of the Train Station

The cheapest hotels in town are northeast of the station (Metro: Termini). Some travelers feel this area is weird and spooky after dark, but these hotels feel plenty safe. With your back to the train tracks, turn right and walk two blocks out of the station.

$ Hotel Fenicia rents 15 decent rooms at a fine price (Sb-€70, Db-€110, Tb-€120, breakfast-€4, air-con-€5/day, 5 percent off with cash, Via Milazzo 20, tel. & fax 06-490-342, www.hotelfenicia.it, info@hotelfenicia.it, Georgio and Anna SE).

$ The Beehive gives vagabonds—old and young—a cheap, clean, and comfy home in Rome. Its artsy-mod double rooms are a great value (D-€60, Db-€80, T-€90, Tb-€120, Q-€120, Qb-€160, cash only, big common kitchen, private garden terrace) and it has an 8-bed dorm (€20 beds). It's thoughtfully run by a friendly young American couple, Steve and Linda (2 blocks north of the train station at Via Marghera 8, tel. 06-447-04553, www.the-beehive.com, info@the-beehive.com). They also run a B&B booking service (private rooms in the old center of Rome, Florence, and Venice, offering comparable quality for €70-110—cheaper than a hotel, www.cross-pollinate.com).

$ Albergo Sileo is a shiny-chandeliered, 10-room place. It has a contract to house train conductors who work the night shift, so its simple, pleasant rooms are rented from 19:00–9:00 only. If you can handle this, it's a wonderful value. During the day, they store your luggage, and though you won't have access to a room, you're welcome to shower or hang out in the lobby or bar (D-€45, Db-€55, Tb-€60, Db for 24 hours-€62 when available, elevator, Via Magenta 39, tel. & fax 06-445-0246, www.hotelsileo.com, info@hotelsileo.com, friendly Alessandro and Maria Savioli NSE, daughter Anna SE).

Near the Colosseum

These places are buried in a Roman world of exhaust-stained, medieval ambience. For Alba and Paba, take the subway one stop from the train station to the Cavour Metro stop. The *elettrico* bus line #117 (San Giovanni in Laterano, Colosseo, Trevi Fountain, Piazza di Spagna, and Piazza del Popolo) connects you with the sights.

$$$ Hotel Capo d'Africa is a new (2002), sleek, business-class place next to the San Clemente Church. It offers 65 of the best rooms that I list, with plush and sprawling public spaces, top-end fine points, and all the extras (Db-€210–235 depending on season, air-con, elevator, sprawling view roof terrace, smoke-free floor, gym, Via Capo d'Africa 54, tel. 06-772-801, fax 06-772-80801, www.hotelcapodafrica.com, info@hotelcapodafrica.com, SE).

$$ Hotel Duca d'Alba, a tight and modern pastel/marble/hardwood place, is more professional than homey (30 rooms, Sb-€134, Db-€120–160 but higher Sept–Oct, extra bed-€20, check Web site for deals, air-con, elevator, Via Leonina 14, tel. 06-484-471, fax 06-488-4840, www.hotelducadalba.com, info@hotelducadalba.com, Angelo SE).

$$ Hotel Paba has six rooms, chocolate box-tidy and lovingly cared for by Alberta and Pasquale Castelli. While overlooking busy Via Cavour just two blocks from the Colosseum, it's quiet enough (Db-€135, extra bed-€35, breakfast served in room, air-con, elevator, Via Cavour 266, tel. 06-4782-4902, fax 06-4788-1225, www.hotelpaba.com, info@hotelpaba.com, SE).

$$ Hotel Lancelot, next to the recommended Hotel Capo d'Africa, is a favorite among United Nations workers. It's quiet, safe, and big (60 rooms), with a shady courtyard, rooftop terrace, bar, and restaurant. Well-run by Faris and Lubna Khan, it's popular with returning guests (Sb-€96–113, Db-€150, Tb-€170, Qb-€185, add €15 for balcony, air-con, elevator, parking-€11/day, behind Colosseum near San Clemente Church at Via Capo d'Africa 47, tel. 06-7045-0615, fax 06-7045-0640, www.lancelothotel.com, info@lancelothotel.com, Lubna S the queen's E).

Near Campo de' Fiori

While you pay a premium to stay in the old center (and endure a little extra night noise), each of these places is romantically set deep in the tangled back streets near the idyllic Campo de' Fiori and, for many, worth the extra money. For locations, see page 948.

$$ Casa di Santa Brigida overlooks the elegant Piazza Farnese. With soft-spoken sisters gliding down polished hallways, and pearly gates instead of doors, this lavish 23-room convent makes exhaust-stained Roman tourists feel like they've died and gone to heaven. If you don't need a double bed, this is worth the splurge (Sb-€95, Db-€170, 3 percent extra with credit card, tasty €15 dinners, roof garden, plush library, air-con, Monserrato 54, tel. 06-6889-2596, fax 06-6889-1573, brigida@mclink.it, many of the sisters are from India and speak English). If you get no response to your fax or e-mail within three days, consider that a "no." Groups are welcome here.

$$ Hotel Smeraldo, with 50 rooms, is thoughtfully run, clean, and a great deal (Sb-€105, Db-€135, Tb-€140, 20 percent less off-season, buffet breakfast-€7, flowery roof terrace, centrally-controlled air-con, elevator, Vicolo dei Chiodaroli 9, midway between Campo de' Fiori and Largo Argentina, tel. 06-687-5929, fax 06-6880-5495, www.smeraldoroma.com, albergosmeraldoroma@tin.it, Massimo SE).

$$ Hotel in Parione, also run by Hotel Smeraldo, crams 16 modern rooms into a tiny, adjacent building. Offering similar amenities and a fabulous location, these rooms are a steal (Sb-€100, Db-€125, €25 less off-season, breakfast-€7, roof terrace, air-con, elevator, Via dei Chiavari 32, tel. 06-6880-2560, fax 06-6834-0904, www.inparione.com, info@inparione.com, SE).

$$ Hotel Arenula is the only hotel in Rome's old Jewish quarter. While it has the ambience of a gym and attracts lots of students, it's a fine value in the thick of old Rome with 50 decent rooms (Sb-€92, Db-€121, Tb-€142, €26 less in July–Aug and winter, air-con, just off Via Arenula at Via Santa Maria de' Calderari 47, tel. 06-687-9454, fax 06-689-6188, www.hotelarenula.com, hotel.arenula@flashnet.it, SE).

Near the Pantheon

These places are buried in the pedestrian-friendly heart of ancient Rome, each within a four-minute walk of the Pantheon. You'll pay more here—but you'll save time and money by being exactly where you want to be for your early and late wandering.

$$$ Hotel Nazionale, a four-star landmark, is a 16th-century palace sharing a well-policed square with the national Parliament. Its 92 rooms are served by lush public spaces, fancy bars, and a uniformed staff. It's a big, stuffy hotel with a revolving front door,

Hotels in the Heart of Rome

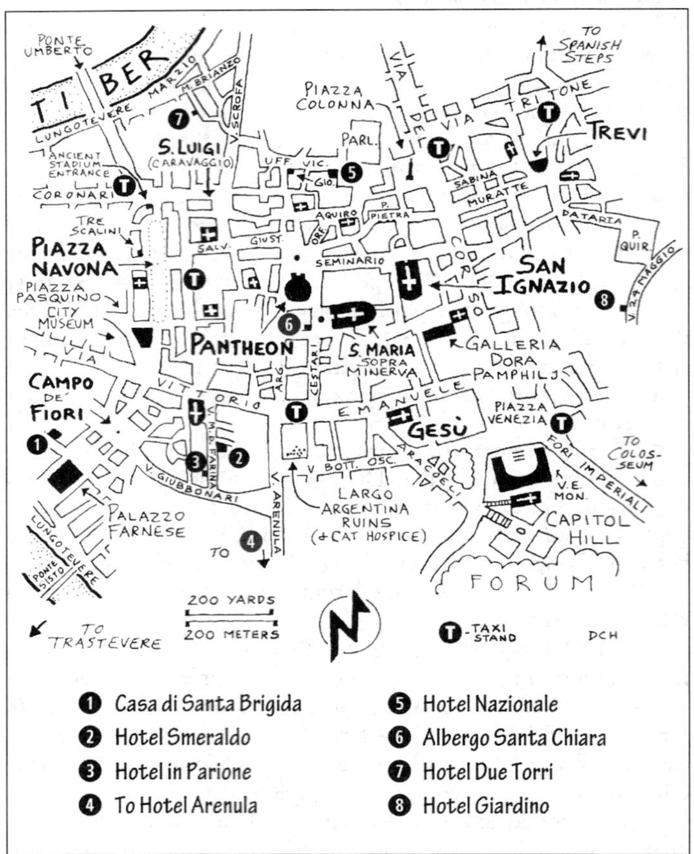

but it's a worthy splurge if you want security, comfort, and ancient Rome at your doorstep (Sb-€203, Db-€303, giant deluxe Db-€420, extra person-€62, less in Aug and winter, air-con, elevator, Piazza Montecitorio 131, tel. 06-695-001, fax 06-678-6677, see Web site for discounts in summer and weekends, www.nazionaleroma.it, hotel@nazionaleroma.it, SE).

$$$ Albergo Santa Chiara is big, solid, and hotelesque, offering marbled elegance and all the hotel services in the old center at an affordable price. Its ample public lounges are dressy and professional and its 100 rooms are quiet and spacious (Sb-€145, Db-€217, Tb-€250, check Web site for deals, elevator, behind Pantheon at Via di Santa Chiara 21, tel. 06-687-2979, fax 06-687-3144, www.albergosantachiara.com, stchiara@tin.it).

$$$ Hotel Due Torri, hiding out on a tiny, quiet street, is a little overpriced but beautifully located. It feels professional yet homey, with an accommodating staff, generous public spaces, and 26 comfortable-if-tight rooms—four with balconies (Sb-€118, Db-€190, family apartment-€250 for 3 and €275 for 4, air-con, Vicolo del Leonetto 23, a block off Via della Scrofa, tel. 06-6880-6956, fax 06-686-5442, www.hotelduetorriroma.com, hotelduetorri@interfree.it, SE).

Near the Spanish Steps

$$ Residenza Frattina is a pink palace—with nine high-ceilinged rooms and a plush living room—in a posh locale. It has an old-fashioned feel and an unbeatable location on a main pedestrian shopping drag near Piazza di Spagna and the Spanish Steps (Db-€180, Tb-€220, prices change with season and are soft, 5 percent cash discount, air-con, Via Frattina 104, tel. 06-679-5509, fax 06-678-3701, www.residenzafrattinacorso.com, residenza.frattina@flashnet.it; to locate hotel, see Dolce Vita Stroll map on page 934).

Near Piazza Venezia

$$ Hotel Giardino, thoughtfully run by Englishwoman Kate, offers 11 pleasant rooms in a central location three blocks northeast of Piazza Venezia (March–June and Sept–Oct: Sb-€90, Db-€130, other times: Sb-€70, Db-€100, check Web site for specials, air-con, double-paned windows, busy street off Piazza di Quirinale, Via XXIV Maggio 51, tel. 06-679-4584, fax 06-679-5155, www.hotel-giardino-roma.com, hotel_giardino@libero.it).

Trastevere

Colorful and genuine in a gritty sort of way, Trastevere is a treat for travelers looking for a less touristy and more bohemian atmosphere. Choices are few here, but by trekking across the Tiber, you can have the experience of living like a temporary Roman. To locate the following two places, see map on page 918.

$$ Hotel Santa Maria sits like a lazy hacienda in the midst of Trastevere. Surrounded by a medieval skyline, you'll feel as if you're on some romantic stage set. Its 20 small but well-equipped, air-conditioned rooms—former cells in a cloister—are all on the ground floor, circling a gravelly courtyard of orange trees and stay-awhile patio furniture. Because this is the only real hotel in Trastevere, it isn't cheap—but for well-heeled poets, it's a deal (Db-€175, Tb-€220, Qb-€260, smaller discounts for shorter stays and credit cards and off-season, suites available for 2–6 people, hearty buffet breakfast, loaner bikes for guests, a block north of Piazza Maria Trastevere at Vicolo del Piede 2, tel. 06-589-4626, fax 06-589-4815, www.htlsantamaria.com, hotelsantamaria@libero.it, Stefano SE).

$ Casa San Giuseppe, better for bohemians on a budget, is down a characteristic, laundry-strewn lane. Friendly nuns offer 25 super-spotless rooms (although only with twin beds) in a peaceful, hotelesque convent (Sb-€70, Db-€95, air-con, elevator, just north of Piazza Trilussa, Vicolo Moroni 22, tel. 06-5833-3490, fax 06-5833-5754, www.casasangiuseppe.it, NSE).

Near the Vatican Museum

To locate hotels, see map on page 951.

$$$ Hotel Sant' Anna is pricey, but located on a charming pedestrian street that fills up with restaurant tables at dinnertime. Its 20 comfy rooms, decorated with classical themes, are somewhere between tasteful and too much (Sb-€150, Db-€200; Db discounted to €145 July–Aug, winter, and slow times; any time of year, ask for a Rick Steves discount; air-con, elevator, courtyard, Borgo Pio 133, near intersection with Mascherino, a couple blocks from entrance to St. Peter's, tel. 06-6880-1602, fax 06-6830-8717, www.hotelsantanna.com, santanna@travel.it, Viscardo SE).

$$$ Hotel Bramante sits like a grand medieval lodge in the shadow of the fortified escape wall that runs from the Vatican to Castel Sant' Angelo. The public spaces and the 16 thoughtfully-appointed rooms are generously sized, with rough wood beams and high ceilings (Sb-€150, Db-€205, Tb-€230, Qb-€240, air-con, no elevator, Vicolo delle Palline 24, tel. 06-6880-6426, fax 06-681-33339, www.hotelbramante.com, hotelbramante@libero.it, Maurizio and Loredana SE).

$$ Hotel Alimandi is a good value, run by the friendly and entrepreneurial Alimandi brothers—Paolo, Enrico, and Luigi—and the next generation, Marta, Irene, Eleanora, and Germano. Their 35 rooms are air-conditioned, modern, and marbled in white (Sb-€90, Db-€155, Tb-€175, closed Jan–mid-Feb, elevator, grand buffet breakfast served in great roof garden, small gym, pool table, piano lounge, down stairs directly in front of Vatican Museum, Via Tunisi 8, near Metro: Cipro-Musei Vaticani, reserve by phone, no reply to fax means they are full, tel. 06-3972-6300, toll-free in Italy tel. 800-122-121, fax06-3972-3943, www.alimandi.com, alimandi@tin.it, SE). They offer free airport pickup and drop-off, though you must reserve when you book your room and wait for a scheduled shuttle (every 2 hours, see their Web site or lobby schedule). They also offer larger, family-friendly rooms at a new, adjacent hotel, Alimandi al Vaticano.

$$ Hotel Spring House, with a hotelesque feel (it's a Best Western), offers 51 attractive rooms—some with balconies or terraces (standard Db-€150, superior Db-€180, Tb-€175, Qb-€190, air-con, elevator, free loaner bikes, Metro: Cipro-Musei Vaticani, Via Mocenigo 7, 2 blocks from Vatican Museum, tel.

Hotels and Restaurants near the Vatican Museum

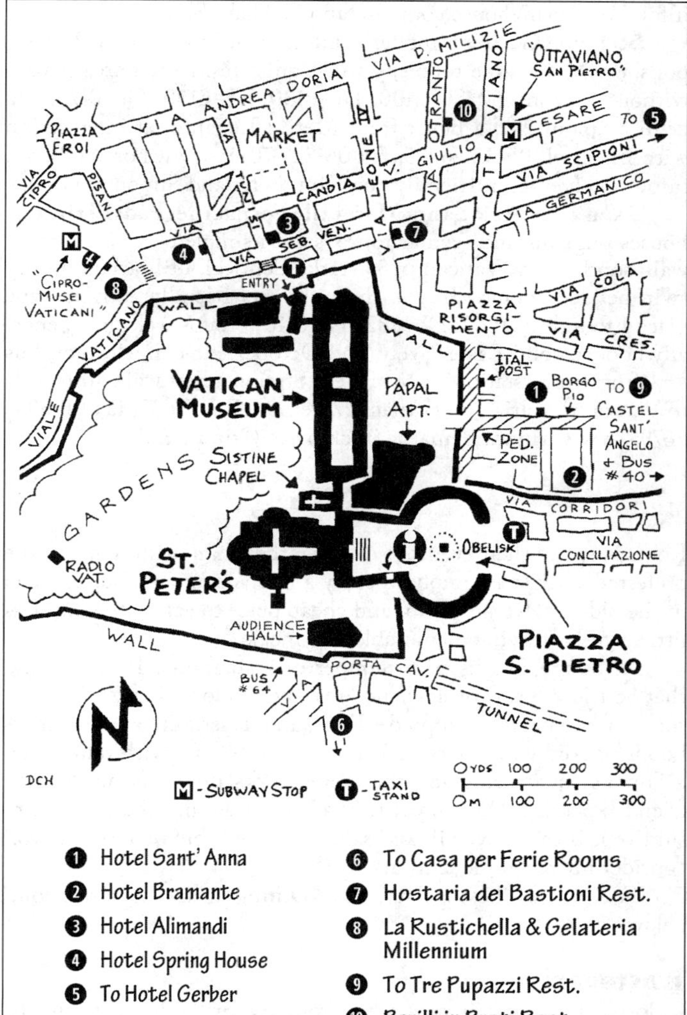

06-3972-0948, fax 06-3972-1047, www.hotelspringhouse.com, info@hotelspringhouse.com, Stefano Gabbani SE).

$$ Hotel Gerber is modern and air-conditioned, with 27 well-polished businesslike rooms, set in a quiet residential area (two S without air-con-€57, Sb-€100, Db-€130, Tb-€150, Qb-€170, Via degli Scipioni 241, a block from Metro: Lepanto, at intersection with Ezio, tel. 06-321-6485, fax 06-321-7048, www.hotelgerber.it, info@hotelgerber.it, friendly dog Kira, Peter and Simonetta SE).

$ Casa per Ferie Santa Maria alle Fornaci dei Padri Trinitari houses pilgrims and secular tourists with simple class just a short walk south of the Vatican in 54 stark, identical, utilitarian, mostly twin-bedded rooms. This is the only user-friendly convent-type place I found (Sb-€62, Db-€82, Tb-€110; groups welcome, generally booked solid Easter, May, and October; air-con, elevator; bus #64 from train station to St. Peters Station, then walk 100 yards to Piazza S. Maria alle Fornaci 27; tel. 06-393-67632, fax 06-393-66795, www.trinitaridematha.it, cffornaci@tin.it, SE).

EATING

Romans spend their evenings eating rather than drinking, and the preferred activity is simply to enjoy a fine, slow meal, buried deep in the old city. Rome's a fun and cheap place to eat, with countless little eateries serving memorable €20 meals.

Although I've listed a number of restaurants, I recommend that you just head for a scenic area and explore. Piazza Navona, the Pantheon area, Campo de' Fiori, and Trastevere are neighborhoods packed with characteristic eateries. Sitting with tourists on a famous square enjoying the scene works fine. (As my Roman friend explained: "When you're in a bad restaurant, the best way to survive is bread, olive oil, and salt.") But for more of a local flavor, consider my recommendations.

For Rome's best gelato, see "Dining near the Pantheon," below.

Trastevere

Colorful Trastevere is now pretty touristy. Still, Romans join the tourists to eat on the rustic side of the Tiber River. Start at the central square (Piazza Santa Maria). Then choose: Eat with tourists enjoying the ambience of the famous square, or wander the back streets in search of a mom-and-pop place with barely a menu. Look over these two places (between Piazza Santa Maria Trastevere and Ponte Sisto, see map on page 918) before making a choice.

Trattoria da Lucia lets you enjoy simple traditional food at a good price in a great scene (Tue–Sun 12:30–15:30 & 19:30–24:00, closed Mon, homey indoor or evocative outdoor seating, Vicolo del

Mattonato 2, tel. 06-580-3601, NSE).

Osteria Ponte Sisto, a rough-and-tumble little place, specializes in traditional Roman cuisine with a menu that changes often. Since it's just outside of the tourist zone, it offers the best value and caters mostly to Romans. It's also easy to find: Crossing Ponte Sisto (pedestrian bridge), continue across the little square (Piazza Trilussa) and you'll see it on the right (daily 12:30–15:00 & 19:30–24:00, Via Ponte Sisto 80, tel. 06-588-3411, SE).

The fine little **Gelateria alla Scala** (across from the church on Piazza della Scala) dishes up delightful cinnamon *(cannella)* and oh-wow pistachio (daily 12:00–24:00, Piazza della Scala 51). Seek this place out.

On and near Campo de' Fiori

While it is touristy, Campo de' Fiori offers a classic and romantic square setting. And, since it is so close to the collective heart of Rome, it remains popular with locals. For greater atmosphere than food value, circle the square, considering each place. Bars and pizzerias seem to overwhelm the square. The **Taverna** and **Vineria** (#16 and #15) offer good perches from which to people-watch and nurse a glass of wine. The only real restaurant is **La Carbonara.** While famous and atmospheric with reasonable prices, it gets mixed reviews (closed Tue, Campo de' Fiori 23, tel. 06-686-4783). Although meals on small surrounding streets are a better value, they lack that Campo de' Fiori magic.

Ostaria da Giovanni ar Galletto—nearby, on the more elegant and peaceful Piazza Farnese—has a dressy local crowd, pleasant outdoor seating, and reasonable prices. Say hi to Angelo, who's committed to serving fine food (Mon–Sat 12:15–15:00 & 19:30–23:00, closed Sun, tucked in corner of Piazza Farnese at #102, tel. 06-686-1714). Of all my listings, this offers perhaps the best alfresco dining experience, but regrettably, single diners are discouraged.

Osteria Enoteca al Bric is a mod bistro-type place run by a man who loves to cook and serve good wine. Wine-case lids decorate the wall like happy memories. With candlelit grace and no tourists, it's perfect for the wine snob in the mood for pasta and fine cheese. Aficionados choose their bottle from the huge selection lining the walls as they enter. Beginners order wine with help from the waiter after they order their meal (open from 19:30, closed Mon, reserve after 20:30, 100 yards off Campo de' Fiori at Via del Pellegrino 51, tel. 06-687-9533). Al Bric offers my readers a special "Taste of Italy for Two" deal (fine plate of mixed cheese and meat with two glasses of full-bodied red wine and a pitcher of water) for €20 from 19:30, but you may need to finish by 20:30. This could be a light meal if you're kicking off an evening stroll, a substantial

Restaurants in the Heart of Rome

appetizer, or a way to check this place out for a serious meal later.

Filetti de Baccala, a tradition for many Romans, is basically a fish bar with paper tablecloths and cheap prices. Its grease-stained, hurried waiters serve old-time favorites—fried cod fillets, a strange bitter *puntarelle* salad, and their antipasto (delightful anchovies with butter)—to nostalgic locals (cash only, Mon–Sat 17:30–23:00, closed Sun, a block east of Campo de' Fiori tumbling onto long tables in a tiny and atmospheric square, Largo dei Librari 88, tel. 06-686-4018). Study what others are eating and order by pointing. Nothing is expensive (see the menu on wall). Urchins can get a cod stick to go and sit on the barnacle church doorsteps just outside.

Trattoria der Pallaro, which has no menu, has a slogan: "Here, you'll eat what we want to feed you." Paola Fazi—with a towel wrapped around her head turban-style—and her family serve up a five-course meal of typically Roman food for €20, including wine, coffee, and a tasty mandarin juice. Make like Oliver Twist asking for more soup and get seconds on the juice (Tue–Sun 12:00–15:00 & 19:00–24:00, closed Mon, indoor/outdoor seating on quiet square, a block south of Corso Vittorio Emanuele, down Largo del Chiavari to Largo del Pallaro 15, tel. 06-6880-1488).

Ristorante Grotte del Teatro di Pompeo, sitting atop an ancient theater, serves good food at fair prices, perfect if you want to dine on a characteristic cobbled street busy with strolling people and musicians (closed Mon and Aug, Via del Biscione 73, tel. 06-6880-3686).

Between Campo de' Fiori and Piazza Navona: **Cul de Sac** is packed with happy locals cobbling together fun meals from the Italian dim sum-type menu of traditional dishes (often crowded, daily 12:00–16:00 & 19:00–24:00, a block southwest of Piazza Navona on Piazza Pasquino). **L'Insalata Ricca,** next door, is a popular chain that specializes in hearty and healthy €7 salads (daily 12:00–15:45 & 18:45–22:00, Piazza Pasquino 72, tel. 06-6830-7881). Another branch is nearby with more spacious outdoor seating (just off Corso Vittorio Emanuele on Largo del Chiavari).

Dining near the Pantheon

Ristorante da Fortunato is an Italian classic, with fresh flowers on the tables, and white-coated, black-tie waiters politely serving good meat and fish to local politicians, foreign dignitaries, and tourists with good taste. Don't leave without perusing the photos of their famous visitors—everyone from Tariq Aziz to Bill Clinton. The outdoor seating is fine for watching the river of Roman street life flow by. The air-conditioned interior has a smoke-free room but I prefer the ambience of the main room. For a dressy night out, this is a good choice. If you're famous you'll be doted over...otherwise, expect brusque service (surprisingly reasonable, plan to spend €30,

Mon–Sat 12:30–15:00 & 19:30–23:30, closed Sun, a block in front of the Pantheon at Via del Pantheon 55, tel. 06-679-2788).

Ristorante Myosotis, an elegant place with dressy waiters and a coat check, is popular with local politicians and diners smart enough to look into the fish locker and make a knowledgeable choice. Secluded and private, it has a traditional yet imaginative menu with a good wine list. Everything here is made on the premises (€35 dinners, Mon 19:30–23:30, Tue–Sat 12:30–15:30 & 19:30–23:30, closed Sun, reservations wise, behind Osteria da Mario—see directions below—at Vicolo Della Vaccarella 3, tel. 06-686-5554).

Eating Cheap and Colorful near the Pantheon

Eating on the square facing the Pantheon is a temptation (there's even a McDonald's offering some of the best outdoor seating in town), and I'd consider it just to relax and enjoy the classic Roman scene. But if you walk a block or two away you'll get less view and better food. Here are some suggestions:

Ristorante Enoteca Corsi is a wine shop that grew into a thriving lunch-only restaurant. The Paiella family serves straightforward, traditional cuisine at great prices to an enthusiastic crowd of office workers. Check the blackboard for daily specials (gnocchi on Thursday, fish on Friday, etc.). Friendly Ilaria and Manuela welcome diners to step into their wine shop and pick out a bottle. For the cheap take-away price plus a euro or two, they'll uncork it at your table. With €5 pastas, €8 main dishes, and fine wine at a third the price you'd pay in normal restaurants, this is a superb value (Mon–Sat 12:00–15:00, closed Sun, a block toward the Pantheon from the Gesu church at Via del Gesu 87, tel. 06-679-0821).

Miscellanea is run by much-loved Michelangelo, who's on a mission to keep foreign students well-fed. You'll find cheap pasta, hearty €3 sandwiches, and a long list of €6 salads. "Mikki" often tosses in a fun little extra (daily 11:00–24:00, indoor/outdoor seating, a block toward Via del Corso from the Pantheon at Via delle Paste 110).

Osteria da Mario, a homey little mom-and-pop joint with a no-stress menu, serves traditional favorites (Mon–Sat 13:00–15:30 & 19:00–23:00, closed Sun, indoor/outdoor, from Pantheon walk 2 blocks up Via Pantheon, go left on Via della Coppelle, take first right to Piazza delle Coppelle 51, tel. 06-6880-6349).

Taverna le Coppelle is good—especially for pizza—with a checkered-tablecloth ambience (closed Tue, Via delle Coppelle 39, tel. 06-688-06557).

Cafeteria Brek, on Largo Argentina just south of the Pantheon, is an appealing self-service restaurant with a modern, efficient atmosphere and really cheap prices (daily 12:00–15:30 & 19:00–22:15, skip the sandwiches and pizza slices downstairs and

Restaurants near the Pantheon

go to the cafeteria upstairs, northwest corner of square, Largo Argentina 1, tel. 06-6821-0353).

The classic **Antica Salumeria** is an old-time *alimentari* (grocery store, daily 9:00–19:00) on the Pantheon square. They sell quality ready-made sandwiches by the weight (€2/*etto*)—ideal for a temple-porch picnic. Sit at the base of a column in the shade and munch lunch.

Non Solo Bevi *enoteca* is a trendy bar several blocks north, tucked into a distant corner of the pedestrian square, Piazza San

Lorenzo in Lucina. Francesco and Lamberto serve fine wine and toothpick munchies free with a glass. Sit at a table (€5 for wine) and enjoy the scene or stand at the bar (€3.50 for wine) and be part of the commotion (open daily, Piazza San Lorenzo in Lucina 15, tel. 06-687-1683; for location, see Dolce Vita Stroll map on page 934).

A block off the same square, at **Vini e Buffet,** Vittorio serves salads, *bruschette*, and wine by the glass (Mon–Sat 12:30–15:00 & 19:30–23:00, closed Sun, Vicolo della Torretta 60, tel. 06-687-1445).

Rome's most famous and venerable ice-cream joint is a minute's walk in front of the Pantheon. **Gelateria Caffè Pasticceria Giolitti** is good, with cheap take-away prices and elegant Old World seating (just off Piazza Colonna and Piazza Monte Citorio at Via Uffici del Vicario 40, tel. 06-699-1243). Another good gelato option nearby is **Gelateria della Palma** (2 blocks directly in front of Pantheon at Via della Maddalena 20). Bright with neon and filled with every type of candy imaginable, kids of all ages will enjoy their huge selection of colorful, tasty gelato.

Near the Spanish Steps

To locate these restaurants, see the Dolce Vita Stroll map on page 934.

Ristorante il Gabriello is inviting and small—modern under medieval arches—offering a peaceful and local-feeling respite from all the top-end fashion shops in the area. Claudio serves with charisma while his brother cooks creative Roman cuisine using fresh, organic products from his wife's farm. Simply close your eyes and point to anything on the menu (pastas-€7, *secondi*-€10, dinner only, get free after-dinner drink with this book, Mon–Sat 19:00–24:00, closed Sun, air-con, reservations smart, Via Vittoria 51, 3 blocks from Spanish Steps, tel. 06-6994-0810).

Ristorante Difronte, with a fresh, stylish ambience, serves big, fun salads (Tue–Sun 12:00–15:30 & 17:30–24:00, closed Mon, Via della Croce 38, tel. 06-678-0355). Stepping next door takes you back about 100 years to the bustling **Fiaschetteria,** serving traditional Italian cuisine (closed Sun, Via della Croce 39). Both places serve €8 plates and offer indoor and outdoor seating.

Ristorante alla Rampa is a classic old restaurant just around the corner from the touristy crush of the Spanish Steps. You'll get quality Roman cooking here, appealing indoor/outdoor seating at a moderate price, and impersonal service. They take no reservations, so arrive by 19:30 or be prepared to wait. For a simple meal, go with the €9 *piatto misto all' ortolana*—a self-service trip to their magnificent antipasto spread with meat, fish, and veggies. Even though you get just one trip to the buffet, this can be a meal in itself (closed Sun, 100 yards east of Spanish Steps at Piazza Mignanelli 18, tel. 06-678-2621).

Near the Trevi Fountain

Ristorante Pizzeria Sacro e Profano fills an old church with spicy south Italian (Calabrian) cuisine and some pricey, exotic dishes. Run by Pasquale and friends, this is just far enough away from the Trevi mobs. Their hearty €13 antipasto plate offers a delightful montage of Calabrian taste treats—plenty of food for a light, memorable meal (daily 12:00–15:00 & 18:00–22:00, a block off Via del Tritone at Via dei Maroniti 29, tel. 06-6791-836).

Around the corner, **Gelateria San Crispino,** well respected by locals, serves particularly tasty, gourmet gelato using creative ingredients such as balsamic vinegar, pear, and cinnamon (Wed–Mon 12:00–24:00, closed Tue, Via della Panetteria 42, tel. 06-679-3924).

Eating Cheaply between the Colosseum and St. Peter-in-Chains Church

You'll find good views but poor value in the restaurants directly behind the Colosseum. To get your money's worth, eat at least a block away. Here are two handy eateries at the top of Terme di Tito (a block uphill from Colosseum, near St. Peter-in-Chains church—of Michelangelo's *Moses* fame).

Caffè dello Studente is a lively spot popular with local engineering students attending the nearby U of Rome. Pina, Mauro, and their daughter Simona (SE) serve typical *bar gastronomia* fare: toasted sandwiches and simple pastas and pizzas. You can get your food to go *(da portar via)* if needed; stand up and eat at the crowded bar; sit at an outdoor table and wait for a menu; or—if it's not busy—show this book when you order at the bar and sit without paying extra at a table (Mon–Sat 7:30–21:00, Sun 9:00–18:00, tel. 06-488-3240).

Ostaria da Nerone, next door, is less friendly and more aggressive, but it's still a good bet for a meal in the area. Their €7 antipasti plate is the best value (Mon–Sat 12:00–15:00 & 19:00–23:00, closed Sun, indoor/outdoor seating, Via delle Terme di Tito 96, tel. 06-481-7952).

Munching near Via Firenze

You have plenty of eating options near my recommended hotels on Via Firenze.

Hostaria Romana is a great place for traditional Roman cuisine served by a fun-loving gang who seem to really enjoy their work. For an air-conditioned, classy, local favorite, eat here (closed Sun, midway between Trevi Fountain and Piazza Barberini, Via del Boccaccio 1, at intersection with Via Rasella, reservations smart, tel. 06-474-5284). Their *antipasti misto della casa* can make a tasty meal by itself—just go to the antipasti bar and fill a €8 plate with a collection of local delights. Take a hard look at their *Specialità Romane* list.

Restaurants in East Rome

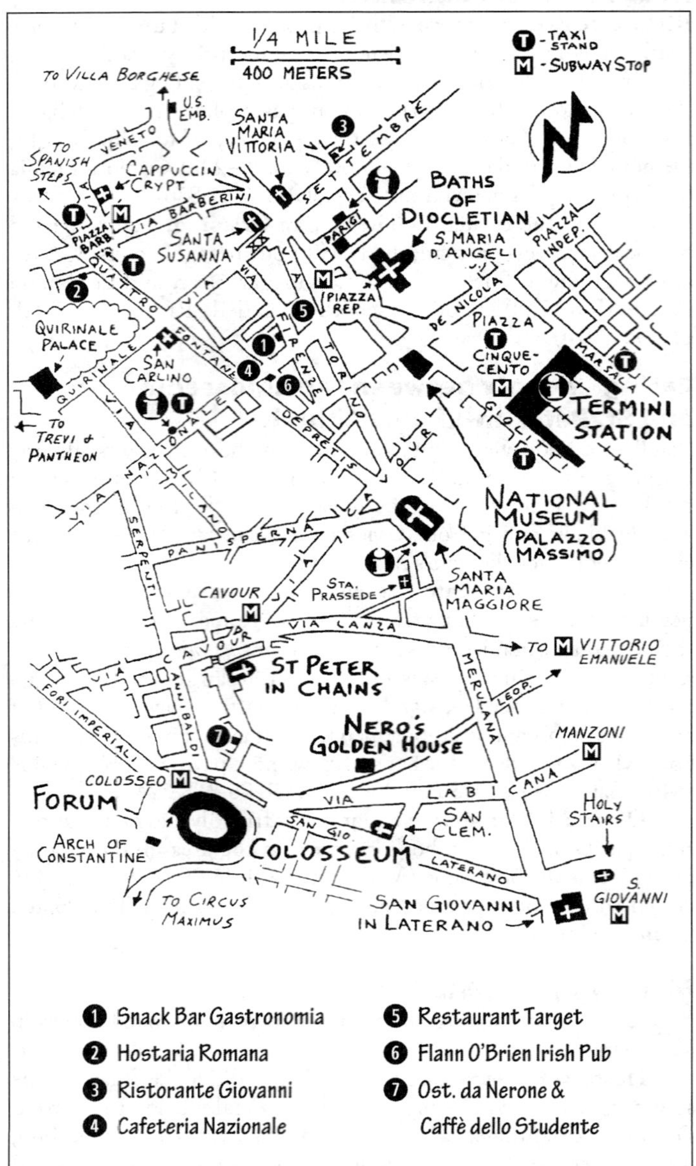

Ristorante da Giovanni is a reasonable, budget option feeding locals and hungry travelers now for 50 years (tired but filling €13 *menu*, Mon–Sat 12:00–15:00 & 19:00–22:30, closed Sun and in Aug, just off Via XX Settembre at Via Antonio Salandra 1, tel. 06-485-950).

Cafeteria Nazionale, with woody elegance, offers light lunches—including salads—at fair prices. It's noisy with local office workers being served by frantic red-vested waitstaff (Mon–Sat 7:00–20:00, closed Sun, Via Nazionale 26-27, at intersection with Via Agostino de Pretis, tel. 06-4899-1716). Their lunch buffet is a delight but gets picked over early (€7.50, Mon–Fri 12:00–15:00, smaller buffet on weekend).

Restaurant Target is a soulless, modern, but handy place serving decent pizza and pasta near recommended hotels (Mon–Sat 12:00–15:30 & 19:00–24:00, Sun 19:00–24:00, indoor/outdoor seating, don't expect great service, Via Torino 33, tel. 06-474-0066).

The **McDonald's** restaurants on Piazza della Repubblica (free piazza seating outside), Piazza Barberini, and Via Firenze offer air-conditioned interiors and salad bars.

Flann O'Brien Irish Pub is an entertaining place for a light meal (of pasta or something *other* than pasta, such as grilled beef, served early or late when other places are closed), fine Irish beer, live sporting events on TV, and perhaps the most Italian crowd of all. Walk way back before choosing a table (daily 7:30–24:00, Via Nazionale 17, at intersection with Via Napoli, tel. 06-488-0418).

Snack Bar Gastronomia is a local joint with one table and a booming take-out business—especially popular for its Greek-style yogurt with fruit and honey (€2–4, confirm price before ordering as there are several versions; fresh meat or veggie sandwiches, freshly squeezed juices, daily 7:00–24:00, Via Firenze 34). An old-fashioned ***alimentari*** (grocery), with everything you'd need for a picnic, is across the street (7:00–19:30), just uphill from the McDonald's.

Near the Vatican Museum and St. Peter's

Avoid the restaurant pushers handing out fliers near the Vatican: bad food, expensive menu tricks. Try any of these instead (see map on page 951).

Perilli in Prati is bright and modern, and just far enough away from the tourist hordes. While friendly Lucia and Massimo specialize in pizza and grilled meats, the highlight is their excellent lunch buffet on weekdays (€5 small plate or €9 for large, closed for lunch Sat–Sun, open daily for dinner, 1 block from Ottaviano Metro stop, Via Otranto 9, tel. 06-370-0156).

Antonio's Hostaria dei Bastioni is tasty and friendly. It's conveniently located midway on your hike from St. Peters' to the

Vatican Museum, with noisy street-side seating and a quiet interior (pastas-€6, *secondi*-€8, no cover charge, Mon–Sat 12:00–15:00 & 19:00–23:30, closed Sun, at corner of Vatican wall, Via Leone IV 29, tel. 06-3972-3034). Antonio is your gracious host.

La Rustichella serves a sprawling antipasti buffet (€7 for a single meal-sized plate). Arrive when they open at 19:30 to avoid a line and have the pristine buffet to yourself (Tue–Sun 12:30–15:00 & 19:30–23:00, closed Mon, near Metro: Cipro-Musei Vaticani, opposite church at end of Via Candia, Via Angelo Emo 1, tel. 06-3972-0649). Consider the fun and fruity **Gelateria Millennium** next door.

Viale Giulio Cesare is lined with cheap **Pizza Rustica** shops, self-serve places, and fun eateries. Restaurants such as **Tre Pupazzi** (closed Sun, tel. 06-686-8371), which line the pedestrian-only Borgo Pio—a block from Piazza San Pietro—are worth a look.

Turn your nose loose in the wonderful Via Andrea Doria **open-air market,** three blocks north of the Vatican Museum (Mon–Sat roughly 7:00–13:30, until 16:30 Tue and Fri except summer, corner of Via Tunisi and Via Andrea Doria). If the market is closed, try the nearby **IN's supermarket** (Mon–Sat 8:30–13:30 & 16:00–20:00, closed Thu eve and Sun, a half block straight out from Via Tunisi entrance of open-air market, Via Francesco Caracciolo 18).

Eating in the Testaccio Neighborhood

Trattoria "Da Oio" A Casa Mia serves a local crowd good quality, inexpensive, traditional cuisine. It's a fun little eatery where you understand the Testaccio passion for the "fifth quarter." (Testaccio, dominated for centuries by its slaughterhouses, is noted for restaurants expert at preparing undesirable meat parts.) The menu is a minefield of soft meats (closed Sun, Via Galvani 43, tel. 06-578-2680).

TRANSPORTATION CONNECTIONS

Termini is the central station (see "Arrival in Rome" on page 878; Metro: Termini). Tiburtina is the bus station (4 Metro stops away from train station; Metro: Tiburtina).

From Rome by Train to: **Venice** (6/day, 5–8 hrs, overnight possible), **Florence** (12/day, 2 hrs, most stop at Orvieto en route), **Pisa** (8/day, 3–4 hrs), **Genoa** (7/day, 6 hrs, overnight option), **Milan** (12/day, 5 hrs, overnight possible), **Naples** (6/day, 2 hrs), **Brindisi** (2/day, 9 hrs, overnight available), **Amsterdam** (2/day, 20 hrs, overnight unavoidable), **Bern** (5/day, 10 hrs, overnight possible), **Frankfurt** (4/day, 14 hrs, overnight available), **Munich** (5/day, 12 hrs, overnight option), **Nice** (2/day, 10 hrs, overnight possible), **Paris** (5/day, 16 hrs, overnight available), **Vienna** (3/day, 13–15 hrs, overnight option).

By Bus to: Assisi (3/day, 3 hrs), **Siena** (7/day, 3 hrs), **Sorrento** (1–2/day: Mon–Sat at 15:00, Fri–Sun at 7:00; 4 hrs, €16, tel. 0805-790-111, www.marozzivt.it; this is the quickest and easiest way to go straight to Sorrento).

Airports

Rome's two airports—Fiumicino (a.k.a. Leonardo da Vinci) and the small Ciampino—share the same Web site (www.adr.it).

Fiumicino Airport: Rome's major airport has a TI (daily 8:00–19:00, tel. 06-6595-4471), ATMs, banks, luggage storage, shops, and bars.

A slick, direct **train** connects the airport and Rome's central Termini train station in 30 minutes. Trains run twice hourly in both directions from roughly 6:00–23:00. From the airport, trains depart at :07 and :37 past the hour. From the airport's arrival gate, follow signs to "Stazione/Railway Station." Buy your ticket from a machine or the Biglietteria office (€9.50). Make sure the train you board is going to "Roma Termini," not "Roma Orte" or others.

Going from the Termini train station to the airport, trains depart at :20 and :50 past the hour, usually from track 25 or 26; to reach these tracks, take a 10-minute walk along track 24 to the end of the station (moving walkways are inside the building to the right on the lower level). Check the departure boards for "Fiumicino Aeroporto"—the local name for the airport—and confirm with an official or a local on the platform that the train is indeed going to the airport (€9.50, buy ticket from computerized yellow ticket machines, any *tabacchi* shop in station, or at the desk near entrance to track 26). Read your ticket: If it requires validation, stamp it in the yellow machine near the platform before boarding.

Shuttle van services run to and from the airport. Consider **Rome Airport Shuttle** (€23/person, 30 percent more late night or early morning, tel. 06-4201-4507, www.airportshuttle.it). **Terravision** shuttles travelers between the airport and Rome's train station, with a few intermediate stops (€9/person, 70 min, 7/day, departs about every 2 hours, tel. 06-6595-8646, schedule and more info at www.terravision.it).

Your hotel can arrange a taxi to the airport at any hour for about €40. To get from the airport into town cheaply by taxi, try teaming up with any tourist also just arriving (most are heading for hotels near yours in the center). Be sure to wait at the taxi stand. Avoid unmarked, unmetered taxis; these guys will try to tempt you away from the taxi stand line-up by offering an immediate (rip-off) ride.

For **airport information,** call 06-65951. To inquire about flights, call 06-6595-3640 (Alitalia: tel. 06-65643, British Air: toll-free tel. 848-812-266, Delta: toll-free tel. 800-864-114,

KLM/Northwest: tel. 06-6501-1441, Lufthansa: tel. 06-6595-4156, SAS: tel. 06-954-070, Swiss International: tel. 848-868-120, United: tel. 848-800-692, Air Europa: tel. 06-6595-5854).

Ciampino Airport: Rome's smaller airport (tel. 06-794-941) handles budget airlines, such as easyJet or Ryanair, and charter flights. To get to downtown Rome from the airport, you can take the LILA/Cotral bus (2/hr, 40 min) to the Anagnina Metro stop, where you can connect by Metro to the stop nearest your hotel. Rome Airport Shuttle and Terravision (both listed above) also offer service to and from Ciampino.

VENICE

(Venezia)

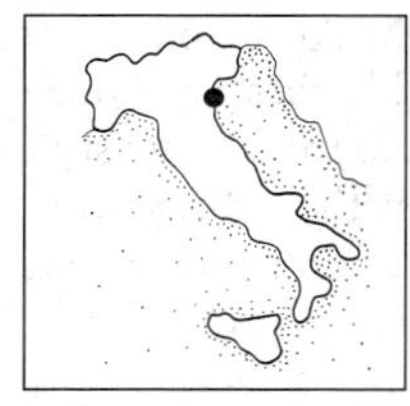

Soak all day in this puddle of elegant decay. Venice is Europe's best-preserved big city. This car-free urban wonderland of a hundred islands—laced together by 400 bridges and 2,000 alleys—survives on the artificial respirator of tourism.

Born in a lagoon 1,500 years ago as a refuge from barbarians, Venice is overloaded with tourists and is slowly sinking (unrelated facts). In the Middle Ages, the Venetians, becoming Europe's clever middlemen for East-West trade, created a great trading empire. By smuggling in the bones of St. Mark (San Marco, A.D. 828), Venice gained religious importance as well. With the discovery of America and new trading routes to the Orient, Venetian power ebbed. But as Venice fell, her appetite for decadence grew. Through the 17th and 18th centuries, Venice partied on the wealth accumulated through earlier centuries as a trading power.

Today, Venice is home to about 65,000 people in its old city, down from a peak population of nearly 200,000. While there are about 500,000 in greater Venice (counting the mainland, not counting tourists), the old town has a small-town feel. Locals seem to know everyone. To see small-town Venice away from the touristic flak, escape the Rialto-San Marco tourist zone and savor the town early and late without the hordes of vacationers day-tripping in from cruise ships and nearby beach resorts. A 10-minute walk from the madness puts you in an idyllic Venice few tourists see.

Planning Your Time

Venice is worth at least a day on even the speediest tour. Hyperefficient train travelers take the night train in and/or out. Sleep in the old center to experience Venice at its best: early and late. For a one-day visit, cruise the Grand Canal, do the major sights on St. Mark's Square (the square itself, Doge's Palace, and St. Mark's Basilica), see the Church of the Frari (Chiesa dei Frari) for art, and wander the backstreets on a pub crawl (described in "Eating," page 1014). Venice's greatest sight is the city itself. Make time to simply wander. While doable in a day, Venice is worth two. It's a medieval cookie jar, and nobody's looking.

ORIENTATION

The island city of Venice is shaped like a fish. Its major thoroughfares are canals. The Grand Canal winds through the middle of the fish, starting at the mouth where all the people and food enter, passing under the Rialto Bridge, and ending at St. Mark's Square (Piazza San Marco). Park your 21st-century perspective at the mouth and let Venice swallow you whole.

Venice is a car-less kaleidoscope of people, bridges, and odorless canals. The city has no real streets, and addresses are hopelessly confusing. There are six districts: San Marco (most touristy), Castello (behind San Marco), Cannaregio (from the train station to the Rialto), San Polo (other side of the Rialto), Santa Croce, and Dorsoduro. Each district has about 6,000 address numbers.

To find your way, navigate by landmarks, not streets. Many street corners have a sign pointing you to *(per)* the nearest major landmark, such as San Marco, Accademia, Rialto, and Ferrovia (train station). Obedient visitors stick to the main thoroughfares as directed by these signs and miss the charm of backstreet Venice.

Tourist Information

There are three main TIs: at the train station (daily 8:00–18:30, crowded and surly); at St. Mark's Square (Mon–Sat 9:00–15:30, closed Sun; with your back to St. Mark's Basilica, it's in far left corner of square); and near St. Mark's Square vaporetto boat stop on the lagoon (daily 10:00–18:00, sells vaporetto tickets, rents audioguides at €3.65/hr for self-guided walking tours). Smaller offices are at Piazzale Roma and the airport (daily 9:30–19:30). For a quick question, save time by phoning 041-529-8711. The TI's offical Web site is www.turismovenezia.it.

At any TI, pick up a free city map and the free *Leo* bimonthly magazine, which comes with an insert, *Leo Bussola,* listing museum hours, exhibitions, and musical events (in Italian and English). Confirm your sightseeing plans. Ask for the fine brochures outlining three offbeat Venice walks. The free periodical entertainment guide *Un Ospite di Venezia* (a monthly listing of events, nightlife, museum hours, train and vaporetto schedules, emergency telephone numbers, and so on) is available at the TI or fancy hotel

Venice Overview

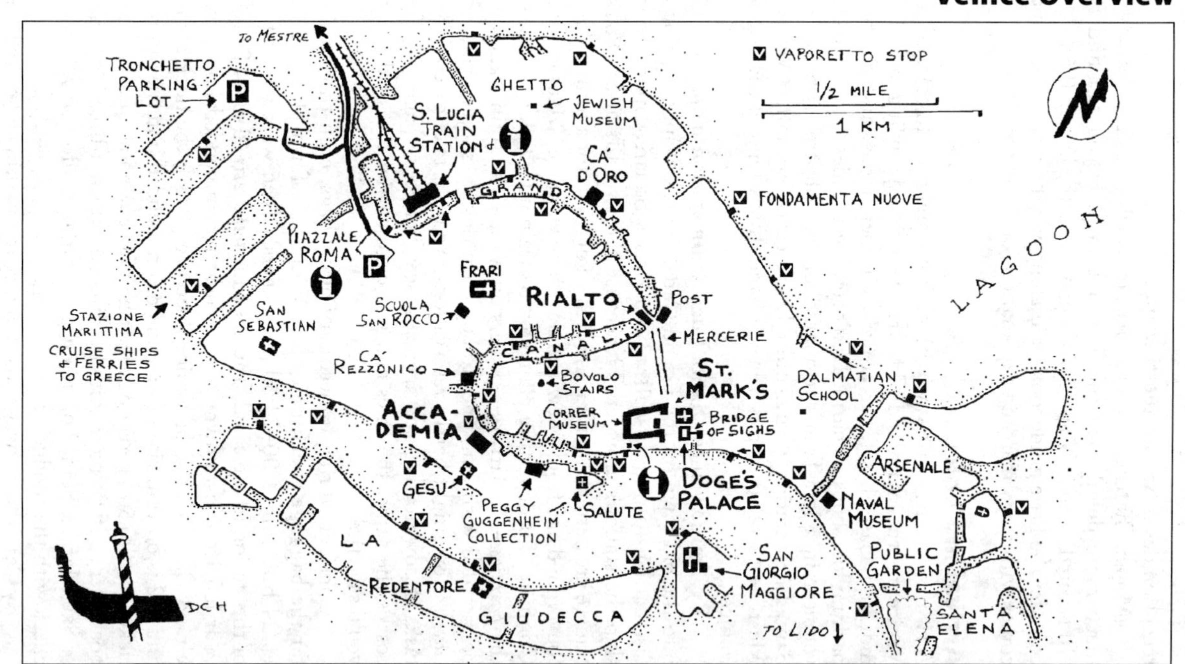

reception desks (www.aguestinvenice.com).

Maps: The cheap Venice map on sale at postcard racks has much more detail than the TI's free map. If you can find the "Illustrated Venice Map" by Magnetic North, buy it (€6). Also consider the little guidebook (sold alongside the postcards), which comes with a city map and explanations of the major sights.

Arrival in Venice

A two-mile-long causeway (with highway and train lines) connects Venice to the mainland. Mestre, Venice's sprawling mainland industrial base, has fewer crowds, cheaper hotels, and plenty of parking lots, but no charm. Don't stop here, unless you're parking your car in a lot. Trains regularly connect Mestre with Venice's Santa Lucia station (6/hr, 5 min). Don't leave your train at Venezia-Mestre—the next stop is Venezia Santa Lucia (end of the line for Venice).

By Train: Venice's **Santa Lucia train station** plops you right into the old town on the Grand Canal, an easy vaporetto ride or fascinating 40-minute walk to St. Mark's Square. Upon arrival, skip the station's crowded TI because the two TIs at St. Mark's Square are better, and it's not worth a long wait for a minimal map (buy a good one from a newsstand with no wait; see "Maps," above). Confirm your departure plan (stop by train info desk or just study the *partenze*—departure—posters on walls). The train station can be crowded with long lines to buy train tickets, supplements, and *cuccetta* (overnight berth) reservations. You can take care of these tasks at downtown travel agencies (see "Services," page 972). The cost is the same, the lines and language barrier are smaller, and you'll save time.

Consider storing unnecessary heavy bags, even though lines for the **baggage check** may be very long (platform 14, €3/12 hrs, €5/24 hrs, daily 6:00–24:00; no lockers). Then walk straight out of the station to the canal. The dock for ***vaporetti*** #1 and #82 is on your left (for downtown Venice, most recommended hotels, and Grand Canal Cruise of Venice—see page 978); the dock for #51 and #52 is on your right (for some recommended hotels). Buy a €5 ticket (or €10.50 all-day pass) at the ticket window and hop on a boat after confirming that it's heading downtown (direction: Rialto or San Marco). Some boats only go as far as Rialto *(solo Rialto),* so check with the conductor.

By Car: The freeway ends at Venice in a parking lot on the edge of the island. Follow the green lights directing you to a parking lot with space, probably Tronchetto (across the causeway and on the right), which has a huge, multistoried garage (€18/day, tel. 041-520-7555). From there, you'll find travel agencies masquerading as TIs and vaporetto docks for the boat connection (#82) to the town

Arrival in Venice

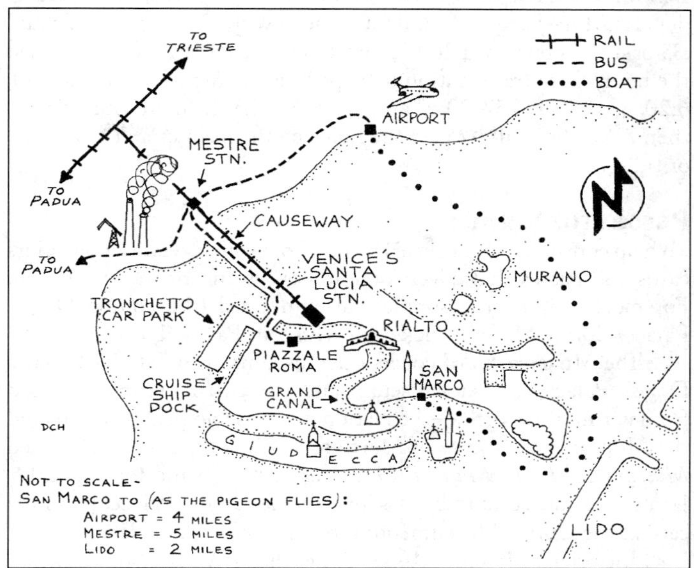

center. Don't let taxi boatmen con you out of the relatively cheap €5 vaporetto ride. Parking in Mestre is easy and cheap (open-air lots €4/day, €5/day garage across from Mestre train station, easy shuttle-train connections to Venice's Santa Lucia Station—6/hr, 5 min). There are also huge and economical lots in Verona, Padua, and Vicenza.

By Plane: Venice's sleek, modern Marco Polo Airport on the mainland, six miles north of the city, has a brand-new wood-beam-and-glass terminal, with a TI, cash machines, car-rental agencies, a few shops and eateries, and easy connections by bus and boat to the city center. Airport info: tel. 041-260-611, flight info: tel. 041-260-9240.

You can get to St. Mark's Square by Alilaguna **boat,** the most direct transportation to the historical center (€10, 2/hr, 70 min, runs 6:15–24:00 from airport, generally departs airport around :10 and :40 after the hour; runs 4:20–22:50 from Venice starting in Zattere, the Dorsoduro hotels; continuing to San Marco/Giardinetti and San Zaccaria around 4:30; tel. 041-523-5775, www.alilaguna.com). A **water taxi** zips you directly to your hotel in 30 minutes for €80. The blue ATVO **shuttle buses** connect the airport and the Piazzale Roma vaporetto stop (€3, 2/hr, 20 min, 5:30–20:40 to airport, 8:20–24:00 from airport, schedule listed in *Un Ospite di Venezia*, www.atvo.it). The cheaper orange ACTV **bus** #5 links the airport with the train station (€1, 2/hr Mon–Sat,

1/hr on Sun and holidays, 20–40 min; from airport to train station departs Mon–Sat at 5:25 and 6:07, then every 30 minutes at :05 and :35 past the hour until 20:05; Sun 1/hr from 7:05–20:05 at :05 past the hour; from train station to airport departing Mon–Sat at 5:30, 6:20, 6:48, then 6:57–20:27 at :27 and :57 past the hour; Sun at 6:30, then 7:02–20:02 at :02 past the hour; confirm times at TI, airport, or train station).

Passes for Venice

To help control (and confuse?) its flood of visitors, Venice now offers cards and passes that cover some museums and/or transportation. For most visitors, the simple Museum Card (the combo Doge's Palace/Correr Museum ticket) or Museum Pass will do.

The **Museum Card** covers the museums of St. Mark's Square: Doge's Palace, Correr Museum, and the two museums accessed from within the Correr—the National Archaeological Museum and the Monumental Rooms of Marciana National Library (€11, called *Museum Card per i Musei di Piazza San Marco*, valid for 3 months, 1 entry per museum; to bypass long line at Doge's Palace, purchase card at the Correr Museum, and then enter Doge's Palace).

The pricier **Museum Pass** includes the St. Mark's Square museums listed above, plus Ca' Rezzonico (Museum of 18th-Century Venice), Mocenigo Palace museum (textiles and costumes), Casa Goldoni (home of the Italian playwright), and museums on the islands—Murano's Glass Museum and Burano's Lace Museum (€15.50, valid for 3 months, 1 entry per museum).

The **Chorus Pass** gives access to 15 of Venice's churches (including San Polo and the Frari, covered in this book) and their works of art (€8, or pay €2.50 per church). You'd need to visit four churches to save money.

Venice also pointlessly offers two other Museum Cards: €8 for the museums of the 18th century (called *Museum Card per area del Settecento*; the museums are Ca' Rezzonico, Casa Goldoni, and Palazzo Mocenigo) and €6 for the island museums (called "*Museum Card per i Musei delle Isole,*" covering Murano's Glass Museum and Burano's Lace Museum).

No cards or passes cover these top attractions: Accademia, Peggy Guggenheim Collection, Scuola Grande di San Rocco, Campanile bell tower, and the three sights within St. Mark's Basilica that charge admission.

Venice Cards: Personally, I don't think these are worth the bother, but here's the information. These cards include Venice's public transportation, public toilets, and, if you get the "orange" version, some sights. To order either card, book online at www.venicecard.com (tel. 041-2424).

The **Blue Venice Card** covers all your vaporetto rides—plus entry to public toilets: one day-€11, three days-€23, seven days-€41; cheaper for "Juniors" under 30. If all you want is a vaporetto pass, you can get a 24-hour pass for €10.50 at any vaporetto dock (described under "Getting Around Venice," below.)

The **Orange Venice Card,** which also includes transportation and toilets, gets you into the museums covered by the Museum Pass. It's like getting a Blue Venice Card and a Museum Pass for one day-€26, three days-€43, and seven days-€58; cheaper for "Juniors" under 30.

"Rolling Venice" Youth Discount Pass: This worthwhile €3 pass gives those under 30 discounts on sights and transportation, plus information on cheap eating and sleeping. It is sold at kiosks at major vaporetto stops, including Ferrovia (train station), Rialto, Accademia, and San Marco/Vallaresso (St. Mark's Square).

Helpful Hints

Venice is expensive for locals as well as tourists. The demand is huge, supply is limited, and running a business is costly. Things just cost more here; everything must be shipped in and hand-trucked to its destination. Perhaps the best way to enjoy Venice is to just succumb to its charms and blow a lot of money.

Get Lost: Accept the fact that Venice was a tourist town 400 years ago. It was, is, and always will be crowded. While 80 percent of Venice is, in fact, not touristy, 80 percent of the tourists never notice. Hit the backstreets.

Venice is the ideal town to explore on foot. Walk and walk to the far reaches of the town. Don't worry about getting lost. Get as lost as possible. Keep reminding yourself, "I'm on an island, and I can't get off." When it comes time to find your way, just follow the directional arrows on building corners or simply ask a local, "*Dov'è San Marco*?" ("Where is St. Mark's?") People in the tourist business (that's most Venetians) speak some English. If they don't, listen politely, watching where their hands point, say "*Grazie*," and head off in that direction. If you're lost, pop into a hotel and ask for their business card—it comes with a map and a prominent "you are here."

Take Breaks: Venice's endless pavement, crowds, and tight spaces are hard on the tourist. Schedule breaks in your sightseeing. Grab a cool place to sit down, relax, and recoup—meditate on a pew in an uncrowded church or buy a cappuccino and a fruit cup in a café.

Etiquette: Walk on the right and don't loiter on bridges. Picnicking is technically forbidden (keep a low profile). Dress modestly. Men should keep their shirts on. When visiting St. Mark's Basilica or other major churches, men, women, and even children should cover their knees and shoulders (or risk being turned away).

Pigeon Poop: If bombed by a pigeon, resist the initial response to wipe it off immediately—it'll just smear into your hair. Wait until it dries and flake it off cleanly.

Public Toilets: There are handy public WCs near St. Mark's Square, the Rialto, and the Accademia Bridge. You'll find public pay toilets near most major landmarks. Use free toilets—in a museum you're visiting or a café you're eating in—when you can.

Water: Venetians pride themselves on having pure, safe, and tasty tap water piped in from the foothills of the Alps; you can actually see the mountains from Venice bell towers on crisp, clear winter days.

Lingo: *Campo* means square, *campiello* is a small square, *calle* is street, *fondamenta* is the road running along a canal, *rio* is a small canal, *rio terra* is a street that was once a canal and has been filled in, and *ponte* is a bridge.

Services

Money: ATMs are plentiful and the easiest way to go. Bank rates for changing traveler's checks vary. The American Express change desk is just off St. Mark's Square (see "Travel Agencies," below). Non-bank exchange bureaus, such as Exacto, will cost you $10 more than a bank for a $200 exchange.

Travel Agencies: If you need to get train tickets, pay supplements, make reservations, or arrange a *cuccetta* (berth on overnight train), avoid the time-consuming trip to the crowded train station by using a downtown travel agency. While American Express charges railpass holders a €5 service fee for reservations, the other agencies do basically everything the train station does for the same price with no fee. All can give advice on cheap flights. Remember, you'll get a far better price if you're able to book at least a week in advance. Consider booking flights for later in your trip while you're here (and remember that in Europe, you don't have to buy a round-trip ticket to get the best price).

Kele & Teo Viaggi e Turismo is good and handy (Mon–Fri 8:30–19:00, Sat 9:00–12:00, closed Sun, at Ponte dei Bareteri on the Mercerie midway between Rialto and St. Mark's Square, tel. 041-520-8722, incoming@keleteo.com).

American Express books flights, sells train tickets, and makes train reservations (travel agency services: Mon–Fri 9:00–17:30, none Sat, finances services: Mon–Fri 9:00–17:30, Sat–9:00–12:30, closed Sun, about 2 blocks off St. Mark's Square at 1471 San Marco, en route to Accademia, tel. 041-520-0844).

Rip-offs, Theft, and Help: While pickpockets work the crowded main streets, docks, and *vaporetti* (wear your money belt and carry your daybag in front), the dark, late-night streets of Venice are safe. A service called Counter of Tourist Mediation handles complaints, but does not give out information (tel. 041-529-8710, complaint@turismovenezia.it).

Church Services: The **San Zulian Church** (the only church in Venice that you can actually walk around) offers a Mass in English at 9:30 on Sunday (May–Sept, 2 blocks toward Rialto off St. Mark's Square). Gregorians enjoy the sung Gregorian Mass on Sundays at 11:00 (plus Mon–Sat at 8:00) at the Church of **San Giorgio Maggiore** (on island of San Giorgio Maggiore, visible from Doge's Palace; see "Venice Lagoon," page 994). Call 041-522-7827 to confirm times.

Laundry: I list several below, but your hotelier can direct you to one near your hotel.

There are two self-service launderettes: One is near St. Mark's Square on Ruga Giuffa at #4826 (daily 8:30–23:00, next to Hotel al Piave, see hotel listing on page 1000 for directions, tel. 041-241-1223, run by Massimo). The other is near the train station (daily 7:30–22:30, #665A/B, San Polo, on Campiello delle Muneghe, a few steps from recommended Albergo Marin—see page 1012 for directions, tel. 348-301-7457).

At either of the following full-service laundries, you can get a nine-pound load washed and dried for €16—confirm price carefully. Drop it off in the morning and pick it up that afternoon. (Call to be sure they're open.) Don't expect to get your clothes back ironed, folded, or even entirely dry. **Lavanderia Gabriella** is near St. Mark's Square (Mon–Fri 8:00–12:30, closed Sat–Sun, 985 Rio Terra Colonne, from San Zulian Church go over Ponte dei Ferali, and then take first right down Calle dei Armeni, tel. 041-522-1758). **Lavanderia S.S. Apostoli** is close to the Rialto Bridge on the St. Mark's side (Mon–Fri 9:00–12:00 & 15:30–19:00, closed Sat–Sun, just off Campo S.S. Apostoli on Salizada del Pistor, tel. 041-522-6650).

Internet Access: The **Net House** isn't cheap but has dozens of terminals (daily 8:00–24:00, on Campo San Stefano, just north of Accademia Bridge, photocopy of your passport required before you start surfing). **Rialtonet** is near the Rialto fish market (Mon–Sat 10:00–20:00, closed Sun, San Polo 278, on north side of Rialto, first square on your right under portico, tel. 041-241-3862).

Post Office: Use post offices only as a last resort, as simple transactions can take 45 minutes if you get in the wrong line. You can buy stamps from tobacco shops and mail postcards from any of the red postboxes around town. A large post office

Daily Reminder

Sunday: The Church of San Giorgio Maggiore (on an island near St. Mark's Square) hosts a Gregorian Mass at 11:00. The Rialto open-air market consists mainly of souvenir stalls today (fish and produce sections closed). These sights are open only in the afternoon: Frari Church (13:00–18:00, closed Sun in Aug) and St. Mark's Basilica (14:00–17:00). It's a bad day for a pub crawl, as most pubs are closed. (Need a calendar? See the appendix.)

Monday: All sights are open except for the Rialto fish market, Dalmatian School, the skippable Palazzo Mocenigo (textiles), and Torcello Museum (on Torcello island). The Accademia and Ca' d'Oro (House of Gold) close at 14:00.

Tuesday: All sights are open except the Peggy Guggenheim Collection, Ca' Rezzonico (Museum of 18th-Century Venice), and the Lace Museum (on Burano island).

Wednesday: All sights are open except the Glass Museum (on Murano Island).

Thursday/Friday: All sights are open.

Saturday: All sights are open (Peggy Guggenheim Collection until 22:00 June–July), except the Jewish Museum.

Notes: The Accademia is open earlier (daily at 8:15) and closes later (19:15 Tue–Sun) than most sights in Venice. Some sights

is just outside the far end of St. Mark's Square—the end farthest from the basilica (Mon–Fri 8:30–14:00, Sat 8:30–13:00, closed Sun, shorter hours off-season). The main P.O. is near the Rialto Bridge (on St. Mark's side, Mon–Fri 8:10–13:30, Sat 8:10–12:30, closed Sun).

Haircuts: I've been getting my hair cut at Coiffeur Benito for 15 years. Benito has been keeping local men and women trim for 25 years. He's an artist—actually a "hair sculptor"—and a cut here is a fun diversion from the tourist grind (€19.50 for women, €16.50 for men, Tue–Sat 8:30–13:00 & 15:30–19:30, closed Sun–Mon, behind San Zulian Church near St. Mark's Square, Calle S. Zulian Gia del Strazzanol 592A, tel. 041-528-6221).

Getting Around Venice

By Vaporetto: The public transit system is a fleet of motorized bus-boats called *vaporetti.* They work like city buses except that they never get a flat, the stops are docks, and if you get off between stops, you may drown.

For most travelers, only two lines matter: #1 is the slow boat, taking 45 minutes to make every stop along the entire length of the Grand Canal; #82 is the fast boat that zips down the Grand close earlier off-season (e.g., Doge's Palace, Correr Museum, Campanile bell tower, and St. Mark's Museum, Treasury, and Golden Altarpiece).

Churches: Modest dress is recommended at churches and required at St. Mark's Basilica for everyone—no bare shoulders, shorts, or short skirts. Some churches are closed to sightseers on Sunday morning (e.g., St. Mark's Basilica and Frari Church) and many are closed from roughly 12:00–15:00 Monday through Saturday (e.g., La Salute and San Giorgio Maggiore).

Crowd Control: Crowds can be a serious problem at the Accademia (to minimize crowds, go early or late or call 041-520-0345 to reserve tickets in advance); St. Mark's Basilica (try going early or late); Campanile bell tower (go early or late—it's open until 21:00 in the summer); and the Doge's Palace. For the Doge's Palace, you have three options for avoiding the ticket-sales line: Buy your Museum Card or Museum Pass at the Correr Museum (then step right up to the Doge's Palace turnstile, skipping the long line); visit the Doge's Palace at 17:00 (if it's April–Oct) when lines disappear; or book a "Secret Itineraries" tour (see page 990).

Canal in 25 minutes, stopping mainly at Tronchetto (parking lot), Piazzale Roma (bus station), Ferrovia (train station), Rialto Bridge, San Tomà (Frari Church), the Accademia Bridge, and St. Mark's Square (specifically, the San Marco/Vallaresso dock). Some #82 boats go only as far as Rialto *("solo Rialto")*—check with the conductor before boarding.

It's a simple system, but there are a few quirks. Some stops have just one dock for boats going in different directions—confirm before you board.

Some lines don't run early or late. For example, the #82 fast vaporetto doesn't leave the San Marco/Vallaresso stop (at St. Mark's Square) until 9:30; if you're trying to get from St. Mark's Square to the train station to catch an early train, you'd need to take slow #1 instead. If there's any doubt, ask a ticket-seller or conductor. If you plan to ride a lot of *vaporetti,* consider picking up the most current ACTV timetable (€0.60, in English and Italian, www.actv.it).

Tickets are €5 to travel up or down the Grand Canal, and €3.50 for other routes. Tickets are good for 90 minutes—enough time for a round-trip cruise. Buy tickets at the dock from ticket booths or from a conductor on board. To avoid a fine, make sure your ticket is stamped with a time before boarding. Tickets come stamped unless you specify otherwise, but to be safe, I stick mine into a time-stamping yellow machine before boarding. Riding free? There's a 1-in-10 chance a conductor will fine you €23.

A 24-hour pass (€10.50) saves money after two trips. Also consider the 72-hour (€22) pass. It's fun to be able to hop on and off spontaneously. There are also two round-trip tickets available: one for €6 (good for any route that doesn't go on the Grand Canal) and another for €7 (includes one trip on the Grand Canal and lines #3 and #4, stopping at San Marco, Rialto, Ferrovia, Piazzale Roma, Tronchetto). Technically, luggage costs the same as dogs—€3.50—but I've never been charged for either.

For vaporetto fun, take the Grand Canal Cruise of Venice (see page 978). Avoid the trip around 9:00 in the morning, when tourists and tour groups are flocking to St. Mark's Square. If you like joyriding on *vaporetti,* ride a boat around the city and out into the lagoon and back. Ask for the circular route—*circulare* (cheer-koo-LAH-ray). It's usually the #51 or #52, leaving from the San Zaccaria vaporetto stop (near the Doge's Palace) and from all the stops along the perimeter of Venice.

By *Traghetto*: Only three bridges cross the Grand Canal, but *traghetti* (gondolas) shuttle locals and in-the-know tourists across the Grand Canal at several handy locations (see map on page 980; routes also marked on pricier maps sold in Venice). Take advantage of these time-savers. They can also save money. For instance, while most tourists take the €5 vaporetto to connect St. Mark's with La Salute Church, a €0.40 *traghetto* does the job just as well. Most people stand while riding (generally 6:00–20:00, sometimes until 23:00).

By Water Taxi: Venetian taxis, like speedboat limos, hang out at most busy points along the Grand Canal. Prices, which average €40 (about €80 to the airport, €50 to the train station, with extra fees for very early or late runs), are a bit soft. Negotiate and settle before stepping in. For travelers with lots of luggage or small groups who can split the cost, taxi rides can be a worthwhile and time-saving convenience—and skipping across the lagoon in a classic wooden motorboat is a cool indulgence.

By Gondola: To hire a gondolier for your own private cruise, see "Gondola Rides," page 996.

TOURS

Walking Tours

Audioguide Tours—At the Campanile bell tower and the TI (the one on the lagoon near St. Mark's Square), you can rent audioguides for self-guided walking tours of Venice (2-hr audioguide-€5/person or €7/double set, 24-hrs €10/person or €14/double set, just punch the number of what you'd like described—exteriors only). The commentary is boring, and if you're reading this chapter, unnecessary.

Venice Walks and Tours—This company offers a selection of historic and entertaining walks, including the basic St. Mark's Square introduction, Cannaregio and the Jewish Ghetto, San Polo and Dorsoduro, Ghosts and Legends, Casanova, and Secret Gardens (€20 per person, cheaper for returnees and students, group size 8–20, English language only, 2 hours each, rain or shine, also day trips into the mainland). For details, see www.venicewalksandtours.com or call Monica or Jonathan at 041-520-8616 or mobile 340-050-2444.

Classic Venice Bars Tour—Debonair local guide Alessandro Schezzini is a connoisseur of Venetian *bacari*—classic old bars serving traditional *cicchetti* (local munchies). He offers evening tours that involve stopping and sampling a snack and a glass of wine at three of these. The fee—about €30 per person—includes wine, *cicchetti*, and a chat with Alessandro, who will answer all your questions about Venice (April–Sept Wed and Sat at 18:00, other evenings by request and with demand, 6–8 per group, tours must have at least 6, call or e-mail a day or two in advance to confirm, meet at top of Rialto Bridge, tel. & fax 041-534-5367, mobile 33-5530-9024, venische@tiscalinet.it).

Venicescapes—Michael Broderick's private theme tours of Venice are intellectually demanding and beyond the attention span of most mortal tourists. While some find him "disinterested and overly intellectual," the curious with stamina can find him enthralling. Michael's challenge: to help visitors gain a more solid understanding of Venice. For a description of his various itineraries, see www.venicescapes.org (book well in advance, 4–6-hr tour: €275 for 2, €50 per person after that, plus admissions and transportation, tel. 041-520-6361, info@venicescapes.org).

Local Guides—Licensed guides are carefully trained and love explaining Venice to visitors. The following companies and guides give excellent tours to individuals, families, and small groups. If you organize a small group from your hotel at breakfast to split the cost (€65/hour with 2-hour minimum), the fee becomes quite reasonable.

Elisabetta Morelli is reliable, personable, and informative, giving good insight into daily life in Venice (€60/hr for Rick Steves' readers, usually 2–3-hour tours, tel. 041-526-7816, mobile 328-753-5220, bettamorelli@inwind.it). **Venice With a Guide** is a co-op of 10 equally good guides (www.venicewithaguide.com). **Walks Inside Venice** is a group of three women enthusiastic about their teaching (Roberta Curiel, tel. 041-524-1706, mobile 347-253-0560, www.walksinsidevenice.com, info@walksinsidevenice.com).

Alessandro Schezzini isn't a licensed Italian guide (and is therefore unable to take you into actual sights), but he does a great job getting you beyond the clichés and into offbeat Venice (€90, 2.5 hrs, listed above in "Classic Venice Bars Tour"). He also does Ghost Tours for spooky evening fun.

Grand Canal Cruise of Venice

For a ▲▲▲ joyride, introduce yourself to Venice by boat. Cruise the Canal Grande from Tronchetto (car park) or Ferrovia (Santa Lucia train station) all the way to San Marco. You can ride boat #1 (slow and ideal, 45 min) or #82 (too fast to comfortably follow this tour, 25 min). When catching either boat, confirm that you're on a "San Marco via Rialto" boat (some boats finish at the Rialto Bridge and others take a non-scenic outside route). The conductor announces *"Solo Rialto!"* for boats going only as far as Rialto. You do not want boats heading for Piazzale Roma. Note that the San Marco vaporetto stop is actually called "San Marco/Vallaresso."

If you can't snag a front seat, lurk nearby and take one when it becomes available or find an outside seat in the stern. This ride has the best light and fewest crowds early or late. Twilight is magic. After dark, chandeliers light up the building interiors. While Venice is a barrage on the senses that hardly needs a narration, these notes give the cruise a little meaning and help orient you to this great city. Some city maps (on sale at postcard racks) have a handy Grand Canal map on the back.

Overview

The Grand Canal is Venice's "Main Street." At over two miles long, nearly 150 feet wide, and nearly 15 feet deep, it's the biggest canal with the most impressive palaces. The canal is the remnant of a river that once spilled from the mainland into the Adriatic. The sediment it carried formed barrier islands that cut off the sea, forming a lagoon.

The Tour Begins

Venice is a city of **palaces,** dating from the days when Venice was the world's richest city. The most lavish formed a grand chorus line along the Grand Canal. Once painted in reds and blues, with black-and-white borders and gold-leaf trim, they made Venice a city of dazzling color. This cruise is the only way to really appreciate the palaces, approaching them at water level, where their main entrances were located. Today, strict laws prohibit any changes in these buildings, so while landowners gnash their teeth, we can enjoy Europe's best-preserved medieval city—slowly rotting. Many of the grand buildings are now vacant. Others harbor chandeliered elegance above mossy, empty ground floors.

Start at the **train station** or **Tronchetto** parking lot. We'll orient by the vaporetto stops.

Venice

FERROVIA (TRAIN STN.)
S. SIMON
RIO FOND. MARIN
PIAZZALE ROMA
AMAI
LACA
CAMPO S. STIN
FRARI
TINT.
SCUOLA SAN ROCCO
CAMPO SANTA MARG.
FOSC.
CAP.
CA' REZZ.
CAMPO SAN BARNABA
TOLETTA
GAMB.
ACCADEMIA
TO ZATTERE
AGNESE
PEGGY GUG. COL.
BAST.
CAMPO MAUR.
CAMPO S. MARIA
LA SALUTE
CUSTOMS HOUSE
BASIN OF SAN MARCO
DCH
SAN MARCO
DOGE'S PALACE
BRIDGE OF SIGHS
RIVA SCHIAV.
SAN ZAC.
OSMAR.
RIM.
S. MARCO
PIAZZA
CORRER MUS.
FREZZ.
VALL.
S. MOISE
22 MARZO
VESTE
LA FENICE
SPEZ.
CAMPO S. STEF.
S. SAM. BOT.
PAL. GRASSI
VERONA
MANDOLA
CAMPO S. ANG.
CAMPO MANIN
S. LUCA
FABBRI
MERCERIE
APR.
GRAND CANAL
S. TOMA
SAON.
CAMPO S. POLO
MAD.
CAMPO S. APONAL
RUGA
S. SILV.
FOND. VIN
MKT.
RIALTO
CAMPO S. BART.
SAL. S. LIO
GIUFFA
CIC.
CAMPO S. MARIA FORMOSA
SAN ZANIPOLO
HOSPITAL
TO FOND. NUOVE
S. CANC.
CAMPO S.S. APOSTOLI
TO TRAIN STN.
FISH MARKET
CAMPO SAN BECC.
200 YARDS
200 METERS
T TRAGHETTO CROSSING
V VAPORETTO STOP
G GONDOLA STATION

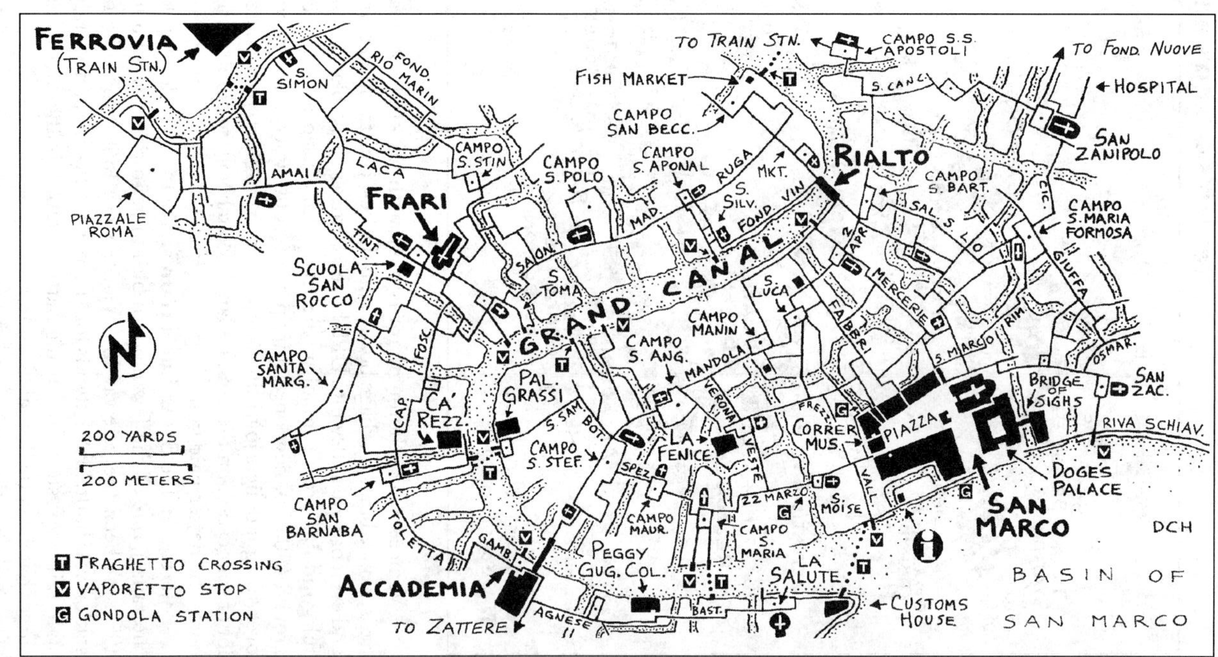

Venice's Grand Canal

Venice's main thoroughfare is busy with all kinds of **boats:** taxis, police boats, garbage boats, ambulances, construction cranes, and even brown-and-white UPS boats. Venice's sleek, black, graceful **gondolas** are a symbol of the city. While used gondolas cost around €10,000, new ones run up to €65,000 apiece. Today, with over 400 gondoliers joyriding amid the churning *vaporetti,* there's a lot of congestion on the Grand Canal. Watch your vaporetto driver curse the better-paid gondoliers.

Ferrovia: The **Santa Lucia train station** (on the left bank of the canal), one of the few modern buildings in town, was built in 1954. It's been the gateway into Venice since 1860, when the first station was built. "F.S." stands for "Ferrovia dello Stato," the Italian state railway system. The **bridge** at the station is the first of only three that cross the Canal Grande.

Opposite the train station, atop the green dome of **San Simeone Piccolo** church, Saint Simon waves *ciao* to whoever enters or leaves the "old" city.

Riva di Biasio: Just past the Riva di Biasio stop, look left down the broad **Cannaregio Canal.** The twin pale-pink six-story "skyscrapers" are a reminder of how densely populated the world's original **ghetto** was. Set aside as the local Jewish quarter in 1516, the area (located behind the San Marcuola stop) became extremely crowded. This urban island developed into one of the most closely knit business and cultural quarters of all the Jewish communities in Italy, and gave us our word ghetto (from *getto,* the copper foundry located here). For more information, visit the Jewish Museum in this neighborhood (see page 993).

San Marcuola: The gray **Turkish Exchange** (right side, opposite the vaporetto stop), is considered the oldest house in Venice. Its horseshoe arches and roofline of triangles-and-dingleballs is Byzantine. Turkish traders in turbans docked here, unloaded their goods into the warehouse on the bottom story, then went upstairs for a home-style meal and a place to sleep. Venice in the 1500s was very cosmopolitan, welcoming people of every religion and ethnicity, so long as they carried cash.

Venice's **Casino** (left-hand side) is housed in the palace where German composer Richard *(The Ring)* Wagner died in 1883. See his distinct, strong-jawed profile in the white plaque on the brick wall. In the 1700s, Venice was Europe's Vegas, with casinos and prostitutes everywhere. Today, this elegant Casino welcomes men in ties and ladies in dresses.

San Stae: Opposite the San Stae stop, look for the **faded frescoes** (left bank, on lower story). Imagine the facades of the Grand Canal at their finest. As colorful as the city is today, it's still only a sepia-toned snapshot of a Technicolor era.

Ca' d'Oro: The lacy **Ca' d'Oro,** or "House of Gold," (left bank, next to the vaporetto stop) is the best example of "Venetian Gothic" on the canal. Its three stories offer different variations on balcony design, topped with a spiny white roofline. Venetian Gothic mixes traditional Gothic (pointed arches and round medallions stamped with a four-leaf clover) with Byzantine styles (tall, narrow arches atop thin columns), filled in with Islamic frills. Like all the palaces, this was originally painted and gilded to make it even more glorious than it is now. Today the Ca' d'Oro is a museum but, other than temporary exhibits, there's little to see inside.

Farther along, on the right, the outdoor arcade of the **fish and produce market** bustles with people in the morning but is quiet the rest of the day. This is a great scene to wander through—even though new European hygiene standards recently required a less-colorful remodeling job. Find the ***traghetto*** gondola ferrying shoppers—standing like Washington crossing the Delaware—back and forth.

Venice at a Glance

▲▲▲St. Mark's Square Venice's grand main square. **Hours:** Always open.

▲▲▲St. Mark's Basilica Cathedral with mosaics, saint's bones, treasury, museum, and viewpoint of square. **Hours:** Mon–Sat 9:45–16:30, Sun 14:00–16:00.

▲▲▲Doge's Palace Art-splashed palace of former rulers, with prison accessible through Bridge of Sighs. **Hours:** Daily April–Oct 9:00–19:00, Nov–March 9:00–17:00.

▲▲Correr Museum Venetian history and art. **Hours:** Daily April–Oct 9:00–19:00, Nov–March 9:00–17:00.

▲▲Frari Church Franciscan church featuring Renaissance masters. **Hours:** Mon–Sat 9:00–18:00, Sun 13:00–18:00, closed Sun in Aug.

▲▲Scuola Grande di San Rocco Tintoretto's "Sistine Chapel." **Hours:** Daily April–Oct 9:00–17:30, Nov–March 10:00–16:00.

▲▲Accademia Venice's top art museum. **Hours:** Mon 8:15–14:00, Tue–Sun 8:15–19:15, shorter hours off-season.

▲▲Peggy Guggenheim Collection Popular showcase of 20th-century art. **Hours:** Wed–Mon 10:00–18:00, June–July open until 22:00 on Sat, closed Tue.

The huge **post office** (left side, just before the Rialto Bridge), with *servizio postale* boats moored at its blue posts, was once the German Exchange, the trading center for German metal merchants. The building's top story has a rare sight in frilly Venice—square windows. Rising above the post office, you can see in the distance the golden angel of the Campanile bell tower at St. Mark's Square, where this tour will end.

As the canal bends, we pass beneath the impressive Rialto Bridge. Singing gondoliers love the acoustics here: "*O sole mio...*"

Rialto: A major landmark of Venice, the **Rialto Bridge** is lined with shops and tourists. Constructed in 1588, it's the third bridge built on this spot. With a span of 160 feet and foundations stretching 650 feet on either side, the Rialto was an impressive engineering feat in its day. Earlier Rialto Bridges could open to let in big ships, but not this one. When this new bridge was completed, much of the Grand Canal was closed to shipping and

▲Campanile Dramatic bell tower with elevator to top. **Hours:** Daily June–Sept 9:00–21:00, Oct–May 9:00–19:00.

▲Ca' Rezzonico Posh Grand Canal palazzo with 18th-century Venetian art. **Hours:** April–Oct Wed–Mon 10:00–18:00, Nov–March Wed–Mon 10:00–17:00, closed Tue.

▲San Giorgio Maggiore Island across the lagoon featuring church with worth-the-trip bell-tower view of Venice. **Hours:** Daily May–Sept 9:30–12:30 & 14:30–18:30, Oct–April until 16:30, closed for sightseeing during Mass on Sun.

La Salute Church Striking church dedicated to the Virgin Mary. **Hours:** Daily 9:00–12:00 & 15:00–17:30.

Jewish Ghetto Neighborhood and Jewish Museum. **Hours:** June–Sept Sun–Fri 10:00–19:00, Oct–May Sun–Fri 10:00–17:30, closed Sat and Jewish holidays.

Dalmatian School Exquisite Renaissance meeting house. **Hours:** Tue–Sat 9:30–12:30 & 15:30–18:30, Sun 9:30–12:30, closed Mon.

Santa Elena 100-year-old neighborhood with few tourists. **Hours:** Always open.

became a canal of palaces. Locals call the summit of this bridge the "icebox of Venice" for its cool breeze. Tourists call it a great place to kiss.

Rialto, a separate town in the early days of Venice, has always been the commercial district, while San Marco was the religious and governmental center. Today, a winding street called the Mercerie connects the two, providing travelers with human traffic jams and a mesmerizing gauntlet of shopping temptations. The restaurants that line the canal feature great views, midrange prices, and low-quality food.

San Silvestro: On the left side, opposite the vaporetto stop, **two palaces stand side by side,** with stories the same height, creating the effect of one long balcony.

We now enter a long stretch of important **merchants' palaces,** each with proud and different facades. Since ships couldn't navigate beyond the Rialto Bridge to reach the section of the Grand Canal you just came from, the biggest palaces—with the major shipping needs—lie ahead. Many feature the Roman country villa design of twin towers flanking a huge set of central windows. These were showrooms designed to let in maximum sunlight.

Just past the Sant'Angelo stop on the right stands the **palace of a 15th-century captain general** of the sea. The Venetian equivalents of five-star admirals were honored with twin obelisks decorating their palaces. This palace flies three flags: those of Italy (green-white-red), the European Union (blue with ring of stars), and Venice (the lion).

Sant' Angelo: Notice how many buildings have a foundation of waterproof white stone *(pietra d'Istria)* upon which the bricks sit high and dry. Many canal-level floors are abandoned; the rising water level takes its toll. The **posts**—historically painted with the gaily-colored equivalent of family coats of arms—don't rot under water. But the wood at the waterline does rot.

Take a deep whiff of Venice. What's all this nonsense about stinky canals? All I smell is my shirt. By the way, how's your captain? Smooth dockings? To get to know him, stand up in the bow and block his view.

San Tomà: After the San Tomà stop, look down the side canal (on the right, before the bridge) to see the traffic light, the **fire station,** and the fireboats ready to go.

We now prepare to round the corner and double back toward St. Mark's. The impressive **Ca' Foscari** (right side) dominates the bend in the canal. Its four stories get increasingly ornate as they rise from the water—from simple Gothic arches at water level, to Gothic with a point, to Venetian Gothic arches topped with four-leaf clovers, to still more medallions and laciness that look almost Moorish. Wow.

Ca' Rezzonico: The grand, heavy, white **Ca' Rezzonico,** directly at the stop of the same name, houses the Museum of 18th-Century Venice. Across the canal is the cleaner and leaner **Palazzo Grassi,** which often showcases special exhibitions.

These days, when buildings are being renovated, huge murals with images of the building mask the ugly scaffolding. Corporations hide the scaffolding for the goodwill—and the publicity.

Accademia: The wooden **Accademia Bridge** crosses the Grand Canal and leads to the **Accademia Gallery** (right side), filled with the best Venetian paintings. The bridge was put up in 1932 as a temporary one. Locals liked it, so it stayed. Cruising under the bridge, you'll get a classic view of the domed La Salute Church ahead.

The low white building among greenery (on the right, between the bridge and the church) is the **Peggy Guggenheim Collection.** The American heiress "retired" here, sprucing up the palace that had been abandoned in mid-construction; the locals call it the "*palazzo non finito.*" Peggy willed the city her fine collection of modern art (described under "Dorsoduro District," page 991).

Salute: A crown-shaped dome supported by scrolls stands atop **La Salute Church.** This Church of Saint Mary of Good Health was built to coax God into delivering Venice from the devastating plague of 1630 (which eventually killed about a third of the city's population).

Across the canal (left side), several **fancy hotels** have painted facades that hint at the canal's former glory.

As the Grand Canal opens up into the lagoon, the last building on the right with the golden ball is the 16th-century **Customs House** (Dogana da Mar, not open to the public). Its two bronze Atlases hold a statue of Fortune riding the ball. Arriving ships stopped here to pay their tolls.

As you prepare to disembark at the San Marco/Vallaresso stop, look from left to right out over the lagoon. On the left, a wide harborfront walk leads past the town's most elegant hotels to the green area in the distance. This is the public garden, the largest of Venice's few parks, which hosts the Biennale art show. Farther in the distance is the **Lido,** the island with Venice's beach. It's tempting, with sand and casinos, but its car traffic breaks into the medieval charm of Venice.

The ghostly white church that seems to float is the architect Palladio's **San Giorgio Maggiore.** It's just a vaporetto ride away (#82 from the "San Zaccaria Jolanda" stop, just past the Bridge of Sighs; see "Venice Lagoon," page 994). Across the lagoon (to your right) is a residential island called **Giudecca.**

San Marco/Vallaresso: Get off at the San Marco/Vallaresso stop. Directly ahead is **Harry's Bar.** Hemingway drank here when it was a characteristic no-name *osteria* and the gondoliers' hangout. Today, of course, it's the overpriced hangout of well-dressed Americans who don't mind paying triple for their Bellinis (peach juice with Prosecco wine) to make the scene. St. Mark's Square is just around the corner.

SIGHTS

St. Mark's Square

For information on Venice's Museum Card and pricier Museum Pass, which cover most of the sights on the square, see page 970.

▲▲▲St. Mark's Square (Piazza San Marco)—Surrounded by splashy and historic buildings, Piazza San Marco is filled with music, lovers, pigeons, and tourists by day, and is your private rendezvous with the Middle Ages late at night. Europe's greatest dance floor is the romantic place to be. St. Mark's Square is about the first place in Venice to flood (you might see stacked wooden

St. Mark's Square

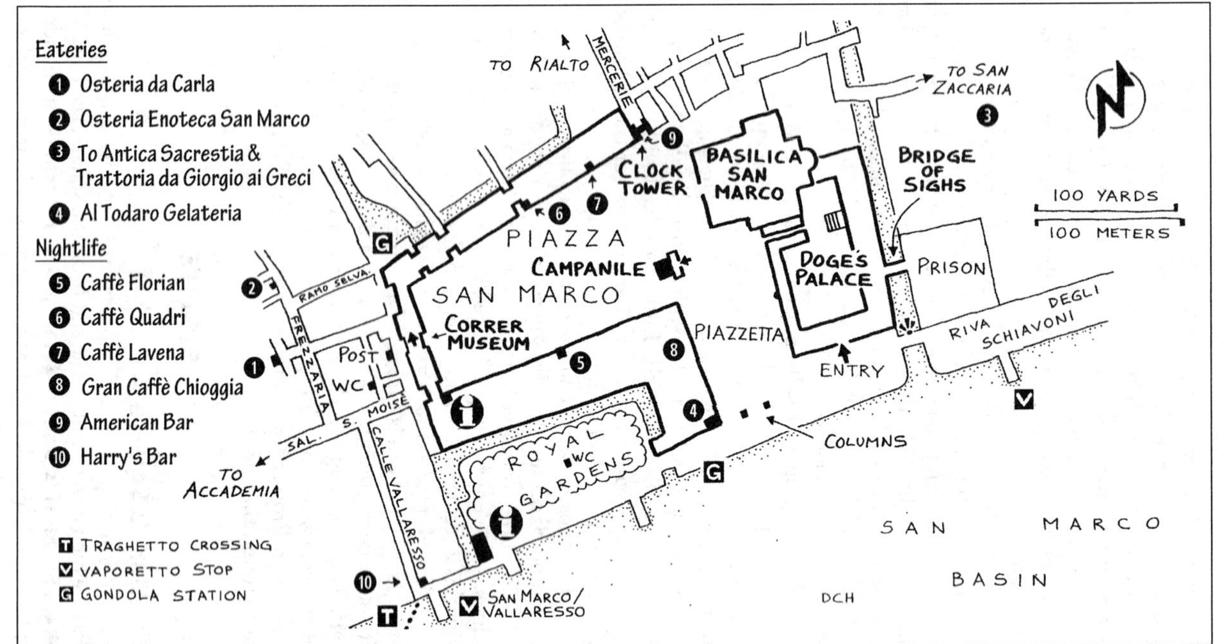

benches; when the square floods, these are put end to end to make elevated sidewalks).

With your back to the church, survey one of Europe's great urban spaces, and the only square in Venice to merit the title "Piazza." Nearly two football fields long, it's surrounded by the offices of the republic. On the right are the "old offices" (16th-century Renaissance). At left are the "new offices" (17th-century Baroque). Napoleon, after enclosing the square with the more simple and austere neoclassical wing across the far end, called this "the most beautiful drawing room in Europe."

For a slow and pricey evening thrill, invest about €15 (including the cover charge for the music) in a glass of wine or coffee at one of the elegant cafés with the dueling orchestras (see Caffè Florian listing, page 999). For an unmatched experience offering the best people-watching, it's worth the small splurge. But if all you have is €1, buy a bag of pigeon feed and become popular in a flurry. (To control the poopulation, the city adds bird birth control to the feed.) To get the flock airborne, toss your sweater in the air.

The clock tower, a Renaissance tower built in 1496, marks the entry to the main shopping drag, called the Mercerie, which connects St. Mark's Square with the Rialto. From the piazza you can see the bronze men (Moors) swing their huge clappers at the top of each hour. In the 17th century one of them knocked an unsuspecting worker off the top and to his death—probably the first-ever killing by a robot. Notice the world's first "digital" clock on the tower facing the square (with dramatic flips every 5 min). The clock tower is slated to open in early 2006.

Venice's best TI is in the far left corner of the square (Mon–Sat 9:00–15:30, closed Sun; a €0.50 WC is nearby, located a few steps beyond St. Mark's Square en route to the American Express office and the Accademia—see *Albergo Diorno* sign marked on pavement, daily 9:00–17:30). The other TI is on the lagoon (daily 10:00–18:00, walk toward the water by the Doge's Palace, go right; pay WCs nearby open daily 10:00–20:00).

▲▲▲St. Mark's Basilica—Built in the 11th century to replace an earlier church, this basilica's distinctly Eastern-style architecture underlines Venice's connection with Byzantium (which protected it from the ambition of Charlemagne and his Holy Roman Empire). It's decorated with booty from returning sea captains—a kind of architectural Venetian trophy chest. The interior glows mysteriously with gold mosaics and colored marble. Since about A.D. 830, the saint's bones have been housed on this site.

Before entering the church, you'll need to check your daybag (small purses are fine). The free bag-check service is just around the corner to the left of the facade, second door on your right down Calle S. Basso at Ateneo S. Basso, a former church (open approximately Mon–Sat 9:45–16:30, Sun 14:00–16:30).

To enter St. Mark's, modest dress is required of everyone, even kids: no shorts, short skirts, or bare shoulders. In peak season, there can be long lines of people waiting to get into the church. People who ignore the dress code hold up the line while they plead fruitlessly with—or put on extra clothes under the watchful eyes of—the dress-code police.

The church has 43,000 square feet of Byzantine mosaics, the best and oldest of which are in the atrium (turn right as you enter and stop under the last dome—this may be roped off, but dome is still visible). Facing the church, gape up (it's OK, no pigeons) and read the story of Adam and Eve that rings the bottom of the dome. Now, facing the piazza, look domeward for the story of Noah, the ark, and the flood (two by two, the wicked being drowned, Noah sending out the dove, a happy rainbow, and a sacrifice of thanks).

Step inside the church (the stairs on the right lead to the bronze horses—save these for later). The interior glows mysteriously with gold mosaics and colored marble. Notice the marble floor richly decorated in mosaics. As in many Venetian buildings, because the best foundation pilings were made around the perimeter, the floor rolls. As you shuffle under the central dome, look up for the Ascension.

Cost, Hours, Tours: The church is free (except for sights listed below) and open Mon–Sat 9:45–16:30, Sun 14:00–16:00, tel. 041-522-5205). The line can be very long during peak season. See the schedule board in the atrium, listing free English guided **tours** (schedules vary, but May–Oct generally Tue and Wed at 10:45, 60 min, meet guide at 10:25 just to the right of main doors, tel. 041-270-2421). The church is particularly beautiful when lit (unpredictable schedule but worth trying to see, often Mon–Fri 11:30–12:30, Sat–Sun all day). No photos are allowed inside the church.

Additional Sights in the Church: Three sights within St. Mark's—the San Marco Museum, Treasury, and Golden Altarpiece—each require small admission fees (€2–3) and share the same opening hours (Mon–Sat 9:45–16:00, Sun 9:45–15:30):

In the **San Marco Museum (Museo di San Marco)** upstairs, you can see an up-close mosaic exhibition, a fine view of the church interior, a view of the square from the balcony with bronze horses, and (inside, in their own room) the newly restored original horses. These well-traveled horses, made during the days of Alexander the Great (4th century B.C.), were taken to Rome by Nero, to Constantinople/Istanbul by Constantine, to Venice by crusaders, to Paris by Napoleon, back "home" to Venice when Napoleon fell, and finally indoors and out of the acidic air. The staircase up to the museum is in the atrium, near the basilica's entrance, marked by a sign that says *Loggia dei Cavalli, Museo.*

San Marco's **Treasury** (with included and informative

audioguide free for the asking) and **Golden Altarpiece** give you the best chance outside of Istanbul or Ravenna to see the glories of Byzantium. Venetian crusaders looted the Christian city of Constantinople and brought home piles of lavish loot (perhaps the lowest point in Christian history until the advent of TV evangelism). Much of this plunder is stored in the Treasury (Tesoro) of San Marco. As you view these treasures, remember that most were made around A.D. 500, while western Europe was stuck in the Dark Ages. Beneath the high altar lies the body of St. Mark ("Marce") and the Golden Altarpiece (Pala d'Oro), made of 250 blue-backed enamels with religious scenes, all set in a gold frame and studded with 15 hefty rubies, 300 emeralds, 1,500 pearls, and assorted sapphires, amethysts, and topaz (c. 1100). Both of these sights are interesting and historic, but neither is as much fun as two bags of pigeon feed.

▲▲▲Doge's Palace (Palazzo Ducale)—The seat of the Venetian government and home of its ruling duke, or doge, this was the most powerful half-acre in Europe for 400 years.

The Doge's Palace was built to show off the power and wealth of the republic and remind all visitors that Venice was number one. In typical Venetian Gothic style, the bottom has pointy arches and the top has an Eastern or Islamic flavor. Its columns sat on pedestals, but in the thousand years since they were erected, the palace has settled into the mud and the bases have vanished.

Enjoy the newly restored facades from the courtyard. Notice a grand staircase (with nearly naked Moses and Paul Newman at the top). Even the most powerful visitors climbed this to meet the doge. This was the beginning of an architectural power trip. The doge, the elected-for-life duke or leader of this "dictatorship of the aristocracy," lived with his family on the first floor near the halls of power. From his living quarters (once lavish, now sparsely furnished), you'll follow the one-way route through the public rooms of the top floor, finishing with the Bridge of Sighs and the prison. The place is wallpapered with masterpieces by Veronese and Tintoretto. Don't worry much about the great art. Enjoy the building.

In room 12, the Senate Room, the 120 senators met, debated, and passed laws. From the center of the ceiling, Tintoretto's *Triumph of Venice* shows the city in all her glory. Lady Venice, in heaven with the Greek gods, stands high above the lesser nations, who swirl respectfully at her feet with gifts.

The Armory—a dazzling display originally assembled to intimidate potential adversaries—shows remnants of the military might that the empire employed to keep the East-West trade lines open (and the local economy booming). Squint out the window to see Palladio's San Giorgio Maggiore and, to the left in the distance, the tiny green dome at Venice's Lido (beach).

The giant Hall of the Grand Council (175 feet long, capacity 2,600) is where the entire nobility met to elect the senate and doge. Ringing the room are portraits of 76 doges (in chronological order). One, a doge who opposed the will of the Grand Council, is blacked out. Behind the doge's throne, you can't miss Tintoretto's monster-piece, *Paradise*, the largest oil painting in the world. Christ and Mary are surrounded by a heavenly host of 500 saints. Its message to electors who met here: Make wise decisions and you'll ultimately join that holy crowd.

Cross the covered Bridge of Sighs over the canal to the prisons (at the fork in the route, descend the stairs rather than continuing right into a cell or you'll miss the basement altogether and end up at the bookshop at the end of the palace visit). In the privacy of his own home, a doge could sentence, torture, and jail his opponents secretly. Circle the cells. Notice the carvings made by prisoners—from olden days up until 1930—on some of the stone windowsills of the cells, especially in the far corner of the building.

As you walk back over the bridge, squeeze your arm through the marble lattice window and wave to the gang of tourists gawking at you.

Cost: €11 (combo-ticket includes admission to the Correr Museum). If the line is very long at the Doge's Palace, buy your ticket at the Correr Museum across the square. With that, you can go directly through the Doge's Palace turnstile without waiting in the long line.

Hours: Daily April–Oct 9:00–19:00, Nov–March 9:00–17:00, last entry 60 min before closing.

Tours: Consider the €5.50 audioguide or "Secret Itineraries Tour," which follows the doge's footsteps through rooms not included in the general admission price. Tours must be booked in advance (€12.50, at 9:55, 10:45 and 11:35 in English, 75 min, arrive 20 min early to check in, no need to wait in line, just *"scusi"* your way to the information desk in the room before the ticket counter). To reserve the tour on the same day or the day before, call 041-291-5911; to book several or more days in advance, call 041-520-9070. While the tour skips the main halls inside, it finishes inside the palace and you're welcome to visit the halls on your own.

▲▲Correr Museum (Museo Civico Correr)— This uncrowded museum gives you a good overview of Venetian history and art. In the Napoleon Wing, you'll see fine neoclassical sculpture by Canova. Then peruse armor, banners, and paintings re-creating festive days of the Venetian republic. The top floor lays out a good overview of Venetian art, including several paintings by the Bellini family. And just before the cafeteria is a room filled with traditional games. There are English descriptions and great Piazza San Marco views throughout (€11 combo-ticket includes Doge's Palace, daily

April–Oct 9:00–19:00, Nov–March 9:00–17:00, last entry 70 min before closing, enter at far end of square directly opposite church, tel. 041-240-5211).

▲Campanile (Campanile di San Marco)—This dramatic bell tower replaced a shorter lighthouse, once part of the original fortress/palace that guarded the entry of the Grand Canal. The lighthouse crumbled into a pile of bricks in 1902, a thousand years after it was built. Ride the elevator 300 feet to the top of the reconstructed bell tower for the best view in Venice. For an ear-shattering experience, be on top when the bells ring (€6, daily June–Sept 9:00–21:00, Oct–May 9:00–19:00). The golden angel at its top always faces into the wind. Beat the crowds and enjoy crisp morning air at 9:00.

Dorsoduro District

▲▲Accademia (Galleria dell' Accademia)—Venice's top art museum, packed with highlights of the Venetian Renaissance, features paintings by the Bellini family, Titian, Tintoretto, Veronese, Tiepolo, Giorgione, Testosterone, and Canaletto. It's just over the wooden Accademia Bridge. Expect long lines in the late morning because they allow only 300 visitors in at a time; to avoid crowds, visit early or late or call 041-520-0345 to reserve tickets in advance (€6.50 entry, Mon 8:15–14:00, Tue–Sun 8:15–19:15, shorter hours off-season, ticket window closes 45 min early, no photos allowed, tel. 041-522-2247). The dull audioguide doesn't let you fast-forward to works you want to hear about; you have to listen to the whole spiel for each room (€4/person, €6/double set, or €6/palm pilot).

At the Accademia Bridge, there's a decent pizzeria canalside (Pizzeria Accademia Foscarini; see "Eating," page 1019), a public WC under it, and usually a classic shell game being played on top (study the system as partners in the crowd win big money, inspiring suckers to lose the same). Nearby sights include the Peggy Guggenheim Collection and La Salute Church.

▲▲Peggy Guggenheim Collection—This popular collection of far-out art, housed in the American heiress' former retirement palazzo, offers one of Europe's best reviews of the art of the first half of the 20th century. Stroll through styles represented by artists whom Peggy knew personally—cubism (Picasso, Braque), surrealism (Dalí, Ernst), futurism (Boccione), American abstract expressionism (Pollock), and a sprinkling of Klee, Calder, and Chagall (€10, Wed–Mon 10:00–18:00, closed Tue, June–July open until 22:00 on Sat, last entry 15 min before closing, audioguide-€5, guidebook-€18, free and mandatory baggage check, pricey café, photos allowed only in garden and terrace—a fine and relaxing perch overlooking Grand Canal, free concerts in summer in garden, see ticket counter or www.guggenheim-venice.it for schedule, near Accademia, tel.

041-240-5411). The place is staffed by international interns working on art-related degrees.

La Salute Church (Santa Maria delle Salute)—This impressive church with a crown-shaped dome was built and dedicated to the Virgin Mary by grateful survivors of the 1630 plague (free, daily 9:00–12:00 & 15:00–17:30, tel. 041-522-5558 to confirm). It's a 10-minute walk from Accademia Bridge. You can also get there by vaporetto (stop: Salute) or via an inexpensive *traghetto* crossing from near St. Mark's Square—catch it on the lagoon next to the TI and Harry's Bar.

▲Ca' Rezzonico (Museum of 18th-Century Venice)—This grand Grand Canal palazzo, Ca' Rezzonico (ret-ZON-ee-koh) offers the best look in town at the life of Venice's rich and famous in the 1700s. Wander under ceilings by Tiepolo, among furnishings from that most decadent century, enjoying views of the canal and paintings by Guardi, Canaletto, and Longhi (€6.50, covered by Museum Pass, April–Oct Wed–Mon 10:00–18:00, Nov–March Wed–Mon 10:00–17:00, closed Tue, ticket office closes 1 hour early, audioguide-€4/person or €6/double set, located at Ca' Rezzonico vaporetto stop, tel. 041-241-0100).

San Polo District

▲▲Frari Church (Chiesa dei Frari)—My favorite art experience in Venice is seeing art *in situ*—the setting for which it was designed—and my favorite example is the Chiesa dei Frari. The Franciscan "church of the friars" and the art that decorates it are warmed by the spirit of St. Francis. It features the work of three great Renaissance masters: Donatello, Bellini, and Titian, each showing worshipers the glory of God in human terms.

In Donatello's wood carving of St. John the Baptist (just to the right of the high altar), the prophet of the desert—dressed in animal skins and nearly starving from his diet of bugs 'n' honey—announces the coming of the Messiah. Donatello was a Florentine working at the dawn of the Renaissance.

Bellini's *Madonna and Child with Saints and Angels* painting (in the chapel farther to the right) came later, done by a Venetian in a more Venetian style—soft focus without Donatello's harsh realism. While Renaissance humanism demanded Madonnas and saints that were accessible and human, Bellini places them in a physical setting so beautiful it creates its own mood of serene holiness. The genius of Bellini, perhaps the greatest Venetian painter, is obvious in the pristine clarity, rich colors (notice Mary's clothing), believable depth, and reassuring calm of this three-paneled altarpiece. It's so good to see a painting in its natural setting.

Finally, glowing red and gold like a stained-glass window over the high altar, Titian's *The Assumption of Mary* sets the tone of exuberant beauty found in the otherwise sparse church. Titian the Venetian—a student of Bellini—painted steadily for 60 years... you'll see a lot of his art. As stunned apostles look up past the swirl of arms and legs, the complex composition of this painting draws you right to the radiant face of the once dying, now triumphant Mary as she joins God in heaven.

Be comfortable discreetly freeloading off passing tours. For many, these three pieces of art make a visit to the Accademia Gallery unnecessary (or they may whet your appetite for more). Before leaving, check out the neoclassical, pyramid-shaped tomb of Canova and (opposite that) the grandiose tomb of Titian. Compare the carved marble Assumption behind Titian's tombstone portrait with the painted original above the high altar.

Cost and Hours: €2.50, covered by Chorus Pass, Mon–Sat 9:00–18:00, Sun 13:00–18:00 but closed Sun in Aug (last entry 15 min before closing, no visits during services, audioguides-€1.60/ person or €2.60/double set). Modest dress is recommended.

The church often hosts evening **concerts;** for details, check for fliers, call 041-272-8611, or visit www.basilicadeifrari.it. (Church info tel. 041-2728-6118.)

▲▲Scuola Grande di San Rocco—Sometimes called "Tintoretto's Sistine Chapel," this lavish meeting hall (next to the Frari Church) has some 50 large, colorful Tintoretto paintings plastered to the walls and ceilings. The best paintings are upstairs, especially the *Crucifixion* in the smaller room. View the neck-breaking splendor with one of the mirrors *(specchio)* available at the entrance (€5.50, includes free and informative audioguide, daily April–Oct 9:00–17:30, Nov–March 10:00–16:00, last entry 30 min before closing, or see a concert here and enjoy the art as an evening bonus, www.scuolagrandesanrocco.it).

Cannaregio District

Jewish Ghetto—The word "ghetto" is Venetian for foundry, and was inherited by Venice's Jewish community when it was confined to the site of Venice's former copper foundries in 1516. Notice how an island—dominated by the Campo del Ghetto Nuovo square and connected with the rest of Venice by only two bridges—would be easy to isolate. While little survives from that time, in its day the square was densely populated, lined with proto-skyscrapers seven to nine stories high. This original ghetto becomes most interesting after touring the **Jewish Museum** (€3, June–Sept Sun–Fri 10:00–19:00, Oct–May Sun–Fri 10:00–17:30, closed Sat and Jewish holidays, Campo di Ghetto Nuovo, tel. 041-715-359). Synagogue tours in English are offered hourly (€8, 30 min, Sun–Fri 10:00–17:30, until 16:30 in winter, contact museum).

Castello District

Dalmatian School (Scuola Dalmata di San Giorgio)—This "school," a fraternal organization, is a reminder that Venice was Europe's most cosmopolitan place in its heyday. It was here that the Dalmatians (from the present-day region of Croatia) worshiped in their own way, held neighborhood meetings, and worked to preserve their culture. The chapel on the ground floor happens to have the most exquisite Renaissance interior in Venice, with a cycle painted by Carpaccio ringing the room (€3, Tue–Sat 9:30–12:30 & 15:30–18:30, Sun 9:30–12:30, closed Mon, between St. Mark's Square and Arsenale, on Calle dei Furlani, 3 blocks southeast of Campo San Lorenzo, tel. 041-522-8828).

Santa Elena—For a pleasant peek into a completely non-touristy, residential side of Venice, walk or catch vaporetto #1 or #82 from St. Mark's Square to the neighborhood of Santa Elena (at the fish's tail). This 100-year-old suburb lives as if there were no tourism. You'll find a kid-friendly park, a few lazy restaurants, and beautiful sunsets over San Marco.

Venice Lagoon

The island of Venice sits in a lagoon—a calm section of the Adriatic protected from wind and waves by the neutral breakwater of the Lido. Four interesting islands hide out in the lagoon.

San Giorgio Maggiore, rated ▲, is the dreamy island you can see from the waterfront by St. Mark's Square. The striking church, designed by Palladio, features art by Tintoretto and a bell tower with oh-wow views of Venice (free entry to church, daily May–Sept 9:30–12:30 & 14:30–18:30, Oct–April closes at 16:30, closed Sun to sightseers during Mass, Gregorian Mass sung at 8:00 Mon–Sat and at 11:00 on Sun—confirm times at TI). The bell tower elevator costs €3 and stops running 30 minutes before the church closes. To reach the island from St. Mark's Square, take the five-minute vaporetto ride on #82 from the San Zaccaria Jolanda stop, just past the Bridge of Sighs, closest to the big statue. (Note: This is not the same vaporetto stop as San Marco/Vallaresso.)

The islands of **Murano, Burano,** and **Torcello** are reached easily, cheaply, and slowly by vaporetto. Pick up a free map of the islands from any TI. Depart from the San Zaccaria Jolanda dock, past the Bridge of Sighs and near the big statue. Line #12 connects all three islands, or take #41 to Murano (get off at "Murano Colonna"), then #12 to the other islands. If you plan to visit even two of these islands, get a 24-hour €10.50 vaporetto pass or a 12-hour €8.50 "Laguna Tour" pass for convenience. Speedboat tours (3–5 hrs) of these three lagoon destinations leave twice a day from the dock past the Doge's Palace near the Cipriani Hotel shuttle dock (look for the signs and booth); the tours are speedy indeed,

Venice Lagoon

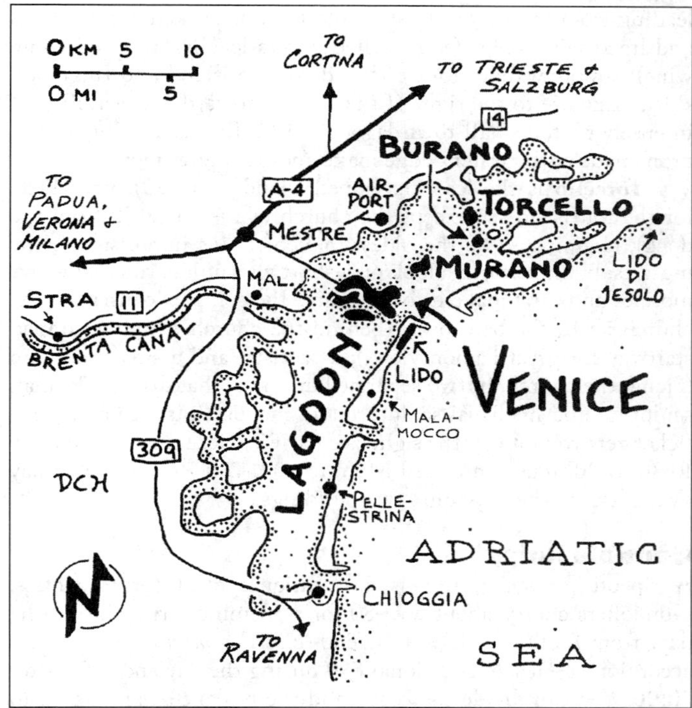

stopping for roughly 35 minutes at each island (€20, April–Oct usually at 9:30 and 14:30, Nov–March 14:30 only, tel. 041-523-8835).

Murano, famous for its glass factories, has the Glass Museum, which displays the very best of 700 years of Venetian glassmaking and exhibits of ancient and modern glass art (Museo Vetrario, €4, covered by €15.50 Museum Pass, Thu–Tue 10:00–17:00, Nov–March 10:00–16:00, last entry 30 min before closing, closed Wed, tel. 041-739-586). You'll be tempted by salesmen offering free speedboat shuttles from St. Mark's Square to Murano. If you're interested in glass, it's handy. You must watch the 20-minute glassmaking show, but then you're free to buy or escape and see the rest of the island. Numerous glass factories (*fabbrica* or *fornace*) offer demonstrations all over the island—check one out. When you're ready to go, head to the "Faro" vaporetto stop and take the #12 to either Burano or Torcello or the #41 back to San Zaccaria.

Burano, famous for its lace, is a sleepy island with a sleepy community—village Venice without the glitz. Lace fans enjoy the Lace Museum (Scuola di Merletti, €4, covered by €15.50 Museum Pass, April–Oct Wed–Mon 10:00–17:00, Nov–March Wed–Mon

10:00–16:00, closed Tue, tel. 041-730-034). While the main drag leading from the vaporetto stop into town is packed with tourists and lined with shops (some sell Burano's locally-produced white wine), simply wander to the far side of the island and the mood shifts. Explore to the right of the leaning tower for a peaceful yet intensely pastel, small-town lagoon world. Benches lining a little promenade at the water's edge make another pretty picnic spot.

Torcello is the least-developed island (pop. 20), with little for the tourist to see except the church (a 10-min walk from the dock), claiming to be the oldest in Venice. It's impressive for its mosaics, but not worth a look on a short visit unless you really love mosaics and can't make it to Ravenna. The complex consists of the church itself, the bell tower (behind the church, climb a ramped stairway for great lagoon views), a sacristy, and a small museum (facing the church, in two separate buildings) that displays Roman sculpture and medieval sculpture and manuscripts. A €6 combo-ticket gets you into all the sights, or pay €2 apiece (most open daily 10:30–17:30, museum closed Mon, tel. 041-730-761). There's a pay WC between the museum's two buildings.

Gondola Rides

A rip-off for some, this is a traditional must for romantics. Gondoliers charge about €65–80 for a 50-minute ride during the day; from 20:00 on, figure on €80–105. For *musica*—singer and accordionist—it's an additional €90 during the day and €100 after 20:00. You can divide the cost—and the romance—among up to six people per boat. Note that only two seats (the ones in back) are next to each other. If you want to haggle, you'll find softer prices on back lanes where single gondoliers hang out than at the bigger departure points.

Though they cost nearly double after dark, gondolas are triply romantic and relaxing under the moon. Glide through nighttime Venice with your head on someone's shoulder. Follow the moon as it sails past otherwise unseen buildings. Silhouettes gaze down from bridges while window glitter spills onto the black water. You're anonymous in the city of masks as the rhythmic thrust of your striped-shirted gondolier turns old crows into songbirds. This is extremely relaxing. Since you might get a narration plus conversation with your gondolier, talk with several and choose one you like who speaks English well. Women, beware...while gondoliers can be extremely charming, local women say anyone who falls for one of these Romeos "has slices of ham over her eyes."

For cheap gondola thrills during the day, stick to the €0.40 one-minute ferry ride on a Grand Canal *traghetto*. At night, vaporettos are nearly empty, and it's a great time to cruise the Grand Canal on the slow boat #1. Or hang out on a bridge along the gondola route and wave at—or drop leftover pigeon feed on—romantics.

Festivals

Venice's most famous festival is **Carnevale,** the celebration Americans call Mardi Gras (Feb, see www.carnevale.venezia.it for dates). Carnevale, which means "farewell to meat," originated centuries ago as a wild two-month-long party leading up to the austerity of Lent. In Carnevale's heyday—the 1600s and 1700s—you could do pretty much anything with anybody from any social class if you were wearing a mask. These days it's a tamer 10-day celebration, culminating in a huge dance lit with fireworks on St. Mark's Square. Sporting masks and costumes, Venetians from kids to businessmen join in the fun. Drawing the biggest crowds of the year, Carnevale has nearly been a victim of its own success, driving away many Venetians (who skip out on the craziness to go ski in the Dolomites).

Every odd year, the city hosts the **Venice Biennale International Art Exhibition,** a world-class contemporary fair. Artists representing 65 nations from around the world send their best and most outrageous art—video, computer art, performance art, digital photography, painting, and sculpture—to be displayed in buildings and pavilions in the Arsenale and adjacent park (May–Nov, take vaporettos #1 or #82 to "Giardini/Biennale;" for the latest, see www.labiennale.org).

Other typically Venetian festival days filling the city's hotels with visitors and its canals with decked-out boats are: **Feast of the Ascension Day** (May 25 in 2006), **Feast and Regatta of the Redeemer** (parade and fireworks, July 16), and the **Historical Regatta** (old-time boats and pageantry, Sept 3). Smaller regattas include the **Murano Regatta** (July 3) and the **Burano Regatta** (Sept 17).

Venice's patron saint, **St. Mark,** is commemorated every April 25. Venetian men celebrate the day by presenting roses to the women in their lives (mothers, wives, and lovers).

Every November 21 is the **Feast of Our Lady of Good Health.** On this local "Thanksgiving," a bridge is built over the Grand Canal so the city can pile into the Salute Church and remember how Venice survived the gruesome plague of 1630. On this day, Venetians eat smoked lamb from Dalmatia (which was the cargo of the first ship admitted when the plague lifted).

Venice is always busy with special musical and artistic events. The free monthly ***Un Ospite di Venezia*** lists all the latest in English (free at TI or from fancy hotels). For a comprehensive list of festivals, contact the Italian tourist information office in the United States (see the appendix) and visit www.turismovenezia.it.

SHOPPING

Shoppers like Murano glass, Burano lace (fun lace umbrellas for little girls), Carnevale masks (fine shops and local artisans all over town), art reproductions (posters, postcards, and books), prints of Venice scenes, traditional stationery (pens and marbled paper products of all kinds), calendars with Venice scenes, silk ties, scarves, and plenty of goofy knickknacks (Titian mousepads, gondolier T-shirts, and little plastic gondolas).

If you're buying a substantial amount from nearly any shop, bargain. It's accepted and almost expected. Offer less and offer to pay cash; merchants are very conscious of the bite taken by credit-card companies.

Popular **Venetian glass** is available in many forms: vases, tea sets, decanters, glasses, jewelry, lamps, mod sculptures (such as solid-glass aquariums), and on and on. Shops will ship it home for you (snap a photo of it before it's packed up). For a cheap, packable souvenir, consider the glass-bead necklaces sold at vendors' stalls throughout Venice.

If you're serious about glass, visit the small shops on **Murano Island.** Murano's glass-blowing demonstrations are fun; you'll usually see a vase and a "leetle 'orse" made from molten glass.

Various companies offer glass-blowing demos for tour groups around St. Mark's Square. **Galleria San Marco,** a tour-group staple, offers great demos just off St. Mark's Square every few minutes. They have agreed to let individual travelers flashing this book sneak in with tour groups to see the show (and sales pitch). And, if you buy anything, show this book and they'll take 20 percent off the listed price. The gallery faces the square behind the orchestra nearest the church; at #139, go through the shop and climb the stairs (daily 9:00–17:30, tel. 041-271-8650, manager Walter Brunello).

Along Venice's many shopping streets, you'll notice fly-by-night vendors selling knockoffs of famous-maker handbags (Louis Vuitton, Gucci, etc.). These vendors are willing to bargain. But beware—police are considering prosecuting the buyers.

NIGHTLIFE

Venice is quiet at night, as tour groups are back in the cheaper hotels of Mestre on the mainland, and the masses of day-trippers return to their beach resorts. **Gondolas** can cost nearly double, but are worth the extra expense. Vaporettos are uncrowded, and it's a great time to cruise the Grand Canal on slow boat #1.

Check at the TI for entertainment listings in publications such as the free *Leo Bussola* magazine (bimonthly, in Italian and English) and in the free *Un Ospite di Venezia* magazine (monthly, bilingual, also available at top-end hotels).

Concerts—Take your pick of traditional Vivaldi concerts in churches throughout town. Homegrown Vivaldi is as trendy here as Strauss in Vienna and Mozart in Salzburg. In fact, you'll find frilly young Vivaldis all over town hawking concert tickets. The TI has a list of this week's Baroque concerts (tickets from €18, shows start at 21:00 and generally last 90 min). There's music most nights at Scuola San Teodoro (east side of Rialto Bridge) and San Vitale Church (north end of Accademia Bridge), among others. If you see a concert at Scuola di San Rocco (tickets €15–30), you can enjoy the art (which you're likely to pay €5.50 for during the day) for free during the intermission. Another unique music experience is a Rondo Veneziano concert—classically inspired music with a modern electronic sound. The general rule of thumb: musicians in wigs and tights offer better spectacle, and musicians in black-and-white suits are better performers. Consider the venue carefully. For information on church concerts, see www.musicinvenice.com or call 041-962-9999. On summer Saturdays, the Guggenheim hosts evening concerts of contemporary music in the museum's garden (June–July, starts about 20:30, included with €10 museum entry, www.guggenheim-venice.it).

St. Mark's Square—For tourists, Venice's main square is the highlight, with lantern light and live music echoing from the cafés. Just being here after dark is a thrill, as **dueling café orchestras** entertain. (See map on page 986.) Every night, enthusiastic musicians play the same songs, creating the same irresistible magic. Hang out for free behind the tables (which allows you to easily move on to the next orchestra when the musicians take a break) or spring for a seat and enjoy a fun and gorgeously set concert. If you sit a while, it can be €15 well spent (for a drink and the cover charge for music). Dancing on the square is free (and encouraged).

Caffè Florian (on the right as you face the church) is the most famous Venetian café and one of the first places in Europe to serve coffee. It's been a popular spot for a discreet rendezvous in Venice since 1720. The orchestra plays a more classical repertoire than the other cafés. The outside tables are the main action, but do walk inside through the richly decorated, 18th-century rooms where Casanova, Lord Byron, Charles Dickens, and Woody Allen have all paid too much for a drink (reasonable prices at bar in back).

Caffè Quadri, exactly opposite the Florian, has an equally illustrous history of famous clientele, including the writers Stendhal and Dumas, and composer Wagner. **Caffè Lavena,** near the clock tower, is newer and less prestigious.

Gran Caffè Chioggia, on the Piazzetta facing the Doge's Palace, charges slightly less, with one or two musicians playing cocktail jazz.

You're not a tourist, you're a living part of a soft Venetian night...an alley cat with money. Streetlamp halos, live music, floodlit history, and a ceiling of stars make St. Mark's magic at midnight. In the misty light, the moon has a golden hue. Shine with the old lanterns on the gondola piers where the sloppy Grand Canal splashes at the Doge's Palace...reminiscing. Comfort the small statues of the four frightened Byzantine emperors where the Doge's Palace hits the basilica. Cuddle history.

SLEEPING

Hotels in Venice are usually booked up on Carnevale (Feb), Easter (April 16 in 2006), April 25, May 1, Nov 1, and on Fridays and Saturdays year-round.

Reserve a room as soon as you know when you'll be in town. Book direct—not through any tourist agency. Most places take a credit-card number for a deposit. If everything's full, don't despair. Call a day or two in advance and fill in a cancellation. If you arrive on an overnight train, your room may not be ready. Drop your bag at the hotel and dive right into Venice.

I've listed prices for peak season: April, May, June, September, and October. Prices can get soft in July, August, and winter. Hotels sometimes give discounts if you stay at least three nights and/or pay cash. If on a budget, ask for a cheaper room or a discount. Always ask.

Virtually all of these hotels are central. See the map on page 1002 for hotel locations. I've listed rooms mainly in two neighborhoods: in the Rialto-San Marco action and in a quiet Dorsoduro area behind the Accademia Gallery. If a hotel has a Web site, check it. Hotel Web sites are particularly valuable for Venice, because they often come with a map that at least gives you the illusion you can easily find the place.

Between St. Mark's Square and Campo Santa Maria di Formosa

$$ Hotel al Piave, with 27 fine air-conditioned rooms above a bright and classy lobby, is fresh, modern, and comfortable (Db-€150, Tb-€195, family suites-€255 for 4, €285 for 5, credit cards ok but gives discount for cash, take vaporetto #82 or #51 to Rialto, find your way to Campo Santa Maria Formosa and it's straight down Ruga Giuffa to #4838/40, Castello, tel. 041-528-5174, fax 041-523-8512, www.hotelalpiave.com, info@hotelpiave.com, Mirella, Paolo, and Ilaria SE, faithful Molly NSE).

$$ Locanda al Leon has nine renovated, spacious, 18th-century Venice-style rooms, many with views overlooking the Doge's Palace and the square, Campo S.S. Filippo e Giacomo. It has

Sleep Code

(€1 = about $1.20, country code: 39)
S = Single, **D** = Double/Twin, **T** = Triple, **Q** = Quad, **b** = bathroom, **s** = shower only, **SE** = Speaks English, **NSE** = No English. Breakfast is included and credit cards are accepted unless otherwise noted. Air-conditioning, when available, is usually only turned on in summer.

To help you sort easily through these listings, I've divided the rooms into three categories based on the price for a standard double room with bath:

$$$ **Higher Priced**—Most rooms €180 or more.
$$ **Moderately Priced**—Most rooms between €130–180.
$ **Lower Priced**—Most rooms €130 or less.

another five rooms in an annex (Db-€120–150, for off-season deals see Web site, triple-paned windows shut out noise, tel. 041-277-0393, fax 041-521-0348, www.hotelalleon.com, leon@hotelalleon.com). From the San Zaccaria vaporetto stop, take Calle della Rasse (to left of pink Hotel Danieli) to Salizada S. Provolo, turn left, then right to get to Campo S.S. Filippo e Giacomo. The hotel is located on the corner of the square and Calle Rimpeto la Sacrestia.

$$ Locanda Correr is a tight and tiny five-room place buried in the old center and up a long stairway. Newly opened and proudly run by Roberto, it features open-beamed ceilings and Venetian-style furnishings along with air-conditioning and modern comforts (Db-€150, Castello 4370, tel. 041-277-7847, fax 041-277-5939, www.locandacorrer.com, info@locandacorrer.com). Take vaporetto #51 to the San Zaccaria stop, head down Calle della Rasse to the left of Hotel Danieli, take a left on Campo San Provolo, a right on Calle Rimpeto la Sacrestia (which turns into Calle Drio della Chiesa), and a left onto Calle del Figher, and it's hiding just past the well-signed Hotel Castello.

$$ Locanda Casa Querini has 11 plush rooms on a quiet square tucked away behind St. Mark's (Db-€130–150 with cash, €5 more for view rooms, €10 more during festivals, air-con, exactly halfway between San Zaccaria vaporetto stop and Campo Santa Maria Formosa at Campo San Giovanni in Oleo 4388, Castello, tel. 041-241-1294, fax 041-241-4231, www.locandaquerini.com, casaquerini@hotmail.com, Silvia SE). Take the street to the right of the Bridge of Sighs to Campo S.S. Fillipo e Giacomo, continue on Calle Rimpeto la Sacrestia, take the second left, and curl around to the left into the little square.

Hotels near St. Mark's Square

$ Hotel Riva, with gleaming marble hallways and bright modern rooms, is romantically situated on a canal along the gondola serenade route. You could actually dunk your breakfast rolls in the canal (but don't). Sandro may hold a corner *(angolo)* room if you ask, and there are also a few rooms overlooking the canal. Confirm prices and reconfirm reservations, as readers have had trouble with both (32 rooms, Sb-€90, 2 D with adjacent showers-€100, Db-€120, Tb-€170, €10 extra for view, cash only, reserve with traveler's check—mail to hotel at Ponte dell' Angelo, Castello 5310, 30122 Venezia, tel. 041-522-7034, fax 041-528-5551). Face St. Mark's Basilica, walk behind it on the left along Calle de la Canonica, take the first left (at blue "Pauly & C" mosaic in street), continue straight, go over the bridge (may be marked Angelo or Anzolo), and angle right to hotel.

$ Corte Campana B&B, run by enthusiastic and helpful Riccardo, rents three comfy, quiet rooms just behind St. Mark's Square (Db-€80–130, Tb-€105–165, Qb-€140–200, Calle del Remedio #4410, Castello, tel. 041-523-3603, mobile 389-272-6500, www.cortecampana.com, info@cortecampana.com). Facing St. Mark's Basilica, take Calle Canonica (to the far left of the church) and turn left before the canal on Calle dell' Anzolo. Take the second right on Calle del Remedio, cross the bridge, and follow signs to Locanda Remedio. Ring the bell at the black gate (#4410) and enter the little courtyard; the door is straight ahead on the left wall and the B&B is up three flights of steps.

On or near the Waterfront, East of St. Mark's Square

These places, located near the Bridge of Sighs, just off the Riva degli Schiavoni waterfront promenade, rub drainpipes with Venice's most palatial five-star hotels. The first, while a bit pricey because of its location, is professional and comfortable. Ride the vaporetto to San Zaccaria (#51 from train station, #82 from Tronchetto car park).

$$ Hotel Campiello, with 16 lacy and bright rooms, was once part of a 19th-century convent, but now has an elevator and air-conditioning. It's ideally located 50 yards off the waterfront (Sb-€70–120, Db-€103–190, 8 percent discount with cash; if you must cancel, do so at least 5 days before your reservation or be charged for the first night; from the waterfront street—Riva degli Schiavoni—take Calle del Vin, between Hotel Danieli and Hotel Savoia e Jolanda, to #4647, tel. 041-520-5764, fax 041-520-5798, www.hcampiello.it, campiello@hcampiello.it, family-run for 4 generations, sisters Monica and Nicoletta, and Thomas).

$ Ca' del Dose is a homey, spotless B&B graciously run by Anna and Marco. Of their seven air-conditioned rooms, one has a terrace with a little view of the waterfront and nearby square and another has a private courtyard (Sb-€60–85, Db-€90–120, see Web site for off-season deals, located 50 yards off Riva degli Schiavoni on Calle del Dose #3801, the first street after the third bridge west of Bridge of Sighs, tel. & fax 041-520-9887, www.cadeldose.com, info@cadeldose.com).

$$ Hotel Fontana is a two-star, family-run place with 14 rooms and lots of stairs on a touristy square two bridges behind St. Mark's Square (Sb-€55–110, Db-€80–170 depending on season and length of stay, family rooms, air-con, 10 percent discount with cash, quieter rooms on garden side, piazza views can be noisy, two rooms have terraces, see Web site for off-season deals, fans in all rooms, vaporetto #51 to San Zaccaria, find Calle de le Rasse—to left of Hotel Danieli—take it, turn right at end, continue to first square, Campo San Provolo 4701, Castello, tel. 041-522-0579, fax 041-523-1040, www.hotelfontana.it, htlcasa@gpnet.it).

$ Albergo Doni is a dark, hardwood, clean, and quiet place—a bit of a time-warp—with 13 dim but classy rooms run by a likable smart aleck named Gina (D-€90, Db-€115, T-€120, Tb-€153, ceiling fans, secure telephone reservations with CC but must pay in cash, Castello 4656, tel. & fax 041-522-4267, www.albergodoni.it, albergodoni@libero.it, Nicolo, Tessa, and Gina SE). From the San Zaccharia vaporetto stop, cross one bridge to the right, take the first left past the historic Hotel Danieli, then turn left at the little square named Fondamenta del Vin.

North of St. Mark's Square

$$ Hotel Orion has 18 neat-as-a-pin, relaxing, and ideally situated rooms. It's a tranquil haven from the bustling streets around St. Mark's Square (Sb-€50–130, Db-€60–165, air-con, from St. Mark's Square walk to left of facade and then left on Spadari, hotel is just before timbered overpass, Spadaria 700/A, 30100 San Marco, tel. 041-522-3053, fax 041-523-8866, www.hotelorion.it, reservations@hotelorion.it).

$$ Locanda Gambero, with 26 rooms, is a comfortable and very central three-star hotel run by Sandro (Sb-€50–130, Db-€65–210, Tb-€90–260, Internet access, air-con, 5 percent discount for payment in cash; from Rialto vaporetto dock walk away from the Rialto bridge, cross one bridge, take first left down skinny Calle le Bembo/Calle del Fabbri; or from St. Mark's Square go through Sotoportego dei Dai then down Calle dei Fabbri to #4687, tel. 041-522-4384, fax 041-520-0431, www.locandaalgambero.com, hotelgambero@tin.it, cheery Gianni covers the night shift, all SE). Gambero runs the pleasant, Art Deco-style La Bistrot on the corner, which serves old-time Venetian cuisine.

$$ Hotel Astoria has 24 simple, tidy rooms tucked away a few blocks off St. Mark's Square (small bed Db-€125, Db-€150, some air-con suites available, 2 blocks from San Zulian Church at Calle Fiubera 951; from Rialto vaporetto #1 dock, go straight inland on Calle le Bembo, which becomes Calle dei Fabbri, turn left on Calle Fiubera; tel. 041-522-5381, fax 041-528-8981, www.hotelastoriavenezia.it, info@hotelastoriavenezia.it, Giorgia SE).

$ Hotel Ai Do Mori, in a central location one block from St. Mark's Square, offers 11 pleasant, comfortable rooms with timbered ceilings (Sb-€40–100, Db-€60–135, a nearby annex of 3 rooms with a shared kitchenette, 3 floors and no elevator, some rooms with views of St. Mark's campanile; from Piazzetta dei Leoni on left of the church facade, take Spadaria one block and turn right; Calle Larga S. Marco 658, 30124, tel. 041-520-4817, fax 041-520-5328, www.hotelaidomori.com, reception@hotelaidomori.com).

$ Home in Venice is a small, tidy apartment (sleeps up to four) with a kitchenette and French doors that open to a gondolier's canal between Rialto and St. Mark's. Maria Antonietta will come and get you wherever you arrive to take you to her place (Db-€90/night, Qb-€120, mobile 339-417-6567, her English isn't great, so try reserving through her friend Giuseppe, mobile 335-548-3054, www.homeinvenice.com).

West of St. Mark's Square

$$$ Hotel Bel Sito, friendly for a three-star hotel, has Old World character and a picturesque location—facing a church on a small square between St. Mark's Square and the Accademia. With solid wood furniture, its 38 rooms feel elegant. Those on the back side are more charming because of a view of a courtyard terrace (Sb-€83–125, Db-€115–192, Tb-€162–248, air-con, elevator, some rooms with canal or church views, vaporetto #1 to Santa Maria del Giglio stop, take narrow alley to square, hotel at far end to your right, Santa Maria del Giglio 2517, San Marco, tel. 041-522-3365, fax 041-520-4083, www.hotelbelsito.info, info@hotelbelsito.info).

$ Alloggi alla Scala, a seven-room place run by gracious Signora Andreina della Fiorentina, is homey, central, and hidden away on a quiet square that features a famous spiral stairway called Scala Contarini del Bovolo (Db-€90, extra bed-€30, breakfast-€9, reserve with credit card, 6 percent discount for payment in cash, take vaporetto #1 to Rialto; to find the hotel from Campo Manin, follow signs on statue's left to "Scala Contarini del Bovolo"; Campo Manin 4306, San Marco, tel. 041-521-0629, fax 041-522-6451, speaks English *"un po"*).

Near the Rialto Bridge

The first three hotels are on the west side of the Rialto Bridge (away from St. Mark's Square) and the last three are on the east side of the bridge (on St. Mark's side). Vaporetto #82 quickly connects the Rialto with both the train station and the Tronchetto car park.

On West Side of Rialto Bridge

$$$ Hotel Locanda Ovidius has a classy Grand Canal view terrace, a breakfast room with a wood-beamed ceiling, and nine bright, comfortable rooms (Sb-€77–190, Db-€130–230, Db with view-€185–280, check Web site for special offers, air-con, Calle del Sturion 677a, tel. 041-523-7970, fax 041-520-4101, www.hotelovidius.com, info@hotelovidius.com).

$$$ Locanda Sturion, with air-conditioning and all the modern comforts, is pricey and popular with all the guidebooks, because it overlooks the Grand Canal (Db-€170–220, Tb-€180–280, family

Hotels near the Rialto Bridge

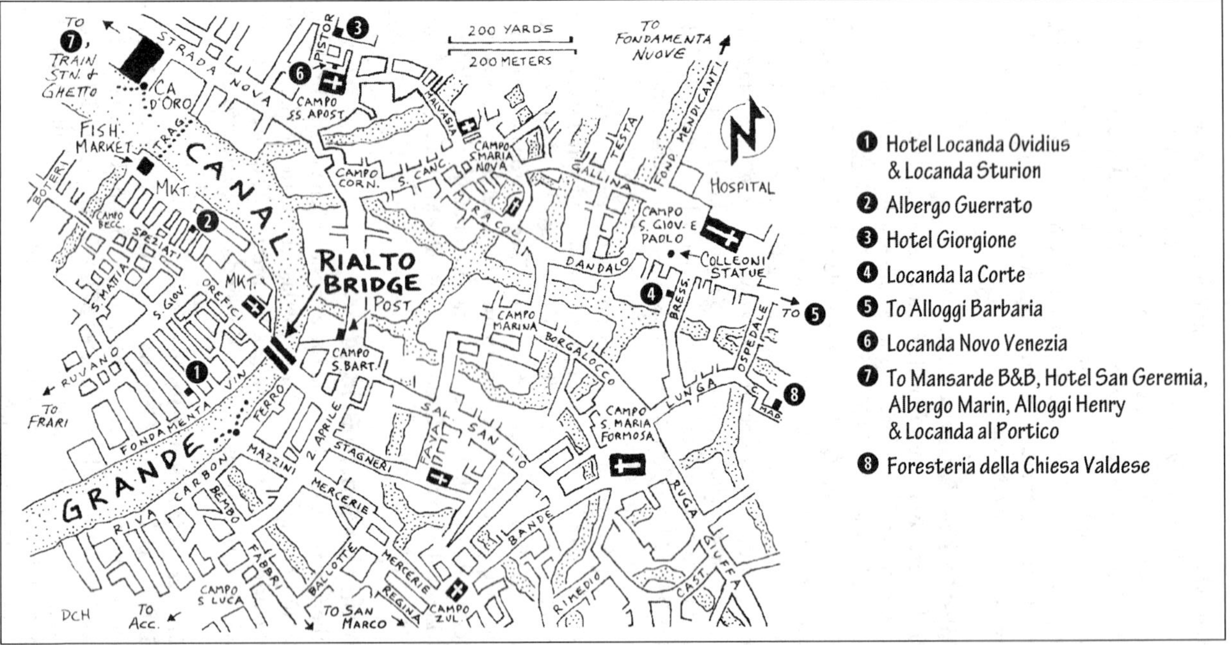

deals, canal-view rooms cost €25 extra, piles of stairs, 100 yards from Rialto Bridge, opposite vaporetto dock, Calle Sturion 679, San Polo, Rialto, tel. 041-523-6243, fax 041-522-8378, www.locandasturion .com, info@locandasturion.com, SE).

$ Albergo Guerrato, above a handy and colorful produce market two minutes from the Rialto action, is run by friendly, creative, and hardworking Roberto and Piero. Giorgio takes the night shift. Their 800-year-old building is Old World simple, airy, and wonderfully characteristic (D-€90, Db-€115, top floor "Guerratino" rooms go for Db-€135, Tb-€145, Qb-€170, cash only; walk over the Rialto away from St. Mark's Square, go straight about 3 blocks, turn right on Calle drio la Scimia—not simply Scimia, the block before—and you'll see the hotel sign, Calle drio la Scimia 240a; tel. 041-522-7131 or 041-528-5927, fax 041-241-1408, hguerrat@tin.it, SE). My tour groups book this place for 50 nights each year. Sorry. Call to determine availability before you fax (otherwise, they won't return the fax). They rent family apartments in the old center (great for groups of 4–8) for around €55 per person.

On East Side of Rialto Bridge

$$$ Hotel Giorgione, a four-star hotel in a 15th-century palace on a quiet lane, is super-professional, with plush public spaces, pool tables, Internet access, a garden terrace, and 76 spacious, over-the-top rooms with all the comforts (Sb-€105–173, Db-€150–265, pricier superior rooms and suites available, extra bed-€60, occasional discount with Web reservations, elevator, air-con, 200 yards off Campo S.S. Apostoli on Salizada del Pistor, #4587, tel. 041-522-5810, fax 041-523-9092, www.hotelgiorgione.com, giorgione @hotelgiorgione.com).

$$ Locanda la Corte, a three-star hotel, has 18 attractive, high-ceilinged, wood-beamed rooms—done in pastels—bordering a small, quiet courtyard (Sb-€90–120, standard Db-€120–150, superior Db-€140–170, suites available, air-con; vaporetto #52 from train station to Fondamente Nove, exit boat to your left, follow waterfront, turn right after second bridge to get to S.S. Giovanni e Paolo square, facing Rosa Salva bar, take street to left—Calle Bressana, hotel is a short block away at #6317 bridge; Castello, tel. 041-241-1300, fax 041-241-5982, www.locandalacorte.it, info@locandalacorte.it).

$$ Locanda Novo Venezia, a charming eight-room place in a 15th-century palazzo run by industrious Claudio and Ivan, is just off a super square—Campo dei S.S. Apostoli, north of the Rialto Bridge (Db-€140, family deals for up to 6 in a room, air-con; from Campo dei S.S. Apostoli head down Salizada del Pistor, take first right on Calle dei Preti to #4529, Cannaregio; tel. 041-241-1496, fax 041-241-5989, www.locandanovo.it, locandanovo@tin.it).

$ Alloggi Barbaria's six quiet, simple rooms have basic comforts (hairdryer, room safe, TV). Near untouristy Campo S.S. Giovanni e Paolo and Fondamenta Nove, it's a good value and a 10-minute walk from St. Mark's Square (Sb-€40–120, Db-€60–150, air-con, tel. 041-522-2750, fax 041-277-5540, www.alloggibarbaria.it, info@alloggibarbaria.it). Take #52 vaporetto to Ospedale stop, turn left as you get off the boat, then right down Calle de le Capucine to #6573 (Castello).

Near the Accademia Bridge

When you step over the Accademia Bridge, the commotion of touristy Venice is replaced by a sleepy village laced with canals. This quiet area, next to the best painting gallery in town, is a 15-minute walk from St. Mark's Square and the Rialto, or you can take the Santa Maria del Giglio or Salute traghetto for a shortcut to St. Mark's. The fast vaporetto #82 connects the Accademia Bridge with both the train station (15 min) and St. Mark's Square (5 min).

On South Side of Accademia Bridge

To reach any of the first four hotels if you're coming from the train station, you can take a vaporetto to the Accademia stop (more scenic, down Grand Canal) or the Zattere stop (less scenic, around outskirts of Venice, but cheaper and faster).

$$$ Hotel Belle Arti is a good bet if you want to be in the old center without the tourist hordes. With a grand entry and all the American hotel comforts, it's a big, 67-room, modern, three-star place sitting on a former schoolyard (Sb-€114–150, Db-€150–215, Tb-€186-265, ask for the Rick Steves discount, plush public areas, air-con, elevator, 100 yards behind Accademia art museum; facing museum, take left, then forced right, Via Dorsoduro 912; tel. 041-522-6230, fax 041-528-0043, www.hotelbellearti.com, info@hotelbellearti.com, SE).

$$ Pensione Accademia fills the 17th-century Villa Maravege. Its 27 rooms are comfortable, elegant, and air-conditioned. You'll feel aristocratic gliding through its grand public spaces and lounging in its breezy garden (Sb-€80–125, standard Db-€130–180, bigger "superior" Db-€170–233, family deals; facing Accademia art museum, take first right, cross first bridge, go right, Dorsoduro 1058; tel. 041-523-7846, fax 041-523-9152, www.pensioneaccademia.it, info@pensioneaccademia.it).

$$ Hotel Galleria has nine tight, velvety, nonsmoking rooms, most with views of the Grand Canal. Some rooms are quite narrow; ask for a larger room (S-€80, D-€110, Db-€120–155, big canal-view rooms #8 and #10, includes scant breakfast in room, fans, near Accademia art museum, and next to recommended

Hotels near the Accademia Bridge

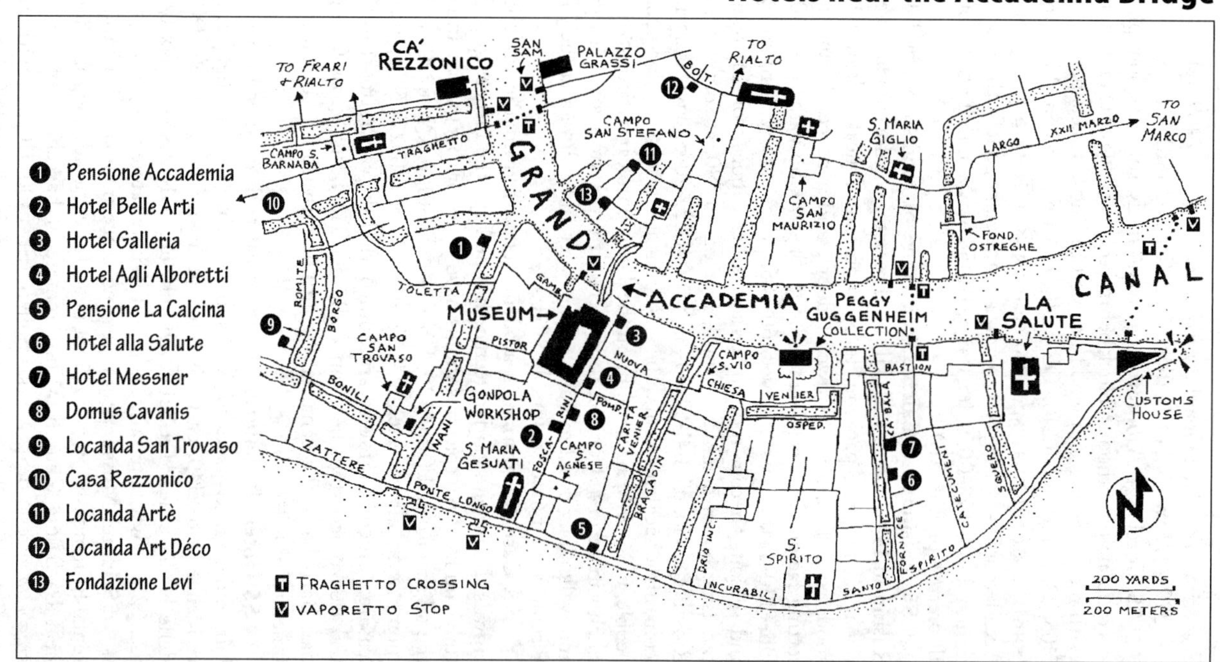

Foscarini pizzeria, Dorsoduro 878a, tel. 041-523-2489, tel. & fax 041-520-4172, www.hotelgalleria.it, galleria@tin.it).

$$ Hotel Agli Alboretti is a cozy, family-run, 23-room place in a quiet neighborhood a block behind the Accademia art museum. With red carpeting and wood-beamed ceilings, it feels plush (Sb-€105, Db-€180, Tb-€210, Qb-€240, elevator, air-con; 100 yards from the Accademia vaporetto stop on Rio Terra a Foscarini at Accademia 884; facing Accademia art museum, go left, then forced right; tel. 041-523-0058, fax 041-521-0158, www.aglialboretti.com, alborett@gpnet.it, SE).

$$ Pensione La Calcina, the home of English writer John Ruskin in 1876, comes with all the three-star comforts in a professional yet intimate package. Its 33 rooms are squeaky clean, with good wood furniture, hardwood floors, and a peaceful canalside setting facing Giudecca Island (S-€75, Sb-€96, Sb with view-€106, Db-€130–145, Db with view-€160–185, prices vary with room size and season, air-con, rooftop terrace, killer sundeck on canal and canalside buffet-breakfast terrace, Dorsoduro 780, at south end of Rio di San Vio, tel. 041-520-6466, fax 041-522-7045, www.lacalcina.com, info@lacalcina.com). They also rent apartments nearby (max 2 people, €136–240, air-con). From the Tronchetto car park or station, catch vaporetto #51 or #82 to Zattere (at vaporetto stop, exit right and walk along canal to hotel). Guests get a fine dinner at their La Piscina restaurant discounted to €20.

$$ Casa Rezzonico is a silent getaway from the madding crowds. Its private garden terrace has perhaps the lushest grass in Italy and its seven spacious rooms have views of this garden and of the adjacent canal (Sb-€120, Db-€140, Tb-€180, Qb-€220, some rooms with air-con, tel. 041-277-0653, fax 041-277-5435, www.casarezzonico.it, info@casarezzonico.it). Take vaporetto #1 to the Ca' Rezzonico stop, head up Calle del Traghetto, cross Campo San Barnaba to the canal, and continue forward on Fondamenta Gherardini to #2813.

$$ Hotel alla Salute, a basic retreat with indifferent owners buried deep in Dorsoduro, works for those wanting a quiet Venice residence (Db-€140, cash discount, air-con, facing the canal Rio delle Fornace near La Salute church, tel. 041-523-5404, fax 041-522-2271, www.hotelsalute.com, info@hotelsalute.com).

$$ Hotel Messner, a sprawling place popular with groups, rents 40 nondescript rooms in a peaceful canalside neighborhood near La Salute Church. While remote, it has cheap and handy *traghetto* access to St. Mark's Square (Sb-€100–110, Db with air-con-€140–160, Db without air-con in simpler annex-€90–115, Tb-€130–145, Qb-€140–160, peaceful garden, midway between lagoon and Grand Canal on Rio delle Fornace canal, tel. 041-522-7443, fax 041-522-7266, www.hotelmessner.it, messnerinfo@tin.it).

$ Locanda San Trovaso is sparkling new, with 14 classy, spacious rooms split between the main hotel and nearby annex and a peaceful location on a small canal (Sb-€90, Db-€115–130, Tb-€145, breakfast in your room, fans, small roof terrace; take vaporetto #82 from Tronchetto or #51 from Piazzale Roma or train station, get off at Zattere, exit left, turn right at tiny Calle Trevisan, cross bridge, cross adjacent bridge, take immediate right, then first left, Dorsoduro 1350/51; tel. 041-277-1146, fax 041-277-7190, www.casantrovaso.com, s.trovaso@tin.it, Mark and his son Alessandro SE).

$ Domus Cavanis, across the street from—and owned by—Hotel Belle Arti, is a big, practical, stark place with a garden, renting 30 quiet, simple, and spacious rooms (Sb-€60, Db-€103, Tb-€150, family rooms, includes breakfast at Hotel Belle Arti, air-con, elevator, Dorsoduro 895, tel. 041-528-7374, fax 041-522-8505).

On North Side of Accademia Bridge

$ Locanda Artè has eight homey rooms with high ceilings, old-style Venetian furnishings, air-conditioning, and thoughtful touches (Sb-€70–110, Db-€100–140, 10 percent cash discount, family room sleeps up to 6, just north of Accademia Bridge, 100 yards west of Campo San Stefano on Calle de Frutariol, San Marco 2900, tel. 041-520-0882, fax 041-277-8395, www.casaarte.info, info@casaarte.info, Alberto SE).

$ Locanda Art Déco is a charming place run by accommodating and equally charming Judith. While the Art Deco theme is scant, a wrought-iron staircase leads from her inviting lobby to seven thoughtfully decorated rooms (Db-€100–160, 3-night minimum on weekends, cash discount, 2 family rooms, air-con, just north of the Accademia Bridge off Campo Santo Stefano at 2966 Calle delle Botteghe, tel. 041-277-0558, fax 041-270-2891, www.locandaartdeco.com, info@locandaartdeco.com).

$ Fondazione Levi, a dorm run by a foundation that promotes research on Venetian music, offers 18 quiet, institutional yet comfortable and spacious rooms (Sb-€65, Db-€108, Tb-€124, Qb-€145, twin beds only, elevator, 80 yards from base of Accademia Bridge on St. Mark's side; from Accademia vaporetto stop, cross Accademia Bridge, take immediate left—crossing the bridge Ponte Giustinian and going down Calle Giustinian directly to the Fondazione, buzz the "Foresteria" door to the right, San Vidal 2893; tel. 041-786-711, fax 041-786-766, foresterialevi@libero.it, SE).

Near the Train Station

$$ Hotel San Geremia, a three-minute walk from the station, offers 20 clean and simple rooms at decent prices near a self-service laundry, Internet café, and the Ferrovia vaporetto stop (one small Db-€80, Db-€115–145, head left outside the station and follow

Lista di Spagna to Campo San Geremia #290/A, tel. 041-716-245, fax 041-524-2342, www.sangeremia.com, Claudio SE).

$ Mansarde B&B has charming apartments lovingly cared for by Anna Maria Andreola in the heart of Cannaregio. She offers babysitting for a fee, free laundry service, and one free cooking lesson—tell her how much you want to spend and what you want to prepare and she can do the shopping (Db-€80–100, Qb-€135; from the train station, turn left onto Lista di Spagna, cross Campo San Geremia, cross the bridge—apartments are located next to the San Paolo Bank on the left, ring bell marked Cazzaro, #1353/A Rio Tera S. Leonardo; tel. 041-718-826, mobile 338-868-8935, cazzar .ola@libero.it).

$ Albergo Marin and his friendly, helpful staff offers 17 good-value, immaculate, quiet rooms handy to the train station (Sb-€50–80, Db-€60–95; cross the Grand Canal and turn immediately right—walking along water, take the third left, pass church, go down Calle del Traghetto di S. Lucia, then jog left again to Campiello delle Muneghe #670/B; tel. 041-718-022, fax 041-721-485, www.albergomarin.it, info@albergomarin.it).

$ Alloggi Henry has eight basic, peaceful rooms in a family-owned hotel a few minute's walk from the train station, in untouristy Cannaregio (Db-€90–130, Tb-€150–170, plus off-season deals on their Web site, no breakfast, but they'll send you to any number of *pasticcerie* in the neighborhood for fresh pastries, some rooms air-con, tel. 041-523-6675, fax 041-715-680, www.alloggihenry .com, yuri2000@libero.it). From the station, exit left and follow Lista di Spagna to the Cannaregio canal, cross the bridge, and follow main street until it forks. Take the left fork, then the second left on Calle Ormesini, following it around to the right until you get to the hotel at #1506/A.

$ Locanda al Portico's nine comfortable rooms are in a quiet alley just off the Grand Canal, near the San Marcuola vaporetto stop close to the train station (Sb-€50–90, Db-€80–120; from vaporetto stop, walk around church and turn left, then immediately right, turn right again on Calle del Cristo and find hotel under Sotoportego del Pegolotto #1804, Cannaregio, tel. 041-275-9202, fax 041-275-7659).

Cheap Dormitory Accommodations

$ Foresteria della Chiesa Valdese, warmly run by the Methodist church, offers 33 beds in dorms and doubles, halfway between St. Mark's Square and the Rialto Bridge. This run-down but charming old place has elegant ceiling paintings (dorm bed-€22, D-€57, Db-€75, family apartment-€116 for 5, must check in and out when office is open: 9:00–13:00 & 18:00–20:00, from Campo Santa Maria Formosa, walk past Bar all' Orologio to end of Calle Lunga and cross bridge, Castello 5170, reservation by phone only, reservations for single beds are not accepted, tel. 041-528-6797, fax 041-241-6238, foresteriavenezia@diaconiavaldese.org).

$ Venice's **youth hostel** on Giudecca Island is crowded and inexpensive (€18 beds with sheets and breakfast in 10- to 16-bed rooms, membership required, office open daily 7:00–9:30 & 13:30–23:30, catch vaporetto #82 from station to Zittele, tel. 041-523-8211, www.ostellionline.org, can reserve in advance through Web site). The budget cafeteria welcomes non-hostelers (nightly 17:00–23:30).

EATING

While touristy restaurants are the scourge of Venice, and most restaurateurs believe you can't survive in Venice without catering to tourists, there are plenty of places that are still popular with locals and respect the tourists who happen in. First trick: Walk away from triple-language menus. Second trick: Order the daily special. Third trick: Most seafood dishes are the local catch-of-the-day.

For romantic—and usually pricey—meals along the water, see "Eating with a Romantic Canalside Setting," page 1021. For dessert, it's gelato (see end of this chapter).

Between Campo Santi Apostoli and Campo S.S. Giovanni e Paolo

Trattoria da Bepi is a classy, family-run place where mama scours the market for just the best ingredients and son, Loris, takes good care of the hungry clientele (€30 meals, Fri–Wed 12:00–14:30 & 19:00–22:00, closed Thu, near Rialto, half a block north of Campo Santi Apostoli on Salizada Pistor, tel. 041-528-5031).

The following colorful *osterias* are good for *cicchetti* (munchies), wine-tasting, or a simple, rustic, sit-down meal surrounded by a boisterous local ambience:

Osteria da Alberto serves *cicchetti* (18:15–19:30) and great €20 seafood dinners (Mon–Sat 12:00–15:00 & 19:30–23:00, closed Sun, midway between Campo Santi Apostoli and Campo S.S. Giovanni e Paolo, next to Ponte de la Panada on Calle Larga Giacinto Gallina, tel. 041-523-8153).

Osteria ai Promessi Sposi does *cicchetti* with gusto—the best selection I found—and offers a little garden for sit-down meals. The ambience is Venetian shipwreck (Thu–Tue 9:00–23:00, closed Wed, a block off Campo S.S. Apostoli and a block inland from Strada Nova at Calle dell' Oca, tel. 041-522-8609).

Osteria al Bomba is run attentively by Sr. Filippi and his two sons. Ask for the menu and stand or sit at the very long table. The place is less ye olde and has a fun list of Bollicine—the local champagne (Tue–Sun from 18:00, closed Mon, near Campo S.S. Apostoli a block off the Strada Nuova on Calle de l'Oca, tel. 041-520-5175). You'll find more pubs nearby, in the side streets opposite Campo St. Sofia across Strada Nova.

East of the Rialto Bridge, near Campo San Bartolomeo

Osteria di Santa Marina is a dressy new place rapidly gaining fame for its mission to reinvent traditional dishes with a creative twist. They serve only the finest seasonal produce (fun-if-pricey menu with €14 pastas and €25 *secondi,* Tue–Sat 12:30–14:30 & 19:30–21:30, closed Sun lunch and Mon all day, eat indoors or outdoors on pleasant little square, midway between Rialto and Campo Santa Maria Formosa on Campo Marina, tel. 041-528-5239).

Osteria il Milion, with bow-tied waiters and dressy candlelit tables indoors and out, is quietly situated next to Marco Polo's home. It serves traditional Italian meals for around €25 (Thu–Tue 12:00–15:00 & 18:30–23:00, closed Wed; near Rialto, head north from Campo San Bartolomeo, over one bridge, take first right off San Giovanni Grisostomo before the church, walk under the sign Corte Prima del Milion o del forno, it's at #5841; tel. 041-522-9302).

The **Devil's Forest Pub,** an air-conditioned bit of England tucked away a block from the crowds, is, strangely, more Venetian these days than the *tipico* places. Locals come here for good English and Irish beer on tap, big salads (€7.50, lunch only), hot bar snacks, and an easygoing ambience (fine prices, daily 10:00–24:00, meals 12:00–15:30, bar snacks all the time, closed Sun in Aug, no cover or service charge, smoky, backgammon and chess boards available-€2, a block off Campo San Bartolomeo on Calle dei Stagneri, tel. 041-520-0623).

The Stand-Up Progressive Venetian Pub-Crawl Dinner

My favorite Venetian dinner is a pub crawl. A *giro d'ombra* (pub crawl) is a tradition unique to Venice—ideal in a city with no cars. (*Ombra*—slang for a glass of wine—means shade, from the old days when a portable wine bar scooted with the shadow of the Campanile bell tower across St. Mark's Square.)

Venice's residential back streets hide plenty of characteristic bars *(baccari)* with countless trays of interesting toothpick munchies *(cicchetti)* and blackboards listing which wines are uncorked and served by the glass. This is a great way to mingle and have fun with the Venetians.

Cicchetti bars have a social stand-up zone and a cozy gaggle of tables where you can generally sit down with your *cicchetti* or order

Restaurants near the Rialto Bridge

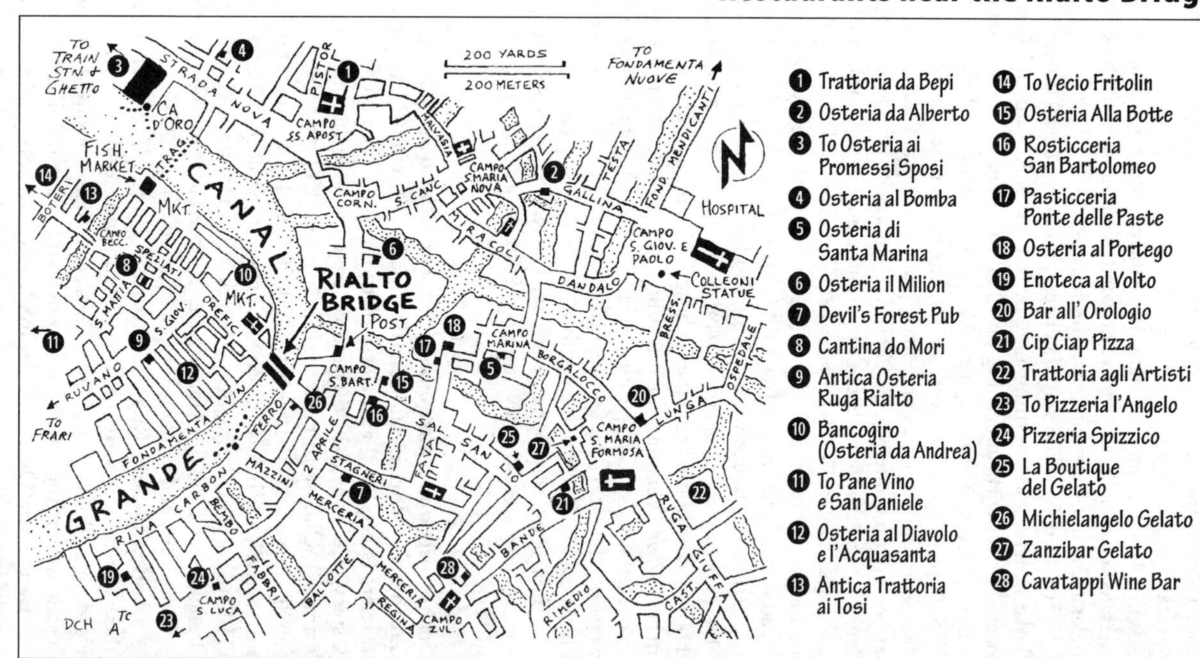

from a simple menu. Food generally costs the same price whether you stand or sit.

I've listed plenty of pubs in walking order for a quick or extended crawl below. If you've crawled enough, most of these bars make a fine one-stop, sit-down dinner.

Try deep-fried mozzarella cheese, gorgonzola, calamari, artichoke hearts, and anything ugly on a toothpick. Crostini (small toasted bread with something on it) are popular, as are marinated seafood, olives, and prosciutto with melon. Meat and fish (*pesce*; PESH-shay) munchies can be expensive; veggies *(verdure)* are cheap, around €3 for a meal-sized plate. In many places, there's a set price per food item (e.g., €1.50). To get a plate of assorted appetizers for €8 (or more, depending on how hungry you are), ask for: "*Un piatto classico di cicchetti misti da* €8" (oon pee-AH-toh KLAH-see-koh dee cheh-KET-tee MEE-stee da OH-toh ay-OO-roh). Bread sticks *(grissini)* are free for the asking.

Drink the house wines. A small glass of house red or white wine *(ombra rosso* or *ombra bianco)* or a small beer *(birrino)* costs about €1. The house keg wine is cheap—€1 per glass, around €4 per liter. *Vin bon,* Venetian for fine wine, may run you from €1.50 to €6 per little glass. *Corposo* means full-bodied. A good last drink is *fragolino,* the local sweet wine—*bianco* or *rosso.* It often comes with a little cookie *(biscotto)* for dipping.

Bars don't stay open very late, and the *cicchetti* selection is best early, so start your evening by 18:00. Most bars are closed on Sunday.

Cicchetterie *and Light Meals West of the Rialto Bridge*

Cantina do Mori is famous with locals (since 1462) and savvy travelers (since 1982) as a classy place for fine wine and *francobolli* (a spicy selection of 20 tiny mayo-soaked sandwiches nicknamed "stamps"). Choose from the featured wines. Confirm the price or they'll rip you off (Mon–Sat 17:00–20:30, closed Sun, stand-up only, arrive early before the *cicchetti* are gone, San Polo 429, tel. 041-522-5401). From Rialto Bridge, walk 200 yards down Ruga degli Orefici, away from St. Mark's Square—then left on Ruga Vecchia S. Giovanni, then right at Sotoportego Do' Mori.

Antica Osteria Ruga Rialto, "the Ruga," is a local fixture where Marco serves great bar snacks and wine to his devoted clientele (daily 11:00–14:30 & 19:00–24:00, easy to find, just past Chinese Restaurant on Ruga Vecchia S. Giovanni #692, tel. 041-521-1243).

Bancogiro (Osteria da Andrea), a simple bar behind the Rialto market, has stark yet powerfully atmospheric outdoor seating overlooking the Grand Canal. Peruse their wine list and basic menu at the bar (strong local cheeses are a forte), order, and grab a table—worth the reasonable cover charge (Tue–Sat 10:30–15:00 & 18:30–24:00, closed Sun eve and Mon, less than 200 yards from Rialto Bridge on Campo San Giacometto, San Polo 122, tel. 041-523-2061).

Pane Vino e San Daniele means bread, wine and the very best ham. While its tables are rustic, the jazz and decor give the bar a trendy feel. They offer free little bruschetti, a rich cheese plate, refreshing and substantial wine *spritz,* fine trios of explosive little ham sandwiches, a helpful menu, and a blackboard of great wine by the glass (Tue–Sun 10:30–16:00 & 18:00–24:00, closed Mon, from Rialto it's a quarter of the way to the train station on Calle dei Boteri 1544—worth the walk, mobile 380-410-8446).

Osteria al Diavolo e l'Acquasanta, three blocks west of the Rialto, serves good—if pricey—pasta and makes a handy lunch stop for sightseers and gondoliers (Mon 12:00–15:00, Wed–Sun 12:00–15:00 & 19:00–23:00, closed Tue, hiding on a quiet street just off Rua Vecchia S. Giovanni, on Calle della Madonna, tel. 041-277-0307). While they list *cicchetti* and wine by the glass on the wall, I'd come here for a light meal rather than tapas.

Antica Trattoria ai Tosi, a small, classy place near the Rialto fish market, offers simple €15, two-course *menus* for *turisticos*—the seafood one is great. Add wine/water and you'll get out for about €20–25 per person. With its pleasant stay-awhile atmosphere, it's good for a quiet, romantic dinner (closed Mon, near Sora al Ponte, Rialto San Polo 1586, tel. 041-524-1086).

Vecio Fritolin is a worthwhile splurge for fresh seafood prepared with care. Mamma Irina brags that they don't even have a freezer. Figure on €30 without wine (Tue–Sun 12:00–14:30 & 19:00–22:30, closed Sun eve and Mon, a few blocks north of the Rialto fish market on Calle della Regina #2262, tel. 041-522-2881, reservations smart).

Cicchetterie *and Light Meals East of the Rialto Bridge, near Campo San Bartolomeo*

Osteria "Alla Botte" Cicchetteria is an atmospheric place packed with a young, local, bohemian-jazz clientele. It's good for a *cicchetti* snack with wine at the bar (see the posted, enticing selection of wines by the glass) or for a light meal in the small back room (Fri–Tue 10:00–15:00 & 17:00–23:00, closed Thu and Sun eve, 2 short blocks off Campo San Bartolomeo in the corner behind the statue—down Calle de la Bissa, notice the "day after" photo showing a debris-covered Venice after the notorious 1989 Pink Floyd open-air concert, tel. 041-520-9775).

If the statue on the Campo San Bartolomeo walked backward 20 yards, turned left, and went under a passageway, he'd hit **Rosticceria San Bartolomeo.** This cheap—if confusing—self-service restaurant has a likeably surly staff (good €6–7 pasta, great fried *mozzarella al prosciutto* for €1.40, delightful fruit salad, €2 glasses of wine, prices listed on wall behind counter, no cover or service charge, daily 9:00–21:30, tel. 041-522-3569). Take out, grab a table, or munch at the bar.

From Rosticceria San Bartolomeo, continue over a bridge to Campo San Lio. Here, turn left, passing Hotel Canada on your right and following Calle Carminati straight about 50 yards over another bridge. On the right is the pastry shop *(pasticceria)* and straight ahead is Osteria Al Portego (at #6015). Both are listed below:

Pasticceria Ponte delle Paste is a feminine and pastel *salon de tè,* popular for its pastries and aperitifs. Italians love taking 15-minute breaks to sip a *spritz* aperitif with friends after a long day's work, before heading home. Ask sprightly Monica for a *spritz al bitter* (white wine, *amaro*, and soda water, €1.55; or choose from the menu on the wall) and munch some of the free goodies at the bar around 18:00 (daily 7:00–20:30, Ponte delle Paste).

Osteria al Portego is a friendly, local-style bar serving great *cicchetti* and good meals (Mon–Fri 9:00–21:00, closed Sat–Sun, tel. 041-522-9038). The *cicchetti* here can make a great meal, but you should also consider sitting down for an actual dinner. They have a fine menu.

Enoteca al Volto offers a vast assortment of Italian wines by the glass and comes with a commitment to good *cicchetti* (the best selection of munchies is 17:00–20:00, fresh seafood and pasta for sit-down meals, Mon–Sat 12:00–14:30 & 17:00–22:00, closed Sun, from Rialto vaporetto stop walk along the canal away from the bridge, take last left before road ends, on Calle Cavalli #4081, tel. 041-522-8945, Andrea).

On or near Campo Santa Maria di Formosa

Campo Santa Maria Formosa is just plain atmospheric (as most squares with a Socialist Party office seem to be). For a balmy outdoor meal, have a pizza with wine on the square. **Bar all' Orologio** has a good setting and friendly service but mediocre "freezer" pizza (they're happy to let you split a pizza, Mon–Sat 6:00–23:00, closed Sun). To have a great pizza picnic on the square, cross the bridge behind the canalside *gelateria* and grab a slice to go from **Cip Ciap Pizza** (Wed–Mon 9:00–21:00, closed Tue; facing *gelateria,* take bridge to the right; Calle del Mondo Novo).

Trattoria agli Artisti is efficient and friendly, with good food, especially the spaghetti *frutti di mare* (dinner from 18:00, closed Wed, half block off square down Ruga Giuffa, tel. 041-277-0029).

At Campo Santa Maria Formosa, pub-crawlers can get a salad course at the fruit-and-vegetable stand next to the water fountain (Mon–Sat, closes about 19:30 and on Sun). The *gelateria* **Zanzibar** on the square seems to wish the tourists would go away...but is very well-situated (open 8:00–24:00, 8:00–20:30 in winter).

Cavatappi wine bar has €8 big gourmet salads, several pasta choices for €7, and entrees with side dishes and wine for €10 (Tue–Sun 9:00–24:00, closed Mon, between Campo Santa Maria di Formosa and St. Mark's Square—near S. Zulian Church in Campo della Guerra #525, tel. 041-296-0252).

Near the Accademia Bridge

For location, see the map on page 1020.

Restaurant/Pizzeria Accademia Foscarini, next to the Accademia Bridge and Galleria, offers decent €7–8 pizzas in a great canalside setting (Wed–Mon 7:00–22:00 in summer, until 21:00 in winter, closed Tue, Dorsoduro 878C, tel. 041-522-7281).

Enoteca Cantine del Vino Gia Schiavi—much loved for its *cicchetti*—is a good place for a glass of wine and appetizers (Mon–Sat 8:00–14:30 & 15:30–20:00, closed Sun, 100 yards from Accademia Gallery on San Trovaso canal; facing Accademia, take a right and then a forced left at canal to the second bridge—S. Trovaso 992, tel. 041-523-0034). You're welcome to enjoy your wine and finger-food while sitting on the bridge.

Ai Gondolieri is considered one of the best restaurants for meat—not fish—in Venice. Its sauces are heavy and prices are high, but carnivores love it (Wed–Mon 12:00–13:00 & 19:00–22:00, closed Tue and for lunch July–Aug, reservations smart, Dorsoduro 366 San Vio, behind Peggy Guggenheim Collection on west end of Rio delle Torreselle, tel. 041-528-6396).

Cantinone Storico, also in this neighborhood, and **Ristorante da Raffaele** (on St. Mark's side of Accademia Bridge) are described below, under "Eating with a Romantic Canalside Setting."

Vino Vino is a small, simple place that seats about 25 (pasta-€5, *secondi*-€9–12, Wed–Mon 10:30–24:00, closed Tue, between Accademia Bridge and St. Mark's Square, just south of La Fenice on Ponte delle Veste, #2007/A, tel. 041-241-7688). From S. Moise, head east on Calle Larga XXIII Marzo, then north on Calle del Sartor da Veste—it's on your left after the bridge.

Near Campo San Barnaba

A number of less-touristed restaurants cluster around this small square. From the Accademia, head northwest, following the curve of the Grand Canal. In five minutes, you'll spill out onto Campo San Barnaba (and the nearby Campo Santa Margherita). Follow the straight and narrow path (Calle Lunga di San Barnaba) west of the square for more restaurants.

Casin dei Nobili has a diverse, reasonably-priced menu in an informal setting (closed Mon, a half-block south of Campo San Barnaba, tel. 041-241-1841). The name means "pleasure-palace (Casino) of the nobles."

Restaurants near the Accademia Bridge

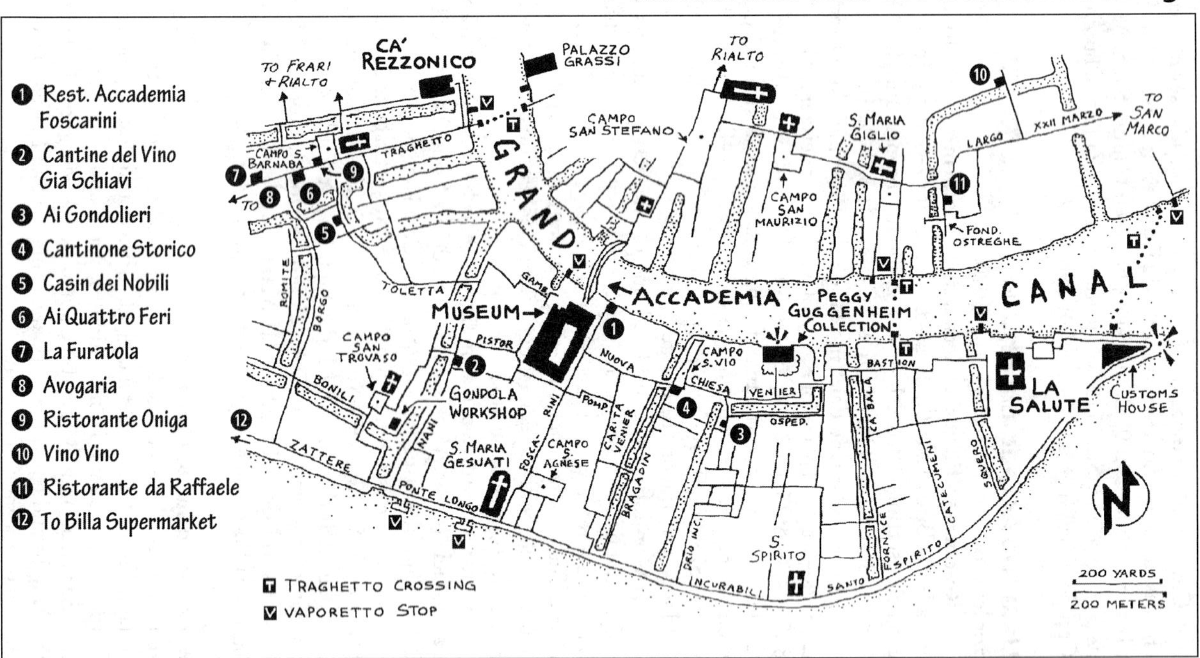

Ai Quattro Feri is a trattoria-style noisy, bustling place for catch-of-the-day seafood, with excellent grilled fish, but very few non-seafood items (closed Sun, just off the square on Calle Lunga di San Barnaba #2757, tel. 041-520-6978).

La Furatola is more upscale, with an extensive seafood menu (closed Thu, farther west on Calle Lunga di San Barnaba at #2869/A, tel. 041-520-8594).

Avogaria is a hip, modern, goateed-waiter wine bar and restaurant. You can have a full meal, or just sit at the tiny bar and drink a glass of Soave Classico while you build a meal of appetizers and delicious desserts. The small outside terrace was made for warm evenings (closed Tue, several hundred yards west of Campo San Barnaba on Calle Lunga San Barnaba, near San Sebastian church, tel. 041-296-0491).

Ristorante Oniga, right on Campo San Barnaba, is a wine bar/restaurant serving up Italian cuisine with a modern twist (closed Tue, tel. 041-522-4410).

Eating with a Romantic Canalside Setting

Of course, if you want a canal view, it comes with lower quality or a higher price. But the memory is sometimes most important.

Ristorante da Raffaele is *the* place for classy food on a quiet canal. It's filled with top-end tourists sent by the fancy hotels. The place was a haunt of the avant-garde a few generations ago. Today it's on a main gondolier thoroughfare—in fact, many guests arrive or depart by gondola. Make a reservation if you want a canalside table (you do). While the multilingual menu is designed for the tourists, locals stick with the daily specials (expensive—plan on €60, Fri–Wed 12:00–15:00 & 19:00–22:30, closed Thu, exactly halfway between Piazza San Marco and the Accademia Bridge at Ponte delle Ostreghe, tel. 041-523-2317). Before leaving, wander around inside to see the owner's intriguing old weapons collection.

Ristorante Cantinone Storico sits on a peaceful canal in Dorsoduro between the Accademia Bridge and the Peggy Guggenheim Collection. It's dressy, specializes in fish, has six or eight tables on the canal, and is worth the splurge (Mon–Sat 12:30–14:30 & 19:30–21:30, closed Sun, reservations wise, on the canal Rio de S. Vio, tel. 041-523-9577).

Rialto Bridge Tourist Traps: Locals are embarrassed by the lousy food and aggressive "service" of the string of joints dominating the best romantic Grand Canal real estate in town. Still, if you want to linger over dinner with a view of the most famous bridge and the romantic song of gondoliers oaring by (and don't mind eating with other tourists), this can be enjoyable. Don't trust the waiter's recommendations for special meals. Just get a simple pizza or pasta and a drink, and you'll savor the ambience without being ripped off.

Near St. Mark's Square

For the location of these restaurants, see the map on page 986.

Osteria da Carla, two blocks west of St. Mark's Square, is a fun and very local hole-in-the-wall where the food is good and the price is right (€8–12 dishes). They have hearty tuna salads and a daily pasta special along with traditional antipasti, polenta, and decent wine by the glass (see blackboard). Seafood-lovers might try their "triple fish and polenta" plate (sardine, squid, and cod, €10). While you can eat outside, table #3 comes with a flushing soundtrack (Mon–Sat 8:00–22:00, closed Sun; from American Express head toward St. Mark's Square, first left down Frezzeria, first left again through "Contarina" tunnel, at Sotoportego e Corte Contarina, sign over door says "Pietro Panizzolo"—it's historic and can't be removed, tel. 041-523-7855, Michela SE).

Osteria Enoteca San Marco offers beautifully-presented "creative new Italian" cuisine with a mod ambience in a classic medieval shell. They proudly offer fine wine by the glass (€20 meals, Mon–Sat 12:30–3:00 & 19:30–22:30, closed Sun, a long block west of St. Mark's Square at #1610 Frezzeria, tel. 041-528-5242, Carlo and his hard-working staff SE).

Antica Sacrestia, a local institution, has à la carte choices and several different fixed-price menus: vegetarian, Venetian, tourist, seafood, and house specialties (€14.50–62, Tue–Sun 12:00–15:00 & 18:30–22:30, closed Mon, on Calle della Sacrestia #4442, two blocks behind St. Mark's, tel. 041-523-0749, www.anticasacrestia.com).

At **Trattoria da Giorgio ai Greci,** also a few blocks behind St. Mark's, Giorgio and his sons serve homemade pastas and fresh seafood. Eat outside, on the canal, or indoors (daily 12:00–24:00, closed Mon in winter, two canals east of St. Mark's on Ponte dei Greci, #4988, tel. 041-528-9780).

The **cafés on St. Mark's Square** offer music and an unbeatable setting for an atmospheric drink or light meal (see "Nightlife," page 999).

Near the Train Station

For fast, cheap food near the station, consider **Brek,** a popular self-service cafeteria (after serving breakfast, it's open 11:30–22:00; with back to station, facing canal, go left on Rio Terra—it becomes Lista di Spagna in 2 short blocks, Lista di Spagna 124, tel. 041-244-0158).

Elsewhere in Venice

Ristorante Acqua Pazza (literally, "crazy water") provides good pizza in a wonderful setting on Campo San Angelo (check out the leaning tower over your shoulder) midway between the Rialto, Accademia, and St. Mark's. The owner is from Naples and he delights locals with Amalfi/Naples cuisine. That means perhaps the best—and most expensive—pizza in Venice (Tue–Sun 12:00–15:00 & 19:00–23:00, closed Mon, Campo S. Angelo 3809, tel. 041-277-0688).

Osteria al Bacco, far beyond the crowds in a rustic Venetian setting, is worth the hike for its local cuisine (€35 for 3 courses and wine, Tue–Sun 12:00–14:00 & 19:00–22:00, closed Mon, reservations recommended, halfway between train station and northernmost tip of Venice, Fondamenta Cappuccine, Cannaregio 3054, tel. 041-717-493).

Osteria la Zucca is a hardworking, homey place on the Rio del Megio canal away from the crowds. You'll get good, typical Venetian cuisine at a moderate price (€20 meals, Mon–Sat 12:30–14:30 for lunch, dinner guests usually have 2 seating choices—19:00 or 21:00, closed Sun, mostly indoors, reserve for canal windows, a few outdoor tables with one on the canal, midway between train station and Rialto Bridge at San Giacomo dell'Orio, Calle Larga, Santa Croce 1762, tel. 041-524-1570). A short block away is the square called San Giacomo dell'Orio—a breezy scene with trees, families at play, and a couple of simple trattorias offering basic food and classic non-touristy outdoor seating.

Cheap Meals

A key to cheap eating in Venice is **bar snacks,** especially stand-up mini-meals in out-of-the-way bars. Order by pointing. *Panini* (sandwiches) are sold fast and cheap at bars everywhere. Basic reliable ham-and-cheese sandwiches (white bread, crusts trimmed) come toasted—simply ask for "toast"; these make a great supplement to Venice's skimpy hotel breakfasts.

For budget eating, I like small ***cicchetti*** **bars** (see "The Stand-Up Progressive Venetian Pub-Crawl Dinner," page 1014); for speed, value, and ambience, you can get a filling plate of local appetizers at nearly any of the bars.

Pizzerias are cheap and easy—try for a sidewalk table at a scenic location. (See the map on page 1015 for the following locales.)

Pizzeria l'Angelo serves up piping-hot pizza by the slice for under €2 or whole pizzas to go. Grab a beer or a soda and find a bench in nearby Campos Manin or Sant'Angelo (Tue–Sun 11:30–22:00, Mon 11:30–16:30, Calle della Mandola #3711, tel. 041-277-1126). **Spizzico** is a cheap fast-food pizza shop on Campo San Luca (between St. Mark's Square and the Rialto Bridge).

The **produce market** that sprawls for a few blocks just past the Rialto Bridge is a great place to assemble a picnic (best 8:00–13:00, closed Sun). The adjacent fish market is wonderfully slimy. Side lanes in this area are speckled with fine little hole-in-the-wall munchie bars, bakeries, and cheese shops.

Gelato

For locations, see the map on page 1015.

La Boutique del Gelato is considered the best *gelateria* in Venice (daily 10:00–20:30, closed Dec–Jan, 2 blocks off Campo Santa Maria di Formosa on corner of Salizada San Lio and Calle Paradiso, next to Hotel Bruno, #5727—just look for the crowd).

Late-night Gelato: At the Rialto, try **Michielangelo,** just off Campo San Bartolomeo, on the St. Mark's side of the Rialto Bridge on Salizada Pio X (daily 10:00–23:00). At St. Mark's Square, the **Al Todaro** *gelateria* opposite the Doge's Palace is open late (daily 8:00–22:00, closes at 20:00 and on Mon in winter).

TRANSPORTATION CONNECTIONS

From Venice by Train to: Padua (3–5/hr, 30 min), **Vicenza** (2/hr, 1 hr), **Verona** (1/hr, 90 min), **Ravenna** (1/hr, 3–4 hrs, transfer in Ferrara or Bologna), **Florence** (9/day, 3 hrs), **Dolomites** (8/day to Bolzano, about hrly, 4 hrs with 1 transfer; catch bus from Bolzano into mountains), **Milan** (1/hr, 3–4 hrs), **Monterosso/La Spezia/ Cinque Terre** (2/day, 6 hrs, departs Venice at 10:00 and 15:00), **Rome** (8/day, 5 hrs, slower overnight), **Naples** (3/day, more with change in Rome, about 8–9 hrs), **Brindisi** (3/day, 11 hrs, change in Bologna), **Bern** (3/day, change in Milan, 8 hrs), **Munich** (2/day, 8 hrs), **Paris** (4/day, 11 hrs), and **Vienna** (3/day, 9 hrs). Train and *cuccetta* reservations (about €18) are easily made at a downtown travel agency, such as Kele & Teo Viaggie Turismo or American Express (see "Travel Agencies" page 972).

FLORENCE

(Firenze)

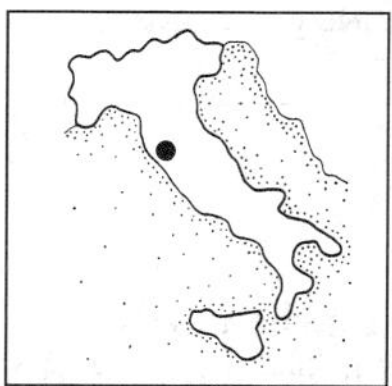

Florence, the home of the Renaissance and birthplace of our modern world, is a "supermarket sweep," and the groceries are the best Renaissance art in Europe.

Get your bearings with a Renaissance walk. Florentine art goes beyond paintings and statues—there's food, fashion, and handicrafts. You can lick Italy's best gelato while enjoying some of Europe's best people-watching.

Planning Your Time

If you're in Italy for three weeks, Florence deserves a well-organized day. Make reservations in advance for the Uffizi Gallery (best Italian paintings anywhere) and Accademia (Michelangelo's *David*). For a day in Florence, see the Accademia, tour the Uffizi Gallery, visit the underrated Bargello (best statues), and do the Renaissance ramble (explained below).

Art-lovers will want to chisel out another day of their itinerary for the many other Florentine cultural treasures. Shoppers and ice cream-lovers may need to do the same.

Plan your sightseeing carefully. Some sights close Mondays and afternoons. While many spend several hours a day in lines, thoughtful travelers avoid this by making reservations or going late in the day. Places open at night are virtually empty.

Connoisseurs of smaller towns should consider taking the bus to Siena for a day or evening trip (75-min one-way, confirm when last bus returns). Siena is magic after dark. For more information, see the Siena chapter.

Florence Overview

ORIENTATION

The Florence that we're interested in lies mostly on the north bank of the Arno River. The main historical sights cluster around the red-brick dome of the cathedral (Duomo). Everything is within a 20-minute walk of the train station, cathedral, or Ponte Vecchio (Old Bridge). The less impressive but more characteristic Oltrarno (south bank) area is just over the bridge. Though small, Florence is intense. Prepare for scorching summer heat, kamikaze motorscooters, slick pickpockets, few WCs, and erratic museum hours.

Tourist Information

There are three TIs in Florence: across from the train station, near Santa Croce Church, and on Via Cavour.

The TI across the square from the train station is most crowded—expect long lines (Mon–Sat 8:30–19:00, Sun 8:30–13:30; with your back to tracks, exit the station—it's across the square in wall near corner of church, Piazza Stazione; tel. 055-212-245). In the train station, avoid the Hotel Reservations "Tourist Information" window (marked *Informazioni Turistiche Alberghiere*) near the McDonald's; it's not a real TI but a hotel reservation business.

The TI near Santa Croce Church is pleasant, helpful, and uncrowded (Mon–Sat 9:00–19:00, Sun 9:00–14:00, shorter hours off-season, Borgo Santa Croce 29 red, tel. 055-234-0444).

Another winner is the TI three blocks north of the Duomo (Mon–Sat 8:30–18:30, Sun 8:30–13:30, closed Sun in winter, Via

Cavour 1 red, tel. 055-290-832 or 055-276-0383, international bookstore across street).

At any TI, pick up a map, a current museum-hours listing (extremely important, since no guidebook—including this one—has ever been able to accurately predict the hours of Florence's sights), and any information on entertainment. The free monthly *Florence Concierge Information* magazine lists museums, plus lots that I don't: concerts and events, markets, sporting events, church services, shopping ideas, bus and train connections, and an entire similar section on Siena. Get yours at the TI or from any expensive hotel (pick one up, as if you're staying there).

Arrival in Florence

By Train: The station soaks up time and generates dazed and sweaty crowds. If you arrive by train, there's no need to linger at the station. Extremely user-friendly, coin-operated gray-and-yellow machines can display schedules, issue tickets, and even make reservations for railpass holders. Otherwise, get tickets and train information for your new destination from travel agencies away from the congested station (e.g., American Express, see page 1030). The fake "Tourist Information" office in the station (next to McDonald's) is actually a room-booking service funded by the hotels. The real TI is across the square from the station (see "American Express," page 1030).

With your back to the tracks, look left to see many of my recommended hotels, a 24-hour pharmacy (*Farmacia Comunale,* near McDonald's), city buses, and the entrance to the underground mall/passage that goes across the square to the Church of Santa Maria Novella. (Note: Pickpockets frequent this tunnel, especially the surface point near the church.) Baggage check is near track 16.

By Car: If you're taking the autostrada (north or south) to Florence, get off at the Certosa exit and follow signs to *Centro;* at Porta Romana, go to the left of the arch and down Via Francesco Petrarca. You'll soon understand why Leonardo never invented the car. Cars flatten the charm of Florence.

Don't drive into the historic core of the city. A new system photographs every car entering the center. You must register your car with your hotel, whether you just drove in to drop off luggage or if you have parking reserved at your hotel. If you don't, a hefty fine will appear on your rental-car statement. If you go into the city beyond the ring road, even accidentally, you need to report your license-plate number to avoid the fine.

Non-residents are not allowed to park on the streets anywhere near or in the old center. Many hotels listed in this book have a few parking spots they can rent to guests in the center—most charge €15–20 per day. In addition, the city has plenty of **parking lots.**

Greater Florence

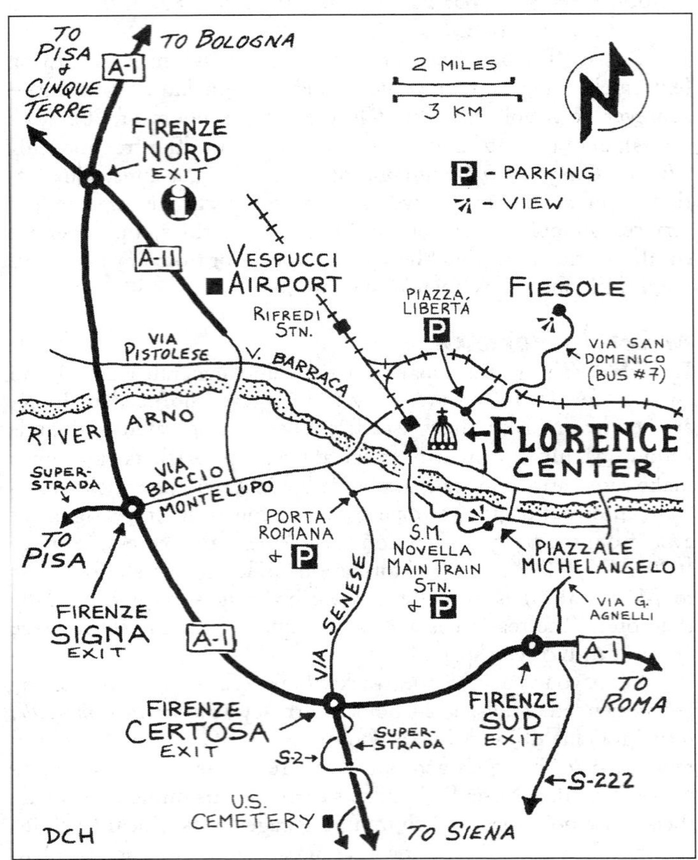

For a short stay, park underground at the train station (€2/hr). The best options for a longer stay are parking at Piazza della Libertà (€15/24 hrs, perhaps cheaper with hotel reservation, 4 blocks east of Fortezza di Basso on the inner ring road) and Porta Romana (exit A1 at Firenze-Certosa, follow signs to Porta Romana, €15 per day). For parking information, ask your hotelier, call 800-055-055 in Italy, or consult the useful Web site, www.firenzeparcheggi.it.

By Plane: Florence has its own airport and Pisa's is nearby. See "Transportation Connections," on page 1084, for details.

Helpful Hints

Theft Alert: Florence has particularly hardworking thief gangs. They specialize in tourists and hang out where you do: near the train station, the station's underpass (especially where the

Make Reservations to Avoid Lines

Florence has a reservation system for its top five sights—Uffizi, Accademia, Bargello, Medici Chapels, and the Pitti Palace. Two of these sights always have long lines: the Accademia (Michelangelo's *David*) and the Uffizi (Renaissance paintings). To avoid long waits—up to two hours at the Uffizi—reserve by phone. Frankly, it's stupid not to.

Make your reservation as soon as you know when you'll be in Florence (ideally at least a month in advance). You dial 055-294-883 (Mon–Fri 8:30–18:30, Sat 8:30–12:30, closed Sun), an English-speaking operator walks you through the process, and two minutes later you say *grazie,* with appointments (15-min entry window) and six-digit confirmation numbers for each of the top museums and galleries. The ticket phone number is often busy; be persistent. If you call months in advance during the off-season or request your hotel to make the appointment for you (when you confirm your hotel booking), you may save some frustration. Some booking agencies offer reservations online for a fee (such as www.weekendafirenze.it).

If you haven't booked ahead, you can make reservations for the top sights at the minor, less-crowded sights (such as the Museum of San Marco or Museum of Precious Stones). Clerks at the ticket booths at these sleepy sights can reserve and sell tickets to the major sights, often for admission the same day, allowing you to skip right past the dreary mob scene.

Lines occasionally form at the Uffizi even for those with reservations who are waiting to pick up tickets. If you have reservations, consider picking up your Uffizi ticket at a less-crowded sight (any ticket office can issue reserved tickets).

tunnel surfaces), and major sights. Also be on guard at two squares frequented by drug pushers (Santa Maria Novella and Santo Spirito). American tourists—especially older ones—are considered easy targets.

Medical Help: To track down a doctor who speaks English, call 055-475-411 (reasonable hotel calls, cheaper if you go to the clinic at Via L. Magnifico 59, near Piazza Libertà) or get a list of English-speaking doctors from the TI. There are 24-hour pharmacies at the train station and near the Duomo on Borgo San Lorenzo.

Addresses: Street addresses list businesses in red and residences in black or blue (color-coded on the actual street number and indicated by a letter following the number in printed addresses: r = red, no indication = black). *Pensioni* are usually black but can be either. The red and black numbers each appear in roughly consecutive order on streets but bear no apparent connection

Daily Reminder

Sunday: Today the Duomo's dome, Science Museum, and Museum of Precious Stones are closed. These sights close early: Duomo Museum (at 13:40) and the Baptistery's interior (at 14:00). A few sights are open only in the afternoon: Duomo (13:30–16:45), Santa Croce Church (13:00–17:30), and Brancacci Chapel and the Church of Santa Maria Novella (both 13:00–17:00).

The Museum of San Marco, which is open on the second and fourth Sunday of the month until 19:00, closes entirely—as does the Bargello—on the first, third, and fifth Sunday. The Medici Chapels and the Modern Art Gallery (in the Pitti Palace) close on the second and fourth Sunday. (Need a calendar? Look in the appendix.)

It's not possible to reserve tickets today by phone for the major sights (Accademia, Uffizi Gallery) because the booking office is closed; see page 1029 for alternatives.

Monday: The biggies are closed—Accademia *(David)* and Uffizi Gallery—as well as the Palatine Gallery/Royal Apartments in the Pitti Palace.

The Medici Chapels and the Modern Art Gallery (in the Pitti Palace) close on the first, third, and fifth Monday of the month. The Museum of San Marco and the Bargello close on the second and fourth Monday. Boboli Gardens

with each other. I'm lazy and don't concern myself with the distinction (if one number's wrong, I look for the other) and can easily find my way around.

American Express: American Express offers all the normal services, but is most helpful as an easy place to get your train tickets, reservations, supplements (all the same price as at the station), or even just information on train schedules (Mon–Fri 9:00–17:30, Sat money exchange only 9:00–12:30, 3 short blocks north of Palazzo Vecchio on Via Dante Alighieri 22 red, tel. 055-50981).

Long-Distance Telephoning: Small newsstand kiosks sell phone cards (denominations of €5, €10, etc.) that give you cheap international rates (see "Telephones," page 1343).

Books: Feltrinelli International, a fine bookstore that sells fiction and guidebooks in English, is a few blocks north of the Duomo and across the street from the TI on Via Cavour (Mon–Sat 9:00–19:30, closed Sun, Via Cavour 20 red, tel. 055-219-524). Edison Bookstore sells CDs and novels on the Renaissance (daily 9:00–24:00, facing Piazza della Repubblica, tel. 055-213-110). Paperback Exchange also sells fiction and close on the first and last Monday. The Palazzo Vecchio may stay open until 23:00 in summer.

Target these sights on Mondays: Duomo Museum, Giotto's Tower, Brancacci Chapel, Michelangelo's House, Science Museum, Palazzo Vecchio, and churches. Or take a walking tour.

Tuesday: All sights are open except for Michelangelo's House and the Brancacci Chapel. The Science Museum closes early (13:00).

Wednesday: All sights are open except for Medici-Riccardi Palace and Santo Spirito Church (closed in afternoon).

Thursday: All sights are open. The Museum of Precious Stones stays open late (19:00) while these sights close early: Duomo (15:30) and Palazzo Vecchio (14:00).

Friday: All sights are open. The Church of Santa Maria Novella opens late (13:00–17:00) and Palazzo Vecchio closes late (may be open until 23:00 in summer).

Saturday: All sights are open, but the Science Museum closes at 13:00. These sights close early on the first Saturday of the month: Duomo (15:30) and the Duomo's dome (16:00). The Museum of San Marco stays open until 19:00. The Accademia, Uffizi, and Palatine Gallery/Royal Apartments may stay open until 22:00 in summer.

guidebooks (cheaper but smaller selection, Mon–Fri 9:00–19:30, Sat 10:00–13:00 & 15:30–19:30, closed Sun, shorter hours in Aug, Via Fiesolana 31 red, at corner of Via Fiesolana and Via dei Pilastri, 6 blocks east of Duomo, tel. 055-247-8154).

Laundry: The Wash & Dry Lavarapido chain offers long hours and efficient, self-service launderettes at several locations (about €6.20 for wash and dry, daily 8:00–22:00, tel. 055-580-480). These are close to recommended hotels: Via dei Servi 105 (and a rival launderette at Via Guelfa 22 red, off Via Cavour; both near *David*); Via del Sole 29 red and Via della Scala 52 red (between train station and river); and Via dei Serragli 87 red (across the river in Oltrarno neighborhood).

Getting Around Florence

I organize my sightseeing geographically and do it all on foot.

If you take **buses,** a €1 ticket gets you one hour (€1.80/3 hrs, €4/24 hrs, tickets not sold on bus before 21:00—buy in *tabacchi* shops or newsstands, validate on bus, after 21:00 buy tickets on bus, route map available at TI). Multi-day passes are also available.

Florence at a Glance

▲▲▲**Uffizi Gallery** Greatest collection of Italian paintings anywhere—reserve ahead. **Hours:** Tue–Sun 8:15–18:50, 8:15–22:00 on holidays and maybe on summer Sat, closed Mon.

▲▲▲**Accademia** Michelangelo's *David* and powerful (unfinished) *Prisoners*—reserve ahead. **Hours:** Tue–Sun 8:15–18:50, 8:15–22:00 on holidays and maybe on summer Sat, closed Mon.

▲▲▲**Bargello** Underappreciated sculpture museum with Michelangelo, Donatello, and Medici treasures. **Hours:** Daily 8:15–13:50; closed first, third, and fifth Sun and second and fourth Mon of each month.

▲▲**Museum of San Marco** Best collection anywhere of frescoes and paintings by the early Renaissance master Fra Angelico. **Hours:** Mon–Fri 8:15–13:50, Sat–Sun 8:15–19:00; closed first, third, and fifth Sun and second and fourth Mon of each month.

▲▲**Medici Chapels** Tombs of Florence's great ruling family, designed and carved by Michelangelo. **Hours:** Daily 8:15–16:50; closed the second and fourth Sun and the first, third, and fifth Mon of each month.

▲▲**Church of Santa Maria Novella** 13th-century Dominican church with Masaccio's famous 3-D painting. **Hours:** Mon–Thu and Sat 9:30–17:00, Fri and Sun 13:00–17:00.

▲▲**Santa Croce Church** 14th-century Franciscan church with precious art, tombs of famous Florentines, and Brunelleschi's Pazzi Chapel. **Hours:** Mon–Sat 9:30–17:30, Sun 13:00–17:30; winter Mon–Sat 9:30–12:30 & 15:00–17:30, Sun 13:00–17:30.

▲▲**Science Museum** Fascinating collection of old clocks, telescopes, maps, and Galileo's finger. **Hours:** Mon and Wed–Fri 9:30–17:00, Tue and Sat 9:30–13:00, closed Sun.

▲▲**Pitti Palace** Three museums in lavish palace: Palatine Gallery (Raphael art), Modern Art Gallery, Grand Ducal Treasures (Medici treasure chest), plus sprawling Boboli Gardens. **Hours:** Palatine: Tue–Sun 8:15–18:50, closed Mon; Modern Art: daily 8:15–13:50; closed second and fourth Sun and first, third, and fifth Mon; Treasures and Boboli: daily 9:00–19:30 June–Aug, 9:00–18:30 fall and spring, 9:00–16:30 in winter, closed first and last Mon of month.

▲▲**Brancacci Chapel** Works of Masaccio, early Renaissance master who reinvented perspective. **Hours:** Mon and Wed–Sat 10:00–17:00, Sun 13:00–17:00, closed Tue.

▲▲**Duomo (Santa Maria del Fiore)** Gothic Cathedral with colorful facade, long nave, and the first dome built since ancient Roman times. **Hours:** Mon–Wed and Fri–Sat 10:00–17:00 except first Sat of month 10:00–15:30, Thu 10:00–15:30, Sun 13:30–16:45.

▲▲**Duomo Museum** Underrated cathedral museum with great sculpture. **Hours:** Mon–Sat 9:00–19:30, Sun 9:00–13:40.

▲**Climbing Duomo's Dome** Grand view into the cathedral, close-up of dome architecture, and, after 463 steps, a glorious Florence vista. **Hours:** Mon–Fri 8:30–19:00, Sat 8:30–17:40 except first Sat of month 8:30–16:00, closed Sun.

▲**Giotto's Tower** Bell tower with views equaling Duomo's, 50 fewer steps, and fewer lines. **Hours:** Daily 8:30–19:30.

▲**Baptistery** Bronze doors fit to be the gates of Paradise. **Hours:** Doors always viewable; Baptistery open Mon–Sat 12:00–19:00, Sun 8:30–14:00.

▲**Medici-Riccardi Palace** Lorenzo the Magnificent's home, with fine art, frescoed ceilings, and a lovely Chapel of the Magi. **Hours:** Tue–Thu 9:00–19:00, closed Wed.

▲**Palazzo Vecchio** Fortified palace once the home of the Medici family, wallpapered with mediocre art. **Hours:** Fri–Wed 9:00–19:00, Thu 9:00–14:00, in summer maybe 9:00–23:00 on Mon and Fri.

▲**Ponte Vecchio** Famous bridge lined with gold and silver shops. **Hours:** Bridge always open.

▲**Mercato Nuovo** Bustling market in loggia. **Hours:** Open daily.

▲**Michelangelo's House** Museum featuring early, lesser-known works of the master. **Hours:** Wed–Mon 9:30–14:00, closed Tue.

▲**Piazzale Michelangelo** Hilltop square in south Florence offering stunning view of city and Duomo. **Hours:** Always open.

The minimum cost for a **taxi** ride is €4 during the day or €5 after 22:00 (rides in the center of town should be charged as tariff #1). A taxi ride from the train station to Ponte Vecchio costs about €8. Taxi fares and supplements (e.g., €2 extra if you telephone a cab) are clearly explained on signs in each taxi.

TOURS

Walking Tours of Florence—This company offers a variety of tours (up to 12/day Mon–Sat year-round plus summer Sundays) featuring downtown Florence, Uffizi highlights, or Tuscany (countryside, Siena, San Gimignano, Pisa, or the Cinque Terre), presented by informative, entertaining, native English-speaking guides. The "Original Florence" walk hits the main sights but gets off-beat to weave a picture of Florentine life in medieval and Renaissance times. You can expect lots of talking, which is great if you like history. Tours, offered throughout the year regardless of the weather, start at their office and are limited to 22 people but will go with as few as two participants. Extra guides are available if more people show up (€25 for 3-hr Original Florence walk, daily at 9:30, office open Mon–Sat 8:30–18:00, Sun 8:30–13:30 but off-season closed on Sun and for lunch, tours depart from office, Via dei Sassetti 1, on Piazza Davanzati, above Odeon Cinema on 2nd floor, a couple blocks southwest of Piazza della Repubblica: booking necessary for all tours, private tours available, tel. 055-264-5033, mobile 329-613-2730, www.artviva.com, staff@artviva.com). For all the schedule details, pick up their extensive brochure in your hotel lobby.

Florentia—Top-notch, private walking tours—geared for thoughtful, well-heeled travelers with good attention spans—are led by local scholars. The tours range from introductory city walks and museum visits to in-depth thematic walks such as the Golden Age of Florence, Medici Dynasty, and more. Excursions to Siena, Lucca, and Tuscan countryside are available (tours start at €175 for a half-day tour, reserve in advance, tel. 338-890-8625, U.S. tel. 510-549-1707, www.florentia.org, info@florentia.org).

Local Guide—**Paola Migliorini** offers museum tours, city walking tours, and Tuscan excursions by van. You (and your group) can tailor tours as you like. The van allows slow walkers to enjoy the city nearly sweat-free (€50/hr, or €65/hr with 8-seat van, Via S. Gallo 120, tel. 055-472-448, mobile 347-657-2611, www.florencetour.com, info@florencetour.com).

A Renaissance Walk through Florence

Even during the Dark Ages, people knew they were in a "middle time." It was especially obvious to the people of Italy—sitting on the rubble of Rome—that there was a brighter age before them. The long-awaited rebirth, or Renaissance, began in Florence for good reason. Wealthy because of its cloth industry, trade, and banking; powered by a fierce city-state pride (locals would pee into the Arno with gusto, knowing rival city-state Pisa was downstream); and fertile with more than its share of artistic genius (imagine guys like Michelangelo and Leonardo attending the same high school)—Florence was a natural home for this cultural explosion.

Take a walk through the core of Renaissance Florence by starting at the Accademia (home of Michelangelo's *David*) and cutting through the heart of the city to Ponte Vecchio on the Arno River.

At the Accademia, you'll look into the eyes of Renaissance man—humanism at its confident peak. Then walk to the cathedral (Duomo) to see the dome that kicked off the architectural Renaissance. Step inside the Baptistery to view a ceiling covered with preachy, flat, 2-D, medieval mosaic art. Then, to learn what happened when art met math, check out the realistic 3-D reliefs on the doors. The painter, Giotto, also designed the bell tower—an early example of a Renaissance genius excelling in many areas. Continue toward the river on Florence's great pedestrian mall, Via de' Calzaiuoli (or "Via Calz")—part of the original grid plan given to the city by the ancient Romans. Down a few blocks, compare medieval and Renaissance statues on the exterior of the Orsanmichele Church. Via Calz connects the cathedral with the central square (Piazza della Signoria), the city palace (Palazzo Vecchio), and the Uffizi Gallery, which contains the greatest collection of Italian Renaissance paintings in captivity. Finally, walk through the Uffizi courtyard—a statuary think tank of Renaissance greats—to the Arno River and Ponte Vecchio.

Sights on a Renaissance Walk through Florence

▲▲▲Accademia (Galleria dell' Accademia)—This museum houses Michelangelo's *David* and powerful (unfinished) *Prisoners*. Eavesdrop as tour guides explain these masterpieces. More than with any other work of art, when you look into the eyes of *David*, you're looking into the eyes of Renaissance man. This was a radical break with the past. Hello, humanism. Man was now a confident individual, no longer a plaything of the supernatural. And life was now more than just a preparation for what happened after you died.

The Renaissance was the merging of art, science, and humanism. In a humanist vein, *David* is looking at the crude giant of medieval darkness and thinking, "I can take this guy." (David was an apt mascot for a town surrounded by big bully city-states.) Back on a religious track, notice *David*'s large and overdeveloped right hand. This is symbolic of the hand of God that powered David to slay the giant...and enabled Florence to rise above its crude neighboring city-states.

Florence

400 METERS
400 YARDS
TO FORTEZZA DA BASSO
TRAIN STN.
PIAZZA ADUA
BUS STN.
FAENZA
GUELFA
FIUME
NAZ.
MERCATO CENTRALE
SAN LORENZO CHURCH & STREET MKT.
MUSEUM OF SAN MARCO
TO PIAZZA LIBERTÁ
ACCADEMIA (DAVID)
PIAZZA S.S. ANNUNZIATA
PRECIOUS STONES MUSEUM
MEDICI CHAPELS
CAVOUR
VIA RICASOLI
MEDICI RICCARDI PALACE
S. MARIA NOVELLA
VIA PANZANI
LAUR. LIB.
PERFUMERY
D. SCALA
CERRETANI
SERVI
DUOMO
DUOMO MUSEUM
BAPT.
AGLI
SOLE
FOSSI
PIAZZA REPUB BLICA
CALZAIUOLI
CORSO
ORI.
STUDIO
DANTE'S HOUSE
BARGELLO
PROCONSOLO
MICHELANGELO'S HOUSE
GHIB.
VIGNA NUOVA
TORNABUONI
S. TRINITA
ORSAN-MICHELE
PORTA ROSSA
MERC. NUOVO
CARRAIA
RIVER
B. D. GRECI
P. S. CROCE
TO BRANCACCI CHAPEL
OLTRARNO
TRIN.
PALAZZO VECCHIO
SCIENCE MUSEUM
B. S. JACOPO
S. SPIRITO
GUICCI.
TINTORI
SANTA CROCE
PONTE VECCHIO
MAGGIO
MAZETTA
GRAZIE
ARNO
UFFIZI
PITTI PALACE
VIA SAN NICCOLO
BOBOLI GARDENS
DCH
FORTE BELVEDERE
PIAZZALE MICHELANGELO
PIAZZA SIGNORIA
VIEW
G = GELATERIA

Beyond the magic marble are two floors of interesting pre-Renaissance and Renaissance paintings, including a couple of lighter-than-air Botticellis.

Cost, Hours, Location: €6.50 (plus €3 reservation fee), Tue–Sun 8:15–18:50, until 22:00 on holidays and maybe on summer Sat, closed Mon (last entry 45 min before closing, Via Ricasoli 60, tel. 055-238-8609). No photos or videos are allowed. The museum is most crowded on Sun, Tue, and the first thing in the morning. It's easy to reserve ahead; see page 1029 for details.

Nearby: Piazza Santissima Annunziata, behind the Accademia, displays lovely Renaissance harmony. Facing the square are two fine buildings: the 15th-century Santissima Annunziata church (worth a peek) and Brunelleschi's Hospital of the Innocents (*Spedale degli Innocenti,* not worth going inside), with terra-cotta medallions by Luca della Robbia. Built in the 1420s, the hospital is considered the first Renaissance building.

▲▲Duomo—Florence's Gothic Santa Maria del Fiori cathedral has the third-longest nave in Christendom (free, Mon–Wed and Fri–Sat 10:00–17:00 except first Sat of month 10:00–15:30, Thu 10:00–15:30, Sun 13:30–16:45, modest dress code enforced, tel. 055-230-2885). Note: The massive crowds that overwhelm the entrance in the morning clear out by afternoon.

The church's noisy neo-Gothic facade from the 1870s is covered with pink, green, and white Tuscan marble. Since nearly all of its great art is stored in the Museo dell' Opera del Duomo (behind the church), the best thing about the interior is the shade. The inside of the dome is decorated by one of the largest paintings of the Renaissance, a huge (and newly restored) *Last Judgment* by Vasari and Zucarri.

Think of the confidence of the age: The Duomo was built with a hole awaiting a dome in its roof. This was before the technology to span it with a dome was available. No matter. They knew that someone soon could handle the challenge...and the local architect Brunelleschi did. The cathedral's claim to artistic fame is Brunelleschi's magnificent dome—the first Renaissance dome and the model for domes to follow.

▲Climbing the Cathedral's Dome—For a grand view into the cathedral from the base of the dome, a peek at some of the tools used in the dome's construction, a chance to see Brunelleschi's "dome-within-a-dome" construction, a glorious Florence view from the top, and the equivalent of 463 plunges on a Stairmaster, climb the dome. When planning St. Peter's in Rome, Michelangelo rhymed (not in English), "I can build its sister—bigger, but not more beautiful, than the dome of Florence."

To avoid the long, dreadfully slow-moving line, arrive by 8:30 (€6, Mon–Fri 8:30–19:00, Sat 8:30–17:40 except first Sat of month

8:30–16:00, closed Sun and holidays; enter from outside church on new north-side entrance, though entry could be switched back to south side; tel. 055-230-2885).

▲Giotto's Tower (Campanile)—If you're not interested in experiencing dome-within-a-dome architecture, you'll likely feel that climbing Giotto's 270-foot bell tower beats scaling the neighboring Duomo's dome because it's 50 fewer steps, faster, and offers the same view plus the dome (€6, daily 8:30–19:30, last entry 40 min before closing).

▲▲Duomo Museum (Museo dell' Opera del Duomo)—The underrated cathedral museum, behind the church, is great if you like sculpture. It has masterpieces by Donatello (a gruesome wood carving of Mary Magdalene clothed in her matted hair, and the *cantoria,* a delightful choir loft bursting with happy children) and by Luca della Robbia (another choir loft, lined with the dreamy faces of musicians praising the Lord). Look for a late Michelangelo *Pietà* (Nicodemus, on top, is a self-portrait), Brunelleschi's models for his dome, and the original restored panels of Ghiberti's doors to the Baptistery. This is one of the few museums in Florence open on Monday (€6, Mon–Sat 9:00–19:30, Sun 9:00–13:40, closed on holidays, Via del Proconsolo 9, tel. 055-230-2885).

If you find all this church art intriguing, look through the open doorway of the Duomo art studio, which has been making and restoring church art since the days of Brunelleschi (a block toward the river from the Duomo at 23a Via dello Studio).

▲Baptistery—Michelangelo said its bronze doors were fit to be the gates of Paradise. Check out the gleaming copies of Lorenzo Ghiberti's bronze doors facing the Duomo. Making a breakthrough in perspective, Ghiberti used mathematical laws to create the illusion of receding distance on a basically flat surface.

The doors on the north side of the building were designed by Ghiberti when he was young; he'd won the honor and opportunity by beating Brunelleschi in a competition (the rivals' original entries are in the Bargello, see below).

Inside, sit and savor the medieval mosaic ceiling where it's Judgment Day. Jesus is giving the ultimate thumbs up and thumbs down (€3; interior open Mon–Sat 12:00–19:00, Sun 8:30–14:00, bronze doors are on the outside, so always "open"; original panels are in the Duomo Museum).

Orsanmichele Church—In the 9th century, this loggia (a covered courtyard) was a market used for selling grain (stored upstairs). Later, it was closed in to make a church. Notice the grain spouts on the pillars inside.

Outside, check out the dynamic statue-filled niches. You can see man stepping out of the literal and figurative shadow of the Church in the great Renaissance sculptor Donatello's *St. George,* on the northwest corner. The predella (panels) at the base of this statue shows St. George slaying the dragon to protect the wispy, melodramatic maiden. This was groundbreaking Renaissance emotion and perspective. Compare this with Nanni's smaller-scale, deeply set, and less sophisticated *Four Saints* statue to its left.

The interior of the church, viewable only during evening concerts, has a glorious Gothic tabernacle (1359) by Orcagna.

A block away, you'll find the...

▲Mercato Nuovo (a.k.a. the Straw Market)—This market loggia is how Orsanmichele looked before it became a church. Originally a silk and straw market, Mercato Nuovo still functions as a rustic market today (at the intersection of Via Calimala and Via Porta Rossa). Prices are soft. Notice the circled X in the center, marking the spot where people hit after being hoisted up to the top and dropped as punishment for bankruptcy. You'll also find *Porcellino* (a statue of a wild boar nicknamed "little pig"), which people rub and give coins in order to ensure their return to Florence. Nearby, a wagon sells tripe (cow innards) sandwiches.

▲Palazzo Vecchio—With its distinctive castle turret, this fortified palace, once the home of the Medici family, is a Florentine landmark. But if you're visiting only one palace interior in town, the Pitti Palace is better. The Palazzo Vecchio interior is worthwhile only if you're a real fan of Florentine history or of the artist Giorgio Vasari, who wallpapered the place with mediocre magnificence. The museum's most famous statues are Michelangelo's *Victory* and Donatello's bronze statue of *Judith and Holerfernes* (€5.70, €8 combo-ticket with Brancacci Chapel, Fri–Wed 9:00–19:00, Thu 9:00–14:00, in summer maybe open 9:00–23:00 on Mon and Fri, ticket office closes 1 hour earlier, tel. 055-276-8465).

Even if you don't go to the museum, do step into the free courtyard (behind the fake *David*) just to feel the essence of the Medicis. Until 1873, Michelangelo's *David* stood at the entrance, where the copy is today. While the huge statues in the square are important only as the whipping boys of art critics and rest stops for pigeons, the nearby Loggia dei Lanzi has several important statues. Look for Cellini's bronze statue of Perseus holding the head of Medusa. The plaque on the pavement in front of the fountain marks the spot where the monk Savonarola was burned in MCDXCVIII (for more on the monk, see "Museum of San Marco" listing, page 1042).

The square fronting the Palazzo Vecchio, Piazza della Signoria, is a tourist's world with pigeons, postcards, horse buggies, and tired hubbies. And, if it would make your tired hubby happy, the ritzy Café Rivoire—with the best view seats in town—is famous for its fancy desserts and hot chocolate (closed Mon).

▲▲▲Uffizi Gallery—This greatest collection of Italian paintings anywhere features works by Giotto, Leonardo, Raphael,

Uffizi Gallery

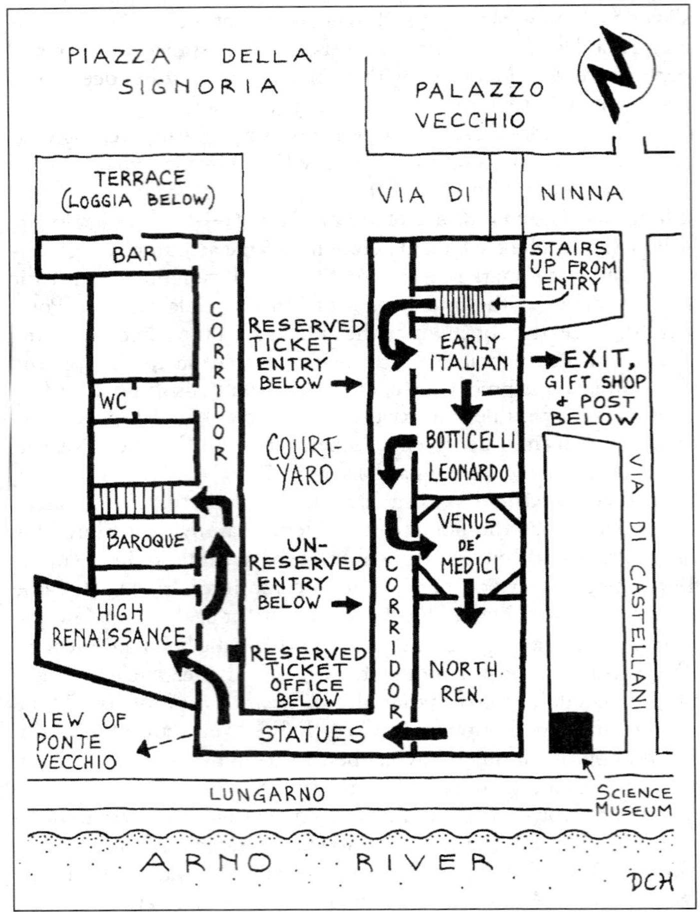

Caravaggio, Rubens, Titian, and Michelangelo, and a roomful of Botticellis, including his *Birth of Venus*.

The museum is nowhere near as big as it is great. Few tourists spend more than two hours inside. The paintings are displayed on one comfortable U-shaped floor in chronological order, from the 13th through 17th centuries. The left wing—starring the Florentine Middle Ages to the Renaissance—is the best. The connecting corridor contains sculpture, and the right wing focuses on High Renaissance and Baroque.

Essential stops are (in this order): Gothic altarpieces (narrative, pre-Realism, no real concern for believable depth) including Giotto's altarpiece, which progressed beyond "totem-pole angels";

Uccello's *Battle of San Romano,* an early study in perspective (with a few obvious flubs); Fra Filippo Lippi's cuddly Madonnas; the Botticelli room, filled with masterpieces, including a pantheon of classical fleshiness and the small *La Calumnia,* showing the glasnost of Renaissance free-thinking being clubbed back into the darker age of Savonarola; two minor works by Leonardo; the octagonal classical sculpture room with an early painting of Bob Hope and a copy of Praxiteles' *Venus de' Medici*—considered the epitome of beauty in Elizabethan Europe; a view through the window of Ponte Vecchio—dreamy at sunset; Michelangelo's only surviving easel painting, the round *Holy Family;* Raphael's noble *Madonna of the Goldfinch;* Titian's voluptuous *Venus of Urbino;* and Duomo views from the café terrace (WC near café).

Cost, Hours, Reservations: €9.50, plus €3 for recommended reservation, Tue–Sun 8:15–18:50, 8:15–22:00 on holidays and maybe on summer Sat, closed Mon, last entry 45 min before closing, after entering take elevator or climb four long flights of stairs.

Because only 780 visitors are allowed inside the building at any one time, there's generally a very long wait (up to two hours). The good news: You can—and should—make a telephone reservation to avoid the long line. It's easy, slick, and costs only €3 (tel. 055-294-883, explained more on page 1029). At the Uffizi, walk briskly past the 200-yard-long line—pondering the IQ of this gang—to the special entrance for those with reservations (labeled in English "Entrance for Reservations Only"), give your number, pay (cash only), and scoot right in.

If you haven't called ahead, there are other ways to make an Uffizi reservation—sometimes for the same day, depending on luck and availability: 1) buy Uffizi tickets with reservations at the Museum of San Marco, the Museum of Precious Stones, or another Florence sight; 2) try booking directly at the Uffizi (ask the clerk who stands at the reservations entrance if you can reserve in person—he may direct you to the ticket office); or 3) take a tour of the museum with Walking Tours of Florence (booking required, see "Tours" page 1034).

In Courtyard of Uffizi: Enjoy the Uffizi's courtyard (free), full of artists and souvenir stalls. The surrounding statues honor earthshaking Florentines: artists (Michelangelo and Leonardo), philosophers (Machiavelli), scientists (Galileo), writers (Dante), and explorers (Amerigo Vespucci), and the great patron of so much Renaissance thinking, Lorenzo "the Magnificent" de Medici.

▲Ponte Vecchio—Florence's most famous bridge is lined with shops that have traditionally sold gold and silver. A statue of Cellini, the master goldsmith of the Renaissance, stands in the center, ignored by the flood of tacky tourism. This is a romantic spot late at night. In fact, hanging over the edge of the bridge (on either side of the Cellini bust) are piles of padlocks. Guys demonstrate the enduring quality of their love by ceremonially taking their girls here, locking a lock, and throwing the key into the Arno. (But what's with the combination lock?)

Notice the "prince's passageway" above the bridge. In less secure times, the city leaders had a fortified passageway connecting the Vecchio Palace and Uffizi with the mighty Pitti Palace, to which they could flee in times of attack. This passageway, called the **Vasari Corridor,** is technically open to the public, but good luck getting an appointment (open "seasonally," try the museum reservation line, tel. 055-294-883).

SIGHTS

Near the Accademia

▲▲Museum of San Marco (Museo di San Marco)—One block north of the Accademia, this 15th-century museum houses the greatest collection anywhere of frescoes and paintings by the early Renaissance master Fra Angelico. You'll see why he thought of painting as a form of prayer, and couldn't paint a crucifix without shedding tears. The ground floor features the monk's paintings, along with some works by Fra Bartolomeo. Upstairs are 43 cells decorated by Fra Angelico and his assistants. While the monk/painter was trained in the medievalreligious style, he also learned and adopted Renaissance techniques and sensibilities, producing works that blended Christian symbols and Renaissance realism. Don't miss the cell of Savonarola, the charismatic monk who rode in from the Christian right, threw out the Medicis, turned Florence into a theocracy, sponsored "bonfires of the vanities" (burning books, paintings, and so on), and was finally burned himself when Florence decided to change channels (€4, daily 8:15–13:50, Sat–Sun 8:15–19:00, but closed first, third, and fifth Sun and second and fourth Mon of each month, tel. 055-238-8608). The ticket office can issue reserved tickets, and even sell tickets (often with immediate reservation) to the Uffizi and Accademia.

Museum of Precious Stones (Museo dell' Opificio delle Pietre Dure)—This unusual gem of a museum features mosaics of inlaid marble and stones. You'll see remnants of the Medici workshop from 1588, including 500 different precious stones, the tools used to cut and inlay them, and room after room of the sumptuous finished product. The fine loaner booklet describes it all in English (€2, Mon–Sat 8:15–14:00, Thu until 19:00, closed Sun, Via degli Alfani 78, around corner from Accademia). This ticket booth can also sell tickets with reservations (often for the same day) to the Uffizi and Accademia.

Heart of Florence

▲▲▲Bargello (Museo Nazionale)—This under-appreciated sculpture museum is in a former police-station-turned-prison that looks like a mini-Palazzo Vecchio. It has Donatello's painfully beautiful *David* (the very influential first male nude to be sculpted in a thousand years), works by Michelangelo, and rooms of Medici treasures cruelly explained in Italian only (politely suggest to the staff that English descriptions would be wonderful). Moody Donatello, who embraced realism with his lifelike statues, set the personal and artistic style for many Renaissance artists to follow. The best works are in the ground-floor room at the foot of the outdoor staircase and in the room directly above (€4, daily 8:15–13:50 but closed first, third, and fifth Sun and second and fourth Mon of each month, last entry 40 min before closing, Via del Proconsolo 4, tel. 055-238-8606).

▲▲Medici Chapels (Cappelle dei Medici)—The chapel, containing Medici tombs, is drenched in lavish High Renaissance architecture and sculpture. The highlight is a chapel with interior decoration by Michelangelo, including the brooding *Night, Day, Dawn,* and *Dusk* statues (€6, daily 8:15–16:50 but closed the second and fourth Sun and the first, third, and fifth Mon of each month, tel. 055-238-8602).

Nearby: Behind the chapels on Piazza Madonna di degli Aldobrandini is a lively market scene that I find just as interesting. Take a stroll through the huge double-decker Mercato Centrale (central food market) one block north.

▲Medici-Riccardi Palace (Palazzo Medici-Riccardi)—Lorenzo the Magnificent's home is worth a look for its art. The tiny Chapel of the Magi contains colorful Renaissance gems such as the *Procession of the Magi* frescoes by Benozzo Gozzoli. The former library has a Baroque ceiling fresco by Luca Giordano, a prolific artist from Naples known as Fast Luke (Luca fa presto) for his ambidextrous painting abilities. While the Medicis originally occupied this 1444 house, in the 1700s it became home to the Riccardi family, who added the Baroque flourishes (€4, Thu–Tue 9:00–19:00, closed Wed, Via Cavour 3, kitty-corner from San Lorenzo Church, 1 long block north of Baptistery, tel. 055-276-0340).

▲Piazza della Repubblica—The large square sits on the site of Florence's original Roman Forum. The lone column—nicknamed the belly button of Florence—is the only remaining bit of Roman Florence except for its grid street plan. Look at the map (by the benches—where the old boys hang out to talk sports and politics) to see the ghost of Rome. Roman Florence was a garrison town—a rectangular fort with this square marking the intersection of the two main roads (Via Corso and Via Roma).

Today's piazza, framed by a triumphal arch, is really a nationalistic statement celebrating the unification of Italy. Florence, the capital of the country (1865–1870) until Rome was liberated, lacked a square worthy of this grand new country. So the neighborhood here was razed to open up a grand modern forum surrounded by grand circa-1890 buildings.

Between here and the river you'll find characteristic parts of the medieval city that give a sense of what this neighborhood felt like before it was bulldozed. Back in the Middle Ages, writers described Florence as so densely built up that when it rained, pedestrians didn't get wet. Torches were used to light the lanes in midday. The city was prickly with noble family towers (like San Gimignano) and had Romeo-and-Juliet-type family feuds. But with the rise of the Medicis (c. 1300), no noble family was allowed to have an architectural ego trip taller then theirs, and nearly all other towers were taken down.

The fancy La Rinascente department store, facing the Piazza della Repubblica, is one of the city's finest (WC on 4th floor, view terrace in small pricey bar above that).

▲▲Science Museum (Istituto e Museo di Storia della Scienza)—This is a fascinating collection of Renaissance and later clocks, telescopes, maps, and ingenious gadgets. Trace the technical innovations as modern science emerges from 1000 to 1900. One of the most talked-about bottles in Florence is the one here containing Galileo's finger. Loaner English guidebooklets are available to supplement the English pamphlets they'll give you. It's friendly, comfortably cool, never crowded, and just a block east of the Uffizi on the Arno River (€6.50, Mon and Wed–Fri 9:30–17:00, Tue and Sat 9:30–13:00, closed Sun, Piazza dei Giudici 1, tel. 055-265-311).

▲▲Church of Santa Maria Novella—The 13th-century Dominican church, just south of the train station, is rich in art. Along with crucifixes by Giotto and Brunelleschi, there's every textbook's example of the early Renaissance mastery of perspective: *The Holy Trinity* by Masaccio; it's opposite the side entrance. The exquisite chapels trace art in Florence from medieval times to early Baroque. The outside of the church features a dash of Romanesque (horizontal stripes), Gothic (pointed arches), Renaissance (geometric shapes), and Baroque (scrolls). Step in and look down the 330-foot nave for a 14th-century optical illusion (€2.50, Mon–Thu and Sat 9:30–17:00, Fri and Sun 13:00–17:00). No photos are allowed.

Nearby: Art lovers can seek out the adjacent **cloisters** (separate fee and entry to the left of the church's facade); the Chapel of the Spaniards—currently under restoration—is notable for Bonaiuto's fresco *Allegory of the Dominican Order.* A palatial **perfumery** is around the corner 100 yards down Via della Scala at #16 (free but shopping encouraged, Mon–Sat 9:30–19:30, closed Sun, tel. 055-216-276). Thick with the lingering aroma of centuries of spritzes, it started as the herb garden of the Santa Maria Novella monks.

Well-known even today for its top-quality products, it is extremely Florentine. Pick up the history sheet at the desk and wander deep into the shop. From the back room, you can peek at Santa Maria Novella's cloister with its dreamy frescoes and imagine a time before Vespas and tourists.

Dante's House (Casa di Dante)—Dante's house is closed indefinitely for restoration. It's actually a copy built near his house just a hundred years ago, consisting of five rooms in an old building with lots of documents and photos relating to his life and work. Well-described in English, it's interesting to literary buffs (across the street and around the corner from Bargello, at Via S. Margherita 1, tel. 055-219-416).

Santa Croce and Nearby

▲▲Santa Croce Church—This 14th-century Franciscan church, decorated with centuries of precious art, holds the tombs of great Florentines (€4, Mon–Sat 9:30–17:30, Sun 13:00–17:30, in winter Mon–Sat 9:30–12:30 & 15:00–17:30, Sun 13:00–17:30, modest dress code enforced, tel. 055-246-6105). The loud 19th-century Victorian Gothic facade faces a huge square ringed with tempting shops and littered with tired tourists. Escape into the church and admire its sheer height and spaciousness.

On your left as you enter is the tomb of Galileo Galilei (1564–1642), the Pisan who lived his last years under house arrest near Florence. Having defied the Church by saying the earth revolved around the sun, his heretical remains were only allowed in the church long after his death.

Directly opposite—on the right side of the nave—find the tomb of Michelangelo Buonarroti (with the allegorical figures of painting, architecture, and sculpture); a memorial to Dante (no body...he was banished by his hometown because of political differences); the tomb of Machiavelli (who wrote the book on hardball politics); a relief by Donatello of the Annunciation; and the tomb of the composer of the *William Tell Overture* (a.k.a. the *Lone Ranger* theme), Rossini.

To the right of the altar, step into the sacristy where you'll find a bit of St. Francis' cowl and old sheets of music. In the bookshop, notice the photos of the devastating flood of 1966 high on the wall. Beyond that is a touristy—but mildly interesting—"leather school." The chapels lining the front of the church are richly frescoed. The chapel to the right of the main altar is a masterpiece by Giotto featuring scenes from the life of St. Francis.

Exit between the Rossini and Machiavelli tombs into the cloisters. On the left enter Brunelleschi's **Pazzi Chapel,** considered one of the finest pieces of Florentine Renaissance architecture.

▲Michelangelo's House (Casa Buonarroti)—Fans enjoy a house built on property once owned by Michelangelo. The house was built by his grand-nephew, who turned it into a little museum honoring his famous relative. You'll see some of Michelangelo's sketches and his early, much-less-monumental statues. Look for his earliest known sculptures, the two relief panels he did as a teenager: *The Madonna of the Stairs* (c. 1490) and the *Battle of the Centaurs* (1490–1492), a squirming tangle of battling nudes (€6.50, Wed–Mon 9:30–14:00, closed Tue, English descriptions, Via Ghibellina 70, tel. 055-241-752).

South of the Arno River

To locate these sights, see map on page 1036.

▲▲Pitti Palace—From the Uffizi, follow the course of the elevated passageway (closed to non-Medicis) across the Ponte Vecchio to the gargantuan Pitti Palace, which has several separate museums.

The **Palatine Gallery/Royal Apartments (Galleria Palatina)** is the biggie, featuring palatial room after chandeliered room, its walls sagging with masterpieces by minor artists and minor pieces by masters. Its Raphael collection is the biggest anywhere (first floor, €8.50, Tue–Sun 8:15–18:50, closed Mon, buy tickets on right-hand side of courtyard, tel. 055-238-8614).

The **Modern Art Gallery** features Romanticism, neoclassicism, and Impressionism by 19th- and 20th-century Tuscan painters (second floor, €5, admission includes Costume Museum, daily 8:15–13:50 but closed second and fourth Sun and first, third, and fifth Mon).

The **Grand Ducal Treasures (Museo degli Argenti)** is the Medici treasure chest, with jeweled crucifixes, exotic porcelain, gilded ostrich eggs, and so on, made to entertain fans of applied arts (ground floor, €6, includes Porcelain Museum and Boboli Gardens, same hours as Boboli Gardens, listed below).

Behind the palace, the huge landscaped **Boboli Gardens** offer a shady refuge from the city heat (€4, daily 9:00–18:30 in fall and spring, 9:00–19:30 June–Aug, 9:00–16:30 winter, but closed first and last Mon of month).

▲▲Brancacci Chapel—For the best look at Masaccio's works (he's the early Renaissance master who reinvented perspective), see his restored frescoes at the Brancacci (brahn-KAH-chee) Chapel. Instead of medieval religious symbols, Masaccio's paintings feature simple, strong human figures with facial expressions that reflect their emotions. The accompanying works of Masolino and Filippino Lippi provide illuminating contrasts

Call the chapel for free, mandatory **reservations** in English, often available for the same day (tel. 055-276-8224). Reservation times begin every 15 minutes, with a maximum of 30 visitors per time slot. You have 15 minutes in the actual chapel. Visits on the top of each hour include a free 40-minute video in English;

ask about this when booking your visit.

Cost, Hours, Location: €4, €8 combo-ticket with Palazzo Vecchio, Mon and Wed–Sat 10:00–17:00, Sun 13:00–17:00, closed Tue, ticket office closes at 16:30, cross Ponte Vecchio and turn right and hike to Piazza del Carmine).

The neighborhoods around the church are considered the last surviving bits of old Florence.

Santo Spirito Church—This has a classic Brunelleschi interior and a very early Michelangelo crucifix, painted on carved wood, given by the sculptor to the monastery in appreciation for the opportunity that they gave him to dissect and learn about bodies. Pop in here for a delightful Renaissance space and a chance to marvel at a Michelangelo all alone (free, most days 10:00–12:00 & 16:00–17:30, Sat–Sun only 16:00–17:30, closed Wed afternoon, Piazza Santo Spirito, tel. 055-210-030).

▲Piazzale Michelangelo—Overlooking the city from across the river (look for the huge statue of David), this square is worth the 30-minute hike, drive, or bus ride (either #12 or #13 from the train station) for the view of Florence and the stunning dome of the Duomo. After dark, it's packed with local schoolkids feeding their dates slices of watermelon and then licking them clean. Just beyond it is the stark, beautiful, crowd-free, Romanesque San Miniato Church.

EXPERIENCES

Gelato

Gelato is an edible art form. Italy's best ice cream is in Florence—one souvenir that can't break and won't clutter your luggage. But beware of scams at touristy joints on busy streets that turn a simple request for a cone into a €10 "tourist special." A key to gelato-appreciation is sampling liberally and choosing flavors that go well together. Ask, as the locals do, for "*Un assaggio, per favore?*" (A taste, please?) and "*Quali si sposano bene?*" (What marries well?).

Gelateria Carrozze is very good (daily 11:00–24:00, closes at 21:00 in winter; on riverfront 30 yards from Ponte Vecchio toward the Uffizi, Via del Pesce 3; also has decent sandwiches to go). **Gelateria dei Neri** is another local favorite worth tracking down (daily in summer 12:00–23:00, closed Wed in winter, 2 blocks east of Palazzo Vecchio at Via dei Neri 20 red).

Vivoli's, which serves "only today's production" is the most famous (Tue–Sun 8:00–1:00; closed Mon, the last 3 weeks in Aug, and winter; opposite the Church of Santa Croce, go down Via Torta a block, turn right on Via Stinche). Before ordering, try a free sample of their *riso* flavor—rice.

If you want an excuse to check out the little village-like

neighborhood across the river from Santa Croce, enjoy a gelato at the tiny **no-name gelateria** at Via San Miniato 5 red (just before Porta San Miniato).

SHOPPING

Florence is a great shopping town. Busy street scenes and markets abound, especially near San Lorenzo, near Santa Croce, on Ponte Vecchio, and at Mercato Nuovo (a covered market square 3 blocks north of Ponte Vecchio, listed on page 1039). Leather (often better quality for less than the U.S. price), gold, silver, art prints, and tacky plaster mini-*Davids* are most popular. Shops usually have promotional stalls in the market squares. Prices are soft in markets. Many visitors spend entire days shopping.

For ritzy Italian fashions, browse along Via de Tornabuoni, Via della Vigna Nuova, and Via Strozzi. Typical chain department stores are **Coin,** the local Macy's (Mon–Sat 9:30–20:00, Sun 11:00–20:00, on Via Calzaiuoli, near Orsanmichele Church); **Oviesse,** the local Penney's, a discount clothing/grocery store (Mon–Sat 9:00–19:55, closed Sun; at intersection of Via Panzani and Via del Giglio, near train station); and the upscale **La Rinascente,** the local Nordstrom's (Mon–Sat 9:00–21:00, Sun 10:30–20:00, on Piazza della Repubblica, expensive café and view terrace on 4th floor).

For shopping ideas, ads, and a list of markets, see the *Florence Concierge Information* magazine described under "Tourist Information," page 1026 (free from TI and many hotels).

SLEEPING

The accommodations scene varies wildly with the season. Spring and fall are very tight and expensive, while mid-July through August is wide open and discounted. November through February is also generally empty. I've listed prices for peak season: April, May, June, September, and October. If a price range is listed, the lower end reflects off-season (Aug, Nov–March) and the higher end, peak season.

With good information and an e-mail or phone call beforehand, you can find a stark, clean, and comfortable double with breakfast and a shower down the hall for about €80 (for the room, not per person). A typical room with a private bath costs around €100 (less at the smaller places, such as the *soggiornos*). You get elegance in peak season for €150. Some places listed are old and rickety, and described as such. Virtually all of the accommodations are central, within minutes of the great sights. Few hotels escape Vespa noise at night.

Sleep Code

(€1 = about $1.20, country code: 39)
S = Single, **D** = Double/Twin, **T** = Triple, **Q** = Quad, **b** = bathroom, **s** = shower only, **SE** = Speaks English, **NSE** = No English. Unless otherwise noted, breakfast is included (but usually optional) and credit cards are accepted. English is generally spoken.

To help you sort easily through these listings, I've divided the rooms into three categories based on the price for a standard double room with bath:

$$$ **Higher Priced**—Most rooms €160 or more.
$$ **Moderately Priced**—Most rooms between €110–160.
$ **Lower Priced**—Most rooms €110 or less.

Book direct—not through a tourist agency. Tourist information room-finding services cannot give opinions on quality. If you're traveling off-season, you can show up without reservations and find huge discounts. Ask if you'll get a discount for paying in cash or for staying for three or more nights (or both). And ask if you can skip breakfast (the overpriced breakfasts are legally optional, though some hotels pretend otherwise).

Book ahead. I repeat, book ahead (by e-mail, fax, or phone). Places will hold a room until early afternoon.

Between the Station and Duomo

$$$ Palazzo Castiglioni offers 16 grand rooms with all the conveniences and a peaceful, *palazzo* decor. Most rooms are spacious, several have frescoes, and all make a fine splurge (Db-€170, Db suite-€200, Tb-€210, 5 percent discount with cash, air-con, elevator, Via del Giglio 8, tel. 055-214-886, fax 055-274-0521, pal.cast@flashnet.it, Laura SE).

$$ Hotel Accademia is an elegant place with marble stairs, parquet floors, attractive public areas, 21 pleasant rooms, and a floor plan that defies logic (Db-€150, Tb-€180, 5 percent additional discount with cash, air-con, tiny courtyard, Via Faenza 7, tel. 055-293-451, fax 055-219-771, www.accademiahotel.net, info@accademiahotel.net, Tea SE).

$$ Hotel Bellettini rents 30 bright, cool, well-cared-for rooms with inviting lounges (S-€78, Sb-€100, D-€105, Db-€140, Tb-€170, Qb-€210; air-con, Via de' Conti 7, tel. 055-213-561, fax 055-283-551, www.hotelbellettini.com, info@hotelbellettini.com, frisky Gina SE). Be warned, they rent much higher-priced rooms in a nearby annex.

Hotels in Florence

1. Palazzo Castiglioni & Hotel Aldobrandini
2. Hotel Accademia
3. Hotel Bellettini
4. Residenza dei Pucci
5. Hotel Basilea
6. Casa Rabatti
7. Affitacamere Lucia Freda
8. Soggiorno Magliani
9. Hotel Loggiato dei Serviti
10. Hotel Morandi alla Crocetta
11. Hotel Le Due Fontane
12. Oblate Sisters of the Assumption
13. Hotel Pendini
14. Residenza Giotto
15. Pensione Maxim
16. Soggiorno Battistero
17. Albergo Firenze
18. Hotel Torre Guelfa & Hotel Pensione Alessandra
19. In Piazza della Signoria B&B
20. Hotel Davanzati
21. Hotel Pensione Elite
22. Bellevue House
23. Hotel Sole
24. Hotel Bargellino

$$ Residenza dei Pucci, a block north of the Duomo, has 12 tastefully decorated rooms—in soothing earth tones—with aristocratic furniture and tweed carpeting. It's fresh and bright (Sb-€130, Db-€145, Db in Aug and much of winter-€105, Tb-€165, suite with grand Duomo view-€207 for 2 people, €233 for 4, breakfast served in room, Via dei Pucci 9, tel. 055-281-886, fax 055-264-314, http://residenzapucci.interfree.it, residenzapucci@interfree.it, SE).

$ Hotel Aldobrandini, a budget choice in a drab old palazzo, has 15 basic, clean rooms, with the San Lorenzo market at its doorstep and the entrance to the Medici Chapels a few steps away (Ss-€50, Sb-€60, D-€75, Db-€90, lots of night noise but has double-paned windows, fans, hiding behind market stalls and mopeds at Piazza Madonna degli Aldobrandini 8, tel. 055-211-866, fax 055-267-6281, www.hotelaldobrandini.it, info@hotelaldobrandini.it, Ignazio SE, though his one-legged mother in wheelchair, who often greets people, speaks Italian).

Near the Central Market

$$ Hotel Basilea offers predictable three-star, air-conditioned comfort in its 38 modern rooms (Sb-€80–110, Db-€110–150, Tb-€150–210, lower prices Aug and Nov–March, elevator, terrace, Via Guelfa 41, at intersection with Nazionale—a busy street, ask for a room in the back, tel. 055-214-587, fax 055-268-350, www.hotelbasilea.net, basilea@florenceitaly.net, SE).

$ Casa Rabatti is the ultimate if you always wanted to be a part of a Florentine family. Its four simple, clean rooms are run with motherly warmth by Marcella, who speaks minimal English. Seeing 10 years of my family Christmas cards on their walls, I'm reminded of how long the Rabattis have been keeping budget travelers happy (D-€60, Db-€70, €25 per bed in shared quad or quint, no breakfast, cash only, fans, no sign other than on doorbell, 5 blocks from station, Via San Zanobi 48 black, tel. 055-212-393, casarabatti@inwind.it). If booked up, Marcella will refer to her daughter's place nearby on Via Nazionale.

$ Affitacamere Lucia Freda is basic, clean, and cheap. Its four ground floor-yet-quiet rooms share two bathrooms, a kitchenette, and a leafy garden terrace (S-€45, D-€55, T-€70, €5 less for 2 or more days, discounts in winter, cash only, no breakfast, Via San Zanobi 76, but ring at #31, tel. 055-487-533, luciafreda@libero.it, kind Lucia and son Claudio).

$ Soggiorno Magliani, central and humble with seven rooms, feels and smells like a great-grandmother's place (S-€38, D-€49, T-€65, cash only but secure reservation with credit card, no breakfast, double-paned windows, near Via Guelfa at Via Reparata 1, tel. 055-287-378, hotel-magliani@libero.it, run by friendly family duo Vincenza and English-speaking daughter Cristina).

East of the Duomo

$$$ Hotel Loggiato dei Serviti, at the most prestigious address in Florence on the most Renaissance square in town, gives you Old World romance with hair dryers. Stone stairways lead you under open-beam ceilings through this 16th-century monastery's classy public rooms. The 38 cells, with air-conditioning, TVs, mini-bars, and telephones, wouldn't be recognized by their original inhabitants. The hotel staff is both professional and friendly (Sb-€146, Db-€210, family suites from €263, 30 percent discount in Aug and late Nov–Feb, 5 elegant rooms in 17th-century annex, elevator, Piazza S.S. Annuziata 3, tel. 055-289-592, fax 055-289-595, www.loggiatodeiservitihotel.it, info@loggiatodeiservitihotel.it, Simonetta, Francesca, and Andrea SE). Ask for a backside room to avoid piazza night noise.

$$$ Hotel Morandi alla Crocetta, another former convent, envelops you in a 16th-century cocoon. Located on a quiet street, with period furnishings, parquet floors, and wood-beamed ceilings, it takes you back (10 rooms, Sb-€110, Db-€170, breakfast-€11, a block off Piazza S.S. Annunziata at Via Laura 50, tel. 055-234-4747, fax 055-248-0954, www.hotelmorandi.it, welcome@hotelmorandi.it, Claudio SE).

$$$ Hotel Le Due Fontane faces the Renaissance Piazza S.S. Annunziata but fills its old building with a smoky, 1970s, business-class ambience. Its 57 air-conditioned rooms are big and comfortable (Sb-€120, Db-€170, Tb-€210, elevator, Piazza S.S. Annunziata 14, tel. 055-210-185, fax 055-294-461, www.leduefontane.it, info@leduefontane.it, SE).

$ Oblate Sisters of the Assumption run an institutional 20-room hotel in a Renaissance building with a dreamy garden and a quiet, nice-place-to-relax-after-you-die feel. Not a hint of English spoken here (€37 per person, elevator, cash only, Borgo Pinti 15, tel. 055-248-0582, fax 055-234-6291).

Near Piazza Repubblica

These are the most central of my accommodations recommendations (and therefore a little overpriced). While worth the extra cost for many, given Florence's walkable core, nearly every hotel can be considered central.

$$ Hotel Pendini, a well-run and well-worn three-star hotel with Old World tiles, chandeliers, and 42 rooms, is popular and central, overlooking the grand Piazza Repubblica (Sb-€86–110, Db-€110–150 depending on season, elevator, fine lounge and breakfast room, air-con, Via Strozzi 2, tel. 055-211-170, fax 055-281-807, www.florenceitaly.net, Barbara SE).

$$ Residenza Giotto has six colorful, modern rooms, and a terrace so close to the Duomo you can almost touch it (Sb-€120,

Db-€140, Tb-€155, breakfast in room, elevator, Via Roma 6, 4th floor, tel. 055-214-593, fax 055-264-8568, www.residenzagiotto.it, residenzagiotto@tin.it, SE).

$$ Pensione Maxim, right on Via dei Calzaiuoli, is a big, institutional-feeling place as close to the sights as possible. Its halls are narrow, but the 29 basic rooms are comfortable and well-maintained (Sb-€75, Db-€105, Tb-€113, Qb-€155, dorm bed-€30, takes credit cards but pay first night in cash, air-con, elevator, Via dei Calzaiuoli 11, tel. 055-217-474, fax 055-283-729, www.hotelmaximfirenze.it, hotmaxim@tin.it, Paolo Maioli SE).

$ Soggiorno Battistero, next door to the Baptistery, has seven simple, airy rooms, most with great views, overlooking the Baptistery and square. You're in the heart of Florence (Sb-€85, Db-€108, Tb-€145, Qb-€155, 5 percent discount with cash, breakfast served in room, air-con,double-paned windows, Piazza San Giovanni 1, 3rd floor, no elevator, tel. 055-295-143, fax 055-268-189, www.soggiornobattistero.it, battistero@dada.it, lovingly run by Italian Luca and his American wife, Kelly).

$ Albergo Firenze, a big, efficient place, offers 58 good, basic rooms in a wonderfully central, reasonably quiet locale two blocks behind the Duomo (Sb-€80, Db-€100, Tb-€147, Qb-€170, cash only; prepay first night with traveler's check, bank draft, or international money order; elevator, air-con, off Via del Corso at Piazza Donati 4, tel. 055-214-203, fax 055-212-370, www.hotelfirenze-fi.it, firenze.albergo@tiscali.it, SE).

Near Piazza della Signoria and Ponte Vecchio

$$$ Hotel Torre Guelfa is topped by a fun medieval tower with a panoramic rooftop terrace and a huge living room. Its 29 rooms vary wildly in size (Sb-€110, small Db-€145, standard Db-€180, Db junior suite-€230, family deals). Room #15, with a private terrace—€210—is worth reserving several months in advance (elevator, air-con, a couple blocks northwest of Ponte Vecchio, Borgo S.S. Apostoli 8, tel. 055-239-6338, fax 055-239-8577, www.hoteltorreguelfa.com, torre.guelfa@flashnet.it, Sabina, Giancarlo, Carlo, and Sandro all SE).

$$$ In Piazza della Signoria B&B is peaceful, classy, and homey at the same time and overlooks Piazza della Signoria. It comes with all the special touches—much like a top-end American B&B. Each of its eight rooms has a huge and lavish bathroom (Sb-€170–210, Db-€200–260, Tb-€280, lower prices without view, family apartments, tiny elevator, air-con, Via dei Magazzini 2, tel. 055-239-9546, fax 055-267-6616, mobile 348-321-0565, www.inpiazzadellasignoria.it, info@inpiazzadellasignoria.it, Sonia SE).

$$ Hotel Pensione Alessandra is a 16th-century, tranquil place with 27 big, modern rooms (S-€72, Sb-€113, D-€113,

Db-€150, T-€150, Tb-€196, Q-€165, Qb-€217, 5 percent discount with cash, air-con, Borgo S.S. Apostoli 17, tel. 055-283-438, fax 055-210-619, www.hotelalessandra.com, info@hotelalessandra.com, SE).

$$ Hotel Davanzati, bright and shiny with artistic touches, has 21 cheery rooms with all the comforts. A family affair, friendly Tomasso and father Fabrizio also book dinners, museums, and excursions (Sb-€95, Db-€150, Tb-€195, prices soft in slow times and off-season, elevator, air-con, Via Porta Rossa 5, tel. 055-286-666, fax 055-265-8252, www.hoteldavanzati.it, info@hoteldavanzati.it, Laura and Stefano SE).

Near the Train Station

Note: As with any big Italian city, the area around the train station is a magnet for hardworking pickpockets on alert for lost, vulnerable tourists with bulging moneybelts hanging out of their khakis.

$ Hotel Pensione Elite, run warmly by sunny Nadia, is a fine value. It has 10 comfortable—if plainly furnished—rooms and a charm rare in this price range (Ss-€70, Sb-€80, Ds-€75, Db-€90, Tb-€110, Qb-€130, breakfast-€6, air-con, fans, Via della Scala 12, 2nd floor, tel. & fax 055-215-395, easy reservations by phone, SE).

$ Bellevue House is a fourth-floor oasis (no elevator) with six spacious rooms flanking a long, mellow yellow lobby. It's a peaceful time-warp run by Rosanna and Antonio Di Grazia (Db-maximum €110 in April–June, Sept, and Oct, Db-maximum €90 off-season, 5 percent cash discount, includes breakfast in a street level bar, oversized modern bathrooms, Via della Scala 21, tel. 055-260-8932, fax 055-265-5315, mobile 333-612-5973, www.bellevuehouse.it, info@bellevuehouse.it).

$ Hotel Sole, a clean, cozy, family-run place with eight bright, modern rooms, is just off Santa Maria Novella square toward the river. Friendly Anna makes you feel like a guest of the family (Sb-€50, Db-€80, Tb-€110, no breakfast, cash only, air-con, elevator, 1:00 curfew, Via del Sole 8, 3rd floor, tel. & fax 055-239-6094, NSE).

$ Hotel Bargellino, run by Bostonian Carmel and her Italian husband Pino, has a traditional faded-paint charm and funky antique furniture just a few blocks north of the train station. Some rooms face a large, peaceful common terrace complete with a tiny greenhouse (S-€43, D-€65, Db-€75, T-€100, credit cards OK but send deposit check to Carmel's sister in Boston to reserve, no breakfast, Via Guelfa 87, tel. 055-238-2658, fax 055-238-2698, www.ilbargellino.com, Carmel SE with a Boston accent).

Oltrarno, South of the River

Across the river in the Oltrarno area, between the Pitti Palace and Ponte Vecchio, you'll still find small traditional crafts shops, neighborly piazzas, and family eateries. All of the following

Hotels in Oltrarno

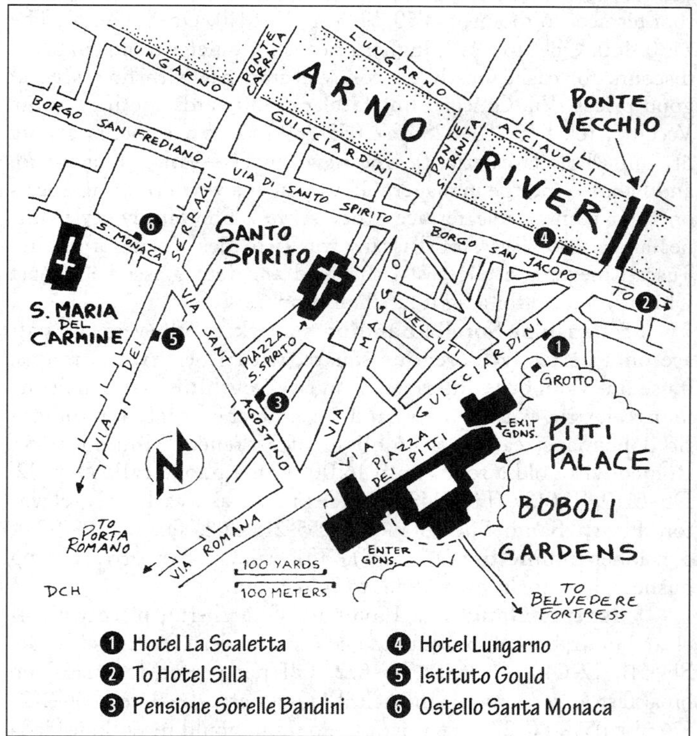

hotels and pensiones are an easy walk from the Ponte Vecchio.

$$$ Hotel Lungarno is *the* place to stay if money is no object. This deluxe, four-star hotel with 74 rooms strains anything stressful or rough out of Italy, and gives you (sometimes snooty) service, physical elegance everywhere you look, and fine views over the Arno and Ponte Vecchio (Sb-€250, Db-€400, Db facing river-€510, fancier suites, great riverside public spaces, air-con, elevator, 100 yards from Ponte Vecchio at Borgo San Jacopo 14, tel. 055-27261, fax 055-272-64-444, www.lungarnohotels.com, bookings@lungarnohotels.com, SE).

$$$ Hotel Silla, a classic three-star hotel with 36 cheery, spacious, pastel, and modern rooms, is a fine value. It faces the river and overlooks a park opposite the Santa Croce Church (Db-€170, Tb-€210, elevator, air-con, Via dei Renai 5, tel. 055-234-2888, fax 055-234-1437, www.hotelsilla.it, hotelsilla@tin.it, Laura and Stefano SE).

$$ Hotel La Scaletta, ramshackle and reeking in character, is a dark, cool place with a labyrinthine floor plan, senseless stairs, loose tiles, lots of Old World lounges, and a romantic, panoramic roof terrace (16 rooms, S-€50, Sb-€95, D-€110, Db-€115–130, Tb-€130–160, Qb-€160–170, higher price is for quieter rooms in back, discount for cash, mostly air-con, elevator, bar with fine wine at good prices, Via Guicciardini 13 black, 150 yards south of Ponte Vecchio, tel. 055-283-028, fax 055-289-562, www.hotellascaletta.it, info@hotellascaletta.it). The new owners—Andrea, Fabrizio, and Paolo—and the manager, Giovanna, enjoy entertaining guests on their comfortable terrace. They serve a fine family-style dinner and a €15 "Taste of Tuscany for Two" deal (plate of quality Tuscan meats and cheeses with bread and four glasses of robust Chianti)—ideal for a light lunch or dinner.

$$ Pensione Sorelle Bandini is a rickety 500-year-old palace on a perfectly Florentine square, with 12 cavernous rooms, museum-warehouse interiors, a musty youthfulness, a balcony lounge-loggia with a view, and an ambience that, for romantic bohemians, can be a highlight of Florence. Mimmo or Sr. Romeo will hold a room until 16:00 with a phone call (D-€102, Db-€110, T-€137, Tb-€149, includes breakfast, cash only, elevator, Piazza Santo Spirito 9, tel. 055-215-308, fax 055-282-761, pensionebandini@tiscali.it, SE). This square can attract drug pushers; just don't invite them to your room.

$ Istituto Gould is a Protestant Church-run place with 41 clean but drab rooms with twin beds and modern facilities (S-€36, Sb-€41, D-€46, Db-€58, Tb-€72, €21 per person in quads, no breakfast, quieter rooms in back, Via dei Serragli 49, tel. 055-212-576, fax 055-280-274, www.istitutogould.it, gould.reception@dada.it). You must arrive when the office is open (Mon–Fri 9:00–13:00 & 15:00–19:00, Sat 9:00–13:00, no check-in Sun or holidays, SE).

$ Ostello Santa Monaca, a cheap hostel, is a long block south of the Brancacci Chapel and attracts a young backpacking crowd (€17 beds with sheets, 4- to 20-bed rooms, 1:00 curfew, Via Santa Monaca 6, tel. 055-268-338, fax 055-280-185, www.ostello.it, info@ostello.it).

EATING

To save money and time for sights, you can keep lunches fast and simple, eating in one of the countless self-service places and pizzerias or just picnicking (try juice, yogurt, cheese, and a roll for €5). For good sit-down meals, consider the following. Remember, restaurants like to serve what's fresh. If you're into flavor, go for the seasonal best bets—featured in the *Piatti del Giorno* ("special of the day") sections of the menus.

Restaurants in Florence

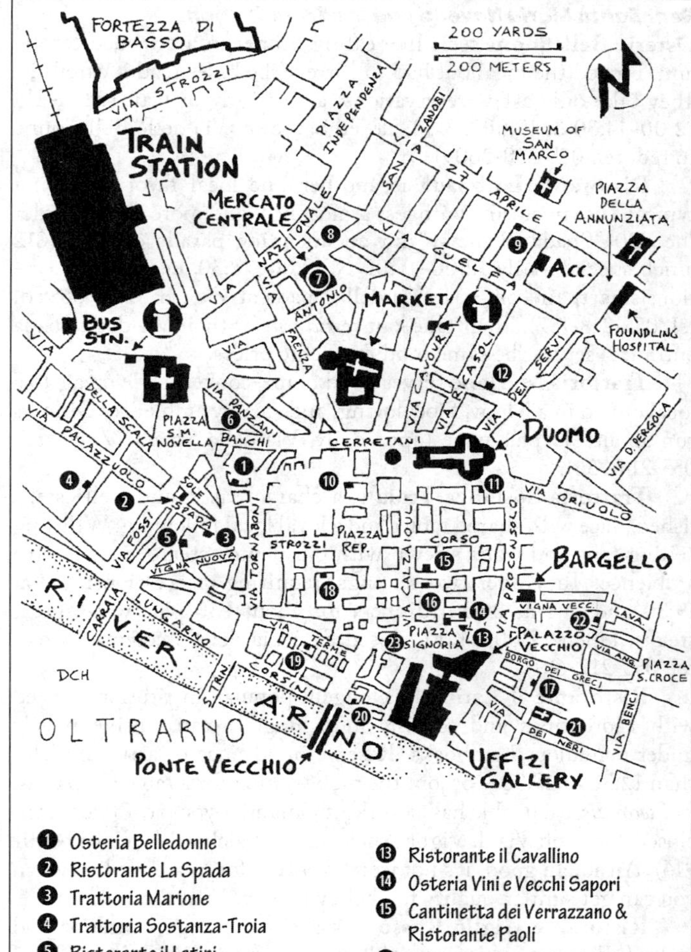

1. Osteria Belledonne
2. Ristorante La Spada
3. Trattoria Marione
4. Trattoria Sostanza-Troia
5. Ristorante il Latini
6. Ristorante Giglio Rosso
7. Mercato Centrale (Market)
8. Trattoria la Burrasca & Osteria la Congrega
9. Gran Caffè San Marco
10. Self-Service Rist. Leonardo
11. Antico Ristorante il Sasso di Dante
12. Ristorante il Ritrovo
13. Ristorante il Cavallino
14. Osteria Vini e Vecchi Sapori
15. Cantinetta dei Verrazzano & Ristorante Paoli
16. I Fratellini Wine & Sandwich Shop
17. Trattoria Icche C'è C'è
18. Osteria del Porcellino
19. Trattoria Nella
20. Gelateria Carrozze
21. Gelateria dei Neri
22. Vivoli's Gelateria
23. Café Rivoire

North of the River

Near Santa Maria Novella and the Train Station

Osteria Belledonne feels like eating dinner in a crowded terrarium. I loved the meal but had to correct the bill—read it carefully. They take only a few reservations; arrive early or wait (Mon–Fri 12:00–14:30 & 19:00–23:30, closed Sat–Sun, Via delle Belledonne 16 red, tel. 055-238-2609).

Ristorante La Spada is another fine local favorite serving typical Tuscan cuisine with less atmosphere and more menu. Order the €20 "Spada's Fantasy" for an unending parade of food (€12 lunch special, daily 12:00–15:00 & 19:00–22:30, evening reservations smart, air-con, near Via della Spada at Via del Moro 66 red, tel. 055-218-757). Their take-out *rosticcerìa* (at their Via della Spada entrance) serves the same food for picnic prices.

Trattoria Marione serves good home-cooked-style meals to a local crowd in a happy, food-loving, and steamy ambience. Dinners run about €15 plus wine (open daily, Via della Spada 27 red, tel. 055-214-756).

Trattoria Sostanza-Troia is a characteristic and well-established place with shared tables and a loyal local following. Whirling ceiling fans and walls strewn with old photos create a time-warp ambience. They offer two seatings, requiring reservations: one at 19:30 and one at 21:00 (dinners for about €30 plus wine, great steaks, lunch 12:00–14:00, closed Sat, Via del Porcellana 25 red, tel. 055-212-691).

Ristorante il Latini is a hugely popular institution packed with Florentines and tourists munching Tuscan cuisine noisily under pendulous hamhocks. Reserve in advance or arrive no later than 12:30 or 19:30—or join the mob waiting for a table (€7 pastas, €15 *secondis*, each table has a bottle of Chianti—you pay €1 per glass, closed Mon, off Via d. Vigna Nuova at Via Palchetti 6, tel. 055-210-916). Although good, it's not worth waiting for in a huge line when you can get similar-quality food elsewhere without the wait.

Ristorante Giglio Rosso has a sleek, modern interior and beautifully-presented, reasonably-priced dishes. Hip Italians, local clergy, and the occasional tourist all enjoy the homemade pasta, flambéed roasts, and luscious dessert cart (open daily, pasta and *secondi* under €10 each, Via Panzani 35 red, tel. 055-211-795).

Near the Central and San Lorenzo Markets

For piles of picnic produce, people-watching, or just a rustic sandwich, try the huge **Central Market,** called Mercato Centrale (Mon–Sat 7:00–14:00, a block north of San Lorenzo street market).

Trattoria la Burrasca is a Flintstone-chic, family-run place ideal for Tuscan home cooking. It's small—10 tables—and often filled with our readers. Anna and Antonio Genzano have cooked and served here with passion since 1982. If Andy Capp were Italian, he'd eat here for special nights out. Everything is homemade except the desserts. And if you want good wine cheap, order it here (Fri–Wed 12:00–15:00 & 19:00–22:00, closed Thu, Via Panicale 6b, at north corner of Central Market, tel. 055-215-827, NSE).

Osteria la Congrega brags it's "a Tuscan wine bar designed to help you lose track of time." In a fresh and romantic two-level setting, chef/owner Mahyar takes pride in his fun, easy menu featuring modern Tuscan cuisine, with top-notch meat and seasonal produce. He offers quality vegetarian dishes, creative salads, and an inexpensive but excellent house wine. With just 10 uncrowded tables, reservations are required for dinner (€5–6 pasta, €12 nightly specials, daily 12:00–15:00 & 19:00–23:00, Via Panicale 43 red, tel. 055-264-5027).

Near the Accademia and Museum of San Marco

Gran Caffè San Marco, conveniently located on Piazza San Marco across from the entrance of the San Marco Museum, churns out cheap but tired cafeteria fare to cheap but tired tourists (no cover charge, self-service and restaurant, Piazza San Marco 11 but enter around the corner on Via Cavour near #50, tel. 055-215-833).

Near the Duomo

Self-Service Ristorante Leonardo is fast, cheap, air-conditioned, and handy, just a block from the Duomo, southwest of the Baptistery (€3 pastas, €4 main courses, Sun–Fri 11:45–14:45 & 18:45–21:45, closed Sat, upstairs at Via Pecori 5, tel. 055-284-446). Luciano (like Pavarotti) runs the place with enthusiasm.

Antico Ristorante il Sasso di Dante serves standard Tuscan fare in a surprisingly pleasant indoor/outdoor setting in the shadow of the Duomo (€20 meals, always good vegetarian dishes and special menu of the day, daily 12:00–14:30 & 19:00–22:30, come early to snare front-row view seats, Piazza delle Pallottole 6, tel. 055-282-113).

Cavernous **Ristorante il Ritrovo** offers a bright, dressy ambience and meaty Tuscan cuisine cooked with family pride (€25 meals, Tue–Sun 12:30–15:00 & 19:00–23:00, closed Mon, 12 tables, air-con, a long block north of the Duomo at Via dei Pucci 4, tel. 055-281-688, Marco SE).

Near Palazzo Vecchio

Piazza della Signoria, the square facing Palazzo Vecchio, is ringed by beautifully situated yet touristy eateries. Any will do for a reasonably priced pizza. Perhaps the least of these evils is **Ristorante il Cavallino** with its glum crowd of tourists, dumbed-down menu, and great outdoor seating in the shadow of the palace (€18 fixed-price dinner *menu*, open daily, tel. 055-215-818). For a fancy dessert and hot chocolate, consider **Café Rivoire** (closed Mon).

Osteria Vini e Vecchi Sapori, half a block north of Palazzo Vecchio, is a colorful hole-in-the-wall serving traditional food, including plates of mixed *crostini* (€1 each—step right up and choose at the bar) and €10 daily specials (Tue–Sun 11:00–22:00, closed Mon, Via dei Magazzini 3 red, facing the bronze equestrian statue in Piazza della Signoria, go behind its tail into the corner and to your left, gruff Giorgio SE).

Cantinetta dei Verrazzano is a long-established bakery/café/wine bar, serving delightful sandwich plates in an elegant old-time setting, and hot focaccia sandwiches to go. Their *Specialita Verrazzano* is a fine plate of four little *crostini* (like mini *bruschetta*) featuring different local breads, cheeses, and meats (€7). The *Tagliere di Focacce,* a sampler plate of mini-focaccia sandwiches, is also fun. Either of these dishes with a glass of Chianti makes a fine light meal. Paolo describes things to make eating educational. As office workers pop in for a quick bite, it's traditional to share tables at lunchtime (Mon–Sat 8:00–21:00, closed Sun, just off Via Calzaiuoli on a side street across from Orsanmichele Church at Via dei Tavolini 18, tel. 055-268-590).

I Fratellini is a rustic little place where the "little brothers" have served peasants 27 different kinds of sandwiches and cheap glasses of Chianti wine (see list on wall) since 1875. Join the local crowd, then sit on a nearby curb or windowsill to munch, placing your glass on the wall rack before you leave (€4 for sandwich and wine, daily 8:00–20:00, 20 yards in front of Orsanmichele church on Via dei Cimatori).

Ristorante Paoli serves great local cuisine to piles of happy eaters under a richly frescoed Gothic vault. Because of its fame and central location, it's filled mostly with tourists, but for a dressy, traditional splurge meal, this is my choice (Wed–Mon 12:00–14:00 & 19:00–22:00, closed Tue, reserve for dinner, €20 tourist *menu,* à la carte is pricier, midway between old square and Duomo at Via de Tavolini 12 red, tel. 055-216-215). Salads are flamboyantly cut and mixed from a trolley right at your table.

Trattoria Icche C'è C'è (ee-kay chay chay; dialect for "whatever is, is") is a small, family-style eatery where fun-loving Gino serves good traditional meals (3-course €11 meals, not too touristy, Tue–Sun 11:00–15:00 & 19:00–24:00, closed Mon, midway between Bargello and river at Via Magalotti 11 red, tel. 055-216-589).

Osteria del Porcellino has a romantic ambience and a fresh, seasonal menu. A rare place that serves late, this dark, dense, candlelit place is packed with a mix of locals and tourists and run with style and enthusiasm by friendly chef Enzo (daily 12:00–14:30 &

19:00–1:00, reserve for dinner, outdoor seating in summer, Via Val di Lamona 7 red, half a block behind Mercato Nuovo, tel. 055-264-148).

Trattoria Nella serves good, typical Tuscan cuisine at affordable prices. Arrive early or be disappointed—it's understandably popular (€20 meals, Mon–Sat 12:00–14:30 & 19:00–22:00, closed Sun, 3 blocks northwest of Ponte Vecchio, Via delle Terme 19 red, tel. 055-218-925).

Oltrarno, South of the River

Near Ponte Vecchio

Ristorante Bibo serves *cucina tipica Fiorentina* with a pink-tablecloth-and-black-bowtie dressiness and leafy, candlelit outdoor seating (good €15 3-course meal, Wed–Mon 12:00–14:30 & 19:00–22:30, reserve for outdoor seating, Piazza Santa Felicita 6 red, tel. 055-239-8554, enthusiastic Tonino SE).

Golden View Open Bar is a lively, trendy place good for a salad, pizza, or pasta with a view of Ponte Vecchio and the Arno River. Reservations for window tables are recommended (reasonable prices, daily 11:30–24:00, impressive wine bar, Internet access, 50 yards upstream from Ponte Vecchio at Via dei Bardi 58, tel. 055-214-502). They have live jazz Mondays and Wednesdays at 21:00.

Via Santo Spirito and Borgo San Jacopo

Several good and colorful restaurants line this multinamed street a block off the river in Oltrarno. I'd survey the scene before making a choice.

Trattoria Cammillo was formerly run by Cammillo, who is now slurping spaghetti in heaven. But his granddaughter Chiara carries on the tradition, mixing traditional Tuscan and creative, modern cuisine. With a charcoal grill and a team of white-aproned waiters cranking out wonderful food in a fun, dressy-but-down-to-earth ambience, this place is a hit (full dinners about €36 plus wine, Thu–Tue 12:00–14:30 & 19:30–22:30, closed Wed, reservations smart, Borgo San Jacopo 57 red, tel. 055-212-427).

Trattoria Angiolino serves good, old-fashioned local cuisine. Sit in the main hall rather than the stuffy side rooms (€20 for dinner plus wine, Tue–Sun 12:00–14:30 & 19:30–22:30, closed Mon, Via di Santo Spirito 36 red, tel. 055-239-8976).

Trattoria Sabatino, farthest away and least touristy, is spacious and disturbingly cheap, with family character, red-checkered tablecloths, and a simple menu. A wonderful place to watch locals munch, it's just outside the Porta San Frediano (medieval gate), a 15-minute walk from Ponte Vecchio (Mon–Fri 12:00–14:30 & 19:20–22:00, closed Sat–Sun, Via Pisana 2 red, tel. 055-225-955, NSE).

Restaurants in Oltrarno

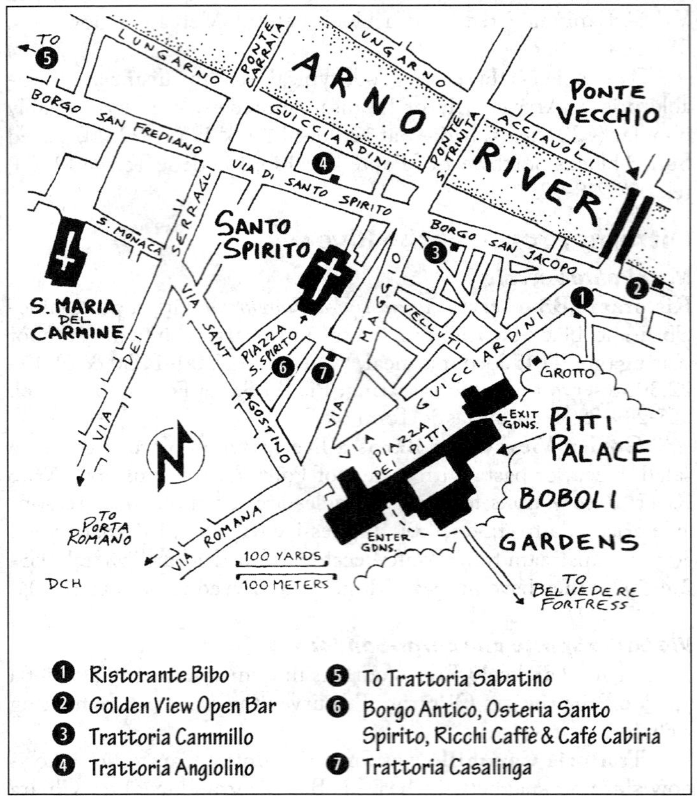

1 Ristorante Bibo
2 Golden View Open Bar
3 Trattoria Cammillo
4 Trattoria Angiolino
5 To Trattoria Sabatino
6 Borgo Antico, Osteria Santo Spirito, Ricchi Caffè & Café Cabiria
7 Trattoria Casalinga

Piazza Santo Spirito

This classic Florentine square (lately a hangout for drug pushers, therefore a bit seedy-feeling and plagued by bag-snatchers on mopeds) has several popular little restaurants and bars that are open nightly. They offer good local cuisine, moderate prices, and impersonal service, with a choice of indoor or romantic on-the-square seating (reservations smart): lively **Borgo Antico** (Piazza Santo Spirito 6 red, tel. 055-210-437) and the quieter yet more bohemian **Osteria Santo Spirito** (Piazza Santo Spirito 16 red, tel. 055-238-2383).

Ricchi Caffè, next to Borgo Antico, has fine gelato and shaded outdoor tables. After noting the plain facade of the Brunelleschi church facing the square, step inside the café and pick your favorite of the many ways it might be finished. **Café Cabiria,** on the other side of Borgo Antico, is a trendy local hangout with good light meals and a cozy Florentine funky room in back. If you're a scene crasher, try it here.

Trattoria Casalinga, an inexpensive standby, comes with aproned women bustling around the kitchen. You'll find more tourists than locals, but all seem to leave full and happy, with euros to spare for gelato (Mon–Sat 12:00–14:30 & 19:00–21:45, after 20:00 reserve or wait, closed Sun and all of Aug, just off Piazza Santo Spirito, near the church at Via dei Michelozzi 9 red, tel. 055-218-624).

TRANSPORTATION CONNECTIONS

From Florence by Train to: Pisa (2/hr, 1.25 hrs), **Lucca** (9/day, 1.5 hrs), **Siena** (9/day, 1.75 hrs, more with transfer in Empoli; bus is better), **La Spezia** (for the Cinque Terre, 2/day direct, 2 hrs, or change in Pisa), **Milan** (12/day, 3–5 hrs), **Venice** (7/day, 3 hrs), **Assisi** (3/day, 2 hrs, more frequent with transfers, direction: Foligno), **Orvieto** (6/day, 2 hrs), **Rome** (hrly, 2.5 hrs), **Naples** (10/day, 4 hrs), **Brindisi** (3/day, 11 hrs with change in Bologna), **Frankfurt** (3/day, 12 hrs), **Paris** (1/day, 12 hrs overnight), **Vienna** (4/day, 9–10 hrs).

Buses: The SITA bus station, a block west of the Florence train station, is user-friendly. Schedules are posted everywhere, with TV monitors indicating imminent departures. Bus service drops dramatically on Sunday. You'll find buses to: **San Gimignano** (€6, hrly, 1.75 hrs), **Siena** (€6.50, hrly, 75-min *corse rapide* fast buses are faster than the train, avoid the 2.5-hr *diretta* slow buses), and the **airport** (€4, hrly, 15 min). Bus info: tel. 800-373760 or 055-214-721 from 9:30–12:30; some schedules are in the *Florence Concierge Information* magazine.

Taxi to Siena: For around €100, you can arrange a ride directly from your Florence hotel to your Siena hotel. For a small group or for people with more money than time, this can be a good value.

Airports

The **Amerigo Vespucci Airport** (www.aeroporto.firenze.it), several miles northwest of Florence, has a TI, cash machines, car-rental agencies, and easy connections by airport shuttle bus with Florence's bus station, a block west of the train station (€4, 2/hr, 30 min, from Florence runs 5:30–23:00, from airport 6:00–23:30). Airport info: 055-306-1300, flight info: 055-306-1700 (domestic), 055-306-1702 (international). Allow about €16–20 for a taxi.

Many international flights land at Pisa's **Galileo Galilei Airport** (also has TI and car-rental agencies, www.pisa-airport.com), an hour from Florence by train (runs hourly; if you're leaving Florence for this airport, catch the train at Florence's train station at platform #5). Flight info: 050-849-300.

SIENA

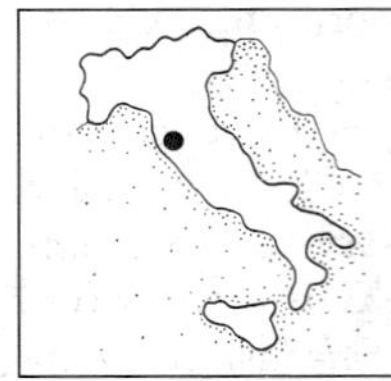

Siena was medieval Florence's archrival. And while Florence ultimately won the battle, Siena still competes for the tourists. Sure, Florence has the most heavyweight sights. But Siena seems to be every Italy connoisseur's pet town. In my office, whenever Siena is mentioned, someone moans, "Siena? I looove Siena!"

Seven hundred years ago (from about 1260–1348), Siena was a major banking and trade center, and a military power in a class with Florence, Venice, and Genoa. With a population of 60,000, it was even bigger than Paris. Situated on the north–south road to Rome (the Via Francigena), Siena traded with all Europe. Then in 1348, the Black Plague that swept through Europe hit Siena and cut the population by a third. Siena never recovered. In the 1550s, her bitter rival, Florence, really "salted" her, forever making Siena a nonthreatening backwater. Siena's loss became our sightseeing gain, as its political and economic irrelevance pickled it purely medieval. Today, Siena's population is still 60,000, compared to Florence's 420,000.

Siena's thriving historic center, with red-brick lanes cascading every which way, offers Italy's best medieval city experience. Most people do Siena, just 30 miles south of Florence, as a day trip, but it's best experienced at twilight. While Florence has the blockbuster museums, Siena has an easy-to-enjoy soul: Courtyards sport flower-decked wells, alleys dead-end at rooftop views, and the sky is a rich blue dome.

For those who dream of a Fiat-free Italy, pedestrians rule in the old center of Siena. Sit at a café on the red-brick main square. Wander narrow streets lined with colorful flags and iron rings to tether horses. Take time to savor the first European city to eliminate automobile traffic from its main square (1966) and then, just to be silly, wonder what would happen if they did it in your city.

Planning Your Time

On a quick trip, consider spending three nights in Siena (with a whole-day side-trip into Florence and a day to relax and enjoy Siena). Whatever you do, enjoy a sleepy medieval evening in Siena. After an evening in Siena, you can see its major sights in half a day.

ORIENTATION

Siena lounges atop a hill, stretching its three legs out from Il Campo. This main square, the historic meeting point of Siena's neighborhoods, is for pedestrians only. And most of those pedestrians are students from the local university.

Everything I mention is within a 15-minute stroll from the square. Navigate by three major landmarks (Campo, Duomo, and church of San Domenico), following the excellent system of street-corner signs. The typical visitor sticks to the San Domenico–Il Campo axis. Make a point to stray from the current of this main artery.

Siena itself is one big sight. Its individual sights come in two little clusters: the square (Civic Museum and City Tower) and the cathedral (Baptistery and Duomo Museum with its surprise viewpoint). Check these sights off, and you're free to wander.

Tourist Information

This is an exasperating place. TI employees claim that transit officials and museum officials don't want them to know anything about the town's sights or buses. They do offer a decent free map (#56 on Il Campo, daily 9:00–19:00, tel. 0577-280-551, www.terresiena.it in Italian only, info@terresiena.it). The helpful booklet *Terre di Siena* lists current hours and prices for sights in Siena and outlying towns. The little TI at San Domenico, while primarily for hotel promotion, sells a €.50 Siena map and organizes daily walking tours of the old town and San Gimignano (across street from church).

Arrival in Siena

By Train: The small train station, located on the edge of town, has a bar and bus office (no baggage check or lockers). To get from the station to the city center, hike about 20 minutes uphill or catch a city bus or taxi. The **taxi stand** is to your far right as you exit the station (about €8 to Il Campo, taxi tel. 0577-49222—keep ringing and someone should answer eventually, or try 0577-289-350, though it's often busy).

By City Bus: Before leaving the train station, buy a €1 ticket from the Bus Ticket Office in the station lobby (daily 6:15–19:30, ask for a city map—it's free and just a bus route map, but it helps get you started), or the newsstand or from the blue machine in the lobby (touch screen for English and select "urban" for type of ticket). Then cross the parking lot and the street to reach the sheltered bus stop. The station fronts a wide roundabout. Buses only drop off passengers at the station—they pick up travelers on the far side (at a covered stop 100 yards across from the station). Buses run about every 15 minutes (fewer on Sun and after 21:00).

Every orange bus goes from here to the center. (Caution: Blue ones go to other cities.) Confirm by asking "*Centro*?" (CHEHN-troh), punch ticket in machine on bus to validate it, and ride to the last stop. (Buses go to Piazza Gramsci/Lizza, Piazza Sale, or Via Stufa Secca—all within several blocks of each other.)

When leaving Siena, you can catch the city bus to the train station from Piazza Gramsci, Piazza del Sale, or Via Stufa Secca (bus stops are marked with a posted schedule and sometimes with yellow lines painted on the pavement, showing a bus-sized rectangle and the word "bus"). Confirm with the driver that the bus is going to the *stazione* (stat-zee-OH-nay). Remember to purchase your ticket in advance from a *tabacchi* shop.

By Intercity Bus: Some buses arrive in Siena at the train station (see "By Train," above), others at Piazza Gramsci (a few blocks from city center), and some stop at both. The main bus companies are Sena and the confusingly named Tra-in (TRAAH-in). You can store baggage underneath Piazza Gramsci in Sotopassaggio la Lizza (€3.50, daily 7:00–19:45, not overnight).

By Car: Drivers coming from the autostrada take the Siena Ovest exit and follow signs for *Centro,* then *Stadio* (stadium, soccer ball). The soccer-ball signs take you to the stadium lot (Parcheggio Stadio, €1.50/hr, €12.50/day) at the huge, bare-brick San Domenico Church. The Fortezza lot nearby charges the same amount, or park in the lot under the train station. Technically, hotel customers are allowed to drop bags at their hotel, but I wouldn't bother. You can park free in the lot below the Albergo Lea, in white-striped spots behind Hotel Villa Liberty, behind the Fortezza, and overnight in most city lots 20:00–8:00. (The signs showing a street cleaner and a day of the week indicate which day the street is cleaned; there's a €100 tow-fee incentive to learn the days of the week in Italian.)

Helpful Hints

Local Guide: Roberto Bechi, a hardworking Sienese guide, specializes in off-the-beaten-path tours of the surrounding countryside (mini-bus, up to six passengers, convenient pick-up at hotel). Married to an American (Patti) and having run restaurants in Siena and the United States, Roberto communicates well with Americans. His passions are Sienese culture, Tuscan history, and local cuisine. Book well in advance (full-day tours from €65–95 per person, half-day tours from €30–60 per person, mobile 328-727-3186 or 328-425-5648, www.toursbyroberto.com, tourrob @tin.it). Roberto has a line on other good city guides.

Internet Access: In this university town, there are lots of places to get plugged in. **Internet Point** is just off Piazza Matteotti, on Via Paradiso (across street from McDonald's) and **Internet Train** is near Il Campo, at Via di Città 121 (tel. 0577-226-366).

Launderettes: Two modern, self-service places are Lavarapido Wash and Dry (daily 8:00–22:00; Via di Pantaneto 38, near Logge del Papa) and Onda Blu (daily 8:00–21:00; Via del Casato di Sotto 17, 50 yards from Il Campo).

Travel Agency: Palio Viaggi on Piazza Gramsci sells train and plane tickets but no bus tickets (Mon–Fri 9:00–13:00 & 15:00–18:00, closed Sat–Sun, La Lizza 12, tel. 0577-280-828, info@palioviaggi.it).

Wednesday Morning Market: The weekly market, consisting mainly of clothes, knickknacks, and food, sprawls between the Fortress and Piazza Gramsci along Viale Cesare Maccabi and the adjacent Viale XXV Aprile.

Combo-Tickets: A deranged person cobbled together a pile of illogically paired combo-tickets to give some travelers a small savings. Nothing covers everything and most are conflicting. You can buy a combo-ticket at the City Tower that also covers the Civic Museum (€10, saves €3). A different combo-ticket gets you into the Duomo Museum and Baptistery (€7.50, saves €2), but doesn't cover the actual Duomo (cathedral). Yet another is for the Civic Museum and Santa Maria della Scala Museum (€10, saves €2.50). There's also a big €16 combo-ticket that doesn't quite cover everything.

SIGHTS

Siena's Main Square

▲▲▲Il Campo—This sight is the heart—geographically and metaphorically—of Siena. Seen from the top of the City Tower, this "heart" appears to pump people through the busy city's veins. The square fans out from the City Hall (Palazzo Pubblico) to create an amphitheater, where the citizens are the stars.

Il Campo is the historic junction of Siena's various competing districts, or *contrade*. The brick surface is divided into nine sections, representing the council of nine merchants and city bigwigs who ruled medieval Siena. The square and its buildings are the color of the soil upon which they stand...a color known to artists and Crayola-users as "Burnt Sienna."

Siena at a Glance

▲▲▲**Il Campo** Best square in Italy. **Hours:** Always open.

▲▲▲**Duomo** Art-packed cathedral with mosaic floors and statues by Michelangelo and Bernini. **Hours:** Mid-March–Oct Mon–Sat 7:30–19:30, Sun 10:15–14:00 worship only, Nov–mid-March Mon–Sat 7:30–17:00, Sun 14:30–17:30.

▲▲**Duomo Museum** Displays cathedral art (Duccio's *Maestà*) and offers sweeping Tuscan view. **Hours:** Daily mid-March–Sept 9:00–19:30, Oct 9:00–18:00, Nov–mid-March 9:00–13:30.

▲**Baptistery** Cave-like building has baptismal font decorated by Ghiberti and Donatello. **Hours:** Daily mid-March–Sept 9:00–19:30, Oct 9:00–18:00, Nov–mid-March 10:00–13:00 & 14:00–17:00.

▲**Civic Museum** City museum in City Hall with Sienese frescoes *Effects of Good and Bad Government*. **Hours:** Daily 10:00–19:00, Nov–Feb 10:00–16:00. May be open summer evenings.

▲**City Tower** 330-foot tower climb. **Hours:** Same as Civic Museum.

▲**Pinacoteca** Fine Sienese paintings. **Hours:** Sun–Mon 8:30–13:15, Tue–Sat 8:15–19:15.

▲**Santa Maria della Scala** Museum with art, medieval hospital displays, and exhibitions. **Hours:** Daily 10:30–18:30, off-season 10:30–16:30.

Church of San Domenico Huge brick church with St. Catherine's head and finger. **Hours:** Daily March–Oct 7:00–13:00 & 14:30–18:30, Nov–Feb 9:00–13:00 & 15:00–18:00.

Sanctuary of Saint Catherine Home of St. Catherine. **Hours:** Daily 9:00–12:30 & 15:00–18:30.

The square is dominated by **City Hall** and its 330-foot tower. In medieval Siena, this secular building was the center of the city, and the whole focus of the Campo flows down to it.

The City Hall's 330-foot-tall **Torre del Mangia**—Italy's tallest secular tower—was named after a hedonistic watchman who consumed his earnings like a glutton consumes food. His chewed-up statue is in the courtyard, to the left as you enter.

Siena

(Tower admission details are below.)

The chapel located at the base of the tower was built in 1348 as thanks to God for ending the Black Plague (after it killed more than a third of the population). It should also be used to thank God that the tower—just plunked onto the building with no extra foundation—still stands. These days, the chapel is only used to bless the Palio contestants and the City Tower's bell only rings for the race.

The ***Fountain of Joy*** *(Fonte di Gaia)* by Jacopo della Quercia marks the square's high point. Find the snake-handler woman, the two naked guys about to be tossed in, and the pigeons politely waiting their turn to gingerly tightrope down slippery spouts to slurp a drink from wolves' snouts. The relief panel on the left (as you face the fountain) shows God creating Adam by helping him to his feet. It's said that this reclining Adam influenced Michelangelo when he painted his Sistine Ceiling. This fountain is a copy. You can see parts of the original fountain in an interesting exhibit at Siena's Santa Maria della Scala Museum, listed on page 1075.

To say Siena and Florence have always been competitive is an understatement. In medieval times, a statue of Venus stood on Il Campo. After the plague hit Siena, the monks blamed the pagan statue. The people cut it to pieces and buried it along the walls of Florence.

The "heart" of Siena beats fastest at Palio time. Picture the Campo when the famous horse races are held on July 2 and August 16 (see page 1071). Ten snorting horses and their nervous riders line up near the "Antica Siena" shop (right side of square) to await the starting signal. Then, they race like crazy three times around the perimeter (the gray pavement), which is covered with dirt. Mattresses pad the sharpest turns. Spectators waving the banners of their neighborhoods cram (for free) into the center of the square or watch from temporary bleachers, or, if they have the money, from the balconies. The winner crosses the line, and 1/17th of Siena goes berserk for the next 365 days.

▲Civic Museum (Museo Civico)—At the base of the City Tower is Siena's City Hall (Palazzo Pubblico), the spot where secular government got its start in early Renaissance Europe. There, you'll find city government still at work, along with a sampling of local art.

In the following order, you'll see: the Sala Risorgimento, with dramatic scenes of Victor Emmanuel's unification of Italy (surrounded by statues that don't seem to care); the chapel, with impressive inlaid wood chairs in the choir; and the Sala del Mappamondo, with Siena's first fresco, Simone Martini's *Maestà* (*Enthroned Virgin*—a groundbreaking, down-to-earth Madonna), facing the faded *Guidoriccio da Folignano* (a mercenary providing a more concrete form of protection).

Next is the Sala della Pace—where the city's fat cats met. Looking down on the oligarchy during their meetings were two interesting frescoes, *Effects of Good and Bad Government*. Notice the whistle-while-you-work happiness of the utopian community ruled by the utopian government (in the better-preserved fresco) and the fate of a community ruled by politicians with more typical values (in a terrible state of repair). The message: Without justice, there can be no prosperity.

Take a moment to savor one of those to-sigh-for rural panoramas out the window of the Sala della Pace. The view out the window is essentially the same as that from the top of the big stairs (€7, €10 combo-ticket includes City Tower—sold only at tower,

Siena's Palio

In the Palio, the feisty spirit of Siena's 17 *contrade* (neighborhoods) lives on. These neighborhoods celebrate, worship, and compete together. Each even has its own historical museum. *Contrada* pride is evident any time of year in the colorful neighborhood banners and parades. (If you hear distant drumming, run to it for some medieval action, often featuring flag-throwers.) But *contrada* passion is most visible twice a year—on July 2 and August 16—when they have their world-famous horse race, the Palio di Siena.

Ten of the 17 neighborhoods compete (chosen by rotation and lot), hurling themselves with medieval abandon into several days of trial races and traditional revelry. Jockeys are considered hired guns...paid mercenaries. But on the big day, the horses are taken into their *contrada*'s church to be blessed. ("Go and win," says the priest.) It's considered a sign of luck if a horse leaves droppings in the church.

On the evening of the big day, Il Campo is stuffed to the brim with locals and tourists, as the horses charge wildly around the square in this literally no-holds-barred race. A horse can win even if its rider has fallen off. Of course, the winning neighborhood is the scene of grand celebrations afterward. Winners receive a *palio* (banner), typically painted by a local artist and always featuring the Virgin Mary. But the true prize is simply proving your *contrada* is numero uno. All over town, sketches and posters depict the Palio. This is not some folkloristic event. It's a real medieval moment. If you're packed onto the square with 15,000 people who each really want to win, you won't see much, but you'll feel it. While the actual Palio packs the city, you could side-trip in from Florence to see horse-race trials each of the three days before the big day (usually at 9:00 and around 19:30). For more information, visit www.ilpalio.org.

▲***Palio al Cinema***—This 20-minute film, *Siena, the Palio, and its History,* helps recreate the craziness. See it at the Cinema Moderno in Piazza Tolomei, two blocks from Il Campo (€5.25; runs May–Oct only, Mon–Sat 9:30–17:30, closed Sun, English showings generally hrly at :30 past the hour—schedule posted on door, air-con, tel. 0577-289-201). Call or drop by to confirm when the next English showing is scheduled—there are usually nine a day.

March–Oct daily 10:00–19:00, Nov–Feb daily 10:00–16:00, last entry 45 min before closing, audioguide-€3.75/person and €5.25/2, tel. 0577-292-111).

▲City Tower (Torre del Mangia)—Siena gathers around its City Hall, not its church. It was a proud republic and this tall tower is the exclamation point of its "declaration of independence." Its 300 steps get pretty skinny at the top, but the reward is one of Italy's best views (€6, €10 combo-ticket with Civic Museum only sold here, March–Oct daily 10:00–19:00, Nov–Feb daily 10:00–16:00, closed in rain, sometimes long lines, avoid midday crowd, limit of 30 tourists at a time, often sold out).

▲Pinacoteca—Siena was a power in Gothic art. But the average tourist, wrapped up in a love affair with the Renaissance, hardly notices. This museum takes you on a walk through Siena's art, chronologically from the 12th through the 15th centuries. For the casual sightseer, the Sienese art in the Civic and Duomo Museums is adequate. But art fans enjoy this opportunity to trace the evolution of Siena's delicate and elegant works, from stiff, gold-backed icon-like Madonnas to curvy, graceful Madonnas to Italian Renaissance. Concentrate on pieces by Duccio (artist of the *Maestà* in the Duomo Museum), Simone Martini (who did the *Maestà* in the Civic Museum), the brothers Ambrogio and Pietro Lorenzetti (Ambrogio did the *Effects of Good and Bad Government* in the Civic Museum), Pinturicchio (who did the Piccolomini Library in the Duomo), and Domenico Beccafumi (who inlaid pavement in the Duomo). From Il Campo, walk out Via di Città and go left on Via San Pietro (€4, Sun–Mon 8:30–13:15, Tue–Sat 8:15–19:15, audioguide-€4, tel. 0577-281-161).

Siena's Cathedral Area

▲▲▲Duomo—If the Campo is the heart of Siena, the Duomo (or cathedral) is its soul. The white and dark-green striped church, sitting on an artificial platform atop Siena's highest point, is visible for miles around. The current structure dates from 1215, with the major decoration done during Siena's heyday from 1250–1350. This ornate but surprisingly secular shrine to the Virgin Mary is stacked with colorful art inside and out, from the inlaid-marble floors to the stained glass windows. Along with sculptures by Bernini and Michelangelo, the church features the Piccolomini Library. The Library holds a series of captivating Pinturicchio frescoes telling the story of Siena's consummate Renaissance man, who later became Pope Pius II.

Cost and Hours: €3, includes Cathedral and Piccolomini Library, mid-March–Oct Mon–Sat 7:30–19:30, Sun 10:15–14:00 worship only; Nov–mid-March Mon–Sat 7:30–17:00, Sun 14:30–17:30, tel. 0577-283-048. Modest dress is required to enter.

Audioguides: Audioguide for church-€3.50, add the library-€4, add the Duomo Museum-€5.50. Church and museum only-€4.50. Two headphones are available at a price break.

Self-Guided Tour: In the **nave**, the heads of 172 popes peer down from above, looking over the fine inlaid art on the floor. With a forest of striped columns, a coffered dome, a large stained-glass window at the far end, and a museum's worth of early Renaissance art, this is one busy interior. Looking closer at the popes, you see the same four faces repeated over and over.

For almost two centuries (1373–1547), 40 artists paved the marble floor with scenes from the Old Testament, allegories, and intricate patterns. The earliest are simple black-and-white, with engraved details, but the later ones use inlay technique with many colored marbles. The series starts with historical allegories near the entrance. The larger, more elaborate scenes surrounding the altar are mostly stories from the Old Testament. Many of the floor panels may be protected with sheet flooring when you visit.

Grab a seat under the **dome**. It sits on a 12-sided base but its "coffered" ceiling is actually a painted illusion. Get oriented to the vast church's array of sights by thinking of the floor as a big clock. You're the middle, and the altar is high noon: You'll find the *Slaughter of the Innocents* pavement panel roped off on the floor at 10:00, Pisano's pulpit between two pillars at 11:00, Duccio's round stained glass window at high noon, Bernini's chapel at 3:00, the Piccolomini Altar with a Michelangelo statue (next to doorway leading to a shop, snacks, and WC) at 7:00, the Piccolomini Library at 8:00, and a Donatello statue at 9:00.

Look for the ***Slaughter of the Innocents*** inlaid pavement panel. Herod (left), standing amid Renaissance arches, orders the massacre of all babies to prevent the coming of the promised Messiah. It's a chaotic scene of angry soldiers, grieving mothers, and dead babies, reminding locals that a republic ruled by a tyrant will experience misery.

Nicola Pisano's octagonal Carrara marble **pulpit** (1268) rests on the backs of lions—symbols of Christianity triumphant. Like the lions, the Church eats its catch (devouring paganism) and nurses its cubs. The seven relief panels tell the life of Christ in rich detail. (Buy light from a coin-op machine.)

To understand why Bernini is considered the greatest Baroque sculptor, step into his sumptuous chapel, ***Cappella della Madonna del Voto***. This last work in the cathedral, from 1659, is enough to make even a Lutheran light a candle. Move up to the altar and look back at the two Bernini statues: Mary Magdalene in a state of spiritual ecstasy and St. Jerome playing the crucifix like a violinist lost in beautiful music.

Over the chapel's altar is the *Madonna del Voto*, a Madonna and Child painted by Duccio and adorned with a real crown of gold and jewels. Tilting her head, she looks out sympathetically. This is the Mary that the Palio is dedicated to, special in the hearts of the Sienese. The faithful's prayers to Mary are accompanied by offerings, found outside the chapel, hanging on the wall to the left, as you exit.

The **Piccolomini Altar** (left wall, marble altarpiece decorated with statues), designed for the tomb of the Sienese-born Pope Pius III, is most interesting for Michelangelo's statue of Paul (lower right, who is clearly more interesting than the bland, bored popes above him). Paul has the look of Michelangelo's *Moses,* the broken-nosed self-portrait of the sculptor himself, and the dangling hand of his *David.* It was the chance to sculpt *David* in Florence that enticed Michelangelo to abandon the Siena project.

The brilliantly-frescoed **Piccolomini Library** captures the exuberant, optimistic spirit of the 1400s, when humanism and the Renaissance were born. The painter Pinturicchio (c. 1454–1513) was hired to celebrate the life of one of Siena's hometown boys. Start from the window and work clockwise, following 10 scenes in the life of the man many call "the first humanist," Aeneas Piccolomini (1405–1464). The library also contains intricately decorated, illuminated music scores, and a statue (a Roman copy of a Greek original) of the Three Graces.

Donatello's rugged ***St. John the Baptist*** (1457), wearing his famous rags, stands in a chapel to the right of the library.

Exit the Duomo, and make a U-turn to the left, walking alongside the church to Piazza Jacopo della Quercia. In a grand plan that fizzled, the nave of the Duomo was supposed to be where the piazza is today. When rival republic Florence began its grand cathedral, proud Siena decided to build the biggest church in all Christendom. The existing cathedral would be used as a transept. Some of the nave's green-and-white-striped columns were built, but are now filled in with a brick wall. The wall, connecting the Duomo with the museum of the cathedral, was as far as Siena got before a plague killed the city's ability to finish the project. Round white stones in the pavement mark the place where columns would have stood. Look through the unfinished entrance facade, seeing blue sky where the stained glass windows might have been, and ponder the struggles, triumphs, and failures of the human spirit... or humanism.

▲▲Duomo Museum (Museo dell' Opera e Panorama)—Siena's most enjoyable museum, on the Campo side of the church (look for the yellow signs), was built to house the cathedral's art. The ground floor is filled with the cathedral's original Gothic sculpture by Giovanni Pisano (who spent 10 years in the late 1200s carving and orchestrating the decoration of the cathedral) and a fine

Donatello *Madonna and Child.* A slender, tender Mary gazes down at her chubby-cheeked baby, and her sad eyes say she knows the eventual fate of her son.

Upstairs to the left awaits a private audience with Duccio's *Maestà* (*Enthroned Virgin*, 1311). Pull up a chair and study one of the great pieces of medieval art. The flip side of the *Maestà* (displayed on the opposite wall), with 26 panels—the medieval equivalent of pages—shows scenes from the Passion of Christ.

Climb onto the "Panorama del Facciatone." For a surprise view of Siena, leave the landing on the top floor and walk to the end of the room on the right—the entrance is through the small doorway. Climb down the steps and then up the claustrophobic spiral staircase to the viewpoint. Look back over the Duomo and consider this: If the grandiose plan for the church had been completed, you'd be looking straight down the nave.

Cost and Hours: €5.50, €7.50 combo-ticket with Baptistery, worthwhile 40-minute audioguide-€3, daily mid-March–Sept 9:00–19:30, Oct 9:00–18:00, Nov–mid-March 9:00–13:30, tel. 0577-283-048.

▲Baptistery—Siena is so hilly that there wasn't enough flat ground on which to build a big church. What to do? Build a big church and prop up the overhanging edge with the Baptistery. This dark and quietly tucked-away cave of art is worth a look (and €2.50) for its cool tranquility and the bronze panels and angels—by Ghiberti, Donatello, and others—adorning the pedestal of the baptismal font (daily mid-March–Sept 9:00–19:30, Oct 9:00–18:00, Nov–mid-March 10:00–13:00 & 14:00–17:00). Note: The "crypt" of the cathedral (entrance above the Baptistery) is important archeologically, but of little interest to the average tourist. I'd skip it.

▲Santa Maria della Scala Museum—This museum (opposite the Duomo entrance) was used as a hospital as recently as the 1980s. Now it displays a lavishly frescoed hall, a worthwhile exhibit on Quercia's *Fountain of Joy* (downstairs), and a so-so archaeological museum (subterranean, in labyrinthine tunnels). The entire museum is a maze, with various exhibitions and paintings plugged in to fill the gaps.

The frescoes in the **Pellegrinaio Hall** show medieval Siena's innovative health care and social welfare system in action (c. 1442, wonderfully described in English). The hospital was functioning as early as the 11th century, nursing the sick and caring for abandoned children (see frescoes). The good work paid off, as bequests and donations poured in, creating the wealth that's evident in the chapels elsewhere on this floor. The Old Sacristy was built to house precious relics, including a "Holy Nail" thought to be from Jesus' cross.

Downstairs, the engaging exhibit on Jacopo della Quercia's early-15th-century ***Fountain of Joy*** doesn't need much English description, fortunately, because there isn't much. In the 19th century, the *Fountain of Joy* in Il Campo was deteriorating. It was dismantled and plaster casts were made of the originals. The Fountain of Joy that stands in Il Campo today is a replica. In this exhibit, you'll see the plaster casts of the original, eroded panels paired with their restored twins, along with the statues that originally stood on the edges of the fountain. In general, the pieces at the beginning and end of the exhibit are original. If there's a piece in a dim room near the exit of the exhibit, it's likely an original chunk awaiting cleaning.

The **Archaeological Museum,** way downstairs, consists mainly of pottery fragments in cases lining tunnel after tunnel. It's like being lost in a wine cellar without the wine. Unless there's a special exhibit, it's not worth the trip.

Cost and Hours: €6, €10 combo-ticket with Civic Museum, daily 10:30–18:30, off-season 10:30–16:30. The chapel just inside the door to your left is free (English description inside chapel entrance).

Siena's San Domenico Area

Church of San Domenico—This huge brick church is worth a quick look. The bland interior (except for the colorful flags of the city's 17 *contrade* or neighborhoods) fits the austere philosophy of the Dominicans. Walk up the steps in the rear for paintings from the life of Saint Catherine, patron saint of Siena. Halfway up the church on the right, find a metal bust of Saint Catherine and a small case containing her finger (sometimes loaned out to other churches). In the chapel (5 yards to the left), surrounded with candles, you'll see Catherine's actual head atop the altar (free, daily March–Oct 7:00–13:00 & 14:30–18:30, Nov–Feb 9:00–13:00 & 15:00–18:00; WC for €0.50 at far end of parking lot—facing church entrance, it's to your right).

Sanctuary of Saint Catherine—Step into Catherine's cool and peaceful home. Siena remembers its favorite hometown gal, a simple, unschooled, but mystically devout soul who, in the mid-1300s, helped convince the pope to return from France to Rome. This schism split the continent in the 14th century, but because of her intervention, Catherine is honored today as Europe's patron saint. Pilgrims have come to her home since 1464. Since then, architects and artists have greatly embellished what was probably a humble home (her family worked as wool-dyers). Enter through the courtyard and walk to the far end. The chapel on your right contains the wooden crucifix upon which Catherine was meditating when she received the stigmata. The chapel on your left used to be the kitchen. Go down the stairs to the left of the chapel/kitchen to reach the saint's room. Catherine's bare cell is behind see-through doors. Much of the art throughout the sanctuary depicts scenes from her life (free, daily 9:00–12:30 & 15:00–18:30, Via Tiratoio). It's a few downhill blocks toward the center from San Domenico (follow signs to Santuario di Santa Caterina).

SHOPPING AND NIGHTLIFE

Shopping

Siena has long been an important trade crossroads. Its two main streets—Via Banci di Sopra and Via Banci di Sotto—are literally named the upper street of banks and the lower street of banks. Via Banchi di Sopra, Siena's top *passeggiata* route, is a can-can of fancy shops today. The big local department store is Upim (Mon–Sat 9:30–19:50, closed Sun, Piazza Matteotti). The Feltrinelli bookstore closest to the Campo sells books and magazines in English (daily 9:00–19:30, Banchi di Sopra 52). The large, colorful scarves/flags, each depicting the symbol of one of Siena's 17 different neighborhoods (such as the wolf, the turtle, and the snail), are easy-to-pack souvenirs, fun for decorating your home (€7 apiece for large size, sold at souvenir stands).

Nightlife

Join the evening *passeggiata* (peak strolling time is 19:00) along Via Banchi di Sopra with gelato in hand.

The **Enoteca Italiana** is a good wine bar in a cellar in the Fortezza/Fortress (sample glasses in 3 different price ranges: €2, €3, €5.50; Mon 12:00–20:00, Tue–Sat 12:00–24:00, closed Sun, bottles and snacks available; cross bridge and enter fortress, go left down ramp, don't confuse this place with Enoteca Toscana—same location but not as nice; tel. 0577-288-497).

Sightseeing geeks take note: Museums are often open late on summer Fridays and Saturdays (check with the TI for current hours).

SLEEPING

Finding a room is tough during Easter or the Palio in early July and mid-August. Call ahead any time of year, as all the guidebooks list Siena's few budget places. While day-tripping tour groups turn the town into a Gothic amusement park in midsummer, Siena is basically yours in the evenings and off-season.

Most of the listed hotels lie between Il Campo and the Church of San Domenico. Part of Siena's charm is its lively, festive character—this means that all hotels can be plagued with noise, even (and sometimes especially) the hotels in the pedestrian-only zone. If tranquility is important for your sanity, ask for a room that's off

Sleep Code

(€1 = about $1.20, country code: 39)
S = Single, **D** = Double/Twin, **T** = Triple, **Q** = Quad,**b** = bathroom, **s** = shower only, **SE** = Speaks English, **NSE** = No English. Breakfast is generally not included. Have breakfast on Il Campo or in a nearby bar. Credit cards are accepted unless otherwise noted.

To help you sort easily through these listings, I've divided the rooms into three categories based on the price for a standard double room with bath:

$$$ **Higher Priced**—Most rooms €120 or more.
$$ **Moderately Priced**—Most rooms between €90–120.
$ **Lower Priced**—Most rooms €90 or less.

the street or consider staying at the recommended places outside the center.

Near Il Campo

Each of these listings is forgettable but inexpensive, and just a horse wreck away from one of Italy's most wonderful civic spaces.

$ Albergo Tre Donzelle is a fine budget value with 28 plain, institutional rooms. Don't hang out here...think of Il Campo, a block away, as your terrace (S-€33, D-€46, Db-€60, T-€65, Tb-€82, no breakfast; with your back to the City Tower, leave Il Campo to the right at 2:00; Via Donzelle 5, tel. 0577-280-358, fax 0577-223-933, Signora Valentina SE).

$ Piccolo Hotel Etruria, with 19 decent rooms but not much soul, is a bit overpriced but well-located and sleepable (S-€43, Sb-€48, Db-€78, Tb-€105, Qb-€127, breakfast-€5, curfew at 00:30, next to Albergo Tre Donzelle at Via Donzelle 1-3, tel. 0577-288-088, fax 0577-288-461, info@hoteletruria.com, Fattorini family SE).

$ Locanda Garibaldi is a modest, very Sienese restaurant/*albergo*. Gentle Marcello wears two hats, running a busy restaurant downstairs and renting seven pleasant rooms up a funky, artsy staircase (Db-€75, Tb-€95, family deals, cash only, takes reservations only a week in advance, half a block downhill off the square at Via Giovanni Dupre 18, tel. 0577-284-204, NSE).

$ Hotel Cannon d'Oro, a few blocks up Via Banchi di Sopra, is spacious and comfortable—if a bit noisy and group-friendly (30 rooms, Sb-€79, Db-€89, Tb-€119, Qb-€138, family deals, breakfast-€6, Via Montanini 28, tel. 0577-44321, fax 0577-280-868, cannondoro@libero.it, Maurizio and Debora SE). This is just a couple blocks from the bus station.

Sleeping Fancy, Southwest of Il Campo

These two classy and well-run places are a 10-minute walk from Il Campo.

$$$ Hotel Duomo, with 23 spacious rooms and a bizarre floor plan, is a great value (Sb-€110, Db-€130, Tb-€175, Qb-€200, includes breakfast, air-con, elevator, picnic-friendly roof terrace, free parking; follow Via di Città, which becomes Via Stalloreggi, to Via Stalloreggi 38; tel. 0577-289-088, fax 0577-43043, www.hotelduomo.it, booking@hotelduomo.it, Alessandra SE). If you arrive by train, take a taxi (€8); if you drive, go to Porta San Marco and follow the signs to the hotel, drop off your bags, and then park in nearby "Il Campo" lot.

$$$ Pensione Palazzo Ravizza, elegant and friendly, with an aristocratic feel and a peaceful garden, is a worthwhile splurge (Sb-€130, small loft Db-€120, standard Db-€160, superior Db-€180—see Web for differences, Tb-€220–310, suites available, includes breakfast, cheaper mid-Nov–Feb, air-con, elevator, free Internet access, back rooms face open country, good restaurant, free parking, Via Pian dei Mantellini 34, tel. 0577-280-462, fax 0577-221-597, www.palazzoravizza.it, bureau@palazzoravizza.it, SE).

Near San Domenico Church

These hotels are within a 10-minute walk northeast of Il Campo. Albergo Bernini and Alma Domus, which enjoy views of the old town and cathedral, are about the best values in town.

$$$ Hotel Chiusarelli, a proper hotel with 49 rooms in a beautiful building with a handy location, comes with traffic noise at night—ask for a quieter room in the back (S-€64, Sb-€82, Db-€121, Tb-€164, includes buffet breakfast, suites available, air-con, pleasant garden terrace, €4 rental bikes, reasonable dinner menu, across from San Domenico at Viale Curtatone 15, tel. 0577-280-562, fax 0577-271-177, www.chiusarelli.com, info@chiusarelli.com, Barbara SE).

$ Alma Domus is ideal—unless nuns make you nervous, you need a double bed, or you plan on staying out past the 23:30 curfew (no mercy given). This quasi-hotel (not a convent) is run with firm but angelic smiles by sisters who offer clean and quiet rooms for a steal and save the best views for foreigners. Bright lamps, quaint balconies, fine views, grand public rooms, top security, and a friendly atmosphere make this a great value. The checkout time is strictly 10:00, but they will store your luggage in their secure courtyard (Db-€60, Tb-€70, Qb-€90, cash only, ask for view room—*con vista,* elevator; from San Domenico walk downhill with the church on your right toward the view, turn left down Via Camporegio, make a U-turn at the little chapel down the brick steps to Via Camporegio 37; tel. 0577-44177, fax 0577-47601, NSE).

Siena Hotels, Restaurants, and Services

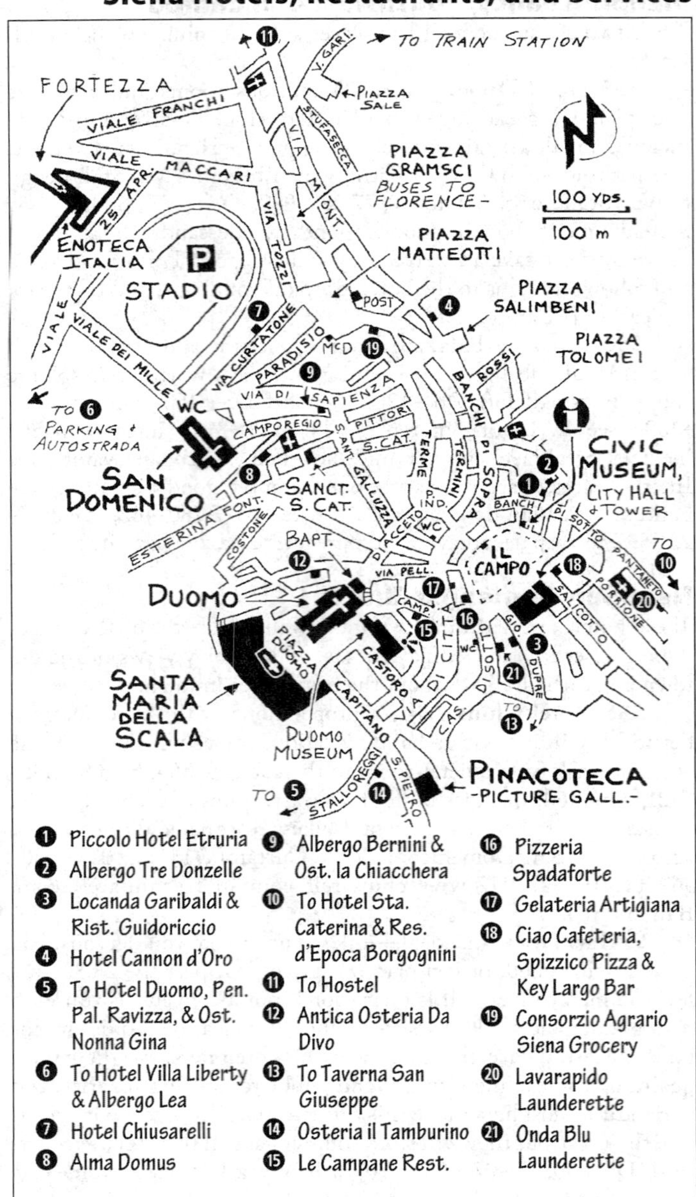

$ Albergo Bernini makes you part of a Sienese family in a modest, clean home with nine fine rooms. Friendly Nadia and Mauro welcome you to their spectacular view terrace for breakfast and picnic lunches and dinners. Outside of breakfast and check-out time, Mauro, an accomplished accordionist, might play a song for you if you ask (Sb-€77, D-€62, Db-€82, breakfast-€7, less in winter, cash only, midnight curfew, on the main San Domenico–Il Campo drag at Via Sapienza 15, tel. & fax 0577-289-047, www.albergobernini.com, hbernin@tin.it, son Alessandro SE). When full, they recommend their bigger but more expensive, less central, and less charming apartments.

Near the Fortezza

$$$ Hotel Villa Liberty has 18 big, bright, comfortable rooms and lots of street noise (S-€75, Db-€130, includes breakfast, only one room with twin beds, elevator, bar, air-con, TVs, courtyard, free and easy street parking, facing fortress at Viale V. Veneto 11, tel. 0577-44966, fax 0577-44770, www.villaliberty.it, info@villaliberty.it, SE).

$$ Albergo Lea is a creaky, old-fashioned place in a residential neighborhood a few blocks past San Domenico with 11 rooms and easy parking (S-€50, Db-€90, Tb-€110, cheaper in winter, includes breakfast, yard and rooftop terrace, Viale XXIV Maggio 10, tel. & fax 0577-283-207, hotellea@libero.it, SE).

Southeast of Il Campo, farther from the Center

The first two places are near each other, in the direction of Porta Romana city gate. The last two are well-served by city buses, but are less convenient.

$$$ Hotel Santa Caterina is a three-star, 18th-century place, great for drivers who need air-conditioning. Professionally run with real attention to quality, it has 22 comfortable rooms with a delightful garden (Sb-€115, small Db-€115, Db-€150, Tb-€200, includes buffet breakfast, elevator; garden side is quieter, but street side—with multi-paned windows—isn't bad; fridge in room, parking-€15/day—request when you reserve, 100 yards outside Porta Romana at Via E.S. Piccolomini 7, tel. 0577-221-105, fax 0577-271-087, www.hscsiena.it, info@hscsiena.it, Lorenza SE). A city shuttle bus runs frequently (4/hr) to the town center.

$ Residenza d'Epoca Borgognini is a grand old building with seven cool, solid, and tastefully decorated rooms. You'll find high ceilings, lots of stairs, and a warm welcome from Maria Antonietta (D-€70, €110 in July–Aug, Db-€80, €120 July–Aug, Tb-€110–140, includes breakfast at nearby bar, Via Pantaneto 160, tel. & fax 0577-44055, mobile 338-7640933, www.hotelborgognini.it, hotelborgognini@yahoo.it).

EATING

Sienese restaurants are reasonable by Florentine and Venetian standards. Enjoy ordering high on the menu here without going broke.

Antica Osteria Da Divo is *the* place for a fine €40 meal. The kitchen is creative, the ambience is candlelit, and the food is fresh and top-notch. The lamb goes *baaa* in your mouth. They offer a basket of exotic fresh breads and excellent seasonal dishes. And the chef is understandably proud of his desserts (daily 12:00–14:30 & 19:00–22:00, reserve for summer eves, Via Franciosa 29; facing Baptistery door, take the far right and walk one long curving block; tel. 0577-286-054).

Ristorante Guidoriccio—just a few steps below Il Campo—feels warm, dressy, and inviting, with friendly service by Ercole and Elis and prices good for the locale (pastas-€7, *secondi*-€13, closed Sun, air-con, Via G. Dupre 2, tel. 0577-44350).

Taverna San Giuseppe, a local favorite, offers modern Tuscan cuisine in a dressy grotto atmosphere. Check the posters tacked around the entry for daily specials. Reserve or arrive early to get a table (Mon–Sat 12:15–14:30 & 19:15–22:00, closed Sun, 7-min walk up street to the right of City Hall, Via Giovanni Dupre 132, tel. 0577-42286).

Osteria il Tamburino is friendly, popular, and serves up tasty, inexpensive meals in a narrow dining room (Mon–Sat 12:00–14:30 & 19:00–21:30, closed Sun; follow Via di Città off Il Campo, becomes Stalloreggi, Via Stalloreggi 11; tel. 0577-280-306).

Le Campane, two blocks off Il Campo, is more formal. It features modern Tuscan fare with a dressy interior and a outdoor tables on a quiet square (pastas-€8, *secondi*-€13, daily 12:15–14:30 & 19:15–22:00, closed Mon in winter, indoor/outdoor seating, a few steps off Via di Città at Via delle Campane 6, tel. 0577-284-035, reservations smart).

Osteria Nonna Gina wins praise from locals for its good quality and prices (Tue–Sun 12:30–14:30 & 19:30–22:30, closed Mon, 10-min walk from Il Campo, 2 blocks beyond Hotel Duomo, Piano dei Mantellini 2, tel. 0577-287-247).

Osteria la Chiacchera is a youthful hole-in-the-brick-wall playing hip music and serving "peasant food" at peasant prices on rustic tables and paper place mats (pastas-€3, *secondi*-€5, daily 12:00–15:30 & 19:00–23:00, reservations wise, understandably proud of their cakes, skip the *trippa*—tripe, 2 rooms, below Pension Bernini at Costa di San Antonio 4, tel. 0577-280-631). Their outside tables cling to a steep lane.

Locanda Garibaldi offers authentic Sienese dining at a fair price (pastas-€6, *secondi*-€9, €20 *menu*, Sun–Fri 12:00–14:00 &

19:00–21:00, closed Sat, arrive early to get a table, within a block of Il Campo down Via Giovanni Dupre at #18). Marcello does a little *piatto misto dolce* for €4, featuring several local desserts with sweet wine.

Even with higher prices, lousy service, and lower-quality food, consider eating on Il Campo—a classic European experience. Considering the real estate, the prices (if you order carefully and are treated fairly) are actually pretty good. Wander across the square and sit wherever your stomach and heart tell you to. **Pizzeria Spadaforte,** at the edge of Il Campo, has a fine perch, decent food, and slanted tables (€7 pizza and pasta, daily 12:00–16:00 & 19:30–22:30, to far right of City Tower as you face it, tel. 0577-281-123).

Drinks or Snacks Overlooking Il Campo

Three places have skinny balconies with benches overlooking the main square for their customers. Sipping a coffee or nibbling a pastry here while marveling at the Il Campo scene is one of my favorite European experiences. And it's very cheap. Survey these three places from Il Campo (from the base of the City Tower, they are at 10:00, high noon, and 3:00 respectively).

Gelateria Artigiana has good ice cream, drinks, and light snacks (off Via di Città). **Bar Paninoteca,** with a youthful pub ambience, has a row of stools overlooking the square and serves 50 kinds of sandwiches (hot and cold, €3 each, €0.50 extra if you sit outside, on Vicolo di S. Paolo on the stairs leading down to Il Campo). **Key Largo Bar** has two benches in the corner offering a great secret perch (Mon–Sat 7:00–22:00 or 23:00, closed Sun, corner left of the tower). Buy your drink or snack at the bar (no extra charge to sit), climb upstairs, and slide the ancient bar to open the door and suddenly...you're imagining Palio ponies zipping wildly around your corner.

Eating Cheaply in the Center

At the bottom of Il Campo, a **Ciao** cafeteria offers easy self-service meals, no ambience, and no views. The crowded **Spizzico,** a pizza counter in the front half of Ciao, serves huge, inexpensive quarter pizzas; on sunny days, people take the pizza, trays and all, out on Il Campo for a picnic (daily 11:00–22:00, non-smoking section—*non fumatori*—in back, to left of City Tower as you face it).

Budget eaters look for *pizza al taglio* shops, scattered throughout Siena, selling pizza by the slice. Of the grocery shops scattered throughout town, the biggest is **Consorzio Agrario Siena** (Mon–Sat 8:00–19:30, a one block off Piazza Matteotti, toward Il Campo at Via Pianigiani 5).

Local Sweets

All over town, **Prodotti Tipici** shops sell Sienese specialties. Siena's claim to caloric fame is its *panforte,* a rich, chewy concoction of nuts, honey, and candied fruits that impresses even fruitcake-haters. There are a few varieties to try: *margherita,* dusted in powdered sugar, is more fruity; *panpepato* has a spicy, peppery crust. Locals prefer a chewy white macaroon-and-almond cookie called *ricciarelli.*

TRANSPORTATION CONNECTIONS

Siena has sparse trains connections, but is a great hub for buses to the hill towns.

From Siena by Train to: Florence (9/day, 1.75 hrs, more with transfer in Empoli). **Rome** (every 2 hrs, 2.75–4 hrs, transfer in Florence or Chiusi).

By Bus to: Florence (2/hr, 1.25–2.5 hrs, by Tra-in bus, last bus at 20:45), **San Gimignano** (6/day, 1.25 hrs, by Tra-in bus, more frequent with transfer in Poggibonsi), **Assisi** (2/day, 2 hrs, €9, by Sena bus; the morning bus goes direct to Assisi, the afternoon bus might terminate at Santa Maria degli Angeli, from here catch a local bus to Assisi, 2/hr, 20 min), **Rome** (7/day, 3 hrs, by Sena bus, arrives at Rome's Tiburtina station), **Milan** (4/day, 5 hrs). Schedules get sparse on Sundays and holidays.

Buses depart Siena from Piazza Gramsci, the train station, or both; confirm when you purchase your ticket. You can get tickets for Tra-in buses or Sena buses at the train station (there's a ticket window for both companies at the station, Mon–Sat 5:50–20:00), or more centrally, under Piazza Gramsci at Sottopassaggio La Lizza (Tra-in bus office: daily 5:50–20:00, tel. 0577-204-246, toll-free tel. 800-570-530, www.trainspa.it; Sena bus office: Mon–Sat 7:45–19:45, closed Sun, tel. 800-930-960, www.senabus.it).

Sottopassaggio La Lizza, under Piazza Gramsci, has a cash machine (neither bus office accepts credit cards), luggage storage (€3.50/day, daily 7:00–19:45, no overnight storage), posted bus schedules, TV monitors (listing imminent departures for all three companies), an elevator, and expensive WCs (€0.55). Those departing Siena after the bus offices close can buy the ticket directly from the driver (and pay a supplement). On schedules, the fastest buses are marked *corse rapide.* I'd stick with these. Note that if a schedule lists your departure point as Via Tozzi or La Lizza, you catch the bus at Piazza Gramsci (Via Tozzi is the street that runs alongside Piazza Gramsci and La Lizza is the name of the bus station).

THE CINQUE TERRE

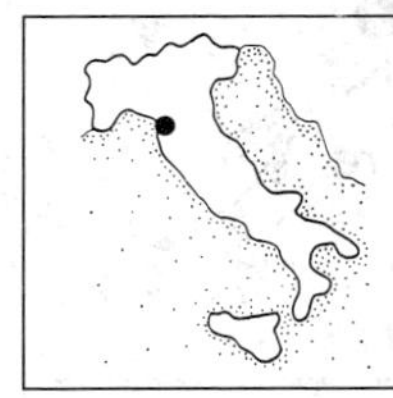

The Cinque Terre (CHINK-weh TAY-reh), a remote chunk of the Italian Riviera, is the traffic-free, lowbrow, underappreciated alternative to the French Riviera. There's not a museum in sight. Just sun, sea, sand (well, pebbles), wine, and pure, unadulterated Italy. Enjoy the villages, swimming, hiking, and evening romance of one of God's great gifts to tourism. For a home base, choose among five villages, each of which fills a ravine with a lazy hive of human activity—callused locals, sunburned travelers, and no Vespas. While the Cinque Terre is now well-discovered (www.cinqueterre.it), I've never seen happier, more relaxed tourists.

The chunk of coast was first described in medieval times as "the five lands." In feudal times, this land was watched over by castles; tiny communities grew up in their protective shadows, ready to run inside at the first hint of a Turkish Saracen pirate raid. Many locals were kidnapped and ransomed or sold into slavery. As the threat of pirates faded, the villages grew, with economies based on fish and grapes. Until the advent of tourism in this generation, the towns were remote. Even today, traditions survive, and each of the five villages comes with a distinct dialect and its own proud heritage. The region has become a national park, and its natural and cultural wonders will be carefully preserved.

Over the next decade, Italy has ambitious plans for the Cinque Terre. In Vernazza, for example, a new waterfront piazza is being built, the church is being refurbished, and a disabled-access elevator is being installed at the train station.

Sadly, a few ugly, noisy Americans are giving tourism a bad name here. Even hip, young locals are put off by loud, drunken tourists. They say, and I agree, that the Cinque Terre is an exceptional

The Cinque Terre

place. It deserves a special dignity. Party in Viareggio or Portofino, but be mellow in the Cinque Terre. Talk softly. Help keep it clean. In spite of the tourist crowds, it's still a real community, and we are guests.

In this chapter, I cover the five towns in order from east to west, from Riomaggiore to Monterosso. Since I still get the names of the towns mixed up, I think of them by number: #1. Riomaggiore (a workaday town), #2. Manarola (picturesque), #3. Corniglia (on a hilltop), #4. Vernazza (the region's cover girl, the most touristy and dramatic), and #5. Monterosso (the closest thing to a beach resort of the five towns).

Planning Your Time

The ideal minimum stay is two nights and a completely uninterrupted day. The Cinque Terre is served by the local train from Genoa and La Spezia. Speed demons arrive in the morning, check

2006 Events on the Cinque Terre

For more festival information, check www.cinqueterre.it and www.5terre.com.

April 16	Easter
May	Monterosso: Lemon Festival
Mid-June	Monterosso: Corpus Domini (procession on carpet of flowers at 18:00)
June 24	Riomaggiore and Monterosso: Festival in honor of St. John the Baptist (procession and fireworks; big fire on old town beach the day before)
June 29	Corniglia: Festival of St. Peter and St. Paul
July 20	Vernazza: Festival for patron St. Margaret
Aug 10	Manarola: Festival for patron St. Lawrence
Aug 15	All towns: Ascension of Mary
early Sept	Monterosso: Maria Nascente, or "Birth of Mary" (fair with handicrafts)

their bags in La Spezia, take the five-hour hike through all five towns, laze away the afternoon on the beach or rock of their choice, and zoom away on the overnight train to somewhere back in the real world. But be warned: The Cinque Terre has a strange way of messing up your momentum. Frankly, anything less than two nights is a mistake that you'll likely regret.

The towns are just a few minutes apart by hourly train or boat. There's no checklist of sights or experiences—just a hike, the towns themselves, and your fondest vacation desires. Study this chapter in advance and piece together your best day, mixing hiking, swimming, trains, and a boat ride. For the best light and coolest temperatures, start your hike early.

Market days perk up the towns from 8:00 to 13:00 on Tuesday in Vernazza, Wednesday in nearby Levanto, Thursday in Monterosso, and Friday in La Spezia. The winter is really dead—hotels mostly close in December and January. Mid-May through mid-June is peak of peak, the only tough time to find rooms.

The Cinque Terre National Park

Now that the region is a national park, there are tighter restrictions on development, a push for sensitive management of the environment, and money for maintenance and improvement of the area. The director of the park (famous for his grandiose visions) is doing impressive things. There are well-staffed information offices in each town (generally offering baggage check, Internet access, maps, hiking tips, souvenirs, and various passes for sale). At the mountain station above Riomaggiore, can rent mountain bikes and arrange horse rides. For all the latest, see www.parconazionale5terre.it or stop by a local TI.

Cinque Terre Cards and Passes

Visitors hiking between the towns need to pay a **park entrance fee.** This fee keeps the trails safe and open, and pays for building fine viewpoints, picnic spots, WCs, and more. The popular coastal trail generates enough revenue to subsidize the development of trails and outdoor activities higher in the hills.

You have several options (all valid until midnight of the expiration date):

The **Hiking Pass** costs €3 (comes with map, kids under 4 free). It's valid for one day and covers all trails (but no buses or trains). Buy it at trailheads, at national park offices, and usually at train stations (no validation required).

The **Cinque Terre Card** combines hiking privileges with free transportation. It covers the park entrance fee, local trains (from Levanto to La Spezia, including all Cinque Terre towns), and shuttle buses (see page 1090). It's sold at TIs inside train stations, but not at trailheads (€5.40/1 day, €13/3 days, €20.60/week, kids 4–12 half-price, under 4 free). The card comes with a map, information brochure, and train schedule. Validate your Cinque Terre Card at a train station by punching it in the yellow machine. The pass pays for itself if you hike, ride a train, and use a shuttle bus in a single day.

The **Cinque Terre Card Plus Boats** includes all of the above, plus unlimited passage on Cinque Terre boats (€13.60/1 day; skip the boats-only pass).

For most travelers, the best option is to buy the Cinque Terre Card and pay out of pocket for boat trips.

Getting Around the Cinque Terre

Within the Cinque Terre, you'll get around the villages more cheaply by train, but more scenically by boat.

By Train: At La Spezia, the gateway to the Cinque Terre, you'll transfer to the milk-run Cinque Terre train. Don't bother with the TI in La Spezia. At the station, buy your train ticket (€1) or Cinque Terre Card, and take the half-hour train ride into the town of your choice. To orient yourself, remember that directions are "*per* (to) Genova" (the Italian spelling of Genoa) or "*per* La Spezia." Assuming you're on vacation, accept the unpredictability of Cinque Terre trains (you're often early, they're often late). Relax while you wait—buy a cup of coffee at a station bar. When the train comes (know which direction to look for), casually walk over and hop on. This is especially easy in Monterosso, with its fine café-with-a-view on track #1 (direction Milano/Genova).

By train, the five towns are several minutes apart. Know your stop. After the train leaves the town before your destination, go to the door and get ready to slip out before mobs pack in. Words to the wise for novice tourists, who often miss their stop: The stations are small and the trains are long, so you might have to get off deep in a tunnel. The doors don't open automatically; you might have to flip open the handle of the door yourself.

It's cheap to buy individual train tickets to travel between the towns. Since a one-town hop costs the same as a five-town hop (around €1) and every ticket is good for six hours with stopovers, save money and explore the region in one direction on one ticket. Stamp the ticket at the station machine before you board. If you have a Eurailpass, don't spend one of your valuable flexi-days on the cheap Cinque Terre.

Cinque Terre Train Schedule: Since the train is the Cinque Terre's lifeline, many shops and restaurants post the current schedule. Carry a copy of it—it'll come in handy (comes with Cinque Terre Card). Note that many trains leaving La Spezia zip right through the Cinque Terre, or stop only in Monterosso. But the trains on the following schedule will stop at all five Cinque Terre towns. All of the below times are accurate as of 2005; most are daily and a few run daily except Sunday, while others (not listed here) operate only on Sundays.

Trains leave La Spezia for the Cinque Terre villages at 7:12, 8:13, 10:08, 11:20, 12:23, 12:55, 13:19, 14:37, 15:02, 16:35, 17:22, 18:15, 19:02, 19:35, 20:20, 21:10, 22:30, and 24:20.

Going back to La Spezia, trains leave Monterosso al Mare at 6:33, 8:12, 10:17, 12:11, 13:00, 13:33, 14:12, 15:16, 16:17, 17:13, 18:40, 19:14, 20:20, 20:27, 22:32, 23:21, and 23:57 (same trains depart Vernazza about 4 min later).

By Boat: From Easter through October (into Nov if weather's good), a daily boat service connects Monterosso, Vernazza, Manarola, Riomaggiore, and Portovenere. Boats provide a scenic way to get from town to town and survey what you just hiked. And boats offer the only efficient way to visit the nearby resort of Portovenere (the alternative is a tedious train/bus connection via La Spezia). In peaceful weather, the boats can be more reliable than the trains, but if seas are rough, they don't run at all. Because the boats nose in and tourists have to gingerly disembark along little more than a plank, even a small chop can cancel some or all of the stops.

I see the tour boats as a syringe, injecting each town with a boost of euros. The towns are addicted, and they shoot up hourly through the summer. (Between 10:00 and 15:00—especially on weekends—masses of tour-bus gawkers inundate the villages, changing the tenor of the region.)

Boats depart Monterosso about hourly (10:00–18:00), stopping at the Cinque Terre towns (except at Corniglia) and ending an hour later in Portovenere. (The Portovenere-Monterosso boats run 9:00–17:00.) Single hops cost about €3. Some towns are also connected by smaller boats and may honor the same tickets—ask. You can buy tickets at little stands at each town's harbor (tel. 0187-732-987 and 0187-818-440). An all-day boat pass, which covers the Cinque Terre towns, costs around €12 (price depends on time of year; the Cinque Terre Card Plus Boats pass is a better value—sold only at TIs, see page 1088). Boat schedules are posted at docks, harbor bars, Cinque Terre Park offices, and hotels.

By Shuttle Bus: Shuttle buses connect each Cinque Terre town with distant parking lots and various points in the hills (for example, from Corniglia's beach and train station to its hilltop town center). Most rides cost €1.50.

Hiking the Cinque Terre

All five towns are connected by good trails. You'll experience the area's best by hiking all the way from one end to the other. While you can detour to dramatic hilltop sanctuaries, I'd keep it simple by following the easy red-and-white-marked low trail between the villages. This entire seven-mile hike can be done in about four hours, but allow five for dawdling. Germans (with their task-oriented *Alpenstock*—walking sticks) are notorious for marching too fast through the region. (The non-German record for the entire five-town hike is by one of my tour guides: 1 hour, 52 minutes.)

Trails can be closed in bad weather. Remember that hikers need to pay a fee to enter the trails (see "Cinque Terre Cards and Passes," page 1088). If hiking the entire five-town route, consider that the trails between towns Riomaggiore (#1), Manarola (#2), and Corniglia (#3) are easiest. The trail from Vernazza (#4) to Monterosso (#5) is the most challenging. You might want to start in Monterosso in order to tackle the toughest section while you're fresh.

Maps aren't necessary for the basic coastal hike described here. But for the expanded version of this hike (from Portovenere to Levanto) and more serious hikes in the high country, pick up a good hiking map (about €5, sold everywhere). To leave the park cleaner than when you found it, request a plastic bag *(sacchetto di plastica)* at any park information booth and pick up a little trail trash along the way. It would be great if American visitors—who get so much joy out of this region—were known for this good deed.

Riomaggiore–Manarola (20 min): Facing the front of the train station in Riomaggiore (#1), go up the stairs to the right, following signs for the Via dell' Amore. The film-gobbling promenade—wide enough for baby strollers—leads down the coast to Manarola (#2). While there's no beach here, stairs lead down to sunbathing rocks. A long tunnel and mega-nets protect hikers from mean-spirited rocks. There's a classy park-run Bar & Vini wine bar at the Riomaggiore trailhead (light meals, awesome town views, clever boat storage under train tracks) and a scenic and peaceful bar midway.

Manarola–Corniglia (45 min): The walk from Manarola (#2) to Corniglia (#3) is a little longer and more rugged than that from #1 to #2. A shuttle bus zips the lazy from the Corniglia station up to the hill-capping town (2/hr).

Corniglia–Vernazza (90 min): The hike from Corniglia (#3) to Vernazza (#4)—the wildest and greenest of the coast—is most rewarding. From the Corniglia station and beach, zigzag up to the town (taking the shorter-but-steeper corkscrew stairs, the longer road, or the shuttle bus). Ten minutes past Corniglia, toward Vernazza, you'll see Guvano beach far beneath you (the region's nude beach, see page 1102). The trail leads past a bar and picnic tables, through lots of fragrant and flowery vegetation, scenically into Vernazza. If you need a break before reaching Vernazza, Franco's Ristorante "La Torre" has a small menu, but big views.

Vernazza–Monterosso (90 min): The trail from Vernazza (#4) to Monterosso (#5) is a scenic up-and-down-a-lot trek. Trails are rough (some readers report "very dangerous") and narrow, but easy to follow. Locals frown on camping at the picnic tables located midway. The views just out of Vernazza are spectacular.

Longer Hikes: Above the trails that run between the towns, higher-elevation hikes crisscross the region. Shuttle buses make the going easier, connecting villages and trailheads in the hills. Ask locally about the more difficult six-mile inland hike to Volastra. This tiny village, perched between Manarola and Corniglia, hosts the Five-Terre wine co-op. The Cantina Sociale is a third of a mile away, in the hamlet of Groppo. If you take this high road between Manarola and Corniglia, allow two hours. In return, you'll get sweeping views and a closer look at the vineyards. Shuttle buses run hourly to Volastra from Manarola and Corniglia (€2.50 or free with Cinque Terre Card); consider taking the bus up and hiking down.

Swimming and Kayaking

Every town has a beach. Monterosso has the biggest and sandiest, with paddleboats, beach umbrellas, and beach-use fees (but it's free where there are no umbrellas). Riomaggiore has a fine beach just outside town. Vernazza's is tiny—better for sunning than swimming. Manarola has the worst beach (no sand), but offers the best deep-water swimming.

Wear your walking shoes and pack your swim gear. Several of the beaches have showers (no shampoo, please). Underwater sightseeing is full of fish—goggles are sold in local shops. Sea urchins can be a problem if you walk on the rocks.

You can rent kayaks in Riomaggiore, Vernazza, and Monterosso (details listed below per town). Mountain biking is possible (park info booths have details on rentals and a map with bike trails high above the coast).

Riomaggiore
(Town #1)

The most substantial non-resort town of the group, Riomaggiore is a disappointment from the train station. But walk through the tunnel next to the train tracks (or ride the elevator through the hillside to the top of town), and you land in a fascinating tangle of pastel homes leaning on each other as if someone stole their crutches.

ORIENTATION

Tourist Information: The TI is inside the train station (daily 6:30–20:00 in winter, until 22:00 in summer, tel. 0187-920-633). The Cinque Terre Park office is next to the TI (daily 8:00–23:30 in summer, until 20:00 in winter, Internet access). A less formal information source is friendly and helpful Ivo, who runs the Bar Centrale (see "Eating," page 1097).

Helpful Hints

Laundry: A self-service launderette is on the main street (daily 8:00–22:00, €3.50 wash, €3.50 dry, next to Edi's Rooms on Via Columbo 111).

Bus Service: The bus shuttles locals and tourists up and down Riomaggiore's steep main street and continues to the parking lot outside of town. It runs twice an hour—just flag it down as it passes (€1.50, free with Cinque Terre Card). The bus heads into the hills, where you'll find the region's top high-country activities.

Introductory Riomaggiore Walk

Here's an easy loop trip that maximizes views and minimizes uphill walking. Start at the train station (if you arrive by boat, take the tunnel alongside the tracks to get to the station). From the station, walk past the colorful murals glorifying the nameless workers (modeled after real-life Riomaggiorians) who constructed the nearly 300 million cubic feet of dry stone walls (without cement) throughout the Cinque Terre, giving the region its characteristic *muri a secco* terracing for vineyards and olive groves. The murals, done by Argentinean artist Silvio Benedetto, are well-explained in English.

At the entrance of the railway tunnel, ride the elevator to the top of town (€1, free with Cinque Terre Card, daily 8:00–20:00). At the top, go right, following the walkway—with spectacular sea views—around the cliff. Ignore the steps marked *Marina Seacoast* (harbor). Instead, continue along the path; it's a five-minute, fairly level stroll to the church. While the church was rebuilt in 1870, it originally dates from 1340. When it was built, the disparate hamlets of this stretch of coastline coalesced into what is today known as Riomaggiore. Continue past the church and then take a right, down a stepped lane to Via Colombo, Riomaggiore's main street.

Stroll down Via Colombo. Just past the WC, you'll see flower boxes on the street, which sometimes block it—these slide back electronically to let the shuttle bus get past. On your way down the hill, you'll pass colorful, small shops, including a bakery, a couple of grocery shops, and the self-service laundry. There's homemade gelato next to the Bar Centrale. When Via Colombo dead-ends, on your left you'll find the stairs down to "The Marina" neighborhood, with the harbor, the boat dock, a 200-yard trail to the beach (*spiaggia*), and an inviting little art gallery (Galleria d'Arte Sciaccheart, with local scenes, Via Giacomo 51). To your right is the tunnel, running alongside the tracks, which takes you directly back to the station and the trail to the other towns. From here, you can take a train, hop a boat, or hike to your next destination.

ACTIVITIES

Beach—Riomaggiore's beach is rocky, but it's clean and peaceful. Take a two-minute walk from the harbor: Face the harbor, then follow the path to your left. At the La Conchiglia bar, go down the stairs to the right and stay on the path to the beach.

Kayaks and Water Sports—Mar Mar rents kayaks (€4/hr for 1-person kayak, €8/hr for 2-person kayak) and offers boat excursions (fishing or cruising, €30/day per person for up to 8 people, see their listing under "Sleeping," below). The town also has a diving center (scuba, snorkeling, boats, and kayaks; under the tracks on Via San Giacomo, tel. 0187-920-011).

Hikes—Consider the cliff-hanging trail that leads from the beach to old World War II bunkers and a hilltop botanical garden (free entrance with Cinque Terre Card). Another trail climbs scenically to the Madonna di Montenero sanctuary, high above the town. If you don't feel like hiking, take the green shuttle-bus up. The bus stops at the starting point of the oversized *trenino* (grape-pickers train), which then shuttles you up to the sanctuary (12-min trip, details at park office). This new park center and bar also offer horse rides and bike rentals.

Riomaggiore

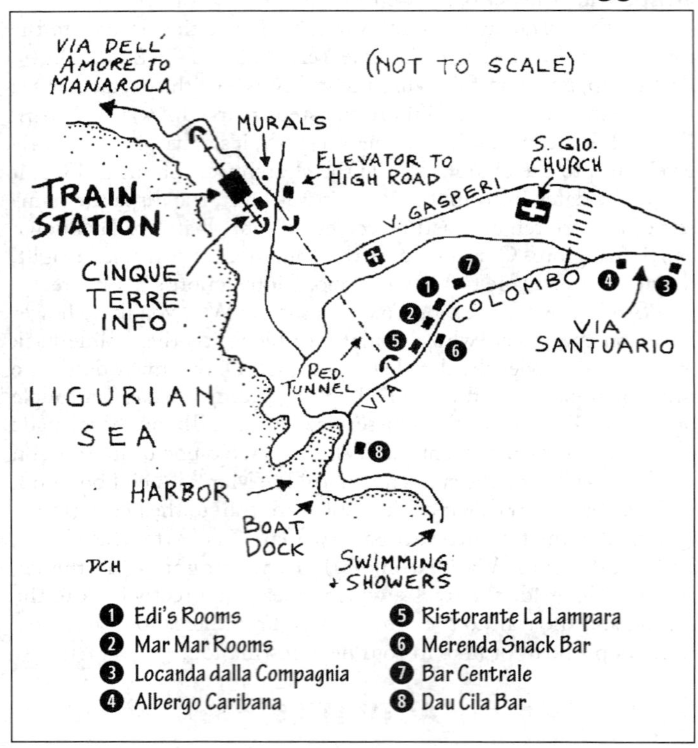

SLEEPING

Riomaggiore has arranged its private-room rental system better than its neighbors. But with organization (and middlemen) come higher prices. Several agencies— with regular office hours, English-speaking staff, and e-mail addresses—line up within a few yards of each other on the main drag. Each manages a corral of local rooms for rent. These offices can close unexpectedly, so it's smart to settle up the day before you leave in case they're closed when you have to depart. Expect lots of stairs.

Room-Finding Services

$$ Edi's Rooms has 20 fine rooms and apartments—half with views. Edi and her partner Luana get my "best business practices" award for this town (non-view Db-€52, apartment Db-€90, apartment Qb-€124, office open daily 9:00–20:00 in summer, otherwise 9:00–13:00 & 15:00–19:00, Via Colombo 111, tel. 0187-760-842, tel. & fax 0187-920-325, edi-vesigna@iol.it).

Sleep Code

(€1 = about $1.20, country code: 39)
S = Single, **D** = Double/Twin, **T** = Triple, **Q** = Quad, **b** = bathroom, **s** = shower only, **SE** = Speaks English, **NSE** = No English. Breakfast is rarely, if ever, included. Unless otherwise noted, credit cards are accepted.

To help you sort easily through these listings, I've divided the rooms into three categories based on the price for a standard double room with bath:

$$$ **Higher Priced**—Most rooms €100 or more.
$$ **Moderately Priced**—Most rooms between €50–100.
$ **Lower Priced**—Most rooms €50 or less.

$$ At **Mar Mar Rooms,** Mario rents 12 rooms, 10 apartments, and a mini-hostel, with American ex-pat Amy smoothing communications (dorm bed-€20 per person, Db-€60–90 depending on view, reception open 9:00–19:00 in season, 30 yards above train tracks on main drag next to Lampara restaurant, Via Malborghetto 4, tel. & fax 0187-920-932, www.marmar.5terre.com in Italian only, marmar@5terre.com). Mar Mar also rents kayaks and runs fishing trips.

$$ **Luciano and Roberto Fazioli** rent nine rooms and a basic eight-bed mini-hostel (dorm bed-€20, €25 on Fri–Sat or for 1-night stays; D-€50–70, Db-€50–80, office open daily 9:00–20:00, Via Colombo 94, tel. 0187-920-904, robertofazioli@libero.it). The apartments are overpriced and the rooms vary in quality; ask to see a room before you commit.

$$ **La Dolce Vita,** across from Edi's, offers five rooms and eight apartments (€20–30 per person; open daily 9:30–19:30—if they're closed, they're full; Via Colombo 120, tel. & fax 0187-760-044, www.dolcevitarooms.com, agonatal@tin.it, Giacomo SE).

Private Rooms and Hotels on Riomaggiore's Main Drag

$$ **Locanda dalla Compagnia** rents five modern rooms—each with air-conditioning, a mini-fridge, and no view—at the top of town, just 300 yards below the parking lot. All rooms are on the same airy ground floor, sharing an inviting lounge. Franca runs it with the help of an American named Lorraine (Db-€75, includes breakfast, Via del Santuario 32, tel. 0187-760-050, fax 0187-760700, www.dallacompagnia.com, lacomp@libero.it).

$$ **Anna Michielini** rents four attractive apartments in the center with no views (Db-€56, Tb-€99, Qb-€110, cheaper

Sleeping on the Cinque Terre

If you think too many people have my book, avoid Vernazza. Monterosso is a good choice for the younger crowd (more nightlife) and rich, sun-worshiping softies (who prefer the comfort and ease of a real hotel). Hermits, anarchists, wine-lovers, and mountain goats like Corniglia. Sophisticated Italians and Germans choose Manarola. Riomaggiore is bigger than Vernazza and less resorty than Monterosso.

While the Cinque Terre is too rugged for the mobs that ravage the Spanish and French coasts, it's popular with Italians, Germans, and in-the-know Americans. Hotels charge more and are packed on Easter, mid-May through Mid-June, in August, and on Fridays and Saturdays all summer. August weekends are worst. But €65 doubles abound throughout the year. For a terrace or view, you might pay an extra €20 or more.

If visiting in July, August, or on a weekend, book ahead. At other times, you can land a double room on any day by just arriving in town (ideally by noon) and asking around at bars and restaurants, or simply by approaching locals on the street. Many travelers enjoy the opportunity to shop around a bit and get the best price by bargaining. Private rooms—called *affitta camere*—are no longer an intimate stay with a family. They are generally comfortable apartments (often with small kitchens) where you get the key and come and go as you like, rarely seeing your landlord. Often landowners rent the buildings by the year to local managers, who then attempt to make a profit by filling them night after night with tourists.

For the best value, visit three private rooms and snare the best. Going direct cuts out a middleman and softens prices. Plan on paying cash. Private rooms are generally bigger and more comfortable than those offered by the pensions and they offer the same privacy as a hotel room.

If you want the security of a reservation, make it at a hotel long in advance (small places generally don't take reservations that far ahead). If you don't get a reply to your faxed request for a room, assume the place is fully booked. If you do reserve, honor your reservation (or, if you must cancel, do it as early as possible). Since people renting rooms usually don't take deposits, they lose money if you don't show up. Cutthroat room hawkers at the train stations might try to lure you away with offers of cheaper rates from a room that you've already reserved. Don't do it. You owe it to your hosts to stick with your original reservation.

Oct–mid-April and for longer stays, 2 nights preferred June–Sept, reserve with credit card but pay cash, across from Bar Centrale at Colombo 143, ring bell to open door, friendly Daniela speaks good English—mobile 328-131-1032—and her mother speaks *solo Italiano*—tel. & fax 0187-920-411, michielinis@yahoo.it).

$$ Albergo Caribana has 10 basic rooms with shared terraces. At the utilitarian edge of town, it's a five-minute walk to the center. The free and easy parking makes this especially appealing to drivers (Db-€90, includes breakfast, Via Santuario 114, tel. 0187-920-773, tel. & fax 0187-920-932, marmar@5terre.com, Alberto SE). The same people run Mar Mar, a room-finding service (see above), using the same e-mail address. Specify which place you want when you reserve.

EATING

Ristorante La Lampara, decorated like a ship, serves a *frutti di mare* pizza, *trenette al pesto,* and the aromatic *spaghetti al cartoccio*—spaghetti with mixed seafood cooked in foil (€15 tourist *menu,* daily 12:00–15:00 & 18:30–22:30, closed Tue in winter, on Via Malborghetto 10 just above tracks off Via Colombo, tel. 0187-920-120).

La Lanterna is a dressier, more expensive place with better food than La Lampara. It's wedged into a niche in the "Marina," overlooking the harbor under the tracks (tel. 0187-920-589).

For a snack or good takeout, try **Te la Do Io la Merenda** ("I'll give you a snack"). Their counter is piled with an assortment of munchies, and they have pastas, roasted chicken, and focaccia to go (daily 8:30–21:30, tel. 0187-920-148, Via Colombo 171). For cheap sit-down pizza, try **Gigi's.** The **Bar & Vini,** at the trailhead on the Manarola end of town, is great for a scenic light meal or quiet drink at night. **Groceries and delis** on Via Colombo sell food to go, including pizza slices, for a picnic at the harbor or beach.

Bar Centrale, run by friendly Ivo and his gang, is a good stop for breakfast, Internet access, and music. Ivo lived in San Francisco and speaks good English. He fills his bar with only the best San Franciscan rock and hosts a big party on the Fourth of July. During the day, Bar Centrale is a shaded place to relax with other travelers. At night, it offers younger travelers the liveliest action in town (daily 7:30–24:00, closed Mon in winter, confirm prices, Via Colombo 144, tel. 0187-920-208, barcentrale1969@libero.it). For the best gelato in town, go next door.

While the late-night fun is at Ivo's Bar Centrale, take a walk down to the harborside **Dau Cila Bar** for jazz, nets, and mellow *limoncino* (called *limoncello* elsewhere in Italy)—a drink of lemon juice, sugar, and pure alcohol (Wed–Mon 10:30–24:30, closed Tue, tel. 0187-760-032).

Manarola

Manarola

(Town #2)

Like Riomaggiore, Manarola is attached to its station by a 200-yard-long tunnel. During WWII air raids, these tunnels provided refuge and a safe place for rattled villagers to sleep.

The town is tiny and picturesque, a tumble of buildings bunny-hopping down its ravine to the fun-loving harbor. Notice how the I-beam crane launches the boats.

Facing the harbor, look at the hillside to your right, dotted with a bar in the middle. It's Punta Bonfiglio, an entertaining park/game area/bar with the best view playground on the coast. From here you can get poster-perfect views of Manarola (2-min walk from the harbor on path to Corniglia) while you sip a coffee or munch a light lunch. The gate farther up the hillside is the entrance to the cemetery. At the top of the town, you'll find great views, the church, and a cluster of accommodations, including a super hostel.

The simple, wooden religious scenes that you'll likely see on the hillside are the work of local resident Mario Andreoli. Before his father died, Mario promised him he'd replace the old cross on the family's vineyard. Mario's been adding figures ever since. After recovering from a rare illness, he redoubled his efforts. On religious holidays, everything's lit up: the Nativity, the Last Supper, the Crucifixion, the Resurrection, and more. The scenes are sometimes left up year-round.

ORIENTATION

Helpful Hints

Park Info: The Cinque Terre Park office is in the train station (daily 7:00–22:00, 8:00–20:00 in winter, €0.50/hr bag storage).

Bus Service: A shuttle bus runs between the main street and the parking lot (€1.50/one-way, €2.50/round-trip, free with Cinque Terre Card, 2/hr, just flag it down).

ACTIVITIES

Beach—Manarola has no sand, but offers the best deep-water swimming in the area. The first "beach" has a shower, ladder, and wonderful rocks. The second has tougher access and no shower, but feels more remote and pristine (follow paved path toward Corniglia just around the point).

SLEEPING

(€1 = about $1.20, country code: 39)

Manarola has plenty of private rooms. Ask in bars and restaurants. There's a modern three-star place halfway up the main drag, a pricey hotel on the harbor, and a cluster of options around the church at the peaceful top of the town (a 5-min hike from the train tracks). Manarola's handy shuttle-bus service makes it easy to get to and from your car (see above).

$$ Albergo ca' d'Andrean is quiet, comfortable, modern, and like a normal hotel. It has 10 big, sunny rooms and a cool garden oasis, complete with lemon trees (Sb-€65, Db-€88, breakfast-€6, closed Nov, up the hill at Via A. Discovolo 101, tel. 0187-920-040, fax 0187-920-452, www.cadandrean.it, cadandrean@libero.it, Simone SE).

$$ Marina Piccola offers 13 bright, modern rooms on the water—so they figure a warm welcome is unnecessary (Db-€90, no breakfast, 3-night minimum July–Aug, air-con, Via allo Scalo 16, tel. 0187-920-103, fax 0187-920-966, www.hotelmarinapiccola.com, info@hotelmarinapiccola.com).

$$ Affitta Camere de Baranin (Via Rollandi 29, tel. & fax 0187-920-595, www.baranin.com; Sara, Silvia, and Andrea SE) and **La Torretta** (Piazza della Chiesa, Vico Volto 14, tel. & fax 0187-920-327, www.cinqueterre.net/torretta, torretta@cdh.it) have a complex pricing system for their pricey rooms.

$ Casa Capellini rents four fine rooms. One has a view balcony, another a 360-degree terrace (Db-€46; €60 for the *alta camera* on the top, with a kitchen, private terrace, and knockout view; 2 doors down the hill from the church, with your back to the church, it's at 2 o'clock, Via Ettore Cozzani 12; tel. 0187-920-823 or 0187-736-765, www.casacapellini-5terre.it, casa.capellini@tin.it, Gianni and Franca NSE).

$ Ostello 5-Terre, Manarola's modern and well-run hostel, stands like a Monopoly hotel behind the church square. It's smart to reserve well in advance in high season. You book with your credit-card number; if you cancel with less than three days' notice, you'll be charged for one night. This is not a party hostel—quiet is greatly appreciated (May–Sept dorm beds-€22, Qb-€88; off-season dorm beds-€17, Qb-€64; closed Dec–mid-Feb, 48 beds in 4- to 6-bed rooms, not coed except for couples and families, optional €3.50 breakfast and €6 dinner; in summer, office closed 13:00–17:00, rooms closed 10:00–17:00, curfew-1:00; during off-season, office and rooms closed until 16:00, curfew at 24:00; open to anyone of any age, laundry, safes, phone cards, Internet, book exchange, elevator, great roof terrace and sunset views, Via B. Riccobaldi 21, tel. 0187-920-215, fax 0187-920-218, www.hostel5terre.com, ostello@cdh.it, well-managed by Nicola).

EATING

Many hardworking places line the main drag. I liked the Botto family's friendly **Trattoria Il Porticciolo** (€6 pastas, closed Wed off-season, just below the train tracks at Via R. Birolli 92, tel. 0187-920-083). For harborside dining, **Marina Piccola** is the winner. While less friendly and a little more expensive, it's worth it for the setting. The bar in the Punta Bonfiglio park offers light meals and the best views of Manarola.

Corniglia
(Town #3)

This is the quiet town—the only one of the five not on the water—with a mellow main square. From the station, a footpath zigzags up nearly 400 stairs to the town. Or take the shuttle bus, which is generally timed to meet arriving trains (€1.50, free with Cinque Terre Card, 2/hr).

Originally settled by a Roman farmer who named it for his mother, Cornelia (how Corniglia is pronounced), the town and its ancient residents produced a wine so famous that—according to legend—vases found at Pompeii touted its virtues. Today, wine is

Corniglia

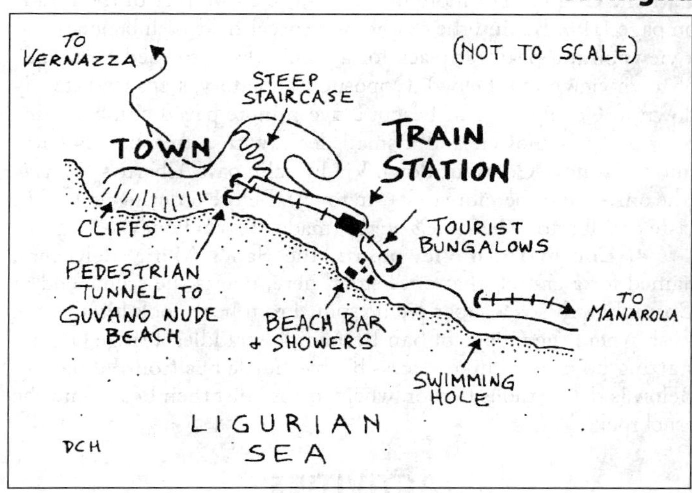

still its lifeblood. Follow the pungent smell of ripe grapes into an alley cellar and get a local to let you dip a straw into a keg. Remote and less visited than the other Cinque Terre towns, Corniglia has fewer tourists, cooler temperatures, a few restaurants, a windy overlook on its promontory, and plenty of private rooms for rent (ask at any bar or shop).

TOURS

Corniglia Town Walk

1. Bus Stop/Town Square: The gateway to this community of 240 people is "Ciappa" square, with an ATM, phone booth, and bus stop. The national park designation has sparked a revitalization of the town, and Corniglia's young generation is now staying put rather than migrating into big cities.

2. Main Street: Stroll the spine of Corniglia, Via Fiaschi. In the fall, the smell of grapes (on their way to becoming wine) wafts from busy cellars. At the Butiega shop (#142), Vincenzo and Lorenzo sell organic local specialties (daily 8:00–20:00). For picnickers, they offer €2.50 made-to-order sandwiches and a fun €3.50 *antipasto misto* to go.

3. Main Square: On Largo Taragio, tables from two bars and a trattoria spill around a memorial to World War I and the town's old well, which once piped in natural spring water from the hillside to locals living without plumbing. What looks like a church is the Oratory of Santa Caterina. (An oratory is a kind of a spiritual clubhouse for a service group doing social work in the name of the

Catholic Church. For more information see "Oratory of the Dead" on page 1119.) Behind the oratory is a soccer field with benches and a viewpoint, a peaceful place for a picnic (less crowded than end-of-town viewpoint, below). Opposite the oratory, steps lead steeply down to Corniglia's non-beach, a five-minute paved climb to sunning rocks, a shower, and a small deck (with a treacherous entry into the water). Continue down Via Fiaschi, past Alberto's *gelateria* (the only—and therefore best—in town). Before ordering, get a free taste of Alberto's *miele di Corniglia* (made of local honey).

4. End-of-Town Viewpoint: The Santa Maria Belvedere, named for a church that once stood here, marks the scenic end of Corniglia. This is a super picnic spot. From here, look high to the west, where the village of San Bernadino straddles a ridge (a good starting point for a hike; accessible by shuttle bus from Vernazza). Below is the tortuous harbor, where locals hoist their boats onto the cruel rocks.

ACTIVITIES

Beaches—This hilltop town has a rocky, man-made beach below its station (toward Manarola). It's clean and uncrowded, and the beach bar has showers, drinks, and snacks.

The nude Guvano (GOO-vah-noh) beach is in the opposite direction (toward Vernazza). Guvano made headlines in Italy in the 1970s, as clothed locals in a makeshift armada of dinghies and fishing boats retook their town beach. But big-city nudists still work on all-over tans in this remote setting. To reach the beach from the Corniglia train station, follow the road north, go over the tracks, and then zigzag below the tracks, following signs to the tunnel in the cliff (walk past the *proprietà privata* sign). When you buzz the intercom, the hydraulic *Get Smart*-type door is opened from the other end. After a 15-minute hike through a cool, moist, and dimly lit and unused train tunnel, you'll emerge at the Guvano beach—and get charged €3. The beach has drinking water, but no WC. A steep (free) trail leads from the beach up to the Corniglia-Vernazza trail. The crowd is Italian counterculture: pierced nipples, tattooed punks, hippie drummers in dreads, and exhibitionist men. The ratio of men to women is about three to two. About half the people on the pebbly beach keep their swimsuits on. With new national park standards, the future of Guvano is in doubt.

SLEEPING

(€1 = about $1.20, country code: 39)

Perched high above the sea on a hilltop, Corniglia has plenty of private rooms (generally Db-€60). To get to the town from the station, catch the shuttle bus or take a 15-minute uphill hike. The town—riddled with meager places charging too much for their rooms—is almost never full.

$$ Cristiana Ricci (not the movie star) rents four rooms just inland from the bus stop (Db-€60, Qb-€90, tel. 0187-812-541, tel. & fax 0187-812-236, mobile 338-937-6547, cri_affittacamere@virgilio.it). She works at Bar Matteo, on the main square, and can meet you there. Her mom rents a few places in town for same price. Cristiana gives guests with this year's book a free coffee-and-brioche breakfast along with their room.

$$ Villa Cecio, more like a hotel, rents eight well-worn rooms on the outskirts of town, all with no character or warmth (Db-€60, cash preferred, views, on main road 200 yards toward Vernazza, tel. 0187-812-043).

$ Pellegrini, on a quiet side street, offers three rooms (one with balcony) that share two baths and a rooftop terrace. You are actually taking a room in someone's home here (D-€45; going up Via Fieschi, take a left at Via Solferino, then go right, left, and left again to find #34; tel. 0187-812-184 or 0187-821-176, Romina).

$$ La Lanterna, a bar on the main square, rents 12 sleepable rooms. It's a last resort (D-€60, Db-€70, tel. 0187-812-291, Via Fieschi 164).

EATING

Corniglia has three decent restaurants. **Cecio,** above the town, is known for its homemade pasta and fresh pesto. The **trattoria** on the main square is most atmospheric. Neither come with particularly charming service. At **Bar Matteo,** Cristiana and Stefano offer light meals and Internet access (also on the main square).

Vernazza
(Town #4)

With the closest thing to a natural harbor—overseen by a ruined castle and an old church—Vernazza is the jewel of the Cinque Terre. Only the occasional noisy slurping up of the train by the mountain reminds you of the modern world.

The action is at the harbor, where you'll find outdoor restaurants, a bar hanging on the edge of the castle, a breakwater with a promenade, and a tailgate-party street market every Tuesday morning. In the summer, the beach becomes a soccer field, where teams fielded by local bars and restaurants provide late-night entertainment. In the dark, locals fish off the promontory, using glowing bobs that shine in the waves.

The town's 500 residents, proud of their Vernazzan heritage, brag, "Vernazza is locally owned. Portofino has sold out." Fearing the change it would bring, keep-Vernazza-small proponents stopped the construction of a major road into the town and region. Families are tight and go back centuries; several generations stay together. In the winter, the population shrinks, as many people move to more comfortable big-city apartments.

Leisure time is devoted to the *passeggiata*—strolling lazily together up and down the main street. Sit on a bench and study the passersby. Explore the characteristic alleys, called *carugi*. Learn—and live—the phrase, "*vita pigra di Vernazza*" (the lazy life of Vernazza).

ORIENTATION

Tourist Information: The TI/park information booth is in the train station (daily 6:30–22:00 in summer, 8:00–20:00 in winter, baggage-check, tel. 0187-812-533).

Helpful Hints

Money: The town has two ATMs (in center and top of town) and a bank.

Bus Service: A shuttle bus, generally with friendly English-speaking Beppe or Simone behind the wheel, runs from the top of the main street to the non-resident parking lot about 500 yards above Vernazza (€1.50 or free with Cinque Terre Card, runs 7:20–19:30, 4/hr). You can also catch the bus to the two sanctuaries in the hills above town (€2.50 each way or free with Cinque Terre Card, schedule posted in train station, 5/day). This high-country 40-minute loop gives you lots of scenery without having to hike.

Best Views: A steep five-minute hike in either direction from Vernazza gives you a classic village photo op (for the best light, head toward Corniglia in the morning, toward Monterosso in the evening). Ristorante "La Torre," with a panoramic terrace, is at the tower on the trail toward Corniglia.

Internet Access: The slick **Internet Point,** run by Alberto and Isabella, is in the village center (daily 9:30–20:00, until 23:00 in summer, HDSL line, will burn CDs for a back-up of your digital photos for €8, international phone cards, tel. 0187-812-949). The **Blue Marlin Bar,** run by Massimo and Carmen, offers Internet access as well (Fri–Wed 7:00–24:00, closed Thu, see "Eating," page 1113).

Laundry: The Blue Marlin Bar (see above) also runs a self-service laundry. Buy tokens at the bar (€4.50 wash, €4.50 dry,

Vernazza

Note: Not to scale Train Station to the Breakwater is a 5-Minute Stroll
Bus Stop
P
Post
Bank + ATM
Rocks
Trail to Monterosso
Cemetery
Boat to Monterosso
Sunning + Swimming
Church
Harbor
Rocks
Break-water
Beach
Shower
Piazza Marconi
Tunnel
Cinque Terre Boats Dock Here
Via Roma
Chapel
Train Station
Castle
Rocks and Cliffs
Trail to Corniglia
Ligurian Sea
1 Trattoria Gianni
2 Albergo Barbara
3 Tonino Basso Rooms & Il Pirata Café
4 Camere Fontana Vecchia
5 Giuliano Basso Rooms
6 Ananasso Bar
7 Bar Baia Saracena
8 Blue Marlin Bar & Café
9 Castello Restaurant
10 Gambero Rosso Restaurant
11 Trattoria del Capitano
12 Ristorante Pizzeria Vulnetia
13 Ristorante Bar Belforte
14 Trattoria da Sandro
15 Trattoria da Piva
16 Ristorante "La Torre"
17 Forno (Bakery)
18 La Cantina del Molo Wine Shop

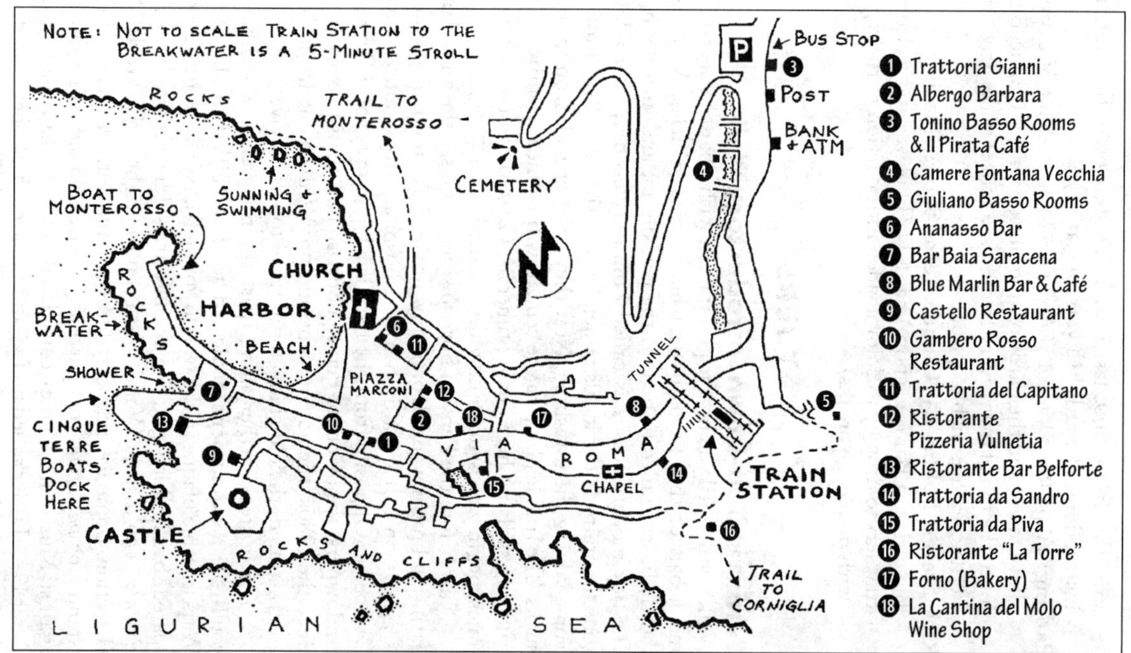

Fri–Wed from 8:00, last load at 22:00, closed Thu, English instructions, 30 yards below train station).

Parking: A parking lot (€1.50/hr, €12/24 hrs, about 500 yards above town) and the hardworking shuttle service (connects the lot to the top of town every 15 min, see above) make driving to Vernazza a reasonable option.

Rick Steves' Public TV Cinque Terre Show: The industrious Blue Marlin Bar (see above) has a DVD player and welcomes travelers to drop by to enjoy a video introduction to the region (with no pledge breaks).

TOURS

Vernazza Top-Down Introductory Walk

Walk uphill until you hit the parking lot, with a bank, a post office, and a barrier that keeps out all but service vehicles. Vernazza's shuttle buses run from here to the parking lot and into the hills. The tidy modern square is called **Fontana Vecchia,** after a long-gone fountain. Older locals remember the river filled with townswomen doing their washing. Now they enjoy checking on the baby ducks. The trail leads up to the cemetery. Imagine the entire village trudging sadly up here during funerals. Glad to be here in happier times, begin your saunter downhill to the harbor.

Just before the Pension Sorriso sign, you'll see the **ambulance** barn (big brown wood doors) on your right. A group of volunteers is always on call for a dash to the hospital, 40 minutes away in La Spezia. Opposite from the barn is a big, empty lot. Like many landowners, the owner of Pension Sorriso had plans to expand, but since the 1980s, the government said no. While some landowners are frustrated, the old character of these towns survives.

A few steps farther along (past the town clinic and library), you'll see a **monument** dedicated to those killed in the World Wars (marble plaque in the wall to your left). Not a family here was spared. Study this sight: On the left are soldiers *morti in combattimento,* who died in World War I; on the right is the World War II section. Some were deported to *Germania;* others—labeled *Part* (stands for *partigiani,* or "partisans")—were killed while fighting against Mussolini. Cynics considered partisans less than heroes. After 1943, Hitler called up Italian boys over 15. Rather than die on the front for Hitler, they escaped to the hills. They become "resistance fighters" in order to remain free.

Perhaps your knees are pressing against the track of the tiny monorail ***trenino.*** The little train is kept up on the wall on your right, except in September and October, when it's busy helping locals bring down the grapes. (Sorry, no rides for the public.) After the harvest, the cantinas in Vernazza are draped with drying grapes. The path to Corniglia leaves from here (behind and above the plaque). Behind you is a tiny square and playground, decorated with three millstones, which no longer grind local olives into oil. From here, Vernazza's tiny river goes underground. Until the 1950s, Vernazza's river ran openly through the center of town. Old-timers recall the days before the breakwater, when the river cascaded down and the surf crashed along Vernazza's main drag. Back then, the town was nicknamed "Little Venice."

Before the tracks (on the left), the wall has 10 spaces, one reserved for each party's political ads during elections—a kind of local pollution control. The **map** on the right, under the railway tracks, shows the region's hiking trails. Number two is the basic favorite. The second set of tracks (nearer the harbor) was recently renovated to lessen the disruptive noise, but locals say it made no difference. Follow the road downhill.

Wandering through this main business center, you'll pass many locals doing their *vasca* (laps) past the entrepreneurial Blue Marlin Bar and the tiny **Chapel of Santa Marta** (the small stone chapel with iron grillwork over the window), where Mass is celebrated only on special Sundays. Next you'll see a grocery, *gelateria*, bakery, pharmacy, another grocery, and another *gelateria*.

On the left, in front of the second *gelateria*, an arch leads to what was a beach, where the town's stream used to hit the sea. Continue down to the **harbor square** and breakwater. Vernazza, with the only natural harbor of the Cinque Terre, was established as the sole place boats could pick up the fine local wine. Peek into the tiny street (behind the Vulnetia restaurant) with the commotion of arches. Vernazza's most characteristic side streets, called *carugi*, lead up from here. The trail (above the church, toward Monterosso) leads to the classic view of Vernazza (see "Best Views," above).

The Burned-Out Sightseer's Visual Tour of Vernazza

Sit at the end of the harbor breakwater (perhaps with a glass of local white wine or something more interesting from a nearby bar—borrow the glass, they don't mind), face the town, and see...

The Harbor—In a moderate storm, you'd be soaked, as waves routinely crash over the *molo* (breakwater, built in 1972). Waves can even wash away tourists squinting excitedly into their cameras. (I've seen it happen.)

The train line (to your left), constructed 130 years ago to tie together a newly united Italy, linked Turin and Genoa with Rome. A second line (hidden in a tunnel at this point) was built in the 1960s. The yellow building alongside the tracks was Vernazza's first train station. You can see the four bricked-up alcoves where people once waited for trains.

Vernazza's fishing fleet is down to just a couple of fishing boats (with the net spools). Vernazzans are more likely to own a boat than a car. Boats are on buoys, except in winter or when the red flag on the pole indicates stormy seas (in which case, they're allowed to be pulled up onto the square—usually reserved for restaurant tables). In the 1970s tiny Vernazza had one of the top water polo teams in Italy, and the harbor was their "pool." Later, when the league required a real pool, Vernazza dropped out.

The Castle—On the far right, the castle, which is now a grassy park with great views, still guards the town (€1, daily 10:00–19:00; from harbor, take stairs by Trattoria Gianni and follow signs to Castello restaurant, tower is a few steps beyond; see the photo and painting gallery rooms). It was the town's lookout back in pirate days. The highest umbrellas mark the recommended Ristorante Castello (see "Eating," page 1113). The squat tower on the water is great for a glass of wine or a bite to eat. Follow the rope to the Ristorante Bar Belforte (see "Eating," page 1115), and pop inside the submarine-strength door. A photo of a major storm shows the entire tower under a wave.

The Town—Vernazza has two halves. *Sciuiu* (literally, "flowery") is the sunny side (on the left), and *luvegu* (literally, "dank") is the shady side (on the right). The houses below the castle were connected by an interior arcade—ideal for fleeing attacks. The "Ligurian pastel" colors are regulated by a commissioner of good taste in the community government. The square before you is locally famous for some of the region's finest restaurants. The big, red, central house—on the site where Genoan warships were built in the 12th century—used to be a kind of guardhouse. Gaze across the windows and notice inhabitants quietly gazing back.

Above the Town—The small, round tower above the guardhouse—another part of the city fortifications—reminds us of Vernazza's importance in the Middle Ages, when it was a key ally of Genoa (whose archenemies were the other maritime republics, especially Pisa). Ristorante "La Torre," just behind the tower, welcomes hikers finishing, starting, or simply contemplating the Corniglia–Vernazza hike, with great town views. Vineyards fill the mountainside beyond the town. Notice the many terraces. Someone—probably after too much of that local wine—calculated that the vineyard terraces of the Cinque Terre have the same amount of stonework as the Great Wall of China. Wine production is down nowadays, as the younger residents choose less physical work. But locals still maintain their plots and proudly serve their family wines. A single steel train line winds up the gully behind the tower. This is for the vintner's *trenino*, the tiny service train. Play "Where's *trenino*?" and see if you can find two. The vineyards once stretched as high as you can see, but since fewer people sweat in the fields these days, the most distant terraces have gone wild again.

The Church, School, and City Hall—Vernazza's Ligurian Gothic church, built with black stones quarried from Punta Mesco (the distant point behind you), dates from 1318. The gray-and-red house above the spire is the local elementary school (which about 25 children attend). High-schoolers go to the "big city," La Spezia. The red building to the right of the schoolhouse, a former monastery, is the city hall. Vernazza and Corniglia function as one community. Through most of the 1990s, the local government was communist. In 1999, they elected a coalition of many parties working to rise above ideologies and simply make Vernazza a better place. Finally, on the top of the hill, with the best view of all, is the town cemetery.

ACTIVITIES

Beach—The harbor's sandy cove has sunning rocks and showers by the breakwater. There's also a ladder on the breakwater for deep-water access. The tiny *acqua pendente* (waterfall) cove, between Vernazza and Monterosso, is accessible only by a small, hired boat. Locals call it their *laguna blu*.

Kayaks—The harbor also has one-person or two-person kayaks available by the hour, as well as dinghy and taxi-boat rentals (June–Sept only, €4/hr for 1, €7/hr for 2).

Massage—Six years ago, Kate Allen moved her massage table from London to Cinque Terre. She provides a good therapeutic rub-down for €45 an hour. Head to the clinic across from Pension Sorriso (100 yards above Vernazza's train tracks) or, for women, arrange for an in-room massage at your hotel rooms while in Vernazza or Monterosso (call for an appointment, cash only, mobile 333-568-4653, katarinaallen@hotmail.com).

SLEEPING

(€1 = about $1.20, country code: 39)

Vernazza, the essence of the Cinque Terre, is my top choice for a home base. There are two recommended pensions and piles of private rooms for rent.

These days, with so many rooms available, you can generally arrive without a reservation and find a place. In fact, you'll save money this way—or gain the chance to shop around and land a place with a terrace and a view for less. Drop by any shop or bar and ask; most locals know someone who rents rooms.

Anywhere you stay here requires some climbing. Night noises can be a problem if you're near the station. Rooms on the harbor come with church bells (but only from 7:00–22:00). Prices do not include breakfast unless otherwise noted. For details on "Sleeping on the Cinque Terre," see page 1096.

Pensions

$$ Trattoria Gianni rents 23 small rooms just under the castle. The funky ones are artfully decorated à la shipwreck and are up lots of tight, winding, spiral stairs. Most have tiny balconies and grand views. The new, comfy rooms lack views but have modern bathrooms and a super-scenic, cliff-hanging private garden. Steely Marisa, who rarely smiles at anyone (not just you), requires check-in before 16:00 (or a phone call to explain when you're coming). Her staff, Giovanni and Simona, both smile and speak a little English (S-€42, D-€60, D with small balcony-€64, Db-€76, Tb-€99, 10 percent discount for cash, Piazza Marconi 5, closed Jan–Feb, tel. & fax 0187-812-228, tel. 0187-821-003, www.giannifranzi.it, info@giannifranzi.it). Pick up your keys at Trattoria Gianni's restaurant/reception on the harbor square and hike up dozens of stairs to #41 (funky, *con vista sul mare*) or #47 (new, *nuovo*) at the top. If you arrive on Wednesday, when the restaurant is closed, pick up your keys at the big *gelateria* by the grotto. (Note: My tour company books this place 50 nights of the season.)

$ Albergo Barbara, on the harbor square, is run by kindly Giuseppe and his Swiss wife, Patricia. Most of their 10 clean, modern rooms share two public showers and WCs (S-€45–48, Db without view-€60, D without view-€45, D with small view-€48, big Db with grand view-€80, Tb-€90; fax or e-mail credit-card information to hold room, but pay cash; 2-night stay preferred, closed Dec–Feb, fans, Piazza Marconi 30, tel. & fax 0187-812-398, mobile 338-793-3261, albergobarbara@libero.it, SE). The two big doubles on the main floor come with grand harbor views (top-floor doubles have small windows and small views). The office is on the top floor of the big, red, vacant-looking building facing the harbor.

Private Rooms *(Affitta Camere)*

The town is honeycombed year-round with private rooms, offering the best values in Vernazza. The owners are usually reluctant to reserve rooms far in advance. It's easiest to call a day or two ahead or simply show up in the morning and look around. Doubles cost €45–70, depending on the view, season, and plumbing. Most places accept only cash. Some have killer views, come with lots of stairs, and cost the same as a small dark place on a back lane over the train tracks. Little English is spoken at many of these places. If you call to let them know your arrival time (or call when you arrive, using the phone just below the station), they'll meet you at the train station.

Especially Well-Managed and Well-Appointed Rooms at the Top of Town

$$ Tonino Basso rents four super, clean, modern rooms, each with its own computer for free Internet access. He's located near the post office, in the only building in Vernazza with an elevator. You get tranquility and air-conditioning, but no views (Sb-€60, Db-€80, Tb-€110, Qb-€130, only B&B to take credit cards, call Tonino's mobile number upon arrival and he'll meet you, mobile 335-269-436, tel. 0187-821-264, fax 0187-821-260, toninobasso@libero.it). If you can't locate Tonino, his wife (Tania) works at the harborside Gambero Rosso restaurant.

$$ Camere Fontana Vecchia is a delightful place, with four bright, spacious, quiet rooms near the post office (no view). It's the only place in Vernazza with almost no stairs to climb (D-€50–60, Db-€60–70, T-€80, Tb-€100, fans and heat, open year-round, Via Gavino 15, tel. 0187-821-130, mobile 333-454-9371, m.annamaria@libero.it, youthful and efficient Annamaria SE).

$$ Giuliano Basso rents four fine rooms that share a large view balcony, allowing you to survey the whole town and Giuliano's own terraced gardens below (but no sea views). Straddling a *trenino* line among orange trees, it's an artfully decorated, Robinson Crusoe-chic wonderland, proudly built out of stone by Giuliano (Db-€75 with breakfast, one family room, open year-round, fridge access, above train station—and therefore with more train noise than others, mobile 333-341-4792, www.cdh.it/giuliano, giuliano@cdh.it). From Pension Sorriso, hike up the trail at the sign to Corniglia; 100 yards later, at the second Corniglia sign, follow the narrow lane left.

Other Reliable Places Scattered through Town and Harborside

$$$ Egi Rooms, run by friendly Egi Verduschi (pronounced "edgy," SE), offers three rooms right in the center on the main drag (S-€65, D-€80, plush and designer Db-€110, Tb-€135, across the street from *gelateria* just before harbor square on main drag at Via Visconti 9, tel. 0187-703-905, mobile 338-822-3202, egidioverduschi@libero.it).

$$ Memo Rooms offers three newly-renovated, immaculate rooms overlooking the main street, in what feels like a miniature hotel (Db-€65, Via Roma 15, tel. 0187-812-360, mobile 338-285-2385).

$$ Martina Callo rents four lofty rooms overlooking the square, up plenty of steps near the silent-at-night church tower (room #1: Qb with harbor view-€110; room #2: huge Qb family room with no view-€110; room #3: Db with grand view terrace-€70: room #4: roomy Db with no view-€55; ring bell at Piazza Marconi 26, tel. & fax 0187-812-365, mobile 329-435-5344, www.roomartina.com, roomartina@supereva.it).

$$ Affitta Camere da Annamaria offers three basic rooms with barnacled ambience up a series of comically tight spiral staircases. Your reward: the best views in town (Db-€75 with town views and terrace, Db-€85 for the top room with the vast sea-view terrace, at pharmacy climb Via Carattino to #64, tel. 0187-821-082).

$$ Nicolina rents four decent rooms: a large one with a view, two overlooking Vernazza's main drag (one comes with frescoed ceiling and a washing machine she'll let you use), and one without any view. Inquire at Pizzeria Vulnetia on the harbor square or reserve in advance by phone (Db-€65, Qb with terrace and view-€130, Piazza Marconi 29, tel. & fax 0187-821-193, www.camerenicolina.it).

$$ Rosa Vitali rents two apartments overlooking the main street. One, for up to three people, has a terrace and fridge (top floor); the other, for four, has windows and a full kitchen (Db-€75, Tb-€100, Qb-€120, small discount for 2 nights or more, reception at Via Visconti 10 next to *gelateria*, tel. 0187-821-181, mobile 340-267-5009, rosa.vitali@libero.it, SE).

$$ Francamaria rents four sharp, comfortable rooms (Db-€60–100, Qb-€100–145, prices depend on view and season, Piazza Marconi 30, tel. 0187-812-002, fax 0187-812-956, mobile 328-711-9728, www.francamaria.com, francamaria@francamaria.com). Son Giovanni has three rooms of his own to rent (same prices but no views).

$$ Rooms by Rosalba rents two no-character, utilitarian rooms 50 yards below the station, overlooking the main street. They're managed by Sonia, who works across the street at the Blue Marlin Bar (Db-€60, family Qb-€70, mobile 338-1136-560, soniazarkovic@yahoo.com).

Other Private Rooms in Vernazza

Here are other places to consider: **Filippo Rooms** (lots of rooms, tel. 0187-812-244), **Eva's Rooms** (Db-€50–60, air-con, tel. 0187-821-134, massimoeva@libero.it), **Sergio Callo Rooms** (apartment Db-€70, tel. 0187-812-284, gemmina@5terre.com), **Armanda** (€65, no view, near castle, Piazza Marconi 15, tel. 0187-812-218, mobile 347-306-4760), **Manuela Moggia** (Db-€70, top of town, Via Gavino 22, tel. 0187-812-397, mobile 333-413-6374), **Elisabetta's Villino Azzurro** (Db-€50–60, view terraces, Via Carattino 62, mobile 347-451-1834 or 333-422-1245, www.elisabettacarro.it, carroelisabetta@hotmail.com), **Tilde's** (Db-€70, sea view, Via Mazzini 9, mobile 339-298-9323), **Patrizia** (Db-€65–70, on main street, tel. 0187-821-231, mobile 335-653-1563, fax 0187-812-907, bemili@libero.it), **Renaldo Leonardini** (Db-€60–75, Via Visconti 15, tel. 0187-821-065, NSE), and **Villa Antonia** (Db-€75, on main drag, tel. 0187-821-143).

EATING

Breakfast

Locals take breakfast about as seriously as flossing. A cappuccino and a pastry or a piece of focaccia does it. No accommodations come with breakfast. Instead, you have several fun options.

The two harborfront bars offer the most ambience. **Ananasso Bar** feels Old World, with low energy but a great location (toasted *panini*, pastries). Eat a bit cheaper at the bar (you're welcome to picnic on a bench or rock) or enjoy the best-situated tables in town. **Bar Baia Saracena** has a chalkboard explaining their various €5 breakfast *menus*. Lucca, the owner, promises a free slice of *bucellato* (the local coffee cake) for breakfast as a bonus for anyone with this year's book taking a breakfast here (located out on the breakwater, tel. 0187-812-113).

The **Blue Marlin Bar** (mid-town) serves a good array of clearly-priced à la carte items (Fri–Wed 7:00–24:00, closed Thu, open daily in Aug, just below station, tel. 0187-821-149). If awaiting a train, its outdoor seats beat the platform. The nearby bakery opens early, offering freshly-made focaccia.

At **Il Pirata delle Cinque Terre,** dynamic Sicilian duo Gianluca and Massimo—and their trusty sidekick Sonia—enthusiastically offer a great assortment of handcrafted, authentic-Sicilian pastries. Gianluca is a pastry artist, hand-painting fanciful sculptured marzipan. Their sweet pastry breakfasts are a hit, with a stunning array of hot-out-of-the-oven treats like *panzerotto*, made of ricotta, cinnamon, and vanilla (€1.20). Other favorites include their *granitas*, slushees made from fresh fruit and garnished with thick whipped cream (daily 6:30–24:00, by post office at top of town, Via Gavino 36, tel. 0187-812-047). While the atmosphere of the place seems like suburban Milano, it has a curious charisma among its customers—bringing Vernazza a welcome bit of Sicily.

Lunch and Dinner

If you enjoy Italian cuisine, Vernazza's restaurants are worth the splurge. All take pride in their cooking and have similar prices. Wander around at about 20:00 and compare the ambience. Expect to spend €8 for pastas and €12 for *secondi*. Harborside restaurants and bars are easygoing. You're welcome to grab a cup of coffee or glass of wine and disappear somewhere on the breakwater, returning your glass when you're done.

Ristorante Castello is run by gracious and English-speaking Monica, her husband Massimo, kind Mario, dashing Francesco, and the rest of her family (you won't see mamma—she's busy personally cooking each *secondo*). Hike high above town to just below the castle for great seafood and regional specialties with commanding

Cinque Terre Cuisine 101

Local Specialities: *Accuighe* (ah-CHOO-gay) are anchovies, a local specialty—always served the day they're caught. If you've always hated anchovies (the harsh, cured-in-salt American kind), try them fresh here. *Tegame alla Vernazza* is the most typical main course in Vernazza: anchovies, potatoes, tomatoes, white wine, oil, and herbs. *Pansotti* are ravioli with ricotta and spinach, often served with a hazelnut or walnut sauce...delightful and filling. While antipasto means cheese and salami in Tuscany, here you'll get *antipasti di mare,* a plate of mixed "fruits of the sea" and a fine way to start a meal. For many, splitting this and a pasta dish is plenty. Try the fun local dessert: *torta della nonna* (grandmother's cake), with a glass of *sciacchetrà* for dunking (see "Wine," below).

Pesto: This region is the birthplace of pesto. Basil, which loves the temperate Ligurian climate, is mixed with cheese (half *Parmigiano* cow cheese and half pecorino sheep cheese), garlic, olive oil, and pine nuts, and then poured over pasta. Try it on spaghetti, *trenette,* or *trofie* (made of flour with a bit of potato, designed specifically for pesto). Many also like pesto lasagna. If you become addicted, small jars of pesto are sold in the local grocery stores (you can take it home or spread it on focaccia here).

Focaccia: This tasty bread also originates from here in Liguria. Locals say the best focaccia is made between the Cinque Terre and Genoa. It's simply bread with olive oil and salt. The baker roughs up the dough with finger holes, then bakes it. Focaccia comes plain or with onions, sage, and olive bits, and is a local favorite for a snack on the beach. Bakeries sell it in rounds or slices by the weight (a portion is about 100 grams, or *un etto*).

Wine: The *vino delle Cinque Terre,* respected throughout Italy, flows cheap and easy throughout the region. It's white—great with the local seafood. *D.O.C.* is the mark of top quality. Red wine is better elsewhere. For a sweet dessert wine, the local *sciacchetrà* wine is worth the splurge (€2.60 per glass, often served with a cookie). While 10 kilos of grapes yield seven liters of local wine, *sciacchetrà* is made from near-raisins, and 10 kilos of grapes make only 1.5 liters of *sciacchetrà.* The word means "push and pull"—push in lots of grapes, pull out the best wine. If your room is up a lot of steps, be warned: *sciacchetrà* is 18 percent alcohol, while regular wine is only 11 percent. In the cool, calm evening, sit on the Vernazza breakwater with a glass of wine and watch the phosphorescence in the waves.

views (Thu–Tue 12:00–15:00 for lunch, 15:00–19:00 for drinks and snacks on cliff-hugging terrace, 19:30–22:00 for dinner, closed Wed and Nov–April, tel. 0187-812-296). Their *lasagna al pesto* and *ravioli di pesce* are time-honored family specialties.

Four places fill the harborfront with happy eaters: **Gambero Rosso,** considered Vernazza's best restaurant, feels classy and costs only a few euros more than the others (Tue–Sun 12:00–15:00 & 19:00–22:00, closed Mon and Dec–Feb, Piazza Marconi 7, tel. 0187-812-265). **Trattoria del Capitano** might serve the best food for the money, including *tagliolini sul pesce*—white fish and delicate pasta—and their *zuppa provenzale,* a hearty Ligurian bouillabaisse (Wed–Mon 12:00–15:00 & 19:00–22:00, closed Tue except in Aug, closed Dec–Jan, tel. 0187-812-201; Paolo, his American wife Julia, and Barbara SE, grandpa Giacomo doesn't need to). **Trattoria Gianni** is an old standby for locals and tourists alike, especially for well-prepared seafood (Thu–Tue 12:00–15:00 & 19:30–22:00, closed Wed except July–Aug, tel. 0187-812-228). **Ristorante Pizzeria Vulnetia** serves regional specialties and pizza (Tue–Sun 12:00–15:00 & 18:30–22:00, closed Mon, Piazza Marconi 29, tel. 0187-821-193).

From the breakwater, a rope leads up and around to the little **Ristorante Bar Belforte,** embedded in the lower part of the old castle. While they serve meals, it's a good spot outside of mealtime for a romantic and/or late-night drink (closed Tue, Seattleite Ryan married into the town and now works here).

Several inland places, without the harbor ambience, manage to compete: **Trattoria da Sandro,** on the main drag, mixes Genovese and Ligurian cuisine with friendly service. It can be a peaceful alternative to the harborside scene (Wed–Mon 12:00–15:00 & 19:00–22:00, closed Tue, just below train station, Via Roma 60, tel. 0187-812-223, Gabriella SE). The more offbeat and intimate **Trattoria da Piva** may come with late-night guitar strumming and Piva's songs in local dialect (Tue–Sun 12:00–14:30 & 19:00–22:00, closed Mon, Via Carattino 6, around corner from pharmacy, tel. 0187-812-194). **Il Pirata delle Cinque Terre,** a haven of heavenly pastry, is popular for good meals and late-night desserts and drinks (see listing under "Breakfast," above).

For a grand view and perfect peace, hike to Franco's **Ristorante "La Torre"** for a dinner at sunset (Wed–Mon 12:00–21:30, kitchen closes from 15:00–19:30 but drinks are served, closed Tue, on trail toward Corniglia, tel. 0187-821-082).

The waiters at **Bar Baia Saracena** ("Saracen Bay") take the pirate theme to heart, swinging in with earrings that blow in the wind. The bar has a dozen plastic tables on the breakwater and serves light meals (€5 salads, €7 pizza, €3.50 glasses of *sciacchetrà*—sweet dessert wine; also see listing under "Breakfast," above).

The main street is creatively filling tourists' needs. The **Blue Marlin** bar offers a good selection of sandwiches, salads, and *bruschetta.* The **Forno** bakery has good focaccia and veggie tarts, and several bars sell sandwiches and pizza by the slice. **Grocery stores** also make inexpensive sandwiches to order (Mon–Sat 8:00–13:00 & 17:00–19:30, Sun 7:30–13:00). The town's two ***gelaterias*** are good.

La Cantina del Molo, the wine shop, will uncork the bottle you buy and supply cups to go (daily 10:30–20:00, until 22:00 in summer, owner makes 5 of the wines, tasting possible).

Monterosso al Mare
(Town #5)

This is a resort with cars, hotels, rentable beach umbrellas, crowds, and a thriving late-night scene. Monterosso has two parts: A new town (called Fegina) with a parking lot, train station, and the TI; and an old town *(centro storico),* cradling the Old World charm with small, crooked lanes, hole-in-the-wall shops, pastel townscapes, and a new generation of creative small businesspeople eager to keep their visitors happy. A pedestrian tunnel connects the old with the new.

Strolling the waterfront promenade, you can pick out each of the Cinque Terre towns decorating the coast. After dark they sparkle. This town is the most enjoyable of the five for young travelers wanting to connect with other young travelers and looking for a little action after dark. Even still, Monterosso is not a full-blown Portofino-style resort—and locals appreciate quiet, sensitive guests.

ORIENTATION

Tourist Information: The TI Proloco is next to the train station (Easter-Oct Mon–Sat 9:30–12:00 & 14:30–18:40, Sun 9:30–12:00, closed Nov–Easter, exit station and go left a few doors, tel. 0187-817-506). The Cinque Terre has park offices on Piazza Garibaldi in the old town and in the train station in the new town (daily 8:00–22:00, until 20:00 in winter, baggage-check, tel. 0187-817-059, www.parconazionale5terre.it, parconazionale5terre@libero.it).

Arrival in Monterosso al Mare

Monterosso is 30 minutes off the freeway (exit: Carrodano). Parking is easy (except Aug and summer weekends) in the huge beachfront guarded lot (€9/day). As you approach, save six miles of needless driving by deciding ahead of time whether to head into the old or new town. Pay attention to the fork that pops up three miles above town, directing cars to *centro storico* (old center, no parking available except for Villa Steno guests) or Fegina (the new town, parking, most likely where you want to go). Train travelers arrive in the new town, where it's a scenic 10-minute stroll to all the old-town action (leave station to the left, but for hotels in the new town, turn right out of station).

Helpful Hints

Bus Service: Shuttle buses run along the waterfront between the old town (Piazza Garibaldi, just beyond the tunnel), the train station, and the parking lot at the end of Via Fegina (Campo Sportivo stop). While the buses can be convenient, saving you a 10-minute schlep with your bags, they only go twice per hour and are likely not worth the trouble (€1, free with Cinque Terre Card).

Medical Help: The town's bike-riding, leather-bag-toting doctor is Dr. Vitone (mobile 338-853-0949).

Internet Access: The Net, a few steps off the main drag (Via Roma) on Via Vittorio Emanuele, offers free coffee to patrons, 10 high-speed computers, and classical music (if Renato's on duty). Renato and Enzo happily provide information on the Cinque Terre, helping visitors book accommodations and schedule tours or scuba-diving excursions (Via Vittorio Emanuele 55, tel. 0187-817-288, www.monterossonet.com). To view my Cinque Terre public television show on their DVD player for free, show them this year's book.

Laundry: A self-service launderette is at Via Mazzini 4 (daily 9:30–13:00 & 15:00–20:00, 13 pounds wash and dry for €11 full-service, allow 2 hrs, just off main drag below L'Alta Marea restaurant).

Boats: From the old-town harbor, boats run nearly hourly (10:30–17:00) to Vernazza, Manarola, Riomaggiore, and Portovenere. Schedules are posted in Cinque Terre park offices (for details, see page 1090).

TOURS

Monterosso Town Tour

Breakwater—Hike out and climb a few rough steps to the very top of the breakwater. (If you're visiting by boat, you'll start here anyway.) From this point, you can survey the old town and the new town (stretching to the left, with train station and parking lot). The little fort above is a private home. The harbor now hosts more paddleboats than fishing boats. Sand erosion is a major problem here. While old-timers remember a vast beach, their grandchildren

Monterosso al Mare

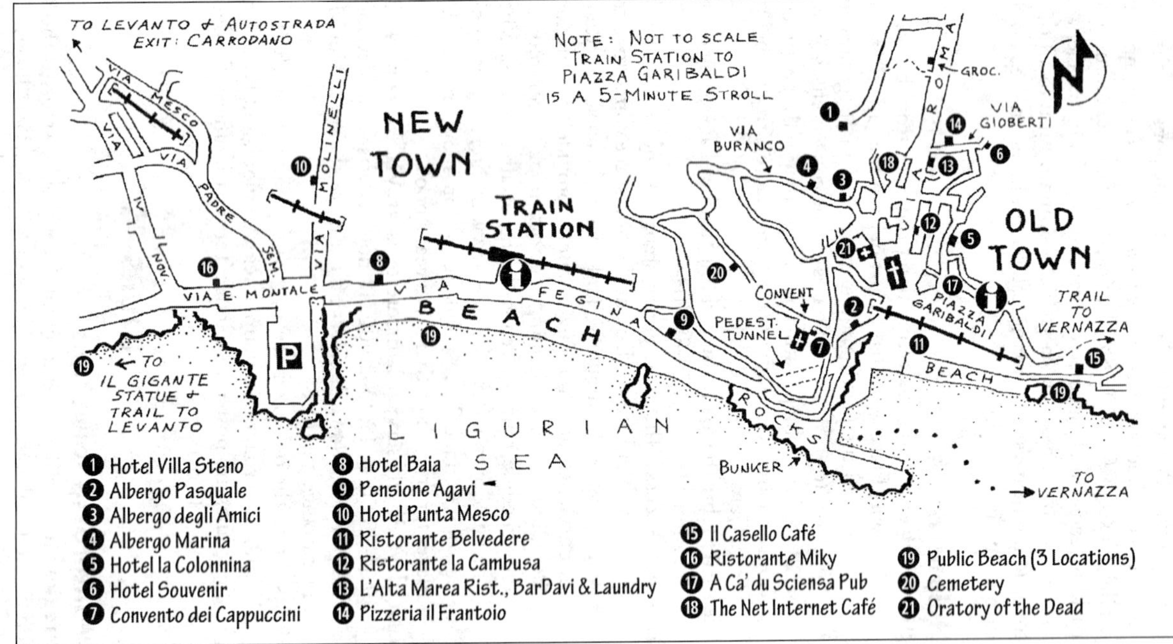

truck in sand each spring to give tourists something to lie on. (The Nazis liked the Cinque Terre, too—find two of their bomb-hardened bungalows, near left and far right.)

The fancy €300-a-night, four-star Hotel Porto Roco (on the far right) marks the trail to Vernazza. High above, you see the costly road built in the 1980s to connect Cinque Terre towns with the freeway over the hills. The two capes (Punta di Montenero and Punta Mesco) define the Cinque Terre region—you can just about make out the towns from here. The closer cape, Punta Mesco, marks an important sea-life sanctuary, home to a rare sea grass that provides an ideal home for fish eggs. Buoys keep fishing boats away. The cape was once a quarry, providing employment to locals who chipped out the stones used to cobble the streets of Genoa. On the far end of the new town you can just see the statue named *Il Gigante*. It's 45 feet tall and once held a trident. While it looks as if it was hewn from the rocky cliff, it's actually made of reinforced concrete and dates from the beginning of the 20th century.

From the breakwater, walk to the old-town square (just past the train tracks and beyond the beach). Find the statue of a dandy holding what looks like a box cutter.

Piazza Garibaldi—The statue honors the dashing firebrand revolutionary who, in 1870, helped unite the people of Italy into a modern nation. Facing Garibaldi, with your back to the sea, you'll see (from right to left) the City Hall (with the now-required European Union flag aside the Italian one), a big home for poor and homeless elderly, and the park information center (in a building bombed in 1945 by the Allies, who were attempting to take out the train line). You'll also see the A Ca' du Sciensa pub (with historic town photos inside and upstairs—see "Nightlife," page 1121), covered arcades where the old-timers hang out (they know all), and the crenellated bell tower of the town church (originally part of a fort that predated the Romanesque Church of St. John the Baptist). Go to church.

Church of St. John the Baptist—This black-and-white church, with marble from Carrara, is typical of this region's Romanesque style. The church dates from 1307—the proud inscription on the middle column inside reads "MilleCCCVII." Leaving the church, turn immediately left and go to church again.

Oratory of the Dead—During the Counter-Reformation, the Catholic Church offset the rising influence of the Lutherans by creating brotherhoods of good works. These religious Rotary clubs were called "confraternities." Monterosso had two, nicknamed White and Black. This building is the oratory of the Black group, whose mission—as the macabre decor indicates—was to arrange for funerals and take care of widows, orphans, the shipwrecked, and those who ignore the request for a €1 donation. It dates from the 16th century, and membership has passed from father to son for generations. Notice the fine 17th-century carved choir stalls just inside the door.

Return to the beach and find the brick steps leading up to the hill-capping convent (starting between the train tracks and the pedestrian tunnel).

The Switchbacks of the Monks—Follow the yellow brick road (OK, it's orange...but I couldn't help singing as I skipped skyward). Go constantly uphill until you reach a convent church, then a cemetery, in a ruined castle at the summit. The lane (Salita dei Cappuccini) is nicknamed "Zii di Frati" (switchbacks of the monks). Midway up the switchbacks, you'll see a statue of St. Francis and a wolf enjoying a grand view. From here, backtrack 20 yards and continue uphill. When you reach a gate marked *Convento e Chiesa Cappuccini* you have arrived. Go to church.

Church of the Cappuccin Monks—The convent is now a tranquil guesthouse (see "Sleeping," page 1123). Before stepping inside, notice the church's striped Romanesque facade. It's all fake. Tap it—no marble, just cheap 18th-century stucco. Sit in the rear pew. The high altarpiece painting of St. Frances can be rolled up on special days to reveal a statue of Mary, which stands behind it. Look at the statue of St. Anthony to the right and smile (you're on convent camera). Wave at the security camera—they're nervous about the precious painting to your left.

This fine painting of the crucifixion is attributed to Van Dyck, the Flemish master who lived and worked for years in nearby Genoa. When Jesus died, the earth went dark. Notice the eclipsed sun in the painting, just to the right of the cross. Do the electric candles work? Pick one up, pray for peace, and plug it in. (Leave €0.50, or unplug it and put it back.) From the church, hike uphill to the cemetery that fills the remains of the castle, capping the hill. Look out from the gate and enjoy the view.

Cemetery—In the Dark Ages, the village huddled within this castle. Slowly it expanded. Notice the town view from here—no sea. You're looking at the oldest part of Monterosso, huddled behind the hill, out of view of 13th-century pirates. Explore the cemetery, but remember that cemeteries are sacred and treasured places (as is clear by the abundance of fresh flowers). Ponder the B&W photos of grandparents past. Q.R.P. is *Qui Riposa in Pace* (a.k.a. R.I.P.). Rich families had their own little tomb buildings. Climb to the very summit—the castle's keep, or place of last refuge. Priests are buried in a line of graves closest to the sea, but facing inland—the town's holy sanctuary high on the hillside (above the road, hiding behind trees). Each Cinque Terre town has a lofty sanctuary, dedicated to Mary and dear to the village hearts. From here, your tour's over—any trail leads you back into town.

ACTIVITIES

Beaches—Monterosso's beaches, immediately in front of the train station, are easily the Cinque Terre's best and most crowded. This town is a sandy resort with everything rentable: lounge chairs, umbrellas, and paddleboats. Beaches are free only where you see no umbrellas. It's often worth the euros to enjoy a private beach. The local hidden beach (free and generally less crowded) is tucked away under Il Casello restaurant at the east end of town (near Vernazza trailhead).

Kayaks, Tours, and Rentals—For information on hiking tours, boat excursions/rentals, chartered fishing, and other tourist services, check out American expatriate Kate Little's Travel Services Web site (tel. 328-842-6885, www.fishnet.it, kate@fishnet.it).

Shuttle Buses for High Country Hikes—Monterosso's bus service (described in "Helpful Hints," above) continues beyond the town limits. They do the heavy lifting, taking hikers to interesting trailheads in the nearby hills. They also go to Colle di Gritta, where you can hike back down to Monterosso via the Sanctuary of Soviore (1 hr, easy) or to Levanto via Punta Mesco (2 hrs, strenuous). Rides costs €1 (free with Cinque Terre Card). For hiking details, ask at either park info booth (at the train station or Piazza Garibaldi).

NIGHTLIFE

Wander up to **Il Casello** for nightlife with a sea view. It's the best on-the-beach drinking spot—inexpensive and hip—with a creative and fun drink list. Built in about 1870 as the town's first train station, it overlooks the beach on the road toward Vernazza, with outdoor tables sandwiched between the old-town beaches. It's also a great place for a salad or sandwich during the day (Wed–Mon 10:30–3:00, closed Tue and Oct–March, tel. 0187-818-330).

A Ca' du Sciensa ("The House of Sciensa") fills an old mansion with an antique dumbwaiter—a remnant from the days when servants toiled downstairs while the big shots wined and dined up top. This classy-yet-laid-back pub offers breezy square seating, bar action on the ground level, an intimate lounge upstairs, and discreet balconies to share with your best travel buddy. It's a good place for light meals and plenty of drinks. Luca and Diego encourage you to wander around the place and enjoy the old Cinque Terre photo collection (daily 9:00–24:00, Piazza Garibaldi 17, tel. 0187-818-233).

Enoteca Eliseo, the first wine bar in town, comes with operatic ambience. Eliseo and his wife Mary love music and wine. You can select a fine bottle from their shop shelf, and for €6 extra, enjoy it and the village action from their cozy tables. They serve munchies and light snacks. Wines sold by the glass *(bicchiere)* are posted (closed Tue in winter, Piazza Matteotti 3, a few blocks inland behind church, tel. 0187-817-308).

BarDavi showcases owners Daniele's and Valeria's stylish knack for delicious entertainment. Each day after 17:00, they offer an amazing "cocktails *con tapas*" deal: Buy a €6 drink and get a light meal's worth of good, local appetizers for free (daily 7:30–22:00, under the arch on main drag, Via Roma 34, tel. 0187-817-019).

Fast Bar, where young travelers and night owls gather, is located on Via Roma in the old town. Customers mix travel tales with big, cold beers (sandwiches and snacks served until midnight, open nightly until 1:30, closed Mon Oct–May).

SLEEPING

(€1 = about $1.20, country code: 39)
Monterosso al Mare, the most beach-resorty of the five Cinque Terre towns, offers maximum comfort and ease. The TI (Proloco) just outside the train station can give you a list of €30–35 per-person double rooms. You can also check with The Net Internet café in town (see page 1118).

To locate the hotels, see the map on page 1118. To get to the old town from the station, exit left, walk along the waterfront, and go through the tunnel.

In the Old Town

$$$ Hotel Villa Steno is lovingly managed and features great view balconies, private gardens off some rooms, air-conditioning, and the friendly help of English-speaking Matteo and his wife Carla. Of their 16 rooms, 12 have view balconies (Sb-€90, Db-€135, Tb-€155, Qb-€175, includes hearty buffet breakfast, Internet, self-service laundry for guests, Via Roma 109, tel. 0187-817-028 or 0187-818-336, fax 0187-817-354, www.pasini.com, steno@pasini.com). It's a 10-minute hike (or €7 taxi ride) from the train station to the top of the old town. They have my Cinque Terre public television show and other Italy episodes for their lobby DVD player. The Steno has a tiny parking lot (free, but call to reserve a spot).

$$$ Albergo Pasquale is a modern, comfortable place, run by the same family that owns Hotel Villa Steno (see above). It's just a few steps from the beach, boat dock, tunnel entrance (to new town), and train tracks. Noise is not a problem (same prices, welcome drink, and Italy DVD as Villa Steno, above; air-con, all rooms with sea view, Via Fegina 8, tel. 0187-817-550 or 0187-817-477, fax 0187-817-056, pasquale@pasini.com, Felicita and Marco SE).

$$$ Two places, next door to each other on a quiet street, both push half-pension by bloating their B&B prices and offering dinner for just a few euros more. The fancy **Albergo degli Amici** has

40 modern rooms (Db-€100–131, includes breakfast, Db with half-pension-€140; no views from rooms, but peaceful above-it-all view garden with "sun beds"—lawn chairs with movable sun shades; Via Buranco 36, tel. 0187-817-544, fax 0187-817-424, www.hotelamici.it, amici@cinqueterre.it). The less-fancy **Albergo Marina** has 23 decent rooms and a garden with lemon trees (Db-€108, €130 with dinner July–Aug, 5 percent discount with cash, elevator, air-con, next door at Via Buranco 40, tel. & fax 0187-817-242 or 0187-817-613, www.hotelmarinacinqueterre.it, marina@cinqueterre.it). To get there from the old-town harbor, go to the left of the arcaded building with the bell tower, walk a block, and turn left.

$$ Hotel La Colonnina, a comfy, modern place with big rooms, is on a sleepy side street and takes reservations in advance only for three-night stays. For a shorter stay, call a day or two ahead (Db-€80–95, cash only, breakfast extra, air-con, elevator, rooftop terrace, garden, Via Zuecca 6, tel. 0187-817-439, fax 0187-817788, www.lacolonninacinqueterre.it, info@lacolonninacinqueterre.it). The hotel is in the old town by the train tracks, directly behind the statue of Garibaldi (one block up, to the right).

$$ Hotel Souvenir is Monterosso's cash-only backpacker's hotel. It has two buildings, each utilitarian but comfortable (one more stark than the other). The first is for students (S-€25, Sb-€30, D-€50, Db-€60, T-€75, no breakfast); the other one is nicer and pricier, with a lounge and pleasant, leafy courtyard (Sb-€40, Db-€80, Tb-€120, includes breakfast). Walk three blocks inland from the main old-town square to Via Gioberti 30 (tel. 0187-817-822, tel. & fax 0187-817-595, www.monterossonet.com, hotel_souvenir@yahoo.com).

$ Casa Manuel B&B is a ramshackle place run by a ramshackle artist with big, basic youth-hostel-type rooms and a good view (€25 per person in Sb, Db, and Tb; family and student deals, cash only, includes self-serve breakfast; in old town, up stepped lane, behind church at top of town, Via San Martino 39; to book, contact Kate at mobile 328-842-6885 or kate@fishnet.it).

Between the Old and New Towns

$$ Convento dei Cappuccini, which may close in 2006, rents 16 spartan rooms on the hill that divides the old and new parts of Monterosso. The terrace has a tremendous panoramic view. Meals are served in a stark old refectory, surrounded by musty, faith-bolstering paintings. It's a long, steep, 15-minute hike from the station (follow the signs from just before the tunnel). You can taxi to within 200 yards (the cemetery) for €7. Rooms, named for monks, come with killer views, a 23:00 curfew, and angelic twin beds with footboards (bad news for those over 6'2"). The gardens, cloisters, views, and rustic elegance all contribute to the dreamy-retreat atmosphere

Sergio and Jerri Redaelli like to give their guests (S-€35, D-€70, Db-€80, all twin beds, includes breakfast, optional dinner-€15, reserve by leaving credit-card number but pay cash, 2-night minimum, tel. 0187-817-531, monterosso.convento@libero.it).

In the New Town

To reach the following listings, turn right as you leave the station. The first two are on the beach, with great views.

$$$ Hotel Baia (by-yah), overlooking the beach near the station, has appealing, high-ceilinged rooms, but impersonal staff. Of the hotel's 28 rooms, the best little two-chair view balconies are on top floors. No matter what, request a view room, since it's the same price (Db-€100–140, includes breakfast, slow elevator, Via Fegina 88, tel. 0187-817-512, fax 0187-818-322, www.baiahotel.it, baiahotel@libero.it).

$$$ Pensione Agavi has 10 bright, airy rooms overlooking the beach near the big rock (S-€35, Sb-€60, D-€80, Db-€100, no breakfast, refrigerators, turn left out of station to Fegina 30, tel. 0187-817-171, fax 0187-818-264, mobile 333-697-4071, www.paginegialle.it /hotelagavi, agavi@libero.it, spunky Hillary SE).

$$$ Hotel Punta Mesco has 17 quiet, modern rooms without views, but some have little terraces (Db-€120, includes breakfast, 5 percent discount with cash, air-con, free parking; exit right from station, take first right to Via Molinelli 35; tel. 0187-817-495, www.hotelpuntamesco.it, info@hotelpuntamesco.it).

EATING

Ristorante Belvedere is *the* place for a good-value meal on the harborfront. Their *amphora di pesce*—mixed seafood stew—is huge, and can easily be shared by up to four (€43/2 people, extra for *antipasti* or pasta). The place is energetically run by Fredrico and Roberto (Wed–Mon 12:00–14:30 & 19:00–22:00, closed Tue off-season, on the harbor in the old town, tel. 0187-817-033).

L'Alta Marea offers a specialty fish ravioli, the catch of the day, and huge crocks of fresh, steamed mussels. Marco is the young chef who cooks with charisma. His wife Anna takes good care of their guests (Thu–Tue 12:00–15:00 & 18:30–22:00, closed Wed, Via Roma 54, tel. 0187-817-170). This place is quieter, buried in old town two blocks off the beach.

Nearby, **La Cambusa** serves up traditional Ligurian cuisine to hungry locals and tourists alike (Tue–Sun 12:00–14:30 & 18:45–22:00, closed Mon except July–Aug, Via Roma 6, tel. 0187-817-546).

Miky is packed with locals who know their seafood and want to eat in a classy environment, but don't want to spend a fortune. For great food, this could be the best value in the entire Cinque Terre. It's clearly a family operation: Miky (dad), Simonetta (mom), and charming Sara (the daughter) all work hard. All their pasta is "pizza pasta"—cooked normally but finished in a bowl that's encased in a thin pizza crust. They cook the concoction in a wood-fire oven to keep in the aroma. This place also has the best wine list in the area, with most available by the glass if you ask (pastas-€10, *secondi*-€18, sweets-€5, Wed–Mon 12:00–15:00 & 19:00–23:00, closed Tue, reservations wise in summer, in the new town, 100 yards north of train station at Via Fegina 104, tel. 0187-817-608).

Light Meals, Take-Out Food, and Breakfast

Lots of shops and bakeries sell pizza and focaccia for an easy picnic at the beach or on the trail. At **Il Frantoio,** Simone makes tasty pizza to go or to munch perched on a stool (daily 9:00–14:00 & 16:00–20:00 but closed Thu in winter, Via Gioberti 1, just off Via Roma, tel. 0187-818-333). For a fun, light meal on a terrace overlooking the beach, try **Il Casello** (see "Nightlife," page 1121).

BarDavi serves the best breakfast in town, a great €10 "international" buffet (also see "Nightlife," page 1122).

TRANSPORTATION CONNECTIONS

Trains

The five towns of the Cinque Terre are on a milk-run train line (described in "Getting Around the Cinque Terre," page 1088). Hourly trains connect each town with the others, La Spezia, and Genoa. While a few of these local trains go to more distant points (Milan or Pisa), it's much faster to change in La Spezia or Monterosso to a bigger train. For train info, call 0187-817-458.

From La Spezia by Train to: Rome (10/day, 4 hrs), **Pisa** (hrly, 1 hr, direction: Livorno, Rome, Salerno, Naples, etc.), **Florence** (nearly hrly, 2.5 hrs, change in Pisa), **Milan** (hrly, 3 hrs direct or 4 hrs with change in Genoa), **Venice** (2/day, 6 hrs, with change in Pisa and Florence; or 2/day, 6 hrs, with change in Milan; or 1 direct/day, in summer only).

From Monterosso by Train to: Venice (2/day, 5.5 hrs, with change in Florence and Pisa; or 2/day, 6 hrs, with change in Milan), **Milan** (11/day, 3 hrs, with change in Genoa), **Genoa** (hrly, 1.25 hrs), **Turin** (7/day, 3 hrs), **Pisa** (8/day, 1.5 hrs), **Sestri Levante** (hrly, 15 min, most trains to Genoa stop here), **La Spezia** (nearly hrly, 20 min), **Levanto** (nearly hrly, 6 min).

AMSTERDAM

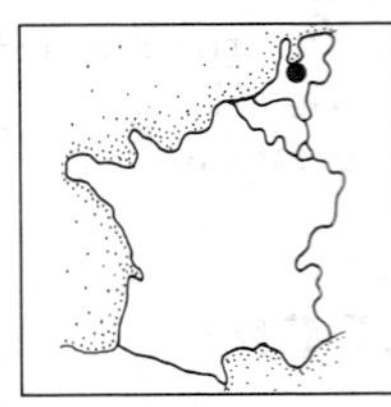

Amsterdam is a progressive way of life housed in Europe's most 17th-century city. Physically, it's built upon millions of pilings. But more than that, it's built on good living, cozy cafés, great art, street-corner jazz, stately history, and a spirit of live-and-let-live. It has 737,000 people and almost as many bikes. It also has more canals than Venice...and about as many tourists.

During its Golden Age in the 1600s, Amsterdam was the world's richest city, an international sea-trading port, and the cradle of capitalism. Wealthy, democratic burghers built a planned city of canals lined with trees and townhouses topped with fancy gables. Immigrants, Jews, outcasts, and political rebels were drawn here by its tolerant atmosphere, while painters like young Rembrandt captured that atmosphere on canvas. But all this history is only the beginning.

Approach the city not as a historian but as an ethnologist observing a strange culture. Stroll through any neighborhood, and see things that are commonplace here but rarely found elsewhere. Carillons chime quaintly in neighborhoods selling sex, as young professionals smoke pot with impunity next to old ladies in bonnets selling flowers. Observe the neighborhood's "social control," where a man feels safe in his home knowing he's being watched by the hookers next door.

The Dutch are unique. They may be the world's most handsome people—tall, healthy, and with good posture—and the most open, honest, and refreshingly blunt. They like to laugh. As connoisseurs of world culture, they appreciate Rembrandt paintings, Indonesian food, and the latest French film—but with an unsnooty, blue-jeans attitude.

Be warned: Amsterdam, a bold experiment in freedom, may box your Puritan ears. Take it all in, then pause to watch the sunset—at 10:00 p.m.—and see the Golden Age reflected in a quiet canal.

Planning Your Time

Amsterdam is worth a full day of sightseeing on even the busiest itinerary. While the city has a couple of must-see museums, its best attraction is its own breezy ambience. The city's a joy on foot—and a breezier and faster joy by bike. Here are the essential stops for a day in Amsterdam:

In the morning, see the city's two great art museums: the Van Gogh and the Rijksmuseum (cafeteria lunch). Walk from the museums to the Singel flower market, then take a relaxing hour-long, round-trip canal cruise from the dock at Spui (see "Tours," below). After the cruise, stroll through the peaceful Begijnhof courtyard and tour the nearby Amsterdam History Museum. Visiting the Anne Frank House after 18:00 will save you an hour in line (last entry is 20:30, or 18:30 Sept–March). Have a memorable dinner: try Dutch pancakes or a rijstafel—an Indonesian smorgasbord.

On a balmy evening, Amsterdam has a Greek-island ambience. Stroll through the Jordaan neighborhood for the idyllic side of town and wander down Leidsestraat to Leidseplein for the roaring café and people scene. Tour the Red Light District while you're at it.

With extra time: With two days in Holland, I'd side-trip by bike, bus, or train to an open-air folk museum and visit Edam or Haarlem. With a third day, I'd do the other great Amsterdam museums. With four days, I'd visit The Hague (for details, see "Netherlands Day Trips" in the next chapter).

ORIENTATION

(area code: 020)

Amsterdam's central train station, on the north edge of the city, is your starting point, with the TI, bike rental, and trams fanning out to all points. Damrak is the main north–south street axis, connecting the station with Dam Square (people-watching and hangout center) and its Royal Palace. From this spine, the city spreads out like a fan, with 90 islands, hundreds of bridges, and a series of concentric canals—named "Gentleman's" (Herengracht), "Emperor's" (Keizersgracht), and "Prince's" (Prinsengracht)—that were laid out in the 17th century, Holland's Golden Age. Amsterdam's major sights are within walking distance of Dam Square.

To the east of Damrak is the oldest part of the city (today's Red Light District), and to the west is the newer part, where you'll find the Anne Frank House and the Jordaan neighborhood. Museums and Leidseplein nightlife cluster at the southern edge of the city center.

Tourist Information

There are four VVV offices ("VVV" is Dutch for TI—tourist information office): inside the train station at track 2 (Mon–Sat 8:00–20:00, Sun 9:00–17:00), in front of the train station (daily 9:00–17:00), on Leidsestraat (less crowded, daily 9:00–19:00), and at the airport (daily 7:00–22:00).

Avoid the crowded, inefficient offices if you can. For €0.60 a minute, you can save yourself a trip by calling the TI toll line at 0900-400-4040 (Mon–Fri 9:00–17:00). If you're staying in nearby Haarlem, ask your Amsterdam questions and pick up the brochures at the helpful, friendly, and rarely crowded Haarlem TI (see next chapter).

At Amsterdam's TIs, consider buying a city map (€2), and any of the walking-tour brochures (€1.50 each, including *Discovery Tour Through the Center, The Former Jewish Quarter,* and *Walks Through Jordaan*). For entertainment, pick up the *Day by Day* calendar (€1.75), call the Last Minute Ticket Shop (tickets for theater, classical music, and major rock shows, tel. 0900-0191), or check out "Nightlife" on page 1147.

At Amsterdam's Central Station, GWK Change has hotel-reservation windows whose clerks sell local and international phone cards and cheaper city maps (€1.60) and can answer basic tourist questions, with shorter lines (in west tunnel, at right end of station as you leave platform, tel. 020/627-2731).

Don't use the TI or GWK to book a room; you'll pay €5 per person and your host loses 13 percent—meaning you'll likely pay a higher rate. The phone system is easy, everyone speaks English, and the listings in this book are a better value than the potluck booking you'd get from the TI.

Passes: The **Museumkaart**—marketed to locals but available to anyone—is a great deal if you're staying several days. It covers the major museums (except for the Anne Frank House)—plus a dozen others in Amsterdam and many more throughout the Netherlands. Knowing a museum is "free" with your pass can suddenly make even minor sights a serendipitous joy (€29.95, good for 1 year, sold at most participating museums, www.museumkaart.nl).

The pricier **Amsterdam Pass,** which covers most museums and all public transportation, is a far lesser value (€31/24 hrs, €41/48 hrs, €51/72 hrs, sold at TIs).

Tourist Information Online: Try www.visitamsterdam.nl (Amsterdam Tourism Board), www.amsterdam.nl (City of Amsterdam), and www.holland.com (Netherlands Board of Tourism).

Amsterdam

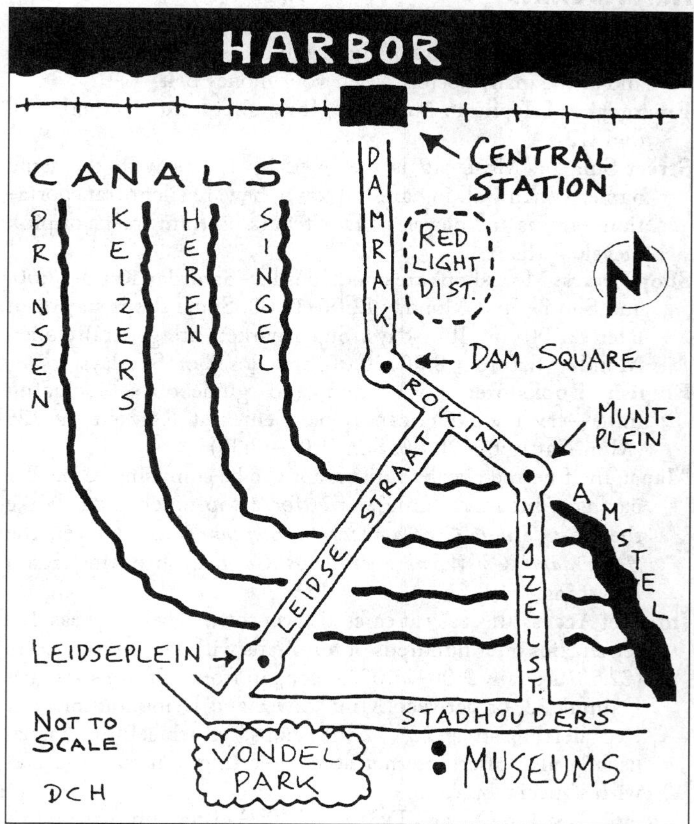

Arrival in Amsterdam

By Train: Amsterdam swings, and the hinge that connects it to the world is its perfectly central Central Station. Expect a chaotic construction zone—the station is being renovated through 2010. The international ticket office should be at track 2, and luggage lockers are at the far east end of the building (from €3.30/24 hrs, daily 7:00–23:00).

Walk out the door of the station, and you're in the heart of the city. You'll nearly trip over trams ready to take you anywhere your feet won't. Straight ahead is Damrak street, leading to Dam Square. With your back to the entrance of the station, the TI and GVB public-transit offices are just ahead and to your left. And on your right is a vast, multistoried bike garage.

By Plane: For details on getting from Schiphol Airport into downtown Amsterdam, see page 1163.

Helpful Hints

Theft Alert: Tourists are considered green and rich, and the city has more than its share of hungry thieves—especially on trams and at the many hostels. Wear your money belt.

Emergency Telephone Number: Throughout the Netherlands, dial 112.

Street Smarts: Most canals are lined by streets with the same name. When walking around town, beware silent transportation—trams and bicycles. (Don't walk on tram tracks or pink bicycle paths.)

Shop Hours: Most shops are open Tuesday–Saturday 10:00–18:00, and Sunday and Monday 12:00–18:00. Some shops stay open later (21:00) on Thursdays. Supermarkets are generally open Monday–Saturday 8:00–20:00, and closed on Sundays.

English Bookstore: For fiction and guidebooks—including mine—try the American Book Center at Kalverstraat 125 (Mon–Sat 10:00–20:00, Sun 11:00–18:30).

Maps: The free and cheap tourist maps can be confusing. Consider paying a bit more (around €2) for a top-notch map. I like the *Carto Studio Centrumkaart Amsterdam* or, better yet, the *Amsterdam: Go Where the Locals Go* map by Amsterdam Anything.

Internet Access: It's easy at cafés all over town. Two huge easyInternetcafés offer hundreds of terminals with fast, cheap access (€2.50/hr, daily 9:00–21:00, a block in front of train station at Damrak 33, or between Mint Tower and Rembrandtplein at Reguliersbreestraat 22). "Coffeeshops," which sell marijuana, usually also offer Internet access—letting you surf the Net with a special bravado.

Queen's Day: On Queen's Day, April 30, Amsterdam turns into a gigantic garage sale/street market.

Getting Around Amsterdam

The helpful GVB public-transit information office is in front of the train station (next to TI). Its free, multilingual *Public Transport Amsterdam Tourist Guide* includes a transit map and explains ticket options and tram connections to all the sights.

By Bus, Tram, and Métro: Trams #2 and #5 travel the north–south axis from Central Station to Dam Square to Leidseplein to Museumplein. Tram #14 goes east–west (Westerkerk–Dam Square–Muntplein–Waterlooplein–Plantage). If you get lost in Amsterdam, 10 of the city's 17 trams take you back to Central Station. The Métro (underground train) is used mostly for commuting to the suburbs, but it does connect Central Station with some sights east of Damrak (Nieuwmarkt–Waterlooplein–Weesperplein).

You have various ticket options:

• **Individual tickets** cost €1.70 and give you an hour on the buses, trams, and Métro system (pay as you board on trams and buses; for the Métro, buy tickets from machines).

• The **24-hour** (€6.50), **48-hour** (€10), or **72-hour** (€13) **tickets** give you unlimited transportation on Amsterdam's public transit network. Buy them at the GVB public-transit office (all versions available) or as you board (24-hr version only, may cost €0.50 extra).

• **Strip tickets** *(strippenkaart)*, cheaper than individual tickets, are good on buses, trams, and the Métro in Amsterdam and throughout the Netherlands. The further you go, the more strips you'll use: Any downtown ride in Amsterdam costs two strips (good for 1 hr of transfers), and you'll need six strips to get from Haarlem to the airport (see next chapter). A card with 15 strips costs €6.80 (you can share them with your partner). Shorter strip tickets (2, 3, and 8 strips) are sold on some buses and trams, but the per-strip cost is about double. It's cheapest to buy the 15-strip tickets at the GVB public-transit office, machines at the train station, post offices, airport, or tobacco shops throughout the country.

By Foot: The longest walk a tourist would take is 45 minutes from the station to the Rijksmuseum. Watch out for silent but potentially painful bikes, trams, and crotch-high curb posts.

By Bike: Everyone—bank managers, students, pizza delivery boys, and police—uses this mode of transport. It's *the* smart way to travel in a city where 40 percent of all traffic rolls on two wheels. You'll get around town by bike faster than you can by taxi. On my last visit, I rented a bike for five days, parked it outside my hotel, and enjoyed wonderful mobility. I highly encourage this for anyone who wants to get maximum fun per hour in Amsterdam. One-speed bikes, with "*brrringing*" bells and two locks (use them both; bike thieves are bold and brazen here), rent for about €7–10 per day (cheaper for longer periods) at any number of places. Hotels can send you to the nearest spot.

MacBike is the bike rental powerhouse, with a huge and efficient outlet at Central Station (daily 9:00–17:45, €4/2 hrs, €7/day, €10/24 hrs, more for 3 gears, €50 deposit plus passport or credit-card imprint, at west end of station just before Ibis Hotel, Stationsplein 33, tel. 020/620-0985, can reserve online, www.macbike.nl). MacBike gives out a free, basic *Great Waterland Bicycle Tour* brochure (3 hrs, 12 miles) and sells several booklets outlining bike tours in and around Amsterdam for €1. For those staying near the Anne Frank House, Frederic Rent-a-Bike is also good (€10/24 hrs, daily 9:00–18:00, Brouwersgracht 78, tel. 020/624-5509, www.frederic.nl).

No one wears helmets. For safety: Use arm signals, stay in the obvious and omnipresent bike lanes, yield to traffic on the right, and fear tram tracks. Cross tram tracks at a perpendicular angle to avoid catching your tire in the rut. You must walk your bike through pedestrian zones. Warning: Police ticket bikers as drivers. Obey traffic signals.

By Boat: While the city is great on foot or bike, another option is the Museum Boat, which shuttles tourists from sight to sight on an all-day ticket. Tickets cost €13.50 (includes sight discounts worth about €2.25). The sales booths in front of the Central Station (and the boats) offer handy free brochures with museum times and admission prices. The narrated ride takes 90 minutes if you don't get off (every 30 min in summer, every 45 min off-season, 7 stops, live quadrilingual guide, departures daily 9:30–17:00, discounted after 13:00 to €11.50, tel. 020/530-1090).

The similar Canal Bus is nearby (€16, ticket is valid until 12:00 the following day, departures daily 10:00–18:00, longer hours in summer, tel. 020/623-9886, www.canal.nl).

If you're looking for a floating nonstop tour, the regular canal tour boats (without the stops) give more information, cover more ground, and cost less (see "Tours," below). For do-it-yourself canal tours, Canal Boat also rents "canal bikes" (a.k.a. paddleboats) near the Anne Frank House and Rijksmuseum (€8/hr per person, July–Aug daily 10:00–21:30, Sept–June daily 10:00–18:00).

By Taxi: Amsterdam's taxis are expensive (€2.50 drop, €1.50 per kilometer). You can wave them down, find a rare taxi stand, or call one (tel. 020/677-7777). Given the fine tram system, taxis are rarely a good value.

By Car: Forget it—all you'll find are frustrating one-ways, terrible parking, and meter maids with a passion for booting cars wrongly parked.

TOURS

▲▲Canal Boat Tours—These long, low, tourist-laden boats leave continually from several docks around the town for a relaxing, if uninspiring, one-hour introduction to the city (with a live quadrilingual guide or recorded headphone commentary). Cruises are operated by **Rondvaart Kooij** (€6.50, 2/hr in summer 10:00–22:00, 2/hr in winter 10:00–17:00, at corner of Spui and Rokin streets, about 5 min from Dam Square, tel. 020/623-3810, www.rederijkooij.nl), **Rederij Noord-Zuid** (€9, 2/hr April–Oct 10:00–18:00, 1/hr Nov–March 10:00–17:00, depart from near Leidseplein, tel. 020/679-1370, www.canal-cruises.nl), and **Holland International** (€8.50, 4/hr mid-March–Oct 9:00–22:00, 2/hr Nov–mid-March 10:00–18:00, blue boats depart from in front of Central Station, tel. 020/622-7788). No fishing allowed—but bring your camera. Some prefer to cruise at night, when the bridges are illuminated.

Amsterdam Overview

Bike Tours—Yellow Bike Guided Tours offers a three-hour city tour (€17, April–Oct Sun–Fri at 9:30 and 13:00, Sat at 9:30 and 14:00) and a six-hour, 22-mile tour of the countryside (€23, April–Oct daily at 11:00, €100 deposit or credit-card imprint; both tours leave from Nieuwezijds Kolk 29, 3 blocks from Central Station, tel. 020/620-6940, www.yellowbike.nl).

Wetlands Safari, Nature Canoe Tours near Amsterdam—If you'd like to get some exercise and a dose of the *polder* country and village life, consider this tour. Majel Tromp, a friendly villager who speaks great English, takes groups limited to 15 people. The program: Meet at the VVV tourist office outside Central

Amsterdam at a Glance

▲▲▲**Rijksmuseum** Best collection anywhere of the Dutch masters: Rembrandt, Hals, Vermeer, and Steen. **Hours:** Daily 9:00–18:00.

▲▲▲**Van Gogh Museum** 200 paintings by the angst-ridden artist. **Hours:** Daily 10:00–18:00, Fri until 22:00.

▲▲▲**Anne Frank House** Young Anne's hideaway during the Nazi occupation. **Hours:** April–Aug daily 9:00–21:00, Sept–March daily 9:00–19:00.

▲▲**Dutch Resistance Museum** History of the Dutch struggle against the Nazis. **Hours:** Tue–Fri 10:00–17:00, Sat–Mon 12:00–17:00.

▲▲**Amstelkring Museum** Catholic church hidden in the attic of a 17th-century merchant's house. **Hours:** Mon–Sat 10:00–17:00, Sun 13:00–17:00.

▲▲**Red Light District** Women of the world's oldest profession on the job. **Hours:** Best between noon and night—avoid late night.

▲▲**Vondelpark** City park and concert venue. **Hours:** Always open.

▲**Amsterdam History Museum** Shows city's growth from fishing village to trading capital to today, including some Rembrandts and a playable carillon. **Hours:** Mon–Fri 10:00–17:00, Sat–Sun 11:00–17:00.

Station at 9:30, catch a public bus, stop for coffee, take a 3.5-hour canoe trip (2–3 people per canoe) with several stops, tour a village by canoe, munch a rural canalside picnic lunch (included), then canoe and bus back into the big city by 14:30 (€30, ask for discount with this book, May–mid-Sept Mon–Fri, reservations required, tel. 020/686-3445, mobile 06-5355-2669, www.wetlandssafari.nl, info@wetlandssafari.nl).

Adam's Apple Tours—This walking tour offers a 90-minute, English-only look at the historic roots of Amsterdam. You'll have a small group and a caring guide, starting at Central Station and ending at the Dam Square (€19, Fri–Sun at 10:00, 12:30, and 15:00, call 020/616-7867 to confirm times and book, www.adamsapple.nl).

Private Guide—Ab Walet is a likeable, hardworking, and

▲**Rembrandt's House** The master's reconstructed house, displaying his etchings. **Hours:** Mon–Sat 10:00–17:00, Sun 13:00–17:00.

▲**Dutch Theater** Moving memorial in former Jewish detention center. **Hours:** Daily 11:00–16:00.

▲**Tropical Museum** Re-creations of tropical-life scenes. **Hours:** Daily 10:00–17:00.

▲**Herengracht Canal Mansion** Elegant 17th-century house. **Hours:** Mon–Fri 10:00–17:00, Sat–Sun 11:00–17:00.

▲**Begijnhof** Quiet courtyard lined with picturesque houses. **Hours:** Daily 8:00–13:00.

▲**Leidseplein** Lively square with cafés and street musicians. **Hours:** Always open, best on sunny afternoons.

▲**Museumplein** Square with art museums, street musicians, crafts, and nearby diamond demos. **Hours:** Always open.

▲**Diamonds** Tours at shops throughout the city. **Hours:** Generally daily 9:00–17:00.

▲**Heineken Brewery** Best beer tour in Europe. **Hours:** Tue–Sun 10:00–18:00, closed Mon.

▲**Hash, Marijuana, and Hemp Museum** All the dope, from history and science to memorabilia. **Hours:** Daily 11:00–22:00.

knowledgeable local guide who enjoys personalizing tours for Americans interested in knowing his city better. He specializes in history and architecture and exudes a passion for Amsterdam (€40/2 hrs, €80/4 hrs, for small groups of up to 4 people, on foot or by bike, tel. 020/671-2588, mobile 06/2069-7882, abwalet@yahoo.com).

Do-It-Yourself Bike Tour of Amsterdam—A day enjoying the bridges, bike lanes, and sleepy, off-the-beaten-path canals on your own one-speed is an essential Amsterdam experience. The real joys of Europe's best-preserved 17th-century city are the countless intimate glimpses it offers: the laid-back locals sunning on their porches under elegant gables, rusted bikes that look as if they've been lashed to the same lamppost since the 1960s, wasted hedonists planted on canalside benches, and happy sailors permanently moored, but still manning the deck.

For a good day, rent a bike at Central Station (see "By Bike" on page 1131). Head west down Haarlemmerstraat, working your wide-eyed way down the Prinsengracht (drop into Café 't Papeneiland at Prinsengracht 2) and detouring through the gentrified small streets of the Jordaan neighborhood before popping out at Westerkerk under the tallest spire in the city.

Pedal out to the lush and peaceful Vondelpark, then cut back through the center of town (Leidseplein to the Mint Tower, down Rokin street to Dam Square). From there, cruise the Red Light District, following Oudezijds Voorburgwal past the Old Church (Oude Kerk) to Zeedijk street, and return to the train station.

From Central Station, you can escape into the countryside by hopping on the free ferry behind the station. In five minutes, Amsterdam will be gone, and you'll be rolling through your very own Dutch painting (get free *Great Waterland Bicycle Tour* brochure from MacBike rental shop, described on page 1131).

SIGHTS

One of Amsterdam's delights is that it has perhaps more small specialty museums than any other city its size. From houseboats to sex, from cannabis to costumes, you can find a museum to suit your interests. The following sights are arranged by neighborhood for handy sightseeing.

Southwest Amsterdam

▲▲▲Rijksmuseum—Built to house the nation's great art, the Rijksmuseum owns several thousand paintings, including an incomparable collection of Dutch masters: Rembrandt, Vermeer, Hals, and Steen. The museum has made it easy for you to focus on the highlights, because that's all that is on display while most of the building undergoes several years of renovation (due to reopen in the summer of 2008). Wander through the Rijksmuseum's Philips Wing for a wonderful, concentrated dose of 17th-century Dutch masterpieces (€9, covered by Museumkaart, €4 audioguide, daily 9:00–18:00, tram #2 or #5 from train station to Hobbemastraat, tel. 020/674-7047, www.rijksmuseum.com). The Philips Wing entrance is near the corner of Hobbemastraat and Jan Luijkenstraat on the south side of the Rijks—the part of the huge building nearest the Van Gogh Museum.

▲▲▲Van Gogh Museum—Near the Rijksmuseum, this remarkable museum showcases works by the troubled Dutch artist whose art seemed to mirror his life. Vincent, who killed himself in 1890 at age 37, is best known for sunny, Impressionist canvases that vibrate and pulse with life. The 200 paintings, a stroll through

Southwest Amsterdam

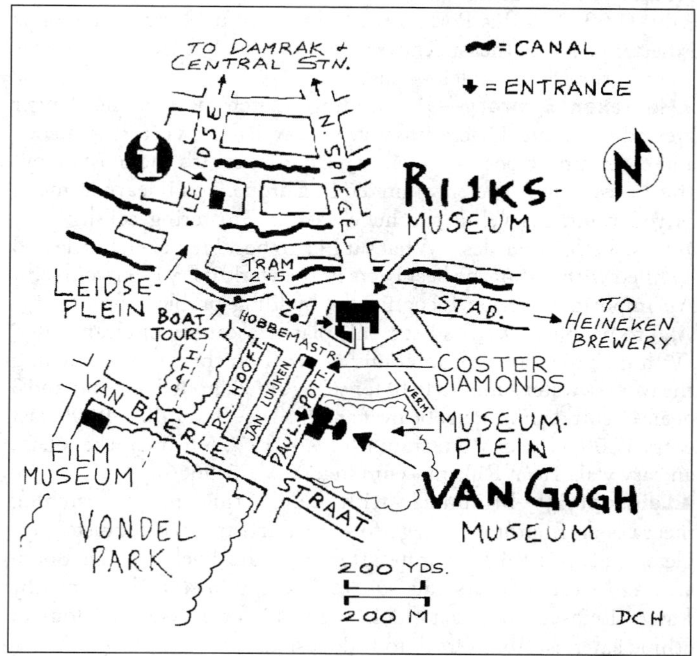

the artist's work and life, were owned by Theo, Vincent's younger, art-dealer brother. Highlights include *Sunflowers*, *The Bedroom*, *The Potato Eaters*, and many brooding self-portraits. The third floor shows works that influenced Vincent, from Monet and Pissarro to Gauguin, Cézanne, and Toulouse-Lautrec. Temporary exhibitions of late 19th- and early 20th-century art fill the new wing, down the escalator from the ground floor lobby. The worthwhile €4 audioguide includes insightful commentaries and quotes from Vincent himself (€9, €2.50 if under 18, covered by Museumkaart, €4 audioguide, daily 10:00–18:00, Fri until 22:00, Paulus Potterstraat 7, tel. 020/570-5200, www.vangoghmuseum.nl).

▲Museumplein—Bordered by the Rijks, Van Gogh, and the Concertgebouw (classical music hall), this square is interesting even to art-haters. Street musicians perform everything from chamber music to Mongolian throat singing. Mimes, human statues, and crafts booths dot the square. Skateboarders careen across a concrete tube, while locals enjoy a park bench or a coffee at the Cobra Café.

Nearby is **Coster Diamonds,** a handy place to see a diamond-cutting and -polishing demo (free and interesting 30-min tours on request followed by sales pitch, popular for decades with tour groups, prices marked up to include tour guide kickbacks, daily 9:00–17:00, 2 Paulus Potterstraat). The tour at Gassan Diamonds is better (see "Southeast Amsterdam," below), but Coster is convenient to the Museumplein scene.

▲Heineken Brewery—The leading Dutch beer is no longer brewed here, but this old brewery now welcomes visitors to a slick and entertaining beer-appreciation experience. It's the most enjoyable brewery tour I've encountered in Europe. You'll learn as much as you want, marvel at the huge vats and towering ceilings, see videos, and go on rides. "What's it like to be a Heineken bottle and be filled with one of the best beers in the world? Try it for yourself." An important section recognizes a budding problem of our age, vital to people as well as beer: this planet's scarcity of clean water. With globalization, corporations are well on their way to owning the world's water supplies (€10 for self-guided, hour-long tour and 3 beers or soft drinks, must be over age 18, Tue–Sun 10:00–18:00, last entry 17:00, closed Mon, tram #16, #24, or #25 to Heinekenplein, an easy walk from Rijksmuseum, tel. 020/523-9666).

▲Leidseplein—Brimming with cafés, this people-watching mecca is an impromptu stage for street artists, accordionists, jugglers, and unicyclists. Sunny afternoons are liveliest. The Boom Chicago theater fronts this square (see page 1148). Stroll nearby Lange Leidsedwarsstraat (1 block north) for a taste-bud tour of ethnic eateries, from Greek to Indonesian.

▲▲Vondelpark—This huge and lively city park is popular with the Dutch—families with little kids, romantic couples, strolling seniors, and hippies sharing blankets and beers. It's a favored venue for free summer concerts. On a sunny afternoon, it's a hedonistic scene that seems to say, "parents...relax."

Amsterdam Film Museum—This is actually not a museum, but a movie theater. In its three 80-seat theaters, it shows several films a day, from small foreign productions to 70-mm classics drawn from its massive archives (€8, always in the original language, often English subtitles, Vondelpark 3, tel. 020/589-1400, www.filmmuseum.nl).

Houseboat Museum (Woonbootmuseum)—In the 1930s, modern cargo ships came into widespread use, making small, sail-powered cargo boats obsolete. In danger of extinction, these little vessels found new life as houseboats lining the canals of Amsterdam. Today, 2,500 such boats—their cargo holds turned into classy, comfortable living rooms—are called home by locals. For a peek into this *gezellig* (cozy) world, visit this tiny museum. Captain Vincent enjoys showing visitors around the houseboat, which feels lived-in because, until 1997, it was (€3, March–Oct Tue–Sun 11:00–17:00, closed Mon; Nov–Feb Fri–Sun 11:00–17:00, closed Mon–Thu; on Prinsengracht, opposite #296 facing Elandsgracht, tel. 020/427-0750, www.houseboatmuseum.nl).

Central Amsterdam, near Dam Square

▲▲▲Anne Frank House—A pilgrimage for many, this house offers a fascinating look at the hideaway of young Anne during the Nazi occupation of the Netherlands. Anne, her parents, an older sister, and four others spent just over two years in a "Secret Annex" behind her father's business. While in hiding, 13-year-old Anne kept a diary chronicling her extraordinary experience. Acting on a tip, the Nazis arrested them in August 1944 and sent the group to concentration camps in Poland and Germany. Anne and her sister died of typhus in March 1945, only weeks before their camp was liberated. Of the eight inhabitants of the Secret Annex, only Anne's father, Otto Frank, survived. He returned to Amsterdam and arranged for his daughter's diary to be published in 1947. It was followed by many translations, a play, and a movie.

Pick up the English pamphlet at the door. The exhibit offers thorough coverage of the Frank family, the diary, the stories of others who hid, and the Holocaust. In summer, skip the hour-long daytime lines by arriving after 18:00 (last entry is 20:30) and visit after dinner (€7.50, April–Aug daily 9:00–21:00, Sept–March daily 9:00–19:00, last entry 30 min before closing, Prinsengracht 267, near Westerkerk, tel. 020/556-7100, www.annefrank.org).

For an interesting glimpse of Holland under the Nazis, rent the powerful movie *Soldier of Orange* before you leave home.

Westerkerk—Near the Anne Frank House, this landmark church (generally open April–Sept Mon–Sat 11:00–15:00) has a barren interior, Rembrandt's body buried somewhere under the pews, and Amsterdam's tallest steeple. The tower is open by tour only (small groups—only 5 people—so lines can be long). The mandatory €3 guided tour (in English and Dutch) tells of the church and its carillon (45 min, departures on the hour, April–Sept Mon–Sat 10:00–17:00, last tour leaves at 17:00, closed Sun and Oct–March).

Royal Palace (Koninklijk Paleis)—The palace, right on Dam Square, was built as a lavish City Hall for Amsterdam, when the country was a proud new republic and Amsterdam was awash in profit from trade. When constructed in 1648, this building was one of Europe's finest. Today, it's the official (but not actual) residence of the queen and has a sumptuous interior. While it pretends that it's open to the public, this is rare (tel. 020/620-4060, www.koninklijkhuis.nl).

New Church (Nieuwe Kerk)—Barely newer than the "Old" Church (which is located in the Red Light District), this 15th-century church has an intentionally dull interior, after the decoration was removed by 16th-century iconoclastic Protestants seeking to unclutter their communion with God. This is where Dutch royal weddings and coronations take place, and it hosts temporary exhibits (fee if exhibition scheduled, covered by Museumkaart, Mon–Sat

Central Amsterdam

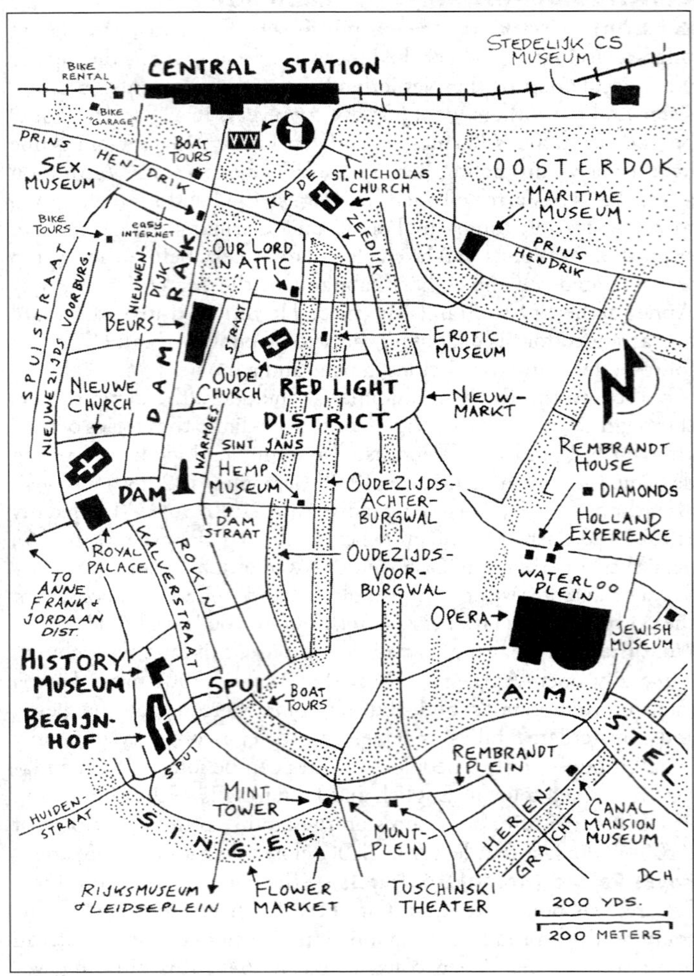

10:00–18:00, Sun 13:00–18:00, on Dam Square, tel. 020/638-6909, www.nieuwekerk.nl).

▲Begijnhof—Stepping into this tiny, idyllic courtyard in the city center, you escape into the charm of old Amsterdam. Notice house #34, a 500-year-old wooden structure (rare, since repeated fires taught city fathers a trick called brick). Peek into the hidden Catholic church, dating from the time when post-Reformation Dutch Catholics couldn't worship in public. It's opposite the English Reformed church, where the Pilgrims worshipped while waiting for their voyage to the New World (marked by a plaque near the door). Be considerate of the people who live around the courtyard (free, daily 8:00–13:00, on Begijnensteeg lane, just off Kalverstraat between #130 and #132, pick up flier at office near entrance).

▲Amsterdam History Museum (Amsterdams Historisch Museum)—Follow the city's growth from fishing village to world trader to hippie haven. Housed in a 500-year-old former orphanage, this creative and hardworking museum features Rembrandt's paintings, fine English descriptions, and a carillon loft. The loft comes with push-button recordings of the town bell tower's greatest hits, and a self-serve carillon "keyboard" that lets you ring a few bells yourself (€6.50, covered by Museumkaart, Mon–Fri 10:00–17:00, Sat–Sun 11:00–17:00, good-value restaurant, next to Begijnhof, Kalverstraat 92, tel. 020/523-1822, www.ahm.nl). The museum's free pedestrian corridor—lined with old-time group portraits—is a powerful teaser.

Stedelijk Museum CS—The modern art museum, temporarily located on the second and third floors of the towering post office building, features art that would normally be displayed at the main Stedelijk Museum building (near the Rijksmuseum), but it's under renovation until 2008. The fun, far-out, refreshing collection consists mainly of post-1945 art, but also includes work by Picasso, Chagall, Cézanne, Kandinsky, and Mondrian, plus special exhibitions (€8, covered by Museumkaart, daily 10:00–18:00, Thu until 21:00, just east of Central Station—to the left as you exit—at Oosterdokskade 5, tel. 020/573-2911, www.stedelijk.nl).

Southeast Amsterdam

To reach these sights from the train station, take tram #9 or #14. All of these sights except the last two (Tropical Museum and Maritime Museum) are close to each other and could easily be connected into an interesting walk.

Waterlooplein Flea Market—For more than a hundred years, the Jewish Quarter flea market has raged daily except Sunday behind the Rembrandt House. The long, narrow park is filled with stalls selling cheap clothes, hippie stuff, old records, tourist knickknacks, and garage-sale junk.

▲Rembrandt's House (Rembrandthuis Museum)—A middle-aged Rembrandt lived here after his wife's death, as his wealth and popularity dwindled down to obscurity and bankruptcy (1639–1658). Tour the place this way: See the 10-minute introductory video (Dutch and English showings alternate); explore Rembrandt's reconstructed house (filled with exactly what his bankruptcy inventory of 1656 said he owned); imagine him at work in his reconstructed studio; marvel at his personal collection of exotic objects, many of which he included in paintings; ask the printer to explain the etching process

Southeast Amsterdam

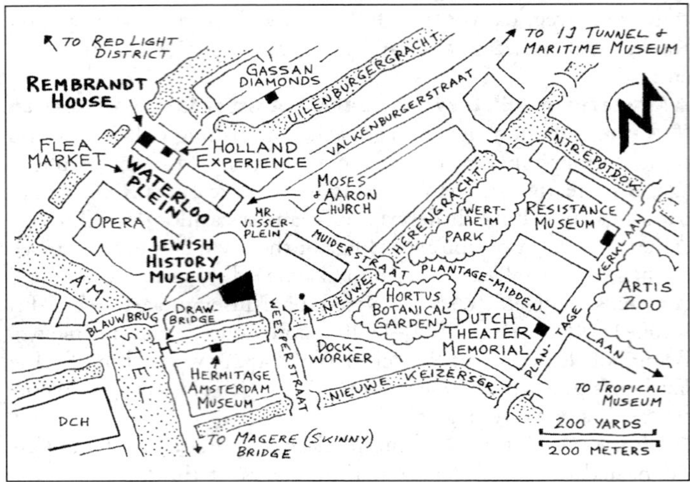

(drawing in soft wax on a metal plate that's then dipped in acid, inked up, and printed); then, for the finale, enjoy several rooms of original Rembrandt etchings. You'll find no Rembrandt paintings, but the etchings are marvelous and well-described. I came away wanting to know more about the man and his art (€7, covered by Museumkaart, €13.50 combo-ticket includes *Holland Experience*—see below, Mon–Sat 10:00–17:00, Sun 13:00–17:00, Jodenbreestraat 4, tel. 020/520-0400, www.rembrandthuis.nl).

Holland Experience—Bragging "Experience Holland in 30 minutes," this 3-D movie takes you traveling with three clowns through an idealized montage of Dutch clichés. There are no words but lots of images and special effects as you rock with the boat and get spritzed with perfume while viewing the tulips (€8.50, ask for discount with this book, €13.50 combo-ticket includes Rembrandt's House, daily 10:00–18:00 on the hour, adjacent to Rembrandt's House at Jodenbreestraat 8, tel. 020/422-2233, www.holland-experience.nl). The men's urinal is a trip to the beach. Plan for it.

▲Diamonds—Many shops in the "city of diamonds" offer tours. These tours come with two parts: a chance to see experts behind magnifying glasses polishing the facets of precious diamonds, followed by a visit to an intimate sales room to see (and perhaps buy) a tiny, shiny souvenir.

The handy and professional **Gassan Diamonds** facility fills a huge warehouse a block from Rembrandt's House. You'll get a security sticker and join a tour to see a polisher at work and hear a general explanation of the process (free, 15 min). Then you'll have an opportunity to sit down and have color and clarity described and illustrated with diamonds ranging in value from $100 to $30,000. Afterward, you can bring your free cup of coffee from the café to the Delftware painting exhibit across the parking lot (daily 9:00–17:00, Nieuwe Uilenburgerstraat 173, tel. 020/622-5333, www.gassandiamonds.com). Another company, Coster, also offers diamond demos, not as good as Gassan's, but handy if you're near the Rijksmuseum (see page 1136).

Jewish Historical Museum (Joods Historisch Museum)—Four historic synagogues have been joined by steel and glass to make one modern complex telling the story of the Jews in Amsterdam through the centuries (€6.50, covered by Museumkaart, daily 11:00–17:00, good kosher café, Jonas Daniel Meijerplein 2, tel. 020/626-9945, www.jhm.nl).

Hermitage Amsterdam Museum—The famous Hermitage Museum in St. Petersburg, Russia, loans Amsterdam art to display in the Amstelhof, a 17th-century former nursing home on the Amstel River (€6, covered by Museumkaart, daily 10:00–17:00, Nieuwe Herengracht 14, tram #4 to Rembrandtplein or #9 to Waterlooplein, tel. 020/531-8751, www.hermitage.nl).

De Hortus Botanical Garden—This is a unique oasis of tranquility within the city (no mobile phones are allowed, because "our collection of plants is a precious community—treat it with respect"). One of the oldest botanical gardens in the world, it dates from 1638, when medicinal herbs were grown here. Today, among its 6,000 different kinds of plants—most of which were collected by the Dutch East India Company in the 17th and 18th centuries—you'll find medicinal herbs, cacti, several greenhouses (one with a fluttery butterfly house—a hit with kids), and a tropical palm house. Much of it is described in English: "A Dutch merchant snuck a coffee plant out of Ethiopia, which ended up in this garden in 1706. This first coffee plant in Europe was the literal granddaddy of the coffee cultures of Brazil—long the world's biggest coffee producer" (€6, Mon–Fri 9:00–17:00, Sat–Sun 11:00–17:00, until 16:00 in winter, Plantage Middenlaan 2A, tel. 020/625-9021, www.hortus-botanicus.nl).

▲Dutch Theater (Hollandsche Schouwburg)—Once a lively theater in the Jewish neighborhood, and today a moving memorial, this building was used as an assembly hall for local Jews destined for Nazi concentration camps. On the wall, 6,700 family names pay tribute to the 104,000 Jews deported and killed by the Nazis. Some 70,000 victims spent time here, awaiting transfer to concentration camps. Upstairs is a small history exhibit with photos and memorabilia of some victims, putting a human face on the staggering numbers. Press the buttons on a model of the neighborhood to see round-up spots from the Nazi occupation. The ruined theater actually offers little to see, but plenty to think about—notice the hopeful messages that visiting school groups attach to the wooden tulips (free, daily 11:00–16:00, Plantage Middenlaan 24, tel. 020/626-9945, www.hollandscheschouwburg.nl).

▲▲Dutch Resistance Museum (Verzetsmuseum)—This is an impressive look at how the Dutch resisted their Nazi occupiers from 1940 to 1945. You'll see propaganda movie clips, study forged ID cards under a magnifying glass, and read about ingenious and courageous efforts—big and small—to hide local Jews from the Germans and undermine the Nazi regime. At the end of the war, Nazi helmets were turned into bedpans.

Besides the history lesson, this thought-provoking exhibit examines the moral dilemmas of life under oppressive rule. Is it right to give money to poor people if the charity is run by Nazis? Should I quit my government job when the Nazis take control, or stay on to do what good I can? If I disagree with my government, is it okay to lie? To vandalize? To kill? (€5, covered by Museumkaart, Tue–Fri 10:00–17:00, Sat–Mon 12:00–17:00, well-described in English, tram #9 from station, Plantage Kerklaan 61, tel. 020/620-2535, www.verzetsmuseum.org.) The recommended Restaurant Plancius is adjacent to the museum (see page 1160), and Amsterdam's famous zoo is just across the street.

▲Tropical Museum (Tropenmuseum)—As close to the Third World as you'll get without lots of vaccinations, this imaginative museum offers wonderful re-creations of tropical-life scenes and explanations of Third World problems. Ride the elevator to the top floor, and circle your way down through this immense collection opened in 1926 to give the Dutch a peek at their vast colonial holdings. Don't miss the display case allowing you to see and hear the world's most exotic musical instruments. The Ekeko cafeteria serves tropical food (€7, covered by Museumkaart, daily 10:00–17:00, tram #9 to Linnaeusstraat 2, tel. 020/568-8215).

Netherlands Maritime Museum (Nederlands Scheepvaart-museum) —This huge collection of model ships, maps, and sea-battle paintings fills the 300-year-old Dutch Navy Arsenal. Given Dutch seafaring heritage, I expected a more interesting museum. Sailors may disagree, but—even with its re-creation of an 18th-century Dutch East India Company ship manned by characters in old costumes—I found the place pretty lifeless (€7.50, covered by Museumkaart; mid-June–mid-Sept daily 10:00–17:00; mid-Sept–mid-June Tue–Sun 10:00–17:00, closed Mon; English explanations, don't waste your time with 30-min movie, bus #22 or #32 to Kattenburgerplein 1, tel. 020/523-2222, www.scheepvaartmuseum.nl).

Rembrandtplein and Neighborhood

One of the city's premier nightlife spots is the leafy Rembrandtplein (the artist's modest statue stands here) and the adjoining Thorbeckeplein. Several late-night dance clubs (such as IT, a half block east down Amstelstraat) keep the area lively into the wee hours. Utrechtsestraat is lined with upscale shops and restaurants.

▲Herengracht Canal Mansion (Museum Willet Holthuysen)—This 1687 patrician house offers a fine look at old Amsterdam's wealthy, with a good 15-minute English introductory film and a 17th-century garden in back (€4, covered by Museumkaart, Mon–Fri 10:00–17:00, Sat–Sun 11:00–17:00, tram #4 or #9 to Herengracht 605, 1 block southeast of Rembrandtplein, tel. 020/523-1870, www.willetholthuysen.nl).

Tuschinski Theater—This movie palace from the 1920s (a half block from Rembrandtplein down Reguliersbreestraat) glitters inside and out. Still a working theater, it's a delightful old place to see first-run movies. The exterior is an interesting hybrid of styles, forcing the round peg of Art Nouveau into the square hole of Art Deco. The stone-and-tile facade features stripped down, functional Art Deco squares and rectangles, but is ornamented with Art Nouveau elements—Tiffany-style windows, garlands, curvy iron lamps, Egyptian pharaohs, and exotic gold lettering over the door. Inside, the sumptuous decor features red carpets, nymphs on the walls, and semi-abstract designs. Grab a seat in the lobby and watch the ceiling morph (Reguliersbreestraat 26–28).

Red Light District

▲▲Amstelkring Museum (Our Lord in the Attic)—While Amsterdam has long been known for its tolerant attitudes, 16th-century politics forced Dutch Catholics to worship discreetly. Near the train station in the Red Light District, you'll find a fascinating hidden Catholic church filling the attic of three 17th-century merchants' houses. When hard-line Protestants took power in 1578, Catholics were forbidden to worship openly, so worshippers gathered secretly to say Mass in homes and offices. In 1663, a wealthy merchant built Our Lord in the Attic, one of a handful of such places in Amsterdam serving as a secret parish church until Catholics were allowed in 1795 to once again worship in public. This unique church comes with a little bonus: a rare glimpse inside an historic Amsterdam home. Don't miss the silver collection and other exhibits of daily life 300 years ago (€7, covered by Museumkaart, Mon–Sat 10:00–17:00, Sun 13:00–17:00, Oudezijds Voorburgwal 40, tel. 020/624-6604, www.museumamstelkring.nl).

▲▲Red Light District—Europe's most touristed ladies of the night shiver and shimmy, as they have since 1200, in 450 display-case windows around Oudezijds Achterburgwal and Oudezijds

Voorburgwal, surrounding the Oude Kerk (Old Church, see below). Drunks and druggies make the streets uncomfortable late at night after the gawking tour groups leave (around 22:30), but it's a fascinating walk between noon and nightfall.

The neighborhood, one of Amsterdam's oldest, has had prostitutes since 1200. Prostitution is entirely legal here, and the prostitutes are generally entrepreneurs, renting space and running their own businesses. Popular prostitutes net around €500 a day (S&F, €25–50) and fill out tax returns.

The **Prostitution Information Center,** open to the public, offers a small €1.50 booklet that answers most of the questions tourists have about the Red Light District (free, Tue–Sat 12:00–17:00, closed Sun–Mon, facing Oude Kerk at Enge Kerksteeg 3, www.pic-amsterdam.com).

Sex Museums—Amsterdam has two sex museums: one in the Red Light District, and another a block in front of the train station on Damrak. While visiting one can be called sightseeing, visiting both is hard to explain. Here's a comparison:

The **Erotic Museum** in the Red Light District is less offensive. Its five floors rely heavily on badly dressed dummies of prostitutes in various acts. It also has a lot of uninspired paintings, videos, phone sex, old photos, and sculpture (€5, daily 11:00–24:00, along the canal at Oudezijds Achterburgwal 54, tel. 020/624-7303).

The **Damrak Sex Museum** goes farther, telling the story of pornography from Roman times through 1960. Every sexual deviation is revealed in various displays, and the nude and pornographic art is a cut above that of the other sex museum. Also interesting are the early French pornographic photos and memorabilia from Europe, India, and Asia. You'll find a Marilyn Monroe tribute and some S&M displays, too (€2.50, daily 10:00–23:30, Damrak 18, a block in front of station).

Old Church (Oude Kerk)—This 14th-century landmark—the needle around which the Red Light District spins—has served as a reassuring welcome-home symbol to sailors, a refuge to the downtrodden, an ideological battlefield of the Counter-Reformation, and today, a tourist sight with a dull interior (€4, covered by Museumkaart, Mon–Sat 11:00–17:00, Sun 13:00–17:00, www.oudekerk.nl).

▲Hash, Marijuana, and Hemp Museum—This is a collection of dope facts, history, science, and memorabilia (€6, daily 11:00–22:00, Oudezijds Achterburgwal 148, tel. 020/623-5961, www.hashmuseum.com).

The **Cannabis College**, "dedicated to ending the global war against the cannabis plant through public education," is a half block away at #124 (free, daily 11:00–19:00, tel. 020/423-4420, www.cannabiscollege.com).

SHOPPING

Amsterdam brings out the browser even in those who were not born to shop. Ten general markets, open six days a week (closed Sun), keep folks who brake for garage sales pulling U-turns. Shopping highlights include Waterlooplein (the flea market); the huge Albert Cuyp street market; various flower markets (such as the Singel Canal market near Mint Tower/Munttoren, which is open daily); diamond dealers (free cutting and polishing demos, including Coster near the Rijksmuseum—see page 1136, and Gassan near Rembrandt's House—see page 1142); and Kalverstraat, Amsterdam's soulless but teeming pedestrian/shopping street (parallel to Damrak).

For something a little different, stroll The Nine Little Streets (De Negen Straatjes), home to 190 diverse shops mixing festive, creative, nostalgic, practical, and artistic items. The cross streets make a tic-tac-toe with a couple of canals just west of Kalverstraat. (Look for the zone where Hartenstraat, Wolvenstraat, and Huidenstraat cross Keizersgracht and Herrengracht canals.)

To experience a Dutch shopping mall, drop by the Magna Plaza Shopping Center. This former main post office in a grand 19th-century building has been transformed into a stylish mall with 40 boutiques. You'll find fashion, luxury goods, and gift shops galore. It's just behind the Royal Palace a block off Dam Square.

NIGHTLIFE

On summer evenings, people flock to the main squares for drinks at outdoor tables. Leidseplein is the glitziest, surrounded by theaters, restaurants, and nightclubs. The slightly quieter Rembrandtplein (with adjoining Thorbeckeplein) is the center of gay discos. Spui features a full city block of bars. And Nieuwmarkt, on the east edge of the Red Light District, is a bit rough, but is probably the most local.

Boom! and *Uitkrant* are two free publications (available at TIs and many bars) that list festivals and performances of theater, film, dance, cabaret, and live rock, pop, jazz, and classical music. The irreverent **Boom!**, which has the best lowdown on the youth and nightlife scene, is packed with practical tips and countercultural insights (includes €3 discount on the Boom Chicago R-rated comedy theater act described below). **Uitkrant** is in Dutch, but it's just a calendar of events, and anyone can figure out the name of the event and its date, time, and location. There's also *What's On in Amsterdam, Time Out Amsterdam,* the Thursday edition of many Dutch papers, and the *International Herald Tribune*'s special Netherlands inserts (all sold at newsstands). The **Last Minute Ticket Shop** at Stadsschouwburg Theater (Leidseplein 26, tel.

0900-0191) is the best one-stop-shopping box office for theater, classical music, and major rock shows.

Music—You'll find classical music at the Concertgebouw (free 12:30 lunch concerts on Wed, at far south end of Museumplein, tel. 020/671-8345, www.concertgebouw.nl) and at the former Beurs (on Damrak, tel. 020/627-0466). For opera and dance, try the new opera house on Waterlooplein (tel. 020/551-8100). In the summer, Vondelpark hosts open-air concerts.

Two rock music (and hip-hop) clubs near Leidseplein are Melkweg (Lijnbaansgracht 234a, tel. 020/531-8181, www.melkweg.nl) and Paradiso (Weteringschans 6, tel. 020/626-4521, www.paradiso.nl). They present big-name acts that you might recognize if you're younger than I am.

Jazz has a long tradition at the Bimhuis nightclub, east of the Red Light District (concerts Thu–Sat, Oude Schans 73-77, box office tel. 020/623-1361, www.bimhuis.nl).

The nearby town of Haarlem offers free pipe organ concerts on Tuesdays in summer at its 15th-century church, the Grote Kerk (at 20:15 mid-May–mid Oct, see page 1168).

Comedy—An R-rated comedy theater act, **Boom Chicago,** was started 10 years ago by a group of Americans on a graduation tour. They have been entertaining tourists and locals alike ever since. The show is a series of rude, clever, and high-powered skits offering a raucous look at Dutch culture and local tourism (€18–20, Sun–Fri at 20:15, Fri also at 23:30, Sat at 19:30 and 22:45, in 300-seat Leidseplein Theater, Leidseplein 12, tel. 020/423-0101, www.boomchicago.nl). They do various shows: *Best of Boom* (a collection of their greatest hits over the years), new shows for locals and return customers, and improv. Meals are optional and a good value.

Movies—Catch modern movies in the 1920s setting of the classic Tuschinski Theater (between Muntplein and Rembrandtplein, described on page 1145). The Amsterdam Film Museum, which has some evening showings, is also worth checking out (€8, covered by Museumkaart, Vondelstraat 69, near Vondelpark, tel. 020/589-1400, www.filmmuseum.nl, see page 1138). It's not unusual for movies at many cinemas to be sold out—consider buying tickets during the day.

Museums—Several of Amsterdam's museums stay open late. The Anne Frank House is open daily until 21:00 in summer (April–Aug) and until 19:00 the rest of the year (last entry 30 min before closing). The Van Gogh Museum is open on Fridays until 22:00. The Hash, Marijuana, and Hemp Museum is open daily until 22:00.

SLEEPING

Greeting a new day by descending steep stairs and stepping into a leafy canalside scene—graceful bridges, historic gables, and bikes clattering on cobbles—is a fun part of experiencing Amsterdam. But Amsterdam is a tough city for budget accommodations, and any room under €140 will have rough edges. Still, you can sleep well and safely in a great location for €80 per double.

Amsterdam is jammed during convention periods, Queen's Day (April 30), and on summer weekends. Many hotels will not take weekend bookings for people staying fewer than three nights.

Parking in Amsterdam is even worse than driving. You'll pay €32 a day to park safely in a garage—and then hike to your hotel.

While I prefer sleeping in cozy Haarlem (see next chapter), those into more urban charms will find that, with the exception of the times noted above, Amsterdam has plenty of beds.

Near the Train Station

$$ Ibis Amsterdam Hotel is a modern and efficient, 187-room place towering over the station and a multistory bicycle garage. It offers a central location, comfort, and good value, without a hint of charm (Sb-€122, Db-€137, family-€189, €10 extra on weekends, skip breakfast and save €13 per person, book long in advance, air-con, smoke-free rooms on request, Stationsplein 49, tel. 020/638-9999, fax 020/620-0156, www.ibishotel.com, H1556-FO@accor-hotels.com).

$$ Amstel Botel, the city's only remaining "boat hotel," is a shipshape, bright, and clean floating hotel with 175 rooms (Sb/Db-€87, Tb-€117, worth the extra €5 per room for canal view, breakfast-€10, elevator, 400 yards from train station, on your left as you leave station, you'll see the sign and the big white boat at Oosterdokskade 2-4, tel. 020/626-4247, fax 020/639-1952,

Sleep Code

(€1 = about $1.20, country code: 31, area code: 020)
S = Single, **D** = Double/Twin, **T** = Triple, **Q** = Quad, **b** = bathroom, **s** = shower only. Nearly everyone speaks English in the Netherlands. Credit cards are accepted, and prices include breakfast unless otherwise noted.

To help you easily sort through these listings, I've divided the rooms into three categories, based on the price for a standard double room with bath:

$$$ Higher Priced—Most rooms €140 or more.
$$ Moderately Priced—Most rooms between €80–140.
$ Lower Priced—Most rooms €80 or less.

Amsterdam Hotels

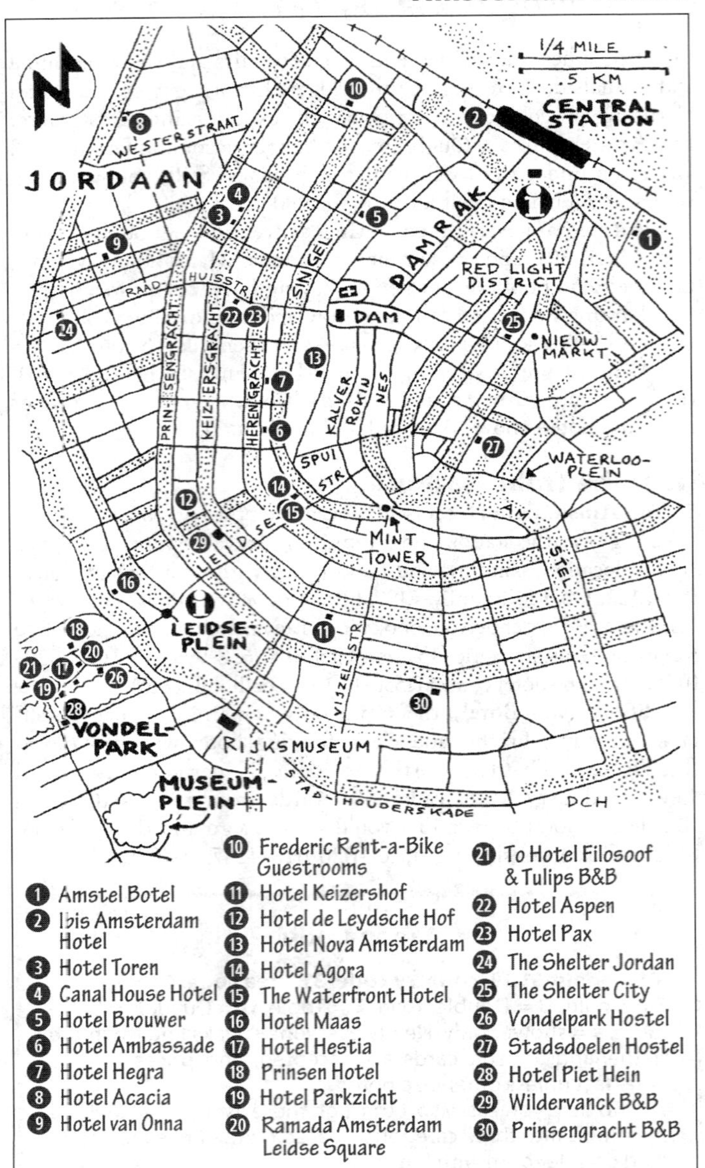

www.amstelbotel.nl). Some construction will occur in the train station behind the hotel in 2006; ask for a room on the canal or on the third or fourth floor, street side.

Between Dam Square and the Anne Frank House

$$$ Hotel Toren is a chandeliered, historic mansion in a pleasant, quiet, canalside setting in downtown Amsterdam. This splurge, run by Eric and Petra Toren, is classy yet friendly, and two blocks northeast of the Anne Frank House. The least expensive four-star in town, it's a great value (Sb-€115–130, Db-€125–185, deluxe canalside Db-€200–230, Tb-€160–205, "bridal suites"-€220–250, prices vary with season, ask for discount with this book when reserving, breakfast buffet-€12, air-con, Keizersgracht 164, tel. 020/622-6352, fax 020/626-9705, www.toren.nl). The staff is a great source of local advice.

$$$ Canal House Hotel, a few doors down, offers a rich 17th-century atmosphere. Above generous and elegant public spaces, tangled, antique-filled halls lead to 26 tastefully appointed rooms. Evenings come with candlelight and soft music (Sb-€140, Db-€150, big Db-€190, elevator, Keizersgracht 148, tel. 020/622-5182, fax 020/624-1317, www.canalhouse.nl, info@canalhouse.nl).

$$$ Hotel Ambassade, lacing together 60 rooms in 10 houses, is amazingly elegant and fresh, sitting aristocratically but daintily on the Herengracht. Its public rooms are palatial, with a library, plush antique furnishings, and modern art. A family-run hotel this size is unusual (Sb-€165, Db-€195, Db suite-€270, Tb-€227, extra bed-€35, 5 percent tax, breakfast-€16—and actually worth it, elevator, free Internet access, Herengracht 341, tel. 020/555-0222, www.ambassade-hotel.nl, info@ambassade-hotel.nl).

$$ Hotel Brouwer, a woody and homey, old-time place situated peacefully but centrally on the Singel canal, rents eight rooms up lots of very steep stairs (Sb-€50, Db-€85, Tb-€105, small elevator, located between train station and Dam Square, near Lijnbaanssteeg at Singel 83, tel. 020/624-6358, fax 020/520-6264, www.hotelbrouwer.nl, akita@hotelbrouwer.nl).

$$ Hotel Hegra is a rare, simple yet comfy, sedate, and cat-friendly place with 11 rooms, run by Robert de Vries. The place is well-worn, but feels safe (D-€70, Ds-€80, Db-€95, includes breakfast, Herengracht 269, tel. 020/623-7877, fax 020/623-8159, www.hegrahotelamsterdam.com).

In the Jordaan

$$ Hotel van Onna is a smoke-free, professional-feeling place renting 41 simple, industrial-strength rooms. Some beds are a bit springy—but the price is unbeatable, and the location makes you want to crack out your easel. The hotel is run by Loek van Onna, who has lived in the building all of his life (Sb-€40, Db-€80, Tb-€120, cash only, reserve only by phone, Bloemgracht 104, tel. 020/626-5801, www.hotelvanonna.com).

$$ Hotel Acacia's 20 plain, rundown rooms fill a funky, cheese-wedge-shaped building on a canal and a workaday square, buried deep in the Jordaan (Sb-€70, Db-€85, Tb-€105, Qb-€125, Quint/b-€135, 5 percent extra to pay with credit card, 3-night minimum on weekends, some larger studios, lots of steep stairs, absentee owners, bus #18 from station, Lindengracht 251, tel. 020/622-1460, fax 020/638-0748, www.hotelacacia.nl, acacia.nl@wxs.nl).

The Acacia also rents four rooms or apartments in two **$$ Acacia Houseboats** moored adjacent to the hotel. This is a good opportunity for that old-time, Amsterdam-houseboat experience in the quintessential Amsterdam neighborhood (Db-€100–115, Tb-€120, Qb-€135, see www.hotelacacia.nl for details).

Near the Jordaan

$ Frederic Rent-a-Bike Guestrooms, with a bike-rental shop as the reception, is a collection of private rooms on a gorgeous canal just outside the Jordaan, a five-minute walk from the train station. Frederic has amassed about 100 beds, ranging from dumpy €70 doubles to spacious and elegant apartments (from €40 per person, plus additional 15 percent reservation fee). Some places are ideal for families and groups of up to six. He also rents houseboat apartments. All are displayed in living color on his Web site (cash only, Brouwersgracht 78, tel. 020/624-5509, www.frederic.nl). His bike shop is open daily 9:00–18:00 (€10/24 hrs).

Spui and Leidseplein Neighborhoods

The area around Amsterdam's rip-roaring nightlife center (Leidseplein) is colorful, comfortable, and convenient. These canalside places are within a five-minute walk of Leidseplein, but in generally quiet and characteristic settings.

$$$ Hotel Nova Amsterdam, a bright, spacious place offering professional service and reliability, rents 60 stark, yellow and beechwood rooms in a great locale (Sb-€109, Db-€149, Tb-€185, Qb-€220, elevator, midway between Dam Square and Spui at Nieuwezijds Voorburgwal 276, tel. 020/623-0066, fax 020/627-2026, www.novahotel.nl, reservations@novahotel.nl).

$$$ Hotel Maas is a big, quiet, and stiffly hotelesque place. Though it's on a busy street rather than a canal, it's a handy option (S-€90, Sb-€105, Db-€145–165, Tb-€200, suite-€205, prices vary with view and room size, breakfast extra, elevator, tram #1, #2, or #5 from station; Leidsekade 91, tel. 020/623-3868, fax 020/622-2613, www.hotelmaas.nl, info@hotelmaas.nl).

$$ Hotel Keizershof is wonderfully Dutch, with six bright, airy rooms in a 17th-century canal house. A steep spiral staircase leads to rooms named after old-time Hollywood stars. The enthusiastic hospitality of the de Vries family gives this place a friendly, almost small-town charm (S-€45, D-€65–70, Ds-€80, Db-€100, 2-night minimum, fine family-style breakfast around a big table, strictly non-smoking; tram #16, #24, or #25 from train station; Keizersgracht 618, where Keizers canal crosses Nieuwe Spiegelstraat, tel. 020/622-2855, fax 020/624-8412, www.hotelkeizershof.nl).

$$ Wildervanck B&B, run by Helene and Sjoerd Wildervanck, offers two rooms in an elegant, 17th-century canal house (big Db on first floor-€120, Db with twin beds on ground floor-€100, extra bed-€25, includes breakfast in their pleasant dining room, family has 3 little girls, Keizersgracht 498, on Keizersgracht canal just west of Leidsestraat, tel. 020/623-3846, fax 020/421-6575, www.wildervanck.com, info@wildervanck.com).

Two well-located places offering mediocre value are side by side overlooking the Singel canal where it hits Koningsplein: **$$ The Waterfront Hotel** feels cozy, with 10 rustic yet nice rooms and lots of steep stairs (Sb-€95, Db-€110, view Db-€135, Tb-€150, Singel 458, tel. & fax 020/421-6621, www.waterfront.demon.nl, info@hotelwaterfront.nl). **$$ Hotel Agora** has 16 rooms (D-€88, Db-€122, view Db-€135, Singel 462, tel. 020/627-2200, fax 020/627-2202, www.hotelagora.nl, info@hotelagora.nl).

$ Hotel de Leydsche Hof, canalside with simple rooms, is open only from Easter through mid-September. Its peaceful atmosphere almost allows you to overlook the flimsy cots and old carpets (Ds-€60, Ts-€90, Qs-€110, no breakfast, cash only, 10-min walk from Leidseplein, Leidsegracht 14, near where it hits Keizersgracht, tel. 020/623-2148, run by friendly Mr. Piller).

$ Prinsengracht B&B, a pretty, recently renovated basement apartment in an 18th-century canal house, has a super location. It's well-run by Liesbeth and her family (€80–85, cash only, 2-night minimum, self-service supplies in kitchen for first breakfast only, Prinsengracht 728, tel. 020/420-3314, fax 020/420-3354, Aronson@xs4all.nl).

Near Vondelpark

These options cluster around Vondelpark in a safe neighborhood that lacks the canal flavor, but is only a short walk from the action.

Between Leidseplein and Vondelpark

These places are in a pleasant nook between the rollicking Leidseplein and the park. They are easily connected with the train station by trams #1, #2, and #5. (The good Vondelpark hostel is also in this neighborhood, listed under "Cheap Hotels and Hostels," below.)

$$$ Ramada Amsterdam Leidse Square is an 89-room, American-style hotel well-situated on a quiet street, just across the bridge from the Leidseplein (Sb-€139–179, Db-€149–189, prices vary depending on season and air-con, elevator, Tesselschadestraat 23, tel. 020/612-6876, fax 020/683-8313, www.ams.nl).

$$ Hotel Hestia, on a safe and sane street, is efficient and family-run, with 18 clean, bright, and generally spacious rooms (Sb-€80, very small Db-€95, Db-€107–133, Tb-€160, Qb-€188, elevator, Roemer Visscherstraat 7, tel. 020/618-0801, fax 020/685-1382, www.hotel-hestia.nl, info@hotel-hestia.nl).

$$ Prinsen Hotel, with 45 nicely appointed but generally cramped rooms, has a peaceful garden and a secure, professional feel (Sun–Thu Sb-€90, Db-€120–135, Tb-€160; Fri–Sat Sb-€105, Db-€130–135, Tb-€170; 4 percent more if you pay with credit card, elevator, Vondelstraat 36-38, tel. 020/616-2323, fax 020/616-6112, www.prinsenhotel.nl, info@prinsenhotel.nl).

$$ Hotel Parkzicht, an old-fashioned place with extremely steep stairs, rents 13 big, plain rooms on a quiet street bordering Vondelpark (S-€39, Sb-€49, Db-€78–90, Tb-€110–120, Qb-€120–130, closed Nov–March, Roemer Visscherstraat 33, tel. 020/618-1954, fax 020/618-0897, hotel@parkzicht.nl).

More near Vondelpark

Hotel Piet Hein is between Vondelpark and the Museumplein; Hotel Filosoof is north of Vondelpark; and Tulips B&B is a few blocks west of Vondelpark, just across a canal.

$$$ Hotel Piet Hein offers comfortable, renovated rooms with a warm, nautical atmosphere (Sb-€92–112, Db-€145–165, extra bed-€30, Vossiusstraat 52–53, tel. 020/6627205, www.hotelpiethein.nl, info@hotelpiethein.nl).

$$ Hotel Filosoof greets you with Aristotle and Plato in the foyer and classical music in its generous lobby. Its 38 rooms are decorated with themes; the Egyptian room has a frieze of hieroglyphics. Philosophers' sayings hang on the walls, and thoughtful travelers wander down the halls or sit in the garden, rooted in deep discussion. The rooms are small, but the hotel is endearing (Db-€111–138, Tb-€150–185, elevator, 3-min walk from tram line #1, get off at Jan Pieter Heijestraat, Anna Vondelstraat 6, tel. 020/683-3013, fax 020/685-3750, www.hotelfilosoof.nl, reservations@hotelfilosoof.nl).

$$ Tulips B&B, with three cozy rooms in a shoes-off home, is run by a friendly Englishwoman, Karen, and her Dutch husband, Paul. Rooms are clean, white, and bright, with red carpeting and green plants. The top-floor room is a lovely suite. They also offer similar rooms—one with a rooftop patio—around the corner on the third floor (no reception desk) on busy Zeilstraat 22 (D-€55–75,

Db-€85, suite-€110, third person-€20, includes milk and cereal breakfast, cash only, non-smoking, Sloterkade 65, they send directions when you book, tel. 020/679-2753, fax 020/408-3028, www.bedandbreakfastamsterdam.net).

Cheap Hotels and Hostels

Inexpensive hotels line the convenient but noisy main drag between City Hall and the Anne Frank House. Expect a long, steep, and depressing stairway, noisy rooms in the front, and quieter rooms in the back.

Hotel Aspen, a good value for a budget hotel, is tidy, stark, and well-maintained (8 rooms, S-€35, D-€46, Db-€65–70, Tb-€75–80, Qb-€95, no breakfast, Raadhuisstraat 31, tel. 020/626-6714, fax 020/620-0866, www.hotelaspen.nl, info@hotelaspen.nl, run by Esam and his family). **Hotel Pax,** a few doors away, has large and plain, but airy rooms (S-€25–34, D-€37–57, Db-€55–85, T-€50–68, Tb-€60–100, Q-€55–77, no breakfast, prices vary with size and season, 2 showers and 2 toilets for 6 rooms, Raadhuisstraat 37, tel. 020/624-9735, run by 2 young brothers: Philip and Pieter).

The Shelter Jordan is a scruffy, friendly, Christian-run, 100-bed place in a great neighborhood. While most of Amsterdam's hostels are pretty wild, this place is drug-free and alcohol-free, with boys on one floor and girls on another. These are Amsterdam's best budget beds, in 14- to 20-bed dorms (€17.50–19.50, includes sheets and breakfast, maximum age 35, Internet access, non-smoking, 02:00 curfew, near Anne Frank House, Bloemstraat 179, tel. 020/624-4717, www.shelter.nl, jordan@shelter.nl). The Shelter serves hot meals, runs a snack bar, offers lockers, leads nightly Bible studies, and closes the dorms from 10:30–13:00. Its sister hostel, **The Shelter City** in the Red Light District, is similar, but definitely not preaching to the choir (€17.50–19.50, includes breakfast and sheets, maximum age 35, curfew, Barndesteeg 21, tel. 020/625-3230, fax 020/623-2282, www.shelter.nl, city@shelter.nl).

The city's two official hostels are **Vondelpark,** Amsterdam's top hostel (€19.50–27 with breakfast, D-€68–80, higher prices are for April–Oct, nonmembers pay €2.50 extra, cash only, lots of school groups, 4–20 beds per room, right on the park at Zandpad 5, tel. 020/589-8996, fax 020/589-8955, www.stayokay.com), and **Stadsdoelen** (€19.50–23.50 with breakfast, nonmembers pay €2.50 extra, cash only, just past Dam Square, Kloveniersburgwal 97, tel. 020/624-6832, fax 020/639-1035, www.stayokay.com). While these hostels are generally booked long in advance, a few beds open up each day at 11:00.

EATING

Traditional Dutch food is basic and hearty, with lots of bread, cheese, soup, and fish. Lunch and dinner are served at American times (roughly 12:00–14:00 and 18:00–21:00).

Dutch treats include cheese, pancakes *(pannenkoeken)*, gin *(jenever)*, light, pilsner-type beer, and "syrup waffles" *(stroopwafel)*.

Experiences you owe your tongue in Holland: trying a raw herring at an outdoor herring stand, lingering over coffee in a "brown café," sipping an old *jenever* with a new friend, and consuming an Indonesian feast—a rijstafel.

Budget Tips: Get a sandwich to go, and grab a park bench on a canal. Sandwiches *(broodjes)* of delicious cheese on fresh bread are cheap at snack bars, delis, and *broodjes* restaurants. Ethnic fast-food stands abound, offering a variety of meats wrapped in pita bread. Easy to buy at grocery stores, yogurt in the Netherlands (and throughout northern Europe) is delicious and often drinkable right out of its plastic container.

Restaurants: Of Amsterdam's thousand-plus restaurants, no one knows which are best. I'd pick an area and wander. The rowdy food ghetto thrives around Leidseplein; wander along Leidsedwarsstraat, Restaurant Row. The area around Spui canal and that end of Spuistraat is also trendy and not as noisy. For fewer crowds and more charm, find something in the Jordaan district. The best advice: your hotelier's. Most keep a reliable eating list for their neighborhood and know which places keep their travelers happy. I've listed some handy places to consider.

Near Spui, in the Center

The first four places cluster along the colorful, student-filled Grimburgwal lane, near the intersection of Spui and Rokin (midway between Dam Square and the Mint Tower).

The city university's **Atrium** is a great budget cafeteria (€6 meals, Mon–Fri 11:00–15:00 & 17:00–19:00, closed Sat–Sun) with an adjoining cheap café (Mon–Fri 15:30–24:00, closed Sat–Sun; from Spui, walk west down Landebrug Steeg past canalside Café 't Gasthuys 3 blocks to Oudezijds Achterburgwal 237, go through arched doorway on the right; tel. 020/525-3999).

Café 't Gasthuys, one of Amsterdam's many brown cafés (so called for their smoke-stained walls), serves light lunches, good sandwiches, and reasonably priced dinners. It offers indoor or peaceful canalside seating and sometimes slow service (daily 12:00–16:30 & 17:30–22:00, Grimburgwal 7, tel. 020/624-8230).

Pannenkoekenhuis Upstairs is a tiny and characteristic perch up some extremely steep stairs, where Arno Jakobs cooks and serves delicious €7 pancakes to four tables (daily 12:00–18:00,

Amsterdam Restaurants

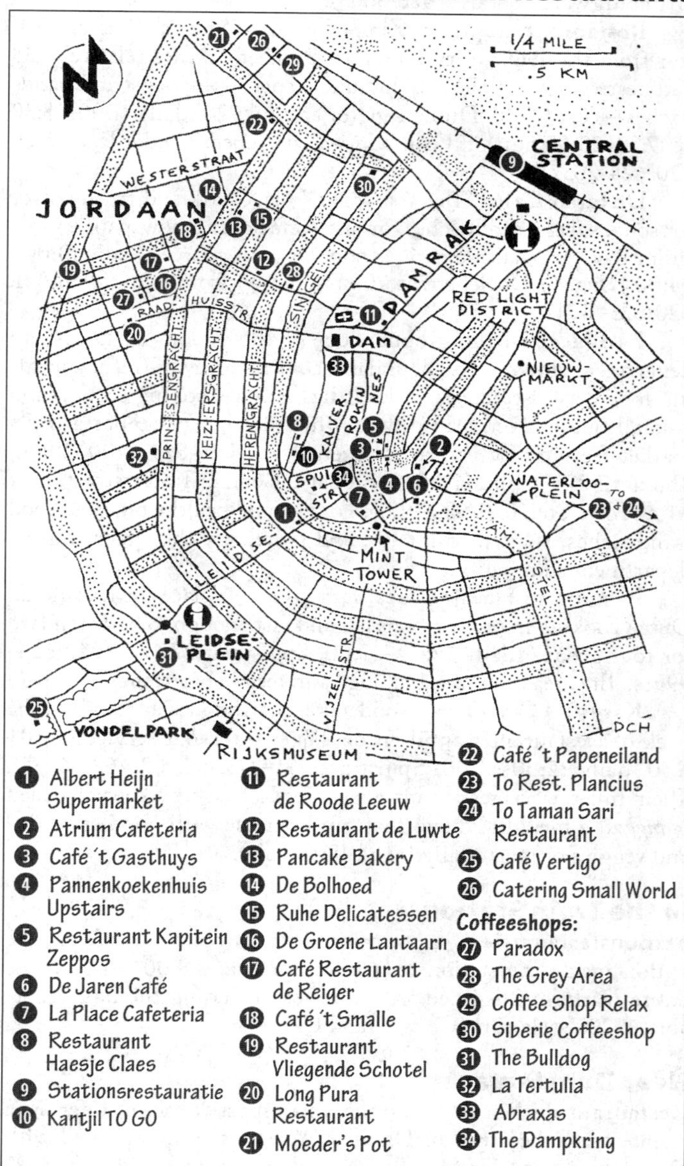

Grimburgwal 2, tel. 020/626-5603).

Restaurant Kapitein Zeppos, named for a Belgian TV star from the 1960s, serves French-Dutch food in a relatively big and festive setting. The light lunch specials—soups and sandwiches—cost €5–10. Dinners go for around €20 (daily 11:00–15:30 & 17:30–23:00, just off Grimburgwal at Gebed Zonder End 5, tel. 020/624-2057).

De Jaren Café ("The Years Café") is a stark and trendy place for soup, salads, sandwiches, or just coffee over a newspaper. On a sunny day, its canalside patio is popular with yuppies (daily 10:00–24:00, Nieuwe Doelenstraat 20–22, just up from Muntplein, tel. 020/625-5771).

La Place, on the ground floor of the Vroom & Dreesman department store, has an abundant, colorful array of fresh, appealing food served cafeteria-style. It has a non-smoking section and a small outdoor terrace upstairs. This thriving place has a lively market feel and lots of great vegetables (Mon–Sat 10:00–20:00, Thu until 21:00, Sun 12:00–20:00, at the end of Kalverstraat, near Mint Tower, tel. 020/622-0171). For fast and healthy take-out food (sandwiches, yogurt, fruit cups, and more), try the bakery on the department store's ground floor.

Restaurant Haesje Claes, famous as *the* place for traditional Dutch cooking in the center, is big and fast enough to be a standard for tour groups (daily 12:00–22:00, Spuistraat 275, tel. 020/624-9998). The area around it is a huge and festive bar scene.

Kantjil TO GO has good take-out Indonesian food in the back of Restaurant Kantjil en de Tijger (take-out service €3.50–6.50, daily 12:00–21:00, Spuistraat 291–293, tel. 020/622-2994). Their full-service restaurant also offers a tasty €9 special called *mangkok,* a meal in a bowl that can be made with noodles or rice and veggies or meat (daily 16:30–18:45 only).

In the Train Station

Stationsrestauratie is a surprisingly good budget, self-service option inside the station on platform 2 (daily 8:00–20:00). The entire platform 2 is lined with eateries, including the tall, venerable, 1920s-style First Class Grand Café.

Near Dam Square

Restaurant de Roode Leeuw is an impressive place, offering a respite from the crush of Damrak. You'll get a menu filled with Dutch traditions, dressy service, and plenty of tourists (€18–23 main dish, 3-course menu with lots of intriguing choices for €30, daily 12:00–22:00, Damrak 93-94, tel. 020/555-0666).

Near the Anne Frank House and in the Jordaan District

All these places, except for the last two, are within a few scenic blocks of the Anne Frank House, providing handy lunches and atmospheric dinners in Amsterdam's most characteristic neighborhood.

Restaurant de Luwte is painfully romantic, on a picturesque street overlooking a canal, with lots of candles, a muted but fresh modern interior, and French Mediterranean cuisine (€18 main courses, €27 for a 3-course set menu, big dinner salads for €15, non-smoking section, daily 18:00–22:00, Leliegracht 26-28, tel. 020/625-8548).

The **Pancake Bakery** serves good pancakes in a nothing special, family atmosphere. The menu features a fun selection of ethnic-themed pancakes—including Indonesian, for those who want two experiences in one (€8–11 pancakes, splitting is OK, daily 12:00–21:30, Prinsengracht 191, tel. 020/625-1333).

De Bolhoed, across the canal, serves serious vegetarian and vegan food in a colorful setting that Buddha would dig (€13 meals, daily 12:00–22:00, Prinsengracht 60, tel. 020/626-1803).

De Groene Lantaarn (The Green Lantern) is fun for fondue. The menu offers fish, meat, and cheese (Dutch and Swiss) with salad and fruit for €17–25 (Thu–Sun from 18:00, closed Mon–Wed, a few blocks into the Jordaan at Bloemgracht 47, tel. 020/620-2088).

Café Restaurant de Reiger must offer the best cooking of any *eetcafé* in the Jordaan. It's famous for its fresh ingredients and delightful bistro ambience. In addition to an English menu, ask for a translation of the €16 daily specials on the chalkboard. The café, which is crowded late and on weekends, takes no reservations, but you're welcome to have a drink at the bar while you wait (daily 11:00–15:30 & 18:00–22:30, glass of house wine-€2.50, veggie options, non-smoking section in front, Nieuwe Leliestraat 34, tel. 020/624-7426).

Café 't Smalle is extremely charming, with three zones where you can enjoy a light lunch or a drink: canalside, inside around the bar, and up some steep stairs in a quaint little loft. While the café is open daily until midnight, food is served only at lunch from 12:00–17:00 (plenty of interesting wines by the glass posted, at Egelantiersgracht 12 where it hits Prinsengracht, tel. 020/623-9617).

Restaurant Vliegende Schotel is a folksy, unvarnished little Jordaan eatery decorated with children's crayon art. Its cheap and fun, meatless menu features fish and vegetarian fare. Choose a table, and then order at the counter. Nothing trendy about this place—just locals who like food and don't want to cook (plates €8–11, daily 17:00–23:00, non-smoking section, wine by the glass, Nieuwe Leliestraat 162, tel. 020/625-2041).

Long Pura is a good place for authentic Indonesian. Though pricey, filled with tourists, and on a noisy street, it's conveniently located and friendly, and proudly serves reliably delicious rice-table extravaganzas in a tasteful Indonesian setting (€31 for *rijsttafel,* €37.50 with appetizer and dessert, daily 18:00–23:00, Rozengracht 46, tel. 020/623-8950).

Moeder's Pot, a six-table neighborhood eatery with great character and charm, is gruff, with the smell of fried food and cigarettes. Hearty main courses come with fried potatoes and vegetables, applesauce, and salad. The place is not central, but puts you in a charming little neighborhood at the seaside edge of the Jordaan (€7–15, Mon–Sat 17:00–22:00, closed Sun and holidays, Vinkenstraat 119, tel. 020/623-7643).

Café 't Papeneiland is a classic brown café. With Delft tiles, an evocative old stove, and a stay-awhile perch overlooking a canal with welcoming benches, it's been the neighborhood hangout since the 17th century (overlooking northwest end of Prinsengracht at #2, tel. 020/624-1989). Though the café serves light meals, most patrons come here to nurse a drink and chat. Once a refuge for Catholics (the name means "Papists' Island"), it once had an escape tunnel for priests on the run.

Catering Small World is a cozy sandwich bar with good coffee, the best muffins in town, and only a few seats (€4–10, Mon–Sat 10:30–20:00, Sun 12:00–20:00, Binnen Oranjestraat 14).

Ruhe Delicatessen, run for decades by Mr. Ruhe, is the perfect late-night deli for a quick, cheap picnic dinner (a block from the recommended Hotel Toren at Prinsenstraat 13, daily 12:00–22:00, tel. 020/626-7438).

Near the Botanical Garden and Dutch Resistance Museum

Restaurant Plancius, adjacent to the Dutch Resistance Museum, is a mod, handy spot for lunch. With good indoor and outdoor seating, it's popular with the broadcasters from the nearby local TV studios (creative breakfasts, light €4–8 lunches and €15–18 dinners, daily 10:00–22:00, Plantage Kerklaan 61a, tel. 020/330-9469).

Taman Sari Restaurant is the local choice for Indonesian, serving hearty, quality €9.50 dinners and *rijsttafel* dinners for €16–22.50 (daily 17:00–23:00, Plantage Kerklaan 32, tel. 020/623-7130).

Near Vondelpark

Café Vertigo offers a fun selection of excellent soups and sandwiches. The service can be slow, but if you grab an outdoor table, you can watch the world spin by (daily 11:00–24:00, beneath Film Museum, Vondelpark 3, tel. 020/612-3021).

EXPERIENCES

Drugs and Coffeeshops

Amsterdam, Europe's counterculture mecca, thinks the concept of a "victimless crime" is a contradiction in terms. Heroin and cocaine are strictly illegal in the Netherlands, and the police stringently enforce laws prohibiting their sale and use. But, while hard drugs are definitely out, marijuana causes about as much excitement as a bottle of beer. If tourists call an ambulance after smoking too much pot, medics just say, "Drink something sweet and walk it off."

Throughout the Netherlands, you'll see "coffeeshops"—pubs selling marijuana. The minimum age for purchase is 18. Coffeeshops can sell up to five grams of marijuana per person per day. Locals buy marijuana by asking, "Can I see the cannabis menu?" The menu looks like the inventory of a drug bust. Display cases show various joints or baggies for sale. The Dutch usually include a little tobacco in their pre-rolled joints (though a few coffeeshops sell joints of pure marijuana). To avoid the tobacco, smokers roll their own (cigarette papers are free with the purchase, dispensed like toothpicks) or borrow a pipe or bong. Baggies of marijuana usually cost €10–15, and a smaller amount means better quality.

Most of downtown Amsterdam's coffeeshops feel grungy and foreboding to anyone over 30. The neighborhood places (and those in small towns around the countryside) are much more inviting to people without piercings, tattoos, and favorite techno artists. I've listed a few places with a more pub-like ambience for Americans wanting to go local, but within reason. For locations, see the map on page 1157.

Paradox is the most *gezellig* (cozy) coffeeshop I found—a mellow, graceful place. The managers, Ludo and Jan, are patient with descriptions and happy to walk you through all your options. This is a rare coffeeshop that serves light meals. The juice is fresh, the music is easy, and the neighborhood is charming. Colorful murals with bright blue skies are all over the walls, creating a fresh and open feeling (loaner bongs, games, daily 10:00–20:00, 2 blocks from Anne Frank House at 1e Bloemdwarsstraat 2, tel. 020/623-5639, www.paradoxamsterdam.demon.nl).

The Grey Area coffeeshop is a cool, welcoming, and smoky hole-in-the-wall appreciated among local aficionados as winner of Amsterdam's Cannabis Cup awards. Judging by the proud autographed photos on the wall, many famous Americans have dropped in. You're welcome to just nurse a bottomless cup of coffee (open Tue–Sun high noon to 20:00, closed Mon, between Dam Square and Anne Frank House at Oude Leliestraat 2, tel. 020/420-4301, www.greyarea.nl, run by two friendly Americans, Steven and Jon).

Coffee Shop Relax is simply the neighborhood pub serving a different drug. It's relaxed and has a helpful staff and homey atmosphere, with plants, couches, and bar seating. The great, straightforward menu chalked onto the board details what it has to offer (daily 10:00–24:00, a bit out of the way, but a pleasant Jordaan walk to Binnen Orangestraat 9).

Siberie Coffeeshop is central, but feels cozy, with a friendly canalside ambience (daily 11:00–23:00, Internet access, helpful staff, fun English menu that explains the personality of each item, Brouwersgracht 11, www.siberie.net).

La Tertulia is a sweet little mother-and-daughter-run place with pastel decor and a cheery terrarium ambience (Tue–Sat 11:00–19:00, closed Sun–Mon, sandwiches, brownies, games, Prinsengracht 312, www.coffeeshopamsterdam.com).

Abraxas Coffeeshop is a mellow and mature nook where butterflies roost and aging hippies check their e-mail (daily 10:00–24:00, just off Kalverstraat, a half block off Dam Square at J. Roelensteeg 12, tel. 020-625-5763).

The Bulldog is the high profile, leading touristy chain of coffeeshops. These establishments are young but welcoming, with reliable selections. They're pretty comfortable for green tourists wanting to just hang out for a while. The flagship branch, in a former police station right on Leidseplein, is very handy, offering fun outdoor seating where you can watch the world skateboard by (daily 9:00–01:00, Leidseplein 17, tel. 020/625-6278, www.bulldog.nl).

The Dampkring is one of very few coffeeshops that also serve alcohol. It's a high profile and busy place, filled with a young clientele, but the owners still take the time to explain what they offer. Scenes from the movie *Ocean's Twelve* were filmed here (daily 11:00–1:00 in the morning, close to Spui at Handboogstraat 29).

TRANSPORTATION CONNECTIONS

Amsterdam's train-information center requires a long wait. Save lots of time by getting train tickets and information in a small-town station, at the airport upon arrival, or from a travel agency. For phone information, dial 0900-9292 for local trains or 0900-9296 for international trains (€0.50/min, daily 7:00–24:00, wait through recording and hold...hold...hold...).

From Amsterdam by Train to: Schiphol Airport (6/hr, 20 min, €3.30), **Haarlem** (6/hr, 15 min, €3.20 one-way, €5.50 same-day round-trip), **The Hague** (2/hr, 45 min), **Delft** (2/hr, 1 hr), **Rotterdam** (4/hr, 1 hr), **Bruges** (hrly, 3.5 hrs, transfer in Antwerp's central station; transfer can be timed closely—be alert and check with conductor), **Brussels** (2/hr, 3 hrs, €30), **Ostende** (hrly, 4 hrs, change in Antwerp), **London** (8/day, 6 hrs, with transfer to

Eurostar Chunnel train in Brussels, Eurostar discounted with railpass, www.eurostar.com), **Copenhagen** (5/day, 11 hrs, transfer in Osnabrück and Hamburg), **Frankfurt** (8/day, 3–4 hrs, some are direct, others involve transfer in Köln or Duisburg), **Munich** (7/day, 7–8 hrs, transfer in Frankfurt; one 11-hr direct night train), **Bonn** (10/day, 3 hrs, some direct but most transfer in Köln), **Bern** (5/day, 9 hrs, one direct but most transfer in Mannheim), **Paris** (5/day, 5 hrs, requires fast Thalys train from Brussels with €11 supplement, www.thalys.com).

By Bus: If you don't have a railpass, the cheapest way to get to Paris is by bus (Eurolines buses make the 8-hour trip 5 times daily, about €40–60 round-trip, compared to €100 second-class by train; bus station in Amsterdam at Julianaplein 5, Amstel Station, 5 stops by Métro from Central Station, tel. 020/560-8788, www.eurolines.com).

Schiphol Airport

Schiphol (SKIP-pol) Airport, like most of Holland, is English-speaking, user-friendly, and below sea level.

Information: Schiphol flight information (tel. 0900-7244-7465) can give you flight times and your airline's Amsterdam phone number for reconfirmation before going home (€0.45/min to climb through its phone tree—or visit www.schiphol.nl). To reach the airlines directly, call: KLM and Northwest, tel. 020/649-9123 or 020/474-7747; Martinair, tel. 020/601-1222; SAS, tel. 0900-746-63727; American Airlines, tel. 06/022-7844; British Air, tel. 023/554-7555; and easyJet, tel. 023/568-4880.

Services: The ABN/AMRO **banks** offer fair rates (in arrivals and lounge area). The GWK **public-transit office** is located in Schiphol Plaza. Surf the **Internet** and make phone calls at the Communication Centre on the top level of lounge 2 (daily 6:00–20:00). Convenient luggage **lockers**, at various points around the terminal, allow you to leave your bag at the airport on a lengthy layover...or for up to a week.

If you have extra time to kill at Schiphol, check out some **fine art**, actual Dutch Masters by Rembrandt, Vermeer, and others. The Rijksmuseum loans a dozen or so of its minor masterpieces from the Golden Age to the unique airport museum "Rijksmuseum Amsterdam Schiphol," a little art gallery behind the passport check at Holland Boulevard between piers E and F. Yes, this is really true (free, daily 7:00–20:00).

Transportation Connections: The airport has a train station of its own. You can validate your Eurailpass and hit the rails immediately, or, to stretch your railpass, buy an inexpensive ticket into Amsterdam today and start the pass later.

From the airport to Amsterdam: There's a direct **train** to Amsterdam's Central Station (6/hr, 20 min, €3.30). The Connexxion **shuttle bus** takes you to your hotel neighborhood; since there are various routes, ask the attendant which works best for your hotel (2/hr, 20 min, €11, one route stops at Westerkerk near Anne Frank House and many recommended hotels, bus to other hotels may cost a couple euros more, departs from lane A7 in front of airport, tel. 020/653-4975, www.airporthotelshuttle.nl). Allow about €40 for a **taxi** to downtown Amsterdam.

From the airport to Haarlem (see next chapter): The **bus** is direct, stopping at Haarlem's train station and near the Market Square (4/hr, 40 min, €5.80, bus #300, departs from lane B2 in front of airport). The **train** is slightly cheaper and just as quick, but you'll have to transfer at the Amsterdam-Sloterdijk station (4/hr, 40 min, €4.55). Figure about €45 to Haarlem by taxi.

From the airport by train to: The Hague (4/hr, 30 min), **Delft** (4/hr, 45 min, transfer in The Hague or Leiden), **Rotterdam** (4/hr, 45 min), **Brussels** (hrly, 2.5 hrs), **Bruges** (hrly, 3.25 hrs, change in Antwerp).

HAARLEM

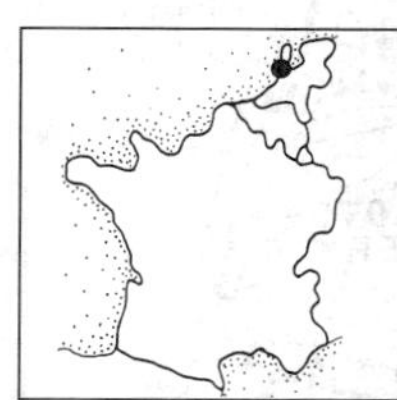

Cute and cozy, yet authentic and handy to the airport, Haarlem is a fine home base, giving you small-town warmth overnight, with easy access (15 min by train) to wild and crazy Amsterdam during the day.

Bustling Haarlem gave America's Harlem its name back when New York was New Amsterdam, a Dutch colony. For centuries, Haarlem has been a market town, buzzing with shoppers heading home with fresh bouquets, nowadays by bike.

Enjoy the market on Monday (clothing) or Saturday (general), when the square bustles like a Brueghel painting, with cheese, fish, flowers, and families. Make yourself at home; buy some flowers to brighten your hotel room.

With extra time, visit some of the Netherlands' fun day-trip destinations: lovely Delft, sleepy Edam, cheesy Alkmaar, flowery Aalsmeer, bustling open-air museums, and more.

ORIENTATION

(area code: 023)

Tourist Information

Haarlem's TI (VVV), at the train station, is friendlier, more helpful, and less crowded than Amsterdam's. Ask your Amsterdam questions here (April–Sept Mon–Fri 9:00–17:30, Sat 10:00–16:00, closed Sun; Oct–March Mon–Fri 9:30–17:00, Sat 10:00–14:00, closed Sun; tel. 0900-616-1600, €0.50/min, helpful parking brochure). The €1 *Holiday Magazine* is not necessary, but it's free if you buy the fine €2 town map. The TI also sells a €2 self-guided

Haarlem

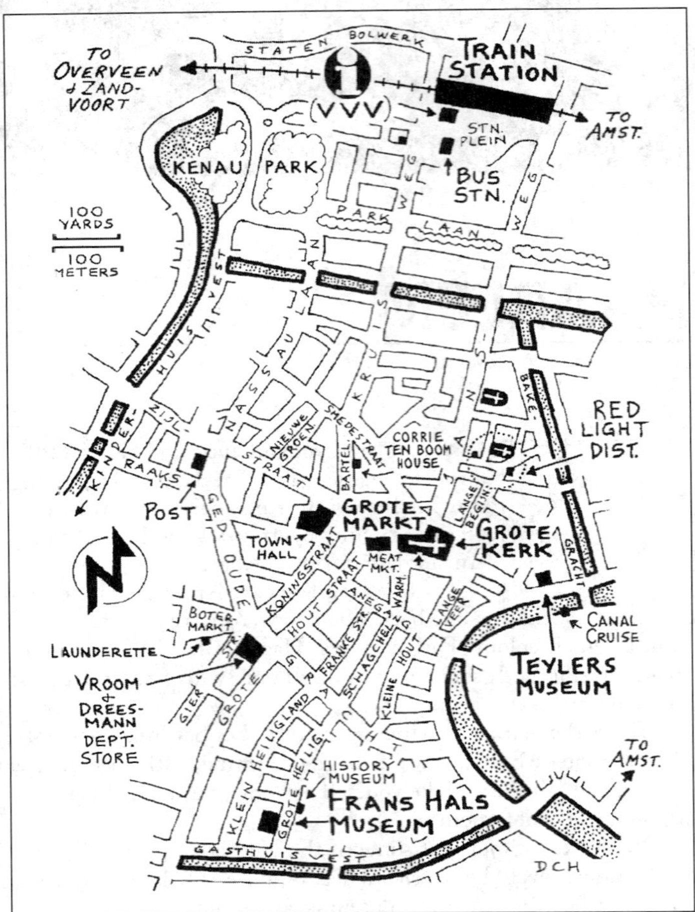

walking-tour map for overachievers. The little computer terminal on the curb outside the TI prints out free maps anytime.

Arrival in Haarlem

By Train: As you walk out of Haarlem's train station (lockers available), the TI is on your right and the bus station is across the street. Two parallel streets flank the train station (Kruisweg and Jansweg). Head up either street, and you'll reach the town square and church within 10 minutes. If you need help, ask a local to point you toward the Grote Markt (Market Square).

By Car: Parking is expensive on the streets (€2.50/hr) and cheaper in several central garages (€1.50/hr). Two main garages let you park overnight for €2 (at the train station and near Die Raeckse Hotel).

By Plane: For details on getting from Schiphol Airport into Haarlem, see page 1164.

Helpful Hints

Bike Rental: You can rent bikes at the train station (€7.50/day, €50 deposit and passport number, Mon–Sat 6:00–24:00, Sun 7:30–24:00).

Currency Exchange: The handy GWK change office at the train station offers fair rates (Mon–Fri 8:00–20:00, Sat 9:00–17:00, Sun 10:00–17:00).

Internet Access: Try Internet Café Amadeus (in Hotel Amadeus overlooking Market Square, €1.20/15 min, ask for discount with this book) or nearly any coffeeshop (if you don't mind marijuana smoke).

Post Office: It's at Gedempte Oude Gracht 2 (Mon–Fri 9:00–18:00, Sat 10:00–13:30, closed Sun, has ATM).

Laundry: My Beautiful Launderette is handy and cheap (€5 self-service wash and dry, bring change, daily 8:30–20:30, €8 full service available Mon–Fri 9:00–17:00, near Vroom & Dreesmann department store at Boter Markt 20).

Flower Parade: On a Saturday in late April (call TI for details), an all-day Flower Parade of floats, decorated with blossoms instead of crepe paper, will waft through eight towns, including Haarlem. The floats are parked in Haarlem at Gedempte Oude Gracht overnight, when they're illuminated, and through the next day.

Local Guide: For a historical look at Haarlem, consider hiring Walter Schelfhout (€75/2-hr walk, tel. 023/535-5715, schelfhout@dutch.nl).

SIGHTS

▲▲Market Square (Grote Markt)—Haarlem's Market Square, where 10 streets converge, is the town's delightful centerpiece...as it has been for 700 years. To enjoy a coffee or beer here, simmering in Dutch good living, is a quintessential European experience. In a recent study, the Dutch were found to be the most content people in Europe. In another study, the people of Haarlem were found to be the most content in the Netherlands. Observe. Sit and gaze at the church, appreciating the same scene Dutch artists captured in oil paintings that now hang in museums.

Just a few years ago, trolleys ran through the square and cars were parked everywhere. But today, it's a people zone, with market stalls filling the square on Mondays and Saturdays and café tables on other days.

This is a great place to build a picnic with Haarlem finger foods—raw herring, local cheese (Gouda and Edam), a *frikandel* (little corn-dog sausage), french fries with mayonnaise, *stroopwafels* (waffles with syrup), and *poffertjes* (little sugar doughnuts).

▲Church (Grote Kerk)—One of the best-known landmarks in the Netherlands, this church is visible from miles around, rising above the flat plain that surrounds it. The church was built over a 150-year period (c. 1390–1540) in the late Gothic style of red and gray brick, topped with a lead-covered wood roof and a stacked tower with a golden crown and a rooster weathervane. The interior is worth a look, if only for its Oz-like organ (from 1738, 100 feet high, its 5,000 pipes impressed both Handel and Mozart). Note how the organ, which fills the west end, seems to steal the show from the altar. Quirky highlights include a replica of Foucault's pendulum, the "Dog-Whipper's Chapel," and a 400-year-old cannonball. To enter, find the small *Entrée* sign behind the church at Oude Groenmarkt 23 (€1.50, Mon–Sat 10:00–16:00, closed Sun to tourists, tel. 023/553-2040). Consider attending (even part of) a concert to hear Holland's greatest pipe organ (regular free concerts Tue at 20:15 mid-May–mid-Oct, additional concerts Thu at 15:00 July–Aug, confirm schedule at TI or at www.bavo.nl; bring a sweater—the church isn't heated).

▲▲Frans Hals Museum— Haarlem is the hometown of Frans Hals, the foremost Dutch portrait painter of the 17th-century Golden Age. This refreshing museum—an almshouse for old men back in 1610—displays many of his greatest paintings, done in his nearly Impressionistic style. Stand eye-to-eye with life-size, life-like portraits of Haarlem's citizens—brewers, preachers, workers, bureaucrats, and housewives—and see the people who built the Golden Age, then watched it start to fade.

Along with Frans Hals' work, the museum features Pieter Breughel's painting *Proverbs,* illustrating 72 Dutch proverbs. To peek into old Dutch ways, identify some with the help of the English-language key. Also look for the 250-year-old dollhouse on display in a former chapel (€5.40, Tue–Sat 11:00–17:00, Sun 12:00–17:00, closed Mon, Groot Heiligland 62, tel. 023/511-5775, www.franshalsmuseum.nl).

History Museum—This small museum, across the street from the Frans Hals Museum, offers a glimpse of old Haarlem. Request the English version of the 10-minute video. Study the large-scale model of Haarlem in 1822 (when its fortifications were still intact), and enjoy the "time machine" computer and video display that shows you various aspects of life in Haarlem at different points in history (€1, Tue–Sat 12:00–17:00, Sun 13:00–17:00, closed Mon, Groot Heiligland 47, tel. 023/542-2427). The adjacent architecture center (free) may be of interest to architects.

Corrie Ten Boom House—Haarlem is home to Corrie Ten Boom, popularized by *The Hiding Place,* an inspirational book and movie about the Ten Boom family's experience protecting Jews from the Nazis. Corrie Ten Boom gives the other half of the Anne Frank story—the point of view of those who risked their lives to hide Dutch Jews during the Nazi occupation (1940–1945).

The clock shop was the Ten Boom family business. The elderly father and his two daughters—Corrie and Betsy, both in their 50s—lived above the store and in the brick building attached in back (along Schoutensteeg alley). Corrie's bedroom was on the top floor at the back. This room was tiny to start with, but the family built a second, secret room (only about a foot deep) at the very back—the hiding place, where they could hide six or seven Jews at a time.

Devoutly religious, the family had a long tradition of tolerance, having for generations hosted prayer meetings here in their home for both Jews and Christians.

The Gestapo, tipped off that the family was harboring Jews, burst into the Ten Boom house. Finding a suspicious number of ration coupons, the Nazis arrested the family, but failed to find the six Jews in the hiding place (who later escaped). Corrie's father and sister died while in prison, but Corrie survived the Ravensbruck concentration camp to tell her story in her memoir.

The Ten Boom House is open for 60-minute English tours; the tours are sometimes mixed with preaching (donation accepted, April–Oct Tue–Sat 10:00–16:00, Nov–March Tue–Sat 11:00–15:00, closed Mon, 50 yards north of Market Square at Barteljorisstraat 19; the clock-shop people get all wound up if you go inside—wait in the little side street at the door, where tour times are posted; tel. 023/531-0823, www.corrietenboom.com).

▲Teylers Museum—Famous as the oldest museum in Holland, Teylers is interesting mainly as a look at a 200-year-old museum—fossils, minerals, and primitive electronic gadgetry. New exhibition halls have freshened up the place with rotating exhibits. Stop by if you enjoy mixing, say, Renaissance art with extinct fish (€5.50, Tue–Sat 10:00–17:00, Sun 12:00–17:00, Spaarne 16, tel. 023/531-9010, www.teylersmuseum.nl).

Canal Cruise—Making a scenic 70-minute loop through and around Haarlem, these little trips by Woltheus Cruises are more relaxing than informative (€7, 4/day, May–Oct daily 10:00–17:00, closed Mon in May and Oct, no tours Nov–April, across canal from Teylers Museum at Spaarne 11a, tel. 023/535-7723).

Red Light District—Wander through a little Red Light District as precious as a Barbie doll—and legal since the 1980s (2 blocks northeast of Market Square, off Lange Begijnestraat, no senior or student discounts). Don't miss the mall marked by the red neon sign reading *t'Steegje.* The nearby *t'Poortje* (office park) costs €6.

NIGHTLIFE

Haarlem's evening scene is great. The bars around the Grote Kerk and Lange Veerstraat are colorful and lively. You'll find plenty of music. The best show in town: the café scene on Market Square. In good weather, café tables tumble happily out of the bars.

For trendy local crowds, sip a drink at **Café Studio** on Market Square (daily 12:00–4:00, next to Hotel Carillon, tel. 023/531-0033). **Grand Café XO** is another hip nightspot on the square (daily 10:00–24:00, Grote Markt 8, 023/551-1350). Tourists gawk at the old-fashioned, belt-driven ceiling fans in **Café 1900** across from the Corrie Ten Boom House (daily 9:00–00:30, live music Sun night except in July, Barteljorisstraat 10, tel. 023/531-8283).

SLEEPING

The helpful Haarlem TI, just outside the train station, can nearly always find you a €20 bed in a private home (for a €6-per-person fee, plus a cut of your host's money, 2-night minimum). Avoid this if you can; it's cheaper to reserve by calling direct.

Haarlem is most crowded in April and May (particularly Easter weekend) and in July and August.

The listed prices include breakfast (unless otherwise noted) and usually include the €1.80-per-person-per-day tourist tax. To avoid this town's louder-than-normal street noises, forgo views for a room in the back. Hotels and the TI have a useful parking brochure.

In the Center

$$$ Hotel Lion D'Or is a classy, 34-room business hotel with all the professional comforts and a handy location. But don't expect a warm welcome (Sb-€135–155, Db-€165–185, extra bed-€30, elevator, some non-smoking rooms, across the street from train station at Kruisweg 34, tel. 023/532-1750, fax 023/532-9543, www.goldentulip.com).

$$ Hotel Amadeus, on Market Square, has 15 small, bright, and basic rooms. Some have views of the square. This characteristic hotel, ideally located above an early-20th-century dinner café, is relatively quiet, especially if you take a room in the back. Its lush old lounge/breakfast room on the second floor overlooks the square, and Mike and Inez take good care of their guests (Sb-€60, Db-€80–85, Tb-€105, includes tax, 2-night stay and cash get you a 5 percent discount, 10-min walk from train station, steep climb to lounge, then an elevator, Grote Markt 10, tel. 023/532-4530, fax 023/532-2328, www.amadeus-hotel.com, info@amadeus-hotel.com). The hotel also runs a six-terminal Internet café (€1.20/15 min, ask for discount with this book).

Sleep Code

(€1 = about $1.20, country code: 31, area code: 023)
S = Single, **D** = Double/Twin, **T** = Triple, **Q** = Quad, **b** = bathroom, **s** = shower only. Credit cards are accepted unless otherwise noted. Nearly every Dutch person you'll encounter speaks English.

To help you easily sort through these listings, I've divided the rooms into three categories, based on the price for a standard double room with bath:

$$$ **Higher Priced**—Most rooms €100 or more.
$$ **Moderately Priced**—Most rooms between €65–100.
$ **Lower Priced**—Most rooms €65 or less.

$$ Hotel Carillon also overlooks the town square, but comes with a little more traffic and bell-tower noise. Many of the 20 well-worn rooms are small, and the stairs are ste-e-e-p. The front rooms come with great town-square views and street noise (tiny loft singles-€33, Db-€76, Tb-€92.50, Qb-€99, includes breakfast, 10-min walk from train station, no elevator, Grote Markt 27, tel. 023/531-0591, fax 023/531-4909, www.hotelcarillon.com, info@hotelcarillon.com).

$$ Joops Hotel, with 26 comfortable rooms, is located just behind the Grote Kerk church (Db-€80–90, breakfast buffet-€9.50, Internet access, Oude Groenmarkt 20, tel. 023/532-2008, fax 023/532-9549, www.joopshotel.com, Joops@easynet.nl). In nearby Hotel Arendshoek, they rent studios with kitchenettes for two to four people (€65–130, elevator, contact Joops Hotel).

$$ Die Raeckse Hotel, family-run and friendly, is not as central as the others and has less character and more traffic noise, but its 21 rooms are decent and comfortable (Sb-€55, Db-€70–80 depending upon size, Tb-€98, Qb-€115, 10 percent discount for 2-night stay Nov–March, Raaks Straat 1, tel. 023/532-6629, fax 023/531-7937, www.die-raeckse.nl, dieraeckse@zonnet.nl). A big, cheap garage is across the street.

$ Bed-and-Breakfast House de Kiefte is your get-into-a-local-home budget option. Marjet (mar-yet) and Hans, a frank, interesting Dutch couple who speak English well, rent four bright, cheery, non-smoking rooms (rates include breakfast and travel advice) in their quiet 1892 home (Ds-€52, T-€73, Qs-€94, cash only, 2-night min, very steep stairs, family loft sleeps up to 5, kids over 4 welcome, Coornhertstraat 3, tel. 023/532-2980, mobile 06-5474-5272). It's a 15-minute walk or €7 taxi ride from the train station and a five-minute walk from the center. From Grote Markt,

Haarlem Hotels and Restaurants

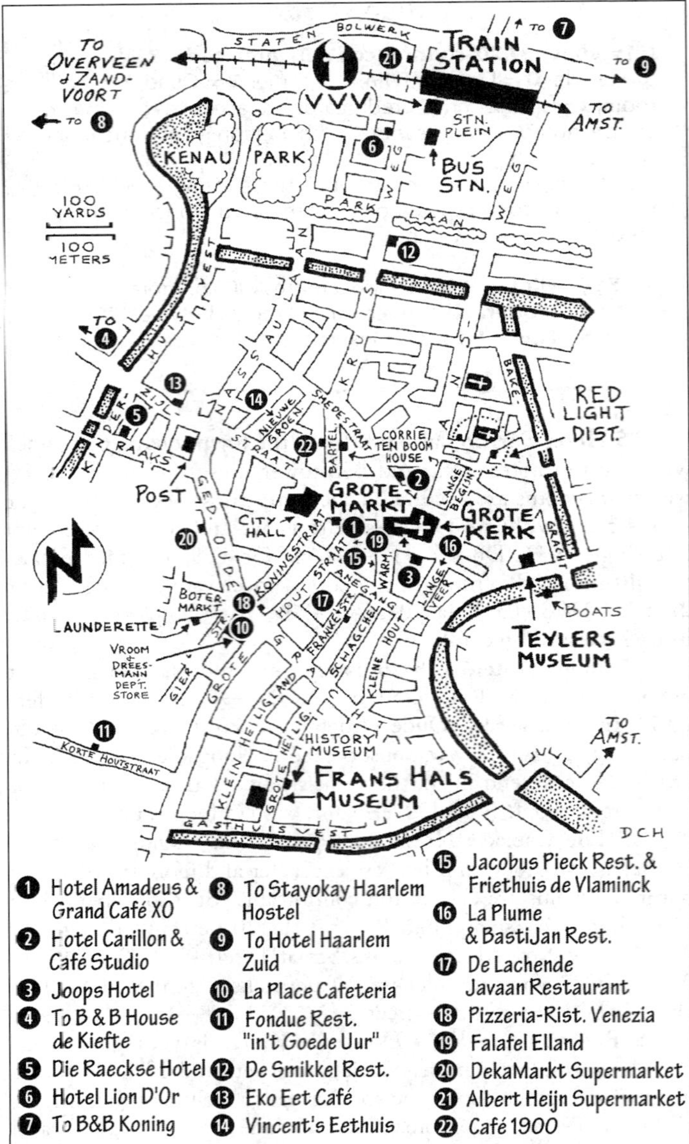

walk to the right of the town hall, straight out Zijlstraat, over the bridge, and take a left on the fourth street.

Near Haarlem

$$ Hotel Haarlem Zuid, with 300 rooms and very American, is sterile, but a good value for those interested only in sleeping and eating. It sits in an industrial zone a 20-minute walk from the center, on the road to the airport (Db-€80, breakfast-€12, elevator, free parking, laundry service, fitness center, inexpensive hotel restaurant, Toekanweg 2, tel. 023/536-7500, fax 023/536-7980, www.hotelhaarlemzuid.nl, info@hotelhaarlemzuid.nl). Buses #70, #71, and #72 connect the hotel with the train station and Market Square every 10 minutes. Bus #80 makes runs to the beach or Amsterdam. Fast airport bus #300 stops at the hotel.

$ B&B Koning, a 15-minute walk north of the train station or a quick jaunt on bus #2 or #71, has five simple rooms in a rowhouse in a residential area (S-€25, D-€50, T-€75, 2-night min, includes breakfast, cash only, Kleverlaan 179, tel. 023/526-1456).

$ Stayokay Haarlem, completely renovated and with all the youth-hostel comforts, charges €19–23 for beds in eight-bed dorms (€2.50 extra for nonmembers, includes sheets and breakfast, daily 7:30–24:00, Jan Gijzenpad 3, 2 miles from Haarlem station—take bus #2 from platform A1, or a 5-min walk from Santpoort Zuid train station, tel. 023/537-3793, fax 023/537-1176, www.stayokay.com/haarlem, haarlem@stayokay.com).

EATING

Between Market Square and the Train Station

Pancakes for lunch or dinner? **Pannenkoekhuis De Smikkel** serves a selection of over 50 pancakes for a meal (meat, cheese, etc.) and dessert. The €7.25 pancakes are filling; smaller sizes are available (daily 12:00–21:00, Sun from 16:00, closed Mon in winter, 2 blocks in front of station, Kruisweg 57, tel. 023/532-0631).

Enjoy a sandwich or coffee surrounded by trains and 1908 architecture in the **Foodcourt Haarlem Station** (daily 7:30–20:00, between tracks #3 and #6 at the station).

On or near Zijlstraat

Eko Eet Café is great for a cheery, tasty vegetarian meal (€11 menu, daily 17:30–21:30, Zijlstraat 39, tel. 023/532-6568).

Vincent's Eethuis, the cheapest restaurant in town, offers basic Dutch food and a friendly staff. This former St. Vincent's soup kitchen now feeds more gainfully employed locals than poor (daily plate-€5.50, specials-€7.25, Mon–Fri 16:30–19:30, closed Sat–Sun, Nieuwe Groenmarkt 22).

Between the Market Square and Frans Hals Museum

Jacobus Pieck Eetlokaal is popular with locals for its fine value "global cuisine" (plate of the day-€9.50, great €5 sandwiches, Mon 10:00–17:00, Tue–Sat 10:00–22:00, closed Sun, Warmoesstraat 18, behind church, tel. 023/532-6144).

Friethuis de Vlaminck is the place for a cone of old-fashioned fresh "Flemish fries" (€1.75, Tue–Sat until 18:00, closed Sun–Mon, Warmoesstraat 3, behind church).

Looking for pizza or pasta? Try **Pizzeria-Ristorante Venezia,** run for 10 years by the same Italian family from Bari (€8–17 meals, pizza from €7.50, daily 13:00–23:00, facing Vroom & Dreesmann department store at Verwulft 7, 023/531-7753).

La Plume steakhouse is noisy, with a happy, local, and carnivorous crowd (€12–18 meals, daily from 17:30, Lange Veerstraat 1, tel. 023/531-3202).

BastiJan serves good Mediterranean cuisine in a classy atmosphere (€16 meals, 4-course dinner for €23, Tue–Sun from 18:00, closed Mon, Lange Veerstraat 8, tel. 023/532-6006).

De Lachende Javaan (The Laughing Javanese) serves the best Indonesian food in town. Their €18–22 *rijsttafels* are excellent (Tue–Sun from 17:00, closed Mon, Frankestraat 27, tel. 023/532-8792).

Fondue Restaurant "in't Goede Uur" is a romantic, 12-table place with classical music on the most charming street in Haarlem. Reservations are required (€17 cheese fondue, Tue–Sun 17:00–24:00, closed Mon, cash only, Korte Houtstraat 1, tel. 023/531-1174).

La Place serves fresh, healthy, budget food with Haarlem's best view. Sit on the top floor or roof garden of the Vroom & Dreesmann department store (Mon 11:00–18:00, Tue–Sat 9:30–18:00, Thu until 21:00, closed Sun except for first Sun of month 12:00–17:00, large non-smoking section, Grote Houtstraat 70, on corner of Gedempte Oude Gracht, 023/515-8700).

Falafel Elland has a salad bar and the best falafel in Haarlem (€4–9 dishes, daily until 21:00, Grote Houtstraat 5a).

Picnic Shopping: You have two good choices: the **DekaMarkt supermarket** near Market Square (Mon 11:00–20:00, Tue–Sat 8:30–20:00, Thu until 21:00, closed Sun, Gedempte Oude Gracht 54, between Vroom & Dreesmann department store and post office) or the new **Albert Heijn supermarket** near the train station (Mon–Sat 8:00–20:00, closed Sun, Kruisweg 10).

TRANSPORTATION CONNECTIONS

From Haarlem by Train to: Amsterdam (6/hr, 15 min, €3.20 one-way, €5.50 same-day round-trip), **The Hague** (4/hr, 35 min), **Delft** (2/hr, 40 min), **Rotterdam** (2/hr, 50 min), **Hoorn** (4/hr, 1 hr), **Alkmaar** (2/hr, 30 min), **Brussels** (hrly, 2.75 hrs, transfer in Rotterdam), **Bruges** (hrly, 3.5 hrs, transfer in Rotterdam and Antwerp).

To Schiphol Airport: Your options are the **bus** (4/hr, 40 min, €5.80, bus #300, departs from Haarlem's train station in *Zuidtangent* lane), **train** (4/hr, 40 min, transfer at Amsterdam-Sloterdijk station, €4.55), or **taxi** (about €45).

NETHERLANDS DAY TRIPS

Holland is tiny. The sights listed below are easy day trips by bus or train from Amsterdam or Haarlem. Match your interest with the village's specialty: flower auctions, folk museums, cheese, Delft porcelain, beaches, or modern art.

Delft

Peaceful as a Vermeer painting (he was born here) and lovely as its porcelain, Delft is a typically Dutch town with a special soul. Enjoy it best by simply wandering around, watching people, munching local syrup waffles, or daydreaming from the canal bridges.

Tourist Information: This TI is a tourist's dream, offering a good brochure on Delft (which includes an excellent map). They sell four different brochures for €1.50 apiece, describing self-guided walking tours (Sun–Mon 11:00–15:00, Tue–Fri 9:00–18:00, Sat 9:00-17:00, free Internet access, 2-min walk north of Markt to Hyppolytusbuurt 4, tel. 015/215-4051, www.delft.nl).

Arrival in Delft: From the train station (€0.50 WCs, ATM on left as you leave), walk across the canal and follow blue-and-white signs to the town center. Drivers take the Delft exit 9 off the A-13 expressway.

Market Days: Multiple all-day markets are held on Thursdays (general on Market Square, flower market on Hippolytusbuurt Square) and on Saturdays (general on Brabantse Turfmarkt and Burgwal, flea market at Hippolytusbuurt Square, and sometimes an art market at Heilige Geestkerkhof).

Netherlands Day Trips

SIGHTS

Royal Dutch Delftware Manufactory—The blue earthenware made at Delft's Koninklijke Porceleyne Fles is famous worldwide and the biggest tourist attraction in town. The Dutch East India Company, headquartered here, had imported many exotic goods, including Chinese porcelain. The Chinese designs became trendy and were copied by many of the local potters. Three centuries later, their descendants are still going strong, and you can see them at work in this factory. Catch an English-language tour (prices vary depending on tour—April–Oct 10:00, 11:00, 14:00, and 15:00), or take a self-guided tour at any time: Watch the short video, follow the small tile arrows, and feel free to stop and chat with any of the artisans (€4, April–Oct daily 9:00–17:00, Nov–March daily 9:00–17:00, Nov–March closed Sun, Rotterdamsweg 196; from train station, catch bus #63, #121, or #129 and get off at TU Aula bus stop—5-min walk from tram or bus stop; tel. 015/251-2030).

SLEEPING

(€1 = about $1.20, country code: 31, area code: 015)

$$ Herberg de Emauspoort, a picture-perfect, family-run hotel, is relaxed, friendly, and ideally located around the family's 82-year-old bakery. Rooms overlook the canal or peek into the courtyard. Romantics can stay in one of their Gypsy caravans ("Pipo de Clown" or "Mammaloe"). Borrow bikes for free (22 rooms, Sb-€77.50, Db-€87.50, Tb-€115, Qb-€140, taxes extra, includes breakfast, some non-smoking rooms, near main square at Vrouwenregt 9-11, tel. 015/219-0219, fax 015/214-8251, www.emauspoort.nl, emauspoort@emauspoort.nl).

$$ Hotel Leeuwenbrug, a former warehouse, has 36 clean rooms, an Old World atmosphere, and a helpful staff (Sb-€75–109, Db-€90–125, prices vary seasonally, ask for off-season pricing, includes breakfast, strictly non-smoking, free 15-minute Internet access, Koornmarkt 16, tel. 015/214-7741, fax 015/215-9759, www.leeuwenbrug.nl, sales@leeuwenbrug.nl).

$'T Raedthuys, a hotel and café/restaurant, is located in the heart of Delft on the main square, with six tired, basic rooms (S-€38, Ss-€42, D-€45, Ds-€55, Qb-€90, no breakfast, €4.50–8 lunches in a great setting, Markt 38-40, tel. 015/212-5115, fax 015/213-6069, www.raadhuisdelft.nl).

TRANSPORTATION CONNECTIONS

From Delft to: Amsterdam (2 trains/hr, 40 min), **The Hague** (you can take the train, but the tram is easier: catch tram #1—Scheveningen to The Hague's city center, purchase tickets at TI).

Edam

For the ultimate in cuteness and peace, make tiny Edam your home. It's sweet but palatable, and 30 minutes by bus from Amsterdam (2/hr).

While Edam is known today for cheese, it was once an industrious shipyard and port. But having a canal to the sea caused such severe flooding in town—cracking walls and spilling into homes—that one frustrated resident even built a floating cellar (now in Edam Museum). To stop the flooding, the harbor was closed off with locked gates (you'll see the gates in Dam Square next to TI). The harbor silted up, forcing the decline of the shipbuilding trade.

Edam's Wednesday market is held year-round, but it's best in July and early August, when the focus is on cheese. You, along with piles of other tourists, can meet the cheese traders and local farmers.

Picnickers stock up at the Topper Supermarket (to the left of Edam Museum).

Tourist Information: The TI, often staffed by volunteers, is on Dam Square. Pick up the €0.50 *Edam Holland* brochure and consider the €2.50 *A Stroll Through Edam* brochure outlining a self-guided walking tour (April–Sept Mon–Sat 10:00–17:00, Oct–March Mon–Sat 10:00–15:00, closed Sun, WC and ATM just outside, tel. 0299/315-125, www.vvv-edam.nl, info@vvv-edam.nl).

Arrival in Edam: To get from the bus station to Dam Square and the TI, it's a five-minute walk: Leaving the station, head for the "Station-Zuid" Restaurant. From there, turn left on Zuidervesting, turn right at the first canal onto Schepenmakersdijk, then left over the first walking bridge onto Lingerzijde; follow this street until you pass the leaning bell tower and take a right onto Kleine Kerkstraat, which leads to Dam Square.

SLEEPING

The TI (tel. 0299/315-125) has a list of inexpensive rooms in private homes.

$$ Hotel de Fortuna is an eccentric, canalside place with flowers and duck and bird noises, offering steep stairs and low-ceilinged rooms in several ancient buildings in the old center of Edam. It's been run by the Dekker family for more than 30 years (Db-€90–100, includes breakfast, Spuistraat 3, tel. 0299/371-671, fax 0299/371-469, www.fortuna-edam.nl, fortuna@fortuna-edam.nl). Try lunch on their garden patio or dinner in their romantic restaurant (3-course meal-€32.50).

$$ Damhotel, centrally located on a canal around the corner from the TI, has attractive, comfortable rooms with a plush feel (Sb-€55, Db-€90, Tb-€125, Qb-€170, includes breakfast, attached café and restaurant, Keizersgracht 1, tel. 0299/371-766, fax 0299/374-031, www.damhotel.nl, info@damhotel.nl).

$ B&B De Gravin, also called "the Duchesse," is an authentic little house run by friendly Greetje. You'll find breakfast in the kitchen (Db-€60, cash only, Kapsteeg 3, 2-min walk from Dam Square, tel. 0299/372-725, reilingh@wxs.nl).

TRANSPORTATION CONNECTIONS

From Amsterdam to Edam, take direct bus #114 (2/hr, 30 min), or slower bus #110 for a scenic route through the town of Volendam (45 min).

Arnhem

Arnhem, an hour southeast of Amsterdam, has two fine sights: the Arnhem Open-Air Dutch Folk Museum and the Kröller-Müller Museum, featuring modern art in a huge park.

Tourist Information: Arnhem's TI is at the train station (Mon 11:00–17:30, Tue–Thu 9:00–17:30, Fri 10:00–16:00, closed Sat–Sun, tel. 026/442-6767).

SIGHTS

▲▲Kröller-Müller Museum and Nationaal Park De Hoge Veluwe—Near Arnhem, Nationaal Park De Hoge Veluwe is the Netherlands' largest national park (13,000 acres) and is famous for its Kröller-Müller Museum. This huge, striking modern art collection, including 55 paintings by Vincent van Gogh, is set deep in the forest. The park has 1,500 white bikes that you're free to use to make your explorations more fun. At the Bezoekerscentrum (visitors center), you'll find maps, WCs, the self-service restaurant Monsieur Jacques, and a playground for children. While riding through the vast green woods, make a point of getting off your bike to climb an inland sand dune (€6 to enter park, €6 more for museum, museum open Tue–Sun 10:00–17:00, closed Mon, easy parking-€6, tel. 055/378-8100).

Getting There: To reach the museum from **Amsterdam**, take the train to Ede-Wageningen, where bus #110 goes directly into Nationaal Park De Hoge Veluwe. Ask the driver where to get off for the visitors center or the art museum. To get to the park from the **Arnhem train station**, catch the bus to Otterlo, then switch to bus #110, which will take you into the park (1/hr).

At this time, there is no direct connection between Arnhem and the Kröller-Müller Museum. Consider a taxi (have the visitors center call for you).

▲▲Arnhem Open-Air Dutch Folk Museum—Arnhem has the Netherlands' first and biggest folk museum. You'll enjoy a huge park of windmills, old farmhouses (gathered from throughout the Netherlands and reassembled here), traditional crafts in action, and a pleasant education-by-immersion in Dutch culture.

Visit the Entrance Pavilion to get a free map or the English guidebook (€4). See the multimedia exhibit, *HollandRama.* At the entrance, ask about special events and activities, especially for kids (€11.70, Easter–Oct daily 10:00–17:00, tel. 026/357-6111, www.openluchtmuseum.nl).

Hit the **highlights**: any farmhouse, the drawbridge, little village (with bakery and old-time toys in the main square), the laundry, paper mill (usually a demo in progress), and the Freia Steam-Dairy Factory (where you can sample free cheese).

The park has several good budget **restaurants** and covered picnic areas. Its rustic Pancake House serves hearty and sweet (split-table) Dutch flapjacks. The De Kasteelboerderij Café-Restaurant at the Oud-Beijerland Manor (traditional €8 *dagmenu,* or plate of the day) is a friendly place that can feed 300 visitors at once.

Getting There: To reach the open-air museum *(openluchtmuseum)* from the Arnhem train station, take bus #3 (direction: Alteveer) or the faster #13 (4/hr, 15 min, runs July–Aug only).

TRANSPORTATION CONNECTIONS

Trains connect Arnhem with Amsterdam (2/hr, 70 min, likely transfer in Utrecht).

By **Car** from Amsterdam, take A-2 south to Utrecht, then A-12 east to Arnhem. Just before Arnhem, take the Arnhem Nord exit Openluchtmuseum (exit #26) and follow signs to the nearby museum. (If driving from Haarlem, skirt Amsterdam to the south on E-9, then follow signs to Utrecht).

MORE SIGHTS IN THE NETHERLANDS

Zaanse Schans Open-Air Museum—This re-created 17th-century town puts Dutch culture—from cheesemaking to wooden-shoe-carving—on a lazy Susan.

Located in the town of Zaandijk, this is your easiest one-stop look at traditional Dutch culture. At the visitors' center, pick up the free brochure/map and ask about the day's scheduled events (bike rentals, lockers, WC). The park hosts the Netherlands' best collection of windmills. Take an inspiring climb to the top of a whirring windmill; gather a group and ask for a tour. Visit the bakery, take a boat tour, sample cheese, and see a wooden shoe being made.

Zaanse Schans' museum, with a multimedia presentation and included audioguide, explains Holland's industrial past and present (€4.50, Tue–Sat 10:00–17:00, Sun 12:00–17:00, closed Mon, tel. 075/616-2862). Pannenkoeken Restaurant De Kraai offers delicious and traditional sweet and/or savory pancakes (€5–8, cash only, closes daily at 18:00 and in Jan).

Cost and Hours: The entrance to the grounds is free, but you must pay up to €5 to go in the windmills and other sights in the park (daily 8:30–17:30, until 17:00 in winter, parking €3.50/first hr, €7 max, tel. 075/616-8218, www.zaanseschans.nl). Zaanse Schans is your typical big-bus tour stop. To avoid the masses, visit early or late.

Getting There: The park is 15 minutes by train north of Amsterdam. Take the Alkmaar-bound **train** to Station Koog-Zaandijk and then walk, following the teal signs—past a fragrant chocolate factory—for 15 minutes. If **driving** from Amsterdam, take A-8 (direction: Zaanstad/Purmerend), turn off at Purmerend A-7, then follow signs to Zaanse Schans.

▲▲Enkhuizen Zuiderzee Museum—This lively, open-air folk museum in the salty old town of Enkhuizen has a "Living on Urk" village (patterned after an old Dutch fishing town), populated by people who do a convincing job of role-playing no-nonsense 1905 Dutch villagers. No one said "Have a nice day" back then. You can eat herring hot out of the old smoker, and see barrels and rope made. Children enjoy playing at the dress-up chest, trying out old-time games, and making sailing ships out of old wooden shoes (€10, early April–late Oct daily 10:00–17:00, July–Aug free tours at 13:30, private guide for €45, closed off-season, tel. 0228/351-111, www.zuiderzeemuseum.nl).

Getting There: Take the train from Amsterdam direct to Enkhuizen (2/hr, 1 hr). To get to the museum from the station, catch a shuttle boat (4/hr) or take a pleasant 15-minute walk.

▲▲Aalsmeer Flower Auction—Get a bird's-eye view of the huge Dutch flower industry. Wander on elevated walkways (through what's claimed to be the biggest commercial building on earth) over literally trainloads of freshly cut flowers. About half of all the flowers exported from Holland are auctioned off here in four huge auditoriums. Stop at one of the "listening posts" for on-the-spot information (€4.50, Mon–Fri 7:30–11:00, closed Sat–Sun, the auction wilts after 9:30 and on Thu, gift shop, cafeteria, tel. 0297/392-185).

Getting There: You can get to the flower auction from Amsterdam (bus #172 from train station, 4/hr, 60 min) or from Haarlem (take bus #198 or #140 and transfer to bus #172 in Aalsmeer, 2/hr, 60 min). Aalsmeer, which is close to the airport, makes a handy last fling before catching a late-morning weekday flight out (direct bus #198 to Schiphol Airport).

▲▲▲Keukenhof—This is the greatest bulb-flower garden on earth. Each spring, 7 million flowers, enjoying the sandy soil of the Dutch dunes and *polderland,* conspire to make even a total garden-hater enjoy them. This 80-acre park is packed with tour groups daily (€12, open late March 23–May 19, daily 8:00–19:30, last tickets sold at 18:00, tel. 0252/465-555, www.keukenhof.com).

Getting There: To get to Keukenhof from Amsterdam, take the train to Leiden, then catch bus #54 to the garden (allow 75 min total). From Haarlem, go by train to Leiden, then take bus #54 to Keukenhof (allow 45 min total). Go late in the day for the best light and the fewest groups.

▲**Alkmaar**—Holland's cheese capital is especially fun (and touristy) during its weekly cheese market (April–Aug only, Fri 10:00–12:30, TI tel. 072/511-4284).

▲▲**The Hague (Den Haag)**—Locals say the money is made in Rotterdam, divided in The Hague, and spent in Amsterdam. The Hague is the Netherlands' seat of government and the home of several engaging museums. The Hague's TI is at the train station (Mon–Sat 9:00–17:30, later in summer, Sun 10:00–17:00; toll tel. 0900-340-3505 costs €0.45/min).

The **Mauritshuis'** delightful, easy-to-tour art collection stars Vermeer and Rembrandt (€7.50, Tue–Sat 10:00–17:00, Sun 11:00–17:00, closed Mon, Korte Vijverberg 8, tel. 070/302-3456). Across the pond, the **Torture Museum** (Gevangenpoort) shows the medieval mind at its worst (€4, Tue–Fri 11:00–17:00, Sat–Sun 12:00–17:00, closed Mon, required tours on the hour, last one at 16:00, ask ticket-taker if film and talk will be in English before you commit, tel. 070/346-0861, www.gevangenpoort.nl).

For a look at the 19th century's attempt at virtual reality, tour **Panorama Mesdag,** a 360-degree painting of nearby Scheveningen in the 1880s, with a 3-D, sandy-beach foreground (€4, Mon–Sat 10:00–17:00, Sun 12:00–17:00, Zeestraat 65, tel. 070/310-6665). The nearby **Peace Palace,** a gift from Andrew Carnegie, houses the International Court of Justice (€5; Mon–Fri: Required guided tours at 10:00, 11:00, 14:00, or 15:00; closes Sat–Sun and without warning—call ahead or check at TI and make reservation, tram #1 or #10 from station, tel. 070/302-4137).

Scheveningen, the Dutch Coney Island, has a newly renovated pier and is liveliest on sunny summer afternoons (from Hague train station, take tram #8 or #9 to Gevers Deynootplein/Kurhaus and walk via Palace Promenade to the Boulevard).

Madurodam, a mini-Holland amusement park, is fun for kids (adults-€12, kids 4–11-€9, Sept–mid-March daily 9:00–18:00, mid-March–June until 20:00, July–Aug until 22:00, George Maduroplein 1, tram #9 from Hague train station, tel. 070/416-2400, www.madurodam.nl).

BARCELONA

Barcelona is Spain's second city and the capital of the proud and distinct region of Catalunya. With Franco's fascism now ancient history, Catalan flags wave once again. Language and culture are on a roll in Spain's most cosmopolitan and European corner.

Barcelona bubbles with life in its narrow Gothic Quarter alleys, along the grand boulevards, and throughout the chic, grid-planned, new part of town called Eixample. While Barcelona had an illustrious past as a Roman colony, Visigothic capital, 14th-century maritime power, and—in more modern times—a top Mediterranean trading and manufacturing center, it's most enjoyable to throw out the history books and just drift through the city. If you're in the mood to surrender to a city's charms, let it be in Barcelona.

Planning Your Time

Sandwich Barcelona between flights or overnight train rides. There's little of earthshaking importance within eight hours by train. It's as easy to fly into Barcelona as it is to fly into Madrid, Lisbon, or Paris for most travelers from the United States. Those renting a car can cleverly start here, fly to Madrid, see Madrid and Toledo, and pick up the car as they leave Madrid.

On the shortest visit, Barcelona is worth one night, one day, and an overnight train or evening flight out. The Ramblas is two different streets by day and by night. Stroll it from top to bottom in the evening and again the next morning, grabbing breakfast on a stool in a market café. Wander the Gothic Quarter, see the cathedral, and have lunch in the Eixample (eye-SHAM-plah). The top two sights in town, Antoni Gaudí's Sagrada Família Church

Barcelona

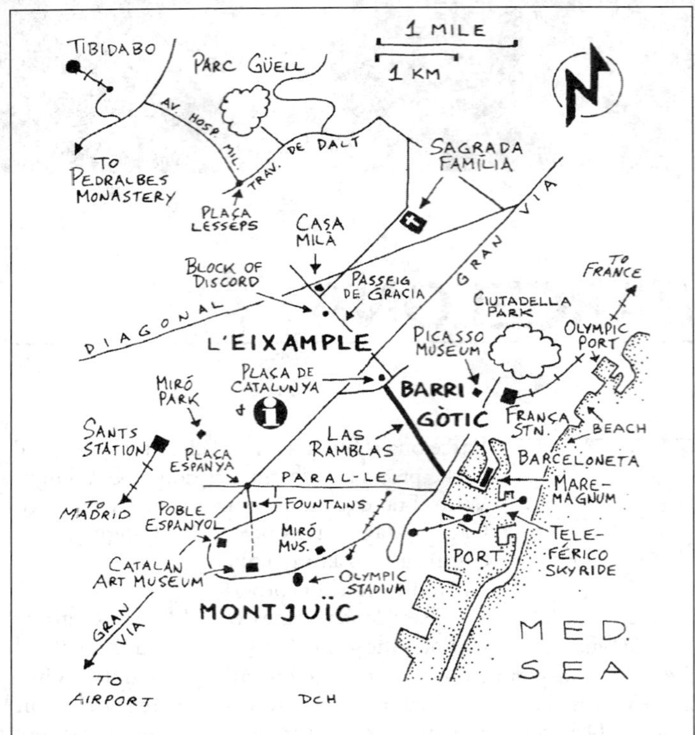

and the Picasso Museum, are usually open until 20:00 during the summer (Picasso closes at 15:00 on Sun and all day Mon). The illuminated fountains on Montjuïc make a good finale for your day.

Of course, Barcelona in a day is insane. To better appreciate the city's ample charm, spread your visit over two or three days.

ORIENTATION

The large square, Plaça de Catalunya, sits at the center of Barcelona, dividing the older and newer parts of town. Sloping downhill from the Plaça is the old town (Barri Gòtic, or Gothic Quarter), with the boulevard called the Ramblas running down to the harbor. Above Plaça de Catalunya is the modern residential area called the Eixample. A hill called Montjuïc overlooks the harbor.

The soul of Barcelona is in its compact core—the old town and the Ramblas. This is your strolling, shopping, and people-watching nucleus. The city's sights are widely scattered, but with a map and a willingness to figure out the sleek subway system (or a few euros for taxis), everything is quite manageable.

Mentally, you'll need to orient yourself to a different language—Catalan. While Spanish ("Castilian") is widely spoken, the native tongue in this region is Catalan, as different as Spanish is from Italian.

Tourist Information

There are several useful **TIs** in Barcelona: at the **airport** (daily 9:00–21:00, offices in both terminal A and terminal B, free room-finding service, tel. 934-784-704); at the **Sants Train Station** (Mon–Fri 8:00–20:00, Sat–Sun 8:00–14:00, near track 6); and **Plaça de Catalunya** (daily 9:00–21:00; on main square near recommended hotels, look for red sign; also has room-finding service). Most of the TIs sell phone cards and tickets for the Tourist Bus (described in "Getting Around Barcelona," below).

The **Barcelona Card** covers public transportation (buses, Metro, Montjuïc funicular, and *golondrina* harbor tours). It offers free admission to minor sights and discounts on major sights (available from 1–5 days, €17/1 day, up to €27/5 days, sold at TIs and El Corte Inglés department store). The **Tourist Bus ticket** offers smaller discounts on sights, but is more convenient since it provides direct transportation right to the sights (see "Getting Around Barcelona," below).

Note that the two-day version of either the Barcelona Card or the Tourist Bus ticket offers a better value than the one-day version.

On weekends, the TI at Plaça de Catalunya offers two **walking tours** in English. One tour concentrates on the Gothic Quarter (€8, April–Sept Fri–Mon at 10:00, Oct–March Sat–Sun at 10:00, 2 hrs, meet at TI, call to reserve) and the other focuses on the Picasso Museum (€10 includes museum fee, €8 on first Sun of month, Sat–Sun at 10:30). To reserve a spot on either tour, call the TI's toll number (tel. 906-301-282, €0.40/min), or book online at www.barcelonaturisme.com. The same TI also has a half-price ticket booth—"Tiquet 3"—where you can drop by in the early evening (3 hours before showtime) to see what tickets are available.

The all-Catalunya TI offices are at **Passeig de Gràcia** (Mon–Sat 10:00–19:00, Sun 10:00–14:00, #107, tel. 932-384-000) and on **Plaça de Sant Jaume** (Mon–Fri 9:00–20:00, Sat 10:00–20:00, Sun 10:00–14:00; in the City Hall Ajuntament building, last-minute room-finding service, less crowded than other TIs).

At any TI, pick up the free small map or the large city map (€1), the brochure on public transport, and the free quarterly *See Barcelona* guide with practical information on museum hours, restaurants, transportation, history, festivals, and so on.

Throughout the summer, you'll see young red-jacketed tourist-info helpers on the streets in the touristed areas of town.

Barcelona at a Glance

▲▲▲**Ramblas** Barcelona's colorful, gritty pedestrian thoroughfare. **Hours:** Always open.

▲▲▲**Picasso Museum** Extensive collection offering insight into the brilliant Spanish artist's early years. **Hours:** Tue–Sat 10:00–20:00, Sun 10:00–15:00, closed Mon.

▲▲▲**Sagrada Família** Gaudí's remarkable, unfinished cathedral. **Hours:** Daily April–Oct 9:00–20:00, Nov–March 9:00–18:00.

▲▲**Casa Milà** Barcelona's quintessential modernist building, the famous melting-ice-cream Gaudí creation. **Hours:** daily 10:00–20:00.

▲▲**Catalan Art Museum** World-class collection of this region's art, including a substantial Romanesque collection. **Hours:** Tue–Sat 10:00–19:00, Sun 10:00–14:30, closed Mon.

▲▲**Catalan Concert Hall** Best modernist interior in Barcelona. **Hours:** 50-minute English tours daily every 30 minutes 10:00–15:30.

▲**Cathedral** Colossal Gothic cathedral. **Hours:** Daily 8:00–13:30 & 16:30–19:30.

Palau de la Virreina, an arts-and-culture TI, offers information on Barcelona cultural events—music, opera, and theater (Mon–Sat 10:00–20:00, Sun 10:00–15:00, Ramblas 99).

Arrival in Barcelona

By Train: Although many international trains use the França Station, all domestic (and some international) trains use Sants Station. Both França and Sants have baggage lockers and subway stations: França's subway is Barceloneta (2 blocks away), and Sants' is Sants Estació (under the station). Sants Station has a good TI, a world of handy shops and eateries, and a classy, quiet Sala Euromed lounge for travelers with first-class reservations (TV, free drinks, study tables, and coffee bar). Take the Metro or a taxi to your hotel. Most trains to or from France stop at the subway station Passeig de Gràcia, just a short walk from the center (Plaça de Catalunya, TI, hotels).

By Plane: Barcelona's **El Prat de Llobregat Airport,** eight miles southwest of town, is connected cheaply and quickly by **Aerobus** (immediately in front of arrivals lobby, 4/hr until 24:00, 30 min to Plaça de Catalunya, buy €3.45 ticket from driver) or by the RENFE **train** (at airport, walk through overpass to train

▲**City History Museum** Tracing Barcelona's history, from Roman times through the Middle Ages to today. **Hours:** June–Sept Tue–Sat 10:00–20:00, Sun 10:00–14:00, closed Mon; Oct–May Tue–Sat 10:00–14:00 & 16:00–20:00, Sun 10:00–14:00, closed Mon.

▲***Sardana* Dances** Patriotic dance where proud Catalans join hands in a circle (usually Sat at 18:00, Sun at 12:00).

▲**Palau Güell** Exquisitely curvy Gaudí interior. **Hours:** Mon–Sat 10:00–20:00, closed Sun, closes at 18:00 Nov–April.

▲**Block of Discord** Noisy block of competing modernist facades by Gaudí and his rivals. **Hours:** Always open.

▲**Parc Güell** Colorful park at the center of the unfinished Gaudí-designed housing project. **Hours:** Daily 9:00–20:00.

▲**Fundació Joan Miró** World's best collection of art by Catalan native Joan Miró. **Hours:** July–Sept Tue–Sat 10:00–20:00, Thu until 21:30, Sun 10:00–14:30, closed Mon, Oct–June Tue–Sat closes at 19:00.

station, 2/hr at :13 and :43 after the hour, 20 min to Sants Station and Plaça de Catalunya; €2.30 or buy a T10 card at the airport and use it for this trip—see below). A **taxi** to or from the airport costs less than €20. The airport has a post office, pharmacy, left-luggage office, and ATMs (avoid the gimmicky machines before the baggage carousels; instead use the bank-affiliated ATMs at the far-left end of arrival hall as you face the street). Airport info: tel. 932-983-467 or 932-983-465.

Getting Around Barcelona

By Subway: Barcelona's Metro, among Europe's best, connects just about every place you'll visit. It has five color-coded lines. Rides cost €1.10. The T10 Card for €6 gives you 10 tickets, good for all local bus and Metro lines as well as the separate FGC line and RENFE train lines (including the airport). Pick up the TI's guide to public transport. One-, two-, and three-day passes are available (for €4.80, €7.20, and €9.15).

By Tourist Bus: The handy Tourist Bus (Bus Turistic) offers two multi-stop circuits in colorful double-decker buses (red route covers north Barcelona—most Gaudí sights; blue route covers

"You're not in Spain, You're in Catalunya!"

This is a popular pro-nationalist refrain you might see on T-shirts or stickers around town. Catalunya is *not* the land of bullfighting and flamenco that many visitors envision when they think of Spain (best to wait until you're in Madrid for those).

The region of Catalunya—with Barcelona as its capital—has its own language, history, and culture, and the people have a proud, independent spirit. Historically, Catalunya has often been at odds with the central Spanish government in Madrid. The Catalan language and culture have been repressed or outlawed at various times in Spanish history, as Catalunya often chose the wrong side in wars and rebellions against the kings in Madrid. In the Spanish Civil War (1936–1939), Catalunya was one of the last pockets of democratic resistance against the military coup of the fascist dictator Francisco Franco, who punished the region with four decades of repression. Three of Barcelona's monuments are reminders of that suppression: The Parc de la Ciutadella was originally a much-despised military citadel, constructed in the 18th century to keep locals in line. The Castle of Montjuïc, built for similar reasons, has been the site of numerous political executions, including hundreds during the Franco era. The Sacred Heart Church atop Tibidabo, completed under Franco, was meant to atone for the sins of Barcelonians during the Spanish Civil War—the main sin being opposition to Franco. Although rivalry between Barcelona and Madrid has calmed down in recent times, it rages any time the two cities' football clubs meet.

To see real Catalan culture, look for the *sardana* dance (described on page 1200) or an exhibition of *castellers*. These teams of human-castle builders come together for festivals throughout the year to build towers of flesh that can reach more than 50 feet high, topped off by the bravest member of the team—a child!

south—Gothic Quarter, Montjuïc) with live multilingual guides (28 stops, 2 hrs per route, 9:00–22:00 in summer, 9:00–21:00 in winter, buses run every 6–30 min, most frequent in summer, buy tickets on bus or at TI). Ask for a brochure (which has a good city map) at the TI or at a pick-up point. One-day (€16) and two-day (€20) tickets include 10–20 percent discounts on the city's major sights and walking tours (leaving from TI at Plaça de Catalunya), which will likely reimburse you for half the Tourist Bus cost over the course of your visit.

By Taxi: Barcelona is one of Europe's best taxi towns. Taxis are plentiful and honest (€1.40 drop charge, €0.88/km, luggage-€0.85/piece, these "*Tarif* 2" rates are in effect 6:00–22:00, pay higher "*Tarif* 1" rates off-hours, other fees posted in window). Save time by hopping a cab (figure €4 from Ramblas to Sants Station).

The Gràcia festival in August and the Mercè festival in September are good times to catch the castellers.

The Catalan language is irrevocably tied to the history and spirit of the people here. Since the end of the Franco era in the mid-1970s, the language has made a huge resurgence. Now most school-age children learn Catalan first and Spanish second. Although Spanish is understood here (and the basic survival words are the same), Barcelona speaks Catalan. Here are the essential Catalan phrases:

Hello	**Hola**	(OH-lah)
Please	**Si us plau**	(see oos plow)
Thank you	**Gracies**	(GRAH-see-es)
Goodbye	**Adéu**	(ah-DAY-oo)
Exit	**Sortida**	(sor-TEE-dah)
Long live Catalunya!	**¡Visca Catalunya!**	(BEE-skah...)

Most place-names in this chapter are listed in Catalan. Here is a pronunciation guide:

Plaça de Catalunya	PLAS-sah duh cat-ah-LOON-yah
Eixample	eye-SHAM-plah
Passeig de Gràcia	PAH-sage duh grass-EE-ah
Catedral	CAH-tah-dral
Barri Gòtic	BAH-rrree GAH-teek
Montjuïc	MOHN-jew-eek

Helpful Hints

Theft Alert: You're more likely to be pickpocketed here—especially on the Ramblas—than about anywhere else in Europe. Most of the crime is nonviolent, but muggings do occur. Be on guard. Leave valuables in your hotel and wear a money belt.

Here are a few common street scams, easy to avoid if you recognize them. Most common is the too-friendly local who tries to engage you in conversation by asking for the time, whether you speak English, and so on. If you suspect the person is more interested in your money than your time, ignore him and move on. A common street gambling scam is the pea-and-carrot game, a variation on the shell game. The people winning are all ringers and you can be sure that you'll lose if you play. Also beware of groups of women aggressively selling carnations, people offering to clean off a stain from your shirt, and people picking things up in front of you on escalators. If you stop for any commotion or show on the Ramblas, put your hands in your pockets before someone else does. Assume any scuffle is simply a distraction by a team of thieves.

U.S. Consulate: Passeig Reina Elisenda 23 (tel. 932-802-227).

Emergency Phone Numbers: Police—092, Emergency—061, directory assistance—010.

24-hour Pharmacy: Near the Boquería Market at #98 on the Ramblas.

American Express: AmEx offices are at Passeig de Gràcia 101 (Mon–Fri 9:30–18:00, Sat 10:00–12:00, closed Sun, includes all travel-agency services, Metro: Diagonal, tel. 932-170-070) and at Las Ramblas 74 (daily 9:00–24:00, banking services only, opposite Liceu Metro station, tel. 933-011-166, toll-free tel. 900-994-426).

Internet Access: When **easyInternetcafé** arrived, prices for Internet access fell all over town. Europe's favorite Internet-access venue—with piles of computers, drinks, and munchies—is open daily 8:00–24:00 and offers zippy access (€1.50/hr) at two central locations: One is half a block west of Plaça de Catalunya on Ronda Universitat, and another is near the seedy bottom of the Ramblas at #31. Or try **Cybermundo** (2 locations near Placa de Catalunya: at Carrer Bergara 3 and at Carrer Balmes 8).

Local Guides: The Barcelona Guide Bureau is a co-op with plenty of excellent local guides who give personalized four-hour tours for €150; Joanna Wilhelm is good (Via Laietana 54, tel. 932-682-422 or 933-107-778, www.bgb.es). Also see the TI's walking tours, described above.

Introductory Walk: From Plaça de Catalunya down the Ramblas

A ▲▲▲ sight, Barcelona's central square and main boulevard exert a powerful pull. Many visitors spend a major part of their time here, doing laps on the Ramblas. Here's a top-to-bottom orientation walk:

Plaça de Catalunya—This vast central square divides old and new Barcelona. It's also the hub for the Metro, bus, airport shuttle, and both Tourist Bus routes (red northern route leaves from El Corte Inglés, blue southern route from west side of Plaça). The grass around its fountain is the best public place in town for serious necking. Overlooking the square, the huge **El Corte Inglés** department store offers everything from bonsai trees to a travel agency, plus one-hour photo developing, haircuts, and cheap souvenirs (Mon–Sat 10:00–22:00, closed Sun, pick up English directory

From Plaça de Catalunya down the Ramblas

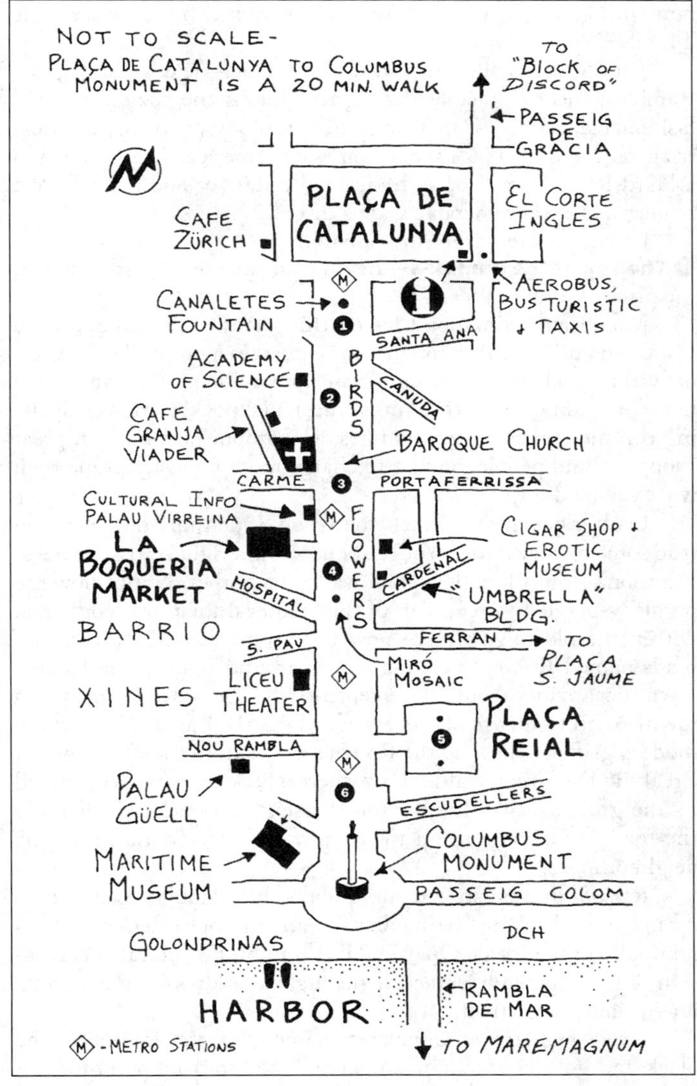

flier, supermarket in basement, 9th-floor terrace cafeteria/restaurant with great city view—take elevator from entrance nearest the TI, tel. 933-063-800).

Four great boulevards start from Plaça de Catalunya: the Ramblas; the fashionable Passeig de Gràcia; the cozier, but still fashionable, Rambla Catalunya; and the stubby, shop-filled, pedestrian-only Portal de l'Angel. Homesick Americans can even find a Hard Rock Café. Locals traditionally start or end a downtown rendezvous at the venerable Café Zürich.

Cross the street from the café to...

❶ The Top of the Ramblas—Begin your ramble 20 yards down at the ornate fountain (near #129).

More than a Champs-Elysées, this grand boulevard takes you from rich (at the top) to rough (at the port) in a one-mile, 20-minute walk. You'll raft the river of Barcelonian life past a grand opera house, elegant cafés, retread prostitutes, pickpockets, power-dressing con men, artists, street mimes, an outdoor bird market, great shopping, and people looking to charge more for a shoeshine than what you paid for the shoes.

Grab a bench and watch the scene. Open up your map and read some history into it: You're about to walk right across medieval Barcelona from Plaça de Catalunya to the harbor. Notice how the higgledy-piggledy street plan of the medieval town was contained within the old town walls—now gone, but traced by a series of roads named Ronda (meaning "to go around"). Find the Roman town, occupying about 10 percent of what became the medieval town—with tighter roads yet around the cathedral. The sprawling, modern grid plan beyond the Ronda roads is from the 19th century. Breaks in this urban waffle show where a little town was consumed by the growing city. The popular Passeig de Gràcia was literally the road to Gràcia (once a town, now a characteristic Barcelona neighborhood).

Rambla means "stream" in Arabic. The Ramblas used to be a drainage ditch along the medieval wall that once defined what's now called the Gothic Quarter. "Las Ramblas" is plural, a succession of five separately named segments, but address numbers treat it as a single long street.

You're at Rambla Canaletes, named for the fountain. The black-and-gold Fountain of Canaletes is the starting point for celebrations and demonstrations. Legend says that a drink from the fountain ensures that you'll return to Barcelona one day. All along the Ramblas, you'll see newspaper stands (open 24 hrs, selling phone cards) and ONCE booths (selling lottery tickets that support Spain's organization of the blind, a powerful advocate for the needs of people with disabilities).

Got some change? As you wander downhill, drop coins into

the cans of the human statues (the money often kicks them into entertaining gear). Warning: Wherever people stop to gawk, pickpockets are at work.

Walk 100 yards downhill to #115 and the...

❷ **Rambla of the Little Birds**—Traditionally, kids bring their parents here to buy pets, especially on Sundays. Apartment-dwellers find birds, turtles, and fish easier to handle than dogs and cats. Buildings with balconies that have flowers are generally living spaces; balconies with air-conditioners generally indicate offices. The Academy of Science's clock (at #115) marks official Barcelona time—synchronize. The Champion supermarket (at #113) has cheap groceries and a handy deli with cooked food to go.

A recently-discovered Roman necropolis is in a park across the street, 50 yards behind the big, modern Citadines Hotel (go through the passageway at #122). Local apartment-dwellers blew the whistle on contractors, who hoped they could finish their building before anyone noticed the antiquities they had unearthed. Imagine the tomb-lined road leading into the Roman city of Barcino 2,000 years ago.

Another 100 yards takes you to Carrer del Carme (at #2), and...

❸ **Baroque Church**—The big, plain Betlem church fronting the boulevard is Baroque, unusual in Barcelona. While Barcelona's Gothic age was rich (with buildings to prove it), the Baroque age hardly left a mark. (The city's importance dropped when New World discoveries shifted lucrative trade to ports on the Atlantic.) The Bagues jewelry shop, across Carrer del Carme from the church, is known for its Art Nouveau jewelry (exactingly duplicated from the c. 1898 molds of Masriera displayed in the window, buzz to get inside). At the shop's side entrance, step on the old-fashioned scales (free, in kilos) and head down the narrow lane opposite (behind the church, 30 yards) to a place expert in making you heavier. Café Granja Viader (see "Eating," page 1221) has specialized in baked and dairy delights since 1870. (For more sweets, follow "A Short, Sweet Walk," listed in "Eating"—page 1227, which begins at the intersection in front of the church.)

Stroll through the Ramblas of Flowers to the subway stop marked by the red M (near #100), and...

❹ **La Boquería**—This lively produce market is an explosion of chicken legs, bags of live snails, stiff fish, delicious oranges, and sleeping dogs (#91, Mon–Sat 8:00–20:00, best mornings after 9:00, closed Sun). The Conserves shop sells 25 kinds of olives (straight in, near back on right, 100-gram minimum, €0.20–0.40). Full legs of ham *(jamón serrano)* abound; *Paleta Ibérica de Bellota* are the best, and cost about €120 each. Beware: *Huevos del toro* are bull testicles—surprisingly inexpensive...and oh so good. Drop by a cafe for an *espresso con leche* or breakfast (*tortilla española*—potato omelet). For lunch and dinner options, consider La Gardunya, located at the back of the market (see "Eating," page 1221), Kiosko Universal (also listed under "Eating"), or any bar at the market.

The **Museum of Erotica** is your standard European sex museum—neat if you like nudes and a chance to hear phone sex in four languages (€7.50, daily June–Sept 10:00–24:00, shorter hours Oct–May, across from market at #96).

At #100, Gimeno sells cigars (appreciate the dying art of cigar boxes). Go ahead, do something forbidden in America but perfectly legal here...buy a Cuban (singles from €1). Tobacco shops sell stamps and phone cards.

Farther down the Ramblas at #83, the **Art Nouveau Escriba Café** is an ornate world of pastries, little sandwiches, locally popular chocolates, and fine coffee. Opened in 1820 as shown on the facade, it was remodeled in the modernist style (daily 8:30–21:00, indoor/outdoor seating, tel. 933-016-027).

Fifty yards farther, find the much-trod-upon anchor mosaic, a reminder of the city's attachment to the sea. Created by noted abstract artist Joan Miró, it marks the midpoint of the Ramblas. (The towering statue of Columbus in the distance is at the end of this hike.) From here, walk down to the **Liceu Opera House** (tickets on sale Mon–Fri 14:00–20:30, tel. 902-332-211; 45-minute €5 tour in English daily at 10:00; 20-min €2.50 version from upper balcony—sometimes with no light—daily at 11:00, 12:00, 13:00; reserve in advance, tel. 934-859-914, www.liceubarcelona.com). From the Opera House, cross the Ramblas to Café de l'Opera for a beverage (#74, tel. 933-177-585). This bustling café, with modernist (that is, old-timey) decor and a historic atmosphere, boasts that it's been open since 1929, even during the Spanish Civil War.

Continue to #46; turn left down an arcaded lane to a square filled with palm trees...

❺ Plaça Reial—This elegant, neoclassical square comes complete with old-fashioned taverns, modern bars with patio seating, a Sunday coin and stamp market (10:00–14:00), Gaudí's first public works (the two colorful helmeted lampposts), and characters who don't need the palm trees to be shady. **Herbolari Ferran** is a fine and aromatic shop of herbs, with fun souvenirs such as top-quality saffron, or *safra* (Mon–Sat 9:30–14:00 & 16:30–20:00, closed Sun, downstairs at Plaça Reial 18). The small streets stretching toward the water from the square are intriguing, but less safe.

Back across the Ramblas, **Palau Güell** offers an enjoyable look at a Gaudí interior (€3 for 60-min English/Spanish tour, usually open Mon–Sat 10:00–20:00, closed Sun, last tickets sold at 15:00, closes at 18:00 Nov–April, Carrer Nou de la Rambla 3–5, tel. 933-173-974). This apartment was the first (1886) of Gaudí's innovative buildings, with a parabolic front doorway that signaled his emerging, non-rectangular style. If you plan to see Casa Milà, skip the climb to this less-interesting rooftop.

Farther downhill, on the right-hand side, is...

❻ Bottom of the Ramblas—The neighborhood to your right, Barri Xines, is the world's only Chinatown with nothing even remotely Chinese in or near it. Named for the prejudiced notion that Chinese immigrants go hand in hand with poverty, prostitution, and drug dealing, the actual inhabitants are poor Spanish, Arab, and Gypsy people. At night, the Barri Xines is frequented by prostitutes, many of them transvestites, who cater to sailors wandering up from the port. A nighttime visit gets you a street-corner massage—look out. Better yet—stay out.

The bottom of the Ramblas is marked by the Columbus Monument (see next listing). And just beyond that, **La Rambla del Mar** ("Rambla of the Sea") is a modern extension of the boulevard into the harbor. A popular wooden pedestrian bridge—with waves like the sea—leads to Maremagnum, a soulless Spanish mall with a cinema, huge aquarium, restaurants (including the recommended Tapasbar Maremagnum; see "Eating," page 1224), and piles of people. Late at night, it's a rollicking youth hangout. It's a worthwhile stroll.

SIGHTS

Ramblas Sights at the Harbor

Columbus Monument (Monument a Colóm)—Marking the point where the Ramblas hits the harbor, this 200-foot-tall monument built for an 1888 exposition offers an elevator-assisted view from its top (€2, April–May daily 9:00–19:30, June–Sept daily 9:00–20:30, Oct–March Mon–Fri 10:00–13:30 & 15:30–18:30, Sat–Sun 10:00–18:30, the harbor cable car offers a better—if less handy—view). It's interesting that Barcelona would so honor the man whose discoveries ultimately led to its downfall as a great trading power. It was here in Barcelona that Ferdinand and Isabel welcomed Columbus home after his first trip to America.

Maritime Museum (Museu Marítim)—Housed in the old royal shipyards, this museum covers the salty history of ships and navigation from the 13th to the 20th century, showing off the Catalan role in the development of maritime technology (for example, the first submarine is claimed to be Catalan). With fleets of seemingly unimportant replicas of old boats explained in Catalan and Spanish, landlubbers may find it dull—but the free audioguide livens it up for sailors (€5.40, daily 10:00–19:00, closed Mon off-season, www.diba.es/mmaritim). For just €0.60 more, visit the old-fashioned sailing ship *Santa Eulàlia*, docked in the harbor across the street.

Cruises—At the foot of the Columbus Monument, tourist boats called *golondrinas* offer 30-minute harbor tours (€3.70, daily 11:45–19:00, until 17:00 Dec–Feb). A glass-bottom catamaran takes longer tours up the coast (€8.80 for 75 min, 6/day, daily 11:30–17:30). For a picnic place, consider one of these rides or the harbor steps.

Cable Car to Montjuïc—You'll see the *teleférico* carrying tourists up to the hill of Montjuïc, which offers views, a castle, and several museums (military, Catalan art, and Joan Miró's art); see "Barcelona's Montjuïc," page 1210.

Gothic Quarter (Barri Gòtic): The Cathedral and Nearby

The Barri Gòtic is a bustling world of shops, bars, and nightlife packed between hard-to-be-thrilled-about 14th- and 15th-century buildings. The area around the port is seedy. But the area around the cathedral is a tangled yet inviting grab bag of undiscovered courtyards, grand squares, schoolyards, Art Nouveau storefronts, baby flea markets (Thursdays), musty junk shops, classy antique shops (on Carrer de la Palla), street musicians strumming Catalan folk songs, and balconies with domestic jungles behind wrought-iron bars. Go on a cultural scavenger hunt. Write a poem.

▲Cathedral (Catedral de Barcelona)—As you stand in the square looking at the cathedral, you're facing what was Roman Barcelona. On the ground to your right, letters spell out BARCINO—the city's Roman name. The three towers on the building to the right are mostly Roman.

The colossal **cathedral,** started in 1298, took 600 years to complete. Rather than stretching toward heaven, it makes a point of being simply massive (similar to the Gothic churches of Italy). The west front, though built according to the original plan, is only 100 years old (note the fancy, undulating rose window). The cathedral welcomes visitors daily (8:00–13:30 & 16:30–19:30; cloisters open daily 9:00–13:00 & 17:00–19:00; tel. 933-151-554).

The spacious interior—characteristic of Catalan Gothic buildings—is supported by buttresses. These provide walls for 28 richly ornamented **chapels.** While the main part of the church is fairly plain, the chapels, sponsored by local guilds, show great wealth. Located in the community's most high-profile space, they provided a kind of advertising to illiterate worshipers. Find the logos and symbols of the various trades represented. The Native Americans that Columbus brought to town were supposedly baptized in the first chapel on the left.

The chapels ring a finely carved 15th-century **choir** *(coro).* Pay €1 for a close-up look (with the lights on) at the ornately carved stalls and the emblems representing the various Knights of the Golden Fleece who once sat here. The chairs were folded up, giving VIPs stools to lean on during the standing parts of the Mass.

Barcelona's Cathedral

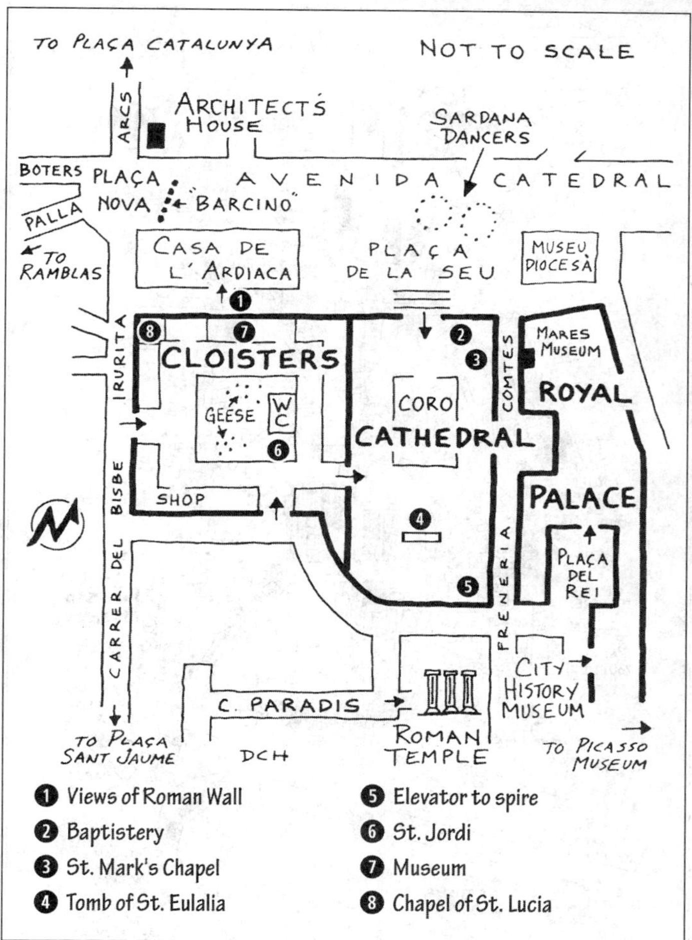

Each was creatively carved and—since you couldn't sit on sacred things—the artists were free to enjoy some secular fun here. Study the upper tier of carvings.

The **high altar** sits upon the tomb of Barcelona's patron saint, Eulàlia. She was a 13-year-old local girl tortured 13 times by Romans for her faith and finally crucified on an X-shaped cross. Her X symbol is carved on the pews. Climb down the stairs for a close look at her exquisite marble sarcophagus.

Ride the **elevator** to the roof and climb a tight spiral staircase up the spire for a commanding view (€1.40, Mon–Fri 10:30–12:30 & 16:30–18:00, closed Sat–Sun, start from chapel left of high altar).

Barcelona's Gothic Quarter Sights

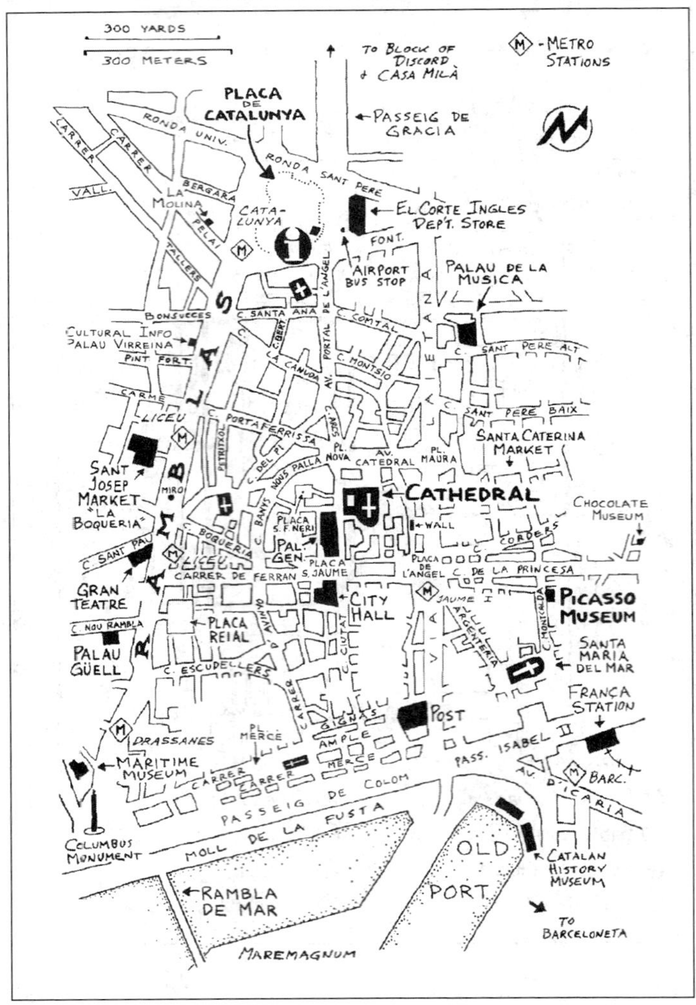

Enter the **cloister** (through arch, right of high altar). From there, look back at the arch, an impressive mix of Romanesque and Gothic. A tiny statue of St. George slaying the dragon stands in the garden. Jordi (George) is one of the patron saints of Catalunya and by far the most popular boy's name here. Though cloisters are generally found in monasteries, this church added one to accommodate more chapels—good for business. Again, notice the symbols of the trades or guilds. Even the pavement is filled with symbols—similar to Americans getting their name on a brick for helping to pay for something.

Long ago the resident geese—there are always 13, in memory of Eulàlia—functioned as an alarm system. Any commotion would get them honking, alerting the monk in charge.

From the statue of St. Jordi, circle to the right (past a WC hidden on the left). The skippable little €0.60 **museum** (far corner) is one plush room with a dozen old religious paintings. In the corner, built into the cloister, is the dark, barrel-vaulted, Romanesque Chapel of Santa Lucía, a small church that predates the cathedral. People hoping for good eyesight (Santa Lucía's specialty) leave candles outside. Farther along, the Chapel of Santa Rita (her forte: impossible causes) usually has the most candles. Complete the circle and exit at the door just before the place you entered.

Walk uphill, following the church. From the end of the apse, turn right 50 yards up Carrer del Paradis to the **Roman Temple** (Temple Roma d'August). In the corner, a sign above a millstone in the pavement marks "Mont Tabor, 16.9 meters." Step into the courtyard for a peek at a surviving corner of the imposing temple, which once stood here on the city's highest hill, keeping a protective watch over Barcino (free, daily 10:00–14:00 & 16:00–20:00).

To locate the next three sights, see the map on page 1197.

Plaça del Rei—The Royal Palace sat on King's Square (a block from the cathedral) until Catalunya became part of Spain in the 15th century. Then it was the headquarters of the local Inquisition. In 1493, a triumphant Christopher Columbus, accompanied by six New World natives (which he called "Indians") and several pure-gold statues, entered the Royal Palace. King Ferdinand and Queen Isabel rose to welcome him home, and honored him with the title "Admiral of the Oceans."

▲City History Museum—For a walk through the history of the city, take an elevator down 65 feet (and 2,000 years) to stroll the streets of Roman Barcelona. You'll see sewers, models of domestic life, and bits of an early Christian church. Then, an exhibit in the 11th-century count's palace shows you Barcelona through the Middle Ages (€4 includes museum, presentation, and visits to Pedralbes Monastery, Parc Güell's Center for Interpretation, and Verdaguer House Museum—see museum pamphlet for details; June–Sept Tue–Sat 10:00–20:00, Sun 10:00–14:00, closed Mon; Oct–May Tue–Sat 10:00–14:00 & 16:00–20:00, Sun 10:00–14:00, closed Mon, Plaça del Rei, tel. 933-151-111).

Frederic Marès Museum—This classy collection combines medieval religious art with a quirky bundle of more modern artifacts—old pipes, pinups, toys, and so on (Tue–Sat 10:00–15:00, Sun 10:00–14:00, closed Mon, Carrer del Comtes, off Plaça de la Seu, next to cathedral, tel. 933-105-800).

▲***Sardana* Dances**—The patriotic *sardana* dances are held at the cathedral (usually Sat at 18:00, Sun at 12:00) and at Plaça de Sant Jaume (often on Sun at 18:00 in spring and summer, 18:30 in fall and winter, none in Aug). Locals of all ages seem to spontaneously appear. For some, it's a highly symbolic, politically charged action representing Catalan unity—for most, it's just a fun chance to kick up their heels. Participants gather in circles after putting their things in the center—symbolic of community and sharing (and the ever-present risk of theft). All are welcome, even tourists cursed with two left feet. Holding hands, they raise their arms Zorba-the-Greek-style as they hop and sway gracefully to the band. The band *(cobla)* consists of a long flute, tenor and soprano oboes, strange-looking brass instruments, and a tiny bongo-like drum *(tambori)*. The rest of Spain mocks this lazy circle dance, but, considering what it takes for a culture to survive within another culture's country, it is a stirring display of local pride and patriotism.

Shoe Museum (Museu del Calçat)—Shoe-lovers enjoy this two-room shoe museum (with a we-try-harder attendant) on the delightful Plaça de Sant Felip Neri (€1.20, Tue–Sun 11:00–14:00, closed Mon, 1 block beyond outside door of cathedral cloister, behind Plaça de G. Bachs, tel. 933-014-533). The huge shoe at the entry is designed to fit the foot of the Columbus Monument at the bottom of the Ramblas.

Plaça de Sant Jaume—On this stately central square (pronounced jow-mah) of the Gothic Quarter, two of the top governmental buildings in Catalunya face each other: The Barcelona city hall (Ajuntament; free, Sun 10:00–13:30), and the seat of the autonomous government of Catalunya (Palau de la Generalitat). *Sardana* dances take place here many Sundays (see "*Sardana* Dances," above).

▲▲**Catalan Concert Hall (Palau de la Música Catalana)**—This concert hall, finished in 1908, features the best modernist interior in town. Inviting arches lead you into the 2,000-seat hall. A kaleidoscopic skylight features a choir singing around the sun, while playful carvings and mosaics celebrate music and Catalan culture. Admission is by tour only and starts with a relaxing 20-minute video (€7, 50-min tours in English, daily every 30 min 10:00–15:30, maybe later, about 6 blocks northeast of cathedral, tel. 932-957-200). Ask about concerts (300 per year, inexpensive tickets, www.palaumusica.org).

Gothic Quarter: The Picasso Museum and Nearby

▲▲▲**Picasso Museum (Museu Picasso)**—This is the best collection in the country of the work of Spaniard Pablo Picasso (1881–1973), and—since he spent his formative years (age 14–21) in Barcelona—it's the best collection of his early works anywhere. By seeing his youthful, realistic art, you can more fully appreciate the artist's genius and better understand his later, more challenging art. It's scattered through two Gothic palaces, six blocks from the cathedral.

Cost, Hours, and Location: €5, or €8 including temporary exhibit on Picasso or his contemporaries, free on first Sun of month, Tue–Sat 10:00–20:00, Sun 10:00–15:00, closed Mon, last entry 30 min before closing, free and required bag check, Montcada 15–23, ticket office at #21, Metro: Jaume I, tel. 933-196-310, www.museupicasso.bcn.es. The ground floor offers a handy array of services (bookshop, WC, bag check, and cafeteria). This generally crowded museum is quieter on sunny days Wed–Sat at about 14:00 and 18:00. For a good lunch, see "Eating—Near the Picasso Museum," page 1224.

Background: Picasso's personal secretary amassed a huge collection of his work and bequeathed it to the city. Picasso, happy to have a fine museum showing off his work in the city of his youth, added to the collection throughout his life. (Sadly, since Picasso vowed never to set foot in a fascist, Franco-ruled Spain, and died two years before Franco, the artist never saw the museum.)

Self-Guided Tour: While the rooms are constantly rearranged, the collection (291 paintings) is always presented chronologically. With the help of thoughtful English descriptions for each stage, it's easy to follow the evolution of Picasso's work. The room numbers in parentheses—though not exact—can help you get oriented in the museum. You'll see his art evolve in these 12 stages:

Rooms 1, 2, 3—Boy wonder, age 12–14, 1895–1897: Pablo's earliest art is realistic and serious. A budding genius emerges at age 12 as Pablo moves to Barcelona and gets serious about art. Even this young, his portraits of grizzled peasants show great psychological insight and flawless technique. You'll see portraits of Pablo's first teacher, his father *(Padre del Artista)*. Displays show his art-school work. Every time Pablo starts breaking rules, he's sent back to the standard classic style. The assignment: Sketch nude models to capture human anatomy accurately. Three self-portraits (1896) show the self-awareness of a blossoming intellect. When Pablo was 13, his father quit painting to nurture his young prodigy. Look closely at the portrait of his mother *(Retrato de la Madre del Artista)*. Pablo, then age 15, is working on the fine details and gradients of white in her blouse and the expression in her cameo-like face. Notice the signature. Spaniards keep both parents' surnames, with the father's first, followed by the mother's: Pablo Ruiz Picasso. Pablo was closer to his mom than his dad. Eventually he kept just her name.

Rooms 4, 5, 6—Málaga, exploration of nature: During a short trip to Málaga, Picasso dabbles in Impressionism (unknown in Spain at the time).

Rooms 7, 8—A sponge, influenced by local painters: As a 15-year-old, Pablo dutifully enters art-school competitions. His first big work—while forced to show a religious subject (*Primera Comunión,* or *First Communion,* Room 7)—is more an excuse to paint his family. Notice his sister Lola's exquisitely painted veil. This painting was heavily influenced by local painters.

In Room 8, *Cienca y Caridad (Science and Charity),* which won second prize at a fine-arts exhibition, got Picasso the chance to study in Madrid. Now Picasso conveys real feeling. The doctor (Pablo's father) represents science. The nun represents charity and religion. But nothing can help, as the woman is clearly dead (notice her face and lifeless hand). Pablo painted a little perspective trick: Walk back and forth across the room to see the bed stretch and shrink. Four small studies for this painting, hanging in the back of the room, show how this was an exploratory work. The frontier: light.

Picasso travels to Madrid for further study. Finding the stuffy fine-arts school in Madrid stifling, Pablo hangs out in the Prado museum and learns by copying the masters. Notice his nearly perfect copy of Felipe IV by Diego Velázquez.

Rooms 4, 8—Independence: Having absorbed the wisdom of the ages, in 1898, Pablo visits Horta, a rural Catalan village, and finds his artistic independence.

Rooms 9, 10—Sadness, 1899–1900: Pablo—poor and without love—returns to Barcelona. It's 1900, and Art Nouveau is the rage. Upsetting his dad, Pablo quits art school and falls in with the avant-garde crowd. These bohemians congregate daily at Els Quatre Gats ("the Four Cats," slang for "a few crazy people"—see "Eating," page 1224). Further establishing his artistic freedom, he paints portraits—no longer of his family...but of his new friends. Still a teenager, Pablo puts on his first one-man show.

Room 10—Paris, 1900–1901: Nineteen-year-old Picasso arrives in Paris, a city bursting with life, light, and love. Dropping the paternal surname Ruiz, Pablo establishes his commercial brand name: "Picasso." Here the explorer Picasso goes bohemian and befriends poets, prostitutes, and artists. He paints Impressionist landscapes like Claude Monet, posters like Henri de Toulouse-Lautrec, still lifes like Paul Cézanne, and bright-colored Fauvist works like Henri Matisse. (*La Espera*—with her bold outline and strong gaze—pops out from the Impressionistic background.) It was Cézanne's technique of "building" a figure with "cubes" of paint that inspired Picasso to soon invent Cubism.

Room 11—Blue Period, 1901–1904: The bleak Paris weather, the suicide of his best friend, and his own poverty lead Picasso to his "Blue Period." He cranks out piles of blue art just to stay housed and fed. With blue backgrounds (the coldest color) and depressing subjects, this period was revolutionary in art history. Now the artist is painting not what he sees but what he feels. The touching portrait of a mother and child, *Desamparados* (*Despair*, 1903), captures the period well. Painting misfits and street people, Picasso, like Velázquez and Toulouse-Lautrec, sees "the beauty in ugliness." Back home in Barcelona, Picasso paints his hometown at night from rooftops *(Terrats de Barcelona)*. Still blue, here we see proto-Cubism...five years before the first real Cubist painting.

Room 11—Rose: The woman in pink *(Retrato de la Sra. Canals)*, painted with classic "Spanish melancholy," finally lifts Picasso out of his funk, moving him out of the blue and into a happier "Rose Period" (of which this museum has only the one painting).

Rooms 12, 13, 14—Cubism, 1907–1920: Pablo's invention in Paris of the shocking Cubist style is well-known—at least I hope so, since this museum has no true Cubist paintings. In the age of the camera, the Cubist gives just the basics (a man with a bowl of fruit) and lets you finish it.

Rooms 12, 13, 14—Eclectic, 1920–1950: Picasso is a painter of many styles. We see a little post-Impressionistic Pointillism in a portrait that looks like a classical statue. After a trip to Rome, he paints beefy women, inspired by the three-dimensional sturdiness of ancient statues. To Spaniards, the expressionist horse symbolizes the innocent victim. In bullfights, the horse—clad with blinders and pummeled by the bull—has nothing to do with the fight. To Picasso, the horse symbolized the feminine and the bull, the masculine. Picasso would mix all these styles and symbols—including this image of the horse—in his masterpiece *Guernica* (in Madrid) to show the horror and chaos of modern war.

Rooms 15, 16, 17—Picasso and Velázquez, 1957: Notice the print of Velázquez's *Las Meninas* (in Madrid's Prado) that introduces this section. Picasso, who had great respect for Velázquez, painted more than 50 interpretations of this work that many consider the greatest painting by anyone, ever. These two Spanish geniuses were artistic equals. Picasso seems to enjoy a relationship with Velázquez. Like artistic soulmates, they spar and tease. He dissects Velázquez, and then injects playful uses of light, color, and perspective to horse around with the earlier masterpiece. In the big black-and-white canvas, the king and queen (reflected in the mirror in the back of the room) are hardly seen, while the self-portrait of the painter towers above everyone. The two women of the court on the right look like they're in a tomb—but they're wearing party shoes. In these rooms, see the fun Picasso had playing paddleball with Velázquez's masterpiece—filtering Velázquez's realism through the kaleidoscope of Cubism.

Room 17—Windows, 1957: All his life, Picasso said, "Paintings are like windows open to the world." Here we see the French Riviera—with simple black outlines and Crayola colors, he paints sun-splashed nature and the joys of the beach. He died with brush in hand, still growing. To the end, through his art Picasso continued exploring and loving life. As a child, he was taught to paint as an adult. Now, as an old man (with little kids of his own and an also-childlike artist Marc Chagall for a friend), he paints like a child.

As a wrap-up, notice 41 works in Rooms 18 and 19, representing Picasso's ceramics made during his later years (1947).

Textile and Garment Museum (Museu Tèxtil i d'Indumentària)—If fabrics from the 12th to 20th centuries leave you cold, have a *café con leche* on the museum's beautiful patio (€3.50, Tue–Sat 10:00–18:00, Sun 10:00–15:00, closed Mon, free entrance to patio—an inviting courtyard with a WC and coffeeshop, which is outside museum but within the walls, 30 yards from Picasso Museum at Montcada 12–14, www.museutextil.bcn.es).

Chocolate Museum (Museu de la Xocolata)—This museum, only a couple of blocks from the Picasso Museum, is a delight for chocolate lovers. It tells the story of chocolate from Aztecs to Europeans via the port of Barcelona, where it was first unloaded and processed. Even if you're into architecture more than calories, don't miss this opportunity to see the Sagrada Família church finished—and ready to eat (€3.80, Mon and Wed–Sat 10:00–19:00, Sun 10:00–15:00, closed Tue, Carrer Comerç 36, tel. 932-687-878, www.museuxocolata.com).

Eixample

Wide sidewalks, hardy shade trees, chic shops, and plenty of Art Nouveau fun make the Eixample a refreshing break from the old town. Uptown Barcelona is a unique variation on the common grid-plan city. Barcelona snipped off the building corners to create light and spacious eight-sided squares at every intersection. For the best Eixample example, ramble Rambla Catalunya (unrelated to the more famous Ramblas) and pass through Passeig de Gràcia (described below, Metro: Passeig de Gràcia for Block of Discord, or Diagonal for Casa Milà).

The 19th century was a boom time for Barcelona. By 1850, the city was busting out of its medieval walls. A new town was planned to follow a gridlike layout. The intersection of three major thoroughfares—Gran Vía, Diagonal, and Meridiana—would shift the city's focus uptown.

The Eixample, or "Expansion," was a progressive plan in which everything was made accessible to everyone. Each 20-block-square district would have its own hospital and large park, each 10-block-square area would have its own market and general services, and each five-block-square grid would house its own schools and daycare centers. The hollow space found inside each "block" of apartments would form a neighborhood park.

While much of that vision never quite panned out, the Eixample was an urban success. Rich and artsy big shots bought plots along the grid. The richest landowners built as close to the center as possible. For this reason, the best buildings are near the Passeig de Gràcia. While adhering to the height, width, and depth limitations, they built as they pleased—often in the trendy new modernist style.

Gaudí's Art and Architecture

Barcelona is an architectural scrapbook of the galloping gables and organic curves of hometown boy Antoni Gaudí (1852–1926). A devoted Catalan and Catholic, he immersed himself in each project, often living on-site. At various times, he called Parc Güell, Casa Milà, and the Sagrada Família home.

▲▲▲Sagrada Família (Holy Family) Church—Gaudí's most famous and persistent work is this unfinished landmark. He worked on the church from 1883 to 1926. Since then, construction has moved forward in fits and starts. (But over 30 years of visits, I've seen considerable progress.) Even today, the half-finished church is not expected to be completed for another 50 years. One reason it's taking so long is that the temple is funded exclusively by private donations and entry fees. Your admission helps pay for the ongoing construction (€8, €6 with Tourist Bus ticket, daily April–Oct 9:00–20:00, Nov–March 9:00–18:00; €3 extra for English tours: 6/day April–Oct, Nov–March usually Fri–Mon only; audioguide-€3; Metro: Sagrada Família, tel. 932-073-031, www.sagradafamilia.org).

When the church is finished, a dozen 330-foot spires (representing the apostles) will stand in groups of four and mark the three entry facades of the building. The center tower (honoring Jesus) will reach 580 feet up and be flanked by 400-foot-tall towers of Mary and the four Evangelists. A unique exterior ambulatory will circle the building, like a cloister turned inside out.

1. Passion Facade (on the western side where you enter): It's full of symbolism from the Bible. Find the stylized Alpha and Omega over the door, Jesus—hanging on the cross—with an open book for hair, and the grid of numbers adding up to 33 (Jesus' age at the time of his death). The distinct face of the man on the lower left is a memorial to Gaudí.

The facade and sculpture are inspired by Gaudí's vision but designed and executed by others. Gaudí knew he wouldn't live to complete the church and recognized that later architects and artists would rely on their own muses for inspiration. This artistic freedom was amplified in 1936 when Civil War shelling burned many of Gaudí's blueprints. Judge for yourself how the recently completed and controversial Passion facade by Josep María Subirachs (b. 1927) fits with Gaudí's original formulation.

Modernist Sights

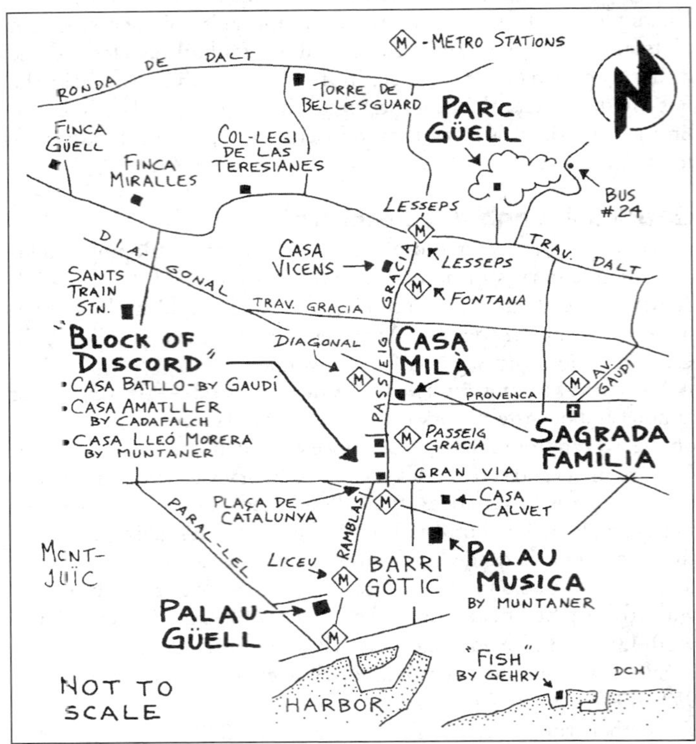

Now look high above: The colorful ceramic caps of the columns symbolize the mitres (formal hats) of bishops. This is only a side entrance. The nine-story apartment flat to the right will be torn down to accommodate the grand front entry of this church. The three facades—Passion, Nativity, and Glory—will chronicle Christ's life from birth to death to resurrection.

Now walk down to your right to the...

2. Museum (in church basement, or crypt): The museum displays physical models used for the church's construction. As you wander, you'll notice that they don't always match the finished product—these are ideas, not blueprints set in stone. See how the church's design is a fusion of nature, architecture, and religion. The columns seem light, with branches springing forth and capitals that look like palm trees. The U-shaped choir hovers above the nave, tethered halfway up the columns. Find the hanging model showing how Gaudí used gravity to calculate the perfect parabolas incorporated into the church design (the mirror above this model shows how the right-side-up church is derived from this).

Modernisme

The Renaixensa (Catalan cultural revival) gave birth to Modernisme (Catalan Art Nouveau) at the end of the 19th century. Barcelona is its capital. Its Eixample neighborhood shimmers with the colorful, leafy, flowing, blooming shapes of Modernisme in doorways, entrances, facades, and ceilings.

Meaning "a taste for what is modern"—things like streetcars, electric lights, and big-wheeled bicycles—this free-flowing organic style lasted from 1888 to 1906. Breaking with tradition, artists experimented with glass, tile, iron, and brick. The structure was fully modern, using rebar and concrete, but the decoration was a clip-art collage of nature images, exotic Moorish or Chinese themes, and fanciful Gothic crosses and knights to celebrate Catalunya's medieval glory days. It's Barcelona's unique contribution to the Europe-wide Art Nouveau movement. Modernisme was a way of life as Barcelona burst into the 20th century.

Antoni Gaudí (1852–1926), Barcelona's most famous modernist artist, was descended from four generations of metalworkers, a lineage of which he was quite proud. He incorporated ironwork into his architecture and came up with novel approaches to architectural structure and space.

Two more modernist architects famous for their unique style are Lluís Domènech i Muntaner and Josep Puig i Cadafalch. You'll see their work on the Block of Discord.

Gaudí lived on the site for more than a decade and is buried in the crypt. When he died in 1926, only the stubs of four spires stood above the building site. A window allows you to look down into the neo-Gothic 19th-century crypt (which is how the church began) to see the tomb of Gaudí. There's a move afoot to make Gaudí a saint. Perhaps some day, this tomb will be a place of pilgrimage. Gaudí—a faithful Catholic whose medieval-style mysticism belied his modernist architecture career—was certainly driven to greatness by his passion for God. When undertaking a lengthy project, he said, "My client"—meaning God—"is not in a hurry." You'll peek into a busy workshop where the slow and steady building pace is maintained.

Outside, just after leaving the building, you'll encounter the...

3. Nativity Facade (east side): This, the only part of the church finished in his lifetime, shows Gaudí's original vision. Mixing Gothic-style symbolism, images from nature, and modernist asymmetry, it is the best example of Gaudí's unmistakable cake-in-the-rain style. The sculpture shows scenes from the birth and childhood of Jesus, along with angels playing musical instruments.

You can love it, hate it, or adopt a love/hate attitude to it, but you can't deny that it's unique.

Finally you walk through the actual...

4. **Construction Zone:** The cranking cranes, rusty forests of rebar, and scaffolding require a powerful faith, but the Sagrada Família church offers a fun look at a living, growing, bigger-than-life building. It's estimated that the proposed central tower (550 feet tall) will require four underground pylons of support, each consisting of 8,000 tons of cement. Take the elevator on the Passion side (€2) or the stairs on the Nativity side (free but often miserably congested) up to the dizzy lookout that bridges two spires. You'll get a great view of the city and a gargoyle's-eye perspective of the loopy church. If there's any building on earth I'd like to see, it's the Sagrada Família...finished.

▲Palau Güell—This is a good chance to enjoy a Gaudí interior (see "Introductory Walk: From Plaça de Catalunya down the Ramblas," page 1194). Curvy.

▲▲Casa Milà (La Pedrera)—This Gaudí exterior laughs down on the crowds filling Passeig de Gràcia. Casa Milà, also called La Pedrera ("The Quarry"), has a much-photographed roller coaster of melting-ice-cream eaves. This is Barcelona's quintessential modernist building and Gaudí's last major work (1906–1910) before dedicating his final years to the Sagrada Família.

You can visit three sections: the apartment, attic, and rooftop. Buy the €7 ticket to see all three. Starting with the apartment, an elevator whisks you to the *Life in Barcelona 1905–1929* exhibit (good English descriptions). Then, walk through a sumptuously furnished Art Nouveau apartment. Upstairs in the attic, wander under parabola-shaped brick arches and enjoy a multimedia exhibit of models, photos, and videos of Gaudí's works. A stairway leads to the fanciful rooftop, where chimneys play volleyball with the clouds. From here, you can see Gaudí's other principal works, the Sagrada Família to the west, Casa Batllò to the south, and Parc Güell to the north (daily 10:00–20:00; free tour in English Mon–Fri at 16:00, or rent the €3 audioguide; Passeig de Gràcia 92, Metro: Diagonal, tel. 934-845-530).

At the ground level of Casa Milà, poke into the dreamily-painted original entrance courtyard (free). The first floor hosts free art exhibits. During the summer, a concert series called "Pedrera by Night" features live music—jazz, flamenco, tango—a glass of champagne, and the chance to see the rooftop illuminated (€10, July–Sept Fri–Sat at 22:00, tel. 934-845-900).

▲Block of Discord—Four blocks from Casa Milà, you can survey a noisy block of competing, late-19th-century facades. Several of Barcelona's top modernist mansions line Passeig de Gràcia (Metro: Passeig de Gràcia). Because the structures look as though they are trying to outdo each other in creative twists, locals nicknamed the block between Consell de Cent and Arago the "Block of Discord." First (at #43) and most famous is Gaudí's Casa Batllò, with skull-like balconies and a tile roof that suggests a cresting dragon's back; Gaudí based the work on the popular St. Jordi/George-slays-the-dragon legend (€16 includes main floor, roof, and decent audioguide). By the way, if you're tempted to snap your photos from the middle of the street, be careful—Gaudí died under a streetcar.

Next door, at Casa Amatller (#41), check out architect Josep Puig i Cadafalch's creative mix of Moorish- and Gothic-inspired architecture and iron grillwork, which decorates a step-gable like those in the Netherlands.

On the corner (at #35) Casa Lleó Morera has a wonderful interior highlighted by the dining room's fabulous stained glass. The architect, Lluís Domènech i Muntaner, also did the Catalan Concert Hall (you'll see similarities).

The perfume shop halfway down the street has a free and interesting little perfume museum in the back. The Hostal de Rita restaurant, just around the corner on Carrer Arago, serves a fine three-course lunch for a great price at 13:00 (see "Eating," page 1225).

▲Parc Güell—Gaudí fans enjoy the artist's magic in this colorful park (free, daily 9:00–20:00). The Center for Interpretation of Parc Güell (Centre d'Interpretació) at the park entrance is a new visitors center, showing Gaudí's building methods plus maps, photos, and models of the park (€2, or €4 combo-ticket including City History Museum, daily 11:00–15:00, red Tourist Bus or bus #24 from Plaça de Catalunya, €8 by taxi, tel. 933-190-222, www.museuhistoria.bcn.es). The small Gaudí Museum is the middle of the park is less interesting than the Center (€4, daily 10:00–20:00, closes at 18:00 Oct–March; red Tourist Bus or bus #24 from Plaça de Catalunya; €6 by taxi, tel. 932-130-488).

Gaudí intended this 30-acre garden to be a 60-residence housing project—a kind of gated community—rather than a park. As a high-income housing development, it flopped. As a park, it's a delight, offering another peek into the eccentric genius of Gaudí. From the bus stop, you'll hike uphill three blocks to the main (lower) entry to the park. (Taxis take you right there.) Notice the mosaic medallions that say "park" in English, reminding folks that this is modeled on an English garden.

Imagine living here 100 years ago, when this gated community was filled with Barcelona's wealthy. Stepping past fancy gate houses (which now hold a good bookshop and an audiovisual intro), you walk by Gaudí's wrought-iron gas lamps (1900–1914)—his dad was a blacksmith, and he always enjoyed this medium. Climb the grand stairway past the ceramic dragon fountain. At the top, drop by the Hall of 100 Columns, a produce market for the neighborhood's 60 (never-completed) mansions. The fun columns—each different, made from concrete and rebar, topped with colorful ceramic, and studded with broken bottles and bric-a-brac—add to the market's vitality. After shopping, continue up. Look left, down the playful "pathway of columns" that support a long arcade. Gaudí drew his inspiration from nature, and this arcade is like a surfer's perfect "tube." From here, continue up to the terrace. Sit on a colorful bench—designed to fit your body ergonomically—and enjoy one of Barcelona's best views. Look for the Sagrada Família church in the distance.

When considering the failure of Parc Güell, also consider that it was an idea just a hundred years ahead of its time. Back then, high-society ladies didn't want to live so far from the cultural action. Today, the surrounding neighborhoods are some of the wealthiest in town, and a gated community here would be a big hit.

Barcelona's Montjuïc

The Montjuïc ("Mount of the Jews"), overlooking Barcelona's hazy port, has always been a show-off. Ages ago it had an impressive fortress. In 1929, it hosted an international fair, from which most of today's sights originated. And in 1992, the Summer Olympics directed the world's attention to this pincushion of attractions.

Getting to Montjuïc: You have several options—the simplest is to take a taxi directly to your destination (about €7). From the port, the fastest and most scenic way to Montjuïc is via the gondola, called the 1929 Transbordador Aereo (€9 round-trip, daily June–mid-Sept 11:00–20:00, mid-Sept–May 10:45–19:00, 4/hr; at tower in port next to World Trade Center, ride elevator up to catch dangling gondola; tel. 934-430-859).

Otherwise, there are three options, all of which drop you off at the base of a funicular/cable car below the Castle of Montjuïc: on the blue Tourist Bus route (see "Getting around Barcelona," page 1187); by bus #50 from the corner of Gran Vía and Passeig de Gràcia (€1, every 10 min), #55 from Plaça de Catalunya (next to Caja de Madrid building); or by Metro to the Parallel stop (funicular covered by T10 transit pass and Barcelona Card). The cable car *(teleférico)* takes you the last stretch up to the Castle of Montjuïc (€3.40 one-way, €4.80 round-trip, daily 11:15–21:00, fewer trips Nov–March, tel. 934-430-859). Alternately, from the same spot you can walk uphill 20 minutes through the pleasant park.

Castle of Montjuïc—The castle offers great city views and a military museum (€2.50, €1 for views from fortress only, daily 9:30–20:00). The seemingly endless museum houses a dull collection of guns, swords, and toy soldiers. An interesting section on the Spanish-American War of 1898 covers Spain's valiant fight against American aggression (from its perspective). Unfortunately, there

Montjuïc

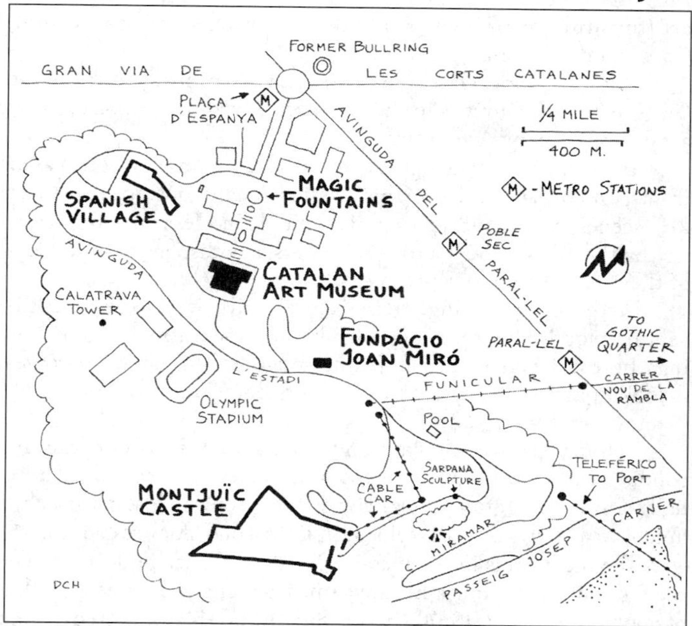

are no English descriptions. Those interested in Jewish history will find a fascinating collection of ninth-century Jewish tombstones. The castle itself has a fascist past. It was built in the 18th century by the central Spanish government to keep an eye on Barcelona and stifle citizen revolt. When Franco was in power, the castle was the site of hundreds of political executions.

▲Fountains (Font Màgica)—Music, colored lights, and huge amounts of water make an artistic and coordinated splash on summer nights at Plaça Espanya (20-min shows start on the half hour Fri–Sat 19:00–21:00, Thu and Sat in summer until 23:00; from the Plaça Espanya Metro station, walk toward the towering National Palace).

Spanish Village (Poble Espanyol)—This tacky five-acre model village uses fake traditional architecture from all over Spain as a shell to contain gift shops. Craftspeople do their clichéd thing only in the morning (not worth your time or €7, www.poble-espanyol.com). After hours, it's a popular local nightspot.

▲▲Catalan Art Museum (Museu Nacional d'Art de Catalunya)—This museum, often called "the Prado of Romanesque art," presents art from the 10th to the mid-20th centuries. The exhibits include Romanesque, Renaissance, and Baroque works; the Cambo and Thyssen collections; and, on the second floor,

19th- and 20th-century works including lesser-known modernist art (furniture, paintings, and sculpture by artists such as Gaudí, Casas, and Llimona).

This rare, world-class collection of art came mostly from remote Catalan village churches in the Pyrenees (saved from unscrupulous art dealers—many American).

The Romanesque wing features frescoes, painted wooden altar fronts, and ornate statuary. This classic Romanesque art—with flat 2-D scenes, each saint holding his symbol, and Jesus (easy to identify by the cross in his halo)—is impressively displayed on replicas of the original church ceilings.

In the Gothic wing, fresco murals give way to vivid 14th-century wood-panel paintings of Bible stories. A roomful of paintings by the Catalan master Jaume Huguet (1412–1492) deserves a look, particularly his altarpiece of Barcelona's patron saint, George.

Before you leave, ice-skate under the huge dome over to the air-conditioned cafeteria. This was the prime ceremony room and dance hall for the 1929 International Exposition. You can also have a chic lunch, with views over Barcelona, in the second-floor restaurant.

The museum is in the massive National Palace building above the fountains, near Plaça Espanya (museum entry-€6, free first Thu of month, Tue–Sat 10:00–19:00, Sun 10:00–14:30, closed Mon, audioguide, on Tourist Bus ticket, take escalators up, tel. 936-622-0376, www.mnac.es).

▲Fundació Joan Miró—For something more up-to-date, this museum—showcasing the modern-art talents of yet another Catalan artist—has the best collection of Joan Miró art anywhere. You'll also see works by other modern artists (such as the American Alexander Calder's *Mercury Fountain*). If you don't like abstract art, you'll leave here scratching your head, but those who love this place are not faking it...they understand the genius of Miró and the fun of abstract art.

As you wander, consider this: Miró believed that everything in the cosmos is linked—colors, sky, stars, love, time, music, dogs, men, women, dirt, and the void. He mixed childlike symbols of these things creatively, as a poet uses words. It's as liberating for the visual artist to be abstract as it is for the poet: Both can use metaphors rather than being confined to concrete explanations. Miró would listen to music and paint. It's interactive, free interpretation. He said, "For me, simplicity is freedom."

To enjoy Miró's art: 1) meditate on it; 2) read the title (for example, *The Smile of a Tear*); 3) meditate on it again. Repeat until epiphany. There's no correct answer—it's pure poetry. Devotees of Miró say they fly with him and don't even need drugs. Take advantage of the wonderful audioguide, included with admission (€7.20,

July–Sept Tue–Sat 10:00–20:00, Thu until 21:30, Sun 10:00–14:30, closed Mon; Oct–June Tue–Sat closes at 19:00, Parc de Montjuïc, tel. 934-439-470, www.bcn.fjmiro.es).

More Sights in Barcelona

Citadel Park (Parc de la Ciutadella)—Barcelona's biggest, greenest park, originally the site of a much-hated military citadel, was transformed in 1888 for a World's Fair (Universal Exhibition). The stately Triumphal Arch at the top of the park was built as the main entrance. Inside, you'll find wide pathways, plenty of trees and grass, the zoo, and the geology and zoology museums. In Barcelona, which suffers from a lack of real green space, this park is a haven. Enjoy the ornamental fountain that the young Antoni Gaudí helped design, and consider a jaunt in a rowboat on the lake in the center of the park (€1.20/person for 30 min). Check out the tropical Umbracle greenhouse and the Hivernacle winter garden, which has a pleasant café-bar (daily 8:00–20:00, Metro: Arc de Triomf, east of França train station).

Barcelona's Beach—Take the trek through the charming Barceloneta neighborhood to the tip of this man-made peninsula. The beaches begin here and stretch for 2.5 miles up the coast to the Olympic Port and beyond. Everything you see here—palm trees, cement walkways, and tons of sand—was installed in the mid-1980s in an effort to shape up the city for the 1992 Summer Olympic Games. The beaches are fine for sunbathing (beach chair rental-€3/day), but the water quality is questionable for swimming. Take a lazy stroll down the seafront promenade to the Olympic Port, where you'll find bars, restaurants, and, at night, dance clubs.

Away from the Center

Monastery of Pedralbes—The museum shows off the monastery's six centuries of history (with a peaceful cloister and cells set up for worship, giving a peek into the everyday life of the cloistered nuns). Unfortunately, it's far from the center (€4, Tue–Sun 10:00–14:00, closed Mon, buses: #22, #63, #64, #75, tel. 932-801-434).

Tibidabo—Tibidabo comes from the Latin for "to thee I shall give," the words the devil used when he was tempting Christ. It's still an enticing offer: At the top of Barcelona's highest peak, you're offered the city's oldest fun-fair (erratic hours, tel. 932-117-942), the neo-Gothic Sacred Heart Church, and—if the weather and air quality are good—an almost limitless view of the city and the Mediterranean.

Getting there is part of the fun: Start by taking the FGC line—similar to, but separate from, the Metro (also covered by the T10 ticket)—from the Plaça de Catalunya station (under Café Zürich) to the Tibidabo stop. The red Tourist Bus stops here, too.

Then take Barcelona's only remaining tram—the Tramvía Blau—from Plaça John F. Kennedy to Plaça Dr. Andreu (€2.90, 2–4/hr). From there, take the funicular to the top (€3, tel. 906-427-017).

NIGHTLIFE

Refer to the *See Barcelona* guide (free from TI) and find out the latest at a TI. Sights open daily until 20:00 include the Picasso Museum (closes at 15:00 on Sun), Casa Milà, Gaudí's Sagrada Família, and Parc Güell. On Thursday, the Joan Miró museum stays open until 21:30. On Montjuïc, the fountains on Plaça Espanya make a splash on weekend evenings (Fri–Sat, plus Thu in summer).

For music, consider a performance at Casa Milà ("Pedrera by Night" summer concert series, see page 1208), the Liceu Opera House (page 1194), or the Catalan Concert Hall (page 1200). Two decent music clubs are La Boite (477 Diagonal, near El Corte Inglés) and Jamboree (on Plaça Reial).

SLEEPING

Book ahead. If necessary, the TI at Plaça de Catalunya has a room-finding service. Barcelona is Spain's most expensive city. Still, it has reasonable rooms. Cheap places are more crowded in summer; fancier business-class places fill up in winter and offer discounts on weekends and in summer. Prices listed do not include the 7 percent tax or breakfast (ranging from simple €3 spreads to €13.25 buffets) unless otherwise noted. While many recommended places are on pedestrian streets, night noise is a problem almost everywhere (especially in cheap places, which have single-pane windows). For a quiet night, ask for "*tranquilo*" rather than "*con vista.*"

Eixample

For an uptown, boulevard-like neighborhood, sleep in the Eixample, a 10-minute walk from the Ramblas action.

$$ Hotel Gran Vía, filling a palatial mansion built in the 1870s, offers Botticelli and chandeliers in the public rooms; a sprawling, peaceful sun garden; and 54 spacious, comfy, air-conditioned rooms. While borderline ramshackle, it's charming and an excellent value (Sb-€75, Db-€125, Tb-€150, elevator, Internet access, quiet, Gran Vía de les Corts Catalanes 642, tel. 933-181-900, fax 933-189-997, www.nnhotels.es, hgranvia@nnhotels.es, Juan Gomez SE).

$$ Hotel Continental Palacete fills a 100-year-old chandeliered mansion. With flowery wallpaper and cheap but fancy furniture under ornately gilded stucco, it's gaudy in the city of Gaudí. But it's friendly, clean, quiet, and well-located, and the beds are good.

Sleep Code

(€1 = about $1.20, country code: 34)
S = Single, **D** = Double/Twin, **T** = Triple, **Q** = Quad, **b** = bathroom, **s** = shower only, **SE** = Speaks English, **NSE** = No English. Unlessotherwise noted, credit cards are accepted.

To help you easily sort through these listings, I've divided the rooms into three categories, based on the price for a standard double room with bath (during high season):

$$$ **Higher Priced**—Most rooms €150 or more.
$$ **Moderately Priced**—Most rooms between €100–150.
$ **Lower Priced**—Most rooms €100 or less.

Owner Señora Vallet (whose son, José, runs the recommended Hotel Continental—see "Hotels with 'Personality' on or near the Ramblas," below) has a creative vision for this 19-room hotel (Sb-€90–150, Db-€110–150, Tb-€150–180, includes breakfast and free fruit-and-drink buffet all day, air-con, 2 blocks north of Plaça de Catalunya at corner of Carrer Diputació, Rambla Catalunya 30, tel. 934-457-657, fax 934-450-050, www.hotelcontinental.com, palacete @hotelcontinental.com).

$ Hostal Residencia Neutral, with a classic Eixample address and 28 very basic rooms, is a family-run time warp (tiny Ss-€30, Ds-€46, Db-€52, extra bed-€9.50, €5 breakfast in pleasant breakfast room, elevator, fans, thin walls and some street noise, elegantly located 2 blocks north of Gran Vía at Rambla Catalunya 42, tel. 934-876-390, fax 934-876-848, hostalneutral@arrakis.es, owner Ramón SE). Its sister hotel, **Hotel Universal,** with 18 noisy rooms, lacks the friendly feel and is stark but well-located (Sb-€45, Db-€60, Tb-€70, no breakfast, 4 quieter rooms in interior, Arago 281, tel. 934-879-762, fax 934-874-028, hoteluniversal@arrakis.es).

Business-Class Comfort near Plaça de Catalunya and the Top of the Ramblas

These nine places have sliding glass doors leading to plush reception areas, air-conditioning, and renovated modern rooms. Most are on big streets within two blocks of Barcelona's exuberant central square. As business hotels, they have hard-to-pin-down prices fluctuating wildly with demand.

$$$ Hotel Catalonia Albinoni, the best located of all these places, elegantly fills a renovated old palace with wide halls, hardwood floors, and 74 modern rooms with all the comforts. It overlooks a thriving pedestrian boulevard. Front rooms have views; balcony rooms on the back are quiet and come with sun terraces

Hotels near the Ramblas

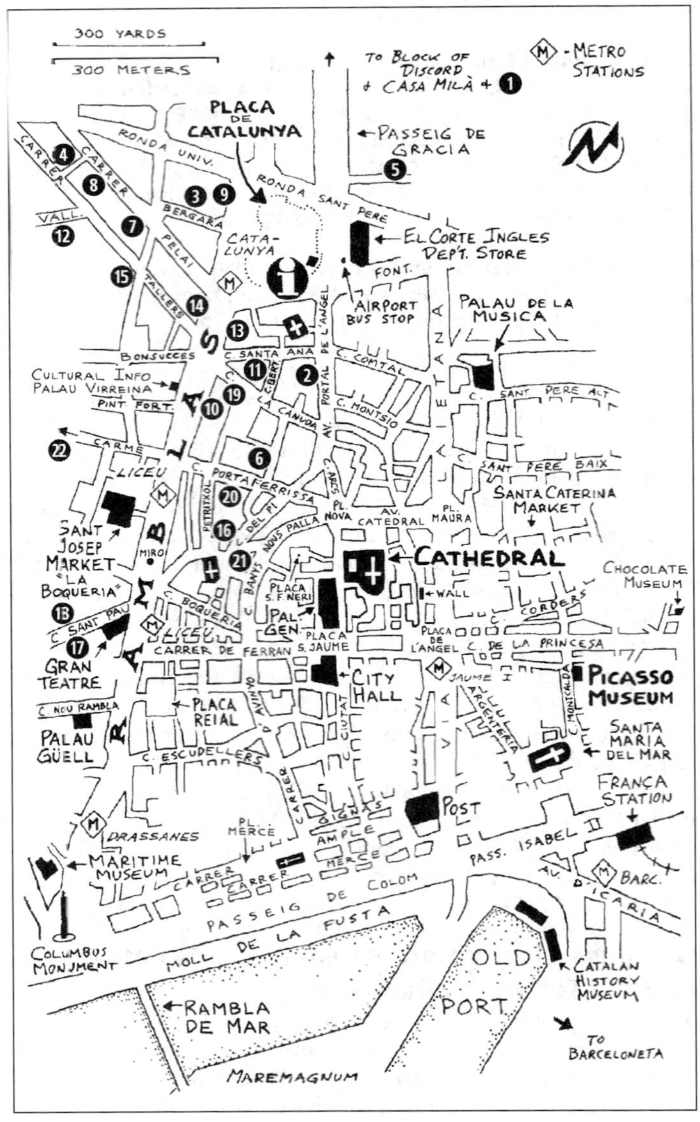

1. To Hotel Gran Vía, Hotel Continental Palacete, Hotel Residencia Neutral & Hotel Universal
2. Hotel Catalonia Albinoni
3. Hotel Duques de Bergara
4. Hotel Occidental Reding
5. Hotel Barcelona
6. Hotel Duc de la Victoria
7. Hotel Lleó
8. Hotel Atlantis
9. Hotel H10 Catalunya Plaza
10. Citadines Ramblas Aparthotel
11. Nouvel Hotel
12. Meson Castilla
13. Hotel Toledano, Hostal Residencia Capitol & Hotel Continental
14. Hotel Lloret
15. Hostería Grau
16. Hotel Jardi
17. Hotel España
18. Hotel Peninsular & Hostal Opera
19. Hostal Campi
20. Pension Fina
21. Pension Vitoria
22. To Hotel Aneto

(Db-€170, extra bed-€35 family rooms, great buffet breakfast free when you book direct and show this book, elevator, air-con, a block down from Plaça de Catalunya at Portal de l'Angel 17, tel. 933-184-141, fax 933-012-631, www.hoteles-catalonia.com, albinoni.reservas @hoteles-catalonia.es).

$$$ Hotel Duques de Bergara boasts four stars. It has splashy public spaces, slick marble and hardwood floors, 150 comfortable rooms, and a garden courtyard with a pool a world away from the big-city noise (Sb-€143, Db-€171, Tb-€201, air-con, elevator, a half block off Plaça de Catalunya at Bergara 11, tel. 933-015-151, fax 933-173-442, www.hoteles-catalonia.es, duques@hoteles-catalonia.es).

$$$ Hotel Occidental Reding, on a quiet street and a five-minute walk west of the Ramblas and Plaça de Catalunya action, rents 44 modern business-class rooms (Db-€118 in low season, €170 in high, extra bed-€51, air-con, elevator, near Metro: Universitat at Gravina 5-7, tel. 934-121-097, fax 932-683-482, www.occidental-hoteles.com, reding@occidentalhoteles.com).

$$$ Hotel Barcelona is another big, American-style hotel with 72 bright, prefab, comfy rooms (Sb-€150, Db-€170, Db with terrace-€215, air-con, elevator, a block from Plaça de Catalunya at Caspe 1–13, tel. 933-025-858, fax 933-018-674, www.husa.es, hotelbarcelona@husa.es).

$$$ Hotel Duc de la Victoria, with 156 rooms, is a professional-yet-friendly business-class hotel, buried in the Gothic Quarter but only three blocks off the Ramblas (Sb/Db-€175 Mon–Thu or €132 Fri–Sun, Aug rate: Db-€100, superior rooms—bigger and on a corner with windows on 2 sides—are worth €15 extra, air-con, elevator, groups get weekend rate, Duc de la Victoria 15, tel. 932-703-410, fax

934-127-747, www.nh-hotels.com, nhducdelavictoria@nh-hotels.com).

$$$ H10 Catalunya Plaza, a business hotel right on the square, was redone in 2003 and has 47 tight, mod rooms with all the air-conditioning and minibar comforts (Sb-€126–180, Db-€150–210 in busy times, elevator, Plaça de Catalunya 7, tel. 933-177-171, fax 933-177-855, www.h10.es, catalunya.plaza@h10.es).

$$ Hotel Lleó is a well-run business hotel with 90 big, bright, and comfortable rooms and a great lounge (Db-€130–160, on weekends-€144, summer Db special-€100, add about €25 for extra person, air-con, elevator, 2 blocks west of Plaça de Catalunya at Pelai 22, tel. 933-181-312, fax 934-122-657, www.hotel-lleo.es, reservas@hotel-lleo.es).

$$ Hotel Atlantis is a solid business-class hotel with 50 rooms and great prices for the area (Sb-€85, Db-€105, Tb-€125, air-con, elevator, Pelayo 20, tel. 933-189-012, fax 934-120-914, www.hotelatlantis-bcn.com, inf@hotelatlantis-bcn.com).

$$ Citadines Ramblas Aparthotel is a clever concept, offering daily rentals of 131 apartments in a bright, modern building right on the Ramblas. Prices range with seasonal demand and rooms come in two categories (studio apartment for 2 with sofa bed or twin and kitchenette-€131–160, apartment with real bed and sofa bed for up to 4 people-€195–240, includes tax, laundry-€9, Ramblas 122, tel. 932-701-111, fax 934-127-421, www.citadines.com, barcelona@citadines.com).

Hotels with "Personality" on or near the Ramblas

The first two listings are hoteleque and comfortable. Hotels Toledano, Residencia Capitol, Continental, and Lloret overlook the Ramblas (at the top, very near Plaça de Catalunya) and offer classic tiny view-balcony opportunities if you don't mind the noise. The last five (Jardi, España, Peninsular, Opera, and Aneto) are a few blocks away from the boulevard at about its midpoint. These places are generally family-run with ad-lib furnishings, more character, and much lower prices.

$$$ Nouvel Hotel, an elegant, Victorian-style building on a handy pedestrian street, has royal lounges and 78 comfy rooms (Sb-€93–105, Db-€152–199, includes breakfast, air-con, Carrer de Santa Ana 18, tel. 933-018-274, fax 933-018-370, www.hotelnouvel.com, info@hotelnouvel.com).

$$ Meson Castilla is well-located, with 57 clean rooms, but also pricey, a bit sterile (less quirky), and in all the American guidebooks. It's three blocks off the Ramblas in an appealing university neighborhood (Sb-€95, Db-€122, Tb-€160, Qb apartment-€190, includes buffet breakfast, elevator, air-con, Valldoncella

5, tel. 933-182-182, fax 934-124-020, www.mesoncastilla.com, hmesoncastilla@teleline.es).

$ Hotel Toledano, overlooking the Ramblas, is suitable for backpackers and is popular with dust-bunnies. Small, folksy, and with new furniture, it's warmly run by Albert Sanz, his father Juan, Juanma, and trusty Daniel on the night shift (Sb-€34, Db-€56, Tb-€71, Qb-€80, some with air-con, front rooms have Ramblas-view terraces, back rooms have no noise—request your choice when you call; Internet access; Rambla de Canaletas 138, tel. 933-010-872, fax 934-123-142, www.hoteltoledano.com, reservas@hoteltoledano.com). The Sanz family also runs **Hostal Residencia Capitol** one floor above—quiet, plain, cheaper, and also appropriate for backpackers (S-€26, D-€38, Ds-€44, Q-€58, 5-bed room-€63).

$ Hotel Continental Barcelona has comfortable rooms, double-thick mattresses, and wildly clashing carpets and wallpaper. To celebrate 100 years in the family, José includes a free breakfast and an all-day complimentary coffee bar. Choose a Ramblas-view balcony or quiet back room (Db with double bed-€75, with twin-€85, with balcony-€95, extra bed-€20, includes tax, special family room, air-con, elevator, Internet access, Ramblas 138, tel. 933-012-570, fax 933-027-360, www.hotelcontinental.com, barcelona@hotelcontinental.com).

$ Hotel Lloret is a big, dark, Old World place on the Ramblas with plain, neon-lit rooms. A dark, dusty elevator cage fills the stairwell like Darth Vader—but on a hot day, you're glad it's there (Sb-€48, Db-€85, Tb-€95, Qb-€110, choose a noisy Ramblas balcony or *tranquilo* in the back, air-con in summer, Rambla de Canaletas 125, tel. 933-173-366, fax 933-019-283, www.hlloret.com, info@lloret.com).

$ Hostería Grau is a homey, almost alpine place, family-run with 27 clean and woody rooms just far enough off the Ramblas (S-€29, D-€50, Ds-€55, Db-€66, family suites with 2 bedrooms-€120, €6 extra charged July–Sept, fans, Internet, 200 yards up Carrer dels Tallers from Ramblas at Ramelleres 27, tel. 933-018-135, fax 933-176-825, www.hostalgrau.com, reservas@hostalgrau.com, Monica SE).

$ Hotel Jardi offers 40 clean and remodeled rooms on a breezy square in the Gothic Quarter. Rooms with tight, little balconies (€15 extra) enjoy an almost Parisian ambience and minimal noise (Sb-€68, Db-€78, Sb/Db with square view-€83, breakfast-€5, air-con, elevator, halfway between Ramblas and cathedral on Plaça Sant Josep Oriol #1, tel. 933-015-900, fax 933-425-733, hoteljardi@retemail.es).

$ Hotel España is a big, creaky, circa-1900 place with lavish public spaces still sweet with Art Nouveau decor by locally popular modernist architect Domènech i Muntaner. While it's 50 yards off the Ramblas on a borderline seedy street, it feels safe (84 rooms, Sb-€50, Db-€98, Tb-€130, includes tax and breakfast, air-con, elevator, near Metro: Liceu at Sant Pau 9, tel. 933-181-758, fax 933-171-134, www.hotelespanya.com, hotelespanya@hotelespanya .com).

$ Hotel Peninsular, farther down the same street, is a unique and thoughtfully-run value in the old center. A former convent, the 80 still-basic and thinly-furnished rooms—once nuns' cells—gather prayerfully around a bright, peaceful courtyard (S-€30, Sb-€50, D-€50, Db-€70, Tb-€80, prices include tax and breakfast and are the same year-round, air-con, elevator, Carrer Sant Pau 34, tel. 933-023-138, fax 934-123-699, Alex and Augustin SE).

$ Hostal Opera, with 70 rooms 20 yards off the Ramblas is simple but modern, clean and comfortable (Sb-€40, Db-€60, Tb-€90, air-con only in summer, elevator, no breakfast, Internet, at Carrer San Pau 20, Tel 933188201, info@hostalopera.com)

$ Hotel Aneto offers 18 clean, functional, and a little over-priced rooms, some with balconies 100 yards off the Ramblas (Sb-€60, Db-€80, air-con, elevator after a few steps, next to a little park behind Boqueria market, Carmen 38, tel. 933-019-989, fax 933-019-862, aneto@hotelaneto.com).

Humble Cheaper Places Buried in the Gothic Quarter

$ Hostal Campi—big, quiet, and ramshackle—is a few doors off the top of the Ramblas. The streets can be noisy, so request a quiet room in the back (24 rooms, D-€44, Db-€52, T-€60, Tb-€70, cash only, Canuda 4, tel. & fax 933-013-545, hcampi@terra.es, friendly Sonia and Margarita SE).

$ Pension Fina offers more cheap sleeps (24 rooms, S-€32, D-€54, Db-€60, Portaferrissa 11, tel. & fax 933-179-787, hostalfina@hotmail.com).

$ Pension Vitoria has loose tile floors and 12 basic rooms, each with a tiny balcony. It's more dumpy than homey, but consider the price (D-€30, Db-€35, T-€40, cheaper off-season, a block off day-dreamy Plaça del Pi at Carrer de la Palla 8, tel. & fax 933-020-834, Mary Cruz SE).

EATING

Barcelona, the capital of Catalan cuisine—featuring seafood and Basque tapas—offers a tremendous variety of colorful places to eat. Many restaurants close in August (or July), when the owners vacation.

Eating Simply yet Memorably near the Ramblas and in the Gothic Quarter

Taverna Basca Irati serves 40 kinds of hot and cold Basque *pintxos* for €1.10 each. These are open-faced sandwiches—like Basque sushi but on bread. Muscle in through the hungry local crowd. Get an empty plate from the waiter, and then help yourself. It's a Basque honor system: You'll be charged by the number of toothpicks left on your plate when you're done. Wash it down with a €1.40 glass of Rioja (full-bodied red wine), €1.40 Txakoli (sprightly Basque white wine), or €1.20 *sidra* (apple wine) poured from on high to add oxygen and bring out the flavor (daily 12:00–24:00, a block off the Ramblas, behind arcade at Carrer Cardenal Casanyes 17, near Metro: Liceu, tel. 933-023-084).

Juicy Jones, next door, is a tutti-frutti vegan/vegetarian place with garish colors, a hip veggie menu (served downstairs), and a stunning array of fresh-squeezed juices served at the bar (lunch and dinner *menu*-€8.75, daily 12:00–24:30, Carrer Cardenal Casanyes 7). Pop in for a quick €3 "juice of the day."

Restaurant Elisabets is a happy little neighborhood eatery packed with antique radios and popular with locals for its "home-cooked" three-course €7.60 lunch special. Stop by for lunch, survey what those around you are enjoying, and order what looks best (Mon–Sat 13:00–16:00, Fri also 21:00–1:00, closed Sun, €12 tapas *menu* only in the evening, 2 blocks west of Ramblas on far corner of Plaça Bonsucces at Carrer Elisabets 2, tel. 933-175-826, run by Pilar).

Café Granja Viader is a quaint time warp, family-run since 1870. They boast to be the first dairy business to bottle and distribute milk in Spain. This feminine place—specializing in baked and dairy delights, toasted sandwiches, and light meals—is ideal for a traditional breakfast (note the "Esmorzars" specials posted). Try a glass of *orxata* (*horchata*—almond milk, summer only), *llet mallorquina* (Majorca-style milk with cinnamon, lemon, and sugar), *crema catalana* (crème brûlée, their specialty) or *suis* (literally, "Switzerland"—hot chocolate with a snowcap of whipped cream). Mentioned on the Ramblas walk on page 1193, it's a block off the boulevard behind El Carme church (Mon 17:00–20:45, Tue–Sat 9:00–13:45 & 17:00–20:45, closed Sun, Xucla 4, tel. 933-183-486).

Try eating at **La Boquería market** at least once. Locals fill the market's bars, munching at the counter. The best—and worth the wait—is **Kiosko Universal** (€9 *menus* with different fresh-fish options, better before 12:30 but always packed, tel. 933-178-286). As you enter market from the Ramblas, it's all the way to the left on the first alley—if you see people waiting, ask who's the last in line *("El último?")*. **La Gardunya,** located at the back of La Boquería market, offers tasty meat and seafood meals made with

Barcelona's Gothic Quarter Restaurants

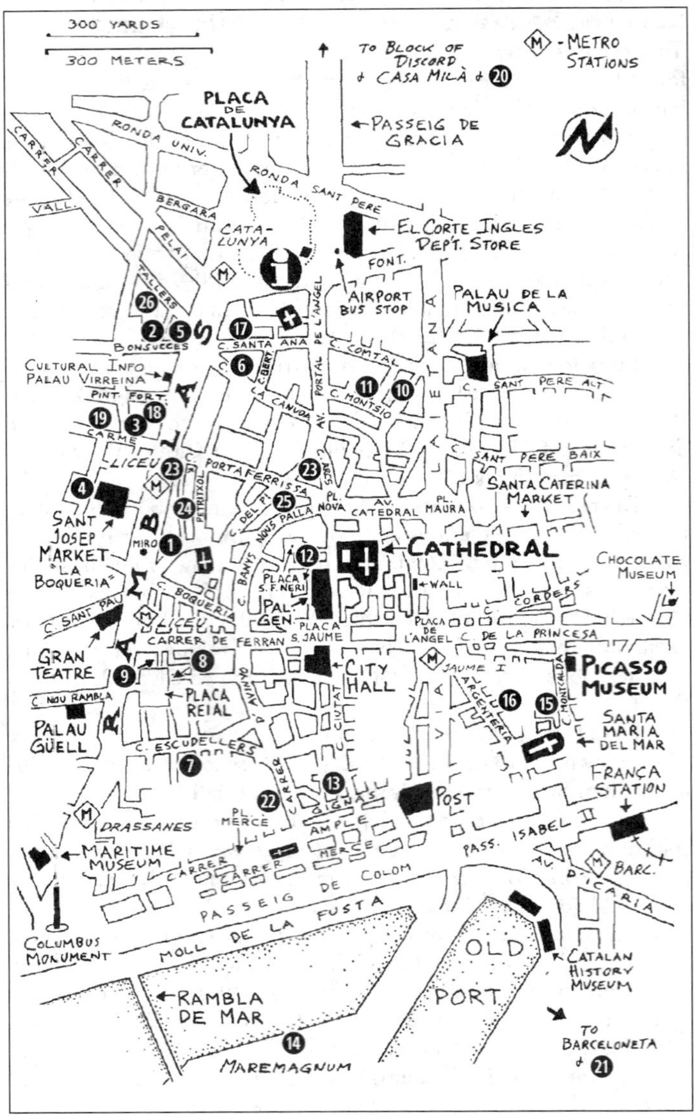

1 Taverna Basca Irati & Juicy Jones	14 Tapasbar Maremagnum
2 Restaurant Elisabets	15 El Xampanyet Tapas Bar
3 Café Granja Viader	16 Celestial Restaurant
4 La Gardunya	17 Self Naturista Veggie Buffet
5 La Poma Rest. & Champion Supermarket	18 Bio Center Veggie Café
6 The Bagel Shop	19 Fresc Co Veggie Cafeteria
7 La Fonda	20 To La Bodegueta, Hostal de Rita & Quasi Queviures
8 Les Quinze Nits	21 To Cova Fumada & Bar Electricitat
9 La Crema Canela	22 Carrer Merce tapas bars
10 La Dolca Herminia	23 Casa Colomina Sweet Shops (2)
11 Els Quatre Gats	24 La Pallaresa Granja-Xocolateria
12 El Pintor Restaurante	25 Fargas Chocolate Shop
13 Restaurante Agut	26 Ganpatti

fresh ingredients bought directly from the market (€9.50 lunch *menus* include wine and bread, €13.50 dinner *menus* don't include wine, Mon–Sat 13:00–16:00 & 20:00–24:00, closed Sun, Carrer Jerusalem 18, tel. 933-024-323).

Tired tourists like **La Poma** for a good pizza, pasta, and salads in a bright modern setting at the top of the Ramblas with comfortable views of all the street action (daily 9:00–24:00, Ramblas 117, tel. 933-019-400).

Homesick tourists flock to **The Bagel Shop** for fresh bagels and brownies (Mon–Sat 9:30–21:30, Sun 11:00–16:00, Carrer Canuda 25, tel. 933-024-161).

Shoestring tourists buy **groceries** at El Corte Inglés (Mon–Sat 10:00–22:00, closed Sun, supermarket in basement, Plaça de Catalunya) and Champion Supermarket (Mon–Sat 9:00–22:00, closed Sun, Ramblas 113).

Dining in the Gothic Quarter

A chain of five bright, modern restaurants with traditional cuisine in classy bistro settings with great prices has stormed Barcelona. Because of their three-course €7.30 lunches and €15–20 dinners (both with wine), all are crowded with locals and tourists in the know. They take no reservations and are marked by long lines at the door. Arrive 30 minutes before opening or be prepared to wait. The first three are within a block of the Plaça Reial, the fourth is near the Catalan Concert Hall, and the fifth **(Hostal de Rita)** is described in the Eixample section below: **La Fonda** (daily 13:00–15:30 & 20:30–23:30, a block from Plaça Reial at Escudellers 10, tel. 933-017-515); **Les Quinze Nits** (daily 13:00–15:45 & 20:30–23:30, on

Plaça Reial at #6—you'll see the line, tel. 933-173-075); **La Crema Canela** (feels cozier than the others in this chain, daily 13:30–15:45 & 20:00–23:30, Ptge. Madoz 6, 30 yards north of Plaça Reial, tel. 933-182-744); and **La Dolça Herminia** (2 blocks toward Ramblas from Catalan Concert Hall at Magdalenes 27, tel. 933-170-676).

Els Quatre Gats, Picasso's hangout (and the place he first showed off his paintings), still has a bohemian feel in spite of its tourist crowds. Before the place was founded in 1897, the idea of a café for artists was mocked as a place where only *quatre gats*—"four cats," meaning "crazies"—would go (€10 3-course lunch, daily 8:30–24:00, live piano from 21:00, Montsio 3, tel. 933-024-140).

El Pintor Restaurante serves perhaps the best €30 dinner in town. Under medieval arches and rough brick, with candles and friendly service, you'll enjoy Catalan and Mediterranean cuisine (daily 13:30–16:30 & 20:00–24:00, from Plaça de Sant Jaume walk north on Carrer Sant Honorat to #7, reserve for evening, tel. 933-014-065).

Restaurante Agut, buried deep in the Gothic Quarter four blocks off the harbor, is a fine place with an enticing menu (in English) for local-style food in a local-style setting. It's almost dressy, with white tablecloths and candles (Tue–Sun 13:30–16:00 & 21:00–24:00, closed Mon and Aug, reservations smart for dinner, Carrer Gignas 16, tel. 933-151-709).

At the intersection of **Carrer de Banys Nous** and **Carrer de la Palla,** several places offer great coffee, local cheeses, ham, sausage, and *cava* (sparkling wine).

Out at Sea—Maremagnum

Tapasbar Maremagnum is a big, rollicking, sports-bar kind of tapas restaurant, great for large groups. It's a fun way to end your Ramblas walk, a 10-minute stroll past the Columbus Monument straight out the dock, with breezy harbor views and good local food with emphasis on the sea (daily 11:00–24:00, Moll d'Espanya, tel. 932-258-180).

Near the Picasso Museum

El Xampanyet, a fun and characteristic bar, specializes in tapas and anchovies. A *sortido* (assorted plate) of *carne* (meat) or *pescado* (fish) costs about €6 with *pa amb tomaquet* (pah ahm too-MAH-kaht), bread topped with a mix of crushed tomato and olive oil (Mon–Sat 12:00–15:30 & 19:00–24:00, closed Sun, half a block beyond Picasso Museum at Montcada 22, tel. 933-197-003).

Celestial, close to Santa María church, is an easy option with a lunch and dinner buffet (lunch-€7.60, dinner-€9.65, weekends-€11.60, daily 12:30–16:00 & 20:00–24:00, Argentaria 53, tel. 933-104-294).

Vegetarian Places near Plaça de Catalunya and off the Ramblas

Self Naturista is a quick, no-stress buffet that makes vegetarians and health-food lovers feel right at home. Others may find a few unidentifiable plates and drinks. The food seems tired—pick what you like and microwave it—but the place is very handy (Mon–Sat 11:30–22:00, closed Sun, near several recommended hotels, just off the top of Ramblas at Carrer de Santa Ana 11–17).

Bio Center, a Catalan soup-and-salad place popular with local vegetarians, is better but not as handy (€7.75 lunches, Mon–Sat 13:00–17:00, closed Sun, Pintor Fortuny 25, Metro: Catalunya, tel. 933-014-583). This street has several other good vegetarian places.

Fresc Co is a healthy and hearty buffet in a sleek and efficient cafeteria. For one cheap price (€7 for lunch, €9.70 for dinner and on weekends), you get a drink and all the salad, pasta, soup, pizza, and dessert you want. Choose from two locations: west of Plaça de Catalunya at Ronda Universitat 29, or a block off the Ramblas (near La Boquería market) at Carme 16 (daily 12:45–24:00, tel. 914-474-388).

Juicy Jones is a juice bar with a modern, fun veggie restaurant in back (just off the Ramblas at midpoint, described above).

Ganpatti welcomes those who miss their local organic co-op. Run by Natalia and Alex, this environmentally friendly, fair-commerce place dishes up veggie moussaka, basmati rice, good desserts, and more (Tue–Sat 12:00–21:00, Thu–Sat until 24:00, near the top of the Ramblas at Tallers 29, tel. 933-022-501, SE).

In the Eixample

The people-packed boulevards of the Eixample (Passeig de Gràcia and Rambla Catalunya) are lined with appetizing places with breezy outdoor seating. Many trendy and touristic tapas bars offer a cheery welcome and slam out the appetizers.

La Bodegueta is an unbelievably atmospheric below-street-level bodega serving hearty wines, homemade vermouth, *anchoas* (anchovies), tapas, and *flautas*—sandwiches made with flute-thin baguettes. Its daily €8.50 lunch special (3 courses with wine) is served from 13:00 to 16:00 (Mon–Sat 8:00–24:00, Sun 19:00–24:00, Rambla Catalunya 100, at intersection with Provenza, Metro: Diagonal, tel. 932-154-894). A long block from Gaudí's Casa Milà, this makes a fine sightseeing break.

Hostal de Rita is a fresh and dressy little place serving Catalan cuisine near the Block of Discord. Their lunches (3 courses with wine-€7, Mon–Fri from 13:00) and dinners (€15, à la carte, daily from 20:30) are a great value (a block from the Passeig de Gràcia Metro stop, near corner of Carrer de Pau Claris and Carrer Arago at Arago 279, tel. 934-872-376). Like its four sister restaurants described above, its prices attract long lines, so arrive just before the doors open...or wait.

Quasi Queviures serves upscale tapas, sandwiches, or the whole nine yards—classic food served fast from a fun menu with modern decor and a sports-bar ambience (daily 7:00–24:00, between Gran Vía and Vía Diputació at Passeig de Gràcia 24, tel. 933-174-512).

Sandwich Shops

Bright, clean, and inexpensive sandwich shops are proudly holding the cultural line against the fast-food invasion hamburgerizing the rest of Europe. You'll find great sandwiches at **Pans & Company** and **Bocatta,** two chains with outlets all over town. Catalan sandwiches are made to order with crunchy French bread. Rather than butter, locals prefer *pa amb tomaquet*—tomato sauce on bread. Study the instructive multilingual menu fliers to understand your options.

Near the Harbor in Barceloneta

Barceloneta is a charming beach suburb of the big city with a village ambience. A grid plan of long, narrow, laundry-strewn streets surrounds the central Plaça Poeta Boscan. For an entertaining evening, wander around the perimeter of this slice-of-life square. Plenty of bakeries, pastry shops, and tapas bars ring a colorful covered produce market. Drop by the two places listed here or find your own restaurant (an unpleasant 15-min walk from the Columbus Monument, Metro: Barceloneta, or taxi). During the day, a lively produce market fills one end of the square. At night, kids play soccer and Ping-Pong.

Cova Fumada, with unmarked wooden doors at #56, is the neighborhood eatery. Josep María and his family serve famously fresh fish (Mon–Fri 9:00–15:00 & 18:30–20:30, closed Sat–Sun and Aug, Carrer del Baluarte 56, on corner at Carrer Sant Carles, tel. 932-214-061). Their *sardinas a la plancha* (grilled sardines-€3) are fresh and tasty. *Calamar a la plancha* (sautéed whole calamari-€4.50) and *bombas* (potato croquets with pork-€1.10) are the house specialty. It's macho to eat your *bombas picante* (spicy with chili sauce); gentler taste buds prefer it *alioli* (with garlic cream). Catalan *bruschetta* is *pa amb tomaquet* (tomato-ey bread, €1). Wash it down with *vino tinto* (house red wine, €0.60).

At **Bar Electricitat,** Lozano is the neighborhood source for cheap wine. Drop in. It's €1.05 per liter; the empty plastic water bottles are for take-away. Try a €0.70 glass of Torroja Tinto, the best local red; Priorato Dulce, a wonderfully sweet red; or the homemade candy-in-heaven vermouth. Owner Agapito can fix a plate of sheep cheese and almonds for €3.50 (Tue–Sun 8:00–15:00 & 18:00–21:00, closed Mon, across square from Cova Fumada,

Plaça del Poeta Boscà 61, tel. 932-215-017, NSE).

The Olympic Port, a swank marina district, is lined with harborside restaurants and people enjoying what locals claim is the freshest fish in town (a short taxi ride past Barceloneta from the center).

Tapas on Carrer Mercè in the Gothic Quarter

Tapas aren't as popular in Catalunya as they are in the rest of Spain, but Barcelona boasts great *tascas*—colorful local tapas bars. Get small plates (for maximum sampling) by asking for "*tapas,*" not the bigger "*raciones.*" Glasses of *vino tinto* go for about €0.50.

While trendy uptown places are safer, better lit, and come with English menus and less grease, these places will stain your journal.

From the bottom of the Ramblas (near the Columbus Monument), hike east along Carrer Clave. Then follow the small street that runs along the right side of the church (Carrer Mercè), stopping at the *tascas* that look fun. For restaurant dining in the area, Restaurante Agut (described above) comes with tablecloths and polite service. But for a montage of edible memories, wander Carrer Mercè west to east and consider these places, stopping wherever looks most inviting:

La Pulpería serves up fried fish, octopus, and *patatas bravas,* all with Galician Ribeiro wine. A block down the street, at **Casa del Molinero,** you can sauté your chorizo *al diablo* (sausage from hell). It's great with the regional specialty, *pa amb tomaquet* (tomato bread). Across the street, **La Plata** keeps things wonderfully simple, serving extremely cheap plates of sardines (€1.25), little salads (€1.10), and small glasses of keg wine (€0.50). **Tasca el Corral** serves mountain favorites from northern Spain, such as *queso de cabrales* (very moldy cheese) and chorizo (spicy sausage) with *sidra* (apple wine sold by the €4 bottle). **Sidrería Tasca La Socarrena** (at #21), is the only place that serves hard cider by the glass. At the end of Carrer Mercè, **Bar Vendimia** serves up tasty clams and mussels (hearty *raciones* for €3 a plate—they don't do smaller portions, so order sparingly). Their *pulpo* (octopus) is more expensive and is the house specialty. Carrer Ample and Carrer Gignas, the streets parallel to Carrer Mercè inland, have more refined barhopping possibilities.

A Short, Sweet Walk

To sample three Barcelona sweets, follow this quick walk. Start at the corner of Carrer Portaferrissa midway down the Ramblas. For the best atmosphere, begin your walk at about 18:00.

Walk down Carrer Portaferrissa to #8. **Casa Colomina,** founded in 1908, sells ice cream and the refreshing *orxata* (almond drink) in summer. In winter they sell homemade *turrón*—a variation of nougat made of almond, honey, and sugar, brought to Spain by the Moors 1,200 years ago. Ask for a sample *(muestra)* of *blando, duro,* and *yema* (soft, hard, and yolk). They sell sizable slabs for €6 (Mon–Sat 10:00–20:30, Sun 12:30–20:30, tel. 933-122-511; in summer you can sample *turrón* at their other shop at nearby Cucurulla 2).

Continue down Carrer Portaferrissa, taking a right at Carrer Petrixol to **La Pallaresa Granja-Xocolatería,** dating from 1800. Older, elegant ladies gather here for the Spanish equivalent of tea time: *chocolate con churros* (€3.30 for 5 *churros*—sweet thick french fries—and a small chocolate, Mon–Sat 9:00–13:00 & 16:00–21:00, Sun 9:00–13:00 & 17:00–21:00, Petritxol 11, tel. 933-022-036).

For your last stop, head for the ornate **Fargas** chocolate shop (daily 9:30–13:30 & 16:00–20:00, a couple blocks farther toward cathedral at Carrer del Pi 16, tel. 933-020-342). Founded in 1827, this is one of the oldest and most traditional chocolate places in Barcelona. Ask if you can see the old chocolate mill *("¿Puedo ver el molino?").*

TRANSPORTATION CONNECTIONS

By Train to: Lisbon (1/day, 17 hrs with change in Madrid, €113), **Madrid** (6/day, 4.5–5.5 hrs, €59, plus 2 night trains, 9 hrs, €33.50–41.50 plus berth cost), **Paris** (1/day, 12 hrs, €127, night train, reservation required), **Sevilla** (3/day, 11 hrs, €49), **Granada** (2/day, 12 hrs, €48), **Málaga** (2/day, 14 hrs, €50), **San Sebastián** (1/day, 8 hrs, plus 1 direct night train, 9 hrs), **Nice** (1/day, 12 hrs, €58, change in Cerbère), **Avignon** (5/day, 6–9 hrs, €38). Train info: tel. 902-240-202.

By Bus to: Madrid (12/day, 8 hrs, half the price of a train ticket, departs from station Barcelona Nord at Metro: Marina). Sarfa buses serve all the coastal resorts (tel. 902-302-025).

By Plane: To avoid 10-hour train trips, check the reasonable flights from Barcelona to Sevilla or Madrid. Iberia (tel. 902-400-500) and Air Europa (tel. 902-401-501 or 932-983-907) offer $80 flights to Madrid. Airport info: tel. 932-983-467.

MADRID

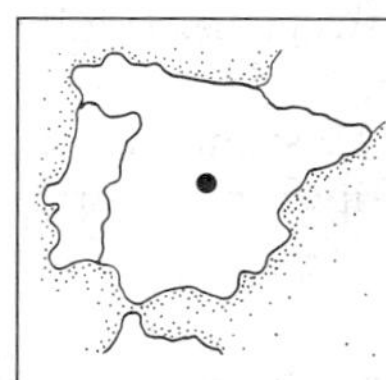

Today's Madrid is upbeat and vibrant, still enjoying a post-Franco renaissance. You'll feel it. Even the living-statue beggars have a twinkle in their eyes.

Madrid is the hub of Spain. This modern capital—Europe's highest, at more than 2,000 feet—has a population of more than four million and is young by European standards. As recently as 1561, King Philip II decided to move the capital of his empire from Toledo to Madrid. One hundred years ago, Madrid had only 400,000 people—so 90 percent of the city is modern sprawl surrounding an intact, easy-to-navigate historic core.

Dive headlong into the grandeur and intimate charm of Madrid. The lavish Royal Palace, with its gilded rooms and frescoed ceilings, rivals Versailles. The Prado has Europe's top collection of paintings. The city's huge Retiro Park invites you for a shady siesta and a hopscotch through a mosaic of lovers, families, skateboarders, pets walking their masters, and expert bench-sitters. Save time for Madrid's elegant shops and people-friendly pedestrian zones.

The city's latest plans include the creation of a pedestrian street crossing the city from the Prado to the Royal Palace (already partly completed) and a new macro-train station in Puerta del Sol (which will keep that subway station under construction until 2008).

By installing posts to keep cars off sidewalks, making the streets safer after dark, and restoring old buildings, Madrid is working hard to make the city more livable...and fun to visit.

On Sundays, cheer for the bull at a bullfight or bargain like mad at a mega-size flea market. Lively Madrid has enough street-singing, bar-hopping, and people-watching vitality to give any visitor a boost of youth.

Planning Your Time

Madrid's top two sights, the Prado and the palace, are each worth a half day. On a Sunday (Easter–Oct), consider allotting extra time for a bullfight. Ideally, give Madrid two days and spend them this way:

Day 1: Breakfast of *churros* (see "Eating," page 1265) before a brisk, 20-minute good-morning-Madrid walk from Puerta del Sol to the Prado (from Puerta del Sol, walk three blocks south to Plaza Ángel, then take the pedestrian walkway to the Prado along Huertas street); spend the rest of the morning at the Prado; take an afternoon siesta in Retiro Park, or tackle modern art at Centro Arte de Reina Sofía *(Guernica)* and/or Thyssen-Bornemisza Museum; dinner at 20:00, with tapas around Plaza Santa Ana.

Day 2: Follow this chapter's "Puerta del Sol to Royal Palace Walk"; tour the Royal Palace, lunch near Plaza Mayor; afternoon free for other sights, shopping, or side trip to El Escorial (open until 19:00). Be out at the magic hour—before sunset—when beautifully lit people fill Madrid.

Note that the Prado, Thyssen-Bornemisza Museum, and El Escorial all close on Monday. For a good day trip from Madrid, visit Toledo (see next chapter).

ORIENTATION

The Puerta del Sol marks the center of Madrid. The Royal Palace (to the west) and the Prado Museum and Retiro Park (to the east) frame Madrid's historic center. Southwest of Puerta del Sol is a 17th-century district with the slow-down-and-smell-the-cobbles Plaza Mayor and memories of pre-industrial Spain. North of Puerta del Sol runs Gran Vía, and between the two are lively pedestrian shopping streets. Gran Vía, bubbling with expensive shops and cinemas, leads to the modern Plaza de España. North of Gran Vía is the gritty Malasaña quarter (sleazy-looking *hombres*).

The historic center can be covered on foot. No major sight is more than a 20-minute walk or a €3.50 taxi ride from Puerta del Sol, Madrid's central square. Divide your time between the city's top three attractions: the Royal Palace, the Prado, and its bar-hopping contemporary scene.

Tourist Information

Madrid has five TIs: **Plaza Mayor** at #3 (it may move to the opposite side, Mon–Sat 10:00–20:00, Sun 10:00–15:00, tel. 915-881-636); **near the Prado Museum** (Mon–Sat 9:00–19:00, Sun 9:00–15:00, Duque de Medinaceli 2, behind Palace Hotel, tel. 914-293-705); **Chamartín** train station (Mon–Sat 8:00–20:00, Sun 8:00–15:00, tel. 913-159-976); **Atocha** train station (daily 9:00–21:00); and at the **airport** (daily 8:00–20:00, tel. 913-058-656). During the summer, small temporary stands with yellow umbrellas pop up at touristed places such as Puerta del Sol, and their yellow-shirted student guides are happy to help out lost tourists.

The general tourist information number is 915-881-636 (or pricier toll call—902-100-007, www.munimadrid.es).

At any TI, pick up a map and confirm your sightseeing plans. Only the most hyperactive travelers could save money buying the TIs' **Madrid Card,** which covers 40 museums, unlimited public transportation, and the Madrid Vision bus tour mentioned in "Tours" below (€28/1 day, €42/2 days, €55/3 days). The free bus map has the most detailed map of the center. Get the three-part brochure on taxi, bus, and Metro costs. TIs have the latest on bullfights and zarzuela, the local light opera.

For entertainment listings, the TI's free *En Madrid/What's On* is not as good as the easy-to-decipher Spanish-language weekly entertainment guide *Guía del Ocio* (€1, sold at newsstands), which lists events, restaurants, and movies ("v.o." means a movie is in its original language, rather than dubbed).

Arrival in Madrid

By Train: Madrid's two train stations, Chamartín and Atocha, are both on subway lines with easy access to downtown Madrid. Each station has all the services. Chamartín handles most international trains. Atocha generally covers southern Spain including the AVE trains to Sevilla. Both stations offer long-distance trains *(largo recorrido)* as well as smaller, local trains (*regionales* and *cercanías*) to nearby destinations. To travel between Chamartín and Atocha, don't bother with the subway (which involves a transfer)—the *cercanías* trains are faster (6/hr, 12 min, €1.20, free with railpass, show it at ticket window in the middle of the turnstiles, departs from Atocha's track 2 and generally Chamartín's track 2 or 3—but check the *Salidas Inmediatas* board to be sure).

At the **Chamartín Station,** the TI is opposite track 19. The impressively large Centro de Viajes/Travel Center customer-service office is in the middle of the building. You can relax in the Sala VIP Club if you have a first-class railpass and first-class seat or sleeper reservations (near track 12, next to Centro de Viajes). The *cercanías* platforms cluster around track 5. The station's Metro stop is Chamartín. (If you arrive by Metro at Chamartín, follow signs to *Información* to get to the lobby rather than signs to *Vías,* which send you directly to the platforms.)

The **Atocha Station** is split into two halves—it's easiest to think of the station as having an AVE side (mostly long-distance trains) and a *cercanías* side (mostly local trains), connected by a corridor of shops. Each side of the station has separate schedules

Greater Madrid

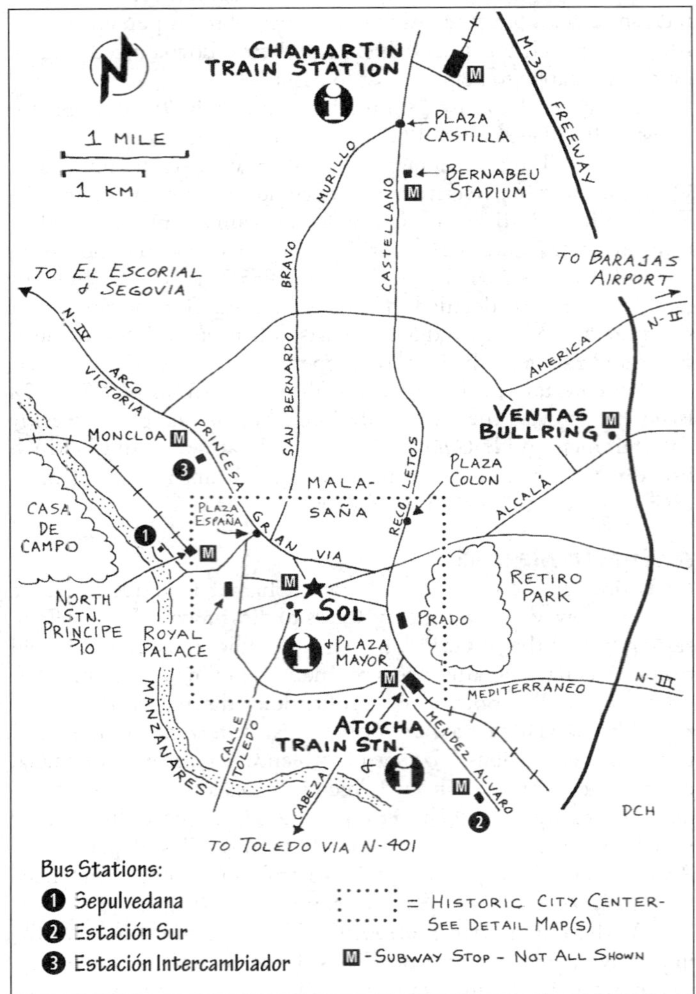

and customer-service offices; this can be confusing if you're in the wrong end of the building. The **TI,** located in the AVE side, handles tourist info only—not train info (daily 9:00–21:00, near the interior botanical garden).

Atocha's AVE side, which is in the towering old-station building, has the slick AVE trains, other fast trains, a pharmacy (daily 8:00–23:00), a cafeteria, and the good Samarcanda restaurant (Mon–Fri 13:00–20:00, Sat–Sun 11:00–20:00).

On the AVE side, the long-distance trains—AVE and Grandes Líneas (grand lines)—depart from the upper floor only. For information on these, try the *Información* counter (daily 6:30–23:30), next to Centro Servicios AVE (this office handles only AVE changes and problems). Both offices are opposite the *Atención al Cliente* office, which deals with problems on Grandes Líneas (daily 6:30–23:30). Also on the AVE side is Atocha's Club AVE, a lounge reserved solely for AVE business-class travelers and for first-class ticket-holders or Eurailers with a first-class reservation (upstairs, past the security check on right, free drinks, newspapers, showers, and info service).

On the *cercanías* side of Atocha Station, you'll find the local *cercanías* trains, *regionales* trains, some eastbound faster trains, and the Metro stop named "Atocha RENFE." (Note that the stop named simply "Atocha" is a different Metro stop in Madrid—not at the train station.) The *Atención al Cliente* office in the *cercanías* section has information only on trains for destinations bordering Madrid.

To buy tickets at Atocha for the local *cercanías* trains (for example, to Toledo), go to the middle of the *cercanías* side and get your ticket from ticket windows in the small rectangular offices (marked *Venta de Billetes sin reserva*). You can buy AVE and other long-distance train tickets in the bigger ticket offices in either half of the building; the airier *Taquillas* office on the AVE side is more pleasant. Since station ticket offices can get really crowded, it's often quicker to buy your ticket at an English-speaking travel agency, such as the El Corte Inglés Travel Agency at Atocha (Mon–Fri 7:00–22:00, weekends only for urgent arrangements, on ground floor of AVE side at the far end) or at the branch within the El Corte Inglés department store at Puerta del Sol (see "Helpful Hints," below). You could also try the downtown RENFE office, which offers train information, reservations, tickets, and minimal English (Mon–Fri 9:30–20:00, closed Sat–Sun, accepts credit cards, go in person, 2 blocks north of the Prado at Calle Alcalá 44, tel. 902-240-202, www.renfe.es). For train travel to points onward, see "Transportation Connections," at the end of this chapter.

By Bus: Madrid's three key bus stations, all connected by Metro, are Sepulvedana (for Segovia, Metro: Príncipe Pío, garage next to Florida Norte Hotel), Estación Sur Autobuses (for Toledo, Ávila, and Granada, on top of Metro: Méndez Álvaro, cash machines, TI open during summer, fast food for sale, tel. 914-684-200), and Estación Intercambiador (for El Escorial, in Metro: Moncloa). For details, see "Transportation Connections" at the end of this chapter.

By Plane: For information on Madrid's Barajas Airport, see "Transportation Connections" page 1267.

Getting Around Madrid

By Subway: Madrid's subway is simple, speedy, and cheap (€1.15/ride, runs from 6:00 to 1:30 in the morning, www.metromadrid.es or www.ctm-madrid.es). The 10-ride Metrobus ticket can be shared by several travelers and works on both the Metro and buses (€5.35, sold at kiosks, tobacco shops, and in Metro). The city's broad streets can be hot and exhausting. A subway trip of even a stop or two saves time and energy. Most stations offer free maps *(navegamadrid)*—navigate by subway stops (shown on city maps). To transfer, follow signs to the next subway line (numbered and color-coded). The names of the end stops are used to indicate directions. Insert your ticket in the turnstile, then retrieve it as you pass through. Green *Salida* signs point to the exit. Using neighborhood maps and street signs to exit smartly can save lots of walking.

By Bus: City buses, while not as easy as the Metro, can be useful (bus maps at TI or info booth on Puerta del Sol, €1.15 tickets sold on bus, or €5.35 for a 10-ride Metrobus ticket—see "By Subway," above; buses run 6:00–24:00). For an easy hop-on, hop-off bus tour, see "Tours," below.

By Taxi: Madrid's 15,000 taxis are reasonably priced and easy to hail (€1.55 drop, €0.70 *Tarifa 1* rates per kilometer on weekdays, €0.88 *Tarifa 2* rates on weekday nights and weekends, more outside of Madrid, €4.20 supplement for airport, €2.20 supplement for train/bus stations, €13.30/hour waiting). If your cabbie uses anything rather than *Tarifa 1* (shown as an isolated "1" on the meter) during Mon–Fri 6:00–22:00, you're being cheated. Threesomes travel as cheaply by taxi as by subway. A ride from the Royal Palace to the Prado costs about €3.50.

Helpful Hints

Theft Alert: Be wary of pickpockets, anywhere, anytime, but particularly on Puerta del Sol (main square), the subway, and crowded streets. Assume a fight or any commotion is a scam to distract people about to become victims of a pickpocket. Wear your money belt. The small streets north of Gran Vía are particularly dangerous, even before nightfall. Muggings occur, but are rare. Victims of theft can call 902-102-112 for help (English spoken, once you get connected to a person).

Embassies: The U.S. Embassy is at Serrano 75 (tel. 915-872-200); the Canadian Embassy is at Nuñez de Balboa 35 (tel. 914-233-250).

Travel Agencies and Free Maps: The grand department store, El Corte Inglés, has two travel agencies (on first and seventh floors, Mon–Sat 10:00–22:00, just off Puerta del Sol) and gives out free Madrid maps (at information desk, immediately inside door, just off Puerta del Sol at intersection of Preciados and Tetuán; has post office and supermarket in basement). El

Madrid

Corte Inglés is taking over the entire intersection; the main store is the tallest building, with the biggest sign.

American Express: The AmEx office at Plaza Cortes 2 sells train and plane tickets, and even accepts Visa and MasterCard (Mon–Fri 9:00–19:30, Sat 9:00–14:00, closed Sun, 2 blocks from Metro: Banco de España, opposite Palace Hotel, tel. 913-225-445).

Books: For books in English, try **Fnac Callao** (Calle Preciados 8, tel. 915-956-190), **Casa del Libro** (English on ground floor in back, Gran Vía 29, tel. 915-212-219), and **El Corte Inglés** (guidebooks and some fiction, in its Librería branch kitty-corner from main store, see listing within "Travel Agencies and Free Maps," above).

Laundry: The impeccable **Onda Blue** will wash, dry, and fold your laundry for €8 plus soap (daily 9:00–22:30, self-service available, change machine, 4 Internet terminals, León 3, south of Plaza Santa Ana, tel. 913-695-071). The mostly self-service **Lavamatique,** across the street and half a block up, is a less attractive option—older, fewer machines, no Internet—but it'll do in a pinch (full-service Mon–Fri 9:00–14:00, self-service Mon–Sat 9:00–20:00, closed Sun, León 6).

Internet Access: The popular **easyInternetcafé** offers 250 fast, cheap terminals at Calle de la Montera, a block above Puerta del Sol and a block below piles of tattoo shops and prostitutes (daily 8:00–24:00). **NavegaWeb,** centrally located at Gran Vía 30, is also good (daily 9:00–24:00). **Zahara**'s Internet café is at the corner of Gran Vía and Mesoneros (Mon–Fri 9:00–24:00, Sat–Sun 9:00–24:00).

TOURS

Madrid Vision Hop-On, Hop-Off Bus Tours—Madrid Vision offers three different hop-on, hop-off circuits of the city (historic, modern, and monuments). Buy a ticket (€10.60/1 day, €13.60/2 days) and you can hop from sight to sight and route to route as you like, listening to a recorded English commentary along the way. Each route has about 15 stops and takes about 90 minutes, with buses departing every 10 or 15 minutes. The three routes intersect at the south side of Puerta del Sol (daily 10:00–21:00, shorter in winter, tel. 917-791-888).

Walking Tours—British expatriate Stephen Drake-Jones gives entertaining, informative walks of historic old Madrid almost nightly (along with more specialized walks, such as Hemingway, Civil War, and Bloody Madrid). A historian with a passion for the memory of the Duke of Wellington (the man who stopped Napoleon), Stephen is the founder and chairman of the Wellington Society. For €25, you become a member of the society for one year and get a free two-hour tour that includes stops at two bars for local drinks and tapas. Eccentric Stephen takes you back in time to sort out Madrid's Hapsburg and Bourbon history. Chairman Stephen likes his wine. If that's a problem, skip the tour. Tours start at the statue on Puerta del Sol (maximum 10 people, tel. 609-143-203 to confirm tour and reserve a spot, www.wellsoc.org, chairman@wellsoc.org). Members of the Wellington Society can take advantage of Stephen's helpline (if you're in a Spanish jam, call him to translate and intervene) and assistance by e-mail (for questions on Spain, your itinerary, and so on). Stephen also does private tours and day trips to great spots in the countryside for small groups (about €350 per group per day, explained on his Web site).

LeTango Tourist Services—Carlos Galvin, a Spaniard who speaks flawless English (and has led tours for me since 1998), offers private tours when he's in Madrid. If he's out, his American wife, Jennifer, also works as a guide. Carlos mixes a city drive (for the big Madrid picture) with a historic walk (to get intimate with the old center and its ways). This gives a fine three-hour orientation and introduction to Madrid (€79 for individuals and groups up to 3...4 if you'll squeeze). Carlos and Jennifer can also arrange longer tours of both the city and the region (tel. 914-293-790, mobile 661-752-458, www.letango.com, info@letango.com).

Typical Big Bus City Sightseeing Tours—Juliatours offers standard, inexpensive guided bus tours departing from Gran Vía 68 (no reservations required—just show up 15 min before departure, tel. 915-599-605). Consider these tours: a three-hour city tour (€19, daily at 9:45 and 15:00); Madrid by Night (€12.50, a 2-hour floodlit overview, nightly at 20:30); Valley of the Fallen and El Escorial (€43, makes the day trip easy, covering both sights adequately with commentary en route, Tue–Sun at 8:45 and 15:00); and a marathon tour of El Escorial, Valley of the Fallen, and Toledo (€87, Tue–Sun at 8:30). If you want to pick up a rental car in Toledo, you could take this tour, stow your luggage under the bus, and then leave the tour at Toledo.

Introductory Walk: From Madrid's Puerta del Sol to the Royal Palace

Connect the sights with the following walking tour. Allow an hour for this half-mile walk, not including your palace visit.

▲▲Puerta del Sol—Named for a long-gone medieval gate with the sun carved onto it, Puerta del Sol is ground zero for Madrid. It's a hub for the Metro, buses, political demonstrations, and pickpockets.

Stand by the statue of King Charles III and survey the square. Because of his enlightened urban policies, Charles III (who ruled until 1788) is affectionately called the "best mayor of Madrid." He decorated the city squares with fine fountains, got those meddlesome Jesuits out of city government, established the public school system, made the Retiro a public park rather than a royal retreat, and generally cleaned up Madrid.

Look behind the king. The statue of the bear pawing the strawberry bush and the madroño trees in the big planter boxes are symbols of the city. Bears used to live in the royal hunting grounds outside Madrid. And the madroño trees produce a berry that makes the traditional *madroño* liqueur.

The king faces a red-and-white building with a bell tower. This was Madrid's first post office, established by Charles III in the 1760s. Today it's the governor's office, though it's notorious for having been Franco's police headquarters. An amazing number of those detained and interrogated by the Franco police "tried to escape" by jumping out the windows to their deaths. Notice the hats of the civil guardsmen at the entry. It's said the hats have square backsides so the men can lean against the wall while enjoying a cigarette.

Crowds fill the square on New Year's Eve as the rest of Madrid

Madrid at a Glance

▲▲▲**Prado Museum** One of the world's great museums, loaded with masterpieces by Diego Velázquez, Francisco Goya, El Greco, and Hieronymus Bosch. **Hours:** Tue–Sun 9:00–19:00, closed Mon.

▲▲▲**Bullfight** Spain's controversial pastime. **Hours:** Sundays and holidays March–mid-Oct, plus daily May–mid-June.

▲▲**Thyssen-Bornemisza Museum** A great complement to the Prado, with lesser-known yet still impressive works (especially good Impressionist collection). **Hours:** Tue–Sun 10:00–19:00, closed Mon.

▲▲**Centro Arte de Reina Sofía** Modern-art museum featuring Picasso's epic masterpiece *Guernica.* **Hours:** Mon and Wed–Sat 10:00–21:00, Sun 10:00–14:30, closed Tue.

▲▲**Royal Palace** Spain's sumptuous national palace, lavishly furnished. **Hours:** April–Sept Mon–Sat 9:00–19:00, Sun 9:00–16:00; Oct–March Mon–Sat 9:30–18:00, Sun 9:00–15:00.

▲▲**Zarzuela** Madrid's delightful light opera. **Hours:** Evenings.

▲**Retiro Park** Festive green escape from the city, with rental rowboats and great people-watching. **Hours:** Always open.

watches the action on TV. As Spain's "Big Ben" atop the governor's office chimes 12 times, Madrileños eat one grape for each ring to bring good luck through the coming year.

Cross Calle Mayor. Look at the curb directly in front of the entrance of the governor's office. The scuffed-up marker is "kilometer zero," marking the center of Spain. To the right of the entrance, the plaque on the wall marks the spot where the war against Napoleon started. Napoleon wanted his brother to be king of Spain. Trying to finagle this, he brought nearly the entire Spanish royal family to France for negotiations. An anxious crowd gathered outside this building awaiting word of the fate of their royal family. This was just after the French Revolution, and there was a general nervousness between France and Spain. When locals heard that Napoleon had appointed his brother as the new king of Spain, they gathered angrily in the streets. The French guard simply massacred the mob. Goya, who worked just up the street, observed the event and captured the tragedy in his paintings *2nd of May, 1808* and *3rd of May, 1808*, now in the Prado.

▲El Rastro Europe's biggest flea market. **Hours:** Sun and holidays 9:00–15:00, best before 11:00.

Charles III's Botanical Garden A relaxing museum of plants, with specimens from around the world. **Hours:** Daily 10:00–21:00, until 18:00 in winter.

Naval Museum Seafaring history of a country famous for its Armada. **Hours:** Tue–Sun 10:00–14:00, closed Mon.

Chapel San Antonio de la Florida Church with Goya's tomb, plus frescoes by the artist. **Hours:** Tue–Fri 10:00–14:00 & 16:00–20:00, Sat–Sun 10:00–14:00, closed Mon, July and Aug only 10:00–14:00.

Royal Tapestry Factory Where you can see traditional tapestries being made. **Hours:** Mon–Fri 10:00–14:40, closed Sat–Sun and Aug.

Moncloa Tower Elevator whisks you up to the best view in town. **Hours:** Tue–Fri 10:00–14:00 & 17:00–19:00, Sat–Sun 10:30–18:00, closed Mon.

Teleférico Cable car dangling over Madrid's city park. **Hours:** Daily July–Aug from 11:00, Sept–June from 12:00.

Walking from Puerta del Sol to Plaza Mayor: On the corner of Calle Mayor and Puerta del Sol, across from McDonald's, is the busy *confitería* Salon la Mallorquina (daily 9:00–21:15). Cross Calle Mayor to go inside. The shop is famous for its sweet Napolitana cream-filled pastry (€1) and savory, beef-filled *agujas* pastries (€1.50). See the racks with goodies hot out of the oven. Look back toward the entrance and notice the tile above the door with the 18th-century view of the Puerta del Sol. Compare this with today's view out the door. This was before the square was widened, when a church stood where the *Tío Pepe* sign stands today. The French used this church to detain local patriots awaiting execution. (The venerable *Tío Pepe* sign, advertising a famous sherry for more than 100 years, was Madrid's first billboard.)

Cross busy Calle Mayor (again), round McDonald's, and veer left up the pedestrian alley called Calle de Postas. The street sign shows the post coach heading for that famous first post office. Medieval street signs included pictures so the illiterate could "read" them. Fifty yards up the street, at Calle San Cristóbal, drop into

Heart of Madrid

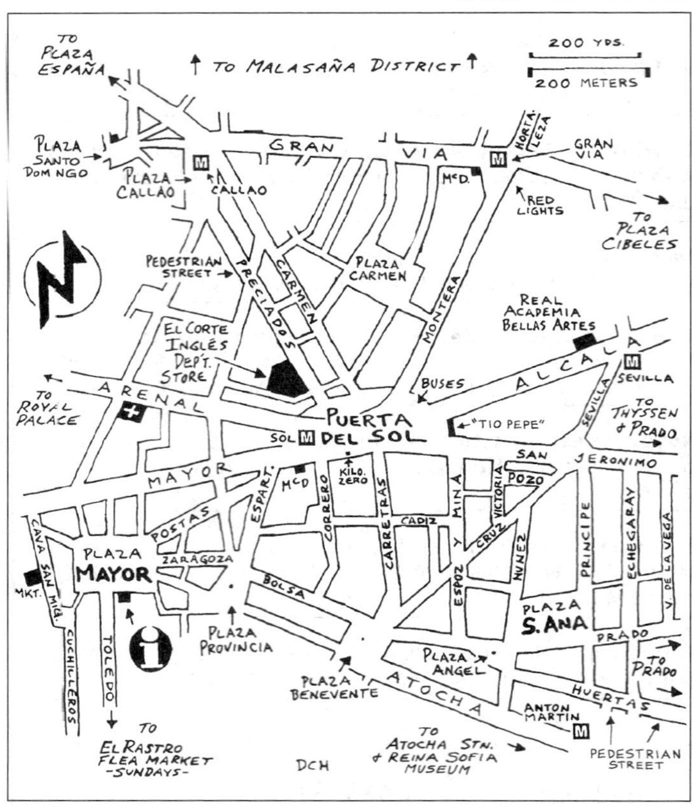

Pans & Company, a popular sandwich chain. Pick up their translated flier illustrating that Spain is a country of four languages: Catalan (spoken in and around Barcelona), Euskera (Basque), Galego (a Portuguese-like language spoken in northwestern Spain—Galicia), and Castilian (what we call Spanish). From here, hike up Calle San Cristóbal. Within two blocks, you'll pass the local feminist bookshop (Librería Mujeres) and reach a small square. At the square, notice the big, brick 17th-century Ministry of Foreign Affairs building (with the pointed spire)—originally a jail for rich prisoners who could afford the cushy cells. Turn right and walk down Calle de Zaragoza under the arcade into...

▲Plaza Mayor—This square, built in 1619, is a vast, cobbled, traffic-free chunk of 17th-century Spain. Each side of the square is uniform, as if a grand palace were turned inside out. The statue is of Philip III, who ordered the square's construction. Upon this stage, much Spanish history was played out: bullfights, fires, royal pageantry, and events of the gruesome Inquisition. Reliefs serving as seatbacks under the lampposts tell the story. During the Inquisition, many were tried here—suspected heretics, Protestants, Jews, and Muslims whose "conversion" to Christianity was dubious. The guilty were paraded around the square (bleachers were built for bigger audiences, while the wealthy rented balconies) with billboards listing their many sins. They were then burned. The fortunate were slowly strangled as they held a crucifix, hearing the reassuring words of a priest as this life was squeezed out of them.

The square is painted a democratic shade of burgundy—the result of a citywide vote. Since Franco's death in 1975, there's been a passion for voting here. Three different colors were painted as samples on the walls of this square, and the city voted for its favorite.

A stamp-and-coin market bustles here on Sundays from 10:00 to 14:00, and on any day it's a colorful and affordable place to enjoy a cup of coffee. Throughout Spain, lesser *plazas mayores* provide peaceful pools in the river of Spanish life. The TI is at #3, on the south side of the square. The building decorated with painted figures, on the north side of the square, is the Casa de la Panadería, which used to house the Bakers' Guild (interior closed to public).

The Torre del Oro Bar Andalu is a good place for a drink to finish off your Plaza Mayor visit (northwest corner of square, to the left of the Bakers' Guild, daily 8:00–15:00 & 18:00–24:00). This bar is a temple to bullfighting. Warning: They push expensive tapas on tourists. A *caña* (small beer) shouldn't cost more than €1.50. The bar's ambience is *Andalu* (Andalusian). Look under the stuffed head of Barbero the bull. At eye level, you'll see a *puntilla,* the knife used to put Barbero out of his misery in the arena.

Notice the breathtaking action captured in the bar's many photographs. At the end of the bar in a glass case is the "suit of lights" the great El Cordobes wore in his ill-fated 1967 fight. With Franco in attendance, El Cordobes—a working-class hero, the Elvis of bullfighters—went on and on, long after he could have ended the fight, until finally the bull gored him. El Cordobes survived; the bull didn't. Find Franco with El Cordobes at the far end, to the left of Segador the bull. Under the bull is a photo of El Cordobes' illegitimate son, El Cordobes, kissing a bull. Disowned by El Cordobes and using his dad's famous name after a court battle, El Cordobes is one of this generation's top fighters.

Walking from Plaza Mayor to the Royal Palace: Leave Plaza Mayor on Calle Ciudad Rodrigo (far right corner from where you entered the square, and to your right as you exit Torre del Oro). You'll pass a series of fine turn-of-the-20th-century storefronts and shops, such as the recommended Casa Rúa, famous for its cheap *bocadillos de calamares*—fried squid-ring sandwiches.

From Plaza Mayor to the Royal Palace

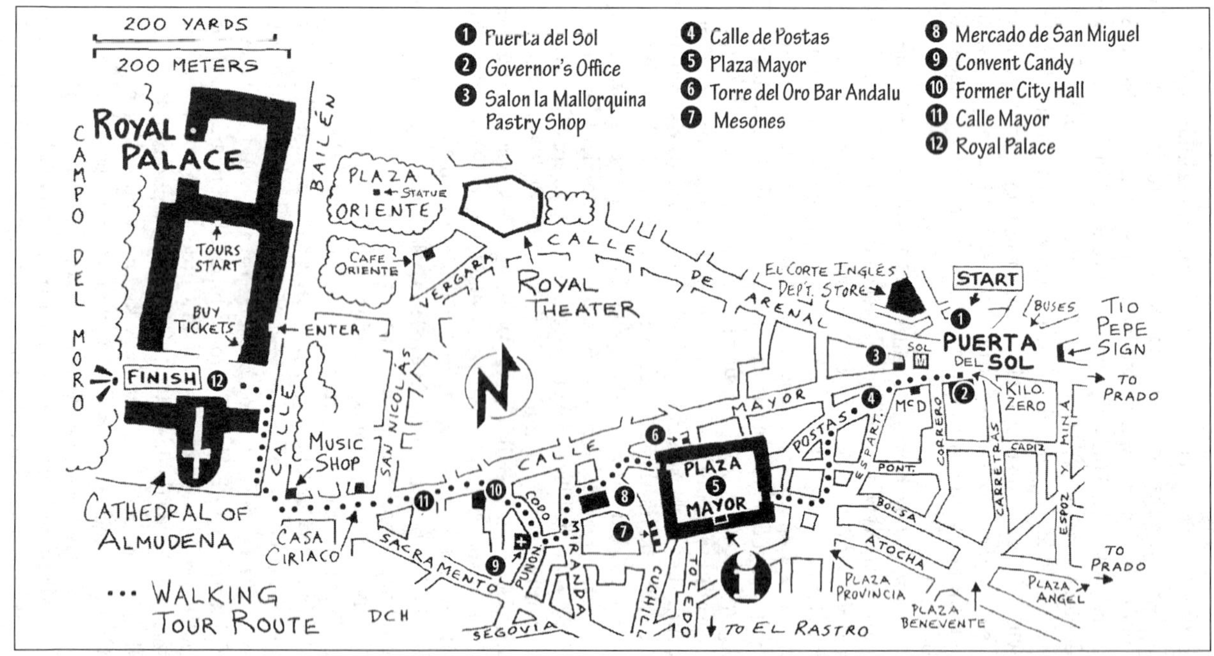

From the archway you'll see the covered Mercado de San Miguel (green iron posts, on left). Before you enter the market, look left down the street Cava de San Miguel. If you like sangria and singing, come back at about 22:00 and visit one of the *mesones* that line the street. These cave-like bars stretch way back and get packed with locals who—emboldened by sangria, the setting, and Spain—might suddenly just start singing. It's a lowbrow, electric-keyboard, karaoke-type ambience, best on Friday and Saturday nights.

Wander through the produce market and consider buying some fruit (Mon–Fri 9:00–14:30 & 17:15–20:15, Sat 9:00–14:30, closed Sun). Leave the market on the opposite (downhill) side and follow the pedestrian lane left. At the first corner, turn right, and cross the small plaza to the modern brick convent. The door on the right says *venta de dulces;* to buy inexpensive sweets from the cloistered nuns, buzz the *monjas* button, then wait patiently for the sister to respond over the intercom. Say "*dulces*" (DOOL-thays) and she'll let you in (Mon–Sat 9:30–13:00 & 16:00–18:30, closed Sun). When the lock buzzes, push open the door and follow the sign to *torno,* the lazy Susan that lets the sisters sell their baked goods without being seen (smallest quantities: half, or *medio,* kilo). Of the many choices (all good), consider *pastas de almendra* (crumbly) or *mantecados de yema* (moist and eggy).

Follow Calle del Codo (where those in need of bits of armor shopped—see the street sign) uphill around the convent to Plaza de la Villa, the square where City Hall was located until 2004 (when it moved to Plaza de Cibeles). The statue in the garden is of Don Bazán—mastermind of the Christian victory over the Muslims at the naval battle of Lepanto in 1571. This pivotal battle, fought off the coast of Greece, ended the Muslim threat to Christian Europe.

From here, busy Calle Mayor leads downhill for a couple more blocks to the Royal Palace. Halfway down (on the left), there's a tiny square opposite the recommended Casa Ciriaco restaurant (#84). The statue memorializes the 1906 anarchist bombing that killed 23 people as the royal couple paraded by on their wedding day. While the crowd was throwing flowers, an anarchist threw a bouquet lashed to a bomb from a balcony of #84 (the building was a hotel at the time). Photos of the event hang just inside the door of the restaurant.

Continue down Calle Mayor. Within a couple of blocks you'll come to a busy street, Calle de Bailen. (The Garrido-Bailen music store is *the* place to stock up on castanets, unusual flutes, and Galician bagpipes.) Across the busy street is the **Cathedral of Almudena,** Madrid's cathedral. Built between 1883 and 1993, its exterior is a contemporary mix and its interior is neo-Gothic, with a colorful ceiling, glittering 5,000-pipe organ, and the 12th-century coffin (empty, painted leather on wood, in a chapel behind the altar) of Madrid's patron saint, Isidro. Isidro, a humble peasant, loved the handicapped and performed miracles. Forty years after he died, this coffin was opened and his body was found unrotted, which convinced the pope to canonize him as the patron saint of Madrid and of farmers, with May 15 as his feast day. Next to the cathedral is the...

▲▲Royal Palace (Palacio Real)—Europe's third-greatest palace (after Versailles and Vienna's Schönbrunn), with arguably the most sumptuous original interior, is packed with tourists and royal antiques. After a fortress burned down on this site, King Phillip V commissioned this huge 18th-century palace as a replacement. Though he ruled Spain for 40 years, Phillip V was very French. (The grandson of Louis XIV, he was born in Versailles, and spoke French most of the time.) He ordered this palace to be built as his own Versailles (although his wife's Italian origin had a tremendous impact in the style). It's big—more than 2,000 rooms, with tons of luxurious tapestries, a king's ransom of chandeliers, priceless porcelain, and bronze decor covered in gold leaf. While these days the royal family lives in a mansion a few miles away, this place still functions as a royal palace and is used for formal state receptions and tourists' daydreams.

Cost, Hours, and Information: €8 without a tour, €9 with a tour, April–Sept Mon–Sat 9:00–19:00, Sun 9:00–16:00; Oct–March Mon–Sat 9:30–18:00, Sun 9:00–15:00, last tickets sold one hour before closing, palace can close without warning if needed for a royal function (you can call a day ahead to check, tel. 915-475-350). The palace is most crowded on Wednesdays, when it's free for locals. Metro: Opera. (Notice the beer-stein urinals—the rage in Madrid—in the WC just past the ticket booth.)

Touring the Palace: A simple one-floor, 24-room, one-way circuit is open to the public. You can wander on your own or join an English-language tour (check time of next tour and decide as you buy your ticket; tours depart about every 20 min). The tour guides, like the museum guidebook, show a passion for meaningless data. Your ticket includes the armory and the pharmacy, both on the courtyard and worth a quick look. The €2.30 audioguides cover only marginally more of interest than what I describe below (and would never mention beer-stein urinals).

Self-Guided Tour: If you tour the palace on your own, here are a few details beyond what you'll find on the little English descriptions posted in each room:

1. The Palace Lobby: In the old days, horse-drawn carriages would drop you off here. Today, a sign divides the visitors waiting for a tour and those going in alone.

2. The Grand Stairs: Fancy carpets are rolled down (notice the little metal bar-holding hooks) for formal occasions. At the top of the first landing, the blue-and-red coat of arms is of the current—and popular—constitutional monarch, Juan Carlos. While Franco chose him to be his successor, J.C. knew Spain was ripe for democracy. Rather than become "Juan the Brief" (as some were nicknaming him), he turned real power over to the parliament. You'll see his (figure) head on the back of the Spanish euro coin. At the top of the stairs (before entering first room, right of door) is a white marble bust of J.C.'s great-great-g-g-g-great-grandfather Phillip V, who began the Bourbon dynasty in Spain in 1700. That dynasty survives today with Juan Carlos.

3. Guard Room: The guards hung out here. Notice the clocks. Charles IV, a great collector, amassed more than 700—the 150 displayed in this palace are all in working order.

4. Hall of Columns: Originally a ballroom and dining room, today this room is used for formal ceremonies. (For example, this is where Spain formally joined the European Union in 1985—see plaque on far wall.) The tapestries (like most you'll see in the palace) are 17th-century Belgian.

5. Throne Room: Red velvet walls, lions, and frescoes of Spanish scenes symbolize the monarchy in this rococo riot. The chandeliers are the best in the house. The throne is only from 1977. This is where the king's guests salute the king prior to dinner. He receives them relatively informally...standing rather than seated on the throne.

The ceiling fresco (1764), the last great work by Venetian painter Giambattista Tiepolo, celebrates the days of the vast Spanish empire—upon which the sun also never set. Find the Native American (hint: follow the rainbow to the macho, red-caped conquistador). Two rooms later you'll find the...

6. Antechamber: The four paintings are of King Charles IV (looking a bit like a dim-witted George Washington) and his wife, María Luisa (who wore the pants in the palace)—all originals by Goya. The clock—showing Cronus, god of time, in marble, bronze, and wood—sits on a music box. The gilded decor you see throughout the palace is bronze with gold leaf.

7. Gasparini Room: This room was meant to be Charles III's bedroom, but was unfinished when he died. Instead, with its painted stucco ceiling and inlaid Spanish marble floor (restored in 1992), it was the royal dressing room. The Asian influence was trendy at the time. Dressing, for a divine monarch, was a public affair. The court bigwigs would assemble here as the king, standing on a platform—notice the height of the mirrors—would pull on his leotards. In the next room, the silk wallpaper is new; notice the *J.C.S.* initials of King Juan Carlos and Queen Sofía. Passing through the silk room, you reach the...

8. Charles III Bedroom: Decorated in 19th-century neoclassical style, a chandelier in the shape of the fleur-de-lis (symbol of the Bourbon family) dominates the room. The thick walls separating each room hide service corridors for servants who scurried about generally unseen.

9. Porcelain Room: The 300 separate plates that line this room were disassembled for safety during the Spanish Civil War. (Find the little screws in the greenery that hide the seams.) The Yellow Room leads to the...

10. Gala Dining Room: Up to 12 times a year, the king entertains up to 150 guests at this bowling-lane-size table—which can be extended to the length of the room. Find the two royal chairs. (Hint: With the modesty necessary for 21st-century monarchs, they are just a tad higher than the rest.) The parquet floor was the preferred dancing surface when balls were held in this fabulous room, decorated with vases from China and a fresco depicting the arrival of Christopher Columbus in Barcelona. The table in the next room would be lined with an exorbitantly caloric dessert buffet.

11. Cinema Room (Sala de Monedas y Medallas): In the early 20th century, the royal family enjoyed "Sunday afternoons at the movies" here. Today, it stores glass cases filled with coins and medals.

12. Silver Room: A collection of silver tableware from different periods is presented in this room.

13. Stradivarius Room: The queen likes classical music. When you perform for her, do it with these precious 350-year-old violins. About 300 Antonius Stradivarius–made instruments survive. This is the only matching quartet: two violins, a viola, and a cello. The next room was the children's room—with kid-size musical instruments.

14. China Rooms: Several collections of China from different kings (some from China, others from Sèvres and Meissen) are displayed in this room.

15. Royal Chapel: The Royal Chapel is used for private concerts and funerals. The royal coffin sits here before making the sad trip to El Escorial to join the rest of Spain's past royalty.

16. Queen's Boudoir: This room was for the ladies, unlike the next...

17. Billiards and Smoking Rooms: The billiards room and the smoking room were for men only. The porcelain and silk of the smoking room imitates a Chinese opium den, which, in its day, was furnished only with pillows.

18. Charles IV Bedroom: Small for a king's room, the neoclassical decoration stands out.

19. Fine Woods Room: Fine 18th- and 19th-century French inlaid-wood pieces decorate this room.

You'll exit down the same grand stairway you climbed 24 rooms ago.

Across the courtyard is the **armory,** which displays the armor and swords of El Cid (Christian warrior fighting the Moors), Ferdinand (husband of Isabel), Charles V (ruler of Spain at its peak of power), and Phillip II (Charles' son who watched Spain start its long slide downward). Near the exit is a cafeteria and a bookstore, which has a variety of books on Spanish history.

As you leave the palace, walk around the corner to the left, along the palace exterior, to the grand yet people-friendly Plaza de Oriente. Throughout Europe, energetic governments are turning formerly car-congested wastelands into public spaces like this. Madrid's latest mayor is nicknamed "The Mole" for all the digging he's doing. Where's all the traffic? Under your feet.

To return to Puerta del Sol: With your back to the palace, face the equestrian statue of Philip IV and (behind the statue) the Royal Theater (*Teatro Real,* neoclassical, rebuilt in 1997, open for 30-minute, €4 visits in English Mon and Wed–Fri 10:30–11:00, Sat–Sun at 11:00–13:30, closed Tue, tel. 915-160-660). Walk behind the Royal Theater (on the right, passing Café de Oriente—a favorite with theatergoers) to another square, where you'll find the Opera Metro stop and Calle Arenal—which leads back to Puerta del Sol.

SIGHTS

Madrid's Museum Neighborhood

Three great museums are in east Madrid. A five-minute walk connects the Prado to the Thyssen-Bornemisza Museum; from the Prado to Centro Arte de Reina Sofía is a 10-minute walk. All three have brand-new modern extensions by well-known architects.

Museum Pass: If you plan to visit all three museums, you'll save 25 percent by buying the Paseo del Arte combo-ticket (€7.66, sold at each museum, valid for 1 year). Note that the Prado and Centro Arte de Reina Sofía museums are free on Sunday (and anytime for those under 18 and over 65); the Prado and Thyssen-Bornemisza are closed Monday; and the Reina Sofía is closed Tuesday.

▲▲▲Prado Museum—The Prado holds my favorite collection of paintings anywhere. With more than 3,000 canvases, including entire rooms of masterpieces by Velázquez, Goya, El Greco, and Bosch, it's overwhelming. Pick up the English-language floor plan as you enter. Take a tour or buy a guidebook (or use my self-guided walking tour at www.ricksteves.com/prado). Focus on the Flemish and northern (Bosch, Albrecht Dürer, Peter Paul Rubens), the Italian (Fra Angelico, Raphael, Titian), and the Spanish art (El Greco, Velázquez, Goya).

Follow Goya through his stages, from cheery *(The Parasol)* to political (*2nd of May, 1808* and *3rd of May, 1808*) to dark ("Negras de Goya": e.g., *Saturn Devouring His Children*). In each stage,

Madrid's Museum Neighborhood

Goya asserted his independence from artistic conventions. Even the standard court portraits from his "first" stage reflect his politically liberal viewpoint, subtly showing the vanity and stupidity of his royal patrons by the looks in their goony eyes. His political stage makes him one of the first artists with a social conscience. His highly-charged painting of the *3rd of May, 1808* depicts a massacre of Spaniards by Napoleon's troops. Finally, in his gloomy "dark stage," Goya probed the inner world of fears and nightmares, anticipating our modern-day preoccupation with dreams.

Don't miss Velázquez's famous *Las Meninas,* a behind-the-scenes glimpse at royal life, showing Princess Margarita, her two attendants *(meninas)*, a jester, a female dwarf, the family dog, and the painter himself—with King Phillip and his wife looking on as they're being painted.

Seek out Bosch's *The Garden of Earthly Delights*—a three-paneled altarpiece showing creation, the "transparency of earthly pleasures," and the resulting hell. Bosch's self-portrait looks out from hell (with the birds leading naked people around the brim of his hat), surrounded by people suffering eternal punishments appropriate to their primary earthly excesses.

The art is constantly rearranged by the Prado's management, so even the museum's own maps and guidebooks are out of date. Regardless of the latest location, most art is grouped by painter, and better guards can point you in the right direction if you say, "*¿Dónde está...?*" and the painter's name as Españoled as you can (e.g., Titian is "Ticiano," and Bosch is "El Bosco"). The Murillo (south) entrance—at the end closest to the Atocha train station—often has shorter lines. Lunchtime, from 14:00 to 16:00, is least crowded.

Cost, Hours, Location: €3; free all day Sun and to anyone under 18 and over 65; covered by €7.66 Paseo del Arte combo-ticket; Tue–Sun 9:00–19:00, closed Mon, last entry 30 min before closing (€3 audioguide; free and mandatory baggage check after your things are scanned, just like at the airport; no water bottles inside, photos allowed but no flash, cafeteria in basement at Murillo end); Paseo del Prado, Metro: Banco de España or Atocha—each a 5-min walk from the museum, tel. 913-302-800, http://museoprado.mcu.es. Cabs picking you up at the Prado are likely to overcharge. Insist on the fare meter.

While you're in the neighborhood, consider a visit to the Charles III Botanical Garden (listed under "Near the Prado," on the next page).

▲▲Thyssen-Bornemisza Museum—Locals call this stunning museum simply the Thyssen (TEE-sun). It displays the impressive collection that Baron Thyssen (a wealthy German married to a former Miss Spain) sold to Spain for $350 million. It's basically minor works by major artists and major works by minor artists (major works by major artists are in the Prado). In 2004, a new collection belonging to the baron's widow was added in the brand-new building annexed to the museum. Art lovers appreciate how the good baron's art complements the Prado's collection by filling in where the Prado is weak (such as Impressionism). For a delightful walk through art history, ride the elevator to the top floor and do the rooms in numerical order from Primitive Italian (room 1) to Surrealism and Pop Art (room 48). The museum is kitty-corner from the Prado at Paseo del Prado 8 in Palacio de Villahermosa (€6, or €10 to add current exhibition; covered by €7.66 Paseo del Arte combo-ticket, children under 12 enter free, Tue–Sun 10:00–19:00, closed Mon, ticket office closes at 18:30, audioguide-€3, free baggage check, café, shop, no photos, Metro: Banco de España or Atocha, tel. 914-203-944, www.museothyssen.org). If you're heading to Centro Arte de Reina Sofía and you're tired, hail a cab at the gate to zip straight there.

▲▲Centro Arte de Reina Sofía—In this exceptional modern-art museum, ride the fancy glass elevator to the second floor and follow the room numbers for art from 1900 to 1950. The fourth floor continues the collection, from 1950 to 1980. The museum is most famous for Pablo Picasso's *Guernica* (second floor, room 6), an epic painting showing the horror of modern war. Guernica, a village in northern

Spain, was the target of the world's first saturation-bombing raid (1937), approved by Franco and carried out by Hitler. Picasso, a Spaniard living in Paris at the time, heard news reports of the event and immediately set to work on this stark black-and-white painting that alerted the world to the growing peril of fascism. Notice the two rooms of studies Picasso did for *Guernica,* filled with iron-nail tears and screaming mouths. *Guernica* was exiled to America until Franco's death, and now it reigns as Spain's national piece of art.

The museum also houses an easy-to-enjoy collection by other modern artists, including more of Picasso (3 rooms divide his art into pre–Civil War, *Guernica,* and post–Civil War) and a mind-bending room of Dalís (room 10). Enjoy a break in the shady courtyard before leaving (€3, free Sat afternoon after 14:30 and all day Sun, always free to those under 18 and over 65; covered by €7.66 Paseo del Arte combo-ticket; Mon and Wed–Sat 10:00–21:00, Sun 10:00–14:30, closed Tue, good brochure, hardworking audioguide-€2.50, no photos, no tours in English, free baggage check, Santa Isabel 52, Metro: Atocha, across from Atocha train station, look for exterior glass elevators, tel. 914-675-062, http://museoreinasofia.mcu.es).

Near the Prado

▲Retiro Park—Siesta in this 300-acre green and breezy escape from the city. At midday on Saturday and Sunday, the area around the lake becomes a street carnival, with jugglers, puppeteers, and lots of local color. These peaceful gardens offer great picnicking and people-watching. From the Retiro Metro stop, walk to the big lake (El Estanque), where you can cheaply rent a rowboat. Past the lake, a grand boulevard of statues leads to the Prado.

Charles III's Botanical Garden (Real Jardín Botánico)—After your Prado visit, you can take a lush and fragrant break in this sculpted park, wandering among trees from around the world. The flier in English explains that this is actually more than a park—it's a museum of plants (€1.50, daily 10:00–21:00, until 18:00 in winter, entry opposite Prado's Murillo entry, Plaza de Murillo 2).

Naval Museum—This tells the story of Spain's navy from the Armada to today (free, Tue–Sun 10:00–14:00, closed Mon, a block north of the Prado across boulevard from Thyssen-Bornemisza Museum, Paseo del Prado 5, entrance at Calle de Montalbán 2, 913-795-299).

More Sights in Madrid

National Archaeological Museum (Museo Arqueológico Nacional)—If you're intrigued by prehistoric cave paintings, you'll dig this place. Located underground in the museum's garden, the paintings are replicas from northern Spain's Altamira Caves. The ancient art, big on bison, gives you a thrill at the skill of the cave artists who created the originals 14,000 years ago. This museum, displaying Iberian art from prehistory to the 19th century, also boasts the marble bust of a woman with an elaborate headress—*Dama de Elche,* dating from the 4th century B.C. (€3, free Sat afternoon and Sun, Tue–Sat 10:00–21:00, Sun 10:00–14:30, closed Mon, Calle Serrano 13, Metro: Serrano or Colón, tel. 915-777-912, www.man.es). The National Library, which shares the same building, has a first-edition copy of *Don Quixote* by Cervantes.

Chapel San Antonio de la Florida—Goya's tomb stares up at a splendid cupola filled with his own frescoes. On June 13, local ladies line up here to ask St. Anthony for a boyfriend, while outside a festival rages, with street musicians, food, and fun (free entry, Tue–Fri 10:00–14:00 & 16:00–20:00, Sat–Sun 10:00–14:00, closed Mon, July and Aug only 10:00–14:00, Glorieta de San Antonio de la Florida, Metro: Príncipe Pío, tel. 915-420-722). This chapel is near the Sepulvedana bus station with service to Segovia. If you're day-tripping to Segovia, it's easy to stop by before or after your trip.

Hungry? Next door to the chapel is **Restaurante Casa Mingo**, popular for its cheap chicken, chorizo, and *cabrales* cheese served with cider. Ask the waiter to pour the cider for you. For dessert, try the *tarta de Santiago* almond cake (daily 11:00–24:00, Paseo de la Florida 34, tel. 915-477-918).

Royal Tapestry Factory (Real Fábrica de Tapices)—Have a look at traditional tapestry-making (€3, Mon–Fri 10:00–14:00, closed Sat–Sun and Aug, some English tours, Calle Fuenterrabia 2, Metro: Menendez Pelayo, take Gutenberg exit, tel. 914-340-551). You can actually order a tailor-made tapestry (starting at $10,000).

Moncloa Tower (Faro de Moncloa)—This tower's elevator zips you up 300 feet to the best skyscraper view in town (€1, Tue–Fri 10:00–14:00 & 17:00–19:00, Sat–Sun 10:30–18:00, closed Mon, Metro: Moncloa, tel. 915-448-104). If you're going to El Escorial by bus, this is a convenient sight near the bus station.

Teleférico—For city views, ride this cable car from downtown over Madrid's sprawling city park to Casa de Campo (€2.90 one-way, €4.20 round-trip, daily July–Aug from 11:00, Sept–June from 12:00, departs from Paseo del Pintor Rosales, Metro: Arguelles, tel. 915-417-450, www.teleferico.com). Do an immediate round-trip to skip Casa de Campo's strange mix of rental rowboats, prostitutes, addicts, a zoo, and an amusement park.

SHOPPING

Shoppers focus on the colorful pedestrian area between Gran Vía and Puerta del Sol. The giant Spanish department store El Corte Inglés, a block off Puerta del Sol, is a handy place to pick up just about anything you need (Mon–Sat 10:00–21:30, closed Sun, free maps at info desk, supermarket in basement).

▲El Rastro—Europe's biggest flea market, held on Sundays and holidays, is a field day for shoppers, people-watchers, and thieves (9:00–15:00, best before 11:00). Thousands of stalls titillate more than a million browsers with mostly new junk. If you brake for garage sales, you'll pull a U-turn for El Rastro. Start at the Plaza Mayor, with its gentle coin-collectors market, and head south or take the subway to Tirso de Molina. Hang on to your wallet. Spin the wheel to try for two cookies for the price of one. Munch on a *pepito* (meat-filled pastry). Europe's biggest stamp market thrives simultaneously on Plaza Mayor.

NIGHTLIFE

Just walking the streets of Madrid seems to be the way the locals spend their evenings. Even past midnight on a hot summer night, whole families with little kids are strolling, licking ice cream, and greeting their neighbors. Start at Puerta del Sol and explore. (See "Tapas: the Madrid Pub-Crawl Dinner," page 1265.)

Disco dancers may have to wait until after midnight for the most popular clubs to even open, much less start hopping. Spain has a reputation for partying very late, not ending until offices open in the morning.

▲▲▲Bullfight—Madrid's Plaza de Toros hosts Spain's top bullfights on Sundays and holidays from March through mid-October and nearly every day during the San Isidro festival (May through mid-June—generally sold out long in advance). Fights start between 17:00 and 19:00 (early in spring and fall, late in summer). Tickets range from €3.50 to €100. There are no bad seats at the Plaza de Toros; paying more gets you in the shade and/or closer to the gore. (The action often intentionally occurs in the shade to reward the expensive-ticket holders.) To be close to the bullring, choose areas 8, 9, or 10; for shade: 1, 2, 9, or 10; for shade/sun: 3 or 8; for the sun and cheapest seats: 4, 5, 6, or 7. (Note that fights advertised as *Gran Novillada con Picadores* feature younger bulls and rookie matadors.)

Hotels and booking offices are convenient, but they add 20 percent or more and don't sell the cheap seats. Call both offices before you buy (Plaza Carmen 1—daily 9:30–13:30 & 16:00–19:00, tel. 915-312-732; and Calle Victoria 3—daily 10:00–14:00 & 17:00–19:00, tel. 915-211-213). To save money, stand in the bullring ticket line, except for important bullfights or during the San Isidro festival. About a thousand tickets are held back to be sold on the five days leading up to a fight, including the day of the fight. The bullring is at Calle Alcalá 237 (Metro: Ventas, tel. 913-562-200, www.las-ventas.com in Spanish).

Madrid's **bullfighting museum** (Museo Taurino) is not as good as Sevilla's or Ronda's (free, Tue–Fri and Sun 9:30–14:30, closed Sat and Mon and early on fight days, at the back of bullring, tel. 917-251-857).

▲▲Zarzuela—For a delightful look at Spanish light opera that even English speakers can enjoy, try zarzuela. Guitar-strumming Napoleons in red capes; buxom women with masks, fans, and castanets; Spanish-speaking pharaohs; melodramatic spotlights; and aficionados clapping and singing along from the cheap seats, where the acoustics are best—this is zarzuela...the people's opera. Originating in Madrid, zarzuela is known for its satiric humor and surprisingly good music. You can buy tickets at Theater Zarzuela, which alternates between zarzuela, ballet, and opera throughout the year (€10–30, box office open 12:00–18:00 for advance tickets or until showtime for that day, Jovellanos 4, near the Prado, Metro: Banco de España, tel. 915-245-400, http://teatrodelazarzuela.mcu.es). The TI's monthly guide has a special zarzuela listing.

▲Flamenco—While Sevilla is the capital of flamenco, Madrid has two easy and affordable options.

Taberna Casa Patas attracts big-name flamenco artists. You'll quickly understand why this intimate (30-table) and smoky venue is named, literally, "the house of legs." Since this is for locals as well as tour groups, the flamenco is contemporary and may be jazzier than your notion—it depends on who's performing (€25 for Mon–Thu at 22:30, €30 for Fri–Sat at 21:00 and 24:00, closed Sun, 75–90 min, price includes cover and first drink, reservations smart, no flash cameras, Cañizares 10, tel. 914-298-471 or 913-690-496, www.casapatas.com). Its restaurant is a logical place for dinner before the show (€20 dinners, Mon–Sat from 20:00). Or, since this place is three blocks south of the recommended Plaza Santa Ana tapas bars, this could be your post-tapas-crawl entertainment.

Las Carboneras is more downscale—an easygoing, folksy little place a few steps from Plaza Mayor with a nightly 60-minute flamenco show (€22 includes a entry and a drink, €45 gets you a table up-front with dinner and unlimited cheap drinks if you reserve ahead, Mon–Thu at 22:30, Fri–Sat at 21:00 and 23:00, closed Sun, earlier shows possible if a group books, reservations recommended, Plaza del Conde de Miranda 1, tel. 915-428-677, Ronan SE).

Regardless of what your hotel receptionist may want to sell you, other flamenco places like Arco de Cuchilleros (Calle de los Cuchilleros 7), Café de Chinitas (Calle Torija 7, just off Plaza Mayor), Corral de la Morería (Calle de Morería 17) and Torres Bermejas (off Gran Vía) are filled with tourists and pushy waiters.

Mesones—Just west of Plaza Mayor, the lane called Cava de San Miguel is lined with *mesones:* long, skinny, cave-like bars famous for drinking and singing late into the night. Toss lowbrow locals, Spanish karaoke, electric keyboards, crass tourists, cheap sangria, and greasy calamari into a late-night blender and turn it on. Probably lively only on Friday and Saturday, but you're welcome to pop in to several places (such as Guitarra, Tortilla, or Boquerón) and see what you can find.

SLEEPING

Madrid has plenty of centrally located budget hotels and *pensiones.* You'll have no trouble finding a sleepable double for €30, a good double for €60, and a modern air-conditioned double with all the comforts for €100. Prices are the same throughout the year, and it's almost always easy to find a place. Anticipate full hotels from May 15 to May 25 (the festival of Madrid's patron saint, Isidro) and the last week in September (conventions). In July and August prices can be softer—ask about promotional deals. All of the accommodations I've listed are within a few minutes' walk of Puerta del Sol.

The Pedestrian Zone between Puerta del Sol and Gran Vía

Reliable and away from the seediness, these hotels are good values for those wanting to spend a little more. Their formal prices may be inflated, and some offer weekend and summer discounts whenever it's slow. Use Metro: Sol for all but Hotel Opera (Metro: Opera). See the map on page 1256 for locations.

$$$ Hotel Regente is a big and traditional place with 154 tastefully decorated and comfortable air-conditioned rooms, a great location, and a great value (Sb-€63, Db-€105, Tb-€128, tax not included, breakfast-€4.50, parking-€13, midway between Puerta del Sol and Plaza del Callao at Mesonero Romanos 9, tel. 915-212-941, fax 915-323-014, www.hotelregente.com, info@hotelregente.com).

$$$ Hotel Arosa charges the same for all of its 134 rooms, whether they're sleekly remodeled Art Deco or just aging gracefully. Ask for a remodeled room with a terrace (Sb-€116, Db-€178, Tb-€240, 20 percent cheaper July–Aug, tax not included, breakfast-€13, air-con, memorably tiny triangular elevator, a block off Plaza del Carmen, Calle Salud 21, tel. 915-321-600, fax 915-313-127, arosa@hotelarosa.com).

$$$ The huge, business-class **Hotel Liabeny** has 220 plush, spacious rooms and all the comforts (Sb-€100, Db-€135, Tb-€155, 10 percent cheaper July–Aug, tax not included, breakfast-€14, air-con, if one room is smoky ask for another, sauna, gym, off Plaza

Sleep Code

(€1 = about $1.20, country code: 34)
S = Single, **D** = Double/Twin, **T** = Triple, **Q** = Quad, **b** = bathroom, **s** = shower only, **SE** = Speaks English, **NSE** = No English. Breakfast is not included unless noted; credit cards are accepted unless noted. In Madrid, the 7 percent IVA tax is sometimes included in the price.

To help you easily sort through these listings, I've divided the rooms into three categories, based on the price for a standard double room with bath during high season:

$$$ **Higher Priced**—Most rooms €100 or more.
$$ **Moderately Priced**—Most between €60–100.
$ **Lower Priced**—Most rooms €60 or less.

del Carmen at Salud 3, tel. 915-319-000, fax 915-327-421, www.liabeny.es, reservas@hotelliabeny.es).

$$$ Hotel Opera, a serious and modern hotel with 79 classy rooms, is located just off Plaza Isabel II, a four-block walk from Puerta del Sol toward the Royal Palace (Sb-€99, Db-€132, Db with big view terrace-€145, Tb-€170, tax not included, buffet breakfast-€10, air-con, elevator, free Internet access, ask for a higher floor—there are 8—to avoid street noise; consider their "singing dinners" offered nightly at 21:30—average price €55, reservations wise; Cuesta de Santo Domingo 2, Metro: Opera, tel. 915-412-800, fax 915-416-923, www.hotelopera.com, reservas@hotelopera.com). Hotel Opera's cafeteria is understandably popular.

$$$ Hotel Santo Domingo has artsy paintings, an inviting lounge, and 121 rooms, each decorated differently (Sb-€127, Db-€184, tax not included, pricier superior rooms are not necessary, air-con, elevator, non-smoking floor, facing Metro: Santo Domingo, Plaza de Santo Domingo 13, tel. 915-479-800, fax 915-475-995, www.hotelsantodomingo.net, reserva@hotelsantodomingo.net). Prices drop €30—and breakfast is included—on weekends (Fri–Sun) and July–Aug.

$$ Hotel Europa has red-carpet charm: a royal salon, plush halls with happy Muzak, polished wood floors, an attentive staff, and 80 squeaky-clean rooms with balconies overlooking the pedestrian zone or an inner courtyard (Sb-€59, Db-€75–95, Tb-€105, Qb-€120, Quint/b-€135, tax not included, breakfast-€5.50, easy phone reservations with credit card, fans or air-con, elevator, fine lounge on 2nd floor, Calle del Carmen 4, tel. 915-212-900, fax 915-214-696, www.hoteleuropa.net, info@hoteleuropa.net, Antonio and Fernando Garaban and their helpful and jovial staff, Javi and

Madrid's Center—Hotels and Restaurants

Jim, SE). The convenient Europa cafeteria/restaurant next door is a great scene, fun for breakfast, and a fine value any time of day.

$$ Hotel Carlos V, a Best Western place with 67 classy high-ceiling rooms and an elegant breakfast and lounge, is a fair value. Its central location off Preciados pedestrian street makes it convenient (Sb-€94, Db-€124, Tb-€167, air-con, elevator, Maestro Victoria 5, tel. 915-314-100, fax 915-313-761, www.hotelcarlosv.com, recepcion@hotelcarlosv.com).

$$ Euromadrid Hotel—like a cross between a Motel 6 and an old hospital—rents 35 white rooms in a modern but well-worn shell (big Sb-€60, Db-€80, tight Tb-€96, includes continental breakfast but not tax, air-con, Mesonero Romanos 7, tel. 915-217-200, fax 915-214-582, clasit@infonegocio.com).

$$ The basic **Hotel Anaco** has a drab color scheme and a dreary lobby, but offers 39 quiet, comfortable rooms in a central location (Sb-€78, Db-€97, Tb-€131, bed extra €34, tax not included, breakfast-€5, air-con, elevator, non-smoking floor, Tres Cruces 3, a few steps off Plaza del Carmen and its underground parking lot-€13.80/day, tel. 915-224-604, fax 915-316-484, www.anacohotel.com, info@anacohotel.com).

$$ Hotel Plaza Mayor, with 32 solidly outfitted rooms, is beautifully situated a block off Plaza Mayor (Sb-€48, Db-€70–80, corner "suite" Db-€85, Tb-€85, air-con, elevator, buffet breakfast-€7, Calle Atocha 2, tel. 913-600-606, fax 913-600-610, www.h-plazamayor.com, info@h-plazamayor.com, Fedra SE).

$ Hostal Acapulco, overlooking the fine little Plaza del Carmen, rents 16 bright rooms with air-conditioning and all the big hotel gear. The neighborhood is quiet enough that it's smart to request a room with a balcony (Sb-€43, Db-€53, Tb-€67, elevator, Salud 13, 4th floor, tel. 915-311-945, fax 915-322-329, hostal_acapulco@yahoo.es, Marco SE).

$ Hostal Triana, at the same address as Acapulco and also a fine deal, is bigger—with 40 rooms—and offers a little less charm for a little less money (Sb-€37, Db-€50, Tb-€65, €3 extra for air-con, taxes included, half the rooms have only fans, elevator, Calle de la Salud 13, 1st floor, tel. 915-326-812, fax 915-229-729, www.hostaltriana.com, triana@hostaltriana.com, Victor González SE).

$ ***Hostales at Gran Vía 44:*** The next three are in the same building at Gran Vía 44, overlooking the busy street. All are cheap and work in a jam. **Hostal Helena,** on the ninth floor, is a homey burgundy-under-heavy-drapes kind of place, renting 10 fine rooms. Enjoy the great little roof garden (S-€30, Ds-€42, Db-€45, Tb-€60, elevator, fans, Internet access, Gran Vía 44, tel. & fax 915-217-585, www.geocities.com/hostalhelena, hostalhelena@yahoo.es, José Luis, SE). The next two are well-worn with stark rooms and traffic noise: **Hostal Residencia Valencia** with 30 rooms (Sb-€40,

Ds-€50, Db-€53, Tb-€68, includes tax, 5th floor, tel. 915-221-115, fax 915-221-113, www.hostal-valencia.com, info@hostal-valencia.com, Antonio SE) and **Hostal Residencia Continental** with 34 rooms (Sb-€37, Db-€48, Tb-€66, includes tax, fans, 3rd floor, tel. 915-214-640, fax 915-214-649, www.hostalcontinental.com, continental@mundivia.es, Andres SE).

On or near Plaza Santa Ana

The Plaza Santa Ana area has small, cheap places mixed in with fancy hotels. While the neighborhood is noisy at night, it has a rough but charming ambience, with colorful bars and a central location (3 min from Puerta del Sol's *Tío Pepe* sign; walk down Calle San Jerónimo and turn right on Príncipe; Metro: Sol). To locate hotels, see map on page 1259.

$$$ Suite Prado, two blocks toward the Prado from Plaza Santa Ana, is a good value, offering 18 sprawling, elegant, air-conditioned suites with a modern yet homey feel (suites are all the same size, charging €122 for single, €153 double, and €176 triple occupancy; sitting rooms, refrigerators, kitchens, 2nd kid free, breakfast at café next door-€4, elevator, Manuel Fernández y González 10, at intersection with Venture de la Vega, tel. 914-202-318, fax 914-200-559, www.suiteprado.com, hotel@suiteprado.com, Paula and Elena SE).

$ Residencia Hostal Lisboa, across the street from Suite Prado (above), is a good budget place (25 rooms, Sb-€44, Db-€54, Tb-€75, interior rooms quieter on weekends, air-con, elevator, Ventura de la Vega 17, tel. 914-294-676, fax 914-299-894, www.hostallisboa.com, hostallisboa@inves.es, SE).

$ Hostal R. Veracruz II, between Plaza Santa Ana and Puerta del Sol, rents 22 decent, quiet rooms (Sb-€36, Db-€50, Tb-€63, no breakfast, elevator, air-con, Victoria 1, 3rd floor, tel. 915-227-635, fax 915-226-749, hostalveracruz@yahoo.es, NSE).

$ ***Cheap Hostel Alternative:*** Because of the following place, I don't list a youth hostel for Madrid. For supercheap beds in a dingy time warp, consider **Hostal Lucense.** Bathrooms are down the hall and there's no heat during winter (13 rooms, S-€15–18, D-€18–25, Db-€28–36, T-€38, €1.20 per shower, cash only, Nuñez de Arce 15, 1st floor, tel. 915-224-888, run by not-so-friendly Sr. and Sra. Michaela García, both interesting characters, Señor SE).

Near the Prado

$$$ Hotel Green Lope de Vega is your best business-class hotel value near the Prado. A four-star place that opened in 2000, it's a "cultural-themed" hotel inspired by the 17th-century writer Lope de Vega. It feels cozy and friendly for a formal business-class hotel (60 rooms, Sb-€108, Db-€135, Tb-€182, 1 child sleeps free, prices about

Plaza Santa Ana Area

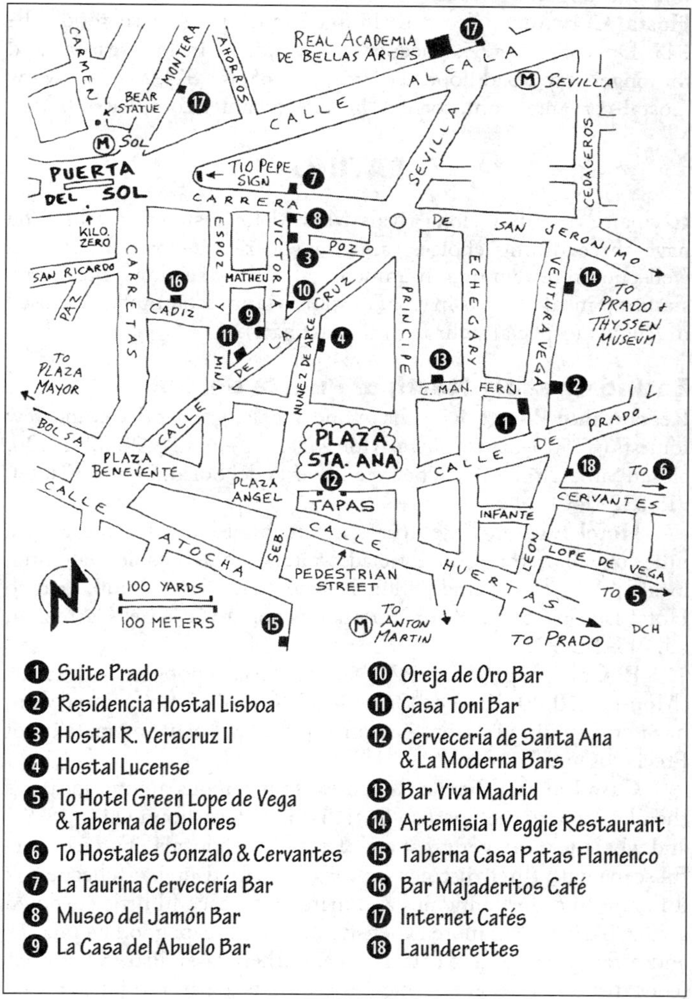

20 percent lower on weekends and during most of the summer, elevator, air-con, Internet access, parking-€18/day, Calle Lope de Vega 49, tel. 913-600-011, fax 914-292-391, www.hotellopedevega.com, lopedevega@hotellopedevega.com, SE).

$ ***At Cervantes 34:*** Two fine budget places are at Cervantes 34 (Metro: Anton Martín). **Hostal Gonzalo**—with 15 spotless, comfortable rooms, well run by friendly and helpful Javier—is deservedly in all the guidebooks. Reserve in advance (Sb-€45, Db-€52, Tb-€63, elevator, 3rd floor, tel. 914-292-714, fax 914-202-007, www.hostalgonzalo.com). Downstairs, the nearly as polished **Hostal Cervantes,** also with 15 fine rooms, is likewise good (Sb-€45, Db-€55, Tb-€65; cheaper on weekdays, in low season, and for longer stays; 2nd floor, tel. 914-298-365, fax 914-292-745, www.hostal-cervantes.com, correo@hostal-cervantes.com, Fabio SE).

EATING

In Spain, only Barcelona rivals Madrid for tastebud thrills. You have three dining choices: an atmospheric sit-down meal in a well-chosen restaurant, an unmemorable basic sit-down meal, or a stand-up meal of tapas in a bar or four. Many restaurants are closed in August (especially through the last half).

Eating Cheaply North of Puerta del Sol

Restaurante Puerto Rico has good meals, great prices, and few tourists (€7.50 3-course *menu,* Mon–Sat 3:00–16:30 & 20:30–24:00, closed Sun, Chinchilla 2, between Puerta del Sol and Gran Vía, tel. 915-322-040).

Hotel Europa Cafetería is a fun, high-energy scene with a mile-long bar, traditionally-clad waiters, great people-watching, local cuisine, and a fine €8 lunch *menu* (daily 7:30–24:00, next to Hotel Europa, 50 yards off Puerta del Sol at Calle del Carmen 4, tel. 915-212-900).

El Corte Inglés' seventh-floor cafeteria is popular with locals (Mon–Sat 10:00–11:30 & 13:00–16:15 & 17:30–20:00, closed Sun, has non-smoking section, just off Puerta del Sol at intersection of Preciados and Tetuán).

Casa Labra Taberna Restaurante is famous among locals as the place where the Spanish Socialist Party was founded in 1879... and where you can get great cod. Packed with locals, it's a wonderful scene with three distinct sections: the stand-up bar (cheapest, 2 different lines for munchies and drinks), a peaceful little sit-down area in back (a little more expensive but still cheap; good €4 salads), and a fancy restaurant (€15 lunches). Their tasty little €1 *bacalao* (cod) dishes put it on the map. The waiters are fun to joke around with (daily 11:00–15:30 & 18:00–23:00, a block off Puerta del Sol at Calle Tetuán 12, tel. 915-310-081).

Vegetarian: **Artemisia II** is a hit with vegetarians who like good, healthy food in a smoke-free room (great €9.50 three-course lunch *menu* Mon–Fri only, daily 13:30–16:00 & 21:00–24:00, 2 blocks north of Puerta del Sol at Tres Cruces 4, a few steps off Plaza Carmen, tel. 915-218-721). **Artemisia I,** II's older sister, is located two blocks east of Plaza Santa Ana at Ventura de la Vega 4, off San Jerónimo (same hours, tel. 914-295-092).

Eating near Plaza Mayor

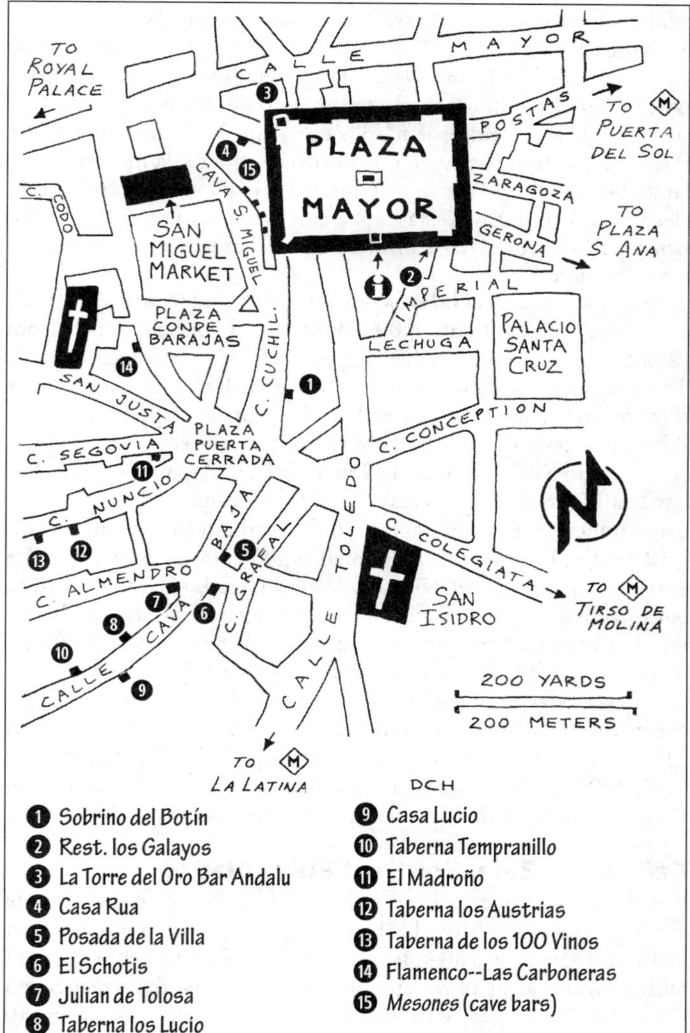

On or near Plaza Mayor

Many Americans are drawn to Ernest Hemingway's favorite, **Sobrino del Botín** (daily 13:00–16:00 & 20:00–24:00, Cuchilleros 17, a block downhill from Plaza Mayor, tel. 913-664-217). It's touristy, pricey (€24–30 average), and the last place he'd go now...but still, people love it and the food is excellent. If phoning to make a reservation, choose between the downstairs (for dark, medieval-cellar ambience) or upstairs (for a still-traditional but airier and lighter elegance). While this restaurant boasts that it's the oldest in the world (dating from 1725), a nearby restaurant teases, "Hemingway never ate here."

Restaurante los Galayos is less touristy and plenty *típico,* with good local cuisine (daily 8:00–24:00, lunch specials, lunch from 12:00, dinner anytime, arrive early or make a reservation, 30 yards off Plaza Mayor at Botoneras 5, tel. 913-663-028). For many, dinner right on the square at a sidewalk café is worth the premium (consider Cervecería Pulpito, southwest corner of the square at #10).

La Torre del Oro Bar Andalu on Plaza Mayor has soul. Diehard bullfight aficionados hate the gimmicky bull bar (La Taurina) listed under "Tapas" on page 1266. Here the walls are lined with grisly bullfight photos from annual photo competitions (read the gory description in "Introductory Walk," page 1241). Have a drink, but establish all prices first. Don't let the aggressive staff bully you into high-priced tapas you don't want (daily 8:00–15:00 & 18:00–24:00, closed Jan, Plaza Mayor 26, tel. 913-665-016).

Plaza Mayor is famous for its *bocadillos de calamares.* For a cheap and tasty squid-ring sandwich, line up at **Casa Rúa** at Plaza Mayor's northwest corner, a few steps up Calle Ciudad Rodrigo (daily 9:00–23:00). Hanging up behind the bar is a photo/ad of Plaza Mayor from the 1950s, when the square contained a park.

Calle Cava Baja, South of Plaza Mayor

Few tourists frequent this traditional neighborhood—Barrio de los Austrias, named for the Hapsburgs. It's three minutes south of Plaza Mayor, or a 10-minute walk from Puerta del Sol. Lined with a diverse array of restaurants and tapas bars, the street called Cava Baja is clogged with locals out in search of a special meal. For a good, authentic Madrileño dinner experience, take time to survey the many places along this street—between the first and last listings described below—and choose your favorite. A key wine-drinking phrase is *mucho cuerpo* (full-bodied).

Posada de la Villa serves Castilian cuisine in a 17th-century posada. Peek into the big oven to see what's cooking (€30 meals, Mon–Sat 13:00–16:00 & 20:00–24:00, closed Sun and Aug, Calle Cava Baja 9, tel. 913-661-860).

El Schotis is less expensive and specializes in meat and fish dishes. Named after a popular local dance, the restaurant retains the traditional character of old Madrid (daily 12:00–17:00 & 20:00–24:00, Calle Cava Baja 11, tel. 913-653-230).

Julian de Tolosa, a classy, pricey, elegantly simple place popular with locals who know good food, offers a small, quality menu of Navarra's regional cuisine from T-bone steak *(chuletón)* to red *tolosa* beans (Mon–Sat 13:30–16:00 & 21:00–24:00, Sun 13:30–16:00, Calle Cava Baja 18, tel. 913-658-210).

Taberna los Lucio has good tapas, salads, *huevos estrellados* (scrambled eggs with potatoes), and wine (Wed–Mon 13:00–16:00 & 20:30–24:00, closed Tue, Calle Cava Baja 30, tel. 913-662-984).

For a splurge, dine with power-dressing locals at **Casa Lucio.** While the king and queen of Spain eat here, it's more stuffy than expensive (daily 13:00–17:00 & 21:00–24:00, Calle Cava Baja 35; unless you're the king or queen, reserve several days in advance, tel. 913-653-252).

Taberna Tempranillo, ideal for hungry wine-lovers, offers tapas and 250 kinds of wine. Use their fascinating English menu to assemble your dream meal. Arrive by 20:00 or wait (daily 13:00–15:30 & 20:00–24:00, closed Aug, Cava Baja 38, tel. 913-641-532).

Tapa-Hopping on Calle del Nuncio (near Calle Cava Baja)

El Madroño ("The Strawberry Tree," a symbol of Madrid) is a fun tapas bar that preserves chunks of old Madrid. A tile copy of Velázquez's famous *Drinkers* grins from its facade. Inside, look above the stairs for photos of 1902 Madrid. Study the coats of arms of Madrid through the centuries as you try a *vermut* on tap and a €2 sandwich, or ask to try the *licor de madroño* (€7.80 lunch *menu* also available, Tue–Sun 9:00–17:00 & 20:00–24:00, closed Mon, Plaza Puerta Cerrada 7, tel. 913-645-629).

Taberna los Austrias, two blocks away, serves tapas, salads, and light meals on wood-barrel tables (daily 12:00–16:00 & 20:00–24:00, Calle Nuncio 17).

Next door is the very hip and popular **Taberna de los 100 Vinos** ("Tavern of 100 Wines"), a classy wine bar serving top-end tapas and fine wine by the glass—see the chalkboard. Eat delicious €3.25 *pinchos* standing up, or sit down for excellent €10 *raciones* (Tue–Sat 13:00–16:00 & 20:00–24:00, closed Sun–Mon, Calle Nuncio 17).

Near the Royal Palace

Casa Ciriaco is popular with locals who appreciate good traditional cooking (€30 meals, Thu–Tue 13:30–16:00 & 20:30–24:00, closed Wed and Aug, halfway between Puerta del Sol and the Royal Palace at Calle Mayor 84, tel. 915-480-620). It was from this building in 1906 that an anarchist bombed the royal couple on their wedding day (for details, see "Introductory Walk," page 1243). A photo of the carnage is inside the front door.

La Bola Taberna, touristy but friendly and tastefully elegant, specializes in *cocido Madrileño*—Madrid stew. The €15 stew consists of various meats, carrots, and garbanzo beans in earthen jugs. It's big enough to split and is served as two courses; first you enjoy the broth as a soup (weekdays 13:00–16:00 & 20:30–23:00, often closed Sat–Sun, cash only, midway between the Royal Palace and Gran Vía at Calle Bola 5, tel. 915-476-930).

Café Ricordi, just a block from the Royal Theater, is a delightfully romantic little spot, perfect for theatergoers. You can enjoy tiny sandwiches with a glass of wine, coffee, and an elegant sweet, or a full meal in this café/bar/restaurant (Tue–Sat 12:00–24:00, closed Sun-Mon, Calle Arrieta 5, tel. 915-479-200).

Near the Prado

Each of the big-three art museums has a decent cafeteria. Or choose from these three places, all within a block of the Prado:

La Platería Bar Museo is a hardworking little café/wine bar with a good menu for tapas, light meals, and hearty salads (listed as *raciones* and 1/2 *raciones* on the chalkboard). Its tables spill onto the leafy little Plaza de Platerías de Martínez (daily 7:30–24:00, directly across busy boulevard Paseo del Prado from Atocha end of Prado, tel. 914-291-722).

Taberna de Dolores, a winning formula since 1908, is a commotion of locals enjoying €2 *canapés* (open-face sandwiches), tasty *almejas* (clams), and *cañas* (small beers) at the bar or at a few tables in the back (daily 13:00–24:00, Plaza de Jesús 4, tel. 914-292-243).

VIPS is where good-looking young tour guides eat cheap and filling salads. This bright, popular chain restaurant is engulfed in a big bookstore (daily 9:00–3:00 in morning, across Paseo del Prado boulevard from northern end of Prado in Galería del Prado under Palace Hotel facing Plaza Canovas). Spain's first Starbucks opened in April 2001, just next door.

Fast Food and Picnics

Fast Food: For an easy, light, cheap meal, try **Rodilla**—a popular sandwich chain with a shop on the northeast corner of Puerta del Sol at #13 (Mon–Fri 9:30–23:00, Sat 10:00–23:00, Sun 11:00–23:00). **Pans & Company,** with shops throughout Madrid and Spain, offers healthy, tasty sandwiches and chef's salads (daily 9:00–24:00, on Puerta del Sol, Plaza Callao, Gran Vía 30, and many more).

Picnics: The department store **El Corte Inglés** has a well-stocked **deli** downstairs (Mon–Sat 10:00–22:00, closed Sun). A perfect place to assemble a cheap picnic is downtown Madrid's neighborhood market, **Mercado de San Miguel.** How about breakfast surrounded by early-morning shoppers in the market's café? (Mon–Fri 9:00–14:30 & 17:15–20:15, Sat 9:00–14:30, closed Sun; to reach the market from Plaza Mayor, face the colorfully painted building and exit from the upper left-hand corner.) The **Museo del Jamón** (Museum of Ham) sells cheap picnics to go (see "Tapas: The Madrid Pub-Crawl Dinner," below).

Churros con Chocolate

Those not watching their cholesterol will want to try the deep-fried doughy treats called *churros* (or the thicker *porras*), best enjoyed by dipping them in pudding-like hot chocolate. **Bar Majaderitos** is a good bet (daily 7:00–24:00, Sun from 9:00, best in morning, 2 blocks off Tío Pepe end of Puerta del Sol, south on Espoz y Mina, turn right on Calle de Cádiz). Their tasty grilled cheese sandwich (with ham and/or egg) rounds out your breakfast. With luck, the *churros* machine in the back will be cooking. Notice the expressive WC signs.

The classy **Chocolatería San Ginés** is much loved by locals for its *churros* and chocolate (Tue–Sun 18:00–7:00, closed Mon). While empty before midnight, it's packed with the disco crowd in the wee hours; the popular dance club Joy Eslava is next door. Dunk your *churros* into the chocolate pudding, as locals have done here for more than 100 years (from Puerta del Sol, take Calle Arenal 2 blocks west, turn left on book-lined Pasadizo de San Ginés, you'll see the café—it's at #5, tel. 933-656-546).

Tapas: The Madrid Pub-Crawl Dinner

For maximum fun, people, and atmosphere, go mobile and do the "tapa tango," a local tradition of going from one bar to the next, munching, drinking, and socializing. Tapas are the toothpick appetizers, salads, and deep-fried foods served in most bars. Madrid is Spain's tapas capital—tapas just don't get any better than here. Grab a toothpick and stab something strange, but establish the prices first, especially if you're on a tight budget or at a possible tourist trap. Some items are very pricey, and most bars push larger *raciones,* rather than smaller tapas. The real action begins late (around 20:00). But for beginners, an earlier start, with less commotion, can be easier. The litter on the floor is normal; that's where people traditionally toss their trash and shells. Don't worry about paying until you're ready to go. Then ask for *la cuenta* (the bill).

Prowl the area between Puerta del Sol and Plaza Santa Ana. There's no ideal route, but the little streets between Puerta del Sol, San Jerónimo, and Plaza Santa Ana hold tasty surprises (see map on page 1259). Nearby, the street Jesús de Medinaceli is also lined with popular tapas bars. Below is a five-stop tapa crawl. These places are good, but don't be afraid to make some discoveries of your own.

1. From Puerta del Sol, walk east a block down Carrera de San Jerónimo to the corner of Calle Victoria. Across from the Museo del Jamón, you'll find **La Taurina Cervecería,** a bullfighters' Planet Hollywood (daily 8:00–24:00). Wander among trophies and historic photographs. Each stuffed bull's head is named, along with its farm, awards, and who killed him. Among the many gory photos, study the first post: It's Che Guevara, Orson Welles, and Salvador Dalí, all enjoying a good fight. Around the corner, the Babe Ruth of bullfighters, El Cordobes, lies wounded in bed. The photo below shows him in action. Kick off your pub crawl with a drink here. Inspired, I went for the *rabo de toro* (bull-tail stew, €10.50)—and regretted it. If a fight's on, the place will be packed with aficionados gathered around the TV. Across the street at San Jerónimo 5 is the...

2. Museo del Jamón (Museum of Ham), tastefully decorated—unless you're a pig (or a vegetarian). This frenetic, cheap, stand-up bar is an assembly line of fast and simple *bocadillos* and *raciones.* Photos show various dishes and their prices. For a small sandwich, ask for a *chiquito* (€0.60, unadvertised). The best ham is the pricey *jamón ibérico*—from pigs who led stress-free lives in acorn-strewn valleys. Just point and eat, but be specific: A *jamón blanco* portion costs only €5, while *jamón ibérico* costs €12 (daily 9:00–24:00, sit-down restaurant upstairs). Next, forage halfway up Calle Victoria to the tiny...

3. La Casa del Abuelo, for seafood-lovers who savor sizzling plates of tasty little *gambas* (shrimp) and *langostinos* (prawns). Try *gambas a la plancha* (grilled shrimp, €4.15) or *gambas al ajillo* (ahh-HHEEE-yoh, shrimp version of escargot, cooked in oil and garlic and ideal for bread dipping, €5.80), and a €1.20 glass of red wine (daily 11:30–15:30 & 18:30–23:30, Calle Victoria 12). Across the street is...

4. Oreja de Oro ("Golden Ear"), named for what it sells—sautéed pigs' ears (*oreja,* €2.50). While pigs' ears are a Madrid specialty, this place is Galician, so people also come here for *pulpo* (octopus, €8.50), *pimientos de Padrón* (green peppers...some sweet and a few hot surprises, €3), and the distinctive *ribeiro* (ree-BAY-roh) wine, served Galician-style, in characteristic little ceramic bowls (to disguise its lack of clarity). Jaime is a frantic one-man show who somehow gets everything just right. Have fun at this place. For a perfect finale, continue uphill and around the corner to...

5. Casa Toni, for refreshing bowls of gazpacho—the cold tomato-and-garlic soup (€1.50, available all year but only popular when temperatures soar). Their specialties are *berenjena* (deep-fried slices of eggplant, €3.60) and *champiñones* (sautéed mushrooms, €3.70; open daily 11:30–16:00 & 18:00–23:30, closed July, Calle Cruz 14).

More Options: If you're hungry for more, and want a trendy, up-to-date tapas scene, head for Plaza Santa Ana. The south side of the square is lined with lively bars offering good tapas, drinks, and a classic setting right on the square. Consider **Cervecería de Santa Ana** (tasty tapas with two zones: rowdy beer-hall and classier sit-down) and **La Moderna** (wine, pâté, and cheese plates).

If you're picking up speed and looking for a place filled with old tiles and young people, power into **Bar Viva Madrid** (daily 13:00–3:00, Calle Manuel Fernández y González, tel. 914-293-640). The same street has other late-night bars filled with music.

TRANSPORTATION CONNECTIONS

By Train to: Toledo (5/day on weekdays, 3/day on weekends, 1.25 hr, change to bus in Algodor; from Madrid's Atocha station leave from *cercanías* [theyr-kah-NEE-ahz] section, not the AVE section, though an AVE link is being built between Madrid and Toledo—ask if it's been completed), **Segovia** (9/day, 2 hrs, both Chamartín and Atocha stations), **Ávila** (hrly, 90–120 min, from Chamartín, and Atocha), **Salamanca** (6/day, 2.5 hrs, from Chamartín), **Santiago** (3/day, 8–9 hrs, includes night train from Chamartín), **San Sebastián** (2/day, 6.5 hrs, plus 1 night train, 8.25 hrs, all from Chamartín), **Barcelona** (6/day, 4.5-5.5 hrs, mostly from Chamartín, plus 2 night trains, 9 hrs), **Granada** (2/day, 6 hrs, both Chamartín and Atocha Stations), **Sevilla** (18/day, 2.5 hrs by AVE; 2 slower TALGO trains/day, 3.5 hrs; both from Atocha), **Córdoba** (18 AVE trains/day, 2 hrs, from Atocha, 12 TALGO trains/day, 2 hrs), **Málaga** (7/day, 4 hrs, from Atocha), **Lisbon** (1/day departing at 22:45, 10 hrs, pricey overnight Hotel Train from Chamartín), **Paris** (1/day, 13.5 hrs, 1 direct overnight—a €130 Hotel Train, €119 in winter, from Chamartín).

By Bus to: Ávila (€10.02 return, 2/hr, 90 min), **Toledo** (€3.89 one-way, 2/hr, 60–75 min, Continental Auto bus company at office #45, tel. 917-456-300), **Santiago** (6/day, 7–9 hrs, includes hourly 24:00–8:30 night bus), and **Granada** (11/day, 5.25 hrs, Continental Auto, tel. 915-272-961). Catch the bus at Estación Sur Autobuses, which sits squarely atop Metro: Méndez Álvaro and has eateries and a small TI open daily 9:00–20:45 (Avenida de Méndez Álvaro, tel. 914-684-200).

Madrid's Barajas Airport

Ten miles east of downtown, Madrid's modern airport has three terminals, connected by long indoor walkways (an 8-minute walk apart). The Metro is in Terminal 2.

If you are flying internationally, you'll likely land at Terminal 1, which has the following: a helpful English-speaking **TI** (marked *Oficina de Información Turística,* daily 8:00–20:00, tel. 913-058-

656); an **ATM** (part of the BBVA bank where you can also buy Alhambra tickets) that's far busier than the lonely American Express window; a 24-hour **exchange office** (plus shorter-hour exchange offices); a **flight info office** (marked simply *Information* in airport lobby, open 24 hrs/day, tel. 902-353-570); a **post-office** window; a **pharmacy;** lots of **phones** (buy a phone card from the machine near the phones); a few scattered **Internet** terminals (small fee); **eateries;** a **RENFE office** (where you can get train info and buy train tickets; daily 8:00–21:00, tel. 913-058-544); and on-the-spot **car-rental agencies** (see above).

Iberia, Spanair, and Air Europa are Spain's airlines, connecting a reasonable number of cities in Spain, as well as international destinations (ask for best rates at travel agencies).

Getting between the Airport and Downtown: By public transport, consider an affordable, efficient **airport bus/taxi combination.** Take the airport bus #89 (no number on bus, but sign *Plaza de Colón-Aeropuerto,* usually blue, ignore bus #101 that goes to the outskirts) from the airport to Madrid's Plaza Colón (€2.50, 4/hr, 20–30 min, leaves Madrid 4:45–1:30 in morning, leaves airport 4:45–2:00 in morning, stops at both Terminals 1 and 2; at the airport, the bus stop is outside Terminal 1's arrivals door, all the way to the right; at Plaza Colón, the stop is underground—marked at top of stairs on square as *Terminal Bus Aeropuerto*). Then, to reach your hotel from Plaza Colón, catch a taxi (insist on meter, ride to hotel should be less than €6; to avoid €2.20 supplement charge for rides from a bus station, it's a little cheaper to go upstairs and flag down a taxi). Or from Plaza Colón, take the subway (from the underground bus stop, walk up the stairs and face the blue *URBIS* sign high on a building—the subway stop, M. Serrano, is 50 yards to your right; it takes one transfer at Bilbao to reach Puerta del Sol).

Consider the simpler **AeroCity shuttle bus service,** which provides door-to-door transport. The fee of €17 covers up to three people per trip; extra passengers pay more (runs 24 hrs, price includes one piece of luggage and one carry-on per person, can book at one of their desks at the airport: Terminal 1—near arrival gate 2; Terminal 2—between arrival gates 5 and 6; or reserve in advance online or by phone or fax; credit card holds reservation but payment required in cash; tel. 917-477-570, fax 917-481-114, www.aerocity.com).

The **Metro** is the cheapest way to get downtown, but involves two transfers (€1.15, or get a shareable 10-pack—10 *viajes*—for €5.35). The airport's futuristic Aeropuerto Metro stop (notice the cash machines, subway info booth, and huge lighted map of Madrid) is in Terminal 2. Access the Metro at the check-in level; to reach the Metro from Terminal 1's arrivals level, stand with your back to the baggage claim, then go to your far right, up the stairs, and follow red-and-blue Metro diamond signs to the station (8-min walk). To get to Puerta del Sol, take line #8 for 12 minutes to Nuevos Ministerios, then continue on line #10 to Tribunal, then line #1 to Puerto del Sol (30 min more total); or exit at Nuevos Ministerios and take a €5 taxi or bus #150 straight to Puerto del Sol.

For a **taxi** to or from the airport, allow €20 during the day or €30 at night and on weekends. Insist on the meter. The €4.20 airport supplement is legal.

TOLEDO

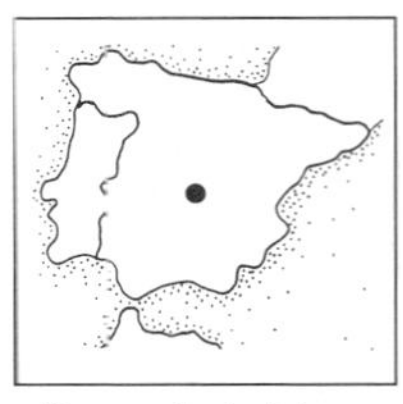

An hour south of Madrid, Toledo teems with tourists, souvenirs, and great art by day, delicious roast suckling pig, echoes of El Greco, and medieval magic by night. Incredibly well-preserved and full of cultural wonder, the entire city has been declared a national monument.

Spain's former capital crowds 3,500 years of tangled history—Roman, Jewish, Visigothic, Moorish, and Christian—onto a high, rocky perch protected on three sides by the Tajo (Tagus) River. It's so well-preserved that the Spanish government has forbidden any modern exteriors. The rich mix of Jewish, Moorish, and Christian heritages makes it one of Europe's art capitals.

Perched strategically in the center of Iberia, Toledo was for centuries a Roman transportation hub with a thriving Jewish population. After Rome fell, the city became a Visigothic capital (A.D. 554). In 711, the Moors (Muslims) made it a regional center. In 1085, the city was reconquered by the Christians, but many Moors remained in Toledo, tolerated and respected as scholars and craftsmen. And from Toledo's earliest times, the city was a haven for Sephardic Jews—educated, wealthy, and cosmopolitan—who were commonly persecuted elsewhere in Europe.

During its medieval heyday (c. 1350), Toledo was famous for intellectual tolerance—a city for the humanities, where God was known by many names. It was a *Sesame Street* world of cultural diversity, home to Jews, Muslims, and Christians, living together in harmony.

Toledo remained Spain's political capital until 1561, when it reached its natural limits of growth as defined by the Tajo River Gorge. When the king moved to more-spacious Madrid, Toledo

Greater Toledo

was mothballed, only to be rediscovered by 19th-century Romantic travelers who wrote of it as a mystical place.

Today, Toledo thrives as a provincial capital and a busy tourist attraction. It remains the historic, artistic, and spiritual center of Spain. In spite of tremendous tourist crowds, Toledo sits enthroned on its history, much as it was when Europe's most powerful king and El Greco called it home.

Planning Your Time

To properly see Toledo's museums (great El Greco), cathedral (best in Spain), and medieval atmosphere (best after dark), you'll need two nights and a day. Plan carefully for lunch closings, and note that a few sights are closed Monday (including Museo El Greco and Sinagoga del Tránsito).

Toledo is just 60 minutes away from Madrid by bus (2/hr), train (3/day), or taxi (about €65 one-way from Puerta del Sol—negotiate ride without a meter). The new high-speed AVE connection will cut the journey by rail to just 15–20 minutes, when it ever gets finished. A car is useless in Toledo. Ideally, see the town outside of car-rental time; pick up or drop off your car here. **Hertz** is at the train station (tel. 925-253-890) and **Avis** is on Calle Venancio González, below the main square (Mon–Fri 9:30–13:30 & 16:30–20:00, Sat 9:30–14:00, closed Sun, tel. 925-214-535).

ORIENTATION

Toledo sits atop a circular hill, with the cathedral roughly dead center. Lassoed into a tight tangle of streets by the sharp bend of the Tajo River (called the Tejo in Portugal, where it hits the Atlantic at Lisbon), Toledo has Spain's most confusing medieval street plan. But it's a small town of 70,000, the major sights are well-signposted, and most locals will politely point you in the right direction.

Those driving into Toledo can enjoy a scenic big-picture orientation by following the *Ronda de Toledo* signs on a big circular drive around the city. The best time for this is the magic hour before sunset, when the top viewpoints are busy with tired old folks and frisky young lovers.

Look at the map and take a mental orientation walk past Toledo's main sights. Starting in the Plaza Zocódover (zoh-KOH-doh-ver), go southwest along the Calle Comercio. After passing the cathedral on your left, follow the signs to Santo Tomé and the cluster of other sights. The visitor's city lies basically along one small but central street—and most tourists never stray from this axis. Make a point to get lost. The town is small and bounded on three sides by the river. When it's time to get somewhere, I pull out the map or ask, "*¿Dónde está Plaza Zocódover?*"

Tourist Information

Toledo has three TIs. The one that covers Toledo, as well as the region, is in a free-standing brick building just outside the Bisagra Gate (the last surviving gate of the 10th-century fortifications), where those arriving by train or bus enter the old town (Mon–Fri 9:00–18:00, Sat 9:00–19:00, Sun 9:00–15:00, longer hours in summer, tel. 925-220-843).

The second TI is in front of the cathedral on Plaza Ayuntamiento (Mon 10:30–14:30, Tue–Sun 10:30–14:30 & 16:30–19:00, tel. 925-254-030). A handier, third TI, which includes a convenience store and restaurant, is close to Plaza Zocódover at Sillería 14 (daily 10:30–19:00, closes at 18:00 Oct–March, tel. 925-220-300).

Toledo

Consider the readable local guidebook, *Toledo: Its Art and Its History* (small version for €5, sold all over town). It explains all of the sights (which generally provide no on-site information) and gives you a photo to point at and say, "*¿Dónde está...?*"

Arrival in Toledo

"Arriving" in Toledo means getting uphill to Plaza Zocódover. From the **train station,** that's a 20-minute hike, €3 taxi ride, or easy bus ride (#5 or #6, €0.80, pay on bus, confirm by asking, "*¿Para Plaza Zocódover?*"). You can stow extra baggage at the station. Consider buying a city map at the kiosk; it's better than the free one at the TI. If you're walking, turn right as you leave the station, cross the bridge, pass the bus station, go straight through the roundabout, and continue uphill to the TI and the Bisagra Gate.

If you arrive by **bus,** go upstairs to the station lobby. You'll find the luggage storage and a small bus-information office opposite the cafeteria. Confirm your departure time (probably every half hour on the hour to Madrid). When you buy your return ticket

Toledo at a Glance

▲▲▲Cathedral One of Europe's best, with a marvelously vast interior and great art. **Hours:** Cathedral—daily 8:00–12:00 & 16:00–18:00; sights inside—daily 10:30–18:00.

▲▲Santa Cruz Museum Renaissance building housing wonderful artwork, including 15 El Grecos. **Hours:** Unpredictable.

▲Alcázar Imposing former imperial residence that dominates Toledo's skyline. **Hours:** Interior currently closed for renovation.

▲Santo Tomé Simple chapel with El Greco's masterpiece, *The Burial of the Count of Orgaz.* **Hours:** Daily 10:00–18:45, until 17:45 mid-Oct–March.

Museo El Greco and "El Greco's House" Replica of El Greco–era home, featuring 20 works by the painter. **Hours:** Tue–Sat 10:00–14:00 & 16:00–21:00 (closes Tue–Sat at 18:00 Dec–Feb), Sun 10:00–13:45, closed Mon.

Sinagoga del Tránsito Museum of Toledo's Jewish past. **Hours:** Tue–Sat 10:00–14:00 & 16:00–17:45, Sun 10:00–13:45, closed Mon.

Sinagoga de Santa María Blanca Harmoniously combines Toledo's three religious influences: Jewish, Christian, and Moorish. **Hours:** Daily April–Sept 10:00–18:45, Oct–March 10:00–17:45.

Museo Victorio Macho Collection of the 20th-century Toledo sculptor's works, with expansive river-gorge view. **Hours:** Mon–Sat 10:00–19:00, Sun 10:00–15:00.

San Juan de los Reyes Monasterio Church/monastery that was to be the final resting place of Isabel and Ferdinand. **Hours:** Daily 10:00–19:00, until 18:00 in winter.

to Madrid—which you can put off until just minutes before you leave—specify you'd like a *directo* bus; the *ruta* trip takes longer (60 min vs. 75 min). From the bus station, Plaza Zocódover is a 15-minute walk (see directions from train station, above), €3 taxi ride, or short bus ride (catch #5 downstairs, underneath the lobby, €0.80, pay on bus).

A series of **escalators** runs near the Bisagra Gate, giving you a free ride up, up, up into town (daily 8:00–22:00). You'll end up near the synagogues and far from Plaza Zocódover, but this doesn't matter. It's great for drivers, who can park free in the streets near the base of the escalator or for a fee (€12.50/day) in the parking lot across from it. Toledo is no fun to drive in. If you don't park near the escalator, drive into town and park in the Garage Alcázar (opposite the Alcázar in the old town—€1.20/hr, €12.50/day).

SIGHTS

▲▲▲Cathedral—Holy Toledo! Spain's leading Catholic city has a magnificent cathedral. Shoehorned into the old center, its exterior is hard to appreciate. But the interior is so lofty, rich, and vast that it'll have you wandering around like a Pez dispenser stuck open, whispering "Wow."

Cost and Hours: While the basic cathedral is free, seeing the great art—located in four separate places within the cathedral (the choir, chapter house, sacristy, and treasury)—requires a €5.50 ticket sold in the Tienda la Catedral shop opposite the church entrance (shop open Mon–Sat 10:30–18:00, Sun 14:00–18:00; also rents audioguides for €3). The strict dress-code sign covers even your attitude: no shorts, no tank tops...and no slouching.

The cathedral itself is free and open to the public (daily 8:00–12:00 & 16:00–18:00, no WC in cathedral or cathedral shop). The four sights inside are open 10:30–18:00. Even though the cathedral closes from 12:00 to 16:00, if you have a ticket you can get in and tour the cathedral as well, with fewer crowds. (Note that the cloister is closed to everyone 13:00–15:30.)

Self-Guided Tour: Holy redwood forest, Batman! Wander among the pillars. Sit under one and imagine a time when the light bulbs were candles and the tourists were pilgrims—before the *No Photo* signs, when every window provided spiritual as well as physical light. The cathedral is primarily Gothic, but since it took more than 250 years to build (1226–1495), you'll see a mix of styles—Gothic, Renaissance, and Baroque. Enjoy the elaborate wrought-iron work, lavish wood carvings, window after colorful window of 500-year-old stained glass, and a sacristy with a collection of paintings that would put any museum on the map.

Toledo's Cathedral

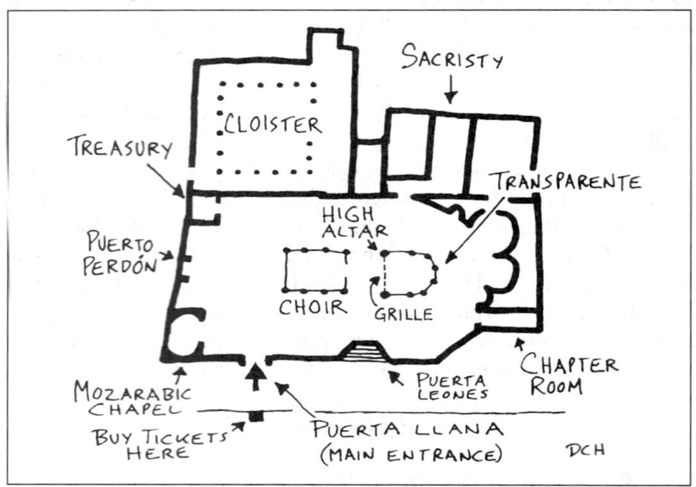

This confusing collage of great Spanish art deserves a close look. Hire a private guide, freeload on a tour (they come by every few minutes during peak season), or follow this quick tour. Here's a framework for your visit:

1. High Altar: First, walk to the high altar to marvel through the iron grille at one of the most stunning altars in Spain. Real gold on pine wood, by Flemish, French, and local artists, it's one of the country's best pieces of Gothic art. About-face to the...

2. Choir: Facing the high altar, the choir is famous for its fine carving and requires a piece of your four-part ticket. The lower wooden stalls are decorated with scenes celebrating the slow one-city-at-a-time Christian victory as the Muslims were pushed back into Africa. Each idealized castle has the reconquered town's name on it, culminating with the final victory at Granada in 1492. The upper stalls (which flank the grand throne of the archbishop) feature Old Testament figures carved out of alabaster. And, as is typical of choir decoration, the carvings on the misericords (the tiny seats allowing tired worshippers to lean while they "stand") feature the frisky, folksy, sexy, profane art of the day. Apparently, since you sat on it, it could never be sacred anyway. There are two fine pipe organs: one 18th-century Baroque and the other 19th-century neoclassical. Note the serene beauty of the 13th-century Madonna and Child at the front, thought to be a gift from the French king to Spain.

The iron grille of the choir is notable for the dedication of the man who built it. Domingo de Céspedes, a Toledo ironworker, accepted the commission to build the grille for 6,000 ducats. The project, which took from 1541 to 1548, was far more costly than he anticipated. The medieval Church didn't accept cost overruns, so to finish it, he sold everything he owned and went into debt. He died a poor—but honorable—man.

3. Chapter House: Face the altar and go around it to your right to the chapter house *(sala capitular)*. Its lavish ceiling celebrates Italian Renaissance humanism with a groundbreaking fresco. You're surrounded by interesting Bible-storytelling frescoes and a pictorial review of 1,900 years of Toledo archbishops. Though the upper row of portraits were not painted from life, the lower portraits were, and therefore are of more historic and artistic interest. Imagine sitting down to church business surrounded by all this tradition and theology. As you leave, notice the iron-pumping cupids carved into the pear-tree panels lining the walls.

The ***transparente,*** behind the high altar, is a unique feature of the cathedral. In the 1700s, a hole was cut into the ceiling to let a sunbeam brighten the Mass. Melding this big hole into the Gothic church presented a challenge that resulted in a Baroque masterpiece. Gape up at this riot of angels doing flip-flops, babies breathing thin air, bottoms of feet, and gilded sunbursts. Study the altar, which looks chaotic but is actually thoughtfully structured: The good news of salvation springs from baby Jesus, up past the angel (who knows how to hold a big fish correctly) to the Last Supper high above, and beyond into the light-filled dome. I like it, as did, I guess, the long-dead cardinal whose faded red hat hangs from the edge of the hole. (A perk that only cardinals enjoy is choosing the place in the cathedral where their hat will hang until it rots.)

4. Sacristy: The cathedral's sacristy has 20 El Grecos as well as masterpieces by Francisco de Goya, Titian, Peter Paul Rubens, Diego Velázquez, Michelangelo Caravaggio, and Giovanni Bellini. First, notice the fine perspective work on the 18th-century ceiling (frescoed by Lucca Giordano from Naples). Then walk to the end of the room for the most important painting in the collection, El Greco's *The Spoliation* (a.k.a. *The Denuding of Christ*).

Spain's first great painter was Greek, and this is his first masterpiece (1579) after arriving in Toledo. El Greco's painting, which hangs above a marble altar that he may have personally designed, shows Jesus surrounded by a sinister mob and suffering the humiliation of being stripped in public before his execution.

The scarlet robe is about to be yanked off, and the women (lower left) avert their eyes, turning to watch a carpenter at work (lower right) who bores the holes for nailing Jesus to the cross. While the carpenter bears down, Jesus—the other carpenter—looks up to heaven, with a "Why me?" expression. The contrast between the motley crowd gambling for his clothes and Jesus' noble face underscores the quiet dignity with which he endures the humiliation. Jesus' delicate white hand stands out from the flaming red tunic with an odd gesture that's common in El Greco's paintings. Some say this was the way Christians of the day swore they were true believers, not merely Christians-for-convenience, like former Muslims or Jews who converted out of necessity.

On the right is a rare religious painting by Goya, the *Betrayal of Christ,* which shows Judas preparing to kiss Jesus, thus identifying him to the Roman soldiers. Enjoy the many other El Grecos. Find the small but lifelike 17th-century carving of St. Francis by Pedro de Mena (to your right as you entered the door).

5. Treasury: The *tesoro* has plenty to see. The highlight is the 10-foot-high, 430-pound monstrance—the tower designed to hold the Holy Communion bread (the Host) during the festival of Corpus Christi (body of Christ) as it parades through the city. Built in 1517 by Enrique de Arfe, it's made of 5,000 individual pieces held together by 12,500 screws. There are diamonds, emeralds, rubies, and 400 pounds of gold-plated silver. The inner part is 35 pounds of solid gold. Yeow. The base is a later addition from the Baroque period. Traditionally, it's thought that much of this gold and silver arrived in Columbus' first load home.

To the right of the monstrance, find the fancy sword of Franco. To the right of that is a gift from St. Louis, the king of France—a 700-year-old Bible printed and beautifully illustrated by French monks. (It's actually a copy, and the precious original is stored elsewhere.) Imagine the exquisite experience for medieval eyes of reading this, with its lavish illustrations. The finely-painted small crucifix on the opposite side—by the great Gothic Florentine painter Fra Angelico—depicts Jesus alive on the back and dead on the front. This was a gift from Mussolini to Franco. Hmmm. There's even a gift in this room from Toledo's sister city, Toledo, Ohio.

If you're at the cathedral between 9:00 and 9:15, you can peek into the otherwise-locked **Mozarabic Chapel** (Capilla Mozárabe). The Visigothic Mass, the oldest surviving Christian ritual in Western Europe, starts at 9:15 (9:45 on Sun). You're welcome to partake in this stirring example of peaceful coexistence of faiths—but once the door closes, you're a Visigoth for 30 minutes.

▲▲Santa Cruz Museum—For years, this museum has been in a confused state of renovation—not really open, not really closed. During renovation, the museum's cloister and a room full of its best art will be open and free. If the core of the building is filled with a temporary exhibit, you can generally wander in for a free look. The building's Plateresque facade is worth seeing anytime.

This great Renaissance building was an orphanage and hospital, built from money left by the humanist and diplomat Cardinal Mendoza when he died in 1495. The cardinal, confirmed as Chancellor of Castile by Queen Isabel, was so influential he was called "the third king." The building is in the form of a Greek cross under a Moorish dome. After renovation, the arms of the building—formerly wards—will be filled with 16th-century art, tapestries, furniture, armor, and documents. It'll be a stately, classical, music-filled setting with a cruel lack of English information (Mon–Sat 10:00–18:30, Sun 10:00–14:00, just off Plaza Zocódover, go through arch, Cervantes 3).

The collection includes 15 El Grecos. The highlight: the impressive *Assumption of Mary,* a spiritual poem on canvas. This altarpiece, finished one year before El Greco's death (in 1614), is the culmination of his unique style, combining all of his techniques to express an other-worldly event.

While on earth, the city of Toledo sleeps, a vision taking place overhead. An angel in a billowing robe spreads his wings and flies up, supporting Mary, the mother of Christ. She floats up through warped space, to be serenaded by angels and wrapped in the radiant light of the Holy Spirit. Mary flickers and ripples, charged from within by her spiritual ecstasy, caught up in a vision that takes her breath away. No painter before or since has captured the supernatural world better than El Greco.

Find the lavish but faded Astrolabe Tapestry (c. 1480, Belgian) which shows a new world view at the dawn of the Renaissance and the age of discovery: God oversees all, as Atlas spins the Cosmos containing the circular Earth, and the wisdom gang (far right) heralds the new age.

An enormous blue banner hangs like a long, skinny tooth opposite the entry. This flew from the flagship of Don Juan of Austria and recalls the pivotal 1571 naval victory over the Muslims at the Battle of Lepanto off the coast of Greece. Lepanto was a key victory in the centuries-long struggle of Christian Europe against the Muslim threat.

▲Alcázar—This huge former imperial residence—built on the site of Roman, Visigothic, and Moorish fortresses—dominates the Toledo skyline. Currently closed for renovation, it will be the National Military Museum when it reopens, likely in 2007. The Alcázar became a kind of right-wing Alamo during Spain's civil war, when a force of Franco's Nationalists (and hundreds of hostages) were besieged for two months in 1936. Finally, after many fierce but futile Republican attacks, Franco sent in an army that took Toledo and freed the Alcázar. The place was rebuilt and glorified under Franco.

▲Tourist Train—For great city views, hop on the cheesy Tren Imperial Tourist Tram. Crass as it feels, you get a 50-minute putt-putt through Toledo and around the Tajo River Gorge. It's a great way to get a general city overview and for non-drivers to enjoy views of the city from across the Tajo Gorge (€3.60, buy ticket from TI at Sillería 14, daily from 11:00, leaves Plaza Zocódover on the hour, tape-recorded English/Spanish commentary, no photo stops but it goes slow; for the best views of Toledo across the gorge, sit on right side, not behind driver; tel. 925-220-300).

Southwest Toledo

▲Santo Tomé—A simple chapel holds El Greco's most-loved painting. *The Burial of the Count of Orgaz* couples Heaven and Earth in a way only The Greek could. It feels so right to see a painting left in situ where the artist put it 400 years ago. Take this slow. Stay a while—let it perform.

The year is 1312. You're at the burial of the good count, who's being laid to rest right here in this chapel. He was so holy, even saints Augustine and Stephen have come down from Heaven to be pallbearers. (The painting's subtitle is "Such is the reward for those who serve God and his saints.")

More than 250 years later, in 1586, a priest hired El Greco to make a painting of the burial to hang over the count's tomb. The funeral is attended by all of Toledo's most distinguished citizens. The painting is divided in two by a serene line of noble faces—Heaven above and Earth below. Above the line of long, somber faces, the count's soul, symbolized by a little baby, rises up through a mystical birth canal to be reborn in Heaven, where he's greeted by Jesus, Mary, and all the saints. A spiritual wind blows through as colors change and shapes stretch. This is Counter-Reformation propaganda—notice Jesus pointing to St. Peter, the symbol of the pope in Rome, who controls the keys to the Pearly Gates. Each face is a detailed portrait. El Greco himself (eyeballing you, 7th figure in from the left) is the only one not involved in the burial. The boy in the foreground—pointing to the two saints as if to say, "One's from the first century, the other's from the fourth...it's a miracle!"—is El Greco's son. On the handkerchief in the boy's pocket is El Greco's signature, written in Greek (€1.50, daily 10:00–18:45, until 17:45 mid-Oct–March, free audioguide, tel. 925-256-098).

Museo El Greco and "El Greco's House"—While many call this El Greco's House, it's actually a traditionally-furnished Renaissance "monument house" built near where he likely lived. You'll see about 20 El Greco paintings, including his masterful *View of Toledo* and portraits of the Apostles. Period pottery and furniture recreate the home and studio of this sophisticated foreigner, who hung out with Spain's writers, bishops, and philosophers (€2.40, free Sat afternoon from 14:30 and all day Sun; Tue–Sat 10:00–14:00 & 16:00–21:00, until 18:00 in winter, Sun 10:00–13:45, closed Mon, Samuel Levi 3).

Sinagoga del Tránsito (Museo Sefardí)—Built in 1361, this is the best surviving slice of Toledo's Jewish past. The museum displays

El Greco
(1541–1614)

Born on Crete and trained in Venice, Doménikos Theotokópoulos (tongue-tied friends just called him "The Greek") came to Spain to get a job decorating El Escorial. He failed there, but succeeded in Toledo, where he spent the last 37 years of his life. He mixed all three regional influences into his palette. From his Greek homeland, he absorbed the solemn, abstract style of icons. In Italy, he learned the bold use of color, elongated figures, twisting poses, and dramatic style of the later Renaissance. These styles were then fused in the fires of fanatic Spanish-Catholic devotion.

Not bound by the realism so important to his 16th-century contemporaries, El Greco painted dramatic visions of striking colors and figures—bodies unnatural and lengthened as though stretched between Heaven and Earth. He painted souls, not faces. His work is on display at nearly every sight in Toledo. Thoroughly modern in his disregard of realism, he didn't impress the austere Spanish king. But his art seems as fresh as contemporary art today.

Jewish artifacts, including costumes, menorahs, and books (€2.40, free Sat afternoon from 14:30 and all day Sun, audioguide-€3; Tue–Sat 10:00–14:00 & 16:00–21:00, Sun 10:00–13:45, Dec–Feb closes Tue–Sat at 18:00, closed Mon, near Museo El Greco, with same price and hours, on Calle de los Reyes Católicos).

The synagogue's interior decor looks more Muslim than Jewish. After Christians reconquered the city in 1085, many Moorish workmen stayed on, beautifying the city with their unique style called Mudejar. The synagogue's intricate, geometrical carving (in alabaster) features leaves, vines, and flowers, but no human shapes, since that would violate the Koran's prohibition on making "graven images." In the frieze (running along the upper wall, just below the ceiling), the Arabic-looking script is actually Hebrew, quoting psalms from the Bible. The back-wall balcony is the traditional separate worship area for women.

This 14th-century synagogue was built at the peak of Toledo's enlightened tolerance—built for Jews, with Christian approval, by Moorish craftsmen. Nowhere else in the city does Toledo's three-culture legacy—Christians, Muslims, and Jews—shine brighter than at this synagogue. But in 1391, just a few decades after it was built, Spanish kings began a violent campaign to unite Spain as a Christian nation, forcing Jews and Muslims to convert or leave. In 1492, Ferdinand and Isabel exiled Spain's remaining Jews. It's estimated that, in the 15th century, a third of Spain's Jews were

Toledo's Muslim Legacy

You can see the Moorish influence in the:

- Sinagoga del Tránsito's Mudejar plasterwork
- Sinagoga de Santa María Blanca's mosque-like horseshoe arches
- Bisagra Gate's horseshoe arch
- Square minaret-like towers (like on the Alcázar, originally built by the Moors)
- The city's labyrinthine, medina-like streets

killed, a third survived by converting to Christianity, and a third moved elsewhere.

Sinagoga de Santa María Blanca—This synagogue-turned-church with Moorish horseshoe arches and wall carvings is an eclectic but harmonious gem, and a vivid reminder of the religious cultures that shared this city (€1.50, daily 10:00–18:45, Oct–March until 17:45, no photos allowed, Calle de los Reyes Católicos 2–4).

Museo Victorio Macho—After *mucho* El Greco, try Macho. Overlooking the gorge, this small, attractive museum—once the home and workshop of the early-20th-century sculptor Victorio Macho—offers several rooms of his bold work interspersed with view terraces. The highlight is *La Madre,* Macho's life-size sculpture of an older woman sitting in a chair. But the big draw for many is the air-conditioned theater featuring two fast-moving nine-minute videos. One sweeps through Toledo's history, while the other focuses on Jews in Toledo (€3, half-price for young and old, Mon–Sat 10:00–19:00, Sun 10:00–15:00, request video showing in English, longer 29-minute history video available, Plaza de Victorio Macho 2, between the two *sinagogas* listed above, tel. 925-284-225).

The **river gorge view** from the Museo Vitorio Macho terrace (or free terraces nearby) shows well how the River Tajo served as a formidable moat protecting the city. Imagine trying to attack from this side. The 14th-century bridge on the right and the remains of a bridge on the left connected the town with the region's *cigarrales*—mansions of wealthy families with orchards of figs and apricots that dot the hillside even today.

San Juan de los Reyes Monasterio—St. John of the Monarchs is a grand, generally Flemish-style monastery, church, and cloisters—thought-provoking because the Catholic Monarchs (Isabel and Ferdinand) planned to be buried here. But after the Moors were expelled in 1492 from Granada, their royal bodies were planted there to show Spain's commitment to maintaining a Moor-free peninsula. Today the courtyard is a delightful spot where happy critters carved into the columns seem to chirp with the birds in the trees. Notice the arrows and yoke representing the kingdom's unity achieved by the Royal Monarchs (€1.50, daily 10:00–19:00, until 18:00 in winter, San Juan de los Reyes 2, tel. 925-223-802).

SHOPPING

Toledo probably sells as many souvenirs as any city in Spain. This is the place to buy medieval-looking swords, armor, maces, three-legged stools, lethal-looking letter-openers, and other nouveau antiques. It's also Spain's damascene center, where, for centuries, craftspeople have inlaid black steel with gold, silver, and copper wire.

At the workshop of English-speaking **Mariano Zamorano,** you can see swords and knives being made. Judging by what's left of Mariano's hand, his knives are among the sharpest (Mon–Sat 9:00–14:00 & 16:00–19:00, closed Sat afternoon and Sun, Calle Ciudad 19, near cathedral and Plaza Ayuntamiento, tel. 925-222-634, www.marianozamorano.com).

El Martes, Toledo's colorful outdoor flea market, bustles on Paseo de Marchen, better known to locals as "La Vega" (near TI at Bisagra Gate), on Tuesdays from 9:00 to 14:00.

SLEEPING

Madrid day-trippers darken the sunlit cobbles, but few stay to see Toledo's medieval moonrise. Spend the night. Spring and fall are high season; November through March and July and August are less busy. There are no private rooms for rent.

Sleep Code

(€1 = about $1.20, country code: 34)
S = Single, **D** = Double/Twin, **T** = Triple, **Q** = Quad, **b** = bathroom, **s** = shower only, **SE** = Speaks English, **NSE** = No English. Breakfast and the 7 percent IVA tax are not included unless noted. Credit cards are accepted unless otherwise noted.

To help you easily sort through these listings, I've divided the rooms into three categories, based on the price for a standard double room with bath during high season:

$$$ **Higher Priced**—Most rooms €90 or more.
$$ **Moderately Priced**—Most rooms between €60–90.
$ **Lower Priced**—Most rooms €60 or less.

Toledo's Plaza Zocódover

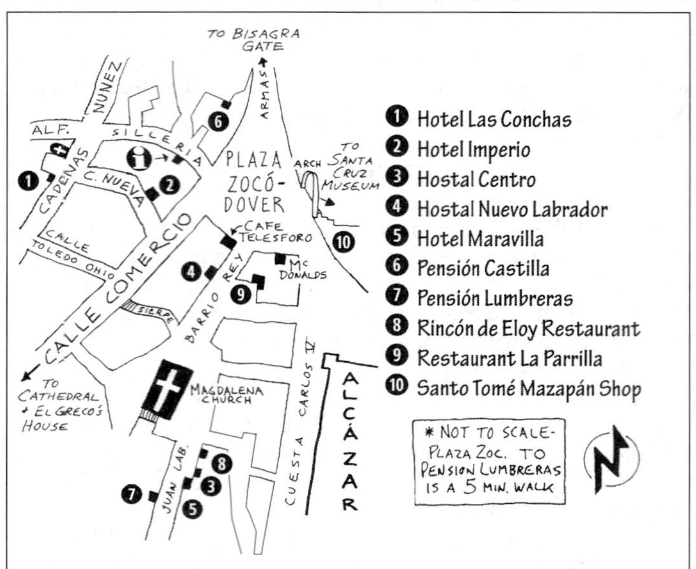

Near Plaza Zocódover

$$ Hotel Las Conchas, a three-star hotel, gleams with marble and sheer pride. It's so sleek and slick it almost feels more like a hospital than a hotel. Its 35 rooms are plenty comfortable (Sb-€55, Db-€75, Db with terrace-€85, breakfast-€5, includes tax, air-con, near the Alcázar at Juan Labrador 8, tel. 925-210-760, fax 925-224-271, www.lasconchas.com, lasconchas@ctv.es, Sole SE).

$ Hotel Imperio is well run, offering 21 basic air-conditioned rooms with marginal beds in a handy old-town location. Weekends can be noisy; ask for a *tranquilo* room (Sb-€28, Db-€42, Tb-€57, includes tax, elevator, cheery café, from Calle Comercio at #38 go a block uphill to Calle Cadenas 5, tel. 925-227-650, fax 925-253-183, www.terra.es/personal/himperio, himperio@teleline.es, friendly Pablo and Esther SE).

$ Hostal Centro rents 28 modern, clean, and comfy rooms just around the corner (Sb-€30, Db-€45, Tb-€60, roof garden, 50 yards off Plaza Zocódover, first right off Calle Comercio at Calle Nueva 13, tel. 925-257-091, fax 925-257-848, www.hostalcentro.com, hostalcentro@telefonica.net, Asun or Ángel, SE).

$ The quiet, modern **Hostal Nuevo Labrador,** with 14 clean, shiny, and spacious rooms, is another good value (Sb-€28, Db-€42, Tb-€55, Qb-€65, includes tax, no breakfast, elevator, Juan Labrador 10, half-board possible in next-door restaurant Rincón de Eloy, tel. 925-222-620, fax 925-229-399, hostalcentro@telefonica

.net, NSE, jointly owned with Hostal Centro, above).

$ Hotel Maravilla, wonderfully central and convenient, has gloomy, claustrophobic halls and 18 simple rooms (Sb-€33, Db-€50, Tb-€67, Qb-€80, includes tax, back rooms are quieter, air-con, a block behind Plaza Zocódover at Plaza de Barrio Rey 5, tel. 925-228-317, fax 925-228-155, hostalmaravilla@infonegocio.com, Felisa María SE).

$ Pensión Castilla, a family-run cheapie, has seven basic rooms (S-€18, Db-€28, extra bed possible, cash only, fans, Calle Recoletos 6, tel. 925-256-318, Teresa NSE).

$ Pensión Lumbreras has a tranquil courtyard and 12 simple rooms, some with views, including rooms 3, 6, and 7 (S-€19, D-€33, reception is at Carlo V Hotel around the corner, air-con, Juan Labrador 9, tel. 925-221-571).

Near the Bisagra Gate

$$$ Hostal del Cardenal, a 17th-century cardinal's palace built into Toledo's wall, is quiet and elegant with a cool garden and a stuffy restaurant. This poor-man's parador, at the dusty old gate of Toledo, is closest to the station but below all the old-town action—however, the new escalator takes the sweat out of getting into town (Sb-€63, Db-€102, Tb-€133, 20 percent cheaper mid-Dec through mid-March, breakfast-€7.28, air-con, nearby parking-€12.50/day, *serioso* staff, enter through town wall 100 yards below Bisagra Gate, Paseo de Recaredo 24, tel. 925-224-900, fax 925-222-991, www.hostaldelcardenal.com, cardenal@hostaldelcardenal.com).

$ Hotel Sol, with 25 newly-decorated rooms in tasteful colors, is a great value. It's on a quiet street halfway between the Bisagra Gate and Plaza Zocódover (Sb-€40, Db-€55, Tb-€68, includes tax, breakfast-€3.60, air-con, parking-€8/day, 50 yards down lane off busy main drag at Hotel Real, Azacanes 8, tel. 925-213-650, fax 925-216-159, www.fedeto.es/hotel-sol, hotel.sol@to.adade.es, José Carlos SE). Their "Hostal Sol" annex across the street is just as comfortable and a bit cheaper. A handy launderette is next door.

$ Hostal Hospedería de los Reyes, good for drivers, has 15 colorful and thoughtfully-appointed rooms in a new, attractive, yellow building 100 yards north of the Bisagra Gate, outside the wall (Sb-€38, Db-€50, includes breakfast, air-con, elevator, Perala 37, tel. 925-283-667, fax 925-283-668, www.hospederiadelosreyes.com).

Deep in Toledo

$$$ Hotel Pintor El Greco, at the far end of the old town, has 33 plush and rustic-feeling rooms with all the comforts, yet it's in a historic 17th-century building. A block from Santo Tomé in a Jewish Quarter garden, it's very quiet (Sb-€83, Db-€103, Tb-€122, tax not included, elevator, air-con, Alamillos del Tránsito

Toledo Hotels and Restaurants

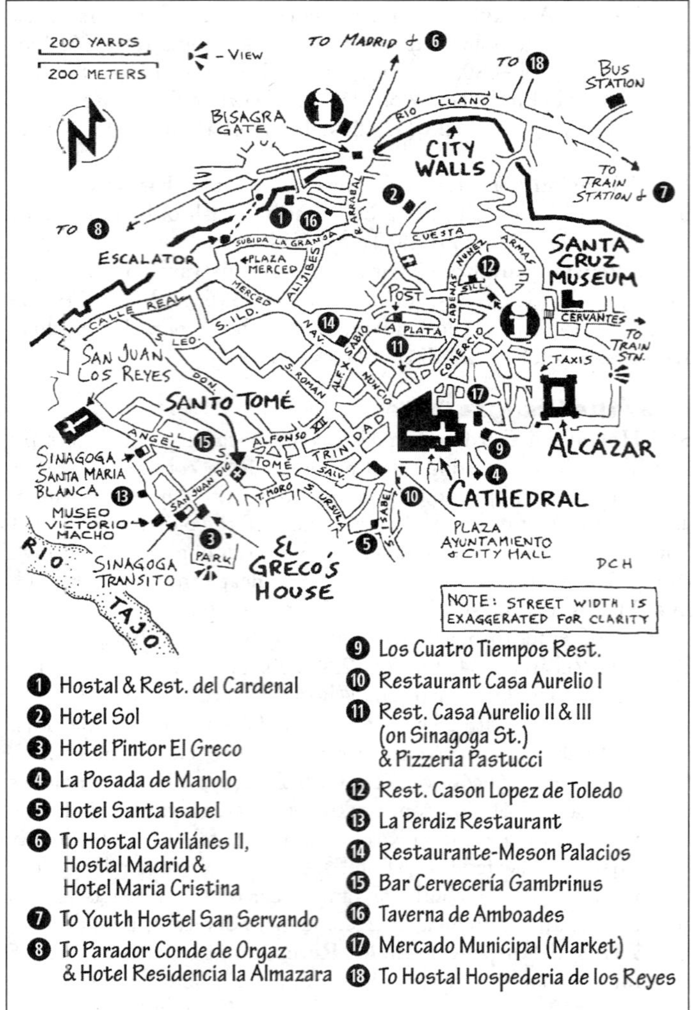

13, tel. 925-285-191, fax 925-215-819, www.hotelpintorelgreco.com, info@hotelpintorelgreco.com).

$$ La Posada de Manolo rents 14 thoughtfully-furnished rooms across from the downhill corner of the cathedral. Manolo Junior recently opened "The House of Manolo" according to his father's vision: a comfortable place with each of its three floors themed a little differently—Moorish, Jewish, and Christian (Sb-€42, Db-€66, big Db-€72–84, includes buffet breakfast, no elevator, air-con, 2 nice view terraces, Calle Sixto Ramón Parro 8, tel. 925-282-250, fax 925-282-251, www.laposadademanolo.com, laposadademanolo@wanadoo.es).

$ Hotel Santa Isabel, in a 15th-century building two blocks from the cathedral, has 42 clean, modern, and comfortable rooms and squeaky tile hallways (Sb-€30, Db-€45, Tb-€62, includes tax, breakfast-€4, elevator, air-con, great roof terrace; buried deep in old town so take a taxi instead of the bus; drivers enter from Calle Pozo Amargo, parking-€6; Calle Santa Isabel 24, tel. 925-253-120, fax 925-253-136, www.santa-isabel.com, santa-isabel@arrakis.es, Andres SE).

Outside of Town

$$$ Hotel María Cristina, next to the bullring, is part 15th-century and all modern. This sprawling 74-room hotel has all the comforts under a thin layer of prefab tradition (Sb-€62, Db-€97, Tb-€130, €154 suites available, tax not included, breakfast-€6, elevator, air-con, attached restaurant, parking-€9.35/day, Marqués de Mendigorría 1, tel. 925-213-202, fax 925-212-650, www.hotelmariacristina.com, informacion@hotelmariacristina.com, SE).

$ ***On the road to Madrid (near bullring):*** There's a conspiracy of clean, modern, and hardworking little hotels with comfy rooms a five-minute walk beyond the Bisagra Gate near the bus station and bullring (Plaza de Toros, bullfights only on holidays). Drivers enjoy easy parking here. While it's a 15-minute uphill hike to the old-town action, buses #4 and #6 go from just west of Hostal Madrid directly to Plaza de Zocódover. Two good bets are **Hostal Gaviláncs II** (18 renovated rooms, Sb-€33, Db-€42, Db suite-€81, Tb-€56, Qb-€65, includes taxes, breakfast-€2.50, parking-€5.50/day, air-con, Marqués de Mendigorría 14, tel. & fax 925-211-628, www.gavilanes.to, hostallosgavilanes2@hotmail.com or javi@acceso0.es, NSE) and **Hostal Madrid** (20 rooms, Sb-€27, Db-€39, Tb-€53, includes tax, café next door, parking-€6/day, air-con, Marqués de Mendigorría 7, tel. 925-221-114, fax 925-228-113, NSE). This *hostal* rents nine lesser rooms in an annex across the street.

$ ***Hostel:*** The **Albergue Juvenil San Servando** youth hostel is lavish and newly-renovated but cheap, with small rooms for two, three, or four people; a swimming pool; views; cafeteria; and good management (95 beds, €8.60 per bed if under age 26, €11.30 if age 26 or older, hostel membership required—you can buy it here for €11, add €2.10 to include breakfast, in 10th-century Arab castle of San Servando, 10-min walk from train station, 15-min hike from town center, over Puente Viejo outside town, tel. 925-224-554, reservations tel. 925-267-729, ralberguesto@jccm.es, NSE).

Outside of Town with the Grand Toledo View

$$$ Toledo's **Parador Nacional Conde de Orgaz** is one of Spain's best-known inns, enjoying the same Toledo view El Greco made famous from across the Tajo Gorge (76 rooms, Sb-€58, Db-€120, Db with view-€136, Tb with view-€179, breakfast-€10, €26 *menus* in their fine restaurant overlooking Toledo, 2 windy miles from town at Cerro del Emperador, tel. 925-221-850, fax 925-225-166, www.parador.es/english/index.jsp, toledo@parador.es, SE).

$ Hotel Residencia La Almazara was the summer residence of a 16th-century archbishop of Toledo. A friend of the cardinal and fond of this location's classic Toledo view, El Greco hung out here for inspiration. A lumbering old place with cushy public rooms, 28 simple bedrooms, and a sprawling garden, it's truly in the country but just 1.5 miles out of Toledo (Sb-€30, Db-€41, Db with view-€57, Tb-€48, 10 rooms have view, air-con, Ctra. de Arges 47, follow signs from circular Ronda de Toledo road, tel. 925-223-866, fax 925-250-562, www.hotelalmazara.com, reservas@hotelalmazara.com).

EATING

Dining in Traditional Elegance

A day full of El Greco and the romance of Toledo after dark puts me in the mood for game. Typical Toledo dishes include partridge *(perdiz)*, venison *(venado)*, wild boar *(jabalí)*, roast suckling pig *(cochinillo asado)*, or baby lamb *(cordero)* similarly roasted after a few weeks of mother's milk. After dinner, find a *mazapán* place (such as Santo Tomé) for dessert.

Los Cuatro Tiempos Restaurante specializes in local game and roasts, proficiently served in a tasteful and elegant setting (€18 set menu lunches, €25–30 à la carte dinners, daily 13:30–16:00 & 20:30–23:00, at downhill corner of cathedral at Sixto Ramón Parro 5, tel. 925-223-782).

Toledo's three **Casa Aurelio** restaurants all offer traditional cooking (game, roast suckling pig, traditional soup), with a classy atmosphere more memorable than the meals (13:00–16:30 & 20:00–23:30, 2 closed Sun night, each closed either Mon, Tue, or Wed, air-con). All are within three blocks of the cathedral: Plaza Ayuntamiento 4 is festive (tel. 925-227-716), Sinagoga 6 is most *típico* (tel. 925-222-097), and Sinagoga 1 is the newest and dressiest, with a wine cellar (popular with Toledo's political class, tel. 925-221-392).

Restaurante Casón López de Toledo, a fancy restaurant located in an old noble palace, specializes in Castilian food, particularly venison and partridge. Its character unfolds upstairs (€18 meals, Mon–Sat 13:30–16:00 & 20:30–23:30, closed Sun, Calle Sillería 3, near Plaza Zocódover, tel. 925-254-774).

Hostal del Cardenal Restaurante, a classic hotel restaurant near the Bisagra Gate at the bottom of town, is understandably popular with tourists for its decent traditional roast dishes (daily 13:00–16:00 & 20:30–23:30, Puerto de Recaredo 24, tel. 925-220-862).

For a splurge near the Santa Tomé sights, consider the classy **La Perdiz,** which offers partridge (as the restaurant's name suggests), venison, suckling pig, fish, and more (Tue–Sat 13:00–16:00 & 20:00–23:00, closes Sun about 16:00, closed Mon and first half of Aug, Calle de los Reyes Católicos 7, tel. 925-214-658).

Eating Simply but Well

Restaurante-Mesón Palacios serves good regional food at reasonable prices in a warm and friendly atmosphere. Their bean soup with partridge *(judías con perdiz)* and fish-stuffed peppers *(pimientos de piquillo rellenos de pescado)* are the most popular appetizers among locals (Mon–Sat from 13:00 and from 19:30, closed Sun, Alfonso X 3, near Plaza de San Vicente, tel. 925-215-972, Jesús is appropriately friendly).

Rincón de Eloy is bright, modern, and a cool refuge for lunch on a hot day (€9.50 *menu,* Mon–Sat 13:00–16:00 & 20:00–22:30, closed Sun night, air-con, Juan Labrador 10, near Alcázar, tel. 925-229-399).

Bar Cervecería Gambrinus is a good tapas bar (try their local veal stew *carcamusas* in small frying pans). Restaurant seating is available in its leafy courtyard or in the more elegant upstairs area (daily 9:00–24:00, near Santo Tomé at Santo Tomé 10, tel. 925-214-440).

Restaurante La Parrilla is on a tiny square behind Plaza Zocódover (facing the Casa Telesforo on Plaza Zocódover, go left down alley 30 yards to Plaza de Barrio Rey). The bars and cafés on Plaza Zocódover are reasonable, seasoned with some fine people-watching.

At **Taverna de Amboades,** a humble but earnest wine-and-tapas bar near the Bisagra Gate, expert Miguel Ángel enjoys explaining the differences among Spanish wines. To try some really good wines with quality local cheese and meat, drop by and let Miguel impress you (2 quality wines and a plate of cheese and meat for €7, Tue–Sat 19:30–24:00, also Thu–Sun 12:30–16:00, closed Mon, Alfonso VI 5, mobile 678-483-749).

Pizzeria Pastucci is the local favorite for pizza (Tue–Sun 12:00–16:00 & 19:00–24:00, closed Mon, near cathedral at Calle de la Sinagoga 10).

Picnics are best assembled at the **Mercado Municipal** on Plaza Mayor (on the Alcázar side of cathedral, with a supermarket inside open Mon–Sat 9:00–20:00 and stalls open mostly in the mornings until 14:00, closed Sun). This is a fun market to prowl, even if you don't need food. If you feel like munching a paper-plate-size Communion wafer, one of the stalls sells crispy bags of *obleas*—a great gift for your favorite pastor.

And for Dessert: *Mazapán*

Toledo's famous almond-fruity-sweet *mazapán* is sold all over town. Locals say the best is made by **Santo Tomé** (several outlets, including a handy one on Plaza Zocódover, daily 9:00–22:22). Browse their tempting window displays. They sell *mazapán* goodies individually (2 for about €1, *sin relleno*—without filling—is for purists, *de piñon* has pine nuts, *imperiales* is with almonds, others have fruit fillings) or in small mixed boxes. Their *Toledanas* is a crumbly cookie favorite with a subtle thread of pumpkin filling.

For a sweet and romantic evening moment, pick up a few pastries and head down to the cathedral. Sit on the Plaza Ayuntamiento's benches (or stretch out on the stone wall to the right of the TI). The fountain is on your right, Spain's best-looking city hall is behind you, and there before you: her top cathedral, built back when Toledo was Spain's capital, shining brightly against the black night sky.

TRANSPORTATION CONNECTIONS

Far more buses than trains connect Toledo with Madrid—take the bus.

To Madrid: by Bus (2/hr, 60–75 min, *directo* is faster than *ruta*, Madrid's Estación sur Autobuses, Metro: Mendez Álvaro, Continental Auto bus company, tel. 925-223-641), **by train** (5/day weekdays, 3/day weekends 1.25 hrs; while new AVE fast train is being completed, you need to bus from Toledo to Algodor, then take the train to Madrid's Atocha station), **by car** (40 miles, 1 hr). Toledo bus info: tel. 925-215-850; train info: tel. 902-240-202.

Interlaken

When the 19th-century Romantics redefined mountains as something more than cold and troublesome obstacles, Interlaken became the original Alpine resort. Ever since, tourists have flocked to the Alps "because they're there." Interlaken's glory days are long gone, its elegant old hotels eclipsed by the new, more jet-setty Alpine resorts. Today, its shops are filled with chocolate bars, Swiss Army knives, and sunburned backpackers.

ORIENTATION

Efficient Interlaken (pop. 5,500) is a good administrative and shopping center. Take care of business, give the town a quick look, and view the live TV coverage of the Jungfrau and Schilthorn weather in the window of the Schilthornbahn office on the main street (at Höheweg 2). Then head for the hills. Stay in Interlaken only if you suffer from Alptitude sickness.

Tourist Information: The **TI** has good information for the region, advice on Alpine lift discounts, and a room-finding service (July–Sept Mon–Fri 8:00–18:30, Sat 8:00–17:00, Sun 10:00–12:00 & 16:00–18:00; Oct–June Mon–Fri 8:00–12:00 & 13:30–18:00, Sat 9:00–12:00, closed Sun; Höheweg 37, tel. 033-826-5300, www.interlakentourism.ch; attached to Hotel Metropole on the main street between West and East stations, a 10-min stroll from either). While the Interlaken/Jungfrau region map costs 2 SF, good mini-versions are included in the many free transportation and hiking brochures. Pick up a Bern map if that's your next destination. The TI organizes free daily walks at 17:00 in the summer (call to confirm).

Arrival in Interlaken

Interlaken has two train stations: East (Ost) and West. All trains stop at both the Ost and West stations. If heading for higher villages, get off at the Ost station. For hotels in Interlaken, get off at the West station. The West station also has a helpful and friendly train information desk (travel center for in-depth rail questions: Mon–Fri 8:00–18:00, Sat–Sun 8:00–12:00 & 14:00–18:00, Nov–March closed Mon–Fri 12:00–14:00; ticket windows open daily 6:00–20:45; tel. 033-826-4750). Ask about discount passes, special fares, railpass discounts, and schedules for the scenic mountain trains. There's a fair exchange booth next to the ticket windows (daily 6:30–20:00).

It's a pleasant 20-minute walk between the West and East stations, or there's an easy, frequent train connection (2/hr, 3.20

SF). From the Interlaken-Ost station, private trains take you deep into the mountainous Jungfrau region (see "Transportation Connections," page 1305).

Helpful Hints

Warning: On Sundays and holidays, small-town Switzerland is quiet. Hotels are open, and lifts and trains run, but many stores are closed.

Telephone: Phone booths cluster outside the post office near the West station. For efficiency, buy a phone card from a newsstand or train station ticket window. (Gimmelwald's sole public phone—at the gondola station—takes only cards, not coins.)

Laundry: Friendly Helen Schmocker's *Wäscherei* has a change machine, soap, English instructions, and a riverside location (open daily 7:00–22:00 for self-service; for full service: Mon–Fri 8:00–12:00 & 13:30–18:00, Sat 8:00–16:00, closed Sun, drop off in the morning and pick up that afternoon, from the main street take Marktgasse over 2 bridges to Beatenbergstrasse 5, tel. 033-822-1566).

Local Guidebook: Don Chmura's Lauterbrunnen guidebook gives history, folk life, flora, fauna, and hiking information (sold throughout the Lauterbrunnen Valley, 8 SF).

Stores: The Migros supermarket is across the street from Interlaken-West train station (Mon–Thu 8:00–18:30, Fri 8:00–21:00, Sat 7:30–16:00, closed Sun). The **Co-op Pronto** mini-market has longer hours (daily 6:00–22:00, across from TI). As Switzerland attempts to buck American pressure and decriminalize pot, there's a buzz surrounding Interlaken's **Hanf Center,** a small shop selling a wide selection of products made from hemp, including clothes, paper, noodles, tea, and beer (Mon 13:30–18:30, Tue–Fri 10:00–12:00 & 13:30–18:30, Sat 10:00–16:00, closed Sun, Rosenstrasse 5, near end of Höhematte Park closest to West station, tel. 033-823-1552).

Interlaken Town Walk

Most visitors use Interlaken as a springboard for high-altitude thrills (and rightly so). But the town itself has history and scenic charm, and is worth a short walk. This 45-minute stroll circles from the West train station down the main drag to the big meadow, past the casino, along the river to the oldest part of town (historically a neighboring town called Unterseen), and back to the station.

Bahnhofstrasse: This main drag, which turns into Höheweg as it continues east, cuts straight through the town center from the West train station to the East. The best Swiss souvenir shopping is along this Bahnhofstrasse stretch (things get more expensive on the Höheweg stretch, near the fancy hotels). Tchibo makes the best take-away coffee in town (Starbucks-style). At the roundabout is the handy post office and Loeb, Interlaken's only department store. Just behind the post office on Marktgasse, the hardware store stocks real cowbells (both ornate and plain). At Höheweg 2, the TV in the window of the Schilthornbahn office shows the weather up top.

Höhematte Park: This "high meadow," or Höhematte (but generally referred to simply as "the park"), marks the beginning of Interlaken's fancy hotel row. Hotels like the Victoria-Jungfrau hearken back to the days when Interlaken was *the* original Alpine resort. The first grand hotels were built here to enjoy the views of the Jungfrau in the distance. (Today, the Jungfraus getting the most attention are next door, at Hooters.)

The park originated as farmland of the monastery that predated the town (marked today by the steeples of both the Catholic and Protestant churches—neither of any sightseeing interest). The actual **monastery site** is now home to the City Hall, courthouse, and city administration building. With the Reformation in 1528, the monastery was shut down and its land was taken by the state. Later, when the land was being eyed by developers, the town's leading hotels and business families bought it and established that it would never be used for commercial buildings (a very early example of smart town planning). There was talk of building a parking lot under it, but the water table here, between the two lakes, is too high. Today, this is a fine place to stroll, hang out on the park benches or at Restaurant Schuh, and watch the parasailors gracefully land.

From the park, turn left into the grounds of **Casino Kursaal** where, at the top of each hour, dwarfs ring the toadstools on the flower clock. The Kursaal, originally a kind of 19th-century fat farm, is now both a casino (passport but no tie required) and a convention center that hosts musical events and nightly folklore shows through the summer (fun yodeling with lots of audience participation, details at the TI).

Follow the path left of the Kursaal to the river (huge public swimming pool just over the river). Walk downstream under the train track and cross the pedestrian bridge, stopping in the middle to enjoy the view.

Aare River: The Aare River is Switzerland's longest. It connects Lake Brienz and Lake Thun (with an 18-foot altitude difference—this short stretch has quite a flow). Then it tumbles out of Lake Thun, heading for Bern and ultimately into the Rhine. Its level is controlled by several sluices. In the distance, a church bell tower marks a different parish and the neighborhood of Unterseen, which shares the town's name, but in German: "Unterseen" is German for "Interlaken" (which is Latin for "between the lakes"). Behind the spire is the pointy summit of the Niesen (like so many

What's What in the Berner Oberland

Allmendhubel (AHL-mehnd-hoo-behl): Funicular from Mürren, leading to good hikes at the top (see page 1315).

Ballenberg: Swiss Open-Air Folk Museum, on Lake Brienz (see page 1300).

Berner Oberland: The mountainous part of the canton of Bern, sometimes referred to as "Jungfrau region." Everything else on this list is in the Berner Oberland.

Birg (beerg): Cable-car stop between Mürren and the Schilthorn, with a trail leading steeply down to Gimmelwald and more (see page 1325).

Brienz (bree-ENTS): Lake on the east side of Interlaken (Brienzersee); also the name of a town on that lake.

Eiger (EYE-gehr): "Ogre," one of the three big mountains in the area (with the Mönch and Jungfrau); famous as a treacherous climbing destination.

First: Overlook point accessible by lift from Grindelwald; endpoint of hike from Schynige Platte (see page 1332).

Gimmelwald (GIM-mehl-vahlt): Wonderfully rustic time-warp village overlooking the Lauterbrunnen Valley; good home-base option (see page 1306).

Grindelwald (GRIN-dehl-vahlt): Expensive resort town, not to be confused with Gimmelwald.

Grütschalp (GREWTSH-alp): Station at the top of the funicular from Lauterbrunnen. It's connected by train and a trail to Mürren (see page 1313).

Interlaken (IN-tehr-lah-kehn): Big town at the "entrance" to the Berner Oberland; you'll go through here to get anywhere else in this chapter (see page 1293).

Jungfrau (YOONG-frow): "Maiden," the region's highest peak (13,642 feet).

Jungfraubahnen (YOONG-frow-bah-nehn): Company that runs all of the trains and lifts in the area (except for the Schilthorn).

Jungfraujoch (YOONG-frow-yoke): High-altitude (11,300 feet) observation deck near the Jungfrau peak, accessible by train from Kleine Scheidegg.

Kleine Scheidegg (KLY-neh SHY-dehk): Viewpoint with breathtaking Eiger, Mönch, and Jungfrau views; has several hotels and restaurants (see page 1336), plus the train station that offers pricey rides to the Jungfraujoch (page 1323).

Lauterbrunnen (LOUT-ehr-broo-nehn): Small town in the middle of the Lauterbrunnen Valley. From here, a funicular goes up to Grütschalp (with connections to Mürren and Gimmelwald) and the train runs up to Wengen and Kleine Scheidegg. For hotels and restaurants, see page 1319.

Lauterbrunnen Valley: Valley at the heart of the Berner Oberland; most towns and activities in this chapter overlook this valley.

Männlichen (MAYN-likh-ehn): Overlook point with pastoral meadow and dramatic views, connected to Wengen and also to Grund (near Grindelwald) by lifts; also the starting point of an easy hike to Kleine Scheidegg with nonstop mountain views (see page 1330).

Mönch (munkh): "Monk," one of the three major peaks of the region (along with Eiger and Jungfrau).

Mürren (MEW-rehn): Pleasant resort town near Gimmelwald, midway up the Schilthorn cable-car line; a good high-mountain home base for those who find Gimmelwald too small and rustic (see page 1313).

Schilthorn (SHILT-horn): The 10,000-foot peak across the Lauterbrunnen Valley from the Jungfrau, reached by cable car from Stechelberg (in the valley), Mürren, and Gimmelwald; features spectacular views and the Piz Gloria revolving restaurant made famous by James Bond (see page 1321).

Schilthornbahn: Cable-car company that operates the lift on the west side of the Lauterbrunnen Valley, connecting Stechelberg (on the valley floor) with Gimmelwald, Mürren, Birg, and the Schilthorn.

Schynige Platte (SHIH-nih-geh PLAH-teh): High-altitude observation point near the entrance to Lauterbrunnen Valley, reached by funicular from Wilderswil; starting point of a long but scenic hike to First (see page 1332).

Sefinen Valley (seh-FEE-nehn): Branches off the Lauterbrunnen Valley beyond Stechelberg and Gimmelwald; good for a hike (see page 1309).

Stechelberg (SHTEH-khehl-behrk): At the end of the Lauterbrunnen Valley, it's the starting point of the cable car leading up to Gimmelwald, Mürren, and on to the Schilthorn (for accommodations, see page 1336).

Thun (toon): Lake to the west of Interlaken (Thunersee), and the name of a town on that lake.

Trümmelbach (TREW-mehl-bahkh): Striking series of waterfalls near Lauterbrunnen (see page 1334).

Wengen (VAYNG-ehn): Resort town on Jungfrau side of Lauterbrunnen Valley; on the train line between Lauterbrunnen and Kleine Scheidegg (for hotels, see page 1334).

Wilderswil (VIHL-dehrs-vihl): Village near entrance of the Lauterbrunnen Valley; on the train line between Interlaken and Lauterbrunnen; has funicular to Schynige Platte and trailhead to First (see page 1332).

Swiss peaks, capped with a restaurant and accessible by a lift). Stroll downstream along the far side of the river to the church spire. The delightful riverside walk is lined by fine residences. Notice that now your Jungfrau view includes the Jungfraujoch observation deck (the little brown bump in the ridge just left of the peak).

Unterseen: At the next bridge, turn right to the town square lined with 17th-century houses on one side and a modern strip on the other. Unterseen was a town when Interlaken was only a monastery. The church is not worth touring. A block away, the (generally empty) **Town History Museum** shows off classic posters, fascinating photos of the construction of the Jungfraujoch, and exhibits on folk life, crafts, and winter sports—all well-described in English (5 SF, May–mid-Oct Tue–Sun 14:00–17:00, closed Mon and mid-Oct–April, Obergasse 26).

Return to Station: From Unterseen, cross the river on Spielmatte, and you're a few minutes' walk from your starting point. On the second bridge, notice the border between the two towns, or parishes, marked by their respective heraldic emblems (each with an ibex, or wild mountain goat). A block or so later, on the left, is the Marktplatz. The river originally ran through this square. The town used to be called "Aaremühle" ("Aare mill") for the mill that was here. But in the 19th century, town fathers made a key marketing decision: Since "Aaremühle" was too difficult for English tourists to pronounce, they changed the name to "Interlaken."

SIGHTS AND ACTIVITIES

Near Interlaken

Boat Trips—"Interlaken" is literally "between the lakes" of Thun and Brienz. You can explore these lakes on a lazy boat trip (8/day mid-June–mid-Sept, fewer off-season, free with Eurail/Eurail Selectpass but uses a flexi-day, schedules at TI or at BLS Travel Center in West station, tel. 033-826-4750 or 033-334-5211). The boats on **Lake Thun** (10/day, 2 hrs to Thun, 4 hrs return, 40 SF round-trip) stop at the St. Beatus Höhlen caves (30 min away, see below) and two visit-worthy towns: Spiez (1 hr) and Thun (1.75 hrs). The boats on **Lake Brienz** (3 hrs, 32 SF round-trip) stop at the super-cute village of Iseltwald (45 min away) and at Brienz (1.25 hrs away, near Ballenberg Open-Air Folk Museum—described below).

St. Beatus Höhlen caves on Lake Thun can be visited with a guided tour (2/hr, 60-min tours, 16 SF, April–mid-Oct daily 10:30–17:00, closed mid-Oct–March, tel. 033-841-1643, www.beatushoehlen.ch). The best excursion plan: Ride the bus from Interlaken (20-min ride, line #21, depart West station at :45 past the hour); tour the caves; take the short, steep hike down to lake;

Interlaken

FUNICULAR TO HARDERKULM
SLOW ROAD TO BRIENZ
CASINO & BIG, RITZY HOTELS
UNTER-SEEN
BRIENZ STRASSE
BOAT DOCK
EAST (OST) STN.
AARE
BEATEN.
TO THUN
UNTER.
MARKT.
HÖHEWEG
LINDENALLEE
HÖHE MATTE PARK
BAHNHOF STRASSE
GASSE
POST
SEESTR.
HELV.
BAHNHOF-STR.
TO 2
ALPEN STRASSE
OELE STRASSE
OB. JUNG.
GEN. GUIS.
WEST STATION
RUGENPARK STRASSE
WYCHEL STR.
HAUPT STR.
TO BRIENZ, LUZERN & SUSTENPASS
BOAT DOCK
WALDEGG
TELL THEATER
HEIMWEHFLUH
N-8 AUTOBAHN
N-8 AUTOBAHN
TO SPIEZ & BERN
TO LAUTERBRUNNEN & EIGER, MÖNCH & JUNGFRAU
* 15 MIN. WALK BETWEEN W & E STATIONS
1 Hotel Lotschberg, Susi's B&B & Villa Heimgarten
2 Sunny Days B&B
3 Hotel Aarburg & Launderette
4 Villa Margaretha
5 Backpackers' Villa Sonnenhof
6 Balmer's Herberge
7 Happy Inn Lodge
8 Restaurant Bären
9 Goldener Anker
10 Città Vecchia
11 Restaurant Löwen
12 La Pastateca
13 Restaurant Schuh
14 Funny Farm Bar
15 Migros Grocery
16 Hanf Center Hemp Shop
17 Town History Museum

and return by boat (30 min to Interlaken, see above).

Adventure Trips—For the adventurer with money and little concern for personal safety, several companies offer high-adrenaline trips such as rafting, canyoning (rappelling down watery gorges), bungee jumping, and paragliding. Costs range from 90 SF to 190 SF (river rafting-95 SF, paragliding-160 SF, hang gliding-185 SF). Interlaken companies include Alpin Raft (tel. 033-823-4100, www.alpinraft.ch), Alpin Center (at Wilderswil station and across from Balmer's youth hostel, tel. 033-823-5523, www.alpincenter.ch), and Outdoor Interlaken (tel. 033-826-7719, www.outdoor-interlaken.ch). For an overview of your options, visit www.interlakenadventure.com or study the racks of brochures at most TIs and hotels (everyone's getting a cut of this lucrative industry).

Recent fatal accidents jolted the adventure-sport business in the Berner Oberland, leading to a more professional respect for the risks involved. In May 2000, an American died bungee jumping from the Stechelberg-Mürren gondola (the operator used a 180-meter rope for a 100-meter jump). In July 1999, 21 tourists died canyoning on the Saxetenbach River, 10 miles from Interlaken; they were battered and drowned by a flash flood filled with debris. (The monument just outside Wilderswil on the Saxeten Road is stirring.) Enjoying nature up close comes with risks. Adventure sports increase those risks dramatically. Use good judgment.

River Rafting: The three-hour Grindelwald-to-Zweilutschinen rafting trips (offered by all the adventure companies) are most exciting. Swiss Adventures is the only outfit leading raft tours down the Aare River from Thun to Bern (2–3 hrs, no white water, tel. 033-773-7373, www.swissadventures.ch).

Helicopter Touring: Air-Glaciers of Lauterbrunnen offers short and pricey tours with landings on glaciers. If you have more money than time, or can assemble a group of four to six tourists to split the cost and lower the price, this might be worth considering. Trips cost 100 SF to 400 SF, depending on the duration and number of people (tel. 033-856-0560, www.airglaciers.ch).

▲▲Swiss Open-Air Folk Museum at Ballenberg—Across Lake Brienz from Interlaken, the Swiss Open-Air Museum of Vernacular Architecture, Country Life, and Crafts in the Bernese Oberland is a rich collection of traditional and historic farmhouses from every region of the country. Each house is carefully furnished, and many feature traditional craftspeople at work. The sprawling 50-acre park, laid out roughly as a huge Swiss map (Italian Swiss in the south, Appenzell in the east, and so on), is a natural preserve providing a wonderful setting for this culture-on-a-lazy-Susan look at Switzerland.

The Thurgau house (#621) has an interesting wattle-and-daub (half-timbered construction) display, and house #331 has a fun bread museum and farmers' shop. There's cheesemaking (near the east entry), traditional farm animals (like very furry-legged roosters, near the merry-go-round in the center), and a chocolate shop (under the restaurant on the east side).

An outdoor cafeteria with reasonable prices is inside the west entrance, and fresh bread, sausage, mountain cheese, and other goodies are on sale in several houses. Picnic tables and grills with free firewood are scattered throughout the park.

The little wooden village of Brienzwiler (near the east entrance) is a museum in itself, with a lovely pint-sized church.

Cost, Hours, Information: 16 SF, half price after 16:00, covered by Swiss Museum Passport. A RailAway combo-ticket, available at either Interlaken station, includes transportation to and from Ballenberg and your admission (32 SF from West, 30.40 SF from Ost, add 9.40 SF to return by boat instead). The houses are open May–Oct daily 10:00–17:00, but the park stays open later. Craft demonstration schedules are listed just inside entry. Use the 2-SF map/guide. The more expensive picture book is a better souvenir than guide. Tel. 033-952-1030, www.ballenberg.ch.

Getting There from Interlaken: Take the train from Interlaken to Brienz (hrly, 30 min, 7.20 SF one-way from West station). From Brienz, catch a bus to Ballenberg (10 min, 3 SF one-way) or hike (45 min, slightly uphill). Consider returning by boat (Brienz boat dock next to train station, one-way to Interlaken-16 SF). Trains also run occasionally from Interlaken to Brienzwiler, a 20-min uphill walk to the museum (every 2 hrs, 30 min, 9.20 SF one-way from West station).

NIGHTLIFE

For counterculture with a reggae beat, check out **Funny Farm** (past Balmer's Youth Hostel, in Matten). The young frat-party dance scene rages at **Balmer's Metro Bar** (their bomb-shelter disco bar thrives, with cheap drinks and a friendly if loud atmosphere). For a stylish wine bar with local yuppies, check in at the **Vinothek,** across from Città Vecchia in Unterseen (see "Eating," below). If you can't sleep and are waiting for your prunes, try **Restaurant Schuh** on the park.

SLEEPING

I'd head for Gimmelwald, or at least Lauterbrunnen (20 min by train or car). Interlaken is not the Alps. But if you must stay...

$$$ Hotel Lotschberg, with a sun terrace and 21 wonderful rooms, is run by English-speaking Susi and Fritz and is the best real hotel value in town. Happy to dispense information, these

Sleep Code

(1.25 SF = about $1, country code: 41)
S = Single, **D** = Double/Twin, **T** = Triple, **Q** = Quad, **b** = bathroom, **s** = shower only, **SE** = Speaks English, **NSE** = No English. Unless otherwise noted, credit cards are accepted, English is spoken, and breakfast is included.

To help you sort easily through these listings, I've divided the rooms into three categories, based on the price for a standard double room with bath:

- **$$$ Higher Priced**—Most rooms 150 SF or more.
- **$$ Moderately Priced**—Most rooms between 90–150 SF.
- **$ Lower Priced**—Most rooms 90 SF or less.

gregarious folks pride themselves on a personal touch that sets them apart from other hotels (Sb-112 SF, Db-155 SF, big Db-175 SF, extra bed-25 SF, family deals, rates about 15 percent cheaper mid-Oct–April, closed Nov and Jan, non-smoking, elevator, Internet access, laundry service, bike rental; 5-min walk from West station: leaving station, turn right, after Migros at the circle go left to General Guisanstrasse 31; tel. 033-822-2545, fax 033-822-2579, www.lotschberg.ch, hotel@lotschberg.ch). Effervescent Fritz loves organizing guided adventures. He tandem parasails almost every day with one of his guests (guests "Fly with Fritz" at a discount, about 20 SF cheaper than any other deal in town).

$$ Guest House Susi's B&B is Hotel Lotschberg's no-frills, cash-only annex, run by Fritz and Susi, offering nicely furnished, cozy rooms (Sb-95 SF, Db-125 SF, apartments with kitchenettes for 2 people-100 SF; for 4–5 people-180 SF, prices about 20 percent cheaper mid-Oct–April, closed Nov and Jan, same contact information as Hotel Lotschberg, above).

$$ Villa Heimgarten is a fine house from 1902 in a quiet and handy location, renting seven basic rooms for a good price. While not particularly warm, it's a fine value (Sb-45–55 SF, Db-90–110 SF, higher prices are for June–Aug, garden, playground, 5 min from West Station, across from Hotel Lotschberg at Bernastrasse 7, tel. 033-822-7477, fax 033-822-7479, www.villaheimgarten.ch, info@villaheimgarten.com).

$$ Sunny Days B&B, a homey, nine-room place in a residential neighborhood, is run by Dave from Britain (Sb-98–110 SF, Db-110–148 SF, prices vary with season and view, extra bed about 40 SF, Nov–March all rooms 100 SF; exit left out of West station and take first bridge to your left, after crossing the bridges turn left on Helvetiastrasse and go 3 blocks to #29; tel. 033-822-8343, fax

033-823-8343, www.sunnydays.ch, mail@sunnydays.ch).

$$ Hotel Aarburg offers 13 plain, peaceful rooms in a beautifully located but run-down old building a 10-minute walk from the West station (Sb-70 SF, Db-120 SF, next to launderette at Beatenbergstrasse 1, tel. 033-822-2615, fax 033-822-6397, hotel-aarburg@tcnet.ch).

$ Villa Margaretha, run by English-speaking Frau Kunz-Joerin, offers the best cheap beds in town. It's like grandma's big Victorian house on a quiet residential street. Keep your room tidy, and you'll have a friend for life (D-86 SF, T-129 SF, Q-172 SF, the 3 rooms share a big bathroom, 2-night minimum, closed Oct–April, no CC, no breakfast served but dishes and kitchenette available, lots of rules to abide by, go up small street directly in front of West station to Aarmühlestrasse 13, tel. 033-822-1813).

$ Backpackers' Villa (Sonnenhof) Interlaken is a creative guest house run by a Methodist church group. It's fun, youthful, and great for families, without the frat-party ambience of Balmer's (listed below). Travelers of any age feel comfortable here. Rooms are comfy, and half come with Jungfrau-view balconies (D-88 SF, T-120 SF, Q-144 SF, dorm beds in 5- to 7-bed rooms with lockers and sheets-32 SF per person, 5 SF more per person for rooms with toilets and Jungfrau-view balconies, includes breakfast, kitchen, garden, movies, small game room, Internet access, laundry, bike rental, no curfew, open all day but reception open only 7:00–11:00 & 16:00–22:00, 10-min walk from either station, across the park from TI, Alpenstrasse 16, tel. 033-826-7171, fax 033-826-7172, www.villa.ch, mail@villa.ch).

$ Balmer's Herberge is many people's idea of backpacker heaven. This Interlaken institution comes with movies, table tennis, a cheap launderette (4 SF/load), bar, restaurant, swapping library, Internet access, tiny grocery, bike rental, excursions, a shuttle-bus service (which meets important arriving trains), and a friendly, hardworking staff. This little Nebraska is home for those who miss their fraternity. It can be a mob scene, especially on summer weekends (dorm beds-24 SF, S-40 SF; D, T, or Q-30–34 SF per person; includes sheets and breakfast, non-smoking rooms, open year-round, easy Internet reservations recommended 5 days in advance except for dorm beds, Hauptstrasse 23, in Matten, 15-min walk from either Interlaken station, tel. 033-822-1961, fax 033-823-3261, www.balmers.com, balmers@tcnet.ch).

$ Happy Inn Lodge has 15 cheap backpacker rooms above a lively, noisy restaurant a five-minute walk from the West station (S-38 SF, D-76 SF, bunk in 4- to 8-bed dorm-22 SF, breakfast-8 SF, Rosenstrasse 17, tel. 033-822-3225, fax 033-822-3268, www.happyinn.com, info@happyinn.com).

EATING

In Unterseen, the Old Town across the River

Restaurant Bären, in a classic low-ceilinged building with cozy indoor and fine outdoor seating, is a great value for *Rösti*, fondue, raclette, fish, traditional sausage, and salads (20-SF plates, open daily except closed Mon off-season, from West station turn left on Bahnhofstrasse and go over the river a block to Seestrasse 2, tel. 033-822-7526).

Goldener Anker is the local hangout—smoky, with a pool table and a few unsavory types. If you thought Interlaken was sterile, you haven't been here. Jeannette serves and Rene cooks, just as they have for 25 years (hearty 20-SF salads, fresh vegetables, 3 courses for 17 SF, Marktgasse 57, tel. 033-822-1672). This place sometimes hosts small concerts, and has launched some of Switzerland's top bands.

Città Vecchia serves the best Italian food in town, with seating indoors or out, on a leafy square (pizza-15 SF, pasta-20 SF, plates-30 SF, Italian wines, open daily except closed Tue off-season, on main square in Unterseen at Untere Gasse 5, tel. 033-822-1754, Rinaldo).

On or near the Main Drag

Restaurant Löwen has an inviting terrace with reasonably priced food. If Goldener Anker, above, has too much character (or too many characters), this is a more relaxing bet—especially when it's hot and you want to sit outside (dinners for 15–20 SF, open daily, a block behind the post office at Marktplatz 10, tel. 033-821-0505).

La Pastateca, at the top hotel in town (Victoria-Jungfrau), is *très* elegant. To sit on its terrace and watch the Jungfrau is one of the great Interlaken treats. To do it affordably, go with the super antipasto buffet (all you like from a huge spread of Italian-style treats, including lots of meat and seafood, 25 SF), or come for the "business lunch" (the buffet, plus a pasta of your choice, great bread and olive oil, bottled water, and coffee for 27 SF, available Mon–Fri 11:30–14:00). The service is formal and can be slow (daily 11:30–23:00, a block past TI, facing the park, tel. 033-828-2620).

Restaurant Schuh, formerly the Grand Café Schuh, retains its grand-café ambience on the best real estate in town (at the corner of the park, across from Hotel Metropole and TI). Meals are disappointing, but desserts are wonderful, and there's no better place to nurse a drink or coffee and watch the parasailors glide into the park (live schmaltzy music, newspapers, elegant indoor and outdoor seating).

TRANSPORTATION CONNECTIONS

Train info: toll tel. 0900-300-3004 (www.rail.ch).

From Interlaken by Train to: Lauterbrunnen (hrly, 30 min, 9 SF each way, from East station only), **Spiez** (2/hr, 20 min), **Brienz** (hrly, 30 min, from East station only), **Bern** (hrly, 50 min), **Zürich** and **Zürich Airport** (hrly, 2.25 hrs, most direct but some with transfer in Bern), **Luzern** (hrly, 2 hrs direct from East station; departures from West station require transfer in Bern).

From Bern by Train to: Lausanne (2/hr, 70 min), **Murten** (hrly, 30 min, most transfer in Kerzers), **Zürich** (2/hr, 70 min), **Zermatt** (hrly, 3.5 hrs, transfer in Brig), **Appenzell** (hrly, 3.25 hrs, transfer in Gossau), **Munich** (4/day, 5.5 hrs), **Frankfurt** (hrly, 4.5 hrs), **Salzburg** (4/day, 7.25 hrs, transfer in Zürich), **Paris** (4/day, 4.5 hrs).

From Interlaken to Gimmelwald

By public transportation: Take the train from the Interlaken Ost station to Lauterbrunnen. From here, you have two options.

1. The faster, easier way—best in bad weather or at the end of a long day with lots of luggage—is to ride the post bus from Lauterbrunnen station (4 SF, hrly bus departure coordinated with arrival of train, stop: Schilthornbahn) to Stechelberg and the base of the Schilthornbahn gondola station, where the gondola will whisk you in five thrilling minutes up to Gimmelwald (7.80 SF, departing at :25 and :55).

2. The more scenic route is to ride the train to Lauterbrunnen and catch the funicular to Mürren (across the street from the train station). Ride up to Grütschalp, where a special scenic train *(Panorama Fahrt)* will roll you along the cliff into Mürren (total trip from Lauterbrunnen to Mürren: 30 min, 9.80 SF). From there, either walk a paved 30 minutes downhill to Gimmelwald, or walk 10 minutes across Mürren to catch the gondola down to Gimmelwald (costs 7.80 SF).

By car: You can drive to Lauterbrunnen and to Stechelberg, but not to Gimmelwald (park in Stechelberg and take the gondola) or to Mürren, Wengen, or Kleine Scheidegg (park in Lauterbrunnen and take the train/funicular). For drivers, the most direct route to Gimmelwald is via the gondola at Stechelberg. It's a 30-minute drive from Interlaken to the Stechelberg gondola station (parking lot: 2 SF/2 hrs, 6 SF/day). Gimmelwald is the first stop above Stechelberg on the Schilthorn gondola (7.80 SF, 2/hr at :25 and :55). Note that for a week in early May and from mid-November through early December, the Schilthornbahn is closed for servicing. During this time, you'll ride the cargo cable car directly from Stechelberg to Mürren, where a small bus shuttles you down to Gimmelwald.

Gimmelwald

Saved from developers by its "avalanche zone" classification, Gimmelwald was (before tourism) one of the poorest places in Switzerland. Its traditional economy was stuck in the hay, and its farmers, unable to make it in their disadvantaged trade, survived only by Swiss government subsidies (and working the ski lifts in the winter). For some travelers, there's little to see in the village. Others (like me) enjoy a fascinating day sitting on a bench and learning why they say, "If Heaven isn't what it's cracked up to be, send me back to Gimmelwald."

Take a walk through the town. While its population has dropped in the last century from 200 to about 100 residents, traditions survive. Most Gimmelwalders have one of two last names: von Allmen or Feutz. They are tough and proud. Raising hay in this rugged terrain is labor-intensive. One family harvests enough to feed only about 15 cows. But they'd have it no other way, and, unlike the absentee-landlord town of Mürren, Gimmelwald is locally owned. (When word got out that urban planners wished to develop Gimmelwald into a town of 1,000, locals pulled some strings to secure the town's bogus avalanche-zone building code.) Those same folks are happy the masses go to touristy and commercialized Grindelwald, just over the Kleine Scheidegg ridge. Don't confuse Gimmelwald and Grindelwald—they couldn't be more different.

ORIENTATION

The huge, sheer cliff face that dominates your mountain views from Gimmelwald is the Schwarzmönch ("Black Monk"). The three peaks above (or behind) it are, left to right, the Eiger, Mönch, and Jungfrau.

A Walk Through Gimmelwald

Gimmelwald, though tiny, with one zigzag street, gives a fine look at a traditional mountain Swiss community. Here's a quick walking tour:

Gondola Station: When the lift came in the 1960s, the village's back end became its front door. Gimmelwald was, and still is, a farm village. Stepping off the gondola, you see a sweet little hut. Set on stilts to keep out mice, the hut was used for storing cheese (the rocks on the rooftop keep the shingles on through wild winter winds). Behind the cheese hut stands the village schoolhouse. In Catholic Swiss towns, the biggest building is the church. In Protestant towns, it's the school. Gimmelwald's biggest building is the

Gimmelwald

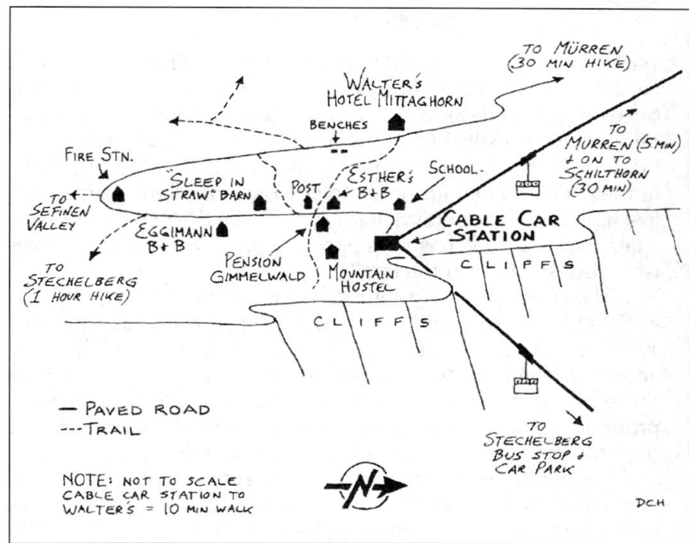

school (2 teachers share one teaching position, 17 students, and a room that doubles as a chapel when the Protestant pastor makes his monthly visit). Don't let Gimmelwald's low-tech look fool you: In this school, each kid has his or her own Web site. In the opposite direction, just beyond the little playground, is Gimmelwald's Mountain Hostel (listed below).

Walk up the lane 50 yards, past the shower in the phone booth, to Gimmelwald's...

"Times Square": The yellow Alpine "street sign" shows where you are, the altitude (4,470 feet), and how many hours *(Std.)* and minutes it takes to walk to nearby points. Most of the buildings used to house two families and are divided vertically right down the middle. The writing on the post office building is a folksy blessing: "Summer brings green, winter brings snow. The sun greets the day, the stars greet the night. This house will keep you warm. May God give us his blessings." The date indicates when it was built or rebuilt (1911). Gimmelwald has a strict building code. For instance, shutters can only be natural, green, or white. Esther's farmer shop (10 yards uphill, always open, buy things on the honor system) is worth a look. From this tiny intersection, we'll follow the town's main street (away from gondola station).

Main Street: Walk up the road. Notice the announcement board: one side for tourist news, the other for local news. Cross the street and peek into the big new barn, dated 1995. This is part of the Sleep in Straw association, which rents out barn spots to

Swiss Cow Culture

Traditional Swiss cow farmers could make more money for much easier work in another profession. In a good year, farmers produce enough cheese to break even—they support their families on government subsidies. (The government supports traditional farming as much for the tourism as for the cheese.) But these farmers have made a lifestyle choice to keep tradition alive and to live high in the mountains. Rather than lose their children to the cities, Swiss farmers have the opposite problem: Kids argue over who gets to take over the family herd.

The cows' grazing ground can range in elevation by as much as 5,000 feet throughout the year. In the summer (usually mid-June), the farmer straps elaborate ceremonial bells on his cows and takes them up to a hut at high elevations. The cows hate these big bells, which can cost upwards of 2,000 SF apiece—a proud investment for a humble farmer. When the cows arrive at their summer home, the bells are hung under the eaves.

These high-elevation summer stables are called "alps." Try to find some on a Berner Oberland tourist map (e.g., Wengernalp, Grütschalp, Schiltalp). The cows stay at the alps for about 100 days. The farmers hire a team of cheesemakers to work at each alp—mostly hippies, students, and city slickers eager to spend three summer months in the mountains. Each morning, the hired hands get up at 5:00 to milk the cows, take them to pasture, and make the cheese—milking the cows again when they come home

travelers when the cows are in the high country. To the left of the door is a cow-scratcher. Swiss cows have legal rights (for example, in the winter, they must be taken out for exercise at least 3 times a week). This big barn is built in a modern style. Traditionally, barns were small (like those on the hillside high above) and closer to the hay. But with trucks and paved roads, hay can be moved more easily, and farm businesses need more cows to be viable. Still, even a well-run big farm hopes just to break even. The industry survives only with government subsidies (see "Swiss Cow Culture" sidebar, above). Go just beyond the next barn. On your right is the...

Water Fountain/Trough: This is the site of the town's historic water supply. Local kids love to bathe and wage water wars in this when the cows aren't drinking from it. From here, detour left down a lane about 50 yards (along a wooden fence and past pea-patch gardens) to the next trough and the oldest building in town, Husmättli, from 1658. (The town's 17th-century buildings are mostly on the road zigzagging below town.) Study the log-cabin construction. Many are built without nails. The wood was logged up the valley and cut on the water-powered village mill (also below in the evening. In summer, all the milk makes alp cheese (it's too difficult to get it down to the market). In the winter, with the cows at lower altitudes, the fresh milk is sold as milk.

Every alp also has a resident herd of pigs. Cheesemaking leftovers (*Molke,* or whey) can damage the ecosystem if thrown out—but pigs love the stuff. The pigs parade up with the cows... but no one notices. Cheesemakers claim that bathing in whey improves the complexion...but maybe that's just the altitude talking.

Meanwhile, the farmers—glad to be free of their bovine responsibilities—turn their attention to making hay. The average farmer has a few huts at various altitudes, each surrounded by small hay fields. The farmer follows the seasons up into the mountains, making hay and storing it above the huts. In the fall, the cows come down from the alps and spend the winter moving from hut to hut, eating the hay the farmer spent the summer preparing for them.

Throughout the year, you'll see farmers moving their herds to various elevations. If snow is in the way, farmers sometimes use tourist gondolas to move their cows. Every two months or so, Gimmelwald farmers bring together cows that aren't doing so well and herd them into the gondola to meet the butcher in the valley below.

town). Gimmelwald heats with wood and, since the wood needs to age a couple of years to burn well, it's stacked everywhere.

Back on the paved road, continue uphill. Notice the cute cheese hut on the right (with Alpine cheese for sale). It's full of strong cheese—up to three years old. On the left (at the B&B sign) is the home of Olle and Maria, the village schoolteachers. Maria runs the Lilliput shop (the "smallest shop with the greatest gifts"—handmade delights from the town and region, just ring the bell and meet Maria). Her son does a booming trade in sugar-coated almonds; her daughter competes with cookies. Fifty yards farther along is the...

Alpenrose: At the old schoolhouse, notice the big ceremonial cowbells hanging under the uphill eave. These swing from the necks of cows during the procession from the town to the high Alps (mid-June) and back down (around Sept 20). If the cows are gone, so are the bells—hanging from similar posts under the eves of mountain huts in the high meadows.

Sefinen Valley: At the end of town, notice the dramatic Sefinen Valley. All the old homes in town are made from local wood cut from the left-hand side of this valley (shady side, slow-growing, better timber). The road switches back at the...

Gimmelwald Fire Station: The *Föhnwacht Reglement* sheet, posted on the fire station building, explains rules to keep the village from burning down during the fierce dry wind of the Föhn season. During this time, there's a 24-hour fire watch, and even smoking cigarettes outdoors is forbidden. Mürren was devastated by a Föhn-caused fire in the 1920s. Because villagers in Gimmelwald—mindful of the quality of their volunteer fire department—are particularly careful with fire, this is a rare village to not have had a terrible fire in its history.

Check out the other posted notices. This year's Swiss Army calendar tells reservists when and where to go. Every Swiss male does a year in the military, then a few days a year in the reserves until about age 40. The *Schiessübungen* poster details the shooting exercises required this year. In keeping with the William Tell heritage, each Swiss man does shooting practice annually for the military (or spends 3 days in jail).

High Road: Follow the high road to Hotel Mittaghorn. The resort town of Mürren hovers in the distance. And high on the left, notice the hay field with terraces. These are from WWII days, when Switzerland, wanting self-sufficiency, required all farmers to grow potatoes. Today, this is a festival of Alpine flowers in season (best at this altitude in May and June). From Hotel Mittaghorn, you can return to Gimmelwald's "Times Square" via the stepped path.

"NIGHTLIFE"

Evening fun in Gimmelwald is found at the hostel (offering a pool table, Internet access, lots of young Alp-aholics, and a good chance to share information on the surrounding mountains) or at **Pension Gimmelwald's** terrace restaurant next door. **Walter's bar** (in Hotel Mittaghorn) is a local farmers' hangout. When they've made their hay, they come here to play. Although they look like what some people would call hicks, they speak some English and can be fun to get to know. Sit outside (benches just below the rails, 100 yards down the lane from Walter's) and watch the sun tuck the mountaintops into bed as the moon rises over the Jungfrau. If this isn't your idea of nightlife, stay in Interlaken.

SLEEPING

(4,593 feet, 1.25 SF = about $1, country code: 41)
Gimmelwald is my home base in the Berner Oberland. To inhale the Alps and really hold them in, you'll sleep high in Gimmelwald, too. Poor but pleasantly stuck in the past, the village has a creaky hotel, happy hostel, decent pension, a couple of B&Bs, and even a

Web site (www.gimmelwald.ch). The only bad news is that the lift costs 7.80 SF each way to get here.

$$ Maria and Olle Eggimann rent two rooms—Gimmelwald's most comfortable—in their quirky but Alpine-sleek chalet. Maria and Olle, who job-share the village's only teaching position and raise three kids of their own, offer visitors a rare and intimate peek at this community (D-110 SF, Db with kitchenette-180 SF for 2 or 3 people, optional breakfast-18 SF, no CC, last check-in 19:30, 3-night minimum, from gondola continue straight for 200 yards along the town's only road, B&B on left, tel. 033-855-3575, oeggimann@bluewin.ch, SE fluently).

$$ Pension Restaurant Gimmelwald offers 13 basic rooms under low, creaky ceilings (D-100 SF, Db-120 SF, T-135 SF, Q-170 SF, 10 percent less for 3-night stays). It also has sheetless backpacker beds (35 SF in small dorm rooms, 6 SF for sheets). The pension has a scenic terrace overlooking the Jungfrau and the hostel (below), and is the village's only restaurant, offering good meals (closed late Oct–Christmas and mid-April–mid-May, non-smoking rooms but restaurant can get smoky, 50 yards from gondola station; reserve by phone, plus obligatory reconfirmation by phone 2–3 days before arrival; tel. 033-855-1730, fax 033-855-1925, www.pensiongimmelwald.ch, Liesi and Mäni).

$ Hotel Mittaghorn, the treasure of Gimmelwald, is run by Walter Mittler, a perfect Swiss gentleman. Walter's hotel is a classic, creaky, Alpine-style place with memorable beds (if too lumpy or short, consider putting mattress on floor), ancient down comforters (short and fat; wear socks and drape the blanket over your feet), and a million-dollar view of the Jungfrau Alps. The loft has a dozen real beds, several sinks, down comforters, and a fire ladder out the back window. The hotel has one shower for 10 rooms (1 SF/5 min). Walter is careful not to let his place get too hectic or big, and he enjoys sensitive Back Door travelers. He runs the hotel with a little help from Rosemarie, from the village. To some, Hotel Mittaghorn is a fire waiting to happen, with a kitchen that would never pass code, bumpy beds, teeny towels, and minimal plumbing, run by an eccentric old grouch. These people enjoy Mürren, Interlaken, or Wengen, and that's where they should sleep. Be warned, you'll see more of my readers than locals here, but it's a fun crowd—an extended family (D-70 SF, Db-80 SF, T-100 SF, Q-125 SF, loft beds-25 SF, 6-SF surcharge per person for 1-night stays, no CC, closed Nov–March, tel. 033-855-1658, www.ricksteves.com/mittaghorn). Reserve by telephone only, then reconfirm by phone the day before your arrival. Walter usually offers his guests a hearty 15-SF dinner (salad, main course, and dessert, served at 19:30, by reservation only). Hotel Mittaghorn is at the top of Gimmelwald, a five-minute climb up the steps from the village intersection.

$ Mountain Hostel is a beehive of activity, as clean as its guests, cheap, and friendly. Phone ahead, or, to secure one of its 50 dorm beds the same day, call after 9:30 and leave your name. The hostel has low ceilings, a self-service kitchen, a mini-grocery, a free pool table, and healthy plumbing. It's mostly a college-age crowd; families and older travelers will probably feel more comfortable elsewhere. Petra Brunner has lined the porch with flowers. This relaxed hostel survives with the help of its guests. Read the signs (Please Clean the Kitchen), respect Petra's rules, and leave it tidier than you found it. The place is one of those rare spots where a congenial atmosphere spontaneously combusts, and spaghetti becomes communal as it cooks (20 SF per bed in 6- to 15-bed rooms, includes sheets, showers-1 SF, no breakfast, hostel membership not required, no CC, Internet access, laundry, 20 yards from lift station, tel. & fax 033-855-1704, www.mountainhostel.com, mountainhostel@tcnet.ch).

$ Esther's B&B, overlooking the main intersection of the village, is like an upscale mini-hostel, with five clean, basic, and comfortable rooms sharing two bathrooms and a great kitchen (S-40 SF, D-80 SF, big D-95 SF, T-100 SF, big T-120 SF, Q-160 SF, family room for up to 5, no CC, 2-night stays preferred, breakfast-12 SF, non-smoking, tel. 033-855-5488, fax 033-855-5492, www.esthersguesthouse.ch, info@esthersguesthouse.ch, some English spoken).

$ Schlaf im Stroh ("Sleep in Straw") offers exactly that, in an actual barn. After the cows head for higher ground in the summer, the friendly von Allmen family hoses out their barn and fills it with straw and budget travelers. Blankets are free, but bring your own sheet, sleep sack, or sleeping bag. No beds, no bunks, no mattresses, no kidding. Esther fluffs up your hay each night (21 SF, 10 SF for kids up to 10, thereafter kids pay their age plus 1 SF, no CC, includes breakfast "barn service" and a modern bathroom, showers-2 SF, open late-June–mid-Oct depending on grass and snow levels, almost never full; from lift, continue straight through intersection to big modern barn marked 1995 on the right, run by Esther with same contact information as above).

EATING

Pension Gimmelwald, the only restaurant in town, serves a hearty breakfast buffet for 13.50 SF, good lunches, and dinners (15–20 SF). The menu features cheese fondue, *Rösti,* local organic produce, homemade pies, and unforgettable (no matter how you try) brownies (daily 8:00–23:00).

Other Options: The hostel has a decent members' kitchen and makes great pizzas in the evenings (non-guests welcome). Hotel Mittaghorn serves dinner only to its guests (15 SF). Consider packing in a picnic meal from the larger towns. If you need a few groceries and want to skip the hike to Mürren, you can buy the essentials—noodles, spaghetti sauce, and candy bars—at the Mountain Hostel's reception desk.

The local farmers sell their produce. Esther (at the main intersection of the village) sells cheese, sausage, bread, and Gimmelwald's best yogurt—but only until the cows go up in June.

Mürren

Mürren—pleasant as an Alpine resort can be—is traffic-free and filled with bakeries, cafés, souvenirs, old-timers with walking sticks, GE employees enjoying incentive trips, and Japanese tourists making movies of each other with a Fujichrome backdrop. Its chalets are prefab-rustic. With help from a gondola, train, and funicular, hiking options are endless from Mürren. Sitting on a ledge 2,000 feet above the Lauterbrunnen Valley, surrounded by a fortissimo chorus of mountains, the town has all the comforts of home (for a price) without the pretentiousness of more famous resorts.

Historic Mürren, which dates from 1384, has been overwhelmed by development. Still, it's a peaceful town. There's no full-time doctor, no police officer (they call Lauterbrunnen if there's a problem), and no resident priest or pastor. (The Protestant church—up by the TI—posts a sign showing where the region's roving pastor preaches each Sunday.) There's not even enough business to keep a bakery open full-time (Mürren's bakery is open mid-June–Sept and Dec–April)—a clear indication that this town is either lively or completely dead, depending on the season. Keep an eye open for the "Milch Express," a tiny cart that delivers fresh milk and eggs to hotels and homes throughout town.

ORIENTATION

Mürren sits high on a ledge, overlooking the Lauterbrunnen Valley. You can walk from one end of town to the other in about 10 minutes.

There are two basic ways to get to Mürren: on the panoramic train from Grütschalp (connects via funicular to Lauterbrunnen); or on the gondola from Stechelberg (in the valley), which stops at Gimmelwald, Mürren, and continues up to the Schilthorn. The train and gondola stations (which both have lockers) are at opposite ends of town.

Tourist Information: Mürren's **TI** can help you find a room and give hiking advice (July–Sept daily 8:30–19:00, Thu until 20:30, less off-season, above the village, follow signs to Sportzentrum, tel.

033-856-8686, www.wengen-muerren.ch). You can change money at the TI, or even better, use the ATM by the Co-op grocery.

Helpful Hints

R & R: The slick **Sportzentrum** (sports center) that houses the TI offers a world of indoor activities (13 SF to use pool and whirlpool; 8 SF for Gimmelwald, Lauterbrunnen, and Interlaken hotel guests; free for guests at Mürren hotels—ask your hotelier for a voucher; pool open Mon–Sat 14:00–18:45, Thu until 20:30, closed Sun, May, and Nov–mid-Dec). In season, they offer squash, mini-golf, table tennis, and a fitness room.

Bike Rental: You can rent mountain bikes and hiking boots at Stäger Sport (bikes with helmets-35 SF/day, boots-12 SF/day, daily 9:00–17:00, closed mid-Sept–mid-June, across from TI/Sportzentrum, tel. 033-855-2355, www.staegersport.ch).

Internet Access: Connect at the TI (see above) or Eiger Guesthouse (daily 8:00–23:00, across from train station, see "Sleeping," below, tel. 033-856-5460).

Laundry: Top Apartments will do your laundry by request (25 SF per load, unreliable hours: Mon–Sat 9:00–11:00 & 15:00–17:00, closed Sun, behind and across from Hotel Bellevue, look for blue triangle, call first to drop off in morning, tel. 033-855-3706).

Mürren Town Walk

Mürren has long been a top ski resort, but a walk across town offers a glimpse into its past. This stroll takes you through town on the main drag, from the train station (where you'll arrive if coming from Lauterbrunnen) to the gondola station, then back up to the Allmendhubel funicular station.

Train Station: The first trains pulled into Mürren in 1891. (A circa-1911 car is permanently parked at the Grütschalp station.) A display case inside the station shows an original car from the narrow-gauge, horse-powered line that rolled fancy visitors from here into town. The current station, built in 1964, comes with impressive engineering for heavy cargo. Look out back, where a small truck can be loaded up and drive away.

Stroll under the Anfi Palace Hotel: Wander into town along the main road. The towering Anfi Palace Hotel was the "Grand Palace Hotel" until it burned in 1928. Its Jugendstil Hall is the finest room in Mürren. The small wooden platform on the left—looking like a suicide springboard—is the place where snow removal trucks dump their loads over the cliff in the winter. Look back at the meadow below the station: This is a favorite grazing spot for chamois (the animals, not the rags for washing cars). Ahead, at Edelweiss Hotel, step to the far corner of the restaurant terrace for a breathtaking view stretching from the big three (Eiger, Mönch, and Jungfrau) to the lonely cattle farm in the high alp on the right. Then look down.

Next, the Haus Montana was where Kandahar ski boots were first made in 1933 (to give the necessary support to daredevils racing from the Schilthorn to the valley floor in Mürren's infamous Inferno race). Today, the still-respected Kandahar boots are made in nearby Thun.

Downtown Mürren: You'll pass the main intersection (where the small service road leads down to Gimmelwald) and the only grocery store in town (Co-op). The tiny fire barn (Feuerwehr) has a list showing the leaders of the volunteer force and their responsibilities. The old barn behind it on the right evokes the day, not so long ago, when the town's barns housed cows. Imagine Mürren with more cows than people.

Gondola Station: Reaching the far end of Mürren, you come to the gondola station. The first gondola (goes directly to Stechelberg) is for cargo, garbage, and the (reputedly) longest bungee jumping in the world. The other takes hikers and skiers up to the Schilthorn and down to Stechelberg via Gimmelwald.

Upper Mürren: Hiking back along the high road, you pass Mürren's two churches, the mountain bike rental office, the Allmendhubel funicular station, and the Sportzentrum (with swimming pool and TI).

Mürren's Allmendhubel Funicular: A quaint-looking but surprisingly rewarding funicular (1912, renovated in 1999) carries nature lovers from Mürren to a perch offering a Jungfrau view that (while much lower) rivals the Schilthorn. At the station, notice the 1920s bobsled. The restaurants here (full- and self-service) have awesome views.

Allmendhubel is particularly good for families: It's cheaper than the Schilthorn. The restaurant overlooks a great playground. And the entertaining children's hike—with rough and thrilling, kid-friendly Alpine rides along the way—departs from here. This is also the departure point for the North Face hike and walks to Grütschalp (see "Hikes," page 1324).

SLEEPING

(5,381 feet, 1.25 SF = about $1, country code: 41)

Prices for accommodations are often higher during the ski season. Many hotels and restaurants close in spring, roughly from Easter to early June, and any time between late September and mid-December.

$$$ Hotel Alpina is a simple, modern place with 24 comfortable rooms and a concrete feeling—a good thing, given its

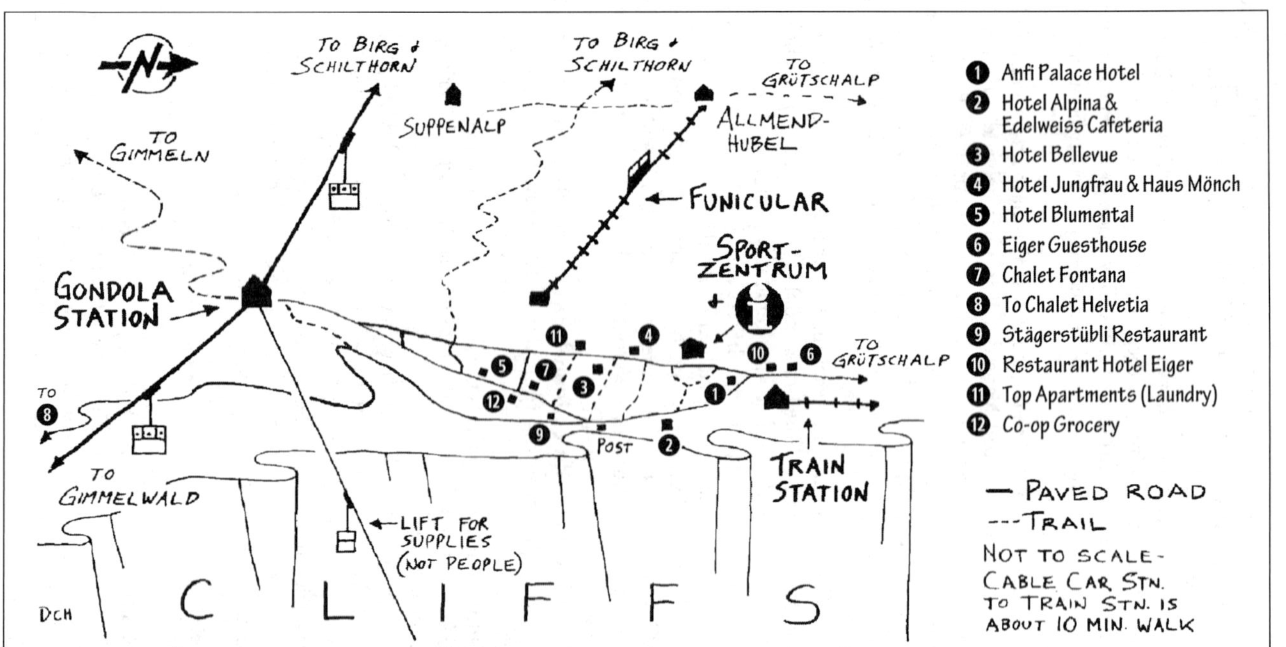
Mürren
1 Anfi Palace Hotel
2 Hotel Alpina & Edelweiss Cafeteria
3 Hotel Bellevue
4 Hotel Jungfrau & Haus Mönch
5 Hotel Blumental
6 Eiger Guesthouse
7 Chalet Fontana
8 To Chalet Helvetia
9 Stägerstübli Restaurant
10 Restaurant Hotel Eiger
11 Top Apartments (Laundry)
12 Co-op Grocery
— PAVED ROAD
--- TRAIL
NOT TO SCALE - CABLE CAR STN. TO TRAIN STN. IS ABOUT 10 MIN. WALK
TO BIRG & SCHILTHORN
TO BIRG & SCHILTHORN
TO GRÜTSCHALP
SUPPENALP
ALLMEND-HUBEL
TO GIMMELN
FUNICULAR
SPORT-ZENTRUM
GONDOLA STATION
TO GRÜTSCHALP
TO 8
POST
TO GIMMELWALD
TRAIN STATION
LIFT FOR SUPPLIES (NOT PEOPLE)
CLIFFS
DCH

cliff-edge position (Sb-85 SF, Db-160 SF, Tb-200 SF, Qb-220 SF with awesome Jungfrau views and balconies, prices less off-season and without a view, outside mid-June–mid-Aug, family rooms, homey lounge, exit left from train station, walk 2 min downhill, tel. 033-855-1361, fax 033-855-1049, www.muerren.ch/alpina, alpina @muerren.ch, Cecilia and her son Roger SE).

$$$ Hotel Bellevue has a homey lounge, solid woodsy furniture, a great view terrace, the hunter-themed Jägerstübli restaurant, and 17 great rooms at fair rates, all with balconies and views (Sb-110 SF, Db-190 SF; Internet, tel. 033-855-1401, fax 033-855-1490, www.muerren.ch/bellevue, bellevue-crystal@bluewin.ch, Ruth and Othmar Suter).

$$$ Hotel Jungfrau offers 29 modern and comfortable rooms (with view: Sb-95–110 SF, Db-190–210 SF; no view: Sb-90–110 SF, Db-170–200 SF; elevator, near TI/Sportzentrum, tel. 033-856-6464, fax 033-856-6465, www.hoteljungfrau.ch, mail @hoteljungfrau.ch, Anne-Marie and Andres).

$$$ Hotel Blumental has 16 older but nicely furnished rooms and a fun, woodsy game/TV lounge (Sb-75–80 SF, Db-150–170 SF, higher prices are for July–Aug, plush but smoky lobby, attached restaurant, tel. 033-855-1826, fax 033-855-3686, www.muerren.ch /blumental, blumental@muerren.ch, Rolf and Heidi, fourth generation in the von Allmen family).

$$ Eiger Guesthouse offers 14 good budget rooms. This is a friendly, creaky, easygoing home away from home (S-60–65 SF, Sb-80–85 SF, D-100–110 SF, Db-130–140 SF, 39- to 45-SF beds in 2- and 4-bunk rooms, includes sheets and breakfast; Internet, closed Nov and for one month after Easter, across from train station, tel. 033-856-5460, fax 033-856-5461, www.eigerguesthouse .com, info@eigerguesthouse.com, well run by Scotsman Alan and Swiss Véronique). The restaurant serves good, reasonably priced dinners. Its poolroom—with public Internet access—is a popular local hangout. They have my Switzerland Alps TV show on DVD available in the lobby.

$$ Haus Mönch, a basic, blocky lodge run by Hotel Jungfrau, offers 20 woodsy, well-worn, but fine rooms, plus good Jungfrau views (Db-140–144 SF, Tb-180 SF, near TI and Sportzentrum, tel. 033-856-6464, fax 033-856-6465, www.hoteljungfrau.ch, mail @hoteljungfrau.ch).

$ Chalet Fontana, run by charming Englishwoman Denise Fussell, is a rare budget option in Mürren, with simple, crispy-clean, and comfortable rooms (35–45 SF per person in small doubles or triples with breakfast and shared bathrooms, price varies with size of room, 5 SF cheaper without breakfast, 1 apartment with kitchen and bathroom-110 SF for 2 people, 145 SF for 4, no CC, closed Nov–April, across street from Stägerstübli restaurant in town center, tel.

033-855-4385, mobile 078-642-3485, chaletfontana@muerren.ch). If no one's home, check at the Ed Abegglen shop next door (tel. 033-855-1245, off-season only).

$ Chalet Helvetia, run by Frau Hunziker, offers a homey, clean, two-bedroom apartment with bathroom, kitchen, separate entrance, and balcony for 40 SF per person (up to 5 people, no breakfast, 2-night minimum preferred, more expensive for 1-night stays, 200 yards below cable-car station on path to Gimmelwald, look for red *Zimmer* sign on right, tel. 033-855-4169, mobile 079-234-7867, kurthunziker105@msn.com).

EATING

Many of these restaurants are in or near my recommended hotels. Outside of summer and ski season, it can be hard to find any place that's open (ask around).

Stägerstübli is, hands down, *the* place to eat in town. It's the only real restaurant not associated with a hotel. Located in the town center, this 1902 building was once a tea room for rich tourists, while locals were limited to the room in the back—the nicest dining area today (lunches and dinners for 15–30 SF, daily 11:30–22:00, Lydia SE). Sitting on its terrace, you know just who's out and about in town.

Pasci's Snack Bar Bistro has fun, creative, and inexpensive light meals; a good selection of salads, vegetarian dishes, coffees, teas, and pastries; and impressive views (take-out available, run by a serious chef—Pasci—and Franzi, daily 10:00–18:00, at the Sportzentrum, overlooking the ice rink).

Restaurant Hotel Jungfrau is a dressy ski lodge with a modern octagonal dining room and a fine view terrace (nightly from 18:30, always a 10.50-SF salad bar, 50-SF 4-course meal, vegetarian options, 23-SF cheese fondue, near TI/Sportzentrum, tel. 033-855-4545, see "Sleeping," above).

The **Edelweiss self-serve restaurant** offers lunch with the most cliff-hanging dining in town—incredible views (daily 10:30–18:00, next to Hotel Alpina, see "Sleeping," above).

Restaurant Hotel Eiger is considered one of the better places in town, with a good chef, classy indoor seating, and a terrace with a view obstructed by the station (open daily, 20-SF plates, 29-SF *menu*, an enticing variety of meat fondue dinners for 45 SF, tel. 033-856-5454). Note that this is not the same as **Eiger Guesthouse**—which also serves good, but simpler, food (see "Sleeping," above).

Hotel Bellevue is pricey but atmospheric, with three dining zones: view terrace, elegant indoor, and the Jägerstübli—a cozy, well-antlered hunters' room guaranteed to disgust vegetarians. This is your best bet for game, as they buy chamois and deer direct from local hunters (mid-June–Oct from 18:00, 35-SF meals, tel. 033-855-1401, see "Sleeping," above).

The **Co-op** is the only grocery store in town, with good picnic fixings and sandwiches (Mon–Fri 8:00–12:00 & 14:00–18:00, Sat until 16:00, closed Sun). Given restaurant prices, this place is a godsend for those on a tight budget.

Lauterbrunnen

Lauterbrunnen—with a train station (has lockers), funicular, bank, shops, and lots of hotels—is the valley's commercial center. This is the jumping-off point for Jungfrau and Schilthorn adventures. It's idyllic, in spite of the busy road and big buildings.

ORIENTATION

Tourist Information: Stop by the friendly TI to check the weather forecast, use the Internet, and buy any regional train or lift tickets you need (June–Aug Mon–Sat 10:00–12:00 & 15:00–18:30, closed Sun, shorter hours off-season, 1 block up from station, tel. 033-856-8568, www.wengen-muerren.ch).

Helpful Hints

Bike Rental: You can rent mountain bikes at Imboden Bike on the main street (25-SF/4 hrs, 35-SF/full day, full-suspension—reserve ahead—45-SF/half day, 65-SF/full day, daily 8:00–18:30, tel. 033-855-2114).

Internet and Laundry: The Valley Hostel on the main street runs an Internet café and a small launderette (10-SF/load, don't open dryer door until machine is finished, or you'll have to pay another 5-SF to start it again; both daily 8:00–22:00, shorter hours Nov–April, tel. 033-855-2008).

SLEEPING

(2,612 feet, 1.25 SF = about $1, country code: 41)

$$ Hotel Staubbach, a big, Old World place—one of the first hotels in the valley (1890)—is being lovingly restored by hardworking American Craig and his Swiss wife, Corinne. Its 30 plain, comfortable rooms are family-friendly, there's a kids' play area, and the parking is free. Many rooms have great views (10 SF extra). They keep their prices down by cleaning the rooms only after every third night (S-60 SF, Ss-70 SF, Sb-90 SF, D-80 SF, Db-110 SF, figure 45 SF per person in family rooms sleeping up to 4, 10 SF extra per room for 1-night stays or for valley-view rooms June–Sept, elevator,

4 blocks up from station on the left, tel. 033-855-5454, fax 033-855-5484, www.staubbach.ch, hotel@staubbach.ch). Guests can watch a DVD of my TV show on the region in the lounge.

$ Valley Hostel is practical, friendly, and comfortable, offering 70 inexpensive beds for quieter travelers of all ages, with a pleasant garden and the welcoming Abegglen family: Martha, Alfred, Stefan, and Fränzi (D with bunk beds-56 SF, twin D-64 SF, beds in larger family-friendly rooms-28 SF per person, breakfast-5 SF, kitchen available, no CC, most rooms have no sinks, 16-SF cheese fondue on request for guests 18:00–20:00, non-smoking, Internet access, laundry, 2 blocks up from train station, tel. & fax 033-855-2008, www.valleyhostel.ch, info@valleyhostel.ch).

$ Chalet im Rohr—a creaky, old, woody firetrap of a place—has oodles of character (spiced with lots of Asian groups) and 50 26-SF beds in big one- to four-bed rooms that share six showers (no breakfast, common kitchen, no CC, closed for 3 weeks after Easter, below church on main drag, tel. & fax 033-855-2182).

$ Matratzenlager Stocki is rustic and humble, with the cheapest beds in town (14 SF with sheets in easygoing little 30-bed coed dorm with kitchen, closed Nov–Dec, across river from station, tel. 033-855-1754, Frau Graf SE).

$ *Camping:* Two campgrounds just south of town provide 15- to 35-SF beds (in dorms and 2-, 4-, and 6-bed bungalows, no sheets, kitchen facilities, no CC, big English-speaking tour groups): **Mountain Holiday Park-Camping Jungfrau,** romantically situated beyond Staubbach Falls, is huge and well organized by Hans (tel. 033-856-2010, fax 033-856-2020, www.camping-jungfrau.ch). It also has fancier cabins (25 SF per person). **Schützenbach Retreat,** on the left just past Lauterbrunnen toward Stechelberg, is simpler (tel. 033-855-1268, www.schutzenbach-retreat.ch).

EATING

At **Hotel Restaurant Oberland,** the Nolan family takes pride in serving tasty meals from a fun menu (daily 11:30–16:00 & 17:30–21:00, tel. 033-855-1241).

Hotel Restaurant Jungfrau, along the main street on the right-hand side, offers a wide range of specialties served by a friendly staff (daily 12:00–14:00 & 18:00–20:00, tel. 033-855-3434, run by Brigitte Melliger).

Hotel Restaurant Silberhorn is the local choice for a fancy meal out (fine indoor and outdoor seating, above the funicular station, tel. 033-856-2210).

MORE IN THE BERNER OBERLAND

SIGHTS AND ACTIVITIES

Lifts and Trains

The following lifts are both rated ▲▲▲. Doing at least one of them is an essential Berner Oberland experience.

The Schilthorn and a 10,000-Foot Breakfast

The Schilthornbahn carries skiers, hikers, and sightseers effortlessly to the 10,000-foot summit of the Schilthorn, where the Piz Gloria station awaits, with a solar-powered revolving restaurant, shop, and panorama terrace. Linger on top. Piz Gloria has a free "touristorama" film room with a multi-screen slide show and explosive highlights from the James Bond thriller that featured the Schilthorn (*On Her Majesty's Secret Service;* if it's not running, press the 007 button on the column in the middle of the room).

Watch paragliders set up, psych up, and take off, flying 45 minutes with the birds to distant Interlaken. (This is a tough launch point, but generally safe in the morning and late in the summer.) Walk along the ridge out back. This is a great place for a photo of you, the mountain-climber.

When you ascend in the gondola, take a look at the altitude meter. (The Gimmelwald-Schilthorn hike is free, if you don't mind a 5,000-foot altitude gain.) Ask at the Schilthorn station for a gondola souvenir decal (Schilthornbahn station in Stechelberg, tel. 033-856-2141). For another cheap thrill, ask the gondola attendant to crank down the window (easiest on the Mürren-Birg section). Then stick your head out the window...and you're hang-gliding.

You can ride up to the Schilthorn and hike down, but it's tough. For information on **hikes** from lift stations along the Schilthorn cable-car line, see "Hikes," page 1324. My favorite "hike" from the Schilthorn is simply along the ridge out back, to get away from the station and be all alone on top of an Alp.

Youth hostelers—not realizing that rocks may hide just under the snow—scream down the ice fields on plastic-bag sleds from the Schilthorn mountaintop. (English-speaking doctor in Lauterbrunnen.)

Cost and Hours: The early-bird and afternoon-special gondola tickets (60 SF round-trip, before 9:00 or after 15:30) take you from Gimmelwald to the Schilthorn and back at a discount (normal rate-80 SF, or 94 SF from the Stechelberg car park; parking-2 SF/2 hrs, 6 SF/day). These same discounted fares are available all day long in the shoulder season (roughly May and Oct). Eurailpass and Swiss railpass holders—who get a 25 percent discount (a better

Alpine Lifts in the Berner Oberland

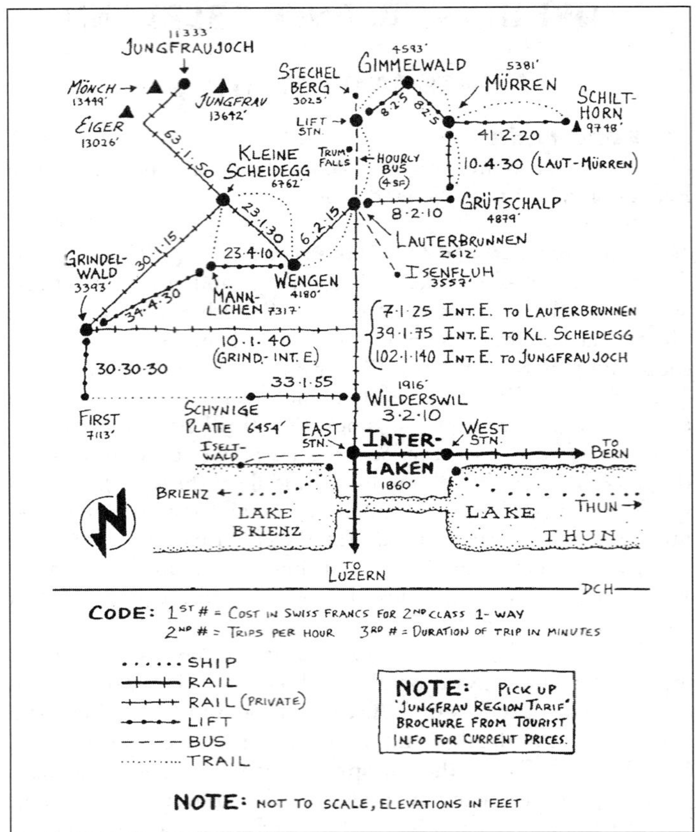

deal than the early/late specials)—might as well go whenever they like, because there's no double discount. Lifts go twice hourly, and the ride (including 2 transfers) to the Schilthorn takes 30 minutes. For more information, including current weather conditions, see www.schilthorn.ch.

Breakfast at 10,000 Feet: There's no à la carte—only a fixed meal for 15 SF (rolls and hot chocolate or coffee) or 22.50 SF (add egg, ham, and champagne; breakfast served 8:00–11:00). If you're going for breakfast before 9:00, consider an early-bird-plus-breakfast combo-ticket to save a few francs (73 SF round-trip from Gimmelwald, 84 SF from Stechelberg). Ask for more hot drinks if necessary. If you're not revolving, ask them to turn it on.

Jungfraujoch

The literal high point of any trip to the Swiss Alps is a train ride

Berner Oberland

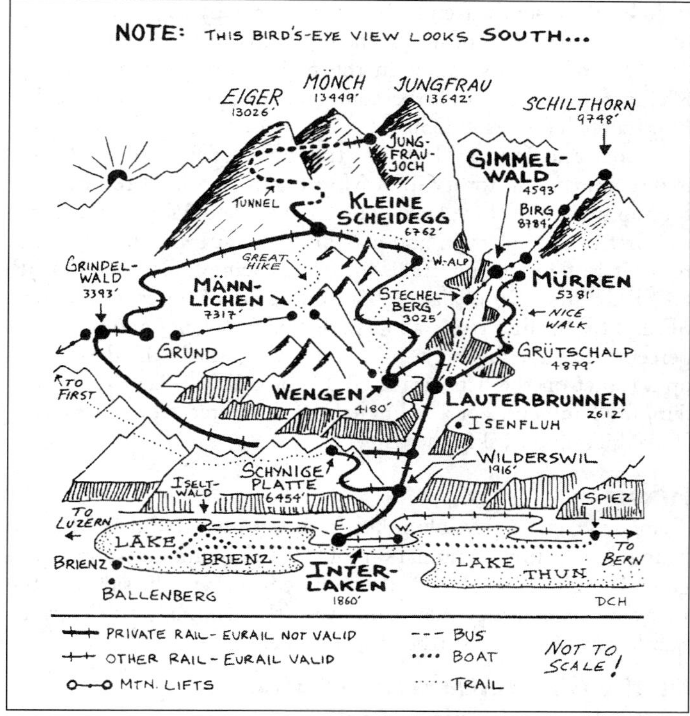

through the Eiger to the Jungfraujoch (but worth it only in good weather). At 11,300 feet, it's Europe's highest train station. The ride from Kleine Scheidegg takes about an hour (sit on right side for better views), including two five-minute stops at stations actually halfway up the notorious North Face of the Eiger. You have time to look out windows and marvel at how people could climb the Eiger—and how the Swiss built this train more than a hundred years ago. The second half of the ride takes you through a tunnel inside the Eiger (some newer train cars run multilingual videos about the history of the train line).

Once you reach the top, study the Jungfraujoch chart to see your options (many of them are weather-dependent). There's a restaurant, history exhibit, ice palace (a cavern with a gallery of ice statues), and a 20-minute video that plays continuously. A tunnel leads outside, where you can ski (30 SF for gear and lift ticket), sled (free loaner discs with deposit), ride in a dog sled (6 SF, mornings only), or hike 45 minutes across the ice to Mönchsjochhütte (a mountain hut with a small restaurant). An elevator leads to the Sphinx observatory for the highest viewing point, from which you can see Aletsch Glacier—Europe's longest, at nearly 11 miles—stretch to the south. Remember that your body isn't used to such high altitudes. Signs posted at the top remind you to take it easy.

One of the best hikes in the region—from Männlichen to Kleine Scheidegg—could be combined with your trip up to the Jungfraujoch (see page 1330).

Cost and Hours: The first trip of the day to Jungfraujoch is discounted; ask for a Good Morning Ticket, and return from the top by noon (Nov–April you can get Good Morning rates for the first or second train and stay after noon; train runs all year; round-trip fares to Jungfraujoch: from Kleine Scheidegg-104 SF, 80 SF for first trip of day—about 8:02; from Lauterbrunnen-154 SF, 130 SF for first trip—about 7:08, confirm times and prices, 25 percent discount for Eurailpass and Swiss railpass holders). Pick up a leaflet on the lifts at a local TI, or call 033-828-7233 (www.jungfraubahn.ch). For a trilingual weather forecast, call 033-828-7931; if it's cloudy, skip the trip.

Hikes

There are days of possible hikes from Gimmelwald and Mürren. Many are a fun combination of trails, mountain trains, and gondola rides. I've listed them based on which side of the Lauterbrunnen Valley they're on: west (the Gimmelwald/Mürren/Schilthorn side) or east (the Jungfrau side).

On the Gimmelwald (West) Side of the Lauterbrunnen Valley

Hikes from the Schilthorn

While several tough trails lead down from the Schilthorn, most visitors take the cable car round-trip simply for the views (see "Lifts and Trains," above). But if you're a serious hiker, consider walking all the way down (first hike) or part of the way down (second hike) back into Gimmelwald. Don't attempt to hike down from the Schilthorn unless the trail is clear of snow. Adequate shoes and clothing (weather can change quickly) and good knees are required. (If you want to visit the Sprutz Waterfall on your way to Gimmelwald, see page 1329.)

From the Top of the Schilthorn—To hike downhill from the Piz Gloria revolving restaurant at the peak, start at the steps to the right of the cable, which lead along a ridge between a cliff and the bowl. As you pass huge rocks and shale fields, keep an eye out for the painted rocks that mark the scant trail. Eventually, you'll hit the service road (a ski run in the winter), which is steep and not very pleasant. Passing a memorial to a woman killed by lightning in 1865, you come to the small lake called Grauseeli. Leave the gravel road and hike along the lake. From there, follow the trail (with the help of cables when necessary) to scamper along the shale in the direction of Rotstockhütte (to Gimmelwald, see next hike) or Schilttal (the valley leading directly to Mürren; follow Mürren/Rotstockhütte sign painted on the rock at the junction).

▲▲Birg to Gimmelwald via Brünli—Rather than the very long hike all the way back down into Gimmelwald, I prefer the easier (but still strenuous) hike from the intermediate cable-car station at Birg. This is efficiently combined with a visit to the Schilthorn (from Schilthorn summit, ride cable car halfway down, get off at Birg, and hike down from there; buy the round-trip excursion early-bird fare—which is cheaper than the Gimmelwald-Schilthorn-Birg ticket—and decide at Birg if you want to hike or ride down).

The most interesting trail from Birg to Gimmelwald is the high one via Grauseeli Lake and Wasenegg Ridge to Brünli, then down to Spielbodenalp and the Sprutz waterfall. Warning: This trail is quite steep and slippery in places, and can take four hours. Locals take their kindergartners on this hike, but it can seem dangerous to Americans unused to Alpine hikes. Do not attempt this hike in snow—which you might find at this altitude, even in the peak of summer. (Get local advice.)

From the Birg lift, hike toward the Schilthorn, taking your first left down and passing along the left side of the little Grauseeli lake. From the lake, a gravelly trail leads down rough switchbacks (including a stretch where the path narrows and you can hang onto a guide cable against the cliff face) until it levels out. When you see a rock painted with arrows pointing to Mürren and Rotstockhütte, follow the path to Rotstockhütte (traditional old farm with light meals and drinks, mattress loft with cheap beds), traversing the cow-grazed mountainside.

For a thrill, follow Wasenegg Ridge. It's more scary than dangerous if you're sure-footed and can handle the 50-foot-long "tightrope" section along an extremely narrow ledge with a thousand-foot drop. This trail gets you to Brünli with the least altitude drop. (The safer, well-signposted approach to Brünli is to drop down to Rotstockhütte, then climb back up to Brünli.) The barbed-wire fence leads to the knobby little summit, where you'll enjoy an incredible 360-degree view and a chance to sign your name on the register stored in the little wooden box.

A steep trail winds directly down from Brünli toward Gimmelwald and soon hits a bigger, easy trail. The trail bends right (just before the farm/restaurant at Spielbodenalp), leading to Sprutz. Walk under the Sprutz waterfall, then follow a steep, wooded trail that deposits you in a meadow of flowers at the top side of Gimmelwald.

Hiking in the Berner Oberland

This region is a wonderful place to hike, and I've listed my favorite excursions. The super-scenic walk from Männlichen to Kleine Scheidegg is the best of all worlds: It's both dramatic and relatively easy. The hike from Schynige Platte to First is spectacular, but much more challenging, as is the hike from the Birg cable-car station down to Gimmelwald—don't try either of these in bad weather. In case of rain, the lower hikes (North Face Trail from Allmendhubel; the walk from Mürren or Allmendhubel to Grütschalp; the Sefinen Valley hike from Gimmelwald; and the stroll along the Lauterbrunnen Valley) are better bets.

To do any serious hiking, you should invest in a real hiking map. Hikers can get specifics at the Mürren TI or from hoteliers. For a description of six diverse hikes on the west side of Lauterbrunnen, pick up the fine and free *Mürren-Schilthorn Hikes* brochure. This 3-D map of the Mürren mountainside makes a useful and attractive souvenir. For the other side of the valley, get the *Wandern Jungfraubahnen* brochure, which also has a handy 3-D map of hiking trails (both brochures free at stations, hotels, and TIs).

Once underway, don't mind the fences (although wires can be solar-powered electric); a hiker has the right of way in Switzerland. Don't forget a water bottle and some munchies. Trails are well-marked, with yellow signs listing destinations and the estimated time it'll take you to walk there. Refer to maps (within this chapter) as you read about the hikes.

Weather Concerns: Locals always seem to know the weather report (as much of their income depends on it). Clouds can roll in anytime, but skies are usually clearest in the morning. All over the region, TV sets are tuned to the local weather station, with real-time views from all the famous peaks. The same station

Hikes from Gimmelwald

▲Up Sefinen Valley to Kilchbalm—An easy trail from Gimmelwald is up the Sefinen Valley (Sefinental). This is a good rainy-weather hike, as you can go as far as you like. After two hours and a gain of only 800 feet, you hit the end of the trail and Kilchbalm, a dramatic bowl of glacier fields. Note that snow can make this trail unsafe, even into the summer (ask locally for information), and there's no food or drink along the way—so plan accordingly.

From the Gimmelwald fire station, walk about 100 yards down the paved Stechelberg road. Leave it on the dirt Sefinental road, which becomes a lane, then a trail. You'll cross a raging river and pass a firing range where locals practice their marksmanship (Fri and Sat evenings; the "danger of fire" sign refers to live bullets). Follow signs to airs a travelogue on the region each evening around 21:30. You can also check the weather at www.swisspanorama.com.

Snow: As late as July, snow can curtail your hiking plans (the Männlichen lift doesn't even open until the first week in June). Before setting out on any hike, get advice from a knowledgeable local. Well into the spring, and sometimes also in early fall, the high trails (Männlichen to Kleine Scheidegg, Schynige Platte to First, and anything from Schilthorn or Birg) are likely to be impassible.

Wildlife: As hunting is not allowed in the vicinity of any lifts, animals find comfort in places you're likely to be. Keep an eye out for chamois (called *Gemse* here)—the sure-footed "goat antelope" that lives at the top of the treeline, and goes a little lower when hungry. Spotting an ibex—a wild goat with horns, scrambling along the rocky terrain—is another Berner Oberland thrill. You'll also encounter marmot, big Alpine mice (like 2 pound squirrels) who get really fat each summer, planning to sleep underground for six months through the winter. These burrowing rodents are fun to watch, and if you sit still, they don't see you. You'll hear them whistle. Your best viewing place is above Allmendhubel, in the meadow above the highest hut in Blumental.

Nordic Walking: You may wonder about the Germans you'll see with their walking sticks *(Alpenstock)*. This is trying to be the next craze: Nordic walking. Enthusiasts claim Nordic walking is an all-body workout, activating 90 percent of your muscles and burning a third more calories than "normal" walking, while cutting way back on the strain on your back and knees when going downhill. To do it right requires proper instruction. Sticks can be rented at some outdoor shops.

Kilchbalm into a forest, along a river, and finally to the glacier fields.

▲Gimmelwald-Tanzbodeli-Obersteinberg-Stechelberg/Gimmelwald—This eight-hour, 11-mile hike is extremely rewarding, offering perfect peace, very few people, traditional Alpine culture, and spectacular views. (There's no food or drink for 5 hours, so pack accordingly.) As the trail can be a bit confusing, this is best done with a good map (buy locally).

About 100 yards below the Gimmelwald firehouse, take the Sefinental dirt road (described above). As the dirt road switches back after about 30 minutes, take the right turn across the river and start your ascent, following signs to Obersteinberg. After 90 minutes of hard climbing, you have the option of a side-trip to Busenalp. This is fun if the goat and cow herder is there, as you can watch the traditional cheesemaking in action. (He appreciates a bottle of wine

Gimmelwald Area Hikes

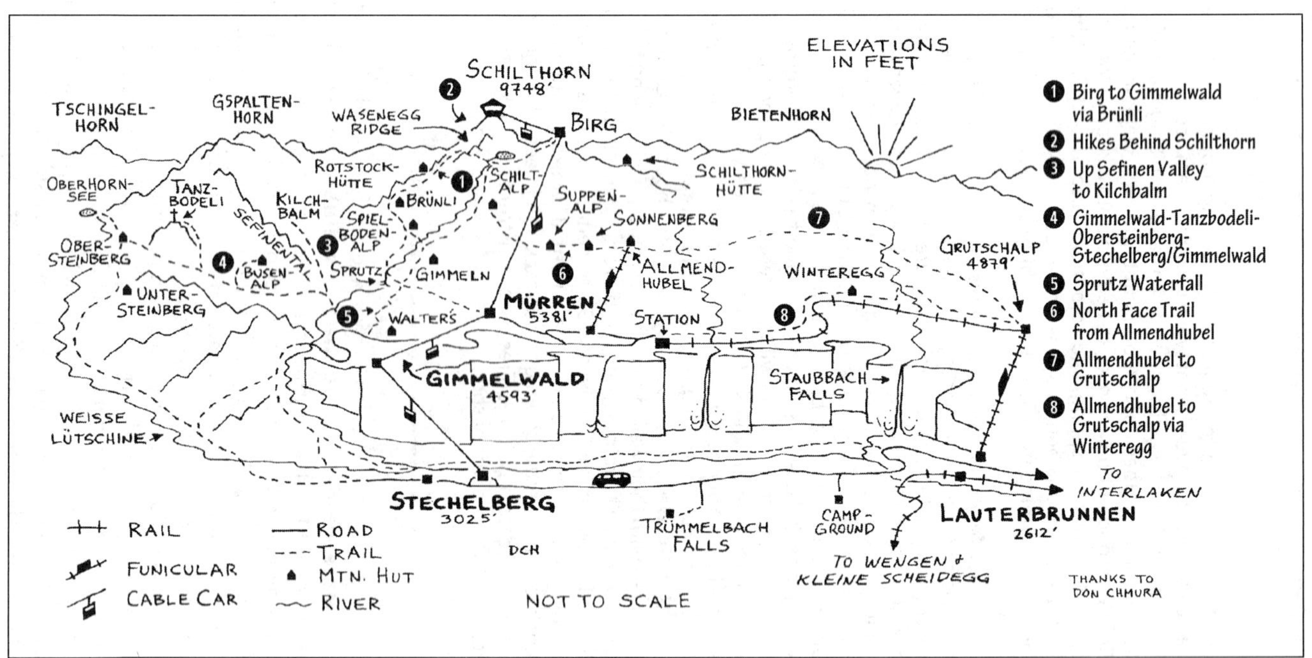

from hikers.) Trail markers are painted onto rocks—watch carefully. After visiting Busenalp, return to the main path.

At the "Obersteinberg 50 min/Tanzbodeli 20 min" signpost, head for Tanzbodeli (literally, "Dancing Floor"). This is everyone's favorite Alpine perch—great for a little romance, or a picnic with breathtaking views of the Obersteinberg valley. From here, you enter a natural reserve, so you're likely to see chamois and other Alpine critters. From Tanzbodeli, you return to the main trail (there's no other way out) and continue to Obersteinberg. You'll eventually hit the Mountain Hotel Obersteinberg (see "Sleeping," page 1337; American expat Vickie will serve you a meal or drink).

From there, the trail leads to Hotel Tschingelhorn and back to Gimmelwald (2 hrs total) or Stechelberg (bottom of Schilthorn cable car, 90 min total). About an hour later, you hit a fork in the trail and choose where you'd like your hike to end.

▲Sprutz Waterfall—The forest above Gimmelwald hides a powerful waterfall with a trail snaking behind it, offering a fun gorge experience. While the waterfall itself is not well-signed, it's on the Gimmelwald-Spielbodenalp trail. It's steep, through a forest, and can be very slippery when wet, but the actual crossing under the waterfall is just misty.

The hike up to Sprutz from Gimmelwald isn't worth the trip in itself, but it's handy when combined with the hike down from Birg and Brünli (see above) or the North Face Trail (see below). As you descend on either of these two hikes, the trail down to Gimmelwald splits at Spielbodenalp—to the right for the forest and the waterfall; to the left for more meadows, the hamlet of Gimmeln, and more gracefully back into Gimmelwald.

Hikes from Mürren/Allmendhubel

▲▲North Face Trail from Allmendhubel—For a pleasant, mainly downhill, two-hour hike (4 miles, from 6,385 feet to 5,375 feet), ride the Allmendhubel funicular up from Mürren (7.40 SF, much cheaper than Schilthorn, good restaurant at top). From there, follow the well-signed route circling around to Mürren (or cut off at Spielbodenalp, near the end, and descend into Gimmelwald via the Sprutz Waterfall). Just follow the blue signs. You'll enjoy great views, flowery meadows, mountain huts, and a dozen information boards along the way, describing the fascinating climbing history of the great peaks around you.

Along the trail, you'll pass four farms (technically "alps," as they are only open in the summer) that serve meals and drinks. Sonnenberg was allowed to break the all-wood code with concrete for protection against avalanches. Suppenalp is quainter. Lean against the house with a salad, soup, or sandwich and enjoy the view.

Notice how older huts are built into the protected side of rocks and cutcroppings, in anticipation of avalanches. Above Suppenalp, Blumental ("Flower Valley") is hopping with marmots. Because hunters are not allowed near lifts, animals have learned that these are safe places to hang out—giving tourists a better chance of spotting them.

The trail leads up and over to a group of huts called Schiltalp. If the poles under the eve have bells, the cows are up. If not, the cows are still at the lower farm. Half the cows in Gimmelwald (about 100) spend their summers here. In July, August, and September, you can watch them making cheese and have a snack or drink. Thirty years ago, each family had its own hut. Labor was cheap and available. Today, it's a communal thing, with several families sharing the expense of a single cow herder. Cow herders are master cheesemakers, and have veterinary skills, too.

From Schiltalp, the trail winds gracefully down to Spielbodenalp—a farm with lots going on (open May–mid-Oct Fri–Wed, closed Thu, good menu, 31-SF dorm beds with breakfast). From there, you can finish the North Face trail (continuing down and left through meadows and the hamlet of Gimmeln, then back to Mürren, with more historic signposts); or cut off right (descending steeply through a thick forest and under the dramatic Sprutz Waterfall into Gimmelwald—see Sprutz Waterfall, above, for details).

▲Allmendhubel/Mürren to Grutschalp—For a not-too-tough, three-hour walk with great Jungfrau views, ride the funicular from Mürren to Allmendhubel (6,344 feet) and walk to Grütschalp (a drop of about 1,500 feet), where you can catch the panorama train back to Mürren. An easier version is the lower Bergweg from Allmendhubel to Grütschalp via Winteregg and its cheese farm. For a super-easy family stroll with grand views, walk from Mürren just above the train tracks to either Winteregg (40 min, restaurant, playground, train station) or Grütschalp (60 min, train station), then catch the panorama train back to Mürren.

Hikes on the Jungfrau (East) Side of the Lauterbrunnen Valley

▲▲▲The Männlichen-Kleine Scheidegg Hike—This is my favorite easy Alpine hike (2.5 miles, 1.5 hours, 900-foot altitude drop to Kleine Scheidegg). It's entertaining all the way, with glorious Jungfrau, Eiger, and Mönch views. That's the Young Maiden being protected from the Ogre by the Monk. (These days, that could be problematic.) Trails may be snowbound into June; ask about conditions at the lift stations or local TIs. If the Männlichen lift is closed, you can take the train straight from Lauterbrunnen to Kleine Scheidegg (see Jungfraujoch under "Lifts and Trains," page 1322).

If the weather's good, descend from Gimmelwald bright and early to Stechelberg. From here, get to the Lauterbrunnen train station by post bus (4 SF, bus is synchronized to depart with the arrival of each lift) or by car (parking at the large, multistory pay lot behind the Lauterbrunnen station-2 SF/2 hrs, 9 SF/day). At Lauterbrunnen, buy a train ticket to Männlichen (29 SF one-way). If hiking from Männlichen to Wengen via Kleine Scheidegg (this complete hike), you'll buy a ticket from Lauterbrunnen to Männlichen, then from Wengen back to Lauterbrunnen, for 51 SF. Sit on the right side of the train for great waterfall views on your way up to Wengen. In Wengen, walk across town (buy a picnic, but don't waste time here if it's sunny—you can linger after your hike) and catch the Männlichen lift to the top of the ridge high above you (lift departs every 15 min, beginning the first week of June). Note that the lift can be open even if the trail is closed; confirm that the trail is open before ascending.

From the top of Wengen-Männlichen lift station, turn left and hike uphill 20 minutes to the little peak (Männlichen Gipfel, 7,500 feet) for that king- or queen-of-the-mountain feeling. Then take an easy hour's walk—facing spectacular Alpine panorama views—to Kleine Scheidegg for a picnic or restaurant lunch. To start the hike, leave the Wengen-Männlichen lift station to the right. Walk past the second Männlichen lift station (this one leads to Grindelwald, the touristy town in the valley to your left). Ahead of you in the distance, left to right, are the north faces of the Eiger, Mönch, and Jungfrau; in the foreground is the Tschuggen peak, and just behind it, the Lauberhorn. This hike takes you around the left (east) side of this ridge. Simply follow the signs for Kleine Scheidegg, and you'll be there in about an hour—a little more for gawkers, picnickers, and photographers. You might have to tiptoe through streams of melted snow—or some small snow banks, even well into the summer—but the path is well-marked, well-maintained, and mostly level all the way to Kleine Scheidegg.

About 35 minutes into the hike, you'll reach a bunch of benches and a shelter with incredible unobstructed views of all three peaks—the perfect picnic spot. Fifteen minutes later on the left, you'll see the first sign of civilization: Restaurant Grindelwaldblick, offering a handy terrace lunch stop with tasty, hearty, and reasonable food (open daily, closed Dec and May, see "Sleeping and Eating in Kleine Scheidegg," page 1336). After 10 more minutes, you'll be at the Kleine Scheidegg train station, with plenty of other lunch options (including Bahnhof Buffet, see "Sleeping and Eating in Kleine Scheidegg," page 1336).

From Kleine Scheidegg, you can catch the train to "the top of Europe" (see Jungfraujoch information, page 1323). Or head downhill, riding the train or hiking (30 gorgeous min to Wengernalp station, a little further to the Allmend stop; 60 more steep min from there into the town of Wengen). The Alpine views might be accompanied by the valley-filling mellow sound of alphorns and distant avalanches.

If the weather turns bad or you run out of steam, catch the train at any of the stations along the way. After Wengernalp, the trail to Wengen is steep and, though not dangerous, requires a good set of knees. Wengen is a good shopping town. (For accommodations, see "Sleeping in Wengen," page 1334.) The boring final descent from Wengen to Lauterbrunnen is knee-killer steep—catch the train.

▲▲Schynige Platte to First—The best day I've had hiking in the Berner Oberland was when I made this demanding six-hour ridge walk, with Lake Brienz on one side and all that Jungfrau beauty on the other. Start at Wilderswil train station (just above Interlaken) and catch the little train up to Schynige Platte (6,560 feet). The high point is Faulhorn (8,790 feet, with its famous mountaintop hotel). Hike to a small mini-gondola called "First" (7,110 feet), then ride down to Grindelwald and catch a train back to your starting point, Wilderswil. Or, if you have a regional train pass (or no car but endless money), take the long, scenic return trip to Gimmelwald: From Grindelwald, take the lift up to Männlichen, do the hike to Kleine Scheidegg and Wengen (see above), then head down into Lauterbrunnen and on to Gimmelwald.

For a shorter (3-hr) ridge walk, consider the well-signposted Panoramaweg, a loop from Schynige Platte to Daub Peak.

The Alpine flower park (5 SF, at the Schynige Platte station) offers a delightful stroll through several hundred Alpine flowers (best in summer) including a chance to see Edelweiss growing in the wild.

Lowa, a leading local manufacturer of top-end hiking boots, has a promotional booth at the Schynige Platte station providing free loaner boots to hikers who'd like to give their boots a try. They are already broken in, but bring thick socks (or buy them there).

If hiking here, be mindful of the last lifts (which can be as early as 16:30). Climbing from First (7,113 feet) to Schynige Platte (6,454 feet) gives you a later departure down and less climbing.

Mountain Biking

Mountain biking is popular and accepted, as long as you stay on the clearly marked mountain-bike paths. A good ride is the round-trip Mürren Loop that runs from Mürren to Gimmelwald, down the Sefinen Valley to Stechelberg, along the dreamy bike path left of the river to Lauterbrunnen, up by funicular to Grütschalp (bike costs same as person-7.80 SF), and back through a working cheese farm to Mürren. You can rent bikes in Mürren (Stäger Sport, 35 SF/day includes helmet, daily 9:00–17:00, closed mid-Sept–mid-

June, across from TI/Sportzentrum, tel. 033-855-2355, www.staegersport.ch) or in Lauterbrunnen (Imboden Bike, 25 SF/4 hrs, 35 SF/day; call ahead to reserve a full-suspension bike: 45 SF/half day, 65 SF/full day; daily 8:30–18:30, tel. 033-855-2114). The Lauterbrunnen shop is often open when the Mürren one isn't. It costs 2.50 SF per segment to take a bike onto the gondola.

You can also bike the Lauterbrunnen Valley from Lauterbrunnen to Interlaken. It's a gentle downhill ride via a peaceful bike path across the river from the road (don't bike on the road). Rent a bike at Lauterbrunnen (see above), bike to Interlaken, and return to Lauterbrunnen by train (to take bike on train, pay about 4 SF extra). Or rent a bike at either Interlaken station, take the train to Lauterbrunnen, and ride back.

Rainy-Day Options

When it rains here, locals joke that they're washing the mountains. If clouds roll in, don't despair. They can roll out just as quickly. With good rain gear and the right choice of trail, a hike in the rain can be thoroughly enjoyable, with surprise views popping out all around you as the clouds break. And there are plenty of good bad-weather options.

▲▲Cloudy-Day Lauterbrunnen Valley Walk—Try the easy trails and pleasant walks along the floor of the Lauterbrunnen Valley. For a smell-the-cows-and-flowers lowland walk—ideal for a cloudy day, weary body, or tight budget—follow the riverside trail from Stechelberg's Schilthornbahn station (left of river) for three miles downhill to Lauterbrunnen's Staubbach Falls, near the town church (you can reverse the route, but it's a gradual uphill to Stechelberg). Detour to Trümmelbach Falls (described below) en route. There's a fine, paved, car-free, riverside path all the way (popular with bikers). In this "Valley of Many Waterfalls" (literally), you'll see cone-like mounds piled against the sides of the cliffs, formed by centuries of rocks hurled by tumbling rivers.

If you're staying in Gimmelwald: Take the lift down to Stechelberg (5 min), then walk to Lauterbrunnen, detouring to Trümmelbach Falls shortly after Stechelberg (15 min to falls, another 45 min to Lauterbrunnen). To return to Gimmelwald from Lauterbrunnen, take the funicular up to Grütschalp (10 min), then either walk (90 min to Gimmelwald) or take the panorama train (15 min) to Mürren. From Mürren, it's a downhill walk (30 min) to Gimmelwald. (This loop trip can be reversed.)

Note that this is an El Dorado of base-jumping (parachuting off of cliffs), and each season the bodies of dead thrill-seekers plummet to the valley floor. They hike to the top of a cliff, leap off—falling as long as they can (this provides the rush)—and then pull the ripcord to release a tiny parachute, hoping it will break their fall and a gust won't dash them into the mountainside.

▲Trümmelbach Falls—If all the waterfalls have you intrigued, sneak a behind-the-scenes look at the valley's most powerful, Trümmelbach Falls (10 SF, daily July–Aug 8:30–18:00, June 9:00–17:30, Easter-May and Sept–mid-Nov 9:00–17:00, closed mid-Nov–Easter, on Lauterbrunnen-Stechelberg road, take post bus from Lauterbrunnen TI or Stechelberg gondola station, tel. 033-855-3232). You'll ride an elevator up through the mountain and climb through several caves (wet, with lots of stairs, and—for some—claustrophobic) to see the melt from the Eiger, Mönch, and Jungfrau grinding like God's bandsaw through the mountain at the rate of up to 5,200 gallons a second (that's 20,000 liters—nearly double the beer consumption at Oktoberfest). The upper area is the best; if your legs ache, skip the lower falls and ride down on the elevator.

Lauterbrunnen Folk Museum (Heimatmuseum)—This humble collection, in Lauterbrunnen, shows off the local folk culture and two centuries of mountaineering. You'll see lots of lace, exhibits on cheese and woodworking, and classic old photos (free if you're staying in the region, 3 SF otherwise, mid-June–mid-Oct Tue, Thu, and Sat–Sun 14:00–17:00, closed off-season, just over bridge and below church at the far end of town, tel. 033-855-3586 or 033-855-1388).

Mürren Activities—This low-key Alpine resort town offers a variety of rainy-day options, from its shops to its slick Sportzentrum (sports center) with pools, steam baths, squash, and a fitness center (details on page 1314). On Wednesday nights at 20:30 from June through August, Mürren's Sportzentrum hosts a lively free cultural night with alpenhorns, folk music, and local wine.

Interlaken Activities—For more bad-weather ideas, see "Sights and Activities—Near Interlaken," page 1298.

SLEEPING AND EATING

In addition to my listings in Interlaken, Gimmelwald, Mürren, and Lauterbrunnen, consider these nearby places.

Sleeping in Wengen

(4,180 feet, 1.25 SF = about $1, country code: 41)

Wengen—a bigger, fancier Mürren on the other side of the valley—has plenty of grand hotels, many shops, tennis courts, minigolf, and terrific views. This traffic-free resort is an easy train ride above Lauterbrunnen and halfway up to Kleine Scheidegg and Männlichen, and offers more activities for those needing distraction from the scenery. Hiking is better from Mürren and Gimmelwald. The **TI** is one block from the station; go up to the main drag, turn left, and look ahead on the left (June–Sept and Dec–mid-April daily 9:00–18:00; mid-April–May and Oct–Nov Mon–Fri 9:00–18:00, closed Sat–Sun; Internet access; tel. 033-855-1414, www.wengen-muerren.ch).

Sleeping Above the Train Station

$$$ Hotel Berghaus, in a quiet area a five-minute walk from the main street, offers 19 rooms above a fine restaurant specializing in fish (Sb-82–117 SF, Db-164–234 SF, elevator, guests can use pool at Park Hotel for free; call on phone at station hotel board for free pickup, or walk up street across from Bernerhof Hotel, bear right and then left at fork, 200 yards more past church on the left; tel. 033-855-2151, fax 033-855-3820, www.wengen.com/hotel/berghaus, berghaus@wengen.com, Fontana family).

$$$ Hotel Schönegg is a centrally located splurge, right on Wengen's main drag (Sb-100–110 SF, Db-200–220 SF; higher July–Aug: Sb-115–125 SF, Db-230–250 SF; non-smoking rooms, all rooms have balconies and great views, cozy family room with fireplace, Internet access, good restaurant with big terrace, look for big yellow hotel on main drag near TI, tel. 033-855-3422, fax 033-855-4233, www.hotel-schoenegg.ch, schoenegg@tcnet.ch, Herr und Frau Berthod).

Sleeping Below the Train Station

The first two listings are bright, cheery, family-friendly, and five minutes below the station: Leave the station toward the Co-op store, turn right and go under the rail bridge, bear right (paved path) at the fork, and follow the road down and around.

$$ Bären Hotel, run by friendly Therese and Willy Brunner, offers 14 tidy rooms with perky, bright-orange bathrooms (Sb-80 SF, Db-150 SF, Tb-210 SF, dinner-20 SF more, family rooms, tel. 033-855-1419, fax 033-855-1525, www.baeren-wengen.ch, info@baeren-wengen.ch).

$$ Familienhotel Edelweiss has 25 bright rooms, lots of fun public spaces, a Christian emphasis, and a jittery Chihuahua named Speedy (Sb-65–75 SF, Db-130–150 SF, non-smoking, great family rooms, elevator, TV lounge, game room, meeting room, kids' playroom, tel. 033-855-2388, fax 033-855-4288, www.vch.ch/edelweiss, edelweiss@vch.ch, Bärtschi family).

$$ Clare and Andy's Chalet (Trogihalten) offers three rustic, low-ceilinged rooms (1-room studio: Sb-52 SF, Db-80 SF; 2-room suite: Sb/Db-98 SF, Tb-131 SF, Qb-172 SF; 4-room flat: Tb-147 SF, Qb-176 SF; breakfast-15 SF, dinner by request-30 SF, 4-night minimum preferred, prices higher for shorter stays, no CC, all rooms with balconies, leave station to the left and follow paved path next to Bernerhof Hotel downhill, steep 5-min hike, tel. &

fax 033-855-1712, mobile 079-423-7813, www.chaletwengen.ch, info@chaletwengen.ch, Clare's English, Andy's Swiss).

$ Backpackers' Wengen Lodge is an old former schoolhouse offering cheap beds a steep 10-minute hike below the station (25 SF per bed with sheets in a 10-bed, often empty dorm; S-30 SF, D-60 SF, no breakfast, kitchens, follow the signs from the station, tel. 033-855-1573, www.wengenlodge.ch, info@wengenlodge.ch, Angela).

Sleeping and Eating at Kleine Scheidegg

(6,762 feet, 1.25 SF = about $1, country code: 41)

Confirm price and availability before ascending. Both places serve meals.

$$ Bahnhof Buffet invites you to sleep face-to-face with the Eiger (dorm bed-50 SF with breakfast, 68 SF with dinner too, D-167 SF with breakfast and dinner, in the train station building, tel. 033-828-7828, fax 033-828-7830, www.bahnhof-scheidegg.ch).

$ Restaurant Grindelwaldblick, a 10-minute hike from the train station, really gets you up into the mountains (38 SF per bed in 12-bed room, includes sheets, closed Nov and May, tel. 033-855-1374, fax 033-855-4205, www.grindelwaldblick.ch).

Sleeping in Stechelberg

(3,025 feet, 1.25 SF = about $1, country code: 41)

Stechelberg is the hamlet at the end of Lauterbrunnen Valley, at the base of the lift to Gimmelwald, Mürren, and the Schilthorn.

$$ Hotel Stechelberg, at road's end, is surrounded by waterfalls and vertical rock, with a garden terrace and 20 quiet rooms—half in a creaky old building, half in a concrete, no-character new building (D-86–104 SF, Db-130, Db with balcony-158 SF, T-147 SF, Tb-186 SF, Q-168 SF, Qb-234 SF, post bus stops here, tel. 033-855-2921, fax 033-855-4438, www.stechelberg.ch, hotel@stechelberg.ch).

$ Nelli Beer, renting three rooms in a quiet, scenic, and folksy setting, is your best Stechelberg option (S-35 SF, D-60 SF, 2-night min, no CC, over river behind Stechelberg post office at big *Zimmer* sign, get off post bus at post office, tel. 033-855-3930, some English spoken).

$ Naturfreundehaus Alpenhof is a homey, cozy Alpine lodge for hikers. Owners Marc (English) and Diane (Australian) have made it a quiet and peaceful place to relax (60 beds, 2–8 people per co-ed room, 22 SF per bed, D-44 SF, breakfast-9 SF extra, laundry-10 SF, no CC, tel. 033-855-1202, alpenhof@naturfreunde.ch). Behind Hotel Stechelberg (post bus stop), take the path to the right across the river.

Sleeping in Obersteinberg

(5,900 feet, 1.25 SF = about $1, country code: 41)

$ Here's a wild idea: **Mountain Hotel Obersteinberg** is a working Alpine farm with cheese, cows, a mule shuttling up food once a day, and an American (Vickie) who fell in love with a mountain man. It's a 2.5-hour hike from either Stechelberg or Gimmelwald. They rent 12 primitive rooms and a bunch of loft beds. There's no shower, no hot water, and only meager solar-panel electricity. Candles light up the night, and you can take a hot-water bottle to bed if necessary (S-81 SF, D-162 SF, includes linen, sheetless dorm beds-64 SF, these prices include breakfast and dinner, without meals S-37 SF, D-73 SF, dorm beds-20 SF, closed Oct–May, tel. 033-855-2033). The place is filled with locals and Germans on weekends, but it's all yours on weekdays. Why not hike there from Gimmelwald and leave the Alps a day later?

Sleeping in Isenfluh

(3,560 feet, 1.25 SF = about $1, country code: 41)

The tiny hamlet of Isenfluh is even smaller than Gimmelwald and offers better views.

$$ Pension Waldrand has a decent restaurant (including great fresh salads) and four reasonable rooms (Db-120–130 SF, Tb-150 SF, includes breakfast, hrly bus from Lauterbrunnen, 4/day from Interlaken, tel. 033-855-1227, fax 033-855-1392, www.waldrand.com, booking@waldrand.com).

APPENDIX

European National Tourist Offices in the U.S.

Austrian Tourist Office: P.O. Box 1142, New York, NY 10108-1142, tel. 212/944-6880, fax 212/730-4568, www.austria.info, travel@austria.info. Ask for their "Austria Kit" with map. Fine hikes and city information.

Belgian Tourist Office: 220 E. 42nd St. #3402, New York, NY 10017, tel. 212/758-8130, fax 212/355-7675, www.visitbelgium.com, info@visitbelgium.com. Hotel and city guides; brochures for ABC lovers—antiques, beer, and chocolates; map of Brussels; information on WWI and WWII battlefields; and a list of Jewish sights.

Czech Tourist Office: 1109 Madison Ave., New York, NY 10028, tel. 212/288-0830, fax 212/288-0971, www.czechtourism.com/usa, info-usa@czechtourism.com. Basic information and map are free; additional materials are $4 (prepaid by check).

Denmark (see Scandinavian Tourist Office)

French Tourist Office: 444 Madison Ave., 16th floor, New York, NY 10022, fax 212/838-7855, www.franceguide.com, info.us@franceguide.com. For questions and brochures (on regions, barging, wine country, etc.), call 410/286-8310 or order online. One brochure and the France Guide magazine are free; additional brochures are $0.50 each, with a handling fee of $2 per order. Order will arrive in 2–3 weeks; rush delivery is extra.

German National Tourist Office: Maps, Rhine schedules, castles, biking, genealogical information, and city and regional information. Visit www.cometogermany.com and contact the nearest office:

In New York: 122 E. 42nd St. #2000, New York, NY 10168, tel. 800-651-7010 or 212/661-7200, fax 212/661-7174, gntonyc@d-z-t.com.

In Illinois: P.O. Box 59594, Chicago, IL 60659, tel. 773/539-6303, fax 773/539-6378, gntoch@aol.com.

In California: 501 Santa Monica Blvd. #607, Santa Monica, CA

90401, tel. 310/394-2580, fax 310/260-2923, info@gntolax.com.

Great Britain Tourist Office: 551 Fifth Ave. #701, New York, NY 10176, tel. 800-462-2748, fax 212/986-1188, www.visitbritain.com, travelinfo@visit britain.org. Free maps of London and Britain. Regional information, garden-tour map, urban cultural-activities brochures.

Greece Tourist Office: 645 Fifth Ave. #903, New York, NY 10022, tel. 212/421-5777, fax 212/826-6940, www.greektourism.com, info@greektourism.com. General how-to booklet, maps of Athens and Greece, and plenty on the islands.

Ireland Tourist Office: 345 Park Ave., 17th floor, New York, NY 10154, tel. 800-223-6470 or 212/418-0800, fax 212/371-9052, www.tourismireland.com, info.us@tourismireland.com, events calendar, golfing, outdoor activities, and historic sights. Tourism Ireland also provides information to travelers who wish to visit Northern Ireland. Learn more about sightseeing opportunities and ask about a vacation planner packet, maps, walking routes, and horseback riding.

Italian Tourist Offices: Check www.italiantourism.com and contact the nearest office...

In New York: 630 Fifth Ave. #1565, New York, NY 10111, brochure hotline tel. 212/245-4822, tel. 212/245-5618, fax 212/586-9249, enitny@italiantourism.com.

In Illinois: 500 N. Michigan Ave. #2240, Chicago, IL 60611, tel. 312/644-0996, fax 312/644-3019, enitch@italiantourism.com

In California: 12400 Wilshire Blvd. #550, Los Angeles, CA 90025, brochure hotline tel. 310/820-0098, tel. 310/820-4498, fax 310/820-6357, enitla@italiantourism.com.

Netherlands Tourist Office: 355 Lexington Ave., 19th floor, New York, NY 10017, tel. 212/557-3500, fax 212/370-9507, www.holland.com, information@holland.com. They no longer distribute printed material; all information is now available only on the Internet.

Scandinavian Tourist Office: P.O. Box 4649, Grand Central Station, New York, NY 10163, tel. 212/885-9700, fax 212/885-9710, www.goscandinavia.com, info@goscandinavia.com. Good general booklets on all the Scandinavian countries. Ask for specific country info and city maps.

Spain Tourist Offices: Check their Web sites (www.okspain.org and www.spain.info) and contact their nearest office...

In New York: 666 Fifth Ave., 35th floor, New York, NY 10103, tel. 212/265-8822, fax 212/265-8864, oetny@tourspain.es.

In Illinois: 845 N. Michigan Ave. #915E, Chicago, IL 60611, tel. 312/642-1992, fax 312/642-9817, chicago@tourspain.es.

In Florida: 1395 Brickell Ave. #1130, Miami, FL 33131, tel. 305/358-1992, fax 305/358-8223, oetmiami@tourspain.es.

In California: 8383 Wilshire Blvd. #956, Beverly Hills, CA 90211, tel. 323/658-7188, fax 323/658-1061, losangeles@tourspain.es.

2006

JANUARY

S	M	T	W	T	F	S
1	2	3	4	5	6	7
8	9	10	11	12	13	14
15	16	17	18	19	20	21
22	23	24	25	26	27	28
29	30	31				

FEBRUARY

S	M	T	W	T	F	S
			1	2	3	4
5	6	7	8	9	10	11
12	13	14	15	16	17	18
19	20	21	22	23	24	25
26	27	28				

MARCH

S	M	T	W	T	F	S
			1	2	3	4
5	6	7	8	9	10	11
12	13	14	15	16	17	18
19	20	21	22	23	24	25
26	27	28	29	30	31	

APRIL

S	M	T	W	T	F	S
						1
2	3	4	5	6	7	8
9	10	11	12	13	14	15
16	17	18	19	20	21	22
23/30	24	25	26	27	28	29

MAY

S	M	T	W	T	F	S
	1	2	3	4	5	6
7	8	9	10	11	12	13
14	15	16	17	18	19	20
21	22	23	24	25	26	27
28	29	30	31			

JUNE

S	M	T	W	T	F	S
				1	2	3
4	5	6	7	8	9	10
11	12	13	14	15	16	17
18	19	20	21	22	23	24
25	26	27	28	29	30	

JULY

S	M	T	W	T	F	S
						1
2	3	4	5	6	7	8
9	10	11	12	13	14	15
16	17	18	19	20	21	22
23/30	24/31	25	26	27	28	29

AUGUST

S	M	T	W	T	F	S
		1	2	3	4	5
6	7	8	9	10	11	12
13	14	15	16	17	18	19
20	21	22	23	24	25	26
27	28	29	30	31		

SEPTEMBER

S	M	T	W	T	F	S
					1	2
3	4	5	6	7	8	9
10	11	12	13	14	15	16
17	18	19	20	21	22	23
24	25	26	27	28	29	30

OCTOBER

S	M	T	W	T	F	S
1	2	3	4	5	6	7
8	9	10	11	12	13	14
15	16	17	18	19	20	21
22	23	24	25	26	27	28
29	30	31				

NOVEMBER

S	M	T	W	T	F	S
			1	2	3	4
5	6	7	8	9	10	11
12	13	14	15	16	17	18
19	20	21	22	23	24	25
26	27	28	29	30		

DECEMBER

S	M	T	W	T	F	S
					1	2
3	4	5	6	7	8	9
10	11	12	13	14	15	16
17	18	19	20	21	22	23
24/31	25	26	27	28	29	30

Swiss Tourist Office: For questions and brochures call 877-794-8037. Comprehensive brochures, great maps, and hiking material. Or contact 608 Fifth Ave., New York, NY 10020, fax 212/262-6116, www.myswitzerland.com, info.usa@myswitzerland.com.

U.S. Embassies and Consulates

Austria: U.S. Embassy, Boltzmanngasse 16, Vienna, tel. 01/313-390, www.usembassy.at.

Belgium: U.S. Embassy, Regentlaan 27 Boulevard du Regent, Brussels (Mon–Fri 9:00–18:00, closed Sat–Sun, tel. 02/508-2111, www.usembassy.be).

Czech Republic: U.S. Embassy, Tržiště 15, Prague, tel. 257-530-663, www.usembassy.cz.

Denmark: U.S. Embassy, Dag Hammarskjölds Allé 24, Copenhagen, tel. 35 55 31 44, www.usembassy.dk

France: U.S. Embassy at 2 avenue Gabriel—to the left as you face Hôtel Crillon (Mo: Concorde, tel. 01 43 12 22 22, www.amb-usa.fr).

Germany: U.S. Embassy, Neustädtische Kirchstrasse 4-5, Berlin, tel. 030/83050, www.usembassy.de.
Great Britain: U.S. Embassy, 24 Grosvenor Square, Tube: Bond Street, tel. 020/7499-9000, www.usembassy.org.uk. (also see Scotland, below)
Greece: U.S. Embassy, Leoforos Vasilissis Sofias 91, near the Megalo Musikis Metro station, tel. 210-721-2951, www.usembassy.gr.
Ireland: U.S. Embassy 42 Elgin Road, Dublin, tel. 01/668-7122 or 01/668-8777, www.usembassy.ie.
Italy: U.S. Embassy at Via Vittorio Veneto 119/A (Mon–Fri 8:30–13:00 & 14:00–17:30, closed Sat–Sun, tel. 06-46741, www.usembassy.it); U.S. Consulate General at Lungarno Vespucci 38, Florence, tel. 055-266-951, www.usembassy.it/florence.
The Netherlands: U.S. Embassy at Lange Voorhout 102, The Hague (Mon–Fri 8:15–17:00, closed Sat–Sun, tel. 070/310-9209, www.usemb.nl); U.S. Consulate at Museumplein 19, Amsterdam (Mon–Fri 8:30–11:30, closed Sat–Sun, tel. 020/575-5309, www.usemb.nl/consul.htm).
Scotland: U.S. Consulate General, 3 Regent Terrace, Edinburgh, tel. 0131/556-8315, emergency tel. 0122/485-7097, www.usembassy.org.uk/scotland
Spain: U.S. Embassy, Calle Serrano 75, Madrid, tel. 915-872-240, emergency tel. 915-872-200, www.embusa.es/cons/services.html.
Switzerland: U.S. Embassy, Jubilaeumsstrasse 93, tel. 031-357-7234, http://bern.usembassy.gov.

VAT Rates and Minimum Purchases Required to Qualify for Refunds

COUNTRY OF PURCHASE	VAT STANDARD RATE*	MINIMUM IN LOCAL CURRENCY	MINIMUM IN U.S. DOLLARS
Austria	20%	€75.01	$98
Belgium	21%	€125.01	$163
Czech Republic	19%	1,000 K_	$45
Denmark	25%	300 DKK	$54
France	19.6%	€175	$227.50
Germany	16%	€25	$32.50
Great Britain	17.5%	£20	$39
Greece	18%	€120	$156
Ireland	21%	—	—
Italy	20%	€155	$202
Netherlands	19%	€137	$178
Spain	16%	€90.15	$118
Switzerland	7.6%	400 SF	$344

** The VAT Standard Rates listed above—while listed as exact amounts—are intended to give you an idea of the rates and minimums involved. But VAT rates fluctuate based on many factors, including what kind of item you are buying. Your refund will also likely be less than the above rate, especially if it's subject to processing fees. For more information and all the fine print, visit http://europa.eu.int.*

Let's Talk Telephones

To make international calls, you need to break the codes: the international access codes and country codes (see below). For information on making local, long-distance, and international calls, see "Telephones" in this book's introduction.

Country Codes

After you've dialed the international access code (011 if you're calling from the U.S.A. or Canada; 00 if you're calling from Europe), dial the code of the country you're calling.

Austria—43
Belgium—32
Britain—44
Canada—1
Croatia—385
Czech Rep.—420
Denmark—45
Estonia—372
Finland—358
France—33
Germany—49
Gibraltar—350
Greece—30
Ireland—353
Italy—39
Morocco—212
Netherlands—31
Norway—47
Poland—48
Portugal—351
Slovakia—421
Slovenia—386
Spain—34
Sweden—46
Switzerland—41
Turkey—90
U.S.A.—1

Numbers and Stumblers

- Europeans write a few of their numbers differently than we do: 1 = 1, 4 = 4, 7 = 7. Learn the difference or miss your train.
- Europeans write dates as day/month/year (Christmas is 25/12/06).
- Except in Great Britain and Ireland, commas are decimal points, and decimals are commas. A dollar and a half is 1,50. There are 5.280 feet in a mile.
- When counting with fingers, start with your thumb. If you hold up your first finger to request one item, you'll probably get two.
- What we Americans call the second floor of a building is the first floor in Europe.
- Europeans keep the left "lane" open for passing on escalators and moving sidewalks. Keep to the right.

Metric Conversion (approximate)

1 inch = 25 millimeters
1 foot = 0.3 meter
1 yard = 0.9 meter
1 mile = 1.6 kilometers
1 centimeter = 0.4 inch
1 meter = 39.4 inches
1 kilometer = 0.62 mile
32 degrees F = 0 degrees C
82 degrees F = about 28 degrees C
1 ounce = 28 grams
1 kilogram = 2.2 pounds
1 quart = 0.95 liter
1 square yard = 0.8 square meter
1 acre = 0.4 hectare

Temperature Conversion: Fahrenheit and Celsius

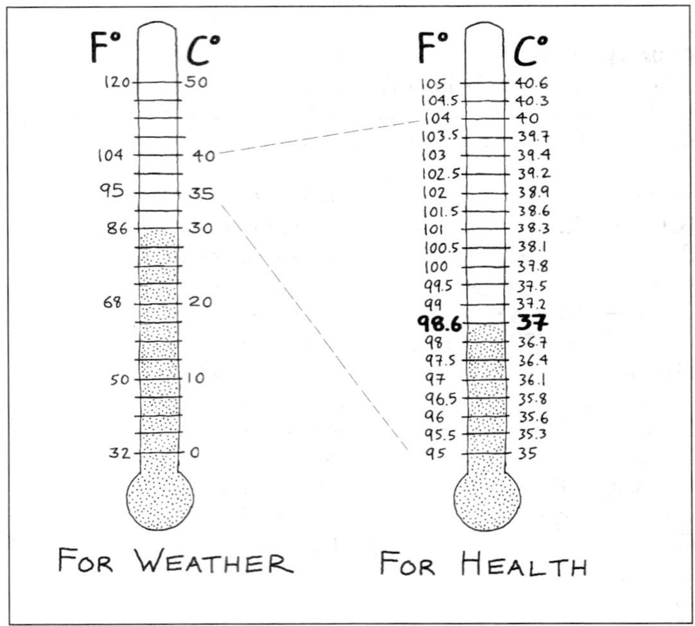

Climate

Here is a list of average temperatures (first line—average daily low; second line—average daily high; third line—days of no rain). This can be helpful in planning your itinerary, but I have never found European weather to be particularly predictable, and these charts ignore humidity.

	J	F	M	A	M	J	J	A	S	O	N	D
AUSTRIA • Vienna												
	25°	28°	30°	42°	50°	56°	60°	59°	53°	44°	37°	30°
	34°	38°	47°	58°	67°	73°	76°	75°	68°	56°	45°	37°
	16	17	18	17	18	16	18	18	20	18	16	16

J	F	M	A	M	J	J	A	S	O	N	D

BELGIUM • Brussels

J	F	M	A	M	J	J	A	S	O	N	D
30°	32°	36°	41°	46°	52°	54°	54°	51°	45°	38°	32°
40°	44°	51°	58°	65°	72°	73°	72°	69°	60°	48°	42°
10	11	14	12	15	15	14	13	17	14	10	12

CZECH REPUBLIC • Prague

J	F	M	A	M	J	J	A	S	O	N	D
23°	24°	30°	38°	46°	52°	55°	55°	49°	41°	33°	27°
31°	34°	44°	54°	64°	70°	73°	72°	65°	53°	42°	34°
18	17	21	19	18	18	18	19	20	18	18	18

DENMARK • Copenhagen

J	F	M	A	M	J	J	A	S	O	N	D
29°	28°	31°	37°	45°	51°	56°	56°	51°	44°	38°	33°
37°	37°	42°	51°	60°	66°	70°	69°	64°	55°	46°	41°
14	15	19	18	20	18	17	16	14	14	11	12

FRANCE • Paris

J	F	M	A	M	J	J	A	S	O	N	D
34°	34°	39°	43°	49°	55°	58°	58°	53°	46°	40°	36°
43°	45°	54°	60°	68°	73°	76°	75°	70°	60°	50°	44°
14	14	19	17	19	18	19	18	17	18	15	15

GERMANY • Berlin

J	F	M	A	M	J	J	A	S	O	N	D
23°	23°	30°	38°	45°	51°	55°	54°	48°	40°	33°	26°
35°	38°	48°	56°	64°	70°	74°	73°	67°	56°	44°	36°
15	12	18	15	16	13	15	15	17	18	15	16

GREAT BRITAIN • London

J	F	M	A	M	J	J	A	S	O	N	D
36°	36°	38°	42°	47°	53°	56°	56°	52°	46°	42°	38°
43°	44°	50°	56°	62°	69°	71°	71°	65°	58°	50°	45°
16	15	20	18	19	19	19	20	17	18	15	16

GREECE • Athens

J	F	M	A	M	J	J	A	S	O	N	D
44°	44°	46°	52°	61°	68°	73°	73°	67°	60°	53°	47°
55°	57°	60°	68°	77°	86°	92°	92°	84°	75°	66°	58°
15	17	20	21	23	26	29	28	26	23	18	16

IRELAND • Dublin

J	F	M	A	M	J	J	A	S	O	N	D
34°	35°	37°	39°	43°	48°	52°	51°	48°	43°	39°	37°
46°	47°	51°	55°	60°	65°	67°	67°	63°	57°	51°	47°
18	18	21	19	21	19	18	19	18	20	18	17

ITALY • Rome

J	F	M	A	M	J	J	A	S	O	N	D
40°	42°	45°	50°	56°	63°	67°	67°	62°	55°	49°	44°
52°	55°	59°	66°	74°	82°	87°	86°	79°	71°	61°	55°
13	19	23	24	26	26	30	29	25	23	19	21

European Calling Chart

Just smile and dial, using this key:
AC = Area Code, LN = Local Number.

European Country	Calling long distance within...	Calling from the U.S.A./ Canada to...	Calling from a European country to...
Austria	AC + LN	011 + 43 + AC (without the initial zero) + LN	00 + 43 + AC (without the initial zero) + LN
Belgium	LN	011 + 32 + LN (without initial zero)	00 + 32 + LN (without initial zero)
Britain	AC + LN	011 + 44 + AC (without initial zero) + LN	00 + 44 + AC (without initial zero) + LN
Croatia	AC + LN	011 + 385 + AC (without initial zero) + LN	00 + 385 + AC (without initial zero) + LN
Czech Republic	LN	011 + 420 + LN	00 + 420 + LN
Denmark	LN	011 + 45 + LN	00 + 45 + LN
Finland	AC + LN	011 + 358 + AC (without initial zero) + LN	00 + 358 + AC (without initial zero) + LN
France	LN	011 + 33 + LN (without initial zero)	00 + 33 + LN (without initial zero)
Germany	AC + LN	011 + 49 + AC (without initial zero) + LN	00 + 49 + AC (without initial zero) + LN
Greece	LN	011 + 30 + LN	00 + 30 + LN
Hungary	06 + AC + LN	011 + 36 + AC + LN	00 + 36 + AC + LN
Ireland	AC + LN	011 + 353 + AC (without initial zero) + LN	00 + 353 + AC (without initial zero) + LN
Italy	LN	011 + 39 + LN	00 + 39 + LN
Netherlands	AC + LN	011 + 31 + AC (without initial zero) + LN	00 + 31 + AC (without initial zero) + LN

European Country	Calling long distance within...	Calling from the U.S.A./ Canada to...	Calling from a European country to...
Norway	LN	011 + 47 + LN	00 + 47 + LN
Poland	AC + LN	011 + 48 + AC (without initial zero) + LN	00 + 48 + AC (without initial zero) + LN
Portugal	LN	011 + 351 + LN	00 + 351 + LN
Slovakia	AC + LN	011 + 421 + AC (without initial zero) + LN	00 + 421 + AC (without initial zero) + LN
Slovenia	AC + LN	011 + 386 + AC (without initial zero) + LN	00 + 386 + AC (without initial zero) + LN
Spain	LN	011 + 34 + LN	00 + 34 + LN
Sweden	AC + LN	011 + 46 + AC (without initial zero) + LN	00 + 46 + AC (without initial zero) + LN
Switzerland	LN	011 + 41 + LN (without initial zero)	00 + 41 + LN (without initial zero)
Turkey	AC (if no initial zero is included, add one) + LN	011 + 90 + AC (without initial zero) + LN	00 + 90 + AC (without initial zero) + LN

- The instructions above apply whether you're calling a fixed phone or mobile phone.
- The international access codes (the first numbers you dial when making an international call) are 011 if you're calling from the U.S.A./Canada, or 00 if you're calling from anywhere in Europe.
- To call the U.S.A. or Canada from Europe, dial 00, then 1 (the country code for the U.S.A. and Canada), then the area code and number. In short, 00 + 1 + AC + LN = Hi, Mom!

	J	F	M	A	M	J	J	A	S	O	N	D
NETHERLANDS • Amsterdam												
	31°	31°	34°	40°	46°	51°	55°	55°	50°	44°	38°	33°
	40°	42°	49°	56°	64°	70°	72°	71°	67°	57°	48°	42°
	9	9	15	14	17	16	14	13	11	11	9	10
SPAIN • Madrid												
	35°	36°	41°	45°	50°	58°	63°	63°	57°	49°	42°	36°
	47°	52°	59°	65°	70°	80°	87°	85°	77°	65°	55°	48°
	23	21	21	21	21	25	29	28	24	23	21	21
SWITZERLAND • Bern												
	29°	30°	36°	42°	49°	55°	58°	58°	53°	44°	37°	31°
	38°	42°	51°	59°	66°	73°	77°	76°	69°	58°	47°	40°
	20	19	22	21	20	19	22	20	20	21	19	21

Making Your Hotel Reservation

Most hotel managers know basic "hotel English." Faxing or e-mailing are the preferred methods for reserving a room. They're more accurate than telephoning and much faster than writing a letter. Use this handy form for your fax or find it online at www.ricksteves.com/reservation. Photocopy and fax away.

One-Page Fax

To: ______________________ @ ______________________
hotel *fax*

From: ______________________ @ ______________________
name *fax*

Today's date: _____ /_____ /_____
day *month* *year*

Dear Hotel ______________________________,
Please make this reservation for me:

Name: ______________________________

Total # of people: ________ # of rooms: ________ # of nights: ________

Arriving: _____ /_____ /_____ My time of arrival (24-hr clock): ________
day *month* *year* (I will telephone if I will be late)

Departing: _____ /_____ /_____
day *month* *year*

Room(s): Single _____ Double _____ Twin _____ Triple _____ Quad _____

With: Toilet _____ Shower _____ Bath _____ Sink only _____

Special needs: View _____ Quiet _____ Cheapest _____ Ground Floor _____

Please fax, mail, or e-mail confirmation of my reservation, along with the type of room reserved and the price. Please also inform me of your cancellation policy. After I hear from you, I will quickly send my credit-card information as a deposit to hold the room. Thank you.

____
Signature

____
Name

____
Address

____
City ***State*** ***Zip Code*** ***Country***

____
E-mail Address

German Survival Phrases

When using the phonetics, pronounce ī as the long I sound in "light."

Good day.	**Guten Tag.**	**goo**-tehn tahg
Do you speak English?	**Sprechen Sie Englisch?**	**shprehkh**-ehn zee **ehng**-lish
Yes. / No.	**Ja. / Nein.**	yah / nīn
I (don't) understand.	**Ich verstehe (nicht).**	ikh fehr-**shtay**-heh (nikht)
Please.	**Bitte.**	**bit**-teh
Thank you.	**Danke.**	**dahng**-keh
I'm sorry.	**Es tut mir leid.**	ehs toot meer līt
Excuse me.	**Entschuldigung.**	ehnt-**shool**-dig-oong
(No) problem.	**(Kein) Problem.**	(kīn) proh-**blaym**
(Very) good.	**(Sehr) gut.**	(zehr) goot
Goodbye.	**Auf Wiedersehen.**	owf **vee**-der-zayn
one / two	**eins / zwei**	īns / tsvī
three / four	**drei / vier**	drī / feer
five / six	**fünf / sechs**	fewnf / zehkhs
seven / eight	**sieben / acht**	**zee**-behn / ahkht
nine / ten	**neun / zehn**	noyn / tsayn
How much is it?	**Wieviel kostet das?**	**vee**-feel **kohs**-teht dahs
Write it?	**Schreiben?**	**shrī**-behn
Is it free?	**Ist es umsonst?**	ist ehs oom-**zohnst**
Included?	**Inklusive?**	in-kloo-**zee**-veh
Where can I buy / find...?	**Wo kann ich kaufen / finden...?**	voh kahn ikh **kow**-fehn / **fin**-dehn
I'd like / We'd like...	**Ich hätte gern / Wir hätten gern...**	ikh **heh**-teh gehrn / veer **heh**-tehn gehrn
...a room.	**...ein Zimmer.**	īn **tsim**-mer
...a ticket to ___.	**...eine Fahrkarte nach ___.**	ī-neh **far**-kar-teh nahkh
Is it possible?	**Ist es möglich?**	ist ehs **mur**-glikh
Where is...?	**Wo ist...?**	voh ist
...the train station	**...der Bahnhof**	dehr **bahn**-hohf
...the bus station	**...der Busbahnhof**	dehr **boos**-bahn-hohf
...tourist information	**...das Touristen-informationsbüro**	dahs too-**ris**-tehn-in-for-maht-see-**ohns**-**bew**-roh
...toilet	**...die Toilette**	dee toh-**leh**-teh
men	**Herren**	**hehr**-rehn
women	**Damen**	**dah**-mehn
left / right	**links / rechts**	links / rehkhts
straight	**geradeaus**	geh-**rah**-deh-**ows**
When is this open / closed?	**Um wieviel Uhr ist hier geöffnet / geschlossen?**	oom **vee**-feel oor ist heer geh-**urf**-neht / geh-**shloh**-sehn
At what time?	**Um wieviel Uhr?**	oom **vee**-feel oor
Just a moment.	**Moment.**	moh-**mehnt**
now / soon / later	**jetzt / bald / später**	yehtst / bahld / **shpay**-ter
today / tomorrow	**heute / morgen**	**hoy**-teh / **mor**-gehn

In the Restaurant

I'd like / We'd like...	**Ich hätte gern / Wir hätten gern...**	ikh **heh**-teh gehrn / veer **heh**-tehn gehrn
...a reservation for...	**...eine Reservierung für...**	ī-neh reh-zer-**feer**-oong fewr
...a table for one / two.	**...einen Tisch für ein / zwei.**	ī-nehn tish fewr īn / tsvī
Non-smoking.	**Nichtraucher.**	**nikht**-rowkh-er
Is this seat free?	**Ist hier frei?**	ist heer frī
Menu (in English), please.	**Speisekarte (in Englisch), bitte.**	**shpī**-zeh-kar-teh (in **ehng**-lish) **bit**-teh
service (not) included	**Trinkgeld (nicht) inklusive**	**trink**-gehlt (nikht) in-kloo-**zee**-veh
cover charge	**Eintritt**	**īn**-trit
to go	**zum Mitnehmen**	tsoom **mit**-nay-mehn
with / without	**mit / ohne**	mit / **oh**-neh
and / or	**und / oder**	oont / **oh**-der
menu (of the day)	**(Tages-) Karte**	**(tah**-gehs-) **kar**-teh
set meal for tourists	**Touristenmenü**	too-**ris**-tehn-meh-**new**
specialty of the house	**Spezialität des Hauses**	**shpayt**-see-ah-lee-**tayt** dehs **how**-zehs
appetizers	**Vorspeise**	**for**-shpī-zeh
bread	**Brot**	broht
cheese	**Käse**	**kay**-zeh
sandwich	**Sandwich**	**zahnd**-vich
soup	**Suppe**	**zup**-peh
salad	**Salat**	zah-**laht**
meat	**Fleisch**	flīsh
poultry	**Geflügel**	geh-**flew**-gehl
fish	**Fisch**	fish
seafood	**Meeresfrüchte**	**meh**-rehs-**frewkh**-teh
fruit	**Obst**	ohpst
vegetables	**Gemüse**	geh-**mew**-zeh
dessert	**Nachspeise**	**nahkh**-shpī-zeh
mineral water	**Mineralwasser**	min-eh-**rahl**-vah-ser
tap water	**Leitungswasser**	**lī**-toongs-vah-ser
milk	**Milch**	milkh
(orange) juice	**(Orangen-) Saft**	(oh-**rahn**-zhehn-) zahft
coffee	**Kaffee**	kah-**fay**
tea	**Tee**	tay
wine	**Wein**	vīn
red / white	**rot / weiß**	roht / vīs
glass / bottle	**Glas / Flasche**	glahs / **flah**-sheh
beer	**Bier**	beer
Cheers!	**Prost!**	prohst
More. / Another.	**Mehr. / Noch ein.**	mehr / nohkh īn
The same.	**Das gleiche.**	dahs **glīkh**-eh
Bill, please.	**Rechnung, bitte.**	**rehkh**-noong **bit**-teh
tip	**Trinkgeld**	**trink**-gehlt
Delicious!	**Lecker!**	**lehk**-er

For more user-friendly German phrases, check out *Rick Steves' German Phrase Book and Dictionary* or *Rick Steves' French, Italian & German Phrase Book.*

French Survival Phrases

When using the phonetics, try to nasalize the n sound.

Good day.	**Bonjour.**	bohn-zhoor
Mrs. / Mr.	**Madame / Monsieur**	mah-dahm / muhs-yur
Do you speak English?	**Parlez-vous anglais?**	par-lay-voo ahn-glay
Yes. / No.	**Oui. / Non.**	wee / nohn
I understand.	**Je comprends.**	zhuh kohn-prahn
I don't understand.	**Je ne comprends pas.**	zhuh nuh kohn-prahn pah
Please.	**S'il vous plaît.**	see voo play
Thank you.	**Merci.**	mehr-see
I'm sorry.	**Désolé.**	day-zoh-lay
Excuse me.	**Pardon.**	par-dohn
(No) problem.	**(Pas de) problème.**	(pah duh) proh-blehm
It's good.	**C'est bon.**	say bohn
Goodbye.	**Au revoir.**	oh vwahr
one / two	**un / deux**	uhn / duh
three / four	**trois / quatre**	twah / kah-truh
five / six	**cinq / six**	sank / sees
seven / eight	**sept / huit**	seht / weet
nine / ten	**neuf / dix**	nuhf / dees
How much is it?	**Combien?**	kohn-bee-an
Write it?	**Ecrivez?**	ay-kree-vay
Is it free?	**C'est gratuit?**	say grah-twee
Included?	**Inclus?**	an-klew
Where can I buy / find...?	**Où puis-je acheter / trouver...?**	oo pwee-zhuh ah-shuh-tay / troo-vay
I'd like / We'd like...	**Je voudrais / Nous voudrions...**	zhuh voo-dray / noo voo-dree-ohn
...a room.	**...une chambre.**	ewn shahn-bruh
...a ticket to ___.	**...un billet pour ___.**	uhn bee-yay poor
Is it possible?	**C'est possible?**	say poh-see-bluh
Where is...?	**Où est...?**	oo ay
...the train station	**...la gare**	lah gar
...the bus station	**...la gare routière**	lah gar root-yehr
...tourist information	**...l'office du tourisme**	loh-fees dew too-reez-muh
Where are the toilets?	**Où sont les toilettes?**	oo sohn lay twah-leht
men	**hommes**	ohm
women	**dames**	dahm
left / right	**à gauche / à droite**	ah gohsh / ah dwaht
straight	**tout droit**	too dwah
When does this open / close?	**Ça ouvre / ferme à quelle heure?**	sah oo-vruh / fehrm ah kehl ur
At what time?	**À quelle heure?**	ah kehl ur
Just a moment.	**Un moment.**	uhn moh-mahn
now / soon / later	**maintenant / bientôt / plus tard**	man-tuh-nahn / bee-an-toh / plew tar
today / tomorrow	**aujourd'hui / demain**	oh-zhoor-dwee / duh-man

In the Restaurant

I'd like / We'd like...	**Je voudrais / Nous voudrions...**	zhuh voo-dray / noo voo-dree-ohn
...to reserve...	**...réserver...**	ray-zehr-vay
...a table for one / two.	**...une table pour un / deux.**	ewn tah-bluh poor uhn / duh
Non-smoking.	**Non fumeur.**	nohn few-mur
Is this seat free?	**C'est libre?**	say lee-bruh
The menu (in English), please.	**La carte (en anglais), s'il vous plaît.**	lah kart (ahn ahn-glay) see voo play
service (not) included	**service (non) compris**	sehr-vees (nohn) kohn-pree
to go	**à emporter**	ah ahn-por-tay
with / without	**avec / sans**	ah-vehk / sahn
and / or	**et / ou**	ay / oo
special of the day	**plat du jour**	plah dew zhoor
specialty of the house	**spécialité de la maison**	spay-see-ah-lee-tay duh lah may-zohn
appetizers	**hors-d'oeuvre**	or-duh-vruh
first course (soup, salad)	**entrée**	ahn-tray
main course (meat, fish)	**plat principal**	plah pran-see-pahl
bread	**pain**	pan
cheese	**fromage**	froh-mahzh
sandwich	**sandwich**	sahnd-weech
soup	**soupe**	soop
salad	**salade**	sah-lahd
meat	**viande**	vee-ahnd
chicken	**poulet**	poo-lay
fish	**poisson**	pwah-sohn
seafood	**fruits de mer**	frwee duh mehr
fruit	**fruit**	frwee
vegetables	**légumes**	lay-gewm
dessert	**dessert**	duh-sehr
mineral water	**eau minérale**	oh mee-nay-rahl
tap water	**l'eau du robinet**	loh dew roh-bee-nay
milk	**lait**	lay
(orange) juice	**jus (d'orange)**	zhew (doh-rahnzh)
coffee	**café**	kah-fay
tea	**thé**	tay
wine	**vin**	van
red / white	**rouge / blanc**	roozh / blahn
glass / bottle	**verre / bouteille**	vehr / boo-teh-ee
beer	**bière**	bee-ehr
Cheers!	**Santé!**	sahn-tay
More. / Another.	**Plus. / Un autre.**	plew / uhn oh-truh
The same.	**La même chose.**	lah mehm shohz
The bill, please.	**L'addition, s'il vous plaît.**	lah-dee-see-ohn see voo play
tip	**pourboire**	poor-bwar
Delicious!	**Délicieux!**	day-lee-see-uh

For more user-friendly French phrases, check out *Rick Steves' French Phrase Book and Dictionary* or *Rick Steves' French, Italian & German Phrase Book*.

Italian Survival Phrases

English	Italian	Pronunciation
Good day.	**Buon giorno.**	bwohn JOR-noh
Do you speak English?	**Parla inglese?**	PAR-lah een-GLAY-zay
Yes. / No.	**Si. / No.**	see / noh
I (don't) understand.	**(Non) capisco.**	(nohn) kah-PEES-koh
Please.	**Per favore.**	pehr fah-VOH-ray
Thank you.	**Grazie.**	GRAHT-seeay
I'm sorry.	**Mi dispiace.**	mee dee-speeAH-chay
Excuse me.	**Mi scusi.**	mee SKOO-zee
(No) problem.	**(Non) c'è un problema.**	(nohn) cheh oon proh-BLAY-mah
Good.	**Va bene.**	vah BEHN-ay
Goodbye.	**Arrivederci.**	ah-ree-vay-DEHR-chee
one / two	**uno / due**	OO-noh / DOO-ay
three / four	**tre / quattro**	tray / KWAH-troh
five / six	**cinque / sei**	CHEENG-kway / SEHee
seven / eight	**sette / otto**	SEHT-tay / OT-toh
nine / ten	**nove / dieci**	NOV-ay / deeAY-chee
How much is it?	**Quanto costa?**	KWAHN-toh KOS-tah
Write it?	**Me lo scrive?**	may loh SKREE-vay
Is it free?	**È gratis?**	eh GRAH-tees
Is it included?	**È incluso?**	eh een-KLOO-zoh
Where can I buy / find...?	**Dove posso comprare / trovare...?**	DOH-vay POS-soh kohm-PRAH-ray / troh-VAH-ray
I'd like / We'd like...	**Vorrei / Vorremmo...**	vor-REHee / vor-RAY-moh
...a room.	**...una camera.**	OO-nah KAH-meh-rah
...a ticket to ___.	**...un biglietto per ___.**	oon beel-YEHT-toh pehr
Is it possible?	**È possibile?**	eh poh-SEE-bee-lay
Where is...?	**Dov'è...?**	DOH-veh
...the train station	**...la stazione**	lah staht-seeOH-nay
...the bus station	**...la stazione degli autobus**	lah staht-seeOH-nay DAYL-yee OW-toh-boos
...tourist information	**...informazioni per turisti**	een-for-maht-seeOH-nee pehr too-REE-stee
...the toilet	**...la toilette**	lah twah-LEHT-tay
men	**uomini, signori**	WOH-mee-nee, seen-YOH-ree
women	**donne, signore**	DON-nay, seen-YOH-ray
left / right	**sinistra / destra**	see-NEE-strah / DEHS-trah
straight	**sempre diritto**	SEHM-pray dee-REE-toh
When do you open / close?	**A che ora aprite / chiudete?**	ah kay OH-rah ah-PREE-tay / keeoo-DAY-tay
At what time?	**A che ora?**	ah kay OH-rah
Just a moment.	**Un momento.**	oon moh-MAYN-toh
now / soon / later	**adesso / presto / tardi**	ah-DEHS-soh / PREHS-toh / TAR-dee
today / tomorrow	**oggi / domani**	OH-jee / doh-MAH-nee

In the Restaurant

English	Italian	Pronunciation
I'd like...	**Vorrei...**	vor-REHee
We'd like...	**Vorremmo...**	vor-RAY-moh
...to reserve...	**...prenotare...**	pray-noh-TAH-ray
...a table for one / two.	**...un tavolo per uno / due.**	oon TAH-voh-loh pehr OO-noh / DOO-ay
Non-smoking.	**Non fumare.**	nohn foo-MAH-ray
Is this seat free?	**È libero questo posto?**	eh LEE-bay-roh KWEHS-toh POH-stoh
The menu (in English), please.	**Il menù (in inglese), per favore.**	eel may-NOO (een een-GLAY-zay) pehr fah-VOH-ray
service (not) included	**servizio (non) incluso**	sehr-VEET-seeoh (nohn) een-KLOO-zoh
cover charge	**pane e coperto**	PAH-nay ay koh-PEHR-toh
to go	**da portar via**	dah POR-tar VEE-ah
with / without	**con / senza**	kohn / SEHN-sah
and / or	**e / o**	ay / oh
menu (of the day)	**menù (del giorno)**	may-NOO (dayl JOR-noh)
specialty of the house	**specialità della casa**	spay-chah-lee-TAH DEHL-lah KAH-zah
first course (pasta, soup)	**primo piatto**	PREE-moh peeAH-toh
main course (meat, fish)	**secondo piatto**	say-KOHN-doh peeAH-toh
side dishes	**contorni**	kohn-TOR-nee
bread	**pane**	PAH-nay
cheese	**formaggio**	for-MAH-joh
sandwich	**panino**	pah-NEE-noh
soup	**minestra, zuppa**	mee-NEHS-trah, TSOO-pah
salad	**insalata**	een-sah-LAH-tah
meat	**carne**	KAR-nay
chicken	**pollo**	POH-loh
fish	**pesce**	PEH-shay
seafood	**frutti di mare**	FROO-tee dee MAH-ray
fruit / vegetables	**frutta / legumi**	FROO-tah / lay-GOO-mee
dessert	**dolci**	DOHL-chee
tap water	**acqua del rubinetto**	AH-kwah dayl roo-bee-NAY-toh
mineral water	**acqua minerale**	AH-kwah mee-nay-RAH-lay
milk	**latte**	LAH-tay
(orange) juice	**succo (d'arancia)**	SOO-koh (dah-RAHN-chah)
coffee / tea	**caffè / tè**	kah-FEH / teh
wine	**vino**	VEE-noh
red / white	**rosso / bianco**	ROH-soh / beeAHN-koh
glass / bottle	**bicchiere / bottiglia**	bee-keeAY-ray / boh-TEEL-yah
beer	**birra**	BEE-rah
Cheers!	**Cin cin!**	cheen cheen
More. / Another.	**Ancora un po.' / Un altro.**	ahn-KOH-rah oon poh / oon AHL-troh
The same.	**Lo stesso.**	loh STEHS-soh
The bill, please.	**Il conto, per favore.**	eel KOHN-toh pehr fah-VOH-ray
tip	**mancia**	MAHN-chah
Delicious	**Delizioso!**	day-leet-seeOH-zoh

For hundreds more pages of survival phrases for your trip to Italy, check out *Rick Steves' Italian Phrase Book & Dictionary* or *Rick Steves' French, Italian, and German Phrase Book.*

Spanish Survival Phrases

Spanish has a guttural sound similar to the J in Baja California. In the phonetics, the symbol for this clearing-your-throat sound is the italicized *h*.

Good day.	**Buenos días.**	**bway**-nohs **dee**-ahs
Do you speak English?	**¿Habla usted inglés?**	**ah**-blah oo-**stehd** een-**glays**
Yes. / No.	**Sí. / No.**	see / noh
I (don't) understand.	**(No) comprendo.**	(noh) kohm-**prehn**-doh
Please.	**Por favor.**	por fah-**bor**
Thank you.	**Gracias.**	**grah**-thee-ahs
I'm sorry.	**Lo siento.**	loh see-**ehn**-toh
Excuse me.	**Perdóneme.**	pehr-**doh**-nay-may
(No) problem.	**(No) problema.**	(noh) proh-**blay**-mah
Good.	**Bueno.**	**bway**-noh
Goodbye.	**Adiós.**	ah-dee-**ohs**
one / two	**uno / dos**	**oo**-noh / dohs
three / four	**tres / cuatro**	trays / **kwah**-troh
five / six	**cinco / seis**	**theen**-koh / says
seven / eight	**siete / ocho**	see-**eh**-tay / **oh**-choh
nine / ten	**nueve / diez**	**nway**-bay / dee-**ayth**
How much is it?	**¿Cuánto cuesta?**	**kwahn**-toh **kway**-stah
Write it?	**¿Me lo escribe?**	may loh ay-**skree**-bay
Is it free?	**¿Es gratis?**	ays **grah**-tees
Is it included?	**¿Está incluido?**	ay-**stah** een-kloo-**ee**-doh
Where can I buy / find...?	**¿Dónde puedo comprar / encontrar...?**	**dohn**-day **pway**-doh kohm-**prar** / ayn-kohn-**trar**
I'd like / We'd like...	**Quiero / Queremos...**	kee-**ehr**-oh / kehr-**ay**-mohs
...a room.	**...una habitación.**	**oo**-nah ah-bee-tah-thee-**ohn**
...a ticket to ___.	**...un billete para ___.**	oon bee-**yeh**-tay **pah**-rah
Is it possible?	**¿Es posible?**	ays poh-**see**-blay
Where is...?	**¿Dónde está...?**	**dohn**-day ay-**stah**
...the train station	**...la estación de trenes**	lah ay-stah-thee-**ohn** day **tray**-nays
...the bus station	**...la estación de autobuses**	lah ay-stah-thee-**ohn** day ow-toh-**boo**-says
...the tourist information office	**...la oficina de turismo**	lah oh-fee-**thee**-nah day too-**rees**-moh
Where are the toilets?	**¿Dónde están los servicios?**	**dohn**-day ay-**stahn** lohs sehr-**bee**-thee-ohs
men	**hombres, caballeros**	**ohm**-brays, kah-bah-**yay**-rohs
women	**mujeres, damas**	moo-***heh***-rays, **dah**-mahs
left / right	**izquierda / derecha**	eeth-kee-**ehr**-dah / day-**ray**-chah
straight	**derecho**	day-**ray**-choh
When do you open / close?	**¿A qué hora abren / cierran?**	ah kay **oh**-rah **ah**-brehn / thee-**ay**-rahn
At what time?	**¿A qué hora?**	ah kay **oh**-rah
Just a moment.	**Un momento.**	oon moh-**mehn**-toh
now / soon / later	**ahora / pronto / más tarde**	ah-**oh**-rah / **prohn**-toh / mahs **tar**-day
today / tomorrow	**hoy / mañana**	oy / mahn-**yah**-nah

In the Restaurant

I'd like / We'd like...	**Quiero / Queremos...**	kee-**ehr**-oh / kehr-**ay**-mohs
...to reserve...	**...reservar...**	ray-sehr-**bar**
...a table for one / two.	**...una mesa para uno / dos.**	**oo**-nah **may**-sah **pah**-rah **oo**-noh / dohs
Non-smoking.	**No fumadores.**	noh foo-mah-**doh**-rays
Is this table free?	**¿Está esta mesa libre?**	ay-**stah** **ay**-stah **may**-sah **lee**-bray
The menu (in English), please.	**La carta (en inglés), por favor.**	lah **kar**-tah (ayn een-**glays**) por fah-**bor**
service (not) included	**servicio (no) incluido**	sehr-**bee**-thee-oh (noh) een-kloo-**ee**-doh
cover charge	**precio de entrada**	**pray**-thee-oh day ayn-**trah**-dah
to go	**para llevar**	**pah**-rah yay-**bar**
with / without	**con / sin**	kohn / seen
and / or	**y / o**	ee / oh
menu (of the day)	**menú (del día)**	may-**noo** (dayl **dee**-ah)
specialty of the house	**especialidad de la casa**	ay-spay-thee-ah-lee-**dahd** day lah **kah**-sah
tourist menu	**menú de turista**	meh-**noo** day too-**ree**-stah
combination plate	**plato combinado**	**plah**-toh kohm-bee-**nah**-doh
appetizers	**tapas**	**tah**-pahs
bread	**pan**	pahn
cheese	**queso**	**kay**-soh
sandwich	**bocadillo**	boh-kah-**dee**-yoh
soup	**sopa**	**soh**-pah
salad	**ensalada**	ayn-sah-**lah**-dah
meat	**carne**	**kar**-nay
poultry	**aves**	**ah**-bays
fish	**pescado**	pay-**skah**-doh
seafood	**marisco**	mah-**ree**-skoh
fruit	**fruta**	**froo**-tah
vegetables	**verduras**	behr-**doo**-rahs
dessert	**postres**	**poh**-strays
tap water	**agua del grifo**	**ah**-gwah dayl **gree**-foh
mineral water	**agua mineral**	**ah**-gwah mee-nay-**rahl**
milk	**leche**	**lay**-chay
(orange) juice	**zumo (de naranja)**	**thoo**-moh (day nah-**rahn**-*h*ah)
coffee	**café**	kah-**feh**
tea	**té**	tay
wine	**vino**	**bee**-noh
red / white	**tinto / blanco**	**teen**-toh / **blahn**-koh
glass / bottle	**vaso / botella**	**bah**-soh / boh-**tay**-yah
beer	**cerveza**	thehr-**bay**-thah
Cheers!	**¡Salud!**	sah-**lood**
More. / Another.	**Más. / Otro.**	mahs / **oh**-troh
The same.	**El mismo.**	ehl **mees**-moh
The bill, please.	**La cuenta, por favor.**	lah **kwayn**-tah por fah-**bor**
tip	**propina**	proh-**pee**-nah
Delicious!	**¡Delicioso!**	day-lee-thee-**oh**-soh

For hundreds more pages of survival phrases for your trip to Spain, check out *Rick Steves' Spanish Phrase Book*.

INDEX

Aalsmeer Flower Auction: 1181

Panoramic Image Credits

Location	Photographer
Austria	
Vienna—Schönbrunn Palace	Cameron Hewitt
Salzburg	Rick Steves
Hallstatt	Dave Hoerlein
Belgium	
Bruges	Dave Hoerlein
Czech Republic	
Prague—View of Prague Castle	Cameron Hewitt
Denmark	
Copenhagen—Nyhavn	Cameron Hewitt
France	
Paris—Louvre	Rick Steves
Provence—Pont du Gard	Rick Steves
The French Riviera—Nice	Dave Hoerlein
Germany	
Bavaria—Neuschwanstein Castle	Dominic Bonuccelli
Rothenburg	Dave Hoerlein
Rhine River	Dominic Bonuccelli
Berlin—Gendarmenmarkt	Cameron Hewitt
Great Britain	
London—Houses of Parliament	Rick Steves
Bath—Pulteney Bridge	Lauren Mills
York—York Minster	Dave Hoerlein
Edinburgh—Edinburgh Castle	Rick Steves
Greece	
Athens—Acropolis	Dave Hoerlein
Ireland	
Dublin—Ha' Penny Bridge	Pat O'Connor
Dingle Peninsula—Blasket Islands	Pat O'Connor

Location	**Photographer**
Italy	
Rome—Piazza Navona	Rick Steves
Venice—Church of San Giorgio Maggiore	Dave Hoerlein
Florence—Piazzale Michelangelo	Rick Steves
Siena—Il Campo	Dave Hoerlein
The Cinque Terre—Corniglia	Rick Steves
Netherlands	
Amsterdam	Rick Steves
Haarlem—Market Square	Rick Steves
Spain	
Barcelona—Montjuïc	Dave Hoerlein
Madrid—Retiro Park	Dave Hoerlein
Toledo	Rick Steves
Switzerland	
Gimmelwald	Dominic Bonuccelli

Start your trip at
www.ricksteves.com

Rick Steves' website is packed with over 3,000 pages of timely travel information. It's also your gateway to getting FREE monthly travel news from Rick—and more!

Free Monthly European Travel News

Fresh articles on Europe's most interesting destinations and happenings. Rick will even send you an e-mail every month (often direct from Europe) with his latest discoveries!

Timely Travel Tips

Rick Steves' best money-and-stress-saving tips on trip planning, packing, transportation, hotels, health, safety, finances, hurdling the language barrier...and more.

Travelers' Graffiti Wall

Candid advice and opinions from thousands of travelers on everything listed above, plus whatever topics are hot at the moment (discount flights, packing tips, scams...you name it).

Rick's Annual Guide to European Railpasses

The clearest, most comprehensive guide to the confusing array of railpass options out there, and how to choo-choose the railpass that best fits your itinerary and budget. Then you can order your railpass (and get a bunch of great freebies) online from us!

Great Gear at the Rick Steves Travel Store

Enjoy bargains on Rick's guidebooks, planning maps and TV series DVDs—and on his custom-designed carry-on bags, wheeled bags, day bags and light-packing accessories.

Rick Steves Tours

Every year more than 6,000 lucky travelers explore Europe on a Rick Steves tour. Learn more about our 30 different one-to-three-week itineraries, read uncensored feedback from our tour alums, and sign up for your dream trip online!

Rick on Radio and TV

Read the scripts and run clips from public television's "Rick Steves' Europe" and public radio's "Travel with Rick Steves."

Respect for Your Privacy

Ordering online from us is secure. When you buy something from us, join a tour, or subscribe to Rick's free monthly travel news e-mails, we promise to never share your name, information, or e-mail address with anyone else. You won't be spammed!

Have fun raising your Travel I.Q. at
www.ricksteves.com

Travel smart...carry on!

The latest generation of Rick Steves' carry-on travel bags is easily the best—benefiting from two decades of on-the-road attention to what really matters: maximum quality and strength; practical, flexible features; and no unnecessary frills. You won't find a better value anywhere!

Convertible, expandable, and carry-on-size:

Rick Steves' Back Door Bag $99

This is the same bag that Rick Steves lives out of for three months every summer. It's made of rugged water-resistant 1000 denier Cordura nylon, and best of all, it converts easily from a smart-looking suitcase to a handy backpack with comfortably-curved shoulder straps and a padded waistbelt.

This roomy, versatile 9" x 21" x 14" bag has a large 2600 cubic-inch main compartment, plus three outside pockets (small, medium and huge) that are perfect for often-used items. And the cinch-tight compression straps will keep your load compact and close to your back—not sagging like a sack of potatoes.

Wishing you had even more room to bring home souvenirs? Pull open the full-perimeter expando-zipper and its capacity jumps from 2600 to 3000 cubic inches. When you want to use it as a suitcase or check it as luggage (required when "expanded"), the straps and belt hide away in a zippered compartment in the back.

Attention travelers under 5'4" tall: This bag also comes in an inch-shorter version, for a compact-friendlier fit between the waistbelt and shoulder straps.

Convenient, expandable, and carry-on-size:

Rick Steves' Wheeled Bag $129

At 9" x 21" x 14" our sturdy Rick Steves' Wheeled Bag is rucksack-soft in front, but the rest is lined with a hard ABS-lexan shell to give maximum protection to your belongings. We've spared no expense on moving parts, splurging on an extra-long button-release handle and big, tough inline skate wheels for easy rolling on rough surfaces.

Wishing you had even more room to bring home souvenirs? Pull open the full-perimeter expando-zipper and its capacity jumps from 2600 to 3000 cubic inches.

Rick Steves' Wheeled Bag has exactly the same three-outside-pocket configuration as our Back Door Bag, plus a handy "add-a-bag" strap and full lining.

Our Back Door Bags and Wheeled Bags come in black, navy, blue spruce, evergreen and merlot.

For great deals on a wide selection of travel goodies, begin your next trip at the Rick Steves Travel Store!

Visit the Rick Steves Travel Store at
www.ricksteves.com

As the #1 authority on European travel, Rick gives you inside information on what to visit, where to stay, and how to get there—economically and hassle-free.

www.ricksteves.com

PHRASE BOOKS & DICTIONARIES

French
French, Italian & German
German
Italian
Portuguese
Spanish

MORE EUROPE FROM RICK STEVES

Easy Access Europe
Europe 101
Europe Through the Back Door
Postcards from Europe

RICK STEVES' EUROPE DVDs

All 43 Shows 2000-2005
Britain
Eastern Europe
France & Benelux
Germany, The Swiss Alps & Travel Skills
Ireland
Italy
Spain & Portugal

PLANNING MAPS

Britain & Ireland
Europe
France
Germany, Austria & Switzerland
Italy
Spain & Portugal

For a complete listing of Rick Steves' books, see page 7.

Avalon Travel Publishing
1400 65th Street, Suite 250
Emeryville, CA 94608

Avalon Travel Publishing
An Imprint of Avalon Publishing Group.

Printed in the U.S.A. by Worzalla
Second printing April 2006

For the latest on Rick Steves' lectures, guidebooks, tours, and public television series, contact Europe Through the Back Door, Box 2009, Edmonds, WA 98020, 425/771-8303, fax 425/771-0833, www.ricksteves.com, rick@ricksteves.com.

ISBN-10: 1-56691-720-4
ISBN-13: 978-1-56691-720-9
ISSN: 1096-7702

Europe Through the Back Door Managing Editor: Risa Laib
ETBD Editors: Cameron Hewitt, Lauren Mills, Jennifer Hauseman, Gene Openshaw
Avalon Travel Publishing Editor and Series Manager: Patrick Collins
Avalon Travel Publishing Project Editor: Madhu Prasher
Research Assistance: Rolinka Bloeming, Carlos Galvin, Sonja Groset, Darbi Macy, Susana Minich, Sarah Murdoch, Pat O'Connor, Heidi Sewell, Steve Smith, Karoline Vass, Honza Vihan, David Willett
Production & Typesetting: Patrick David Barber
Interior Design: Laura Mazer, Jane Musser, Amber Pirker
Cover Design: Kari Gim, Laura Mazer
Maps and Graphics: David C. Hoerlein, Laura VanDeventer, Lauren Mills, Mike Morgenfeld
Front Matter Color Photos: Page i: Venice, Italy © Rick Steves; page xvi: Koln Cathedral, Germany © Andrea Johnson
Cover Photos: Front image: Eiffel Tower, Paris © Dominic Bonuccelli; back image: Sunflower field, Tuscany, Italy. © David Tomlinson / Lonely Planet Images

Distributed to the book trade by Publishers Group West, Berkeley, California